CHILDREN'S CATALOG

FOURTEENTH EDITION

1981

STANDARD CATALOG SERIES

GARY L. BOGART, GENERAL EDITOR

CHILDREN'S CATALOG
FICTION CATALOG
JUNIOR HIGH SCHOOL LIBRARY CATALOG
PUBLIC LIBRARY CATALOG
SENIOR HIGH SCHOOL LIBRARY CATALOG

CHILDREN'S CATALOG

FOURTEENTH EDITION 1981

EDITED BY

RICHARD H. ISAACSON
and
GARY L. BOGART

NEW YORK
THE H. W. WILSON COMPANY
1981

Copyright © 1981

By The H. W. Wilson Company

Printed in the United States of America

Library of Congress Cataloging in Publication Data
    Children's catalog.

    (Standard catalog series)
    Includes index.

    1. Children's literature—Bibliography—Catalogs. I. Isaacson,
Richard H. II. Bogart, Gary L. III. H. W. Wilson Company.
IV. Series.

Z1037.C5443   1981   011.62   81-7550

ISBN 0-8242-0662-2   AACR2

PREFACE

The seventy fifth anniversary of its first appearance will occur during the life of this, the fourteenth, edition of Children's Catalog. Begun in 1909 as the inaugural venture of The H. W. Wilson Company in selective bibliography, successive editions of the Catalog have reflected the cultural and educational styles of three generations. The initial effort—modest when compared with the present edition—revealed the great progress made in the publishing of children's books during the nineteenth century.

At the beginning of that century such rudimentary learning tools as hornbooks and battledores were still in use. But the tide had already turned against the moralizing tone, so characteristic of early children's books. The true children's book, written to delight as well as instruct, gradually superseded the cruder school primers. As text and illustration were united with increasing skill, the genre attracted leading writers and artists. By the end of the century and the time of the first edition of Children's Catalog, the children's book had attained a distinguished place in British and American publishing.* In the years since that first edition, the children's book has grown steadily in popularity. The history of that growth is chronicled in the many editions of Children's Catalog, including this fourteenth edition.

Preparation. In preparing this edition, The H. W. Wilson Company has had the benefit of an advisory committee of distinguished librarians. The committee reexamined the previous edition of the Catalog and its supplements and also proposed new titles. The list resulting from the committee's deliberations was then submitted to a group of experienced children's librarians from dispersed geographical areas, who did the actual election of titles.

Scope and Purpose. The Catalog includes books for children from pre-school through the sixth grade. And, in addition to the bound volume of the fourteenth edition itself, the service unit includes four supplements to be published in 1982, 1983, 1984, and 1985. Since it is difficult to take care of all the needs of the precocious child, this edition should be used with the fourth edition of Junior High School Library Catalog, published in 1980.

Although it can be considered a basic collection, the list will undoubtedly have to be supplemented by those libraries serving large systems, and those that must satisfy the special needs of their patrons. The fourteenth edition includes 5,901 titles and 11,256 analytical entries. Regrettably, it needs to be said, that some good books, once in print, are no longer available, and other books, sorely needed, remain to be written. Out-of-print books have not been included, but titles brought back into print later will be considered for one of the supplements. Certain sections of the Catalog reveal a dearth of good materials. This is true, for example, in the geography and history areas.

The general features of the last edition have been retained, with the exception of books in series. In this fourteenth edition, only the first book in a series is given in full, the others in the sequence are listed briefly, without annotation. Paperbacks are again included, when no hardcover version is available, and they are also mentioned when available from the publisher of the hardcover version; foreign language and bilingual editions are listed when available from the publisher of the English language version. The use of uniform titles, begun in the previous edition, is continued so that variant forms of individual folk and fairy tales can be brought together under one heading. These headings have been established from the second edition of Mary H. Eastman's *Index to Fairy Tales, Myths and Legends* (Faxon, 1926) and its four supplements published in 1937, 1952, 1973, and 1979, respectively. There are also materials for the professional librarian: books on the history and development of children's literature; book selection; the operation of media centers; and periodicals on library science, reviewing, and education.

*For a more detailed historical account, the interested reader is referred to J. H. Plumb's "The First Flourishing of Children's Books" in *Early Children's Books and their Illustration* (New York, The Pierpont Morgan Library, 1975)

Organization. The Catalog is organized for effective use. It consists of three parts: Classified Catalog; Author, Title, Subject, and Analytical Index; and Directory of Publishers and Distributors. To gain the greatest benefit from the Catalog it is advisable to peruse the next section: How to Use Children's Catalog.

Acknowledgments. The H. W. Wilson Company expresses its appreciation to those publishers who generously supplied copies of their books and information on editions and prices. The Company also wishes to acknowledge its debt to the two groups of librarians who gave so generously of their time and energy: the advisory committee and the consultants. Their names appear below.

The advisory committee comprised:

Margaret Drew, Chairperson
Librarian
Lincoln School
Brookline, MA

Margaret Bush, formerly Network
Consultant, National Library
Service for the Blind and
Physically Handicapped
The Library of Congress
Washington, D.C.

Carol N. Euller, Librarian
Schlegel Road Elementary School
Webster, NY

Julanne M. Goode, Senior Subject
Specialist in Children's Literature
St. Louis Public Library
St. Louis, MO

Ruth H. Hadlow, Coordinator of Children's
Services
Cleveland Public Library
Cleveland, OH

Barbara Miller, formerly Coordinator of
Children's Services
Louisville Free Public Library
Louisville, KY

Diana Young, Public Library Consultant
on Children's Services
North Carolina State Library
Raleigh, NC

The following consultants participated in the voting:

Joyce E. Batchelder, Librarian
District Library Coordinator
Katonah-Lewisboro School District
Katonah, NY

Christine A. Behrmann, Children's
Materials Specialist
The New York Public Library
New York, NY

Elizabeth Breting, Director,
Children's Services
Kansas City Public Library
Kansas City, MO

Juanita Carter, Supervisor of
Library Services
Little Rock Public School District
Little Rock, AR

Julie A. Cummins, Children's
Services Consultant
Monroe County Library System
Rochester, NY

Frances C. Dean, Director
Division of Instructional Materials
Montgomery County Public Schools
Rockville, MD

Laurie Dudley, Special Services
Librarian
Abilene Public Library
Abilene, TX

Beth Greggs, Area Children's
Librarian
King County Library Dept.
Seattle, WA

Marilyn Kaye, Instructor
College of Librarianship
University of South Carolina
Columbia, SC

Amy Kellman, Head,
Children's Department
Carnegie Library of Pittsburgh
Pittsburgh, PA

Elizabeth B. Murphy, Coordinator,
Children's Services
District of Columbia Public Library
Washington, D.C.

Marylett R. Robertson, Librarian
West Hills Elementary School
Knoxville, TN

Marian Schroether, Children's Librarian
Waukegan Public Library
Waukegan, IL

Helen Tyler, Media Services Specialist
Eugene School District
Eugene, OR

Caroljean L. Wagner, Librarian
Public Library
Milwaukee, WI

Jane Walsh, Librarian
Newton Public School
Newtonville, MA

TABLE OF CONTENTS

HOW TO USE CHILDREN'S CATALOG

CHILDREN'S CATALOG is arranged in three parts: Part 1. Classified Catalog; Part 2. Author, Title, Subject, and Analytical Index; Part 3. Directory of Publishers and Distributors.

USES OF THE CATALOG

CHILDREN'S CATALOG is designed to serve several purposes:

As an aid in purchasing. The CATALOG is designed to assist in the selection and ordering of titles. Annotations are provided for each title and information is given concerning publisher and price as well as varying editions. Since Part 1 is arranged by the Dewey Decimal Classification, the CATALOG may be used as a checklist to determine those parts of the library collection which are weak and require additional material. It is important to mention that many books are susceptible to classification in more than one area. If a particular title is not found where it might be expected in the Classification, the Index in Part 2 should be checked to make certain the title is not classified elsewhere in the schedules.

It is not expected, nor would it be advisable, for a library to depend upon a single aid in book selection. Each library will have to take into account the special character of its own school and community.

As a cataloging aid. For this purpose full bibliographical information is provided in Part 1. This includes recommended subject headings based upon *Sears List of Subject Headings* and a suggested classification based upon the *Abridged Dewey Decimal Classification*.

As a reference aid. Reference work is facilitated both through the annotations in Part 1 and by the subject and analytical approach in Part 2.

As an aid in rebinding, discarding, and replacing. It is possible to see what other titles on a subject are available, a factor which often influences the decision whether to discard, rebind, or replace a book.

As an aid in library schools. The CATALOG is of use in courses which deal with book selection, particularly on the preschool and elementary levels.

Part 1.   Classified Catalog

The Classified   Catalog is arranged with the non-fiction books first, classified by the Dewey Decimal Classification in numerical order from 000 to 999. Fiction books follow and are designated by the symbol "Fic." These are then followed by the short story collections denoted by the symbol "S C" and finally the easy books which are marked "E."

Each book is listed under its main entry, which will usually be the author. For some books, however, the main entry will be under the editor, and, for others, under title. The following is a typical entry:

> **Pringle, Laurence**
> Animals and their niches; how species share resources; illus. by Leslie Morrill. Morrow 1977 64p illus $6.25, lib. bdg. $6 (3-5)
> **591.5**
>
> 1 Animals—Habits and behavior 2 Ecology
> ISBN 0-688-22127-0; 0-688-32127-5   LC 77-3636
>
> "Given limited resources in a wildlife community, how do similar species live together in the same habitat? . . . [The author] explains how each inhabitant occupies a special place that has few overlaps with others of a similar kind. It feeds on certain foods, moves at certain levels, builds its home in specific places. Thus three species of garter snakes that live on the same portion of land or five species of warblers that live in evergreen trees are not really in direct competition. Studies that set forth these and several other related findings are cited by Pringle, who in a final chapter also reflects on some unanswered questions, such as why animal niches are arranged the way they are." Booklist
>
> "The text is lucid and accurate; Pringle shows, more clearly than if he had made a statement on the subject, how painstaking and objective the scientific method is and how a body of knowledge grows through a diversity of research findings. The print is large, the realistic wash drawings are adequately captioned, and a relative index is appended." Chicago. Children's Bk Center
> Glossary: p59-60. Further reading: p61-62

In this entry the name of the author is given in the form in which it appears on the title page of the book. It is inverted and is printed in dark or bold face type.

The first part of the main body of the entry gives the title of the book *Animals and their niches*.

The information that the book is published by Morrow follows (reference to Part 3 will show that this publisher is William Morow & Company, Inc. located at 105 Madison Ave, New York, N.Y. 10016). This information, with the price, is useful in ordering books. The date 1977 is the date when this book was published. Further information records that it contains 64 pages and illustrations. It currently sells in a trade edition for $6.25 and in a library binding edition for $6. As the CATALOG grows older, however, prices should be rechecked with the publisher for possible changes. The figures (3-5) indicate that this book is useful for children in the 3d to 5th grades. It is difficult to make gereralizations as to the reading ability of children and for this reason the grading given is rather flexible. Most listings are graded, except for Easy books, professional tools for the librarian, and some reference books.

At the end of the last line in the body of the entry is the figure 591.5 in dark type. This is the classification number according to the *Abridged Dewey Decimal Classification*. 591.5 is the classification for ecology of animals.

The line "1 Animals—Habits and behavior 2 Ecology" gives the recommended subject headings for this book. All subject headings are based upon *Sears List of Subject Headings*.

Sometimes the subject or subjects assigned to the entire book will not show that there are portions of the book which deal with more specific subjects. In this case analytics are made. The book listed above contains a section dealing with Minnows. In Part 2 there will be an entry for this portion of the book under the subject heading Minnows.

There are then three notes giving a brief description of the book and its contents. The descriptive note for this example ·was taken from Booklist and the critical note was taken from the University of Chicago's Bulletin of the Center for Children's Books. Additional notes describe special features, such as the glossary and bibliography in the example. Annotations are useful in evaluating books for book selection. They are also useful in determining which of several books on the same subject are best suited for the individual reader.

Part 2. Author, Title, Subject, and Analytical Index

This is an alphabetical index of all the books entered in the CATALOG. Each book is entered under author, title if distinctive, subject, and under joint author and illustrator if any. Also included are the subject, author and title analytics for the books analyzed. The classification number is the key to the main entry of the book in Part 1. The following are index entries for the book cited above:

Author	**Pringle, Laurence** Animals and their niches (3-5)	**591.5**
Title	**Animals** and their niches. Pringle, L.	**591.5**
Subject	**Ecology** Pringle, L. Animals and their niches	**591.5**
Subject Analytic	**Minnows** *See pages in the following book*: Pringle, L. Animals and their niches p30-40 (3-5)	**591.5**
Illustrator	**Morrill, Leslie** (illus) Pringle, L. Animals and their niches	**591.5**

Examples of other types of entries:

Joint Author	**Adamson, Wendy Wriston** (jt. auth.) Gadler, S. J. Sun power: facts about solar energy	**621.47**
Author Analytic	**Alexander, Lloyd** How the cat swallowed thunder *In* Just for fun p3-12	**S C**
Title Analytic	**How** the cat swallowed thunder. Alexander, L. *In* Just for fun p3-12	**S C**
Uniform Title	**Brave little tailor** Grimm, J. The brave little tailor *In* The Andrew Lang Fairy tale treasury p64-72 **398.2** *In* Blue fairy book p306-16 **398.2** Grimm, J. The gallant tailor *In* Grimm, J. Household stories p109-17 **398.2** Grimm, J. The valiant little tailor *In* Grimm, J. The complete Grimm's fairy tales p112-20 **398.2** *In* Grimm, J. Fairy tales of the Brothers Grimm p71-80 **398.2** Grimm, J. The valiant tailor *In* Grimm, J. Grimm's Fairy tales p44-53 **398.2** Thane, A. The brave little tailor *In* Thane, A. Plays from famous stories and fairy tales p397-413 **812** *See also* Jack and the varmints; Johnny Gloke	

Part 3. Directory of Publishers and Distributors

The name of the publisher or distributor is given in abbreviated form in each entry. This Directory lists the abbreviation and then provides the full name and address of the publisher or distributor.

PART 1

CLASSIFIED CATALOG

Outline of Classification

Reproduced below is the Second Summary of the Dewey Decimal Classification.* As Part 1 of this Catalog is arranged according to this classification, the outline will serve as a table of contents for it. Please note, however, that the inclusion of this outline is not to be considered as a substitute for consulting the Dewey Decimal Classification itself.

*Reproduced from the Abridged DEWEY Decimal Classification, Edition 11 (1979) by permission of Forest Press Division, Lake Placid Education Foundation, owner of copyright.

CHILDREN'S CATALOG

FOURTEENTH EDITION, 1981

CLASSIFIED CATALOG

000 GENERALITIES

001.51 Communication

Neal, Harry Edward
Communication: from stone age to space age; illus. with photographs. [Rev. ed.] Messner 1974 192p illus lib. bdg. $7.29 (5 and up) 000.51

1 Communication—History
ISBN 0-671-32652-X   LC 74-156858
First published 1960
This historical survey of human communications describes the development and functions of languages, alphabets, numbers, writing, printing, newspapers, radio, telegraph, various forms of telecommunication visual arts, and music
Bibliography: p183-84. Sources of further information: p185

Stewig, John Warren
Sending messages; Richard D. Bradley, photographer. Houghton 1978 64p illus lib bdg. $6.95 (2-4)   001.51

1 Communication
ISBN 0-395-24387-4   LC 77-26110
"Various means of communication are presented in pictures and words—from the most primitive cave paintings to the sophisticated Labanotation used in dance choreography. Both personal and professional message systems are explored: talking, writing, mime, braille, chemical symbols, traffic signals, and an orchestra conductor's hand movements, among others." Horn Bk
"There are multiple visuals per page, and potential use for class or group presentations makes this worthwhile as a resource." Booklist

001.53 Cybernetics

Silverstein, Alvin
The world of bionics [by] Alvin Silverstein and Virginia Silverstein. Methuen [1980 c1979] 116p illus $7.95 (5 and up)   001.53

1 Bionics
ISBN 0-416-30221-1   LC 79-19024
The authors "begin by focusing on Steve Austin, television's 'Six Million Dollar Man,' and discuss the various bionic attributes of this fictional superhero. Following this catchy introduction, they get down to serious science as they present a historical review of medical progress in the creation and use of artificial organs. From 'seeing' machines to working robots, realities and possibilities are described in fairly technical terms, but with sufficient explanation to make the elaborate and complicated research and experimentation understandable to the intelligent reader." Booklist

001.56 Nonlinguistic communication

Adkins, Jan
Symbols: a silent language; written, designed and illus. by Jan Adkins. Walker & Co. 1978 31p illus $7.95, lib. bdg. $7.85 (4-6)   001.56

1 Signs and symbols
ISBN 0-8027-6330-8; 0-8027-6331-6   LC 78-2977
"Symbols play a bigger role in our lives than we realize, says Adkins, and submits hundreds of examples to prove his point: the dashboard of a car, road signs, weather maps, blueprints . . .

coats of arms, and corporate trademarks. He depicts the symbols in red, white, and black, including a written label and brief narrative with each. Some confusion results from combining semaphores and Braille markings for different letters on the same page, or musical notations and playing cards; and a few of the inclusions (black criss-crossed lines on a red field supposedly signifying 'house') are puzzling because they lack explanation. However, the variety is entertaining." Booklist

Amon, Aline
Talking hands; Indian sign language; written and illus. by Aline Amon. Doubleday 1968 80p illus map $4.95, lib. bdg. $5.90 (3-6)   001.56

1 Indians of North America—Sign language
ISBN 0-385-08891-4; 0-385-09425-6   LC 68-10123
"Beginning with the names of the fingers and basic positions of the hands, the author shows how to put words together into sentences, ask questions, tell stories and carry on conversations in sign language. The illustrations throughout are clear and explicit, and the index lists slightly more than 200 words." Sch Library J
"Irresistible as a combination of fun and education, [this book] is a godsend to both harried parents and restless offspring." NY Times Bk Rev

Fronval, George
Indian signs and signals, by George Fronval and Daniel Dubois. Sterling [1979 c1978] 80p illus $12.95, lib. bdg. $11.69 (4-6)   001.56

1 Indians of North America—Sign language
ISBN 0-8069-2720-8; 0-8069-2721-6   LC 78-57792
Original French edition, 1976
"Translated by E. W. Egan; photographs by George C. Hight; illustrations by Jean Marcellin; period paintings by George Catlin." Verso of title page
This is "an important and valuable book in large format on American Indian sign language, much of which is still used today by native Americans. The signs are clearly illustrated by photographs of members of a contemporary Kiowa family demonstrating their use. At the end of the book is a small section covering smoke signals, trail signs, the language of feathers, the language of blankets, and the use of body paint. This book belongs in the library of everyone interested in Indians." Children's Bk Rev Serv

Hofsinde, Robert
Indian sign language; written and illus. by Robert Hofsinde (Gray-Wolf). Morrow 1956 96p illus lib.. bdg. $5.52 (3-6)   001.56

1 Indians of North America—Sign language
ISBN 0-688-31610-7   LC 56-5178
"This book shows how to form the gestures representing about five hundred words [in Indian sign language] ranging from familiar terms, such as 'man,' 'beaver,' and 'rapids,' to modern additions like 'motion picture' and 'coffee.' The key words are printed in heavy type, and are accompanied by concise directions and explanatory sketches. Words related in meaning are arranged in groups, and there is an alphabetical index." Ontario Library Rev

Lubell, Winifred
Picture signs & symbols, by Winifred & Cecil Lubell. Parents Mag. Press 1972 64p illus maps lib. bdg. $5.41 (2-4)   001.56

1 Signs and symbols
ISBN 0-8193-0577-4   LC 76-39742
"A Stepping-stone book"
The authors "explain the use of pictures as symbols of information and communication. Beginning with a general introduction, the . . . text progresses to highway signs, Olympic game symbols,

1

Lubell, Winifred—*Continued*

Indian signs, etc. Why flags, mascots, animals, and hands are used in symbols is discussed. There are also chapters on holiday and map symbols and a final section of the newly created ecology signs." Sch Library J

"Clear and attractive drawings are carefully integrated with the text in a book that is useful as well as interesting, and that may stimulate readers to a further interest in symbols and communication." Chicago. Children's Bk Center

Myller, Rolf

Symbols & their meaning. Atheneum Pubs. 1978 unp illus $9.95 (4 and up)   001.56

1 Signs and symbols
ISBN 0-689-30638-5   LC 77-17015

Title on cover: Symbols
Illustrated by the author

"Forty types of symbols are illustrated, with explanations of their meanings and origins appearing on the facing page. Included are Morse Code, braille, hand language, semaphore, musical and chemical notation, chess pieces and coats of arms, signs of the zodiac, and religious symbols. Examples of Chinese writing and even a story w[...] in hieroglyphics are also pictured. Flags are discussed, but since the book's illustrations are in black, white, red, grey, and pink, the U.S. flag is not pictured." Sch Library J

"This isn't the first or only book about signs and symbols, but it's one of the best, for several reasons: the text moves from simple symbols to more complicated ones, it's written with clarity and humor, it gives a broad conception of the many different kinds of symbols used for quick communication or labeling, and it is very handsome. The pages are . . . laid out with a fine sense of design." Chicago. Children's Bk Center

001.64   Electronic data processing

Halacy, D. S.

What makes a computer work? By D. S. Halacy, Jr. Pictures by Nat Goldstein. Little 1973 64p illus lib. bdg. $5.95 (2-4)   001.64

1 Computers
ISBN 0-316-33830-3   LC 73-7909

"An Atlantic Monthly Press book"

This "survey explains computer functions to beginners. The essential mechanisms of computer operations—arithmetic, memory, input-output, and control—are outlined while short explanations of the binary number system, the programming process, the development of counting machines, and some jobs of modern computers are given. For use in classrooms, particularly as a push-off point for study undertaken at higher age levels. Black-and-white drawings supplement the text; a combination index and glossary is appended." Booklist

Lewis, Bruce

Meet the computer; pictures by Leonard Kessler. Dodd 1977 47p illus lib. bdg. $5.25 (3-5)   001.64

1 Computers
ISBN 0-396-07456-1   LC 77-2856

This is an "introductory treatment of computers and computer processing (but not computer languages). . . . There is an explanation of the number system used by computers (not identified as the binary number system) plus . . . simplified descriptions of many positive scientific and non-scientific applications of computers." Sch Library J

"Technical aspects of computers remain in the background. . . . Lewis spends time dispelling awe of the machines ('. . . there is nothing magic about a computer') and pointing out how 'computers today are part of just about everything you do.' Mundane pen cartoons provide ordinary illustrations." Booklist

Srivastava, Jane Jonas

Computers; illus. by James and Ruth McCrea. Crowell 1972 32p illus (Young math bks) $6.95, lib. bdg. $6.89 (2-4)   001.64

1 Computers
ISBN 0-690-20850-2; 0-690-20851-0   LC 70-171009

"The computer is compared to a five-ring circus —the five essential parts being input, binary language, memory bank, output, and control units. The reader is told about flowcharts, for example, and then asked to make his own. Throughout the book the information is reinforced by activities or concrete examples shown by good illustrations. All in all, a young reader would have his curiosity whetted after reading 'Computers.' " Appraisal

001.9   Controversial knowledge

Baumann, Elwood D.

The Devil's Triangle. Watts, F. 1979 117p illus maps lib. bdg. $6.90 (6 and up)   001.9

1 Bermuda Triangle
ISBN 0-531-01094-5   LC 75-22020

"Baumann relates some of the many disappearances of planes, boats, and ships, plus accounts of unexplained explosions in the now-infamous Bermuda Triangle. Recounted are the mysterious losses of five U.S. Navy bombers in December of 1945, the disappearance of the ships 'Cyclops' and the 'Carroll A. Deering.' . . . To his credit, the author offers no farfetched answers to the mysteries. . . . This is presented without the sensationalism that often accompanies such titles." Sch Library J

Bibliography: p113-14

Bendick, Jeanne

The mystery of the Loch Ness monster. McGraw 1976 128p illus maps $5.95, lib. bdg. $6.95 (5 and up)   001.9

1 Loch Ness monster
ISBN 0-07-004496; 0-07-004497-X   LC 76-18083

Provided is "information about early sightings, the stirring of wide belief and of scientific investigations that began in the 1930's, and the apparent corroboration by computer-sharpened photographs, experiments with sonar and echo-sounding equipment, and underwater television cameras of 'some' kind of creature living in the cold waters of the loch." Chicago. Children's Bk Center

The author "does a fine job of applying scientific research to such an ephemeral subject as monster-tracking." Booklist

Bibliography: p123-25

Blumberg, Rhoda

UFO. Watts, F. 1977 63p illus lib. bdg. $5.90 (5 and up)   001.9

1 Flying saucers
ISBN 0-531-00397-3   LC 76-50931

"A First book"

"Starting with bizarre news stories, Blumberg proceeds to ask six key questions around which much of the book revolves. Tracing UFOs through history from an Egyptian description dating back 3500 years ago to the Romans, to Scotland and through the Middle Ages, the author finally notes that in the United States, UFO sightings date back 100 years." AAAS Sci Bks & Films

"Although a few pages at the end of the book suggest that many scientists have open minds about unidentified flying objects and wish to pursue observation and investigation, most of this book is devoted to reporting on the history and debunking of those reports that have been logged, both in the past and in contemporary sightings. . . . Blumberg also points out some obviously invented reports by pranksters, or faked objects. While the subject is always intriguing, the book offers little that is new." Chicago. Children's Bk Center

Bibliography: p60-61

Branley, Franklyn M.

A book of flying saucers for you; illus. by Leonard Kessler. Crowell 1973 72p illus lib. bdg. $8.79 (2-4)   001.9

1 Flying saucers
ISBN 0-690-15189-6   LC 72-78278

The author describes and offers some explanations of unidentified flying objects, and considers the possibility of life on other planets

"Cheerful, appealing wash drawings full of point, looking rather like the paintings on the schoolroom walls, and a clear, brief text to match make up this small book for young grade school readers. There are photographs of flying hats and a Mars crater and useful lists of the dates of bright planet apparitions and meteor showers. The whole vexed

Branley, Franklyn M.—*Continued*
topic—hoaxes, the will to believe, Ezekiel, balloons, St Elmo's fire and all—is spelled out in simple language without either rancor or credulousness. . . . The experienced astronomical author has made a model of honest approach and genuine content." Scientific Am

Cohen, Daniel
The ancient visitors. Doubleday 1976 213p illus $6.95 (6 and up) 001.9
1 Civilization. Ancient 2 Flying saucers
ISBN 0-385-09786-7 LC 75-21220
"An impartial, objective and critical analysis of various theories that earth has been visited by 'extraterrestrial intelligences' (ETIs). With a colloquial, personal writing style, Cohen skims the speculations of Fort, Lowell, Downing and other ETI believers; but he concentrates on the major-domo of ETI visitation—Erich von Dániken." AAAS Sci Bks & Films
Bibliography: p203-06

The world of UFOs. Lippincott 1978 160p illus $7.95 (6 and up) 001.9
1 Flying saucers
ISBN 0-397-31780-8 LC 77-11659
Cohen discusses some of the incidents and controversies connected with reports of unidentified flying objects. He "supports official explanations for reported sightings (temperature inversions, ball lightning, etc.). He elaborates on the investigative work of individuals and groups . . . [and presents] the conclusions of the Condon Committee and the Air Force's Project Bluebook researchers." Sch Library J
"The author seems to have written a balanced as well as entertaining book on the history of the UFO social phenomenon. It is not a definitive work, but it is complete enough to give the reader a solidly based and reasonable opinion of what has gone on." Horn Bk
Selected bibliography: p154-56

Cusack, Michael J.
Is there a Bermuda Triangle? Science and sea mysteries; photographs, maps. Messner 1976 126p illus maps lib. bdg. $7.29 (5 and up) 001.9
1 Bermuda Triangle
ISBN 0-671-32783-6 LC 76-2717
The author "describes, in the first four chapters of the book, the highly dramatic losses of air and ocean ships, all in mysterious circumstances, over many decades, and goes on to discuss the theories of a 'Bermuda Triangle.' Each theory proposed an area of the sea (usually triangular) in which inexplicable, sudden forces caused ships and airplanes to vanish. But the author goes on to report on the detailed examinations made by doubting researchers and scientists (one 'lost' ship never existed, another sailed from one Pacific port to another, etc.) and to explain the various meteorological and oceanographic phenomena of the area: sudden waterspouts, nova storms, ocean eddies, hurricanes, and marine and magnetic disruptions. His thesis is that all or any of these may account for the lost craft, and that all of the 'Bermuda Triangle' theories that imply supernatural or extraterrestrial forces are not valid." Chicago. Children's Bk Center
"Lucid and to the point, the text informs but doesn't purport to have all the answers and deliberately avoids much of the sensationalism that has characterized so many . . . titles on the subject." Booklist
Suggested further reading: p120-22

Knight, David C.
Those mysterious UFOs; the story of unidentified flying objects; illus. with photographs. Parents Mag. Press 1975 64p illus $5.95, lib. bdg. $5.41 (4 and up) 001.9
1 Flying saucers
ISBN 0-8193-0959-1; 0-8193-0820-X LC 74-31465
"Finding-out books"
"This book is a compilation of UFO sightings including: the Ezekiel story, the 'airship' of 1897, the 'foo' fighters, the Mt. Rainier sightings, the Mantell incident, Project Blue Book, the Condon Report, man-made satellites, the Washington flap of 1952, Father Gill's humanoids, the Hopkinsville monster, and the Georgia gray-skinned creatures of 1973." Sci and Children

"Excellent use is made of photographs and drawings, and an index is provided. The text is interesting and clearly written, and the book tends to convince the reader that many UFOs are real and have not been adequately explained." AAAS Sci Bks & Films

UFOs: a pictorial history from antiquity to the present. McGraw 1979 192p illus $7.95 (5 and up) 001.9
1 Flying saucers
ISBN 0-07-035103-1 LC 78-23653
The author has compiled an "extensive collection of UFO photographs . . . along with brief recapitulations of the history of sightings from the ancient 'astronauts' of Biblical times through the 19th-Century sightings of mysterious 'air ships' to sightings since the 1950s. Well over 100 photographs, many from the recently declassified Project Blue Book files, are reproduced here: many are acknowledged fakes, others were designated hoaxes, reflections, processing errors, and the like by Blue Book investigators. The majority were simply written off as inexplicable because of 'insufficient data' and several were actually accepted as genuine sightings of 'unidentified flying objects' (although not necessarily of an extraterrestrial nature). While the text is scanty and the captions often frustratingly incomplete, the photographs alone make this a worthwhile addition to collections on UFO phenomena." Sch Library J
Bibliography: p187. Glossary: p188

Place, Marian T.
On the track of Bigfoot; illus. with photographs. Dodd 1974 156p illus map $4.95 (5 and up) 001.9
1 Sasquatch
ISBN 0-396-06883-9 LC 73-15375
This is a "book about 'monsters' of the Pacific Northwest, which have long been the object of much curiosity and search by many people, including some scientists. [The creature is] variously known as Bigfoot, Sasquatch and Oh-Mah. . . . [It] is, reportedly, huge (over 8ft. tall), humanlike, two-legged, covered with hair, a resident of remote forests and very shy of humans." Sci Bks
"By collecting many of the stories people have been telling each other about the bigfoot over the years and retelling them in readable detail, Marian T. Place has produced a fascinating book for young readers. . . . [Her] accounts—without much attempt at scholarly assessment—become redundant; but, for once, that is part of the point: If all of those different people at all those different times were hallucinating, why did they all describe such similar creatures? In fact the book has substance." NY Times Bk Rev
Bibliography: p151-52

Rabinowich, Ellen
The Loch Ness monster; illus. by Sally Law. Watts, F. 1979 47p illus map lib. bdg. $5.90 (3-5) 001.9
1 Loch Ness monster
ISBN 0-531-02274-9 LC 78-21880
"An Easy-read fact book"
"Rabinowich briefly and simply discusses various theories and facts surrounding the possible existence of the 'most famous monster in the world.' Accounts of eye-witness reports, old legends, and actual underwater explorations are given along with ideas of how the monster got into Loch Ness and why conditions there make tracking difficult. In addition to black-and-white and color photographs (supposedly of the monster) and diagrams showing location and terrain, unlabeled drawings of grotesque creatures depict, one must assume, various imagined monsters of the ages. The easy-to-read style facilitates use by upper elementary students with reading problems." Booklist

011 General bibliographies

American Library Association. Children's Services Division. 1940-1970 Notable Children's Book Committee
Notable children's books, 1940-1970. A.L.A. 1974 84p pa $3 011
1 Children's literature—Bibliography 2 Books and reading—Best books
ISBN 0-8389-3182-0 LC 77-641

American Library Association. Children's Services Division. 1940-1970 Notable Children's Book Committee—*Continued*

Replaces: Notable children's books, 1940-1959, published 1966

"Titles chosen as Notable Children's Books in the years 1940-1970 have been reevaluated as to enduring qualities by the ALA/CSD 1940-1970 Notable Children's Book Committee and listed here alphabetically by the author with short annotations. Included is a title and illustrator index." Booklist

Association for Childhood Education International

Bibliography: books for children. The Association pa $3.75   011

1 Children's literature—Bibliography   2 Books and reading—Best books

Triennial. First published 1937 with title: Bibliography of books for children. Frequency of publication varies

This is a selected list of books, classified and annotated. The books are grouped by subject or form and suggested age levels are given. An index of titles and authors and a directory of publishers are included

Best books for children; preschool through the middle grades; ed. by John T. Gillespie and Christine B. Gilbert. 2d ed. Bowker 1981 635p $29.95   011

1 Children's literature—Bibliography
ISBN 0-8352-1332-3   LC 80-29095

First published 1959; in new format 1978

This bibliography includes over 10,000 books. Each entry includes bibliographic information and a brief annotation. The book is divided into sections by broad subject

"Although this volume has many of the problems that librarians find in the 'best' lists on which it is based, perhaps the strengths and weaknesses of the lists balance each other, so that those who want composite judgments will find this work a convenient source of advice." Cur Ref Bks [review of 1978 edition]

The Best in children's books; the University of Chicago guide to children's literature, 1966-1972. Univ. of Chicago Press 1973 484p $12.50, pa $6.50   011

1 Children's literature—Bibliography   2 Books and reading—Best books 3 Books—Reviews
ISBN 0-226-78057-0; 0-226-78058-9   LC 73-77140

"A guide designed to aid librarians, teachers and parents in selecting from the best children's literature published 1966-1972. The 1400 reviews, done by the editor of the University of Chicago's 'Bulletin of the Center for Children's Books,' are listed alphabetically by author, give full bibliographic information, and are annotated. The appendix gives addresses of American and British publishers of listed children's books and there are several indexes for different approaches to the literature: title, curricular, reading level, subject and type of literature." Wis Library Bul

"The book has not been planned as a balanced list in respect to an individual grade or age, or to subject or genre. The editor's selections have been made primarily on the basis of literary quality, with representation of subjects as a secondary consideration." Introduction

The Best in children's books; the University of Chicago guide to children's literature, 1973-1978; written and ed. by Zena Sutherland. Univ. of Chicago Press 1980 547p $17.50 011

1 Children's literature—Bibliography   2 Books and reading—Best books 3 Books—Reviews
ISBN 0-226-78059-7   LC 79-24331

Similar in format to the first volume, entered above, this volume covers an additional 1400 titles published between 1973 and 1978

"The reviews included here have been selected by the editor from those already published in the 'Bulletin of the Center for Children's Books.' . . . Since some of the late titles of 1972 were not available for inclusion in the previous edition, they have been included here. . . . The practice of using an asterisk to denote books of special distinction was not instituted until September 1975 (the first issue of volume 29), and is therefore missing from some earlier titles which surely merit such recognition." Suggestions for Using This Book

The Best of the best; picture, children's and youth books from 110 countries or languages. 2d enl. ed. Verlag Dokumentation [distributed by Bowker] 1976 344p illus $19.95   011

1 Children's literature—Bibliography   2 Books and reading—Best books
ISBN 0-7940-3253-5   LC 77-142169

First published 1971

Edited by Walter Scherf for the International Jugendbibliothek, Munich

"A compilation of more than 4,000 titles representing some 60 languages and selected by librarians at the International Youth Library in Munich and by children's literature specialists throughout the world. Entries are organized alphabetically by country, and within each section are arranged by author in groupings by age: 3-6, 7-9, 10-12, and 13-15. Imprints include author, title in the original language as well as in German and English, publication date, and name and city of publisher. There are no annotations. Sample illustrations are interspersed throughout." Booklist

"Librarians will find this a valuable selection tool of international scope for development of foreign language collections." Top of the News

Booklist

Reference and subscription books reviews. A.L.A.   011

1 Reference books—Bibliography   2 Reference books—Reviews

Reprinted from issues of the Booklist

Volumes covering the years 1956-1968 published beginning 1961 with title: Subscription Books Bulletin reviews. First published with this title 1970

Starting with volume covering the years 1974-1975 biennial publication pattern changed to annual format

Volumes 1956-1960, 1960-1962, 1962-1964, 1964-1966, 1966-1968 o.p. 1980; 1968-1970 pa $3 (ISBN 0-8389-0092-5); 1970-1972 pa $4 (ISBN 0-8389-0143-3); 1972-1974 pa $8.50 (ISBN 0-8389-0194-8); 1974-1975 pa $10 (ISBN 0-8389-0229-4); 1975-1976 pa $10 (ISBN 0-8389-0231-6); 1976-1977 pa $11 (ISBN 0-8389-3207-X); 1977-1978 pa $15 (ISBN 0-8389-3221-5); 1978-1979 pa $20 (ISBN 0-8389-3237-1)

These reviews prepared by the Reference and Subscription Books Review Committee of the A.L.A. describe and evaluate encyclopedias, dictionaries, biographical reference works, atlases and gazeteers, directories, yearbooks and annuals and statistical compendia as well as bibliographical reference sources and periodical indexes

Booklist. A.L.A. $32 per year   011

1 Books and reading—Best books   2 Books—Reviews
ISSN 0006-7385

A semi-monthly guide to current books except for August, which has a single issue—the annual index. The Booklist was first published 1905 with title: A.L.A. Booklist. It combined in September, 1956 with Subscription Books Bulletin. In September 1969 it resumed the title: Booklist

This "is a selected, annotated list of recent publications recommended especially for small and medium-sized libraries. Arranged by broad classes, fiction, books for young adults, children's books, new editions and series, U.S. government publications, pamphlets and paperbacks. Beginning with v66 (1969) audiovisual materials are reviewed regularly. Complete bibliographical information is given for each entry, including price. Annotations describe, evaluate, and indicate the kind of library for which the book is recommended." Sheehy. Guide to Ref Bks. 9th edition

Books for children, 1960-1965; as selected and reviewed by The Booklist and Subscription Books Bulletin, September 1960 through August 1965. A.L.A. 1966 [c1965] 477p $10   011

1 Catalogs, Classified   2 Children's literature—Bibliography 3 Books and reading—Best books
ISBN 0-8389-0016-X   LC 66-29507

A compilation of 3,068 titles listed and recommended for purchase in the Children's Books section of: The Booklist and Subscription Books Bulletin. The original "Booklist" information is given for each title

"Arranged by a modified Dewey Decimal classification, with a separate biography section and two sections on fiction, one being on easy and picture

Books for children, 1960-1965—*Continued*
books, it provides a useful source of bibliographical
information, with annotations of content and a
critical and comparative evaluation for each title.
Reader interest, grade level, classification number,
and subject headings are also supplied. A dictionary index to author, subject, and title is appended." Cur Ref Bks
Continued from 1966 to 1972 by the following
annual supplements, also available from A.L.A.,
with the title: Books for children, preschool
through junior high school: 1965-1966 pa $2 (ISBN
0-8389-0017-8); 1966-1967 pa $2.25 (ISBN 0-8389-
0018-6); 1967-1968 pa $3 (ISBN 0-8389-0019-4); 1968-
1969 pa $3.50 (ISBN 0-8389-0082-8); 1969-1970 pa
$3.50 (ISBN 0-8389-0099-2; 1970-1971 pa $5 (ISBN
0-8389-0119-0)

Building a children's literature collection. A
suggested basic reference collection for academic libraries, and A suggested basic collection of children's books. Rev. ed. by
Harriet B. Quimby & Rosemary Weber.
Choice 1978 42p (Choice Bibliographical essay
ser) pa $4.75   011
1 Children's literature—Bibliography
ISBN 0-914492-04-7   LC 78-15886
First published 1975
These two essays, which first appeared in the
November and December 1974 issues of Choice,
"were designed to give professional, knowledgeable
guidance to librarians in charge of collections which
support academic programs in children's literature.
The first essay discussed reference books in the
field of children's literature under such headings as
Texts, History of Children's Literature, Authors,
Illustrators and Illustration, Awards and Prizes,
and International Childen's Literature. The second
essay was concerned with actual books for children and encompassed Fiction, Picture and Easy
Books, Folklore, Biography, Poetry, and non-fiction. . . . Over one thousand titles, with complete
bibliographic information, are included; author and
title indexes have been added." Horn Bk [re-
view of 1975 edition]

Children's books. Library of Congress [for
sale by Supt. of Docs] pa $1.25   011
1 Children's literature—Bibliography   2 Books
and reading—Best books
ISSN 0069-3464   LC 65-60015
Annual. First published 1964
Compiled by Virginia Haviland, chief of the Children's Literature Center, Library of Congress, with
the assistance of a committee of children's librarians and media specialists
This annotated list of books for preschool through
junior high school age children is arranged by
categories such as: picture books and picture stories; stories for the middle group; fiction for older
readers; folklore; poetry, rhymes, songs and plays;
arts and hobbies; biography; history, people, and
places; nature and science. Reading levels are indicated

Children's books of international interest; a
selection from four decades of American publishing. 2d ed. Virginia Haviland, editor.
A.L.A. 1978 77p pa $4   011
1 Children's literature—Bibliography   2 Books
and reading—Best books
ISBN 0-8389-0258-8   LC 77-18509
First published 1972
Based on the annual lists prepared by the International Relations Committee of the American Library Association's Association for Library Service
to children (formerly the Children's Services Division) entitled: U.S.A. children's books of international interest (previously entitled: Books recommended for translation), which are intended to promote the international exchange of children's books
published in the United States which are considered to have both literary value and universality
of interest
"The list has been updated and reevaluated, and
titles no longer in print have been deleted. Entries, divided into books for younger and older
children and categorized by subject [including picture books; first reading; fiction; folklore; poetry;
biography; history; peoples, and places; the arts;
science and nature] have short annotations and list
grade levels." Booklist

Children's books too good to miss [by] May
Hill Arbuthnot [and others]. Press of Case
Western Reserve Univ. [distributed by Univ.
Press Book Service] illus pa $4.95   011
1 Children's literature—Bibliography   2 Books
and reading—Best books
First published 1948. Periodically revised
"A highly selective list with critical appraisals
of 230 books of 'outstanding merit.' Introductory
matter discusses the evaluation of children's books.
An other section briefly discusses 'the artist and
children's books.' Small format. Illustrated with
black and white reproduction from children's
books." Wynar. Guide to Ref Bks for Sch Media
Centers [review of 1971 edition]

Children's literature; a guide to reference
sources; prepared under the direction of
Virginia Haviland. Lib. of Congress [distri-
buted by Supt. of Docs.] 1966 341p illus
$5.45   011
1 Children's literature—Bibliography   2 Reference books   LC 66-62734
"As a guide to reference sources for children's
literature, this annotated bibliography describes
books, articles, and pamphlets selected on the
basis of their estimated usefulness to adults concerned with the creation, reading, or study of
children's books. Children's literature is here considered to be books for boys and girls up to 14
years of age, or in grades through the eighth."
Preface
"The volume is well organized under such topics
as history and criticism, authorship, illustration,
bibliography, books and children, with briefer sections on international and national studies from
other countries. The clarity of its annotations, the
analytical entries for important parts of general
works, the inclusion of Library of Congress location symbols, the author, title, subject indexes,
and the discriminating judgment with which the
selections were made make this an indispensable
bibliography for all interested in children's literature." Cur Ref Bks

Children's literature; a guide to reference
sources; first supplement; comp. by Virginia
Haviland with the assistance of Margaret N.
Coughlan. Lib. of Congress [distributed by
Supt. of Docs.] 1972 315p illus $5.50   011
1 Children's literature—Bibliography   2 Reference books
ISBN 0-8444-0022-X   LC 66-62734
A supplement to: Children's literature, entered
above, this contains the same type of bibliographic
information
This "new selective annotated list contains 746
titles issued from 1966 through 1969 and older
items not available [for the earlier volume. It also]
. . . describes books, articles, and pamphlets related to the creation, reading, or study of children's books, citing both domestic and foreign
publications. The Library of Congress plans regular supplements to the first volume at perhaps
five-year intervals." Top of the News

Children's literature; a guide to reference
sources; second supplement; comp. by Virginia Haviland with the assistance of Margaret N. Coughlan. Lib. of Congress [dis-
tributed by Supt. of Docs.] 1977 413p illus
$7.75   011
1 Children's literature—Bibliography   2 Reference books
ISBN 0-8444-0215-X   LC 66-62734
A continuation, in the same format, of the main
volume and first supplement entered above, this
volume lists an additional 929 titles, mostly published from 1970 to 1974 but also including some
1969 titles omitted from the previous supplement

Dreyer, Sharon Spredemann
The bookfinder; a guide to children's literature about the needs and problems of youth
aged 2-15. Am. Guidance Service 1977 various
pagings $28.50   011
1 Children's literature—Bibliography   2 Bibliotherapy 3 Child psychology—Bibliography
ISBN 0-913476-45-5   LC 78-105919

Dreyer, Sharon S.—*Continued*

This volume consists of "two separately paged parts bound side-by-side as a 'split-page' book. The top section (pp. 1-649) contains the table of contents, subject index, author index, and title index (plus publishers directory) to all titles described in the section below. . . . The main section contains the introduction to the guide and its use and the 1,031 annotations, arranged alphabetically by author. The guide describes and categorizes current children's books according to some 450 psychological, behavioral, and developmental topics of concern to children and young adolescents (ages 2 through 15). . . . Each annotation contains a full bibliographic entry; the main subject heading (primary theme) followed by secondary themes; synopsis; commentary on the book's potential uses, limitations or strengths, literary merit, or special qualifications of the author, sequels, etc.; reading level; adaptations into other formats." Am Ref Bks Annual, 1978

"Most of the volumes described are fiction, although some significant biographies and other nonfiction books are included. Also includes . . . an explanation of the history and uses of bibliotherapy; a professional reading list of selected books and articles for further reading about bibliotherapy; a listing of other subject bibliographies of children's books; and examples of use of 'The Bookfinder' with individuals and groups." Rdng Teacher

"This is a big book, both in size and in what it attempts to do, and it is worth every cent of its substantial price. Anyone who deals with books and children—librarians, teachers, parents, counselors, others—will find in its [annotations and subject index] . . . a gold mine of information." Top of the News

The **Elementary** school library collection; a guide to books and other media, phases 1-2-3. Bro-Dart Foundation $39.95   **011**

1 Catalogs, Classified   2 Children's literature—Bibliography   3 Audio-visual materials—Catalogs   4 School libraries—Catalogs

Annual. First published 1965

Editors: 1st-8th editions: Mary V. Gaver; 9th-10th editions: Phyllis Van Orden; 11th edition: Phyllis Van Orden and Lois Winkel; 12th edition: Lois Winkel

This bibliography lists trade books, "audio-visual titles, plus periodicals, reference books, and professional tools. Keyed for first, second, and third purchase, it is arranged by Dewey classification. Entries provide bibliographic information, a brief annotation, approximate reading level, and suggested subject headings to be used by the cataloger. Three separate indexes appear in Section II: Author Index, Title Index, and Subject Index." Peterson. Ref Bks for Elem and Jr High Sch Libraries [review of 1973 edition]

For younger readers: braille and talking books. Lib. of Congress. National Library Service for the Blind and Physically Handicapped pa gratis   **011**

1 Blind, Books for the   2 Talking books   3 Children's literature—Bibliography
ISSN 0093-2825   LC 73-4220

Biennial. First published 1964 for the Library of Congress, Division for the Blind and Physically Handicapped, by the American Foundation for the Blind

"The National Library Service for the Blind and Physically Handicapped provides books and magazines for individuals who have problems reading because of a visual or physical limitation, temporary or permanent. Thousands of books on cassette, disc, and in braille are available on loan through a network of cooperating libraries. . . . Books and equipment are delivered by mail. No postage is required to borrow or return any materials. 'Talking Book Topics and Braille Book Review,' two bi-monthly magazines, inform readers of books and magazines added to the program. . . . Eligibility for the program is determined by the inability to see well enough to read a conventional print book or to hold a book and turn pages." About the Free Reading Program

This catalog lists braille, disc, and cassette books which have been announced in Braille Book Review and Talking Book Topics. Its annotated entries, which include grading (preschool to 9), are arranged in a non-fiction section, which is subdivided into broad subject areas, a fiction section

subdivided by themes and genres, a section of materials for very young readers, and a Spanish language section. Author/title indexes for each type of material (cassette, disc, and braille) are included, as are loan order forms

Jordan, Alice M.

Children's classics; with lsit of recommended editions by Paul Heins. 5th ed. Horn Bk. 1976 16p illus pa $2   **011**

1 Children's literature—Bibliography   2 Books and reading—Best book   3 Children's literature—History and criticism
ISBN 0-87675-136-2   LC 78-274608

This article first appeared in The Horn Book Magazine of February 1947. The booklist of classics first prepared by Alice M. Jordan was revised by Helen Adams Masten in 1952, 1960, and 1967, and by Paul Heins in 1976

"An aid in selecting editions of the classics to buy for school or library. The list contains an article by Miss Jordan, illustrations from some of the books, as well as a list of recommended editions . . . with publication dates and prices [given]." Library J [review of the 1967 edition]

Junior high school library catalog. 4th ed. 1980 Ed. by Gary L. Bogart and Richard H. Isaacson. Wilson, H.W. 1980 939p $62   **011**

1 Catalogs, Classified   2 School libraries—Catalogs   4 School libraries (High school)—Catalogs
ISBN 0-8242-10652-5   LC 80-53462

"Standard catalog series"

Kept up to date by annual supplements which are included in the cost of the main catalog

First published 1965

Contents: Part 1. Classified catalog, Part 2. Author, title, subject, and analytical index; Part 3. Directory of publishers and distributors

he fourth edition catalogs 3,775 books and includes 9,061 subject and author and title analytical entries. The voting list for this edition was compiled by an advisory committee of distinguished librarians and was then submitted to a group of consultants who made the final selection of titles. The format is similar to that of Children's Catalog

This catalog "attempts to bridge the gap between elementary and senior high level reading materials. In this volume the analytical entries in the Author, Title, Subject, and Analytical index are valuable for locating specific titles in collected works." Peterson. Ref Bks for Elem and Jr High Sch Libraries [review of 1970 edition]

In this edition uniform title entries have been used where they could be ascertained to bring together variant titles of folk tales in Part 2

Meacham, Mary

Information sources in children's literature; practical reference guide for children's librarians, elementary school teachers, and students of children's literature. Greenwood Press 1978 256p illus (Contributions in librarianship and information science) lib. bdg. $18.95   **011**

1 Children's literature—Bibliography
ISBN 0-313-20045-9   LC 77-91107

This guide to books and periodicals about children's literature is intended as "a key to the vast resources available in dealing with the numerous questions, problems, and decisions in the area of children's trade books and other materials that librarians and teachers face daily in an ordinary elementary school library or children's section of a public library. Hopefully, it will help in deciding what children's resource materials to buy (and keep), and how to use them in answering reference questions posed by children or adults; it should help adults find out more about children's books and other media from preschool to approximately the sixth-grade level. Its scope is comprehensive, with much of it being a bibliography of bibliographies." Preface

Contents: Building the basic collection; Keeping up-to-date, science books, indexes and abstracts; Special help for special fields; Illustrators, authors and awards; Using books with children; Technical processes; Appendix 1: Organizing and running the library/media center; Appendix 2: Criteria for evaluating a children's book; Appendix 3: Further reading

A **Multimedia** approach to children's literature; a selective list of films, filmstrips, and recordings based on children's books; comp. and ed. by Ellin Greene and Madalynne Schoenfeld. 2d ed. A.L.A. 1977 xxiii, 182p pa $6   011

1 Children's literature—Bibliography 2 Audiovisual materials—Bibliography 3 Motion pictures —Catalogs 4 Children's literature—Discography
ISBN 0-8389-0249-9   LC 77-10802
First published 1972
"Contains annotated listings of more than 500 children's books, each followed by separately annotated listings of 16mm films, filmstrips and recordings (disc and tape) based upon the books. All selections are the result of first-hand evaluation and use of the materials with children from preschool age to grade 6. Selections are arranged alphabetically by book title and include buying information. There is a special section on authors and illustrators and an annotated listing of resources including related readings, selection aids, program aids, and realia. Author, subject, and media indexes are also included, as is a directory of distributors." Publisher's note

National Council of Teachers of English. Committee on the Elementary School Booklist
Adventuring with books; a booklist for pre-K—grade 8. New ed. prepared by Patricia Cianciolo, editorial chair, and the Committee on the Elementary School Booklist of the National Council of Teachers of English. The Council 1977 500p pa $3.95   011

1 Children's literature—Bibliography 2 Books and reading—Best books
ISBN 0-8141-0074-0   LC 77-8348
First published 1950
"This annotated bibliography is divided into 13 broad subject areas such as Traditional Literature, Religion and Holidays, and Physical Sciences. Both fiction and non-fiction are included. Most entries have been published since 1970. . . . Author, title, illustrator if any, publisher, publication date, age range of readers, and a brief annotation are given for each major entry. An unannotated list of other recommended and mostly well-known titles is given at the end of each section. The annotations adequately summarize the books and compare titles when appropriate. All entries are books that the selectors recommend. A directory of publishers, and author and title indexes complete the book." Am Ref Bks Annual, 1978

National Council of Teachers of English. Picture Book Committee
Picture books for children [by] Patricia Jean Cianciolo, editor, and the Picture Book Committee, National Council of Teachers of English. The Council 1973 159p illus pa $7.50   011

1 Picture books for children—Bibliography 2 Books and reading—Best books
"Devised as a book selection tool for teachers, librarians, and those concerned with children's picture books, this graded, annotated bibliography contains more than 375 titles for the pre-schooler through the [young] teenager. The books chosen exemplify story and illustration acting in combination emphasizing aesthetic as well as educational value. Cianciolo has written a 22-page introduction followed by a booklist arranged in broad categories such as 'Me and My Family,' 'Other People,' 'The Imaginative World.' There is an index of authors. illustrators, and titles." Cur Ref Bks

Peterson, Carolyn Sue
Reference books for elementary and junior high school libraries. 2d ed. Scarecrow 1975 314p $11   011

1 Reference books—Bibliography
ISBN 0-8108-0816-1   LC 78-8537
First published 1970
"Peterson has compiled a collection of almost 900 titles from which individual schools may select the ones that are suited to their specific needs. The titles included represent qualitative suggestions, and attention has been paid to books published in the 1970s. Titles are arranged by type (encyclopedias, yearbooks, indexes, atlases, etc.) and by subject (biography, foreign language, history, social

science, ethnic groups, natural science and mathematics, applied science, recreation and hobbies). Titles are arranged alphabetically except where level of difficulty is important. The very full annotations given are quite valuable for choosing among several books in the same field. . . . Of additional help are three sample lists in the introduction for primary, intermediate, and junior high schools." Am Ref Bks Annual, 1976

Richardson, Selma K.
(ed.) Periodicals for school media programs. A.L.A. 1978 xxii, 397p pa $8.50   011

1 Periodicals—Bibliography
ISBN 0-8389-0243-X   LC 77-25069
First published 1969 under the editorship of Marian H. Scott with title: Periodicals for school libraries
"The directory is a buying list of recommended periodicals for all grade levels, K-12. . . . The alphabetically arranged list of periodicals is supplemented by an annotated list of periodical indexes and a subject index. Entries give address, grade level, frequency, price, annotation describing general content, and where abstracted. Highly selective it will be most valuable in small libraries." Wynar. Guide to Ref Bks for Sch Media Centers [review of 1973 edition]

Rosenbach, A. S. W.
Early American children's books; with bibliographical descriptions of the books in his private collection. Foreword by A. Edward Newton. Kraus Reprint Corp. 1966 lix, 354p illus with color illus $30, without color $17   011

1 Children's literature—Bibliography 2 Book collecting
ISBN 0-527-77000-0; 0-527-77002-7   LC 77-10180
First published 1933 by Southworth Press
"The book contains titles, with descriptive and historical notes, for 816 books, with 104 illustrations. Each title is complete with city of publication, publisher and date, size, number of leaves, signature numbers, illustrations, binding and record of mention in Sabin or Evans; there is a fine set of indexes." NY Her Trib Bks
"Dr. Rosenbach's introduction is amusing and informative, and his notes describe the contents and character of each of the items in his collection, with copious and well-chosen quotations." Times (London) Lit Sup
Bibliography: p353-54

Rosenberg, Judith K.
Young people's literature in series: fiction, non-fiction, and publishers' series, 1973-1975. Libs. Unlimited 1977 234p lib. bdg. $13.50   011

1 Children's literature—Bibliography
ISBN 0-87287-140-1   LC 76-57963
Supplements Young people's literature in series: fiction and Young people's literature in series: publishers' and non-fiction series, both o.p. This supplement updates the earlier volumes "with inclusion of 263 new fiction titles and 2,614 non-fiction and publishers' series books. This new volume combines fiction and nonfiction, listing those published after 1972, those inadvertently omitted in the earlier volume, and those in continuing series. Helpful notations allow cross-referencing back to the earlier volumes. Fiction titles are arranged by author and cover grades 3-9; nonfiction and publisher series are arranged by series and cover grades 3-12. Both have special designations for suggested use with reluctant readers. Annotations are descriptive with brief evaluative comments on style and quality." Booklist

Schon, Isabel
Books in Spanish for children and young adults: an annotated guide. Scarecrow Press 1978 153p $7   011

1 Latin American literature—Bibliography 2 Spanish literature—Bibliography 3 Children's literature—Bibliography
ISBN 0-8108-1176-6   LC 78-10299
A selection guide for "books in Spanish written by Hispanic authors for children of preschool through high school age. Most of the books included in this guide were published after 1973, and come from Argentina, Chile, Colombia, Costa Rica, Cuba,

Schon, Isabel—*Continued*

Ecuador, Guatemala, Mexico, Peru, Puerto Rico, Spain, Uruguay and Venezuela. I have identified books for children and young adults that highlight the lifestyle, folklore, heroes, history, fiction, poetry, theatre, and classical literature of Hispanic cultures as expressed by Hispanic authors. . . . I have also indicated a tentative grade level for each book, but the individual student's Spanish reading ability, interest, taste, and purpose should be the main criteria for determining the true level of each book. . . . To assist selectors in ordering these books, I have included in Appendix I the names and addresses of dealers in Spanish-speaking countries that in my experience will expedite shipment of any order . . . I have also included in Appendix II a list of book dealers in the United States that specialize in books from Spanish-speaking countries." Preface

Spache, George Daniel

Good reading for the disadvantaged reader; multi-ethnic resources. Rev. ed. Garrard 1975 311p pa $5.75   011

1 Socially handicapped children, Books for—Bibliography 2 Minorities in literature and art—Bibliography
ISBN 0-8116-6012-5   LC 75-328163

First published 1970
"Emphasizing the need for an individual's positive self-concept, this book presents guidelines for aiding a minority child in developing one. Lists of books and other resources ranging from primary to secondary levels in all subject areas are presented. Minority groups receiving special attention are Black Americans, American Indians, Mexican Americans, Oriental Americans, and Puerto Ricans." Ref Bks for Elem and Jr High Sch Libraries [review of 1970 edition]

Withrow, Dorothy E.

Gateways to readable books. . . . 5th ed. By Dorothy E. Withrow, Helen B. Carey [and] Bertha M. Hirzel. Wilson, H.W. 1975 299p $12
                                              011

1 Children's literature—Bibliography 2 Slow learning children, Books for—Bibliography
ISBN 0-8242-0566-9   LC 75-12933

First edition, 1944 by Ruth Strang, Alice Checkovitz, Christine Gilbert and Margaret Scoggin
"An annotated graded list of books in many fields for adolescents who are reluctant to read or find reading difficult." Subtitle
This bibliography lists over 1,000 titles in broad subject categories, giving full bibliographic information and grade level of difficulty for each book. Indexed by author, title and grade level of reading difficulty
"Only books below the tenth-grade level of difficulty were included. . . . The estimated grade level is indicated after each title. The majority of books included are of fifth- and sixth-grade level of difficulty." Booklist

Wynar, Christine L.

Guide to reference books for school media centers. Libs. Unlimited 1973 473p lib. bdg. $18.50   011

1 Reference books—Bibliography
ISBN 0-87287-069-3   LC 73-87523

This volume contains 2,575 annotated entries for reference books and selection tools for use in elementary, junior, and senior high schools. The subjects treated are those generally included in school curricula plus extracurricular topics such as pets, hobbies, clubs, etc. Entries are arranged alphabetically by author under 54 main subject headings. Paperback editions and prices are shown. Index includes author, title and subject entries
"The main advantage here will be breadth and up-to-dateness. . . . One could quibble that some titles are too specialized for school libraries or that some very useful titles are omitted. However, this will be a useful list for collection building and for reminding librarians or patrons of sources to use on particular problems." Cur Ref Bks

Guide to reference books for school media centers: 1974-75 supplement. Libs. Unlimited 1976 131p $8   011

1 Reference books—Bibliography
ISBN 0-82787-121-5   LC 73-87523

This "Supplement adds 518 reference books published from the cut off date of the base volume, July 1973, through December 1975. . . . Together, the Supplement and base volume include 3,094 titles, plus several hundred additional titles that are cited in the annotation." Introduction

Yonkers, N.Y. Public Library. Children's Services

A guide to subjects & concepts in picture book format. 2d ed. Oceana 1979 163p illus lib. bdg. $12.50   011

1 Picture books for children—Bibliography
ISBN 0-379-20276-X   LC 78-31811

First published 1974
"Intended as a finding tool, not a buying guide for material, this index is limited to titles specifically classified as 'picture books' in the Yonkers (N.Y.) Public Library. Divided into 52 categories and subdivisions, some 2,000 entries cover title, author, publisher, and year of publication. . . . As a supplement to the card catalog for parents, teachers, and library school students, this book is recommended for comprehensive collections." Cur Ref Bks [review of 1974 edition]
Bibliography: p161-63

015.71 Bibliographies and catalogs of works issued or printed in Canada

Canadian books for young people [and] Livres canadiens pour la jeunesse; ed. by Irma McDonough. Univ. of Toronto Press 1980 205p illus pa $15   015.71

1 Canadian literature—Bibliography 2 French Canadian literature—Bibliography 3 Children's literature—Bibliography
ISPN 0-8020-4594-4

First published 1976 with title: Canadian books for children [and] Livres canadiens pour enfants
This is a listing of in-print Canadian books and magazines in English and French ranging in level from preschool to ninth grade. . . . English and French sections are arranged in double columns under . . . broad subject headings such as 'Folklore,' 'Social Sciences,' 'Sports and Recreation,' 'Biography,' and 'Literature,' some of which are subdivided. . . . Full bibliographical descriptions and brief, uncritical annotations are provided for most titles; specific reading levels are given for French works while many English-language entries are described as being 'for younger, middle, older or mature readers.' It should be noted that adult titles are included in this catalog where Canadian books specifically for children do not exist. A few government publications are listed." Ref & Subscription Bks Revs [review of the 1978 edition]

015.73 Bibliographies and catalogs of works issued or printed in the U.S.

Children's books in print. Bowker $32.50 015.73

1 Children's literature—Bibliography
ISSN 0069-3480   LC 70-101705

Annual. First published 1969, expanded from and replacing: Children's books for schools and libraries
"Three separate alphabets are incorporated in the volume: author index, title index, and illustrator index. The entries in each section are arranged alphabetically by word. Difficulties in the grouping of some authors' names is experienced due to computer limitations. All entries include author, coauthor, co-editor, illustrator, translator, title, price, imprint, publisher, year of publication, plus other data where warranted (e.g., order number, ISBN, edition, number of volumes, grade range, type of binding). A key to abbreviations is in the front of the volume, along with an instructive 'How to Use' section. An alphabetical index of publishers is in an unpaged section at the end that provides short form, full name, address, and ISBN prefix." Wynar. Guide to Ref Bks for Sch Media Centers

Subject guide to Children's books in print. Bowker $32.50   015.73

1 Children's literature—Bibliography 2 Catalogs, Subject
ISSN 0000-0167   LC 70-101705

Annual. First published 1970

A subject arranged companion to Children's books in print, entered above. Headings used are derived from the Sears List of subject headings, entered in class 025.4

"The author and title entries provide full bibliographic, price, and binding data—the same as that given in 'Children's Guide to Books in Print.' A key to abbreviations is at the front, and a directory of publishers is located at the back of the volume. The 'Subject Guide' has been criticized for inconsistencies in headings and their assignment and for a dearth of cross references." Wynar. Guide to Ref Bks for Sch Media Centers [review of third edition]

Vertical file index; a subject and title index to selected pamphlet material. Wilson, H.W. pa $18 a year   015.73

1 Pamphlets—Bibliography 2 Pamphlets—Indexes
ISSN 0042-4439

First published 1932 with title: Vertical file service catalog
Issued monthly except August

This index is a subject and title index to selected pamphlets considered to be of interest to general libraries. It is not intended to be a complete list of all pamphlet material, nor does inclusion of a pamphlet constitute recommendation. Each issue contains a list of current, available pamphlets, booklets, leaflets, and mimeographed material arranged alphabetically by subject; each entry includes title, paging, publisher, publication date, descriptive note, and price or condition under which it may be obtained. A title index, giving the subject heading under which each title may be found, follows the subject list. Each issue contains a list of subject headings used, which is cumulated each quarter

Wittig, Alice J.

U.S. government publications for the school media center. Libs. Unlimited 1979 121p illus $9.50   015.73

1 U.S.—Government publications—Bibliography
ISBN 0-87287-214-9   LC 79-24798

"The purpose of this book is to provide a quick introduction for those people working in school libraries to whom this is a largely unexplored subject and to be a time conserving source of reference and a checklist for librarians who feel that they may be overlooking and/or underutilizing some areas in this rich field of information. The well over 300 documents included here have been chosen on the basis of their potential usefulness to patrons of school libraries and media centers. To insure easy access to information concerning individual documents, a list alphabetized by title is provided for each of 41 general topics. Each entry includes the date of publication and the price of the document as well as the Superintendent of Documents classification number and the stock number which must be included when ordering documents from the GPO." Introduction

016 Bibliographies of general encyclopedia works

Encyclopedia buying guide; a consumer guide to general encyclopedias in print. Bowker $19.25   016

1 Encyclopedias—Bibliography
ISSN 0-361-1094   LC 76-645701

Successor to General encyclopedias in print, compiled by S. Padraig Walsh
First published 1976, planned as a biennial. Editor 1976— Kenneth F. Kister

This book "provides evaluations of . . . nonspecialized encyclopedias . . . on the American market. These include adult sets, those geared to school curricula and family use, works intended for very young readers, one- or two-volume works, 'supermarket' sets, and British encyclopedias distributed in this country. For each set Kister

provides basic bibliographic and purchasing information, along with descriptive and critical comments on purpose and scope, authority, reliability, objectivity, recency, arrangement and accessibility, writing style and level, bibliographies, graphics, physical format, and special features. A summary comment makes straightforward comparisons with similar sets and tells whether the set is generally a good or bad buy. Introductory material covers encyclopedias and their use, sales practices, and consumer protection information." Cur Ref Bks [review of 1976 edition]

For fuller review see: American Reference Books Annual, 1977

016.07 Bibliographies of journalism and publishing

Gottlieb, Robin

Publishing children's books in America, 1919-1976: an annotated bibliography. Children's Bk. Council 1978 195p illus $15   016.07

1 Publishers and publishing—Bibliography 2 Children's literature—Bibliography
LC 78-113505

"Arranged chronologically under many subject categories, the more than seven hundred annotated entries 'deal with the publishing of trade books only' and were chosen for what they reveal of the philosophy behind juvenile publishing or the actual process of book publishing. Entries 'include whole books and parts of books, as well as periodical, newspaper, and newsletter articles . . . monographs, exhibition catalogues, and statistical tables.' The subjects [treated include] . . . editorial [matters]; illustration, design, and production; publicity, promotion, and advertising; sales; financial matters; individual publishing houses and editors; special kinds of publishing; trends in the past as well as predictions for the future." Horn Bk

016.302 Bibliographies of social interaction

Reading ladders for human relations. 5th ed. [by] Virginia M. Reid, editor, and the Committee on Reading Ladders for Human Relations of the National Council of Teachers of English. Am. Council on Educ. 1972 346p $10.50, pa $4.50   016.302

1 Human relations—Bibliography 2 Intercultural education—Bibliography 3 Children's literature—Bibliography
ISBN 0-8268-1375-5, 0-8268-1373-9   LC 72-87462

First published 1947. 1st-3d editions edited by Margaret H. Heaton. 4th edition edited by Muriel Crosby

The books annotated in this work "develop four themes. The themes explore the individual's concept of himself; his relationship to his family, peers, and others, or his alienation from those groups; his appreciation or lack of appreciation of persons from other socio-economic, cultural or ethnic groups; and his need to cope with change, including all of the traumatic experiences change can produce. . . . Within each theme books are arranged by maturity level and then listed alphabetically by author. The assignment or cross-reference of a given title to a given ladder or a given sequence is only suggestive; any complex work will have more facets than can be reflected here." Design of the Rdng Ladders

016.3058 Bibliographies of racial, ethnic, national groups

The **Black** experience in children's audiovisual materials. Sponsored by North Manhattan Project. Countee Cullen Regional Branch. N.Y. Pub. Lib. 1973 32p pa $1   016.3058

1 Black studies—Audio-visual aids 2 Audio-visual materials—Bibliography
ISBN 0-87104-610-5   LC 74-158993

The Black experience in children's audiovisual materials—*Continued*

Compiled by Diane DeVeaux, Marilyn Berg Iarusso and Viola Jones Clark

"Designed as a supplement to 'The Black Experience in Children's Books' [entered below] this bibliography is a well organized list of audio-visual materials depicting Black life. It is divided into the following sections: records and cassettes, films, filmstrips, and multi-media kits. It also contains a directory of sources. Each section lists materials held by the North Manhattan and Countee Cullen branch libraries which have proved popular with children." Peterson. Ref Bks for Elem and Jr High Sch Libraries

The **Black** experience in children's books; selected by Barbara Rollock. N.Y. Pub. Lib. 1974 122p pa $2.50　　**016.3058**

1 Blacks—Bibliography

ISBN 0-87104-614-8　　LC 75-324201

First published 1957 with title: Books about Negro life for children. Previous editions were compiled by Augusta Baker

"This booklist contains selected stories portraying Black life for children from preschool to age twelve. Arranged geographically (United States, South and Central America, the Caribbean, Africa, and England), the list is further subdivided by subjects with titles alphabetically arranged under each heading. Subjects include picture books, readers, stories for younger children, stories for older boys and girls, folklore, poetry and verse, music and art, sports, science, Civil Rights, Frederick Douglass, Dr. Martin Luther King, Jr., biography, history, the way it is, references, and periodicals. Each entry gives the title, author, illustrator, publisher, date, price, and brief annotation." Peterson. Ref Bks for Elem and Jr High Sch Libraries

Buttlar, Lois

Building ethnic collections; an annotated guide for school media centers and public libraries [by] Lois Buttlar [and] Lubomyr R. Wynar. Libs. Unlimited 1977 434p lib. bdg. $18.50　　**016.3058**

1 Ethnic groups—Bibliography　2 Minorities—Bibliography

ISBN 0-87287-130-4　　LC 76-55398

"This guide provides a comprehensive listing of available resources covering a broad spectrum of materials dealing with ethnic groups and ethnic topics. The first part contains general titles on ethnicity and the second part includes sections listing materials related to 44 different groups, which are arranged in alphabetical order. The materials are divided into five basic categories: reference sources, teaching methodology and curriculum materials, nonfiction, fiction, and audiovisual materials. All of the entries within each category provide complete bibliographic descriptions, prices, and grade levels for which the title is best suited. Adult titles and books for teachers are designated as such. . . . Following the 2,286 numbered entries is a directory of producers and distributors of audiovisual materials." Sch Library J

Duran, Daniel Flores

Latino materials; a multimedia guide for children and young adults. Am. Bibl. Center-CLIO Press 1979 249p (Selection guide ser) $14.95　　**016.3058**

1 Mexican Americans—Bibliography　2 Puerto Ricans in the U.S.—Bibliography　3 Latin Americans—Bibliography　4 Audio-visual materials—Bibliography

ISBN 0-87436-262-8　　LC 78-18470

This annotated guide includes general Latino resources and Mexican American and Puerto Rican resources arranged by audience level (elementary, secondary and professional materials). Includes a glossary and a directory of publishers and distributors

Multi-ethnic media; selected bibliographies in print; David Cohen, coordinator, Task Force on Ethnic Materials Information Exchange, Social Responsibilities Roundtable. Office for Library Service to the Disadvantaged. A.L.A. 1975 33p pa $2　　**016.3058**

1 Ethnic groups—Bibliography　2 Minorities—Bibliography

ISBN 0-8389-3170-7

"The first section includes bibliographic essays in which the author has explained in detail the criteria and other bases for the selection of the recommended materials. The second section deals with bibliographic materials to be used primarily with children and young adults. The third section, while relatively small, contains important sources of information about new materials available for most ethnic groups. A source of multicultural, multi-ethnic and multiracial media." Wis Library Bul

Schon, Isabel

A bicultural heritage: themes for the exploration of Mexican and Mexican-American culture in books for children and adolescents. Scarecrow 1978 158p lib. bdg. $8　　**016.3058**

1 Mexican Americans—Bibliography　2 Mexico—Civilization—Bibliography

ISBN 0-8108-1128-6　　LC 78-4332

This bibliography and study guide "is designed to expose students to the customs, life-styles, heroes, folklore, and history of Mexican and Mexican-American cultures. The readings and activities are intended to be entertaining as well as informative." Overview

"This title is a must for those interested in cultural pluralism, in ethnic studies, and in providing reading guidance to students in bicultural and multicultural communities." Am Ref Bks Annual, 1979

016.3627　Bibliography of problems of and services to young people

Bernstein, Joanne E.

Books to help children cope with separation and loss. Bowker 1977 255p $16.25　　**016.3627**

1 Child psychology—Bibliography　2 Children's literature—Bibliography　3 Bibliotherapy　4 Bereavement—Bibliography

ISBN 0-8352-0837-0　　LC 77-23970

"Annotated listing of books that [the author feels] can be used to help children cope with the trauma that often accompanies separation and loss. The first part of the book defines bibliotherapy and reviews its history. Criteria for selection of titles in the bibliography and a discussion of children's responses to separation and loss are also presented in the opening pages. Part II, the bibliography, lists and describes 438 books for children between the ages of 3 and 16. Titles, most of them published after 1970, are arranged in three major categories with subdivisions. The categories are 'Learning to Face Separation,' 'Coping with Tragic Loss,' and 'Who Will Take Care of Me?' . . . Most of the books are realistic fiction. Fantasy, history, biography and folk tales, are accorded only slight representation as is nonfiction. No short stories or poetry are included. More titles are recommended for the younger (3-11-year-old) than for the adolescent reader. Annotations are clear and concise, averaging about 150 words. Interest and reading levels are indicated. . . . Part III offers two bibliographies for adults: one on separation and loss, the other on bibliotherapy." Booklist

Includes author, title, subject, interest level and reading level indexes

Fassler, Joan

Helping children cope; illus. by William B. Hogan. Free Press 1978 162p illus $12.95　　**016.3627**

1 Stress (Psychology)—Bibliography　2 Child psychology—Bibliography　3 Children's literature—Bibliography　4 Bibliotherapy

ISBN 0-02-693500-7　　LC 77-6943

"This publication concentrates on certain areas of potential stress, such as hospitalization, illness, death, separation experiences, moving, adoption, divorce, birth of a baby in the family, and other situations that may strain a child's coping skills. Each chapter presents an initial discussion of professional viewpoints concerning the topic under consideration, followed by a discussion of selected children's books that may help them gain mastery of the situation. Many of the books discussed have been used at the Yale University Child Study

Fassler, Joan—*Continued*
Center and nearby hospitals and schools. . . . Difficulties with certain books, as well as serious areas of neglect in the children's book field, are noted as well. Each chapter concludes with a list of professional references concerning the chapter topic, or topics, followed by separate listings of recommended juvenile books. The emphasis here is on books for children in the four-to-eight-year age range." Preface

Gillis, Ruth J.
Children's books for times of stress; an annotated bibliography [by] Ruth J. Gillis; with technical assistance by Louise S. Spear. Indiana Univ. Press 1978 xxiii, 322p $15   016.3627
1 Stress (Psychology)—Bibliography 2 Child psychology—Bibliography 3 Children's literature—Bibliography 4 Bibliotherapy
ISBN 0-253-31348-1   LC 76-48517
Listing titles appropriate for children from preschool to age nine, "this bibliography serves as a guide to the growing number of books dealing with emotionally stressful situations. As such it will be welcomed by teachers, parents, and others who work with children. Seven broad categories are used in the bibliography: (1) emotions, (2) behavior, (3) family, (4) difficult situations, (5) new situations, (6) self concepts, (7) friendship. These are further subdivided as 'Emotions: Anger, Boredom, Rejection'; 'Difficult situations: Adoption, Death, Death of Pet, Handicaps,' etc. In all there are 85 different subject headings under which the 261 titles are listed. If a story treats several subjects, it may be listed under each of the pertinent topics. . . . Alphabetically arranged annotations make up the main body of the book. Although review sources are named, the annotations are not copied or excerpted. Instead Gillis offers her own description and evaluation of the book as it realtes to the subject heading under which it is listed. There are occasional notes on the illustrations and age levels. Full bibliographic information is given for each title, and following each annotation is a list of all the subjects under which the book can be found. . . . Title, author, and illustrator indexes are included after the subject index. . . . [Because of the computer-assisted indexing] the entire book resembles a computer printout. Solid capitals, uneven inking, and spacing make reading a slow process." Ref & Subscription Bks Revs

016.3713 Bibliographies of instructional materials

Brown, Lucy Gregor
Core media collection for elementary schools [by] Lucy Gregor Brown; assisted by Betty McDavid. Bowker 1978 224p $17.50   016.3713
1 Audio-visual materials—Catalogs
ISBN 0-8352-1096-0   LC 78-11674
Replaces: Resources for learning; a core media collection for elementary schools; edited by Roderick McDaniel
"Selection guide to nonprint media titles. The majority of the titles in this book are for sound or captioned filmstrips, kits, recordings, and some 16mm films; however, study prints, art prints, 8mm loops, slides, and transparencies are also listed. They cover a wide variety of subject and ability levels. . . . This collection was developed with the school curriculum needs of students in grades K-6 in mind. . . . Only a few titles produced before 1973 are listed, since many titles are by nature subject to rapid obsolescence." Preface
"Easy to use, the entries, complete with annotations, are listed in the main index by subject, with appropriate cross-references. A title index and a producer/distributor directory are useful additional features. . . . Because it focuses on a core audiovisual collection, this book would be convenient for one starting a new collection." Choice

Educational Film Library Association
Film evaluation guide. The Association
016.3713
1 Motion pictures—Catalogs
Volume covering 1946-1964 o.p. 1980 (available in microfilm from University Microfilm Inc.); Supplement covering September 1, 1964-August 31, 1967 and Supplement two covering September 1, 1967-August 31, 1971 each $12

The basic volume is a compilation of 4500 evaluations of 16mm films. Annotations provide "information on subject, running time, price, distributor, age level, possible audience, and rating. Intended for universities, school systems, public libraries, church groups, labor organizations, and youth-serving agencies with film libraries or film programs." Pub W
Evaluation sets are available since 1971 to members of the Association

Educational film locator of the Consortium of University Film Centers and R. R. Bowker Company. Bowker [1979 c1978] xxxv, 2178p $45   016.3713
1 Motion pictures—Catalogs 2 Motion pictures in education 3 Libraries and motion pictures
ISBN 0-8352-0956-3   LC 78-67185
The Locator is a union list of 37,000 films held in 50 university library film centers. They have been selected by staff members on the basis of user demand. The main listing is alphabetical by film title. Information given in the entry includes color or black & white, running time, sound or silent, producer/distributor, production or copyright year, subject, audience level, ISBN number, descriptive annotation, and symbol for each library holding film. Film titles are also listed by LC subject headings with indication of audience level and running time. An index to these headings with cross references precedes this section. In another list the subject headings used in the directory are arranged by 29 broad classes. There are also lists of the participating film libraries, producer/distributors, film series and an index of foreign film titles
"The volume is essential for all libraries that rent, borrow, or lend films. It even includes the library lending policies of all contributing institutions to aid users in gaining access to the films listed." Choice

Educators guide to free films. Educators Progress Service pa $16.25   016.3713
1 Motion pictures—Catalogs
ISSN 0070-9395   LC 45-412
Annual. First published 1941
"This list of sponsored films available to schools free (or for cost of postage) is well annotated. It is indexed by title and by subject." Ref Materials for Sch Libraries

El-hi textbooks in print. Bowker $32.50
016.3713
1 Textbooks—Bibliography
ISSN 0070-9565   LC 70-105104
Annual. First issued in 1872 as part of Publisher's Weekly. Formerly published with titles: The American educational catalog, and later, Textbooks in print. First published under present title 1970
This volume lists "elementary, junior high, and senior high texts, published by . . . American textbook companies, plus data on programmed learning materials in book form, professional books for teachers and auxiliary AV aids. The subject index lists texts under curriculum headings . . . providing author, title, grade level, publication date, binding, ISBN, price, related teaching material, and publisher. Series are grouped together under the series title. Author, title, and series indexes and a directory of publishers are also provided." Wynar. Guide to Ref Bks for Sch Media Centers

Gaffney, Maureen
(comp.) More films kids like; a catalog of short films for children. Comp. and ed. by Maureen Gaffney; assisted in research by Gerry Bond Laybourne and Kay Weidemann Scott. A.L.A. 1977 159p illus pa $8.95   016.3713
1 Motion pictures—Catalogs
ISBN 0-8389-0250-2   LC 77-12174
Companion volume to: Films kids like, edited by Susan Rice, o.p. 1981
An "annotated list of 200 short 16mm general interest films that were found to be successful with children, three to twelve, by the Children's Film Theater Project of New York. Each listing contains pertinent data such as running time, distributor, technique, and production data if available, followed by a lively brief synopsis of the film and reactions of the kids grouped according to three

Gaffney, Maureen—*Continued*
age ranges. The book presents a detailed explanation of the methods used to determine the children's reactions to the films. Technical information on how to run a successful film program, including some creative follow-up activities, is presented. A subject index, sorely lacking in the first catalog, incorporates titles from both." Top of the News

George Peabody College for Teachers, Nashville, Tenn.
Free and inexpensive learning materials. The College [distributed by Incentive Pubs] pa $4.50   016.3713
1 Teaching—Aids and devices—Bibliography
2 Pamphlets—Bibliography

Biennial. First published 1941
"The annotated entries are listed under 85 alphabetically arranged subject categories. . . . The headings generally parallel units taught in elementary and secondary schools. Cross references are provided to connect subject groups. . . . Each entry provides the name of the source or the type of material, the address, and a brief description of the type of material, prices, grade level, and other useful information. Many entries are followed by lists of specific titles including dates, pages, and prices. Some but not all items are briefly described. There is no index. The book lists pamphlets, posters, paperback books, charts, teaching units, some selected catalogs of instructional media, newsletters, journal and encyclopedia offprints, slides and films, simulation games, and other materials for student use. Catalogs issued by professional associations are included, as well as paperback books for teachers." Am Ref Bks Annual, 1977 [review of 1976 edition]

Landers Film reviews. Landers Associates $45 a year   016.3713
1 Motion pictures—Reviews
ISSN 0023-785X   LC 67-6334
Published five times a year. First published 1956 with title: Bertha Landers Film reviews
Loose-leaf, with binder
"In addition to coverage of instructional films of all types for kindergarten through adult viewing, it includes training films, experimental films, TV documentary and short subject films, and children's fiction films. About 700 to 800 titles from nearly 600 producers (major companies and small independent firms) are reviewed annually. . . . Arrangement of 16mm films is alphabetical by title; other media are arranged by producer. Entries give title, producer/distributor (address is included if the name is not listed in the Source Directory), year of release, running time, sound, color/black and white, price (sale, rental, or free loan), credits, intended audience (e, jh, sh, c, ad) subject area, purpose, and review of about 150 words. Each review provides a synopsis of the film, followed by a short evaluation. Title and subject indexes are included in each issue, and annual cumulative indexes are provided in the last issue of the volume." Wynar, Guide to Ref Bks for Sch Media Centers

National Information Center for Educational Media
[NICEM Indexes to nonbook media] The Center   016.3713
1 Audio-visual materials—Catalogs

Also available in microfiche
Most of the volumes in the series are periodically revised and are kept up to date by NICEM Update of nonbook media. Apply to publisher for subscription options
Contains indexes to: 16mm educational films (4v) $126; 35mm educational filmstrips (3v) $99; Educational overhead transparencies (2v) $61; Educational audio tapes $54; Educational video tapes $34; Educational records $54; 8mm motion cartridges $54; Education slides $49; Producers and distributors $24; Psychology—multimedia $55; Vocational and technical education—multimedia $55; Health and safety education—multimedia $55; Environmental studies—multimedia $40; Nonprint special education materials—multimedia (learner volume) $47; Nonprint special education materials —multimedia (professional volume) $15

New York Library Association. Children's and Young Adult Services Section
Films for children; a selected list. Prepared by New York Library Association, Children's and Young Alult Services Section. Committee: Films for children, Julie Cummins [and others] 4th ed. The Association 1977 27p pa $3 016.3713
1 Motion pictures—Catalogs
First published 1966
"This list consists of more than one hundred films which children have seen and enjoyed over a period of years. It is not a 'basic' list, but rather a highly selective list of films which have been used successfully by librarians. In general, the Committee did not include 'classroom' films except where the factual material was presented in an imaginative artistic way." Introduction to the second edition
The annotated list of films, with information on subject, running time, price, distributor, color, series, and date of production is preceded by a short introduction giving guidelines for the planning and presentation of library film programs for children and a bibliography

016.3726 Bibliographies of storytelling

Association for Library Service to Children
Storytelling; readings/bibliographies/resources, prepared by an ad hoc committee of the Association for Library Service to Children. American Library Association. A.L.A. 1978 16p pa $1   016.3726
1 Storytelling—Bibliography   2 Storytelling— Audio-visual aids
ISBN 0-8389-3216-9   LC 78-105802
"The section on Preparation and Storytelling includes lists of books, articles and excerpts, recordings, films, and videotapes to provide background information. The section on the Art of Storytelling contains listings of like resources. Finally, under Sources of Stories, are included indexes, bibliographies, and available lists of stories." Publisher's note

Stories to tell to children; a selected list. Published for Carnegie Library of Pittsburgh Children's Services by the Univ. of Pittsburgh Press illus pa $3.95   016.3726
1 Storytelling—Bibliography 2 Children's literature—Bibliography 3 Holidays—Bibliography
First published 1916. Periodically revised. Editors vary
"An invaluable guide for pre-service and inservice teachers as well as for librarians, the book is logically arranged, beginning with an extensive listing of stories appropriate for three age groups: preschoolers, children from six to ten, and older boys and girls. Stories for Holiday Programs offer en excellent potpourri of tales for all seasons, while a classified list of stories—incorporating such diverse subjects as Afro-Americans, Ecology, Ghosts, Toys—indicates both the range as well as the relevancy of the collection. Also included is a selective list of Aids for the Storyteller—a short guide to articles and books treating various aspects of selection and presentation. Professionally sound, attractive in format and price, the compilation should satisfy many needs." Horn Bk
Includes an alphabetical and a classified list of stories

016.398 Bibliographies of folklore

Folklore from Africa to the United States; an annotated bibliography; comp. by Margaret N. Coughlan. Library of Congress [for sale by the Supt. of Docs.] 1976 161p illus $4.50
016.398
1 Folklore, Black—Bibliography 2 Folklore— Africa—Bibliography
ISBN 0-8444-0175-7   LC 75-43905
This selective "bibliography, comprising one hundred ninety items, describes works available in the collections of the Library of Congress,

Folklore from Africa to the United States —Continued

but single-tale picture books have generally been excluded. Divided into sections devoted to Sub-Saharan Africa, West Africa, Southern Africa, Central Africa, East Africa, the West Indies, and the United States, the annotations make judicious distinctions between studies and collections for children. Many of the entries are enriched with significant quotations, analogies are constantly drawn between African folklore motifs and those found in classical European folklore, and such items as the Anansi tales and the Brer Rabbit stories are correlated with their African sources. The reproductions from such illustrators of African folklore as Ashley Bryan, Leo and Diane Dillon, and Trina Schart Hyman add a touch of elegance to the thoughtful and stimulating entries. With an [author and title] index keyed to entry numbers." Horn Bk

Folklore of the North American Indians; an annotated bibliography; comp. by Judith C. Ullom, Children's Book Section. Library of Congress [for sale by Supt. of Docs] 1969 126p illus map $4.05   **016.398**

1 Folklore, Indian—Bibliography 2 Indians of North America—Legends—Bibliography
LC 70-601462

This bibliography of Indian tales from North America "is organized into 11 culture areas, according to the order set forth by folklorist Stith Thompson: Eskimo, Mackenzie, Plateau, North Pacific, California, Plains, Central Woodland, Northeast Woodland, Iroquois, Southeast, Southwest. Each area is introduced with a statement concerning the tales in relation to the particular culture area and lists separately representative studies, anthologies, and children's anthologies. Each entry is comprehensively annotated indicating scope and purpose of the work. An index to authors, compilers, title entries, and tribal names increases the usefulness of this fine compilation. The moods and spirit of Indian lore are captured in well chosen black-and-white reproductions taken from books represented." Top of the News

"An invaluable compilation." Horn Bk

016.423 Bibliographies of English language dictionaries

Kister, Kenneth F.

Dictionary buying guide; a consumer guide to general English-language wordbooks in print. Bowker 1977 xx, 358p $16.50   **016.423**

1 English language—Dictionaries—Bibliography
ISBN 0-8352-1038-3   LC 77-15010

This work "reviews 58 general English-language dictionaries, evaluates 60 school and children's dictionaries, and critically examines 225 special purpose dictionaries and wordbooks. The latter group includes etymological, usage, rhyming, slang, semiotic, and abbreviations dictionaries, thesauri, and secretarial handbooks. All works included were in print in August 1977." Ref & Subscription Bks Revs

"The profiles contain full bibliographic and price information, descriptive details, Kister's evaluation, and citations to other evaluations. Supplementary sections include a list of recently discontinued titles, a bibliography of articles about dictionaries, a directory of publishers and distributors, and a title-author-subject index. Designed for the general public, this guide is interestingly written and provides clear evaluations." Cur Ref Bks

016.5 Bibliographies of science

AAAS Science film catalog. Ann Seltz-Petrash, project editor and compiler, and Kathryn Wolff, managing editor. AAAS Publications Program; prepared with the assistance of the National Science Foundation. Am. Assn. for the Advancement of Science [distributed by Bowker] 1975 xxi, 398p $18.50   **016.5**

1 Science—Motion pictures—Catalogs 2 Motion pictures in education—Catalogs
ISBN 0-8352-0860-5   LC 75-11536

This catalog, updated through September 1974, identifies "approximately 5,000 16mm films in the sciences and social sciences. . . . Two main sections, one for junior high and adult films, and one for elementary schools, constitute the main body of the work. In volume, the latter section occupies about one-sixth. Each section is arranged by the Dewey Decimal System and has an alphabetical, cross-referenced list of subject headings to ease its use. Cross-references also accompany many of the classification numbers in the text. Each entry tells us whether the film is in black and white or color and provides the title, intended audience, running time, rental and sale prices, description, release date, distributor's order number, and a distribution code: this code refers to the directory of producers and distributors at the rear, which provides addresses for the various commercial, governmental, university, and industrial sources consulted. Suitably bound, attractively laid out, and reasonably priced, this comprehensive work deserves high marks." Choice

For a fuller review see: The Booklist, July, 1976

Appraisal; children's science books. Children's Science Book Review Committee $6 a year   **016.5**

1 Science—Bibliography—Periodicals 2 Books—Reviews
ISSN 0003-7052   LC 75-10816

Triennial. First published 1967

"Supported by the Harvard Graduate School of Education and New England libraries, this is an objective book review service. It offers a rating system for science books that qualify for inclusion in elementary through high school collections. Some 50 to 75 books are analyzed in each issue. A dual approach is usually offered, i.e., first a subject expert places the work within his or her area; second, a librarian describes how it will fit into the total collection. The two 50-to 100-word descriptions are used to give the book a rating from 'Excellent' to 'Unsatisfactory.' This is far superior to most services for children's and teen-agers' books, and deserves wider backing than it is now getting." Katz. Magazines for Libraries. 3d edition

Science Books & Films. Am. Assn. for the Advancement of Science $17.50 a year   **016.5**

1 Science—Bibliography—Periodicals 2 Science—Motion pictures—Periodicals 3 Books—Reviews 4 Motion pictures—Reviews
ISSN 0036-8253   LC 75-645493

Quarterly. First published 1965 with title: Science Books

This periodical reviews trade books, textbooks, reference books and 16mm films in the pure and applied sciences "for all age/grade levels, primary through adult. Arrangement is by Dewey Decimal numbers. Entries provide full bibliographic data, including a grade level code and evaluative annotations aimed at laymen." Wynar. Guide to Ref Bks for Sch Media Centers

016.51 Bibliographies of mathematics

Matthias, Margaret

Children's mathematics books; a critical bibliography, by Margaret Matthias and Diane Thiessen. A.L.A. 1979 61p pa $4.50   **016.51**

1 Mathematics—Bibliography
ISBN 0-8389-0285-5   LC 79-11896

This is a listing of almost 200 books, suitable for pre-school to sixth grade children, grouped by these headings: counting, geometry, measurement, number concepts, time and miscellaneous. Besides commenting on content, accuracy, style, and grade level, the authors give ratings for each book, ranging from highly recommended to not recommended

016.7899   Bibliographies of recordings

New York Library Association. Children's and Young Adult Services Section
Recordings for children; a selected list of records and cassettes. 3d ed. The Association 1972 40p pa $2.50   **016.7899**

1 Sound recordings—Bibliography   2 Magnetic recorders and recording—Bibliography   3 Children's songs—Discography   4 Children's literature—Discography

"Committee: Recordings for Children. Marilyn Iarusso, co-chairman; Mary Nicholaou, co-chairman; Mary Strang [and] Clara Hulton." Title page

First published 1961

"Approximately 450 highly selective titles are included in this subject arranged bibliography. Both disc recordings and cassettes are chosen for children ranging in age from preschool to age 13. Prepared with emphasis on recordings for home and recreational use, the list covers a wide range of subjects and includes both musical and nonmusical recordings. Entries give album title, composer/author, performing group, narrator, producer/recording company, record number, and a brief annotation." Peterson. Ref Bks for Elem and Jr High Sch Libraries

016.8   Bibliographies of literature

Baskin, Barbara H.
Notes from a different drummer; a guide to juvenile fiction portraying the handicapped, by Barbara H. Baskin and Karen H. Harris. Bowker [1978 c1977] 375p illus $17.50   **016.8**

1 Handicapped—Fiction—Bibliography   2 Children's literature—Bibliography
ISBN 0-8352-0978-4   LC 77-15067

"The authors intended their book to be a 'comprehensive guide to juvenile fiction written between 1940 and 1975 that depicts handicapped characters.' They have succeeded admirably. The 100-page introduction should be required reading for everyone working with young people. The heart of the work consists of descriptions and analysis—favorable and unfavorable—of 311 titles. Entries [under authors] contain full bibliographic information, a reading level designation, an indication of the disability portrayed, and a critical and descriptive annotation. The plot summaries are accurate and well done, analyses are written from both the literary and special-education points of view, and critical comments are clear, direct, and useful. There is a detailed subject index [and a title index]." Cur Ref Bks

Children & poetry: a selective, annotated bibliography, comp. by Virginia Haviland, Head, Children's Literature Center, and William Jay Smith, Consultant in Poetry, 1968-70. 2d ed., rev. Library of Congress [for sale by Supt. of Docs] 1979 84p illus $3   **016.8**

1 Children's poetry—Bibliography
ISBN 0-8444-0267-2   LC 78-57071

First published 1969

"This selective, annotated bibliography 'comprises rhymes and more serious poetry, the old and the new, works originating in English and translations from all over the world.' Omitted are traditional ballads and Mother Goose rhymes, textbooks and collections intended for classroom use. . . . Many black-and-white reproductions add to the handsomeness of the publication, which is indexed." Haviland. Children's Lit. First supplement [review of the 1969 edition]

Children's books: awards and prizes. Children's Bk. Council pa $8.95   **016.8**

1 Literary prizes—Bibliography   2 Children's literature—Bibliography

Biennial. First published 1969 under sponsorship of Children's Book Council; earlier editions prepared by Westchester Library System

"A compilation of honors awarded in the childrens book field including major international and foreign awards of English-speaking, and some non-English speaking countries. . . . The awards are separated into three categories: Part I, United States Awards: Part II, British Commonwealth Awards: Part III, International Awards. Within these sections the awards are arranged alphabetically. Each entry includes a brief history of the award. . . . Honor books are noted for the Newbery and Caldecott Medals and 'Other Finalists' for the National Book Award. Illustrators are named only when the award is specifically for illustrations or design. In such listings, if only one name appears, the same person wrote and illustrated the book." Introduction [1977 edition]

"This is the most complete, up-to-date source on the subject of children's book awards and prizes." Am Ref Bks Annual. 1978 [review of 1977 edition]

Hotchkiss, Jeanette
American historical fiction and biography for children and young people. Scarecrow 1973 318p $9.50   **016.8**

1 U.S.—History—Fiction—Bibliography   2 U.S.—Biography—Bibliography   3 America—History—Fiction—Bibliography
ISBN 0-8108-0650-9   LC 73-13715

"An annotated bibliography of 1,600 titles, designed to aid teachers, librarians, and students themselves in locating authentic and exciting novels and biographies concerning the history of both Americas [with emphasis on the United States]. Arranged chronologically in the first section and topically in the second one, the list contains symbols indicating reader ability and interest levels from kindergarten through high school." Peterson. Ref Bks for Elem and Jr High Sch Libraries

European historical fiction and bibliography for children and young people. 2d ed. Scarecrow 1972 272p $9.50   **016.8**

1 Europe—History—Fiction—Bibliography   2 Europe—Biography—Bibliography
ISBN 0-8108-0515-4   LC 72-1599

First published 1967 with title: European historical fiction for children and young people

This bibliography "lists 1,341 books set in the British Isles and continental Europe, including some juvenile history as well as fiction and biography, grouped under geographical regions by historical period. Titles, selected on the basis of historical accuracy, literary merit, readability, and good taste, are briefly annotated, with general age level given. Separate author, title, and biographical indexes are appended." Booklist

Lynn, Ruth Nadelman
Fantasy for children; an annotated checklist. Bowker 1979 288p $17.95   **016.8**

1 Fantastic fiction—Bibliography   2 Fairy tales—Bibliography
ISBN 0-8352-1232-7   LC 79-21401

This book, "a comprehensive bibliographic guide to more than 1,650 recommended fantasies for children in grades three through eight, is intended for use by librarians, teachers, and parents. Approximately 1,200 titles are main entries; the remainder are sequels or related works that are mentioned in the annotations and are useful with the main entry. All titles were published in English in the United States (including translations into English) between 1900 and 1978, although a number of earlier classics, such as 'Alice in Wonderland,' have also been included. . . . Titles have been arranged in 13 chapters by type of fantasy, such as alternative worlds and imaginary lands, magical toys, mythical beings and creatures, and time travel. In general, science fiction, particularly books about space travel, technology, or scientific phenomena, is outside the scope of this book and has been omitted." Preface

Wilkin, Binnie Tate
Survival themes in fiction for children and young people; with a foreword by Jerome Cushman. Scarecrow 1978 256p $11   **016.8**

1 Fiction—Bibliography   2 Fiction—History and criticism   3 Children's literature—Bibliography   4 Children's literature—History and criticism
ISBN 0-8108-1048-4   LC 77-14295

Synopses of fiction books for children and adolescents are arranged in three main sections: the individual, pairings and groupings, and views of the world. Each entry includes analysis of the book's value in addressing contemporary problems of young people. Includes an introductory history of children's literature and an annotated source list." Ref Serv Rev

Wilkin, Binnie T.—*Continued*

Under the umbrella of 'survival' are subheadings embracing aloneness and loneliness, feelings, sexuality, images, for 'the individual'; friendship, peer pressures, families, for 'pairings and groupings'; and man and the environment, religion and politics, war and peace, celebration of life and death, for the enlarged 'views of the world.' The 'sources and notes' section is a gold mine with pungent insights appended to most of the titles. Title, author, and subject combine within a single alphabetized index. A respected librarian-professor-author, Wilkin cuts a new swath in the genre bibliography. This slim volume, because of its incisiveness outpaces any previous listing. A product of love and dignity, it demands sharing." Choice

016.9   Bibliographies of history

Metzner, Seymour

World history in juvenile books: a geographical and chronological guide. Wilson, H.W. 1973 356p $12   016.9

1 History—Bibliography 2 Historical fiction—Bibliography 3 Biography—Bibliography
ISBN 0-8242-0441-7   LC 72-11598

Companion volume to: American history in juvenile books, op 1981

"This bibliography lists around 2,700 titles for elementary and junior high school age groups relating to political and social aspects of world history. Each of ten chapters covers a large geographical area (e.g., Africa). The last chapter covers subjects of international interest. Books under each country are categorized as fiction, nonfiction and biography. Where there are many books available, chronological subheadings are used. Author, title, publisher, year, grade level and a brief annotation (when needed to disclose the subject) are provided. Selection was made from 'Books in Print', publishers' catalogs, and review journals." Cur Ref Bks

016.970004   Bibliographies of American Indians

Books on American Indians and Eskimos; a selection guide for children and young adults; Mary Jo Lass-Woodfin, editor. A.L.A. 1978 237p $20   016.970004

1 Indians of North America—Bibliography
ISBN 0-8389-0241-3   LC 77-17271

An annotated bibliography of "807 fiction and nonfiction books for young people about Native Americans in the United States. The materials, including some from denominational and little known publishers, reflect a wide spectrum of attitudes and outlooks. The lengthy annotations include grade-level estimates and quality indicators of 'Good,' 'Adequate,' and 'Poor'. . . . [Its index] provides access by tribes, persons, and events." Cur Ref Bks

"Each book listed was read by at least two reviewers, with the resulting comments summarizing their thoughts. Occasionally the reviewers' comments showed marked differences; therefore both reports are included. There are capsule notes on the reviewers. . . . [This book] is a useful, needed bibliography that can offer sound guidelines for the selection of books about Eskimos and native Americans for children and young adults." Booklist

Stensland, Anna Lee

Literature by and about the American Indian; an annotated bibliography; with contributions by Aune M. Fadum. 2d ed. Natl. Council of Teachers of English 1979 382p pa $6.95
                                              016.970004

1 Indians of North America—Bibliography 2 American literature—American Indian authors—Bibliography
ISBN 0-8141-2984-6   LC 79-18073

First published 1973

This bibliography "devotes Section I to teaching suggestions and Section II to the annotated bibliography itself under seven headings: Myth,

Legend, Oratory, and Poetry; Fiction; Biography and Autobiography, History; Traditional Life and Culture; Modern Life and Problems; and Music, Art, and Crafts. There is a foreword by a native American and the book ends with a directory of publishers and author-title indexes. Recommendations range from elementary school level to college and adult. The teaching section includes a basic list of Native American literature, sources of additional materials, and discussions of themes and stereotypes in the literature. There is also a list of biographies of selected American Indian authors. . . . This sets a model for this kind of publication and it would be useful for classroom English and social studies teachers, for librarians in collection building, reader's advisory or reference work, and also for youthworkers with a Native American clientele." VOYA

016.9733 Bibliographies of the American Revolution

Creating independence, 1763-1789; background reading for young people; a selected annotated bibliography. Comp. by Margaret N. Coughlan, Children's Book Section. Library of Congress [for sale by Supt. of Docs] 1972 62p illus pa $1.45   016.9733

1 U.S.—History—Revolution, 1775-1783—Bibliography
ISBN 0-8444-0029-7   LC 72-3573

This "attractively designed publication is an invaluable resource for librarians and teachers. Scholarly, readable annotations indicate the importance of the works selected and testify to meticulous research. The Preface by Virginia Haviland lists the criteria used for selection. The significance of these criteria is further developed in the pithy introduction by Richard B. Morris . . . which sets the American Revolution in historical perspective. Of particular interest to educators are the instructions for ordering photocopies of all illustrations—including reproductions of colonial currency—from the Library's photoduplication department. A unique contribution; a fundamental acquisition." Horn Bk

016.977   Bibliographies of the Middle West

Hinman, Dorothy

Reading for young people: the Midwest [by] Dorothy Hinman [and] Ruth Zimmerman. A.L.A. 1979 244p pa $10.50   016.977

1 Middle West—Bibliography
ISBN 0-8389-0271-5   LC 78-24479

"Describes the best available fiction, history, and biography pertaining to the Midwest states of Ohio, Indiana, Illinois, Iowa, and Missouri for readers in grades 4 through 10. Each entry in this bibliography provides an annotation emphasizing the book's strengths and weaknesses, the grades in which it may be used, and the state or states it covers. . . . [In the index] the subjects covered in the books are listed together with references to their exact location in those books." Publisher's note

016.978   Bibliographies of the Great Plains

Laughlin, Mildred

Reading for young people: the Great Plains. A.L.A. 1979 159p pa $7.50   016.978

1 Great Plains—Bibliography
ISBN 0-8389-0265   LC 78-27242

"A regionally-oriented list of books selected and annotated by a committee of librarians from Kansas, Nebraska, North Dakota, and South Dakota. The 368 books selected for inclusion reflect the adventures of those who followed the Santa Fe and Oregon Trails, the culture of the Plains Indians, heroes of fact and fiction, and the unsung settlers whose courageous spirit brought civilization to the

Laughlin, Mildred—*Continued*
region. . . . Each annotation opens with a short
quote to identify a unique style, theme, strong
character, or general mood. Brief descriptive resumes indicate each book's content, scope, and
general grade level. Access to the bibliography is
provided through a simple author, title, and subject index." Publisher's note

023 Library personnel

**American Association of School Librarians.
Certification of School Media Specialists
Committee**
Certification model for professional school
media personnel. A.L.A. 1976 32p pa $2   **023**

1 Instructional materials centers   2 Library education
ISBN 0-8389-3179-0   LC 76-366554

"Existing certification requirements for school
media specialists are determined by the separate
states and have become unduly diversified, if not
confusing. The present work introduces the basis
for rationalizing certification requirements by identifying the three criteria that must be integrated
into all the local systems of certification. Doing so
will make possible reevaluation and modernization
of the certification requirements in each state."
Publisher's note
Glossary: p29-30. Bibliography: p31-32

025.3 Bibliographic analysis and control

ALA Filing rules [prepared by the] Filing
Committee, Resources and Technical Services
Division, American Library Association.
A.L.A. 1980 50p pa $3.50   **025.3**

1 Files and filing   2 Catalogs, Card
ISBN 0-8389-3255-X   LC 80-22186

"The filing rules that follow offer guidelines for
the arrangement of displays of bibliographic records representing library materials. . . . 'ALA
Filing Rules' is the successor to 'A.L.A. Rules
for Filing Catalog Cards' (1942) and 'ALA Rules
for Filing Catalog Cards', second edition (1968).
Since the present rules are based to a much
greater extent than their predecessors on the
'file-as-is' principle, and since the new rules are
applicable to bibliographic displays in other than
card formats, the work should be considered as
new, and not as another edition. . . . The rules
reflect, with very few exceptions, the 'file-as-is'
principle; that is, that character strings (one or
more characters set off by spaces, dashes, hyphens,
diagonal slashes, or periods) to be considered for
filing should be considered in exactly the form
and order in which they appear. This principle
emphasizes the way character strings look rather
than the way they sound or their meaning.
. . . The basic order of filing is word by word.
. . . The present rules are intended to be applicable to the arrangement of bibliographic records, whether by manual or automated means."
Introduction

Akers, Susan Grey
Akers' Simple library cataloging. 6th ed.
completely rev. and rewritten by Arthur Curley
and Jana Varlejs. Scarecrow 1977 338p illus
$8.50   **025.3**

1 Cataloging
ISBN 0-8108-0978-8   LC 76-26897

First published 1927 by American Library Association
This manual of library classification and cataloging has been designed for the inexperienced or
untrained librarian working in a small library,
although it can also serve as an introduction for
library school students. Fundamental classification
and cataloging rules are presented with numerous
illustrations and an appendix of sample catalog
cards. The volume surveys the use of the Dewey
Decimal Classification tables, Sears List of Subject Headings, the Anglo-American Cataloging
Rules, and the A.L.A. Rules for Filing Catalog
Cards. There is also a section dealing with central-
ized and cooperative cataloging
Appendices include abbreviations, definitions of
technical terms, and a bibliography

Anglo-American cataloging rules. 2d ed. prepared by the American Library Association,
the British Library, the Canadian, Committee
on Cataloguing, the Library Association, the
Library of Congress. Ed. by Michael Gorman
and Paul W. Winkler. A.L.A. 1978 620p $15
pa $10   **025.3**

1 Cataloging
ISBN 0-8389-3210-X; 0-8389-3211-8
       LC 78-13789
First published 1967
"These rules are designed for use in the construction of catalogues and other lists in general
libraries of all sizes. . . . The rules cover the
description and entry of all library materials commonly collected at the present time, and the integrated structure of the text will facilitate the use
of the general rules as a basis for cataloguing un-
comonly collected materials of all kinds and library
materials yet unknown. This edition of the rules
incorporates numerous agreements on the development of rules in the first edition and is based on
a reconciliation of the British and North American
texts of that edition. The reconciliation extends
to style, which in this edition is generally in ac-
cordance with the University of Chicago Press
'A Manual of Style', and to spellings, which are
those of 'Webster's New International Dictionary.'
. . . The rules follow the sequence of cataloguers'
operations in most present-day libraries and bibliographic agencies, in that Part I deals with the
provision of information describing the item being
catalogued and Part II deals with the determination and establishment of headings, or access points
in the catalogue, under which the descriptive information is to be presented to catalogue users,
and with the making of reference to those headings. . . . In both parts the rules proceed from the
general to the specific." General introduction
Appendices include capitalization, abbreviations,
numerals and glossary

Piercy, Esther J.
Commonsense cataloging; a manual for the
organization of books and other materials in
school and small public libraries. 2d ed. rev.
by M. Sanner. Wilson, H.W. 1974 233p illus $9
    025.3

1 Cataloging
ISBN 0-8242-0009-8   LC 73-7573

First published 1965
Designed as a practical manual for the beginning
cataloger, the book proceeds from the general to
the specific, from principles to practice. The appendixes include routines, a glossary and a bibliography

Weihs, Jean
Nonbook materials: the organization of integrated collections. 2d ed. [by] Jean Weihs
with Shirley Lewis [and] Janet Macdonald in
consultation with the CLA/ALA/AECT/AM-
TEC Advisory Committee on the Cataloguing
of Nonbook Materials. Canadian Lib. Assn.
1979 134p illus pa $8   **025.3**

1 Cataloging—Audio-visual materials
ISBN 0-88802-130-5

Also available from the American Library Association (ISBN 0-8389-3244-4)
First published 1973
This volume discusses rules pertaining to nonbook materials including art originals, charts, dio-
ramas, filmstrips, flash cards, games, globes, kits,
machine-readable data files, maps, microforms,
microscope slides, models, motion pictures, pictures, realia, slides, sound recordings, technical
drawings, transparencies, and videorecordings.
Cataloging policy, subject analysis, filing, and
storage are discussed and alternatives considered
Glossary: p109-10. Bibliography: p128-32

025.4 Subject analysis and control

Dewey, Melvil
Abridged Dewey Decimal classification and relative index; devised by Melvil Dewey. Edition 11. Ed. under the direction of Benjamin A. Custer. Forest Press 1979 618p $24   **025.4**
1 Classification, Dewey Decimal
ISBN 0-910608-13-X   LC 78-12514
Also available from The H. W. Wilson Company
First abridged edition published 1894
Based on the 19th Unabridged Edition, the 11th Abridged Edition is an abridgment in contrast to the 10th Edition which was an adaptation. Intended to meet the needs of small and growing libraries, the 11th Abridged Edition is designed primarily for school and public libraries with collections of up to 20,000 titles. There are 2,516 entries in the schedules and auxiliary tables, compared to 29,528 in the 19th Unabridged Edition on which it is based. Changes in this edition include expansions in the Social Sciences, Pure Sciences, and the Arts. The schedules and tables for Sociology, Political Process and the British Isles have been completely revised
This is the classification system used for this catalog

Sears List of subject headings. 11th ed. Edited by Barbara M. Westby. Wilson, H.W. 1977 xli, 617p illus $18   **025.4**
1 Subject headings
ISBN 0-8242-0610-X   LC 77-807
First published 1923 with title: List of subject headings for small libraries, by Minnie Earl Sears
This list of headings follows the Library of Congress form of headings with appropriate adaptations to meet the needs of smaller libraries. This edition features suggested classification numbers for the subject headings. The numbers are based upon the Tenth Edition of the Abridged Dewey classification and relative index. The Eleventh edition of the latter title, providing recent changes in classification numbers, is entered above
Materials for further reference: pxxxiii-xxxiv

Sears List of subject headings: Canadian companion; comp. by Ken Haycock and Lynne Isberg. Wilson, H.W. 1978 50p $5.50   **025.4**
1 Subject headings
ISBN 0-8242-0629-0   LC 78-13687
"The principles and practices of subject cataloging are clearly outlined in the introduction to 'Sears List of Subject Headings [entered above].' . . . It is essential that these be reviewed before proceeding to use this companion volume. 'As a companion volume to Sears, this list is in no way to be regarded as a comprehensive list of subject headings or as a Canadian substitute for Sears.' Only Canadian references are given for headings in this list. The cataloger must still consult 'Sears' under the appropriate heading(s) to identify what general references might also be suggested, advisable or necessary. . . . The lists are compatible. Nevertheless, due to the Canadian context, some headings do break 'Sears' niles. . . . 'Sears headings have been duplicated in the companion volume only if there are different classification numbers or subdivisions or cross-references from a Canadian topic. Some Canadian topics, e.g. Maple sugar, are not in the companion volume since they are already in 'Sears.' . . . Primary sources for the development of the Canadian companion include 'Sears List of Subject Headings.' 11th edition (H.W. Wilson, 1977). 'A list of Canadian Subject Headings' (Canadian Library Association. 1968) and 'Columbo's Canadian References' (Oxford University Press, 1976). Additional indexes and reference works were consulted for current headings and historical periods especially." Introduction

027 General libraries

Hardendorff, Jeanne B.
Libraries and how to use them. Watts, F. 1979 61p illus lib. bdg. $5.45 (3-6)   **027**
1 Libraries
ISBN 0-531-02259-5   LC 78-12992

"A First book"
"Brief introductory material is provided on the history of libraries, Dewey and Library of Congress classification systems, catalogs, and reference books. Technical terms such as 'shelf list,' 'inter-library loan,' and 'microfiche' appear in bold print and are defined in context. . . . Although the author uses a traditional introduction to the card catalog, alternatives are cited." Sch Library J
"A former librarian and teacher of library science provides an explicit and well-organized text for the child who needs information on organization and use of library materials. . . . A useful book, written with crisp authority." Chicago. Children's Bk Center

Wilson Library Bulletin. Wilson, H.W. $17 per year   **027**
1 Library science—Periodicals 2 Libraries—Periodicals 3 Books and reading—Periodicals
ISSN 0043-5651
Monthly except July and August. First published 1914 with title: The Wilson Bulletin
"With 'Library Journal,' the only substantial national library magazine published by an independent publisher with an interest in all aspects of the profession. The result is a publication outstanding in its quality. Each issue contains either two to three substantial articles on varied topics (e.g., the art of book binding, user problems in a historical society library, and publicity ideas for the small public library—all in one recent issue) or a series of articles on one central topic (e.g., library education, prison library services). The writing style is professional, lively, informative, and quite often controversial. There are many departments, including excellent reference book reviews and reviews of films for small and medium-sized public libraries. The makeup from the cover to the last page is as imaginative as are the contents. Essential for all libraries." Katz Magazines for libraries. 3d edition

027.4 Public libraries

Rockwell, Anne
I like the library. Dutton 1977 unp illus $6.50 (k-1)   **027.4**
1 Public libraries
ISBN 0-525-32528-X   LC 77-6365
"In a brief text printed beneath explicit pictures, a small boy tells of his weekly visit to the public library. While his mother selects her own books, he participates in a story hour and in an audio-visual session, chooses picture books and a recording to take home, observes a baby in a library playpen and some older children absorbed in a chess game, and watches the charging machine." Horn Bk
"The element most often missing in children's books about libraries is delight. It's here in abundance. Pictures [by the author] and story line blend to relate the experiences of a preschool child. . . . The book has a bright future as a staple for picture book programs (capable of generating additional 'I like . . .' ideas from youngsters), and parents will find it pleasant and positive for sharing on a one-to-one basis." Booklist

027.62 Libraries for children and young adults

Broderick, Dorothy M.
An introduction to children's work in public libraries. Wilson, H.W. 1965 176p $6   **027.62**
1 Libraries, Children's 2 Children's literature
ISBN 0-8242-0027-6   LC 64-22813
Building a proper collection of books for children and insuring maximum use of that collection is the subject of this book, the first half of which treats the philosophy of service to children, problems of book selection, organization and administration of children's rooms, and the relation of the library to the community. The second half deals with the various areas in children's literature, and closes with a chapter on books about children's books, an appendix listing books mentioned in the text, and an index

Broderick, Dorothy M.—*Continued*

Library work with children. Wilson, H.W. 1977 197p $10   **027.62**

1 Libraries, Children's
ISBN 0-8242-0620-7   LC 77-14288

"Originally meant as a revision of the author's 'An introduction to children's work in public libraries' [entered above] this work developed into an entirely new text, reflecting the many changes in children's librarianship. The content is organized into two basic sections: the collection, and library services. Within the first, the author presents the basic elements of building a children's collection and discusses some of the issues surrounding materials for children. There are separate chapters on selection standards, 'the ism controversy,' and sex and sexuality in children's books. Part two on library services opens with a description of the child in the library. Children's programs and the library's relationship to its community are discused. In a chapter on areas related to children's work, the author discusses the theories of Jean Piaget, death and moral judgment, and the influence of television. Finally, the author outlines the needs for continuing professional education in children's work." J Academic Librarianship

"There is no definitive work on library service to children, but in many respects this book can fill the gap until one does appear. It addresses itself to children's librarians in public libraries, to school librarians, to young adult librarians (the word 'children' in the title is somewhat misleading), and to their Canadian counterparts. It will cause its readers to think and to rethink and therein lies its value." Top of the News
Bibliography: p168-82

Children's services of public libraries; Selma K. Richardson, editor. Univ. of Ill. Graduate Sch. of Library Science 1978 178p $9
027.62

1 Libraries, Children's 2 Library service
ISBN 0-87845-049-1   LC 78-11503

"Papers presented at the Allerton Park Institute sponsored by University of Illinois Graduate School of Libary Science, held November 13-16, 1977, Allerton House, Monticello, Illinois"

Following the editor's introduction and a discussion of the goals of public library services for children this volume presents papers on the following topics: the child, the children's librarian, services, facilities, materials, research, and evaluations of the Institute program

Dyer, Esther R.

Cooperation in library service to children. Scarecrow 1978 152p $8   **027.62**

1 Libraries, Children's 2 Libraries and schools
3 Library cooperation
ISBN 0-8108-1111-1   LC 77-28190

"The administration and governance of two tax-supported public institutions, the public school and the public library, and their common client group is the subject of this book. It is, therefore, not a book about children's services in public libraries and media services in public schools as separate entities but rather about the driving and restraining forces which affect the probability and desirability of interaction between these two institutions. Undeniably a study of administrative constraints, institutional rigidity and vested interests, this research also provides fresh insights into and a different perpective on an old problem. In the chapters which follow the comments of individual participating experts, and statistical breakdowns of total panel reactions are woven together to provide a clearer picture of the current thinking of the leadership level of the profession." Preface

Partial contents: Cooperative patterns (Actual and proposed); The urban outlook; The non-urban outlook; Inter-institutional relations; The coordinators and supervisors; Location of facilities; Alternative administrative patterns; Manpower; Program alternatives: internal coordination by agreement; Program alternatives: joint provision of services by contract; Program alternatives: division of responsibility; Program alternatives: telecommunications
Bibliography: p143-48

Hill, Janet

Children are people; the librarian in the community. Crowell [1974 c1973] 163p illus $8.95   **027.62**

1 Libraries, Children's 2 Libraries and community 3 Children's literature
ISBN 0-690-00475-3   LC 73-16277
First published 1973 in England

"The author, a London children's librarian, shares her insight on the work of the librarian in the community, with suggestions on storytelling, book selection and concerns of minority groups." Wis Library Bul

"The book is interesting because the author has done a fine job in her career as a children's librarian in Lambeth, but the problems of British librarians are not the problems of those in the U.S.A. Her philosophy, however, is one that librarians everywhere can adopt, 'taking library services out to those who use them least and possibly need them most.'" Cath Library World

Renfro, Nancy

A puppet corner in every library. Nancy Renfro Studios 1978 110p illus pa $8.95 **027.62**

1 Puppets and puppet plays 2 Libraries, Children's
ISBN 0-931044-01-4   LC 78-1808

Contents: Using puppets in the library; A library mascot or symbol; A get-acquainted friend; An informal puppet-corner; A way to teach library concepts and functions to children; A media-loan service; An aid to story-telling; For play productions by children and/or librarians; For children's workshops; A cultural enrichment program by professional puppeteers for the community as a whole; The stage; The puppets; Articles—puppets in the library; Resources

The **Special** child in the library. Barbara Holland Baskin and Karen H. Harris, editors. A.L.A. 1976 199p $9   **027.62**

1 Libraries, Children's 2 Exceptional children 3 Library service
ISBN 0-8389-0222-7

There are certain "adaptations necessary to adequately serve the exceptional child. Because of progress in technology and the increasing level of involvement of the special child in the library program, the librarian needs to have readily available a handbook which will cogently present a philosophical base for procedures, a compendium of information on materials, examples of creative, unusual and effective programs, and guidelines for environmental modifications. This book of readings is offered in the hope that the new practitioners, in addition to experienced librarians who wish to increase their knowledge and competency vis à vis the exceptional child, will find herein exciting ideas and the means to implement them." Introduction

Start early for an early start; you and the young child; [prepared by] Preschool Services and Parent Education Committee, Children's Services Division, American Library Association with the cooperation of Early Childhood Education Committee, American Association of School Librarians; Ferne Johnson, editor. A.L.A. 1976 181p illus pa $7.50   **027.62**

1 Libraries, Children's 2 Children's literature
ISBN 0-8389-3185-5   LC 76-44237

"The purpose of this book is to provide tested, effective methods, techniques, and resources to help all those interested in the intellectual growth and development of young children. . . . The contributors, all actively engaged in careers directly related to the welfare of young children, have consistently emphasized the why and how of library-related service to preschoolers and to adults responsible for their welfare. The sources of additional information cited in reference lists and bibliographies are selective and meant to be suggestive only. The programs described are current; their value has been, and in most cases continues to be, documented. Entire projects or selected elements may be adapted with confidence by public and school libraries of any size." Preface

"Because books on library work with pre-school children are few and far between and because articles on the topic are scattered in library and

Start early for an early start—*Continued*
education periodical literature [this book] is a
good investment for everyone planning programs
with parents and very young children. The background information on child development and the
many suggested reading lists and bibliographies
extend the usefulness of this compact reference
source for children's librarians." Sch Library J

027.6205 Libraries for children and young adults—Periodicals

Top of the News. A.L.A. $15 per year   027.6205
1 Libraries, Children's—Periodicals
ISSN 0040-9286
Quarterly. First published 1942
"Journal of the Association for Library Service
to Children and the Young Adult Services Division of the American Library Association"
"This and 'School Library Journal' [entered in
class 027.805] are the best general magazines covering the field of school librarianship from the elementary through the high school scene. It has improved with the years, and while the writing is
uneven, the overall feeling is of dedication with a
dash of realism, and a dash of cynicism about
instant cures for anything. Most of the authors
are practicing librarians who know of what they
speak. Brief reviews of magazines, books (including new editions), and media in 'The Top' and
lengthier ones in 'Added Entries,' along with much
association and other news, add to the usefulness
of this highly recommended journal." Katz. Magazines for Libraries, 3d edition

027.8 School libraries

Cultural pluralism & children's media. Esther
R. Dyer, compiler; Jane Anne Hannigan, series
editor. A.L.A. 1978 [i.e. 1979] 77p (School
media centers: focus on trends and issues)
pa $4.50   027.8
1 School libraries   2 Instructional materials centers 3 Library service 4 Minorities
ISBN 0-8389-3218-5   LC 78-25845
Contents: Children's media for a culturally pluralistic society, by E. R. Dyer; American Indian
people and children's resources, by C. A. Metoyer;
The Afro-American heritage in children's fiction,
by C. M. Annelli; The Asian American: divergent
elements of cultural pluralism, by F. M. Yoshiwara
and V. Kobayashi; The role of media centers in
bilingual education, by R. A. Thomas
"The unifying theme of this work is the value of
culturally pluralistic materials and service for library programs. Within a legislative and societal
framework, Esther Dyer discusses the potential
role of the media center in smoothing transition
from a melting pot to a multicultural philosophy.
. . . Whereas the first chapter in this book is general in nature, the succeeding chapters address the
specific client needs, programs, and materials of
four cultural or ethnic groups: American Indian,
Asian American, Afro-American and Spanish-speaking peoples. While this book is not a comprehensive
treatment of the variety of cultural and ethnic
groups comprising the American mosaic, the problems, issues, and concerns about materials and
services for these major groups provide valuable
information for those professionals who seek to
develop culturally pluralistic programs and collections." Introduction
Includes chapter bibliographies

Davies, Ruth Ann
The school library media program; instructional force for excellence. 3d ed. Bowker 1979
580p illus $16.95   027.8
1 School libraries   2 Instructional materials
centers
ISBN 0-8352-1244-0   LC 79-20358
First published 1969 with title: The school library
Partial contents: The teaching role of the library
media specialist; The curriculum support role
of the library media specialist; The library media

specialist's role as instructional technologist; The
library media program supports the English program; The lbrary media program supports the
social studies program; The library media program
supports the science and mathematics programs;
The library media program supports the human-
ities program; The library media program implements the developmental skills program; Evaluating the effectiveness of the school library media
program; Basic background readings; A sample
interdisciplinary unit; A guide for constructing
mini-courses; Media evaluation guidelines; How
to use ERIC; Thinking-learning-communicating
skills continuum, K-12; Facilities planning; Terminology; Bibliography
"The goals and services of the school media
center should focus on the needs of the students
and activities must be closely related to the curriculum, says the author and she provides practical, meaningful help to the library media specialist. . . . This is done thoroughly and should be
most helpful to educators interested in the total
involvement of students, teachers, and librarians.
. . . I am enthusiastic about the book; I appreciate authors who deal with the day-to-day issues
and offer practical assistance. I recommend it
heartily to media specialists, future media specialists and educators in general." Cath Library World

Gillespie, John T.
Creating a school media program [by] John
T. Gillespie [and] Diana L. Spirt. Bowker 1973
236p $16.25   027.8
1 School libraries   2 Instructional materials centers
ISBN 0-8352-0484-7   LC 77-164032
This book discusses the "basic principles and
practices involved in creating, organizing, and ad-
ministering an individual school media center. The
focus is on practical considerations, especially in
regard to problems to be anticipated in converting
a school library to a media center. Part one is a
very brief history of the development of the school
media center concept; part two discusses the
nature, elements, and evaluation of media programs; and part three concentrates on specific
aspects of management of a media center-budget,
staff facilities, selection, and acquisition and
organization. . . . The whole book is noteworthy
for its precise text, with no unnecessary verbiage,
its illustrations, and its lists." Am Ref Bks
Annual, 1975
Selected readings: p223-26

The young phenomenon: paperbacks in our
schools [by] John T. Gillespie [and] Diana L.
Spirt. A.L.A. 1972 140p (ALA Studies in
librarianship) pa $5   027.8
1 Paperback books   2 School libraries
ISBN 0-8389-0133-6   LC 72-2653
Companion volume to: Paperback books for young
people, entered in class 070.5025
"A survey of the use of paperbacks in elementary
and secondary schools based on an interpretation
and analysis of the computer data from a 1967
school paperback survey conducted by the School
Improvement Committee of the American Association of School Librarians, augmented by a 1970
follow-up survey designed by the authors to update the earlier questionnaire. The book highlights
effective programs and treats book selection, administration of paperback collections, and the sale
of paperbacks in schools. A practical guide to
dealing with paperbacks this . . . will be useful
. . . for librarians, teachers, and others concerned
with paperbacks." Booklist
Selected bibliography: p113-18

Lowrie, Jean Elizabeth
Elementary school libraries. 2d ed. Scarecrow 1970 238p $7   027.8
1 School libraries
ISBN 0-8108-0305-4
First published 1961
Partial contents: Curriculum supportive experiences in the middle grades; Reading guidance in
the middle grades library program; "How do I
find—"; The teacher and the school library; Role
of the school administrator; Community relationships; Children's books mentioned in text; Bibliography

Media center facilities design; comp. and ed. by Jane Anne Hannigan and Glenn E. Estes. A.L.A. 1978 117p illus pa $10.50   027.8
1 Instructional materials centers   2 School libraries
ISBN 0-8389-3212-6   LC 78-93336
"This work describes in detail the architectural features, facilities, and equipment needed for an effective media center. The role of staff and students is outlined with emphasis on introducing the media specialist to planning sessions. Planning considerations requiring tradeoffs to design and architecture are explained, and the relation between educational program and physical facilities is shown." Publisher's note
Resources: p113-14

Nickel, Mildred L.
Steps to service; a handbook of procedures for the school library media center. A.L.A. 1975 124p illus pa $4.50   027.8
1 School libraries   2 Instructional materials centers
ISBN 0-8389-0161-1   LC 74-19420
"This handbook is a source of help to the beginning librarian and a review for the experienced librarian seeking to reevaluate his/her program. It also serves as an instructional and procedural handbook for paraprofessionals, clerks and volunteers. Under appropriate headings, the author treats basic concerns: budget, evaluation and selection of materials, ordering and receiving, processing, use of materials, mending, rebinding, discarding, inventory, reports, supplies, instruction in the use of media, staff relationships and technological developments. Also included is a glossary and a directory of publishers, producers and suppliers." Wis Library Bul

Peterson, Ralph
A place for caring and celebration: the school media center. A.L.A. 1979 33p (School media centers: focus on issues and trends) pa $3   027.8
1 School libraries   2 Instructional materials centers
ISBN 0-8389-3229-0   LC 78-31809
"Identifies the qualities that give the media center its special educational value—its openness to students, its suitability for a wide variety of activities, and its range of resources that encourages exercise of imagination for both the individual and the group." Publisher's note

Sullivan, Peggy
Problems in school media management. Bowker 1971 245p (Bowker Ser. in problem-centered approaches to librarianship) $14.95   027.8
1 School libraries   2 Instructional materials centers
ISBN 0-8352-0427-8   LC 78-126023
The author presents thirty case studies for librarians and library students reviewing current problems involving the administration and organization of school media programs
"Undoubtedly the book will prove invaluable as a supplementary text, as it can provide the basis for discussions, for role playing, and for simulation exercises. It covers a vast range of problems, from those related to teaching library skills, to censorship, and covers numerous critical areas. The cases are germane and representative, but are not intended to be comprehensive." Sch Library J

Vandergrift, Kay
The teaching role of the school media specialist. A.L.A. 1979 56p (School media centers: focus on trends and issues) pa $4   027.8
1 School libraries   2 Instructional materials centers   3 Library service
ISBN 0-8389-3222-3   LC 78-27401
"Discusses the three instructional functions of the media specialist. Starting from the distinction between teaching and instruction, this work describes the importance of the media specialist in making a place conducive to education and in planning functions." Publisher's note

027.805   School libraries— Periodicals

SLJ/School Library Journal; for children's, young adult, and school librarians. Bowker $23 per year   027.805
1 School libraries—Periodicals   2 Books—Reviews
ISSN 0000-0035
Monthly August through May. First published 1954 with title: Junior libraries
"The best of the magazines devoted to work with children and teenagers in libraries. Articles cover all aspects of work with young people, but the magazine has gained a deserved reputation for publishing material (both from librarians and from staffers) that leads, rather than follows, the movements in the library field. There are usually four excellent, well-written articles per issue, three regular columns, a number of departments (news, professional reading, some lively letters to the editor, etc.), and first-rate book reviews. An essential purchase for all school and public libraries." Katz. Magazines for Libraries, 3d edition

School Librarian. School Library Assn. $30 per year   027.805
1 School libraries—Periodicals   2 Books—Reviews
ISSN 0036-6595
Quarterly. First published 1937
"The official voice of the British School Library Association, this quarterly consists of two major parts. The first section includes three to four articles of interest to readers. The second consists of 60 to 70 pages (out of approximately 90 to 100 pages in an issue) of book reviews. The signed reviews are well written, descriptive, evaluative, and often critical. Emphasis is on British books, but notes on AV materials, professional reading, etc., are included. The reviews of 150 to 200 words are grouped by subject and by age level. An index, arranged alphabetically by author, facilitates the search for a particular selection. The reviews are as good as any found in the standard American works such as 'Hornbook' or 'School Library Journal.'" Katz. Magazines for libraries, 3d edition

School Media Quarterly. A.L.A. $15 per year   027.805
1 School libraries—Periodicals   2 Instructional materials centers—Periodicals
First published 1972. Formerly School libraries
"Journal of the American Association of School Librarians"
"Another attractive and well-edited ALA division publication, each 60- to 70-page issue contains four or five articles by practicing librarians, a number of departments, book reviews (including reviews of government publications), and, of course, news of the Association. The articles are deeply involved with change in elementary and high school libraries. Along with 'School Library Journal' and 'Top of the News' [entered in classes 027.805 and 027.6205 respectively] this is essential for all school librarians." Katz. Magazines for Libraries. 3d edition

028.1   Book reviews

Chicago. University. Graduate Library School
Bulletin of the Center for Children's Books Univ. of Chicago Press $10 per year   028.1
1 Books—Reviews   2 Children's literature—Periodicals
ISSN 0008-9036
Monthly except August. First published 1945
"Both recommended and not recommended titles are included in this review periodical. Highly regarded for its critical evaluations of books, this source contains reviews for about 70 books in each issue. Entries contain grade level indications and ratings including the following: recommended, additional book of acceptable quality for collections needing more material in this area, marginal book that is slight in content or weak in style or format, not recommended, subject matter or treatment will tend to limit the book to specialized collections, and a book that will have appeal for the unusual reader only." Peterson. Ref Bks for Elem and Jr High Sch Libraries

Children's book review index. Gale Res. $42

028.1

1 Books—Reviews—Indexes 2 Children's literature—Reviews—Indexes LC 75-27408

Annual. First published 1975
Editor: 1975— Gary C. Tarbert
"An index citing all reviews about children's books listed in Gale Research's 'Book Review Index' (BRI). Compiled by the same editorial staff which has responsibility for BRI. . . . Reviews cited appear in periodicals devoted to children's literature such as 'Horn Book' and in general education and literary journals such as 'Instructor' and 'Saturday Review' as well as in journals concentrating on specialized fields of interest such as social studies. Reviews from prestigious newspapers are also included. In total, more than 250 periodicals and newspapers are indexed. Coverage of titles runs from preschool up to and including eighth grade. . . . Each entry is arranged alphabetically by author, giving book title, abbreviation of the published review, volume number, date of issue and page number." Ref Serv Rev
Title index, absent in volume one, added in later volumes

Gillespie, John
Introducing books; a guide for the middle grades, by John Gillespie and Diana Lembo. Bowker 1970 318p $13.95 **028.1**

1 Books—Reviews 2 Literature—Stories, plots, etc. 3 Books and reading
ISBN 0-8352-0215-1 LC 74-94512

Companion volume: Introducing more books, by Diana L. Spirt, entered below
"Over 80 titles suitable for readers from about age 9 to 14 receive detailed treatment in this book for teachers and librarians, a companion volume to the authors' 'Juniorplots' [entered below]. The titles have been classified according to generally accepted development goals which are expressed by 11 headings such as Making Friends, Developing Values, etc. The material for each title is arranged in four parts: Plot Analysis, Thematic Material, Book Talk Material, and Additional Suggestions (including related books). There is an author-title index; the subject index rearranges the titles under topics rather than themes." Wynar. Guide to Ref Bks for Sch Media Centers

Juniorplots; a book talk manual for teachers and librarians, by John Gillespie and Diana Lembo. Bowker 1967 222p $13.95 **028.1**

1 Books—Reviews 2 Literature—Stories, plots, etc. 3 Books and reading
ISBN 0-8352-0063-9 LC 67-18146

"Similar in goals and arrangement to the authors' 'Introducing Books' [entered above] 'Juniorplots' analyzes books, according to the authors, for youngsters 9 to 16. However, a close look at the material included reveals very few titles appealing to either the 9 or the 16 year old, for most seem geared to the middle school level. The choices, however, are good, and can be easily located in either the author-title index or the subject index." Peterson. Ref Bks for Elem and Jr High Sch Libraries

More juniorplots; a guide for teachers and librarians. Bowker 1977 xxv, 253p lib. bdg. $12.95

028.1

1 Books—Reviews 2 Literature—Stories, plots, etc. 3 Books and reading
ISBN 0-8352-1002-2 LC 77-8786

Companion volume to Juniorplots, entered above
"This book consists primarily of plots and related material on 72 books. The titles have been organized under nine developmental goals associated with adolescence. In a supplementary index, the books are also listed under conventional subject headings (e.g., Adventure Stories, Animal Stories). The nine developmental goals are: (1) getting along in the family; (2) developing lasting values; (3) understanding social problems; (4) developing an understanding of the past and other cultures; (5) understanding physical and emotional problems; (6) becoming self-reliant; (7) developing relationships with both sexes; (8) developing a wholesome self-image; and (9 developing a respect for nature and living things." Preface

The **Junior** Bookshelf; a review of children's books. Marsh Hall $10 per year **028.1**

1 Books—Reviews 2 Children's literature—Periodicals
ISSN 0022-6505

6 issues per year. First published 1936
"An English magazine that reviews some 125 to 150 children's books (i.e., preschool through about the eighth grade). The reviews are well written, critical, and descriptive. Most, although not all, titles are published in the United Kingdom. There are excellent articles on all aspects of children's reading and books." Katz. Magazines for Libraries, 3d edition

Kirkus Reviews. Kirkus Service apply to publisher for price **028.1**

1 Books—Reviews
ISSN 0042-6598

Juvenile reviews may be subscribed to separately
Loose-leaf
Semimonthly. First published 1934
"Highly critical reviews of about 70 children's books and 140 adult books are contained in each issue of this book review service. A major advantage of this source is that it reviews titles early, often before publication of the book. Each issue is indexed with indexes cumulating at three and six month intervals." Peterson. Ref Bks for Elem and Jr High Sch Libraries

The **New** York Times Book Review. N.Y. Times Co. illus $15 per year **028.1**

1 Books—Reviews
ISSN 0028-7806

Weekly. First published 1896
" 'The New York Times Book Review' is a section of the Sunday 'New York Times' and is available separately by subscription. The coverage is broad, aiming at new adult books of literary and cultural interest and books on contemporary political, economic, and social problems. Biography, popular history, and literature are emphasized. A moderate number of children's books are also reviewed. . . . All reviews give author, title, place and publisher, pages, price, and name of the reviewer. The young reader's page reviews from two to six books each week (about 200 or more books per year) plus additional titles contained in two Special Children's Book Issues. Picture books, fiction, and nonfiction are all included. The purpose of these reviews is to inform parents, children's librarians, and bookstore operators of those children's books most likely to be favorites or at least substantial choices for a child's home reading; some books that receive less than favorable evaluations are also reviewed." Wynar. Guide to Ref Bks for Sch Media Centers

Spirt, Diana L.
Introducing more books; a guide for the middle grades. Bowker 1978 240p $13.95 **028.1**

1 Books—Reviews 2 Literature—Stories, plots, etc. 3 Books and reading
ISBN 0-8352-0988-1 LC 78-13490

Companion volume to: Introducing books, by John Gillespie and the author, entered above
"In this volume, there are plot summaries of 72 books, which together with the 6 or 7 related materials suggested for reading, viewing, or listening make a listing of almost 500 titles. The titles have been carefully read and put under an appropriate developmental goal for middle childhood. . . . Each of the main titles is divided into these sections: 1. 'Plot Summary.' The story is summarized emphasizing the important characters and situations and hopefully retaining some of the author's flavor. Brief references to the author and illustrator, as well as age appeal, are given in the beginning paragraphs. 2. 'Thematic Analysis.' Both main and subthemes are stated to encourage multiple uses in presenting the title. 3. 'Discussion Materials.' Various ways of introducing the book are suggested. Pages and illustrations that are suitable for reading aloud, describing or displaying, book talking, or discussing are also given. 4. 'Related Materials.' Included are books and audio-visual titles on similar themes or topics that may interest the same readers." Preface

028.5   Reading of children and young adults

Andrews, Siri
  (ed.) The Hewins lectures, 1947-1962; introduction by Frederic G. Melcher. Horn Bk. 1963 375p pa $5   **028.5**
  1 Children's literature—History and criticism
  2 American literature—History and criticism
  ISBN 0-87675-056-0   LC 63-21644
  Suggested in 1946 by Frederic G. Melcher, this is "a series of lectures on New England books for children, by New England residents. . . . The first fifteen are included in this volume, and invite both a backward and forward look at children's literature. All but one of the Lectures are on some aspect of writing for children; the one exception is that on New England folklore." The editor

Authors and illustrators of children's books; writings on their lives and works [ed. by] Miriam Hoffman and Eva Samuels. Bowker 1972 471p $17.95   **028.5**
  1 Children's literature—History and criticism
  2 Authors 3 Illustrators
  ISBN 0-8352-0523-1   LC 76-38607
  A collection of articles, culled from periodicals and newspapers, about fifty authors and illustrators of children's literature
  "The title is somewhat misleading, since illustrators who are not also authors are omitted, as are poets. Although a number of journals are represented, the bulk of the articles originally appeared in 'Elementary English.' The articles are arranged alphabetically by biographee. Editors' notes following each article offer some updating, although this is not always consistently handled. Notes also indicate honors and awards given to the biographees and books published since the date of the original article. An appendix lists each author-illustrator's works. In spite of the wide variation in coverage, style, and length of the articles, this biographical reader is of importance to all children's literature collections." Wynar. Guide to Ref Bks for Sch Media Centers

Bechtel, Louise Seaman
  Books in search of children; speeches and essays; selected and with an introduction by Virginia Haviland. Macmillan Pub. Co. 1969 xx, 268p illus $6.95   **028.5**
  1 Children's literature—History and criticism
  2 Books and reading
  ISBN 0-02-508290-6   LC 79-78078
  "The growth and diversity of publishing for children is reflected in the pieces chosen to celebrate the 50th anniversary of the Children's Book Department of the Macmillan Company which was the pioneering effort of Louise Seaman Bechtel. After a graceful introduction by Virginia Haviland touching on the highlights of Bechtel's career, the selections, from 'Horn Book', 'Library Journal', and other periodicals and from her speeches, cover individual authors and illustrators, the heritage of children's literature, preparation of a publisher's catalog, and books for children under five years. The title essay is a study of the professions that contribute to books for children. Illustrations are taken from early Macmillan catalogs for boys and girls." Booklist
  Index of titles, authors and artists: p256-68

The **Black** American in books for children: readings in racism; ed. and with an introduction by Donnarae MacCann and Gloria Woodard. Scarecrow 1972 223p $8.50   **028.5**
  1 Racism in literature 2 Blacks in literature and art 3 Children's literature—History and criticism
  ISBN 0-8108-0526-X   LC 72-4490
  "Intended to make schools and libraries more conscious of their responsibilities in 'alleviating the negative racial attitudes and behavior of white Americans toward black Americans and to nurture the self-esteem and racial pride of black Americans,' these 23 reprints of articles from library and education journals of the late '60's and early '70's include such well-known contributors as Augusta Baker, Binnie Tate, and Nancy Larrick. Minority publishing and the portrayal of the Black in children's literature are the principal

themes, treated in both general terms and in the analysis of individual works, such as 'The "Real" Doctor Dolittle.' Indexes to titles and authors of children's books mentioned in the articles are appended." Ref Serv Rev
  "Though the articles vary greatly in style, coherence, logic, and polemics, the selection is an important one for anyone who is interested in what is considered racist in children's books." Horn Bk

Boy Scouts of America
  Reading. The Author illus pa 55¢   **028.5**
  1 Books and reading 2 Books and reading—Best books
  "Merit badge series"
  Intended as a guide for Boy Scouts working toward a merit badge in reading, this pamphlet encourages balance in the book fare of older boys in news, technical fields, travel, fiction, poetry and other areas

Broderick, Dorothy M.
  Image of the black in children's fiction. Bowker 1973 219p illus $15.95   **028.5**
  1 Children's literature—History and criticism
  2 Blacks in literature and art
  ISBN 0-8352-0550-9   LC 72-1741
  "Over 100 children's books from 1909 to 1968 are analyzed by Dr. Broderick to determine the image of blacks presented in juvenile writings. She concludes that most of them were condescendingly racist and gave a distorted picture of the black heritage. . . . The early books analyzed in the study were listed in Jacob Blanck's popular juvenile bibliography 'Peter Parly to Penrod: A Bibliographic Description of the Best-Loved American Juvenile Books, 1827-1926 (Bowker, 1938). Other children's titles are from the 1908 to 1968 editions of the H. W. Wilson Company's 'Children's Catalog.' . . . Notes, a lengthy bibliography, and an index are additional valuable features of this well-researched work." Wynar. Guide to Ref Bks for Sch Media Centers

Caldecott Medal books: 1938-1957; with the artist's acceptance papers & related material chiefly from the Horn Book Magazine. Ed. by Bertha Mahony Miller and Elinor Whitney Field. Horn Bk. 1957 329p illus $15   **028.5**
  1 Caldecott Medal books 2 Illustrators 3 Children's literature—History and criticism
  ISBN 0-87675-001-3   LC 57-11582
  "Horn Book Papers"
  "A companion volume to the editors' 'Newbery Medal books: 1922-1955' [entered below]. A short study of Randolph Caldecott, for whom the award is named, prefaces the chronological listing of the award books. With this listing are given the acceptance speech of each artist and a biographical sketch of each. The illustrations—one from each book—are grouped together in the middle of the volume. In the concluding chapter Esther Averill evaluates the award books as picture books." Booklist
  Followed by: Newbery and Caldecott Medal books: 1956-1965, entered below

Cameron, Eleanor
  The green and burning tree; on the writing and enjoyment of children's books. Little 1969 377p pa $3.95   **028.5**
  1 Children's literature—History and criticism
  ISBN 0-316-12522-9   LC 69-11780
  "An Atlantic Monthly Press book"
  The author's "essays explore imagination versus 'realism' in writing for children, the roles of inspiration, technique and style. She is particularly interested in time fantasy, but by no means limits herself to this kind of juvenile writing. . . Among authors she discusses are H. C. Andersen, E. Nesbit, Kennth Grahame, Hugh Lofting, Beatrix Potter, Lucy Boston, Eleanor Farjeon, Wanda Gag and Mark Twain. . . . Excellent index and bibliography." Pub W

Carlson, Ruth Kearney
  Enrichment ideas. 2d ed. Brown, W.C. 1976 166p illus (Literature for children) pa $4.95   **028.5**
  1 Books and reading 2 Children's literature—History and criticism
  ISBN 0-697-06209-0   LC 75-25232

Carlson, Ruth K.—*Continued*

First published 1970

"Provides background material for teachers on the development of language and the forms of creative literature. Suggests books for teachers and ways to promote an interest in various modes of communication, including how to introduce books for children. Includes bibliographies. Covers K-12, although the emphasis is on elementary grades." Wynar. Guide to Ref Bks for Sch Media Centers [review of 1970 edition]

Chambers, Aidan

Introducing books to children. Heinemann Educational Bks. [distributed by Horn Bk] 1973 152p pa $6.50   028.5

1 Books and reading 2 Reading 3 Children's literature—History and criticism
ISBN 0-435-80261-5   LC 74-154759

"This book has been written for teachers, particularly student-teachers and beginners in the profession, and for anyone who is concerned about how to help children become avid, willing, enthusiastic readers. It is an attempt to take a straightforward and practical look at ideas, methods, varying approaches which bring books and young people into contact." Preface

Contents: Why bother? The making of a literary reader; The set and the setting; Storytelling and reading aloud; Adult recommendations; Friends and peers; Undirected reading; Book buying: book owning; Star performers; Worrying about the rubbish; A list of books and sources of information; Appendices: Readings that relate to some aspects of the text

Includes annotated chapter bibliographies

Chicago. University. Graduate Library School

A critical approach to children's literature; the thirty-first annual conference of the Graduate Library School, August 1-3, 1966. Ed. by Sara Innis Fenwick. Univ. of Chicago Press [1976 c1967] 129p (Univ. of Chicago Studies in lib. science) pa $6   028.5

1 Children's literature—History and criticism
ISBN 0-226-24162-9

"Midway Reprint series"

First published 1967 and analyzed in Essay and general literature index

"Twelve essays ranging from such general topics as poetry for children and a psychologist's view of children's literature to such specialized subjects as children's responses to humor, machine animism in children's literature, and current reviewing of children's books. . . . Originally published as the January 1967 issue of 'Library Quarterly' " Booklist

Children and literature; views and reviews; [comp.] by Virginia Haviland. Scott 1973 461p illus pa $6.95   028.5

1 Children's literature—History and criticism
ISBN 0-673-07676-8   LC 72-77507

"An excellent background book for students and teachers of children's literature, the author-compiler has assembled, in one handy volume, essays, articles, and excerpts from books on the history, development, and evaluation of children's literature. . . . Sendak's 'Mother Goose's garnishings,' Walter de la Mare's essay on Lewis Carroll, and Frances Clarke Sayers' stinging commentary on Walt Disney are only a few of the many spirited articles that add sprightliness and vigor to the book. Perennial controversial topics such as fantasy vs. realism, literary works vs. pedestrian writing and comics, and standards for children's reading, are presented. Criticism and reviewing of children's books as well as the awards given writers and illustrators both here and abroad—are all covered in detail." Choice

Includes bibliographical references

Children's literature review; excerpts from reviews, criticism, and commentary on books for children and young people. Gale Res. ea $40   028.5

1 Children's literature—History and criticism
2 Books—Reviews
ISSN 0362-4145   LC 76-643301

First published 1976. Irregular. Editors vary

This work provides "excerpts from contemporary criticism and commentary on past and present authors of children's books (preschool through teens. Each volume is to include 40 to 50 authors. . . . A typical entry covers several pages and consists of brief biographical information, excerpts from general commentary on the author, excerpts pertaining to individual titles, and citations to other review information." Cur Ref Bks

In volume 3 the background sections were lengthened, cross-references to entries in other Gale Research publications were expanded to cover additional titles (now including: Something about the author, Contemporary authors, Contemporary literary criticism, and Yesterday's authors of books for children), author's commentaries on their own work was added for some entries, and representation of non-fiction writers was increased. Each new volume will contain cumulative indexes of authors, titles and critics

Chosen for children . . . ed. by Marcus Crouch and Alec Ellis. 3d ed. Library Assoc. [distributed by Oryx Press] 1977 180p illus lib. bdg. $15.50   028.5

1 Library Association Carnegie Medal 2 Children's literature—History and criticism
ISBN 0-85365-349-6   LC 78-303207

First published 1957 in England

"An account of the books which have been awarded the Library Association Carnegie Medal, 1936-1975." Title page

The Carnegie Medal is awarded annually by the British Library Association to a children's book of outstanding merit published in English in the United Kingdom during the preceding year. In this volume, the editors' appraisal of each book is followed by a brief excerpt and comments by the author. Illustrated with pictures from the books and photographs of the authors

Cleary, Florence Damon

Blueprints for better reading; school programs for promoting skill and interest in reading. 2d ed. Wilson, H.W. 1972 312p $14   028.5

1 Books and reading 2 Reading
ISBN 0-8242-0406-9   LC 69-15806

First published 1957

This book explores ways teachers and librarians can improve their reading programs in areas of selection and evaluation of books and other instructional materials

"Part I identifies the problems involved in improving reading guidance programs, and describes the forces and factors that influence the reader and the understandings required of the person who guides the reading of youth. Part II delineates the kind of organization and schedules essential in promoting effective reading guidance programs in the schools, lists the criteria for the selection and evaluation of learning materials, and explores and describes a variety of directive and nondirective approaches to reading guidance. Part III describes programs, procedures, activities, and devices for teaching young pople to read critically, to acquire and use information and knowledge, to build values, appreciations, and the attendant skills that promote lasting habits of reading and reflection." Preface

Includes bibliographies

Cook, Elizabeth

The ordinary and the fabulous; an introduction to myths, legends and fairy tales. 2d ed. Cambridge 1976 xx, 182p $19.50, pa $6.95   028.5

1 Children's literature—History and criticism
2 Mythology 3 Fairy tales—History and criticism
4 Storytelling
ISBN 0-521-20825-4; 0-521-09961-7   LC 75-7213

First published 1962

The author's "discussions include the significance and values found in myths and fairy tales; suggest various myths for different age groups with comments on children's responses; deal with practical problems of the storyteller, and reproduce and dissect parallel passages from children's book versions and their original sources. The annotated selective bibliography, though excellent, is British oriented." Booklist

"A comprehensive and knowledgeable analysis of the legends of the Greek and Norse gods, the European myths, the traditional and literary fairy tales—and how to select, interpret, and use these stories with children. While the main body of this

Cook, Elizabeth—*Continued*

second edition differs only slightly from the first, it offers an enlarged, updated, annotated bibliography of books of tales, myths, and legends that contains new sections on stories collected from the Third World and Eastern Europe, on books describing techniques of presenting these stories to children, and on books that interpret the stories and their place in Western civilization. . . . Cook deals emphatically with 'trendy' interests,' such as our growing awareness of the Third World, our concern with the 'education of the eye,' our neglect in giving literature of substance to children, and our worship of 'relevance.' A significant, sensitive analysis of the literature that often lies at the heart of our being, whether we know it or not." Choice

Council on Interracial Books for Children. Racism and Sexism Resources Center for Educators
Human—and anti-human—values in children's books; a content rating instrument for educators and concerned parents; guidelines for the future. The Center 1976 280p $14.95, pa $7.95
      028.5
1 Children's literature—History and criticism 2 Children's literature—Bibliography 3 Minorities —Bibliography 4 Sex role—Bibliography
      LC 76-11665
"The first section of the book identifies the societal targets: a number of 'isms,' which when present in children's books may serve to limit human potential. Racism, sexism, ageism, elitism, materialism, individualism, escapism and conformism are all defined as negatives and explored from the perspectives of the language used as well as the societal implications. . . . The major portion of the text contains a brief analysis of 235 children's books, published in 1975, which range from preschool through high school, and selected for their minority, feminist and/or social themes. The content of each book, both the art and words, was scored on a Values Rating Checklist in the categories of racism, sexism or whatever category was important to that reviewer. Books about particular cultures were examined by a person of that culture." Rdng Teacher
"This work presents a viewpoint not readily available in other reviewing media which will be useful to all concerned about the selection of literature for children." Library J

A **Critical** history of children's literature; a survey of children's books in English prepared in four parts under the editorship of Cornelia Meigs. Rev. ed. by Cornelia Meigs [and others] Decorations by Vera Bock. Macmillan Pub. Co. 1969 xxviii, 708p $14.95
      028.5
1 Children's literature—History and criticism
ISBN 0-02-583900-4   LC 67-10271
First published 1953
Contents: Part 1 Roots in the past, up to 1840, by C. Meigs; Part 2 Widening horizons, 1840-1890, by A. T. Eaton; Part 3 A rightful heritage, 1890-1920, by Elizabeth Nesbitt; Part 4 Golden years and time of tumult, 1920-1967, by R. H. Viguers.
"While it is obviously a valuable reference book for libraries, schools, and teacher-training institutions, it makes fascinating reading not only for those adults who were fortunate enough to have grown up among books, but for those parents who wish to provide such a background for their own children." Cath World
Includes bibliographies

Egoff, Sheila
The republic of childhood; a critical guide to Canadian children's literature in English. 2d ed. Oxford 1975 335p $13.50, pa $9.50 **028.5**
1 Children's literature—History and criticism 2 Children's literature—Bibliography 3 Canadian literature—History and criticism
ISBN 0-19-540231-6; 0-19-540232-2   LC 75-329954
First published 1967
Covering important children's books published to October 1974 this study is divided as follows: Indian and Eskimo legends; Folktales; Fantasy; Historical fiction; The realistic animal story; Realistic fiction; History and biography; Poetry and plays; Illustration and design; Picture-books and picture-storybooks

"Written by a distinguished children's librarian this excellent guide provides lengthy analysis and criticism of children's books by Canadian authors. . . . Both American and English books are drawn into the discussion to emphasize areas of weakness or strength of Canadian works. Annotated lists at the end of each chapter are limited to Canadian titles." Wynar. Guide to Ref Bks for Sch Media Centers [review of 1967 edition]
Includes an index of authors, titles and illustrators

Fisher, Margery
Who's who in children's books; a treasury of the familiar characters of childhood. Holt 1975 399p illus $22.95   **028.5**
1 Children's literature—History and criticism 2 Characters and characteristics in literature—Dictionaries
ISBN 0-03-015091-4   LC 75-5463
"Entries include personalized animals, toys, and vehicles, and fairy and folktale characters as well as historical and contemporary personalities but exclude nursery-rhyme and most mythological figures. Each listing describes the character's appearance, mannerisms, background, and most importantly, role in the development of the story. As Fisher states in her introduction, this is not intended as a comprehensive checklist, but as a personal guide to those characters she has found absorbing during her many years of living with children's books. Approximately 400 illustrations accompany the text, from original illustrations to photographs of scenes from films. A book that teachers, librarians, children, and parents will use as a reference tool, a motivation for encouraging reading, and a browsing item. Organized alphabetically by character with a title and author index appended." Booklist

Halsey, Rosalie V.
Forgotten books of the American nursery: a history of the development of the American storybook. Singing Tree 1969 244p illus $10.50
      028.5
1 Children's literature—History and criticism
ISBN 0-8103-3483-6   LC 68-31084
A reissue of the title first published 1911 by Goodspeed
"A historical survey covering the period of 1647-1840, touching upon many authors and publishers, and replete with interesting and appropriate quotations from U.S. and British critics. A very readable and important landmark in the history of children's literature." Pellowski. The World of Children's Lit

Hazard, Paul
Books, children & men; tr. by Marguerite Mitchell. [4th ed.] Horn Bk. 1960 xxvi, 176p $7.50, pa $5   **028.5**
1 Children's literature—History and criticism 2 Books and reading
ISBN 0-87675-050-1; 0-87675-051-X   LC 60-52244
Original French edition, 1932. First American edition, 1944
"Literature for children is given its place among the literatures of the world in this series of brilliant essays, by a distinguished French scholar, who discusses, with evident enjoyment, children's books in terms of the cultures of various peoples." NY Pub Library
Bibliography: p173-76

Horn Book Reflections on children's books and reading; selected from eighteen years of The Horn Book Magazine, 1949-1966; ed. By Elinor Whitney Field. Horn Bk. 1969 367p pa $4.50   **028.5**
1 Children's literature—History and criticism
ISBN 0-87675-033-1   LC 75-89793
Companion volume to A Horn Book Sampler on children's books and reading, entered below
A collection of "articles and essays relating to various aspects of children's reading and literature includes material by authors, illustrators, parents, teachers, and librarians. Sections devoted to authors' own descriptions of writing experiences and to recollections of visits to famous authors are especially engaging." Booklist

A **Horn** Book Sampler on children's books and reading; selected from twenty-five years of The Horn Book Magazine, 1924-1948. Ed. by Norma R. Fryatt; introduction by Bertha Mahony Miller. Horn Bk. 1959 261p $7, pa $4.50 **028.5**

1 Children's literature—History and criticism
ISBN 0-87675-030-7; 0-87675-031-5   LC 59-15028
Companion volume to Horn Book Reflections on children's books and reading, entered above
Analyzed in Essay and general literature index
"Articles, editorials, book reviews, and a few poems reprinted from the 'Horn Book' from its founding in 1924 to 1948. The sampler includes essays by authors on how certain of their stories came to be written, evaluations of the work of such illustrators as Kate Greenaway, Arthur Rackham, and Leslie Brooke, criticisms of single books and of trends in children's literature, discussions of fairy tales and books for small children, and a group of papers addressed to parents. Appended to two of the selections are 1959 commentaries by the original authors. Of particular interest to children's librarians and connoiseurs of children's literature." Booklist
"Miss Fryatt has exercised a very nice sense of the relationship of these papers to each other. . . . Insight is I think, the key word to this sampler." NY Times Bk Rev

Huck, Charlotte S.
Children's literature in the elementary school. 3d ed., updated. Holt 1979 788p illus $15.95
028.5

1 Children's literature—History and criticism
2 Books and reading   3 Children's literature—Bibliography
ISBN 0-03-046086-7   LC 78-21081
First published 1961
"An excellent guide for teachers and librarians, covering criteria for selection of books in many fields, children's characteristics and interests at various ages, ways of using books with children, and extensive subject bibliographies. Supplementary material includes children's book awards, children's book clubs, and other topics related to children's books." Hodges. Bks for Elem Sch Libraries [review of the 1968 edition]

Issues in children's book selection; a School Library Journal/Library Journal anthology; with an introduction by Lillian Gerhardt. Bowker 1973 216p $11.95   **028.5**

1 Book selection 2 Children's literature—History and criticism
ISBN 0-8352-0688-2   LC 73-13553
"Twenty-nine articles, first printed in 'School Library Journal,' underscore recent issues of children's book selection for librarians: the tension between censorship and selection; bias and prejudice in children's books; genre defenses and criticisms. By juxtaposing articles of different perspectives, the book provides a starting point for discussion and evaluation. . . . As an introduction to the problems of book selection or as an account of the gamut of issues affecting the contemporary children's book world, the compilation only lacks an indication that the quality of the book as a piece of literature might be an issue in children's book selection." Horn Bk

Jan, Isabella
On children's literature; ed. by Catherine Storr; with a preface by Anne Pellowski. Schocken 1974 189p $8   **028.5**

1 Children's literature—History and criticism
ISBN 0-8052-3564-7   LC 74-9143
Original French edition published 1969. This translation first published 1973 in England
The author considers the sources and types of children's literature, with particular emphasis on such themes as the hero, animals, adventure, and the family
This book reads "like a series of lectures, each one perceptive and persuasively argued, but lacking a central unity. Professor Jan's strength lies in her range. She cites relevantly and with ease examples from a dozen countries. The depth of her critical penetration varies greatly. . . . As usual with critics in this field, her judgments rest on psychological and sociological principles rather than on stylistic qualities." Times (London) Lit Sup

Jordan, Alice M.
From Rollo to Tom Sawyer, and other papers; decorations by Nora S. Unwin. Horn Bk. 1948 160p pa $5   **028.5**

1 Children's literature—History and criticism
ISBN 0-87675-058-7   LC 48-9996
Analyzed in Essay and general literature index
"Three essays in the book concern children's magazines of the Nineteenth Century, one is a lecture given by Miss Jordan in 1940, and five essays are about important [19th century] authors and editors of children's books." Sch Library J

Karl, Jean
From childhood to childhood; children's books and their creators. Day 1970 175p $8.95   **028.5**

1 Children's literature—History and criticism
ISBN 0-381-98131-2   LC 71-107207
The author "describes some of the characteristics of a group of successful children's book writers and how they get their works down on paper, following their work from manuscript to mill, including the functions of literary agents, book designing and some fascinating information about the illustrations and the problems of matching illustrators with authors. She also offers a fine section on the history of children's books, which really began when an 18th century printer-bookseller, John Newbery, issued 'A Pretty Little Pocketbook.'" Pub W
Bibliography: p171-75

Lanes, Selma G.
Down the rabbit hole; adventures & misadventures in the realm of children's literature. Atheneum Pubs. 1976 [c1971] 241p illus pa $4.95
028.5

1 Children's literature—History and criticism
ISBN 0-689-70533-6   LC 73-135575
First published 1971
This "informative collection of essays on picture books and children's stories, is a handsomely illustrated, thoroughly indexed source for parents and teachers who want to know more about the expanding field of children's literature. Much attention is given to illustrators, with separate essays on fairy tales, series books, and books with black themes." Wis Library Bul
Bibliography: p214-31

Larrick, Nancy
A parent's guide to children's reading. 4th ed. With illustrations from fifty favorite children's books. Doubleday 1975 432p illus $8.95
028.5

1 Books and reading   2 Children's literature—History and criticism   3 Children's literature—Bibliography
ISBN 0-385-02564-5   LC 74-18815
First published 1958
In addition to providing bibliographies the author covers such topics as television and children, oral language in early childhood, developing children's interests, poetry, the audio-visual bridge to reading, how reading is taught, using reference books, buying books and building a home library, the paperback bonanza, magazines, and audio-visual materials
"An up-to-date bibliography of hundreds of standard book titles is arranged by subject; selected recordings, films, and filmstrips based on children's books are listed separately." Horn Bk

Lepman, Jella
A bridge of children's books; tr from the German by Edith McCormick; with a foreword by J. E. Morpurgo. A.L.A. 1969 155p $5
028.5

1 Libraries, Children's   2 Children's literature
ISBN 0-8389-0070-4   LC 68-54215
Original German edition, 1964
"In an anecdotal, personal account of her efforts to build international understanding through children's books [the author] reconstructs the events leading to the 1946 Munich International Children's Book Exhibition, the establishment of the International Youth Library in Munich, and the subsequent founding, in 1951 in Switzerland, of the International Board of Books for Young People, which now awards the Hans Christian Andersen prize." Library J

Lepman, Jella—*Continued*

"The campaign for children's books after World War II, which has never before been described, has an important place in the history of children's literature. Since it is interwoven with the unusual experiences of an extraordinary woman and reported with great vitality, the result is an absorbing book." Horn Bk

Literature and young children. Bernice E. Cullinan and Carolyn W. Carmichael, editors. Natl. Council of Teachers of English 1977 180p illus pa $8.95   **028.5**

1 Children's literature—History and criticism
2 Books and reading   LC 77-4870

"The content, scope, and the many means of reaching preschool children by the use of literature are the major emphases in this collection. This book is aimed at the teacher, school librarian, preservice teacher, or librarian who is interested in bringing to the preschool child the best that is available in appropriate and distinguished books, storytelling, arts, prose and poetry exploration, audio-visual materials usage, and strategies in presentation as well as evaluating the responses of children to literature which lie in the affective domain. The format of the book is attractive, and the selections of poetry and prose clearly demonstrate the author's intent. Accompanying samples of illustrations highlight the essays. The cohesive chapters lead to the final children's book reference lists found at the end of each section, and the high point of the volume is the annotated list of the 100 best books and authors for young children." Choice

Lukens, Rebecca

A critical handbook of children's literature. Scott 1976 214p illus pa $5.50   **028.5**

1 Children's literature—History and criticism
ISBN 0-673-15007-0   LC 75-35858

The author "states and then demonstrates that literature for children differs from literature for adults in degree, not kind, and that it should be judged by the same standards. Failure to apply critical standards to children's literature demeans it as though it were inferior to adult literature. Techniques of literary criticism are applied to children's books through analysis of character, plot, setting, theme, point of view, style and tone." Children's Bk Rev Serv

"Each chapter ends with suggestions for reading and evaluating specific titles and a list of books mentioned. Extremely helpful for teachers and librarians working with children's books as well as teachers of children's literature courses." Booklist

MacCann, Donnarae

The child's first books; a critical study of pictures and texts, by Donnarae MacCann and Olga Richard. Wilson, H.W. 1973 135p illus $12   **028.5**

1 Picture books for children 2 Children's literature—History and criticism
ISBN 0-8242-0501-4   LC 73-3224

"A carefully written analysis of picture books, designed for critics and book selectors, emphasizing the study of both literary and graphic aspects. Beginning with the proposition that during a child's first eight years no 'cultural or intellectual deprivation must occur . . . if the child is to reach his full potential in later years,' the authors go on to relate illustration to the graphic arts, and to consider texts an graphics separately. They provide provocative discussions in chapters entitled: Stereotypes in Illustration; Graphic Elements; Outstanding Contemporary Illustrators; Book Design; Literary Elements; Outstanding Narrative Writers; Specialized Texts (e.g. alphabet and counting books, concept and nature books); The Caldecott Award; and The Child, the Librarian, and the Critic. Backed by a liberal number of philosophical quotations about art and writing, and with a bibliography of books recommended in the study, the work will serve admirably as background reading for students. The beautifully designed volume with forty illustrations, seven in full color, includes two large foldouts." Horn Bk

Newbery and Caldecott Medal books: 1956-1965; with acceptance papers, biographies & related material chiefly from The Horn Book Magazine. Ed. by Lee Kingman. Horn Bk. 1965 300p illus $15   **028.5**

1 Newbery Medal books 2 Caldecott Medal books
3 Children's literature—History and criticism
4 Authors 5 Illustrators
ISBN 0-87675-002-1   LC 65-26759

"Horn Book Papers"

This compilation continues the coverage begun in: Newbery Medal books, 1922-1955, entered below, and Caldecott Medal books, 1938-1957, entered above

"The pattern in the new collection is the same as in the earlier [ones]: a brief description of format, a short book note, the acceptance speech, and a biographical note. . . . An added bonus is the listing of runners-up from the beginning of each medal through 1965. . . . [This book] will be useful to librarians, teachers and other adults interested in children's books. It will so be used by some older boys and girls who are readers of the books, especially those who want to know more about the authors." Top of the News

Newbery and Caldecott Medal books: 1966-1975; with acceptance papers, biographies and related material chiefly from The Horn Book Magazine. Ed. by Lee Kingman. Horn Bk. 1975 xx, 321p illus $15   **028.5**

1 Newbery Medal books 2 Caldecott Medal books 3 Children's literature—History and criticism 4 Authors 5 Illustrators
ISBN 0-87675-003-X   LC 75-20167

"Brings up to date the volumes, 'Newbery Medal books: 1922-1955 [entered below], Caldecott Medal books: 1938-1957,' and 'Newbery and Caldecott Medal books: 1956-1965 [entered above].' Gives for each Newbery or Caldecott award winner his acceptance speech, a biographical note, and a book note. An excerpt from each Newbery book gives an example of the writer's style; a sample illustration from each Caldecott book is supplemented by notes on size, medium, printing process, number of illustrations and type used. Valuable not only as a reference tool, but also for focus on the creative process. Acceptance speeches and biographies reveal philosophies about children and about writing and illustrating for them. Editing, publishing, and book production fall into perspective." Choice

Newbery Medal books: 1922-1955; with their authors' acceptance papers & related material chiefly from the Horn Book Magazine. Ed. by Bertha Mahony Miller and Elinor Whitney Field. Horn Bk. 1955 458p illus $15   **028.5**

1 Newbery Medal books 2 Authors 3 Children's literature—History and criticism
ISBN 0-87675-000-5   LC 55-13968

Companion volume to: Caldecott Medal books: 1938-1957, entered above

"The first volume of a series . . . [of] papers originally published in numbers of the 'Horn Book' that are now out of print. This collection constitutes a history of the Newbery Medal awards to date [1955]; the winning books are presented in chronological order, and for each there is a book note [a short excerpt] and an acceptance paper. [There are also brief biographies of the authors.] Introductory essays on Frederic Melcher and John Newbery add to the value of a book that will be prized by librarians and connoisseurs of children's literature." Booklist

Followed by: Newbery and Caldecott Medal books: 1956-1965, entered above

Only connect; readings on children's literature. 2d ed. Edited by Sheila Egoff, G. T. Stubbs, and L. F. Ashley. Oxford 1980 457p illus pa $8.95   **028.5**

1 Children's literature—History and criticism
ISBN 0-19-540309-6

Firs published 1969 and analyzed in Essay and general literature index

A collection of 38 essays on children's literature, mostly reprinted from articles published in periodicals in the 1960's and 1970's, arranged under the following headings: Books and children; Fairy tales, fantasy, animals; Some writers

Only connect—*Continued*

and their books; Illustration; The modern scene. Among the contributors are: Roger Lancelyn Green, John Rowe Townsend, J. R. R. Tolkien, Donnarae MacCann, P. L. Travers, C. S. Lewis, T. S. Eliot, Graham Greene, Edward Ardizzone, Roger Duvoisin, Maurice Sendak and Sylvia Engdahl

"Anyone creating, selecting, reviewing, or teaching children's literature [will find] this compilation . . . distinctive, rich, and truly critical." Horn Bk

Pierpont Morgan Library, New York

Early children's books and their illustration. Godine 1975 263p illus $35   028.5

1 Children's literature—History and criticism
2 Illustration of books—History
ISBN 0-87923-158-0   LC 75-24968

This "volume is the catalog of a 1975 exhibition held at The Pierpont Morgan Library in New York City. It was organized by the Library's Curator of Early Children's Books, Gerald Gottlieb, who has written the Foreword, brief introductions to the 34 main sections and has provided abbreviated bibliographic descriptions and additional . . . annotations about over 225 items including over 100 taken from the Elizabeth Ball Collection. . . 'Aesop's Fables,' the first chapter, starts with a description of a third-century papyrus fragment written in Greek which was found in Egypt and concludes with a first edition of the famous 1912

Polette, Nancy

E is for everybody: a manual for bringing fine picture books into the hands and hearts of children; with an introduction by Marjorie Hamlin; art consultant, Patricia Gilmore. Scarecrow 1976 xviii, 147p illus $8   028.5

1 Picture books for children—Bibliography
2 Books and reading 3 Arts
ISBN 0-8108-0966-4   LC 76-16199

"Dispelling the idea that picture books are only for primary grades, Polette, . . . offers a multitude of ways to use these books with all elementary and junior high students as well. Choosing 147 titles with wide range and interest, the author summarizes plot and describes suggested activities such as dramatizations, art and science projects, creative writing, media production, and games. . . . [She] suggests drawing, collages, book making, puppetry, and making slides and filmstrips as ways to assure an enjoyable art/literature experience. A useful manual for librarians and teachers and one that might be suggested to other adults working with children." Booklist

Sadker, Myra Pollack

Now upon a time; a contemporary view of children's literature [by] Myra Pollack Sadker [and] David Miller Sadker. Harper 1977 475p illus $14.50   028.5

1 Children's literature—History and criticism
2 Books and reading
ISBN 0-06-045693-0   LC 76-46423

"Stating in the preface that their main emphasis is on the issues contained in children's books and their subsequent impact on the child, the authors have centered their discussions on four main themes: 'Life's Cycle' (family, sex, age), 'The American Mosaic' (blacks, Jew, women), 'Save Our Planet—Save Ourselves' (ecology, humor war), and 'Approaches to Working with Children and Books' (censorship, teaching). Titles are used liberally throughout; and bibliographies appear at each chapter's end, although their choice, according to the authors, is dependent on contemporary mood rather than lasting literary quality alone, as their purpose is not to be a comprehensive reference volume. . . . Appendixes include an annotated bibliography of books depicting the handicapped, publishers' addresses, and children's book awards. Subject (with author) and title index." Booklist

Smith, Lillian H.

The unreluctant years; a critical approach to children's literature. A.L.A. 1953 193p $5   028.5

1 Children's literature—History and criticism
2 Book selection
ISBN 0-8389-0065-8   LC 52-13520

"The aim of this book is to consider children's books as literature and to discover some of the standards by which they can be so judged." Foreword

Contents: The case for children's literature; The lineage of children's literature; An approach to criticism; The art of the fairy tale; Gods and men; Heroes of epic and saga; Poetry; Picture books; Stories; Fantasy; Historical fiction; Books of knowledge; Envoy

Includes bibliographies

Suitable for children? Controversies in children's literature; ed. and introduced by Nicholas Tucker. Univ. of Calif. Press 1976 224p $15.95

028.5

1 Children's literature—History and criticism
ISBN 0-520-03236-5   LC 76-6016

"A collection of British essays on controversial aspects of children's literature centers here on five specific topics: fairy tales, comics, children's books and the arousal of fear, classics, and the value of children's literature. Authors range from Charles Lamb, J. B. Priestley, and Dickens to the more contemporary persuasions of Jill Paton Walsh, Catherine Storr, and Janet Hill. The lasting effects of literature on children runs as a motif thread throughout these discussions. Areas such as language, sexual references, and sexism—of recent concern in the U.S.—are not touched; the issue of racism appears however in connection with 'Little Black Sambo,' and violence is dealth with briefly." Booklist

The editor's "excellent introductions point to further critical works and to authors of children's books and reinforce his basic point that children's writers can offer something to all ages. . . . In such arguments as he and others set forth, the book can offer comfort and reinforcement to harried librarians marshalling their defenses against the pressure groups and the individuals who lodge complaints; in other directions it speaks to those seeking to raise the consciousness of adults who fail to give children's books their due importance in the literary world. . . . With selected bibliographies for each section." Horn Bk

Sutherland, Zena

Children & books. 6th ed. [by] Zena Sutherland, Dianne L. Monson [and] May Hill Arbuthnot. . . . Scott 1981 678p illus $16.95

028.5

1 Children's literature—History and criticism
2 Children's literature—Bibliography
ISBN 0-673-15377-0   LC 80-23537

First published 1947

"Part five: Areas and issues edited by Dorothy M. Broderick; cover and part opening illustrations by Charles Mikolaycak." Title page

"Part One is an overview of children's needs and interests, the range of books for children, types of and criteria for evaluation of children's literature, and history and trends. . . . Part Two discusses artists and their illustrations, and includes a chapter on books for the youngest, reflecting a growing area of emphasis. . . . In Part Three, the types of literature are explored: folk tales, including tall tales; fables, myths, and epics; modern fantasy; poetry; modern fiction and historical fiction; and biography and informational books. . . . Part Four deals with methodology, discussing the role of the adult and the techniques to be used in introducing children to literature. . . . Part Five . . . considers areas and issues relating to children and their books . . . [including] censorship, research, children and television, and mainstreaming." Preface to the Sixth Edition

This "standard textbook on children's books . . . provides discussions of children's needs, types of materials with a heavy emphasis on synopses and some analyses of stories, reproductions of illustrations from books, and lists of books and authors in each category. . . . Its emphasis is on acquainting teachers with forms of literature and with specific titles, authors and illustrators of books for children from preschool through junior high school." Wynar. Guide to Ref Bks for Sch Media Centers [review of 4th edition]

Thwaite, Mary F.

From primer to pleasure in reading; an introduction to the history of children's books in England from the invention of printing to 1914 with an outline of some developments in other countries. Horn Bk. 1972 340p illus $12.50
    028.5

1 Children's literature—History and criticism
ISBN 0-87675-275-X   LC 72-82182

First published 1963 in England with title: From primer to pleasure
"The main object of this comprehensive work is 'to provide a general introduction to scholarly histories of the subject for the benefit of [people] interested in the link between children's books of today and those of the past.' This it does very well. Chronologically following the developments of children's books and their different genres, the author puts them into proper historical perspective, highlights especially influential works and makes comparative evaluations. The prolific nineteenth century is interestingly analyzed, using a classified arrangement (e.g. fairy lore and fantasy, the tale of adventure, periodicals, etc.). The main body of this work focuses on England, drawing occasional parallels to German and French events. . . . [This] is a throughly researched and stimulating reference tool for the student and teacher of children's literature." Top of the News
Bibliography: p283-313

Townsend, John Rowe

A sounding of storytellers; new and rev. essays on contemporary writers for children. Lippincott 1979 218p $13.95   **028.5**

1 Children's literature—History and criticism
ISBN 0-397-31882-0

Analyzed in Essay and general literature index
The author has taken seven of the nineteen essays from his earlier book: A sense of story (1971), and combined them with seven new essays to produce "a literate, stimulating and up-to-date view of contemporary children's fiction. The new essays included here deal with the work of Nina Bawden, Vera and Bill Cleaver, Peter Dickinson, Virginia Hamilton, E. L. Konigsburg, Penelope Lively and Jill Paton Walsh. These, combined with updated essays on Paula Fox, Leon Garfield, Alan Garner, William Mayne, K. M. Peyton, Ivan Southall and Patricia Wrightson, result in a book that is a must for those involved in children's literature. Townsend's criticism is knowledgeable, concise, and eminently readable." Children's Bk Rev Serv

Written for children; an outline of English-language children's literature. [Rev. ed.] Lippincott [1975 c1974] 368p illus $11.95   **028.5**

1 Children's literature—History and criticism
ISBN 0-397-31528-7   LC 74-695

First published 1965 in England. First American edition published 1967 by Lothrop. This edition first published 1974 in England
The author "covers fiction from England, the United States, Australia, and a few other parts of the English-speaking world, as well as poetry, picture books, and the art of book illustrations. . . . The book ends with notes on the sources of all quotations, an impressive seven-page bibliography of works on children's literature, and an index." Horn Bk
"The writing style is very relaxed and almost chatty with the author providing anecdotes and personal comments and reactions which make the book very alive and entertaining reading. It is for the serious student of children's literature, but one most all of them will enjoy." Children's Bk Rev Serv

Whaley, Joyce Irene

Cobwebs to catch flies; illustrated books for the nursery and schoolroom, 1700-1900. Univ. of Calif. Press 1975 [c1974] 163p illus $16.50
    028.5

1 Children's literature—History and criticism
2 Illustration of books—History
ISBN 0-520-02931-3   LC 74-27298

First published 1974 in England
An "overview of illustrated books for young children published during the 18th and, primarily, the 19th centuries, mostly in England. . . . The books discussed are classified according to type (alphabet, counting, reading, geography, etc.) and are so discussed." Choice
"Illustrated with reproductions. The author states that her intent was to produce a study of 'The illustrated educational books which were used to instruct children during their earliest gears, in the home rather than the school.' All but a few of the books noted are from the Victoria and Albert Museum Library's collection of children's books. The thesis is well-supported that social history is to be gleaned from examination of early children's books, but the scholar notes that fairy tales, poetry, and fiction have to be studied beyond these pages. . . . The book has a strong internationality with American, French, and German publications included in the discussion, the illustrations, and the extensive bibliography of children's books and works about children's literature. For a wide range of readers, a substantial work of history and criticism with a fresh focus." Horn Bk

Yankee Doodle's literary sampler of prose, poetry, and pictures; being an anthology of diverse works published for the edification and/or entertainment of young readers in America before 1900; selected from the rare book collections of the Library of Congress and introduced by Virginia Haviland and Margaret N. Coughlan. Crowell 1974 466p illus $18.95   **028.5**

1 Literature—Collections   2 Children's literature—History and criticism
ISBN 0-690-00269-6   LC 74-12217

"Included are the familiar and the little known in a chronological assortment of readings expected to be instructive and entertaining to the young. Initially influenced by British models, the assertion of indigenous American character and style is shown early. The collection provides a composite introduction to the quality and variety available to children prior to the twentieth century from a growing book industry as well as in juvenile magazines. Facsimile pages with original illustrations, some in color, add charm to a sourcebook that also offers insights into earlier social and moral values." Booklist
Selected bibliography: p451-58

028.505   Children's reading—Periodicals

Bookbird. Hermann Schaffstein Verlag $16.75 per year   **028.505**

1 Children's literature—Periodicals 2 Books—Reviews 3 Books and reading—Best books
ISSN 0006-7377

Quarterly. First published 1962 in Austria by Verlag für Jugend und Volk
Issued by the International Board on Books for Young People and the International Institute for Children's Literature and Reading Research
This periodical "contains articles of interest to anyone working in the field of children's books. Lists of recommended books for translation . . . appear regularly in almost each issue. There is also a very helpful review of recent publications about children's books and libraries. . . . Awards, congresses, special meetings, exhibits, seminars and many other types of activities throughout the world are reported on in brief news items. Occasional longer articles cover the various aspects of children's books in depth." Pellowski. The World of Children's Lit
"Approximately 40 countries contribute material to the journal through the associate editor named from each country." Katz. Magazines for Libaries. 3d edition

Children's Literature. Yale Univ. Press [distributed by Children's Literature Foundation] $20   **028.505**

1 Children's literature—Periodicals 2 Children's literature—History and criticism

Annual. First published 1972 by the English Department of the University of Connecticut with cover title: The great excluded. Title and publisher varies

Children's Literature—*Continued*

Journal of the Modern Language Association Group on Children's Literature and the Children's Literature Association

"A 250-plus-page scholarly annual of articles on aspects, national and international, of children's literature. The journal is divided into three sections: —'Articles,' approximately 18 essays dealing with segments of the broad theme set for each issue, e.g., 1976 issue features essays on American children's literature from the colonial age to the present; 'Reviews,' short essays that examine trends and issues in children's literature by citing and analyzing exemplary works, and not necessarily very new publications; and 'Varia,' which includes 'Dissertations of Note' and a list of suggested 'Topics for Research.' The contributors are scholars, educators, writers, critics, and librarians. The journal is highly recommended as a resource for students and professionals." Katz. Magazines for Libraries. 3d edition

Children's Literature in Education. Agathon Press [distributed by APS Publications, Inc.] $20 per year   028.505

1 Children's literature—Periodicals   2 Children's literature—History and criticism
ISSN 0045-6713

Quarterly. First published 1970
"A basic title for children's librarians and teachers in elementary and junior high schools. Worldwide in scope, this originates in England, is published in the United States, and has an American editor, Joan Blos, a children's literature expert from the University of Michigan. An average 60-page issue moves from articles on the history of children's literature, opinion pieces, and editorials to subject bibliographies. It is all quite scholarly, yet with a firm footing in reality, as informative as it often is entertaining." Katz. Magazines for Libraries. 3d edition

Growing Point. Ed. and distributed by Margery Fisher, Ashton Manor, Northampton NN7 2JL, Eng. $5 per year   028.505

1 Children's literature—Periodicals   2 Books—Reviews
ISSN 0046-6506

6 issues per year. First published 1962
This is "Margery Fisher's regular review of books for the growing families of the English reading world, and for parents, teachers, librarians and other guardians"

The **Horn** Book Magazine. Horn Bk. $15 per year   028.505

1 Children's literature—Periodicals   2 Books—Reviews
ISSN 0018-5708

Bimonthly. First published 1924 with title: The Horn Book
"This is one of the most important publications in the field of children's literature. It includes [signed] reviews of current children's books. These are classified by subject and age level. Reproductions of many illustrations from the newest books are incorporated into the text. Articles about authors, illustrators, award books, history of children's literature are frequently featured." Huck. Children's Lit in the Elem Sch

Interracial Books for Children Bulletin. Council of Interracial Books for Children $15 per year   028.505

1 Children's literature—Periodicals   2 Minorities in literature and art   3 Racism in literature   4 Books—Reviews
ISSN 0020-9708

8 issues per year. First published 1970
"Confronts head-on the longstanding, extremely critical problems of racism and sexism in both education and children's literature. . . . Holding that 'children's books are not toys,' but rather 'powerful tools by which a society perpetuates its values,' the Council's bulletin features incisive analyses of defamatory stereotyping and blatant omission in textbooks and juvenile trade titles, energetically promotes authentic minority group publishing, and abounds with otherwise hard-to-find data on pertinent resource groups and materials, domestic and international." Katz. Magazines for Libraries 3d ed.

The Bulletin "contains articles as well as reviews of books. Reviews are forcefully written and do not reflect the opinions of other review sources. . . . This periodical is valuable for selecting books through junior high school." Peterson. Ref Bks for Elem and Jr High Sch Libraries. 2d ed

Phaedrus; an international journal of children's literature research. Phaedrus, Inc. $12 per year   028.505

1 Children's literature—Periodicals   2 Children's literature—History and criticism
ISSN 0098-3365

Biennial. First published 1973
"What began as a newsletter is now an impressive interdisciplinary and international journal 'concerned with theoretical inquiry into the media environment of the child and the adolescent.' It draws attention to research and research sources by citing selected dissertations and journal articles, and by reviewing published studies, bibliographies, and catalogs. There is also periodically a section that surveys special collections of children's books and research materials available in a particular geographic area. Further, each issue features a central theme discussed in several articles, e.g., children's literature of the U.S.S.R., management of children's literature research collections. . . . Contributors are children's literature specialists in their own countries, and the illustrative material consists of a few black-and-white photos and illustrations reproduced from material discussed. A must for scholars and researchers and all libraries concerned." Katz. Magazines for Libraries. 3d ed.

Signal; approaches to children's books. Thimble Press $10.50 per year   028.505

1 Children's literature—Periodicals   2 Children's literature—History and criticism
ISSN 0037-4954

3 issues per year, January, May and September. First published 1970
"A journal 'published to provide a voice for writers whose ideas about, and interests in, children's books cannot be contained in brief reviews and articles, or in periodicals whose purposes are basically pragmatic or educational.' A typical 45-page issue contains three to seven thoughful and well-written articles, often including one reprint. . . . Although the articles are concerned primarily with British poets, authors, and illustrators, many are on general topics (e.g., genre studies, book reviewing) or deal with classics familiar to American readers. The informative, scholarly presentations should be enjoyed by those with a serious interest in children's literature." Katz. Magazines for Libraries. 3d ed.

028.7   Use of books and other media as sources of information

Cleary, Florence Damon
Discovering books and libraries; a handbook for students in the middle and upper grades. 2d ed. Wilson, H.W. 1977 196p illus pa $5   028.7

1 Reference books   2 Libraries—Handbooks, manuals, etc.
ISBN 0-8242-0594-4   LC 76-55368

First published 1966
"A handbook designed for sixth- to ninth-graders as a self-teaching or teacher/librarian-directed text in the appreciation and use of books and libraries. Each chapter provides a brief history of its topic, an explanation accompanied by diagrams and directed activities, and an exercise for practicing skills. The material proceeds from the 'anatomy' of books and libraries through the 'physiology' of card catalogs, basic reference materials, and mass media. The final chapter synthesizes the skills taught through guiding their use in extensive research." Top of the News

031   American encyclopedias

Britannica Junior encyclopaedia for boys and girls. Encyclopaedia Britannica Educ. Corp. 15v illus maps apply to publisher for price   031

1 Encyclopedias

Britannica Junior encyclopaedia for boys and
girls—*Continued*

First published 1934 in 12 volumes

"The set is organized into 15 separately paged
volumes, using the unit letter plan (one or more
complete letters per volume). Articles are arranged
alphabetically letter by letter. Volume 1 is the
Ready Reference Index containing, in addition to
the 664-page index, the list of contributing editors
and writers and a nine-page introduction to the
index. . . . Annual revisions are made in some
articles and the reference index is also revised
yearly. Much illustrated matter is included in the
encyclopedia. In fact, few pages are without some
color or black and white photo, sketch, map, graph,
or diagram. Color is also used to highlight the fact
boxes in an attempt to brighten such usually drab
presentations of data. However, state flowers, symbols, etc., in articles on the states—usually colorful
features in juvenile encyclopedias—are small and
unattractive. Maps are liberally distributed through
the set to show political/physical features, distribution of people, land use, and economic factors.
Volume 15, in addition to containing letters X, Y,
and Z, offers a complete world atlas section with
its own index." Wynar. Guide to Ref Bks for Sch
Media Centers

For a fuller review see: The Booklist, December 1, 1978

Collier's encyclopedia; with bibliography and
index. Macmillan Educ. Corp. 24v illus maps
apply to publisher for price   031

1 Encyclopedias

First published 1949-1951 by Crowell-Collier Educ.
Corp.

The articles in this set "are well developed,
well presented, and well illustrated. Arrangement
is alphabetical, letter by letter. The scholarly,
signed articles vary in length according to importance of subject treated. The set is especially useful
for its coverage of politics, biography, fine arts,
religion, philosophy, the classics, science, and technology. Small topical maps and large (many multi-
colored) maps with adjacent gazetteer information
accompany articles on states, provinces, and countries. The list of contributors appears in Volume 1
and notes the qualifications and writings of each
specialist. Volume 24 contains the bibliography;
a comprehensive, analytical index; and a study
guide designed to aid the reader seeking to enlarge
his knowledge on a particular subject. Bibliographies are listed under broad subject fields, explicitly sub-divided, with title entries arranged
under broad or narrow subjects according to the
scope of the books listed; generally the books begin
at high school level and progress through college
and postcollege levels, with easier or general works
treated first. Continuous revision program, with
several printings a year, assures up-to-dateness."
ALA Ref Bks for Small and Medium-Sized Pub
Libraries

"Principally designed to be used by junior and
senior high school, college and university students,
it appeals to and can readily be used by upper
elementary grade children. . . . It is probably the
easiest adult set for children to use and therefore
provides a smooth transition from encyclopedias coordinated with school curricula to those designed for
mature users." Peterson. Ref Bks for Elem and
Jr High Sch Libraries

Supplemented by: Collier's encyclopedia year
book

For a fuller review see: The Booklist, February 1, 1979

Compton's Encyclopedia and fact-index. Compton 26v illus maps apply to publisher for price
031

1 Encyclopedias

First published 1922 with title: Compton's Pictured encyclopedia

"Arrangement of articles is alphabetical, letter
by letter. At the beginning of each volume is a
section, 'Here and There in This Volume,' that
serves as a guide to some of the more interesting
items and that provides a stimulus to browse. The
remainder of each volume is divided into text
and Fact-Index. The Fact-Index provides references to the exact location of related information
in all volumes of the set; it is handy as a ready
reference tool because it includes dictionary-type
information on specific topics that do not merit
inclusion as regular articles. . . . In each article
basic information is given first, followed by a
progression toward more complex areas of specialization. Following many of the main text articles
are reference outlines and bibliographies. There are
study guides and reading guides that lead the

reader to a systematic survey of fields of interest
too large or too detailed to have been included in
a single article." Wynar. Guide to Ref Bks for
Sch Media Centers

"Extensive use of photographs, drawings, graphs,
maps (with liberal use of color) add interest and
provide experience in learning from illustrations.
As usual, the text is well organized, clear in style,
and concise. The books, as always, are packed with
excellent learning aids." Sci Teacher

Supplemented by: Compton yearbook

For a fuller review see: The Booklist, December 15, 1978

Kane, Joseph Nathan

Famous first facts; a record of first happenings, discoveries and inventions in the United
States. 3d ed. Wilson, H.W. 1964 1165p $25
031

1 Encyclopedias

ISBN 0-8242-0015-2   LC 63-14893

First published 1933

This volume "includes 6,652 first happenings,
discoveries and inventions in the United States,
listed and described under general subject-head-
ings, with appropriate subheads; an index by years,
from 1007 to July 10, 1962, the date of the first
trans-oceanic television program; an index by
days of the month, so useful in planning displays
and exhibits; an index to personal names; and a
geographical index. . . . Reference librarians may
wish that there were more citations to the sources
of information, but the compiler's long years of
effort, involving, in many cases, unpublished
sources, inspire a good deal of confidence in the
volume as a source of ready reference." Cur Ref
Bks

Merit students encyclopedia. Macmillan Educ.
Corp. 20v illus maps apply to publisher for
price   031

1 Encyclopedias

First published 1967 by Crowell-Collier Educ.
Corp.

This encyclopedia is "created for children from
fifth grade through high school and is geared to
curriculum materials from all states. Its subject
coverage, while outstanding in all areas, is especially strong on states and countries, particularly
Canada, science, technology, fine arts, literature,
and vocational guidance. The articles are clearly
written and are prepared primarily for the grade
levels at which the subject is taught. Exceedingly
accurate, each article is reviewed or written and
signed by one of the many contributing specialists.
The encyclopedia is continuously revised and is
reprinted at least once each year to include important happenings. . . . Articles, arranged alphabetically letter by letter under specific entry, each
begins with a dictionary definition, including pronunciation. Using extensive cross references to
link related material, the set includes a 400-page
index with 125,000 entries. 'Fact Boxes' and 'Student Guides' further assist in quick location of
essential data. Bibliographies of graded titles
appear with major articles. The outstanding format
features clear printing with bold headings on fine
quality paper." Peterson. Ref Bks for Elem and
Jr High Sch Libraries

Supplemented by: Merit students year book

For fuller review see: The Booklist, Dec. 15, 1978

The **New** book of knowledge; the children's
encyclopedia. Grolier 20v illus maps apply
to publisher for price   031

1 Encyclopedias

Supersedes The Book of knowledge. This title
first published 1966

"It is designed primarily for the elementary
grades, but it can also be of some assistance to
slower developing children in junior high schools.
The material is arranged alphabetically, letter by
letter, by broad topics. Each volume contains an
index that is cross-referenced to the entire content of the set. In addition to the conventional
entries, this index also contains many brief notes
and informational items, particularly useful for
quick reference. The Dale-Chall readability formula
is used to test the reading level of every article
and, in general, the material is presented in clear
and simple style, with helpful pronunciation guides.
. . . In terms of revision policy, 'The New Book
of Knowledge' follows the policy of continuing revision; the set is printed three or four times a year

The **New** book of knowledge—*Continued*
to incorporate some of the most important information. All in all, this is one of the best encyclopedias for this age group; it is highly recommended by all major reviewing journals." Wynar. Guide to Ref Bks for Sch Media Centers
"This children's encyclopedia is strongly oriented toward the sciences and mathematics throughout and has many suggestions for individual projects and teaching procedures. Although the text is intended primarily for students in Grade 3 and upward, younger children can use the set to advantage." The AAAS Sci Bk List for Children
Supplemented by: The New book of knowledge annual
For fuller review see: The Booklist, December 1, 1978

The **New** Lincoln Library encyclopedia. Frontier Press 3v illus maps $99.95   031
1 Encyclopedias
First published 1924 in one volume with title: The Lincoln Library of essential information
"A serviceable compendium of varied information, now revised with every printing. Non-alphabetical. Materials are grouped by subject field in compact form, often using graphs, charts, and tables. Alphabetical index." Sheehy. Guide to Ref Bks. 9th edition

The **World** Book encyclopedia. World Book-Childcraft Int. 22v illus maps apply to publisher for price   031
1 Encyclopedias
First published 1917-1918 by Field Enterprises
"A good juvenile encyclopedia, one of the leading American works in the field; approximates the form and treatment of the standard works for adults and so is especially good for the older child who is nearly ready to use adult material. Alphabeting is word by word. For the most part the work has short articles on narrow topics, although some long articles are also included. Articles are signed. There are many cross references to related subjects. Pronunciation is indicated for unusual names and words. Bibliographies are brief but well chosen, sometimes with short annotations. Illustrations and graphs, in color and black-and-white, are clear and pertinent." Sheehy. Guide to Ref Bks. 9th edition
Supplemented by: The World book year book
For a fuller review see: The Booklist, May 1, 1979

032   English encyclopedias

Guinness Book of world records. Sterling illus $9.95, lib. bdg. $9.89   032
1 Encyclopedias   2 Curiosities and wonders
LC 65-24391
First published 1955 in England with title: The Guinness Book of records; in the United States, 1962. Frequently revised
Lists records of all kinds, including the smallest fish ever caught, the most expensive wine, the greatest weight lifted by a man, the world's longest horse race and the longest river in the world
A "compilation of facts, including both the significant and trivial which young people may find intriguing." Booklist

051   American periodicals

Abridged Readers' guide to periodical literature. Wilson, H.W. $30 a year   051
1 American periodicals—Indexes
ISSN 0001-334X   LC 38-34737
First published July 1935. Monthly except June, July, and August (The indexing for these months is included in the September issue) Permanent bound annual cumulations
An index to 59 periodicals of general interest which have been chosen by the subscribers to the index from the approximately 180 periodicals covered by the unabridged Readers' Guide to Periodical Literature [entered below]. The form of indexing is the same as that used in the unabridged Readers' Guide with all the bibliographic information provided that is necessary for locating any article

An index "designed especially for school and small public libraries unable to afford the regular Readers' guide. For the public library which is growing and can possibly afford the greater expense, the unabridged Guide is the better investment." Sheehy. Guide to Ref Bks. 9th edition

Cricket; the literary magazine for children. Open Court Pub. Co. $15 a year   051
1 Children's literature—Periodicals
ISSN 0090-6034
Monthly. First published 1973
"'Cricket' is the only truly literary magazine for children ages 6-12. The editorial board includes Isaac Singer, Paul Heins, Lloyd Alexander, Virginia Haviland, and others. Internationally known writers and illustrators are contributors of never-before-published stories, poems and articles, which make up the major portion of each issue. Also included are some reprinted materials, craft ideas, book reviews, and letters to 'Cricket'. There is a section devoted to contributions from young readers. The excellent format is complemented by predominantly black-and-white illustrations (cover in full color), and there is no advertising. Highly recommended also to all storytellers as a source for new and exciting literature to share with children." Katz. Magazines for Libraries. 3d edition

Ebony Jr. Johnson Pub. Co. $7 a year   051
1 Children's literature—Periodicals
ISSN 0091-8660
10 issues per year. First published 1973
"Based on the idea that reading opens the door to opportunity and that learning is fun, its purpose is to stimulate pride in and knowledge of black history. It is much like the average children's magazines for ages 6-12, a sort of 'Jack and Jill' for black children. There are games, fiction, articles on black personalities and historical events, recipes, arts and crafts, a book review, a calendar of important dates in black history, and writings submitted by readers. All in all, a worthy contribution to this genre." Katz. Magazines for Libraries. 3d edition

How to use the Readers' guide to periodical literature. Wilson, H.W. pa gratis   051
1 Reader's guide to periodical literature
First published 1962. Frequently revised
This pamphlet is designed for teaching the use of Readers' guide to elementary and secondary school students. Reasonable quantities for class use are free

Readers' guide to periodical literature. Wilson, H.W. $62 a year   051
1 American periodicals—Indexes
ISSN 0034-0464   LC 6-8232
First published 1900. Published semimonthly, monthly February, July and August. Quarterly and permanent bound annual cumulations
A cumulative author and subject index to approximately 180 periodicals specifically chosen to represent all the important areas of contemporary interest. Reference value has been increased with expanded coverage in current events, history, political science, health, and recreation. Periodicals have been selected that best serve the needs of students, librarians, and researchers, a swell as general readers. Articles indexed are given author and appropriate subject entries, both located in a single alphabetical list. Criticisms of individual works of ballet, drama, musical comedy and opera are indexed by the title of work, with the full entry under the name of the author or composer of the work. Short stories are indexed by the name of the author and under the heading "Short stories." Author and subject entries include all the necessary information needed to find the article cited
"This is a modern index of the best type." Sheehy. Guide to Ref Bks. 9th edition

Subject index to children's magazines. Ed. and distributed by Gladys Cavanagh, 2020 University Ave, Suite 6, Madison, Wis. 53705 $12 a year   051
1 American periodicals—Indexes   2 Children's literature—Periodicals—Indexes
ISSN 0039-4251
Monthly with semi-annual commulations in February and August. First published 1949
Formerly published by Meribah Hazen, now edited and published by Gladys Cavanagh

Subject index to children's magazines—*Cont.*

"This monthly periodical index is essential for an elementary school library. Using the same form of entry as the 'Readers' Guide,' it indexes the valuable children's publications which contain invaluable information. Its list includes the juvenile weekly newspapers, e.g., 'Newstime' and 'My Weekly Reader;' varied titles, such as 'Boys' Life,' 'Jack and Jill,' 'Cricket,' 'Humpty_Dumpty,' 'Highlights for Children,' 'Arizona Highways,' 'Man and His Music,' 'Ranger Rick's Nature Magazine,' and regional historical magazines, for example, 'Illinois History' and 'Wisconsin Trails.' Indexing stories, poems, and plays as well as factual material. 'Subject Index to Children's Magazines' is an indispensable tool for both children and teachers." Peterson. Ref Bks for Elem and Jr High Sch Libraries. 2d edition

060.4   General rules of order

Robert, Henry M. 1837-1923
Robert's Rules of order; newly rev. A new and enl. ed. by Sarah Corbin Robert, with the assistance of Henry M. Robert, III, James W. Cleary [and] William J. Evans. Scott 1970 xlii, 594p $9.95   060.4

1 Parliamentary practice
ISBN 0-673-05714-3   LC 71-106451

First published 1876 as: Pocket manual of rules of order for deliberative assemblies
"This book embodies a codification of the present-day general parliamentary law (omitting provisions having no application outside legislative bodies). The book is also designed as a manual to be adopted by organizations or assemblies as their parliamentary authority." Introduction
"The standard handbook, although not necessarily the easiest to use . . . a 48-page section of 'charts, tables, and lists' printed on tinted paper has been inserted in the middle of the volume for easy reference." Sheehy. Guide to Ref Bks 9th edition

069   Museum science

Thomson, Peggy
Museum people; collectors and keepers at the Smithsonian; illus. by Joseph Low. Prentice-Hall 1977 305p illus $8.95 (5 and up)   069

1 Smithsonian Institution   2 Museums
ISBN 0-13-606889-8   LC 77-3175

A survey of activities at the Washington, D.C. based Smithsonian Institution whose resources include many museums and a zoo
"Divided into three areas, [this book] presents the physical plant(s) of the Smithsonian, the people employed there (from curator to carpenter), and the work done (from collecting sea mud cores to keeping track of over 200,000 foraminifera). Lightly written, with a warm approach to the people involved, it is a fascinating view into the complex world of a unique institution." Sch Library J
Glossary: p290-92. Bibliography: p304-05

070.4   Specific journalistic activities and types of journalism

Weiss, Ann E.
News or not? Facts and feelings in the news media; illus. with photographs. Dutton 1977 136p illus $8.95 (6 and up)   070.4

1 Journalism   2 Reporters and reporting
ISBN 0-525-35795-5   LC 76-54920

The author "discusses the complex subject of what the news is and how it is presented today in the print and electronic media. She points out that the selection and content of news reports are affected by the attitudes of reporters, editors, and news managers; those of owners, stockholders, advertisers, and government officials, and those of readers and viewers themselves." Sch Library J
"Weiss is specific about examples, candid about people, and usually objective, aware throughout of the responsibility of the news media and of the conflicting theories about the public's right to know." Chicago. Children's Bk Center
Bibliography: p131

070.5   Publishing

Greenfeld, Howard
Books: from writer to reader. Crown 1976 211p illus $8.95, pa $4.95 (6 and up)   070.5

1 Books   2 Book industries and trade   3 Printing
ISBN 0-517-52620-4; 0-517-53493-2   LC 76-15991

"A comprehensive survey of the many roles involved in the extremely complex process of carrying a book through the stages of production from writer to reader. Every facet of bookmaking—from selection of the typeface to indexing, from editing to binding—receives careful, evenhanded coverage. . . . The author maintains a particularly good balance between the often opposing demands of commercial success and artistic integrity and includes an excellent discussion of the financial problems involved in the publication of a book. The book itself—and especially the page layout—is a handsome example of design. Useful and informative, with glossary, bibliography, and index." Horn Bk

070.5025   Publishing—Directories

Children's media market place; ed. by Deirdre Boyle & Stephen Calvert; Lillian Shapiro, consultant. Gaylord 1978 411p pa $15.95   070.5025

1 Publishers and publishing—Directories   2 Audio-visual materials—Directories
ISBN 0-915794-17-9   LC 77-93720

This "volume is intended to be a comprehensive directory of sources of children's materials in all formats and media. The listings are grouped in 20 categories—e.g., publishers, audiovisual producers and distributors, reviewers, book clubs, sources of children's TV programs, state and local library personnel and services connected with children's services, and a bibliography of selection and reference tools. . . . The data provided for the sources include address and telephone numbers, types and subjects of materials offered, intended audience, and discounts. There is a name and numbers index to all the listings, and some sections have subject and special-interest indexes. Despite some omissions, out-of-date information, and overlap with other guides, this volume contains a great deal of material conveniently arranged, and it will be very useful to a variety of librarians and patrons who work with children." Cur Ref Bks
For a fuller review see: Booklist, September 15, 1978

Gillespie, John T.
Paperback books for young people; an annotated guide to publishers and distributors. 2d ed. A.L.A. 1977 223p pa $9   070.5025

1 Publishers and publishing—Directories   2 Paperback books—Directories
ISBN 0-8389-0248-0   .   LC 77-21627

First published 1972
Companion volume to: The young phenomenon: paperbacks in our schools, entered in class 027.8
"The book is organized into three parts. The first is an introduction to and directory of the leading publishers of paperbacks and their imprints. The second is a list of paperback distributors in the United States and their services. The third part comprises a brief discussion and an annotated listing of selection aids for paperback books. . . . It is my hope that this book will aid the librarian and educator to choose and acquire the best, most suitable paperbacks for their media programs." Introduction
"The purpose of this book is to give libraries, teachers and others concerned with young people's reading an introduction to important paperback publishers. It lists and describes the leading publishers and their imprints, paperback distribution by state, and in addition to addresses, gives specialty of the publishers, series (if any) for young people, pricing and other information including statements as to whether a publisher's paperbacks can be ordered directly." Wis Library Bul [review of the 1972 edition]

Literary market place: LMP; with Names & numbers; the directory of American book publishing. Bowker pa $26.95 **070.5025**

1 Publishers and publishing—Directories
ISSN 0075-9899 LC 41-51571

A combined edition of the titles first published 1940 and 1952/1953 respectively, and issued annually

"Eighty-two alphabetically arranged sections provide names, addresses, phone numbers and other data on literary agents, associations, book manufacturers, review services, editorial services, exporters, book clubs, typesetters, book wholesalers, and many other specialized production and promotional services of essential interest to the trade. Librarians will be more concerned with the directory information on American and Canadian publishers, lists of awards, associations, and prizes." Wynar. Guide to Ref Bks for Sch Media Centers

070.505 Publishing—Periodicals

Publishers Weekly. Bowker $38 per year **070.505**

1 Publishers and publishing—Periodicals 2 Books —Reviews
ISSN 0000-0019

Weekly. First published 1872 with title: The Publishers' and Stationers' Weekly Trade Circular

This journal provides news of the book industry and trade. Its features cover publishing news throughout the world and its forecasts section contains reviews of forthcoming adult, juvenile and paperback titles

100 PHILOSOPHY AND RELATED DISCIPLINES

113 Cosmology (Philosophy of nature)

Fisher, Aileen

I stood upon a mountain; pictures by Blair Lent. Crowell 1979 unp illus $9.95, lib. bdg. $9.79 (k-3) **113**

1 Universe
ISBN 0-690-03977-8; 0-690-03978-6 LC 79-3983

"During each of the seasons, a little girl looks at the world and wonders how it came into being. Every time, she encounters someone who offers another explanation of the earth's origin. Did the world start as an egg or a fire? Did it begin at the impulse of the Word of God or because an explosion wracked the universe? What existed before the fire, the egg, the Word, the mass of matter? The girl concludes that the wonder she experiencs in viewing the world is more important than a precise answer about earth's beginning." Sch Library J

"The luminous watercolor illustrations, a departure in style for the artist, underscore the controlled emotion of the text, at the same time conveying the splendor of a mountain landscape in spring, a pulsing ocean in summer, a rich-hued desert in autumn, and a snow-clad village in winter. In contrast to the magnificence of the double-page spreads which depict the seasonable vistas, other pages delineate the child and her companions in subtle character studies. A celebration of nature, childhood, and beauty." Horn Bk

121 Epistemology (Theory of knowledge)

Moorman, Thomas

What is it really like out there? Objective knowing. Atheneum Pubs. 1977 87p $5.95 (6 and up) **121**

1 Knowledge, Theory of 2 Truth
ISBN 0-689-30557-5 LC 76-25466

The author "translates basic philosophy and objective ways of thinking into simple language for beginners. He examines the obstacles which must be overcome and the tools needed to determine truth for oneself. After clear explanations of brainwashing and 'braintwisting,' ethnocentric prejudices, theories of truth, etc., Moorman gives project suggestions, carefully explaining the strengths and weaknesses of survey investigations (good for social science projects). . . . Moorman understands the uncertainties of truth seeking, has the sense to reveal his own bias, and has a definite knack for simplifying difficult concepts." Sch Library J

128 Humankind

Bernstein, Joanne E.

When people die [by] Joanne E. Bernstein and Stephen V. Gullo; photographs by Rosemarie Hausherr. Dutton 1977 unp illus $7.50 (k-3) **128**

1 Death
ISBN 0-525-4255-4 LC 76-23099

"The authors attempt to explain in simple terms the reasons for death, theories on afterlife, burial practices, grief and the naturalness of death as a process of life." AAAS Sci Bks & Films

"This is a factual book with an honest outlook. It would probably not appeal to its young audience soon after the death of a loved one—it is too analytic and matter of fact. It might well fascinate this age group when not concerned with an immediate death, or once the healing process has started. The black-and-white photographs are excellent artistically and impressive in their portrayal of many ages and races." Children's Bk Rev Serv

Zim, Herbert S.

Life and death [by] Herbert S. Zim [and] Sonia Bleeker; illus. By Rene Martin. Morrow 1970 63p illus lib. bdg. $5.52 (4 and up) **128**

1 Death
ISBN 0-688-31553-4 LC 73-91211

The text is "invested with the attitude that the cessation of life is a part of life itself. The authors consider man's life span in relation to other living things. Having discussed the nature of the latter, they describe the process of aging and dying, the technicalities of burial and cremation, and some of the funeral practices of other times and other lands. The one significant piece of information that is not included is the fact that the services of a funeral director and the choice between cremation and earth burial are not absolute, but that it is possible to bequeath a body to an institution for medical research. An index is appended." Sutherland. The Best in Children's Bks

"Psychologists, psychiatrists, educators, members of the medical professions, social worker, and parents were among those consulted by the authors. This worthwhile book has been needed for a long time." Sci Bks

133 Parapsychology and occultism

Cohen, Daniel

In search of ghosts; illus. with photographs and reproductions. Dodd 1972 182p illus $5.95 (6 and up) **133**

1 Psychical research 2 Ghosts
ISBN 0-396-06485-X LC 70-175312

Here is a description of alleged occurrences of ghosts and other supernatural phenomena, and an account of psychical research, including seances, tracking poltergeists, and taking spirit photographs

The author has broadened "the traditional definition of ghosts to include almost any alleged occurrence involving 'spirits.' . . . For anyone seeking an introduction to various views of life 'beyond the grave' there are certainly some intriguing snippets of information (and some well-chosen illustrations) here." NY Times Bk Rev

A selected bibliography: p174-78

133.1   Apparitions. Ghosts

Cohen, Daniel
Real ghosts; illus. with photographs and
prints. Dodd 1977 125p illus $5.95 (4-6)   **133.1**

1 Ghosts
ISBN 0-396-07454-5   LC 77-6502
A "collection of famous hauntings, mainly
British, taken from the files of psychical researchers. Possible scientific explanations for many
of the hauntings, accounts of follow-up investigations, and the reasons for doubting the reports of
witnesses are also included. Treatment throughout
is simple and reasonable." Sch Library J
"Black-and-white photographs, especially of the
'ghosts,' will attract attention, and ghost detectives wanting proof should find room for research
here." Booklist

The world's most famous ghosts; illus. with
photographs and prints. Dodd 1978 112p illus
$5.95 (4 and up)   **133.1**

1 Ghosts
ISBN 0-396-07543-6   LC 77-16857
"Cohen presents accounts of ghostly apparitions of Abraham Lincoln, Anne Boleyn, Aaron
Burr and other . . . figures from history. The
potpourri also includes tales of the nameless . . .
Man in Gray, the Flying Dutchman, and the Horror
of No. 50 Berkeley Square in London." Sch Library J
"Though these untaxing accounts appear rather
slapdash, students of unnatural history will probably have some fun looking up their favorite
haunts." NY Times Bk Rev

Kettelkamp, Larry
Haunted houses; written and illus. by Larry
Kettelkamp. Morrow 1969 94p illus $6.25, lib.
bdg. $6 (4 and up)   **133.1**

1 Ghosts
ISBN 0-688-21377-4; 0-688-31377-9   LC 69-16269
The author "analyzes 10 documented cases of
hauntings and poltergeist activity in England and
America and discusses various scientific theories
which have been suggested as possible explanations
for such phenomena. Illustrated with black-and-
white drawings and three authentic photographs
of ghosts." Booklist
"As a matter-of-fact look at spectral phenomena,
the book serves its purpose. . . . It's all bound to be
interesting to a young reader on the phantom trail,
but don't look for goose pimples." NY Times Bk
Rev

Simon, Seymour
Ghosts; drawings by Stephen Gammell. Lippincott 1976 79p illus (The Eerie ser) $7.95,
pa $2.95 (4-6)   **133.1**

1 Ghosts
ISBN 0-397-31664-X; 0-397-31665-8   LC 75-37520
Contents: The noisy ghosts of Calvados Castle;
The nameless horror of Berkeley Square; A Long
Island spirit; The restless coffins; The brown lady
of Raynham Hall; The ghostly hitchhikers; The
S. S. Watertown phantoms; The hounds of death;
Haunted American history
"Tales of poltergeists, moving coffins, ghostly
hitchhikers, and even hauntings in the White
House are told; much of the material can be found
in other collections. Two intriguing photographs
of ghosts appear, and the drawings . . . help to
raise the hair on the back of the reader's neck."
Horn Bk

133.3   Divinatory arts

Aylesworth, Thomas G.
Astrology and foretelling the future; illus.
by J. H. Breslow. Watts, F. 1973 63p illus
lib. bdg. $4.90 (5 and up)   **133.3**

1 Astrology 2 Fortune telling
ISBN 0-531-02606-X   LC 72-8797
"A Concise guide"
The author describes the principles of astrology
and the zodiac, explaining how to prepare a simple
horoscope. He also provides information about

reading tarot cards and tea leaves, as well as predicting the future with dominoes. One chapter contains brief definitions of over twenty-five more
obscure kinds of fortune telling and divination
"Since a mystic lurks in almost every young
person these days, the book should attract much
interest. The illustrations are marvelous." Pub W

133.4   Magic, witchcraft, demonology

Kohn, Bernice
Out of the cauldron; a short history of
witchcraft. Holt 1972 119p illus $5.95 (5 and
up)   **133.4**

1 Witchcraft
ISBN 0-03-088367-9   LC 74-150030
"A concise, easy-to-read survey of witchcraft, its
origins in pagan religion, its practices, and the witch
hysteria that swept Western Europe in the fifteenth
and sixteenth centuries and Salem in the seventeenth. The author describes the lore of the coven
and the sabbat, very briefly profiles some famous
witches and warlocks, and gives a few charms and
recipes from white and black magic concluding with
a quick look at witchcraft today. Appended are
several pertinent documents, a glossary, and a bibliography." Booklist

Starkey, Marion L.
The tall man from Boston; illus. by Charles
Mikolaycak. Crown 1975 46p illus lib. bdg. $5.95
(3-5)   **133.4**

1 Witchcraft 2 Salem, Mass.
ISBN 0-517-52187-3   LC 75-9970
"A compressed and simplified account of the
Salem witch trials, revealing how narrowly John
Alden escaped death after he was unjustly ac-
cused of being a 'witch.' " LC. Children's Bks
1975
"Mikolaycak has illustrated the account with
dramatic black and white pictures that are as
subtly simple as posters, strongly outlined, with
no background detail, and stark in mood." Chicago.
Children's Bk Center

133.8   Psychic phenomena and extrasensory perception

Hall, Elizabeth
Possible impossibilities; a look at parapsychology. Houghton 1977 169p $6.95 (6 and
up)   **133.8**

1 Psychical research
ISBN 0-395-25299-7   LC 76-58529
"All of the familiar topics—clairvoyance, precognition, psychokinesis, and telepathy—are given
fair and judicious treatment in this . . . account
of paranormal phenomena. In addition, there is a
dispassionate analysis of parapsychological research,
animal psychics (usually outright frauds), psychic
surgery, and Uri Geller's purported psychic powers."
Sch Library J
"Perhaps its most valuable asset is that it contains no misinformation concerning a topic to
which a great disservice has been done by hack
writers and narrow-minded scientists. . . . The
enlightening, attractively produced book consistently demonstrates thoughtfulness and impartiality
and is, therefore, a sufficient introduction to the
subject." Horn Bk

Kettelkamp, Larry
Investigating psychics; five life histories
illus. with photographs. Morrow 1977 128p
illus $6.25, lib. bdg. $6 (5 and up)   **133.8**

1 Extrasensory perception 2 Clairvoyance
ISBN 0-688-22123-8; 0-688-32123-2   LC 77-23975
"This provides an overview of current developments and future directions in the new science
of psi or parapsychology plus profiles of five gifted
psychics. Results of controlled laboratory experiments are outlined to document the claims of Ingo
Swann, an astral traveller famous for his psychic
probes of Jupiter and Mercury; Olga and Ambrose
Worrall, psychic healers; Rosemary Brown, a musical medium; and Matthew Manning, a multi-
talented psychic." Sch Library J

Kettelkamp, Larry—*Continued*

"Kettelkamp's new book is an interesting primer on parapsychology. He writes clearly and gives a concise definition of the 'sixth sense!' The five people discussed here do indeed come across as having experienced super-normal lives." Pub W

Sixth sense; written and illus. by Larry Kettelkamp. Morrow 1970 95p illus lib. bdg. $6 (5 and up)   **133.8**

1 Extrasensory perception 2 Clairvoyance
ISBN 0-688-31463-5   LC 76-119845

"The author clearly explains the nature of telepathy, clairvoyance, and precognition, and also discusses psychometry, retrocognition, astral projections, mediums, possession, psychokinesis, psychic photography and healing, and the tricks of phony mediums and mentalists. . . . [He gives] a generally accurate and balanced picture of present knowledge about parapsychology." Sch Library J

152.1 Sensory perception

Brenner, Barbara

Faces; photographs by George Ancona. Dutton 1970 unp illus lib. bdg. $8.95 (k-2)   **152.1**

1 Senses and sensation
ISBN 0-525-29518-6   LC 70-102737

"Big, clear photographs illustrate with joyous vitality the things we see, hear, smell, and taste, and show how each sense operates separately, so that we can shut off perception and use some parts of our faces for different things. More subtly, the book points out the kinship of all peoples. It can be read aloud to very young children and used as a springboard for discussion, but the easy vocabulary, large print, and short sentences make the book an excellent choice for independent readers." Sat Rev

Kettelkamp, Larry

A partnership of mind and body: biofeedback; illus. with photographs. Morrow 1976 96p illus $6.25, lib. bidg. $6 (5 and up)   **152.1**

1 Biofeedback training 2 Mind and body
ISBN 0-688-22088-6; 0-688-32088-0   LC 76-24818

"Biofeedback refers to controlling presumed involuntary body mechanisms with the aid of an outside monitor. The book has five major chapters covering control of skin temperature, heart rate and blood pressure, involuntary muscles, brain waves, and the measuring of changes in electrical resistance in the skin. The author incorporates early discoveries and numerous remarkable instances of control and describes possible medical or psychological applications." Horn Bk

"Kettelkamp's books are always authoritative and objective, and in this lucid examination of a provocative and still controversial subject, he carefully restricts discussion to recorded scientific research. . . . A stimulating subject; a fine survey." Chicago. Children's Bk Center

Simon, Seymour

The optical illusion book; drawings by Constance Ftera. Four Winds 1976 78p illus lib. bdg. $7.95 (4 and up)   **152.1**

1 Optical illusions
ISBN 0-590-07403-7   LC 75-33873

The author "discusses how what we think we see may be affected by past experience, familiarity with perspective, how light or color can effect illusion, and how much of our visual impression may be determined by the brain rather than the eye. There is also an interesting chapter on optical illusions in art, and several suggestions for readers' experiments." Chicago. Children's Bk Center

152.3 Movements and motor functions

Silverstein, Alvin

The left-hander's world [by] Alvin Silverstein and Virginia B. Silverstein. Follett 1977 96p illus lib. bdg. $5.95 (4 and up)   **152.3**

1 Left- and right-handedness
ISBN 0-695-40752-X   LC 76-50325

"This book describes the many inconveniences suffered by this group living in a world where almost everything is designed for the right-handers." Children's Bk Rev Serv

"Along with much general information about handedness (a trait peculiar to humans), there are interesting and safe experiments and observations to determine whether an individual's left or right brain hemisphere is dominant. A useful appendix lists catalogs and stores serving south-paw needs." Sch Library J

152.4 Emotions and feelings

LeShan, Eda

What makes me feel this way? Growing up with human emotions; illus. by Lisl Weil. Macmillan Pub. Co. 1972 128p illus $6.95, pa $1.95 (3-6)   **152.4**

1 Emotions
ISBN 0-02-757320-6; 0-02-044340-4   LC 71-165573

The author uses specific situations involving such emotions as love, hate, fear, anger and jealousy to illustrate the conflicts and confusion every child experiences and to help the child understand and accept his feelings

"A straightforward, thorough presentation of emotions which covers a wide range of feelings and attitudes and how to handle them. The treatment is . . . comprehensive . . . and includes feelings about sex and death. Rather than an exclusive focus on self, the discussion of feelings of parents, teachers, and children in the past broadens reader understanding . . . Children will surely identify with some of the hundreds of examples, and the examination of accepting feelings and learning to cope effectively is very readable. Cartoon-type illustrations keep the tone light but do not add to the explanations." Library J

Miles, Betty

Around and around—love. Knopf 1975 42p illus lib. bdg. $4.99, pa $2.50 (k-3)   **152.4**

1 Love
ISBN 0-394-93111-4; 0-394-73137-9   LC 75-2539

"People of all sizes and shapes, ages and stages are shown together—happy, glad, troubled, sad—whispering it, shouting it, feeling good about love." Booklist

"A slight poetic text is used with photographs by many photographers to show the multi-faceted faces and actions of love. The pictures are exceptional. . . . The text is wonderfully light and avoids the temptation to tell what's going on in the pictures." Children's Bk Rev Serv

Stein, Mark L.

Good and bad feelings; illus. by Richard Cuffari. Morrow 1976 96p illus $5.75, lib. bdg. $5.52 (3-6)   **152.4**

1 Emotions
ISBN 0-688-22061-4; 0-688-32061-9   LC 75-28353

"Explains the origins and manifestations of anger, love, fear, happiness, and sadness. There is good specific information on a number of scientific experiments—both ones with people and ones with animals—which have helped to explain human emotions and reactions. The tone of this book is precise, though somewhat pedantic. I think the manner in which lobotomies are presented is frightening and no longer entirely valid. Otherwise, this is a book which may appeal to some children, and perhaps be of value to teachers and parents in explaining feelings to children. The gray tone illustrations are charming and effective." Children's Bk Rev Serv

153.4 Knowledge (Cognition)

Burns, Marilyn

The book of think; (or how to solve a problem twice your size); illus. by Martha Weston. Little 1976 125p illus $7.95, pa $4.95 (4 and up)   **153.4**

1 Thought and thinking 2 Problem solving
ISBN 0-316-11742-0; 0-316-11743-9 LC 76-17848

Burns, Marilyn—*Continued*

"The Brown paper school series"

"Divided into three general sections—Getting Out of Your Own Way, Knowing a Problem When You See It, and Brain Push-ups—the book, although undoubtedly inspired by current adult interest in self-improvement through non-traditional thinking patterns, maintains a youthful perspective in its discussion of the various conditions which determine success or failure in problem solving: the inhibiting influence of preconceived notions and habits, the need to define the exact nature of the problem, the importance of seeking alternative solutions, and the difference between reasonable logic and sophistic argumentation." Horn Bk

153.6　Communication

Castle, Sue

Face talk, hand talk, body talk; photographs by Frances McLaughlin-Gill. Doubleday 1977 unp illus $7.95, lib. bdg. $8.90 (k-2)　　153.6

1 Nonverbal communication　2 Body language
ISBN 0-385-11018-9; 0-385-11019-7　　LC 75-46529

"The author and photographer have created a book recognizing, interpreting, and using facial and body clues as a means of communication." Children's Bk Rev Serv

"The book will be most appealing to preschoolers; but its length makes it necessary to use only sections at a time with younger children. The attractive black-and-white photographs show both boys and girls expressing a wide range of emotions and becoming involved in active play. Though the majority of the children pictured are white, a number of black and oriental children are also shown. The author's helpful introduction suggests ways to use the book and the 'Body Talk' game with groups of children through early elementary school." AAAS Sci Bks & Films

153.7　Perceptual processes

Bendick, Jeanne

Observation; written and illus. by Jeanne Bendick. Watts, F. 1972 71p illus (Science experiences) lib. bdg. $5.90 (3-5)　　153.7

1 Perception
ISBN 0-531-01440-1　　LC 72-6053

Using reader-participation pictures and questions, the author discusses how man observes the world around him, examining what senses he uses and what qualities are important in the perception of objects—including shape, color, size, motion, temperature, weight, smell and sound. The concept of change and some techniques of observation and record keeping are also considered

"The reader becomes a detective looking for the answers to posed questions. The illustrations are well drawn and aid the written material. Because it is a question and answer book with no set answers, a child can read it over and over and still find it an enjoyable experience." Appraisal

154.6　Sleep phenomena. Dreams

Kettelkamp, Larry

Dreams; written and illus. by Larry Kettelkamp. Morrow 1968 94p illus lib. bdg. $6 (5 and up)　　154.6

1 Dreams
ISBN 0-688-21245-X　　LC 68-14803

This account "includes a history of attitudes toward dreams, from ancient Egypt to modern psychoanalysis; a . . . report on contemporary sleep research; a discussion of parapsychology; and some practical suggestions for the interpretation of one's own dreams." Commonweal

"A good first book on the subject. . . . In discussing both the psychological aspects of dreaming and the studies of physiological processes, the author goes into the subjects only enough to make them comprehensible, so that the amount of information given is not too heavy for the understanding of the intended audience." Chicago. Children's Bk Center

Silverstein, Alvin

Sleep and dreams [by] Alvin Silverstein and Virginia B. Silverstein. Lippincott 1974 159p illus map $7.95 (6 and up)　　154.6

1 Sleep
ISBN 0-397-31325-X　　LC 73-13825

This examination of sleep and dreams "includes experiments conducted with animals and humans; circadian rhythms; dream theories (pre-Freud to the present); a technical explanation of the brain's functioning during sleep; sleep learning and therapy; and current and future sleep research." Library J

"The authors have come up with an informative and well-written summary of . . . data, which they have presented clearly and non-technically and yet in sufficient detail to answer questions arising in the minds of readers. . . . Photographs and charts are well selected and helpful. This slender volume is excellent as collateral reading and for classroom use as an introduction to the subject." Sci Bks

155.4　Child psychology

Harris, Robie H.

Before you were three; how you began to walk, talk, explore, and have feelings, by Robie H. Harris & Elizabeth Levy; with photographs by Henry E. F. Gordillo. Delacorte Press 1977 142p illus $7.95, ilb. bdg. $7.45　　155.4

1 Child development
ISBN 0-440-00522-1; 0-440-00527-2　　LC 76-5587

"Following two subjects, Hillary and Tommy, through their first three years, the authors . . . explicate the processes of early growth and development. After each vignette, the elements of learning and maturation involved are explained and related to readers' own probable experiences." Sch Library J

"The authors consulted highly competent early-childhood educators on the content of this book, an illustrated narrative of the child's first three years of life. The sensitive photos capture the child in his accomplishments, fears, aggressions, and happiness. The authors speak to children and adults alike in simple forthright language about the milestones we all pass. Each reader, young or old, will become actively engaged in reconstructing his or her own beginning." Children's Bk Rev Serv

Stein, Sara Bonnett

About phobias; an open family book for parents and children together; Thomas R. Holman, consultant; photographs by Erika Stone. Walker & Co. 1979 47p illus $6.95 (k-3)　　155.4

1 Fear　2 Child psychology
ISBN 0-8027-6348-0　　LC 78-65615

This book has "two separate texts running parallel down the page. One is the story meant for parent and child to share; the other is an interpretive commentary for the adult—uniformly substantial, lucid analyses in child psychology and behavior. . . . Stone's many black-and-white photos are unusually natural and well integrated with the texts. In 'About Phobias' Susie's subconscious desire to have Daddy to herself underlies the development of a phobic fear of dogs. But her mother's sensitive handling of Susie's feelings about her father effectively eases her phobia. . . . [About phobias] enlightens and reassures without resorting to pat final answers." Sch Library J

Williams, Gurney

Twins [by] Gurney Williams III. Watts, F. 1979 64p illus lib. bdg. $6.45 (5 and up)　　155.4

1 Twins
ISBN 0-531-02265-X　　LC 78-9954

"A First book"

Beginning with the biological explanation of how twins occur, both fraternal and identical, the author proceeds to the characteristics, feelings and development of individual twin children. The book also contains twin lore and legend, a chapter on use of twins in heredity vs. environment research, a section on Siamese twins, and discussion of other multiple births including the Dionne quintuplets. There is a bibliography of recommended articles and books and information on two major twin organizations

155.5 Psychology of adolescents

LeShan, Eda
You and your feelings. Macmillan Pub. Co. 1975 117p $5.95 (6 and up)   155.5

1 Adolescent psychology 2 Emotions
ISBN 0-02-757330-3   LC 74-22254

"Some reassuring insights for adolescents who are trying to cope with roller coaster feelings. Family, school, peers, dating, sex, love, drugs, alcohol, and other teen troubles are tacked; responsibility for actions is also stressed with pragmatic ideas on how to develop and cope with adult problems. In a few areas—e.g. sex and drugs—books for further reading are suggested. Other books on teenage feelings are usually more like standard psychology tests; LeShan's use of quotes from young adults gives this a personal tone, a sense of immediacy, and greater validity." Sch Library J

155.9 Environmental psychology. Influence and effect of death

Bernstein, Joanne E.
Loss and how to cope with it. Seabury [distributed by Houghton] 1977 151p $7.95 (5 and up)   155.9

1 Bereavement 2 Death—Psychological aspects
ISBN 0-395-28891-6   LC 76-50027

"A Clarion book"
"The book focuses on what it feels like when someone you know or love dies. It discusses the effects of mourning on one's physical, mental, and emotional well-being. 'Loss' has quite a number of case studies depicting actual reactions to death. Despite some repetition and rambling, the book seems to be unique among children's books and would be a worthy addition to the collection." Children's Bk Rev Serv
Bibliography: p121-34. Filmography: p133-37

Bradley, Buff
Endings; a book about death. Addison-Wesley 1979 191p $7.95 (6 and up)   155.9

1 Death—Psychological aspects
ISBN 0-201-00422-4   LC 78-31624

"While Bradley summarizes legal and scientific debate on the determination and definition of death and describes funeral customs, his emphasis is on emotional and philosophical responses to death. He discusses ways individuals face death (their own or that of loved ones) and reviews some of the more common fears concerning death and the emotional stages individuals go through upon learning they are dying. He also treats views on immortality, longevity, life after death, and death on purpose—murder, capital punishment, war, abortion, suicide, and euthanasia. He includes case histories and literary and mythological references in a provocative but balanced introductory overview." Booklist
Selected bibliography: p185-88

LeShan, Eda
Learning to say good-by; when a parent dies; illus. by Paul Giovanopoulos. Macmillan Pub. Co. 1976 85p illus $6.95 (4 and up)   155.9

1 Bereavement 2 Death—Psychological aspects
ISBN 0-02-756360-X   LC 76-15155

The author "puts the bereaved children in touch with their grief. She then proceeds to explain the universality and validity of these feelings and how to cope with them healthfully. Actual examples illustrate many of her points." Sch Library J
"Here is the outspoken and unequivocal book that has been needed for what seems like forever. . . . In her introduction . . . [LeShan] states that some people might find her message shocking; they feel children should be protected from the agony of loss. But she stresses that children must not be shut out. They must grieve and mourn just as adults do when death strikes. The sharing of sorrow is a needed part of the healing process for everyone. This book, with its graphic illustrations, is immeasurably valuable." Pub W
Further reading: p83-85

Stein, Sara Bonnett
About dying; an open family book for parents and children together, by Sara Bonnett Stein, in cooperation with Gilbert W. Kliman [and others]; photography by Dick Frank; graphic design, Michael Goldberg. Walker & Co. 1977 47p illus $5.95 (k-3)   155.9

1 Death—Psychological aspects
ISBN 0-8027-6170-0   LC 73-15268

"A book with two running texts, one addressed to parents and the other to be read aloud to small children, is illustrated with photographs. The text for adults discusses children's needs and fears, the ways in which a parent can describe death, help a child grow in understanding, and the behavior patterns that can show a child's fears or confusion in reacting to the death of a pet or a person. The attitude stressed is that of being open and natural." Chicago. Children's Bk Center

158 Applied psychology

Kalb, Jonah
What every kid should know, by Jonah Kalb and David Viscott. Houghton 1976 127p illus $5.95 (5 and up)   158

1 Human relations
ISBN 0-395-24386-6   LC 75-45123

The authors offer "commonsense advice on helping youngsters identify and deal with the basic emotions that might be prompting their worries about themselves and their relationships with others. A significant portion of the text counsels on coping with parents; how children's rights—among them privacy, property, and the right to an explanation—are balanced against their responsibilities as well as the rights and responsibilities of their parents. Information on the nature of friendships and advice on 'finding yourself' offer further guidance in sorting things out. The final section on how a child might better cope with parents' decision to divorce might be of particular help to many." Booklist
"This self-help guide covers territory familiar to adult readers of pop psychology but is far superior to the usual run of how-to-find-a-friend fare produced for this age level. The advice is realistic and balanced, according rights to parents and peers as well. Although pronouns used are exclusively male or neuter, there are no sexist innuendos or inferences. . . . Useful assistance with the problems that loom large." Sch Library J

Richards, Arlene Kramer
Boy friends, girl friends, just friends, by Arlene Kramer Richards and Irene Willis. Atheneum Pubs. 1979 155p $6.95 (6 and up)   158

1 Friendship
ISBN 0-689-30695-4   LC 78-14257

"What makes a friend, how to get and keep friends, how to handle rejection by and loss of friends, and how to grow with friends are some of the major topics of this book. The book is written for teens and includes anecdotes about teens. The authors emphasize the importance of friends and the effects of friends on growth and development. They begin each chapter with an anecdote and then discuss the reasons for the behavior of the various characters in the example." VOYA
"Although rather talky and inclined to repetition (things are frequently explained several times and ways, lending a patronizing air), the treatment does portray a variety of interpersonal relationships and will promote thought about friendships." Booklist

179 Treatment of animals

McCoy, J. J.
In defense of animals; illus. with photographs. Seabury [distributed by Houghton] 1978 192p illus $8.95 (5 and up)   179

1 Animals—Treatment
ISBN 0-395-28864-9   LC 76-58508

McCoy, J. J.—*Continued*

"A Clarion book"

"McCoy's lucidly written book wins points for, above all, his reasonable arguments on behalf of animals. Not even hunters, scientists who experiment on animals or any persons usually condemned by conservationists can object to the author's demands for merciful methods in dealing with creatures wild and domestic. The text begins with a report on England's Richard Martin ('Humanity Dick'), sponsor of the first law governing the treatment of animals. In succeeding chapters are details on the use and abuse of animals and the efforts of humane societies to protect them. Photos of mistreated creatures are added, effective pleas for their protection. Although written for young people, the book should be required reading for all ages." Pub W

Suggested reading: p187-88

200 RELIGION

211 Concepts of God

Fitch, Florence Mary

A book about God; illus. by Leonard Weisgard. Lothrop 1953 unp illus lib. bdg. $7.92 (k-3)   **211**

1 God
ISBN 0-688-51253-4   LC 53-6735

In terms of the beauties and wonders of nature—the sky, stars, mountains and hills, rain, and the sea—author and artist explain to the wondering child what God is like. Simple poetic text and lovely pictures; a reassuring, unsentimental book." Booklist

"Written for believers of all faiths, it necessarily shuns specific doctrines, such as the uniqueness of Christ. It provides a foundation on which any parent can help his child build a more definite structure of faith." NY Times Bk Rev

220.3 Bible—Encyclopedias and dictionaries

Northcott, Cecil

Bible encyclopedia for children; designed and illus. by Denis Wrigley. Westminster Press 1964 174p illus $8.95 (5 and up)   **220.3**

1 Bible—Encyclopedias
ISBN 0-664-20494-5   LC 64-10800

"A readable book of reference which seems to achieve its purpose of providing basic information about 'the chief people, the main events, and the leading ideas of the Bible.' A wealth of background material is adroitly contained within the concise entries which despite their brevity have clarity and sufficient liveliness to encourage children to read further in the Scriptures. Bible references are chiefly to the Authorized Version. Cross references . . . enhance the book's usefulness." Toronto Boys and Girls House

220.5 Bible. Modern versions

Bible

The Holy Bible; containing the old and New Testaments; tr. out of the original tongues: and with the former translations diligently compared and rev. by King James's special command, 1611. Oxford prices vary   **220.5**

The authorized or King James version originally published 1611

The Holy Bible. Revised standard version; 2nd ed. containing the Old and New Testaments . . . . Reference ed. Nelson 1971 1296, 94p maps prices vary   **220.5**

"Translated from the original languages: being the version set forth A.D. 1611, revised A.D. 1881-1885 and A.D. 1901, compared with the most ancient authorities and revised A.D. 1946-1952. Second edition of the New Testament A.D. 1971." Title page

"In this Reference Edition, cross references that refer the student of the Bible to passages having a common motif or theme are placed in the center column of each page. There is also a Concise Concordance divided into references to key words and references to proper names, and there are twelve maps in color." Pub W [review of 1959 edition]

Includes a reader's guide, reader's concordance and index to Nelson's Bible atlas

Bible. Selections

A first Bible; illus. by Helen Sewell [Selected and arranged by Jean West Maury] Walck, H.Z. 1934 109p illus $8.95 (4 and up)   **220.5**

ISBN 0-8098-2302-0

First published by Oxford

"Fourteen stories from the Old Testament and almost twice as many from the New, told in the words of the King James Bible." Booklist

"Helen Sewells work is always finely sincere: in these pictures it rises to a high level of strength and beauty. There is poetry in these gravely lovely drawings, and in their sweep and rhythm, their reverent simplicity, they are a very fitting aid to a child's enjoyment of the magnificent literature which the Bible offers him." NY Times Bk Rev

The Holy Bible for children; a simplified version of the Old and New Testaments; ed. by Allan Hart Jahsmann; illus. and maps by Don Kueker. Concordia 1977 415p illus maps $10.95 (3 and up)   **220.5**

ISBN 0-570-03465-5   LC 77-3226

A simplified retelling of selected portions of each book in the Bible, including maps and pictures

220.8 Nonreligious subjects treated in Bible

Asimov, Isaac

Animals of the Bible; illus. by Howard Berelson. Doubeday 1978 unp illus $6.95, lib. bdg. $7.90 (3-6)   **220.8**

1 Bible—Natural history
ISBN 0-385-07195-7; 0-385-07215-5   LC 77-16893

The author writes about forty-five animals mentioned in the Old and New Testaments. He "gives some attention to the ancient use of animal symbolism in the Bible, but primarily focuses on the employment and distribution of animals in Biblical times." Sch Library J

Asimov "sparks a page-turning expedition as he reveals the books of the Bible where each animal may be found, offering his best guesses as to what a leviathan or behemoth may have been, besides giving the animals' habitats and uses in Biblical times. He hopes the book 'will make the Bible mean just a little more' to eight- to 12-year-olds, but this could easily prove a charming reference work for adults. Berelson's animated two-color illustrations warm up each page." Christian Sci Monitor

Bible. Selections

Animals of the Bible; a picture book by Dorothy P. Lathrop; with text selected by Helen Dean Fish from the King James Bible. Lippincott 1937 65p illus $8.95 (1-4)   **220.8**

1 Bible—Natural history
ISBN 0-397-31536-8

Awarded the Caldecott Medal, 1938

Illustrations of the animals mentioned in the Bible. "The creatures sometimes appear in double-page procession, as when they enter the Ark with a pair of tortoises cheerfully trotting at the head of the line, or as they emerge from the mists of creation; sometimes humans are in the picture, as with Elijah's ravens or the Peaceable Kingdom; sometimes there are angels, as with Balaam and the ass." NY Her Trib Bks

"Dorothy Lathrop's love and understanding of animals, the sensitiveness and joy with which she draws them, make her the ideal artist for such a volume. It is more than a beautiful picture book, for she has studied the fauna and flora of Bible lands until each animal and bird, each flower and tree, is true to natural history." NY Times Bk Rev

Farb, Peter
The land, wildlife, and peoples of the Bible; illus. by Harry McNaught. Harper 1967 171p illus maps $6.95, lib. bdg. $7.89 (5 and up)
220.8

1 Bible—Natural history
ISBN 0-06-021863-0; 0-06-021864-9 LC 67-17105
This book provides "scientific data on the land, people, plants and animals of the Bible lands. . . . [The] author used the Bible as a guide and constantly related what he observed on his trip to the Holy Land to incidents in the Bible. Useful in geography, history and literature classes." Bruno. Bks for Sch Libraries
The author "knows the land well, and . . . writes about the Holy Land with authority and good sense. He is especially informative when he discusses the animals and birds of the Bible, and in this he is helped by the wonderfully precise drawings." NY Times Bk Rev
Suggested readings: p160-62. Index of Biblical references: p163-64

220.9 Bible—Geography, history, biography, stories

Northcott, Cecil
People of the Bible; designed and illus. by Denis Wrigley. Westminster Press 1967 157p illus $4.95 (5 and up)
220.9

1 Bible stories 2 Bible—Biography
ISBN 0-664-20764-2 LC 67-12336
"A companion to the author's Bible Encyclopedia for Children [entered in class 220.3] this . . . collection of stories is based on the Revised Standard Version and is organized around significant biblical personalities . . . [in] both the Old and New Testaments from Genesis to Revelation. . . . Each story [is] preceded by an appropriate biblical quote." Library J

The **Taizé** Picture Bible: stories from the Scriptures; adapted from the text of the Jerusalem Bible; with illus. by Brother Eric de Saussure of the Taizé Community. Fortress Press [1969 c1968] 277p illus $9.95
220.9

1 Bible stories
ISBN 0-8006-0005-3 LC 69-11860
"First published 1968 in England with title: Bible stories for children
Includes 143 old and new Testament stories from the creation of earth to the conversion of Saul
"The text of the Jerusalem translation has been altered for young readers or listeners." Book jacket
Map on lining-papers

Turner, Philip
Brian Wildsmith's Illustrated Bible stories; as told by Philip Turner. Watts, F. [1969 c1968] 134p illus lib. bdg. $8.95, pa $5.95 (2-6)
220.9

1 Bible stories
ISBN 0-531-01529-7; 0-531-02374-5 LC 68-14250
First published 1968 in England
The author's "Biblical adaptations, compact and dignified, give the Old and New Testament stories in a sweeping chronological continuum." Sutherland. The Best in Children's Bks
This "is a combination of art work and text which is almost too good to be true. [Wildsmith's] jewel-like illustrations, pen-and-ink drawings, rainbow washes, explosions of brilliant color, are matched by a beautiful text." NY Times Bk Rev

221.9 Bible. Old Testament— Stories

Bolliger, Max
Noah and the rainbow; an ancient story retold by Max Bolliger. Tr. by Clyde Robert Bulla; with pictures by Helga Aichinger. Crowell 1972 unp illus $8.79, pa $2.95 (k-3) **221.9**

1 Noah's ark 2 Bible stories
ISBN 0-690-58448-2; 0-690-03814-3 LC 72-76361

Original German language edition published in Switzerland
"A beautifully rhythmic text, Biblical in cadence, retells the ancient story of the flood. . . . The Austrian artist's eleven full-page paintings face spaciously set verses. Stylized animals, a cubist Mount Ararat, and a brilliant climactic rainbow emerge with grandeur from sweeping lines and colors, which change from dark tones and deep greens to soft aqua and apricot." Horn Bk

Brodsky, Beverly
Jonah; an Old Testament story. Lippincott 1977 unp illus $8.95 (k-3) **221.9**

1 Jonah, the prophet 2 Bible stories
ISBN 0-397-31733-6 LC 77-5925
"Jonah himself tells the story of his initial refusal to announce God's retribution against the people of Nineveh and of his punishment—being swallowed by a great fish. . . . Jonah is depicted as a proud man throughout; it is not fear of Nineveh that causes him to disobey God but disdain. . . . His prayer to God from the fish's belly follows the substance of the Old Testament and his anger at God for proving him a false prophet by saving Nineveh is realized as wounded pride. Jonah's final capitulation to God's omniscience is especially moving." Horn Bk
"Massive paintings [by the author] in wonderful hues depict archaic times faithfully. They are highly stylized illustrations, especially those of people captured in statuesque poses. All the action in the story is ingeniously suggested rather than emphasized." Pub W

Bulla, Clyde Robert
Jonah and the great fish; illus. by Helga Aichinger. Crowell 1970 unp illus $7.95 (k-3)
221.9

1 Jonah, the prophet 2 Bible stories
ISBN 0-690-46430-4 LC 69-13636
"A direct and simplified version of the Bible story in an edition particularly notable for the stunning use of color and the bold composition of the illustrations. . . . It reads aloud well, and the illustrations are varied and subtle." Sutherland. The Best in Children's Bks

DeJong, Meindert
The mighty ones (great men and women of early Bible days); pictures by Harvey Schmidt. Harper 1959 282p illus lib. bdg. $9.98 (6 and up)
221.9

1 Bible stories
ISBN 0-06-021521-6 LC 59-5314
Using Hebrews 11 as a focal point—"Now faith is the substance of things hoped for, the evidence of things not seen" the author tells the stories of those men and women for whom these words were true. Here are Noah and his sons, Abraham, Isaac, Sarah, David, Cain, Abel, and many others—living men and women whose faith was the evidence of things not seen

De La Mare, Walter
Stories from the Bible; illus. by Edward Ardizzone. Knopf 1961 420p illus lib. bdg. $8.99 (5 and up)
221.9

1 Bible stories
ISBN 0-394-91676-X LC 61-6048
First published 1929 in England
Here are thirty-four stories retold from the first nine books of the Bible. "New drawings in Ardizzone's typical pen-and-ink style, although not so dramatic as the stories themselves, make an attractive volume. The retellings are outstanding for the beauty of their prose style, rendered with Biblical cadence and dignity fitting the many passages interwoven from the King James Bible. Unsurpassed for stories of the Garden of Eden, Noah's Ark, and such Old Testament heroes as Joseph, Moses, and David." Horn Bk

Graham, Lorenz
David he no fear; pictures by Ann Grifalconi. Crowell 1971 unp illus lib. bdg. $6.89 (1-4)
221.9

1 David, King of Israel 2 Bible stories
ISBN 0-690-2365-9 LC 71-109898
Text first published 1946 as part of the author's: How God fix Jonah
This is the Biblical story of David and Goliath retold in Liberian English dialect

Graham, Lorenz—*Continued*

"Strongly and economically retold . . . in the manner of African storytellers, Ann Grifalconi's beautifully rendered double-page woodcuts (black-and-white spreads alternating with others in black, mustard, and deep orange) powerfully interpret the text and will enhance children's appreciation of the familiar story." Sch Library J

Hutton, Warwick

Noah and the great flood; retold and illus. by Warwick Hutton. Atheneum Pubs. 1977 unp illus $7.95 (k-3)   **221.9**

1 Noah's ark 2 Bible stories
ISBN 0-689-50098-X   LC 77-3217

"A Margaret K. McElderry book"
A retelling of the story of Noah, based on the King James version of the book of Genesis
"The artist uses muted, often somber, water-colors to evoke his atmosphere. Storm scenes in deep grays and blues symbolize the outpouring of God's wrath; animals, two-by-two, depict orderliness and purpose; and the loneliness of the journey is emphasized in the sparing detail. A thoughtful and beautiful introduction to an old biblical tale." Booklist

Singer, Isaac Bashevis

The wicked city; pictures by Leonard Everett Fisher; tr. by the author and Elizabeth Shub. Farrar, Straus 1972 unp illus $6.95 (3-6)   **221.9**

1 Bible stories 2 Sodom 3 Lot (Biblical character)
ISBN 0-374-38426-6   LC 72-175144

The author retells the Biblical story of the destruction of Sodom and its inhabitants with the exception of Abraham's nephew Lot and his family
"The drama of the story is heightened by the deep-red monotone of the full-page illustrations. With details supplied only by a skillful use of white lines and cross-hatching, the illustrations are particularly effective in character portrayal, and together with the somber story, form a remarkable unified whole." Horn Bk

222 Historical books

Asimov, Isaac

Words from the Exodus; decorations by William Barss. Houghton 1963 203p illus maps $7.95 (6 and up)   **222**

1 Bible. Old Testament 2 English language—Etymology
ISBN 0-395-06570-4   LC 63-7136

The author traces the Biblical origins of words and phrases from Exodus, Leviticus, Numbers and Deuteronomy
"This etymology of Bible words . . . awakens interest in history, language study and the Bible itself. Young people will find this an exciting treasure hunt." Commonweal

232.9 Family and life of Jesus

Aichinger, Helga

The shepherd. Crowell [1967 c1966] unp illus $8.95 (k-3)   **232.9**

1 Jesus Christ—Nativity
ISBN 0-690-73021-7   LC 67-18394

Original German edition published 1966 in Switzerland

This retelling of the Christmas story "is a simple one. A single shepherd seeks the Christ child, first in a beautiful town, then in a magnificent castle, finally finding him in an old hut. The illustrations [by the author] . . . exude the warmth inherent in the Christmas story." Horn Bk

Bible. New Testament. Selections

The Christ child; as told by Matthew and Luke; made by Maud and Miska Petersham. Doubleday 1931 unp illus lib. bdg. $8.95, pa $3.95 (k-3)   **232.9**

1 Jesus Christ—Biography
ISBN 0-385-07319-4; 0-385-15841-6   LC 31-28341

The artists "have interpreted through pictures the spirit of the Holy Land which was the background of the childhood of Jesus. With the exception of the prophecy from the book of Isaiah, the text is from the gospels of Matthew and Luke. A picture book of unusual beauty." Cleveland

The "simplicity [of the Bible text is] unspoiled by adaptation. . . . The paper, type, and entire make-up of the book show an almost perfect accord of subject matter and format." Booklist

The Christmas story from the Gospels of Matthew & Luke; ed. by Marguerite Northrup. Metropolitan Mus. distributed by N.Y. Graphic 1966 32p illus $5.95   **232.9**

1 Jesus Christ—Nativity
ISBN 0-87099-047-0   LC 65-23504

First published 1950 by Pantheon Books
"A very handsome book indeed, the text comprising selections from the King James Version of the Bible. The layout is spacious and dignified, each page that has print on it being faced by a full-page reproduction in color of a painting appropriate to that part of the Christmas story being told. The page of print has, in addition to the title of the painting, a small reproduction of a woodcut in black and white." Sutherland. The Best in Children's Bks
Bibliography: p32

Blanco, Tomás

The Child's gifts; a twelfth night tale. Tr. by Harriet de Onís; with musical ornaments by Jack Delano and illustrations by Irene Delano. Westminster Press 1976 [c1962] 33p illus music $8.95 (5 and up)   **232.9**

1 Magi 2 Bilingual books—Spanish-English
ISBN 0-664-32595-5   LC 75-46530

First published 1962 in Puerto Rico
This book features side-by-side Spanish and English versions of the story of the three kings' journey to bring gifts to the infant Jesus. The music, which appears intermittently throughout the book, is a synopsis of that which was used to accompany the orginal radio broadcast of the text [in 1954] in Puerto Rico. In this version each king rules a nation rich in one of the qualities of faith, hope, or charity, but lacking in the other two. Their gifts to the Christ Child embody those qualities and on the return journey each discovers that he has received replicas of all three gifts. But according to the narrator, they apparently have not yet completed the journey home

Brown, Margaret Wise

Christmas in the barn; pictures by Barbara Cooney. Crowell 1952 unp illus $7.95 (k-2)   **232.9**

1 Jesus Christ—Nativity 2 Bible stories
ISBN 0-690-19272-X   LC 52-7858

A retelling of the Nativity story in simple rhyme. The illustrations are large and detailed
There is "use of modern dress in the pictures instead of the traditional Biblical costume, but this does not detract from the spirit of Barbara Cooney's illustrations. They are lovely." Library J

De Paola, Tomie

The Lady of Guadalupe; written and illus. by Tomie de Paola. Holiday House 1980 unp illus lib. bdg. $10.95, pa $4.95 (k-3)   **232.9**

1 Mary, Virgin 2 Legends—Mexico
ISBN 0-8234-0373-4; 0-8234-0403-X   LC 79- 19610

Also available in a Spanish language edition (ISBN 0-8234-0374-2; 0-8234-0404-8)
"In 1531, Juan Diego, a simple Indian peasant, was visited by the Virgin Mary and instructed to tell the bishop of Mexico to build a church in her honor. The bishop, however, was reluctant to follow the poor farmer's words until, in her third visitation, she provided Juan with a special sign—a picture of the Lady, as he saw her, indelibly inscribed into his rough cactus-fiber tilma. This piece of cloth, which can be seen today at the Lady of Guadalupe shrine in Mexico City, is the source of the legend of the patron saint of Mexico." Booklist
"The story is a simply told and well-developed narrative. The accompanying pencil, ink, and watercolor illustrations in soft, muted tones are appealing and appropriate." Children's Bk Rev Serv

Graham, Lorenz
Every man heart lay down; pictures by Colleen Browning. Crowell 1970 unp illus $8.95
(1-4)
232.9

1 Jesus Christ—Nativity 2 Bible stories
ISBN 0-690-27134-4   LC 75-109899
Text first published 1946 as part of the author's:
How God fix Jonah
Retold in Liberian English dialect, this is the story of the birth of Jesus
"Told with great dignity, vitality, and simplicity. The African speech patterns and the striking pictures give a new meaning and beauty to the timeless story." Commonweal

Hoffmann, Felix
The story of Christmas; a picture book. Atheneum Pubs. 1975 unp illus $6.95 (k-3)
232.9

1 Jesus Christ—Nativity 2 Bible stories
ISBN 0-689-50031-9   LC 75-6921
"A Margaret K. McElderry book"
"Although this picturebook version of the Nativity eschews Biblical language, it adheres closely to the original. . . . The text begins with the appearance of the Angel Gabriel to Mary and concludes with the Holy Family's return to Nazareth after the death of King Herod." Chicago. Children's Bk Center
Hoffman "interprets the Nativity in subtle lithographs of great beauty and feeling. Matched by his graceful retelling, these strong images make the familiar story seem freshly heard." LC. Children's Bks 1975

Kurelek, William
A northern nativity; Christmas dreams of a prairie boy. Tundra Bks. 1976 unp illus $12.95, pa $6.95 (4 and up)
232.9

1 Jesus Christ—Nativity 2 Canada—Social life and customs
ISBN 0-88776-071-6; 0-88776-009-6   LC 76-23274
Each of "20 anecdotal accounts is accompanied by a painting and recalls [the author/artist's] personal dreams of watching the Holy Family as they seek shelter and succor from farmers, fishermen, lumbermen, truckers, skiers and rod riders; from Eskimos, blacks, Indians and Mennonites, Mr Kurelek is of course retelling the story of the first Nativity, updating it as we still search for our own peace and perfection." NY Times Bk Rev
"Presented as a series of dreams experienced by the boy William . . . the familiar events are revitalized and given added dimension when relocated in Canada during the Depression years. . . . The noted Canadian artist has interpreted the Nativity, Epiphany and Flight in twenty different settings and portrayed the Holy Family in each instance as belonging to an ethnic or working group appropriate to that setting. . . . The magnificent representational paintings, in combination with a nonsentimental but moving text, place religious experience in the context of daily life." Horn Bk

Lindgren, Astrid
Christmas in the stable; pictures by Harald Wiberg. Coward-McCann 1962 unp illus lib. bdg. $5.89, pa $2.50 (k-2)
232.9

1 Jesus Christ—Nativity
ISBN 0-698-30042-4;0-698-20489-1   LC 62-14449
A "tender telling of the Christmas story by a Swedish mother to her small child, who visualizes the birth of Jesus as happening now on a farm like their own." Wis Library Bul
"Beautiful paintings of the Swedish countryside interpret the . . . story." NY Pub Library

242 Devotional literature

Field, Rachel
Prayer for a child; pictures by Elizabeth Orton Jones. Macmillan Pub. Co. 1944 unp illus $5.95 (k-3)
242

1 Prayers
ISBN 0-02-735190-4   LC 44-47191
Awarded the Caldecott Medal, 1945
One of Rachel Field's "greatest legacies to [children] has been this [brief] prayer. It was written for her own daughter, but now belongs to all boys and girls everywhere. It is a prayer, beautifully written and . . . bespeaking the faith, love, hopes, and the trust of little children." Library J
"The pictures have a freshness and childlikeness which match the text perfectly." Boston Globe

First graces; illus. by Tasha Tudor. Walck, H.Z. [1959 c1955] 47p illus $2.95 (k-3)   242

1 Prayers
ISBN 0-8098-1953-8   LC 59-12017
First published 1955 by Oxford
Companion volume to: First prayers, entered below
"A diminutive book of short graces, some from standard authors and some for special occasions such as birthday, UN Day, Thanksgiving Day and others. Illustrations are the author's usual soft pencil sketches and water color paintings." Chicago. Children's Bk Center

First prayers; illus. by Tasha Tudor. Walck, H.Z. [1959 c1952] 48p illus $2.95 (k-3)   242

1 Prayers
ISBN 0-8098-1952-X   LC 52-12780
"Protestant edition"
Companion volume to: First graces, entered above
First published 1952 by Oxford in both Catholic and Protestant editions
"Although its small size makes it more suitable for home purchase, many libraries will want this tiny gem of a book. There are prayers for morning, evening, and meals, some less familiar, but all within the understanding of a child. Delicately and tenderly illustrated." Booklist

274.15 Christian Church in Ireland

Corfe, Tom
St Patrick and Irish Christianity; published in cooperation with Cambrdge Univ. Press. Lerner Publications [1979 c1973] 51p illus maps lib. bdg. $4.49 (5 and up)
274.15

1 Patrick, Saint 2 Ireland—Church history
ISBN 0-8225-1217-3   LC 78-56811
"A Cambridge Topic Book"
First published 1973 in England
Contents: How Patrick came to Ireland; How Patrick brought Christianity to Ireland; Irish monks and monasteries; Missionary monks in Britain and Europe

289 Other denominations and sects. Shakers

Faber, Doris
The perfect life; the Shakers in America Farrar, Straus 1974 215p illus $6.95 (6 and up)
289

1 Shakers
ISBN 0-374-35819-2   LC 73-90968
A history of the Shakers who "came to America to found communities based on religious idealism. And from the time Mother Ann Lee of Manchester sailed from England in 1774, Shaker settlements in New York, New England, and Ohio expanded and developed through the nineteenth century. But by the beginning of the twentieth century, these communities began to dwindle until the women remaining at Canterbury, New Hampshire, decreed—in 1964—an end to all Shaker recruiting. Based on the principles of celibacy, communal living, and obedience to a spiritual leader, reinforced by personal contacts with Deity and by songs and dancing in worship, the Shakers regarded the perfect life as attainable by women as well as by men, by blacks as well as by whites." Horn Bk
"This book is a delight to read. It is interesting [and] informative. . . . The Shaker way of life is sympathetically recreated, and the personalities of Shaker leaders are portrayed with vigor and realism." Children's Bk Rev Serv
Shaker museums and public collections: p201-05.
Suggestions for further reading: p207-08

Yolen, Jane

Simple gifts; the story of the Shakers; illus. by Betty Fraser. Viking 1976 115p illus $6.95 (5 and up)   **289**

1 Shakers
ISBN 0-670-64584-2   LC 76-14420

The author explores the history of Shakerism and discusses Shaker beliefs, worship, and life style. She "presents a sympathetic picture of this enigmatic group, with descriptions of their songs, dances, distinctive household furniture, and tools. A final chapter gives a personal look at one of the two communities surviving now, at Sabbathday Lake, Maine." Booklist

Books for further reading: p110-11

291 Comparative religion and religious mythology

Bulfinch, Thomas

Bulfinch's Mythology: The age of fable; The age of chivalry; Legends of Charlemagne (6 and up)   **291**

1 Mythology 2 Folklore—Europe 3 Chivalry 4 Charlemagne

Some editions are:

Crowell $11.95 (ISBN 0-690-57260-3)
Modern Lib. (Modern Lib. Giants) $6.95 (ISBN 0-394-60437-7) Has title: Mythology

This book contains the myths of Greece, Rome, Egypt, and the Far East, as well as German and Norse myths, and the legends of King Arthur, Charlemagne and the Mabinogion

Fitch, Florence Mary

Their search for God; ways of worship in the Orient; illus. with photographs selected by Edith Bozyan, Beatrice Creighton and the author. Lothrop 1947 160p illus lib. bdg. $7.92 (4 and up)   **291**

1 Religions 2 Asia—Religion
ISBN 0-688-51599-1   LC 47-11705

The author describes beliefs, ceremonies and festivals of Hinduism, Confucianism, Taoism, Shinto, and Buddhism

"The book is not only an introductory study of comparative religions . . . but is also a valuable contribution to our understanding of the Orient." NY Times Bk Rev

"The excellent photographs would make this book attractive even to a reader not naturally drawn to the subject." Sat Rev

Kettelkamp, Larry

Religions, East and West. Morrow 1972 128p illus lib. bdg. $6.96 (5 and up)   **291**

1 Religions
ISBN 0-688-31926-2   LC 72-75805

"A broad survey of world religions which briefly explains the development and major tenets of ancient Egyptian beliefs, Hinduism, Buddhism, Taoism, Confucianism, Shintoism, Parsiism (Zoroastrianism), Judaism, Christianity, and Islam as well as new trends in faith. Also included are the relationship of science and religion, psychic science, archaeological findings, and religious experiments. The black-and-white illustrations are generally of religious symbols." Sch Library J

Moskin, Marietta D.

In search of God; the story of religion. Atheneum Pubs. 1979 142p illus map $10.95 (6 and up)   **291**

1 Religions 2 Religion
ISBN 0-689-30719-5   LC 79-10493

"Instead of the common practice of devoting one chapter to each major religion, Moskin explores their common themes. She tries to explain why people use religion to deal with mysteries of life such as creation, evil, and death and to point out similarities in the way people respond to God. In her view, religions change, develop, and influence each other. What people believe about God is tied to their entire culture." Sch Library J

"Written from a universal rather than from a sectarian point of view, the book is clear and precise. . . . Black-and-white reproductions of murals and paintings with religious themes are drawn from such sources as the Metropolitan Museum of Art, the Pierpoint Morgan Library, and the British Museum." Horn Bk

Selected bibliography: p134-36

Seeger, Elizabeth

Eastern religions, illus. with photographs. Crowell 1973 213p illus map $10 (6 and up) **291**

1 Religions 2 Asia—Religion
ISBN 0-690-25342-7   LC 73-10206

"Giving full due to the mythological concepts native to India, China, and Japan [the author] has traced the rise and development of Far Eastern philosophical or mystical religions as revealed by the lives and teachings of the Buddha, Confucius, or Laotse. Doctrines and principles are quoted as well as exemplified in occasional poems strategically placd: and stories and anecdotes are chosen to illustrate the tenets of the various Oriental religions and beliefs. Carried on in a vital geographic and historical context, the discussions give an account of the spread of Buddhism in the Far East as well as a sense of the significance of Western influence on Oriental life and thought. Ramakrishna and Gandhi are presented as modern exemplars of Hinduism; and the mythology of Shintoism is related to aspects of life in modern Japan. The book is pervaded by understanding and respect." Horn Bk

291.03 Comparative religion and religious mythology— Encyclopedias and dictionaries

Barber, Richard

A companion to world mythology; illus. by Pauline Baynes. Delacorte Press [1980 c1979] 312p illus maps $14.95 (5 and up)   **291.03**

1 Mythology—Encyclopedias
ISBN 0-440-00750-X   LC 79-16843

First published 1979 in England

This "volume is not merely a reference book but a collection of tales. Mythical materials are drawn from every continent but Antarctica. . . . Some of the items identify characters or places; others are full accounts of events associated with divinities or heroes. The edge of each page is decorated with vertical panels of black-and-white or full-color illustrations, in which gods and legendary men and women are presented—for the most part—'as they had been imagined by the people of the countries concerned.' The pictures of mythological characters are not individually identified, but their origin may be inferred from the accompanying texts. A mine of precise information and rich with authentic images, the book satisfies the curiosity while stimulating the imagination. With maps, a list of literary and musical works inspired by myths, and indexes of subjects, persons, and places." Horn Bk

Sedgwick, Paulita

Mythological creatures; a pictorial dictionary. Holt 1974 unp illus $6.95 (5 and up)   **291.03**

1 Mythology—Dictionaries 2 Animals, Mythical—Dictionaries
ISBN 0-03-012946-X   LC 74-8004

"Characters from familiar Greek, Roman, and Norse mythology are joined in this volume by creatures from the folklore of cultures as diverse as Libya, Peru and the Netherlands. The inclusion of animals as commonplace as toads and pelicans which have traditionally been endowed with extra-ordinary connections does indeed give a mythology fan much new territory to explore. . . . This would be a much more valuable tool if the definition included the name of the myth or folklore tradition where the creature is mentioned, or perhaps an index in which the creatures were divided by country of origin." Mass YA Coop Bk Rev Group

"The fanciful pen illustrations, reminiscent of the drawings in medieval bestiaries, add to the book's browsing appeal." Library J

Includes a selected bibliography

291.4 Religious experience, life, practice

Baylor, Byrd

The way to start a day; illus. by Peter Parnall. Scribner 1978 unp illus lib. bdg. $8.95 (1-3)   **291.4**

1 Sun 2 Worship
ISBN 0-684-15651-2   LC 78-113

"The author's sensitive singing prose will certainly convince readers that the way to start the day is to go outside, face the east, greet the sun with some kind of 'blessing or chant or song that you made yourself and keep for early morning.' Throughout the book, she gives examples of cavemen and cavewomen, of Peruvian Indians, of Egyptians and others who have celebrated the dawn—with drum beats, ringing of bells, gift gold or flowers—different peoples in different ways. Parnall's glittering paintings alternate between swirling shapes in the vibrant hues of the sunrise and strong, equally stunning geometrics that depict Pharoahs, Indians, Congolese and all whom Baylor offers as examples in this beautiful work." Pub W
"While the format is that of a picture book, the concepts in the poetic text of this handsome volume are more appropriate for independent readers who can grasp the historic and ritual values of Baylor's thoughts." Chicago. Children's Bk Center

292 Classical religion and religious mythology

Asimov, Isaac

Words from the myths: decorations by William Barss. Houghton 1961 225p illus $8.95 (6 and up)   **292**

1 Mythology, Classical 2 English language—Etymology
ISBN 0-395-06568-2   LC 61-5137

The author's "informal retelling and discussion of the myths to point out the scores of words rooted in mythology and to explain their usage in the English language provide a fresh look at the myths and a better understanding of the words and expressions derived from them." Booklist
Mythological index: p222-25

Aulaire, Ingri d'

Ingri and Edgar Parin d'Aulaire's Book of Greek myths. Doubleday 1962 192p illus maps lib. bdg. $9.95 (3-6)   **292**

1 Mythology, Classical
ISBN 0-385-07108-6   LC 62-15877

A "book for first readers in the field of mythology. . . . [The myths] are related as one continuous story, roughly divided into four sections: The Titans, Zeus and his Family, Minor Gods and Goddesses, and Mortal Descendants of Zeus." Best Sellers
"Written in a smooth, uncluttered style, the stories are brief, though not spare, and will probably have more appeal than the more ornate traditional retellings presently available in most libraries. Though the text is well written, this volume is most notable for its illustrations. Some of the lithographs are in soft colors, and a number are full-page. The d'Aulaires' distinctive stylized technique is ideally suited to the subject and captures the strength, grandeur, and heroism of these tales. . . . A distinguished piece of bookmaking." Sch Library J

Benson, Sally

Stories of the gods and heroes; illus. by Steele Savage. Dial Press 1940 256p illus $7.95 (5 and up)   **292**

1 Mythology, Classical
ISBN 0-8037-8291-8   LC 40-33522

This is "a fine collection of Greek myths based on Bulfinch's 'Age of Fable', some edited and others entirely rewritten." Adventuring With Bks. 2d edition

Bulfinch, Thomas

A book of myths; selections from Bulfinch's Age of fable; with illus. by Helen Sewell. Macmillan Pub. Co. 1942 126p illus $5.95 (5 and up)   **292**

1 Mythology, Classical
ISBN 0-02-782280-X   LC 42-25450

"Thirty Greek myths, the text adapted with few changes from Bulfinch's Age of Fable, including such well known myths as 'The golden fleece' and 'Perseus' as well as many less easily available to boys and girls, such as 'Castor and Pollux' and 'Niobe'." Ontario Library Rev
"Without illustrations, this would be a most usable collection of Greek myths. . . . With the illustrations, this is a truly distinguished book. Helen Sewell's clear-cut, sculptural lines achieve a modern and a classical effect at the same time, in perfect keeping with the text; they too, are simple, restrained, and dignified." Library J

Colum, Padraic

The Golden Fleece and the heroes who lived before Achilles; illus. by Willy Pogany. Macmillan Pub. Co. 1962 [c1921] 317p illus $8.95 (5 and up)   **292**

1 Argonauts 2 Mythology, Classical
ISBN 0-02-723620-X

A reissue of a book first published 1921; copyright renewed 1949
Contents: The voyage to Colchis; The return to Greece; The heroes of the quest
"With the adventures of Jason, who sought the famous golden fleece, are interwoven other myths and hero stories—of Orpheus the minstrel, who knew the ways and histories of the gods, of Pandora, the Golden Maid, and Atalanta, the huntress of Peleus who won a bride from the sea, and of Theseus who slew the Minotaur." Pittsburgh
"Mr Colum preserves the spirit of the Greek tales and weaves them into a magic whole. In this he is aided by the spirited drawings." Booklist

Farmer, Penelope

The story of Persephone; illus. by Graham McCallum. Morrow 1973 unp illus $6.75, lib. bdg. $6.48 (3-5)   **292**

1 Demeter 2 Persephone
ISBN 0-688-20084-2; 0-688-30084-7   LC 73-4923

"The strong and simple prose in this effective retelling of the ancient [Greek] myth conveys the drama of goddess Demeter's loss of her lovely daughter Persephone. Accompanying illustrations, which alternate between stark black-and-white and brilliant color spreads, evoke the surreal quality of this myth on the changing of the seasons." Library J

Gates, Doris

A fair wind for Troy; drawings by Charles Mikolaycak. Viking 1976 84p illus lib. bdg. $6.95 (4 and up)   **292**

1 Mythology, Classical
ISBN 0-670-30505-7   LC 76-27738

The author "recounts the events that led up to the Trojan War; the wooing of Helen, the oaths of the suitors, the judgment of Paris, the abduction of Helen, the madness of Odysseus, and the conscripting of Achilles." Horn Bk
"The complicated gods' hierarchy falls easily into place, tension is high, and small parts played by Achilles, Odysseus, and other humans may well motivate additional reading. Mikolaycak's gray-shaded drawings add tremendous power." Booklist
Glossary: p83-84

The golden god: Apollo; illus. by Constantinos CoConis. Viking 1973 110p illus lib. bdg. $7.95 (4 and up)   **292**

1 Apollo
ISBN 0-670-34412-5   LC 72-91397

"Sixteen stories involving Apollo which treat his birth, his victory over the serpent, Python, his fruitless pursuit of Daphne, the loss of his son Phaethon, and his relationship with his twin sister Artemis." Sch Library J
"The illustrations emerge as the most significant accomplishment for they sometimes capture the horror and the strength of the myths, which the text often fails to convey." Horn Bk
Glossary: p109-10

Gates, Doris—*Continued*

Lord of the sky: Zeus; illus. By Robert Handville. Viking 1972 126p illus lib. bdg. $7.95 (4 and up)   **292**

1 Zeus
ISBN 0-670-44051-6   LC 72-80514

A retelling of myths in which Zeus plays a part. Included are stories about Io, Deucalion, Baucis and Philemon, Europa, Cadmus, Theseus, Ariadne, Minos and Dionysus

"Although the myths related to Zeus are many, complicated, and often erotic, Gates has managed to distill readable stories without distorting the spirit of the original too much." Booklist
Glossary: p125-26

Mightiest of mortals: Hercules; illus. by Richard Cuffari. Viking 1975 94p illus lib. bdg. $6.95 (4 and up)   **292**

1 Hercules
ISBN 0-670-47556-4   LC 75-16374

A retelling of the Greek myths in which the demi-god Heracles plays a part, including the tales of the twelve labors imposed upon him by Hera

"The narrative provides an admirable preparation for many classical allusions which children will encounter in subsequent readings. A glossary is thoughtfully provided, and Cuffari's stylized 'Grecian urn' drawings of action and heroism are most appropriate." Sch Library J

Two queens of heaven: Aphrodite [and] Demeter; illus. by Trina Schart Hyman. Viking 1974 94p illus lib. bdg. $7.95 (4 and up)   **292**

1 Aphrodite 2 Demeter
ISBN 0-670-73680-5   LC 73-17423

A retelling of some Greek myths in which the goddesses of love and fertility play a major role. Included are the stories of Adonis, Anchises and Aphrodite, Pygmalion, Atalanta, Cupid and Psyche, Hero and Leander, Pyramus and Thisbe, Demeter and Persephone, and Aphrodite's birth from the sea foam

"Trina Hyman's artistic conception of the deities is classical, and her fine-boned, bared figures, executed in flowing pencil drawings, actively project the emotional pitch of the text." Booklist
Glossary: p93-94

The warrior goddess: Athena; illus. by Don Bolognese. Viking 1972 121p illus lib. bdg. $7.95 (4 and up)   **292**

1 Athena
ISBN 0-670-74996-6   LC 72-80515

A retelling of the story of Athena's birth along with other myths in which the Greek goddess plays a part. Included are stories about Aglauros, Perseus, Medusa, Andromeda, Bellerophone, Jason, Heracles, Medea, and Arachne

"A simplified, highly readable version of Greek myths. . . . Strong, black-and-white pictures accompany the text." Pub W
Glossary: p119-21

Guerber, H. A.

The myths of Greece & Rome. Rev. by Dorothy Margaret Stuart; with forty-nine reproductions from famous pictures and statues. London House & Maxwell 1963 316p illus maps $14.95 (5 and up)   **292**

1 Mythology, Classical
ISBN 0-8277-0035-0

First published 1907 by Harrap
Contents: The beginning: Zeus; Hera; Athene; Apollo; Artemis; Aphrodite; Hermes; Ares; Hephaestus; Poseidon; Pluto; Bacchus (Dionysus); Demeter and Persephone; Hestia; Ceyx and Halcyone; Aeolus; Herakles; Perseus; Theseus; Jason and the Golden Fleece; The Calydonian Hunt; Oedipus; King of Thebes; Bellerophone; The Trojan War; The Adventures of Odysseus; Agamemnon and his family; Virgil's "Aeneid"; The lesser gods of the Romans; Interpretation; Glossary and Index; Map of Greece of the myths; Map of Mediterranean countries in mythical times; Genealogical table

"A standard reference book for identification of names and allusions from classical mythology. Includes a genealogical table, a glossary, and an index." Hodges. Bks for Elm Sch Libraries

Hamilton, Edith

Mythology; illus. by Steele Savage. Little 1942 497p illus $7.95 (6 and up)   **292**

1 Mythology, Classical 2 Mythology, Norse
ISBN 0-316-34114-2   LC 42-12948

Contents: The gods; the creation and the earliest heroes; Stories of love and adventure; Great heroes before the Trojan War; Heroes of the Trojan War; Great families of mythology; Less important myths; Mythology of the Norsemen; Genealogical tables

"In her distinguished re-telling of the stories, the author has kept very close in style to the originals. . . . Each story is prefaced by a brief descriptive and informative introduction in italics." Bookmark

Hawthorne, Nathaniel

A wonder-book, and Tanglewood tales; illus. by Gustaf Tenggren. Houghton 1951 421p illus $9.95 (5 and up)   **292**

1 Mythology, Classical
ISBN 0-395-07079-1

"Greek myths retold as fairy tales for nineteenth-century children, lighter in tone and with moral implications, suitable as an introduction to classical mythology for younger children." Hodges. Bks for Elem Sch Libraries

Hodges, Margaret

Persephone and the springtime; a Greek myth; retold by Margaret Hodges; illus. by Arvis Stewart. Little 1973 32p illus (Myths of the world) lib. bdg. $5.95 (k-3)   **292**

1 Persephone
ISBN 0-316-36786-9   LC 72-7492

This is the retelling of the myth of Persephone, how she was abducted to Hades by Pluto, and how her return to earth for part of the year became our springtime

"Here the focus is not on the anguished goddess Demeter hunting the daughter who has disappeared, taken as a captive bride to Pluto's underworld kingdom, but on Persephone." Chicago. Children's Bk Center

"An excellent retelling, with rich, detailed illustrations." New Bks for Young Readers

Newman, Robert

The twelve labors of Hercules; told by Robert Newman; illus. by Charles Keeping. Crowell 1972 150p illus (Crowell Hero tales) $7.95 (4-6)   **292**

1 Hercules
ISBN 0-690-83920-0   LC 75-132300

Included in this retelling of the twelve labors imposed on the Greek god Hercules are his killing and flaying of a lion whose skin is impenetrable; his slaying of the nine-headed Hydra; and his cleaning of the huge Augean stables in a single day

The tale is told "in readable format with dramatic drawings." NY Pub Library. Children's Bks & Recordings, 1972
Glossary: p146-50. Map on lining-papers

Serraillier, Ian

A fall from the sky; the story of Daedalus; illus. by William Stobbs. Walck, H.Z. 1966 [c1965] 61p illus $4.95 (4-6)   **292**

1 Daedalus 2 Icarus
ISBN 0-8098-2361-6   LC 66-13953

First published 1965 in England
A retelling of the legend of Daedalus, the master craftsman of ancient Athens, whose attempt to fly led to the tragic death of his son Icarus, who came too near the sun

"Without doing violence to the basic outlines of various stories related to Daedalus, the author has established a logical sequence and well-developed plot. Literary style, format, and strong, simple illustrations are in keeping with the subject." Sch Library J

Bibliography included in Acknowledgments: p5

292.03 Classical mythology— Encyclopedias

Kravitz, David
Who's who in Greek and Roman mythology; illus. by Lynne S. Mayo. Potter C.N. [1976 c1975] 246p illus $10, pa $3.95   **292.03**
1 Mythology, Classical—Encyclopedias
ISBN 0-517-52746-4; 0-517-52747-2   LC 76-29730

First published 1975 in England with title: The dictionary of Greek & Roman mythology
"This double-columned work consists of about 3,600 entries, mostly names of mythological persons, with explanations running from one line to half a page. Besides names of persons, there are entries for such topics as 'Seven Wonders of the World,' 'Seven Hills of Rome,' and also entries for beasts . . . which were sacred to, or in some way connected with, one of the divinities. There are also entries . . . such as marriage, god of; justice, goddess of Greek; and crops, divinities of as well as references wherever a topic is associated with several different characters. . . . Synopses of major Greek and Roman legends (e.g., Trojan War, Golden Fleece, Wandering of Aeneas) and entries for classic poets Homer, Virgil, and Horace [are included]. . . . An Appendix contains a calendar of festivals celebrated at Rome. . . . Names which refer to essentially the same divinity, but which differ in the Roman or Greek language, such as Jupiter (Zeus) . . . are entered twice, under each form of the name, with commentary on the Roman or Greek veneration, legends, or tradition. Cross-references are provided between entries because their content varies." Booklist

Tripp, Edward
Crowell's Handbook of classical mythology. Crowell 1970 631p maps $16.95   **292.03**
1 Mythology, Classical—Encyclopedias
ISBN 0-690-22608-X   LC 74-127614

"A Crowell Reference Book"
This alphabetical guide to the myths of Greece and Rome includes the characters, events, and places mentioned in the myths, the constellations named for mythological personages, and brief descriptions of the principal classical works in which the myths are found
"I can without hesitation recommend this title as a worthy addition to reference collections dealing with the imaginative world of the ancient Greek pantheon. It is thoroughly comprehensive, and though admittedly aimed at the general reader, it will nonetheless prove useful to teacher, student, and librarians." Library J
Pronouncing index: p611-31

293 Germanic religion and mythology

Aulaire, Ingri d'
Norse gods and giants [by] Ingri and Edgar Parin d'Aulaire. Doubleday 1967 154p illus $9.95, lib. bdg $10.90 (4-6)   **293**
1 Mythology, Norse
ISBN 0-385-04908-0; 0-385-07235-X   LC 67-19109

Illustrated by the authors, this collection of Norse myths depicts raging giants, horrible monsters, and all-too-human gods. It includes stories about such personages as one-eyed Odin, mischievous Loki, enormous Thor and the beautiful Freya
The illustrations "reveal the d'Aulaires' intimate acquaintance with Nordic landscape and folk art and establish brilliant pictorial atmosphere. . . . All the creatures in the mythological hierarchy are clearly established, and their stories are told in a smooth, colorful prose." Horn Bk
"It is not usual that a book which is essentially a good reference volume can be recommended as a storybook as well. . . . There is a 'Reader's Companion' that is both glossary and index. . . . The d'Aulaires' new volume is a big, handsome book and fit companion to their excellent [Book of Greek myths, listed in class 292]." NY Times Bk Rev

Barth, Edna
Balder and the mistletoe; a story for the winter holidays; retold by Edna Barth; pictures by Richard Cuffari. Seabury [distributed by Houghton 1979 64p illus $7.95 (3-5)   **293**
1 Mythology, Norse 2 Balder
ISBN 0-395-28956-4   LC 78-4523

"A Clarion book"
"The goddess Frigga asks every living and non-living thing in the world to swear they will not harm her son Balder when he says he has dreamt of his own death—everything but the mistletoe. That information is cunningly drawn from her by the wicked Loki, and he uses it to kill Balder. The story ends with Balder in the underworld, doomed to stay until the final battle between the gods and the frost giants who threaten the world; a brief author's note describes the ways in which Balder was remembered in the rites of Norse, Celtic, and Germanic peoples and the symbolic use of mistletoe." Chicago. Children's Bk Center
"The narrative style is clear and lively, and the characterization of Balder has both grace and sharpness; he is presented as 'fairest of all the gods . . . free of any arrogance' and one who 'radiated peace and well-being.' The atmosphere of the story has an almost palpable quality of contrasting darkness and light. The drawings, among the artist's last work, have a notable strength and beauty appropriate to the other worldliness of the ancient tale." Horn Bk

Hodges, Margaret
Baldur and the mistletoe; a myth of the Vikings; retold by Margaret Hodges; illus. by Gerry Hoover. Little [1973 c1974] 30p illus (Myths of the world) $6.95 (4-6)   **293**
1 Mythology, Norse 2 Balder
ISBN 0-316-36787-7   LC 73-608

"When Baldur, best and brightest of the gods, dreams of his death, his mother exacts a promise from all things touching the earth that they will not harm her son. Jealous Loki, the mischief-maker who desires Baldur's death, learns that only the weak young mistletoe has not taken the oath. From this plant Loki fashions a fatal arrow and Baldur's dream comes to pass; his death signals the Twilight of the Gods but also a new world and the birth of hope. The smooth, sober retelling is illustrated with sweeping charcoal drawings that impart a serious mood, even one of horror in some grotesque, skeleton-filled scenes of death and the underworld." Booklist

Hosford, Dorothy G.
Thunder of the gods; illus. by Claire & George Louden. Holt 1952 115p illus lib. bdg. $5.95 (5 and up)   **293**
1 Mythology, Norse
ISBN 0-03-015691-2   LC 52-9038

"A retelling of the Norse myths . . . which recreates the spare beauty and simple dignity, the humor and pathos of these stories as they are told in the Eddas. In this version, the terse, dramatic form of the folk tale is used throughout, yet the heightened language in which they are told preserves the remoteness necessary to mythical stories of the gods." Ontario Library Rev
Line drawings "catch and emphasize the spirit of the legends. A book to suggest for home libraries as well as public and school libraries." Library J
Includes: Note on the Norse myths [and] Pronunciation of proper names

294.3 Buddhism

Edmonds, I. G.
Buddhism. Watts, F. 1978 65p illus lib. bdg. $6.45 (4 and up)   **294.3**
1 Buddhism
ISBN 0-531-01349-9   LC 77-12407

"A First book"
An introduction to Buddhism in which "the religion's basic tenets come through well enough with mystical aspects often clarified by a Buddhist story-lesson. Edmonds also scans major and minor divisions existing currently, and assesses the role of Buddhism today—including where and how it survives social upheaval: in China it co-exists

Edmonds, I. G.—*Continued*
with the government; in Cambodia it is founder-
ing under Khmer Rouge repression. A functional
introductory outline with a glossary, list of important dates, and a few suggestions for further
reading. Black-and-white photographs." Booklist

Rawding, F. W.
The Buddha; published in cooperation with
Cambridge Univ. Press. Lerner Publications
[1979 c1975] 51p illus maps lib. bdg. $4.49
(5 and up)   **294.3**
  1 Buddhism 2 Gautama Buddha
  ISBN 0-8225-1212-2   LC 78-56789
  "A Cambridge Topic Book"
  First published 1975 in paperback by Cambridge
University Press
  Contents: How we know about the Buddha;
Prince Siddhartha Gotama; The ancient civilization
of India; The Buddha; Buddhism becomes organ-
ized; The Buddha's later years; Ahoka; The expansion of Buddhism
  "Early on, Rawding acknowledges that legend
provides a goodly portion of what's known of the
Buddha, and legendary parts alluded to in the
course of this biography appear in italicized print.
Bolstering these information threads is a cultural
exposition of Hindu life before and during the
Buddha's time. Fictionalization becomes unnecessary and Siddhartha's movements better clarified
in the supplied context. With maps, diagrams, and
photographs of religious sculpture and contemporary Indian scenes." Booklist

294.5   Hinduism

Edmonds, I. G.
Hinduism. Watts, F. 1979 64p illus $6.45
(5 and up)   **294.5**
  1 Hinduism
  ISBN 0-531-02943-3   LC 79-10349
  "A First book"
  The author focuses "on theological and cultural
aspects of Hinduism with emphasis on the former.
Deities, sacred writings, and beliefs are explained
in simple, understandable terms. There is some
discussion of the caste system and its origins
and religious basis; mention is made of Mahatma
Gandhi's attempts to have 'untouchability' out-
lawed in the Indian constitution. The author notes
other religions, such as Buddhism and Jainism,
which have their roots in Hinduism, and comments on present social reforms to elevate the
role of women. There is a glossary, index, and
short bibliography." Booklist

296   Judaism

Rossel, Seymour
Judaism. Watts, F. 1976 61p illus. lib.
bdg. $6.45 (4 and up)   **296**
  1 Judaism
  ISBN 0-531-00841-X   LC 75-31561
  "A First book"
  The author "touches briefly on almost all major
facets of Judaism, including Biblical history, religious prayers and practices, Zionism, holidays
and festivals, dietary laws, bar mitzvah, etc. The
current status of rabbinical education for women
is noted. Good black-and-white photographs complement the text, and a short list of suggested
reading and an adequate index are included.
Though by no means a comprehensive guide to
Jewish belief and practice, this does provide broad,
well-organized coverage for middle-grade children
with little or no knowledge of Judaism." Sch Library J

296.4   Traditions, rites, public services

Cone, Molly
The Jewish New Year; illus. by Jerome
Snyder. Crowell 1966 unp illus. (A Crowell
Holiday bk) lib. bdg. $7.89 (1-3)   **296.4**
  1 Rosh ha-Shanah 2 Yom Kippur
  ISBN 0-690-46041-4   LC 66-7314

The author "tells of the origin and significance
of the 10-day observance of the New Year, from
Rosh Hashonah to Yom Kippur, and then notes
the many customs that have grown up in various
countries in connection with these ancient holy
days." NY Times Bk Rev
  "A simple but dignified telling. . . . Striking
illustrations add to a book that can be read and
understood by children of all faiths and backgrounds." Sch Library J

Purim; illus. by Helen Borten. Crowell 1967
unp illus (A Crowell Holiday bk) lib. bdg. $7.89
(1-3)   **296.4**
  1 Purim (Feast of Esther) 2 Esther, Queen of
Persia
  ISBN 0-690-65922-9   LC 67-817
  "Through a simple retelling of the story of
Esther, the author explains the origin and significance of Purim, followed by a description of
the special foods and ceremonies with which the
Jewish day of rest is celebrated." Hodges. Bks
for Elem Sch Libraries

Epstein, Morris
All about Jewish holidays and customs; illus.
by Arnold Lobel. Rev. ed. Ktav 1970 142p illus
pa $4.50 (4-6)   **296.4**
  1 Fasts and feasts—Judaism
  ISBN 0-87068-500-7   LC 71-106522
  First Published 1959
  This description of Jewish holidays reveals the
joys and the sorrows, the traditions and the ceremonies of the Jewish people
  Partial contents: The Jewish year; Everything
starts with a calendar; The synagogue; Bar Mitzvah; The Jewish home; The world of Jewish books;
Bibliography

Greenfeld, Howard
Chanukah; designed by Bea Feitler. Holt 1976
39p illus $5.95 (4 and up)   **296.4**
  1 Hanukkah (Feast of Lights) 2 Maccabees
  ISBN 0-03-015566-5   LC 76-6527
  A "retelling of the episode in Jewish history
that is commemorated by Chanukah, the Festival
of Lights. Greenfeld describes the persecution
ordered by Antiochus in his attempt to eradicate
Judaism and Hellenize his kingdom, the resistance
movement led by Mattathias and his son Judah,
and the three-year struggle that culminated in
victory by Judah's troops." Chicago. Children's
Bk Center
  "Decorated with emblems rather than illustrations . . . this handsome book is really more like
an extended Chanukah greeting card." Sch Library J

Passover; illus. by Elaine Grove; designed
by Bea Feitler. Holt 1978 32p illus lib. bdg. $5.95
(4 and up)   **296.4**
  1 Passover
  ISBN 0-03-039921-1   LC 77-13910
  The author "describes the celebration of a major
Jewish holiday, giving both details of the celebratory meal and the reasons for each traditional
observance. This is prefaced by a retelling of Biblical events that led to the flight of Jews from
Egypt and to the miracle of the passing over, the
parting of the waters of the Red Sea. In keeping
with the dignity of the text, the black and white
illustrations are framed and stiffly decorative in
the style of early woodcuts." Chicago. Children's
Bk Center

Rosh Hashanah and Yom Kippur; illus. by
Elaine Grove. Holt 1979 31p illus lib. bdg. $5.95
(4 and up)   **296.4**
  1 Rosh ha-Shanah 2 Yom Kippur
  ISBN 0-03-044756-9   LC 79-4818
  "Greenfeld captures the intense spiritual significance of the two holiest days in the Jewish
religion, Rosh Hashanah, the New Year's Day and
a day of remembrance, and Yom Kippur, the day
of atonement, on which Jews repent for all sins
and pray for forgiveness. The fundamental beliefs,
the symbols, and the formal religious service are
set forth simply and clearly. The text explains
the meaning of certain rituals, such as the blowing
of the shofar, and includes specific prayers, such
as the Kol Nidre. . . . Woodcut-style illustrations
depict scenes from the Bible and from temple worship." Booklist

Hirsh, Marilyn

The Hanukkah story. Bonim Bks. 1977 unp illus $7.95 (1-3)   **296.4**

1 Hanukkah (Feast of Lights)   2 Maccabees
ISBN 0-88482-756-9   LC 77-22183

"To explain the origin of Hanukkah, the author-artist has derived a simplified narrative from some of the events related in the book of Maccabees. . . . Double-page spreads and full-page illustrations with inserted texts tell of the tyranny of Antichus the Fourth, King of Syria, who wished to destroy the Jewish religion and desecrated the Temple in Jerusalem; but most of the story is concerned with the rebellion of Mattathias and his sons and with the exploits of Judah and Maccabee. The line drawings overlaid with tones of red, yellow, and gray are dramatically animated, depicting the violence and confusion of war and invasion and glorifying the jubilation of the people at the reconsecration of the Temple. Brief mention is made of the legend of the single day's supply of oil which miraculously lasted for eight days." Horn Bk

One little goat; a Passover song; adapted and illus. by Marilyn Hirst. Holiday House 1979 unp illus music lib. bdg. $6.95 (k-2)   **296.4**

1 Passover   2 Jews—Songs and music
ISBN 0-8234-0345-9   LC 78-24354

"Lively red-and-black illustrations depict children in costumes acting out a Passover song about a little goat eaten by a dog, which is beaten by a stick, which is burned by fire, and so on." Children's Bk Rev Serv

"The song itself is rather like 'The House That Jack Built,' with each new verse building on its predecessor, and the pictures are graphic enough to allow for easy copying of action and costumes. . . . The melody for the song is included at the back—a very attractive, haunting melody—and two author's notes explain the meaning of Passover and the song itself." NY Times Bk Rev

Simon, Norma

Hanukkah; illus. by Symeon Shimin. Crowell 1966 unp illus (A Crowell Holiday bk) lib. bdg. $7.89 (1-4)   **296.4**

1 Hanukkah (Feast of Lights)
ISBN 0-690-36953-0   LC 66-7618

The author has told the story of Hanukkah, the Festival of Lights, which commemorates the battle of the Maccabees for religious freedom—its history, customs, and significance

The information is "presented with dignity in a simple text and pleasing black-and-white and colored drawings." Booklist

Passover; illus. by Symeon Shimin. Crowell 1965 unp illus (A Crowell Holiday bk.) lib. bdg. $7.89 (1-3)   **296.4**

1 Passover
ISBN 0-690-61094-7   LC 65-11644

"Simply written and attractively illustrated, this is a good addition to the series of books about holidays. The author describes the origin of the Passover celebration, and explains in detail the procedures of the ritual dinner; there is a brief description, also, of observances in Israel and in Jordan today." Chicago. Children's Bk Center

296.7 Religious experience, life, practice

Greene, Laura

I am an Orthodox Jew; illus. by Lisa C. Wesson. Holt 1979 unp illus $5.95 (2-4)   **296.7**

1 Judaism   2 Jews—Social life and customs
3 Jews—Rites and ceremonies
ISBN 0-03-044661-9   LC 78-14094

"Greene allows her fictional narrator, Aaron Katz, to describe his daily life as an Orthodox Jew. Aaron tells the reader about Hebrew Day School, his special clothing, Sabbath preparations, synagogue services, and his bar mitzvah. The fact that children who are Orthodox Jews can be part of a rich religious tradition and yet share many experiences with non-Jewish friends is expressed both in the text and in the line drawings. . . . Although the book may seem simplistic to those already familiar with Orthodox Judaism, it provides a good introduction to a religious way of life that is unfamiliar to many readers." Sch Library J

297 Islam

Edmonds, I. G.

Islam. Watts, F. 1977 65p illus lib. bdg. $6.45 (5 and up)   **297**

1 Islam
ISBN 0-531-01288-3   LC 77-2664

"A First book"

"A crisp, factual account of the Islamic tradition and religion that seems geared to class assignments. Edmonds briefly recounts events in the life of the prophet Mohammed, the influence that Judeo-Christian traditions had on his philosophy and teachings, and his drive to make converts by means of the sword. The tenets of the Islamic faith, and the religious duties set down in the Koran, are clearly enumerated, and there are sections on the role of Islam in the Middle East today, the place of women in Moslem society, and the various sects that practice the teachings of the prophet differently." Sch Library J

Glossary: p60-62. For further reading: p64

299 Other religions

Kristos, Kyle

Voodoo. Lippincott 1976 112p illus $6.95, pa $2.95 (6 and up)   **299**

1 Voodooism
ISBN 0-397-31706-9; 0-397-31707-7   LC 76-18989

"A balanced, skillfully written introduction to Voodoo belief and its practice (particularly in Haiti). The author carefully dispells popular misconceptions in describing the rituals of this pseudo-religion which is still practiced by the majority of Haiti's population. Although the sensational aspects of the subject are not emphasized, a typical Voodoo ceremony is described which includes the slaughter of sacrificial animals and the drinking of blood. Kristos views Voodoo as fulfilling basic human needs, and its power in the lives of its adherents is recognized though no tacit approval is given to its methods or doctrine. Well-researched, informative coverage." Sch Library J

Bibliography: p108

300 SOCIAL SCIENCES

304.2 Human ecology

Gregor, Arthur S.

Man's mark on the land; the changing environment from the Stone Age to the age of smog, sewage, and tar on your feet; illus. with photographs, maps, and charts. Scribner 1974 120p illus maps lib. bdg. $5.95 (4 and up)   **304.2**

1 Man—Influence on nature   2 Human ecology
ISBN 0-684-13740-2   LC 73-19367

"Maps, charts, and illustrations by Jean Simpson." Verso of title page

In this historical look at man's interaction with his environment, the author discusses the discovery of farming, the coming of the city, and the rise of civilization. He then describes the effects each had on the environment

"His writing is descriptive, and it is well sprinkled with pictures and illustrations to hold the elementary reader's attention. Gregor briefly covers most major cultures of the world. He has undertaken a written history which just skims a few ideas but is educational and of value to the student." Sci Bks

Dictionary for the environment: p112-15. For further reading: p116-17

304.6   Population (Demography)

Asimov, Isaac
Earth: our crowded spaceship. Day 1974 160p
illus $8.95 (5 and up)   304.6
1 Population 2 Conservation of natural resources
ISBN 0-381-99625-5   LC 74-8967
"Asimov discusses how Earth became overpopulated and measures for coping with and/or
putting a stop to population growth (new forms
of energy, major wars, etc.). The psychology of
having babies and the need to educate people about
the necessity of birth control are explained, however, methods are not. Although written in a
casual style, the text is full of carefully indexed
facts, statistics (given in metric measures with a
conversion table appended), and definitions of
terms such as "standard of living" and "gross
national product." Although the author's advocacy
of birth control may run counter to that of some
groups, this timely book is . . . useful." Sch Library J
Bibliography: p155

305.2   Age levels

Ancona, George
Growing older. Dutton 1978 unp illus $7.95
(3-6)   305.2
1 Elderly
ISBN 0-525-31050-9   LC 78-7605
"Ancona has gracefully caught the experience of
aging in these 13 mini-portraits ranging from a
Texas trader to a 95-year-old accountant in New
York City and back again to Nicodemus, Kansas,
where 100-year-old Lulu Mae Craig reminisces
about the early homesteading of ex-slaves. This is
walking history. Native American, Mexican, Anglo,
and European immigrant faces all show up here,
often side by side with pictures of them as babies
or young people. Summarizing their own lives and
aging, they create an eloquent text: 'I go over
the trails of the past ofen, very often.' The interviews are intelligently edited to a few pages each,
which, together with warm, candid black-and-
white photographs, show active friendly old people,
sometimes coping with painful physical problems,
to be a precious resource. Children will want to
garner their own grandparents' story, perhaps to
contribute to a class book along similar lines."
Booklist

Berger, Terry
Special friends; photographs by David Hechtlinger. Messner 1979 63p illus lib. bdg. $6.97
(1-3)   305.2
1 Old age 2 Friendship
ISBN 0-671-33091-8   LC 79-13059
"Photographs and a simple text describe a 10-
year-old girl's relationship with an elderly woman
who lives in the neighborhood. Told from the girl's
point of view, the story offers a glimpse into the
feelings and problems of the elderly: the small
pleasures, the loneliness, and the physical inability
to do certain things. The give-and-take between
the two is warm and cheerful but not cloying.
. . . The firendship is portrayed in a natural,
nondidactic way, and there's a healthy amiable tone
to the text." Booklist

Burns, Marilyn
I am not a short adult! Getting good at
being a kid; illus. by Martha Weston. Little
1977 125p illus $7.95, pa $4.95 (3-6)   305.2
1 Children 2 Human behavior
ISBN 0-316-11746-3; 0-316-17745-5   LC 77-24486
"A Brown paper school book"
"A scatter gun approach, but nonetheless one
of the few available, to discussing the state of
childhood with children. There are some opening
nudges to help find out 'what kind of kid you are'
with lists and games; a brief social history of
children's treatment by adults; an examination of
children's legal status; a look at the influences and
institutions that most affect children (the family,
school, television); facts about work, finances and
protection from child abuse; and suggestions about
communication with adults." Booklist

"Designed as a scrapbook with humorous spot
drawings, this potpourri of information is sure
to boost the ego of kids besieged by the expectations of their elders and, like Louis XIII, encouraged to relinquish hobby horses too soon." Sch
Library J

Silverstein, Alvin
Aging, by Alvin, Virginia, and Glenn Silverstein. Watts F. 1979 86p illus lib. bdg. $6.90
(5 and up)   305.2
1 Aging
ISBN 0-531-02863-1   LC 79-11890
"This is a much-needed account of the aging
process, for young readers. Here, the meaning of
growing old is explored in many ways—psychological, physical, and social. Young people are introduced to the feelings of older people in candid
and realistic situations." Children's Bk Rev Serv
Further reading: p81-82

305.4   Women

Carlson, Dale
Girls are equal too; the women's movement
for teenagers; decorations by Carol Nicklaus.
Atheneum Pubs. 1973 146p illus $6.95, pa $1.95
(6 and up)   305.4
1 Women—Social conditions 2 Women—Civil
rights 3 Women's Liberation Movement
ISBN 0-689-30106-5; 0-689-70433-X   LC 73-76333
This is a "discussion of what causes sexist attitudes and how females are discriminated against
in their personal, academic, professional, and social
roles." Chicago. Children's Bk Center
"The section on the history of the movement is
superb and comprehensive with excellent relevant
statistics. The last section discusses topical information for the teenage girl (boys, marriage, work,
etc.) with exceptional insight. And throughout
[the author's message] (that what women are
fighting for is the freedom of personal choice)
comes through loud and clear." Children's Bk
Rev Serv
"Carol Nicklaus' amusing pen-and-ink drawings
spark this provocative treatment of the women's
movement." Sch Library J
Suggested reading: p144-46

De Pauw, Linda Grant
Founding mothers; women in America in the
Revolutionary era; wood engravings by Michael
McCurdy. Houghton 1975 228p illus $6.95 (6
and up)   305.4
1 Women—U.S—History 2 Women—Social conditions 3 U.S.—Social life and customs—Colonial
period, 1600-1775
ISBN 0-395-21408-4   LC 75-17031
"Viewing roles of women who lived during the
Revolutionary era from a contemporary feminist
perspective . . . [the author] examines Black,
white and Native American women as well as
women of all social classes, including slaves. She
uncovers unusual and previously ignored historical
facts and dispels commonly held myths (e.g. Betsy
Ross' claim to fame) while detailing the untold
tales of women soldiers, spies, organizers, couriers
and political activists." Sch Library J
"Quotes from primary sources abound and are
the spice of this briskly methodical report; the
author's care in providing relative perspective
often adds insight and demolishes stereotypes;
certainly this is a notable contribution toward dust-
ing off women's history for young people." Booklist
Suggestions for further reading: p220-22

Ingraham, Claire R.
An album of women in American history
[by] Claire R. & Leonard W. Ingraham. Watts,
F. 1972 88p illus $4.90 (5 and up)   305.4
1 Women—U.S.—History 2 Women—Social con-
ditions 3 Women—Civil rights
ISBN 0-531-01515-7   LC 72-6138
"This brief survey discusses women in the United
States from Indian women at the time of coloni-
zation to the current drive for equal rights."
Notable Children's Trade Bks (Social Studies)

Ingraham, Claire R.—*Continued*

"Many biographies are noted, but individuals are always viewed as part of women's larger fight for equality. The numerous drawings and photos effectively break up the text and make it a good reference source . . . however the reading list is aimed at older grades." Sch Library J
Suggestions for further reading: p81-82

Levenson, Dorothy
Women of the West. Watts, F. 1973 88p illus lib. bdg. $3.90 (4 and up)　　305.4

1 Women—The West (U.S.)　2 Frontier and pioneer life—The West (U.S.)　3 The West (U.S.)—History
ISBN 0-531-00793-6　　LC 72-10441

"A First book"
"This covers the role of 19th-Century women—primarily blacks and native American Indians—in the Western U.S. No individual woman is discussed in depth, and only a few receive one or two paragraphs. The lives of these pioneer women are treated realistically, especially the hardships of the prairie, and the U.S. Army's harsh treatment of the Indians is also described. The text is clear and unbiased, and the focus on minority women will be particularly useful." Sch Library J
Bibliography: p86

Warren, Ruth
A pictorial history of women in America. Crown 1975 228p illus $7.95 (6 and up)　305.4

1 Women—U.S.—History　2 Women—Social conditions
ISBN 0-517-51845-7　　LC 74-83212

"Although the book is profusely illustrated with print reproductions and photographs, it is not a picture history but an extensive survey of the role of women and the contributions of individual women to all aspects of life in the United States, from colonial times to today. Despite the recurrent note of fulsome praise, the book provides varied and interesting information about well-known and lesser-known women in all fields, with emphasis on those who participated in the battle for the vote. A lengthy bibliography and a full index add to reference use." Chicago. Children's Bk Center

305.8　Racial, ethnic and national groups

Avakian, Arra S.
The Armenians in America. Lerner Publications 1977 87p illus maps (The In America ser) blg. $5.95 (5 and up)　　305.8

1 Armenian Americans
ISBN 0-8225-0228-3　　LC 77-73739

Illustrated with black and white photographs, this book begins "with a historical profile charting the forces that prompted immigration or general contact with America; middle portions explore the immigrants' integration into the labor force and the degree to which they've assimilated over the years. Concluding sections call attention to prominent Americans of . . . [Armenian] background." Booklist

Bagai, Leona B.
The East Indians and the Pakistanis in America. Lerner Publications 1967 63p illus map (The In America ser) lib. bdg. $5.95 (5 and up)　　305.8

1 East Indian Americans　2 Pakistani Americans
ISBN 0-8225-0210-0　　LC 67-15680

"A history of Americans from India, with emphasis on their contributions in science, education, the arts, and philosophy. Hindus, Sikhs, and Muslims are covered in this description of East Indians and Pakistanis and their experience in the United States. Indexed." Buttlar. Building Ethnic Collections

Cates, Edwin H.
The English in America. Lerner Publications 1966 70p illus (The In America ser) lib. bdg. $5.95 (5 and up)　　305.8

1 British Americans
ISBN 0-8225-0205-4　　LC 66-5730

"This history of the English in America emphasizes the life style and customs established in the Colonies and the contributions and influence of outstanding Americans of English background." Buttlar. Building Ethnic Collections

Clifton, Lucille
The Black B C's. illus. by Don Miller. Dutton 1970 45p illus $5.95 (k-2)　　305.8

1 Blacks　2 Alphabet
ISBN 0-525-26596-1　　LC 70-121589

"Brief verses for each letter of the alphabet, appropriately illustrated, lead into short commentaries about black Americans and their contributions to our national life. Other minorities are included in the text and illustrations, but black personalities and accomplishments are stressed. Excellent for Black Studies at elementary levels." Keating. Building Bridges of Understanding Between Cultures

Engle, Eloise
The Finns in America. Lerner Publications 1977 110p illus map (The In America ser) lib. bdg. $5.95 (5 and up)　　305.8

1 Finnish Americans
ISBN 0-8225-0229-1　　LC 77-73740

This is a survey of the Finns' immigration to America including their reasons for leaving their homeland, problems of adjustment in the United States, and their contributions to American life. Illustrated with black and white photographs

Eubank, Nancy
The Russians in America. Lerner Publications 1973 94p illus (The In America ser) lib. bdg. $5.95 (5 and up)　　305.8

1 Russian Americans
ISBN 0-8225-0226-7　　LC 72-3589

This is "a history of Russian immigration to the United States, with particular attention to early settlements in Alaska. Reasons for leaving the Russian homeland, the living conditions existent among the early settlers, and unique aspects of their Russian culture and customs are covered. The various waves of Russian immigration are explained and the Russian contributions to America are described. Many individual biographical sketches of those well-known in the arts, sciences, government, etc., are included." Buttlar. Building Ethnic Collections

Gracza, Rezsoe
The Hungarians in America, by Rezsoe and Margaret Gracza; photo selection and captions by Miriam Butwin. Lerner Publications 1969 76p illus maps (The In America ser) lib. bdg. $5.95 (5 and up)　　305.8

1 Hungarian Americans
ISBN 0-8225-0216-X　　LC 68-31503

"A chronology of the history of the Hungarians in America is presented from the days of the early explorations of Leif Ericson's crew, which is said to have included one Hungarian. The various waves of immigration are described and famous Hungarians throughout the period are discussed. Individuals of outstanding achievement and those who have made contributions to American society are indicated. Many photographs document the work." Buttlar. Building Ethnic Collections

Greenfeld, Howard
Gypsies. Crown 1977 109p illus $6.95 (5 and up)　　305.8

1 Gypsies
ISBN 0-517-52842-8　　LC 77-23746

"The first part is a discussion of the many myths connected to the rootless tribes, legends they themselves have invented or encouraged as a protection of their privacy. The author also tells us that it was not until the 19th century that some neat detective work proved that the nomads went

Greenfeld, Howard—*Continued*

to Europe from India, several hundred years earlier. Their way of surviving as deliberate outsiders is explored in this ... account." Pub W

"Well-designed with black-and-white photos which, however, add little to the informative narrative, this is a clearly written and dispassionate introduction to a fascinating ethnic group." Sch Library J

Bibliography: p105-06

Griffin, John Howard

A time to be human. Macmillan Pub. Co. 1977 102p illus $6.95 (5 and up)   **305.8**

1 Blacks—Civil rights   2 U.S.—Race relations
ISBN 0-02-737200-4   LC 76-47468

"In 1959 Griffin had his skin medically treated so that, for a while, he appeared black. He then traveled through the South and wrote about his travels in the book 'Black Like Me.' Now, almost 20 years later, he has incorporated his reflections on that experience and many others in a discussion of the causes and effects of prejudice as he feels it exists at present." NY Times Bk Rev

"Illustrated with photographs. . . . Set in large type and easy to read, 'A Time to Be Human' is easily accessible to young readers. It presents a wise, mature philosophy formulated over the years by a man who believes that it is for the good of all that the cycle of prejudice must be stopped." Horn Bk

Grossman, Ronald P.

The Italians in America. Lerner Publications 1966 62p illus (The In America ser) lib. bdg. $5.95 (5 and up)   **305.8**

1 Italian Americans
ISBN 0-8225-0202-X   LC 66-4212

"The history of the Italian-Americans is told, beginning with fifteenth-century explorers and sixteenth-century colonists. Part II details the heavy migration from 1831 through 1950. Part III gives biographical data about prominent immigrants and cites the prejudice and discrimination endured by this nationality group. The last part informs readers about Italian-Americans achievements and contributions to our society. The breezy style of the text holds reader interest and includes rich anecdotal material." Keating. Building Bridges of Understanding Between Cultures

Hillbrand, Percie V.

The Norwegians in America. Lerner Publications 1967 79p illus maps (The In America ser) lib. bdg. $5.95 (5 and up)   **305.8**

1 Norwegian Americans
ISBN 0-8225-0212-7   LC 62-15683

"Norwegian history in America is covered [in this book] with emphasis on the earliest immigrants and their settlements including the Viking sailors. Some Norwegians are noted for their outstanding achievements or talents in various fields; contributions of the group as a whole are also indicated." Buttlar. Building Ethnic Collections

The Swedes in America. Lerner Publications 1966 79p illus (The In America ser) lib. bdg. $5.95 (5 and up)   **305.8**

1 Swedish Americans
ISBN 0-8225-0201-1   LC 66-4205

The author "presents a background of Swedish history and the reasons why the Swedes left their homeland. The years of immigration and life in the New World are then described. The last section of the book, the major part, describes Swedish contributions to American life and culture. Outstanding Swedish Americans are indicated." Buttlar. Building Ethnic Collections

Ifkovic, Edward

The Yugoslavs in America. Lerner Publications 1977 102p illus maps (The In America ser) lib. bdg. $5.95 (5 and up)   **305.8**

1 Yugoslav Americans
ISBN 0-8225-0231-3   LC 77-73742

The author examines Yugoslav immigration to the United States and discusses the contributions made by the Yugoslavs to America's culture. Illustrated with photographs

Jackson, Jesse

Black in America; a fight for freedom, by Jesse Jackson & Elaine Landau. Messner 1973 112p illus $5.29 (6 and up)   **305.8**

1 Blacks—History   2 Slavery in the U.S.
3 Blacks—Civil rights
ISBN 0-671-32362-8   LC 73-5397

"A short, readable history of the struggle of blacks in the U.S. from colonial times to today. The book should serve as an excellent introduction to all youny readers who have been deprived of this basic information." Adventuring with Bks

Johnson, James E.

The Irish in America. 1976 rev. ed. Lerner Publications 1976 80p illus (The In America ser) lib. bdg. $5.95 (5 and up)   **305.8**

1 Irish Americans
ISBN 0-8225-0203-8   LC 76 370487

First published 1966

This study of the Irish in the United States examines the conditions in 19th century Ireland which led to the Irish migration, describes the arduous journey, the discrimination faced by the new arrivals, and the Irish participation in the Civil War. Famous Americans of Irish ancestry are portrayed and Irish participation in politics is dealt with

The Scots & Scotch-Irish in America. Lerner Publications 1966 86p illus (The In America ser) lib. bdg. $5.95 (5 and up)   **305.8**

1 Scottish Americans   2 Scotch-Irish Americans
ISBN 0-8225-0206-2   LC 66-5729

"The history and contributions of the Scotch and the Scotch-Irish are covered [in this book] with an explanation of the term Scotch-Irish and the Scotch people who immigrated to America via Ulster, Ireland. Prominent personalities and their specific achievements are indicated, including the soldiers in the American Revolution of Scottish descent." Buttlar. Building Ethnic Collections

Jones, Claire

The Chinese in America. Lerner Publications 1972 95p illus (The In America ser) lib. bdg. $5.95 (5 and up)   **305.8**

1 Chinese Americans
ISBN 0-8225-0223-2   LC 72-3585

The author discusses the reasons behind the immigration of the Chinese to the United States, describing also the problems they have met here and the contributions they have made to American life

Jones, Jayne Clark

The Greeks in America. Lerner Publications 1969 78p illus maps (The In America ser) lib. bdg. $5.95 (5 and up)   **305.8**

1 Greek Americans
ISBN 0-8225-0215-1   LC 68-31504

This book traces the history of Greek emigration from classical times to the present day, emphasizing the problems of Greek immigrants in the United States and their contributions to America's history and culture

Kunz, Virginia Brainard

The French in America. Lerner Publications 1966 94p illus (The In America ser) lib. bdg. $5.95 (5 and up)   **305.8**

1 French Americans
ISBN 0-8225-0204-6   LC 66-10146

"Teachers should find this especially helpful in developing an appreciation of the French role in the early exploration and settlement of America. The text begins with Cartier and covers the migration of French Huguenots, the Revolutionary Wars of France and the United States, and the settlement of New Orleans and St. Louis. Biographical data about Anthony Benezet, a prominent abolitionist, caught my special attention." Keating. Building Bridges of Understanding Between Cultures

Kunz, Virginia B.—*Continued*

The Germans in America. Lerner Publications 1966 86p illus (The In America ser) lib. bdg. $5.95 (5 and up)   305.8

  1 German Americans
ISBN 0-8225-0208-9   LC 66-10147

"This history of the Germans in America includes a brief account of their life in Germany and describes their reasons for immigration to the United States, the experiences and adjustments they had to make, the contributions they made to the development of America, and unique aspects of the German cultural heritage. Some of the most outstanding German Americans and their achievements are indicated." Buttlar. Building Ethnic Collections

"Part I, The Germans in Colonial America, includes material about the Amish and other religious sects included among those classified as Pennsylvania Dutch." Keating. Building Bridges of Understanding Between Cultures

Kuropas, Myron B.

The Ukrainians in America. Lerner Publications 1972 86p illus (The In America ser) lib. bdg. $5.95 (5 and up)   305.8

  1 Ukrainian Americans
ISBN 0-8225-0221-6   LC 72-3588

This book "presents four major areas of emphasis: 1) background history of the Ukraine; 2) Ukrainian immigration to the United States; 3) the Ukrainian-American community and its religion, education, organizations, and experience; and 4) contributions by Ukrainians in various fields, arts and professions." Buttlar. Building Ethnic Collections

Kurtis, Arlene Harris

The Jews helped build America; illus. with photographs. [Rev. ed] Messner 1974 95p illus lib. bdg. $4.64 (4 and up)   305.8

  1 Jews in the U.S.
ISBN 0-671-32707-0   LC 74-19114

First published 1970

"An account of the Jewish experience in America from the early days of the German and East European immigration to the present. Includes information about Jewish customs, holidays, and leaders. A helpful reference for both the Jewish and non-Jewish child." Wolfe. About 100 Books

Larsen, Ronald J.

The Puerto Ricans in America. Lerner Publications 1973 87p illus (The In America ser) lib. bdg. $5.95 (5 and up)   305.8

  1 Puerto Ricans in the U.S.
ISBN 0-8225-0225-9   LC 72-3590

This book "describes Puerto Rican immigration to the mainland and life in the Puerto Rican communities there. Emphasis is on the Puerto Rican cultural heritage and its influence on American society." Buttlar. Building Ethnic Collections

Leathers, Noel L.

The Japanese in America. Lerner Publications 1967 70p illus (The In America ser) lib. bdg. $5.95 (5 and up)   305.8

  1 Japanese Americans
ISBN 0-8225-0211-9   LC 67-15684

"Every aspect of the movement of Japanese to the West is covered in this excellent history, beginning with Perry's contact with Japan during the nineteenth century. Parts III and IV merit special attention since prejudice and discrimination and the shameful treatment of Japanese-Americans during World War II are covered in detail. Heroic military service of these people is cited in Part V. The influence of Japanese in Hawaiian culture is outlined in the last section." Keating. Building Bridges of Understanding Between Cultures

Meltzer, Milton

(ed.) In their own words; a history of the American Negro. Crowell 1964-1967 3v illus each $8.95, pa v 1 $2.95, v2 & 3 $1.65   305.8

  1 Blacks—History

Contents: v1 1619-1865 (ISBN 0-690-44691-8; 0-8152-0348-9); v2 1865-1916 (ISBN 0-690-44692-6; 0-8152-0349-7); v3 1916-1966 (ISBN 0-690-44693-4; 0-8152-0350-0)

A "history of the American Negro from 1619 to [1966] is told in his own words through selections from letters, diaries, journals, speeches, and other documents. Helpful background information and commentary introduce each of the pieces, some of which have been edited for easier reading, and the source is given at the end of each document. A calendar of Negro history . . . and an annotated reading list are appended [in each of the three volumes]." Booklist

"The collection is occasionally distinguished by a simple eloquence and despite the underlying sadness, is notably lacking in bitterness. . . . [Many will find] inspiration to work for solutions to current problems]." Horn Bk

Remember the days; a short history of the Jewish Americans; illus. by Harvey Dinnersten Doubleday 1974 114p illus pa $4.95 (6 and up)   305.8

  1 Jews in the U.S.
ISBN 0-385-05946-9   LC 74-5532

"Zenith books"

"An introduction to Jewish settlement in America, beginning in 1654 with the arrival of 23 Dutch Jewish refugees from Brazil and continuing through several waves of immigration from Central and Eastern Europe. The author relates the immigrants' new life to situations in the countries they left and ties their absorption into the U.S. to contemporaneous events in American history, especially the fate of other minority groups. Factual and to the point." Booklist

Taking root; Jewish immigrants in America. Farrar, Straus 1976 262p illus map $7.95 (6 and up)   305.8

  1 Jews in the U.S.   2 Jews—Social conditions
ISBN 0-374-37369-8   LC 76-18169

Companion volume to: World of our fathers, entered below

"America appeared to be the promised land, the solution to all problems [for starving Eastern European Jews]. But the enormous numbers of immigrants were to find new trials as well as new opportunities. After overcoming legal difficulties in leaving their homelands, enduring the filthy, uncomfortable voyage, and receiving an unencouraging reception at Ellis Island, the new settlers had to find housing and employment in a completely unfamiliar environment. From many sources, including the experiences of his own family, the author has assembled a detailed picture of the daily life of the newcomers, containing descriptions of the horrors of child labor, sweatshops, and tenement life, and also an account of the immigrants' remarkable assimilation into American society with the help of settlement houses, libraries, and special foundations. . . . The author discusses the contributions of immigrants to literature, drama, and journalism, and stresses the role of garment workers in the formation and acceptance of trade unions." Horn Bk

An "historical narrative, well researched and written, which integrates primary and secondary sources. It is a safe, familiar text about making it or not in the promised land of America. The Jacob Riis photographs are the same ones always used to document tenement life in New York City at the turn of the century." Children's Bk Rev Serv

Bibliography: p251-56

World of our fathers; the Jews of Eastern Europe. Farrar, Straus 1974 274p illus maps $7.95 (6 and up)   305.8

  1 Jews in Eastern Europe
ISBN 0-374-38530-0   LC 74-14755

"In part a history of the Jews during the Christian era, the account is chiefly concerned with the life and fate of Eastern European Jews before and after the partition of Poland and especially under the restrictive and repressive rule of the Russian Czarist government. . . . The author conveys a sense of daily life as well as of the fundamental cultural conflicts among the Eastern European Jews during the 18th, 19th, and [early] 20th centuries. Conventional Orthodoxy and Hasidism; the Enlightenment, socialism, and Zionism; the creation of two bodies of literature (one in Hebrew and one in Yiddish)—all are explored and clarified. Many quotations from firsthand accounts give existential reality to the historical and cultural topics of the book. Glossary of Yiddish words, an extensive bibliography, and an index." Horn Bk

"The author's research is thorough and his style is compelling." Pub W

Patterson, Wayne

The Koreans in America [by] Wayne Patterson [and] Hyung-chan Kim. Lerner Publications 1977 62p illus map (The In America ser) lib. bdg. $5.95 (5 and up)   **305.8**

1 Korean Americans
ISBN 0-8225-0230-5   LC 77-73741

The authors discuss the history of the Koreans' immigration to the United States, describing the problems they have met and the contributions they have made to American life. Illustrated with photographs   •

Pinchot, Jane

The Mexicans in America. Lerner Publications 1973 99p illus (The In America ser) lib. bdg. $5.95 (5 and up)   **305.8**

1 Mexican Americans
ISBN 0-8225-0222-4   LC 72-3587

This book starts with the life of the Mexicans living in the American Southwest before statehood, then continues on to the United States acquisition of their land and their contributions to American life

Roucek, Joseph S.

The Czechs and Slovaks in America. Lerner Publications 1967 70p illus maps (The In America ser) lib. bdg. $5.95 (5 and up)   **305.8**

1 Czech Americans 2 Slovak Americans
ISBN 0-8225-0209-7   LC 67-15685

"This history of the movement of these people to our country and their contribution to American culture is presented with a concise text and black-and-white photographs. Information about early Moravian colonies was of particular interest to me." Keating. Building Bridges of Understanding Between Our Cultures

Sung, Betty Lee

The Chinese in America. Macmillan Pub. Co. 1972 120p illus map $6.95 (5 and up)   **305.8**

1 Chinese Americans
ISBN 0-02-788670-0   LC 78-188774

"A simple history of Chinese people in the United States, which begins with the arrival of the first Chinese to work in the California gold mines. It briefly covers their problems, reveals their other occupations, and discusses their life and customs today. Hard work, desire for education, and willingness to take jobs unwanted by others are cited as the keys to their gradual acceptance by American society. Most other books on the subject are either stories of one person's experiences or of a single phase of Chinese life; however, this account provides an overall view of Chinese-Americans as well as their history." Sch Library J
A list of books for further reading is appended

Swift, Hildegarde Hoyt

North star shining; a pictorial history of the American Negro; illus. by Lynd Ward. Morrow 1947 44p illus $6.95 (5 and up)   **305.8**

1 Blacks—History
ISBN 0-688-21904-7   LC 47-30086

Brief pictorial history of Blacks in the United States from early slave days to the 1940's, written in free verse, and picking out a succession of great moments to carry the theme. The illustrations are lithographs
The many characters make this useful for verse choir, individual dramatic readers, or assembly programs." We Build Together

TenZythoff, Gerrit J.

The Dutch in America. Lerner Publications 1969 98p illus maps (The In America ser) lib. bdg. $5.95 (5 and up)   **305.8**

1 Dutch Americans
ISBN 0-8225-0220-8   LC 68-31505

"A history of the Dutch in America beginning with the earliest explorers, then immigrants and early settlements. The author describes the physical and social atmosphere of New Netherland and indicates political, religious, and cultural contributions of the Dutch Americans. Some individuals who have made outstanding achievements are named, and places important in the history of the Dutch in America are discussed." Buttlar. Building Ethnic Collections

Wolf, Bernard

In this proud land: the story of a Mexican American family. Lippincott 1978 95p illus $8.95 (4 and up)   **305.8**

1 Mexican Americans 2 Migrant labor
ISBN 0-397-31815-4   LC 78-9680

"A sympathetic, documentary rendering of the life of a family of Mexican-American migrant workers, David and Maria Hernandez and their seven children, aged thirteen to twenty-four. Although Mr. Hernandez has part-time work as a carpenter's assistant and the older children contribute some of their earnings from various jobs, it is necessary to supplement the family income by migrant farm work. The family leaves its home in Texas and drives to Minnesota to work on a sugar beet farm. . . . But in spite of the financial situation and the fact that the parents do not speak English, they wholeheartedly support higher education for their children." Horn Bk
The author's "photographs have an eloquence and immediacy that the long, diffuse, unfocused text lacks; and, while the strength and cohesiveness of the Hernandez family unit is evident, the glowingly described family members are barely individualized. Still, Wolf is to be commended for departing from the stereotypes of Chicanos as victims or activists. . . . For its "all-American' message of minorities making it in today's society through the old-fashioned virtues of hard work and higher education, the book belongs in any library on inspirational grounds alone." Sch Library J

Wytrwal, Joseph A.

The Poles in America. Lerner Publications 1969 84p illus maps (The In America ser) lib. bdg. $5.95 (5 and up)   **305.8**

1 Polish Americans
ISBN 0-8225-0218-6   LC 68-31506

In this book there is "a brief survey of the land and history of Poland as well as a more thorough discussion of the Poles in America, their individual contributions, and their reasons for coming to a new homeland." Buttlar. Building Ethnic Collections

306   Culture and institutions. Anthropology

Marcus, Rebecca B.

Survivors of the Stone Age; nine tribes today; illus. with photographs. Hastings House 1975 124p illus lib. bdg. $6.95 (5 and up)   **306**

1 Society, Nonliterate folk
ISBN 0-8038-6726-3   LC 75-6843

"The Ik, Bushman, and Pygmy of Africa; the Jivaro and Kranhacrore of South America; the Arunta of Australia; and the Tasaday, Onge, and Papuan of the greater Southeast Asia area are presented as nine tribes still maintaining a Stone Age existence. Fascinating insights into their cultures, problems and future are provided. While these peoples are not truly living in the Stone Age, they do maintain a very basic and relatively primitive way of life. Characteristic of all nine groups is a reliance upon a nonmetal-based technology; they do not produce metal objects, but rely upon outsiders to provide them. In addition, these nine groups share something more important and, ultimately, more significant: they are experiencing the negative impact of contact with the outside world." AAAS Sci Bks & Films
"The book is free of unnecessary anthropological terms. . . . Black-and-white photographs and a good bibliography contribute to a highly readable book." Horn Bk

306.8   Marriage and family

Berger, Terry

How does it feel when your parents get divorced? Photographs by Miriam Shapiro. Messner 1977 62p illus lib. bdg. $6.64 (3-6)   **306.8**

1 Divorce
ISBN 0-671-32883-2   LC 77-332

Berger, Terry—*Continued*

"A preadolescent girl recalls her parents' divorce, exploring her reactions past and present and bringing to the surface the wide range of feeling most children experience in similar circumstances. Although no real effort is made to show the means for coping with guilt, loneliness, and anger, these emotions are all accurately expressed and apparently dealt with by the narrator. Also, incidents do much to show the girl's developing awareness of the continuity of her parents' love for her." Booklist

"Opposite each page of brief text is a black-and-white photograph that underlines the child narrator's memories and reactions. An honest job, and the child-to-child approach is useful for initiating discussions of the subject." Sch Library J

Gardner, Richard

The boys and girls book about divorce; with an introduction for parents; foreword by Louise Bates Ames; illus. by Alfred Lowenheim. Aronson, J. 1970 159p illus $12.50 (4 and up)
306.8

1 Divorce
ISBN 0-87668-032-5   LC 72-110254
First published by Science House

"Although marred by excessive repetition, this book is frank and honest in treatment and fills the need of providing children with valid information and guidance for dealing with divorce situations. . . . Gardner's clear, candid discussion of common childhood fears and worries attendant on divorce is designed to help the child understand his disquieting thoughts and feelings and to face his problems realistically. . . . Illustrated with amusing supplemental drawings." Booklist

LeShan, Eda

What's going to happen to me? When parents separate or divorce; illus. by Richard Cuffari. Four Winds 1978 134p illus $6.95 (4-6)
306.8

1 Divorce
ISBN 0-590-07535-7   LC 78-4340
The author provides advice for children whose parents are or will be divorced. Her "message is that feelings of fear, anger, and loss are natural and should not be repressed; she advises seeking help and being patient in waiting for the new pattern to be established. The text is divided into such sections as 'Before It Happens,' 'When It Happens,' 'Life Goes On,' and so on; it includes discussions of tension between parent and child, adjusting to the fact that divorced parents date and many remarry, accepting stepparents, understanding legal stipulations." Chicago. Children's Bk Center

Naylor, Phyllis Reynolds

Getting along in your family; drawings by Rick Cooley. Abingdon 1976 112p illus lib. bdg. $5.50 (4 and up)
306.8

1 Family life
ISBN 0-687-14120-6   LC 75-44295
"A readable description of some typical family tensions emphasizes acceptance of the family as a diverse group of individuals bound together by ties of love, experience, and practical considerations that make it important for everybody to show as much tolerant understanding as possible. The predominant slant here is toward children adjusting —the reader should try going that extra mile— and the author assumes reasonable, caring parents and strong, articulate children. There are no therapeutic solutions outside the theme that love goes a long way. . . . Altogether, this offers commonsense perspective on the minor irritations of basically healthy relationships." Booklist

Richards, Arlene

How to get it together when your parents are coming apart [by] Arlene Richards and Irene Willis. McKay 1976 170p $7.95 (5 and up)
306.8

1 Divorce
ISBN 0-679-20322-2   LC 76-12746
"A practical, sensible handbook for young people whose parents are having marital problems. The down-to-earth advice can also be used by many other people (such as parents, teachers, counselors and the clergy) who are involved in helping the young with the effects of parents' troubles. The authors cover troubles before, during, and after divorce, illustrating their points with interesting personal vignettes featuring both boys and girls. Along with the explanations, the authors emphasize that the marital problems are their parents', not the young people's. The last section has suggestions about where to turn for help." Children's Bk Rev Serv

Simon, Norma

All kinds of families; pictures by Joe Lasker. Whitman, A. 1976 unp illus $6.50 (k-3)
306.8

1 Family
ISBN 0-8075-0282-0   LC 75-42283
"The diversity of family structures in our multiethnic society is warmly and positively conveyed in this picture book, which stresses the supportive nature of the family, whether together or apart. That families are for 'caring . . . loving . . . sharing' in good as well as sad times is iterated joyously in flowing text and soft, expressive illustrations—alternating color with black-and-white spreads—of a great variey of family units and experiences. Primary teachers will find this Concept Book an excellent discussion starter for social studies units; second- and third- grade children will find it appealing and easy to read. Parents of preschoolers will find it a happy read-aloud experience which invites listener participation." Booklist

Sobol, Harriet Langsam

My other-mother, my other-father; photographs by Patricia Agre. Macmillan Pub. Co. 1979 34p illus $6.95 (3-5)
306.8

1 Stepchildren
ISBN 0-02-785960-6   LC 78-24165
"Andrea is the child of divorced parents, each of whom has remarried. As a child with two parents, two stepparents, four sets of grandparents, a brother, a stepsister, and a stepbrother, her family relationships are quite complicated. Despite minimal conflict between her natural parents, Andrea and her brother often find themselves torn between loyalties. In a simple, straightforward manner this book attempts to explore the feelings, tensions, and problems created in the lives of children whose family life has been disrupted in this manner." Sch Library J

Stein, Sara Bonnett

On divorce; an open family book for parents and children together; Thomas R. Holman, consultant; photographs by Erika Stone. Walker & Co. 1979 47p illus $6.95 (k-3)
306.8

1 Divorce
ISBN 0-8027-6344-8   LC 78-19687
Two separate texts appear on each page. One, in large type, is written on a child's level. The other, intended for adults, presents psychological explanations of the family's behavior

"The scope of 'On Divorce,' makes it a perceptive book to share with children whose own families are intact. The parents of Becky's friends were recently divorced. This is enough to set off her fears. She's afraid that her mother's irritation at her father for constantly working late will lead to their divorce. Only after a blow-up between her parents at the breakfast table does she ask the terrifying question 'Are you getting a divorce?' They answer, 'No,' and respond to her and each other with sensitivity." Sch Library J

White, Ann S.

Divorce. Watts, F. 1979 55p illus $6.45 (3-6)
306.8

1 Divorce
ISBN 0-531-02254-4   LC 78-10464
"A First book"

"This is a kind of briefing that may answer some of the factual questions children have as to what is going on legally, financially, and custodially—questions their parents may be unable to discuss as objectively as the child needs. The examples of several fictional children's living arrangements seem more distracting than informational, but basics such as grounds, alimony, and visiting rights—terms that may be battered about within hearing but never explained—are defined here on a basic, simplified level." Booklist

307.7   Specific kinds of communities

Müller, Jörg

The changing city. Atheneum Pubs. [1977 c1976] unp illus $11.95   **307.7**

1 Cities and towns—Pictorial works
ISBN 0-689-50084-X   LC 76-46646

"A Margaret K. McElderry book"
First published 1976 in Switzerland

Companion volume to: The changing countryside, entered below

This portfolio of "eight fold-out prints spanning 13 years, shows how a quaint neighborhood is gradually renovated into an impersonal area of highrises, parking lots, and freeways. In the process, clearly visible from print to print, the area loses all character and personality." Sch Library J

"A cold but telling commentary on social changes and destruction of the natural environment, the pictures are stunning in themselves and offer a broad range of subjects for discussion. Easily comprehensible, they can also be used by individual children for browsing. And, one hopes, thinking. This may cause problems of storage and circulation, but it should be a very useful supplemental teaching aid for art, social studies, and other areas." Chicago. Children's Bk Center

The changing countryside. Atheneum Pubs. [1977 c1973] unp illus $11.95   **307.7**

1 Man—Influence on nature   2 Urbanization—Pictorial works
ISBN 0-689-50085-8   LC 76-46647

"A Margaret K. McElderry book"
First published 1973 in Switzerland

This companion volume to: The changing city, entered above, presents a portfolio of seven fold-out pictures in full color showing the changes wrought by industrialization and urbanization on what was once a tranquil country landscape

"Muller's realistic paintings are colorful and appealing, and even though they detail devastation, they contain humorous asides. . . . Unique and unparalleled." Sch Library J

Ross, Pat

What ever happened to the Baxter place? Illus. by Roger Duvoisin. Pantheon Bks. 1976 unp illus $5.99, lib. bdg. $4.95 (2-4)   **307.7**

1 Farm life   2 Urbanization
ISBN 0-394-93178-5   LC 75-22251

The story and illustrations show "how population has moved, changing the land. The Baxter family owned a large, attractive and profitable farm. As needs arose, and builders and others pressured them, bit by bit, parts of the farm were sold." Children's Bk Rev Serv

This "book takes one into an area of crushing sadness. Along with a text remarkable for clarity and a matter-of-fact handling, the Caldecott artist's pictures reveal the step-by-step destruction of a once thriving farm in Maryland." Pub W

Schwartz, Alvin

Central city/spread city; the metropolitan regions where more and more of us spend our lives. Macmillan Pub. Co. 1973 132p illus maps lib. bdg. $4.95 (5 and up)   **307.7**

1 Metropolitan areas   2 Regional planning
ISBN 0-02-781320-7   LC 72-81068

"A depressing, yet true picture of the living and working conditions existing in most central cities and their surrounding suburbs. Although not called by name, the inner city and suburbs described are in the vast metropolitan area surrounding Philadelphia, where five million people live and work. Dilapidated and inadequate housing, lack of schools, playgrounds, health services and jobs, and the rising crime rate (especially crimes against persons) sum up the sense of futility and frustration of the seven hundred thousand predominantly black people who live in the inner city (Tioga-Nicetown neighborhood). Contrasting with this bleak picture are the conditions, different but also depressing, in the 'typical' new, almost all white suburbs (Upper Merion Township) of split levels and ranch houses, apartments, vast shopping centers, industrial parks, rising crime rates (mostly crimes against property) and boredom for most

young people. Some small rays of hope are offered for the future, through the possibilities of good planning. . . . The book is liberally illustrated with photographs, maps and charts; and a supplementary reading list of over one hundred references [both nonfiction and fiction] is appended, including many specifically directed toward teachers." Sci Bks

Ventura, Piero

Piero Ventura's Book of cities. Random House 1975 unp illus $4.95, lib. bdg. $5.99 (2-4)   **307.7**

1 Cities and towns
ISBN 0-394-82744-9; 0-394-92744-3   LC 74-4927

An "introduction to the wonders of cities. By selecting cities like London, New York, Kyoto and Venice, the author shows how cities can vary widely in form. . . . [He] highlights the differing lifestyles found in the cities of the world while introducing subjects such as city living, transportation, employment, economics, and leisure and recreation activities." AAAS Sci Bks & Films

The author/artist's "subtle watercolors 'are not exact reproductions. . . . They are instead an attempt to combine the special elements and colorful impressions that [make] each city a unique experience.' . . . [The illustrations] are replete with fascinating detail and humorous activities; the drawings capture the feeling of the different locales." Horn Bk

310   Statistics

Riedel, Manfred

Winning with numbers; a kid's guide to statistics; illus. by Paul Coker, Jr. Prentice-Hall 1978 64p illus $5.95 (6 and up)   **310**

1 Statistics
ISBN 0-13-961466-4   LC 77-26729

The author "covers the definition of statistics, how to gather facts, how to treat them, and how to graph them to better understand the results. Measurements of the mean, median, mode, and range are explained and different situations are used to illustrate how these are used in almost every field." Sch Library J.

"A fine introduction to statistical information as it is generally made available to the public. It illustrates extremely well how figures can lie—and often do." Appraisal

310.5   Statistics—Yearbooks

The **Statesman's** year-book; statistical and historical annual of the states of the world. St Martins $30   **310.5**

1 Statistics—Yearbooks   2 Political science—Yearbooks   3 Encyclopedias
ISBN 0-312-76093-0   LC 4-3776

Annual. First published 1864

"Not an almanac of miscellaneous statistics but a concise and reliable manual of descriptive and statistical information about the governments of the world. Contents vary somewhat but usually give: (1) British Commonwealth and Empire; (2) United States; (3) Other countries, arranged alphabetically. [Recent issues have included a section on international organizations.] For each country [this] gives information about its ruler, constitution and government, area, population, religion, social welfare, instruction, justice and crime, state finance, defense, production and industry, agriculture, commerce, navigation, communications, banking and credit, money, weights and measures, diplomatic representatives, etc. A valuable feature is the selected bibliography of statistical and other books of reference given for each country. . . . The most useful of all the general yearbooks; indispensable in any type of library." Sheehy. Guide to Ref Bks. 9th edition

317.3   General statistics of the United States

Information please almanac; atlas & yearbook. Simon & Schuster $7.95, pa $3.95   **317.3**

1 U.S.—Statistics   2 Statistics—Yearbooks   3 Almanacs   LC 47-845

Information please almanac—*Continued*

Annual. First published 1947 by Doubleday with John Kieran as editor

"An almanac of miscellaneous information, with a general topic arrangement and a subject index. Includes extensive statistical and historical information on the United States; chronology of the year's events; statistical and historical descriptions of the various countries of the world; sports records; motion picture, theatrical, and literary awards, etc.; and many kinds of general information. Sources for many of the tables and special articles are noted." Sheehy. Guide to Ref Bks. 9th edition

"A useful annual compilation of facts which supplements the 'World Almanac,' [entered below] each including information not in the other. More legible than the latter, and therefore easier to consult." Enoch Pratt. Ref Bks. 1978

The **World** almanac and book of facts. Newspaper Enterprise Assn. [distributed by Doubleday] $7.95 **317.3**

1 U.S.—Statistics 2 Statistics—Yearbooks 3 Almanacs
ISBN 0-385-15711-8 LC 4-3781

Annual. First issued 1868
"The most comprehensive and most frequently useful of the American almanacs of miscellaneous information. Contains statistics on social, industrial, political, financial, religious, educational, and other subjects; political organizations; societies; historical lists of famous events, etc. Well up to date and, in general, reliable; sources for many of the statistics are given. A useful handbook. . . . Alphabetical index at the front of each volume." Sheehy. Guide to Ref Bks. 9th edition

323.4 Civil rights

Kohn, Bernice

The spirit and the letter; the struggle for rights in America. Viking 1974 175p illus $6.95 (5 and up) **323.4**

1 Civil rights 2 U.S. Constitution—Amendments
ISBN 0-670-66301-8 LC 73-22306

This discussion of civil rights as guaranteed by the Constitution and its Amendments examines individual issues of freedom of worship, speech, privacy, and assembly, as well as the problem of segregation and rights of Blacks

"The inherent flexibility of the Constitution and the changing nature of public and judicial opinion are emphasized throughout. Also, such . . . matters as the Watergate wire-taps, the Pentagon Papers, and the proposed Equal Rights Amendment are filtered through the author's philosophy, consistent with that of the Warren court. With the Declaration of Independence and the Constitution appended, this volume can serve as valuable discussion material for school projects." Booklist
Biography: p167-68

Meltzer, Milton

The human rights book. Farrar, Straus 1979 264p $8.95 (6 and up) **323.4**

1 Civil rights 2 Political prisoners
ISBN 0-374-31700-3 LC 79-13017

"Meltzer offers an historical perspective as well as detailed chapters typifying violations of rights in the countries of Argentina, Iran, South Africa, Indonesia, the U.S.S.R. and the U.S. More than one-third of the book is devoted to selected documents on Human Rights which makes this a ready-reference tool. Presented in a readable and interesting style." VOYA
Bibliography: p157-62

Sterling, Dorothy

Tear down the walls! A history of the American civil rights movement. Doubleday 1968 259p illus map lib. bdg. $6.95 (6 and up) **323.4**

1 Blacks—Civil rights 2 Blacks—History
ISBN 0-385-09436-1 LC 68-14212

"The author describes the African beginnings of black Americans, the slave trade, the abolitionists and the Civil War, such familiar figures in Negro history as Carver, Douglass and DuBois, the Klan, and black stereotype, and the accelerated pressures of recent years: legislation, school integration, riots, voter-registration drives, and new leaders." Chicago. Children's Bk Center

"The significance of events is pointedly underscored by numerous anecdotes citing the personal experiences of ordinary men and women as well as famous personages. Illustrated with photographs and drawings." Booklist
Suggested reading. p251-52

323.44 Freedom of action

American Library Association. Office For Intellectual Freedom

Intellectual freedom manual; comp. by the Office for Intellectual Freedom of the American Library Association. A.L.A. 1974 various pagings pa $5 **323.44**

1 Intellectual freedom 2 Libraries—Censorship
ISBN 0-8389-3181-2 LC 73-22336

"This manual is designed to answer the many practical questions that confront librarians in applying the principles of intellectual freedom to library service. It is our hope that every librarian will keep this volume on his desk as a convenient reference work." Preface
Contents: Library Bill of Rights; Freedom to read; Intellectual freedom; Intellectual freedom and the law; Assistance from ALA
Includes bibliography

Newsletter on Intellectual Freedom. A.L.A. $8 per year **323.44**

1 Intellectual freedom—Periodicals 2 Censorship—Periodicals
ISSN 0028-9485

Bimonthly. First published 1952
"A 20-page newsletter which attempts to give objective current information on censorship. There are usually one or two introductory articles, and then 'Censorship Dateline' which traces activities in various regions and states. 'From the Bench' gives current legal opinions, followed by 'Is it Legal?' and 'Success Stories.' There is a minimum of ALA business. Unfortunately, this does not enjoy a wide circulation. It should be brought to the attention of nonlibrarians, and certainly is a required item in any library, regardless of size, type, or location." Katz. Magazines for Libraries

324.273 Political parties of the United States

Cook, Fred J.

The rise of American political parties. Watts, F. 1971 90p illus lib. bdg. $6.45, pa $1.25 (5 and up) **324.273**

1 Political parties 2 U.S.—Politics and government
ISBN 0-531-00741-3; 0-531-02362-1 LC 77-161834

"A First book"
This book examines the American political system as it evolved from the views of Jefferson and Hamilton in the early days of the republic to the current basic two-party structure. Political parties of historical note, including the Federalists, Whigs, Populists, Know-Nothings and today's Democrats and Republicans, are discussed

"Reproductions of many contemporary drawings and photographs add interest." Booklist

324.6 Elections

Gray, Lee Learner

How we choose a President; the election year. 4th ed. St Martins 1976 167p $6.50 (5 and up) **324.6**

1 Presidents—U.S.—Election
ISBN 0-312-39410-1 LC 76-12610

First published 1964
The author describes and explains the activities of the Presidential election year including the search for candidates, the nomination of candidates, the campaign and election day. He also presents an historical background of the laws which affect the election process

Gray, Lee L.—*Continued*
This book includes "a section titled 'Campaign Tricks,' which addresses some of the legitimate and illegitimate ploys political tacticians use; later a sum-up chapter on presidential campaigns recaps Watergate's beginnings and raises further questions on campaigning tactics and financing." Booklist
Glossary: p134-39; Books about politics and the Presidency: p159-62

Lindop, Edmund
The first book of elections. Rev. ed. Illus. by Gustave C. Nebel. Watts, F. 1972 84p illus lib. bdg. $6.45 (4 and up)   **324.6**
1 Elections—U.S.
ISBN 0-531-00521-6   LC 72-182978
First published 1968
This book "analyzes the American election process, explaining who has the right to vote; what an election is; what is involved in local, state, and national elections; and why the Australian ballot was adopted for use in the United States. The author discusses why some people fail to vote or lose their right to vote when they move; however, no mention is made of criminals losing their right to vote." Library J [review of 1968 edition]
"Cartoon-style drawings add little that is informative, but gives some glimpses of familiar scenes that enliven the . . . approach of this timely book." Sat Rev [review of 1968 edition]

Weingast, David E.
We elect a President; illus. with photographs. [Rev. ed.] Messner 1977 255p illus lib. bdg. $8.29 (6 and up)   **324.6**
1 Presidents—U.S.—Election
ISBN 0-671-32839-5   LC 77-2658
First published 1962
"This reviewer was impressed by the non-partisanship displayed throughout this historical presentation of aspirants for candidacy for the presidency, what they do to get there and what their position is when they succeed. Well researched, yet anecdotal. Absorbing reading." Best Sellers [review of 1973 edition]
Glossary: p239-45. Suggested further reading: p246-47

326   Slavery and emancipation

Buckmaster, Henrietta
Flight to freedom; the story of the underground railroad. Crowell 1958 217p $8.95 (5 and up)   **326**
1 Slavery in the U.S.   2 Underground railroad
ISBN 0-690-30846-9   LC 58-9731
"An historical survey of the formation and operation of the Underground Railroad that is made more vivid by fictionalized examples of escape episodes. . . . The status of slavery and growth of the abolition movement . . . the leadership of men and women of both races, and the role of the Negro after the Civil War are described." Chicago. Children's Bk Center
"Equally interesting are the stories of the great figures . . . Garrison, Douglass, Lovejoy, Wendell Phillips, etc.—and of the many less familiar men and women who played dramatic and heroic roles in the long struggle." Horn Bk
Bibliography: p209-11

Commager, Henry Steele
The great Proclamation; a book for young Americans. Bobbs 1960 112p illus $5.95 (6 and up)   **326**
1 Emancipation proclamation   2 Slavery in the U.S.   3 Lincoln, Abraham, President U.S.
ISBN 0-672-50304-2   LC 60-7170
This book covers "the background of Abraham Lincoln's writing of the Emancipation Proclamation; his boyhood feelings about slavery, the Lincoln-Douglas debates, and the great dilemmas facing the President in the midst of Civil War. Told partly in Lincoln's own words or in the words of contemporary documents." Pub W
"This book, fair and just in its appraisal of slavery, and containing many fine reproductions of paintings and photographs, is a valuable aid to understanding the man and the issues." NY Times Bk Rev

Ingraham, Leonard W.
Slavery in the United States; illus. with photographs and drawings. Watts, F. 1968 89p illus lib. bdg. $6.45 (5 and up)   **326**
1 Slavery in the U.S.
ISBN 0-531-00630-1   LC 68-27402
This book traces the early history of the black man in America, beginning with the arrival of twenty African indentured servants brought to Jamestown, Virginia, in 1619. The story goes on to the establishment of slavery and finally to its abolition, as black Americans gained legal freedom with the passage of the Thirteenth Amendment to the Constitution
"The author's writing on the whole is lucid. The book is enhanced by capsule sketches of distinguished black men and women, by numerous well-correlated photographs, drawings and diagrams, and by quotations from original sources." Sch Library J
Suggestions for further reading: p85-86

Lester, Julius
To be a slave; illus. by Tom Feelings. Dial Press 1968 160p illus $5.95 (6 and up)   **326**
1 Slavery in the U.S.
ISBN 0-8037-8955-6   LC 68-28738
"Through the words of the slave, interwoven with strongly sympathetic commentary, the reader learns what it is to be another man's property; how the slave feels about himself; and how he feels about others. Every aspect of slavery, regardless of how grim, has been painfully and unrelentingly described." Rdng Ladders
"Striking black-and-white drawings add to the mood and effectiveness of the presentation." Booklist
Bibliography: p159-60

328.73   Legislative branch of U.S. government

Johnson, Gerald W.
The Congress; illus. by Leonard Everett Fisher. Morrow 1963 128p illus lib. bdg. $7.44 (5 and up)   **328.73**
1 U.S. Congress
ISBN 0-688-31182-2   LC 63-7878
"The author explains how the legislative branch of the government functions, discusses its beginnings, and, by citing famous cases in history, shows how the constitutional system of checks and balances operates. Appended are listings of speakers of the House, Vice-Presidents, and standing committees of the Senate and House." Booklist
"Mr. Johnson has the gift of telling a complex matter in a readable vigorous way, making it stimulating and dramatic. . . . Mr. Fisher's woodcut-style illustrations are strong and interpretative." Christian Sci Monitor

Stevens Leonard A.
How a law is made; the story of a bill against air pollution; illus. by Robert Galster. Crowell 1970 109p illus $7.97 (5 and up)   **328.73**
1 Legislation   2 Air—Pollution—Law and legislation
ISBN 0-609-40609-6   LC 74-101934
In this account of a state law against air pollution, the process of law-making takes nearly two years of work by a citizens' committee and legislators. There are times when party politics, public apathy, and pressure from industrial interests threaten to undermine the bill. Compromise is necessary. Step by step, the author shows how citizens can change the law and thereby improve the environment in which they live
"This is an intelligent book for youngsters seeking an understanding of the political process on the state level." Library J

Weiss, Ann E.
Save the mustangs! How a federal law is passed; illus. with photographs. Messner 1974 96p illus. lib. bdg. $6.29 (3-5)   **328.73**
1 Horses—Law and legislation   2 Legislation
ISBN 0-671-32648-1   LC 73-18355

Weiss, Ann E.—*Continued*

A class of fourth graders wages a "pencil war" by writing to their Congressman to introduce a strong save-the-mustangs bill. The author of this book takes readers behind the scenes of this project "as she documents the bill's journey through congressional houses and committee's until its signing into law by President Nixon. The plight of the mustangs—sent by 'mustangers' to pet food factories at the going rate of six cents a pound—will serve well in holding the interest of those trying to absorb their lessons in the mechanics of federal government legislation." Booklist

"The author has done a lucid job of explaining the federal lawmaking process, while dealing with an issue which has meaning to young readers. Numerous photographs of the horses and people who supported the bill add to the book's readability." Babbling Bookworm

Glossary: p91-93

330.973 U.S.—Economic conditions

Katz, William Loren

An album of the Great Depression. Watts, F. 1978 96p illus lib. bdg. $7.90 (5 and up)
330.973

1 Depressions, Economic 2 U.S.—Economic conditions—1919-1933 3 U.S.—Economic conditions—1933-1945 4 U.S.—Social conditions
ISBN 0-531-02914-X   LC 77-21413

"The grim story of the Great Depression that began with the crash of the stock market in 1929 is effectively told here through captioned photographs and a text that is broken down into smaller, specific subjects such as the march of the war veterans on Washington, the plight of sharecroppers, the 1932 election, the growth of popular culture, and the beginnings of the social security system. The author gives some background information about the economic situation that led to the crash, describes Hoover's attitude, Roosevelt's election and the various relief measures taken by the New Deal government, and ends with the looming problems of the war in Europe and the declaration of war by the United States after the attack on Pearl Harbor." Chicago. Children's Bk Center

Bibliography: p94

331.09 Historical and geographical treatment of industrial relations

Sandler, Martin W.

The way we lived; a photographic record of work in a vanished America. Little 1977 120p illus $8.95 (4 and up)   331.09

1 Labor and laboring classes—U.S. 2 U.S.—Social conditions 3 Occupations—History
ISBN 0-316-77020-5   LC 77-10810

"An assemblage of fascinating photographs that together catalog common occupations as they were in the years spanning, roughly, 1880 to 1920. . . . The pictures form a linear view of changing times, of the rise of mechanization and a changing economy. With each study (shipping, farming, mining, factories, construction, and child labor are some of the fourteen areas) comes a narrative commentary, plus interesting excerpts from contemporary autobiographical accounts. At the end is a 'vanished occupations' sequence, showing workers at now extinct activities and inviting readers to guess what they are. . . . The photographs are aesthetic as well as instructive; it's an intriguing record useful to browser as well as students of history." Booklist

331.4 Women workers

Saul, Wendy

Butcher, baker, cabinetmaker; photographs of women at work. Photography by Abigail Heyman; text by Wendy Saul. Crowell 1978 44p illus $8.95, lib. bdg. $8.79 (k-2)   331.4

1 Women—Employment
ISBN 0-690-03899-2; 0-690-03900-X   LC 77-27668

"A series of photographs of good quality is accompanied by a minimal amount of print and plenty of white space; the pictures show women in a wide variety of jobs: astronaut, artist, lawyer, mother, butcher, legislator, carpenter, athlete, coal miner, and so on." Chicago. Children's Bk Center

"Saul and Heyman have produced an excellent primer on nonsexism. The uncomplicated text makes it a snap for little ones to comprehend—reading it alone or with the help of grown-ups. . . . An added attraction of this book is that it depicts black women in various professions, thus arguing against another kind of crippling discrimination." Pub W

331.5 Migrant workers

Weiner, Sandra

Small hands, big hands; seven profiles of Chicano migrant workers and their families. Pantheon Bks. 1970 55p illus lib. bdg. $5.99 (4 and up)   331.5

1 Migrant labor 2 Mexican Americans
ISBN 0-394-90442-7   LC 75-122925

The seven profiles in this book are based on taped interviews with Mexican-American migrant workers ranging in age from eleven to sixty-seven. Through photographs and first-person accounts, the life of a farm laborer in this country is portrayed

"In some cases, the photographs reveal more than the text does. This kind of first-hand, primary source information is valuable to have: children are enabled to see the facts and draw their own conclusions. The text is within the grasp of third-grade readers, but the book will probably be much more useful for slightly older children with incipient social consciences." Library J

331.7 Labor by industry and occupation

Ancona, George

And what do you do? A book about people and their work; written and photographed by George Ancona. Dutton 1976 47p illus $7.95 (3-6)   331.7

1 Occupations 2 Vocational guidance
ISBN 0-525-25605-9   LC 75-40285

"Casting aside familiar occupations such as teacher, doctor, and fireman, this book explores the world of everyday workers. All of the jobs described can be done by either men or women; none require a college degree. . . . The author describes jobs such as barber, zookeeper, mechanic, and day-care center worker. The reader learns how a person trains for the job and future employment that may result from the job." Children's Bk Rev Serv

"After giving a brief but accurate description of each occupation, Ancona offers much needed advice about how to obtain such positions. In many cases, he goes a step further and discusses how one can advance within a particular field. . . . Photographs accompany each job description and strengthen the text by depicting men and women—including minorities—in various nonstereotyped roles. This is a useful and easy-to-use reference for young students interested in exploring career possibilities." AAAS Sci Bks & Films

332.4 Money

Forman, James

Inflation. Watts, F. 1977 115p lib. bdg. $6.90 (5 and up)   332.4

1 Inflation (Finance)
ISBN 0-531-00392-2   LC 76-53763

"An introduction to inflation—its causes and history from the inception of U.S. monetary policy through the two World Wars to today. Forman summarizes the theories of economists Smith and Keynes, the architects of our current policy which has proven inadequate in the post-war period. The pressure to acquire armaments, the increasing power of developing countries, and devaluation of

Forman, James—*Continued*
the dollar are presented in a text that is, as a whole, balanced and objective; the author gives the basic material a refreshing and appropriate point of view by suggesting in conclusion that there is a need for a new social ethic to stave off world inflation." Sch Library J
Glossary: p103-05. Bibliography: p107-09

333.79 Energy and energy resources

Kiefer, Irene
Energy for America; illus. with photographs, diagrams, charts, and maps. Atheneum Pubs. 1979 199p illus maps $10.95 (6 and up)   **333.79**

1 Power resources 2 Energy policy
ISBN 0-689-30713-6   LC 79-14656

In this survey of America's energy outlook, the author considers the need for improved methods of finding and extracting fossil fuels; new technologies for using wind and water power; continued development of solar energy, nuclear power, biomass; and, finally, saving energy by conservation
Glossary: p185-92. Sources of additional information: p193-94

Shuttlesworth, Dorothy E.
Disappearing energy; can we end the crisis? By Dorothy E. Shuttlesworth with Lee Ann Williams. Doubleday 1974 95p illus $6.95, lib. bdg. $7.90 (5 and up)   **333.79**

1 Power resources 2 Energy conservation
ISBN 0-385-04862-9; 0-385-04863-7   LC 73-20943

"This is a good resource book presenting factual data on the use and misuse of energy. Interesting descriptions of how coal, oil, and other fuels are searched for and found are included. The reader is left with an idea of not only the need for but also the 'how' of exploring for energy-producing fields. The authors spend significant time on the topic of conservation and energy misuse, although the development of this subject is more a review of what has been done rather than an inquiry into what could be done in the future to solve the problem. The photographs are dated and do not add much to the book." Sci and Children

Smith, Norman F.
Sun power; illus. by Don Madden. Coward, McCann & Geoghegan 1976 46p illus (Science is what and why books) lib. bdg. $5.99 (1-3)   **333.79**

1 Power resources 2 Solar energy
ISBN 0-698-30626-0   LC 76-3493

"Orange, gray, and black illustrations (the orange always represents the sun or heat) demonstrate the many uses of energy. New uses for solar heat are examined, and a simple explanation of nuclear fission is included. There is a double-page of 'facts about the sun' and good descriptions of the formation of coal, oil, and electricity. A fine early science book about a difficult subject." Adventuring with Bks

Watson, Jane Werner
Alternate energy sources. Watts, F. 1979 62p illus lib. bdg. $5.45 (4 and up)   **333.79**

1 Power resources
ISBN 0-531-022252-8   LC 78-10872

"A First book"
"Sources of energy that are mentioned include nuclear, solar, geothermal, and unusual uses of wind and water. Wood or dried plant matter are mentioned as possible alternatives." Sci and Children
"The writing is accurate, informative, and dry; the material is well-organized and accessible through an index; the close-set print is a visual handicap. A glossary is included." Chicago. Children's Bk Center

333.95 Biological resources

Ricciuti, Edward R.
Plants in danger; illus. by Ann Zwinger. Harper 1979 86p illus $8.95, lib. bdg. $8.99 (5 and up)   **333.95**

1 Rare plants
ISBN 0-06-024978-1   LC 77-25669

"Ricciuti discusses various endangered plants around the world, stating that more than 20,000 species (in contrast to 1,000 animals) are in danger of extinction. Explanations of how this began (rise of agriculture, building of cities, advance of technology, collecting by individuals) include descriptions of the imperiled grasslands of Africa, coastal wetlands of the Amazon, and highlands of the Himalayas, with emphasis on threatened U.S. plants such as California's redwood forests, eastern U.S. chestnut trees, and Florida's Everglades. . . . Accounts of steps being taken on a national and international level and the importance of this work conclude with a word on how individual plant fanciers can help rather than hinder those efforts. Detailed, softly shaded pencil drawings will add to the understanding of this thoughtful and clearly presented text." Booklist
Bibliography: p81

336.2 Taxes and taxation

Liston, Robert A.
Who shall pay? Taxes and tax reform in America. [Rev. ed.] Messner 1976 159p lib. bdg. $6.29 (5 and up)   **336.2**

1 Taxation—U.S.
ISBN 0-671-32795-X   LC 76-2519

First published 1972
"Provides an excellent summary of the reasons for the tax crisis and the reluctance of American taxpayers in voting new subsidies. The variety of taxes, e.g., income, social security, unemployment compensation, etc., are well outlined. Inequities are clearly explained in terms of the legal, economic, and psychological justifications and possible solutions are reviewed. . . . This also contains a pertinent chapter on revenue sharing as well as an index." Sch Library J
Suggested further reading: p156-57

338.09 Historical and geographical treatment of production

Fisher, Leonard Everett
The factories; written and illus. by Leonard Everett Fisher. Holiday House 1979 62p illus (Nineteenth century America) lib. bdg. $6.95 (5 and up)   **338.09**

1 Factories—History 2 U.S.—Industries
ISBN 0-8234-0367-X   LC 79-2092

The author "describes how New England became the manufacturing center of the country and what influences led to the spread of these industries across the nation. Names of specific companies—Singer, Steinway, Eastman Kodak—and their products dot the narrative as forerunners of today's giant corporations. Mention is also made of the working conditions and human exploitation that existed as America fumbled its way toward becoming an industrialized giant." Booklist
This book is "characterized by excellent design, well-spaced, readable type, and Fisher's dramatic black-and-white scratchboard illustrations." Sch Library J

338.1 Agriculture. Food supply

Archer, Jules
Hunger on planet Earth; illus. with photographs. Crowell 1977 216p illus $10 (6 and up)   **338.1**

1 Food supply 2 Famines
ISBN 0-690-01126-1   LC 76-3603

Archer, Jules—*Continued*

The author "paints a grim and appalling world picture of malnutrition and starvation, laying blame, in great part, on overpopulation. He explains both the Malthusian theory and the 'Green Revolution'; then, continent by continent, he reviews the hunger problem and efforts (often negated by bureaucratic snarls, politics, greed, and/or weather) to combat it. He does not stint in describing the widespread hunger in the U.S. or in naming prominent persons who have worked for or against alleviating the situation, stressing that feeding America's hungry is not politically popular among voters. He also considers both sides of the pesticide and chemical fertilizer question and spells out ways in which the race between food and population might be won. Although at times belabored and repetitive, the account is fact packed, hard hitting, and eye opening." Booklist

Bibliography and suggested further reading: p206-09

Gemming, Elizabeth

Wool gathering; sheep raising in old New England; illus. with prints and photographs. Coward, McCann & Geoghegan 1979 47p illus $6.95 (4-6) **338.1**

1 Wool trade and industry—History 2 Sheep
ISBN 0-698-20482-4   LC 78-24377

This "volume of information and regional lore presents an inviting view of a bygone cottage industry in New England. It also reveals today's movement to revive the homespun way of life as craftsmen again work with wool. Included in the text are instructions for spinning, weaving, and knitting. Scientific facts are integrated with the history, which describes how 'the quality of life changed' when 'the colonial "cottage industry" became big business' and how later the sheep moved westward, bringing an end to the New England wool industry. With an index and instructions for designing and knitting a muffler." Horn Bk

"Many of the black-and-white photographs show scenes presumably enacted at a recreated colonial village. That true-life backdrop strengthens the text's holding power and drives home the reality of the information." Booklist

Perl, Lila

The global food shortage; food scarcity on our planet and what we can do about it. Morrow 1976 128p illus lib. bdg. $6 (6 and up) **338.1**

1 Food supply 2 Power resources
ISBN 0-688-32068-6   LC 75-35860

"A stream of statistics effectively describes the dimensions of the world's food shortage, while Perl identifies some of the major factors that bear on the problem—the burgeoning world population, the effects of the energy crisis and droughts on food production, and the political and economic realities that too often lead to inhumane distribution policies. . . . The overall assessment is not optimistic, and viable solutions—which require careful consideration before implementation—can't really be dealt with here. What Perl does do is affirm the interdependency of have and have not nations and reiterate the oft-heard plea for affluent societies to re-evaluate their consumption patterns with an eye toward conservation; suitable as a starting point for investigation into the subject." Booklist

Pringle, Laurence

Our hungry Earth; the world food crisis. Macmillan Pub. Co. 1976 119p illus map (Science for survival ser) $6.95 (5 and up) **338.1**

1 Food supply
ISBN 0-02-775290-9   LC 76-10828

"This up-to-date report on the world food crisis concentrates on the 1970's, discussing starvation, food production, population control, politics, and attitudes. In covering the enormity and complexity of the food problem, Pringle lays blame on the United States' wasteful methods of farming, cooking, and eating for part of the problem." Sch Library J

"The text is gripping, and the information about current events may be new to many readers. . . . Not only the subject matter but the manner of presentation is outstanding: Striking photographs emphasize the text; statistics are well-placed; the pages are spaciously designed; the bibliography is graded and annotated; and a helpful glossary is included." Horn Bk

338.2 Mineral industries

Rutland, Jonathan

See inside an oil rig and tanker [author: Jonathan Rutland; editor: Anita Townsend; illustrations: Doug Harker and others] Warwick Press [1979 c1978] 29p illus lib. bdg. $6.90 (5 and up) **338.2**

1 Artificial islands 2 Petroleum 3 Tankers
ISBN 0-531-09121-X   LC 78-66167

First published 1978 in England

"By devoting each double-page spread to a particular aspect of oil production, this book briefly but competently explores how the world gets its petroleum. Operation and structure of drilling rigs, production platforms, oil tankers, and refineries are discussed along with comments about the people who work and sometimes live there. Color photographs and diagrams (e.g., cross section of a tanker and pictures of laying an undersea pipeline) supplement the brief text." Booklist

Glossary of terms: p28

341.23 United Nations

Sasek, M.

This is the United Nations; published with the co-operation of the United Nations. Macmillan Pub. Co. 1968 60p illus $5.95 (3-6) **341.23**

1 United Nations
ISBN 0-02-778400-2   LC 68-12093

"An entertaining guide to the United Nations, the organization of which is briefly explained. The various rooms, art objects, and items of interest—like gifts from member countries—are pictured, and stories told about them. A chart shows the flags of the 122 nations that make up the United Nations [1968]; and the specialized agencies—UNESCO, UNICEF, WHO, and the rest—are listed and identified." Horn Bk

"As always, M. Sasek is smoothly passing along the odd bits and pieces of data children seem to enjoy. . . . But there is plenty of basic historical information in the slim volume. The style is whimsical but not so whimsical that the read-aloud experience is a bore. Inevitably U.N. fans will grumble that there is . . . not enough about the unique status of the U.N.'s staff as international civil servants, or the U.N.'s Peace Force accomplishments in the Middle East and Cyprus and the Congo. But this is such an attractive introduction to the U.N. it seems a pity to carp. It's gay. It's informative. A book to be read once and again, handed down in the family, borrowed—and returned." NY Times Bk Rev

342 Constitutional and administrative law

Commager, Henry Steele

The great Constitution; a book for young Americans. Bobbs 1961 128p illus $7.50 (5 and up) **342**

1 U.S.—Constitutional history
ISBN 0-672-50299-2   LC 61-7914

This description of the Constitution tells of the work and ideals of George Washington, James Madison, Alexander Hamilton, and the others who were a part of its creation. It describes the many difficulties of preparing a document that would provide a better government than the Articles of Confederation had, and indicates the attitudes of the states to the new Constitution

The "style is informal, as the author tries to make the members of the Constitutional Convention real individuals, and the issues as exciting and the discussions as lively to young Americans as they ought to be. . . . [There are] many direct quotations from source materials, and the book is amply illustrated in black and white. . . . The text of the Constitution itself is not included in the book." Sch Library J

"A unique and valuable approach to the study of our history." NY Her Trib Bks

Fincher, E. B.
The Bill of rights. Watts, F. 1978 65p illus lib. bdg. $5.90 (5 and up)   **342**

1 U.S. Constitution—Amendments   2 Civil rights
ISBN 0-531-01347-2   LC 77-10890

"A First book"
"Fincher launches his outline-like introduction to the Bill of Rights with an account of the death of abolitionist editor Elijah P. Lovejoy at the hands of a mob bent on destroying his printing presses. Then back-tracking a bit, he considers the legal precedents and philosophical currents that influenced the Constitution's framers: the Magna Carta; the 1689 British Bill of Rights; and the ideas of Rousseau, Voltaire, and Locke. The Bill of Rights itself is considered amendment by amendment, with explanations ranging from paragraph length to several pages defining the context in which the article was conceived. Later portions review its interpretation through the years via Supreme Court decisions; here the role of public opinion comes into play, buttressing the concluding comment warning that the rights expressed depend more on the public than the government. With black-and-white photographs and a multipart appendix that features the Bill of Rights." Booklist
Glossary: p56-57. Bibliography: p61-62

Katz, William Loren
The Constitutional amendments, by William Loren Katz and Bernard Gaughran; illus. with contemporary prints and photographs. Watts, F. 1974 87p illus lib. bdg. $5.90, pa $1.25 (4 and up)   **342**

1 U.S. Constitution—Amendments
ISBN 0-531-02360-5   LC 73-14794

"A First book"
This book describes each of the twenty-six amendments to the Constitution. The historical background and the rights and privileges guaranteed by each amendment are discussed as well as the process of amending the Constitution
Bibliography: p84

345   Criminal law

Aymar, Brandt
Laws and trials that created history, by Brandt Aymar and Edward Sagarin. Crown 1974 214p illus $7.95 (6 and up)   **345**

1 Trials—History
ISBN 0-517-50535-5   LC 73-78876

The authors offer "informative commentary on 24 trials that span over two millenia. The selection of cases is unusual and includes those of Socrates, Galileo, Andrew Johnson, Oscar Wilde, Sacco and Vanzetti, Jomo Kenyatta, Eichmann, the Chicago Seven and Angela Davis. Although the selections lack focus and are not necessarily 'history making,' the book is a convenient introduction for students of civilization. Events leading up to each trial are described, as well as the trial itself and its aftermath, with editorial comments included; in many cases transcripts are excerpted. Black-and-white photographs and reproductions are plentiful, and a bibliography organized by case indicates research efforts by the authors." Booklist

David, Andrew
Famous criminal trials. Lerner Publications 1979 128p illus (On trial) lib. bdg. $6.95 (5 and up)   **345**

1 Trials
ISBN 0-8225-1427-3   LC 79-17543

"Brief definitions of law, crime, and U.S. criminal law introduce a fascinating, occasionally disturbing, discussion of eight familiar criminal cases. A chapter each is devoted to the trials of Sacco and Vanzetti, Leopold and Loeb, John T. Scopes, Bruno Hauptmann, the Rosenbergs, the Chicago Eight, Sirhan Sirhan, and James Earl Ray. The criminal action that instigated each trial and the nature of the evidence against the suspect are described, and the account includes comments on personalities involved in each case. . . . Readers will be caught up in this exciting and informative exposition of human drama." Booklist

346   Private law

Englebardt, Leland S.
You have a right; a guide for minors. Lothrop 1979 128p $7.50, lib. bdg. $7.20 (6 and up)   **346**

1 Children—Law and legislation   2 Children—Civil rights   3 Youth—Law and legislation   4 Youth—Civil rights
ISBN 0-688-41893-7; 0-688-51893-1   LC 79-4678

"What kind of legal or constitutional rights do young people have? Do minors have any civil rights at all? These questions and others are dealt with in a straightforward discussion of the various problems children and adolescents can encounter in everyday living. Examples of typical situations in which the rights of a young person are abused or ignored are provided, along with commentary and analysis. Activities of inexperienced young people described in examples serve to make each point; with advice on everything from contracts to child abuse, on how to protect rights and avoid losing those special privileges accorded youth, this is a solid introduction and guide. In conclusion, Englebardt suggests and lists places where youth can seek legal aid." Booklist

349   Law of individual states and nations

Seuling, Barbara
You can't eat peanuts in church and other little-known laws; written and illus. by Barbara Seuling. Doubleday 1975 64p illus $4.95, lib. bdg. $5.90, pa $1.75 (4 and up)   **349**

1 Law—U.S.
ISBN 0-385-01383-0; 0-385-01435-X; 0-385-12137-7   LC 74-19384

A "collection of off-beat laws (e.g., 'In Colorado Springs, Colorado, the law upholds a dog's right to one bite') gathered from all parts of the United States. Most are one-liners, and some are illustrated by cartoons which point out the incongruities of the law. An introduction provides useful background information." Sch Library J

352   Local governments

Eichner, James R.
The first book of local government; illus. by Dan Nevins. Rev. ed. Watts, F. 1976 lib. bdg. $5.90 (4 and up)   **352**

1 Local government   2 U.S.—Politics and government
ISBN 0-531-00571-2   LC 75-43728

"A First book"
First published 1964 with illustrations by Bruce Bacon
An introduction to the most common forms of local government including organization, responsibilities, and duties of the specific departments
Glossary: p56-58

353.04   The cabinet in federal government

Parker, Nancy Winslow
The President's Cabinet and how it grew; with an introduction by the Honorable Dean Rusk. Parents Mag. Press [distributed by Four Winds] 1978 unp illus $6.50, lib. bdg. $6.19 (3-5)   **353.04**

1 Cabinet officers   2 Presidents—U.S.
ISBN 0-8193-0923-0; 0-8193-0924-9   LC 77-10090

"Beginning with the disclaimer that the President's Cabinet is not a piece of furniture, Parker delves into the practical duality of the Cabinet, that group of federal officials which not only advises the President on matters of national policy, but which also administers the various departments of the Executive Branch. Foregoing an administration-by-administration approach, 13 major developments in the growth and specialization of

Parker, Nancy W.—_Continued_
the Cabinet are cited, from Washington through
Carter. Then each . . . officer receives an additional half-page treatment before the conclusion
describing his/her responsibilities and the various
offices, bureaus, and organizations which comprise
each department." Sch Library J
"Colorful, cartoon-like illustrations play a major
role in relating the history of the cabinet and each
department's responsibilities. The innovative format makes learning a treat in this book which
captures the reader's attention from the introduction by Dean Rusk to the last page. The information is up-to-date, including Carter's administration. Clearly written and informative (did you
know that Cabinet members take their chairs with
them when they leave office?). 'The President's
Cabinet' is definitely one of the best books available on this subject." Children's Bk Rev Serv

355 Military art and science

Wakin, Edward
Black fighting men in U.S. history; illus.
with photographs. Lothrop 1971 192p illus lib.
bdg. $6 (5 and up)   355

1 U.S.—History, Military 2 Black soldiers
ISBN 0-688-51264-X   LC 75-101480
In this assessment of the black man's role in
American wars, the author shows that while
blacks have taken part in every major war, battle
and campaign, their rights were abused even while
they fought—and died. And when the battle was
done, the black man was forgotten, his contribution to the country overlooked
Bibliography: p185-87

355.8 Military equipment and supplies

Colby, C. B.
Fighting gear of World War II; equipment
and weapons of the American G.I. Coward-
McCann 1961 48p illus lib. bdg. $5.19 (4 and up)
                                              355.8
1 U.S. Army—Ordnance and ordnance stores
2 World War, 1939-1945—U.S.
ISBN 0-698-30078-5   LC 61-13403
A photographic essay describing fighting equipment used by American soldiers against the Germans and Japanese

359.3 Organization of naval forces

Van Orden, M. D.
The book of United States Navy ships. 3d
ed. fully rev. Dodd 1979 94p illus $5.95 (5 and
up)   359.3
1 U.S. Navy 2 Ships 3 Warships
ISBN 0-396-07661-0   LC 78-25600
First published 1969
The most representative types and classes of
U.S. Navy ships—carriers, battleships, cruisers,
frigates, destroyers, submarines, mine sweepers,
amphibious warfare ships—are discussed and illustrated. Included also is Navy terminology, the
rules and requirements for naming ships and
specifications of individual ships arranged by type
"Succinct and easy-to-use, this will be popular
with military ship enthusiasts." Sch Library J

361 Social problems and social welfare

Sechrist, Elizabeth Hough
It's time for brotherhood, by Elizabeth
Hough Sechrist and Janette Woolsey; illus.
by John R. Gibson. [Rev. ed] Macrae Smith
Co. 1973 296p illus lib. bdg. $7.97 (5 and up)
                                              361
1 Social work 2 Human relations 3 Biography
ISBN 0-8255-8191-5   LC 72-11098

First published 1962
This book discusses organizations and individuals that have worked to promote the concept of
brotherhood, including religious and charitable
organizations, civil rights movements, service agencies, foundations, exchange programs, and the
United Nations
Bibliography: p271-79

361.6 Public action

Myers, Walter Dean
Social welfare. Watts, F. 1976 65p illus
lib. bdg. $6.95 (4 and up)   361.6
1 Public welfare
ISBN 0-531-00340-X   LC 76-16552
"A First book"
"This is not a history of social welfare or of
the reformers who have influenced institutions
and legislation, but an examination of the welfare
system in the United States today. It discusses
Social Security, Aid to Dependent Children, the
procedure for getting on (or off) welfare rolls, the
costs to municipalities, and the differing viewpoints on solutions to the intricate problems of
funding social welfare. Myers provides some historical background in a brief survey of changes since
the Depression Era, and gives very concrete
examples of such problems as disparate taxing, the
dilemma of the welfare mother, and the possible
alternatives to public welfare; he concludes with
a question-and-answer section on attitudes and
aspects of the welfare program." Chicago. Children's Bk Center
"Throughout the text, certain myths are de-
molished—that blacks are the primary recipients
of welfare or that the more children a welfare
mother has, the easier she has it—and a series of
questions and answers at the conclusion confronts
commonly held prejudices with reasoned responses.
. . . Overall, a case is made for social welfare,
but the hard look at its shortcomings supports the
author's call for changes. Black-and-white photographs throughout." Booklist

362.1 Physical illness

Beame, Rona
Emergency! Written and photographed by
Rona Beame. Messner 1977 64p illus lib.
bdg. $6.97 (3-6)   362.1
1 Hospitals
ISBN 0-671-32824-7   LC 76-57778
"A description of the emergency services at New
York's Bellevue Hospital: ambulance service, pedi-
atric emergency service, adult emergency service,
and emergency ward. In each case, the chapter includes a running account of patients who come in,
sequentially, through a medical team's shift. The
book certainly gives . . . [an] impression of the
tempo and tension of emergency work, and it gives
many facts about staff and procedures." Chicago.
Children's Bk Center
"Exciting is the only way to describe this book.
. . . Rona Beame has caught the excitement and
tension of the ambulance, emergency room, and
the personnel who staff them. The photographs are
superb; the text is well-written." Appraisal

Marino, Barbara Pavis
Eric needs stitches; photographs by Richard
Rudinski. Addison-Wesley 1979 28p illus $6.95
(k-3)   362.1
1 Hospitals 2 Medical care
ISBN 0-201-04401-3   LC 78-31694
"When Eric has a bicycle accident and needs
stitches, he's frightened. [The book] follows him
through the entire process, from home to
emergency room, ministrations by nurse and doctor, and finally, out for ice cream." Appraisal
"With the aid of numerous black-and-white
photos (which add to the book's realism without
dwelling upon gore), the author takes us step-by-
step through a typical emergency room visit.
Marino does not sugar-coat any of her presentation, but her calm matter-of-fact style should be
reassuring to young readers." Sch Library J

Sobol, Harriet Langsam

Jeff's hospital book; photographs by Patricia Agre. Walck, H.Z. 1975 unp illus $6.95 (k-3)
362.1

1 Hospitals 2 Children—Medical care 3 Eye-Surgery
ISBN 0-8098-1229-0   LC 74-25982

"The author efficiently and empathetically documents young Jeff's hospital stay, during which time he undergoes an operation that uncrosses his eyes. The black-and-white photographs and simple text follow Jeff through admissions procedures, doctors' visits, the operation itself, and its aftermath. Routine practices that might frighten children have been perceptively incorporated into the dialog and commentary. Thus readers become familiar with details like an anesthetic's effect of drying the mouth or the reasons for raising bedside bars: just prior to surgery they see Jeff being strapped onto a stretcher and then later being administered oxygen through a facial mask. An honest portrayal with much to say to children harboring their own private apprehensions." Booklist

Weber, Alfons

Elizabeth gets well; pictures by Jacqueline Blass. Crowell 1970 28p illus lib. bdg. $8.79 (k-3)
362.1

1 Hospitals
ISBN 0-690-25839-9   LC 78-120996

Originally published 1969 in Switzerland

Elizabeth must go to the hospital to have her appendix out. Since she has never been in the hospital before, she is a bit frightened. This book, written to allay the child's fear of hospitals, describes Elizabeth's experiences before her operation and during her recovery

"An interesting account that can be read to small children or which others can read. The text is on the left-hand pages and on the right-hand pages are reproduced watercolors which let the reader see what is happening at each stage of the story. Each step is explained: the process of admission, examination, going to the operating room, awakening after it is all over, intravenous feeding, recovery, a precautionary chest x-ray, the meeting of new friends, and the joyous return home." Sci Bks

362.3   Mental retardation

Dunbar, Robert E.

Mental retardation. Watts, F. 1978 63p illus lib. bdg. $6.45 (4 and up)
362.3

1 Mentally retarded
ISBN 0-531-01491-6   LC 78-8689

"A First book"

An "account of the various causes and forms of retardation and its effect on the individual learning to cope in society. The 'complications' of mental retardation figure importantly—not only frequently accompanying physical handicaps, but emotional problems arising out of poor adjustments to school demands and inadequate guidance from the 'normal' world." Booklist

Sobel, Harriet Langsam

My brother Steve is retarded; photographs by Patricia Agre. Macmillan Pub. Co. 1977 26p illus $5.95 (3-5)
362.3

1 Mentally retarded children
ISBN 0-02-785990-2   LC 76-46996

"Beth is 11 and, as the title says, has a brother Steven who is retarded. . . . [The photographs and text depict] Beth in the midst of normal, everyday affairs as she articulates her mixed feelings about herself, her brother, and her relationship to him. He's older than she but looks smaller and acts younger; sometimes she finds it hard to love him; she gets angry at him, but his pleasure when she spends time with him is a reward; she wonders about his future—probably as a worker in a sheltered home—and hopes he will be happy." Booklist

The author "is obviously writing about experiences she well understands. This is a completely 'up-front', honest book about a retarded child. . . . The photographs are excellent: varied, intriguing, touching, and, in some cases, haunting.

This book is a worthwhile addition to any library, to increase every child's understanding, whether or not he or she has direct contact with those who are retarded." Children's Bk Rev Serv

362.4   Problems of and services to people with physical handicaps and disabilities regardless of cause

Adams, Barbara

Like it is: facts and feelings about handicaps from kids who know; photographs by James Stanfield. Walker & Co. 1979 96p illus $8.95, lib. bdg. $8.85 (4-6)
362.4

1 Physically handicapped children 2 Mentally handicapped children
ISBN 0-8027-6374-X; 0-8027-6375-8   LC 79-2201

"With one exception each section of the book is a first-person narrative in which a child with a particular kind of handicap talks about his or her own problems and about children with related problems; the sections are on hearing and speech impairment, visual impairment, orthopedic handicaps, developmental/mental disabilities, retardation, and learning disabilities. Several examples of behavior disorders are described in the final section, in third person, with a first-person commentary by a school principal who is concerned and helpful. . . . [This book gives] a broad view of how children cope with various kinds of handicaps, the range of differences in disabilities, the special needs of handicapped children, and their feelings about how they would like to be treated by others." Chicago. Children's Bk Center

Glossary: p92-96

Berger, Gilda

Physical disabilities Watts, F. 1979 119p illus $6.90 (6 and up)
362.4

1 Physically handicapped
ISBN 0-531-02927-1   LC 78-10106

"Berger surveys the whole range of physical disabilities—nerve and muscle disorders, bone and joint disorders, chronic health impairments, and sensory impairments. Opening chapters explore attitudes toward the disabled, current and past; the body of the text explains specific disabilities, their history and treatment; and the closing section emphasizes the 'new day' resulting from more enlightened views and strong federal legislation to protect the disabled citizen's rights." VOYA

The author "has approached her topic with clarity and simplicity. . . . [She] never loses sight of her intended audience; her explanations are concrete and the legible type size makes for comfortable reading." Sch Library J

Bibliography: p113. Further reading: p114-15

Haskins, James

The quiet revolution; the struggle for the rights of disabled Americans, by James Haskins with J. M. Stifle. Crowell 1979 147p illus $7.95, lib. bdg. $7.89 (5 and up)
362.4

1 Physically handicapped—Civil rights
ISBN 0-690-03981-6; 0-690-03982-4   LC 77-27664

"A John Day book"

"This book on the movement to provide disabled Americans with their basic civil rights is an . . . overview of the efforts made by organizations and individuals in this area. The book is structured around the United Cerebral Palsy's 'Bills of Rights for the Handicapped,' with chapters covering the medical, educational, and economic aspects of these rights, as well as the problem of accessibility." Children's Bk Rev Serv

"The text gives a greater understanding of the militant attitudes of some handicapped people and of the apathetic and sometimes hostile attitudes of the non-handicapped society. New terms are explained well and a concise synopsis of the myriad laws affecting the handicapped passed in the last decade is included. A seven-page bibliography and numerous photographs round out an excellent beginning text for this highly current and controversial subject." Sch Library J

Kamien, Janet
What if you couldn't. . . ? A book about special needs; illus. by Signe Hanson. Scribner 1979 83p illus $7.95 (4-6)   362.4
1 Handicapped
ISBN 0-684-15970-8   LC 78-26659

"Based on the premise that antipathy and condescension toward people who are different arise from ignorance rather than from innate dislike, the book introduces and explains six handicaps—blindness, deafness, dyslexia, emotional problems, impaired mobility, and mental retardation. Clear descriptions are provided for their causes, if known, as well as for their characteristics and consequences. Appropriate terms are integrated into a direct, unsentimental text, which also introduces experiments so that nonhandicapped readers can, by simulating a given disability, become more knowledgeable and thus more understanding." Horn Bk

Peter, Diana
Claire and Emma; photographs by Jeremy Finlay. Day [1977 c1976] unp illus lib. bdg. $5.79 (2-4)   362.4
1 Deaf   2 Deaf—Means of communication   3 Sisters
ISBN 0-381-90059-2   LC 77-629

First published 1976 in England
"Color photographs show two small sisters, both born deaf, who are lively and playful, enjoy the same things that other children do, but need special training because of their handicap. The text describes some of the equipment and training that help the girls talk or read lips, and it suggests helpful patience on the part of the reader: 'If you don't quite understand her, try to help her explain. Don't be in a hurry and don't walk away if you cannot understand at first. Just give her a little longer.' Whether or not readers will relate to a pictured child is debatable, but the book . . . certainly makes it clear that deaf children have normal intelligence, ability, and interests." Chicago. Children's Bk Center

Petersen, Palle
Sally can't see. Day [1977 c1974] unp illus lib. bdg. $5.79 (2-4)   362.4
1 Blind
ISBN 0-381-90058-4   LC 77-628

First published 1974 in Denmark
"This simply written book about a blind twelve-year-old is illustrated with color photographs and a Braille chart. Sally, blind from birth, compensates for lack of eyesight by patient training in learning by touch and hearing. The book stresses the fact that Sally enjoys the same things as do other children of her age, and that she wants to be treated, insofar as possible, in the same way. The text is fairly positive in approach, citing what Sally can do rather than what she can't, but it is a bit lifeless; despite the photographs, there's no development of Sally's personality." Chicago. Children's Bk Center

Peterson, Jeanne Whitehouse
I have a sister—my sister is deaf; pictures by Deborah Ray. Harper 1977 unp illus $6.95, lib. bdg. $6.89 (k-3)   362.4
1 Deaf   2 Sisters
ISBN 0-06-024701-0; 0-06-024702-9   LC 76-24306

"Being deaf has some assets as well as liabilities. This book helps to point out some ways a deaf child compensates and some ways that other senses are developed more fully. It has an appreciation for accomplishments and strengths. It gives a picture of a warm relationship between a girl and her younger deaf sister." Children's Bk Rev Serv
"A lovely, tender story, with a sense of poetry that is quite captivating. The pencil sketch illustrations by Deborah Ray aptly evoke the mood of the text. Especially to be recommended to those who are deaf or who have a close relationship with someone who has this difficulty." Babbling Bookworm

Stein, Sara Bonnett
About handicaps; an open family book for parents and children together, by Sara Bonnett Stein, in cooperation with Gilbert W. Kliman. . . . [and others]; photography by Dick Frank; graphic design, Michel Goldberg. Walker & Co. 1974 47p illus $5.95 (k-3)   362.4
1 Physically handicapped   2 Physically handicapped children
ISBN 0-8027-6174-7   LC 73-15270

"An explanatory text for adults runs alongside a large-print photo-story for young children. . . . [The story concerns] a superhealthy child, Matthew, [who] is upset by encounters with Joe, a little boy with cerebral palsy, and a man whose arm has been replaced with a hook. Matthew overcomes his aversions when the man explains how the hook works and Joe proves to be a good playmate." Sch Library J

Sullivan, Mary Beth
Feeling free [by] Mary Beth Sullivan, Alan J. Brightman [and] Joseph Blatt; with Margaret Roberts [and] JoAnn Williams Fiske. Illustrations: Marci Davis [and] Linda Bourke; photographs: Alan J. Brightman. Addison-Wesley 1979 186p illus lib. bdg. $9.95, pa $5.95 (3 and up)   362.4
1 Physically handicapped children
ISBN 0-201-07479-6; 0-201-07485-0   LC 79-4315

Based on the television series of the same title
"This is a collection of interviews, cartoons, skits, games, puzzles, and stories, aimed at dispelling myths about disabled people. It deals with five handicaps specifically: blindness, deafness, learning disabilities, dwarfism, and cerebral palsy." Sch Library J
"Most of the text consists of statements by children with disabilities. . . . Their comments are candid and extensive, and the book certainly fulfills the function of informing other children what it's like to be handicapped, and certainly it has a high potential for awakening understanding rather than pity. Just as certainly, it may assuage the feelings of handicapped readers that their problems are unique." Chicago. Children's Bk Center

White, Paul
Janet at school; photographs by Jeremy Finlay. Crowell 1978 unp illus lib. bdg. $5.79 (k-3)   362.4
1 Physically handicapped children
ISBN 0-381-99557-7   LC 77-26681

"A John Day book"
"The author and artist present a frank portrait of Janet, who suffers from 'spina bifida,' a congenital defect that confines her to a wheelchair. Janet's buoyant personality comes through, as do her daily pitfalls and accomplishments." Booklist
"White includes interesting details about Janet that all children can easily identify with and understand. He further involves readers by suggesting that they try feeling down their backs as he explains about the normal functioning of the spine and Janet's spinal damage. The spirited color photos and text blend nicely together in this engaging, positive portrait for young children." Sch Library J

Wolf, Bernard
Anna's silent world. Lippincott 1977 48p illus $8.95 (2-4)   362.4
1 Deaf
ISBN 0-397-31739-5   LC 76-52943

Also available in a Spanish language edition (ISBN 0-397-31847-2, $6.95)
"Anna, born deaf, leads for all intents and purposes a normal life. This has been possible because of family support, special training, and sound-amplifying technology that maximizes what little hearing she does possess. Wolf's photographs and running text take us into Anna's life, showing her in a round of activities with family, friends, teachers, and pets. Information on deafness and the kinds of therapy that work to overcome it twine through the text; questioning reactions of other children crop up when Anna's mother explains to a young visitor why her daughter's speech is sometimes hard to understand and how Anna is able to understand what's being spoken around her." Booklist

Wolf, Bernard—*Continued*

The text, with "photographs by Bernard Wolf, is a particularly appropriate book for a situation where a deaf child might by trying to cope with other children. It gives a clear documented picture of the active life, limitations, yet perfectly normal attitudes of the child who cannot hear. If could be a very important book to have, not for the one who is handicapped solely by a lack of hearing ability, but also for those who might be handicapped by a lack of understanding. Good for the public or school library." Babbling Bookworm

Connie's new eyes; written and photographed by Bernard Wolf. Lippincott 1976 95p illus $8.95 (4 and up)   362.4

1 Blind 2 Guide dogs
ISBN 0-397-31797-6   LC 76-17014

"Wolf presents the everyday experiences of a highly productive young person who is handicapped. The book begins with the training of Blythe, the golden retriever puppy who becomes Connie's guide dog, and then follows 22-year-old Connie—blind from birth—through her training at The Seeing Eye with Blythe and her first year as a teacher. Wolf's excellent candid photographs have the familiarity of a family album, and his straightforward text conveys the feeling that he is telling about a friend." Sch Library J

Don't feel sorry for Paul; written and photographed by Bernard Wolf. Lippincott 1974 94p illus $8.95 (3-6)   362.4

1 Physically handicapped children
ISBN 0-397-31588-0   LC 74-9925

"Written in the form of a documentary, [this book] presents the highlights of several weeks in the life of Paul Jockimo, a child born without a right hand and foot, and with a deformed left hand and left foot. In stark pictures, with accompanying text, we see Paul's deformities and watch as he puts on the three prosthetic devices. We follow him bicycling, playing, going to school, celebrating his seventh birthday, and, finally, winning second prize in a horse show. We also follow him through a session at the Institute for Rehabilitative Medicine after he has broken two of his prostheses, and we learn how artificial devices that substitute for feet are made." NY Times Bk Rev

"Photographs of superb quality illustrate a text written with candor and dignity. . . . No mincing of words, no sentimentality, no appeal for sympathy in this text. It's a fine way to acquaint readers with the problems of the handicapped; even more, it is a beautifully conceived book." Chicago. Children's Bk Center

362.7 Problems of and services to young people

Bunin, Catherine

Is that your sister? A true story of adoption, by Catherine and Sherry Bunin. Pantheon Bks. 1976 35p illus lib. bdg. $5.99 (k-3)
362.7

1 Adoption
ISBN 0-394-93230-7   LC 76-60

"In this true account, a six-year-old girl tells what it is like to be adopted, to have dark skin unlike her parents and older siblings, and to have a younger sister who is also adopted. She gives her impressions of the social worker's initial visit, the foster home, the court proceedings. But more important, it's the story of two young children who have found a home with a loving family that wants them." Adventuring with Bks

362.8 Problems of and services to other groups

Seixas, Judith S.

Living with a parent who drinks too much. Greenwillow Bks. 1979 116p $6.95, lib. bdg. $6.67 (4 and up)   362.8

1 Alcoholism 2 Alcoholics 3 Parent and child
ISBN 0-688-80196-X; 0-677-84196-1   LC 78-1108

"Most books on the subject of alcoholism deal only with the physiological effects of alcohol on the body. Seixas has taken a different approach, stressing coping strategies for the children of alcoholic parents. Using case histories, the author tries to help readers understand that alcoholism is an illness and that alcoholics cannot restrain their behavior. Young people are further urged not to feel guilty or ashamed, as alcoholism is not a problem that they caused, nor is it one that they can control." Sch Library J

"The straightforward, second-person writing approach is supportive and unflinching. For example, readers are told to preplan where to call for emergency medical help in their area; and those victimized by beatings or sexual abuse are advised that, if no help is available at home, outside aid is important to them. . . . Also important is the notion of taking responsibility for 'your own life' and separating oneself from a parent's drinking problem. There is considerable information on Alateen, and a final discussion talks about the personal choice of whether or not to drink. The candor throughout is effective, underscoring the message that youngsters with problem-drinking parent(s) are neither alone nor need be helpless." Booklist

363.2 Police services

Demuth, Jack

City horse, by Jack and Patricia Demuth. Dodd 1979 79p illus lib. bdg. $6.95 (3-6)   363.2

1 New York (City)—Police 2 Horses
ISBN 0-396-07650-5   LC 78-23651

"Hannon is the city horse, a purebred Tennessee Walker donated to the NYPD Mounted Unit. His rider is Mike Sicignano, a Mounted Unit member who picked Hannon for his own despite the horse's slow adjustment to city surprises. The authors do an excellent job of filling readers in on what mounted police and their animals are all about. Matters of training, routine duties, special events, and equine upkeep are all included, with plenty of excellent black-and-white photographs to show specifics." Booklist

Millimaki, Robert H.

Fingerprint detective. Lippincott 1973 96p illus lib. bdg. $10.95 (5 and up)   363.2

1 Fingerprints
ISBN 0-397-31484-1   LC 73-7861

After giving a brief history of fingerprinting, the author shows how to make a set of prints and classify them. He also discusses the importance of fingerprints in criminal investigations and describes how to locate, develop, lift, classify and analyze prints

"The subject will no doubt appeal to young sleuths inundated with TV detective work, but just how far they'll get will depend on their perseverance. . . . Classifying the prints is intimidating, and only dedicated would-be technicians will master the numerical system; this is not to fault the presentation but merely to indicate that readers can do as much or as little as they wish and still have learned about the subject." Booklist

363.3 Other aspects of public safety

Beame, Rona

Ladder Company 108; written and photographed by Rona Beame. Messner 1973 62p illus lib. bdg. $6.64 (3-5)   363.3

1 Fire departments 2 New York (City)—Fires and fire prevention
ISBN 0-671-32642-2   LC 73-7173

"This details the activities of Ladder Company 108 in New York City over a three-day period. The dangers and discomforts involved in fire fighting are brought out and on-the-scene black-and-white photographs are provided." Sch Library J

"The straightforward and informal text and clear, unposed photographs describe the division of labor within the unit, the way the men spend their time in the firehouse, the company's response to different kinds of alarms, from time-consuming false alarms to refuse fires and big fires that necessitate life-saving and calling in other units." Chicago. Children's Bk Center

363.7 Environmental problems and services

Elliott, Sarah M.

Our dirty water; illus. with photographs; maps and drawings by the author. Messner 1973 64p illus lib. bdg. $5.29 (4-6)   363.7

1 Water—Pollution
ISBN 0-671-32576-0   LC 73-5399

"The causes of water pollution, the dangers of using dirty water, and the actions being taken to rectify the situation are clearly presented in this well-organized treatment accompanied by black-and-white photographs. Weak, laxly enforced anti-pollution laws on the national and local level, industrial lobbying against such laws, and campaign money given to politicians by big business are mentioned. However, while some industries are identified as major polluters, specific companies are not named. A final chapter includes questions about community treatment plants, an experiment for testing fresh water sources, and other suggestions. Unfortunately, the biological process involved in pollution is scarcely mentioned." Sch Library J

Miles, Betty

Save the Earth! An ecology handbook for kids; illus. by Claire A. Nivola. Knopf 1974 91p illus lib. bdg. $5.97, pa $2.50 (4 and up)   363.7

1 Pollution 2 Conservation of natural resources 3 Ecology
ISBN 0-394-92658-7; 0-394-82658-2   LC 73-15116

This book contains information and "activities for children on topics of town planning, paper waste, space vs. population, pollution of air and water, noise control, and home conservation practices. Some activities are short ones, such as keeping a log of water use, planning a 'new town,' and identifying noise pollution sources. Others are long-range, such as taking daily photographs of industrial pollution." Sci and Children

"The book's major strength is in its emphasis on involvement for change. The author encourages students to fight pollution not only as individuals but as citizens working through a variety of channels. Samples of ways to proceed are included. The text is somewhat choppy, but the book contains specific information which is helpful—a chart measuring common sounds in decibels, a list of ecology organizations, and a bibliography which includes newsletters. It is well-organized, and the format is interestingly varied with squiggly line drawings and well-selected black-and-white photographs." Appraisal

Milgrom, Harry

ABC of ecology; photographs and designs by Donald Crews. Macmillan Pub. Co. 1972 unp illus $4.95 (k-2)   363.7

1 Pollution 2 Alphabet
ISBN 0-02-766920-3; 0-02-044740-X   LC 76-175598

" 'ABC of Ecology' is a somewhat deceptive title, the book deals specifically with urban pollution, not ecology. It runs through the alphabet (A atmosphere, B bottle, etc.) making a brief statement about each example and asking a question or suggesting an activity for the reader. The author has relied heavily on visual impact, using strong black and white pictures and occasionally two colors in the layout. In the back is a section for parents and teachers describing the conditions to be stressed with the child reader. This allows even the most uninformed adult to deal effectively with the subject." Sci Bks

Showers, Paul

Where does the garbage go? Illus. by Loretta Lustig. Crowell 1974 33p illus (Let's-read-and-find-out science bks) $7.95, lib. bdg. $7.89 (1-3)   363.7

1 Refuse and refuse disposal
ISBN 0-690-00392-7; 0-690-00402-8   LC 73-14881

"Problems of sanitation, conservation, and recycling are seen from the child's viewpoint. . . . The child points out that it's different in the country: garbage goes to the pigs and trash is buried. After discussing the problems of the mess and the vermin of city dumps, the pollution of water from garbage, and the possibilities of separating garbage components for recycling, the text comes back to the child's viewpoint. One can help by making less trash and one can mend old toys." Chicago. Children's Bk Center

"The illustrations are an excelltnt addition to a good book on the important role that garbage plays in the life cycle of the community." Sci Teacher

369.43 Boy Scouts

Blassingame, Wyatt

Story of the Boy Scouts; illus. by David Hodges. Garrard 1968 96p illus lib. bdg. $4.78 (4 and up)   369.43

1 Boy Scouts—History 2 Boy Scouts of America
ISBN 0-8116-6500-3   LC 68-13593

"Here is a book which should interest most young boys and certainly their scoutmasters. Mr. Blassingame successfully traces the beginnings of scouting in several nations, showing how various similar groups were eventually merged into the present-day Boy Scout organization. Several true stories of rescues, hiking, and even an Antarctic exploration are included, while helping others, attending jamborees, and working on conservation projects are portrayed as those activities of scouting which lead to international understanding and friendship. The lack of an index dampens neither the appeal of nor the need for this book, as the subjects until now [have] been covered solely in official Scout handbooks." Sch Library J

Boy Scouts of America

Bear Cub Scout book. The author illus pa $1.50 (3-4)   369.43

1 Boy Scouts—Handbooks, manuals, etc.

Sequel to: Wolf Cub Scout book, entered below
Copyright 1967. Frequently reprinted with minor revisions

This is a Cub book for the 9 year old Scout containing Cub literature and including a parents' supplement

Followed by: Webelos Scout book, entered below

Fieldbook; for Boy Scouts, explorers, scouters, educators, and outdoorsmen. [2d ed] The author 1967 565p illus maps flexible bdg. $3.35   369.43

1 Outdoor life
ISBN 0-8395-3201-6

First edition 1944 by James E. West and William Hillcourt published with title: Scout field book. Subtitle varies with reprintings

"This excellent guide covers hiking, camping, swimming, safety, and first aid, survival, nature, conservation, astronomy, weather, and many other topics. Illustrated with outstanding photographs on nearly every page, this book is not limited to use by Boy Scouts, but is universal in content and appeal. Following the explicit instructions, even an amateur could perform well. Well organized and easy to use, it contains an extensive bibliography and a detailed index." Peterson. Ref Bks for Elem and Jr High Sch Libraries

The official Boy Scout handbook. The author [distributed by Simon & Schuster] illus $9.95, pa $3   369.43

1 Boy Scouts—Handbooks, manuals, etc.

First published 1910 with title: Official handbook for boys. Frequently revised with varying titles. Ninth edition (1979) by William Hillcourt in association with the Boy Scouts of America

"Material on scouting, good citizenship, badge requirements, and opportunities in the organization is presented for members; but others can also benefit from information on camping, wildlife, first aid, signaling, and weather." Booklist [review of the ninth edition]

Webelos Scout book. The author illus pa $1.50 (4-5)   369.43

1 Boy Scouts—Handbooks, manuals, etc.

Sequel to: Bear Cub Scout book, entered above
Copyright 1967. Frequently reprinted with minor revisions

This handbook is designed for the 10 year old boy who is between Cub Scouting and Scouting and includes all the literature on the program

Boy Scouts of America—*Continued*
Wolf Cub Scout book. The author illus pa $1.25 (2-3)   **369.43**
1 Boy Scouts—Handbooks, manuals, etc.
Copyright 1967. Frequently reprinted with minor revisions
This handbook of Cub Scout information for the 8 year old includes a parents' supplement
Followed by: Bear Cub Scout book, entered above

369.463   Girl Scouts and Girl Guides

De Leeuw, Adèle
The Girl Scout story; illus. by Robert Doremus. Garrard 1965 95p illus lib. bdg. $4.78 (2-5)   **369.463**
1 Girl Scouts—History   2 Girl Scouts of the United States of America
ISBN 0-8116-6501-1   LC 65-14549
"A simply written history of the Girl Scout movement, stressing its importance in promoting international goodwill." Hodges. Bks for Elem Sch Libraries

Girl Scouts of the United States of America
Worlds to explore: handbook for Brownie and Junior Girl Scouts. The author 1977 392p illus pa $2.75   **369.463**
1 Girl Scouts—Handbooks, manuals, etc.
ISBN 0-88441-316-0   LC 77-152656
This handbook presents the history of girl scouting, the programs for Brownie and Junior Girl Scouts, and activities in 5 areas: the home, the world, the future, the arts and the out-of-doors

World Association of Girl Guides and Girl Scouts
Trefoil round the world; girl guiding and girl scouting in many lands. The author [distributed by the Girl Scouts of the United States of America] illus pa $4   **369.463**
1 Girl Scouts
ISBN 0-88441-362-4
First published 1958. Periodically revised
This history of girl scouting tells how the World Association of Girl Guides and Girl Scouts began, and includes words of promise and law, mottos, and programs of the 90 member countries

369.47   Camp Fire Girls

Camp Fire Girls, Inc.
Adventure. The author 1973 181p illus music pa $2.25 (4-6)   **369.47**
1 Camp Fire Girls—Handbooks, manuals, etc.
"Written by Laurie James. . . . Illustrated by Beth Charney." Verso of title page
This book outlines the Camp Fire Adventure program, its aims and activities, designed for girls in the 4th, 5th or 6th grades

The Blue Bird wish. The author 1970 64p illus music pa $1.75 (1-3)   **369.47**
1 Camp Fire Girls—Handbooks, manuals, etc.
"Written by Laurie James, illustrated by Margaret A. Hartelius." Verso of title page
This book is designed for six, seven or eight year old girls who want to be Blue Birds. It outlines the history of the organization and describes meetings and activities

The Camp Fire Blue Bird Series; written by Lila Phillips Walz; illus. by Margaret A. Hartelius. The author 1973 3v illus bk3 pa $2 (1-3)   **369.47**
1 Camp Fire Girls—Handbooks, manuals, etc.
Contents: bk. 1 It's all about me (o.p. 1980); bk.2 Here I am (o.p. 1980); bk.3 I can do lots of things
These three books include activities and projects designed for girls aged six, seven and eight

Discovery; written by Laurie James. The author 1971 95p illus music pa $2.95 (6 and up)   **369.47**
1 Camp Fire Girls—Handbooks, manuals, etc.
This book is designed for 7th and 8th grade girls who are members of the Discovery Club. It outlines the club's activities and aims as well as those of the national organization of Camp Fire Girls of which it is part

370.5   Education—Periodicals

Learning; magazine for creative teaching. Education Today Co. $14 per year   **370.5**
1 Education—Periodicals   2 Teaching—Periodicals
ISSN 0090-3167
Nine issues a year. First published 1972
This periodical is designed for "elementary and junior high school teachers looking for new ideas on how to teach. . . . Articles, usually by teachers, tell of successful curriculum planning, 'how-to-do-it' ideas, and methods of dealing with typical problems. A good feature: profiles and interviews with the world's leaders in education. Also, a concerted effort is made through the writings of well-known authorities to consider basic questions of education and society, e.g., there have been articles on drugs in the school, sexism, and a theory of values. In addition to book reviews, there are notes on new equipment and teaching materials. The magazine is lively, [and] well illustrated." Katz. Magazines for Libraries

Teacher. Macmillan Professional Magazines $15 per year   **370.5**
1 Education—Periodicals   2 Teaching—Periodicals
ISSN 0017-2782
Monthly except July and August (May-June combined issue). First published 1883. Publisher varies. Former title: Grade teacher
"Includes articles on all subject fields in elementary and junior high schools." Camp. Guide to Periodicals in Educ

371.3   Methods of instruction and study

Bell, Irene Wood
Basic media skills through games [by] Irene Wood Bell [and] Jeanne E. Wieckert; Warren G. Wieckert, illustrator. Libs. Unlimited 1979 242p illus $13.50   **371.3**
1 Instructional materials centers—Handbooks, manuals, etc.   2 Libraries and readers
ISBN 0-87287-194-0   LC 79-941
This is a book of 74 games designed to aid in teaching elementary school students the skills necessary to use an instructional materials center effectively. Topics covered by these games include the card catalog, the Dewey Decimal Classification, reference books, and the use of audiovisual equipment. Each game description includes instructions, materials, time required to play, grade level, method of checking, and illustrations of boards, cards or other necessary materials

Center for Understanding Media
Doing the media; a portfolio of activities, ideas and resources. New rev. ed. Edited by Kit Laybourne [and] Pauline Cianciolo. A.L.A. [1979 c1978] 212p illus lib. bdg. $15   **371.3**
1 Audio-visual education
ISBN 0-8389-0275-8   LC 78-9076
"A Dantree Press book"
First published 1972
"The work provides step-by-step instruction in the use of media through an emphasis on particular projects—from the creation of a storyboard to the production of a mixed media festival. Grouped under major sections on Photography, Film, Video, Sound, and Other Media, each of 17 chapters in the book concentrates on a single medium and suggests activities for its instructional use. Other chapters provide general guidance on introducing media into the classroom and on curriculum design. A resource list of books and nonprint materials, periodicals, organizations, and media distributors is also included." Publisher's note

Hug, William E.
Instructional design and the media program
A.L.A. 1975 148p illus pa $6.50 **371.3**

1 Audio-visual education 2 Instructional materials centers
ISBN 0-8389-0207-3 LC 75-40425

"A foundation for organizing a school media program and coordinating it with the curriculum is established by this publication. Information as an educational utility, knowledge, general curriculum movements, and systems designs are related for the development of school media programs. Functions, responsibilities, and goals are analyzed schematically in the work to make the media program both an effective, self-contained unit and a component of the instructional program. . . . Discussion questions and sample learning activities are presented at the end of each chapter." Publisher's note

Kemp, Jerrold E.
Planning and producing audiovisual materials, by Jerrold E. Kemp with the assistance of Ron Carraher, Richard F. Szumski [and] Willard R. Card. 3d ed. Crowell 1975 320p illus $14.95 **371.3**

1 Audio-visual materials 2 Audio-visual education
ISBN 0-690-00805-8 LC 75-16470

First published 1963 by Chandler Publishing Company
"This book is designed to provide information and experiences that will enable the reader to gain competencies relative to. . .selecting the most appropriate medium to serve instructional needs for group teaching or individualized learning; applying necessary planning steps prior to production; using fundamental skills in photography, graphics, and sound recording for preparing materials; applying techniqques for producing photographic print series, slide series, filmstrips, overhead transparencies, tape recordings, motion pictures, visual materials for television, and multi-image/multimedia materials." Preface
Appendices include: Correlated still/motion super-8 mm films; Books, films, pamphlets, and periodicals; Sources for equipment and materials; Services; Glossary

Media programs: district and school. Prepared by the American Association of School Librarians, ALA, and Association for Educational Communications and Technology. A.L.A./Assn. for Educational Communications & Technology 1975 128p pa $2.95 **371.3**

1 Audio-visual education 2 Audio-visual materials 3 Instructional materials centers
ISBN 0-8389-3159-6 LC 74-32316

Replaces: Standards for school media programs
This book "delineates guidelines and recommendations for media programs and resources essential for quality education. . . . It describes programs designed to respond to both district and school objectives and reflects the vital interrelationships between those operations. The quantitative statements that follow provide corresponding standards for the staff, collections, and facilities that are required to implement the programs. . . . [The] recommendations are based on a module of 250 students and multiples thereof." Introduction
Terminology: p109-13

Nardini, Mary Lois
Fundamentals of bulletin board design; 123 bulletin board ideas for teachers; designed for opaque projector tracing by Mary Lois Nardini and Patricia Quinett. Denison 1979 155p illus spiral bdg. $7.95 **371.3**

1 Bulletin boards
ISBN 0-513-01659-7 LC 78-75212

This book provides practical suggestions for creating bulletin boards. Topics covered include idea files, resources and materials; line drawings, flat pictures and lettering; captions, color schemes and layout. Sample designs for various subject areas are illustrated and described

Thomas, James L.
Turning kids on to print using nonprint; illus. by Carol H. Thomas, and photographs by James L. Thomas. Libs. Unlimited 1978 168p illus $11.50 **371.3**

1 Audio-visual education
ISBN 0-87287-184-3 LC 78-9075

This discussion of student AV media production starts with a chapter on "storyboarding" and goes on to demonstrate the procedures involved in planning and producing simple projects in various media. "Each chapter is systematically arranged for easy reading so that at a glance the reader can determine 1) the specific objectives of the process, 2) the strategies to be used in winning over the student, 3) the definition of any terms which the reader might not be familiar with, 4) the materials to be used and the maximum costs expected, 5) the exact step by step procedure to use in producing the item, 6) a sample format from an actual graphic produced by students, 7) suggested follow-up activities, 8) a bibliography with page references for further information, and 9) a list of possible suppliers of the equipment and software items used in each production." Introduction

Weisburg, Hilda K.
Elementary school librarian's almanac; a complete media program for every month of the school year [by] Hilda K. Weisburg [and] Ruth Toor. Center for Applied Res. in Educ. 1979 286p illus $22.95 **371.3**

1 Audio-visual education 2 Audio-visual materials 3 Instructional materials centers
ISBN 0-87628-299-0 LC 78-31808

Designed as a tool for library media specialists, this book provides suggestions for programs from September through June. It includes birthdates of famous authors and illustrators, ideas for bulletin boards, library art activities, storytelling suggestions, library skills teaching units and games, descriptions of areas of professional responsibility, and other practical advice for dealing with audio-visual materials

371.3025 Methods of instruction and study—Directories

Audiovisual market place; a multimedia guide. Bowker illus pa $23.50 **371.3025**

1 Audio-visual materials—Directories
ISSN 0067-0553 LC 69-18201

Annual. First published 1969
At head of title: AVMP
This is a listing of audio-visual hardware and software resources that includes producers, distributors, production companies, production services, cataloging services, equipment manufacturers and dealers, a calendar of exhibitions and conferences, associations, reference books and directories, awards and festivals, a glossary

371.305 Methods of instruction and study—Periodicals

Instructional Innovator. Assn. for Educational Communications and Technology $18 per year **371.305**

1 Audio-visual education—Periodicals
ISSN 0106-6979

Formerly published with title: Audio Visual Instruction
Monthly September through May. First published 1956
"Includes articles, reports, and other information intended to help improve instruction through more effective use of audio-visual materials and technology. Each issue contains articles devoted to a single theme. . . . Ten to fifteen major articles are published per issue. Book and film reviews are included." Camp Guide to Periodicals in Educ
The "exploration of themes . . . is complemented by departments and features on new products, research notes, copyright, new books, etc. . . . A good format and lively writing style make this a required item for most libraries." Katz. Magazines for Libraries. 3d edition

Media & methods; exploration in education. North American Pub. Co. $11 per year
371.305

1 Audio-visual education—Periodicals 2 Teaching
—Periodicals
ISSN 0025-6897

9 issues a year September through May. First published 1965
This "is a first choice for any library, and while of primary interest to the schools, should be considered by public libraries too. Teachers are primary contributors, tend to write articles which shakeup the established view of education. There is a great emphasis on new approaches to learning. And while a good deal of the material covers films, video, television, etc., there are usually one or two articles on the book. In fact, the book is never forgotten, and what makes this magazine fascinating is that it can stress audiovisual without resorting to dumping everything for the machine. Nor is it all pie in the sky. The articles tend to be practical, give down to earth hints on materials, methods and practices. There are regular departments which review both feature and educational films, television programs, recordings, tapes, books, etc." Katz. Magazines for Libraries. 2d edition

371.905   Special education— Periodicals

Exceptional Children. Council for Exceptional Children $20 per year
371.905

1 Exceptional children—Education—Periodicals
ISSN 0014-4029

Monthly October through May. First published 1934
"Covers not only the bright child and his or her other educational problems but is concerned with any exceptional child, i.e., handicapped psychologically or physiologically. Experienced educators and teachers contribute articles on planning curriculum, classroom hints, organization of programs, and report on current developments in all areas; also included are information on new teaching aids, news notes, a calendar of events, and some book reviews." Katz. Magazines for libraries. 3d edition

372.05   Elementary education— Periodicals

Childhood Education; a journal for teachers, administrators, church-school workers, librarians, pediatricians. Assn. for Childhood Educ. $18 per year
372.05

1 Education, Elementary—Periodicals
ISSN 0009-4056

Monthly September through May. First published 1924
"This journal, while covering many aspects of childhood education in scholarly articles, contains sections of book reviews. The rather long reviews are arranged by broad subjects in the curriculum." Peterson. Ref Bks for Elem and Jr High Sch Libraries

Early Years; a magazine for teachers of preschool through grade three. Allen Raymond $11 per year
372.05

1 Education, Elementary—Periodicals 2 Education, Preschool—Periodicals
ISSN 0094-6532

Nine issues a year. First published 1971
"Edited for teachers at the preschool through third-grade level, this periodical . . . has . . . 'how-to-do-it' articles written by and for teachers, feature articles on developments in eductaion, notes on federal and state legislation, and just about anything to make the teacher's life a bit easier. Good book reviews and descriptive notes on new materials and equipment." Katz. Magazines for Libraries. 3d edition

Instructor. Instructor Publications $14 per year
372.05

1 Education, Elementary—Periodicals 2 Teaching —Periodicals
ISSN 0020-4285

Nine times yearly with May/June and August/September issues. First published 1891
"Directed primarily to the elementary school teacher, principal, and special staff. The large, colorful format is familiar to almost any librarian or teacher. Each issue includes articles 'dealing with trends in educational theory and practice, and sections on arts and crafts and teaching suggestions for all subjects.' Each area is supplemented with diagrams, illustrations, and photographs." Katz Magazines for Libraries

372.1   Generalities of elementary education

Blake, Jim
The great perpetual learning machine; being a stupendous collection of ideas, games, experiments, activities, and recommendations for further exploration, by Jim Blake and Barbara Ernst; with tons of illustrations. Little [1977 c1976] 308p illus $12.95, pa $7.95
372.1

1 Education, Elementary 2 Education, Preschool 3 Children's literature—Bibliography
ISBN 0-316-09938-4; 0-396-09937-6   LC 76-24124

"This source book—organized around general subject categories of nature and ecology, mathematics, arts and crafts, music and movement, ourselves, and language—introduces ideas, evaluates juvenile trade books and materials, and suggests additional relevant topics for motivating children. Each large topic is subdivided: under Nature and Ecology, for example, there are General Resources, Animals, Plants, Our Planet Earth, and Astronomy." Booklist
"Chock full of photos, drawings, and diagrams and includes detailed bibliographies (with publisher's addresses and prices) of text books, children's books, handbooks, and manuals. There is also an index. Fascinating browsing and certain to make teaching interesting and learning fun." Children's Bk Rev Serv

I saw a purple cow, and 100 other recipes for learning, by Ann Cole [and others]; illus. by True Kelley. Little 1972 96p illus $7.95, pa $4.95
372.1

1 Education, Preschool
ISBN 0-316-15174-2; 0-316-15175-0   LC 72-404

This book "is geared to the important first six years of children's lives and attempts to help the untrained mother during this period. The table of contents is keyed to indicate which activities are appropriate for such special situations as 'Sick in bed,' 'Traveling or waiting,' 'Math readiness,' and 'Reading readiness.' Especially needed is the section entitled 'The Basics' which gives recipes for paste, finger paint, fun dough, and cornstarch clay. The authors show how such simple ideas as a stroll around the block or a visit to the supermarket can be good learning-by-observing experiences. The helpful section on music and rhythm includes dramatic games and simple instructions for more advanced projects. Ideas for party decorations, food, and games that young children can help prepare are included. The illustrations are busy but add to the text." Sch Library J

Mulac, Margaret E.
Educational games for fun. Harper 1971 180p $10.95
372.1

1 Games 2 Education, Elementary
ISBN 0-06-013099-7   LC 77-138752

"A collection of individual and team games primarily for children of elementary school age, including exercises in math, spelling, history, geography, nature, and science, and a variety of word games. Each game is graded and the suggested variations range from simple to more difficult forms. While intended for use by both teachers and recreational leaders the material is largely didactic in substance and will be more useful for classroom diversion than as party fun." Booklist

372.4 Reading

McGuffey, William H.
Old favorites from the McGuffey readers, 1836-1936; ed. by Harvey C. Minnich; associate editors: Henry Ford [and others]. Singing Tree [1969 c1936] 482p $12   **372.4**
1 Reading materials
ISBN 0-8103-3854-8   LC 79-76081
First published 1936 by the American Book Company
This "is an anthology of selections from the famous Readers which substituted healthy if preachy morality for the gloomy theological selections of the day." Booklist

372.405 Reading—Periodicals

The **Reading** Teacher. Int. Reading Assn. $25 per year   **372.405**
1 Reading—Periodicals
ISSN 0034-0561
8 issues a year October through May. First published 1947
"Deals with all aspects of the teaching of elementary and secondary reading, but concentrates on the elementary level. Each issue carries signed articles which range from scholarly studies of reading habits to semi-popular contributions on the woes and joys of teaching the subject. Regular departments include notes on current research, magazine articles and books worth examining, a list of materials particularly suited for children, 'Crossfire,' 'Interchange,' 'Critically Speaking,' 'ERIC/CRIER' and 'The Membership Card.' Particularly useful for the teacher who is searching for new methods of improving reading." Katz. Magazines for Libraries

372.6 Language arts (Communication skills). Storytelling

Baker, Augusta
Storytelling: art and technique by Augusta Baker and Ellin Greene. Bowker 1977 142p illus pa $8.25   **372.6**
1 Storytelling
ISBN 0-8352-0840-0   LC 77-16481
"More basic and limited in scope than Pellowski's 'World of Storytelling.' [entered below] is Baker and Greene's practical manual for school and public librarians. Range of information includes a brief history of storytelling as practiced in the U.S., purpose and value of storytelling, types of literature usable, basic techniques of preparation and presentation, program planning with sample story hours, administration of programs. Appendid are practical guidelines for in-service sessions and sources for the storyteller (an extensive bibliography of stories, recordings, and books about storytelling). Numerous examples interspersed throughout make this a worthwhile guide." Booklist
"This book was written primarily for librarians serving children in public and school libraries, but teachers, recreation workers, and other adults interested in the art of storytelling also will find it helpful. Our emphasis throughout is on storytelling as an oral art." Preface
Sources for the storyteller: p113-33. Glossary: p134-35.

Bauer, Caroline Feller
Handbook for story tellers. A.L.A. 1977 381p illus music $15, pa $8.50   **372.6**
1 Storytelling—Handbooks, manuals, etc.
ISBN 0-8389-0225-1; 0-8389-0293-6   LC 76-56385
"Design by Vladimir Reichl. Pen-and-ink drawings by Kevin Royt"
"Bauer presents multitudinous simple but ingenious ideas for the storyteller—magnetic boards, puppets, paper cut-outs, videotapes, picture posters, costumes, favors, music, and much more. Divided into four parts, the book covers (1) planning, preparation, and promotion; (2) sources for storytelling; (3) multimedia storytelling; and (4) programs for specific age and interest groups. This volume complements other works in the field, such as Ruth Sawyer's 'The way of the storyteller,' Marie Shedlock's 'The art of the storyteller,' and Sylvia Ziskind's 'Telling stories to children,' [all entered below]. It expands upon these basic works by adding multimedia storytelling techniques and a great variety of mechanical aids, as well as illustrations and examples of appropriate materials. The excellent bibliographies, placed at the end of each chapter would be more useful if combined at the end of the book or if indexed." Choice

Carlson, Bernice Wells
Listen! And help tell the story; illus. by Burmah Burris. Abingdon 1965 176p illus $6.50   **372.6**
1 Storytelling 2 Literature—Collections
ISBN 0-687-22096-3   LC 65-14090
"Pre-schoolers learn first to listen and then to participate in these finger-plays, action verses and poems with sound effects and choruses which may be used with either a single child or any sized group." Ontario
"Though Miss Carlson states that the book is for the child's own use, its basic value will be to teachers and parents. . . . The art work is uneven in quality but has the merit of showing racial integration." Sch Library J

De Wit, Dorothy
Children's faces looking up; program building for the storyteller. A.L.A. 1979 156p $11   **372.6**
1 Storytelling
ISBN 0-8389-0272-3   LC 78-10702
"A valuable guide for new storytellers who want to enrich their programming with imaginative themes. Discussion of storytelling's evolution, a definition of the tellable tale, and recognition of quality material precede the six sample programs. These center on motifs such as magic, holidays, animals, and feasting. An extensive bibliography of sources is appended." Booklist
Bibliography: p133-49

It's time for story hour; comp. by Elizabeth Hough Sechrist and Janette Woolsey; illus. by Elsie Jane McCorkell. Macrae Smith Co. 1964 258p illus lib. bdg. $6.97   **372.6**
1 Storytelling 2 Literature—Collections
ISBN 0-8255-8211-3   LC 64-23918
"A fine anthology of 40 stories—some humorous, some romantic, and others about strange happenings —which the [editors] . . . have found from their own experience as storytellers to be favorites with children. Enjoyable for individual reading and particularly suitable for library storytelling and for reading aloud. Illustrated with attractive line drawings." Booklist

Juba this and Juba that; story hour stretches for large or small groups; selected by Virginia A. Tashjian; with illustrations by Victoria de Larrea. Little 1969 116p illus $6.95   **372.6**
1 Storytelling 2 Literature—Collections
ISBN 0-316-83230-8   LC 69-10666
"A useful source of chants, poetry and rhyme, stories, finger plays, riddles, songs, tongue twisters, and jokes. The selections accompanied by lively orange and black illustrations, are all suitably silly. They require and inspire audience participation." Sch Library J
"The short, funny tales and games are guaranteed to dispel restlessness, relax listeners, and add variety to any story hour. The illustrations are as full of fun and nonsense as the book." Horn Bk

Moore, Vardine
Pre-school story hour. 2d ed. Scarecrow 1972 174p illus $7   **372.6**
1 Storytelling
ISBN 0-8108-0474-3   LC 78-188549
First published 1966
This book discusses "some of the essentials required to relate a story and conduct a program; story hour location; some recommended physical arrangements; practical measures to deal with the perennial problem of what to do with parents; specific techniques and examples of program planning and extended activities; what makes a story good to tell, in terms of subject and interest areas, type of material, format, and design of the books; and an extensive bibliography of recommended

Moore, Vardine—*Continued*
stories and 'related activities.' In the last, the author details a short but effective collection of finger plays, action stories and games with an appended list of recommended books and recordings." Sch Library J

"Even experienced storytellers can benefit from the inspiration and practical advice covering all aspects of this recognized important type of programming." ALA. CSD. Mother Hubbard's cupboard [review of 1966 edition]

Pellowski, Anne
The world of storytelling. Bowker [1978 c1977] 296p illus $15.95   **372.6**
1 Storytelling
ISBN 0-8352-1024-3   LC 77-16492
The author provides a history of storytelling, including discussion of types of storytelling format and style, the training of storytellers, and a multilingual dictionary of storytelling terms
Bibliography: p259-79

Ross, Eulalie Steinmetz
(ed.) The lost half-hour; a collection of stories; illus. by Enrico Arno. Harcourt 1963 191p illus $5.95   **372.6**
1 Storytelling 2 Literature—Collections 3 Folklore
ISBN 0-15-249360-3   LC 65-23537
The editor "has told all seventeen of these stories [many of which are folk tales] again and again to children. . . . They are not difficult for the beginning storyteller to prepare, and their success with children has been proved. . . . Concluding the book is a valuable and practical essay on storytelling." Horn Bk

Sawyer, Ruth
The way of the storyteller. Penguin [1977 c1962] 356p illus pa $3.95   **372.6**
1 Storytelling 2 Literature—Collections
ISBN 0-14-004436-1   LC 76-48214
First published 1942 by Viking
"This is not primarily a book on how to tell stories; it is rather the whole philosophy of story telling as a creative art. From her own rich experience the author writes inspiringly of the background, experience, creative imagination, technique and selection essential to this art." Booklist
"This book is the expression of a generous spirit. . . . The book will appeal to the creative artist in any field. The storyteller will welcome the group of [eleven] selected stories for telling and the reading lists which reflect the range and variety of the author's interests." NY Pub Library
Bibliography: p334-39

Shedlock, Marie L.
The art of the story-teller; foreword by Anne Carroll Moore. 3d ed. rev. with a new bibliography by Eulalie Steinmetz. Dover 1951 xxi, 290p front pa $3.50   **372.6**
1 Storytelling 2 Literature—Collections
ISBN 0-486-20635-1   LC 52-9976
First published 1915
"Suggestions for selecting and for telling stories are included as well as eighteen of Miss Shedlock's own favorites." Horn Bk

Siks, Geraldine Brain
Drama with children. Harper 1977 252p illus $10.95   **372.6**
1 Drama in education
ISBN 0-06-046151-9   LC 76-43301
The author "demonstrates how drama (playacting, role playing, improvisation, etc.) can be incorporated into the basic educational program of an elementary school. The book is divided into three parts: 'Drama in education,' 'Teaching the art of drama,' and 'Teaching through drama.' Each chapter includes concrete examples of how the activities have been and can be effectively practiced. (For such presentations, composite accounts from actual reports, tapes, etc. are used.) Extremely valuable for drama students who plan to teach, it will also greatly help experienced teachers seeking new approaches in their methodology. Some first-hand accounts of successful experiences with special groups, e.g., religious classes, the physically handicapped, are included. A selective, but excellent bibliography, index, and three short plays conclude the volume." Choice

Stories to dramatize; selected and ed. by Winifred Ward. The Children's Theatre Press 1952 389p $6   **372.6**
1 Drama in education 2 Literature—Collections
LC 52-11569
"This excellent collection of stories, chosen from classic and modern literature, is arranged by age levels from kindergarten through junior high school. There are suggestions for evaluating stories for dramatization and pointers on dramatizing them. Useful to camp counselors and recreation leaders as well as teachers of creative dramatics." Booklist
Bibliography: p381-83. Some good books for integrated projects: p384-86

With a deep sea smile; story hour stretches for large or small groups; selected by Virginia A. Tashjian; illus. by Rosemary Wells. Little 1974 132p illus music $6.95   **372.6**
1 Storytelling 2 Literature—Collections
ISBN 0-316-83216-2   LC 72-8874
This is a collection of chants, poetry, rhymes, stories, finger plays, riddles, songs, tongue twisters and jokes planned for use as story hour activities. They are taken from a wide variety of sources
"Hints are offered on using the material. Prefacing each selection, and of even greater value, are specific suggestions for stimulating participation. Lively illustrations capture the fun of the contents, making the book attractive to children as well as to adults." Horn Bk
Includes an index of titles

Ziskind, Sylvia
Telling stories to children. Wilson, H.W. 1976 162p $10   **372.6**
1 Storytelling
ISBN 0-8242-0588-X   LC 75-42003
A basic introduction. "Guidelines on selecting stories stress the importance of being comfortable with the tale; carefully kept file cards are suggested as a key to fastening the story firmly in mind. There's advice on presenting poetry and using creative dramatics; and a chapter on planning the story hour provides sample introductions and run-throughs for several age groups and audience types. Throughout, there are numerous examples of stories and poems that have worked well for Ziskind, and her extensive bibliography includes source collections of both poetry and stories plus lists of personal favorites. Professional materials on voice and speech, creative dramatics, and puppetry, as well as foreign-language story books, are also listed." Booklist
Bibliography: p113-57

380.5 Transportation

Billout, Guy
By camel or by car; a look at transportation. Prentice-Hall 1979 unp illus lib. bdg. $7.95 (1-4)   **380.5**
1 Transportation
ISBN 0-13-109603-6   LC 78-26120
"The illustrations in Guy Billout's picture book on transportation are wonderful: clear, simple nearly to the point of austere yet meticulous in detail, with a bold use of color, and a linear perspective that is long and expansive. . . . Opposite each drawing is a page with a short factual paragraph on the particular mode of transportation, followed by a paragraph of personal memories or sentiments, sometimes relating to his coming to the United States from France or to his experiences in the war. While the personal touch is interesting and vivid, it may not easily be understood by the very young and is not written in a vocabulary they readily could comprehend. But this matters not, as the illustrations redeem all and even young children will enjoy them." Sch Library J

Hellman, Hal
Transportation in the world of the future. New, rev. ed. Evans, M.&Co. 1974 187p $6.95 (5 and up)   **380.5**
1 Transportation
ISBN 0-87131-155-0   LC 73-86220

Hellman, Hal—*Continued*

First published 1968
This discussion of the function and operation of a variety of vehicles that may be in use in the future includes chapters on rail rapid transit, high speed ground transportation, tunnels and tubes, the electric car and aircraft
Bibliography: p177-80

Hofsinde, Robert

Indians on the move; written and illus. by Robert Hofsinde (Gray-Wolf). Morrow 1970 95p illus lib. bdg. $6.48 (4-6)   **380.5**

1 Indians of North America—Social life and customs 2 Transportation
ISBN 0-688-31615-8   LC 72-102191

"A concise, readable introduction to Indian modes of travel presented in clear, simple text, drawings, and diagrams. . . . [The author] discusses the daily, seasonal, and migratory movement of various tribes, the design and construction of equipment used to transport people and goods, and the tribal customs and environmental circumstances that influenced type and method of transportation. He concludes with a chapter on Indian travel today." Booklist

381 Internal commerce (Domestic trade)

Schwartz, Alvin

Stores; photographs by Samuel Nocella, Jr. Macmillan Pub. Co. 1977 106p illus $7.95 (3-6)   **381**

1 Retail trade
ISBN 0-02-781310-X   LC 76-47451

"The author focuses on 37 of the more than 300 stores in his home town of Princeton, N. J. Beginning at the beginning of a working day he describes what each store does and how it is done. At the Acme supermarket it is midnight when four men start to unpack and mark the produce for the next day. At the Baltic Bakery the night kitchen is bright as the bakers begin beating batter at 3 A.M. The text is straightforward, succinct, filled with answers to the kind of questions children ask and adults fumble: how eyeglasses are made, how gas is pumped, etc." NY Times Bk Rev
"The pleasant photos and personalized text which is chock full of extras (e.g., how to read medicine prescriptions; a recipe for 'The Big Bux' Banana split) make this far more entertaining than typical career information guides." Sch Library J

382.09 International commerce (Foreign trade)—History

Tamarin, Alfred

Voyaging to Cathay; Americans in the China trade [by] Alfred Tamarin and Shirley Glubok. Viking 1976 202p illus maps $10 (5 and up)   **382.09**

1 U.S.—Commerce—History 2 China—Commerce —History
ISBN 0-670-74857-9   LC 75-14415

This book describes the growth of the trade between the United States and China from the years following the American Revolution through the era of clipper ships
"The days of the China clippers and worldwide piracy come alive in this carefully researched and skillfully written history. The distinctions of the various types of teas and ships and the steps in making Chinaware are especially informative. The regrettable aspects of the China trade—opium smuggling and the wholesale slaughter of sea otters and fur seals—are also treated without moralizing. The fascinating paintings, engravings, maps, reproductions of porcelain pieces and other objects make up almost half of the book." Sch Library J
Includes bibliography

382.9 Trade agreements and their implementation

Rothkopf, Carol Z.

The common market; uniting the European community, by Carol Z. Rothkopf and David J. Rothkopf. Watts, F. 1977 85p illus maps lib. bdg. $4.90 (5 and up)   **382.9**

1 European Economic Community
ISBN 0-531-01272-7   LC 77-3732

"An Impact book"
"An introduction to the nine-member European Economic Community, otherwise known as the Common Market, scans its history and reviews its efforts toward unifying Europe. The authors explain the working structure of the organization, briefly survey its commercial and scientific policies and goals, and measure its achievements against Europe's current background of economic instability, political discord, and intense nationalism." Booklist
"Maps, contemporary photographs, a useful list of European organizations, and a chronology of important dates round out the coverage which is concise and informative." Sch Library J

383 Postal communication

Adams, Samuel Hopkins

The pony express; illus. by Lee J. Ames. Random House 1950 185p illus lib. bdg. $5.99 (5 and up)   **383**

1 Pony express 2 The West (U.S.)—History
ISBN 0-394-90307-2   LC 50-10533

"Landmark books"
"All the excitement of Indian attacks, holdups by outlaws, and buffeting by storms is caught in this story of the riders who carried the mail from Missouri to California." Hodges. Bks for Elem Sch Libraries
Map on lining-papers

Pinkerton, Robert

The first overland mail; illus. by Paul Lantz. Random House 1953 185p illus lib. bdg. $5.99 (5 and up)   **383**

1 Postal service—U.S. 2 Butterfield, John
ISBN 0-394-90340-4   LC 53-6259

"Landmark books"
"A narrative history of the first overland delivery of mail by stagecoach from Misouri to California, and of John Butterfield—the man who undertook the impossible—to cover the 2,800 mile route in 25 days—and succeeded." Booklist

384.55 Television

Jones, Eurfron Gwynne

Television magic. Viking 1978 61p illus $5.95 (4 and up)   **384.55**

1 Television 2 Television—Production and direction 3 Television broadcasting
ISBN 0-670-69514-9   LC 78-2225

Editor: Ruth Thomson, Art editor: Joanna Dale
The "books in this series originating in England are simply chock-a-block with facts, illustrations, clear diagrams, and interesting projects and experiments outlined in red. All follow the same format, with 29 topics each covered in a double page spread. . . . [This volume] includes everything from the techniques of production to TV equipment to the amazing complexities of sending color pictures through the air. Some of the possibilities mentioned are realities already, e.g., electronic games to play on the home TV set. Sample projects include: making a 'whirlen' to fool the eye, trying out lighting effects, and arranging a sequence of stills to tell a story." Sch Library J

385   Railroad transportation

Navarra, John Gabriel
Supertrains. Doubleday 1976 79p illus lib.
bdg. $7.95 (3-6)   **385**

1 Railroads
ISBN 0-385-02024-4   LC 74-18820

"The author discusses the growing need for public transportation systems which are fast, convenient, and comfortable—compatible with other requirements, such as preserving the countryside and
reducing pollution. We learn with interest what
is being done to provide transportation via superb
trains in Japan, France and other countries. We
also find that inflation has killed many exciting
plans for the construction of effective systems."
Pub W

"Although some of the topics are treated so
briefly (a page or two of text) that they leave
questions unanswered, the book is on the whole
informative and the prospects it raises are exciting." Chicago. Children's Bk Center

Sattler, Helen Roney
Train whistles; language in code; illus. by
Tom Funk. Lothrop 1977 31p illus $8.25, lib.
bdg. $7.92 (k-1)   **385**

1 Railroads—Signaling 2 Locomotives
ISBN 0-688-41808-2; 0-688-51808-7   LC 77-2163

"How whistle codes function to communicate with
the train's crew, with animals, people, and with
other trains is explained. . . . Along with the
meaning of the signals (two longs, one short, and
another long indicates that a train is coming down
the track) interesting facts about railroad personnel and procedures are included. Funk's yellow,
red, and black drawings of trains en route and
amiable children, pets, and adults will attract and
hold pre-schoolers' attention. Informative and entertaining." Sch Library J

385.09   Railroad transportation—
History

Ault, Phil
"All aboard!" The story of passenger trains
in America; illus. with photographs and old
prints. Dodd 1976 183p illus maps $5.95 (5 and
up)   **385.09**

1 Railroads—History
ISBN 0-396-07350-6   LC 76-12505

This "informal history focuses on the amenities,
discomforts and dangers of American passenger
trains. The 20th-Century Limited, a luxury train
of the 1930's, is highlighted in the opening chapters, and colorful accounts by Greeley, Nordhoff,
Stevenson, and Dickens stoke authenticity into
descriptions of 19th-Century train travel. There
are stories about private, 'whistle-stop,' circus,
funeral, excursion, 'milk-shake,' and local trains
as well as train wrecks, robberies, and rescues.
Ault ends with the arrival of diesels and Amtrak,
and the conversion of stations into restaurants,
schools, and even a winery." Sch Library J
Acknowledgments and bibliography: p179-80

Fisher, Leonard Everett
The railroads; written and illus. by Leonard
Everett Fisher. Holiday House 1979 62p illus
map (Nineteenth century America) lib.
bdg. $6.95 (5 and up)   **385.09**

1 Railroads—History
ISBN 0-8234-0352-1   LC 79-1458

This book "tells how the coming of the railroads
changed America forever during the 1800s. Readers
discover that linking the country via transconti-
nental tracks involved violence as well as progress.
Indians whose lands were usurped by the iron
horse were incited to bloody warfare; bandits made
careers of robbing the trains; tycoons built fortunes just as illegally if less flagrantly as the
marauding James brothers, the Reno gang and
other outlaws." Pub W

"Intricate, precisely worked woodcuts set a
powerful, even awesome tone." Booklist

Snow, Richard F.
The iron road; a portrait of American rail-
roading. Text by Richard Snow; photographs
by David Plowden. Four Winds 1978 90p illus
lib. bdg. $9.95 (6 and up)   **385.09**

1 Railroads—History
ISBN 0-590-07523-3   LC 78-5388

"An anecdotal history of the invention and development of trains and tracks in the U.S. Snow
provides [a] perspective by comparing the early
U.S. railroad to its counterpart in England. The
role played by the railroad in the 19th Century is
described including its part in the Civil War. The
evolution of the steam locomotive is described as
are the railroad's opponents. Cross country expansion and the rivalries between the Chinese and
the Irish immigrants are also covered as well as
the activities of railroad freeloaders, hoboes, and
profit-hungry robber barons. . . . The status of
the railroad in the 20th Century and its future is
evaluated." Sch Library J

"From the photograph on the front of the jacket
. . . to the photograph on the back . . . you have
all the magic and beauty of the American train,
properly dedicated to 'the railroad men who built
the iron road and who run it today.' It's all in
black and white, and the selection of photographs
is superb." NY Times Bk Rev

386   Inland waterway and
ferry transportation

Franchere, Ruth
Westward by canal. Macmillan Pub. Co. 1972
149p illus map $4.95 (5 and up)   **386**

1 Canals—History 2 U.S.—History—1783-1865
ISBN 0-02-735700-7   LC 71-185217

"Map by Rafael Palacios." Verso of title page
"In a lively and informative account of the beginning of the canal era, the author describes the construction of the canals, the people who initiated the
plans and those who took part in the digging, and
the life on and around the waterways. The canal
era, a brief but important period in this country's
history, is treated as an influential factor in the
westward migration from the crowded eastern
seaboard and in the mass emigration from other
countries to this land." Top of the News
For further reading: p145-46

387.1   Ports. Lighthouses

Berenstain, Michael
The lighthouse book. McKay 1979 unp illus
$6.95 (2-4)   **387.1**

1 Lighthouses
ISBN 0-679-20777-5   LC 78-23175

"This combines black-and-white drawings on
every page with a brief text touching on the
history, construction, and function of lighthouses.
Several illustrations are cutaway exposures of
buildings, and the writer is straightforwardly informative. While there are other books on lighthouses available, none of them really focuses on
this age group, in transition from picture books to
more in-depth coverage, as Merenstain does."
Booklist

Smith, Arthur
Lighthouses; written and illus. by Arthur
Smith. Houghton 1971 146p illus $4.95 (5 and
up)   **387.1**

1 Lighthouses
ISBN 0-395-12371-2   LC 79-98515

"From the ancient beacons guiding ships in the
Mediterranean Sea, this delightful book proceeds
to describe in words and pictures the individual
United States lighthouses from Maine to Florida
on the Atlantic Coast, from California to Alaska
on the Pacific Coast, in the Hawaiian Islands, and
on to Midway and Guam before coming back to
the lighthouses on those fresh water giants—
the Great Lakes. The writing style combines
history, technology, geography, sea lore, and anecdotes to hold the reader's interest and attention. . . . The book is certainly useful for collateral reading in seafaring history, construction
methodology, and United States geography." Sci
Bks

387.2 Ships

Berenstain, Michael
The ship book. McKay 1978 unp illus $6.95
(k-3)   387.2
1 Ships—History
ISBN 0-679-20449-0   LC 77-14915

"Beginning with an explanation of how sailing
ships evolved from primitive times when humans
learned to navigate on floating logs, the text and
pictures go on to cover the majestic seagoing vessels of later eras. Readers learn about boats manned
by ancient Egyptians, the galleys connected with
the conquering Romans, Columbus's ships, the
Spanish Armada and other historic ships." Pub W

"Berenstain gives much basic information in a
fluid style that does not suffer when spanning eras
or nations. By far the most interesting portion
of the book deals with a description of the 'U.S.S.
Constitution,' with cutaway diagrams and a recounting of duties aboard ship. Black-and-white
drawings add much to the text to produce a worthy
book for basic information." Sch Library J

Colby, C. B.
Sailing ships; great ships before the age
of steam. Coward-McCann 1970 48p illus lib.
bdg. $5.29 (3-6)   387.2
1 Ships—History
ISBN 0-698-30301-6   LC 70-97608

A pictorial history of sailing ships of all types,
from all ages. The illustrations range from ship
models at the Smithsonian to restored ships at
Mystic, Connecticut, to contemporary crafts. Information about rigging, masts, and sails is included

Knight, Frank
Ships. Crowell-Collier Press [1971 c1969]
63p illus $4.95 (5 and up)   387.2
1 Ships—History
ISBN 0-02-75089-0   LC 70-124418

First published 1969 in England

"Brisk text copiously illustrated with black-and-
white and colored photographs traces the evolution of water transport in reverse chronological
order beginning with nuclear submarines and
specialized cargo carriers of today and going back
through the eras of steam and sail to the galleys
of ancient Rome and the dugout canoes and basket
boats of primitive man. Although broad rather than
thorough in coverage, the book contains many
enlightening historical facts which highlight some
of the social, economic, and practical considerations
as well as technological advances that affected the
development and use of ships." Booklist

"Though the photographs and reproductions are
small, they are excellent and numerous, many in
full color, with explanatory notes. In fact, the
illustrations are worth the price of the book because there are few volumes with such visual appeal for this age level." Sch Library J

Lasky, Kathryn
Tall ships; photographs by Christopher G.
Knight. Scribner 1978 64p illus $9.95 (5 and
up)   387.2
1 Ships 2 Seafaring life
ISBN 0-684-15964-3   LC 78-14580

"Focusing initially on 'Operation Sail,' the race
from Plymouth, England, to Newport, Rhode
Island, in celebration of America's bicentennial, the
book recreates . . . the era when the great clipper ships 'followed the wind routes of the water
world to China, Australia, and India to bring home
the goods Americans wanted.'" Horn Bk

"Using information from old diaries, logs, letters,
and books, the author personalizes her discussion
with details on how the ships were built, who designed and captained them, and what life was like
for the seamen who climbed the masts, cooked the
meals, and mended the torn sails. Historical prints
combine with Knight's black-and-white and four-
color pages of striking photographs (some of which
lose their full effect through unfortunate cropping)
of the contemporary tall ships that he took during
a recent excursion on the 'Regina Maris.' One can
almost feel the salt spray as pages turn and vessels
pass by in this nostalgic but informative review."
Booklist

Navarra, John Gabriel
Superboats. Doubleday 1977 79p illus maps
(Museum of science and industry/Chicago
ser) $5.95, lib. bdg. $6.90 (4 and up) 387.2
1 Ships
ISBN 0-385-12043-5; 0-385-12044-3   LC 76-23784

A "compilation of information about the numerous unusual and very large seagoing craft now in
use throughout the world. From hovercraft, hydro-
foils and large passenger ships to supertankers,
other modern types of cargo vessels, projected sail-
powered cargo vessels and specialized craft such
as ice-breakers and oil-drilling ships, the author
provides a wealth of diverse information. In addition, the characteristics and limitations of deep-
water ports and the Suez and Panama Canals are
discussed in some detail." AAAS Sci Bks & Films

"A cutaway section of a bulk-cargo ship, a
working-parts diagram for a hydrofoil, a placement
map for a deep-water port, and numerous black-
and-white photographs may be helpful to researchers." Booklist

Plowden, David
Tugboat; text & photographs by David
Plowden. Macmillan Pub. Co. 1976 unp illus
$7.95 (3-6)   387.2
1 Tugboats
ISBN 0-02-774550-3   LC 76-13464

"A chronicle of a typical day in the work week
of the Julia C. Moran, a modern diesel-electric
powered New York Harbor tug. On the Saturday
described, the Julia participates in six dockings
and embarkations of various cruise ships, a container ship, and a freighter." Sch Library J

"Photographs of high calibre illustrate [the]
text. . . . Plowden gives a great deal of information about harbor vessels particularly the liners
and tankers the tugs assist: he describes details
of docking and undocking procedures and supplies
a list of bell signals, a chart of the harbor, and
an explanation of the marine time system. Text and
pictures are nicely integrated, the writing style is
clear, and the material is well organized." Chicago.
Children's Bk Center

Sullivan, George
Supertanker! The story of the world's biggest ships; illus. with photographs and maps.
Dodd 1978 144p illus maps lib. bdg. $6.95 (5
and up)   387.2
1 Tankers 2 Petroleum industry and trade
ISBN 0-396-07527-4   LC 77-16870

The author "gives a history of the oil industry, the shipping lanes used since the introduction of oil in the world market, the United State's
energy needs, and, in more detail, the supertanker
and its predecessors. The focus, as the title suggests, is on the supertankers of today, their construction, their use, and their hazards." Best Sellers

"This book is not only about Supertankers, but
also covers related problems and issues, such as
superports, safety at sea, crew training, pollution,
and others. The photographs are superb, and convey not only the immense size of these ships, but
also the immensity of both the industrial effort
needed to manufacture them and the facilities
needed to operate them. This is a well organized,
complete book on a topic of current interest."
Appraisal

Glossary: p137-39

Zim, Herbert S.
Cargo ships [by] Herbert S. Zim [and]
James R. Skelly; illus. by Richard Cuffari.
Morrow 1970 62p illus lib. bdg. $5.71 (3-6)
                                       387.2
1 Ships 2 Merchant marine
ISBN 0-688-31143-1   LC 70-89599

The authors describe "the construction and equipment of cargo ships and the ways in which they
may be powered, the function and operation of the
three basic cargo ships in use today—freighter,
tanker, and bulk carrier—and the duties of the
crew and career possibilities on cargo ships. The
writing style is clear and simplified, the information specific, the print large; the precise line drawings on almost every page are an essential feature
of the book." Booklist

387.7   Air transportation

Wilson, Mike
Jet journey. Consultant: Captain A. J. Hanley-Browne; authors: Mike Wilson and Robin Scagell; editorial team: Robin Scagell and Vanessa Galvin; art editor: Adrian Gray; editor-in-chief: Beverley Hilton. Viking 1978 59p illus $5.95 (3 and up)   **387.7**
1 Aeronautics, Commercial   2 Airports   3 Jet planes
ISBN 0-670-40671-6   LC 78-2405
This book is part of a series in which "full-color photographs, meticulous, well-labeled diagrams, clear, concise descriptions, and detailed drawings set in large, attractive format offer young readers close-up looks at . . . areas of high interest. . . . [It contains] oft-searched-for but seldom found information as well as related projects and experiments. . . . Passenger and crew preliminary procedures such as reservations, check-in, refueling, and flight plans are presented along with material on control towers, navigational know-how, landing patterns, and supersonic flights. Instructions for building a [paper] model Concorde are included. Unfortunately, the index and glossary are bound into the back cover. Packed solid with fascinating information, the visuals alone should catch the reluctant and satisfy the inveterate reader with no trouble at all." Booklist

388.3   Vehicular transportation

Tunis, Edwin
Wheels; a pictorial history; written and illus. by Edwin Tunis. Crowell [1977 c1955] 96p illus $12.95 (5 and up)   **388.3**
1 Carriages and carts   2 Transportation—History
ISBN 0-690-01341-8   LC 76-25809
This is a reissue of the title first published in 1955 by World Publishing Company
Beginning with the first primitive roller, this history of land transportation, exclusive of railroads, progresses to the earliest known wheeled vehicle, the Elamite chariot, through Egyptian, Greek, Roman and Oriental chariots and carts, through the development of the road coaches of Europe and on to modern automobiles and buses
"Emphasizes wagons and carriages rather than automobiles. . . . Many illustrations on every page. Attractive and very readable, it may also have reference value although there is no index." Minnesota

388.5   Pipeline transportation

Shumaker, Virginia O.
The Alaska pipeline; illus. with photographs and maps. Messner 1979 64p illus maps lib. bdg. $6.97 (4-6)   **388.5**
1 Alaska pipeline
ISBN 0-671-32975-8   LC 79-13696
"This beginner's introduction to the Alaska pipeline continually balances oft-opposing environmental and energy concerns as it describes the great physical problems that had to be overcome in pipeline construction. . . . There are plentiful black-and-white photographs showing the rugged terrain, weather conditions, heavy equipment and living quarters of pipeline workers." Booklist

389   Metrology and standardization

Adler, Peggy
Metric puzzles, by Peggy Adler and Irving Adler; illus. by Peggy Adler. Watts, F. 1977 66p illus lib. bdg. $6.90 (4-6)   **389**
1 Metric system
ISBN 0-531-01295-6   LC 77-1948
"Fifty-two carefully developed games including mathematical computations, anagrams, and word puzzles teach the metric units for determining area, volume, and temperature. . . . Peggy Adler's black-and-white pen drawings add to the fun of these well-conceived exercises which help readers to learn important metric relationships through discovery and analysis." Sch Library J

Bitter, Gary G.
Exploring with metrics, by Gary G. Bitter and Thomas H. Metos; cartoons by Kevin Callahan. Messner 1975 64p illus lib. bdg. $6.29 (3-5)   **389**
1 Metric system
ISBN 0-671-32745-3   LC 75-25520
"Like most on the metric system, this delightfully illustrated math book accurately explains the history and basic principles of the metric system. What makes it most pleasing to the reader are the numerous photographs illustrating the principles discussed in the text. Also, a peanut-like cartoon figure jumps from one page to another, stressing the basic measurement facts explained. The author nicely introduces the ideas of distance, weight, and capacity measurement in the metric system, then allows the reader to explore these topics further." Appraisal

Branley, Franklyn M.
How little and how much; a book about scales; illus. by Byron Barton. Crowell 1976 33p illus (Young math bks) lib. bdg. $7.89 (2-4)   **389**
1 Weights and measures
ISBN 0-690-01058-3   LC 75-43643
"A beginning book about scale and the need for units of measure. The common scales of length are discussed, and the history of Fahrenheit's efforts to perfect a scale for temperature is explained. Metric units are mentioned in passing." Sch Library J
"Quite a lot of handy information in a short text. Color and black-and-white illustrations and diagrams [are included]." Booklist

Measure with metric; illus. by Loretta Lustig. Crowell 1975 33p illus lib. bdg. $7.89, pa $2.95 (2-4)   **389**
1 Metric system
ISBN 0-690-01117-2; 0-690-01265-9   LC 74-4056
"A direct approach to the challenge of familiarizing students with metric measurement. Readers can, in minutes, make a cardboard meter stick, a simple balance with homemade gram weights, and a plastic bag-lined liter box for liquid measurement. After measuring familiar household items with the help of this book, children will have some functional understanding of metrics. Illustrated with cheerful black-and-white and color pictures." Booklist

Think metric! Illus. by Graham Booth. Crowell [1973 c1972] 53p illus maps $7.95, lib. bdg. $7.89 (3-6)   **389**
1 Metric system
ISBN 0-690-81861-0; 0-690-81862-9   LC 72-78279
The author explains how the metric system works and "describes its advantages over our present system of measurement both in terms of efficiency and of translation. The text begins with historical background, goes on to the establishment of the metric system, and presents translation problems that can familiarize the reader with the metric system." Chicago. Children's Bk Center
into the text, and English-metric equivalents are
"Problem solving and examples are well integrated listed at the end. The clarity of the writing and of the often amusing illustrations make this a good introduction." Booklist

Hirsh, S. Carl
Meter means measure; the story of the metric system. Viking 1973 126p lib. bdg. $5.95 (5 and up)   **389**
1 Metric system
ISBN 0-670-47365-0   LC 72-91398
In this book "the controversies and efforts that have occurred in initiating the use of the metric system as a universal measuring standard are described. . . . The influence of persons like Thomas Jefferson, John Quincy Adams, Alexander Graham Bell, Albert Michelson and others is shown in historical perspective as America moves toward the utilization of the metric system of measure." Top of the News
"Well-researched and readable, this also explains the pressures and counter-pressures involved in the reluctance of the United States to adopt the metric system—a dimension which is not covered by other books on the subject." Sch Library J
Suggestions for further reading: p121

Leaf, Munro

Metric can be fun! Written and illus. by Munro Leaf. Lippincott 1976 63p illus $6.79, pa $1.95 (2-4) **389**

1 Metric system
ISBN 0-397-31679-8; 0-397-31680-1   LC 75-29223

"Starting with a decimeter [the author] moves logically through linear, square and cubic measures; quantities (dry and liquid); weights (avoirdupois) and temperatures in centigrade instead of Fahrenheit." Pub W

"What Leaf has done is provide a skillful mix of assumed prior knowledge and new information. . . . [He] invites reader participation and suggests activities. The pen-and-ink illustrations resemble humorous decorations in a science notebook." NY Times Bk Rev

Pine, Tillie S.

Measurements and how we use them, by Tillie S. Pine and Joseph Levine; pictures by Harriet Sherman. [Rev. ed] McGraw 1977 48p illus $6.95 (2-4) **389**

1 Measurement 2 Measuring instruments
ISBN 0-07-050085-1   LC 76-56131
First published 1974

This "book attracts the reader's attention with its bright colors and imaginative layout. The book begins with examples of measurement problems encountered in everyday life. . . . The authors deal with spatial measurements, time, weight and temperature. In each case, the reader is told exactly how to use the measuring device to determine the quantity of units desired. The authors also describe how each measuring device is constructed. In addition, they cite several experiments that can be performed when primary measuring tools are not available. . . . Many examples are cited showing the importance of measurement in a variety of jobs." Sci Bks

"Sherman's cartoon-like pen-and-ink illustrations complement and enliven the text. . . . This [book] will fill the need for concept and skill deveopment material in an easy-to-read format." Sch Library J

Rahn, Joan E.

The metric system; illus. by Ginny Linville Winter. Atheneum Pubs. 1966 79p illus $6.95 (6 and up) **389**

1 Metric system
ISBN 0-689-30510-9   LC 75-29445

The author "emphasizes that a more meaningful approach to the metric system can be obtained through use and understanding of metrics rather than constant conversion from our current system. She describes specific ways to measure distance, time, and objects in metrics, an exercise which she feels will result in familiarity with the terms. An introduction sketching the history and current status of metrics in the world is followed by individual chapters devoted to length, area, volume, weight, temperature, and time. Clear examples and well-drawn diagrams insure textual clarity. A valuable appendix lists definitions of metric units, conversion tables, and an explanation of exponents and how to use them." Booklist

Srivastava, Jane Jonas

Weighing & balancing; illus. by Aliki. Crowell 1970 32p illus (Young math bks) $7.95 (1-3) **389**

1 Weights and measures
ISBN 0-690-87114-7   LC 73-106579

"A brief, uncomplicated text and attractive, often humourous drawings ably explain the difficult concepts of weight, balance, and density to young children. Directions are given for making a simple balance, and the reader is encouraged to experiment with it using marbles, pennies, pencils, and objects of known weight to discover which object is heavier. An easy-to-do experiment using the balance, a stick, a stone, and a glass of water to demonstrate density is also included." Booklist

Zim, Herbert S.

Metric measure [by] Herbert S. Zim [and] James R. Skelly; illus. by Timothy Evans. Morrow 1974 63p illus maps lib. bdg. $6.48 (3-6) **389**

1 Metric system
ISBN 0-688-30118-5   LC 74-702

The authors discuss the history and applications of the metric system of measurement and give examples of its use in common situations. They explain how scientific standards of measurement have been developed for determining length, weight, time and temperature and tell briefly about other units of measurement

391 Costume and personal appearance

Barwell, Eve

Disguises you can make; illus. by Richard Rosenblum. Lothrop 1977 111p illus lib. bdg. $6.96 (4-6) **391**

1 Costume 2 Makeup, Theatrical 3 Masks (Facial)
ISBN 0-688-51810-9   LC 77-24998

"Here are instructions for becoming a clown (happy and sad), a devil, a pirate, Santa Claus, a monster, etc., including such costume requirements as yarn wigs and masks molded from newspapers, burlap and other materials. There is also a brief introduction to theatrical makeup. Some of the costumes require nothing more than paper bags and magic markers." Sch Library J

"Besides clever black-and-white illustrations and a clear text, Ms. Barwell includes tips on using theatrical make-up and suggestions for role playing to make your disguise really come to life. While perfect for Halloween, have this book around for some creative 'dress-up' play all year round." Babbling Bookworm

Baylor, Byrd

They put on masks; illus. by Jerry Ingram. Scribner 1974 46p illus lib. bdg. $7.95 (1-4) **391**

1 Masks (Facial) 2 Indians of North America
ISBN 0-684-13767-4   LC 73-19557

The "text describes the masks used by some Indian tribes, chiefly those of the Southwest, in their ceremonial rites and dances, giving details about the way the masks are made as well as about how they are used. . . . The text incorporates some of the beautiful song poetry that is used by the masked dancers, but it does more than that; it explains how the masks evoke the spirits of those they portray, how wearing a mask invests the person with the powers of the god or the creature he has become." Chicago. Children's Bk Center

"This truly outstanding book is beautifully illustrated by Jerry Ingram with dozens of Indian figures and actual masks in brilliant colors and of authentic design. The intangible spirit of beauty and love of the soil which motivate the Indian people are remarkably captured in this book. Children of all ages, and adults as well, will learn of a variety of Indian customs from many tribes and with masks as the theme, as well as actual chants which accompany the rituals in which the masks appear. After seeing the many types of masks, the child will be able to copy the ones illustrated, recreate Indian lore for himself, and finally design a personal mask with individual meaning." Rdng Teacher

Chernoff, Goldie Taub

Easy costumes you don't have to sew; costumes designed and illus. by Margaret A. Hartelius. Four Winds 1975 41p illus $6.95 (3-5) **391**

1 Costume 2 Paper crafts
ISBN 0-590-07491-1   LC 76-46428

"Garbage bags, cartons, cardboard, paper bags, and old white sheets provide the basis for a variety of easy-to-make costumes. At-hand materials (newspaper, milk cartons, string) and clear directions result in simply constructed snowmen, mice, shaggy dogs, turtles, ladybugs, bats, skeletons, robots, totem poles, and even a group dragon. Each two-page spread is devoted to one costume, with careful diagrams, lists of necessary materials, precise instructions for each part, and guidelines for putting on the costume. Suggestions for appropriate hats (witch, pilgrim, crown), wigs, beards, and other disguises are also included. As the costumes can easily be adapted (some examples are shown), the book will be helpful for party, play, and parade preparations." Booklist

Cosner, Shaaron

Masks around the world, and how to make them; drawings by Ann George. McKay 1979 120p illus $7.95 (5 and up)   391

1 Masks (Facial)   2 Handicraft
ISBN 0-679-20802-X   LC 78-20328

In this book "specifics about the sizes, materials, and facial expressions of masks in different geographical areas are woven into the discussion of their use in funeral and birth celebrations, religious rites, plays, folktale dramatizations, holiday festivals, and other important events. Updating the subject, the author talks briefly about masks used today for protection (football), terrorist tactics (Ku Klux Klan), recreation (Halloween), and parades (Mardi Gras). The instructions for making 10 masks are brief and students may need adult help. . . . Materials are easily obtainable and the large drawings will facilitate the work. Black-and-white photographs from galleries and museums further supplement the text. Bibliography appended." Booklist

Eisner, Vivienne

Quick and easy holiday costumes; illus. by Carolyn Bentley. Lothrop 1977 154p illus $8.25, lib. bdg. $7.92 (3-6)   391

1 Costume   2 Handicraft
ISBN 0-688-41809-0; 0-688-51809-5   LC 77-21987

"Twenty-three holidays (some very minor) provide the excuse for these costumes. All are based on five basic parts—headband, tunic, full skirt, cape, and sandwich sign—and can be thrown together almost instantly with no sewing and no paint (staples, glue, and magic markers are used instead)." Sch Library J

"This book is unique in that the more than 60 costumes are inexpensive to make and none requires sewing. However, many of them are so oversimplified that they consist of a headband and a sign which is necessary to recognize the identity of the wearer. Though these costumes won't win any prizes, the book would be useful in a fifth or sixth-grade class when everyone must have a costume for a special occasion." Children's Bk Rev Serv

Gilbreath, Alice

Making costumes for parties, plays, and holidays; pictures by Timothy Evans. Morrow 1974 93p illus lib. bdg. $6 (4-6)   391

1 Costume
ISBN 0-688-30103-7   LC 74-13996

This book contains step-by-step instructions for constructing twenty-one costumes from readily available materials. Presented in their order of difficulty, there are directions for making ghost, scarecrow, octopus, robot, gingerbread boy, valentine, firecracker, and poodle costumes

"Clear directions, accompanied by black-and-white drawings and diagrams, provide all necessary information." Booklist

Hofsinde, Robert

Indian costumes; written and illus. by Robert Hofsinde (Gray-Wolf). Morrow 1968 94p illus lib. bdg. $5.25 (3-6)   391

1 Indians of North America—Costume and adornment
ISBN 0-688-31614-X   LC 68-11895

"The distinctive costumes of ten different North American Indian tribal groups are here illustrated, showing their ceremonial, warring or everyday apparel. Black and white drawings help in explaining how they were made." Bruno, Bks for Sch Libraries, 1968

The tribes represented are the Apache, Blackfoot, Crow, Iroquois, Navaho, Northwest Coast Indians, Ojibwa, Pubelo, Seminole and Sioux Indians

Hunt, Kari

(Masks and mask makers [by] Kari Hunt and Bernice Wells Carlson. Abingdon 1961 67p illus $5.95 (5 and up)   391

1 Masks (Facial)   2 Masks (Sculpture)
ISBN 0-687-23705-X   LC 61-5097

"An interesting survey of different types of masks worn by man since primitive times. The authors tell what peoples have used the various

masks, and what social and symbolic functions masks have served. Legends and ceremonies associated with their use are described, and instructions are given for homemade masks." The AAAS Sci Bk List for Children

"Could be much used by teachers . . . and by the boys and girls themselves in accelerated lower grades for special reports. Whether interested in theatre, art, or ethnology, there is something here for older readers, too." Library J

Includes bibliography

Leeming, Joseph

The costume book; drawings by Hilda Richman. Lippincott 1938 123p illus lib. bdg. $8.95   391

1 Costume
ISBN 0-397-30052-2   LC 38-27654

Title on cover: The costume book for parties and plays

Descriptions and illustrations are given for folk costumes of twenty-seven nations, for fanciful and fairy tales costumes, and for historic costumes of Ancient Egypt, Palestine, Greece and Rome, Medieval Europe, Sixteenth century Europe and Elizabethan England, Seventeenth century Europe and America, Eighteenth century Europe and American colonial, Early nineteenth century or empire period, Mid-Victorian England, and American Civil War period

"There are practical directions for making costumes, on how to cut and use a pattern, and hints on inexpensive material that will give the desired effect. . . . Black-and-white drawings illustrate the costumes." Booklist

Meyer, Carolyn

Mask magic; illus. by Melanie Gaines Arwin. Harcourt 1978 90p illus $7.95 (4-6)   391

1 Masks (Facial)   2 Handicraft
ISBN 0-15-253107-6   LC 77-14080

"Though basically a guide to mask making, this also provides background information on the whys and whens of mask wearing. In an opening chapter, the author relates the use of these age-old disguises in primitive dance rituals, Greek drama, Japanese Noh, and seventeenth-century mumming plays. Following are instructions on preparing and decorating half-masks, helmet and stick masks, and head and face masks with notes on celebrations for Midsummer Night's Eve, Halloween, and Carnival. Suggested materials are inexpensive and easily obtained; but though written instructions are clear, use of diagrams is skimpy." Booklist

Parish, Peggy

Costumes to make; illus. by Lynn Sweat. Macmillan Pub. Co. 111p illus $6.95 (4-6)   391

1 Costume   2 Sewing
ISBN 0-02-76950-1   LC 75-102969

A "book that gives instructions for making very simple costumes, many of them using in part a basic commercial pattern and describing only the frills or accessories. For a toy soldier, for example, the costume is based on a pajama pattern, with instruction given for trim and for making a hat. While the step-by-step directions are clear, and the costumes uncomplicated, the user would need to be familiar with patterns and sewing." Chicago. Children's Bk Center

"The directions are neither so brief that important information is left out or assumed to be known, nor so complex that heads spin and arms flail in exasperation. The 50 costumes are childlike—Indian boys and girls, cowboys, angels and a long list of storybook characters starting with Mother Goose and ending with animals of different kinds. The drawings are appealing to the browser and illuminating to the seamstress." Sch Library J

Price, Christine

The mystery of masks. Scribner 1978 64p illus map lib. bdg. $7.95 (5 and up)   391

1 Masks (Facial)
ISBN 0-684-15653-9   LC 77-27558

The author "describes the power masks have held in various cultures throughout history. . . . Both geographical and social origins are explored among peoples such as Eskimos, Bushmen, and Iroquois Indians. The author points out that the tremendous time and care necessary for the construction of masks has been made prohibitive by social and economic changes in modern times." Horn Bk

Price, Christine—*Continued*

"'Masks' appears to be carefully researched, with the information concise enough to hold reader interest and detailed enough to give a real sense of the art and ritual of masks. The pencil illustrations are beautifully done, with excellent detail and an amazing feeling of strength. This book, while probably not suitable to read straight through, would be well used to supplement a history program or as an impetus for art projects." Children's Bk Rev Serv

Purdy, Susan

Costumes for you to make. Lippincott 1971 121p illus $8.95 (4 and up)   391

1 Costume
ISBN 0-397-31317-9   LC 77-151470

There are "directions for each costume part, including collars, cuffs, wings, hats, capes, tunics, medals, and even wolf muzzles and dog snouts. Every item is accompanied by detailed drawings, directions for measuring and for reducing patterns in some cases." Library J

"Presenting suggestions for all types of costumes, the book contains brief sections on theatrical make-up and costume material. . . . Excellent ideas and simple instructions for theatrical productions or for parties." Horn Bk

391.09 Costume—History

Fox, Lilla M.

Folk costume of Southern Europe; illus. by the author. Plays, Inc. [1973 c1972] 64p illus maps $4.95 (4 and up)   391.09

1 Costume—History
ISBN 0-8238-0088-1   LC 74-150101

First published 1972 in England

The author "describes in detail the costumes of Italy, Switzerland, Spain, and the Mediterranean Islands." Library J

The author's "illustrations are excellent and very detailed, and her text is simple and clear. She provides an index and a map of the region and one of the Swiss Cantons." Jr Bookshelf

Folk costume of Western Europe; illus. by the author. Plays, Inc. [1971 c1969] 64p illus map $4.95 (4 and up)   391.09

1 Costume—History
ISBN 0-8238-0087-3   LC 76-107602

First published 1969 in England

"Presenting a wide range of the traditional folk dress of Western Europe, this book is particularly useful as a guide for the costuming of folk dances and plays. Fox describes how climate, geography and historical events influenced styles of national expression and points up the diversity of costumes within the same country. . . . Great Britain France, Belgium, the Netherlands, Western Germany, Denmark, Sweden, Norway, Finland, and Lapland are each treated in a separate capter; however, . . . Fox concentrates on regional rather than national dress. Though the author's line drawings, done in black and white with touches of red and yellow, sometimes fail to capture the distinctiveness of the costumes, a helpful map of Western Europe with the relevant regions indicated is a redeeming accompaniment to the brief, authoritative text." Sch Library J

Schnurnberger, Lynn Edelman

Kings, queens, knights & jesters: making medieval costumes, by Lynn Edelman Schnurnberger in association with The Metropolitan Museum of Art; drawings by Alan Robert Showe; photographs by Barbara Brooks and Pamela Hort. Harper 1978 113p $7.95, lib. bdg. $8.49 (4 and up)   391.09

1 Costume—History 2 Civilization, Medieval
ISBN 0-06-025241-3; 0-06-025242-1   LC 77-25682

The author "presents a close look at the wearing apparel of the people of the period and provides simple directions for creating usable copies. Dividing the book into three sections, the author explains the construction of the three basic shapes (the T, the tunic, and the circle) comments on the fashions and life-styles of the various classes of people (royalty, noblemen, peasants, clergy), and suggests ways to appropriately decorate and accessorize the costumes." Booklist

"An outgrowth of the medieval festival held each year at the Cloisters, the book reaches for beyond the average craft guide in combining the practical and aesthetic aspects of costume design. An attractive format displays numerous photographs of the children in the festival as well as reproductions of medieval art—woodcuts, stained glass, and tapestries. One section of reproductions consists of handsome color plates, each illustrating authentic costumes of the period. Contained within the text are anecdotes about historical figures and their style of dress. . . . The dress of peasants, monks, craftsmen, wizards, and others is presented along with that of the royalty. Three simple patterns form the basis of each costume described; the reader is left to his own inventiveness in the selection of decoration and fabric. Instructions are clearly stated and illustrated." Horn Bk

392 Customs of life cycle and domestic life

Lasker, Joe

Merry ever after; the story of two medieval weddings; written and illus. by Joe Lasker. Viking 1976 unp illus lib. bdg. $7.95, Penguin Bks. pa $2.95 (3-5)   392

1 Marriage customs and rites 2 Civilization, Medieval
ISBN 0-670-47257-3; 0-14-050280-7   LC 75-22017

"Set in medieval Europe, the story tells of the arranged marriage of Anne and Gilbert and, coincidentally, of the marriage of the rather coarser-looking Martha and Simon. The first couple were very rich; the second, peasants." Sat Rev

"Basing his richly colored and detailed pictures on medieval paintings, Lasker has illustrated his text in a way that can help readers visualize the costumes, architecture, and customs of aristocrats and peasants of medieval Europe. . . . The text, like the illustrations, gives many facts about medieval life styles; the writing is direct and informal; the pictures are handsome." Chicago. Children's Bk Center

Price, Christine

Happy days; a UNICEF book of birthdays, name days and growing days; written and illus. by Christine Price. Dutton [1970 c1969] 128p illus $3 (4-6)   392

1 Birthdays 2 Rites and ceremonies
ISBN 0-525-31453-9   LC 77-95577

"By organizing the material by type of event rather than by country or location Price gives a cultural perspective on observances and rituals that differ widely but share common themes—celebration of a child's birth, various significant states in his development, or his initiation into adulthood. The text is enriched by effective illustrations in color and black and white and by poetry and chants connected with some of the celebrations. An appendix includes the music for several birthday songs, a section on children's names around the world, and suggestions for further reading." Booklist

393 Death customs

Glubok, Shirley

The mummy of Ramose; the life and death of an ancient Egyptian nobleman, by Shirley Glubok and Alfred Tamarin. Harper 1978 82p illus $6.95, lib. bdg. $7.89 (5 and up)   393

1 Mummies 2 Egypt—Antiquities 3 Ramose 4 Funeral rites and ceremonies
ISBN 0-06-022039-2; 0-06-022042-2   LC 76-21392

"Illustrated with photographs and reproductions in black and white. Ramose was a historical person, an Egyptian nobleman of high position, who lived at an important time; he was vizier to Amenhotep III, the father of Akhenaten and Tutankhamun. . . . Against a background of the dynastic and economic history and the religious beliefs of the era, the authors have skillfully reconstructed the last day of his life. Of particular interest is a careful description of the process of mummification, which required great skill; in the case of a high official like Ramose, the work took

Glubok, Shirley—*Continued*
seventy days. Each detail of the procedure and
the funeral had its source in some aspect of the
Egyptian's belief in an afterlife. The book contains a postscript on sources, a selected bibliography, and an index." Horn Bk

McHargue, Georgess
Mummies. Lippincott 1972 160p illus map
(The Weird and horrible lib) $7.95 (5 and up)
                      393

  1 Mummies
  ISBN 0-397-31516-3   LC 72-2324

A discussion of natural and embalmed mummies
from the frozen mastodons of Siberia to the mummies of ancient Egypt, Polynesia, South America
and Europe. The author describes why mummies
were made, how they have been preserved and
found, and attitudes and superstitions about them
  "The many photographs, some rather gruesome,
complement a concise overview which concludes
with a look at a few present-day mummies and
cryonic sleep." Booklist
  Suggestions for further reading: p155

Pace, M. M.
Wrapped for eternity; the story of the Egyptian mummy; Egyptologist and content consultant: Kenneth Jay Linsner; line drawings
by Tom Huffman. McGraw 1974 192p illus
map $6.95 (5 and up)   **393**

  1 Mummies   2 Egypt—Antiquities
  ISBN 0-07-048053-2   LC 73-14539

In this study of mummification, the author
"describes the highly advanced embalming techniques used by the Egyptians, the religious significance of the burial ceremony, and the historical
and medical facts that have been discovered with
the unearthing and unwrapping of these ancient
remains." Babbling Bookworm
  "The writing style is crisp and informal, the
organization of material into and within chapters
is logical, and the easily-incorporated research
is evident in the extensive bibliography." Chicago.
Children's Bk Center

394.2 Customs— Special occasions

The **Animals'** Christmas; poems, carols, and
stories chosen by Anne Thaxter Eaton; decorated by Valenti Angelo. Viking 1944 124p
illus lib. bdg. $5.95 (4 and up)   **394.2**

  1 Christmas—Fiction   2 Christmas—Poetry
  3 Animals—Fiction 3 Animals—Poetry
  ISBN 0-670-12800-7   LC 44-9296

An anthology of Christmas poems and stories,
in each of which animals have an important role
  The compiler "has brought together here a collection of such legends, in both prose and verse,
making a distinguished addition to the shelf of
Christmas material. . . . The decorative illustrations in green and white . . . have a pleasing simplicity." Wis Library Bul   z
  Bibliographical references included in Acknowledgments

Barksdale, Lena
The first Thanksgiving; illus. by Lois Lenski.
Knopf 1942 57p illus lib. bdg. $4.99 (3-5)   **394.2**

  1 Thanksgiving Day
  ISBN 0-394-81156-9   LC 42-21306

"Hannah, who lives with her parents and older
brothers in Maine, comes down to Massachusetts
to make the acquaintance of her cousins and to
eat Thanksgiving dinner with Grandma and
Grandpa. After the dinner is over she hears Grandma tell the story of that first Thanksgiving in
which she and Grandpa had taken part, all of
forty years ago, in Plymouth." Wis Library Bul
  "The book is warmly human and the pictures by
Lois Lenski are full of the atmosphere of New
England." Bookmark

Barth, Edna
Hearts, cupids, and red roses; the story of
the Valentine symbols; illus. by Ursula Arndt.
Seabury [distributed by Houghton] 1974 64p
illus $8.95 (3-6)   **394.2**

  1 Valentine's Day 2 Signs and symbols
  ISBN 0-395-28841-X   LC 73-7128

"A Clarion book"
  "Beginning with the origins of St. Valentine's
Day, Barth traces the celebration of the holiday
from the Roman 'Lupercalia' (a pagan festival)
to present-day practices. Included are descriptions of the many different types of valentines
and the meanings of the colors red, white, and
pink as well as such symbols as flowers, doves,
hearts, and cupids." Sch Library J
  "Interesting, concise text and lists of stories,
poems and sources about St. Valentine's Day make
this [book] superior." Minnesota
  Bibliography: p62-63

Holly, reindeer, and colored lights; the story
of the Christmas symbols; illus. by Ursula
Arndt. Seabury [distributed by Houghton]
1971 96p illus $7.95 (3-6)   **394.2**

  1 Christmas 2 Signs and symbols
  ISBN 0-395-28842-X   LC 71-157731

"A Clarion book"
  "A collection of Christmas customs from around
the world. . . . The book considers each of the
symbols , traces its historical roots—whether
pagan, Christian, or mythological—and tells of
the part it plays in present-day Christmas celebrations. The customs associated with plants,
flowers, foods, and lights are just a few of the
traditions explained. The book also contains many
Christmas legends." Horn Bk
  "The well-written text is concise and interesting and the two-colored marginal drawings are
festive. A selected list of books containing Christmas stories and poems is appended." Booklist

Lilies, rabbits, and painted eggs; the story
of the Easter symbols; illus. by Ursula Arndt.
Seabury [distributed by Houghton] 1970 63p
illus $7.95 (3-6)   **394.2**

  1 Eastern 2 Signs and symbols
  ISBN 0-395-28844-4   LC 74-97033

"A Clarion book"
  "By revealing the ancient—often pagan—roots of
Easter traditions, the book [indicates] how similar man's desires have always been, especially in
the celebration of the miracle of new life in artistic
and religious ways. [It] also explains Easter
games, chants, and rituals as performed all over
the world. . . . Some of the stories are funny, some
dramatic; all will add to the appreciation of the
season. The small pen drawings which illustrate
the symbols and the celebrations will please the
children, and an index and a bibliography of other
Easter books will please the librarian." Horn Bk

Shamrocks, harps, and shillelaghs; the story
of the St Patrick's Day symbols; illus. by
Ursula Arndt. Seabury [distributed by Hough-
ton] 1977 95p illus $8.95 (3-6)   **394.2**

  1 St Patrick's Day 2 Signs and symbols
  ISBN 0-395-28845-2   LC 77-369

"A Clarion book"
  "Irish history, lore, and legend are part of a
wealth of information provided about Patrick the
real missionary, St. Patrick's Day, and its celebration. Includes lists of stories for St. Patrick's
Day and sources." L.C. Children's Bks, 1977

Turkeys Pilgrims, and Indian corn; the
story of the Thanksgiving symbols; illus. by
Ursula Arndt. Seabury [distributed by Hough-
ton] 1975 96p illus $8.95 (3-6)   **394.2**

  1 Thanksgiving Day 2 Pilgrims (New England
  colonists) 3 Signs and symbols
  ISBN 0-395-28846-0   LC 75-4703

"A Clarion book"
  This discussion of the American celebration
of Thanksgiving "includes details on why the
Pilgrims left England and speculates about their
journey across the ocean on the 'Mayflower.'
In a lively, warm text the author describes such
aspects as family life (including a separate chapter on Pilgrim mothers), clothing, houses, and
Indian neighbors. The real strength of this work

Barth, Edna—*Continued*

lies in the information on various symbols we associate with Thanksgiving—Indian corn, turkey, cranberries, and cornucopias. Gold-and-black margin illustrations decorate the text. Selected bibliography and source lists for further study are appended." Booklist

Witches, pumpkins, and grinning ghosts; the story of the Halloween symbols; illus. by Ursula Arndt. Seabury [distributed by Houghton] 1972 95p illus $8.95 (3-6)   **394.2**

1 Halloween 2 Signs and symbols
ISBN 0-395-28847-9   LC 72-75705

"A Clarion book"
"This discusses the origins of Halloween and the way it is celebrated today in different countries. Witches (male and female), bats, toads, ghosts, traditional foods, and other customs and symbols related to All Saint's Day are covered. Barth also touches on the incorporation of pagan beliefs into Christianity." Sch Library J
"A diverting as well as useful account appropriately illustrated with drawings in black and orange." Booklist
Stories for Halloween: p95

Bartlett, Robert Merrill

Thanksgiving Day; illus. by W. T. Mars. Crowell 1965 unp illus (A Crowell Holiday bk) lib. bdg. $7.89 (1-3)   **394.2**

1 Thanksgiving Day 2 Pilgrims (New England colonists)
ISBN 0-690-81045-8   LC 65-16178

Here is "a simple, brief history of the custom of giving thanks at harvest time from the days of ancient Greece to the present with emphasis on the Pilgrims and their thanksgiving celebrations of 1621 and 1623." Booklist
A "book to use as an introduction to further study and discussion of the early settlers in our country." Wis Library Bul

Borten, Helen

Halloween; written and illus. by Helen Borten. Crowell 1965 unp illus (A Crowell Holiday bk) lib. bdg. $7.89 (1-3)   **394.2**

1 Halloween
ISBN 0-690-36314-1   LC 65-16184

The magic and fun of Halloween is found in this attractively illustrated book which covers the early customs and superstitions and our own modern celebrations." Chicago

Bulla, Clyde Robert

St Valentine's Day; illus. by Valenti Angelo. Crowell 1965 unp illus (A Crowell Holiday bk) lib. bdg. $7.89 (1-3)   **394.2**

1 Valentine's Day
ISBN 0-690-71744-X   LC 65-11643

"A brief and simple text about the origins of the legends and celebration of St. Valentine's Day and about the way the holiday is observed today." Chicago. Children's Bk Center

Burnett, Bernice

The first book of holidays. Rev. ed. Watts, F. 1974 87p illus lib. bdg. $6.45 (4 and up) **394.2**

1 Holidays
ISBN 0-531-00548-8   LC 74-3075

First published 1955
This book "not only covers standard American holidays but also celebrations of ethnic minorities in the U.S. and holidays in foreign nations—e.g., Mexico, Canada, France, Japan. In describing the origins of these traditions, Burnett shows how vestiges of the past have been incorporated into present-day celebrations, and excellent black-and-white illustrations and photos add authenticity. A list of holidays around the world, a bibliography, and a thorough index complete the coverage." Sch Library J

Cantwell, Mary

St Patrick's Day; illus. by Ursula Arndt. Crowell 1967 unp illus (A Crowell Holiday bk) lib. bdg. $6.89 (1-3)   **394.2**

1 St Patrick's Day 2 Patrick, Saint
ISBN 0-690-71673-7   LC 67-846

"The author tells the origin of St. Patrick's Day, how he became a much-loved saint and how his day has been celebrated by different countries. The illustrator brightens his story with pleasant sketches." Pub W

Cheng, Hou-tien

The Chinese New Year; scissor cuts by the author. Holt 1976 unp illus lib. bdg. $5.50 (1-4)   **394.2**

1 New Year—China 2 China—Social life and customs
ISBN 0-03-017511-9   LC 76-8229

"Cheng Hou-tien describes the events of each of the days of the Little New Year, the five-day celebration of the New Year that follows, and the three-day Festival of Lanterns that takes place ten days later, with the first full moon of the new year. The Chinese New Year, a movable holiday, falls between January 21 and February 20, and has been celebrated for five thousand years; the book concludes with an explanation of the twelve-year cycle of animal signs. Cheng is a master of the art of papercutting and his illustrations, each page cut from a single sheet of paper in intricate style, are handsome but, as printed on the page, give no real sense of the medium since they could as well have been painted." Chicago. Children's Bk Center

Cooney, Barbara

Christmas; written and illus. by Barbara Cooney. Crowell 1967 unp illus (A Crowell Holiday bk) lib. bdg. $7.89 (1-3)   **394.2**

1 Christmas
ISBN 0-690-19201-0   LC 67-18510

A "lovely and thoughtful book, which begins with the traditional preparations for the holiday; tells very simply of the birth of Christ; pursues the story into its Jewish background, and ties in some of our customs to the Roman Saturnalia. At the end the book returns to modern holiday customs in various lands, including our own." Bruno Bks for Sch Libraries, 1968

Cuyler, Margery

Jewish holidays; illus. by Lisa C. Wesson. Holt 1978 64p illus $5.95 (2-6)   **394.2**

1 Fasts and feasts—Judaism 2 Handicraft
ISBN 0-03-039936-X   LC 77-10801

The author "describes the significance of each of the nine major Jewish holidays and the way they are commemorated. Weekly Shabbat counts as a holiday too, and a closing 'Other Holidays' chapter calls attention to Yom ha-Azma'ut, Israel's Independence day, as well as Lag Baomer and Tishah be-Av, lesser-known but noted days." Booklist
"A clear, factual, and useful book for teaching children the significance of the Jewish holidays. . . . The illustrations done in black-and-white pertain to the excellent text but are not particularly interesting. . . . At the end of each chapter is an easy-to-do arts and crafts project which relates to the holiday described." Sch Library J
Glossary: p58-61

Dalgliesh, Alice

The Thanksgiving story; with illus. by Helen Sewell. Scribner 1954 unp illus map lib. bdg. $8.95, pa $2.95 (k-2)   **394.2**

1 Thanksgiving Day 2 Pilgrims (New England colonists)
ISBN 0-684-12230-4; 0-684-16005-6   LC 54-8785

A "picture book that tells the story of Thanksgiving through the experiences of one family on the Mayflower, the hardships of their first winter, the birth of the new baby, spring planting, harvest, and the giving of thanks." Wis Library Bul
"It is told briefly and directly in the words that will be easy for the youngest readers to enjoy for themselves and in pictures which are in the character of American primitives and at the same time have strength and drama. From the somber tones of the earlier heart of the story the pictures work up to a climax of glowing autumn colors in the illustration for the Thanksgiving feast." Sat Rev

De Paola, Tomie
Things to make and do for Valentine's Day.
Watts. F. 1976 48p illus (Things to make and
do bks) lib. bdg. $7.90 (1-3)   394.2
  1 Valentine's Day 2 Handicraft 3 Cookery
  4 Games
  ISBN 0-531-00187-9   LC 75-38974
  Illustrated by the author, this book includes
activities such as "making cards, playing games,
creating Valentine lockets from baker's clay. None
of the ideas is especially remarkable or unique, but
the presentation is attractive and this can be
enjoyed by holiday celebrants of early elementary
age." Sch Library J
  "A boisterous array of youngsters (and a few
animals) add their suggestions in colorful comic-
book-type illustrations that convey a great deal
of information and amplify the book's child
appeal." Booklist

Dobler, Lavinia
National holidays around the world; illus.
& designed by Vivian Browne. Fleet Press 1968
234p illus $7.95 (5 and up)   394.2
  1 Holidays
  ISBN 0-8303-0044-9   LC 66-16525
  "Arranged by day under each month, national
holidays of 137 countries are described in this
. . . very useful reference tool. Miss Dobler includes a brief history of each land and how its
independence was gained, including important
dates, how it is governed today, how the holiday
is celebrated, the appearance of its flag and em-
blem or seal, and the title of its national anthem." Sch Library J
  Bibliography: p231

Epstein, Sam
A year of Japanese festivals, by Sam and
Beryl Epstein; illus. by Gordon Laite. Garrard
1974 96p illus (An Around the world holiday
bk) lib. bdg. $4.48 (4-6)   394.2
  1 Festivals—Japan 2 Japan—Social life and
  customs
  ISBN 0-8116-4954-7   LC 73-22045
  Includes the celebration descriptions of such
festivals as: Hi Matsuri, Girls Day, The One
Thousand Person Procession, the Okunchi Festival
and the Peace Festival
  "Representative Japanese festivals, arbitrarily
divided into five categories, are described in short,
simple sentences with special attention to the
fascinating mechanics of preparing floats, etc.
However, the piecemeal treatment of the religious
elements in the festivals results in a confusing
and misleading picture of the Japanese as primitive and superstitious people." Sch Library J

Festivals; comp. by Ruth Manning-Sanders;
illus. by Raymond Briggs. Dutton [1973
c1972] 188p illus $7.25 (3-6)   394.2
  1 Festivals 2 Holidays
  ISBN 0-525-29675-1   LC 72-78084
  First published 1972 in England
  "This anthology is a month-by-month journey
through major celebrations throughout the world.
The young reader learns about Christmas in India,
Guy Fawkes Day in England, Easter in Athens
and so on. The book includes poetry and prose by
Tennyson, Dylan Thomas, Robert Herrick, Jan
and Rumer Godden, P. L. Travers, Laura Ingalls
Wilder and the anthologist." Pub W
  This book "is a delicious dip even for some
of the more reluctant readers. . . . It can hardly
fail to please many children, and would be a mar-
vellous ideas book for an enterprising but hard-
pressed primary school teacher. Briggs' pictures
are aptly cheerful and festive in feel." Times (London) Lit Sup

Festivals in Asia. Kodansha [distributed by
Harper] 1975 66p illus $6.95 (2-5)   394.2
  1 Festivals—Asia
  ISBN 0-87011-265-1   LC 75-30415
  "Asian copublication programme series 2. Spon-
sored by the Asian Cultural Centre for UNESCO"
  "Some of the [nine] festivals [from China, Iran,
Japan, Bangladesh, Burma, Cambodia, Laos, Sri
Lanka and the Philippines] are religious; some
are seasonal; all are traditional. The stories have

been selected and edited by a five-country editorial board with the help of Unesco member
states in Asia.' Both the text and the illustrations
were done by people indigenous to the various
countries." Horn Bk
  Supplemented by: More Festivals in Asia, entered below

Fisher, Aileen
Easter; illus. by Ati Forberg. Crowell 1968
unp illus (A Crowell Holiday bk) lib. bdg. $7.89
(1-3)   394.2
  1 Easter 2 Jesus Christ
  ISBN 0-690-25236-6   LC 67-23666
  An "account of the events of Holy Week and
of the ways in which they are observed is preceded by a more general discussion of Easter
customs in the Christian faith. Some of these,
seeming secular, have religious origins; some have
been incorporated from pre-Christian celebrations
of the springtime." Chicago. Children's Bk Center
  "Large, clear print on yellow and white pages
and many bright, stylized drawings make it an
attractive book which conveys the optimism and
happiness of the season." Bruno. Bks for Sch
Libraries. 1968

Foley, Daniel J.
Christmas the world over. . . . Line drawings
by Charlotte Edmands Bowden. Chilton Bk.
Co. 1963 128p illus $10, pa $6.95   394.2
  1 Christmas
  ISBN 0-8019-1277-6; 0-8019-6363-X LC 63-21171
  "How the season of joy and good will is ob-
served and enjoyed by peoples here and every-
where." Title page
  Includes celebrations and customs from the
United States, Australia, and many countries of
Europe, Latin America, and Asia
  "A useful addition to holiday collections be-
cause of its unusually broad coverage." Booklist

Gregory, Ruth W.
Anniversaries and holidays. 3d ed. . . .
A.L.A. 1975 246p $10.50   394.2
  1 Holidays 2 Calendars 3 Holidays—Bibliog-
  raphy 4 Birthdays—Bibliography
  ISBN 0-8389-0200-6   LC 75-23163
  "A revision of the work by Mary Emogene
Hazeltine." Title page
  First published 1928
  This volume covers 152 countries and "includes
2,736 entries for holidays, special-events days and
birthdays. . . . 'Calendar of fixed dates' the
largest portion of the book, is based on the solar
Gregorian calendar and includes civic, religious,
and special-events days and commemorative days
for notable people. . . . [Also included] are five
'Calendars of movable days': Christian, Islamic,
Jewish, and festivals in the Eastern and in the
Western worlds. An annotated, classified bibliography of over 1,000 titles is correlated to the holidays in the Gregorian calendar. Approximately
one calendar entry in every four refers to book(s),
most with recent imprint dates. Gives no alphabetical listing of books by author. Complete index
to holidays. The introductory essay explains the
history and characteristics of different calendars.
Highly recommended for all libraries." Choice

Holiday ring; festival stories and poems;
chosen and introduced by Adeline Corrigan;
illus. by Rainey Bennett. Whitman, A. 1975
256p illus lib. bdg. $10.95 (4 and up)   394.2
  1 Holidays 2 Holidays—Fiction 3 Holidays—
  Poetry
  ISBN 0-8075-3356-4   LC 75-15975
  Arranged chronologically, this anthology includes
poems, essays, and short stories for the celebration of major American and Canadian holidays
  "This anthology promises to be a tremendous
resource to teachers everywhere. . . . [It includes]
interesting tidbits that will provide many enriching supplementary activities for the classroom."
Instructor

It's time for Christmas; written and comp. by Elizabeth Hough Sechrist and Janette Woolsey; decorations by Reisie Lonette. Macrae Smith Co. 1959 256p illus $6.50 lib. bdg. $5.97 (4 and up)   394.2
1 Christmas
ISBN 0-8255-8222-9; 0-8255-8223-7   LC 59-13255
"In trying to 'present Christmas as Christ's birthday rather than from the Santa Claus point of view', the authors start off with the story of the Nativity according to St. Luke and continue with a history of Christmas, legends and traditional stories about St. Francis, La Befana, St. Nicholas, and others. . . . [Includes a] section on Christmas customs [and symbols] the words of 10 favorite carols and how they came to be written and finally [a] . . . collection of poems and stories." Chicago Sunday Trib
"This collection is a welcome addition in planning the true celebration of Christmas in the home, classroom, or club. Indexed." Lutheran Educ

It's time for Easter; written and comp. by Elizabeth Hough Sechrist and Janette Woolsey; illus. by Elsie Jan McCorkell. Macrae Smith Co. 1961 255p illus $8.50 (4 and up)   394.2
1 Easter
ISBN 0-8255-8198-2   LC 61-8299
"Beginning with a shortened version of Biblical Easter story as told in the Gospels an excellent and welcome anthology gives a brief history of Easter, explains the origin and meanings of Easter symbols, describes Lenten and Easter customs around the world, and includes Easter legends, music, poems, and stories. Illustrated with attractive line drawings, some in color." Booklist
Most of the material "should be very useful to teachers and group leaders. So may the section on composers of Easter music and authors of famous hymns, although it is not very inspiringly presented. The section of fiction is for a rather younger audience than is the first part of the anthology but good stories of Easter are hard to find and this includes some charming ones." NY Times Bk Rev

It's time for Thanksgiving; written and comp. by Elizabeth Hough Sechrist and Janette Woolsey; decorations by Guy Fry. Macrae Smith Co. 1957 251p illus lib. bdg. $5.97 (4 and up)   394.2
1 Thanksgiving Day
ISBN 0-8255-8215-6   LC 57-12005
"Pleasant stories, producible plays, traditional and modern poems, recipes, and games for Thanksgiving are brought together here in a useful . . . volume. The [editors] have frequently turned author to give us some always needed, fresh holiday material." Library J

Lazar, Wendy
The Jewish holiday book; illus. by Marion Behr. Doubleday 1977 143p illus $8.95, lib. bdg. $9.90 (3-6)   394.2
1 Fasts and feasts—Judaism 2 Handicraft 3 Cookery, Jewish
ISBN 0-385-11426-5; 0-385-11427-3   LC 76-42342
"Easy handicrafts, quick games, and cooking ideas are given for the 10 major Jewish holidays, weekly Shabbat celebration, and Israel Independence Day. Beginning with Rosh Hashanah, the start of the Jewish year, each holiday is briefly described as to its religious or historical significance, followed by projects such as apple compote for Yom Kippur, seed mosaics for Sukkot, menorahs and potato latkes for Chanukah, masks for Purim, and jam puffs for Passover. A short introductory note to parents gives directional and motivational guidelines." Booklist
The book "focuses on craft products. Few are difficult, some not even requiring step-by-step instructions; for example, a box for spices is made by covering a large match box with any of a variety of decorative materials. While the games and recipes are usually specifically related to Jewish holidays, many of the craft projects are not: a baby's bib, a macaroni necklace, a painted rock doorstop, et cetera." Chicago. Children's Bk Center

Les Tina, Dorothy
May Day; illus. by Hope Meryman. Crowell 1967 unp illus (A Crowell Holiday bk) lib. bdg. $7.89 (1-3)   394.2
1 May Day
ISBN 0-690-52645-8   LC 67-3776
"An interesting résumé of the ways in which May Day has been celebrated through the centuries, with special emphasis on the Roman rites and the traditional customs of rural England. There is also a brief mention of the fact that the first of May is celebrated in some places today by worker's marches, and several pages are devoted to May Day customs in countries around the world. The illustrations, attractive woodcuts, are sedate in color but full of movement." Chicago. Children's Bk Center

McGovern, Ann
Squeals & squiggles & ghostly giggles; illus. by Jeffrey Higginbotton. Four Winds 1973 unp illus $6.95 (2-5)   394.2
1 Halloween 2 Magic 3 Ghosts—Fiction
ISBN 0-590-17306-5   LC 72-87083
"A Halloween book, with spooky games, poems, scarey ghost stories, clever tricks and fortunes to tell, 'limer-eeks,' and even a skit with ghouls and demons." New Bks for Young Readers
"The four short stories are appropriately spooky and well suited to retelling. Diagrams for tricks are clear, and the black-and-white illustrations depict large-faced, floppy-haired children engaged in amusing antics. While there is no general discussion of Halloween, this collection offers good fun for that holiday and all year round." Sch Library J

More Festivals in Asia. Kodansha [distributed by Harper] 1975 65p illus $6.95 (2-5)   394.2
1 Festivals—Asia
ISBN 0-87011-273-2   LC 75-34740
"Asian copublication programme series 2. Sponsored by the Asian Cultural Centre for UNESCO"
An additional nine narrative descriptions of festivals, in similar format to Festivals in Asia, listed above. The countries covered include Korea, Pakistan, Indonesia, Malaysia, Vietnam, Nepal, India, Thailand and Afghanistan

Phelan, Mary Kay
The Fourth of July; illus. by Symeon Shimin. Crowell 1966 unp illus (A Crowell Holiday bk) lib. bdg. $7.89 (1-3)   394.2
1 Fourth of July
ISBN 0-690-31415-9   LC 65-25909
"This account begins with a brief history of the events leading up to the Declaration of Independence and mention of some of the key leaders in the Continental Congress. How news of the Declaration was spread throughout the colonies and celebrations by the people are described. There is also mention of many events that have taken place on the anniversary of Independence Day." Sch Library J
"Symeon Shimin's light wash illustrations are soberly, historically patriotic." NY Times Bk Rev

Purdy, Susan Gold
Jewish holidays; facts, activities, and crafts. Lippincott 1969 94p illus $8.95 (4 and up)   394.2
1 Fasts and feasts—Judaism 2 Handicraft
ISBN 0-397-31076-5   LC 75-84360
"Each holiday is described, both as to its origins and in the traditional ways in which it is celebrated. Each is followed by directions for some project associated with the holiday: a table decoration, a toy, a recipe, puppets and costumes, greeting cards, etc. The instructions are clear, with a note that adult supervision is needed for handling any sharp tools. The body of the text is preceded by a Jewish calendar and a brief discussion of the Jewish religion. Notes on pronunciation are included; a list of materials and foods used in the projects, and an index are appended. Particularly useful for religious education or for craft groups." Chicago. Children's Bk Center

Rollins, Charlemae

(comp.) Christmas gif'. . . . Line drawings by Tom O'Sullivan; book design by Stan Williamson. Follett 1963 119p illus $7.95 (4 and up)   394.2

1 Christmas 2 American literature—Black authors 3 Blacks in literature and art
ISBN 0-695-81190-8   LC 63-17805

"An anthology of Christmas poems, songs, and stories, written by and about Negroes." Title page
This book "gets its title from a joyful Christmas Day custom widespread among the plantation slaves. Included are . . . some special recipes, many of . . . [which] come from the [compiler's] grandmother who was born a slave. A lovely collection of the new and the old enhanced by spirited line drawings." Pub W
Includes author and title indexes

Sawyer, Ruth

Joy to the world; Christmas legends; illus. by Trina Schart Hyman. Little 1966 102p illus $5.95 (3-6)   394.2

1 Christmas—Fiction 2 Legends 3 Carols
ISBN 0-316-77177-5   LC 66-14905

Ancient Arabia, Serbia, Ireland and Spain are the sources for these six Christmas stories, each accompanied by a carol
These are "unusual and varied Christmas legends. . . . Narrations convey the cultural tone of each country; some of the shorter selections will make good holiday dramatization." Wis Library Bul
"The illustrations in black and white and tones of golden tan makes a book that matches in appearance the glowing spirit of the tales. A beautiful book for family sharing." Horn Bk

Sechrist, Elizabeth Hough

Christmas everywhere; a book of Christmas customs of many lands; written and comp. by Elizabeth Hough Sechrist; illus. by Elsie Jane McCorkell. New rev. and enl. ed. Macrae Smith Co. 1962 186p illus $6.95, lib. bdg. $6.71   394.2

1 Christmas
ISBN 0-8255-8130-3; 0-8255-8131-1   LC 62-13303

"First published 1931"
"The Christmas customs of 20 countries are discussed. Activities, food, and beliefs of the people make this a good resource book." Adventuring with Bks. 2d edition

Red letter days; a book of holiday customs; illus. by Elsie Jane McCorkell. Rev. ed. Macrae Smith Co. 1965 253p illus $6.67, lib. bdg. $6.47   394.2

1 Holidays
ISBN 0-8255-8162-1; 0-8255-8163-X   LC 65-16332

"Text first published 1940"
Beginning "with a chapter on the story of the calendar, there follow interesting accounts of the holidays, their historical significance, and some explanation of the methods of celebration in different parts of the world. The days [are arranged] in chronological order. . . .A bibliography and index add to the usefulness [of the book]." Wis Library Bul [review of the 1940 edition]

Showers, Paul

Indian festivals; illus. by Lorence Bjorklund. Crowell 1969 unp illus (A Crowell Holiday bk) $6.95, lib. bdg. $7.89 (1-3)   394.2

1 Indians of North America—Rites and ceremonies 2 Festivals—North America 3 Holidays
ISBN 0-690-43697-1; 0-690-43698-X   LC 70-78266

The author describes the festivals and holidays of American Indian tribes such as the Seminoles, Zuñis, Sioux and Cheyennes, and the religious beliefs which they reflect
"Transitions are occasionally abrupt, but the text is clear and non-fictionalized. Soft flesh-colored and black crayon drawings adequately depict customs, costumes and individual faces." Sch Library J

Spicer, Dorothy Gladys

46 days of Christmas; a cycle of Old World songs, legends and customs; illus. by Anne Marie Jauss. Coward-McCann 1960 96p illus lib. bdg. $4.99 (4 and up)   394.2

1 Christmas
ISBN 0--698-30091-2   LC 60-12497

Some of this material has been adapted from the author's Festivals of Western Europe, published 1958
Christmas "celebrations in 18 European and Asiatic countries. Arranged in chronological order from Saint Barbara's Day in Syria on December 4th, to the old Twelfth Night, January 18, in England. A . . . carol, prayer, or hymn precedes each chapter." Library J
Indexed by countries, song titles, and special days

Take joy! The Tasha Tudor Christmas book; selected, ed. and illus. by Tasha Tudor. Collins [distributed by Philomel Bks.] 1966 157p illus music $9.95, lib. bdg. $9.99   394.2

1 Christmas
ISBN 0-529-04962-7; 0-529-00208-6   LC 66-31200

"A collection of Christmas stories, poems, customs, and carols and their music, celebrating both the religious and the secular aspects of the holiday. Included are the particular traditions and recipes of the Tudor family." Adventuring with Bks. 2d edition
Generously illustrated with tenderness and reverence in full-color and black-and-white pictures. . . . Of special interest to children who enjoy homely, old-fashioned pleasures, parents and grandparents wanting to preserve family Christmas traditions, and to Tasha Tudor fans of all ages." Booklist

Thanksgiving; feast and festival; comp. by Mildred Corell Luckhardt; illus. by Ralph McDonald. Abingdon 1966 352p illus $12.95 (4 and up)   394.2

1 Thanksgiving Day 2 Thanksgiving Day—Fiction 3 Thanksgiving Day—Poetry
ISBN 0-687-41404-0   LC 66-16996

"An anthology of prose and poetry about the Thanksgiving holiday in the United States and about other observances of giving thanks or of harvest time. The first section of the book is entitled 'The Pilgrims and Thanksgiving'; the second, and longer, section is called 'Thanksgiving and Harvest Time, Near and Far.' Some of the excerpts from books have been abridged or adapted; there are some pages of background information about holiday customs by the editor. Most of the selections are good, and the book should be useful as an additional source of material; it is weakened somewhat by the pedestrian illustrations. A bibliography and an author-title index are appended." Chicago. Children's Bk Center

Tudor, Tasha

A time to keep; the Tasha Tudor book of holidays; written and illus. by Tasha Tudor. Rand McNally 1977 unp illus $6.95, lib. bdg. $6.97 (k-3)   394.2

1 Holidays
ISBN 0-528-82019-2; 0-528-80213-5   LC 77-9067

"Nostalgic memories of days long ago shimmer across the pages, as Tasha Tudor reminisces about her family's early New England festivities. Twelfth Night charades, Valentine's Day cards, maple sugaring, Easter egg trees, maypoles, Fourth of July picnics, Halloween pumpkins, Thanksgiving turkeys, and Christmas crèches are remembered in brief narrative and depicted in soft delicate watercolors. Twinings of pines, grasses, and herbs border the pictures, which are filled with the Corgis, cats, looms, marionettes, wheelbarrows, cider presses, lanterns, and fascinating minutiae found in the artist's own home." Booklist

395   Etiquette

Joslin, Sesyle

What do you do, dear? Pictures by Maurice Sendak. Young Scott Bks. 1961 unp illus lib. bdg. $5.95 (k-2)   395

1 Etiquette
ISBN 0-201-09387-1   LC 61-19972

Joslin, Sesyle—*Continued*

Companion volume to the author's: What do you say, dear? entered below

A "handbook of etiquette for young ladies and gentlemen to be used as a guide for everyday social behavior." The author

"The propriety of what the well-mannered child will do is related to extraordinary situations, as for example: The Sheriff of Nottingham interrupts you while you are reading, to take you to jail; you will, naturally, 'Find a bookmark to save your place.' Sendak's pictures account for a great share of the fun." Horn Bk

A "wonderful spoof on manners in a hilarious picture-book made for laughing aloud." Child Study Assn of Am

What do you say, dear? Pictures by Maurice Sendak. Young Scott Bks. 1958 unp illus lib. bdg. $5.95 (k-2)   395

1 Etiquette
ISBN 0-201-09391-X   LC 58-3616

Companion volume to the author's: What do you do, dear? entered above

"A handbook of etiquette for young ladies and gentlemen to be used as a guide for everyday social behavior." Preceding title page

"A rollicking introduction to manners for the very young. A series of delightfully absurd situations being introduced to a baby elephant, bumping into a crocodile, being rescued from a dragon—are posed and appropriately answered. The illustrations are among Sendak's best—and funniest." Chicago, Children's Bk Center

This "funny and imaginative picture book . . . may stimulate children to invent situations of their own." Booklist

398 Folklore

The **American** riddle book, [comp.] by Carl Withers and Sula Benet; illus. by Marc Simont. Abelard-Schuman 1954 157p illus lib. bdg. $8.79 (5 and up)   398

1 Riddles
ISBN 0-200-71842-8   LC 53-10845

"A collection of over a thousand riddles, conundrums, and other riddling nonsense, old and new, compiled by two anthropologists. . . . Includes numerous special categories such as arithmetic riddles, kinship riddles, Bible riddles, word charades, and Little Moron riddles, and a separate section of representative riddles from other nations, regions, and tribal groups. Amusing illustrations. Of interest to sociologists as well as to children." Booklist

"The title refers to the audience rather than the sources." NY Times Bk Rev

"The authors have classified the entries for ready reference, but readers may begin on any page for a chuckle." Wis Library Bul

And so my garden grows; illus. by Peter Spier. Doubleday 1969 unp illus (The Mother Goose lib) $5.95, lib. bdg. $6.90 (k-3)   398

1 Nursery rhymes
ISBN 0-385-08757-8; 0-385-05156-5   LC 68-25599

Pictures from Italian cities, parks, vineyards, monasteries, farms and great estates provide the background to such nursery rhymes as "Mistress Mary, quite contrary," "This is the key to the kingdom," "Rosemary green, and lavender blue," and "Mother, may I go and bathe?"

"As children pore over the extraordinary depth of these pictures, as they surely will, they may even feel that they already have half a foot in this magical land, so brilliantly has it been brought to life in these pages." Times (London) Lit Sup

The **Annotated** Mother Goose, nursery rhymes old and new; arranged and explained by William S. Baring-Gould & Ceil Baring-Gould; illus. by Walter Crane [and others] with chapter decorations by E. M. Simon. Potter, C.N. 1962 350p illus $10   398

1 Nursery rhymes
ISBN 0-517-02959-6   LC 62-21606

A fully annotated edition containing more than 1,000 rhymes—originals, variations, allusions and sources. Includes over 200 illustrations by various artists

Bibliography: p333-40

Aulaire, Ingri d'

D'Aulaires' Trolls [by Ingri and Edgar Parin d'Aulaire]. Doubleday 1972 62p illus $5.95, lib. bdg. $6.70 (3-6)   398

1 Folklore—Norway
ISBN 0-385-08255-X; 0-385-01275-6   LC 76-158897

Illustrated by the authors

The d'Aulaires "present a kind of dissertation on trolls, and children wil revel in the glorious array: forest trolls and water and sea trolls, along with their trollhag wives and their troll-brat offspring; little, mischievous gnome-trolls; and the biggest, most nightmarish of all—the mountain trolls, often twelve-headed, which had magical powers and the strength of fifty men. . . . The commodious pages —black-and-white stone lithographs alternating with full-color illustrations prepared on acetate overlays—are alive with vigor and imagination and a full measure of grotesque detail." Horn Bk

Aylesworth, Thomas G.

The story of vampires; illus. with photographs and old prints. McGraw 1977 85p illus $6.95 (4 and up)   398

1 Vampires
ISBN 0-07-002647-5   LC 76-53581

"This outline of vampire lore covers the history of vampirism in legend (mainly Eastern European beliefs and customs), literature, and film as well as real-life counterparts." Sch Library J

"This book, illustrated with photos (mostly from the many movies about vampires) and old prints, is an engrossing account. . . . The author's style is engagingly light and humorous but by no means offhand. He goes into all the myths, legends and histories of real people responsible for the belief in vampires." Pub W

Other books about vampires: p79-80

Bodecker, N. M.

It's raining, said John Twaining; Danish nursery rhymes; tr. and illus. by N. M. Bodecker. Atheneum Pubs. 1973 unp illus $6.95, pa $1.95 (k-2)   398

1 Nursery rhymes
ISBN 0-689-30316-5; 0-689-70437-2   LC 72-85912

"A Margaret K. McElderry book"

These "nursery rhymes are quite different from what we are used to, but they read easily and well. Almost immediately they begin to seem familiar to us in their warmth and simplicity. . . . [The] full-color pictures set different moods to evoke the particular feelings of a rhyme, and which are always rather unexpected. . . . Here are tender, simple, silly nursery rhymes that Danish men and women have grown up with, each specially interpreted for us in an enormously varied and well-constructed picture book. They give us another slant and great pleasure." NY Times Bk Rev

Brian Wildsmith's Mother Goose; a collection of nursery rhymes. Watts, F. [1965 c1964] 80p illus. lib. bdg. $7.90, pa $4.95 (k-2)   398

1 Nursery rhymes
ISBN 0-531-01535-1; 0-531-02372-9   LC 65-10040

First published 1964 in England

These eighty-six verses "are well selected and include many quaint and lesser-known verses." Bk Week

"The artist's wholly original, sophisticated yet childlike interpretation of long-familiar material is revealed in his clever composition, unconventional humor, and characteristic watercolor technique with its use of geometric patterns and brilliant chromatic modulations." Horn Bk

Index of first lines: p80

Cakes and custard: children's rhymes; chosen by Brian Alderson; illus. by Helen Oxenbury. Morrow 1975 [c1974] 156p illus $9.95, lib. bdg. $9.55 (k-2)   398

1 Nursery rhymes 2 Poetry—Collections
ISBN 0-688-22050-9; 0-688-32050-3   LC 75-24523

Cakes and custard: children's rhymes——Cont.

First published 1974 in England

The editor "has brought together Mother Goose, jump-rope and counting-out rhymes worn smooth and renewed by children over the centuries, and for good measure, a few contemporary verses by James Reeves and Robert Graves to show, as Alderson stresses, the continuance of the nursery rhyme tradition." NY Times Bk Rev

"Original and dynamic in layout and design, the book is illustrated by a masterful artist. . . . Emphasizing the agelessness of the rhymes, [Oxenbury] has dealt with time settings eclectically, making some of the characters look unexpectedly contemporary. A superb colorist and draftswoman, she has created a compendium of artistic possibilities and moods—from tiny vignettes to vigorous full-page pictures, from reticent lyricism to earthy, sardonic, even grotesque humor." Horn Bk

Includes an Index of first lines

Chorao, Kay

The baby's lap book. Dutton 1977 58p illus lib. bdg. $6.95 (k-1)   398

1 Nursery rhymes
ISBN 0-525-26100-1   LC 77-23534

A collection of more than fifty traditional nursery rhymes accompanied by "Chorao's soft, eminently careful pencil drawings of the characters and their situations. Innocence is all pervasive, in the alternating pastel pink and yellow pages that nicely counter the light grays of the framed drawings; in the young faces, both animal and human; and in the fullness of cozy interiors and bucolic outdoor field and forest scenes. The artist's light hand is right for her interpretation, unabashedly, uncloyingly sweet, and admirably suited to its purpose." Booklist

Includes an index of first lines

Emberley, Barbara

Drummer Hoff; adapted by Barbara Emberley; illus. by Ed Emberley. Prentice-Hall 1967 unp illus $8.95, pa $1.95 (k-3)   398

1 Nursery rhymes
ISBN 0-13-220822-9; 0-13-220855-5   LC 67-28189

Awarded the Caldecott Medal, 1968

In this version of "a rhyming folk verse a cannon is assembled by a team of soldiers, while poker-faced Drummer Hoff stands at the ready [to fire it off] and the ornate headgear of the militia protrudes like ramrods from a trench below. . . . The firing is shown in a double-page spread . . . and the last picture displays a . . . scene in which time has erased all scars and the cannon is covered with flowers and spiderwebs." Sat Rev

"Stylized woodcuts in brilliant hues develop this martial folk rhyme into a sprightly book which the young child will enjoy again and again. The pictures are to be re-examined for their entertaining details (birds, ladybugs, and flowers appear and reappear), and the lines of the brief text are to be chanted for their alliterative nonsense." Horn Bk

Emrich, Duncan

(comp.) The hodgepodge book; an almanac of American folklore. . . . Illus. by Ib Ohlsson. Four Winds 1972 367p illus lib. bdg. $8.95   398

1 Folklore—U.S.
ISBN 0-590-07250-1   LC 72-77811

"Containing all manner of curious, interesting, and out-of-the-way information drawn from American folklore, and not to be found anywhere else in the world; as well as jokes, conundrums, riddles, puzzles, and other matter designed to amuse and entertain; all of it most instructive and delightful." Title page

"Children, who love the absurd, will be pleased by the size of the volume and its twenty-one alluring topical areas such as Cumulative Stories ('The Little Old Lady Who Swallowed a Fly'), Love and Kisses ('I Love You Better Than a Pig Loves Slop'), and Mind Your Manners! ('Temper, Temper!'). Following the folklorist's notes for the various sections, an impressive fifty-two-page bibliography of sources is appended for scholars. References are keyed to a list of folklore journals. The scribbly pen-and-ink sketches are pert and suitably appropriate to the text." Horn Bk

Emrich, Duncan

(comp.) The nonsense book of riddles, rhymes, tongue twisters, puzzles and jokes from American folklore; illus. by Ib Ohlsson. Four Winds 1970 266p illus lib. bdg. $8.95 (3 and up)   398

1 Folklore—U.S.
ISBN 0-590-17157-7   LC 77-105339

An "extensive collection of traditional American nonsense, funsense, and sentiment. Whatever the occasion or mood, there is a verse or a chant to fit it—from the tongue-tingling tangler 'This is a zither' to the unabashed sentimentality of 'When in my lonely grave I sleep/And bending willows o'er me weep,'/'Tis then, dear friend, and not before,/I think of thee no more, no more.' The compiler . . . has enhanced the value of the collection with a succinct, incisive summary of the history of nonsense together with an extensive bibliography of studies relating to its various forms. But, as the introduction points out, the compilation is first of all 'a reminder of the wonderful world of play and rhyme and beautiful nonsense.' The skillfully executed line drawings add to the fun." Horn Bk

Granfa' Grig had a pig, and other rhymes without reason from Mother Goose; comp. and illus. by Wallace Tripp. Little 1976 96p illus $9.95, pa $5.95 (k-3)   398

1 Nursery rhymes
ISBN 0-316-85282-1; 0-316-85284-8   LC 76-25234

An "ambitious, oversized collection. . . . Tripp has energetically penned a menagerie of animal 'people' whose faces are, as always, keenly expressive of the matter at hand. Most spreads feature several rhymes with accompanying illustration, but periodically there's an eye-grabbing double-page spread for one rhyme, the fiendishly evil giant for 'Fee, Fie, Fo, Fum!' on page one being the first knockout example." Booklist

Index of first lines: p96

Gregory Griggs and other nursery rhyme people; selected & illus. by Arnold Lobel. Greenwillow Bks. 1978 47p illus $8.25, lib. bdg. $7.92 (k-2)   398

1 Nursery rhymes
ISBN 0-688-80128-5; 0-688-84128-7   LC 77-22209

"The author has collected thirty-four little-known nursery rhymes and embellished them with strong, expressive illustrations done in pastel colored wash. Included are many unusual characters with very human problems: Joshua Lane, who couldn't seem to catch his train; the dejected little man who always expected bad weather; Clotilda, whose party was a flop because nobody came; and Gregory Griggs, who was indecisive about his favorite among twenty-seven wigs." Horn Bk

Hark! Hark! The dogs do bark, and other rhymes about dogs; chosen by Lenore Blegvad; illus. by Erik Blegvad. Atheneum Pubs. 1976 [c1975] unp illus lib. bdg. $5.95 (k-2)   398

1 Nursery rhymes   2 Dogs—Poetry
ISBN 0-689-50035-1   LC 75-9788

"A Margaret K. McElderry book"

First published 1975 in England

This "collection of English and Scottish nursery rhymes is a companion to 'Mittens for Kittens' [entered below]. Included, of course, is Mother Hubbard's famous pet as well as the little dog who 'laughed to see such sport.' But readers will also meet 'Rover,' 'Buff,' 'Sandy,' 'Poor Dog Bright,' 'Blue Bell' (whose antics rival those of Mother Hubbard's dog) and assorted other canine characters." Pub W

"Most of the poems share a single page with an illustration in black and white or in color. . . . Some of the meticulous line drawings suggest miniature toys; and the simplicity and cleanness of line, color, and composition create idealized British settings for the inquisitive, pert, or excited dogs that inhabit the pages of the book." Horn Bk

Heaps, Willard A.
Superstition! Elsevier/Nelson Bks. 1972
204p $7.95 (6 and up)   398
1 Superstition
ISBN 0-525-66226-X   LC 72-8114
First published by Thomas Nelson
An examination of the history of and bases
for superstitions in such areas as theater, gambling, sports, medicine, courtship, marriage, and
death
This is "an entertaining catalog of superstitions
to delight and intrigue believer or skeptic." Booklist
Sources and readings: p192-97

Helfman, Elizabeth S.
Maypoles and wood demons; the meaning
of trees; drawings by Richard Cuffari. Seabury [distributed by Houghton] 1972 128p
illus $6.95 (3-6)   398
1 Plant lore 2 Trees
ISBN 0-395-28859-2   LC 72-75706
"A Clarion book"
The author explores the folklore of trees, and
relates tree legends and ceremonies from different
parts of the world, from ancient to modern times
"This is an educational and absorbing book, with
lively pictures." Pub W
Books for further reading: p123-24

Signs & symbols of the sun. Seabury [distributed by Houghton] 1974 192p illus $8.95
(5 and up)   398
1 Sun 2 Folklore
ISBN 0-395-28860-8   LC 73-20121
"A Clarion book"
"With objectivity and understanding Helfman
presents an interesting look at sun worship, mythology about the sun, and sun symbols. Ceremonies,
beliefs, and customs of various cultures and periods in history are covered including Persian, Far
Eastern, American Indian, European, Incan and
Aztec. Final chapters cover scientific knowledge
about the sun and symbols used in modern times.
Well organized and simply written." Sch Library J

Hot cross buns, and other old street cries;
chosen especially for children by John
Landstaff; pictures by Nancy Winslow
Parker. Atheneum Pubs. 1978 26p illus
music lib. bdg. $7.95 (3-5)   398
1 Folk songs, English
ISBN 0-689-50103-X   LC 77-14426
"A Margaret K. McElderry book"
"A collection of thirty traditional street cries—
such as 'Chairs to Mend,' 'Seville Oranges,' . . .
'Knives or Scissors to Grind'—which are from one
hundred to three hundred years old. Both the words
and the music are printed one cry or more to a
page and illustrated with ingenuously humorous
black-and-tan drawings of the peddlers. At least
two of the cries can be sung together, a number
of them can be sung simultaneously in groups of
three, and one lends itself to performance as a
three-part round. The brief introduction highlights
the cultural and musical significance of the old
street calls and suggests entertaining ways for
children to use them." Horn Bk
Young singers may find this collection "a little
harder to sink their teeth into than Langstaff's
earlier gathering of rounds, 'Sweetly Sings the
Donkey' but sheer curiosity about 'olden day ads'
may attract children who can sing all of today's
commercials. The melodies, true to their original
form, come with no suggested accompaniment and
some have rather tricky rhythms. . . . Historical
setting might have been deepened for greater
interest, but Parker's brown-black-and-white illustrations supply charm and some of the needed
sense of context. As much a music and drama resource book as a let's-all-get-together-and-sing
volume." Booklist

The **House** that Jack built; pictures by Paul
Galdone. McGraw 1961 32p illus lib.
bdg. $7.95 (k-2)   398
1 Nursery rhymes
ISBN 0-07-022719-5   LC 61-7577

"Whittlesey House Publications"
"A picture book that gives a joyful interpretation
of the familiar nursery rhyme. The rhyme has been
left intact, and the illustrations are delightful: the
fiirst picture of the cow with a crumpled horn
shows the dog being tossed, not hurt but completely surprised, into the grass; a second picture,
when the lines recur, shows the cow benignly licking the dog, with only one startled eye visible in
the dog's rather apprehensive face." Chicago. Children's Bk Center

The **House** that Jack built; la maison que
Jacques a bâtie. A picture book in two
languages [by] Antonio Frasconi. Harcourt
1958 unp illus $6.50 (1-4)   398
1 Nursery rhymes 2 Bilingual books—French-
English
ISBN 0-15-236300-9   LC 58-8625
"On each page the lines cumulate separately in
French and in English until the end of the tale is
reached; then the story is reiterated, with French
and English in coupled lines. A third section asks a
question in English and answers in French." Chicago. Children's Bk Center
"A refreshing way to learn vocabulary in a
second language. . . . Mr. Frasconi's modern
woodcuts deserve a review all their own, alive as
they are with imaginative action, variety of expression and texture, and expert use of three
colors plus black." Horn Bk

I saw a ship a-sailing; pictures by Janina
Domanska. Macmillan Pub. Co. 1972 unp
illus $4.95 (k-1)   398
1 Nursery rhymes
ISBN 0-02-732940-2   LC 75-185147
An illustrated presentation of the traditional
Mother Goose rhyme about a magical ship with
its delectable cargo, an irrepressible crew of four-
and-twenty white mice, and the stalwart captain
duck
The book "is illustrated by pictures that are composed with a high sense of design and a deft use
of color. The patterns are often geometric, the
details intricate, and the bold colors of the ship,
her crew, and the cargo effectively set off by the
cool pastel shades of water or a patterned background. The illustrations are not primarily humorous, but there are amusing conceits like the clouds
that emanate from a giant pipe smoked by the
man in the moon." Sutherland. The Best in Children's Bks

If all the seas were one sea; etchings by
Janina Domanska. Macmillan Pub. Co. 1971
unp illus $6.95 (k-2)   398
1 Nursery rhymes
ISBN 0-02-732930-5   LC 73-146621
"The familiar nursery rhyme about a tree made
of all the trees in the world falling into a sea
made of all the seas in the world ('. . . what a
splish splash that would be!') is illustrated with
the intricate but not too-busy geometric figures
that are distinctively Domanska's style. The designs are stunning and sophisticated and color is
used with enough restraint so that the two do not
compete." Sutherland. The Best in Children's Bks

Ivimey, John W.
Complete version of Ye three blind mice;
illus. by Walton Corbould. Warne 1979 unp
illus music $6.95 (k-3)   398
1 Nursery rhymes 2 Mice—Poetry
ISBN 0-7232-2256-8   LC 79-65174
First published 1904 in England
"This reproduction gives little children the gift
of Ivimey's 1904 invention in its entirety. The
opener is a simple musical arrangement of the
round for three voices. There follow verses describing events in the lives of three gentlemen
rodents that will certainly surprise readers who
know only stanzas about the blind mice and the
farmer's wife cutting off their tails with a carving knife." Pub W
"The black line sketches and full-color drawings,
which perfectly complement the story, are executed with enthusiastic vigor." Booklist
"The book falsely equates a disability such as
blindness with illness . . . it also implies that
disability is a bizarre and/or amusing sight." Interracial Bks for Children Bul

James Marshall's Mother Goose. Farrar, Straus 1979 unp illus $8.95 (k-3) 398

1 Nursery rhymes
ISBN 0-374-33653-9 LC 79-2574

"Clean, translucent pastel colors and jolly cartoon figures give this limited collection [of thirty-five rhymes] a cheerful countenance. Marshall's interpretations of familiar nursery rhyme figures are sometimes flat but more often amusing, especially in the case of a debonair Humpty Dumpty and a positively lascivious dish (that ran away with the spoon.) Several of the old favorites are here, plus a number of lesser known rhymes such as little Poll Parrot and Little Tommy Tittlemouse. The illustrations depict the action in a literal way, with a breezy, occasionally offbeat humor, as when Mother Hubbard's hungry dog responds to the empty cupboard with 'I can scarcely believe it.' " Booklist

Jeffers, Susan

Three jovial huntsmen; adapted and illus. by Susan Jeffers. Bradbury Press 1973 unp illus $7.95 (k-2) 398

1 Nursery rhymes
ISBN 0-87888-023-2 LC 70-122739

Title on cover: Mother Goose—Three jovial huntsmen

"The story involves three dimwits who hunt through a forest full of game without ever seeing any. However, viewers will have the pleasure of spotting all the nearly hidden animals the huntsmen either fail to see or mistake for something else." Sch Library J

"It's main attraction lies in the book's physical beauty: The subdued tones of the illustrations—created by yellow, red, blue, and black overlays on pen-and-ink drawings—have been masterfully blended and differentiated. In some of the night scenes, the twisted branches and muted blues are reminiscent of Arthur Rackham's work." Horn Bk

"A sloppy binding occasionally interrupts beautiful visual effects of the double-page spreads." Booklist

Leach, Maria

Noodles, nitwits, and numskulls; drawings by Kurt Werth. Collins [distributed by Philomel Bks.] 1961 96p illus lib. bdg. $6.99 (4 and up) 398

1 Wit and humor 2 Riddles 3 Folklore
ISBN 0-529-03662-2 LC 61-14112

A "collection of time-honored jokes, riddles and funny stories that go way back into the folklore of various countries. There are . . . notes about the origins of these [at the end of the book]." Pub W

"The illustrations have a light humor, and the book is made attractive by good type size and plenty of space on the pages. Not the sort of book for continuous reading, but very useful as a source of material in this genre." Chicago. Children's Bk Center

Bibliography: p96

Riddle me, riddle me, ree; illus. by William Wiesner. Viking 1970 142p illus $4.95, Penguin Bks. pa $1.50 (3-6) 398

1 Riddles 2 Folklore
ISBN 0-670-05065-2; 0-14-030960-8 LC 74-106922

"A more scholarly collection than most, this is devoted entirely to riddles from around the world. . . . [The more than 200 riddles included] are divided into sections by subject, and the country of origin is given for each one. In addition, each riddle is fully annotated in the 'Notes and Bibliography' section at the back of the book. Told from the viewpoint of the folklorist, some of the riddles will be in a form unfamiliar to American children . . . but the U.S. entries include elephant jokes and state name riddles." Sch Library J

McHargue, Georgess

The beasts of never; a history natural & unnatural of monsters mythical & magical; illus. by Frank Bozzo. Bobbs 1968 112p illus $5.95 (5 and up) 398

1 Animals, Mythical
ISBN 0-672-50217-8 LC 67-18651

Companion volume to the author's: The impossible people, entered below

"This is a book about legendary animals, especially those whose history is connected with western Europe and the country near the Mediterranean Sea. The various species of the beasts and their evolution are explored; their myths are explained in terms of the people by whom they were invented. A thoroughly fascinating account of almost-true magical beasts including unicorns, dragons, phoenix, basilisks, winged and sea monsters and the Loch Ness monster." Wis Library Bul

"An oversize book (8⅝" × 11⅜") with full page illustration for each chapter and numerous smaller drawings within the text." Library J

Bibliography: p108-09

Meet the vampire; drawings by Stephen Gammell. Lippincott 1979 80p illus (The Eerie ser.) $6.95, pa $3.95 (5 and up) 398

1 Vampires
ISBN 0-397-31833-2; 0-397-31851-0 LC 78-20393

"This book includes myths and legends, information about the real Dracula, and tells how to recognize and banish vampires." Rdng Teacher

"This homage to the bloodsuckers will undoubtedly find a receptive audience. There's a lot of information here. . . . McHargue includes a history of Vlad the Impaler, alleged to be the real Dracula, and notes vampire traditions in parts of the world other than Transylvania. She explores the symbolic significance of blood and suggests reasons why certain actual historical events could give rise to a belief in vampires. . . . The matter-of-fact tone seems to give credence to the existence of these monsters—an attitude that will surely please the diehard vampire devotee. Illustrations include photographs from films." Booklist

Meet the werewolf; drawings by Stephen Gammell. Lippincott 1976 79p illus (The Eerie ser.) $7.95, pa $2.95 (4 and up) 398

1 Werwolves 2 Animals, Mythical
ISBN 0-397-31662-3; 0-397-31663-1 LC 75-34046

In addition to werewolves, "other protean creatures of folk literature such as swans, selchies or seal folk, the badgers and foxes of Japan, Scandinavia's berserkers, and the were-jaguars of South America are described. Readers are then regaled with stories as well as some real people who were believed to be werewolves and sentenced as such. There is also a discussion of the 'reality' of werewolves and the historical conditions which gave rise to beliefs in them. McHargue finishes off with a blood-thirsty tale entitled 'The Worst Werewolf Story of All' which is sure to raise gooseflesh on even the staunchest non-believers. For young readers who love to be terrified and are old enough to handle the gore, this is choice. The illustrations are excellent as well." Sch Library J

Marguerite de Angeli's Book of nursery and Mother Goose rhymes. Doubleday 1954 192p illus $8.95, lib. bdg. $9.90 (k-2) 398

1 Nursery rhymes
ISBN 0-385-07232-5; 0-385-06246-X LC 54-9838

Marguerite de Angeli "has compiled and illustrated a beautiful edition that offers nearly 400 rhymes, all the old favorites and the less familiar, and over 250 lovely, imaginative pictures, both in full color and in black and white." Wis Library Bul

Mittens for kittens, and other rhymes about cats; chosen by Lenore Blegvad; illus. by Erik Blegvad. Atheneum Pubs. 1974 unp illus lib. bdg. $5.95 (k-2) 398

1 Nursery rhymes 2 Cats—Poetry
ISBN 0-689-50003-3 LC 74-76269

"A Margaret K. McElderry book"

Companion volume to: Hark! Hark! The dogs do bark, entered above

A selection of 25 brief English rhymes about cats and kittens

The illustrator "has created pages full of his uniquely appealing pictures (some in color, others in black and white) to accompany the verses selected by his wife. . . . The poems are many and various, ranging from the well-known 'Ding, Dong, Bell' and 'I Love Little Pussy' to others which will be new to young readers." Pub W

Morrison, Lillian
(comp.) Black within and red without; a book of riddles; illus. by Jo Spier. Crowell 1953 120p illus $7.95 (4 and up)   **398**
1 Riddles
ISBN 0-690-14656-6   LC 53-8420
"This is a collection of almost 200 traditional riddles, most of them in rhyme. . . . There are some 'pun riddles' but the most common are those in which the answers are hidden in metaphors, some strongly imaginative or strangely evocative, others making up in sound or vitality what they lack in sense. . . . The sources of the riddles in this book are shown in the bibliography at the end." Preface
"There is fun and poetry and echoes of the past in these gay riddles, which will keep a child happy puzzling friends and relatives for the answers." Chicago Sunday Trib

Mother Goose; pictures by Gyo Fujikawa. Grosset 1968 125p llius $5.95 (k-2)   **398**
1 Nursery rhymes
ISBN 0-448-01810-1   LC 69-29949
"An oversize book that contains 300 rhymes." Best Bks for Children

Mother Goose; re-arranged and ed. in this form by Eulalie Osgood Grover; illus. by Frederick Richardson. The classic Volland ed. Rand McNally [1976] c1971 159p illus $7.95 (k-2)   **398**
1 Nursery rhymes
ISBN 0-528-82800-2   LC 76-16156
First published 1915 by P. F. Volland & Co. This is a reprint of the edition published 1971 by Hubbard
"Full-page, old fashioned paintings make a charming edition of this classic book." Best Bks for Children
"According to the publisher [Hubbard] this re-vised edition of a book originally published in 1915 contains 140 additional rhymes, a new in-troduction, and an index." Booklist (review of 1971 edition)

Mother Goose; seventy-seven verses with pic-tures by Tasha Tudor. Walck, H.Z. 1944 87p illus $6.95 (k-2)   **398**
1 Nursery rhymes
ISBN 0-8098-1901-5
First published by Oxford
A lovely "Mother Goose, fresh in its interpreta-tion both as to selection and illustration. . . . The book is smaller than usual for Mother Goose; the pictures in soft colors and in black and white are quaint and charming." Booklist
"Perfect in flavor and spirit for the young child and delightful from the adult standpoint." Li-brary J

Mother Goose; or, The old nursery rhymes; illus. in colour by Kate Greenaway. Warne 1964 52p illus $4.95 (k-2)   **398**
1 Nursery rhymes
ISBN 0-7232-0591-4   LC 64-3665
A reprint of the title first published 1881 by G. Routledge and Sons
"This tiny little book contains but a limited num-ber of rhymes but its charming illustrations have delighted many children. The artist, Kate Greena-way, has kept to her usual type of English chil-dren rather than adapting herself to the accepted Mother Gose style." Right Bk for the Right Child

Mother Goose and nursery rhymes; wood engravings by Philip Reed. Regnery/Gate-way [1979 c1963] 57p illus $9.95 (k-2)   **398**
1 Nursery rhymes
ISBN 0-89526-098-0   LC 79-65853
First published 1963 by Atheneum
A collection of almost 70 "long rhymes, short ones, some most familiar, others less so. . . . The characters are 18th century in costume." Pub W
The selection is "highly individual [and] fresh. . . . The artist-designer has provided beautifully printed wood engraving in six clear colors. With superb execution, quaintness, and humor, they make a volume for the lover of fine books; for the nursery age, [there are] the details and amusing traits of personality." Horn Bk
Index of first lines: p55-56

The Mother Goose book; illus. by Alice and Martin Provensen. Random House 1976 60p illus $6.95, lib. bdg. $7.99 (k-2)   **398**
1 Nursery rhymes
ISBN 0-394-82122-X; 0-394-92122-4   LC 76-8548
"Most of these 150 rhymes are familiar but there are a few little-used rhymes as well. They are grouped by subject and illustrated in one big double-page spread for each subject." Children's Bk Rev Serv
"In putting together this extensive collection of nursery rhymes, familiar and not so well known, the couple have been generous to the point of lavishness. Here are more than 150 entries, illus-trated in pleasing pastels. . . . They offer, in short, one of the most comprehensive and attrac-tive collections of the traditional verses available." Pub W
Includes an index of first lines

Mother Goose nursery rhymes; illus. by Arthur Rackham. Viking 1975 153p illus $7.95 (k-2)   **398**
ISBN 0-670-49003-2   LC 75-16242
"A Studio book"
A reprint of the edition first published 1913 with title, Mother Goose: the old nursery rhymes
A collection of 162 nursery rhymes which were Rackham's childhood favorites. "The pictures re-produced faithfully here are as full of enchantment as ever. Some are in lovely colors, most in black-and-white, all lively and true to the themes." Pub W

The Mother Goose treasury; [illus. by] Raymond Briggs. Coward-McCann 1966 217p illus lib. bdg. $9.99 (k-2)   **398**
1 Nursery rhymes
ISBN 0-698-30243-5   LC 66-12045
The versions of these 408 verses were done by Iona and Peter Opie. They include "from four-liners to 12, 13 and 14-stanza rhymes, such as 'The House that Jack Built' or 'The Old Woman and her Pig' and 'The Twelve Days of Chrismas.' Here you will find the complete text of 'The Bells of London,' 'The Death and Burial of Cock Robin,' 'The Love-sick Frog,' 'Little Bo-Peep' to say noth-ing at all of the many other familiar and not-at-all familiar shorter rhymes. What is special about this edition is that it has been illustrated by Ray-mond Briggs, who made some 890 drawings and paintings that are a delight, especially in color." Best Sellers
Index to first lines and titles: p[218-20]

Nicola Bayley's Book of nursery rhymes. Knopf [1977] c1975 unp illus $4.95, lib. bdg. $5.99 (k-1)   **398**
1 Nursery rhymes
ISBN 0-394-83561-1; 0-394-93561-6   LC 76-57923
First published 1976 in England
"Nicola Bayley has created illustrations for 22 familiar nursery rhymes. Some echo the richly detailed Victorian scenes of her first book, 'Tyger Voyage.' Some are lavish two-page spreads. Some depict each verse of a rhyme with a tiny cameo." West Coast Rev of Bks
"The selection, order, and art in this book are brilliant. How often do you find the complete poem of Cock Robin? Or Simple Simon? Or Old Mother Hubbard in a small, thirty-two page col-lection? The variety and harmony of design is astonishing. And the full-color art of Nicola Bay-ley is—exquisite." Children's Bk Rev Serv

Old Mother Hubbard and her dog; illus. by Evaline Ness. Holt 1972 unp illus lib. bdg. $4.95 (k-2)   **398**
1 Nursery rhymes
ISBN 0-03-088369-5   LC 74-182788
"Using a baker's dozen of verses found in the Opies' 'The Oxford Nursery Rhyme Book' (Oxford) [entered below under title] the artist has pro-duced the most splendid of all picture-book con-ceptions of the adventures of the incongruous pair. A huge, shaggy white sheepdog dominates the brilliant full-color pictures; and while his gaunt, dead-pan mistress runs about the town buy-ing him all sorts of delicacies, he romps about the house, smoking a pipe, playing the flute, dancing a jig, and standing on his head." Horn Bk

Old Mother Hubbard and her dog; pictures by Paul Galdone. McGraw 1960 32p illus. lib. bdg. $7.95 (k-2)   **398**

1 Nursery rhymes
ISBN 0-07-022723-3   LC 60-12769

"Whittlesey House publications"
"The entire rhymed tale of Mother Hubbard is illustrated by Paul Galdone in lovely, humorous black-and-white pictures with touches of red. Spirited addition to Mother Goose and picture book collections and attractive for reading aloud." Library J

One I love, two I love, and other loving Mother Goose rhymes; illus. by Nonny Hogrogian. Dutton 1972 unp illus $5.95 (k-2)   **398**

1 Nursery rhymes
ISBN 0-525-36420-X   LC 79-179047

Seventeen Mother Goose rhymes chosen for their theme of love. Among those included are: Peter pumpkin eater, Georgie Porgie, and Willy, Willy Wilkin
"Some of the choices ('Daffy-down dilly' for example) seem only remotely related to the scope indicated by the subtitle, but the attractive drawings add appeal to the durable verses, so there seems little for complaint." Chicago. Children's Bk Center

One misty moisty morning; rhymes from Mother Goose; pictures by Mitchell Miller. Farrar, Straus 1971 unp illus $2.95   **398**

1 Nursery rhymes
ISBN 0-374-35647-5   LC 70-149215

"For a small child the rhymes mean only what they say. They don't mean it too seriously, either; otherwise a few of them would sound a little grim. Most sound charming. . . . Even if we already knew that 'Little Tommy Tittlemouse/Lived in a little house,' did we know that the house was little enough for Mr. Tittlemouse to wear it like a garment gable roof and all? And the 'old man/Clothed all in leather'who'd have expected his costume to be the pelt of the versatile buffalizard (or is it a crocadonkey?). Mr. Miller expected it—and drew it. . . . The flavor is subtle and as real and ambiguous as a dreamy grin." Christian Sci Monitor
This "is rich, evocative, mysterious in its terror. It is for an audience that is invited to go far into the transformations of everything called up by the rhymes. The parrot who does 'not like thee, Doctor Fell' wears a man's head and a wig; the King (and Queen) of the Cannibal Islands are most domestic, and you will not forget them; St. Dunstan pulling the devil's nose with red-hot tongs is here. . . . This one lets you follow dread and enchantment: Mitchell Miller has made another book at which one stares and stares." NY Times Bk Rev

Opie, Iona
The lore and language of schoolchildren, by Iona and Peter Opie. Clarendon Press [1960 c1959] 417p illus maps $22   **398**

1 Folklore—Great Britain
ISBN 0-19-827206-5   LC 60-905

"Rhymes, riddles, incantations, jeers, torments, parodies, nicknames, holiday customs, and other types of lore that is current among school children today and is transmited orally, some of it over a period of hundreds of years. The basic study was made in Great Britain and detailed analysis of geographic usage is made for Great Britain but some usage in other countries is also noted. Chiefly of interest to folklorists, teachers, librarians, and others who work with children but nostalgic appeal for the general reader." Booklist
Includes index to first lines, and geographical index

The **Oxford** Dictionary of nursery rhymes; ed. by Iona and Peter Opie. Oxford 1951 xxvii, 467p illus $22.50   **398**

1 Nursery rhymes
ISBN 0-19-869111-4   LC 51-14126

"A collection of 550 rhymes, songs and riddles which through the years, have come to be associated with childhood. While some are printed here with variations, notes on all of them list approximate age, first appearance in print, literary and historical associations, and parallels in other languages. . . . Arrangement is alphabetical according to the most important word. Nearly 100 reproductions scattered through the text show the changes in illustration of nursery literature during the past two centuries. An index of notable figures and an index of first lines make for easy reference. A comprehensive and authoritative study of the subject, this is an essential tool for all who are engaged in the study or teaching of children's literature." Cvr Ref Bks
Bibliography: pxxv-xxvii

The **Oxford** Nursery rhyme book; assembled by Iona and Peter Opie; with additional illustrations by Joan Hassall. Oxford 1955 223p illus $15.95   **398**

1 Nursery rhymes
ISBN 0-19-869112-2   LC 55-12050

"Gathered here are 800 rhymes and ditties. They are the infant jingles, riddles, catches, tongue-trippers, baby games, toe names, maxims, alphabets, counting rhymes, prayers, and lullabies, with which generation after generation of mothers and nurses have attempted to please the youngest." Preface
"Freely illustrated with reproductions and specially designed wood engravings in the traditional style. Unlike the scholarly 'The Oxford Dictionary of nursery rhymes' [entered above] this is intended mainly for reading to children; it will, however, probably be of more value as a source book." Booklist
Includes: Sources of the illustrations; Index of first lines, refrains, and familiar titles

Potter, Beatrix
Cecily Parsley's nursery rhymes. Warne [1964?] 34p illus $3.50 (k-3)   **398**

1 Nursery rhymes
ISBN 0-7232-0614-7   LC 66-4155

First published 1922
Illustrated by the author, this book consists of rhymes about Cecily Parsley, a rabbit who "brewed good ale for gentlemen" until she ran away; Goosey, goosey, gander; A little pig who couldn't find his way home; Mistress Pussy; Three blind mice; Little Tom Tinker's dog, etc.

The **Puffin** Book of nursery rhymes; gathered by Iona and Peter Opie; with illus. by Pauline Baynes. Penguin Bks. 1963 220p illus pa $1.95   **398**

1 Nursery rhymes
ISBN 0-14-030200-X   LC 64-1118

Hardcover edition published 1964 by Oxford with title: A family book of nursery rhymes, o.p. 1980
"This collection of [over] two hundred verses is intended as a companion volume to 'The Oxford Nursery Rhyme Book' [entered above]. The book contains an excellent section of notes on some of the rhymes; within the body of the text there are some instances of comparative versions—seven versions of Humpty Dumpty, for example. The small black-and-white illustrations are appropriate and attractive. A fine and useful book, not divided into sections, but with the selections so arranged that there are affinitive relationships. An index of first lines and an index of principal subjects are appended." Chicago. Children's Bk Center

Randolph Caldecott's John Gilpin, and other stories; containing: The diverting history of John Gilpin; The house that Jack built; The frog he would a-wooing go; The milkmaid. Warne 1977 80p illus lib. bdg. $9.95 (k-3)   **398**

1 Nursery rhymes
ISBN 0-7232-2062-X   LC 77-081562

These four works illustrated by Randolph Caldecott were originally published separately, the first two, a humorous ballad by William Cowper and a nursery rhyme, in 1878, and the last two, a folk-song and another nursery rhyme, in 1883 and 1882 respectively
"Four of Caldecott's works collected here offer exemplary samples of the robust action, economy of line, and attention to detail that the nineteenth-century artist brought to his work. Alternating brown line sketches with rich, full-color illustrations, Caldecott's representative art infuses nuances

Randolph Caldecott's John Gilpin, and other stories—*Continued*

of humor that add extra dimensions to [William Cowper's story of] John Gilpin's ruinous ride, Jack's burgeoning house, the frog's disastrous courting session, and the milkmaid's timely revenge. Authentic backgrounds accurately portray the surroundings of the artist's own world, while his sly wit and innate ability to entertain reach easily across the span of time." Booklist

The **Real** Mother Goose; illus. by Blanche Fisher Wright. Rand McNally 1916 128p illus $5.95, lib. bdg. $5.97 (k-2)   398

1 Nursery rhymes
ISBN 0-528-82322-1; 0-528-80177-5
Copyright renewed 1944
This large volume of over 300 Mother Goose verses "is one of the most popular. It has colorful pictures on every page—pictures so clear and simple that they appeal to the young child." Larrick. A Parent's Guide to Children's Reading
Includes a list of titles and an alphabetical list of first lines

Rees, Ennis
Riddles, riddles everywhere; illus. by Quentin Blake. Abelard-Schuman 1964 125p illus lib. bdg. $6.79 (3-6)   398

1 Riddles 2 Folklore
ISBN 0-200-71915-7   LC 64-12744
The author states that "most of the verse riddles included in this book, I have made from prose originals that have for generations been part of American and British folklore." In recreating riddles in rhyme Dr. Rees has tried to capture and further the fun children have experienced when reading and riddling prose riddles. . . . Attractive in format with modern but childishly humorous ink drawings, some with green or orange added, this new collection should prove to be popular. . . . The riddles aren't arranged in any set order, and there is no index." Sch Library J

Riddles of many lands [comp.] by Carl Withers and Sula Benet; illus. by Lili Cassel. Abelard-Schuman 1956 160p illus lib. bdg. $7.89 (5 and up)   398

1 Riddles
ISBN 0-200-00099-3   LC 56-5101
"Contains eight hundred riddles from over ninety countries, regions and tribal or ethnic groups." The compilers
This volume is divided into seven major divisions: North America, South America, the British Isles, Europe, Africa, Asia and Oceania. Includes sources
"Children love riddles, and they will love this compiler team for expanding their favorite horizons. Folklorists and teachers of social studies will also welcome such a collection. Lili Cassel's illustrations are gay and pertinent." Library J
Map on lining-papers

Ring o'roses; a nursery rhyme picture book; with numerous drawings in color and black and white by L. Leslie Brooke. Warne 1976 193p illus $7.95 (k-3)   398

1 Nursery rhymes
ISBN 0-7232-1980-X
A reprint of the title first published 1922
"Leslie Brooke provides an imaginative and broadly humorous pictorial interpretation of the traditional [Mother Goose] verses. The characters are in English period costumes and are utterly satisfying interpretations. Simple Simon is Simple Simon, daft and delightful. But above all you will remember Leslie Brooke's pigs—after chuckling over them you will never again see pigs as plain pigs. This is, after all, the test of great illustrations: they do more than illustrate—they interpret the text so vividly that they become the embodiment of the words." Sutherland. Children and Bks. 5th ed.

The **Rooster** crows; a book of American rhymes and jingles [comp. and illus. by] Maud and Miska Petersham. Macmillan Pub. Co. 1945 unp illus $5.95 (k-2)   398

1 Nursery rhymes 2 Folklore—U.S.
ISBN 0-02-773100-6
                                   LC 46-446

Awarded the Caldecot Medal, 1946
A "collection of the familiar rhymes and jingles known to succeeding generations of children and chanted in their play, such as game rhymes, counting-out rhymes, rope-skipping rhymes." Wis Library Bul
"The Petershams have made delightful pictures in soft harmonious colors, with plenty of humor for these . . . rhymes that American children chant freely. They have made a beautiful book and the publishers have given it clear large type for young readers." Horn Bk

Sarnoff, Jane
Take warning! A book of superstitions, by Jane Sarnoff and Reynold Ruffins. Scribner 1978 159p illus lib. bdg. $8.95 (5 and up)   398

1 Superstition
ISBN 0-684-15550-8   LC 77-26295
"The authors have listed hundreds of superstitions, in alphabetical order with many cross references. Some superstitions are beliefs and some are practices and many are known around the world in varying forms. The superstitions deal with many topics, including food, weather, colors, health, marriage, and love." Children's Bk Rev Serv
"Illustrated by Reynold Ruffins. Odd beliefs about everything from sneezing cats to crowing roosters are included in a fascinating collection. . . . The humor of the book arises not only from the amusing origins of some of the beliefs but also from the frequent juxtaposition of contradictory superstitions. Black silhouettes add an appropriate touch of spookiness to the text. With a list of books for further reading." Horn Bk

Schwartz, Alvin
(comp.) Cross your fingers, spit in your hat; superstitions and other beliefs; collected by Alvin Schwartz; illus. by Glen Rounds. Lippincott 1974 161p illus $7.95, pa $2.95 (4 and up)   398

1 Superstition
ISBN 0-397-31530-9; 0-397-31531-7 LC 73-21912
This is a compilation of superstitions about such subjects as love and marriage, food and drink, witches, travel, the human body, ailments and curses, plants and animals, and death
"This delightful book reveals the sometimes humorous but always interesting ideas people have about what's happening. There's even an explanation of the 12 signs of the zodiac plus a brief description of their particular characteristics for budding astrologists. Comically illustrated by Glen Rounds, this book will give hours of fun and fascinating information about people and their beliefs." Children's Bk Rev Serv
Bibliography: p154-60

(comp.) Kickle snifters and other fearsome critters; collected from American folklore; illus. by Glen Rounds. Lippincott 1976 63p illus $9.95 (2-5)   398

1 Folklore—U.S. 2 Animals, Mythical
ISBN 0-397-31645-3   LC 75-29048
The compiler and illustrator "have collaborated on an imaginary bestiary, a collection of grotesque creatures—some of them illusions of fear and terror, others the pure, tall-tale inventions of frontiersmen, woodsmen, cowboys, and carnival sharps to prank the tenderfoot and pass the time.' " Horn Bk
"This is a list of illustrated definitions, with notes on sources included at the back of the book. The scratchy, vigorous illustrations by Rounds extend the text and often add a humorous note." Chicago. Children's Bk Center
Bibliography: p63

(comp.) Tomfoolery; trickery and foolery with words; collected from American folklore; illus. by Glen Rounds. Lippincott 1973 127p illus $7.95, pa $2.50 (4 and up)   398

1 American wit and humor—U.S. 2 Riddles 3 Folklore—U.S.
ISBN 0-397-31466-3; 0-397-31467-1 LC 72-12900
"This is a sampling of verbal trickery garnered not only from folklore archives, publications, and folklorists but also from Schwartz's childhood, his children, and other children. Rounds' amusing line drawings add visual interest to the collection which

Schwartz, Alvin—*Continued*

includes wisecracks, riddles, practical jokes, double talk, endless tales, and anecdotes with trick endings. Appended are notes, sources, and a bibliography." Booklist

(comp.) Witcracks: jokes and jests from American folklore; illus. by Glen Rounds. Lippincott 1973 128p illus $6.95, pa $2.50 (4 and up)   398

1 American wit and humor 2 Folklore—U.S.
ISBN 0-397-31475-2; 0-397-31476-0   LC 73-7630

A collection of American humor including "riddles, shaggy dog stories, Tom Swifties, hate jokes, noodle-head humor, ethnic humor, and knock-knock jokes." Chicago. Children's Bk Center

"Short explanations about when and why such jokes are told precede each section; copious notes gives the origins of jokes and stories; and black-and-white line drawings add to the humor. It is unfortunate, however, that hate or ethnic jokes as well as sick jokes popular in the '50's have been included." Sch Library J

Bibliography: p121-25

Sendak, Maurice

Hector Protector, and As I went over the water; two nursery rhymes with pictures. Harper 1965 unp illus $8.95, lib. bdg. $8.79 (k-1)   398

1 Nursery rhymes
ISBN 0-06-025485-8; 0-06-0256486-6   LC 65-8256

"Sendak has chosen two of the briefest Mother Goose rhymes to expand with drawings, adding 'surprising dimensions.' . . . The little boy Hector Protector works out his hatred of wearing a green suit and being made to visit the queen by acquiring as companions a huge but benign lion and a great snake. In victorious spirit, all present themselves to the queen and the king. The creature conquered in the second rhyme is a boat-swallowing dragon." Horn Bk

He "again proves that the grotesque can be combined with the humorous and appealing in the same creatures." Minnesota

Sing a song of sixpence; illus. by Randolph Caldecott. Hart 1977 30p illus $3.95 (k-2)   398

1 Nursery rhymes
ISBN 0-8055-0359-5   LC 77-153296

This is a reprint of "one of Randolph Caldecott's original books, published between 1876 and 1886. . . . Both the black-and-white drawings and color reproductions show why the artist has been singled out for setting such high standards of picture book illustration. Of more than historical interest, the action, precision, and individuality of his work will please youngest nursery rhyme fanciers of today as much as those of a century ago." Booklist

The **Snow** and the sun; la nieve y el sol; woodcuts by Antonio Frasconi. Harcourt 1961 unp illus $6.95 (1-4)   398

1 Nursery rhymes 2 Folklore—Latin America 3 Bilingual books—Spanish-English
ISBN 0-15-276565-4   LC 61-12342

At head of title: A South American folk rhyme in two languages

"The rhyme is in Spanish and in English (translated by Mr. Frasconi) and is one of the many resembling 'The House that Jack Built,' both in its accumulation and in its series of relationships. But in mood it is very different; 'Cloud that covers the sun,/Sun that melts the snow,/Snow that hurts my feet,/why are you bad?/I am not bad;/The Wind is bad/that blows me away.' As in his 'The House that Jack Built' [entered above under title] Mr. Frasconi proves again that the repetition of the accumulative folk tales makes them ideal for helping young children to a very natural enjoyment of a second language." Horn Bk

"The book can be used for independent reading, but it may also be used for reading aloud to both English-speaking and Spanish-speaking children." Chicago. Children's Bk Center

"Mr. Frasconi's woodcuts are so evocative that they cause the verse to seem more poetic than it really is." NY Times Bk Rev

Still, James

Way down yonder on Troublesome Creek; Appalachian riddles & rusties; pictures by Janet McCaffery. Putnam 1974 unp illus lib. bdg. $4.49 (3-6)   398

1 American wit and humor 2 Riddles 3 Folklore—Appalachian region
ISBN 0-399-60850-8   LC 73-76133

"This joke collection presents a fine assortment of riddles and rusties (wise cracks or pranks) that are [in most cases] unavailable elsewhere. Mountain colloquialisms abound giving the spirit of Appalachia. . . . Most unfamiliar terms are defined on the page where they appear, but many riddles are understood easily without any explanation. . . . Janet McCaffery's strong woodcuts illustrate the collection with imagination and humor." Sch Library J

The **Tall** book of Mother Goose; pictured by Feodor Rojankovsky. Harper 1942 120p illus $5.95, lib. bdg. $6.89 (k-2)   398

1 Nursery rhymes
ISBN 0-06-025055-0; 0-06-025056-9   LC 42-36352

This tall, narrow book of about 100 of the familiar rhymes is illustrated with over 150 illustrations, more than 50 of them in color

The book's size "makes it easy to hold and look at; its colored pictures are gay, humorous [and] interesting." New Yorker

This little pig-a-wig, and other rhymes about pigs; chosen by Lenore Blegvad; illus. by Erik Blegvad. Atheneum Pubs. 1978 unp illus lib. bdg. $7.95 (k-2)   398

1 Nursery rhymes 2 Pigs—Poetry
ISBN 0-689-50110-2   LC 78-7015

"A Margaret K. McElderry book"

"Lenore's selections of verses from English and American lore show that porkers have always enjoyed a place in the poetic imagination. 'To Market, to Market,' 'Tom, Tom, the Piper's Son,' 'This Little Piggy Went to Market' and other familiar rhymes appear along with . . . chants not so well known." Pub W

"Some of the pigs in these 22 nursery rhymes bear a subtle but startling resemblance to humans in their behavior, particularly small humans. The rhymes are tantalizingly silly, of course, and hop along with sounds children will enjoy repeating out loud. . . . The artist's full-color illustrations alternating with black and white have a satisfying rural charm—he obviously has a good grip on his pigs. In fact, all the two-and four-legged animals show up humorously well in delicate line and cross-hatching. For early play and bed-time chanting." Booklist

To market! To market! Illus. by Peter Spier. Doubleday 1967 unp illus (The Mother Goose lib) $5.95, lib. bdg. $6.90 (k-2)   398

1 Nursery rhymes
ISBN 0-385-08755-1; 0-385-09081-1   LC 67-18664

"Nineteen traditional rhymes and proverbs have been woven into a charming tapestry of 19th century American rural life. Countless small details engage the imagination in pictures of water wheels, town squares, smithies, and barnyards, with historical and geographical background provided in a closing section. Most of the rhymes date back to English sorces, but they seem quite at home in the New England setting." Sch Library J

What do you feed your donkey on? Rhymes from a Belfast childhood; collected by Colette O'Hare; illus. by Jenny Rodwell. Collins [distributed by Philomel Bks] 1978 32p illus $6.95, lib. bdg. $6.91 (k-3)   398

1 Nursery rhymes 2 Folklore—Ireland
ISBN 0-00-183703-6; 0-00-183734-6   LC 77-17155

"These twenty-three short jump rope rhymes, street chants, ballads, and limericks were set down as they were heard by the collector on the streets of Belfast, Ireland. Teasing, mock serious, rueful, mostly comic in tone, they have the roughness of language and rhythm and the rowdiness of subject and situation that identifies them as being of the folk." Children's Bk Rev Serv

"The illustrations in full color or in black and white are stippled and luminous; ranging from animated street scenes to cozy interiors, they portray with delightful realism the familiar background of everyday, unsophisticated living." Horn Bk

The **Whim**-wham book; contributed by youngsters, college students, mothers, and aunts and uncles from San Jose, California, to Fort Lauderdale, Florida, and from Yarmouth, Maine, to San Antonio, Texas; collected by Duncan Emrich; illus. by Ib Ohlsson. Four Winds 1975 335p illus $8.95

398

1 Folklore—U.S. 2 American wit and humor
ISBN 0-590-07315-X   LC 75-9872

This is a collection of riddles and jokes, superstitions and wishes, games, camp songs, jump rope jingles, minute mystries and more, contributed by children and adults from across the United States
"There's plenty of new material, elephant jokes and rank outs, but they're variations on old themes. Whether it's culled from the past or created today, if it's in current use Duncan Emrich calls it American folklore. . . . [This is] a jam-packed, thoroughly delightful compendium of contemporary Americana. . . . Ib Ohlsson has decorated the book in perfect synch with the fun and fanciful theme." NY Times Bk Rev
Bibliographical notes: p335

398.03 Folklore—Encyclopedias and dictionaries

Briggs, Katharine
An encyclopedia of fairies: hobgoblins, brownies, bogies, and other supernatural creatures. Pantheon Bks. [1977 c1976] 481p illus $12.95, pa $4.95

398.03

1 Fairies—Encyclopedias 2 Folklore—Great Britain—Encyclopedias
ISBN 0-394-40918-3; 0-394-73467-X   LC 76-12939

Originally published in England with title: A dictionary of fairies
"This eclectic encyclopedia covers British fairy lore, broadly constituted as 'that whole area of the supernatural which is not claimed by angels, devils, or ghosts.' Entries are alphabetically arranged, and terms are capitalized in the text to indicate that they have separate entries. Items included range from names of specific supernatural beings, to names of stories concerning fairies (occasionally including the text of one version of the story), to persons in some way important to the study of fairy lore, to concepts and customs regarding fairies. . . . Supplementary material includes a selected reading list and indexes of tale types and motifs mentioned in the text." Library J

Palmer, Robin
A dictionary of mythical places; illus. by Richard Cuffari. Walck, H.Z. 1975 118p illus $7.95 (5 and up)

398.03

1 Geographical myths—Encyclopedias
ISBN 0-8098-2431-0   LC 75-6018

"Arranged alphabetically by name with the cultural origin of each designated—Greek, Persian, Celtic, Teutonic, Japanese, American Indian, etc.—the places are described in a section between one sentence and several pages in length, usually a paragraph, which also relates their mythological or literary context. Included along with more obscure entries such as Hamistaken (Iranian), Yalaing (Oceanian), and Adivun (Eskimo) are old familiars like Big Rock Candy Mountain, Hobbiton-Across-the-Water, and Narnia." Booklist
"This appears to be less a reference than an introduction to lead browsers on to further reading." Sch Libbrary J

398.2 Folk literature

Sagas, romances, legends, ballads, and fables in prose form, and fairy tales, folk tales, and tall tales are included here, instead of with the literature of the country of origin, to keep the traditional material together and to make it more readily accessible. Modern fairy tales are classified with Fiction or Story collections (SC)

Aardema, Verna
Behind the back of the mountain; black folktales from southern Africa; retold by Verna Aardema; pictures by Leo and Diane Dillon. Dial Press 1973 85p illus $5.95, lib. bdg. $5.47 (4-6)

398.2

1 Folklore—Africa, Southern
ISBN 0-8037-0613-8; 0-8037-0617-0   LC 72-7602

A collection of "folk legends from half a dozen language groups of South Africa; trickster tales, witches outwitted, talking animals and magical sky-maidens, stories of love and charity and hunger that reflect the concerns of people who live close to the land and are governed by the mores of their cultures." Chicago. Children's Bk Center
The stories "may have a touch of violence—about on a par with Hansel and Gretel—but they open up exotic vistas. . . . Here, too, are frameable illustrations—gray, black and white in primitive-style patterns on patterns." Christian Sci Monitor
Glossary: p81-82

Half-a-ball-of-kenki; an Ashanti tale retold by Verna Aardema and with pictures by Diane Stanley Zuromskis. Warne 1979 unp illus lib. bdg. $8.95 (k-2)

398.2

1 Folklore, Ashanti
ISBN 0-7232-6158-X   LC 78-16135

"Adapted from Akan-Ashanti folk-tales by R. S. Rattray"
"Leopard and Fly go looking for girls to marry. Handsome and jaunty Fly gets all the attention, so Leopard, enraged, ties him to a tree. Neither the peanut nor the banana will free him. An unconventional heroine arrives—half a ball of cornmeal mush, called Kenki by the Ashanti. She frees Fly and fights the Leopard. A tumble into the campfire produces Leopard's spots, and to this day, flies cluster around balls of Kenki, saying thank you." Sch Library J
The story "is illustrated with colorful blocked pictures, some framed, that have bold, full use of space and have decorative details based on Ashanti motifs. . . . Nice to read aloud or use for storytelling, the tale has representations of sounds ('Leopard leaped 'harr' out of the bushes . . . she unwound the creeper kpung, kpung, kpung. . . . She was stepping daintily pip, pip, pip . . .'), repetition, and the victory of the weak over the strong as appeals, and it's told with verve and humor." Chicago. Children's Bk Center

The riddle of the drum; a tale from Tizapán, Mexico; tr. and retold by Verna Aardema; illus. by Tony Chen. Four Winds 1979 unp illus lib. bdg. $7.95 (k-2)

398.2

1 Folklore—Mexico
ISBN 0-590-07489-X   LC 78-23791

"Translated and retold from 'El aro de hinojo y el cuero de piojo' in Tales from Jalisco, Mexico, by Howard T. Wheeler"
"A young prince attempts to solve a riddle devised by a king for anyone wishing to marry his daughter. On the way to the palace, the prince meets several characters whose help he enlists: a runner, an archer, a hearer, a blower, and an eater. The entire troupe arrives to answer the question: What is the top of the king's drum made of? But when the prince guesses the answer correctly, the king reneges and creates further challenges." Horn Bk
This "traditional Mexican folktale is illustrated with paintings that alternate color and black and white on sets of facing pages, and that are distinctive for their bright colors and clean lines; the pictures incorporate splendid floral and costume details, although there's an old mix of contemporary and pre-Columbian clothing. . . . The tale is retold in a brisk conversational style and includes many devices of the oral tradition: magic, the three tasks, verse, cumulation, the quest, and the winning of a princess; it is a good choice for storytelling or for reading aloud." Chicago. Children's Bk Center
Includes glossary

Tales from the story hat; illus. by Elton Fax; introduction by Augusta Baker. Coward-McCann 1960 72p illus lib. bdg. $4.99 (3-6)

398.2

1 Folklore—Africa 2 Animals—Fiction
ISBN 0-698-30348-2   LC 60-6852

Aardema, Verna—*Continued*

"Nine African tales of clever animals who out-wit their adversaries are retold with zest and illustrated with humor. Helpful notes for the story-teller, a glossary, and a bibliography are included." Hodges. Bks for Elem Sch Libraries

Who's in Rabbit's house? A Masai tale; retold by Verna Aardema; pictures by Leo and Diane Dillon. Dial Press 1977 unp illus $7.95, lib. bdg. $7.45, pa $2.50 (k-3)   398.2

1 Folklore, Masai 2 Animals—Fiction
ISBN 0-8037-9550-5; 0-8037-9551-3, 0-8037-9549-1
LC 77-71514

This tale is presented "in the form of a play, acted by Masai villagers wearing expressive animal masks (a piece of artistic license, by the way). . . . After Leopard, Elephant and Rhino have bungled the job, it is none other than Frog who flushes the monster that has holed up in Rabbit's house. That the much feared 'Long One turns out to be merely a boastful caterpillar is double confirmation of the power of bluff." NY Times Bk Rev

"The illustrations, double-page spreads rich with color, are beautifully composed, although young children may be confused by the fact that there are three images of Jackal, for example, shown on the page that refers to a single Jackal. The story is deftly told, with the action and humor that appeal to children, and the text is extended by the vitality of the illustrations." Chicago. Children's Bk Center

Why mosquitoes buzz in people's ears; a West African tale retold; pictures by Leo and Diane Dillon. Dial Press 1975 unp illus $7.95, lib. bdg. $7.45, pa $2.50 (k-3)   398.2

1 Folklore—Africa, West 2 Mosquitoes—Fiction
3 Animals—Fiction
ISBN 0-8037-6089-2; 0-8037-6087-6; 0-8037-6088-4
LC 74-2886

Awarded the Caldecott Medal, 1976
This story "begins with a mosquito teasing an iguana and te iguana inadvertently alarming a python. The panic is contagious, passed on from one forest animal to another, until a monkey, swinging wildly through the trees, breaks a branch that kills a baby owl, and Mother Owl refuses to hoot for the sun to rise. At King Lion's investi-gation into the tragedy, the chain of events is unraveled in a singsong, this-is-the-house-that-Jack-built rhythm that traces all the trouble right back to the lowly mosquito." NY Times Bk Rev

"Stunning full-color illustrations—watercolor sprayed with air gun, overlayed with pastel, cut out and repasted—give an eye-catching abstract effect and tell the story with humor and power." Sch Library J

Afanas'ev, Aleksandr

Russian fairy tales. tr. by Norbert Guterman from the collections of Aleksandr Afanas'ev; illus. by Alexander Alexeieff; folkloristic com-mentary by Roman Jakobson. Pantheon Bks. [1975 c1945] 661p illus $12.95, pa $5.95   398.2

1 Folklore—Russia 2 Fairy tales
ISBN 0-394-49914-X; 0-394-73090-9   LC 75-327368

Reprint of the title first published 1945. Copy-right renewed 1973

"The Brothers Grimm allowed themselves to make radical changes in the stories which they recreated. Afanasyev might have allowed himself to combine variations of the same tale, but as a rule he remained faithful to the story as he heard it. His tales carry the reader to faraway Russian villages, long winter nights, deep snow, thatched huts, forests teeming with wild animals and muzhiks (peasants), who have never pro-gressed beyond the very beginnings of human civilization. . . . [This is a] beautiful book. I recommend it to all readers, young and old who are interested in the folktale and its unique qualities." NY Times Bk Rev

Includes bibliographical notes

Aliki

Three gold pieces; a Greek folk tale retold and illus. by Aliki. Pantheon Bks. 1967 unp illus lib. bdg. $5.99 (k-2)   398.2

1 Folklore—Greece, Modern
ISBN 0-394-91737-5   LC 67-14228

"A Greek folktale concerning a peasant who, after working for 10 years far from home, ex-changes his total earnings of three gold pieces for three pieces of advice. So well does he heed the good advice that he avoids death twice and returns home with pockets and bundle filled with gold." Booklist

"Colorful and bright, [the illustrations] give one the feeling of Greece and its people." Pub W

The twelve months; a Greek folktale retold and illus. by Aliki. Greenwillow Bks. 1978 unp illus $7.95, lib. bdg. $7.63 (k-2)   398.2

1 Folklore—Greece
ISBN 0-688-80164-1; 0-688-84164-3   LC 78-3554

"A humble woman who sees good in all the seasons is rewarded, while a greedy woman, ex-pecting the same but only able to find fault, is punished." Sch Library J

"Aliki's pen drawings for the Greek tale show a soft-eyed heroine and unmistakenly nasty neigh-bor; scenes are simple but strongly evocative—always in tune with the story's emotional ups and downs." Booklist

Anderson, Jean

The haunting of America; ghost stories from our past; illus. by Eric von Schmidt. Houghton 1973 171p illus $6.95 (5 and up)   398.2

1 Ghosts 2 Legends—U.S.
ISBN 0-395-17518-6   LC 73-5864

The author presents accounts of ghosts, polter-geists and supernatural beings who have become part of American folklore. Among those included are Ocean-Born Mary, the Golden Girl of Apple-dore Island, the Lady in Black of Boston Harbor, the ghost of Abraham Lincoln, the Galloping Ghost of Laramie, Bigfoot, and Marie Laveau, Queen of the Voodoos

"The ghosts collected here hail from a variety of times and places, and all should intrigue fanciers of the supernatural. . . . Anderson makes no claims to authenticity but only tantalizingly relates what 'oldtimers' recall and what scientific investiga-tions have been unable to explain." Booklist

Anderson, Lonzo

Arion and the dolphins; based on an ancient Greek legend; illus. by Adrienne Adams. Scribner 1978 unp illus lib. bdg. $7.95 (k-3)   398.2

1 Legends—Greece
ISBN 0-684-15128-6   LC 77-16564

This is the "story of Arion, who spends his days entertaining playful dolphins with the lilting music of his lute. When he hears of a contest in Sicily he decides he must enter. Of course he wins the prize and starts his journey home, laden with gold. During the return voyage greedy sailors attempt to rob and kill him. He makes a final request, to be allowed to sing one last song. His request is granted and at the song's conclusion, he leaps overboard where his friends the dolphins carry him home to Corinth. When the sailors arrive home they are met by . . . Arion and the king, who forces them to return the gold and then pun-ishes them for their crime." Bibliophile

"In a simple, graceful retelling of a Greek legend, Anderson comunicates a sense of bubbling joy, and the lightness is echoed in Adams' pastel-sunny watercolor paintings of sea and sky, of the ebullient boy Arion and the leaping dolphins who are his friends. Interior scenes have exquisite de-tails of Grecian costume and architecture." Chi-cago. Children's Bk Center

The **Andrew Lang** Fairy tale treasury; ed. and with an introduction by Cary Wilkins; with numerous illustrations by H. J. Ford, G. P. Jacomb Hood, and Lancelot Speed. Avenel Bks. 1979 614p illus $4.98 (4-6)   398.2

1 Fairy tales 2 Folklore
ISBN 0-517-27928-2   LC 79-10836

"The stories in this collection have been selected from nine of [Andrew Lang's] fairy books—the Red, Blue, Green, Yellow, Brown, Grey, Violet, Pink, and Olive. Lang chose stories from all over the world and used the original printed or oral sources whenever possible. He refused to censor or bowdlerize them, insisting that their magic

The **Andrew** Lang Fairy tale treasury—*Cont.*
and horror were important in keeping the imagination of children alive. Lang himself retold hardly any of the stories. In fact, most of the retelling and translating was done by his wife, his cousins, his wife's nieces, and other literary young women. . . . In addition to selecting the most popular tales, I have usually weeded out stories in which the same faces reappear with different names." Introduction

These 52 tales from the folklore of various countries throughout the world include stories by the Brothers Grimm, Charles Perrault, Madame d'Aulnoy, Compte de Caylus and Hans Christian Anderson as well as anonymous versions

The **Arabian** nights; their best-known tales; ed. by Kate Douglas Wiggin and Nora A. Smith; illus. by Maxfield Parrish. Scribner [1974 c1909] 340p illus pa $3.95 (5 and up)   398.2

1 Folklore, Arabic 2 Fairy tales
ISBN 0-684-13809-3

"The Scribner Illustrated classics"
A paperback reissue of the title first published in 1909

A collection of ten tales, from the Arabian nights, of talking birds, genies, Sinbad, Ali Baba, and Aladdin

"Twelve full-page plates, individual, highly imaginative, and unsurpassed in richness of color." Pittsburgh

The **Arabian** nights entertainments; selected and ed. by Andrew Lang; with numerous illus. by H. J. Ford. Dover 1969 424p illus pa $4 (5 and up)   398.2

1 Folklore, Arabic 2 Fairy tales
ISBN 0-486-22289-6   LC 69-17098

Also available for $7.50 in hardcover from Peter Smith (ISBN 0-8446-0752-5)

First published 1898 in England

A selection of 26 of the tales with which Scheherazade purportedly beguiled the Persian Sultan Schahriar in order to end his execution of his wives. These fairy tales, folk tales, legends and romances of Arabia and the East include the stories of Aladdin, Sindbad the Sailor, The three calenders, Noureddin and the fair Persian, Prince Camaralzaman and Princess Badoura, and The enchanted horse. The preface states that they have been translated from French versions by Monsieur Galland, who omitted the poetry and some other material, and have been further shortened in places. Pieces considered unsuitable for young people were omitted

Arkhurst, Joyce Cooper
The adventures of Spider; West African folk tales; retold by Joyce Cooper Arkhurst; illus. by Jerry Pinkney. Little 1964 58p illus. lib. bdg. $6.95 (2-5)   398.2

1 Folklore—Africa, West 2 Spiders—Fiction
ISBN 0-316-05016-3   LC 64-13975

"Spider (usually called Anansi), popular and cunning trickster of West African folk tales, is the hero of six humorous how-and-why stories. . . . Modern illustrations, many in bold color, amplify Spider's amusing character and the West African background." Horn Bk

These Anansi tales "are slightly simpler than the retellings by . . . Courlander. . . . The less difficult text, open format, and attractive illustrations will encourage some children to read them who would not be attracted to other editions. Quite suitable for storytelling, although Courlander's [see his: The hat-shaking dance, entered below] are still the preferred versions." Sch Library J

Arnott, Kathleen
African myths and legends; retold by Kathleen Arnott; illus. by Joan Kiddell Monroe. Oxford 1962 211p illus (Oxford Myths and legends) $10.95 (4 and up) 398.2

1 Folklore—Africa 2 Legends—Africa
ISBN 0-19-274115-2

Here are thirty-four "well-retold tales, characteristic of [nineteen countries and] a number of different tribes south of the Sahara. Some are animal stories, some are stories of wise and wicked humans, and several are 'why' stories. . . . Distinguished in illustration and format." Horn Bk

Bibliography: p[212]

The **Arthur** Rackham Fairy book; a book of old favorites with new illustrations. Lippincott 1950 286p illus $10 (3-6)   398.2

1 Folklore 2 Fairy tales
ISBN 0-397-30218-5

First published 1933

Twenty-three "old favorites gathered from Grimm, Andersen, Arabian nights, Perrault, Washington Irving and other sources. Exquisite new Rackham illustrations, eight in color. 53 in black and white interpret the spirit and action of the tales." NY Libraries

Artzybasheff, Boris
Seven Simeons; a Russian tale; retold and illus. by Boris Artzybasheff. Viking [1961 c1937] unp illus $3.95 (3-6)   398.2

1 Folklore—Russia
ISBN 0-670-63574-X   LC 61-16181

A reissue of a book first published 1937

This is an old Russian folk tale about great King Douda and seven brothers with remarkable abilities. The King commissioned six of the brothers to find him a princess, but the seventh he locked up. However, without the seventh Simeon the brothers would never have been able to give the King beautiful Princess Helena

"The airy delicacy of the drawings in three colors, the beauty of paper and print, all complement the romantic, gay and ironic tale." Sch Library J

Aruego, Jose
A crocodile's tale; a Philippine folk story, by Jose & Ariane Aruego. Scholastic [1975 c1972] unp illus pa $1.50 (k-3)   398.2

1 Folklore—Philippine Islands 2 Crocodiles—Fiction
ISBN 0-590-09899-3

First published 1972 by Scribner

Illustrated by the authors

A crocodile decides to eat Juan, the boy who has just saved his life. Juan's appeals to a worn-out basket and a hat which float by are received without sympathy, because both have suffered from man's ingratitude. Saved at last by a clever monkey, Juan shows that he has learned the importance of being grateful

"An amusing Philippine folktale written in clear colloquial language. . . . Warm browns, greens and oranges predominate in the cartoon-like illustrations of the jungle and the village." Wis Library Bul

Asbjørnsen, Peter Christen
East of the sun and west of the moon; old tales from the North; illus. by Kay Nielsen. Doubleday [1977 c1976] 108p illus $8.95, lib. bdg. $9.90 (3-6)   398.2

1 Folklore—Norway 2 Fairy tales
ISBN 0-385-13213-1; 0-385-13214-X   LC 77-74791

First published 1976 in England

"Six of the 15 Norwegian stories in this famous collection, first published in 1914, are reprinted here with Nielsen's blackand-white drawings and 13 of his paintings. The reproductions lack the delicacy of color and line that marked the originals but still make striking illustrations. The translations have been slightly edited to modern usage. . . . A preface about the stories (collected by Asbjörnsen and Moe) and a brief biography of Nielsen introduce the tales: 'East of the Sun and West of the Moon,' 'The Blue Belt,' 'The Lassie and her Godmother,' 'The Three Princesses of Whiteland,' 'The Widow's Son,' and 'The Three Princesses in the Blue Mountain.' " Booklist

The squire's bride; a Norwegian folk tale originally collected and told by P. C. Asbjornsen; illus. by Marcia Sewall. Atheneum Pubs. 1975 unp illus lib. bdg. $6.95 (1-4)   398.2

1 Folklore—Norway
ISBN 0-689-30463-3   LC 74-19316

This "version of a Norwegian folktale is based on the H. L. Broekstad translation and is illustrated with pencil drawings that have warmth,

Asbjörnsen, Peter C.—*Continued*
vitality, and a great sense of the comic. The pictures suit the tale admirably, since the story of an obdurate peasant girl who outwits an equally determined elderly suitor ends on a note of comedy. The story, which is as good for storytelling as it is for reading aloud or alone, gives the reader that special pleasure of being in on the joke, since only the squire assumes that the bride who is being forcibly summoned and dressed for the wedding is the girl; everyone else knows it's a horse." Chicago. Children's Bk Center

The three Billy Goats Gruff [by] P. C. Asbjornsen and J. E. Moe; pictures by Marcia Brown. Harcourt 1957 unp illus $6.50, pa $2.50 (k-3) **398.2**

1 Folklore—Norway 2 Goats—Fiction
ISBN 0-15-286399-0; 0-15-690150-1 LC 57-5265
Taken from the translation of G. W. Dasent
A picture book version of the familiar tale of the troll who attempts to devour each of three goats but who meets his match in Big Billy Gruff
"With the originality and imagination which she brings to all her work the artist has interpreted the story in striking pictures which admirably reflect the strength, simplicity, and excitement of the tale." Booklist

Aulnoy, Comtesse d'
The White Cat, and other old French fairy tales; arranged by Rachel Field and drawn by E. MacKinstry. Macmillan Pub. Co. [1967 c1928] 150p illus $4.95 (3-6) **398.2**

ISBN 0-02-726250-2 LC 68-849
A reprint of the title first published 1928
"More romantic and less elemental than the classic retellings of French folktales by Perrault are the original tales told by Madame D'Aulnoy, first recorded in the late 1600's." Bruno. Bks for Sch Libraries, 1968
"Charming book. . . . [The] full-page illustrations have the romantic, rather bloodless grace that is in the tradition of seventeenth century France. The [five] tales themselves are old favorites." NY Evening Post

Babbitt, Ellen C.
Jataka tales; animal stories re-told by Ellen C. Babbitt; with illus. by Ellsworth Young. Prentice-Hall 1940 92p illus $5.95 (1-3) **398.2**

1 Folklore—India 2 Fables
ISBN 0-13-509729-0
First published 1912 by Century with title: Jataka tales retold
The Jatakas are fables about Buddha in his various incarnations, mostly in animal form. Many of them are humorous and all teach a lesson. Eighteen of these fables are retold here
"They are simply and acceptably told for children and illustrated with delightful silhouettes." Booklist

Baker, Betty
At the center of the world; based on Papago and Pima myths; illus. by Murray Tinkelman. Macmillan Pub. Co. 1973 53p illus lib. bdg. $4.95 (4-6) **398.2**

1 Papago Indians—Legends 2 Pima Indans—Legends 3 Creation
ISBN 0-02-708290-3 LC 72-88820
"A stately narrative of six myths woven together by the author from records made by early anthropologists. These include Southern Arizona Indians' stories about how the world was created by Earth Magician, how Coyote caused a great flood, how Eetoi, son of Earth and Sky, saved men from an evil pot and a monster eagle, how he was later judged and killed for his misdeeds, and finally how he returned from the Underworld to win the first war. The illustrations have a dark, epic quality, and the text is smoothly-paced for reading in Indian and comparative mythology studies." Booklist

Baldwin, James, 1841-1925
The story of Roland; illus. by Peter Hurd. Scribner 1930 347p illus $12.50 (6 and up) **398.2**

1 Roland (Legendary hero) 2 Legends—France 3 Charlemagne—Romances
ISBN 0-684-20731-1 LC 30-26892

"The Scribner Illustrated classics"
First published 1883
"Roland, the nephew of the Charlemagne of romance, and his companion in all great enterprises, is unknown to history. Yet he is the typical knight, the greatest hero of the middle ages. His story, as I shall tell it to you, is not a mere transcript of the old romances. The main incidents have been derived from a great variety of sources, while the arrangement and the connecting parts are of my own invention." Foreword
The story "is told in a stirring narrative and illustrated with richly colored paintings." Hodges. Bks for Elem Sch Libraries

The story of Siegfried; with pictures by Peter Hurd. Scribner 1931 279p illus $12.50 (6 and up) **398.2**

1 Siegfried 2 Legends, Germanic
ISBN 0-684-20732-X LC 41-28113
"The Scribner Illustrated classics"
First published 1882
Here is the story of the adventures of Siegfried, or Sigurd, the Germanic hero whose exploits are described in the sagas of many Northern lands. Apprenticed to a master smith as a young prince, Siegfried forges the sword Balmung and goes forth to fight evil and defend the weak. He slays the dragon Fafnir, gains a gold hoard, wins a beautiful princess, and is treacherously slain
"In spite of the fact that Baldwin used many versions to bring together the complete story, the writing has unity. The language is not that of the saga but it does reflect its spirit." Ontario Library Rev

Bang, Betsy
The old woman and the rice thief; adapted from a Bengali folktale; illus. by Molly Garrett Bang. Greenwillow Bks. 1978 unp illus $7.95, lib. bdg. $7.63 (k-2) **398.2**

1 Folklore—India
ISBN 0-688-80098-X; 0-688-84098-1 LC 76-30671
"An old woman's domestic serenity is threatened by the discovery that a thief has stolen her rice. Outraged, she hobbles off to complain to the raja, passing along the way 'a scorpion fish,' a 'wood-apple,' a razor, a 'cowpat,' and an alligator—all of whom urge her to take them with her on the return journey. Regrettably, the raja is out hunting tigers, and the old woman is forced to retrace her steps. Her self-appointed helpers tell her where to secrete them about her house and garden, and when the thief returns—unnamed, but pictured as a rodent—they conspire to ambush the creature and drive it from the village." Horn Bk
"The amusing and beguiling cumulative tale, simply and dramatically told, is accompanied by a series of double-page drawings which have a wealth of authentic detail showing life in Bengali villages. . . . The decorative pictures and the endpapers, which are drawn as a folk-weave tapestry displaying the story's motifs, are rich with harmonious colors and reminiscent of traditional Indian folk art." Sch Library J

Bang, Molly Garrett
Wiley and the Hairy Man; adapted from an American folk tale. Macmillan Pub. Co. 1976 64p illus lib. bdg. $6.95 (1-4) **398.2**

1 Folklore—Southern States
ISBN 0-02-708370-5 LC 75-28581
"A Ready-to-read book"
In this adaptation of an Alabama folk yarn "the swamp-dwelling Hairy Man must be tricked three times before a person is safe from being caught and carried off by him. Wiley, a Black boy, twice meets the Hairy Man in the swamp, and both times quick thinking and his hound dogs save him. On the critical third time, Wiley's mother traps the conjure man into taking a piglet instead of her son." Sch Library J
"Ms. Bang has created through the text and her magnificent illustrations a book that should be noted by all who work with the older reluctant reader because it does not have the 'baby' look of so many series books." Children's Bk Rev Serv

Barth, Edna
Jack-o'-lantern; pictures by Paul Galdone. Seabury [distributed by Houghton] 1974 unp illus $6.95 (2-4) **398.2**

1 Folklore 2 Halloween—Fiction
ISBN 0-395-28763-4 LC 73-20194

Barth, Edna—*Continued*

"A Clarion book"
The author "retells an old European tale brought to the United States by some of our first settlers. Jack, a stubborn blacksmith, is kind one day to an old man, who is St. Peter in disguise. Given three wishes, Jack desires not the good of his soul but the ability to trick his fellows. He uses his new power to best the Devil's children and finally the Devil himself. After Jack is dead, he tries to sneak into heaven, but St. Peter rejects him. Jack makes his way to Hell, but the Devil locks the gate against him, relenting only enough to give him a few coals to light his path. Jack wanders the world forever, his glowing embers encased in a pumpkin. Although this is presented in a picture book format, the tale is enjoyed by children of all ages and by adults and is an excellent choice for storytelling. Paul Galdone's pictures in orange and brown add humor and atmosphere to this Halloween-oriented version." Rdng Teacher

Baumann, Hans
The stolen fire; legends of heroes and rebels from around the world; tr. by Stella Humphries; illus. by Herbert Holzing. Pantheon Bks. 1974 150p illus lib. bdg. $6.39 (4-6)   398.2

1 Folklore 2 Legends 3 Heroes and heroines—Fiction
ISBN 0-394-92675-7   LC 73-15107

Original German edition 1972
These twenty-seven "legends are about heroes who fight dragons, resist the oppressor and conquer fear—adventures where everyone must prove himself in his own way. . . . They come from Africa and India, China and Australia, North America and Mexico, Russia and Polynesia. They tell of Sumerian, Indian, Kara-Kirghiz, Tibetan, Ainu and Pygmy heroes, not forgetting the heroines of the various continents. Just as Siegfried and Theseus kill terrifying monsters, so do Mbega and Onkoito, Kara Khan's daughter and Nana Miriam." Introduction
"The stories are brief and fast-paced, retaining their ethnic flavor without additional literary flourishes from the author. Some of the unfamiliar selections are symbol-laden myths, while a few are didactic fables; others, particularly the Slavic and Asian stories, are more suitable to general storytelling sessions." Booklist

Belpré, Pura
Dance of the animals; a Puerto Rican folk tale. Paul Galdone drew the pictures. Warne 1972 30p illus lib. bdg. $4.95 (k-2)   398.2

1 Folklore—Puerto Rico 2 Animals—Fiction
ISBN 0-7232-6039-7   LC 72-83126

Text first published 1946 in Pura Belpré's: The Tiger and the Rabbit, and other tales
"A lion and his lioness are desperately hungry for meat; their favorite prey, goats, have been too wily for them. But Senor and Senora Lioness have a plan: they invite all the forest animals to a dance and fill a pit with a roaring fire into which they hope to maneuver the goats." Pub W
The illustrator "elaborates Belpré's pithy animal satire with black-and-white and color sketches. He employs sly humor in the animals' posture and facial characteristics (e.g., the smirk on the triumphant dog's face, the grace of the dancing donkeys) but he doesn't anthropomorphize them. In all, an enjoyable addition to Caribbean folklore collections." Sch Library J

Once in Puerto Rico; illus. by Christine Price. Warne 1973 96p illus map $7.95 (3-6)
398.2

1 Folklore—Puerto Rico
ISBN 0-7232-6101-6   LC 73-84896

These 17 tales "are a mixture of historical and magical incidents. The stories of heroes and the supernatural . . . will have appeal for story hours or for individual reading. Other tales about specific places—Ponce, San Juan, and certain small villages—and about the historical conflicts of Indians and Spaniards will hold particular interest for young Puerto Ricans. In the storyteller's informative opening chapter, she sketches the background of these legends which are a mixture of Indian, Spanish, and Negro lore." Horn Bk

Perez and Maritina; a Portorican folk tale; illus. by Carlos Sanchez. M. [New ed] Warne [1961 c1960] unp illus $5.95 (2-4)   398.2

1 Folklore—Puerto Rico 2 Mice—Fiction
3 Cockroaches—Fiction
ISBN 0-7232-6017-6   LC 61-294079

Also available in a Spanish language edition for $5.95 (ISBN 0-7232-6018-4)
First published 1932
This Puerto Rican folk tale describes the adventures of the sprightly Señorita Martina, a Spanish cockroach of high degree, and her many suitors. After turning away the suitors she did not like, Señorita Martina married Perez the gallant mouse and they were very happy until Perez came to grief
"Here is a picture book with an authentic background, for this droll nonsense tale has long been beloved of Spanish-speaking children. . . . The pictures are full colored and decorative while keeping the realistic quality to which young children always respond." NY Her Trib Bks

Belting, Natalia
Whirlwind is a ghost dancing; illus. by Leo and Diane Dillon. Dutton 1974 unp illus maps $7.50 (3-6)   398.2

1 Indians of North America—Legends 2 American poetry—American Indian authors
ISBN 0-525-42625-6   LC 73-77464

Poetic versions of American Indian lore from tribes including the Iroquois, Shoshon, Dakota and Micmac
"Since each brief piece is identified by nation and general location, the influence of environmental conditions is readily apparent. . . . Each of these vivid images is matched by handsome, stylized illustrations developed from authentic Indian motifs; the colors are rich and deep, suggesting the natural dyes available to the Indians." Horn Bk

Berger, Terry
Black fairy tales; drawings by David Omar White. Atheneum Pubs. 1969 137p illus lib. bdg. $5.95, pa $1.25 (4 and up)   398.2

1 Folklore—Africa, Southern 2 Fairy tales
ISBN 0-689-20622-4; 0-689-70402-X LC 70-75517

Adapted from "Fairy tales from South Africa" by E. J. Bourhill, published 1908 in England
These ten folk and fairy tales from the Swazi, Shangani, Msuto and other Black peoples of South Africa "are filled with ogres, enchanted beasts, and giants. A glossary explains unfamiliar words. These stories would be of particular interest to those preparing Black Heritage curricula." Keating, Building Bridges of Understanding Between Cultures
"The stories, some of them familiar, tell of the customs and of the daily life of South African people, while the superb black-and-white illustrations add their own distinct touch." Pub W

Berson, Harold
Kassim's shoes; adapted and illus. by Harold Berson. Crown 1977 unp illus lib. bdg. $5.95 (k-3)   398.2

1 Folklore—Morocco
ISBN 0-517-53063-5   LC 77-4688

"Kassim loves his old patched, nailed-together shoes, but they are an affront to his neighbors, who present him with a fine new pair. . . . Kassim knows he will have to get rid of his old shoes lest he be tempted to wear them. His attempts to throw them away end in disaster: First they are netted by fishermen from the river below his house, and then they drop onto a villager's head from the window-ledge. Finally, after Kassim places them in a palm tree, they fall onto a donkey, who kicks the market to pieces. In desperation the villagers listen to the advice of a small boy who recommends that the shoes be returned to Kassim." Horn Bk
Berson has adapted this Moroccan folk tale "with all its charm and wisdom. . . . His precise illustrations kindle fond images of that fascinating country and should entice even the most reluctant audience." Babbling Bookworm

Bishop, Claire Huchet
The five Chinese brothers, by Claire Huchet Bishop and Kurt Wiese. Coward-McCann 1938 unp illus $5.95, lib. bdg. $4.79 (1-3)   398.2
1 Fairy tales 2 Folklore—China
ISBN 0-698-20044-6; 0-698-30089-0   LC 38-27908
"Each of five identical Chinese brothers has a special talent which he uses to save the lives of all." Hodges. Bks for Elem Sch Libraries
"The cleverness of . . . [the five brothers who find their] similarity a great help in outwitting the executioner is described in a picture-story book which has the flavor of a folk tale, and the repetition and rhythm that appeal to little children. Kurt Wiese's gaily exaggerated illustrations in black and yellow capture the blithe quality of the story. Excellent for storytelling." NY Libraries

Blue fairy book; collected by Andrew Lang; ed. by Brian Alderson; illus. by John Lawrence. [Rev. ed.] Kestrel Bks. [distributed by Viking 1978 c1975] 373p illus $14.95 (4-6)   398.2
1 Folklore 2 Fairy tales
ISBN 0-670-17481-5   LC 77-28843
First published 1889 by Longmans. This edition first published 1975 in England
"Invaluable as reference books, storytelling sources, or absorbing reading for children, [the Blue, Green and Red Fairy books] have been intelligently revised from their 1889, 1890, and 1892 editions. Alderson has excluded a few literary selections in favor of folkloric content, has strengthened translations to adhere more faithfully to early sources, rearranged some of the stories for a smoother flow, but in all maintained a sense of Lang's work, including his original introductions, placed here at the end of the book with notes on each story. Black-and-white drawings by a different illustrator for each volume show consistently old-style, high-quality draftsmanship." Booklist
Bibliographical references included in Notes: p364-73

Bowden, Joan Chase
The bean boy; pictures by Sal Murdocca. Macmillan Pub. Co. 1979 62p illus lib. bdg. $6.95 (1-3)   398.2
1 Folklore—Italy
ISBN 0-02-711800-2   LC 78-12150
"Ready-to-read"
"In hopes of a son who will make them rich, a poor old couple carve a boy from a bean, but the lad just sits in his bowl. So the old woman, taking the tiny boy, goes out in the world to try her luck. She meets a man whose rooster swallows the bean boy, bowl and all, and he's so ashamed that he gives her the bird to make up the loss. The old woman trudges on, losing her sole asset with each person she meets but gaining bigger animals, until she winds up with a mule. Then she runs afoul of her king. He says she's so silly, she should be clapped in jail. At that, the bean boy makes a move, deep inside all the swallowed animals, and saves the day. Not only that, he charms the monarch, who makes the old couple rich indeed." Pub W

Why the tides ebb and flow; illus. by Marc Brown. Houghton 1979 unp illus $6.95 (k-2)   398.2
1 Folklore 2 Tides—Fiction
ISBN 0-395-28378-7   LC 79-12359
"Old Woman defies the Sky Spirit by taking from the sea a rock to use for shelter. This action causes the waters to pour down the hole left by the removal of the rock. To save the sea, the Sky Spirit sends a dog, woman, and man—all of whom join Old Woman and become a family. Grateful for their company, Old Woman replaces the rock and agrees to borrow it only twice a day." Booklist
The book's "attractiveness rests not only on its rhythmic and idiomatic style, but also on the eye pleasing design and detail of the simple and expressive illustrations. . . . Perfectly harmonizing with text, the pictures underscore its humor and drama, giving it a special ethnic character without diminishing the universality of its appeal." Sch Library J
Although the source and setting of the tale is unspecified, the geometric border of the illustrations suggests African folk art and the final illustration appears to be set in an African village

Bowman, James Cloyd
Tales from a Finnish tupa; by James Cloyd Bowman and Margery Bianco; from a translation by Aili Kolehmainen; pictured by Laura Bannon. Whitman, A. 1936 273p illus $5.95 (4 and up)   398.2
1 Folklore—Finland 2 Fairy tales
ISBN 0-8075-7756-1   LC 36-17727
Forty-three "folk tales and legends translated from authentic Finnish sources, arranged under the headings: Tales of magic, Droll stories, Fables. Some are easily traced variants of well-known tales from other countries, others are fresh and unusual in plot and characterization. The unfamiliar proper names may offer some hindrance to children's own reading, which will not exist if the stories are read or told to them. Attractive, highly imaginative illustrations." Booklist

Brown, Marcia
The bun; a tale from Russia. Harcourt 1972 unp illus $6.95 (k-2)   398.2
1 Folklore—Russia
ISBN 0-15-213450-6   LC 75-167832
"The author-illustrator retells a long-time favorite folktale and captures the essence of its Russian background in her hearty bright drawings. A rollicking read-aloud tale of the runaway bun, a counterpart of the Gingerbread Man and Johnny Cake." Wis Library Bul
"The amount of text and illustration varies on each page. Brown, gold, and turquoise drawings, some with bright scarlet added for accent, give a superb sense of movement and spirit." Horn Bk

Dick Whittington and his cat; told and cut in linoleum by Marcia Brown. Scribner 1950 unp illus lib. bdg. $7.95 (k-3)   398.2
1 Legends—Great Britain 2 Whittington, Richard —Fiction
ISBN 0-684-13210-9   LC 50-9157
This retelling of the English legend about the merchant Dick Whittington who became Lord Mayor of London tells how young Dick achieved fame and fortune by selling his cat to a king who was plagued by rats
"The print, black and clear, balances the bold lines of the linoleum blocks; the pictures combine strength of line, and a sense of design with vigorous action. The version is complete in the thread of the story but simpler and less wordy in places than in some of those given in the fairy tale collections." Ontario Library

Once a mouse; a fable cut in wood. Scribner 1961 unp illus lib. bdg. $5.95 (k-3)   398.2
1 Folklore—India 2 Fables
ISBN 0-684-12662-1   LC 61-14769
Awarded the Caldecott Medal, 1962
At head of title: From ancient India
A "fable from the Indian 'Hitopadesa.' There is lively action in spreads showing how a hermit 'thinking about big and little' suddenly saves a mouse from a crow and then from larger enemies by turning the little creature into the forms of bigger and bigger animals—until as a royal tiger it has to be humbled." Horn Bk
"The illustrations are remarkably beautiful. The emotional elements of the story . . . are conveyed with just as much intensity as the purely visual ones." New Yorker
"For children the pleasure is in the transformations; older children will understand the meaning of the fable. For adults, some of the interesting features of this book are its color, its pictorial economy, and the method of reproduction." Sat Rev

Stone soup; an old tale; told and pictured by Marcia Brown. Scribner 1947 unp illus lib. bdg. $7.95, pa $1.25 (k-3)   398.2
1 Folklore—France
ISBN 0-684-92296-7; 0-684-12631-1   LC 47-11630
"When the people in a French village heard that three soldiers were coming, they hid all their food for they knew what soldiers are. However, when the soldiers began to make soup with water and stones the pot gradually filled with all the vegetables which had been hidden away. The simple language and quiet humour of this old folk tale are amplified and enriched by gay and witty drawings of clever lighthearted soldiers, and the gullible 'lightwitted' peasants." Ontario Library Rev

Bryan, Ashley

The adventures of Aku; or, How it came about that we shall always see Okra the cat lying on a velvet cushion, while Okraman the dog sleeps among the ashes; retold and illus. by Ashley Bryan. Atheneum Pubs 1976 70p illus $7.95 (3-5)   398.2

1 Folklore—Africa
ISBN 0-689-30519-2   LC 75-44245

"Illustrated with dramatic, stylized pictures in black and white or in black, red, and gold, this synthesis of African folktales into one story that contains other tales is smooth and effective. Basically it is a 'why' story that explains the different ways people treat dogs and cats, but it also contains many familiar folklore patterns; the child who comes magically to a lonely childless person; the dolt who forgets his errand; the crafty creature (Spider Ananse, in this case) who is outwitted; the kind deed rewarded, and others. Bryan's style is direct and colloquial in the best storytelling tradition. The child, Aku, who foolishly buys a dog, a cat, and a bird when given gold dust to buy food, is rewarded for his kindness by the bird, a bewitched ruler. He gives Aku a magic ring. Aku becomes a chief and falls in love with Ananse's niece, who has been sent by her uncle to steal the ring. She succeeds, Aku sends his cat and dog to retrieve the ring and the dog proves useless while the faithful, clever cat brings home the magical ring. And that's why Cat sleeps on a velvet cushion, and Dog sleeps among the ashes." Chicago. Children's Bk Center

The dancing granny; retold and illus. by Ashley Bryan. Atheneum Pubs. 1977 unp illus lib. bdg. $6.95 (1-4)   398.2

1 Folklore—West Indies
ISBN 0-689-30548-6   LC 76-25847

"Granny Anika is a lively old woman who wakes up singing every morning and dances in her garden every day. Her vegetables grow to the rhythm of the pat-a-pat of her dancing feet against the earth. . . . Spider Ananse decides that he must have some. Each day, he sings a song that makes Granny dance away from her garden, and steals her luscious vegetables. But one day Granny catches Ananse and makes him dance with her." Children's Bk Rev Serv

'A touch of rhyming talk and the visual portrayal of Ananse as a slouch-hatted dude spice Bryan's exuberant, musical retelling of a trickster story from the Antilles. Both Granny Anika . . . and Ananse himself are heartily evoked in visual and verbal terms; freewheeling, loosely lined studies of Granny in motion novelly extend the story's powerful sense of life and movement, and the overall text with its song chants and snatches of dialogue is rich for reading aloud." Booklist

Calhoun, Mary

The witch's pig; a Cornish folktale; adapted by Mary Calhoun; illus. by Lady McCrady. Morrow 1977 unp illus lib. bdg. $7.92 (k-3)   398.2

1 Folklore—Great Britain   2 Witches—Fiction
3 Pigs—Fiction
ISBN 0-688-32092-9   LC 76-27321

"Betty Trenoweth is a staple of Cornish legend, a canny woman credited with supernatural powers. . . . Betty's cousin Tom despises her as 'naught but a noddy old woman'. . . . Tom buys the pig Betty has her eye on and refuses to give it up. And then his woes begin. The pig refuses to fatten, escapes and damages the property of Tom and neighbors and becomes altogether worthless. Still the stubborn man won't give up his porker until Betty's trump card, an awesome hex, changes his mind." Pub W

"Lady McCrady's pencil-on-board illustrations (full-color spreads alternate with ones that are aqua-green and black) are themselves appropriately noddy: bats hover around the margins; the sun hangs from a string; the pig looks unabashedly devilish; and Tom appears increasingly more frazzled and bedraggled. This adaptation of a Cornish tale is lilting and bursting with sly humor and a must for folklore collections." Sch Library J

Carpenter, Frances

Tales of a Chinese grandmother; illus. by Malthé Hasselriis. Tuttle 1973 261p illus pa $5.95 (4 and up)   398.2

1 Folklore—China. 2 Fairy tales
ISBN 0-8048-1042-7   LC 72-77514

"Tut books"
A paperback reprint of the title first published 1937 in hardcover by Doubleday

"Thirty Chinese folk stories and legends from various sources are retold with the full flavor of the Orient. . . . They are told to a boy and girl by their grandmother on occasions in their daily life which suggest a story. Useful for storytelling." Booklist

"Phrased with grace and charm, the stories are revelatory of Chinese beliefs in years past, and of customs and home life. Drawings in color and black and white." NY Libraries

Carrick, Malcolm

The wise men of Gotham; adapted and illus. by Malcolm Carrick. Viking 1975 [c1973] unp illus lib. bdg. $6.95 (3-5)   398.2

1 Folklore—Great Britain
ISBN 0-670-77520-7   LC 74-10832

First published 1973 in England

"A selection of tales from a chapbook version of 'The Foles of Gotyam' is adapted and illustrated with vigorous, busy pictures, some in color and some in black and white. Almost every culture has a set of tales like these, a collection of stories about the noodleheads of a particular town. The retellings are blithe and bouncy, the pictures captivating in their humor and vitality. The study Gotham folk love spring, so they capture a spring bird, the cuckoo, so that it will always be spring; when a huge eel eats all the fish in the net, they punish him by putting him in the river to drown; the blacksmith burns down his forge to rid it of wasps." Chicago. Children's Bk Center

Carter, Dorothy Sharp

Greedy Mariani, and other folktales of the Antilles; selected and adapted by Dorothy Sharp Carter; illus. by Trina Schart Hyman. Atheneum Pubs. 1974 131p illus lib. bdg. $5.50 (3 and up)   398.2

1 Folklore—West Indies
ISBN 0-689-30425-0   LC 73-85318

"A Margaret K. McElderry book"

"Here are twenty folktales from the group of islands which include Jamaica, Haiti, Cuba, Puerto Rico, and the Dominican Republic. One finds among these stories a few familiar faces and variants of timeless themes—a wily Jamaican Annancy, a Montserra Brer Rabbit, a classic fool named Juan Bobo, and the doctor who made a deal with Death." Booklist

"One of the most delightful collections of folktales to appear in a long, long time, these stories from the West Indies are illustrated with black and white drawings that are handsome and dramatic. The stories are entertaining in themselves, but they are made delectable by the adapter's style, which captures to perfection the conversational tone of the oral tradition, extracts every ounce of humor from the stories, and handles deftly the use of other languages in dialogue." Chicago. Children's Bk Center

The Cat on the Dovrefell; a Christmas tale; tr. from the Norse by Sir George Webbe Dasent; illus. by Tomie de Paola. Putnam 1979 unp illus $8.95, pa $3.95 (k-2)   398.2

1 Folklore—Norway   2 Christmas—Fiction
ISBN 0-399-20680-9; 0-399-20685-X   LC 78-26340

Translated by Dasent from the version of the Norwegian folktale by Peter Christen Asbjornsen and Jorgen E. Moe

"Bedeviled by trolls each Christmas Eve, Halvor and his family are forced to flee their home. Regardless of this knowledge, a forester and his huge white bear take refuge in the house. On schedule, the trolls invade, eating and drinking everything in sight, and mistaking the bear snoozing under the stove for a cat. They offer it a sausage, whereupon the growling bear arises and drives the trolls away. The following Christmas, a troll appears and hesitantly inquires about the 'cat's' presence, to which Halvor replies, 'She's lying at home under the stove . . . [with] seven kittens, far bigger and fiercer than she is herself.' From that time on, trolls have never been seen at Dovrefell Mountain on Christmas Eve." Booklist

"Suggesting folk art, the robustly stiff figures set against stylized backgrounds appropriately interpret the traditional tale. The full-color illustrations, remarkable for clarity and scale, are carefully integrated with the narrative. The result is a droll tale presented with gusto. Storytellers will find it an excellent choice for picture-book presentations." Horn Bk

Cheney, Cora

Tales from a Taiwan kitchen; illus. with Chinese paper cuttings by Teng Kung Yun-chang (Grandma Teng) and others. Dodd 1976 160p illus $5.95 (4-6)   **398.2**

1 Folklore—Taiwan 2 Festivals—Taiwan
ISBN 0-396-07291-7   LC 75-38364

A collection of Taiwanese tales arranged according to the Chinese cycle of the year. "The 21 stories include tales about how a woman tricked a dragon to save her son, how a man was repayed in kindness for helping insects escape a flood, how a man went to live in a beautiful undersea world with a princess, how a simple fish was able to become a mighty dragon, and how a weaving maid, cowherder, and ox got into the starry sky. Many of the illustrations are from the paper cuttings of the late Taiwanese folk artist, Teng Kung Yun-chang, and offer an unusual but appropriate touch to the text." Booklist

Cheng, Hou-tien

Six Chinese brothers; an ancient tale; illus. with scissor cuts by the author. Holt 1979 unp illus lib. bdg. $5.95 (k-3)   **398.2**

1 Folklore—China
ISBN 0-03-048311-5   LC 79-1218

"Similar in concept to Claire Huchet Bishop's, 'Five Chinese Brothers' [entered above] this ancient tale deals with a family of brothers, each of whom has a special ability—one has a hard head, one has skin like iron, another can withstand heat, etc. When their father becomes ill, one brother steals the king's magic pearl, which can cure the father. Upon discovering the theft, the king orders the boy's execution, but the six brothers outwit him by exchanging one brother for another over whom the mode of execution is powerless, and so on. The tale is illustrated with black-and-red scissor cuts; this style makes it inevitable that all characters look alike, although each has a different hairstyle and clothes. Unlike the Bishop version, the king here absolves the brothers not for their cleverness, but for their filial devotion. But the essential appeal of the earlier book is still present, and his version may appease those who objected to the alleged stereotyping in the Bishop story." Booklist

Clark, Ann Nolan

In the Land of Small Dragon; a Vietnamese folktale; told by Dang Manh Kha to Ann Nolan Clark; illus. by Tony Chen. Viking 1979 unp illus lib. bdg. $8.95 (2-4)   **398.2**

1 Folklore—Vietnam 2 Fairy tales
ISBN 0-670-39697-4   LC 78-26233

"An unusual Cinderella story from Vietnam is retold in blank verse. . . . Cấm is consumed with jealousy of her beautiful older step-sister Tâm, and the mother, siding with her own child, works Tâm to the bone. When Tâm appeals to her father, he sets his daughters to task to determine who shall be Number One. Cấm, of course, tricks Tâm in whatever she tries to do until finally magic intervenes and secretly rewards the long suffering Tâm with a pair of jewelled slippers. A blackbird flies off with one of them and drops it in front of the Emperor's son as he walks in the Palace's moonlit garden. The Prince declares he will marry the owner of the matching shoe and all ends happily ever afterwards as fairy stories should." Sch Library J

"Chen's black-and-white illustrations and opulent, full-color paintings are as delicate as the lyric language that tells about the woes and eventual victory of good, lovely Tâm." Pub W

The **Classic** fairy tales [ed. by] Iona and Peter Opie. Oxford 1974 255p illus $15.95, pa $7.95   **398.2**

1 Fairy tales
ISBN 0-19-211559-6; 0-19-520219-8   LC 73-90332

This "surely must be the definitive scholarly edition of the classic fairy tales, those 24 tales that are the most familiar. For the first time in one volume, the reader is able to find the earliest known printed versions of these tales as well as brief but packed analyses of the origins and histories of the stories. Not necessarily for today's children (several of these are taken from somewhat bawdy 18th-century chapbooks), this book will delight every adult who cares about authentic folk material and recognizes its impact on Western thinking. In addition to the faultless text, the reproductions (woodcuts, wood engravings, oils, etc.) of some of the greatest illustrators of these tales (Evans, Doré, Cruikshank, Dulac, Crane, and others) make this book one that must be owned by every library. Helpful indexing, bibliography, list of sources of illustrations." Choice

Colum, Padraic

The girl who sat by the ashes; illus. by Imero Gobbato. Macmillan Pub. Co. 1968 117p illus $3.95 (4-6)   **398.2**

1 Fairy tales
ISBN 0-02-723980-2   LC 68-12080

The author presents his own version of the Cinderella story with a Celtic flavor. Girl-go-with-the-goats becomes the Matchless Maiden and wins the heart and hand of the prince. In this version the traditional fairy godmother appears as an ancient dame dressed in a cloak of crow feathers. Irish turns of speech are employed, and some new details are added, but the main features of the old story are preserved

"Beautiful literary style and imaginative story telling have created a marvelous version of the Cinderella story. The illustrations in this new edition . . . are placed perfectly within the story to enhance a truly charming telling." Bruno. Bks for Sch Libraries, 1968

Colwell, Eileen

Round about and long ago; retold by Eileen Colwell; illus. with lino-cuts by A. Colbert. Houghton 1974 [c1972] $4.95 (3-6)   **398.2**

1 Folklore—Great Britain
ISBN 0-395-18515-7   LC 73-21962

First published 1972 in England

"Almost all the stories in this book have been retold from collections of folklore made in the period between 1840 and 1900 from oral tradition. I have tried to retain the directions and flavour of the original while at the same time telling the stories in a more modern idiom so that present-day children may enjoy them as did their ancestors so long ago." Author's note

"There is a most appealing distinctive bluntness, an earthiness, a doggedness about these stories along with the usual dose of humour and tenderness; difficult to pin down, but it's there all right. Anthony Colbert's fine strong lino-cuts of boggarts and giants and green children define this mood too. All in all, this is a well-written, well-illustrated and well-produced book." New Statesman

Coombs, Patricia

The magic pot; Lothrop 1977 unp illus lib. bdg. $6.96 (k-3)   **398.2**

1 Folklore—Denmark
ISBN 0-688-51792-7   LC 76-54876

The retelling of a folk tale in which a demon in the guise of a magic pot outwits a greedy, rich man and brings wealth and happiness to a poor old fellow and his wife

"This retelling of the old Danish tale is brief but effective. . . . The vocabulary is simple enough and the print large enough for independent readers in the second or third grades. Coombs' gentle, humorous drawings . . . reinforce and blend perfectly with the text." Sch Library J

Courlander, Harold

The hat-shaking dance, and other tales from the Gold Coast; by Harold Courlander with Albert Kofi Prempeh; illus. by Enrico Arno. Harcourt 1957 115p illus $5.75 (3-6)   **398.2**

1 Folklore—Ghana 2 Folklore, Ashanti 3 Spiders —Fiction
ISBN 0-15-233615-X   LC 56-5872

Here are twenty-one tales from the Ashanti people of the Gold Coast (now Ghana) about the "wiley spider, Anansi. Storytellers and students of folklore will appreciate this additional highly tellable material and be glad for the section of notes concerning origins and variants of the tales. Each [story] . . . portrays the amoral character of Anansi, his perennial gluttony and ruthless guile, in 'how' stories, 'tall tales,' and riddle stories, with fable-like lessons or reasons why today certain animals or things are as they are. . . . Clever and decorative sketches." Horn Bk

Courlander, Harold—*Continued*

The king's drum, and other African stories; illus. by Enrico Arno. Harcourt 1962 125p illus $6.50, pa 75¢ (4-6)   **398.2**

1 Folklore—Africa
ISBN 0-15-242925-5; 0-15-647190-6   LC 62-14242

"A good collection of [twenty-nine] African folk tales, each very short, told in a style that has restraint and simplicity. Some of the tales are quietly humorous: some are realistic, some are fables; many are perceptive commentaries on the foibles of the human race. Good for reading aloud, and a good source for storytelling. The tales come from many parts of the continent; an appendage gives excellent notes on each story; sources, adaptations, and background information." Chicago. Children's Bk Center

"Enrico Arno's diverting combination of interestingly drawn animals and figures spotted with geometrical designs in the most unexpected areas are most effective." NY Her Trib Bks

Olode the hunter, and other tales from Nigeria; by Harold Courlander with Ezekiel A. Eshugbayi; illus. by Enrico Arno. Harcourt 1968 153p illus $4.50 (4-6)   **398.2**

1 Folklore—Nigeria 2 Folklore. Yoruba
ISBN 0-15-257826-9   LC 68-13370

"These tales are mostly from the Yoruba people with a few from the Ibos and Hausas. There are stories of Ijapa the tortoise, who in Nigeria plays the role given to Anansi the spider in other African cultures. Many of the tales illustrate proverbs, others are how and why stories. All are beautifully retold with the simplicity of true folk tales which brings out the universality of the themes." Sch Library J

"There is a concluding section of notes on the stories, in some cases, comparing them with similar ones in other cultures. Glossary and pronunciation guide. The pictures strongly convey the spirit of the stories." Pub W

The piece of fire, and other Haitian tales; illus. by Beth and Joe Krush. Harcourt 1964 128p illus $4.95 (4-6)   **398.2**

1 Folklore—Haiti
ISBN 0-15-261610-1   LC 64-12507

A collection of twenty-six Haitian folk tales, among them "are animal fables; tales of trickery, wisdom, and foolishness; and wildly exaggerated tall tales. An abundance of peasant humor, as well as excellent notes from the author's scholarly research, makes the collection equally valuable for the young reader, the storyteller, and the folklorist." Horn Bk

The tiger's whisker, and other tales and legends from Asia and the Pacific; illus. by Enrico Arno. Harcourt 1959 152p illus $5.25 (4-6)   **398.2**

1 Folklore—Asia
ISBN 0-15-287652-9   LC 59-10172

Included here are thirty-one tales collected from Korea, Burma, China, India, Kashmir, Japan, Arabia, Persia, Laos, Indonesia, Malaya, Polynesia, and Yap, followed by notes on the stories

The "stories, short, humorous or subtle with meaning, reflect the culture of regions from which it is so often difficult to find storytelling material. Notably lacking in sorcery, supernatural creatures, and magic which are common in European folklore, the tales present human and animal characters as heroes, tricksters, fools or villains. Good for telling and most welcome in library folklore collections. Able line drawings by Enrico Arno add luster to the stories." Library J

Craig, M. Jean

The donkey prince; adapted from Grimm by M. Jean Craig; illus. by Barbara Cooney. Doubleday 1977 unp illus $6.95, lib. bdg. $7.90 pa $2.95 (k-3)   **398.2**

1 Folklore—Germany 2 Fairy tales
ISBN 0-385-11294-7; 0-385-11295-5; 0-385-15189-6
LC 75-45477

"The king and queen beg the Wizard for a child. When they try to save money and trick the Wizard, a donkey rather than a baby is born to

them. The king and queen reject him and give him no love because he is ugly. But the prince is charming, and . . . he runs off and finds acceptance and caring in a new kingdom. The princess' love turns him into a handsome prince, and they live happily ever after." Children's Bk Rev Serv

"A Grimm tale, 'The Donkey,' has undergone extensive modifications with overtones of 'Beauty and the Beast'; nonetheless it is a delightful setting for the bright watercolors which adorn the book. Particularly fine are her depictions of the attitudes and expressions of the pensive donkey-prince and of the landscapes." Horn Bk

Credle, Ellis

Tall tales from the high hills, and other stories; illus. by Richard Bennett. Elsevier/Nelson Bks. 1957 156p illus $6.95 (4 and up)   **398.2**

1 Folklore—Blue Ridge Mountains
ISBN 0-525-66088-7   LC 57-10019

First published by Thomas Nelson

"Twenty tales gathered from the folk of the Blue Ridge Mountains and handed down from one generation to another. Two of them, about pioneer days, have been written by Miss Credle, but the rest are [retellings]." Ontario Library Rev

"Chiefly they tell of poor farmers and their wives and children in hilarious domestic comedies dealing with animal and agricultural problems. . . . With color in the rich vernacular as well as in the subjects themselves, these tales are superb for telling and reading aloud to groups combining younger and older listeners." Horn Bk

Crompton, Anne Eliot

The winter wife; an Abenaki folktale; retold by Anne Eliot Crompton; illus. by Robert Andrew Parker. Little 1975 47p illus lib. bdg. $6.95 (1-3)   **398.2**

1 Abnaki Indians—Legends
ISBN 0-316-16143-8   LC 74-19061

"An Atlantic Monthly Press book"

"An Indian hunter is alone in the cold; he traps animals to sell their pelts and to eat their meat. On the day he follows a young cow moose, his life changes. She turns into a young squaw, his 'winter wife,' who warns him to marry no one when he returns to his people in the spring. When the hunter marries and acquires a summer wife, the story takes on . . . suspense." Pub W

"Parker's illustrations, in loose line washed with soft blues and tans, are in keeping with the barren setting of the story." Booklist

Curtis, Edward S.

The girl who married a ghost, and other tales from the North American Indian; collected, and with photographs, by Edward S. Curtis; ed. by John Bierhorst. Four Winds 1978 114p illus $10.95 (4 and up)   **398.2**

1 Indians of North America—Legends
ISBN 0-590-07505-5   LC 77-21515

"The nine tales included are as varied as their origins; one is a sacred Navajo narrative that explains how twin brothers rid the world of the people-destroying monsters who ruled it. An Eskimo story relates how two lost boys are reunited with their families via the help of a powerful old medicine woman. A trickster tale of the Apaches tells of a fox outwitting a bear, who rightly believes the fox family ate the body of his dead brother. . . . An annotated list of books 'By and About Edward Curtis' is appended." Booklist

"These nine haunting stories and the marvelous photos are taken from the 'The North American Indian' (a twenty-volume series begun in 1907, which is an invaluable reference work) by Curtis, who was a student and photographer of Indians in the early 1900's. The editor, John Bierhorst, has grouped these stories by nine geographical and tribal sources with a brief summary for each of the nine sections. The stories are stark and fearful, unlike many young people's books about Indians which dilute and soften reality in the legends. . . . Beautiful authentic photographs and excellent book design all contribute to this highly recommended book." Babbling Bookworm

Davis, Robert

Padre Porko, the gentlemanly pig; illus. by Fritz Eichenberg. Holiday House 1948 197p illus $6.95 (4-6)   398.2

1 Folklore—Spain 2 Pigs—Fiction 3 Animals—Fiction
ISBN 0-8234-0085-9   LC 48-8251

First published 1939

These eleven tales from Spanish folklore tell about the chivalrous pig who uses his wisdom to aid both animals and humans in distress

"Davis has kept the fluency of the voices which told him these stories. He has kept the humor, the emotion of despair, the elation of those who work together, the spiritual and earthy qualities of everyday life. Each of the Padre's rescues is so quietly thrilling that you long for a Spanish grandmother who knows more and more of his tales." Chicago Sun

"An excellent reading aloud book." Wis Library Bul

Dawood, N. J.

Tales from the Arabian nights; retold from the original Arabic by N. J. Dawood; illus. by Ed Young. Doubleday 1978 320p illus $12.95 (5 and up)   398.2

1 Folklore, Arabic 2 Fairy tales
ISBN 0-385-12365-5   LC 77-16886

"Newly translated from the Arabic by a Middle East specialist, these 30 tales are given a contemporary and literate telling that avoids both archaisms and colloquialisms. The frame is kept, with Shahrazad, 33 months and three children later, receiving loving pardon of the King. In between are tales of Ali Baba; the Ebony (flying) horse; Sinbad; Aladdin (including the roc-egg); the Fisherman and the Jinnee—leading to the Tale of the Enchanted King. In addition, there are 11 tales not in Wiggins'. Lang's or Colum's editions [the first two of which are entered above under the titles: the Arabian nights tales, and the Arabian nights entertainments]. . . . The apt choice of illustrator and the excellent telling make this a good first purchase for small collections—and a very readable new one for large." Sch Library J

"Children will find that the style is less stilted than Andrew Lang's translations and that, despite its wordiness at times, it readily lends itself to reading aloud or alone. . . . Young's full-color paintings are elaborately done in dark, often pseudo-impressionistic colors that lack the artist's usual precise technique." Booklist

Dayrell, Elphinstone

Why the sun and the moon live in the sky; an African folktale; illus. by Blair Lent. Houghton 1968 26p illus $7.95 (k-2)   398.2

1 Folklore—Nigeria 2 Sun—Fiction 3 Moon—Fiction
ISBN 0-395-25381-0   LC 68-14293

First told by the author in his book: Folk stories from Southern Nigeria, West Africa, published 1910 in England

"When the Sun and the Moon extended an invitation to Water and his people to visit their earthly home, they underestimated the number of Water's followers and thus were forced to seek a habitation in the sky." Sch Library J

"It was an inspiration to bring [this tale] back with Blair Lent's illustrations, for its fanciful, childlike quality offers marvelous scope for his creative talents. Here are the superb sense of design and color, originality and humor that distinguished his earlier books. . . . Pictures in mustard yellow and brown, blue and green, reflect the whole range of African art but are uniquely the artist's own: they tell the story as though it were acted out by African tribesmen dressed to represent the sun and the moon, the water and its creatures." Bk World

De Paola, Tomie

The clown of God; an old story; told and illus. by Tomie de Paola. Harcourt 1978 unp illus $8.95, pa $3.96 (k-3)   398.2

1 Legends 2 Miracles—Fiction 3 Christmas—Fiction
ISBN 0-15-219175-5; 0-15-618192-4   LC 78-3845

"The anonymous story of the juggler of Notre Dame was set down in the thirteenth century—one of a body of miracle tales popular in medieval France. The original French manuscript was written in verse and had no connection with Christmas; Anatole France retold it and Massenet made it into an opera. In recent years, however, the narrative has been known as a Christmas story of reverence, compassion, and naive faith. . . . Giving his version as Italian background, [the author] tells of the orphan Giovanni, so adroit at juggling that he became a travelling entertainer delighting people wherever he went. But Giovanni eventually grew old and clumsy, and the crowds began to mock him; weak and hungry, he returned as a beggar to the town of his childhood. There, on Christmas Eve a miracle came to pass, as the juggler, awe-stricken in the monastery church, summoned his last strength to make his only possible offering." Horn Bk

"Mr. de Paola has written the tale with love, tenderness, and joy. He has executed authentic Renaissance illustrations that are magnificent in design and beauty. The little juggler will once again be known and loved by today's children and this version will become a classic." Children's Bk Rev Serv

Strega Nona; an old tale retold and illus. by Tomie de Paola. Prentice-Hall 1975 unp illus. $7.95, pa $3.95 (k-3)   398.2

1 Folklore—Italy
ISBN 0-13-851600-6; 0-13-851592-1   LC 75-11565

In this Italian folk-tale set in Calabria. "Strega Nona, 'Grandma Witch,' leaves Big Anthony alone with her magic pasta pot. He decides to give the townspeople a treat. . . . Big Anthony doesn't know how to make the pot stop. The town is practically buried in spaghetti before Strega Nona returns to save the day." Sch Library J

"In this picturebook version of an Italian folk-tale. Tomie de Paola has used simple colors, simple line, and medieval costume and architecture in his spaciously composed humorous pictures. The tale of Strega Nona ('Grandmother Witch') is told in modest but fluent style, and the familiar theme of a self-filling magical object used to good effect." Chicago. Children's Bk Center

Followed by: Big Anthony and the magic ring, an original tale involving the same characters, entered in class E

De Regniers, Beatrice Schenk

Little Sister and the Month Brothers; retold by Beatrice Schenk de Regniers; pictures by Margot Tomes. Seabury [distributed by Houghton] 1976 unp illus $8 (k-3)   398.2

1 Folklore, Slavic 2 Fairy tales
ISBN 0-395-28623-1   LC 75-4594

"A Clarion book"

"Orphaned. Little Sister is overworked and abused by her stepmother and stepsister sent to find violets in midwinter, she appeals to the Month Brothers, who bring a quick and magical springtime flowering; when the stepsister goes off for 'her' violets and is rude to Brother January, she gets lost in a snowstorm and so does her mother when she goes looking for the girl. Neither is ever seen again. Little Sister, on the other hand, has a happy marriage and a fruitful life. The tone is light, nicely geared for younger readers." Chicago. Children's Bk Center

"Beatrice Schenk de Regniers's retelling of this Slavic tale is skilled, affectionate and happily in harmony with Margot Tomes's illustrations. These are witty and expressive, leaping easily from homeyness to humor to mystery, even to grandeur, and back." NY Times Bk Rev

Red Riding Hood; retold in verse for boys and girls to read themselves; drawings by Edward Gorey. Atheneum Pubs. 1972 42p illus lib. bdg. $5.95, pa $1.95 (1-3)   398.2

1 Folklore—Germany 2 Wolves—Fiction 3 Stories in rhyme
ISBN 0-689-30036-0; 0-689-70435-6   LC 79-175561

This retelling of the old folktale in verse is "based on the Brothers Grimm version, in which a hunter slices open the sleeping wolf to rescue the already-swallowed Grandma and Red, fills the animal's belly with stones, and sews him up without waking him." NY Times Bk Rev

This "is stronger fare than the standard version told to nursery age children. . . . Fittingly accompanied by Edward Gorey's illustrations (pen-and-ink sketches in gray with red accents) of the wonderfully sly, wicked wolf and the plain little girl, this brisk retelling in simple words will brighten the 'easy reading' shelves." Sch Library J

Domanska, Janina

The best of the bargain; adapted from a Polish folktale. Greenwillow Bks. 1977 unp illus $8.95, lib. bdg. $8.59 (k-2)   398.2

1 Folklore—Poland 2 Animals—Fiction
ISBN 0-688-80062-9; 0-688-84062-0   LC 76-13010

"Olek the fox, who owned the apple orchard, and Hugo the hedgehog, who owned the field, made an agreement to work together and to share the crop as well as the fruit. When Olek decided to take the half that grew above ground, Hugo suggested they plant potatoes. The next year Olek decided to take the half that grew beneath the earth, and Hugo suggested they plant wheat. Cheated a second time, Olek refused to be the hedgehog's partner again when the third spring came around." Horn Bk

"The story is perkily told and pictured, mainly in shades of greens and golds, pinks and purples, the incised waves in the magenta fox's tail visually echoing the undulating furrows amid patterned fans of trees. The simple, clear text and eye-leading double-spreads make this useful both for telling and independent reading." Sch Library J

King Krakus and the dragon. Greenwillow Bks. 1979 unp illus $8.95, lib. bdg. $8.59 (k-2)   398.2

1 Folklore—Poland 2 Dragons—Fiction
ISBN 0-688-80189-7; 0-688-84189-9   LC 78-12934

A retelling of a "Polish legend. The city of Krakow is named for King Krakus who loves the grand mountains in his realm and establishes his capital on the peak of Wavel, beside the Vistula. The settlement grows and life is good to the ruler, his daughter Princess Wanda and his subjects. Then a monstrous dragon threatens to destroy inhabitants, animals and buildings. Thanks to a wise youth, Dratevka, the shoemaker, the bully is vanquished and peace reigns along with King Krakus again. Equally wise is the king who rewards Dratevka with an honored post, 'not' his daughter's hand, a beau geste that proves he has the sense not to turn a woman into a trophy." Pub W

"From the first of the book's striking end papers —both dominated by a tondo showing stylized medieval towers—the eye of the reader is carried along from page to page by continuing horizontal deep-red borders embellished with symbols and motifs. For the first time the artist has used solid, simplified forms to achieve representational effects in dramatic storytelling pictures matched by handsome pages of text, each one with an appropriately decorated initial letter. Janina Domanska has never made a more beautiful book—a triumph of unity, color, and design." Horn Bk

Downing, Charles

Russian tales and legends; retold by Charles Downing; illus. by Joan Kiddell-Monroe. Oxford 1957 231p illus (Oxford Myths and legends) $10.95 (4 and up)   398.2

1 Folklore—Russia 2 Legends—Russia
ISBN 0-19-274106-3   LC 57-3755

"Charles Downing tells with skill and sprightliness a generous selection of the colorful and fantastic folk and hero tales from the heritage of the Russian people.... The illustrations are outstanding." Chicago Sunday Trib

Duff, Maggie

Rum pum pum; a folk tale from India; retold by Maggie Duff; pictures by Jose Aruego and Ariane Dewey. Macmillan Pub. Co. 1978 unp illus $7.95 (k-3)   398.2

1 Folklore—India
ISBN 0-02-732950-X   LC 77-12389

"When the king ordered his men to capture a 'sweet-singing blackbird,' her mate promptly declared war on the ruler. Marching along the road and beating his drum, the bird picked up a variety of willing allies, all of whom he miraculously hid in his ear—a cat, some ants, a stick, and a river— until he required their assistance. With text and graphics printed on variegated pages and with the artists' characteristic brilliant, motion-filled illustrations, the book presents a flamboyant appearance—a kaleidoscope of color." Horn Bk

"A retelling of a variant of 'Drakestail.'.... The illustrations truly extend this funny story, with the cat in the bird's ear seen in a sequence of balloon-pictures, as ants, stick, and river crowd in on him; and Blackbird himself, laughably armed to the beak, wily and audacious. . . . This veiled poke at an oppressor is a high-spirited tale." Sch Library J

Duvoisin, Roger

The three sneezes, and other Swiss tales, written and illus. by Roger Duvoisin. Knopf 1941 244p illus lib. bdg. $5.99 (4-6)   398.2

1 Folklore—Switzerland
ISBN 0-394-91746-4   LC 41-16603

Thirty-seven tales "made up partly of variants of familiar stories and partly of those that are purely local. Many of the latter are short legends explaining the origin of an unusual mountain, lake, or stream." Library J

"The stories are divided into 'Swiss French Tales' and 'Tales from German Switzerland' [and] all have a hearty peasant flavor. Simple, dramatic and full of humor, they will be welcomed by children and by the story teller. Mr. Duvoisin, who was brought up in Switzerland and heard these tales as a child, has caught their lively humor in his drawings." NY Times Bk Rev

Map on lining-papers

Elkin, Benjamin

Six foolish fishermen; based on a folktale in Ashton's Chap-books of the eighteenth century, 1882; illus. by Katherine Evans. Childrens Press 1957 unp illus lib. bdg. $5.95 (1-3)   398.2

1 Folklore
ISBN 0-516-03601-7   LC 57-3198

"In simple fashion for beginning readers ... [this book] describes how a small boy relieves the bewilderment of six fishing brothers who fear one of their number is lost because each, counting in turn, overlooks himself. Folk-style drawings in full color considerably enhance the humor of the tale and the attractiveness of the book." Horn Bk

Eskimo songs and stories; collected by Knud Rasmussen on the Fifth Thule Expedition; selected and tr. by Edward Field; with illus. by Kiakshuk and Pudlo. Delacorte Press 1973 102p illus $6.95 (3 and up)   398.2

1 Folklore, Eskimo 2 Eskimo poetry—Collections
ISBN 0-440-02336-X   LC 73-3263

"A Merloyd Lawrence book"

"This collection contains 34 brief free-verse translations taken from the Eskimo oral tradition as recorded in the annals of a historic Arctic expedition during the 1920s." Booklist

"By excellently arranging the poems, the author moves from stories of creation to tales of sickness, of death, and of afterlife. Even though constructed on such universal themes, many of the items may seem oblique to readers unfamiliar with the customs and lore of the Eskimo, and the book probably will have to be introduced and read aloud to children. The bold stonecuts by two Eskimo artists intensify the legends, adding a stark beauty to the book." Horn Bk

Suggested reading: p101-02

Evans, C. S.

Cinderella; retold by C. S. Evans and illus. by Arthur Rackham. Penguin Bks. 1978 110p illus pa $4.95 (3-5)   398.2

1 Fairy tales
ISBN 0-14-004907-X   LC 78-18392

First published 1919 by Lippincott. This is a paperback reprint of the edition published 1972 in hardcover by Viking

Here is the fairy tale about the poor, beautiful, but mistreated kitchen maid who wins the heart of the prince with the aid of her fairy godmother. A briefer version of the tale is entered below under Charles Perrault

"C. S. Evans elaborated the old folktale of Cinderella into a miniature novel for older children. . . . The original Rackham silhouette illustrations . . . are still fresh and appealing." Booklist

The sleeping beauty; told by C. S. Evans and illus. by Arthur Rackham. Viking 1972 110p illus $5.95 (3-5)   398.2

1 Fairy tales
ISBN 0-670-65096-X   LC 72-81682

Evans, C. S.—_Continued_

"A Studio book"
A reissue of the title first published 1920 by Lippincott
This is an expanded, novel-length version of the popular fairy tale about the beautiful princess who is put into an enchanted sleep for one hundred years, until the kiss of a prince awakens her. Earlier, briefer versions of the story appear in the collected tales of Charles Perrault and the Brothers Grimm
This edition contains "the black-and-white (mostly) illustrations which Rackham prepared in silhouette fashion for the edition he originally illustrated. It . . . is charming." Best Sellers

Evslin, Bernard

The green hero; early adventures of Finn McCool; illus. by Barbara Bascove. Four Winds 1975 181p illus $8.95 (5 and up)   **398.2**

1 Folklore—Ireland 2 Finn Mac Cumaill
ISBN 0-590-07121-1   LC 74-23851

A retelling of some of the adventures of a legendary Celtic giant. "The author extends and invents, introducing a wonderful pair of hags, and gives Finn a talking cat and hawk for companions. He also shifts names or terms and episodes for ironic purposes." Sch Library J
"In retelling the story of a mythical hero, an author is not necessarily limited by a classical text. . . . The lineaments of the story of Finn, however, are recognizable. . . . The black-and-white woodcuts are decorative as well as expressive of the buoyant mood of the teller." Horn Bk

The **Fairy** tale treasury; [illus. by] Raymond Briggs; selected by Virginia Haviland. Coward, McCann & Geoghegan 1972 192p illus lib. bdg. $7.49 (k-3)   **398.2**

1 Fairy tales
ISBN 0-698-30438-1   LC 72-76706

Companion volume to: The Mother Goose treasury entered in class 398
"Thirty-two fairy tales chosen from many sources, but chiefly from Perrault, Jacobs, Grimm, and Andersen. In addition to many well-known tales ('The Story of the Three Little Pigs,' 'The History of Tom Thumb,' 'Puss in Boots,' and 'The Ugly Duckling'—to name only a few), there are two African stories and the by-now-familiar Japanese 'One-Inch Fellow.'. . . Pictures on practically every page—either filling the wide margins, or appearing in doublespread or full-page drawings—alternate color with black and white; and much caricaturing of character and activity is used to embellish the narratives with humor." Horn Bk

Fairy tales from many lands; illus. by Arthur Rackham. Penguin Bks. 1978 121p illus pa $5.95 (4-6)   **398.2**

1 Fairy tales 2 Folklore
ISBN 0-14-004914-2   LC 78-16789

First published 1916 by Lippincott with title: The Allies' fairy book. This is a paperback reprint of the edition published 1974 in hardcover by Viking
"Thirteen folk tales told in a traditional way. . . . The florid, formal style of such classics as Joseph Jacobs' 'Jack the Giant-Killer' and Perrault's 'Sleeping Beauty' stand colorfully beside a robust Russian 'Frost,' three spare Japanese tales, and the complexly ethical, haunting Belgian story of 'The Last Adventure of Thyl Ulenspiegel.' These are all complemented in Rackham's masterful, unique manner with numerous black-and-white line drawings and 12 full-color plates." Booklist
"It should be noted . . . that these are original versions of the traditional tales, and contain some gory sequences." Pub W

Faulkner, William J.

The days when the animals talked; black American folktales and how they came to be; illustrations by Troy Howell. Follett 1977 190p illus $7.95, lib. bdg. $7.98 (5 and up)   **398.2**

1 Folklore, Black 2 Slavery in the U.S.
ISBN 0-695-80755-2; 0-695-40755-4   LC 76-50315

"Although the title gives no indication of it, the book contains not only animal tales but, in a separate section, a series of anecdotes about his days of slavery told by Simon Brown to Faulkner, an eminent black folklorist. The several forewords and introductions are addressed, clearly, to adult readers, while the reminiscences and the folktales . . . are scaled for younger audiences.' Chicago. Children's Bk Center
"The narratives, showing the quick wit required for survival, are either direct or symbolic stories of protest. Eleven plantation tales describe the injustices, suffering, and frustrations endured by the slaves; twenty-two animal tales tell of the exploits of the trickster Brer Rabbit, somewhat in the pattern of the Uncle Remus stories. . . . The author explains his sacrifice of dialectal speech for standard English in order to discourage children's use of such language patterns and the perpetuation of an Uncle Remus image." Horn Bk

Felton, Harold W.

John Henry and his hammer; illus. by Aldren A. Watson. Knopf 1950 82p illus lib. bdg. $5.99 (5 and up)   **398.2**

1 Legends—U.S. 2 John Henry 3 Railroads—Fiction
ISBN 0-394-91291-8   LC 50-10105

"The vigorous tale of the American folk hero, whose magnificent strength and skill with the hammer helped build the country's railroads, is matched by dramatic drawings in black, gray, and white. . . . The book ends with the completion of the Big Bend Tunnel and John Henry's death after his contest with the steam drill." Booklist
"The swing of John Henry's hammer echoes in this rhythmic telling of his mighty deeds. The illustrations and the format add to the book's distinction. This version lends itself to the storyteller's art." NY Pub Library
"A John Henry ballad": p[83-85]

Finger, Charles

Tales from silver lands; woodcuts by Paul Honoré. Doubleday 1924 225p illus $8.95, lib. bdg. $9.90 (5 and up)   **398.2**

1 Folklore—South America 2 Indians of South America—Legends
ISBN 0-385-07513-8; 0-385-04815-7   LC 24-26940

Awarded the Newbery Medal, 1925
The author "has here transcribed legendary stories out of South America, based upon tales that he took down at first hand from the Indians he met in his wanderings. . . . There are nineteen tales in this book and all reflect the flavor of the lands of their origin. Mr. Finger's service in gathering them is a valuable one, and in the telling he remains a self-effacing troubadour, never diverting the interest of the reader from his story to himself." NY Her Trib Bks
"The wood cuts by Paul Honoré are exceedingly fine, and carry an atmosphere of the country." Bookman

The **Firebird**, and other Russian fairy tales; illus. by Boris Zvorykin; ed. and with an introduction by Jacqueline Onassis. Viking 1978 78p illus $12.95 (5 and up)   **398.2**

1 Folklore—Russia 2 Fairy tales
ISBN 0-670-31544-3   LC 78-5235

"A Studio book"
"Although the stories treat variously of honor, obedience, loyalty, etc., all center around courtship. In 'The Firebird' and 'Maria Morevna,' the young hero wins a bride, passing even through death before the happy ending in marriage. In 'Vassilissa the Fair' a Russian Cinderella wins the Tsar as her husband with the help of her mother's spirit, her own skills and goodness. Only 'The Snow Maiden' ends unhappily, as two young women fall victim to the fickle affections and the power of men, to nature and human nature." Sch Library J
"Of the four stories, the first two—'The Firebird' and 'Maria Morevna'—are conventional retellings, while the others—'The Snow Maiden' and 'Vassilissa the Fair'—have a poignant, moving quality. The elaborate illustrations, too, vary though all are illuminated by intense color and meticulous design detail. Some, however, (especially of 'The Snow Maiden') show unity of composition and emotional depth, while others ('The Firebird') seem coldly impressive. Art and stories together form a rich background of Russian motifs and magic that children will absorb to great advantage." Booklist

Fisher, Anne B.

Stories California Indians told. illus. by Ruth Robbins. Parnassus Press 1957 109p illus map $6.95 (3-5) **398.2**

1 Indians of North America—Legends
ISBN 0-395-27664-0

Twelve "stories telling how the Great Spirit created California, how light, fire and the mountains were made; and how the god Coyote helped the people overcome the hardship of their lives." Hodges. Bks for Elem Sch Libraries

They are "retold with animation and presented in a well-designed, effectively illustrated book." Booklist

Fritz, Jean

Brendan the Navigator; a history mystery about the discovery of America; illus. by Enrico Arno. Coward, McCann & Geoghegan 1979 31p illus maps $6.95 (3-5) **398.2**

1 Brendan, Saint—Legends 2 Legends—Ireland 3 America—Exploration
ISBN 0-698-20473-5   LC 78-13247

"Ireland's St. Brendan, called The Navigator, was evidently at once a real man (who may or may not have sailed to North America in a skin boat around A.D. 550), a Catholic religious figure and a hero of Celtic mythological tradition, nor is it at all easy to disentangle the three elements of his story. Perhaps wisely, author Jean Fritz does not try (at least not very hard). Her Brendan grows rather engagingly from a holy little boy into a holy terror. . . . Brendan's nephew Barinthus tells him about a visit he (Barinthus) has made to a fair and fragrant land to the west, called Paradise. . . . Brendan sails off to look for Paradise, encountering en route all sorts of marvels. . . . Jean Fritz's narrative is beautifully cadenced, lively and wry. Her historical postscript is all right, too, and the two-color illustrations are appropriately convoluted and Celtic." NY Times Bk Rev

Gaer, Joseph

The fables of India; illus. by Randy Monk. Little 1955 176p illus $6.95 (5 and up) **398.2**

1 Folklore—India 2 Fables
ISBN 0-316-30153-1   LC 55-5184

The fables of India which are retold in this book have been selected from three great collections: The Panchatantra, or The book of five headings; The Hitopadesa, or The book of good counsel; The Jatakas, or The book of Buddha's birth stories

"Originally told orally to instruct the young, they are rich in source material for the story-teller in search of animal folklore. They make a fine supplement to the Greek fables of Aesop, the French fables of La Fontaine, and the Indian fairy tales collected by Joseph Jacobs." Sat Rev

Books to read: p173-76

Gág, Wanda

Gone is gone; or, The story of a man who wanted to do housework; retold and illus. by Wanda Gág. Coward-McCann 1935 unp illus lib. bdg. $4.49 (k-3) **398.2**

1 Folklore—Bohemia
ISBN 0-698-30179-X   LC 35-27311

The author retells a humorous folk tale which she heard as a child in Bohemia. "Told in informal conversational style, it follows one catastrophe after another as they happen in the brief space of a morning when a peasant farmer takes over what he calls the 'puttering and pottering' of housework in order that his wife might toil in the fields and learn how hard 'his' work is. The full flavor of the tale is conveyed in the numerous small drawings by the author. Excellent version for use in story-telling." NY Libraries

Wanda Gág's The sorcerer's apprentice; illus. by Margot Tomes. Coward, McCann & Geoghegan 1979 unp illus $6.95 (k-3) **398.2**

1 Folklore—Germany 2 Fairy tales
ISBN 0-698-20481-6   LC 78-23990

Companion volume to: Wanda Gág's Jorinda and Joringel, entered under Grimm, Jacob, below

"The text was adapted by W. Gág from several sources, and originally appeared in the collection More Tales from Grimm [entered below]." Verso of title page

"A boy, pretending he cannot read or write, is accepted as the apprentice of a wicked sorcerer; and studying his master's books in secret, he not only outwits the magician but saves his own life." Horn Bk

"This small book has a macabre note that is nicely echoed by the pictures (alternately in color and in black and white) which combine eerie details with a sort of peasant scruffiness. While the vocabulary is fairly sophisticated, the story . . . can be read with discretion to younger children." Chicago. Children's Bk Center

Galdone, Joanna

The tailypo; a ghost story; illus. by Paul Galdone. Seabury [distributed by Houghton] 1977 unp illus $8.95 (k-3) **398.2**

1 Folklore—U.S.
ISBN 0-395-28809-6   LC 77-23289

"A Clarion book"

"An old man lives in the Tennessee backwoods with his three hunting dogs, Uno, Ino and Cumptico-Calico. . . . The old man sees an odd animal squeezing through a crack in his cabin and grabs it. All he gets is its tail but he makes a snack of that and gets into bed with a satisfied appetite. But the dismembered ghost wants its tail back. When he haunts the old man with his keening, 'Tailypo, tailypo, all I want is my tailypo' in vain, he settles for vengeance instead." Pub W

"The energetic postures of the old man and his dogs form a strong accompaniment to the clean, vigorous storytelling, and the subtly underplayed color in the paintings not only suggests the ghostliness of the story but is pleasing in itself." Horn Bk

"The violent ending of the story (in which the farmer is 'scratched . . . to pieces' and his cabin destroyed) may bother some young children." Sch Library J

Galdone, Paul

Cinderella. McGraw 1978 unp illus $7.95 (k-2) **398.2**

1 Folklore—France 2 Fairy tales
ISBN 0-07-022684-9   LC 78-7614

Based on Perrault's French version of the fairy tale about the mistreated kitchen maid who attends the royal ball with the aid of her fairy godmother. "Galdone's telling is kinder to the wicked stepmother and stepsisters than Roger's [translation of Grimm, entered below]. When the scullery maid gets her prince, she forgives her selfish relatives, after they abase themselves and plead for pardon." Pub W

"This is an eminently robust version of the story, in contrast to the quieter, more romantic tone of, say, Marcia Brown's classic work [entered below under Perrault]. . . . Moreover, the ambitious spreads reflect Galdone's essential lightheartedness of style; comedy seeps through in the pompous, snobby faces of the stepmother and sisters. Dialogue gives the text an informal feeling but does adhere to folktale conventions. . . . Visually, this has surefire child appeal; it's a good working interpretation." Booklist

The gingerbread boy. Seabury [distributed by Houghton] 1975 unp illus $8.95 (k-2) **398.2**

1 Folklore 2 Fairy tales
ISBN 0-395-28799-5   LC 74-11461

"A Clarion book"

"A lively version of the tale of the gingerbread boy who sprang into action as soon as he was baked and gleefully eluded all would-be captors until he was finally outwitted by a fox. The artist's gingerbread boy is a strong-legged, cocky individual, who sets out on a merry race through the countryside. The action of the tale is well-paced; large, humorous illustrations with stone fences, a covered bridge, and hearty rural folk suggest a New England background, while the triumphant fox is the epitome of all slyness.' Horn Bk

Henny Penny; retold and illus. by Paul Galdone. Seabury [distributed by Houghton] 1968 unp illus $6.95 (k-2) **398.2**

1 Folklore 2 Poultry—Fiction 3 Animals—Fiction
ISBN 0-395-28800-2   LC 68-24735

"A Clarion book"

A folktale also popularly known as Chicken Little. "The simple retelling has a different ending which makes the fox seem somewhat less villainous—when Henny Penny and her credulous friends follow Foxy Loxy into the cave they are

Galdone, Paul—*Continued*

never seen again and the king is never told that
the sky is falling, but Foxy Loxy, his wife, and
seven little foxes (appealingly portrayed in a picture as a family group) still remember the fine
feast they had that day." Booklist
"Paul Galdone here brings to life with vivid
pictures the old favorite. . . . Henny Penny, Cocky
Locky, Ducky Lucky, Goosey Loosey, and Turkey
Lurkey are clearly and individually portrayed with
characteristic details and expressive facial features.
Probably the most animated character in this version is Foxy Loxy, who wears a conniving grin as
he offers to show the way to the king's palace."
Sch Library J

The little red hen. Seabury [distributed by
Houghton] 1973 unp illus $6.95 (k-1)   **398.2**
    1 Folklore   2 Chickens—Fiction
    ISBN 0-395-28803-7   LC 72-97770

"A Clarion book"
"In a light-hearted interpretation of the old tale,
a domesticated little hen, complete with mobcap
and apron busies herself in a picturesquely shabby
cottage while her three house mates—a cat, a dog,
and a mouse—doze blissfully. The industry of the
little hen produces a cake; and only when 'a delicious smell filled the cozy little house,' do her
lazy companions come to life." Horn Bk
"The large, clear, colorful pictures perfectly suit
the book for pre-school story hours; the simple
text, with one or two lines per page, will make
it a success with beginning readers." Sch Library J
"Galdone's is a more fully developed story than
Domanska's bare bones version, [entered under
title] below, and in addition is fleshed out by his
more traditional warm-hued illustrations." Booklist

Little Red Riding Hood; adapted from the
retelling by the Brothers Grimm [by] Paul
Galdone. McGraw 1974 unp illus $6.95, lib.
bdg. $7.95 (k-2)   **398.2**
    1 Folklore—Germany   2 Wolves—Fiction
    ISBN 0-07-022731-4; 0-07-022732-2   LC 74-6426
The folktale about the innocent little girl's encounter with a villainous wolf is illustrated by
the adapter "in a retelling that adheres to the
Grimm version with both Grandmother and Red
Riding Hood eaten up and later rescued by a
passing huntsman." Booklist
"The appealing format—comfortable size, attractive (though sometimes slapdash) full-color illustrations—and a traditional happy ending will make
this version a favorite with small children. Both
Grandma and Red Riding Hood escape in the
Grimm version illustrated by Pincus [entered
below] whose stumpy 'Little Red Riding Hood'
resembles a dwarf in a snow-suit, and in De-
Regniers' rhymed, humorous 'Red Riding Hood'
[entered above] wittily illustrated by Gorey; however, Galdone's larger, bright illustrations make
this better for showing to groups." Sch Library J

The monkey and the crocodile; a Jataka
tale from India. Seabury [distributed by
Houghton] 1969 unp illus $8.95 (k-2)   **398.2**
    1 Folklore—India   2 Fables   3 Monkeys—Fiction
    4 Crocodiles—Fiction
    ISBN 0-395-28806-1   LC 78-79939

"A Clarion book"
Illustrated by Galdone, this is a retelling of one
of the Jataka fables about Buddha in his animal
incarnations. "The crocodile wants a meal of
monkey, but the intended prey is far wilier than
his antagonist. When the monkey eludes the crocodile one more time, by telling him to open his
mouth (which means that he must close his eyes),
the monkey leaps on to his head, and from there
to the river bank, his tree, and safety." Sch Library J
The story "has the humor, plot, and movement
to make it a good book for any young child, even
one unused to stories; the brilliant colors, clear
pictures, and brief text should make it very successful for sharing with groups of children." Horn
Bk

Puss in Boots. Seabury [distributed by
Houghton] 1976 unp illus $7.95 (k-2)   **398.2**
    1 Folklore—France   2 Fairy tales
    ISBN 0-395-28808-8   LC 75-25505

"A Clarion book"
This retelling of Charles Perrault's version of
the French fairy tale tells of the miller's youngest
son who receives Puss as his only inheritance. He

soon learns that Puss is no ordinary cat. After
being provided with boots and a sack with a cord,
Puss outwits a giant, acquires land and a castle
for his master, and helps him win the King's
daughter as his wife
"Galdone follows Perrault's story line faithfully,
as Puss works mischief to obtain a fortune for
his master. The writing, fluid and readable, makes
even this familiar tale sound fresh—no mean feat.
Galdone's large, humorous caricatures—easily seen
for story hour—have great gusto, and Puss is the
embodiment of cleverness and knavery." Sch Library J

The table, the donkey and the stick; adapted
from a retelling by the Brothers Grimm.
McGraw 1976 unp illus $6.95, lib. bdg. $7.95
(k-3)   **398.2**
    1 Folklore—Germany   2 Fairy tales
    ISBN 0-07-022700-4; 0-07-022701-2   LC 76-15559

"The story concerns three sons who, upon leaving the masters, receive respectively a table that
will set itself, a donkey which spews gold coins,
a stick which attacks upon command. The local
innkeeper steals table and donkey from the first
two youths while the third, with his stick, delivers
a just reward." Sch Library J
"A minor episode and the irrelevant coda in the
original version have been judiciously omitted by
the artist whose typically entertaining illustrations
—full of verve, exaggerated characterizations, and
earthy humor—make a well-balanced picture book."
Horn Bk

Three Aesop fox fables. Seabury [distributed
by Houghton] 1971 unp illus $6.95 (k-3)
    398.2
    1 Fables   2 Foxes—Fiction
    ISBN 0-395-28810-X   LC 79-133061

"A Clarion book"
In two of the three fables retold and illustrated
by Galdone: The fox and the grapes and The fox
and stork, the fox is outsmarted. In The fox and
the crow, however, the fox's cunning triumphs
"Paul Galdone's bright-eyed fox is the quintes-
sence of merry cunning. . . . The pictures, full of
movement and humor, are especially good for
showing to a group because of the large animal
figures and simple composition." Sat Rev

The three bears. Seabury [distributed by
Houghton] 1972 unp illus $8.95 (k-2)   **398.2**
    1 Folklore   2 Bears—Fiction
    ISBN 0-395-28811-8   LC 78-158833

"A Clarion book"
In Galdone's illustrations for his retelling of the
tale of Goldilocks, "his three bears are beautifully
groomed, civilized creatures, living a life of rustic
contentment in an astonishingly verdant forest,
while his Goldilocks is a horrid, be-ringletted, over-
dressed child who rampages wantonly through the
bears' tidy home. . . . The brief simple text manages to avoid tedium without omitting any of the
traditional elements, and Mr Galdone must be
congratulated on bringing freshness and vitality
to a story that almost every English speaker over
the age of four must know by heart." Times (London) Lit Sup
"Big clear drawings that can be seen easily from
a distance make it a good choice for groups as
well as for lap-sitters. The use of print size that
is correlated with wee, middle-sized, and great
big voices will help incipient readers learn to
identify words." Sat Rev

The three Billy Goats Gruff. Seabury [dis-
tributed by Houghton] 1973 unp illus $7.95
(k-2)   **398.2**
    1 Folklore—Norway   2 Goats—Fiction
    ISBN 0-395-28812-6   LC 72-85338

In this retelling of the old Norwegian folk tale,
"the goats flummox the wicked troll and send him
over the rickety bridge to a watery grave." Pub W
"Galdone's illustrations are in his usual bold,
clear style. The three Billy Goats Gruff are expressively drawn, and the troll looks appropriately
ferocious and ugly. The large, lively, double-page
spreads are sure to win a responsive audience at
story hour; however, storytellers may prefer the
version illustrated by Marcia Brown [entered above
under Asbjornsen] as the text is written in more
colorful language." Sch Library J

Galdone, Paul—*Continued*

The three little pigs. Seabury [distributed by Houghton] 1970 unp illus $6.95 (k-2) 398.2

1 Folklore—Great Britain 2 Pigs—Fiction
3 Wolves—Fiction
ISBN 0-395-28813-4 LC 75-115780

A retelling of the classic English folktale about two little pigs whose poorly built houses are inadequate to protect them from a hungry wolf and their brother whose sturdily constructed brick house enables him to survive and triumph over the wolf

"The illustrator has adapted Joseph Jacobs' well-loved version of the tale and brought it to life in vibrant line-and-watercolor drawings. . . . Small touches—the framed illustrations of each pig building his house, the portraits of Mama and his two brothers on the third little pig's wall, and the four-leaf clovers hidden on the dust jacket and in the end papers—help make for a balanced, sunnily attractive picture book." Horn Bk

Gauch, Patricia Lee

On to Widecombe Fair; illus. by Trina Schart Hyman. Putnam 1978 unp illus music $7.95 (k-3) 398.2

1 Folklore—Great Britain
ISBN 0-399-20563-2 LC 76-48151

"The tale about seven men and their travels to and from the fair presents the flavor of the [Devonshire] countryside and the fair, while explaining a local legend. On their way to the fair various modes of transportation break down and in desperation they borrow Tom Pearse's old gray mare. Promising to take good care of her they set off once more for the fair, each man taking his turn riding the mare and walking. . . . On the return trip they are much the worse for their revels and unwisely decide that all seven will ride the mare together. The old mare valiantly tries to carry them home, but the strain is too much for her and she collapses and dies. . . . The seven men are suitably rewarded for their thoughtless act by being doomed to ride forever on the back of the ghostly mare. . . . The traditional song which was written about this legend, complete with the musical score is included at the back of the book." Bibliophile

"There is an infectious lilt to the language . . . and Trina Schart Hyman has given the loose-jointed tale a grandiose . . . graphic production. Sketching on location at Widecombe in Devon, the artist recreates the village. . . . [and] provides loving, close-up vignettes of local flora, fauna and architecture. In addition, she presents us with a septet of memorable country bumpkins, each individualized with raffish charm. Yet the ultimate effect of her busy alternating full-color and black-and-white spreads is of surfeit—overblown action and detail almost smothering the frail narrative." NY Times Bk Rev

Gerson, Mary-Joan

Why the sky is far away; a folktale from Nigeria; retold by Mary-Joan Gerson; illus. by Hope Meryman. Harcourt 1974 unp illus $4.95 (1-3) 398.2

1 Folklore—Nigeria
ISBN 0-15-296310-3 LC 73-17343

"Vigorous woodcuts in black and bright blue, accented by white, add excitement to a compelling fantasy. African legend has it that the sky, long ago, was close to the earth and that it provided all the food humans needed. One had only to reach up and break off a piece of blue that tasted sometimes like stew or corn, sometimes like delectable pineapple. But the sky grew angry when people began wasting his bounty, taking more than they needed and creating garbage. Thus it was that the sky moved far out of reach and man was forced to plant and reap, to work for his daily bread." Pub W

Giants & witches and a dragon or two; selected by Phyllis R. Fenner; with illus. by Henry C. Pitz. Knopf 1943 208p illus lib. bdg. $5.99 (4-6) 398.2

1 Folklore 2 Fairy tales
ISBN 0-394-91183-0 LC 43-16225

A collection of seventeen stories from various countries involving magical creatures such as the Russian Baba Yaga, Scandinavian trolls and Welsh giants. "All in excellent versions, from such sources as Pyle, MacManus, Lang, and Jacobs. Attractive in title, make-up and selection." Ontario Library Rev

"Good story-telling material, especially for occasions like Hallowe'en. . . . Some are the familiar tales you would expect; others are new." Wis Library Bul

"This is one of the best. . . . All made pleasantly scary with marvelous drawings." Bk Week

Ginsburg, Mirra

How the sun was brought back to the sky; adapted from a Slovenian folk tale; pictures by Jose Aruego and Ariane Dewey. Macmillan Pub. Co. 1975 unp illus $6.95 (k-2) 398.2

1 Folklore, Slovenian 2 Sun—Fiction
ISBN 0-02-735750-3 LC 74-19060

"Several chicks and friends (a snail, a duck, a rabbit and other animals) ascend to the heavens to learn why the sun has disappeared. They find the sun ashamed to be seen, for clouds have dirtied its countenance and made the great star irritable. So the litle band of helpers sets to work to take away all the smudges and coax the sun to shine again." Pub W

"Brilliant, full-color pictures outlined in pen and ink and executed in the artists' characteristically luxuriant color, are the compelling feature of a slight but appealing cumulative picture-story. The simple saga . . . is more universal than Slovenian." Horn Bk

The proud maiden, Tungak, and the Sun; a Russian Eskimo tale; retold by Mirra Ginsburg; illus. by Igor Galanin. Macmillan Pub. Co. 1974 31p illus $4.95 (1-3) 398.2

1 Folklore—Russia 2 Folklore, Eskimo
ISBN 0-02-736260-4 LC 73-19060

A retelling of A Russian Eskimo folk tale which illustrates the cycle of arctic days and nights. Tungak, the evil spirit, is destroyed and the proud maiden finds happiness in her marriage to the Sun

"A sense of remoteness is vividly conveyed in full-page and doublespread illustrations, whose blues and whites suggest the arctic chill. Although a slightly stylized treatment is given to all the figures, only Tungak has a frightening mask for a face." Horn Bk

Striding slippers; adapted from an Udmurt tale by Mirra Ginsburg; pictures by Sal Murdocca. Macmillan Pub. Co. 1978 unp illus $7.95 (k-3) 398.2

1 Folklore—Russia
ISBN 0-02-736370-8 LC 77-12035

"Crime does not pay in this humorous adaptation of a Russian morality tale. A poor shepherd weaves himself a pair of bark 'striding slippers' that allow him to cross a field in a single bound, making herd-tending an easier job. A stranger, stealing the slippers, finds that his feet are out of control. After stumbling around the countryside, the slippers are finally removed, only to have them fall into the hands of another thief! A similar fate awaits all wearers until the footgear is returned to its original owner." Sch Library J

The illustrations feature "brisk navy lines with subdued clay-toned swatches of blue, tan, and salmon shades. Faces are cartoon-expressive, with a vitality that exceeds that of the color tones." Booklist

The strongest one of all; based on a Caucasian folktale; pictures by Jose Aruego & Ariane Dewey. Greenwillow Bks. 1977 unp illus $8.25, lib. bdg. $7.92 (k-3) 398.2

1 Folklore—Caucasus
ISBN 0-688-80081-5; 0-688-84081-7 LC 76-44326

"A lamb slips on the ice and figures that ice must be 'the strongest one of all.' But the ice says that the sun melts it, so the sun must be stronger. Going to the sun, the lamb learns that a cloud can cover the fiery star, and so he travels on, meeting stronger things. Then he learns the powerful earth is pierced by grass, which the lamb eats, so lamb must be the mightiest." Pub W

"The large print should be inviting to beginning readers. Soft but clear colors edged in black line conform to the subjects described—blue ice, orange-yellow sun, gray clouds—and convey to children a joy in their natural surroundings." Horn Bk

Ginsburg, Mirra—*Continued*

The twelve clever brothers, and other fools; folktales from Russia collected and adapted by Mirra Ginsburg; illus. by Charles Mikolaycak. Lippincott 1979 89p illus $8.95, lib. bdg. $8.79 (3-5)   398.2

1 Folklore—Russia
ISBN 0-397-31822-7; 0-397-31862-6   LC 79-2409

"This tidy assortment of Russian fool tales is thoroughly appealing. As Ginsberg tells them, they are punchy and pared down, with as much slapstick silliness as sly, quick humor. Once in a while the fool even wins out. Mikolaycak's robust black-and-white scenes have a life of their own; they are rich in character and novel detail, with bold, close-up compositions that demand attention. The collection is a good entertainment package, rewarding when read either alone or aloud." Booklist

Grandfather tales; American-English folk tales; selected and ed. by Richard Chase; illus. by Berkeley Williams, Jr. Houghton 1948 239p illus $8.95 (4 and up)   398.2

1 Folklore—Southern States
ISBN 0-395-06692-1   LC 48-7912

Folklore gathered in Alabama, "North Carolina, Virginia and Kentucky. Written down only after many tellings, these [twenty-four] humorous tales are told in the vernacular of the region with added touches of local color provided by the storytellers as they meet together to keep Old-Christmas Eve. . . . Of special interest to storytellers." Booklist

"Here is a real contribution to American folklore, one of the many made by Mr. Chase, who has gathered old songs and tunes, rhymes and stories from the mountain people. There is an interesting appendix which gives the source for each story as well as some parallels, types and suggestions for the telling of the tales." NY Her Trib Bks

Grasshopper to the rescue; a Georgian story; tr. from the Russian by Bonnie Carey; illus. by Lady McCrady. Morrow 1979 unp illus $6.95, lib. bdg. $6.67 (k-3)   398.2

1 Folklore—Russia
ISBN 0-688-22172-6; 0-688-32172-0   LC 78-11824

"In this Georgian folktale an ant journeying with a grasshopper friend falls into a river; his companion begs a pig along the bank for some bristles to plait a rescue line. But the pig wants some acorns, the oak tree wants a service in return for them, and the chain of action proper to the cumulative tale spins out." Sch Library J

"In an original and effective large-page design, the storytelling proceeds in horizontal parallels: The text narrates the grasshopper's danger-filled adventures while the pictures dramatize the ant's adventures with predators. Fanciful and attractive in soft colors, the illustrations reflect the story's Russian origin." Horn Bk

Green fairy book; collected by Andrew Lang; ed. by Brian Alderson; illus. by Antony Maitland. [Rev. ed] Viking 1978 408p illus $14.95 (4-6)   398.2

1 Folklore 2 Fairy tales
ISBN 0-670-35420-1   LC 77-28223

First published 1892 by Longmans. For a description of this edition, see note for Blue fairy book, entered above

Bibliographical references included in Notes: p398-408

Greene, Ellin

(comp.) Clever cooks; a concoction of stories, charms, recipes and riddles; illus. by Trina Schart Hyman. Lothrop 1973 154p illus lib. bdg. $7.92 (3-6)   398.2

1 Folklore 2 Cookery
ISBN 0-688-51519-3   LC 72-7280

This collection of folk and fairy tales involving clever cooks and food is interspersed with charms, riddles and recipes for items such as butter cookies, cherry dumplings, marzipan, roast chicken, pancakes, pumpkin pie and hearty soup

"The pen-and-ink illustrations are crisp and lively, and the collection—the only one with this theme—makes a good addition to the folk lore shelf." Sch Library J

Grimm, Jacob

About wise men and simpletons; twelve tales from Grimm; tr. by Elizabeth Shub; etchings by Nonny Hogrogian. Macmillan Pub. Co. 1971 118p illus $5.95 (3-6)   398.2

1 Folklore—Germany 2 Fairy tales
ISBN 0-02-737290-1   LC 79-146628

"Newly translated from the first edition [with one exception] of the Grimms' stories, this collection includes such favorites as 'Hansel and Gretel,' 'The Bremen Town Musicians,' and 'Rumpelstiltskin.' The versions are brief, less ornamented than they are in familiar versions, and chosen because, Elizabeth Shub says in her preface, 'here, even more than in later editions, the storyteller's voice is omnipresent.'" Sutherland. The Best in Children's Bks

"The translator has presented three short narratives under the heading of 'About Elves' and four more under the heading of 'About Simpletons,' so that she has really translated [seventeen stories]." Horn Bk

"Nonny Hogrogian's etchings, spare and deft, are beautifully appropriate for the ingeneous simplicity of the writing." Sat Rev

The **bear** and the kingbird; a tale from the Brothers Grimm; tr. by Lore Segal; pictures by Chris Conover. Farrar, Straus 1979 unp illus $7.95 (k-3)   398.2

1 Folklore—Germany 2 Fairy tales
ISBN 0-374-30618-4   LC 79-118605

"A simple and smooth translation of the story in which the creatures of the air war with those of land. . . . The reason? The bear has insulted the kingbird's nestlings, who threaten a hunger strike unless their honor is satisfied. The outcome? A wasp stings the fox under his tail, the tail droops, the bear's forces know that this is the agreed signal for retreat. Later, the bear apologies." Chicago. Children's Bk Center

"This is one of the more curious and lesser known Grimm tales and has not a human character in it. Conover has not so much illustrated the tale as made an illuminated edition of it. Her paintings are rich in color, detail, and quiet humor. Even finer are her borders—elaborate and varied. She has also solved the visual problem of depicting both bears and fleas in the same illustration by providing a personalized magnifying glass over the insects. . . . The book's old world design makes it best for one-to-one sharing or individual reading rather than group presentation. As such it could well become for many a 'favorite all-time book.'" Sch Library J

The **bearskinner**; a story by the Brothers Grimm; with pictures by Felix Hoffmann. Atheneum Pubs. 1978 unp illus $8.95 (1-4)   398.2

1 Folklore—Germany
ISBN 0-689-50123-4   LC 77-92742

"A Margaret K. McElderry book"

German language edition of this version originally published 1977 in Switzerland

"For limitless pocket money the devil will supply him, a penniless ex-soldier agrees to wear a bearskin and go unkempt and unwashed for seven years, but to forfeit his soul if he dies before the time is up. The youngest daughter of a debtor he saves staunchly promises to marry him despite her sisters' taunts, and is handsomely rewarded when the soldier wins his release and comes for her in santorial splendor. The simplified retelling of this lesser-known tale deletes several somber elements of the original: the sisters' suicide and the devil's consolation of getting two souls for the one lost." Sch Library J

"The Swiss artist was in the process of completing the illustrations for the tale at the time of his death. His preliminary sketches, brush drawings, and color studies have been used in the finished book, giving it a vibrant, spontaneous quality. The classical features and expressive attitudes of the characters are shown in angular line splashed with brilliant color; and the roughhewn look of some of the pictures does not detract from the effect." Horn Bk

Grimm, Jacob—*Continued*

The best of Grimm's fairy tales; illus. by Svend Otto S; tr. by Anthea Bell and Anne Rogers. Larousse 1979 unp illus $9.95, lib. bdg. $10.95 (1-4)   **398.2**

1 Folklore—Germany 2 Fairy tales
ISBN 0-88332-150-5; 0-88332-122-X   LC 79-63439

"Bell and Rogers do yeoman service in the translations of 'Snow White and the Seven Dwarfs,' 'The Wolf and the Seven Little Kids,' 'The Musicians of Bremen,' 'Tom Thumb' and 'Puss in Boots.' But it's the ineffable marvels by the Danish artist, Svend Otto S. that one is drawn to over and over again. . . . He depicts happenings in the old tales with such ingenuity that they convey a fresh and much livelier feeling." Pub W

The Bremen town musicians; from the collection of the Brothers Grimm; Paul Galdone drew the pictures. McGraw 1968 32p illus $7.95 (k-3)   **398.2**

1 Folklore—Germany 2 Animals—Fiction
ISBN 0-07-022705-5   LC 68-15736

"With new warm rhythmic illustrations Paul Galdone revives Grimm's tale of the four lonely old animals, about to be done away with, who, for a place to live, rout some robbers from their den. The illustrations of the ass, dog, cat, and cock have form, body and substance as they plod on their way or relax near a tree. The eyes of the robbers and the animals are unusually expressive. Excellent for story telling." Bruno. Bks for Sch Libraries, 1968

The Brothers Grimm: popular folk tales; newly tr. by Brian Alderson; illus. by Michael Foreman. Doubleday 1978 192p illus $8.95 (4 and up)   **398.2**

1 Folklore—Germany 2 Fairy tales
ISBN 0-385-14356-7   LC 77-17748

In this collection of tales from Grimm the translator "shuns the prettified speech of some early translations and aims for the (British) ear in a work that emphasizes the tales' oral nature. To give the feeling of some of the original dialects, he uses North Country speech for the Low German of 'Fisherman and His Wife,' which has the pair living in a 'piss-pot down by the sea.' Three other tales he links into one ('Lazy 'Arry') and casts it in music-hall Cockney for good humored effect. Only a few of the colloquialisms jar, and overall he has been most successful in conveying immediacy while retaining wonder. (The tales would be great read aloud.)" Sch Library J

"Michael Foreman provides a black and white sketch for the beginning of each story and a full-page, full-color painting for each. The paintings are either in the romantic or the grotesque mood: they are varied, imaginative, and deft in composition and use of color." Chicago. Children's Bk Center

Cinderella; illus. by Svend Otto S.; tr. by Anne Rogers. Larousse 1978 unp illus lib. bdg. $6.95 (1-3)   **398.2**

1 Folklore—Germany 2 Fairy tales
ISBN 0-88332-093-2   LC 78-50997

"Perrault's French court version of the Cinderella story [entered above] is the one most familiar to American audiences. Illustrator [Svend] Otto S. has chosen the Grimm rendition, which differs significantly from Perrault. . . . Cinderella here has no godmother; instead her finery is bestowed by a bird on the tree she planted over her mother's grave. Nor must she flee by midnight; rather, she chooses freely to leave but runs to escape the prince, who is curious about her and her family. . . . The harshness inherent in the Grimm tale is here: Cinderella's stepsisters cut off parts of their feet in efforts to fit the slipper (a gold one) and, in the end, lose their sight when the doves who are Cinderella's benefactors peck their eyes out. The text has been acceptably modernized, a plus for younger readers; [Svend] Otto S.'s illustrations are quiet but graceful in a roughcut way, with a wash-over pencil medium that makes for soft lines and a dusty cast to the pages. Useful as an important variant to a popular story." Booklist

"Rogers offers a version of the fairytale that some squeamish adults may feel is too bloodthirsty for little ones. Children, however, seem able to cope with gory details in the original versions of the classics, especially when villains are punished." Pub W

The complete Grimm's fairy tales; introduction by Padraic Colum; folkloristic commentary by Joseph Campbell; 212 illustrations by Josef Scharl. Pantheon Bks. [1974 c1972] 863p illus $12.95, pa $5.95 (4 and up)   **398.2**

1 Folklore—Germany 2 Fairy tales
ISBN 0-394-49415-6; 0-395-70930-6

A reissue of the edition first published 1944 with title: Grimm's Fairy tales. Copyright renewed 1972

"The text of this edition is based on the translation of Margaret Hunt. It has been thoroughly revised, corrected and completed by James Stern." Verso of title page

"A standard edition of the collected household tales. A discussion of folk literature, with examples from the Grimm's stories, adds to the value of the book." Chicago. Children's Bk Center

This "complete, and lovely Grimm should be in every school, that the teacher may learn anew the magic art of story-telling." Cath World

One tale in this collection: The Jew among thorns, is anti-Semitic in tone

Fairy tales of the Brothers Grimm; illus. by Kay Nielsen; with an introduction by Bryan Holme. Metropolitan Mus. of Art and Viking 1979 121p illus $12.95 (4 and up)   **398.2**

1 Folklore—Germany 2 Fairy tales
ISBN 0-670-30565-0   LC 79-12945

"A Studio book"

"Translation of 12 of the Kinder-und Hausmärchen, with the illustrations originally published in Fleur-de-Neige et d'autres contes de Grimm. Paris, 1925." Verso of title page

"The existence of this book of folk tales is due to the 12 watercolor paintings by Kay Nielsen. The translations of the 12 well-known Grimm tales are fine and the book is indeed a handsome edition." Sch Library J

The fisherman and his wife, by the Brothers Grimm; tr. by Elizabeth Shub; illus. by Monika Laimgruber. Greenwillow Bks. 1978 unp illus $8.95 (1-4)   **398.2**

1 Folklore—Germany 2 Fairy tales
ISBN 0-688-86003-6   LC 78-8133

"A poor fisherman catches a magic fish and releases him when the fish pleads for his life. The man's wife sends him back to the enchanted flounder to ask a wish in return. The fisherman continues to visit the fish with his wife's demands —which become more and more extravagant. Finally, she asks to be 'like God' and loses everything." Sch Library J

"Artist Monika Laimgruber has made the most of the opportunity to depict the unlovely wife ensconced in a variety of opulent and fantastic throne rooms. . . . The irridescent spotted flounder emerges from a roiling sea that looks to be truly a cauldron of magic spells, and even the couple's original home in a cracked porcelain 'night pot' looks picturesquely poor. In short, folklore's most unflattering portrait of a nagging wife has never been more handsomely decked out." NY Times Bk Rev

The goose girl; a new translation illus. by Marguerite de Angeli. Doubleday 1964 31p illus $4.95 (2-4)   **398.2**

1 Folklore—Germany 2 Fairy tales
ISBN 0-385-05148-4   LC 64-10043

This is "the Grimms' tale about the princess who tended the geese while the serving maid who betrayed her married the prince." Booklist

"Lovely picture book with many full-color illustrations and a few pencil sketches done in the typical manner of the artist. The translation [by De Angeli] adheres to the usually accepted ones of this popular fairy tale. This will be useful in introducing younger children to the world of Grimm." Sch Library J

Grimm's Fairy tales; twenty stories; illus. by Arthur Rackham. Penguin Bks. 1978 127p illus $5.95 (3-6)   **398.2**

1 Folklore—Germany 2 Fairy tales
ISBN 0-14-004908-8   LC 78-7011

Grimm, Jacob—*Continued*

First published 1973 by Viking

A collection of "20 familiar stories illustrated by Rackham from the out-of-print 1909 Constable edition of Grimm's fairy tales. The selections keep their original form, and the sometimes harsh opposition of good and evil is faithfully left unsoftened." Booklist

"The illustrations include some full-color plates, some black and white drawings, some silhouettes. More romantic and conventional than Sendak's interpretation [in The juniper tree, and other tales from Grimm, entered below], Rackham's pictures have a beauty and—in some pictures—a vigor that are perennially delectable." Chicago. Children's Bk Center

Hans in luck, by the Brothers Grimm; pictures by Felix Hoffmann. Atheneum Pubs. 1975 unp illus $7.95 (k-2)   **398.2**

1 Folklore—Germany
ISBN 0-689-50020-3   LC 74-18184

"A Margaret K. McElderry book"

German language edition of this version originally published in Switzerland

"The silly tale of young Hans who trades his seven years' wages for one thing after another until he arrives home empty-handed, but convinced that he's lucky." Babbling Bookworm

"The story by the Brothers Grimm has been considerably curtailed and adapted so that only a single line of text appears on each page of the picture book; but the highly stylized humor remains intact. . . . The white pages supply a perfect foil for the animals and people which are solidly drawn and richly embellished with watercolor, creating a story-telling frieze that moves steadily from page to page. The interplay of the restless or stolid animal forms with the angular, gauche, yet expressive human figures perfectly embodies the rustic humor of the original tale." Horn Bk

Hansel and Gretel [by] the Brothers Grimm; illus. by Lisbeth Zwerger; tr. from the German by Elizabeth D. Crawford. Morrow 1979 unp illus $7.95, lib. bdg. $7.63 (k-3)   **398.2**

1 Folklore—Germany   2 Fairy tales
ISBN 0-688-22198-X; 0-688-32198-4   LC 79-989

A retelling of the folk tale about the two children who were abandoned in the woods by their father and stepmother. There they encountered a witch who lived in a house made of cookies and candy

"A finely crafted treatment of the popular folktale, with a direct text and more somber artwork that will tend to attract an older audience than the version illustrated by Adrienne Adams [entered below]. . . . The young Austrian illustrator has done 11 pleasing line-and-wash paintings in low-key color and shrouded backgrounds. . . The sure sketches have nice details—the children's hungry, expectant faces at the witch's table, or the hag's clutch at the oven doorjamb as Gretel shoves determinedly." Sch Library J

Hansel and Gretel, by the Brothers Grimm; tr. by Charles Scribner, Jr.; illus. by Adrienne Adams. Scribner 1975 unp illus $6.95, pa $2.95 (k-3)   **398.2**

1 Folklore—Germany   2 Fairy tales
ISBN 0-684-14400-X; 0-684-16006-4   LC 74-14080

Another version of the traditional German tale entered above

"The illustrations are handsome, particularly the night scenes; Adams is skilled at using color to create atmosphere: the trees loom, a greenish light sifts through the dark forest. When the children escape, it is into a sunny, open landscape of lake, sky, and clouds. The paintings are deftly composed and dramatic, closely fitted to the incidents of the story." Chicago. Children's Bk Center

Hansel and Gretel; story by the Brothers Grimm; illus. by Arnold Lobel. Delacorte Press 1971 37p illus lib. bdg. $6.46 (1-3)   **398.2**

1 Folklore—Germany   2 Fairy tales
ISBN 0-440-03466-3   LC 75-11729-6

First published 1970 in England. Text copyright by Kathleen Lines

Another version of the traditional German tale entered above

"In moss green or ocher washed drawings, the illustrator . . . captures the element of intuitive mystery in the story without over-emphasizing the possible element of horror: The pictures of the children listening in the loft to their stepmother's plan to get rid of them, of the finding of the witch's little house in the deep forest, of the fattening of the children for the witch's feast, and of the final destruction of the witch herself are skillfully controlled and successfully lead to the protection and warmth of the reunion scene between father and children. A quiet, completely effective interpretation." Horn Bk

Household stories; from the collection of the Bros. Grimm. Tr. from the German by Lucy Crane, and done into pictures by Walter Crane. Dover [1963] 269p illus pa $3 (4-6)   **398.2**

1 Folklore—Germany   2 Fairy tales
ISBN 0-8446-2167-6   LC 64-16327

Also available in hardcover from Peter Smith (ISBN 0-8446-2167-6) for $6.75

This collection of over fifty fairy tales "is an unabridged republication of the work first published by Macmillan and Company in 1886." Verso of title page

It "preserves the flavor of the original and is illustrated by a famous nineteenth-century artist." Hodges. Bks for Elem Sch Libraries

The juniper tree, and other tales from Grimm; selected by Lore Segal and Maurice Sendak. Tr. by Lore Segal; with four tales tr. by Randall Jarrell; pictures by Maurice Sendak. Farrar, Straus 1973 2v (332p) boxed set $15 (4 and up)   **398.2**

1 Folklore—Germany   2 Fairy tales
ISBN 0-374-18057-1   LC 73-82698

"Through 27 selections, Segal and Sendak brilliantly expose the underside of Grimms' fairy tale world. The happily-ever-after tinkering re-tellers will gasp at some of the grizzly goings-on—a stepmother slices and stews her son for dinner in the title story. . . . However, the collection, which contains many unfamiliar tales, is not monotonously morbid. Peasants still marry princes; simpletons find success and fame; and devils get their due. . . . The translations, smooth and chatty, echo the tales' oral origins, but it is the artwork which is unforgettable. The superbly detailed pen-and-ink drawings are reminiscent of German woodcuts. . . . Sendak pictures his people in provocative poses—viewers eavesdrop on a startled and semi-nude couple; the devil's grandmother cradles sleeping Satan in a mock Pietà. . . . Although not for the timid, this is a truly towering achievement in good book-making for children." Sch Library J

King Grisly-Beard [a tale from the Brothers Grimm] tr. by Edgar Taylor; pictures by Maurice Sendak. Farrar, Straus 1973 unp illus $2.95 (k-3)   **398.2**

1 Folklore—Germany   2 Fairy tales
ISBN 0-374-34134-6   LC 73-77911

This translation first published 1823 in German popular tales

Another version of the folktale entered below with title: King Thrushbeard, this is illustrated as a stage production acted by two children, with their humorous comments given in balloons

"With a minimum of props and scenery, Sendak deftly stages the production in wryly humorous watercolor cartoons that run below the 1823 Edgar Taylor translation. Fortunately, the illustrations upstage and undercut the sexist tale. An uppity princess learns humility after she's forced to marry a beggar, actually King Grisly-Beard, one of her rejected suitors. The potato-faced princess and her equally homely husband steal the show. . . . Young children will applaud these pint-sized stars, and hopefully readers will be as unmoved by the message as Sendak's unflappable little girl who exits triumphant." Library J

King Thrushbeard; a story by the Brothers Grimm; with pictures by Felix Hoffmann. Harcourt 1970 unp illus $5.95 (1-3)   **398.2**

1 Folklore—Germany   2 Fairy tales
ISBN 0-15-242940-9   LC 74-123890

German language edition of this version originally published 1969 in Switzerland

"A beautiful and haughty princess mocks the suitors presented to her, so her father forces her

Grimm, Jacob—*Continued*

to marry the first vagabond who comes to the palace door. Once she has been systematically humbled by being made to live as a peasant wife and kitchen servant, her husband reveals himself as King Thrushbeard, one of the noble suitors she formerly disdained." NY Times Bk Rev

"The story of the comeuppance of the proud princess here unfolds in a somber tone that would have a Woman's Liberation Mover frothing. . . . However, Mr. Hoffmann's imaginative beauty of composition and richness of expression and detail make inclusion of this along with his other individual titles . . . essential to a good collection." Sch Library J

Another version is entered above with title: King Grisly-Beard

Little Red Riding Hood; a story by the Brothers Grimm; with pictures by Harriet Pincus. Harcourt 1968 unp illus $6.95 (k-3)   398.2

1 Folklore—Germany 2 Fairy tales
ISBN 0-15-247132-4   LC 68-11505

"A humorously stocky, pudding-faced Little Red Riding Hood comes to her encounter with the wolf via the usual forest route carrying her basket of cakes and honey. At Grandmother's house she is eaten in one gulp, the text reports, by the wolf who has just dispatched her grandmother in the same way. In the end, a passing huntsman slits open the wolf to release the still-spry prisoners and kills the beast. . . . The retelling is longer and more robust than that of 'The Renowned history of Little Red Riding-Hood' [entered below under title]." Booklist

"The captivating illustrations for this old tale are filled with droll humor. . . . The delicate blending of soft color gives the effect of textural variety." Sch Library J

More Tales from Grimm; freely tr. and illus. by Wanda Gág. Coward. McCann & Geoghegan 1947 257p illus $6.95 (4-6)   398.2

1 Folklore—Germany 2 Fairy tales
ISBN 0-698-20093-4   LC 47-11377

Sequel to: Tales from Grimm, entered below
A collection of 32 tales from Grimm including many lesser-known tales "presented with this author's fresh and zestful interpretation, freely translated yet retaining the essence of the original tales. This is the book which Wanda Gág was working on at the time of her death. Although the translation of the text was ready for the press, the drawings were in varying stages of completeness. . . . Many of the drawings which existed only in their preliminary stages have been included without any retouching or correction." Booklist

The pictures are "drawn with humor and charm. Finely made, the book is a pleasure to hold in the hand and a joy to read." Horn Bk

Rapunzel; a story by the Brothers Grimm; with pictures by Felix Hoffmann. Harcourt 1961 [c1960] unp illus $5.50 (1-4)   398.2

1 Folklore—Germany 2 Fairy tales
ISBN 0-15-265656-1   LC 61-2865

German language edition of this version originally published 1949 in Switzerland. This translation first published 1960 in England
The classic folk tale of a beautiful girl named Rapunzel, held prisoner at the top of a high tower by a witch, and how, by means of her long golden hair, a prince was able to rescue her
The artist's lithographs "are often beautiful; they combine clarity of line and colouring with a romantic strangeness, a sense of distance and time. . . . But Mr. Hoffmann also responds to what is harsh and cruel." Times (London) Lit Sup

The seven ravens; a story by the Brothers Grimm; with pictures by Felix Hoffmann. Harcourt 1963 unp illus $6.95 (k-3)   398.2

1 Folklore—Germany 2 Fairy tales
ISBN 0-15-272920-8   LC 63-2506

German language edition of this version first published 1962 in Switzerland
"The tale of a man whose impatient curse changed his seven boys into ravens. Their little sister, who had been the unwitting cause of their misfortune, traveled a weary way to break the spell." America

"A delightfully illustrated version of an old favorite; the pictures are invariably lovely, but have variety in their mood and execution, some of the illustrations of the ravens being strong and bold while those of the ice palace and the walk to the end of the world have a charming fragility." Chicago. Children's Bk Center

Snow White, by the Brothers Grimm; freely tr. from the German by Paul Heins; with illus. by Trina Schart Hyman. Little 1974 unp illus $7.95, pa $3.95 (k-3)   398.2

1 Folklore—Germany 2 Fairy tales
ISBN 0-316-35450-3; 0-316-35451-1   LC 73-13585

"An Atlantic Monthly Press book"
Another version of the tale entered below with title: Snow-White and the seven dwarfs
"The language of the translation is idiomatic, direct, and graceful. And the pictures interpret the story as thoroughly and carefully as does the text, adding depth and dimension to the characters, which are visually memorable. Snow White is not cloyingly sweet nor is she a vapid beauty, but a lively pretty child, who grows into a grave and beautiful woman. The dwarfs are sober and kind, misshapen but not grotesque; each is distinctively characterized. . . . The illustrator's characteristic line is visible, but the vigorous imagination of the full-color double-spreads surpasses that of all her previous work." Horn Bk

Snow White and Rose Red [by] the Brothers Grimm; illus. by Adrienne Adams. Scribner 1964 unp illus lib. bdg. $5.95 (1-3)   398.2

1 Folklore—Germany 2 Fairy tales
ISBN 0-684-20717-6   LC 64-21290

Here is the "tale of the two sisters, the kind brown bear who is a prince under a wicked enchantment, and the ungrateful dwarf, illustrated in delicate colors with charm and significant detail." Children's Bks, 1964

Snow-White and the seven dwarfs; a tale from the Brothers Grimm; tr. by Randall Jarrell; pictures by Nancy Ekholm Burkert. Farrar, Straus 1972 unp illus $7.95 (k-3) 398.2

1 Folklore—Germany 2 Fairy tales
ISBN 0-374-37099-0   LC 72-81489

"In a large picture book of beauty and distinction, the traditional fairy tale is given a setting of noteworthy stature. All but one of the illustrations—medieval in tone, mood, and detail—cover two-page spreads. . . . Richly detailed medieval motifs are used to decorate the end papers and the illustrations, and the colors used throughout have both clarity and depth. The text is true to its Germanic sources; and the end is not softened." Horn Bk

Snow White and the seven dwarfs; freely tr. and illus. by Wanda Gág. Coward-McCann 1938 43p illus lib. bdg. $5.49 (1-4)   398.2

1 Folklore—Germany 2 Fairy tales
ISBN 0-698-30320-2   LC 38-27575

The beloved story of the little princess who wandered into the home of the seven dwarfs and of how she eluded the schemes of her wicked step-mother, bent on destroying her
Miss Gág "has gone to the German for her text and with her own inimitable drawings, and a translation faithful to the original, has kept the spirit and the beauty of the tale." Wis Library Bul

Tales from Grimm; freely tr. and illus. by Wanda Gág. Coward-McCann 1936 237p illus $7.95 (4-6)   398.2

1 Folklore—Germany 2 Fairy tales
ISBN 0-698-20139-6   LC 36-28509

"Sixteen of the Grimm fairy and household tales ranging from the familiar Cinderella, Rapunzel, and The fisherman and his wife, to the less known Six servants . . . and Lean Liesl and Lanky Lenz." NY Libraries

"Miss Gág has made a thoroughly satisfying book, and one that children will at once feel belongs to them. In her translations and in her drawings Miss Gág has caught the essence of the folktale, its drama, its wonder, its humor, its joy,

Grimm, Jacob—*Continued*

and with a fine freshness and zest she is bringing these qualities to boys and girls." NY Times Bk Rev

Includes glossary

Followed by: More tales from Grimm, entered above

Tom Thumb; the story by the Brothers Grimm; with pictures by Felix Hoffmann. Atheneum Pubs. 1973 unp illus $7.95 (k-3)
                                398.2

1 Folklore—Germany   2 Fairy tales
ISBN 0-689-30318-1   LC 72-85917

"A Margaret K. McElderry book"

German language edition of this version first published 1972 in Switzerland

"Tom, the wish-fulfillment child of poor farmers, is tiny in size but large in cunning. He persuades his parents to sell him to two sharpies who plan to feature him in a sideshow. He has his own plans for outwitting his owners and they are successful, as are his other schemes for getting the best of other adversaries and incidentally getting rich." Pub W

"The illustrator's animals are sturdily lifelike, his rustic characters full of spirit, his panoramas and treatment of changing light masterful. Children will be captivated by the invention of window-like views of Tom inside his captors." Horn Bk

The twelve dancing princesses; retold from a story by the Brothers Grimm; illus. by Errol Le Cain. Viking 1978 unp illus lib. bdg. $8.95 (k-3)
                                398.2

1 Folklore—Germany   2 Fairy tales
ISBN 0-670-73358-X   LC 78-8578

A retelling of the "classic German tale of an old soldier who discovers the secret of the 12 princesses and so wins himself a wife and kingdom is given new life by Le Cain who sets the story . . . in a resplendent baroque court." Sch Library J

"Le Cain's skillfully elaborate artwork, faulty only from occasional clutter or clash in design between double-page spreads, raises a question of appropriateness in illustrating folktales. While technically admirable, the richly colored paintings are almost devoid of emotional tension. . . . The underground forest scenes are stunning, whereas several other ornate spreads leave the story cold. Nevertheless, they are successful as decoration, and the adaptation is smooth, with only minor changes—unsuccessful princes are dismissed from the palace instead of losing their heads, for instance. A carefully defined vision of enchantment for fairy tale connoisseurs." Booklist

Wanda Gág's Jorinda and Joringel; illus. by Margot Tomes. Coward, McCann & Geoghegan 1978 unp illus $6.95 (k-3)   398.2

1 Folklore—Germany   2 Fairy tales
ISBN 0-698-20440-9   LC 77-26680

In this translation of the Grimm Brothers' tale, a witch changes Jorinda into a nightingale. Her sweetheart Joringel discovers through a dream how to save her. This translation appeared previously in Gág's More Tales from Grimm, entered above

"Wanda Gág's flowing translation . . . is the inspiration for a small, beautifully crafted book in which full-color illustrations alternating with detailed pen-and-ink drawings complement the ingeniousness of the narrative. . . . The pictures show the relationship between the central characters as youthful friendship rather than romantic love. The childlike quality is emphasized in the delineation of Joringel's devotion as he searches for the 'red, red flower' with which he will release Jorinda from the evil sorceress. Meticulously detailed backgrounds, remarkable for their evanescent coloration, suggest an enchanted landscape against which the sturdily limned figures recall the tale's folk origin." Horn Bk

The wolf and the seven little kids; a story by the Brothers Grimm; with pictures by Felix Hoffmann. Harcourt 1959 unp illus $6.95 (k-3)
                                398.2

1 Folklore—Germany   2 Goats—Fiction   3 Wolves —Fiction
ISBN 0-15-299108-5   LC 59-16357

German language editions of this version originally published 1957 in Switzerland. This translation first published 1958 in England

The tale of a clever mother goat who, assisted by the youngest of her seven little kids, recovers the other six from the wolf

"A distinguished picture book by a noted Swiss artist. Interpreting the beloved folk tale with just the right blend of fantasy and realism, the beautiful lithographs are strong and simple in line and restrained in color. A pure delight for young children." Booklist

Haley, Gail E.

A story, a story; an African tale retold and illus. by Gail E. Haley. Atheneum Pubs. 1970 unp illus $5.95, lib. bdg. $7.89 pa $2.95 (k-3)
                                398.2

1 Folklore—Africa   2 Spiders—Fiction
ISBN 0-689-20510-4; 0-689-20511-2; 0-689-70423-2
                               LC 69-18961

Awarded the Caldecott Medal, 1971

"The story explains the origin of that favorite African folk material, the spider tale. Here Ananse, the old spider man, wanting to buy the Sky God's stories, completes by his cleverness three seemingly impossible tasks set as the price for the golden box of stories which he takes back to earth." Sutherland. The Best in Children's Bks

"The magnificent, big woodcut illustrations in rich, bold colors and the poetic text . . . combine to make a truly distinguished version of an ancient African tale." Commonweal

The **Hare** and the tortoise; pictures by Paul Galdone. McGraw 1962 unp illus lib. bdg. $7.95 (k-3)   398.2

1 Fables   2 Rabbits—Fiction   3 Turtles—Fiction
ISBN 0-07-022713-6   LC 62-9988

"Whittlesey House publications"

A fable about the boastful, swift hare who, because he is overconfident and stops to take a nap, loses a race to the slow but steady tortoise

"An ingratiating picture-book treatment of Aesop's fable. The drawings mingle lively forest animals with flowers and grasses done in green, brown, and yellow. Although a little undisciplined in composition, the double-page spreads provide plenty of visual entertainment. Text, in large print, is from Joseph Jacobs." Sch Library J

Harper, Wilhelmina

(comp.) Ghosts and goblins; stories for Halloween; illus. by William Wiesner. New, rev. ed. Dutton 1965 250p illus $6.95   398.2

1 Folklore   2 Halloween—Fiction   3 Ghosts— Fiction
ISBN 0-525-30516-5   LC 65-21281

First published 1936

"A welcome collection of [twenty-six] tales [and some poems] with a shiver in them, drawn from the folklore of several different countries. Many of them are for young children." Horn Bk

"Its use will doubtless not be restricted to this season alone. . . . There is no element of terror in these stories to leave its mark of fear and nightmare on sensitive minds, but each has its share of magic and mystery to stir the imagination." NY Times Bk Rev

The Gunniwolf; retold by Wilhelmina Harper; illus. by William Wiesner. Dutton 1967 unp illus $7.95 (k-1)   398.2

1 Folklore
ISBN 0-525-31139-4   LC 67-22387

A retelling of the folktale about Little Girl who ignores her mother's warnings, wanders into the jungle searching for pretty flowers, and encounters the fierce Gunniwolf

"Pictures are green and orange with numerous black lines." Bruno. Bks for Sch Libraries, 1968

Harris, Christie

Mouse Woman and the mischief-makers; drawings by Douglas Tait. Atheneum Pubs. 1977 114p illus $7.95 (4 and up)   398.2

1 Indians of North America—Legends
ISBN 0-689-30554-0   LC 76-25846

"In a companion to 'Mouse Woman and the Vanished Princesses' [entered below] Harris presents seven more stories of this sharply characterized, grandmotherly narnauk, or spirit being, who determinedly makes it her business to set things

Harris, Christie—*Continued*
right when mischief-makers of either the spirit or mortal world disturb the natural order of things. There are greedy humans, pompous spirit creatures, and an assortment of victims whom Mouse Woman chooses to deal with or aid. . . . There's a concluding story . . . that features Mouse as an imperfect little girl narnauk who once got into trouble for lying." Booklist
"The black and white illustrations are impressive, having the precision of Fisher's scratchboard work with some of the drama of early Keeping illustration. Sources for the tales are cited." Chicago. Children's Bk Center

Mouse Woman and the muddleheads; drawings by Douglas Tait. Atheneum Pubs. 1979 131p illus $7.95 (4 and up)   398.2
1 Indians of North America—Legends
ISBN 0-689-30682-2   LC 78-13402
Companion volume to: Mouse Woman and the vanished princesses, entered below and Mouse Woman and the mischief-makers, entered above
"The tiny narnauk directs her wit and supernatural powers to correcting the result of stupidity, whether on the part of humans or other narnauks. And stupidity most often lies in breaking the rules of correct behavior. When narnauk and human meet in marriage, as they do in several stories, trouble results even where intentions are good: ambition out of hand brings death; a princess who carries out her childbearing duty for the future is rewarded." Booklist
"The narratives are rich in descriptions of folkways—taboos, charms, and superstitions. The artist uses black line and stippling for strong, handsome effects contrasting light and dark. Authenticating the tales is a list of five source collections published between 1899 and 1953." Horn Bk

Mouse Woman and the vanished princesses; drawings by Douglas Tait. Atheneum Pubs. 1976 155p illus. $7.95 (4 and up)   398.2
1 Indians of North America—Legends
ISBN 0-689-30502-8   LC 75-23147
"From Haida and Tsimshian Indian folklore come six . . . stories about Mouse Woman, a supernatural being. Sometimes a mouse, sometimes a tiny woman, always sympathetic, enterprising and very proper, she is especially interested in young people in trouble. In each story a different princess is lured from her village by other supernatural beings and helped to return to her family by Mouse Woman who is rewarded with her favorite gift of long woolen ear tassles." Sch Library J
"The tellings are aggressive, if occasionally coy, while meticulous pen drawings give striking form to characters in the text." Booklist

Once more upon a totem; illus. by Douglas Tait. Atheneum Pubs. 1973 195p illus $5.95 (4 and up)   398.2
1 Indians of North America—Legends
ISBN 0-689-30088-3   LC 72-86939
The following three legends of the Indians of the Pacific Northwest are prefaced by brief introductions with background information on culture and traditions: The prince who was taken away by the salmon; Raven traveling; Ghost story
"Striking illustrations accompany the stories, which reveal the Indians' humor, strong family ties, exemplary noblesse oblige, profound veneration of all life (including their prey and the spirit world) ecologically perceptive religion, and acceptance of death." Sch Library J

Harris, Rosemary
Beauty and the beast; retold by Rosemary Harris; illus. by Errol Le Cain. Doubleday [1980 c1979] unp illus $7.95 lib. bdg. $8.90 (2-4)   398.2
1 Fairy tales 2 Folklore—France
ISBN 0-385-15482-8; 0-385-15483-6   LC 79-7482
First published 1979 in England
"Even though editions of the enduring fairy tale are many and some extremely popular, the collaboration by Harris and Le Cain will surely stand up to competition. The author's exquisite style emphasizes the moods in the classic and harmonizes with the awesome paintings. . . Even those who have frequently read the tale of how Beauty's unselfishness and love for Beast conquer all should find unexpected nuances and depth in this lovely book." Pub W

The elaborate and stylized representations provide just the right distance from the tale, complementing its sophistication and drama. Beauty is not conventionally pretty, and the elegant costumes and settings resemble opera sets or baroque paintings. Each page of text facing a full-page illustration is framed in a rich border of paisley-like pattern, and the tones of the illustrations are appropriately muted lavender, azure, rose, and rust. There is sumptuous detail and depth in the backgrounds, clever caricature in the faces. LeCain delays a direct portrayal of the Beast until the climactic moment when Beauty reluctantly leaves him and first admits her feelings: our shock at her ability to love such a monster is thus intensified. An admirable production." Sch Library J

Hatch, Mary C.
13 Danish tales; retold by Mary C. Hatch; illus. by Edgun. Harcourt 1947 169p illus $4.50 (3-5)   398.2
1 Folklore—Denmark 2 Fairy tales
ISBN 0-15-285683-8   LC 47-30505
A collection of thirteen tales based on J. C. Bay's Danish fairy & folk tales, published in 1899
The stories "deal largely with everyday objects touched with magic—talking pots, enchanted cats and knapsacks that are never empty." Christian Sci Monitor
"Engaging and humorous. . . . They are the real 'peasant' tales—homely, funny, sometimes a bit sly and cryptic. It is a gay-looking book with apt illustrations." Sat Rev

Haviland, Virginia
Favorite fairy tales told in Czechoslovakia; retold by Virginia Haviland; illus. by Trina Schart Hyman. Little 1966 90p illus $6.95 (2-5)   398.2
1 Folklore—Czechoslovakia 2 Fairy tales
ISBN 0-316-35083-4   LC 65-13713
"The illustrations—some in black and white, others in tomato red, olive green, and black—combine finely detailed drawing with strong, vigorous characterizations which heighten the forthright drama and the humor of the stories; the use of Slavic patterns and designs adds a sense of rightness and authenticity. Three of the tales are familiar favorites: 'Kuratko the Terrible' (magnificently pictured as a great strutting tyrant), 'The Shepherd's Nosegay,' and 'The Twelve Months'; the other two, 'The Wood Fairy' and 'The Three Golden Hairs of Grandfather Know All,' contain many traditional folklore motifs." Horn Bk

Favorite fairy tales told in Denmark; retold by Virginia Haviland; illus. by Margot Zemach. Little 1971 90p illus lib. bdg. $6.95 (3-5)   398.2
1 Folklore—Denmark 2 Fairy tales
ISBN 0-316-35058-3   LC 73-117022
These "six Danish stories depict greed, craftiness, and common sense." Christian Sci Monitor
"A certain generosity of spirit and good humor pervade the collection, along with a very definite sense of justice. . . . The pencil-sketched line drawings with their plum and mustard washes perfectly reflect the good-natured mood of the stories." Horn Bk

Favorite fairy tales told in France; retold from Charles Perrault and other French storytellers, by Virginia Haviland; illus. by Roger Duvoisin. Little 1959 91p illus lib. bdg. $6.95 (2-5)   398.2
1 Folklore—France 2 Fairy tales
ISBN 0-316-35054-0   LC 59-7346
"Five French fairy tales translated from original sources and retold by the author with style and grace. . . . Beautiful illustrations. . . . are in perfect complement with the text." Library J

Favorite fairy tales told in Greece; retold by Virginia Haviland; illus. by Nonny Hogrogian. Little 1970 90p illus lib. bdg. $6.95 (2-5)   398.2
1 Folklore—Greece. Modern 2 Fairy tales
ISBN 0-316-35060-5   LC 79-77448
"Among the eight representative Greek tales in this collection are a version of the story about the

Haviland, Virginia—*Continued*

king's daughter who 'loved her father like salt,' a variant of 'The three sillies,' and several stories in which the exquisite Greek fairies either gain control over a mortal by magic or lose their magic powers to a mortal who acquires possessions of one of their personal belongings. This welcome addition to Haviland's popular series of traditional tales for young readers is illustrated with piquant line drawings some of which are accented with color." Booklist

Favorite fairy tales told in India; retold by Virginia Haviland; illus. by Blair Lent. Little 1973 95p illus lib. bdg. $6.95 (2-5)   398.2

1 Folklore—India 2 Fairy tales
ISBN 0-316-35055-9   LC 71-117019

These eight tales tell of clever jackals who outwit lions, tigers, and alligators; a cat who discovers the danger of eating everything you see; a pot-maker who accidentally becomes the saviour of his kingdom; a magical little man who helps a solider's son win a princess; a blind man and a deaf man who overcome demons and accidentally cure each other

The selections have been "chosen from late-nineteenth and early-twentieth century versions of Hindu folk tales and fables. . . . The stories are marked by the humorous situations and the ingenious solutions of universal folklore. The handsome illustrations by the winner of the 1972 Caldecott Award range from the meticulous to the bold. Black-and-white line drawings alternate with three-color illustrations in cream, green, and mauve. Foliage, architecture, and decorative motifs suggest the exuberance of Hindu art." Horn Bk

Favorite fairy tales told in Ireland; retold from Irish storytellers by Virginia Haviland; illus. by Arthur Marokvia. Little 1961 91p illus lib. bdg. $7.95 (2-5)   398.2

1 Folklore—Ireland 2 Fairy tales
ISBN 0-316-35051-6   LC 61-9282

A collection of 5 tales involving humans, animals and a leprechaun. The stories can be read independently by the children in the age range to which they appeal, and they serve as an incentive to explore further as reading ability improves." Library J

The illustrations "are exuberant and colorful." Horn Bk

Favorite fairy tales told in Italy; retold by Virginia Haviland; illus. by Evaline Ness. Little 1965 90p illus lib. bdg. $6.95 (2-5) 398.2

1 Folklore—Italy 2 Fairy tales
ISBN 0-316-35076-1   LC 65-13715

This retelling of six stories selected from older sources which are out of print has "attractive illustrations and format that entice the young reader. In this volume, three stories follow particularly familiar story patterns: 'Cenerentola,' a Cinderella story; 'The Three Goslings,' reminiscent of the three pigs; and 'Bastianelo,' about three sillies." Horn Bk

Favorite fairy tales told in Japan; retold by Virginia Haviland; illus. by George Suyeoka. Little 1967 89p illus $7.95 (2-5)   398.2

1 Folklore—Japan 2 Fairy tales
ISBN 0-316-35091-5   LC 67-18112

"A fine literary and visual experience for younger readers. The retellings of 'One-Inch Fellow,' 'The Good Fortune Kettle,' 'The Tongue-Cut Sparrow,' 'Momotaro,' and 'The White Hare and the Crocodile' have retained their oriental aspects, and the full-page illustrations in orange, green, black, and white are up to the standard expected for this series." Sch Library J

Favorite fairy tales told in Norway; retold from Norse folklore by Virginia Haviland; illus. by Leonard Weisgard. Little 1961 88p illus lib. bdg. $7.95 (2-5)   398.2

1 Folklore—Norway 2 Fairy tales
ISBN 0-316-35053-2   LC 61-9283

These seven "stories have been adapted from the 1859 translation by Sir George Webb Dasent of Norwegian folk tales gathered by Peter Christian Asbjornsen and Jorgen E. Moe." Verso of title page

Compared with several other of Miss Haviland's collections, "the Norwegian volume is, perhaps, the prettiest with its neat precise pictures some of which recall designs in Scandinavian folk art." Pub W

Favorite fairy tales told in Scotland; retold by Virginia Haviland; illus. by Adrienne Adams. Little 1963 92p illus $6.95 (2-5)   398.2

1 Folklore—Scotland 2 Fairy tales
ISBN 0-316-35043-5   LC 63-7676

"Six lively tales of peasants and pages, serpents and fairies in this useful series of stories." Ontario Library Rev

"The retelling is direct and simple, the print is large and clear, the illustrations are attractive. Sources for tales are cited, and the book should be as useful for storytelling as it is for the individual reader." Chicago. Children's Bk Center

Favorite fairy tales told in Spain; retold by Virginia Haviland; illus. by Barbara Cooney. Little 1963 87p illus lib. bdg. $6.95 (2-5)   398.2

1 Folklore—Spain 2 Fairy tales
ISBN 0-316-35047-8   LC 63-7677

These six tales concern such characters as an enchanted mule, four wise and foolish brothers, a flea, and a half-chick

"As in other volumes in the series, this collection of retellings is handsomely illustrated and is printed in large, clear type. The stories are told with a true feeling for the genre and a true feeling of the country of origin; the style is direct and vivacious. A good book for storytelling, for reading aloud, or for independent reading." Chicago. Children's Bk Center

Favorite fairy tales told in Sweden; retold by Virginia Haviland; illus. by Ronni Solbert. Little 1966 92p illus lib. bdg. $6.95 (2-5)   398.2

1 Folklore—Sweden 2 Fairy tales
ISBN 0-316-35052-4   LC 65-13714

"Plain, plucky heroes—peasant or prince—gain good fortune with good sense in six tales told with simplicity and humor. The Swedish stories are less well-known than some, but their themes will be familiar. Vigorous, sweeping lines intensified with vibrant yellow and orange suggest the rustic strength and blazing brilliance of a land of the midnight sun." Horn Bk

"Excellent for storytelling." Sch Library J

Hieatt, Constance

The Castle of Ladies; retold by Constance Hieatt; illus. by Norman Laliberte. Crowell 1973 72p illus $8.95 (4 and up)   398.2

1 Gawain 2 Arthur, King
ISBN 0-690-18064-0   LC 75-187945

"Mistaking Sir Gawain for a scullion, Lady Maudisante scorns his pledge to rescue her sister from imprisonment. Unmindful of her, he sets out and soon finds he requires the Sword of the Strange Scabbard, housed in the Castle of Ladies forbidden to men. Undaunted, Sir Gawain enters and withstands attacks on his life, at last receiving the sword and the blessings of his aunt Morgan Le Fay, Mistress of the castle. Now properly armed and respected by Maudisante, he easily effects the rescue and returns to Camelot with Maudisante as his bride to be. Hieatt has drawn on Arthurian and other medieval source material to weave her own apt tale of romance and magic." Booklist

The knight of the cart; retold by Constance Hieatt; illus. by John Gretzer. Crowell 1969 85p illus lib. bdg. $8.79 (4-7)   398.2

1 Lancelot 2 Arthur, King
ISBN 0-690-47532-2   LC 70-78263

The author "confesses to adding her own interpretations to the versions of Chrétien de Troyes and Malory, thus giving a fresh and vivid cast to the familiar Arthurian legends. The king, already troubled by the disappearance of many good men of Camelot, is struck with dismay when a messenger comes to report that the queen and her ladies have been taken captive by the evil Sir Malagant and transported to the Land of Gorre. Sir Lancelot, hot in pursuit, submits to the indignity of riding in a cart (a disgrace usually meted out

Hieatt, Constance—*Continued*

to criminals) to save his queen, an episode that is only the first of his adventures. The writing style is wonderfully fluent and appropriately romantic." Sutherland. The Best in Children's Bks

"The lively and effective black, white, and gray illustrations seem to be somewhat indebted in style to Evelyn Ness." Horn Bk

Hirsh, Marilyn

Could anything be worse? A Yiddish tale retold and illus. by Marilyn Hirsh. Holiday House 1974 unp illus lib. bdg. $7.95 (k-3)
398.2

1 Folklore, Jewish
ISBN 0-8234-0239-8   LC 73-17364

"A tale found in many cultures, here adapted from the Yiddish version, is nicely told and illustrated. Dissatisfied with the way his family behaves, a man takes the advice of a friend and goes to the Rabbi for counsel. The Rabbi will answer no questions, but tells the man to bring chickens into the house, then a cow, then some relatives. The small house is noisy and crowded. Again the man goes to the Rabbi; the relatives are sent off, then the cow, then the chickens. The family throws open the windows and cleans and polishes, and settles down in peace. . . . One of the most durable of the count-your-blessings tales, gently humorous, is pleasant to read alone or aloud, although the format indicates wider read-aloud use." Chicago. Children's Bk Center

Hodges, Margaret

The Fire Bringer; a Paiute Indian legend; retold by Margaret Hodges; illus. by Peter Parnall. Little 1972 31p illus lib. bdg. $6.95 (2-4)
398.2

1 Paiute Indians—Legends   2 Fire—Fiction
3 Coyotes—Fiction
ISBN 0-316-36783-4   LC 70-182247

Adapted from the version by Mary Austin in: The basket woman, published 1904

"The coyote is the true hero of the tale, as he helps the Paiute boy who is his friend alleviate the winter suffering of his tribe. Choosing the hundred best runners, who are stationed at intervals along the trail to the mountain of the Fire Spirits, Coyote steals a burning brand, runs to the first station, and passes the fire on; the runners speed along in relay fashion, the Fire Spirits chase to no avail." Chicago. Children's Bk Center

"The Promethean myth is frequently found in American Indian folklore. However, unlike other tellings in which animals form the relay team and humorous elements are stressed, this version emphasizes the nobility of the deed. Peter Parnall's handsome pen-and-ink drawings washed with flat spreads of muted color contrast the stark coldness of the world to the power and beauty of the stolen fire." Sch Library J

The wave; adapted from Lafcadio Hearn's Gleanings in Buddha-fields; illus. by Blair Lent. Houghton 1964 45p illus $3.50, lib. bdg. $3.23 (3-5)
398.2

1 Folklore—Japan
ISBN 0-395-06817-7; 0-395-06818-5   LC 63-14524

This "Japanese folktale was designed for reading aloud. It tells of an old man who set fire to his own rice fields to warn a village of an approaching tidal wave." Wis Library Bul

"Strong, dramatic illustrations in muted colors have the feeling and flow of Japanese art and turn the story into a handsome picture book." Horn Bk

Hogrogian, Nonny

The contest; adapted and illus. by Nonny Hogrogian. Greenwillow Bks. 1976 unp illus $8.95, lib. bdg. $8.59 (1-3)
398.2

1 Folklore—Armenia
ISBN 0-688-80042-4; 0-688-84042-6   LC 75-40389

A "gently humorous retelling of an Armenian folk tale about two robbers who not only share the same occupation but are engaged to the same girl." Sch Library J

"The symmetrical elements of the tale, which create arabesques of humor, are well-served by the full-color, full-page illustrations and by the

pencil drawings scattered through the text. Some of the colored illustrations are bordered by oriental rug patterns, and all of the paintings and drawings are strong in their depiction of Armenian physiognomy. The uncluttered line drawings economically state the actions of the thieves and their horses." Horn Bk

One fine day. Macmillan Pub. Co. 1971 unp illus $6.95, pa $1.95 (k-3)
398.2

1 Folklore—Armenia   2 Foxes—Fiction
ISBN 0-02-744000-1; 0-02-043620-3   LC 75-119834

Awarded the Caldecott Medal, 1972

"A picture story book based on an Armenian folk tale is illustrated [by the author] with bold, simple compositions in soft colors, the pictures echoing the humor of the story. Nicely told, the tale uses a familiar cumulative pattern: when a fox drinks all the milk from an old woman's pail, she cuts off his tail; he begs her to sew it on so that his friends won't laugh at him. She agrees—if he will return her milk. So the fox goes from one creature to another, each asking for a reciprocal favor, until a kind man takes pity, and gives him grain to take to the hen to get the egg to pay the peddler, etc. A charming picture book that is just right for reading aloud to small children, the scale of the pictures also appropriate for group use." Sutherland. The Best in Children's Bks

Holman, Felice

The Drac; French tales of dragons and demons, by Felice Holman and Nanine Valen; drawings by Stephen Walker. Scribner 1975 84p illus map lib. bdg. $6.95 (5 and up) 398.2

1 Folklore—France   2 Legends—France
ISBN 0-684-14334-8   LC 75-4029

"Five little-known tales have been carefully researched from primary sources and sifted through to get at the heart of the legend. The authors have retold the stories skillfully, making them ideal for telling and reading aloud. All revolve around demons or dragons in France and the terror they struck in people's hearts. In each case a short history of the legend and a bibliography of professional interest are included. A map of France designates the areas where the stories originated. In his black-and-white line drawings Walker exercises great imagination in capturing the fierce mythical animals." Booklist

Hooke, Hilda Mary

Thunder in the mountains; legends of Canada; illus. by Clare Bice. Oxford 1947 223p illus $10.50 (5 and up)
398.2

1 Indians of North America—Legends   2 Legends
—Canada
ISBN 0-19-540043-7   LC 48-204

A collection of seventeen Canadian folk tales gathered from existing source material. The book is arranged in three sections. In the first, The garden of Gitche Manitou, the author retells the Indian legends of the early inhabitants of the garden created by Gitche Manitou, the Great Spirit. The second section has three tales of the coming of the white men to Canada; and the third section deals with the white men's stories of magic, witches, pixies, saints and the legend which explains why Montreal is such a windy city

"The book fills a gap in our national folklore collections." Library J
Bibliography: p221-23

Houston, James

Kiviok's magic journey; an Eskimo legend; written and illus. by James Houston. Atheneum Pubs. 1973 unp illus lib. bdg. $5.25 (1-4)
398.2

1 Legends, Eskimo
ISBN 0-689-30419-6   LC 73-75435

"A Margaret K. McElderry book"

"Kiviok, an Eskimo folk hero, marries Kungo, one of the five snow geese left behind as a maiden because an evil raven stole her feather coat. They live happily together until the raven returns and casts a spell which turns Kungo and her two children into snow geese. Inukpuk, a giant, helps Kiviok pursue the flock south by giving him the power to follow them [under water]." Sch Library J

"A legend unusual for both its suspense and poignancy. . . . The vivid text describes Kiviok's

Houston, James—*Continued*

lonely hundred-day journey of searching for Kungo and his meeting with . . . Inukpuk and with the helpful Kaka, the father of all fish. Sienna-and-black drawings suggest the broad dimensions of the magic and the boldness of the Eskimo background." Horn Bk

Tikta'liktak; an Eskimo legend; written and illus. by James Houston. Harcourt 1965 63p illus $6.25 (4-6)   **398.2**

1 Legends, Eskimo
ISBN 0-15-287745-2   LC 65-21696

The author retells a "legend that celebrates man's will to survive. Tikta'liktak, a young hunter, is trapped on an ice floe and marooned on a barren island. Feeling certain that the island is to be his grave, he prepares a stony coffin. A dream foretells the lucky appearance of an unlucky seal, restoring the hunter's strength and desire to live. . . . [He] survives freezing weather, an attack by a polar bear and the long journey that brings him safely home." NY Times Bk Rev

"A book that has all the appeal of the Crusoe situation plus the embellishment of the exotic setting. The illustrations, strong and stark in black and white, enhance the mood of solitude and isolation." Sutherland. The Best in Children's Bks

How Djadja-em-ankh saved the day; a tale from ancient Egypt; tr. from the original hieratic, with illus. and commentary by Lise Manniche. Crowell 1977 c1976 unp illus slip cased pa $6.95 (4 and up)   **398.2**

1 Folklore—Egypt 2 Snofru, King of Egypt
3 Egypt—Civilization 4 Hieroglyphics
ISBN 0-690-01280-2   LC 76-26919

Also available in special edition rolled in tube for $8.95 (ISBN 0-690-01281-0)

"An unusual book offering an introduction to Egyptian culture through folktale and fact. Opening up into one long sheet in the manner of a scroll, this allows readers to experience the story from right to left as Egyptians did. Set in the reign of Seneferu about 4,500 years ago, the simple tale [translated from the Papyrus Westcar] is about 20 women on an afternoon boat trip. The rowing stops when the helmswoman loses her amulet in the water, but Djadja-Em-Ankh saves the day by rolling back the water and recovering the amulet. Having read the story children can turn the pages left to right and find clearly written information about Egyptian culture and language, including a detailed description on making scrolls from papyrus and a discussion of hieroglyphics and the hieratic script of the Egyptians. Attractive pen-and-ink drawings are copies from Egyptian tombs with minor changes to fit the story (the source is given for each drawing)." Sch Library J

"Format is not durable, but is extremely interesting and stimulating for classroom use. The complete hieratic text is also presented. Beautifully done and illustrated by a noted Egyptologist. The regular slip-covered edition unfolds in accordian fashion." Children's Bk Rev Serv

Hume, Lotta Carswell

Favorite children's stories from China and Tibet; illus. by Lo Koon-chiu. Tuttle 1962 119p illus $7.50 (3-6)   **398.2**

1 Folklore—China 2 Folklore—Tibet
ISBN 0-8048-0179-7   LC 61-6219

"Nineteen traditional stories from various sections of China and from Tibet, heard and retold by an American woman who lived for 22 years in central China. Most of these enjoyable tales, filled with humor and wisdom are about animals, and many have counterparts in other countries. Illustrated with many attractive black-and-white drawings and full-color pictures done in the Chinese brush style. Suitable for storytelling." Booklist

Hürlimann, Ruth

The proud white cat; tr. from the German by Anthea Bell. Morrow 1977 unp illus $7.75, lib. bdg. $7.44 (k-3)   **398.2**

1 Folklore—Germany 2 Cats—Fiction
ISBN 0-688-22095-9; 0-688-32095-3   LC 76-51807

This "translation of a German folk tale is about a vain tom cat who thinks that he will never find a wife good enough for him. To aid him in

his search for the perfect mate he seeks out 'Mrs. Vixen.' This oh-so-clever fox leads him through the book in a series of adventures and finally cures him of his conceit." Children's Bk Rev Serv

"Stylized spreads, given meticulous texture with misty cross-hatchings, breathe earthy color against plentiful white space." Booklist

Hutton, Warwick

The sleeping beauty; retold and illus. by Warwick Hutton. Atheneum Pubs. 1979 unp illus lib. bdg. $9.95 (1-4)   **398.2**

1 Folklore—Germany 2 Fairy tales
ISBN 0-689-50131-5   LC 78-64772

"A Margaret K. McElderry book"

This version of the well-known folk tale "is distinguished by gentle, beautiful illustrations. Although the figures occasionally show a slight awkwardness, the watercolor paintings . . . are simple in line and coolly elegant in muted greens and blues. Two double-page panoramas of the widespread land and the distant castle are particularly noteworthy, showing the same scene, first with columns of smoke from the burning spindles and later with the prince approaching the briar-encircled castle. The spacious illustrations have a remote, tranquil quality reinforcing the theme of sleep and complement the unadorned simplicity of the well-known story." Horn Bk

"Hutton's retelling of the Briar Rose story is close to the traditional Grimm version." Booklist

Index to fairy tales, myths and legends; [comp.] by Mary Huse Eastman. 2d ed. rev. and enl. Faxon 1926 610p (Useful reference ser) lib. bdg. $14   **398.2**

1 Folklore—Indexes 2 Fairy tales—Indexes
3 Legends—Indexes 4 Mythology—Indexes
ISBN 0-87305-028-2   LC 26-11491

First published 1915 by the Boston Book Company

This reference work indexes about 700 collections of "fairy tales and fables, the stories from Greek and Norse mythology which seemed most likely to be called for, also hero stories and some [popular] modern stories like the 'Leak in the dyke.' . . . A special effort has been made to include folk stories of as many nationalities as possible. . . . Since inquiries for stories are mainly by title this is first of all a title index. When the same story appears under various titles, it is indexed under the best known or under the one that seemed most descriptive of the story, and references are made from all the other titles. . . . [There are also selected] cross references from subjects—holidays, stars, flowers, etc." Preface

There are also a list of books analyzed, a geographical and racial index to collections analyzed, and a bibliography

Index to fairy tales, myths and legends; supplement [comp.] by Mary Huse Eastman. Faxon 1937 566p (Useful reference ser) lib. bdg. $12   **398.2**

1 Folklore—Indexes 2 Fairy tales—Indexes
3 Legends—Indexes 4 Mythology—Indexes
ISBN 0-87305-061-4   LC 26-11491

This volume indexes 500 volumes published from 1926 to 1937, as well as some older books omitted from the second edition. New features include catch word title cross references and a title list of books indexed. Subject indexing has been expanded. The subjects now appear in a separate Subject List, with the exception of a few, like holidays, which still appear in the main body of the index

Index to fairy tales, myths and legends; second supplement [comp.] by Mary Huse Eastman. Faxon 1952 370p (Useful reference ser) lib. bdg. $11   **398.2**

1 Folklore—Indexes 2 Fairy tales—Indexes
3 Legends—Indexes 4 Mythology—Indexes
ISBN 0-87305-082-7

Indexes 270 volumes published since the first supplementary volume

"The lists of stories for holidays and other days have been moved from the Title Index to the Subject List. However titles beginning with the subject 'catch word' . . . have been omitted." Preface

Followed by: Index to fairy tales, 1949-1972, entered below

Index to fairy tales, 1949-1972; including folklore, legends, & myths, in collections [comp.] by Norma Olin Ireland. Faxon 1973 xxxviii, 741p (Useful reference ser) lib. bdg. $18   398.2

1 Folklore—Indexes 2 Fairy tales—Indexes
3 Legends—Indexes 4 Mythology—Indexes
ISBN 0-87305-101-7   LC 73-173454

Compiled as a continuation of Eastman's Index to fairy tales, and the first and second supplements

"406 books have been indexed, under title and subject, with authors included only when specifically mentioned in the collection. Stories in collections 'only' are included, not individual-story books. We have included a few older titles which have come out in new [editions] or were not included in the earlier indexes. . . . Variant titles are cross-referenced only if mentioned in the books indexed; Eastman has a very complete list of variants and should be referred to, if needed. Our first innovation is the comprehensive subject indexing of stories. . . . All entries are combined into a single alphabet, unlike the Eastman books, as we feel that such an arrangement is easier to use. . . . We have tried to analyze stories according to the 'importance' of subjects (not always every subject) and towards that purpose we have personally read most every one of these stories." Foreword

Index to fairy tales, 1973-1977; including folklore, legends and myths in collections; fourth supplement; comp. by Norma Olin Ireland. Faxon 1979 259p (Useful reference ser) $20   398.2

1 Folklore—Indexes 2 Fairy tales—Indexes
3 Legends—Indexes 4 Mythology—Indexes
ISBN 0-87305-111-4   LC 79-16150

A continuation of Index to fairy tales, myths and legends, compiled by Mary Huse Eastman, its first and second supplements, and Index to fairy tales, 1949-1972, compiled by Norma Olin Ireland, all entered above

"This volume includes collections published from 1973-1977, plus a few reprints of works not included in the earlier indexes, collections of special geographic interest (e.g., Torres Straits), and some works of interest to adults as well. . . . 130 titles (collections only) have been indexed. . . . In general, the headings used in the previous Index are repeated here, with some additions and a few changes." Foreword

Indian fairy tales; selected and ed. by Joseph Jacobs; illus. by John D. Batten. Dover [1969] 255p illus pa $3.50 (4-6)   398.2

1 Folklore—India 2 Fairy tales
ISBN 0-486-21828-7   LC 68-55534

Also available in hardcover from Peter Smith for $6.50 (ISBN 0-8446-0723-1)
A reprint of the title first published 1892 in England. A Putnam edition, o.p. 1980, had title: Indian folk and fairy tales

"From all these sources—from the Jatakas, from the Bidpai, and from the more recent [19th century] collections—I have selected those [twenty-nine] stories which throw most light on the origin of Fable and Folk-tales, and at the same time are most likely to attract English children. . . . The stories existing in Pali and Sanskrit I have taken from translations." Preface
Includes notes and references

Ish-Kishor, Sulamith
The carpet of Solomon; a Hebrew legend; pictures by Uri Shulevitz. Pantheon Bks. 1966 57p illus lib. bdg. $4.99 (4-6)   398.2

1 Solomon, King of Israel 2 Legends, Jewish
ISBN 0-394-91131-8   LC 65-20658

"Discarding a diabolical gift which gave him a false sense of omnipotence, King Solomon learns the value of humility in a symbolic series of mystical adventures. Rare sensitivity in visual and textual imagery." Top of the News

The **Jack** tales . . . with an appendix comp. by Herbert Halpert; and illus. by Berkeley Williams, Jr. Houghton 1971 201p illus $7.95 (4-6)   398.2

1 Folklore—Southern States
ISBN 0-395-06694-8   LC 43-12028

First published 1943. Copyright renewed 1971
"Told by R. M. Ward and his kindred in the Beech Mountain section of Western North Carolina and by other descendants of Council Harmon (1803-1896) elsewhere in The Southern Mountains; with three tales from Wise County, Virginia. Set down from these sources and edited by Richard Chase." Title page
"Humor, freshness, colorful American background, and the use of one character as a central figure in the cycle mark these 18 folk tales, told here in the dialect of the mountain country of North Carolina. A scholarly appendix by Herbert Halpert, giving sources and parallels, increases the book's value as a contribution to American folklore. Black-and-white illustrations in the spirit of the text." Booklist
These stories "show how European tales took on coloration of their new background." Library J
Glossary: p201-[02]

Jacobs, Joseph
English fairy tales; collected by Joseph Jacobs; illus. by John D. Batten. [3d ed.] Dover 1967 261p illus pa $3 (4-6)   398.2

1 Folklore—Great Britain 2 Fairy tales
ISBN 0-486-21818-X

Also available in hardcover from Peter Smith for $6.75 (ISBN 0-8446-2303-2)
First published 1890 in England. First American edition published 1891 by Putnam. This edition is a reprint of the 1898 Putnam edition. Also published with title: English folk and fairy tales
"As outstanding as the best collections of fairy tales of any country, are those of the folk-lore of the British Isles made by Joseph Jacobs. In his re-writing of the [forty-one] stories, he has preserved their humour and dramatic power, and while simplifying dialect, has retained its full flavor. He intends his stories to be read aloud, and while children enjoy them for their own reading, this makes them invaluable for the story-teller who appreciates a colloquial, conversational style." Toronto
Includes notes and references

The **fables of Aesop** (4 and up)   398.2

1 Fables
ISBN 0-8317-3115-X

Some editions are:
Mayflower Bks. (Fascimile classics ser) $5.95 (ISBN 0-8317-3115-X) Edited by Joseph Jacobs; illustrated by Richard Heighway. Fascimile reprint of 1894 Macmillan edition with new added title page giving title as: Jacob's Fables of Aesop
Schocken Bks. $6, pa $3.95 (ISBN 0-8052-3068-8; 0-8052-0138-6) Selected, told anew, and their history traced by Joseph Jacobs; done into pictures by Richard Heighway
First published 1894 by Macmillan
A collection of 82 fables considered by Jacobs to be among the most effective and familiar of the hundreds attributed to Aesop
"There is no fixed text even for the nucleus collection contained in this book . . . . What we call [Aesop's] fables can in most cases be traced back to the fables of other people, notably of Phaedrus and Babrius. . . . I have therefore felt at liberty to retell the fables in such a way as would interest children, and have adopted from the various versions that which seemed most suitable in each case, telling the fable anew in my own way. . . . I have attached to the 'Fables' in the obscurity of small print at the end a series of notes, summing up what is known as to the 'provenance' of each fable." Preface

Johnny-cake; illus. by Emma L. Brock. Putnam [1967 c1933] unp illus lib. bdg. $4.29 (k-3)   398.2

1 Folklore—Great Britain
ISBN 0-399-60324-7   LC 33-27395

A reissue of a book first published 1933
A "lively cumulative nursery tale of the johnny-cake that leaps out of the oven to outrun the farmer, his wife, his little boy, and a succession of other human and animal characters until he meets the fox—and disaster. Emma Brock's black-and-white drawings express the homely quality of the

Jacobs, Joseph—*Continued*
English folk tale. A basic book for storytelling with younger children." Sch Library J
The American counterpart of this story is generally known as The gingerbread boy

Jagendorf, M. A.
Folk stories of the South; illus. by Michael Parks. Vanguard [1973 c1972] xx, 355p illus $8.95 (4 and up)   398.2
1 Folklore—Southern States 2 Legends—Southern States
ISBN 0-8149-0000-3   LC 70-134672
"The noted folklore anthologist has selected 95 items from the 11 states of the old Confederacy. . . . [Included are] a potpourri of pirate tales, Indian legends, ghost stories, Civil and Revolutionary War stories, and local anecdotes. Some tales, like 'The Arkansas Traveler' and that of 'Kate, the Bell Witch' are well known; others are recognizable variants or widely told; but most here have not appeared before at this level. Many would enliven a story hour. . . . Arrangement is alphabetical by state; format is attractive; and Jagendorf's notes are helpful and suggest further sources." Sch Library J

The gypsies' fiddle, and other gypsy tales, by M. A. Jagendorf and C. H. Tillhagen; illus. by Hans Helweg. Vanguard 1956 186p illus $7.95 (5 and up)   398.2
1 Folklore, Gypsy
ISBN 0-8149-0339-8   LC 56-7891
"Some of the nineteen fairy tales and legends have no parallel elsewhere, but a few are variants of the widespread 'noodle stories' about foolish peasants. They . . . reveal many gypsy characteristics." Horn Bk
Includes sources

New England bean-pot; American folk stories to read and to tell; illus. by Donald McKay; introduction by B. A. Botkin. Vanguard 1948 272p illus $7.95 (5 and up)   398.2
1 Folklore—New England 2 Legends—New England
ISBN 0-8149-0336-3   LC 48-9145
"A collection of New England folklore which will be of special interest to storytellers and folklorists. . . . Short retellings; dry humor." Booklist
These "are legends, tales, yarns, jokes, incidents arranged as [46] 'Folk Stories' to read and tell. For that reason they are salted with folksayings and larded with sidelights of the localities from where they come. I have added proverbs, customs, and weather lore, and sometimes even local happenings." Foreword
"There are merry stories of the devil confounded, discomfited witch-hunters, sailors and pirates which have not hitherto appeared in juvenile collections and for which we are the richer. Donald McKay has illustrated them with imagination and skill." NY Times Bk Rev

Noodlehead stories from around the world; with illus. by Shane Miller. Vanguard 1957 302p illus $7.95 (4-6)   398.2
1 Folklore 2 Wit and humor
ISBN 0-8149-0329-0   LC 57-12266
This collection contains 64 humorous stories selected from the folk tales of 36 lands and peoples. These stories, all meant for laughter, are about the fools who are sometimes wise, and the wise who are sometimes foolish

Tyll Ulenspiegel's merry pranks; illus. by Fritz Eichenberg. Vanguard 1938 188p illus $7.95 (4-6)   398.2
1 Eulenspiegel 2 Legends—Germany 3 Legends—Flanders
ISBN 0-8149-0337-1   LC 38-9511
Tyll Ulenspiegel is "a legendary figure of Germany and Flanders. . . . There are thirty-seven stories or episodes, in all of which Tyll plays his jokes and discomforts his enemies, but is always kind and helpful to the poor and the good people with whom he comes in contact." Library J

"The eight full-page illustrations and smaller decorative drawings by Fritz Eichenberg have caught exactly the jovial humor of the tales and add a fine flavor of the period." NY Times Bk Rev

Jameson, Cynthia
The clay pot boy; adapted from a Russian tale; pictures by Arnold Lobel. Coward, McCann & Geoghegan 1973 unp illus lib. bdg. $6.59 (k-2)   398.2
1 Folklore—Russia
ISBN 0-698-30479-9   LC 72-183554
This is a retelling of a Russian folktale about "a childless couple who create a son out of clay. The clay pot boy comes alive and greedily swallows everything and everyone in sight. However, he gets his comeuppance when a billy goat smashes him to bits and frees all that he has gobbled. The boy's cumulative boasting makes the story easy to master; however, this same repetition factor limits the development of the theme." Sch Library J
"A favorite tale for storytellers is nicely adapted here and given added dimensions by the illustrations. Lobel's clay pot boy looks like a piece of pottery, and he grows larger and larger as he goes on his voracious path." Chicago. Children's Bk Center

Jataka tales; ed. by Nancy DeRoin; with original drawings by Ellen Lanyon. Houghton 1975 82p illus $5.95 (3-5)   398.2
1 Folklore—India 2 Fables 3 Animals—Fiction
ISBN 0-395-20281-7   LC 74-20981
The editor has selected thirty of the Jataka tales, "animal fables attributed to the Buddha. Their morals speak of vices and foibles with varying effectiveness to a reader more used to Aesop's directness. There is sharp irony in the story of a drunken dung beetle who challenges an elephant to a battle and is quickly squelched not by an elephant foot, but a giant dropping. Other stories are more subtly indicative of their Eastern origins. . . . But such differences in flavor shouldn't deter librarians from purchasing this introductory group of tales largely unfamiliar to U.S. audiences. . . . Illustrated with brown-and-white drawings which have some awkward angles of perspective but project a feel of age and echo the stories' Indian setting." Booklist

Keats, Ezra Jack
John Henry; an American legend; story and pictures by Ezra Jack Keats. Pantheon Bks. 1965 unp illus $3.95, lib. bdg. $5.99 (k-3)   398.2
1 John Henry 2 Legends—U.S.
ISBN 0-394-91302-7   LC 65-11444
"John Henry lived and died with a hammer in his hand. Mr. Keats has adapted legends into a picturebook introduction to the famous Negro folk hero and his high-spirited adventures. The dynamic power with which he wields his hammer is matched by the strong illustrations: brilliant oranges and reds contrast with grays and blacks that are often silhouettes; unusual backgrounds produce startling effects. A good picture-story to show to a group." Horn Bk

Kendall, Carol
Sweet and sour; tales from China, retold by Carol Kendall and Yao-wen Li; drawings by Shirley Felts. Seabury [distributed by Houghton 1979 c1978] 111p illus $7.95 (4-6)   398.2
1 Folklore—China
ISBN 0-395-28958-0   LC 78-24349
"A Clarion book"
First published 1978 in England
This is a "collection of twenty-four Chinese tales of every kind and from many eras. There are stories of wise fools, clever magistrates, the unpredictability of Fate, and the greediness of man—all very suitable for storytelling." Horn Bk
"The style of the retellings is brisk and readable and echoes the condensed style of the original Chinese, retaining their humor and succinct qualities. The black-and-white illustrations, accurate in their delineation of local color and background, are well drawn and have a delicacy of their own produced with fine line and stipple." Sch Library J

Kim, So-un

The story bag; a collection of Korean folk tales; tr. by Setsu Higashi; illus. by Kim Eui-hwan. Tuttle 1955 229p illus pa $3.25 (4 and up) **398.2**

1 Folklore—Korea
ISBN 0-8048-0548-2   LC 55-13738
Original Japanese edition, 1953

This collection contains retellings of thirty Korean folk tales including ones about animals which repay human kindness, the origins of earthquakes and eclipses, a conspiracy by stories to destroy the man who has kept them confined in a bag, insects who get drunk at a feast, a warrior who rescues three princesses from an ogre, a little mouse whose care for its blind mother leads to a spoiled girl's reformation, and others

Kirkup, James

The magic drum; told by James Kirkup; illus. by Võ-Dinh. Knopf 1973 58p illus $4.50 lib. bdg. $5.99 (3-5) **398.2**

1 Folklore—Far East
ISBN 0-394-82672-8; 0-394-92672-2   LC 73-5510

A tale set in ancient China, adapted from the traditional Japanese Noh play: Tenko. The son of a peasant couple, whose birth was miraculously foretold in a dream involving a magic drum, finds his destiny linked to the drum both in life and after death

"A number of strong, impressionistic wash drawings by a Vietnamese-born artist add to the beauty of the book. The perfect telling makes this a unique story to share with children on a special occasion. Its strangeness and its poetry will linger." Horn Bk

The **Lazies**; tales of the peoples of Russia; tr. and ed. by Mirra Ginsburg; illus. by Marian Parry. Macmillan Pub. Co. 1973 70p illus $4.95 (3-5) **398.2**

1 Folklore—Russia
ISBN 0-02-735840-2   LC 72-92437

"Fifteen variations on the theme of laziness have been culled from the folklore of the U.S.S.R. . . . that indolence is not limited to the rich, to the poor, or to human beings is revealed in the selections, which include talking-beast tales, drolls, and fables as well as stories of princesses and peasants." Horn Bk

"The retellings are brisk, sprightly and complemented by amusing black-and-white line drawings." Sch Library J

Leach, Maria

The lion sneezed; folktales and myths of the cat; illus. by Helen Siegl. Crowell 1977 102p illus $7.95 (4-6) **398.2**

1 Folklore 2 Cats—Fiction
ISBN 0-690-01364-7   LC 77-3665

"In this cat-oriented collection of folktales, stories, poems, riddles, and old sayings, Leach draws from the lore of places such as England, Ireland, Italy, India, and the U.S. The tales are short (some only one page) and wittily told, including a story of the cat on Noah's Ark, who was tossed from a lion; a kitten and a baby rat who became friends; a mouser who frightened the people of Schildburg, Germany; and a magical cat named Gattomammone. . . . The author has included comprehensive notes and an extensive bibliography." Booklist

"Distinctive animated woodcut illustrations—at least one for each of the twenty short tales and several for the groups of proverbs and riddles—make this a handsome book. Showing cats in a variety of characteristic postures, the pictures enhance the humor and liveliness of the selections." Horn Bk

Whistle in the graveyard; folktales to chill your bones; illus. by Ken Rinciari. Viking 1974 128p illus $6.95 (4-6) **398.2**

1 Folklore 2 Ghosts—Fiction
ISBN 0-670-76245-8   LC 73-22255

These "stories, drawn from many cultures and far-distant lands, deal with bogeys and bugaboos, ghosts, witch lore, supernatural manifestations, and haunted places from the White House to the Tower of London. Directions for playing 'a scary game' in the dark of a Halloween night appear at the end of the book. Of interest to adults are the bibliography and the ample notes." Horn Bk

The author "has authenticated each tale, and Rinciari's pen-and-ink sketches add a spine-tingling touch." Sch Library J

Lent, Blair

John Tabor's ride; story and pictures by Blair Lent. Little 1966 48p illus maps $6.95 (k-3) **398.2**

1 Legends—New England 2 Sea stories 3 Whales—Fiction
ISBN 0-316-52086-1   LC 66-12818

"An Atlantic Monthly Press book"

"A tall tale based on a New England legend about a shipwrecked sailor from Nantucket. Picked up by a strange old man. —John Tabor was taken on a long, wild ride on the back of a whale. . . . John played cribbage with King Neptune and came to a lighthouse manned by a walrus and an albatross. Eventually he was delivered by the whale to the very heart of town; grateful, John Tabor had his whale towed back to the sea and freedom." Sutherland. The Best in Children's Bks

"The pictures are as full of fun and movement as the story and catch both the sea in action and the look of Nantucket." Sch Library J

Le Prince de Beaumont, Marie

Beauty and the beast; tr. from the French of Madame de Beaumont and illus. by Diane Goode. Bradbury Press 1978 unp illus $7.95 **398.2**

1 Folklore—France 2 Fairy tales
ISBN 0-87888-119-0   LC 76-57884

"Beauty is ultimate perfection, appreciated by her father, deprecated by her sisters. The father discovers the Beast in the castle when he loses his way on a journey to improve his economic lot for the sake of his daughters. The story has more than the usual twisting denouements, but Beauty's caring and her promise to marry Beast returns him to the handsome prince guise." Children's Bk Rev Serv

"A flexible but faithful translation of de Beaumont's French fairy tale carries the formal court style into a graphic interpretation entirely different from Mercer Mayer's [entered below]. Goode's elegant line work, conscious architectural planes, sharpened color, and delicate, coiffured characters place the story clearly in the realm of magic. Poses are dramatic in the manner of an eighteenth-century royal play, and the discrete, structured tone of both art and language leaves much to the imagination. A worthwhile version that shows considerable care." Booklist

Lester, Julius

The knee-high man, and other tales; pictures by Ralph Pinto. Dial Press 1972 28p illus $5.95, lib. bdg. $5.47 (k-3) **398.2**

1 Folklore, Black 2 Folklore—U.S. 3 Animals—Fiction
ISBN 0-8037-4593-1; 0-8037-4607-5   LC 72-181785

"Rural scenes in quiet colors are a background for nicely-detailed creatures in an appealing collection of six animal stories from black folklore. The clever Mr. Rabbit outwits Mr. Bear and a farmer in two of the tales; two are 'Why' stories, another proves that you should never trust a snake, and the sixth is on the familiar theme of the person (sometimes it's an animal) who is dissatisfied with himself, tries to change, and gratefully accepts what he can't do anything about—in this case, the knee-high man resigns himself after consultation with a wise owl." Chicago. Children's Bk Center

"These are excellent for story telling and should be so presented for the greatest impact. . . . Handling the book is pleasurable as the pictures, rich in warmth and color, complement the text and trigger an emotional empathy with the stories." NY Times Bk Rev

Lexau, Joan M.

Crocodile and Hen; retold by Joan M. Lexau; pictures by Joan Sandin. Harper 1969 unp illus lib. bdg. $7.89 (k-1) **398.2**

1 Folklore—Congo (Brazzaville) 2 Fables
ISBN 0-06-023867-4   LC 70-85017

"An adaptation of the tale entitled 'Why the crocodile does not eat the hen.'" Verso of title page

Lexau, Joan M.—*Continued*

Based on a folktale from Africa, in which the hen deters the crocodile from eating her by always calling him brother. The crocodile puzzles over their brotherhod until a lizard explains it to him

"Both text and pictures are simple in presentation but rich in suggestion." Sch Library J

Little Red Hen; pictures by Janina Domanska. Macmillan Pub. Co. 1973 unp illus $7.95 (k-1)   398.2

1 Folklore 2 Chickens—Fiction
ISBN 0-02-732820-1   LC 72-92436

"To illustrate a terse and compact telling of the old nursery tale, the artist has made some of her most animated pictures. The enterprising hen busies herself with planting the wheat; cutting, threshing, and carrying it to the mill; and finally baking the flour into bread; while the uncooperative cat, goose, and rat stage a side show of high jinks and capers. Still characteristically stylized, with bold geometric patterns against brilliant reds, yellows, and greens, the illustrations clearly display a welcome vitality and humor not often found in the artist's beautifully designed pages." Horn Bk

The illustrations here are "in vivid contrast to the warm, realistic pictures in Paul Galdone's version . . . [entered above]. Both Mr. Galdone and Ms. Domanska have done full justice to the classic; to choose between them is impossible so why not have both?" Pub W

Littledale, Freya

The elves and the shoemaker; retold by Freya Littledale; pictures by Brinton Turkle. Four Winds 1975 unp illus $4.95 (k-3)   398.2

1 Folklore—Germany 2 Fairy tales
ISBN 0-590-07426-1   LC 75-12500

Based on the version by the Brothers Grimm, this is "a picture-book version of the famous tale about the destitute shoemaker who is rescued from poverty by the aid of two energetic elves, who appear at midnight to make shoes." Sch Library J

"Few illustrators could infuse the familiar fairy-tale with so much charm as Brinton Turkle has. His pictures dance with life and color in an authentic 19th century setting. And Ms. Littledale's retelling is equally compelling." Pub W

Lobel, Anita

King Rooster, Queen Hen. Greenwillow Bks. 1975 48p illus lib. bdg. $5.71 (1-3)   398.2

1 Folklore—Denmark 2 Animals—Fiction
ISBN 0-688-84008-6   LC 75-9787

"Greenwillow Read-alone"
Based on a Danish folk tale

"No sooner has the cock decided that they will leave their cosy thatched-cottage pecking ground for worldlier fields than we see them attired as King Rooster and Queen Hen under a weight of jewelled crowns and ermine-trimmed robes. Soon, too, a carriage (an old shoe) and horses (field mice) materialize and a proper retinue to support them in their social climbing—a sparrow as queen's maid, duck as cook, and crow as butler (the sartorial image of old Cock Robin). A danger-filled climax introduces a wily fox, but then a perfect denouement." Washington Post Children's Bk World

"Lobel has reduced the reading effort considerably by working word and phrase repetition into a nicely paced story. Book design is wholly appealing—from the clean, well-spaced type and layout to [the author's] amusingly stylized illustrations in gold, brown, and rose tones that carry a rustic air." Booklist

The pancake. Greenwillow Bks. 1978 48p illus $5.95, lib bdg. $5.71 (1-3)   398.2

1 Folklore—Norway
ISBN 0-688-80125-0; 0-688-84125-2   LC 77-24970

"Greenwillow Read-alone"

"A simplified but fluent version of the familiar folktale is illustrated with decorative, framed paintings in pastel tones. Hearing that it is going to be eaten by the cook's seven hungry children, a pancake rolls off to escape its fate. Invited to stop and be nibbled on by a series of animals, the pancake retorts by boasting (cumulatively) of its escape—and then it meets a wily pig. Those who are chasing the pancake are disappointed, but the woman offers to make a new and even better pancake, and in the end there's a throng

around the table enjoying the second pancake. With, some may be glad to see, father scrubbing the pot in the last frame." Chicago. Children's Bk Center

"Anita Lobel has freely adapted the original Norse tale using short lines of text for easy reading and throughout the book has given prominence [in her illustrations] to the children." Horn Bk

Lowe, Patricia Tracy

The tale of Czar Saltan; or, The prince and the swan princess [by] Alexander Pushkin; illus. by I. Bilibin; tr. and retold by Patricia Tracy Lowe. Crowell 1975 unp illus $5.95 (3-5)   398.2

1 Folklore—Russia 2 Fairy tales
ISBN 0-690-00792-2   LC 75-5655

"In this prose version of Pushkin's poetic retelling of a Russian folktale, the youngest of three sisters "wins the hand of Czar Saltan. But, due to the malicious scheming of her jealous elder siblings, the czarina and her handsome son are ordered to be abandoned at sea. The prince, who magically reaches full maturity, coaxes the waves to take the royal pair to the shore of a faraway island where, through the help of a white swan (later transformed into a princess), a joyous reunion with Czar Saltan results." Sch Library J

"It is difficult to ascertain whether any of Pushkin's poetic fluidity of style has been preserved. . . . The rich, full-colored illustrations create sumptuous and evocative images, and the artist, respectfully cooperating with the poet, has remembered the Czar's dog and the palace cat—naturalistic touches that offer just the right contrast to the general atmosphere of magnificence." Horn Bk

The tale of the golden cockerel [by] Alexander Pushkin; illus. by I. Bilibin; tr. and retold by Patricia Tracy Lowe. Crowell 1975 unp illus $5.95 (3-5)   398.2

1 Folklore—Russia 2 Fairy tales
ISBN 0-690-00790-6   LC 75-4623

Based on Pushkin's poetic retelling of a Russian folktale, this prose version "tells of a golden cockerel which is able to tell the Czar from which direction trouble is coming. When the Czar ignores the cockerel, the Czar dies." Children's Bk Rev Serv

The illustrations "are spectacular; richly embroidered and ornate, the pictures have intricate details of costumes and furnishings; they have a quality of Oriental opulence, a similarity to Persian miniatures, and a romantic, almost medieval aura, especially in those pictures that are in frieze form." Chicago. Children's Bk Center

Lubin, Leonard B.

The white cat, by Madame d'Aulnoy; adapted and illus. by Leonard B. Lubin. Little 1978 unp illus $7.95 (1-3)   398.2

1 Folklore—France 2 Fairy tales
ISBN 0-316-53490-0   LC 77-5845

"Lubin effectively alternates elaborate black-and-white silhouettes with highly stylized . . . candied-pastel paintings in his retelling of Madame d'Aulnoy's classic French fairy tale. . . . The story, summarized by rhymed captions after every three pages of text, concerns the three quests of the king's youngest son as he fulfills his father's demands for the tiniest dog in the world, a piece of muslin so fine it could be drawn through the eye of a needle, and the loveliest princess in the kingdom. The youngest prince succeeds with the help of a magnificent white cat, who is in turn transformed by his love into a beautiful princess. The formality of the French court is highlighted in the artist's precise attention to detail and elegant depiction of dress, furnishings, and backgrounds." Booklist

McCormick, Dell J.

Paul Bunyan swings his axe. Caxton Ptrs. 1936 111p illus $6.95 (4-6)   398.2

1 Legends—U.S. 2 Bunyan, Paul 3 Lumber and lumbering—Fiction
ISBN 0-87004-093-6   LC 36-33409

Tales about the legendary exploits of the giant logger and his blue ox, Babe

"Paul's pranks blithely play havoc with the natural laws. . . . Science teachers may not approve, but these stories, retold with gusto and

McCormick, Dell J.—*Continued*
embellished with drolly imaginative drawings, are a tremendous lot of fun." NY Times Bk Rev

McDermott, Beverly Brodsky
The Golem; a Jewish legend. Lippincott 1976 unp illus $8.95 (2-5)   **398.2**
1 Legends, Jewish 2 Golem
ISBN 0-397-31674-7   LC 75-29136
This is "the legend of the Golem, a clay creature created and brought to life, long ago, by a Prague Rabbi, to protect his people against persecution. . . . The Golem has the Name of God in his mouth, but he is mute. Silent and watchful, he guards the ghetto; when a shouting crowd advances with 'Kill the Jews!' the Golem grows into a giant, crushing people, leveling houses, and hurling rocks. The Rabbi commands that the Golem return to the dust from which he came; the Golem opens his mouth, the Name of God tumbles out, and he dies. And the Rabbi mourns, and puts the sacred clay away." Chicago. Children's Bk Center
"The paintings are monumental in keeping with their theme and are laced with Hebrew letters and motifs. There is a profound contrast between the full-page brooding face of the Golem just before the pogrom begins and the wild release of clashing colors and movement in succeeding double-page spreads, followed finally by a sober diffusion of energy lighted by a single window in the dark. A complex graphic and narrative translation of East European Jewish tradition, this is worth some careful work with children ranging from primary grade listeners to intermediate students of folklore." Booklist
Bibliography: p[4]

McDermott, Gerald
Anansi the spider; a tale from the Ashanti; adapted and illus. by Gerald McDermott. Holt 1972 unp illus lib. bdg. $6.95 (k-3)   **398.2**
1 Folklore—Ghana 2 Folklore, Ashanti 3 Spiders—Fiction
ISBN 0-03-088368-7   LC 76-150028
The adaptation of this traditional tale of Ghana is based on an animated film by McDermott. It tells of Anansi, a spider, who is saved from terrible fates by his six sons and is unable to decide which of them to reward. The solution to his predicament is also an explanation for how the moon was put into the sky
"This folk tale is illustrated with strikingly stylized, boldly colored designs based on the traditional geometric forms of Ashanti art." Sat Rev
"The simplicity of the writing style makes this a good adaptation for reading aloud to young children or as a source for storytelling." Chicago. Children's Bk Center

Arrow to the sun; a Pueblo Indian tale; adapted and illus. by Gerald McDermott. Viking 1974 unp illus lib. bdg. $10.95, Penguin Bks. pa $2.50 (k-3)   **398.2**
1 Pueblo Indians—Legends
ISBN 0-670-13369-8; 0-14-050211-4   LC 73-16172
Awarded the Caldecott Medal, 1975
This myth tells how Boy searches for his immortal father, the Lord of the Sun, in order to substantiate his paternal heritage. Shot as an arrow to the sun, Boy passes through the four chambers of ceremony to prove himself. Accepted by his father, he returns to earth to bring the Lord of the Sun's spirit to the world of men
"The simple, brief text—which suggests similar stories in religion and folklore—is amply illustrated in full-page and doublespread pictures. . . . The strong colors and the bold angular forms powerfully accompany the text, and even on those pages where there is no text, both colors and form are visually eloquent." Horn Bk

The magic tree; a tale from the Congo; adapted and illus. by Gerald McDermott. Holt 1973 unp illus lib. bdg. $5.95 (k-3)   **398.2**
1 Folklore—Zaïre
ISBN 0-03-015061-2   LC 72-76567
"The brilliant colors, the stunning designs based on African motifs, and the dignity of the stylized figures combine to illustrate effectively, a Congolese tale that has many elements traditional in the folk genre. Rejected, a young man whose twin brother has been loved and favored leaves home. He releases an enchanted people from the magic tree in which each had been a leaf, and he weds the princess and lives in wealth, having promised never to reveal this. Visiting his family, Mavungu tells of his experiences: suddenly he remembers that he has sworn secrecy and he rushes back to his wife and the beautiful village she magically created. But there is nothing left—only a grove of silent trees. The adaptation is terse and simple, the ending abrupt but with great visual impact." Chicago. Children's Bk Center

The stonecutter; a Japanese folk tale; adapted and illus. by Gerald McDermott. Viking 1975 unp illus lib. bdg. $7.50, Penguin Bks. pa $2.50 (k-3)   **398.2**
1 Folklore—Japan
ISBN 0-670-67074-X; 0-14-050289-0   LC 74-26823
"Tasaku is a poor stonecutter. One day, he sees a prince and his rich retinue ride by, and makes the wish that he might equal the noble youth in wealth and power. The spirit of the mountain where Tasaku is working grants the stonecutter's wish. But . . . Tasaku is unsatisfied. He wants more power—to be the sun, then the cloud which can obscure the sun and, at last, the mountain. . . . At last, the once lowly stonecutter feels that, as the mountain, he will stand forever, strong and immutable. Then he feels a stonecutter chipping away at his base." Pub W
"A restrained text, suggesting the subtle brevity of haiku, is combined with brilliant, four-color illustrations. Utilizing the motifs of traditional Japanese prints, the artist has produced a dazzling picture-story, reminiscent of its folklore origin yet contemporary in feeling and original in execution. Designed initially as an animated film, the tale—for which no source is given—adapts easily from one visual medium to another." Horn Bk

McGovern, Ann
Too much noise; illus. by Simms Taback. Houghton 1967 44p illus lib. bdg. $8.95 (k-3)   **398.2**
1 Folklore
ISBN 0-395-18110-0   LC 67-4450
"The too crowded house of a familiar old tale becomes a too noisy house in this entertaining picture-book story. Bothered by the noises in his house, an old man follows the advice of the village wise man by first acquiring and then getting rid of a cow, donkey, sheep, hen, dog, and cat. Only then can he appreciate how quiet his house is. The simplicity and straightforwardness of the folktale are evident in both the telling of the cumulative story and in the amusing colored illustrations." Booklist

MacManus, Seumas
Hibernian nights; introduced by Padraic Colum; illus. by Paul Kennedy. Macmillan Pub. Co. 1963 263p illus lib. bdg. $5.95 (4 and up)   **398.2**
1 Folklore—Ireland 2 Fairy tales
ISBN 0-02-762090-5   LC 62-16316
"The 22 Irish folk and fairy tales in this superior collection were chosen by a master storyteller as the cream of his story lore. . . . Told with a strong and charming Irish flavor and handsomely printed and illustrated, these stories of the little people, kings and queens, cruel stepmothers, and youngest sons will be a delight to read, to read aloud, or to tell." Booklist

Malcolmson, Anne
Yankee Doodle's cousins; illus. by Robert McCloskey. Houghton 1941 267p illus $7.95 (4 and up)   **398.2**
1 Legends—U.S.
ISBN 0-395-06896-7   LC 41-24262
Copyright renewed 1969
These are retellings of stories about some of the real and legendary characters who have become part of American folklore. Among the twenty-eight stories are tales of Captain Kidd, Ichabod Paddock, Johnny Appleseed, Mike Fink, Daniel Boone, Pirate Jean Laffite, Brer Rabbit,

Malcolmson, Anne—*Continued*
Pecos Bill and Paul Bunyan. The tales are arranged by region: the East, the South, the
Mississippi Valley, and the West
   The tales "are part of the legendary lore of
every young America. Their robust humor, absurdities, and exaggerations are a never-failing
delight, and Robert McCloskey's drawings reflect
these qualities to perfection." Children's Bks Too
Good to Miss
   Glossary: p261-[68]

Manning-Sanders, Ruth
A book of charms and changelings; illus.
by Robin Jacques. Dutton [1972 c1971] 124p
illus $7.95 (3-6)   **398.2**
   1 Folklore 2 Fairy tales
   ISBN 0-525-26775-1   LC 71-179053
   First published 1971 in England
   A "collection of worldwide fairy stories dealing with the dual themes of charms and changelings. . . . Although many familiar symbols and
motifs are called up, these particular stories are
not commonly available. In [some stories]
charms—a piece of amber, a handmill, the bones
of an ox, and an amulet respectively—work for
their owners' good. In other stories, the spells
are of evil intent." Sch Library J
   These fifteen tales are illustrated with "deft
and distinctive black and white drawings. . . .
Like other compilations by Manning-Sanders, this
is a joy to read aloud; the magical fairy changelings and human pawns are described in a light,
flavorful style that has a sense of humor even
when the tales are not humorous. Good for storytelling, too." Chicago. Children's Bk Center

A book of dragons; drawings by Robin
Jacques. Dutton [1965 c1964] 128p illus lib.
bdg. $7.95 (3-6)   **398.2**
   1 Folklore 2 Fairy tales 3 Dragons—Fiction
   ISBN 0-525-26824-3   LC 65-19578
   First published 1964 in England
   This volume "contains fourteen fairy tales—
many of them unfamiliar—gathered from Greece,
China, Japan, Macedonia, Rumania, Ireland, Germany and Slovakia. No sources are listed but
all are good tales, interesting and unusual in
their use of incident. . . . Some of the stories
are concerned with kindly dragons while others
are about dragons bad and savage, to be either
killed or outwitted." Toronto
   "Smooth storytelling versions attractively illustrated." Children's Bks, 1965

A book of enchantments and curses; illus.
by Robin Jacques. Dutton [1977 c1976] 128p
illus lib. bdg. $7.99 (4-6)   **398.2**
   1 Folklore
   ISBN 0-525-28670-7   LC 76-58423
   First published 1976 in England
   "Things are not what they seem in these 13
tales of magical transformations wrought in
gratitude or malice, for good or ill. In a German tale, thwarted desire makes an ill-tempered
mannikin change a king and his daughter into
horses, and in a chaste Pomeranian tale an absent king who refused to kiss a witch has to
hop home a frog. But, in a Swiss 'Tinderbox'
variant, an 'Enchanted Candle' has a mind of
its own and aids the handsome young hero.
Tales from Africa, Sicily, Jamaica, Spain, and
Transylvania round out, and 13 illustrations top
off a . . . collection of unusual folktales." Sch
Library J
   "The author's skilled style of storytelling is
again evident in this latest collection of tales. . . .
Delicate black-and-white drawings provide occasional illustration." Booklist

A book of ghosts & goblins; illus. by Robin
Jacques. Dutton [1969 c1968] 126p illus
pa $1.25 (3-6)   **398.2**
   1 Folklore 2 Ghosts—Fiction
   ISBN 0-525-45014-9   LC 71-81719
   First published 1968 in England
   A collection of twenty-one stories, funny or
frightening, about all kinds of ghosts and goblins
   "Lively content, smooth storytelling, and inviting format will make the collection of twenty-
one stories, gathered from many different nations,
highly popular. The foreword lists the origin of
all the stories by country—from Africa to Siberia,
from Spain to Ireland. . . . The humor, eeriness,

and suspense of the book create a superior collection for sharing aloud or for a child's own
reading. Two thirds of the selections are about
ghosts—restlessly seeking to right a wrong, to
regain something missing, or merely wandering.
The goblin tales, including three amusing ones
from Estonia, are particularly entertaining. The
illustrator's skillful line drawings give apt individuality to the characters, and supply humorous
detail." Horn Bk

A book of kings and queens; illus. by Robin
Jacques. Dutton [1978 c1977] 125p illus lib.
bdg. $7.95 (3-6)   **398.2**
   1 Folklore 2 Kings and rulers—Fiction 3 Queens
   —Fiction
   ISB 0-525-26925-8   LC 77-16462
   First published 1977 in England
   "Manning-Sanders focuses on royalty in this
10-story collection from places such as Greece,
Russia, Sicily, Czechoslovakia, and Ireland. Feats
and foibles of all kinds engage a variety of
monarchs as a snake-queen grants a young flute
player a tree that bears apples and oranges on
alternating days; King Eagle outwits the Devil,
saving his friend from a foolish pact with the
Lord of Hell; a young girl dreams herself Queen
and sees it come true; and a stolen bowl of
dough frustrates a young queen on her wedding
day." Booklist
   "As with the many other collections in the
Manning-Sanders series of retold tales, no sources
are given for the stories, and little or no national background or atmosphere are reflected in
them. Their deserved popularity rests on the
rhythmic storytelling style and on the judicious
mixture of everyday and magic happenings. 'King
Eagle' is the most exciting of the tales and
has one of the best of Robin Jacques' masterly
[black-and-white] illustrations, showing the devil
breaking down the stable door." Sch Library J

A book of monsters; illus. by Robin Jacques.
Dutton [1976 c1975] 128p illus lib. bdg. $7.95
(3-6)   **398.2**
   1 Folklore 2 Monsters—Fiction
   ISBN 0-525-26951-7   LC 75-33252
   First published 1975 in England
   The monsters in this "folktale collection are of
three sorts as noted in the foreword: transformed
humans who are monsters in shape only (e.g.,
'Singing Leaves'); good-natured monsters whose
appetite for humans is only an unfortunate habit
(e.g., 'Dunber' and 'The Great Golloping Wolf');
and the truly horrible, gluttonous monsters (e.g.
'Ubir') that are children's favorite kind. From
such disparate places as Sicily, Sweden, West
Africa, and South Russia, Manning-Sanders has
assembled an impressive crew of unlovely creatures." Sch Library J
   "The author creates clever dialogue and individualized characters. Illustrated with pen-and-
ink drawings." Booklist

A book of ogres and trolls; illus. by Robin
Jacques. Dutton [1973 c1972] illus lib.
bdg. $7.95 (3-6)   **398.2**
   1 Folklore 2 Fairy tales
   ISBN 0-525-26998-3   LC 73-77454
   First published 1972 in England
   These 13 "folk tales from Russia, Iceland, Sicily
and other European countries prove that agreeable ogres are a rarity, while trolls, though mischievous, often help humans out of trouble and
even into wealth." Pub W
   "Excellent stories. . . . All are retold in the
selector's characteristically rhythmic and folksy
style. Teamed with Robin Jacques' comic pen-
and-ink drawings, this is a book to be shared."
Sch Library J

A book of spooks and spectres; illus. by
Robin Jacques. Dutton [1980 c1979] 127p
illus $7.95 (3-6)   **398.2**
   1 Folklore 2 Ghosts—Fiction
   ISBN 0-525-27045-0   LC 79-17673
   "Spooks, Manning-Sanders says in her introduction, have 'always been Spooks,' while spectres
were 'once creatures of flesh and blood . . . who
after death, find the gates of heaven and hell
shut against them, and so must return to earth.'
She further categorizes spooks as generally happy
beings, while spectres are cheerless ones, and
substantiates these thoughts with 23 rousing tales

Manning-Sanders, Ruth—*Continued*

from around the world. Short—often only a few pages in length—the selections are sometimes amusing, sometimes ghoulish, making good choices for reading or telling aloud." Booklist
"The book is illustrated by Jacques with black and white drawings that are graceful, distinctive for the fine detail achieved by broken parallel lines." Chicago. Children's Bk Center

A book of witches; drawings by Robin Jacques. Dutton [1966 c1965] 126p illus lib. bdg. $7.95 (3-6)   398.2
1 Folklore 2 Fairy tales 3 Witches—Fiction
ISBN 0-525-27054-X   LC 66-14685
First published 1965 in England
"The bad witches in this collection of twelve stories are the kind children expect to encounter on Halloween. Some—the witches in 'Rapunzel' and 'Hansel and Gretel'—are already known, while others are not as familiar but just as scary. . . . The tales come from several European countries." Horn Bk
"A nicely illustrated compilation. . . . The writing style is smooth and colloquial, with just enough of that turn of phrase appropriate to the genre to give the stories color without burdening them with either quaintness or floridity. Useful for reading aloud or for storytelling." Sutherland. The Best in Children's Bks

Marriott, Alice
American Indian mythology [by] Alice Marriott and Carol K. Rachlin. Crowell 1968 211p illus $12.50, pa $4.95   398.2
1 Indians of North America—Legends
ISBN 0-690-07201-5, 0-8152-0335-7   LC 68-21613
"A fascinating collection of myths, legends and contemporary folklore which the authors have obtained in most cases directly from Indians. . . . With each tale there is a brief introduction to the tribe. Subjects include myths of creation; the world and the hereafter; 'how-and-why' stories told to children; historic legends and witchcraft. Among the tribes represented are Cheyenne, Modoc, Ponca, Hopi, Kiowa, Comanche and Zuñi." Pub W
The authors "seek to present the best of two worlds, accurate background on the main Indian groups in America, and a sort of literary telling of their myths and legends. The viewpoint is that of the anthropologist rather than of the folklorist. The stories do not have an Indian flavor but this makes for somewhat smoother reading." Library J
Bibliography: p207-11

Mayer, Marianna
Beauty and the beast; retold by Marianna Mayer; illus. by Mercer Mayer. Four Winds 1978 unp illus $9.95   398.2
1 Folklore—France 2 Fairy tales
ISBN 0-590-07497-0   LC 78-54679
"Apparently based on the Lang version of the story first made popular by Madame Leprince de Beaumont, this is adequately told; it is illustrated in a richly ornamented, romantic style that has echoes of Rackham (particularly in the trees) and of Hyman in use of color and composition. Occasionally the pictures seem to conflict with the text, as when Beauty comments on the Beast's sad eyes, while the picture shows them glowing fiercely. Nevertheless, the story of a daughter's sacrifice and her reward when the Beast is revealed, through her love, as an enchanted prince, loses none of its appeal, and the illustrations are appropriately magical and ornamented with the fine details." Chicago. Children's Bk Center
"A simpler version than Goode's translation of de Beaumont [entered above under Le Prince de Beaumont]. . . . A lushly romantic picture book that will find avid readers in a wide age-range." Sch Library J

Mehdevi, Anne Sinclair
Persian folk and fairy tales; retold by Anne Sinclair Mehdevi; illus. by Paul E. Kennedy. Knopf 1965 117p illus lib. bdg. $5.99 (4-6)   398.2
1 Folklore—Iran 2 Fairy tales
ISBN 0-394-91496-1   LC 65-11969

"This is a fine collection of [eleven] stories straight out of the oral tradition, retold with grace and authority. . . . Storytellers will recognize variants of European and English stories in ['The pumpkin child' ('Cinderella')] 'Mistress Cockroach' ('Perez and Martina') and 'Simpletons' ('The Three Sillies'). Some stories have an 'Arabian Nights' flavor, some [are] beast tales." Sch Library J
"Unusually compatible illustrations lend cultural as well as artistic distinction. Patterned after old Persian paintings, they have flowing lines and intricate designs." Horn Bk

Midsummer magic; a garland of stories, charms and recipes; comp. by Ellin Greene; illus. by Barbara Cooney. Lothrop 1977 158p illus $8.25, lib. bdg. $7.92 (4-6)   398.2
1 Folklore 2 Summer—Fiction
ISBN 0-688-41800-7; 0-688-51800-1   LC 77-7313
"The compiler has assembled around a central theme a potpourri of folk tales, traditional customs, herbal lore, and cookery. The selections chiefly represent Scandinavia, Great Britain, and Ireland; among the northern Europeans for whom winter is a long, dark season, 'Midsummer is a time of merriment and joy, and Midsummer Eve a night of magic and enchantment.' Many of the rites and ceremonies of the summer solstice were originally pagan, but as was often the case, the festival eventually became overlaid with Christian symbolism; both aspects of the observance are reflected in the book. The material, inevitably a bit miscellaneous, is packaged handsomely and unified by graceful, highly decorative drawings." Horn Bk

Mobley, Jane
The star husband; illus. by Anna Vojtech. Doubleday 1979 32p illus $6.95, lib. bdg. $7.90 (1-3)   398.2
1 Indians of North America—Legends
ISBN 0-385-14282-X; 0-385-14283-8   LC 78-1213
"A version of the legend about the American Indian maiden who marries a star, moves to the sky, and bears a son who becomes the Moon. Although she lives a carefree life in the sky, where creatures do not grow old, she becomes very bored and lonely for her people on earth. She digs a hole in floor of the sky and descends to earth. There she spends her life like other Indians and, finally, grows old and dies. Upon her earthly death, she returns to her husband and son in the sky." Children's Bk Rev Serv
"Vojtech's splendid paintings in full color depict characters as well as the natural and supernatural episodes impressively." Pub W

Mosel, Arlene
The funny little woman; retold by Arlene Mosel; pictures by Blair Lent. Dutton 1972 unp illus lib. bdg. $8.95, pa $1.95 (k-2)   398.2
1 Folklore—Japan
ISBN 0-525-30265-4; 0-525-45036-X   LC 75-179046
Awarded the Caldecott Medal, 1973
Based on Lafcadio Hearn's The old woman and her dumpling
"A Japanese folk tale about a funny little woman who laughs 'Tee-he-he-he' all the time and makes rice dumplings. One of her dumplings rolls away and she chases it into the domain of the fearful 'oni,' a monster. The 'oni' sets the giggling woman to work, cooking for him and his friends, until the day she escapes with their magic paddle that lets her create a potful of rice with only one grain." Pub W
"The tale unfolds in a simple tellable style. . . . Using elements of traditional Japanese art, the illustrator has made marvelously imaginative pictures. . . . All the inherent drama and humor of the story are manifest in the illustrations: the toothy, fearsome 'oni,' their weird, watery-green subterranean house contrasting with tiny drawings of the deserted little house aboveground; the swirling [underground] river . . . and the ever merry, dauntless figure of the little woman in her gay orange kimono." Horn Bk

Tikki Tikki Tembo; retold by Arlene Mosel; illus. by Blair Lent. Holt 1968 unp illus lib. bdg. $7.95 (k-2)   398.2
1 Folklore—China 2 Names, Personal—Fiction
ISBN 0-03-012711-4   LC 68-11839
A "Chinese folk tale about a first son with a very long name. When Tikki Tikki Tembo-No Sa

Mosel, Arlene—*Continued*

Rembo-Chari Bari Ruchi-Pip Peri Pembo fell into the well. it took his little brother so long to say his name and get help that Tikki almost drowned." Hodges. Best Bks for Elem Sch Libraries
"In this polished version of a story hour favorite, beautifully stylized wash drawings of serene Oriental landscapes are in comic contrast to amusingly visualized folk and the active disasters accruing to the possessor of a 21-syllable, irresistibly chantable name." Best Bks of the Year, 1968

North American legends; ed. by Virginia Haviland; illus. by Ann Strugnell. Collins [distributed by Philomel Bks.] 1979 214p illus $8.95 (5 and up) 398.2

1 Folklore—U.S. 2 Indians of North America—Legends
ISBN 0-529-05457-4 LC 78-26999
"A collection containing a broad range of stories reflecting different cultures found in North America. The most satisfying section is the first—fourteen Indian and Eskimo legends—including hero tales, creation stories, and stories with humorous elements. A smaller group, five Black folk tales, deals with magic, trickery, and the wise fool. In the section 'European Tales Brought by Immigrants' four are Appalachian stories and one is from New England, leaving non-British cultures under-represented. The final section—Tall Tales—includes material of literary origin; the editor states that while such stories are not true folklore they have become part of American legend. Although most of the chosen texts succeed in representing the material 'attractively as well as accurately,' many are drawn from familiar sources. The handsome black-and-white illustrations are based on decorative motifs reflecting the cultures of different peoples." Horn Bk
Some suggestions for further reading: p211-14

The **Old** woman and her pig; pictures by Paul Galdone. McGraw 1960 32p illus lib. bdg. $7.95 (k-2) 398.2

1 Folklore
ISBN 0-07-022721-7 LC 59-14958
"Whittlesey House publications"
"A retelling of the old [cumulative] tale about the woman who had difficulty getting her pig home from market and had to enlist the aid of a cat, a rat, a rope, a butcher, an ox, water. fire a stick and a dog." Pub W
"Paul Galdone has done an outstanding piece of work in providing the delightful illustrations and artistic book designs for this dearly loved folk tale. The whole is dramatic in appearance, appropriately quaint, and full of warm-hearted humor. Young children will enjoy it and many will memorize the text." Library J

Olenius, Elsa

(comp.) Great Swedish fairy tales; illus. by John Bauer; tr. by Holger Lundburgh. Delacorte Press/Seymour Lawrence 1973 238p illus $10, pa $6.95 (4 and up) 398.2

1 Folklore—Sweden 2 Fairy tales
ISBN 0-440-03043-9; 0-440-03041-2 LC 73-132364
"A Merloyd Lawrence book"
Original Swedish edition 1966
"A double delight for American readers—21 Swedish fairy tales virtually unknown in this country with artwork by a major Swedish illustrator. Of the nine authors whose tales reflect 19th-Century morality, Elsa Beskow is best known. . . . The illustrations which are reminiscent of Bauer's contemporary, Arthur Rackham, have a wonderful clarity of detail even though most depict dark scenes of night, caves, and deep forests. Like the tales, the pictures swarm with princes and princesses, harmless tomte; and vicious, wild trolls. The only complaint is that a few tales for which illustrations appear . . . are not included in the present collection." Sch Library J

One trick too many; fox stories from Russia; tr. by Mirra Ginsburg; pictures by Helen Siegel. Dial Press 1973 39p illus $5.95, lib. bdg. $5.47 (1-3) 398.2

1 Folklore—Russia 2 Foxes—Fiction
ISBN 0-8037-6670-X; 0-8037-6671-8 LC 72-711
This collection includes nine Russian fox stories "derived from both European and Asiatic sources.

The style is bright and succinct, and the cunning of the fox is evident in all of the tales as he succeeds in outwitting the peasants and the other animals. Although sometimes, as in the stories of 'The Red Fox and the Walking Stick' and 'The Fox and the Quail,' he attempts one trick too many and loses out altogether. Full-page woodcuts in handsome shades—predominately red and yellow—give lively expression to each tale." Horn Bk

The **Peasant's** pea patch; a Russian folktale; tr. by Guy Daniels; illus. by Robert Quackenbush. Delacorte Press 1971 unp illus $5.95, lib. bdg. $5.47 (k-3) 398.2

1 Folklore—Russia
ISBN 0-440-06897-5; 0-440-06826-6 LC 70-132355
"A picture book version of a Russian folktale about a peasant whose efforts to capture a flock of cranes by placing a trough of vodka and honey in his pea patch lead to a series of hilarious misadventures. Vividly colored illustrations mirror the robust humor of the fast-paced story. A good read-aloud choice." Booklist

Perrault, Charles

Cinderella; or, The little glass slipper. A free translation from the French of Charles Perrault; with pictures by Marcia Brown. Scribner 1954 unp illus lib. bdg. $9.95 (k-3) 398.2

1 Folklore—France 2 Fairy tales
ISBN 0-684-12676-1 LC 54-12897
Awarded the Caldecott Medal, 1955
This is the classic story of the poor, good-natured girl who works for her selfish step-sisters until a fairy godmother transforms her into a beautiful "princess" for just one night
"A distinguished picture book. . . . The story can be used for telling, but it is perfect for the picture-book hour. With soft, delicate colors and lines that subtly suggest, Miss Brown creates a thoroughly fairyland atmosphere, at the same time recreating the sophistication of the French Court with its golden coach, canopied bed, dazzling chandeliers, liveried footmen, curled and pompadoured ladies, and peruked [bewigged] courtiers." Library J

Perrault's Complete fairy tales; tr. from the French by A. E. Johnson and others; with illus. by W. Heath Robinson. Dodd 1961 183p illus $5.95 (4-6) 398.2

1 Folklore—France 2 Fairy tales
ISBN 0-396-07496-0 LC 61-6938
"Of the fourteen tales which comprise the present volume, the first eleven are from the master-hand of Charles Perrault. . . . Three of the tales, 'The Ridiculous Wishes,' 'Donkey Skin' and 'Patient Griselda' . . . are reproduced here by paraphrase rather than literal translation [of their original verse form]. . . . To the eleven tales of Perrault, three others have been added here: 'Beauty and the Beast,' by Mme. Leprince de Beaumont (1711-1781) . . . [and] 'Princess Rosette' and 'The Friendly Frog' . . . from the prolific pen of Mme. d'Aulnoy (1650-1705)." Prefatory note
"This is an excellent group to have in one well-printed volume, especially as the 'moralities' of Perrault have not been omitted, and as the fine old illustrations of W. Heath Robinson are used." NY Her Trib Bks

Puss in Boots; a free translation from the French; with pictures by Marcia Brown. Scribner 1952 unp illus lib. bdg. $8.95 398.2

1 Folklore—France 2 Fairy tales
ISBN 0-684-12988-4 LC 52-12026
This is the story of the poor miller's son, whose fortune was made by the cleverness of his loyal cat
"A beautiful, gay, very French picture book. Miss Brown has made her own free translation, which is humorous and spirited. She has created such a Master Sly-boots as never before has helped to turn a youngest son into a marquis." NY Her Trib Bks
"The colors, chiefly coral pink, yellow and gray, are brilliantly handled, lush without being in the least vulgar. This effect is one of gaiety and wit." NY Times Bk Rev

Picard, Barbara Leonie

Stories of King Arthur and his knights; retold by Barbara Leonie Picard; with wood engravings by Roy Morgan. Oxford 1955 291p illus $12.95 (5 and up)   **398.2**

1 Arthur, King 2 Legends—Great Britain
ISBN 0-19-274510-7   LC 55-14947

"Oxford illustrated classics"
"Miss Picard consulted many sources for this retelling of the Arthurian legends, and, without using archaic words, has turned phrases to recall the grace and vigor of an earlier idiom. Since Arthur's reign is her primary concern, only a few chapters are devoted to his birth and rise to the throne. . . . But to include too many stories would be to crowd out the detail which makes the adventures real, and the best-known stories of the knights are all here. This will make an excellent introduction to Camelot for children who find the language of Lanier's Malory and of Howard Pyle still too difficult. . . . The wood engravings . . . are fittingly strong and medieval." Horn Bk

Price, Christine

The valiant chattee-maker; a folktale of India; retold by Christine Price. Warne 1965 unp illus $4.95 (k-3)   **398.2**

1 Folklore—India
ISBN 0-7232-0348-2   LC 65-10030

"Through a series of accidents the [village potter] . . . earns a reputation for bravery and is mistakenly considered a hero." Chicago
"Handsome, lively illustrations that include a magnificent golden tiger complement the story." Horn Bk

Pyle, Howard

King Stork; illus. by Trina Schart Hyman. Little 1973 48p illus $8.95 (k-3)   **398.2**

1 Fairy tales
ISBN 0-316-72440-8   LC 78-182249

Text first published 1888 in the author's collection: The wonder clock, entered below
Pyle's story of a poor drummer youth who wins a beautiful but wicked princess "with the help of King Stork's magic and 'tames' her with a beating is fluidly illustrated with medieval scenes. . . . [It is] a story in the devious-female, dominating-male tradition." Booklist
"The illustrations fit the various moods of the story. . . . The princess is scantily-clad yet certainly beautiful. Children will enjoy the detailed illustrations and the simplicity and magical qualities of the story." Sch Library J

The merry adventures of Robin Hood of great renown in Nottinghamshire, as written & illus. by Howard Pyle. Scribner 1976 288p illus lib. bdg. $17.50 (5 and up)   **398.2**

1 Legends—Great Britain 2 Robin Hood
ISBN 0-684-14838-2   LC 46-11873

On spine: "Hudson River editions"
Twenty-two stories of Robin Hood and his adventures with the king's foresters in Sherwood Forest. This band of outlaws made a practice of robbing the rich to help the poor. Set during the reign of Henry II of England
"Of all the books of Robin Hood this is best for literary style, adherence to the spirit and events of the old ballads and wealth of historical background." Toronto
"The author illustrates [this adventure] in a most appropriately picturesque style for young people." Baker's Best

Pepper & salt; or, Seasoning for young folk, prepared by Howard Pyle. Harper 1923 109p illus lib. bdg. $9.89 (4-6)   **398.2**

1 Folklore 2 Fairy tales
ISBN 0-06-024811-4   LC 24-712

A companion volume to: The wonder clock, entered below
First published 1885
This book, with its eight modern retellings of old fairy tales, interspersed with ballads and rhymes, and its drawings by the author, has long been a favorite with children and with storytellers

Some merry adventures of Robin Hood of great renown in Nottinghamshire; written and illus. by Howard Pyle. Scribner 1954 212p illus $4.95 (5 and up)   **398.2**

1 Legends—Great Britain 2 Robin Hood
ISBN 0-684-13066-1   LC 54-11823

Adapted by Pyle from his longer work: The merry adventures of Robin Hood, entered above. This contains 12 stories while the other has 22. Although some of the remaining stories are shortened or condensed, the style and spirit remain the same and the changes make this edition easier reading than the original version

The wonder clock; or, Four & twenty marvelous tales, being one for each hour of the day; written & illus. by Howard Pyle. Embellished with verses by Katharine Pyle. Harper 1915 318p illus lib. bdg. $4.79 (4-6)   **398.2**

1 Folklore 2 Fairy tales
ISBN 0-06-024821-1   LC 74-18938

First published 1887
"Tales told by the puppet figures of an old clock found in Time's garret." Hodges. Bks for Elem Sch Libraries
"Pyle adapted tales from Grimm and other legends in his own lively and humorous way." Adventuring With Bks. 2d edition

Quigley, Lillian

The blind men and the elephant; an old tale from the land of India, re-told by Lillian Quigley; illus. by Janice Holland. Scribner 1959 unp illus lib. bdg. $5.95, pa 95¢ (k-3)   **398.2**

1 Folklore—India 2 Fables
ISBN 0-684-13276-1; 0-684-12782-2   LC 59-7209

"Retelling of the Indian fable of six blind men who cannot agree on a single description of an elephant, which underlines the sage moral that to get a true picture of the whole one must include all its parts." NY Times Bk Rev
"The tale takes on new humor and charm. The journey of the six men to the palace of an Indian Rajah is delightfully comic, yet the world which frames the journey is filled with exquisite colors and the ornate designs of Indian architecture and fabrics." Chicago Sunday Trib

Ransome, Arthur

The Fool of the World and the flying ship; a Russian tale retold by Arthur Ransome; pictures by Uri Shulevitz, Farrar, Straus 1968 unp illus $4.95 (k-3)   **398.2**

1 Folklore—Russia
ISBN 0-374-32442-5   LC 68-54105

"An Ariel book"
Awarded the Caldecott Medal, 1969
Text first published 1916 in Ransome's Old Peter's Russian tales
The Fool of the World, was the third and youngest son whose parents thought little of him. When the Czar announced that his daughter would marry the hero who could bring him a flying ship, Fool of the World went looking and found one. Aided in surprising ways by eight peasants with magical powers, he then had to outwit the treacherous Czar
This "is a fascinating tale, told with humor and grace and brought vividly to life by Uri Shulevitz's illustrations. Using a palette of rainbow colors, [he] has set the Fool and his ship against a large airy format—helping create a book that will impress grownups and delight the young." NY Times Bk Rev

Red fairy book; collected by Andrew Lang; ed. by Brian Alderson; illus. by Faith Jaques. [Rev. ed.] Kestrel Bks. [distributed by Viking 1978 c1976] 371p illus $14.95 (4-6)   **398.2**

1 Folklore 2 Fairy tales
ISBN 0-670-59110-6   LC 77-28770

First published 1890 by Longmans. This edition first published 1976 in England. For a description of this edition see note for Blue fairy book, entered above
Bibliographical references included in Notes: p361-[72]

Reeves, James

English fables and fairy stories; retold by
James Reeves; illus. by Joan Kiddell-Monroe.
Oxford 1954 234p illus (Oxford Myths and
legends) $10.95 (4-6)   **398.2**

1 Folklore—Great Britain 2 Fairy tales
ISBN 0-19-274101-2   LC 54-39522

A "collection of nineteen English tales, told in
language beautiful for either reading or telling.
Several familiar tales are included with old
favorites such as 'Molly Whipple,' 'Dick Whittington', and 'Jack and the Beanstalk.' " Secondary
Educ Board

These stories "do not make use of the vernacular found in Jacobs' [English fairy tales, entered
above] a factor which sometimes puzzles young
readers. Style is more polished, similar to that
of Perrault." Library J

The shadow of the hawk, and other stories;
by Marie de France; retold by James Reeves;
pictures by Anne Dalton. Seabury [distributed
by Houghton] 1977 154p illus $7.95 (5 and
up)   **398.2**

1 Legends, Celtic 2 Knights and knighthood—
Fiction
ISBN 0-395-28820-7   LC 76-28949

"A Clarion book"
First published 1975 in England
"Six tales from the little-known 12th-century
poems of Marie de France, evoking the age of
the 'courts of love' when knighthood flowered,
are retold here in prose. Several of the stories
involve King Arthur's court and all are about
love (not always chaste), honor, adventure, and
magic. The title story concerns a beautiful girl,
married to a sour old man who finds true love
in the guise of an enchanted hawk. Another
features Lord Elfan, condemned by heredity to
become a werewolf. 'The Nightingale' is a short,
bittersweet account of the doomed love between
a young bachelor and his neighbor's wife, while
'Launfal' (Lancelot) tells of the knight's devotion to the mysterious Rosamund." Sch Library J

The lais, or verse legends, "of Marie de France,
originally written in French at the court of
Henry II of England, have been extended and
adapted to appeal to modern readers. The plots
of the narratives . . . have been essentially respected and retain Marie de France's keen psychological insights into human emotions and pas-
sions. . . . For the purposes of dramatic storytelling, the author has admittedly transformed
indirect conversation into spoken dialogue." Horn
Bk

Reyher, Becky

My mother is the most beautiful woman
in the world; a Russian folktale retold by
Becky Reyher; pictures by Ruth Gannett.
Lothrop 1945 39p illus lib. bdg. $7.44 (1-4)
                                              398.2

1 Folklore—Russia
ISBN 0-688-51251-8

First published by Howell, Soskin
A Russian folktale about a little peasant girl,
lost in the wheat fields, who tried to describe
her mother as the "most beautiful woman in
the world." When an exceptionally ugly woman
claimed the little girl, they remembered the
proverb: "We do not love people because they
are beautiful, but they seem beautiful to us
because we love them"

"Though its people are Russian peasants a
long time ago, and though Ruth Gannett has
brought them to us in brilliant, convincing pictures, there is not a little listening child to
whom it is read that will not claim it for his
own. These are just the right pictures for a
story told in just the right way." NY Her Trib
Bks

Rice, Eve

Once in a wood: ten tales from Aesop;
adapted and illus. by Eve Rice. Greenwillow
Bks. 1979 64p illus $5.95, lib. bdg. $5.71
(1-3)   **398.2**

1 Fables
ISBN 0-688-80191-9; 0-688-84191-0   LC 78-16294

"Greenwillow Read-alone"
"The brief and essentially simple statements
of the fable are admirably suitable as a text

for the beginning reader. Included are such tales
as 'Belling the Cat,' 'The Crow and the Water
Jug,' and 'The Hare Who Had Many Friends.'
The point of each tale is well made within
the confines of the form, adhering to the disciplines
of brevity and precision without sacrificing flavor."
Horn Bk

Most of the fables contain "a rhyming conclusion that helps point out the moral. The illustrations are gravely decorative, black and white
pictures of flora and fauna, deftly textured and
composed and resembling old lithographs in style
and mood." Chicago. Children's Bk Center

Riordan, James

Tales from Central Russia; retold by James
Riordan; illus. by Krystyna Turska. Kestrel
Bks. [distributed by Viking 1979 c1976] 285p
illus map (Russian tales, v 1) $12.50 (5 and
up)   **398.2**

1 Folklore—Russia 2 Fairy tales
ISBN 0-670-69154-2

Companion volume to: Tales from Tartary, entered below
First published 1976 in England
This "volume contains an ample selection from
Afanasiev's more than six hundred stories, which
are newly translated and illustrated. The collection includes many well-known tales, told with
flavor and directness. An atmosphere of fantasy
derives from the settings of steppes and forests
inhabited by demons, and the detailed drawings
explicate the often bizarre and amusing creatures
of folklore. An eighteen-page commentary sketches
the historical background of the tales and the
enormous contribution of Afanasiev, who saw folk
tales as 'primitive man's story of Nature.' " Horn
Bk

Tales from Tartary; retold by James
Riordan; illus. by Anthony Colbert. Viking
[1979 c1978] 170p illus maps (Russian tales,
v2) $12.50 (5 and up)   **398.2**

1 Folklore—Russia 2 Fairy tales
ISBN 0-670-69156-9   LC 77-27871

First published 1978 in England
" 'Kahns' instead of 'kings,' 'auls' instead of
'villages,' and heroes with names like Aldar-Kose
instead of Jack—these are the special features of
'Tales from Tartary.' . . . Some of the tales are
derived from 'Books Consulted' and some are
tales collected by Riordan during his travels in
Tartarstan, that area of Russia where Oriental
and European cultures meet. . . . The 29 selections include riddles ('Which is Biggest?'),
'pourquoi' stories ('How the Bear Lost His Tail'),
drolls ("Two Lazy Brothers'), and fairy tales
('Aldar-Kose and Shigai-Bai')." Sch Library J
"In his extensive commentary Riordan refers
to the Tartars as 'a hardy, courageous and cultivated people,' and he points out that, as in
'The Arabian Nights,' Oriental influences are
apparent in the sensuous fantasies and legends.
Many of the stories, he adds, have their origins
in actual history. The book is superbly illustrated
with pictures that are strong in design and full
of humor and action." Horn Bk

Glossary: p161-62

Robbins, Ruth

Baboushka and the three kings; illus. by
Nicholas Sidjakov; adapted from a Russian
folk tale. Parnassus Press 1960 unp illus lib.
bdg. $5.95 (1-4)   **398.2**

1 Legends—Russia 2 Christmas—Fiction
ISBN 0-395-37672-1   LC 60-15036

Awarded the Caldecott Medal, 1961
"A retelling of the Christmas legend about the
old woman who declined to accompany the three
kings on their search for the Christ Child and
has ever since then searched for the Child on
her own. Each year as she renews her search
she leaves gifts at the homes she visits, acting,
in this respect, as a Russian equivalent to Santa
Claus

"Mystery and dignity are in the retelling. . . .
At the end of the book is the story in verse set
to original music. Extraordinary modern drawings, some in rich colors, and a handsome type
face . . . combine to make a beautiful picture
book." Horn Bk

Robbins, Ruth—*Continued*

Taliesin and King Arthur; written and illus. by Ruth Robbins. Parnassus Press 1970 unp illus $4.75 (3-5)   398.2

1 Legends—Wales 2 Taliesin 3 Arthur, King
ISBN 0-395-27721-3   LC 75-129540

"Ornately detailed and deftly composed illustrations show the small figures of a feudal court, stylized and romantic. The young poet Taliesin has come [from northern Wales] to Arthur's court at Caerlon, delighting the king and his retinue with strange tales and with his rare wisdom. At the Grand Contest of Poets on Christmas Eve, Taliesin tells the dramatic and magical story of his birth, King Arthur proclaims him the greatest bard of all, and the audience rejoices. The story mingles fact and legend, the style is poetic, and the tale within a tale should please readers addicted to folklore and legend." Chicago. Children's Bk Center

Robinson, Adjai

Singing tales of Africa; retold by Adjai Robinson; illus. by Christine Price. Scribner 1974 80p illus music lib. bdg. $5.95 (3-5)   398.2

1 Folklore—Africa 2 Songs, African
ISBN 0-684-13683-X   LC 73-1378

"Seven rhythmic and poetic African folktales that are a pleasure to read aloud. Each story is preceded by music and lyrics (in native languages and with English translations) to a chant which reappears in the tale. Sources at the back of the book give the origin of each tale: e.g., 'Why the Baboon Has a Shining Seat' is from the Krio people in Sierra Leone; and 'Why There Is Death in the World' is an Ibo legend. Striking and humorous black-and-white woodcuts capture the vitality of everyday life." Sch Library J

Three African tales; illus. by Carole Byard Putnam 1979 47p illus $6.95 (3-6)   398.2

1 Folklore—Sierra Leone 2 Folklore—Kenya
ISBN 0-399-20656-6   LC 78-13927

These three tales are more like authentic anecdotes than the usual folklore, full of tribal reference, chants, and with sometimes anti-climactic endings. One speaks of rivalry between a shooter and a trapper of game. . . . The second tells how the village clown tries to trick a maiden into speech and thus force her to become his wife. . . . The third tells of a nephew wrestling for kingship with his evil uncle who has inherited the throne. Magic and song make the narrations (no scores are given) which are illustrated in alternate single and double spreads." Sch Library J
The "stories are cleanly told, with fresh language turns and contents that dwell on human rather than animal characters. An author's note elaborates on the Sierra Leone and Kenyan origins of the stories, thereby giving greater context to the tales' operating values. These are culture bound and distinctly regional. . . . Byard's charcoal illustrations are dark and sweeping but uneven, while detail and shadings tend to be sloppy; faces, on the other hand, can be especially dramatic." Booklist

Rockwell, Anne

The old woman and her pig, & 10 other stories; told and illus. by Anne Rockwell. Crowell 1979 87p illus $10.95, lib. bdg. $10.79 (k-3)   398.2

1 Folklore
ISBN 0-690-03927-1; 0-690-02929-X   LC 78-13901

"The author has gathered together eleven folk tales and added colorful, humorous illustrations. Included are 'The Three Sillies,' 'The Tortoise and the Hare,' 'The Bremen Town Musicians,' and other well-known tales from such sources as the Grimm Brothers, Aesop, and Asbjørnsen and Moe. One or two less well-known tales appear, such as 'The Shepherd Boy' and 'The Travels of a Fox.' All of the stories are retold in a simple manner for younger readers. The table of contents has a distinctive illustration next to the title of each story so that a small listener can easily identify his choice." Horn Bk

Poor Goose: a French Folktale; retold and illus. by Anne Rockwell. Crowell 1976 unp illus $7.95, lib. bdg. $7.89 (1-3)   398.2

1 Folklore—France
ISBN 0-690-00912-7; 0-690-01014-1   LC 75-4886

This tale recounts how Goose "set off for the castle in search of a headache remedy and is joined along the way by a cat, a lamb, and a cow. When night comes and the four friends fear the wolf will find them, they take refuge with a lonely old woman who needs them all." Sch Library J
"This is a short, easy-to-read cumulative story. . . . [The conclusion] will satisfy young readers and audiences at story hours; the precisely executed watercolor illustrations have an appropriate Gallic flair. Unfortunately, the text is superimposed on provincial textile patterns which border the pictures—an embellishment which may make it difficult for beginning readers to discern the exact configuration of the letters and the continuity of the phrases." Horn Bk

The three bears & 15 other stories; selected [retold] and illus. by Anne Rockwell. Crowell 1975 116p illus $9.95 (k-3)   398.2

1 Folklore 2 Fairy tales
ISBN 0-690-00597-0   LC 74-5381

"Besides familiar favorites like 'The Three Bears,' 'The Gingerbread Man,' 'The Three Little Pigs' and others, . . . readers will find a few that will be new to them. These include a brisk run-through of the comic-suspense tale, 'The Water-Nixie,' in which a boy and girl are enslaved by an evil creature who lives in a well and 'The Star Money,' about a generous little girl who is blessed a hundred-fold for her kindnesses." Pub W
This is "a square, solid volume that is inviting to look at and comfortable to hold. . . . Since the sources, though well-known, are not indicated in the book, the stories take on a certain anonymity; and no feeling of period or nationality can be observed in the bright and cheerful, firmly limned, full-color paintings that are scattered generously through the book." Horn Bk

Rounds, Glen

Ol' Paul, the mighty logger. . . . [Rev] Holiday House 1976 93p illus $8.95 (3-6)   398.2

1 Legends—U.S. 2 Bunyan, Paul 3 Lumber and lumbering—Fiction
ISBN 0-8234-0269-X   LC 75-22163

First published 1936
"Being a true account of the seemingly incredible exploits and inventions of the great Paul Bunyan, profusely illustrated by drawings made at the scene by the author, Glen Rounds, and now republished in this special fortieth anniversary edition." Subtitle
"Ever since their first appearance in 1936, Glen Rounds' tall tales of the doughty American folk hero, Paul Bunyan, and his super-ox Babe have been read-aloud favorites. Now reissued with text from the enlarged 1949 edition, the book has a larger format, with crisp, clear type, wider margins, and zany new pen-and-ink sketches by the author." Sch Library J

Sakade, Florence

(ed.) Japanese children's favorite stories; illus. by Yoshisuke Kurosaki. [2d ed. rev] Tuttle 1958 120p illus $9.50 (2-4)   398.2

1 Folklore—Japan 2 Fairy tales
ISBN 0-8084-0284-X   LC 58-11620

First published 1953
A collection of twenty folk tales "traditionally told to Japanese children. The gay illustrations will appeal to younger children." Asia: A Guide to Bks for Children

San Souci, Robert

The legend of Scarface; a Blackfoot Indian tale; adapted by Robert San Souci; illus. by Daniel San Souci. Doubleday 1978 unp illus $7.95, lib. bdg. $8.90 (2-4)   398.2

1 Siksika Indians—Legends
ISBN 0-385-13247-6; 0-385-13248-4   LC 77-15170

"The hero of this Blackfeet Indian folktale is a young man who is despised because of his poverty and particularly because of the scar on his face that has given him his name. Scarface is a courageous youth, and he dares to love the chief's daughter. She . . . returns his love. But she has promised the Sun that she will never marry. Perhaps the Sun would release Singing Rain from her vow? Scarface resolves to ask him.

San Souci, Robert—*Continued*

So he journeys the long way to the Sun's lodge, guided by animals, for he is known to them as a brother and true friend." America

"A greatly abbreviated retelling of the classic hero tales so well set down by George Grinnell in his 'Blackfoot Lodge Tales.' As a précis, it is skillful, keeping the mood and spirit of the original, but it necessarily sacrifices details, incidents, and minor characters. . . . The retelling ends as Scarface is married . . . rather than continuing until the couple dies in old age. The twelve large full-color paintings have a dramatic strength, realistically interpreting the action, the Indian characters, and the animals." Horn Bk

Sawyer, Ruth

Journey cake, ho! Illus. by Robert Mc-Closkey. Viking 1953 45p illus lib. bdg. $5.95, Penguin Bks. pa $1.95 (k-2)   398.2

1 Folklore
ISBN 0-670-40943-X; 0-14-050275-0   LC 53-3366

In this new version of the old folk tale about Johnny-cake, Johnny has to leave his mountain home because his foster parents are too poor to keep him. But his parting present, a journey cake, leads the boy into adventures and brings him back home along with a flock of pursuing animals. The cake is then renamed Johnny-cake

Johnny is "drawn with that rollicking bold humor that has made Mr. McCloskey popular. The story is rather odd, but probably good fun for small children who will laugh at a cake that rolls and sings a repeated verse." NY Her Trib Bks

Say, Allen

Once under the cherry blossom tree; an old Japanese tale; retold and illus. by Allen Say. Harper 1974 31p illus lib. bdg. $6.89 (1-3)   398.2

1 Folklore—Japan
ISBN 0-06-025217-0   LC 73-14336

"A miserly old landlord sat grumbling on a fine spring day, watching the villagers dance and sing; he swallowed a cherry pit, and a tree grew out of his head. In desperation he pulled it out, leaving a cavity where fish soon appeared. Angry at some boys who were fishing in his head, the old man jumped up, tripped on a rock, and tumbled. His feet went into his head, and soon nothing was left of him but a pond, a lovely pond near which the villagers danced and sang." Chicago. Children's Bk Center

"The intricately textured pen drawings are finely done with the same odd humor that makes this tale unique." NY Times Bk Rev

Schwartz, Alvin

Whoppers; tall tales and other lies; collected from American folklore by Alvin Schwartz; illus. by Glen Rounds. Lippincott 1975 127p illus $8.95, pa $2.95 (4 and up)   398.2

1 Folklore—U. S.
ISBN 0-397-31575-9; 0-397-31612-7   LC 74-32024

Excerpted and adapted from a variety of sources, this is an "assemblage of tall tales and whoppers from American folklore. They range from brief one-liners, some of which are strung into tall stories, to rambling discourses on preposterous turns of events. The humor is marked with both sly subtlety and broad slapstick. . . . Curious readers will find the appended notes and sources thoughtfully informative, and storytellers who aren't intimidated by the various dialects will find good raw material for telling." Booklist

The tales are "divided by topics such as people, animals, weather, and Rounds' scribbly sketches add a quiet folksy humor of their own." Sch Library J

Bibliography: p119-25

Scribner, Charles

The devil's bridge; a legend retold by Charles Scribner, Jr; illus. by Evaline Ness. Scribner 1978 unp illus $7.95 (2-4)   398.2

1 Legends—France 2 Devil—Fiction
ISBN 0-684-15034-4   LC 77-12722

A retelling "of a legend that has survived in France since the Middle Ages. When the bridge between the village and the town where the farmers sell their produce collapses, Satan appears

with an offer the villagers can't refuse. The devil restores their lifeline instantly, but demands an awesome sacrifice, his usual: a human soul. Thanks to the local, canny stone-mason, however, the devil loses again." Pub W

A beautifully retold legend with colorful, textured block print illustrations." Children's Bk Rev Serv

Sechrist, Elizabeth Hough

Once in the first times; folk tales from the Philipines, retold by Elizabeth Hough Sechrist; illus. by John Sheppard. Macrae Smith Co. 1969 213p illus map $6.50, lib. bdg. $5.97 (4-6)   398.2

1 Folklore—Philippine Islands
ISBN 0-8255-8140-0; 0-8255-8141-9   LC 69-18630

First published 1949

These fifty-one "tales range from the simple why and how myths . . . to the more sophisticated stories including variants of some familiar western tales. The book is accordingly divided into two sections: the first and most lengthy deals with the stories of the early peoples of the islands from the Negritos to the Malayan and Chinese settlers; the second reflects Spanish and American influences. . . . Sources (Igorot, Tagalong, Visayan, etc.) are given for almost every tale. Pen and ink sketches enhance the attractive format, making this good folktale fare for libraries not possessing the now out of print 1949 edition [from which one story has been deleted]." Sch Library J

Seuling, Barbara

The teeny tiny woman; an old English ghost tale; retold and illus. by Barbara Seuling. Viking 1976 unp illus lib. bdg. $6.95, Penguin Bks. pa $1.95 (k-2)   398.2

1 Folklore—Great Britain 2 Ghosts—Fiction
ISBN 0-670-69505-X; 0-14-050266-1   LC 75-22160

"A retelling of the famous English ghost tale of the bitty woman who finds a stray bone and puts it in her cupboard." Sat Rev

"The soft-pencil drawings with plum-color overlays on small but spacious pages have a neatness that allows each detail its precise place in pictures appropriate to lines filled with 'teeny tiny.' " Horn Bk

Sewall, Marcia

The wee, wee mannie and the big, big coo; a Scottish folk tale; illus. by Marcia Sewall. Little 1977 32p illus lib. bdg. $4.95 (k-2)   398.2

1 Folklore—Scotland 2 Cows—Fiction
ISBN 0-316-78180-0   LC 76-48947

"An Atlantic Monthly Press book"

"A witty tale of a wee, wee mannie who finally gets the best of his contrary cow by telling her to do the opposite of what he really wants." Booklist

"The incongruity of tiny man and huge cow should appeal to children, and the story (despite the brashness of 'Hoot,' 'Mither,' or 'Coo' passing as Scottish speech cadence) should appeal to children because of its pattern and denouement. The illustrations are vigorous with slightly dulled reds and pinks contrasting with black, white and greys in formally framed pictures out of which, at times, burst the limbs of the exuberant cow." Chicago. Children's Bk Center

Shapiro, Irwin

Heroes in American folklore; illus. by James Daugherty and Donald McKay. Messner 1962 256p illus lib. bdg. $6.29 (4 and up)   398.2

1 Legends—U.S. 2 Heroes and heroines—Fiction
ISBN 0-671-32054-8   LC 62-10205

This book contains five tales about legendary American heroes originally published as separate volumes: Casey Jones and Locomotive No. 638; How old Storm-along captured Mocha Dick; John Henry and the double-jointed steam drill; Steamboat Bill and the captain's top hat; Joe Magarac and his U.S.A. citizens papers. Includes the original illustrations

The author writes "in a vigorous style well suited to heroic deeds. . . . James Daugherty and Donald McKay must have grown up with these heroes, judging from their free swinging rollicking, whoopin' and hollerin' illustrations." Chicago Sunday Trib

Sherlock, Philip M.

Anansi, the spider man; Jamaican folk tales; told by Philip M. Sherlock; illus. by Marcia Brown. Crowell 1954 112p illus $9.95 (4-6) **398.2**

1 Folklore—Jamaica
ISBN 0-690-08905-8   LC 54-5619

Fifteen West Indian stories about the Caribbean folk hero Anansi "who was a man when things went well, but who became a spider when he was in great danger. They are of West African origin, and the animal characters include Tiger, 'the strongest of all,' Snake, Kisander the cat, Old Owl, Rat and Turtle. The author tells the stories simply and directly, with respect for their 'folk' quality. Line illustrations by Marcia Brown are excellent, and have caught the gaiety of the tales." Ontario Library Rev

This collection has been "retold in a form that will be useful for the storyteller and fun for independent reading." Chicago. Children's Bk Center

West Indian folk-tales, retold by Philip Sherlock; illus. by Joan Kiddell-Monroe. Oxford 1966 151p illus (Oxford Myths and legends) $10.95 (4-6) **398.2**

1 Folklore—West Indies
ISBN 0-19-274116-0   LC 66-70268

"Twenty-one tales of the ancient peoples, the Caribs and the Arawaks, are intertwined here with the folklore of the African slaves. Simply structured and ably retold, the collection includes the familiar 'pourquoi' (why) stories, several tales of Anansi, the spiderman, and other legends that recount the trials and successes of the West Indian birds and animals." Sch Library J

Shub, Elizabeth

Clever Kate; adapted from a story by the Brothers Grimm; pictures by Anita Lobel. Macmillan Pub. Co. 1973 unp illus $5.95 (1-3) **398.2**

1 Folklore—Germany
ISBN 0-02-782490-X   LC 72-81063

"Ready-to-read"

"A credit to the easy-to-read genre, this retains the absurdity of the original folktale in a new framework of simple but uncondescending short sentences. Kate's mistakes—flooding the basement with beer, soaking up the beer with flour, exchanging gold pieces for clay pots, sending the cheeses to chase after each other down the hill, carrying the door with her as a safer measure than locking it, and dropping her burdens on the thieves under the tree she and her husband are hiding in—will make as funny reading as they have listening for children. Every page has either a floral-framed drawing on it or a full-page illustration opposite, providing plenty of visual action in tones of blue, green, and yellow." Booklist

Shulevitz, Uri

The magician; an adaptation from the Yiddish of I. L. Peretz. Macmillan Pub. Co. 1973 32p illus $7.95, pa $1.95 (k-2) **398.2**

1 Elijah, the prophet—Fiction 2 Legends, Jewish 3 Passover—Fiction
ISBN 0-02-782510-8; 0-02-045320-5   LC 72-85186

In this story based on a Yiddish folk legend about the prophet Elijah, "a ragged magician appears in a village on the eve of Passover and astounds a pious, needy couple by giving them all they need for the feast." Chicago Pub Library. What's New In Bks

Shulevitz's drawings "are snapshot-sized meticulously executed in black and white [and] . . . occasionally spotlighted by patches of untouched white paper. . . . [They] provide archetypal vignettes of a now-extinct Jewish community life. At once both somber and gay . . . bleak yet exuding an ethnic warmth, the illustrations have a dreamlike, mythic quality." NY Times Bk Rev

"Nicely retold . . . a story to read alone, read aloud, and tell." Chicago. Children's Bk Center

The treasure. Farrar, Straus 1978 unp illus $7.95 (k-3) **398.2**

1 Folklore
ISBN 0-374-37740-5   LC 78-12952

This folk tale "tells of an old man who dreams thrice that a treasure is buried under a bridge in a far-off city. He makes the long journey to investigate, and when a bridge guard questions his wandering about the bridge so often, Isaac tells him of his dream. The guard laughs and tells his own dream of treasure buried under a stove in the house of a man named Isaac. Whereupon the old man returns to find the treasure in his own home." Babbling Bookworm

"Although the story is known in many cultures, the retelling suggests the Hassidic tradition, when the grateful Isaac, having found the treasure, builds a house of prayer and inscribes: 'Sometimes one must travel far to discover what is near.' The precept is logically integrated into the narrative, so the tale does not seem didactic. The eastern European influence is extended in the illustrations, which depict the aging Isaac against constantly changing backdrops while documenting his travels, through vast timberlands and fields, to royal dwellings. . . . Thoughtfully designed, the book is modestly scaled to suit the essential simplicity of the story." Horn Bk

Simon, Solomon

More Wise men of Helm and their merry tales; ed. by Hannah Grad Goodman; illus. by Stephen Kraft. Behrman 1965 119p illus pa $3.95 (4 and up) **398.2**

1 Folklore, Jewish 2 Folklore—Poland
ISBN 0-87441-126-2   LC 65-14594

"A wonderful companion to the The Wise Men of Helm this second collection of tales about the mythical Jewish community in Poland is great fun to read. . . . All are delightful and will make excellent reading aloud and storytelling material." Library J

The wise men of Helm and their merry tales; illus. by Lillian Fischel. Behrman 1945 135p illus pa $3.95 (4 and up) **398.2**

1 Folklore, Jewish 2 Folklore—Poland
ISBN 0-87441-125-4   LC 46-25130

Originally published 1942 in Yiddish. Translated by Ben Bengal and David Simon

An "attractively designed [book] which relates the misadventures of the [Jewish] people who lived in the town of Helm deep in the forests of Poland. While all the world looked upon them as fools, the Helmites believed themselves wondrously wise. The foolishness of Helm was fabulous only because 'foolish things were always happening to them.' Rich in humor, folklore quality—and in the underlying truths of life." Booklist

Singer, Isaac Bashevis

Mazel and Shlimazel; or, The milk of a lioness; pictures by Margot Zemach; tr. from the Yiddish by the author and Elizabeth Shub. Farrar, Straus 1967 42p illus $8.95 (2-5) **398.2**

1 Folklore, Jewish
ISBN 0-374-34884-7   LC 67-19887

"An Ariel book"

The happiness of Tam, a poor peasant lad, and lovely Crown Princess Nesika depends upon the outcome of a battle of wits between Mazel, the spirit of good luck, and Shlimazel, the spirit of bad luck

This story "is based on a Jewish folk tale. . . . The way Shlimazel contrives to win the wager is a witty surprise, and how, moreover, the storyteller arranges to have the story end happily after all is also ingenious and satisfying. The colored illustrations . . . have the flavor of folk art but, like the text, are anything but artless." New Yorker

When Shlemiel went to Warsaw & other stories; pictures by Margot Zemach; tr. by the author and Elizabeth Shub. Farrar, Straus 1968 115p illus $8.95 (4 and up) **398.2**

1 Folklore, Jewish
ISBN 0-374-38316-2   LC 68-30982

"An Ariel book"

"A fine collection of five retold traditional Yiddish folk tales and three original stories. The foolish people of Chelm, that indomitable Eastern European town known for its inverted wisdom, are so lovingly presented that readers will laugh with and not at them: Utzel, whose daughter Poverty's feet grow larger in proportion to the time wasted

Singer, Isaac B.—*Continued*

by his lazy refusals to work; Lyzer the Miser, who learns that if a silver tablespoon can give birth to a teaspoon, silver candlesticks can die; and, of course, Shlemiel himself, whose attempted trip to Warsaw has incredible repercussions. The original stories—'Tsirtsur and Peziza' 'Rabbi Leib and the Witch Cunegunde,' and 'Menaseh's Dream' —blend well with the reworked tales, and Margot Zemach's delightful black-and-white illustrations fittingly capture moods and protagonists." Sch Library J

"The writing has a cadence that is especially evident when the tales are read aloud; the length, the style, and the humor make them a happy source for storytelling." Chicago. Children's Bk Center

Zlateh the goat, and other stories; pictures by Maurice Sendak; tr. from the Yiddish by the author and Elizabeth Shub. Harper 1966 90p illus $10, lib. bdg. $9.98 (4 and up)   **398.2**

1 Folklore, Jewish
ISBN 0-06-025698-2; 0-06-025699-0   LC 66-8114

These seven tales which draw upon the Jewish folklore of Poland "will have wide appeal for the excellence of their interpretation; they have the poetic power of folk tales—a quality of timelessness in the wisdom imparted and a feeling for the essense of human nature. Devils and everyday people, adults and children inhabit stories about the first shlemiel; the village of Chelm, 'a village of fools'; the devil who made a mistake on Hanukkah; the lovely goat that survived a snowstorm on her way to the butcher." Horn Bk

"Their humor, mysticism, and a quiet acceptance of fate are perfectly interpreted in Sendak's fineline sketches." Children's Bks 1966

Sleator, William

The angry moon; retold by William Sleator; with pictures by Blair Lent. Little 1970 45p illus $6.95 (k-3)   **398.2**

1 Tlingit Indians—Legends
ISBN 0-316-79735-9   LC 74-91230

"An Atlantic Monthly Press book"
"The original legend . . . was first recorded by Dr. John R. Swanton in Bulletin 39 of the Bureau of American Ethnology, Tlingit myths and texts"

"An adaptation of a legend of the Tlingit Indians of Alaska, the writing simple and staccato; the illustrations combine colorful, sometimes misty backgrounds and details of costumes or totems that are based on Tlingit designs. When Lapowinsa laughs at the moon, she disappears, leaving her friend Lupan desolate. He shoots arrows at the stars . . . and they form a ladder up which Lupan climbs. With the help of the grandmother of a tiny sky boy, he rescues Lapowinsa, using the four magic objects the grandmother had given him to foil the angry moon in pursuit of his escaped prisoner. An attractive book and an interesting legend useful for storytelling, but rather stilted when read aloud." Sutherland. The Best in Children's Bks

Small, Ernest

Baba Yaga; illus. by Blair Lent. Houghton 1966 48p illus lib. bdg. $7.95 (k-3)   **398.2**

1 Folklore—Russia
ISBN 0-395-16975-5   LC 66-12098

"Little Marusia searching for turnips in the forest comes on the house of a wicked witch. . . . Baba Yaga takes little Marusia captive, but Marusia shows herself more than a match for the witch's evil . . . ways. The story is a composite of many of the Baba Yaga stories told to Russian children." Christian Sci Monitor

"While rather cursory this tale is redeemed by illustrations that sweep, tumble and soar through the environs of Baba Yaga's haunted forest." NY Times Bk Rev

The **Sound** of flutes, and other Indian legends; told by Lame Deer, Jenny Leading Cloud, Leonard Crow Dog, and others; transcribed and ed. by Richard Erdoes; pictures by Paul Goble. Pantheon Bks. 1976 129p illus lib. bdg. $6.99 (5 and up)   **398.2**

1 Indians of North America—Legends   2 Indians of North America—Great Plains
ISBN 0-394-93181-5   LC 76-8660

This collection "is from storytellers of Plains Indian tribes, some tales remembered and some

transcribed from tapes by Erdoes. Goble's illustrations, stylized and handsome in color or in black and white, are used both as full-page pictures and as marginal ornamentation, and the stories have variety and vitality. They include historical material (the death of Sitting Bull), dignified legends, brief humorous tales, 'pourquoi' tales, and stories of creation. A fine collection." Chicago. Children's Bk Center

Stalder, Valerie

Even the devil is afraid of a shrew; a folktale of Lapland; retold by Valerie Stalder; adapted by Ray Broekel; illus. by Richard Brown. Addison-Wesley [1972] unp illus lib. bdg. $6.95 (k-3)   **398.2**

1 Folklore—Lapland   2 Devil—Fiction
ISBN 0-201-07188-6   LC 70-177415

"An Addisonian Press book"
"Pava Jalvi is a peaceful man whose life is made miserable by the bad temper and nagging of his shrewish wife. One day he takes the opportunity of pushing her down a deep hole. Peace! But he is conscience-stricken. He ties some strong plants together to make a rope. . . . Up comes the devil, delighted to get away from the shrew, but the devil's subsequent mischief leads Pava Jalvi to try a trick: he pretends his wife has gotten free and frightens the devil back below ground." Chicago. Children's Bk Center

A "lively, amusing readaloud. . . . Brown's illustrations of the characters—humorous, grotesque, Punch-and-Judy-like caricatures in brightly colored Lapp costumes—are effectively contrasted with the peaceful mountain setting." Sch Library J

Steel, Flora Annie

Tattercoats; an old English tale; pictures by Diane Goode. Bradbury Press 1976 unp illus $8.95 (k-3)   **398.2**

1 Folklore—Great Britain   2 Fairy tales
ISBN 0-87888-109-3   LC 76-9947

"Tattercoats is the grandchild of a bitter old lord who has sworn never to look upon the child. His beloved daughter has died in bearing her. Tattercoats grows up neglected, almost friendless. Her old nurse and a mysterious gooseherd are the only ones who care for her. The gooseherd works haunting magic on the pipes he plays to entertain the sad girl. The music is the key to a glorious future for her, as it attracts a rich prince who falls in love with Tattercoats and makes her his bride." Pub W

"A romantic tale from Steel's [1918] collection, 'English Fairy tales,' is beautifully illustrated in soft, floating pastel watercolors. All the paraphernalia of the Cinderella theme are here [in this variant]: the beautiful waif, the besotted royal suitor, and the magic that changes the rags Tattercoats is wearing to ballgown and crown. . . . Goode picks up every nuance of the story, including one picture in which the geese, who have accompanied the gooseherd to the ball, are echoed by a group of simpering courtiers." Chicago. Children's Bk Center

Stephens, James

Irish fairy tales; illus. by Arthur Rackham. Macmillan Pub. Co. [1968 c1948] 318p illus $6.95 (6 and up)   **398.2**

1 Folklore—Ireland   2 Legends—Ireland   3 Fairy tales
ISBN 0-02-788000-1

First published 1920; copyright renewed 1948
The collection includes ten hero tales and legends from Ireland. Among them are tales of Fionn and Fianna, the Carl of the Drab Coat, and Becuma

"There is much good narrative, much humour, and, usually, unstrained simplicity in the book, but above all there are passages of enchanting beauty." Times (London) Lit Sup

"Children may enjoy it but, like Arthur Rackham's exquisite illustrations, it will be fully appreciated only by more sophisicated readers." Review

Stern, Simon

The Hobyahs; an old story told and illus. by Simon Stern. Prentice-Hall 1977 unp illus $5.95 (k-2)   **398.2**

1 Folklore—Great Britain   2 Fairy tales
ISBN 0-13-392522-6   LC 76-39985

"In this story adapted from an English folktale, Turpie the dog saves the master's family

Stern, Simon—*Continued*

from the dreaded Hobyahs. They all live together in a turnip house—the old man, the old woman, the little girl, and Turpie." Children's Bk Rev Serv

"Stern has softened the story taken from Joseph Jacobs' 'More English Fairy Tales' with whimsy, humor, and a happy ending, and accompanied it with meticulously colored, lighthearted drawings. The result lacks the punch of the grisly original, but the changes do make it more suitable for very young children." Sch Library J

Stoutenburg, Adrien

American tall-tale animals; illus. by Glen Rounds, Viking 1968 128p illus lib. bdg. $8.95, Penguin Bks. pa 95¢ (4-6)   398.2

1 Folklore—U.S. 2 Animals—Fiction
ISBN 0-670-12066-9; 0-14-030928-4   LC 68-18124

"Whiffle-poofles, gillygaloos, bears of incredible size and wit, talented rattlesnakes, fur-bearing trout, water-toting, humped-backed desert fish, and spirited hoss-mackerel are among the curious creatures that appear in Miss Stoutenburg's collection of fantastic American fauna. Drawn from old newspapers, periodicals, out-of-print books and authentic regional sources, these entertaining descriptive accounts of rare animal life and unique hunting tactics add a new dimension to American folklore." Booklist

"Many of these stories can be found scattered throughout B. A. Botkin's 'A Treasury of American Folklore,' but . . . [Stoutenburg's] carefully organized, entertainingly folksy retellings and Glen Rounds' amusing, backwoodsy sketches add greatly to their appeal for children." Sch Library J

Synge, Ursula

Land of heroes; a retelling of the Kalevala. Atheneum Pubs. 1978 [c1977] 221p $6.95 (5 and up)   398.2

1 Legends—Finland
ISBN 0-689-50094-7   LC 77-14489

"A Margaret K. McElderry book"
First published 1977 in England with title: Kalevala: heroic tales from Finland

A "prose retelling of the 'Kalevala,' the Finnish epic poem, which describes the adventures of the three heroes: Vainamoinen, the singer and poet; Ilmarinen, the smith; and Lemminkainen, the warrior. Kalevala (which means land of heroes) is their home, a country pitted against the rival land of Pohja, ruled by the sly and evil sorceress Louhi. All three heroes are competitors for the hand of the Maiden of Pohja, Louhi's daughter, and undergo many tests of strength and cunning to win her. Ilmarinen becomes the victor after forging the 'sampo', a mill which magically grinds out corn, salt, and coins. Into this framework are introduced other episodes, including the story of Kullervo, a vengeful servant." Horn Bk

"Leaving out extraneous details, Synge never loses sight of the poem's mythic undertones or its tragic flow. Her lively prose captures the sparkling quality of northern nature and heroic life, with rich colors, precise landscapes, and breathless travel and action." Sch Library J

The **Tall** book of nursery tales; pictures by Feodor Rojankovsky. Artists and Writers Guild, inc. [distributed by Harper] 1944 120p illus $5.95, lib. bdg. $6.89 (k-2)   398.2

1 Folklore 2 Fairy tales
ISBN 0-06-025065-8; 0-06-025066-6   LC 44-3881

"Twenty-four well told traditional tales. The illustrations, with the 'tall' pages used to the best advantage, are . . . fresh and delightful. . . . The table of contents with vignettes for each title is as much fun as the rest of the book. Perfect table book if shelving is a problem." Booklist

Tatterhood, and other tales; stories of magic and adventure; ed. by Ethel Johnston Phelps; with illus. by Pamela Baldwin Ford. Feminist Press 1978 xxi, 165p illus $11.95, pa $5.95 (3-6)   398.2

1 Folklore 2 Fairy tales
ISBN 0-912670-49-5; 0-912670-50-9   LC 78-9352

"Phelps devoted herself to researching fairy tales and folklore to collect stories for this anthology. Her purpose was to celebrate canny,

resourceful, admirable girls and women instead of the wan, passive females in most classic stories starring brave heroes. After the learned discourse in the introduction (addressed to adults), the reader finds 'Tatterhood,' a defiantly sloppy maiden whose courage helps her outwit dreadful ogres and release her sister from their spell. . . . This Norwegian tale is followed by retellings of old favorites from Ireland, Scotland, Africa, India, and other parts of the globe. America is represented by a fable relished by the Indians of California." Pub W

"The international selection makes for a witty, varied portrayal of both men and women, and the illustrations capture the national characteristics of each story, both in the people and the local flora and fauna." Sch Library J
Suggested reading: p165

Thompson, Vivian L.

Hawaiian myths of earth, sea, and sky; illus. by Leonard Weisgard. Holiday House 1966 83p illus lib. bdg. $7.95 (3-6)   398.2

1 Folklore—Hawaii 2 Mythology, Hawaiian
ISBN 0-8234-0042-5   LC 66-3206

The twelve "tales are concerned with the gods Hina, Maui, Pele, Kane, God of creation, and others; old beliefs of the creation, the sun, moon, and stars, the volcanoes, the winds and other natural phenomena are related. An interesting group of stories tells how tapa cloth was first made." Library J

This "is a useful supplementary book for school units on Hawaii. The Weisgard illustrations in orange, green, and black are a nice complement to the book." Wis Library Bul
Includes glossary and bibliography

Hawaiian tales of heroes and champions; illus. by Herbert Kawainui Kane. Holiday House 1971 128p illus lib. bdg. $7.95 (4-6)   398.2

1 Folklore—Hawaii
ISBN 0-8234-0192-8   LC 72-151757

Included among these twelve tall tales of Old Hawaii are stories of shape-shifters who could change their form from one object to another; the supernatural kupua who roamed the islands, challenging kings and chiefs, tricking men, women and boys; and men with rare and special weapons

"The feats of chiefs and gods are recounted in a straightforward, dignified manner and illustrated in dark sepia wash drawings with strong line and Polynesian detail by an artist who once lived in Hawaii." Horn Bk
Glossary: p122-26. Bibliography: p127-28

The **Three** little pigs; illus. by Benvenuti; tr. from the French by Ann Sperber. Knopf 1979 20p illus $1.75 (k-1)   398.2

1 Folklore 2 Pigs—Fiction 3 Wolves—Fiction
ISBN 0-394-84104-2   LC 78-12526

A small format version of the well-known tale about the wolf who easily overcomes two careless pigs but is defeated by the cleverer third pig whose brick house withstands his attack

The **Three** wishes; pictures by Paul Galdone. McGraw 1961 32p illus lib. bdg. $7.95 (k-2)   398.2

1 Folklore—Great Britain 2 Fairy tales
ISBN 0-07-022714-4   LC 61-15909

"A Whittlesey House publication"
"The Three Wishes dates all the way back to Greek mythology. . . . This telling is from 'More English Fairy Tales,' edited by Joseph Jacobs." Verso of title page

"The old folk-tale about a woodman receiving three wishes for sparing an oak tree is illustrated with drawings that echo the simplicity and humour of the story to perfection." Ontario Library Rev

Time for old magic; comp. by May Hill Arbuthnot and Mark Taylor; illus. by John Averill [and others]. . . . Scott 1970 389p illus $11.95   398.2

1 Folklore 2 Storytelling—Collections
ISBN 0-673-05844-1   LC 73-91952

An expansion of the section: Old magic, in Arbuthnot's: Time for fairy tales, old and new, first published 1952

Time for old magic—*Continued*

"A representative collection of folk tales, fables, myths, and epics to be used in the classroom, home, or camp; especially planned for college classes in children's literature; with section introductions, headnotes for the individual stories, and a special section titled 'Old Magic and Children.'" Title page

Bibliography: p366-83. Glossary and pronunciation guide: p384-86

Titiev, Estelle

How the Moolah was taught a lesson & other tales from Russia; tr. and adapted by Estelle Titiev and Lila Pargment; pictures by Ray Cruz. Dial Press 1976 53p illus $5.95, lib. bdg. $5.47 (2-4)   **398.2**

1 Folklore—Russia
ISBN 0-8037-5744-1; 0-8037-5746-8   LC 75-9200

"In the four stories, each taken from a different area of Russia, familiar motifs appear in unfamiliar settings. Greed and power are conquered by virtue; a wicked witch is foiled by a courageous youth; a wife as wise as she is beautiful magically helps her husband solve impossible problems; a miraculous blanket can stretch to cover a thousand men; and a wonderful kettle can feed an army. Full-page illustrations are executed in finely detailed pen-and-ink drawings which convey the varying backgrounds and the stories." Horn Bk

"Good for reading aloud or alone, this will be a welcome addition to the storyteller's sources." Chicago. Children's Bk Center

Told under the green umbrella; favorite folk tales, fairy tales, and legends; selected by the Literature Committee of the Association for Childhood Education International; illus. by Grace Gilkison. Macmillan Pub. Co. 1930 188p illus $6.95 (1-4)   **398.2**

1 Folklore 2 Fairy tales
ISBN 0-02-706830-7   LC 78-101086

"The Umbrella books"
"This collection includes twenty-six familiar stories which range in length and difficulty from 'The pancake' to 'The princess on the glass hill.' Acceptable versions have been used throughout. . . . Good format and many illustrations." Booklist

Toye, William

The fire stealer; pictures by Elizabeth Cleaver; retold by William Toye. Oxford [1980 c1979] unp illus $6.95 (k-3)   **398.2**

1 Indians of North America—Legends
ISBN 0-19-540321-5   LC 79-67169

"One of the tales of Nanabozho, hero of many Canadian Indian legends, is simply retold for younger children and is illustrated in handsome, bright collages by Cleaver. . . . In this story, Nanabozho uses his magic to change shape, and is thereby able to steal fire and bring it home to ease his grandmother's last years. Thus his people learn to use fire, yet be alert to its dangerous quality; too, the story explains the bright colors of fall foliage, for Nanabozho asked his people to remember him and how the torch he carried had lit the trees with red and gold. A good choice for reading aloud or telling to young children." Chicago. Children's Bk Center

How summer came to Canada; pictures by Elizabeth Cleaver; retold by William Toye. Oxford [1979 c1969] 32p illus pa $4.95 (k-3)   **398.2**

1 Micmac Indians—Legends 2 Legends—Canada
3 Seasons—Fiction
ISBN 0-19-540290-1

First published 1969 by H. Z. Walck
"A legend of the Micmac Indians of eastern Canada is retold in simple rhythmic prose. The people of a once fertile land held in the grip of Giant Winter are saved by their lord Glooskap who goes in search of Summer, the Queen of 'where it is always warm.' Double page illustrations are alive with rich, glowing colors." Cane. Selected Media about the Am Indian for Young Children

The loon's necklace: retold by William Toye; pictures by Elizabeth Cleaver. Oxford 1977 unp illus $5.95 (1-3)   **398.2**

1 Tsimshian Indians—Legends
ISBN 0-19-540278-2   LC 77-82683

A Tsimshian Indian legend explaining the origin of the loon's white feather markings. "An old man who cannot provide for his family because of blindness appeals to the loon, regains his sight by swimming on its back under the lake, and rewards it with his shell necklace, which makes a permanent pattern on its feathers. . . . A dramatic choice for storytelling and folklore units." Booklist

"The beauty of the book lies in its artwork. Ms. Cleaver's rich pictures are actually collages of torn paper, paper cutouts, and linocuts, which turn this quiet tale into a vivid essay on nature in British Columbia." Babbling Bookworm

Traven, B.

The creation of the sun and the moon; illus. by Alberto Beltrán. Hill & Co./Creative Arts Bk. Co. 1977 [c1968] 65p illus pa $3.95 (5 and up)   **398.2**

1 Indians of Mexico—Legends 2 Sun—Fiction
ISBN 0-88208-087-3

First published 1968 by Hill & Wang
The first part of this retelling of a Mexican Indian legend "recounts the adventures of Chicovaneg who, aided by the Quetzal bird and the Feathered Serpent, borrows light from the stars to rekindle the sun destroyed by evil spirits; the second part tells how his son Hauchinog-va-neg, with the help of the rabbit Tul, creates a moon to bring light and comfort to mankind at night." Booklist

"Traven's sonorous prose, the spirited illustrations in black and terracotta by the Mexican artist Alberto Beltrán, and the attractive format that make this an outstanding book that belongs in all folklore collections." Library J

Tresselt, Alvin

The mitten; an old Ukrainian folktale, retold by Alvin Tresselt; illus. by Yaroslava. Adapted from the version by E. Rachev. Lothrop 1964 unp illus $5.50 (k-2)   **398.2**

1 Folklore—Ukraine 2 Animals—Fiction
ISBN 0-688-51053-1   LC 64-14436

"On the coldest day of the year a little Ukrainian boy loses his fur-lined mitten, which becomes so overcrowded with animals seeking a snug shelter that it finally bursts. Brightly colored pictures show the animals dressed in typical Ukrainian costumes." Hodges. Bks for Elem Sch Libraries

Turska, Krystyna

The magician of Cracow. Greenwillow Bks. 1975 unp illus $9.25 (k-3)   **398.2**

1 Folklore—Poland 2 Devil—Fiction
ISBN 0-688-80010-6   LC 75-8846

"A magician who coveted power and omniscience made a pact with the devil. For a while he enjoyed his mastery over the Evil One and amassed great wealth and fame. But the devil grew tired of his ignominious role and managed finally by trickery to regain the upper hand; while the magician, knowing that 'the devil of course is banned from all heavenly realms,' made the best of a bad bargain and took refuge on the moon." Horn Bk

"Striking illustrations, many looking like perfect backdrops for an opera stage, come alive with the vibrant, glowing colors and rich details of Turska's painting. The border motifs, akin to tapestry work, add a folk-art flavor to the entire book." Booklist

The **Twelve** dancing princesses; illus. by Adrienne Adams. Holt [1980 c1966] unp illus lib. bdg. $3.59, pa $2.95 (k-3)   **398.2**

1 Folklore—France 2 Fairy tales
ISBN 0-03-057493-5   LC 66-10104

A reprint of the title first published with these illustrations 1966

In this retelling of a fairy tale based on the French version included in Andrew Lang's Red fairy book, entered above, a young cowherd uses a cloak of invisibility to free twelve princesses from a mysterious enchantment

The **Twelve** dancing princesses—*Continued*

This is "longer and more romantic [than the Grimm version]. . . . The illustrations, in colors that are rich and warm, are as romantic as the story." Horn Bk

Uchida, Yoshiko

The magic listening cap; more folk tales from Japan; retold and illus. by Yoshiko Uchida. Harcourt 1955 146p illus pa $1.95 (3-6)   398.2

1 Folklore—Japan 2 Fairy tales
ISBN 0-15-655119-5   LC 55-5240

These fourteen Japanese folk tales are retold "with charm and humor and display those universal elements of folk lore that will give them wide appeal. Several of the stories have counterparts in other folk lore. The stories are suitable for reading aloud, or for telling, and will also be of interest to students of comparative folk lore." Chicago. Children's Bk Center
Includes a glossary

Valen, Nanine

The Devil's tail; based on an old French legend; illus. by David McPhail. Scribner 1978 61p illus lib. bdg. $7.95 (2-4)   398.2

1 Legends—France 2 Devil—Fiction
ISBN 0-684-15292-4   LC 77-24135

An adaptation of a legend explaining how a French town acquired its name and hilly terrain and why its inhabitants speak through their noses
"Three brothers discover a figure frozen in the snow and carry him home for thawing out in the oven. It's not long before they notice a tail coming out of the oven door slot and learn it's the Devil they've brought home. Refusing to let him out at first, the boys then give in to his 'usual offer' of three wishes in return for his freedom. Their desires include a sled and a hill to use it on: this last causes havoc as people and belongings slide down the suddenly tilting terrain. Moreover, when folk discover how their hill came to be, greed for their own wishes takes over. They besiege the still oven-bound demon, sorely stretching his tail till it snaps and all tumble down." Booklist
"An amusing tale, illustrated with detailed line drawings full of droll humor." Horn Bk

Van Woerkom, Dorothy O.

The friends of Abu Ali; three more tales of the Middle East, retold by Dorothy O. Van Woerkom; illus. by Harold Berson. Macmillan Pub. Co. 1978 64p illus $6.95 (k-3)
398.2

1 Folklore—Turkey 2 Nasr al-Dīn, Khwājah
ISBN 0-02-791320-1   LC 77-12624

"Ready-to-read"
"These stories are freely adapted from tales told of Nasr-ed-Din Hodja, one of the most celebrated personalities of the Middle East." Verso of title page
"In three short tales for the beginning independent reader, Von Woerkom adapts some Middle Eastern noodlehead stories in a style that has vitality and humor despite its simplicity. Abu Ali, Musa, Nouri, and Hamid bicker about such weighty matters as who should be entitled to sit in a donkey's shadow (while the donkey runs away), whether or not too much sniffing will make a cake fall (the cake falls), and whether or not Musa's [imaginary] donkey should be allowed to cross Hamid's bridge, which he doesn't really own. . . . Berson's illustrations, distinctive for their fluid line, echo the humor of the stories." Chicago. Children's Bk Center

The queen who couldn't bake gingerbread; an adaptation of a German folk tale; illus. by Paul Galdone. Knopf 1975 unp illus lib. bdg. $5.99 (k-3)   398.2

1 Folklore—Germany 2 Fairy tales
ISBN 0-394-93033-9   LC 74-15302

"King Pilaf's search for a wife that can bake gingerbread brings him to wise Princess Calliope, who is searching for a husband that can play the slide trombone. No agreement is to be had, but months of fruitless searching on the part of the king cause him to reconsider: 'A wife who is wise . . . does not need to know how to bake gingerbread.' Calliope likewise relents: 'It seems to me that a husband who is kind . . . is more to be loved than one who can play on the slide trombone.' The two vow never to mention each other's shortcomings, but of course the inevitable happens and a royal freeze ensues, until once again each softens and opts for practical solutions. Pilaf learns to bake gingerbread and Calliope masters the trombone. Van Woerkom's updated rendition of an old German tale leaves hardly a semblance of folk flavor, but in its stead is a hearty humor graphically exploited by Galdone's robust lines and full-color washes." Booklist

Tit for tat; pictures by Douglas Florian. Greenwillow Bks. 1977 56p illus lib. bdg. $5.71 (1-3)   398.2

1 Folklore
ISBN 0-688-84076-0   LC 76-28454

"Greenwillow Read-alone"
"The old woman's generosity to a ragged stranger nets her a pile of gold while all the miser gets for his stinginess is a big head cold." Sch Library J
"This well-done retelling of a universal folk theme seems to have no particular ethnic identity but carries its message with style nevertheless. . . . A carefully limited vocabulary is handled quite ably, and the parable will hold up under any test of honest telling. Warm, spacious drawings with earth-tone coloring have a rough, folk character and charming details." Booklist

Vasilisa

Vasilisa the beautiful; tr. from the Russian by Thomas P. Whitney; illus. by Nonny Hogrogian. Macmillan Pub. Co. 1970 unp illus $4.95 (k-3)   398.2

1 Folklore—Russia
ISBN 0-02-792540-4   LC 73-102971

"In this Russian equivalent of Cinderella, Vasilisa has a doll, the gift of her dying mother, instead of a godmother to advise and help her and the plot is more inclusive than that of the fairy tale as it is known to Western readers. By prevailing over the witch Baba Yaga, to whom she has been sent to fetch a light, Vasilisa triumphs over her evil stepmother and jealous stepsisters—and marries the king." Booklist
"From the Afanasiev collection of traditional tales . . . translated in good style to read smoothly for reading aloud or independently. The illustrations are handsome: soft colors, comic details, effective composition." Chicago. Children's Bk Center

Walker, Barbara

Teeny-Tiny and the witch-woman; illus. by Michael Foreman. Pantheon Bks. 1975 unp illus lib. bdg. $5.99 (k-3)   398.2

1 Folklore—Turkey
ISBN 0-394-93088-6   LC 74-15297

"In a Turkish version of 'Hansel and Gretel,' Teeny-Tiny saves himself and his two brothers from 'kind Auntie,' a witch whose knobby fence is made of 'little people bones.' Foreman pictures the tale in a fairyland setting in which minarets, thatched cottages, medieval garb, and pickle-faced witches are mixed together in an appropriately humorous-scary blend. Primary graders will enjoy this at storyhour or on their own." Sch Library J

Wiesner, William

Turnabout; a Norwegian tale retold and illus. by William Wiesner. Seabury [distributed by Houghton] 1972 unp illus $5.95 (k-3)
398.2

1 Folklore—Norway
ISBN 0-395-28832-0   LC 72-190380

"A Clarion book"
"This text has been adapted from the version of Edouard Laboulaye." Verso of title page
"Broad humor marks this brisk, pithy retelling of a Norwegian version of the folktale about a farmer who swaps jobs with his wife and discovers that keeping house is not as easy as he thought it was. A new twist is given to the ending for though both go back to their accustomed tasks, the wife sometimes joins her husband in the fields because she enjoys working outdoors

Wiesner, William—*Continued*
and the farmer sometimes helps his wife with
the housework without making so many mistakes."
Booklist
"The artist has drawn many doublespreads
which depict—on the left-hand page—the wife
calmly raking row after row in the field, while the
husband smashes eggs, fails to put the stopper in
the cider barrel, and gets stuck in the chimney—a
victim of his own ineptitude. The line drawings—
washed in tones of red, green, blue, yellow, gray,
and brown—are direct, fresh, and sprightly." Horn
Bk

Wildsmith, Brian
The miller, the boy and the donkey. Oxford
[1980 c1969] unp illus pa $4.95 (k-2)   398.2
1 Fables
ISBN 0-19-272114
"Based on a fable by La Fontaine." Half-title
page
First published 1969
Adapted and illustrated by Brian Wildsmith
The miller and his son take their donkey to
market to sell him. To keep him clean they decide
to carry him, but a passing farmer laughs at them
and they ride the donkey instead. Thus begins a
series of suggestions from other people they meet
as to who should ride the donkey. The poor miller
is utterly confused trying to please everyone and
in the end decides that next time he will only
please himself
"A spirited and attractive picture book." Childrens' Bks 1970

The rich man and the shoe-maker; a fable
by La Fontaine; [retold and] illus. by Brian
Wildsmith. Oxford [1980 c1965] unp illus
pa $3.95 (k-2)   398.2
1 Fables
ISBN 0-19-272104-6
First published 1965
This "fable—the tale of the poor but carefree
shoemaker to whom sudden wealth brought only
anxiety and distress—has been freely adapted into
simple prose. Amplifying the story with an imaginative life of their own, the pictures are full of
shapes, angles, and rhythmic patterns, while the
sheer glory of dynamic color carries its own emotional impact." Horn Bk

Williams, Jay
The surprising things Maui did; illus. by
Charles Mikolaycak. Four Winds 1979 unp
illus $8.95 (1-3)   398.2
1 Legends—Hawaii 2 Maui (Polynesian deity)
3 Mythology, Polynesian
ISBN 0-590-07553-5   LC 79-5069
"When Maui is born, the crops have failed so
he is sent to be raised by his uncle, the God of
the Sea. Maui grows to be strong but lazy. He is,
however, endowed with special gifts. He raises
the low sky so that it no longer presses upon
the world, and he slows the sun in its course to
make the land warmer and more productive. He
hooks an island up out of the sea and discovers
the secret, from some tricky mudhens, of making
fire." Sch Library J
"The Hawaiian myth is accompanied by lavish
full-color illustrations that alternate repeatedly
with the same (notably lackluster) sepia-and-
white painting. In general Mikolaycak's colors
swirl and flow, the darkened browns, greens, and
poppy reds set off by accenting brights. Composition is especially striking; the pictures are almost
larger than life and project a sense of power
that sometimes nearly overwhelms the story."
Booklist

The wicked tricks of Tyl Uilenspiegel;
illus. by Frisco Henstra. Four Winds 1978
51p illus $8.95 (3-5)   398.2
1 Legends—Flanders 2 Eulenspiegel
ISBN 0-590-07478-4   LC 77-7884
"The rogue Tyl Uilenspiegel—known in English
as Till Owlglass and in German as Tyll Eulenspiegel—was famous in Flemish as well as in
German folklore. Four stories, three of which
originally appeared in 'Cricket' magazine, tell of
Tyl's cunning tricks and devices during the sixteenth century in the Low Countries when the

Netherlanders were fighting against Spain for
their independence. Playing a daring role—as
tight-rope walker, doctor, or thief—Tyl employed
his talents in deceiving the Spaniards and in aiding the Netherlanders." Horn Bk
"Crosshatched sketches, half in black-and-white,
half in color or washes, lend flair and droll authenticity to these humorous stories." Sch Library J

Winter-telling stories; comp. by Alice
Marriott; illus. by Richard Cuffari. Crowell
1969 82p illus lib. bdg. $7.89 (3-6)   398.2
1 Kiowa Indians—Legends
ISBN 0-690-89636-0   LC 73-78264
First published 1947 by William Sloane Associates, illustrated by Roland Whitehorse
"Based on the Kiowa Indian stories about Saynday, the man who made the world the way it is,
this is a delightful collection of brief stories of the
good and sometimes bad things Saynday brought
to the Indians." Pub W
Pleasing format with many attractive black-and-
white drawings. The writing style is informal and
full of colloquial dialogue, which, along with the
appealing subject and humor, make this useful
for junior high remedial reading as well as good
entertainment for older elementary school children. The quality of the stories varies throughout,
but always remains in the average to superior
range." Sch Library J

Winthrop, Elizabeth
Journey to the bright kingdom; illus. by
Charles Mikolaycak. Holiday House 1979 unp
illus lib. bdg. $7.95 (2-4)   398.2
1 Folklore—Japan 2 Mice—Fiction 3 Blind—
Fiction
ISBN 0-8234-0357-2   LC 78-23261
A "story based on the Japanese folk tale 'The
Rolling Rice Cakes.' A woman, who was a gifted
and sensitive artist, loved nature and had a
particular fondness for the little mice which
scampered around her as she sketched. When she
lost her sight, her personality changed, and people
found her strange. In vain, her husband took her
to doctor after doctor; the blindness was incurable. The birth of a daughter, Kiyo, was a temporary source of joy, but eventually the woman
grew sadder and weaker, and it seemed she would
die. Then one day Kiyo was able to bring her
mother to the legendary kingdom of Kakure-sato,
a beautiful place ruled by mice, where no one
was blind. They were allowed to spend one day
there, and the mother saw her daughter for the
first time. Afterward the magic of the place remained with them, for though the mother was
still sightless, she had regained her will to live."
Horn Bk
"The book is beautifully designed and printed,
the softly graded tones of Mikolaycak's black-and-
white illustrations perfectly balancing the text."
Sch Library J

Wolkstein, Diane
Lazy stories; retold by Diane Wolkstein;
pictures by James Marshall. Seabury [dis-
tributed by Houghton] 1976 39p illus $6.95
(3-5)   398.2
1 Folklore
ISBN 0-395-28833-9   LC 75-25781
"A Clarion book"
Wolkstein "retells three short humorous folk-
tales from Japan, Mexico, and Laos, all with the
theme of laziness: Hiroko has so many servants
she never even washes her own hands; Mario
refuses to work, saying 'If God wishes to give,
He will give, even if He has to push it in through
the window'; Khotan even refuses to feed himself.
Helpful storyteller's notes conclude with hints for
telling, suggestions for age levels, and length of
time needed for each story. Marshall's amusing
pen-and-ink caricatures are a refreshing departure from his usual style." Booklist

Wyndham, Robert
Tales the people tell in China; illus. by
Jay Yang; consulting editor: Doris K.
Coburn. Messner 1971 92p illus lib. bdg. $7.29
(3-6)   398.2
1 Folklore—China
ISBN 0-671-32428-4   LC 74-154971
A "collection of 15 simply told Chinese legends,
stories, and anecdotes including a traditional tale

Wyndham, Robert—*Continued*

that, according to Wyndham, has been rewritten for propaganda purposes by the government of the People's Republic of China. In addition, there are stories of scholars, ghosts, generals, peasants, Confucius, and the emperor, and a selection of short sayings. Sources and notes are appended." Booklist
"Gracefully illustrated in the classical Chinese style, the ancient stories offer considerable insight to Chinese culture and customs." Pub W

Yellow fairy book; collected by Andrew Lang; ed. by Brian Alderson; illus. by Erik Blegvad. [Rev. ed.] Viking 1980 329p illus $14.95 (4-6)   **398.2**
1 Folklore 2 Fairy tales
ISBN 0-670-79385-X   LC 79-4118
First published 1894 by Longmans
A collection of 44 tales from the folklore of England, France, Germany, Hungary, Iceland, Poland, Russia, and the American Indians. Sources for the tales are provided by the editor

Yellow Robe, Rosebud

Tonweya and the eagles, and other Lakota Indian tales; retold by Rosebud Yellow Robe; pictures by Jerry Pinkney. Dial Press 1979 118p illus $7.95, lib. bdg. $7.45 (4-6)   **398.2**
1 Teton Indians—Legends
ISBN 0-8037-8973-4; 0-8037-8974-2   LC 78-72470
"The eldest daughter of Chauncey Yellow Robe, a hereditary chief of the Lakota-oyate tribe, re-tells stories she heard from her father as a child. . . . The stories in the collection feature her father as the young boy Chano going on his first buffalo hunt and listening to stories told by his parents, whom he loved deeply. The stories feature animal characters such as the beaver and the red-eyed ducks. Folk customs, such as rubbing blood on a young pony's nose to allay a fear of blood, are woven into the narratives. The tales are direct and simple, and the distinctive line drawings done in pencil interpret both the action and feeling of the stories in fine detail." Horn Bk
Glossary and pronunciation guide: p117-18

Yolen, Jane

The emperor and the kite; pictures by Ed Young. Collins [distributed by Philomel Bks] 1967 unp illus lib. bdg. $6.99 (k-3)   **398.2**
1 Folklore—China
ISBN 0-529-00255-8   LC 67-13816
A retelling of an old Chinese tale. "Princess Djeow Seow, the smallest one, largely ignored by her father the Emperor and her brothers, took solace from her kite. When the Emperor was imprisoned in a tower by wicked men, the tiny girl devised his escape by braiding a rope, attaching it to the kite, and flying it up to her father." Bruno. Bks for Sch Libraries, 1968
This book "is especially distinguished by its Chinese artist's modern use of the Old Oriental paper-cut style. Vividly colored, choreographic figures move across open white pages and grace the equally distinctive poetic rhythm and balance of the text. Small children will be captivated by the emperor's youngest daughter." Bk World

Young, Ed

The terrible Nung Gwama; a Chinese folktale adapted by Ed Young from the retelling by Leslie Bonnet; illus. by Ed. Young. Collins, in cooperation with the U.S. Committee for UNICEF [distributed by Philomel Bks.] $5.95, lib. bdg. $5.99 (k-3)   **398.2**
1 Folklore—China
ISBN 0-529-05444-2; 0-529-05445-0   LC 78-18766
"A Unicef storycraft book"
"On white pages, Young painted the same bamboo-fan shape in pale brown. The figures and the landscape glow with color against the dun background, especially the graceful figure of a woman, in a soft-pink gown. She meets the dread Nung Gwama while she's taking cakes to her venerable parents. The monster swears he will slay and eat her in her home that night because she refuses to give it the cakes. Sobbing by the roadside, the woman gets a variety of unlikely weapons to battle Nung Gwama with, all of which work in a way that makes the tale both side-splitting and fearful." Pub W

Zemach, Harve

Duffy and the devil; a Cornish tale retold by Harve Zemach; with pictures by Margot Zemach. Farrar, Straus 1973 unp illus $7.95 (k-3)   **398.2**
1 Folklore—Great Britain
ISBN 0-374-31887-5   LC 72-81491
Awarded the Caldecott Medal, 1974
"In this Cornish variation on Rumpelstiltskin Squire Lovel brings the maid Duffy home to help his housekeeper Old Jone, who can no longer do the work that needs 'sharp eyes and quick fingers.' But in truth Duffy can neither spin, knit nor weave until the devil comes to her aid. They strike a bargain whereby Duffy must discover the devil's name at the end of three years—which she does through the help of Old Jone." Booklist
"The artist employs her typical pastel coloring, but the use of shading and perspective to create entire scenes is highly unusual for her, and the illustrations far surpass anything she has done to date. The author embues the story with wry humor, invented words, and slightly edgy statements, which are perfectly exploited in the illustrations: Duffy sitting 'herself ladylike' on the horse, and the witches taking a swig of beer. The legend of Rumpelstiltskin has probably never seemed as funny as in this version by the author-artist team." Horn Bk

A penny a look; an old story retold by Harve Zemach; pictures by Margot Zemach. Farrar, Straus 1971 unp illus $6.95 (k-3)   **398.2**
1 Folklore
ISBN 0-374-35793-5   LC 71-161373
"An insensitive and aggressive man has heard about the land of one-eyed people, and he persuades his do-nothing but merciful brother to come along on a trek to get there. Object: to capture one man, bring him back, exhibit him, and get rich. The gentler brother will be allowed to collect penny fees. But the tables are turned: surrounded by one-eyed men, the malfeasant is captured and exhibited, since he is a rarity, a man with two eyes. The brother (even one-eyed men could see he'd never amount to much) is no threat, so he is permited to collect fees." Sutherland. The Best in Children's Bks
"Zemach's style is low-key and pseudo-serious, his dialogue droll. But it's really his wife Margot who never misses a chance to make you laugh. She has drawn a series of slapstick scenes, like a silent-movie pantomime, that follow the brothers on their Phineas Foggish trek. . . . With a gesture here, a posture there, she draws with a master humorist's touch. . . . Behind the laugh is a lesson: cruelty and avarice don't pay." NY Times Bk Rev

Zemach, Kaethe

The beautiful rat; written and illus. by Kaethe Zemach. Four Winds 1979 unp illus $7.95 (k-3)   **398.2**
1 Folklore—Japan 2 Marriage—Fiction 3 Rats —Fiction
ISBN 0-590-07584-5   LC 79-11752
"Zemach has adapted and simplified a traditional tale (of which there are many variants) about a rat (more often the character is a mouse) whose proud mother thinks no husband in the world is too good for her daughter; offered in turn to the sun, a cloud, the wind, and a stone wall (more often a mountain), all of whom refuse, the lovely Yoshiko weds her old friend Toshio. After all, rats are so powerful they can destroy a stone wall, which can stop a wind, which can blow away a cloud, which can obscure the sun." Chicago. Children's Bk Center
The story "focuses upon events culminating in the wedding festivities and makes the abstract characters less so by personifying them. The interpretive illustrations, swirling and rhythmic, are executed in shades of blues and oranges to accompany the brief cumulative text. Although Japanese motifs are suggested in the exaggerated drawings, the effect is one of a free and original response to traditional material." Horn Bk

Zemach, Margot

It could always be worse; a Yiddish folk tale retold and with pictures by Margot Zemach. Farrar, Straus 1976 unp illus $7.95 (k-3)   **398.2**

1 Folklore, Jewish
ISBN 0-374-33650-4   LC 76-53895

The author-illustrator retells "the familiar tale of the simple villager whose house was so crowded and noisy, he went to the Rabbi for help. On orders from the wise one, the frantic man brought his livestock into the house, only to be told to remove them when the commotion became predictably unbearable." Horn Bk

"Important here are Margot Zemach's illustrations, which show all the rumpus and ruckus, all the accouterments of Old World peasantry. . . . The colors are stronger, bolder than those the illustrator has done for 'Duffy and the Devil,' [by Harve Zemach, entered above]. . . . It could always be worse, indeed. But never before has it been done better." NY Times Bk Rev

400 LANGUAGE

410   Linguistics. Multilingual books

Adler, Irving

Language and man [by] Irving and Joyce Adler; illus. by Laurie Jo Lambie. Day 1970 48p illus $7.89 (3-5)   **410**

1 Language and languages
ISBN 0-381-99978-5   LC 78-109148

"The Reason why series"

"A discussion of the importance of speech and of the transmission and diffusion of culture across barriers of time and space, emphasizing the fact that all men are capable of acquiring any language and that infants everywhere make the same sounds, refining their speech to meet approval of the adults with whom they first communicate. There is a competent introduction to the facts that some words resemble each other in many languages and that English has been influenced both by proximity and importation of words from other languages. The writing is clear but staid, the book distracting on a few pages because of the difficulty of reading print against a background of pattern in color." Chicago. Children's Bk Center
Word list: p47

Frasconi, Antonio

See and say; guada e parla, mira y habla, regarde et parle; a picture book in four languages; woodcuts by Antonio Frasconi. Harcourt 1955 unp illus $6.95, pa $1.35 (3 and up)   **410**

1 Language and languages 2 Multilingual books
ISBN 0-15-272454-0; 0-15-680350-X   LC 55-8675

"Striking three- and four-color woodcuts in modern design accompany words [for the familiar objects pictured] in English (always printed in black), Italian (blue), French (red) and Spanish (green). The words selected are important to children and their pronunciations are given. The last page, also illustrated, has four parallel columns of everyday expressions. For the very youngest this will succeed as a bright picture book, but it is the next older, more interested today in foreign words, who will find it of special interest, though it is not a book for teaching language." Horn Bk

Hautzig, Esther

At home; a visit in four languages; illus. by Aliki. Macmillan Pub. Co. 1968 unp illus $4.95 (k-3)   **410**

1 Language and languages 2 Multilingual books 3 Home
ISBN 0-02-743470-2   LC 68-23063

Vocabularies in English, French, Spanish and Russian are presented in this book depicting home scenes "in Chicago, Marseilles, Barcelona, and Leningrad in which families are enjoying each other and the relatives and friends who come to visit. . . . Some additional words and the Russian alphabet are appended and phonetic equivalents are given for all foreign words in the book." Booklist

In school; learning in four languages; pictures by Nonny Hogrogian. Macmillan Pub. Co. 1969 unp illus $4.95 (k-3)   **410**

1 Language and languages 2 Multilingual books 3 Schools
ISBN 0-02-743360-9   LC 69-18236

The author "introduces children to the Spanish, French, and Russian equivalents of some three dozen words used in the classroom. Hautzig's brief text and Hogrogian's sprightly colored illustrations make it clear that children, whether in San Francisco, San Sebastian, Cherbourg, or Odessa, go to school to study and learn and to have fun, too. Some additional words and the Russian alphabet are appended and a few given names are identified on the endpapers. Phonetic pronunciation is given for all non-English words in the book." Booklist

"The text is stilted and dull; but the pictures are bright and lively, full of humor and mischief, and have universal appeal." Horn Bk

In the park; an excursion in four languages; pictures by Ezra Jack Keats. Macmillan Pub. Co. 1968 unp illus $4.95 (k-3)   **410**

1 Language and languages 2 Multilingual books 3 Parks
ISBN 0-02-743450-8   LC 68-10067

"A sunny day in the park in New York, Paris, Moscow or Madrid and what to do, see and eat in English, French, Russian and Spanish. The introductory and closing statements are in English and the objects found in the park are presented in all four languages with pronunciation." Library J

"Very simple, very functional, very attractive. . . . The pictures are gay, the word-comparison can be fun, and the universality of children's interests is an implicit additional message. . . . A list of additional words and a pronunciation guide to the Russian alphabet are appended." Chicago. Children's Bk Center

411   Notations (alphabets and ideographs)

Fisher, Leonard Everett

Alphabet art; 13 ABCs from around the world; written and illus. by Leonard Everett Fisher. Four Winds 1978 61p illus $8.95 (4 and up)   **411**

1 Alphabet
ISBN 0-590-07420-9   LC 78-6148

"An introductory section, 'The ABCD of Language' gives meaning to such terms as hieroglyphs, hieratic and demotic writing, and syllabaries. A brief text for each alphabet provides information on the people and events that originated it. A full-page scratchboard illustration, representing some aspect of the individual culture, accompanies each essay. Except for the text, which is printed in black, the book is printed in rosy brick red. Each of the thirteen alphabets is presented in full: Arabic, Cherokee, Chinese, Cyrillic, Eskimo, Gaelic, Gothic, German, Greek, Hebrew, Japanese, Sanskrit, Thai, and Tibetan." Horn Bk

A "well-written and nicely designed book. . . . The letters of each alphabet are used to form decorative captions for [the] illustrations. Unfortunately, the English translations of these captions are inconveniently located, all on one page. But the visual representations make up for just about any flaw in the book: Fisher does a fine job in making all 13 alphabets vibrant and beautiful." Sch Library J

Ogg, Oscar

The 26 letters. Rev. ed. Crowell 1971 294p illus $11.95   **411**

1 Alphabet 2 Writing—History 3 Printing—History
ISBN 0-690-84115-9   LC 70-140646

First published 1948

Beginning with the earliest man 35,000-15,000 B.C.), his implements and his culture, this . . . book traces through the centuries the development of writing from the earliest cave drawings

Ogg, Oscar—*Continued*
in northern Spain to the modern linotype." Library J
"A fascinating evolution of writing characters, enlivened with historical anecdotes and numerous drawings. . . . An attractive book that cannot fail to arouse interest in alphabets and type faces." Massachusetts
"Simply and clearly told. . . . One example of fine bookmaking to use with young people and adults." Booklist

413 Lexicography

Kraske, Robert
The story of the dictionary; illus. with photographs. Harcourt 1975 67p illus $6.50 (5 and up)   413
1 English language—Dictionaries—History
ISBN 0-15-280850-7   LC 74-23177
The author "begins with a history of the dictionary—when and why it came into being; methods of dictionary-making; changes in format; current methods of compilation—and concludes with chapters on 'Dictionaries for Boys and Girls' and the effects that English dictionaries have had on changes in spelling and word usage." Sch Library J
"Separate chapters are devoted to the great lexicographers, Dr. Johnson and Noah Webster, and to the 'king of dictionaries,' The Oxford English Dictionary.' A once-over-lightly history of the English language traces the manifold roots of today's living language. . . . Children are endlessly fascinated by words, facts, and statistics; fortunately, the author deals with all three in a brisk, inviting style." Horn Bk
Selected bibliography: p63-64

419 Verbal language other than spoken and written

Charlip, Remy
Handtalk; an ABC of finger spelling & sign language [by] Remy Charlip, Mary Beth [and] George Ancona. Four Winds [1980] unp illus $9.95   419
1 Deaf—Means of communication 2 Alphabet
ISBN 0-590-07766-X
First published 1974 by Parents Magazine Press
This book provides an "introduction to the two modes of manual communication used primarily by the deaf: signs (gestures which represent words) and fingerspelling (the process by which words are spelled using the letters of the manual alphabet). . . . The format includes full-page scenes of persons making various signs, with insets at the bottom of each page which illustrate the fingerspelling of the word represented by the sign. Thus, the learner may test his memory of the manual alphabet to discover the word being shown. While the book could be used as a basic text in learning the manual alphabet, it would be only of supplemental value in the learning of signs because of the more animated nature of signing. Its most basic function would be that of educating children and adults about the language and comunication methods of a little-known minority group. For these purposes, 'Handtalk' is highly recommended. It comes as close as any inanimate medium can to capturing the liveliness and sparkle of a beautiful, expressive and often humorous method of comunication." AAAS Sci Bks

420.5 English language— Periodicals

Language Arts. Natl. Council of Teachers of English $20 per year   420.5
1 English language—Periodicals 2 English language—Study and teaching—Periodicals
ISSN 0360-9170
8 issues a year. First published 1924 with title: Elementary English review. Also published previously with title: Elementary English

Reading, composition, speaking, and listening skills are emphasized in this journal. Effective teaching is encouraged by coverage of such areas as ethnic studies, humanistic education, language development, and creativity. Among the topics featured regularly are children's literature, educational research, instructional materials and strategies, plus a children's page

422 Etymology of standard English

Kohn, Bernice
What a funny thing to say! Pictures by R. O. Blechman. Dial Press 1974 87p illus $5.95, lib. bdg. $5.47 (5 and up)   422
1 English language—Etymology
ISBN 0-8037-9048-1; 0-8037-9079-1   LC 73-6023
"After a brief but informative survey of the English language's development from its ancient beginnings, the author reveals curiosities of modern usage. She shows how we update by adding foreign words and fabricating others, and deftly explains the differences between colloquialisms, slang, and jargon. The 'hippie subculture' may differ with some of Kohn's interpretations of its 1960s' vocabulary, while the ironic comments on Pidgin English may be lost on young readers; however, these discussions and others on cockney rhyming slang, cliches, and pig latin word games provide an informal digression from heavier language study material. A partial table of language families is appended." Booklist
Bibliography: p84

423 English language— Dictionaries

The **American** Heritage School dictionary. Houghton 1977 xxviii, 992p illus $9.95 (4 and up)   423
1 English language—Dictionaries
ISBN 0-395-24792-6   LC 77-361042
"This is a reprint of the first edition (1972) with some changes incorporated into the introductory sections." Am Ref Bks Annual, 1979
The 35,000 entry words defined in this "school dictionary were selected from a computerized corpus. . . . [The designers] set out to identify in an objective way words which are actually encountered by students in American schools in grades 4 through 8. Overall the selection of words covers all areas and topics and should be satisfactory for most classroom work for grades 4 through 8, although obviously many words will have to be located in unabridged dictionaries. The page format is clear and well designed. . . . [It includes a] center column for small photos and drawings and etymological notes. . . . A pronunciation key is printed at the bottom of each left-hand page. Definitions are arranged on the same principle as in 'The American Heritage Dictionary of the English Language'. Examples are supplied where these are useful for illustrating figurative senses and multiple senses of words. Definition by example is also employed where needed. Most variants are separately entered. . . . [Geographic] and biographic entries are included on a highly selective basis." Wynar. Guide to Ref Bks for Sch Media Centers [review of the 1972 edition]

The **Cat** in the hat Beginner book dictionary, by the Cat himself and P. D. Eastman. Beginner Bks. 1964 133p illus $4.95, lib. bdg. $5.99 (k-3)   423
1 English language—Dictionaries
ISBN 0-394-81009-0; 0-394-91009-5   LC 64-11457
Also available in a French language edition, LC 65-22650 (ISBN 0-394-81063-5) for $7.95 and a Spanish language edition, LC 66-8588 (ISBN 0-394-81542-4; 0-394-91542-9) for $8.95, lib. bdg. $8.99
"A dictionary written only as the Cat Himself can, it is an illustrated explanation of the meanings of words. Simple sentences and pictures explain word meanings. Interest level is not restricted to the primary grade readers." Wynar. Guide to Ref Bks for Sch Media Centers

Children's dictionary. Houghton 1979 xxxii, 816p illus $10.95 (3-6) **423**

1 English language—Dictionaries
ISBN 0-395-27512-1   LC 78-27636

"The entries include phonetic pronunciation, part of speech, other forms of the word (plural forms of nouns, tenses of verbs), definitions, and —usually—examples. All forms of the entry word are in boldface; examples are printed in italics. A pronunciation key is repeated at the bottom of each verso column. Derivations are not included; variant meanings and explanations of idiomatic use are. . . . [Includes] over 30,000 entries." Chicago. Children's Bk Center

"Both practical and attractive, this competently put together dictionary comprises a very well-written introductory section on the English language and its development, and a guide to the dictionary which even the youngest and slowest will be able to negotiate with no problem. Many entries are illustrated with either monochrome photographs or colored drawings." Sch Library J

Macmillan Dictionary for children. [Rev. ed.] William D. Halsey, editorial director; Christopher G. Morris, editor. Macmillan Pub. Co. 1977 724p illus $10.95 **423**

1 English language—Dictionaries
ISBN 0-02-578750-0   LC 77-152717

First published 1975. Text edition, with a different introduction, has title: Macmillan Beginning dictionary

This dictionary "designed for the primary and elementary grades, contains about 30,000 American entries which include derived and compound forms. Arrangement is alphabetic, letter by letter. There are geographical entries for the states of the U.S., for continents, and for major countries of the world. There are no biographical entries, no foreign words or phrases, and no slang terms. . . . The publisher states that this 'is the first dictionary to list entries without breaking for syllables, allowing a child to find words printed the same way they appear in other books.' . . . Different meanings of the word are numbered in order, with the first meaning the most important or most frequently used. . . . Contractions, prefixes, and suffixes are entered. No synonyms or antonyms are provided. Homonyms are provided. Homonyms are indicated in the following manner: 'leak.' . . . Another word that sounds like this is leek.' . . . There are about 260 brief language notes or word stories. These are marked by a small blue triangle and are printed between two heavy blue lines. The months and states have such a word history. Each letter of the alphabet has an illustrated note about its evolution." Ref & Subscription Bks Rev

The **Magic** world of words; a very first dictionary; William D. Halsey, editorial director; Christopher G. Morris, editor. Macmillan Pub. Co. 1977 256p illus $8.95 (1-3) **423**

1 English language—Dictionaries
ISBN 0-02-578770-5   LC 77-9188

"Clear, concise definitions (1500 of them) printed in large type comprise this dictionary. The entries—chosen from a computerized survey of the words young children most frequently encounter' —are explained in a conversational manner with references to friends, school, and familiar activities; all of the words defined are used in sentences. It's too bad there aren't more illustrations, but there is a game (after each letter, several items are pictured with page numbers and students are asked to find the definitions in the text) and an easy-to-follow 'how to' section in the front. A good addition to the classroom library or for the beginning reader section of the public library." Sch Library J

For a fuller review see: Booklist, February 15, 1979

The **Merriam**-Webster Dictionary for large print users. Hall, G.K.&Co. [1977 c1975] 1119p lib. bdg. $27.50 **423**

1 English language—Dictionaries
ISBN 0-8161-6459-2   LC 77-1497

"A Merriam-Webster"

"This dictionary, which has been approved by the Production Review Committee of the National Association of Visually Handicapped, contains more than 57,000 entries and several additional sections such as a list of foreign words and phrases, a table of signs and symbols, etc. The typography: 18-point type guide words, 14-point type word entries, and 12-point type definitions; supplementary sections are in 16-point type." Library J

"For the visually handicapped who want basic information and brief definitions, this dictionary will be quite adequate. However, for . . . [those] who expect derivations, full definitions and more comprehensive scope, the only way to go is still a good magnifying device used with other dictionaries. The publisher is to be complimented on the format; clear black print with no fuzziness, superb leading, nonglare and high-opacity paper." Cur Ref Bks

The **Random** House School dictionary; Stuart Berg Flexner, editor-in-chief; Eugene F. Shewmaker, managing editor. Random House illus maps $7.98 (4 and up) **423**

1 English language—Dictionaries
ISBN 0-394-00044-7   LC 77-29053

First published 1970 with title: The Random House Dictionary of the English language, school edition. Frequently reprinted with minor corrections

"Based on the unabridged and college editions of the 'Random House Dictionary of the English Language,' the School Edition also uses word frequency lists to determine its entries. It contains a single alphabetical sequence of more than 47,500 entries, including biographical and geographical entries, abbreviations, and contractions. Entries include the pronunciation, part of speech, definitions, and examples used in sentences and phrases. Meanings of words appear in order of frequency with the most common meaning first. A lengthy section called the 'Student's Guide to the Dictionary' and the 'Explanatory Notes for a Specimen Page' will be beneficial to the user. The 15 pages of maps by Rand McNally and the tables of weights and measures further extend the usefulness of this dictionary. Designed for fourth to eighth grade students, it should definitely have a space on the school reference shelf." Peterson. Ref Bks for Elem and Jr High Sch Libraries [review of 1973 edition]

Schiller, Andrew

In other words; a beginning thesaurus [by] Andrew Schiller [and] William A. Jenkins. Rev. ed. Lothrop [1978 c1977] 240p illus $8.50, lib. bdg. $8.16 (3-5) **423**

1 English language—Synonyms and antonyms
ISBN 0-688-41847-3; 0-688-51847-8   LC 77-90370

Companion volume to the authors': Junior thesaurus, entered below

First published 1969 under the authorship of W. Cabell Greet, William A. Jenkins, and Andrew Schiller

"The authors have culled the 100 words most frequently used by grade school students (including what they aptly call 'tired words,' such as awful, cute, nice, etc.), and provided over 1000 synonyms for them. . . . There are a dozen pages explaining how to look up words, how to use cross references, etc. Examples for each entry word are provided, and synonyms are elucidated by full sentences that are always crystal clear yet never trite. Multiple examples are given to illustrate various nuances of meaning and idioms are by no means neglected. Each attractively laid out page is embellished by one or more full color pictures: some are photographs (mostly good), some original drawings, generally mildly humourous and unobtrusive." Sch Library J

Junior thesaurus; In other words II [by] Andrew Schiller [and] William A. Jenkins. Rev. ed. Lothrop [1978 c1977] 448p illus lib. bdg. $9.36 (5 and up) **423**

1 English language—Synonyms and antonyms
ISBN 0-688-51827-3   LC 77-84159

First published 1970 under the authorship of W. Cabell Greet, William A. Jenkins and Andrew Schiller. Companion volume to the authors': In other words, entered above

"Illustrated in full color, this thesaurus gives 2,000 synonyms for 300 over-used words and idioms. Examples are given in sentence context. Antonyms are also included

Schulz, Charles M.
The Charlie Brown dictionary; based on The rainbow dictionary by Wendell W. Wright assisted by Helene Laird. Random House 1973 399p illus $8.95, lib. bdg. $8.99 (k-3)   **423**

1 English language—Dictionaries
ISBN 0-394-83041-5; 0-394-93041-X   LC 72-12135

"Illustrated with cartoons of Charlie Brown, Snoopy, Lucy, et al., this picture dictionary will be chosen by primary students for the popular drawings alone. They will, however, be getting a bargain, for this dictionary is a new one based on the 'Rainbow Dictionary' [entered below under Wendell Wright]. Both the illustrations and definitions are new, but in general the vocabulary is that of the earlier book. Additions and deletions were made to reflect changes in the language that children speak, read, and hear, especially on television. Altogether, this book contains 2,400 entries, consisting of both main entries and related forms, and has over 580 pictures in full color." Peterson. Ref Bks for Elem and Jr High Sch Libraries. 2d edition

Scott, Foresman Beginning dictionary, by E. L. Thorndike [and] Clarence L. Barnhart. Doubleday illus $12.95 (3-5)   **423**

1 English language—Dictionaries
Also available in a text edition from Scott, Foresman for $9.93

First published 1945 by Scott, Foresman with title: Thorndike Century Beginning dictionary, based on the Thorndike Century Junior dictionary, first published 1935 by Appleton-Century. 1952-1972 editions have title: Thorndike-Barnhart Beginning dictionary. First published with this title 1976. Frequently revised

"Each citation in this basic dictionary includes pronunciation, syllabication, definition, examples of the word used in sentences, and parts of speech (etymologies for most of the words are not included). An extensive introduction gives tips on reading a citation, alphabetizing, finding plurals as well as using guide words and the pronunciation key which is placed at the top right of each page. The print is widely spaced and there are many effective illustrations with the size of pictured animals given in both standard and metric measure." Sch Library J [review of 1976 edition]

Scott, Foresman Intermediate dictionary, by E. L. Thorndike [and] Clarence L. Barnhart. Doubleday illus $12.95 (5 and up)   **423**

1 English language—Dictionaries
Also available in a text edition from Scott, Foresman for $9.99

First published 1971 by Scott, Foresman with title: Thorndike-Barnhart Intermediate dictionary. Based on the Thorndike-Barnhart Junior dictionary (first published 1952 and based, in turn, on the Thorndike Century Junior dictionary, first published 1935 by Appleton-Century) and on the Thorndike-Barnhart Advanced Junior dictionary (first published 1957). Frequently revised

Designed especially for the junior high school student. The introductory material explains how to use the different kinds of information included in each entry

6,000 words; a supplement to Webster's Third New International dictionary. Merriam 1976 20, 220p $8.50   **423**

1 English language—Dictionaries 2 Words, New —Dictionaries
ISBN 0-87779-007-8   LC 75-45066

"A Merriam-Webster"
This "is essentially the most recent Addenda section of Webster's Third New International Dictionary [entered below]. The Addenda section serves two purposes: to record as many as space will permit of the new words and meanings that have become established since Webster's Third was edited and to enter those older words that for various reasons had been passed over in the earlier editing." Preface

Webster's Intermediate dictionary; a new school dictionary. Merriam 1977 24, 910p illus $7.50 (5 and up)   **423**

1 English language—Dictionaries
ISBN 0-87779-279-8   LC 76-39925

"A Merriam-Webster"
First published 1972

This dictionary "is aimed at the young teenager. It has some 57,000 entries. . . . In pronunciation, syllabication, and format this dictionary has the excellence associated with the Merriam-Webster name. An excellent 'Using your Dictionary' section is included. Checking reveals some very current words from various fields of interest to young people. . . . Some definitions seem quite technical, containing words that would have to be looked up themselves." Cur Ref Bks [review of 1972 edition]

"Although the dictionary carries a 1977 copyright date, no information is provided in the prefatory material concerning any changes that have been made since the previous (1972) copyright, and this printing can be considered a 'new edition' only in a minimal sense." Am Ref Bks Annual, 1979

Includes "supplementary material on presidents, states, nations, and signs and symbols." Wynar. Guide to Ref Bks for Sch Media Centers [review of 1972 edition]

Webster's New Elementary dictionary. Merriam 1975 16a, 612p illus $5.95 (4 and up)   **423**

1 English language—Dictionaries
ISBN 0-87779-275-5   LC 75-312223

A successor to Webster's Elementary dictionary, which was first published in 1956

This volume contains over 32,000 entries, directions for using the dictionary, and tables of special information

Webster's New Students dictionary. Merriam illus $7.95 (5 and up)   **423**

1 English language—Dictionaries
"A Merriam-Webster"
First published 1964 with title: Webster's Students dictionary. Periodically revised

Designed to meet the needs of advanced elementary, junior and senior high school students and teachers, this dictionary contains over 81,000 vocabulary sections. Special sections are included on abbreviations, signs, and symbols. Over 600 synonym paragraphs are included to explain the differences in meaning between related words. More than 15,000 etymologies and 534 illustrations complete the volume

"This dictionary is easy to use, clear, and readable. Its excellent format, numerous etymologies and vocabulary entries, and employment of usage examples are of great value." Booklist

Webster's New World dictionary for young readers; David G. Guralnik, editor-in-chief. New rev. ed. Collins [distributed by Simon & Schuster] 1979 48, 880p illus $9.95 (4 and up)   **423**

1 English language—Dictionaries
ISBN 0-671-41821-1   LC 79-110224

First published 1961 with title: Webster's New World dictionary; elementary edition

This dictionary contains over 46,000 entries set in large type and over 19,000 illustrations including 30 pages in full color. Other features include: color tinted word histories, synonym paragraphs, biographical entries, usage notes, idiomatic phrases and full color reference sections which include how to use the dictionary, firsts in space and metric conversion tables among others

Webster's Third New International dictionary of the English language; unabridged. Merriam illus   **423**

1 English language—Dictionaries
"A Merriam-Webster"
Prices vary according to binding

First published 1828 by S. Converse as: An American dictionary of the English language, by Noah Webster. Also appeared with titles: Webster's Unabridged dictionary, Webster's International dictionary of the English language, and Webster's New International dictionary of the English language. This edition first published 1961. Frequently reprinted with additions and changes to keep it up to date

Editor in chief: 1961- Philip Babcock Gove and the Merriam Webster editorial staff

This work "is evidently intended as a dictionary for our times, for its more than 450,000 entries

Webster's Third New International dictionary of the English language—*Continued*

include 100,000 newly added terms and exclude words obsolete before 1755. Its more than 200,000 quotat̶i̶o̶ns illustrate contemporary usage, drawing on many modern writers. Instead of encyclopedic treatment at one place of a group of related terms, each term is defined at its own place in the alphabet with an analytical one-phrase definition. . . . Gone are the biographical and geographical sections, the key to pronunciation at the bottom of each page, while only 3,000 new illustrations replace the 12,000 found in the earlier edition. . . . Thus the dictionary must stand on its true dictionary features—as a source of etymology, pronunciation, syllabication and definition." Cur Ref Bks

"Much is included, often without qualification, which may be regarded by many as colloquial, vulgar, or incorrect. . . . Regardless of varying opinions of editorial judgment, this edition will be essential in most American libraries, though the 2d edition will be wisely retained as well." Sheehy. Guide to Ref Bks. 9th edition

For a fuller review see: The Booklist and Subscription Books Bulletin, July 1, 1963

The **World** Book dictionary; ed. by Clarence L. Barnhart [and] Robert K. Barnhart; prepared in cooperation with World Book-Childcraft International, Inc. World Book-Childcraft Int. 2v illus $74   **423**

1 English language—Dictionaries

"A Thorndike-Barnhart dictionary"

First published 1963 with title: The World book encyclopedia dictionary. Revised annually

"This dictionary was prepared for use with 'The World Book Encyclopedia' [entered in class 031] and for this reason biographical and geographical entries are omitted. In place of such encyclopedic material, the dictionary concentrates on providing word meanings, usage notes, and word history. Supplementary sections cover vocabulary development and use, language rules and references, and a guide to use of the dictionary. . . . The 200,000 entries include idioms, new words and foreign words in general use. Each entry in bold face is followed by the pronunciation (an adaptation of the International Phonetic Alphabet); parts of speech with separate definitions; definitions of various meanings, arranged by frequency; homographs; restrictive labels (e.g., obsolete); inflections; variant spellings; usage notes; illustrative sentences; word origins; synonyms and antonyms. About 2,000 small black and white illustrations placed within the text area are clear. . . . The entries are well prepared, concise, and easy to locate and read. . . . [The supplementary sections contain over 100 pages and] are more simply written than similar ones in other general dictionaries." Wynar. Guide to Ref Bks for Sch Media Centers [review of the 1973 edition]

For a fuller review see: The Booklist and Subscription Books Bulletin Reviews, September 1, 1963

Wright, Wendell W.

The rainbow dictionary, by Wendell W. Wright; assisted by Helene Laird; illus. by Joseph Low. Newly rev. ed. Collins [distributed by Simon & Schuster] 1978 463p illus $8.95 (1-4)   **423**

1 English language—Dictionaries
ISBN 0-671-41842-4   LC 77-89609

Title on spine: The rainbow dictionary for young readers

First published 1947. The 1978 edition has been revised and updated by the editorial staff of Webster's New World dictionary, second college edition

A dictionary in picture book format which "contains 2300 entries consisting of 2000 main entries and related forms, which children use in speaking and recognize when reading. The words chosen are those that occur most frequently in a consolidation of eight word lists for [young] children." An explanation

"The big pages are not overcrowded, the type is large and well spaced, and best of all, each page has a number of small pictures in color o give force to the definitions." Horn Bk

438   Standard German usage

Cooper, Lee

Fun with German; illus. by Elizabeth M. Githens. Little 1965 119p illus lib. bdg. $6.95 (4 and up)   **438**

1 German language
ISBN 0-316-15588-8   LC 65-18362

"Using a circus motif [the author] begins with [German] phrases and sentence sequences to introduce vowel and consonant sounds and a few essentials of grammar, and then presents stories, games, songs, and ideas and activities for a German club. Includes a guide to pronunciation symbols and a German-English vocabulary." Booklist

An "introduction to the German language. . . . The phonetic symbols are excellent, especially for those sounds which do not have exact English equivalents." Sch Library J

443   French language— Dictionaries

Fonteneau, M.

Mon premier Larousse en couleurs [par] M. Fonteneau et S. Theureau. Larousse illus $25.25   **443**

1 French language—Dictionaries
First published 1953. Frequently revised

"Nearly 4,000 words are defined in this French dictionary. Pictures and words are effectively used to aid the student in understanding meanings. The dictionary is not bilingual but is written entirely in French with no English equivalents. Designed for children aged 5 to 8, it includes conjugations of verbs, and sentences for definitions and plurals." Peterson. Ref Bks for Elem and Jr High Sch Libraries. 2nd edition

448   Standard French usage

Brunhoff, Laurent de

Babar's French lessons; Les lecons de Français de Babar. Random House 1963 14 [i.e.28]p illus $5.95 (1-3)   **448**

1 Bilingual books—French-English
ISBN 0-394-80587-9   LC 63-18288

"This is not a new adventure of Babar but a word and phrase book in French and English in which Babar teaches fourteen French lessons to the reader. It is conversational French about such subjects as a birthday party, fun at the seaside, a morning shower bath. Probably a very useful and acceptable addition to the French collection, but must be confined to that. It would be a disappointment to the child if mistaken for a new Babar." Toronto

Cooper, Lee

Fun with French, by Lee Cooper and Clifton McIntosh; illus. by Ann Atene. Little 1963 120p illus $5.95, lib. bdg. $6.95 (4 and up)   **448**

1 French language
ISBN 0-316-15607-8   LC 62-12374

An elementary text which makes use of pictures, stories, songs, and phrases to introduce French words

"Humorous drawings on almost every page. Pronunciation key provides excellent approximations of French sounds." Library J

Le dictionnaire: p100-20

Joslin, Sesyle

There is a dragon in my bed; il y a un dragon dans mon lit; and other useful phrases in French and English for young ladies and gentlemen going abroad or staying at home; illus. by Irene Haas. Harcourt 1961 unp illus $4.95 (3-6)   **448**

1 Bilingual books—French-English
ISBN 0-15-285146-1   LC 61-6118

Joslin, Sesyle—*Continued*

"Contains simple English phrases, and their French equivalents, with a line giving the phonetic pronunciation and each keyed to a picture, taking children on an imaginary trip from America to France." Spring'f'd Republican

"The book is delightfully humorous; adults will enjoy reading it aloud and small children will enjoy having it read aloud. The humor is in the choice of situation and phrase and in the zany illustrations of nonsensical situations." Chicago. Children's Bk Center

468 Standard Spanish usage

Cooper, Lee

Fun with Spanish; illus. by Ann Atene. Little 1960 118p illus lib. bdg. $6.95 (4 and up)   **468**

1 Spanish language
ISBN 0-316-15589-6   LC 59-7341

Pronunciation is Mexican rather than Castilian in this elementary text which makes use of pictures, stories, games and phrases to introduce over 500 Spanish words

"Any child who can read English can gallop through it and at the end find himself reading and speaking simple Spanish with comparative ease." Horn Bk

More Fun with Spanish; illus. by Ann Atene. Little 1967 120p illus lib. bdg. $6.95 (4 and up)   **468**

1 Spanish language
ISBN 0-316-15616-7   LC 67-17287

A second volume to supplement the author's Fun with Spanish, listed above. This one "is only slightly more difficult than the first. It contains 11 entertaining stories each of which introduces a new point of grammar, but without the reader's awareness until the end of the story when the grammar point is summarized for emphasis. The text is entirely in Spanish, the only English appearing in the pronunciation guide and 24-page vocabulary. Copiously illustrated with lively two-color drawings." Booklist
El diccionario: p99-117

Joslin, Sesyle

There is a bull on my balcony; hay un toro en mi balcón; and other useful phrases in Spanish and English for young ladies and gentlemen abroad or staying at home; illus. by Katharina Barry. Harcourt 1966 unp illus $5.95 (2-5)   **468**

1 Bilingual books—Spanish-English
ISBN 0-15-285057-0   LC 66-11202

"In a series of zany episodes, two boy-travelers in Mexico introduce Spanish phrases and their English counterparts." Minnesota

495.1 Chinese language

Wolff, Diane

Chinese writing; an introduction. Calligraphy by Jeanette Chien; photographs: collection of C. C. Wang. Holt 1975 46p illus lib. bdg. $5.95 (5 and up)   **495.1**

1 Chinese language 2 Calligraphy
ISBN 0-03-013006-9   LC 74-20579

"The book introduces material about the different styles of calligraphy, the way it reflects the heart and mind of the scribe, and the materials used; it also includes instructions for practicing the art of Chinese writing." Horn Bk

"The direction in which each stroke should be made—an important aspect of calligraphy—is discussed elsewhere in the book, but, unfortunately, there are no directional arrows on the practice pages. Still, this only slightly diminishes the value of a well-executed and unusual offering." Sch Library J

Other sources: p46. Bibliography: p46

500 PURE SCIENCES. NATURAL HISTORY

Allison, Linda

The reasons for seasons; the great cosmic megagalactic trip without moving from your chair. Little 1975 121p illus $8.95, pa $5.95 (5 and up)   **500**

1 Seasons 2 Nature study 3 Handicraft
ISBN 0-316-03439-8; 0-316-03440-1   LC 75-5930

"The Brown paper school series"

"Loosely categorized into sections on the four seasons, this appealing book is chockfull of projects, recipes, ideas, experiments, scientific and historical information, and fun. There are explanations of the origins of Groundhog Day and the nature of a virus, directions for making a Christmas tree for birds, and a timetable telling when shooting stars (Meteor swarms) will be most visible. The reader will learn how to make a worm farm, a crystal garden, spore prints, and much more. Enthusiasm for doing things and learning about the cycles and life processes around us is communicated on every page. Droll line drawings add to the general good humor of the text." Appraisal

The wild inside; Sierra Club's guide to the great indoors; written and illus. by Linda Allison. Sierra Club Bks/Scribner 1979 144p illus $9.95, pa $5.95 (5 and up)   **500**

1 Science 2 Science—Experiments
ISBN 0-684-16108-7; 0-684-16119-2   LC 79-937

"A Yolly Bolly Press book"

"A compendium of miscellaneous information about the complex science laboratories that lurk within modern dwelling houses. One section of the book deals with animals and insects—pests as well as pets—and the parasites thereof, along with such biological phenomena as molds and fungi, bacteria and other 'microlife,' and the ramifications of plant growth and indoor gardens. 'House Happenings' considers all sorts of things from fuel and fire to oxidation and humidity and introduces some fascinating facts about the interior waterways of sewage and plumbing. 'Indoor Geology' discusses the scores of minerals found in everyday domestic use: talcum powder, scouring cleansers, concrete, plaster, and table salt—to name but a few." Horn Bk

"This is a crowded, busy book exploring science inside the house. It is a jumble of things: activities, experiments, information, questions, all crowded together into four very general sections. Written in the second person, this encourages children to experiment and investigate different things inside their houses in order to learn different scientific and ecological facts. Its tone is humorous, and it is illustrated with funny sketches." Appraisal

Beer, Kathleen Costello

What happens in the spring. Natl. Geographic Soc. 1977 32p illus (k-3)   **500**

1 Spring 2 Nature study
ISBN 0-87044-242-2   LC 77-76970

Obtainable only as part of a set for $9.95 with: The blue whale, by Donna K. Grosvenor, class 599.5; Creatures of the night, by Judith E. Rinard, class 591.5; and Let's go to the moon, by Janis Knudsen Wheat, class 629.45

"Books for young explorers"

Prepared by the Special Publications Division of the National Geographic Society

This book describes the changes in plants and animals in the spring

Brown, Marcia

Listen to a shape; text and photographs by Marcia Brown. Watts, F. 1979 unp illus $4.95, lib. bdg. $7.90 (1-4)   **500**

1 Size and shape 2 Nature study
ISBN 0-531-02383-4; 0-531-02930-1   LC 78-31616

"Marcia Brown Concept library"

"Brown imaginatively trains her camera on everyday nature scenes. . . . Each image takes on new dimension as the suggestions for careful appraisal result in greater awareness of the environment and oneself." Booklist

Brown, Marcia—*Continued*

Touch will tell; text and photographs by Marcia Brown. Watts, F. 1979 unp illus $4.95, lib. bdg. $7.90 (1-3)   **500**

1 Touch   2 Nature study
ISBN 0-531-02384-2 0-531-02931-X   LC 78-27260
"Marcia Brown Concept library"
Text and color photographs suggest ways in which the sense of touch may help people experience the world around them
"Children sharing these with adults, especially in preparation for a nature walk, will best realize the full potential of this uplifting visual experience." Booklist

Walk with your eyes; text and photographs by Marcia Brown. Watts, F. 1979 unp illus $4.95, lib. bdg. $7.90 (1-4)   **500**

1 Nature study   2 Perception
ISBN 0-531-02385-0; 0-531-02925-5   LC 78-27688
"Marcia Brown Concept library"
"'Walk with your eyes' encourages visual perception and looking beyond the obvious to really 'see' the world around." Children's Bk Rev Serv

Clement, Roland C.

Hammond Nature atlas of America. . . . Hammond 1973 255p illus maps $19.95, pa $8.95   **500**

1 Natural history—U.S.
ISBN 0-8437-3513-9; 0-8437-3512-0   LC 73-7524
"A Ridge Press book"
This title supersedes: Hammond's Nature atlas of America, by E. L. Jordan
"Reptiles & amphibians, insects, birds, wildflowers, trees, rocks & minerals, fishes, mammals." Title page
"This book is essentially a color photo sampler covering geologic, botanical, and zoological features of America; clearly written description (about 150 words each) accompany each pictured example. The claim to the title 'atlas' lies in the range maps, which show regional distributions for a sampling of animals, plants, minerals, weather conditions, and physiographic features." Library J
"The illustrations are colorful, accurate, and graphic. Particularly noteworthy are the special maps. . . . Written in clear, succinct language readily understood by the student or layman [this work] is an excellent introduction to the ecology of the United States." Booklist
Glossary: p249. Suggested reading: p251
For a fuller review see: Reference and Subscription Books Reviews, February 1, 1974

Grillone, Lisa

Small worlds close up [by] Lisa Grillone & Joseph Gennaro. Crown 1978 unp illus $7.95 (5 and up)   **500**

1 Science—Pictorial works   2 Electron microscopy and microscopy   3 Photomicrography
ISBN 0-517-53289-1   LC 77-15860
"A wide variety of everyday materials (e.g., salt crystals, chalk, cork, newspaper, moth wings, skin, etc.) seen in intricate and surprising detail through the telling eye of an electron microscope. Each item is presented in very clear black-and-white photographs accompanied by a paragraph describing characteristics and special properties. Magnifying strengths vary from 60x to 6000x and are cited for each picture. The objects are grouped by animal, vegetable, and mineral." Sch Library J
"Young readers with a strong sense of wonder are sure to respond instantly to Grillone and Gennaro. Their book, graced with an eye-catching cover in black and gold, is a triumph of photographic techniques. . . . [The authors], both professional biologists and teachers, present interesting information in a text remarkable for clarity and style." Pub W

Selsam, Millicent E.

Land of the giant tortoise; the story of the Galápagos; illus. with photographs by Les Line. Four Winds 1977 55p illus map lib. bdg. $7.95 (3-5)   **500**

1 Natural history—Galápagos Islands   2 Galápagos Islands
ISBN 0-590-07416-4   LC 77-4897
"The author describes the early discovery of these unique islands and explains to beginning students of evolution how and why certain types of animals and birds may be found here and nowhere else in the world. How the islands were formed, how the natural inhabitants came to thrive, what Charles Darwin found on his famous voyage, and why some species were almost exterminated are discussed in relation to their present state." Appraisal
"Finches that have different kinds of beaks, tortoises that vary from island to island, and the near absence of mammals figure into the scientific and clearly stated discussion. Recent ecological preservation measures are touched on briefly. Strikingly clear black-and-white and full-color photographs (plus a line drawn map) enhance the discerning text. A top-notch example of natural history for younger readers." Booklist

Wilkins, Marne

The long ago lake; a child's book of nature lore and crafts; illus. by Martha Weston. Sierra Club Bks./Scribner 1978 160p illus map lib. bdg. $8.95, pa $5.95 (5 and up)   **500**

1 Natural history—Wisconsin   2 Country life—Wisconsin   3 Handicraft
ISBN 0-684-15614-8; 0-684-15613-X   LC 77-18173
"Wilkins combines recollections of her northern Wisconsin childhood summers in the 1930s with tidbits of nature lore and particulars about crafts that she and her family enjoyed. Individual chapters bring to life events such as May Day festivities, country fairs, canoeing excursions, song fests and storytelling by campfire, along with frightening experiences with a forest fire, a runaway horse, and an iceboat. Craft instructions, many emanating from Chippewa Indian neighbors, include such diverse areas as making rope swings, shell jewelry, bird houses, tassel dolls, pine needle baskets, signaling devices, sun dials, lichen dyes, casts of animal tracks, and simple looms." Booklist
"The mixture of practical and philosophical wisdom is expressed in spontaneous and readable prose. . . . A deep respect for the knowledge and skills learned during a life spent close to nature underlies the text. Black-and-white illustrations match the spirit and exuberance of the writing." Horn Bk
More books to read: p157-58

500.5   Space sciences

Couper, Heather

Space frontiers. Viking 1978 61p illus lib. bdg. $5.95 (3 and up)   **500.5**

1 Outer space—Exploration   2 Space sciences
ISBN 0-670-65954-1   LC 78-6180
Authors: Heather Couper and Nigel Henbest; editor: Christopher Cooper
This book "begins with a 'moon colony' and ends with 'starships' for generation travel. . . . The rest of the book is . . . [concerned] with encapsulations of past and present space missions, astronomy, space hardware and space-program accomplishments." Appraisal
This oversize book conveys "a wealth of fascinating information, mainly by means of very large and extremely clear, colored drawings. . . . The explanations are mainly oversimplified, superficial, and almost worthless as teaching materials for students of meager background. But the readers will be as hypnotized by the 'life-size' pictures as I was. A worthwhile addition to any library." Children's Bk Rev Serv

502.8   Scientific apparatus and equipment

Selsam, Millicent

Greg's microscope; pictures by Arnold Lobel. Harper 1963 64p illus (A Science I can read bk) lib. bdg. $6.89 (1-3)   **502.8**

1 Microscope and microscopy
ISBN 0-06-025296-0   LC 63-8002

"The acquisition of a microscope entices Greg into looking at anything tiny, so he prepares his own slides of salt and sugar, water and flour, and bits of many other household things. Eventu-

Selsam, Millicent—*Continued*
ally he isolates some amoebae from his fish tank, but finds himself third in the microscope line—Mother and Dad are in front." NY Times Bk Rev
"There is a lively, here-and-now quality to [the] conversations and to the drawings." Horn Bk

503 Science—Encyclopedias and dictionaries

Asimov, Isaac
More Words of science; decorations by William Barss. Houghton 1972 267p $6.95 (6 and up)   **503**
1 Science—Terminology 2 English language—Etymology
ISBN 0-395-13722-5   LC 79-187422
Companion volume to: Words of science and the history behind them, entered below
The author combines scientific information with etymology as he explains the meaning and historical background of 250 scientific terms
"Asimov's clear and lively prose is informative and enjoyable even when the terms are known to the reader." Chicago. Children's Bk Center

Words of science and the history behind them; illus. by William Barss. Houghton 1959 266p illus $10.95 (6 and up)   **503**
1 Science—Terminology 2 English language—Etymology
ISBN 0-395-06571-2   LC 59-5198
A book "both for the reader interested in science and the reader interested in language and words. Two hundred and fifty words [arranged alphabetically] are given one-page explanations, but each word is used as a starting point for giving the histories and derivations of other words related by concept or etymology. The choice of words is, of necessity, rather arbitrary, but the selection is well-balanced and comprehensive; the author has defined his field broadly. . . . Format is attractive, and [there is an] excellent index." Chicago. Children's Bk Center

The **New** Book of popular science. Grolier illus maps apply to publisher for price   **503**
1 Science—Encyclopedias 2 Natural history—Encyclopedias 3 Technology—Encyclopedias
First published 1924 with title: The Book of popular science. Changed to present title 1978. Revised annually
The 1979 edition consisted of six volumes covering the following areas: Astronomy & space sciences; Computers & mathematics; Earth sciences; Energy; Environmental sciences; Physical sciences; Plant life; Animal life; Mammals; Human sciences; Technology

505 Science—Serial publications

Owl. The Young Naturalist Foundation $6 per year   **505**
1 Natural history—Periodicals
ISSN 0382-6627
Ten issues a year. First published 1976
"There are few Canadian magazines for children, and even if there were, this one would stand near the top. The whole thing is full of information on the world around us. There are news, jokes and riddles, articles on how to do just about any outdoor activity, from gardening and kite making to mushroom identification, puzzles, games, and things to make. There is even a pull-out animal poster. Most photographs are in color and done in a professional manner that will delight any child, and a lot of adults too! A must for any school or public library." Katz. Magazines for Libraries

Ranger Rick's Nature magazine. National Wildlife Federation $8 per year (2-6)   **505**
1 Natural history—Periodicals
ISSN 0033-9229   LC 73-12298

Monthly. First published 1967
Color illustrations, including photographs, accompany articles, stories, riddles, games, crossword puzzles, projects, and reviews of books concerning nature
"The writing is informative and lively. . . . Ranger Rick, the raccoon, supplies helpful information at the end of some articles and is quick to mention ways to help protect endangered species. . . . Some stories and illustrations by children are printed. The color photographs, especially the close-ups, are the magnificent feature of this magazine. . . . This is one of the few periodicals meriting inclusion in any collection serving children." Richardson. Periodicals for Sch Media Programs

Science year; the World book science annual. A review of science and technology during the [preceding] school year. Field Enterprises illus apply to publisher for price   **505**
1 Science—Yearbooks 2 Technology—Yearbooks
    LC 65-21776
Annual. First published 1965
The first section of this volume contains over a dozen signed "special reports" about recent scientific and technological developments. The second section, Science file, presents over 40 signed, briefer articles in alphabetical order which survey fields from agriculture and anthropology to transportation and zoology. An annotated bibliography is included. The section entitled Men and women of science offers descriptions of the work of two scientists, lists and descriptions of major science awards, and a necrology. There is also a 3 year cumulative index
For a fuller review see: Reference and subscription Books Reviews, June 1, 1975

507 Science—Study and teaching

Cobb, Vicki
More Science experiments you can eat; illus. by Giulio Maestro. Lippincott 1979 126p illus $7.95, pa $3.95 (5 and up)   **507**
1 Science—Experiments 2 Food
ISBN 0-397-31828-6; 0-397-31853-7   LC 78-12732
"In Cobb's former book, 'Science Experiments You Can Eat' [entered below] emphasis was on using food to understand basic scientific principles; here the author changes focus, using the principles to learn about food. Experiments designed to investigate spoilage, dehydration, ripening, acidity, freezing, extraction, and flavor potentiation are presented in an easy-to-follow format; there is an introduction to each subject followed by sections on materials and equipment, procedures, observations, and further study. Readers can find out what makes bananas get ripe, how textures of home and commercially frozen zucchini differ, which foods contain vitamin C, what the effect of adding acid is to whipped dessert topping, and if the taste of Coke and other colas is different or recognizable. Although not a cookbook, this provides worthwhile laboratory projects for home economics classes and science units, along with opportunities for individual fun or family sharing in the kitchen." Booklist
"Some readers may be disturbed by Cobb's attitude toward food additives and her firm reliance on the FDA and their GRAS (Generally Regarded As Safe) list. However, she states her position, and this could provide a springboard for discussions, especially if the book is used in the classroom." Sch Library J

Science experiments you can eat; illus. by Peter Lippman. Lippincott 1972 127p illus $7.89, pa $4.95 (5 and up)   **507**
1 Science—Experiments 2 Cookery 3 Food
ISBN 0-397-31487-6; 0-397-31179-6   LC 71-151474
"Few cooks think of themselves as chemists, but Vicki Cobb is one who did. The result is an excellent 'lab manual' of experiments utilizing readily available materials and frequently seen processes. Ms. Cobb demonstrates physical states such as solution, suspension and emulsion by giving recipes for popsicles, borscht and strawberry bombe, while discussing the Tyndall effect and suppression of freezing point by solute. She also presents chemistry experiments (in recipe form) to demonstrate such processes as protein denaturation (sour milk biscuits) and coagulation (custard), and the

Cobb, Vicki—*Continued*

sol-gel transformation (jello). There's also a section on biology, using such experiments as striped celery (by osmotic pressure, color changes in spinach chlorophyll (use of buffered boiling solutions), and measuring moisture content of seeds (diameter of popped corn). And best of all, when the experiments are finished, the young scientist can eat them! ((There are a few exceptions, but Ms. Cobb is careful to use clear warnings of safety. All in all, the book is a delightful combination of learning by doing, and of relating common activities to basic scientific principles." Sci Bks

Cooper, Elizabeth K.

Science in your own back yard; with illus. by the author. Harcourt 1970 192p illus $6.95, pa $1.35 (5 and up)   507

1 Nature study
ISBN 0-15-270664-X; 0-15-679596-5   LC 76-19412

A reissue of the title first published 1958

A "stimulating out-of-doors book opening up all sorts of nature activities, practicable even on a 50-foot lot. Beginning with soil and rock, it continues with chapters on grass, water, flowers, plant forms, earthworms and insects, birds, clouds, weather, stars, and outer space. Pen-and-ink sketches by the author [with an index included.]" Library J

Milgrom, Harry

Adventures with a cardboard tube; illus. by Tom Funk. Dutton 1972 31p illus (First science experiments) $7.95 (k-2)   507

1 Science—Experiments
ISBN 0-525-25150-2   LC 71-179045

This book "spells out simple activities designed to reveal the properties and possibilities of a cardboard tube. Besides being a cylinder, it rolls in a straight line, acts like a spring, bounces, and can act as a weight-mover, light-blocker, sound-collector, and sound-maker." Appraisal

The author's "technique of asking and answering questions would be particularly effective if the book were used with supervision; the child could attempt to answer the questions himself before seeing Milgrom's answers. The most elaborate activity described is the construction of a balance scale which is ingenious and leads to other scientific activity. A summary at the end of the book lists the surprisingly numerous ideas presented." Sci Bks

Adventures with a straw; illus. by Leonard Kessler. Dutton 1967 32p illus (First science experiments) $7.95 (k-2)   507

1 Science—Experiments
ISBN 0-525-25229-0   LC 67-14133

"This is a greatly needed participation book which leads a child to observe, reason, and discover. A straw is used to show simple science concepts, such as that light travels in a straight line, that air takes up space, that a vibrating column of air can produce a sound, and that air has pressure. The clear text is expanded in clever, informative illustrations, and there is a concluding summary in words and pictures of the concepts offered." Library J

Egg-ventures; first science experiments; illus. by Giulio Maestro. Dutton 1974 31p illus $6.95 (1-3)   507

1 Eggs 2 Science—Experiments
ISBN 0-525-29160-1   LC 74-5231

"Using simple kitchen utensils, young readers are shown how to conduct simple scientific experiments with eggs. Differences in size, color, weight, and content are discussed as well as the different parts of eggs and how chicks hatch. Milgrom also explains how to tell rotten eggs from fresh ones; how eggs are graded; and how to decorate shells. Maestro's friendly tiger family who demonstrate the projects add humor to this lively presentation which concludes with an excellent summary of the material." Sch Library J

Moorman, Thomas

How to make your science project scientific. Atheneum Pubs. 1974 94p illus lib. bdg. $9.95, pa $1.95 (5 and up)   507

1 Science—Experiments 2 Science—Methodology
ISBN 0-689-30436-6; 0-689-70452-6   LC 74-75568

This book describes the scientific method of experimentation, including its use in simple experiments, controlled experiments, case study, blind and double-blind experiments, naturalistic observation and survey methods. There is a discussion of statistics, record keeping and reporting to others

"This is an easily read book that treats a topic about which there is much talk but not much real effort on the part of many students. . . . There are line drawings and charts which illustrate the examples developed in the text." Sci Teacher

Glossary: p80-88. Bibliography: p91-92

Renner, Al G.

Experimental fun with the yo-yo, and other science projects; written and illus. by Al G. Renner. Dodd 1979 128p illus lib. bdg. $5.95 (3-6)   507

1 Science—Experiments
ISBN 0-396-07657-2   LC 78-23569

"The principles, techniques, and tools of scientific method are introduced in the context of six projects built around the yo-yo, wind wagon, sailboat, inverted tumbler, Cartesian diver, and hang glider. Readers are encouraged to test a wide variety of suggested and do-it-yourself hypotheses, always adhering to fundamentally sound scientific process. Unfortunately, some of the projects require prior understanding, an adult guide, and/or unusual ability to interpret spare directions. If one can work around that, the amateurish illustrations probably won't be too bothersome." Booklist

Bibliography: p127

How to build a better mousetrap car—and other experimental science fun; written and illus. by Al G. Renner. Dodd 1977 128p illus lib. bdg. $5.95 (4-6)   507

1 Science—Experiments 2 Models and model making
ISBN 0-396-07419-7   LC 76-48912

"This creative compendium leads students through intriguing experiments such as building a 'car' out of mousetrap parts, a fire with fire bows, a better frisbee, etc. In each case, the basic problem is defined, materials listed, a method described, and elaborations suggested." Sch Library J

"The author emphasizes throughout how the experimenter can learn much about the scientific method through the building and testing of the models. Modifications in the models cause changes in their performance and lead the experimenter to verify hypotheses and develop scientific laws. Renner notes which of the projects are the easiest and the most difficult. Easily available and inexpensive objects (milk cartons, metal coat hangers) are suggested for use in the construction of the models. For more inquisitive readers wishing further information, encyclopedia articles are referenced. Books for further study are also listed." AAAS Sci Bks & Films

Schneider, Herman

Science fun for you in a minute or two; quick science experiments you can do, by Herman and Nina Schneider; pictures by Leonard Kessler. McGraw 1975 64p illus lib. bdg. $6.95 (2-4)   507

1 Science—Experiments 2 Scientific recreations
ISBN 0-07-055432-3   LC 75-20175

How nice to have a book of experiments and home demonstrations that are simple to do, require little equipment, and take only a few minutes. The authors have grouped their suggestions; things to make, things to do at bath time, quick tricks, etc. Some of the projects are explained, some are open-ended, and they demonstrate physical phenomena without getting too technical. An index 'for adults only' gives labels to the principles, phenomena, or devices covered, including fluid friction, equal expansion, Bernoulli's Law, surface tension, electrolytic action, and differential vision." Chicago. Children's Bk Center

"Reference to additional sources is encouraged by the inclusion of a special index which provides the scientific term for each phenomenon. . . . Often an additional experiment is suggested at the end of each activity. Elementary science teachers will also find these experiments useful." AAAS Sci Bks & Films

Simon, Seymour

Exploring fields and lots; easy science projects; pictures by Arabelle Wheatley. Garrard 1978 63p illus lib. bdg. $4.74 (3-5)
507

1 Nature study 2 Biology—Experiments
ISBN 0-8116-6108-3   LC 77-4477

"Simplicity is the essence of Simon's beginner's list of scientific projects geared for the backyard or nearby lots or fields. He counsels careful note-taking no matter what the enterprise; those he suggests aim to sensitize readers to the complexity of their surroundings without much ado: for example, taking the temperature at various eleva-tions—close to ground, higher up, in shade or out, can point to subtle habitat-influencing differences. . . . Some activities are familiar; e.g., to find out the effects of sunlight on plants, grow one in sun, one in shade sit very quietly and observe the animal life (including insects) that goes on around you. There are easily recognizable line drawings of common weeds and insects for several identifi-cation projects. The text is widely spaced; cartoon drawings with green accents provide illustration. A useful, easy-to-follow introduction to environ-mental science." Booklist

Science in a vacant lot; illus. by Kiyo Komoda. Viking 1970 64p illus lib. bdg. $4.95 (2-5)
507

1 Nature study
ISBN 0-670-62163-3   LC 78-102924

Given here are "many ideas for natural science projects in urban vacant lots. Several of the ideas could be adapted to the suburban backyard also. Subjects explored are rocks and soil, insects, plants, birds, and other animals, and the questions raised are open ended. That observations can be made at a site being bulldozed is one interesting suggestion for a science study. The reproductions of pencil sketches that illustrate the book are pleasant and helpful. Some children will be stimu-lated to begin scientific observation by this book, most will use it best if there is teacher or par-ental encouragement. It should be useful for class projects in the middle grades." Sci Bks
Books for reading and research: p61-62

Webster, David

How to do a science project; illus. with photographs and drawings. Watts, F. 1974 61p illus lib. bdg. $6.45 (4 and up)
507

1 Science—Experiments
ISBN 0-531-00817-7   LC 73-12214

"A First book"
The author "outlines the three major types of projects that could be selected—reports, demon-strations and research, gives suggestions for each category and then proceeds to carefully and sequentially outline how to go about carrying out the project. The print of the book is especially clear and uncrowded. Each chapter heading is prominent and the sub-headings in these chapters are also obvious. The illustrations are excellent and varied, ranging from photographs, to cartoons to graphs and charts. All give the child help in planning, doing and presenting his own project. There is a large bibliography at the end which would be of great help when a particular project has been chosen." Sci Bks

More brain-boosters; with photographs by the author. Doubleday 1975 127p illus lib. bdg. $5.95 (4 and up)
507

1 Science—Experiments 2 Scientific recreations
ISBN 0-385-02497-5   LC 73-78092

Companion volume to the author's: Brain boost-ers, o.p. 1980
A "collection of science brain teasers. The scope of the activities includes the various sciences, and the experiments and puzzles are adaptable to a wide . . . range of interests and talents. . . . [The author] includes puzzles about structures (bridges, buildings and such) which relate to the physical laws, many experiments with air and water, 'mystery' photographs of shadows and other unusual patterns, kitchen chemistry and electricity experiments and some number puzzles. The illustrations are clever and the indicated solutions are very well done." AAAS Sci Bks & Films

White, Laurence B.

Investigating science with coins, by Laurence B. White, Jr. Addison-Wesley 1969 95p illus lib. bdg. $5.95 (4 and up)
507

1 Science—Experiments
ISBN 0-201-08654-9   LC 69-15796

"An Addisonian Press book"
"A considerable number of investigations are described which produce interesting phenomena using coins and a few common household items. The effects are directly related to such ideas as surface tension, sensory perception, chemical reac-tions of metals, energy, momentum, friction, re-fraction, and several mathematical concepts. The explanations are generally adequate (some of the chemistry is questionable), but are sometimes too quickly offered and too final. Some good-natured chicanery adds to the fun without detracting from the science. Illustrations are effective." Sci Bks

Investigating science with nails, by Laurence B. White, Jr. Addison-Wesley 1970 108p illus lib. bdg. $5.95 (4 and up)
507

1 Science—Experiments 2 Nails and spikes
ISBN 0-201-08651-4   LC 74-124880

"In this book young scientists are using nails in a number of experiments ranging from heat transfer to magnetism to magic. The text is clearly written with great pedagogical insight, and the illustrations cannot be misunderstood." The AAAS Sci Bk List for Children

Investigating science with rubber bands, by Laurence B. White, Jr. Addison-Wesley 1969 95p illus lib. bdg. $5.95 (4 and up)
507

1 Science—Experiments
ISBN 0-201-08656-5   LC 72-80505

"In a clear, unpretentious style, simple experi-ences are set up to illustrate surface tension, chemical bonds, Hooke's Law, sound, molecular models, physiology and the production of 'rubber' from milkweed or dandelions. The experiences 'invite themselves' to be performed, and the simple diagrams illustrate the materials needed and what is to be done." Sci Bks

Science puzzles [by] Laurence B. White, Jr. Drawings by Marc Tolon Brown. Addison-Wesley 1975 unp illus lib. bdg. $5.95 (k-3)
507

1 Science—Experiments
ISBN 0-201-08602-6   LC 74-2155

"An Addisonian Press book"
Simple science puzzles and experiments include experiments with mirrors, footprints, ice cubes, soup cans and water
This book has "obvious appeal with easily mastered techniques, brief, simple, large-type in-structions, and attractive, cartoonish, black-and-white drawings against colored backgrounds." Booklist

Wyler, Rose

Prove it! By Rose Wyler and Gerald Ames; pictures by Tālivaldis Stubis. Harper 1963 64p illus lib. bdg. $6.89 (1-3)
507

1 Science—Experiments
ISBN 0-06-020051-0   LC 62-21288

"A Science I can read book"
Simple experiments performed with ordinary objects
"Beginners will have no difficulty in reading and following the instructions—and certainly they will be pleased with the illustrations, which are not only clear but original in concept and in use of color." Horn Bk

507.05   Science—Study and teaching—Periodicals

The Science Teacher. Natl. Science Teacher's Assn. $28 per year
507.05

1 Science—Study and teaching—Periodicals
ISSN 0036-8555

Monthly September through May. First published 1934
"Includes articles which relate to the teaching of science, administration and supervision of science programs, and science teacher education." Camp. Guide to Periodicals in Educ

510.28 Mathematics—Techniques, apparatus, equipment, materials

Bitter, Gary G.

Exploring with pocket calculators [by] Gary G. Bitter and Thomas H. Metos; and Jeffrey T. Metos. Messner 1977 64p illus lib. bdg. $6.64 (3-6)   **510.28**

1 Calculating machines
ISBN 0-671-32822-0   LC 77-351

"This book offers a very clear explanation of the mechanics of calculators for young mathematicians. The first half of the text is devoted to how past computing devices worked from the ancient abacus to 19th century mechanical monsters. The latter half deals with how to operate the typical simple calculators of today that are small enough to fit in one's hand. Throughout the book the authors give directions for many easy problems to solve and their answers. Illustrated with photographs and line drawings and indexed." Appraisal

"This book is adequate for presenting a few elementary facts about the development and use of pocket calculators. It does not have enough depth to be of value for reference or classroom use for the frequent user of a pocket calculator." AAAS Sci Bks

Madison, Arnold

Pocket calculators: how to use and enjoy them [by] Arnold Madison and David L. Drotar. Elsevier/Nelson Bks. 1978 144p illus $6.95 (5 and up)   **510.28**

1 Calculating machines
ISBN 0-525-66580-0   LC 78-707

First published by Thomas Nelson

"The authors attend first to the practical—identifying five general machine types (four-function, memory, slide rule, scientific, and business), explaining functions and features for prospective purchasers, simplifying calculator mechanics, describing the instrument's use as a classroom aid in figuring circumferences, percentages, square roots, metric equivalents, etc., and suggesting uses outside a school situation. Later sections offer a selection of puzzles, tricks, and competitive games to test calculator agility. Manufacturers listing and bibliography of books and periodical articles appended." Booklist

511 Mathematics—Generalities

Bendick, Jeanne

Names, sets and numbers; written and illus. by Jeanne Bendick. Watts, F. 1971 65p illus (Science experiences) lib. bdg. $5.90, pa $1.25 (2-5)   **511**

1 Set theory 2 Mathematics
ISBN 0-531-01436-3   LC 73-137151

"In an informal, simply written explanation, Bendick explores the importance of names and numbers and then introduces some basic concepts of set theory, including empty sets and subsets. Exercises which utilize the concepts presented or stimulate further thinking are interspersed throughout the text: answers are given in the back of the book. Illustrated with lively, occasionally humorous drawings." Booklist

Lowenstein, Dyno

Graphs; written and illus. by Dyno Lowenstein. Rev. ed. Watts, F. 1976 65p illus lib. bdg. $5.90 (5 and up)   **511**

1 Graphic methods 2 Statistics—Graphic methods
ISBN 0-531-00679-4   LC 76-29347

"A First book"
First published 1969

"This introduction to graphs is well organized and has a superior format, making it useful for a wide age range. Construction details, use, limitations, and adequate examples are given for the line, pie, bar graph, and pictograph. A short history of graphs is included as well as a discussion of their usefulness in making statistics comprehensible. The composite bar graph and sliding bar graph are also explained; a percentage protractor which can be constructed by readers is included for the pie graph, and sets of figures for pictographs can be reproduced. Perhaps most interesting of all is the chapter on how statistics and graphs can lie which makes use of data and graphs shown throughout the book." Sch Library J

512 Algebra

Sitomer, Mindel

Zero is not nothing, by Mindel and Harry Sitomer; illus. by Richard Cuffari. Crowell 1978 34p illus lib. bdg. $6.89 (2-4)   **512**

1 Zero (The number)
ISBN 0-690-03829-1   LC 77-11562

This "is a math concept book in which the Sitomer team skillfully presents and defends the idea that zero is definitely 'something.' Zero as a starting point, as a separation point, as a break-even point, and as a place holder in a place value system are explained by association with activities familiar to children. The history of the symbol for zero is also discussed. The break-even concept seems not to be relevant for the age group intended, but the clear explanation of zero as a place holder is a big plus and the pen-and-ink drawings help to reinforce the main ideas." Sch Library J

Weiss, Malcolm E.

666 jellybeans! All that? An introduction to algebra; illus. by Judith Hoffman Corwin. Crowell 1976 33p illus (Young math bks) lib. bdg. $5.95 (3-5)   **512**

1 Algebra
ISBN 0-690-00914-3   LC 75-9528

"Weiss utilizes sound technique in introducing the most fundamental tenets of algebra; the symbol as an unknown number and the equation. Starting with a concrete example (and adding punch by formulating it in terms of a trick to try on one's friends), the author eases the transition from numbers to written letter symbols with explanations along the way. A careful breaking down of simple equations demonstrates their principles. Clean, three-color illustrations are helpful and reflect the light but reasoned tone of the text." Booklist

513 Arithmetic

Adler, David A.

Roman numerals; illus. by Byron Barton. Crowell 1977 33p illus (Young math bks) lib. bdg. $6.89 (2-4)   **513**

1 Arithmetic
ISBN 0-690-01302-7   LC 77-2270

"Adler provides exercises on how to write Roman numerals and handle the subscription principle involved in writing the symbols representing four and nine. He also explains the historical origins of the symbols for five and ten plus the uses and development of Roman numerals—information difficult to obtain for this age level." Sch Library J

"A simple demonstration with labeled cards clearly explains how the symbols are ordered; another practice lesson tests readers' comprehension of when to use subtraction symbols. . . . A jaunty cartoon figure acts out textual descriptions against an orange-and-brown backdrop. It's light, lucid, good-humored lesson." Booklist

Adler, Irving

Integers: positive and negative; illus. by Laurie Jo Lambie. Day 1972 47p illus lib. bdg. $6.89 (4 and up)   **513**

1 Arithmetic 2 Number theory
ISBN 0-381-99988-2   LC 78-162589

"The Reason why books"

This book explains the meaning and uses of integers, describing how numbers may be positive or negative by comparing them with rewards and penalties. It shows how to add and substract

Adler, Irving—*Continued*

integers using checkers, arrows, and a number line. Directions for making a slide rule and a simple adding machine are also given

"The author must be complimented for his skillful treatment of this basic topic, and the publishers for producing a sturdy and attractive little book." Sci Bks

Charosh, Mannis

Number ideas through pictures; illus. by Giulio Maestro. Crowell 1974 33p illus (Young math bks) $3.95, lib. bdg. $6.89 (2-4)   513

1 Arithmetic   2 Number theory
ISBN 0-690-00156-8   LC 73-4370

Using pictures of familiar things, this book presents information on several number concepts. "Even-odd number states are defined and explored briefly; square numbers are constructed, based on consecutive adding of odd numbers; and triangular numbers are made by the consecutive addition of even and odd numbers. Various relationships of arithmetic squares and triangles are discussed and diagrammed." Booklist

"This book is a lovely introduction at an elementary level to some important concepts in number theory. . . . The text reads nicely and is handsomely complemented by good illustrations. All in all, a very nice job and a fine addition to the elementary school literature in good mathematics." Sci Bks

Dennis, J. Richard

Fractions are parts of things; illus. by Donald Crews. Crowell 1971 33p illus (Young math bks) $6.95, lib. bdg. $6.89, pa $1.45 (2-4)   513

1 Arithmetic
ISBN 0-690-31520-1; 0-690-31521-X; 0-600-31522-8
                                       LC 73-127603

The author "makes clear by the clever use of colored mathematical shapes the relationships that are one-half, one-third, two-thirds, one-fourth, and three-fourths. The text contains questions, suggests activities, and invites discussion and group learning." Sci Bks

Froman, Robert

The greatest guessing game; a book about dividing; illus. by Gioia Fiammenghi. Crowell 1978 33p illus (Young math bks) lib. bdg. $7.79 (2-4)   513

1 Arithmetic
ISBN 0-690-01376-0   LC 77-5463

"A therapeutic book for children with deep-seated fear of division. Froman points out that division answers can be guessed at and, if the guess is wrong, can always be adjusted as many times as necessary. No arithmetic notation at all is used." Sch Library J

"Several examples are given to show that there are different ways of solving real-life problems: if you can't divide books exactly among members of a group, the remaining books can be the start of a library; five people having two cents left over when paid for doing a job could use the two cents to buy candy and divide it, etc. The text does not attempt to teach division of numbers but to arouse interest and lay the groundwork for working with numbers. The illustrations are perky and humorous line drawings." Chicago. Children's Bk Center

Linn, Charles F.

Estimation; illus. by Don Madden. Crowell 1970 34p illus (Young math bks) lib. bdg. $6.89 (2-4)   513

1 Arithmetic
ISBN 0-690-27028-3   LC 75-106574

"By a series of open-ended experiments the young reader is taught to check his estimates of dimensions, quantity, distance and number. Questions are asked that emphasize importance and practical uses of estimates in human activity. Some of the questions may require help from the teacher or parent in analyzing them." The AAAS Sci Bk List for Children

O'Brien, Thomas C.

Odds and evens; illus. by Allan Eitzen. Crowell 1971 33p illus (Young math bks) $4.50, lib. bdg. $5.25, pa $1.45 (2-4)   513

1 Arithmetic   2 Number theory
ISBN 0-690-00207-6   LC 79-106575

"Instead of defining odd and even numbers and discussing their properties, [the author] encourages the reader to discover for himself the differences betwen the two typs of numbers and some of the characteristics through the examples, questions, and experiments that are presented in the book." Booklist

"The book will perhaps be more fun if an older person shares it with a child, or a group of children. The reading is a little difficult for nursery school and kindergarten youngsters yet they can comprehend the illustrations and participate in the exercises." Sci Bks

St John, Glory

How to count like a Martian. Walck, H.Z. 1975 66p illus $7.95 (4-6)   513

1 Number theory   2 Counting
ISBN 0-8098-3125-2   LC 74-19714

This short text "develops central number concepts (base, place, zero, symbols). The unifying thread is the need to decipher a message, containing four distinct symbols, being received from Mars (it is never deciphered, unfortunately). The investigation proceeds historically, looking for precedent in terrestrial cultures. Systems discussed are those used by Egyptians, Babylonians, Mayans, Greeks, Chinese, Hindus, an abacus and a computer." AAAS Sci Bks & Films

"This book demonstrates that it is certainly possible to write an abstract mathematical treatise which is fun for nonmathematicians to read. It is an eye-catching book from the point of view of design. From the reader's viewpoint, the fact that everything printed in red turns out to be some kind of number becomes apparent rather slowly and contributes to the development of what is, in a sense, a mystery story." Horn Bk

Sitomer, Mindel

How did numbers begin? [By] Mindel and Harry Sitomer; illus. by Richard Cuffari. Crowell 1976 33p illus (Young math bks) lib. bdg. $6.89 (1-3)   513

1 Number theory
ISBN 0-690-00794-9   LC 75-11756

The authors "take us back to a time in history when there were no names for numbers and no real numbers either. Then, reconstructing by informed conjecture, the authors describe the first use of counting symbols that formed the basis of words. Numbers such as two, five, ten, and others really do have a history, as we learn. Ordering of numbers and the way we count by matching a number to the object being counted are also shown to be key elements in the story." Booklist

"An excellent introduction. . . . Richard Cuffari's line drawings are well executed and designed to add color and continuity. An especially useful title because little else is available on the subject for this age level." Sch Library J

Srivastava, Jane Jonas

Number families; illus. by Lois Ehlert. Crowell 1979 40p illus lib. bdg. $6.89 (2-4)   513

1 Number theory
ISBN 0-690-03924-7   LC 78-19511

"Picture-book format is used to explain, through simple text and collage-style illustrations, how numbers work in groups. After comparing them to human families, the author develops the idea of number families by discussing the concepts of even, odd, times, prime, square, and triangle. Multiple examples and questions are asked to involve young mathematicians in the process." Booklist

"The illustrations are good—ink blot raccoons, rabbits, and deer cavort across the pages in colors of blue, gray, and black. Some ideas will be above students' heads but this can serve as a first exposure." Sch Library J

Watson, Clyde
Binary numbers; illus. by Wendy Watson. Crowell 1977 33p illus (Young math bks) lib. bdg. $6.89 (2-4)   513

1 Binary system (Mathematics)
ISBN 0-690-00993-3   LC 75-29161

The author explains "what the binary number system is and how it can be used. Initially, string and measured cardboard lengths help readers see for themselves the relationships within the binary sequence. Then charts are constructed (to be completed by readers), and finally Watson shows the 'on-off,' 'one-zero' form of expression which duplicates basic computer language." Booklist
"This stands as one of the simplest descriptions of the binary system yet published for beginners, and the text is nicely integrated with the helpful illustrations." Chicago. Children's Bk Center

513.028   Arithmetic—Techniques, apparatus, equipment, materials

Dilson, Jesse
The abacus: a pocket computer; drawings by Angela Pozzi. St Martins 1968 143p illus $6.95, pa $2.95 (5 and up)   513.028

1 Abacus
ISBN 0-312-00105-3; 0-312-00140-1   LC 68-17463

"A practical introduction to the use of the abacus, along with an anecdotal history of the device is provided in this entertaining book. There are ample clear diagrams, including a chapter showing the young reader how to build his own abacus with beads, wire, and a cigar box. One of the more interesting sections explains how one can do binary calculations on an abacus using the same number systems employed in modern computers. There is a good amount of simple mathematics in this little book." Sci Bks

514   Topology

Froman, Robert
Rubber bands, baseballs and doughnuts; a book about topology; illus. by Harvey Weiss. Crowell 1972 33p illus (Young math bks) $6.95, lib. bdg. $6.89 (2-4)   514

1 Topology
ISBN 0-690-71353-3; 0-690-71354-1   LC 74-158690

"A clear introduction to topology for primary school children. Simple experiments reveal the concepts of distortion and invariance, and the genus concept. . . . Although the topic of topology is peripheral to most elementary curriculums, this would provide enjoyable recreational reading for young math buffs." Sch Library J
This book "reaps all the advantages that come from being the first to explain an extremely complex subject to a layman. In some cases—and this is one—no amount of erudite exposition can beat a little playing around with rubber bands, balloons, and a teacup or two. . . . Froman manages to convey with intelligence some basic principles of topology." Bk World

Holt, Michael
Maps, tracks, and the bridges of Königsberg; a book about networks; pictures by Wendy Watson. Crowell 1975 33p illus (Young math bks) $6.95, lib. bdg. $6.89 (3-5)   514

1 Topology
ISBN 0-690-00746-9; 0-690-00753-1   LC 74-31176

"An attractive concept book which introduces several problems of topology. Seemingly complicated problems of linking cities or crossing each of the bridges of Königsberg only once before returning home are simplified by connecting points to form networks. Rules of topology are introduced to help solve the problems and explain traceable networks. Watson's orange-and-green illustrations are lively and well adapted to the text, as are the many diagrams." Sch Library J

516   Geometry

Charosh, Mannis
The ellipse; illus. by Leonard Kessler. Crowell 1971 33p illus (Young math bks) lib. bdg. $7.89 (2-4)   516

1 Geometry
ISBN 0-690-25857-7   LC 73-132293

The author describes the ellipse and, through a series of experiments to be performed by the young reader, explains its relationship to straight lines and to other curves—hyperbolas, parabolas, and circles
The book "is delightful. The illustrations are amusing; the faces within the curves, the animals formed only by the use of the ellipse, and the diagrams all deserve special commendation." Sci Bks

Straight lines, parallel lines, perpendicular lines; illus. by Enrico Arno. Crowell 1970 33p illus (Young math bks) $7.95, lib. bdg. $7.89, pa $1.45 (2-4)   516

1 Geometry
ISBN 0-690-77992-5; 0-690-77993-3; 0-690-77994-1
     LC 76-106569

"Using string, a checker set and board, pencil, and paper, the reader can follow suggestions for investigating straight, parallel, and perpendicular lines. The text, brisk and straight-forward, also points out some of the familiar objects that illustrate these phenomena: the edge of the table, the corner of a rug, the opposite sides of a blackboard. The illustrations, like the print, are large and clear, with good correlation between pictures and text." Chicago. Children's Bk Center

Diggins, Julia E.
String, straightedge, and shadow; the story of geometry; illus. by Corydon Bell. Viking 1965 160p illus maps $7.95 (6 and up)   516

1 Geometry—History
ISBN 0-670-67858-9   LC 64-13597

The author "relates how early scientists used only three simple tools—the string, the straightedge, and the shadow—to discover the basic principles of geometry, and tells how these discoveries affected the civilizations of ancient Egypt, Greece, and Mesopotamia." Hodges. Bks for Elem Sch Libraries
"Some of the illustrations are informative, some merely decorative. The geometric principles and problems are presented as though their discoverers were explaining them." Chicago. Children's Bk Center
Suggestions for further reading: p156

Froman, Robert
Angles are easy as pie; illus. by Byron Barton. Crowell [1976 c1975] 33p illus (Young math bks) lib. bdg. $7.89 (2-4)   516

1 Geometry
ISBN 0-690-00916-X   LC 75-6608

"Angles are invitingly defined as delicious pieces of pie which are divided among Barton's hungry-looking and Hester-like alligators. Other everyday angles are pointed out and are used to build triangles, quadrangles, and various polygons. Instructions for cutting out angles and making figures are clearly incorporated into the text." Appraisal
"Froman works without numbers and degrees, so that expertise in these is not required of the reader. Colorful, uncomplicated illustrations put friendly reptilian creatures to work demonstrating the ideas and directions in the text." Booklist

Phillips, Jo
Exploring triangles; paper-folding geometry; illus. by Jim Rolling. Crowell 1975 34p illus (Young math bks) lib. bdg. $7.89 (2-4)   516

1 Geometry 2 Paper crafts
ISBN 0-690-00645-4   LC 74-14862

"This well-planned book introduces and explores triangles. Definitions of vertex, angle, ray, bisector, median, and center of gravity are clearly presented, with each definition accompanied by paper folding exercises. Using bisectors of the

Phillips, Jo—*Continued*

vertices and perpendicular bisectors of the sides, readers construct circles that fit inside and outside the triangles. Lastly, properties of the equilateral triangle are introduced. The illustrations and design by Jim Rolling in orange, red, green, and black are winning." Sch Library J

Russell, Solveig Paulson

Lines and shapes; a first look at geometry; illus. by Arnold Spilka. Walck, H.Z. 1965 31p illus lib. bdg. $5.95 (2-4)   516

1 Geometry 2 Size and shape
ISBN 0-8098-1112-X   LC 65-13224

"The author introduces the young reader to geometry by guiding him to examine his environment for lines and shapes. Simple, clear statements, such as 'When a line or a number of lines enclose space, a shape is made' lead the reader from one idea to related ideas in logical sequence. Some of the related concepts introduced . . . are: perpendicular, horizontal, vertical, parallel; right, acute and obtuse angles; triangle, rectangle, square, and other polygons; circle, oval, crescent, arc, semi-circle, sphere, cone, pyramid, and cube." Sch Library J

"Certainly this initial glimpse should prove useful—not to say exciting—to children . . . for they are shown how to observe line and shape in every area of the world around them. Arnold Spilka's line drawings are lively and helpful." America

Sitomer, Mindel

Circles, by Mindel and Harry Sitomer; illus. by George Giusti. Crowell 1971 33p illus (Young math bks) lib. bdg. $7.89, pa $1.45 (2-4)   516

1 Size and shape 2 Geometry
ISBN 0-690-19431-5; 0-690-00206-8   LC 71-113856

"Basic mathematical principles of circles are explored. . . . [The book] explains, by examples, the meaning of the terms circle, radius, diameter, and semicircle, gives a number of experiments to do and designs to make using a compass and ruler, and shows how squares, right angles, regular hexagons, and triangles can be formed from circles." Booklist

"Attractive drawings, simple and large-scale, illustrate clearly the ideas presented in a good introduction to the manipulative charms of the 'perfect' figure. . . . The text is straightforward and lucid, an admirable example of science writing." Chicago. Children's Bk Center

What is symmetry? By Mindel and Harry Sitomer; illus. by Ed Emberley. Crowell 1970 33p illus (Young math bks) pa $1.45 (2-4)   516

1 Geometry
ISBN 0-690-87618-1   LC 70-101933

"The authors present for young children an understandable explanation of the nature and occurence of line, point, and plane symmetry. The explicit, well-developed text is complemented by apt pictorial examples and enlivened with drawings of playful alligators demonstrating some important points. The book will be most effective when used with adult help." Booklist

Srivastava, Jane Jonas

Area; illus. by Shelley Freshman. Crowell 1974 33p illus. (Young math bks) $7.95, lib. bdg. $7.89 (2-4)   516

1 Measurement
ISBN 0-690-00404-4; 0-690-00405-2   LC 73-18057

The author "touches upon such diverse topics as units of measurement (both British and metric) and the measurement of surface areas, both planar and spherical. The book consists largely of brief statements followed by unanswered questions. . . . The author's use of the term 'standard unit of measurement,' while technically correct, is at variance with the conventional one with which the student may already be familiar. As enrichment material, especially in the classroom, the book does suggest some useful activities." Sci Bks

The "illustrations visualize the concepts explained in the text and are especially helpful in showing readers how to construct and use graph paper." Sch Library J

519.2 Probabilities

Linn, Charles F.

Probability; illus. by Wendy Watson. Crowell 1972 33p illus (Young math bks.) lib. bdg. $7.89 (2-4)   519.2

1 Probabilities
ISBN 0-690-65602-5   LC 79-171006

"An elementary introduction to the probability theory including several experiments for the reader to try." Minnesota

"A light, informal style and lucid explanations are used in conjunction with humorous pictures in cartoon-strip style. . . The materials are simple, the instructions for doing the experiments, keeping records, and drawing inferences are clear, and the text covers enough material to enable young readers to grasp basic principles but not so much that they may feel overwhelmed." Chicago. Children's Bk Center

519.5 Statistical mathematics

James, Elizabeth

What do you mean by "average"? Means, medians, and modes [by] Elizabeth James & Carol Barkin; illus. by Joel Schick. Lothrop 1978 60p illus $6.50, lib. bdg. $6.24 (4-6)   519.5

1 Mathematics
ISBN 0-688-41854-6; 0-688-51854-0   LC 78-7227

"In launching her campaign for Student Council, Jill, hoping to prove she is the most average person in school, plans some strategy sessions with her friends. This gimmick provides the take-off for James and Barkin's explanations of mean, median, mode, sampling, and percentages. Each concept is introduced as a hurdle to a successful campaign and then presented in clear mathematical terms. Additional information is given on how to take a survey and how to question slanted advertising campaigns. The fictionalization may be objectionable to some, but the brisk presentation does treat an otherwise dry subject in a clear, understandable manner, effectively eliminating any mystery. Cartoon drawings accompany the text." Booklist

Srivastava, Jane Jonas

Averages; illus. by Aliki. Crowell 1975 33p illus (Young math bks) $7.95, lib. bdg. $7.89 (2-4)   519.5

1 Mathematics
ISBN 0-690-00742-6; 0-690-00743-4   LC 75-5927

"The text is lucid and simply written, describing the differences in the terms 'median,' 'mode,' and 'mean,' explaining how each is deduced and how it is used. Aliki's pictures extend the text, and they are also amusing, often using cartoon-style balloon comments to add humor." Chicago. Children's Bk Center

Statistics; illus. by John J. Reiss. Crowell 1973 31p illus (Young math bks) lib. bdg. $7.89 (2-4)   519.5

1 Statistics
ISBN 0-690-77300-5   LC 72-7559

The author introduces the mathematical concepts of statistics and tells "how to assemble numerical facts, classify them into significant information, display findings, and interpret results in addition to drawing up and using various types of graphs." Booklist

"The uses as well as the dangers of statistics . . . are explained in the clear and simple text which is accompanied by John Reiss' amusing, colorful pen-and-ink drawings." Sch Library J

523 Descriptive astronomy

Berger, Melvin

Quasars, pulsars and black holes in space. Putnam 1977 57p illus lib. bdg. $5.29 (4 and up)   523

1 Astronomy
ISBN 0-399-61051-0
LC 76-50057

Berger, Melvin—Continued

"Berger's book leaves out technical explanations and opts for generalized definitions that use easily understandable analogies to clarify certain points or principles. The described capabilities of optical and radio telescopes suffice to give an idea of how scientists found out what they know about the universe; and there's an uncomplicated explanation of the spectroscope, which separates light into color and gives an idea of a star's chemical makeup. After that, an explanatory chapter is devoted to each title subject, including reportage on scientific processes of discovery and puzzles still to be researched. A glossary pins down technical terms." Booklist

Freeman, Mae

The sun, the moon, and the stars. Rev. ed. by Mae and Ira Freeman; illus. by René Martin. Random House 1979 59p illus $3.95, lib bdg. $4.99 (2-4)   523

1 Astronomy
ISBN 0-394-80110-5; 0-394-90110-X   LC 78-64604

First published 1959
"An introduction to astronomy for younger elementary students. Basic facts and concepts about the Earth, sun, moon, planets, stars, and deep space objects are covered. Easily understood analogies on space, time, and distance are included. Several experiments are included in the text that young readers can understand and perform. The astronomy facts are up-to-date with the exception of the number of Jupiter's and Saturn's natural satellites. The book would be an excellent supplement to elementary school reading." Sci and Children

Jobb, Jamie

The night sky book; an everyday guide to every night; illus. by Linda Bennett. Little 1977 127p illus $8.95, pa $5.95 (4 and up)   523

1 Astronomy
ISBN 0-316-46551-8; 0-316-46552-6   LC 77-24602

"A Brown paper school book"
This book "has directions on how to make dozens of things including a tin can planetarium, an anywhere stick sundial and a basketball earth. There's information about stars, planets, altitudes, 'quasars, pulsars and other oddballs.' Along with puzzles, history and myths, there are simple drawings and professional photographs from the Aeronautics and Space Administration." West Coast Rev of Bks
"This has the remarkable capacity to satisfy the youngest as well as older astronomy novitiates. Clear descriptive prose and line illustrations convey the functioning of the four-dimensional world of space and draw readers into observations and experiments." Sch Library J

McGowen, Tom

Album of astronomy; illus. by Rod Ruth. Rand McNally 1979 64p illus $6.95, lib. bdg. $6.97 (4-6)   523

1 Astronomy 2 Solar system
ISBN 0-528-82048-6; 0-528-80048-5   LC 79-9485

"This devotes 10 of its 14 short chapters to the solar system. The remaining four discuss the origin of the universe, types of stars, and what makes a constellation. This is designed to be fun first and an information source second. Each chapter explores one feature of its topic at some length, then mentions general information; each is illustrated with one full page, full-color painting and several marginal drawings." Sch Library J

Simon, Seymour

Look to the night sky; an introduction to star watching. Viking 1977 87p illus $6.95, Penguin Bks pa $2.95 (4 and up)   523

1 Astronomy
ISBN 0-670-43993-2; 0-14-049185-6   LC 77-24181

"An experienced stargazer gives practical advice to beginners of an enjoyable hobby. Various schemes are explained for finding constellations. Also discussed are the moon, planets, comets, meteorites, eclipses and other heavenly phenomena. In the appendix are sources of materials, an index, a simple bibliography and . . . a section on astrology." Children's Bk Rev Serv

"The text is simple, straightforward, and well organized. Small diagrams picture the constellations individually as well as in relation to each other at various times of the year." Booklist

Zim, Herbert S.

Stars; a guide to the constellations, sun, moon, planets, and other features of the heavens, by Herbert S. Zim and Robert H. Baker; illus. by James Gordon Irving; 150 paintings in color. [Rev. ed.] Golden Press 1956 160p illus maps (A Golden Nature guide) lib. bdg. $9.15, pa $1.95 (4 and up)   523

1 Astronomy 2 Stars—Atlases
ISBN 0-307-63507-4; 0-307-24493-8   LC 56-4594

First published 1951 by Simon & Schuster
"A gem of a field guide for the novice, this little book tells how to scan the heavens, where to look and when. Authoritative, carefully organized, here is a wealth of data for quick reference. Divided into three sections: stars, constellations, and solar system. Every page is beautifully illustrated. . . . Binding good for the size." Library J
Includes a bibliography

523.1   Universe

Knight, David C.

Galaxies, islands in space. Morrow 1979 94p illus $5.95, lib. bdg. $5.71 (5 and up)   523.1

1 Galaxies
ISBN 0-688-22180-7; 0-688-32180-1   LC 78-21625

"In this book galaxies are used as steppingstones through a history of modern astronomical discoveries to current theories about the origin and future of the universe. A great deal of new information is presented, especially the reasoning behind popularized theories of quasars and black holes (the author makes clear how much is still speculation). Various new means of observation such as spectroscopes and radio telescopes are discussed. . . . Knight's book will not only update the collection, but will broaden readers' understanding of astronomy." Sch Library J

Simon, Seymour

The long view into space. Crown 1979 unp illus $7.95 (4-6)   523.1

1 Universe 2 Solar system
ISBN 0-517-53659-5   LC 79-11388

"This is an illustrated tour of the solar system beginning with earth and gradually moving out into the universe. The moon, sun, planets, and stars are included as are comets, meteoroids, nebulae and galaxies
"Profusely illustrated with photographs of astronomical bodies and of phenomena peculiar to them, this lucid and serious text serves as a good introduction to the universe for middle grade readers." Chicago. Children's Bk Center

Smith, Norman F.

Space: what's out there? Illus. by Murray Tinkelman. Coward, McCann & Geoghegan 1976 30p illus lib. bdg. $5.59 (2-5)   523.1

1 Outer space
ISBN 0-698-30585-X   LC 76-4855

The author "explains both facts and suppositions about solar winds, meteors, comets, radiation belts, and gravity of planets. In his discussion of the last, he tells about Deimos, a moon of the planet Mars, and how easy it would be to jump its highest mountain. Speculation on intelligent life in space and what is being done to trace any possibilities of it concludes the text." Booklist
"This book is not about our solar system or the United States space program but, as the title suggests, about space and the things which are out there. . . . The handsome two-color crosshatched illustrations have a haunting quality and capture the stark and mysterious quality of space in just the right manner." Appraisal

523.1

Zim, Herbert S.
The universe. Newly rev. ed. Illus. with drawings by Gustav Schrotter and René Martin and photographs. Morrow 1973 63p illus maps lib. bdg. $6.48, pa $1.25 (4-6)
523.1

1 Universe 2 Astronomy
ISBN 0-688-31976-9; 0-688-25096-3   LC 72-14200
First published 1961
"Zim surveys man's conception of the nature and size of the universe from ancient times to the present. He clearly and accurately discusses such topics as galaxies, clusters, variable stars, and how vast distances are measured. . . . [Includes] material on radio telescopes . . . moon landings and interplanetary probes." Sch Library J

523.2 Solar system

Asimov, Isaac
The solar system; with illus. by David Cunningham and photographs. Follett 1975 32p illus (A Follett Beginning science bk) lib. bdg. $3.39 (3-5)
523.2

1 Solar system 2 Planets
ISBN 0-695-40473-3   LC 73-93548
In this book the author "relates postulated theories about the origin of the solar system and smoothly bridges enormous concepts from universe to galaxy to solar system. Gravity and its relationship to the orbits of planets, their satellites, asteroids, and comets are made clear and simple. Although individual planets are not covered extensively, the author provides an excellent overview of the subject. He does award detail to several specific phenomena such as eclipses and meteorites. Briefly explored are the possibilities of life within our solar system, with the conclusion that although some forms of life may exist on Mars, more exciting possibilities lie beyond our solar system on the planets of distant stars. Color photographs and charts both explain and amplify the text. Projects are listed, but not described in detail. However, combined with the text, they may encourage the interested to explore in greater depth the mysteries of space." Appraisal

Branley, Franklyn M.
Comets, meteoroids, and asteroids; mavericks of the solar system; illus. by Helmut K. Wimmer. Crowell 1974 115p illus (Exploring our universe) $8.95 (6 and up)
523.2

1 Solar system
ISBN 0-690-20176-1   LC 73-16043
A "book about the many other smaller bodies that move among our nine planets and their thirty-two satellites. This is the book for one who is looking for concise, accurate descriptions of meteorites, asteroids, tektites, comets, the zodiacal light, the solar wind, and cosmic rays." Best Sellers
"The author introduces these relatively well-known phenomena, surveys myths, theories, and studies, and offers knowledgeable arguments on some scientific issues. Excellent black-and-white drawings and photographs, useful charts, and careful instructions for observing and recording the presence of meteors complete this resource, which will supplement astronomy studies. Suggestions for further reading are appended." Booklist

523.3 Moon

Shuttlesworth, Dorothy E.
The moon; steppingstone to outer space [by] Dorothy E. Shuttlesworth and Lee Ann Williams. Doubleday 1977 117p illus $5.95, lib. bdg. $6.90 (5 and up)
523.3

1 Moon
ISBN 0-385-12118-0; 0-385-12119-9   LC 76-50787
The authors discuss theories of the moon's origin beginning with pre-scientific myths and superstition to modern theories. They move on to space programs and lunar explorations that have determined the physical makeup of the moon

A book of "fascinating facts and myths about this readily perceived orb in our night sky. The illustrations, mainly photographs, are pertinent to the text and enhance its readability." Babbling Bookworm
Glossary: p111-13

523.4 Planets

Asimov, Isaac
Jupiter; the largest planet; illus. with photographs. Rev. ed. Lothrop 1976 224p illus lib. bdg. $7.63 (6 and up)
523.4

1 Jupiter (Planet)
ISBN 0-688-51728-5   LC 75-30294
First published 1973
Asimov delves into every aspect of what is known about Jupiter, theories of the past, present knowledge, and conjectures about future probes and findings. The text is firmly organized and is written with a lucid informality. . . . Jupiter is compared to other planets in reference to whiteness, oblateness, speed of rotation, axial tilt, mass, density, orbital speed, etc. The same close scrutiny is applied to the planet's satellites, and all of the information is summarized in tables, fifty-four of them. There are discussions of the problems yet to be explored, descriptions of what is visible from Jupiter's surface and from its satellites, and theories of Jupiter's formation. A thorough treatment, a good introduction for the layman, and a demonstration of how exciting scientific inquiry can be." Chicago. Children's Bk Center
Glossary: p214-19

Branley, Franklyn M.
A book of Mars for you; illus. by Leonard Kessler. Crowell 1975 56p illus lib. bdg. $8.79 (2-4)
523.4

1 Mars (Planet)
ISBN 0-690-15296-5   LC 77-355663
First published 1968
The author discusses Mars and the ways that information gathered by Mariner IV has expanded our knowledge of this planet. He discusses "the canals," craters and composition of Mars, and the latest scientific ideas about the possibility of life on the planet

The nine planets. New rev. ed. Illus. by Helmut K. Wimmer. Crowell 1978 99p illus (Exploring our universe) $8.95, lib. bdg. $8.79 (6 and up)
523.4

1 Planets
ISBN 0-690-03848-8; 0-690-03849-6   LC 77-26604
First published 1958
"After a discussion of the planets as a group—their origins, treatment throughout history, and place in the universe—each planet is discussed separately in order of its distance from the sun. Physical characteristics are given, accompanied by anecdotes in the history of man's observation of the planets and his speculations. The inclusion (last chapter) of the proposed-but-unconfirmed planets is unusual: Vulcan, suspected to be closest to the sun, and #10, a huge planet supposed to be beyond Pluto. The text is clear, appropriately technical, and amply illustrated." Sch Library J
Further reading: p95

Knight, David C.
The tiny planets; asteroids of our solar system; with 21 photographs and diagrams. Morrow 1973 95p illus lib. bdg. $6.96 (4 and up)
523.4

1 Planets, Minor
ISBN 0-688-30072-3   LC 72-12946
"The author defines asteroids and then launches into a history of their discovery and naming, noting that after the excitement attending the first flurry of their discovery between 1890 and 1940, their novelty waned. The specifics of their physical nature and theories of origin are outlined, and a final chapter describes their usefulness to contemporary astronomical investigations." Booklist
"The subject is introduced in a stimulating manner and developed logically. Mr. Knight adheres totally to facts and is painstakingly careful to

Knight, David C.—Continued

explain new terms or concepts. His information is
scientifically accurate. He has produced a work
which will inform some members of his intended
audience. Others it will surely stimulate to further
study and will linger as a reference." Appraisal
Glossary: p88-91

Nourse, Alan E.

The asteroids. Watts, F. 1975 59p illus lib.
bdg. $6.45 (5 and up)   **523.4**

1 Planets, Minor
ISBN 0-531-00822-3   LC 74-12020

"A First book"
Nourse "describes how asteroids were discovered,
what is known about them, current theories of
their origin, and the hope that asteroids will
yield evidence about the origin of the solar system. . . . This is an accurate and readable introductory book on astronomy." Sch Library J
Additional reading: p55

The giant planets. Watts, F. 1974 62p illus
lib. bdg. $6.45 (5 and up)   **523.4**

1 Planets
ISBN 0-531-00816-9   LC 73-14515

"A First book"
"An imaginary space voyage to the giant planets
is described in this book which introduces one to
the vocabulary, such as planet, orbit and ellipse,
by citing examples of origin or explaining the
terms. In the descriptions of the various planets,
it is of particular interest that their atmospheres,
surface temperatures and cloud covers are compared with the more familiar domain of Earth. In
presenting various facts about the closer planets
to the Earth, time and speed comparisons are presented to illustrate possibilities of space travel. In
addition to the telescope, other means of gathering
information regarding the planets, such as the
radio-radar telescope and rockets, are explained."
Sci Bks
"This is a highly readable, five-chapter book for
the young astronomer. . . . Black and white
photographs enhance the text material." Sci
Teacher

523.7 Sun

Asimov, Isaac

What makes the sun shine? Illus. by Marc
Brown. Little 1971 57p illus lib. bdg. $5.95
(4-6)   **523.7**

1 Sun
ISBN 0-316-05462-3   LC 77-129905

"An Atlantic Monthly Press book"
"Simple experiments throughout the text on the
formation of the solar system complement the
step-by-step explanation of what the sun's energy
consists of, how it works, and what it does. The
glossary/index and the illustrations offer further
clarification." Appraisal
"The questions that this excellent book will raise
in the minds of young readers will tax even our
better teachers. The book puts the elementary
student on the brink of inquiry into cosmology,
quantum theory, and chemistry." Sci Bks
Index and glossary: p55-57

Branley, Franklyn M.

Eclipse; darkness in daytime; illus. by
Donald Crews. Crowell 1973 33p illus (Let's-
read-and-find-out science bk) lib. bdg. $7.89
(2-4)   **523.7**

1 Eclipses, Solar
ISBN 0-690-25414-8   LC 73-3492

The author "explains the phenomenon of the
total solar eclipse, defining terminology and explaining why it is possible for the moon to obscure
the larger sun. There's some discussion of the
effect of the eclipse on animals and on the people
of ancient times, and a home demonstration project that will enable the reader to see the image
of the eclipse in safety. Succinct, lucid, and
authoritative, the text is attractively illustrated."
Chicago. Children's Bk Center

Shapp, Martha

Let's find out about the sun, by Martha
and Charles Shapp; pictures by Stephanie
Later. Rev. full color ed. Watts, F. 1975 39p
illus lib. bdg. $6.45 (1-3)   **523.7**

1 Sun
ISBN 0-531-00104-0   LC 74-2996

First published 1965
This book tells the dependence of all living
things on the sun for light and warmth. The
earth's rotation on its axis about the sun and
the changing seasons are also explained through
text and pictures
"The authors avoid the trap of providing every
bit of information available. . . . Most of the
text is descriptive. . . . There isn't much attempt
at explaining, which, I believe, at this age is just
right. . . . The activities, though few in number,
are simple and fun to perform. The illustrations
are delightful." Appraisal

Zim, Herbert S.

The sun; illus. by Larry Kettelkamp and
photographs. Newly rev. ed. Morrow 1975 60p
illus map lib. bdg. $6.48 (3-5)   **523.7**

1 Sun
ISBN 0-688-32033-3   LC 74-34461

First published 1953
This "treatment of the sun for beginners covers
its size, distance from earth, temperature, and
structure; the nature and effects of the radiation; and its function." Sch Library J
"Although this book presumes some prior scientific knowledge on the part of the young reader,
it should offer no difficulty to the average student
curious enough to pick it up. The content is
accurate with numerous figures and photographs
to help out. In spite of the title, it branches out
to cover some topics of the whole solar system
and the rest of the universe. A few very simple
related experiments are described." Appraisal

523.8 Stars

Asimov, Isaac

How did we find out about black holes?
Illus. by David Wool. Walker & Co. 1978
64p illus (How did we find out) $6.95, lib.
bdg. $6.85 (5 and up)   **523.8**

1 Black holes (Astronomy) 2 Stars
ISBN 0-8027-6336-7; 0-8027-6337-5   LC 78-4320

"First describing the ways in which astronomers
observe and analyze aberrant behavior in stellar
bodies, [the author] explains the several ways
in which stars change as they age, and how—
having lost its ability to emit light—the dense,
collapsed star appears as a black hole in space."
Chicago. Children's Bk Center
"From white dwarfs to neutron stars to black
holes, Asimov clearly and simply discusses how
it was first found or conjectured to exist, what
it is, and how it fits into the scheme of the universe. Without being dogmatic about whether
their existence is proven or not, Asimov gives
the best explanation to date of where and why
astronomers are looking for black holes." Sch
Library J

Branley, Franklyn M.

The Big Dipper; illus. by Ed Emberley.
Crowell 1962 unp illus (Let's-read-and-find-
out science bks) lib. bdg. $7.89 (k-2)   **523.8**

1 Stars
ISBN 0-690-01116-4   LC 62-10999

"This book for the youngest skywatchers gives
directions for locating the Big Dipper and the
Little Dipper, explains how they show direction,
and relates facts and legends concerning the two
constellations." Hodges. Bks for Elem Sch Libraries
"While the scope of subjects exceeds that indicated by the title, it is not too complicated for
the age of the reader. The text is, however, not
always clarified by the illustrations." Chicago.
Children's Bk Center

Branley, Franklyn M.—*Continued*

A book of stars for you; illus. by Leonard Kessler. Crowell 1967 unp illus $8.95, lib. bdg. $8.79 (2-4)   **523.8**

1 Stars
ISBN 0-690-157215; 0-690-15722-3   LC 67-18509

The author "explains the place and importance of the solar system in the galaxy; the numbers, distances, motions, and properties of stars; and even describes something of the way stars are formed and evolve. . . . Some younger children may require explanation of some of the technical terms." Sci Bks

"Overwhelming as any consideration of astronomy may seem, when introduced in a concise picture-book style the subject has a fascinating appeal for a child just beginning to understand something of the vastness of our universe." Cincinnati

Gallant, Roy A.

The constellations; how they came to be. Four Winds 1979 203p illus $11.95 (5 and up)   **523.8**

1 Stars 2 Mythology
ISBN 0-590-07552-7   LC 79-12816

"A welter of myths from all over the world is combined with guidance on what amateur astronomers should look for where with eye, binoculars, or small telescopes in 44 northern hemisphere constellations. Each constellation appears in an area star map which indicates star magnitudes and again in its own diagram with the imaginary figure laid over the stars and at least its two brightest stars named. There is a wealth of information here . . . but it isn't always well digested. The text has choppy spots and there are some discrepancies between text and diagrams. Still, this is an appealing guide, longer than tall (10″ × 8″), with open format and many black-and-white photos of what those spots and blurs would look like if one had a 200 inch telescope in one's backyard." Sch Library J
Glossary: p189-96

Fires in the sky; the birth and death of stars. Four Winds 1978 162p illus $7.95 (5 and up)   **523.8**

1 Stars 2 Sun
ISBN 0-590-07475-X   LC 78-4339

This book provides a "history of our knowledge of the nature of stars and their life cycles, emphasizing the sun and giving a few experiments readers can try to make their own solar observations. The development is clear and well planned, showing that Gallant has frequently used and carefully refined the lecture notes on which the book is based. He does oversimplify some points, but this may be necessary to keep it accessible to young readers." Sch Library J
Glossary: p131-44

Joseph, Joseph Maron

Point to the stars [by] Joseph Maron Joseph and Sarah Lee Lippincott; illus. with photographs and line drawings. Rev. 2d ed. McGraw 1977 96p illus lib. bdg. $6.95 (6 and up)   **523.8**

1 Stars 2 Planets
ISBN 0-07-033050-6   LC 76-53737

First published 1963
This is an "excellent guide for locating and identifying stars and constellations . . . its tables on the positions of planets cover the period 1977 to 1981. A section on each constellation includes a sketch of the object lending its name to the star group, a drawing showing the constellation as it appears in the the sky, instructions for finding the constellation, a bit of mythology, and comments on what to look for with the naked eye, binoculars, and a telescope. The method advised for designating the location of a star is the one used by professional astronomers, and readers will need no special equipment to explore the skies with the aid of this book." Sch Library J
Glossary: p92-93

Rey, H. A.

Find the constellations. Rev. ed. Houghton 1976 72p illus lib. bdg. $9.95, pa $4.95 (3-6)   **523.8**

1 Stars
ISBN 0-395-24509-5; 0-395-24418-8   LC 76-370489

First published 1954
"Constellation diagrams are presented with and without connecting lines and are drawn for 40° N. Latitude to cover the continental United States. The use of color in these diagrams is a refreshing change from the black-and-white usually used. Key words in the text are also highlighted in color, and the text includes at critical points several self-tests with inverted answer keys. Scientific accuracy is stressed, stellar magnitudes are indicated on the diagrams, and the concept of light year is discussed. Some of the myths surrounding the names of the constellations are given. A planet finder to the year 1985 is included, as well as an index and glossary." AAAS Sci Bks & Films

"This is unquestionably a readable, enjoyable, and informative guide. . . . It is not imperative to have this update, but some edition of the guide is essential." Sch Library J

The stars; a new way to see them. Enl. world-wide ed. Houghton 1967 160p illus maps $10.95, pa $5.95 (5 and up)   **523.8**

1 Stars
ISBN 0-395-08121-1; 0-395-24830-2   LC 60-13609

First published 1952
In addition to charts and line drawings that suggest to the reader the mythological figures for which the constellations were named, this book "contains 40 charts showing the sky throughout the year as far north as Alaska and as far south as Australia and New Zealand." Pub W

"A second section of the book explains phases of the moon, celestial movement, equinoxes, etc." Hodges. Bks for Elem Sch Libraries

525 Earth (Astronomical geography)

Asimov, Isaac

How did we find out the earth is round? Illus. by Matthew Kalmenoff. Walker & Co. 1972 59p illus $4.95, lib. bdg. $5.85 (4-6)   **525**

1 Earth
ISBN 0-8027-6121-6; 0-8027-6122-4   LC 72-81378

"Early theories of the shape and structure of the earth are discussed, ending with the proof supplied by the explorations of Columbus and Magellan." Best Bks for Children

"Well written, authentic, readily understood. This book should appeal to a wide range of readers." Adventuring with Bks

Branley, Franklyn M.

The end of the world; illus. by David Palladini. Crowell 1974 39p illus lib. bdg. $8.79 (5 and up)   **525**

1 End of the world 2 Earth
ISBN 0-690-26608-1   LC 72-13264

The author describes the inevitable natural destruction of our planet by means of energy flashes from other stars, aging from the sun's rays, or changes in the earth's relationship to the moon. He believes that by the time this happens man will have found another life-supporting planet

"Informative, depressing, authoritative, and fascinating, the book is illustrated with imaginative and dramatic pictures." Chicago. Children's Bk Center

Sunshine makes the seasons; illus. by Shelley Freshman. Crowell 1974 33p illus maps (Let's-read-and-find-out science bks) lib. bdg. $3.89 (2-4)   **525**

1 Seasons
ISBN 0-690-00438-9   LC 73-19694

"This picture book for younger readers explains the cycle of seasons as an effect of the earth-sun relationship. . . . The text is generally clear in describing the progress of the tilted earth and the changes in amounts of daylight and dark or heat and cold as we revolve around the sun. Large black-and-white and three-color illustrations and diagrams help make the abstract concepts accessible." Booklist

Cartwright, Sally
The tide; illus. by Marilyn Miller. Coward-McCann 1971 46p illus (The Science is what and why bks) lib. bdg. $4.49 (1-3)   525

1 Tides
ISBN 0-698-30367-9   LC 79-127949

"The difficult concept of tidal movement is presented here simply and understandably. In some 15 illustrated pages with minimal text on each, the author discusses phenomena a child can observe for himself at the ocean side (high tide, low tide, etc.). From this logical beginning she leads readers farther away to the moon's changing influence. Now the text becomes longer, scientifically correct but still uncomplicated and never taking up more than half a page." Sch Library J
"Delightful, almost poetic prose has been successfully combined with appealing illustrations." Sci Bks

Polgreen, John
Sunlight and shadows [by] John and Cathleen Polgreen. Doubleday 1967 57p illus lib. bdg. $4.95 (1-3)   525

1 Earth   2 Solar radiation   3 Shades and shadows
ISBN 0-385-06417-9   LC 67-10681

"The Polgreens have written a straightforward, no-nonsense presentation of the subject. Changing shadows are explained in terms of the changing location of the sun, and the changing locations are related to rotation and revolution of the earth. The authors suggest things to do: to chart the shadows, and to observe the sun safely with a viewing box." The AAAS Sci Bk List for Children
"Realistic illustrations in color and black-and-white provide excellent clarification of the text in this concept book. . . . This is an attractive picture book for use in the primary grades." Library J

Tresselt, Alvin
It's time now! Illus. by Roger Duvoisin. Lothrop 1969 unp illus lib. bdg. $7.75 (k-2)   525

1 Seasons 2 City life
ISBN 0-688-41619-5   LC 69-14313

The author portrays the sights, sounds, and smells of the changing seasons in the city
"The illustrations, bright with color and movement, show city streets and parks; the text has a light and easy tone as it describes seasonal activities; the games, the holidays, the family outings, and the changing weather and foliage." Chicago. Children's Bk Center

526   Mathematical geography. Cartography

Branley, Franklyn M.
North, south, east, and west; illus. by Robert Galster. Crowell 1966 unp illus map (Let's-read-and-find-out science bks) $4.50 lib. bdg. $5.25 (1-3)   526

1 Compass
ISBN 0-690-58609-4   LC 66-14486

In this book "the young reader learns that left is left and right is right no matter what direction he is facing, up is away from earth and down is toward the earth no matter whether he stands on his feet or on his head, and down continues to the center of the earth. The directions are taught by the position of the rising and setting sun. Observation of shadows and their changing direction during the day is the 'do-it-yourself activity' that reinforces learning. Finally the reader is introduced to the magnetic compass and the compass 'rose' on maps that indicates North." Sci Bks
The book consists of "simple text and cheery, strong drawings." Scientific Am

Brown, Lloyd A.
Map making; the art that became a science. Little 1960 217p illus maps $6.95 (5 and up)   526

1 Map drawing 2 Maps
ISBN 0-316-11115-5   LC 60-9338

"An outstanding survey of the development of cartography from earliest times to the beginning of the twentieth century. The discussion takes into account discovery and geography, measuring instruments, compasses, clocks, navigation by the stars and related topics. Authenticated with reproductions of old prints." Sci Bks

Oliver, John E.
What we find when we look at maps; illus. by Robert Galster. McGraw 1970 39p illus maps lib. bdg. $6.95 (3-5)   526

1 Map drawing 2 Maps
ISBN 0-07-047677-2   LC 72-107293

"A good book for encouraging spatial awareness and careful observation as well as for introducing the basic concepts used in map-making. The idea of a map is very deftly presented by the first few photographs, which show a close-up of a baseball diamond, then a view from high in the stands, then a view from a helicopter and last, the final view translated into a map. This comparison of photographs and diagrams proves useful several times during the book, as the author explains the use of symbols, scale drawing, grids and labels, and the various things that maps show, such as location, dimension, direction, etc." Chicago. Children's Bk Center

529   Time (Chronology)

Adler, Irving
The calendar [by] Irving and Ruth Adler. Day 1967 48p illus lib. bdg. $6.89 (3-5)   529

1 Calendars
ISBN 0-381-99975-0   LC 67-23865

"The Reason why books"
This "introduction to the calendar explains solar and lunar cycles and relates mathematical attempts to make days, weeks, months, and years coincide with these cycles. Directions for making a 50-year calendar and many diagrams and sketches are included. Slightly more matter-of-fact than is Brindze's 'The story of our calendar' [entered below] but otherwise similar in scope and coverage." Booklist

Brindze, Ruth
The story of our calendars; illus. by Helene Carter. Vanguard 1949 63p illus maps $5.95 (4 and up)   529

1 Calendars
ISBN 0-8149-0278-2   LC 49-8710

"An expedition back into time to explore the real story behind the neat little calendar we use today. There are some nice bits of information about the early races who were concerned with the calendar—the Babylonians, the Egyptians and the Romans. The illustrations in blue with touches of yellow carry out the calendar's link with the heavens." Ontario Library Rev
"Useful in reference work, this book is also a pleasure to handle." Horn Bk

Burns, Marilyn
This book is about time; illus. by Martha Weston. Little 1978 127p illus maps $7.95, pa $4.95 (5 and up)   529

1 Time
ISBN 0-316-11752-8; 0-316-11750-1   LC 78-6614

"A Brown paper school book"
"Burns explores the subject of time—and many of its complexities—in a lively way that should give readers pause at the next strike of the clock. The oft taken-for-granted concepts of reaction time, waking-up schedules, length of a second, and blooming of flowers are discussed with titillating experiments and investigations that give new awareness of the subject. Historical coverage is included with explanations of the Mayan and Egyptian calendars, the impact of railroads on time zones, and the determination of the international date line. Bringing her discussion to a more personal level, the author comments on jet lag, biorhythms, and day and night people." Booklist

Trivett, Daphne
Time for clocks [by] Daphne and John Trivett; pictures by Giulio Maestro. Crowell 1979 33p illus lib. bdg. $6.89 (1-3)　　**529**

1 Time　2 Clocks and watches
ISBN 0-690-03896-8　　LC 78-4782

"In a book to help primary grades children become familiar with time concepts and heighten their ability to tell time easily, Trivett uses a great deal of reinforcement-by-repetition. Her suggestions for home demonstrations are usually open-ended ('Does the sun go from your left to your right, or the opposite way?') or give instructions for making a paper-plate clock. Most of the simply written text is devoted to explanations and more explanations of telling time, enabling the reader to practice such intricacies as a quarter past the hour, or understanding that 2:52 is the same thing as eight minutes to three." Chicago. Children's Bk Center
"Maestro's penguin demonstrators set a cheery, benign mood as they act out textual directives." Booklist

530.8　Physical units, dimensions, constants

Adler, David A.
3D, 2D, 1D; illus. by Harvey Weiss. Crowell 1975 33p illus (Young math bks) $7.95, lib. bdg. $7.89 (2-4)　　**530.8**

1 Dimensions　2 Measurement
ISBN 0-690-00456-7; 0-690-00543-1　　LC 74-5156

"An introduction to perspective for young readers through experimentation with common household objects and objects at hand, e.g., the page being read and books. Harvey Weiss' illustrations add levity and color. A clever commentary by two bearded men and a goat accompanies the basic text, adding to readers' understanding and amusement. The material on area and volume is covered in many other sources, but the emphasis on understanding the three dimensions is not readily available." Sch Library J

531　Mechanics

Adler, Irving
Energy; illus. by Ellen Viereck. Day 1970 48p illus lib. bdg. $7.89 (3-5)　　**531**

1 Force and energy
ISBN 0-381-99609-3　　LC 71-101463

"The Reason why books"
"Covered are energy's many different forms: inertia, force, friction, heat, electrical, chemical, and nuclear—all adding up to the energy of work. Illustrations are simple and helpful. There is also a word list, as well as a very useful, specific table of contents—really needed since the book is so crammed full of information." Sch Library J

Branley, Franklyn M.
Gravity is a mystery; illus. by Don Madden. Crowell 1970 33p illus (Let's-read-and-find-out science bks) $7.95, lib. bdg. $7.89 (1-3)　　**531**

1 Gravitation
ISBN 0-690-35071-6; 0-690-35072-4　　LC 70-101922

"The force of gravity is explained with the aid of amusing color illustrations. The differences in gravitational forces on the sun, on the earth, and on other planets are carefully explained." The AAAS Sci Bk List for Children
"Mainly of value as a supplemental science book which primary-grade children can read for themselves, the account describes basic concepts." Booklist

Weight and weightlessness; illus. by Graham Booth. Crowell [1972 c1971] 33p illus (Let's-read-and-find-out science bks) lib. bdg. $7.89 (1-3)　　**531**

1 Gravitation　2 Weightlessness
ISBN 0-690-87329-8　　LC 70-132292

The author provides a simple explanation of the subjects of gravity and weightlessness, drawing examples from both everyday life and the world of space. The principles behind how a spaceship is sent into orbit are also discussed
"There are few science books for children which can effectively simplify a difficult concept with a creative approach to the topic. This is one of the few. . . . [It combines] succinct text and appealing and clear pictures. . . . There is no comparable book on the subject for this grade level and few science books with such universal appeal." Sch Library J

Hellman, Hal
The lever and the pulley; illus. by Lynn Sweat. Evans, M.&Co. 1971 45p illus $4.95 (3-5)　　**531**

1 Machinery　2 Mechanics
ISBN 0-87131-072-4　　LC 74-161363

"The text leads easily from the basic principles of the lever into its use in the seesaw and into other applications in scissors, pliers, pumps, beam balances, wheelbarrows, bottle openers, nutcrackers, the human arm, and various toys like bats and golf clubs. The reader is helped to see the lever in a ship's or car's wheel, a faucet handle, a screwdriver, and a door knob. . . . The concept of the pulley is next introduced and its advantages in flexibility of applications to moving loads is illustrated with experiments to be carried out with a single fixed pulley, a movable pulley, and with other more complicated arrangements." Sci Bks
"Clear diagrams, well-placed in relation to textual references to the principles they illustrate, add to the usefulness of a text that is simple and clear." Chicago. Children's Bk Center

Kaufmann, John
Streamlined; written and illus. by John Kaufmann. Crowell 1974 33p illus (Let's-read-and-find-out science bks) lib. bdg. $7.89 (2-4)　　**531**

1 Aerodynamics　2 Hydrodynamics
ISBN 0-690-00565-2　　LC 74-2357

The author explains the nature of streamlining as it occurs in nature and as man has applied it to vehicles. Experiments are given to show how shape affects motion through air and water
"A well-focused, self-contained presentation that explains a fundamental physical concept. . . . The text offers simple explanations and is coordinated with uncomplicated drawings." Booklist

532　Mechanics of fluids

Branley, Franklyn M.
Floating and sinking; illus. by Robert Galster. Crowell 1967 unp illus (Let's-read-and-find-out science bks) lib. bdg. $7.89 (1-3)　　**532**

1 Hydrodynamics
ISBN 0-690-30918-X　　LC 67-15396

The author "invites the young reader to experiment and so to discover why things float and sink. Information for this age group is simplified in the text and attractively and effectively presented in illustrations." Adventuring With Bks. 2d edition

Corbett, Scott
What makes a boat float? Pictures by Victor Mays. Little 1970 42p illus lib. bdg. $5.95 (3-5)　　**532**

1 Hydrodynamics　2 Boats and boating　3 Marine engineering
ISBN 0-316-15713-9　　LC 76-94498

"An Atlantic Monthly Press book"
"The physical properties of water, gravity, density and the principles of buoyancy are explained as the fundamentals of naval engineering, and in particular for designing hulls for various types of surface and subsurface vessels. Good drawings clarify a well-written text. Good collateral reading for elementary science students." Sci Bks
Index and glossary: p39-42

534   Sound and related vibrations

Branley, Franklyn M.

High sounds, low sounds; illus. by Paul Galdone. Crowell 1967 unp illus (Let's-read-and-find-out science bks) lib. bdg. $7.89, pa $1.45 (1-3)   **534**

1. Sound
ISBN 0-690-38018-6; 0-690-00638-1   I.C 67-23662

"This book describing sounds and how they are made also contains several experiments that illustrate the basic concepts of physics involved." Chicago

"Humorous illustrations reinforce the ideas expressed in a very simple text." Booklist

535   Visible light (Optics)

Beeler, Nelson F.

Experiments in optical illusion [by] Nelson F. Beeler and Franklyn M. Branley; illus. by Fred H. Lyon. Crowell 1951 114p illus $7.95 (5 and up)   **535**

1 Optics—Experiments 2 Optical illusions
ISBN 0-690-27507-2   LC 51-5642

"Numerous diagrams and drawings here prove that seeing is not always believing. The authors explain 'why' our eyes deceive us and show how optical illusions and psychological patterns in sight play a part in everyday experience. Includes plans for home projects." AAAS Sci Bk List for Children

Branley, Franklyn M.

Light and darkness; illus. by Reynold Ruffins. Crowell 1975 33p illus (Let's-read-and-find-out science bks) lib. bdg. $7.89 (1-3)   **535**

1 Light
ISBN 0-690-01122-9   LC 74-23938

"Children learn how light helps them see the world. They locate objects that produce their own light and compare these with objects that reflect light. They learn that light is everywhere, even under bedcovers or inside 'a dark closet in a dark room on a dark night.' " Sci and Children

"These basic facts about light, actually an introduction to physics, are very simply presented and are repeated at various points. The text is further clarified by careful, pleasant drawings, resulting in an effective beginner's book on a complex subject." Appraisal

Gardner, Robert

Shadow science; Robert Gardner and David Webster. Doubleday 1976 124p illus lib. bdg. $5.95 (4-6)   **535**

1 Shades and shadows
ISBN 0-385-09591-0   LC 74-18797

"An exploration of a familiar phenomenon with multiple suggestions for ways of looking at shadows and the objects that make them. Including more than 100 black-and-white photographs, the authors incorporate into their text experiments, puzzles, tricks, and games dealing with the subject. In many cases, photographs depict a situation, such as the shadow of a house, with a captioned question asking what time it was taken, what direction it was taken from, or how to identify the object when only a shadow is seen. Answers are given separately. Although much of the book will be best for individual browsing, the demonstrations on time and seasonal changes and the experiments on making, reflecting, and shaping shadows could be used in science classrooms." Booklist

Kettelkamp, Larry

Tricks of eye and mind; the story of optical illusion; with illus. by the author. Morrow 1974 127p illus lib. bdg. $6.96 (4 and up)   **535**

1 Optical illusions
ISBN 0-688-31829-0   LC 74-5935

This "book explains the how, the why, and the use we make of optical illusions. Chapter one discusses the biology of the eye and how the mind interprets information. Chapter two explores the more commonly known optical illusions. The final chapter considers the application of illusions to camouflage, motion pictures, art, and architecture." Appraisal

"There are a lot of ideas here for individual or class projects, experiments, and library research; a balanced blend of science, art, and entertainment. The illustrations are black and white." Sci and Children

Schneider, Herman

Science fun with a flashlight, by Herman and Nina Schneider; pictures by Harriet Sherman. McGraw 1975 unp illus lib. bdg. $6.95 (1-4)   **535**

1 Light 2 Shades and shadows 3 Science—Experiments
ISBN 0-07-055455-2   LC 74-9982

"The concept of shadows is explored in depth. Some aspects of light such as the rainbow, prisms, reflected light, and heat of light are also presented. In all, the book combines some simple activities using a flashlight with information about light and shadow. . . . The three-color illustrations add to the eye appeal of the book." Sci and Children

535.5   Beams and their modification

Lewis, Bruce

What is a laser? Pictures by Tom Huffman. Dodd 1979 48p illus lib. bdg. $5.95 (4 and up)   **535.5**

1 Lasers
ISBN 0-396-07646-7   LC 78-11100

"Gently humorous illustrations make clear for beginners the scientific concepts necessary to an understanding of lasers. Stimulation emission, for example, is shown as air escaping from an inflated football when a player stomps on it. The author explains what laser means, its basic design, the generation of coherent light, and the various types and uses of lasers. Scientific terms like photons are explained in the text, but only to the extent needed to grasp the subject." Sch Library J

"I would have hesitated before taking on the job of getting the concept of lasers across to primary-grade children. The author and the illustrator may possibly have hesitated, but they certainly carried the task through very effectively. They use analogy, of course. . . . The analogies are, however, well chosen from the pedagogic familiar-to-unfamiliar standard; and where the familiarity might be doubtful, the illustrations close the gap. I can recommend the book highly." Horn Bk

535.6 Color

Adler, Irving

Color in your life; illus. by Ruth Adler. Day 1962 127p illus lib. bdg. $7.89 (5 and up)   **535.6**

1 Color
ISBN 0-381-9995-5   LC 62-7784

The author explains "the basic structure and characteristics (e.g.: reflection and diffraction) of light, and the more complex phenomena (polarization, the Doppler effect, etc.). [He] discusses sources of color in nature and the role of color in printing, television, and photography. Scientific explanations are given for phenomena such as the coloring of soap bubbles, [and] the sunset." The AAAS Sci Bk List for Children

Another of the author's "accurate, clear, and entertaining books based on recent scientific knowledge and theory. . . . [He] touches on aspects of organic chemistry and quantum theory without overwhelming or talking down. He gives abundant examples and a few experiments. Good, clear drawings." Library J

"Unlike most science books, it should appeal strongly to young people who have an artistic bent." Pub W

Branley, Franklyn M.
Color, from rainbows to lasers; illus. by Henry Roth. Crowell 1978 87p illus lib. bdg $8.79 (6 and up)   535.6
1 Color
ISBN 0-690-03847-X   LC 76-46304
"A scientifically accurate book for children explaining that fascinating property of light which we call color. [The author] presents a basic introduction to the principles of the color spectrum and theories of color vision. Well-illustrated with drawings and simple diagrams, many in beautiful color, Mr. Branley answers that age-old question 'Why is the sky blue?' Older children, however, may be more interested in his colorful optical illusions and his explanation of color television." Babbling Bookworm
Further readings: p81

Emberly, Ed
Green says go. Little 1968 32p illus lib. bdg. $5.95 (k-3)   535.6
1 Color
ISBN 0-316-23599-7   LC 68-21165
The author "first shows primary, secondary and complementary colors and then demonstrates how the addition of black or white can darken or lighten colors. The second part of the book plays with some of the color-associated terms in common use . . . and points out various ways in which color is used for communication." Sat Rev

536   Heat

Adler, Irving
Hot and cold; illus. by Peggy Adler. Rev. ed. Day 1975 128p illus lib. bdg. $7.89 (4-6)   536
1 Heat 2 Cold 3 Temperature
ISBN 0-381-99990-4   LC 74-9357
First published 1959
The author "explains the nature of heat and cold, examines theories of heat and its behavior, discusses methods of producing and practical uses of very high and very low temperatures, and describes devices used in measuring temperature. A methodical and understandable treatment of the subject." Booklist [review of the 1959 edition]

Balestrino, Philip
Hot as an ice cube; illus. by Tomie de Paola. Crowell 1971 33p illus (Let's-read-and-find-out science bks) lib. bdg. $7.89 (k-3)   536
1 Heat
ISBN 0-690-40415-8   LC 70-139092
"Basic information about heat and cold is clearly and simply presented in attractive picture-book format. Balestrino explains that there is heat in everything, even icebergs, discusses the relationship between heat and molecular motion, and gives several easy experiments. He also tells why some objects expand when heated and mentions that heat flows from a hot object to a cooler one." Booklist

537   Electricity and electronics

Epstein, Sam
The first book of electricity, by Sam and Beryl Epstein; illus. by Rod Slater. Rev. 3d ed. Watts, F. 1977 64p illus lib. bdg. $6.45 (4-6)   537
1 Electricity
ISBN 0-531-00522-4   LC 76-41317
First published 1953
"This extremely well-written book throws much light on the nature of electricity and applications of its everyday use. Black-and-white diagrams and photos on every page complement the text. Although the authors explain electricity succinctly and clearly, emphasis is on description of familiar electrical uses: house wiring, meter reading, fuses, wall switches, toasters, TV, etc. Three simple experiments are given, including directions for making a telegraph set. Definitely a first choice for elementary science collections." Sch Library J
Glossary: p61-62

539   Modern physics. Atomic structure. Chemical physics

Bronowski, J.
Biography of an atom, by J. Bronowski and Millicent E. Selsam; illus. with pictures by Weimer Pursell and with photographs. Harper 1965 43p illus lib. bdg. $6.79 (4 and up)   539
1 Atoms 2 Carbon
ISBN 0-06-020641-1   LC 64-19708
"This is the biography of a single atom—what is it like, where it came from, and its place in the world. There are about one hundred different kinds of atoms, but this story will be about an atom of carbon because carbon is found in every living cell, and its atoms therefore enter into your life and mine." p6
"The very best kind of science writing: simple, lucid, dignified, well-organized and stripped of nonessentials. The diagrams are placed and labelled carefully and there is, out of this matter-of-fact and scientific approach, an honest feeling of wonder communicated: a sense of the marvel of design and continuity in the world about us." Chicago. Children's Bk Center

539.7   Atomic and nuclear physics

Asimov, Isaac
How did we find out about nuclear power? Illus. by David Wool. Walker & Co. 1976 64p illus $6.95, lib. bdg. $6.85 (5 and up)   539.7
1 Atomic energy
ISBN 0-8027-6265-4; 0-8027-6266-2   LC 76-12057
"Asimov describes the accrued knowledge that, over a century, made it possible for scientists to perfect techniques of nuclear fusion and fission. The material is chronologically arranged, so that the reader can understand how each new discovery about atomic structure contributed to the body of nuclear knowledge, and can appreciate how discoveries in science may be based on the work of predecessors. The author concludes with a discussion of controlled nuclear fusion that could give new resources to an energy-starved world." Chicago. Children's Bk Center
This book "moves quickly and presents information in a style that is streamlined and compact but clear. . . . [It] is brief, and the vocabulary is not difficult (pronunciations are given for the scientific words). . . . Ample illustrations and diagrams are included, as well as an index." Appraisal

540   Chemistry and allied sciences

Morgan, Alfred
First chemistry book for boys and girls; illus. by Bradford Babbitt and Terry Smith. [Rev. ed.] Scribner 1977 175p illus pa $2.95 (5 and up)   540
1 Chemistry
ISBN 0-684-14755-6   LC 76-49992
First published 1962
"An introduction to this science with accompanying interesting projects and activities." Best Bks for Children

540.1   Chemistry and allied sciences—Philosophy and theory. Alchemy

Aylesworth, Thomas G.
The alchemists: magic into science. Addison-Wesley 1973 128p illus lib. bdg. $6.95 (6 and up)   540.1
1 Alchemy
ISBN 0-201-00143-8   LC 72-7295

Aylesworth, Thomas G.—*Continued*

"An Addisonian Press book"
"This is a well-written account of the rogues, rascals, magicians and scientists who from ancient Egypt to contemporary times have been smitten (for a number of reasons) with the desire to change metals into precious gold. The author presents brief biographies of notorious alchemists and describes interesting situations involving them and their discoveries, including chemicals used in dyes, medicine, glass, waterproofing, sleeping potions and a pain-killing drug. The author points out that the age-old attempt to develop a little man grown in a bottle, the feverish search for the philosopher's stone and the hope of discovering an elixir of life are not such crazy ideas in the light of what modern science is accomplishing today." Sci Bks
"It's an engrossing book, written with verve and wit; the period illustrations are arresting." Pub W
Bibliographic references included in Acknowledgements: p123-24

540.7 Chemistry—Experiments

Shalit, Nathan
Cup and saucer chemistry; illus. by Charles Waterhouse. Grosset [1972] 93p illus pa $2.95 (4-6)   **540.7**
1 Chemistry—Experiments
ISBN 0-448-11690-1   LC 72-158766
The author provides "an opportunity to explore and investigate chemical elements and compounds in common foods and cleansing agents. Precise directions, which call for ingredients found in storage cupboards and in the refrigerator, are given for some exciting chemical determination for reactants, acids, bases, salts, precipitates, crystalizations, formation of gases and some fun things such as mystery writing." Sci Bks
Here are "chemical experiments intended for young scientists at the kitchen sink, but also suitable for the classroom. . . . The experiments are clearly illustrated, explained, and simple, but most still require supervision and not all are guaranteed successes." Sch Library J

541.3 Physical chemistry

Haines, Gail Kay
Fire; pictures by Jacqueline Chwast. Morrow 1975 unp illus lib. bdg. $6.48 (1-3)   **541.3**
1 Fire
ISBN 0-688-32009-0   LC 74-13396
"After briefly tracing the discovery and uses of fire in ancient times, the author . . . describes the chemistry of burning. Several . . . experiments using a candle, jar and matches allow readers to observe scientific principles at work. A short discussion of the varied uses of heat energy in modern technology and a comment on fire safety conclude the account." Sch Library J
"Striking black cutout forms and jagged-edged areas of fiery red are all there is to the strong and splendidly appropriate illustrations that dramatize this simple text for early readers." Sci Am

Zubrowski, Bernie
Bubbles; illus. by Joan Drescher. Little 1979 64p illus $6.95, pa $3.95 (3-5)   **541.3**
1 Soap bubbles
ISBN 0-316-98880-4; 0-316-98881-2   LC 78-27497
"A Children's Museum activity book"
The author "discusses the various properties of soap and water and the best mixture for making bubbles. The book shows different ways of blowing bubbles, creating bubble sculptures, measuring and shrinking bubbles, and more. It also contains a brief list for further reading on the mathematical and scientific aspects of bubble-making. . . . The text integrates questions with discussion and provides experiments which will help the reader learn answers as well as raise questions of his own. The black-and-white photographs and the clear line drawings are presented in an attractive format." Horn Bk

548 Crystallography

Gans, Roma
Millions and millions of crystals; illus. by Giulio Maestro. Crowell 1973 33p illus (Let's-read-and-find-out science bks) lib. bdg. $6.89 (2-4)   **548**
1 Crystallography
ISBN 0-690-54030-2   LC 72-7547
An introduction to the characteristics, formation, and uses of crystals. Examples include sugar, salt, snowflakes, sand, jewels, and rock crystals which are found in caves in the form of stalagmites and stalactites
"The black-and-white line drawings are a perfect complement to and extension of the text. Simple activities are described, such as pulling off layers of mica with a pin and examining sugar and salt crystals on dark paper in the sunlight or through a magnifying glass. This is a fine book, highly recommended as a supplementary classroom book and for pleasure reading." Sci Bks

549 Mineralogy

Chesterman, Charles W.
The Audubon Society Field guide to North American rocks and minerals [by] Charles W. Chesterman [and] Kurt E. Lowe. Knopf [1979 c1978] 850p illus $9.95   **549**
1 Rocks 2 Mineralogy
ISBN 0-394-50269-8   LC 78-54893
"Among the features of this guide are: a visual key arranged by color, a descriptive key to ease identification, a review of North America's minerals and rocks, a visual key to rocks by rock type, a guide to mineral environments, a glossary, and name and locality indexes. All minerals and rocks mentioned are illustrated with color photographs of excellent quality. Thick but otherwise pocket sized, this highly recommended handbook will be valuable to field collectors, amateur and pro. The identification keys seem clear enough to use: the information given is more than most amateurs will need." Library J
Bibliography: p799-801

Fenton, Carroll Lane
Rocks and their stories, by Carroll Lane Fenton and Mildred Adams Fenton. Doubleday 1951 112p illus lib. bdg. $5.95 (4-6)   **549**
1 Mineralogy 2 Rocks 3 Petrology
ISBN 0-385-07113-2   LC 51-12152
"An introduction to petrology, distinguishing rocks, stones, and minerals; explaining methods of identification; and discussing 40 basic minerals." Hodges. Bks for Elem Sch libraries
"Its brief 112 pages contain fine information under alluring titles and the many photographic illustrations are superbly chosen and reproduced." NY Her Trib Bks

Keen, Martin L.
Be a rockhound; illus. with drawings and photographs by the author. Messner 1979 64p illus lib. bdg. $6.97 (4 and up)   **549**
1 Mineralogy 2 Rocks—Collectors and collecting
ISBN 0-671-32820-4   LC 79-17969
"Collecting rocks for fun and knowledge is the focus of this readable, well-organized introduction. The essential skills discussed include identification of rocks and minerals, cleaning methods, and tools and equipment necessary for hunting rocks. Along with basic information on the formation of rocks and their composition, there is a table of rocks and minerals, a list of the best North American mineral collections, a bibliography that includes magazines, and a modified 'Code of Ethics of the American Federation of Mineralogical Societies.'" Booklist

Kerrod, Robin
Rocks and minerals. Warwick Press [1978 c1977] 44p illus $3.95, lib. bdg. $5.90 (5 and up)   **549**
1 Rocks 2 Mineralogy
ISBN 0-531-09083-3; 0-531-09058-2   LC 77-85249

Kerrod, Robin—*Continued*

"Modern knowledge library"
First published 1977 in England
"Editorial consultant: David George; illustrators: Ross Wardle, John Mariott." Verso of title page
Besides discussing igneous, sedimentary, and metamorphic rocks, the book introduces the reader to "Rocks from Other Worlds," meteorites, and tektites. Mineral ores and nonmetallic minerals are compared and summarized in tables presenting the scientific names, with the common names in parentheses. An index is included." Sci Teacher
"Tall, slim and colorful, with photographs and naturalistic drawings and diagrams liberally placed about the pages, this can function as a browsing item as well as an information resource." Booklist

Pough, Frederick H.

A field guide to rocks and minerals. 4th ed. Houghton 1976 317p illus $10.95, pa $5.95
549

1 Mineralogy 2 Rocks
ISBN 0-395-24047-6; 0-395-24049-2   LC 75-22364

"The Peterson Field guide series"
First published 1953
This "well-illustrated identification handbook . . . includes chapters on crystallography, mineralogy, and collecting techniques. The chief value of the guide is in identification of specimens. The photos of rocks and minerals are accompanied by drawings of the crystal structures and description of physical properties, composition, tests, and distinguishing characteristics. Also explains procedures for distinguishing between similar materials." Wynar. Guide to Ref Bks for Sch Media Centers [review of 3d edition]
Glossary: p297-302. Annotated bibliography: p303-05

Shuttlesworth, Dorothy

The story of rocks; illus. by Su Zan N. Swain. Rev. ed. Doubleday 1966 57p illus (Nature bks. for young people) lib. bdg. $5.95 (5 and up)
549

1 Rocks 2 Mineralogy
ISBN 0-385-06929-4   LC 55-12319

First published 1956
This book for the rock collector not only tells how rocks are formed and gives various tests for their identification, but also discusses beautiful and practical minerals, metals with strange properties, and rock oddities
"A well written, beautifully illustrated and practical book, packed with information." Chicago Sunday Trib
Books to take on collecting trips for good reading: p55. Likely hunting grounds: p56

Simon, Seymour

The rock-hound's book; illus. by Tony Chen. Viking 1973 80p illus lib. bdg. $5.95, Penguin Bks. pa $1.95 (4 and up)
549

1 Mineralogy 2 Rocks
ISBN 0-670-60240-X; 0-670-05104-7   LC 72-91396

The text "deals with some of the elementary facts and concepts about rocks, minerals and ores. Definitions of 'mineral,' 'rock' and 'ore' and explanations of the formation of igneous, sedimentary and metamorphic rock are given. The author describes searching for novel rocks, using tools to take rock samples, avoiding fracturing rocks unnecessarily and making rock collections. There are also discussions of clues for identifying rocks and minerals and use of Mohr's scale for detecting hardness. The book ends with a 'mineral check list' for identification." Sci Bks
"Safety precautions are given, and information is reinforced by occasional repetition. Also included are: an index, reading list, and a section on where to buy materials. The book is well designed with wide margins, ample spacing between lines, and handsome titles. The minerals and rocks are shown in full color, while other illustrations of . . . children are in black, gray, and white." Sch Library J

Zim, Herbert S.

Rocks and minerals; a guide to familiar minerals, gems, ores and rocks, by Herbert S. Zim and Paul R. Shaffer; illus. by Raymond Perlman. Golden Press 1957 160p illus maps (A Golden Nature guide) lib. bdg. $9.15, pa $1.95 (4 and up)
549

1 Mineralogy 2 Rocks
ISBN 0-307-63502-3; 0-307-24499-7   LC 57-3710

First published by Simon & Schuster
A pocket "handbook that is educational for amateurs and useful for quick reference for professionals. Introductory material on the earth and its rocks gives basic geological information and activities for amateurs are suggested in identifying, collecting and studying rocks and minerals. Colored diagrams and pictures of specimens aid in identification. Description [of over 400 specimens] include information on formation, structure, use and importance." Chicago. Children's Bk Center
More information: p156. Museums and exhibits: p157

551 Physical and dynamic geology

Ames, Gerald

The earth's story, by Gerald Ames & Rose Wyler. Creative Educ. Soc. in cooperation with the Am. Mus. of Natural Hist. 1967 224p illus map (Creative science ser) lib. bdg. $6.95 (4 and up)
551

1 Geology
ISBN 0-87191-012-8   LC 66-30640

First published 1957
The contents of this volume include: The ever changing land; Building and rebuilding; The parade of life; Treasures of our planet; Guides to discovery
Glossary: p221

Branley, Franklyn M.

The beginning of the earth; illus. by Giulio Maestro. Crowell 1972 33p illus (Let's-read-and-find-out science bks) $6.95, lib. bdg. $6.89 (1-3)
551

1 Earth 2 Geology
ISBN 0-690-12987-4; 0-690-12988-2   LC 79-184979

The author "presents theories of the earth's formation from clouds of dust and gasses billions of years ago at about the time other planets and the sun were forming. He conveys a sense of immense time by his slowly built descriptions of the earth's materials packing together, cooling under constant rains, and hardening into solid rock on the surface. . . . The illustrations in purple, blue, and black show amorphous masses changing into more identifiable shapes." Booklist
"Whilst there is no extraneous material in this description of the evolution of the earth through the long millennia of whirling dust, heat and rain, the text has an almost lyric cadence and is imbued with an appreciation of the slow, slow passage of time during which the earth formed." Chicago. Children's Bk Center

Lauber, Patricia

This restless earth; illus. by John Polgreen. Random House 1970 129p illus maps (Random House Science lib) lib. bdg. $4.99 (5 and up)
551

1 Geology
ISBN 0-394-90802-3   LC 75-102387

Replaces the author's: All about the planet earth, published 1962
Using the birth of the island of Surtsey as an example of how our seemingly solid earth is constantly changing, the author describes the phenomena that account for these changes: volcanoes, earthquakes and continental drift

Ruchlis, Hy
Your changing earth; illus. by Janet and Alex D'Amato. Harvey House 1963 40p illus (A Science parade bk) lib. bdg. $5.09 (2-4) **551**

1 Geology
ISBN 0-8178-3462-1   LC 63-15191
"Beginning with the origin of the earth and solar system, the author tells how the land, sea, and air developed, how mountains formed and changed, and how landscapes are transformed as a result of natural forces." The AAAS Sci Bk List for Children
"With pictures on almost every page . . . and over-simplified text, this will be useful as a first book on the subject for primary grades." Sch Library J

Wyckoff, Jerome
The story of geology; our changing earth through the ages; illus. with photographs and with paintings by William Sayles, Harry McNaught, and Raymond Perlman. Rev. ed. Golden Press 1976 177p illus maps $7.95, lib. bdg. $13.77 (5 and up) **551**

1 Geology
ISBN 0-307-17750-5; 0-307-67750-8   LC 76-374531
First published 1960. Published 1967 with title: Geology
"In introductory chapters, Wyckoff explains the concept of geological time and reviews the changes taking place in the configuration of the solid earth. In the second section, he discusses the development of landforms, as related to volcanic activity and to erosion and deposition by wind, water and ice. Topics in the last part are, in sequence, sedimentary rocks, structural geology, earthquakes, minerals, seascapes, plate tectonics, planetary geology and fossils. Although this arrangement seems illogical, the author achieves continuity and engages the attention of the reader from beginning to end. This success is due to the clearly written and lively text, the excellent illustrations, and, above all, the author's treatment of the earth as a dynamic body." AAAS Sci Bks & Films

551.023   Physical and dynamic geology—Vocational guidance

Fodor, R. V.
What does a geologist do? Illus. with photographs and diagrams. Dodd 1977 62p illus lib. bdg. $5.25 (4 and up) **551.023**

1 Geology—Vocational guidance
ISBN 0-396-07481-2   LC 77-6483
An overview of the geology field which "defines the many specialty areas—paleontology, volcanology, sedimentology, etc.—briefly describing the activities of each specialist, whether in the field or in the lab, and noting the knowledge pooling that brings diverse pieces of information together to further overall understanding of the earth's surface and substructure. Educational requirements are only briefly noted (an M.A. degree, preferably a Ph.D.) and employment possibilities are primarily found with the government or various oil and mining corporations. Throughout, descriptions of geological exploration are necessarily explained in terms of their concerns. With black-and-white photographs." Booklist

551.1   Gross structure and properties of earth and other worlds

Branley, Franklyn M.
Shakes, quakes, and shifts: earth tectonics; illus. by Daniel Maffia. Crowell 1974 33p illus $8.95, lib. bdg. $8.79 (5 and up) **551.1**

1 Continental drift 2 Plate tectonics
ISBN 0-690-00422-2; 0-690-00423-0   LC 73-18059
"Mr. Branley explains how our planet is still shifting and changing as it has been doing for millions of years due to atmospheric gases and the inner core of the earth itself. He devotes much of the text to a discussion of geologists' ideas of how the land was once one mass, Pangaea, how it split off into separate continents, and how it is still moving at the rate of about one inch a year. . . . It is a very short book and as such only whets the appetite for more." Appraisal
Bibliography: p29

Fodor, R. V.
Earth in motion; the concept of plate tectonics; with diagrams by John C. Holden and photographs. Morrow 1978 95p illus maps $5.95, lib. bdg. $5.71 (5 and up) **551.1**

1 Plate tectonics 2 Continental drift
ISBN 0-688-22135-1; 0-688-32135-6   LC 77-12568
"In a brief introduction to the theory of continental drift, Fodor, a geologist, discusses the historical background of plate tectonics, describes the makeup of the earth, and cites the evidence that scientists have accumulated to back up their beliefs. Information on the more practical aspects —search for oil and gas deposits, as well as earthquake warning systems—is given in a final chapter." Booklist
"The book holds the reader's interest every minute as it is clear, logically developed, and well-written, with scientific terminology used economically. The diagrams are helpful in clarifying and reinforcing the text." Children's Bk Rev Serv

Kiefer, Irene
Global jigsaw puzzle; the story of continental drift; illus. by Barbara Levine and with photographs. Atheneum Pubs. 1978 79p illus maps $6.95 (6 and up) **551.1**

1 Continental drift 2 Plate tectonics
ISBN 0-689-30621-0   LC 77-16188
This book "is intended for a readership already familiar with the concepts of plate tectonics (the generally held current theory which accounts for the shapes of continents, volcanic action, earthquakes, and strings of islands). The first half of the book is devoted to the history of relevant theories, as well as techniques of echo sounding and core sampling that have documented and validated the theory. Whereas most books begin with the breakup of Pangaea, the super-continent whose fragments today constitute the seven continents of the world, Kiefer elaborates, if only glancingly, the forces which preceeded the formation of Pangaea, resulting in the 400-million-year-old Appalachians and 250-million-year-old Urals. Coverage is enriched by an excellent glossary as well as by a useful index." Sch Library J

McNulty, Faith
How to dig a hole to the other side of the world; pictures by Marc Simont. Harper 1979 32p illus $8.95, lib. bdg. $8.79 (2-4) **551.1**

1 Earth—Internal structure 2 Geology
ISBN 0-06-024147-0; 0-06-024148-9   LC 78-22479
"This book for young readers provides an amusing, simplified discussion of the internal structure of the earth. McNulty indicates the various layers encountered as the digging progresses, their composition and temperature, and the problems the diggers might face. Humorous drawings reinforce the discussion, such as the depiction of a 'no-spaceship' necessary for penetrating the hot interior of the globe. The material will be useful collateral reading for students studying the internal structure of our planet." AAAS Sci Bks & Films
"Advice on what to do in emergencies such as striking oil and on how to avoid volcanoes, geysers, and sharks (in the Indian Ocean, where you come out) adds humor to a careful scientific description with simple definitions smoothly integrated into the text. A funny but earnest combination of science and science fiction with lively, amusing illustrations." Horn Bk

551.2   Earthquakes. Volcanoes

Asimov, Isaac
How did we find out about earthquakes? Illus. by David Wool. Walker & Co. 1978 58p illus maps $5.95, lib. bdg. $5.85 (5 and up) **551.2**

1 Earthquakes
ISBN 0-8027-6305-7; 0-8027-6306-5   LC 78-4098

Asimov, Isaac—*Continued*

"Humankind's attempts to understand the causes of earthquakes, from mythology to present-day scientific theory, are explained in a clear lucid style. Asimov demonstrates how each subsequent discovery helped scientists in developing the current theory of plate tectonics. Asimov concentrates on theories advanced by western scientists, using the Lisbon quake of 1755 as the starting point for his examination of European earthquakes. This introductory survey explains the concepts of surface and body waves, the structure of the earth and gives credit to the scientists who introduced the various theories." Sch Library J

Brown, Billye Walker

Historical catastrophes: earthquakes, by Billye Walker Brown and Walter R. Brown. Addison-Wesley 1974 191p illus lib. bdg. $7.95 (5 and up)   **551.2**

1 Earthquakes
ISBN 0-201-00546-8   LC 73-15617
"An Addisonian Press book"
This is a "chronological account of earthquakes from the Lisbon quake of 1755 to the Alaskan disaster of 1964. In addition to discussion of ancient beliefs and theories of tremors and quakes, scientific explanations of the causes of earthquakes are also provided. The black-and-white photographs are interesting." Sch Library J

Lauber, Patricia

Earthquakes; new scientific ideas about how and why the earth shakes; illus. with maps and diagrams by Cal Sacks and with photographs. Random House 1972 81p illus maps lib. bdg. $5.39 (4-6)   **551.2**

1 Earthquakes
ISBN 0-394-92373-1   LC 72-1808
"Covered are the origins of earthquakes, tsunami, Pangaea, and the history of earthquakes in Alaska, California and Japan. Definitions of terms are provided in the text." Sch Library J
"Errors are few and insignificant; the arrangement and balance of the presentation is commendable. . . . [Readers] who want to know what new earth science terms like 'continental drift' and 'plate tectonics' are all about, will come away from this well illustrated and easily read volume with a much improved appreciation of this ever-changing planet and an understanding of why these earthquake-caused changes will always be with us." Sci Bks

Marcus, Rebecca B.

The first book of volcanoes & earthquakes. Rev. ed. Watts, F. 1972 86p illus maps lib. bdg. $5.90 (5 and up)   **551.2**

1 Volcanoes 2 Earthquakes
ISBN 0-531-00799-5   LC 72-2301
"A First book"
First published 1963
This book "is profusely illustrated and interestingly written. The presentation of the genesis of Paricutin Volcano and the discussions of the interrelationships between volcanoes, earthquakes and plate tectonic theory are presented in simple enough vocabulary to reach upper elementary and high school students, and the presentation is complete enough that the student should have a good understanding of the subject. . . . Among other materials related to volcanoes, the text covers geysers and hot springs and touches on the potential power to be developed from these sources, such as is presently done in California and Iceland. Another of the interesting discussions involves the history of the seismometer and its early use in China and Japan. Altogether the book provides a very complete and interesting presentation of its subject." Sci Bks
Glossary: p78-82

Mercer, Charles

Monsters in the earth; the story of earthquakes. Putnam 1978 157p illus $7.95 (5 and up)   **551.2**

1 Earthquakes
ISBN 0-399-20642-6   LC 78-3755
"The author recreates two disasters: the 1976 quake in China and the 1906 upheaval in San Francisco. Besides a report on the monstrous effects in these places, the text provides anecdotes about people, famous and obscure, and their surprising reactions to the overwhelming forces of nature. Of chief importance, however, are Mercer's explanation of what causes earthquakes, discussions of scientific discoveries and speculations about dealing with the threat." Pub W
"A basic knowledge of geography and geology is presupposed and there are no illustrations demonstrating scientific concepts. But the consideration of the sociological and political impact of earthquakes found here is not included in other juvenile titles on the subject." Sch Library J
Bibliography: p147-49. Glossary: p151-52

Nixon, Hershell H.

Volcanoes; nature's fireworks [by] Hershell H. Nixon and Joan Lowery Nixon; illus. with photographs. Dodd 1978 48p illus lib. bdg. $4.95 (3-5)   **551.2**

1 Volcanoes
ISBN 0-396-07559-2   LC 77-16873
"This discussion defines various kinds of volcanoes, gives reasons for their eruptions, describe the formative process, and explains their effects. Examples of actual disasters such as Kilauea in Hawaii and Krakatoa in the East Indies are depicted in black-and-white photographs. In addition to a brief history of volcanoes, the authors also comment on use of tiltmeters and seismographs, the work of volcanologists, and the ways scientists have used volcanic activity beneficially. A well-rounded information source." Booklist

Simon, Seymour

Danger from below: earthquakes, past, present, and future. Four Winds 1979 86p illus maps $7.95 (4 and up)   **551.2**

1 Earthquakes
ISBN 0-590-07514-4   LC 78-22283
"The author interweaves descriptions of earthquakes with the latest discoveries about earthquakes—how and why they happen, how they can be predicted, and how warning systems can save lives. Simon also tells how scientists can measure the energy released by a quake using the Richter Scale and the degree of its damage using the Mercali Intensity Scale. Suggestions follow about what to do for your personal safety in an earthquake. Many excellent black-and-white photographs and simplified drawings complement the lively text. A thorough index lets you locate important points made in the 11 short chapters." Sci and Children

551.3 Glaciers. Icebergs

Gans, Roma

Icebergs; illus. by Bobri. Crowell 1964 unp illus (Let's-read-and-find-out science bks) lib. bdg. $6.89 (1-3)   **551.3**

1 Icebergs
ISBN 0-690-42775-1   LC 64-18163
The text explains "for the young child what icebergs are, where they come from, and the dangers they present to ships." Hodges. Bks for Elem Sch Libraries
Young children "will welcome a book they can read themselves. . . . Bold illustrations augment the text nicely." Sch Library J

Matthews, William H.

The story of glaciers and the ice age, by William H. Matthews, III. Harvey House 1974 142p illus maps lib. bdg. $6.29 (5 and up)   **551.3**

1 Glaciers
ISBN 0-8178-5142-9   LC 73-79452
"The author explains how glaciers form and flow, how their movements affect life on earth, and what scientists are currently theorizing and researching in regard to glaciers—past, present, and future." Booklist
"The book has a colorful and attractive cover and is generously illustrated with photos, maps, and diagrams. It has a glossary of over 100 terms, is

Matthews, William H.—*Continued*

well indexed, and includes a relatively complete list of other books on the topic. It will best serve as a reference source in the earth sciences; however, a student will pick up the book as an assignment and find himself reading for pleasure." Sci and Children

Schultz, Gwen

Icebergs and their voyages. Morrow 1975 95p illus maps lib. bdg. $6 (5 and up)   **551.3**

1 Icebergs
ISBN 0-688-32047-3   LC 75-9958

"The book traces the story of icebergs from the geological origin and physical characteristics, through their history as a fearsome menace to navigation, to their present status as objects of scientific inquiry and their potential future as a commodity of commerce and a boon to mankind." Appraisal

This book "is very readable, thorough, balanced, and well illustrated. A valuable addition to earth science classes." Sci Teacher

551.4   Geomorphology and general hydrology

Atwood, Ann

The wild young desert; text and photographs by Ann Atwood. Scribner 1970 unp illus lib. bdg. $5.95 (4 and up)   **551.4**

1 Deserts
ISBN 0-684-12625-7   LC 73-106536

The author depicts the desert's slow cycle of geologic change, the effects of wind and water, and the plants and animals which have adapted to the desert environment

"The text is sensitively, even poetically, written and will stir the imagination of some children; others may find it too generalized and unspecific and wish for more factual detail. There won't be any disagreement over Miss Atwood's dramatically juxtaposed color photographs, majestic long views alternating with close-ups of dazzling flowers, formations of agate and quartz, animals resting in shadows out of the sun. They are superbly beautiful and excellently reproduced." NY Times Bk Rev

Coburn, Doris

A spit is a piece of land; landforms in the U.S.A. Illus. with photographs; maps and drawings by William Jaber. Messner 1978 127p illus maps lib. bdg. $7.79 (4-6)   **551.4**

1 Physical geography—U.S.
ISBN 0-671-32844-1   LC 77-17605

The author "discusses various landforms that shape the earth, commenting on their creation, physical characteristics, and tectonic forces. Individual sections describe the coastlines (beaches, spits, dunes); lowlands (delta, marshes, inland plains); highlands (cliffs, mountains, volcanoes); and valleys (canyons, passes, gaps), as well as islands, caves, glaciers, and deserts. Passing mention of flora and fauna found in these areas is included, along with examples and peculiarities of specific geographic areas." Booklist

Gans, Roma

Caves; illus. by Giulio Maestro. Crowell 1976 32p illus (Let's-read-and-find-out science bks) lib. bdg. $6.89 (1-3)   **551.4**

1 Caves
ISBN 0-690-01070-2   LC 76-4881

The author describes "the ways in which caves are formed, the range of size from a small animal's lair to an enormous cavern, and the lure of cave exploration to amateurs (spelunkers) and scientists (speleologists) alike. . . . Gauged in extent and difficulty for a young independent reader, the book describes stalactites and stalagmites, cave tunnels, and the blind fish that inhabit the water in some caves." Chicago. Children's Bk Center

"The book is illustrated with water color drawings in blue, gray, and black which help suggest the damp darkness of the cave's interior." Appraisal

Goetz, Delia

Valleys; illus. by Leslie Morrill. Morrow 1976 64p illus $6.25, lib bdg $6 (3-6)   **551.4**

1 Valleys   2 U.S.—Geography
ISBN 0-688-22059-2; 0-688-32059-7   LC 75-26980

"The Shenandoah, Tennessee, Red River, Death, and the Ten Thousand Smokes. The great valleys of the United States, ranging across the continent from Virginia to California and Alaska are explored and discussed in a simple narrative style by Ms. Goetz. The formation of valleys and their impact upon the development of the country are also explained. The text is splendidly illustrated with detailed sketches of the valleys and maps of the areas." Adventuring With Bks

Laycock, George

Caves; illus. by DeVere E. Burt. Four Winds 1976 101p illus $6.95 (5 and up)   **551.4**

1 Caves
ISBN 0-590-07392-3   LC 76-15194

The author "describes cave formation, well-known caves, cave animals, and the fascinating uses man has found for caves from the time of the Indians to the present. Final pages give practical information on spelunking: precautions, lists of government-owned caves, and a bibliography." Horn Bk

"Although the black-and-white drawings are striking and lend an appropriate mysterious air to the subject, researchers will wish for photographs." Booklist

551.46   Oceanography

Berger, Melvin

Oceanography lab. Day 1973 126p illus maps (Scientists at work) lib. bdg. $8.79 (4-6)   **551.46**

1 Oceanography—Research   2 Oceanography—Vocational guidance   3 Woods Hole, Mass. Oceanographic Institute
ISBN 0-381-99940-8   LC 72-2417

"Woods Hole Oceanographic Institution on Cape Cod is the setting for the story of what an oceanographer does . . . . The early chapters discuss the reasons for establishing research bases, how research projects are initiated, how developed and how financed. The succeeding chapters each discuss the work of one type of scientist: the geologist, the bacteriologist, the chemist, the biologist, etc. There is a chapter on a ten-day expedition aboard the research vessel 'Knorr'; another on the work of the submarine 'Alvin'." Appraisal

"Excellent photographs of the Institute and its research activities on Cape Cod and at sea add to the effectiveness of this generally well-conceived and well-executed presentation." Library J
Further reading: p123-24

Jacobs, Francine

The Red Sea; illus. by Elsie Wrigley. Morrow 1978 79p illus $6.50, lib. bdg. $6.24 (4-6)   **551.46**

1 Red Sea
ISBN 0-688-22150-5; 0-688-32150-X   LC 77-25927

The author "combines information on the historical, economic, and biological aspects of the Red Sea, bringing into focus a well-balanced picture of the importance of this strategic body of water. Emphasis, however, is on the sea life, with careful attention given to the coral reefs and the wide assortment of fish, invertebrates, and mammals that live there in close relationships. Brief mention is made of the danger of pollution. Recent discoveries of mineral deposits and how they should be explored are discussed, and in closing the author links the plate tectonics theory to the continual widening of the Red Sea." Booklist

"Some of the topics are covered in depth, while others are dealt with superficially. The various conditions (salinity, temperature, geological and life processes) are explained thoroughly, but the political ramifications of location and potential wealth needs more elucidation. It is unfortunate that there are no color illustrations; however, the pen-and-ink drawings lend themselves gracefully and impressively to the text. As a supplement to geography classes, and for science classes studying marine life, this book would be useful." Sch Library J

551.47 Dynamic oceanography

Brindze, Ruth
The rise and fall of the seas; the story of the tides; illus. with photographs and with diagrams by Felix Cooper. Harcourt 1964 96p illus maps $5.95 (4 and up)   551.47

1 Tides
ISBN 0-15-267380-6   LC 64-11491

An "explanation of tides, and the effect of the moon's and sun's gravity on air, water, and the land masses of earth. Methods for predicting tides, the hazards of tides, and their potential value to man are presented." Children's Bks, 1964
"In this brief book, beautifully illustrated, the author [writes] in a clear and interesting manner. Young readers will find how the effects of the tide can be easily observed at the seashore. . . . It is a well written, instructive book." Best Sellers

Clemons, Elizabeth
Waves, tides, and currents; illus. with maps, diagrams & photographs. Knopf 1967 112p illus maps lib. bdg. $5.99 (3-5)   551.47

1 Tides 2 Ocean waves
ISBN 0-394-91824-X   LC 66-13786

"A general definition of the tide is followed by a discussion of the force of gravity that leads into an explanation of the causes of the tides, their ranges and differences. Wave action, ground swells, tsunamis, and currents are explained." The AAAS-Sci Bk List for Children
"This beginners' book on oceanography delights the eye with its unity of text, illustration and design." NY Times Bk Rev
Glossary: p105-06. Bibliography: p107-08

Zim, Herbert S.
Waves; illus. by René Martin. Morrow 1967 62p illus maps lib. bdg. $6.48 (3-5)   551.47

1 Ocean waves
ISBN 0-688-31479-1   LC 67-21734

"A very simple account of ocean waves, describing their origin, physical characteristics, and the natural forces that modify them. . . . The author discusses techniques that scientists use to measure waves and programs they have developed to handle the vast amounts of sand that are continually being shifted along the shore. One section is devoted to a description of the tsunami or tidal wave resulting from a seismic disturbance." Sch Library J
"The book was prepared for the use of elementary school students in their introduction to the oceans. It should serve that purpose well, being a highly readable discourse on a complex subject. If the book has a fault it lies in its brevity." Sci Bks

551.48 Hydrology

Gans, Roma
Water for dinosaurs and you; illus. by Richard Cuffari. Crowell 1972 33p illus (Let's-read-and-find-out science bks) lib. bdg. $6.89, pa $2.95 (1-3)   551.48

1 Water 2 Water supply
ISBN 0-690-87027-2; 0-690-00202-5   LC 78-158691

"Stressing the use and reuse of water over millions of years, this is . . . [an] account of the water cycle. The sources of water—oceans, lakes, rivers, underground water, rain—are simply described. Pollution is also briefly covered." Appraisal
"The pictures are generally accurate; and the text descriptions are excellent in spite of the necessarily limited vocabulary." Sci Bks

551.5 Meteorology

Bendick, Jeanne
How to make a cloud. Parents Mag. Press [distributed by Enslow Pubs.] 1971 64p illus lib. bdg. $6.45 (1-3)   551.5

1 Clouds 2 Meteorology
ISBN 0-8193-0441-7   LC 74-134834

"A Stepping-stone book"
In order to explain "how to make a cloud," the author-illustrator presents a brief discussion on the composition of air as well as the phenomenon of hot air rising and cold air sinking. Included also are sections devoted to simple experiments, the identification of major types of clouds, and directions for 'making' rain, smog, sleet and snow
"What may seem an oversimplified explanation of clouds, their formation, appearance and effects on the weather is adequate for the age intended and can be read independently. . . . Black, white and blue cartoon-like drawings support the text. An index makes this a possible reference tool for the very young scientist." Appraisal

Branley, Franklyn M.
Flash, crash, rumble, and roll; illus. by Ed Emberley. Crowell 1964 unp illus (Let's-read-and-find-out science bks) lib. bdg. $6.89 (k-3)   551.5

1 Thunderstorms 2 Lightning 3 Rain and rainfall
ISBN 0-690-30563-X   LC 64-18161

"This reassuring book makes thunderstorms interesting instead of frightening by explaining their causes, nature, and effects. Includes safety rules and directions for telling how far away a storm is." Hodges. Bks for Elem Sch Libraries

Brindze, Ruth
Hurricanes; monster storms from the sea; illus. with photographs. Atheneum Pubs. 1973 106p illus maps lib. bdg. $7.95 (5 and up)   551.5

1 Hurricanes
ISBN 0-689-30423-4   LC 72-85915

"A Margaret K. McElderry book"
Contents: When Great Hurricane Camille hit the Gulf Coast; What we know about hurricanes; Columbus discovered hurricanes; Some hurricanes that shaped American history; A tour of the National Hurricane Center; Flights into hurricanes; Can earth's greatest storms be tamed; Anyone can track the course of a hurricane; Official safety rules; Terms to know; Lists of names used for hurricanes
The book's "chapters are well done and might serve to entice a student into some further inquiry into the historical events mentioned. The book reinforces the notion that science and technology stem from social needs and interactions with the natural world. . . . Hurricanes, like volcanoes and other major natural occurrences, are intrinsically interesting to children, and this book should lead them to a better understanding of such events." Sci Bks

Brown, Billye Walker
Historical catastrophes: hurricanes & tornadoes, by Billye Walker Brown and Walter R. Brown. Addison-Wesley [1972] 223p illus lib. bdg. $7.95 (5 and up)   551.5

1 Hurricanes 2 Tornadoes
ISBN 0-201-00777-0   LC 72-1980

"An Addisonian Press book"
"Beginning with the destruction of Galveston in 1900 by a hurricane the authors . . . show how over the years the development of a tracking and warning system has saved many lives when hurricanes and tornadoes have struck, and graphically describe the major storms from 1935 to 1970. They discuss the work of the Hurricane Hunters and scientific experiments with seeding a hurricane to decrease its violence and explain how hurricanes and tornadoes probably develop." Booklist
"Interesting stories about the effects of storms on people make this a good bet for older reluctant readers." Sch Library J

Buehr, Walter
Storm warning; the story of hurricanes and tornadoes; written and illus. by Walter Buehr. Morrow 1972 62p illus $6.75, lib. bdg. $6.48 (3-6)   551.5

1 Hurricanes 2 Tornadoes 3 Storms
ISBN 0-688-21921-7; 0-688-31921-1   LC 71-175815

The author describes hurricanes he has encountered, explains the conditions that can spawn a

Buehr, Walter—Continued

tropical storm, and discusses the techniques that
have been developed to establish effective storm
forecasting
"Not a comprehensive treatment, but a good
introduction to the topic, written in an informal
but dignified style." Chicago. Children's Bk Center

Heuer, Kenneth

Rainbows, halos, and other wonders; light
and color in the atmosphere; illus. with
photographs and prints. Dodd 1978 108p illus
lib. bdg. $5.95 (6 and up)   551.5

1 Meteorology 2 Optics
ISBN 0-396-07557-6   LC 77-16865

"This book on atmospheric optics should help
you to see and appreciate the wonders of light
and color in the open air. The features of the
atmosphere are arranged here, for the most part,
according to the physical processes causing them.
. . . The book is illustrated with photographs and
prints. . . . Some of the best pictures of these
effects were made in the nineteenth century and
are included in these pages. For anyone who has
ever wondered why the stars twinkle, or if you
can walk under the arch of a rainbow, or why the
sky is blue, this book has been written." Preface
Annotated bibliography: p105-06

Jennings, Gary

The killer storms; hurricanes, typhoons,
and tornadoes. Lippincott 1970 207p illus
maps $8.95 (5 and up)   551.5

1 Hurricanes 2 Typhoons 3 Tornadoes
ISBN 0-397-31128-1   LC 78-101899

The author "describes briefly the creation
of these storms and then details interesting
phenomena associated with them . . . . The de-
cription of the physics of storm formation is brief
and quite clear. Concludes with a description of
forecasting tracking facilities of the Environmental Science Services Administration and the
U.S. Air Force and a few things you may do
to survive a killer storm." The AAAS Sci Bk List
for Children
"Excellent photographs and drawings elucidate
the text." Library J

Laycock, George

Tornadoes, killer storms. McKay 1979 58p
illus $6.95 (4 and up)   551.5

1 Tornadoes
ISBN 0-679-20979-4   LC 78-20326

The author explains how tornadoes form, where
they occur, the damage they do, and ways of
surviving them. He also presents U.S. government
research attempts at "unraveling tornado secrets"
"The book also explains how tornadoes create
stress and despair for people and leave pets and
wildlife homeless. A collection of stories by persons having lived through tornado experiences are
vivid and fascinating, written in language for
young readers. Includes black-and-white photographs." Sci and Children

Weiss, Malcolm E.

Storms—from the inside out; illus. by
Lloyd Birmingham, and with photographs.
Messner 1973 96p illus maps lib. bdg. $5.79
(4-6)   551.5

1 Storms
ISBN 0-671-32612-0   LC 73-5396

This is an "introduction to cloud-storm relationships, causes and effects of lightning, tornado and
hurricane formation, and cold/warm front interaction." Sch Library J
"This reviewer wishes there had been more
material on formation processes and global
weather patterns. . . . The illustrations and photographs are well conceived and executed, and
the word descriptions of the formation of the
weather processes tie in well with the pictures."
Sci Bks
Glossary: p89-90

551.57   Hydrometeorology

Branley, Franklyn M.

Rain and hail; illus. by Helen Borten.
Crowell 1963 unp illus (Let's-read-and-find-
out science bks) $6.95 (k-3)   551.57

1 Rain and rainfall 2 Hail
ISBN 0-690-66844-9   LC 63-12469

An elementary explanation of what causes rain
and how hail forms. Pictures and text tell of the
part played by clouds, droplets and water vapor,
in these processes

Snow is falling; illus. by Helen Stone.
Crowell 1963 unp illus (Let's-read-and-find-
out science bks) $6.95, lib. bdg. $6.89 (k-3)
    551.57

1 Snow
ISBN 0-690-74299-1; 0-690-74300-9   LC 63-15084

An explanation of what makes snow, the shape
of snowflakes, the appearance and uses of snow,
and how it affects plants and animals
"Attractively illustrated, a good science book
for beginning independent readers. . . . [An]
introduction to the topics of weather or seasons."
Chicago. Children's Bk Center

Busch, Phyllis S.

A walk in the snow; photographs by
Mary M. Thacher. Lippincott 1971 40p illus
$7.95 (1-4)   551.57

1 Snow 2 Nature study
ISBN 0-397-31233-4   LC 79-151476

"Photographs are used both to show the beauty
of winter and the ways in which an observant
child can find clues to wind direction, read animal
tracks, make a plastic copy of a snowflake, test the
effect of color on temperature (a piece of dark
cloth and a piece of white sink to different depths),
or see the evidence of repeated snowfalls in the
layers of a snowbank." Sat Rev
"The photographs make this book. It is unfortunate that the text is rather ordinary. Activities are those traditionally used in most elementary schools. Certainly, however, the book
does encourage exploration and observation, particularly that of the sounds of different snows.
Thus it will be a useful experience." Appraisal

De Paola, Tomie

The cloud book; words and pictures by
Tomie de Paola. Holiday House 1975 30p
illus lib. bdg. $7.95 (k-3)   551.57

1 Clouds
ISBN 0-8234-0259-2   LC 74-34493

The author "instructs young readers about the
ten most common types of clouds, how they were
named, and what they mean in terms of changing weather. Actually a very good text to use
for early science instruction. Includes a scattering
of traditional myths that have clouds as a basis."
Adventuring With Bks

551.6   Climatology and weather

Bova, Ben

The weather changes man. Addison-Wesley
1974 139p illus lib. bdg. $6.95 (5 and up)
    551.6

1 Climate 2 Man—Influence of environment
ISBN 0-201-00555-7   LC 73-16480

"An Addisonian Press book"
The author "explores the effect of weather on
man: the original formation of a liveable environment on earth, the weather's role in agriculture,
the physiological effects of climate, and some
recent discoveries about weather's influence on
modern living." Booklist

Gallant, Roy A.

Earth's changing climate. Four Winds 1979
226p illus $9.95 (6 and up)   551.6

1 Climate
ISBN 0-590-07447-4   LC 78-22124

"According to Gallant, climatologists are in general agreement that earth is due for a change

Gallant, Roy A.—*Continued*

of climate after a relatively warm and stable first half of the twentieth century, but they disagree somewhat on what kind of change and when it will occur. To enable readers to understand climate, he explains earth's atmosphere and some of the more important ingredients of climate (seasons, ocean currents, wind systems, etc.) the reconstruction of past climates throughout the geological time scale, ice ages and natural and technological factors that influence climate change. He concludes with a look at various large-scale projects proposed to control climate. Gallant handles a complex subject with dexterity, clarity, and even a certain liveliness, and complements his text with many good diagrams and charts. Still some background knowledge of earth science will aid the reader." Booklist

Bibliography: p207-10. Glossary: p211-20

Hays, James D.

Our changing climate. Atheneum Pubs. 1977 101p illus $6.95 (5 and up)   551.6

1 Climate
ISBN 0-689-30586-9   LC 77-5055

"This exposition of climate-shaping forces concentrates on making processes and mechanisms clear. Chapters on global temperature controls and local and regional climate elaborate on how factors of solar radiation, tilt of the earth's axis, differing heat capacities of land and water and the movement of air all mesh to create varying temperature and climate zones." Booklist

"A well-written account of the changes in the earth's climate. . . . The illustrations add much to the impact of the text, most dramatically in the depiction of Rhone Valley glaciation in the 19th Century and today." Sch Library J

A **January** fog will freeze a hog, and other weather folklore; comp. and ed. by Hubert Davis; illus. by John Wallner. Crown 1977 unp illus lib. bdg. $6.95 (1-3)   551.6

1 Weather lore
ISBN 0-517-52811-8   LC 76-54333

The editor "chose many obscure and earthy sayings from folklore to make up his text which is jolly entertaining if not always reliable weather forecasting: 'When you see a beaver/ Carrying sticks in its mouth,/ 'Twill be a hard winter—/ You'd better go south.' . . . Notes at the end of the book tell about the origins of beliefs on what is portended by various natural phenomena. Davis points out that some, like the title verse, were made up just for fun." Pub W

"Wallner's vivid . . . illustrations reflect the intensity and diversity of nature and reveal in fine detail the integration of people, animals, and plants with the weather. Presented in two-page spreads of complicated design in which fair and foul skies and various birds and beasts move in and out of bordered vignettes, the artwork dominates the simple text." Sch Library J

Milgrom, Harry

Understanding weather. Rev. ed. Illus. by Lloyd Birmingham. Crowell-Collier Press 1970 84p illus map lib. bdg. $4.95 (5 and up)   551.6

1 Weather 2 Weather forecasting
ISBN 0-02-766940-8   LC 77-97756

First published 1959 by Capitol Pub. with title: The adventure book of weather

This book "is informative, inspirational and experimental, providing good background in the how and why of the weather, the water cycle, the classification of clouds and a cloud chart, explanations of the principles of meteorological instruments, and a description of the organization and work of meteorological services. . . . Information on the use of weather satellites and . . . suggestions to anyone interested in exploring meteorology as a career [are also included]. . . . The black-and-white illustrations are well labeled and are keyed to the text." Sci Bks

For further reading: p79-80

Sattler, Helen R.

Nature's weather forecasters. Elsevier/ Nelson Bks. 1978 158p illus $6.95 (5 and up)   551.6

1 Weather lore 2 Weather forecasting 3 Nature study
ISBN 0-525-66594-3   LC 78-1694

First published by Thomas Nelson

A book "on observing and interpreting weather signs. Readers are alerted to signs that reveal changes in humidity, temperature, winds, and clouds and to what those signs portend. Attempts are also made to illustrate the effects of weather on people and their social environment." Sch Library J

Weiss, Malcolm E.

What's happening to our climate? Illus. by Paul Plumer. Messner 1978 93p illus maps lib. bdg. $7.29 (5 and up)   551.6

1 Climate
ISBN 0-671-32846-8   LC 78-15684

"Weiss surveys the climate question ably for younger readers, first explaining how weather is created and then exploring some of the theories and counter theories as to why past and certain presently discernable trends have happened. The significance of all this relates to world food production capacities, which have benefited by the past 50 years of 'unusually warm' weather and stand in jeopardy if planning doesn't take into account inevitable climate shifts. Interesting and easily digested, this could have benefited from more aesthetic design; its purely functional look locks it into the classroom assignment sourcebook category." Booklist

Glossary: p81-85

552 Rocks (Petrology)

Branley, Franklyn M.

Pieces of another world; the story of moon rocks; illus. by Herbert Danska. Crowell 1972 58p illus lib. bdg. $9.89 (5 and up)   552

1 Lunar petrology
ISBN 0-690-62566-9   LC 71-158684

"The title of this attractively produced book refers to the material brought back by Apollo 11, 12 and 14, and Luna 16. The astronauts' tools and collection methods and the quarantine and analysis procedures employed at the Lunar Receiving Laboratory are described. Current theories about the origin of the samples and of the moon itself are discussed. The illustrations are well chosen and executed; the exposition is clear and well organized." Sch Library J

For further reading p55

De Paola, Tomie

The quicksand book. Holiday House 1977 unp illus lib. bdg. $8.95 (k-3)   552

1 Quicksand
ISBN 0-8234-0291-6   LC 76-28762

Illustrated by the author

"Jungle Girl, swinging on a vine from her tree house, falls into a patch of . . . [quicksand] but, fortunately, is observed by Jungle Boy. As she slowly sinks, her scholarly, bespectacled young Tarzan delivers a long but interesting lecture on the properties of and useful means of rescue from quicksand. Meanwhile, Jungle Boy's attendant monkey is setting up a delightfully civilized tea table. Rescued not a moment too soon, Jungle Girl is soon leisurely enjoying her tea, while observing Jungle Boy, who has now fallen in himself. Helpful instructions on making a jolly bog in a bucket are added." Horn Bk

"A deft blend of fact and fiction is illustrated with ebullient paintings framed in enormous leaves that remind the lap audience of the jungle setting and that provide a corner for silent action that gives a third dimension. . . . And the information about quicksand is accurate, too. Very nice." Chicago. Children's Bk Center

Gallob, Edward

City rocks, city blocks, and the moon; photographs by the author. Scribner 1973 48p illus lib. bdg. $6.95 (3-5)   552

1 Rocks 2 Lunar petrology
ISBN 0-684-13542-6   LC 73-1333

This photoessay brings "elementary geology to the city dweller's doorstep by leading readers to the streets to search out such items as granite curbstones, marble steps, or sandy brownstones.

Gallob, Edward—*Continued*

These and other commonly encountered stone surfaces serve as easily accessible illustrations of igneous, sedimentary, and metamorphic rocks—the three broad rock groupings Gallob describes. Within each group the author explains the ongoing formative processes and illustrates various specific rock types, including man-made and moon rocks. Not an in-depth book, but an attractive starting point for budding rock hounds confined to an urban setting." Booklist

Ruchlis, Hy

How a rock came to be in a fence on a road near a town; illus. by Mamoru Funai. Walker & Co. [1974 c1973] unp illus $4.85 (2-4)   552

1 Rocks
ISBN 0-8027-6161-5   LC 73-81790

"The story traces the development of sedimentary rocks from their origin to the kinds of rocks in the fence. It begins with the layers of shells at the bottom of the sea and continues with the elevation of the bottom of the sea, the weathering of exposed rock, and the movement of pieces of rock by glaciers. The collection of rocks is then arranged in a fence row by a farmer and his sons who farm the land and need to clear it of the rocks." Sci and Children
"Written with simplicity and grace, nicely illustrated. . . . The text is accurate but does not digress to discuss such subjects as the different kinds of rocks or the cause of the land rising from the ocean floor, although the illustration shows volcanic action. Deftly compartmentalized in treatment, the book gives a good picture of the slow, inexorable changes in nature." Chicago. Children's Bk Center

553.2   Carbonaceous materials

Kraft, Betsy Harvey

Coal. Watts, F. 1976 66p illus lib. bdg. $6.45 (4-6)   553.2

1 Coal 2 Coal mines and mining
ISBN 0-531-00336-1   LC 76-16203

"A First book"
This book "provides basic information about the history and uses, geologic origins, mining practice and hazards, and effects on the environment of mining and burning coal." AAAS Sci Bks & Films
"The accompanying black-and-white photographs are particularly well done. No collection should be without this introduction to an important resource." Sch Library J
Glossary: p62-64

553.6   Earthy materials

Goldin, Augusta

Salt; illus. by Robert Galster. Crowell [1966 c1965] unp illus (Let's-read-and-find-out science bks) lib. bdg. $7.89 (1-3)   553.6

1 Salt
ISBN 0-690-71815-2   LC 65-18696

"Starting with a simple experiment to demonstrate how salt crystals can be grown, this book proceeds to explain the importance of salt, where it is found, how it is mined and its uses. An attractively illustrated [book]." Ontario Library Rev

553.7   Water and aqueous deposits

Berger, Melvin

The new water book; illus. by Leonard Kessler. Crowell 1973 111p illus $6.95 (4-6)   553.7

1 Water 2 Water—Pollution
ISBN 0-690-58146-7   LC 73-3395

"A treatment of the subject that is comprehensive in scope, simple in style, lucid in explanation, and given added interest by the inclusion

throughout the text of home demonstrations, helpfully illustrated and clearly outlined. The text discusses the composition of water, its three states (liquid, solid, and gas), and some of the unusual properties of water; it describes the need for water in plants, human beings, and other animal life; it surveys water in agriculture and industry, describes the water cycle, and discusses the water supply and water pollution." Chicago. Children's Bk Center
"A list of more advanced books for further reading is appended." Booklist

560   Paleontology. Paleozoology

Aliki

Fossils tell of long ago. Crowell 1972 33p illus (Let's-read-and-find-out science bks) lib. bdg. $6.89 (1-3)   560

1 Fossils
ISBN 0-690-31379-9   LC 78-170999

"Emphasizing what fossils are, how they were formed, and what they reveal about past life, the author . . . describes various ways in which fossils can be formed, tells where to look for them, and suggests making an instant fossil—a handprint in clay." Booklist
"Lively and amusing drawings [by the author] add to the informational value of a good introduction to the subject of fossils, the writing and the scope of the book making it simple enough to read to preschool children although it is intended for the independent reader." Chicago. Children's Bk Center

Hussey, Lois J.

Collecting small fossils, by Lois J. Hussey and Catherine Pessino; illus. by Anne Marie Jauss. Crowell [1971 c1970] 57p illus $6.95 (3-6)   560

1 Fossils—Collection and preservation
ISBN 0-690-19733-0   LC 77-101932

"Simply written and well organized, this short how-to-do-it manual describes the formation of fossils, their likely locations, necessary equipment and procedures for collecting them. The general instructions are practical. . . . Drawings are accurate, there is a good annotated bibliography, and addresses for obtaining topographic and geologic maps are included." Sch Library J

Rhodes, Frank H. T.

Fossils; a guide to prehistoric life, by Frank H. T. Rhodes, Herbert S. Zim and Paul R. Shaffer; illus. by Raymond Perlman. Golden Press 1962 160p illus (A Golden Nature guide) lib. bdg. $9.15 pa $1.95 (6 and up)   560

1 Fossils
ISBN 0-307-63515-5; 0-307-24411-3   LC 62-21640

At head of title: 480 illustrations in color
"Introductory material on fossil hunting is followed by a survey of life of the past; then invertebrate and vertebrate animal fossils are described and a brief account of fossil plants is given." The AAAS Sci Bk List for Children
"The last section, a rather condensed treatment of fossil plants, could easily have been enlarged. However, this book is crammed full of information for the fossil collector and is recommended for any school or public library as an inexpensive, colorful guidebook." Library J

567.9   Fossil reptiles. Dinosaurs

Aliki

My visit to the dinosaurs. Crowell 1969 33p illus (Let's-read-and-find-out science bks) $6.95, lib. bdg. $6.89, pa $1.45 (k-3)   567.9

1 Dinosaurs
ISBN 0-690-57401-0; 0-690-57402-9; 0-690-57403-7
                                      LC 70-78255

Illustrated by the author, this "first-person account of a little boy's visit to a museum, presented in clear pictures and easy-reading text,

Aliki—*Continued*

gives simple facts about the work of paleontologists and the skeletal structure, appearance, and eating habits of such dinosaurs as the brontosaurus, allosaurus, stegosaurus, and triceratops. Limited in scope but contains useful introductory information." Booklist

Cohen, Daniel

What really happened to the dinosaurs? Illus. by Haru Wells. Dutton 1977 70p illus $8.50 (4-6)   **567.9**

1 Dinosaurs
ISBN 0-525-42472-5   LC 77-7545

"Cohen's excellent book provides . . . a statement of question, evidence and conclusions for the various theories of dinosaur extinction. Other great extinctions, such as that of the Pleistocene, are briefly discussed. While emphasizing that evolutionary change is slow and our evidence for the rapidity of evolution incomplete, he discusses climate and habitat change, catastrophe, competition and disease as causes of extinction. In the final pages he considers the popular view of dinosaurs as warm-blooded animals, and the possibility that birds are their descendants, meaning that dinosaurs may not have become extinct after all. This book is useful in presenting the idea of multiple working hypotheses, the incompleteness of our data, and the fact that the problem of extinction is far from being solved. . . . The illustrations are mood pieces in wash, except for three scientific drawings which serve as backgound to the text." AAAS Sci Bks & Films
Suggested reading: p67

Cole, Joanna

Dinosaur story; illus. by Mort Kunstler. Morrow 1974 unp illus lib. bdg. $6 (k-3)   **567.9**

1 Dinosaurs
ISBN 0-688-31826-6   LC 74-5831

"Beginning with scientists' work on bones, the author gives facts about 10 different dinosaurs, relating them to each other in terms of food cycle and time period. Each prehistoric animal is pictured in accurate, black-and-white drawings projecting a sense of action." Booklist
"This will be helpful to fill requests of the very young who never have enough dinosaur books. Style and clarity will interest adults reading aloud to preschoolers and older children able to read on their own." Children's Bk Rev Serv

Darling, Lois

Before and after dinosaurs; written and illus. by Lois and Louis Darling. Morrow 1959 95p illus map lib. bdg. $5.52 (5 and up)   **567.9**

1 Reptiles, Fossil
ISBN 0-688-31077-X   LC 59-9439

"The evolution of vertebrate animals is traced for hundreds of millions of years, emphasis is on Class Reptilia and its five subclasses: turtles, mammal-like reptiles, icthyosaurs, sauroteryglans, and the ruling reptiles which included the dinosaurs." The AAAS Sci Bk List for Children
Includes pronunciation list. "Good pictures, charts, and readable text. . . . This is a good addition to a collection." Library J

Halstead, Beverly

A closer look at prehistoric reptiles; illus. by Richard Orr. Gloucester Press 1978 c1977 30p illus pa $1.95 (4-6)   **567.9**

1 Reptiles, Fossil 2 Dinosaurs
ISBN 0-531-02487-3   LC 77-10464

"A Closer look book"
First published 1977 in England
"Well-designed charts and striking full-color illustrations of familiar and lesser-known prehistoric creatures in action augment the lucid text. Topics covered include how we know about prehistoric reptiles, what a reptile is, which ones lived during the different prehistoric periods, and the evolution of flight. An index adds to the book's usefulness." Sch Library J

Jackson, Kathryn

Dinosaurs; paintings by Jay H. Matternes. Natl. Geographic Soc. 1972 31p illus (k-3)

1 Dinosaurs
ISBN 0-87044-123-X   LC 72-91418

Obtainable only as part of a set for $9.95 with: Dogs working for people, by Joanna Foster, class 636.7; Lion cubs, by the National Geographic Society, class 599.74, and Treasures in the sea, by Robert M. McClung, class 910.4
"Books for young explorers"
Prepared by the Special Publications Division of the National Geographic Society
Title on spine: Days of the dinosaurs
This book describes the various types of dinosaurs which evolved in the distant past and what scientists learn about them by studying fossils

Kaufmann, John

Flying reptiles in the age of dinosaurs. Morrow 1976 unp illus $6, lib. bdg. $5.52 (1-4)   **567.9**

1 Pterosaurs
ISBN 0-688-22073-8; 0-688-32073-2   LC 76-1919

An "account of the pterosaurs written for the young. The story line follows their probable course of evolution from four-legged terrestrial beasts to winged monsters of the sky. . . . Brief accounts of each of the major types of pterosaurs are followed by a full discussion of how pterosaurs stayed aloft. The story concludes with an account of the recent discovery of 'Quetzalcoatlus,' the 747 of pterosaurs, with a 51-foot wing spread." AAAS Sci Bks & Films
"Fine charcoal drawings visualize the author-artist's conception of how these reptiles looked, and labeled illustrations detail the bones of such fossils as the 51-foot Quetzalcoatlus found in Texas. A clear distinction of factual material and scientifically based assumptions makes this a worthwhile addition to the always popular dinosaur books for young readers." Booklist

Knight, David C.

Dinosaur days; illus. by Joel Schick. McGraw 1977 unp illus $6.95 (k-3)   **567.9**

1 Dinosaurs
ISBN 0-07-035101-5   LC 77-7917

This "brief introduction to the age of dinosaurs describes the physical world in which the creatures lived and explains how scientists, through the study of fossils, have come to their conclusions. . . . Especially helpful is the breakdown of 18 different kinds (with pronunciations), such as brontosaurus, diplodocus, stegosaurus, and pteranodon, which gives specific details concerning size, eating habits, movement, and method of attacking enemies." Booklist
The "text is simple, easily assimilated and never condescending. . . . And Schick's drawings are marvels of accuracy and professionalism, set against landscapes as they must have been, millions of years ago, before the arrival of the first humans on earth." Pub W

McGowen, Tom

Album of dinosaurs; illus. by Rod Ruth. Rand McNally 1972 60p illus $5.95, lib. bdg. $5.79 (3-5)   **567.9**

1 Dinosaurs
ISBN 0-528-82024-9; 0-528-80152-X

"Following an introductory sketch of the history and general characteristics of dinosaurs, each of twelve succeeding chapters focuses upon a particular genus—its peculiarities, presumed habits, and relationships to contemporary life." Sci Bks
"The mention of differing scientific opinions regarding the habits and behavior of dinosaurs as well as tales of some noteworthy fossil finds heighten the educational value of this book. . . . The colorful, full-page illustrations and smaller, black-and-white drawings accurately portray prehistoric creatures." Sch Library J

Dinosaurs & other prehistoric animals; illus. by Rod Ruth. Rand McNally 1978 110p illus $6.95 (3-6)   **567.9**

1 Dinosaurs 2 Mammals, Fossil
ISBN 0-528-82078-8   LC 78-54737

Contains the author's Album of dinosaurs, first published 1972 and entered separately above and his Album of prehistoric animals, first published 1974

McGowen, Tom—*Continued*

"The various species are discussed as to their age, physical characteristics, eating habits, predatory instincts, et al., each in three pages of text accompanied by black-and-white sketches in the margins and a one-page, full-color illustration of the creature in dramatic, often life-and-death, situations. Included in the 25 varieties are the Stegosaurus, Protoceratops, and Tyrannosaurus from the dinosaur era and the Eohippus, Mammoth, and Ursus spelaeus from the mammalian period that followed." Booklist

"Thanks to Ruth's colorful paintings, McGowen's clear text, and the balanced format, this remains one of the most attractive and accessible books for young prehistoric animal enthusiasts." Sch Library J

Parish, Peggy

Dinosaur time; pictures by Arnold Lobel. Harper 1974 30p illus $5.95, lib. bdg. $6.89 (k-2)   **567.9**

1 Dinosaurs
ISBN 0-06-024653-7; 0-06-024654-5   LC 73-14331

"An Early I can read book"

"Excellent illustrations, big print and not too much of it, good page layout, and a simple, accurate presentation make a fine first book on the subject. There's a bit of background information, and then specific material on eleven dinosaurs, each topic beginning with the pronunciation ('BRACHIOSAURUS. This is how to say it—brack-ee-oh-SAW-russ.') and describing each kind of dinosaur." Chicago. Children's Bk Center

Pringle, Laurence

Dinosaurs and people; fossils, facts, and fantasies; illus. with photographs and drawings. Harcourt [1979 c1978] 64p illus $6.95 (4 and up)   **567.9**

1 Dinosaurs
ISBN 0-15-260501-0   LC 78-52810

"An excellent story of dinosaur fossil gathering, reconstruction, and interpretation, including lucid descriptions of the recent 'warmblooded dinosaur' theory. Black-and-white illustrations show paleontologists at work, as well as reconstructed dinosaurs. . . . The book contains an index and a list of further readings. Though the latter contains references which are above the age level for whom the book is intended, one is made aware of the top-notch resources consulted in the writing of the book. An excellent library resource, useful for individualized student reports." Sci Teacher

Dinosaurs and their world; illus. with photographs and drawings. Harcourt 1968 63p illus lib. bdg. $4.95, pa $1.95 (3-5)   **567.9**

1 Dinosaurs
ISBN 0-15-223520-5; 0-15-626060-3   LC 68-11506

"A well-researched and carefully written narrative illustrated with photographs of paintings, restorations, fossils, field sites, and museum preparations. There are explanatory drawings of anatomical features and a geological timetable. It is easy to read and the lucid descriptions should hold the interest of any young reader. The text describes evolutionary history, morphology, representative specimens, field work, and museum study methods. The final chapter lists museums of North America that have dinosaur exhibits." Sci Bks

"Of particular interest is the description of how fossil clues are used by paleontologists to reconstruct the appearance and trace the life cycles of dinosaurs." Library J

Selsam, Millicent E.

Sea monsters of long ago; pictures by John Hamberger. Four Winds [1978 c1977] unp illus lib. bdg. $6.95 (1-3)   **567.9**

1 Reptiles, Fossil
ISBN 0-590-07567-5   LC 78-5385

"Selsam presents a variety of creatures that inhabited the seas during the dinosaurian era, explaining in simple-to-understand language their physical appearance, reproduction techniques, and aquatic abilities. The author discusses the Ichthyosaurs, which resembled fish; Plesiosaurs, which looked like turtles with long necks; and Mosasaurs, which had a lizard appearance; she also

talks about discovery of the fossils that enabled scientists to make their present-day conclusions. Vivid full-color illustrations support the informative text." Booklist

Tyrannosaurus rex. Harper 1978 41p illus $5.95, lib. bdg. $5.79 (3-5)   **567.9**

1 Tyrannosaurus rex
ISBN 0-06-025423-8; 0-06-025424-6   LC 77-25677

"In 1902, following the discovery of a dinosaur horn, three scientists traveled to Montana and excavated the fossilized bones of a 'Tyrannosaurus rex, the largest meat-eating animal ever to live on earth. Selsam discusses the recovery and resulting reconstruction work of this and a 1908 finding, describing the difficulties due to the size and weight of the skeleton. Explaining that many deductions can be made about this monstrous creature's food, enemies, and physical characteristics, the author also . . . points out questions that remain unanswered and speculates on the purpose of the animal's small front legs and body color, some possible reasons for its extinction, and the question of whether it was warm or cold blooded. Black-and-white photographs and reproductions of paintings accompany the text." Booklist

"A simple, informative account that should appeal to all young dinosaur enthusiasts, though the accompanying bibliography would be more useful to teachers than to third or fourth graders." Sch Library J

Shuttlesworth, Dorothy E.

Dodos and dinosaurs. Hastings House 1968 64p illus map lib. bdg. $3.99 (4-6)   **567.9**

1 Dinosaurs 2 Reptiles, Fossil
ISBN 0-8038-1532-8   LC 68-25626

"Famous museums"

"By narrating the history of some unusual exhibits in the American Museum of Natural History, Mrs. Shuttlesworth relates clearly and concisely the story of the now extinct dodos and auks. She also tells of the famed early 20th-Century dinosaur hunts headed by Dr. Barnum Brown and Dr. Roy Chapman Andrews, searches which resulted in the uncovering of dinosaur skeletons, Protoceratops eggs, and a mummified Trachodont, all of which are now in the museum. Well-chosen, carefully placed photographs enhance the text . . . and hint at the formidable obstacles encountered by the dinosaur hunters. The accounts of the expeditions are dramatic, and the author's accurate, unemotional description of the extinction of auks and dodos is effective." Sch Library J

To find a dinosaur. Doubleday 1973 113p illus lib. bdg. $5.95 (5 and up)   **567.9**

1 Dinosaurs
ISBN 0-385-08890-6   LC 73-78093

Illustrated with drawings and photographs

"Beginning with an account of recent fossil footprint discoveries in New Jersey and Connecticut, the book goes on to review the history of 'dinosaur hunting' from earliest discoveries in England to the results of landmark expeditions in North America and Asia, with a brief and general account of the procedures involved in transforming dinosaur fossils into finished museum exhibits." Appraisal

"The author, who has long worked in the field of natural history, writes with easy competence and communicates her sense of excitement about the satisfactions of fossil-collecting. A relative index is appended." Chicago. Children's Bk Center

568 Fossil birds

Kaufmann, John

Little dinosaurs and early birds; written and illus. by John Kaufmann. Crowell 1977 32p illus (Let's-read-and-find-out science bks) lib. bdg. $6.89 (1-3)   **568**

1 Birds 2 Reptiles, Fossil
ISBN 0-690-01110-5   LC 75-37575

"The text describes the major fossil remains of prehistoric birds. It also discusses body temperature, feathers, bone structure, and two theories of the evolution of flight." Horn Bk

The "illustrations are both functional and interesting, ably depicting the theories described. Pronunciation guides are given for the various

Kaufmann, John—*Continued*
creatures discussed, making this an excellent addition to a fine beginning reader science series."
Sch Library J

569 Fossil mammals

Aliki
Wild and woolly mammoths; written and illus. by Aliki. Crowell 1977 unp illus (Let's-read-and-find-out science bks) lib. bdg. $6.89 (1-3) **569**

1 Mammoth
ISBN 0-690-01276-4   LC 76-18082
"Aliki describes the woolly mammoth's structure, its herbivorous habits, and the ways in which it was hunted by early man, having first discussed the changes brought by the ice age to living creatures. She brings in just enough material about how specimens were preserved and how they were pictured or captured in prehistoric times to clarify for the reader the ways that archeologists gain their knowledge." Chicago. Children's Bk Center
"With such imagination and integration of related subject matter, the book is a model of interesting factual writing for children." Horn Bk

572 Human races

Cohen, Robert
The color of man; with an afterword by Juan Comas; illus. by Ken Heyman. Random House 1968 109p illus $4.95, lib. bdg. $6.99 (5 and up) **572**

1 Race 2 Color of people
ISBN 0-394-81039-2; 0-394-91039-7   LC 68-103551
This "volume provides a sound, objective introduction to the physical and social significance of skin color. Cohen dispels the myths of color prejudice with facts which explain the biological basis of skin color, the evolution of color variations throughout the world, and the historical background of many false concepts about race. A brief afterword by a noted Mexican anthropologist stresses the need for racial understanding." Booklist
"A lucid book, the writing straightforward and the material rather loosely organized. The photographs are truly impressive, pictures of people from many parts of the world, pictures that amplify the text's message of brotherhood." Sutherland. The Best in Children's Bks

McKern, Sharon S.
The many faces of man; illus. with photographs. Lothrop 1972 192p illus lib. bdg. $7.92 (5 and up) **572**

1 Race 2 Anthropology
ISBN 0-688-50062-5   LC 72-1100
The author "explains the techniques utilized by physical and cultural anthropologists and discusses the facts and theories concerning racial differences and similarities revealed by their findings. McKern cites some of the factors which influence physical and cultural differences and stresses the fallacy of looking upon these differences as an indication of either superiority or inferiority. The account is lucidly presented, contains numerous interesting facts about different behavior patterns, and is well illustrated with photographs." Booklist
Further reading: p187-88

573.2 Organic evolution and genetics of humankind

Asimov, Isaac
How did we find out about our human roots? Illus. by David Wool. Walker & Co. 1979 57p illus $6.95, lib. bdg. $6.85 (4 and up) **573.2**

1 Man—Origin and antiquity 2 Man, Prehistoric 3 Evolution
ISBN 0-8027-6360-X; 0-8027-6361-8   LC 78-74161

"This clear, succinct essay reviews the chain of hominoid discoveries that point out the evolutionary path 'Homo sapiens' appear to have followed. It is organized chronologically, beginning with Bible-based creation theories that give way to nineteenth-century geological discoveries, and following through to recent African and Egyptian fossil finds that might be the common ancestor of both humans and African apes: the so-called missing link." Booklist

573.3 Prehistoric man

Goode, Ruth
People of the Ice Age; illus. by David Palladini. Crowell-Collier Press 1973 151p illus map lib. bdg. $5.95 (5 and up) **573.3**

1 Man—Origin and antiquity 2 Man, Prehistoric
ISBN 0-02-736420-8   LC 72-85191
"Seven gifts set man apart: upright posture, a long-striding walk; free-moving arms five-fingered hands, eyes that look forward, a reasoning brain, and the power of speech. The evolution of these attributes and the advances man has made with them are the foundation on which Goode bases this fascinating account of the human species from the first man-ape to the beginnings of prehistoric agrarian society." Booklist
This book is "sure to stimulate a young reader's interest in anthropology. The author's examination of cultural factors is particularly effective. . . . [She presents a] refreshingly clear explanation of the role of mutation and natural selection in the evolutionary process." Sci Bks

574 Biology

Selsam, Millicent E.
Is this a baby dinosaur? And other science picture-puzzles; illus. with photographs. Harper [1972 c1971] 32p illus lib. bdg. $7.89 (k-3) **574**

1 Nature study 2 Biology
ISBN 0-06-025303-7   LC 72-76508
First published 1971 by Scholastic in a paperbound edition
"In this science book for small children, a photograph of an unidentified object or a portion of one is followed by a photograph showing the object in context. The photos are accompanied by questions and answers: e.g., 'Is this an old broken tire? No. It is the horn of a desert bighorn sheep.' Short explanations expand each answer and impart simple scientific information. . . . This title provides an interesting way for young readers to learn specific facts." Sch Library J

574.1 Physiology

Branley, Franklyn M.
Oxygen keeps you alive; illus. by Don Madden. Crowell 1971 33p illus (Let's-read-and-find-out science bks) $7.95, lib. bdg. $7.89, pa $2.95 (1-3) **574.1**

1 Respiration 2 Oxygen
ISBN 0-690-60702-4; 0-690-60703-2; 0-690-60708-3   LC 73-139093
"The importance of oxygen to man, animals, and plants is emphasized in an easy-to-read account which gives brief, elementary descriptions of human respiration and of photosynthesis in plants, an explanation of how fish breathe, and a simple experiment to show the presence of dissolved oxygen in water. The picture book is enhanced by cheerful drawings in color and in black and white." Booklist

Meeks, Esther K.
How new life begins [by] Esther K. Meeks and Elizabeth Bagwell. Follett 1969 46p illus (Follett Family life education program) lib. bdg. $3.48 (k-3) **574.1**

1 Reproduction 2 Growth
ISBN 0-695-43855-7   LC 69-13381
Illustrated with color photographs, this book "reveals the variety and uniqueness of living

Meeks, Esther K.—*Continued*

things and the continuous renewal of life through the production of young. Simple facts about animal reproduction are given." Booklist

Silverstein, Alvin

The excretory system; how living creatures get rid of wastes [by] Alvin Silverstein and Virginia B. Silverstein; illus. by Lee J. Ames. Prentice-Hall 1972 74p illus $6.95 (4-6)
574.1

1 Excretion 2 Physiology, Comparative
ISBN 0-13-293654-2   LC 72-4190

The authors describe and compare the roles of the skin, the lungs, the urinary system and the digestive system in the disposal of waste in man and animals

"Especially useful for reference work on the human body, this also covers excretion in animals and plants and relates these waste removal systems to pollution problems." Booklist

The muscular system; how living creatures move [by] Alvin Silverstein and Virginia B. Silverstein; illus. by Lee J. Ames. Prentice-Hall 1972 76p illus $4.95 (4-6)   **574.1**

1 Animal locomotion 2 Physiology, Comparative 3 Muscles
ISBN 0-13-606947-9   LC 70-37600

An "examination of the human muscular system and how it works. The Silversteins also discuss locomotion in other animals and in the plant world, making frequent comparisons between the human muscular system and that of lower animals." Booklist

"Although somewhat misleading in title, since movement of plants, ciliated protozoa and various hydraulic structures are included, this is an interesting, quite well-illustrated and very readable account of movement in various species. . . . A very good feature is the large number of simple experiments, using the reader's own body or readily available materials, interspersed through the text." Sci Bks

The respiratory system; how living creatures breathe, by Alvin Silverstein and Virginia B. Silverstein; illus. by George Bakacs. Prentice-Hall 1969 60p illus $4.95 (4-6)   **574.1**

1 Respiration 2 Physiology, Comparative
ISBN 0-13-774547-8   LC 68-28376

"A concise, accurate treatment of the respiratory system of man and other life forms. . . . The authors discuss, in logical progression: the purpose of such structures as the nose, epiglottis, bronchi, lungs, and diaphragm; the composition of air; the nature of fish, insect, and plant breathing; gas cycles; etc. Technical terms used are immediately followed by pronunciation aids, and the accompanying illustrations (in black, white and turquoise) are generally well captioned." Sch Library J

The skin; coverings and linings of living things [by] Alvin Silverstein and Virginia B. Silverstein; illus. by Lee J. Ames. Prentice-Hall 1972 90p illus $4.95 (4-6)   **574.1**

1 Skin 2 Physiology, Comparative
ISBN 0-13-812776-X   LC 72-2004

An "introductory explanation of the structure and function of human skin and the outer coverings and inner linings of blood vessels, nerves, and organs of the human body. [The authors] also discuss, in brief, the protective coverings of protozoa, insects, birds, mammals, and plants and touch on current research in human skin grafting and treatment of burns. The account includes the pronunciation of technical terms and is ably complemented by numerous cross-section drawings and diagrams." Booklist

"Well-organized, clearly written, and illustrated with drawings that are carefully captioned and placed." Chicago. Children's Bk Center

Simon, Seymour

The secret clocks; time senses of living things; illus. by Jan Brett. Viking 1979 74p illus $8.95 (5 and up)   **574.1**

1 Biology—Periodicity
ISBN 0-670-62892-1   LC 78-31910

This is a "presentation of the time senses of living things—the daily and seasonal rhythms of plants and animals—and the total harmony of the rhythms of the earth. Simon touches on the fascinating arctic tern and its migratory pattern, the grunions, fish who come onto California beaches regularly as clock-work every two weeks in spawning season, and the fiddler crab, to name but a few." Sch Library J

The book also "covers bio-rhythms of humans with discussions of day and night people, suggestions for self-tests, and directions for scientific experiments based on preceding chapters. The straightforward, lively writing is marked by careful delineation between fact and theory and is supplemented with black line drawings." Booklist

For further reading and research: p69-70

574.19 Biophysics and biochemistry

Berger, Melvin

Enzymes in action. Crowell 1971 151p illus $7.95 (6 and up)   **574.19**

1 Enzymes
ISBN 0-690-26735-5   LC 76-132291

"This is a short up-to-date review of enzymology and its practical application in industry. Berger covers adequately such topics as the role of enzymes in digestion, food production, and preparation of beverages, enzymes as drugs; enzymes and diseases; and enzymes at work. He describes historic and salient discoveries including the latest achievement in enzymology." Sci Bks

"In a fascinating survey of research and findings, the author makes a complicated subject clear. . . . Lively, informal, and informative, this is not only good science . . . but also a good picture of scientific method. A divided bibliography and an index are appended." Chicago. Children's Bk Center

574.2 Pathology

Pringle, Laurence

Death is natural. Four Winds 1977 54p illus lib. bdg. $6.95 (4 and up)   **574.2**

1 Death
ISBN 0-590-07440-7   LC 76-48923

"Using as a theme the death of a rabbit hit by a car, the text explains how its body is recycled by means of scavengers and decay. Death is necessary so that elements and atoms can be passed on to other forms of life. Characteristics, genes, extinct species, and the balance of nature are discussed. The emphasis is on death as it affects the world as a whole rather than the individual, and the interdependence of various forms of life." Appraisal

"This unusual book about death is well illustrated with soft, black-and-white photographs of plants and animals—both living and dead—to go along with the reading material. Elementary students should find this book fascinating reading about one of the natural occurrences of life (i.e., death)." AAAS Sci Bks & Films

Glossary: p48-50. Further reading: p51-52

574.3 Development and maturation

Zappler, Georg

From one cell to many cells; illus. by Elise Piquet; science consultant: Stanley R. Wachs. Messner 1970 54p illus lib. bdg. $7.29 (2-4)   **574.3**

1 Embryology 2 Cells
ISBN 0-671-32251-6   LC 73-107060

"A Center for Media Development, Inc. book"

"The author explains the basics of embryology with finesse: fertilization, cell division, formulation of the blastula and the gastrula, the formation of the germ layers and the differentiation of the various kinds of tissues." Sci Bks

574.4 Anatomy and morphology

Patent, Dorothy Hinshaw
Sizes and shapes in nature—what they mean. Holiday House 1979 160p illus $7.95 (5 and up)   **574.4**
1 Anatomy
ISBN 0-8234-0340-8   LC 78-12554

The author "deals with the subject of morphology (the study of form and structure) and how it relates to the environment and daily life of animals and plants. Many creatures, as well as a variety of plants, are discussed, including paramecia, bees, cows, birds, kangaroos, squids, corn and mushrooms. . . . It becomes clear that each living thing has evolved a body structure suitable to its particular life. Even the type of stem a plant has is determined by whether it is an aquatic plant supported by the denser medium of water or a land dweller supported by the less dense medium of air. Because horses are grazers, they have evolved hoofs to withstand the constant weight of standing." Best Sellers
"The prose is clear, straightforward, brisk. Excellent, pertinent black-and-white photographs and clear line drawings accent the text." Sch Library J
Bibliography: p153-56

574.5 Ecology

Batten, Mary
The tropical forest; ants, ants, animals & plants; illus. by Betty Fraser. Crowell 1973 130p illus maps $9.95 (5 and up)   **574.5**
1 Tropics 2 Forest ecology
ISBN 0-690-00138-X   LC 73-4196

The author "starts by noting what a tropical forest is not—in terms of our commonly-heard clichés—then goes on to enlarge upon the characteristics of tropical forests. Ecology is the connecting thread in the book's discussion of plant relationships, layers of life, techniques for survival, ants, reptiles and amphibians, birds, bats, monkeys, and science and tropical forests. Contrasts are drawn between New World tropics (which have more arboreal animals) and Old World tropics (where there are larger and more terrestrial animals). Throughout the book, black-and-white drawings are both textually enlightening and aesthetically satisfying. One of the most pleasing aspects of the book is the author's ability to develop an idea and then to draw comparisons from it to apply to other situations. . . The book is very well written; the information presented doesn't get in the way of the flow and readability of the book. It is more than a compendium of well-known facts about the tropics." Sci Bks
For further reading: p125-26

Baylor, Byrd
The desert is theirs; illus. by Peter Parnall. Scribner 1975 unp illus lib. bdg. $6.95 (1-4)   **574.5**
1 Desert ecology 2 Papago Indians
ISBN 0-684-14266-X   LC 74-24417

"Poetic interpretations of Papago Indians' ecological and spiritual relationships with desert resources. . . . Illustrations add to the usefulness of this mood piece for sensitizing children to respect for nature, reading aloud, studying Indian cultures and techniques of using line, space and color." Rdng Teacher
"Parnall's multi-dimensional illustrations are sparse, like the desert, but as you stroll among them, they bloom, like the desert. More colorful than his previous art, they blend earth-tones and brilliant sky turquoise. Baylor's poetic understanding evokes warmth as one lingers over each page. She has known the wisdom of the desert and recreates with words the hushed, harmonious sharing that occurs among those who feel the 'rightness' of belonging in the desert." Children's Bk Rev Serv

Billington, Elizabeth T.
Understanding ecology; illus. by Robert Galster. Warne 1971 88p illus $6.95 (5 and up)   **574.5**
1 Ecology
ISBN 0-7232-6022-2   LC 69-10306

First published 1968
Among the topics considered are environment, ecosystems, biomes of the world, habitat, niches, food chains and chemical cycles
"This introduction to ecology will introduce the young biologist to a new approach to the out-of-doors, focusing not on isolated species but on the entire skein of nature. The young reader's horizons will be broadened by this clear approach to a most fascinating field. Not to be overlooked are the numerous practical projects suggested by which the reader may practice developing his or her observational skill and sensitivity to nature's relationships." Appraisal [review of the 1968 edition]

Cortesi, Wendy W.
Explore a spooky swamp; photographs by Joseph H. Bailey. Natl. Geographic Soc. 1978 32p illus (k-3)   **574.5**
1 Marshes 2 Marsh ecology
ISBN 0-87044-263-5   LC 77-95414

Available only as part of 4v set for $7.95 with: Animals in danger (591.5); Animals that live at sea, by J. A. Straker (591.92); and Zoo babies, by D. K. Grosvenor (590.74)
"Books for young explorers"
Prepared by the Special Publications Division of the National Geographic Society
Two children tour the Okefenokee Swamp and discover the animals and plants that live there. Color photographs highlight simple text

Graham, Ada
The milkweed and its world of animals, by Ada and Frank Graham; photographs by Les Line. Doubleday 1976 103p illus lib. bdg. $5.95 (5 and up)   **574.5**
1 Ecology 2 Milkweed
ISBN 0-385-09933-9   LC 74-18801

The authors seek to show "how the qualities of the milkweed fix the lives of the monarch butterfly and the milkweed beetle, the aphid and the ladybug, the ant and the honeybee, the katydid, more butterflies still and a legion of spiders." Sci Am
"Written in a direct, informal style. . . . Illustrated by good magnified photographs . . . [the authors] give a clear picture of much of the ecology of a meadow, excluding only larger forms of wildlife." Chicago. Children's Bk Center

Kane, Henry B.
The tale of a pond; written and illus. by Henry B. Kane. Knopf 1960 110p illus (Borzoi Nature study bks) $3.50, lib. bdg. $5.39 (4 and up)   **574.5**
1 Pond ecology 2 Fresh water biology
ISBN 0-394-81720-6; 0-394-91720-0   LC 60-8604

"A boy watches the strange and interesting inhabitants of a pond through the four seasons. In words, photographs, and expressive drawings of Mr. Kane, we see the teeming, changing life of fish, frogs, turtles, birds, small animals, insects, and plants and learn how to care for many of these creatures in home terrariums and aquariums." Library J

Laycock, George
Exploring the great swamp. McKay 1978 58p illus $6.95 (4-6)   **574.5**
1 Marshes 2 Marsh ecology
ISBN 0-679-20600-0   LC 78-54044

"An introductory chapter defines and describes the various kinds of swamps, and in succeeding chapters Laycock discusses individual swamps and their distinguishing features—the Okefenokee in Georgia, with its floating islands and festoons of Spanish moss; the Great Dismal, south of Washington, D.C., a refuge for many forms of wild life; the Alakai, a mountaintop swamp in Hawaii on which rain falls almost every day. The text includes anecdotes and legends, carefully distinguishing between these and the facts it provides about the flora and fauna, the topology, and the climate of such areas. Laycock includes information about discoverers, marauders, and preservers in a book that is informative, well-organized, and written in a practiced, competent style." Chicago. Children's Bk Center

Laycock, George—*Continued*

Islands and their mysteries. Four Winds
1977 106p illus $7.95 (5 and up)   **574.5**

1 Islands 2 Island ecology
ISBN 0-590-07455-5   LC 77-6265

"Laycock explores various islands around the
world, commenting on their formation, plant and
animal life, as well as their ecological peculiarities.
Introductory chapters describe how islands are
born, how life comes to islands, and what kind of
unusual animals are found on them: detailed information is given about Hawaii, the Aleutians,
the Florida Keys, the Galápagos, Turtle Island (off
the South Carolina coast), and the islands of Lake
Erie." Booklist

"First-hand travel experiences and clearly captioned black-and-white photographs enhance this
account. . . . There is . . . a valuable chapter on
America's seagirt national parks." Sch Library J

Lerner, Carol

On the forest edge. Morrow 1978 unp illus
$5.95, lib. bdg. $5.71 (3-5)   **574.5**

1 Forests and forestry 2 Forest ecology
3 Ecology
ISBN 0-688-22162-9; 0-688-32162-3   LC 78-6209

"Here is an example of that all-too-rare combination; a book which painlessly imparts a good
deal of interesting information and is a visual and
esthetic delight as well. The subject is the fringe
area between deep woodland and open fields. This
narrow, shifting border, which at first glance appears to be little more than a tangled, weedy
thicket, supports an amazingly varied and numerous population of mammals, birds, insects and
plant life. . . . The author points out that a similar 'edge effect' may appear along unmowed
roadsides and railroad rights-of-way in suburbs
and cities. Exquisite pen and ink drawings, large
clear print, and an elegant text make an eloquent
case for the preservation of these border habitats.
A brief glossary is included." Appraisal

List, Albert

A walk in the forest; the woodlands of
North America [by] Albert List, Jr. [and]
Ilka List; illus. with photographs and draw-
ings by the authors. Crowell 1977 197p illus
$9.95 (5 and up)   **574.5**

1 Forest ecology 2 Forests and forestry—North
America
ISBN 0-690-00990-9   LC 76-40171

This work "is aimed directly at young readers,
particularly those who might now and again . . .
take a long walk in the American woodlands. It
begins with a general overview of what a forest is
and how and where forests are found, and of the
complex turnover within them. One device is used
throughout: the text is a series of very informal
questions and answers written at grade school
level. . . . The book follows . . . the life of the
high canopy, of leaves, katydids and the flash
of the tanager, the middle layers of woodpeckers
and berries, the ground cover of moss, eft and
deer, down to the soil of the earthworm and the
starnosed mole." Sci Am

"An unusual book, artistic yet factual, with
magnificent photographs and drawings. . . . As an
antithesis to the textbook approach, it is a triumph. . . . Much knowledge is imparted, from the
identification of trillium and the function of roots
to the delineation of the layers of a forest. I doubt
many readers will go straight through the book,
but they should delight in sampling passages here
and there, comparing description with what they
have seen. Pictures appear on nearly every page."
Horn Bk

Bibliography: p188-90

Nature at work; introducing ecology. British
Museum (Natural History)/Cambridge 1978
83p illus $15.95, pa $4.95 (4-6)   **574.5**

1 Ecology
ISBN 0-521-22390-3; 0-521-29469-X   LC 78-66795

Prepared by the staff of the British Museum
(Natural History) in conjunction with the exhibition: Introducing ecology

This book introduces the concept of ecosystems
by illustrating the interactions of the animals and
plants with the non-living surroundings of an oak

woodland and a rocky seashore. Full color photographs, drawings, and diagrams illustrate the
function of food chains, food webs and pyramids
of stored energy. There are keys to plants and
animals in the book and a bibliography

Pringle, Laurence

Chains, webs & pyramids; the flow of
energy in nature; illus. by Jan Adkins.
Crowell 1975 33p illus $7.95, lib. bdg. $7.89
(4-6)   **574.5**

1 Food chains (Ecology)
ISBN 0-690-00562-8; 0-690-00563-6   LC 75-1084

"The author makes his readers dramatically
aware of man's role in his own survival. Through
discussions, charts, and illustrations, the author
explores the 'flow of life's energy on Earth.' He
points out that while most nutrients are ultimately returned to the soil, air, or water for recycling, the resulting energy supplied to the members of a food chain, web, or pyramid decreases
in amount as it is transferred from one member
to the next. Therefore, more energy is constantly
required. The primary energy source is the sun
which is vital to green plants in photosynthesis."
Sci and Children

"In clear and vivid terms the author clarifies
a complex subject and explains some of the
methods that ecologists use to trace the flow of
food energy in nature. Jan Adkins's handsome and
yet delicate black-and-white illustrations are
superb. Indexed." Appraisal

Estuaries; where rivers meet the sea.
Macmillan Pub. Co. 1973 55p illus map lib.
bdg. $5.95 (4-6)   **574.5**

1 Estuarine ecology
ISBN 0-02-775300-X   LC 72-86506

Through text and photographs, the book describes the ecosystem of estuarine bays and salt
marshes, and the many varieties of plant and animal life found in it—including grasses, snails,
oysters, fish and birds

"The text is neatly organized, simply written,
lucid, and informative; the quality of the photographs is excellent. A glossary and an index are
appended." Chicago. Children's Bk Center

The gentle desert; exploring an ecosystem.
Macmillan Pub. Co. 1977 58p illus maps lib.
bdgs. $6.95 (4-6)   **574.5**

1 Desert ecology
ISBN 0-02-775380-8   LC 77-5875

The author "examines the great variety of
[desert] plant and animal life and their essential
interrelatedness. The aim of course, is to correct
the notion that deserts are harsh, empty waste-
lands. In keeping with that, he questions the
common attitude that the desert is 'a place to be
used and changed.' The damaging effects of those
uses—stripmining, illegal motorcycling that tears
up the turf, and growing populations that draw
on limited water supplies and continually lower
the water table—underscore Pringle's belief that
the desert should be appreciated on its own
terms." Booklist

"Through superb photography and vivid description, Pringle manages to convey the mysterious,
delicate beauty of the North American desert.
. . . His description of the importance of the
saguaro cactus in the desert food chain is especially instructive. . . . Phonetic pronunciation and
a glossary are included to help younger readers."
Sci Teacher

Further reading: p55-56

The hidden world; life under a rock.
Macmillan Pub. Co. 1977 64p illus $6.95
(4-6)   **574.5**

1 Invertebrates 2 Plants 3 Ecology
ISBN 0-02-775340-9   LC 76-47641

"In the cool, dark places under rocks or boards,
the relatively stable temperature and humidity, as
well as the protection of the object on the ground,
afford an inviting home to all kinds of creatures.
This is the cryptosphere, the hidden world that is
one kind of miniature ecosystem. Suggesting ways
to investigate such hidden worlds with least damage to the investigator or the inhabitants, Pringle
goes on to give detailed descriptions of some of
the most common creatures found under objects
on earth or in water." Chicago. Children's Bk
Center

Pringle, Laurence—*Continued*

"Illustrated with drawings by Erick Ingraham and with photographs. Eye-catching, larger-than-life black-and-white photographs of an assortment of creatures, such as salamanders, millipedes, slugs, wolf spiders, beetle larvae, and ants, are the strong features of the book, which should interest even the children who usually say 'ugh.' The author describes not only commonly found land animals that hide, but water animals such as crayfish, leeches, hellgrammites, and caddis flies. If, after reading the book, a child doesn't lift a stone or a log on his next walk, I doubt he ever will." Horn Bk
Further reading: p61-62

Into the woods; exploring the forest ecosystem. Macmillan Pub. Co. 1973 54p illus lib. bdg. $4.95 (4-6)
574.5
1 Forest ecology 2 Forests and forestry
ISBN 0-02-775320-4   LC 72-92448
The author "presents an elementary explanation of forest ecosystems. The interrelationships between forest zones and the life they support are described, as well as the process of plant succession and the effects—not always bad—of forest fires. A few words on the national forests and an admonition to care for them and all woodlands round out the smooth presentation, abundantly illustrated with clear, black-and-white photographs." Booklist
"A few concepts are overly sophisticated for young readers, and even some of the simpler ones might be difficult for children more familiar with concrete than with humus." Sch Library J
Glossary: p49-50. Further reading: p51

Natural fire; its ecology in forests. Morrow 1979 63p illus $5.95, lib. bdg. $5.71 (5 and up)
574.5
1 Forest fires 2 Forest ecology 3 Forests and forestry
ISBN 0-688-22210-2; 0-688-32210-7   LC 79-13606
"Forest fires aren't all bad; in fact, under the right circumstances they can be quite good, a natural force whose effect is necessary for certain forest balances to be maintained. . . .Pringle effectively traces the course of events that led to current pro-fire forest-management schools of thought. He cites a number of favorable fire-caused effects; certain plant communities depend on fire for their survival; some animals depend on the new growth that follows. Also, the idea that fires kill great numbers of forest animals is labeled myth. . . . The summing-up thought is that if some fires are allowed to perform their function, they will restore rather than destroy the land. With good-quality black-and-white photographs." Booklist
Glossary: p56-58. Further reading p59-60

This is a river; exploring an ecosystem. Macmillan Pub. Co. 1972 55p illus $4.95 (4-6)
574.5
1 Rivers 2 Ecology 3 Water—Pollution
ISBN 0-02-775240-2   LC 70-160074
"A useful introduction. As its subtitle suggests, the author sketches the interdependencies of the creatures in and around rivers—including man—and shows rivers to be not mere bodies of water connecting points on a map, but total life systems embracing fish, fowl, animals, vegetables, minerals, and human beings far beyond their banks." Bk World
"Straightforward writing style, well-organized material, and authoritative information simply presented make 'This is a river' an excellent introduction to the subject." Chicago. Children's Bk Center
Glossary: p50-52. Further reading: p53

Roach, Marilynne K.

Dune fox; written and illus. by Marilynne K. Roach. Little 1977 32p illus $6.95 (1-3)
574.5
1 Sand dune ecology 2 Foxes 3 Natural history—Massachusetts
ISBN 0-316-74870-6   LC 76-54755
"An Atlantic Monthly Press book"
"Roach's simple story of a fox living among the dunes in the Northeast and experiencing the seasons of the year takes second place to her abundant illustrations of dune ecology. Flora and fauna are all neatly labeled for readers in pictures which show sand blowing, birds flying, plants growing, rain falling, and the wind smoothing away animal tracks on the beach. The text is blocked off within rectangular borders and sometimes the drawings, several to a page, are boxed as well, creating visually pleasing effects." Sch Library J

Tresselt, Alvin

The beaver pond; illus. by Roger Duvoisin. Lothrop 1970 unp illus lib. bdg. $7.92 (k-3)
574.5
1 Pond ecology 2 Beavers
ISBN 0-688-51123-6   LC 72-120161
"Beautiful pictures in full color, bright and delicate, show the abundance of wildlife in the pond from the first invasion of the industrious beavers who have dammed a small stream, through the changing colors of the season, to the abandonment of the dam years later. The colony grows and prospers, the beavers raise their families and fight enemies, and the friendly animals flourish in a balanced ecology. Written with quiet dignity, this is unobtrusively informative and lovely to look at." Sat Rev

Van Soelen, Philip

Cricket in the grass, and other stories. Sierra Club Books/Scribner 1979 128p illus $9.95 (1-5)
574.5
1 Ecology—Pictorial works 2 Food chains (Ecology)—Pictorial works
ISBN 0-684-16110-9   LC 79-4108
"A Yolla Bolly Press book"
"A series of five wordless picture 'stories' shows unobtrusively the life-sustaining food chain patterns as they might operate in five different habitats." Booklist
"In the introduction and afterword, the author discusses the ecosystems, the fundamentals of life, and encourages readers to develop their powers of perception and understanding of nature. The lessons and the dramatic pictures are effective indeed." Pub W

Zim, Herbert S.

Caves and life; illus. by Richard Cuffari. Morrow 1978 62p illus $5.95, lib. bdg. $5.71 (4-6)
574.5
1 Cave ecology 2 Caves
ISBN 0-688-22112-2; 0-688-32112-7   LC 77-337
"The book treats the formation, structure, and location of caves. Mention is also made of the world-famous caves at Lascaux as well as caves in Turkey and in New Mexico. Much of the book is devoted to the cave environment and the plants and animals that dwell in it. Among those included are the blind, white flatworm that is less than two centimeters long, blind cave fish, bats and birds as well as the prehistoric cave dwellers." Sch Library J
"This brief, easily read book contains a wealth of scientific fact, highlighted by excellent, true-to-nature illustrations that will fascinate the young nature lover. The simple format and the large type should not deceive readers into thinking that the material is intended for a younger age group. . . . All measurements are given in metric and a short paragraph in the beginning provides conversion information. The book contains much new and attractive material." AAAS Sci Bks & Films

574.8 Tissue, cellular, molecular biology

Silverstein, Alvin

Cells: building blocks of life, by Alvin Silverstein and Virginia B. Silverstein; illus. by George Bakacs. Prentice-Hall 1969 60p illus $5.95 (4 and up)
574.8
1 Cells
ISBN 0-13-121715-1   LC 69-14810
"This comprehensive discussion of cells—both plant and animal—gives young readers an elementary understanding of cells, how they work

Silverstein, Alvin—*Continued*
and grow, and a description of instruments and
techniques used to study them." The AAAS Sci
Bk List for Children
"Pronunciation and definition of biological terms
are incorporated in the lucid text which is complemented by labelled drawings." Booklist

574.9   Geographical treatment of organisms

Clark, Ann Nolan
Along sandy trails; photographs by Alfred
A. Cohn. Viking 1969 31p illus lib. bdg. $5.95
(2-5)   **574.9**
1 Natural history—Arizona 2 Deserts 3 Papago
Indians
ISBN 0-670-11485-5   LC 69-13076
Excellent color photographs combined with poetic
text describe the wild plant and animal life observed by a small Papago Indian girl and her
grandmother while on a walk in the Arizona
desert. Written in the first person, the text expresses the little girl's delight in what she sees
and in what her wise grandmother tells her about
desert wild life. Identification of the plants included is given at the back of the book." Booklist

Lewin, Ted
World within a world: Baja; written and
illus. by Ted Lewin. Dodd [1979 c1978] 73p
illus $5.95 (4-6)   **574.9**
1 Natural history—Baja California
ISBN 0-396-07615-7   LC 78-7740
"Lewin records his impressions of the flora and
fauna of Baja California while waiting for the
annual migration of the California gray whales.
His text is impressionistic, lyric, and acute in
observation of behavioral details, particularly of
seals and sea lions; finally the whales come,
breeching and leaping in awesome beauty. Beautifully textured, soft pencil drawings of plants and
animals are as vivid as the textual comments."
Chicago. Children's Bk Center
"Little science will be learned here, but an important appreciation for nature in the wild cannot
help but be instilled in the young reader." Appraisal

Rinard, Judith E.
Wonders of the desert world. Natl.
Geographic Soc. 1976 30p illus (k-3)   **574.9**
1 Desert animals 2 Desert plants 3 Deserts
ISBN 0-87044-197-3   LC 76-2221
Obtainable only as part of a set for $9.95 with:
Animals that build their homes, by Robert M. Mc-
Clung, class 591.5; Camping adventure, by William
R. Gray, class 796.45; and The playful dolphins,
by Linda McCarter Bridge, class 599.5
"Books for young explorers"
Prepared by the Special Publications Division
of the National Geographic Society
Through text and color photographs, this book
"explores the desert by night and day, depicting
coyotes, snakes, lizards, as well as creeping devil,
cholla cacti, and the flowering hedgehog and
prickly pear." Booklist
"The color photographs are outstanding and
enhance the text. The writing is clear, simple, and
easy to understand. Both the non-reader and
beginning reader should enjoy this book." Appraisal

574.92   Marine and fresh-water biology

Buck, Margaret Waring
Along the seashore; written and illus. by
Margaret Waring Buck. Abingdon 1964 72p
illus map $5.95 (3-6)   **574.92**
1 Seashore 2 Marine biology
ISBN 0-687-01114-0   LC 63-10808

"Beginning with the plants and simple forms of
sea life that live near the shore, and continuing
through the fish and the most common birds, Miss
Buck presents the flora and fauna of the U.S.
coastline in the form of a guide book. Careful
black-and-white drawings, small but quite clear,
accompany the short factual entries." Pub W
More to read: p72

Burgess, Robert F.
Exploring a coral reef; illus. by Ronald
Himler; science consultant: Harry Milgrom;
experiments and investigations by Leon Dorf-
man. Macmillan Pub. Co. 1972 56p illus lib.
bdg. $4.95 (4-6)   **574.92**
1 Coral reefs and islands 2 Coral reef ecology
ISBN 0-02-716130-7   LC 74-161426
Contents: Let's look at a reef; Building blocks of
the reef; Where does coral grow; The most important plants; Is it a plant or an animal; Creeping, swimming, clinging creatures; Little Fish, big
fish; The reef at night; Some interesting alliances;
The food chain; Experiments and investigations;
Glossary
"A descriptive study of the organisms and ecology of a coral reef. . . . The excellent glossary
includes pronunciation aids. However, although the
black-and-white illustrations and diagrams complement the text, the use of color would have been
more effective." Sch Library J

Cooper, Elizabeth K.
Science on the shores and banks; with
illus. by the author. Harcourt 1960 187p illus
$4.95, pa $1.50 (5 and up)   **574.92**
1 Marine biology 2 Fresh water biology
ISBN 0-15-270843-X; 0-15-679609-0   LC 60-8411
A "provocative science hobby book, in which
[the author] invites the young reader to do some
scientific exploring, observing, and collecting of
many forms of small [insect and animal] creatures
and plants that live at the water's edge, on bank
or shore, and in tide pools. He is encouraged to
experiment, following scientific method in handling
his problem and also later in setting up displays.
Clearly illustrated with line sketches and diagrams." Horn Bk
"It will be an ideal book for children who spend
their summer vacations at the beach, even those
whose reading is generally confined to less factual
material." Pub W

Goldin, Augusta
The sunlit sea; illus. by Paul Galdone.
Crowell 1968 33p illus (Let's-read-and-find-
out science bks) $7.95, lib. bdg. $7.89,
pa $1.95 (1-3)   **574.92**
1 Marine biology 2 Marine ecology
ISBN 0-690-79411-8; 0-690-79412-6; 0-690-79413-4
         LC 68-17075
This book "describes the plant and animal life
that inhabits the sunlit area of the sea which
extends downward from the surface to approximately 200 feet in depth. The simple text and appealing, accurate illustrations depict different
types of marine life and indicate the role of each
in nature's food chain." Booklist

McGovern, Ann
The underwater world of the coral reef.
Four Winds [1977 c1976] 40p illus map lib.
bdg. $6.95, pa $1.50 (2-4)   **574.92**
1 Coral reefs and islands 2 Coral reef ecology
3 Marine biology
ISBN 0-590-07467-9; 0-590-10255-9   LC 75-44305
The author "describes the exotic undersea world,
building of reefs, inhabitants (both night and day),
scenes at feeding time, dangers that prevail, interdependence of various plants and animals, and
reasons for the variety of color. McGovern, a scuba
diver, concludes her narrative with brief remarks
about divers who come to explore. Full-color photographs introduce young readers to intriguing
species such as barracuda, squirrelfish, foureye
butterfly fish, and vase sponges." Booklist

Reid, George K.

Pond life; a guide to common plants and animals of North American ponds and lakes, by George K. Reid, under the editorship of Herbert S. Kim and George S. Fichter; illus. by Sally D. Kaicher and Tom Dolan. Golden Press 1967 160p illus (A Golden Nature guide) lib. bdg. $9.15, pa $1.95 (6 and up)
574.92

1 Fresh water animals 2 Fresh water plants
ISBN 0-307-63535-X; 0-307-24017-7   LC 67-16477

This guide "explains the dynamics of a pond or lake, shows some of the plants, animals, insects, and fishes likely to be found in or near it, and tells how to collect specimens." Pub W
For more information: p155

Selsam, Millicent E.

See along the shore; pictures by Leonard Weisgard. Harper 1961 unp illus lib. bdg. $6.89 (3-5)
574.92

1 Seashore 2 Marine biology
ISBN 0-06-025336-3   LC 61-12007

The author "answers questions that arise when a child goes to the seashore, and suggests some things he can do while there. Queries such as why driftwood burns different colors, why the tides come and go, and why waves glow at night are pursued and some plants and animals of the shore are pictured." The AAAS Sci Bk List for Children

"Illustrated with attractive drawings in color or in black and white on every page the book should encourage firsthand exploration and further reading on the subject." Booklist

Zim, Herbert S.

Seashores; a guide to animals and plants along the beaches, by Herbert S. Zim and Lester Ingle; illus. by Dorothea and Sy Barlowe. Sponsored by the Wildlife Management Institute. Golden Press 1955 160p illus (A Golden Nature guide) lib. bdg. $9.15, pa $1.95 (5 and up)
574.92

1 Seashore 2 Marine animals 3 Marine plants
ISBN 0-307-63512-0; 0-307-24496-2   LC 55-2608

"A comprehensive pocket guide for identifying 'plant and animal life found in North American tidal waters.' Algae, sponges, corals, shellfish, birds, flowering plants, etc. are included with brief descriptive text and illustrations in full color. Index." Horn Bk

575 Organic evolution and genetics

Merrill, Margaret W.

Skeletons that fit; illus. by Pamela Carroll. Coward, McCann & Geoghegan [1979 c1978] 63p illus lib. bdg. $5.29 (4-6)
575

1 Evolution 2 Bones
ISBN 0-698-30677-5   LC 77-24155

This book "traces bone differences in fish, amphibians, reptiles, birds, and mammals, suggesting ways of looking at familiar animals to heighten understanding. In a final chapter, reasons for the demise of extinct creatures such as the Irish elk and giant sloth are described. Facts about the particular ways in which the bone structures of animals and humans serve them in today's environment are threaded throughout the text." Booklist

"Elegant line-drawings here form an effective complement, realizing the text with details: an early amphibian walks; below it its skeleton appears in motion. The comparison of a human skeleton with a marionette similarly posed reinforces the text's analogy of bones to levers. Altogether an effective introduction to both skeletal structures and evolution for the middle-grade reader. A glossary and an index are appended." Appraisal
Books for further reading: p60-61

575.1 Genetics. Heredity

Facklam, Margery

From cell to clone; the story of genetic engineering by Margery and Howard Facklam; illus. with diagrams by Paul Facklam and with photographs. Harcourt 1979 128p illus $7.95 (6 and up)
575.1

1 Genetics 2 Cloning
ISBN 0-15-230262-X   LC 79-87515

"Beginning with Aristotle, the Facklams trace the scientific discoveries that have led to the development of genetics and genetic engineering. The work of Mendel, Watson and Crick, and many other scientists is described in fascinating detail. The second half of the book deals with the practical capabilities of scientists today: bacteria which can produce human insulin, in vitro fertilization (England's test tube baby), and the ability to clone entire forests, herds of cattle, and animals for laboratory research." Sch Library J

"A fine synopsis of a large subject, in terms understandable by many, many readers, this book concludes by urging young people to elect biological research as their life-work. Well illustrated, the book also boasts a useful glossary of technical terms (which should also have pronunciation indicated). Recommended without reservation." Best Sellers
Bibliography: p123-24

Pomerantz, Charlotte

Why you look like you, whereas I tend to look like me; pictures by Rosemary Wells and Susan Jeffers. Young Scott Bks. 1969 64p illus lib. bdg. $6.95 (4-6)
575.1

1 Mendel's law 2 Heredity
ISBN 0-201-09409-6   LC 68-27028

"Zany poetry and cartoons explain how Mendel's experiments with garden peas led to the modern theory of heredity. Dry discoveries are made interesting and understandable. A description with supporting diagrams of Mendel's cross pollination process and a short biography of his life supplement the verse." Adventuring with Bks. 2d edition

Showers, Paul

Me and my family tree; illus. by Don Madden. Crowell 1978 33p illus (Let's-read-and-find-out science bks) $6.95, lib. bdg. $6.79 (k-3)
575.1

1 Heredity
ISBN 0-690-03886-0; 0-690-03887-9   LC 77-26595

"The basic introduction on the process of heredity should help unravel the often confusing concept of ancestral relationships for young readers. Showers uses a lively tone to discuss what a family tree is and how genetic traits are inherited. Background material on Mendel's pea plant experiments and how these led to an understanding of heredity traits is incorporated into the text. Perky line drawings awash in bright shades of red and yellow expand the information and should motivate interest in digging up family roots." Booklist

Silverstein, Alvin

The code of life [by] Alvin and Virginia Silverstein; illus. by Kenneth Gosner. Atheneum Pubs. 1972 89p illus $6.95 (6 and up)
575.1

1 Genetics 2 DNA
ISBN 0-689-30038-7   LC 77-175558

The authors investigate the genetic code—in the chromosomes, the genes, the DNA bases—detailing how they, along with RNA, "work together to direct the activities of living cells. They describe the inheritance or mutation of traits from generation to generation and discuss genetic research from the study of fruit flies and work done with clones of bacteria to the isolation of a single gene and the synthesis of genes, concluding with a look at progress and prospects in the growing new science of genetic engineering. Many captioned scientific drawings and diagrams complement the text." Booklist

"In tackling a tough subject, the Silversteins occasionally get over-technical, but the rewards are worth the effort." Bk World

576   Microbes

Nourse, Alan E.
Viruses. Watts, F. 1976 65p illus lib.
bdg. $4.90 (5 and up)   **576**

1 Viruses
ISBN 0-531-00839-8   LC 75-19142

"A First book"
"Nourse ranges from the 18th century (Jenner's work with smallpox and Pasteur's with rabies) to present-day knowledge and research. In an introductory fashion, he discusses the discovery and study of viruses, viral diseases and their effect on humans, and the search for vaccines (including how immunity works, the antigen-antibody reaction and the uses of gamma globulin). Modern virus research is presented in a rational fashion, current ideas are discussed in the light of supporting evidence, and the author makes it clear that further research may alter or disprove present theories. There is a good index and an additional reading list, and the text is interspersed with photographs and excellent explanatory diagrams. This is a most recommendable book for the students interested in medical science." AAAS Sci Bks & Films

Silverstein, Alvin
A world in a drop of water [by] Alvin and Virginia Silverstein. Atheneum Pubs. 1969 58p illus $4.95 (3-5)   **576**

1 Microbiology
ISBN 0-689-20632-1   LC 69-13524

An introduction to microbiology which describes the life processes of the amoeba, the paramecium, the hydra, the flatworm and other organisms which live in a drop of pond water
"The superbly detailed photographs of tiny plants and animals are worth the purchase price of this book." Sch Library J

579   Collection and preservation of biological specimens

Rahn, Joan Elma
Seven ways to collect plants; with illustrations prepared by the author. Atheneum Pubs. 1978 83p illus $5.95 (4 and up)   **579**

1 Plants—Collection and preservation 2 Photography of plants
ISBN 0-689-30640-7   LC 77-21181

"The seven ways of collecting plants described in this how-to book are making leaf prints with ink, making xerox copies of leaves, collecting dry plant specimens, photographing plants, and collecting living plants." Chicago. Children's Bk Center
"In each instance, techniques and equipment are thoroughly explained, and all directions are clear, logical, and concise. Photographs and diagrams are helpful, along with good definitions of botanical terms. Practical suggestions, combined with scientific information, make this a valuable title for those interested in preserving some of nature's delicate creations." Sch Library J

581   Botany

Cole, Joanna
Plants in winter; illus. by Kazue Mizumura. Crowell 1973 33p illus (Let's-read-and-find-out science bks) $6.95, lib. bdg. $6.89 (1-3)   **581**

1 Trees 2 Plants
ISBN 0-690-62885-4; 0-690-62886-2   LC 73-1771

"The author describes clearly and simply the different ways that plants have adapted for survival during the adverse conditions of winter. The text explains the function of tree leaves and movement of plant materials and water within the plant. Also discussed are the winter dormancy period, leaf fall which protects the deciduous trees, and the leaf structure and thick, tough coats which protect evergreen plants. Underground roots and stems—bulbs, rhizomes and runners —as well as seeds, which can tolerate cold temperatures, are discussed as adaptations which help plants survive." Sci Bks

"The text is clear and simple and is accompanied by wash drawings. Considering how slight a volume this is, it covers a wide range of plants. . . . This is an attractive and informative introduction to plant life." Appraisal

Rahn, Joan Elma
Seeing what plants do; illus. by Ginny Linville Winter. Atheneum Pubs. 1972 58p illus $4.95 (3-5)   **581**

1 Plants 2 Botany—Experiments
ISBN 0-689-30034-4   LC 70-175559

The author offers "twenty-one basic experiments which will provide information about the functioning parts of plants. The experiments are graded from simple to complex. All are easy to perform and require little specialized equipment. Through the directions for setting up the experiments the child is also introduced to the correct botanical names for the parts of plants. The approach is not didactic; instead, Ms. Rahn's well-placed questions encourage the young experimenter to develop a discovery method approach to botanical studies. The answer section which follows the last experiment enables the child to check his or her own responses. The concluding statement encourages the readers to experiment further in the area of botany." Sci Bks
Followed by: More about what plants do, entered in class 581.3

Selsam, Millicent E.
A first look at the world of plants, by Millicent E. Selsam and Joyce Hunt; illus. by Harriett Springer. Walker & Co. 1978 32p illus $5.95, lib. bdg. $5.85 (1-3)   **581**

1 Plants
ISBN 0-8027-6298-0; 0-8027-6299-9   LC 77-78088

This introduction to plant study, intended for the youngest readers, includes illustrated pages on bacteria, algae, bryophytes, fungi, ferns, gymnosperms, and angiosperms. The author shows how each class differs from the others, and provides games where the reader is invited to match names and pictures
"Just enough material, just enough classification in the plant world is included in an excellent book for the primary-grades reader. . . . The text and illustrations are nicely coordinated." Chicago. Children's Bk Center

Play with plants. Newly rev. ed. Photographs by Jerome Wexler. Morrow 1978 95p illus lib. bdg. $7.20 (3-6)   **581**

1 Plants 2 Botany—Experiments
ISBN 0-688-32167-4   LC 78-8509

First published 1949
This book provides directions for growing plants from the roots, stems, leaves, or seeds of common potatoes, beans, and house plants. It also tells how a seed grows and presents simple gardening experiments
This "is a painless introduction to some basic botany (osmosis, photosynthesis, germination, etc.). None of the projects are unique to this book, nor are they complicated. Growing sweet potatoes in water, rooting geranium cuttings, or growing avocado or pineapple plants are unspectacular but apt demonstrations of living breathing chloroplasm au natural. Directions are clearly outlined and easy to follow, although the instructions for punching holes in plastic containers with stove-heated ice picks might make more than a few parents uncomfortable. . . . This sample of the Selsam-Wexler collaboration is a happy one and can be relied on to spur interest in the green world and leave readers with some sound and practical knowledge and an appetite for more." Sch Library J

Stonehouse, Bernard
A closer look at plant life; illus. by Richard Orr, Philip Weare [and] Gary Hincks. Gloucester Press 1978 c1977 32p illus lib. bdg. $5.90 (5 and up)   **581**

1 Botany
ISBN 0-531-01430-4   LC 77-14978

"A Closer look book"
First published 1977 in England
This book introduces the world of plants and their part in the food chain. Among the topics

Stonehouse, Bernard—*Continued*
covered are the evolution of plants; the function of flowers and pollen; fruits and seeds; photosynthesis and pollination

The author "does an excellent job of interweaving basic ideas of plant biology with the evolutionary story of the plant kingdom. Each pair of facing pages presents an idea that is developed by a brief text and complemented by a beautiful color painting that flows across both pages; the visual impact is strong. Captions expand textual concepts, interpret the paintings and explain information presented in diagrammatic illustrations." AAAS Sci Bks & Films

581.1 Physiology of plants

Branley, Franklyn M.
Roots are food finders; illus. by Joseph Low. Crowell 1975 33p illus map (Let's-read-and-find-out science bks) lib. bdg. $6.89 (2-4)
581.1
1 Plants—Nutrition
ISBN 0-690-00703-5   LC 74-23924
"Without technical terminology the author explores the external structure of roots and compares the advantages of different types. The relationship between these types and ecological principles is clearly described. Branley's method of calling on the reader to do things with familiar objects rather than only to read about them should prove to be popular with children and certainly will stimulate their interest in science." AAAS Sci Bks & Films

Rahn, Joan Elma
How plants are pollinated; illus. by Ginny Linville Winter. Atheneum Pubs. 1975 135p illus $7.95 (5 and up)
581.1
1 Fertilization of plants   2 Flowers
ISBN 0-689-30482-X   LC 75-9526
This book is "scientifically accurate, and written in a very clear and concise style. Plant pollination is covered in detail with the emphasis on mechanisms of pollination. The introductory chapters on why pollination occurs and how to recognize flower parts are complete and well done. The primary emphasis is on means of pollination, such as by wind, animals, bees, butterflies, birds, bats or water. Several of these topics are covered in great detail, emphasizing the physical interaction of the pollinating agent and the pollinating organ of the plant. The illustrations are outstanding and beautifully complement the text. The author continually reminds the reader of the value of observation, and she also suggests that the reader plant and observe a garden. Finally, there is an excellent glossary." AAAS Sci Bks & Films

581.3 Development and maturation of plants

Rahn, Joan E.
More about what plants do; illus. by Ginny Linville Winter. Atheneum Pubs. 1975 74p illus lib. bdg. $6.95 (5 and up)   581.3
1 Botany—Experiments   2 Growth (Plants)
ISBN 0-689-30454-4   LC 74-19280
Sequel to the author's Seeing what plants do, entered in class 581
A collection of twenty experiments designed to help readers understand how plants grow
These experiments "have been attractively illustrated and arranged in a well-designed book. The operations include such things as charting a growth curve; raising plants from seeds, stems, roots, leaves, bulbs; and measuring the effects of salt on plants. The procedures are simple, instructions clear, and materials easy to obtain." Horn Bk

Watch it grow, watch it change; written and illus. by Joan Elma Rahn. Atheneum Pubs. 1978 88p illus $7.95 (5 and up)   581.3
1 Growth (Plants)   2 Germination
ISBN 0-689-30665-2
     LC 78-6287

"Using lilac, apple, sunchoke, squash, and pea seeds as her prototypes, Rahn discusses the formation and growth patterns of plants. Presented in diary format and supplemented with label, line-drawn diagrams, details are recorded for the opening of a bud into a leafy twig that produces its own leaf bud, development of a bud through flower and fruit stages, opening of a bud on a tuber, and germination of seeds. The author carefully and smoothly integrates explanations of botanical terms, cautions that variations in season or climates will alter growing time, and encourages further experiments. Interested botanists may wish for photographs but will find this an unusual approach to plant study." Booklist

581.4 Anatomy and morphology of plants

Zim, Herbert S.
What's inside of plants? Illus. by Herschel Wartik. Morrow 1953 32p illus lib. bdg. $6 (2-4)
581.4
1 Botany—Anatomy
ISBN 0-688-31490-2   LC 52-5943
"A general discussion of plants and their roots, stems, leaves, flowers and fruits. The pages are alternately in large and small type, the former intended for beginners and the latter offering slightly more advanced information." The AAAS Sci Bk List for Children
"The material is expertly geared to children's interest in these subjects and presented in concise text and in excellent illustrations." Booklist

581.5 Botany—Ecology

Selsam, Millicent E.
Birth of a forest; illus. with pictures by Barbara Wolff and with photographs. Harper 1964 unp illus lib. bdg. $7.89 (4-6)   581.5
1 Botany—Ecology   2 Forests and forestry 3 Forest ecology
ISBN 0-06-025276-6   LC 63-17281
"The fact that 'the world of nature is always changing' is demonstrated through the story of the progression of plant life in a meadow pond. Beginning with the minute plants floating in the waters of the pond, the author traces the slow changes through which the pond gradually fills with plants, becomes a swamp which is able to support a swamp forest, until, in the course of time these trees are superceded by the 'beech-maple forest,' which is the 'climax community' of the area. Photographs and delicate pen-and-ink-drawings complement the text which is clear and straightforward." Toronto

581.6 Economic botany

Fenton, Carroll Lane
Plants we live on; the story of grains and vegetables [by] Carroll Lane Fenton [and] Herminie B. Kitchen; illus. by Carroll Lane Fenton. [Rev. and enl. ed] Day 1971 128p illus map lib. bdg. $7.89 (4-6)   581.6
1 Plants, Edible   2 Grain   3 Vegetables
ISBN 0-381-99819-3   LC 78-89322
First published 1956 with title: Plants that feed us
This book tells the story of grains and vegetables, of the people who grew them in ancient times and of the influence of these food plants on the progress of mankind
"The material is treated in a nontechnical manner yet it provides the essential facts for developing the curiosity of the young." Sci Bks
Books, articles, and illustrations: p124-25

Limbing, Peter R.
Poisonous plants; illus. by Marjorie Zaum. Messner 1976 93p illus map lib. bdg. $7.29 (4 and up)
581.6
1 Poisonous plants
ISBN 0-671-32805-0   LC 76-25804
"Although pleasing to look at and useful as medicine, many common plants are poisonous if

Limburg, Peter R.—_Continued_
eaten. Categorizing these under the headings of
House Plants, Plants of Gardens and Yards, and
Plants of Woods, Fields, and Roadsides, Limburg
discusses each variety separately. Information is
included about the plant's appearance, historical
origins, locations, use, and the symptoms and
reactions of humans or animals upon eating them.
. . . Black-and-white sketches of the species are
not suitable for identification purposes. A glossary
and a map of the natural range of 50 kinds of
poisonous plants in North America are appended."
Booklist

Watch out, it's poison ivy! Photographs by
the author; drawings by Haris Petie. Messner
1973 96p illus lib. bdg. $5.79 (3-6)   **581.6**

1 Poison ivy
ISBN 0-671-32564-7   LC 72-11964
This book "serves both as an identification source
and as a compilation of information about recognizing symptoms and treating poison ivy. The
text stresses safety measures in both treatment
of poisoning and in eradicating the plant, and
warns repeatedly of the necessity of getting professional attention if the case is severe or the
poison is near a victim's eyes. There is also discussion of other plants that are harmless but
resemble poison ivy and of poison oak and poison
sumac; with both text and pictures giving details
that enable the reader to recognize each plant."
Chicago. Children's Bk Center
"Clearly written and profusely illustrated with
. . . drawings, and photographs, this account
offers broader coverage of the subject than is
found in scout, camping, and first aid handbooks
or in more general treatments of plant life." Sch
Library J
Glossary: p91-92

Pringle, Laurence
Wild foods; a beginners guide to identifying, harvesting and cooking safe and tasty
plants from the outdoors; text and photographs by Laurence Pringle; illus. by
Paul Breeden. Four Winds 1978 182p illus
$9.95 (5 and up)   **581.6**

1 Plants. Edible   2 Cookery
ISBN 0-590-07511-X   LC 78-1910
The author's "purpose is to turn doubt into
enthusiasm as he invites readers to find, cook,
and eat parts of 19 plants which can be found
in most areas of the United States. Each plant
is shown in a photograph and drawing and described as to most likely location, common and
scientific names, edible part, and seasonal availability. The processes of harvesting the food and
preparing the recipes are clearly described, and
many of the dishes are tasty; however, as Pringle
warns, some of them are definitely acquired tastes.
Caution is suggested when there is danger of
mistaking a poisonous plant for the one sought,
or when parts of a plant are inedible. The author's
care and thoroughness are evident in the text,
and the excellent black-and-white drawings are
attractive as well as useful." Sch Library J
Glossary: p173-74. Further reading: p175-78

Schaeffer, Elizabeth
Dandelion, pokeweed, and goosefoot; how
the early settlers used plants for food,
medicine, and in the home; with illus. by
Grambs Miller. Young Scott Bks. 1979 94p
illus pa $5.95 (4 and up)   **581.6**

1 Botany, Economic   2 Botany, Medical   3 Plants,
Edible
ISB 0-201-09306-5   LC 72-17852
First published 1972
"Not all the wild plants known and used by
early settlers in North America were native; some
had been deliberately imported while others had
made the journey to the New World as hitchhikers.
In this book, the plants are first divided by habitat
into three groups: woodland, pastureland, and
swampland. In each section the plants are further
grouped according to the purpose for which they
were gathered: medicine, food, or household use.
Historical allusions and nature lore are included
in the general descriptions and in the explanations
of Latin and common names. . . . A Bibliography
and an Index are to be found in the well-
researched, carefully prepared, and accurately
illustrated book." Horn Bk

Selsam, Millicent E.
Plants that heal; illus. by Kathleen Elgin.
Morrow 1959 96p illus lib. bdg. $6.48 (4-6)
    581.6

1 Botany, Medical
ISBN 0-688-31486-4   LC 59-5513
" 'The plant kingdom was man's only drugstore
for countless centuries.' Thus opens a brief and
fascinating history of man's use of roots, stems,
leaves, and seeds of plants to heal (and some to
poison, too). A résumé of superstitions and magic,
prescriptions in medieval herbals and Indian folk
medicine (now being studied anew) precedes description and recent discoveries of antibiotics and
vitamins. Clear botanical sketches; a list of common and scientific plant names, and an index."
Horn Bk

581.92   Marine and fresh-water botany

Earle, Olive L.
Pond and marsh plants; written and illus.
by Olive L. Earle. Morrow 1972 64p illus lib.
bdg. $5.52 (3-6)   **581.92**

1 Fresh water plants
ISBN 0-688-31779-0   LC 72-168472
"An easy-to-read reference on wild water plants.
Explicit information and accurate black-and-white
drawings help young readers understand these
plants and identify which ones have edible parts.
Examples are culled from a wide range of pond
and marsh plants, including those that grow in,
near, on and under water. Unfortunately, Earle
does not indicate where plants are commonly
found. The 45 plants included are indexed by
common name; scientific names are not used."
Sch Library J

Pringle, Laurence
Water plants; illus. by Kazue Mizumura.
Crowell 1975 32p illus (Let's-read-and-find-
out science bks) lib. bdg. $6.89 (1-3)   **581.92**

1 Fresh water plants
ISB 0-690-00738-8   LC 74-23942
"Using the devise of a food chain (a frog,
eaten by a pickerel, is in turn gulped by a blue
heron), Laurence Pringle leads the young reader
through the rushes and cattail to the water's edge;
then through the wild rice, pickerel weeds, and
arrowheads that live in a foot of water; into the
deeper water where floating plants and carnivorous
bladderworts, water lilies, crowfoots, fanworts, and
celery plants flourish. The text is aimed at younger
children and tells something interesting about most
of the plants mentioned. The clearly labeled watercolor illustrations will be useful to older children
for field identification and nicely complement this
introduction to the most common fresh water
plants." Appraisal

582   Seed-bearing plants

Day, Jenifer W.
What is a fruit? Illus. by Enid Kotschnig.
Golden Press 1976 29p illus lib. bdg. $6.08
(1-3)   **582**

1 Fruit
ISB 0-307-61801-3   LC 74-80879
"An interesting, and probably successful, attempt
to teach basic biology through induction. Each
double-page spread describes a particular form
of the general subject (single-seed fruits with a
fleshy exterior [etc.]) . . . noting unique characteristics as well as those held in common with
others in the book. Most useful of all, species are
color illustrated and carefully labeled. By the end,
a reader has retained enough information to
follow the short discussion about the general subject and its typical forms. Although vocabulary
is difficult and certain anatomical terms and
biological functions are not explained, it is commendable that real terms are used. Frequent
word, phrase, and sentence repetition, while
clumsy, reinforces meaning in context; a word
list is appended for study." Booklist

Hutchins, Ross E.
The amazing seeds; photographs by the author. Dodd 1965 159p illus lib. bdg. $5.95 (5 and up) **582**

1 Seeds
ISBN 0-396-06478-7   LC 65-19215

Starting with an initial chapter on seedless plants, the book then "describes pollination, seed production, germination, plant growth, dispersal of seeds, and other botanical processes. Many forms of common and uncommon seeds are described and illustrated, and the book closes with a brief instruction of collecting wild flower seeds." Sci Bks

Jordan, Helene J.
How a seed grows; illus. by Joseph Low. Crowell 1960 unp illus (Let's-read-and-find-out science bks) lib. bdg. $6.89, pa $1.95 (k-2) **582**

1 Seeds
ISBN 0-690-40645-2; 0-690-40646-0   LC 60-11541

"Begins by explaining that the seeds of different plants are different and grow differently. Then suggests that the student plant and care for some bean seeds in order to observe how they develop; thus it effectively teaches the beginner how a seed grows into a plant." The AAAS Sci Bk List for Children

"For beginning independent readers. Large print, plenty of white space, and information given with simplicity implement the appropriate level of sentence length and vocabulary difficulty." Chicago. Children's Bk Center

Seeds by wind and water; illus. by Nils Hogner. Crowell 1962 unp illus (Let's-read-and-find-out science bks) $6.95, lib. bdg. $6.89 (k-2) **582**

1 Seeds
ISBN 0-690-72452-7; 0-690-72453-5   LC 62-12820

This is "an elementary explanation of the variety of ways in which seeds are distributed. [It] shows how wind, animals, water and even airplanes carry seeds from place to place. Color and black-and-white drawings of each seed and plant help in identifying the plants discussed." The AAAS Sci Bk List for Children

"A very brief account . . . useful for elementary science projects." NY Times Bk Rev

Selsam, Millicent E.
Play with seeds; illus. by Helen Ludwig. Morrow 1957 93p illus lib. bdg. $6.48 (3-6) **582**

1 Seeds
ISBN 0-688-31489-9   LC 57-6080

"Excellent informative introduction to the study of plants and seeds. . . . Traces their evolution on earth from their beginnings 100 million years ago. Clear explanations, accompanied by detailed black-and-white drawings show the development of the seed in a wide variety of plants. The travel of seeds, both useful and harmful, aided by birds, wind, and man, is described with interesting details. Numerous simple but enlightening experiments are suggested. Index adds to the usefulness." Library J

Shuttlesworth, Dorothy E.
The hidden magic of seeds; illus. by John Hamberger. Rodale 1976 44p illus $6.95 (2-4) **582**

1 Seeds
ISBN 0-87857-128-0   LC 76-3328

"A basic introduction to the subject of seeds— what they are and how they grow. The text shows that seeds are moved by wind, animals, and birds and that they are used to provide food, clothing, and more plants of their own kind. The simple text is combined with carefully drawn and labeled pictures in full color, allowing readers to easily grasp the substance of the text." Booklist

582.1 Herbaceous and woody plants

Petrides, George A.
A field guide to trees and shrubs. . . . Illus. by George Petrides [and] Roger Tory Peterson. 2d ed. Houghton 1972 xxxii, 428p illus $9.95, pa $5.95 **582.1**

1 Trees 2 Shrubs 3 Climbing plants
ISBN 0-395-13651-2; 0-395-17579-8   LC 76-157132

"The Peterson Field guide series"
First published 1958
"Field marks of all trees, shrubs, and woody vines that grow wild in the northeastern and north-central United States and in southeastern and south-central Canada." Title page

"Written primarily for the amateur naturalist who wants a quick method of identifying woody plants based on easily observed characteristics. . . . The extensive coverage of shrubs and woody vines adds greatly to the value of this guide. . . . There are silhouettes of tree shapes for many common trees, a key to the hickories, and keys for winter identification. Important information on wildlife values, and uses for furniture, dyes, and emergency food add to the readability of the volume." Choice

582.13 Herbaceous flowering plants

Busch, Phyllis S.
Wildflowers and the stories behind their names; paintings by Anne Ophelia Dowden. Scribner 1977 88p illus lib. bdg. $9.95 (4-6) **582.13**

1 Wild flowers 2 Plant names. Popular
ISBN 0-684-14820-X   LC 73-1351

"The distinguished botanical artist has provided beautiful, realistic paintings, chiefly full page or spreading in part over a second page and alternating between handsome full color and almost equally pleasing black and white. With a scientist's precision she has drawn her fifty species to a scale stated to be 'exactly 4/5 actual size' and added enlarged details as separate sketches on her pages. The author, a science educator, combines straight-forward botanical information (including scientific as well as descriptive names) with legends, superstitions, and customs of plant use, many from the lore of American Indians and early settlers and some from ancient myths." Horn Bk

"Although this is not a field guide . . . 46 common wildflowers can easily be identified. . . . The enticing paintings makes this a treat for beginners and enthusiasts alike." Sch Library J

Dowden, Anne Ophelia
Look at a flower; illus. by the author. Crowell 1963 120p illus $8.95 (6 and up) **582.13**

1 Flowers 2 Botany
ISBN 0-690-50656-2   LC 63-12650

This book presents "the evolution, structure and reproduction of common North American plants and flowers, grouped into ten families." Toronto

"Exquisitely detailed botanical drawings will lead the holder of this book first to read the pictures and thus to find introduction to a highly scientific and readable text. It is an excellent treatment of basic botany . . . in a handsomely produced volume, complete with general index and an index of plants referred to in illustration and text." Horn Bk

State flowers; illus. by the author. Crowell 1978 86p illus $7.95, lib. bdg. $7.89 (5 and up) **582.13**

1 State flowers
ISBN 0-690-01339-6; 0-690-03884-4   LC 78-51927

"Artist Dowden's careful hand has meticulously etched the leaves, stems, petals, and stamens, capturing the intricate individuality of each flower in its natural shades and colors. Statutes enacting the state flower laws are given verbatim along with historical and other background information

Dowden, Anne O.—*Continued*

appearing in the brief text juxtaposed with the paintings. Except in a few cases where two states have the same flower and thus are placed together, an alphabetical order by state is observed." Booklist

"The radiant botanical illustrations add beauty to a small but useful compendium." Horn Bk

Wild green things in the city; a book of weeds; illus. by the author. Crowell 1972 56p illus $8.95 (4 and up)   **582.13**

1 Wild flowers 2 Weeds
ISBN 0-690-89067-2   LC 72-158687

The author describes "city weeds and their development—roots in April, leaves in May, flowers in June, composites and grasses in summer, and seeds in autumn. She discusses plant survival in a man-made environment and man's dependence on oxygen-manufacturing plant life." Booklist

"Beautifully illustrated with meticulously realistic drawings of plants and plant parts, this is not only an excellent book for identification and appreciation of weeds, but gives a great deal of information about botanical structure, photosynthesis, and propagation. The plants described are those found in three urban areas: Manhattan, Denver, and Los Angeles. Lucidly written, the text is followed by lists of plants for each of the three areas, each list divided into rare, common, and very common weeds. An index is appended." Chicago. Children's Bk Center

Milne, Lorus J.

Because of a flower [by] Lorus J. Milne & Margery Milne; drawings by Kenneth Gosner. Atheneum Pubs. 1975 152p illus $6.95 (5 and up)   **582.13**

1 Flowers 2 Botany—Ecology
ISBN 0-689-30452-8   LC 74-19292

The authors "have selected a varied cross-section of flowering plants: water lilies, orchids, yucca plants, oak trees, cacti, milkweed, etc.—all with unusual, sometimes unique, interdependence on one or several animals and insects. Each flower is dealt with separately in its own chapter. Each is illustrated in soft, delicate and realistic black and white drawings. . . . They have chosen to tell the most intriguing and unusual things about the formation, pollination, seeds, and flowering of each plant and the sometimes bizarre habits of the animals who either depend on or are depended on by the flower. There are chapters at the front and back about flowering plants in general, a list of further reading, and an index, as well as a family tree of ancient plants 200 million years ago—ancestors of those flowers in the book." Appraisal

"Each chapter may be read separately for its own story, but interest mounts with each new plant and its attendant life. The authors, eminent ecologists, succeed in portraying vividly their stated theme in a style which is for the most part simple and colorful." Children's Bk Rev Serv

Selsam, Millicent E.

A first look at flowers, by Millicent E. Selsam and Joyce Hunt; illus. by Harriett Springer. Walker & Co. [1976 c1977] 31p illus $5.95, lib. bdg. $6.85 (1-3)   **582.13**

1 Flowers
ISBN 0-8027-6281-6; 0-8027-6282-4   LC 76-57063

"Text and corresponding black-and-white illustrations direct children's attention to flower shape, arrangement on the stalk, petal formation, location and number of stamens and pistils, etc. Nine flowers pictured in the text appear again on the last pages for a recognition test." Sch Library J

"Meticulously drawn pictures . . . of flowers and flower parts add to the usefulness of a succinctly written introduction to the subject, and the authors incorporate into the text such basic scientific principles as observation, identification, and comparison. The writing is direct and simple, occasionally asking such questions as 'Which has six and which has ten stamens?' when the illustrations below are obvious and labelled." Chicago. Children's Bk Center

Stupka, Arthur

Wildflowers in color, by Arthur Stupka with the assistance of Donald H. Robinson. Harper 1965 144p illus $9.95   **582.13**

1 Wild flowers
ISBN 0-06-071860-9   LC 65-21010

This is "a combination field guide to identification and full-color picture book portraying 250 species common in the eastern United States, with full botanical information and an excellent color photograph of each." Hodges. Bks for Elem Sch Libraries

"True, the wildflowers listed and notes here are found mostly in the Southern Appalachian Mountains, (in the Shenandoah, Blue Ridge, and Great Smokey National Parks); but they occur frequently enough in a large number of instances further north into New York State and Massachusetts for this to be a helpful guide. The pictures with their accompanying notes, are presented in rather haphazard order, it would seem, but can be located by the Index." Best Sellers

Suggested readings: p135-36

Zim, Herbert S.

Flowers; a guide to familiar American wildflowers, by Herbert S. Zim and Alexander C. Martin; illus. by Rudolf Freund. 134 paintings in full color. Sponsored by the Wildlife Management Institute. Golden Press 1950 157p illus maps (A Golden Nature guide) $9.15, pa $1.95   **582.13**

1 Wild flowers
ISBN 0-307-63511-2; 0-307-24491-1   LC 50-8172

First published by Simon & Schuster

"This is an extremely practical beginner's guide. . . . To facilitate identification the flowers are arranged in four groups according to color. Each flower is pictured in color with a range map. . . . Brief descriptive text gives characteristics, habitat, growing season and family." Booklist

"It is not only a very informing book. It is attractive and easy to carry in a coat pocket." Sat Rev

582.16   Trees

Anderson, Margaret J.

Exploring city trees and the need for urban forests; illus. with photographs and line drawings. McGraw 1976 102p illus lib. bdg. $6.95 (4-6)   **582.16**

1 Trees—U.S.
ISBN 0-07-001695-X   LC 75-20481

The author "focuses on changes in northeastern hardwoods during the span of four seasons, she also discusses the problems and use of urban forests. There is repeated emphasis on taxonomy and on trees in an ecological context." AAAS Sci Bks & Films

"Black and white photographs and line drawings enhance the text, which is written in easily understood language. A well-organized index and bibliography are provided." Sci and Children

Bulla, Clyde Robert

A tree is a plant; illus. by Lois Lignell. Crowell 1960 unp illus (Let's-read-and-find-out bks) lib. bdg. $6.89, pa $2.95 (k-2)   **582.16**

1 Trees
ISBN 0-690-83529-9; 0-690-00201-7   LC 60-11540

"The text presents very simply the fact that there are many kinds of trees, that they reproduce by seeding and that an apple tree will be chosen as an example of a tree. The cycle of growth and the seasonal changes, the structure and the functioning of the parts are then described in terms of the apple tree. . . . The greatest asset of the book is the limitation of information: there is no extraneous information or terminology that might confuse the reader." Chicago. Children's Bk Center

"Lois Lignell's illustrations, each stretching across two pages, are informative as well as beautiful in color and design." Horn Bk

Collingwood, G. H.

Knowing your trees, by G. H. Collingwood and Warren D. Brush. Am. Forestry Assn. illus maps $8.50   **582.16**

1 Trees—U.S.
First published 1937. Revised with each printing

"The appearance of the tree is described, its economic importance is indicated, and its range is shown on a small map of the United States.

Collingwood, G. H.—*Continued*
Good photographs show a mature tree and the leaf and bark. Deciduous broadleafed trees are pictured in summer and winter. Index of scientific and common names." Am Forests

Dowden, Anne Ophelia
The blossom on the bough; a book of trees; illus. by the author. Crowell 1975 71p illus $8.95 (5 and up) 582.16
1 Trees—U.S. 2 Forests and forestry
ISBN 0-690-00384-6 LC 74-6192
An "introduction to the unfamiliar flowers and fruits of our country's trees. Discussed are the importance of forests, the tree as a woody plant, growth, cycles, chemical activity, the parts and functions of tree flowers and fruits distinctive features of conifers, and the geographical forest regions of the U.S. (a map of these forest regions lists trees by both Latin and common names)." Sch Library J
Surely Ms. Dowden has no peer in botanical drawing; her pictures have the beauty and precision of Audubon's bird paintings, and the color reproduction is marvelously faithful in hues and shadings. While less formal in style than a textbook, this can serve as a beginning text in botany. The pictures can be used for identifying species . . . A list, divided by forest regions, of common trees, and an index that gives scientific and common names are appended." Chicago. Children's Bk Center

Earle, Olive L.
Nuts, by Olive L. Earle with Michael Kantor; illus. by Olive L. Earle. Morrow 1975 63p illus $5.75, lib. bdg. $5.52 (3-6) 582.16
1 Nuts
ISBN 0-688-22025-8; 0-688-32025-2 LC 74-26800
"The authors list 34 of the more familiar nut species, telling where they are found, how they grow, and what they are used for. A beginning chapter explains the botanical terminology that appears throughout and clarifies the scientific definition of the term 'nut'. Illustrated with Earle's pencil sketches showing the leaves, flowers, and nuts of each plant." Booklist
"This will be of interest considering the upsurge in natural foods and forest foraging." Sch Library J

State trees. Newly rev. ed. Written and illus. by Olive L. Earle. Morrow 1973 unp illus lib. bdg. $5.52 (4 and up) 582.16
1 State trees
ISBN 0-688-31956-4 LC 73-4932
First published 1960
"Describes in brief text the appearance, growth, [legends about] and use of the [39] trees chosen as state trees and shows in detailed drawings the seed, flower, leaf, bark, and shape of the tree. While the same information can be found in encyclopedias many libraries will find it convenient to have the material in a single volume. Arranged alphabetically by tree with an index by state." Booklist [review of 1960 edition]
"A good book for the young naturalist who has tramped beyond the novice field. . . . Lucid text and dignified drawings." NY Times Bk Rev [review of 1960 edition]

Riedman, Sarah R.
Trees alive; illus. by Giulio Maestro. Lothrop 1974 128p illus $7.25, lib. bdg. $6.96 (5 and up) 582.16
1 Trees
ISBN 0-688-41574-1; 0-688-51574-6 LC 74-1382
The author "presents fascinating information about one of our greatest resources. The history of the use of trees is examined, as well as latest scientific findings. Chapters explore such topics as: structure and function of tree parts; how trees breathe, grow, reproduce, age, and die; how they convert solar energy to chemical energy; and the process by which trees purify and renew our air. The concluding chapter poses a sober question for us all: Will trees forever remain a renewable resource if continued cutting depletes our forests?" Sci Teacher
Suggestions for further reading: p125

Selsam, Millicent E.
Maple tree; photographs by Jerome Wexler. Morrow 1968 46p illus lib. bdg. $7.44 (2-4) 582.16
1 Maple
ISBN 0-688-31496-1 LC 68-25933
"Using the Norway maple to demonstrate the principles of growth, the author and photographer describe the step-by-step development of a seed into a tree from the winged fruit which puts roots into the ground, produces buds, leaves and stems to the trunk and branches." Pub W
"Clear photographs, many enlarged close-ups, in black and white and some in color (and beautiful), add to the appeal of a lucid and informative botany book for the primary grades reader." Chicago. Children's Bk Center

Play with trees; pictures by Fred F. Scherer. Morrow 1950 64p illus lib. bdg. $6.48 (3-5) 582.16
1 Trees
ISBN 0-688-31495-3 LC 50-8832
"A good introduction to the study of trees [and how they grow] showing how they can be distinguished by their shapes, bark, buds and leaves. It gives the methods for collecting and preserving leaves and twigs, and it is illustrated by numerous black and white drawings." Ontario Library Rev
"Growing a miniature forest in a windowsill-size aquarium glass is one of the most fascinating experiments included in this book. . . . There are many other experiments too and much information for the gradeschool science classes either in city or country schools." Horn Bk

Zim, Herbert S.
Trees; a guide to familiar American trees, by Herbert S. Zim and Alexander C. Martin; illus. by Dorothea and Sy Barlowe. 143 species in color. Sponsored by the Wildlife Management Institute. [Rev. ed] Golden Press 1956 160p illus maps (A Golden Nature Guide) lib. bdg. $9.15, pa $1.95 582.16
1 Trees
ISBN 0-307-63509-0; 0-307-24494-6 LC 57-3009
First published 1952 by Simon & Schuster
"A beginner's pocket-size guidebook, uniform with . . . other titles in the Golden Nature series; illustrates in color and describes . . . American trees, pointing up the features important in identification—form and height of tree, leaves, bark, fruit, flowers, buds—and including, in most cases, a range map." Booklist
"The authors' aim is to make tree study easy. . . . The nature fan has to read only about 100 words to get complete information about a tree he's trying to identify." Chicago Sunday Trib

583 Dicotyledons

Busch, Phyllis S.
Cactus in the desert; illus. by Harriet Barton. Crowell 1979 34p illus (Let's-read-and-find-out science bk) $6.95, lib. bdg. $6.89 (1-3) 583
1 Cactus
ISBN 0-690-00292-0; 0-690-01336-1 LC 78-4771
"The text explains how cactus plants survive without much rainfall, and describes the ways in which people and animals use the stored juice of cactus or the plant itself for drink or food. In closing, Busch suggests varieties of cactus available as house plants." Chicago. Children's Bk Center
The author "skillfully presents information about cactus and livens it with anecdotes such as this: 'Indians used to break off the curved spines of cactus and use them as fishhooks.' Best of all, Busch follows all size and bulk measurements with comparisons youngster can understand. . . . Bright illustrations spark this carefully researched and carefully worded book about cactus. Strong oranges, sand colors, ochers and browns define the drawings. Each drawing strengthens a point made in the text." Christian Sci Monitor

Earle, Olive L.

Peas, beans, and licorice; written and illus. by Olive L. Earle. Morrow 1971 63p illus $5.75 (4-6)　　**583**

1 Legumes

ISBN 0-688-21570-X　　LC 77-126737

This "introduction to the small plants and the trees of the legume family . . . describes the distinguishing characteristics of legumes and the appearance and practical and ornamental uses of different species. In addition to the three species mentioned in the title, the book covers alfalfa, loco weed, wisteria, peanuts, Scotch broom, the laburnum tree, and many other legumes. A service supplement to plant studies and, with the author's clear, accurate drawings, a helpful guide to identification." Booklist

The rose family; written and illus. by Olive L. Earle. Morrow 1970 63p illus lib. bdg. $5.52 (4-6)　　**583**

ISBN 0-688-31491-0　　LC 72-90270

"Clearly written survey of the wide variety of members of the rose family. . . . The text points out the similarities and differences among the 20,000 species, illustrating these with exotic as well as familiar flowers, bushes, and trees." Sat Rev

"Each page of the book includes an illustration appropriate for the text on that page. The drawings, by the author, are accurate, labeled, and offer added interest to the text. A discussion on the economic uses of the members of the rose family helps children realize that although many rose family plants are usually appreciated solely for aesthetic beauty, they also may have practical uses as wood products and food sources. For example, a consideration is provided of rose family fruits that belong to the botanical groupings known as drupes, true berries, and pomes. [The author] indicated many botanical terms and their origins that are of concern when offering a scientific account of the rose family." Sci Bks

Rahn, Joan Elma

Alfalfa, beans & clover; illus. by Ginny Linville Winter. Atheneum Pubs. 1976 119p illus $6.50 (6 and up)　　**583**

1 Legumes

ISBN 0-689-30528-1　　LC 76-67

The author "limits her discussion to 60 of the 14,000 kinds [of legumes] concentrating on their various characteristics and importance to the world. Descriptions relate similarities and differences of flowers, leaves, pods, and seeds, with well-labeled diagrams supplying visual support. Included is information on the uses of this bean family as a food source as well as for forage, timber, medicinal products, and its special property for putting nitrogen into the soil. Scientific names are explained in an appendix." Booklist

Selsam, Millicent E.

The amazing dandelion [by] Millicent E. Selsam and Jerome Wexler. Morrow 1977 46p illus $6.75, lib. bdg. $6.48 (2-4)　　**583**

1 Dandelions

ISBN 0-688-22129-7; 0-688-32129-1　　LC 77-9029

"Selsam describes the dandelion's structure and life cycle, stressing the many ways of reproduction that make the plant so tenacious a weed, a pest to most people but a source of food to many." Chicago. Children's Bk Center

"Though all but a few special photographs are black and white, Wexler's close-ups of dandelions and their parts ably illustrate Selsam's lucid examination." Booklist

The apple and other fruits; photographs by Jerome Wexler. Morrow 1973 48p illus $6.95, lib. bdg. $7.44 (3-5)　　**583**

1 Apple 2 Fruit 3 Trees

ISBN 0-688-20089-3; 0-688-30089-8　　LC 73-4928

The book combines photographs "with clear, uncompromising explanations of the apple blossoms' pollination, the fruit's growth from a flower ovary, grafting and budding, and the comparable development of pears, peaches, plums, cherries, and oranges." Booklist

This is "a model of botanical instruction. . . . There is no extraneous text, and the magnified photographs are handsome, clear, and nicely placed." Chicago. Children's Bk Center

Mimosa, the sensitive plant [by] Millicent E. Selsam and Jerome Wexler. Morrow 1978 48p illus $7.50, lib. bdg. $7.20 (3-5)　　**583**

1 Mimosas

ISBN 0-688-22167-X; 0-688-32167-4　　LC 78-15090

"The beautifully clear photographs here (both color and black and white) have been so expertly chosen and placed that other problems fold up and seem to evaporate. This photo-essay aimed at students in the middle elementary grades focuses on the thigmotropism phenomenon as seen in one of nature's most outstanding performers. . . . The accompanying text explains the carefully documented actions and gives instructions for growing a plant from seed. Although the large and generously spaced prints seem to be intended for the very young, the concepts and vocabulary are not for the uninitiated. As a supplementary science assignment this might work, but few early elementary grade children could grasp this information unless spoonfed by an adult. However, 'Mimosa' is worth the tab just for the photographs, and with some guidance and selectivity could be used for a great range of levels and abilities." Sch Library J

Peanut; photographs by Jerome Wexler. Morrow 1969 46p illus lib. bdg. $7.44 (2-4)　　**583**

1 Peanuts

ISBN 0-688-31803-7　　LC 70-81886

"A clear, accurate text and outstanding close-up photographs, seven in color, describe the development of the self-pollinating peanut plant from seed to maturity. This excellent science book . . . also notes the peanut's value as food, some of its other uses, and the harvesting of peanuts." Booklist

Svatos, Ladislav

Dandelion. Doubleday 1976 unp illus $5.95, lib. bdg. $6.90 (k-2)　　**583**

1 Dandelions

ISBN 0-385-02913-6; 0-385-04629-4　　LC 73-20911

"A spare narrative and bold color illustrations recount the life cycle of the familiar dandelion in a clear and inviting manner. The text begins with the little parachutes which carry the seeds of new plants and emphasizes the role of the wind, soil, rain, and sunshine in the development of the flower. An attractive beginning science book for the story hour set." Sch Library J

584　Monocotyledons

Goldin, Augusta

Grass; the everything, everywhere plant. Elsevier/Nelson Bks. 1977 176p illus $7.95 (5 and up)　　**584**

1 Grasses

ISBN 0-525-66453-X　　LC 76-52502

First published by Thomas Nelson

"The importance of grasses to human civilization is described in this . . . book. Various food- and non-food grasses, including wheat, corn, oats, barley, rye, millet, sorghum, rice, and sugar are discussed, as well as their products, such as bread, cereal, vegetable oil, sugar, beer, and other alcoholic beverages. The use of grasses as animal feed is also discussed. (The author argues that meat animals consume only a small fraction of the amount of grain consumed by humans; however, this view is not adequately supported.) The black-and-white photographs are excellent. The book includes an appendix of common and scientific names of grasses, a bibliography, and an index." Sci Teacher

Selsam, Millicent E.

Bulbs, corms, and such; photographs by Jerome Wexler. Morrow 1974 48p illus $7.75, lib. bdg. $7.44 (2-5)　　**584**

1 Bulbs

ISBN 0-688-21822-9; 0-688-31822-3　　LC 74-5939

This book explains "the reproductive, life-sustaining function of the fleshy, underground parts of

Selsam, Millicent E.—*Continued*

non-seedbearing plants. Spring flowers like daffodils and hyacinths serve to illustrate bulbs; gladiolas, begonias, canna plants, sweet potatoes, and dahlias are examples of corms, tubers, rhizomes, and tuberous roots. Directions for growing each flower are appended." Booklist

The book is illustrated with "full-color pictures of plants in bloom contrasting dramatically with black and white pictures—often with plants parts cut away—of stages in the growth of bulbs, corms, tubers, tuberous roots, and rhizomes. . . . This is an example of the best kind of science writing: clear and informative, with the text and illustrations nicely integrated." Chicago. Children's Bk Center

Popcorn; photographs by Jerome Wexler. Morrow 1976 48p illus map $6.75, lib. bdg. $6.48 (3-5) **584**

1 Popcorn
ISBN 0-688-22083-5; 0-688-32083-X   LC 76-26627

"After giving some facts about evidence of corn in pre-Columbian times and distinguishing popcorn from other varieties, the text suggests a home experiment in which the reader can grow a popcorn plant. Excellent enlarged photographs show plant parts as the author explains structure, fertilization, and development of the plant; the text concludes with a discussion of some of the many uses of corn in foods, as animal fodder, in manufactured products, in medicine, in chemicals. Impeccably organized and lucidly written . . . this is also outstanding for the quality of the photography and the handsomeness of the format." Chicago. Children's Bk Center

585 Gymnosperms (Naked-seed plants)

Adler, David A.

Redwoods are the tallest trees in the world; illus. by Kazue Mizumura. Crowell 1978 32p illus map (Let's-read-and-find-out science bks) lib. bdg. $6.89 (2-3) **585**

1 Redwood
ISBN 0-690-01368-X   LC 77-4713

"In a gently informative first-person narrative a young boy tells what he knows about the redwood trees he saw in a California national park. There a ranger explained about them and the kind of habitat they require. . . . Where they fit in the tree spectrum, how they reproduce, the protective function of the bark and the trees' timber value are noted . . . along with the Save-The-Redwoods League efforts to buy threatened redwood forests and make them into parks. Informative and admiring in an understated way; if only some of the olive drab and mud brown watercolor illustrations showed more spirit." Booklist

586 Seedless plants

Hutchins, Ross E.

Plants without leaves; lichens, fungi, mosses, liverworts, slime-molds, algae, horsetails; photographs by the author. Dodd 1966 152p illus lib. bdg. $5.95 (5 and up) **586**

1 Plants
ISBN 0-396-06653-4   LC 66-20449

"Algae, fungi, slime-molds, lichens, liverworts, mosses, and horse-tails can be quite exciting when examined by a 10-power hand lens, preferably in the woods during the rainy season. Mr Hutchins explains their growth habits, uses to man, and manner of survival. His excellent macrophotographs add depth to the lively text." Sch Library J

Lists of manuals for further study of leafless plants: p145-47

588 Bryophyta. Mosses

Davis, Bette J.

The world of mosses; written and illus. by Bette J. Davis. Lothrop 1975 64p illus $6.25, lib. bdg. $6 (6 and up) **588**

1 Mosses
ISBN 0-688-41667-5; 0-688-51667-X   LC 74-10606

The author "gives detailed anatomical and life cycle information on mosses in general, noting also many variations in the shapes of parts and in overall formation of different orders of the class Musci. Other sections are included on plants that are mistaken for mosses, on the uses of peat and mosses' role in the making of soil, and on setting up a terrarium for gathered specimens." Booklist

"Dignified, solidly informative, and meticulously illustrated, the book concludes with a glossary, a brief bibliography, and an index." Chicago. Children's Bk Center

589.2 Fungi

Froman, Robert

Mushrooms and molds; illus. by Grambs Miller. Crowell 1972 33p illus (Let's-read-and-find-out science bks) lib. bdg. $6.89 (1-3) **589.2**

1 Mushrooms 2 Molds
ISBN 0-690-56603-4   LC 71-187936

The book gives "information on fungi covering their growth from mycelium, their manufacture of soil for green plants, and their reproduction by spores. Suggestions for growing bread molds and making mushroom spore patterns are intriguing and practical for small children." Booklist

"The definitions included within the text are scientifically accurate, yet very simple. The drawings on each page clearly show what the author is explaining. Because there is little available on the subject, this will provide good supplementary material for elementary science collections." Sch Library J

Kavaler, Lucy

The wonders of fungi; illus. with photographs and with drawings by Richard Ott. Day 1964 128p illus lib. bdg. $6.89 (5 and up) **589.2**

1 Fungi
ISBN 0-381-99770-7   LC 64-10450

An introduction to "the study of molds, mushrooms, yeasts, and other kinds of fungi, explaining their useful and harmful effects in food and medicine." Hodges. Bks for Elem Sch Libraries

"A final chapter conjectures about the fungi that may be found in space." Chicago. Children's Bk Center

590.74 Zoological museums, collections, exhibits

Grosvenor, Donna K.

Zoo babies; with photographs by the author. Natl. Geographic Soc. 1978 31p illus (k-3) **590.74**

1 Zoological gardens 2 Animals—Infancy
ISBN 0-87044-262-7   LC 77-95413

Available only as part of 4v set for $7.95 with: Animals that live at sea, by J. A. Straker (591.92), Explore a spooky swamp, by W. W. Cortesi (574.5), Animals in danger (591.5)

"Books for young explorers"

Prepared by the Special Publications Division of the National Geographic Society

Through color photographs 17 varieties of baby animals are introduced. The text explains how the zoo personnel meet their special needs

Halmi, Robert

Zoos of the world. Four Winds 1975 117p illus lib. bdg. $6.95 (5 and up) **590.74**

1 Zoological gardens
ISBN 0-590-07247-1   LC 72-87078

The author "presents his personal observations about the purposes, problems, and design of zoos. He discusses the aspects of taming, housing, feeding, and displaying animals that are common to most zoos citing specific zoos as examples. Criticism of zoos has been made in other books but Halmi makes a stronger plea for more sensible and natural treatment of animals through thought-provoking descriptions of some well-known zoos which provide poor facilities." Sch Library J

Hewett, Joan

Watching them grow; inside a zoo nursery; photographs by Richard Hewett. Little 1979 64p illus $7.95 (3-6)   **590.74**

1 Animals—Infancy   2 San Diego, California. Zoological Garden
ISBN 0-316-35968-8   LC 79-13345

"Chronologically arranged episodes covering a four-month period in the animal nursery at the San Diego Zoo. Loretta Owens is 'night nurse' from 3:30 to midnight, and during this period has a pygmy chimpanzee (Kalind), twin orangutans (Lisa and Lock), a spider monkey (Drainola), and an aardvark (A-seven, better known as Piggy) under her care. Without exhaustive detail, Hewett introduces us to the care and concern expended on the comfort and upbringing of these delightful babies. . . . Illustrated with engaging photographs." Sch Library J

Scott, Jack Denton

City of birds and beasts; behind the scenes at the Bronx Zoo; with photographs by Ozzie Sweet. Putnam 1978 120p illus $8.95 (6 and up)   **590.74**

1 New York (City). Zoological Park
ISBN 0-399-20633-7   LC 77-13888

The author "describes, almost moment by moment, the incredible events during one day at the . . . [Bronx Zoo]. At dawn, the staff is alerted by screams from the rheas (ostrichlike birds) and arrest a man who is caught pulling out the creatures' tail feathers. At 6:20 a.m., the curator of reptiles solves the mystery of 30 timber rattlers found in a shopping center. From sunup to sundown, incidents infuriating, amusing, worrying, and sometimes tragic keep the people on the alert." Pub W

"This gives many facts about animal care and feeding, accommodations and the work of the zoo staff; the anecdotal approach gives the book vitality, and the writing style and photography are up to the usual high standards of Scott and Sweet." Chicago. Children's Bk Center

591   Zoology

Discovering nature indoors; a nature and science guide to investigations with small animals; ed. by Laurence Pringle. Natural Hist. Press 1970 128p illus $4.95 (5 and up)   **591**

1 Zoology   2 Nature study
ISBN 0-385-01000-1   LC 70-103134

"This book is comprised of articles from 'Nature and Science' magazine. Dealing with snails, turtles, guppies, mealworms, cockroaches, houseflies, ants, shrimp, gerbils, mice, and other small animals it offers information on how to keep them successfully and suggests projects and investigations for studying them. It also includes instructions on how to make and use a microscope. With many clear photographs and diagrams, a helpful and stimulating books. A list of books for further reading and the names and addresses of supply houses are appended." Booklist

Selsam, Millicent E.

Benny's animals, and how he put them in order; pictures by Arnold Lobel. Harper 1966 60p illus (A Science I can read bk) lib. bdg. $6.89 (1-3)   **591**

1 Zoology—Terminology
ISBN 0-06-025273-1   LC 66-10725

"Benny, whose passion for tidiness rather worried his mother, became curious about animals after bringing some specimens home from the beach. With some guidance from a museum zoologist Benny and his friend learned something about the major divisions in zoological classification." Chicago. Children's Bk Center

"This is a readable book, basically accurate and informative. . . . It teaches fundamental processes of observation, comparison,—classification, and reasoning." Sci Bks

Simon, Seymour

Animal fact/animal fable; illus. by Diane de Groat. Crown 1979 unp illus $7.95, pa $3.95 (1-4)   **591**

1 Animals
ISBN 0-517-53474-6; 0-517-53794-X   LC 78-14866

"After a brief explanation of the terms 'fact' and 'fable,' the author proceeds to either verify or dispel many common beliefs about animals. Each fable is accompanied by a full-color illustration, a comical exaggeration of the belief. Following the factual statement is another picture and a short explanation of the actual behavior of the animal." Children's Bk Rev Serv

"The amusement comes from the outrageously, ridiculously anthropomorphic illustrations of the questioned statements. . . . The de Groat style is highly sophisticated while the depiction is unflinchingly silly, and the effect is happily preposterous. The illustrations which accompany the serious explanations are straightforward, realistic, and quite beautiful. Done in watercolors of muted tones, the pictures are admirable and the text is informative. A very fine collaboration." Sch Library J

Ylla

Animal babies. Story by Arthur Gregor; designed by Luc Bouchage. Harper 1959 unp illus lib. bdg. $8.79, pa $1.95 (k-3)   **591**

1 Animal—Pictorial works   2 Animals—Infancy
ISBN 0-06-026741-0; 0-06-443013-8   LC 58-9783

"These artistically sympathetic, uncluttered photographs of animal babies with their mothers will be studied with wonder and enjoyment by kindergarten and primary age children, who find the reality of uncolored photographs absorbing in a way that the younger picture-book ages do not. And the older child's greater familiarity with the animals of farm and zoo will give him an interest with which to approach this beautiful book." Horn Bk

"Accompanying each photograph are a few lines of text which do little more than identify the animals." Booklist

Whose eye am I? Story by Crosby Bonsall; planned by Charles Rado; designed by Luc Bouchage. Harper 1968 unp illus $8.95 (k-3)   **591**

1 Animals—Pictorial works   2 Eye
ISBN 0-06-020563-6   LC 68-24336

"'A small boy sees the eye of an animal in a hole in the fence on a farm.' He goes around the farm seeking the owner of the eye and having conversations with the animals he encounters. . . . Black-and-white pictures, from full-page to very small, are stunning—superbly contrasted, cleverly angled, and marvelously successful in evoking the different animal personalities. . . . A fine read-aloud for preschoolers, this will appeal to independent readers in the second and third grades too." Sch Library J

591.1   Physiology of animals

Freedman, Russell

Getting born; drawings by Corbett Jones. Holiday House 1978 unp illus lib. bdg. $6.95 (2-4)   **591.1**

1 Reproduction   2 Animals—Habits and behavior
ISBN 0-8234-0336-X   LC 78-6673

"Captioned black-and-white photographs, diagrams, and descriptive text give the details of various fish, frogs, turtles, snakes, chicks, cats, dolphins, and horses in the process of hatching or live birth." Booklist

"The photography throughout the book is outstanding. Pictures depicting the developmental stages of all species at birth provide excellent detail. 'Getting Born' can serve as an introduction to the subject of reproduction or as a supplement to the discussion of human reproduction, a topic not covered. The information is advanced, yet understandable. A very worthwhile library addition, this book also could be used when a child begins to question the process of development and birth." AAAS Sci Bks & Films

May, Julian

Living things and their young. Follett 1969 48p illus (Follett Family life education program) lib. bdg. $3.48 (4-6)   591.1

1 Reproduction
ISBN 0-695-45294-0   LC 68-10481

This book details "the process of reproduction in a variety of animals, from those with one cell to complex mammals." Princeton Pub. Library. Hello, Baby.

The author "stresses the importance of the family in the care and protection of the young. Illustrated with photographs and schematic drawings; a glossary is appended." Booklist

591.3 Development and maturation of animals

Brady, Irene

Wild babies; a canyon sketchbook; written and illus. by Irene Brady. Houghton 1979 50p illus $8.95 (4-6)   591.3

1 Animals—Infancy
ISBN 0-395-27464-8   LC 79-12655

"A thin narrative thread shows the separateness and suggests the interactions of six animal families (bobcat, squirrel, bat, deer, hawk, bear) living in the same canyon. . . . In each family the young are shown from birth to young adulthood. Meticulously detailed black-and-white sketches are informational; lightly sentimentalized, sepia illustrations are handsome and appealing." Sch Library J

Cosgrove, Margaret

Eggs—and what happens inside them; illus. by the author. Dodd 1966 63p illus lib. bdg. $5.95 (3-6)   591.3

1 Embryology 2 Eggs
ISBN 0-396-06507-4   LC 66-14147

"Clear, scientific text and well-labeled drawings explain the life-producing process of eggs and describe the way in which an embryo develops. The book traces the development of different types of eggs from the simple jelly-encased eggs of birds and reptiles to the eggs of mammals. There is a detailed account of the growth of a frog and chicken embryo. The development of insect larva is not given but insect eggs are described. Kinds of eggs which may be studied at home or in school and the methods of embryologists are briefly mentioned. Pronunciation and definition of scientific terms are given in the text and explanations are simple enough to be used with primary children." Booklist

Lauber, Patricia

What's hatching out of that egg? Crown 1979 60p illus $7.95 (2-4)   591.3

1 Animals—Infancy 2 Reproduction 3 Eggs
ISBN 0-517-53724-9   LC 79-12054

This book involves the reader in a "guessing game as they follow clues to what's pecking its determined way out of 11 eggs of various sizes and shapes. Once the newborn creature breaks its shell, its identity becomes obvious. The text then goes into details about how the young are cared for or manage on their own. The wildlings discussed are alligators, butterflies, frogs, octopuses, ostriches, penguins, platypuses, pythons, salmon, spiders and turtles." Pub W

"The close-up views allow children to observe these natural phenomena as though present, and the format is extremely adaptable to classroom or individual exploration." Booklist

Selsam, Millicent E.

All kinds of babies; pictures by Symeon Shimin. Four Winds [1969 c1967] unp illus lib. bdg. $5.95 (k-3)   591.3

1 Animals—Infancy
ISBN 0-590-07156-4   LC 69-17248

First published 1953 by Scott with title: All kinds of babies and how they grow. Helen Ludwig was the illustrator

"An attractive picture book for the very young explains and shows, by means of attractive illustrations, that the young of many species closely resemble their parents (particularly most mammals), but the young of other species do not resemble their parents at all (butterflies, frogs, eels). However, no matter what the young look like, 'Every kind of living thing in the world makes more of its own kind. This is true of fish, insects, birds, and every kind of animal.' Fundamental biological facts are acquired pleasantly by the child." Sci Bks

When an animal grows; pictures by John Kaufmann. Harper 1966 64p illus (A Science I can read bk) $5.95, lib. bdg. $6.89 (k-3)   591.3

1 Growth 2 Animals—Infancy
ISBN 0-06-025460-2; 0-06-025461-0   LC 66-7288

"In concurrent narratives which compare the babyhood and maturation first of a gorilla and a lamb, and then of a sparrow and a mallard duck, the author describes some basic factors common to all growing animals as well as variations in rate of growth and time of dependency on parental care in different species. The attractive, realistic illustrations [in black and white] supplement the text and add to the book's appeal." Booklist

591.4 Anatomy and morphology of animals

Cooper, Gale

Inside animals; written and illus. by Gale Cooper. Little 1978 64p illus lib. bdg. $7.95 (4-6)   591.4

1 Anatomy, Comparative
ISBN 0-316-15618-3   LC 76-50919

"An Atlantic Monthly Press book"

The author describes "the internal anatomy and functioning of animals. The book begins with simple one-celled organisms and proceeds to more complex species, culminating with mammals. The final third of the book is devoted to specialized organs of 20 different animals, including the poison gland of the snake and the shell of the ladybug." AAAS Sci Bks & Films

"The drawings are very clearly presented in black, white, and red, and will be sought by all ages." Appraisal

Zim, Herbert S.

What's inside of animals? Illus. by Herschel Wartik. Morrow 1953 32p illus lib. bdg. $6.96 (2-5)   591.4

1 Anatomy, Comparative
ISBN 0-688-26518-9   LC 52-12123

"The comparative anatomy of representatives of various animal phyla, with simplified internal and external views. Contains information about each animal's structure, habitat, and life cycle. Colorful, attractive format helps the child understand how life developed, and man's place in the animal kingdom." The AAAS Sci Bk List for Children

591.5 Ecology of animals

Animals in danger; trying to save our wildlife. Natl. Geographic Soc. 1978 32p illus (2-4)   591.5

1 Wildlife—Conservation 2 Rare animals 3 Man —Influence on nature
ISBN 0-87044-261-9   LC 77-95411

Available only as part of 4v set for $7.95 with: Animals that live at sea, by J. A. Straker (591.92); Zoo babies, by D. K. Grosvenor (590.74); and Explore a spooky swamp, by W. W. Cortesi (574.5)

"Books for young explorers"

"Prepared by The Special Publications Division; Robert L. Breeden, ed., Peggy D. Winston, writer." p32

A survey of 11 endangered animals, portrayed by color photographs and brief text. Efforts to save the animals are shown in cartoons

Arnosky, Jim

Crinkleroot's book of animal tracks and wildlife signs. Putnam 1979 unp illus $7.95 (2-4)   **591.5**

1 Animal tracks 2 Tracking and trailing 3 Animals—Habits and behavior
ISBN 0-399-20663-9   LC 78-13081

"Arnosky's Crinkleroot, a sort of Grizzly Adams sans grizzly, gives a folksy introduction to the habits, habitats, and hoof-paw-claw prints of a variety of relatively common wild 'critters'— beaver, otter, raccoon, bobcat, red fox et al.— plus a bird or two in illustrated mini-mysteries. There are lots of clear illustrations by the author washed in woodsy browns and greys." Sch Library J

A kettle of hawks and other wildlife groups; written and illus. by Jim Arnosky. Coward, McCann & Geoghegan 1979 unp illus $7.50 (2-4)   **591.5**

1 Animals—Habits and behavior
ISBN 0-698-20469-7   LC 78-10212

"This is a handsome and fascinating book, simple enough for the young, yet rich in detail. Using the poetic and evocative group terminology of a species as a springboard, Mr. Arnosky describes the behavior behind the often curious appellations. A kettle of hawks boil upwards on a thermal; startled tadpoles stir up the pond into a cloud; a gaggle of geese fly in an energy saving formation, leaving them strength to honk. The text and illustrations are well integrated and beautifully designed, with a large yet elegant typeface and spacious layout." Appraisal

Baylor, Byrd

We walk in sandy places; photographs by Marilyn Schweitzer. Scribner 1976 unp illus lib. bdg. $6.95 (k-2)   **591.5**

1 Animal tracks 2 Desert animals
ISBN 0-684-14526-X   LC 75-8341

"Excellent sepia-toned photographs create a warm desert mood for sparse free verse about animals. . . . Large double-page spreads which bleed off the edges of pages varied with occasional spot pictures show the tracks of animals (only a beetle, horned toad, squirrel, and desert tortoise are actually shown in the photographs. . . This is a pleasant offering that successfully communicates the fact that humans only 'share' the earth with other forms of life." Sch Library J

Berrill, Jacquelyn

Wonders of the woods and desert at night; illus. by the author. Dodd 1963 78p illus lib. bdg. $5.95 (4-6)   **591.5**

1 Animals—Habits and behavior
ISBN 0-396-06395-0   LC 63-7626

The author "describes and illustrates animals who sleep by day and forage for food by night. . . . There are owls . . . skunks, mice, wood and pack rats, coyotes, cougars, opossums and bobcats. But there are also animals, birds, and insects one sees by day as well, such as frogs, foxes, ground squirrels, moose, bears and deer." Christian Sci Monitor

The illustrations "are bold, strong, attractively designed portraits of a great variety of animals, every hair or feather in place. Those done on black in white line are especially effective." NY Her Trib Bks

Branley, Franklyn M.

Big tracks, little tracks; illus. by Leonard Kessler. Crowell 1960 unp illus (Let's-read-and-find-out science bks) lib. bdg. $6.89 (k-2)   **591.5**

1 Animal tracks 2 Tracking and trailing 3 Animals—Habits and behavior
ISBN 0-690-14371-0   LC 60-51146

"A first exercise in nature detection. Author and illustrator make [a] game of watching for and identifying animal tracks and those of humans too." NY Times Bk Rev

"This volume is clearly written, attractively illustrated, and full of the excitement of first explorations in science." Sat Rev

Buck, Margaret Waring

Where they go in winter; written and illus. by Margaret Waring Buck. Abingdon 1968 72p illus maps $4.95, pa $1.95 (3-6)   **591.5**

1 Animals—Habits and behavior
ISBN 0-687-45176-0; 0-687-45177-9   LC 68-15404

The "author-illustrator tells how various creatures survive the winter months. The six sections —insects and spiders, fishes, amphibians, reptiles, birds and mammals—describe the winter habits of various species with drawings that border the pages depicting them as they are usually seen and as they look during the winter." Pub W

"The illustrations are detailed enough to be used as identification guides, and maps indicate usual habitat." Adventuring with Bks. 2d edition
More to read: p72

Cartwright, Sally

Animal homes; illus. by Ben F. Stahl. Coward, McCann & Geoghegan 1973 46p illus (The Science is what and why bks) lib. bdg. $5.99 (1-3)   **591.5**

1 Animals—Habitations
ISBN 0-698-30492-6   LC 72-89755

Selecting the habitations of the squirrel, porcupine, woodchuck and beaver as representative of various homes in the forest, the author describes both the materials used to build the homes and the lives of the creatures which inhabit them

"This is a good introduction which emphasizes that each animal home suits the animal who uses it. The warm and earthy illustrations will help young children visualize the interiors of the animal homes, and there is an excellent chart on the dwelling habits of other small forest creatures." Sch Library J

Cohen, Daniel

Night animals; illus. by Haris Petie. Messner 1970 95p illus lib. bdg. $4.79 (4-6)   **591.5**

1 Animals—Habits and behavior
ISBN 0-671-32259-1   LC 78-107064

The author introduces his book with a description of two unusual displays at the Bronx Zoo in New York which use special lighting to give visitors the opportunity of observing, during daylight hours, the active night-time period of nocturnal animals. He then discusses these "animals, and their activities, the diurnal rhythms of life, biological 'alarm clocks,' the adaptation of eyes to vision at night, hearing as a substitute for vision in some animals, kinesthetic senses, echo location, bioluminescence, and other topics. Experimental evidence is offered in support of some discussions. The survey is very rapid, yet will certainly interest the reader who is aided in understanding the technical terms by reference to the glossary. Since many young readers will desire to read more information, there should be a list of references, but there is not. The book is indexed. The illustrations are good." Sci Bks

Dean, Anabel

How animals communicate; drawings by Haris Petie. Messner 1977 63p illus lib. bdg. $6.97 (4-6)   **591.5**

1 Animal communication
ISBN 0-671-32818-2   LC 77-23281

"After a general discussion of the nature of communication and a chapter on methods of communication, each succeeding chapter focuses on motives for communication: staying alive (getting food and having a place to live), raising a family (finding a mate, raising the young), and living with others (protection, defense, or functioning as part of a group). Under these headings, the text describes visual signals, touch signals, sound signals, etc. A glossary and an index are appended." Chicago. Children's Bk Center

"Pleasantly written and generously illustrated . . . [this book] contains simple vocabulary and sentence structure. The author maintains the reader's interest by dramatic presentation and by excluding unnecessary information." AAAS Sci Bks & Films

Freedman, Russell

Animal games; illus. by St. Tamara. Holiday House 1976 unp illus lib. bdg. $5.95 (1-3)   591.5

1 Animals—Infancy 2 Animals—Habits and behavior
ISBN 0-8234-0284-3   LC 76-10975

"The play and exercise games of sixteen wild animals are described in one and two page accounts. Included are the gorilla, bear, beaver, wolf, bobcat, antelope, langur, eagle, dolphin, duck, penguin, elephant, hawk, lion, seal and chimpanzee. Black-and-white line drawings depict real-life situations and surroundings. Each story discusses the type of activity conducted by the animal and, whenever appropriate, gives an explanation of the purpose served by the play such as training to hunt, protection, or just play." Appraisal

"Unfortunately, [the author] does not delve deeply enough into the purpose and benefits of animal game playing and the text ends abruptly with no conclusion. However, this is an unusual topic and the black-and-white line drawings are very attractive." Sch Library J

Hanging on; how animals carry their young. Holiday House 1977 32p illus lib. bdg. $5.95 (1-3)   591.5

1 Animals—Habits and behavior 2 Animals—Infancy
ISBN 0-8234-0292-4   LC 76-41822

"Freedman demonstrates the variety of ways animals transport their young. Baby animals are carried to feeding grounds, moved from danger, and taken along for a ride in the pouches of kangaroos, on the backs of scorpions and opossums, against the bellies of gibbons, and in the arms of beavers. Members of the cat family are conveyed by the scruff of the neck, baby swans hitch rides in their mother's feathers, and, in the case of marmosets, it's the father that bears the load." Booklist

"Effective inclusions are the excellent black-and-white photographs taken from different sources. . . . Every animal discussed is clearly shown carrying its young. Some photographs detail development of the young, pouches in the mother and carrying techniques. Young readers will enjoy the pictures of the koala and of the brush-tailed opossums riding on their mothers' backs. An excellent aid for readers is the inclusion of phonetic pronunciations of some of the more difficult names." AAAS Sci Bks & Films

How animals defend their young. Dutton 1978 87p illus $7.95 (5 and up)   591.5

1 Animals—Habits and behavior 2 Animals—Infancy
ISBN 0-525-32382-1   LC 78-7251

"Although their reactions are stimulated by instinct rather than human emotions, most animals act swiftly to protect their young. Defense tactics vary, and Freedman describes several measures in a straightforward text, peppered with examples. Behavior patterns of birds, fish, insects, reptiles, and mammals are discussed in chapters covering ways in which parents use shelters and hiding places, danger signals, flight, camouflage, deception, attack, and group assemblage as methods of protection. A final note reminds readers that while wild creatures can defend themselves against natural enemies, they are helpless against human destructiveness. Black-and-white photographs supplement the narrative. Further reading appended." Booklist

How animals learn [by] Russell Freedman and James E. Morriss. Holiday House 1969 159p illus $6.95 (5 and up)   591.5

1 Animal intelligence
ISBN 0-8234-0050-6   LC 77-3492

The authors discuss the difference between animal instinct and learning while describing the pioneer work of Skinner, Pavlov and Lorenz

"Fine photographs harmonize well with the text, and a book list and simple experiments to be done with animals are included for especially interested readers. An entertaining exposition, particularly useful in school libraries." Sch Library J

Hopf, Alice L.

Nature's pretenders. Putnam 1979 95p illus $8.95 (6 and up)   591.5

1 Camouflage (Biology) 2 Animals—Habits and behavior
ISBN 0-399-20671-X   LC 78-31560

"Hopf's explanations of the defenses and deceptions used by animals provide worthwhile material for research. Disguises in appearance as well as changes in behavior take place for diverse reasons—self-defense, surprising enemies, and protection during the mating process. In detailing the particular abilities of deceivers such as the viceroy butterfly, walkingstick, octopus, grouse, opossum, and praying mantis, the author comments on habitats, life cycles, behavioral characteristics, and physical appearances of the 18 different species included, along with various scientific studies of them. Black-and-white photographs sharply illustrate the text's major points." Booklist
Bibliography: p91-92

Kohl, Judith

The view from the oak; the private worlds of other creatures, by Judith and Herbert Kohl; illus. by Roger Bayless. Sierra Club Bks./Scribner 1977 110p illus lib. bdg. $8.95, pa $4.95 (6 and up)   591.5

1 Animals—Habits and behavior 2 Senses and sensation
ISBN 0-684-15016-6; 0-684-15017-4   LC 76-57680

"An oak tree may be home to a fox, a nest for a beetle, and a source of food for a woodpecker. How a bee senses a flavor differs from the way an ant or person sees, touches, or smells it. With simple, clearly phrased examples, the Kohls describe an animal's world of experience or its 'unwelt.' Sprinkling in scientific, literary, and philosophical references . . . the authors gracefully introduce the subject of ethology." Sch Library J

"An excellent treatment of an abstract topic. This book is not for skimming by the casual young reader. It contains activities and games for further understanding of how living things sense their environment." Children's Bk Rev Serv
If you liked this book: p110

McClung, Robert M.

Animals that build their homes. Natl. Geographic Soc. 1976 26p illus (k-3)   591.5

1 Animals—Habitations 2 Birds—Habitations
3 Insects—Habitations
ISBN 0-87044-198-1   LC 76-2117

Obtainable only as part of a set for $9.95 with: Camping adventure, by William R. Gray, class 796.54; The playful dolphins, by Linda McCarter Bridge, class 599.5; and Wonders of the desert world, by Judith E. Rinard, class 574.9
"Books for young explorers"
Prepared by the Special Publications Division of the National Geographic Society

"The variety of ways different animals provide homes for themselves is pointed up in . . . [this book] as camera and text probe the hows and whys of the habitats of creatures such as the badger, crayfish, woodpecker, weaverbird, wasp, termite, and honeybee." Booklist

"The excellent color photographs are visually instructive and closely correlated with the text. . . . The writing is simple, clear, and down-to-earth. Both the non-reader and beginning reader should enjoy this scientifically accurate book." Appraisal

How animals hide. Natl. Geographic Soc. 1973 40p illus (k-3)   591.5

1 Camouflage (Biology)
ISBN 0-87044-144-2   LC 73-7112

Obtainable only as part of a set for $9.95 with: Honeybees, by Jane Lecht, class 595.7; Namu, by Ronald M. Fisher, class 599.5; and Pandas, by Donna K. Grosvenor, class 599.74
"Books for young explorers"
Prepared by the Special Publications Division of the National Geographic Society

In color photographs and text, this book shows how animals can hide to avoid their enemies or to trap their prey by using their color and shape to blend in with their environment or by using other types of disguise and protection

"It takes photographers as skilled and well-directed as the contributors to this book to reveal the beauty and mastery of nature's works of

McClung, Robert M.—*Continued*

camouflage. In stunning color, the pictures offer a broad but graspable scope of biological wonders, from the varying hare to the crab spider and from the peacock flounder to the magnificent pink and white flower mantid. . . . The text is simple, straightforward, and uncompromising in informational value and support of the illustrative matter. An elegant book, its visual impact is unfortunately marred by a binding that resists page-flattening." Booklist

Mice, moose, and men; how their populations rise and fall; written and illus. by Robert M. McClung. Morrow 1973 64p illus $7.25, lib. bdg. $6.96 (4 and up)   **591.5**

1 Animal populations
ISBN 0-688-20087-7; 0-688-30087-1   LC 73-4926

This "survey of animal population patterns cites the conditions—good and bad, natural and artificial —that affect nature's cyclic balancing mechanisms. To elucidate the notions of balance and change, [the author] defines the determining factors surrounding fertility rates, life span of species, animal explosions, and invasions into new territories, with specific animal, insect, and bird examples for each concept or fact introduced." Booklist
The book "imparts information through supportive anecdotes of the believe-it-or-not sort that attract middle graders. . . . Clearly illustrated in line drawings." Sch Library J
Suggestions for further reading: p60-62

Mason, George F.

Animal tracks. Morrow 1943 95p illus lib. bdg. $6.48 (4 and up)   **591.5**

1 Animal tracks 2 Tracking and trailing
ISBN 0-688-31041-9   LC 43-11275

"A guidebook designed to aid in the identification of the tracks of more than 40 common North American animals. There is a full-page drawing [by the author] of each animal, with descriptive text on its tracks, habits, and range. Tracks are pictured in marginal drawings, giving dimensions and showing both the perfect footprints and those of the animal in motion." Booklist

May, Julian

How the animals came to North America; illus. by Lorence F. Bjorklund. Holiday House 1974 37p illus maps lib. bdg. $4.50 (2-4)   **591.5**

1 Animals—North America 2 Animals—Migration 3 Evolution
ISBN 0-8234-0234-7   LC 73-17145

"The content is interwoven around the precise and accurate illustrations of various animals presented throughout this book in one continuous story. The author has recorded in an entertaining and informative way how the Earth gradually separated into several continents and how various animals spread from one land mass to another, thus inhabiting the land in North America. The theory of continental drift is used to explain why some wild animals had to swim or fly from continent to continent. The book also provides an explanation of how the Ice Ages contributed to the dissemination of species on the North American continent. The reader is introduced to the idea that many tame animals were brought to North America by the first settlers from Europe." Sci Teacher

Murie, Olaus J.

A field guide to animal tracks; text and illus. by Olaus J. Murie. 2d ed. Houghton 1975 [c1974] xxi, 375p illus $9.95, pa $5.95   **591.5**

1 Animal tracks 2 Tracking and trailing
ISBN 0-395-19978-6; 0-395-18323-5   LC 74-6294

"The Peterson Field guide series"
First published 1954
This is a "handbook of the tracks, droppings, trails, and nests of many common mammals, birds, insects, reptiles, and amphibians of the Western Hemisphere. Each animal is fully described and illustrated, showing how to identify tell-tale evidence of its presence." The AAAS Sci Bk List for Children [review of the first edition]
"A comprehensive volume which serves as both an identification handbook and a manual of ecology." Booklist [review of the first edition]
Bibliography: p359-67

Pringle, Laurence

Animals and their niches; how species share resources; illus. by Leslie Morrill. 1977 64p illus $6.25, lib. bdg. $6 (3-5)   **591.5**

1 Animals—Habits and behavior 2 Ecology
ISBN 0-688-22127-0; 0-688-32127-5   LC 77-3636

"Given limited resources in a wildlife community, how do similar species live together in the same habitat? . . . [The author] explains how each inhabitant occupies a special place that has few overlaps with others of a similar kind. It feeds on certain foods, moves at certain levels, builds its home in specific places. Thus three species of garter snakes that live on the same portion of land or five species of warblers that live in evergreen trees are not really in direct competition. Studies that set forth these and several other related findings are cited by Pringle, who in a final chapter also reflects on some unanswered questions, such as why animal niches are arranged the way they are." Booklist
"The text is lucid and accurate; Pringle shows, more clearly than if he had made a statement on the subject, how painstaking and objective the scientific method is and how a body of knowledge grows through a diversity of research findings. The print is large, the realistic wash drawings are adequately captioned, and a relative index is appended." Chicago. Children's Bk Center
Glossary: p59-60. Further reading: p61-62

Ricciuti, Edward R.

Sounds of animals at night; illus. with photographs. Harper 1977 56p illus lib. bdg. $7.89 (3-5)   **591.5**

1 Animals—Habits and behavior 2 Animal communication
ISBN 0-06-024981-1   LC 76-3843

"The book discusses the night sounds of such animals as frogs, toads, night birds, night insects, and night mammals. It is scientifically accurate, and gives just the right amount of information at the right level to interest all students and to whet the appetite of the biologically-oriented student. There is even a formula given to calculate air temperature based on number of cricket chirps. The book has a table of contents, bibliography, and index. The text is illustrated with excellent photographs of nocturnal animals." Appraisal

Rinard, Judith E.

Creatures of the night. Natl. Geographic Soc. 1977 31p illus (k-3)   **591.5**

1 Animals—Habits and behavior
ISBN 0-87044-214-4   LC 77-76968

Obtainable only as part of a set for $9.95 with: The blue whale, by Donna K. Grosvenor, class 599.5; Let's go to the moon, by Janis Knudsen Wheat, class 629.45; and What happens in the spring, by Kathleen Costello Beer, class 500
"Books for young explorers"
Prepared by the Special Publications Division of the National Geographic Society
This book describes the after-dark activities of a number of nocturnal animals in simple text and color photographs

Rounds, Glen

Wildlife at your doorstep; text and drawings by Glen Rounds. . . . Holiday House 1974 [c1958] 96p illus $4.95 (4 and up)   **591.5**

1 Animals—Habits and behavior
ISBN 0-8234-0238-X   LC 73-17402

"An illustrated almanac of curious doings . . . dealing with wasps . . . spiders . . . snakes . . . toads . . . birds . . . ants . . . squirrels and other kinds of small wildlife that can be found working at complicated trades within sight of my doorstep." Title page
A reissue of a title first published 1958. "The full-page pen-and-ink drawings which appeared in the 1958 edition have been reduced here to spot size and delicately complement these observant sketches of animal life." Sch Library J

Sarasy, Phyllis

Winter-sleepers; illus. by Edna Miller. Prentice-Hall 1962 64p illus $4.95 (3-5)   **591.5**

1 Animals—Hibernation
ISBN 0-13-961490-7   LC 62-15797

This book "tells where snakes and groundhogs, turtles and carp go in winter, how bats and humming-birds conserve fuel by lowering their own

Sarasy, Phyllis—*Continued*
body temperatures while asleep, and introduces the use of cold sleep for people undergoing surgery without anesthetics." NY Times Bk Rev
"With abundant and attractive sketches of wildlife, this little book for younger readers is straight information on hibernation. . . . The tale is direct and conversational, with a good sense of adventure and suspense." Christian Sci Monitor

Selsam, Millicent E.
Hidden animals; illus with photographs. [Rev. ed] Harper 1969 63p illus (A Science I can read bk) $5.95, lib. bdg. $6.89 (k-3)
591.5
1 Camouflage (Biology)
ISBN 0-06-025281-2; 0-06-025282-0   LC 72-85020
First published 1947
By searching for the stonefish hidden in the coral, or the snowshoe rabbit in his winter habitat, young readers learn the concepts of protective coloration and natural selection as they apply to these and many other animals
"The photographs are effective in encouraging readers to discover insects and animals in their surroundings." Pub W

How animals live together. Newly rev. ed. Illus. with photographs. Morrow 1979 95p illus lib. bdg. $6.67 (5 and up)   591.5
1 Animals—Habits and behavior
ISBN 0-688-32212-3   LC 79-13308
First published 1963
This book "discusses some of the many kinds of animal relationships: grouping together for warmth and protection, classes and 'pecking orders,' the organization of herds and other mammal groups, insect societies, and association between species (symbiotic and parasitic)." AAAS Sci Bk List for Children [review of first edition]
Bibliography: p89-91

How animals tell time; illus. by John Kaufmann. Morrow 1967 94p illus lib. bdg. $7.95 (5 and up)   591.5
1 Animals—Habits and behavior 2 Biology— Periodicity
ISBN 0-688-31407-4   LC 67-450
"In a fascinating study of biological clocks, Mrs. Selsam discusses the relationship between the earth's daily, seasonal, and tidal rhythms and animal breeding, hibernation, migration, and other behavior. Her simple, lucid analyses of numerous scientific experiments explains current theories about time-related behavior and describes research being done on the unsolved problem of the internal location of biological clocks. Contains clear, accurate drawings and diagrams and a short list of books for further reading." Booklist

The language of animals; illus. by Kathleen Elgin. Morrow 1962 96p illus lib. bdg. $7.92 (5 and up)   591.5
1 Animal communication
ISBN 0-688-31515-1   LC 62-7714
In this study the "author examines the means by which animals communicate emotion and information, stressing the fallacy of thinking that animals communicate in the same manner and for the same purposes as human beings." Hodges. Bks for Elem Sch Libraries
"Good scientific writing: objective, simple, dignified, but never dry. Mrs. Selsam gives to the reader, in addition to the information in the text, a consistency of scientific attitude that is most valuable. . . . A bibliography is appended; the index is starred to indicate location of illustrations." Chicago. Children's Bk Center

Shuttlesworth, Dorothy E.
Animals that frighten people; fact versus myth; illus. with photographs. Dutton 1973 122p illus $6.95 (5 and up)   591.5
1 Animals—Habits and behavior
ISBN 0-525-25745-4   LC 73-77458
"Some members of the animal world have long lived with reputations for being dangerous and frightening. In these ten chapters the author presents the basis for these myths and the facts

as we know them today. Some of the dreaded creatures included are the tarantula, scorpion, wolf, octopus, and bat. The accounts make good reading and the black-and-white photographs add to the book's appeal. This is a good browsing item. An index makes it useful as a source of specific information." Appraisal

How wild animals fight. Doubleday 1976 95p illus $5.95 (4 and up)   591.5
1 Animals—Habits and behavior
ISBN 0-385-08599-0   LC 75-19144
"After a brief discussion of the problems of survival for wild creatures, the author describes the ways in which they struggle against predators, fight for food, or battle for a mate or for territorial rights. The text is divided into chapters based on physical attributes that help wild creatures survive, such as antlers, horns, teeth, claws, the ability to wound by such devices as quills or poison, or emitting a bad smell." Chicago. Children's Bk Center
"In every respect, it is a superb treatment of aggression in wild animals. . . . The writing is not only lucid, straightforward and accurate, but also colorful, interesting and enlightening. This book . . . [also includes] 27 full-page black-and-white photographs of high quality." AAAS Sci Bks & Films

Silverstein, Alvin
Animal invaders; the story of imported wildlife [by] Alvin and Virginia Silverstein. Atheneum Pubs. 1974 124p illus lib. bdg. $6.95 (5 and up)   591.5
1 Geographical distribution of animals and plants 2 Ecology
ISBN 0-689-30146-4   LC 73-84835
This book describes animals which man has introduced into new environments, accidentally or deliberately, as pets, or as predators to control existing problems. Because these animals lack natural enemies in their new environments, they eventually cause damage to the ecosystem. The authors cite cases involving birds, mammals, fish, insects and snails
"This is a provocative and informative introduction to an overlooked aspect of ecology." Sch Library J

Swift, David
Animal travelers. Greenwillow Bks. 1977 55p illus $5.95, lib. bdg. $5.71 (1-3)   591.5
1 Animals—Migration
ISBN 0-688-80044-0; 0-688-84044-2   LC 75-43931
"Greenwillow Read-alone"
"The migration patterns of caribou, barn swallows, painted lady butterflies and . . . [gray] whales are explained, accompanied by maps showing the various migration patterns." AAAS Sci Bks & Films
"Although the print is smallish for a second grade reader, he surely will be able to read and comprehend this good little study of migration. . . . The author has illustrated his own work in soft colors, a minimum of detail, and a definite feeling of motion that is just right. Mr Swift has made sure to include the astonishing feats of endurance of these migratory animals, enough to intrigue not only the young, but also the adult who will want to read this book with a child or class. Interesting, very informative, attractive, and definitely recommended for any library or nature study group." Appraisal

591.6 Economic zoology

Brenner, Barbara
Beware! These animals are poison; illus. by Jim Spanfeller. Coward, McCann & Geoghegan 1979 63p illus $7.95 (3-5)   591.6
1 Poisonous animals
ISBN 0-698-20438-7   LC 77-27591
"An articulate, sensible description of animals that are poisonous and sometimes deadly. The creatures are grouped by the means through which their venom is distributed—stings, fangs, teeth, etc. Many of the dangerous animals, such as wasps, some snakes, and black widow spiders, are familiar; but others, such as a certain kind of toad, are not as notorious. Brenner emphasizes

Brenner, Barbara—*Continued*

that these animals do not use their poison indiscriminately, but that the poison serves as a means through which such creatures survive and defend themselves. Although the subjects are often frightening, the author avoids using scare tactics and simply informs the reader of potential danger. Spanfeller's fine line drawings have a graceful elegance and precise rendering of detail." Booklist

591.9   Geographical treatment of animals

McClung, Robert M.

Lost wild worlds; the story of extinct and vanishing wildlife of the Eastern Hemisphere; with illus. by Bob Hines. Morrow 1976 288p illus maps $9.50 (6 and up)   **591.9**

1 Rare animals 2 Wildlife—Conservation 3 Extinct animals 4 Man—Influence on nature
ISBN 0-688-22090-8   LC 76-25851

This account "tells briefly of man's rise to civilization, how he spread over the earth and explored it, and how he finally came to dominate it and alter it to his own uses. Through narrative accounts of wildlife species, continent-by-continent, this book relates how man has brought about the extinction of many kinds of wildlife and endangered the survival of others. It also tells how organizations and individuals of goodwill in many countries are endeavoring to reverse these destructive trends and save our fellow creatures." Foreword

"The pen drawings are small but more than adequate representations of the animals. An excellent source of information that is greater in breadth and depth than most other materials available." Sch Library J
Selected bibliography: p269-78

Nayman, Jacqueline

Atlas of wildlife; illus. by Adrian Williams & David Nockels; maps by Geographical Projects, London. Consultant: Maurice Burton. Day 1972 124p illus maps $11.95 (5 and up)   **591.9**

1 Geographical distribution of animals and plants
ISBN 0-381-98162-2   LC 78-38034

This work deals mostly with mammals but also includes a few birds, reptiles, amphibians and lungfishes. The opening chapter is a "discussion of the origin of the continents and thus of the six major regions. Each region receives a chapter with up to three double-page maps . . . [showing] the distribution of the most characteristic animals, many of which have been illustrated in colour in the text; for each region there is also a chart indicating the occurence of the animals in other regions. Two final chapters deal with Antarctica and with certain islands or island groups, followed by a map of the 200 major wildlife parks in the world." Times (London) Lit Sup

The **Rand** McNally Atlas of world wildlife; with a foreword by Sir Julian Huxley. Rand McNally 1973 208p illus maps $16.95   **591.9**

1 Geographical distribution of animals and plants
2 Ecology
ISBN 0-528-83014-7   LC 73-3724

"Produced in consultation with the Zoological Society of London and with contributions from leading zoologists throughout the world." Verso of title page
This book "presents tremendous amounts of material on the eight zoogeographical regions of the earth. Fourteen pages are devoted to species inhabiting reefs and islands of the oceans; one section analyzes the effects of man's activities on wildlife. Special features include panoramas of some key species in each region treated, endangered species, and maps showing major parks and reserves. The quality of reproductions, paintings, graphs, charts and photographs of animals and plant associates are outstanding. The only difficulty is that some people may experience is correlating colors and keys with maps and graphs. In some

cases, the colors are too much alike in tone for easy differentiation. No similar publication is as extensive as this one as far as subject matter is concerned. . . . It will be of great value to anyone interested in geography, oceanography, or ecology, as well as any phase of wildlife resources." Choice
Glossary: p205. Sources of reference: p207-08

Shuttlesworth, Dorothy E.

The wildlife of South America; illus. by George Frederick Mason; foreword by Philip K. Crowe. Hastings House 1974 120p illus maps (The Hastings House World wildlife conservation ser) lib. bdg. $6.95 (5 and up)   **591.9**

1 Animals—South America 2 Wildlife—Conservation
ISBN 0-8038-8069-3   LC 74-817
First published 1966
An "overall picture of South American fauna is communicated verbally, and the author weaves in timely information and commentary on wildlife destruction and conservation. A list of rare and endangered species and a map indicating national parks of South America are included." Booklist
Bibliography: p116-17

591.92   Marine zoology

Jacobs, Francine

Sounds in the sea; illus. by Jean Zallinger. Morrow 1977 95p illus $5.75, lib. bdg. $5.52 (4-6)   **591.92**

1 Animal communication 2 Marine animals
ISBN 0-688-22113-0; 0-688-32113-5   LC 77-345

A study of underwater sounds and of the hearing abilities of marine animals, and of how man uses this knowledge
"This is an excellent, fast-reading description of the variety of animals in the sea that produce sound. Scientists have learned that snapping shrmp, spiny lobsters, fiddler and ghost crabs, even sessile barnacles and mussels, spiny sea urchins, drumfish, groupers, toadfish, seahorses, sea lions, seals, sea otters, whales and of course porpoises and dolphins all generate sound. The author describes the types of sounds produced by each of these organisms, their habitats and the work of scientists in attempting to understand and adapt to this noisy undersea realm. Black and white illustrations augment the text, helping readers to better visualize each creature and where it lives beneath the sea." Appraisal

Selsam, Millicent

See through the sea, by Millicent Selsam and Betty Morrow; pictures by Winifred Lubell. Harper 1955 unp illus lib. bdg. $7.89 (2-4)   **591.92**

1 Marine animals 2 Ocean
ISBN 0-06-025456-4   LC 54-8990

"'In each part of the sea, the plants and animals are different. Turn the pages of this book, and you will see through the sea where it is shallow, deeper and deepest.' A description of the teeming life [mainly animals] of the sea, from the seashore, down through the various levels of the ocean, to its depths. It is amplified by arresting pictures and diagrams in predominating tones of green, yellow and black." Ontario Library Rev
"The artist's contrasts between surface light and dark depths create atmospheres of beauty and wonder and suggest the excitement of diving with goggles, helmet, or bathysphere." Horn Bk

Straker, Joan Ann

Animals that live in the sea. Natl. Geographic Soc. 1978 31p illus (1-3)   **591.92**

1 Marine animals 2 Marine ecology
ISBN 0-87044-264-3   LC 77-95415

Available only as part of 4v set for $7.95 with: Animals in danger (591.5); Zoo babies, by D. K. Grosvenor (590.74); and Explore a spooky swamp, by W. W. Cortesi (574.5).
"Books for young explorers"
Prepared by the Special Publications Division of the National Geographic Society
This book introduces through color photographs and simple text a variety of sea creatures, ranging from sharks to crabs to anemones

592 Invertebrates

Selsam, Millicent E.
A first look at animals without backbones, by Millicent E. Selsam and Joyce Hunt; illus. by Harriett Springer. Walker & Co. [1977 c1976] 32p illus lib. bdg. $6.85 (2-4)
592

1 Invertebrates
ISBN 0-8027-6269-7   LC 76-12056

"A concise introduction to the taxonomy of the 50,000 spineless animals in the world. Such groups of invertebrates as arthropods, echinoderms, mollusks, worms, coelenterates, sponges, and protozoa are clearly and logically examined in a careful presentation which includes pronunciations of the multisyllabic terms introduced. With its informative text and neat, explanatory pencil drawings, this can help promote an interest in scientific classification and nomenclature." Sch Library J

593.1 Amoeba

Morrison, Sean
The amoeba; photomicrographs by Nina Stromgren Allen; consultant: Robert D. Allen. Coward, McCann & Geoghegan 1971 46p illus (Science is what and why) lib. bdg. $4.69 (3-6)
593.1

1 Amoeba
ISBN 0-698-30010-6   LC 75-156884

"The life history, morphology, physiology, and ecology of 'Amoeba proteus' are explained by the use of good photographs and photomicrographs with appropriate legends, and labeling of anatomical detail where necessary. Because the amoeba is such a primordial animal, the explanation of its biological makeup and its feeding and reproductive processes have provided the author with an opportunity to give a brief introduction to microscopy and to explain some of the basic elements of cytology. Scientific terms are used where needed throughout the book and are defined in a glossary. The book is carefully indexed. Its excellence is proof that accurate scientific writing can interest children. This is an essential book for children's libraries and will be very useful in elementary science classrooms for collateral study and reference." Sci Bks

593.4 Sponges

Jacobson, Morris K.
Wonders of sponges [by] Morris K. Jacobson and Rosemary K. Pang; illus. with photographs Dodd 1976 79p illus $5.95 (5 and up)
593.4

1 Sponges
ISBN 0-396-07300-X   LC 75-38363

"Dodd, Mead Wonders books"

"A survey of the various types of sponges, their differing characteristics, life functions, and usefulness to man. Included are descriptions of a fresh-water sponge that grows around a twig, the Cliona sponge that bores holes into shells and coral, stinging and poisonous varieties, and the suberitid sponge, which is often inhabited by the hermit crab. The authors explore the ways sponges are harvested commercially, uses of the product, and problems encountered by the sponge fishermen; they end their text with a brief mention of collecting, preserving, and identifying specimens. Black-and-white photographs depict the various species preserved or in natural habitats." Booklist

"The large number of scientific terms with derivations introduced into the text is unusual for this series and makes mastery of the complex subject matter . . . difficult despite the glossary. . . . But all in all a competent treatment of a difficult subject. . . . A two-page bibliography is included." Appraisal

593.6 Corals

Zim, Herbert S.
Corals; illus. by René Martin. Morrow 1966 63p illus maps lib. bdg. $6.48 (3-5) **593.6**

1 Corals
ISBN 0-688-31186-5   LC 66-16402

The author "describes these interesting animals, their habitat, representative living and fossil specimens, the location of major coral islands and reefs, and some of the other invertebrates and fishes that live in association with the corals, and the formation of coral reefs and atolls." Sci Bks

"Coral animals that look like flowering plants are depicted in drawings of photographic clarity and supplemented by readable text." Sch Library J

593.7 Jellyfish

Waters, John F.
A jellyfish is not a fish; illus. by Kazue Mizumura. Crowell 1979 34p illus (Let's-read-and-find-out science bks) $6.95, lib. bdg. $6.89 (2-4)
593.7

1 Jellyfishes
ISBN 0-690-03888-7; 0-690-03889-5   LC 77-26594

In this book "a few different species [of jellyfish] are described, as well as the basic patterns for anatomical structure, eating methods, and locomotion. Waters is careful to warn readers more than once of the dangers of handling unidentified (potentially poisonous) species. . . . While it is misleading to state that 'jellyfish have very few parts, other than their big gaping mouths,' there is more here that is clear than not." Booklist

"Pleasant watercolor drawings in grey, blue, and red are . . . imprecise. . . . However, this book is attractive and may stimulate children to ask for something more on a subject inherently interesting." Sch Library J

593.9 Starfish

Hurd, Edith Thacher
Starfish; illus. by Lucienne Bloch. Crowell 1962 unp illus (Let's-read-and-find-out science bks) lib. bdg. $7.89 (k-3) **593.9**

1 Starfishes
ISBN 0-690-77069-3   LC 62-7742

"An easy introduction to the world of starfish. Touches on the feeding habits, life cycle, structure and power of regeneration of these interesting creatures." The AAAS Sci Bk List for Children

"The full-page illustrations are like sections of a decorative mural in greens, grays, and mauve. The information is concise, interesting, and authentic, with the emphasis on personal discovery. The whole has a poetic feeling associated with beachcombing and the sea." Christian Sci Monitor

McClung, Robert M.
Sea star; written and illus. by Robert M. McClung. Morrow 1975 47p illus lib. bdg. $6.96 (2-4)
593.9

1 Starfishes
ISBN 0-688-32034-1   LC 75-2247

"A storybook approach to the life of a starfish. The author describes the habitat, anatomy, diet, and life cycle of the common starfish. Marine organisms that live in the same habitat are noted, and briefly described. Each page contains clear artist's illustrations of the various organisms and processes discussed in the narrative. The print is large, clear, and properly proportioned on the page for easy reading." Sci and Children

"Throughout, the viewpoint is strictly that of an observer, and the information is authentic and adequate. Almost half the page space is taken up by illustrations, both color and black and white, showing starfish and other echinoderms in their environments and in various activities and stages of growth. A teacher could use this book as an introduction to ecology, for the emphasis is on relationships among living things and the environment." AAAS Sci Bks & Films

Zim, Herbert S.

Sea stars and their kin, by Herbert S. Zim and Lucretia Krantz; illus. by René Martin. Morrow 1976 64p illus lib. bdg. $6.25 (4 and up)   **593.9**

1 Starfishes 2 Marine animals
ISBN 0-688-22053-3; 0-688-32053-8   LC 75-17633

"A detailed description of the morphology and physiology of the creatures commonly known as starfish and of other echinoderms. The authors discuss reproduction, regeneration, habitats, and—distinguishing between larval and adult stages—the functioning of digestive and water-vascular systems." Chicago. Children's Bk Center

"For the uninformed, the book provides a wealth of information and the excellent illustrations coordinate with the narrative." Sci and Children

594   Mollusks and mollusk-like animals. Shells

Abbott, R. Tucker

Sea shells of the world; a guide to the better-known species; under the editorship of Herbert S. Zim; illus. by George and Marita Sandström. Golden Press 1962 160p illus maps $9.15, pa $1.95 (5 and up)   **594**

1 Shells 2 Shells—Collection and preservation
ISBN 0-307-63514-7; 0-307-24410-5   LC 62-9852

"A Golden Nature guide"

"Emphasizing attractive and better-known species, this handy collector's guide identifies 562 sea shells of the world. An introductory section classifies mollusks, briefly describes the major groups of marine shells, locates shell regions or provinces, and offers tips on collecting and keeping sea shells. Illustrated with hundreds of colored drawings." Booklist

Includes bibliographies

Carrick, Carol

Octopus; illus. by Donald Carrick. Seabury [distributed] by Houghton 1978 unp illus lib. bdg. $6.95 (2-4)   **594**

1 Octopus
ISBN 0-395-28777-4   LC 77-12769

"A Clarion book"

"Carrick follows a female octopus as she skims along the ocean floor, finding meals of lobster and crab and encountering her enemy, the moray eel. A male octopus comes to her, they mate, and she moves away to feed and prepare a place to lay her eggs. As she waits for her young to hatch, she rarely stirs, slowly starving to death. The thoughtfully written text is complemented by expressive pen-and-wash drawings in cool sea colors." Sch Library J

Goudey, Alice E.

Houses from the sea; illus. by Adrienne Adams. Scribner 1959 unp illus lib. bdg. $8.95, pa 95¢ (k-3)   **594**

1 Shells
ISBN 0-684-12458-0; 0-684-12783-0   LC 59-6932

"A scientifically accurate introduction to shells . . . which is at the same time an idyllic tale of two children filling their pails with these treasures while playing at the beach. The short lines of rhythmic prose describe a great variety of shells; their names, how they look, and how they serve as houses for animals of the sea. . . . Even without pictures the text would give clear impressions; but the handsome, detailed color drawings of seashore life and activity turn it into a valuable and distinctive science picture book for kindergarten and beginning readers. Teachers have shown special interest in it." Horn Bk

There is "a quality of delicacy in both writing and the pastel shades of sky, sea and shells. All the shells collected by the children are pictured and labeled at the end of the book." Bookmark

Hess, Lilo

A snail's pace. Scribner 1974 48p illus lib. bdg. $4.95 (3-5)   **594**

1 Snails
ISBN 0-684-13568-9   LC 73-1384

"Hess begins her survey of snails by following one particular creature, 'our land snail,' through its feeding habits, mating procedure, etc. [She then presents] . . facts on various species of snails—their care and feeding as pets, their habits, and their relatives." Sch Library J

The author's "beautifully detailed black-and-white photographs are the highlights of this combination pet-keeper's and nature student's source book on snails. The text is clear and thoughtfully selective . . . but it is frequently not well-coordinated with the illustrations and digresses to extended discussions on the relatives of snails and on sea shell collecting. Despite its loose organization, however, the book will be valuable for juvenile naturalists." Booklist

Shaw, Evelyn

Octopus; pictures by Ralph Carpentier. Harper 1971 61p illus (A Science I can read bk) lib. bdg. $6.89 (1-2)   **594**

1 Octopus
ISBN 0-06-025559-5   LC 74-135779

A book about the "life cycle of the octopus as well as her food, enemies, protective devices and habits. Water color washes create the ocean scene." Appraisal

"A good first science book. Although the behavior of an octopus is described in sequence . . . this is not fictionalized. The writing is direct and simple, the information interesting, the illustrations attractive but not always clear in detail." Chicago. Children's Bk Center

Vevers, Gwynne

Octopus, cuttlefish & squid; illus. by Joyce Bee. McGraw [1978 c1977] 48p illus (A McGraw-Hill New biology) lib. bdg. $7.95 (4-6)   **594**

1 Octopus 2 Squid 3 Cuttlefish
ISBN 0-07-067405-1   LC 77-25083

First published 1977 in England

"Clearly stated material, labeled diagrams, and colorful naturalistic drawings provide basic information on three members of the mollusk family. The octopus, squid and cuttlefish are explored in relation to their digestive processes, breathing apparatuses, mobility techniques, and breeding characteristics. Their unusual protective systems in the form of coloration and size changes are explained, especially the cuttlefish's camouflage abilities through use of pigmented secretions. Young scientists will find the straightforward presentation satisfactory for research." Booklist

Zim, Herbert S.

Snails [by] Herbert S. Zim [and] Lucretia Krantz; illus. by René Martin. Morrow 1975 64p illus $6.75, lib. bdg. $6.48 (4 and up)   **594**

1 Snails
ISBN 0-688-22012-6; 0-688-32012-0   LC 74-16262

"Physical characteristics of snails, including the interesting process of shell formation, are clearly described with scientific terms well defined. There are many detailed diagrams, and the line drawings depicting distinctive shapes of land and ocean species will be useful to shell collectors. Utilitarian in appearance (there are no color photographs though the beautiful hues of the shells are frequently mentioned) this is otherwise quite thorough and informative." Sch Library J

595   Other invertebrates

Rhine, Richard

Life in a bucket of soil; illus. by Elsie Wrigley. Lothrop 1972 96p illus $6.75, lib. bdg. $6.48 (5 and up)   **595**

1 Invertebrates 2 Soil ecology
ISBN 0-688-41514-8; 0-688-51514-2   LC 72-155756

The author describes soil inhabitants which can be found in the average backyard, such as beetles,

Rhine, Richard—*Continued*
worms, snails, spiders, and centipedes. He tells
how they live and interreact, how they affect the
soil, and how they can be collected and studied
'Ms. Wrigley has drawn excellent reproductions
of the animals discussed as well as labelled their
various parts. This fits in wonderfully with Mr.
Rhine's scientific discussion of each animal. . . .
The young reader will find in this book information and activities to bring him to a greater
understanding of the relationship between the
soil and its inhabitants." Appraisal
Further reading: p94

595.1 Worms and related animals

Darling, Lois
Worms [by] Lois and Louis Darling.
Morrow 1972 64p illus lib. bdg. $6.48 (1-3)
595.1
1 Earthworms
ISBN 0-688-31773-1   LC 77-102408

Illustrated by the authors, this book explains
the structure of the earthworm, describes its behavior and provides instructions on how to keep
earthworms alive in a container
"The drawings are both imaginative and informative, and beautifully integrated with the clear,
simple text." Horn Bk

Hess, Lilo
The amazing earthworm. Scribner 1979 48p
illus lib. bdg. $7.95 (3-5)   595.1
1 Earthworms
ISBN 0-684-16079-X   LC 78-24321

This book is an "exploration of the characteristics, life cycle, and beneficial aspects of earthworms. A complete account of how to raise earthworms at home is also included." Appraisal
"Hess' straightforward style covers anatomical
and environmental basics that turn out to be surprisingly interesting (a worm has five hearts),
with some simple, humane direction for further
investigation. This could stir interest in an ecological study, an outdoors project, or a science
fair experiment." Booklist

Lauber, Patricia
Earthworms, underground farmers. Garrard
1976 64p illus lib. bdg. $5.10 (3-5)   595.1
1 Earthworms   2 Soils
ISBN 0-8116-6104-0   LC 75-25820

"The introduction begins on a note of mystery
at a farm and slides gently into a description of
earthworms in terms of their usefulness for such
things as fishing and soil improvement. . . . The
text examines the anatomy, physiology and life
history of earthworms in an entertaining and
reasonably complete way. The interactions of
worms and the environment are discussed to show
worms as a part of the biotic cycle and also as a
part of the geologic and agricultural cycles. The
final chapter illustrates how one species of earthworm can be harnessed to work for people. Patricia
Lauber gives several good ideas for experimenting
with earthworms and gardening." AAAS Sci Bks
& Films
"The prose is neither dry nor cute; black-and-
white and color photographs, while often less than
spectacular, include a few rare and amazing
shots." Booklist

Pringle, Laurence
Twist, wiggle, and squirm; a book about
earthworms; illus. by Peter Parnall. Crowell
1973 33p illus (Let's-read-and-find-out science
bks) $7.95, lib. bdg. $7.89 (1-3)   595.1
1 Earthworms
ISBN 0-690-84154-X; 0-690-84155-8   LC 74-184983

"A well-designed, uncluttered book that relates
the facts about earthworms—their movements,
regenerative powers, skin breathing apparatus,
mating habits, enemies, and value to plants and
soil." Booklist

"Artist Peter Parnall's view of life in the underground is enormously appealing. His sinewy earthworms dig long tunnels through the soil, curl up
sleepily in the burrows at wintertime, wiggle to
the surface of the earth [and] tie themselves in
knots." Christian Sci Monitor

Simon, Seymour
Discovering what earthworms do; illus. by
Jean Zallinger. McGraw 1969 47p illus lib.
bdg. $6.95 (3-5)   595.1
1 Earthworms
ISBN 0-07-057404-9   LC 69-17191

"The earthworm is an interesting creature to
young children and this book will answer many of
their questions and stimulate them to find answers
to other questions through a number of simple
observations and experiments. Simon describes
his subject in adequate detail for his young reader
and tells them how to keep earthworms, study
their food habits, their regeneration ability, and
their reaction to different environments and learning situations. The simple style of the text and the
good illustrations will sustain the reader's interest." Sci Bks

595.3 Lobsters. Crabs

Cook, Joseph J.
The nocturnal world of the lobster; illus.
with diagrams and drawings by Jan Cook
and with photographs. Dodd 1972 89p illus
lib. bdg. $5.95 (4-6)   595.3
1 Lobsters   2 Crayfish
ISBN 0-396-04620-5   LC 70-143289

"In a straightforward, rather stolid style that
is occasionaly lightened by informality, Cook describes the structure of the lobster, its life cycle,
the ways in which different species live, and the
ways in which the crustaceans are trapped and—
since the lobster supply is shrinking—the ways in
which they are now being selectively bred and
tagged. One catch-all chapter describes 'The Lobster and Crayfish in Fact and Fiction,' with many
small and not always relevant bits of information,
but there is some truly fascinating material scattered throughout the book." Chicago. Children's
Bk Center
Selected bibliography: p78

Holling, Holling Clancy
Pagoo; illus. by the author and Lucille
Webster Holling. Houghton 1957 86p illus
$10.95, lib. bdg. $4.95 (4 and up)   595.3
1 Crabs   2 Marine animals
ISBN 0-395-06826-6; 0-395-29927-6   LC 56-5551

"The life cycle of the hermit crab and a close-up
of the teeming life of the tide pool are presented,
as in the author's earlier books, in an animated
narrative, scientifically detailed marginal drawings,
and handsome full-page colored pictures. Although
adults are likely to feel that the crab is too
humanized and to be irritated by the facetious,
overly colorful writing, children will find the story
of Pagoo both exciting and informative." Booklist

Zim, Herbert S.
Crabs, by Herbert S. Zim and Lucretia
Krantz; illus. by René Martin. Morrow 1974
63p illus $6.95, lib. bdg. $6.48 (3-5)   595.3
1 Crabs
ISBN 0-688-20114-8; 0-688-30114-2   LC 73-16328

"The authors introduce young readers to the
many crab families and tell how the different
species live. In non-technical language, they describe the general physical structure of crabs
and some of the basic facts about their behavior.
The authors explain how crabs court and mate,
raise their young, feed, secure oxygen, and protect themselves. The molting process is described
in interesting detail as is the crab's regeneration
of a lost appendage. The authors conclude with a
brief discussion of the industry which harvests and
markets edible crabs commercially. Realistic pen
and ink drawings contribute much of the informational value of the text." Sci and Children

595.4   Spiders

Bason, Lillian
Spiders. Natl. Geographic Soc. 1974 32p illus (k-3)   **595.4**

1 Spiders
ISBN 0-87044-156-6   LC 74-10109

Obtainable only as part of a set for $9.95 with: Cats: little tigers in the house, by Linda McCarter Bridge, class 636.8; Creepy crawly things, by the National Geographic Society, class 597.6, and Three litle Indians, by Gene S. Stuart
"Books for young explorers"
Prepared by the Special Publications Division of the National Geographic Society
This book illustrates the physical appearance, habitats, behavior and natural enemies of spiders. Construction of webs and trapdoors as means of catching food are also described
This book "offers remarkable color photographs, a brief general text of considerable value, and a minimum of gimmickry." Booklist

Chenery, Janet
Wolfie; pictures by Marc Simont. Harper 1969 63p illus (A Science I can read bk) $5.95, lib. bdg. $6.89 (k-3)   **595.4**

1 Spiders
ISBN 0-06-021261-6; 0-06-021264-0   LC 78-77950

"Wolfie is a wolf spider that Harry and his friend George keep in a jar in an unused doghouse, away from the prying eyes of Harry's little sister who is promised a view of Wolfie after she has brought him 100 flies. What the boys learn about their spider and spiders in general from Miss Rose at the Nature Center and what Harry learns about little sisters is told in a lively story with easy-to-read text and expressive drawings." Booklist

Conklin, Gladys
Black widow spider—danger! Illus. by Leslie Morrill. Holiday House 1979 unp illus lib. bdg. $4.95 (1-3)   **595.4**

1 Black widow spider
ISBN 0-8234-0342-4   LC 78-2556

In this book "we watch a female building her net, catching food, mating, laying eggs, and dying after her spiderlings' departure. Line drawings effectively enliven the text. In an introduction the author describes the geographical distribution of the black widow and gives warning of the potency of her venom—but in general, the '—danger' of the title is underplayed. A brief bibliography lists several general books for children about spiders." Appraisal

Tarantula: the giant spider; illus. by Glen Rounds. Holiday House 1972 unp illus lib. bdg. $5.95 (1-3)   **595.4**

1 Tarantulas
ISBN 0-8234-0208-8   LC 72-75596

The author describes the life cycle of the male and female California tarantula. Not poisonous to man, this spider is portrayed as a gentle, useful member of the natural world
"The text is simple, understandable and convincing. . . . [The] illustrations, in black-and-white, add immensely to the appeal of the story." Pub W
Bibliography included in Author's note

Goldin, Augusta
Spider silk; illus. by Joseph Low. Crowell 1964 unp illus (Let's-read-and-find-out science bks) lib. bdg. $7.89, pa $1.45 (1-3)   **595.4**

1 Spiders
ISBN 0-690-76075-2; 0-690-01262-4   LC 64-18164

"The story of how a spider spins his web and uses it to trap insects and cradle its eggs makes fascinating reading." Chicago. Children's Bk Center
"This tells the whole story very well. The pen-and-ink sketches with color wash are most effective." Sch Library J

Hawes, Judy
My daddy longlegs; illus. by Walter Lorraine. Crowell 1972 31p illus (Let's-read-and-find-out science bks) $7.95, lib. bdg. $7.89 (1-3)   **595.4**

1 Daddy longlegs
ISBN 0-690-56655-7; 0-690-56656-5   LC 74-175107

"Big print, engaging style, lively illustrations and fascinating information combine to make this an altogether charming book. The reader is urged to catch a few Daddy Longlegs and is told how, when, and where to do this, how to observe them, what to look for and how to build a home for them while the study is in progress. Youngsters may well find this an embarkation point for an enthusiastic study of nature." Appraisal

Lexau, Joan M.
The spider makes a web; pictures by Arabelle Wheatley. Hastings House 1979 40p illus $5.95 (1-3)   **595.4**

1 Spiders
ISBN 0-8038-6766-2   LC 78-75103

"This picture-book science title shows the process one spider might go through in spinning its web. Designating the spider a young female allows a picture of spider mating, egg laying, and birth to emerge. The text is clean and straightforward, its shape growing out of natural events. The pen-and-ink illustrations, highlighted with greens and salmon-like shades of pink, aren't meticulous, but are effective enough at showing actions the text can't take time to describe." Booklist

The **Spider's** web, by Oxford Scientific Films; photographs by John Cooke. Putnam [1978 c1977] unp illus $5.95 (3-6)   **595.4**

1 Spiders
ISBN 0-399-20621-3   LC 77-8322

First published 1977 in England
This book presents "photographs of a garden spider's orb web in the stages of being woven and also a shot of a net-throwing spider that hunts by dropping a small, neat rectangular array of threads right over an unwary passing beetle." Sci Am
There are "four pages of simple background information followed by two dozen pages of color photographs. . . . The spiders spinning webs have a certain elegance." NY Times Bk Rev

595.7   Insects

Anderson, Margaret J.
Exploring the insect world. McGraw 1974 160p illus lib. bdg. $6.95 (5 and up)   **595.7**

1 Insects
ISBN 0-07-001625-9   LC 73-17412

"Several of the 15 chapters focus on environmental settings (e.g., 'Insects on the Night Shift,' 'Exploring a Pond'), others on a few species of particular interest (e.g., bees and wasps, ants, dragonflies, caddisflies), and still others are used to round out the picture (e.g., general anatomical features, friends, enemies). But the real value of the book is not merely in its content (fine as it is: but in the way the material is presented. Ms. Anderson is an engaging writer and particularly adept at leading the reader to significant questions that are answerable by diligent observation or simple experimentation. The tools and equipment needed for the suggested experiments are readily available, for the most part, in any kitchen or garage. . . . The illustrations are straightforward and useful, the bibliography is simple and the index extensive enough to be useful." Sci Bks

Ault, Phil
Wonders of the mosquito world; illus. with photographs and charts. Dodd 1970 64p illus $5.95 (5 and up)   **595.7**

1 Mosquitoes
ISBN 0-396-07154-6   LC 70-114242

"Dodd, Mead Wonders books"
This is the story of one of nature's villains and of man's fight to conquer it. The author delves into the history of the mosquito, which goes back

Ault, Phil—*Continued*

millions of years, and examines the insect's body structure, as well as its role as a carrier of yellow fever, malaria, and other diseases

"The life cycle of mosquitoes is explained, including the sex differences. Three principal species are differentiated: the yellow-fever mosquito, the malaria mosquito; and the ordinary nuisance house msquito of temperate zones. There is a historical summary of control programs, but the most interesting part is a description of experimental work at Notre Dame." The AAAS Sci Bk List for Children

Bees and honey, by Oxford Scientific Films; photographs by David Thompson. Putnam [1977 c1976] unp illus $7.95 (3-6)   595.7

1 Bees
ISBN 0-399-20589-6   LC 76-45849
First published 1976 in England

"A six-page text, divided into brief topics ('The Hive,' 'The Queen,' 'Foraging,' etc.) and crisply written, is followed by captioned full-page color photographs, most of which are greatly enlarged. Text and captions give information about division of labor, communication and cooperation, food-making, life-cycle, and the role of the beekeeper." Chicago. Children's Bk Center

"Special photographic equipment was used to obtain the remarkably clear enlargements. Such high-quality photography is rarely found in children's books." Children's Bk Rev Serv

Bronson, Wilfrid S.

Beetles; written and illus. by Wilfrid S. Bronson. Harcourt 1963 160p illus $5.50 (4 and up)   595.7

1 Beetles 2 Beetles—Collection and preservation
ISBN 0-15-206260-2   LC 63-15397
This study of beetles introduces the reader to the different varieties, including the Scarab, the deathwatch beetle, the firefly and glowworm, the water-beetle, and the locust. The author also gives information on collecting, preserving and showing specimens

The author is "humorous, and chatty in telling of his 'bugs' and has a gift for passing along serious scientific information in an almost casual way, full of anecdotes and informal experiments." Christian Sci Monitor

Includes bibliography

The **Butterfly** cycle, by Oxford Scientific Films; photographs by Dr John Cooke. Putnam [1977 c1976] unp illus $7.95 (3-6)   595.7

1 Butterflies
ISBN 0-399-20590-X   LC 76-45850
First published 1976 in England

The introduction provides background on the life cycle of the butterfly. This "is followed by full-page color photographs with a single line of text. The photographs . . . magnify each stage—laying of eggs, development of the caterpillar, creation of the chrysalis, emergence of the cabbage white butterfly." Sch Library J

"Cooke's exciting, full-color photos are the result of . . . recently developed camera techniques. . . . The book is truly an adventure." Pub W

Cole, Joanna

Cockroaches; illus. by Jean Zallinger. Morrow 1971 62p illus lib. bdg. $6 (3-6)   595.7

1 Cockroaches
ISBN 0-688-31177-6   LC 74-128784
Although the cockroach is an unloved insect, the author contends that its reputation may be worse than it deserves. She describes the origins of the cockroach, its various species, and its life cycle. She also explains why it is the ideal creature for scientific research and briefly summarizes the experiments in which it has proved useful

"Clearly written and copiously illustrated with accurate drawings on almost every page, the brief study is absorbing despite its unpopular subject." Booklist

Find the hidden insect [by] Joanna Cole & Jerome Wexler. Morrow 1979 39p illus $6.95, lib. bdg. $6.67 (k-3)   595.7

1 Insects 2 Camouflage (Biology)
ISBN 0-688-22203-X; 0-688-32203-4   LC 79-18648

"Good black-and-white photographs of insects illustrate how insects are able to blend into their environments. Examples show how blending into the background can give an insect a safe place to live or can help it acquire food. Other photographs illustrate insects that use their bodies for camouflage, such as the woolly aphid and the spit bug. The text is simple and to the point. Most of the insects pictured are common and readily observed in most parts of the country; children will want to find their own examples after looking at this book." AAAS Sci Bks & Films

"This book communicates a sense of wonder about these remarkable adaptations. It is well-written at a low readability level. The black-and-white photographs are effective and dramatic." Children's Bk Rev Serv

Fleas; illus. by Elsie Wrigley. Morrow 1973 62p illus lib. bdg. $5.52 (3-6)   595.7

1 Fleas
ISBN 0-688-31844-4   LC 72-5795
The author "discusses the evolution of fleas, the varieties (separate kinds for cats, dogs, man, etc), the pestilence caused by fleas, and flea circuses (which are horrible). Marvelous and frequent illustrations accompany the text. When drawings are enlarged, actual size is so noted." Appraisal

Conklin, Gladys

The bug club book; a handbook for young bug collectors; illus. by Girard Goodenow. Holiday House 1966 96p illus $5.95 (3-6)   595.7

1 Insects—Collection and preservation
ISBN 0-8234-0017-4   LC 66-31932
The author's easy-to-follow directions for collecting, raising, preserving, mounting, studying, and displaying insects will be useful to many young amateurs. The organization of clubs to study insects, suggestons for involvement of parents, and the preparation of exhibits for public display are useful." Sci Bks

More books to read: p93

I like beetles; pictures by Jean Zallinger. Holiday House 1975 unp illus lib. bdg. $6.95 (k-3)   595.7

1 Beetles
ISBN 0-8234-0262-2   LC 75-4728
"The artist's full colors help to make understandable the anatomies of a wide variety of beetles. The author has selected twenty-nine species to describe in a few short lines of text, indicating biological activities and habitats. Most of the species appear magnified—like the stag beetle sucking sap from an oak tree and the Goliath beetle of Africa seen as 'almost as big as my hand'; in contrast the pine sawyer beetle, the Colorado potato beetle, and the ladybug are shown in approximate life size. Written as if spoken by a child, the text concludes, 'Beetles are fun to watch. I wonder how many beetles are watching me.'" Horn Bk

Praying mantis: the garden dinosaur; illus. by Glen Rounds. Holiday House 1978 unp illus lib. bdg. $4.95 (2-4)   595.7

1 Praying mantis
ISBN 0-8234-0323-8   LC 77-27007
"A friendly first-person narrative begins by affirming that it's fun to watch a praying mantis grow up. The phases of that genially recounted process aptly unfold in Rounds' sly pen drawings, which picture such events as tiny mantises emerging from their egg case and a female laying a new egg case. Conklin's introductory note and concluding comments on what it's like to own a pet mantis further personalize this well-crafted beginner's introduction." Booklist

Ewbank, Constance

Insect zoo; how to collect and care for insects; illus. by Barbara Wolff. Walker & Co. 1973 96p illus $4.95, lib. bdg. $5.85 (4 and up)   595.7

1 Insects—Collection and preservation
ISBN 0-8027-6145-3; 0-8027-6146-1
The author describes the characteristics of various types of insects and offers instructions for the

Ewbank, Constance—*Continued*

collection, care, and study of living and dead specimens. True bugs, beetles, water insects, noisy insects, butterflies and moths are among the insects considered

Illustrated with "clear black-and-white drawings. . . . There is just enough interesting information given about the insects to inspire one to want to begin 'insect watching.' This book would be helpful for a budding entomologist, an individual child, a class of youngsters, or an interested adult." Appraisal

Bibliography: p91

George, Jean Craighead

All upon a sidewalk; illus. by Don Bolognese. Dutton 1974 unp illus $7.95 (2-4)

595.7

1 Ants
ISBN 0-525-25462-5   LC 74-5229

The author describes a day in the life of a common yellow ant, " 'Lasius Flavus', who searches the city streets for a treat to bring home to her queen. Climbing out of a crack, over a huge bottle cap, 'Lasius' lays down a chemical scent which she counts on to guide her home. But what perils are in her path as she tracks down the treasure! She's trapped in a soda straw, attacked by a bee and by a sparrow, involved in a fight with ants of another species." Pub W

"This ant's eye view of a city sidewalk presents ecology to children in a palatable fashion. The author, Jean George, has a way with words. . . . Good readers will find this factual yet creative account absorbing and challenging. Less able readers will surely find pleasure in the superb illustrations." Rdng Teacher

All upon a stone; illus. by Don Bolognese. Crowell 1971 unp illus lib. bdg. $7.49 (1-3)

595.7

1 Crickets
ISBN 0-690-05533-1   LC 75-101929

This is "the story of a mole cricket who crawls from the earth deep under the stone, spends a summer day exploring, and after a brief, festive encounter with a host of other mole crickets, returns." Horn Bk

This book "reveals unsuspected color and life in a seemingly barren rock. . . . [The] illustrations make an uninterrupted block print of fabric, weaving the pages into a background for the mole cricket's universe." Christian Sci Monitor

Hawes, Judy

Bees and beelines; illus. by Aliki. Crowell 1964 unp illus (Let's-read-and-find-out science bks) $6.95, lib. bdg. $6.89, pa $1.45 (k-2)

595.7

1 Bees
ISBN 0-690-12739-1; 0-690-12740-5; 0-690-12745-6
LC 64-10864

"Young children are told how bees can go great distances, find their way home, and then dance a message about where the nectar is to be found."

"An amazing little book in that it gives so much information about a very specific subject in simple language. . . . The line drawings of bees are both attractive and scientifically correct." Sch Library J

Fireflies in the night; illus. by Kazue Mizumura. Crowell 1963 unp illus (Let's-read-and-find-out science bks) lib. bdg. $5.79, pa $1.45 (k-3)

595.7

1 Fireflies
ISBN 0-690-30065-4; 0-690-01259-4   LC 63-15088

The author "fills this sprightly little volume [on fireflies] with information about their history, their biological functions and even directions on how to make a firefly lantern." NY Times Bk Rev

"A most satisfying presentation of a subject unfamiliar to most very young children. . . . The pictures are lovely." Bk Week

Ladybug, ladybug, fly away home; illus. by Ed Emberley. Crowell 1967 unp illus (Let's-read-and-find-out science bks) $6.95, lib. bdg. $6.89, pa $1.45 (k-2)

595.7

1 Ladybugs
ISBN 0-690-48383-X; 0-690-48384-3; 0-690-00200-9
LC 67-15399

The author "tells of the importation of ladybugs from Australia, where they had been found to be instrumental in controlling the pest that was damaging orange trees; and briefly describes their morphology and habits." Sat Rev

"A good first book about the small beetle familiar to most children; the text is written in a crisp, informal style with an occasional note of pleasantry. The illustrations are quite effective: large, clear diagrams or attractive embellishments that make good use of black, white, red, and green." Chicago. Children's Bk Center

Hogner, Dorothy Childs

Grasshoppers and crickets; illus. by Nils Hogner. Crowell 1960 61p illus $7.95, lib bdg. $7.89 (2-5)

595.7

1 Locusts 2 Crickets
ISBN 0-690-35035-X; 0-690-35036-8   LC 60-9219

"Differentiates between grasshoppers, locusts and crickets with the aid of labelled diagrams showing the principal anatomical features, and relates important details of their natural history." The AAAS Sci Bk List for Children

"Good science writing: simple, succinct, and accurate; illustrations are clearly detailed. . . . Large print." Chicago. Children's Bk Center

Hughes, Jill

A closer look at bees and wasps; illus. by Tony Swift and Norman Weaver. Watts, F. 1977 c1976 31p illus lib. bdg. $6.90 (4 and up)

595.7

1 Bees 2 Wasps
ISBN 0-531-00369-8   LC 76-27972

"A Closer look book"

First published 1976 in England

The book "focuses on bumblebees, honeybees, and various types of wasps as it shows how the anatomy of queen bees, drones, and workers, for example, is adapted to their particular work function. Details depicting pollen gathering, honeycomb construction, and honey production show the highly programmed system under which bees live." Booklist

An "inviting, well-organized format. . . . Excellent full-color illustrations and precise well-labeled diagrams add greatly to the book's appeal. I suspect this will whet the appetite of many youngsters and send them on to further field work and research." Appraisal

Hussey, Lois J.

Collecting cocoons [by] Lois J. Hussey and Catherine Pessino; illus. by Isabel Sherwin Harris. Crowell 1953 73p illus lib. bdg. $6.89 (4-6)

595.7

1 Moths—Collection and preservation
ISBN 0-690-19698-9   LC 53-5086

This book "describes the four stages in the development of the moth, how cocoons are made, where and when to look for cocoons, how to collect and care for them, how to breed moths, and how to keep a collection of cocoons. The last half of the book consists of identification data on 19 moths. . . . A good basic book for beginners." Booklist

Where to go for other information: p70

Hutchins, Ross E.

The bug clan; illus. with photographs by the author. Dodd 1973 127p illus lib. bdg. $5.50 (5 and up)

595.7

1 Insects
ISBN 0-396-06771-9   LC 72-11254

"This comprehensive and well-organized survey of the insect orders Hemiptera and Homoptera provides a ready reference guide and superb magnified photographs that can be used for identification. The author, after making distinctions between the true bug and other orders of insects, methodically describes the families of the two orders of bugs, giving facts about the life cycle, habitat, habits, and the usefulness (or harmlessness) to people or plants. Succinct and lucid, the text is a model of its kind: a classification outline, a bibliography, and an index are appended." Chicago. Children's Bk Center

Hutchins, Ross E.—*Continued*

Insects and their young; illus. with photographs by the author. Dodd 1975 125p illus $6.95 (5 and up)   **595.7**

1 Insects
ISBN 0-396-07062-0   LC 74-20862
In this book's introduction, the author "clarifies and simplifies the rather complicated classification system used by naturalists. . . . Sections two through five are divided into four types of insect life histories: primitive, gradual, incomplete, and complete, and within each of these types of life histories, the Latin order name followed by the familiar name of the insect is placed above the brief . . . text." Appraisal
"The text is profusely illustrated with 175 excellent black-and-white close-up photographs of insects at all stages of development. Thus, when compared to other books at comparable prices, this one not only provides an insight into a fascinating aspect of entomology, it is also a real bargain." NY Times Bk Rev

A look at ants; with photographs by the author. Dodd 1978 48p illus lib. bdg. $4.95 (3-5)   **595.7**

1 Ants
ISBN 0-396-07539-8   LC 77-16867
The author "also has supplied the many photographs for a simply written text that describes the structure and life cycle of ants, discusses their classification, and then focuses on some of the many varieties of ants. In so doing, he makes clear the complexity of the social structure in the ant world, the division of labor and the several roles (workers, queens, soldiers) played by individual ants, and the amazing varieties of life styles of different ant communities." Chicago. Children's Bk Center

The world of dragonflies and damselflies; illus. with photographs by the author. Dodd 1969 127p illus $4.50 (5 and up)   **595.7**

1 Dragonflies 2 Damsel flies
ISBN 0-396-07163-5   LC 69-15910
This introduction to the life cycles of the dragonfly and damselfly describes their coloration and distribution and the giant dragonflies of the past.
"This life history and ecological study of dragonflies and damselflies is . . . since the subject is sufficiently limited in scope to facilitate handling in adequate depth. It contains directions for those who wish to collect and mount these insects for study; keys and identification of families, and references for more detailed study. Libraries who are building good natural history collections for young people should purchase it." Sci Bks

Kaufmann, John

Insect travelers. Morrow 1972 126p illus maps $7.25, lib. bdg. $6.96 (6 and up)   **595.7**

1 Insects—Migration
ISBN 0-688-20036-2; 0-688-30036-7   LC 72-1546
"This covers how and why insects travel, distances they attempt, their power of flight, and how they find their way. . . . The account is well written and absorbing on the whole and will be useful for libraries trying to build a large, diversified collection of insect lore." Sch Library J
Bibliography: p119-21

Klots, Alexander B.

A field guide to the butterflies of North America, east of the Great Plains; illus. with color paintings of 247 species by Marjorie Statham and 232 photographs by Florence Longworth. Houghton 1951 349p illus $13.95, pa $6.95   **595.7**

1 Butterflies
ISBN 0-395-07865-2; 0-395-25859-6   LC 51-10190
"The Peterson Field guide series"
The author describes and tells the reader how to identify butterflies found east of the Great Plains from Greenland to Mexico. He tells about the habits, the range, the food plant of the caterpillar and the type of country in which the butterfly is likely to be found
"It is scientific without being pedantic." NY Times Bk Rev
Bibliography: p301-08. Checklist of butterflies: p308-28

Lecht, Jane

Honeybees. Natl. Geographic Soc. 1973 31p illus (k-3)   **595.7**

1 Bees
ISBN 0-87044-141-8   LC 73-7111
Obtainable only as part of a set for $9.95 with: How animals hide, by Robert M. McClung, class 591.5; Namu, by Ronald M. Fisher, class 599.5; and Pandas, by Donna K. Grosvenor, class 599.74
"Books for young explorers"
Prepared by the Special Publications Division of the National Geographic Society
In color photographs and text, this book describes the life of a honeybee hive, noting the differences between the queen bee, the drone and the worker. It tells how bees gather nectar to make honey and pollinate flowers, and deals briefly with man's treatment of bees
"The superb, color macrophotographs, clear, large print and explanatory illustrations are boldly arranged in poster-style format. Each page reaches out to the reader in a way similar to but even more aggressive than some of the best of television for children. This book represents an exciting approach to science for the younger set and demonstrates the information resource capacity of the picturebook medium." Booklist

Lutz, Frank E.

Field book of insects of the United States and Canada, aiming to answer common questions. 3d ed. rewritten to include much additional materials with about 800 illustrations, many in color. Putnam 1935 510p illus (Putnam's Nature field bks) $5.95   **595.7**

1 Insects
ISBN 0-399-10289-2   LC 35-27036
First published 1918
This "is intended to be an introduction to commonly observed species and to the larger groups (genera and particularly families) of insects. Although the species mentioned are, for the most part, inhabitants of northeastern United States, many of them have a wide distribution in this country and some of them in other continents. . . . I have made an effort in this book to record the real names correctly and have given the nicknames when I knew them." Introduction
"Though not intended for children this is a most valuable handbook for younger as well as older amateur entomologists." Toronto

McClung, Robert M.

Bees, wasps, and hornets and how they live; written and illus. by Robert M. McClung. Morrow 1971 64p illus $6.25, lib. bdg. $6 (3-6)   **595.7**

1 Bees 2 Wasps 3 Hornets
ISBN 0-688-21075-9; 0-688-31075-3   LC 73-151942
The author explores the differences and similarities of the membrane winged insects, dividing them into four groups; parasitic wasps, solitary hunting wasps, social wasps, and bees. He concludes with a chapter on the ecological value of bees and wasps
"Packed with relevant information, easy to read, it has the plus of a pleasing format and well-captioned, detailed illustrations." Sch Library J

Caterpillars and how they live; written and illus. by Robert M. McClung. Morrow 1965 63p illus lib. bdg. $6.98 (2-4)   **595.7**

1 Caterpillars
ISBN 0-688-31152-0   LC 65-20949
"The anatomy and life of the caterpillar, the many different kinds of caterpillars, methods of controlling the harmful varieties, and how to raise caterpillars—all aspects are covered." Horn Bk
"The information on shelter, protection and camouflage, is good, as is the brief mention of useful and harmful caterpillars. The final chapter on raising caterpillars is commendable." Sci Bks
"Clear, soft-pencil drawings of caterpillars, in all stages of the life cycle, enhance the [book's] scientific value." Children's Bks, 1965

Luna; the story of a moth; written and illus. by Robert M. McClung. Morrow 1957 unp illus lib. bdg. $6 (2-4)   **595.7**

1 Moths
ISBN 0-688-31523-2   LC 57-8561

McClung, Robert M.—*Continued*

This is a life cycle story of the Luna moth as it evolves from its cocoon, lays hundreds of eggs, and lives just a few days. Because of the constant danger from other insects and small animals, only one of the six eggs laid on the walnut tree survives to become a caterpillar and pupa

"A beautiful and poetic treatment. . . . Each page or double page is effectively designed with type and decoration as a unit, and the information, told simply enough for young children, is authentic enough for any age." Christian Sci Monitor

Mitchell, Robert T.

Butterflies and moths; a guide to the more common American species, by Robert Mitchell and Herbert S. Zim; illus. by Andre Durenceau. 423 illus. in full color. Golden Press 1964 160p illus (A Golden Nature guide) lib. bdg. $9.15, pa $1.95 (4 and up)   595.7

1 Butterflies 2 Moths
ISBN 0-307-63524-4; 0-307-24413-X   LC 64-24907

"So numerous are North American species that only about three per cent have been included, but these were selected to include the most common, widespread, important, or unusual kinds. . . . [Includes] range maps which show distribution." Foreword

"No other book shows so many butterflies and moths with their caterpillars, chrysalises, and cocoons. The oft neglected states west of the Rockies appear to be fully covered." Sch Library J Books: p18

Patent, Dorothy Hinshaw

Butterflies and moths; how they function. Holiday House 1979 160p illus $7.95 (5 and up)   595.7

1 Butterflies 2 Moths
ISBN 0-8234-0350-5   LC 78-20614

This book "examines almost every aspect of lepidopterans: Mating, reproduction, feeding, morphology, physiology, defenses against predators, life stages, coloration, and the ways in which moths and butterflies, in their various stages, are considered pests or benefactors by people." Chicago. Children's Bk Center

"Terms are well defined in the text, and a glossary and bibliography are included. Visual aspects of the book are unfortunately weak. The format is pleasing and the drawings adequate but not as inclusive or precise as they should be to complement and augment the text. The black-and-white photographs are well chosen but sometimes muddy in the reproduction." Sch Library J

Pringle, Laurence

Cockroaches: here, there, and everywhere; illus. by James and Ruth McCrea. Crowell 1971 32p illus (Let's-read-and-find-out science bks) lib. bdg. $6.89 (k-3)   595.7

1 Cockroaches
ISBN 0-690-19680-6   LC 79-132301

"The presentation given the roach is simple and straightforward. It starts with history and proceeds through the ecological place of the roach to the inevitable conclusion that the roach will be living with mankind for the future. Both good and bad points in the life of the roach are given. Precautions are given in relation to food spoilage. The book is well-illustrated." Sci Bks

Ripper, Charles L.

Mosquitoes; written and illus. by Charles L. Ripper. Morrow 1969 63p illus lib. bdg. $6.48 (3-5)   595.7

1 Mosquitoes
ISBN 0-688-31801-0   LC 69-14628

This book describes the research work and control methods used on mosquitoes and gives a "detailed description of anatomy, appearance and life cycle of 3 genera. Excellent illustrations." Minnesota

Ryder, Joanne

Fireflies; pictures by Don Bolognese. Harper 1977 61p illus (A Science I can read bk) $5.95, lib. bdg. $6.89 (1-3)   595.7

1 Fireflies
ISBN 0-06-025153-0; 0-06-025154-9   LC 76-58695

"The text describes a firefly from the time it is a glowworm through its adulthood." Sch Library J

"Unfortunately, the three-color illustrations are largely garish in hue . . . although careful scrutiny is rewarded with visual information. The writing is accurate while sensitively tuned to young people's vocabularies." Booklist

Selsam, Millicent E.

A first look at insects, by Millicent E. Selsam and Joyce Hunt; illus. by Harriett Springer. Walker & Co. 1975 31p $5.50, lib. bdg. $5.39 (2-4)   595.7

1 Insects
ISBN 0-8027-6181-X; 0-8027-6182-8   LC 73-92451

"The basic characteristics of insects (six legs and a three-part body) are presented, then other animals, such as the spider and crayfish, are introduced and the reader is asked to determine if they fit into the insect classification. Insects are further distinguished by different types of antenae and wing and mouth parts. After giving the reader the basic background for identifying insects, several pages of pictures are included with activity suggestions. . . . The common name of the insect is always given beside its illustration, and at the end of the book a summary of parts is given to see if the reader knows which wings go with which body or if he or she can identify various insects from pictures." AAAS Sci Bks & Films

"The careful drawings are nicely integrated with the text, and the authors use them to suggest matching words and pictures. . . . The book, useful but less fluid than Selsam's solo work, concludes with suggestions for ways to collect and care for insects." Chicago. Children's Bk Center

The harlequin moth; its life story; with photographs by Jerome Wexler. Morrow 1975 48p illus $7.75, lib. bdg. $7.44 (2-5)   595.7

1 Moths
ISBN 0-688-22049-5; 0-688-32049-X   LC 75-17862

Text and photographs detail the four stages in the development of the harlequin moth

"Insect development is shown in a series of striking, enlarged photographs, a few of which are in color. No student will need to memorize the stages of metamorphosis after reading this books; he will know them. In the rapidly-occurring stages, such as molting, pupation, and adult emergence, every small change is represented, and anyone who has missed these transformations in rearing his own insects will enjoy seeing them. The text is brief and simple." Horn Bk

Terry and the caterpillars; pictures by Arnold Lobel. Harper 1962 64p illus (A Science I can read bk) lib. bdg. $6.89 (k-2)   595.7

1 Caterpillars
ISBN 0-06-025406-8   LC 62-13309

Also available in a Spanish language edition (ISBN 0-06-025409-2), lib. bdg. $3.79

"A little girl finds three caterpillars, puts them into a jar, and watches all the stages of their life: caterpillar to cocoon to moth to egg and back to caterpillar again." Hodges. Bks for Elem Sch Libraries

"The child gets a good idea of the continuity of reproduction . . . and the attractive presentation may persuade him to do some collecting himself." Library J

"A good sensible easy science book with lively pictures." NY Her Trib Bks

Shuttlesworth, Dorothy E.

All kinds of bees; illus. by Su Zan Noguchi Swain. Random House 1967 62p illus lib. bdg. $4.99 (4-6)   595.7

1 Bees
ISBN 0-394-90143-6   LC 67-9156

"Gateway books"

"An overall summary of the families of bees; their anatomy, ways, dances, and relationship to plants and animals. The book has just enough of the facts yet makes interesting reading. The drawings even though black and white, are excellent." Appraisal

"An appendix on classification gives scientific names for all of the families and some of the species of bees." Booklist

This "is a good systematic reference book for young readers." NY Times Bk Rev

Simon, Hilda

Dragonflies; illus. by the author. Viking 1972 95p illus lib. bdg. $4.95 (5 and up) **595.7**

1 Dragonflies 2 Damsel flies
ISBN 0-670-28147-6   LC 71-185347

The author explores every aspect of the life of a dragonfly and includes an identification guide to North American dragonflies

"Seventy realistic and colorful drawings perfectly complement the text. Although this is a rather technical subject and the writer has aimed at young readers, there is no trace of condescension. The facts are stated simply, accurately and adequately." Sci Bks

Simon, Seymour

Deadly ants; illus. by William R. Downey. Four Winds 1979 49p illus $7.95 (4-6) **595.7**

1 Ants
ISBN 0-590-07610-8   LC 79-14705

This "book describes the life history, social life and the activities inside a colony of two most dangerous kinds of ants—fire ants and army ants. . . . The author describes how the ants sting, the symptoms they cause, the construction of colonies, different castes of ants and their functions, different ways of foraging for foods, the care of developing eggs, the formation of a new colony, and the marching of ants in large hordes." AAAS Sci Bks & Films

"The illustrations—attractive black-and-white drawings well designed for a spacious format—are generally more impressionistic than informative. They tend to emphasize the monstrous quality of the insects, a distorted perspective which is not conveyed by the more balanced point of view of the text." Sch Library J

Teale, Edwin Way

The junior book of insects; illus. with photographs and drawings by the author. 2d rev. ed. Dutton 1972 266p illus $9.95 (6 and up) **595.7**

1 Insects
ISBN 0-525-32925-0   LC 52-12966

First published 1939 with title: The boy's book of insects

"The habits of such insect families as the ants, butterflies, moths, wasps, and beetles are discussed, as are methods of studying insects in nature or in captivity. Though the author unfortunately directs his comments to boys . . . both sexes will be engrossed by the anecdotes and little-known details of insect life and by the interesting and practical suggestions for observing and collecting. This will be a useful addition to basic collections on entomology." Sch Library J
Bibliography: p251-59

Van Woerkom, Dorothy

Hidden messages; illus. by Lynne Cherry. Crown 1979 unp illus lib. bdg. $6.95 (2-4) **595.7**

1 Ants 2 Animal communication
ISBN 0-517-53520-3   LC 78-10705

"Written concisely and clearly, this fine introductory science book describes the ways in which scientists observe natural phenomena, form theories, and test them. It begins with an anecdote about Benjamin Franklin's observation of what seemed to him ant communication, goes on to cite an experiment with moths by Jean Henri Fabre . . . and [continues] with a discussion of the social behavior of ants, the way they secrete grandular liquids to communicate, the fact that these scented liquids are called pheromones, and . . . a conjecture about whether or not human beings have pheromones. . . . The illustrations are clean in composition, subdued in color, and nicely matched to textual references; although they don't give scale, they do show comparative sizes of ant species." Chicago. Children's Bk Center

White, William

A mosquito is born, by William White, Jr. and Sara Jane White. Sterling 1978 80p illus (Sterling Nature ser.) $6.95 (5 and up) **595.7**

1 Mosquitoes
ISBN 0-8069-3534-0   LC 77-93319

Contents: The mosquito: form, biting, mating; Life cycle: egg, larva, pupa, adult; The mosquito and disease; The mosquito in history; Index

"Notable features of the book are the highly magnified photographs, numerous detailed diagrams, and clear explanations of technical material. The result is an uncommonly interesting treatment of a commonly detested subject." Sch Library J

Zim, Herbert S.

Insects; a guide to familiar American insects, by Herbert S. Zim and Clarence Cottam; illus. by James Gordon Irving. Sponsored by The Wildlife Management Institute. 225 species in full color. [Rev. ed] Golden Press [1961 c1956] 160p illus maps (A Golden Nature guide) lib. bdg. $9.15, pa $1.95 (4 and up) **595.7**

1 Insects
ISBN 0-307-63504-X; 0-307-24992-X   LC 61-8325

First published 1951 by Simon & Schuster

"Two hundred and twenty-five species of common, important and showy insects are described here with brief texts and colored illustrations for the novice insect collector." NY Pub Library

"An excellent handbook for the young naturalist. A Key to Insect Groups is included to help in identification and there are colored pictures on every page. Many authorities in the field have been consulted to assure the accuracy of the book." Horn Bk

596 Chordates. Vertebrates

Livaudais, Madeleine

The skeleton book; an inside look at animals, by Madeleine Livaudais and Robert Dunne. Walker & Co [1973 c1972] 31p illus $5.95, lib. bdg. $5.85 (3-6) **596**

1 Vertebrates 2 Anatomy, Comparative
ISBN 0-8027-6125-9; 0-8027-6126-7   LC 72-81381

"The authors present stark photographs—white bones against a black background—of the skeletons of a snake, fish, whale, turtle, frog, bird, penguin, bat, giraffe, horse, elephant, cat, gorilla and human. Distinguishing features of each are singled out, and readers are encouraged to make their own comparisons between related skeletal types." Booklist

Selsam, Millicent E.

A first look at animals with backbones, by Millicent E. Selsam and Joyce Hunt; illus. by Harriet [sic] Springer. Walker & Co. 1978 32p illus $6.95, lib. bdg. $6.85 (1-3) **596**

1 Vertebrates
ISBN 0-8027-6338-3; 0-8027-6339-1   LC 78-4321

"This serves as a good introduction to scientific classification as well as to the subject of vertebrates. The text has large print, good spacing, good placement of illustrations in relation to text, and good sequence of material, moving from the general to the specific. If it occasionally sounds simplistic ("You can feel your backbone . . . Any animal that has a backbone is called a vertebrate . . . Are you a vertebrate?") it may be due to the translation from classroom technique." Chicago. Children's Bk Center

597 Cold-blooded vertebrates. Fishes

Aliki

The long lost coelacanth: and other living fossils; written and illus. by Aliki. Crowell 1973 31p illus (Let's-read-and-find-out science bks) $7.95 (1-3) **597**

1 Coelacanth
ISBN 0-690-50478-0   LC 72-83773

The author describes the coelacanth, a fish thought to have been extinct for 70 million years until one was discovered in 1938, and other "living fossils" such as the horseshoe crab and the Galapagos tortoise

"The simple text gives a clear explanation of how fossil finds enable naturalists to recognize

Aliki—*Continued*
living fossils, and mentions some of the familiar creatures that—although they may have changed in size—are essentially the same as their ancestors of millions of years ago." Chicago. Children's Bk Center

Blumberg, Rhoda

Sharks. Watts, F. 1976 77p illus lib. bdg. $5.90 (4-6)   **597**

1 Sharks
ISBN 0-531-00846-0   LC 75-45120

"A First book"
A straightforward presentation of the various types of sharks, their physical characteristics, habitats, feeding habits, reproduction, and communication abilities. Blumberg talks about the shark's sea companions—pilot fish and suckerfish —as well as its enemies—porcupine fish, porpoises, other sharks, and people who kill it for oil, food, skins, and sport. Material covering individual species such as the basking, blue, tiger, sand, whale, and hammerhead is interspersed with interesting stories." Booklist
"The language is vivid and the stories impressive. . . . Most of the major shark species are represented in the black-and-white photographs which are scattered throughout the book." Horn Bk
Glossary: p69-70. Bibliography: p71

Brown, Anne Ensign

Wonders of sea horses; illus. with photographs and drawings. Dodd 1979 64p illus $5.95 (5 and up)   **597**

1 Sea horses
ISBN 0-396-07665-5   LC 78-22439

"Dodd, Mead Wonders books"
"A background chapter on that intriguing little fish, the sea horse, points out the many ways in which it differs from most fish; succeeding chapters describe many genera and species, and discuss the ways in which the sea horse courts, mates, breeds, and feeds, and the ills and predators from which it suffers. The final chapter gives information on preparing and maintaining a salt water aquarium for sea horses, and gives advice on feeding." Chicago. Children's Bk Center

Carrick, Carol

Sand tiger shark; illus. by Donald Carrick. Seabury [distributed by Houghton] 1977 unp illus $6.95 (2-4)   **597**

1 Sharks
ISBN 0-395-28779-0   LC 76-40206

"A Clarion book"
"Following one nameless creature from its birth in a shallow nursery to its brutal death as victim of a fellow shark, the author . . . presents the life cycle, physical characteristics, and mating patterns." Booklist
The illustrator's "watery paintings catch the eerie, sea-filtered light and almost ghostly presences of creatures whose ancestors were swimming around 'long before dinosaurs, and before flowers and trees.' The accompanying prose is an intelligent unsentimental description of one shark's bloodthirsty life cycle." NY Times Bk Rev

Cook, Joseph J.

The nightmare world of the shark, by Joseph J. Cook and William L. Wisner; illus. with photographs and diagrams. Dodd 1968 96p illus lib. bdg. $5.95 (4 and up)   **597**

1 Sharks
ISBN 0-396-06354-3   LC 68-29808

Both a "factual and fanciful history of sharks is presented. . . . Several species are identified and the characteristics of sharks as dangerous predators to seamen and swimmers, challenging prey for sportsmen, and a source of many products useful to man are discussed by the authors." Booklist
"Many excellent photographs and several simple line drawings complement the text as does the index. The book will interest both serious and casual readers, as well as swimmers who have the normal amount of healthy fear, but it does not include a bibliography or references to enable further study." Sch Library J

Copps, Dale

Savage survivor: 300 million years of the shark. Westwind Press; distributed by Follett 1976 66p illus $5.95, lib. bdg. $5.97 (5 and up)   **597**

1 Sharks
ISBN 0-8172-0502-0; 0-8172-0503-9   LC 75-38744

"Tracing its origin back 400 million years, Copps surveys the fact and legend surrounding the inscrutable shark, examining its virtual resistance to evolutionary change and comparative biological makeup—particularly its unique system of movement and sound detection. He also provides a succinct look at feeding habits, constant companions, and natural enemies along with portraits of seven of the more voracious species, including the hammerhead, great white, and tiger shark. Chapters offer a sampling of efforts toward development of an effective shark repellent and an unusual view of some practical uses for the fish. Distinguished from the many recent treatments by the brevity and excellent photographs." Booklist

Fegely, Thomas D.

The world of freshwater fish; illus. with photographs and drawings. Dodd 1978 128p illus lib. bdg. $6.95 (5 and up)   **597**

1 Fishes—North America 2 Fresh water animals
ISBN 0-396-07562-2   LC 77-16879

"General chapters on physiology, habits and behavior and such dangers as parasites and pollution precede brief discussions of some sixty of the over eight hundred species of freshwater fish found in North America. Because he covers so much ground, the author's treatment of any one topic, while clear, is necessarily very brief. . . . Discussions of individual species touch on geographical distribution, habitat, appearance, feeding habits, and reproductive patterns, as well as the importance of the fish as food or as a source of recreation—all generally in under a page. The book is profusely illustrated with excellent black and white photographs, well chosen and well captioned to illustrate the author's points." Appraisal
Bibliography: p125

Fletcher, Alan Mark

Fishes dangerous to man; illus. by Jane Teiko Oka and Willi Baum. Addison-Wesley 1969 47p illus lib. bdg. $5.95 (4-6)   **597**

1 Fishes
ISBN 0-201-02056-4   LC 71-80502

"An Addisonian Press book"
"The electric eel, great white shark, piranha, stingray, lionfish, and puffer are among the 'shockers,' 'biters,' 'stingers,' and poisonous-to-eat fishes assembled here. The short . . . account identifies approximately 25 fishes and describes the ways in which they are dangerous to man." Booklist
The illustrations "are realistic and approximately labeled." The AAAS Sci Bk List for Children

McGowen, Tom

Album of sharks; illus. by Rod Ruth. Rand McNally 1977 60p illus $5.95, lib. bdg. $5.97 (4-6)   **597**

1 Sharks
ISBN 0-528-82023-0; 0-528-80212-7   LC 77-5172

"Individual chapters are used to describe 11 different types of sharks, such as the hammerhead, mako, blue, thresher, bull, Greenland, and great white shark. Each opens with a dramatically told incident, includes specifics on food, habitat, and size, and captures reader interest with various tidbits of information and lore about these fascinating sea creatures. Differences among the species are stressed; and although McGowen attempts to dispel the myth that sharks are 'simply a kind of big fish that sometimes eats people,' nearly each discussion relates a story concerning a specific attack. The black-and-white line drawings placed in the margin are more in keeping with the text than the vividly colored full-page illustrations that tend to sensationalize. Young shark hunters will devour this!" Booklist

Patent, Dorothy Hinshaw

Fish and how they reproduce; drawings by Matthew Kalmenoff. Holiday House 1976 128p illus $7.95 (5 and up)   **597**

1 Fishes 2 Reproduction
ISBN 0-8234-0285-1   LC 76-10349

Patent, Dorothy H.—_Continued_

"The text gives, in the first two chapters, adequate general information about the variety of fishes, their intelligence and their habitats, the development of the senses in fish, and some facts about hereditary characteristics and adaptation. Succeeding chapters describe some of the many, and often fascinating, ways in which fish court, mate, spawn and breed, and protect their progeny —including facts about migration, color change, sex change, and defense mechanisms." Chicago. Children's Bk Center

"A good general description of kinds of fish and the breeding habits of odd and familiar types. The discussion of the evolution of the modern fish is interesting. Some of the more fascinating aspects of fish reproduction which are presented include the mating of sea horses (the female squirts eggs into the male's brood pouch), the spawning of grunion (which is synchronized with the phases of the moon and tides), the activities of hermaphroditic fish and the breeding habits of mouthbrooders. . . . Good drawings and a satisfactory index, glossary and suggested reading list are provided." AAAS Sci Bks & Films

Selsam, Millicent E.

A first look at sharks, by Millicent E. Selsam and Joyce Hunt; illus. by Harriett Springer. Walker & Co. 1979 32p illus $7.95, lib. bdg. $7.85 (1-3)   **597**

1 Sharks
ISBN 0-8027-6372-3; 0-8027-6373-1   LC 79-2200

"Primary information about the shark is presented both in concise text and in spare pictures that work together to encourage children in their powers of observation. Physical characteristics such as gills, fins, shape of head, and markings are named and described, while carefully drawn black line and gray-shaded drawings, appropriately large and clear, allow easy identification." Booklist

This book "is clear, simply written, and nicely organized, with information limited to an absorbable amount, with clear and carefully placed illustrations, and with a summary of the anatomical features cited in the text that distinguish sharks from bony fish and that differentiate between one shark species and another." Chicago. Children's Bk Center

Waters, John F.

Hungry sharks; illus. by Ann Dalton. Crowell 1973 33p illus (Let's-read-and-find-out science bks) lib. bdg. $7.89 (1-3)   **597**

1 Sharks
ISBN 0-690-01121-0   LLC 72-7563

"A brief examination of the various senses a shark uses to locate food. The shark's sense of smell as a principal means is accompanied by a short profile of the anatomy of a shark's nose. The shark's ability to feel the water movements created by live food is explained via its lateral line system. Likewise, a shark's capacity to hear the vibrations of the water movements and how it sees the food are added to the presentation. . . . As brief as the book is, it definitely conveys the importance of scientific observation and experimentation in a low-keyed way. The authenticity is effectively augmented by a graphic style which is free flowing and communicative." Sci Teacher

Wong, Herbert H.

My goldfish, by Herbert H. Wong and Matthew F. Vessel; illus. by Arvis L. Stewart. Addison-Wesley 1969 30p illus (Science ser. for the young) lib. bdg. $6.95 (k-2)   **597**

1 Goldfish
ISBN 0-2010-8720-0   LC 69-15803

"An Addisonian Press book"

"A book that describes within a fictional framework how a goldfish breathes, sleeps, and eats. A few other facts are given, and the boy, who has won his fish at a school fair, decides that he would rather have his own pretty goldfish than his uncle's impressive collection of fish. The illustrations are very attractive, the text useful both as a beginning science book and as an example of caring for pets. . . . But the text is stiff and not pleasing when read aloud." Chicago. Children's Bk Center

Zim, Herbert S.

Fishes; a guide to fresh-and salt water species, by Herbert S. Zim and Hurst H. Shoemaker; illus. by James Gordon Irving. 278 fishes in full color. Golden Press 1957 160p illus (A Golden Nature guide) lib. bdg. $9.15, pa $1.95   **597**

1 Fishes
ISBN 0-307-63508-2; 0-307-24498-9   LC 61-8322
First published 1956 by Simon & Schuster

"A pocket identification guide with suggestions for collecting, classifying, and photographing fishes." Hodges. Bks for Elem Sch Libraries

The book contains "a glossary of scientific names and a list of public aquaria. The descriptions include interesting and helpful natural history notes." The AAAS Sci Bk List for Children

Books to read: p153-54

Sharks; illus. by Stephen Howe. Morrow 1966 63p illus lib. bdg. $6 (2-5)   **597**

1 Sharks
ISBN 0-688-21810-5   LC 66-10706

"A descriptive account of the evolution of sharks is followed by mention of their chief anatomical features compared with those of bony fishes. A condensed sketch of their activities and feeding habits, individual illustrations and descriptive notes on some of the principal species of sharks, an account of the menace of some species to human life, and other interesting information are included." Sci Bks

"The accuracy of the author's opening statement that 'Sharks are the largest . . . creatures in the sea,' can be questioned; this distinction seems to belong to whales. Nevertheless, this is an interesting, informative, well-illustrated account." Sch Library J

597.6 Amphibians

Conant, Roger

A field guide to reptiles and amphibians of Eastern and Central North America; illus. by Isabelle Hunt Conant. 2d ed. Houghton 1975 429p illus maps $10.95, pa $6.95   **597.6**

1 Reptiles 2 Amphibians
ISBN 0-395-19979-4; 0-395-19977-8   LC 74-13425

"The Peterson Field guide series"

First published 1958 with title: A field guide to reptiles and amphibians of the United States and Canada east of the 100th meridian

This book contains "information on crocodilians, turtles, lizards, snakes, salamanders, and toads and frogs. The information is . . . organized under broad headings, subdivided into specific entries for the 574 species and subspecies covered. . . . Three hundred thirty-one species are covered." Booklist

"Photographic reproductions of live specimens (472 in color; 174 in black-and-white) are included in 48 plates near the middle of the book. When necessary for unequivocal identification, many specimens are shown from more than one view. Line drawings are used judiciously throughout the text to make subtle comparisons in morphology among similar species or between sexes. Over 300 good quality distribution maps are near the end of the book. . . . The written description of each species is concise in capturing its distinguishing attributes, behavioral and vocal as well as morphological. Additional dimensions in this field guide are short, relevant chapters on the capture and care of herpetological specimens and a chapter on snakebite." AAAS Sci Bks & Films

Glossary: p351-53. References: p354-61

National Geographic Society

Creepy crawly things; reptiles and amphibians. The Society 1974 32p illus (k-3)   **597.6**

1 Reptiles 2 Amphibians
ISBN 0-87044-157-4   LC 75-306257

Obtainable only as part of a set for $9.95 with: Cats: little tigers in your house, by Linda McCarter Bridge, class 636.8; Spiders, by Lillian Bason, class 595.4, and Three Little Indians, by Gene S. Stuart

"Books for young explorers"

Prepared by the Special Publications Division of the National Geographic Society

In text and color photographs, this book describes some aspects of anatomy, behavior, habitats and reproduction of salamanders, frogs, toads, alligators, turtles, lizards and snakes

National Geographic Society—Continued

This book "speaks directly to an eager readership in giving generally superb photographic representations of a variety of reptiles and amphibians. The dramatic format, occasionally overdone with slightly askew print or photos, is clean and shows up the animal examples well. . . . A brief text contains factual items of interest." Booklist

Ommanney, F. D.

Frogs, toads & newts; illus. by Deborah Fulford. McGraw [1975 c1973] 48p illus (A McGraw-Hill New biology) lib. bdg. $6.95 (4-6)   **597.6**

1 Frogs 2 Toads 3 Salamanders
ISBN 0-07-047705-1   LC 74-9513

First published 1973 in England
This book briefly discusses the evolution and characteristics of amphibians and then describes the habitats, physical characteristics, mating, reproduction and life cycles of frogs and toads, and of newts and other types of salamanders

"An especially interesting and attractively designed survey. . . . Besides general characteristics of the phylum and its larger subgroups, unusual aspects of common British and U.S. species and examples of lesser-known animals in other countries are called to the reader's attention through clear textual descriptions and exact, full-color illustrations. Captions give generic and scientific names and frequently indicate the animal's actual size in relation to the picture. Wide margins and large type will be helpful to beginning readers." Booklist

Patent, Dorothy Hinshaw

Frogs, toads, salamanders, and how they reproduce; illus. by Matthew Kalmenoff. Holiday House 1975 142p illus $7.95 (5 and up)   **597.6**

1 Amphibians 2 Reproduction
ISBN 0-8234-0255-X   LC 74-26567

"This book delves into the habits and adaptations of amphibians from all over the world, uncovering much curious and little known information. Courtship, mating, egg-laying, embryonic deveoplment, metamorphosis, nest building, and care of the young are treated in detail, with attractive illustrations accompanying." Sci Teacher

"Detailed pencil drawings expand the text. A wide variety of species are covered here that will be of special interest to those already fascinated by these creatures." Sch Library J

Bibliography: p137-38

597.8   Frogs. Toads

Common frog, by Oxford Scientific Films; photographs by George Bernard. Putnam 1979 unp illus $6.95 (3-6)   **597.8**

1 Frogs
ISBN 0-399-20675-2   LC 78-24038

This book begins with a four page introduction which is followed by a shorter, simpler text that accompanies closeup color photographs of frog mating, tadpoles developing, and frogs as both hunter and prey

Hawes, Judy

What I like about toads; illus. by James and Ruth McCrea. Crowell 1969 33p illus (Let's-read-and-find-out science bks) lib. bdg. $7.89, pa $1.25 (k-3)   **597.8**

1 Toads
ISBN 0-690-87577-0; 0-690-87582-7   LC 76-78262

In easy text the author "describes the appearance, habits, and life cycle of toads, dispels the false notion that toads cause warts, and points out the valuable service which these insect-eating amphibians perform for farmers. The appearance and characteristic behavior of a toad are cleverly depicted in the black-and-white and three-color illustrations." Booklist

"Easy enough for very young or reluctant readers, informative and entertaining for all. . . . Pen-and-ink drawings by James and Ruth McCrea complement the text very well, capturing the seemingly smug, introspective look of toads." Sch Library J

Why frogs are wet; illus. by Don Madden. Crowell 1975 35p illus pa $2.95 (k-3)   **597.8**

1 Frogs
ISBN 0-690-00640-3   LC 68-21605

First published 1968
A "scientific introduction to the life of frogs, their adaptation since prehistoric times, physiology, growth cycle and feeding." Sch Library J

An easy-to-read, straightforward text with the marvelously humorous drawings of Don Madden. The result is irresistible—even to the most hesitant young reader." Bk World

McClung, Robert M.

Peeper, first voice of spring; illus. by Carol Lerner. Morrow 1977 unp illus lib. bdg. $6.96 (2-4)   **597.8**

1 Frogs 2 Ecology
ISBN 0-688-32116-X   LC 77-2410

This book gives "a picture of the ecological balance of the peeper's environment as well as an explanation of the stages of its life and reproductive processes." Chicago. Children's Bk Center

The narrative "is smoothly set forth. Lerner's drawings, spread over double pages or facing a body of text, command the eye with their beauty and precision. They're memorable, at once scientific and aesthetically complete. The book sets a striking standard for illustration and design in nonfiction." Booklist

Simon, Hilda

Frogs and toads of the world; written and illus. by Hilda Simon. Lippincott 1975 128p illus $7.95 (5 and up)   **597.8**

1 Frogs 2 Toads
ISBN 0-397-31634-8   LC 75-14095

The author "surveys briefly the origin of amphibians, frog anatomy and development. The succeeding five chapters deal with five groups of frogs: primitive frogs and toads, toads, tree frogs, true frogs and maverick frog families. Each group receives a brief but adequate and accurate coverage. The final chapter contains a discussion of unusual breeding habits, a most fascinating feature of frogs." AAAS Sci Bks & Films

"Brightly illustrated diagrams are found in profusion throughout the book. Also included is a bibliography, an index of scientific names, a general index, and a list of illustrations. This text is aptly suited to middle school students and others with an interest in this unique order of amphibians." Sci and Children

Simon, Seymour

Discovering what frogs do; illus. by Jean Zallinger. McGraw 1969 47p illus lib. bdg. $6.95 (2-4)   **597.8**

1 Frogs
ISBN 0-07-057442-7   LC 77-88330

The book contains information on how to go frog hunting, how to capture frogs and bring them home without hurting them, and how to keep them well-fed and happy in a home-made aquarium. It also describes the development of the frog and offers instructions for unharmful experiments

"A good introduction to the topic. . . . The information given is useful, the illustrations adequate; the writing is marred by an occasional excursion into exclamation points and by some patronizing questions. . . . A final page, headed 'A Note on the Names of Frogs' gives the common and scientific names for the leopard frog described in the text, and for three others." Chicago. Children's Bk Center

Zim, Herbert S.

Frogs and toads; illus. by Joy Buba. Morrow 1950 unp illus map lib. bdg. $6.48 (2-5)   **597.8**

1 Frogs 2 Toads
ISBN 0-688-31316-7   LC 50-5653

"The many fascinating aspects of frog and toad life are presented in a lively, informative manner. Discusses their methods of defense and camouflage and their unique food-getting apparatus. The section on amphibian reproduction is thorough and well written. Common misconceptions about frogs and toads are dispelled." The AAAS Sci Bk List for Children

The "illustrations, beautifully executed, are a very helpful addition to the interesting text." NY Times Bk Rev

597.9 Reptiles

Brenner, Barbara

Lizard tails and cactus spines; photographs by Merritt S. Keasey, III. Harper 1975 84p illus lib. bdg. $7.89 (4-6)   597.9

1 Lizards 2 Desert animals 3 Desert plants
ISBN 0-06-020667-5   LC 75-6297

"Fictional twelve-year-old Alan Pippin and his expeditions in the Arizona desert are the vehicle for the author's casual, informative observations. . . . Alan's interest in the ancient order of lizards, the diversity of the species and their unique characteristics leads him to appreciate the vastness of the desert environment and to gain the knowledge to survive unfamiliar experiences, including a scorpion bite. He demonstrates scientific techniques for recording his observations and collecting specimens with a youthful enthusiasm which will trigger identification feelings in other budding herpetologists. Black-and-white photographs portray the plants and animals he studies, and much information is contained in his ponderings about the nature of life in this particular environment." Appraisal

The author "combines Pip's adventures and conversations with facts about the desert and its creatures so smoothly that the book is truly a coup, a completely successful mesh of fiction and fact." Chicago. Children's Bk Center

A snake-lover's diary; illus. with photographs. Young Scott Bks. 1970 90p illus lib. bdg. $6.95 (5 and up)   597.9

1 Snakes
ISBN 0-201-09349-9   LC 79-98113

"The author, the mother of a young herpetologist, records her son's experiences as if he had described them in a journal. Mark began by discovering a garter snake one April day and decided then and there to 'start a scientific study of snakes, and keep a diary of [his] findings.' Having won over his mother, been abetted by his father, and accompanied and advised by a college-age companion in some of his collecting excursions, Mark enjoyed a spring and summer that netted a number of species. The scientific names, differences, and eating habits of snakes are carefully recorded in a text that contains a mine of fascinating facts relayed informally and with humor. . . . Excellent photographs of collecting scenes and species enliven the book. A glossary, a bibliography, and a list of herpetological organizations are appended." Horn Bk

Darling, Lois

Turtles, by Lois and Louis Darling. Morrow 1962 64p illus lib. bdg. $6.48 (3-5)   597.9

1 Turtles
ISBN 0-688-31547-X   LC 62-8905

"Every teacher who has had a turtle in the classroom will find this the perfect answer to all those questions children ask, for it covers the history and structure of turtles, the life cycle, and the problems of their survival, and ends with an indispensable chapter on turtle keeping with complete and specific instructions which tell why turtles need to be cared for in certain ways." Chicago Sch J

The book is "compact, and lively. . . . [It] is beautiful to look at because of the variety and excellence of the illustrations. The anatomical drawings are particularly useful and interesting." Horn Bk

Freschet, Berniece

Lizard lying in the sun; illus. by Glen Rounds. Scribner 1975 32p illus lib. bdg. $5.95 (1-3)   597.9

1 Lizards
ISBN 0-684-14406-9   LC 75-8344

In this story "readers find out about how the lizard obtains food and how he avoids becoming the dinner of other creatures in his environment." Sch Library J

"An easy-to-read text, complemented by spirited pen-and-ink line drawings. . . . Without emphasizing the notion of nature's violence, the account of the lizard's adventures and escape is imbued with a sense of drama and urgency." Horn Bk

Turtle pond; illus. by Donald Carrick. Scribner 1971 unp illus lib. bdg. $6.95 (k-3)   597.9

1 Turtles
ISBN 0-684-12326-6   LC 75-121751

After two months in a dry, sandy hole near the pond, eleven turtle eggs hatch. The author tells of the dangers the eleven little turtles encounter on their short trip to the water

"A lovely picture book about pond life. . . . In an easy, natural way, the author helps readers understand the many facets of life in one small habitat, including the fact that some animals fall prey to others. . . . The realistic illustrations are beautiful in soft colors, with marvelous natural detail." Sch Library J

Gross, Ruth Belov

Alligators and other crocodilians. Four Winds [1978 c1976] 58p illus $7.95 (2-5)   597.9

1 Alligators 2 Crocodiles
ISBN 0-590-07556-X   LC 77-18310

"Four animals of the crocodilian family—alligators, caimans, gavials, and crocodiles—are explored in short, understandable narrative and full-page, clear black-and-white photographs. Gross explains the differences in the animals' length, physical characteristics, habitats, and behavior, as well as their familial similarities. Old myths about the creatures, such as their living several hundred years and crying tears, are dispelled; and the author answers many oft-asked questions concerning their enemies, food, possible attack on humans, and survival factors. A vivid description of the ecological part they play in the chain-of-life pattern in the Florida Everglades concludes the text. A worthwhile addition to the animal book collection." Booklist

Snakes. Four Winds 1975 [c1973] 63p illus $7.95 (3-5)   597.9

1 Snakes
ISBN 0-590-07385-0   LC 74-13227

"The first part of the book contains illustrated discussions of the fascinating aspects of snakes: reproduction, shedding, food and eating, dealing with enemies, locomotion, and hibernation. The second half presents colored portraits with accompanying descriptions of nonpoisonous and poisonous snakes found in the United States and Canada and of four deadly serpents from other parts of the world. Index and glossary of common and scientific names." Horn Bk

"The writing style is direct and crisp, with short sentences and large print, and with the text arranged in short chapters to facilitate reading ease." Chicago. Children's Bk Center

Huntington, Harriet E.

Let's look at reptiles; written and illus. with photographs by Harriet E. Huntington; drawings by J. Noël. Doubleday 1973 106p illus lib. bdg. $6.90 (4-6)   597.9

1 Reptiles
ISBN 0-385-04853-X   LC 73-76447

"The author explains the reproductive cycles peculiar to lizards, crocodiles, alligators, turtles, and snakes. Descriptions of characteristics are combined with a discussion of eating, sleeping, self-preservation, and growth patterns for each reptile." Booklist

"Plentifully illustrated with marvelous photos, this is a model of clarity and organization. Even without an index, it should prove useful for elementary school reference." Sci and Children

Leen, Nina

Snakes. Holt 1978 80p illus lib. bdg. $6.95 (4 and up)   597.9

1 Snakes
ISBN 0-03-039926-2   LC 77-13917

"Organized by function rather than species, this gives information on senses, habitat, locomotion, defense, hatching, shedding, temperature, eating, hunting, and endangered species, in . . . photo-essay style. . . . An introductory list of snakes in the book gives common name, Latin name, range, venomous/nonvenomous classification, and page numbers." Booklist

"Leen's camera-work is exceptional. Her . . . remarkable shots combine with a pleasing layout and informative text to present a clear account of these ever-fascinating reptiles." Sch Library J
Suggested reading: p78

McClung, Robert M.

Snakes: their place in the sun. Garrard 1979 61p illus lib. bdg. $5.97 (3-5)   597.9

1 Snakes
ISBN 0-8116-6112-1   LC 79-10238

"Basic information about the life cycle of snakes is presented. . . . Descriptions of the eating habits as well as remarks about animals that feed on snakes indicate this reptile's place in the ecological food chain. Other material covers the snake's hibernation, mating, skin-shedding, defenses, and various physical characteristics." Booklist

"The text is simple and understandable, but never dull or dry. The photographs are more variable in quality, but some are excellent." Appraisal

McGowen, Tom

Album of reptiles; illus. by Rod Ruth. Rand McNally 1978 61p illus $5.95, lib. bdg. $5.97 (4-6)   597.9

1 Reptiles
ISBN 0-528-82001-X; 0-528-80014-0   LC 78-9716

"McGowen introduces his text with a concise differentiation between this family and other groups of animals. Various crocodiles, snakes, turtles, tortoises, lizards, and the tuatara, a one-of-a-kind prehistoric survivor that lives in New Zealand, are discussed individually as to their physical characteristics, native habitats, reproduction processes, and defense mechanisms. Comments also include prehistoric origins of the reptiles and their ongoing relationships with humans." Booklist

"Each chapter is illustrated with a large full-color painting of a reptile in action as well as small black and white drawings which are appealing and contribute further detail to the text." Appraisal

Pronunciation guide: p61

Patent, Dorothy Hinshaw

Reptiles and how they reproduce; drawings by Matthew Kalmenoff. Holiday House 1977 127p illus $7.95 (5 and up)   597.9

1 Reptiles 2 Reproduction
ISBN 0-8234-0310-6   LC 77-3817

The author describes "the evolution of reptilian species, the characteristics of each, and the characteristics they have in common. Separate chapters then describe patterns of courting and mating, nest-building, and—in some species—care of young, social organization, establishment of territorial rights or individual dominance. The careful drawings are well-placed and adequately labelled, and the writing is scientifically exemplary, using technical terms when necessary and otherwise avoiding them, distinguishing between fact and theory, communicating a sense of appreciation for the intricacies of life forms without becoming rhapsodical about them." Chicago. Children's Bk Center

Glossary: p120-22. Suggested reading: p123-24

Roever, J. M.

Snake secrets; written and illus. by J. M. Roever. Walker & Co. 1979 155p illus $7.95, lib. bdg. $7.85 (6 and up)   597.9

1 Snakes
ISBN 0-8027-6332-4; 0-8027-6333-2   LC 78-4318

"Roever covers everything from myths and legends to instructions on how to dissect a snake. The book is divided into three sections: the habits of snakes in the wild; snakes as pets; treating snakebite and learning through dissection. The author advises caution and gives good, practical advice for handling even non-venomous snakes. She also makes a case for the value of snakes to mankind and a plea for preservation and conservation. The text is illustrated with drawings (many of dissected anatomies) which are detailed but lack color, a serious drawback in learning to identify snakes." Sch Library J

Bibliography: p147

Scott, Jack Denton

Loggerhead turtle; survivor from the sea; photographs by Ozzie Sweet. Putnam 1974 unp illus $6.95 (4 and up)   597.9

1 Turtles
ISBN 0-399-20379-6   LC 73-83993

"The account focuses on the mating and egg-laying of the female [loggerhead turtle] and then shifts to describe the overwhelming dangers from predators, including man, that conservation groups such as Florida's 'Turtle Boys' are trying to offset. Stunning black-and-white photographs document each of the activities encompassed in the text, and the end result is a stately tribute to the loggerhead's 'miracle of survival.'" Booklist

Shaw, Evelyn

Alligator; pictures by Frances Zweifel. Harper 1972 60p illus (A Science I can read bk) $5.95, lib. bdg. $6.89 (1-2)   597.9

1 Alligators
ISBN 0-06-025556-0; 0-06-02557-9   LC 70-183157

A description of "an alligator's life cycle in narrative form. The female prepares a nest, lays her eggs and covers them with mud and plants; two months later the baby alligators hatch, but—a natural and convincing moment of suspense—the mother is at that moment in hiding from hunters and cannot get back to the nest to uncover the babies. A larger alligator frightens the hunters away, and the mother is able to get back to the nest and rescue the forty babies. The book ends with the young alligators old enough to go off on their own." Chicago. Children's Bk Center

"The drawings and pictures illustrate the environment in which the alligator lives and include both predators and prey. The primary student will find this an interesting reference book on alligators as well as an exciting adventure story." Sci Bks

Simon, Hilda

Snakes; the facts and the folklore; illus. by the author. Viking 1973 128p illus lib. bdg. $8.95 (5 and up)   597.9

1 Snakes
ISBN 0-670-65315-2   LC 73-5154

The author "discusses the role of snakes in Bible stories and in mythology, their evolution from lizards and the behavior patterns of a great variety of snakes. She does much to dispel the universal loathing these creatures inspire but also warns against the deadly nature of some species. A guide to the care of snakes as pets closes the book." Pub W

"Nearly 80 detailed illustrations, most in color, are an excellent addition to the interesting text." Sch Library J

Stonehouse, Bernard

A closer look at reptiles; illus. by Gary Hincks, Alan Male, Phil Weare. Gloucester Press 1979 c1978 unp illus lib. bdg. $5.90 (5 and up)   597.9

1 Reptiles
ISBN 0-531-02495-4; 0-531-03401-1   LC 78-11539

First published 1978 in England

This book discusses "the evolution, habitats, general and specialized structures, breeding habits, and protective mechanisms of reptiles. . . . The book is a plea for humans, reptiles' most destructive enemy, to understand that these animals hold an important niche in the Earth's ecology." Sci and Children

Waters, John F.

Green turtle mysteries; illus. by Mamoru Funai. Crowell 1972 33p illus (Let's-read-and-find-out science bks) $7.95, lib. bdg. $7.89 (1-3)   597.9

1 Turtles
ISBN 0-690-35994-2; 0-690-35995-0   LC 70-158701

"The author of this book explains what green turtles are, where they live and mate and lay their eggs. He points out the unsolved mysteries surrounding the turtle's habits . . . and questions: How do baby turtles always find their way to the ocean on hatching even though they cannot see it? Where do they go once they reach the sea? How do they find the beach of their birth as adult females ready in their turn to lay eggs? Like many other children's books, this one ends with a strong plea for preserving this turtle which is perhaps on its way to extinction." Appraisal

"It is good to see a book which makes a point of presenting questions about nature to which scientists have not yet found solutions. . . . 'Green Turtle Mysteries' is short . . . well-illustrated, and has a brief text in large type." Sci Bks

White, William

The American chameleon [by] William White, Jr. Sterling 1977 80p illus (Sterling Nature ser) $6.95 (4-6)   597.9

1 Chameleons
ISBN 0-8069-3532-4   LC 76-51162

"This overview of the American chameleon, or anole, examines its physical make-up, habits, behavior, and adaptability as a pet. The black-and-white photographs, some clearer than others, and accompanying text explore the animal's life cycle, describing its peculiar characteristics of color change and regeneration. High-power microphotography has been used to capture embryo and egg stages as well as individual body parts of the anole. Six rules are given for caring for chameleons in captivity. Useful for zoology studies." Booklist
"Explanations are accurate and scientific. . . . Both public and school libraries should find this a useful addition since the anole is a separate species not generally covered in other material on chameleons." Sch Library J

Zim, Herbert S.

Alligators and crocodiles. Newly rev. ed. Illus. by Jean Zallinger. Morrow 1978 64p illus lib. bdg. $6.67 (4-6)   597.9

1 Alligators 2 Crocodiles
ISBN 0-688-32170-4   LC 78-6615
First published 1952

"This book provides a brief summary of the evolution, adaptation, ecology and behavior of crocodiles and alligators. Almost two-thirds of the text is filled with accounts of the various living crocodilians from the American alligator to the Indian gharial and Cuban crocodile." AAAS Sci Bks & Films
"The three families of crocodilians—alligators, crocodiles, and gharials—receive thorough coverage; the information is accurate and well presented. The print is large and readable, and the black-and-white drawings illustrate the text admirably." Sch Library J

598   Birds

Amon, Aline

Roadrunners and other cuckoos; written & illus. by Aline Amon. Atheneum Pubs. 1978 87p illus $7.95 (5 and up)   598

1 Cuckoos
ISBN 0-689-30646-6   LC 78-6648

Cuckoos "vary greatly among the 94 to 142 species that range the world. Beginning with the southwestern U.S. variety of roadrunners, Amon describes the physical characteristics and behavior of cuckoos, paying particular attention to their nesting, eating, and migratory habits. The European common cuckoo, for example, is a brood parasite, laying eggs in the nests of host birds, which hatch and care for their young, while the Central American ani develops group nests for communal living. Comments on the birds' adaptability to human environment, references to scientific studies, and naturalistic black-and-white drawings round out the text. . . . The narrative, . . . is smooth and offers young ornithologists an interesting look at an unusual bird." Booklist
Bibliography: p82-84

Audubon, John James

The birds of America; with a foreword and descriptive captions by William Vogt. Macmillan Pub. Co. 1937 xxvi p, 435 plates $19.95   598

1 Birds—North America 2 Birds—Pictorial works
ISBN 0-02-504440-0   LC 37-28771

The 435 plates in this volume were originally published by Audubon, in London, during the years 1827-1838
"William Vogt has written an excellent introduction and a brief descriptive note for each plate. The names, both common and scientific, accompanying each plate, are those found in the 'Check-List' of the American ornithologists' union. Index is to common names only. Fine format." Booklist
In this edition "we have not only an art work and naturalist's handbook, but a monument to one of the great Americans." New Repub

Blassingame, Wyatt

Wonders of crows. Dodd 1979 96p illus $5.95 (5 and up)   598

1 Crows
ISBN 0-396-07649-1   LC 78-21633
"Dodd, Mead Wonders books"

"Blassingame is definitely on the crows' side, and he writes in lively detail about the habits, intelligence, and history of one of the most widespread and well-known birds and its relatives, ravens, rooks, and jackdaws. Descriptions of nesting and care of the young; accounts of crows in the Bible, Roman mythology, and literature; instructions on the care of pet crows (carefully debunking the myth that a crow's tongue must be slit before it can talk); and some anecdotes are included. The crow's bad habits are not overlooked (damage to crops, for example) but it is pointed out that they also eat large numbers of destructive insects. Illustrated with black-and-white photographs and a few drawings." Sch Library J

Brady, Irene

Owlet, the great horned owl; written and illus. by Irene Brady. Houghton 1974 40p illus lib. bdg. $4.95 (2-4)   598

1 Owls
ISBN 0-395-18519-X   LC 74-5483

This book chronicles the life cycle of a great horned owl, from the time he is hatched until he mates and begins his own family

Brenner, Barbara

Baltimore orioles; pictures by J. Winslow Higginbottom. Harper 1974 62p illus (A Science I can read bk) $4.95, lib. bdg. $5.79 (k-2)   598

1 Orioles
ISBN 0-06-020664-0; 0-06-020665-9   LC 73-14327

"Describing one oriole family during the cycle of a year, the text covers courtship, mating, nest-building, hatching, the care and feeding of baby birds, and predators. The print is large, the prose rather more choppy than in many books in this series . . . but the facts are accurate and the book useful both for the information it gives and as an encouraging reading experience." Chicago. Children's Bk Center
"An attractively illustrated account . . . which should appeal to the young reader and may well stimuate more careful observation of bird behavior in general." Appraisal

Cook, Joseph J.

Wonders of the pelican world [by] Joseph J. Cook and Ralph W. Schreiber; illus. with photographs by Ralph W. Schreiber. Dodd 1974 64p illus $5.95 (4 and up)   598

1 Pelicans
ISBN 0-396-06935-5   LC 73-19086
"Dodd, Mead Wonders books"

"The authors present an excellent and concise life story primarily of the brown pelican. The book begins with a description of the habitat, physical characteristics, courtship behavior, breeding, nest-building, and hatching and care of the chicks. Beautiful black and white photographs show different patterns of behavior of this majestic bird. Information is presented which relates the pelican to its role in religion, myths, and legends through time. A detailed process of banding the birds for scientific study by scientists is presented. The book concludes on a note of warning for posterity. It suggests the pelicans are destined for extinction because the fish they eat are polluted with increasing concentrations of DDT." Sci Teacher

Dugdale, Vera

Album of North American birds; illus. by Clark Bronson. Rand McNally 1967 112p illus pa $2.95 (4-6)   598

1 Birds—North America
ISBN 0-528-87010-6   LC 67-18285

Companion volume to: Album of North American animals, class 591.9
"A lively, non-technical text gives the essential information about the appearance, life and habits of fifty-two well-known birds. Twenty-six of these are shown full page and full color. A wide variety

Dugdale, Vera—*Continued*

of species is represented, some unusual ones such as the wild turkey and rare whistling swan, as well as more common ones. Has an excellent index for easy reference." Bruno. Bks for Sch Libraries, 1968

"There are smaller drawings in black and white, precise and delicate, of all the birds. . . . The scientific name for each bird is given." Sutherland. The Best in Children's Bks

Earle, Olive L.

Birds and their nests. Morrow 1952 60p illus lib. bdg. $6.48 (3-6)   598

1 Birds 2 Birds—Eggs and nests
ISBN 0-688-31098-2   LC 52-5931

Fifty-two species of birds and the type of nests they build are presented; for each species, the author describes the nest, where it is built, the eggs, their color and size, song, and habits of the bird." Kansas Sch Naturalist

"Olive L. Earle has made ready reference easy with the index, but the pictures and presentation of the material tempt one to read the whole of this short book." Library J

State birds and flowers. Morrow 1961 64p illus maps lib. bdg. $5.52   598

1 State birds 2 State flowers
ISBN 0-688-31536-4   LC 61-8023

A revised reprint of the title first published 1951
This small book is arranged alphabetically by state. Included for each state are a sketch of the state, indicating capital, and black and white illustrations of the indigenous bird and flower. Information is also included about the appearance, growth, and reproduction of the flowers. For birds a description, the activities, and the off-spring of each are given

"Excellent introduction to the geography of the states as well as a book for nature lovers of all ages." Library J

Eberle, Irmengarde

Penguins live here. Doubleday 1975 36p illus $4.95 (3-5)   598

1 Penguins
ISBN 0-385-05715-6   LC 74-1383

This "description of the migration, mating and nesting patterns of the Adelie penguin . . . includes background material about the penguin's adjustment to its environment and about man's discovery of the penguin during exploration of the antarctic continent. The continuous text focuses on the behavior of a single pair of birds." Chicago. Children's Bk Center

"Descriptions of nest building, incubation, natural enemies, and caring for the young are quietly informative; black-and-white photographs face each page of text, and the omission of an index is compensated for by the book's brevity and narrow focus." Booklist

Eimerl, Sarel

Gulls. Simon & Schuster 1969 64p illus lib. bdg. $3.79 (3-5)   598

1 Gulls
ISBN 0-671-65079-3   LC 76-86944

The author describes the various members of the gull family, their ranges, feeding and hunting habits, migrations, breeding grounds and courtship rites. He also discusses the role instinct plays in the gull's ability to survive

"Graceful design complements the excellent photographs of lovely gulls. Text and photos are well coordinated." Sci Bks

Fisher, Harvey I.

Wonders of the world of the albatross [by] Harvey I. Fisher and Mildred L. Fisher; illus. with photographs by Harvey I. Fisher. Dodd 1974 80p illus lib. bdg. $5.95 (4 and up)   598

1 Albatrosses
ISBN 0-396-06880-4   LC 73-15036

"Dodd, Mead Wonders books"
"This book describes the life of the Laysan Albatross, the 'gooney bird' of Midway Island in the Pacific. With black and white photographs and text appropriate for the upper elementary bird enthusiast, the authors introduce the physical characteristics of these largest of sea birds. Topographical, meteorological and other features of the islands inhabited by the albatross are discussed.

An interesting part of the book deals with the bird-man encounters on these islands. The life cycle of the albatross is treated in detail. Separate chapters describe nesting, the young chicks, maturation of the fledglings, their departure for the sea, flying skills, securing nesting territory, winning a mate, and the first nesting of the young adults." Sci and Children

"The most delightful aspect of the book, making a pleasure of even the briefest perusal, is the abundant selection of black-and-white photographs. Their clarity, beauty, and even humor more than make up for their lack of color." Appraisal

Flanagan, Geraldine Lux

Window into a nest, by Geraldine Lux Flanagan and Sean Morris. Houghton [1976 c1975] 96p illus $10.95 (5 and up)   598

1 Birds—Eggs and nests
ISBN 0-395-21895-0   LC 75-17028

First published 1975 in England
"A nesting box with open back was built against a window, the window was covered with black cloth, and the cloth could be stealthily pulled aside for observation and photography. Thus the authors were able to record minute details of the events of the nest, as the birds imitated nest-cupping, the patterns of egg-brooding, the incessant activity of feeding seven chicks (including solving such problems as coping with an oversize, uncooperative caterpillar), and the preparation for flight." Chicago. Children's Bk Center

Ford, Barbara

How birds learn to sing; illus. with photographs by Bob Combs. Messner 1975 96p illus lib. bdg. $5.79 (4 and up)   598

1 Bird song
ISBN 0-671-32729-1   LC 74-28482

The author "presents the work of several well-known experts in her study of how birds learn to sing. The opening chapter distinguishes the difference between a bird call and a bird song. Both male and female birds use calls to provide information about such items as danger and food. Songs are usually only sung by male birds to call their mates and claim territory. The author presents the results of studies made with various birds. Charts, diagrams, and black and white photographs clarify the text. The types, number, and lengths of bird songs are studied." Appraisal

"The well-written text clearly defines unfamiliar terms which are spelled phonetically, and it is profusely illustrated with photographs of birds in natural habitats and in laboratories. A useful glossary and index conclude the coverage of this heretofore unexplored subject." Sch Library J

Freedman, Russell

How birds fly; drawings by Lorence F. Bjorklund. Holiday House 1977 64p illus $7.95 (4-6)   598

1 Birds—Flight
ISBN 0-8234-0301-7   LC 77-555

An "explanation of bird flight, beginning with anatomy, details of feathers, and various air currents. Freedman also relates the flight of birds to that of airplanes." Sch Library J

"Illustrated by soft pencil drawings, meticulously detailed, a simple, lucid text moves logically from those features of bird anatomy that contribute to the ability to fly, to general principles of flight, and then—in brief chapters—to separate aspects of birds' flight: getting lift, gliding or flapping, taking off or landing, etc. Freedman also discusses the differences between different kinds of birds and their flying speeds. A glossary and an index are appended." Chicago. Children's Bk Center
Bibliography included in Author's note: p4

Freschet, Berniece

The owl and the prairie dog; pictures by Gilbert Riswold. Scribner 1969 unp illus $3.95 (k-4)   598

1 Owls 2 Prairie dogs
ISBN 0-684-20828-8   LC 69-17061

The author "weaves information about the habits of two wild creatures who live in symbiotic harmony into an appealing picturebook nature story about a burrowing owl that builds her nest in an abandoned hole in a prairie-dog town. Illustrations in muted earth shades dramatize the actions of natural friends and enemies in a book suitable for reading aloud and for use in primary grade nature study." Booklist

Gans, Roma

Bird talk; illus. by Jo Polseno. Crowell 1971 33p illus (Let's-read-and-find-out science bks) lib. bdg. $6.89 (k-3)   **598**

1 Bird song
ISBN 0-690-14593-4   LC 71-132298

"Simply written and attractively illustrated, this gives a young reader the fact that birds make different sounds for different purposes, and it explains what some of those purposes are: mating calls, warning sounds, declarations of territorial rights [and] reactions to a specific predator, et cetera." Chicago. Children's Bk Center

Birds at night; illus. by Aliki. Crowell 1968 33p illus (Let's-read-and-find-out science bks) lib. bdg. $6.89, pa $1.45 (k-2)   **598**

1 Birds
ISBN 0-690-14444-X; 0-690-01251-8   LC 68-11062

"This is successful treatment for young listeners and readers of a fascinating subject: how nature has provided for a bird's health and protection. The muted wash illustrations are beautifully matched with large clear type. The interesting text explains and illustrates with simple tables and labelled diagrams such things as why a bird has three eyelids, how a feather is constructed, and the comparative body temperatures of birds and humans." Library J

Birds eat and eat and eat; illus. by Ed Emberley. Crowell 1963 unp illus (Let's-read-and-find-out science bks) $6.95, lib. bdg. $6.89, pa $1.45 (k-2)   **598**

1 Birds
ISBN 0-690-14514-4; 0-690-14515-2; 0-690-00633-0
LC 63-9213

"With a small amount of easy-to-read text set into full-page decorative sketches, some of the pages in green and blue, a great deal of basic information about birds is given—what they eat and how they eat. The young reader is encouraged to make simple home feeders, too, and to observe for himself." Christian Sci Monitor

Hummingbirds in the garden; illus. by Grambs Miller. Crowell 1969 33p illus maps (Let's-read-and-find-out science bks) lib. bdg. $6.89 (1-3)   **598**

1 Hummingbirds
ISB 0-690-42562-7   LC 69-11083

"The ruby-throated hummingbird is the species described in this book, which differentiates between the plumage of males and females, and reviews briefly their morphology, natural history, and flight mechanics. Suggestions are offered as to how hummingbirds may be attracted to a garden and taught to feed on artificial nectar. Their seasonal migration is described." Sci Bks

It's nesting time; illus. by Kazue Mizumura. Crowell 1964 unp illus (Let's-read-and-find-out science bks) lib. bdg. $6.89, pa $1.45 (k-2)   **598**

1 Birds—Eggs and nests
ISBN 0-690-45544-5; 0-690-45549-6   LC 64-10861

"A lot about nests. . . . The author writes mainly of the materials various birds use in their nests and says very little about egglaying and care of the young." NY Times Bk Rev

"A very simply written introduction. . . . Some of the illustrations are in black and white, but many are in color and can be used as a help in identification. The book should be an incitement to bird-watching, and it should be useful in a curricular unit on nature study." Chicago. Children's Bk Center

Garelick, May

About owls; illus. by Tony Chen. Four Winds 1975 39p illus lib. bdg. $7.95 (1-3)   **598**

1 Owls
ISBN 0-590-07389-3   LC 74-31324

"The author describes the life patterns of three owls: the elf owl, the barn owl, and the great horned owl, whose habits and food differ because of their size. The little elf owl will hunt mainly for insects, whereas the great horned owl will capture opossums (misspelled in the text) and large snakes. Differences and similarities of owls

are presented in the text, which proceeds in a pleasant, narrative, sometimes conversational style." Appraisal

"In sepia drawings, the artists captures intriguing owl faces set atop picturesquely mottled bodies, and these illustrations, along with the adequate text, serve as a fine introduction to the wonders of the owl." Horn Bk

Graham, Ada

Falcon flight [by] Ada and Frank Graham; illus. by D. D. Tyler. Delacorte Press 1978 112p illus $6.95, lib. bdg. $6.46 (5 and up)   **598**

1 Falcons
ISBN 0-440-2485-4; 0-440-2486-2   LC 78-50442

"An Audubon reader"

This account of the vanishing peregrine falcon tells how the species has survived shooting, trapping and nest robbery, but almost succumbed to DDT's effect on their eggs. Efforts to breed and raise them in captivity are dealt with as are their mating habits and "family life"

"The Grahams provide a vivid look at the falcon's life in the wild, skillfully integrated with the story of its near-disappearance and the efforts being made to restore it to its former range. . . . D. D. Tyler's fine illustrations are a definite plus. . . . The 'Acknowledgements' could substitute as a bibliography for further reading." Appraisal

Harris, Lorle

Biography of a whooping crane; illus by Kaze Mizumura. Putnam 1977 63p illus lib. bdg. $5.49 (2-4)   **598**

1 Whooping cranes
ISBN 0-399-61063-4   LC 76-23240

This nature biography "follows a year in the life of a family of whooping cranes from their summer home in Canada to their winter home in Texas. The young chick is protected by his parents on the long flight from bears, eagles, high winds and hunters' guns." Babbling Bookworm

"This biography is an accurate and up-to-date account of one of our most endangered species. . . . The account is sympathetic, but not sentimental, each page dealing with the realities of daily life. The Author's Note at the end brings one up to the present on the status of the cranes and the current experiments being carried on by both United States and Canadian Wildlife Services to increase the flocks and to relocate North America's tallest bird." Appraisal

Hogner, Dorothy Childs

Birds of prey; illus. by Nils Hogner. Crowell 1969 132p illus $8.95 (4-6)   **598**

1 Birds of prey
ISBN 0-690-14585-3   LC 79-81954

The author describes nearly fifty birds of prey, telling where they live and nest, what they eat, how they may be identified, and in what parts of the United States they are found. She also discusses the conservation methods being used to save some of them from complete extinction

"Easily read text, carefully drawn, accurate illustrations, and an open-looking format." Booklist

Hoke, Helen

Owls [by] Helen Hoke [and] Valerie Pitt; illus. by Robert Jefferson. Watts, F. 1975 [c1974] 63p illus lib. bdg. $4.47 (4-6)   **598**

1 Owls
ISBN 0-531-00832-0   LC 74-23981

"A First book"

First published 1974 in England

The text gives "coverage to the physiological features that make owls such successful predators, to their hunting habits and their prey, to their patterns of courtship, mating, nesting, and breeding. The last section of the book describes various kinds of owls, giving distinctive habits and habitats. A brief bibliography and an index are appended." Chicago. Children's Bk Center

"A well-organized, well-written general survey of owls that discusses their extraordinarily acute vision and hearing, their unique silent flight, and concludes with a discussion of several of the more interesting species from around the world. The text is generously illustrated with detailed black-and-white line drawings." Sch Library J

Hopf, Alice L.

Biography of a snowy owl; illus. by Fran Stiles. Putnam 1979 62p illus (A Nature biography bk) lib. bdg. $5.49 (3-5)   598

1 Snowy owl
ISBN 0-399-61130-4   LC 78-16533

This book, which follows the life cycle of the snowy owl, provides "information about their natural enemies (fox, jaeger), their food supplies (mice, squirrels), their migration habits, and the peculiar necessity of having lemmings available for food at mating time. . . . [One] particular owl [described in the narrative] experiences contact with humans when it lives for a time near an airport and is saved from destruction by a trapper who uses padded traps to catch the bird and releases it unharmed in a national park." Booklist

"This book is illustrated with attractive line drawings depicting various events in the story." AAAS Sci Bks & Films

Hosie's aviary; pictures by Leonard Baskin; words mostly by Tobias Baskin & [others]. Viking 1979 unp illus $10   598

1 Birds
ISBN 0-670-37965-4   LC 78-27027

These 21 "watercolor paintings, which generally occupy a full page, depict a variety of birds. . . . The brief texts accompanying each painting were mostly supplied by the artist's family." Horn Bk

"The pictures are stunning in their vigor, in the use of color, and in the way the artist has captured the personality of each bird. The layout is handsome and spacious, the text of variable quality: some descriptions have a haiku quality . . . while others . . . serve only as captions, and still others seem obscure . . . or intricate. . . . Younger children can enjoy the beauty of the paintings alone." Chicago. Children's Bk Center

Kaufmann, John

Birds are flying; written and illus. by John Kaufmann. Crowell 1979 34p illus (Let's-read-and-find-out science bk) $6.95, lib. bdg. $6.89 (2-4)   598

1 Birds—Flight
ISBN 0-690-03941-7; 0-690-03942-5   LC 78-22510

"This simple text offers a good deal of accurate information about the different ways in which birds fly. The anatomical and skeletal features that give them this ability and the various flying practices of specific types of birds are demonstrated in elementary terms. The drawings strike a balance between scientific and decorative, with some effective use of gold on black and white. A clear, concise text and functional illustrations make this a useful 'beginner' introduction." Booklist

Birds in flight; written and illus. by John Kaufmann. Morrow 1970 96p illus lib. bdg. $6.48 (5 and up)   598

1 Birds—Flight
ISBN 0-688-31100-8   LC 79-101587

"Text, drawings, and diagrams comprise a fascinating as well as thorough study of bird flight. Kaufmann describes in detail the anatomy of birds and the structure and function of bird wings and feathers. He then discusses them in relation to the principles of aerodynamics, the four major methods of bird flight—gliding, soaring, flapping, and hovering—and basic bird flight maneuvers." Booklist

"This book is good fare for all birdwatchers. . . . It offers some aid in identifying birds in flight." Sci Bks

Bibliography: p92-93

Robins fly north, robins fly south; written and illus. by John Kaufmann. Crowell 1970 unp illus map lib. bdg. $6.89 (3-5)   598

1 Robins 2 Birds—Migration
ISBN 0-690-70643-X   LC 70-109907

"Sharp, clear, delicately detailed pictures of robins fill these pages with movement. The text focuses on the thesis that the movements of robins are guided by the sun's position at different times of the day. Migration, while discussed in detail, is treated as part of the robin's life-cycle and its relationship to the environment, all in the simplest of terms and straightforward style." Sat Rev

Lavine, Sigmund A.

Wonders of the eagle world; illus. with photographs. Dodd 1974 64p illus $5.95 (4 and up)   598

1 Eagles
ISBN 0-396-06911-8   LC 73-17866

"Dodd, Mead Wonders books"

This book relates myths concerning eagles and man's relationship to the birds. It also describes physical characteristics and habits, including hunting methods, migration, courtship, and the raising of young

Martin, Lynne

Peacocks; illus. by Lydia Rosier. Morrow 1975 96p illus lib. bdg. $6.96 (4-6)   598

1 Peafowl
ISBN 0-688-32032-5   LC 74-34179

An "account of many aspects of the peafowl's life. Included are facts about courtship, relationship to other birds, a fine detailed description of plumage, as well as uses by humans. The various myths and religious beliefs, as well as culinary statistics enliven this book. A good index adds to its usefulness." Appraisal

"This competently written text . . . is well complemented by soft but beautifully detailed and realistic pencil illustrations." Sch Library J

Mizumura, Kazue

The emperor penguins. Crowell 1969 35p illus (Let's-read-and-find-out science bks) lib. bdg. $6.89 (k-3)   598

1 Penguins
ISBN 0-690-26088-1   LC 69-10486

This book "describes the habits and habitat of the Emperor Penguins, with particular attention to their unusual methods of feeding and caring for their young." Chicago. Children's Bk Center

"Pre-school children and beginning readers will especially enjoy this book. After finishing the text, the reader, be he adult or child, will know about as much of the life cycle and ecology of the Emperor Penguin as a regular reader of 'Scientific American.'" Appraisal

National Geographic Society

Song and garden birds of North America by Alexander Wetmore and other eminent ornithologists; foreword by Melville Bell Grosvenor. The Society 1964 400p illus (Natural science lib) $11.95   598

1 Birds—North America 2 Birds—Pictorial works
LC 64-23367

Also available as part of a boxed set together with: Water, prey, and game birds of North America, entered below, for $20.95

At head of title: 327 species portrayed in color and fully described

General articles on birds are followed by sections on the different "species—nearly all that breed north of Mexico—[wherein you can] study its picture, and learn its life history, breeding and winter ranges, and characteristics. . . . [There are] 555 illustrations that show each bird to best advantage for identification. Where the female's plumage differs significantly from the male's, both sexes are portrayed." Preface

"Beautiful illustrations, lively and informative text and sturdy binding are combined here in a book for any library. . . . A pocket inside the back cover contains a small album, of 6 vinyl records presenting songs for 70 species." Library J

Map on lining-paper

Water, prey, and game birds of North America, by Alexander Wetmore and other eminent ornithologists; foreword by Melville Bell Grosvenor. The Society 1965 464p illus maps (Natural science lib)   598

1 Birds—North America 2 Water birds 3 Birds of prey 4 Game and game birds
LC 65-25605

Available only as part of a boxed set together with: Song and garden birds of North America, entered above, for $20.95

At head of title: 329 species portrayed in color and fully described

Life histories, breeding and feeding habits, range and characteristics of ducks, seabirds, hawks, geese, vultures and others

National Geographic Society—*Continued*

"Superbly turned out. Hardly a page without one or more photos or paintings reproduced in blazing or muted colors. Action shots, closeups, birds in colonies or caught singly against a full moon. . . . Group by group, the birds are discussed in general terms and characterized by species . . . with anecdotes that reveal more than a story. . . . This . . . book is no ordinary field guide." Sat Rev

Album of 6 vinyl records in pocket contains 97 bird sounds
Acknowledgments: p463

Peterson, Roger Tory

A field guide to the birds; giving field marks of all species found east of the Rockies; text and illus. by Roger Tory Peterson. 2d rev. enl. ed. Sponsored by National Audubon Society. Houghton 1947 xxiv, 290p illus map $9.95, pa $5.95　　598

1 Birds—North America
ISBN 0-395-08082-7; 0-395-08083-5　　LC 47-5163

"The Peterson Field guide series"
Companion volume to: A field guide to Western birds, listed below
First published 1934

A "guide to the field marks of Eastern birds, designed to help in identifying live birds at a distance. . . . The text gives field marks, such as range, habits, manner of flight, etc., that can not be pictured. In addition it mentions birds that might in any instance be confused with a given species." NY Libraries

"This book was written for 'popular' guidance. It is distinctly for amateurs, beginning or advanced. . . . It is, in fact, a fine compendium of 'field marks' and the 'field mark' is as helpful to the wandering bird student as the highway signs are to a motoring tourist." NY Times Bk Rev

Includes 60 plates in color and black and white and many line drawings
Home reference suggestions: p273-74

A field guide to Western birds. . . . Text and illus. by Roger Tory Peterson. 2d ed. rev. and enl. Sponsored by the National Audubon Society and National Wildlife Federation. Houghton 1961 xxvi, 366p illus map $10.95, pa $6.95　　598

1 Birds—The West (U.S.)　2 Birds—North America
ISBN 0-395-08085-1; 0-395-13692-X　　LC 60-12250

"The Peterson Field guide series"
First published 1941
Companion volume to A field guide to the birds, entered above

"Field marks of all species found in North America west of the 100th meridian, with a section on the birds of the Hawaiian Islands." Title page

"This compact, but complete little work employs [a] system of field identification based upon the characteristic features of the birds and facilitating quick recognition at a distance." Springf'd Republican

Pringle, Laurence

Listen to the crows; illus. by Ted Lewin. Crowell 1976 33p illus $7.89 (3-6)　　598

1 Crows
ISBN 0-690-01069-9　　LC 75-43535

The author "introduces readers to the work of several researchers who have pinned down specifics such as assembly and dispersal calls and who speculate on a much wider range of crow 'language.' Aspects of a crow behavior emerge throughout the discussions, although this is not really a comprehensive introduction to the species. It stands as an amiable, narrowly focused study that introduces readers to an intriguing phenomenon for its own sake." Booklist

"The book is well written, and holds the reader's attention, but the various facets of crow communication would be better emphasized if occasional subheadings were given, but an adequate index is included. The book is enhanced by numerous drawings which are well done and true to life." AAAS Sci Bks & Films

Schick, Alice

The peregrine falcons; pictures by Peter Parnall. Dial Press 1975 83p illus $5.95, lib. bdg. $5.47 (5 and up)　　598

1 Falcons
ISBN 0-8037-4917-6; 0-8037-4972-4　　LC 74-18599

"Zeus and Artemis mate in the Palisades of the Hudson River. Their life cycle is complete as three young peregrines hatch, learn to fly, and catch their own food (smaller birds). Then follows the gradual disappearance of the falcons, probably due to DDT. New hope for the peregrine arises from an imaginative project at Cornell, when a scientist brings young peregrines from nests in the Arctic tundra. One learns of the process involved in saving a species, and the plans for their eventual release." Sci and Children

"The clarity of the writing and the excellent illustrations make this book suitable for a comparatively wide age-range, and it can be highly recommended to all children interested in natural history and ecology." AAAS Sci Bks & Films

Bibliography: p[85]

Scott, Jack Denton

Canada geese; photographs by Ozzie Sweet. Putnam 1976 64p illus $6.95 (4 and up)　　598

1 Geese
ISBN 0-399-20492-X　　LC 76-871

"Pictures and text are devoted to the geese's precision flights, the instinct which urges them to flee south before the first killing frosts, the way they choose leaders for their exhausting V-formation flight (which sometimes takes them as high as 9000 feet) and other facts about the superb navigators." Pub W

"There is no obtrusive introduction of facts, but they emerge with quiet authority in a book written with no sentimentality but great appreciation. The photographs, carefully placed in relation to textual references, are clear and handsome, whether they are informative close shots or stunning pictures of a skein of geese silhouetted against a moonlit sky." Chicago. Children's Bk Center

Discovering the mysterious egret; photographs by Ozzie Sweet, with line drawings by Pamela Sweet Distler. Harcourt 1978 53p illus $7.95 (4-6)　　598

1 Herons
ISBN 0-15-223593-0　　LC 77-88967

Text and photographs describe the habits of the enigmatic cattle egret. A native of East Africa, weighing approximately four pounds, it lives amongst herds of grazing cattle, hippopotamus and rhinoceros

"The text is lengthy and very inclusive, covering the egret from birth to maturity to death. The photographs both complement and expand the factual information. An excellent resource for both African and ornithological information." Sch Library J

The gulls of Smuttynose Island; words by Jack Denton Scott; photographs by Ozzie Sweet. Putnam 1977 62p illus $7.95 (4-6)　　598

1 Gulls　2 Smuttynose Island
ISBN 0-399-20618-3　　LC 77-7870

"This book reports on the gull population of an island off the New England coast. Scott tells many interesting facts about the strong bird—unusually adapted for survival by reason of its social habits mainly—and corrects several misconceptions about the 'sea gull.'" Pub W

"Another beautiful, well-written book from this author/photographer team. Striking black-and-white photographs of gulls on Smuttynose, a major nesting area, highlight some surprising information on types of gulls, their mating, nesting, feeding, and flying habits. School libraries will want this inviting, attractive photo essay to tempt nonreaders as well as young wildlife enthusiasts." Sch Library J

Map on lining papers

The submarine bird; photographs by Ozzie Sweet. Putnam 1980 63p illus $8.95 (4 and up)　　598

1 Cormorants
ISBN 0-399-20701-5　　LC 79-18297

This book about the cormorant "describes courting, mating, nesting, the habits and care of the young, the first flights at about six weeks, and the

Scott, Jack D.—*Continued*

social habits and appearance of nestlings and adult birds. Most interesting to the majority of readers may well be the section that describes the way the cormorant, with its keen eyesight and aquatic ability, spots and dives for prey, a talent used by Oriental fishermen to help them gather fish." Chicago. Children's Bk Center

"Scott's polished text is particularly interesting where it describes features of the bird that substantiate the theory of avian evolution from reptiles. . . . The many engrossing facts about the 'submarine bird' are illustrated by Sweet's remarkable photos taken at rookeries where thousands of birds are massed and in various parts of the world. But the most striking, literally in-depth shots are those taken under-water, showing how the sharp-eyed, powerful bird dives below 200 ft., to catch fish for itself or the fishermen." Pub W

That wonderful pelican; photographs by Ozzie Sweet. Putnam 1975 63p illus $6.95 (5 and up) **598**

1 Pelicans
ISBN 0-399-20449-0   LC 74-21064

"The book gives information about the fact that many species are endangered, describes the habitats of species, and goes into full detail about the brown pelicans of Florida's Pelican Island: mating, nesting, parental care, feeding and flight patterns, et cetera." Chicago. Children's Bk Center

"The pelican's life-cycle, habits, and anatomy are covered, and the species is put into historical perspective. The photographs are unusual and add greatly to the appeal of the book, which will inspire many with an appreciation of these amazing birds." Appraisal

Selsam, Millicent E.

A first look at birds, by Millicent E. Selsam and Joyce Hunt; illus. by Harriett Springer. Walker & Co. [1974 c1973] 35p illus lib. bdg. $5.39 (1-3) **598**

1 Birds
ISBN 0-8027-6164-X   LC 73-81404

This book "invites the young child to use his powers of observation and learn to identify birds. Simple questions and matching games encourage the child to notice color, size, shape, feet, and feathers—important factors in bird identification. The illustrations are large, clear and well-labeled. Red and blue are used in the section on colors, but all other illustrations are black and white." Appraisal

"The value of the book lies in its single, uncomplicated purpose and in the simplicity of its approach to the study of birds. A good companion to more colorful, encyclopedic volumes." Booklist

Tony's birds; illus. by Kurt Werth. Harper 1961 64p illus (A Science I can read bk) $5.95, lib. bdg. $6.89 (k-2) **598**

1 Bird watching
ISBN 0-06-025420-3; 0-06-025421-1   LC 61-5775

"Birdwatching is the subject. With the help of his father, Tony learns to use binoculars and a bird guidebook to find and identify birds. Two- and three-color pictures and clear print make an attractive easy-to-read book which makes birdwatching an interesting activity." Horn Bk

Shaw, Evelyn

A nest of wood ducks; pictures by Cherryl Pape. Harper 1976 60p illus (A Science I can read bk) $5.95, lib. bdg. $6.89 (1-3) **598**

1 Ducks
ISBN 0-06-025591-9; 0-06-025592-7   LC 76-3833

A "chronology of major events in the life of the wood duck begins in early spring when a hen makes her nest deep in a tree hole several feet above the ground. She lays eight eggs and, after the ducklings hatch, encourages them to climb out of the nest and float down to the water. Although two of the young fall prey to natural enemies, the rest survive and mature and, when autumn comes, join other ducks migrating for the winter. The account comes full circle the following spring when another young hen in search of a nesting site finds the very tree in which she was hatched; and the cycle begins again. Three-color drawings suggest the magnificent plumage of the drake and the quieter colors of hen and ducklings and give vitality to the many illuminating details of the story." Horn Bk

Simon, Hilda

Bird and flower emblems of the United States. Dodd 1978 128p illus $7.95 (4 and up) **598**

1 State birds 2 State flowers
ISBN 0-396-07581-9   LC 78-7324

"This book is essentially a full-color portrait gallery of all the state flowers and birds of the United States, accompanied by short, informative paragraphs. In order to avoid confusion and assure equal treatment for every state, those birds and flowers that were chosen by more than one were repeated for each state, with only minor variations and additions to both text and pictures." Introduction

"Simon's illustrations are carefully and naturally conceived. Comments on the physical appearance, behavioral characteristics, and reasons for the selection of both flower and bird are given. . . . A general introduction surveys the use of flower and bird emblems throughout history, and a list of scientific names is appended." Booklist

Stemple, David

High ridge gobbler; a story of the American wild turkey; illus. by Ted Lewin. Collins [distributed by Philomel Bks.] 1979 47p illus $7.95 (3-5) **598**

1 Wild turkeys
ISBN 0-529-05524-4   LC 78-24200

This book follows an eastern wild turkey from birth to maturity. Explained along the way are the hatching process, food gathering, mating, territoriality and warning devices taught to the young

"Accompanying the brisk, knowledgeable text are expressive pencil drawings depicting the birds in their natural arena. . . . Author's note on the environmental status of the American turkey is appended." Booklist

Stonehouse, Bernard

Penguins; illus. by Trevor Boyer. McGraw 1979 48p illus (A McGraw-Hill New biology) $7.95 (4 and up) **598**

1 Penguins
ISBN 0-07-061740-6   LC 79-13661

First published 1978 in England

This book discusses the evolution and history of penguins, the characteristics which distinguish them from all other birds, and their enemies on land and in the water. Physical details and behavior patterns are given for the several species of penguins who occur in different environments in the Southern hemisphere in Australia, New Zealand, South America, South Africa and Antarctica. Particular attention is given to the life cycle of the Gentoo penguins on the island of South Georgia in the South Atlantic

Vevers, Gwynne

Birds and their nests; illus. by Colin Threadgall. McGraw [1973 c1971] 32p illus (A McGraw-Hill Natural science picture bk) lib. bdg. $5.72 (1-4) **598**

1 Birds—Eggs and nests
ISBN 0-07-067414-0   LC 72-11452

First published 1971 in England

"Here are descriptions and illustrations of a variety of nests; open, stick, weaver-bird, hangnests, nests of mud and saliva, nests on and in the ground, on water, in tree trunks, in other birds nests, in bowers, in mounds and even penguins' portable ones. One or two examples of birds or families of birds which construct nests of each type are given along with a bit of natural history and geography. On the last page the author discusses conservation. She suggests that one observe and possibly photograph nests but warns against disturbing the nest or the young. The illustrations, colored and black-and-white, all are attractive and realistic." Sci Bks

Zim, Herbert S.
Birds; a guide to the most familiar American birds, by Herbert S. Zim and Ira N. Gabrielson; illus. by James Gordon Irving. 125 birds in full color. Sponsored by The Wildlife Management Institute. [Rev. ed] Golden Press 1956 60p illus maps (A Golden Nature guide) lib. bdg. $9.15, pa $1.95   **598**

1 Birds
ISBN 0-307-63505-8; 0-307-24490-3   LC 56-4593
First published 1949 by Simon & Schuster
This book "pictures 129 well-known American birds in full color, with descriptions in the text of additional species, enabling the reader to identify 250 birds. Includes a table of data on migration, eggs, kinds and locations of nests, and natural food for each illustrated bird." The AAAS Sci Bk List for Children

Owls. Newly rev. ed. Illus. by James Gordon Irving and René Martin. Morrow 1977 60p illus lib. bdg. $6 (3-5)   **598**

1 Owls
ISBN 0-688-32109-7   LC 76-52927
First published 1950
"This small book is a storehouse of information on owls. While written for young audiences and printed in large type with well-spaced lines, anyone with an interest in owls would enjoy it. North American owls are emphasized, although owls from many parts of the world are mentioned. Numerous black-and-white sketches illustrate various aspects of owl natural history, including their unique adaptations for hunting. . . . A few facts presented are oversimplified, but the book is not intended to be a technical treatise. In general 'Owls' is well done . . . and deserving of a place on the shelves of school libraries. The sizes of the owls are given in metric measure." AAAS Sci Bks & Films

599 Mammals

Burt, William Henry
A field guide to the mammals. . . . Text and maps by William Henry Burt; illus. by Richard Philip Grossenheider. 3d ed. Sponsored by the National Audubon Society and National Wildlife Federation. Houghton 1976 xxv, 289p illus maps $9.95, pa $5.95   **599**

1 Mammals
ISBN 0-395-24082-4; 0-395-24084-0   LC 75-26885
"The Peterson Field guide series"
"Field marks of all North American species found north of Mexico." Title page
First published 1952
"Describes 380 terrestrial and marine species and gives, for most of them, life history data, distribution (shown by map) and economic status. Measurements are in metric as well as conventional units. The tracks and the dental formulas for key species are given. A bibliography lists mammal faunas by states and provinces. (Bryde's Whale is misspelled.) The eight plates with black-and-white photographs of 101 skulls are poor because of shadow illumination and black backgrounds. Twenty-eight color plates reproduce quite faithfully the subtle browns and grays of mammalian pelage." AAAS Sci Bks & Films
References: p271-76

Jordan, E. L.
Animal atlas of the world. Hammond 1969 224p illus maps $16.95   **599**

1 Mammals 2 Geographical distribution of animals and plants
ISBN 0-8437-1600-2   LC 75-83276
This book describes the habits and behavior of mammals in the mountains and tundras, deserts and oceans, rain forests and ice caps of the world. It also includes distribution maps, showing the range of the species; a geologic time chart of all orders; an article by the author on the world's major wildlife areas; and a zoological breakdown of the orders of mammals
"The atlas, with an Introduction about the efforts made around the globe to preserve some of the threatened species of wild life, . . . is a superb piece of book making. . . . The short account of each of the 182 different species [included] is succinct and greatly informative." Best Sellers

McClung, Robert M.
Hunted mammals of the sea; illus. by William Downey. Morrow 1978 191p illus maps $7.95, lib. bdg. $7.63 (5 and up)   **599**

1 Marine animals 2 Mammals 3 Rare animals
ISBN 0-688-22146-7; 0-688-32146-1   LC 77-25388
McClung presents "the life cycle of the great whales, along with historical data on whaling and discussion of . . . the danger of overkill. The dolphin, the sea otter, the walrus, the polar bear and other creatures—some of them now exterminated—are described in a similar manner." America
This is "an intelligent, concerned book which avoids the easy emotionalism often surrounding endangered species. . . . The balanced, thoughtful presentation is also highly readable, and is recommended for any collection which needs information on marine life or on endangered animals. There is a list of common and scientific names, a bibliography, and an index, as well as a chart of whale species, characteristics, and status. . . . Downey's illustrations are superb." Appraisal

National Geographic Society
Wild animals of North America. The Society 1979 406p illus maps (Natural science lib) $14.95   **599**

1 Mammals
ISBN 0-87044-292-5   LC 79-18452
First published 1960
"Discusses briefly the characteristics and evolution of mammals in general, then examines the common species in each of the major orders represented in North America. Their appearance, habits, distribution, and frequent personal accounts of observation are included. The beautiful illustrations alone warrant the purchase of this outstanding book . . . and the comprehensive text by . . . leading naturalists is enthusiastically presented and well-integrated." AAAS Sci Bk List for Young Adults [review of first edition]

Zim, Herbert S.
Mammals; a guide to familiar American species, by Herbert S. Zim and Donald F. Hoffmeister; illus. by James Gordon Irving. 218 animals in full color. Sponsored by The Wildlife Management Institute. Golden Press 1955 160p illus maps (A Golden Nature guide) lib. bdg. $9.15, pa $1.95   **599**

1 Mammals
ISBN 0-307-63510-4; 0-307-24497-0   LC 61-8320
First published by Simon & Schuster
This book "gives the appearance, measurements, and distinguishing characteristics of common North American mammals in each major order and family. This handbook also supplies information on mammals in general—traits, evolution, and hints for studying them. Each description is accompanied by a picture and a keyed map showing its present and original ranges, or compares its distribution to that of a related species." Sci Bks

599.2 Marsupials

Darling, Louis
Kangaroos and other animals with pockets; written and illus. by Louis Darling. Morrow 1958 64p illus maps lib. bdg. $5.52 (4-6) **599.2**

1 Kangaroos 2 Marsupials
ISBN 0-688-31501-1   LC 58-8497
"A compact and informative book about marsupial mammals of the world; their evolution from a common ancestor and their isolation on the Australian continent is explained. An unusual feature in this book is the use of paired drawings of marsupial animals and their comparable forms among the pouchless mammals. The distinguishing features and habits of the red kangaroo are described in detail as an example of the marsupial's life." Chicago. Children's Bk Center
"Although easy enough for the beginning reader, it should have appeal for any child interested in these fascinating animals." Library J

Eberle, Irmengarde

Koalas live here. Doubleday 1967 59p illus
lib. bdg. $6.95 (1-3)   **599.2**

1 Koalas

ISBN 0-385-08719-5   LC 67-17779

"Appealing full-page photographs and succinct
text describe the characteristics and natural life
of the koala and the ways in which man contributes to the protection and survival of these
Australian animals in their native habitat." Booklist

Freschet, Berniece

Possum baby; illus. by Jim Arnosky.
Putnam 1978 45p illus lib. bdg. $6.29 (k-3)   **599.2**

1 Opossums

ISBN 0-399-61105-3   LC 77-21000

"A See and read nature story"

The author "has a rare gift for writing about
nature. Without overstepping the fine line into
anthropomorphism, she informs her readers in a
style that is more like storytelling than factual
exposition. It is perfect for telling her young readers about the life and development of a young
opossum. Jim Arnosky's black ink drawings are
the illustrator's parallel to that style. They generally add to the effect, except on those occasions
when his use of cartoon conventions distract from
the book's flow." Children's Bk Rev Serv

Jenkins, Marie M.

Kangaroos, opossums, and other marsupials;
drawings by Matthew Kalmenoff. Holiday
House 1975 160p illus $7.95 (5 and up)   **599.2**

1 Marsupials

ISBN 0-8234-0264-9   LC 75-10798

"A clear, well-organized examination of the
various kinds of marsupials. . . . [The author]
describes kangaroos, which bear only one baby
at a time but keep a second embryo in reserve;
koalas, which eat only leaves from a few species
of eucalyptus trees; and quolls, bandicoots, wom-
bats, and wallabies, all equally unusual and fascinating creatures. With the North American opossum being one of the few exceptions, most marsupials are found in Australia, and the author
cites continental drift theories to explain why. She
also includes several nonmarsupial Australian
mammals such as the duckbill platypus and spiny
anteater, which are monotremes." Booklist

Suggested reading: p151-54

Lavine, Sigmund A.

Wonders of marsupials; illus. with photographs and old prints. Dodd [1979 c1978]
80p illus $5.95 (4 and up)   **599.2**

1 Marsupials

ISBN 0-396-07619-X   LC 78-7745

"Dodd, Mead Wonders books"

"The wombat, numbat, and Tasmanian devil are
but a few of the creatures introduced along with
more commonly known marsupials such as the
kangaroo, koala, and opossum. . . . Readers will
learn the function of the pouch (all marsupials
have them—marsupial means pouch) plus diverse
eating habits and behavior patterns of some of
the approximately 250 living species." Sch Library J

"This highly informative book is illustrated with
well-captioned black-and-white photographs and
drawings; yet there are no illustrations of marsupial pouches." Sci and Children

Rau, Margaret

The gray kangaroo at home; with drawings
by Eva Hülsmann. Knopf 1978 89p illus
map $5.95, lib. bdg. $5.99 (5 and up)   **599.2**

1 Kangaroos

ISBN 0-394-83451-2; 0-394-93451-8   LC 77-14942

The author "focuses on a doe and her 'young-
at-foot,' a joey who at nine months has to live
outside her pouch because she is carrying another
suckling infant inside it. Existence is an acute
struggle for the kangaroo mob and other marsupials because of gunners, animal predators, eagles,
and most dramatic, a dry electric storm resulting
in a fire that burns for days. . . . An epilogue
makes a plea on behalf of endangered species: a
bibliography lists books, scientific papers, periodicals, and interviews." Horn Bk

"A beautifully written nature book. . . . A few
carefully done full page charcoal illustrations add
to the appeal of this thoroughly enjoyable volume." Appraisal

599.32   Rodents. Rabbits

Alston, Eugenia

Come visit a prairie dog town; illus. by
St Tamara. Harcourt 1976 60p illus $4.95,
pa $1.95 (1-4)   **599.32**

1 Prairie dogs

ISBN 0-15-219480-0; 0-15-219481-9   LC 75-37005

"A Let me read book"

This book "describes prairie dog society and its
interactions with the environment and other animals. The contrast between ferrets and prairie
dogs is not developed enough to be very helpful;
however, Alston successfully covers the rearing
of the young, maintenance of mounds and burrows,
food, enemies, and hazards." Sch Library J

"Large type and short, simple sentences make
this book a desirable learning experience for the
early reader. The account of the natural history of
prairie dogs is detailed and factual. The author
recounts many incidents in a typical day of a
prairie dog family without structuring the book
around a central plot. . . . Some words that are
likely to be new to the young reader are defined,
but occasionally a generic term is defined only in
terms of the specific usage of the book. . . . The
many pen-and-ink drawings, which are executed
by an accomplished artist, will charm the reader."
AAAS Sci Bks & Films

Brady, Irene

Wild mouse. Scribner 1976 unp illus $6.95
(2-4)   **599.32**

1 Mice   2 Reproduction

ISBN 0-680-14664-9   LC 76-14912

"This small book introduces us to a wild mouse
in the author's kitchen and through diary entries
follows the small creature through two months
and the birth and early days of three baby mice.
The format is that of a picture book on every
page. The author observes their birth, growth, and
behavior and records it in brief, but descriptive
entries that will inform and entertain children."
Children's Bk Rev Serv

"A delightful exploration in diary form of the
pregnancy of a wild mouse and the birth of her
babies is illustrated [by the author] with delicate,
fine drawings in pale brown and pink. . . . The
author's obvious affection for and gentle treatment
of wild animals combine with careful scientific
observations and graceful pictures to make a
simple and lovely nature book." Horn Bk

Eberle, Irmengarde

Prairie dogs in prairie dog town; illus. by
John Hamberger. Crowell 1974 53p illus
$7.95 (2-5)   **599.32**

1 Prairie dogs

ISBN 0-690-00069-3   LC 73-9921

"Set in one of the nation's state parks, this
satisfactory nature study examines the life of a
family of prairie dogs: how they communicate
through barks and chatterings, their response to
such intruders as owls and snakes, and their cooperative relationships." Sch Library J

"This easily readable book has lavish illustrations on nearly every page which will help to hold
the interest of young readers or even younger
listeners. The book is informative, interesting and
recommended." Sci Bks

Freschet, Berniece

Bear mouse; illus. by Donald Carrick.
Scribner 1973 unp illus lib. bdg. $6.95 (2-4)   **599.32**

1 Mice

ISBN 0-684-13320-2   LC 72-13745

This is the "story of a meadow mouse that ventures forth in the winter snow to feed herself and
thus sustain her nursing brood. She narrowly
escapes an owl and a bobcat, and in her frantic
effort to hide discovers a lifesaving cache of
food." Booklist

"The story of her day with its many small crises,
frustrations, and fears makes a moving narrative,
vivid because of the precise details of surroundings
and actions, and enriched by language both realistic and poetic. Handsome watercolors illustrate
the two worlds of the mouse; the hidden world
safe beneath the snow; and the cold upper world
where fox, owl, hawk, and bobcat are dramatically
pictured as threats to her existence." Horn Bk

Freschet, Berniece—*Continued*

"This is a quiet book, with neither plot nor anthropomorphization, but it is accurate in the information it gives about the mouse and the food-chain of which she is a part, and it also communicates a sense of affection for wild life and natural beauty." Chicago. Children's Bk Center

Porcupine baby; with pictures by Jim Arnosky. Putnam 1978 47p illus (A See and read nature story) lib. bdg. $6.29 (k-3)   **599.32**

1 Porcupines
ISBN 0-399-61101-0   LC 77-4199

"Three interrelated tales, which lie somewhere between story and nature essay. . . . Descriptive information about the physical characteristics, natural environment, and feeding forages make up part one; in the second, Porcupine Baby's mother teaches him about his secret weapon of sharp quills; and in the third, he nearly meets his match in an experienced, crafty fox. Arnosky's black ink drawings are not of the identification guide variety and are most pleasing when capturing the antics of the young animal." Booklist

Hess, Lilo

Mouse and company; story and photographs by Lilo Hess. Scribner 1972 46p illus lib. bdg. $5.95 (3-5)   **599.32**

1 Mice 2 Rodents
ISBN 0-684-12810-1   LC 76-37188

This book "is crammed with useful and interesting information, without seeming stuffed. It begins by giving a brief natural history of a female deer mouse, introducing the concept of territory, giving the gestation period and something of the classification; all as a natural part of the story. Other common rodents, especially mice—wild and domestic, and including rats, gerbils and hamsters, are discussed in the balance of the book. The essentials of rodent raising and maze-building are also covered. Mrs. Hess has written a book that doesn't talk down to intelligent young people and includes pictures that will appeal to all." Sci Bks

McNulty, Faith

Woodchuck; pictures by Joan Sandin. Harper 1974 64p illus (A Science I can read bk) $5.95, lib. bdg. $6.89 (1-3)   **599.32**

1 Marmots
ISBN 0-06-024166-7; 0-06-024167-5   LC 74-3585

"A year in the life of a small creature of fields and meadows is presented with clarity, simplicity, and effectiveness. . . . Accompanied by realistic illustrations containing just enough detail to supplement the text, the activities of a female woodchuck are followed from the end of one hibernation period to the beginning of the next. No hint of anthropomorphism or sentimentality mars the objectivity of the story, as the animal responds to the first stirrings of spring, leaves the security of her underground home to find food, evades enemies, mates, raises a family, and finally, in late autumn, returns once again to another deep, safe sleep." Horn Bk

Newton, James R.

The march of the lemmings; illus. by Charles Robinson. Crowell 1976 34p illus (Let's-read-and-find-out science bks) lib. bdg. $7.89 (2-4)   **599.32**

1 Lemmings
ISBN 0-690-01085-0   LC 75-42491

A description of "the changes in behavior of lemmings in a community that has become overpopulated. Once friendly, the animals are now hostile and restless; they begin their inexorable march across the countryside to the sea, where they drown. And those lemmings left in the colony, with ample room and food, begin the cycle again. Newton discusses briefly the theories held by scientists as to what triggers the suicidal procession, making it clear that there are no answers yet." Chicago. Children's Bk Center

"This is an attractive well-written picture book which describes the life and mystery of the small furry rodents called lemmings. . . . The black-and-white and blue-and-brown illustrations add to the book's appeal and convey the harsh realities of this true life drama very well." Appraisal

Rounds, Glen

The beaver; how he works; written and illus. by Glen Rounds. Holiday House 1976 unp illus lib. bdg. $6.95 (2-4)   **599.32**

1 Beavers
ISBN 0-8234-0287-8   LC 76-15027

This "volume is devoted entirely to the single-minded industry of a beaver as he selects a stream to be the site for his new home, tunnels temporary living quarters into the bank, and then proceeds to dam the stream and eventually to construct a secure, water-tight dwelling in the middle of the pond he has created. Spare pen-and-ink drawings . . . show the beaver in numerous positions as he goes about his work. Despite the untidy aspect of his completed dam and the ecological havoc he has caused in drowning meadows and ruining trees, he earns respect for his use of the materials at hand—shrubs, trees, mud, rotting water plants." Horn Bk

"In a quietly teasing but entirely informative text, artist-storyteller Rounds describes the beaver. . . . His pen drawings, less scratchy here than usual, picture one busy subject." Booklist

Scott, Jack Denton

Little dogs of the prairie; words by Jack Denton Scott; photographs by Ozzie Sweet. Putnam 1977 62p illus $7.95 (5 and up)   **599.32**

1 Prairie dogs
ISBN 0-399-20561-6   LC 76-56217

"Photographs show a host of prairie dogs in various positions, and the text describes their daily activities, burrows, communicative barks, natural enemies, mating habits, sentries, and sub-species; it also discusses the systematic poisoning and the loss of habitat which have resulted in the dwindling population of the animals." Horn Bk

"It is illustrated with black-and-white photographs and a few pencil drawings of the underground tunnel and a family of young 'dogs.' The book has a sensitivity for the place of the prairie dog as a part of nature. It portrays a faithful picture of an interesting little animal." Appraisal

Shuttlesworth, Dorothy E.

The story of rodents; illus. by Lydia Rosier. Doubleday 1971 95p illus lib. bdg. $5.90 (3-6)   **599.32**

1 Rodents
ISBN 0-385-04689-8   LC 71-103922

The book "discusses briefly the physical appearance, behavior, diet, and relationship with man of various species of mice, rats, squirrels, lemmings, beaver, porcupines, and other rodents, and describes the origins of such rodent pets as gerbils, hamsters, and guinea pigs. Black-and-white and colored drawings, more decorative than informative, illustrate the clear, readable text." Booklist

Silverstein, Alvin

Gerbils: all about them, by Alvin Silverstein and Virginia B. Silverstein; with photographs by Frederick J. Breda. Lippincott 1976 159p illus $8.95, pa $3.95 (4 and up)   **599.32**

1 Gerbils
ISBN 0-397-31660-7; 0-397-31661-5   LC 75-34390

"Although this book includes nformation on gerbils in the research field, the major thrust is to provide the novice with information on the care and handling of these animals as pets. The authors . . . present useful and practical information on the physical characteristcs, mating and birth, environmental requirements, types and selection, housing, diet, training, and health of gerbils, as well as simple observation activities and experiments." Sci and Children

"The text is profusely illustrated with more than one hundred black-and-white photos. It succeeds quite well in answering questions about gerbils. . . . [The book is] clearly written and most informative." Best Sellers

For further reading: p155

Silverstein, Alvin—*Continued*

Guinea pigs: all about them [by] Alvin & Virginia Silverstein; with photographs by Roger Kerkham. Lothrop 1972 96p illus $7.25, lib. bdg. $6.96 (3 and up)　　　**599.32**

1 Guinea pigs
ISBN 0-688-41664-0; 0-688-51664-5　　LC 74-148487

"This simple book has three sections: 1) a general orientation about guinea pigs, their origin, morphology, varieties and natural history, including a 'rodent family tree' showing their relatives; 2) 'Guinea pigs as pets,' telling how to select, house and care for them and how to breed them and raise the progeny; and 3) 'Guinea pigs in the laboratory,' describing their use in testing new drugs and investigating the causes of disease and as experimental animals for germ-free research in studies of nutrition, intelligence and heredity." Sci Bks

"Here is an excellent reference book for boys and girls interested in learning more about guinea pigs and how to care for them. The photographs are most apealing. Descriptions of the many uses of guinea pigs in medical research and genetics add depth to the contents of this volume." Appraisal

Hamsters: all about them [by] Alvin & Virginia Silverstein; with photographs by Frederick Breda. Lothrop 1974 126p illus lib. bdg. $6.96 (4 and up)　　　**599.32**

1 Hamsters
ISBN 0-688-50056-0　　　LC 74-8863

This book is a manual for the hamster owner, with information on the care, feeding, housing, and breeding of these pets. Types of hamsters and their use in laboratory research is also discussed

"It's a good, fat volume chock full of excellent photographs . . . [and] should prove to be as popular as hamsters themselves." Pub W

Rabbits: all about them [by] Alvin and Virginia Silverstein; with photographs by Roger Kerkham. Lothrop 1973 160p illus lib. bdg. $6.95 (4 and up)　　　**599.32**

1 Rabbits
ISBN 0-688-51564-9　　　LC 73-4952

"This well-organized compendium of rabbit fact and fancy gives the reader far more than other standard works on the subject. After an admirable section on care and feeding of rabbits as pets, the remaining chapters examine both the hare and rabbits as laboratory research subjects, then describe their zoological, behavioral, and ecological characteristics, and end with a tasteful survey of rabbit legend and lore. There is a bountiful assortment of instructive and endearing photographs throughout. The authors are moderately anecdotal without cheapening their straightforward writing style, which is devoid of condescension toward the young audience. Suggestions for further reading are appended." Booklist

Tunis, Edwin

Chipmunks on the doorstep; written and illus. by Edwin Tunis. Crowell 1971 69p illus lib. bdg. $7.89 (5 and up)　　　**599.32**

1 Chipmunks
ISBN 0-690-19045-X　　　LC 73-13205

"An analysis of chipmunks, their habitats, habits, and ways of making them semi-pets are presented. The author covers the etymology of the word 'chipmunk' and discusses the subspecies that survive in various regions of the world. However, particular emphases are on shape and color, locomotion, grooming habits, breeding, and eating and foraging activities, the latter including a discussion of the ways the chipmunk makes use of its sharp teeth. . . . The latter portion of the book deals with the chipmunk as predator and as prey and the way the animal uses burrows for hibernation and breeding." Sci Bks

"Because he is writing informally and affectionately about creatures he loves, the author adds to acuity of observation and meticulous detail in illustration a humor that enlivens the informative text." Sat Rev

Van Wormer, Joe

Squirrels. Dutton 1978 56p illus lib. bdg. $7.95 (3-5)　　　**599.32**

1 Squirrels
ISBN 0-525-39860-0　　　LC 78-5804

"Good black-and-white photographs [by the author] are a strength here. One to a page, they clearly picture the various squirrel family members introduced and briefly described in the text. These include woodchucks, marmots, and prairie dogs as well as ground and tree squirrels. Information for each of these groups follows generalized lines calling attention to group-held characteristics as well as individual species traits, such as size, coloration, range, and type of food. It's a light once-over, quite useful as a first introduction." Booklist

Wildsmith, Brian

Squirrels. Watts, F. 1975 c1974 unp illus lib. bdg. $5.95 (k-2)　　　**599.32**

1 Squirrels
ISBN 0-531-02754-6　　　LC 74-6193

"Arresting close-ups of furry orange squirrels are the forte of Wildsmith's latest graphic display. . . . While the minimal text is secondary to the color spreads, it imparts enough factual material to constitute a suitable introduction for young listeners." Booklist

599.4　Bats

Kaufmann, John

Bats in the dark; illus. by the author. Crowell 1972 33p illus (Let's-read-and-find-out science bks) $7.89, lib. bdg. $6.95 (1-3)　　　**599.4**

1 Bats
ISBN 0-690-11781-7; 0-690-11780-9　　LC 72-158695

"Information is presented about how [little brown] bats secure their food, give birth and raise their young. A longer section tells how bats use ultrasonic sounds to find food and to avoid objects while in flight. There is some information about the diet of other bats that feed upon fish, fruit and nectar." Sci Bks

"The attractive format in which black-and-white representational studies are alternated with more impressionistic, mixed-media illustrations is at once explicit and exciting." Horn Bk

Lauber, Patricia

Bats; wings in the night; illus. with photographs. Random House 1968 77p illus lib. bdg. $4.99 (4-6)　　　**599.4**

1 Bats
ISBN 0-394-90147-9　　　LC 68-23672

"Gateway books"
"The author discusses the classification of bats, and those habits or abilities that distinguish them from other mammals or, within the order of Chiroptera, from each other." Sutherland. The Best in Children's Bks

"There is also a discussion of a few of the scientists who have worked with bats and how these men experimented with the animals. Some of the animals' remaining mysteries are mentioned to arouse the young reader's curiosity. Although the text treats of bats in general (there are 800-900 species), a chapter is devoted to each of the five more unusual ones—Flying Foxes, Vampire Bats, Cannibal Bats, Flower Bats, and the Fisherman Bats. Excellent black-and-white photographs and an index add to the value as a science book." Sci Bks

Lavine, Sigmund A.

Wonders of the bat world; illus. with photographs. Dodd 1969 64p illus lib. bdg. $5.95 (4 and up)　　　**599.4**

1 Bats
ISBN 0-396-06532-5　　　LC 75-80712

"Dodd, Mead Wonders books"
This book "introduces the various kinds of bats and describes their distribution and morphology. [The author] describes lucidly their extraordinary senses, particularly their hearing and echo-location, smell, and place memory and, where appropriate, mentions research findings that have provided the

Lavine, Sigmund A.—*Continued*
foundation for our knowledge. Peculiarities of bat behavior, particularly their hibernation, migration, and feeding habits are discussed. . . . A concluding chapter offers suggestions on observing bats." Sci Bks

Leen, Nina
The bat. Holt 1976 79p illus $6.95 (4 and up) **599.4**
1 Bats
ISBN 0-03-015581-9   LC 75-32252
This book carries a "conservation message effectively through approximately one hundred black-and-white photographs of 22 different bat species; each picture is accompanied by a concise, informative caption. The author notes that these unique animals serve as effective natural insecticides, consuming thousands of tons of insects annually. A helpful inclusion for bat enthusiasts is a suggested reading list of bat books." AAAS Sci Bks & Films

599.5   Dolphins. Whales

Bridge, Linda McCarter
The playful dolphins; photographs by Lowell Georgia. Natl. Geographic Soc. 1976 32p illus (k-3) **599.5**
1 Dolphins
ISBN 0-87044-100-X   LC 76-2118
Obtainable only as part of a set for $9.95 with: Animals that build their homes, by Robert M. McClung, class 591.5; Camping adventure, by William R. Gray, class 796.54; and Wonders of the desert world, by Judith E. Rinard, class 574.9
"Books for young explorers"
Prepared by the Special Publications Division of the National Geographical Society
These "animals seem to leap from the pages as they perform their pranks from oceanarium stages; information on their care and living habits is also included." Booklist
"The text seems to be of secondary importance to the excellent and large color photographs. . . . While the book does not present facts about the animal's natural habitat and behavior patterns, it serves a useful purpose in exposing youngsters to dolphins in what is probably the only habitat in which they will ever see these playful creatures." Appraisal

Cook, Joseph J.
Blue whale; vanishing leviathan, by Joseph J. Cook and William L. Wisner; illus. with drawings by Jan Cook, photographs, and old prints. Dodd 1973 80p illus lib. bdg. $5.95 (4 and up) **599.5**
1 Whales 2 Rare animals
ISBN 0-396-06739-5   LC 72-7750
"This is an interesting account of the blue whale. Discussed are the evolution, food, anatomy, behavior, and conservation of the earth's largest mammal. The selection of photographs is excellent. . . . This is a timely consideration of a species threatened with extinction." Sch Library J

Cousteau, Jacques-Yves
Dolphins [by] Jacques-Yves Cousteau and Philippe Diolé; tr. by J. F. Bernard. Doubleday 1975 304p illus maps (The Undersea discoveries of Jacques-Yves Cousteau) $12.95 (5 and up) **599.5**
1 Dolphins
ISBN 0-385-00015-4   LC 74-9481
The authors "convey a warm affection along with their scientific regard for that most nearly 'human' and intelligent marine mammal, the dolphin. They have studied dolphins in the freedom of the oceans from Monaco and Mauritania to the Seychelles, and in captivity in various private 'tanks' and public 'marinelands' and labs. Out of their experiences they have pieced together a composite view of a playful sea creature, currently the subject of naval experiments." Pub W
"Popular illusions and myths regarding the dolphin are truthfully explored . . . in this well-documented book. Numerous photographs, most in color, add to the enjoyment. The text is supplemented with appendixes, an illustrated glossary, a bibliography and an index." AAAS Sci Bks & Films

Fisher, R. M.
Namu: making friends with a killer whale. Natl. Geographic Soc. 1973 30p illus (k-3) **599.5**
1 Whales
ISBN 0-87044-142-6   LC 73-7113
Obtainable only as part of a set for $9.95 with: Honeybees, by Jane Lecht, class 595.7; How animals hide, by Robert M. McClung, class 591.5; and Pandas, by Donna K. Grosvenor, class 599.74
"Books for young explorers"
Prepared by the Special Publications Division of the National Geographc Society
In text and color photographs, this book describes how Namu, a killer whale caught by salmon fishermen in the Pacific Ocean, was brought to the aquarium in Seattle, Washington where his new owner, Ted Griffin, made friends with him and scientists studied him to learn more about whale behavior

Graham, Ada
Whale watch [by] Ada and Frank Graham; illus. by D. D. Tyler. Delacorte Press 1978 120p illus $6.95, lib. bdg. $6.46 (5 and up) **599.5**
1 Whales 2 Whaling
ISBN 0-440-09505-0; 0-440-095006-9   LC 77-20532
"An Audubon reader"
This "survey of the dwindling whale population of the oceans describes both the intensive slaughter and the inadequate protective legislation that have led many conservation groups to protest the killing of whales. The Grahams discuss the various kinds of baleen and toothed whales, including their physical differences, habits and habitats, reproductive patterns and care of young; they also describe whales in captivity and some of the information that has been gained by research scientists working with these mammals. The illustrations are excellent; a list of sources and an index are appended." Chicago. Children's Bk Center

Grosvenor, Donna K.
The blue whale; paintings by Larry Foster. Natl. Geographic Soc. 1977 29p illus (k-3) **599.5**
1 Whales
ISBN 0-87044-243-0   LC 77-76971
Obtainable only as part of a set for $9.95 with Creatures of the night, by Judith E. Rinard, class 591.5; Let's go to the moon, by Janis Knudsen Wheat, class 629.45; and What happens in the spring, by Kathleen Costello Beer, class 500
"Books for young explorers"
Prepared by the Special Publications Division of the National Geographic Society
This book presents a year in the life of a female blue whale and her offspring

McGovern, Ann
Little whale; illus. by John Hamberger. Four Winds 1979 unp illus $7.95 (2-4) **599.5**
1 Whales
ISBN 0-590-07630-2   LC 78-31737
The author "follows the life of one particular humpback from the time of its birth to adulthood and includes material on its enemies, food, water acrobatics, migration, and association with humans. Full-color art rendered mainly in deep sea blues and greens depicts the creatures of their watery environment. An author's note comments on the possible extinction of whales. Glossary appended." Booklist

McNulty, Faith
Whales: their life in the sea; illus. by John Schoenherr. Harper 1975 88p illus $5.95, lib. bdg. $7.89 (5 and up) **599.5**
1 Whales
ISBN 0-06-024169-1   LC 74-20395
"Comprehensive coverage of whales, including what they eat, where they live, and how they communicate and care for their young, is woven into a fascinating yet factual explanation. McNulty describes such aspects of the whales' ocean

McNulty, Faith—_Continued_

life as depth and length of dives, echo location, and humanlike sociability. Beginning with a chapter on evolution of whales, the author highlights the outstanding differences between the various species and concludes with a plea to save these creatures of the sea." Booklist

"McNulty is a clear and graceful writer. . . . She avoids anthropomorphizing altogether, yet conveys the marvel of the areas still unknown about whales' intelligence. The black-and-white illustrations by John Schoenherr are fine but not such stuff as will fire a child's imagination. They are nice complements to the text, which itself is directed at kids who already know enough about whales to want to know more." NY Times Bk Rev

For further reading: p86

Mizumura, Kazue

The blue whale. Crowell 1971 32p illus (Let's-read-and-find-out science bks) lib. bdg. $7.89 (k-2)   **599.5**

1 Whales
ISBN 0-690-14994-8   LC 70-139107

The author provides information "about whales in general and about the blue whale in particular which is the largest of all. All of the essentials of the life history of a blue whale are here. . . . [A] two-page spread illustrates how whales swim and how a typical bony fish swims. The birth of a blue whale is illustrated and described, and particularly interesting is the description of a whale nursing—the mother squirts milk into him. . . . There are incidental references to the whaling industry, to the products formerly made of whales (now mostly made of plastics), and to the depletion of the whale resources due to over-exploitation." Sci Bks

"Nicely illustrated and very simply written. . . . There is a rather forced fictional framework (a fishing boat captain tells 'many things about whales') but it detracts little from the book." Chicago. Children's Bk Center

Moffett, Martha

Dolphins, by Martha and Robert Moffett; illus. with photographs. Watts, F. 1971 85p illus lib. bdg. $5.90 (4-6)   **599.5**

1 Dolphins
ISBN 0-531-00723-5   LC 76-134497

"A First book"

A straightforward, factual account describes the better known members of the dolphin family, the physical structure, senses, language, and social organization of dolphins, and current scientific research on the marine mamals. The authors [also] discuss dolphin intelligence." Booklist

"A ratio of approximately three pages of photographs for each five pages of text help to maintain interest and encourage the readers to pursue the information presented in the text." Sci Bks

Morris, Robert A.

Dolphin; pictures by Mamoru Funai. Harper 1975 62p illus (A Science I can read bk) $5.95, lib. bdg. $6.89 (1-3)   **599.5**

1 Dolphins
ISBN 0-06-024337-6; 0-06-024342-2   LC 75-6292

"The book is meant to be read aloud by a young child, and despite necessary vocabulary constraints, the text contains much information about dolphins, including how they are born, how they breathe, what they eat, their natural enemies and how they communicate with one another." AAAS Sci Bks & Films

"The text, in story format, explains the life cycle of the dolphin as well as characteristics that classify the animals as a mammal. Children will learn simple facts easily through the experience of the book. The illustrations utilize color and form for motion and warmth resulting in delightful impressions of the sea." Appraisal

Scheffer, Victor B.

Little Calf; adapted from The year of the whale; decorations by Leonard Everett Fisher. Scribner 1970 140p illus lib. bdg. $5.95 (5 and up)   **599.5**

1 Whales
ISBN 0-684-20939-X   LC 79-123836

The author "tells the story of a year in the life of a sperm whale calf—from its birth in equatorial waters through the first months of its suckling life, its growth, its awareness of the whale herd swimming through thousands of miles of seas (tropical and arctic) and its first recognition of that mysterious creature, man, who comes in ships." Pub W

"This edition for young people omits the interpretive notes and resource materials in the original book, The Year of the Whale. Thus the material too advanced for older grade school students has been omitted and they can enjoy the fascinating story uninterrupted." Sci Bks

Simon, Seymour

Killer whales. Lippincott 1978 96p illus $8.95, pa $3.95 (4-6)   **599.5**

1 Whales
ISBN 0-397-31784-0; 0-397-31792-1   LC 77-20187

"Simon reports on the physical characteristics, habits, natural environment, and life in captivity of the killer whale, detailing its sonar detection devices, communication abilities, and societal structure. The book's emphasis, however, is on dispelling the myth of the killer whale as a bloodthirsty animal and establishing the realistic understanding of a sea creature that must kill for food. Factual accounts about Moby Doll, Skana, and others are cited by aquarium personnel and marine scientists as evidence of the whale's intelligence and friendliness, while stories of whales atacking humans are explained away as a mistake. Black-and-white photographs catch the animal close up as well as in full-length, out-of-the-water movements." Booklist

"A dependable science writer, Simon combines accuracy and logical organization with a smooth writing style and an exemplary scientific objectivity." Chicago. Children's Bk Center

For further reading: p93

Stonehouse, Bernard

A closer look at whales and dolphins; illus. by Norman Weaver. Gloucester Press 1978 c1976 31p illus lib. bdg. $6.90, pa $1.95 (4-6)   **599.5**

1 Dolphins 2 Whales
ISBN 0-531-01484-3; 0-531-02489-X   LC 78-5031

First published 1976 in England

"Insatiable hunters of whale and dolphin information will find the large, colorful pictures, carefully prepared drawings, and well-labeled diagrams that accompany the perfunctory text helpful and interesting. Comparisons of the whale, rabbit, and human brains, cross sections of the heads of the sperm and rorqual whales, classification charts, migratory route maps, and diagrams of how light rays strike the eye of humans and whales add an extra dimension to the presentation. . . . [There are] two to four paragraphs of text per page discussing various kinds of whales, evolutionary backgrounds and habitats." Booklist

599.6 Elephants

Conklin, Gladys

Elephants of Africa; illus. by Joseph Cellini. Holiday House 1972 unp illus lib. bdg. $6.95 (2-4)   **599.6**

1 Elephants
ISBN 0-8234-0201-0   LC 72-179099

"This book is an account of the African elephants and begins with an 'author's note' that describes in general the salient facts of the natural history and distribution of elephants and includes a plea for their conservation. The story itself concerns a herd of elephants on migration in Africa, and the main character, a new calf, is called 'Little Elephant.' The story continues as he grows into an independent young bull. This book, like others by the same author, presents life histories of single groups or species of animals in a straightforward, factual manner." Sci Bks

"The illustrations by Joseph Cellini are worth the price of the book. They are more beautiful than color photographs and portray the animals in accurate, lifelike situations." Appraisal

Holbrook, John

A closer look at elephants; illus. by Peter Barrett. Watts, F. 1977 c1976 29p illus lib. bdg. $6.90, pa $1.95 (4-6)　　　**599.6**

1 Elephants
ISBN 0-531-00370-1; 0-531-02491-1　LC 76-029327

"A Closer look book"
First published 1976 in England
The author examines the elephant's evolution since prehistoric times, anatomy and eating habits, social behavior, courtship and mating, communication within the herd, and their survival in the wild

"The style is pedestrian but lucid, and Holbrook focuses a wealth of detail. Realistic drawings portray situations unlikely to be caught by camera." Appraisal

Van Wormer, Joe

Elephants. Dutton 1976 unp illus lib. bdg. $7.50 (3-6)　　　**599.6**

1 Elephants
ISBN 0-525-29210-1　LC 75-40323

Through text and photographs, the author describes "the physical characteristics, habits, and behavior of elephants. After contrasting Asian and African elephants, the author considers individual features such as hide, feet, tusks and trunk, describing . . . the nature and use of each." Appraisal

"The information is logically arranged and easy to read; the format is open and uncluttered; and the book is profusely illustrated with excellent black-and-white photographs." Sch Library J

599.72　Odd-toed ungulates

Hopf, Alice L.

Biography of a rhino; illus. by Kiyo Komoda. Putnam 1972 63p illus lib. bdg. $5.49 (2-4)　　　**599.72**

1 Rhinoceros
ISBN 0-399-60745-5　LC 70-183548

A life cycle story of Fari, a white rhino in a Uganda national park. It tells of her capture by the rangers, her life in the park, her eventual return to the wilderness for mating and motherhood, and her tragic death

"Fari is killed by poachers, an event that gives the author an opportunity to deplore the extermination of threatened species. The narrative framework is handled with skill, with facts about feeding, mating, symbiotic relationships, and other information about the rhinoceros smoothly incorporated." Chicago. Children's Bk Center

Rounds, Glen

Wild horses of the Red Desert; written and illus. by Glen Rounds. Holiday House 1969 unp illus lib. bdg. $7.95 (2-4)　　　**599.72**

1 Horses　2 The West (U.S.)
ISBN 0-8234-0146-4　LC 77-2897

"Against a background of the 'barren land of high rocky ridges and dusty sagebrush flats' . . . [the author] shows and tells the life of the wild horses who make this place their home through the seasons that bring hot winds in summer, deep snows in the winter, a home that is filled with dangers for them, any season, from other animals and from men." Pub W

"Well-illustrated account of how the wild horses live throughout the year in the Badlands of South Dakota. The reader is filled with feelings of adventure and can sense the wilderness atmosphere." Adventuring with Bks. 2d edition

Scott, Jack Denton

Island of wild horses; words by Jack Denton Scott; photographs by Ozzie Sweet. Putnam 1978 60p illus lib. bdg. $8.95 (4 and up)　　　**599.72**

1 Horses
ISBN 0-399-20648-5　LC 78-17380

This is a "documentary on the sturdy, independent horses that live free on Assateague Island, off Virginia. . . . [Scott] explores the theories of how the staunch horses arrived in the inhospitable area where they have survived, against big odds,

for 300 years. The most logical, if romantic, explanation is that they escaped a wrecked Spanish galleon, to live and breed and change, gradually, while acclimating themselves to the rigorous weather and sparse fodder of the island." Pub W

"Sweet's sharp black-and-white photographs show the tough mustang-like animals engaged in family life—grooming, nudging, biting, swimming, stampeding, neck wrestling, giving birth, nursing, etc. This is a fine, handsomely illustrated and well-designed factual essay on a lively subject bound to be appealing to a wide audience." Sch Library J

599.73　Even-toed ungulates

Cooke, Ann

Giraffes at home; illus. by Robert Quackenbush. Crowell 1972 31p illus (Let's-read-and-find-out science bks) $7.95, lib. bdg. $7.89 (1-3)　　　**599.73**

1 Giraffes
ISBN 0-690-33082-0; 0-690-33083-9　LC 79-158686

The author deals "with the appearance, behavior, and habitat of giraffes in an easy-to-read account illustrated with black-and-white or colored drawings on every page. Included are simple diagrams of the bone structure of a giraffe's neck and of the position of an unborn giraffe within the mother." Booklist

The book is "appropriate for reading aloud and is sufficiently interesting and attractive to hold the younger child's attention." Sci Bks

Eberle, Irmengarde

Moose live here. Doubleday 1971 59p illus lib. bdg. $5.90 (1-3)　　　**599.73**

1 Moose
ISBN 0-385-05665-6　LC 72-105682

This book about a year in the life of a bull moose and her calf "pictures the birth of a calf on an island and his early training to feed and avoid dangerous enemies by his mother. The illustrations are excellent and will appeal to any nature lover. They are unusual and depict different animals in poses that illustrate behavior at particular and important moments in their life; such as listening for danger, feeding, etc. The text is an excellent story of the growth of a young calf toward independence. It is a book that will appeal to young and old naturalists." Appraisal

Hopf, Alice L.

Biography of a giraffe; etchings by Patricia Collins. Putnam 1978 60p illus lib. bdg. $5.49 (3-5)　　　**599.73**

1 Giraffes
ISBN 0-399-61088-X　LC 76-52934

"This features, with the help of velvety etchings opposite every page of a text for younger readers, a detailed look at one animal from birth through growing experiences with the herd to the establishment of his independence and mating. The biographical approach maintains objectivity and sympathy at the same time, a balance rarely kept in this genre. It's too bad that human disturbance of giraffes' environment is only implied with the animal's entanglement in some telephone wires, but all in all this is aesthetic nonfiction as well as practical preparation for a trip to the zoo." Booklist

Jenkins, Marie M.

Goats, sheep, and how they live; drawings by Matthew Kalmenoff. Holiday House 1978 157p illus $7.95 (5 and up)　　　**599.73**

1 Sheep　2 Goats
ISBN 0-8234-0317-3　LC 77-20149

"Jenkins describes goats and sheep and their close relatives from an anatomical viewpoint and also from a practical life cycle approach. . . . The description of the function of hooves and horns on these various ungulates is remarkable. All the near relatives of goats—the ibex, goral, antelope, chamois, takin, musk ox, tahr, aoudad, ram, mouflon, urial and bighorn—are included. Their peculiar features and place in the ecosystems of the world are beautifully explained. This book is a delight to read—I could not put it down. It would be a very good reference for courses in the natural

Jenkins, Marie M.—*Continued*
history of mammals, especially ungulates. The illustrations are excellent, and the book should have wide audience appeal." AAAS Sci Bks & Films
Bibliography: p151-54

Ryden, Hope
The little deer of the Florida Keys; written and photographed by Hope Ryden. Putnam 1978 62p illus $7.95 (3-6)   **599.73**

1 Deer
ISBN 0-399-20635-3   LC 77-20884
"A photo-essay on the delicate Key Deer of Florida. Ryden describes the small bands that the does form and live in throughout adulthood, the cantankerous behavior of bucks during mating season, and the does' affectionate care of fawns. The text lends an historical perspective on the survival of the species, explaining local political and cultural obstacles that ecologists had to overcome in their fight to save the deer." Sch Library J
"The rare key deer from Florida takes on considerable interest as a result of the striking photographs. . . . The author skillfully creates tension by alternating an account of the deer's natural living habits with the story of its near extinction." Horn Bk

Schlein, Miriam
Giraffe: the silent giant; illus. by Betty Fraser. Four Winds 1976 58p illus $6.95 (3-6)   **599.73**

1 Giraffes
ISBN 0-590-07421-0   LC 76-7922
"Chapters deal with the first giraffe brought to Europe; the giraffe's many other names; its classification, evolution, biology, and life habits; and its interaction with man in the wild and in zoos." Horn Bk
"This beautifully written story of the giraffe is illustrated with gorgeous soft pencil drawings that reflect the dignity and gentleness of the giraffe. . . . A lucid lovely book, profusely illustrated." Appraisal

Waters, John F.
Camels: ships of the desert; illus. by Reynold Ruffins. Crowell 1974 33p illus (Let's-read-and-find-out-science bks) $7.95, lib. bdg. $7.89 (1-3)   **599.73**

1 Camels
ISBN 0-690-00394-3; 0-690-00395-1   LC 73-14514
Comparing the camel's physical characteristics to man's, this book explains how camels withstand the desert sand, heat, and lack of water and food
This "is an excellent addition to the elementary science library. Appropriately illustrated in 'water and sand' colors, the book presents a graphic portrait of the 'ship of the desert.' But it does more; it gives a scientific explanation for and refutes theory and superstition about the camel's storage of water. At the same time the basic science principles pertaining to heat and cold, perspiration, the skin and its function and the processes of elimination are all neatly fitted in. Vocabulary is appropriate; and text and pictures have a wonderful invitational quality, asking questions then answering, but carrying the reader along logically and allowing him to make the discovery rather than telling him in so many trite phrases." Sci Bks

599.74 Carnivores

Adamson, Joy
Elsa. . . . Pantheon Bks. 1961 unp illus lib. bdg. $4.99 (2-5)   **599.74**

1 Lions
ISBN 0-391-91117-2   LC 61-10032
"The true story of a lioness who was brought up from cubhood by Joy Adamson and her husband, a senior game warden; they taught her to stalk and kill for herself so that she could be set free into the African jungle." Title page
"The same story as 'Born Free', simplified for young readers. Illustrated with full-page photographs." The AAAS Sci Bk List for Children

Annixter, Jane
The year of the she-grizzly, by Jane and Paul Annixter; drawings by Gilbert Riswold. Coward, McCann & Geoghegan 1978 68p illus $5.95 (4-6)   **599.74**

1 Grizzly bear
ISBN 0-698-20456-5   LC 77-26724
"There is a good deal of information as well as enjoyment included in this tale of a She-Grizzly and her cub—ecology, habits, food, adaptation to environment, breeding, enemies, yearly changes are all an integral part of the animal story. The story begins in October and ends a year later. There will be some objection to the anthropomorphism . . . but children will enjoy this good animal story." Appraisal

Barry, Scott
The kingdom of wolves; written and photographed by Scott Barry. Putnam 1979 63p illus $8.95 (5 and up)   **599.74**

1 Wolves
ISBN 0-399-20657-4   LC 78-9895
"The author explores prejudice toward the wolf and describes many incidents in folklore and literature in which the wolf is maligned. Special functions of certain body parts of this predator are discussed. . . . Other topics covered include the organization and function of the pack, pup rearing, habitats, and wolf communication." Sch Library J
The "text is a potent appeal for the protection of wolves in America and in other countries. Barry's remarkable close-ups and long shots, well-reproduced black-and-white photos, are extra arguments for halting the slaughter and encroachment on the habitats of the wild animals whose numbers have been shockingly reduced." Pub W

Blassingame, Wyatt
Wonders of raccoons; illus. with photographs. Dodd 1977 80p illus lib. bdg. $5.95 (4-6)   **599.74**

1 Raccoons
ISBN 0-396-07485-5   LC 77-6491
"Dodd, Mead Wonders books"
The author gives a "picture of the raccoon as a crafty, playful, yet thoroughly wild creature. Information about physical characteristics feeding and mating habits, care of the young, and general behavior is interspersed with humorous tales of this rambunctious animal's banditlike forays. In addition the author discusses raccoon folktales, coon hunting, relatives of the raccoon (giant pandas and coatimundis), and considerations of the animal as a pet." Booklist
"Blassingame's ease with his subject is apparent in this readable discussion. . . . Attractive black-and-white photographs show the animal in its natural habitat and interacting with people." Sch Library J

Bonners, Susan
Panda; written and illus. by Susan Bonners. Delacorte Press 1978 unp illus $6.95, lib. bdg. $6.46 (k-2)   **599.74**

1 Giant panda
ISBN 0-440-06827-4; 0-440-06835-5   LC 77-86324
"A simple, easy-to-read description of the life and habits of the Panda. Eating, sleeping, cub rearing, growth, mating, lifespan, and habitat are all discussed in easily understood terms and illustrated in soft, expressive watercolors of blue and white." Sch Library J

Brady, Irene
Beaver year; written and illus. by Irene Brady. Houghton 1976 40p illus lib. bdg. $8.95 (3-6)   **599.74**

1 Beavers
ISBN 0-395-24208-8   LC 75-38907
"A narrative of the life cycle of beavers. . . . The book is not indexed, so its role as a reference volume is limited. However, information on the external anatomy, protective devices, enemies, role of male and female in rearing the young, dam building and food storing and other information concerning beaver ecology is all there." AAAS Sci Bks & Films

Brady, Irene—*Continued*

"Although the approach is patterned, the narrative form and authenticity of details give the book substance. Brady's black and white sketches, softly drawn and realistic, are remarkable for their texture." Chicago. Children's Bk Center

Elephants on the beach. Scribner 1979 unp illus lib. bdg. $7.95 (3-5)   599.74

1 Elephant seals
ISBN 0-684-16115-X   LC 79-89

"Author-illustrator Brady has taken her sketchbook to the beach and recorded, in diary form, the events of one day, as she observed the behavior of the northern elephant seal." Sch Library J

"The text records the seals' behavior and some of the other shore creatures which are scattered about (shells, seaweed) or which venture close to the seals (a brush rabbit, a herring gull). Fresh, observant, and provocative, the text is informal and informative; the soft sketches, pencil and wash, are nicely detailed and convey a sense of admiration that echoes the tone of the text." Chicago. Children's Bk Center

Brown, Louise C.

Elephant seals; illus. with photographs by Andrée Abecassis and drawings by Nina Inez Brown. Dodd 1979 40p illus $4.95 (2-4)   599.74

1 Elephant seals
ISBN 0-396-07665-3   LC 78-25623

"A Skylight book"

"Topics include anatomy, feeding habits deep in the ocean, breeding ground social behavior, battles for male dominancy, growth cycle of young pups, and the killer whale as a natural enemy. Unanswered questions are posed about herding habits, use of feeding grounds, migration, and the mystery of where the seals go for two-thirds of a year when they leave the land for the sea." Appraisal

"Some wide-eyed description . . . lends an air of condescension to opening portions of this introduction to elephant seals. But once the prose settles down to its simple explaining of habits, lifestyle, and special features, the tone improves. Black-and-white illustrations show the beasts in active and passive moments. Informative, simple, untaxing, and reasonably attractive." Booklist

Dixon, Paige

Silver Wolf; illus. by Ann Brewster. Atheneum Pubs. 1973 108p illus $5.95, pa $1.95 (4 and up)   599.74

1 Wolves
ISBN 0-689-30083-2; 0-689-70422-4   LC 72-86932

"The author gives a most vivid picture of the life of a wolf and his pack. He follows this young wolf through the seasons of one year in the wilderness. Silver Wolf is very young when the book opens and the winter is almost over. The social structure of the pack, the hierarchy, the organization for survival, all are vividly described, as are the search for food, the meeting with enemies, such as man the trapper, man the observer, man the conservator and man the game hunter. . . There are those who will decide that such a book belongs with fiction and others who feel that such detailed observation and knowledge of wolves warrants placing this tale among books of nature nonfiction. In any case, it is exciting reading." Appraisal

Suggestions for further reading: p107-08

The young grizzly; illus. by Grambs Miller. Atheneum Pubs. 1974 106p illus lib. bdg. $6.95 (4-6)   599.74

1 Grizzly bear
ISBN 0-689-30137-5   LC 73-84827

This story of two grizzy bear cubs and their mother "is a factual account, beginning before the birth of the cubs, following them both for a while, and then the young male to early adulthood. Data are recorded concerning daily happenings: food, wanderings, quarrels, play, how the mother trains and disciplines her young, and the occasional encounters with their only enemy, man. Actually, the bears are described more realistically than the bear-hating hunter and his nature-loving son; they seem somewhat contrived. There are delightful descriptions of the young cubs playing with their mother and with each other. . . . The dozen or so black-and-white sketches by Grambs Miller add to the interest of the book." Sci Bks

Bibliography: p105-06

Fichter, George S.

Cats; illus. by Arthur B. Singer. Golden Press 1973 160p illus (Golden nature guides) lib. bdg. $9.15, pa $1.95 (5 and up)   599.74

1 Cats
ISBN 0-307-64356-5; 0-307-24356-7   LC 72-92486

The author "introduces the varied members of the cat family. There are capsule descriptions of the different breeds of cats, both wild and domestic; physiology, personality, and care of cats; and brief looks at the cat in history, literature, art and legend. The color illustrations are attractive and largely accurate. The work is well organized and indexed with a bibliography for further reading." Appraisal

Fox, Michael

The wolf; illus. by Charles Fracé. Coward, McCann & Geoghegan 1973 95p illus $6.95 (4-6)   599.74

1 Wolves
ISBN 0-698-20200-7   LC 72-76700

The author traces the stories of five wolves of Alaska "from the birth of a litter through the first year of their cubs' lives, giving a sequential picture of the care and training of the cubs, the ways in which the young learn to avoid danger, hunt, and acquire the approved patterns of behavior." Chicago. Children's Bk Center

"Fox emphasizes the intelligence of the animals, their affection and respect for one another, the part wolves play in the balance of nature, and the fact that men have hunted wolves from planes just for the pleasure of killing them. In a note at the end he speaks briefly on the need for protecting wolves and the deep satisfaction which people can feel when they hear or see a free wolf." Booklist

Freschet, Berniece

Grizzly bear; drawings by Donald Carrick. Scribner 1975 unp illus lib. bdg. $7.95 (2-4)   599.74

1 Grizzly bear
ISBN 0-684-14333-X   LC 75-4056

"Beginning with the birth of the cubs, the story line of this informational book takes a mother grizzly and her twin cubs through a season of training for survival that leads to independence. Action-filled watercolor illustrations enhance the already engrossing text which reads aloud effectively as well as giving accurate facts." Rdng Teacher

Skunk baby; illus. by Kazue Mizumura. Crowell 1973 41p illus $3.95, lib. bdg. $7.89 (2-4)   599.74

1 Skunks
ISBN 0-690-74194-4   LC 72-83781

"Attractively illustrated and simply written, the description of the first experiences of a baby skunk are given just enough of a narrative framework to lend impetus to the book. Smallest of his litter, Skunk Baby investigates his small world with adventurous impunity, he knows no fear but obeys the danger signals his mother gives. Skunk Baby learns what fear is when he first encounters a predatory fox. The fox is young also, and he learns from the confrontation what a powerful weapon skunks have. The text and the illustrations have a quiet fidelity to nature." Chicago. Children's Bk Center

Grosvenor, D. K.

Pandas; with photographs by the author; paintings by George Founds. Natl. Geographic Soc. 1973 30p illus (k-3)   599.74

1 Giant panda
ISBN 0-87044-143-4   LC 73-7114

Obtainable only as part of a set for $9.95 with: Honeybees, by Jane Lecht, class 595.7; How animals hide, by Robert M. McClung, class 591.5; and Namu, by Ronald M. Fisher, class 599.4

"Books for young explorers"

Prepared by the Special Publications Division of the National Geographic Society

In color pictures and text, this book describes the habitats and behavior of the giant panda. Included are descriptions of Ling-Ling and Hsing-Hsing, the two young pandas sent as a gift from the people of China to the National Zoo in Washington, D.C.

Harris, John

Endangered predators, by John Harris and Aleta Pahl; illus. by Aleta Pahl; conceived and produced by Whitehall, Hadlyme & Smith, Inc. Doubleday 1976 84p illus $5.95, lib. bdg. $6.90 (5 and up)   599.74

1 Predatory animals 2 Rare animals
ISBN 0-385-08038-7; 0-385-08012-3   LC 75-34051

This book describes "how five predators (wolf, fox, coyote, cougar and bobcat) live. The predators are made likeable by showing that they and their behaviors have evolved as part of natural ecosystems to regulate population numbers and to weed out unfit prey animals. Most of the factual information is accurate, current and presented at a level consistent with the intended audience. There is a good bibliography for further reading. The many pencil drawings by Pahl are beautiful and greatly enhance the written portion." AAAS Sci Bks & Films

Harris, Lorle

Biography of a river otter; illus. by Ruth Kirschner. Putnam [1979 c1978] 62p illus (A Nature biography bk) lib. bdg. $5.49 (3-5)   599.74

1 Otters
ISBN 0-399-61127-4   LC 78-3606

"This fictionalized biography of a mother otter and her cubs encompasses a year in their lives, from the birth of the cubs to their departure to make way for a new litter. It is pleasant and informative in a general way." Appraisal

Hess, Lilo

The curious raccoons; story and photographs by Lilo Hess. Scribner 1968 46p illus lib. bdg. $5.95 (3-5)   599.74

1 Raccoons
ISBN 0-684-12459-9   LC 68-29363

"When a female raccoon is transported by animal-welfare authorities from the suburbs to the countryside, she makes a new home, mates, and raises a family of three kits. This straightforward account of one particular raccoon acquaints the reader with the habits and characteristics of the species." Booklist

"Lilo Hess has snapped some truly expressive photographs of a raccoon family (a mother and three kits) as the bandit-masked, ringtailed creatures poke their noses into garbage cans, corn cribs, running brooks and wasps' nests. There's much nature lore unobtrusively slipped into a sympathetic narrative." NY Times Bk Rev

The misunderstood skunk; story and photographs by Lilo Hess. Scribner 1969 45p illus lib. bdg. $6.95 (3-5)   599.74

1 Skunks
ISBN 0-684-12360-6   LC 79-85271

"Miss Hess tells the story, from birth through the first year of life, of a family of skunks who made their home on her farm. She describes their appearance, musk-releasing defense mechanism, maturation process, feeding habits, qualities as pets, etc. Children will especially delight in the many black-and-white photographs, which depict the beautiful, inquisitive little animals both outdoors and in, sleeping, eating, exploring, and playing." Sch Library J

Hiss, Anthony

The giant panda book; pictures by Greg and Tim Hildebrandt. Golden Press 1973 45p illus maps lib. bdg. $9.15 (3-5)   599.74

1 Giant panda
ISBN 0-307-63753-0   LC 73-78209

"A most interesting and attractive children's book on the popular giant panda. The color illustrations by Greg and Tim Hildebrandt are excellent and appropriately illustrate the story in the text. The three parts of the book are: 'The Wild Giant Pandas of Szechwan,' 'The Story of Chi-Chi,' and 'The Story of Ling-Ling and Hsing-Hsing.' In the first part, the author concentrates on the native habitat of the giant pandas and on their zoological relationships: the second part concerns the female panda at the London Zoo; the third part tells the story of the two pandas who now live at the National Zoo in Washington, D.C. An altogether fine book to be read by or to young children." Sci Bks

Kohn, Bernice

Raccoons; pictures by John Hamberger. Prentice-Hall 1968 unp illus pa $1.50 (1-3)   599.74

1 Raccoons
ISBN 0-13-749903-5   LC 68-14548

The author provides "descriptions of the raccoon's appearance, relationships with other mammals, habits and life history." Sci Bks

"A competent text enhanced by attractive illustrations reproduced in warm colors. The book should prove useful for nature study or for recreational reading." Library J

McDearmon, Kay

Polar bear; illus. with photographs. Dodd 1976 46p illus lib. bdg. $4.50 (3-5)   599.74

1 Polar bears
ISBN 0-396-07331-X   LC 76-8920

"A polar bear mother and her cubs are followed through a two-year period of their life in a simple narrative and appealing photographs. A description of the Arctic world, its inhabitants, and the dangers they face is included along with information about the physical characteristics and behavior of the bears. A competent treatment for intermediate graders of an inherently interesting subject." Sch Library J

Morey, Walt

Operation blue bear; a true story; illus. with photographs. Dutton 1975 87p illus lib. bdg. $8.95 (4-6)   599.74

1 Bears
ISBN 0-525-36445-5   LC 75-12521

A "true tale of the rescue of an extremely rare blue or glacier bear by members of the staff of the San Diego zoo. The bear somehow finds its way to the garbage cans and kitchens of the Coast Guard station at Yakutat, Alaska, where it faces almost certain death at the hands of trophy hunters as soon as it leaves the protection of the government reservation. An alert Coast Guardsman notifies the San Diego Zoo of its plight and the action begins as several dozen people prove that both civilians and government personnel do care about our wildlife. A positive, suspenseful, humorous story that is well above the usual." Sch Library J

National Geographic Society

Lion cubs; growing up in the wild. The Society 1972 31p illus (k-3)   599.74

1 Lions
ISBN 0-87044-121-3   LC 72-91420

Obtainable only as part of a set for $9.95 with: Dinosaurs, by Kathryn Jackson, class 567.9; Dogs working for people, by Joanna Foster, class 636.7; and Treasures in the sea, by Robert M. McClung, class 910.4

"Books for young explorers"

Prepared by the Special Publications Division of the National Geographic Society

"Super photographs. Illustrated is a brief story of lion cubs, their home, dependency on the pride for two years, and their relationship with other animals. Included is a two-page spread showing other members of the cat family. This book is beautiful to see with no depth of information." Appraisal

North, Sterling

Little Rascal; illus. by Carl Burger. Dutton 1965 78p illus $7.95 (3-5)   599.74

1 Raccoons 2 Country life—Wisconsin
ISBN 0-525-33854-3   LC 65-19579

The original book, Rascal, entered below, has been specially illustrated and abridged for young readers

The book "describes a year in the life of a boy in Wisconsin fifty years ago. Rascal is his pet raccoon, and his exploits are comic and sometimes touching, and described without sentimentality." Times (London) Lit Sup

Rascal; a memoir of a better era; illus. by John Schoenherr. Dutton 1963 189p illus $7.95 (5 and up)   599.74

1 Raccoons 2 Country life—Wisconsin
ISBN 0-525-18839-8   LC 63-13882

A book about Rascal "a young raccoon, Sterling North's pet the year he was eleven, in rural Wisconsin. . . . The book calls up a series of marvelous pictures: boy fishing in peaceful company

North, Sterling—*Continued*

of raccoon, boy riding on bike with raccoon (a demon for speed) standing up in bike basket, raccoon with friend, a prize trotting horse, raccoon helping boy to win a pie-eating contest. A central episode is about an idyllic camping trip." Pub W

"Beyond being a charming true animal story, it is also an account of life in a Wisconsin village in 1918. . . . Young readers will cherish it." NY Times Bk Rev

Patent, Dorothy Hinshaw

Raccoons, coatimundis, and their family. Holiday House 1979 127p illus $7.95 (5 and up)   599.74

1 Raccoons 2 Procyonidae
ISBN 0-8234-0360-2   LC 79-10468

This book introduces the reader to raccoons, coatimundis, ringtails, olingos, kinkajous and pandas, all members of the family Procyonidae. Each animal's environment is discussed as well as its habits and likelihood as a pet

"There is also a clear explanation of an ongoing argument: how should pandas be classified, as bears or raccoons? The black-and-white photographs show procyonids in their natural environment, and no species mentioned in the text is neglected. The writing style is highly readable, despite the quantity of information given; a few lighthearted anecdotes break the serious scientific tone." Sch Library J
Suggested reading: p123-24

Weasels, otters, skunks, and their family; illus. by Matthew Kalmenoff. Holiday House 1973 95p illus $7.95 (3-6)   599.74

1 Mustelidae
ISBN 0-8234-0228-2   LC 73-76801

The book describes mammals of the Mustelid family: "Carnivorous weasels, ferrets, minks, and martens; omnivorous skunks, badgers, and wolverines; and the playful and aquatic sea and river otters. [The author] discusses their physical characteristics, eating habits, and reproductive processes, and where necessary, dispels damaging myths about them. She follows these animals through their daily lives showing how they seek out other animals, protect themselves, survive in different environments, cooperate with other animals, and are captured by their predators." Booklist

"Written with grace and precision. . . . Matthew Kalmenoff's pictures (starting with the loving otter mother and baby on the cover) are realistic and reassuringly un-Disneylike." Pub W
Suggested reading: p91

Rau, Margaret

The giant panda at home; with drawings by Eva Hülsmann. Knopf 1977 80p illus map lib. bdg. $5.99 (5 and up)   599.74

1 Giant panda
ISBN 0-394-93248-X   LC 76-40332

This "book describes the mating, birth, habitat, raising of the young, and flora and fauna surrounding the giant panda of China." Appraisal

"While other children's books on the giant panda have focused upon those in captivity, Rau has used accounts of recent Chinese zoological expeditions as well as natural history source material. Thus the complete environmental background (terrain, flora, fauna, climate) which surrounds the panda is provided, making its adaptations and behavior more comprehensible. Hülsmann's soft drawings, interspersed throughout, catch in fine detail the wildlife of the region, the relationships of the pandas, and the tragedies of the wilderness. The prologue, epilogue, and bibliography document sources as well as Rau's concern for preservation of the panda's natural terrain." Booklist

Schaller, George B.

The tiger; its life in the wild, by George B. Schaller and Millicent E. Selsam; illus. with photographs, drawings and maps. Harper 1969 71p illus maps lib. bdg. $8.79 (5 and up)   599.74

1 Tigers
ISBN 0-06-025280-4   LC 69-14447

"The gist of man's knowledge about tigers is contained in this delightful book. It is accurate and tells how an ecologist goes about studying animals in their natural habitat. The book covers life history, behavior, superstitions and the present distribution and abundance of tigers. The chapters on man-eaters and social life are intriguing, and the entire book reflects the excitement of the author's firsthand experiences." Sci Bks

"The book is handsomely illustrated with black-and-white prints of tigers at the beginning of each chapter, clear photographs, and useful maps." Sch Library J
For further reading: p69

Wonders of lions [by] George and Kay Schaller; illus. with photographs by George Schaller and sketches by Richard Keane. Dodd 1977 96p illus maps lib. bdg. $5.95 (5 and up)   599.74

1 Lions
ISBN 0-396-07409-X   LC 76-50551

"Dodd, Mead Wonders books"

The authors include "descriptions of environment, pride, cubs, communication, territory, nomads, and hunting. The tone is straightforward with occasional sidelights of the authors' personal observation. Most importantly, they respect the lion's nature rather than adulate it and show the animals' individuality rather than summing up collective traits into one representative of the species. Closeup black-and-white action photographs show lions in the Serengeti National Park, and several series of pen-and-ink sketches illustrate facial expressions and body positions." Booklist

The "lucid writing is superb. . . . Eight references are listed for further reading. An excellent index is included." AAAS Sci Bks & Films

Schick, Alice

Serengeti cats; illus. by Joel Schick. Lippincott 1977 126p illus $6.95 (4 and up)   599.74

1 Lions 2 Leopards 3 Cheetahs 4 Serengeti National Park
ISBN 0-397-31757-3   LC 77-812

The book "draws young readers into the Serengeti National Park in Tanzania where Africa's wild animals are protected in a natural habitat. Spotlighting a lion, a leopard and a cheetah, the text describes the life cycles of the cat families in an area 'about the size of the state of Connecticut.' The book ends with speculations about the future of the 1000 lions, 600 leopards and 250 cheetahs at home in the preserve." Pub W

"While the book's primary concern is with the habits and behavior patterns of the cat families, it is filled with information about other African wildlife. A timely title, well written and complemented by expressive pencil drawings." Sch Library J

Schlein, Miriam

What's wrong with being a skunk? Illus. by Ray Cruz. Four Winds 1974 unp illus $5.95 (k-3)   599.74

1 Skunks
ISBN 0-590-07305-2   LC 73-88078

"From this book the young reader learns that skunks are really good-natured animals and they only use their special protective weapon of odor when they are in a real crisis. Their eating habits, sleeping habits, and how they spend the winter are described as well as growing to adulthood, and their natural enemies." Sci Teacher

"The provocative title introduces youngsters to the skunks—striped, spotted, hooded, hognosed or pygmy. Black-and-white sketches highlight the text. . . . The informal story format carries the student along, providing interest and motivation through pictures and a readable text. Vocabulary is appropriate and the sentence length varied. The popularity of the animal is mentioned—also its unpopularity—allowing the reader to make his own choice." Sci Bks

Steiner, Barbara

Biography of a Bengal tiger; illus. by Lloyd Bloom. Putnam 1979 63p illus lib. bdg. $5.89 (3-5)   599.74

1 Tigers
ISBN 0-399-61138-X   LC 78-24470

Follows Mohta, a male cub, from birth, through survival training and play, to maturity

"The two color wash over the pen and ink drawings is often too confusing—the colors fighting with and often obliterating the details of the lines. However, it is a fine book—the sort of book that makes zoologists." Appraisal

Zim, Herbert S.

The big cats. Newly rev. ed. Illus. by Dot Barlowe. Morrow 1976 61p illus lib. bdg. $5.52 (3-6)   **599.74**

1 Cats
ISBN 0-688-32072-4   LC 76-819

First published 1955
The book includes an introductory section which "describes common physical characteristics and behavior, and there is a brief section on each of the individual animals—the lion, tiger, leopard, jaguar, cougar, and cheetah." Sch Library J
"In line with current environmental concepts, the emphasis is placed on social behavior of the big cats and particularly their status as endangered species." Booklist

Little cats; illus. by Jean Zallinger. Morrow 1978 62p illus $6.95, lib. bdg. $6.67 (3-5)   **599.74**

1 Cats
ISBN 0-688-22149-1; 0-688-32149-6   LC 77-20257
"Zim describes the characteristics and habits of 11 species of little cats, including the bobcat, lynx, and domestic cat. (About half the book is devoted to the history of the domestic cat.) . . . Zallinger's careful, accurate drawings on each page illuminate the text and add to the book's appeal, and an index adds to its usefulness." Sch Library J

599.8 Primates. Monkeys

Leen, Nina

Monkeys. Holt 1978 80p illus $6.95 (4-6)   **599.8**

1 Monkeys
ISBN 0-03-044001-7   LC 78-4284
"Prefaced by the comments of a staff member of the American Museum of Natural History and by a chart (which also serves as an index, since it gives page numbers) that gives common and scientific names for species mentioned in the text, with habitats and notes on which species are endangered, this book is devoted to monkeys primarily, although there are brief sections on premonkeys (lemurs, lorises, and bushbabies), apes, and great apes. There is about a line or paragraph of print per page, most of the space being devoted to photographs; the text is divided into such topics as the prehensile tail, grooming, family patterns, child care, etc." Chicago. Children's Bk Center
"The approach here generates visual excitement but this same diversity weakens the basis for a unified text. Even the index does not help in finding out how long monkeys live or the gestation period of offspring. The book, however, does stand on its merits as a portfolio of startling clarity and beauty which enhances our appreciation of the monkey family." Sch Library J
Suggested reading: p78

Rau, Margaret

The snow monkey at home; with drawings by Eva Hülsmann. Knopf 1979 101p illus map $6.95, lib. bdg. $6.99 (5 and up)   **599.8**

1 Japanese macaque
ISBN 0-394-83976-5; 0-394-93976-X   LC 78-31550
The author "takes a male Japanese macaque from the moment of birth through leadership of a troop and finally to rejection as a 'solitary.' Attention is given to the development of instincts and the teaching by the mother of life-saving behaviors not instinctive in macaques. The approach is scientific, particularly in descriptions of communicative aspects of behavior, physical appearance of the animal as it changes with seasons and age, and the complex social machinery of the macaque. Sentimentality is avoided; the graphic descriptions of birth and mating are detached and precise." Sch Library J
Bibliography: p93-97

Selsam, Millicent E.

A first look at monkeys and apes, by Millicent E. Selsam and Joyce Hunt; illus. by Harriett Springer. Walker & Co. 1979 32p illus maps $7.95, lib. bdg. $7.85 (1-3)   **599.8**

1 Monkeys 2 Apes
ISBN 0-8027-6358-8; 0-8027-6359-6   LC 79-4701

"Nicely detailed pencil drawings are carefully placed in relation to textual references, especially important here because the text refers to differences between species that can help the reader understand principles of classification. The text is direct, accurate, and simply written; it makes no pretense of being comprehensive, but points out similarities and differences between and among New World and Old World monkeys and among apes." Chicago. Children's Bk Center

Shuttlesworth, Dorothy E.

The story of monkeys, great apes, and small apes. Doubleday 1972 111p illus $5.95, lib. bdg. $6.90 (5 and up)   **599.8**

1 Monkeys 2 Apes
ISBN 0-385-06055-6; 0-385-04724-X   LC 76-150872
Illustrated with photographs, this book examines many of the members of the ape (chimpanzee, gorilla, orangutan) and monkey (baboon, marmoset, rhesus) world. It discusses their distinguished physical characteristics, their environment and way of life, their proper care and feeding, as well as their role in mythology and folklore
"The book has easy-to-read language and print, is well illustrated with many photographs, and has an index. The book conveys a feeling of concern for the well-being of the apes, in their natural habitat or in zoos." Appraisal

Zim, Herbert S.

Monkeys; illus. by Gardell D. Christensen. Morrow 1955 unp illus map lib. bdg. $6 (3-6)   **599.8**

1 Monkeys
ISBN 0-688-31517-8   LC 55-6744
"An interestingly written introduction to monkeys. Beginning with a description of the entire group of primates and showing structural similarities and differences, the author then discusses the various types of monkeys and how they resemble, or differ from, each other. The detailed drawings add interest and information to the book. There is helpful material on choosing and caring for a monkey as a pet. A useful book for nature study or hobby groups, as well as for general reading." Chicago. Children's Bk Center

599.88 Apes

Alston, Eugenia

Growing up chimpanzee; illus. by Haru Wells. Crowell 1975 unp illus $7.95, lib. bdg. $7.89 (2-4)   **599.88**

1 Chimpanzees
ISBN 0-690-00015-4; 0-690-00564-4   LC 74-12307
"The startlingly human-like primates are presented sympathetically in this book. The black-and white pictures by Haru Wells add zest to Ms. Alston's easily mastered and engrossing text. . . . The structure of the [chimpanzee] family and its place in society are explored. We learn how the mother cares for her young, how status is achieved in the community and other fascinating facts." Pub W

Amon, Aline

Orangutan: endangered ape; text & drawings by Aline Amon. Atheneum Pubs. 1977 163p illus maps $7.95 (5 and up)   **599.88**

1 Orangutan 2 Rare animals
ISBN 0-689-30563-X   LC 76-41354
This book discusses "the history, mythology, biology and present status of the orangutan. . . . The author reports on the current movement to save the orangutan in the wild and makes it clear that while man's cruelty has limited the orangutan in the past, the present cause of decline is lumbering operations in the animal's jungle range. She relates the work of zoos to keep the orangutan a breeding species—and points out quite justly that the zoo-bred orangutan may turn out quite unlike the wild bred animal." Appraisal
"Most of the book is really two books skillfully woven together by alternating chapters of each. One tells the story of a wild ape, the other presents the scientific information. Toward the end, both come together as the focus moves on to modern field studies, orangutan rehabilitation centers and conservation efforts. The text, pictures, and index are excellent. The scientific accuracy is flawless, and the author provides useful reference and reading lists for readers interested in further information." AAAS Sci Bks & Films

Amon, Aline—*Continued*

Reading, writing, chattering chimps; text and drawings by Aline Amon. Atheneum Pubs. 1975 118p illus $7.95 (5 and up)   **599.88**

1 Chimpanzees 2 Animal communication
ISBN 0-689-30472-2   LC 75-9524

" 'Talking Animals Fact or Fiction?' is the opening chapter of the book. It becomes more fact than fiction as the text develops. Communicating with apes through visual techniques such as sign language, computer, and plastic symbols is the basis of the study. Through repetitive and patient efforts of scientists and their assistants, using innovative techniques, the apes learn to sign and perform other simple tasks. The studies often compare the growth and development of the ape with that of children of the same age. The importance and value of the psychologists' findings and implications for human development are discussed in the text. It is informative, provocative, and enjoyable to read." Sci and Children

Bibliography: p113-15. Suggestions for further reading: p117-18

Conklin, Gladys

Little apes; illus. by Joseph Cellini. Holiday House 1970 unp illus lib. bdg. $7.95 (k-3)
599.88

1 Apes
ISBN 0-8234-0070-0   LC 73-102431

"Written very simply, a description of a day in the lives of a baby gorilla, chimpanzee, gibbon, and orangutan provides children with an excellent first book on apes, and one that may make it easier for them to distinguish between apes and monkeys. The four diurnal patterns are quite similar, but the illustrations give the book variety: precisely drawn and uncluttered, they have a humorous fidelity and charm." Sat Rev

Fenner, Carol

Gorilla gorilla; illus. by Symeon Shimin. Random House 1973 unp illus $4.95, lib. bdg. $5.99 (1-4)   **599.88**

1 Gorillas
ISBN 0-394-82069-X; 0-394-92069-4   LC 70-136590

"This book describes the birth and early training of a young male gorilla in the eastern Congo until the hunters trap him and ship him to a large zoo. The adjustment to cage-life at the zoo completes this scientifically accurate portrayal of one gorilla's life experience." Top of the News

"The author's free-form poetic style is very effective and makes it easy to empathize with the gorilla as he struggles to adjust to his imprisonment. The sensitive illustrations by a talented artist help create this excellent book." Sci Bks

Kevles, Bettyann

Watching the wild apes; the primate studies of Goodall, Fossey, and Galdikas. Dutton 1976 164p illus maps $8.95 (5 and up)   **599.88**

1 Apes 2 Zoologists
ISBN 0-525-42233-1   LC 75-38939

"Accounts of the amazing and persistent field work recently done by primate scientists (mainly women) to reveal the behavioral patterns of chimpanzees, gorillas and orangutans in their native habitats. Dispels myths and misinformation about these humanlike animals and shows the methods used, and hardships suffered by investigators in inhospitable environments." Children's Bk Rev Serv

"The scholarly studies are made accessible to beginning students through an anecdotal approach to the often exciting and dangerous information-gathering of the scientists and through carefully balanced interpretations of their speculations. Clear photographs and maps are used throughout the book and a table of characteristics together with a selective bibliography and a thorough index are appended." Sch Library J

McDearmon, Kay

Gorillas; illus. with photographs. Dodd 1979 59p illus $4.95 (3-5)   **599.88**

1 Gorillas
ISBN 0-396-07645-9   LC 78-11292

"A Skylight book"

This book is "well organized into clearly marked sections, moving from an arresting start into environment and habits, life cycles, scientific observations, and population decline. An accurate and involving report, flexible as background reading for study of animals, evolution, environment, or just plain trips to the zoo." Booklist

Teleki, Geza

Aerial apes; gibbons of Asia, by Geza Teleki, Lori Baldwin, Meredith Rucks. Coward, McCann & Geoghegan 1979 unp illus map $7.50 (2-4)   **599.88**

1 Gibbons
ISBN 0-698-20477-8   LC 78-10721

"Three pages of introductory text and an accompanying map present the physical appearance, eating habits, and native environment of these Asian apes, explaining how the animals are uniquely equipped for their aerial acrobatics and arboreal lives. Following are 24 pages of black-and-white photographs (some lacking clarity and sharpness) of the gibbons in midair action, close-up, clutching high tree branches and, once in a while to their own surprise, falling to the ground. Short captions describe their movements and colorations." Booklist

Goblin, a wild chimpanzee [by] Geza Teleki and Karen Steffy; with assistance from Lori Baldwin; illus. with photographs. Dutton 1977 56p illus $7.95 (4-6)   **599.88**

1 Chimpanzees
ISBN 0-525-30747-8   LC 77-8833

"Using a day-in-the-life approach, the authors present Goblin, a real chimp, in his natural habitat, Tanzania's Gombe National Park. Clean text and photographs chronicle his routine activities—feeding, napping, meandering—interspersed with periodic drama—playing too roughly with a friend or getting charged by a cape buffalo." Booklist

"The authors have afforded, through lucid text and pictures, an enlightening and rewarding view of chimp society and especially of the life of the alert, bouncy, curious, imitative, high-spirited Goblin and his loving mother." Sch Library J

More about wild primates: p56

600 TECHNOLOGY (APPLIED SCIENCES)

Papallo, George

What makes it work; technical illus. [by] Graham Forsaith. Arco 1976 143p illus $8.95, pa $4.95 (5 and up)   **600**

1 Technology
ISBN 0-668-03962-0; 0-668-03963-9   LC 76-14838

Reprint of 2 works published 1972 in Australia with titles: How it works, and More How it works

"Papallo explains the basic principles of technology behind such inventions as an offshore oil rig, a grain harvester, a refrigerator, a submarine, etc. Over 80 inventions are explained in simple layman's terms with serviceable illustrations. Although not a 'how-to-fix-it' book, nevertheless, this will fascinate tinkerers and gadget lovers." Sch Library J

Pollard, Michael

How things work. Larousse [1979 c1978] 96p illus $7.95 (5 and up)   **600**

1 Technology 2 Inventions
ISBN 0-88332-097-5   LC 78-54638

Mechanical and electronic inventions are described in two or three page chapters. Aircraft, engines, telescopes, scuba equipment, gears, radio, lasers and oil-rigs are among the products of modern technology which are covered here

This book offers "a variety of information for browsers or students needing material for brief reports. There is a wealth of illustration without clutter and a fairly tight organization that compensates for broad scope. Color photographs and diagrams supplement and relieve the three-column text, which is straight-forward and scientific." Booklist

604.6   Waste technology

Pringle, Laurence
Recycling resources. Macmillan Pub. Co.
1974 119p illus $5.95 (6 and up)   **604.6**

1 Recycling (Waste, etc.)
ISBN 0-02-775310-7   LC 72-81062

"In the course of the book, the operations and
problems of incinerators and landfills are discussed, as are the history and problems of throw-
away cans and bottles. Efforts to recycle materials such as paper, plastics, cars, cans, cloth
and glass are outlined in the context of the
total amount that is also wasted. The final chapters deal with plans for the future and the legislative, monetary and attitudinal problems that
have to be faced. Sound suggestions are given
for individuals to follow. Throughout the book,
black-and-white illustrations and cartoons are uncluttered and make their message clear. There is
a list of contents, an index and a graded list of
additional reading materials. The book itself is
printed on recycled paper." AAAS Sci Bks &
Films

Shanks, Ann Zane
About garbage and stuff; with photographs
by the author. Viking 1973 unp illus lib.
bdg. $5.95 (k-3)   **604.6**

1 Recycling (Waste, etc.)   2 Refuse and refuse
disposal
ISBN 0-670-10050-1   LC 73-5147

In this book "a discussion of recycling is cleverly approached from the child's viewpoint; it begins
with a family shopping for groceries, describes
the amount of garbage it throws away each day,
and the problem of garbage disposal: what happens when there is too much to use for landfill?
The family then separates its glass, metal, etc.
and the text describes recycling plants; it concludes by coming back to the two children of
the family. What can they do? Use both sides
of the paper when drawing . . . use disposable
paper instead of plastic, put things in one big
bag instead of many small ones, and so on. The
pictures are large scale, the text is clear and not
too heavy, and tone is brisk and matter-of-fact;
we have a problem, here's what we can do. No
dire threats, no coaxing." Chicago. Children's Bk
Center

608   Inventions and patents

Garrison, Webb
Why didn't I think of that? From alarm
clocks to zippers; illus. by Ray Abel.
Prentice-Hall 1977 120p illus $6.95 (4 and
up)   **608**

1 Inventions
ISBN 0-13-958603-2   LC 77-5806

This book "is a compilation of anecdotes describing innovations which have become a part
of everyday life. The author briefly describes the
problem and circumstances of the inventor or
innovator and the inspiration which led to a
solution. Most of the sketches include the financial reward accrued by the inventor. The title is
apt for most of the items discussed (e.g. book
matches, drive-in movies, ice cream cones, potato
chips, etc.), but the inspiration which led to
ballpoint pens, helicopters, Xerox copying machines, and zippers is beyond armchair musing.
The young reader will be entertained and impressed by these factual accounts of inventions
and discoveries. This book is highly recommended
to the creative and curious youngster." AAAS
Sci Bks & Films

Murphy, Jim
Weird & wacky inventions. Crown 1978
unp illus $7.95 (4 and up)   **608**

1 Inventions   2 Curiosities and wonders
ISBN 0-517-53318-9   LC 77-15859

"Murphy has brought together some of the
oddest of the four million or so inventions granted
patents by the U.S. Patent and Trademark Office
since it opened in 1790." Sch Library J
"The material is interesting, often amusing, and
Murphy has given added interest by showing pictures of each invention, presenting multiple choices
for guessing what it is or does, and giving the

answer and a fuller explanation with a turn of
the page. Quite useless and totally fascinating,
an entertaining book for browsers." Chicago.
Children's Bk Center

609   Technology—Historical and geographical treatment

Cooke, David C.
Inventions that made history. Putnam 1968
70p illus (These made history) lib. bdg. $4.99
(5 and up)   **609**

1 Inventions—History   2 Technology—History
ISBN 0-399-60302-6   LC 68-24508

Here are thirty-two inventions from printing
to the laser which have revolutionized the course
of human life. They are placed in historical perspective, and the long years of labor, the frequent failures and the breakthroughs are described

610.69   Medical personnel

Pelta, Kathy
What does a paramedic do? Illus. with
photographs. Dodd 1978 63p illus lib.
bdg. $5.95 (4-6)   **610.69**

1 Allied health personnel
ISBN 0-396-07541-X   LC 77-16868

This book discusses the work paramedics do
and the training they must undergo. It also
examines the history of emergency medical care
"Plentiful black-and-white photographs show
paramedics (mostly men here, the way the field
presently stands) undergoing training, handling
emergencies, and carrying out public education
programs." Booklist

Rockwell, Harlow
My doctor. Macmillan Pub. Co. 1973 unp
illus lib. bdg. $7.95 (k-1)   **610.69**

1 Physicians   2 Medicine
ISBN 0-02-777480-5   LC 72-92442

This book is intended to "familiarize children
with equipment in a modern doctor's office. Depicted are such items as jars of bandages, a
sphygmomanometer and an otoscope, an eye chart,
a hypodermic syringe and needle, an open refrigerator with jars of medicines, wooden sticks for
tongue depression, and a stethoscope." Sch Library J
"An uncluttered format, poster-like water-color
illustrations, and an economical text are combined
in an uncondescending picture-information book
for the young child anticipating a routine check-
up at the doctor's office. Satisfying and reassuring in its explicit, calm presentation of standard
medical office equipment, the book is also noteworthy for avoiding stereotyped roles without
blatantly advertising the fact. 'My doctor' is
depicted as a woman." Horn Bk

612   Human physiology

Adler, Irving
Taste, touch and smell [by] Irving and
Ruth Adler. Day 1966 48p illus lib. bdg. $6.89
(3-5)   **612**

1 Senses and sensation
ISBN 0-381-99953-X   LC 66-11448

"The Reason why books"
The author describes how the senses of touch,
smell and taste work through the nervous system.
He also discusses the purpose served by each of
these senses
"The vocabulary is sophisticated, precise, and
will expand the language facility of the reader."
Sch Library J
Word list: p47

Your eyes [by] Irving and Ruth Adler.
Day 1962 48p illus lib. bdg. $6.89 (3-5)   **612**

1 Eye   2 Vision
ISBN 0-381-99947-5   LC 62-16223

Adler, Irving—Continued

"The Reason why books"

"A text that comprises discussions of several aspects of sight: normal and abnormal eyesight, color blindness, education for the blind and the partially-sighted, optical illusions, and the structure and function of the human eye." Chicago. Children's Bk Center

"Illustrated with many diagrams and a few drawings and photographs. A glossary is appended." Booklist

Aliki

My five senses. Crowell 1962 unp illus (Let's-read-and-find-out science bks) lib. bdg. $7.89, pa $2.95 (k-2) **612**

1 Senses and sensation
ISBN 0-690-56763-4; 0-690-56768-5   LC 62-7150

"For beginning independent readers, a simply written book about the senses. The [author's] illustrations are lovely, and with light humor they capture a child's delight as he sniffs a flower and his bliss as, with eyes closed, he licks an ice cream cone. While readers will be already familiar with some of the facts established by the text, they will probably become more conscious of the fact that different senses combine in varied ways dependent on the activity at hand." Chicago. Children's Bk Center

Ancona, George

It's a baby. Dutton 1979 unp illus $7.95 (k-2) **612**

1 Infants
ISBN 0-525-32598-0   LC 79-10453

"Charming, candid black-and-white photographs document the growth and learning experiences of a baby boy from birth to age one. Sucking, smiling, crawling, walking—each development of the baby's mental and physical abilities is described in simple terms that express the wonder and joy of watching a baby discover the world. A tender, warm introduction to the miracle of human life." Booklist

Andry, Andrew C.

How babies are made, by Andrew C. Andry and Steven Schepp; illus. by Blake Hampton. Time-Life Bks. 1968 unp illus $5.95 (k-3) **612**

1 Reproduction 2 Sex education   LC 68-55284

"The illustrations give clear physiological information about intercourse, pregnancy and birth, and the text moves from flowers to animals to humans in a brief commentary on each illustration." The AAAS Sci Bk List for Children

"Colorful paper cut-outs illustrate this introduction to reproduction." Princeton Pub Library. Hello, baby

Balestrino, Philip

The skeleton inside you; illus. by Don Bolognese. Crowell 1971 32p illus (Let's-read-and-find-out-science bks) lib. bdg. $7.89, pa $1.45 (1-3) **612**

1 Bones
ISBN 0-690-74123-5; 0-690-01263-2   LC 72-132290

"A very simplified text on skeletal structure this does not describe all the bones in the human body, but discusses the different shapes of bones, something of their structure and their function, cartilage, joints, and ligaments. The text also mentions the foods that are high in calcium, necessary for strong bones, and the fact that bones grow and mend. The writing is matter-of-fact and informal, the amount of coverage right for the primary grades audience. The illustrations are lively and often illuminating." Chicago. Children's Bk Center

Berry, James R.

Why you feel hot, why you feel cold; your body's temperature; illus. by William Ogden. Little 1973 48p illus lib. bdg. $6.95 (2-4) **612**

1 Temperature 2 Fever
ISBN 0-316-09211-8   LC 72-11703

This book "explains why you feel hot and cold and why you may have a fever and chills, along with experiments that help explain the ideas. Large type. Helpful illustrations." Sci and Children

Brenner, Barbara

Bodies; with photographs and design by George Ancona. Dutton 1973 unp illus $8.95 (k-2) **612**

1 Physiology 2 Anatomy, Human
ISBN 0-525-26770-0   LC 72-89838

This book "points out the qualities that make the animal world different from plants or inanimate objects, briefly discusses the components of the human body (blood, flesh, skin, bones—all made of cells) and describes all the things people can do (run, jump, sleep, eliminate, eat, etc.)." Chicago. Children's Bk Center

"Brenner makes clear that though human skin and blood cells are similar, everyone does things in his own way. The crisp, skillfully assembled photographs (including two of undressed children and one of a child sitting on a toilet) are matched by the text which is mature in tone and presents factual material without condescension." Library J

Cole, Joanna

Twins; the story of multiple births, by Joanna Cole & Madeleine Edmondson; with drawings by Salvatore Raciti & photographs. Morrow 1972 64p illus lib. bdg. $6 (3-6) **612**

1 Twins
ISBN 0-688-31981-5   LC 75-168470

"Beginning with an explanation of the difference between fraternal and identical twins, the authors examine the biological development of twins, Siamese twins and supertwins, discuss the relationship between twins as they grow up, and tell of the importance of twins to scientists studying the effects of heredity and environment on human development. The informative wide-ranging account is enlivened by anecdotes and illustrated with numerous photographs and drawings." Booklist

Day, Beth

The secret world of the baby, by Beth Day and Margaret Liley; illus. with photographs by Lennart Nilsson, Suzanne Szasz, and others. Random House 1968 113p illus lib. bdg. $5.69 **612**

1 Embryology 2 Infants
ISBN 0-394-91555-0   LC 68-23670

"From conception through the first few months after birth the baby's physical development and his changing responses are explored." Princeton Pub Library. Hello, baby

"In this successful collaboration by a pediatrician and a layman, a simply written, authoritative text is given added usefulness by photographs of the infant in utero and added charm by photographs of a newborn and very young babies. . . . The final chapters—on the infant's ways of communicating and on the evidences of mental and physical growth—are particularly interesting." Sutherland. The Best in Children's Bks

De Schweinitz, Karl

Growing up; how we become alive, are born, and grow. 4th ed. Macmillan Pub. Co. 1965 54p illus pa $1.50 (2-5) **612**

1 Reproduction 2 Sex education
ISBN 0-02-042870-7   LC 65-20192

First published 1928

An account of the processes of procreation, birth, and early growth. "Well written and thoroughly treated, this book explores the birth process in animals before introducing life and its beginning in humans. Information is treated honestly, simply, and without awkwardness. The photographs accompanying the text have been carefully selected and are in good taste." Adventuring With Bks. 2d edition

Doss, Helen

Your skin holds you in; illus. with drawings by Christine Bondante and photographs. Messner 1978 64p illus lib. bdg. $6.97 (3-5) **612**

1 Skin
ISBN 0-671-32935-9   LC 78-2777

"Doss discusses skin anatomy and function as well as fingerprints, hair, nails, skin color, injuries to the skin, and skin hygiene. The text is clear and accessible with large type, wide margins, and many useful drawings throughout. (Especially interesting are the cross sections of blisters, pimples, and blackheads.)" Sch Library J
Glossary: p62-63

Elgin, Kathleen

The human body: the brain; written and illus. by Kathleen Elgin. Watts, F. [1970 c1967] 51p illus lib. bdg. $6.90 (3-5)   **612**

1 Brain 2 Nervous system
ISBN 0-531-01170-4

First published 1967 with title: Read about the brain

"This is a very simple introduction to the human brain. It is mainly a vocabulary identification of parts of the brain and how it controls the body functions. Due to oversimplification there is not an adequate explanation of current information on how the different parts of the brain operate. The superior capacity of the human brain over those of animals is pointed out. Illustrations are clear." Sch Library J

The human body: the digestive system; written and illus. by Kathleen Elgin. Watts, F. 1973 72p illus lib. bdg. $6.90 (4 and up)   **612**

1 Digestion
ISBN 0-531-01183-6   LC 73-4417

The digestive process is described from the time food enters the mouth to the excretion of waste materials. Medical terms for the parts of the digestive system are included in the text with pronunciations and definitions

The human body: the heart; written and illus. by Kathleen Elgin. Watts, F. 1968 50p illus lib. bdg. $6.90 (3-5)   **612**

1 Heart
ISBN 0-531-01174-7   LC 68-17703

The heart is the powerful pump that sends the blood stream on its way. This is an explanation of how that most critical muscle works to help move the nutrients and oxygen throughout the circulatory system

"An introduction to the topic that is limited in usefulness by some weaknesses of the illustrations, which are very handsome in design, but susceptible to confusion in the way color is used. . . . The text is clear; it is focused on a description of heart action rather than a complete description of the circulatory system." Chicago. Children's Bk Center

The human body: the muscles; written and illus. by Kathleen Elgin. Watts, F. 1973 71p illus lib. bdg. $6.90 (3-6)   **612**

1 Muscles
ISBN 0-531-01181-X   LC 72-8130

"The need for muscles in the human body, the types of muscles—smooth, cardiac, and skeletal—with which people are endowed, and a general description of how these work are covered in clear, concise language in the first third of the book. New terms are defined as they are introduced, and the name and pronunciation are given for each skeletal muscle described. A rather small number of pages of text and illustration . . . deal specifically with cardiac and smooth muscles. The remainder of the book is devoted to selected skeletal muscles. Location of the muscle in the body is ilustrated, and function is explained. The author shows how people are able to smile, eat, swallow, move eyes, lift arms, use legs, breathe and perform numerous other physical activities by using muscles. Illustrations are simple uncomplicated line drawings, and these are used profusely. Children at intermediate and advanced elementary levels with a curiosity about human muscular activity should find this a helpful reference." Sci Bks

The human body: the skeleton; written and illus. by Kathleen Elgin. Watts, F. 1971 66p illus lib. bdg. $6.90 (3-6)   **612**

1 Bones
ISBN 0-531-01180-1   LC 74-152741

This is a lucid straightforward "explanation of the structure and function of the skeleton. It describes the composition and growth of bones, tells how they move, and names and discusses in a few sentences each of the major bones of the body." Booklist

"Liberal paragraphing, careful placement of the large illustrations, a pronunciation guide following each term as it appears, and a complete index make this book extremely useful as an introduction to the skeleton." Sch Library J

Goldin, Augusta

Straight hair, curly hair; illus. by Ed Emberley. Crowell 1966 unp illus (Let's-read-and-find-out science bks) lib. bdg. $7.89, pa $1.45 (k-2)   **612**

1 Hair
ISBN 0-690-77921-6; 0-690-77928-8   LC 66-12669

Also available in a Spanish language edition for $7.89 (ISBN 0-690-77923-2)

To explain why hair can be straight or curly, this "book tells about the cross-sectional shape of hair and about its follicles. It presents genuine experiments . . . [using] hair, Scotch tape, keys and some curiosity." Scientific Am

"An easy-to-read scientific explanation. . . . The humorous drawings add interest to a subject about which most children are curious." We Build Together

Gross, Ruth Belov

A book about your skeleton; pictures by Deborah Robison. Hastings House [1979 c1978] 30p illus (A Science starter bk) $5.95 (k-2)   **612**

1 Bones
ISBN 0-8038-0794-5   LC 78-24168

"This clear and simple text has good-sized print, plenty of space on the pages, and illustrations that are bright and tidy, if seldom informative. The text describes the bones of the human body—without too much detail or too much technical terminology for the young reader—and explains their several functions, how they are constructed, and why diet is a factor in keeping bones strong. A labelled skeleton is pictured at the end of the text." Chicago. Children's Bk Center

Kalina, Sigmund

Your nerves and their messages; illus. by Arabelle Wheatley. Lothrop 1973 48p illus $6.48 (3-5)   **612**

1 Nervous system
ISBN 0-688-50045-5   LC 72-9360

"Less inclusive and less difficult than the Silversteins' 'The Nervous System: the Inner Networks' [entered below] this covers . . . brain structure, simple reflex acts, the nerve network, and the spinal cord." Sch Library J

"The illustrations, always appealing, are of two sorts: simple scenes in the daily life of children pointing to the function of the nervous system and technical illustrations of nerve cells, nerve pathways and portions of the nervous system. The well-written and accurate text stresses the basic functional unit of the nervous system, the reflex arc." Sci Bks

May, Julian

A new baby comes; illus. by Brendan Lynch. Creative Educ. Soc. 1970 unp illus lib. bdg. $6.95 (1-4)   **612**

1 Reproduction 2 Embryology 3 Sex education
ISBN 0-87191-033-0   LC 70-84731

An account of the prenatal development of a baby from ovum to birth in simple text and illustrations

"Worthwhile are actual-size sketches of the embryo through the first five months. Emphasized are the family's preparations for the coming of the baby and, finally, pictures of the baby's growth stages to womanhood with a baby of her own." Appraisal

Nilsson, Lennart

How was I born? A story in pictures. Delacorte Press/Seymour Lawrence 1975 31p illus $6.95 (3-6)   **612**

1 Reproduction 2 Embryology 3 Sex education
ISBN 0-440-05378-1   LC 75-11757

"A Merloyd Lawrence book"

Translated from the original Swedish by Jan Cornell and Rune Pettersson

"The first half of the book deals with the developing human fetus. . . . A brief text describes nutrition and various fetal changes in size, tail, gill slits, and heartbeat. . . . The second part of the book contains a matter-of-fact description of intercourse and fertilization." Horn Bk

Nilsson, Lennart—*Continued*

"The pictures are extremely beautiful color photographs of embryo and fetuses within fetal membranes or with these stripped away; black-and-white photographs of newborn and young babies with parents, and very clear outline diagrams showing genital organs. The text is detailed and clear. . . . This is a book that should be easy to use with children. Although generally attractive in format, the offset printing and color plates on grayish paper make for a certain dreariness." Appraisal

Nourse, Alan E.

Hormones. Watts, F. 1979 87p illus lib. bdg. $6.45 (6 and up)   612

1 Hormones
ISBN 0-531-02892-5   LC 79-11785

"An Impact book"
In this book "clear explanations of the thyroid and pituitary functions, the use of insulin and cortisone, sex hormones and their role in reproduction, and dysfunctions of thyroid hormones are emphasized by informative illustrations. The cover lists clinical-sounding terms; however no glossary is provided; these words are italicized in the text, some are found in the index. This is no real hardship, but may discourage the slower reader who has no quick access to definitions. Recommended as a basic presentation." VOYA
Additional reading: p83

Parker, Stephen

Life before birth: the story of the first nine months; illus. by John Bavosi. Cambridge 1979 48p illus $6.95, pa $2.95 (3-6)   612

1 Fetus 2 Embryology
ISBN 0-521-22382-2; 0-521-29464-9   LC 78-60029

"Adapted from a slide-sound program at the British Museum, this is divided into four parts: the fertilization of the egg, the development of the cells into a human fetus, its growth into a baby ready to be born, and the birth." Booklist
"The color illustrations are superb. The scientifically accurate text is well written, but quite technical. Compressed within 48 pages is a wealth of information." Appraisal

Portal, Colette

The beauty of birth; adapted from the French by Guy Daniels. Knopf 1971 26p illus lib. bdg. $4.99 (3-6)   612

1 Reproduction 2 Embryology 3 Sex education
ISBN 0-394-92287-5   LC 70-155813

"Delicate and precise watercolor illustrations show the development of a baby in utero, from ovulation and conception through the embryonic and fetal stages to parturition. Especially interesting are the pages on which the author-artist shows the growth of individual anatomical features such as the hand, changing from a knobbly bud to the articulated perfection of an infant's hand. The text is accurate, straightforward, and lucid." Sutherland. The Best in Children's Bks

Riedman, Sarah R.

Hormones: how they work. Rev. ed. of Our hormones and how they work. Illus. by Norman Gorbaty. Abelard-Schuman 1973 222p illus $9.95 (6 and up)   612

1 Hormones
ISBN 0-200-00005-5   LC 72-12072

First published 1956
"Explaining complex interconnections between systems of cells and tissues, organs, and organisms requires great patience, a gift for words, and an understanding of what a reader does or does not know. Dr. Riedman has done a creditable job. . . . She writes without the mawkishness characteristic of many books for young people. Beginning with the rather complex discovery of insulin and continuing through cyclic AMP and the prostaglandins, the author describes the discovery of hormones and their discoveries. . . . The technical aspects of the book, the line drawings in a diagrammatic style, the binding, and type style are good; a useful index is appended." Sci Bks

Sheffield, Margaret

Where do babies come from? Illus. by Sheila Bewley. Knopf 1973 [c1972] 33p illus $6.95 (k-3)   612

1 Reproduction 2 Sex education
ISBN 0-394-48482-7   LC 72-10044

First published 1972 in England
Based on a BBC program used throughout the British primary school system, this book is designed to answer the "questions young children pose about how the sperm fertilizes the egg, how it gets into the mother's body, and how the baby gets out. Nearly all the paintings show nude people—infants, a prepubescent boy and girl, grown lovers, a pregnant mother, a baby growing inside the woman's body, a newborn having the cord cut, and finally, a clothed young couple with their new infant." Sch Library J
"The information is given in serious, forthright style, with all the facts included and with the use of correct terminology. What makes this book different from (and, for the most part, better than) other such books is the tone, without a specific reference to the beauty and intricacy of birth, the mood of reverence for life is created in a harmonious complementing of text and illustration." Chicago. Children's Bk Center

Showers, Paul

A baby starts to grow; illus. by Rosalind Fry. Crowell 1969 33p illus (Let's-read-and-find-out science bks) lib. bdg. $7.89, pa $2.95 (k-2)   612

1 Embryology
ISBN 0-690-11320-X; 0-690-11325-0   LC 69-11827

Unlike Showers' other book: Before you were a baby, entered below, this book does not begin with a description of the sexual act leading to conception. It does, however, "go into greater detail on embryonic growth, in a simple, clear, accurate text accompanied by lively illustrations. The material is very basic and much simplified, the format definitely juvenile, making this unsuitable for use beyond the second grade." Sch Library J

Before you were a baby, by Paul Showers and Kay Sperry Showers; illus. by Ingrid Fetz. Crowell 1968 33p illus (Let's-read-and-find-out science bks) lib. bdg. $7.89 (1-3)   612

1 Reproduction 2 Embryology 3 Sex education
ISBN 0-690-12882-7   LC 68-13588

"Here is a well-illustrated book of human reproduction that begins with a description of the sex organs and the process of fertilization. Then it describes the initial stages of cell division, implantation, gastrulations, and weekly stages in development until about 10 weeks when the foetus is fully formed. There is an excellent colored illustration of each stage; also of the four, six, and eight month old foetus, and finally the birth occurs." Sci Bks
"Without fanfare, mystery, coyness, or superfluous information, this gives the facts . . . in a format that is attractive and in language that is clear and simple. The illustrations of children are beguiling, the diagrams helpful, and the print large; the writing is lucid and matter-of-fact." Sat Rev

A drop of blood; illus. by Don Madden. Crowell 1967 unp illus (Let's-read-and-find-out science bks) lib. bdg. $7.89, pa $2.95 (1-3)   612

1 Blood
ISBN 0-690-24526-2; 0-690-24531-9   LC 67-23672

"Crisp, straightforward writing and gay, cartoonlike illustrations combine to make this introduction to the topic of human blood clear, simple, and accurate. The author describes circulation and the protective powers of the blood, the types of cells of which blood is composed, and the reassuring fact that there is constant replenishment of the blood supply—although the details of this process are not given." Sutherland. The Best In Children's Bks

Showers, Paul—*Continued*

Hear your heart; illus. by Joseph Low. Crowell 1968 35p illus (Let's-read-and-find-out science bks) $6.95, lib. bdg. $7.89, pa $2.95 (k-3)   **612**

1 Heart 2 Blood—Circulation
ISBN 0-690-37378-3; 0-690-37379-1; 0-690-00636-5
LC 68-11067

"Simple, graphic sketches with text illustrate the mechanism of the heart, beating day and night, varying its pace with age and pumping blood out of the arteries into the veins. Included are experiments on hearing the heart beat thru a tube and on counting the pulse at given places." Bruno. Bks for Sch Libraries, 1968

How you talk; illus. by Robert Galster. Crowell [1967 c1966] unp illus (Let's-read-and-find-out science bks) lib. bdg. $7.89, pa $1.45 (k-3)   **612**

1 Speech 2 Sounds
ISBN 0-690-42136-2; 0-690-00637-3
LC 66-15766

Simple experiments demonstrate "how humans use the lungs, larynx, mouth, tongue, lips, teeth and nose to produce speech." Minnesota

"The text is simple, the animated drawings are uncomplicated, and the experiments included are both helpful and fun. Parents as well as teachers will find this useful." Booklist

Look at your eyes; illus. by Paul Galdone. Crowell 1962 unp illus (Let's-read-and-find-out science bks) $6.95, lib. bdg. $7.89, pa $1.45 (k-2)   **612**

1 Eye
ISBN 0-690-50727-5; 0-690-50728-3; 0-690-01261-6
LC 62-12821

Also available in a Spanish language edition for $7.95 (ISBN 0-690-50729-1)

"The young reader is asked to observe his eyes in a mirror as he reads about the human eyes and the specifics of eyecolor; the function of eyelids, eyebrows, and eyelashes; of tears; and the reason for the changes in size of the pupil." The AAAS Sci Bk List For Children

The book "is lucid in explaining basic facts . . . and the writing is not any more stilted than a book for beginning independent readers must be. It is unusual, also, in the simplicity with which the text and the illustrations shows the speaker to be a Negro child; he is quite matter-of-fact about brown eyes, quite matter-of-fact about his friends, whose eyes may be blue or brown. And in the last illustrations, waiting in utter boredom for his mother to get back to the car from her shopping and then seeing his mother's smiling eyes between bundles, he is every child." Chicago. Children's Bk Center

Use your brain; illus. by Rosalind Fry. Crowell 1971 33p illus (Let's-read-and-find-out science bks) $7.95, lib. bdg. $7.89, pa $1.95 (1-3)   **612**

1 Brain 2 Nervous system
ISBN 0-690-85410-2; 0-690-85411-0; 0-690-00204-1
LC 79-157646

"A good introduction for the young reader, not going into too much detail but giving facts about the structure and function of the brain and some information about the rest of the nervous system. The text explains very simply the response to stimuli and the role of nerves; the illustrations are lively but less informative than the few diagrams. . . . Several pages are devoted to the effect of drugs on the efficiency of the nervous system." Chicago. Children's Bk Center

What happens to a hamburger; illus. by Anne Rockwell. Crowell 1970 33p illus (Let's-read-and-find-out science bks) $7.95, lib. bdg. $7.89, pa $1.45 (1-3)   **612**

1 Digestion
ISBN 0-690-87540-1; 0-690-87541-X; 0-690-01264-1
LC 70-106578

This book explains how not only hamburgers but all things we eat are turned into bones and muscles and energy. Simple experiments are included

"A simple but quite adequate explanation of the digestive process, with attractive illustrations that only occasionally veer from the factual—such as a conventional heart-shaped symbol in a diagram of the circulatory system. The text does not give all the facts or terms (there is no mention of enzymes) and it does, in some instances, move into peripheral areas, but on the whole it is a competent, simplified treatment of a phenomenon about which most children are curious." Chicago. Children's Bk Center

Your skin and mine; illus. by Paul Galdone. Crowell 1965 unp illus (Let's-read-and-find-out science bks) lib. bdg. $7.89, pa $2.95 (1-3)   **612**

1 Skin
ISBN 0-690-91127-0; 0-690-00205-X   LC 65-16185

"The simple, brief text and attractive illustrations present the basic facts about skin and its functions, including color differences, the dermis and epidermis, hair follicles, pores, sensation and temperature adjustments, etc. The discussion of color differences and the use of boys of different color are natural parts of the text and illustrations. Large print and attractive format." We Build Together

"The information on skin color could be used to develop concepts in the area of racial understanding." Minnesota

Silverstein, Alvin

The digestive system; how living creatures use food, by Alvin Silverstein and Virginia B. Silverstein; illus. by Mel Erikson. Prentice-Hall 1970 74p illus $6.95 (4 and up) **612**

1 Digestion
ISBN 0-13-213009-2   LC 75-102279

"The book explains why digestion is necessary to all living organisms, describes the complex physical and chemical processes involved in human digestion, and compares human digestion with that of lower animals and plants. Difficult words are defined in the text with the pronunciation given the first time the word is used." Booklist

"Readers will need some acquaintance with chemistry and biology; diagrams are clearly drawn but not explicitly explained, nor is the scale indicated. One chapter discusses a balanced diet and the body's need for minerals and vitamins. The final one deals briefly with hunger in the world, the importance of protein in an infant's diet, and the search for new sources of food—but these vital issues call for greater emphasis. . . . This title will be useful since the subject is not treated this extensively elsewhere." Library J

The endocrine system; hormones in the living world [by] Alvin Silverstein and Virginia B. Silverstein; illus. by Mel Erikson. Prentice-Hall 1971 68p illus $6.95 (4 and up) **612**

1 Glands, Ductless 2 Hormones
ISBN 0-13-277152-7   LC 70-135648

This is an "account of the endocrine system and the effects of various hormones on the body. Covered are animal hormones, plant hormones, pheromones (hormones for communication), and hormone research." Sch Library J

"This book is a concise and informative overview of endocrinal systems in living organisms. It should be most useful as a source for reports or for those students in search of material supplemental to classroom presentation. The format and print are excellent and highly readable. A table of contents and index are included. Scientific terminology is given phonetic pronunciation within the context when the term appears for the first time. The illustrations by Mel Erikson are adequate but not inspiring, mostly because of the publisher's decision to run them in black and white with one color." Appraisal

The nervous system; the inner networks [by] Alvin Silverstein and Virginia B. Silverstein; illus. by Mel Erikson. Prentice-Hall 1971 64p illus $6.95 (4 and up) **612**

1 Nervous system
ISBN 0-13-610964-0   LC 76-119514

"In addition to giving information on the structure and function of the brain, spinal cord, and neurons, the Silversteins compare the human nervous system with that of lower animals and touch on the problem of mental illness." Booklist

Silverstein, Alvin—*Continued*

The authors "have skillfully employed the analogies of facets of telecommunications systems to assist in explaining the organization and functioning of the human central, peripheral, and autonomic nervous systems. The illustrations are closely integrated with the text and are well-labeled. Neurological terms are printed in italics and pronunciation is indicated immediately following the first use of a term in the book. . . . Throughout the book, insofar as the rather difficult material permits, the young reader is involved by asking him to perform certain exercises, and this device will maintain his interest." Sci Bks

The sense organs; our link with the world [by] Alvin Silverstein and Virginia B. Silverstein; illus. by Mel Erikson. Prentice-Hall 1971 73p illus $6.95 (4 and up) **612**

1 Senses and sensation
ISBN 0-13-806687-6   LC 75-130373

This book focuses "on the sense organs, describing the structure and function of human eyes, ears, nose, mouth, and skin receptors and comparing them briefly with those of other animals. The Silversteins also discuss the body's inner senses such as those that help maintain balance, perceptive thirst and hunger; and give a number of simple experiments for the reader to perform." Booklist

"For the most part, information is adequate for the very young, but in some instances it is scanty, especially about the middle ear and the elimination of blind spots in our vision. Short chapters are arranged logically. Durable binding, attractive black-and-green illustrations, and large, readable type make for ideal format. The style is interesting and clear, and the book has a very good index." Appraisal

The skeletal system; frameworks for life [by] Alvin Silverstein and Virginia B. Silverstein; illus. by Lee J. Ames. Prentice-Hall 1972 74p illus $5.95 (4 and up) **612**

1 Bones
ISBN 0-13-812701-8   LC 71-39146

"The authors discuss the structure and function of the human skeleton, the growth and changes in the bone structure from birth to adulthood, the internal and external skeletons of other animals and insects, and the importance of fossilized bones in revealing information about past life on earth." Booklist

"An excellent introduction to basic anatomy. . . . The inclusion of standard terminology with good definitions as part of the text provides a stepping stone to more detailed works and introduces advanced concepts without 'talking down' to students. This reviewer highly recommends it as an addition to the general science resources shelf." Sci Bks

Wilson, Ron

How the body works; foreword by Edmund O. Rothschild. Larousse 1978 96p illus $7.95 (4 and up) **612**

1 Physiology 2 Anatomy, Human 3 Medicine
ISBN 0-88332-096-7   LC 78-54036

"This is practically an encyclopedia of the human body, covering all of the various structures and functions (skeleton, muscles, circulation, digestion, etc.) as well as many other related topics (intelligence, [birth, growth, aging, disease] hospitals, spare part surgery, etc.). Each topic is clearly and succinctly explained; many photographs, diagrams, and drawings serve to further amplify the text. Readers should be aware that British word usage (nappier for diaper) and spelling (haemoglobin, oestrogen, oesophogus) predominate. While one or two digarams should be more clearly labeled and the glossary is incomplete, the text as a whole is excellent and the format very appealing." Sch Library J

Zim, Herbert S.

Blood; illus. by René Martin. Morrow 1968 63p illus lib. bdg. $6.48 (4-6) **612**

1 Blood
ISBN 0-688-31109-1   LC 68-12692

This study of blood describes its composition and the processes by which the body makes use of it. Other topics included are the uses of vaccines and antitoxins, beliefs and customs concerning blood, and an explanation of blood groups and the Rh factor

"This book is a clearly superior explanation of blood, its components and functions. . . . With few exceptions, the book is quite readable and comprehensible and the illustrations are generally useful in expanding the contents of the text." Appraisal

Bones; illus. by René Martin. Morrow 1969 63p illus lib. bdg. $6.48 (3-5) **612**

1 Bones
ISBN 0-688-31115-6   LC 69-14482

"A sound, basic explanation of the composition and formation of bones and the parts and function of the human skeleton together with brief comments on the uses of bones, presented in Zim's usual simple lucid style." Booklist

The book "uses René Martin's drawings as pictures—that is, as tools for description—and uses them in striking style. You will never see anyone walking around with his skeleton visible in detail, but after reading this book you should have a pretty good idea of what a person's framework would look like if this were possible." Horn Bk

Our senses and how they work; illus. by Herschel Wartik. Morrow 1956 64p illus lib. bdg. $6.48 (4-6) **612**

1 Senses and sensation
ISBN 0-688-31550-X   LC 56-6364

"An introduction to the senses, what they are, details of the working of the five major senses, and the nervous system in general." Chicago. Children's Bk Center

"Interesting, and concise text with clear drawings. . . . Experiments are suggested." Library J

Your brain and how it works; illus. by René Martin. Morrow 1972 63p illus lib. bdg. $6.48 (4-6) **612**

1 Brain 2 Nervous system
ISBN 0-688-31922-X   LC 78-168479

"The author discusses the growth of the nervous system, its microscopic and macroscopic structure, the functions of its parts, and especially emphasizes interrelationships and interdependencies. He illustrates these with common experiences from daily life, thereby helping to develop a concept of mind. He offers a few standard exercises by which the reader can test his perception and finishes with a little wholesome advice which the development of his text has given him every right to offer. Illustrations, both diagrams and pictures, are helpful." Appraisal

Your skin; illus. by Jean Zallinger. Morrow 1979 62p illus $6.95, lib. bdg. $6.67 (4 and up) **612**

1 Skin 2 Skin—Diseases
ISBN 0-688-22178-5; 0-688-32178-X   LC 78-10878

"This encyclopedic treatment will help children understand the skin's complexity and importance. From its origin in the embryo, to its structure, to differences because of sex and race, to problems that arise, the skin is described and illustrated in detail. Race is treated simply and straightforwardly." Sci and Children

"Common problems of acne, aging, rashes, allergies, and other skin diseases are described with comments about remedies such as cosmetics, surgery, and healthy diet." Booklist

Your stomach and digestive tract; illus. by René Martin. Morrow 1973 63p illus lib. bdg. $6.48 (3-6) **612**

1 Stomach 2 Digestion
ISBN 0-688-31838-X   LC 72-6734

"This step-by-step digestive tract tour assumes no prior knowledge of the area; Zim locates and describes the stomach and then backtracks to the mouth where the process begins. From there he traces the path of food from start to finish, describes chemical actions along the way, and explains the hows and whys of two of the most common stomach disorders, vomiting and ulcers." Booklist

"Each step of the process is described clearly. . . . This explanation of man's alimentary canal, accompanied by black-and-white drawings, will complement the information found in the Silversteins' 'The Digestive System: How Living Creatures Use Food.' [entered above]." Sch Library J

613   General and personal hygiene

Cobb, Vicki

Supersuits; illus. by Peter Lippman. Lippincott 1975 95p illus $7.95, pa $2.95 (3-6)   **613**

1 Clothing and dress—Environmental aspects
ISBN 0-397-31559-7; 0-397-31609-7   LC 74-19083

"Clothes may not exactly make the man, but in the five unusual environments described in this book, specially designed clothes ('supersuits') are vital to man's survival. The intense cold of polar exploration, the extreme heat of fire fighting, the crushing depths of undersea exploration, the rarified altitude of mountain climbing and the hostile environment of outer space all provide hazardous barriers to exploration of these areas. Each chapter is devoted to an interesting analysis of one of these environments and its effects upon the human body. This leads directly into a discussion of the special clothing needed for man to function safely in that environment. Each chapter concludes with an informal but highly communicative sketch of the 'supersuit' designed for that particular service." AAAS Sci Bks & Films

"The drawings while not in color, are imaginative and fit the text well. Of special importance also is the large type size, and the descriptive diagrams of each of the protective suits." Sci and Children

Kozuszek, Jane Eyerly

Hygiene. Watts, F. 1978 64p illus lib. bdg. $6.45 (4-6)   **613**

1 Hygiene 2 Grooming, Personal
ISBN 0-531-01410-X   LC 77-16637

"A First book"

"The author discusses the problems of dirt, how to keep skin clean and free from infection, the body's immunity system, and how to prevent food-related diseases." Sch Library J

"The photographs and illustrations add much to this scientifically accurate, lucidly written text. A book like this is exactly what is needed for this age group." Appraisal

613.2   Dietetics

Asimov, Isaac

How did we find out about vitamins? Illus. by David Wool. Walker & Co. 1974 64p illus lib. bdg. $5.85 (4 and up)   **613.2**

1 Vitamins
ISBN 0-8027-6184-4   LC 73-92453

"The discovery of vitamins provides an excellent case study in the history of science, beginning with the early observation and description of certain human diseases. It proceeds to the experimentation that led to isolating the related vitamins, and concludes with the still incomplete knowledge of the role these substances play in the chemistry of the body. Dr. Asimov unfolds the step-by-step processes which resulted in our modern knowledge of such diseases as scurvy, beri-beri, rickets, and pellagra. This book should be a useful supplement—more importantly, 'an essential part of'—the study of nutrition." Sci and Children

Nourse, Alan E.

Vitamins. Watts, F. 1977 66p illus lib. bdg. $6.45 (5 and up)   **613.2**

1 Vitamins
ISBN 0-531-00096-6   LC 76-47505

"A Concise guide"

In this introduction to vitamins, illustrated with photographs and drawings, the author "recounts the expected stories of deficiency diseases and how, bit by bit, scientists found that vitamins played crucial roles in maintaining body health. A little vitamin chemistry runs through the text as each vitamin's role is described; biological terms are printed in boldface type." Booklist

"This is serious and authoritative, yet written in a direct style. Nourse . . . is objective about controversial topics such as the value of massive doses of vitamin C, his material is organized well, and he includes a brief list of books for further reading and an index. . . . Diagrams are adequate; photographs—especially those paired pictures of before-and-after patients—are dramatic." Chicago. Children's Bk Center

613.7   Physical fitness

Antonacci, Robert J.

Physical fitness for young champions [by] Robert J. Antonacci and Jene Barr; illus. by Frank Mullins. 2d ed. McGraw 1975 144p illus lib. bdg. $7.95 (5 and up)   **613.7**

1 Physical fitness 2 Exercise
ISBN 0-07-002142-2   LC 75-2226

First published 1962

After describing ways of testing physical fitness using the Kraus-Weber Test and the President's Youth Physical Fitness Test, the author describes exercises to develop muscle strength, coordination, and speed and suggests activities for keeping fit. Exercise advice for the physically and mentally handicapped is included

Carr, Rachel

Be a frog, a bird, or a tree; Rachel Carr's creative yoga exercises for children; photographs by Edward Kimball, Jr. Illus. by Don Hedin. Doubleday 1973 95p illus $6.95, lib. bdg. $7.90 (1-4)   **613.7**

1 Yoga 2 Exercise
ISBN 0-385-00339-0; 0-385-02358-8   LC 72-92198

"An excellent introduction to yoga for children begins with a brief explanation and suggestions for starting exercises, proceeding with a two-page spread for each of 30 poses: the first page has inspiring photographs of children taking the position, and the opposite page has a drawing of the animal or object for which the position is named, such as the cat or hare, and underneath it a simple first-person description of the movements and feelings involved." Booklist

"An appended section of notes for parents and teachers describes working with children, gives instructions for using the book, and—a useful addition—explains what each exercise accomplishes." Chicago. Children's Bk Center

Diskin, Eve

Yoga for children. Arco [1977 c1976] 207p illus $8.95 (4 and up)   **613.7**

1 Yoga
ISBN 0-668-04075-0   LC 76-28685

First published 1976 in paperback by Warner Books

Photographs, drawings, and text present beginning, intermediate, and advanced yoga exercises

"Children, parents, and teachers will thoroughly enjoy this well-illustrated guide to yoga. The instructions for each exercise are explicitly given with clear and simple explanations. Each is further described in terms of its benefits for the participant, and plentiful diagrams and photographs enable nonreaders to easily choose one to practice." Sch Library J

Showers, Paul

Sleep is for everyone; illus. by Wendy Watson. Crowell 1974 33p illus (Let's-read-and-find-out science bks) lib. bdg. $7.89 (k-2)   **613.7**

1 Sleep
ISBN 0-690-01118-1   LC 72-83785

The author "writes with simplicity and smoothness about an intricate subject. His text discusses the ways in which different forms of living things sleep, the fact that people need sleep and that their behavior becomes aberrant when they feel that need strongly, and that the amount of sleep need varies among individuals. The illustrations are attractive, adding humor especially to a description of an experiment in which four scientists stayed awake as long as they could. Nicely done." Chicago. Children's Bk Center

Turner, Alice K.

Yoga for beginners; photographs by Meryl Joseph. Watts, F. 1973 64p illus lib. bdg $6.45 (6 and up)   **613.7**

1 Yoga 2 Exercise
ISBN 0-531-02643-4   LC 73-5712

"A Concise guide"

"In a book that can be used at home or in conjunction with classes, the author writes enthusiastically and clearly about the disciplines and rewards of 'hatha-yoga.' The reader learns about the history of yogic 'asanas' (positions), exercises

Turner, Alice K.—*Continued*

that were developed and practiced in India over a thousand years ago. Photographs accompany a text which tells precisely how to perform all the exercises in a beginner's course. A final chapter gives suggestions for further study." Pub W

613.8 Addictions

Gorodetzky, Charles W.

What you should know about drugs [by] Charles W. Gorodetzky and Samuel T. Christian. Harcourt 1970 121p illus $5.95 (5 and up)   **613.8**

1 Drug abuse 2 Drugs
ISBN 0-15-295510-0   LC 74-128366

"Curriculum-related books"
"Although this gives enough coverage to be useful to adults it is so simply written that it serves as an excellent source of information for the young reader. Separate chapters describe the origins, effects, uses, and abuses of narcotics, marijuana, hallucinogens, sedatives, stimulants, alcohol, and organic solvents such as those found in glue. The tone is dispassionate, the style straightforward. Tables give the generic, trade, and slang names for stimulants and sedatives; a glossary of terms and a relative index are appended." Chicago. Children's Bk Center
"The book refrains from moralizing. . . . The most refreshing aspect of the volume is that it has no axe to grind—its purpose is merely to inform." NY Times Bk Rev

Hyde, Margaret O.

Alcohol: drink or drug? McGraw 1974 150p illus $6.95 (6 and up)   **613.8**

1 Alcohol—Physiological effect 2 Alcoholism
ISBN 0-07-031635-X   LC 78-17760

This is "an informative, nonmoralizing introduction to alcohol use and abuse. Hyde gives a quick historical overview of alcohol use and discusses the making and characteristics of beer, wine, and various distilled spirits as well as the effect of alcohol on the human body, social versus problem drinking and driving, alcoholism, research projects, and the prevention and treatment of alcoholism. The suggestions for further reading include books on choosing wines, cooking with alcohol, and making beer and wine together with studies and reports on alcohol and alcoholism." Booklist

Know about alcohol; illus. by Bill Morrison. McGraw 1978 80p illus $6.95 (4 and up)   **613.8**

1 Alcohol 2 Alcoholism
ISBN 0-07-031621-X   LC 78-7988

"Hyde's even-tempered text intends to provide readers with information enough to make their own choice of whether or not to drink. Accordingly there are no moral judgments, only straightforward explanations of what alcoholic beverages are and what effects alcohol has on the body. . . . Common symptoms of alcohol abuse (not necessarily alcoholism) are described, there's special attention given to the question of young problem drinkers—are they growing in number or are people just more aware of problem drinking? Hyde points out a tie-in between a good self image, self-confidence, and sound information with decreased chances of becoming alcoholic. Her final chapter sketches common social situations involving alcohol and suggests ways of coping (a drunken husband offering to drive a babysitter home, an older sibling who drinks) that might not always work but still function as reasonable behavior guideposts." Booklist
Suggestions for further reading; p77

Know about drugs. 2d ed. by Margaret O. Hyde and Bruce G. Hyde; illus. by Bill Morrison. McGraw 1979 63p illus $6.95 (4-6)   **613.8**

1 Drugs 2 Drug abuse
ISBN 0-07-031643-0   LC 79-13288

First published 1972
"Contains basic factual information about drugs and their effect on the human body and mind. Fairly restrained in approach and simple in presentation the book treats the dangers of nicotine, sniffing, marijuana and other hallucinogens, alcohol, coca and cocaine, heroins, barbiturates, and the combining or mixing of drugs." Booklist [review of first edition]

Lee, Essie E.

Alcohol and you, by Essie E. Lee and Elaine Israel; illus. by Jerry Smath. Messner 1975 64p illus lib. bdg. $6.29 (5 and up)   **613.8**

1 Alcohol—Physiological effect 2 Alcoholism
ISBN 0-671-32759-3   LC 75-29429

A discussion of the history, components, and uses of alcohol, and how it affects the body. Also treated are the physical and social problems young drinkers can encounter
Glossary: p56-60

Madison, Arnold

Smoking and you; illus. with photographs and diagrams. Messner 1975 64p illus lib bdg. $6.97 (4 and up)   **613.8**

1 Smoking 2 Tobacco—Physiological effect
ISBN 0-671-32725-9   LC 75-1347

"This book makes a case against smoking and clearly explains smoking's effect on the respiration system and the body's organs. The history of smoking and research on smoking is reviewed." Sci and Children
"Particularly useful for school projects, this is illustrated with black-and-white photographs and diagrams. A glossary is appended." Booklist

Seixas, Judith S.

Alcohol—what it is, what it does; illus. by Tom Huffman. Greenwillow Bks. 1977 56p illus $5.95, lib. bdg. $5.71 (1-3)   **613.8**

1 Alcohol
ISBN 0-688-80080-7; 0-688-84080-9   LC 76-43344

"Greenwillow read-alone"
"Basic information about alcohol is presented, including why people drink or don't drink alcohol, what kinds of liquids contain alcohol, some of the dangers that may be brought on from consuming large doses of alcohol. Alcoholism is discussed as a disease and a social problem, and sources of help for alcoholics and their families are listed. Common misconceptions are discussed." AAAS Sci Bks & Films
"Factually accurate, this uncomplicated, easy-to-read book is illustrated with excellent color cartoons. Books about the use and abuse of alcohol are needed for children in this age group." Appraisal

Silverstein, Alvin

Alcoholism [by] Alvin Silverstein and Virginia B. Silverstein; with an introduction by Gail Gleason Milgram, consulting editor. Lippincott 1975 128p $7.95, pa $3.50 (5 and up)   **613.8**

1 Alcohol—Physiological effect 2 Alcoholism
ISBN 0-397-31648-8; 0-397-31649-6   LC 75-17938

The authors "are concerned with the effects of alcohol on the body and the seriousness of alcoholism today. This is a very readable presentation of the facts which does not preach to young readers. It does impress them with the information that one out of 15 young people will become an alcoholic and the importance of responsible drinking. . . . It includes a discussion of drugs used in treating alcoholics [and] a section on living with an alcoholic parent; and a list of groups such as Alateens which can help." Sch Library J
For further information: p123

Sonnett, Sherry

Smoking. Watts, F. 1977 63p illus lib. bdg. $6.45 (4 and up)   **613.8**

1 Smoking 2 Tobacco—Physiological effect
ISBN 0-531-01299-9   LC 77-5419

"A First book"
"A simple account of the consequences of smoking, describing the adverse effects of tobacco on the normal physiology of the heart and lungs." Sch Library J
"A handy, dispassionate roundup of current knowledge on the popular habit. With photographs, charts, and reproductions of cartoons and old prints." Booklist

Stwertka, Eve

Marijuana, by Eve and Albert Stwertka. Watts, F. 1979 64p illus lib. bdg. $5.90 (5 and up)   613.8

1 Marihuana
ISBN 0-531-02944-1   LC 79-10156

"A First book"
"The cultivation, history, chemistry, uses, and effects of marijuana are explored. . . . The material is carefully organized and presented without lectures. . . . Although the authors admit that the exact effects of the drug are still unknown, they do take note of the possibilities of chromosome, brain, respiration, and hormone damage, as well as possible medicinal uses currently under investigation. There is a chapter exploring legal aspects of the drug and the movement toward possible legalization." Booklist
Bibliography: p59-60. For further reading: p61-62

Woods, Geraldine

Drug use and drug abuse. Watts, F. 1979 65p illus lib. bdg. $5.90 (4 and up)   613.8

1 Drug abuse 2 Drugs
ISBN 0-531-02941-7   LC 79-11739

"A First book"
"This is an easy to read, well organized book, providing necessary information about all types of drugs in a factual, objective manner. It explains the use of drugs to treat illness and the differences between prescription and over-the-counter drugs in a very basic, simple way. There is a chapter on drug addiction and its treatment, as well as chapters dealing with the use and abuse of all the different types of drugs. Tranquilizers, barbiturates, amphetamines, cocaine and hallucinogens are described. . . . There is also a separate chapter devoted to tobacco and alcohol." VOYA
"There are black-and-white photographs of various drugs and several charts that give names, nicknames, descriptions, and methods of use. A glossary, index, and bibliography are included, along with a limited list of drug treatment facilities. Although much attention is given to the dangers of drug use and the potential for abuse and addiction, 'scare' tactics are not employed, and the basic attitude seems to be an appeal for common sense." Booklist
Books for further reading: p62

613.9 Family planning and sex hygiene

Johnson, Corinne Benson

Love and sex and growing up [by] Corinne Benson Johnson [and] Eric W. Johnson; illus. by Visa-Direction Studio, Inc.; foreword by Louise Bates Ames. Updated ed. Lippincott 1977 126p illus $6.95 (4 and up)   613.9

1 Sex education
ISBN 0-397-31768-9   LC 77-22462

First published 1970
"Part one discusses knowledgeably and simply the physical facts of sex and reproduction, love, and marriage in the context of total human life. Part two emphasizes the importance of families, comparing the distinctive family systems of the Iroquois and Japanese with that of Western culture. Part three describes types of reproduction in other animals and in plants. A final short section is devoted to questions of particular interest to preteens and gives addresses for booklets on menstruation. Well illustrated with drawings." Booklist [review of first edition]

Johnson, Eric W.

Love and sex in plain language. 3d rev. ed. Illus. by Russ Hoover; foreword by Emily H. Mudd. Lippincott 1977 143p illus $8.95 (6 and up)   613.9

1 Sex education
ISBN 0-397-01231-4   LC 77-5105

First published 1965
The author considers various aspects of sex; male and female sexual organs and their functions, masturbation, sexual intercourse, fertilization, and how a baby is born. He covers the changing role of women, homosexuality, venereal disease, abortion, and methods of contraception. He also discusses drugs and alcohol and their effects on sexual relations
Includes bibliographical references

614.4 Incidence, distribution, control of disease

Berger, Melvin

Disease detectives; illus. with photographs. Crowell 1978 87p illus (Scientists at work) $8.95, lib. bdg. $8.79 (5 and up)   614.4

1 Legionnaires' disease 2 Center for Disease Control 3 Public health
ISBN 0-690-03907-7; 0-690-03908-5   LC 77-26589

"The Legionnaires' disease, which struck so disastrously in Philadelphia during the American Legion Convention in 1976, provides the basis for Berger's discussion of the Center for Disease Control. He follows the painstaking research of each department—bacteriology, virology, and toxicology—in the race to locate the epidemic's cause, describing the broader scope of their work along the way." Booklist

Wolfe, Louis

Disease detectives. Watts, F. 1979 64p illus lib. bdg. $5.90 (4-6)   614.4

1 Center for Disease Control 2 Public health
ISBN 0-531-02921-2   LC 78-11097

The "story of the world-famous Center for Disease Control, in Atlanta, Georgia. Legionaires Disease, the mysterious ailment that plagued the American Legion veterans and families who attended a convention in Philadelphia in 1976, is the subject of one fascinating story. Diagnosing and treating malaria, tuberculosis, rat control, smoking, venereal disease, and lead poisoning are discussed." Sci and children
For further reading: p60-61

615 Pharmacology and therapeutics

Zim, Herbert S.

Medicine; illus. by Judith Hoffman Corwin. Morrow 1974 62p illus $6.75, lib. bdg. $6.48 (4-6)   615

1 Drugs
ISBN 0-688-21786-9; 0-688-31786-3   LC 74-4299

"Not a survey of the field of medicine but of medicinal products, this discusses the various ways in which medicines are used (taken by mouth, injected by a hypodermic syringe, etc.) and the care with which dosage is decided. Zim describes the dangers of careless use of over-the-counter drugs, while recognizing the usefulness of these for the treatment and relief of symptoms and minor illnesses; he discusses such groups of drugs as antibiotics, tranquilizers, anesthetics, analgesics, etc., in relation to the illnesses for which they are prescribed. The book contains much sensible advice, and the material is authoritative and well organized, the writing style is not difficult to read because of complexity, but it is sedate and the pages quite solid with close although large print. A single-page index is appended." Chicago. Children's Bk Center

615.5 Therapeutics

Kettelkamp, Larry

The healing arts; illus. with photographs and drawings. Morrow 1978 128p illus $5.95, lib. bdg. $5.71 (5 and up)   615.5

1 Medicine 2 Therapeutics
ISBN 0-688-22161-0; 0-688-32161-5   LC 78-12403

"Holistic health principles underlie Kettelkamp's scan of the many ways of healing. These include naturopathy, chiropractic, acupuncture, and spiritual healing as well as various conventional medical practices. The broad definitions of these diverse areas are useful in an introductory sense as their

Kettelkamp, Larry—*Continued*
historical development, underlying principles, and present status are described. Thoughtful readers will rightfully wish for more rigorous interpretation of certain documentation: how valid or widely accepted are cited studies, reports, or research ventures? If Kettelkamp shows a bias, it's toward open-mindedness; implicit in his rundown is the notion that these widely divergent healing practices might complement each other in some ways. Summary portions note growing medical acceptance of the idea that the whole person must be treated." Booklist

615.9 Poisons and poisoning

Haines, Gail Kay
Natural and synthetic poisons; illus. by Giulio Maestro. Morrow 1978 96p illus $6.95, lib. bdg. $6.67 (4-6)   **615.9**
1 Poisons
ISBN 0-688-22157-2; 0-688-32157-7   LC 78-18886

The author "introduces the various kinds of poisons that confront people in their everyday world. . . . [She] proceeds to examine wide-ranging poisons (animal, plant, bacteria, and mineral) according to their source, describing the chemical changes triggered in the body, [and] mentioning possible antidotes. . . . A concluding chapter deals with the science of toxicology, considering the work of poison specialists and the kind of testing and detecting skills they use." Booklist
Each chapter "poses a question for readers to resolve with answers at the end. The illustrations are sparse and not in color; otherwise, this is a good addition to upper elementary school collections." Sch Library J

616 Diseases

Asimov, Isaac
How did we find out about germs? Illus. by David Wool. Walker & Co. 1974 64p illus lib. bdg. $5.85 (5 and up)   **616**
1 Bacteriology—History 2 Microbiology—History
ISBN 0-8027-6166-0   LC 73-81402

This "survey of man's expanding knowledge of germs touches on such highlights as the first microscope, the discovery of bacteria, the theory of spontaneous generation and the experiments by Spallanzani and Pasteur that disproved it. The text also discusses antisepsis and disease, vaccination, and viruses." Chicago. Children's Bk Center
The author "presents the usually dull secondary school biology background material in a readable and fascinating style. The book is simply written yet to the point scientifically. It avoids extraneous terminology and provides information about the origin of the basic terms which are included. Further, longer words are pronounced in a simplified fashion, a boon to the reader encountering them for the first time. A number of halftone illustrations complement the text." Sci and Children

Cobb, Vicki
How the doctor knows you're fine; illus. by Anthony Ravielli. Lippincott 1973 48p illus $7.95 (2-4)   **616**
1 Medicine 2 Medical care
ISBN 0-397-31240-7   LC 73-4758

The author "explains the procedure of and reasons for each portion of a medical examination from the 'outside'—posture, height, skin condition, and genitals—to the 'inside'—eyes, ears, nose, heart and lungs. Diagrams are drawn and labelled to give a general understanding of human anatomy." Booklist
"The illustrations are clear, informative and greatly extend the text." Sch Library J

616.02 First aid and domestic medicine

Gore, Harriet Margolis
What to do when there's no one but you; illus. by David Lindroth. Prentice-Hall 1974 48p illus $4.95 (2-5)   **616.02**
1 First aid
ISBN 0-13-955070-4   LC 73-13939

Through a series of fictional episodes "first aid treatments for 26 common household accidents are explained sensibly and easily. The brief text and cartoon drawings treat knife cuts, nose bleeds, burns, scrapes, eye injuries, etc. The book concludes with an excellent explanation of artificial resuscitation by the nose and mouth methods and an index lists all of the injuries alphabetically." Sch Library J
"The recommended treatment is good medical practice. The physician will especially appreciate the frequently repeated advice that in some situations medical consultation is absolutely necessary. . . . The language is simple and often spiced with prankish remarks. There is no lecturing or preaching, yet children will understand that many accidents are their own fault. The imaginative illustrations intensify the usefulness of the text." Sci Bks

Vandenburg, Mary Lou
Help! Emergencies that could happen to you, and how to handle them; illus. by R. L. Markham. Lerner Publications 1975 71p illus lib. bdg. $3.95 (2-5)   **616.02**
1 First aid 2 Safety education
ISBN 0-8225-0020-5   LC 75-7007

"This book makes children aware of emergencies involving fire, lightning, animal and insect bites, swimming and skating accidents, and getting lost in the wilderness or in crowds. For each class of emergency, there is a general introduction and then a description of the appropriate behavior to be followed to prevent injury or death. There are two main lines of advice: The first is not to panic under any circumstances, and the second is to follow a few common sense rules. Specific advice and the reasons for the action suggested are then given." AAAS Sci Bks & Films
"The format is economical and unexciting, but the text is neatly organized and indexed. It is a book libraries should have—for reference as well as to encourage children to obtain this kind of vital, self-survival information." Appraisal

616.4 Diabetes

Kipnis, Lynne
You can't catch diabetes from a friend, by Lynne Kipnis and Susan Adler; photographs by Richard Benkof. Triad Scientific Publishers 1979 63p illus $9.95 (2-5)   **616.4**
1 Diabetes
ISBN 0-9600472-3-9   LC 79-1165

This book "is divided into four parts, each of which describes a different child [with diabetes]. In describing Karen, the focus is on her insulin shots, the section on Danny focuses on diet ,the section on Colleen on urine testing, and the last part describes Robert and how he and his family handle insulin reaction. The authors stress the facts that every diabetic must have insulin injections, adhere to a food plan, be tested frequently by a doctor, know what to do in case of insulin reaction, and test urine daily, and the fact that all the family is affected when a member is diabetic. The information is given in a clear and straightforward manner, but the book is weakened by deliberate pace, repetition, and contrived dialogue." Chicago. Children's Bk Center

Silverstein, Alvin
The sugar disease: diabetes, by Alvin Silverstein and Virginia B. Silverstein; with an introduction by Charles Nechemias, consulting editor. Lippincott 1980 111p $7.95, lib. bdg. $7.89 (5 and up)   **616.4**
1 Diabetes
ISBN 0-397-31844-8   LC 78-11631

Silverstein, Alvin—*Continued*

"Calling attention to diabetes as a growing health problem that most people know relatively little about, the Silversteins offer a well-written, well-rounded explanation aimed primarily at non-diabetics. They cover physical aspects of the disease, including testing procedures and treatments. There is a bit of medical history in the look at how knowledge of coping with diabetes developed. A chapter about living with the disease is supportive, noting some celebrities who have it and commenting on daily routines and health habits. A report on present research areas sums up the well-organized account." Booklist

For further information: p105-06

616.8   Diseases of nervous system

Silverstein, Alvin

Epilepsy [by] Alvin Silverstein and Virginia B. Silverstein; with an introduction by J. Gordon Millichap, consulting editor. Lippincott 1975 64p illus $5.95 (5 and up)   **616.8**

1 Epilepsy
ISBN 0-397-31615-1   LC 74-31382

"The authors explain the fears and misunderstandings of epilepsy in the past, what is being done now to help patients, and what can be expected through the use of drugs and surgery. They describe in detail the cause and effect of seizures, what onlookers can do to help, and how important it is to realize that in almost all cases there is no danger or after-effects." Appraisal

"This clearly written and generally very accurate book should be helpful to epileptic patients, their families, concerned persons in public institutions (such as teachers, transit workers) and others who are simply curious." AAAS Sci Bks & Films

616.9   Communicable and noncommunicable diseases

Nourse, Alan E.

Lumps, bumps, and rashes; a look at kids' diseases. Watts, F. 1976 65p illus lib. bdg. $6.45 (5 and up)   **616.9**

1 Comunicable diseases
ISBN 0-531-00845-2   LC 75-34276

"A First book"

The author covers common childhood diseases and infections, including "those caused by bacteria as well as viruses. He divides his material logically into the measles diseases, the strep and staph infections, virus diseases, and the preventable destroyers, (pertussis, poliomyelitis, diphtheria, smallpox, tetanus). Then he covers vaccines and how they work and immunization programs. He describes the symptoms and treatment of each of these common childhood diseases and infections and lists basic immunization vaccines. Photographs, diagrams and cartoons are used effectively as an adjunct to the text. There is an excellent glossary and the book is indexed." AAAS Sci Bks & Films

616.95   Venereal diseases

Hyde, Margaret

VD: the silent epidemic. McGraw 1973 63p illus $6.95 (5 and up)   **616.95**

1 Venereal diseases
ISBN 0-07-031638-4   LC 73-1440

"The text describes the major kinds of venereal diseases, their symptoms, their treatment, and the manner in which they are transmitted, and discusses some of the campaigns of help and information that have been mounted by official agencies and volunteers." Chicago. Children's Bk Center

"Hyde's factual approach to venereal disease avoids scare tactics and preaching and provides a very readable account. . . . Intelligent parents should encourage their children to become familiar with the information in this book, and it is a good supplementary source for physical education and hygiene courses." Sci Bks

Johnson, Eric W.

V.D.: venereal disease and what you should do about it. New and rev. ed. With a foreword by King Holmes; Rob Roy MacGregor, medical consultant; clinic and Operation Venus photographs by Eric E. Mitchell. Lippincott 1978 126p illus $7.95 (5 and up)   **616.95**

1 Venereal diseases
ISBN 0-397-31811-1   LC 78-8666

First published 1973

"Every five seconds someone contracts venereal disease. The unsettling statistic is one of many making up the 'straight story' on VD as told in this book by Eric Johnson, one of the best I have seen on the subject for young people. Johnson gives teenagers, as well as the parents, the who, what, when, where, and why in a question-and-answer format. He tells how one gets VD, how to avoid it, how to cure it, and where to go for treatment. . . . A vigorous writing style and good illustrations combine with the jarring facts on VD to make this compelling reading." Sci Teacher

616.97   Allergies

Riedman, Sarah R.

Allergies. Watts, F. 1978 63p illus lib. bdg. $6.45 (4-6)   **616.97**

1 Allergy
ISBN 0-531-01352-9   LC 77-20858

"A First book"

"Here is a detailed discussion of common allergies such as asthma, hay fever, reactions to insect stings, chronic rhinitis, food reactions, and contact dermatitis. The book includes an informative list of preventive measures, as well as details about tests—skin, transfer, and patch—used by doctors to pinpoint the many different causes of allergic reactions. A few photographs accompany the text, as well as a glossary, index, and bibliography." Sci Teacher

Glossary: p56-59. Further reading: p60-61

Silverstein, Alvin

Allergies, by Alvin Silverstein and Virginia B. Silverstein; with an introduction by Sheldon G. Cohen, consulting editor. Lippincott 1977 128p illus $7.95, pa $2.95 (5 and up)   **616.97**

1 Allergy
ISBN 0-397-31758-1; 0-397-31759-X   LC 77-1284

"In nontechnical language, the authors describe the causes and types of allergic response. Common afflictions such as hay fever, asthma, and insect stings are discussed and so are food, skin and drug allergies. An up-to-date report on immunologic research rounds out this thorough, well-written treatment of a widespread problem." Sch Library J

Itch, sniffle & sneeze; all about asthma, hay fever and other allergies, by Alvin Silverstein and Virginia B. Silverstein; illus. by Roy Doty. Four Winds 1978 unp illus lib. bdg. $7.95 (3-5)   **616.97**

1 Allergy
ISBN 0-590-07540-3   LC 77-20791

"Presented in simple-to-understand terms, this brief discussion explains what allergies are, the body's reactions to them, allergenic substances, and how relief can be found. The Silversteins. . . . provide basic understanding for sufferers of dust, pollen, certain foods, and other irritants. The authors touch briefly on tests such as RAST and other research in which scientists are currently involved. Cartoon drawings add splashes of gold and green color, while simplified diagrams show, for example, how allergies affect the body. Glossary of terms appended." Booklist

617   Surgery and related topics

Berger, Melvin

Bionics. Watts, F. 1978 82p illus lib. bdg. $6.90 (6 and up)   **617**

1 Bionics 2 Artificial organs
ISBN 0-531-01354-5   LC 77-17073

Berger, Melvin—*Continued*

"An Impact book"

"Berger explores this designated science's 'bringing together' nature to show how medical, biological, and engineering technologies merge to provide the information researchers rely on to produce lifelike artificial systems, whether they be body parts or specialized machines such as computers or robots. The main emphasis here, though, is on body parts; and existing systems—a variety of artificial limbs, organs, induced senses—plus a quick look at computers and experimental robots demonstrate theories in practice." Booklist

"An excellent introduction to the science. . . . The most advanced medical knowledge and engineering techniques are employed, so that the results often sound like science fiction. A fascinating book." Children's Bk Rev Serv

Nourse, Alan E.

Fractures, dislocations, and sprains. Watts, F. 1978 63p illus lib. bdg. $6.45 (4-6)   **617**

1 Fractures 2 Dislocations 3 Sprains
ISBN 0-531-01494-0   LC 78-6855

"A First book"

The author has written an "explanation of bones and joints and the injuries that can befall them. The author describes each structure making up the skeletal system, tells how each can be injured, and how each heals. Some simple first-aid measures are also included although the author stresses that 'Fractures, Dislocations, and Sprains' are all serious injuries and that a doctor should always be consulted." Sch Library J

"The information flows smoothly. There are diagrams aplenty, photographs, and first aid pointers. Good introductory material, especially useful in health or first aid units." Booklist

Glossary: p55-57. Additional reading: p58

Shapiro, Irwin

The gift of magic sleep; early experiments in anesthesia; illus. by Pat Rotondo. Coward, McCann & Geoghegan 1979 64p illus lib. bdg. $5.49 (4-6)   **617**

1 Anesthetics—History
ISBN 0-698-30694-5   LC 78-24224

"This well-written account of the early development of anesthetics contains many facts, combining biographical information on the four frontrunners in experiments with ether (Crawford Long, Charles Jackson, Horace Wells, and William Morton) with information on early medical practices. It reads smoothly and will hold interest, presenting an accurate introduction to the topic. . . . The carefully drawn black-and-white illustrations are nicely detailed and add to the text." Sch Library J

Selected bibliography: p64

617.6 Dentistry

Barnett, Naomi

I know a dentist; illus. by Linda Boehm. Putnam [1978 c1977] unp illus lib. bdg. $4.29 (1-3)   **617.6**

1 Dentistry
ISBN 0-399-61097-9   LC 77-24968

"Community helper books"

"A clear, easy-to-read account of a trip to the dentist with additional info on proper brushing techniques, good diet, and the role inheritance plays in strong teeth. Common tools and machines used with children, including small hand tools, drill, and X-ray machines, are explained and shown in simple line drawings with blue accents. Correct terms are used for each item and more difficult ones appear in a glossary. . . . A book that will provide useful preparation for children who have not yet been to a dentist." Sch Library J

Nourse, Alan E.

The tooth book. McKay 1977 79p illus $6.95 (5 and up)   **617.6**

1 Teeth 2 Teeth—Diseases
ISBN 0-679-20376-1   LC 77-5239

"In this practical, well organized introduction to teeth and their care, Nourse effectively explains why everyday upkeep and regular dental checks are so important to keeping a whole and healthy set of teeth. Tooth structure, the decay process, and particulars of proper brushing and flossing are well covered; but beyond this Nourse has taken time to explain the hows and whys of various dental problems; brace wearers might find the discussion of alignment problems particularly interesting and appreciate Nourse's acknowledgment that braces are 'not very attractive, never have been, never will be' but are not in vain. Format is unexceptional, and diagrams seem harshly reproduced, but content definitely compensates." Booklist

Rockwell, Harlow

My dentist. Greenwillow Bks. 1975 unp illus $7.50, lib. bdg. $7.20 (k-2)   **617.6**

1 Dentistry
ISBN 0-688-80004-1; 0-688-84004-3   LC 75-6974

This is a "straightforward run-through of a routine trip to the dentist. A young patient describes each of the pieces of standard dental equipment she sees on her visit and explains how her dentist uses them." Sch Library J

"Because of the simple, restrained format, and because of the precise, detailed illustrations, the author-illustrator has been able to turn what can be a frightening experience for a child into an understandable, necessary event." Horn Bk

Silverstein, Alvin

So you're getting braces: a guide to orthodontics [by] Alvin Silverstein and Virginia B. Silverstein; with an introduction by James L. Ackerman; photographs by the authors. Lippincott 1978 112p illus $6.89, pa $3.95 (5 and up)   **617.6**

1 Orthodontics
ISBN 0-397-31786-7; 0-397-31787-5   LC 77-16588

This book describes "how teeth and jaw can go awry and how orthodontists set bands, wires, and devices to work in straightening misaligned teeth. . . . The hindrances braces pose in enjoying gum, certain candy, and food are frankly acknowledged, as are the aches and pains they might give. Warnings are posted on getting broken or loosened parts fixed quickly (see a regular dentist if you or your orthodontist is out of town) lest desired movement be set back, and there is insistence that wearers not shirk in cooperation: 'you can't fool your teeth . . . the better you cooperate, the sooner the treatment will be finished.' " Booklist

The book "is well organized and clearly written, with technical terms defined. Diagrams are clear and 25 photographs show children's case histories in progress. Helpful addresses and books for further information are listed." Sch Library J

617.7 Ophthalmology

Brindze, Ruth

Look how many people wear glasses; the magic of lenses; illus. by photographs and drawings. Atheneum Pubs. 1975 101p illus $7.95 (6 and up)   **617.7**

1 Eyeglasses 2 Lenses
ISBN 0-689-50028-9   LC 75-8947

"A Margaret K. McElderry book"

This book includes an explanation of an eye examination, a "historical account of spectacles worn in the past, and information on selecting glasses. Other chapters discuss lens manufacture, sunglasses, microscopes and telescopes, and eye health." Horn Bk

"Advice on eye care and first-aid concludes the overview, which should prove useful for both assignments and simple browsing. Illustrated with diagrams and black-and-white photographs." Booklist

Kelley, Alberta

Lenses, spectacles, eyeglasses, and contacts; the story of vision aids. Elsevier/Nelson Bks. [1979 c1978] 98p illus $6.95 (5-7)   **617.7**

1 Eyeglasses 2 Contact lenses
ISBN 0-525-66617-6   LC 78-14827

First published by Thomas Nelson

"The history of eyeglasses is presented in a volume that packs plenty of information in a readable format and text. . . . Kelley does a good job of explaining how the eye functions. She also discusses the concept of vision training, although

Kelley, Alberta—*Continued*
her presentation is not a conclusive report on this
fast-growing field of eye therapy. Most timely are
discussions of contact lenses (including the expanding use of soft lenses) and on exciting developments in aids to the blind." Pub W
Bibliography: p92

617.8   Otology and audiology

Levine, Edna S.
Lisa and her soundless world; illus. by
Gloria Kamen. Human Sciences Press 1974
unp illus $7.95 (1-3)   **617.8**
1 Deafness   2 Deaf
ISBN 0-87705-104-6   LC 73-14819

"Intended to help children understand deafness,
this focuses on eight-year-old Lisa whose disability
is undetected until a doctor diagnoses it. Levine
presents useful facts about how the deaf learn to
speak and hear in special schools (through hearing aids, lip reading, feeling vibrations in the
throat, sign language) and encourages readers to
perform simple exercises that promote awareness
of what a deaf person experiences." Sch Library J
"The book accomplishes several things: it makes
the deaf child's plight explicit, it makes clear the
difficulty a deaf child has in learning to speak, it
explains why a child so handicapped may feel
angry and unloved, and it stresses the fact that
the halting speech of the deaf may be governed
by physical limitations, that it is not due to a
lack of intelligence." Chicago. Children's Bk Center

Litchfield, Ada B.
A button in her ear; pictures by Eleanor
Mill. Whitman, A. 1976 unp illus lib.
bdg. $6.50 (1-3)   **617.8**
1 Hearing aids   2 Deafness
ISBN 0-8075-0987-6   LC 75-28390

"Concept book"
"As the story follows Angela from her handi-
cap-caused confusion through her hearing test and
eventually to her adjustment to her new hearing
aid, the reader is informed as well as warned
by the inner feelings of the child experiencing
the hearing loss. A hearing aid is shown to be
as acceptable as eye glasses. This book should
be required reading for all children with hearing
loss as well as their families, friends and classmates." AAAS Sci Bks & Films
"Although this is a 'problem' book, the problem
is treated creatively. There is a lightness and
subtle humor about the statements which are
misinterpreted by Angela and by her decision to
turn down her hearing aid when she chooses 'not'
to hear something. This book may help the thousands of deaf and hard of hearing children develop
a positive attitude toward their hearing aids."
Children's Bk Rev Serv

621.36   Applied optics. Lasers

Kettelkamp, Larry
Lasers, the miracle light; illus. with photographs and diagrams. Morrow 1979 126p illus
$6.95, lib. bdg. $6.67 (5 and up)   **621.36**
1 Lasers
ISBN 0-688-22207-2; 0-688-32207-1   LC 79-17486

The author "discusses those properties of laser
light that make it special. He recounts the discoveries that led to the development of the laser
and explains the construction and theory of operation of solid, gas, liquid and semiconductor lasers.
He . . . [describes laser applications including]
medical instruments, industrial welding and cutting tools, distance measuring devices . . . fiber
optics communication, optical video discs and
holography." AAAS Sci Bks & Films
"The explanations are good, and the uses up-to-
date. Abstractions are well covered by analogies.
The hopeful possibility of using the power of
laser light in nuclear fusion is very well covered.
. . . The photographs have been carefully planned."
Horn Bk

621.38   Electronic and communication engineering

Math, Irwin
Morse, Marconi and you. Scribner 1979
80p illus $8.95 (6 and up)   **621.38**
1 Telecommunication
ISBN 0-684-16081-1   LC 79-1351

"Illustrations by Hal Keith." [Verso of title page]
This "lively and scientifically accurate book, deals
with the show and why of basic electronics. From
a discussion of basic electrical theory in the
opening chapter, the book progresses in clear
sequence through directions for building a telegraph, telephone, and radio set. The theory behind
each of these devices is explained, and there is a
logical progression of information from one project to the next." Sci Teacher
"If you're looking for a nice easy text with
good pictorial directions, and if you have students
who like to do experiments, this is the book. It is
designed to bridge the gap between packaged kits
and the 'how to do it' of popular magazines."
VOYA
For further reading: p78

621.381   Electronic engineering

Bendick, Jeanne
Electronics for young people; including
automation, computers, communications, micro-
circuits, lasers, and more. New 5th ed. by
Jeanne Bendick and R. J. Lefkowitz; illus. by
Jeanne Bendick. McGraw 1973 206p illus lib.
bdg. $6.95 (5 and up)   **621.381**
1 Electronics
ISBN 0-07-004495-3   LC 72-6584

First published 1944 with title: Electronics for
boys and girls
This book traces the development of electronics
from experiments conducted 2600 years ago to
modern technological advances. It describes concepts and operations of electrons, electron tubes,
different kinds of waves, transistors, microelec-
tronic circuits, lasers, computers, photoelec-
phototransistors, radio and television. It also discusses applications in the health, science and telecommunication fields
Electronic terms: p187-99

621.382   Wire telegraphy

Nathan, Adele Gutman
The first transatlantic cable; illus. by
Denver Gillen. Random House 1959 180p illus
maps lib. bdg. $5.99 (5 and up)   **621.382**
1 Cables, Submarine   2 Field, Cyrus West
ISBN 0-394-90388-9   LC 59-6471

"Landmark books"
"Communication across the Atlantic Ocean be-
comes reality in this story of the men [especially
Cyrus Field] who through belief and perseverance
made ocean cables possible." Adventuring with
Bks. 2d edition

621.4   Heat engineering and prime movers. Wind engines

Dennis, Landt
Catch the wind; a book of windmills and
windpower; photographs by Lisl Dennis.
Four Winds 1976 114p illus. lib. bdg. $8.95
(5 and up)   **621.4**
1 Windmills   2 Wind power
ISBN 0-590-07414-8   LC 75-45002

"After explaining how windpower was used
over the centuries and why it should be considered
now because of the limited fossil fuel supply,
Dennis launches into a heavily illustrated discussion of the history of windmills. The text concludes
with the prospects for adopting windpower as a
viable source of energy and some current innovations." Sch Library J

Dennis, Landt—*Continued*

"Striking black-and-white photographs, art reproductions, and early design sketches serve as an integral part of this absorbing and comprehensive presentation. A bibliography and sources of information about building windmills are appended." Booklist

Weiss, Harvey

Motors and engines and how they work. Crowell 1969 62p illus $10.95 (5 and up)
621.4

1 Power (Mechanics) 2 Engines
ISBN 0-690-56478-3   LC 69-11828

The author discusses the different kinds of motors and engines in today's world. He combines text, photographs, and drawings to illustrate the complexities of the principles and operation of: water engines; wind engines; gravity engines; spring engines; steam engines; electric motors; gasoline engines; jet and rocket engines

"The clear accurate text is illustrated with diagrams and photographs. Of practical value to the mechanically minded and useful for science projects." Booklist

621.46 Electric propulsion technology

Renner, Al G.

How to make and use electric motors. Putnam 1974 127p illus lib. bdg. $5.49 (5 and up)
621.46

1 Electric motors
ISBN 0-399-60858-3   LC 73-77421

"Detailed instructions and clear diagrams direct the construction of three types of battery-powered, electromagnetic motors. A special feature is suggestions for varying the materials and design of separate parts after each basic model is put together. The usefulness of this book as a guide in experimentation depends on the availability of supplies—which, should not be a great problem—and the reader's curiosity and manual skill. One drawback to the author's teaching method is that he relies almost totally on readers gaining knowledge from making the projects: explanations and definitions of terms are minimal. Some ideas for putting the motors to work are included. Useful for hobbies and school projects." Booklist

621.47 Solar-energy engineering

Bendick, Jeanne

Putting the sun to work. Garrard 1979 63p illus lib. bdg. $4.74 (3-5)
621.47

1 Solar energy
ISBN 0-8116-6111-3   LC 78-6178

"The book tells what the sun can do for us, how the sun's energy can be harnessed for solar heating and conversion into electricity, and describes solar cells, power stations, panels, collectors, and concentrators. Energy transformations, heat flow, and insulation are briefly treated." Sci and Children

"This book covers solar energy principles concisely and accurately. The large type and simple prose style make it extremely easy to read. Even better than the text are the clear and simple illustrations that provide a ready index to the subjects discussed. Students of all ages can gain a great deal from studying the illustrations. Of particular interest to younger readers are five simple and instructive solar energy experiments." AAAS Sci Bks & Films

Berger, Melvin

Energy from the sun; illus. by Giulio Maestro. Crowell 1976 32p illus (Let's-read-and-find-out science bks) lib. bdg. $7.89 (1-3)
621.47

1 Solar energy
ISBN 0-690-01056-7   LC 75-33310

The emphasis of this very simple book is on the importance of the sun as a source of energy. . . . Berger explains how the food we eat comes indirectly from the sun and stresses the dependence of all living things on energy. Devices that use electricity are mentioned, and mechanical energy is explained as being produced in engines by heat from fuels, which are mainly sun-derived; coal, gas an oil are presented in this context. The author concludes with an optimistic look at new discoveries for capturing, storing and using energy. The solar cell and the solar-heated house are cited as examples of direct use of the sun's energy; the splitting of atoms is listed as a source of nuclear energy; steam trapped in the earth, the blowing wind and ocean tides are mentioned as additional energy sources." AAAS Sci Bks & Films

"Brightly colored poster-type illustrations which alternate with black-and-white ones will surely draw readers and browsers to this well-executed book." Appraisal

Branley, Franklyn M.

Solar energy; Updated ed. Illus. by John Teppich. Crowell 1975 117p illus $7.95 (5 and up)
621.47

1 Solar energy
ISBN 0-690-00719-1   LC 74-17222

First published 1957

This book explains solar energy and its potential utilization as a power resource. It includes simple experiments which demonstrate theories of solar energy

Bibliography: p112

Gadler, Steve J.

Sun power: facts about solar energy [by] Steve J. Gadler [and] Wendy Wriston Adamson. Lerner Publications 1978 103p illus lib. bdg. $6.95 (6 and up)
621.47

1 Solar energy
ISBN 0-8225-0643-2   LC 77-92290

"This is an efficient, readable overview of solar energy and its potential for answering energy needs. Pertinent but not always fully necessary background information takes up the first third of the book: the sun's role in the energy production spectrum is an important point; so are its internal workings. Human attitudes toward it seem like filler, however. The most practically instructive portions explain the ways solar energy is or might be harnessed. Flat-plate, focusing, and parabolic trough collectors are simply and clearly described; so are solar stills and covers. Good, too, are explanations of promising drawing-board schemes that have solar power producing electricity via steam. An interesting final portion uses a question-and-answer format to pinpoint anticipated problems, among them some intriguing legal ones." Booklist

Knight, David C.

Harnessing the sun; the story of solar energy; illus. with photographs and diagrams. Morrow 1976 128p illus lib. bdg. $6 (6 and up)
621.47

1 Solar energy
ISBN 0-688-32070-8   LC 75-44301

The topic of solar energy is explained through a "blend of history, theory, current examples and future possibilities. Many anecdotes and inventions are included to demonstrate the effects and applications of solar energy." Appraisal

"The text is straightforward and, for the most part, easily understandable, though a few explanations of how solar cells transform sunlight into electricity may be too technical for some. Black-and-white photographs and diagrams illustrate the text." Booklist

Glossary: p123-25

621.48 Nuclear engineering

Halacy, Dan

Nuclear energy. Watts, F. 1978 64p illus lib. bdg. $6.45 (4 and up)
621.48

1 Atomic energy
ISBN 0-531-01492-4   LC 78-4659

"A First book"

"The usefulness of Halacy's overview of nuclear energy lies in the fact that there aren't many introductions at this middle-grade level. His general coverage includes a brief look at atomic structure and at some of the early atomic pioneers. Descriptions of the mining and milling of uranium precede the book's most practical feature, a description of how a nuclear power plant operates.

Halacy, Dan—*Continued*
The weakest area comes with a final chapter on
the dangers of nuclear energy; problems with storage are ackowledged but other pollution dangers
are played down, a tone at odds with the record
of minor accidents and nuclear pollution incidents
that have already occurred." Booklist
Glossary of important terms: p58-60. For further
reading: p61

Hyde, Margaret O.
Everyone's trash problem: nuclear wastes
[by] Margaret O. Hyde and Bruce G. Hyde.
McGraw 1979 118p $7.95 (4 and up) **621.48**
1 Atomic power plants—Environmental aspects
2 Radioactivity 3 Waste products
ISBN 0-07-31551-5 LC 78-23859
This book discusses nuclear waste and its potential to cause irreversible damage to the environment. Also discussed are: slow breeders, fast
breeders, and light water reactors; radiation, recycling, and the future of nuclear power plants.
A glossary of atomic language, sources of further
information and suggestions for further reading
are included
"The authors have done an outstanding job of
stripping away the mystery and technical jargon
to explain the essence of the problem. Without
trying to bias the reader either for or against
nuclear power, the authors simply provide the
basic education needed to intelligently discuss the
issue." AAAS Sci Bks & Films

Pringle, Laurence
Nuclear power; from physics to politics.
Macmillan Pub. Co. 1979 133p illus (Science
for survival ser.) $7.95 (6 and up) **621.48**
1 Atomic energy 2 Atomic power plants
ISBN 0-02-775390-5 LC 78-27180
"This organized, up-to-date book discusses
safety, costs, politics, and alternatives to nuclear
energy. Views and arguments are presented from
both proponents and opponents. An excellent introduction to encourage young readers to think
objectively and to involve themselves in further
research. An index, glossary, and bibliography are
included." Sci and Children

621.8 Machine engineering

Hoban, Tana
Dig, drill, dump, fill. Greenwillow Bks.
1975 unp illus lib. bdg. $6.96 (k-2) **621.8**
1 Machinery—Pictorial works
ISBN 0-688-84016-7 LC 75-11987
"Tana Hoban's camera catches heavy-duty
machinery in powerful black-and-white action
shots that will captivate children. Photographed
in on-the-spot locations, the road rollers, fillers,
diggers, and wreckers seem to rumble and roar
as metal twists, cement mixes, and pavement
crumbles. The eye of the camera captures a total
feeling of what is happening, and children will
enjoy supplying the sound effects. A pictorial
glossary serves as an explanatory aid in the otherwise wordless picture book." Booklist

Pine, Tillie S.
Simple machines and how we use them
[by] Tillie S. Pine [and] Joseph Levine;
illus. by Bernice Myers. McGraw 1965 48p
illus lib. bdg. $6.95 (2-4) **621.8**
1 Machinery
ISBN 0-07-050067-3 LC 64-7733
"Whittlesey House publications"
The book "describes simple machines, such as
the wheel and axle, lever, pulley, wedge, and
screw, and discusses their application in doing
the world's work. Basic information presented in
simple text and many pictures." Hodges. Bks for
Elem Sch Libraries

Rockwell, Anne
Machines, by Anne & Harlow Rockwell.
Macmillan Pub. Co. 1972 unp illus lib.
bdg. $5.95 (k-1) **621.8**
1 Machinery
ISBN 0-02-777520-8 LC 72-185149

Illustrated by the authors, this book describes
machines and machine parts: pulley, block and
tackle, gear, jackscrew, sprocket
"One of the highlights of the book is the use of
full-color watercolor paintings as illustrations of
the types of machines. Large primary print is
used describing the simple machines such as the
wheel on gears. The sentences are structured for
primary usage by introducing the terms such as
lever or pulley and not using additional new terminology. A brief explanation of the factors which
make machines work is presented. This book
would be useful as a source of supplementary information in a unit on simple machines since the
reading and comprehension level is well within
the average primary child's abilities." Sci Bks

Weiss, Harvey
What holds it together? Written and illus.
by Harvey Weiss. Little 1977 48p illus lib.
bdg. $6.95 (3-5) **621.8**
1 Fasteners
ISBN 0-316-92888-7 LC 76-54692
"An Atlantic Monthly Press book"
"Weiss provides a practical look at nails, nuts
and bolts, screws, rivets, and glue; he broadens
his base to include magnets and gravity and continues his examination with ways of tying, melting, and interlocking. All of this consecutively
demonstrates the making of larger, stronger, and
more complicated structures. Competent explanations are supplemented with precise black line
drawings, some of which add light touches of
humor. Most discussions include easy experiments
to try individually or in classroom situations. An
engrossing topic for building enthusiasts and pro-
ject-oriented youngsters." Booklist

Zim, Herbert S.
Hoists, cranes, and derricks [by] Herbert
S. Zim [and] James R. Skelly; illus. by Gary
Ruse. Morrow 1969 59p illus lib. bdg. $6.48,
pa $1.25 (3-6) **621.8**
1 Cranes, derricks, etc. 2 Hoisting machinery
ISBN 0-688-31395-7; 0-688-26395-X LC 74-79098
The text "explains in very simple terms the three
basic types of lifting machines—hoists, cranes and
derricks—the kinds of jobs for which they are normally used and some of the things an operator
must do to control them. A fascinating feature
is the explanation of hand signals used to instruct
the operator. At least one illustration of the subject matter is found on each page of the book,
as well as some very simple quizzes about the
mechanics of pulleys. There is a table showing
capacities of typical cranes and derricks. A brief
sketch of the first practical lifting machine built
by the Romans about 1500 years ago is also included. The book is indexed and ought to make
interesting reading." Sci Bks

621.9 Tools and fabricating equipment

Rockwell, Anne
The toolbox, by Anne & Harlow Rockwell.
Macmillan Pub. Co. 1971 unp illus lib.
bdg. $6.95, pa $2.25 (k-1) **621.9**
1 Tools
ISBN 0-02-777540-2; 0-02-044800-7 LC 72-119836
Illustrated by Harlow Rockwell, this book describes the contents of a toolbox and explains the
uses of each tool
"A picture book celebrates with unadorned economy of words and illustrations that simple beauty
of useful tools. The brief text is printed in clear,
handsome type; very little boys—and undoubtedly
some girls as well—will pore over the appreciative
portraits of common implements, which make ingenious use of watercolor to show textures and
surfaces of wood and metal." Horn Bk

Zim, Herbert S.
Machine tools [by] Herbert S. Zim [and]
James R. Skelly; illus. by Gary Ruse. Morrow
1969 63p illus lib. bdg. $6.48, pa $1.25 (3-6)
621.9
1 Machine tools
ISBN 0-685-31555-0; 0-688-26555-3 LC 69-10403
This book "shows the development of modern
hand tools which evolved from Stone Age tools.
Then draft animals, water power, steam, gasoline

Zim, Herbert S.—*Continued*

engines and electricity replaced human power with the resultant capability of performing larger tasks. The machinist and the machine tools with which he works are introduced: the lathe, the giant power press, the twist drill and drill press, shaper, milling machine, planer, multiple or gang drilling machine, boring mill, broaching machine, surface grinders, drop forge, and punch press. There is an illustrated glossary explaining and illustrating the principal mechanical parts of machine tools." Sci Bks

623 Military and nautical engineering

Cummings, Richard

Make your own model forts & castles; written and illus. by Richard Cummings. McKay 1977 122p illus $7.95 (5 and up)   623

1 Fortification—Models 2 Castles—Models
ISBN 0-679-20400-8   LC 77-3970

"Small-scale forts, castles, and other fortifications for use with miniature soldiers are presented with clear, easy-to-follow instructions and helpful diagrams. The seven projects, which range from simple to more complex, are a Roman fort, a Norman castle, a World War I trench defense line, a log fort, a twelfth-century round-towered castle, a reconstruction of the French Maginot Line, and Italy's Monte Cassino fortress. Each project lists necessary tools, materials, and adhesives; delineates step-by-step processes; gives finishing hints; and suggests alternative uses for the constructions." Booklist
Bibliography: p116-18

Peterson, Harold L.

Forts in America; illus. by Daniel D. Feaser. Scribner 1964 61p illus map lib. bdg. $5.95 (4 and up)   623

1 Fortification
ISBN 0-684-12890-X   LC 64-17210

The author "recounts in an interesting and clear manner the role and development of forts built by French, Spanish, English and, later, Americans on what is now U.S. soil. He carefully points out differences between forts in coastal-areas and those in frontier country and includes relevant historical incidents such as the writing of our national anthem. Fonts which can be visited are so noted. Terms are carefully explained in the text. Skillfully executed diagrams and drawings. Well indexed. . . . [Readers] who enjoy military and historical books, or those who like to create their own models will like this; useful also in American history." Sch Library J

623.4 Ordnance

Colby, C. B.

Arms of our fighting men; personal weapons, bazookas, big guns. New and rev. ed. Coward, McCann & Geoghegan 1972 48p illus lib. bdg. $5.29 (4 and up)   623.4

1 Firearms 2 U.S. Army—Ordnance and ordnance stores 3 Tanks (Military science)
ISBN 0-698-30432-2   LC 79-180910

First published 1952

In photographs and brief text, this book describes weapons used by American servicemen: hand guns, shoulder arms, recoilless rifles, grenades, mobile artillery, missiles, tanks, and antiaircraft weapons

Revolutionary War weapons; pole arms, hand guns, shoulder arms and artillery. Coward-McCann 1963 48p illus lib. bdg. $5.29 (4 and up)   623.4

1 Firearms 2 U.S. Army—Ordnance and ordnance stores 3 U.S—History—Revolution, 1775-1783
ISBN 0-698-30290-4   LC 63-15538

Here are photographs and descriptions of weapons used in the Revolutionary War by both sides of the contest as well as by the Indians. Included are spears, lances, halberts, flintlock muskets, pistols, knives, pikes and tomahawks

"It is fortunate that some examples of weapons are still preserved in museums and private collections so that they can be photographed and looked at so many years later. . . . After reading this book, you will have a far better understanding of what the soldier of the Revolution had to be like." p3

Glubok, Shirley

Knights in armor; designed by Gerard Nook. Harper 1969 48p illus lib. bdg. $8.79 (4 and up)   623.4

1 Arms and armor—History 2 Knights and knighthood
ISB 0-06-022038-4   LC 69-10208

"The discussion of knighthood and the craftsmanship of medieval armorers has the directness and clarity of expression and the meaningful selection of content of one who knows children well. Equally as impressive as the selection for text is the choice of illustrations. . . . Illuminated manuscripts, paintings, and museum pieces of armor make graphic in book form the training and ideals of knights, details of armor construction, chivalric exploits, and the period pageantry." Horn Bk

Tunis, Edwin

Weapons; a pictorial history; written and illus. by Edwin Tunis. Crowell [1977 c1954] 151p illus $14.95 (5 and up)   623.4

1 Arms and armor 2 Munitions—History
ISBN 0-690-01340-X   LC 76-29699

A reissue of the title first published 1954 by World Publishing Company

The story, in text and pictures, of arms through the ages—from the first tied stone thrown by prehistoric man to the super bombs of our own day

The author-illustrator "emphasizes the offensive rather than the defensive weapon in his narrative which omits strategy due to space limitations, but does include fortifications. He clearly explains with diagrams and text how the mechanism of the weapons operates. Whether it is used for reference or browsing, this handsomely illustrated book will engage the interest of the nonmilitary-minded as well as the hobbyist or weapons collector." Booklist

623.74 Military vehicles. Airplanes

Cooke, David C.

Famous U.S. Air Force bombers. Dodd 1973 62p illus lib. bdg. $5.95 (5 and up)   623.74

1 Bombers 2 U.S. Air Force
ISBN 0-396-06695   LC 72-5947

"Two pages of text and pictures are devoted to each of approximately 30 aircraft, from the MB-1 of 1918 to the B-66 of 1956. The descriptions generally include a brief history of the origin and employment of the craft, production and performance data." Sch Library J

Famous U.S. Navy fighter planes. Dodd 1972 63p illus lib. bdg. $5.95 (5 and up)   623.74

1 Fighter planes 2 U.S. Navy
ISBN 0-396-06484-1   LC 75-180928

"This book is a progressive history of fighter aircraft in the U.S. Navy following World War I. Every plane described and pictured was designed in this country, and every one—including the failures—was a milestone of progress in man's conquest of the air." Foreword

"Despite its narrow scope and lack of an index, the book is clear and up-to-date and will be popular with children interested in planes." Sch Library J

Delear, Frank J.

Helicopters and airplanes of the U.S. Army; illus. with photographs. Dodd 1977 96p illus lib. bdg. $5.95 (5 and up)   623.74

1 Airplanes, Military 2 Helicopters 3 U.S. Army
ISBN 0-396-07476-6   LC 77-6495

"Helicopters as well as utility, cargo, observation, attack, and training craft are shown in numerous black-and-white photographs (which vary in clarity) and described in a statistics-filled narrative as

Delear, Frank J.—*Continued*

to speed, cruising altitude, dimensions, load, and fuel capacity. Grouping by type, the author includes aircraft from Wright 'Flyer' of 1909 to those used in World War II, the Korean conflict, and Vietnam. A final chapter probes the future, discussing the air fleet that the army is developing and its possible uses. A glossary of general aircraft and helicopter terms is appended." Booklist

623.8 Nautical engineering and seamanship. Nautical craft

Adkins, Jan

Wooden ship; written, designed, and illus. by Jan Adkins. Houghton 1978 47p illus $6.95 (5 and up)   623.8

1 Shipbuilding 2 Whalers
ISBN 0-395-26449-9   LC 78-60497

"A beautifully illustrated story of the building of a wooden whaling ship. . . . The pictures are lovely pencil and ink drawings, the diagrams of the ship's framing and timbers are clear, and the various tools used by the shipwrights of the 1860s are carefully labelled. There is a date at the bottom of the pages to indicate the chronological progress of the ship's construction. Not only are the technical aspects of ship building discussed, but the author presents the economic conditions that fostered the growth of the 19th-Century whaling industry. The text is brief and clear." Sch Library J

Fisher, Leonard Everett

The shipbuilders; written and illus. by Leonard Everett Fisher. Watts, F. 1971 48p illus (Colonial Americans) lib. bdg. $5.90 (4 and up)   623.8

1 Shipbuilding—History
ISBN 0-531-01043-0   LC 72-150733

This account traces the history of shipbuilding in Colonial America and describes with clarity the methods used to construct a wooden sailing ship." Booklist
"Tools are described; technical terms defined; and the many clear illustrations and diagrams graphically detail every aspect of ship construction." Sch Library J

Gilmore, H. H.

Model boats for beginners; pictures and diagrams by the author. Harper 1959 97p illus lib. bdg. $6.89 (5 and up)   623.8

1 Ships—Models
ISBN 0-06-021981-5   LC 59-8969

"Easy-to-follow instructions, illustrated with clear diagrams, for making simplified floating models of 10 boats and ships; included are a motorboat, cruiser, tugboat and barge, ferryboat, ocean liner, sloop, schooner, aircraft carrier, atomic submarine, and Coast Guard cutter. The book also explains how a boat floats and is propelled, shows how to identify boats and the parts of boats, outlines the history of the development of boats, and gives information on navigation aids and a chronological list of a few famous sea adventures." Booklist

Model submarines for beginners; 87 pictures and diagrams by the author. Harper 1962 122p illus lib. bdg. $7.89 (5 and up)   623.8

1 Submarines—Models
ISBN 0-06-022011-2   LC 62-7944

"After presenting briefly the history of the submarine, explaining how a submarine works, and showing how to identify submarines, the author . . . gives easy-to-follow instructions and adequate diagrams for building simplified scale models of 14 submarines from the 'Turtle' of the Revolutionary War period to the nuclear-powered ships of the present." Booklist

Tunis, Edwin

Oars, sails & steam; a picture book of ships; written and illus. by Edwin Tunis. Crowell [1977 c1952] 77p illus $10.95 (5 and up)   623.8

1 Ships
ISBN 0-690-01284-5   LC 76-25453

A reissue of the title first published 1952 by World Publishing Company
This book traces the history of boats from their beginnings to the present, featuring the most interesting and significant designs
"It makes a remarkable reference book for authors and artists. It will also be useful in school libraries, in connection with the great sea battles in which some of these ships took part." NY Her Trib Bks
Glossary of nautical terms: p69-76

Weiss, Harvey

Ship models and how to build them. Crowell 1973 66p illus $8.95 (4 and up)   623.8

1 Ships—Models
ISBN 0-690-73270-8   LC 72-7562

This book contains directions for constructing tug-boat, sailboat, riverboat, submarine, hollow hull and powerboat models
The author's "text, clear and matter-of-fact, gives background information first: tools, materials, using and adapting scale drawings, general tips. Each project begins with a list of materials and overall suggestions, then proceeds with a step-by-step explanation; the projects are of increasing difficulty; the diagrams are labelled, explicit, and well-placed. Throughout the book Weiss stresses safety and careful work but no need for perfection, and he encourages the reader who wants to adapt or vary the designs to suit himself." Chicago. Children's Bk Center

623.88 Seamanship

Adkins, Jan

The craft of sail; written, designed and illus. by Jan Adkins. Walker & Co. 1973 64p illus $6.95 (5 and up)   623.88

1 Sailing
ISBN 0-8027-0401-8   LC 72-87347

With pen, ink and wash pictures and accompanying text, [the author] has produced a handsome small primer on sailing that is also a model of brevity, clarity and simplicity. Starting with the Bernoulli effect (which explains how sailboats move to windward), the book ends with anchoring, having passed through everything from knots to points of sail, from rigging to docking, from man-overboard drills to the rough-weather practice of heaving to. On small craftsmanship and sheer draftsmanship Adkins is hard to beat." Time

624 Civil engineering

Corbett, Scott

Bridges; illus. by Richard Rosenblum. Four Winds 1978 122p illus $8.95 (4 and up)   624

1 Bridges
ISBN 0-590-07464-4   LC 77-13871

"Uncluttered pages and clean line drawings reminiscent of David Macaulay's complement a lucid history of bridge building. The discussion of primitive forms of construction—Indian and Peruvian suspension bridges, the wooden piles of Swiss lake dwellers, and Chinese cantilevers—introduces a variety of engineering notions within their social and historical context. . . . In the chapters which outline Roman, medieval, Renaissance and modern bridges, the discussion of historical necessities and human foibles is nicely balanced by descriptions of engineering innovation. Technical terminology is challenging, but concepts are introduced slowly so as to avoid overwhelming the reader." Horn Bk

Kelly, James E.

The tunnel builders, by James E. Kelly and William R. Park; drawings by Herbert E. Lake. Addison-Wesley 1976 unp illus lib. bdg. $6.95 (2-4)   624

1 Tunnels
ISBN 0-201-03721-1   LC 74-5076

"An Addisonian Press book"
"A basic explanation of the various tunnel-building techniques. In simple terms the authors, both of whom are involved in the construction industry, describe sinking the shaft, blasting the rock, placing the support braces, lining the sides with concrete, and finally ventilating and lighting

Kelly, James E.—*Continued*
the completed tunnel. Cranes, drills, moles, convey-
ors, mucking machines, air locks, pumps, and
compressors are examples of the equipment used
in these construction stages, and detailed instructional drawings are included to explain their function." Booklist

Macaulay, David
Underground. Houghton 1976 109p illus
$9.95 (5 and up)   **624**
1 Civil engineering 2 Building 3 City life
ISBN 0-395-24739-X   LC 76-13688
In this "examination of the intricate support
systems that lie beneath the street levels of our
cities, Macaulay explains the ways in which
foundations for buildings are laid or reinforced,
and how the various utilities or transportation
services are constructed." Chicago. Children's Bk
Center
"That such information is conveyed accurately,
concisely, and artistically is the triumph of an
unusual book which achieves clarity through an
imaginative and ingenious approach. Introduced
by a visual index—a bird's eye view of a busy,
hypothetical intersection with colored indicators
marking the specific locations analyzed in subsequent pages—detailed illustrations are combined
with a clear, precise narrative to make the subject
comprehensible and fascinating. The use of two-
and three-dimensional cutaway views, diagrams,
and a variety of unusual perspectives creates the
illusion of a guided tour beneath as well as
through the underground maze." Horn Bk
Glossary: p112

625.1 Railroads

Weiss, Harvey
How to run a railroad; everything you
need to know about model trains. Crowell
1977 127p illus $8.95 (4 and up)   **625.1**
1 Railroads—Models
ISBN 0-690-01304-3   LC 76-18128
"After an inviting introduction, the author gives
readers a section defining model-train terminology.
Succeeding chapters describe kinds of trains, how
they work, where to get them, etc. The beginner
can go step by step from a modest layout, all the
way through more complicated sets, which involve
elevated railroads, settlements for the trains to
run through (complete with trees, houses and
other authentic details)." Pub W
"In his usual meticulous fashion, Weiss gives a
full and logically arranged sequence of facts about
buying, building, and operating a model railroad.
The diagrams are adequately labelled and are
nicely placed in relation to textual references, and
the writing is clear, informal, and authoritative."
Chicago. Children's Bk Center

625.7 Roads and highways

Oppenheim, Joanne
Have you seen roads? Young Scott Bks.
1969 unp illus lib. bdg. $5.95 (k-2)   **625.7**
1 Roads 2 Transportation
ISBN 0-201-09211-5   LC 69-14566
Design and picture selection by Gerard Nook
From country roads and city streets to super
highways and underwater tunnels, from shipping
channels to pathways to the stars, the author
describes, in photos and verse, the pathways of
the 20th century
"The writing is poetic and evocative, the photographs carefully selected. The book is handsome
to look at, a pleasure to read aloud (save for the
reiteration of the title question), and a good
launching pad for a discussion of various means
of transportation." Sat Rev

Paradis, Adrian A.
From trails to superhighways; the story of
America's roads; illus. by Russell Hoover.
Messner 1971 96p illus map lib. bdg. $5.64
(3-6)   **625.7**
1 Roads
ISBN 0-671-32472-1   LC 74-161513
"Paradis traces the development of roads in the
U.S. from the Indian and animal trails used by the
first settlers to the superhighways of today. He
also explains how corduroy, macadam, asphalt,
and other types of roads are built and discusses
both the advantages of the construction of more
superhighways and the increasing opposition from
conservationists and others to them. . . . The book
is well organized, simply written, and informative. A glossary is appended." Booklist

627 Hydraulic engineering

Farb, Peter
The story of dams; an introduction to
hydrology; foreword by E. C. Itschner; illus.
by George Kanelous. Reviewed for scientific
accuracy by the U.S. Army Corps of Engineers. Harvey House 1961 127p illus maps
(A Story of science ser. bk. for young
people) lib. bdg. $6.29 (5 and up)   **627**
1 Dams
ISBN 0-8173-3252-1   LC 60-14420
"This informal presentation explains the importance, principal types, purpose, construction, and
operation of dams, describes some famous American dams, and offers a number of experiments with
water and dams, and includes a guide to the location of approximately 200 of the largest dams in
the U.S. Many photographs, diagrams, and a few
color plates add considerably to the usefulness of
the book. Suggestions for further reading are
appended." Booklist
"A chapter at the end of the book suggests some
assorted home demonstrations: generating electricity, checking stream sediment, mapping a creek
basin." Chicago. Children's Bk Center

Kelly, James E.
The dam builders, by James E. Kelly and
William R. Park; drawings by Herbert E.
Lake. Addison-Wesley 1977 unp illus lib.
bdg. $6.95 (1-3)   **627**
1 Dams
ISBN 0-201-05727-1   LC 77-5406
"An Addisonian Press book"
"Earthfill and masonry dams are explained in
this . . . book. Headings on each page describe
the separate steps in the building process and
large pictures clearly show the equipment, workers, and construction sites. Trucks and tractors
fill the pages, and are shown in small silhouetted
diagrams across the tops of some of the double
spreads." Sch Library J

628.9 Fire-fighting

Colby, C. B.
Space age fire fighters; new weapons in
the fireman's arsenal. Coward, McCann &
Geoghegan [1974 c1973] 48p illus lib.
bdg. $5.29 (3-6)   **628.9**
1 Fire departments—Equipment and supplies
2 Fire fighting
ISBN 0-698-30531-0   LC 73-82034
The author discusses new techniques in fighting
fires on land, air and sea. He also describes innovative developments in clothing and equipment
which resulted from the space program, such as
astronaut's suits, rocket torches and jet-axes
"Numerous black-and-white photoclips . . .[are
included in this] up-to-date, adulatory look at a
subject with perennial appeal." Booklist

629.13 Aeronautics

Bendick, Jeanne
The first book of airplanes; pictures by
the author. Rev. ed. Watts, F. 1976 65p illus
maps lib. bdg. $5.90 (3-5)   **629.13**
1 Aeronautics
ISBN 0-531-00455-4   LC 75-31880
First published 1958
"In this simple little book, Bendick describes
how airplanes fly and gives some aeronautical
history; she reviews airline operation and describes many of the uses of aircraft. The writing

Bendick, Jeanne—Continued
is simple and clear. Some of the descriptions of principles of aircraft operation are not totally accurate but perhaps more suitable for a juvenile audience than more involved explanations. The illustrations, black-and-white line drawings, are excellent, descriptive and lively. Elementary school children should have no difficulty reading this book; younger children may enjoy hearing it read." AAAS Sci Bks & Films
Some airplane words: a glossary: p60-63

Foster, John T.
The flight of the Lone Eagle; Charles Lindbergh flies nonstop from New York to Paris. Watts, F. 1974 61p illus lib. bdg. $5.90 (5 and up)   **629.13**
1 Lindbergh, Charles Augustus, 1902-1974
2 Spirit of St Louis (Airplane) 3 Aeronautics—Flights
ISBN 0-531-02723-6   LC 75-898
"A Focus book"
"A readable account of Lindbergh's historic solo flight from its inception in the young aviator's mind to its completion. The emphasis is on the flight itself and Lindbergh's ups and downs as he recalls them: period setting, biographical material, and details of the airplane's construction are also present in small doses. The author steers away from sensationalism, offering instead fast-paced, dramatic narrative. Black-and-white photographs add immediacy to a text that should painlessly inform as it entertains." Booklist

629.132   Principles of aerial flight

Corbett, Scott
What makes a plane fly? Pictures by Len Darwin. Little 1967 58p illus lib. bdg. $5.95 (3-6)   **629.132**
1 Aerodynamics 2 Flight
ISBN 0-316-15705-8   LC 67-19793
"An Atlantic Monthly Press book"
"The author discusses the shape of an airplane and of its wings as they add to—or diminish—drag, lift, and speed, and the functioning of air pressure in relation to wing shape. He describes the various methods used to obtain thrust, the aberrations of flight . . . and the balancing forces of lift, thrust, weight, and drag." Sutherland. The Best in Children's Bks
"Labeled diagrams and drawings further clarify every page of text. Combined index and glossary." Booklist

629.133   Aircraft

Barnaby, Ralph S.
How to make & fly paper airplanes; illus. by the author. Four Winds 1968 70p illus $7.95 (5 and up)   **629.133**
1 Airplanes—Models 2 Aerodynamics 3 Paper crafts
ISBN 0-590-07102-5   LC 67-31286
"A clearly illustrated, easily understood guide to making and flying paper airplanes. . . . [The author] not only provides explicit directions for making several different models of paper airplanes but also explains the basic principles of flight and flight control, tells how to analyze and correct flying defects of the models, and gives instructions for aerial maneuvers and tips on holding competitions and airshows." Booklist
Glossary: p65-70

Burchard, Peter
Balloons; from paper bags to skyhooks; designed and illus. by the author; with photographs. Macmillan Pub. Co. 1960 48p illus $5.95 (3-6)   **629.133**
1 Balloons
ISBN 0-02-71560   LC 60-13224
This "book presents highlights in the history of ballooning from the eighteenth-century experiments of the Montgolfier brothers to the space balloons of today. With many captioned drawings and photographs to supplement the sketchy text, the book will serve as an interesting introduction to ballooning." Booklist

Curry, Barbara
Model aircraft. Watts, F. 1979 63p illus lib. bdg. $5.45 (4-6)   **629.133**
1 Airplanes—Models
ISBN 0-531-02260-9   LC 78-11647
"A First book"
"Here is a book on making model planes for true beginners. The author discusses assembling plastic models from kits, making paper airplanes of varying degrees of complexity, constructing balsa wood gliders, and includes an actual-size pattern for a delta-wing Dart. There are suggestions for some models made from unconventional materials, such as a helicopter assembled from a carrot and six ice-cream sticks. There is an introductory chapter on the types of equipment and supplies useful to novices. Exhibiting models on a pegboard, a block stand with braces, or in a mobile is suggested—although the directions here are short on specifics." Sch Library J

Harris, Susan
Helicopters; illus. by E. Smart. Watts, F. 1979 48p illus lib. bdg. $5.90 (2-4)   **629.133**
1 Helicopters
ISBN 0-531-02850-X   LC 79-11533
"An Easy-read fact book"
"Easily understandable descriptions of the operation and structure of helicopters point out the machine's special capacities and contrast its differences with other aircraft. The history of its evolution, along with discussions of various types used today, is peppered with statistics and supplemented by a few diagrams and numerous black-and-white or color photographs. Technical terms such as 'suction, airfoil,' and 'cyclic pitch control column' are explained in the text, making this a drawing card for reluctant readers." Booklist

Jacobs, Lou
The jumbo jets, by Lou Jacobs, Jr. 2d ed. Bobbs 1976 64p illus $7.50 (5 and up)   **629.133**
1 Jet planes
ISBN 0-672-52280-2   LC 76-27278
First published 1969
"Competent coverage of a topic of great current interest is made more useful by photographs, drawings, and charts—particularly the charts that compare various types of jumbo jets that are on the drawing boards or in the air. The author gives some history of jet flight, describes in some detail the planning, testing, assemblage, and components of the jumbo jets, and discusses the problems of noise control, safety, airport accommodations, etc." Chicago. Children's Bk. Center. [review of 1969 edition]

Lopshire, Robert
A beginner's guide to building and flying model airplanes. Harper 1967 128p illus lib. bdg. $8.79 (5 and up)   **629.133**
1 Airplanes—Models
ISBN 0-06-023999-9   LC 66-12885
Illustrated by the author
Partial contents: Four kinds of models; What are the parts called; Why does it fly; Tools; Where shall I work; How to use your new tools; Make it smooth; Timber; Ways with wire; Nuts and bolts; How to solder metals; Power; Let's fly it
"Complete, detailed instructions are given for building planes from the simple glider to the racer. Instructions are clear, well-illustrated and simple enough for the beginner. The book is liberally sprinkled with precautions about the use of special materials such as razor blades, glue and plastic." Bruno. Bks for School Libraries, 1968

Navarra, John Gabriel
Superplanes. Doubleday 1979 79p illus $6.95, lib. bdg. $7.90 (5 and up)   **629.133**
1 Airplanes
ISBN 0-385-12561-5; 0-385-12562-3   LC 77-16936
"This book is part of a Museum of Science & Industry/Chicago series of science books"
"Each day commercial airplanes carry more than one-half million people on giant subsonic aircraft. High-performance military aircraft are streaking across the sky at twice the speed of sound. And commercial supersonic transports are carrying passengers from continent to continent. . . . In this book you will find information about some of the aircraft used in commercial and military aviation. In addition, you will find a section that details the use of aircraft for special purposes such as weather forecasting, astronomical observation, and surveying." Preface

Ross, Frank

Flying paper airplane models [by] Frank Ross. Jr. Illus. with photographs and drawings. Lothrop 1975 128p illus $5.95, lib. bdg. $6.48 (5 and up)   629.133

1 Airplanes—Models 2 Paper crafts
ISBN 0-688-51683-1; 0-688-41683-7   LC 74-22479

"Helping to fill the ever-present demand for paper airplane books, Ross has put together a precise, careful instruction guide containing patterns for eight jet and propeller planes in use today and four flyers of the future: three hypersonic planes and a space shuttle. Aids to building the flyable models include clear patterns (not on the same scale), simple slot-and-glue assembly instructions, and black-and-white photographs of both plane and completed model. Many readers will be interested in Ross' descriptions of the actual vehicles and the lists of their physical characteristics." Booklist
Glossary: p121-4. Books for further reading: p125

Historic plane models; their stories and how to make them [by] Frank Ross, Jr. Illus. with photographs, maps, and drawings. Lothrop 1973 188p illus maps lib. bdg. $7.92, pa $2.95 (5 and up)   629.133

1 Airplanes—Models
ISBN 0-688-50046-3; 0-688-45046-6   LC 72-9361

The author "tells of some memorable flights and pilots—Lindbergh, Blériot, Commander Byrd and Amelia Earhart, among others. Then he provides patterns and directions for creating copies of the planes discussed. In each case, a photo of the model is shown, as well as one of the original planes." Pub W
"Ross suggests the use of household materials or easily and inexpensively purchased supplies and offers tips on coping with difficult procedures and making more realistic recreations. . . . The clarity of instructions on the whole and the capsule flight histories will be useful for model enthusiasts who are interested in early planes." Sch Library J
Further reading: p183

Simon, Seymour

The paper airplane book; illus by Byron Barton. Viking 1971 48p illus lib. bdg. $7.50, Penguin Bks. pa $2.50 (3-5)   629.133

1 Airplanes—Models 2 Aerodynamics 3 Paper crafts
ISBN 0-670-53797-7; 0-14-030925-X   LC 71-162669

"Simple sketches illustrate how to fold a sheet of paper into a fair representation of an airplane. Several variations are illustrated and the reader can choose between an airplane designed for aerobatic maneuvers or one which is a beautiful long-distance glider. The reader is shown how to make rudders, elevators, and flaps with simple cuts in the paper and is encouraged to investigate their effects on the model's flight characteristics." Sci Bks
The directions "are easy to follow, the question and try-it-and-see approach to the experiments is provocative, and the diagrams and drawings showing each step in the construction of the planes and illustrating the experiments are usually clear." Booklist

Weiss, Harvey

Model airplanes and how to build them; illus. with photographs, plans, and drawings. Crowell 1975 90p illus $8.95 (5 and up)   629.133

1 Airplanes—Models
ISBN 0-690-00594-6   LC 74-19451

The author "gives instructions for toy replicas rather than accurate reproductions of specific planes. Some models are suspended on a counter-balanced beam and powered by a one- or two-battery motor, and there are also instructions for simple, rubberband powered flyers and gliders. Written instructions and illustrations of tools, materials, and finishing techniques are clear and are for beginners as well as more advanced model-makers." Sch Library J

Yolen, Jane

World on a string; the story of kites. Collins [distributed by Philomel Bks. 1969 c1968] 143p illus lib. bdg. $5.99 (4 and up)   629.133

1 Kites
ISBN 0-529-00394-5   LC 68-26976

First published by World Publishing Company
"The history of kites, which began at least 2,000 years ago in China, is given in vivid detail. . . . How kites have contributed to weather watching, electricity, bridge building, the airplane, aerial photography, military operations, even rescues; how they have served as religious symbols, art objects, toys, and for sporting use is told with style, enthusiasm and authority." Bk World
"Illustrated with photographs. A volume of fascinating content, produced with distinction. . . . The pages carry a profusion of well-printed reproductions representing the two-thousand year history of kites. As if pulled by a kite string, the title words and the chapter headings are interestingly slanted. The latter have trailing, string-like initial letters as decorative devices below the words." Horn Bk
Books for further reading: p137-38

629.2 Motor land vehicles, and cycles

Alth, Max

Motorcycles & motorcycling. Watts, F. 1979 90p illus lib. bdg. $5.90 (5 and up)   629.2

1 Motorcycles
ISBN 0-531-02945-X   LC 79-12267

"A First book"
"This overview of motorcycles has a wide-ranging scope that includes not only the machine but also its history and past and present uses. Technical information comes primarily from the second chapter that looks at cycle parts, including various engine types, and explains the significance of elements such as RPM and engine displacement. A rundown of today's bikes briefly notes distinctions among street, dirt, and combination bikes, and also places minibikes, mopeds, and other kinds of bikes in the motorcycle hierarchy. A look at competitions and the special requirements they demand rounds off the survey." Booklist

Ancona, George

Monsters on wheels; written and photographed by George Ancona. Dutton 1974 41p illus $7.50 (3-6)   629.2

1 Vehicles 2 Machinery
ISBN 0-525-35155-8   LC 73-20308

"Huge-wheeled movers and shakers have been captured for the edification and delight of children . . . interested in the uses and performances of various vehicles. Ancona's black-and-white pictures show the monsters in action; his text is a lucid explanation of their functions. We must add that we have seldom seen a book so handsomely designed. Separate chapters are devoted to the scrapper, piggy packer, windrower, tractor, crane, bulldozer, paver, straddle carrier and others, fetching up with a discussion of the lunar rover." Pub W

Bendick, Jeanne

The first book of automobiles; pictures by the author. [4th] rev. ed. Watts, F. 1978 66p illus lib. bdg. $5.90 (3-5)   629.2

1 Automobiles
ISBN 0-531-02227-7   LC 78-6252

"A First book"
First published 1955
The author "offers a fundamental explanation of how cars work and distinguishes between various types of vehicles, e.g., RVs ('recreational vehicles'), trucks and sports cars. The very basic information is accurate." Sch Library J
Discussions of CB radios as well as safety and environmental problems created by the automobile are also included
Some automobile words: a Glossary: p62-64

Coombs, Charles

Mopeding. Morrow 1978 125p illus $6.95, lib. bdg. $6.67 (5 and up)   629.2

1 Mopeds
ISBN 0-688-22155-6; 0-688-32155-0   LC 78-18394

The author "writes with authority and interest about a vehicle that is gaining popularity in the U.S. His valuable advice includes tips on what to look for when buying a moped and how to drive the cycle safely; his detailed lessons on the construction of the machine, its operation, and proper maintenance procedures are clear and concise. . . . This informal yet informative and highly readable volume will capably fill a need in library collections." Booklist
Glossary: p121-22

Corbett, Scott
What makes a car go? Pictures by Len Darwin. Little 1963 43p illus lib. bdg. $5.95 (3-6)   629.2

1 Automobiles
ISBN 0-316-156957   LC 62-12377

"An Atlantic Monthly Press book"
This book "explains the parts of the car's mechanism and how they work to make the engine run and the wheels move." Horn Bk
Text "and clear diagrams and drawings are combined to give a complete and readily understood explanation. . . . Easy enough for the interested third grader to read independently and helpful for the older reader, adult included, who requires a simplified explanation." Booklist

Dahnsen, Alan
Bicycles. Watts, F. 1978 48p illus lib. bdg. $5.90 (2-4)   629.2

1 Bicycles and bicycling
ISBN 0-531-01372-3   LC 78-7346

"An Easy-read fact book"
This book discusses changes in bicycles from their invention to the present, their uses and advantages, their parts and how they work, riding and safety tips, and the different types of bicycles. Illustrated with color drawings and photographs

De Waard, E. John
Electric cars, by E. John De Waard and Aaron E Klein. Doubleday 1977 103p illus lib. bdg. $8.90 (5 and up)   629.2

1 Automobiles, Electric
ISBN 0-385-08143-X   LC 74-18790

"Part of a Museum of Science & Industry/Chicago series of science books"
"A timely, lucid introduction to the checkered past and promising future of the electric automobile. The popularity of the quiet, clean electric car is traced back to the beginning of this century. . . . The authors explain the development of the engine, its intricacies, and actual operation. The final chapter plots out why, in these energy conscious times, the acceptance of the electric auto is only a matter of time." Sch Library J

Henkel, Stephen C.
Bikes; a how-to-do-it guide to selection, care, repair, maintenance, decoration, safety, and fun on your bicycle; illus. by the author. Chatham Press [distributed by Devin-Adair] 1972 96p illus $5.95, pa $4.95 (5 and up) 629.2

1 Bicycles and bicycling
ISBN 0-85699-033-7   LC 73-172354

This guide covers such varied aspects of cycling as what size bike to buy, learning to ride it, and the tools and techniques needed for repair operations. Safety on the road is emphasized
"A comprehensive treatment of bikes and bicycling containing clear, concise, accurate information. . . . Although the price information will become dated, this does not detract from the book's overall value. The illustrations are labeled and easy to follow." Library J
Bibliography: p89

Jackson, Robert B.
Antique cars. Walck, H.Z. 1975 64p illus $5.95 (4-6)   629.2

1 Automobiles—History
ISBN 0-8098-2105-2   LC 76-12179

The author "briefly explains the popularity of early automobiles and traces their development through four decades (1893-1932), from infancy to mass production. He focuses on 14 autos which illustrate the variety and individuality of these distinctive machines, including well-known makes (e.g., Maxwell and Hudson) as well as lesser-known but historically significant makes (e.g., Brush and Briscoe). Numerous black-and-white photos are interspersed and a list of antique car museums in the United States and Canada is included. A good companion to Jackson's 'Classic Cars' . . . [entered below] which features cars built between 1925 and 1942." Sch Library J
This book "will appeal to classic car buffs, young and old. Photos of the venerable vehicles certainly explain part of their charm: individuality." Pub W

Classic cars; illus. with photographs. Walck, H.Z. [1974 c1973] 63p illus $6.95 (4-6)   629.2

1 Automobiles—History
ISBN 0-8098-2094-3   LC 73-7530

"Jackson's latest trip into nostalgia includes photographs of the beautiful automobiles that were so much a part of a glamorous scene in the 1930s. . . . The American Duesenberg, the stately British Bentley, the French Hispano-Suiza and the Italian Isotta-Fraschini are all pictured and discussed among many others, in a text and pictures which illustrate details of their construction and intriguing anecdotes about their inventors." Pub W
The author "pays tribute to the men whose craftmanship and creativity produced them. Car buffs will especially appreciate the chart of mechanical specifications and information on classic car museums and model kits." Sch Library J

Lindblom, Steven
The fantastic bicycles book. Houghton 1980 100p illus $8.95, pa $3.95 (5 and up)   629.2

1 Bicycles and bicycling
ISBN 0-395-28481-3; 0-395-28482-1   LC 79-15281

This book discusses how to find inexpensive bikes and parts, how to combine the parts to construct recycled bikes and how to repair them. Detailed plans are included for projects such as racing, moto-cross, ski and tandem bikes
"Some projects are more difficult than others and seem to require—in addition to a large amount of motivation—an above-average mechanical ability; the book, however, includes sensible advice on when and where to seek adult or professional help. . . . The section on repair and maintenance is comprehensive and would be helpful to any bike-owner, regardless of mechanical skill. The simple line drawings and diagrams are useful and detailed, matching the text in spirit and clarity." Horn Bk

Marston, Hope Irwin
Big rigs. Dodd 1980 unp illus $5.95 (4-6)   629.2

1 Trucks
ISBN 0-396-07785-4   LC 79-21356

"Tractor trailers, or 'eighteen wheelers,' the largest trucks on the highways, are the stars of a generously illustrated, attractively produced informational book. Although enthusiastic about her subject, the author uses a straightforward style, honed and explicit. The declarative sentence predominates, and contractions are avoided—two factors which make the brief narrative accessible to beginning readers as well as to the older reluctant reader. And truck buffs, young and old, will be intrigued by the sampling of CB terminology, the suggestions for identifying different makes of trucks, and the detailed descriptions of various tractor-trailer components." Horn Bk

Navarra, John Gabriel
Supercars. Doubleday 1975 63p illus $7.95, lib. bdg. $8.90 (4 and up)   629.2

1 Automobiles
ISBN 0-385-09381-0; 0-385-06827-1   LC 73-10949

"A Chicago Museum of Science & Industry book"
"This is not a continuous text but a series of brief articles, illustrated by photographs, on new or experimental models of cars and the special features that make them more safe or on such aspects of the automobile in our society as controlled parking, pollution, and restricted use of freeways. Navarra also describes the conservation of fossil fuels and alternatives to the internal combustion engine. This doesn't go into any aspect of the subject deeply, but it is a clear and brisk overview." Chicago. Children's Bk Center

Olney, Ross R.
Modern racing cars; illus. with photographs. Dutton 1978 98p illus $8.95 (4 and up) 629.2

1 Automobiles 2 Automobile racing
ISBN 0-525-35130-2   LC 77-17221

"Olney surveys over a dozen different race car types from stock cars to Indy racers. . . . The text informs us that 'racing drivers are naturally very competitive,' and the numerous black-and-white photos sprinkled throughout the book bear out this notion." Sch Library J

Olney, Ross R.—*Continued*

"This book may not tell the reader everything he ever wanted to know about racing cars but it comes close to it. . . . Famous racers are mentioned and so are the important races, but this is mostly a book about cars." West Coast Rev of Bks

Ross, Frank

Antique car models; their stories and how to make them [by] Frank Ross, Jr. Illus. with diagrams by the author and photographs by George A. Haddad. Lothrop 1978 192p illus $8.95, lib. bdg. $8.59 (5 and up) 629.2

1 Automobiles—Models
ISBN 0-688-41833-3; 0-688-51833-8   LC 78-2349

The author presents "instructions for building models of four vintage automobiles—the Stanley Steamer, the Waverly Stanhope Electric, and two gasoline-powered cars. A brief history of each auto precedes the directions for constructing these models made of cardboard, paper, matchsticks, and straws." Sch Library J
"The book is unusual in combining cardboard and construction-paper techniques with fascinating vignettes of early automotive history. . . . As in his earlier volumes on model building, the author provides a descriptive list of necessary materials and tools, excellent directions, and clear, well-labeled diagrams." Horn Bk
Includes glossary and bibliography

Historic racing car models; their stories and how to make them [by] Frank Ross, Jr. Illus. with diagrams and photographs. Lothrop 1976 220p illus $7.75, lib. bdg. $7.44 (5 and up) 629.2

1 Automobiles—Models 2 Automobile racing
ISBN 0-688-41770-1; 0-688-51770-6   LC 76-41168

This book "provides explicit directions, diagrams and photographs for constructing models of six racing cars. In addition, Ross . . . describes the events which brought fame and fortune to the 1895 Panhard-Levassor, the 1904 Mercedes, the 1921 Duesenberg, the 1957 Maserati, the 1963 Lotus-Ford and the 1971 McLaren M16." Booklist
"In constructing the models no plastic materials are used but rather inexpensive and readily available household items such as drinking straws, construction paper, match sticks and marking pens. One of the better crafts books on this topic, young car buffs will appreciate the loving attention to design and detail that man has always lavished on the automobile." Sch Library J
Glossary: p216-17. Further reading: p218

Sarnoff, Jane

A great bicycle book, by Jane Sarnoff and Reynold Ruffins; Rudy "The Bicycle Man" Veselsky, technical consultant. New ed. Scribner 1976 32p illus lib. bdg. $8.95 (4 and up) 629.2

1 Bicycles and bicycling
ISBN 0-684-14580-4   LC 75-33507

First published 1973
This is a "do-it-yourself guide for bicycle owners, which conveys useful information with imagination, verve, and humor. In fact, you don't have to own a bicycle to enjoy it. . . . Clear and precise suggestions for bicycle selection, repair, and maintenance as well as rules for riding, racing, and safety are punctuated with serious and comic bicycle facts and statistics. The text is complemented with vibrant illustrations in a kaleidoscope page format." Horn Bk [review of the 1973 edition]

Stambler, Irwin

Minibikes and small cycles. Putnam 1977 126p illus lib. bdg. $5.89 (5 and up) 629.2

1 Motorcycles
ISB 0-399-61055-3   LC 76-25174

This is "a sound, sensible guide written by a seasoned veteran who doesn't talk down to young readers. In addition to the expected descriptions of mechanical functioning and riding experiences, it offers a fascinating chapter on the engineering

and marketing genius of Soichiro Honda of the Honda Motor Company; a troubleshooting guide suggesting areas in which newcomers might want to try their hand at tinkering; and, a section on features and options of different makes containing enough statistics and specifications to satisfy even the most number-hungry cycle enthusiasts." Sch Library J

Supermachines; editor, Toni Palumbo; contributor, Ralph Hancock. Viking 1978 61p illus $5.95 (4 and up) 629.2

1 Vehicles 2 Machinery
ISBN 0-670-68446-5   LC 78-2202

This book covers "the family car, a motorcycle, a Formula I racer, a combine harvester, a forklift, a hydrofoil, a hovercraft, etc. Various engines, automotive clutch and gear-box, differential and disc brakes are diagrammed and their workings explained. Projects include making an electro-magnet and a rubber-band powered boat." Sch Library J
"From a child's (of any age including adults) point of view [the book is] super; interesting subject well explained, exciting format, full-color photographs and drawings on every page." Appraisal

Weiss, Harvey

Model cars and trucks and how to build them; illus. with photographs, plans, and drawings. Crowell 1974 74p illus $10.95 (4 and up) 629.2

1 Automobiles—Models 2 Trucks—Models
ISBN 0-690-00414-1   LC 74-7403

Included here are instructions for making seven basic wooden model cars and trucks, with ideas for modifications and improvisations to create such other vehicles as racing cars, fire trucks, derricks, tractors, and bulldozers
"The clear text is full of practical suggestions and reminders and is reinforced by the simple plans and drawings. The format of the book is comfortable and convenient, and the photographs of the finished models are a pleasure to behold." Horn Bk

Zim, Herbert S.

Tractors [by] Herbert S. Zim [and] James R. Skelly; illus. with drawings by Lee J. Ames and photographs. Morrow 1972 63p illus lib. bdg. $6.48, pa $1.25 (3-6) 629.2

1 Tractors
ISBN 0-688-31782-0; 0-688-26782-3   LC 78-189893

"How all types of tractors work and the tasks they accomplish are concisely described in this . . . book. Tractor engines, including hydraulic systems, are covered. The last chapter provides brief career information. Farm and industrial tractors with various attachments are shown in drawings and photographs." Sch Library J
"While the print is large, the text is rather technical on subjects like principles of traction and hydraulic power. Carefully labelled diagrams of engine and body parts will attract mechanically minded readers." Booklist

Trucks [by] Herbert S. Zim & James R. Skelly; illus. by Stan Biernacki. Morrow 1970 64p illus lib. bdg. $6.48, pa $1.25 (4-6) 629.2

1 Trucks
ISBN 0-688-31565-8; 0-688-26565-0   LC 75-107973

"Complete illustrated descriptions are provided of trucks of all kinds, the adaptation of the truck body and chassis to the intended cargo is well described. A section on truck engines differentiates among, and explains the principles of, the three types—gasoline, diesel and gas turbine. An explanation of various transmission and braking systems follows. There is a detailed account of the duties and qualifications of the driver of a big truck, and some of the facilities and requirements of a smoothly operating trucking industry. For a young person who may be interested in learning about trucking as a career, this is a readable eye-opener." Sci Bks

629.4 Astronautics

Asimov, Isaac

How did we find out about outer space? Illus. by David Wool. Walker & Co. 1977 62p illus lib. bdg. $6.85   **629.4**

1 Outer space—Exploration
ISBN 0-8027-7284-0   LC 76-57064

In five chapters, the author "fields the question posed in this book's title. The reader is taken from humanity's early dreams of flying through the discovery of the vacuum of space to rockets, liquidfueled rockets and satellites and spaceships." AAAS Sci Bks & Films

"Easily digestible and useful in terms of providing a context for more technical reading. With black-and-white illustrations picturing scientists and/or their apparatuses." Booklist

Branley, Franklyn M.

A book of moon rockets for you; illus. by Leonard Kessler. Rev. ed. Crowell 1970 65p illus lib. bdg. $8.79 (1-3)   **629.4**

1 Rockets (Aeronautics) 2 Lunar probes 3 Space flight to the moon
ISBN 0-690-15438-0   LC 76-101921

First published 1959

Including drawings and photographs of missions up to the Apollo 11 flight, this book "furnishes information on what moon rockets are, how they were used to determine the possibilities for man's survival on the moon and what lunar probes were used to gather the information. . . . At the back of the book there is a list of the lunar probes that were successfully launched and what they accomplished." Appraisal

Experiments in the principles of space travel; illus. by Jeanyee Wong. Rev. ed. Crowell 1973 113p illus $8.95 (5 and up)   **629.4**

1 Space flight 2 Physics—Experiments
ISBN 0-690-27792-X   LC 72-7543

First published 1955

"Scientists' understanding and proper application of basic principles of science can, according to Branley, determine the success or failure of space exploration. The author's succinct presentation of some of these principles is given in tandem with a highly technical yet comprehensible series of experiments. The experiments discuss the principles behind space measurements, rocket design and streamlining, rocket engines, power and pressure in space, temperature control in space, and gravitational force. Clear explanations, illustrations, and charts expose the reader to the scientific tools and framework needed to develop problem-solving abilities while orienting the reader toward research as well." Booklist

629.44 Auxiliary spacecraft

Bergaust, Erik

Colonizing space. Putnam 1978 62p illus lib. bdg. $4.99 (5 and up)   **629.44**

1 Space stations 2 Space colonies
ISBN 0-399-61113-4   LC 77-11147

"In the regions near Earth, space is not the void described by the ancient poets but is packed with elements of pure energy, such as light and heat, thrown off by the sun. . . . In this book [the author] taps the latest serious thinking of space scientists on how to convert this great element of the sun to the aid of an earth that is rapidly running out of energy. The answer . . . put forth by practical engineers and scientists—is to establish human colonies in our solar system which will capture and beam back to Earth this powerful largess of the sun." About the book

"Science-fiction often comes to reality so swiftly that modern youngsters will enjoy being kept up to date by this exciting book. Space engineers have the know-how, and NASA is actually designing 20-mile-long space stations from which solar electrical energy will be beamed to Earth, and factories will produce chemicals and other products under zero-gravity conditions. This stimulating book also answers many questions about how people can live and work in space." Children's Bk Rev Serv

Branley, Franklyn M.

Columbia and beyond; the story of the space shuttle. Collins [distributed by Philomel Bks.] 1979 88p illus $12.95 (4-6)   **629.44**

1 Space vehicles 2 Spacelab Project 3 Space stations
ISBN 0-529-05525-2   LC 78-26891

This book about America's space shuttle includes such details as "the weightless showerstall and rescue balls to be used by escaping passengers in an emergency. There is also information on Europe's Spacelab and a time chart of firsts in space exploration. A section of color illustrations, an easy-to-read format, and wide margins contribute to a readable appearance." Sch Library J

Knight, David C.

Colonies in orbit; the coming age of human settlements in space; illus. with photographs and diagrams. Morrow 1977 94p illus $7.25, lib. bdg. $6.96 (5 and up)   **629.44**

1 Space colonies
ISBN 0-688-22096-7; 0-688-32096-1   LC 76-56086

"After briefly reviewing early ideas about colonizing space, Knight describes in detail a proposal . . . to build and continually replicate 'habitats' in orbit around the earth. These colonies would become so nearly self-sufficient and attractive that most human activity would cease on the earth, which would then become a beautiful park." Sch Library J

"As a popularization, the work is credible. The book is clearly written with good illustrations and a glossary. . . . I suggest this book for those who are interested in visionary applications of science and technology." AAAS Sci Bks & Films

Ross, Frank

The space shuttle; its story and how to make a flying paper model, by Frank Ross, Jr. Lothrop 1979 96p illus $6.50, lib. bdg. $6.24 (5 and up)   **629.44**

1 Space vehicles
ISBN 0-688-41882-1; 0-688-51882-6   LC 79-12155

"A short history of space technology and the development of the shuttle concept precedes a detailed description of the construction of the space shuttle. NASA pictures and Rockwell International's diagrams clarify the function of each part of the space craft. Preliminary testing of the Enterprise and plans for using the shuttles yet to be built are discussed. . . . The author has included, as an added feature, plans for a paper model space shuttle. Unfortunately, the dimensions are not accurate and the directions are insufficient, leaving out important details. The rest of the book will nicely update material on space technology." Sch Library J

Bibliography: p92

Taylor, L. B.

Space shuttle, by L. B. Taylor, Jr. Crowell 1979 119p illus $7.95 (5 and up)   **629.44**

1 Space vehicles 2 Space stations
ISBN 0-690-03897-6   LC 78-4777

"NASA's space shuttle will be operational in the 1980s, according to Taylor, and his text opens with a fictional account of a sample voyage. From there on, the book sticks to a more straightforward presentation with explanations of the shuttle's design and operation, criteria for the shuttle mission candidates, and justification for the program's existence. The major stress is on both national and international benefits (communications, weather knowledge, medical breakthroughs). . . . Taylor devotes a chapter to 'Costs and Critics' (which he explains away) and concludes with comments on industrial possibilities and the eventual building of entire cities in space. Researchers will have to ferret out the facts from Taylor's suppositions and NASA's publicity material, but the author does supply a close look at a new era about to be launched. Illustrated with black-and-white photographs." Booklist

629.45 Manned flight

Collins, Michael
Flying to the moon and other strange places. Farrar, Straus 1976 159p illus $6.95 (5 and up)   **629.45**

1 Space flight to the moon 2 Astronauts
ISBN 0-374-32412-3   LC 76-25496

Based in part on: Carrying the Fire, written by the author for adults
A "report on what it was like to train for and then be part of two manned-space flights. Much of the description is concerned with equipment operations. . . . Through it all, as Collins interprets and clues us in on the expected and unexpected problems, the reader will be newly respectful of the missions' success, and there will be a fresh understanding of the uniqueness of an astronaut's experiences." Booklist
"Many people like to put themselves in the place of someone who has done important things, and Mr Collins does a fine job of supplying the background which makes possible this exercise of the imagination. He is not quite so good at explaining the bits of science which have to be discussed occasionally, but this is hardly a fatal weakness. I enjoyed the book greatly. Bibliography and index." Horn Bk

Fuchs, Erich
Journey to the moon. Delacorte Press 1970 [c1969] unp illus $5.95, lib. bdg. $5.47 (4 and up)   **629.45**

1 Apollo project
ISBN 0-440-4277-1; 0-440-4278-X   LC 74-103151

A "Seymour Lawrence book"
Original German edition 1969
"Twelve stunning doublespread paintings, unencumbered by any text, tell the story of the Apollo 11 from lift off to splashdown, capturing in the full the wonder and excitement of the space mission. Explanatory captions are located on two pages preceding the paintings." Booklist

Wheat, Janis Knudsen
Let's go to the moon; drawings by Bill Burrows. Natl. Geographic Soc. 1977 31p illus (k-3)   **629.45**

1 Apollo project 2 Space flight to the moon
ISBN 0-87044-244-9   LC 77-76972

Obtainable only as part of a set for $9.95 with: The blue whale, by Donna K. Grosvenor, class 599.5; Creatures of the night, by Judith E. Rinard, class 591.5; and What happens in the spring, by Kathleen Costello Beer, class 500
"Books for young explorers"
This book describes the journey of the crew of Apollo 17 from the time they suit up until their return to earth
"The superb full color photographs taken on the journey illustrate every page and small well-done diagrams . . . clarify the workings of the spacecraft itself." Appraisal

630.1 Farm life

Jackson, Louise A.
Grandpa had a windmill, Grandma had a churn; illus. with photographs by George Ancona. Parents Mag. Press [distributed by Four Winds] 1977 unp illus $6.25, lib. bdg. $5.71 (2-4)   **630.1**

1 Farm life—U.S.
ISBN 0-8193-0872-2; 0-8193-0873-0   LC 77-23313

"This sensitive first-person account of a country farmhouse, its special possessions, and the narrator's loving grandparents combines a bucolic setting with a healthy learning experience. The text tells how butter is churned, what a whetstone does, how a windmill operates, and much more. The explanations are interesting and concise, and the book is well designed and attractively illustrated with appropriate sepia photographs. A fine nostalgic contribution to collections of Americana." Sch Library J

631.4 Soil and soil conservation

Goldin, Augusta
Where does your garden grow? Illus. by Helen Borten. Crowell 1967 unp illus (Let's-read-and-find-out science bks) $7.95, lib. bdg. $7.89 (1-3)   **631.4**

1 Soils
ISBN 0-690-88357-9; 0-690-88358-7   LC 67-18517

"The subject of this book is not gardens but soil and, particularly, the topsoil in which plants flourish. Much of the text is concerned with the formation of humus and the part plants and animals play in its creation." Library J
"The basic information concerning horticulture imparted for beginning readers is good and clearly stated. The illustrations are unrealistic, 'arty' embellishments for the most part." Sci Bks

Keen, Martin L.
The world beneath our feet; the story of soil; illus. by Haris Petie and with photographs. Messner 1974 96p illus lib. bdg. $6.64 (4-6)   **631.4**

1 Soils 2 Soil conservation
ISBN 0-671-32674-0   LC 74-7148

"This well-organized volume does a conscientious job of explaining the origins and makeup of soil and the ways in which man and nature can both destroy and protect it. A description of soil formation is followed by chapters which analyze plant and animal content in the earth and show the decay and growth cycles that take place. [Included also are] sections on the farming and grazing practices that lead to soil infertility, the effects of wind and rain on unprotected land, and modern efforts to reclaim and preserve the earth's usefulness." Pub W
"The photographs and diagrams clarify difficult concepts and, overall, this offers an interesting and informative look at the subject." Sch Library J
Glossary: p90-93

631.8 Fertilizers and soil conditioners

Rockwell, Harlow
The compost heap. Doubleday 1974 24p illus lib. bdg. $5.90 (k-1)   **631.8**

1 Compost 2 Fertilizers and manures
ISBN 0-385-08989-9   LC 73-10544

"Not a lesson in organic gardening, but a description of the changes in a compost heap comprising leaves, grass, and vegetable garbage. The story is told, very simply, by a small boy who watches the compost change to earth, steaming and sprouting and filled with worms. Then he and his father spread it on their garden." Chicago. Children's Bk Center
The text is "complemented and extended through explicit, poster-like illustrations in soft pastels. An appealing story, which effectively and accurately introduces to preschoolers the wonders of natural phenomena." Horn Bk

632 Plant injuries, diseases, pests

Graham, Ada
Bug hunters [by] Ada and Frank Graham; illus. by D. D. Tyler. Delacorte Press 1978 100p illus $6.95, lib. bdg. $6.46 (5 and up)   **632**

1 Insects. Injurious and beneficial 2 Pests—Biological control
ISBN 0-440-00909-X; 0-440-00910-3   LC 77-20531

"An Audubon reader"
"Chemical insecticides that have been used in attempts to control insect pests generally have ecologically disastrous side effects. This is not the case when insect pests are combatted by means of biological controls, for example, by encouraging other insects which parasitize the pests. The adventure and tremendous value involved in the development of biological controls should be evident even to the younger readers of this book." Children's Bk Rev Serv
Bibliographical references included in Acknowledgments: p93

Hogner, Dorothy Childs

Good bugs and bad bugs in your garden; backyard ecology; illus. by Grambs Miller. Crowell 1974 86p illus lib. bdg. $7.89 (5 and up)　　**632**

1 Insects. Injurious and beneficial　2 Pests—Biological control
ISBN 0-690-00120-7　　LC 74-6235

This introduction to biological control of insect pests in the home garden discusses the use of natural enemies, companion planting, immune strains of plants, and botanical insecticides as alternatives to harmful pesticides

"Amply illustrated, an informative and simply written text is divided by topic rather than chapter, the brief topics listed in the table of contents [are] grouped so that all of the facts about harmful bugs, about beneficial ones, and about methods of pest control are in sequence." Chicago. Children's Bk Center

Bibliography: p81-82

Pringle, Laurence

Pests and people; the search for sensible pest control. Macmillan Pub. Co. 1972 118p illus lib. bdg. $5.95 (5 and up)　　**632**

1 Pests—Control　2 Pests—Biological control
3 Pesticides—Environmental aspects
ISBN 0-02-775270-4　　LC 71-165104

The author describes the dangers of pesticide usage to plants and animals, and explores possible alternatives which would employ biological rather than chemical means of control

"Present problems and the uphill task in adopting biological control are presented in the book so that the reader is aware that biological control has not yet achieved perfection. . . . The accuracy of the book is above reproach; and the inclusion of a glossary, list of recommended books for further reading and an index at the end of the book enhances its value. It will serve as excellent collateral reading material but cannot be used as a reference." Sci Bks

633.1　Cereals

Aliki

Corn is maize; the gift of the Indians; written and illus. by Aliki. Crowell 1976 33p illus (Let's-read-and-find-out science bks) lib. bdg. $7.89 (1-3)　　**633.1**

1 Corn
ISBN 0-690-00975-5　　LC 75-6928

In this book, the author provides a history of corn, or maize, and "also the life cycle of the plant itself, its growth and reproductive patterns, and its many uses. Excellent illustrations by the author help convey both cultural aspects and technological uses of corn." Sci and Children

633.6　Sugar crops

Gemming, Elizabeth

Maple harvest; the story of maple sugaring. Coward, McCann & Geoghegan 1976 47p illus $5.95 (4-6)　　**633.6**

1 Maple sugar
ISBN 0-698-20360-7　　LC 75-45132

"The author relates the history of maple syrup and sugar from pre-colonial times to the present blending social, economic, botanical, technological and aesthetic considerations. The black-and-white illustrations—photographs, line drawings and reproductions of old paintings and prints—are well integrated with the text and while not compellingly attractive, are clear and instructively pertinent. A short appendix on how to visit a sugar house (mainly addresses of organizations to write for further information) is a helpful, upbeat finishing touch." AAAS Sci Bks & Films

634　Orchards, fruits, nuts, forestry

Johnson, Hannah Lyons

From apple seed to applesauce; photographs by Daniel Dorn, Jr. Lothrop 1977 unp illus lib. bdg. $7.44 (3-5)　　**634**

1 Apple
ISBN 0-688-51790-0　　LC 76-52944

"Not only from apples to applesauce, this book also goes from the beginning to the end of the apple season. Soil preparation, pruning, grafting, pesticide use, fertilization with bees, and the harvest are chronicled." Appraisal

"Clean design and a straightforward writing style brighten this informational look at apples and apple farming. . . . Black-and-white photographs illustrate almost every page." Booklist

634.9　Forestry

Budbill, David

Christmas tree farm; illus. by Donald Carrick. Macmillan Pub. Co. 1974 unp illus lib. bdg. $5.95 (k-2)　　**634.9**

1 Trees　2 Nurseries (Horticulture)
ISBN 0-02-715330-4　　LC 73-6051

The author follows the growth of a Christmas tree, from the spring planting of the seedling, through transplanting and pruning, to the fall harvest

"Children whose only acquaintance with the trees is seeing them on open lots in the city will learn that they are produced on farms and are the result of planning and care. Budbill's quiet, matter-of-fact text narrates the process, pictured in Carrick's panoramic, serene water-color illustrations of one Vermont tree farm." Booklist

Kurelek, William

Lumberjack; paintings and story by William Kurelek. Houghton 1974 unp illus $6.95 (3-5)　　**634.9**

1 Lumber and lumbering
ISBN 0-395-19922-0　　LC 74-9377

"This is an inspired carte-de-visite to the post-War logging camps of Canada's vast wilderness. In a wry and candid introduction, the Canadian artist explains his motivation for working in 'the bush' of Quebec and Ontario, and his text continues in this vein with concise explanations of the rudiments of lumbercamp life. But it is Kurelek's full-color, full-page illustrations which make this book a masterpiece. Full of humour and affectionate detail, the primitivist paintings splendidly evoke the atmosphere of the pre-mechanized lumbercamp." Children's Bk Rev Serv

635　Garden crops (Horticulture)

Baker, Samm Sinclair

The indoor and outdoor grow-it book; illus. by Erik Carle. Random House 1966 65p illus lib. bdg. $4.99, pa $2.95 (1-6)　　**635**

1 Gardening　2 House plants
ISBN 0-394-93457-1; 0-394-83457-7　　LC 66-15409

"Simple, easy-to-follow instructions in text and pictures for growing plants indoors and outdoors for pleasure, gifts, food, decoration, and science projects. The book tells how to grow such things as a pineapple plant, an African violet 'child', herbs, cactus, and insect-eating plants; it gives directions for such activities as growing a garden in a glass bowl or a bottle cap, making an indoor greenhouse, and arranging, pressing, or drying flowers; and, finally, it includes general indoor and outdoor 'grow-it' tips. The two-color illustrations are clearly drawn and attractive. Enticing, workable suggestions for both individual and group projects." Booklist

Cutler, Katherine N.

Growing a garden, indoors or out; illus. by Jacqueline Adato. Lothrop 1973 96p illus lib. bdg. $6.96 (4 and up)   635

1 Gardening 2 House plants
ISBN 0-688-31365-5   LC 73-4936

"Emphasizing that gardening can be fun and is accessible to everyone, this is a clear introduction to indoor and out-door planting. In a straightforward manner, Cutler explains how plants grow and what they need to thrive, e.g., she gives the different light requirements needed for a variety of plants. Both sections of the book—indoor and outdoor gardening—contain detailed information that will be helpful to beginning gardeners. . . . There is also a good glossary, a list of plant and seed catalogs, and a well-selected bibliography." Sch Library J

Davis, Burke

Newer and better organic gardening; drawings by Honi Werner. Putnam 1976 95p illus $5.95 (5 and up)   635

1 Organiculture 2 Vegetable gardening
ISBN 0-399-20510-1   LC 75-42028

This introduction to organic gardening "explains the how and why of gardening without the use of commercial fertilizers and pesticides. Chapters cover the definition of an organic garden, how to prepare the soil and deal with insects, as well as a basic list of vegetables, including specific information on the preferred varieties of each plant, its hardiness, yield, planting instructions, etc." Appraisal

"The directions—from making compost to controlling pests and predators without poisons—are simple as well as practical. . . . The drawings are attractive, precise, and informative. An appendix includes supplementary readings, a list of seed companies, a compilation of sources for obtaining help in insect control, a planting table, and maps showing average frost dates. A balanced, useful guide, attractive in format and easy to understand." Horn Bk

Dowden, Anne Ophelia

This noble harvest; a chronicle of herbs; illus. by the author. Collins [distributed by Philomel Bks.] 1979 80p illus $12.95 (4 and up)   635

1 Herbs
ISBN 0-529-05548-1   LC 79-12021

"Dowden chronicles the history of herb use throughout Europe and the Western world. The importance of herbs in daily life as medicine, dye, magic (black and white) and cooking aides is told accompanied by full color paintings of the herbs—showing leaves and flowers. The illustrations are striking, and the writing style is clear and easy to follow." Sch Library J

Some old herbals available in reprints: p76. Some books about herbs: p77

Fenten, D. X.

Gardening . . . naturally; line drawings by Howard Berelson. Watts, F. 1973 87p illus pa $2.95 (4 and up)   635

1 Organiculture
ISBN 0-531-02338-9   LC 72-13790

This book offers advice to organic gardeners about outdoor and indoor plants. There is information about selecting garden sites, growing vegetables and flowers, soil and light conditions, everyday garden care, biological control of insect pests and diseases, and year-round garden planning. A list of organic gardening suppliers is also included

Here is "a text that gives sensible advice . . . [which is] well-organized and is written in an informal, almost conversational style. . . . An excellent book for the beginning gardener." Chicago. Children's Bk Center

Glossary of gardening terms: p28-83. Other books to read: p84

Herda, D. J.

Vegetables in a pot; illus. with drawings by Kathy Fritz McBride and photographs. Messner 1979 94p illus lib. bdg. $7.29 (3-6)   635

1 Vegetable gardening
ISBN 0-671-32929-4   LC 78-23936

This "is a straightforward gardening book written and illustrated with drawings and photographs to help children get started growing things for themselves quickly and inexpensively. The book gives a short account of how plants grow and considers, in more detail, selection of containers and seed, preparation of containers and soil, planting the seeds, and caring for the plants. Water, light temperature, and humidity are explained briefly. . . . Time-to-maturity, occasional suggestions for use, and minimum pot sizes are included along with short descriptions of the plants. . . . With a little help from an interested adult . . . beginning gardeners of middle and upper elementary-school age should be able to use this book enjoyably and successfully." Appraisal

Johnson, Hannah Lyons

From seed to jack-o'-lantern; photographs by Daniel Dorn. Lothrop 1974 unp illus lib. bdg. $6.48 (1-3)   635

1 Pumpkin
ISBN 0-688-51644-0   LC 74-6458

"The simple text and black-and-white photographs show ground preparation, planting, and growth stages of the pumpkin plants, and the author explains the necessity for weeding and ensuring cross-pollination so that the plants can produce mature fruits. . . . Johnson brings the fruits indoors to show how to carve it and roast its seeds. Those with an inclination for indoor gardening can send for bush pumpkin plants that can be grown in a pot." Booklist

The "text is uncluttered and easy to follow, and we'd like to add that grown-ups can learn from and enjoy this book as well as children." Pub W

From seed to salad; photographs by Daniel Dorn, Jr. Lothrop 1978 unp illus $7.20, lib. bdg. $7.50 (2-4)   635

1 Vegetable gardening 2 Salads
ISBN 0-688-41834-1; 0-688-51834-6   LC 78-2813

"The subject of making salad from scratch is treated in the same format as the author's 'From Apple Seed to Applesauce' [entered in class 634]. Clear black-and-white photographs show children making a garden plan, preparing soil, planting, weeding, dealing with garden pests, harvesting, and finally making salad from their produce. The vegetables grown are tomatoes, peppers, spinach, carrots, radishes, scallions, cucumbers, and lettuce; three recipes for home-made dressings are included." Sch Library J

"Other introductory gardening books contain more information, but few can match the intimacy and good feeling generated by the photo-essay format found here." Booklist

Kohn, Bernice

The organic living book; drawings by Betty Fraser. Viking 1972 91p illus lib. bdg. $7.95, Penguin Bks. pa $1.25 (4 and up)   635

1 Organiculture
ISBN 0-670-52833-1; 0-670-05079-2   LC 78-183936

"Delicate line drawings illustrate the text of a book that speaks with fervor on the topics of organic gardening, unadulterated foods, conservation and recycling of waste materials, and living closer to nature. The author gives advice on shopping, gardening, cooking (including recipes for some gourmet dishes and separate chapters on baking bread and making your own yogurt) and making compost. The final chapter lists ways of conserving materials and avoiding pollution. The tone is moderate, the style of writing direct, the author's viewpoint enthusiastic." Chicago. Children's Bk Center

For further reading: p85-87

Lavine, Sigmund A.

A beginner's book of vegetable gardening; illus. with photographs and with drawings by Jane O'Regan. Dodd 1977 128p illus $5.95 (5 and up)   635

1 Vegetable gardening
ISBN 0-396-07410-3   LC 76-53439

"All phases of vegetable gardening (planning, planting, tending, and harvesting) are discussed fully and accurately though in an overly formal style that is sometimes difficult to read. Alternatives to the use of chemical insecticides are not sufficiently explored, but much sensible information is offered on each of 20 vegetables (including

Lavine, Sigmund A.—*Continued*

recommended varieties) along with facts on seed selection and sowing, transplanting 'starts' and coping with garden pests. Excellent black-and-white photographs plus useful lists and tables support the text." Sch Library J

Wonders of herbs; illus. with photographs. Dodd 1976 64p illus lib. bdg. $5.95 (5 and up)   **635**

1 Herbs 2 Gardening
ISBN 0-396-07294-1   LC 75-38356

"Dodd, Mead Wonders books"
An "introduction to the history of herbs—their uses, their cultivation, the lore surrounding them. There are also directions for raising balm, basil, chives, mint, parsley, rosemary, sage and thyme as well as brief instructions for making herbal beauty aids. With black-and-white photographs that will aid readers in identifying many species, the account is clearly and simply written." Sch Library J

Mintz, Lorelie Miller

Vegetables in patches and pots; a child's guide to organic vegetable gardening; illus. by the author. Farrar, Straus 1976 115p illus $6.95 (3-6)   **635**

1 Vegetable gardening 2 Organiculture
ISBN 0-374-38091-0   LC 76-46998

"The book is characterized by enthusiastic and spirited prose and should inspire the most reluctant city dweller to try a hand at gardening. Full instructions for preparing garden areas as well as informaiton on ordering seeds, discouraging pests, and growing specific vegetables are included. Black-and-gray wash drawings add an aesthetic touch to a practical guide, but they would be even more effective in color." Horn Bk

Paul, Aileen

Kids outdoor gardening; illus. by John DeLulio. Doubleday 1978 80p illus $5.95, lib. bdg. $6.90 (3-6)   **635**

1 Gardening
ISBN 0-385-12757-X; 0-385-12758-8   LC 77-80907

The author describes "all the hows and whys of outdoor gardening. . . . Both chemical and organic methods of fertilization and pest control are discussed, leaving readers to experiment and arrive at their own conclusions. When chemicals are mentioned, appropriate caution is urged. A short chapter is devoted to container gardening, and special projects such as a peanut patch, a 'bean tent,' or flower initials are also suggested." Sch Library J
"A logically organized book for the beginning young gardener. . . . The text is clearly written, and the book includes a list of sources for further information, a glossary, and an index." Chicago. Children's Bk Center

Riedman, Sarah R.

Gardening without soil; illus. by Rod Slater. Watts, F. 1979 64p illus lib. bdg. $5.45 (5 and up)   **635**

1 Plants—Soilless culture
ISBN 0-531-02256-0   LC 78-13088

"A First book"
"Well-organized, direct and dry in style, comprehensive in coverage and explicit in detail, this 'how-to' book is excellent of its kind, discussing many aspects of hydroponic gardening. Riedman gives a brief history of plants grown without soil, and weighs the advantages and disadvantages of plants grown in water or in aggregate. Most of the text is devoted to specific instructions for setting up hydroponic systems, open or closed (in re water supply) and includes information about containers, forms of aggregate, placement of plants, supplying and testing nutrients, and about planting and caring for plants. It also discusses plant diseases and damaging insects, and concludes with a description of a commercial hydroponic greenhouse. A reading list, an index, and lists of suppliers and consultants are appended." Chicago. Children's Bk Center

Selsam, Millicent E.

More potatoes! Pictures by Ben Shecter. Harper 1972 62p illus (A Science I can read bk) lib. bdg. $6.89 (1-3)   **635**

1 Potatoes
ISBN 0-06-025324-X   LC 78-183167

Because of a young girl's curiosity, her teacher arranges for the class to visit a warehouse and a farm in order to learn how potatoes are grown, harvested, and distributed
"Illustrations with a pleasantly casual air follow the investigation of Sue and her classmates as they learn all about potatoes. . . . The fictional framework is nicely balanced by the information in an adroitly written book for beginning readers." Chicago. Children Bk Center

Walsh, Anne Batterberry

A gardening book: indoors and outdoors; written and illus. by Anne Batterberry Walsh. Atheneum Pubs. 1976 100p illus $6.95 (4-6)   **635**

1 Gardening
ISBN 0-689-50042-4   LC 75-28249

"A Margaret K. McElderry book"
In this "how-to book, the author provides good advice and excellent project plans—thus ensuring young readers a positive gardening experience. The instructions range, in graduated steps, from the simple sweet potato in water to a complicated vegetable garden and from the ordinary tomato to the exotic cactus. Each variation is carefully planned—even to requesting adult advice; necessary materials are listed prominently; instructions are given intelligently; there is a glossary of terms; and there are humorous (but helpful) drawings which illustrate the steps." AAAS Sci Bks & Films

635.9 Flowers and ornamental plants

Kramer, Jack

Plant sculptures; making miniature indoors topiaries; photographs by Matthew Barr; drawings by Tom Adams. Morrow 1978 63p illus $6.50, lib. bdg. $6.24 (4-6)   **635.9**

1 Plants, Ornamental 2 House plants
ISBN 0-688-22144-0; 0-688-32144-5   LC 78-2524

Kramer discusses how the art of topiary can be performed indoors with house plants and gives instruction for ten projects
"Given the current interest in house plant horticulture, the subject of indoor topiaries is a timely variation on a popular theme. . . . Selected for their appeal to young hobbyists, the sculptures could also serve as introductory projects for adults; phrases such as 'remove errant stems' suggest that the content might have been adapted from the author's considerable body of work for older audiences. With detailed lists of materials, explicit directions, numerous illustrations, copious suggestions for plant care, and a list of mail order suppliers." Horn Bk

Millard, Adele

Plants for kids to grow indoors; photographs by Glenn Lewis and Bud Millard; drawings by Gregory Thompson. Sterling 1975 124p illus $6.95, lib. bdg. $6.69 (4-6)
                                                          635.9

1 House plants
ISBN 0-8069-3070-5; 0-8069-3071-3   LC 75-14509

Instructions are "presented describing how to grow plants using different techniques. These instructions are precise and simple to follow. Carrot and beet tops, sweet potato vines, and avocado seeds in a jar receive special attention. Procedures are detailed for establishing and maintaining various terraria, rock gardens, and botanical gardens including vegetables and flowers, as well. Basic needs of plants such as light, water, soil, nutrients, and containers provide a background of information for those who wish to experiment." Sci and Children
This is a splendid little book for arousing the interest of children in growing plants indoors. It should also lead them towards consideration of ecological factors outdoors. Details for plant care and the construction of indoor habitats are excellent. Some of the illustrations, both photo and drawing, are somewhat confusing or overpowering because of the scale, which hides details." Appraisal

Parker, Alice

Terrariums; illus. by Marika. Watts, F. 1977 47p illus lib. bdg. $5.45 (2-4)   **635.9**

1 Terrariums
ISBN 0-531-01315-4   LC 77-8554

"An Easy-read fact book"
The author's "instructions will enable young children to understand and participate in terrarium construction. The text begins with a brief explanation of how an enclosed environment functions and directions are then given for three types: woodland, tropical, and desert. . . . Vocabulary is controlled for young readers, and definitions and pronunciations are given for all unfamiliar words. Large illustrations and a clear, uncluttered layout add to the usefulness of this book." Sch Library J

Paul, Aileen

Kids gardening; a first indoor gardening book for children; illus. by Arthur Hawkins. Doubleday 1972 96p illus $4.95 (3-6)   **635.9**

1 House plants
ISBN 0-385-02492-4   LC 73-177239

"A book that gives good coverage, sensible advice, and an encouraging word to the beginning gardener. The directions are clear, although (as in the section on propagation) instructions are not always comprehensive. The author first gives general instructions on preparing potting soils, planting, watering, et cetera, then discusses house plants by type: plants that flower from bulbs, plants with attractive foliage, cacti, waterplants, and so on. . . . Appended are a list of sources for further information, a brief glossary, and a relative index." Chicago. Children's Bk Center

Selsam, Millicent E.

How to grow house plants; illus. by Kathleen Elgin. Morrow 1960 96p illus lib. bdg. $7.44 (4-6)   **635.9**

1 House plants
ISBN 0-688-31410-4   LC 60-6613

"Begins with an explanation of the structure of a plant and the function of its parts, then describes a number of house plants especially suitable for the beginner, and gives practical advice on water, light, temperature, soil, and fertilizer; also discusses plant housekeeping, raising plants from cuttings, seeds, and bulbs and suggests ideas for miniature gardens. Illustrated with many clear drawings. Helpful for plant growers at home or at school." Booklist
"It should tempt more experimenting and bring increased results while stimulating a hobby." Horn Bk
Guide to the culture of some common house plants: p91-96. Includes technical names

636.08 Production, maintenance, training of livestock and other domestic animals. Pets

Chrystie, Frances N.

Pets; a complete handbook on the care, understanding, and appreciation of all kinds of animal pets; 3d rev. ed. With illus. by Gillett Good Griffin. Little 1974 xxi, 269p illus $7.95 (4 and up)   **636.08**

1 Pets
ISBN 0-316-14051-1   LC 73-21819

First published 1953
Contents: Dogs; Cats; Small caged animals; Caged birds; Aquarium and vivarium pets; Wild animals and birds; Farm animals; Ponies and saddle horses; First aid and common diseases
"The author stresses the dependency of pets on their owners and the importance of careful attention to animals' needs. The text is illustrated only with miniscule pen-and-ink drawings, but it provides much useful information on a host of pets from beef steers to woodchucks." Sch Library J

Clemens, Virginia Phelps

Super animals and their unusual careers. Westminster Press 1979 192p illus $8.95 (4 and up)   **636.08**

1 Animals
ISBN 0-664-32649-8   LC 79-10932

"Each chapter presents anecdotes, many photographs, and descriptions of training for each species discussed. Bomb-detecting dogs, horses helping disabled children, life-saving dolphins, and entertaining animal actors are just a few of the services described. Although Clemens has omitted guide dogs for the blind and the rescue work of St. Bernards, she has substituted sections on the use of "aid dogs" for the deaf and crippled and a lengthy chapter on Newfoundland dogs' daring lifesaving feats." Sch Library J
"Clemens's accounts of working animals are unusually interesting and will create a new attitude of respect for many intelligent creatures in the minds of readers." Pub W

Cooper, Kay

All about rabbits as pets; photographs by Alvin E. Staffan. Messner 1974 64p illus lib. bdg. $6.97 (3-6)   **636.08**

1 Rabbits
ISBN 0-671-32694-5   LC 74-7592

"Brief sections are included on physical characteristics, on species of wild rabbits and breeds of domestic ones, and on rabbits in research; these supplement the longer, practical chapters which contain advice on choosing, housing, feeding, and breeding domestic rabbits. Of special value are careful descriptions of mating, pregnancy, and birth as well as directions for sexing rabbits. Explicit black-and-white photographs and a table of information on breeds are included." Booklist

Dobrin, Arnold

Gerbils; written and illus. by Arnold Dobrin. Lothrop 1970 63p illus map lib. bdg. $6.96 (3-6)   **636.08**

1 Gerbils
ISBN 0-688-51636-X   LC 77-82101

"Gerbils, first brought into the United States for experimental purposes less than twenty years ago, have rapidly become one of the most popular of small pets. . . . This first book for young people should prove of great interest. The illustrations are precise, and the text gives information on the gerbil's habits in its natural environment, as well as complete information about feeding and caring for the animal in captivity. Included are advice on breeding, recording experiments, and arranging for the gerbil's comfort when the owner is away." Sat Rev

Shuttlesworth, Dorothy E.

Gerbils, and other small pets; illus. with photographs. Dutton 1970 130p illus $6.95 (3-6)   **636.08**

1 Rodents 2 Pets
ISBN 0-525-30459-2   LC 76-102744

"Helpful advice on how to keep gerbils, hamsters, squirrels, mice, rats, guinea pigs, and rabbits as pets and how to care for and enjoy them. The author points out the importance of understanding the nature and needs of these small rodents in order to keep them healthy and contented and the opportunity such pets offer for learning about animal behavior. The easily read text is enlivened by photographs and a frequent mention of personal experiences with rodent pets. A list of books for further reading is appended." Booklist
The author "is careful to say which animals enjoy being handled and which do not, and which should be left outdoors." NY Times Bk Rev

Simon, Seymour

Discovering what gerbils do; illus. by Jean Zallinger. McGraw 1971 47p illus lib. bdg. $6.95 (2-5)   **636.08**

1 Gerbils
ISBN 0-07-057434-0   LC 75-136184

"This is an excellent book for a boy or girl . . . who has or is thinking about getting a gerbil as a pet. The book not only tells the child how to care for the gerbil, but through open-ended questions allows the child to discover facts about the gerbil's behavior and living patterns. The illustrations are excellent. The presentation is well-organized and the type is large and easy to read." Sci Bks

Stein, Sara Bonnett

Great pets! An extraordinary guide to usual and unusual family pets. Workman Pub. 1976 356p illus $10.95, pa $5.95 (4 and up)   636.08

1 Pets
ISBN 0-911104-71-2; 0-911104-72-0   LC 75-44012

This book contains "practical advice on the care and feeding of more than 50 different pets. Those included vary from common types of dogs, cats, goldfish, canaries, guinea pigs, and hamsters to those pets the author classifies as backyard (geese and goats), unusual apartment (ferrets and skunks), serpentarium (snakes, vivarium iguanas and crickets), overnight (fireflies, salamanders), and pets in the wild (raccoons and ducks). . . . Where applicable, Stein discusses housing, diet, illnesses, general care, and approximate costs involved. Interspersed throughout are black-and-white photographs, useful drawings, and short, often amusing experiences about pet ownership. A final chapter offers detailed diagrams, costs, and instructions for constructing pet homes such as bird cages, hutches, aquariums, and even a goat shed." Booklist

How to raise mice, rats, hamsters, and gerbils; photographs by Robert Weinreb. Random House 1976 48p illus (A Child's book of pet care) $3.95, lib. bdg. $5.99 (3 and up)   636.08

1 Pets 2 Rodents
ISBN 0-394-83224-8; 0-394-93224-2   LC 76-8138

"What to look for in cages and other equipment; what to feed the rodent pet; information about each particular breed—all these questions are answered in this comprehensive pet care manual. There is also an introductory note to parents which gives average prices of animals and cages, as well as other helpful information. Illustrated with photographs, many in color." Adventuring with Bks.

Stevens, Carla

Your first pet; and how to take care of it; illus. and based on an idea by Lisl Weil. Macmillan Pub. Co. 1974 122p illus lib. bdg. $4.95, pa $2.50 (2-4)   636.08

1 Pets
ISBN 0-02-788200-4; 0-02-045240-3   LC 74-2267

"Ready-to-read handbook"
In this handbook of house-pet care, the author gives instructions on the feeding, housing and care of gerbils, guinea pigs, mice, hamsters, goldfish, parakeets, cats, and small dogs
"The print is large, and the vocabulary is generally accessible to independent readers, but Stevens doesn't talk down by oversimplifying terms like 'veterinarian,' 'incisors,' and 'siphon.' Lisl Weil's drawings, appealing in their cartoon-like simplicity, illustrate techniques and equipment with which readers may not be familiar." Sch Library J

Weber, William J.

Care of uncommon pets; rabbits, guinea pigs, hamsters, mice, rats, gerbils, chickens, ducks, frogs, toads and salamanders, turtles and tortoises, snakes and lizards and budgerigars; photographs by the author. Holt 1979 222p illus $7.95 (5 and up)   636.08

1 Pets
ISBN 0-03-022731-3   LC 78-14093

"Clear, detailed advice on housing and breeding of each is provided, including step-by-step directions for building cages. The author, a veterinarian, also discusses diseases common to each type of pet and suggests prevention and treatments. . . . Although amphibian aquariums are described, aquariums for fish have been excluded." Sch Library J

Includes bibliographies. Definitions: p216-17

636.089 Veterinary sciences

Berger, Melvin

Animal hospital. Day 1973 126p illus (Scientists at work) lib. bdg. $8.79 (4 and up)   636.089

1 Veterinary medicine 2 Veterinarians
ISBN 0-381-99941-6   LC 72-2418

The author "discusses the activities of veterinarians with emphasis on small animal practice and of researchers in animal medicine. He describes what goes on in the examination, treatment, laboratory, X-ray, and operating rooms and the work done by the veterinarian's assistants." Booklist

"Sixty black-and-white photographs accompany Mr. Berger's highly informative text. . . . The writing style is simple and the subject matter is clearly presented. . . . The list of suggested readings is well chosen." Appraisal

Curtis, Patricia

Animal doctors; what it's like to be a veterinarian and how to become one; illus. with photographs. Delacorte Press 1977 167p illus $7.95 (6 and up)   636.089

1 Veterinarians 2 Veterinary medicine
ISBN 0-440-0140-4   LC 76-5593

"The chapters are structured as if they were transcripts of actual interviews with specific veterinarians (e.g. a zoo doctor, a horse doctor) yet the acknowledgment explains that with the exception of the circus doctor, the other 'interviewees' are composites based on 19 real veterinarians. To her credit Curtis does not back off from controversial subjects. The equine veterinarian, for instance, speaks out against rodeos, zoos, hunting, racing two year olds, and destroying mustangs. The five female vets discuss their reception in a predominantly male profession. Several vets confess their anxiety about treatment and surgery, and a student tells of his disillusionment at the callousness of some teachers. Chapters on the history of veterinary medicine, on how to seek admission to veterinary school and how to become a veterinary technician are also included." Sch Library J

Gillum, Helen L.

Veterinary medicine. Dillon Press 1976 107p illus (Looking forward to a career) lib. bdg. $6.95 (6 and up)   636.089

1 Veterinary medicine
ISBN 0-87518-106-6   LC 75-29291

"The veterinary field encompasses more than operating neighborhood or rural animal clinics; to her credit Gillum describes many of the lesser-known aspects such as inspecting meat and dairy products for the armed forces or conducting research on animal diseases transmittable to people. Schooling requirements—with blithely supportive advice for women or minority group members trying to break into the field—are included, and two chapters address in a general sense various support jobs that do not require a D.V.M. degree." Booklist

The author "enthusiastically encourages young people to get involved in related activities early in their education, and includes information on qualifications and educational guidance. Enhanced with photographs which will attract many browsers, this is a valuable addition to career collections." Sch Library J
For more information: p103-05

Jaspersohn, William

A day in the life of a veterinarian. Little 1978 74p illus $7.95 (4 and up)   636.089

1 Veterinary medicine 2 Veterinarians
ISBN 0-316-45810-4   LC 78-13584

In photographs and text, "Jaspersohn follows David Sequist, a Vermont country vet, through a composite average day in his busy practice. From a piglet with a cold to a Labrador with a tumor to a 2100 lb. bull with a sore foot, the doctor greets all his patients with equanimity, skill, concern and pure physical strength." Sch Library J

"Most interesting is the unfamiliar; the view of a horse spread out for surgery or a bull neatly turned on his side via a special mechanical table so that his abscessed hoof can be treated. . . . The oversized format allows for unhurried perusing, and that it's all real means built-in appeal." Booklist

Strong, Arline
Veterinarian, doctor for your pet; text and pictures by Arline Strong. Atheneum Pubs. 1977 44p illus $7.95 (2-4)   **636.089**
1 Veterinary medicine   2 Veterinarians
ISBN 0-689-30575-3   LC 76-46948
"Text and photographs follow Barbara Strauss, a veterinarian specializing in 'companion' animals, as she gives her patients general checkups or treats them for specific problems like fleas or, in the case of Jeffrey, a golden retriever, an ear that needed surgery." Booklist
"The text is unbiased and realistic in its portrayal of a veterinarian's job; the photographs of the doctor working on her patients are effective; and, a useful glossary of terms is appended." Sch Library J

636.1   Horses

Anderson, C. W.
C. W. Anderson's Complete book of horses and horsemanship; with over fifty drawings by the author. Macmillan Pub. Co. 1963 182p illus $6.95, pa $2.95 (5 and up)   **636.1**
1 Horses
ISBN 0-02-703340-6; 0-02-041460-9   LC 63-16746
"Beginning with the history and development of the horse, the author discusses breeds of horses, selection, care and training, and techniques of riding. Anatomically correct drawings." Hodges. Bks for Elem Sch Libraries
"A fat book of facts and features on the . . . horse, written with clarity, detail, and the appreciation of the equine always exhibited in any Anderson volume. Although much of the basic information is duplicated in various source books, few write about horses with Anderson's feeling and flair." Sch Library J
Horsemen's talk: p175-79

Balch, Glenn
The book of horses; cover photo: Zimbel-Monkmeyer. Four Winds 1967 96p illus $8.95 (4 and up)   **636.1**
1 Horses   2 Horseback riding
ISBN 0-590-07048-7   LC 67-5092
First copyrighted 1958
"The author presents the history, breeds, care and riding of horses and points out effectively the difference between English and western styles of riding." Bruno. Bks for Sch Libraries, 1968
"The photographs are many, varied, and excellent. The author emphasizes the need for instruction and experience in handling one's own horse, an important point, especially for children." Sch Library J

Berry, Barbara J.
Horse happy; a complete guide to owning your first horse; with photographs by James Dandelski and line illus. by Terry Nell Morris. Bobbs [1979 c1978] 118p illus $8.95, pa $5.95 (5 and up)   **636.1**
1 Horses
ISBN 0-672-52521-6; 0-672-52535-6   LC 78-55671
The author "goes into great detail about the aspects of horse buying and owning which can be picked up from a book, but in the long run, she suggests learning about horses by being around them, and around people who know them. If you can't afford riding lessons, she opines, find a friendly and well-run barn and hang around, clean stables for free, in short immerse yourself in the horse world. She tells readers how to distinguish the expert from the novice and also warns that experienced, professional horse people often disagree. The final chapters describe stabling requirements, and give some tips on riding and handling a horse safely and easily. Berry gives the sort of thorough advice beginning horse owners should have emblazoned on their foreheads (never tie a horse to a rail, never loop a lead around your hand, but which is typically ignored in books of this sort." Sch Library J
Glossary: p106-12. Suggestions for further reading: p113-14

Brady, Irene
America's horses and ponies; written and illus. by Irene Brady. Houghton 1969 202p illus lib. bdg. $12.95, pa $6.95 (5 and up)   **636.1**
1 Horses   2 Ponies
ISBN 0-395-06659-X; 0-395-24050-6   LC 70-86298
"The author covers each breed with a pencil drawing (to scale), a table of outstanding conformations, and a short commentary on the breed's 'character' and 'flavor' as well as its history. The commentaries are generally informative, but not heavy reading. The author has a nice easy style. The drawings are excellent, and the 'poses' are fairly constant, so that one might compare the various horses, ponies, etc. There is a short section on the evolution of the horse, a diagram of the parts of the horse, and a table describing points of conformation to be used in a comparative judging." Sci Bks
Bibliography: p202

Burt, Olive W.
The horse in America; illus. with photographs. Day 1975 192p illus map $8.95 (5 and up)   **636.1**
1 Horses—History   2 U.S.—History
ISBN 0-381-99630-1   LC 73-6187
This book deals with the history of the horse in America and the horse's influence on American history. The author discusses prehistoric fossils, the role of the horse in America's exploration and settlement, its influence on the Indians and importance in frontier life, its relationship to the cowboy, its use in warfare, its role in transportation, communication and industry, and its place in present-day America
Bibliography: p181-83

Darling, Lois
Sixty million years of horses, by Lois and Louis Darling. Morrow 1960 64p illus lib. bdg. $6.48 (4 and up)   **636.1**
1 Horses—History
ISBN 0-688-31000-1   LC 60-8998
This book "tells of the wild ass, the zebra, and the different breeds of modern horses, the uses of horses through the years; and then goes back to the little fossil eohippus and traces the evolution of horses to modern times." Christian Sci Monitor
"For young readers, the history of the horse provides an easy introduction to the complexities of evolution. . . . The handsome drawings reflect the authors' point that man always has loved horses and will continue to, even tho most of our horse power now comes from machines." Chicago Sunday Trib

Edwards, Elwyn Hartley
The Larousse Guide to horses and ponies of the world; illus. by David Nockels. Larousse 1979 238p illus $15.95, pa $7.95   **636.1**
1 Horses
ISBN 0-88332-120-3   LC 79-64108
"Nearly 200 types and breeds of horses are described and pictured in this guidebook. The descriptions include colors, height, uses, origin, appearance, and temperament. Immediately opposite each concise description is a photograph or colored drawing of the animal. Particularly well-known or important breeds have two or three pictures. The contents are arranged by continent and then by country of origin. A short history of the horse, glossary and index are included." Library J

Henry, Marguerite
Album of horses; illus. by Wesley Dennis. Rand McNally 1951 112p illus $6.95, lib. bdg. $6.79 (4 and up)   **636.1**
1 Horses
ISBN 0-528-82050-8; 0-528-80155-4   LC 51-14002
"The names of this author and artist and the word 'horse' on the cover are enough to recommend a book to hundreds of Henry-Dennis fans throughout the country. They will not be disappointed in these beautifully illustrated chapters on horses of many kinds, from Thoroughbred racers to Shetland ponies. And mules and burros have their chapters too. Description, history and interesting anecdotes are included. Twenty-six full-page colored illustrations and many marginal drawings in black and white." Horn Bk

Hess, Lilo

A pony to love; story and photographs by Lilo Hess. Scribner 1975 46p illus lib. bdg. $8.95 (3-6)　　　　636.1

1 Ponies
ISBN 0-684-14236-8　　　　LC 75-614

"Full and sensible advice for those readers who rent, own, or hope to own a pony. Hess discusses the care with which a pony should be assessed before purchase, the different pony breeds, and the expense having a pony entails: food, housing, pasturage, veterinary service, et cetera. She makes suggestions for training a pony and for breeding, for care of a mare in foal and of the foal itself." Chicago. Children's Bk Center

Shetland ponies; story and photographs by Lilo Hess. Crowell 1964 57p illus $8.95 (k-3)　　　　636.1

1 Ponies
ISBN 0-690-73234-1　　　　LC 64-10862

"The growth and development of two Shetland ponies from their birth in the spring to their first winter, affectionately described in . . . photographs and accompanying brief, narrative text." Booklist

The book contains "some gay, frisking photographs. There is little story line but a fair amount of information about this subject matter, which ranks high in appeal for almost every child." Pub W

Isenbart, Hans-Heinrich

A foal is born; photographs by Hanns-Jörg Anders; tr. by Catherine Edwards. Putnam 1976 unp illus $5.95 (k-3)　　　　636.1

1 Horses—Infancy　2 Reproduction
ISBN 0-399-20517-9　　　　LC 76-2605

Original German edition published 1975

"The birth of a foal and its early postnatal period is told by a charming series of black-and-white photographs. . . . The story introduces the concepts of growth, development and parturition. The text and photographs coordinate well and the story unfolds smoothly. Except for an occasional complex term, the vocabulary is suitable for the beginning and intermediate reader. This book could serve as a good introduction to the study of reproduction in animals, leading to a comparison between animals and humans. Explanations of 'sac' and 'umbilical cord' are accompanied by photographs. A feeling of warmth and naturalness associated with the birth process is carried throughout the book." AAAS Sci Bks & Films

Miller, Jane

Birth of a foal. Lippincott 1977 unp illus $6.95 (1-3)　　　　636.1

1 Horses—Infancy
ISBN 0-397-31702-6　　　　LC 76-5402

This is the story of "a newly-born Welsh Mountain pony. Fizz is shaggy, frisky, and round-eyed; the text describes her birth, her mother's tender care, the things she learns in her first days of life: nursing, cantering, scratching, nuzzling." Chicago. Children's Bk Center

"The full-page and two-to-a-page photos . . . expand the spare, simple text, and the large black print will encourage reluctant readers." Sch Library J

Selsam, Millicent E.

Questions and answers about horses; pictures by Robert J. Lee. Four Winds 1973 62p illus $6.95 (2-4)　　　　636.1

1 Horses
ISBN 0-590-07567-5　　　　LC 73-88073

In a question-and-answer format, the author presents an "introduction to how horses evolved, how they live, and how man has made use of them. She also describes the various breeds of horses and how they may be distinguished." Babbling Bookworm

The book "is greatly enhanced and enlarged by brown-and-green water-color paintings and has the text printed in these same colors. Providing browsing material and fodder for simple school reports, this title will also stimulate the interest of older reluctant readers." Sch Library J

Slaughter, Jean

Pony care; photographs by Hugh Rogers. Knopf 1961 115p illus lib. bdg. $5.69 (5 and up)　　　　636.1

1 Ponies
ISBN 0-394-901515-1　　　　LC 61-6054

"The author begins by describing the types of ponies and the purchase of a pony by the young enthusiast. From this point the book is very detailed in the various ways of handling and caring for the pony, treating in separate chapters the elements of feeding and grooming, care during different seasons of the year and the fundamentals of first aid and the signs of illness. The book is intended in the first place for young owners, but will be enjoyed by young horse lovers if for nothing else than vicarious experience and a better understanding of ponies." Best Sellers

Glossary: p109-10

Wright, Dare

Look at a colt. Random House 1969 unp illus lib. bdg. $4.99 (k-2)　　　　636.1

1 Horses
ISBN 0-394-90746-9　　　　LC 69-17441

"The life of a young colt is vividly presented in very good photographs. The brief text, usually just a sentence or two on each page is superimposed on the photographs." Sci Bks

"Children will not find strange the literary device that has the colt telling (interestingly) of his birth, his dependence on his mother, his probable future, the work of a quarter horse, etc." Library J

636.2　Cattle

Cole, Joanna

A calf is born; with photographs by Jerome Wexler. Morrow 1975 unp illus lib. bdg. $6.48 (k-2)　　　　636.2

1 Cows—Infancy　2 Reproduction
ISBN 0-688-32036-8　　　　LC 75-12408

The book explains and shows "eating habits of cows, milking procedures, and the birth of a calf. The actual birth is pictured step-by-step, including the sac covering the newborn and the afterbirth." Babbling Bookworm

"The dramatic photographs of the entire birth process and the first few hours in the calf's life point out vividly the differences and similarities of birth among animals. This is a very honest presentation of a subject that is thankfully no longer a mystery to city children." Instructor

636.3　Sheep and goats

Scott, Jack Denton

The book of the goat; photographs by Ozzie Sweet. Putnam 1979 64p illus $8.95 (4-6)　　　　636.3

1 Goats
ISBN 0-399-20681-7　　　　LC 79-14321

This book "begins with a historical look that posits the goat as one of the earliest domesticated animals. There follows some talk of breeds and the goat's special usefulness, particularly for those with allergies and certain digestive problems. There is also the expected information on goat behavior and breeding, with a summary that notes the animal's special survival abilities. Some of the photographs seem underdeveloped and lose detail, but this remains an informative introduction that is, on balance, fine to look at." Booklist

636.5　Poultry

The **Chicken** and the egg, by Oxford Scientific Films; photographs by George Bernard and Peter Parks. Putnam 1979 unp illus $6.95 (3-6)　　　　636.5

1 Chickens　2 Eggs
ISBN 0-399-20676-0　　　　LC 78-23663

A brief text, followed by large color photographs, describes the farmyard chicken. Among the topics covered are the pecking order, feeding, mating and the development of a chick embryo inside an egg in six stages of growth

Cole, Joanna

A chick hatches; photographs by Jerome Wexler. Morrow 1976 46p illus lib. bdg. $6.96 (k-3)   **636.5**

1 Chickens 2 Reproduction 3 Eggs
ISBN 0-688-32087-2   LC 76-29017

"A simply written account of the development from egg to embryo to fetus to chick is made more meaningful by the accompanying photographs, some in color and almost all enlarged. The writing is matter-of-fact, but the pictures of the developing fetus make the recurrent miracle of reproduction vividly clear." Chicago. Children's Bk Center

Flanagan, Geraldine Lux

Window into an egg; seeing life begin; with photographs. Young Scott Bks. 1969 71p illus lib. bdg. $7.95 (4-6)   **636.5**

1 Chickens 2 Embryology 3 Eggs
ISBN 0-201-09405-3   LC 66-1141

Through text and step-by-step photographs, this book describes the development of a chick embryo, from fertilization to hatching

"Many authors have attempted to explain the embryology of the chick for young readers, but none have been so meticulously accurate and succesful as Mrs. Flanagan who has used remarkably good photographs from many sources. . . . The development of the chick [is presented] as a prototype of all vertebrate embryology. This book is needed in all school and public libraries—multiple copies, please—and in children's book collections at home." Sci Bks

Selsam, Millicent E.

Egg to chick; pictures by Barbara Wolff. [Rev. ed] Harper 1970 63p illus (A Science I can read bk) lib. bdg. $6.89 (k-3)   **636.5**

1 Chickens 2 Embryology 3 Eggs
ISBN 0-06-025290-1   LC 74-85034

First published 1946

The author "factually and clearly presents the development of the chicken until its hatching. The narrative is conversational in tone, allowing the author to suggest in a natural sort of way that the fertilization process is universal in the animal kingdom. Simple line drawings of the ubiquitous egg are supplemented by a ten-page photographic section showing a chick actually pecking its way out of the egg, emerging as a wobbly, wet baby bird, and finally standing dry and fluffy beside the broken shell. The author wisely explains why 'you cannot hatch a chick from your breakfast egg' in the early pages of this informative little book." Horn Bk

Zim, Herbert S.

Homing pigeons; illus. by James Gordon Irving. Morrow 1949 62p illus map lib. bdg. $6.48 (5 and up)   **636.5**

1 Pigeons
ISBN 0-688-31398-1   LC 49-7864

"A guide book to the raising, flying and racing of homing pigeons, with plans for building simple lofts and pens. Further instructions for developing the hobby will be helpful to individuals or leaders, planning pigeon clubs." Wis Library Bul

636.6 Birds other than poultry

Mowat, Farley

Owls in the family; illus. by Robert Frankenberg. Little 1961 103p illus $8.95 (4 and up)   **636.6**

1 Owls 2 Saskatchewan
ISBN 0-316-58641-2   LC 62-7169

"An Atlantic Monthly Press book"

"Two owls, Wol and Weeps, who are found as babies at the beginning of this account, were the author's own pets during his boyhood in Saskatoon. The description of the owls' endearing and humorous traits, their intelligence and mischief in upsetting household and neighbors, is continuously absorbing and provocative of hearty laughter. Their personalities are vividly different. . . . Outstanding for reading aloud." Horn Bk

Mowat's "story is rich with unobtrusive natural history ,and he achieves a rare combination of simplicity, grace and distinction in the writing. Robert Frankenberg's witty illustrations completely capture the spirit of the book." NY Times Bk Rev

Villiard, Paul

Birds as pets; with 75 photographs by the author. Doubleday 1974 177p illus lib. bdg. $7.90 (5 and up)   **636.6**

1 Cage birds 2 Pets
ISBN 0-385-04337-6   LC 73-20722

"Helpful information on the care, feeding, housing, breeding, and training of about 40 bird species which thrive in captivity (e.g., finches, canaries, budgerigars, parrots, love birds). Similar in format to other pet selection guides by the author . . . the text is generously illustrated with captioned black-and-white photographs." Sch Library J

Zim, Herbert S.

Parrakeets; illus. by Larry Kettelkamp. Morrow 1953 59p illus lib. bdg. $6 (4 and up)   **636.6**

1 Budgerigars
ISBN 0-688-31544-5   LC 53-7107

This book contains "everything the young person needs to know about breeding, raising, and training parrakeets, including how to teach them to talk and how to build the right kind of cage for them." Hodges. Bks for Elem Sch Libraries

This "simply presented information . . . will be useful to those who already have these amusing pets and may well encourage others to become owners. Dr. Zim's explanation of color mutations according to the rules of genetics will interest serious young scientists. Plainly labeled drawings." Horn Bk

636.7 Dogs

American Kennel Club

Complete dog book. Howell Bk. House illus $10.95   **636.7**

1 Dogs

First published 1935 by Garden City Books as a combination of: Pure bred dogs, first published 1929 by G. Watt, and The care, handling and feeding of dogs, compiled by E. R. Blamey. Frequently revised and brought up to date

"The photograph, history, and official standard of every breed admitted to AKC registration, and the selection, training, breeding, care, and feeding of pure-bred dogs." Title page of 1979 Golden Anniversary edition

Broderick, Dorothy M.

Training a companion dog; illus. by Haris Petie. Prentice-Hall 1965 72p illus lib. bdg. $4.95, pa $1.25 (4 and up)   **636.7**

1 Dogs—Training
ISBN 0-13-926634-8; 0-13-926626-7   LC 65-10439

"P-H Junior research books"

"An excellent book on training—explicit, detailed, and sensible. The illustrations are helpful; the text is well-organized and is clear enough to need that help only slightly. The author discusses the need for training a dog, the way a dog learns, and the equipment needed and how to use it correctly. The succeeding chapters then describe, step by step, each procedure in the training program —including what not to do and what to do if the dog does not respond. The last chapter discusses Obedience Trials; an index is appended." Chicago. Children's Bk Center

Bronson, Wilfrid S.

Dogs; best breeds for young people; written and illus. by Wilfrid S. Bronson. Harcourt 1969 96p illus $6.50 (3 and up)   **636.7**

1 Dogs
ISBN 0-15-22335-9   LC 69-11594

"There are many good books on choosing and training a dog, but this has additional appeal because of the humorous style, the forthright discussion of minor problems of dogs and owners, and the sensible discussion of safety measures, courtesy, preparation for ownership, and responsibilities as well as the major problems of selection and care. Actually, there is little on the topic of best breeds; there are several picturecharts (small, medium, big, and giant dogs) of 'Congenial K-9's for Young Folks.' The illustrations are crude but lively in comic valentine style, and a divided bibliography is appended." Chicago. Children's Bk Center

Cole, Joanna

My puppy is born; with photographs by Jerome Wexler. Morrow 1973 unp illus lib. bdg. $6.48 (k-3) 636.7

1 Dogs—Infancy 2 Reproduction
ISBN 0-688-30078-2 LC 72-14201

"Graphic photos show details of the birth of several [dachshund] puppies and the early days in their lives. The . . . [young girl narrating the story] chooses one she names Sausage and the book ends happily with him growing slowly, eating on his own, ready to leave his mother at eight weeks, and adjusting to a leash." Pub W

"This is a wonderful opportunity for the child who has never seen the miracle of birth: to see the sac emerging, the mother biting the cord and licking the newborn pup, and the helplessness of infant life. It's also a lesson in being gentle with animal babies, and it's charming in portrayal of the beguiling puppies." Chicago. Children's Bk Center

Fichter, George S.

Working dogs. Watts, F. 1979 64p illus lib. bdg. $5.45 (4-6) 636.7

1 Dogs
ISBN 0-531-02887-9 LC 78-11345

"A First book"

"Organized in chapters by function, this short survey describes the dog's role as shepherd, sled puller, war weapon, in movies, as seeing eye or hearing ear companion, in rescue, police work or space science. Recent examples enliven the clear presentation of facts, useful for brief school research. Much of this information is available elsewhere, but black-and-white photographs on every third page will draw reluctant readers." Sch Library J

Suggested reading: p60-61

Foster, Joanna

Dogs working for people; photographs by James L. Stanfield. Natl. Geographic Soc. 1972 40p illus (k-3) 636.7

1 Dogs
ISBN 0-87044-124-8 LC 72-91419

Obtainable only as part of a set for $9.95 with: Dinosaurs, by Kathryn Jackson, class 567.9, Lion cubs, by the National Geographic Society, class 599.74 and Treasures in the sea, by Robert M. McClung, class 910.4

"Books for young explorers"

Prepared by the Special Publications Division of the National Geographic Society

This book describes in simple text and color photographs retrievers, trackers and hunting dogs, cow and sheep-hearding dogs, seeing-eye dogs, racing greyhounds, police and guard dogs, circus dogs, and Lassie, the television star

Hess, Lilo

A dog by your side. Scribner 1977 89p illus lib. bdg. $9.95 (3-6) 636.7

1 Dogs
ISBN 0-684-14864-1 LC 76-57744

"The author emphasizes the satisfactions of owning and showing purebred dogs. Dividing her subject by groups—sporting dogs, hounds, working dogs, terriers, toys, and non-sporting dogs the author sensibly and enthusiastically points out their origins, behavioral traits, physical conformations, and particular characteristics as pet candidates. Information about kennels, breeding, show points and titles, and readying a dog for showing is also included. . . . The close-up black-and-white photographs of most of the dogs under discussion mark this high as a browsing item or as a sturdy information manual." Booklist

Life begins for puppies. Scribner 1978 34p illus lib. bdg. $6.95 (4-6) 636.7

1 Dogs—Infancy 2 Reproduction
ISBN 0-684-15652-0 LC 77-28256

The "story of the author's Shetland Sheepdog, Poco, and of the birth and first eight weeks of life of her four puppies." Sch Library J

The photographs of the "pups are beguiling, of course, but the book offers a great deal more than the pictures, as it describes gestation and birth, the dog's care and training of her pups, and the changes that occur in the puppies as they grow." Chicago. Children's Bk Center

A puppy for you. Scribner 1976 49p illus lib. bdg. $6.95, pa $2.95 (3-5) 636.7

1 Dogs
ISBN 0-684-14753-X; 0-684-16013-7 LC 76-17842

The author "discusses choice of the proper dog, considerations of purchase (will it be a pet or show dog?), and preparations for bringing it home. Although her descriptions of feeding, training, housebreaking, and grooming make it all sound extremely easy, children will get an overview of many of the responsibilities involved." Booklist

"Informational, entertaining, 'and' humane, the photographs illustrate better than anything what is involved in all aspects of dog care." Babbling Bookworm

Landshoff, Ursula

Okay, good dog. Harper 1978 64p illus $5.95, lib. bdg. $6.89 (1-3) 636.7

1 Dogs—Training
ISBN 0-06-023672-8; 0-06-023673-6 LC 77-25648

"An I can read book"

"The text discusses housebreaking, being gentle but firm, training for cooperative behavior, and teaching a dog tricks. It stresses kindness, mentions getting shots, and using rewards to teach; it does not give information about what to feed a dog or describe coping with illness, save for carsickness." Chicago. Children's Bk Center

"A popular subject dealt with simply but unpatronizingly is successfully contained in the I-Can-Read format. . . . The tone is calm and reassuring, the directions clear, and the illustrations helpful and entertaining." Horn Bk

McCloy, James

Dogs at work; illus. by Sheila Beatty. Crown 1979 74p illus lib. bdg. $7.95 (4-6) 636.7

1 Dogs
ISBN 0-517-53408-8 LC 78-24558

This "browser's introduction to working dogs features astute, realistic charcoal drawings and large, clean, well-spaced type. Almost all of the described breeds are good-sized dogs, and a few, such as the Great Pyrenees or the Bouvier des Flandres, won't be familiar. Each two- to four-page profile includes information on the dog's origin and past working background as well as its contemporary status." Booklist

Pinkwater, Jill

Superpuppy; how to choose, raise, and train the best possible dog for you, by Jill and D. Manus Pinkwater; line drawings by Jill Pinkwater. Seabury [distributed by Houghton] 1977 206p illus $9.95 (5 and up) 636.7

1 Dogs
ISBN 0-395-28878-9 LC 76-8825

"A Clarion book"

"The authors begin by suggesting that you examine your reasons for owning a dog. The rest of the book details all the problems and rewards of caring for a dog and, in short, does everything promised in the title." Pub W

"Here is the most humane, straight-from-the-shoulder dog book around. . . . Lively, personal, and outspoken as to the whys as well as the hows of having a 'Superpuppy,' this is a superbook." Sch Library J

Some books: p197-98

Putnam, Peter

The triumph of the Seeing Eye; ed. by Walter Lord; illus. with 30 photographs, courtesy of the Seeing Eye. Harper 1963 178p illus lib. bdg. $7.89 (5 and up) 636.7

1 Guide dogs 2 Blind 3 Seeing Eye, Incorporated, Morristown, N.J.
ISBN 0-06-024776-2 LC 62-21294

"A Breakthrough book"

The story of Morris Frank, pioneer in the use of guide dogs for the blind, and "of the Seeing Eye organization which includes a description of the education of the dogs before they meet their new masters, and the training of dog and man together." Wis Library Bul

"Young readers will find here an informative tale that will inspire them, as well [as] give insight into the problem of the blind." Best Sellers

Bibliography: p171-73

Sabin, Francene

Dogs of America, by Francene and Louis Sabin; photographs by William P. Gilbert. Putnam 1967 127p illus lib. bdg. $5.97 (5 and up)   636.7

1 Dogs
ISBN 0-399-60131-7   LC 67-14810

While this book recounts the "story of the evolution and origin of the domesticated dog, its main thesis is a description of the various breeds of domesticated dogs—for various tasks and personal tastes—that have been developed over a very long time from the ancestral tamed wolves. The 115 kinds of purebred dogs recognized by the American Kennel Club are discussed and there are suggestions on the care, feeding and training of dogs." Sci Bks

"Although the writing is in places too colloquial and consciously clever, the admiration the authors show for the dogs should lead the reader to an appreciation of many breeds. Clear photographs of show dogs identify almost every breed included." Booklist

Selsam, Millicent E.

How puppies grow; photographs by Esther Bubley. Four Winds [1972 c1971] unp illus lib. bdg. $7.95 (k-3)   636.7

1 Dogs—Infancy
ISBN 0-590-07190-4   LC 72-77803

Originally published 1971 in paperback by Scholastic

"This book traces the growth of a litter of six puppies from when they are one day old until they become self-sufficient at the age of about six weeks. . . . Browsers will find photographs of the puppies nursing and at play endearing." Sch Library J

Written with the author's "usual gift for very simple prose that avoids being stilted; easy enough for beginning independent readers, the text is smooth enough to read aloud well, and can be used with preschool children." Chicago. Children's Bk Center

Simon, Seymour

Discovering what puppies do; illus. by Susan Bonners. McGraw 1977 40p illus lib. bdg. $6.95 (3-5)   636.7

1 Dogs—Infancy
ISBN 0-07-057424-3   LC 76-56421

"This common-sense introduction to canine senses, behavior, and methods of communication, illustrated with soft, charcoal drawings, is gentle in tone. Although the pleasures and responsibilities of having a puppy 'as a playmate, not a play toy' are stressed, this is not a training manual." Sch Library J

Unkelbach, Kurt

Both ends of the leash; selecting and training your dog; illus. by Haris Petie. Prentice-Hall 1968 72p illus $4.95, pa $1.50 (3-6)   636.7

1 Dogs 2 Dogs—Training
ISBN 0-13-080275-1; 0-13-080903-9   LC 68-15000

"A short, concise and useful book. The author presents his personal choice of 10 best breeds for children's pets, explaining why he didn't choose seven other popular breeds. He then deals with the teaching of six basic obedience commands, offers a good chapter on dog shows, and discusses such chestnuts as 'you can't teach an old dog new tricks.'" Sch Library J

Glossary: p65-67

How to bring up your pet dog; choosing, understanding, training, protecting, enjoying; illus. by Sam Savitt. Dodd 1972 119p illus $5.95 (4 and up)   636.7

1 Dogs
ISBN 0-396-06488-4   LC 78-180934

"Drawing on his experience as a breeder, trainer, and exhibitor of Labrador Retrievers the author gives sensible advice on selecting a healthy pup, caring for and training it, taking basic health and safety precautions, and dealing with common ailments. He includes numerous personal anecdotes and answers many representative questions from prospective or actual dog owners. He also provides detailed instructions for building an outdoor run, simple bench for indoor sleeping quarters, puppy playpen, and doghouse and lists of organizations and journals concerned with dogs. Attractive, accurate, and often amusing black-and-white drawings complement the text." Booklist

636.8 Cats

Bridge, Linda McCarter

Cats: little tigers in your house; photographs by Donna K. Grosvenor. Natl. Geographic Soc. 1974 30p illus (k-3)   636.8

1 Cats—Infancy
ISBN 0-87044-159-0   LC 74-10112

Obtainable only as part of a set for $9.95 with: Creepy crawly things, by the National Geographic Society, class 597.6; Spiders, by Lillian Bason, class 595.4; and Three little Indians, by Gene S. Stuart

"Books for young explorers"

Prepared by the Special Publications Division of the National Geographic Society

This book follows the activities of two kittens from the time they are born until they are two months old and are given to their new owners. It describes how their mother cares for them, their play, their eating and sleeping behavior, and their reactions to other animals

"The main appeal of Bridge's book on cats is its excellent photographic documentation. . . . The text here is moderately factual and liberally laced with conversational narrative." Booklist

Burger, Carl

All about cats; illus. with photographs; with a foreword by William Bridges. Random House 1966 143p illus $2.95, lib. bdg. $5.39 (5 and up)   636.8

1 Cats
ISBN 0-394-80258-6; 0-394-90258-0   LC 66-7939

"All about books"

"The evolution of the cat, his role in history and folklore, and his characteristics and personality are discussed in an entertaining and informative book. Includes a classification table, a chart of the cat's family tree, and a bibliography." Hodges. Bks for Elem Sch Libraries

De Paola, Tomie

The kids' cat book; written and illus. by Tomie de Paola. Holiday House 1979 unp illus lib. bdg. $7.95 (2-4)   636.8

1 Cats
ISBN 0-8234-0365-3   LC 79-2090

"Granny Twinkle's house is full of cats and with prompting from an inquisitive young visitor, she introduces all her feline friends. There are the Siamese, who were once used as palace guards and the Abyssinians, who look and act like kittens at any age. There are curly Rex cats and cuddly Persians. Granny also knows cat history, lore, and a famous feline or two. She shares practical information about raising cats, too." Sch Library J

"The illustrations add great touches of humor and show cats being cats everywhere. All those who have new kittens will find useful information. Those who do not have a kitten may want one after reading this." Children's Bk Rev Serv

Leen, Nina

Cats. Holt 1980 77p illus $7.95 (3-5)   636.8

1 Cats
ISBN 0-03-052331-1   LC 79-22137

"Purebreds, house and alley cats, and wild forms are pictured. . . . There is a short section on cats in history and mythology followed by descriptions and [black and white] photographs which illustrate a cat's senses, natural behavior and instincts, family life, intelligence, play, and friendship with other animals." Appraisal

This book is profusely illustrated by photographs of fine quality. The text is clearly by a cat-lover. . . . but there are also some sections ('Kitten at Play,' or 'A Swim in the Bathtub') that verge on calendar-art in appeal. The text concludes with a series of pictures, with descriptive comments, on purebred cats." Chicago. Children's Bk Center

Rockwell, Jane

Cats and kittens; illus. with photographs. Watts, F. 1974 76p illus lib. bdg. $5.90 (4 and up)　　　　　636.8

1 Cats
ISBN 0-531-00812-6　　　　　LC 73-14560

"A First book"
"More instructive than the average pet care book for the middle grades, this volume offers important items of practical concern and curiosity for cat fanciers. Besides chapters on the history of the species and on general care and feeding, there are sctions on anatomy and physiology, social and sexual behavior, choosing and training a kitten, and breeds of cats. Black-and-white photographs and drawings with interesting captions supplement the text, and lists of U.S. cat organizations and cat publications are appended." Booklist

Selsam, Millicent E.

How kittens grow; photographs by Esther Bubley. Four Winds [1975 c1973] unp illus $5.95 (k-2)　　　　　636.8

1 Cats—Infancy
ISBN 0-590-07409-1　　　　　LC 74-13162

First published 1973 in paperback by Scholastic
In text and photographs this book describes the first eight weeks in the lives of four kittens. It tells how their mother nurses them, how they learn to walk and to eat solid food, and how they begin to play with each other and with objects around them
"This is an attractive and informative book which will appeal to young primary graders as well as older reluctant readers." Sch Library J

Silverstein, Alvin

Cats: all about them [by] Alvin & Virginia Silverstein; with photographs by Frederick J. Breda. Lothrop 1978 224p illus $7.95, lib. bdg. $7.63 (4 and up)　　　　　636.8

1 Cats
ISBN 0-688-41841-4; 0-688-51841-9　　　　　LC 77-25182

A "clear description of cat behavior, breeds, care, life cycle, history, use in the laboratory, and wild relatives. . . . This offers access to more scientific research on cats than has previously been available to this age level . . . [and the authors] include their own experiences and observations." Sch Library J

Stevens, Carla

The birth of Sunset's kittens; photographs by Leonard Stevens. Young Scott Bks. 1969 unp illus $6.95 (k-4)　　　　　636.8

1 Cats 2 Reproduction
ISBN 0-201-09119-3　　　　　LC 69-14569

"A series of photographs show every detail of the always-wonderful sight of tiny, blind-eyed kittens being born. The text explains what is happening with matter-of-fact clarity: the muscles of the cat's uterus are contracting, moving the kitten along the birth canal; the kitten emerges, and the clinging amnion is eaten by the cat. The mother cat gently licks and grooms her new family; the kittens nurse. No cute posed pictures, no saccharine comment, just the miraculous facts." Sutherland. The Best in Children's Bks
"The photographs of Sunset and her litter are more than instructive; they arouse affection for the mother and convey her pleasure in the birth of her kittens." NY Times Bk Rev

638　Insect culture

Stevens, Carla

Insect pets; catching and caring for them; illus. by Karl W. Stuecklen. Greenwillow Bks. 1978 96p illus $5.95, lib. bdg. $5.71 (2-4)　　　　　638

1 Insects 2 Pets
ISBN 0-688-80121-8; 0-688-84121-X　　　　　LC 77-9940

"A Greenwillow Read-alone guide"
"Directions are given for capturing and caring for seven insects: whirligigs, waterstriders, praying mantids, ladybird beetles, fireflies, antlions, and field crickets." Horn Bk

This book "may become as necessary as the map and compass for 8- and 9-year-olds on the nature trail, but the index and the clear drawings . . . make this a useful book for all ages. The experiments recommended will harm neither insects nor children ('If the water's depth is over your knees, be sure to ask an adult to help you'), and the book repeats what parents are always telling children who want to keep their crickets and ladybirds forever: 'When you cannot find any more aphids, let your ladybird fly away so that it can seek its own food.'" NY Times Bk Rev

639　Nondomesticated animals and plants

Conklin, Gladys

I caught a lizard; words by Gladys Conklin; pictures by Arthur Marokvia. Holiday House 1967 unp illus lib. bdg. $6.95 (k-3)　　　　　639

1 Animals—Habits and behavior 2 Pets
ISBN 0-8324-0054-9　　　　　LC 67-3392

"Sixteen common small creatures—lizard, salamander, baby bird, snake, praying mantis, among them—are found or bought, one after the other, by a small boy or girl. Some of the creatures are observed in their own habitat; others are brought home, caged, and fed, but most of these are set free again after a short period. The easy-to-read conversational text is full of information, and the food requirements of the small pets are recapitulated in a concluding chart." Horn Bk

Fichter, George S.

Keeping amphibians and reptiles as pets. Watts, F. 1979 64p illus lib. bdg. $5.45 (4 and up)　　　　　639

1 Reptiles 2 Amphibians 3 Pets
ISBN 0-531-02257-9　　　　　LC 78-10813

"A First book"
This book provides information on keeping frogs, toads, salamanders, snakes, lizards and turtles as pets
For more information: p61

Hess, Lilo

Small habitats. Scribner 1976 42p illus lib. bdg. $5.95 (4-6)　　　　　639

1 Terrariums 2 Pets
ISBN 0-684-14579-0　　　　　LC 75-39295

This "guide to the equipping and maintaining of terrariums focuses on the forms of animal life that can adapt with comfort to such enclosed habitats. The continuous text is profusely illustrated with photographs of snakes, turtles, toads, chamelions, and other small creatures. Hess describes the various kinds of terrariums (meadow, woodland, tropical jungle, desert, etc.) and what should go into them; she gives advice on purchasing animals at pet stores and on catching one's own, and on the care and feeding of each kind. Brisk and sensible, a useful book; a chart of habitats and an index are appended." Chicago. Children's Bk Center

Kellner, Esther

Animals come to my house; a story guide to the care of wild animals; drawings by Heidi Palmer. Putnam 1976 160p illus $7.95 (5 and up)　　　　　639

1 Pets 2 Animals—Care and treatment
ISBN 0-399-20500-4　　　　　LC 75-37937

"The book is divided into two major sections. The first section is devoted to many interesting anecdotes about the animal boarders—how they came to the author, the care provided, and the fun of having the animals around. Throughout this section, many excellent ideas are offered on how to handle situations such as how to prepare an animal for its return to the wild. Children will especially enjoy this section which speaks of opossums, squirrels, raccoons, rabbits, and other small animals. The second section provides an excellent manual of general care for animals: emergencies, food and feeding, handling, infections, illnesses, and bathing. Throughout the text are many beautiful pen-and-ink sketches by Heidi Palmer." Sci and Children

McMillan, Bruce

Finestkind o'day; lobstering in Maine. Lippincott 1977 48p illus lib. bdg. $8.95 **639**

1 Fisheries—Maine 2 Lobsters
ISBN 0-397-31763-8   LC 77-3049

"Text and photographs follow Brett, the author's son, as he boards the 'Ruth M.' with Allison Wilson, a veteran lobsterman. The two spend the day along the Maine coast pulling the baiting traps, pegging lobsters, and fishing for halibut. Much basic information about lobsters and lobstering is imparted along the way." Sch Library J

"Sharp black-and-white photographs capture the flavor of young Brett's days as sternman (lobsterman's helper). . . . [The author] keeps his text brief and to the point. Some of the photographs are too dark to see the detail clearly, but the excitement of the day is evident." Booklist

Ricciuti, Edward R.

Shelf pets; how to take care of small wild animals; photographs by Arline Strong. Harper 1971 132p illus lib. bdg. $7.89 (5 and up) **639**

1 Pets 2 Animals—Habits and behavior
ISBN 0-06-024994-3   LC 76-135782

"A how-to book for city and country children. Frogs, salamanders, snakes, turtles, spiders, crickets, guppies, snails, hamsters and guinea pigs are some of the animals described here." Pub W

"This is a useful guide for the young naturalist who wishes to study nature at close range. . . . For each pet the author suggests ways of procuring the animal, methods of providing appropriate housing and kinds of food required. In some cases a brief history of the animal is included. The reader is encouraged to simulate the natural environment as much as possible and is provided with many hints for achieving this end with maximum ease." Appraisal

Recommended books: p127-28

Simon, Seymour

Pets in a jar; collecting and caring for small wild animals; illus. by Betty Fraser. Viking 1975 95p illus $7.95, Penguin pa $2.95 (4 and up) **639**

1 Pets 2 Invertebrates
ISBN 0-670-55060-4; 0-14-049186-4   LC 74-14905

The author "presents fifteen creatures; with preliminary chapters on choosing a pet and assembling the necessary equipment. After discussing the characteristics and habitats of each one, he tells how to go about catching and then caring for them. The responsibility for the creatures' needs and comfort is stressed, as well as safety precautions for the child. Numerous observations and projects are given, such as testing the amount of salt in the jar water with a hydrometer and making one's own net. . . . The final chapter offers ecological guidance on how to release the pet if the child decides he no longer wants it." Appraisal

"Included are hydras . . . planarians, pond snails, water bugs (not the roach kind), tadpoles, newts, toads, earthworms, ants, crickets, praying mantes, butterflies and moths, brine shrimp (as pets?), hermit crabs and starfish. . . . The book is attractively printed, easy to read, pleasantly illustrated, well indexed and deserves a place on the school-room shelf; it could serve as the major reference for a miniature classroom zoo." AAAS Sci Bks & Films

Weber, William J.

Wild orphan babies: mammals and birds; caring for them & setting them free; photographs by the author [2d ed] Holt 1978 159p illus $6.95 (4 and up) **639**

1 Mammals 2 Birds 3 Pets 4 Animals—Infancy
ISBN 0-03-044976-6   LC 78-4352

First published 1975

The book "when it first appeared in 1975, quickly became the standard guide to caring for young wild animals. . . . [It conveys] practical, clearly written advice and instructions for animal care, along with the understanding that surviving orphans are eventually returned to the wild. A must for any library without the original edition." Sch Library J

Suggested for further reading: p152-53

Wong, Herbert H.

Our terrariums, by Herbert H. Wong and Matthew F. Vessel; illus. by Aldren A. Watson. Addison-Wesley 1969 31p illus (Science ser. for the young) lib. bdg. $6.95 (k-3) **639**

1 Terrariums 2 Pets
ISBN 0-201-08722-7   LC 69-15805

"An Addisonian Press book"

This book "shows young children how to make an observation habitat for a toad and a lizard." Christian Sci Monitor

"Good elementary science reading." Sci Bks

Zappler, Georg

Amphibians as pets, by Georg and Lisbeth Zappler; with photographs and drawings by Richard Marshall. Doubleday 1973 159p illus lib. bdg. $6.90 (5 and up) **639**

1 Amphibians
ISBN 0-385-08581-8   LC 72-92252

"A thorough introduction to the world of amphibians with clear and detailed description of the characteristics of each kind found throughout the world, and illustrated with precise diagrams. All aspects are covered: range, description, digestive tract, hearing, sight, courtship, reproduction, development, etc. . . . A most useful guide, it gives information on over 40 different ones. The last third of the book is the section devoted to finding your own pet; suggested field trips with notetaking; how to catch tadpoles, prepare tanks, aquariums, and terrariums. There are detailed instructions on the care of the amphibians, on treating a sick pet, on rearing your own flies and other insects for food; and much more. The book closes with one-paragraph descriptions of some exotic foreign species available at pet stores." Appraisal

Zim, Herbert S.

Commercial fishing [by] Herbert S. Zim [and] Lucretia Krantz; illus. by Lee J. Ames. Morrow 1973 64p illus $6.75, lib. bdg. $6.48, pa $1.25 (3-6) **639**

1 Fisheries
ISBN 0-688-20091-5; 0-688-30091-X; 0-688-05267-3
LC 73-4931

"A skillfully organized explanation of commercial fishing which calls attention to the expanding use of seafood in combating food shortages. Descriptions of the types of boats employed are followed by identification and uses of fish. There is also a section on shellfish. New techniques for locating fish (radio, echo sounders, hydrophones) are discussed along with the familiar hook and line which still works best for catching fish. The text is clear and interesting, and the black-and-white drawings extend the information." Sch Library J

639.3 Fish culture

Axelrod, Herbert R.

Tropical fish as a hobby; a guide to selection, care and breeding. Rev. ed. McGraw 1969 300p illus $12.50 (5 and up) **639.3**

1 Tropical fish 2 Aquariums
ISBN 0-07-002606-8   LC 68-9550

First published 1952

With chapters on How fish get their names, and Aquarium genetics, by Myron Gordon, and a chapter on The balanced aquarium myth, by James W. Atz

The book discusses "rules for the care, feeding and breeding of fish, and maintaining a healthy home aquarium. . . . A tabular chart gives popular and scientific name, source, reproduction of type, aquarium temperature, disposition, facts on breeding for more than 100 fish for ready reference. Information for both beginners and more advanced tropical-fish hobbyists." Booklist

Bibliography: p285-86

Tropical fish in your home, by Herbert R. Axelrod and William Vorderwinkler; G. J. M. Timmerman, photographer. [Rev. ed.] Sterling 1960 144p illus $8.95 (5 and up) **639.3**

1 Tropical fish 2 Aquariums
ISBN 0-8069-3710-6   LC 56-7698

Axelrod, Herbert R.—_Continued_

First published 1956
The authors describe how the beginning aquarist can create a tiny underwater world. They offer information on many varieties of fish from which to choose, citing methods of caring for each. The author's objective is to provide answers for the questions raised by young collectors

Cooper, Kay

All about goldfish as pets; photographs by Alvin E. Staffan. Messner 1976 64p illus lib. bdg. $6.97 (3 and up)   **639.3**

1 Goldfish 2 Aquariums
ISBN 0-671-32801-8   LC 76-26519

"Although there are more than twenty-five kinds of goldfish, two (the common and the comet) are most frequently found in aquariums. Text gives information about the organs of the goldfish that enable it to live for up to twenty years in water. Also tells how to set up an aquarium, maintain it, and keep the fish healthy. Fish reproduction is explained." Adventuring with Bks

Hoke, John

Aquariums. Watts, F. 1975 71p illus lib. bdg. $5.90 (4 and up)   **639.3**

1 Aquariums
ISBN 0-531-02772-4   LC 74-9834

"A First book"
"Viewing aquariums as artificial ecosystems, Hoke emphasizes the tank set-up—light, air, temperature, etc. Aquarium maintenance is covered in detail, but there is only minimal discussion for the fish themselves." Sch Library J
"A useful if undecorated manual for serious beginning fish hobbyists." Booklist

Paige, David

Behind the scenes at the aquarium; photographs by Roger Ruhlin. Whitman, A. 1979 48p illus lib. bdg. $6.95 (4-6)   **639.3**

1 Aquariums
ISBN 0-8075-0607-9   LC 77-24670

"The discussion [of aquariums] opens with a look at the kinds of fish and other water animals that live there and explanations of how and from where these specimens are collected. . . . Information on the special necessities required to keep such a building operating (water pipes, temperature regulations, comfortable habitat areas) leads into a description of the individual jobs of those who work there, along with their qualifications." Booklist
"While Paige has used the Shedd Aquarium in Chicago as an example, he also describes other kinds of aquariums and much of the text applies to any aquarium. Profusely illustrated with photographs, many of which are in color, the book can give readers a fine introduction both to the beauty and interest of the exhibits and to the responsibilities of the administrators, collectors, exhibit designers, lecturers, guides, librarians, and other members of the support staff. The material is adequately organized; the writing style is straightforward." Chicago. Children's Bk Center

Pels, Gertrude

The care of water pets; illus. by Ava Morgan. Crowell 1955 119p illus $8.95, lib. bdg. $8.79 (4-6)   **639.3**

1 Aquariums 2 Fishes 3 Amphibians
ISBN 0-690-17070-X; 0-690-17071-8   LC 54-9768

An "informative introduction to the care of water pets of various kinds: fish, both tropical and native; frogs; turtles; snails; and salamanders and newts. Directions for setting up an aquarium, for choosing fish, for caring for the aquarium, for feeding and caring for the plants and animals, for breeding fish, and for building an outdoor pond are all discussed in clear detail. The book will make an attractive, useful addition to nature study collections." Chicago. Children's Bk Center

Sarnoff, Jane

A great aquarium book; the putting-it-together guide for beginners, by Jane Sarnoff and Reynold Ruffins. Scribner 1977 47p illus lib. bdg. $8.95, pa $3.95 (4 and up)   **639.3**

1 Aquariums 2 Tropical fish
ISBN 0-684-14589-8; 0-684-14630-4   LC 75-39298

Illustrations by Reynold Ruffins
"A beginner's guide to creating a basic aquarium, with information on selecting fish and providing for them a comfortable, healthy environment." Sch Library J
This book "has colorful, useful pictures, comprehensive instructions geared to avoiding mistakes before they are made, and a leavening of perfectly silly fish riddles and fish jokes. Best of all, it is simple without being unscientific or sloppy." NY Times Bk Rev

Selsam, Millicent E.

Plenty of fish; illus. by Erik Blegvad. Harper 1960 61p illus (A Science I can read bk) $6.89 (k-3)   **639.3**

1 Goldfish
ISBN 006-025321-5   LC 60-5786

"By observing his own two goldfish brought home from the five-and-ten in plastic bags and by experimenting—with a little help from his father—a small boy learns how fish eat and breathe and how to house and care for them." Booklist
"Outstanding because of the beauty of its format, the excellence of its illustrations by Erik Blegvad, the humor and lack of condescension in its text." Horn Bk

Simon, Seymour

Tropical saltwater aquariums; how to set them up and keep them going; illus. by Karl Stuecklen. Viking 1976 90p illus $7.95 (4 and up)   **639.3**

1 Marine aquariums
ISBN 0-670-73191-9   LC 76-14447

"Every aspect is thoroughly covered: setting up a tank, getting the seawater, purchasing the fish, providing food, and maintaining a healthy aquarium through daily, weekly, and monthly upkeep. Suggestions for a first purchaser are followed by possibilities for the more advanced aquarium-keeper, including details for adding anemones, crabs, and shrimps. Specific hints in a final chapter suggest choices for both a 20- and 30-gallon aquarium." Booklist
"Enjoyable reading, this is an asset to inexperienced as well as experienced aquarium keepers." Sch Library J
For reading and research: p85

What do you want to know about guppies? Illus. by Susan Bonners. Four Winds 1977 66p illus $7.95 (4-6)   **639.3**

1 Guppies 2 Aquariums
ISBN 0-590-07412-1   LC 77-5930

This book presents basic information on guppies: "their history, reproduction, and diseases; how to establish and maintain an aquarium for them; and how to choose compatible plants and animals. Black-and-white drawings illustrate fish anatomy and identifying characteristics of guppies, snails, and aquatic plants." Sci Teacher
"Readers are likely to find most of their questions answered. . . . Lists of guppy types and further readings close out the introduction." Booklist

Zim, Herbert S.

Goldfish; pictures by Joy Buba. Morrow 1947 unp illus lib. bdg. $6.48 (2-5)   **639.3**

1 Goldfish 2 Aquariums
ISBN 0-688-31340-X   LC 47-31105

"Not children alone but older persons who keep goldfish as pets may find a great deal of help and information in this factual and authentic book. The type is large, the text clear and simple, the illustrations accurate and amusing. . . . Dr. Zim writes interestingly about the different kinds of fish, their habits and their requirements, and why they have reached their great popularity." Horn Bk
"Simply written but sound scientifically." Los Angeles Sch Libraries

640.73   Consumer education

Gay, Kathlyn

Be a smart shopper; photographs by David C. Sassman. Messner 1974 64p illus lib. bdg. $6.64 (4-6)   **640.73**

1 Consumer education
ISBN 0-671-32696-1   LC 74-7593

Gay, Kathlyn—*Continued*
"A short, elementary consumer's lesson that emphasizes the importance of careful consideration and selection in the purchase of goods and services. Gay discusses consumer motivations and how they are influenced by advertising, packaging, and display; she also clues young shoppers in on some common pitfalls and warns them to familiarize themselves with merchandise so they can distinguish between real and false bargains. . . . Welcome advice for the legions of young buyers who are often the special targets of manufacturers." Booklist

641 Food and drink

Berger, Melvin
The new food book; nutrition, diet, consumer tips, and foods of the future [by] Melvin and Gilda Berger; illus. by Byron Barton. Crowell 1978 150p illus $6.95, lib. bdg. $6.79 (4 and up)   641

1 Food 2 Nutrition
ISBN 0-690-01295-0; 0-690-03841-0   LC 77-7976

"The standard information is here—detailed talk of nutrition, digestion, informed food buying, food production and marketing—as well as more unusual subjects such as world hunger, the Green Revolution, and foods of the future. The text is dotted with briefly described experiments." Sch Library J
"Packed with information, this worthwhile resource will be most helpful for assignments concerning food and nutrition." Booklist

641.1 Applied nutrition

Gilbert, Sara
You are what you eat; a common-sense guide to the modern American diet. Macmillan Pub. Co. 1977 144p $7.95 (5 and up)   641.1

1 Nutrition 2 Diet 3 Food
ISBN 0-02-736020-2   LC 76-39806

"Gilbert touches briefly on nutrition, food-related diseases, and the emotional and cultural aspects of food, but her main concern is with the mass-production food industry's tremendous impact on modern eating habits. She urges young people to try new fods and think before they eat." Sch Library J
"Essentially what's here is a skeptical look at the food industry showing how the nutritional quality of food has too often been sacrificed to the cause of bigger industry profits. . . . Schools where consumer education units are taught will find it especially useful." Booklist
Where to find out more: p130-40

Riedman, Sarah R.
Food for people. 2d rev. ed. Introduction by Lord John Boyd Orr; illus. by Robert McGlynn. Abelard-Schuman 1976 228p illus $6.95 (6 and up)   641.1

1 Nutrition 2 Diet 3 Food
ISBN 0-200-00161-2   LC 75-33193

First published 1954
Partial contents: Answers by weighing and measuring; Chemical building blocks; Inorganic nutrients; Vitamins for the best of health; How much food do you need; What food processing hath wrought . . . ; A hungry world
"On the whole, Riedman does foster an understanding of basic nutrition, and if her picture of the global problems could be more incisive, the book still works as a starting point." Booklist
For further reading: p217-19

641.3 Food and foodstuffs

Fenten, Barbara
Natural foods, by Barbara and D. X. Fenten; illus. by Howard Berelson. Watts, F. 1974 66p illus. lib. bdg. $4.47 (5 and up)   641.3

1 Food, Natural
ISBN 0-531-02675-2   LC 73-10381

"A Concise guide"
This book gives guidelines on the selection of natural foods, vitamins, and supplements. The authors tell how to grow and prepare various natural foods and suggest what the inclusion of those foods in the diet can and cannot do for the individual
"A balanced, straight-to-the-point presentation that distinguishes between organic, health, and natural foods and discusses the latter in light of the current concern about overprocessing and chemical additives. . . . No scare tactics here, but a low-keyed reminder that much food bought by Americans is worthless if not harmful and that there is a different way to eat. A few places to buy natural foods are suggested, along with some adult books to read." Booklist

Hays, Wilma P.
Foods the Indians gave us, by Wilma P. Hays and R. Vernon Hays; illus. by Tom O'Sullivan. Washburn 1973 113p illus $5.95 (5 and up)   641.3

1 Food 2 Indians 3 Agriculture
ISBN 0-679-24025-X   LC 72-83041

"The authors have prepared an informative and interesting book concerning foods which originated as wild plants, were cultivated by the Indians of North and South America, and were eventually introduced to and enjoyed by many other nations. There are discussions of the probable origins of potatoes (white and sweet), peanuts, beans, tomatoes, pineapple, chocolate and cocoa, seafoods, maize or corn and a variety of other foods. The text stresses the importance of a stable food supply in building a civilization, the genius of the Indian farmers in cultivating wild plants for food and what modern man has done to improve these foods. The last chapter contains 25 simple recipes adapted from the Indian ways of cooking." Sci Bks

Lavine, Sigmund A.
Indian corn and other gifts; illus. with photographs, drawings, and old prints. Dodd 1974 80p illus $5.95 (4 and up)   641.3

1 Food 2 Indians 3 Agriculture
ISBN 0-396-06777-8   LC 75-12541

"Dealing with the contributions of American Indians to the Western world's diet, Lavine concentrates on five important natural products: potatoes, corn, maple syrup, and varieties of beans and squash. Besides learning of the Indians' cultivation, gathering, and preparation of these and other edibles, one reads about the plants' appearance in legend, ritual, and artifact and also discovers the nature of the white man's first encounter with the vegetation as food. . . . An annotated list of original territories of tribes mentioned in the text and a bibliography are appended." Booklist
"Illustrated with photos and old prints, Lavine's book . . . is not only informative but entertaining. . . . Recommended for students and others who wish to learn more about their country and the Indians." Pub W

Meyer, Carolyn
Milk, butter, and cheese; the story of dairy products; illus. by Giulio Maestro. Morrow 1974 96p illus lib. bdg. $6 (5 and up)   641.3

1 Dairy products 2 Cookery—Dairy products
ISBN 0-688-30100-2   LC 73-13574

This book discusses the dairy industry and its products. Part one surveys milk production, processing, and nutritional value. Part two tells of specific dairy products including butter, cheese, and ice cream. Recipes are included at the end of each chapter
"This look at dairy products covers ground not likely to be familiar to many young readers. . . . A surprise to some will be the recently discovered fact that certain people—especially Africans, Southeast Asians, and Indians of North and South America—after childhood lose the ability to digest milk and so can be made ill by it. Historical facts and a sprinkling of legend also add life to the section on cheesemaking, which describes varying processes." Booklist

641.5 Cookery

Barta, Ginevera
Metric cooking for beginners; illus. by Colette Peters. Enslow Pubs. 1978 95p illus lib. bdg. $6.95 (4 and up)　　**641.5**

1 Cookery 2 Metric system
ISBN 0-89490-009-0　　LC 78-6737

"The first 25 pages of this are devoted to: explaining cooking measurements to beginners; metric measurement by volume, and how-to; metric measurement by weight and how-to; and basic work habits in cooking. Following these sections are the recipes, and lastly, kitchen experiments (which might prove useful to science classes) and an afterword for adults which includes where to purchase metric measures for cooking." VOYA

Chosen for the beginning cook, the recipes "can also be used by those wanting to test their skills with the metric system. Though few children will be motivated to pick this up on their own, home economics teachers should find it a real boon." Booklist

Better Homes and Gardens New Junior cook book; for beginning cooks of all ages. [3d ed. Meredith 1972] 80p illus $3.95 (3-6)　　**641.5**

1 Cookery
ISBN 0-696-00405-4　　LC 78-73183

First published 1955 with title: Better Homes and Gardens Junior cook book

"Close-up, color photographs of tempting dishes such as taco burgers, crunch-top tuna casserole, orange-applesauce salad, French toast, apple nut coffee cake, strawberry shakes, frozen chocolate bananas, and peanut butter cookies make this an appealing beginners' cookbook. Ingredients and needed equipment are listed clearly, directions are simple and easy to follow, adult supervision is noted, and variations to recipes are offered. The 75-plus selections, arranged in groups (sandwiches, main dishes, vegetables and salads, breads, and treats), have been selected with children in mind. . . . An introductory section, 'Welcome to the Kitchen,' discusses menus, measuring, equipment, and clean-up." Booklist

Betty Crocker's Cookbook for boys & girls. Golden Press 1975 160p illus spiral bdg. $5.95, lib. bdg. $9.15, pa $2.95 (3-6) **641.5**

1 Cookery
ISBN 0-307-09647-5; 0-307-69604-9; 0-307-09917-2
LC 74-23006

First published 1957 by Simon & Schuster. Golden Press edition published in 1965 had title: Betty Crocker's New boys and girls cook book

A picture cookbook with step-by-step recipes for breads, main dishes, vegetables, party treats, and snacks

Blanchard, Marjorie Page
The outdoor cookbook; illus. by Rod Slater. Watts, F. 1977 119p illus (A Cooking plus bk.) lib. bdg. $5.95 (6 and up)　　**641.5**

1 Cookery, Outdoor 2 Menus
ISBN 0-531-00381-7　　LC 76-56407

The author's "compilation of inventive recipes and sample menus provides instruction in the techniques and advantages of the various methods of outdoor cooking. The joys of al fresco cooking and dining are explored from a leisurely weekend canoe trip to a beach feast with a minimum of sand. Especially helpful are ideas for plan-ahead menus and suggestions on how to coordinate serving times. The recipes vary in complexity, but all directions are clear and succinct." Sch Library J

Borghese, Anita
The down to earth cookbook. Rev. ed. Illus. by Ray Cruz. Scribner 1980 144p illus $8.95 (4-6)　　**641.5**

1 Cookery—Food, Natural
ISBN 0-684-16618-6　　LC 80-21483

First published 1973

"A natural foods cookbook for middle graders. Cooking terms, utensils, and ingredients are explained, and the recipe directions are clear. The tone is realistic and comforting. . . . There is a good index, the line drawings of boys and girls cooking are pleasant, and the book on the whole stresses that cooking is a creative, enjoyable activity." Sch Library J [review of the 1973 edition]

Cavin, Ruth
1 pinch of sunshine, 1/2 cup of rain; natural food recipes for young people; illus. by Frances Gruse Scott. Atheneum Pubs. 1973 95p illus $7.95 (4-6)　　**641.5**

1 Cookery—Food, Natural
ISBN 0-689-30099-9　　LC 72-86928

"A variety of easy recipes using whole grains, unrefined sweeteners, wheat germ, and unprocessed meats and vegetables. Also has tips for preparing foods for best nutritional value." Chicago

"This natural food cook book gives some variations on familiar recipes plus a few unusual ones. . . . The directions are simple to follow and enlivened with humorous illustrations." Library J

Cooper, Jane
Love at first bite; snacks and mealtime treats the quick and easy way; designed and illus. by Sherry Streeter. Knopf 1977 93p illus lib. bdg. $5.99, pa $3.50 (4 and up)　　**641.5**

1 Cookery—Food, Natural
ISBN 0-394-93399-0; 0-394-83399-6　　LC 76-42246

"This book is a guide to help you prepare tasty, healthy, and quick foods for when you're really hungry and want something right away. You won't find menus for five-course meals, but you will find ideas for breakfasts, bag lunches, afternoon snacks, drinks, and desserts—all no-bake." The Author

"Cooper attempts to steer kids toward healthy foods, freshly prepared, and away from pre-packaged junk. The recipes are simply written, and Cooper prefaces them with a section covering in detail basic rules of the kitchen, equipment, terms used in recipes." Sch Library J

Cooper, Terry Touff
Many hands cooking; an international cookbook for girls and boys, cooked and written by Terry Touff Cooper and Marilyn Ratner; illus. by Tony Chen. Crowell in cooperation with the U.S. Committee for UNICEF 1974 50p illus $6.50 (4 and up)　　**641.5**

1 Cookery
ISBN 0-690-00536-9　　LC 74-11871

Spiral binding

"An intriguing collection of recipes from all over the world ranging from cocoa and maple snow to Guacamole and African stew. Even the simplest fare has new twists such as adding vanilla to cocoa or making herb butter for sweet corn. Directions are clear; the recipes are graded according to difficulty; and the ingredients are easily available. A grade-A cookbook for young gourmets." Sch Library J

Kitchen terms to know: p xi-xiii

Dobrin, Arnold
Peter Rabbit's natural foods cookbook; illus. by Beatrix Potter. Warne 1977 112p illus $6.95 (3-5)　　**641.5**

1 Cookery—Food, Natural
ISBN 0-7232-6142-3　　LC 76-45309

"Format is inviting, with its square shape, heavy paper, and pleasing layout, liberally sprinkled with Potter's drawings and watercolors. The 33 recipes are full of natural foods which are easily available, are clearly written so that they can be followed by beginning cooks, and are just plain delicious." Sch Library J

"This is a book that will be appreciated by collectors of Beatrix Potter memorabilia rather than juvenile cookbook enthusiasts because of its superb reproductions of her art work. . . . It's a luxury item, but it is gorgeous." Children's Bk Rev Serv

Ellison, Virginia H.
The Pooh cook book. . . . Illus. by Ernest H. Shepard. Dutton 1969 120p illus $6.95 (4 and up)　　**641.5**

1 Cookery
ISBN 0-525-37404-3　　LC 75-92616

"Inspired by Winnie-the-Pooh and The house at Pooh Corner, by A. A. Milne." Title page

"A rather special book and not essential but one which lovers of Pooh will find both pleasurable and practical. Recipes for some distinctly Pooh dishes

Ellison, Virginia H.—*Continued*

such as marmalade on a honeycomb, colored honey, Cottleston pie and Cucumber or Mastershalum leaf sandwiches are interspersed between recipes for scrambled eggs, honey buns, hot potato salad with tuna fish, blueberry pie, and Christmas nut cookies. Directions are explicit and easy to follow and the book is enhanced with numerous quotations from 'Winnie the Pooh' and 'The House at Pooh Corner.'" Booklist

Gaeddert, LouAnn

Your night to make dinner; illus. by Ellen Weiss. Watts, F. 1977 116p illus (A Cooking plus bk) lib. bdg. $5.90 (6 and up)   **641.5**

1 Cookery
ISBN 0-531-01297-2   LC 77-5116

"A cookbook designed for teenagers who help with the family cooking, especially the evening meal. . . . Safety tips, meal planning, menus, shopping tips, quick meals, economy, vegetable and fruit selection, and other topics are covered. . . . Metric and standard measurements are given." Children's Bk Rev Serv

"For the most part, the recipes are appetizing and economical. . . . Although it relies heavily on pre-processed and canned foods, this will give beginning cooks confidence." Sch Library J

Girl Scouts of the United States of America

Cooking out-of-doors. The author 1960 216p illus pa $3.25 (4 and up)   **641.5**

1 Cookery, Outdoor
ISBN 0-88441-128-1   LC 60-4009

Spiral binding
First published 1946, this is a revision of Woodland cookery
Compiled by Alice Sanderson Rivoire
Designed for both the novice and the pro camper this book of outdoor cookery contains about 250 recipes indexed-keyed to ingredients, and skill levels

Girl Scout cookbook. Contemporary Bks. 1971 160p illus lib. bdg. $6.95 (4 and up)   **641.5**

1 Cookery
ISBN 0-8092-9144-4   LC 70-144349

First published by Cowles
"Edited by Ely List." Verso of title page
"Beginning with recipes for snacks and beverages, this book provides advice on meal planning with information on party and outdoor cooking, including recipes for main dishes, soups, and salads.

"A very good book for the cook of intermediate status. . . . [The recipes] are interspersed with general comments and bits of ancillary advice. A brief bibliography precedes the relative index." Chicago. Children's Bk Center

Hautzig, Esther

Cool cooking; 16 recipes without a stove; pictures by Jan Pyk. Lothrop 1973 unp illus $6.25, lib. bdg. $6 (2-5)   **641.5**

1 Cookery
ISBN 0-688-41532-6; 0-688-51532-0   LC 73-1389

"Simple kitchen tools (no stove is required) and easily available ingredients will produce no-fail, fun-to-make dishes for budding gourmets in the elementary grades. Instructions for the 16 recipes—ranging from 'Grapefruit Cups' to 'Strawberry Mint Julep'—are simple to follow, and even second graders can prepare anything from an appetizer to a dessert. . . . It is a good additional cooking book with a different viewpoint, perky illustrations, and a lively format." Sch Library J

MacGregor, Carol

The storybook cookbook; illus. by Ray Cruz. Doubleday 1967 96p illus lib. bdg. $4.95 (3-6)   **641.5**

1 Cookery
ISBN 0-385-06329-6   LC 67-15382

The twenty-two "recipes in this cookbook are for foods that favorite storybook characters have eaten—Heidi's Toasted Cheese Sandwiches, Captain Hook's Poison Cake, Hans Brinker's Waffles, Pinocchio's Poached Eggs, and many more. There are brief descriptions of all the stories, quotes from the books about the foods, and then recipes to follow—for cakes, pies, pretzels, fried chicken, and pot pie." NY Times Bk Rev

Glossary: p93-95

Moore, Eva

The Seabury Cook book for boys and girls; easy to read, easy to cook. Pictures by Talivaldis Stubis. Seabury [distributed by Houghton 1971 c1969] 48p illus $5.95 (1-3)   **641.5**

1 Cookery
ISBN 0-395-28818-5   LC 79-129210

"A Clarion book"
First published 1969 in paperback by Scholastic with title: The lucky cook book for boys and girls

"A very good first cook book. It contains nine easy recipes: on one page it lists the ingredients and equipment needed, on the other are listed numbered steps in procedure. The illustrations are big and clear, and safety warnings are given repeatedly. Lists of terms and of tools, also illustrated, are included, and instructions for preparing a dinner and a party (using the recipes in the book) are given." Chicago. Children's Bk Center

Parents' Nursery School

Kids are natural cooks; child-tested recipes for home and school using natural foods. Text by Roz Ault; based on the ideas of Liz Uraneck; illus. by Lady McCrady. Houghton 1974 129p illus $6.95, pa $4.95 (3-6)   **641.5**

1 Cookery—Food, Natural
ISBN 0-395-18508-4; 0-395-18521-1   LC 73-22054

"This is a cookbook that can be used by independent readers or can be used by adults working with young children. The recipes are sensibly grouped by seasons, using ingredients when they are plentiful and suiting the cooking to the weather —especially useful if the book is used for group projects. The instructions are firm but informal, and the recipes use natural foods; cooks are encouraged to be creative. A set of 'Guidelines for Teachers and Parents' gives suggestions for making cooking enjoyable and informative, for equipment and safety measures, and for substituting ingredients." Chicago. Children's Bk Center

Paul, Aileen

Kids cooking; the Aileen Paul Cooking School Cookbook, by Aileen Paul and Arthur Hawkins. Doubleday 1970 128p illus $5.95, lib. bdg. $6.90 (3-6)   **641.5**

1 Cookery
ISBN 0-385-06874-3; 0-385-02219-0   LC 78-89105

"This basic cookbook giving recipes for breakfast, lunch, dinner, dessert and party foods, places importance on the pleasure of cooking by suggesting foods that are established favorites with children. The authors have presented their material in an easily understood format with the ingredients on one page and step-by-step directions opposite." Pub W

"Grouping is by meals or type (dinner or lunch, party or snack dishes), and there are separate prefaces addressed to the adult and the child." Sat Rev

Kids cooking without a stove; a cookbook for young children; illus. by Carol Inouye. Doubleday 1975 63p illus $5.95, lib. bdg. $6.90 (1-3)   **641.5**

1 Cookery
ISBN 0-385-03140-8; 0-385-03172-6   LC 74-3553

"After some general hints on rules to follow and equipment to use, the recipes are divided into desserts, drinks, salads, sandwiches, snacks, and candies. Each recipe begins with 'Here's what you need' and 'Here's what you do.' Where necessary large red print suggests adult help with things like cutting a lemon in half. Old favorites such as lemonade, peanut butter, and chicken salad, are included as well as blackberry-patch salad, Arabian dates, and strawberry whip." Booklist

"A good source of fun ideas in the kitchen. Paul falls short in introducing young cooks to nutritional values. . . . The tasks are carefully adjusted to young capabilities and safety is considered." Sch Library J

Penner, Lucille Recht

The colonial cookbook; illus. with prints and photographs selected and arranged by Laura Geringer. Hastings House 1976 128p illus map $7.95 (5 and up)   **641.5**

1 Cookery   2 U.S.—Social life and customs—Colonial period, 1600-1775
ISBN 0-8038-1202-7   LC 76-26550

"This is a unique book that will introduce young readers to the times and food situation of the American settlers. The forty-nine recipes are from different geographical areas and from poor colonists and wealthy southern plantation owners alike. The recipes are adapted to our modern kitchens, but all are authentic. Each is described and its history told." Children's Bk Rev Serv

"In a well-written and a carefully-researched volume, the author presents a variety of colonial memorabilia. Handsome illustrations are deftly integrated into the text to provide an appropriate setting for the recipes. . . . The book offers a view of the daily lives and customs of those with whom the recipes originated as well as the interesting derivations of several commonly used words like 'dessert' and 'ketchup.'" Horn Bk
Selected bibliography: p122-23

Perl, Lila

Hunter's stew and Hangtown fry; what pioneer America ate and why; pictures by Richard Cuffari. Seabury [distributed by Houghton] 1977 156p illus map $8.95 (4 and up)   **641.5**

1 Cookery   2 U.S.—Social life and customs—19th century
ISBN 0-395-28922-X   LC 77-5366

"A Clarion book"
"A sequel to Perl's excellent 'Slumps, grunts, and snickerdoodles: what Colonial America ate and why,' [entered below] this is a culinary cultural history of the growing United States during the 19th Century. The author divides the country into five sections and, in a readable style, describes the people, the food, and the ambience of the times. There are 20 choice and representative recipes, a few at the end of each chapter." Sch Library J
"Illustrated with atmospheric gray wash over black line drawings. Worthwhile for social history studies." Booklist
Bibliography included in Acknowledgments: pvii-viii

Slumps, grunts, and snickerdoodles; what Colonial America ate and why; drawings by Richard Cuffari. Seabury [distributed by Houghton] 1975 125p illus map $7.95 (4 and up)   **641.5**

1 Cookery   2 U.S.—Social life and customs—Colonial period, 1600-1775
ISBN 0-395-28923-8   LC 75-4894

"A Clarion book"
"The social history of colonial America can be explored with astonishing success in terms of those often oddly-named dishes that steamed, simmered, boiled, and baked in the fireplaces. In this book, thirteen colorfully titled recipes have been chosen to tell not only 'what' the colonists ate and 'why,' but to show the geographical and historical background as well as the intimate domestic surroundings in which these developments took place." p10
"Useful for both home economics and social studies classes." Minnesota
Followed by: Hunter's stew and Hangtown fry, entered above

Purdy, Susan Gold

Christmas cookbook. Watts, F. 1976 94p illus (A Holiday cookbook) lib. bdg. $6.90, pa $2.95 (4 and up)   **641.5**

1 Cookery
ISBN 0-531-01207-7; 0-531-02373-7   LC 76-24884

"Cooking for Christmas is more than just making goodies, according to Purdy's suggestions of what to make and eat during the holidays. Recipes are grouped into areas such as Christmas Trimmings to Make and Eat (molded sugar bells); Festive Breakfasts (Santa Lucia saffron buns); Vegetables and Salads (peas in tomato shells); Potatoes, Rice, and Pasta (rice wreath); Main-Dish Meats (meat balls in pastry pockets); and Treats and Sweets (marzipan, gingerbread men, and wassail punch). Introductory chapters on solid basic skill tips are followed by background tidbits on each dish, listing of needed equipment and food items, ingredients in order of usage, and step-by-step instructions. Safety precautions are frequently noted." Booklist

"Librarians who can never get enough holiday materials should consider this for purchase. It is a well-prepared cookbook, with easy to follow step-by-step instructions for a variety of festive dishes and a few food decorations. There are many small red and black drawings for each recipe illustrating procedures and the finished product. This is a good holiday book." Children's Bk Rev Serv

Halloween cookbook. Watts, F. 1977 96p illus (A Holiday cookbook) lib. bdg. $6.90 (4 and up)   **641.5**

1 Cookery
ISBN 0-531-01320-0   LC 77-6428

"Knowing that Halloween is a popular time for parties and treats, Purdy stacks her selections with appropriate harvest ingredients, uses variations of basic recipes, and devises bewitching touches to match the mood. Edible table decorations include cookie place cards, chocolate-dipped marshmallow cats, and squash centerpieces—all carefully explained with helpful diagrams. Recipes are divided into suggestions for brunch and lunch, vegetable variations, main dish meats, and treats and sweets. . . . Introductory skills and measurement hints preface the recipes, all of which have easy-to-follow directions, metric and standard measures, and helpful hints for would-be gourmets." Booklist

"This book will give youngsters and adults so many hours of pleasure that one can hardly wait to use it! The illustrations by the author (in black and orange) and the easy-to-follow layout ('Equipment, Foods You Will Need, Ingredients, and How To'), plus intriguing recipes, make this book the happiest Halloween gift of all time!" Babbling Bookworm

Jewish holiday cookbook. Watts, F. 1979 96p illus (A Holiday cookbook) lib. bdg. $6.90, pa $2.95 (4-6)   **641.5**

1 Cookery, Jewish   2 Fasts and feasts—Judaism
ISBN 0-531-02281-1; 0-531-03430-5   LC 79-4462

The chapters of this book "follow the Jewish calendar year from Rosh Hashanah to Shavuot, with the Sabbath starting things off. Each holiday is explained in a preface, which is then followed by the recipes representative of the holiday. Breads, cakes, soups, main meals, and specialties are given full treatment from the basic equipment to be kept on hand, the foods one should have, to detailed steps accompanied by pen-and-ink drawings." Children's Bk Rev Serv

"Instructions for basic steps such as measuring, sifting, chopping, rendering chicken fat, and putting together matzoh meal make this [book] usable for beginning as well as for more advanced gourmets. The description of kosher cooking clearly explains dietary laws, and each recipe is keyed for pareve, dairy, meat, or Passover cooking." Booklist

Rombauer, Irma S.

A cookbook for girls and boys; chapter headings by Marion Rombauer Becker. [Rev. ed] Bobbs 1952 243p illus $6.95 (4 and up)   **641.5**

1 Cookery
ISBN 0-672-50258-5   LC 52-2453

First published 1946
This book "defines cooking terms and processes, teaches correct methods of measuring and mixing, and gives hundreds of recipes for the new and the experienced cook." Hodges. Bks for Elem Sch Libraries

Schwartz, Paula Dunaway

You can cook; how to make good food for your family and friends; illus. by Byron Barton. Atheneum Pubs. 1976 192p illus $7.95 (5 and up)   **641.5**

1 Cookery
ISBN 0-689-50065-3   LC 76-12482

Schwartz, Paula D.—*Continued*
"A Margaret K. McElderry book"
"The recipes in this book have been chosen because they are simple but not unsophisticated. Any one of them could be served proudly to guests of any age. They are for 'real' food—fresh food, cooked simply and with care. There are almost no canned or frozen ingredients included, because convenience foods do not taste nearly as good as fresh foods. Suggestions are made as to what may be served with the main courses to make a meal, and some sample menus are included. Preparation and cooking times are given for every recipe. If the meal consists of several parts, steps are indicated in their proper order. A number of dishes can be cooked ahead of time, and this is indicated in the recipes." Foreword
"In a light, conversational tone, the author presents basic recipes for foods. . . . Through a careful ordering of instructions, more complicated recipes are made accessible to beginners; however, a greater number of illustrations would have been helpful and would have enhanced the design." Horn Bk

Shapiro, Rebecca
A whole world of cooking; illus. by the author. Little 1972 70p illus $5.95 (5 and up)   **641.5**
1 Cookery
ISBN 0-316-78286-6   LC 78-169007
"More for the young amateur than for the beginner, these recipes call for uncomplicated cooking procedures and, despite the international flavor, only standard ingredients. Breezy writing introduces each dish, but the instructions that follow are clear and businesslike. The table of contents is arranged by country, the index by type of dish." Sat Rev

Wide world cookbook; illus. by the author. Little 1962 58p illus $5.95 (5 and up)   **641.5**
1 Cookery
ISBN 0-316-78283-1   LC 62-7106
"A collection of recipes listed alphabetically by country of origin in the table of contents, and indexed by type of food. There is one recipe from each country (except for the United States). . . . Some of the recipes are quite simple, some a bit more complicated; the directions given for the latter are adequate for a reader with cooking experience, but not always adequate for the beginner. Each recipe is preceded by a few lines about the country or the dish." Chicago. Children's Bk Center

Van der Linde, Polly
Around the world in 80 dishes, by Polly and Tasha Van der Linde; pictures by Horst Lemke. Scroll Press 1971 85p illus $5.95 (3-6)   **641.5**
1 Cookery
ISBN 0-87592-007-1   LC 71-160447
"Easy-to-follow recipes for 53 dishes from many different countries, which utilize common or readily obtainable ingredients, are presented in a cookbook written by two sisters, ages ten and eight. The cheerfully illustrated book is divided into sections of side dishes, soups, eggs, fish, meats, vegetables and salad, sauces and dressings, desserts, and drinks. There are no indications of the number of servings that each recipe will make, an unfortunate omission for beginning cooks, but the book does include a glossary of cooking terms, notes to parents, general rules, tips for setting the table, an illustrated list of cooking utensils, and the authors' subjective evaluation of the difficulty of each recipe." Booklist

Walker, Barbara Muhs
The Little House cookbook; frontier foods from Laura Ingalls Wilder's classic stories; illus. by Garth Williams. Harper 1979 240p illus $8.95, lib. bdg. $8.79 (5 and up)   **641.5**
1 Cookery 2 Wilder, Laura Ingalls 3 Frontier and pioneer life
ISBN 0-06-026418-7; 0-06-026419-5   LC 76-58733
This book contains "recipes for the frontier foods found in the classic stories of Laura Ingalls Wilder (the 'Little House' books). Also included are essays on the origins, development and characteristics of the various dishes." Bks of the Times

"Using quotations and illustrations from the original stories, Walker discusses food accessibility and preparation on the western frontier, relating these directly to the everyday customs and special occasions of the Ingalls family. The recipes, which have been altered for modern-day measurements, kitchen equipment, and availability, maintain the flavor of the time. Selections include both the familiar (pumpkin pie, buckwheat pancakes, . . . plum preserves) and the unusual (blackbird pie, corn dodgers, vinegar pie). . . . Though children may not be motivated to try the items themselves, these offer outlets for family sharing or classroom experiences as well as excellent source material for research. Glossary, metric conversion table, and chronological bibliography appended." Booklist

641.6 Cookery of and with specific materials

De Paola, Tomie
The popcorn book. Holiday House 1978 unp illus lib. bdg. $7.95 (k-3)   **641.6**
1 Popcorn
ISBN 0-8234-0314-9   LC 77-21456
"While one twin prepares the treat, the other stays close-by and reads aloud what popcorn is, how it's cooked, stored, and made, how the Indians of the Americas discovered it, and who eats the most (Milwaukee, Minneapolis, Chicago, and Seattle). The best thing about popcorn, the twins decide, is eating it. Two recipes are included." Babbling Bookworm
The author-artist's "amusing soft-color pictures —each bordered with a lavender frame—show action in the past or the present while a few lines of text or balloon speeches describe what is happening." Horn Bk

Perl, Lila
The hamburger book; all about hamburgers and hamburger cookery; illus. by Ragna Tischler Goddard. Seabury [distributed by Houghton] 1974 128p illus $7.95 (5 and up)   **641.6**
1 Cookery—Meat
ISBN 0-395-28921-1   LC 73-7173
"A Clarion book"
The author traces the history of man's use of ground meat from thirteenth century Russia through our modern hamburger chains. Also included are twenty-two international recipes which use ground meat
"The recipes are varied, and the step-by-step instructions are given clearly. A considerable portion of the text in each section gives background information of moderate interest, usually including some facts about national eating habits or other national dishes." Chicago. Children's Bk Center

641.8 Cookery of various specific kinds of composite dishes

Adkins, Jan
The bakers; a simple book about the pleasures of baking bread; written, designed, and illus. by Jan Adkins. Scribner 1975 32p illus lib. bdg. $5.95 (4-6)   **641.8**
1 Bread
ISBN 0-684-14387-9   LC 75-17398
"First we learn something of the history of the staff of life, in capsule accounts: cave dwellers made bread from wild grains but it was only 6000 years ago, in Egypt, that the first real bread was baked. The following paragraphs go into Greek, Roman and later cultures and their baking. Ah, but at last we get to the heart of the text. In lucid language, the author tells exactly how to create beautiful, fragrant, nourishing loaves of your very own, and adds, 'if you give some away, the loaf you keep tastes better.'" Pub W
"Adkins examines his topic thoughtfully and respectfully. The book is actually about bread rather than bakers, who are in effect defined as anyone making bread from prehistoric times to the present, including the Egyptians, Greeks, Romans, and early American settlers. . . . Besides

Adkins, Jan—*Continued*

providing a prosy but instructive recipe, Adkins also explains the dynamics of the process. . . . As with his other titles, the design is solid and the format meticulous, even if the illustrations themselves—pen-and-ink drawings often heavily cross-hatched—are not so light and airy as we've seen before." Booklist

Borghese, Anita

The international cookie jar cookbook; drawings by Yaroslava Mills. Scribner 1975 190p illus pa $3.95 (4 and up)　　641.8

1 Cookies
ISBN 0-684-14627-4　　LC 74-14075

"Cookie fanciers will find explicit directions for making virtually every kind they ever heard of and in a real cookbook. No packaged mixes are mentioned here; every treat here is a 'from scratch' project. Some cookies are harder to make than others but all are possible if the instructions are followed. The recipes are arranged by location." Pub W

"The ingredients required for some of the recipes will probably not be available in smaller communities. The general directions on cookie-making methods are thorough. We found most of these cookies less sweet than American children are accustomed to, but their richness and unique flavors made them popular with all ages. This would be an excellent source book for Scout and other youth group leaders." Children's Bk Rev Serv

Johnson, Hannah Lyons

Let's bake bread; photographs by Daniel Dorn. Lothrop 1973 unp illus lib. bdg. $6.48 (2-5)　　641.8

1 Bread
ISBN 0-688-51297-6　　LC 72-10590

"What could be better than a cookbook that tells the most inexperienced reader exactly what he needs to know, and nothing that he doesn't? Here, with photographs that add to its usefulness, is a text that does just that: takes a neophyte step by step through the several procedures of breadbaking, beginning with utensils and ingredients. The photographs show three children mixing, measuring, kneading, and so on; while the pictures and the simple, clear directions make this a book that young cooks can use alone, the text has no note of coyness, so that older readers may feel encouraged to try their hands as well." Chicago. Children's Bk Center

Meyer, Carolyn

The bread book; all about bread and how to make it; illus. by Trina Schart Hyman. Harcourt 1971 96p illus $6.95 (3-6)　　641.8

1 Bread
ISBN 0-15-212040-8　　LC 76-140780

"The author describes the importance of bread in early times after giving a conjectural explanation of the discovery of baked grain, discusses its place in religious ceremonies and the many special forms in which it appears, gives some facts about large baking plants and small neighborhood bakeries. And, of course, gives recipes for several kinds of home-baked bread. An index is appended." Chicago. Children's Bk Center

The recipes "are aimed at beginners, but there is no writing down and no fictionalizing. Useful for foods units, holidays and customs units, social studies, and for generally inquisitive readers who like a fast-moving, fact-filled book." Sch Library J

"Throughout the tale of the loaf, the illustrator's humorous pen-and-ink drawings delightfully highlight the universality of man's need for this staple no matter what shape, type, or texture it—or he—comes in. An unusual and eminently satisfying presentation." Horn Bk

Moore, Eva

The cookie book; illus. by Talivaldis Stubis. Seabury [distributed by Houghton] 1973 64p illus $6.95 (3-5)　　641.8

1 Cookies
ISBN 0-395-28866-5　　LC 76-190381

"A Clarion book"

The author provides beginning bakers with twelve recipes for such favorites as snicker doodles; animal-shaped butter cookies; Christmas ornament cookies; molasses, peanut butter, and oatmeal cookies; and coconut drops, each suggested for a particular month of the year

"The batches are small and manageable—not over two dozen each—and all of the recipes are basic. Important tips, an illustrated cooking dictionary, and an easy conversational style make this collection of recipes as practical as it is readable." Horn Bk

Solomon, Hannah

Bake bread! Photographs by Edward Stevenson. Lippincott 1976 80p illus $7.95, pa $3.95 (4 and up)　　641.8

1 Bread
ISBN 0-397-31670-4; 0-397-31671-2　　LC 76-18807

"Through numerous photographs and detailed explanations, the step-by-step process of bread-making is revealed. The book focuses on procedure but offers several variations on a basic recipe—including cheese bread, cinnamon-raisin loaf, and pizza. A concluding discussion of the chemical reactions which occur during baking is an unusual feature." Horn Bk

Williams, Vera B.

It's a gingerbread house; bake it, build it, eat it! Greenwillow Bks. 1978 47p illus $5.95, lib. bdg. $5.71 (2-4)　　641.8

1 Gingerbread houses
ISBN 0-688-80153-6; 0-688-84153-8　　LC 77-25979

"A Greenwillow Read-alone guide"

In story format, this book provides simple instructions for baking and building a gingerbread house

646.2　Sewing and related operations

Corrigan, Barbara

I love to sew. Doubleday 1974 139p illus lib. bdg. $6.90 (4-6)　　646.2

1 Sewing 2 Handicraft
ISBN 0-385-03163-7　　LC 73-15333

Illustrated by the author

"Attractive, functional items result from these instructive projects that teach sewing basics and require a minimum of stitching expertise. The simplest placemats call for fringing raw edges and perhaps ironing on an applique. Tote bags, purses, belts, and triangle scarves require only straight seams; more impressive looking but just as simple are a set of curtains and a bedspread. Later examples escalate slightly in difficulty by introducing curved seams or simple facings. Commercial patterns are relegated to older sewers, though instructions for using a basic pants pattern are included. A clear, effective guide to first experiences with a needle and thread." Booklist

Inouye, Carol

It's easy to sew with scraps and remnants. Doubleday 1977 123p illus lib. bdg. $7.90 (6 and up)　　646.2

1 Sewing 2 Handicraft
ISBN 0-385-11051-0　　LC 76-2784

"An easy-to-follow guide to sewing simple clothes, gifts, and accessories using recycled and new materials. Information on pattern-making, stitches, tools, and fabrics is included along with detailed instructions for 35 projects ranging from bean bag toys and ice cream-shaped pot holders to halter tops, bikinis, and peasant blouses." Sch Library J

Glossary: p111-13

646.4　Clothing construction

Corrigan, Barbara

Of course you can sew! Basics of sewing for the young beginner; written and illus. by Barbara Corrigan. Doubleday 1971 127p illus $4.95, lib. bdg. $5.90 (5 and up)　　646.4

1 Sewing 2 Dressmaking
ISBN 0-385-07697-5; 0-385-03241-2　　LC 77-110030

Corrigan, Barbara—*Continued*
"A sound and practical guide to fundamental sewing techniques presented in explicit text and clear diagrams and drawings. Information about equipment, fabrics, basic hand stitches, and the operation of a sewing machine is followed by instructions for making accessories from straight pieces of material; ponchos or capes based on simple geometric shapes; shifts or robes from Turkish towels; curtains, gowns, or robes from colorful sheets; and gathered skirts; and for using commercial patterns to make simple, sleeveless dresses and blouses." Booklist

647 Management of public households

Sobol, Harriet Langsam
Cosmo's restaurant; photographs by Patricia Agre. Macmillan Pub. Co. 1978 51p illus $7.95 (2-4) **647**
1 Restaurants, bars, etc.
ISBN 0-02-785970-3   LC 78-9685
"An intriguing present-tense description of a young boy's involvement in his family's Italian restaurant. Helping out is not a burden but a privilege, a coming of age that shows his parents' trust in his future responsibility. Meanwhile, readers are learning specifics of the hard work it takes to run a restaurant—the buying trips, cooking, serving, and cleaning up in which everyone has a part. The writing is immediate and the black-and-white photographs unposed, giving a real sense of these people and their work. They are people worth knowing, and their story offers a refreshing change of pace from more glamorized but less personalized career/people rundowns. It's nice, too, to give youngsters who are learning how to behave in a restaurant some idea of what's going on behind the scenes." Booklist

649 Child rearing

Hautzig, Esther
Life with working parents: practical hints for everyday situations; illus. by Roy Doty. Macmillan Pub. Co. 1976 124p illus $6.95 (5 and up) **649**
1 Parent and child   2 Home economics   3 Children—Care and hygiene
ISBN 0-02-743500-8   LC 76-15223
The author's "sensible directions, which most parents have tried to impress on their children at one time or another, look wonderfully authoritative in print. General hints suggest work priorities and independent entertainment, while subsequent chapters deal with safety precautions, housework, meal preparation, money, pet care, babysitting, and ever-present or ever-absent working parents. The text is very clear and specific, including recipes, craft instructions, and even the ABCs of using household appliances. A good, long reading list is divided by subject, and the book is sprinkled with black-and-white cartoon drawings. Reassurance where it's needed." Booklist
Bibliography: p115-18

Samson, Joan
Watching the new baby; photographs by Gary Gladstone. Atheneum Pubs. 1974 65p illus $7.95 (3-5) **649**
1 Infants   2 Child development
ISBN 0-689-30119-7   LC 73-84833
"This excellent book on infant development provides the . . . child with simple tools for observing the behavior of a new-born baby in his home and understanding the different types of motor and sensory developments occurring in the baby's first 18-24 months of life. Early chapters are devoted to prenatal development, birth, appearance. Subsequent chapters explain developments in touch, movement, sight, andhearing as well as the importatnce of eating, sleeping, and crying. The book not only informs, but suggests ways in which the reader may actively participate in this growth process. Fine black-and-white photography depicts all family members participating in the infant care process. A chart at the back suggests when a baby may be expected to accomplish various motor/sensory tasks." Appraisal
Glossary: p62-64. Sources: p65

Saunders, Rubie
The Franklin Watts Concise guide to babysitting; illus. by Tomie de Paola. Watts, F. 1972 63p illus lib. bdg. $4.90 (5 and up) **649**
1 Baby sitters   2 Children—Care and hygiene
ISBN 0-531-02563-2   LC 71-188479
Title on spine: The concise guide to babysitting
"A concise, useful guide to baby-sitting intended for the novice. It treats baby-sitting in a professional manner and deals briefly with each step taken in preparation for the first job. Covered are how to find a job, how much to charge, the sitter's responsibilities, safety precautions to remember, and, of course, the care and feeding of the child. . . . The drawings which accompany the text are amusing." Sch Library J

652 Processes of written communication. Cryptography

Albert, Burton
Codes for kids [by] Burton Albert, Jr. Illus. by Dev Appleyard. Whitman, A. 1976 32p illus $5.95 (3-6) **652**
1 Cryptography   2 Ciphers
ISBN 0-8075-1239-7   LC 76-25456
"A jungle jumble, Popsticklers, Brainbusters, Zigzaggers, and Jefferson's Nose are but a few examples of the 29 codes explained and illustrated here. Each code offers a practice session to test readers' wits, and an answer key checks out the decoding. Easy-to-understand directions, brown-and-black line drawings, and suggestions for using the codes make this fun for perennial secret-clubbers." Booklist

More codes for kids [by] Burton Albert, Jr. Illus. by Jerry Warshaw. Whitman, A. 1979 32p illus lib. bdg. $5.50 (3-6) **652**
1 Cryptography   2 Ciphers
ISBN 0-8075-5270-4   LC 79-245
"Junior cryptanalysts who delighted in 'Codes for Kids' [entered above] will enjoy sleuthing out more of the same with the 25 codes offered here. Maps, letters, numbers, graphs, line dots, and symbols are used to set up the cipher, with answers often being a riddle or a joke; readers who discover the fun will soon be making their own. A comic Sherlock Holmes and floppy-eared, bespectacled hound cartoon the codes." Booklist

Babson, Walt
All kinds of codes. Four Winds 1976 135p illus $8.95 (5 and up) **652**
1 Cryptography   2 Ciphers
ISBN 0-590-07427-X   LC 76-17529
"Code making and breaking can be challenging and fun when readers follow Babson's clear, smoothly written explanations. His collection ranges from simple mind-teasers to complex bafflers and includes Swiss Cheese Grille, Crisscross, Rail Fence, and more than 50 other codes. Step-by-step directions are given for using invisible writing, code tools, camouflage, and substitution-in-position, as well as for decoding secrets from someone else. Even everyday situations such as grocery shopping and remembering historical dates can provide an opportunity for creating codes, and the author suggests them as a way to improve memory. A final chapter on quickie code games completes the text." Booklist

Gardner, Martin
Codes, ciphers and secret writing. Simon & Schuster 1972 96p illus $5.95 (5 and up) **652**
1 Cryptography   2 Ciphers
ISBN 0-671-65201-X   LC 72-82218
"A book that should delight the puzzle fan, this explains how to code and decode messages, moving from fairly simple transposition and substitution ciphers to increasingly intricate examples using symbols and numbers as well as alphabets. One chapter describes code machines such as telephone dials, wheels, and grilles; another is devoted to invisible writing. Many examples of classic codes and messages are included; answers to practice codes and riddles are not. A divided bibliography is appended." Chicago. Children's Bk. Center

James, Elizabeth

How to keep a secret; writing and talking in code [by] Elizabeth James & Carol Barkin; illus. by Joel Schick. Lothrop 1978 56p illus $5.95, lib. bdg. $5.71 (4-6)   **652**

1 Cryptography   2 Ciphers
ISBN 0-688-41828-7; 0-688-51828-1   LC 77-18295

"Perplexing number substitutions, distorted alphabetical sequences, invisible writing messages, plus secret signaling and language codes should flourish with the arrival of this book on library shelves. Using numerous examples, the authors describe commonly known codes (Pig Latin, Morse code) and suggest various devices (pigpen, fence post cipher, coding sticks) to mystify would-be code breakers. Use of red print for codes and humorous drawings add up to an attractive format." Booklist

Kohn, Bernice

Secret codes and ciphers; illus. by Frank Aloise. Prentice-Hall 1968 63p illus lib. bdg. $4.95, pa $1.50 (4 and up)   **652**

1 Cryptography   2 Ciphers
ISBN 0-13-797399-3; 0-13-797738-7   LC 68-20368

"After explaining the basic differences between codes and ciphers, the author describes various simple and complex types of both including dictionary and machine codes and concealment, transposition, and substitution ciphers. She documents her account with several historic examples and with the work of famous cryptographers and cryptanalysts. Tables showing English letter and word frequencies are appended and the book is illustrated with amusing black-and-white drawings." Booklist

Lamb, Geoffrey

Secret writing tricks. Elsevier/Nelson Bks. 1975 88p illus $6.95 (5 and up)   **652**

1 Cryptography   2 Ciphers
ISBN 0-525-66465-3   LC 75-20473

First published by Thomas Nelson

"A British author explains various systems for writing secret messages, using letters, colors, pinpricks, numbers, and symbols as well as invisible ink. He describes some famous ciphers of the past and suggests ways to break and read encoded messages, giving practice activities in a last section. The material covered in the book is substantially the same as that of Martin Gardner's 'Codes, Ciphers and Secret Writing' [entered above]; this is more formally written although equally lucid." Chicago. Children's Bk Center

"The author stresses the need for care and consistency so the reader can comprehend the sender's message. Bits of history are inserted as Lamb speaks of individuals like Julius Caesar, the Marquis of Worcester, and the Bishop of Chester all of whom used and devised secret codes." Booklist

Peterson, John

How to write codes and send secret messages; illus. by Bernice Myers. Four Winds 1970 64p illus $5.95, pa 95¢ (2-4)   **652**

1 Cryptography   2 Ciphers
ISBN 0-590-07056-8; 0-590-02606-2   LC 68-27278

"A practical little book on encoding and decoding secret messages, specifically geared to the interests of young children. The clear easy text, illustrated with two-color diagrams and drawings, gives directions for writing messages in space, hidden word, Greek, and alphabet codes and in invisible ink made of lemon juice or washing soda. The concluding chapter suggests ways of delivering the secret messages." Booklist

Sarnoff, Jane

The code & cipher book, by Jane Sarnoff and Reynold Ruffins. Scribner 1975 37p illus lib. bdg. $6.95, pa $2.95 (3-6)   **652**

1 Cryptography   2 Ciphers
ISBN 0-684-14246-5; 0-684-16219-9   LC 74-24419

A "compendium of ciphers, codes, and such variants as pig Latin and cockney slang concludes with a page of advice on breaking ciphers and some messages to decode, with keys to the numbers used for cipher systems in the book. Each of the ciphers is explained, and sentences to encode and decode follow. Here and there throughout the

book are double-page spreads that offer little bits of information about codes used in history, rules about who was permitted to use them, signs used by hoboes, etc." Chicago. Children's Bk Center

"The book is a tantalizing smorgasbord of information about secret messages which, as the preface notes, incorporates into the specifics of code-making 'recipes for invisible ink, methods of inkless writing, information about breaking codes, facts about codes in history . . . and more.' A total success." Horn Bk

658   General management

Amazing Life Games Company

Good cents; every kid's guide to making money, by members of The Amazing Life Games Company (and friends); illus. by Martha Hairston and James Robertson. Houghton 1974 128p illus $7.95, pa $3.95 (4 and up)   **658**

1 Business   2 Finance, Personal
ISBN 0-395-19500-4; 0-395-19501-2   LC 74-9378

"Suggestions here are attractively presented with humorous cartoon-type illustrations that make the projects . . . look like lots of fun. Realistic as to the capabilities of middle graders as well as the marketability of the goods or services suggested. 'Good Cents' really is a sensible manual that should provide incentive for youngsters trying to earn cash." Sch Library J

658.85   Personal selling (Salesmanship)

Fisher, Leonard Everett

The peddlers; written & illus. by Leonard Everett Fisher. Watts, F. 1968 45p illus maps lib. bdg. $4.90 (4 and up)   **658.85**

1 Peddlers and peddling   2 U.S.—Social life and customs—Colonial period, 1600-1775
ISBN 0-531-01031-7   LC 68-10335

The author describes Colonial peddlers, "the wares they carried, the routes they followed, the hazards they encountered, and their importance to the settlers." Booklist

"Even more than the text, the strong scratchboard illustrations convey the struggles and strivings of colonial America and the importance of trade to a frontier society." Sch Library J

664   Food technology

Buehr, Walter

Salt, sugar and spice. Morrow 1969 78p illus map lib. bdg. $6 (3-6)   **664**

1 Salt   2 Sugar   3 Spices
ISBN 0-688-31569-0   LC 69-15873

"The first two sections give a brief history of salt and sugar respectively, along with a description of the methods used to obtain and process each. The final section explains the importance of the early spice trade and gives the characteristics and uses of 33 major spices." Booklist

"There is a two-page map showing the Portuguese and Dutch spice routes, the Arab caravan and ship routes, and Columbus' route to the West Indies. The various countries and the spices they supply are also indicated on the map. The attractive book concludes with a descriptive list of spices found in most kitchens. There is an index. This book will be a very useful addition to any collection of children's books." Sci Bks

A spice list: p53-[79]

Jenness, Aylette

The bakery factory: who puts the bread on your table; text and photographs by Aylette Jenness. Crowell 1978 71p illus $5.95, lib. bdg. $5.79 (4 and up)   **664**

1 Bakers and bakeries
ISBN 0-690-03805-4; 0-690-01338-8   LC 77-8094

"Touring a local bread factory, the author-photographer and her daughter observe machinery and procedures, which are illustrated on nearly

Jenness, Aylette—*Continued*
every page. They talk to employees, asking questions about the work done in the factory and the attitudes people have towards their jobs. General questions are also raised about other products we use and buy, where they come from, and how they are made; the reader is encouraged to think about the varied jobs and careers now available and to design other tours." Horn Bk

"Clear photographs and a casual, almost conversational, writing style make this more palatable than most books in the let's-visit category." Chicago. Children's Bk Center

Loeper, John J.
Mr Marley's Main Street confectionery; a history of sweets & treats; illus. with old prints. Atheneum Pubs. 1979 69p illus $6.95 (5 and up) **664**

1 Confectionery—History
ISBN 0-689-30716-0   LC 79-10549

"Evoking a sense of time when confectionery shops were a common sight, Loeper invites readers, via a fictionalized format, back to a small Pennsylvania town in 1895. Glimpses of various customers' lives unfold as visits to Mr. Marley's shop result in mouthwatering purchases of fudge, penny candy, chocolates, ice cream sodas, popcorn, and other treats. Interspersed are explanations of where and how these sweets originated, what they were made of, and what parts they played in holiday and other celebrations. Nostalgic touches to the vigorous writing make a nice balance, and though researchers will find extraction of material difficult without an index, a fascinating and flavorful mood is created. Old prints add a historical note but lack child appeal." Booklist

666 Ceramic and allied technologies

Fisher, Leonard Everett
The glassmakers; written and illus. by Leonard Everett Fisher. Watts, F. 1964 43p illus (Colonial Americans) lib. bdg. $4.90 (4 and up) **666**

1 Glass manufacture   2 U.S.—Social life and customs—Colonial period, 1600-1775
ISBN 0-531-01028-7   LC 64-16320

The author presents the history of glass, the techniques in making it, and the way colonial glassmakers worked

"Well-written text and strong, vibrant illustrations." Sch Library J
Glassmaking terms: p40-41

The potters; written & illus. by Leonard Everett Fisher. Watts, F. 1969 47p illus map (Colonial Americans) lib. bdg. $4.90 (4 and up) **666**

1 Pottery, American   2 U.S.—Social life and customs—Colonial period, 1600-1775
ISBN 0-531-01032-5   LC 69-14499

This "book discusses the basic ingredients necessary for, and processes involved in, making pottery. The coarse utensils the American potters wrought lacked the beauty of china or porcelain pieces but served very well the needs of the early colonists. Mr. Fisher utilizes a historical approach to detail early pottery operations and the contributions of . . . men instrumental in maintaining this colonial craft. The author's precise, substantial black-and-white illustrations are an integral part of the book, graphically showing equipment, processes, and techniques." Sch Library J

669 Metallurgy

Smith, Norman F.
If it shines, clangs & bends, it's metal; drawings by Tom Huffman. Coward, McCann & Geoghegan 1980 47p illus lib. bdg. $5.99 (3-5) **669**

1 Metals
ISBN 0-698-30717-8   LC 79-227

This is "a first look at a basic group of elements, describing origins, properties, and uses of metal. The text is lively, brisk, and clear, and much information, ranging from the Bronze Age and the cave dwellers' metal tools to a nice conservation plug for recycling, is conveyed palatably. The aim is less to be technical or experimental than to encourage awareness of the child's immediate environs. Huffman's pen-and-ink drawings are abundant, consistent, and perhaps the best part of the book. Touches of bright orange amid black and white are as appealing as the touches of wit and humor are entertaining." Sch Library J

670 Manufactures

Colby, C. B.
Early American crafts; tools, shops and products. Coward, McCann & Geoghegan 1967 48p illus lib. bdg. $5.29 (4 and up) **670**

1 Art industries and trade—U.S.   2 U.S.—Social life and customs—Colonial period, 1600-1775
ISBN 0-698-30066-1   LC 67-24212

Photographs "taken at the Colonial Williamsburg, Old Sturbridge Village and Mystic Seaport restorations, add another dimension to [this] study of colonial life. Cabinetmakers, silversmiths, blacksmiths, printers, and others are shown at work as are homecraftsmen doing spinning, weaving and candlemaking. Suitable as a survey or a browsing book." Library J

Fisher, Leonard Everett
The homemakers; written & illus. by Leonard Everett Fisher. Watts, F. 1973 48p illus (Colonial Americans) lib. bdg. $4.90 (4 and up) **670**

1 Art industries and trade—U.S.   2 U.S.—Social life and customs—Colonial period, 1600-1775
ISBN 0-531-01047-3   LC 73-5692

The author explains how in colonial times, "four household items—candles, soap, brooms, and cider—were made by families for their own needs. [He] describes techniques and skills involved in these homemaking chores. [The book has] black-and-white illustrations and diagrams and simple text." Sch Library J

Tunis, Edwin
Colonial craftsmen and the beginnings of American industry; written and illus. by Edwin Tunis. Crowell [1976 c1965] 159p illus $12.95 (5 and up) **670**

1 Art industries and trade—U.S.   2 U.S.—Social life and customs—Colonial period, 1600-1775
ISBN 0-690-01062-1   LC 75-29612

Reprint of the title first published 1965 by World

The author describes the working methods and products, houses and shops, town and country trades, individual and group enterprises by which the early Americans forged the economy of the New World. He discusses such trades as papermaking, glassmaking, shipbuilding, printing, and metalworking, and describes some of the objects that are now heirlooms—silverware of Paul Revere, Queensware pottery, etc.

"An oversize book that is impressively handsome and that should be tremendously useful; well-organized and superbly illustrated, the text is comprehensive, lucid, and detailed. . . . An extensive index is appended." Chicago. Children's Bk Center

675 Leather and fur technologies

Fisher, Leonard Everett
The tanners; written & illus. by Leonard Everett Fisher. Watts, F. 1966 43p illus (Colonial Americans) lib. bdg. $4.90 (4 and up) **675**

1 Tanning   2 U.S.—Social life and customs—Colonial period, 1600-1775
ISBN 0-531-01038-4   LC 66-10136

Fisher, Leonard E.—*Continued*

"This history and description of the preparation and tanning of hides to manufacture leather and parchment . . . provides young readers with accurate and interesting insights into the development of American crafts and industries. The woodcuts are in the spirit of the work and assist in explaining the text." Sci Bks

Tanners' terms: p40-41

676 Pulp and paper technology

Fisher, Leonard Everett

The papermakers; written & illus. by Leonard Everett Fisher. Watts, F. 1965 46p illus (Colonial Americans) lib. bdg. $4.90 (4 and up) **676**

1 Paper making and trade 2 U.S.—Social life and customs—Colonial period, 1600-1775

ISBN 0-531-01030-9 LC 65-13683

The author "explains the techniques of the papermaker and gives a brief glimpse into the historical background, the need for paper in the American colonies and the techniques used by these skilled artisans and patriots." Sch Library J

The book "includes a glossary of terms and identifies a number of paper watermarks. Strong black-and-white illustrations on every other page. Special but attractive." Booklist

677 Textiles

Buehr, Walter

Cloth from fiber to fabric; written and illus. by Walter Buehr. Morrow 1965 96p illus lib. bdg. $6 (5 and up) **677**

1 Textile industry 2 Fabrics

ISBN 0-688-31176-8 LC 65-10260

"The various processes of clothmaking—spinning, weaving, knitting, bleaching, and dyeing—are described by Buehr in this brief historical survey. Different fibers such as wool, linen and cotton, require different methods of preparation. An account of these methods, as well as a description of a modern mill, are included. The text moves rapidly and the information is accurate." Sci Bks

"Clear illustrations and diagrams." Horn Bk

Houck, Carter

Warm as wool, cool as cotton; natural fibers and fabrics and how to work with them; pictures by Nancy Winslow Parker. Seabury [distributed by Houghton] 1975 91p illus $6.95 (3-6) **677**

1 Fibers 2 Textile industry

ISBN 0-395-28861-4 LC 74-18089

"A Clarion book"

"An introduction to natural fibers and their uses begins with a look at the origins and history of wool, cotton, linen, and silk. Other textile materials such as jute, hemp, and various animal fibers find mention in a catchall chapter entitled 'Other Odd Things for Spinning'. Succeeding discussions examine how fibers are transformed into cloth by way of weaving, knitting, or crocheting, or made more attractive with dyes and printing techniques. Project ideas meant to reinforce each chapter touch on major craft areas such as fabric dyeing, batik, knitting, and crocheting, 'but the necessarily narrow scope provides a superficial experience at best; beginners who attempt knitting or crocheting on the basis of the few diagrams will more than likely end up frustrated. Craft projects aside, the simple overview succeeds in providing an introductory perspective, and further questions can be answered by following up the appended selections for further reading.'" Booklist

Raben, Marguerite

Textile mill. Watts, F. 1978 65p illus (Industry at work) lib. bdg. $4.90 (4 and up) **677**

1 Textile industry

ISBN 0-531-02209-9 LC 78-1614

"The nature of natural and synthetic fibers and the steps incurred in transforming them to a finished bolt of cloth are made essentially clear. . . . [The book also points] out the job ranges, skilled and unskilled, in this area." Booklist

"The writing style . . . is simple and concise; the format, well designed for young readers; and the information, especially suitable for school career-awareness programs." Sch Library J

Further reading: p61-62

679 Other products of various specific materials

Fisher, Leonard Everett

The wigmakers; written and illus. by Leonard Everett Fisher. Watts, F. 1965 45p illus (Colonial Americans) lib. bdg. $4.90 (4 and up) **679**

1 Wigs 2 U.S.—Social life and customs—Colonial period, 1600-1775

ISBN 0-531-01039-2 LC 65-21628

"The text is divided into a section on the historical background for the industry and one on the techniques of manufacture. The illustrations are nicely detailed and quite informative. . . . A glossary of terms and an index are appended." Chicago. Children's Bk Center

681.1 Instruments for measuring time

Gibbons, Gail

Clocks and how they go. Crowell 1979 unp illus $6.95, lib. bdg. $6.89 (2-4) **681.1**

1 Clocks and watches

ISBN 0-690-03973-5; 0-690-03974-3 LC 78-22498

This book explains "what makes things tick—literally. The mechanisms for time-telling are shown, gear by gear, each in its own color. . . . It describes in detail the weight-clock and the spring-clock and covers time from the sundial to the digital readout." Bks of the Times

"Bold, straightforward illustrations in clear bright colors accompany simple explanations. . . . An admirable example of the kind of book that explains for the young reader how mechanical things work; it even tells why some clocks go 'tick-tock' and others go 'tick-tick-tick-tick-tick.'" Horn Bk

Johnson, Chester

What makes a clock tick? Pictures by Nathan Goldstein. Little 1969 73p illus lib. bdg. $4.50 (4 and up) **681.1**

1 Clocks and watches

ISBN 0-316-46738-3 LC 68-28704

"An Atlantic Monthly Press book"

The author describes how clocks work by examining the function of each piece and the regulation necessary for achieving the precise time. Readers are encouraged to try and rebuild a clock

"The mechanical details of spring-wound clocks and watches, and of weight-and-pendulum movement clocks are written very lucidly in a step-by-step sequence. The drawings that accompany the descriptive text are clear. . . . In the final part of the book there are brief descriptions of electrically-driven clocks and watches, including the timekeeper of ultimate precision, the cesium atomic clock. . . . The book should have excellent reception in all schools and particularly vocational schools." Sci Bks

Index and glossary: p67-73

682 Blacksmithing

Fisher, Leonard Everett

The blacksmiths; written & illus. by Leonard Everett Fisher. Watts, F. 1976 47p illus (Colonial American craftsmen) lib. bdg. $4.90 (4 and up) **682**

1 Blacksmithing 2 U.S.—Social life and customs—Colonial period, 1600-1775

ISBN 0-531-02901-8 LC 75-26684

Fisher, Leonard E.—*Continued*

"Black and white scratchboard illustrations show tools, processes, and techniques of the colonial smithy; the text is divided . . . into a section that gives historical background about the role of the smith in the colonies, and a somewhat longer section that describes the equipment, procedures, and products of the blacksmith's forge." Chicago. Children's Bk Center

"Explaining the techniques and products (e.g., iron fences, door latches) of this craftsman, this succeeds in providing an accurate account both in a well-written text and [the author's] distinctive full-page illustrations. A glossary of blacksmith's terms is included at the end of the book." Sch Library J

684   Woodworking

Adkins, Jan

Toolchest; written, designed, and illus. by Jan Adkins; carpenter in residence, Joseph Karson. Walker & Co. 1973 48p illus $6.95, lib. bdg. $6.85 (5 and up)   684

1 Carpentry—Tools 2 Woodwork
ISBN 0-8027-6153-4; 0-8027-6154-2   LC 72-81374

"Meticulously illustrated with drawings that show exact details of tools, hardware, wood grains, and techniques, this is a superb first book for the amateur carpenter. Adkins explains the uses of each tool, the ways in which each variety of saw or chisel is fitted for a particular task, such procedures as dowelling, gluing, or cutting a tenon and mortise, and he describes the uses for each kind of nail and screw. This most useful book concludes with advice on the care of tools. A fine piece of craftsmanship, both in example and in execution." Chicago. Children's Bk Center

Lasson, Robert

If I had a hammer; woodworking with seven basic tools; photographs by Jeff Murphy. Dutton 1974 76p illus lib. bdg. $8.95 (4 and up)   684

1 Woodwork 2 Tools
ISBN 0-525-32532-8   LC 74-6457

"The book is divided into two parts. The first is concerned with tools and techniques. Seven tools are described—hammer, try square, saw, C-clamp, tape measure, drill and Surform plane. . . . The second part of the book describes six projects using the tools. They range from a potholder hanger (a short plank of wood with a few screws in it) up to a hanging planter, a carrying box, a pet bed. These are the simplest constructions, basically variations of box forms." NY Times Bk Rev

"An easy introduction to carpentry that could substitute, if necessary, for what a child should have shown to him by an older person working alongside. Large black-and-white photographs clarify each stage of instruction . . . which are sound and simple enough for independent completion by a child capable of reading the text. General tips on handling tools and wood emphasize careful, clean workmanship." Booklist

Torre, Frank D.

Woodworking for kids. Doubleday 1978 132p illus $6.95, lib. bdg. $7.90 (5 and up)   684

1 Woodwork
ISBN 0-385-11430-3; 0-385-11431-1   LC 77-76264

"Initial chapters which describe tools and their uses as well as woods and their finishes, are followed by instructions for sixteen woodworking projects. Simple projects—a slicing board, calendar, bracelet, and shelf—are included with others more complicated in design and construction, such as a checkerboard or a birdhouse. Step-by-step directions are numbered, and each project is accompanied by several photographs showing the stages of production." Horn Bk

"Basic building skills are clearly demonstrated and explored. . . . Although many projects may require adult assistance, most children will find working with wood and real tools an exciting challenge." Babbling Bookworm

684.1   Furniture

Fisher, Leonard Everett

The cabinetmakers; written & illus. by Leonard Everett Fisher. Watts, F. 1966 47p illus (Colonial Americans) lib. bdg. $4.90 (4 and up)   684.1

1 Cabinet work 2 Furniture, American 3 U.S.—Social life and customs—Colonial period, 1600-1775
ISBN 0-531-01026-0   LC 66-10580

The author explains that colonial American furniture is a reflection of the social life of the times and of the history of the craftsmen who designed it. He also discusses how cabinetmakers worked, what tools they used, and what skills were employed to bring about the final product

"Partly because Mr. Fisher's distinctive illustrative style lends itself well to the graining of wood, the pictures seem unusually handsome. [Includes] two pages of photographs of colonial furniture." Chicago. Children's Bk Center

685   Leather and fur goods, and related manufactures

Fisher, Leonard Everett

The shoemakers; written & illus. by Leonard Everett Fisher. Watts, F. 1967 44p illus (Colonial Americans) lib. bdg. $5.90 (4 and up)   685

1 Shoes and shoe industry 2 U.S.—Social life and customs—Colonial period, 1600-1775
ISBN 0-531-01035-X   LC 67-10296

In the New World, the demand for footwear was immense, and shoemaking early became a flourishing business. Here, the author tells the history of the American shoemakers and gives an account of how they went about their work

"Written in a "lucid, graphic manner. . . . A glossary of terms is included and the book is illustrated with carefully drawn, detailed pictures on every other page." Booklist

Hirsch, S .Carl

Stilts; illus. by Betty Fraser. Viking 1972 41p illus lib. bdg. $4.75 (4 and up)   685

1 Stilts
ISBN 0-670-67053-7   LC 72-80512

"With a very interesting approach, this book treats a specific topic—stilts—from historical, utilitarian, literary, and other points of view. The author avoids a pedantic structure and sequence, dealing with the various facets in a refreshing but sometimes confusing eclectic way. The book is well-written, engagingly illustrated, and contains good suggestions for activities." Appraisal

686   Book arts

Purdy, Susan

Books for you to make; written and illus. by Susan Purdy. Lippincott 1973 96p illus lib. bdg. $8.79 (4 and up)   686

1 Books 2 Bookbinding
ISBN 0-397-31318-7   LC 73-4568

"While directing readers through the construction of their own books, Purdy introduces bookbinding vocabulary and, briefly, concepts of book design, layout, and illustration. A lengthy section on preparing bindings includes instructions for a multi-signature, full-bound book as well as examples of various simpler approaches to binding. The shift in final chapters to exploring professionally printed books becomes an easy step for readers who have busily put together their homemade versions; here the author's illustrated explanations of letter-press versus offset printing, camera and color separation, and the assemblage of printed pages allows readers a functional glimpse behind the scenes of book-making." Booklist

Weiss, Harvey

How to make your own books; illus. with photographs and drawings. Crowell 1974 71p illus lib. bdg. $8.95 (4 and up)   686

1 Books 2 Bookbinding
ISBN 0-690-00400-1   LC 73-17267

The author "deals first with practical matters: choosing papers, cutting, folding, binding techniques (sewing, stapling, or glueing), and attaching covers. Creating marbleized paper is one of the fascinating how-to's described and made to seem achievable by the amateur. Suggestions of kinds of books to make fill the second half of the volume, ranging from travel journals, albums, and scrapbooks to experimental books, and books of sketches, prints, or rubbings (the last not only from stone or metal but from frozen fish, tree bark, or driftwood)." Horn Bk

"In a clear, conversational style, Harvey Weiss shares his love of all kinds of personal books and his extensive knowledge of how to create them. . . . Photographs of books Mr. Weiss has done for his own pleasure abound with designing hints, and his step-by-step drawings and instructions are perfect." Children's Bk Rev Serv

686.2   Printing

Barker, Albert

Black on white and read all over; the story of printing; illus. by Anthony D'Adamo and with photographs. Messner 1971 96p illus lib. bdg. $5.79 (4-6)   686.2

1 Printing—History
ISBN 0-671-32394-6   LC 77-141835

"The text traces the history and development of papermaking from its beginnings in China and then carries along with the history of printing up to modern times, with some speculation on the future of printing. The final chapter outlines the various steps in the writing and publishing of a typical book. The various forms of printing—woodblock, letterpress, lithography, photo-offset, and photo-gravure—are explained. . . . In general the book is readable and has good continuity. The illustrations are good and add to the enjoyment of the reader. The glossary and index are good and add to the value of the book for collateral reading and reference." Sci Bks

Berger, Melvin

Printing plant. Watts, F. 1978 66p illus (Industry at work) lib. bdg. $4.90 (4 and up)   686.2

1 Printing
ISBN 0-531-02207-2   LC 78-2529

"Step-by-step processes are clearly defined and explained as the author follows the preparation and printing of books, magazines, and newspapers. Descriptions of the front office work, composing room, platemaking, makeup, paste-up, stripping, pressroom, and bindery are combined with information about the jobs of the people who work there and supplemented by on-site black-and-white photographs. The revolutionary changes within the industry are reflected in the discussion of the use of computers, laser beams, and complex, specially designed cameras." Booklist

"The writing style . . . is simple and concise; the format, well designed for young readers; and the information, especially suitable for school career-awareness programs." Sch Library J
Further reading: p62-63

Epstein, Sam

The first book of printing, by Sam and Beryl Epstein. Rev. ed. Watts, F. 1975 66p illus lib. bdg. $4.90 (5 and up)   686.2

1 Printing
ISBN 0-531-00796-0   LC 72-2294

First published 1955
Illustrated with prints and black and white photographs this book traces the history of printing from the invention of moveable type to modern presses. The authors stress the importance of the print medium in contemporary communication

Fisher, Leonard Everett

The printers; written & illus. by Leonard Everett Fisher. Watts, F. 1965 46p illus (Colonial Americans) lib. bdg. $4.90 (4 and up)   686.2

1 Printing—History 2 U.S.—Social life and customs—Colonial period, 1600-1775
ISBN 0-531-01033-3   LC 65-12774

The first part of the text describes the role of the printer-publishers; the second part describes the presses that they used, the making of type-characters, and the procedures of the printing process." Chicago. Children's Bk Center

"Full-page (some double-page) illustrations show accurately and clearly the main details of the equipment and how the printers used it. Pages of early colonial newsletters and books are legibly reproduced." Sch Library J
Printers' terms: p42-43. Some Colonial American printers: p45

688   Other final products

Maginley, C. J.

Historic models of early America, and how to make them; illus. with numerous diagrams, by James MacDonald. Harcourt 1947 xx, 156p illus $5.95, pa 60¢ (6 and up)   688

1 Models and model making 2 Machinery—Models
ISBN 0-15-234689-9; 0-15-640371-4   LC 47-11432

This book includes "exact specifications, working diagrams, and clear instructions for making Early American models grouped in four categories: transportation, farms, homes, and villages. Especially useful for history projects." Hodges. Bks for Elem Sch Libraries

An historical sketch proceeds each of the models which range in difficulty from a log canoe to the first Ford

"A really challenging book for a young carpenter. Inexpensive tools and materials are easily obtained." Pub W

Models of America's past, and how to make them; illus. by Elisabeth D. McKee. Harcourt 1969 144p illus $6.25 (6 and up)   688

1 Models and model making
ISBN 0-15-255051-8   LC 69-17116

"This book contains precise directions for building simple wooden models of household furniture, school and meetinghouse buildings and equipment, barns, bridges, wagons, and other objects in common use during the seventeenth, eighteenth, and nineteenth centuries. Advice on specific details of modelmaking and lists of the necessary tools and supplies are given in the introduction, and the step-by-step instructions for making each model are supplemented by explanatory diagrams and drawings and preceded by a thumbnail historical sketch of each object. An excellent and practical craft book for home or school use." Booklist

688.6   Nonmotor land vehicles

Gould, Marilyn

Skateboards, scooterboards & seatboards you can make [by] Marilyn Gould & George Gould; drawings by Loring Eutemey; photographs by Lou Jacobs, Jr. Lothrop 1977 75p illus $7.25, lib. bdg. $6.96 (3-6)   688.6

1 Skateboards 2 Scooters
ISBN 0-688-41794-9; 0-688-51794-3   LC 76-52929

This book gives directions for building skateboards, scooterboards, and seatboards, and information on how to ride them
Glossary: p70-71

Maginley, C. J.

Make it and ride it; diagrams by Elisabeth D. McKee. Harcourt 1949 120p illus $5.95 (4 and up)   688.6

1 Vehicles 2 Toys 3 Woodwork
ISBN 0-15-251336-1   LC 49-11081

Maginley, C. J.—*Continued*

"Careful directions and clear diagrams for making an intriguing collection of toys to ride will insure this book a hearty welcome. . . . There are 18 projects of varying difficulty, including models of racers for the famous Soap Box Derby. Most of the projects, however, are not the simplest and would require some experience." Library J

Some of the projects included are: wagons, bike trailers, scooters, jeeps, toys for younger children. Hand tools and scrap materials can be used for most of the projects

Stevenson, Peter

The Buffy-Porson; a car you can build and drive, by Peter and Mike Stevenson. Scribner 1973 63p illus $6.95 (4-6)   **688.6**

1 Coaster cars
ISBN 0-684-13436-5   LC 73-1363

"Clear, sensible directions and a straightforward, informal style characterize an inviting do-it-yourself book produced by a father-and-young son partnership. The Buffy-Porson, 'a small racer of great spirit,' can be constructed with ordinary household tools; but, the young enthusiast is told, 'One building aid that you "will" need once in a while is an Older Person to lend a hand.' Attractive photographs and businesslike diagrams illustrate the proceedings from the very beginning to the point where 'the car stops being a project and starts being a sporting proposition.' Some good lumber and hardware are essential to build a sturdy car and to finish it off with a few stylish accessories; the appendix lists the precise sizes and quantities of the necessary materials." Horn Bk

688.7 Recreational equipment

Glubok, Shirley

Dolls, dolls, dolls; special photography by Alfred Tamarin; designed by Gerard Nook. Follett 1975 64p illus $5.95, lib. bdg. $5.97 (3-6)   **688.7**

1 Dolls
ISBN 0-695-80483-9; 0-695-40483-0   LC 73-93559

"Black-and-white photographs and clear, concise text trace the history of dolls from ancient Greece to modern times. This is their story and includes early carved wooden dolls, stylish fashion dolls, clever mechanical dolls, and celebrity dolls such as Shirley Temple and Mickey Mouse. A special section includes dollhouses and some distinctive Oriental, American Indian, and African samples. Anyone who has ever loved a doll will love this book!" Babbling Bookworm

690 Buildings

Berger, Melvin

Building construction. Watts, F. 1978 66p illus (Industry at work) lib. bdg. $4.90 (4 and up)   **690**

1 Building
ISBN 0-531-02206-4   LC 78-6258

"Berger discusses the various work involved in building homes, factories, and skyscrapers. In logistical progression, the jobs of the planners (architects, engineers), structural workers (excavators, carpenters), finishing crews (roofers, masons), and mechanical workers (plumbers, electricians) are described and related to one another with attention given to the skills necessary for these jobs." Booklist
Further reading: p62-63

Harman, Carter

Skyscraper goes up; illus. with photographs. Random House 1973 137p illus lib. bdg. $5.99 (5 and up)   **690**

1 Skyscrapers 2 Building
ISBN 0-394-92147-X   LC 72-11059

The author follows the whole process of planning and building one skyscraper—the Exxon Building in New York City. He covers such topics as: selecting a site, architectural planning, building a steel superstructure, and operating the finished building

"The text does not go much beyond the single tower, its parking and supplies, but within those limits it is a most readable and informative narrative. Costs are treated sketchily. . . . Floor plans, block maps, sections, elevator schemes and a good set of photographs made over a period of time add to the verisimilitude of this witness's account." Sci Am

Sobol, Harriet Langsam

Pete's house; photographs by Patricia Agre. Macmillan Pub. Co. 1978 58p illus $7.95 (3-5)   **690**

1 Building 2 Houses
ISBN 0-02-785980-0   LC 77-12564

"Pete's father takes him along to watch the family's new house being built, and he's fascinated by the craftsmen who contribute their know-how to the building's construction. Black-and-white photographs record the work of masons, carpenters, plumbers, siding men, tapers, and others who, step by step, push the house toward completion. The simple narrative text personalizes key workers and explains their special activities. The construction pace is ideally steady from the time masons lay the foundation to the excitement as painters finish the rooms—Pete's grin on the final page where the finished product sits on display behind him is understandable. The information is sound, the lesson interesting." Booklist

Stiles, David

The tree house book; designs & illus. by the author. Avon 1979 74p illus pa spiral binding $3.95 (6 and up)   **690**

1 Tree-dwellings
ISBN 0-380-43133-5   LC 78-65887

"Clear instructions on how to build an inventive, practical, sturdy, and safe haven in the branches. How to choose a site, where to secure wood, what tools are needed, and safety procedures in all facets of building are detailed. Free form and planned constructions are explained and basic designs utilizing one to four trees are described and illustrated. A miscellaneous section offers finer touches, e.g., crow's nests, furniture, perspective drawing models, and rope bridges. The spiral notebook format allows [the book] to be hung for easy reference while building. The rough brown paper, engineering lettering, and excellent line drawings (showing clear perspectives) carry out the artistic and professional tone. An original, considerate, thoroughly trustworthy guide." Sch Library J

Walker, Les

Housebuilding for children; written, photographed and illus. by Les Walker; preface by Nonny Hogrogian. Overlook Press 1977 174p illus $10 (2 and up)   **690**

1 Building 2 Houses
ISBN 0-87951-059-5   LC 76-47220

"This book is written for young people who want to build houses just as older people do. I designed six small houses that would educate children in the different 'real-life' ways of building houses." Introduction

"An enthusiastically written and clearly illustrated guide. Preparatory projects are included to help children learn the use of basic tools and methods. The six houses—including a tree house—were all built by children from seven to nine, supervised by an adult. Full-page photographs of the young builders and of houses under construction appear on nearly every other page, adjacent to drawings of materials and the step-by-step procedures. An appendix lists other books and gives the addresses of tool companies." Horn Bk

Weiss, Harvey

Model buildings and how to make them; illus. with photos and drawings by the author. Crowell 1979 95p illus $7.95 (4 and up)   **690**

1 Buildings—Models
ISBN 0-690-01341-8   LC 77-26597

"Divided into two sections, building from cardboard and building from wood, the text . . . leads hobbyists into the proper techniques, complete with tool requirements and procedures for measuring, cutting, bending, scoring, gluing, and planning to scale. Directions for constructing basic houses, elaborate castles, and usable dollhouses include details for finishing porches, chimneys, turrets, windows, and doors." Booklist

Weiss, Harvey—*Continued*

"An excellent introduction to an intriguing hobby. . . . Thoughtfully presented and logically designed, the volume should be useful for hobbyists as well as for the more casual reader whose curiosity has been piqued by the current interest in model building as an art form and as a means of re-creating the past." Horn Bk

693   Construction in specific materials and for specific purposes

Zubrowski, Bernie

Milk carton blocks; illus. by Otto Coontz. Little 1979 62p illus $6.95, pa $3.95 (3-5)   **693**

1 Building   2 Handicraft
ISBN 0-316-98884-7; 0-316-98885-5   LC 78-27215

"A Children's Museum activity book"

The book "employs the principles of physics and engineering in the building of arches, beams, doorways, and windows to make houses and other structures. Directions for making the blocks from squared-off milk cartons filled with sand are included. The text explains how different modes of construction using bricks were employed by various peoples in history." Horn Bk

"Questions and suggested experiments encourage children to learn through observation. While the questions are thought-provoking, they are not expanded upon in the text; no answers are given and there is no follow-up discussion. Because of this, the book would be best used with adult guidance." Sch Library J

696   Utilities

Zim, Herbert S.

Pipes and plumbing systems, by Herbert S. Zim and James R. Skelly; illus. with drawings by Lee J. Ames and Mel Erikson. Morrow 1974 63p illus $6.25, lib. bdg. $6, pa $1.25 (3-6)   **696**

1 Plumbing
ISBN 0-688-20101-6; 0-688-30101-0; 0-688-25101-3
           LC 73-14589

This overview "covers water, sewer, and gas pipes and home heating systems. The authors then describe plumbing uses in industry; the history of plumbing: the manufacture and use of various valves, pipes, and pumps; the training procedure for plumbers and pipe fitters; and the jobs of inspectors, engineers, apprentices, journeymen, and master plumbers. The line illustrations of pipes, fittings, systems, and pumps are meticulously accurate." Sch Library J

700   THE ARTS

701   The arts—Philosophy and theory

Chase, Alice Elizabeth

Looking at art. Crowell 1966 119p illus $8.95 (5 and up)   **701**

1 Art   2 Painting   3 Art appreciation
ISBN 0-690-50869-7   LC 66-11947

"This book will deal chiefly with paintings, although some sculptures and prints will be included." p3

The author has taken several aspects of the artist's craft and shown how each has been used in widely differing times and cultures. There are chapters on perspective, the human figure, landscape, and composition

"Profusely illustrated with reproductions of works of art and with illuminating diagrams, this is a fine introduction to artistic interpretation. . . . Miss Chase, who is authoritative, sensible, and lucid, draws upon a wide range of sources and periods." Sat Rev

Grigson, Geoffrey

Shapes and stories; a book about pictures, by Geoffrey and Jane Grigson. Vanguard [1965 c1964] 65p illus $7.95 (5 and up)   **701**

1 Art   2 Art appreciation
ISBN 0-8149-0311-8   LC 65-25262

First published 1964 in England

This book "deals with the content of a selected group of pictures, rather than being a history of art or giving biographical information about the artists. The collection of art (largely European) begins with 'Adam naming the beasts' by William Blake, proceeds to individual animals, real or imaginary, then to landscapes and architectural subjects. . . . The authors' comments about the pictures and about the artists' intent and craft are well chosen and exciting. . . . Pen, pencil drawings, oils, woodcuts, tapestries, watercolours are represented. . . . The outsize format permits the illustrations (both black and white and in colour) to be large." Toronto

702.8   Art—Techniques

Marks, Mickey Klar

Op-tricks; creating kinetic art; kinetics by Edith Alberts; photographed by David Rosenfeld. Lippincott 1972 unp illus $7.89   **702.8**

1 Kinetic art
ISBN 0-397-31539-2   LC 79-38550

"A brief introduction defining kinetic or 'op art' and its significance in relation to the contemporary scene is followed by a series of suggested projects to stimulate the beginner to explore an exciting area of creative expression. The step-by-step instructions for each project are preceded by a list of materials needed, many of which are part of the everyday equipment of most households. Black-and-white photographic close-ups of construction details, correlating with the directions, plus views of the completed projects extend and clarify the instructions." Horn Bk

"Although the art projects shown present only an opportunity for copying, the techniques used can be adapted for other, original work by the reader. . . . The explanations are clear, the projects not too complicated, the results—as shown in photographs—intriguing." Chicago. Children's Bk Center

708   Galleries and museums

Weisgard, Leonard

Treasures to see; a museum picture-book. Harcourt 1956 unp illus $6.95 (1-4)   **708**

1 Art—Galleries and museums
ISBN 0-15-290337-2   LC 56-10739

"The author explains the purpose of an art museum, its main divisions, and the type of things each contains." Sch Arts

"Excellent drawings. . . . The illustrations are representations of the kinds of things to be found in a museum rather than actual reproductions of works of art. The book should serve a useful purpose in cities where children have access to a museum." Chicago. Children's Bk Center

709   Art—History

Batterberry, Ariane Ruskin

The Pantheon Story of art for young people. A rev. up-to-date ed. Pantheon Bks. 1975 157p illus $12.95 (5 and up)   **709**

1 Art—History
ISBN 0-394-83107-1   LC 74-24717

First published 1964. Author's name appeared as Ariane Ruskin

A history of art from cave painting to Pop Art, illustrated with reproductions in color and black-and-white. The final chapter briefly discusses non-Western art

Batterberry, Ariane R.—*Continued*

"This oversize book is profusely illustrated with reproductions of excellent quality, many in full color. The writing style is simple and informal, the information given with authoritative knowledge; the author discusses details of pictures as well as giving general facts about artists, trends in art history, and the cultural matrices out of which artists or trends emerged. . . . There is no index." Chicago. Children's Bk Center

709.01 Arts of nonliterate peoples and ancient times

Baylor, Byrd

Before you came this way; illus. by Tom Bahti. Dutton 1969 unp illus lib. bdg. $7.95 (1-4)   **709.01**

1 Indians of North America—Art 2 Cave drawings
ISBN 0-525-26312-8   LC 74-81709

"A handsome book, thought-provoking and written with lyric simplicity; the illustrations, on handmade bark paper, are in the style of the prehistoric rock pictures on which the book is based. Walking in the quiet of a canyon in the Southwest, you wonder if you are the first to pass this way . . . then you see that some brother, long-dead, has made a record of his people and their lives: the animals they hunted, the battles and the feasts, the masks of the dancers. The writing style is sensitively attuned to the dignity and mystery of the subject." Sutherland. The Best in Children's Bks

Glubok, Shirley

The art of ancient Mexico; designed by Gerard Nook; special photography by Alfred H. Tamarin. Harper 1968 41p illus lib. bdg. $7.89 (4 and up)   **709.01**

1 Indians of Mexico—Art 2 Mexico—Antiquities
ISBN 0-06-022034-1   LC 68-14921

This book covers the Indian cultures—such as Aztec, Mixtec, Toltec, Olmec, Zapotec—that flourished in Mexico before the Spanish conquest. The author examines these peoples through their art and introduces the reader to Mexico's past. Temples, religious objects, jewelry, weapons and painted books are shown

"Religious and secular art in stone, clay, and metal introduce the Aztec and pre-Aztec world. Fierce gods and warriors abound in photos surging with the spirit of a bellicose and bloodthirsty people; a lighter touch prevails in artifacts depicting the common man at work or play. Heroic and mythical creatures adorn the few examples of architecture." Library J

"The objects are either curious or beautiful enough to provide a varied and interesting picture of the intricacy and craftsmanship of several cultures, although the text is rather choppy." Sat Rev

The art of the North American Indian; designed by Oscar Krauss. Harper 1964 unp illus lib. bdg. $8.79 (4 and up)   **709.01**

1 Indians of North America—Art 2 Indians of North America—Social life and customs
ISBN 0-06-022066-X   LC 64-11829

An "introduction to North American Indian art. . . . Carved masks, baskets, totem poles, wampum, Kachina dolls, pottery, and sand painting are among the examples of Indian art shown in photographs and briefly described as to material, design, and use." Booklist

"A most handsome book, with photographs of varied and beautiful objects in a format of dignified simplicity. The text is clear and direct." Chicago. Children's Bk Center

The art of the Northwest coast Indians; designed by Gerard Nook. Macmillan Pub. Co. 1975 48p illus $7.95 (4 and up)   **709.01**

1 Indians of North America—Art 2 Indians of North America—Northwest, Pacific
ISBN 0-02-736150-0   LC 74-22384

This book concentrates on the crafts of the Indian groups that live along the Pacific coast of the United States and Canada: the Kwakiutl,

Tlingit, Nootka, Haida, Tsimshian, Bella Coola, and Coast Salish. Featured are the decorated totems and house fronts, long canoes, ceremonial masks, feast dishes, baskets, and woven fabrics representative of the artistic heritage of these peoples. Black and white photographs accompany the text

The art of the Plains Indians; designed by Gerard Nook; special photography by Alfred Tamarin. Macmillan Pub. Co. 1975 48p illus $7.95 (4 and up)   **709.01**

1 Indians of North America—Art 2 Indians of North America—Great Plains
ISBN 0-02-736360-0   LC 75-14064

"The author has recreated the Plains Indian culture by focusing on the varied, often intricate, art forms by which these Indians embellished their shelter and clothing and preserved their traditions and history. Descriptions of techniques used in construction and decoration are given as well as explanations indicating the purpose for which each object was made." Horn Bk

"Each illustration carries a label denoting source, and the objects are not only impressive in themselves but give, in conjunction with the text, a great deal of information about the way the tribes lived: what they ate, how they dressed, how they worshipped. Glubok also gives, simply and sympathetically, some of the sad history of the relationships between the Plains Indians and white settlers." Chicago. Children's Bk Center

The art of the Southeastern Indians; designed by Gerard Nook; special photography by Alfred Tamarin. Macmillan Pub. Co. 1978 48p illus $8.95 (4 and up)   **709.01**

1 Indians of North America—Art 2 Indians of North America—Southern States
ISBN 0-02-736480-1   LC 77-20850

"Artifacts from largely prehistoric times graphically illustrate cultural aspects of various southeastern tribal cultures, 'different in many ways but alike in others.' Glubok's commentary describes and explains in a general sense, introducing names and facts and rendering occasional artistic judgments." Booklist

"This is excellent in its assembling of information, covering a wealth of topics from lifestyle to aesthetics, from earliest times to modern days. Photographs, paintings, and reprinted etchings complement and expand the well-written text." Sch Library J

The art of the Southwest Indians; photographs by Alfred Tamarin; designed by Gerard Nook. Macmillan Pub. Co. 1971 48p illus $7.95 (4 and up)   **709.01**

1 Indians of North America—Art 2 Indians of North America—Southwest, New
ISBN 0-02-736120-9   LC 78-133558

"Information about some aspects of tribal cultures is woven into discussions of the works of art of the Apache, Navajo, and Pueblo peoples. The photographs of rock carvings and paintings, pottery and basketwork, weaving, carving, jewelry, sand paintings, ceremonial robes and masks, and kachina dolls are accompanied by an informative . . . text. The large print and dignified design of the pages add to the attractiveness of a useful book." Chicago. Children's Bk Center

The art of the Woodland Indians; designed by Gerard Nook; special photography by Alfred Tamarin. Macmillan Pub. Co. 1976 48p illus $7.95 (4 and up)   **709.01**

1 Woodland Indians—Art
ISBN 0-02-736440-2   LC 76-12434

"Northeast Woodland Indian artifacts are photographed and simply described. . . . Information on individual cultures is woven through the narrative: the time-span is wide, ranging from Adena artifacts of 2,500 years ago to contemporary pieces, but here again craftsmanship is what speaks the loudest." Booklist

Hofsinde, Robert

Indian arts; written and illus. by Robert Hofsinde (Gray-Wolf). Morrow 1971 95p illus lib. bdg. $6 (4-6)   **709.01**

1 Indians of North America—Art
ISBN 0-688-31617-4   LC 73-137100

Hofsinde, Robert—Continued

"This account explains the materials and techniques used by different American Indian tribes in the creation of artistic works for decorative, religious, and practical purposes. A final chapter discusses current interest in Indian arts and the types of artwork being produced today. Well illustrated with many black-and-white drawings." Booklist

Price, Christine

Made in the South Pacific; arts of the sea people; illus. with photographs and drawings. Dutton 1979 134p illus map $11.95 (6 and up) **709.01**

1 Art, Oceanian 2 Islands of the Pacific
ISBN 0-525-34397-0   LC 78-12807

An "account of the artistic skills and accomplishments of the peoples of the South Pacific. Beginning with a chapter on seafaring canoes, the author first indicates how ancient migrants were able to settle scattered islands ranging from New Guinea and New Zealand to Micronesia and the Hawaiian Islands. In separate sections on the use of such materials as clay, wood, stone, fiber, and shell, she discusses the techniques employed in making and decorating traditional artifacts and explains their ritualistic significance in relationship to such activities as warfare, festive dancing, and tattooing. Mention is occasionally made of the influence of the white man on South Pacific life and crafts, and the book ends with a chapter on the development of contemporary painters and artists." Horn Bk

"For the most part the black-and-white photographs which make up a large part of the book are helpful in clarifying the text." Sch Library J

709.02 Art—History, 500-1499

Glubok, Shirley

The art of the Vikings; designed by Gerard Nook. Macmillan Pub. Co. 1978 48p illus $8.95 (4 and up) **709.02**

1 Art, Viking 2 Vikings
ISBN 0-02-736460-7   LC 78-6849

"A brief overview of Scandinavian art covering the period from 800 to 1500 A.D., when Viking trade and exploration flourished. The Vikings did not create works of art for their beauty alone, but were superb craftsmen who ornamented everyday objects. Through black-and-white photographs and a simple text, the author shows the scope of Norse art with examples ranging from primitive fertility figures to intricately carved ships, inlaid jewelry, and weapons. The mythology of the Vikings, an integral part of their art, is interwoven with descriptions of the artifacts." Horn Bk

709.04 Art—History, 20th century

MacAgy, Douglas

Going for a walk with a line; a step into the world of modern art, by Douglas and Elizabeth MacAgy. Doubleday [1973 c1959] unp illus pa $1.95 (3 and up) **709.04**

1 Art, Modern—20th century
ISBN 0-385-05246-4

"A Zephyr book"
First published 1959
The authors "take the child on a guided tour of pictures done by artists with a fresh viewpoint, the infinite variety of the line pointing the way for aesthetic experience ranging from Henri Rousseau on the first page to Paul Klee on the last." Library J

Forty-three "examples of contemporary masterpieces are reproduced here, in full color and in black and white, and linked together by brief, poetic text. . . . It is designed with a balance of educational and artistic experience in interpreting a child's way of thinking and seeing." Horn Bk

709.37 Roman and Etruscan art

Glubok, Shirley

The art of ancient Rome; designed by Oscar Krauss. Harper 1965 40p illus lib. bdg. $8.79 (4 and up) **709.37**

1 Art, Roman 2 Rome—Civilization
ISBN 0-06-022046-5   LC 65-11449

"Young readers are introduced to the classic art of ancient Rome through a clear description of Roman mosaics and murals, portraits and statuary, monuments and buildings. Heroes, games, warfare, school and family life, and worship are represented." Wis Library Bul

"Illustrated with photographs. Those familiar with the author's preceding studies . . . can visualize the makeup of this companion with its superb reproductions of art." Horn Bk

The art of the Etruscans; designed by Gerard Nook; special photography by Alfred H. Tamarin. Harper 1967 40p illus lib. bdg. $8.79 (4 and up) **709.37**

1 Art, Etruscan
ISBN 0-06-022058-9   LC 67-14066

This book "covers the known aspects of the Etruscans and their art; speculation as to their origins, connections with Greece, tomb wall-paintings, urns—works in terra-cotta, bronze, and gold granulation." Christian Sci Monitor

The author "respects her readers by not writing down to them as she identifies fact, myth, and legend. . . . Of superior quality are the graphic designs . . . including aesthetic placement of color and text with the clearly defined photographs." Library J

709.51 Chinese art

Glubok, Shirley

The art of China; designed by Gerard Nook. Macmillan Pub. Co. 1973 48p illus $6.95 (4 and up) **709.51**

1 Art, Chinese
ISBN 0-02-736170-5   LC 72-81059

"The text—by meandering in and out of Chinese history, customs, culture, and religion—helps the reader develop an awareness of the variety and excellence of Chinese art. Touching briefly on the various forms of art—bronze ceremonial vessels, pottery, scroll paintings, calligraphy, religious statues, and temples—the book also explains some of the ancient Chinese inventions—porcelain, silk, and lacquer—which made various new art forms possible." Horn Bk

"Designed with discrimination, the book is . . . both handsome and informative, and it should lead readers to further examination of Chinese art." Chicago. Children's Bk Center

709.52 Japanese art

Glubok, Shirley

The art of Japan; designed by Gerard Nook; special photography by Alfred Tamarin. Macmillan Pub. Co. 1970 48p illus $5.95 (4 and up) **709.52**

1 Art, Japanese
ISBN 0-02-736080-6   LC 75-89584

The author shows how the artistic heritage reflects the history and culture of a country in this "survey of Japanese art from simple teapots to paintings, temples, and gardens." Children's Bks. 1970

This book "panoramically sets forth . . . highlights of Japan's multitudinous, classical art forms. . . . Glubok's text, light as a calligrapher's brush stroke, is economically explicit and designer Gerald Nook ravishes the eye in his clearcut unfussy presentation. The selection of masterpieces cannot be faulted." NY Times Bk Rev

709.54　Indic art

Glubok, Shirley
The art of India; designed by Gerard Nook; special photography by Alfred H. Tamarin and Carol Guyer. Macmillan Pub. Co. 1969 48p illus $5.95 (4 and up)　709.54

1 Art, Indic
ISBN 0-02-736040-7　　　　LC 72-78087
This book "presents a brief introduction to ancient and traditional sculpture and painting, focusing on art objects which represent the three great religions of India. The reader [also] receives . . . a glimpse of the civilization that produced these extraordinary works." Top of the News
"Since almost all Indian art is religious art, most of the text here is either descriptive of the object or structure shown in a photograph or it is an explanation of the religious background. . . . [The book] is handsome in design, clearly written, and extremely useful, since there is comparatively little material available on Indian art for the elementary level. The illustrations are preponderantly sculpture and the lack of color is no limitation, but the miniatures lose effectiveness in black-and white." Sutherland. The Best in Children's Bks

709.6　African art

Glubok, Shirley
The art of Africa; designed by Gerard Nook; special photography by Alfred H. Tamarin. Harper 1965 48p illus $6.95, lib. bdg. $8.79 (4 and up)　709.6

1 Art, African
ISBN 0-06-022035-X; 0-06-022036-8　LC 65-21016
"A fine presentation of representative examples of art and artifacts of various tribes throughout Africa which is interesting, informative and written at a level which is comprehensible for children. The photographs and format are excellent." Africa
"The art is varied and unusual, often strange to American eyes. Shirley Glubok has chosen [wooden] masks, [bronze and brass] figures, rock paintings, gold weights, carved stools, combs, musical instruments, and other objects to illustrate her book." Pub W

Price, Christine
Made in West Africa; illus. with photographs and drawings. Dutton 1975 150p illus map $9.95 (5 and up)　709.6

1 Art, African
ISBN 0-525-34400-4　　　　LC 74-4202
The author's premise is that the arts of Africa are an integral part of the spiritual and everyday lives of the people. Focusing on West Africa, the book contains some "160 black-and-white photographs that show carvers and weavers at work today, along with . . . [art] objects, both ancient and contemporary. The text is organized by craft: textiles, metalwork, decorated calabashes, pottery, sculpture, and carving." Sch Library J
"One of the most beautiful of Price's series of books about the arts and crafts of various countries or regions, in part because the objects shown are so striking, in part because the book itself is handsome and dignified in layout. The photographs and drawings are of high quality, the text written with grave simplicity and as informative about cultural context as about the art forms it describes and pictures." Chicago. Children's Bk Center

Books for further reading: p147

709.73　American art

Batterberry, Ariane Ruskin
The Pantheon Story of American art for young people [by] Ariane Ruskin Batterberry and Michael Batterberry; introduction by Tom Armstrong. Pantheon Bks. 1976 157p illus $14.95 (5 and up)　709.73

1 Art, American
ISBN 0-394-82842-9
LC 75-22249

A "presentation of the splendors of American art, which begins with the Indians, includes the early settlers, the great portraitists, realistic and romantic schools—and ends with contemporary artists. . . . American art, including a few references to crafts and sculpture, is treated chronologically, with enough background and biographical material to illuminate many aspects of the artists' aims. Although the book is, of necessity, an overview of a vast subject, the authors, nonetheless, make comprehensible the typically American influences that are reflected in the various works of art." Horn Bk
"Using high-quality reproductions and well-written text, the Batterberrys interweave the history of American art with the growth of the U.S. . . . The unfortunate lack of an index relegates this otherwise creditable research work, featuring more than 65 color and nearly 100 black-and-white reproductions, to either browsing or cover-to-cover reading." Booklist

Glubok, Shirley
The art of America from Jackson to Lincoln; designed by Gerard Nook. Macmillan Pub. Co. 1973 48p illus $6.95 (4 and up)　709.73

1 Art, American
ISBN 0-02-736250-7　　　　LC 72-81066
The author "imparts much information about American artists at work up to the time of the Civil War. The illustrations—in black and white with some brown tints—include landscapes, rural and urban scenes, individual and family portraits, and photographs showing architectural styles and interior designs and furnishings. Covering only the period from 1820-1860, this concise history provides interesting supplementary material." Sch Library J

The art of America in the early twentieth century; designed by Gerard Nook. Macmillan Pub. Co. 1974 48p illus $6.95 (4 and up)　709.73

1 Art, American　2 Art, Modern—20th century
ISBN 0-02-736180-2　　　　LC 74-6329
The author surveys American art during the first four decades of the twentieth century. Painting is emphasized, but sculpture, architecture and photography are also considered
"The simple text points out various trends and provides an informative commentary on the artists and their work. . . . The reproductions, none in their original color, are sometimes indistinct, but the presentation still works well as basic introductory material." Booklist

The art of America in the gilded age; designed by Gerard Nook. Macmillan Pub. Co. 1974 48p illus $7.95 (4 and up)　709.73

1 Art, American
ISBN 0-02-736100-4　　　　LC 73-6048

"Continuing the author's series of books on American art, this volume reflects the growing wealth and diversity of life in the years between the Civil War and the twentieth century. In addition to the work of the masters who studied abroad, there are genre paintings, examples of the new medium of photography, Sullivan's auditorium and the lavish homes of financial barons, Tiffany glass, and other media that were examples of art nouveau. The text describes the objects pictured and relates them to the life of the 'Gilded Age.'" Chicago. Children's Bk Center
"The author's well-chosen illustrations are bound to appeal to youngsters: family scenes, children at play, sports events. Reproductions are in black and white, but occasional splashes of color brighten the pages." Christian Sci Monitor

The art of America since World War II; designed by Gerard Nook. Macmillan Pub. Co. 1976 47p illus $7.95 (4 and up)　709.73

1 Art, American　2 Art, Modern—20th century
ISBN 0-02-736310-4　　　　LC 74-34453

"Pop art, op art, combines, stabiles, and surrealism are among the intriguing modern art techniques explored in [this book]. . . . Large black-and-white illustrations of works by Jackson Pollock, Andy Warhol, Claes Oldenberg and other well-known contemporary artists [are] coupled with clear, concise explanations." Babbling Bookworm

Glubok, Shirley—*Continued*

The art of colonial America; designed by Gerard Nook. Macmillan Pub. Co. 1970 48p illus $7.95 (4 and up)   709.73

1 Art, American
ISBN 0-02-736070-9   LC 77-102964

This "book shows the development of American arts and crafts from their primitive beginnings in the 1600's to their coming of age in 1776. Growing freedom, affluence and sophistication are reflected in such objects as silver, glass, pottery, needlework, furniture, architecture, and painting. ... Excellent black-and-white photographs illustrate the simple, factual text, which, however, is rather stilted in its museum-catalog style. ... This will be helpful for elementary study of colonial history as well as of American arts and crafts." Sch Library J

The art of the new American nation; designed by Gerard Nook. Macmillan Pub. Co. 1972 48p illus $7.95 (4 and up)   709.73

1 Art, American
ISBN 0-02-736140-3   LC 76-160073

A presentation of American art from 1776 to 1826. Among the forms highlighted are portraits of America's heroes by Gilbert Stuart and Mather Brown; canvases of Revolutionary battles by John Trumbull; and paintings by Samuel F. B. Morse and Robert Fulton—artists as well as inventors. Included also are public and private buildings, furniture, and silver

"Illustrated with photographs and reproductions. ... The photographs are excellent, although a few color plates might have added a new dimension; the brief text is competent if unexciting, perhaps because so slim a volume can only suggest rather than explore so large a topic. A functional compilation." Horn Bk

The art of the Spanish in the United States and Puerto Rico; designed by Gerard Nook; photographs by Alfred Tamarin. Macmillan Pub. Co. 1972 48p illus $7.95 (4 and up)   709.73

1 Art, Latin American
ISBN 0-02-736130-6   LC 75-185218

An examination of the Spanish contribution to art and architecture in Florida, Texas, New Mexico, Colorado, Arizona, California and Puerto Rico, including homes, churches, forts, furniture, tinware, weaving and embroidery

"In the readable style and attractive format of Glubok's other titles, this provides an overview of the rich Spanish influence on art and architecture. ... Of particular interest are the 'santos,' small carved and painted statues representing characters from legends and Bible stories. Brief summaries of these stories add interest to the book which will increase reader understanding and awareness of Spanish art heritage." Sch Library J

709.98 Eskimo art

Glubok, Shirley

The art of the Eskimo; designed by Oscar Krauss; special photography by Alfred H. Tamarin. Harper 1964 48p illus lib. bdg. $8.79 (4 and up)   709.98

1 Eskimos—Art 2 Eskimos—Social life and customs
ISBN 0-06-022056-2   LC 64-16637

This introduction to Eskimo art shows masks, ivory carving, soapstone carving, dolls, decorative pipes, recent graphic arts, and other arts and crafts, covering a span of more than a thousand years

"Once again an excellent selection of museum pieces is displayed in handsome photographs—many set on colored pages—to awaken interest in another culture. ... Partly because so many Eskimo groups are represented, the text suffers from oversimplification and lack of unity." Horn Bk

711 Area planning

Macaulay, David

City; a story of Roman planning and construction. Houghton 1974 112p illus $9.95 (4 and up)   711

1 City planning—Rome 2 Civil engineering 3 Architecture, Roman
ISBN 0-395-19492-X   LC 74-4280

"By following the inception, construction, and development of an imaginary Roman city, the account traces the evolution of Verbonia from the selection of its site under religious auspices in 26 B.C. to its completion in 100 A.D. A military camp set up by soldiers and slaves becomes the basis for an expanding community, which—in the course of its growth—builds roads, a bridge, walls, water and sewage systems, a marketplace, and a religious and civic center, as well as areas for relaxation and entertainment." Horn Bk

"Like his impressive 'Cathedral,' a Caldecott Honor Book of 1973, [entered in class 726] Macaulay's 'City' is large in concept as well as in size, profusely illustrated with fascinatingly detailed drawings, and written with clarity and authority. ... Younger children ... may not understand every detail but can browse through the text and pore over the pictures." Chicago. Children's Bk Center

Glossary: p112

720.9 Architecture—History

Paine, Roberta M.

Looking at architecture. Lothrop 1974 127p illus map lib. bdg. $7.92 (4 and up)   720.9

1 Architecture—History
ISBN 0-688-51553-3   LC 73-17718

This book considers "varied aspects of architecture as exemplified by specific structures: the Parthenon, the Pantheon, the pyramids and temples of Mexico, the Taj Mahal, Gothic churches, and skyscrapers—to mention only a few. ... The architectural mileus include Africa and Asia as well as Europe and America; and structures of the modern world are discussed as well as those of antiquity, the middle ages, and the Renaissance." Horn Bk

"Profuse black-and-white photographs and reproductions illustrate the text." Booklist

Glossary of building materials: p115-19. Notes on the architects: p120-24. For further reading: p125

722 Ancient and Oriental architecture

Leacroft, Helen

The buildings of ancient Egypt [by] Helen and Richard Leacroft. Young Scott Bks. 1963 39p illus map lib. bdg. $7.95 (5 and up)   722

1 Architecture, Egyptian 2 Egypt—Civilization
ISBN 0-201-09141-8   LC 63-24455

This book describes "architectural details, processes of building, and the furnishing of three different styles of pyramid-tombs and other temples ... also houses, from reed and mud-daubed huts to the mud-brick house and estate of nobleman and royalty. Particulars of social structure give insight into the way the Egyptians lived." Horn Bk

"Useful as a supplement to study of architecture through the ages." Wis Library Bul

The buildings of ancient Greece [by] Helen and Richard Leacroft. Young Scott Bks. 1966 40p illus maps lib. bdg. $7.95 (5 and up)   722

1 Architecture, Greek 2 Civilization, Greek
ISBN 0-201-09143-7   LC 66-12056

The book tells of "the domestic and public architecture of Greece, from prehistoric times to 300 B.C., against a background of early Greek life." Hodges. Bks for Elem Sch Libraries

This work "is more technical than the jacket would suggest. It is about 50 per cent illustration, the text is clear and concise and many of the diagrams are highly detailed. Excellent for budding architects as well as historians." Times (London) Literary Sup

Leacroft, Helen—*Continued*

The building of ancient man [by] Helen and Richard Leacroft. Young Scott Bks. 1973 39p illus lib. bdg. $7.95 (5 and up)   722

1 Architecture, Ancient   2 Architecture, Domestic
ISBN 0-201-09150-X   LC 72-5262

"How ancient man developed architecture to build homes, fortifications, settlements, as well as religious monuments is described in this concise and readable account. Architectural styles are explained as the history of housing is traced from simple lean-tos to more complex structures with many rooms. The text is well-written, although advanced, and the informative illustrations, many of which are in full color, feature nude or partially-clad figures." Sch Library J

The buildings of ancient Rome [by] Helen and Richard Leacroft. Young Scott Bks. 1969 40p illus maps lib. bdg. $7.95 (5 and up)   722

1 Architecture, Roman   2 Rome—Civilization
ISBN 0-201-09145-3   LC 69-18971

"In concise, graphic text well correlated with many detailed full-color and line drawings, the authors . . . describe the materials, designs, and construction of Roman temples, public buildings, towns, aqueducts, theaters, and private housing. . . . Information is based on the excavations and reports of archeologists and provides sidelights on the life style and attitudes of the Romans as well as explaining their architectural skill." Booklist

Buildings of early Islam [by] Helen and Richard Leacroft. Young Scott Bks. 1976 40p illus lib. bdg. $7.95 (5 and up)   722

1 Architecture, Islamic   2 Civilization, Islamic
ISBN 0-201-09446-0   LC 76-2463

"Numerous diagrams, cutaway drawings, and some full-color spreads illustrate the architectural specifics that the text describes. Buildings include several mosques; caravanserais, which provided shelter to travelers on trade routes; various houses and palaces; and some schools and hospitals. Among the cited structures are the Alhambra and Istanbul's Topkapi Palaces. The text is instructive, citing not only structural characteristics, but relating the architecture to the culture that produced it." Booklist

"A compact but dry introduction to Western Islamic architecture for readers with stamina. . . . Hardly light reading but useful." Sch Library J

726 Buildings for religious and related purposes

Grant, Neil

Cathedrals; illus. with photographs. Watts, F. 1972 90p illus lib. bdg. $4.90 (4-6)   726

1 Cathedrals   2 Architecture, Gothic   3 Architecture, Romanesque
ISBN 0-531-00755-3   LC 79-183939

"After defining the word 'cathedral' the author discusses briefly the great medieval period of cathedral building and illustrates the two types of architecture used, Romanesque and Gothic. He notes the secular use of cathedrals during the Middle Ages and explains the meaning behind different, sometimes grotesque types of church decoration. Grant describes in a few words the best-known cathedrals of France, England, Germany, Spain, Russia, and the U.S. plus one in Africa and indicates how architects of modern cathedrals have departed from the Gothic style and are using original designs. Copiously illustrated with photographs." Booklist

Hiller, Carl E.

Caves to cathedrals; architecture of the world's great religions. Little 1974 138p illus $8.95 (5 and up)   726

1 Temples   2 Synagogues   3 Mosques   4 Churches
ISBN 0-316-36395-2   LC 74-16188

The author "discusses the basic tenets of each of the major religions of the world in a page or two, describes the building in which their congregations worship in an equivalent amount of space, and devotes the remainder of each chapter to a series of photographs with identifying captions and a brief comment on site, use, architectural detail, or some other feature notable in the picture." Chicago. Children's Bk Center

"The glossary, copiously illustrated to facilitate comprehension of such terms as transept, basilica, etc., is definitely the highlight of this book. Although far too sketchy to be used as a main reference, this could supplement school library collections on architecture and/or theology and possibly stimulate interest for further research." Sch Library J

Bibliography: p133-35

Macaulay, David

Cathedral: the story of its construction. Houghton 1973 77p illus $10.95 (4 and up)   726

1 Cathedrals—Europe   2 Architecture, Gothic
ISBN 0-395-17513-5   LC 73-6634

This is a description, illustrated with black-and-white line drawings, of the construction of a Gothic cathedral "in southern France from its conception in 1252 to its completion in 1338. The spirit that motivated the people, the tools and materials they used, the steps and methods of constructions, all receive measured factual attention." Booklist

The "drawings, some from ground level, some from high in the building itself, reveal the ongoing stages of construction, the interrelation of the parts and the ingenuity and skill of medieval craftsmanship. . . . The fictional Cathedral of Chutreaux—as those real cathedrals of Chartres, Canterbury, Vienna, Ulm, Paris, York, and all the others—achieved that essential blend of beauty and utility that marks all truly functional architecture of the highest order. It is the great virtue of . . . Macaulay's book to reveal this in a pleasing and convincing way." NY Times Bk Rev

Glossary: p[80]

Pyramid. Houghton 1975 80p illus $9.95 (5 and up)   726

1 Pyramids   2 Egypt—Civilization
ISBN 0-395-21407-6   LC 75-9964

The construction of a pyramid in 25th century B.C. Egypt is described —"beginning with the reasons why the ancient Egyptians attached so much importance to the building of permanent, magnificent tombs. Information about selection of the site, drawing of the plans, calculating compass directions, clearing and leveling the ground, and quarrying and hauling the tremendous blocks of granite and limestone is conveyed as much by pictures as by text. It is interesting to note that although the author mentions the many thousands of people recruited to work on the pyramid and the ceremonies conducted from time to time during its construction and after its completion, he makes no attempt to dramatize either the labors of the workers or the pomp and circumstance of the ceremonies. This restraint adds strength to a notable presentation." Horn Bk

"The text is seldom more than 15 lines per page, with the remainder of the page devoted to one or two stylized line drawings. The drawings are excellent and illustrate the text far better than would photographs. A glossary is appended to define the more unfamiliar words and technical terms." AAAS Sci Bks & Films

728 Residential buildings

Hoag, Edwin

American houses: colonial, classic, and contemporary. Lippincott 1964 160p illus $10 (6 and up)   728

1 Architecture, Domestic   2 Architecture, American   3 Houses
ISBN 0-397-30721-7   LC 64-19042

"This is a handsome book, handsomely illustrated, comprehensive and competent; it is written in a straightforward style that is informal without being either jocose or patronizing. The author relates developments always to influences of heritage, of materials and climate, of function, or of period-fashion. The text provides a considerable amount of historic background to the story of houses in America; the book should be of some use to younger readers as a limited reference source, particularly for the illustrations." Chicago. Children's Bk Center

Bibliography: p155-66

Hofsinde, Robert

Indians at home; written and illus. by Robert Hofsinde (Gray-Wolf). Morrow 1964 96p illus lib. bdg. $6 (4 and up)   **728**

1 Indians of North America—Housing 2 Indians of North America—Social life and customs
ISBN 0-688-31611-5   LC 64-10258

This "book describes how Indian homes were built, from the open chikees of the Seminole in the Everglades to the cozy earth lodges of the Mandan. In addition the reader is allowed to investigate the life and customs that went with each home, and the changes that modern times have made in them." Chicago Sch J

"Neatly organized, straightforward in style, and well-illustrated. . . . A map of linguistic-group distribution precedes the text, and a list of tribes within linguistic groups follows it; an index is appended." Chicago. Children's Bk Center

Huntington, Lee Pennock

Simple shelters; illus. by Stefen Bernath. Coward, McCann & Geoghegan 1979 63p illus $5.64 (3-5)   **728**

1 Houses 2 Architecture, Domestic
ISBN 0-698-30690-2   LC 78-23712

"This catalog of elementary shelters bears out the introductory idea that people build houses to suit their needs and living patterns. . . . Lesser-known designs include Amazon river houses, stilt houses of New Guinea, yurts, Bedouin and Berber desert tents, and a variety of mud and adobe brick structures. Each house has a page or two of commentary that describes materials and special features. Neat pen drawings that often spread across both pages give a clear representation of what's being described." Booklist

Glossary p62-63

Myller, Rolf

From idea into house; house designed by Myller & Szwarce; drawings for this book prepared by Henry K. Szwarce. Atheneum Pubs. 1974 64p illus $7.95 (5 and up)   **728**

1 Architecture, Domestic—Designs and plans 2 Houses 3 Building
ISBN 0-689-30144-8   LC 73-84832

This book "describes the building process—buying land, drawing up plans, and constructing the house. The author follows one family's efforts from the idea stage through contact with the realtor, architect, contractor, mortgagor, etc. Detailed floor plans and diagrams used by elecricians, plumbers, and other subcontractors are included." Sch Library J

"Readers may not understand all the minutiae of the drawings, but they will certainly have a thorough introduction to architectural specifications and the order in which a house is constructed." Chicago. Children's Bk Center

Glossary p60-64

Siberell, Anne

Houses; shelters from prehistoric times to today; written and illus. by Anne Siberell. Holt 1979 unp illus $6.95 (2-4)   **728**

1 Houses 2 Architecture, Domestic
ISBN 0-03-044656-2   LC 78-14097

"A description of shelters from caves to today's dwellings, including split-level and solar-heated houses. . . . The book introduces important architectural styles—from house designs associated with certain ethnic groups to skyscrapers and geodesic domes. Buckminster Fuller's plan for a floating city of prefabricated units is also mentioned." Horn Bk

"Minimally lined scenes with rust-colored accents give an immaculate appearance to this picturebook review of housing history. The connection between cultural developments and housing is implicit throughout and representative examples . . . by no means comprehensive, still make clear how varied and culturally unique shelters have been across time." Booklist

Simon, Nancy

American Indian habitats; how to make dwellings and shelters with natural materials [by] Nancy Simon and Evelyn Wolfson; drawings and diagrams by Nancy Poydar. McKay 1978 108p illus $7.95 (5 and up)   **728**

1 Indians of North America—Housing 2 Building
ISBN 0-679-20500-4   LC 78-4416

"Divided according to geographical area (the Plains, the Southwest, etc.) where similar types of Indian homes and materials were found, this serves a dual purpose, briefly conveying information about home construction customs of various tribal groups as well as do-it-yourself directions for building an Indian shelter. The link between Indian shelters and an affinity for natural surroundings is made clear." Sch Library J

"The text is documented with well-reproduced illustrations, among them botanical sketches and construction diagrams, in addition to the photographs." Horn Bk

728.8   Castles

Adkins, Jan

The art and industry of sandcastles; being: an illustrated guide to basic constructions along with divers information devised by one Jan Adkins, a wily fellow. Walker & Co. 1971 xxix p illus map $5.95 (4 and up)   **728.8**

1 Castles
ISBN 0-8027-0336-4   LC 76-141615

"Designed with an unobtrusive mastery of form and line the text and illustrations together serve both as a sophisticated guide to making sandcastles and as a record of the evolution of castle building in Europe. The explanation of various processes used to make sand structures and to build various kinds of actual castles is given in a pleasing, skillfully presented book for all ages, with information included on the duties of major personnel in the traditional castle." Booklist

"Castles conjure up dreams that are deftly captured on sand-colored paper, with hand-lettered text and ink wash drawings." Brooklyn. Art Bks for Children

Duggan, Alfred

The castle book; illus. by Raymond Briggs. Pantheon Bks. 1961 95p illus $2.50 (4 and up)   **728.8**

1 Castles
ISBN 0-394-81001-5   LC 61-7461

First published 1960 in England with title: Look at castles

"A castle is a building that tries to do two things at once: to shelter a great man and his family in some comfort—and to keep out his enemies." Thus begins this account of how castles were built and used from Norman times until their decline six centuries later

"An entertaining and informative book . . . written with humor with an occasional jarring flippancy or a reference that may be confusing to the young reader [and] . . . especially useful because it gives the reasons, in describing architectural details, for their existence." Chicago. Children's Bk Center

Macaulay, David

Castle. Houghton 1977 74p illus $10.95 (5 and up)   **728.8**

1 Castles 2 Fortification
ISBN 0-395-25784-0   LC 77-7159

Macaulay depicts "the history of an imaginary thirteenth-century castle—built to subdue the Welsh hordes—from the age of construction to the age of neglect, when the town of Aberwyfern no longer needs a fortified stronghold." Economist

"It's always been hard to evaluate Macaulay's work without overindulgence in superlatives; it's hard now to find superlatives that haven't been used. They are well-deserved: the line drawings are meticulous in detail, lucidly illustrating architectural features described in the text and injected with a refreshing humor (a series of pictures of workmen on the master engineer's staff concludes with a view of his dog) that is never overdone. The pictures are equally impressive whether they show small stonework details or a broad view of castle and town. The writing is clear, crisp, and informative, with a smooth narrative flow." Chicago. Children's Bk Center

Includes glossary

Unstead, R. J.
British castles. Crowell 1970 92p illus maps
$7.95 (5 and up)   **728.8**
1 Castles
ISBN 0-690-16029-1   LC 74-94224
Originally published in England with title:
Castles
This is a "well-illustrated survey of high points
in the development of the British castle, its
'slighting' under Cromwell, and subsequent demise.
. . . Discussed in brief are construction, design,
castle life, keeps, attack, defence, and 'Z-plan'
castles. The book concludes with suggestions for
visiting castles." Sch Library J
Glossary: p91

See inside a castle. Warwick Press [1979
c1977] 28p illus lib. bdg. $6.90 (5 and up)
                                                      728.8
1 Castles
ISBN 0-531-09119-8   LC 78-63163
First published 1977 in England
"Text and illustrations combine to explain the
castle areas (keeps, kitchen, courtyard, great hall),
the daily work (feeding, arming), and various
activities (amusements, hunting, chapel). Information is included on the defenses and use of the
towers, gatehouses, and moats, with techniques to
inhibit invaders pointed out and a castle at the
height of attack envisioned. Side drawings depict
hoardings, catapults, and drawbridges; a glossary
of terms completes the text." Booklist

731 Processes and representations of sculpture

Brindze, Ruth
The story of the totem pole; illus. by Yeffe
Kimball. Vanguard 1951 62p illus $7.95 (4
and up)   **731**
1 Totems and totemism 2 Indians of North
America—Northwest, Pacific
ISBN 0-8149-0277-4   LC 51-8370
Miss Brindze "writes of the origins and uses of
the poles, and of the American Indians of the
Northwest who carved them. She includes also
brief stories about specific poles and even some
information on how to read the carvings. The
illustrations are striking and in themselves make
a valuable addition to books about America."
Horn Bk

Holz, Loretta
Mobiles you can make; illus. with drawings by the author and photographs by
George and Loretta Holz. Lothrop 1975 128p
illus $7.75, lib. bdg. $7.44 (4 and up)   **731**
1 Mobiles (Sculpture)
ISBN 0-688-41695-0; 0-688-51695-5   LC 75-8994
Diagrams and explanations provide "step-by-
step instructions for making variants of three
kinds of mobiles: string-hung, wire-armed, and
base-hung. The author lists materials and describes
techniques, encouraging the reader to design original mobiles; in the chapters on the three types,
the examples progress from simpler projects to
those more difficult. A bibliography, a list of
sources of supplies, and an index are appended."
Chicago, Children's Bk Center

Parish, Peggy
Beginning mobiles; illus. by Lynn Sweat.
Macmillan Pub. Co. 1979 63p illus $6.95 (1-3)
                                                      731
1 Mobiles (Sculpture)
ISBN 0-02-770030-5   LC 79-9950
"Ready-to-read handbook"
"Simple, explicit, and nicely illustrated with the
diagrams in a step-by-step format. General instructions precede the examples, all of which use
the same base, a circle of oak tag or cardboard;
none of the materials required is expensive or difficult to get: pipe cleaners, construction paper,
staples and glue, scissors, egg cartons, etc. The
print is large and is set off by ample space; the
projects include mobiles that can be used for
holidays and that may, as the author suggests,
prompt children to try their own ideas." Chicago
Children's Bk Center

731.4 Sculpture—Techniques

Fine, Joan
I carve stone; photographs by David
Anderson. Crowell 1979 53p illus $8.95, lib.
bdg. $8.79 (5 and up)   **731.4**
1 Sculpture—Technique
ISBN 0-690-03985-9; 0-690-03986-7   LC 79-63798
"A sculptor explains how she works and how she
feels about her work in a simple written text that
follows—as do the photographs—each step of the
process of making a stone sculpture. Fine begins
with a 350 pound block of Vermont marble, describing the way she plans her work and begins the
carving, discussing the tools she uses, and expressing her satisfaction as the polished, fluent
figure emerges after months of hard work. . . .
Succinct and informative." Chicago, Children's Bk
Center
"A list of necessary materials is appended; however, this is more an appreciation guide than a
how-to manual and will inspire the most enthusiasm among those with an artistic bent."
Booklist

Seidelman, James E.
Creating with clay, by James Seidelman
and Grace Mintonye; illus. by Robert William
Hinds. Crowell-Collier Press 1967 56p illus
$5.95 (4 and up)   **731.4**
1 Clay 2 Modeling
ISBN 0-02-767160-7   LC 67-4637
"A guide to clay modeling covering tools,
materials, basic instructions, a glossary of claying
terms, and a special section on firing, glazing, and
painting the finished product. Illustrated with
photographs, diagrams, and colored line drawings."
Hodges. Bks for Elem Sch Libraries

Creating with papier-mache [by] James E.
Seidelman and Grace Mintonye; illus. by
Christine Randall. Crowell-Collier Press 1971
56p illus $4.95 (4-6)   **731.4**
1 Paper crafts
ISBN 0-02-767190-9   LC 72-138026
"The instructions are clear and complete. The
text discusses types of paper, wet and dry methods, things that can be used for armature or for
decoration, making molds and working with pulp,
and making masks, animal figures, dolls, etc."
Chicago. Children's Bk Center
"The book offers enough ideas, encouragement,
and practical help for individual and group projects to make it satisfactory as an introduction to
the craft." Booklist

Slade, Richard
Modeling in clay, plaster and papier-
mâché; illus. with photographs. Lothrop
[1968 c1967] 64p illus pa $2.95 (3 and up)
                                                      731.4
1 Modeling 2 Paper crafts
ISBN 0-688-45009-1   LC 68-27716
First published 1967 in England with title: Your
book of modeling
"A no-nonsense, practical guide to modeling with
three types of material—clay, plaster, and papier-
mâché—with many excellent photographs that help
to explain the procedures. Extra housekeeping hints
(such as not pouring waste plaster water down
the drain) are a good addition to this easy, concise, and clear introduction." Sch Library J
Books for further reading: p60

732 Nonliterate, ancient, Oriental sculpture

Price, Christine
Dancing masks of Africa. Scribner 1975
unp illus lib. bdg. $6.95 (2-6)   **732**
1 Masks (Facial) 2 Africa, West—Social life
and customs
ISBN 0-684-144332-1   LC 75-4028
This is a "picture book about the dynamic function of masks in [West] African culture. Most
African masks belong to secret societies and are
used in ritual ceremonies of supplication or celebration." Horn Bk

Price, Christine—*Continued*

"Each mask is dramatically described and traditional meanings and functions are briefly stated. This book is best read aloud, as its language is musical and poetic, evoking feelings of dance movement and gaiety. The bold reds, browns, and blacks of the linocut illustrations are alive and complementary to the text." Children's Bk Rev Serv

736   Carving and carvings. Paper cutting and folding

Araki, Chiyo

Origami in the classroom. Tuttle [1965-1968] 2v illus ea $4.75 (4 and up)   **736**

1 Origami 2 Paper crafts
ISBN Bk I 0-8048-0452-1; Bk II 0-8048-0453-2
                             LC 65-13412

Book I has title: Activities for autumn through Christmas. Book II has title: Activities for winter through summer

Original patterns of graduated difficulty are presented for various holidays, events, seasons, etc. Measurements, length of time, and materials necessary are given for most projects

Cheng, Hou-tien

Scissor cutting for beginners. Holt 1978 unp illus $6.50 (1-3)   **736**

1 Paper crafts
ISBN 0-03-039941-6   LC 77-26776

"An almost wholly visual guide for the youngest beginners in the art of paper cutting, this limits itself to numbers and the letters of the alphabet. Palm-sized red and black squares are the start of each letter or numeral; they are progressively shaped in (usually) five or six cuts to their intended end. A brief introduction explains paper cutting's folk-art status, while a seven-step 'how to do it' list offers guidance on holding paper and cutting. Finished pieces can be assembled into the various message posters ('Happy Birthday,' 'Welcome Home') listed in a concluding 'Ideas' section." Booklist

Hawkesworth, Eric

Paper cutting; making all kinds of paper shapes and figures; illus. by Margaret and Eric Hawkesworth. Phillips 1977 95p illus $7.95 (4-6)   **736**

1 Paper crafts 2 Storytelling—Audio-visual aids
ISBN 0-87599-224-2   LC 76-30461

This "is a unique craft book that combines the simple art of paper cutting with the illustrating of well-known children's stories. Not only does the author present clearly illustrated directions for cutting, he includes a section in each chapter on 'what to say' to make you a performer as well as an artist. Similar to paper magic tricks, the projects include chains of Humpty-Dumptys and trolls, Jack's expanding beanstalk, and clever adaptations on the folding paper doll. With just paper, pencil, and scissors, Mr. Hawkesworth adds an exciting dimension to story hour." Babbling Bookworm

Price, Christine

Arts of wood. Scribner 1976 64p illus maps lib. bdg. $6.95 (5 and up)   **736**

1 Wood carving
ISBN 0-684-14665-7   LC 76-13886

Companion volume to: Arts of clay, entered in class 738.3

"In many parts of the world, wood crafting is done for utilitarian purposes much as it has been done for centuries. The resulting products—bowls, stools, ladles, headrests, and pipes are usually made by individuals for their own households and not considered a work of art as designated by the Western world. Descriptions here include whale-shaped feast dishes from the Northwest Coast of the U.S., three-legged stools used as a sign of manhood from West Africa, elegantly carved combs carrying secret messages of love in a design from Surinam, and betel nut mortars for grinding nuts to a chewable state from the Solomon Islands." Booklist

"Almost as remarkable as the items themselves are the illustrations, executed so faithfully the reader can almost feel the patina of the smooth and mellow wood. The concise text explains the function and the craftsmanship of the carvings and the significance of the often elaborate designs. In an impressive list at the end of the book, the source is given of every object pictured." Horn Bk

Sarasas, Claude

The ABC's of origami; paper folding for children; illus. by the author. Tuttle 1964 55p illus $6.25 (4-6)   **736**

1 Origami 2 Alphabet 3 Multilingual books
ISBN 0-8048-0000-6   LC 64-17160

First published 1951 in Japan

Here are "diagramed directions for folding 26 objects from Albatross to Zebra with each heading [first in English and then] translated into French and transliterated Japanese. Color illustrations show finished object against an oriental background." Sch Library J

737.4   Coins

Andrews, Charles J.

Fell's International coin book. Fell illus $7.95, pa $4.95   **737.4**

1 Coins

First edition published 1953 under the authorship of Jacques Del Monte. Periodically revised to amend current values

A "companion to 'Fell's United States coin book' [entered below] ... this brief history of foreign coins is followed by tables showing how to identify and information on how to collect. The coins and paper issues with current values are arranged alphabetically by country." Booklist

Includes bibliography and glossary

Fell's United States coin book. Fell illus pa $4.95   **737.4**

1 Coins

First edition published 1949 under the authorship of Jacques Del Monte. Periodically revised to bring material up to date

This guide contains complete tables showing today's value of every coin minted in the United States. Along with illustrations are information on the history of coins, speculation and investment, how to start a collection, how to sell coins and recognize worthless coins

Reinfeld, Fred

Coin collectors' handbook; rev. by Beatrice Reinfeld. Doubleday illus $7.95   **737.4**

1 Coins

First published 1954 by Sterling. Frequently revised to bring the material on prices and issues up to date

This book tells how to acquire coins for fun and investment, how to store collections, preserve rarities, and sell coins profitably. In the catalog section of the book are up-to-date values for every condition of every United States and Canadian coin, along with the quantities issued

Includes glossary

How to build a coin collection. Rev. by Burton Hobson. Sterling illus pa $1.95   **737.4**

1 Coins

First published 1958. Periodically revised to keep material up to date

Contains information necessary to start, build, and maintain a good coin collection. With a sample collection, the author shows how to select coins, and how to build through careful investment by replacement with coins in superior condition. How to recognize and identify mint marks; how to grade, classify, and determine the condition of coins; and how to care for and store a coin collection are covered

Foreign coins, price lists and glossary are included

Rosenfeld, Sam
The story of coins; illus. by James E. Barry. . . . Harvey House 1968 126p illus (A Story of science series bk) lib. bdg. $6.29 (5 and up) **737.4**
1 Coins
ISBN 0-8178-3922-4 LC 67-16903
"Checked for accuracy by Henry Grunthal, curator of European and modern coins, The American Numismatic Society." Title page
This introduction to the hobby of coin collecting tells the story of coinage, from the beginnings of barter through the development of ancient Greek and Roman civilizations. Included are sections devoted to the techniques of coin collecting and to United States coins
Coin glossary: p116-18. Books about coins: p119-20

738.1 Ceramic arts—Techniques

Weiss, Harvey
Ceramics; from clay to kiln. Young Scott Bks. 1964 63p illus (Beginning artist's lib) lib. bdg. $7.95 (5 and up) **738.1**
1 Pottery
ISBN 0-201-09153-4 LC 64-13583
"A very good book for the beginner. The explanations and the illustrations are clear, the progression of difficulty well-paced. Mr. Weiss strikes a nice balance between detailed, step-by-step instruction and an encouragement of experimentation and creativity. He suggests simple equipment and modest designs, but suggests to the reader that the more complicated procedures should be understood; the reader is referred, for example, to textbooks on glazing, although the method for adding a simple glaze is given." Chicago. Children's Bk Center
Explanation of terms: p[64]

738.3 Earthenware and stoneware

Price, Christine
Arts of clay. Scribner 1977 64p illus map lib. bdg. $6.95 (5 and up) **738.3**
1 Pottery
ISBN 0-684-15120-0 LC 77-23103
Companion to: Arts of wood, entered in class 736
The author's "appreciation of pottery down through time takes the form of a running commentary that compares and contrasts the variety of designs in broad pot groups (i.e., 'Pots for Cooking,' 'Pots for Pouring,' 'Pots to Hold Fire,' etc.). The chosen examples are bounded by neither geography nor time; rather readers are guided to appreciating unities of form that often transcend cultures, though, of course, the special features of a particular group's pottery are noted. . . . Price has made careful, representational drawings and correlated them well with the text; an appended list of illustrations gives the artifacts' actual dimensions and names the museums where they may be found." Booklist
"A handsomely produced and illustrated history of ceramic arts and techniques. . . . The prose is graceful and interesting and reveals a deep appreciation of the potter's craft." Sch Library J

739.2 Work in precious metals

Fisher, Leonard Everett
The silversmiths; written & illus. by Leonard Everett Fisher. Watts, F. 1964 46p illus (Colonial Americans) lib. bdg. $5.90 (4-6) **739.2**
1 Silverwork 2 U.S.—Social life and customs—Colonial period, 1600-1775
ISBN 0-531-01036-8 LC 64-17792
In this discussion of the history and techniques of colonial silversmiths "respect for . . . achievement is reflected in striking full-page scratchboard illustrations and in concise, informative text." Horn Bk
Silversmiths' terms: p40-41. Some Colonial American silversmiths and their marks: p42-44

741.2 Drawing—Techniques

Emberley, Ed
Ed Emberley's Big green drawing book. Little 1979 91p illus lib. bdg. $6.95, pa $3.95 (2-6) **741.2**
1 Drawing
ISBN 0-316-23595-4; 0-316-23596-2 LC 79-16247
The author "combines basic shapes (circles, triangles, lines, squiggles) to create a variety of cartoon people and animals. The crisp green-and-black illustrations on a white background are large and well spaced. . . . As in his other drawing books, Emberley's wordless step-by-step method is easy to follow; even very young children can successfully reproduce the simple but appealing figures." Sch Library J

Hawkinson, John
Pastels are great! Whitman, A. 1968 48p illus lib. bdg. $6.25 (3-6) **741.2**
1 Pastel drawing
ISBN 0-8075-6362-5 LC 68-22193
"A child will benefit most if an adult shares this book on the techniques of using pastel chalks. The various types of strokes are well demonstrated and the blending of colors illustrated." Bruno. Bks for Sch Libraries, 1968

Rauch, Hans-Georg
The lines are coming; a book about drawing. Scribner 1978 56p illus lib. bdg. $7.95 (2-6) **741.2**
1 Pen drawing
ISBN 0-684-15989-9 LC 78-12861
"The parade of pen-and-ink drawings [in this book] is Rauch's way of giving us another means of looking at art; not only does he utilize each type of line (tiny, curly, thick, thin, fat, long, and ugly) with amazing skill and versatility, but he helps us see how effects are created by isolating technical aspects. This is an inspirational work, suggesting the power of the pen stroke rather than directly teaching any methods. . . . Despite a picture-book format, the book could be used with older students." Booklist

Slobodkin, Louis
The first book of drawing. Watts, F. 1958 68p illus lib. bdg. $5.90 (5 and up) **741.2**
1 Drawing 2 Anatomy, Artistic
ISBN 0-531-00516-X LC 58-11352
"Many a child will welcome this book. Brief as it is, there is helpful information about basic techniques and materials for using pencil, pen and ink, charcoal, Conte crayon, or brush. Illustrations, which fill a major part of the book, follow the text closely. They demonstrate what may be accomplished by shading, or 'modeling,' to give third dimension, movement, and tone. Perspective, 'a complicated science,' is limited to two pages. Mr. Slobodkin's own style of book illustration with pen and ink, water-color pencil, and wet brush will be recognized and appreciated as an apparently simple, effective technique." Horn Bk
"This should prove to be an encouraging book for the young artist. It gives a positive approach to art either as a pleasant pastime or in the serious business of becoming an artist." Ontario Library Rev

Weiss, Harvey
Pencil, pen and brush; drawings for beginners. Young Scott Bks. 1961 63p illus lib. bdg. $8.95 (5 and up) **741.2**
1 Drawing
ISBN 0-201-09311-1 LC 61-2895
The author provides "guidance in basic techniques and media and specific step-by-step directions for first efforts to draw from photographs as models. Different methods for capturing the special quality of a subject are illustrated in the work of several artists shown together. Interspersed are examples of ways to suggest textures and tones. . . . actions, and space. . . . Although the coverage is broad and sketchy, it is recommended for stimulus to creative expression and for enjoyment of the illustrations used, from Leonardo to the moderns." Horn Bk
Other books about drawing: p63

Zaidenberg, Arthur
    How to draw with pen & brush; a book
for beginners. Vanguard 1965 61p illus $6.95
(3 and up)   **741.2**

1 Pen drawing 2 Drawing
ISBN 0-8149-0441-6   LC 65-17376

The author demonstrates different effects
achieved with a pen or brush and ink. Scratchboard drawing, pen sketches, dry brush and stick
painting are among the varieties discussed

741.5   Cartoons, caricatures, comics

Ames, Lee J.
    Draw 50 famous cartoons. Doubleday 1979
unp illus $5.95, lib. bdg. $6.90 (4-6)   **741.5**

1 Drawing 2 Cartoons and caricatures
ISBN 0-385-13661-7; 0-385-13662-5   LC 78-1176

Step by step instructions show young artists
how to draw some of their favorite cartoon characters. Included are: The Flintstones, Dick Tracy,
Mickey Mouse, Popeye, Archie and many more

Cummings, Richard
    Make your own comics for fun and profit;
illus. by Richard Cummings, some famous
cartoonists, and some talented young people.
Walck, H.Z. 1976 118p illus $8.95 (5 and up)
                                              741.5

1 Comic books, strips, etc.
ISBN 0-8098-3929-6   LC 75-12181

"A how-to book for budding cartoonists which
combines some solidly useful information on techniques and procedure with examples of comic
strips by young people. Most of the illustrations
are amateur efforts and the four or five professional artists discussed are introduced by examples
of work they did in their own school days. Cummings stresses that it is not drawing ability, but
the idea, the story, and the technical know-how
which make a comic strip exciting and successful.
There are plenty of tips on planning, on placement
of figures, use of symbols, various angles of viewing scenes, and recommended materials for careful
rendering." Sch Library J
Books for supplementary reading: p109-13

Glubok, Shirley
    The art of the comic strip; designed by
Gerard Nook. Macmillan Pub. Co. 1979 53p
illus $8.95 (4-6)   **741.5**

1 Comic books, strips, etc.
ISBN 0-02-736500-X   LC 78-24342

This "book traces the history of the newspaper
comic strip in America. Proceeding largely in
chronological order, the author presents a wide
range of examples—including 'Hogan's Alley,'
'The Katzenjammer Kids,' and 'Peanuts'—and
briefly comments on their place in the evolution
of the genre or on their significance as indications of prevalent social attitudes. . . . A concise
and readable introduction to the subject." Horn
Bk

741.6   Illustration and commercial art

Smith, Jessie Willcox
    The subject was children: the art of Jessie
Willcox Smith; [text by] Gene Mitchell.
Dutton 1979 66p illus $19.95, pa $9.95   **741.6**

1 Children in art
ISBN 0-525-21185-3; 0-525-47601-6   LC 79-51141

An introduction providing biographical material
and an autobiographical note written by Smith herself are followed by reproductions of 68 illustrations of children and nursery rhymes

741.64   Illustration of books and book jackets

Burkert, Nancy Ekholm
    The art of Nancy Ekholm Burkert; ed. by
David Larkin; introduced by Michael Danoff.
Harper 1977 unp illus $15   **741.64**

ISBN 0-06-023699-X   LC 76-54103

"An original Peacock Press/Bantam book"
"Although the tone of the text and the small
print size indicate that this is primarily a book
for adults, it should be of interest to young art
students and, like any art book, can be used for
browsing by children too young to be interested in
the text. It should be especially appealing to children who will recognize some of the pictures from
books like 'The Scroobious Pip' or 'The Nightingale'; also included are some family portraits,
photographs of Burkert's sculpture, some pencil
drawings, and—the majority of selections—brush
and colored ink illustrations in reproduction. Danoff's introduction discusses the artist's career, her
theories about art, and the techniques and qualities of her art. The oversize format of the book
offers a splendid showcase for the plates that
follow." Chicago. Children's Bk Center

The **Illustrator's** notebook; ed. by Lee Kingman. Horn Bk. 1978 153p illus $25   **741.64**

1 Illustration of books 2 Illustrators 3 Children's literature—History and criticism
ISBN 0-87665-013-7   LC 77-20028

This is a collection of excerpts from articles
originally published in "The Horn Book Magazine."
The artists discuss their feelings about book illustration in terms of its history and its significance
as an art form and as a means of communication.
They also discuss various illustration techniques,
including woodcut, lithography, collage and color
separation. The book contains over a hundred illustrations, many in color, that provide examples of
the illustrator's craft
Articles, books and catalogs suggested for reading and reference: p143-44

Illustrators of children's books: 1744-1945;
comp. by Bertha E. Mahony, Louise Payson
Latimer [and] Beulah Folmsbee. Horn Bk.
[1961 c1947] 527p illus $25   **741.64**

1 Illustration of books 2 Illustrators 3 Children's
literature—History and criticism
ISBN 0-87675-015-3   LC 47-21264

"An unabridged republication, without change in
format, of a book first released in 1947." Booklist
Part one consists of 10 chapters by leading
authorities on children's literature, which deal
with the history and development of children's book
illustration. Part two contains brief biographies of
almost 400 illustrators. Part three includes extensive bibliographies

Illustrators of children's books: 1946-1956;
comp. by Ruth Hill Viguers, Marcia
Dalphin [and] Bertha Mahony Miller. A
supplement to Illustrators of children's
books: 1744-1945. Horn Bk. 1958 299p illus
$25   **741.64**

1 Illustration of books 2 Illustrators 3 Children's literature—History and criticism
ISBN 0-87675-016-1   LC 17-31264

Supplement to the title entered above
It brings forward through December 1956 the
biographies and bibliographies of the outstanding
illustrators of children's books. Also included are
three articles: Distinction in picture books, by
M. Brown; The book artist: ideas and techniques,
by L. Ward; The European picture book, by F.
Eichenberg

Illustrators of children's books: 1957-1966;
comp. by Lee Kingman, Joanne Foster and
Ruth Giles Lontoft. Horn Bk. 1968 295p
illus $25   **741.64**

1 Illustration of books 2 Illustrators 3 Children's
literature—History and criticism
ISBN 0-87675-017-X   LC 47-31264

Supplement to: Illustrators of children's books,
1744-1945 and Illustrators of children's books: 1946-
1956, both entered above

Illustrators of children's books: 1957-1966
—Continued
This volume brings forward through 1966 the
biographies and bibliographies of the leading illus-
trators in the field of children's books. It includes
four articles: One wonders, by Marcia Brown;
Color separation, by Adrienne Adams; The artist
and his editor, by Grace Allen Hogarth; and
Beatrix Potter; centenary of an artist-writer, by
Rumer Godden

Illustrators of children's books: 1967-1976;
comp. by Lee Kingman, Grace Allen
Hogarth [and] Harriet Quimby. Horn Bk.
1978 290p illus $32.50   **741.64**
1 Illustration of books 2 Illustrators 3 Children's literature—History and criticism
ISBN 0-87675-018-8   LC 78-13759
"A supplement to Illustrators of children's
books: 1744-1945, Illustrators of children's books:
1946-1956 [and] Illustrators of children's books:
1957-1966 [all entered above]" Facing title page
Brings forward through 1976 the biographies of
children's book illustrators and bibliographies of
illustrators and authors with entries for approximately 500 artists. Includes four articles: Book
illustration: the state of the art, by Walter Lorraine; A view from the island; European picture
books 1967-1976, by Brian Alderson; Where the
old meets the new: the Japanese picture book, by
Teiji Seta and Momoko Ishii; In the beginning was
the word: the illustrated book 1967-1976 by Treld
Pelkey Bicknell. Includes a cumulative index to
volumes 1-4

Potter, Beatrix
The art of Beatrix Potter; with an
appreciation by Anne Carroll Moore and
notes to each section by Enid and Leslie
Linder. [5th ed.] Warne 1972 406p illus $30
                                        741.64
ISBN 0-7232-1457-3   LC 76-358049
First published 1955
This "is not merely a tribute to Beatrix Potter
and her work. It is an attempt, carefully planned
and magnificently carried out, to place in the hands
of those who are charmed by her books a representative selection of all the studies that culminated in the books. Part I traces her development
as an artist from the age of nine. Part II begins
with the first ideas for books and follows, book by
book, with plates that throw light on the preparation of the books and ends with an excellent set
of photographs of the settings in her life and
works. In all there are 167 reproductions in color
and seventy-three in monochrome, as well as
many examples of manuscripts and letters." Sat
Rev [review of first edition]
Bibliography: p400-06

741.9 Collections of drawings

Caldecott, Randolph
The Randolph Caldecott treasury; selected
and ed. by Elizabeth T. Billington; with an
appreciation by Maurice Sendak. Warne 1978
288p illus $30   **741.9**
ISBN 0-7232-6139-3   LC 76-45308
An anthology of Caldecott's "drawings, magazine
and book illustrations, and picture books. . . .
Four of the picture books are reproduced in their
entirety, including The House That Jack Built,
. . . The Diverting History of John Gilpin, The
Milkmaid, and Hey Diddle Diddle. . . . Elizabeth
Billington's biographical essay is interwoven with
an account of her pilgrimage through England and
America to places where the artist lived and
worked. . . . In addition there is an article on
woodblock printing by Michael Hutchins that discusses Caldecott's collaboration with engraver
Edmund Evans." Sch Library J
The accompanying text is "directed toward discriminating grownups, especially those connected
professionally with children's literature. Every boy
and girl, however, should be exposed to the fresh,
comic and beautiful art created by the legendary
Caldecott." Pub W
Bibliography: p285-86

I never saw another butterfly; childrens
drawings and poems from Theresienstadt
Concentration Camp, 1942-1944. McGraw
[1964] 80p illus $8.95   **741.9**
1 Children as artists 2 Children as authors
3 Terezín (Concentration camp)
ISBN 0-07-067570-8
First published 1959 in Czechoslovakia
Edited by Hana Volavková
Title on spine: Children's drawings and poems—
Terezín, 1942-44
"A collection of eloquent, touching poems and
drawings created by Jewish children marked for
death who pased through Theresienstadt Concentration Camp during World War II. A gift to the
children of the world. . . . Epilogue by Jiri Weil."
Keating. Building Bridges of Understanding Be-
tween Cultures

743 Drawing and drawings by subject

Ames, Lee J.
Draw 50 airplanes, aircraft & spacecraft.
Doubleday 1977 unp illus $6.95, lib. bdg. $7.90
(4 and up)   **743**
1 Drawing 2 Airplanes
ISBN 0-385-12235-7; 0-385-12236-5   LC 76-51554
"Step-by-step sketches, originating from circles,
boxes, rectangles, and triangles, show young practitioners how to draw various airborne vehicles.
Included are more than 50 plans for drawing such
aircraft as the Wright brothers' first plane, the
Concord SST, a helicopter, a sailplane, the B-52,
the Saturn V rocket, and various fighter planes
from yesterday and today." Booklist

Draw 50 boats, ships, trucks & trains.
Doubleday 1976 unp illus $6.95, lib. bdg. $7.90
(4-6)   **743**
1 Drawing 2 Vehicles
ISBN 0-385-08903-1; 0-385-08904-X   LC 75-19011
"A short introductory text comprises the only
written part in the book; after that Ames relies
on his easy-to-follow, step-by-step sketches to
show how to draw variations of 50 vehicles. Full-
page sequences with six to eight dawings in various
stages lead the way to the pictures' completion,
shown here in soft blue pencil. . . . Young artists
who aren't sure how or where to begin may find
guidance here." Booklist

Draw 50 buildings and other structures.
Doubleday 1980 unp illus $6.95, lib. bdg. $7.90
(5 and up)   **743**
1 Drawing 2 Buildings
ISBN 0-385-14400-8; 0-385-14401-6   LC 79-7483
This is similar in format to the author's other
books. Step by step procedures enable the reader
to draw houses from the U.S. and Ireland, bridges
and even a torii (a Japanese gateway)

Draw 50 dinosaurs and other prehistoric
animals; with a foreword by George Zappler.
Doubleday 1977 unp illus $6.95, lib. bdg. $7.90
(5 and up)   **743**
1 Drawing 2 Dinosaurs 3 Animal painting and
illustration
ISBN 0-385-11134-7; 0-385-11135-5   LC 76-7285
"A 'how to' guide to drawing 50 prehistoric animals (briefly identified with their size indicated),
using oval and circular shapes as progressive steps
in simulating the animal forms. Although beyond
the duplicating ability of very young dinosaur
freaks, the sketches are skillful and economic in
line." Sch Library J

Bolognese, Don
Drawing horses and foals. Watts, F. 1977
68p illus (A How-to-draw bk) lib. bdg. $5.90
(4-6)   **743**
1 Drawing 2 Horses 3 Animal painting and
illustration
ISBN 0-531-00379-5   LC 77-3688
"This how-to-draw book addresses itself to
horses and foals, calling attention to the changing
proportions of the animal as it grows older and

Bolognese, Don—*Continued*

to the differing musculature and facial features of various breeds. Much more detailed than . . . 'Ed Emberley's Drawing Book of Animals' [entered below] the process of turning out a finished drawing from preliminary sketches is skillfully delineated, and both the anatomical and artistic explanation is interesting and helpful for young artists and horse lovers." Sch Library J

Emberley, Ed

Ed Emberley's Drawing book: make a world. Little 1972 unp illus lib. bdg. $5.95 (2-6)   743

1 Drawing
ISBN 0-316-23598-9   LC 70-154962

"Emberley gives directions for drawing, among a myriad of other things, 10 different kinds of cars, 16 varieties of trucks, and animals of all species including anteaters and dinosaurs." Bk World

"The final three pages, which supply suggestions for making comic strips, posters, mobiles and games, help make the volume particularly appealing. For all developing artists and even for plain scribblers." Horn Bk

Ed Emberley's Drawing book of animals. Little 1970 unp illus lib. bdg. $5.95 (2-6)   743

1 Drawing 2 Animal painting and illustration
ISBN 0-316-23597-0   LC 75-107232

"If children can draw a triangle, a circle and a rectangle, and a few 'Things' such as the 'scratchy scribble' and the 'curly scribble,' and if they can write numbers and letters, then they can, by putting them all together in the book's carefully designated manner, draw any of Ed Emberley's charming animals." Sch Library J

The book "has no literary pretensions at all and may well offend the free-drawing advocates, but it makes an encouraging book for those, adults included, who imagine they can't draw for toffee." Christian Sci Monitor

Ed Emberley's Drawing book of faces. Little 1975 32p illus lib. bdg. $5.95 (2-6)   743

1 Drawing 2 Face 3 Cartoons and caricatures
ISBN 0-316-23609-8   LC 74-32033

Using a "step-by-step illustrative format . . . Emberley shows how to embellish a simple shape so that it becomes an amusing character. . . . One row of instruction shows what to draw and one row shows where to put it. Most people and animal faces are accomplished in six to eight steps and the author maintains that if children can 'draw 7 things, they can draw all kinds of faces.'" Sch Library J

"Also included are sections showing how to put action into full figures and suggestions on how to make cards, posters, masks, puppets and other 'good stuff' from the faces." Pub W

Ed Emberley's Great thumbprint drawing book. Little 1977 37p illus lib. bdg. $5.95 (2-6)   743

1 Drawing
ISBN 0-316-23613-6   LC 76-57346

"The artist shows how to combine thumbprints and simple lines to create a multitude of animals, people, birds, and flowers. In the 'people' section, the artist uses short strokes to show action, change facial expressions, add hats, and make a variety of hair styles. Combining thumbprints results in flower gardens, trains, dragons, and butterflies." Booklist

"There is little text; most of the book consists of illustrations, step-by-step, of making pictures out of thumbprints. A few Emberley embellishments and a page that suggests other ways of making prints (carrot or potato) are included." Chicago. Children's Bk Center

Frame, Paul

Drawing cats and kittens. Watts, F. 1979 71p illus (A How-to-draw book) lib. bdg. $6.90 (5 and up)   743

1 Drawing 2 Animal painting and illustration
ISBN 0-531-02282-X   LC 79-11935

"This is for serious beginners, ones willing to put in the practice time Frame stresses is necessary to develop drawing skills. The overall emphasis is on studied observations of form, with

exercises that allow work on problems such as perspective changes or distribution of light and shadow. . . . Sketches are plentiful and helpful as practice ideals. The parade of completed cats that finishes the presentation gives readers a standard to aim for." Booklist

745.4 Pure and applied design and decoration

Ellison, Elsie C.

Fun with lines and curves; with illus. adapted from author's drawings by Susan Stan. Lothrop 1972 95p illus lib. bdg. $7.44, pa $2.95 (4 and up)   745.4

1 Geometrical drawing 2 Design, Decorative
ISBN 0-688-51527-4; 0-688-45527-1   LC 72-1095

After "explaining the use of ruler, compass, and protractor Ellison gives step-by-step instructions augmented by exemplary drawings for making simple polygons and stars, using only straight lines to produce a curved line working with squares, angles, and circles, and combining techniques to achieve three-dimensional effects." Booklist

"The explanations are expressed in exactly the right terms; clear and accurate statements lead the reader along so cleverly that it is difficult to resist rummaging for the tools to start the designs. . . . With many illustrations and the clear directions children (and teachers) should have no difficulty constructing the designs." Sci Bks

745.5 Handicrafts

Becker, Joyce

Jewish holiday crafts. Bonim Bks. 1977 179p illus $9.95, pa $6.95 (4 and up)   745.5

1 Holiday decorations 2 Handicraft 3 Fasts and feasts—Judaism
ISBN 0-88482-757-7; 0-88482-755-0   LC 77-7478

"A Bonim Activity book"

"This is an excellent resource book for enriching the celebration of the Jewish holidays. A brief description of each holiday and its historical significance is given at the begining of every chapter, and related projects follow. A multitude of excellent craft ideas are described, with attractive black-and-white illustrations offering step-by-step guidance. Projects range in difficulty from simple to quite sophisticated, and all of them are outstanding." Children's Bk Rev Serv

Chernoff, Goldie Taub

Clay-dough play-dough; clay-dough creations and drawings by Margaret A. Hartelius. Walker & Co. 1974 unp illus $3.95 (1-4)   745.5

1 Bread dough craft 2 Modeling
ISBN 0-8027-6178-X   LC 73-92449

A "book of projects made with clay-dough (uncooked flour, salt, and water). Large color photographs of easy-to-make bracelets, animals, baskets, tiles, toys, and decorations accompany the step-by-step directions. Many of the projects are geared for youngest sculptors." Sch Library J

"The instructions are clear, the projects uncomplicated, the illustrations adequate. The text points out that oven-drying should be done only under adult supervision." Chicago. Children's Bk Center

Cobb, Vicki

Arts and crafts you can eat; illus. by Peter Lippman. Lippincott 1974 127p illus $7.95, pa $2.75 (4 and up)   745.5

1 Handicraft 2 Cookery
ISBN 0-397-31391-4; 0-397-31492-2   LC 73-13864

Instructions are included for such creations as chocolate marshmallow scratchboard, inlaid pancakes, stained glass cookies, pulled taffy flowers, a pasta mobile, orange peel pomander, and an edible necklace

"The clear and precise directions make failures unlikely; but if they occur, the author consoles the readers by reminding them that they can always eat their mistakes." Horn Bk

Comins, Jeremy

Art from found objects. Lothrop 1974 126p illus $7.25, lib. bdg. $6.96 (5 and up)   **745.5**
1 Handicraft
ISBN 0-688-41646-2; 0-688-51646-7   LC 74-8220
"A wide variety of techniques for creating sculpture and other art from found objects is explained in this unusual book. The author is careful to leave the aesthetic decisions up to the reader while he lists basic materials and gives instructions for assemblage. The many black-and-white photographs of mobiles, collages, pendants, and standing or framed constructions show Comins' very able students' work as well as some adult art. A chapter on vacuum forming may present technical difficulties for younger readers but is not out of range for others. A glossary is appended."
Booklist

Eskimo crafts, and their cultural backgrounds. Lothrop 1974 126p illus lib. bdg. $6.96 (3-6)   **745.5**
1 Handicraft
ISBN 0-688-51705-6   LC 75-9573
" 'Ookpik' is the Eskimo word for 'owl' and an Ookpik doll is a furry, owl-like figure popular in Eskimo craft. Mr. Comins explains how to make an Ookpik and many other Eskimo-like objects in this well-documented book on their handicraft. Instructions are also included for making stencil prints, applique, and replicas of soapstone sculptures from material at hand. Step-by-step directions for many designs and handsome photos of Eskimo art make this a book to treasure." Adventuring with Bks

Latin American crafts, and their cultural backgrounds. Lothrop 1974 128p illus lib. bdg. $6.96 (4 and up)   **745.5**
1 Handicraft
ISBN 0-688-51582-7   LC 73-17704
"This stresses both an appreciation of native crafts and ways to make items in both the ancient and modern styles. The history of Latin American art forms and a description of how each was originally done precede instructions on how to reproduce them using common materials such as metal, wood, wax, wool, papier-maché and cloth. Especially attractive are the masks, carvings, appliqué work, needlepoint, embroidery, and string designs. Photographs of the original works and student copies are included along yith clear line illustrations and simple, step-by-step directions in this especially useful heritage/how-to book." Sch Library J
Glossary: p121-23. Suggested reading: p124

D'Amato, Janet

African crafts for you to make, by Janet and Alex D'Amato. Messner 1969 65p illus lib. bdg. $7.79 (4 and up)   **745.5**
1 Handicraft 2 Folk art, African
ISBN 0-671-32130-7   LC 70-75690
"Projects giving complete details regarding patterns, construction, and materials are described for items such as musical instruments, miniature houses, dolls, costumes, games, and ceremonial masks." Keating. Building Bridges of Understanding Between Cultures
"Far more than just a collection of diagrams and instructions, this meaty, yet slim volume includes much information on tribal backgrounds and living conditions. While describing the item to be made, the book delves into the significance of the ceremonies and rituals in which the art object is used. Maps of tribal areas add geography to the history, culture, and art which are welded into a compact and intriguing study of a long overlooked area of ancient art forms." Christian Sci Monitor
Suggested further reading: p65. Maps on lining-papers

Algonquian and Iroquois crafts for you to make [by] Janet and Alex D'Amato. Messner 1979 96p illus lib. bdg. $8.29 (4-6)   **745.5**
1 Handicraft 2 Iroquois Indians—Social life and customs 3 Algonquian Indians—Social life and customs
ISBN 0-671-32979-0   LC 79-15487
A discussion of the social life and customs of the Algonquian and Iroquois Indians accompany suggested craft projects divided into six general categories: houses, household, clothing, beads and other decorations; ceremony and religion; games and toys
Sources of supply: p94

American Indian craft inspirations, by Janet and Alex D'Amato; illus. by Janet D'Amato; designed by Alex D'Amato. Evans, M.&Co. 1972 224p illus $7.95 (5 and up)   **745.5**
1 Indians of North America—Costume and adornment 2 Handicraft
ISBN 0-87131-031-7   LC 72-83734
The authors examine the materials and techniques used by the Indians in their crafts, and then outline adaptations for both beginner and expert craftsmen. With emphasis on costume, instructions are included for work with such materials as beads, shells, metals, and bone
"Interesting, well-presented ideas with clear illustrations and instructions. . . . Though authentic, the designs are adapted to easily acquirable materials." Sch Library J

Colonial crafts for you to make, by Janet and Alex D'Amato. Messner 1975 64p illus $8.29 (4 and up)   **745.5**
1 Handicraft 2 U.S.—Social life and customs—Colonial period, 1600-1775
ISBN 0-671-32706-2   LC 74-19005
"This is a book that will appeal strongly to children who like to make things. Following diagrams, patterns and instructions presented here, youngsters can create authentic houses complete with fireplaces, dolls and their colonial costumes, warming pans, patchwork furnishings, candle holders and even period toys. Some help may be needed from adults who will probably be eager to get in on the projects." Pub W

Indian crafts [by] Janet and Alex D'Amato. Foreword by Morton Thompson. Lion 1968 65p illus lib. bdg. $7.21 (4 and up)   **745.5**
1 Handicraft 2 Indians of North America
ISBN 0-87460-088-X   LC 68-19688
"Clear, detailed instructions are given for construction of six models of various tribal dwellings, two canoes and a travois. Directions for clothing, household items, weapons, and objects for ceremony and ritual include some miniature and some full scale projects. Tribes from all parts of the United States are represented. The diagrams and drawings are excellent; the bibliography is short but good and includes mostly adult titles. Background bits of information enrich the text and enlarge the scope of the book's usefulness." Sch Library J

More Colonial crafts for you to make, by Janet and Alex D'Amato. Messner 1977 64p illus lib. bdg. $7.79 (4 and up)   **745.5**
1 Handicraft 2 U.S.—Social life and customs—Colonial period, 1600-1775
ISBN 0-671-32841-7   LC 77-6333
"A follow-up to the authors' 'Colonial Crafts For You To Make' [entered above] using a similar format, this attempts to present colonial crafts in their historical context." Sch Library J
"Sections—designed to coincide with the stages of childhood at that time—include 'Education,' 'Craftsmen and Apprentices,' and 'Private Instructions, Ladies' Amusements and Toys' and feature projects such as model colonial schoolrooms, corncob dolls, hornbooks, battledores, miniature wooden buckets, tole designs, quillery, needlework, and stick hobbyhorses. Unfortunately, the historical information that introduces each chapter is superficial and fails to show how the articles relate to colonial occupations. The simplicity and usefulness of the book as a resource in making colonial replicas compensates, however, where there is a demand. A brief list of museums noted for colonial exhibits is appended." Booklist

Gilbreath, Alice

More beginning crafts for beginning readers; illus. by Joe Rogers. Follett 1976 32p illus $4.95, lib. bdg. $4.98 (k-3)   **745.5**
1 Handicraft
ISBN 0-695-80635-1; 0-695-40635-3   LC 76-367145
"A series of projects, designed for young children, require only the sorts of materials that are likely to be on hand: paper tissue, scissors, and crayons; or that are relatively inexpensive; pipe cleaners, masking tape, or balloons. The objects are simple but not always wholly convincing, i.e., a chain of paper rings with a clothespin head does not really make a realistic alligator, nor a roll

Gilbreath, Alice—*Continued*

of pink paper wrapped in blue paper a very realistic baby for a tinfoil manger. However, the projects are clearly explained, inexpensive, nicely geared for unskilled hands, and possible catalysts for independent creativity." Chicago. Children's Bk Center

"The directions are easy to follow and brightly-colored illustrations are supportive and will attract even youngest crafters." Sch Library J

Hautzig, Esther

Let's make more presents; easy and inexpensive gifts for every occasion; illus. by Ray Skibinski. Macmillan Pub. Co. 1973 150p illus lib. bdg. $5.95 (4 and up)   745.5

1 Handicraft   2 Gifts
ISBN 0-02-743490-7   LC 72-92445

Companion volume to the author's: Let's make presents, entered below

The author presents 70 easy-to-make gifts which can be constructed from inexpensive, readily available materials. Step-by-step instructions are given for making personal presents; gifts for children, the home, and holidays; and a variety of cookies and candies. There are also special sections on sewing and wrapping

"A bonanza for the crafty kid. . . . Mothers will be pleased to find the book contains safety and sanitation advice. Mr. Skibinski's drawings are as direct and economical as the instructions." Pub W

Let's make presents; 100 gifts for less than $1.00; illus. by Ava Morgan. Crowell 1962 191p illus $8.95 (3 and up)   745.5

1 Gifts   2 Handicraft
ISBN 0-690-48951-X   LC 61-14532

Directions and diagrams for making gifts from inexpensive materials for every occasion. There is a section on making foods for gift-giving, and a page of alphabets to trace

"This book with its dozens and dozens of suggestions for home or school-made presents will be a boon to many a harassed teacher at Christmas time or before Father's and Mother's Day." NY Her Trib Bks

Helfman, Harry

Creating things that move; fun with kinetic art; illus. with photographs by the author. Morrow 1975 48p illus lib. bdg. $6 (4-6)   745.5

1 Handicraft   2 Kinetic art
ISBN 0-688-32038-4   LC 75-11719

"A clear description of kinetic art prefaces instructions for making a variety of simple constructions that move—all interesting projects that sound like fun. The instructions are precise, but the old-fashioned format with stiff photos lacks the excitement of the content. Nevertheless, it will be useful for the highly motivated child or teacher in need of ideas." Children's Bk Rev Serv

"The instructions are casual, with emphasis on encouraging readers to use their own imaginations. The materials needed are of the simplest—scraps and discards." Pub W

Hoople, Cheryl G.

The heritage sampler; a book of colonial arts & crafts; pictures and diagrams by Richard Cuffari. Dial Press 1975 132p illus $6.95, lib. bdg. $6.46 (5 and up)   745.5

1 Handicraft   2 U.S.—Social life and customs—Colonial period, 1600-1775
ISBN 0-8037-5414-0; 0-8037-5430-2   LC 75-9203

"This account of many of the social customs and crafts of the colonists is entertaining and educational. This is a delightful blend of history and crafts. Each chapter gives background on a custom or craft followed by recipes or instructions for a project (butter, rugmaking, preserving, etc.). A book to be enjoyed . . . by teachers and students." Children's Bk Rev Serv

Partial contents: Quilting bee; Samplers; Rugmaking; Puppets; An old-fashioned Christmas; Sugaring off; Selected bibliography

Kerina, Jane

African crafts; illus. by Tom Feelings, with diagrams by Marylyn Katzman. Lion 1970 64p illus lib. bdg. $7.21 (4 and up)   745.5

1 Handicraft
ISBN 0-87460-084-7   LC 69-18916

This book includes "directions for making a variety of useful and decorative objects in the tradition of African craftsmen, including pottery, jewelry, wood carvings, calabash kitchen-ware, Akuaba dolls, tie-dyed cloth, a musical instrument, and simple danshiki and other articles of clothing. The objects, which utilize easily obtainable materials, are identified as to their use, history, and region of origin. Clear drawings show the finished objects and some of the steps in their creation. Since the directions are frequently sketchy, children may require adult help in making many of the projects." Bks for Children, 1970-1971

Kohn, Bernice

The beachcomber's book; illus. by Arabelle Wheatley. Puffin Bks. [1976 c1970] 96p illus pa $1.95 (3-6)   745.5

1 Handicraft   2 Seashore   3 Marine biology
ISBN 0-14-049158-9

First published 1970 by Viking

"This book includes advice on shell collecting, a home aquarium, collecting and cooking food, drying flowers, and making objects out of sand, driftwood, pebbles, shells, animal skeletons, et cetera. There are several projects for which adult assistance is suggested, but most of them are fairly simple; some supplies are needed, but these tend to be easily obtainable and not expensive." Sutherland. The Best in Children's Bks

"It is never laboriously instructive, and the wide range of suggestions encourages interests of various kinds. . . . The delicate black-and-white drawings, useful for identification or amplification, are quite charming in themselves." Sat Rev

Some common shells and seaweeds: p86-93. Bibliography: p94

Löfgren, Ulf

Swedish toys, dolls and gifts you can make yourself; traditional Swedish handcrafts. Collins + World [distributed by Philomel Bks.] 1978 32p illus $5.95, lib. bdg. $5.99 (4-6)   745.5

1 Handicraft   2 Sweden—Social life and customs
ISBN 0-529-05448-5; 0-529-05449-3   LC 78-8619

"A Storybook book"

Published "in cooperation with the U.S. Committee for UNICEF." Title page

"Instructions for making 29 traditional Swedish crafts and foods. . . . There are recipes for gingerbread cookies, a gingerbread house, and saffron buns plus directions for making paper snowflakes and stars, angels, tomten, Easter eggs, Viking ships and Dala horses. Measurements are given in metric units, with a conversion formula to inches appended. . . . This is a well-produced, attractively illustrated book." Sch Library J

Newsome, Arden J.

Make it with felt; an art and craft book; written and illus. by Arden J. Newsome. Lothrop 1972 96p illus lib. bdg. $6.96 (4 and up)   745.5

1 Felt work
ISBN 0-688-50984-3   LC 77-181892

The author gives instructions on how to get the best results when working with felt and then follows up with step-by-step directions that steer the reader from raw materials to finished articles. Included are patterns for making games, toys, household articles, gifts, holiday and party items, and accessories for school

"Instructions are easy to follow, the patterns and illustrations are clear, and most of the materials are readily available at home or from one of the sources of supplies listed in the appendix." Booklist

Parish, Peggy

Let's be early settlers with Daniel Boone; drawings by Arnold Lobel. Harper 1967 96p illus lib. bdg. $7.89 (2-5)   745.5

1 Handicraft   2 Frontier and pioneer life   3 Costume
ISBN 0-06-024648-0   LC 67-14068

Parish, Peggy—Continued

"A brief preface to this how-to-make-it book describes the role of early settlers like Boone, explaining that the projects described are for fun and games but will give the reader an idea of some of the things that the early settlers used. Some of the objects or processes: making dyes, building model flatboats or covered wagons, making items of dress, making a hornbook or a diorama of a log cabin. Although the writing seems oversimplified for the audience, the book has value because the materials suggested are easily obtainable (scissors, paste, pipe cleaners, newspaper, straws, salt, clay, et cetera) and the directions clear; the illustrations are sometimes helpful, sometimes decorative, and always amusing." Chicago. Children's Bk Center

Let's be Indians; drawings by Arnold Lobel. Harper 1962 96p illus lib. bdg. $7.89
745.5
1 Handicraft 2 Indians of North America
ISBN 0-06-024651-0   LC 62-13314
Instructions "on how to make Indian costumes, build model Indian villages, play Indian games, etc. The materials recommended are easily available and inexpensive. Profuse attractive black-and-white drawings." Sch Library J
"The book will appeal to many because it is a stimulus for creativity, and it will certainly be suitable for adult use in guiding younger children." Chicago. Children's Bk Center

Pettit, Florence H.

How to make whirligigs and whimmy diddles, and other American folkcraft objects; illus. by Laura Louise Foster. Crowell 1972 349p illus $6.95 (5 and up)   **745.5**
1 Folk art, American 2 Handicraft
ISBN 0-690-41389-0   LC 78-175108
This book contains "instructions for making 17 different types of folkcraft. The author introduces many of the crafts with a short discussion of their history. . . . The projects include two toys, woodcarvings, quilts, candles, cornhusk dolls, decorations composed of seeds, cones, and pods, kachina dolls, and theorem paintings. Pettit also includes suggestions for finding designs and directions for enlarging or reducing designs or changing proportions, and appends a glossary of tools and materials, lists of supply houses [and] museums featuring folk arts." Booklist
"Descriptions for making the objects provide explicit directions accompanied by numerous, attractive, and instructive illustrations." Top of the News
Books you will enjoy: p334-35

Pflug, Betsy

Egg-speriment; easy crafts with eggs and egg cartons. Lippincott 1973 39p illus $7.95 (1-3)   **745.5**
1 Eggshell craft 2 Egg carton craft
ISBN 0-397-31460-4   LC 72-12522
Illustrated by the author
"A collection of art projects which can be done with eggs [mainly blown eggshells] and egg cartons. Using such household supplies as pins, scissors, paper, yarn, and scraps, the author clearly and simply describes how to make items like puppets, dolls, masks, bird feeders, animals, flowers, and party favors. Christmas and Hanukkah decorations are included as well as games constructed from cartons. Colorful line drawings show how the finished product will look." Sch Library J

Rockwell, Harlow

I did it. Macmillian Pub. Co. 1974 56p illus lib. bdg. $4.95 (1-3)   **745.5**
1 Handicraft
ISBN 0-02-777550-X   LC 73-19059
"Ready-to-read"
"A how-to book for the beginning reader has big print, plenty of restful blank space and clean-lined drawings in shades of brown and green. Best of all, it has projects that are truly simple, save for the last, breadmaking, and even that is broken down into easy-to-follow instructions. The projects are varied: making a paper airplane, writing a message in invisible ink, making a picture out of dried foods, making a papier mâché fish, making a paper bag mask, and baking bread. Good format, clear instructions, and a variety of things to do." Chicago. Children's Bk Center

Sattler, Helen Roney

Recipes for art and craft materials; written and illus. by Helen Roney Sattler. Lothrop 1973 128p illus lib. bdg. $6.96 (4 and up)
745.5
1 Handicraft—Equipment and supplies 2 Artists' materials
ISBN 0-688-51557-6   LC 73-4950
"A particularly useful sourcebook for all who work with crafts, whether as hobbyists or as teachers. It contains directions for making a great variety of pastes, modeling and casting compounds, paints and paint mediums, inks, and flower preservatives. Materials needed are inexpensive and easily procured. Directions are succinct, clear, and illustrated with simple, explanatory line drawings." Horn Bk

Sommer, Elyse

The bread dough craft book; illus. by Giulio Maestro. Lothrop 1972 128p illus lib. bdg. $7.44 (3-6)   **745.5**
1 Bread dough craft 2 Modeling
ISBN 0-688-51275-5   LC 79-177330
Here is a how-to book describing the old folk craft which uses a white bread and glue mixture as a sculpture medium. The author provides a recipe for making the dough and explains how to preserve, color, shape, dry and varnish it, and offers suggestions for several projects from toys and gadgets to jewelry and holiday decorations
"Imagination does not play a large part in either the writing or the projects chosen for inclusion; however, the book will most certainly be a godsend for harried mothers on rainy days and for desperate Girl Scout and Brownie leaders in need of ideas for inexpensive amusements and gifts. A list of Sources of Supplies is given at the end." Horn Bk

Wirtenberg, Patricia Z.

All-round-the-house art and craft book; photographs by Patricia Z. Wirtenberg. Houghton 1968 103p illus pa $3.95 (4 and up)   **745.5**
1 Handicraft
ISBN 0-395-19974-3   LC 68-28058
"An unusual 'make-it' book that rates special notice because its products are designed to be not merely gifts nor gadgets but bona fide works of art. . . . Text and numerous black-and-white photographs describe fifty imaginative projects that use materials from kitchen, laundry, attic, garage, and yard to create paintings, collages, mosaics, prints, and sculpture. . . . Directions for the projects are specific but 'not' so specific that they preclude creative variations. The aim—and the success—of the presentations is to induce the reader to look at old objects in new ways. The book will provide hours of exciting activity to stimulate the reader-doer's imagination and enhance his appreciation of art." Horn Bk

Wiseman, Ann

Making things; the hand book of creative discovery. Little 1973 159p illus $7.95, pa $4.95 (5 and up)   **745.5**
1 Handicraft
ISBN 0-316-94847-0; 0-316-94849-7   LC 73-760
"The majority of the ingenious projects here are not found in other craft books. Topics covered include paper cutting and construction, printing, painting, rubbing, simple wooden toys, nature study, weaving, easy-to-sew clothing, batik and tie-dye, costumes, puppets, masks, homemade musical instruments, and the like. None of the projects are excessively difficult, and though adult supervision is expected, 10-year-olds could comprehend many of the suggestions. The hand-printed text is attractive to look at, and the excellent lists of craft titles and 'Books on Ways of Learning' constitute valuable reference tools." Sch Library J

745.51   Wood handicrafts

Seidelman, James E.
Creating with wood [by] James E. Seidelman and Grace Mintonye; illus. by Lynn Sweat. Crowell-Collier Press 1969 56p illus lib. bdg. $4.95 (4 and up)   **745.51**

1 Woodwork 2 Handicraft
ISBN 0-02-767170-4   LC 69-11402

"Describes simple wood projects for beginners using toothpicks, woodscraps, reed, balsa, bark, and driftwood. Includes a section on basic tools and a workshop." Pub W

"Clear, entertaining, logically organized, this stresses the versatility, sturdiness, low costs involved in working with wood, and demonstrates how it may be used in sculpture, mobiles, printing blocks (no utilitarian projects here). The illustrations are generally helpful, though the items shown lack labels; there is no glossary. . . . Limited in scope, this title will be most useful in large collections of craft books." Sch Library J

745.54   Paper handicrafts

Amidon, Eva V.
Easy quillery; projects with paper coils and scrolls; illus. by Charles H. Amidon. Morrow 1977 95p illus $6.75, lib. bdg. $6.48 (3-6)   **745.54**

1 Paper crafts
ISBN 0-688-22130-0; 0-688-32130-5   LC 77-6463

"Quillery, the art of simulating metal filigree with carefully coiled paper strips, takes its name from the quills that colonial women used to complete their projects. Historical notes, guidelines for general procedures, and instructions for making different kinds of coils preface directions for the 12 projects, all child-tested by the author's third-grade class. Ideas range from pendants and bracelets to napkin rings, place cards, and baskets to a Christmas wreath and snowflake designs." Booklist

Miller, Donna
Egg carton critters; photographs by Robert L. Dunne; created by Donna Miller. Walker & Co. 1978 32p illus $5.95, lib. bdg. $5.85 (2-5)   **745.54**

1 Egg carton craft
ISBN 0-8027-6334-0; 0-8027-6335-9   LC 78-4319

"Finding enough egg cartons may be a problem after children, teachers, and parents discover the possibilities this attractive book suggests. Scissors, glue, paint, brushes, and pipe cleaners easily turn the containers into dragons, caterpillars, turtles, rabbits, finger puppets, and 'Martian' mobiles. Availability of materials, simple directions, and inclusion of several black-and-white and many appealing full-color photographs will surely inspire other creations." Booklist

Pflug, Betsy
Funny bags. Van Nostrand 1968 40p illus $8.95 (k-3)   **745.54**

1 Paper crafts 2 Paper bags
ISBN 0-397-31549-X   LC 68-20908

"A colorful, easy-to-use book containing a variety of creative projects that can be made with paper bags, readily obtained or inexpensive decorative materials, and imagination. Masks, puppets, party favors, gift wrap, and games are among the projects presented. Adequate directions are given in a minimum of text and an abundance of helpful drawings [by the author]." Booklist

Sattler, Helen Roney
Kitchen carton crafts; with diagrams by the author. Lothrop 1970 94p illus lib. bdg. $6.96, pa $2.95 (3-5)   **745.54**

1 Paper crafts
ISBN 0-688-51133-3; 0-688-45005-9   LC 77-101478

This "craft book, aimed at primary or intermediate children, or adults working with them, employs easily available materials—milk cartons, salt boxes, egg cartons, etc. It contains concise directions

with excellent diagrams for 45 games, toys, and projects, including many holiday ideas. . . . A welcome compilation, the book features such ideas as recipe racks, bottle cap toss, and bird feeders that suggest workable, well thought out projects; many are adaptable for other projects also." Sch Library J

Weiss, Harvey
Working with cardboard and paper. Addison-Wesley 1978 72p illus (Beginning artist's lib) lib. bdg. $8.95 (5 and up)   **745.54**

1 Paper crafts
ISBN 0-201-09342-1   LC 77-21860

"A Young Scott book"

"Information on different kinds of cardboard, as well as cutting, bending, and joining it, introduces young craftspeople to the fun of working with paper. Would-be architects and designers will find suggestions for constructing houses, castles, villages, airplanes, cars, boats, and trains. . . . Additionally, ideas for completing cardboard sculpture, mobiles, gift boxes, paper mosaics, and geometric shapes offer creative impetus. A final chapter invites the innovative to make their own paper." Booklist

"This is a well organized, informative and attractive treatment with clear photos, crisp print, and wide margins." Sch Library J

745.55   Shell handicrafts

Cutler, Katherine N.
Creative shellcraft; illus. by Giulio Maestro. Lothrop 1971 96p illus lib. bdg. $6.95, pa $2.95 (4-6)   **745.55**

1 Shellcraft
ISBN 0-688-50988-6; 0-688-45011-3   LC 73-148484

"A handy book for young craftsmen living in coastal areas or inlanders with a seashell collection from last summer's vacation. The book includes some simple scientific information on shells and hints on collecting, as well as instructions for making shell jewelry, matchbox covers, Christmas tree ornaments and other decorations." Pub W

The author writes "clearly and with enthusiasm in a person-to-person style . . . [He] distinguishes between collecting for specimens and collecting for shellcraft, urges against taking live shells, and encourages the use of imagination in creating things from shells. A list of books for further reading and a list of shell suppliers are appended." Booklist

745.56   Metal handicrafts

Lidstone, John
Building with wire; photographs by Roger Kerkham. Van Nostrand 1972 95p illus $8.95 (5 and up)   **745.56**

1 Wire craft
ISBN 0-442-24793-1   LC 70-149258

"An experienced art teacher, explains in a conversational style how to find wire and other simple supplies needed, how to work with them, and how to produce bracelets, mobiles, screens, pendants, and abstract sculptural constructs. [The] photos of children in the process of making sculptures equal the text in lucidity. Lack of an index or glossary is not a detriment." Library J

745.58   Handicrafts from beads, found and other objects

Cutler, Katherine N.
From petals to pinecones; a nature art and craft book; illus. by Giulio Maestro. Lothrop 1969 128p illus lib. bdg. $7.92, pa $2.95 (4 and up)   **745.58**

1 Nature craft
ISBN 0-688-51594-0; 0-688-45003-2   LC 79-81753

"A good, solid, attractively illustrated collection of nature-craft ideas. Emphasizing the use of natural materials found in each area of the United

Cutler, Katherine N.—*Continued*

States, and with an eye on conservation rules, this provides ideas for gift, holiday, and school projects. An excellent list of basic tools, clear instructions for pressing and drying the plant materials used in many of the projects, plus imaginative use of materials make this a useful fund of projects, for city as well as suburban rural children." Sch Library J

Books for further reading: p124

Inouye, Carol

Naturecraft. Doubleday 1975 64p illus lib. bdg. $6.90 (4-6)   **745.58**

1 Nature craft
ISBN 0-385-01190-3   LC 74-33681

The author "uses objects from nature—beans, stones, shells, flowers, fruit—to create over 30 traditional craft items which are both functional and fun to make. For each project the materials needed are listed; detailed easily understood instructions are numbered; illustrations show the steps involved; and, for most projects, there are additional suggestions of things to make using the same materials." Sch Library J

745.59 Making specific objects

Alkema, Chester Jay

Monster masks; photographs by the author. Sterling 1973 48p illus (Little craft bk. ser) $4.95, lib. bdg. $5.89   **745.59**

1 Masks (Facial) 2 Handicraft
ISBN 0-8069-5256-3; 0-8069-5257-1   LC 72-95208

This book offers instructions for making a variety of masks for wearing and for decoration. Among the materials suggested are: crayons, paint, drinking straws, yarn, pipe cleaners, seeds, gravel, egg cartons, fiberboard, plastic foam, tinfoil, aluminum, tooled copper, clay and cast sand

Brock, Virginia

Piñatas; illus. by Anne Marie Jauss. Abingdon 1966 112p illus $6.50 (4 and up)
745.59

1 Pinatas 2 Christmas—Fiction
ISBN 0-687-31436-4   LC 66-10567

This "welcome and serviceable addition to holiday and handicraft books gives a brief history of 'piñatas,' suggestions on when and how to use them, explicit instructions supplemented by diagrams for making 11 different 'piñatas' and three stories in which 'piñatas' play an important part. A glossary and pronunciation guide is appended." Booklist

Coskey, Evelyn

Christmas crafts for everyone; illus. by Roy Wallace; photographs unless otherwise indicated are by Sid Dorris. Abingdon 1976 144p illus $8.95 (5 and up)   **745.59**

1 Christmas decorations 2 Handicraft
ISBN 0-687-07815-6   LC 76-4916

"Coskey gives clear and simple directions for making various Christmas decorations and explains a bit of the history behind each and the customs that surround it. There are directions for advent calendars, creche scenes, tree ornaments, baked foods and decorations, yarn crafts, and items made of paper." Library J

Bibliography: p141-42

Crook, Beverly Courtney

Invite a bird to dinner; simple feeders you can make; illus. by Tom Huffman. Lothrop 1978 63p illus $6.67, lib. bdg. $6.24 (4-6)
745.59

1 Bird feeders
ISBN 0-688-41849-X; 0-688-51849-4   LC 78-8657

"A 'Quick Peck Counter,' 'String-along Meals,' and 'Lunch in a Bag' are just a few of the clever but simple ideas for making bird feeders out of easily obtainable (in some cases recycled) materials. Egg cartons, plastic milk jugs, and margarine containers can be turned into serviceable and reasonably attractive feeders. Instructions are very clear with drawings that add a note of humor,

provide interesting background information on birds and their habits, and show exactly how to put the feeders together and what to put in them. Suggestions for menus include some wise precautions, such as combining peanut butter with cornmeal because birds may choke on peanut butter alone. Other timely warnings protect the birds as well as the builder, such as covering all sharp edges with tape, avoiding the use of thread that might entangle birds, and never using containers that may have held poisonous substances." Sch Library J

Bird books: p62-63

Cutler, Katherine N.

Crafts for Christmas, by Katherine N. Cutler and Kate Cutler Bogle; illus. by Jacqueline Adato. Lothrop 1974 95p illus lib. bdg. $6.96 (3 and up)   **745.59**

1 Christmas decorations 2 Handicraft 3 Gifts
ISBN 0-688-51663-7   LC 74-8750

The authors have provided an "assortment of holiday craft projects: gifts, functional or ornamental decorations, and recipes. . . . [The directions make] use of 'found' objects such as shells and pine cones; in general the projects are simple. There is enough diversity . . . to give the hobbyist a choice of techniques and materials, and the instructions are clear. The pages are clean and spacious, the illustrations adequate; an index is appended." Chicago. Children's Bk Center

Gates, Frieda

Easy to make monster masks and disguises. Harvey House 1979 46p illus lib. bdg. $5.39 (1-3)   **745.59**

1 Masks (Facial)
ISBN 0-8178-6165-3   LC 78-73755

Instructions for making over 20 kinds of masks are provided, using materials (cardboard and egg cartons, paper bags, yarn, crayon) that, for the most part, are easily accessible and manipulable. The instructions are generally clear and fun, although the ones for the foam rubber masks do not indicate that the pattern has to be enlarged and the cutting of plastic bottles and containers may be too difficult for this age group. This is a competent basic craft book." Sch Library J

Meyer, Carolyn

Christmas crafts; things to make the 24 days before Christmas; pictures by Anita Lobel. Harper 1974 136p illus $7.95, lib. bdg. $7.89 (5 and up)   **745.59**

1 Christmas decorations 2 Handicraft 3 Cookery
ISBN 0-06-024197-7; 0-06-024198-5   LC 74-2608

Here are instructions for making two dozen crafted objects appropriate to the Christmas season, including egg ornaments, gingerbread sculptures, St Lucia buns, piñatas, and pomander balls

"The author has actually collected Advent and Christmas traditions from many cultures; and she describes the religious symbolism, the historical significance, and the folklore associated with each project. Materials used are inexpensive and accessible; instructions are simple and sensible. An abundance of pen-and-ink drawings clarifies the sequence of every procedure and adds beauty to an unusual book for the whole family." Horn Bk

Parish, Peggy

December decorations; a holiday how-to book; illus. by Barbara Wolff. Macmillan Pub. Co. 1975 64p illus lib. bdg. $6.95 (1-3)
745.59

1 Holiday decorations 2 Handicraft 3 Christmas decorations
ISBN 0-02-769920-X   LC 75-14285

"Ready-to-read handbook"

"Each of 30 holiday-season decorations is explained separately and simply for the youngest readers. Primary-grade children can manage the project alone in many cases, and materials are easily obtained. Macaroni wreaths and gumdrop trees may not be original or automatically inspiring; however, the book's most rewarding benefit will be the reader's satisfaction in having read and followed instructions well enough to produce a pretty item. Illustrations in green and black do a good job of explaining steps." Booklist

Parish, Peggy—*Continued*

Let's celebrate: holiday decorations you can make; illus. by Lynn Sweat. Greenwillow Bks. 1976 56p illus lib. bdg. $5.71 (3-6)   **745.59**

1 Holiday decorations 2 Handicraft
ISBN 0-688-84050-7   LC 76-2726

"Greenwillow Read-alone"
"Easy decorations to make, not just for Christmas and Easter but for lesser known holidays such as Rosh Hashana and Hanukkah. Every month of the year is represented. Numbered directions are simple to follow, and mothers will appreciate the instructions to 'work on old newspapers' and 'clean up when you finish.'" Adventuring with Bks

Pettit, Florence H.

Christmas all around the house; traditional decorations you can make; drawings by Wendy Watson. Crowell 1976 226p illus $12.95 (5 and up)   **745.59**

1 Christmas decorations 2 Handicraft
ISBN 0-690-01013-3   LC 75-37876

"With an emphasis on natural materials or on such common items as aluminum foil food trays, the author has adapted traditional crafts from a variety of world cultures for the enhancement of the Christmas holidays." Horn Bk
"The book is more than just a craft compendium. . . . The author provides fascinating lore concerning the rich legends and traditions of many countries' celebrations. Numerous diagrams, to-scale patterns, and more than 40 photographs accompany this worthwhile volume." Booklist

A **Pumpkin** in a pear tree; creative ideas for twelve months of holiday fun, by Ann Cole [and others]; illus. by Debby Young. Little 1976 112p illus lib. bdg. $8.95, pa $5.95 (1-4)   **745.59**

1 Holiday decorations 2 Handicraft 3 Games
4 Cookery
ISBN 0-316-15110-6; 0-316-15111-4   LC 75-17645

"The authors cover traditional as well as less-celebrated holidays—Moon Day, for example—in this compendium of easy-to-do activities. Traditional recipes (e.g., Mulligan stew for St. Patrick's Day), games (e.g., silly sentences for April Fool's Day), and arts and crafts activities (a compass for Columbus Day) accompany a brief history of each holiday." Sch Library J
"One of its major strengths is the wide range of holidays it covers—including ones from several different ethnic groups. . . . The items used are neither expensive, nor impossible to find." Children's Bk Rev Serv
Bibliography: p112

Purdy, Susan

Christmas gifts for you to make. Lippincott 1976 96p illus $8.79, pa $4.95 (4-6)   **745.59**

1 Gifts 2 Handicraft
ISBN 0-397-31695-X; 0-397-31696-8   LC 76-10160

"Over 40 items which, though titled 'for Christmas,' will be fun to make for birthdays and other gift-giving occasions. After introducing each present, Purdy lists needed materials, gives concise, easy-to-follow instructions, and includes marginal diagrams to help visualize the working process. Examples of suggested gifts include pom pon playmates, paddle wheel boats, a thumb tack trivet, wood candlesticks and dolls, paper beads, a log carrier, dried flower note cards, appliquéd potholders, and even gifts for pets; an added bonus is ideas for inexpensive and original gift wrapping." Booklist
"There is no discernible arrangement of material in this compendium of instructions for simple, homemade gifts; the projects range in difficulty from painting or crayoning a glove to make finger puppets to more complex gifts such as a lap desk or a macramé plant hanger. The author is very careful about safety warnings—'Use oven only with help or permission of an adult' is printed in heavy type when oven use is required. The weakness of the book is that the step-by-step instructions are often compressed and not always adequately illustrated. . . . Information on sources of supplies precedes the text." Chicago. Children's Bk Center

Temko, Florence

Folk crafts for world friendship; illus. by Yaroslava. Doubleday 1976 143p illus $9.95   **745.59**

1 Handicraft 2 Holiday decorations 3 Festivals
ISBN 0-385-11115-0   LC 76-4215

"This craft manual includes instructions for making toys, games, decorations, masks and information on celebrations from such countries as Germany, Japan, Israel, Mexico, Ghana, and Greece. For each of the projects there is a description of its derivation and use today." Sch Library J
"Clear working directions are given, and suggestions are included for adapting the techniques for other purposes. On attractive pages instructive sketches and photographs of finished products recommend the book for children to use unaided. Only the jacket states that the book was published in cooperation with the U.S. Committee for UNICEF." Horn Bk

745.592 Toys, models, related objects

Friedrichsen, Carol S.

The Pooh craft book; inspired by Winnie-the-Pooh and The house at Pooh Corner, by A. A. Milne; illus. by E. H. Shepard; craft ideas and drawings by Carol S. Friedrichsen. Dutton 1976 53p illus $6.95 (3-6)   **745.592**

1 Toys 2 Handicraft 3 Felt work
ISBN 0-525-37410-8   LC 76-10711

"Felt miniatures of Winnie-the-Pooh, Tigger, Eeyore, and other friends of Christopher Robin are created here for stitching and stuffing. Following general instructions, there are listings of needed materials, specific guidelines, and traceable designs for each animal. In a separate section directions are included for felt pictures featuring some of the famous characters, a Hunny Pot made from clay, and a Tiddely-Pom snow scene. Quotations and black-and-white sketches from the original Milne texts are interspersed throughout the text. . . . Instructions given in long paragraphs might look formidable; but young crafters working with adults will collect a colorful menagerie and have fun in the doing." Booklist

Heady, Eleanor B.

Make your own dolls; illus. by Harold F. Heady. Lothrop 1974 94p illus lib. bdg. $6.96 (3-5)   **745.592**

1 Dollmaking
ISBN 0-688-51570-3   LC 73-17712

This book contains "ideas for spool figures; sock dolls and carved soap dolls; as well as dolls made of natural materials such as flowers, grass, and cornhusks." Sch Library J
"Making the 17 kinds of male and female dolls from scratch with the help of this book will provide ungimmicky, creative entertainment. . . . Most of the dolls have costumes which are sewn from patterns included in the instructions. A number of the dolls are complex to make but worthwhile; the author assumes little or no sewing or craft knowledge on the reader's part and adequate diagrams and drawings are included." Booklist

Lane, Jane

How to make play places and secret hidy holes, by Jane and John Lane. Doubleday 1979 45p illus $6.95 (2-4)   **745.592**

1 Handicraft
ISBN 0-385-13048-1; 0-385-13056-2   LC 78-14681

"Most of the play places in this book can be made by children with little adult help. The structures include a puppet theater, a lemonade stand, a teepee, a boat, a train, and a rocket. All the materials needed are free or inexpensive and readily accessible, such as cardboard boxes, newspaper, grocery sacks, hangers, and sheets. Instructions are safety oriented. . . . The last third of the book, however, is dedicated to building a loft bed and listing multiple uses for one. An adult must do most of the work on this project, and at this point in the book, the vocabulary becomes difficult." Sch Library J

Lopshire, Robert

How to make snop snappers, and other fine things. Greenwillow Bks. 1977 54p illus lib. bdg. $5.71 (1-3)   745.592

1 Toys 2 Games 3 Handicraft
ISBN 0-688-84066-3   LC 76-18760

"Greenwillow Read-alone"

"Twenty-three simple games and projects made with materials readily available in most households are described in a format suited to beginning readers. Although several ideas, such as the pin-punched picture or the sock puppet, may be familiar to the constant seeker after simple crafts, the selection is valuable in that all items can be constructed with minimal—if any—adult assistance. Materials needed for each project are listed; a clever literal 'table of contents,' each item carefully set out and labeled with the appropriate page number, serves as an invitation and a stimulus to young imaginations." Horn Bk

Roche, P. K.

Dollhouse magic; how to make and find simple dollhouse furniture; photographs by John Knott; drawings by Richard Cuffari. Dial Press 1977 58p illus $7.95, lib. bdg. $7.45, pa $2.95 (2-4)   745.592

1 Dollhouses 2 Handicraft
ISBN 0-8037-2122-6; 0-8037-2123-4; 0-8037-1769-9
LC 76-42932

"Instructions describe the making of sofas, chairs, beds and other furniture, and small items such as lamps, mirrors, rugs, and curtains. Concluding pages suggest ingenious ways of accommodating dollhouse rooms in boxes, on bookcase shelves, or on steps. Each photograph of a furnished room shows doll-size teddy bears appearing to be comfortable occupants." Horn Bk

"An ideal gift for a child who wants to make his/her own dollhouse furniture. The ideas are very inexpensive. The actual processes of cutting, pinning, and pasting are appropriate for the interests and coordination of the intended age. The author has done an impressive job of writing the directions as simply as possible; nevertheless, any child reading below third-grade level will probably need help with the text. There is good emphasis on the child modifying the directions for his/her own needs and taste. The photographs and illustrations are clear and exact." Children's Bk Rev Serv

Thomson, Neil

Fairground games to make and play, by Neil and Ruth Thomson; illus. by Chris McEwan. Lippincott 1978 45p illus $5.95 (3-5)   745.592

1 Handicraft 2 Games
ISBN 0-397-31770-0   LC 77-23593

"This is a book which has been long awaited. There are approximately twenty-six games and toys, including board games, face painting, and throwing games. It also includes the history of fairs, the materials and tools needed to make the games, and fairground cooking. The directions explain how to play each game as well as the steps involved in its construction. Each step is accompanied by a good-size colorful diagram, making the directions very easy to follow. The large format and attractive, vivid illustrations add to the clarity of the book. This unique volume will be very helpful to the many schools, clubs, and other organizations that sponsor fund-raising carnivals. Also, as the authors suggest, a Fairground Party can be a lot of fun." Children's Bk Rev Serv

745.594 Decorative objects

Coskey, Evelyn

Easter eggs for everyone; drawings by Giorgetta Bell; photographs unless otherwise indicated are by Sid Dorris. Abingdon 1973 191p illus $8.95 (5 and up)   745.594

1 Egg decoration
ISBN 0-687-11492-6   LC 72-6680

This "compendium of information about Easter eggs begins with customs and legends dating from antiquity and continues with explicit directions for decorating eggs in a great variety of ways. Lists to materials and equipment needed for the simplest to the most elaborate Easter eggs are accompanied by instructions for blowing eggs, dyeing with different materials, scratch carving, and batik processing, and for making the beautiful and difficult pysanky, the traditional Ukrainian Easter egg. Cutout, jeweled, peephole, and collage eggs of various kinds are described, as well as such novelties as candles, mobiles, vases, egg animals, and egg trees." Horn Bk

"Simply and lucidly written, helpfully illustrated by diagrams and adorned by photographs of beautifully decorated eggs, this is a book to be enjoyed in home libraries as well as in school and library collections. A bibliography and index are appended." Chicago. Children's Bk Center

Purdy, Susan

Holiday cards for you to make. Lippincott 1976 64p illus $8.95 (5 and up)   745.594

1 Greeting cards 2 Handicraft
ISBN 0-397-31574-0   LC 67-5101

"This colorful book contains instructions for silk screen, stencil, linoleum block, potato, eraser, hand, and string prints, as well as directions on collage, marbleizing, and pressed-flower techniques. Information for cut-out and movable cards is also included. . . . There is a special list of materials needed and a short paragraph on postal mailing regulations. Clear directions and good illustrations make this book a pleasure to use." Sch Library J

Tichenor, Tom

Christmas tree crafts. Lippincott 1975 112p illus $7.95, pa $3.95 (6 and up)   745.594

1 Christmas decorations 2 Handicraft 3 Felt work
ISBN 0-397-31637-2; 0-397-31638-0   LC 75-15777

"All that's needed to make these traditional ornaments is felt, trim, and some imagination. Tichenor explains ideas for each ornament, giving lots of tips for using sewing scraps for trim. Patterns to trace—bells, reindeer, candy canes, etc.—and pictures of the finished decorations are included. Handicrafters will be able to use this sparsely worded workbook to make simple but creative Christmas tree decorations." Sch Library J

745.6 Lettering

Baron, Nancy

Getting started in calligraphy. Sterling 1979 95p illus $12.95, lib. bdg. $11.98, pa $7.89 (5 and up)   745.6

1 Calligraphy
ISBN 0-8069-6392-6; 0-8069-5393-4; 0-8069-5394-2
LC 78-66311

"Early chapters stress preparation: gathering necessary materials, holding and using pens properly, and doing loosening-up exercises. Lessons include chancery cursive, formal, and straight in the italic and straight and rounded in the blackletter style, with helpful, specific suggestions on the do's and don'ts of letter formations given for each. Samples, suggestions of ways to effectively use calligraphy, master sheet guidelines, a glossary, and a brief bibliography round out the text." Booklist

Eager, Fred

Italic handwriting for young people. Collier Bks. 1978 116p illus pa $4.95   745.6

1 Calligraphy
ISBN 0-02-079960-8   LC 78-1945

This guide to the practice of Italic handwriting covers the small letters and capitals, horizontal and diagonal joins, and equipment needed. Many exercises are included, since the book is primarily intended for those who intend to learn this calligraphic hand by themselves

745.92　Floral arts

Cramblit, Joella
Flowers are for keeping; how to dry flowers and make gifts and decorations, by Joella Cramblit and Jo Ann Loebell; illus. with drawings and photographs. Messner 1979 128p illus lib. bdg. $7.79 (5 and up)　　**745.92**
1 Flowers. Drying 2 Flower arrangement
ISBN 0-671-33007-1　　　　　　LC 79-12892
"Imaginative suggestions for drying and keeping flowers, seedpods, berries, and grains. The explicit instructions for picking, drying (with silica gel or air, pressing, and storing these materials lead into the preparation of a generous variety of dried bouquets, framed pictures, and gifts. The enthusiastic authors have included pertinent information such as hints on repairing damaged flowers and choosing proper containers, as well as supplemental diagrams and photographs to make flower crafting an easy enterprise for home or classroom." Booklist
List of books: p128

Munari, Bruno
A flower with love; tr. by Patricia Tracy Lowe. Crowell 1974 unp illus lib. .bdg. $7.89 (4 and up)　　**745.92**
1 Flower arrangement
ISBN 0-690-00571-7　　　　　　LC 74-2059
First published 1973 in Italy
"In a book for beginners, the Japanese art of floral arrangements, 'ikebana', is defined as 'both an art and a philosophy . . . a way of creating beauty out of ordinary things.' Emphasis is placed on looking at natural objects reflectively in order to discover nature's hidden messages and then creating original messages with 'care and love.' Twelve such arrangements have been created by the author and photographed in superb color. The page preceding each photograph usually consists of a descriptive text and line drawings of the materials used. . . . Although 'ikebana' is an art with definite rules, there are no rules for the novice who is introduced to the subject through this book. The whole approach is one of freedom, and arrangements are offered only as ideas, not to be rigidly copied." Horn Bk

746.1　Yarn preparation and weaving

Fisher, Leonard Everett
The weavers; written and illus. by Leonard Everett Fisher. Watts, F. 1966 45p illus (Colonial Americans) lib. bdg. $5.90 (4 and up)　　**746.1**
1 Weaving 2 U.S.—Social life and customs
ISBN 0-531-01037-6　　　　　　LC 66-10581
"The text gives a brief history of the craft in this country; the second, and major part of the book is devoted to a description of weaving itself: the simplest tools and machines first, then such improvements as the foot-power loom and the flying shuttle. The description of patterns also moves from the simplest plain weave to more complicated patterns, showing the positioning of threads in the loom and giving some samples of pattern drafts." Chicago. Children's Bk Center
"The artist's sharp, familiar style of scratchboard drawing is well suited to show clearly the looms and spinning wheel and the tools for carding, spinning, and weaving." Horn Bk
Weavers' terms: p42-43

Gilbreath, Alice
Fun with weaving; illus. by Judith Hoffman Corwin. Morrow 1976 94p illus lib. bdg. $6 (4-6)　　**746.1**
1 Weaving
ISBN 0-688-32063-5　　　　　　LC 75-34006
"The beginning projects here impart basic weaving principles without requiring a loom. Using strips of paper or a tapestry needle, beginners can fashion a simple placemat, bookmark, or wall hanging. Spool and finger weaving which result in cordlike strands are used to make objects such as a necklace, a rug, or, hung together in mass, a curtain. More complex weaving can be done on the simple cardboard loom Gilbreath shows the reader how to make, while elementary basket weaving carries out the same techniques in three-dimensional form. A brief glossary at the outset explains terminology and materials." Booklist
"There is a great variety in the projects, and directions are clearly given; however, as with many craft books for children, the quality of the finished product in relation to the time, effort, and cost required is sometimes questionable. Drawings in black and white illustrate the text." Children's Bk Rev Serv

Rubenstone, Jessie
Weaving for beginners; photographs by Charles Forbes Ward, Jr. Lippincott 1975 80p illus $6.95, pa $2.95 (4 and up)　　**746.1**
1 Weaving
ISBN 0-397-31635-6; 0-397-31636-4　　LC 75-16309
"Beginning with explanations of the most elementary terms (loom, warp, fiber, etc.) Rubenstone shows how to make a simple and inexpensive loom, set up the warp and weft, and start weaving. Three weaves are taught—plain, loop, and knot." Sch Library J
"This book is suitable for teaching weaving to children because it uses clear, simple language, its projects appeal to young people, and its recommended materials are familiar to them." Christian Sci Monitor
Includes glossary

746.4　Needle- and handwork

Meyer, Carolyn
Yarn—the things it makes and how to make them; illus. by Jennifer Perrott. Harcourt 1972 128p illus $5.95 (4 and up)　　**746.4**
1 Needlework
ISBN 0-15-299713-X　　　　　　LC 72-76367
The author "tells a bit about the history of crocheting, knitting, weaving, and macrame, lists the equipment needed, and gives very clear instructions for the beginning steps in each craft. She suggests simple items which can be made when the basic skill is mastered and repeats the first directions before adding other steps. The accompanying drawings and diagrams are also clear." Booklist

746.42　Nonloom weaving and related techniques

Lightbody, Donna M.
Braid craft; illus. with photographs. Lothrop 1976 96p illus $7.25, lib. bdg. $6.96 (4 and up)　　**746.42**
1 Braid
ISBN 0-688-41769-8; 0-688-51769-2　　LC 76-19079
A "guide to braiding and the use of braids in making such items as headbands, lanyards, glasses cases, dog leashes, plant hangers, etc. The author provides a section on the history of braiding (a craft developed by prehistoric man), suggestions for further reading, and a list of supply sources. There is also an index and glossary. Some of the braids are quite complicated, using as many as 16 strands, but the photographs make the steps of interweaving understandable, and readers as young as fourth grade could successfully manage the simpler projects." Sch Library J

746.43　Knitting, crocheting, tatting

Parker, Xenia Ley
A beginner's book of knitting and crocheting; illus. with diagrams and photographs. Dodd 1974 154p illus $5.95 (5 and up)　　**746.43**
1 Knitting 2 Crocheting
ISBN 0-396-06862-6　　　　　　LC 73-11990

Parker, Xenia L.—_Continued_
"A compendium of basic information, the text is liberally supplemented with illustrative material and offers encouragement as well as practical advice to neophyte knitters and crocheters. The beginning chapters in each category focus on materials, equipment, and accessories. Detailed directions for the various processes involved include a comprehensive listing of the abbreviations for stitches used in patterns and conclude with the main feature—several easy-to-make . . . projects: a scarf, a granny square pillow, knitted caps, and a fringed poncho. Explicit and clear, conversational and uncondescending." Horn Bk

Rubenstone, Jessie
Crochet for beginners; photographs by Edward Stevenson. Lippincott 1974 64p illus $7.95, pa $2.95 (3-5)   **746.43**
1 Crocheting
ISBN 0-397-31547-3; 0-397-31548-1   LC 74-4462
The author describes the materials and basic stitches used in crocheting and gives directions for making several articles, including scarves, belts, and pot holders. She also explains how to block, wash, and care for finished items
"A good basic book for beginning crocheters. High contrast black and white photographs are clear." Children's Bk Rev Serv

Knitting for beginners; photographs by Edward Stevenson. Lippincott 1973 64p illus $7.95, pa $2.95 (4 and up)   **746.43**
1 Knitting
ISBN 0-397-31473-6; 0-397-31474-4   LC 73-6755
"Clear photographs are well placed in relation to the text to show, step by step, how to knit a very simple sample square: casting on, knitting, casting off. The author discusses left-handed knitting, recycling old wool, how to make one's own knitting needles, and how to shop for yarn. The instructions that follow are for objects of increasing complexity, but none is very difficult; instructions for purling, ribbing, and making button loops are included. The book concludes with suggestions for caring for knitted articles and some helpful hints. While it may help to have an experienced knitter guide the beginner, this is as clear a book as such guides can be and really can be used for learning alone." Chicago. Children's Bk Center
Glossary: p64

746.44   Embroidery

Enthoven, Jacqueline
Stitchery for children; a manual for teachers, parents, and children. Reinhold 1968 172p illus pa $7.95   **746.44**
1 Needlework
ISBN 0-442-22325-0   LC 67-24702
Here is stitchery for the pre-schooler to the high school student arranged by age and school grade. There are over 200 diagrams and photographs featuring children's stitcheries, 24 in color. Easy ways of doing traditional stitches, transferring designs, and threading needles are presented.

Hodgson, Mary Anne
Fast and easy needlepoint [by] Mary Anne Hodgson and Josephine Ruth Paine; photographs by Michael Pitts and Richard Fowlkes. Doubleday 1978 96p illus lib. bdg. $7.90 (3-6)   **746.44**
1 Needlepoint
ISBN 0-385-12432-5   LC 76-56302
A "beginner's book on the art of needlepoint. The book starts with a list of inexpensive supplies and seven 'learning designs' to demonstrate each new needlepoint stitch. Each project is clearly illustrated with large black-and-white drawings, photographs and stitch charts. Later chapters include suggestions for creating your own designs and tips on combining colors and stitches. Most important is the final unit which demonstrates clearly how to block and line your work so you can make pillows, belts, and other useful items." Babbling Bookworm
"The writing is chatty, but clarity itself, instilling confidence in children essaying the various stitches: Gobelin, Brick, Parisian, etc. The designs are simple geometrics for tracing onto canvas." Pub W

Miller, Irene Preston
The stitchery book; embroidery for beginners, by Irene Preston Miller and Winifred Lubell; drawings by Winifred Lubell. Doubleday 1965 96p illus lib. bdg. $5.90 (5 and up)
                                         746.44
1 Embroidery
ISBN 0-385-05550-1   LC 65-16370
"Embroidery, from the Bayeux Tapestry to the present day, is the subject of a book including both history and explicit directions for basic stitches. Clear illustrations and suggestions for creative projects." Hodges. Bks for Elem Sch Libraries

Wilson, Erica
Fun with crewel embroidery; illus. with photographs and drawings. Scribner 1965 41p illus lib. bdg. $5.95 (3 and up)   **746.44**
1 Crewelwork
ISBN 0-684-12894-2   LC 65-26942
Through text and illustrations, the author explains how to make a number of articles by stitching designs on fabric with wool. She demonstrates the types of stitches, progresses from simple to more difficult projects, and gives instructions for sewing various motifs such as mushrooms, trees, rabbits, and birds. Directions are also furnished for enlarging a design
"Attractive illustrations and simple but useful projects should encourage the young to discover the fun in crewel work." Wis Library Bul
Alphabet of stitches: p41-[48]

746.46   Patchwork and quilting

Choate, Judith
Patchwork, by Judith Choate and Jane Green; illus. by Carol Inouye. Doubleday 1976 64p illus lib. bdg. $7.90 (4 and up)
                                         746.46
1 Patchwork 2 Handicraft
ISBN 0-385-09681-X   LC 74-33982
The authors suggest a variety of ways to use patchwork "in such projects as headbands, shirts, vests, guitar straps, place mats, tote bags, and even sneakers. The friendship wall-hanging pattern can be used for a bedcover although the authors suggest it be undertaken as a group project. General instructions and necessary supplies are listed along with descriptions for making the patterns, cutting the fabric, and learning the stitches to be used. Red, white, and blue drawings illustrate the necessary steps." Booklist

Ratner, Marilyn
Plenty of patches; an introduction to patchwork, quilting, and appliqué; illus. by Chris Conover. Crowell 1978 85p illus $7.95, lib. bdg. $7.49 (5 and up)   **746.46**
1 Quilting 2 Appliqué 3 Patchwork
ISBN 0-690-01329-9; 0-690-03836-4   LC 77-3401
This book presents "simple patchwork projects that introduce basic patch and quilting techniques. A first chapter of how-to's explains preferred fabrics, needles, templates, joining techniques, and sewing stitches (all projects use hand sewing, though a machine is fine, too, if one is available). A nine-patch pillow starts things off; a jeans-pocket patch utilizes a triangle whose patterning calls for centering points; a 48-inch-square 'mini-quilt' gives quilting practice. Perhaps the most difficult project to finish well is a patched work-shirt yoke." Booklist
This "admirably explicit how-to book assumes no previous knowledge on the part of readers but does not oversimplify or talk down to them. . . . Diagrams are nicely placed in relation to pertinent text, and each project is clearly explained, step by step. A metric conversion table, an annotated list of terms, and an index are appended." Chicago. Children's Bk Center

Sommer, Elyse

A patchwork, appliqué, and quilting primer [by] Elyse Sommer, with Joellen Sommer; illus. by Giulio Maestro. Lothrop 1975 128p illus lib. bdg. $6.96 (4 and up)   **746.46**

1 Quilting 2 Appliqué 3 Patchwork
ISBN 0-688-51693-9   LC 74-34152

"Basic techniques of beginning patchwork, appliqué, and quilting are presented through a series of small-scale projects that can be done by hand or on a sewing machine. Patchwork items include a belt, pillow, totebag, and simple child's halter; appliqués are the basis for designing wall hangings and a tote; while directions on quilting and some additional miscellaneous projects round out the lesson." Booklist

"A glossary, list of supply sources, brief suggested reading list (including some more advanced titles), and an index are appended. An especially good selection for parents and teachers looking for inexpensive craft projects which are both functional and fun." Sch Library J

746.5   Bead embroidery

Hofsinde, Robert

Indian beadwork; written and illus. by Robert Hofsinde (Gray-Wolf). Morrow 1958 122p illus lib. bdg. $6 (5 and up)   **746.5**

1 Beadwork 2 Indians of North America—Costume and adornment
ISBN 0-688-31575-5   LC 58-5251

A "handbook on the various types of beading methods and the articles which can be made using beadwork as decoration—belts, jewelry, purses, knife sheaths, book covers, and moccasins. In each case the author recommends ready made articles to be decorated or tells how to make them. . . . Since the work is fairly intricate, and in some cases requires a special frame or leather, most children would probably need some assistance in getting started. However, the instructions and diagrams are, for the most part, clear and detailed." Chicago. Children's Bk Center

746.7   Rugs and carpets

Wiseman, Ann

Rags, rugs and wool pictures; a first book of rug hooking. Scribner 1968 32p illus lib. bdg. $5.95 (5 and up)   **746.7**

1 Rugs, Hooked
ISBN 0-684-13490-X   LC 68-29368

"Ann Wiseman's approach to the subject of rug hooking is simplified with step-by-step directions and diagrams designed for the younger reader to make rugs, samplers and wool pictures." Pub W

"The author stresses the simplicity and originality in children's art and shows how such drawings can be transformed into pleasing rug patterns. The instructions are clear, but most children will need adult help in finding some of the materials." Library J
Glossary: p32

751.4   Painting—Techniques

Seidelman, James E.

Creating with paint [by] James E. Seidelman and Grace Mintonye; illus. by Peter Landa. Crowell-Collier Press 1967 58p illus lib. bdg. $5.95 (4 and up)   **751.4**

1 Painting—Technique
ISBN 0-02-767200-X   LC 67-29359

"This creative approach to painting starts with basic information on materials but offers many ideas to get the young artist started. Paper, textures, brushes, and paints are discussed, followed by suggested projects and techniques. It is well-expressed and well-illustrated." Bruno. Bks for Sch Libraries, 1968

Weiss, Harvey

Paint, brush and palette. Young Scott Bks. 1966 64p illus (The Beginning artist's lib) lib. bdg. $8.95 (5 and up)   **751.4**

1 Painting—Technique
ISBN 0-201-09303-0   LC 66-11410

"An excellent book for the beginner, profusely illustrated with diagrams, charts, sketches and reproductions of works of art. The first half of the book is devoted to color: primary, complementary, and contrasting colors; explanations of values and intensity, of warmth and coolness, and of contrast. The author discusses forms, textures, and shadows. The second half of the book describes media and technique—including a brief explanation of perspective—and gives instructions for making an easel. Not comprehensive, but lucidly written and always encouraging the reader to experiment." Chicago. Children's Bk Center

751.42   Watercolor painting

Hawkinson, John

Collect, print and paint from nature. Whitman, A. 1963 38p illus $5.95 (3-6)   **751.42**

1 Water color painting—Technique 2 Nature study
ISBN 0-8075-1272-9   LC 63-13330

An instruction book "on the use of watercolor in painting flora and fauna, with a few techniques for making prints with media other than the brush. The author does not claim to be teaching everything about painting, but limits himself to instructions on using one medium for one field of subjects. The instructions are very lucid and simple, the illustrations very neatly integrated with the text. The colors are wonderfully clear, a very important asset in a book in which brush strokes and paint saturation are discussed. Particularly useful are the illustrations that show the the reader examples of correct and of incorrect brush strokes." Chicago. Children's Bk Center

Zaidenberg, Arthur

How to paint with water colors; a book for beginners. Vanguard 1968 60p illus $5.95 (4 and up)   **751.42**

1 Water color painting—Technique
ISBN 0-8149-0440-8   LC 66-28885

"An ideal book for children who are interested in painting and who have graduated from the crayon stage. . . . [The author] describes techniques and materials in water colors." Pub W

"The written descriptions and instructions are concise and informative. Comparison of these reproductions with color prints of the same pictures will be an interesting and most helpful exercise for students of the art." Sch Library J

759.85   Swedish painting

Larsson, Carl

A farm; with paintings by Carl Larsson and a text by Lennart Rudstrom based on the artist's original text; tr. by Ernest Edwin Ryden. Putnam 1976 unp illus $7.95 (4-6)   **759.85**

1 Sweden—Social life and customs 2 Farm life—Sweden
ISBN 0-399-20541-1   LC 76-2130
Original Swedish edition published 1966

This book "projects the serenity and charm of a turn-of-the-century way of life in Sweden—an art book, for both adults and children, that is also social history. The famous watercolor paintings, reproduced on large, broad pages, bring to life season by season, the outdoor and indoor labors of workers on the artist's farm. . . . The scenes begin with January logging, February ice-cutting, and springtime carpentering and fishing, proceed through the months of field work to fall activities and, finally to Christmas Eve. The opposite pages of simple, slightly fictionalized, descriptive commentary and parallel narrow columns of technical explanations discuss country living and farm economy of the period. The paintings are evocative with varying lights and moods, clearly detailed action, and lively touches of warmth and humor." Horn Bk

759.9493 Belgian painting

Craft, Ruth
Pieter Brueghel's The fair; story by Ruth Craft. Lippincott [1976] c1975 unp illus $7.95 (2-4)   **759.9493**
1 Fairs—Poetry
ISBN 0-397-31698-4   LC 76-10256
First published 1975 in England
"The doublespread, full-color reproductions of Pieter Brueghel the Younger's 'The Fair,' which introduces the book, is followed by isolated portions of the original panoramic painting accompanied by rough-and-ready verses. From page to page, the poet invites the viewer to concentrate on one of the many separate vignettes which make up the whole painting, and she supports her invitation with lines of poetry varying in length and rhyming intermittently. . . The book is the lively revelation of the pleasure of becoming aware of the contents and details of an art. After the separate views and the bustling verses run their course, all that's left to do is to look at the whole painting again and to marvel at its pyrotechnic display of reds and whites." Horn Bk

760.2 Printmaking—Techniques

Rockwell, Harlow
Printmaking. Doubleday [1974 c1973] 60p illus (Crafts for children) lib. bdg. $5.90 (4-6)   **760.2**
1 Prints—Technique
ISBN 0-385-01816-9   LC 73-78479
This book gives "step-by-step directions for making twelve different kinds of prints, ranging from the simple hand print to the more exacting two-color woodcut and two-color linoleum print." Horn Bk
"The beginning projects are simple enough for children to do alone; however, later techniques, which involve use of knives and gouges or hot objects, will require adult guidance. The introduction lists where to find supplies and the reproductions of children's own handiwork will add incentive for beginning printmakers." Sch Library J

Weiss, Peter
Simple printmaking; illus. by Sally Gralla. Lothrop 1976 122p illus lib. bdg. $6.48 (4 and up)   **760.2**
1 Prints—Technique
ISBN 0-688-51735-8   LC 75-31762
"Profusely illustrated with examples of prints of many kinds, this excellent book for the hobbyist encourages experimentation but gives enough specific advice to make the neophyte experimenter confident. Weiss describes equipment and techniques for printing by roller, stencil, or stamp pad, explains the procedures for making block prints and monotypes, and gives advice for printing on fabric. The explanations are clear, the material varied; a list of books for further reading and an index are appended." Chicago. Children's Bk Center

761 Relief processes (Block printing)

Pettit, Florence H.
The stamp-pad printing book; illus. with designs and drawings by the author and with photographs by Robert M. Pettit. Crowell 1979 153p illus $7.95, lib. bdg. $7.89 (5 and up)   **761**
1 Rubber stamp printing
ISBN 0-690-03967-0; 0-690-03968-9   LC 78-22504
"Explicit directions supplemented by clear diagrams and photographs tell how to cut stamps out of erasers and how to use them—alone or in conjunction with ready-made alphabet sets—to create decorative greeting cards, bookmarks, notepaper, posters, wrapping paper, and cloth banners. The author gives specific advice about tools and necessary supplies and lists their approximate prices. Basic stamp designs to trace are included as well as ideas for simple pattern. A thorough guide to the craft, the attractive book provides a springboard for the beginner's own imagination." Horn Bk

769 Prints

McLoone, Margo
Sports cards; collecting, trading, and playing [by] Margo McLoone & Alice Siegel; foreword by Pete Rose. Holt 1979 78p illus $8.95, pa $4.95 (4 and up)   **769**
1 Sports cards—Collectors and collecting
ISBN 0-03-042696-0; 0-03-049311-0   LC 78-13790
"The authors describe how the cards came into being and offer collectors' guidelines on acquiring and organizing their finds. Sports card games and a gathering of things to make with spare cards finish off the presentation. The format is open, with fairly large type and profuse reproductions of collectible cards. Lists of sports card magazines and sources are included in the body of the text." Booklist

769.56 Postage stamps

Olcheski, Bill
Beginning stamp collecting. Walck, H.Z. 1976 135p illus $8.95 (5 and up)   **769.56**
1 Postage stamps—Collectors and collecting
ISBN 0-8098-2429-9   LC 74-25978
"Aimed at novice stamp collectors, this starts with a discussion of how to acquire and organize stamps, select the right album and specialize in topical collecting. Olcheski also reviews the value of catalogs, stamp dealers, auctions, stamp shows, etc. Compared to the many existing stamp collecting books, this stands up favorably, providing solid foundation in the field as well as information on the postal service, stamp production, and stamp design." Sch Library J

United States Postal Service
Postage stamps of United States. U.S. Govt. Ptg. Off. illus pa $2   **769.56**
1 Postage stamps
Cover title: United States postage stamps
Annual since 1970. Supersedes the publication with the same title first issued 1927 by the United States Post Office Department
"This is a comprehensive catalog of all adhesive stamp series issued since the first in 1847, including commemorative stamps and plates. Lists all designers and engravers with their stamps, date of issue and the number in the first issue. Stamp series are arranged chronologically by denomination with information on subject, colors and dates. Indexed by subjects depicted on stamps." Wynkoop. Subject Guide to Government Ref Bks

Villiard, Paul
Collecting stamps; with 77 photographs by the author. Doubleday 1974 191p illus lib. bdg. $6.95 (5 and up)   **769.56**
1 Postage stamps—Collectors and collecting
ISBN 0-385-08677-6   LC 73-10950
The author "tells readers first how to care for their stamps—since even the slightest damage almost always results in a lower appraisal value—and then goes on to describe the immense variety of collectible items, including types of plate blocks, revenue stamps, first day covers, and numerous other philatelic items. Integrated throughout are explanations of how and why certain stamps rise in value and suggestions on what to watch for when buying. Names and addresses of services and periodicals of help and interest are sprinkled throughout, and an extensive glossary and index provide easy access to specific points of information." Booklist

770.28 Photography—Techniques

Davis, Edward E.
Into the dark; a beginner's guide to developing and printing black and white negatives. Atheneum Pubs. 1979 210p illus $9.95 (6 and up)   **770.28**
1 Photography 2 Photography—Processing
ISBN 0-689-30676-8   LC 78-11284
The first third of the text is "devoted to cameras, film, accessories, shopping in person and by mail and finally picture composition. . . . The rest

Davis, Edward E.—*Continued*
of the book [concerns developing and printing. Beginning with chemicals, it describes] . . . the darkroom setup, photographic development, contact printing, enlargement making and growth in achievement." Sci Am

"Clear, step-by-step guide to darkroom work and equipment, and specific, though not comprehensive information on photography, makes this a worthy addition to all collections." VOYA

Bibliography: p202-04

Forbes, Robin
Click: a first camera book. Macmillan Pub. Co. 1979 unp illus $6.95, pa $2.95 (3-5)
    770.28

1 Photography
ISBN 0-02-043210-0; 0-02-735640-X   LC 78-31756

"A well-conceived and uniquely simple book, this photographic how-to-do-it guide for the uninitiated is informative and fun. The use of a child and a mime as models in the photos to demonstrate each area of discovery is effective. Budding photographers are warned of the pitfalls of standing too close or too far away from what they want to capture. A profusion of photographs are used to note distinctions between the effects of lighting, shadow, vantage point, and subject selection. Lots of ideas are presented for studies utilizing patterns, shapes, colors, shades, seasons, moods and, most importantly, what the photographer feels." Sch Library J

Holland, Viki
How to photograph your world; photographs by the author. Scribner 1974 63p illus lib. bdg. $6.95 (3-5)
    770.28

1 Photography
ISBN 0-684-13709-7   LC 73-19561

"Some thoughts on organization and creative approach rather than instructions on how to work a camera. Holland suggests using a simple camera . . . and then discusses such things as composition, props, and planning, as well as making a photograph into a personal statement or record of a special event. An appealing format fortifies the occasionally choppy text, illustrated with numerous helpful black-and-white photos from the author's own collection. A reasonable prep book for beginners." Booklist

Laycock, George
The complete beginner's guide to photography. Doubleday 1979 149p illus $7.95, lib. bdg. $8.90 (5 and up)
    770.28

1 Photography
ISBN 0-385-13264-6; 0-385-13265-4   LC 78-1207

"The author adeptly guides readers through the maze of problems confronting the novice photographer, starting with advice on choosing the proper camera and continuing through such topics as lenses, filters, film care, artificial light, camera, settings and techniques, developing your own pictures, and making money with your camera. While he includes most of the essential information for the photographer-to-be, even the intermediate or advanced photographer can profit from tidbits of useful techniques. . . . Beginner's books are often apt to turn readers away because they are either too dull, too difficult, too general, or too specific. Laycock, though, correctly anticipates users' needs and reading level so that this is extremely well-balanced; it could almost be a first course in photography." Sch Library J

Weiss, Harvey
Lens and shutter; an introduction to photography. Young Scott Bks. 1971 120p illus (The Beginning artist's lib) lib. bdg. $8.95 (5 and up)
    770.28

1 Photography
ISBN 0-201-09240-9   LC 79-115913

"Young photographers can learn much about good photography from a careful study of the many well-chosen photographs by such persons as Ansel Adams, Dorothea Lange, and Edward Weston which illustrate this book as well as from the author's lucid, stimulating text. Following a discussion of equipment and basic techniques [the author] deals with various types of photography, including action shots, portraits and close-ups. He concludes with a section on darkroom work." Booklist

770.9   Photography—History

Glubok, Shirley
The art of photography; designed by Gerard Nook. Macmillan Pub. Co. 1977 48p illus $7.95 (4 and up)
    770.9

1 Photography—History 2 Photography, Artistic
ISBN 0-02-736680-4   LC 77-4985

"This survey is a quick trip through the selective development of portraiture, social documentation, journalism and abstract illustration as exemplified in the work of photographers whose names are immortal: Julie Margaret Cameron, Arnold Genthe, Atget, Stieglitz, Steichen, Man Ray, Cartier-Bresson and more." Pub W

"The author treats photography as a 'fine art, equal to painting and sculpture' and has chosen well-known pictures to illustrate her commentary. The text focuses more on photographic 'firsts' than on current trends and occasionally borders on the didactic. Still, the book is well designed and integrated and should serve as a useful introduction for the young." Horn Bk

Sandler, Martin W.
The story of American photography; an illustrated history for young people. Little 1979 318p illus $16.95 (6 and up)
    770.9

1 Photography—History
ISBN 0-316-77021-3   LC 78-24025

This is a survey of the development of photography in the U.S. "from its beginnings in the mid-19th century to the present. The author starts his story in Europe, giving credit to Louis Daguerre and the other pioneers. He then moves to Mathew B. Brady and the Civil War, the westward expansion, George Eastman, Alfred Stieglitz, unknown regional masters, documentary photography, news photography and the influence of Life Magazine, and finally to photography today and tomorrow." NY Times Bk Rev

"In both content and design, [this book] treats its young audience like the passionate and capable scholars of American photographic history that they just might be. . . . Sandler is to be credited for bringing to his subject an enthusiasm and scholarship rare in children's book writing of this kind. . . . Best of all there are the photographs themselves: 200 of them, lovely things, the unknown with the familiar, all which taken together form a stunning visual gloss on American life over the past 150 years." Christian Sci Monitor

Bibliography: p313-14

778.5   Motion picture and television photography

Andersen, Yvonne
Make your own animated movies; Yellow Ball Workshop film techniques. Little 1970 101p illus $6.95 (5 and up)
    778.5

1 Motion picture cartoons 2 Motion picture photography
ISBN 0-316-03940-3   LC 74-117025

A "survey of both the preparation techniques in making animated film, and the intricacies of filming itself. Such media as clay figures, cutouts, drawing (directly on the film), pixillation (incorporating live actors), and tearouts are discussed, and the processes of positioning, filming, simulating motion, synchronizing sound and motion, splicing film et cetera are described." Sutherland. The Best in Children's Bks

"All of the techniques are clearly illustrated with black-and-white photos and drawings. The book concludes with lists of film equipment and art supplies plus a filmography. Not for rank amateurs, this is a practical and attractive addition to the hobby shelf, where it will be popular with readers having the requisite interest, time and money." Sch Library J

Horvath, Joan
Filmmaking for beginners. Elsevier/Nelson Bks. 1974 162p illus $7.95 (6 and up)   **778.5**

1 Motion picture photography
ISBN 0-525-66375-4   LC 74-701

Horvath, Joan—*Continued*

This book includes "information for ambitious beginners regarding the making of Super 8 and 8mm films. Subjects covered include film gauges, films available for varying shooting conditions, the parts of a camera, speed of filming and projecting, camera brands and capabilities, approaches to writing scripts, kinds of shots, camera angles, camera movements, lighting effects, maintaining proper screen direction, hints on directing the actors, special effects which can be created with the camera and with simple homemade devices, editing, sound, and chapter on animation techniques." Top of the News

Weiss, Harvey

How to make your own movies; an introduction to filmmaking. Young Scott Bks. 1973 96p illus (The Beginning artist's lib) lib. bdg. $8.95 (5 and up)   778.5

1 Motion picture photography
ISBN 0-201-09310-3   LC 72-11650

"An introduction to the craft of moviemaking that is comprehensive enough to give a novice an understanding of the ways and means of making a film. Written simply and clearly by an author who has a string of craft books to his credit, the book could easily be used by grade-school children." Horn Bk

780.1   Music—Philosophy and aesthetics

Siegmeister, Elie

Invitation to music; preface by Virgil Thomson; illus. by Beatrice Schwartz. Harvey House 1961 193p illus music lib. bdg. $6.69 (6 and up)   780.1

1 Music—Analysis, appreciation
ISBN 0-8178-3182-7   LC 61-15658

The author "explains the basic elements of musical structure, form and style, points out the similarities and differences between folk and composed music and gives examples of all manner of compositions. . . . There are a chapter on orchestral instruments, suggestions for building a record library and a bibliography for further reading." NY Times Bk Rev

"Simple vocabulary, appealing format, sketches of composers, listening tests . . . add to this book's usefulness. Excellent supplementary text for music appreciation courses." Library J

780.3   Music—Encyclopedias and dictionaries

Davis, Marilyn Kornreich

Music dictionary, by Marilyn Kornreich Davis in collaboration with Arnold Broido; illus. by Winifred Greene. Doubleday 1956 63p illus music $5.95 (6 and up)   780.3

1 Music—Dictionaries
ISBN 0-385-07594-4   LC 54-9837

"There are over 800 concise definitions of musical words, foreign terms, and instruments of common and uncommon use, with many illustrations." Christian Sci Monitor

"The pages are large and easily readable off the music rack. Witty black and white sketches are by Winifred Greene. Despite their good cheer, there never is any doubt that a bassoon is a bassoon or that you can work a kettledrum with a pedal to change its tunning. The information is serious." Chicago Sunday Trib

Hurd, Michael

The Oxford Junior companion to music. 2d ed. Based on the original publication by Percy Scholes. Oxford 1979 352p illus music $25 (5 and up)   780.3

1 Music—Encyclopedias
ISBN 0-19-314302-X

"Though based on Percy Scholes' 1954 book of the same title, this text has been completely revised and rewritten by British musicologist Hurd to reflect contemporary changes. Arranged in alphabetical order, the entries contain a wealth of pertinent facts about people, places, instruments, terms, and kinds of music that are amply supplemented by well-chosen photographs, drawings, and diagrams. To draw attention to areas of particular interest, discussion of some materials is drawn together and boxed (facts of operatic history, basic elements, and names of operas, for example, are all grouped together under Opera) with liberal cross-referencing for accessibility. An opening section discusses notation, interpretation, abbreviations, and composition. A worthwhile reference volume." Booklist

781   Music—General principles and considerations. Musical forms

Hawkinson, John

Rhythms, music and instruments to make [by] John Hawkinson and Martha Faulhaber; illus. by John Hawkinson. Whitman, A. 1970 95p illus (Music involvement ser) $5.95 (3-6)   781

1 Music—Theory   2 Musical instruments
3 Rhythm
ISBN 0-8075-6958-5   LC 70-91737

"The book combines text, drawings, and charts to give explicit instructions for making and playing a variety of simple percussion, wind, and string instruments including drums, panpipes, box harps, a metallophone, xylophone, and a wooden guitar. Together with examples of music for both single and combinations of instruments, the authors explain pitch, major and minor scales, and musical notation and offer suggestions for inventing original melodies and rhythms. A stimulating presentation for interested individuals or for group and classroom use." Booklist

Hughes, Langston

The first book of jazz. Updated ed. Watts, F. 1976 64p illus lib. bdg. $4.90 (4 and up)   781

1 Jazz music
ISBN 0-531-00565-8   LC 76-39

First published 1955

"An absorbing history of jazz beginning with some of the early music that later contributed to jazz, such as African drums, work songs, jubilees, the blues, etc. . . . Much of the story is told through the life of Louis Armstrong, since his life is in itself a kind of history of jazz." Chicago. Children's Bk Center [review of 1955 edition]

This edition includes "explanations of more recent forms of jazz (cool, rock, and free form) and a section on Duke Ellington. These changes, together with a new glossary and index, make this a necessary replacement." Booklist

781.7   Music of ethnic and national orientation

Berger, Melvin

The story of folk music. Phillips 1976 127p illus music lib. bdg. $8.95 (5 and up)   781.7

1 Folk music—History and criticism
ISBN 0-87599-215-3   LC 76-18159

The author surveys "the evolution of American folk music [and] includes brief explanations of how folk music is created as well as descriptions of folk instruments and biographies of folk singers and instrumentalists. An unusual feature is the inclusion of instructions on how to make some simple musical instruments at home and compose one's own songs. An index of books and records, first lines and titles of songs are appended." Sch Library J

"The feeling behind folk music is adequately explained by showing how beautiful melodies are born of the labor, joy, misery, legend, and prayer of everyday people. . . . The title is a bit inappropriate, however, for it is mostly a discussion of music of American derivation." Children's Bk Rev Serv

Bierhorst, John

A cry from the earth: music of the North American Indians. Four Winds 1979 113p illus $8.95 (4 and up)   **781.7**

1 Indians of North America—Music
ISBN 0-590-07533-0   LC 78-21538

"A collection of songs which demonstrates how music permeates Native American life. The range encompasses not only wide regional differences but also historical variations from the late 18th Century to the mid-20th. The introductory section describes how songs are made, how the rhythms are conveyed and how the voice is pushed through a tight throat, contrary to European vocal training. Succeeding chapters cover instrumentation, children's songs, storytelling, prayers and magic, dances, war songs, songs of love, songs for the dead, and songs for new life. Addendi include information on musical symbols used, a guide to pronunciation, a short bibliography, source lists, and an index to songs by 'Musical Area and Tribe.' The companion album, A 'Cry from the Earth' (FC7777, Folkway Records), is especially helpful (as all musical experiences are better heard than described) but is not necessary to understanding. The book is fascinating, informative, and excellent for research. The horizontal format is inviting, alternating text, photos, and melodies (with drum music and metronome gauge). Songs are given in English and original language; dance diagrams are supplied." Sch Library J

Songs of the Chippewa; adapted from the collections of Frances Densmore and Henry Rowe Schoolcraft, and arranged for piano and guitar; pictures by Joe Servello. Farrar, Straus 1974 47p illus music $6.95 (3-6)   **781.7**

1 Chippewa Indians—Music
ISBN 0-374-37145-8   LC 74-6040

"The pioneer American ethnographer Schoolcraft collected Indian material in the nineteenth century; less well-known is the ethnomusicologist, Frances Densmore, who worked more than fifty years later. The seventeen songs, originally found near the western shores of the Great Lakes, included lullabies, sacred songs, chants, and love songs; and like most Indian songs, they are brief and precise, encompassing a single idea, emotion, or experience. . . . In a few cases, the original Chippewa words have been retained, but English equivalents are indicated. Schoolcraft recorded words but not music; and the editor has replaced the unknown melodies with tunes carefully selected from Densmore." Horn Bk

"A very valuable and handsomely produced book. . . . Authoritatively edited with a section of valuable notes to explain the various songs, this book can be used in many ways with children and adults who are interested in authentic American music. For each of the 17 songs, the artist has captured the mood in effective pictures that complement the lyrics. A book that will do much to better our understanding of the Indian life style and culture." Children's Bk Rev Serv
Bibliography included in notes: p45-47

Fichter, George S.

American Indian music and musical instruments; with instructions for making the instruments; drawings and diagrams by Marie and Nils Ostberg. McKay 1978 115p illus map music $7.95   **781.7**

1 Indians of North America—Music   2 Musical instruments
ISBN 0-679-20443-1   LC 77-14906

This is a "book on the music of the American Indians covering the songs and music of the major events in their lives—birth, death, harvest, the hunt, warfare, etc." Children's Bk Rev Serv

"An excellent book, including not only descriptions, words, and sometimes music for various types of Indian songs, but also directions, with diagrams, for making and decorating the instruments described. Well written and tastefully illustrated, this is a fine addition to either Native American or Ethnomusicology collections." Sch Library J
Selected bibliography: p111

Hoffmann, Charles

American Indians sing; drawings by Nicholas Amorosi. Day 1967 96p illus music lib. bdg. $12.49 (5 and up)   **781.7**

1 Indians of North America—Music   2 Indians of North America—Dances
ISBN 0-381-99608-5   LC 67-14614

"An extensive study of why and how the Indians made music and how these songs and ceremonies were a part of their lives. The reader is introduced to the instruments used and also to the dances of the major tribes. Profuse illustrations, photographs, musical scores and an accompanying recording help make this book even more interesting." Bruno. Bks for Sch Libraries, 1968
Reading list for students: p92. Reading list for teachers and parents: p92

Hofsinde, Robert

Indian music makers; written and illus. by Robert Hofsinde (Gray-Wolf). Morrow 1967 94p illus music. lib. bdg. $6 (3-6)   **781.7**

1 Indians of North America—Music   2 Musical instruments
ISBN 0-688-31616-6   LC 67-15149

An introductory chapter discusses "the wide variety and great importance of music in the life of the American Indian. Explicit details are given on various tribes' methods of making and using tom-toms, drums, rattles, and courting flutes. Using Chippewa tribal life as an example, Mr. Hofsinde includes nine simple musical scores with his discussion of typical songs, their origins, and the occasions for their use. The differences between Indian songs and the white man's songs are explained briefly as well as the modern changes in traditional Indian songs." Sch Library J

"A short and readable book. . . . His information is made more accessible by an index to instrument types, and by bold but practical drawings in ink." Christian Sci Monitor

781.91   Musical instruments

Dietz, Betty Warner

Musical instruments of Africa; their nature, use, and place in the life of a deeply musical people [by] Betty Warner Dietz and Michael Babatunde Olatunji; illus. by Richard M. Powers. Day 1965 115p illus map music $9.95 (6 and up)   **781.91**

1 Musical instruments   2 Music, African
ISBN 0-381-97013-2   LC 65-13733

"For young people interested in making their own music—and even their own instruments—this fully illustrated study shows how native African instruments are made and used. Includes two songs with words and melody and a long-playing record of African music recorded in Africa by Colin M. Turnbull." Children's Bks. 1965
Books for further reading: p111-12. Additional books for adults: p113-14

Mandell, Muriel

Make your own musical instruments, by Muriel Mandell and Robert E. Wood; illus. by Margaret Krivak. Sterling 1957 126p illus $6.95, lib. bdg. $6.69 (3-6)   **781.91**

1 Musical instruments   2 Handicraft
ISBN 0-8069-5022-6; 0-8069-5023-4   LC 57-11535

The author provides "directions and illustrations for making a variety of musical instruments from things around the home and suggestions for forming a rhythm and a calypso band." Hodges. Bks for Elem Sch Libraries

There are "more than 100 ingenious instruments described . . . The text is concise, the pictures clear, and both are easily understood." Booklist

Posell, Elsa Z.

This is an orchestra. Rev. ed. Illus. with photographs. Houghton 1973 90p illus music $6.95 (5 and up)   **781.91**

1 Musical instruments   2 Orchestra
ISBN 0-395-17712-X   LC 73-7889

Posell, Elsa Z.—*Continued*

First published 1950

"An excellent basic title to buy because of the wealth of information on orchestral instruments [by families] plus pointers on how to choose an instrument . . . how to buy and instrument, find a teacher and form successful practice habits. There is a chapter on famous makers of stringed instruments and one on building a home record library. . . . [Includes] a seating chart of the orchestra." Wis Library Bul [review of 1950 edition]

"Distinguished for its excellent photographs of instruments [and] its clearly written text in large print." Cur Ref Bks [review of 1950 edition]

Wiseman, Ann

Making musical things; improvised instruments. Scribner 1979 63p illus lib. bdg. $8.95 (3-6)   **781.91**

1 Musical instruments 2 Handicraft
ISBN 0-684-16114-1   LC 79-4474

Wiseman's "clever black-and-white drawings and short, clear directions show how to make over fifty basic but ingenius musical instruments. Many of the supplies needed can be found around the house, particularly in the kitchen, and an entire band could be put together in an afternoon!" Babbling Bookworm

Resources: [p64]

782.1   Opera

Grimm, William

Hansel and Gretel; a story of the forest, by William & Jacob Grimm; music by Engelbert Humperdinck and illus. by Warren Chappell. Knopf 1944 unp illus music lib. bdg. $6.99 (3-5)   **782.1**

1 Operas—Stories, plots, etc.
ISBN 0-394-91221-7   LC 44-9580

This libretto follows the familiar tale of the children of a poor wood-cutter lost in the forest and of their encounter with the witch who lives there

"A child's book of the opera, four of whose most melodious airs are reduced to easy playing and put each on a page in a simple piano arrangement." NY Her Trib Bks

"The pictures in color by Warren Chappell have a heavy, peasant-like quality, the dark shades in which they are reproduced contributing to the dread impression of the forest setting." Wis Library Bul

Montresor, Beni

Cinderella; from the opera by Gioacchino Rossini in a version written and illus. by Beni Montresor. Knopf 1965 unp illus lib. bdg. $5.99 (2-4)   **782.1**

1 Operas—Stories, plots, etc.
ISBN 0-394-91055-9   LC 65-21556

Based on Rossini's opera, Cenerentola, which opened in 1817, this version has the young Cinderella transformed into a lovely bride by the Prince's major domo. Illustrations are based on Montresor's set and costume designs for a Metropolitan Opera Company production

The pictures "glow as if the costumes and scenery were in a golden setting, grandiose and artificial but romantic. . . . The tone of the story is more sophisticated than the usual version for the youngest children." Bk Week

Streatfeild, Noel

The first book of the opera; illus. by Hilary Abrahams. Watts, F. 1966 62p illus lib. bdg. $4.90 (4 and up)   **782.1**

1 Opera
ISBN 0-531-00602-6   LC 65-10097

Published in England with title: Enjoying opera

The author "explains the difference between opera, light opera, operettas, and musical plays, outlines the history of opera, tells how operas are composed and produced, gives notes on well-known operas, composers, and performers, and includes a discography. Because of its brevity and enthusiastic tone this compressed account should serve as a useful introduction to opera. The numerous illustrations are colorful though not outstanding." Booklist

Updike, John

The Ring; music by Richard Wagner; adapted and illus. by John Updike and Warren Chappell. Knopf 1964 unp illus music lib. bdg. $5.39 (4 and up)   **782.1**

1 Operas—Stories, plots, etc.
ISBN 0-394-91544-5   LC 64-20169

"In an attempt to simplify the Nibelungenlied's complex characters and incidents, the author has concentrated on the story of the third opera in the Ring, Siegfried. He gives enough detail from earlier and later events to cover the entire range of Wagner's epic. The excellent text will probably have most appeal for the mature young reader and music lover. The musical themes are integrated with the text, and Warren Chappell's illustrations carry out the majestic sweep of the tale." Sch Library J

"An aid in understanding the music and arousing interest in reading the Siegfried legend." Hodges. Bk for Elem Sch Libraries

783.6   Sacred songs. Carols

And it came to pass; Bible verses and carols, selected by Jean Slaughter; illus. by Leonard Weisgard. Macmillan Pub. Co. 1971 unp illus music $4.95 (k-4)   **783.6**

1 Carols 2 Jesus Christ—Nativity
ISBN 0-02-782900-6   LC 70-127471

"Alternating selections from the Gospel of St. Luke and Christmas carols are arranged chronologically to tell the Nativity story. The illustrations, some in pen and ink and some in full-color tempera, are a reverent and graceful extension of the text. Guitar and piano arrangements accompany the carols." Pub W

Baker, Laura Nelson

The friendly beasts; illus. by Nicolas Sidjakov; adapted from an old English Christmas carol of the same title. Parnassus Press 1957 unp illus music $4.95 (k-3)   **783.6**

1 Carols
ISBN 0-87466-045-9   LC 57-12731

An adaptation of the 14th century English Christmas carol which tells "the story of the animals that waited in wonder in the stable in Bethlehem and told of the gifts each would give to the Christ child who was to be born that night in the manger. . . . The words and music of the carol appear at the end of the book." Booklist

"Nicolas Sidjakov's illustrations, rich in color and exciting in design, have a stained glass quality and help make the book a small gem for family and connoisseur." Chicago Sunday Trib

Davis, Katherine

The little drummer boy [illus. by] Ezra Jack Keats; words and music by Katherine Davis, Henry Onorati and Harry Simeone. Macmillan Pub. Co. 1968 unp illus music $7.95, pa $2.50 (k-2)   **783.6**

1 Carols
ISBN 0-02-749530-2; 0-02-044090-1   LC 68-25714

"Katherine Davis' Christmas song, originally called 'The Carol of the Drum,' has become a well-loved favorite with young and old. Now the tender verses, which follow a pattern familiar in Nativity stories and legends, provide the text for a handsome picture book. . . . The drummer's boyish earnestness is beautifully characterized in the pictures; occasional touches of collage add variety and texture to the rich color of the painting. Music and words are printed together at the end of the book." Horn Bk

Includes unaccompanied melody

Ehret, Walter

The international book of Christmas carols; musical arrangements by Walter Ehret. Translations and notes by George K. Evans; illus. by Don Martinetti; foreword by Norman Luboff. Stephen Greene 1980 338p illus music pa $11.95   **783.6**

1 Carols
ISBN 0-8289-0378-6   LC 80-13105

Ehret, Walter—*Continued*

First published 1963 by Prentice-Hall
"Arranged by nationality this excellent collection gives the words and music of a generous number of carols from England, the U.S., France, Germany, Scandinavia, the Slavic countries, Italy, and Spain. Five Latin carols are included. Lyrics of foreign-language songs are accompanied by English translations. Other features: a prefatory essay on Christmas and its songs, appended notes, a chart of guitar chords, and a title and a first-line index." Booklist

Horder, Mervyn

On Christmas day; first carols to play and sing; arranged by Mervyn Horder; illus. by Margaret Gordon. Macmillan Pub. Co. 1969 unp illus music $5.95 (3-6)   **783.6**

1 Carols
ISBN 0-02-74400-7   LC 69-11103

Here are "thirteen carols with simple piano arrangements . . . presented for unison singing by young children. The well-known American carols 'Away in a manger' and 'We three Kings of Orient are' and the English carols 'The first noel' and 'I saw three ships' are included but the others are English and French carols less familiar to American children." Booklist
"The half-page and full-page illustrations in their glowing greeting-card colors and stylized but lively designs richly set the stage." Horn Bk

Pauli, Hertha

Silent night; the story of a song; illus. by Fritz Kredel. Knopf 1943 81p illus music $2.75 (4 and up)   **783.6**

1 Carols 2 Gruber, Franz Xaver
ISBN 0-394-81621-8   LC 43-13486

"The story of one of the best loved Christmas carols—how it came to be written on Christmas eve 1818 in an Austrian village, the mystery which surrounded its authorship for so long, and its spread throughout the world." Booklist

The **Season** for singing; American Christmas songs and carols; comp. by John Langstaff; with music harmonized and arranged by Seymour Barab for piano or guitar accompaniment. Doubleday 1974 124p illus $7.95, lib. bdg. $8.90 (4 and up)   **783.6**

1 Carols
ISBN 0-385-06564-7; 0-385-06566-3   LC 74-4064

This book contains American Christmas carols which reflect the cultural diversity of the nation. Included are folk carols; Shaker, Moravian, Indian, Puerto Rican, and Afro-American carols; shape-note hymns; composed songs; and part songs; all with piano and guitar accompaniments. An index of first lines is appended
"The book will supplement collections exclusively devoted to all-time favorites, providing entertainment and a few diminished lessons in our diverse cultural heritage." Booklist

A **Treasury** of Christmas songs and carols; ed. and annotated by Henry W. Simon. 2d ed. with guitar chords. Illus. by Rafaello Busoni. Piano arrangements by the editor and Rudolph Fellner. Houghton 1973 243p illus music $11.95, pa $6.95   **783.6**

1 Carols 2 Songs
ISBN 0-395-17786-3; 0-395-17785-5

First published 1955
This collection contains over one hundred songs and carols, with arrangements for both piano and guitar. Designed for use by small informal groups who will find many of the familiar carols but also a sampling of foreign traditional airs
Divided into these six parts: British and American carols; Carols from foreign parts; Christmas hymns and chorales; Especially for children; Christmas solo songs; Christmas rounds and canons; Index of titles and first lines; Index of musical and literary sources
"The piano arrangements, except for a few solo songs from the great masters, contain the melody and are both well filled out and easily played. Pleasing illustrations have varied two-color arrangements." Horn Bk [review of 1955 edition]

The **Twelve** days of Christmas; in pictures by Ilonka Karasz. Harper 1949 unp illus music $7.95, lib. bdg. $8.79 (1-5)   **783.6**

1 Carols
ISBN 0-06-023090-8; 0-06-023091-6   LC 49-11875

"Ilonka Karasz has set the verses of [this] lovely old carol against twelve pictures which combine modern technique with the exuberance of the medieval tradition. The first picture is one partridge in a pear tree, then to the succeeding pictures is added, in order, each of those gifts which 'my true love sent to me,' until we see in grand finale the twelve drummers drumming, the lords a-leaping, the maids a-milking and all the other thoughtful presents." NY Times Bk Rev
Presented as "a thing of beauty and a joy forever. . . . The color is soft and rich, and on the last two pages is the music for the song. Here are art and music and an old tradition for young and old, all between the covers of one book." Sat Rev

784   Voice and vocal music

The **Laura** Ingalls Wilder songbook; favorite songs from the "Little house" books comp. and ed. by Eugenia Garson; arranged for piano and guitar by Herbert Haufrecht; illus by Garth Williams. Harper 1968 160p illus music $12.95, lib. bdg. $11.89 (3 and up)   **784**

1 Songs, American
ISBN 0-06-021933-5; 0-06-021934-3   LC 68-24327

A former children's librarian has researched, compiled, and annotated 62 of the songs that appear in Wilder's 'Little house' books. The collection, valuable as representative of a period as well as interesting in connection with the series, contains dancing or singing game tunes, patriotic songs, ballads, minstrel-show and music-hall melodies, hymns, and gospel songs. Brief notes with the music indicate the page of the story on which each song appears and gives, when available, information about the song, composer, or lyricist." Booklist
"Garth Williams' charming illustrations, done originally for the 1953 uniform edition of the Wilder books add to the appeal of a volume that will be a welcome addition to any children's collection that includes the 'Little House' books." Sch Library J

784.1   Choruses and part songs

Rounds about rounds; collected and ed. by Jane Yolen; musical arrangements by Barbara Greene; illus. by Gail Gibbons. Watts, F. 1977 120p illus music lib. bdg. $7.90 (3-6)   **784.1**

1 Songs 2 Folk songs
ISBN 0-531-00125-3   LC 77-7919

"A collection of 57 rounds. . . . Proverbs, stories, and verses are given with each round, and there are also piano accompaniments to aid in teaching the basic melody plus background information on rounds, catches, and canons." Sch Library J
"Some of the songs are serious, some silly, some are favorites, some new, some are lovely, some just noisy and fun! This beautifully bound book rates highly in every respect. The musical arrangements are simple, yet they allow the repeating song to be heard in the accompaniment. The line drawings are appropriate to each selection and are highlighted by a bit of prose or poetry in keeping with the music being illustrated. This is a book to treasure and use!" Children's Bk Rev Serv
Sources of rounds: p116. Sources of additional material: p118

Sweetly sings the donkey; animal rounds for children to sing or play on recorders; selected by John Langstaff; pictures by Nancy Winslow Parker. Atheneum Pubs. 1976 27p illus music $6.95 (2-5)   **784.1**

1 Songs 2 Animals—Songs and music
ISBN 0-689-50063-7   LC 76-9530

Sweetly sings the donkey—*Continued*

The compiler "has gathered together a baker's dozen of easy songs in canon form which are ideal for young children and has written a brief introduction to explain the various ways of performing rounds. The music is well-suited to the recorder; but beginners at the piano will also enjoy the simple tunes." Horn Bk

"The illustrator has chosen a medieval theme for her doll-like figures and dollhouse buildings, all done in a pleasant red-clay color against the white page. In sum, a harmonious contribution, accessible to novice musicians with and without adult assistance." Booklist

784.4 Folk songs

Emberley, Barbara
One wide river to cross; adapted by Barbara Emberley; illus. by Ed Emberley. Prentice-Hall 1966 unp illus music $5.95 (k-3)
784.4

1 Folk songs—U.S. 2 Noah's Ark 3 Counting—Songs and music
ISBN 0-13-636167-6   LC 66-20703

The illustrator depicts "the animals as they file into the ark—snakes on roller skates, elephants doing tricks, and so on, one by one up to ten by ten. The music for this old folk song is included." Children's Bks. 1966

"Processional black woodcut images on solid, bright-colored paper create an exciting, cumulative design of animals. . . . The character of illustrations is striking, and evokes thoughts of Egyptian hieroglyphics or spiritual Negro art." Wis Library Bul

The **Erie** Canal; illus. by Peter Spier. Doubleday 1970 unp illus map music $6.95, lib. bdg. $7.90, pa $1.95 (k-4)   **784.4**

1 Folk songs—U.S.
ISBN 0-385-06777-1; 0-385-05452-1; 0-385-05234-0
                                                      LC 70-102055

An American folk song is recreated in full-color scenes. Historical notes, a map of the canal which served as a busy trade route, and the musical arrangement for the song is included

The illustrator "records detail with the meticulous accuracy of the historian and the appreciative eye of the artist. His characteristic full-color pictures—many of them double-spreads—are full of boats, buildings, animals, and people, all involved in the bustling activity on and along the banks of the canal." Horn Bk

Fireside book of folk songs; selected and ed. by Margaret Bradford Boni; arranged for the piano by Norman Lloyd; illus. by Alice and Martin Provensen. Simon & Schuster [1966 c1947] 323p illus music $17.50   **784.4**

1 Folk songs 2 Songs
ISBN 0-671-25836-2   LC 47-31480

Companion volume to: The Fireside book of favorite American songs, entered in class 784.7

Reprint of the 1947 edition with guitar chords added

"One of the most colorful and charming collections for people who like to sing for the fun of it. . . . Outstanding for the selection exercised in compiling this volume of 147 old favorites, sea chanteys, cowboy songs and hymns, railroad songs, spirituals and Christmas carols. Arrangements for the piano by Norman Lloyd are excellent for their simplicity. Each song is prefaced by a brief introduction and these plus brief statements at the beginning of each category, constitute all the commentary. It is meant for a songbook and used as such it will be most successful. The colored illustrations, 500 of them, are very gay." Cur Ref Bks

Includes notation for guitar accompaniment

The **Fireside** song book of birds and beasts; ed. by Jane Yolen; arranged by Barbara Green; illus. by Peter Parnall. Simon & Schuster 1972 223p illus music $9.95   **784.4**

1 Folk songs 2 Animals—Songs and music
ISBN 0-671-66540-5   LC 75-175047

For each of the nearly one hundred songs assembled here there is a brief introduction, a musical arrangement for piano, and guitar chords. The book is divided into five sections: Farmyard and house, Field and forest, In the air, In the sea, and Other phenomena

"A delightful collection, with many old favorites, is delectably illustrated by the clean-lined drawings of Peter Parnall. They are just right for the animal songs to be used by or with children, and the piano accompaniments are not intricate. . . . An index of titles is appended." Chicago. Children's Bk Center

Fowke, Edith
(comp.) Ring around the moon; illus. by Judith Gwyn Brown. Prentice-Hall 1977 160p illus music $6.95   **784.4**

1 Folk songs, Canadian 2 Humorous poetry
ISBN 0-13-781252-3   LC 76-44207

Most of these 200 rounds, animal songs, circular and cumulative songs, songs about curious characters, ditties, rhyming riddles, "tongue-twisters, answerback songs, omens, and charms, collected from the folk traditions of Canada, are just as familiar in the U.S. . . . Although the format is for the middle grades, some of the material (e.g., 'Three Blind Mice,' 'Row Row Row Your Boat') is for preschoolers." Sch Library J

"This is the sort of fare that all kids love because they can browse around and always find something of interest. The illustrations are excellent line drawings, full of charm. There is a very good reference section [which lists sources] and a valuable bibliography." Children's Bk Rev Serv

The **Fox** went out on a chilly night; an old song illus. by Peter Spier. Doubleday 1961 unp illus music $6.95, lib. bdg. $7.90, pa $1.49 (k-3)   **784.4**

1 Folk songs—U.S.
ISBN 0-385-07990-7; 0-385-00231-9; 0-385-01065-6
                                                      LC 60-7139

Set in New England, this old folk song tells about the trip the fox father made to town to get some of the farmer's plump geese for his family's dinner, and how he manages to evade the farmer who tries to shoot him

"A true picture book in the Caldecott-Brooke tradition. Fine drawings, lovely colors, and pictures so full of amusing details that young viewers will make fresh discoveries every time they scrutinize (as they surely will) these beautiful, action-filled pages." Horn Bk

Includes music

Go tell Aunt Rhody; illus. by Aliki. Macmillan Pub. Co. 1974 32p illus music $5.95 (k-3)   **784.4**

1 Folk songs—U.S.
ISBN 0-02-711920-3   LC 74-681

"A piano arrangement and lyrics are included in this version of the American folk song about the old gray goose." Rdng Teacher

"Rich tasty colors and vivid expressions . . . are found in the illustrations. . . . Capturing unabashedly the rural pleasures of the American past, Aliki has dipped into 18th-century landscapes for just the right settings. The children's faces tell us how it feels to live on a farm, to have an Aunt Rhody and to be excited and a little frightened by the death of a goose." NY Times Bk Rev

Hush, little baby [illus. by] Margot Zemach. Dutton 1976 unp illus music lib. bdg. $7.95 (k-1)   **784.4**

1 Lullabies 2 Folk songs
ISBN 0-525-32510-7   LC 76-5477

The book contains "ridiculously appealing pictures accompanying the verses of the time-honored lullaby. The setting is Victorian with literal representations of a put-upon household where the diamond ring for the little baby turns brass, the mockingbird won't sing, the horse and cart roll over, the other disappointments occur. The pages are full of action and color and one of the funniest shows that dog Rover that won't bark, an outsized beast, taking over a whole bed to the disgust of the family, especially a pet cat and the 'sweetest little baby in town.' " Pub W

Hush, little baby—*Continued*

"The antics of the sturdy figures, limned in energetic black line, are an amusing contrast to the use of tempera, an elegant painterly medium. . . . In this latest version, the lines of the song are arranged so that the conclusions to the speculative clauses are depicted on the following pages, a technique which enhances the sense of movement in the illustrations. A marvelously earthy and zestful interpretation. Words and music are appended." Horn Bk

Langstaff, John

Frog went a-courtin'; retold by John Langstaff; with pictures by Feodor Rojankovsky. Harcourt 1955 unp illus music $6.50, pa $1.95 (k-3)   **784.4**

1 Ballads, Scottish
ISBN 0-15-230214-X; 0-15-633900-5   LC 55-5237

Awarded the Caldecott Medal, 1956
"Picture book version of the old Scottish ballad [also known as: A frog he would a-wooing go]. . . . Each page has a colorful and humorously detailed picture, usually with two lines of the ballad below. The words given here are a composite of several versions. The ending turns out happily when frog and mouse, safely wed despite the old tom cat's interruption at the wedding party, sail for France. The format makes an attractive picture book and good story telling (or singing) material." Chicago. Children's Bk Center

Illustrated in "vivid colours. . . . The accompanying tune is the one sung in the southern Appalachian mountains." Ontario Library Rev.

(ed.) Hi! Ho! The rattlin' bog, and other folk songs for group singing; with piano settings by John Edmunds [and others]; with guitar chords suggested by Happy Traum; illus. by Robin Jacques. Harcourt 1969 112p illus music $5.50 (4 and up)   **784.4**

1 Folk songs
ISBN 0-15-234400-4   LC 75-76616

"An ample and satisfying collection of fifty-three genuine folk songs for group singing at home, school, or camp: work songs, jig tunes, narrative ballads, counting and riddle songs, lullabies, calypsos, and historical songs—a great range, with further variety provided in their settings by four different composers. . . . The title song is not to be found in any other collection, and some of the other selections will seem new to many. The simple accompaniments will tempt young pianists." Horn Bk

"Brief notes explores [the] origin and meanings [of these songs], arrangements are fresh and original and easy to play. . . . Black and white drawings by Robin Jacques are reminiscent of old-fashioned steel engravings and give added appeal to a very rich collection." NY Times Bk Rev

Oh, a-hunting we will go; pictures by Nancy Winslow Parker. Atheneum Pubs. 1974 unp illus music $7.95 (k-2)   **784.4**

1 Folk songs
ISBN 0-689-50007-6   LC 74-76274

"A Margaret K. McElderry book"
The nonsense verses of this folk song trace the hunt for such animals as an armadillo, a fox, and a snake, and describe the imagined treatment of each animal once it is caught

"The 12 stanzas are complemented by Parker's droll crayon illustrations (the fox caught in the box is watching TV), and a score for guitar and piano is appended. An amusing addition to 'song' picture books." Sch Library J

Over in the meadow; with pictures by Feodor Rojankovsky. Harcourt 1957 unp illus music $5.95, pa $1.50 (k-2)   **784.4**

1 Songs 2 Counting—Songs and music
ISBN 0-15-258854-X; 0-15-670500-1   LC 57-8587

"This old counting rhyme [based on a folk song] tells of ten meadow families whose mothers advise them to dig, run, sing, play, hum, build, swim, wink, spin and hop. The illustrations, half in full color, show the combination of realism and imagination which little children like best. The tune arranged simply, is on the last page, and children will have fun acting the whole thing out." Horn Bk

"Mr. Rojankovsky's soft-colored close-ups of the flora and fauna of the meadow seem, somehow, a little static in comparison to his usual robustious pictures. They are, however, very decorative, and they make it easy to count the foxes two, the seven polliwogs and even the spiders nine." NY Times Bk Rev

The two magicians; adapted by John Langstaff from an ancient ballad; pictures by Fritz Eichenberg. Atheneum Pubs. 1973 unp illus music lib. bdg. $4.95 (k-3)   **784.4**

1 Folk songs, English
ISBN 0-689-30319-X   LC 72-85919

"A Margaret K. McElderry book"
Here is an ancient English ballad with the text adapted and the tune modified for children. It is "about a witch who is being pursued by a magician. A full-page illustration accompanies each verse as the witch '. . . became a fish,/a fish all in a creek,/And he became a wading bird/and caught her with his beak.' The story progresses until '. . . she became herself,/as pretty as the day,/And he became a handsome prince/and carried her away.'" Library J

"The melody [is] pleasingly harmonized in a simple piano arrangement [with guitar chords]. . . . The illustrator's lively humor shows in the figures and the background details drawn in four colors." Horn Bk

London Bridge is falling down! Illus. by Peter Spier. Doubleday 1967 unp illus music $6.95, lib. bdg. $7.90, pa $1.49 (k-2)   **784.4**

1 Folk songs, English 2 Nursery rhymes
ISBN 0-385-08717-9; 0-385-08718-7; 0-385-08025-5   LC 67-17695

This picture book illustrated with scenes of eighteenth-century London presents the traditional verses of the Mother Goose nursery rhyme. The musical score is included, as well as a three-page historical sketch of London Bridge through the centuries

"For the child who enjoys big pictures filled with small details, this version of the familiar verses should be a small treasure. Each illustration is a double-page spread teeming with action. The colors are subdued save for a bright red-orange, and the pages are crowded with scenes, containing authentic details (in costume, architecture, signs, etc.) as well as amusing caricatures." Sat Rev

Nic Leodhas, Sorche

Always room for one more; illus. by Nonny Hogrogian. Holt 1965 unp illus music $5.95, pa $1.65 (k-3)   **784.4**

1 Folk songs, Scottish
ISBN 0-03-088343-1; 0-03-088507-8   LC 65-12881

Awarded the Caldecott Medal, 1966
"A picture book based on an old Scottish folk song about hospitable Lachie MacLachlan, who invited in so many guests that his little house finally burst. Rhymed text . . . a glossary of Scottish words, and music for the tune are combined into an effective whole." Hodges. Bks for Elem Sch Libraries

"Pen and ink drawings with chalk and color wash add dimension and humor to the lilting text. An enchanting picture book." Wis Library Bul

Old MacDonald had a farm [illus. by] Robert Quackenbush. Lippincott 1972 unp illus music $8.95 (k-2)   **784.4**

1 Folk songs—U.S.
ISBN 0-397-31262-8   LC 72-172150

A "picture-book version of the familiar folk song about Old MacDonald and the noisy animals on his farm. As each new animal is mentioned in the lyrics printed on the righthand page, that animal is added to brightly colored pictures of the farm on the lefthand page." Booklist

"A joyful treat . . . complete with music and background notes on the origin of the song." Pub W

Quackenbush, Robert

Go tell Aunt Rhody; starring the old gray goose who is a living legend in her own lifetime and the greatest American since the American eagle. Lippincott 1973 unp illus music lib. bdg. $8.95 (k-3)   784.4

1 Folk songs—U.S. 2 Puzzles
ISBN 0-397-31459-0   LC 72-8711

Illustrated by the author

"A combination puzzle, picture and song book. The verses are based on the death of the old grey goose, the one 'Aunt Rhody' is planning to use to make a feather bed and other things. Some of the brain teasers here will be over the heads of the littlest readers but it's a book that can be enjoyed, over and over, with the help of older friends." Pub W

She'll be comin' round the mountain. Lippincott 1973 unp illus music $6.95 (k-3)   784.4

1 Folk songs—U.S.
ISBN 0-397-31480-9   LC 73-2943

"A picture book in play form, this old railroad song is presented in bold purples and blues, golds and oranges. The animated full-page pictures freely interpret the song: a Wild West show, traveling by train, is coming into Pughtown for a one-night stand. Before the train arrives, Sneaky Pete, Rattlesnake Hank and Crumby Joe attempt to rob it. But, the show's star, Little Annie, snares the robbers with her lasso . . . and the show can go on." Babbling Bookworm

"Quackenbush has amiably included a piano accompaniment and a suitably silly number game to decide Annie's future." Booklist

Skip to my Lou. Lippincott 1975 unp illus music $8.95 (k-2)   784.4

1 Folk songs—U.S.
ISBN 0-397-31613-5   LC 74-14585

In this version "Matthew writes a letter to his Cousin George telling of his sister Lou's engagement party and the 'disasters' that happened at it. Robert Quackenbush has taken the folksong 'Skip to My Lou' and made a lively, action-filled picture book for children. He finishes the book with the music to the song and a depiction of how to dance to 'Skip to My Lou.' Colorful, bold illustrations showing life in the 1800's depict the chaos of each disaster." Children's Bk Rev Serv

Simple piano and guitar chord arrangements included

Seeger, Pete

The foolish frog [by] Pete Seeger and Charles Seeger; illus. by Miloslav Jagr; music adapted from an old song; book adapted and designed from Firebird Film by Gene Deitch. Macmillan Pub. Co. 1973 unp illus music $4.95   784.4

1 Folk songs—U.S.
ISBN 0-02-781480-7   LC 73-2121

A farmer makes up a song about a frog and sings it to the storekeeper of the general store. The latter becomes exuberant, treats the customers to pop and soda crackers, and sets up a chain reaction of revelry

The text "is enlivened by splashy, colorful cartoon drawings. The book's usefulness is enhanced by the catchy lyrics and tune included at the end of the book. Where material on folk songs is desired, this would be an adequate addition." Sch Library J

Seeger, Ruth Crawford

American folk songs for children in home, school and nursery school; a book for children, parents and teachers; illus. by Barbara Cooney. Doubleday 1948 190p illus music $9.95, lib. bdg. $10.90   784.4

1 Folk songs—U.S. 2 Singing games
ISBN 0-385-07210-4; 0-385-07316-X   LC 48-9384

A big book of 90 folk songs from all parts of the country that may be sung and acted out with many variations. The tunes and piano accompaniments are simple enough for most adults to play. It is a source book for family fun

"Several introductory chapters discussing the value of folk music for children and how to use the folk songs with children at home and at school give the book added meaning for parents, teachers, and play-group leaders. Excellent classified indexes and index of titles and first lines." Booklist

(comp.) American folk songs for Christmas; illus. by Barbara Cooney. Doubleday 1953 80p illus music lib. bdg. $5.95   784.4

1 Folk songs—U.S. 2 Carols
ISBN 0-385-08299-1   LC 53-9986

Contains more than fifty American folk songs based on Christmas themes. Divided into these categories: Stars and shepherds; Mary and the Baby; Praise and festivity

"In the introduction [the compiler] tells about the sources of the songs and the holy-day and holiday celebrations at which they used to be sung. . . . The songs vary in difficulty and children will, of course, need an adult to use the book with them. It offers great possibilities for interesting Christmas programs." Horn Bk

Serwadda, W. Moses

Songs and stories from Uganda; transcribed and ed. by Hewitt Pantaleoni; illus. by Leo and Diane Dillon. Crowell 1974 80p illus music $6.50, lib. bdg. $7.39   784.4

1 Folk songs, Ugandan 2 Folklore—Uganda
ISBN 0-690-75240-7; 0-690-75241-5   LC 72-7556

This is a collection of storytelling songs from the Luganda, an East African language. "The music is transcribed in Western style; and words are supplied in both English and Luganda, with careful instructions for the pronunciation of Luganda words. To go along with the music, explanations or instructions are included for game songs or for dances. The dynamic two-color woodcuts add strongly to the African flavor of the book." Horn Bk

El **Toro** pinto, and other songs in Spanish; selected and illus. by Anne Rockwell. Macmillan Pub. Co. 1971 52p illus music $7.95 (1-6)   784.4

1 Folk songs, Spanish 2 Bilingual books—Spanish-English
ISBN 0-02-777490-2   LC 70-146623

"Brightly colored illustrations give this diversified collection of 30 songs in Spanish from Latin America, Spain and the Southwestern U.S. a cheerful, attractive appearance. Melody, guitar chords, and Spanish words are given for each of the lullabies, carols, and other songs; English translations, not intended for singing, are appended; and the country of origin of each song is indicated in the table of contents. Brief introductory notes and suggestions for using the songs precede the selections." Booklist

784.6 Songs for specific groups and on specific subjects

Child, Lydia Maria

Over the river and through the wood; pictures by Brinton Turkle. Coward, McCann & Geoghegan 1974 unp illus music $7.95 (1-3)   784.6

1 Thanksgiving Day—Songs and music
ISBN 0-698-20301-1   LC 74-79700

This version of the poem about a family's visit to their grandparents for Thanksgiving, which first appeared in 1844 as "The Boy's Thanksgiving Day," includes usually omitted verses, as well as a musical arrangement for piano and guitar

"The pictures, realistic in period detail, are evocative and are framed so that each looks as though it were in an album. Pictures of the visiting family are in color and alternate with quiet black and white pictures of the grandparents' preparations (bringing in logs, rolling the piecrust, setting the long table) and then the whole family is together." Chicago. Children's Bk Center

Conover, Chris

Six little ducks; retold and illus. by Chris
Conover. Crowell 1976 unp illus music $5.95,
lib. bdg. $6.79 (k-2)   **784.6**

1 Ducks—Songs and music
ISBN 0-690-01036-2; 0-690-01037-0   LC 75-22155

"Music [for piano or guitar] and lyrics are provided at the back of the book for an adaptation
of a children's song. . . . The ducks go to market,
lose their wares, are rejected by a hostile baker
when they ask for bread, go home and bake their
own bread, and go to a party." Chicago. Children's Bk Center

"Miss Conover has not merely illustrated a
song. Her black-and-white drawings and colorful,
double-page panoramas enhance and expand, adding new dimension to the words. What comes
across is a sense of joy, loving care for detail
and a sprinkling of mischief." NY Times Bk Rev

Crofut, William

The moon on the one hand; poetry in
song; arrangements by Kenneth Cooper &
Glenn Shattuck; illus. by Susan Crofut.
Atheneum Pubs. 1975 80p illus music $9.95
(3-6)   **784.6**

1 Songs 2 Poetry—Collections 3 Nature in
poetry
ISBN 0-689-50018-1   LC 74-18179

"A Margaret K. McElderry book"
"A selection of animal and nature poems, by
such well-known poets as E. E. Cummings, Robert
Louis Stevenson, and Randall Jarrell, has been
set to music." LC. Children's Bks. 1975
"The melodies are original and perfectly suited
to the poems, and the arrangements by Kenneth
Cooper and Glenn Shattuck offer a variety of
styles and instrumentation. Basically written for
piano with guitar diagrams, there are opportunities
for flute, recorder, violin, harmonica, obbligato
voice, or harpsichord. Some arrangements are
simple sight reading; others require putting together, but all provide enjoyable pieces for individual or group use." Sch Library J

Engvick, William

(ed.) Lullabies and night songs; music
by Alec Wilder; pictures by Maurice Sendak.
Harper 1965 77p illus music $15, lib.
bdg. $12.89 (k-3)   **784.6**

1 Lullabies 2 Songs
ISBN 0-06-021820-7; 0-06-021821-5   LC 65-22880

"The editor has selected verses, in addition to
some of his own, from poets as notable and varied
as Eleanor Farjeon, Tennyson, Thurber, Stevenson,
Kipling, Walter de la Mare, and William Blake, as
well as many anonymous, traditional poems like
'Sleep, Baby, Sleep,' 'Wee Willie Winkie,' and
'Now the Day is Over.'" Horn Bk
"Wilder's contemporary and original music and
simple arrangements are suitable. Sendak's gay
muted color illustrations capture every mood perfectly." Wis Library Bul

The **Fireside** book of children's songs; collected & ed. by Marie Winn; musical
arrangements by Allan Miller; illus. by
John Alcorn. Simon & Schuster 1966 192p
illus music $9.95   **784.6**

1 Songs 2 Folk songs
ISBN 0-671-25820-6   LC 65-17108

The book is divided into five parts: Good morning and good night, Birds and beasts, Nursery
songs, Silly songs, and Singing games and rounds
"Over 100 songs for preschool and elementary
age children are contained in this most attractive
volume. . . . The accompaniments are simple,
and guitar chords are provided. . . . Stylized
decorations in mustard, rust, and shocking pink
add to the overall appeal of the volume. Highly
recommended for homes, schools, and public libraries." Sch Library J
Index of song titles and first lines: p191

The **Fireside** book of fun and game songs;
collected and ed. by Marie Winn; musical
arrangements by Allan Miller; illus. by
Whitney Darrow, Jr. Simon & Schuster
1974 222p illus music $12.50   **784.6**

1 Songs 2 Singing games
ISBN 0-671-65213-3   LC 74-6957

The songs are divided into ten categories which
include cumulative and diminishing songs, echo
songs, motion and wordplay songs, question and
answer songs, and rounds
"Although many of the individual items could
be found in other books, some would be almost
impossible to locate elsewhere. Musical arrangements and accompaniments are simple, and spirited
drawings add to the innocent merriment." Horn Bk
Title and first line index: p[223-24]

Girl Scouts of the United States of America

Sing together; Girl Scout songbook. 3d ed.
The author 1973 182p illus pa $3 (4 and up)
                                         784.6

1 Songs 2 Folk songs
ISBN 0-88441-309-8

First published 1949
A collection of over 140 songs, including blues,
jazz, contemporary, folk, popular songs, and songs
from other lands, as well as scouting favorites.
Guitar chords and a glossary of terms and instruments add to the illustrated text. Designed to
provide material for ceremonial meetings or smaller
group gatherings

The **Great** song book; ed. by Timothy John;
music ed. by Peter Hankey; illus. by Tomi
Ungerer. Doubleday 1978 112p illus music
$12.50   **784.6**

1 Songs 2 Folk songs
ISBN 0-385-13328-6   LC 77-74707

"The Benn Book collection"
First published 1975 in Switzerland
A collection of songs "long familiar to English-
speaking people. Grouped around such broad categories as nursery rhymes, folk songs, lullabies, and
Christmas, they range from simple unaccompanied
unison selections to part songs with piano accompaniments of varying complexity; guitar chords
are included throughout. Full-page paintings as
well as smaller illustrations, all in color, often
comment upon rather than represent the songs and
display the scope of the artist's many moods—all
the way from a comic spirit, with broad lusty
humor reminiscent of Hogarth and Rowlandson,
to a quiet reverence, even tenderness." Horn Bk

The **Holiday** song book; 100 songs! 27
holidays! Selections, illustrations, and additional lyrics by Robert Quackenbush; all
music arranged for easy piano and guitar
by Harry Buch. Lothrop 1977 128p illus
music $9.95, lib. bdg. $9.55   **784.6**

1 Holidays—Songs and music
ISBN 0-688-41820-1; 0-688-51820-6   LC 77-5895

A "collection of one hundred songs which are
grouped by holidays—over twenty-five in all.
Occasions such as April Fool's Day, Martin Luther
King's birthday, and Earth Day are among those
included. Each section is introduced by a note on
the origins of the holiday and is decorated in
black and gold." Horn Bk
"Arrangements are simple to play for sing-
alongs. The table of contents and an index of
first lines, titles, and holidays make everything
easy to find. There are some problems, chiefly
in editing: the fourth day is missing from 'The
Twelve Days of Christmas'; 'I've Been Working
on the Railroad' stops with 'Dinah, won't you blow
your horn.' For some reason Quackenbush celebrates Martin Luther King, Jr. Day with a version
of 'We Shall Overcome' that King didn't sing.
. . . Despite these annoyances the book is holiday group fun; a pleasant . . . addition to a
children's music collection" Sch Library J

Jim along, Josie; a collection of folk songs
and singing games for young children;
comp. by Nancy and John Langstaff. Piano
arrangements by Seymour Barab; guitar
chords by Happy Traum; optional percussion accompaniments for children; illus. by
Jan Pienkowski. Harcourt 1970 127p illus
music $7.50 (k-4)   **784.6**

1 Folk songs 2 Singing games
ISBN 0-15-240250-0   LC 79-118757

Here are "eighty-one songs chosen for their
freshness and adaptability, with simple piano arrangements, guitar chords, and directions or suggestions for use. Decorated with lively silhouettes." Top of the News

Kapp, Paul
Cock-a-doodle-doo! Cock-a-doodle-dandy! A new songbook for the newest singers; pictures by Anita Lobel. Harper 1966 70p illus music lib. bdg. $8.79 (k-2) **784.6**
1 Songs
ISBN 0-06-022388-X LC 65-22243
This "collection includes, in addition to traditional rhymes, verses by Carroll, Lear, John Bunyan, Blake, Eugene Field, Keats, Herrick, and Christina Rosetti." Horn Bk
"The music is contemporary in feeling, easy to play, and in most cases, easy to sing. For parent or teacher, this is a delightful addition to a song library." NY Times Bk Rev

Peterson, Carolyn Sue
(comp.) Index to children's songs; a title, first line, and subject index; comp. by Carolyn Sue Peterson and Ann D. Fenton. Wilson, H.W. 1979 318p $15 **784.6**
1 Children's songs—Indexes
ISBN 0-8242-0638-X LC 79-14265
"An index to more than 5,000 English and foreign-language children's songs and variations contained (both music and lyrics) in 298 song books published between 1909 and 1977. The work consists of three sections: (1) a list of books indexed, arranged alphabetically by author with a location code number for each book; (2) a title and first line index, merged into one alphabet (first lines printed in italics), tracing variations of titles and lines and giving location code and page number for each entry; and (3) an extensive subject index, which lists song titles under more than 1,000 subject headings and includes a 'Broad topic guide' to the subject headings. . . . This up-to-date and detailed index should prove very useful to teachers, parents, and young people." Choice

784.7 National airs, songs, hymns

Bangs, Edward
Steven Kellogg's Yankee Doodle. Four Winds [1980 c1976] unp illus music lib. bdg. $9.95 (k-3) **784.7**
1 National songs, American
ISBN 0-590-07782-1 LC 80-17024
Reprint of the 1976 edition published by Parents' Magazine Press
An illustrated version of the popular Revolutionary War song, originally penned in 1775 by Harvard student Edward Bangs. "Processions, battlefield action, and a little boy spectator, wearing a feather in his cap and usually waving a flag, fill the pages of a visually satisfying book. Handsome endpapers show first the arrival and later the departure of the British redcoats in full-rigged sailing ships. A commentary about the history of the song and its variations precedes the text; the eight measures of the familiar melody are given at the end of the book." Horn Bk
"The color illustrations are zesty and action filled. . . . But Kellogg's rewording of some of the well-known verses are downright silly. In an attempt to please feminists, for instance, he has changed . . . 'and with the girls be handy' (which meant something) to 'with the folks be handy' (which means nothing)." Pub W

Browne, C. A.
The story of our national ballads; rev. by Willard A. Heaps. Crowell 1960 314p $9.95 (5 and up) **784.7**
1 National songs, American
ISBN 0-690-77707-8 LLC 60-15255
First published 1919
This volume contains stories of patriotic songs and war ballads from Yankee Doodle to songs of World War II with biographies of many of their authors including Francis Scott Key, Julia Ward Howe, Daniel Decatur Emmett, Samuel F. Smith, Stephen Foster, Katharine Lee Bates, and Irving Berlin
Reading list: p287-96

The **Fireside** book of favorite American songs; selected and ed. by Margaret Bradford Boni; arranged for the piano by Norman Lloyd; illus. by Aurelius Battaglia; introductions by Anne Brooks; with a foreword by the late Carl Van Doren. Simon & Schuster 1952 359p illus music $15.95, pa $9.95 **784.7**
1 Songs, American 2 Folk songs—U.S.
ISBN 0-671-24771-9; 0-671-22061-6 LC 52-13624
Companion volume to: Fireside book of folk songs, entered in class 784.4
This book "includes a wide range of ballads, sentimental songs, gospel hymns, and ragtime songs." Hodges. Bks for Elem Sch Libraries

The **Frogs** who wanted a king and other songs from La Fontaine; collected by Edward Smith; illus. by Margot Zemach. Four Winds 1977 58p illus music lib. bdg. $11.95 **784.7**
1 Songs, French 2 Fables 3 Bilingual books—French-English
ISBN 0-590-17294-8 LC 77-5819
"Twenty-nine songs based upon the enduring fables of La Fontaine are revived in the spirit of an eighteenth-century songbook. The original figured bass is presented with a simple piano accompaniment and an additional melody line. The lyrics are in French, but the stories are also told in English." Children's Bk Rev Serv
"Never has the artist used color more sumptuously nor pen and ink more expressively. With eighteenth-century French music 'intended expressly for children,' the distinctive song book can add pleasure to the study of French and offer choral groups of any age fresh and entertaining material." Horn Bk

Key, Francis Scott
The Star-Spangled Banner; illus. by Peter Spier. Doubleday 1973 unp illus map music $7.95, lib. bdg. $8.90 (1-4) **784.7**
1 National songs, American
ISBN 0-385-09458-2; 0-385-07746-7 LC 73-79712
"All of the verses of the national anthem are illustrated. . . . Most of the pictures show the battle scenes that inspired Francis Scott Key to write the words of 'The Star-Spangled Banner' in 1814, but others reflect aspects of life in the United States today. Following the illustrated lyrics are a photograph of the manuscript, a discussion of the War of 1812, the music for the anthem, and a double-page spread that shows official flags for government agencies and officers." Chicago. Children's Bk Center
"At the beginning of the book, the mood is set by the detailed line drawings of sailing vessels and by the panoramic doublespreads vigorous with the flight of rockets. The pastel watercolor tones are never mawkish or sentimental but convey the dramatic feeling for space made possible by the sizable dimensions of the book." Horn Bk

Lyons, John Henry
Stories of our American patriotic songs; illus. by Jacob Landau. Vanguard [1958 c1942] 72p illus music $7.95 (4 and up) **784.7**
1 National songs, American
ISBN 0-8149-0354-1 LC 42-24375
Reissue of a 1942 title in larger format
"The stories behind 10 of America's most popular patriotic songs—when, why, and by whom they were written. . . . Words and music are given for each. A large, flat book, well-illustrated." Booklist
Contents: Star-Spangled Banner; Yankee Doodle; Hail, Columbia; America; Columbia, the gem of the ocean; Dixie; Maryland, my Maryland; Battle cry of Freedom; Battle hymn of the Republic; America, the beautiful

National anthems of the world; ed. by Martin Shaw [and others. 5th ed. enl. and rev] Arco 1978 511p music $24.95 **784.7**
1 National songs
ISBN 0-668-04496-9 LC 78-231
First published 1943 in England with title: National anthems of the United Nations and France

National anthems of the world—*Continued*

This volume contains national anthems of more than 150 nations, including melody and accompaniment. Words are presented in the native language with transliteration provided where necessary. English translations are also provided. Brief historical notes on the adoption of each anthem are included and the book concludes with a list of national days

Sandburg, Carl

(ed.) The American songbag. Harcourt [1970 c1927] xxiii, 495p illus music pa $6.95
784.7

1 Songs, American 2 Folk songs—U.S. 3 Ballads, American
ISBN 0-15-605650-X   LC 74-3218

First published 1927

"The music includes not merely airs and melodies, but complete harmonizations or piano accompaniments." Introduction

This is a collection of 280 songs and ballads from every section of the country which reflects the spirit of the time and place as well as the mood of the singer—songs of the Negro, the pioneer, the Irish immigrant, the southern mountaineer, the Great Lakes bargeman, the hobo, the section hand, the lumberjack, the soldier, the college student. The collection is a commentary on American life with sidelights on American history

"Each song is introduced by Mr. Sandburg who in a few words gives the story of his discovery or of its origin. Those notes make fascinating reading, and they can be enjoyed by those who cannot read notes or who belong to the minority that does not like to sing—or hear singing." Springf'd Republican

Schackburg, Richard

Yankee Doole; woodcuts by Ed Emberley; notes by Barbara Emberley. Prentice- Hall 1965 unp illus music pa $1.50 (k-3)   **784.7**

1 National songs, American
ISBN 0-13-971879-6   LC 65-15000

"Using only the primary colors with black and white, the artist has made illustrations that are vivid, amusing, and very attractive. The text consists of the verses of the song, printed in a running line at the foot of each page; notes on the origin of the lyrics, and of some of the words used, preface the text; the music is appended." Chicago Children's Bk Center

Walk together children; Black American spirituals; selected and illus. by Ashley Bryan. Atheneum Pubs. 1974 53p illus music $7.95   **784.7**

1 Spirituals (Songs)
ISBN 0-689-30131-6   LC 73-84821

"The selector prefaces two dozen spirituals—slave songs and 'sorrow songs'—with a commentary that explains the fusion of African musical culture with free melodic ideas to make 'America's most distinctive contribution to word music.' . . . Melody lines and one or more verses are provided for each selection; and stark, heavy woodcuts illustrate most of the songs." Horn Bk

785.06 Bands

Etkin, Ruth

The rhythm band book; illus. by Bunny Cappiello; with photographs by David Cohen. Sterling 1978 96p illus music $6.95, lib. bdg. $6.69   **785.06**

1 Rhythm bands and orchestras 2 Percussion instruments
ISBN 0-8069-4570-2; 0-8069-4571-0   LC 78-57886

"Children with a music background will welcome Etkin's bok which explains how to set up a band, how to make percussion instruments, and how to follow and write rhythm band scores. . . . Promoted as a means to learning about music and sharing it with friends and family, the contents of the book will be most appreciated by a parent, teacher, or older child leading the band. For each tune, the author supplies simple piano music and the rhythmic accompaniment on adjacent pages. Brief histories of the selected songs (classical and folk) and instructions on how to construct instruments follow the arrangements." Sch Library J

788 Wind instruments

Berger, Melvin

The trumpet book; illus. with photographs. Lothrop 1978 128p illus $7.50, lib. bdg. $7.20 (4 and up)   **788**

1 Trumpet
ISBN 0-688-41832-5; 0-688-51832-X   LC 78-863

"Beginning with the history of trumpets, moving from their origins as hollow tree branches to current three-valve constructions, with related instruments included, we find out about the trumpet's composers, musicians, and the scientific principles of its construction in factories today. Photographs and diagrams are part of the book, and the final chapter tells trumpet students about choosing a trumpet, instruction, and careers. There are also a glossary, list of 'The Trumpet on Records' and index. One couldn't ask for a more helpful description—good for the general reader, essential for school libraries." Babbling Bookworm

789 Percussion, mechanical, electrical instruments

Bailey, Bernadine

Bells, bells, bells; illus. with photographs. Dodd 1978 95p illus $5.95 (4 and up)   **789**

1 Bells
ISBN 0-396-07551-7   LC 77-16859

"The Chinese used bells as far back as 4000 B.C., according to Bailey in her straightforward explanation of the making and use of bells throughout history. As prelude to discussion of the art of bell ringing, the author details the casting, tuning, and hanging of bells and their differences from carillons. Stories about more famous bells—Big Ben of London, the Liberty Bell, Great Tom of Oxford—round out the text. Young musicians will find the 'change ringing' descriptions fascinating, and anecdotal incidents will supply supplementary lore for social studies reports." Booklist

This is "a well-produced work with attractive photographs and two reproductions from old prints." Horn Bk

Kettelkamp, Larry

Drums, rattles, and bells; written and illus. by Larry Kettelkamp. Morrow 1960 47p illus lib. bdg. $6.96 (4 and up)   **789**

1 Percussion instruments
ISBN 0-688-31247-0   LC 60-10159

The author "describes the four basic groups of percussion instruments: drums, rattles, bells, and keyboard. For each group of instruments there is a brief description of the earlier forms, an explanation of the way in which this type of percussion instrument is made, and some description of the various types used today. The instructions for making instruments at home require materials that are inexpensive or free, and ones easy to procure; directions for assembling the instrument are clear." Chicago. Children's Bk Center

Price, Christine

Talking drums of Africa. Scribner 1973 unp illus map lib. bdg. $5.95 (2-5)   **789**

1 Drum 2 Yorubas 3 Ashantis
ISBN 0-684-13492-6   LC 73-6405

This book tells "how various kinds of drums are made and played in a number of countries of western Africa. . . . Poems of the Yoruba people of Nigeria and the Ashanti people of Ghana are interpolated to illustrate uses of the drum for festivals and dances, as well as for messages and summonings." Horn Bk

"Price's rhythmic, repetitive, and mesmerizing prose evokes the sound of drums. The black-and-white prints with bright blue and gold overlays are powerful . . . the interesting format and style make this an attractive addition to African culture collections." Sch Library J

Rothman, Joel

How to play drums; illus. by Jerry Warshaw. Whitman, A. 1977 48p illus (The Music involvement ser) lib. bdg. $5.95 (4-6)

789

1 Drum
ISBN 0-8075-3420-X   LC 76-39937

"Included are instructions for mastering the basic beats, descriptions of each part of the drum set (snare, bass, tom-tom, and cymbals), explanations for setting up a drum set, suggestions for using the drumsticks effectively, and exercises for developing drum techniques. A question-and-answer section covers finding an instructor, length of practice sessions, costs involved, and career possibilities." Booklist

"A useful and unique book, this teaches kids how to play the drums at home without a drum set. . . . Line drawings on virtually every page heighten the appeal." Sch Library J

Yolen, Jane

Ring out! A book of bells; drawings by Richard Cuffari. Seabury [distributed by Houghton] 1974 128p illus $6.95 (5 and up)

789

1 Bells
ISBN 0-395-28886-X   LC 74-4043

"A Clarion book"

Legends and stories help document this historical description of using bells for religious, curative, political, communicative, musical, and other purposes. Bellringing and bellmaking are also considered. The final chapter contains poems and songs about bells

"A nicely illustrated book. . . . The text is adequately organized and is printed in one broad column, with italicized notes in the broad margin." Chicago. Children's Bk Center

Bibliography: p123-24

790.1 Recreational activities

Caney, Steven

Steven Caney's Kids' America. Workman Pub. 1978 414p illus map $12.95, pa $6.95 (4 and up)

790.1

1 Amusements 2 Handicraft 3 U.S.—Social life and customs
ISBN 0-911104-79-8; 0-911104-80-1   LC 77-27465

"In an attempt to help children rediscover those parts of America's past that are fun to know, Caney provides hundreds of things for them to make and do centered around what people wore, studied, ate, and played as well as their superstitions, crafts, and inventions. Organized into 11 broad categories—heritage, know-how, homes, backyards and gardens, fashions, eating, school days, arts and crafts, toys and puzzles, Saturday night entertainment, and business—are individual projects that include genealogies, weather forecasting, stencil wall prints, nature games, tongue twisters, taffy pulling, gravestone rubbing, flower drying, dolls, rope spinning, fortune telling, hex signs, coin collecting, garage sales, and many more. The author has tested all the selections with children." Booklist

"The illustrations are a lively blend of photographs and sketches, and the text is brisk and practical—the author even thoughtfully advises how to avoid inadvertent long-distance calls while using a push-button telephone as a musical instrument. For the sheer volume of innovative, imaginative ideas for kids, this is one of the best bargains." Sch Library J

Hofsinde, Robert

Indian games and crafts; written and illus. by Robert Hofsinde (Gray-Wolf) Morrow 1957 126p illus lib. bdg. $6.24 (4 and up)

790.1

1 Indians of North America—Games
ISBN 0-688-21607-2   LC 56-8479

"These detailed instructions for making and playing 12 North American Indian games are clear, the diagrams and illustrations have exact measurements and the materials to be used are easily obtained." Bookmark

"The book will thus be useful both for the recreation hour and the craft period in summer camps, schools and scout groups." Horn Bk

Lavine, Sigmund A.

The games the Indians played; illus. with photographs and old prints. Dodd 1974 93p illus lib. bdg. $4.95 (5 and up)

790.1

1 Indians—Games
ISBN 0-396-06846-4   LC 73-7093

The author describes the games of chance and of dexterity invented and played by Indians of the Americas, including dice games, lacrosse, football, archery, and cat's-cradle

"Many games of chance and skill are described here, not with a 'how-to' approach but through the eyes of an informed commentator on Indian ceremony and lore. This is a detailed survey, amplified with black-and-white photographs and reproductions of artwork. . . . It will be useful for collections of Indian studies materials." Booklist

McCoy, Elin

The incredible year-round playbook; illus. by Irene Trivas. Random House 1979 96p illus lib. bdg. $5.99, pa $3.95 (2-6)

790.1

1 Amusements 2 Handicraft
ISBN 0-394-93564-0; 0-394-83564-6   LC 78-55909

"Projects to fill leisure hours are presented here in a quasi-seasonal format. Ideas for games, tricks, recipes, experiments, crafts, and activities are explained and illustrated under sections devoted to play in the sun, sand, water, wind, and snow. . . . The projects use easy-to-find ingredients, clear directions, and safety warnings where necessary. Adults working with children as well as youngsters themselves will enjoy collecting solar energy, sending secret sun messages, building sand sculptures, trying beach hopscotch, developing saltwater distillers, using underwater binoculars, planning paper airplane races, constructing kites, playing tug-of-snow-war, and making snow monsters." Booklist

"Illustrations are two-color sketches, with plenty of clear diagrams and instructions. . . . This offers learning as well as doing experiences and should be useful and popular in both public and school libraries." Sch Library J

Savitz, Harriet May

Wheelchair champions; a history of wheelchair sports. Crowell 1978 117p illus $7.95, lib. bdg. $7.79 (5 and up)

790.1

1 Sports 2 Physically handicapped
ISBN 0-381-90057-6; 0-381-99555-0   LC 77-11561

"A John Day book"

This book provides "capsule biographies of several wheelchair bound athletes. After World War II, formerly active men who were paralyzed from wounds received in combat began to be interested in sports, most notably basketball. At about the same time, the University of Illinois started a program called the Division of Rehabilitation Education Services, encouraging athletic participation by wheelchair users. Other schools and athletic organizations followed suit and today there are Wheelchair Olympics which include a wide range of sports." Sch Library J

"Students, whether athletes or not, will enjoy reading this unusual and informative book and be inspired by the accomplishments of these special people." Children's Bk Rev Serv

791.3 Circuses

De Regniers, Beatrice Schenk

Circus; photographs by Al Giese. Viking 1966 unp illus $5.95 (k-3)

791.3

1 Circus
ISBN 0-670-22272-0   LC 66-8230

"Color photographs of performing lions, elephants, clowns, acrobats, and other circus artists together with a minimum of rhythmic text capture remarkably well the glitter, the breathless excitement, and enchantment of the circus." Booklist

Great days of the circus, by the editors of American Heritage, The Magazine of History; narrative by Freeman Hubbard, in consultation with Leonard V. Farley. Am. Heritage [distributed by Harper] 1962 153p illus $9.95 (5 and up)   **791.3**

1 Circus
ISBN 0-06-022630-7   LC 62-12907

"American Heritage Junior library"

A book that is "comprehensive, attractive, and nostalgic. . . . [It is] gay and colorful from blue bareback rider and yellow acrobats on the cover to the old print of an action-filled circus ring which forms the end paper. Particularly valuable to have in one book are the many examples of brilliant circus posters which at one time dotted our national landscape. The first chapter describes in detail a typical day when the circus came to town. Others tell of famous performers [clowns, trapeze artists] and animal acts, of Barnum, of the problems involved in moving a circus from place to place, and much else, all of it fascinating." Horn Bk

For further reading: p149

Krementz, Jill

A very young circus flyer; written and photographed by Jill Krementz. Knopf 1979 unp illus $9.95   **791.3**

1 Circus 2 Acrobats and acrobatics
ISBN 0-394-50574-3   LC 78-20546

This book "details circus life from the viewpoint of the youngest member of a talented and courageous family of trapeze artists. Nine-year-old Tato is a full-fledged professional—one of the four 'Flying Farfans,' who work with the Ringling Bros. and Barnum & Bailey Circus. But this photographic documentary and first-person text introduce much more than the home life, training, and thrilling aerial acts of the high-flying performers; clowns, tightrope walker, ringmaster, costumer, and choreographer as well as animal stunts and circus parades are all included in the commentary of the engaging, knowledgeable child about 'the greatest show on earth.' The volume boasts an innovation—fifteen pages of resplendent colored photographs." Horn Bk

Meyer, Charles R.

How to be a clown. McKay 1977 51p illus (A Ringling Bros. and Barnum & Bailey Circus bk) $6.95 (3-6)   **791.3**

1 Clowns
ISBN 0-679-20406-7   LC 77-2421

The book traces the history of clowning and describes how to become a circus clown, how to develop gags, clown costuming, and how to perfect such useful skills as mime

"The make-up section in this [book] is helpful, listing necessary materials, advising on where to look for them, warning against substitutes, and providing clear, step-by-step instructions for application and removal. . . . Black-and-white photos throughout identify various Ringling Brothers clowns." Sch Library J

Powledge, Fred

Born on the circus; illus. with photographs by the author. Harcourt 1976 94p illus $7.95   **791.3**

1 Circus 2 Cristiani, Armando
ISBN 0-15-209970-0   LC 76-2449

"Behind the smiles and sequins lie years of training and discipline—this is the central theme of an informative documentary which explores the world of the circus from the viewpoint of Armando Cristiani, youngest member of the internationally known family of performers. Beginning with a description of a typical performance, the narrative then traces the history of the Cristiani family before focusing again on Armando as an entertainer and as a growing, curious, active child. The black-and-white photographs of the circus environment, of the Cristianis' two homes—their traveling van and their winter quarters—and of Armando, practicing, performing, playing, and studying, complement the descriptions of a family united in their devotion to one another and to their work." Horn Bk

791.43   Motion pictures

Aylesworth, Thomas G.

Movie monsters. Lippincott 1975 79p illus $7.95, pa $3.95 (4 and up)   **791.43**

1 Motion pictures—History 2 Monsters
ISBN 0-397-31639-9; 0-397-31640-2   LC 75-12997

"Chapters are arranged by 'the greatest,' such as the greatest ape-monster (King Kong) and the greatest 'moon-made monster' (the Wolf Man) with background information provided on both the creation of the monster and the celluloid product. Original black-and-white photo stills (Elsa Lanchester's electrifying pose in 'The Bride of Frankenstein,' John Barrymore's classically evil Mr. Hyde) from studio archives such as RKO and Universal reinforce the authenticity of the text. Trivia fans will also delight in the filmography section (James Arness is listed as a supporting actor in 'The Thing'), and a name/title/subject index rounds out the coverage." Sch Library J.

Edelson, Edward

Funny men of the movies. Doubleday 1976 127p illus lib. bdg. $6.90 (6 and up)   **791.43**

1 Motion pictures—History 2 Comedians
ISBN 0-385-09693-3   LC 75-14817

The author "gives a capsule history of the Hollywood movie industry through this account of the major contributors to film comedy. All of the early greats—Chaplin, Sennett, Fields, the Marx Brothers—are included, and the history is brought up to date with discussions of Jerry Lewis and Woody Allen. The emphasis is on critical evaluation of each actor's comedy techniques (personal life and problems are mentioned only as they affect the actor's career) and on descriptions of best-known films. Primarily concerned with Hollywood comedians, this also discusses the art of Alec Guinness and Jacques Tati." Sch Library J

Great monsters of the movies. Doubleday 1973 101p illus $6.95, lib. bdg. $7.90 (4-6)   **791.43**

1 Monsters 2 Motion pictures—History
ISBN 0-385-00668-3; 0-385-00857-0   LC 72-87499

Here is a collection of movie monsters from the dinosaurs of silent film to the teen-age vampires of more recent films, with an historical narration of horror stories and legends. It is also an account of the actors who played famous monster roles

"The extensive use of film stills—including a shot of Lon Chaney as the Phantom, and King Kong perched atop his favorite building—should please all of those who love a monster." Horn Bk

Great movie spectaculars. Doubleday 1976 150p illus $6.95, lib. bdg. $7.90   **791.43**

1 Motion pictures—History
ISBN 0-385-11179-7; 0-385-11180-0   LC 76-56

The author "covers briefly the classic films of D. W. Griffith and Cecil B. DeMille, John Ford's westerns, Busby Berkeley's musical extravaganzas, the era of the swashbuckling romance, and the disaster films of the 1970's. A major portion of the book deals with the various tricks of the trade used to create special effects, detailing particular scenes in numerous films and describing the hazardous work of stunt people and animals. Black-and-white stills are scattered throughout to invite browsers and whet the appetite for viewing the films themselves." Sch Library J

Finch, Christopher

The art of Walt Disney; from Mickey Mouse to the Magic Kingdoms. New concise ed. Abrams 1975 160p illus $15.95   **791.43**

1 Disney, Walt 2 Disney (Walt) Productions
ISBN 0-8109-0321-0   LC 74-8435

Based on the earlier work first published 1973

The author describes Walt Disney's career and traces the history of Disney Studios. He also comments on Disney's major films, Disney Land, and Walt Disney World. Among the illustrations are sketches, frames, and stills from the animated and live-action films, and photographs of the Disney parks

791.45 Television

The **ACT** Guide to children's television; or, How to treat TV with T.L.C. by Evelyn Kaye, with the cooperation of the American Academy of Pediatrics; illus. by Edward Frascino and additional designs by Richard Lyons and Charles Beier. Rev. ed. Beacon Press 1979 xx, 226p illus $10.95, pa $5.95
791.45

1 Television and children
ISBN 08070-2366-3; 0-8070-2367-1   LC 78-53654

First published 1974 by Pantheon Books with title: The family guide to children's television: what to watch, what to change, and how to do it

This guide is primarily concerned with giving both parents and children a better understanding of television's impact on young viewers and in offering guidelines to enable the viewer to better utilize television

Partial contents: Who is talking to your children; To view or not to view; Television and the classroom; Violence and the FCC; The advertising game—gimme gimme gimme; The Federal Trade Commission and children's advertising; Violence in children's television programs; Bibliography

791.5 Miniature, toy, shadow theaters. Puppetry

Cochrane, Louise

Shadow puppets in color; illus. by Kate Simunek. Plays, Inc. 1972 48p illus (The Puppet lib) $5.95 (2-5)   **791.5**

1 Shadow pantomimes and plays 2 Puppets and puppet plays
ISBN 0-8238-0139-X   LC 72-3700

Published in England with title: Shadows in colour

"Providing an introduction to shadow puppetry, this book fills a gap for primary-school children. Three main styles—Chinese, Greek, and Javanese—are presented along with very short adaptations of traditional plays. The book contains detailed instructions with patterns to trace, an easy-to-follow guide to making shadow theaters, and suggested production techniques. Cochrane's clear text supported by Simunek's illustrations will be useful in school libraries." Sch Library J

Plays included are: Moon Dragon; Karagiosis and the dragon; The story of Rama and Sita

Engler, Larry

Making puppets come alive; a method of learning and teaching hand puppetry [by] Larry Engler and Carol Fijan; photography by David Attie; demonstration puppets designed by Paul Vincent Davis. Taplinger [1974 c1973] 192p illus $9.95, pa $7.95   **791.5**

1 Puppets and puppet plays
ISBN 0-8008-5074-2; 0-8008-5073-4   LC 72-6623

The book "opens with a brief description of puppetry as a performing art, an explanation of what a puppet is and how to make one. Since the text is for beginners, most of the puppets discussed and pictured are those activated by hand, not with rods and strings. Instructions on how to manipulate and control the little fantasy figures are also included." Pub W

Bibliography of recommended books: p190-91

Mendoza, George

Shadowplay [by] George Mendoza with Prasanna Rao; photographs by Marc Mainguy. Holt 1974 unp illus lib. bdg. $5.95 (3-6)   **791.5**

1 Shadow pantomimes and plays
ISBN 0-03-007881-4   LC 72-9958

"Even though readers are encouraged to practice forming these intricate and often stunning shadows with their own hands, this collection of silhouette images functions not as a how-to book but primarily as a record of a fascinating art form. Twenty-six animals, objects, and scenes are created by master artist Prasanna Rao; the silhouette is shown on the right page of the spread, a black-and-white photograph of the hand

configuration on the left. A few hand exercises are demonstrated at the end, but even these require more dexterity than most children or adults can boast. The shadows themselves are nearly all too difficult for a beginner to make successfully, still, this is a rare visual treat." Booklist

Pels, Gertrude

Easy puppets; making and using hand puppets; illus. by Albert Pels. Crowell 1951 104p illus $8.95 (3-6)   **791.5**

1 Puppets and puppet plays
ISBN 0-690-25377-X   LC 51-6331

"The step-by-step processes of making simple puppets and giving puppet plays are clearly explained and illustrated in this practical book. . . . By following the book's diagrams and instructions, children can construct and operate puppets made from such materials as apples, bottle-caps, clothes-pins, and buttons. Directions for making papier-mâché heads and improvised stages are also included." Library J

"Over-all, this how-to book has a wide appeal and will start many a child off on a creative experience." NY Times Bk Rev

Ross, Laura

Finger puppets; easy to make, fun to use; illus. by Laura and Frank Ross, Jr. Lothrop 1971 64p illus lib. bdg. $6.96 (k-3)   **791.5**

1 Puppets and puppet plays
ISBN 0-688-51613-0   LC 78-155752

This book "gives clear step-by-step directions for making nine different types of simple finger puppets. Some of the puppets require only bare hands and paint while others are made from scraps of cloth, cardboard, or other readily obtainable materials. [The author] also includes several folktales and poems and tells how to dramatize them using the finger puppets; a list of books of rhymes, songs, and stories is appended." Booklist

Hand puppets; how to make and use them; written and illus. by Laura Ross. Lothrop 1969 192p illus lib. bdg. $7.63, pa $2.95 (k-2)   **791.5**

1 Puppets and puppet plays
ISBN 0-688-51615-7; 0-688-45015-6   LC 73-82100

For beginners as well as those with some experience, this book provides step-by-step directions and diagrams for making simple paper-bag, rod, and papier-mâché puppets. The book also contains instructions for dressing and handling puppets, setting up a stage, and writing and producing one's own puppet show. It also includes three puppet plays: Rumpelstiltskin, Punch and Judy, and A visit from outer space

"This is one of the clearest, most thorough, and easiest-to-follow presentations on the subject for children. While her instructions are explicit the author encourages the reader to modify and improvise." Booklist

List of terms: p14. Some other useful books: p189

Scrap puppets; how to make and move them; illus. by Frank Ross, Jr. photographs by George Dec. Holt 1978 189p illus $7.95 (4-6)   **791.5**

1 Puppets and puppet plays
ISBN 0-03-018511-4   LC 78-4282

"Construction of four basic types of puppets—hand, rod, shadow, and string—is explained and accessorized here with emphasis on using left-over materials found around home and school. . . . Information on gathering materials, making basic shapes, and manipulating the puppets introduces the text, with detailed comments on the historical aspects heading up each section. Clear, easy directions and suggestions for alternate materials are supplemented with diagrams and photographs of the finished products." Booklist

Reading list: p185

Wiesner, William

Hansel and Gretel: a shadow puppet picture book; adapted from the versions of Ludwig Bechstein and the Brothers Grimm. Seabury [distributed by Houghton] 1971 40p illus $6.50 (1-4)   **791.5**

1 Shadow pantomimes and plays 2 Fairy tales
ISBN 0-395-28829-0   LC 78-154302

Wiesner, William—*Continued*

"A Clarion book"

Presented in the form of a shadow play, this is the tale of the brave children, the gingerbread house, and the wicked witch, with illustrations by the author. Instructions for creating a theatre and puppets and for mounting a production are included along with a list of books about shadows and shadow plays

"A good deal of manual dexterity would seem to be required, which might prove frustrating to many children in the publisher's stipulated age group. This sort of book should inspire children (and teachers) to go on to writing their own scripts and designing their own sets." Pub W

792 Theater (Stage presentations)

Carlson, Bernice Wells

The right play for you; illus. by Georgette Boris. Abingdon 1960 160p illus $3.75 (4 and up)   **792**

1 Amateur theatricals 2 Drama—Collections
ISBN 0-687-36376-4   LC 60-5321

"Original and very useful book. Practical, clear suggestions for producing plays [including casting and staging], for adapting them for particular groups, for writing plays from stories, fables, legends, or true events, and for dramatizing jokes or holiday themes. Twenty original plays are given as examples and, except for an occasional slang expression, are well written. Illustrations in black and white by Georgette Boris are suitable." Library J

A few stage terms: p160

792.3 Pantomime

Howard, Vernon

Pantomimes, charades & skits; with drawings by Shizu. Sterling 1974 128p illus $4.95 (4-6)   **792.3**

1 Charades 2 Pantomimes 3 Skits
ISBN 0-8069-7004-9   LC 74-195093

First published 1959

The author describes the techniques involved in the silent portrayal of dramatic situations using body language, dramatic gesture, and facial expressions

"Included are over 100 games, most with 10 to 20 or more suggestions for play. Howard is thorough on the subject of mime games (not traditional white-face mime) and provides an imaginative collection of popular stunts and games designed for parties, workshops, and classrooms." Sch Library J

Ross, Laura

Mask-making with pantomime and stories from American history; drawings by Frank Ross, Jr.; constructed mask photos by George Haddad. Lothrop 1975 112p illus lib. bdg. $6.96 (5 and up)   **792.3**

1 Pantomimes 2 Masks (Facial) 3 U.S.—History—Drama
ISBN 0-688-51721-8   LC 75-11960

"Clear instructions for creating masks, helpful tips on preparation of pantomime and stories based on historical events are well combined. . . . Beginning with an informative history of these crafts, Ross goes on to discuss possible materials such as aluminum foil pans, which are usable in mask making. Black-and-white photographs and diagrams are useful in carrying out instructions. Well-thought-out suggestions are enumerated so that the wearing of masks, use of mime, and designing of sets and costumes can be coordinated for successful production. The last half of the book suggests four possible skits which the author hopes will stimulate individual creativity in her readers. Reading list included." Booklist

792.8 Ballet

Baylor, Byrd

Sometimes I dance mountains; photographs by Bill Sears; drawings by Ken Longtemps. Scribner 1973 unp illus $5.95 (k-3)   **792.8**

1 Modern dance
ISBN 0-684-13440-3   LC 73-1330

In this introduction to modern dance, the author puts into words the feelings shown by a young girl in her dancing

"The illustrations are innovative in combining photography and sweeping design." Pub W

Bullard, Brian

I can dance, by Brian Bullard and David Charlsen; foreword by Melissa Hayden. Putnam 1979 127p illus $10.95 (4-6)   **792.8**

1 Dancing 2 Ballet
ISBN 0-399-12383-1   LC 79-13759

"This text introduces the rudiments of dance in a descriptive how-to manner. . . . The five basic positions are introduced and carefully explained in a step-by-step fashion with the help of numerous black-and-white photographs, some of which are strikingly executed with 'stroboscopic photography' capturing an entire movement in a single image. Instructions for various exercises (pliés, side stretch, tendus), isolations (shoulder, arm, leg movements), and movements (balancing, jumps) are also included with background remarks about the importance of doing them correctly. . . . A worthwhile addition to the growing collection of ballet books for beginning students and dance admirers alike." Booklist

Chappell, Warren

The Nutcracker; adapted and illus. by Warren Chappell. Knopf 1958 unp illus lib. bdg. $6.99 (2-5)   **792.8**

1 Ballets—Stories, plots, etc. 2 Christmas—Fiction 3 Fairy tales
ISBN 0-394-90742-6   LC 58-11075

"Based on the [Alexandre] Dumas version of E. T. A. Hoffmann's story is the fantasy of the Nutcracker who fights the Mouse King; of the bewitched Princess Pirlipate and her handsome rescuer. All these—and more—adventures are the dreams of Marie, the little girl who received a toy nutcracker for Christmas, and who grew up to wed a handsome young man exactly like the imagined suitor of the Princess." Chicago. Children's Bk Center

"A stunning picture book containing excerpts from the music of the popular Tschaikovsky ballet and a simple retelling of the story on which the ballet is based. The writing is a bit stiff here and there, but the book is primarily of interest, probably, as a guide to the ballet for young music and ballet enthusiasts. The illustrations, done in rich, deep colors, are very striking." Pub W

Draper, Nancy

Ballet for beginners, by Nancy Draper and Margaret F. Atkinson. Knopf 1951 115p illus music $4.95, lib. bdg. $6.99 (5 and up) **792.8**

1 Ballet
ISBN 0-394-80929-7; 0-394-90929-1   LC 51-9406

Children's ballet class photographs by Fred Lyon; drawings by Margaret F. Atkinson; music adapted and arranged by Beatrix B. Woolard

"Photographs and charts along with the clearly written text show the basic ballet positions and tell children how to practice. Included also are several pages with music . . . photographs and briefer biographical sketches of a few famous ballerinas; a history of the ballet; synopses of some of the ballets especially appealing to young people; and a dictionary of ballet terms." Horn Bk

Bibliography: p113-15

Elliott, Donald

Frogs and the ballet; illus. by Clinton Arrowood. Gambit 1979 xxi, 57p illus $9.95 (4 and up)   **792.8**

1 Ballet
ISBN 0-87645-099-0   LC 78-19566

"The book is, first of all, the best guide to the basic foot positions, and steps in ballet to come out in years. The carefully executed full-page ink illustrations precisely depict each page of accurate

Elliott, Donald—*Continued*

description. So what if the dancers are frogs? The straightfaced descriptions give due regard for art while recognizing the fundamental absurdity of the artifice. . . . For balletomanes it is hysterically funny. As for the majority, who are not and couldn't care less, this zany book draws them in, despite themselves." Sch Library J

Jessel, Camilla

Life at the Royal Ballet School; text and photographs by Camilla Jessel. Methuen 1979 143p illus $10.95 (5 and up)   792.8

1 Ballet 2 Royal Ballet School, London
ISBN 0-416-30191-6   LC 79-12162

"A discriminating narrative and more than 300 sharply focused, black-and-white photographs provide an in-depth look into the daily lives of the dancers in training at White Lodge, home of the Lower School of Britain's Royal Ballet. Evidence of the grueling work, physical stamina, artistic acuity, and self-discipline needed to become a ballet dancer unfolds as the pupils experience the tension of auditions, the fear of injuries, the stress of competition, and the continual struggle for growth in their dancing. Information about specific steps, body positions, and the necessity for correct training is interspersed with photographs of professionals gracefully executing the movements in actual performances." Booklist

Krementz, Jill

A very young dancer. Knopf 1976 unp illus $9.95   792.8

1 Ballet—Pictorial works
ISBN 0-394-40885-3   LC 76-13700

"A black-and-white photo essay, depicting the training, selection, and performance of the leading child ballerina for Balanchine's annual New York City Ballet production of 'The Nutcracker.' The large, clear photos follow ten-year-old Stephanie through her lessons, with glimpses of her and her family at home, to the auditions, rehearsals, costume fittings, make-up and performance. The simple text is kept to a minimum. . . . There is no glossary or translation for the French terms; however, the photos clarify most meanings adequately." Sch Library J

"When an outstanding photographer has an equally remarkable subject, the result is a rare treat. . . . Children who respond to the beauty and excitement of ballet will love this book." Pub W

Maiorano, Robert

Backstage, by Robert Maiorano and Rachel Isadora. Greenwillow Bks. 1978 unp illus $6.95, lib. bdg. $6.67 (k-3)   792.8

1 Ballet 2 Theaters—Pictorial works
ISBN 0-688-80130-7; 0-688-84130-9   LC 77-21822

This book presents a small girl "purposefully walking through the stage-door entrance to a ballet rehearsal for 'The Nutcracker.' She continues past costume rooms, wig rooms, rehearsal rooms, onto the catwalk, up to the fly, in front of the proscenium and other magic places, until she finds and announces to her mother, the ballerina, 'Time to go home.' [The story] is a short enchantment with artfully cluttered pictures—perfect in black and white with some lavender washes—written by dancers." Babbling Bookworm

Mara, Thalia

First steps in ballet; basic barre exercises for home practice, by Thalia Mara with Lee Wyndham; illus. by George Bobritzky. Doubleday 1955 64p illus $6.95 (4 and up)   792.8

1 Ballet
ISBN 0-385-02432-0   LC 55-6550

First published by Garden City Bks.
With numerous illustrations, this book explains twelve elementary ballet barre exercises for the beginning student. The correct balletic terms are given in French, with the phonetic pronunciation of each, as well as their meanings; and the purpose and function of each exercise

Streatfeild, Noel

A young person's guide to ballet; drawings by Georgette Bordier. Warne 1975 120p illus $11.95 (6 and up)   792.8

1 Ballet
ISBN 0-7232-1814-5   LC 74-81666

Focusing on two children, Anna and Peter, the author shows how they learn the basic steps of ballet. The book also provides a brief history of ballet and describes some ballet stories and film ballets, leading dancers, and other forms of dancing.

"The author is an expert on her subject. Through her simple, precise text, we learn how much discipline and sweat is required to create the illusion that ballet movements are as easy and natural as breathing. . . . Skillful sketches and photos, along with period illustrations, add to the value of an outstanding contender for self space." Pub W

793   Indoor games and amusements

Carlson, Bernice Wells

Do it yourself! Tricks, stunts, and skits; illus. by Laszlo Matulay. Abingdon 1952 159p illus $4.50, pa $2.95 (4 and up)   793

1 Amusements 2 Tricks 3 Skits
ISBN 0-687-11007-6; 0-687-11008-4   LC 52-1773

A volume for young readers showing how to do a variety of tricks, ranging from the very simple to the more complicated; some stunts, both physical and mental; and some brief dramatizations

"For the planned or impromptu party this collection of tricks, stunts and skits offers fun for both performers and audience." NY Times Bk Rev

Cassell, Sylvia

Indoor games and activities; with 55 drawings by Sylvia S. Cassell. Harper 1960 115p illus $6.95 (3-6)   793

1 Amusements 2 Games
ISBN 0-06-021150-4   LC 60-5776

"A variety of indoor projects and amusements that children can enjoy alone or in groups are included in this practical guide. Suggestions for arts and crafts, puzzles, recipes, games, science experiments, and special parties are described in simply written text." Chicago

Helfman, Harry

Strings on your fingers; how to make string figures [by] Harry and Elizabeth Helfman; illus. by William Meyerriecks. Morrow 1965 47p illus $6.48 (3-6)   793

1 Games 2 String figures
ISBN 0-688-31582-8   LC 65-11329

"When you make a 'cat's cradle' on your fingers you are indulging in one of the oldest forms of amusement—this and other intriguing facts about string are accompanied by instructions for constructing string figures." Cincinnati
Bibliography: p[48]

793.2   Parties and entertainments

Frame, Jean

How to give a party, by Jean and Paul Frame; illus. by Paul Frame. Watts, F. 1972 90p illus lib. bdg. $4.90 (4-6)   793.2

1 Parties
ISBN 0-531-00759-6   LC 74-183296

"A First book"
"In a helpful guide to party giving from planning to entertaining the guests the authors consider nine themes—among them balloon, circus, monster, and winter parties. For each they provide a list of supplies, practical decorating ideas with specific instructions for carrying them out, and somewhat unimaginative menus complete with simple recipes. They also describe a variety of familiar but fun games, some active, others quiet, and a number for beginning or ending a party. The many clear sketches augment the directions." Booklist

793.3   Dancing

Price, Christine
Dance on the dusty earth, Scribner 1979
60p illus map lib. bdg. $8.95 (4 and up)   **793.3**
1 Folk dancing
ISBN 0-684-16088-9   LC 78-25714
"Movement, rhythm, and pattern—the rudiments
of dance language—are the basis upon which Price
examines folk dancing around the world. Organizing her book around particular actions, the
author discusses the traditions and meanings of
the leaping, bending, shuffling, and handwaving
that form an intrinsic part of the rituals." Booklist
"Described in detail are the circle dance of
worship of Benin, West Africa, and the prayer
dance for rain in the shrine of Santo Domingo.
Poetic, evocative words together with clear, dramatic pencil drawings depict both the history
and the variety of world-wide dance traditions.
A dance map indicates with animated figures the
forms of dance found all over the world." Horn Bk

793.7   Games not characterized by action

Adler, Irving
Magic house of numbers; illus. by Ruth
Adler and Peggy Adler. Rev. ed. Day 1974
143p illus lib. bdg. $8.79 (6 and up)   **793.7**
1 Mathematical recreations
ISBN 0-381-99986-6   LC 73-19471
First published 1957
This book presents mathematical puzzles, riddles, tricks, Fibonacci and Lucas numbers, and
number oddities which introduce the basis of our
number system. It also shows different methods
of counting

Adler, Peggy
Geography puzzles; illus. by Peggy Adler.
Watts, F. 1979 64p illus map lib. bdg. $5.90
(4-6)   **793.7**
1 Geography 2 Puzzles
ISBN 0-531-02867-4   LC 79-1483
A "collection of 63 puzzles of various types—
match, word scramble, rebuses, and geograph-o-
grams, with answers given in the final 12 pages.
The hidden-explorer puzzle is made up of a few
statements describing the accomplishments of an
explorer whose name must be discovered in a
caption for a black-and-white cartoon that often
features animals of the woods. The author doesn't
tell whether students are to circle the answers
in the book, write them down on paper, or find,
look, and check the answer with the key all
mentally. . . . The introductory word hunt puts
the general and the particular together—Arctic
and product; but subsequent ones are grouped
around a theme—original colonies, Central and
South American, European, African (South Africa
is excluded), and the Far Eastern countries." Sch
Library J

Math puzzles, by Peggy Adler and Irving
Adler; illus. by Peggy Adler. Watts, F. 1978
64p illus lib. bdg. $6.90 (4-6)   **793.7**
1 Mathematical recreations
ISBN 0-531-02216-1   LC 78-2833
"Several children and hedgehogs are the characters in this collection of 44 story problems. Questions dealing with geometry, measurement of time
and distance, age, money, and magic squares are
illustrated with black-and-white drawings. . . . A
thorough knowledge of the basics of division, algebra, and prime numbers is required . . . but those
who enjoy and have success in solving word problems will relish the challenge of this book." Sch
Library J

Barr, George
Entertaining with number tricks; illus. by
Mildred Waltrip. McGraw 1971 143p illus
lib. bdg. $6.95 (5 and up)   **793.7**
1 Mathematical recreations
ISBN 0-07-003842-2   LC 71-157478

Contents: Showmanship—parading your genius;
What is your favorite number; Guessing Aunt
Tillie's age; Please take a number; The magic
of 1089; Sum addition stunts; Fun with cards,
tickets, and tags; Those fascinating magic squares;
Crazy arithmetic; More baffling tricks; Puzzles,
riddles, and nonsense; Let's talk algebra
The author "describes each trick clearly, step
by step, explaining the mathematical principle
involved and suggesting patter to divert the audience. . . . Line drawings supplement the text."
Booklist

Burns, Marilyn
The I hate mathematics! book; illus. by
Martha Hairston. Little 1975 127p illus $8.95,
pa $5.95 (5 and up)   **793.7**
1 Mathematical recreations
ISBN 0-316-11740-4; 0-316-11741-2   LC 75-6707
"The Brown paper school series"
"This lively collection of puzzles, riddles, magic
tricks, and brain teasers provides a painless introduction to mathematical concepts and terms
through the process of experimentation and discovery. The cartoon-like illustration and breezy
titles—'Fathead,' 'Who Needs a Ceiling?' 'Infinity
Is Not in Vermont'—should appeal to the not-so-
mathematically inclined as well as to puzzle devotees. Required materials are readily available
and inexpensive; the techniques described are
educationally sound and exciting. An excellent
resource for parents, teachers, and children."
Horn Bk

Cerf, Bennett
Bennett Cerf's Book of animal riddles; illus.
by Roy McKie. Beginner Bks. 1964 62p illus
$3.95, lib. bdg. $4.99 (k-3)   **793.7**
1 Riddles
ISBN 0-394-80034-6; 0-394-90034-0   LC 64-11246
Title on spine: Animal riddles
A book of easy-reading riddles about animals
such as "Why are fish so smart? They always
go around in schools"
"The kind of humor that adults find obvious and
absurd but most children think hilarious. . . . Roy
McKie's boldly madcap illustrations have the same
tongue-in-cheek spirit." NY Times Bk Rev

Bennett Cerf's Book of riddles; illus. by
Roy McKie. Beginner Bks. 1960 62p illus
$3.95, lib. bdg. $4.99 (k-3)   **793.7**
1 Riddles
ISBN 0-394-80015-X; 0-394-90015-4   LC 60-13492
These thirty-one riddles are arranged with the
riddles being asked on one page and answered on
the next, to keep the element of surprise
"Mr Cerf has collected riddles which are very
funny to a child and pleasantly nostalgic to an
adult. He has also avoided using the old crutches,
giving new twists to many of the riddles." NY
Times Bk Rev
"Simple cartoonlike drawings use strong colour
for their effect." Ontario Library Rev

Charosh, Mannis
Mathematical games for one or two; illus.
by Lois Ehlert. Crowell 1972 33p illus
(Young math bks) $7.95, lib. bdg. $7.89 (1-4)
793.7
1 Mathematical recreations
ISBN 0690-52324-6; 0-690-52325-4   LC 74-187934
Each of these six groups of games—pyramid
games, shifting games, checker games, take-away
games, nim games, and magic tricks—begins with
an elementary version and continues with more
complex versions in a way that illustrates the
basic logical or mathematical principal so that
the reader may develop the game still further
"Lois Ehlert's colorful, lively illustrations add
humor and her diagrams help to clarify the text.
An enjoyable book which will aid in sharpening
perception of pattern and sequence." Sch Library J

Cricket's Jokes, riddles and other stuff; comp. by Marcia Leonard and the editors of Cricket Magazine; designed by John Grandits. Random House 1977 unp illus $2.95, lib. bdg. $3.99 (1-4)   **793.7**
1 Riddles 2 Wit and humor
ISBN 0-394-8345-X; 0-394-93545-4   LC 77-3164
"Several illustrators have added their cartoons to giggle-makers like 'Why did the three little pigs decide to leave home? 'Because their father was an awful boar'. . . . Contents are divided into elephant jokes, limericks, tongue twisters and other nonsense, the kinds youngsters adore." Pub W
"This collection should have wide appeal. . . . An inexpensive way to add a funny book to the joke shelves." Booklist

De Regniers, Beatrice Schenk
It does not say meow, and other animal riddle rhymes; pictures by Paul Galdone. Seabury [distributed by Houghton] 1972 unp illus $5.95 (k-1)   **793.7**
1 Riddles 2 Animals—Poetry
ISBN 0-395-28822-3   LC 72-75704
A "riddle book for the very young in which clues to the identity of each of nine different animals including a cat, elephant, ant, dog, frog, and mice are given in a short rhyming verse and full-page illustration. The correct answer appears in a captioned double-spread picture on the following pages." Booklist
"Young readers will relate to the children in the book who are pictured visiting the zoo, watching birds, playing Indians, etc. The colorful illustrations are appealing." Sch Library J

Doty, Roy
Puns, gags, quips and riddles; a collection of dreadful jokes. Doubleday 1974 unp illus $5.95, lib. bdg. $6.90 (4-6)   **793.7**
1 Wit and humor 2 Riddles
ISBN 0-385-06051-3; 0-385-06057-2   LC 73-13116
The author's "irreverent brand of humor will appeal to inveterate joke collectors. The generous selection is spaced two to a page and each gag is surrounded by an apropos cartoon. Most follow a simple question-answer form and are drawn, as the title implies, from a mixed bag of puns and riddles. A good choice for replenishing the well-used joke book shelf." Booklist

Fixx, James F.
Solve it! A perplexing profusion of puzzles. Doubleday 1978 94p illus $5.95, lib. bdg. $6.90 (5 and up)   **793.7**
1 Puzzles
ISBN 0-385-13039-2; 0-385-13040-6   LC 77-25589
"A humorous and charming book of simple puzzles that is designed to delight most youngsters. Many have tricky and surprising solutions, though hardly any involve a grasp of mathematics beyond elementary school." Children's Bk Rev Serv

Gilbreath, Alice Thompson
Beginning-to-read riddles and jokes; illus. by Susan Perl. Follett 1967 30p illus $3.39, pa $1.12 (1-3)   **793.7**
1 Riddles 2 Wit and humor
ISBN 0-695-40516-0; 0-695-30516-6   LC 74-83610
"A certain success with beginning readers, this will help fill the never-ending request for joke and riddle books. Susan Perl's unusual and clever illustrations are just right for jokes and riddles." Bruno. Bks for Sch Libraries, 1968

Hoke, Helen
Hoke's Jokes, cartoons & funny things; pictures by Eric Hill. Watts, F. 1975 c1973 unp illus lib. bdg. $4.90 (1-4)   **793.7**
1 Jokes 2 Wit and humor
ISBN 0-531-02682-5   LC 74-7459
First published 1973 in England
"An assortment of jokes and nonsense accompanied by colorful, funny illustrations. 'Mock Meanings' is the cleverest section (e.g., 'Pasteurize: Up to your forehead.', 'Intense: Where Boy Scouts sleep.') The 11 tongue-twisters are fresh, but the few traditional selections like Lewis Carroll's 'Tweedle-Dum and Tweedle-Dee' seem out of place." Sch Library J

Keller, Charles
(comp.) The star spangled banana, and other revolutionary riddles; comp. by Charles Keller and Richard Baker; illus. by Tomie de Paola. Prentice-Hall 1974 unp illus $3.95, pa $1.50 (3-5)   **793.7**
1 Riddles 2 U.S.—History—Revolution, 1775-1783
ISBN 0-13-842971-5; 0-13-842989-8   LC 74-594
"Children's love for outrageously bad puns, riddles, and jokes must, at least, date back to the American Revolution; so it is only fitting that such a group of jokes be collected to commemorate the Spirit of '76. Certainly, the puns and jokes in this selection should cause groans and laughter about everything from the signing of the Declaration of Independence to Paul Revere's ride. . . . [The riddles] do for the Revolution what Art Buchwald does for contemporary American politics." Horn Bk
"De Paola's pencil drawings of the 61 riddles are always a pleasure. His good-natured cartoons take clever pokes at history. . . Children in their first encounter with American history will relish this slightly irreverent portrayal." Sch Library J

Leeming, Joseph
Fun with pencil and paper; games, stunts, puzzles; pictures by Jessie Robinson. Lippincott 1955 91p illus $8.95 (4 and up)   **793.7**
1 Games 2 Puzzles
ISBN 0-397-30300-9   LC 55-5646
The author has gathered "pencil-and-paper games—word, drawing, number, and spelling games, stunts, and puzzles. In each case the number of players is indicated, the verbal pictorial explanations are clear, and answers and solutions are given on the same page with the quizzes and puzzles. The material included varies greatly in degree of difficulty." Booklist

Riddles, riddles, riddles; enigmas, anagrams, puns, puzzles, quizzes, conundrums; illus. by Shane Miller. Watts, F. 1953 244p illus lib. bdg. $6.90 (4 and up)   **793.7**
1 Riddles
ISBN 0-531-01777-X   LC 53-9926
"Terrific triple title series"
"There are a few classic examples . . . but for the most part Mr. Leeming has concentrated on the riddle or the conundrum with the quick, short answer—the kind that makes you wonder. how you could have missed it. The general merriment is heightened by . . . [the] decorations." NY Times Bk Rev
"A good addition to the collection for parties or any moment of fun." Library J

Low, Joseph
Five men under one umbrella, and other ready-to-read riddles. Macmillan Pub. Co. 1975 63p illus $6.95 (1-3)   **793.7**
1 Riddles
ISBN 0-02-761460-3   LC 74-20615
"Ready-to-read books"
Riddle books "easy enough for beginning readers are doubly desirable. . . . [This one] fills the bill. . . . Some of the riddles have been around for eons ('What state is round on the ends and high in the middle? Ohio) but fresher material is included, and even the oldest may be new to primary graders." Sch Library J
"It is not the jokes that are truly humorous, but the wonderfully spirited watercolor illustrations. With great animation, the artist sketches everything from a delightfull hairy monster to an intense counting dog." Horn Bk

A mad wet hen, and other riddles. Greenwillow Bks. 1977 55p illus $5.95, lib. bdg. $5.71 (1-3)   **793.7**
1 Riddles
ISBN 0-688-80082-3; 0-688-84082-5   LC 76-44329
"Greenwillow Read-alone"
Illustrated by the author, the "brief text, apparently designed for beginning readers, contains 24 standard-style riddles, with a question or an answer per single page." Booklist
"The witty pictures [are] drawn in shades of red, yellow, and black with attractively shaded overlays." Horn Bk

Mosler, Gerard

The puzzle school; illus. by Frank C. Smith. Abelard-Schuman 1977 87p illus lib. bdg. $6.89 (5 and up)   **793.7**

1 Puzzles
ISBN 0-200-00168-X   LC 75-45428

"A collection of 85 quizzes, puzzles, and teasers arranged into broad categories of school subjects—math, language arts, science, social studies, and home economics. Learning is not the prime motivation, however, as the emphasis is definitely on the challenge and the fun. Methods of obtaining correct answers vary, requiring a sharp pencil, a shrewd eye, a good memory, and, at times, a lucky guess. Cartoon line drawings decorate the puzzles. Solutions appended. Useful as diversion tactics on rainy days." Booklist

Olney, Ross

Pocket calculator fun & games, by Ross and Pat Olney; illus. by Gretchen Lopez. Watts, F. 1977 86p illus lib. bdg. $6.45 (5 and up)   **793.7**

1 Calculating machines—Problems, exercises, etc.
2 Mathematical recreations
ISBN 0-531-00387-7   LC 76-49079

"Ranging from number sequence tricks to words formed with numbers and group contests such as 'calculator poker,' the activities are described in a comprehensible manner, although answers are not given. A vocabulary list suggested for code sending is also included. A brief introduction describes the inner workings of a pocket calculator, but no mention is made that different brands have individual features prohibiting some of the computations suggested. Whole pages of diagonal lines, some of which frame silly cartoons, detract from the book, but students concentrating on fingering the keys won't notice." Booklist

Rothman, Joel

Which one is different? Designed by Seymour Chwast and Victor Kotowitz. Doubleday 1975 unp illus lib. bdg. $7.90 (2-5)   **793.7**

1 Puzzles
ISBN 0-385-11017-0   LC 74-5

"Twenty-six picture puzzles—each page shows a group of objects, one of which is slightly different from the others in line, shape, color, etc. The varying difficulty of the puzzles makes the book suitable to a broad age group, and the illustrations are very attractive (almost half in full color). Entertaining for kids who like this sort of stumper." Sch Library J

Sarnoff, Jane

I know! A riddle book, by Jane Sarnoff and Reynold Ruffins. Scribner 1976 96p illus lib. bdg. $7.95 (3-5)   **793.7**

1 Riddles
ISBN 0-684-14761-0   LC 76-26505

"The riddles are divided, more or less, into topics such as dogs, mice, school, bugs, flowers, numbers, and pigs, with about 6 to 12 teasers per subject." Booklist

"The answers are found in either blue or brown lettering; some of them are printed upside-down to make the reading more than a simple matter of straightforward looking. [Ruffins'] multicolored illustrations combining weirdness of pattern with quietly blatant combinations of color joyfully add visual to verbal caricature." Horn Bk

The monster riddle book, by Jane Sarnoff and Reynold Ruffins. Rev. ed. Scribner 1978 unp illus lib. bdg. $7.95 (4-6)   **793.7**

1 Riddles 2 Monsters
ISBN 0-684-15660-1   LC 78-50842

First published 1975

"Spread over pages made striking by [Ruffins'] untrammelled sense of design and his use of brilliant, modulating color is a delectable array of monster riddles whose correct answers lean heavily upon double meanings, spoonerisms, and gruesome puns. A monster maze and an illustrated glossary of mythical monsters further enhance the book." Horn Bk [review of first edition]

What? A riddle book, by Jane Sarnoff and Reyold Ruffins; technical consultant: Simms Taback. Scribner 1974 62p illus lib. bdg. $9.95, pa $3.95 (3-5)   **793.7**

1 Riddles
ISBN 0-684-13911-1; 0-684-15273-8   LC 74-9592

Illustrated by Reynold Ruffins, this is a collection of over five hundred one-line riddles on a variety of subjects. The last chapter includes a series of riddles in code with instructions for deciphering them

"The clever word play in this collection adds up to unusual juvenile humor in which a distinction has been made between silly and stupid. Although some of the answers may cause groans, and others, perplexity, some are just plain funny. . . . Visual charm adds a big bonus to the text. While browsers may dip in and out of the pages of straight black-and-brown print, they will pore over the color spreads with riddles angled into comic illustrations." Booklist

Tremain, Ruthven

Fooling around with words. Greenwillow Bks. 1976 56p illus $5.95, lib. bdg. $5.71 (2-4)   **793.7**

1 Word games
ISBN 0-688-80039-4; 0-688-84039-6   LC 75-38673

"Greenwillow Read-alone"

"A collection of puzzles, word and picture games, and problems, with answers in the back of the book. This is more than a game book, however, since almost every entry can teach a child, painlessly, something about the language; words that are spelled differently but sound alike; words that have rhyming answers (Stupid finger? Dumb thumb), scrambled words, phrases that lack one letter (mrecrnnthecbfru? a picture and a textual hint supply the missing 'o'). This is one of the better collections of word games for this reading level." Chicago. Children's Bk Center

Wiesner, William

A pocketful of riddles; collected and illus. by William Wiesner. Dutton [1977 c1966] 119p illus pa $1.50 (2-4)   **793.7**

1 Riddles
ISBN 0-525-45032-7

First published 1966

The author "has made up this collection of over 200 riddles, conundrums, and rebuses by culling old riddle books back as far as the nineteenth century and adding a few riddles of his own. This is a small sized picture book with from one to three riddles with illustrated answers on each page or double spread. For lovers of tiny books and for lovers of riddles." Sch Library J

"Since the answers appear in illustrated columns facing the questions the reader needs a young companion for maximum fun or a group to make it possible to turn the whole business into a game. . . . Bright little drawings." Horn Bk

The riddle pot; collected and illus. by William Wiesner. Dutton 1973 120p illus lib. bdg. $5.95, pa $1.50 (1-3)   **793.7**

1 Riddles 2 Wit and humor
ISBN 0-525-38285-2; 0-525-45033-5   LC 73-77461

A "plump little volume containing a generous gathering of riddles, teasers, and a few puzzles, illustrated with cheerful, breezy drawings." Horn Bk

Williams, Jerome

Science puzzles, by Jerome Williams and Lelia K. Williams; illus. by Myron Grossman. Watts, F. 1969 64p illus lib. bdg. $5.90 (5 and up)   **793.7**

1 Scientific recreations 2 Puzzles
ISBN 0-531-02876-3   LC 79-1236

"Riddles, scrambled word, crossword, word equation, respell, key word, substitution code, unblankit, syllable savvy, reduction code and similar puzzles comprise this challenger for science students. The different types of puzzles are divided into chapters by subject area: biology, weather and climate, chemical, physical, earth and space sciences, with a summary section drawing from all areas. The solution chapter, placed at the end, makes it harder to 'peek' when the

Williams, Jerome—*Continued*

puzzles seem difficult, but both puzzles and solutions are clear and easily read. Although most terms are covered in the intermediate science curriculum, it is too much to assume that most children will recall the 'seven forms of energy' easily enough to choose and combine the proper syllables. Some library users may not heed the directions to 'copy or trace the squares onto a piece of paper' before attempting to solve, causing problems to future borrowers." Sch Library J

793.8 Magic

Arnold, Ned

The great science magic show, by Ned Arnold and Lois Arnold; illus. by Tom Huffman. Watts, F. 1979 99p illus lib. bdg. $6.90 (5 and up)   793.8

1 Magic 2 Scientific recreations
ISBN 0-531-02922-0   LC 78-11089

"You can make a straw cut through a potato, cause a glass of cold water to boil instantaneously, and turn a pencil to rubber—all this, while demonstrating scientific principles to both your audience and yourself. It's all laid out . . . in the form of a complete, 20-trick magic show that groups feats according to the concepts on which they depend (and which they reveal, if you understand the secrets—from inertia and center of gravity to static electricity and optical illusion." Booklist

"The material is presented concisely, with 'what you need,' 'what you do,' 'tips,' and 'how it works' sections for each ploy. Clear photographs in black-and-white and line drawings illustrate each chapter. The materials required can mostly be found at home; the procedures are relatively simple and could be performed successfully without too much practice." Sch Library J

Cobb, Vicki

Magic . . . naturally! Science entertainments & amusements; illus. by Lance R. Miyamoto. Lippincott 1976 159p illus $6.95, pa $2.95 (4 and up)   793.8

1 Magic 2 Scientific recreations
ISBN 0-397-31631-3; 0-397-31632-1   LC 76-13179

"Thirty magic tricks with accompanying scientific explanations are arranged according to phenomena of mechanics, fluids, energy, chemistry, and perception. The emphasis is on fun, however, with the information presented to insure a true understanding of the 'magic.' Each stunt describes what happens, explains the setup and act, and gives tips for the performance. For example, the 'Intelligent Eggs' trick relies on the principle of buoyancy and depends on the audience's unawareness that sugarwater will keep one egg afloat while plain water will sink another. Useful in the classroom as well as a boon to amateur magicians." Booklist

Fleischman, Sid

Mr Mysterious's secrets of magic; illus. by Eric von Schmidt; with diagrams by Mr Mysterious. Little 1975 81p illus lib. bdg. $5.95 (3-6)   793.8

1 Magic 2 Tricks
ISBN 0-316-28584-6   LC 74-28222

"An Atlantic Monthly Press book"
"Twenty-one sleight-of-hand procedures are helpfully presented [by the hero of the author's novel: Mr Mysterious & Company, entered under Fiction] under such attractive titles as 'Frankenstein's Toothache,' 'The Witch's Foot,' and 'The Invisible Man's Money.' The artist's offhand, free-and-easy sketches add their own light-heartedness, and explicit diagrams by the wizard himself elucidate the text." Horn Bk

"What a great positive self-image a child gets by reading the book and putting on his own magic show. Secrets of magic are revealed in such simple language and drawings that even the most reluctant reader wants the book." Rdng Teacher

Helfman, Harry

Tricks with your fingers; illus. by Robert Bartram. Morrow 1967 46p illus lib. bdg. $6.48 (3-6)   793.8

1 Magic 2 Tricks
ISBN 0-688-31583-6   LC 67-1985

"All one needs is fingers, string, coins, hankies, and marbles to do these ten sleight-of-hand tricks which can be performed almost anywhere. Carefully explained and illustrated, they are easy to do." Wis Library Bul

Hutton, Darryl

Ventriloquism; how to put on an act, use the power of suggestion, write a clever accompanying patter, and make your own dummy. Sterling 1975 128p illus $6.95, lib. bdg. $6.69 (6 and up)   793.8

1 Ventriloquism
ISBN 0-8069-7022-7; 0-8069-7023-5   LC 75-14508

Adapted from the book Modern ventriloquism, first published 1974 in England

"Various aspects of perfecting the art of ventriloquism are described in this thorough guide, which includes fundamentals of projecting the voice, manipulating a dummy, planning a routine, and preparing a stage performance. After discussing what ventriloquism is and how it works, the author explains in detail the necessary steps in creating a dummy's voice and exercising for development of lips and vocal chords. Actual skits and dialogue are included, as well as tips for music, lighting, publicity, and usable tricks to accomplish the wanted illusion. Although better ideas for making puppets can be found elsewhere and information regarding professional appearances may be too advanced, young readers intrigued with craft will find help here. Also included are suggestions for using ventriloquism with speech correction, plus appendixes listing recommended materials, suppliers of dummies, and a glossary." Booklist

Kettelkamp, Larry

Magic made easy; written and illus. by Larry Kettelkamp. Morrow 1954 63p illus lib. bdg. $6.67 (4 and up)   793.8

1 Magic 2 Tricks
ISBN 0-688-31579-8   LC 54-5835

"An introduction to magic tricks for young readers. The first tricks are simple ones that can be done with practice and very little equipment. Toward the end of the book some more elaborate tricks are described and some suggestions for patter are given." Chicago. Children's Bk Center

"Although not quite so easy as the title and format would indicate, the tricks in this little book are clearly explained both in text and pictures. . . . Sets down also a few basic rules for all magicians." Booklist

Spooky magic; written and illus. by Larry Kettelkamp. Morrow 1955 64p illus lib. bdg. $6.48 (3-6)   793.8

1 Magic 2 Tricks
ISBN 0-688-31581-X   LC 55-8845

The author tells "how to perform some spooky tricks, such as raising a human body a few feet in the air, making the table move, finding a ghostly spirit in a catchup bottle. Some of the tricks are very simple, some will need patience." Library J

"Mr. Kettelkamp understands his magic and knows how to explain it to youngsters so that they can follow his instructions, and no expensive or hard-to-obtain props are needed to handle these tricks." Sat Rev

Lopshire, Robert

It's magic? Macmillan Pub. Co. 1969 unp illus $6.95, pa $1.25 (k-2)   793.8

1 Magic 2 Tricks
ISBN 0-02-761430-1; 0-02-044360-9   LC 78-78075

"In a first-reading book of the most entertaining variety, Boris, a huge bear, visits a Big Magic Show to witness fourteen easy tricks performed with simple materials by Tad, a great magician-dog. Tad even invites him to be the audience participator. Some of the magic lies in jokes. The results of most are obvious and achieved as illustrated; a few must be tried to satisfy the reader. Children will be entranced into copying

Lopshire, Robert—*Continued*
the performance for anyone whose attention they
can command. The reading alone has entertainment value, for Boris is a naive childlike spectator, repeatedly fooled, and capable of saying, 'I
knew it all the time.' " Horn Bk

Marks, Burton
Give a magic show! By Burton and Rita
Marks; illus. by Don Madden. Lothrop 1977
62p illus $7.25, lib. bdg. $6.96 (3-5)   **793.8**
1 Magic 2 Tricks
ISBN 0-688-41819-8; 0-688-51819-2   LC 77-5436
"This collection of 17 uncomplicated tricks is sure
encouragement for those dabbling in magic. Preparation for the gimmicks is explained simply,
with easy-to-find ingredients such as cards, coins,
scarves, match boxes, and string. The authors suggest that expertise comes with practice and include
careful explanations and diagrams for executing
the tricks. When it's time to perform, instructions
are given for costuming, setting the stage, planning
the program, and developing stage presence. Black-
and-red cartoon drawings add zip to the text."
Booklist

Permin, Ib
Hokus pokus: with wands, water & glasses;
[tr. by Katherine Lunt Fluger; drawings by
Guy Brison-Stack. Rev. ed.] Sterling 1978
72p illus $5.95 (5 and up)   **793.8**
1 Magic 2 Tricks
ISBN 0-8069-4578-8   LC 77-93314
Original Danish edition published 1968. First
American edition published 1969
"Beginning magicians looking for easy tricks to
build into their act will find more than 25 suggestions included here. Focusing on those that use
magic wands, water, and drinking glasses, the
author describes tricks such as making a wand
disappear, changing water to cola, and pounding
a glass through a table. Hints for successful execution are given in brief text, diagrams, and
black-and-white photographs. Practical advice and
suggestions for avoiding likely pitfalls are helpful.
General 'magic tips' appearing in boxed squares
are interspersed throughout." Booklist

Severn, Bill
Bill Severn's Big book of magic; illus. by
Katharine Wood. McKay [1979 c1973] 238p
illus pa $4.95 (6 and up)   **793.8**
1 Magic 2 Tricks
ISBN 0-679-20534-9
First published 1973
The author includes card, rope, money and
handkerchief tricks as well as close-up and stage
magic. He explains the secret, necessary materials, preparation and performance of each trick
"The tricks are as clearly explained as they can
be without a live demonstration." Chicago. Children's Bk Center

Magic with coins and bills; illustrations by
Elizabeth Green. McKay 1977 147p illus $7.95
(6 and up)   **793.8**
1 Magic 2 Coins 3 Tricks
ISBN 0-679-20380-X   LC 76-43541
"The routines, selected for ease of learning and
ease of execution, involve sleight of hand using
coins and bills, and there is also a chapter of
stage 'showtime' tricks including updated versions
of some magic classics. Many sequences of illustrations showing hand manipulation add to the
clarity of the text. Well balanced in trick selection, presentation, magic theory and ease of access, there is no better book for helping kids on
their way to becoming a magician." Sch Library
J

Stoddard, Edward
The first book of magic; illus. by Rod
Slater. Rev. ed. Watts, F. 1977 65p illus lib.
bdg. $5.90 (4-6)   **793.8**
1 Magic 2 Tricks
ISBN 0-531-00575-5   LC 76-47643

First published 1953
Includes tricks of varying difficulty using cards,
paper, coins and balls. The tricks need only inexpensive materials, most of which can be found
at home. Step-by-step illustrations and suggestions
for producing a magic show are included
"Instructions are consistently clear. Rules for
misdirection and for being a good magician are
emphasized." Sch Library J

Van Rensselaer, Alexander
Fun with magic; illus. by John N. Barron.
Doubleday 1957 55p illus $4.95 (4 and up)
793.8
1 Magic 2 Tricks
ISBN 0-385-02428-2   LC 57-9854
"After offering some tips on basic techniques and
equipment the author . . . gives clear instructions
for performing 25 tricks with coins, handker-
chiefs, cards, string, and numbers, most of them
simple enough for beginners." Booklist
"Each trick has helpful step-by-step illustrations, most colorful and attractive in black, white,
and red." Library J

White, Laurence B.
So you want to be a magician? Illus. by
Bill Morrison. Addison-Wesley 1972 224p
illus lib. bdg. $6.95 (5 and up)   **793.8**
1 Magic 2 Tricks
ISBN 0-201-08627-1   LC 70-164400
"An Addisonian Press book"
"Asserting that a magician's purpose is to entertain and that he does so by being a good actor
with well-prepared patter and well-practiced tricks
the author tells how to become a successful amateur magician. Describing over 50 tricks, all of
which require only common household items and
the use of such basic techniques as misdirection
and substitution he gives lucid directions, illustrated with clear drawings, for performing each.
White also indicates how to appeal to different
age groups, encourages the young magician to
try original ideas, and includes practical suggestions on planning a magic show." Booklist

Wyler, Rose
Magic secrets, by Rose Wyler and Gerald
Ames; pictures by Talivaldis Stubis. Harper
[1978 c1967] 63p illus pa $1.95 (1-3)   **793.8**
1 Magic 2 Tricks
ISBN 0-06-444007-9   LC 67-4229
"An I can read book"
First published 1967
"A first book about tricks that can be done by
an amateur. . . . The text suggests that an audience sees that to which its attention is directed,
and shows the small diversionary tactics that add
to illusion." Chicago. Children's Bk Center
"Here we have happily combined a book with
a graded vocabulary, designed to help children
in the initial stages of reading, and a collection
of simple tricks. The book is wittily illustrated."
Times (London) Lit Sup

Spooky tricks, by Rose Wyler and Gerald
Ames; pictures by Talivaldis Stubis. Harper
1968 64p illus $5.95, lib. bdg. $6.89 (1-3)
793.8
1 Magic 2 Tricks
ISBN 0-06-026633-3; 0-06-02634-1   LC 68-16822
"An I can read book"
Readers can learn such tricks as making ghosts
appear, cats sparkle in the dark, girls disappear,
and boys float on air
The book has "easy-to-understand instructions.
The lively tone of the simple text, the imaginative yet clear, illustrative drawings, and the
grouping of the 24 tricks under the headings How
to be a spook, Willie the ghost, and Haunted
house enhance the enjoyment of the book." Booklist

794.1 Chess

Kidder, Harvey
Illustrated chess for children. Doubleday
1970 127p illus $7.95 (4-6)   **794.1**
1 Chess
ISBN 0-385-05764-4   LC 71-116220

Kidder, Harvey—*Continued*

"A really fine book for the beginning chess player; although there seems an undue stress on the relationship of each piece to its real-life equivalent (the pawns were pikemen who fought side by side, the knight's move can be remembered as the charge of a leaping horse, etc.) the concept gives the book an added dimension. Each piece and its moves are explained separately, and a blitzkrieg game is illustrated. There are illustrations of games-in-process, with questions and answers about possible moves and why some are preferred. The clear diagrams are very helpful, as is the proceeding from basic moves to more and more complicated problems." Chicago. Children's Bk Center

Leeming, Joseph

The first book of chess; rev. by Robert S. Fenton. Rev. ed. Watts, F. 1977 63p illus lib. bdg. $5.90 (4-6) **794.1**

1 Chess
ISBN 0-531-01290-5　　　　　LC 77-7229
"A First book"
First published 1953
The book "familiarizes the beginner with the chessmen and their moves, explains the most important basic principles, rules, and strategy and includes several practice games." Booklist [review of the 1953 edition]
"Instructions are easy to follow, type and general format are appealing." Booklist

Lombardy, William

Chess for children, step by step; a new easy way to learn the game [by] William Lombardy and Bette Marshall; photographs by Bette Marshall; chess art by John Schnell. Little 1977 107p illus $8.95, pa $4.95 (4-6) **794.1**

1 Chess
ISBN 0-316-53091-3; 0-316-53090-5　　LC 77-23183
"Through a series of simple 'mini-game[s],' each focusing on a specific piece, the authors have developed a novel and effective approach to the teaching of chess. Carefully outlined and detailed procedures, using algebraic rather than descriptive notation, are accompanied by attractive photographs and clear diagrams, which enable beginners of any age to learn chess by playing it without having their interest short-circuited by an overload of information." Horn Bk

Reinfeld, Fred

Chess for children; with moves and positions pictured in photo and diagram; drawings by Doug Anderson & Dennis Critchlow. [Rev. ed] Sterling 1980 72p illus lib. bdg. $6.69 (5 and up) **794.1**

1 Chess
ISBN 0-8069-4905-8
First published 1958
An "introductory book on chess that can be used alone and will be especially helpful to study as a supplement to personal instruction. The pieces used in the game, the ways in which each piece moves and captures and the conventions of illustration (of the board and of moves in diagram) are explained." Chicago. Children's Bk Center [review of 1958 edition]
"Clear explanation with many photographs and illustrations mark this thoughtfully prepared volume. The step-by-step presentation is easy to understand and inclusive enough to satisfy the bright beginner." Library J [review of 1958 edition]

Sarnoff, Jane

The chess book, by Jane Sarnoff and Reynold Ruffins. Consultant: Bruce Pandolfini. Scribner 1973 39p illus $6.95 (4-6) **794.1**

1 Chess
ISBN 0-684-13494-2　　　　　LC 73-1385
"Clearly laying out the basic rules of chess, the setup of the board, the movement of pieces, a sample game (Scholar's Mate), some simple strategy, and a few chess problems, the book also captures in its format and tone the fun and enjoyment found in the game." Horn Bk
The authors "do a grand job enticing new players into its spell. The thoughtful designs, precise diagrams and witty illustrations make their book an irresistible invitation to play chess." NY Times Bk Rev

794.6　Bowling

Dolan, Edward F.

The complete beginner's guide to bowling [by] Edward F. Dolan, Jr. Doubleday 1974 127p illus lib. bdg. $7.90 (5 and up) **794.6**

1 Bowling
ISBN 0-385-01667-0　　　　　LC 73-15335
In this guide the author discusses the fundamentals of the game from the lanes themselves, to the equipment, the rules, and the actual "steps" involved
"For novices and intermediate bowlers wishing to rid themselves of bad habits, this well-written book may be the next best thing to private lessons." Booklist

Ravielli, Anthony

What is bowling? Written and illus. by Anthony Ravielli. Atheneum Pubs/SMI 1975 unp illus lib. bdg. $6.95 (3-5) **794.6**

1 Bowling
ISBN 0-689-30492-7　　　　　LC 75-13572
"Cavemen playing with stones invented the first bowling game, and from there it has emerged in a variety of adaptations: Roman gladiators played boccie ball, Englishmen invented lawn bowling, and Germans changed it to kegel ball and later ninepins, and the Dutch brought it to America. Along with the history, Ravielli intersperses some legendary lore, such as Rip Van Winkle's thunder, that surrounds the game. The final pages deal with the rules, regulations, and scoring of the sport today as well as tips and techniques for improving one's game." Booklist
This "how-to-do-it book is illustrated with impeccably drawn stop-action figures of bowlers." Chicago. Children's Bk Center

795.1　Backgammon. Other games with dice

Belton, John

Dice games. Authors: John Belton [and] Joella Cramblit. Raintree Pubs. 1976 47p illus $7.33, lib. bdg. $6.60 (4 and up) **795.1**

1 Dice　2 Games
ISBN 0-8172-0024-X; 0-8172-0023-1　LC 75-43625
"Beginning with a vocabulary list for novices, this introduction to easy dice games includes the rules and an illustrative pattern of play for ten games which are suitable for two or more players. 'Craps' is not included, and there is no mention of playing for money. . . . Although best suited for game collections, this is also a fun-filled way to learn number skills." Sch Library J

Stern, Don

Backgammon. Watts, F. 1977 84p illus lib. bdg. $5.90 (5 and up) **795.1**

1 Backgammon
ISBN 0-531-01298-0　　　　　LC 77-6362
"A First book"
This guide for the beginner includes sample games and winning strategies, as well as instructions for the end game, doubles, and how to run a tournament. Diagrams and tables supplement the instructions

795.3　Dominoes

Belton, John

Domino games. Authors: John Belton [and] Joella Cramblit. Raintree Childrens Bks. 1976 48p illus lib. bdg. $7.99 (4 and up) **795.3**

1 Dominoes
ISBN 0-7182-0625-7　　　　　LC 76-8864
"An attractive blue-and-black format provides a background for clear instructions to six different games: Draw Game, Fortress, Concentration, Muggins, Matador, and Eleven-Point Black Tile. A general introduction describes the game pieces and provides a key to terminology." Booklist

795.4   Card games

Belton, John

Card games. Authors: John Belton [and] Joella Cramblit. Raintree Childrens Bks. 1976 48p illus $6.60, lib. bdg. $7.99 (4 and up)   **795.4**

1 Card games
ISBN 0-8172-0022-3; 0-8172-0021-5   LC 75-42319

This book offers "step-by-step directions for Concentration, Thirty-One, Speed, Ninety-Eight, Fan Tan, Crazy Eights, I Doubt It, Kings in the Corner, and Rummy. For each game the author lists number of players, object of the game dealing of the cards, and steps for playing and scoring. In some instances strategy, special rules, and sample game descriptions are included. Throughout the book, layouts of cards in their black-and-red colors help visualize the instructions." Booklist

Solitaire games. Authors: John Belton [and] Joella Cramblit. Raintree Childrens Bks. 1975 47p illus lib. bdg. $7.99 (4 and up)   **795.4**

1 Solitaire (Game)
ISBN 0-8172-0027-4   LC 75-25956

"Containing sample games and step-by-step directions for nine different versions of solitaire, this is arranged in order of increasing difficulty of the games. Although there are occasional mistakes in the diagrams . . . this will provide beginning card players with ammunition." Sch Library J

Reisberg, Ken

Card games. Watts, F. 1979 62p illus lib. bdg. $5.45 (4 and up)   **795.4**

1 Card games
ISBN 0-531-02253-6   LC 78-11646

"A First book"
"Following a brief description of the history and lore of cards, Reisberg provides instructions for 13 popular games such as crazy eights, Yukon, hearts, rummy, spades, solitaire, and casino. The satisfactory directions include number of players and level of difficulty, as well as a rundown on objectives, dealing, leading, strategies, pointers, and scoring techniques, supplemented with some photographs of sample hands and layouts." Sch Library J

796   Athletic and outdoor sports and games

Arthur, Lee

Sportsmath: how it works [by] Lee Arthur, Elizabeth James [and] Judith B. Taylor. Lothrop 1975 96p illus $6.75, lib. bdg. $6.48 (4-6)   **796**

1 Sports—Statistics
ISBN 0-688-41712-4; 0-688-51712-9   LC 75-17714

By describing one actual professional game in football, baseball, basketball, hockey, and tennis, the authors demonstrate how basic mathematical principles are used to produce statistics such as averages, projections, and percentages

"Children liking sports and math will be fascinated, and adults may find the book a useful motivation for young athletes not tuned in to mathematics." Booklist

Barr, George

Young scientist and sports; featuring baseball, football, and basketball; illus. by Mildred Waltrip. McGraw 1962 159p illus lib. bdg. $6.50 (4 and up)   **796**

1 Sports 2 Physics
ISBN 0-07-003806-6   LC 62-12477

"Whittlesey House publications"
The author "applies such scientific principles as action and reaction, gravity, and inertia to sports in general and the three major sports in particular. Useful in science classes as well as in sports." Hodges. Bks for Elem Sch Libraries

Keith, Harold

Sports and games. 6th ed. rev. Crowell 1976 313p illus $9.95 (5 and up)   **796**

1 Athletics 2 Sports
ISBN 0-690-01254-3   LC 76-17585

First published 1941
This introduction to seventeen well known and popular sports includes the history, rules, techniques, and training procedures for each sport

796.03   Sports—Encyclopedias and dictionaries

The **Concise** encyclopedia of sports. 2d rev. ed. Edited by Gerald Newman. Watts, F. 1979 218p illus $8.95, lib. bdg. $10.90   **796.03**

1 Sports—Encyclopedias
ISBN 0-531-02391-5; 0-531-00445-7   LC 79-10260

First published 1970 under the editorship of Keith W. Jennison
This book describes over eighty-five sports. Each entry contains a history of the game, its rules and regulations, statistics, and materials on sports immortals
Includes bibliographical references

Guinness Sports record book [comp. by] Norris McWhirter & Ross McWhirter. Sterling illus $5.95, lib. bdg. $6.69 (4 and up)   **796.03**

1 Sports—Encyclopedias
"Taken from the Guinness Book of world records [entered in class 032]." Title page
First published 1972 and periodically revised to keep material up to date
This compilation presents records set in over sixty sports and games from archery to yachting, including auto racing, bridge, chess, scrabble and tiddleywinks. Material is arranged alphabetically by sport

The **Junior** illustrated encyclopedia of sports. [Rev. and enl.] Willard Mullin, illustrator; Herbert Kamm, editor. Bobbs 1975 681p illus $8.95 (5 and up)   **796.03**

1 Sports—Encyclopedias
ISBN 0-672-52094-4   LC 74-17658

Cover title: The New Junior illustrated encyclopedia of sports
First published 1960 under the editorship of Willard Mullin
For thirteen major sports, this book provides histories, biographical sketches of outstanding participants, records and statistics, and many photographs and drawings

Menke, Frank G.

The encyclopedia of sports. Barnes, A.S. illus $30   **796.03**

1 Sports—Encyclopedias
First published 1939. Periodically revised to bring material up to date
This is a "standard work. . . . It covers a wide variety of sports, e.g. baseball, boxing, football, basketball, hockey and soccer providing brief history, description, basic rules, names and records of champions. . . . [There is also] a tabulation of all current records and statistics." Am Ref Bks Annual, 1970 [review of the 1969 edition]

796.1   Miscellaneous games

Bley, Edgar S.

The best singing games for children of all ages; drawings by Patt Willen, piano arrangements by Margaret Chase. Sterling 1957 96p illus music $7.95, lib. bdg. $7.49   **796.1**

1 Singing games 2 Folk songs
ISBN 0-8069-4550-1; 0-8069-4451-X   LC 57-13285

"More than 50 musical games, jump-rope jingles, and play party games, with words, musical scores, and directions for action. Arranged by age levels and illustrated with helpful drawings." Hodges. Bks for Elem Sch Libraries

Dolan, Edward F.

The complete beginner's guide to making and flying kites, by Edward F. Dolan, Jr. Illus. by John Lane. Doubleday 1977 151p illus $6.95, lib. bdg. $7.90 (5 and up) **796.1**

1 Kites
ISBN 0-385-04905-6; 0-385-04937-4   LC 75-36585

This book includes "a brief history of kites; the appeal of kite flying; kinds of kites, their parts and materials; special flying techniques, races and games; details of design and construction of several types of kites; and an explanation of why kites can fly. Practical information, such as estimating wind speed and judging the height of a kite, in included. The breadth of subject matter is the book's strongest point. There are, however, some weak aspects to the book; in particular, the explanation of why kites fly and the treatment of the nature and behavior of wind." AAAS Sci Bks & Films
Includes bibliography

Downer, Marion

Kites; how to make and fly them. Lothrop 1959 64p illus lib. bdg. $6.48 (4-6) **796.1**

1 Kites
ISBN 0-688-51227-5   LC 58-14497

The author "first discusses tools, materials, and construction methods for making reels, tails, and kite parachutes, as well as kite bodies of many styles. She concludes with requirements for kite contests, tournaments, and a kite-making race. The large photographs, selected from several sources, are evocative of pleasures in the sport." Horn Bk

Fowke, Edith

(comp.) Sally go round the sun; 300 children's songs, rhymes, and games; musical arrangements by Keith MacMillan; illus. by Carlos Marchiori. Doubleday 1970 [c1969] 160p illus music $9.95, lib. bdg. $10.90 **796.1**

1 Singing games 2 Songs
ISBN 0-385-02513-0; 0-385-02956-X   LC 77-87873

First published 1969 in Canada
This selection of children's lore includes "singing games, rhymes used for rope skipping, ball bouncing, and clapping, foot and finger plays, taunts and teases, and silly songs. Directions for the games and the foot and finger plays are given in an appended section of notes along with sources and comparative references; piano and guitar accompaniments are provided for some of the songs." Booklist
"Younger children, too, will appreciate the material in this collection, since the book is ideally suited for adult use with small children in groups. The musical arrangements are simple." Sutherland. The Best in Children's Bks

Glazer, Tom

Do your ears hang low? 50 more musical fingerplays; illus. by Mila Lazarevich. Doubleday 1980 112p illus $8.95, lib. bdg. $9.90 (k-3) **796.1**

1 Singing games 2 Finger play
ISBN 0-385-12602-6; 0-385-12603-4   LC 78-20072

A companion volume to the author's Eye winker, Tom Tinker, Chin chopper, entered below
The author, an "experienced folk singer, performer, and recording artist reiterates the importance of imitation and dramatic expression in the playtime occupations of young children. Some of the selections in the new book are well-known finger-play or activity songs, some are favorite songs adapted for the purpose, and some are original musical settings of finger-play lyrics. A considerable amount of fresh and unfamiliar material is included. The accompaniments may be played on the piano; chords are indicated for use with guitar, banjo, or autoharp. Simple directions and amusing line drawings appear on spacious pages, making the book an attractive and valuable volume uniquely suited for use with young children and with exceptional children of all ages." Horn Bk

Eye winker, Tom Tinker, chin chopper; fifty musical fingerplays; illus. by Ron Himler. Doubleday 1973 91p illus $7.95, lib. bdg. $8.90, pa $1.95 (k-3) **796.1**

1 Singing games 2 Finger play
ISBN 0-385-08200-2; 0-385-09453-1; 0-385-13344-8
    LC 72-97497

This collection of 50 songs, with piano arrangements, guitar chords and instructions for finger and body movements, "represent three distinct groups: fingerplay songs, such as 'Eentsy, Weentsy Spider'; familiar action rhymes 'newly set to music,' like 'Here Is the Church' and 'Pat-A-Cake'; and many songs—both new and traditional—set down with totally new fingerplays." Horn Bk
"The illustrations are frolicsome [and] always attractive. . . . Even without the fingerplay, this is a compilation of songs that anyone working with young children, particularly in groups, should find useful, and older children who can play piano or guitar can use the book for the music alone." Chicago. Children's Bk Center

Grayson, Marion

Let's do fingerplays; illus. by Nancy Weyl. Luce, R.B. 1962 109p illus $8.95 (k-2) **796.1**

1 Finger play
ISBN 0-88331-003-1   LC 62-101217

"Approximately 200 rhymes and songs, with directions for accompanying finger plays, are organized under such headings as Animal Antics, Counting and Counting Out, and Holidays and Special Occasions." Hodges. Bks for Elem Sch Libraries
"Sources are listed, and there is a first-line as well as title index. Format is generous, with the pages well designed and illustrated. Very useful book." Sch Library J

Greenaway, Kate

Kate Greenaway's Book of games; with twenty-four full-page plates. [Merrimack Pub. Corp. n.d.] 63p illus $4.75, pa $3.74 **796.1**

1 Games
ISBN 0-87497-096-2; 0-87497-193-4

"Reproduced just as Kate Greenaway created it in 1889, this charming collection of directions for Follow-My-Leader, Drop the Handkerchief, Blind Man's Bluff, Mulberry Bush, and even Seesaw and Marbles will continue to delight Greenaway fans today. Soft subdued colors, gentle English countrysides, and well mannered, stylishly dressed children characteristically grace the pages." Booklist

Hunt, Sarah Ethridge

Games and sports the world around; illus. by Max Heldman. 3d ed. Ronald 1964 271p illus $11.95 **796.1**

1 Games 2 Sports
ISBN 0-8260-4565-0   LC 64-18466

First published 1941 by A. S. Barnes with title: Games the world around
The author presents "games, sports, and play for developing an understanding of human relationships. Each activity is prefaced with headings indicating age level, number of players, playing area, necessary equipment, type, and intellectual appeal. Addressed to teachers and recreation leaders, but useful also to pupils." Hodges. Bks for Elem Sch Libraries
Definition of terms: p237. Books of games and sports played in the United States: p242

Jump the rope jingles; [collected] by Emma Vietor Worstell; illus. by Sheila Greenwald. Collier Bks. 1972 [c1961] 44p illus pa $1.95 (k-4) **796.1**

1 Jump rope rhymes
ISBN 0-02-045450-3

First published 1961 by Macmillan Publishing Company
"Amusingly illustrated, a compilation of calls and jingles used in jumping rope. Several pages of instructions for jump-rope games are appended, as is an index of first lines. A useful book, and one that can be used by an adult with children too young to read the text independently." Chicago. Children's Bk Center

Kettelkamp, Larry

Kites; written and illus. by Larry Kettelkamp. Morrow 1959 48p illus lib. bdg. $6.96
(3-6)   **796.1**

1 Kites
ISBN 0-688-31584-4   LC 59-7931

"Included in this book are directions for building
various kinds of kites as well as pertinent information on the scientific aspects of kite-flying. The
place of kites in the development of aviation
and in the gathering of weather data is also
discussed briefly." Adventuring With Bks. 2d edition

"Extra ideas, such as adding attachments to the
kite line or glitter to the kite, spark up the book,
as do accounts of the Japanese kite fighting contests and the launching of Chinese dragon kites."
Chicago Sunday Trib

Spinning tops. Morrow 1966 63p illus $6.75,
lib. bdg. $6.48 (3-6)   **796.1**

1 Top
ISBN 0-688-21585-8; 0-688-31585-2   LC 66-10307

Illustrated by the author
A "fresh activity book is this fully illustrated
guide to the making and use of tops. The text
introduces international backgrounds for a variety of tops, some of which, like the popular
yo-yo, have served practical purposes as well as
entertained children. Games and stunts using
hand-spun and string-wound types are clearly
diagramed, and action drawings suggest their
fun. Other pictures show how acorns, gourds,
Tinker-toys, or spools can readily be converted
into tops." Horn Bk

Langstaff, John

Shimmy shimmy coke-ca-pop! A collection
of city children's street games and rhymes,
by John Langstaff and Carol Langstaff; photographs by Don MacSorley. Doubleday 1973
95p illus music lib. bdg. $6.95 (2-5)   **796.1**

1 Singing games 2 Games
ISBN 0-385-05769-5   LC 72-92227

This collection of urban children's chants, some
accompanied by music, is divided into 11 sections:
name calling, ball bouncing, sidewalk drawing
games, circle games, who's it, tag games, jump
rope rhymes, action games, follow the leader,
hand clapping, and dramatic play

"Photographs on almost every page capture the
same energetic action and constant motion generated through the rhymes. For an adult the
book will provide interesting insight into contemporary children's blend of traditional and
current lore, while young readers can see their
own games in print and maybe even learn a few
new ones." Booklist

Millen, Nina

(comp.) Children's games from many lands;
illus. by Allan Eitszen. New and rev. ed. Friendship Press 1965 192p illus music pa $4.95 **796.1**

1 Games
ISBN 0-377-45011-1   LC 65-24039

First published 1943
"This anthology is a survey of two hundred
fifty-eight children's games from sixty-four countries. Readers will find games reflecting the
music and language of people, the way people
earn a living, daily customs and common foods
from various countries. They may also discover
the universality of games and game patterns.
Each geographical section of the book is introduced with comments noting the main characteristics of games of this area." Reading Ladders.
5th edition

Nelson, Esther L.

Singing and dancing games for the very
young; illus. by Minn Matsuda; photographs
by Shirley Zeiberg. Sterling 1977 72p illus
music $7.95, lib. bdg. $7.49   **796.1**

1 Singing games 2 Dancing 3 Finger play
ISBN 0-8069-4568-0; 0-8069-4579-9   LC 77-79513

Over forty songs, with lyrics, simple piano scores
and instructions, are suggested for use with individual children or groups. The selections include
finger plays, folk songs and rhythm games, familiar favorites ("Humpty Dumpty," "Where is
Thumbkin") and original material. Sketches and
photographs show the games being performed

"This book would be a superb choice for the
preschool/primary classroom, but deserves a place
on the home bookshelf as well. The directions are
easy to follow, the melodies tuneful and the games
great fun." Children's Bk Rev Serv

Opie, Iona

Children's games in street and playground
. . . by Iona and Peter Opie. Oxford 1969
xxvi, 371p illus maps $38   **796.1**

1 Games 2 Folklore
ISBN 0-19-827210-3   LC 76-437542

"Chasing; catching; seeking; hunting; racing;
duelling; exerting; daring; guessing; acting; pretending." Title page

"Illustrated with game diagrams and photographs. . . . This volume concerns the 'games that
children, aged about 6-12, play of their own accord when out of doors, and usually out of sight.'
Compared and documented both geographically
and in relation to earlier lore are hundreds of examples of starting-out or counting-out rhymes,
ritualistic folk dialogues, chants of chasing and
catching games, and the many other categories
named in the subtitle. These are helpfully indexed to make the book a useful reference work
as well as fascinating reading." Horn Bk

Rockwell, Anne

Games (and how to play them) [Text and]
pictures by Anne Rockwell. Crowell 1973 43p
illus $9.95, lib. bdg. $9.79 (k-4)   **796.1**

1 Games
ISBN 0-690-32159-7; 0-690-32160-0   LC 72-10936

"A compendium of 43 noisy, quiet, indoor, outdoor activities." NY Times Bk Rev

"A book that can be used with younger children as well as by independent readers. The
explanations are brief but clear; the pictures are
often informative and always attractive with
animals as characters and with intriguing details.
A small bonus: the humor of interpretation, such
as the kilted rabbit for hopscotch, or the octopus-
sailors having a knot contest." Chicago. Cildren's
Bk Center

What shall we do and Allee galloo! Play
songs and singing games for young children. Collected & ed. by Marie Winn;
musical arrangements by Allan Miller;
pictures by Karla Kuskin. Harper 1970 87p
illus music lib. bdg. $7.89 (k-2)   **796.1**

1 Singing games 2 Songs
ISBN 0-06-026537-X   LC 72-85039

These "forty-seven play games and songs, both
familiar and less known, have large-print music
and lyrics (piano and guitar accompaniment) and
instructions for group participation." Children's
Bks. 1970

"A title and first-line index is included, and
cheerful, decorative illustrations appear on every
page." Booklist

796.2   Active games requiring equipment

Olney, Ross R.

Better skateboarding for boys and girls
[by] Ross R. Olney and Chan Bush. Dodd
1977 63p illus $5.95 (5 and up)   **796.2**

1 Skateboarding 2 Skateboards
ISBN 0-396-07433-2   LC 76-53437

Photographs by the authors
"Riding techniques, construction guidelines, competition stakes, and repair tips highlight this
down-to-earth presentation. In both the smoothly
written text and the clear black-and-white photographs, safety precautions and gear (helmets,
wrist braces, and knee pads) are featured. Increased interest in competition has resulted from
the sport's growing popularity, and the authors
describe freestyle, downhill slalom, and cross-
country as the three major events." Booklist

Roller skating! By Ross R. Olney and
Chan Bush. Lothrop 1979 128p illus $6.75,
lib. bdg. $6.48 (4 and up)   **796.2**

1 Roller skating
ISBN 0-688-41892-9; 0-688-51892-3   LC 78-27248

Olney, Ross R.—Continued

This book covers the history of roller skating and the fundamentals of the sport, including care of equipment. It also contains descriptions of new techniques such as bowl skating, trick maneuvers, roller derby and roller disco dancing

Tricky discs: Frisbee saucer flying. Lothrop 1979 128p illus $7.50, lib. bdg. $7.20 (4 and up)   796.2
1 Frisbee (Game)
ISBN 0-688-41891-0; 0-688-51891-5   LC 78-31851
"Facts covered include the history of the sport, an explanation of the scientific factors involved in the flight of the disc, instructions in the basic throws as well as trick throws and catches, games that can be played, and even how to take care of your disc. . . . Illustrated with photographs from championship competition events of the International Frisbee Association, the book also gives current world records." Sch Library J

Shevelson, Joseph F.

Roller skating. Harvey House 1978 62p illus lib. bdg. $6.19 (5 and up)   796.2
1 Roller skating
ISBN 0-8178-5944-6   LC 78-56557
A brief history of the sport is followed by discussion of skates and safety, skating rink attractions (including disco skating) and rules, methods of learning and practicing, and competition

Sullivan, George

Better roller skating for boys and girls. Dodd 1980 64p illus lib. bdg. $5.95 (4 and up)   796.2
1 Roller skating
ISBN 0-396-07784-6   LC 79-22717
The author provides basic information about roller skating, including the sport's history, equipment, techniques, advanced maneuvers and safety. There are also discussions of recreational skating, speed skating, roller skate dancing and roller skate hockey
Glossary: p64

Weir, LaVada

Skateboards and skateboarding; the complete beginner's guide; photographs by Al Moote; illus. by W. E. Hopmans. Messner 1977 128p illus lib. bdg. $7.79 (3-6)   796.2
1 Skateboarding
ISBN 0-671-32828-X   LC 76-51296
The book offers "complete and accurate instructions on how to skateboard and to do some tricks. It will also show you how to have fun and not get hurt. You can learn how to take care of your equipment, get the best for your money, or build your own . . . [and] how skateboarding began and grew." Foreword
List of sources and products: p122-24. Glossary: p125-28

796.32   Basketball. Volleyball

Antonacci, Robert J.

Basketball for young champions [by] Robert J. Antonacci and Jene Barr; illus. by Patti Boyd. 2d ed. McGraw 1979 183p illus (Young champion ser) $7.95 (5 and up) 796.32
1 Basketball
ISBN 0-07-002141-4   LC 78-8029
First published 1960
"Instruction in how to guard, dribble, shoot for the basket, pass and catch the basketball. Within each chapter specific shots, dribbles, passes, etc. are described as well as exercise for both solo and group use that will improve players' skills. A clearly written, detailed, and helpful guide for both boys and girls." Sch Library J

Clark, Steve

Illustrated basketball dictionary for young people; illus. by Frank Baginski. Harvey House 1977 124p illus lib. bdg. $6.79 (3-6)   796.32
1 Basketball—Dictionaries
ISBN 0-8178-5642-0   LC 77-77859

"Capsulized descriptions of plays and definitions of terms are highlighted by light-hearted pen-and-ink drawings in this collection of basketball basics. Handily organized in alphabetical order, the entries are preceded by a brief account of the origins of the sport and concluded with cursory introductions to an elite few of basketball's all-time professional stars, as well as a select group of current court greats." Booklist

Coombs, Charles

Be a winner in basketball. Morrow 1975 126p illus lib. bdg. $6.96, pa $2.45 (5 and up)   796.32
1 Basketball
ISBN 0-688-32039-2; 0-688-22039-5   LC 75-17778
The author gives a brief history of the beginnings of basketball, "then goes into various aspects of offense, defense, and moving and shooting the ball. A basic guide for the would-be player or fan unfortunately includes only one mention of girls as participants, and all but one of the generally good black-and-white action shots show male players in college or professional games." Booklist
Glossary: p121-24

Devaney, John

The story of basketball; illus. with photographs. Random House 1976 150p illus lib. bdg. $5.99 (5 and up)   796.32
1 Basketball—History 2 Basketball—Biography
ISBN 0-394-92806-7   LC 76-8129
This book traces the history of the game from its nineteenth century beginnings through the NBA championship games of 1976. The author describes the careers of past basketball heroes such as Hank Luisetti, George Mikan, and Bill Russell plus heroes of the present such as Kareem Abdul-Jabbar, Rick Barry, and Julius Erving. He also includes stories on such teams as the Minneapolis Lakers of the 1950s, the Boston Celtics of the '60s, and the UCLA Bruins of the '70s
"Biographical data is set off in boxes. Numerous black-and-white photographs fill nearly every page, making this an appealing browsing item, whose index will lead researchers to specific information." Booklist

Gault, Clare

The Harlem Globetrotters and basketball's funniest games, by Clare and Frank Gault; illus. by Charles McGill. Walker [1977 c1976] 41p illus $6.95 (3-6)   796.32
1 Harlem Globetrotters 2 Basketball
ISBN 0-8027-6274-3   LC 76-56611
"Gault traces the history of the Globetrotters' basketball team evaluating both the players' on-court abilities and their talents as comic performers. The text, enlivened with anecdotes and highlighted by numerous black-and-white line drawings, can be handled easily by independent readers in the middle grades." Sch Library J

Knosher, Harley

Basic basketball strategy; foreword by Rick Barry; illus. with diagrams by Leonard Kessler. Doubleday 1972 102p illus $5.95, lib. bdg. $6.90 (4 and up)   796.32
ISBN 0-385-05804-7; 0-385-00008-1   LC 79-171302
The author "covers every aspect of basketball strategy that concerns a young player, from basics to advanced techniques, from shooting and dribbling to setting a fast break, switching and gambling on defense." Foreword
"Drawings and diagrams illustrate the right and wrong way to perform various skills. Knosher also discusses the value of conditioning, practice, and drills, shows clearly the various ways in which fouls are committed, and stresses the importance of knowing the rules." Booklist

Liss, Howard

Basketball talk for beginners; illus. by Frank Robbins. Messner 1970 95p illus lib. bdg. $5.79 (4 and up)   796.32
1 Basketball—Dictionaries
ISBN 0-671-32299-0   LC 72-123163
Accompanied by diagrams and drawings of the action on the court, this book provides explanations both of the rules of basketball and slang expressions used by the players

Monroe, Earl

The basketball skill book [by] Earl Monroe & Wes Unseld; ed. by Ray Siegener. Atheneum Pubs. 1973 114p illus $7.95 (4 and up)   **796.32**

1 Basketball
ISBN 0-689-10528-2   LC 72-862687

Basic basketball fundamentals such as ball handling, dribbling, shooting, passing, and individual and team offensive and defensive play are introduced through text and numerous photographs

Sullivan, George

Better basketball for girls. Dodd 1978 64p illus lib. bdg. $5.95 (5 and up)   **796.32**

1 Basketball
ISBN 0-396-07580-0   LC 78-7732

"Sullivan gives a brief history of women's basketball in the United States, makes some suggestions for getting in condition and choosing sneakers, and launches into a skill-by-skill explanation of techniques and skills (various passes, various shots, screening, getting free, etc.) and concludes with several chapters on team defense and defensive play. Rules of the game and a glossary are appended." Chicago. Children's Bk Center

"The chapter on the struggle of women to achieve parity with men on the court, the photographs of female college players in action, and the consistent use of the feminine pronoun will help to build a sense of pride and solidarity among girls and women involved in the sport." Sch Library J

Better volleyball for girls. Dodd 1979 64p illus $5.95 (5 and up)   **796.32**

1 Volleyball
ISBN 0-396-07697-1   LC 79-12640

This book "is a well-rounded and thorough presentation of history, rules, and a profusion of techniques with well-chosen black-and-white photos included. This will be accessible to most and should make the game more enjoyable through increased skill." Sch Library J

A glossary of volleyball terms is included

This is pro basketball; illus. with photographs and diagrams. Dodd 1977 118p illus lib. bdg. $6.50 (5 and up)   **796.32**

1 Basketball
ISBN 0-396-07455-3   LC 77-6497

The author "highlights some of today's best players plus former greats of the game to illustrate all offensive and defensive skills. The nearly 100 photographs are up to date, and there is an interesting section on 'All-Time NBA Records.' Best of all is the chapter giving insight into the peripatetic lifestyles of these pros, entitled appropriately enough, 'The Travel is Unbelievable.'" Sch Library J

796.332   American football

Anderson, Dick

Defensive football [by] Dick Anderson and Nick Buoniconti; ed. by Bill Bondurant. Atheneum Pubs. 1973 146p illus $7.95 (3-6)   **796.332**

1 Football
ISBN 0-689-10573-8   LC 73-80752

"Written by two members of the Miami Dolphins, this is intended to give aspiring players tips on defensive play. Nick Buoniconti, middle linebacker, handles the defensive line positions; Dick Anderson, safety, describes the defensive back's duties. There are also chapters dealing with tackling, pass coverage, reading keys, meeting runs, interceptions, agility drills, fumbles, and punt returns. Numerous demonstration photographs of Anderson and Buoniconti are included (though some are too small), and there is the usual message about dedication, discipline, etc. Easy to read with many anecdotes and summaries of main points at the end of each chapter." Sch Library J

Antonacci, Robert J.

Football for young champions [by] Robert J. Antonacci and Jene Barr; illus. by Frank Mullins. 2d ed. McGraw 1976 152p illus lib. bdg. $7.95 (4 and up)   **796.332**

1 Football
ISBN 0-07-002154-6   LC 75-10825

First published 1958 by Whittlesey House with illustrations by Rus Anderson

The book "describes various formations and positions and outlines several ways youngsters can test their skills." Sch Library J

Coombs, Charles

Be a winner in football. Morrow 1974 127p illus lib. bdg. $6.96, pa $2.45 (5 and up)   **796.332**

1 Football
ISBN 0-688-30119-3; 0-688-25119-6   LC 74-5832

"A useful guide to football basics. Coombs puts the reader in a team member's shoes and talks him through various plays, giving rules and pointers on the game. Chapters about getting into shape, playing the various positions, passing, and kicking are included. Beginners and more experienced youngsters will be attracted by the generous print size, good black-and-white photographs of pros in action, and down-to-earth, ungimmicky approach. A glossary is appended." Booklist

Dolan, Edward F.

Basic football strategy; an introduction for young players, by Edward F. Dolan, Jr. Foreword by Duffy Daugherty; illus. with diagrams by John Lane. Doubleday 1976 131p illus $6.95, lib. bdg. $7.90 (4 and up)   **796.332**

1 Football
ISBN 0-385-03998-0; 0-385-04184-5   LC 76-3438

"A clearly-written, well-diagrammed book that keeps the physical limitations of its audience in mind. [The author] covers offensive and defensive strategy, mental and physical preparedness, with useful tips at the end of each chapter." Sch Library J

Jackson, C. Paul

How to play better football; illus. by Leonard Kessler. Crowell 1972 233p illus $8.79 (4 and up)   **796.332**

1 Football
ISBN 0-690-41567-2   LC 72-158707

"Covered are the history of the game, basic rules, explanations of offensive and defensive team play, the importance of teamwork, and the skills necessary to execute good play. Descriptions of physical conditioning and proper equipment, a glossary of football terms, and illustrated officials' signals round out the coverage. The large print format, with many diagrams and illustrations, enhances the clearly-written text." Sch Library J

796.334   Soccer

Antonacci, Robert J.

Soccer for young champions [by] Robert J. Antonacci and Anthony J. Puglisi; illus. by Patti Boyd. McGraw 1978 183p illus $7.95 (4 and up)   **796.334**

1 Soccer
ISBN 0-07-002147-3   LC 77-27565

The authors discuss the history, rules, and techniques of soccer including drills, advice on keeping score, and ways of involving the physically handicapped in the sport

"The text is not always clear. . . . Nevertheless, the advice is sound, the illustrations (awkward drawings) show black and white players, men and women; the glossary and index are useful." Chicago. Children's Bk Center

Coombs, Charles

Be a winner in soccer; illus. with 55 photographs and diagrams. Morrow 1977 127p illus $6.75, lib. bdg. $6.48 (5 and up)   **796.334**

1 Soccer
ISBN 0-688-22099-1; 0-688-32099-6   LC 76-39850

Coombs, Charles—*Continued*

"Using an easygoing, personable style, Coombs explains soccer basics—rules of the game, techniques, positions and the special abilities needed for each, and offensive and defensive strategies. He is careful to direct his advice to both boys and girls; numerous black-and-white photographs illustrate points of the text, and the format . . . features attractive, medium-sized print and clean page design." Booklist
Glossary: p121-23

Dolan, Edward F.

Starting soccer; a handbook for boys & girls; photographs by Jameson C. Goldner. Harper 1976 114p illus lib. bdg. $8.79 (5 and up)   796.334

1 Soccer
ISBN 0-06-021683-2   LC 76-3838

Divided into three main sections (The Basics, Game Time and Building Your Skills), this book covers such specifics as kicking, rules and the different playing positions, along with practice minigames and warm-up exercises
The book is "well illustrated with black-and-white photographs [and] features boys and girls executing techniques described in the text, their everyday appearance well in keeping with the book's unintimidating feel." Booklist

Gardner, James B.

Illustrated soccer dictionary for young people; illus. by David Ross. Harvey House 1976 124p illus lib. bdg. $6.79 (5 and up)   796.334

1 Soccer—Dictionaries
ISBN 0-8178-5482-7   LC 76-10044

All the information necessary to play and observe this sport—the positions, penalties, signals, plays, and players—are included here in dictionary format, with amusing cartoon-like drawings
"The simply written definitions successfully explain the terms on a level comprehensible to newcomers to the game." Sch Library J

Gemme, Leila Boyle

Soccer is our game; photographs by Roberta Caliger. Childrens Press 1979 31p illus lib. bdg. $7.35 (k-2)   796.334

1 Soccer
ISBN 0-516-03615-7   LC 79-13245

In short, simple sentences which accompany full page color photographs, this book depicts children playing soccer
This book "is tailor-made for pre-schoolers who play or watch soccer. The color photos here are crisp and well chosen to illustrate the simple text." Sch Library J

Jackson, C. Paul

How to play better soccer; illus. by Don Madden. Crowell 1978 147p illus $8.95, lib. bdg. $8.79 (4 and up)   796.334

1 Soccer
ISBN 0-690-01363-9; 0-690-03828-3   LC 76-51450

The author "gives a history of the game, and explains the rules and techniques for a sport which is growing in popularity with spectators and players in the United States, and which has long been the most popular international sport. Team play and position play are lucidly described and the diagrams illustrating them are well-placed and adequately labelled. A chart of official signals, a glossary, and an index are appended." Chicago. Children's Bk Center
"Exceptionally clever, lighthearted drawings lend flair and a sense of humor to a clarification of the rules and regulations of soccer. Jackson enlivens this thorough coverage of essential information with a vivid account of a hypothetical soccer game, descriptions of exercises to keep players of both sexes in good physical condition, and practice drills to improve players' skills." Booklist

Liss, Howard

The great game of soccer; photographs by Bruce Curtis. Putnam 1979 64p illus $8.95 (5 and up)   796.334

1 Soccer
ISBN 0-399-20644-2   LC 78-9842

This book "gives history and information about stars, rules, and some brief tips on techniques. Its large format and well placed black-and-white photos by Bruce Curtis make it a good starting point for new soccer converts." Sch Library J
A glossary of soccer terms is included

Sullivan, George

Better soccer for boys and girls. Dodd 1978 64p illus map lib. bdg. $5.95 (4 and up)   796.334

1 Soccer
ISBN 0-396-07533-9   LC 77-16869

"Clear diagrams and photographs complement a brisk and comprehensive text that describes the way the game is played, explains the rules, includes a quiz to make sure the reader understands them, and gives detailed advice on each aspect of play. Sullivan begins with a history of the game, and discusses its growing popularity in the United States." Chicago. Children's Bk Center
Glossary: p63-64

This is pro soccer; illus. with photographs and diagrams. Dodd 1979 126p illus lib. bdg. $6.95 (5 and up)   796.334

1 Soccer 2 North American Soccer League
ISBN 0-396-07643-2   LC 78-10729

This book "accents the sport's foremost players (Pelé, Kyle Rote, Jr., Steve David, Georgio Chinaglia, Gordon Banks and others) and includes information on coaching, how the game is played, professional tactics, and how to watch the game. A glossary, all-time NASL records, and index, diagrams and action-packed, black-and-white photographs accompany the text." Sch Library J
Glossary: p116-18

Toye, Clive

Soccer. Rev. ed. Watts, F. 1979 66p illus lib. bdg. $5.90 (4-6)   796.334

1 Soccer
ISBN 0-531-02936-0   LC 78-24314

"A First book"
First published 1968
In this "book, which covers many aspects of the game, both the fan and the player will find explanations (and diagrams) of tactics, techniques, and rules and regulations." Horn Bk
Great names in soccer: p54-58. Glossary of soccer terms: p59-62

796.34 Racket games

Boccaccio, Tony

Racquetball basics; illus. by Bill Gow; photographs by Paul Jacobs; created and produced by Arvid Knudsen. Prentice-Hall 1979 48p illus lib. bdg. $6.95 (4 and up)   796.34

1 Racquetball
ISBN 0-13-129585-3   LC 79-15234

This book "describes the history and development of the sport and the basic rules and variations of the game as well as the equipment used and the racquetball court itself (including dimensions and the placement of the Service Zone). Pointers for play include preparatory exercises, methods of concentration, how to select the racquet, basic strokes, the serve, returning the serve, playing the back wall, offensive and defensive strategy, playing doubles, and how match results are posted." Sch Library J

Fichter, George S.

Racquetball. Watts, F. 1979 64p illus lib. bdg. $5.90 (4 and up)   796.34

1 Racquetball
ISBN 0-531-04078-X   LC 79-11876

"A First book"
Explains the rules and basic strategy of racquetball and discusses the necessary equipment and ways of improving one's game
The author "has good suggestions for strategy and coping with the speed of the game. Illustrations aid in the explanation of body movements and ball handling." Sch Library J
Racquetball talk: p50-55. Racquetball information sources: p59-60

Sullivan, George

Better table tennis for boys and girls. Dodd 1972 64p illus lib. bdg. $5.95 (5 and up)

796.34

1 Ping-pong
ISBN 0-396-06643-7   LC 72-3154

This description of how to play ping-pong includes directions for grips, basic shots, spin, serving, footwork, tactics and strategy of singles and doubles play, advanced shots, scoring, official rules and tournaments

"This gives complete, detailed and, for the most part, clear explanations of equipment, techniques, strategies, and rules of table tennis. Numerous excellent photographs and carefully placed diagrams aid understanding of the often technical text. Photos and discussions of major players of the sport are an effective addition, as is the inclusion of a brief, even-handed treatment of Ping-Pong diplomacy with China in the introduction. Well written with no condescension." Sch Library J

796.342 Tennis

Coombs, Charles

Be a winner in tennis; illus. with photographs. Morrow 1975 128p illus lib. bdg. $6.96, pa $2.45 (5 and up)   **796.342**

1 Tennis
ISBN 0-688-32020-1; 0-688-27020-0   LC 74-23262

The book "starts out with a history of tennis and proceeds to the basics of the game. The explanations are clear; there is a most worthwhile chapter on tennis equipment (ball, shoes, etc.); and many black-and-white photos demonstrate positions and techniques." Sch Library J
Glossary: p124-26

Duroska, Lud

Tennis for beginners; consultant, Charles Lundgren; introduction by Jimmy Connors. Grosset 1975 90p illus $10.15 (3 and up)

796.342

1 Tennis
ISBN 0-448-13236-2   LC 74-94

Using photographs and simple text, the author covers tennis history, racket grips, various strokes, common faults and practice hints. Also discussed are official rules, etiquette, attire, and doubles play

Hopman, Harry

Better tennis for boys and girls. Dodd 1972 95p illus lib. bdg. $5.95 (5 and up)   **796.342**

1 Tennis
ISBN 0-396-06365-9   LC 76-165672

In text, photographs, and diagrams, the author describes the techniques for playing winning tennis. He discusses grips and strokes, tactics and strategy involving court position for singles and doubles, training and preparation, practice in the home, the use of a wall for practice, etiquitte, footwork, and the benefits of tennis as a game for life

"For the serious beginning player who wants practical advice on all aspects of the game." Chicago
Tennis terms: p92-95

McCormick, Bill

Tennis. Watts, F. 1973 66p illus lib. bdg. $5.90 (5 and up)   **796.342**

1 Tennis
ISBN 0-531-00803-7   LC 73-3407

"A First book"

"A diversified look at tennis from various strokes and tactics to a list of past and present greats. . . . Basic playing and scoring information are discussed in simple terms dealing with such items as court dimensions; forehand, backhand, and volley strokes; and tennis etiquette and conditioning. Minor factual errors, such as Chris Evert's incorrect home state, do not detract from the overall appeal of this introductory work." Booklist
Glossary: p62-64

796.352 Golf

Ravielli, Anthony

What is golf? Written and illus. by Anthony Ravielli. Atheneum Pubs./SMI 1976 unp illus $6.95 (3-6)   **796.352**

1 Golf
ISBN 0-689-30518-4   LC 75-38342

The author 'traces the historical aspect of the sport and provides tips for beginning practitioners. Legend attributes golf's beginnings to shepherds swinging their crooks at pebbles during idle hours, but scholars point to written records noting its start in Scotland 500 years ago. Although played avidly in the British Isles ever since, golf did not become popular in the U.S. until the turn of the century. Turning to technical aspects, the author describes the golf course, kinds of clubs and balls, and various swings, using careful, green-shaded drawings of girls and boys in his illustrations. A brief list of dos and don'ts is appended." Booklist

Smith, Parker

Golf techniques: how to improve your game; photographs by Meryl Joseph; illus. by Dom Lupo. Watts, F. 1973 63p illus lib. bdg. $4.90 (5 and up)   **796.352**

1 Golf
ISBN 0-531-02627-2   LC 73-3048

"A Concise guide"

This book contains "elementary lessons on basics such as grip, stance, and swing and tips on common trouble shots and putting. . . . The photographs and diagrams are generally well correlated with the text." Sch Library J
Glossary: p56-58. Bibliography: p59

796.357 Baseball

Antonacci, Robert J.

Baseball for young champions [by] Robert J. Antonacci and Jene Barr; foreword by Yogi Berra; illus. by Patti Boyd. 2d ed. McGraw 1977 158p illus lib. bdg. $7.95 (4 and up)   **796.357**

1 Baseball
ISBN 0-07-002134-1   LC 76-55328

First published 1956

"This book tells the way baseball started and how it grew to be our great national game. It gives you health and training rules that are so necessary if you want to play good baseball. It explains why good sportsmanship and team play are so important and it tells exactly how to play each position on the team. There are drills to practice so that young people may become fine players." Foreword

There are "black-and-white line drawings throughout. Photographs, often a top attraction, are not included." Booklist

Brewster, Benjamin

Baseball; rev. by Bill Gutman. [6th] rev. ed. Watts, F. 1979 64p illus lib. bdg. $5.90 (3-5)   **796.357**

1 Baseball
ISBN 0-531-02932-8   LC 78-24230

"A First book"

First published 1950 with title: The first book of baseball

"The book covers equipment and fundamentals of the game, including how to play different positions and read box scores." Sch Library J

Gemme, Leila Boyle

T-ball is our game; photographs by Richard Marshall. Childrens Press 1978 31p illus lib. bdg. $7.35 (k-2)   **796.357**

1 T-ball
ISBN 0-516-03630-0   LC 77-17273

T-ball is a form of baseball played by first and second graders, using no pitcher—the batter hits from a post, or tee. In this book, photographs and text describe the play of a T-ball game. The rules of T-ball are included

Gemme, Leila B.—*Continued*

"With its extremely large type and bright pictures, this primer-level sports book is a sure winner. The writing is direct and simple; each page has one very short sentence facing a well-chosen photograph. The effect is not monotonous because the illustrations vary in size, shape, and placement." Sch Library J

Kalb, Jonah

The easy baseball book; illus. by Sandy Kossin. Houghton 1976 49p illus $5.95 (1-3)
796.357

1 Baseball
ISBN 0-395-24385-8   LC 75-44085

In short simple sentences, the author "gives directions for hitting . . . as well as fielding and pitching. The basic directions for each skill are followed by sections on common mistakes and practice tips." Sch Library J

"A smooth, well-organized text designed to boost egos while it counsels and corrects. . . Careful touches of humor and the author's identification with fellow ball freaks help make this book a standout. Note, too, the first-rate, light-hearted pen drawings of boys—and girls—at play." Booklist

Robinson, Jackie

Jackie Robinson's Little league baseball book. Prentice-Hall 1972 135p illus $5.95 (4 and up)
796.357

1 Little league baseball
ISBN 0-13-509232-9   LC 74-158193

"Using a conversational approach and including many anecdotal reminiscences . . . [the author] emphasizes the importance of personal attitude, teamwork, and sportsmansship and gives solid advice on improving baseball skills, covering hitting and base running as well as each of the positions in the infield and outfield, pitching, and catching. He also has an admonishing word on the role of the adult, parent and coach, in the functioning of the Little League." Booklist

Sullivan, George

Baseball's art of hitting; illus. with photographs and diagrams. Dodd 1974 128p illus lib. bdg. $5.95 (5 and up)
796.357

1 Baseball
ISBN 0-396-06913-4   LC 73-17864

"Offering sound advice on hitting from several major league and ex-major league ball players, this includes tips on developing a level swing, learning how to sacrifice bunt, going for hits instead of home runs, concentrating on the pitched ball, and learning the strike zone. Material on game improvement is complemented by chapters on the construction of the baseball bat, famous pinch hitters, and thumbnail sketches of modern greats like Pete Rose, Dick Allen, and Henry Aaron." Library J

The catcher, baseball's man in charge; illus. with photographs and diagrams. Dodd 1976 124p illus lib. bdg. $5.95 (5 and up)
796.357

1 Baseball
ISBN 0-396-07278-X   LC 75-37650

"A thorough look, including over 100 black-and-white photographs and diagrams, at baseball catching with descriptions of job requirements; handling pitchers, hitters, and base stealers; and looking in depth at the techniques of the trade. Sullivan bases his material on interviews with major-league managers, scouts, and catchers themselves." Booklist

Home run! Illus. with photographs and diagrams. Dodd 1977 127p illus lib. bdg. $5.95 (4 and up)
796.357

1 Baseball
ISBN 0-396-07402-2   LC 76-53582

"Sullivan's early chapters trace the history of the home run which did not have the foremost place in baseball until Babe Ruth arrived. Other chapters treat the mechanics of hitting homers, modern home run hitters of each league, ball parks that help or hinder home runs, the great home runs in baseball history, who among today's players might break Hank Aaron's record (none

apparently), how a baseball is made, and why there has been a decline of late in the numbers of home runs." Sch Library J

"Baseball fans will relish the numerous archival photographs and charts that further enliven this worthwhile addition to sports collections." Booklist

Pitchers and pitching; illus. with photographs and diagrams. Dodd 1972 123p illus lib. bdg. $5.95 (5 and up)
796.357

1 Baseball
ISBN 0-396-06473-6   LC 70-175307

This book explains and analyzes the art and craft of pitching, describing different types of pitches, grips and deliveries, pitching strategy, control, and how the ball curves. It reveals how pitchers train and keep in condition. Also included are all-time pitching records and brief profiles of baseball's greatest pitchers

Turkin, Hy

The official encyclopedia of baseball, by Hy Turkin and S. C. Thompson. Barnes, A. S. illus $17.95
796.357

1 Baseball—Encyclopedias   LC 78-68004

First published 1951. Periodically revised and updated

The volume includes historical information on the evolution of baseball, data on players, umpires, managers, major leagues, world series games, and records, playing hints and official playing rules; baseball ballads; and a glossary of slang terms

796.4 Athletic exercises and gymnastics. Olympic games

Antonacci, Robert J.

Track and field for young champions, by Robert J. Antonacci and Gene Schoor; illus. by Frank Mullins. McGraw 1974 185p illus $7.95 (4 and up)
796.4

1 Track athletics
ISBN 0-07-002136-8   LC 73-17761

The authors discuss sprinting and distance running; relay racing and hurdle racing; broad jumping and pole vaulting; shot-put, discus and javelin throws; as well as walking, jogging and hiking. The history of each event is covered briefly, rules explained in detail, and valuable tips, drills and exercises are suggested

This "is designed for reluctant readers who are beginners at this sport, but . . . [the authors] skillfully keep both interest and instructional levels on a high plane." Sch Library J

Glossary: p177-81

Asch, Frank

Running with Rachel, by Frank and Jan Asch; photographs by Jan Asch and Robert Michael Buslow. Dial Press 1979 64p illus lib. bdg. $7.28, pa $3.95 (3-5)
796.4

1 Track athletics
ISBN 0-8037-7553-9; 0-8037-7552-0   LC 78-72471

This book follows eleven-year-old Rachel as she shifts from running errands to regular mileage. She discusses the transition and such things as shoes, diet, exercise and competition

"The reader has to forget that when Rachel is alone, she is with a photographer; the reader also, because children are like this, will bear with the fleeting earnestness—organic veggies, vitamin pills and a 97-pound-weakling line like 'Running not only changed how I felt about myself, but it changed how I looked too. I used to have a pot belly,' etc. Otherwise, Rachel is delightful. She appreciates the sun, the wind and the motion; she is bouncy, wholesome, even interesting. Mostly, she is real and the pictures are un-selfconscious." NY Times Bk Rev

Benjamin, Carol Lea

Running basics; written and illus. by Carol Lea Benjamin; photographs by M. Beth Brennan. Prentice-Hall 1979 484p illus $6.95 (4-6)
796.4

1 Track athletics
ISBN 0-13-783928-6   LC 78-31518

Benjamin, Carol L.—*Continued*

This book "is upbeat, short, and crammed with everything you need to know. Information on shoes, clothing, training, maladies, and especially on runner's clubs and marathons is all here. The author is a believer who manages to excite and convince readers about running." Sch Library J

Columbu, Franco

Weight training and bodybuilding; a complete guide for young athletes [by] Franco Columbu, with Dick Tyler. Wanderer Bks. 1979 127p illus pa $4.95 (6 and up)   796.4

1 Weight lifting 2 Physical fitness
ISBN 0-671-33006-3   LC 79-10368

"Columbu tells how he became interested in developing his physique when he was a skinny kid in his native Sardinia, Italy. . . . The payoff was winning the titles, Mr. Italy, Mr. Europe, Mr. World, Mr. International, Mr. Universe and Mr. Olympia. Columbu later became a chiropractic physician with the encouragement of his wife, already established as a specialist in the field. His book outlines programs that he espouses, exercises and mental disciplines which include sane nutritional habits. The sections on training (for beginners through advanced athletes) are illustrated by photos of the formidable expert in action." Pub W

Coombs, Charles

Be a winner in track and field; illus. with photographs. Morrow 1975 [c1976] 128p illus $7.25, lib. bdg. $6.96 (5 and up)   796.4

1 Track ahletics
ISBN 0-688-22064-9; 0-688-30032-4   LC 75-33077

The author "takes readers through the motions required for each of the major track and field events, while photographs of athletes in action graphically demonstrate techniques. Each discussion includes mention of desirable physical traits and ideal times to which a competitor can aspire; the role of mental factors such as dedication and attitude is also emphasized. Coombs gives lip service to the fact that women also compete in track by 'he or she' sprinkled throughout his explanatory passages." Booklist

Dolan, Edward F.

The complete beginner's guide to gymnastics [by] Edward F. Dolan, Jr. With photographs by James Stewart. Doubleday 1980 209p illus $8.95, lib. bdg. $9.90 (5 and up)   796.4

1 Gymnastics
ISBN 0-385-13434-7; 0-385-13435-5   LC 78-60286

The author introduces the reader to gymnastics by describing the basic exercises, equipment, and the eight competitive events (floor exercise, vaulting, rings, side horse, parallel bars, horizontal bar, balance beam and uneven parallel bars) and more than 100 stunts that may be performed in them

Glubok, Shirley

Olympic games in ancient Greece, by Shirley Glubok and Alfred Tamarin. Harper 1976 116p illus lib. bdg. $8.79 (5 and up)   796.4

1 Olympic games 2 Civilization, Greek
ISBN 0-06-22048-1   LC 75-25408

"Illustrated with photographs and reproductions. Based on information gleaned from such sources as pictures on vases, poetry, history, drama, and references to lost lists of ancient Olympic victors, the book considers the games in the context of Greek history and culture. The authors, reconstructing an ideal Olympiad occurring around 400 B.C., review the events of the five-day celebration, which was a religious festival held in honor of Zeus as well as a series of athletic events. They carefully describe horse races, foot races, wrestling, boxing, and discus and javelin throwing; make clear the differences between ancient Greek and modern athletic events; and relate anecdotes about the contestants. They even discuss the growth of professionalism, corruption, and bribery. Briefly tracing the chronology of the Olympic games, which were celebrated for more than a thousand years, they finally touch upon the modern revival of the Olympics. Among the reproductions, the sculpture and the vase paintings reveal the importance of athletics and the well-formed male body in ancient Greek art. With a chronology including a complete list of modern Olympic games and an index." Horn Bk

Krementz, Jill

A very young gymnast; written and photographed by Jill Krementz. Knopf 1978 unp illus $9.95   796.4

1 Gymnastics
ISBN 0-394-50080-6   LC 78-5502

"The author-photographer accompanied ten-year-old Torrance York, aspiring Olympic gymnast, through a year's worth of training and competition. . . . [The book explores] every aspect of the sport, from the endless practices—sometimes fun, sometimes frustrating—to the always exciting competitions." Horn Bk

This "is a beautifully photographed, expertly produced study of a young athlete. While the text (in the young Torrance York's own words) is lively, it is the photographs which most movingly capture the vibrant personality of the very engaging little girl featured. Not an instructional book, but a title certain to please young readers while leading them to new insights and fresh perspectives." Sch Library J

Lyttle, Richard B.

Jogging and running. Watts, F. 1979 62p illus lib. bdg. $5.90 (5 and up)   796.4

1 Track athletics
ISBN 0-531-02949-2   LC 79-10598

"A Concise guide"

This book introduces the young runner to the benefits of running, selection of proper shoes and other gear, pace, style, exercises, aches and pains, and competitive running, including names and addresses of national organizations

This book "is for those just getting started. [The author] is solid on the basics and his tone is of encouragement within the framework of one's own limitations." Sch Library J

For further reading: p59

Olney, Ross R.

The young runner. Lothrop 1978 128p illus $6.50, lib. bdg. $6.24 (4 and up)   796.4

1 Track athletics
ISBN 0-688-41873-2; 0-688-51873-2   LC 78-15902

The author "stresses the slow steady approach that leaves plenty of oxygen for enjoyment. Olney's straightforward tone is right: what he says is clear and understandable for youngsters but applies just as surely to anyone. Warm up, dress down, do it—however and whenever it's comfortable. But his suggestions on regulating pace, time schedules, and muscle tone will help beginners, even if only by supporting them in what feels right or preventing them from the sometimes painful blunders of ignorance. . . . Girls and boys get equal attention throughout. A list of organizations and equipment sources, as well as books and periodicals, is appended. Illustrated with black-and-white photos." Booklist

Prudden, Suzy

See how they run; Suzy Prudden's Running book for kids, by Suzy Prudden and Jeffrey Sussman; photographs by Jeffrey Sussman. Grosset 1979 72p illus lib. bdg. $5.99, pa $3.95 (4-6)   796.4

1 Track athletics
ISBN 0-448-13126-9; 0-448-16828-6   LC 78-71308

This beginner's book on running presents information on proper shoes and dress, physical fitness, locale, weather, hazards, joggers' attitudes and exercises

"The exercise section at the end is the book's clearest and best feature." Sch Library J

Resnick, Michael

Gymnastics and you; the whole story of the sport. Rand McNally 1977 96p illus pa $3.95 (4-6)   796.4

1 Gymnastics
ISBN 0-396-07453-7   LC 77-6484

"A brief history of the sport is combined with descriptions of gymnastic events for women and men. There are chapters on scoring and starting out in gymnastics (stressing safety) plus a list of Olympic gold medalists. The over-size 8½" x 10¾") format with large print and black-and-white photographs on every page is attractive, and the vocabulary is appropriate for upper elementary graders." Sch Library J

Sullivan, George

Better gymnastics for girls. Dodd 1977 62p
illus lib. bdg. $5.95 (4 and up) **796.4**

1 Gymnastics
ISBN 0-396-07453-7   LC 77-6484

"The book opens with a brief survey of historical
developments in international gymnastic competition, highlighting its increasing popularity in recent years. Emphasizing the four areas in which
women compete, the text describes various stunts
and then outlines them with step-by-step instructions beneath the pictures. On two pages, the sequence is not shown accurately. A comprehensive
elementary guide for use by individuals and in-
structors, which includes a glossary and a directory
of organizations and competitions." Horn Bk

Traetta, John

Gymnastics basics, by John and Mary Jean
Traetta; illus. by Bill Gow; photographs by
Don Carter. Ed. and produced by Arvid
Knudsen. Prentice-Hall 1979 64p illus lib.
bdg. $6.95 (4 and up)   **796.4**

1 Gymnastics
ISBN 0-13-37175-7   LC 79-15092

This book "begins with suggestions for choosing
the proper professional and safety-conscious gymnastics program and then examines the essential
movements, positions, exercises, etc. for seven different gymnastics skills: floor exercises, vaulting,
uneven and horizontal bars, balance beam, pom-
mel horse, parallel bars, and still rings, with each
element broken down into a series of line drawings indicating the correct movement. Included
for each skill is a description of equipment needed,
including proper dimensions, placement, height,
padding, etc." Sch Library J

796.5 Outdoor life

Larson, Randy

Backpacking; for fun and glory; photographs & sketches by John R. Henshaw.
Harvey House 1979 77p illus lib. bdg. $6.39
(4-6)   **796.5**

1 Backpacking
ISBN 0-8178-6100-9   LC 78-73747

In this book the author discusses the history
of backpacking, selecting the best equipment,
choosing and setting up a campsite, and cooking
outdoors

Lyttle, Richard B.

The complete beginner's guide to backpacking. Doubleday 1975 148p illus lib.
bdg. $8.90 (5 and up)   **796.5**

1 Backpacking
ISBN 0-385-06885-9   LC 74-18817

"A readable, non-patronizing account of backpacking aimed at beginners. All aspects of this
exciting . . . sport are touched upon—e.g., tips on
health and safety on the trail, planning a short
or long trip, cooking in the open, courtesy on
the road. Advice is also included on selecting and
purchasing equipment (current prices are mentioned), and specific brand names are recommended. The numerous line drawings and black-
and-white photographs are only adequate; however, the bibliography and appended lists of
suppliers and forest, park, and land bureau offices
are especially helpful." Sch Library J

796.54 Camping

Gray, William R.

Camping adventure; photographs by Steve
Raymer. Natl. Geographic Soc. 1976 31p illus
(k-3)   **796.54**

1 Camping
ISBN 0-87044-196-5   LC 76-2116

Obtainable only as part of a set for $9.95 with:
Animals that build their homes, by Robert M.
McClung, class 591.5; The playful dolphins, by
Linda McCarter Bridge, class 599.5; and Wonders
of the desert world, by Judith E. Rinard, class
574.9

"Books for young explorers"
Prepared by the Special Publications Division
of the National Geographic Society
"Hints for good camping safety and suggestions for clothing and equipment needs accompany
the fun and excitement of one family's expedition
into a mountain wilderness area . . . [as] sights
and discoveries of unusual flora and fauna form
a subtle learning part of the holiday." Booklist

Janes, Edward C.

The first book of camping. Rev. ed. Illus.
by Rod Slater. Watts, F. 1977 64p illus lib.
bdg. $5.90 (3-6)   **796.54**

1 Camping
ISBN 0-531-00494-5   LC 76-47479

"A First book"
First published 1963 with pictures by Julio
Granda

Contents: What kind of camping; What to wear;
What equipment do you need; Canteens; For the
camp cook; What's to eat; Cutting tools; Camp
lights; Your compass; Packs; A good night's rest;
Tents; Campcraft; Fires, good and bad; Camp
stoves; Preparing your meals; Index

796.6 Cycling

Coombs, Charles

Bicycling; illus. with 59 photographs and
diagrams. Morrow 1972 127p illus $7.25, lib.
bdg. $6.96 (5 and up)   **796.6**

1 Bicycles and bicycling
ISBN 0-688-20032-X; 0-688-30032-4   LC 72-1547

The author describes the many types of bicycles and tells the prospective buyer what to
look for when choosing his model. He gives guidelines for care, maintenance, home repair, and safe
riding. He discusses the increasing use of the
bicycle as a speedy and efficient tool in commerce
and industry, and its possible future role in community safety. In conclusion, he reports some of
the group and club activities, such as camping,
hosteling, and racing, that are available
Glossary: p123-24

Edmonds, I. G.

BMX! Bicycle motocross for beginners;
illus. with photographs by the author. Holt
1979 207p illus $7.95 (5 and up)   **796.6**

1 Bicycle racing
ISBN 0-03-044321-0   LC 79-4311

The author gives "historical background as well
as riding techniques and safety tips. The style
is simple with subheadings to divide chapters.
Photos help illustrate technical terms. The author
is expert and carefully reveals the highs as well
as the dangers involved." Sch Library J

Frankel, Lillian

Bike-ways (101 things to do with a bike)
by Lillian and Godfrey Frankel. New rev.
ed. Sterling 1972 128p illus $5.95, lib.
bdg. $6.69 (4-6)   **796.6**

1 Bicycles and bicycling
ISBN 0-8069-4004-2; 0-8069-4005-0   LC 72-190650

First published 1961 with title: 101 things to do
with a bike

Bike clubs, trips and tours, camping, selecting a
bike, accessories, and safety are some of the aspects of bicycles and bicycling covered in this
book

Sullivan, George

Better bicycling for boys and girls. Dodd
1974 64p illus map lib. bdg. $5.95 (4 and up)
                                       796.6

1 Bicycles and bicycling
ISBN 0-396-06845-6   LC 73-7092

Aspects covered include maintenance and repair,
rules of the road and safety, equipment and tips
for touring

"There are numerous black-and-white photographs and references to helpful information
sources throughout; a list of mainly U.S. cycling
organizations is appended. The lack of index is
partially compensated for by well-marked sections
and subsections." Booklist

796.7   Driving motor vehicles

Olney, Ross R.
How to understand auto racing. Lothrop 1979 187p illus $6.95, lib. bdg. $6.67 (4 and up)   **796.7**

1 Automobile racing
ISBN 0-688-41913-5; 0-688-51913-X   LC 79-14558

"Automobile racing fans will find this easy-to-understand guide helpful in unraveling the complexities of the sport. The numerous varieties of cars, races, and tracks are unscrambled as Olney explains formation and rules of, as well as function for, the different world federations and U.S. clubs. Well-known faces and cars appear in the many accompanying photographs as discussion ranges over drag, off-road, stock car, Indianapolis, and Grand Prix racing. The author's long association with racing has allowed him insights and observations that add human interest to an otherwise factual text." Booklist

Yaw, John
Motocross motorcycle racing. Lerner Publications 1978 47p illus (Superwheels ser) lib. bdg. $6.95 (4 and up)   **796.7**

1 Motorcycle racing
ISBN 0-8225-0423-5   LC 77-92298

This book describes motocross competition—motorcycle races run on dirt tracks. The difficulty of the sport, the kinds of cycles needed, and some of the top motocross competitors are featured

796.8   Combat sports

Kozuki, Russell
Junior karate; photographs by the author. Sterling 1971 128p illus $5.95, lib. bdg. $5.99 (5 and up)   **796.8**

1 Karate
ISBN 0-8069-4446-3; 0-8069-4447-1   LC 71-167665

Illustrating with pen and camera, the author "renders karate exercises, stances, blocking techniques, strikes, kicks, contests, and Katas vividly—certainly graspable—for young readers." Sch Library J

Reisberg, Ken
The martial arts. Watts, F. 1979 86p illus lib. bdg. $5.90 (4 and up)   **796.8**

1 Self-defense
ISBN 0-531-04077-1   LC 79-10506

"A First book"
The author presents a history of the martial arts and then describes the individual disciplines: Judo, Karate, Kendo, Aikido and Kung Fu. Black-and-white photographs together with line drawings illustrate the moves and equipment. A list of martial arts associations, a glossary and pronunciation guide are included
Books for further reading: p81-82

Ribner, Susan
The martial arts, by Susan Ribner and Richard Chin; drawings by Melanie Arwin. Harper 1978 181p illus $8.95, lib. bdg. $8.79 (5 and up)   **796.8**

1 Self-defense
ISBN 0-06-024999-4; 0-06-025000-3   LC 76-58713

"A general introduction to the martial arts, this provides information about the lesser known types such as kendo as well as karate, judo, etc. Wisely, the authors have not attempted to write a 'how to' manual. They concentrate on the principles behind each form, its history, and underlying philosophy. . . . The book is a readable, accurate account that should prove popular." Sch Library J

796.9   Ice and snow sports

Litsky, Frank
The winter Olympics. Watts, F. 1979 87p illus lib. bdg. $5.90 (4-6)   **796.9**

1 Olympic games
ISBN 0-531-02946-8   LC 79-10600

"A First book"
This book is a "well-organized look at the history and growth of the games. Each game from 1924 on is discussed with highlights and notable personalities. Another section is dedicated to outstanding athletes throughout the history of the games with such stars as Jean-Claude Killy, Peggy Fleming, and Rosi Mittermaier seen close up. Good black-and-white photos accompany the text." Sch Library J

796.91   Ice skating

Krementz, Jill
A very young skater; written and photographed by Jill Krementz. Knopf 1979 unp illus $9.95   **796.91**

1 Ice skating
ISBN 0-394-50833-5   LC 79-2209

This "is a handsomely produced book, profusely illustrated with photographs in black and white, featuring a confident ten-year-old for whom skating is the hub of of existence. Written in the first person, the brief text is an introduction to the various facets of Katherine Healey's life: her home, school, family, friends and, above all, the world of skating—practice sessions, competitions, and ice shows. Well-known professional skaters appear in a number of expert photographs, and John Curry plays a significant role in the girl's training. Although the search for perfection is not minimized, the emphasis is on triumph rather than on trials." Horn Bk

Sullivan, George
Better ice skating for boys and girls. Dodd 1976 64p illus lib. bdg. $5.95 (4 and up)   **796.91**

1 Ice skating
ISBN 0-396-07339-5   LC 76-12425

The author "discusses the three forms of ice skating—figure, speed, and power—in a thorough, clearly written account of this popular sport. Basic techniques of stroking and stopping are described along with more advanced forms of crossover, turns, jumps, and spins. Maintaining that proper, correctly fitted equipment is vital to good skating, the author surveys boots, blades, clothing, and care of equipment. Helpful diagrams of positions and sequential black-and-white photographs are included as well as a brief history of the sport. Glossary appended." Booklist

796.96   Ice hockey

Coombs, Charles
Be a winner in ice hockey. Morrow 1974 128p illus lib. bdg. $6.96, pa $2.45 (5 and up)   **796.96**

1 Ice hockey
ISBN 0-688-30099-5; 0-688-25099-8   LC 73-10769

This book "treats fundamentals of rules, skating, stickhandling, shooting, and passing. The advice is thorough and sound. Photographs of youngsters demonstrating techniques are generally excellent; but, action illustrations of professionals are not nearly as useful." Sch Library J

Kalb, Jonah
The easy hockey book; illus. by Bill Morrison. Houghton 1977 64p illus $6.95 (3-5)   **796.96**

1 Ice hockey
ISBN 0-395-25842-1   LC 77-9917

"This is not, the author states firmly, a book intended to teach readers to play hockey, but a compilation of advice on individual aspects of the game (skating forward, skating backward, passing, shooting, and the most common mistakes in all of these) so that the reader can be a better player. . . . It doesn't give game rules, but it does discuss equipment, it gives sensible advice, and it fills a need for a book about ice hockey techniques for readers in the middle grades." Chicago. Children's Bk Center

Liss, Howard

Hockey talk for beginners; illus. by Frank Robbins. Messner 1973 94p illus lib. bdg. $5.79 (4 and up)   **796.96**

1 Ice hockey—Terminology
ISBN 0-671-32644-9   LC 73-7448

"A series of definitions and explanations, alphabetically arranged and with cross-references, is useful as a handbook for new hockey fans or players, but it doesn't function as well as an introduction to the game because the reader with no background must collate scattered facts while reading. . . . As a companion to a book that explains the game, however, this is very handy." Chicago. Children's Bk Center

Sullivan, George

Better ice hockey for boys. [New and updated ed.] Dodd [1976 c1975] 64p illus lib. bdg. $5.95 (5 and up)   **796.96**

1 Ice hockey
ISBN 0-396-06595-3   LC 65-27389

First published 1965

"Designed for the serious sportsman, the book includes information on the selection and care of skates and other equipment and on playing techniques. The author explains how to develop speed and control on the ice, avoid accidents, play various positions, and execute various game maneuvers. He also discusses playing strategy, teamwork, and sportsmanship and gives rules of the game, official signals and a glossary of ice-hockey terms. Copiously illustrated with diagrams and action photographs." Booklist [review of 1965 edition]
Glossary of ice-hockey terms: p64

797.2 Swimming and diving

Sullivan, George

Better swimming and diving for boys and girls. Dodd 1967 64p illus lib. bdg. $5.95 (5 and up)   **797.2**

1 Swimming 2 Diving
ISBN 0-396-06574-0   LC 67-26143

"This guide to swimming strokes and springboard dives is designed for the young person who wishes to train for competition. The concise text explains precisely how to perform each style of swimming and diving, while clear sequences of photographs illustrate ideal form." Booklist
Glossary: p64

798.2 Horsemanship

Devereux, Frederick L.

Horseback riding, by Frederick L. Devereux, Jr. Illus. by Heather St. Clair Davis. Watts, F. 1976 63p illus lib. bdg. $4.90 (4-6)   **798.2**

1 Horseback riding
ISBN 0-531-00844-4   LC 75-34189

"A First book"

The author "teaches methods of mounting and dismounting; explains and thoroughly compares basic riding styles (hunt seat, saddle seat, Western seat); and gives extra weight to the correct use of hands for restraining and legs for propelling the horse forward. No horse admirer will be able to resist Davis' black-and-white drawings of Arab, hunter, saddlebred, or Quarter horse types, and her excellent diagrams of anatomy, gaits, and tack (a few awkwardly broken at the centerfold) extend the written explanations." Sch Library J
Includes bibliography

Krementz, Jill

A very young rider; written and photographed by Jill Krementz. Knopf 1977 unp illus $9.95   **798.2**

1 Horseback riding
ISBN 0-394-41092-0   LC 77-74996

"Vivi Malloy is a 10-year-old girl who lives a life dreamed about by millions of children. She has her own pony, Ready Penny, with which she spends apparently every minute not demanded by schoolwork or other necessary chores. It's easy to envy Vivi her affluence but Krementz's probing camera and the text prove that the child earns the privilege of owning her own mount. The splendid photo illustrations record not only the thrills of riding and competing but Vivi's grueling work, giving Penny the intensive care the pony needs. It's exciting and instructive to follow the young rider and her family." Pub W

Sports Illustrated Horseback riding, by the editors of Sports Illustrated. [Rev. ed] Lippincott 1971 [c1960] 94p illus (The Sports Illustrated lib) $4.95, pa $2.95 (6 and up)   **798.2**

1 Horseback riding
ISBN 0-397-00736-1; 0-397-00735-3   LC 74-161580

First published 1960 with title: Sports Illustrated Book of horseback riding

Text by Gordon Wright with Alice Higgins. Illustrated by Sam Savitt

This book, designed for the beginning rider, includes instructions on the handling of horses, equipment and the care and feeding of horses

Sullivan, George

Better horseback riding for boys and girls. Dodd 1969 64p illus lib. bdg. $5.95 (5 and up)   **798.2**

1 Horseback riding
ISBN 0-396-06404-3   LC 75-88071

"Many carefully sequenced photographs accompany a clear, informative text. . . . [The book] covers the basics of safe and correct horseback riding for beginners of any age. Each step is clearly developed, including choosing the correct tack and clothing; handling the horse by leading, mounting and riding through the basic gaits; jumping and trail riding; and the personal care of one's own horse." Sch Library J
Glossary: p64

798.4 Horse racing

Anderson, C. W.

Twenty gallant horses. Macmillan Pub. Co. 1965 87p illus $7.95 (5 and up)   **798.4**

1 Horses 2 Horse racing
ISBN 0-02-705530-2   LC 65-16565

Some of these brief horse stories were published 1939, in different versions, in the author's: Black, bay and chestnut

"In handsome full-page lithographs and brief text [the author, who is also the illustrator] portrays a score of the greatest racing and jumping champions of all time, describing the qualities of breeding, courage, and intelligence that accounted for their amazing performances." Booklist

799.1 Fishing

Hofsinde, Robert

Indian fishing and camping; written and illus. by Robert Hofsinde (Gray-Wolf). Morrow 1963 92p illus map lib. bdg. $6 (3-6)   **799.1**

1 Indians of North America 2 Fishing
ISBN 0-688-31797   LC 63-8798

"Factual descriptions of Indian and Eskimo camping and fishing are accompanied by detailed accounts of how to make many different items of Indian fishing equipment, of what bait to use, and of how to cook one's catch. Exact, informative illustrations further instruct the reader in these activities." Wis Library Bul

Liss, Howard

Fishing talk for beginners; illus. by Leonard Cole. Messner 1978 96p illus lib. bdg. $7.29 (5 and up)   **799.1**

1 Fishing
ISBN 0-671-32882-4   LC 77-25258

"Alphabetically arranged, the text gives information on kinds of fish, terms used in fishing, equipment, techniques, special clothing, cooking fish, and occasional odd bits such as Isaak Walton, lily pads, or dog days. The illustrations are well placed and informative, and the book gives many facts about the sport, although the arrangement of material means that a beginner cannot find needed information about equipment or techniques in one location." Chicago. Children's Bk Center

799.2   Hunting

Hofsinde, Robert
  Indian hunting; written and illus. by Robert
Hofsinde (Gray-Wolf). Morrow 1962 96p
illus $6 (3-6)   **799.2**
  1 Indians of North America   2 Hunting
  ISBN 0-688-31608-5   LC 62-8273
  "The division of the text is on the basis of the
game being hunted: large game, small game,
whales and seals; two sections discuss hunting
from canoes and preparing for the hunt. In each
section, there are descriptions of the differences
in tribal techniques, of traps and weapons, and
of the special procedures used with individual
animals." Chicago. Children's Bk Center
  "An anthropological approach to the hunting
and fishing lore of early man. Fine sketches of
traps and weapons." Chicago Sch J

799.3   Archery

Sullivan, George
  Better archery for boys and girls. Dodd
1970 64p illus lib. bdg. $5.95 (5 and up)   **799.3**
  1 Archery
  ISBN 0-396-07173-2   LC 71-102732
  Basic information for the beginning archer is
given—how to choose the proper bow and arrow,
how to brace a bow, nock, draw, hold, air, release and follow through. Tips are also given on
correcting faults, caring for equipment, and safety
measures
  "One interesting section is devoted to self-cor-
rection where several examples of faults are
pointed out with simple techniques for eradication
of the errors. The principle negative-adaptation in
motor learning is well exemplified in this valuable
part." Choice
  Glossary: p64

800   LITERATURE

803   Literature—Encyclopedias and dictionaries

Brewer's Dictionary of phrase and fable.
Centenary ed. Rev. by Ivor H. Evans.
Harper [1971 c1970] 1175p front $22.95   **803**
  1 Literature—Encyclopedias   2 Allusions
  ISBN 0-06-010466-X   LC 79-107024
  First published 1870, edited by Ebenezer Cobham
Brewer
  This book "encompasses real, fictitious, and
mythical names from history, romance, the arts,
science, and fable, and phrases, superstitions, and
customs ancient and contemporary. The 20,000
entries include phrases grouped under key words,
[i.e.] names of saints, giants. Quotations provide
source, etymology, and pronunciation." Wynar.
Guide to Ref Bks for Sch Media Centers
  "Long on trivia. Grand for browsing. Useful for
reference." Choice

808   Rhetoric

Brandt, Sue R.
  How to improve your written English;
illus. by Carolyn Bentley. Watts, F. 1972 87p
illus lib. bdg. $4.90 (4-6)   **808**
  1 English language—Composition and exercises
  2 English language—Grammar
  ISBN 0-531-00772-3   LC 72-5843
  "A First book"
  This book discusses the differences between
spoken and written English and between formal
and everyday speech. Aimed at middle-school
age children, it has sections on vocabulary building, use of verbs and pronouns, sentence structure, spelling, handwriting, capitalization and
punctuation

  How to write a report; illus. by Peter P.
Plascencia. Watts, F. 1968 66p illus lib.
bdg. $4.90 (6 and up)   **808**
  1 Report writing
  ISBN 0-531-00554-2   LC 68-17702
  "A First book"
  Part one of this book offers "helpful information
on understanding the subject, locating information, taking notes, preparing a bibliography, making an outline, and drafting the actual report.
Reference tools and sources, including the card
catalog, are thoroughly explained. Part two, How
to Discover and Share Books, covers written and
oral book reviews, note taking and reading records." Library J

Cassedy, Sylvia
  In your own words; a beginner's guide to
writing. Doubleday 1979 214p $7.95, lib.
bdg. $8.90 (6 and up)   **808**
  1 English language—Composition and exercises
  2 Authorship   3 Poetics
  ISBN 0-385-14036-3; 0-385-14037-1   LC 78-1237
  This book presents "a competent, orderly approach to creative writing—without condescension
or preciosity. The author opens with the premise
that writing starts with awareness and sensual
perception. The two main parts of the book—
prose and poetry—are set out in logical fashion.
Numerous prose forms, from myths, fairy tales,
and science fiction to letters, editorials, and school
reports, are examined along with such technical
matters as characterization, plot, and style. The
lucid, comprehensive section on poetry considers
rhyme and rhythm, imagery, feelings and emotions, figures of speech and other aspects of poetic diction—as well as varieties of poetry, such
as riddles and shaped poems. Particularly effective is the treatment of haiku. . . . Although the
book is well within the grasp of older children,
it could also be used intelligently by teachers
and other adults who work with young people."
Horn Bk

Jackson, Jacqueline
  Turn not pale, beloved snail; a book about
writing among other things. Little 1974 235p
$7.50   **808**
  1 Authorship   2 English language—Composition
and exercises
  ISBN 0-316-45481-8   LC 74-12425
  "Lots of encouragement and sound advice
emerge from this occasionally windy but nonetheless engaging primer on how to write. Jackson's
own experiences coupled with those of her children provide concrete examples of her methods
in action: becoming acutely aware of one's surroundings, learning to recognize a useful or dramatic moment, and quickly getting it down on
paper. Rewrites, grammar, and polish can come
later. Excerpts from the author's favorite stories,
among them 'Charlotte's Web', 'Wind in the Willows', and 'Harriet the Spy', all intermittently
serve as models of various techniques." Booklist
  "Parents and teachers of creative writing could
find this book a great help. Most chapters provide ideas for many lively lessons. Often there
are briefly outlined observations games which
can be used at home or school . . . particularly
appealing to older children and young teens. But
it has value to readers—and writers—of any age."
Christian Sci Monitor

808.06   Writing children's literature

Hunter, Mollie
  Talent is not enough; Mollie Hunter on
writing for children. Harper 1976 126p $7.95
      808.06
  1 Authorship   2 Children's literature—Technique
  ISBN 0-06-022649-8   LC 76-3841
  In this book based on a series of lectures delivered in 1975, the author "speaks succinctly and
wittily about the demanding, satisfying craft of
writing. Her remarks include personal feelings
and rich interpretations of historical fiction, fantasy, and folklore." Booklist

Yolen, Jane

Writing books for children. Writer 1973 150p $8.95 **808.06**

1 Authorship 2 Children's literature—Technique
ISBN 0-87116-101-X LC 73-9527

"Yolen's book is helpful in getting would-be authors started because it offers the security of advice. . . . Her high standards, however, will discourage beginners from the cute or condescending approach to writing for children and will help them think carefully about picture books, folklore, fantasy, nonfiction, realism, animal stories, poetry, and magazine writing. Practical suggestions on how and where to send manuscripts, how to cope with rejections, and how to proceed after acceptance are sprinkled with personal anecdotes. The afterword contains an annotated list for further reading on children's books." Booklist

808.1 Rhetoric of poetry

Cosman, Anna

How to read and write poetry. Watts, F. 1979 64p illus lib. bdg. $5.45 (5 and up) **808.1**

1 Poetics
ISBN 0-531-02261-7 LC 78-11861

"A First book"
"Give Cosman's rally for poetry and minilecture on the craft a special place on the shelf and forgive its faults. What she points out about specific poems is true and revealing. Moving easily among Merriam, Swinburne, Malmsten, and Issa, she takes their work apart, compares stanza setups, and rearranges verse lines into sentences. She shows how a poem develops, using a couple of her own as examples. She encourages readers to try to write concrete poems and haiku and translate common experience. There's a problem with style: the book reads as if it were spoken into a recorder. . . . There's a mismatch between the reading level of the language, what is explained, and the level of the poems presented. . . . However, literary analysis for the elementary group is usually limited to oral, classroom experience. Children could read this book on their own and be enthused." Sch Library J

808.5 Rhetoric of speech

Kettelkamp, Larry

Song, speech, and ventriloquism; written and illus. by Larry Kettelkamp. Morrow 1967 96p illus lib. bdg. $6.48 (5 and up) **808.5**

1 Voice 2 Speech 3 Singing 4 Ventriloquism
ISBN 0-688-31799-5 LC 67-277

"The mechanism of speech is discussed with explanation of the muscles and actions involved in breathing, vibration of the larynx, and articulation. There is a chapter on singing and one on ventriloquism." The AAAS Sci Bk List for Children
"In this combination of scientific text and how-to-do-it manual, the interrelationships between the two parts are not always made clear. However, the book would be very useful to those interested in the subject and the illustrations and charts admirably support the text." Library J
Glossary of terms: p91-93

808.8 Literature—Collections

The Arbuthnot Anthology of children's literature [comp. by] May Hill Arbuthnot and [others]; 4th ed. rev. by Zena Sutherland; special contributors: Sam Leaton Sebesta [and others]; illustrators: Rainey Bennett [and others]. Lothrop 1976 xxii, 1088p illus $23.50 **808.8**

1 Literature—Collections
ISBN 0-688-41725-6

First published 1953 by Scott
An anthology of selections and excerpts from a wide range of literature for children of all ages, this book was originally intended as a source book for classes in children's literature as well as a collection of materials to be used with children in groups or individually. Part one includes over 500 poems. Part two is a collection of folk tales, fables, myths, epics, hero tales and modern fantasy. Part three consists of selections from realistic stories, historical fiction, biographies, and informational books. Part four contains the following: a chronology of important events in the history of children's literature; "Illustrations in children's books," by Donnarae MacCann and Olga Richard—an historical and critical account accompanied by illustrations, a glossary and a bibliography; "Guiding literary experience," by Sam Sebesta and Dianne Monson—a guide to the selection and use of literature with children, including suggestions for reading aloud, storytelling, dramatization and discussion groups, with subsection bibliographies; a listing of children's book award winners; an annotated bibliography including background and reference sources for adults, sources of audiovisual materials, and lists of books for children corresponding to the organization of Parts I to III. The book contains a glossary, a subject index, and an index of authors, illustrators and titles

Includes "many black-and-white illustrations, and a portfolio of color. This is the classic jumbo collection of writing for children. . . . A cornerstone for any children's library." Sat Rev

Association for Childhood Education International

Told under the Christmas tree; stories and poems from around the world; selected by the Literature Committee of the Association for Childhood Education; illus. by Maud and Miska Petersham. Macmillan Pub. Co. 1948 304p illus $6.95 (3-6) **808.8**

1 Literature—Collections 2 Christmas—Fiction 3 Christmas—Poetry
ISBN 0-02-706500-6 LC 48-9525

"The Umbrella books"
"A fine collection of Christmas stories and verse which includes . . . a group of stories and poems related to Hanukkah, the Jewish Festival of Lights, which falls near the Christmas season. Many of the stories are excerpts from longer ones and describe the customs and traditions of the Christmas celebration in many lands. Listed at the end are the titles, with sources, of Christmas stories which have been published in preceding Umbrella books but which are not included here." Booklist
"The book can be enjoyed by Christian and Jew alike, and perhaps draw the two more closely together through an understanding of each other's beliefs." NY Times Bk Rev

Darrell, Margery

(ed.) Once upon a time; the fairy tale world of Arthur Rackham. Viking 1972 296p illus $14.95 (4 and up) **808.8**

1 Literature—Collections
ISBN 0-670-52574-X LC 72-1255

"A Studio book"
This is "a compilation of the full texts of seven works illustrated by Rackham: 'Alice's Adventures in Wonderland,' 'A Christmas Carol,' 'Fables' by 'Aesop,' 'Peter Pan in Kensington Gardens,' 'Rip Van Winkle,' 'Seven Fairy Tales' of the Grimm Brothers and 'Three Tales from Shakespeare,' by the Lambs. The illustrations, in black and white and in color, are valuable both in themselves and for historical reasons, and the editor's preface discusses both Rackham's work and his philosophy of illustration for children." Chicago. Children's Bk Center

The Golden Treasury of children's literature; ed. and selected by Bryna and Louis Untermeyer. Golden Press 1966 544p illus $12.95, lib. bdg. $19.92 **808.8**

1 Literature—Collections
ISBN 0-307-16522-1; 0-307-66522-4 LC 66-114668

Selections from the ten previously published volumes comprising: The Golden Treasury of children's literature
Featured here are modern stories, as well as the classics, ancient myths, folk tales and legends

Gruenberg, Sidonie Matsner

(ed.) Favorite stories old and new. Rev. and enl. ed. Illus. by Kurt Wiese. Doubleday 1955 512p illus $8.95   **808.8**

1 Literature—Collections
ISBN 0-385-07293-7   LC 55-9012

First published 1942
This volume contains "many excellent stories and poems, chosen for appeal to children of all ages, useful for storytelling and reading aloud." Hodges. Bks for Elem Sch Libraries

(comp.) Let's hear a story; 30 stories and poems for today's boys and girls; illus. by Dagmar Wilson. Doubleday 1961 160p illus $7.95   **808.8**

1 Literature—Collections
ISBN 0-385-03316-8   LC 61-6894

Stories and poems by such authors as: Hardie Gramatky, Miriam Schlein, Eleanor Farjeon, Virginia Lee Burton, Alvin Tresselt, Phyllis McGinley and Marjorie Flack. Some of the subjects are "lively boys and girls, birthday parties, kittens, puppies, kangaroos, horses and elephants, trains, tugboats and grandpas." Introduction
"A read-aloud anthology. . . . Some [inclusions] are appropriate for independent reading by second-grade children. The selection is judicious and the book is useful, although the material is available elsewhere." Chicago. Children's Bk Center

Witches, witches, witches; selected by Helen Hoke; pictures by W. R. Lohse. Watts, F. 1958 230p illus lib. bdg. $6.90 (5 and up)   **808.8**

1 Witches 2 Literature—Collections
ISBN 0-531-01823-7   LC 58-10945

"Short stories, fairy tales, poetry, and excerpts from books are included in this collection of material about witches. Some of the authors and editors represented are Oliver Wendell Holmes, Sigrid Undset, the brothers Grimm, Oscar Wilde, Rachel Field, and Eleanor Farjeon. Selection has been made with discrimination." Chicago. Children's Bk Center
"A bonanza for storytellers and Halloween requests. Wonderfully spooky illustrations by W. R. Lohse. Print is clear and well spaced, so 5th-graders on up can read it. All the stories are already in libraries though some in books now out of print, but this is good for those that can afford the luxury of having their witches all together in one brew." Library J

808.81   Poetry—Collections

Beastly boys and ghastly girls; poems collected by William Cole; drawings by Tomi Ungerer. Collins [distributed by Philomel Bks.] 1964 124p illus lib. bdg. $6.99 (5 and up)   **808.81**

1 Poetry—Collections
ISBN 0-529-03903-6   LC 64-20962

Here is "a collection of fiendish rhymes by such humorists as Gelett Burgess, Hilaire Belloc, Shelly Silverstein, A. A. Milne, and Lewis Carroll." Children's Bks. 1964
"In these poems is the naughtiest crew of pre-adults ever assembled. In words and marvelous line drawings they stand ready to gladden the hearts of children." Pub W
Author and title indexes

Brewton, John E.

(comp.) Index to children's poetry . . . Comp. by John E. and Sara W. Brewton. Wilson, H.W. 1942 xxxii, 965p $22   **808.81**

1 Poetry—Indexes
ISBN 0-8242-0021-7   LC 42-20148

"A title, subject, author, and first line index to poetry in collections for children and youth." Title page

An index, in one alphabet, to more than 15,000 poems by approximately 2,500 different authors. The poems, from 130 collections of poems for children and young people, are classified under more than 1,800 subjects. An analysis of the books indexed, noting grade levels of interest, and a directory of publishers are included

(comp.) Index to children's poetry; first supplement. . . . Comp. by John E. and Sara W. Brewton. Wilson, H.W. 1954 xxii, 405p $14   **808.81**

1 Poetry—Indexes
ISBN 0-8242-0022-5   LC 42-20148

"A title, subject, author, and first line index to poetry in collections for children and youth." Title page
Following the form of the main volume, entered above, this volume indexes 66 collections, published between 1938 and 1951, of more than 7,000 poems by about 1,300 different authors. Classified under 1,250 subjects. Each collection is analyzed and graded

(comp.) Index to children's poetry; second supplement. . . . Comp. by John E. and Sara W. Brewton. Wilson, H.W. 1965 xxiv, 453p $14   **808.81**

1 Poetry—Indexes
ISBN 0-8242-0023-3   LC 42-20148

"A title, subject, author, and first line index to poetry in collections for children and youth." Title page
An extension of the basic volume and of the first supplement, published in 1942 and 1954, respectively, and entered above. This volume indexes 85 collections, published between 1949 and 1963, of more than 8,000 poems by approximately 1,400 authors, classified under more than 1,500 subjects

(comp.) Index to poetry for children and young people, 1964-1969. . . . Comp. by John E. and Sara W. Brewton and G. Meredith Blackburn, III. Wilson, H.W. 1972 xxx, 575p $20   **808.81**

1 Poetry—Indexes
ISBN 0-8242-0435-2   LC 71-161574

"A title, subject, author, and first line index to poetry in collections for children and young people." Title page
An extension of the basic volume published with title: Index to children's poetry, and the first and second supplements, all entered above. This volume indexes 117 collections of more than 11,000 poems by approximately 2,000 authors

(comp.) Index to poetry for children and young people, 1970-1975. . . . Comp. by John E. Brewton and G. Meredith Blackburn, III, and Lorraine A. Blackburn. Wilson, H.W. 1978 xxxii, 472p $20   **808.81**

1 Poetry—Indexes
ISBN 0-8242-0618-5   LC 77-26036

"A title, subject, author and first line index to poetry in collections for children and young people." Title page
An extension of the basic volume published with title: Index to children's poetry, its first and second supplements, and Index to poetry for children and young people, 1964-1969, all entered above. This volume covers over 10,000 poems that are found in 110 collections published from 1970 through 1975

Bridled with rainbows; poems about many things of earth and sky; selected by Sara and John E. Brewton; decorations by Vera Bock. Macmillan Pub. Co. 1949 191p illus lib. bdg. $4.95 (3-6)   **808.81**

1 Poetry—Collections
ISBN 0-02-712680-3   LC 49-7721

Nearly 200 poems, arranged according to subject with author, title, and first line indexes
"The anthology includes verses by modern poets as well as the old favorites that tell of the joys of childhood, the earth and sky, the seasons and school, the sea and ships, the day and night." Wis Library Bul

Bridled with rainbows—*Continued*

"This anthology will be a pleasant addition to poetry collections in children's rooms. The compilers have favored the imaginative poems over the humorous or down-to-earth and Vera Bock's excellent black-and-white decorations are very appropriate. Many of the selections are good for reading aloud." Library J

Callooh! Callay! Holiday poems for young readers; ed. by Myra Cohn Livingston; illus. by Janet Stevens. Atheneum Pubs. 1978 131p illus $7.95 (4-6)   **808.81**

1 Holidays—Poetry 2 Poetry—Collections
ISBN 0-689-50117-X   LC 78-8794

"A Margaret K. McElderry book"
This "collection of approximately seven dozen poems offers a variety of forms and styles, ranging from traditional English carols to contemporary works by Felice Holman, David McCord, and John Updike. The list of celebrations is standard; the selection, however, frequently offers new perspectives on familiar events or personalities through fresh material or by juxtaposing contrasting views." Horn Bk
"A fine holiday smorgasbord with author, title, and first line indexes, and a list of translators." Chicago. Children's Bk Center

Christmas bells are ringing; a treasury of Christmas poetry, selected by Sara and John E. Brewton; illus. by Decie Merwin. Macmillan Pub. Co. 1951 114p illus $4.95 (4 and up)   **808.81**

1 Christmas—Poetry
ISBN 0-02-712790-7   LC 51-12401

"About 100 poems are included in this inviting and varied anthology of Christmas poetry. Under such headings as In the week when Christmas comes and Who will kneel them gently down, there are selections for all ages, gay verses as well as reverent poems. Author, title, and first-line indexes." Booklist
"Good for personal ownership and a valuable addition to school and public libraries." Horn Bk

A Christmas feast; poems, sayings, greetings, and wishes; comp. by Edna Barth; etchings by Ursula Arndt. Houghton 1979 xx, 156p illus $9.95 (4-6)   **808.81**

1 Christmas—Poetry
ISBN 0-395-28965-3   LC 79-13282

"A Clarion book"
"Gathered from a span of five centuries, this collection of poems, carols, sayings, rhymes, and superstitions provides a rich sampling for holiday festivities and quiet moments alone. The selections are arranged under broad title categories, such as 'Christmas Is Coming,' 'At Christmas Time We Deck the Hall,' 'A Thousand Bells Ring Out,' 'A Child Is Born,' 'Our Joyful'st Feast,' and 'Welcome, Dear St. Nicholas, Santa Claus, and Father Christmas, and include contemporary authors (Aileen Fisher, Elizabeth Coatsworth), classic writers (Tennyson, Longfellow, Shakespeare) and traditional offerings from folk literature." Booklist

Dinosaurs and beasts of yore; verses selected by William Cole; illus. by Susanna Natti. Collins [distributed by Philomel Bks.] 1979 62p illus $8.95   **808.81**

1 Dinosaurs—Poetry 2 Extinct animals—Poetry 3 Poetry—Collections
ISBN 0-529-05511-2   LC 78-31619

"If interest in dinosaurs extends to the poetry shelves, this compact collection of humorous verse will find eager audiences. Poets such as Shel Silverstein, X. J. Kennedy, Steven Kroll, Jack Prelutsky, Mary Ann Hoberman, and Cole himself bring pterodactyls, brontosauruses, mastodons, and tyrannosauruses alive once again in funny poems that are illustrated with spirited black line drawings that often flow across two-page spreads." Booklist

Favorite poems, old and new; selected for boys and girls by Helen Ferris; illus. by Leonard Weisgard. Doubleday 1957 598p illus $9.95, lib. bdg. $10.90 (4-6)   **808.81**

1 Poetry—Collections
ISBN 0-385-07696-7; 0-385-06249-4   LC 57-11418

An anthology of more than seven hundred poems divided into eighteen sections related to children's interests that enable the reader either to browse or to find a special poem for a special occasion
"This collection with its Leonard Weisgard illustrations is a treasure for the children's library shelves and for the family to own." Wis Library Bul
Includes indexes of authors, titles and first lines

Granger's Index to poetry. 6th ed. completely rev. and enl. indexing anthologies published through December 31, 1970; ed. by William James Smith. Columbia Univ. Press 1973 xxxvii, 2223p $99.50   **808.81**

1 Poetry—Indexes
ISBN 0-231-03641-8

First published 1904 by McClurg with title: Index to poetry and recitations
This "is the best known of poetry indexes. The sixth edition indexes 514 volumes of poetry anthologies containing the works of some 12,000 poets and translators. There is a subject index that lists poems under 5,000 headings, an author index, and a combined first-line and title index." Wynar. Guide to Ref Bks for Sch Media Centers
For a fuller review see: The Booklist and subscription Books Bulletin, April 1, 1974

Granger's Index to poetry, 1970-1977; ed. by William James Smith. Columbia Univ. Press 1978 635p $59.50   **808.81**

1 Poetry—Indexes
ISBN 0-231-0428-5   LC 78-4097

Supplement to: Granger's Index to poetry, 6th edition, entered above
Indexes 120 anthologies of poetry published during the years 1970-1977

I went to the animal fair; a book of animal poems; selected by William Cole; illus. by Colette Rosselli. Collins [distributed by Philomel Bks.] 1958 45p illus $5.95 (k-3)   **808.81**

1 Animals—Poetry 2 Poetry—Collections
ISBN 0-529-03480-8   LC 75-23020

"Thirty-five poems about animals—from frogs and grasshoppers to bears and whales—entrancingly illustrated and presented in picture-book format. Humor and catchy rhythms predominate in the pleasing collection which includes old favorites and many less familiar verses. Among the poets represented are Milne, De la Mare, Coatsworth, Lindsay, Aldis, Laura E. Richards, and William Jay Smith." Booklist
"William Cole, an experienced anthologist, has chosen well. Like the poems, Colette Rosselli's drawings are simple, humorous and direct." NY Times Bk Rev
Title index: p[46]. Author index: p[47]

Life hungers to abound; poems of the family; selected by Helen Plotz. Greenwillow Bks. 1978 181p $7.95, lib. bdg. $7.63 (6 and up)   **808.81**

1 Family—Poetry 2 Poetry—Collections
ISBN 0-688-80176-5; 0-688-84176-7   LC 78-5829

An anthology of 120 poems divided into five categories: marriage, parent to child, brothers and sisters, ancestors and descendants, and child to parent. Sources range from the Bible, Shakespeare, translations of Chinese poems, Wordsworth, Ann Bradstreet, and Emily Dickinson to modern American and English poets such as Allen Ginsberg, W. H. Auden, James Dickey, Theodore Roethke, Elizabeth Bishop and Adrienne Rich. Includes indexes to authors, titles, and first lines

Morrison, Lillian

(comp.) Sprints and distances; sports in poetry and the poetry in sport; illus. by Clare and John Ross. Crowell 1965 211p illus $9.95 (5 and up)   **808.81**

1 Sports—Poetry 2 Poetry—Collections
ISBN 0-690-76571-1   LC 65-14906

Morrison, Lillian—*Continued*

"The poems included here range from memorable newspaper verse to pieces by Pindar, Virgil, Wordsworth, and Yeats. They vary in form from simple quatrains to intricate modern verse. No attempt was made to include every sport though many are represented, from baseball to falconry." Prefatory note

"A very good poetry anthology; discriminating selection, good format, and—considering the limitations of the subtitle—a surprising range of moods and sources. . . . Sources are cited; appended are indexes by author, by first line, by title, and by sport." Chicago. Children's Bk Center

O frabjous day! Poetry for holidays and special occasions; ed. by Myra Cohn Livingston. Atheneum Pubs. 1977 205p $8.95 (5 and up)   **808.81**

1 Holidays—Poetry   2 Poetry—Collections
ISBN 0-689-50076-9   LC 76-28510

"A Margaret K. McElderry book"

This anthology contains poems touching not only upon joyous occasions but also on some more sobering ones, such as the assassinations of American leaders. It "is divided into three sections—celebrating, honoring, and remembering momentous happenings. It ranges from the secular to the religious, touches upon Jewish holy days as well as Christian, and remembers the Buddha's birthday. A selection of poetry including such contrasting sources as David McCord, the Bible, Rilke, Alexander Blok, Issa, Shakespeare, and Gwendolyn Brooks, it reveals the many different ways of regarding and observing special days. With notes on some of the poems and separate indexes of authors, titles and translators." Horn Bk

This book "is unique in that poems from many time periods and cultures are included, offering a variety of perspectives on the same event. The selections are outstanding, but some may require explanation to the unsophisticated . . . reader. . . . An unfortunate oversight is that there are still many unexplained esoteric and ethnic references." Children's Bk Rev Serv

Piping down the valleys wild; poetry for the young of all ages; ed. with an introduction by Nancy Larrick; illus. by Ellen Raskin. Delacorte Press 1968 xxiii, 247p illus $4.95   **808.81**

1 Poetry—Collections
ISBN 0-440-06923-8   LC 67-19762

A collection of poems, from all over the world, arranged in sixteen sections, each one containing poems dealing with a particular subject or experience common to young people. Some of the poets included are: Dylan Thomas, Emily Dickinson, Langston Hughes, John Updike, and William Shakespeare

"A pleasant, quite comprehensive collection that includes little unfamiliar material; the selections range widely in source, somewhat less widely in mood. . . . An index of first lines and an author-title index [are] appended. The compiler's introduction is addressed to adults and discusses reading aloud to the young; this plus the fact that so much of the poetry is for quite young children suggests that the book may be best suited to a home collection, although it should be useful in any collection of books for children." Sutherland. The Best in Children's Bks

Poetry of earth; selected and illus. by Adrienne Adams. Scribner 1972 48p illus lib. bdg. $6.95 (3-6)   **808.81**

1 Nature in poetry. 2 Poetry—Collections
ISBN 0-684-13012-22   LC 70-39577

In this collection of thirty-three poems, such poets as Robert Frost, David McCord, Edna St Vincent Millay, and James Stephens write about the earth and its many creatures

"Handsomely designed and beautifully illustrated with pictures in soft colors, with some of the pages in quiet tones of earth and rock colors, this a compilation of poems that celebrate the beauty of flora and fauna, of the stars and the sea and the snow. The poetry has been chosen with high selectivity. . . . A good choice for reading to younger children as well as for independent readers." Chicago. Children's Bk Center

Room for me and a mountain lion; poetry of open space; selected by Nancy Larrick; illus. with photographs. Evans, M.&Co. 1974 191p illus $6.95 (5 and up)   **808.81**

1 Nature in poetry   2 Poetry—Collections
ISBN 0-87131-124-0   LC 73-87710

This anthology "doesn't merely illustrate a theme, but conveys a feeling of connectedness, of interaction between our inner and outer worlds. The poets represented are mostly contemporary, ranging from Frost and D.H. Lawrence through Roethke and Jarrell to Stafford, Levertov, Kinnell, Swenson (and some lesser names); there are also short selections from Whitman, some Eskimo and Indian songs, [and] an 18th-Century Chinese poem." Library J

It "includes the work of children's poets as well as adult, and although it is perhaps too heavily weighted with William Stafford and, to a lesser degree, Galway Kinnell and Walt Whitman, it is certainly . . . appealing . . . for younger children." NY Times Bk Rev

Indexes of poems and poets and of first lines are included

Subject index to poetry for children and young people, 1957-1975; comp. by Dorothy B. Frizzell Smith and Eva L. Andrews. A.L.A. 1977 1035p $30   **808.81**

1 Poetry—Indexes
ISBN 0-8389-0242-1   LC 77-3296

"Intended to supplement the o.p. 1957 edition, this alphabetically arranged subject index includes over 2,000 headings, indexing poems in 263 anthologies not listed previously, or updating indexing for those editions that have been revised. The books indexed are listed in order of the assigned code, to which the user is referred from the entry. Publisher, date, grade level, and those titles listed in Wilson catalogs are designated. . . . Useful only when searching by subject, this index uses headings primarily from Sears, 10th ed., which has since been updated. However, the collection is enriched with the inclusion of a broad spectrum of ethnic material." Choice

A Tune beyond us; a collection of poetry; ed. by Myra Cohn Livingston; illus. by James J. Spanfeller. Harcourt 1968 280p illus $7.50 (6 and up)   **808.81**

1 Poetry—Collections   LC 68-11502

"For this worldwide collection, ranging in time from the eighth century to the present, the compiler has chosen poems greatly varied in subject, form, and mood but uniformly superior in their felicity of poetic expression. Among the poets represented, usually by little-known selections, are Auden, Brecht, Eliot, Hopkins, Jiménez, Li Po, Pushkin, Rilke, Roethke, Yeats, and Yevtushenko. English translations of poems from other languages are followed by the original in an uncommonly fresh and rewarding anthology for the appreciative reader. Separately indexed by author, translator, title, and first line." Booklist

Under the tent of the sky; a collection of poems about animals large and small; selected by John E. Brewton; with drawings by Robert Lawson. Macmillan Pub. Co. 1937 205p illus $5.95 (3-6)   **808.81**

1 Animals—Poetry   2 Poetry—Collections
ISBN 0-02-712470-3   LC 37-27434

A collection of poems grouped under twenty headings such as: Circus cavalcade; I went to the zoo; Animals never seen in circus or zoo; Let's pretend; In fairy-land; Beneath man's wings; Little folks in the grass; Hurt no living thing

"A charming collection. . . . Children will find much to delight and entertain them. . . . Decorated end pages and pen and ink sketches by Robert Lawson. Indexes of authors, titles and first lines." NY Libraries

What a wonderful bird the frog are; an assortment of humorous poetry and verse; ed. by Myra Cohn Livingston. Harcourt 1973 192p $5.25 (5 and up)   **808.81**

1 Humorous poetry   2 Poetry—Collections
ISBN 0-15-295400-7   LC 72-88171

What a wonderful bird the frog are—*Continued*

"A cheerful anthology comprises poems and jingles chosen from authors who range from the fifth century A.D. to contemporary, and from sources other than the English language. Just as varied are the subjects and styles, from haiku and couplets to extracts from plays and mock-serious odes. There's a title index, an author index that includes birth dates, an index of first lines, and—small but significant—an index of translators." Chicago. Children's Bk Center

This book "presents interesting material not found in similar collections for young people. . . . [It] will afford children many hours of pleasurable reading, either independently or in groups." Sch Library J

The **Year** around; poems for children; selected by Alice I. Hazeltine & Elva S. Smith; decorations by Paula Hutchison. Arno Press [1973] 192p illus $15 (4 and up)   **808.81**
1 Seasons—Poetry 2 Holidays—Poetry 3 Poetry —Collections
ISBN 0-8369-6403-9   LC 72-11921
"Granger index reprint series"
Reprint of the 1956 Abingdon edition
A "volume of poems about the seasons, special days and nature. Divisions are by the four seasons, and then by the individual months within each season." Chicago. Children's Bk Center
"The selections are from familiar authors, modern favorites, and some less-familiar poets, but all with appeal to children." Sat Rev
"Nicely illustrated with spot drawings. Author and title index." Booklist

Zero makes me hungry; a collection of poems for today; comp. by Edward Lueders and Primus St John. Art and design: John Reuter-Pacyna. Lothrop 1976 143p illus $8.95, lib. bdg. $8.59   **808.81**
1 Poetry—Collections
ISBN 0-688-41745-0; 0-688-51745-5   LC 75-33543
Drawn from modern twentieth century output, this collection covers a wide range of ethnic and cultural traditions, including Eskimo, Chinese, African and Japanese. There are "114 poems arranged in 10 generally homogeneous sections concerning modern technology, creativity, death, sports, animals, love, and other aspects of daily living. Most of the selections are contemporary. . . . John Ciardi, Al Young, Denise Levertov, Paul Goodman, Maxine Kumin, Alice Walker, Robert Graves, and Ogden Nash are among the poets represented. The colorful graphics may invite readers; the appeal of the poems will hold them." Booklist

808.82 Drama—Collections

Kreider, Barbara A.
(comp.) Index to children's plays in collections. 2d ed. Scarecrow 1977 227p $10.50
          808.82
1 Drama—Indexes
ISBN 0-8108-0992-3   LC 76-49666
First published 1972
This work indexes "a total of 1,450 one-act plays, skits, monologues, and dialogues from 66 collections published between 1965 and 1974. . . . The index is arranged in one alphabetical order by author, title, and subject. There is no indication of a play's merit. Additional listings include subject headings, cast analysis (by sex and number of characters), directory of publishers, and bibliography of collections." Booklist

One hundred plays for children; an anthology of non-royalty one-act plays, ed. by A. S. Burack. Plays, Inc. 1970 886p $11.95   **808.82**
1 One act plays 2 College and school drama—Collections
ISBN 0-8238-0002-4   LC 75-99964
First published 1949
These plays "appeared originally in 'Plays,' the drama magazine for young people. Providing a varied collection for both classroom and special assembly programs, the four sections cover holidays, legends, historical plays, and a general

group of about thirty. A valuable feature is the appended instruction for production with playing time, costumes, properties, and setting given." Cur Ref Bks

Play index. Wilson, H.W. 1953-1978   **808.82**
1 Drama—Indexes
ISSN 0554-3037
First published 1953, covering the years 1949-1952, and edited by Dorothy Herbert West and Dorothy Margaret Peake, $10. Additional volumes are: 1953-1960 $14 Edited by Estelle A. Fidell and Dorothy Margaret Peake; 1961-1967 $16 Edited by Estelle A. Fidell; 1968-1972 $20 Edited by Estelle A. Fidell; 1973-1977 $28 Edited by Estelle A. Fidell
Play index indexes plays in collections and single plays; one-act and full-length plays; radio, television, and Broadway plays; plays for amateur production; plays for children, young adults, and adults. It is divided into four parts. Part I is an author, title, and subject index; the author or main entry includes the title of the play, brief synopsis of the plot, number of acts and scenes, size of cast, number of sets, and bibliographic information. Part II is a list of collections indexed, and Part III, a cast analysis, lists plays by the type of cast and number of players required. Part IV is a directory of publishers and distributors

Plays, the Drama Magazine for Young People. Plays, Inc. $13 per year, 2 years $25   **808.82**
1 Drama—Collections—Periodicals 2 College and school drama—Collections—Periodicals
ISSN 0032-1540   LC 45-27696
Monthly October through May. First published 1941
"Features eight to ten plays per issue designated for lower, middle grades, junior, and senior high. Most are original, unimaginative one act plays which may be performed in less than an hour. A few plays represent adaptations of better known classics. There are often skit or puppet programs. For each play production notes are included (number and sex of characters, costumes, time, and properties)." Katz. Magazines for Libraries. 2d edition

Popular plays for classroom reading; ed. by A. S. Burack and B. Alice Crossley. Plays, Inc. 1974 xx, 353p $7.95 (4-6)   **808.82**
1 One act plays 2 College and school drama—Collections
ISBN 0-8238-0151-9   LC 74-998
Among the twenty-four one-act plays in this collection are comedies, mysteries, adventure plays, and dramatizations of classic stories and novels

808.87 Humor—Collections

The **Big** book of jokes; selected and told by Helen Hoke; pictures by Richard Erdoes. Watts, F. 1971 200p illus lib. bdg. $6.90 (4 and up)   **808.87**
1 Jokes 2 Riddles
ISBN 0-531-01990-X   LC 78-161837
A collection of jokes and anecdotes, quips, and crazy stories listed under such categories as: Animal antics; Goofy girls; Kute kids; Legal laughs; Medical madness; Neurotic nonsense; Vacation vagaries; Youthful yarns; Zestful zoology
"Young people will certainly appreciate the humor in the jokes and in the equally amusing black-and-white Lear-like sketches." Library J

Jokes for children, comp. by Marguerite Kohl [and] Frederica Young; illus. by Bob Patterson. Hill & Wang 1963 116p illus $6.95 (3-5)   **808.87**
1 Jokes
ISBN 0-8090-6181-3   LC 63-11056
"A collection of more than 650 jokes including jokes told by children as well as jokes selected by them for their school publications and theatrical productions. The book is divided into the following categories: Teachers and pupils, Melissa, Rhymes, Gruesomes, Riddles, The little moron, Whoppers and insults, Puns, Alfie and Archie, Family style, Wildlife; Sign language, and Mishmash. Will fill a need for books of humor." Booklist

Jokes, giggles & guffaws; selected by Helen Hoke; pictures by Haro. Watts, F. 1975 [c1973] 158p illus lib. bdg. $6.90 (3-6)
                                                        808.87

1 Jokes 2 Riddles
ISBN 0-531-02844-5   LC 75-6047
First published 1973 in England with title: Jokes, jokes, jokes 2
"A better-than-average collection of limericks, riddles, 'fractured' nursery rhymes, and short poems." Sch Library J
"The quality ranges from dismally lacking in humor to impressively witty. A large percentage of this material is rather sophisticated, suggesting that this book might be more popular among junior high students than those in upper elementary grades. Also, the use of English English, and English cultural patterns might be difficult for younger children. Fortunately, the selector avoided ethnic jokes and did not include a large number of sexist ones. Simple black cartoon-style drawings are funny." Children's Bk Rev Serv

Laughing together; giggles and grins from around the globe; comp. by Barbara K. Walker with everybody else's help; designed and illus. by Simms Taback. Four Winds, in association with the U.S. Committee for UNICEF 1977 106p illus lib. bdg. $8.95 (3-6)   **808.87**

1 Jokes 2 Riddles
ISBN 0-590-07486-5   LC 77-7789
"This collection of children's jokes from nearly 100 countries . . . includes droodles, jingles, jokes, counting rhymes, tongue twisters, [short tales] and riddles . . . divided into such categories as 'Family Funnies,' 'School Snickers,' 'Fun with Friends,' etc. An introduction to each section points out the similarities between the jests of various cultures. Although few children will be able to read the drolleries in their original languages, the compiler frequently includes the foreign versions (of interest to children intrigued by strange alphabets) along with the English translations. An inviting format (cartoons appear on every page) plus humor well-selected for its child-appeal combine to make this a fine choice for school and public libraries." Sch Library J
Where necessary, selections "include short explanatory statements. An afterword invites children's suggestions for a proposed second volume." Booklist

808.88 Collections of miscellaneous writings

Bartlett, John
(comp.) Familiar quotations. Little $17.50
                                                        808.88

1 Quotations
First published 1855. Periodically revised and brought up to date. Editors vary
"A collection of passages, phrases and proverbs traced to their sources in ancient and modern literature." Subtitle [of 14th edition]
Authors are arranged in chronological order from ancient times to the present so that the quotations may be considered in the context of the author's work and period. Includes author and key word indexes
"A standard collection, comprehensive and well selected. . . . One of the best books of quotations with a long history." Sheehy. Guide to Ref Bks. 9th edition

Brandreth, Gyles
The biggest tongue twister book in the world; illus. by Alex Chin. Sterling 1978 128p illus $5.95 (4 and up)   **808.88**

1 Tongue twisters
ISBN 0-8069-4594-X   LC 78-7784
Text first published 1977 in England with title: Tongue twisters
"Hundreds of linguistic acrobatics test the flexibility of agile tongues in this collection of challenging twisters. Arranged in broad alphabetical order, the selections range from short one-liners ('Shipshape suit shops ship shapely suits') to longer ones of 4, 8, and even 20 lines. In addition to the amusement that is offered, an afterword

reprinted from Instructor Magazine describes ways to use tongue twisters in strengthening language art skills. Cartoon line drawings embellish the pages." Booklist

The **Home** book of quotations; classical and modern; selected and arranged by Burton Stevenson. Dodd $40   **808.88**

1 Quotations
First published 1934 and periodically revised
"A comprehensive and well-chosen collection of more than 50,000 quotations arranged alphabetically by subject with subarrangement by smaller topics. Usually gives exact citation. Includes an index of authors—giving full name, identifying phrase, and dates of birth and death, with reference to all quotations cited—and a word index, which indexes the quotation by leading words, usually nouns, though in some case verbs and adjectives are also used. Boldface entries are given for some of the smaller subjects. The quotations under these are not indexed separately, and one must, therefore, turn to the subject and run through the entries. This practice must be remembered when using this index." Sheehy. Guide to Ref Bks. 9th edition

Morrison, Lillian
(comp.) Best wishes, amen; a new collection of autograph verses; illus. by Loretta Lustig. Crowell 1974 195p illus $6.95 (5 and up)   **808.88**

1 Epigrams
ISBN 0-690-00579-2   LC 74-2456
A companion volume to Morrison's earlier collections of autographs, "this comprises over three hundred new bon mots, jibes [and] complimentary verses. . . . There are many that demonstrate the self-conscious humor of young autographers who felt comfortable only when taking a dig at a friend's expense, some impersonal quips, a few that reflect the changing times, and a modest number that admit to affection: in fact, exactly what one finds in children's autograph books." Chicago. Children's Bk Center
"A final section contains Spanish autograph rhymes, plus translations, again gathered from actual albums of Spanish-speaking children in New York City. A guaranteed hit with elementary graders, this won't gather any dust on the shelves—especially at promotion/graduation time." Sch Library J

(comp.) A diller, a dollar; rhymes and sayings for the ten o'clock scholar; illus. by Marj Bauernschmidt. Crowell 1955 150p illus $8.95 (5 and up)   **808.88**

1 Epigrams
ISBN 0-690-23957-2   LC 55-9213
"A collection of schoolroom plaints and schoolyard taunts, mnemonics, proverbs and parodies, jokes and jingles, admonitions, game rhymes, and chants. Garnered from old-time primers, chapbooks, nursery rhymes, and folk journals, from adults' remembrances of rhymes known in childhood, and from children and teenagers themselves, the rhymes included here were selected on the basis of inventiveness, sound, fun, and freshness today. Arranged under subject categories and decorated with amusing illustrations. Sources given." Booklist
Bibliography: p149-50

(comp.) Remember me when this you see; a new collection of autograph verses; illus. by Marjorie Bauernschmidt. Crowell 1961 182p illus $8.95 (5 and up)   **808.88**

1 Epigrams
ISBN 0-690-69613-2   LC 60-11536
This book includes poems about love, friendship, sincerity, and success, as well as nonsense poems. All are suitable for autograph albums
"A new bonanza of the tender sentiments, the jokes, and puns . . . the friendly insults and good advice that our grandfathers and grandmothers may well have written in their albums." NY Times Bk Rev

Rosenbloom, Joseph

Twist these on your tongue; illus. by Joyce Behr. Elsevier/Nelson Bks. 1978 91p illus $6.95 (4 and up)   **808.88**

1 Tongue twisters
ISBN 0-525-66612-5   LC 78-16776

First published by Thomas Nelson
"It would be hard to imagine a more extensive compendium of tongue twisters. This is a collection to be dipped into, tried out, shared, and admired. All of the oldies are here (rubber baby buggy bumpers) along with the author's own originals. . . . The hundreds of entries, some of which are old jingles and word-play rhymes, are listed alphabetically and the text is leavened by black-and-white drawings." Sch Library J

Schwartz, Alvin

(comp.) A twister of twists, a tangler of tongues; tongue twisters; illus. by Glen Rounds. Lippincott 1972 125p illus $8.95, pa $1.95 (4 and up)   **808.88**

1 Tongue twisters
ISBN 0-397-31387-X; 0-397-31412-X   LC 72-1434

This is a collection of tongue twisters in both prose and verse, including several in other languages
"A grand gathering guaranteed to gag a gaggle of garrulous gossips, the selection of well-known and not-so-well-known tongue twisters should provide endless hours of elocutionary diversion for young and old alike. . . . A helpful series of notes, sources, and bibliographic references give added dimension to a light-hearted, yet incisive, compilation, highlighted by the jovial line drawings." Horn Bk

810.8 American literature— Collections

Free to be . . . you and me; conceived by Marlo Thomas; developed and ed. by Carole Hart [and others] Editor: Francine Klagsbrun; art director: Samuel N. Antupit. McGraw 1974 143p illus music $8.95, pa $6.95 (k-3)   **810.8**

1 American literature—Collections
ISBN 0-07-064223-0; 0-07-064224-9   LC 73-14784

"A project of the Ms. Foundation, Inc." Title page
The theme of this collection of twenty-five songs, stories, poems and a dialogue is that children should develop as individuals and be independent of obsolete sexual and racial role myths. Fifteen of the selections originally were recorded on a 1973 album of the same title
This collection "is a significant step toward filling the need for nonsexist material for children. . . . The total adds up to a qualitatively uneven but still useful endeavor at encouraging children to be themselves." Booklist

811 American poetry

Adoff, Arnold

Big sister tells me that I'm black; illus. by Lorenzo Lynch. Holt 1976 unp illus lib. bdg. $4.95 (1-3)   **811**

1 Blacks—Poetry
ISBN 0-03-01456-5   LC 75-32249

This book is a "celebration of blackness, as big sister tells her brother that they are smart and proud and strong, that they will grow and stand tall and be free." Chicago. Children's Bk Center
"Written in vigorous free verse, the rhythms seem at times to echo a cheering squad. . . . Written with no punctuation and with no upper case letters, the typography is clearly part of the poetic design. The art, done with a black felt tip pen and ink wash, is spirited and consistent without being dull." Rdng Teacher

I am the running girl; pictures by Ronald Himler. Harper 1979 unp illus $6.95, lib. bdg. $6.89 (3-5)   **811**

1 Track athletics—Poetry
ISBN 0-06-020094-4; 0-06-020095-2   LC 78-14083

A free-verse prose-poem that describes the pride and joy that running provides a young girl
"The loosely strung verse fashions a welcome paean, one that's nicely grounded in Himler's observant, softly shaded pencil drawings." Booklist

Under the early morning trees; poems. Illus. by Ronald Himler. Dutton 1978 unp illus lib. bdg. $7.50 (4-6)   **811**

1 Trees—Poetry 2 Nature in poetry
ISBN 0-525-41860-1   LC 78-5561

"In picture-book format this is a long, prosy poem about a girl's early morning walk along a hundred-tree, hundred-year-old hedge that bounds the farm where she lives. She notices the different kinds of trees that make up the hedge and encounters various insects, birds, and animals there. The mood is quiet and appreciative. Despite the subtitle 'Poems,' however, individual pages or spreads cannot really stand alone. . . . Children will need some familiarity with poetry patterns to read this book successfully." Sch Library J
"Himler has caught and held the experience with line, texture, play of light and dark in impressively composed black-and-white drawings. This is some of Adoff's best work; the inner rhyme is startling, as are the sensory images and the flashes of color contrast woven together or apart. There is a natural ring and flow to the verse arrangement that fits the core of meaning and word working." Booklist

Aiken, Conrad

Cats and bats and things with wings; poems. Drawings by Milton Glaser. Atheneum Pubs. 1965 unp illus $6.95 (k-4)   **811**

1 Animals—Poetry
ISBN 0-689-30017-4   LC 65-21724

These "poems about sixteen different members of the animal kingdom are all but overshadowed by sixteen astonishingly imaginative drawings. . . . Poem and picture have each a page to themselves; each poem also makes a picture in its typographical arrangement. Conrad Aiken clearly enjoyed writing the verses. [However] here and there the poems peter out at the end." Horn Bk

Aldis, Dorothy

All together; a child's treasury of verse. . . . Illus. by Helen D. Jameson, Marjorie Flack, and Margaret Freeman. Putnam 1952 192p illus $7.95 (k-3)   **811**

ISBN 0-399-20006-1   LC 52-9826

"Including selections from Everything and anything; Here, there and everywhere; Hop, skip and jump; Before things happen; with poems previously unpublished in book form." Title page
"These are poems that the author herself has chosen from her store and they are the ones that have been most loved through the years. The joy of childhood lies within these pages, and the pathos; the magic and the energy." Christian Sci Monitor
"Many of the familiar illustrations have been printed in color, adding to the appeal of the book." Library J

Asch, Frank

Country pie. Greenwillow Bks. 1979 32p illus $6.95, lib bdg. $6.67 (1-4)   **811**

1 Country life—Poetry
ISBN 0-688-80188-9; 0-688-84188-0   LC 78-14837

Illustrated by the author
"Light-hearted poems, relating to nature and the weather in the countryside. . . . Young readers and listeners will find it hard to resist 'Sunflakes' in which, if 'sunlight fell like snowflakes we could build a sunman' or have a 'sunball fight,' or the one about trying to whistle like the winter wind. The poems are also just right to move to and say aloud, making this a valuable addition to collections." Sch Library J

Asch, Frank—*Continued*

"Each of the fourteen poems is roundly reflected by a facing illustration, both pages framed in a common border of stylized undergrowth that won't seem to let your eyes go. The pictures themselves continue the ornate black-and-white line work in contrasting patterns and textures, with sun-yellow highlights reflecting off a simple frame of the same color." Booklist

Atwood, Ann

Haiku: the mood of earth. Scribner 1971 unp illus lib. bdg. $9.95, pa $4.95 (5 and up) **811**

1 Haiku 2 Nature photography 3 Nature in poetry
ISBN 0-684-12494-7; 0-684-16214-8   LC 70-162737

"Stating in her brief introductory analysis of Haiku that the oriental verse form is primarily a visual experience which achieves direct contact with nature through the use of specific techniques, the author suggests that the same principles can be applied in art or photography to capture a timeless moment of wonder. She then presents 25 such moments, drawn from the moods of earth and the cycles of the seasons, each consisting of two color photographs, one frequently a closeup or magnification of detail in the other, accompanied by a single unifying Haiku. A striking volume for any young reader inclined toward poetry, photography, or nature." Booklist

My own rhythm; an approach to haiku. Scribner 1973 unp illus lib. bdg. $6.95 (5 and up) **811**

1 Haiku 2 Nature photography 3 Nature in poetry
ISBN 0-684-13248-6   LC 72-9037

"Introducing this lovely book, Ann Atwood offers a brief history of haiku and points out the differences among three Japanese masters of the form: Buson, Issa and Bashō. The rest of the book consists of her own haiku, each one her reaction to splendors in nature which she has photographed in full color. This is a volume to treasure." Pub W

Behn, Harry

The little hill; poems & pictures by Harry Behn. Harcourt 1949 58p illus $4.50 (1-4) **811**
ISBN 0-15-245966-9   LC 49-10198

"This small book of poems about nature and familiar things to childhood is unusual both as to the different and unexpected rhythms and the decorative and imaginative drawings." Booklist

"Gardens, raindrops, the merry-go-on, the caterpillar, Undine's garden and Hallowe'en among the varied subjects included." Horn Bk

Benét, Rosemary

A book of Americans, by Rosemary and Stephen Vincent Benét; illus. by Charles Child. Holt 1933 114p illus lib. bdg. $5.95 (5 and up) **811**

1 U.S.—History—Poetry 2 U.S.—Biography—Poetry
ISBN 0-03-015041-8   LC 33-27433

"Fifty-six poems of varied moods and meters describe cleverly and often with gusto the life and character of famous men and women from Columbus to Woodrow Wilson. Humorously illustrated . . . in red, white and blue, and black and white." NY Libraries

"The verse bids fair to give fresh life to boys and girls who have been starving for living words of American history. It is a book of fine ideas and true associations, as well as one of amusing characterization of American idiosyncrasies." Atlantic Bookshelf

Bodecker, N. M.

Hurry, hurry, Mary dear! And other nonsense poems; written and illus. with pen sketches by N. M. Bodecker. Atheneum Pubs. 1976 118p illus $6.95 (2-5) **811**

1 Nonsense verses
ISBN 0-689-50067-X   LC 76-14841

"A Margaret K. McElderry book"
"This wholehearted nonsense is worth some quiet giggles, and a quiet giggle is worth a lot —especially attached to word playing. Bodecker has a roving imagination that enlarges on itself and just gets sillier and sillier, page after page, especially in juxtaposition with black-and-white line drawings which exaggerate or give a funny twist to the verses. There are 43 in all, and generally they are fresh." Booklist

"As light as soufflé, this will go down easily —even among kids who claim to be staunch poetry haters." Sch Library J

Let's marry said the cherry, and other nonsense poems; written and illus. by N. M. Bodecker. Atheneum Pubs. 1974 79p illus $5.95 (2-5) **811**

1 Nonsense verses
ISBN 0-689-50004-1   LC 74-76271

"A Margaret K. McElderry book"
Here are thirty-two short nonsense poems, ranging from "The Porcupine," about a girl who pats a porcupine, to "Mr. Beecher," a poem describing an offbeat Spanish teacher

The verses "are immediately inviting for their combination of syllabic nonsense and topsy-turvy logic. . . . Secondly, they are always full of rhyme if not of reason, and their rhythm echoes familiar cadences. The poems are profusely illustrated with line drawings elegantly and humorously expressive, and delicately ornamented with patterns and hatchings. When read aloud, they must be said trippingly on the tongue, lest they trip up on the unwary reader." Horn Bk

Brooks, Gwendolyn

Bronzeville boys and girls; pictures by Ronni Solbert. Harper 1956 40p illus $5.95, lib. bdg. $7.89 (2-5) **811**

1 Blacks—Poetry
ISBN 0-06-020650-0; 0-06-020651-9   LC 56-8152

A collection of thirty-six poems about everyday experiences of children. "While the children are black and the place is Chicago, the place might be anywhere and the children, any children." Adventuring with Bks. 2d edition

"The poems are gay, carefree, and serious—but none is sad. . . . Ronni Solbert's sensitive and expressive drawings reflect and extend the mood and beauty of the poetry." Chicago Sunday Trib

Brown, Margaret Wise

Nibble, nibble; poems for children; illus. by Leonard Weisgard. Young Scott Bks. 1959 unp illus lib. bdg. $7.95 (k-3) **811**

1 Nature in poetry
ISBN 0-201-09291-3   LC 59-4895

"A posthumous collection of [25] nature poems, 14 of which are published here for the first time. The pleasingly cadenced verses are fresh and childlike, and the illustrations in black, white, and cool green are lovely; together they make a harmonious, evocative whole which young children will enjoy." Booklist

Carmer, Carl

The boy drummer of Vincennes; illus. by Seymour Fleishman. Harvey House 1972 unp illus map lib. bdg. $5.49 (2-4) **811**

1 U.S.—History—Revolution, 1775-1783—Poetry
ISBN 0-8178-4932-7   LC 72-76398

"A narrative poem in first person celebrates a facet of the American Revolution. Based on a true incident, the story is told by a drummer boy on the Western frontier; in 1779, a band of patriotic volunteers led by George Rogers Clarke marched across the soggy lands of Illinois to take from the British a small French outpost they had won— Vincennes. The poem has a swinging rhythm that fits the jaunty mood of the lad who defiantly thumps his drum and it is faithful in its language to the speech of the period. Nice to read aloud, useful for its historical as well as its poetic appeal, the poem incorporates some of the folklore and the contemporary lyrics of the time." Chicago. Children's Bk Center

Caudill, Rebecca

Wind, sand and sky; illus. by Donald Carrick. Dutton 1976 unp illus lib. bdg. $6.95 (1-4) **811**

1 Deserts—Poetry
ISBN 0-525-42899-2   LC 75-34113

Caudill, Rebecca—*Continued*

"Despite the picture-book format, middle grade children, who are themselves writing haiku, would be a more appreciative audience for Caudill's 24 mood-setting verses about the Arizona desert where she spends the winters." Sch Library J

"Caudill's poetry has abundant, melodic wording; few children will recognize it as Haiku but can follow it as a girl's statement of feeling for the land, especially with the help of Carrick's graceful watercolors in shades of blue and gold." Booklist

Ciardi, John

I met a man; illus. by Robert Osborn. Houghton 1961 74p illus lib. bdg. $8.95, pa $2.95 (1-3)   811

1 Nonsense verses
ISBN 0-395-18018-X; 3-395-17447-3   LC 60-9094

"These poems were written for a special pleasure: I wanted to write the first book my daughter read herself. To bring them within her first-grade range, I based them on the two most elementary word lists in general use. . . . The basic devices of these poems for leading the child to new words are rhyme, riddles, context, and word games." Author's note

Ciardi's "imagination, fluency in rhyme, and delight in plays on words lift the results of his intention above the limitation of the first-grade word lists. . . . The cartoonish drawings admirably suit the moods of his fantastic sequences. . . . An honest and original attempt to make both poetry and learning fun." Horn Bk

The man who sang the sillies; drawings by Edward Gorey. Lippincott 1961 63p illus $7.95 (2-5)   811

1 Nonsense verses
ISBN 0-397-30568-0   LC 61-11734

"Twenty-four nonsense poems, appropriately illustrated by exaggeratedly zany line drawings. Some of the selections are flagrant and elaborate playing with words and sounds, others are narrative-nonsense verse in the vein of Lewis Carroll. . . . Variable in quality; none of the verse is mediocre but a good deal of it seems to strain for humorous effect." Chicago. Children's Bk Center

You read to me, I'll read to you; drawings by Edward Gorey. Lippincott 1962 64p illus lib. bdg. $8.95 (1-4)   811

1 Humorous poetry
ISBN 0-397-30645-8   LC 62-16296

Thirty-five "imaginative and humorous poems for an adult and a child to read aloud together. Written in a basic first-grade vocabulary, the poems to be read by the child alternate with poems to be read by the adult." Booklist

"With few exceptions, the poems are humorous: some in a nonsense vein, some tongue-in-cheek about parents or children, some playing imaginatively with words or ideas. Here and there the poetry seems to strain for effect, but for the most part it is gay and imaginative. The selections are good for reading aloud." Chicago. Children's Bk Center

Clifton, Lucille

Everett Anderson's Christmas coming; illus. by Evaline Ness. Holt 1971 unp illus lib. bdg. $3.95 (k-3)   811

1 Christmas—Poetry
ISBN 0-03-089507-3   LC 75-150025

A young black boy "gives readers his thoughts and feelings about the Christmas season in nine brief poems. And Evaline Ness has . . . created the illustrations (three color line-and-wash drawings), that reflect the quiet spirit of Christmas. From his city apartment world, Everett spreads warm wishes and cheer to young readers everywhere." Pub W

Everett Anderson's friend; illus. by Ann Grifalconi. Holt 1976 unp illus lib. bdg. $6.95 (k-3)   811

1 Friendship—Poetry
ISBN 0-03-015161-9   LC 75-32251

"Everett Anderson, a small black boy who is the protagonist of earlier Clifton books, is delighted to see a new family move in across the

hall but disappointed, at first, when he learns that all the children are girls. He thinks Maria is too proficient at playing ball, he thinks three (two male friends and he) are just the right number and he thinks things would be better if Daddy were there. But it's nice to be welcomed when you've lost your apartment key—and Maria's mother distributes tacos and kisses—and Maria proves to be a compatible fourth in Everett Anderson's group of friends." Chicago. Children's Bk Center

"For the first time, a book in the series is not illustrated with woodcuts; instead, brown ink sketches, drawn on rice paper and reproduced on cream-colored stock, capture very well the expressions of the characters and the fluid movements of athletic Maria." Horn Bk

"Clifton's poem has a nice easy swing to it, forced only in a few places, which is unusual for a rhymed story." Booklist

Everett Anderson's nine month long; illus. by Ann Grifalconi. Holt 1978 unp illus $6.95 (k-3)   811

1 Infants—Poetry 2 Brothers and sisters—Poetry
ISBN 0-03-043536-6   LC 78-4202

"Everett Anderson is a very observant young Black boy whose mother has recently remarried. He seems to adjust very well to the idea of having another person in the family. When Everett begins to notice that something special seems to be going on, his mother tells him that a baby is on the way. . . . His questions are answered, and concerns are laid to rest. The story ends with Everett very excited about the new arrival to the family. This book, written in wonderful poetic style with beautiful soft, charcoal and pencil illustrations, projects a warm, loving, understanding and supportive family." Interracial Bks for Children Bul

Everett Anderson's 1 2 3; illus. by Ann Grifalconi. Holt 1977 unp illus $6.95 (k-3)   811

1 Parent and child—Poetry
ISBN 0-03-017441-4   LC 76-25866

This tells, in verse, how a "worried little boy gradually became reconciled to the idea of a new father joining the family." Horn Bk

"The illustrations, strongly drawn with bold, broken lines, are large in scale, almost all pictures of the three characters with only minimal background details. The text is tender, artful in the simplicity and brevity with which it gets to the gist of the matter." Chicago. Children's Bk Center

Everett Anderson's year; illus. by Ann Grifalconi. Holt 1974 unp illus lib. bdg. $4.95 (k-3)   811

1 Seasons—Poetry
ISBN 0-03-012736-X   LC 73-2244

In this book, "the reader is guided through a poetic view of Everett's own distinctive outlook on a year in his life. Everett, a seven year old, lives alone with his working mother in apartment 14A. Each month offers him a different kind of excitement, experience, reminiscence, or apprehension. Despite the activity of the moment, one theme persists—love—that's what it's all about." Rdng Teacher

"The best of these verses will cause smiles of understanding and feelings of camaraderie with the small black boy. Large woodcuts in black and white with alternating orange and light blue accents and backgrounds are traditional and pleasing to the eye." Booklist

De Regniers, Beatrice Schenk

Something special; drawings by Irene Haas. Harcourt 1958 unp illus $5.95 (k-2)   811

ISBN 0-15-277101-8   LC 58-9745

"A collection of [nine] poems in varied styles. Some are rollicking entertainment, such as the cumulative chanting game, 'What Did You Put In Your Pocket?' with the humor of incongruity; others are gently evocative ('If You Find a Little Feather'); and 'If I Were Teeny Tiny' is pure fantasy." Chicago. Children's Bk Center

"This is a delightful book of poems that has caught the spirit of a child's world with humor, sounds, smell, and color. The fine drawings complement the text." Atlantic

Dickinson, Emily

I'm nobody! Who are you? Poems of Emily Dickinson for children; illus. by Rex Schneider; with an introduction by Richard B. Sewall. Stemmer House 1978 84p illus $11.95, pa $5.95 (3-6)   811

ISBN 0-916144-21-6; 0-916144-22-4   LC 78-6828

"A Barbara Holdridge book"
This collection of Emily Dickinson's poetry is illustrated with full color drawings depicting life in nineteenth century New England
Glossary: p81-84

Poems for youth; ed. by Alfred Leete Hampson; foreword by May Lamberton Becker; illus. by George and Doris Hauman. Little 1934 unp illus $5.95 (5 and up)   811

ISBN 0-316-18418-7   LC 34-40845

"Poems written by Emily Dickinson for her young niece and nephews serve as an excellent introduction to the poet. Indexed by first lines." Hodges. Bks for Elem Sch Libraries
"The fact that of the seventy-eight poems in this group many were written for special children does not narrow their appeal. On the contrary, it seems to widen it." Boston Transcript
"The illustrations have a grace and delicacy that is most appropriate." NY Times Bk Rev

Dunbar, Paul Laurence

I greet the dawn; poems of Paul Laurence Dunbar; selected and illus. by Ashley Bryan. Atheneum Pubs. 1978 170p illus $7.95 (6 and up)   811

1 Blacks—Poetry
ISBN 0-689-30613-X   LC 77-21232

"Concentrating principally on Dunbar's standard English poems rather than on his more acclaimed black dialect poetry, Bryan offers a collection of more than 100 pieces in which Dunbar addresses himself to broadly human concerns such as love, death, and the mysteries of life. A sketch of Dunbar's literary career prefaces the selection, which demonstrates the further versatility of a celebrated American poet and provides a complement to anthologies focusing on the writer's folk dialect poems. Title and first-line indexes appended." Booklist

Farber, Norma

How does it feel to be old? Illus. by Trina Schart Hyman. Dutton 1979 unp illus $7.95 (2-4)   811

1 Old age—Poetry
ISBN 0-525-32414-3   LC 79-11516

"A Unicorn book"
"A woman's poetic monologue is couched in drawings that breathe lifelike detail within a telescopic framework of her past and present. Both pictures and poem invite lingering, the one for sight and the other sound. The woman's memories are illustrated in antique brown, her realities, including a happy visit with her granddaughter, in black and white. There is intimate sympathy for her as an individual experiencing what makes an old person different and sometimes lonely—or similar and sometimes close—to anyone younger." Booklist

Small wonders; poems. Woodcuts by Kazue Mizumura. Coward, McCann & Geoghegan 1979 31p illus $6.50 (2-5)   811

ISBN 0-698-20484-0   LC 78-31282

"Norma Farber focuses on small items in nature and on the city street. Using various rhythmic forms, she concentrates on one aspect of each 'wonder,' providing original and intriguing metaphors to define every image. Stars become 'silver keys/to open up the night'; cherries are 'marbles that grow on trees.' Such images have a precision that casts a unique perspective on the item described. Decorative woodcuts unobtrusively complement the poems." Booklist

Field, Eugene

Poems of childhood. Airmont 1970 221p illus pa $1.50   811

ISBN 0-8049-0211-9

"An Airmont classic"
First published 1896 by Scribner
This is a collection of poems both grave and gay, from "Love-songs of childhood" and "With trumpet and drum" which were first published 1894 and 1892 respectively

Field, Rachel

Poems; decorations by the author. Macmillan Pub. Co. 1957 118p illus $3.95 (2-5)   811

ISBN 0-02-735060-6   LC 57-9894

A collection of poems, most of them taken from the author's books, several of which are out of print. A few are reprinted from magazines, and six of the poems are here printed for the first time
"Most of Rachel Field's lilting 'poems' are tiny, about tiny things. . . . Their delicacy is admirably expressed in the agile, silhouetted figures that illustrate them." Christian Sci Monitor
Includes an Index of first lines

Fisher, Aileen

Cricket in a thicket; illus. by Feodor Rojankovsky. Scribner 1963 63p illus lib. bdg. $4.95, pa 95¢ (k-3)   811

1 Nature in poetry
ISBN 0-684-13456-X; 0-684-12784-9   LC 63-14337

"Poems about grasshoppers, and ladybugs, and ducklings, and turtledoves, and other outdoor things that delight the eye of children." Pub W
Short "poems fitted into capricious categories such as six legs and eight, four legs and two, and warm days and cold, make wonderful read-aloud material. Soft charcoal drawings and easy vocabulary. Variations of rhythms and themes stimulate the urge to read the complete volume, and brevity assures it." Chicago Sch J
Includes an index of titles

Do bears have mothers, too? [Illus. by] Eric Carle. Crowell 1973 unp illus lib. bdg. $8.29 (k-2)   811

1 Animals—Poetry
ISBN 0-690-00167-3   LC 73-4721

This collection of short poems describes "mother-and-child life among the animals. Features are a white swan and her cygnets, a bear and cubs, a deer and her fawn, alligator mom and [babies] along with several others." Pub W
"Eric Carle's distinctive and ebullient collages dominate this poetry book about 12 animal mothers and their young. . . . Although the verses are competent, they are not as spontaneous as many of Fisher's other poems. Used as a lap book, however, this would be good for sharing with a small group of children." Sch Library J

In one door and out the other; a book of poems; illus. by Lillian Hoban. Crowell 1969 65p illus $7.89 (1-3)   811

ISBN 0-690-43555-X   LC 70-81949

A selection of poetry which embraces the adventures, joys and frustrations of childhood as it touches upon such subjects as father, mother, playmates, pets, and the wonders of nature
"The poems are aptly illustrated with a profusion of small black-and-white drawings, which young readers will identify with and delight in." Sch Library J

My cat has eyes of sapphire blue; pictures by Marie Angel. Crowell 1973 24p illus $7.95, lib. bdg. $7.49 (2-4)   811

1 Cats—Poetry
ISBN 0-690-56637-9; 0-690-56638-7   LC 72-13925

Twenty-four short poems describe "the multi-faceted nature of cats and their activities." Booklist
"A pair of cat-lovers—a poet-naturalist and a nature painter—have combined their talents to create a tour de force that cannot fail to surprise and delight other feline fanciers. . . . The exquisitely meticulous cat portraits—which so easily could have strayed into sentimentality—are totally representational, yet strikingly expressive." Horn Bk

Fox, Siv Cedering

The blue horse, and other night poems; pictures by Donald Carrick. Seabury [distributed by Houghton] 1979 30p illus $8.95 (k-3)   811

1 Sleep—Poetry 2 Dreams—Poetry
ISBN 0-395-28952-1   LC 78-12793
"A Clarion book"

"The poems begin with "In the evening/I pull the shade/of my eyes/to see/what the night/will show me.' The others express what the child experiences in the dark: vagrant thoughts, memories, visions, sometimes fears crowding in as she drifts into sleep. The last entry is, appropriately, a hymn to morning." Pub W

"New poetry is welcome, especially when it contains evocative images which speak directly to the child and which are accompanied by illuminating but not overpowering drawings. Donald Carrick's spacious pictures convey the wondrous and sometimes terrifying concepts of the imagistic phrases. . . . The poems convey a quiet, dreamlike atmosphere of nighttime." Horn Bk

Frost, Robert

Stopping by woods on a snowy evening; illus. by Susan Jeffers. Dutton 1978 unp illus $7.95 (k-3)   811

1 Winter—Poetry
ISBN 0-525-40115-6   LC 78-8134

"The well-known lines of Frost's poem inspire Jeffers to a dreamily benign winter landscape: clean, soft, and shining from the heavily fallen snow and radiating an almost palpable serenity. In the heart of this pristine world moves Frost's narrator, realized here as a jovial, rotund old man, who pauses to savor deeply the special mood of the woods and to leave behind a jumble of seed and twiggy shelter for invisibly hovering wild creatures. . . . Scenes are fully and carefully built, with each essentially black-and-white spread allotted a quiet infusion of color. . . . The visual interpretation preserves—even strengthens—the poem's underlying wonder; the only dispute is with the sweetening of some of the animals, the horse in particular." Booklist

"Because Mr. Frost's famous poem is open to many interpretations, this version, which hints so of Santa traveling through magnificent woods, could start wondrous conversations." Babbling Bookworm

You come too; favorite poems for young readers; with wood engravings by Thomas W. Nason. Holt 1959 94p illus lib. bdg. $5.95 (5 and up)   811

ISBN 0-03-089530-8   LC 59-12940

This volume features "Frost's own selection of his poems to be read to and by young people." Hodges. Bks for Elem Sch Libraries

Frost's "simplicity, wisdom, and humanity, as well as his craftsmanship, come clear in some half-hundred poems, among them 'Mending Wall,' 'The Death of the Hired Man,' and 'Tree at My Window.' The foreword by Hyde Cox, one of Frost's younger friends, introduces the ageless poet and his poetry with sensitive skill. Format is distinctive, and Thomas W. Nason's wood engravings will surely sharpen reader's pleasure and perception." Library J

Index to titles: p93-94

Gardner, John

A child's bestiary; with additional poems by Lucy Gardner & Eugene Rudzewicz, & drawings by Lucy, Joel, Joan & John Gardner. Knopf 1977 69p illus $4.95, lib. bdg. $5.99 (4-6)   811

1 Animals—Poetry
ISBN 0-394-83483-6; 0-394-93483-0   LC 77-3945

"In the tradition of Hilaire Belloc and Ogden Nash, the author has written sixty poems about animals, from the African Wild Dog to, predictably, the Zebra. Included in the book, rather peculiarly, is a brief article about the hognosed snake, originally published in 1947. Humorous and wryly sophisticated, the poems celebrate the Creation—with frequent reference to the inventive capabilities of the Father and the Son—and make many sly digs at the folly of man. The poems are sometimes pithy: 'Never grab a Crab'; sometimes funny: 'The Tiger is a perfect saint/As long as you respect

him;/But if he happens to say 'ain't.'/You'd better not correct him'; and sometimes pointed: 'It's a Man's tender care that makes Turkeys thrive;/If we'd eaten the dodo he'd still be alive.' The line drawings, done by both adults and children —vary from simple but pleasing to amusing and skillful." Horn Bk

Giovanni, Nikki

Spin a soft black song; poems for children; illus. by Charles Bible. Hill & Wang 1971 unp illus $7.95 (k-3)   811

1 Blacks—Poetry
ISBN 0-8090-8795-2   LC 76-163572

"A beautifully illustrated book of poems about black children for children of all ages. . . . Simple in theme but a very moving collection nonetheless." Rdng Ladders. 5th edition

Greenfield, Eloise

Honey, I love, and other love poems; pictures by Diane and Leo Dillon. Crowell 1978 unp illus $5.95, lib. bdg. $6.49 (2-4)   811

1 Blacks—Poetry 2 Love poetry
ISBN 0-690-01334-5; 0-690-03845-3   LC 77-2845

"These 16 poems explore facets of warm, loving relationships as experienced by a young Black girl. Central to the theme of the book is the idea that the child loves herself and is very confident in expressing that love." Interracial Bks for Children Bul

"From the cover on, [this book] reaches out and pulls you in to a warm place. The poems . . . show you that you don't have to go on forever to say a lot. [Greenfield] writes this about a child's view on an elderly aunt: 'What do people think about/When they sit and dream/All wrapped up in quiet/and old sweaters.' The illustrations . . . are a fine combination of sophisticated realistic drawings superimposed over happy little pictures that look childrawn." NY Times Bk Rev

Grimes, Nikki

Something on my mind; [illus. by] Tom Feelings; words by Nikki Grimes. Dial Press 1978 32p illus $7.50, lib. bdg. $7.28   811

1 Blacks—Poetry
ISBN 0-8037-8229-2; 0-8037-8225-X   LC 77-86266

"The black and white drawings of black children by Feelings were used by Grimes as bases for prose poems that interpret the pictures. The drawings are sensitive portraits, some beautifully shaded and soft, others looking like deft, unfinished sketches. The poems vary in depth and treatment, some fragmentary and others imbued with poignant emotion; all are serious, some reflecting the black experience and others—most of the selections —capturing universal longings or reactions of childhood." Chicago. Children's Bk Center

Hoban, Russell

Egg thoughts, and other Frances songs; pictures by Lillian Hoban. Harper 1972 31p illus $6.95, lib. bdg. $6.89 (k-2)   811

ISBN 0-06-022331-6; 0-06-022332-4   LC 70-183162

In this collection of poems, Frances the badger focuses "on eggs cooked in various ways, a well-worn favorite doll, string, homework, little sister Gloria, and other joys and tribulations of childhood. All of the verses are new except for 'Soft boiled' which is taken from 'Bread and jam for Frances' [entered in class E]." Booklist

"'Frances' thoughts and observations though not always fluidly expressed, are childlike and unselfconsciously amusing, and the verse is complemented by illustrations that are equally down-to-earth and appealing." Sch Library J

Hoberman, Mary Ann

Nuts to you & nuts to me; an alphabet of poems; illus. by Ronni Solbert. Knopf 1974 unp illus lib. bdg. $5.99 (k-2)   811

1 Alphabet
ISBN 0-394-92742-7   LC 74-734

This book contains a brief rhyme for each letter of the alphabet about such things as ants, balloons, cookies, and ducks

"A blend of lilting rhythms, unforced rhymes, and freshly conceived, child-like imagery cast in a variety of poetic forms. Some of the poems are tongue twisters . . . others are just plain nonsense . . . while still others offer an unexpected yet wondrously logical twist. . . . [The book is] ingenious, unpretentious, and appealing." Horn Bk

Hughes, Langston

Don't you turn back; poems. Selected by Lee Bennett Hopkins; woodcuts by Ann Grifalconi. Knopf [1970 c1969] 78p illus lib. bdg. $5.69 (5 and up)   811

1 Blacks—Poetry
ISBN 0-394-90846-5   LC 78-82549

This selection of Langston Hughes' poetry is divided into four parts: My people, Prayers and dreams, Out to sea, and I am a Negro. The 45 poems "celebrate the dreams and sorrows, the joys and aspirations of his people, prideful of being Black." Best Sellers

"Dramatic woodcuts and dignified format help make this a tribute to a fine poet." Sat Rev

Includes an index of titles and an Index of first lines

The dream keeper, and other poems; with illus. by Helen Sewell. Knopf 1932 77p illus lib. bdg. $5.69 (5 and up)   811

1 Blacks—Poetry
ISBN 0-394-91096-6   LC 32-19486

This volume contains "the author's own selection of his poems, including lyrics, songs, and several typical Negro blues." Hodges. Bks for Elem Sch Libraries

Ichikawa, Satomi

A child's book of seasons. Parents Mag. Press [distributed by Four Winds 1976 c1975] unp illus $5.95, lib. bdg. $5.41 (k-3)   811

1 Seasons—Poetry
ISBN 0-8193-0795-5; 0-8193-0796-3   LC 74-31047

Illustrated by the author

"Full-color, full-page paintings and simple verses offer young readers a glimpse at many facets of the ever-changing seasons. The rhymed couplets on each page are secondary to the illustrations, particularly the outdoor scenes." Adventuring with Bks

Jordan, June

Who look at me; illus. with twenty-seven paintings. Crowell 1969 97p illus $9.95 (6 and up)   811

1 Blacks—Poetry 2 Blacks in literature and art
3 Painting, American
ISBN 0-690-88854-6   LC 69-13641

"Twenty seven paintings of black people are accompanied by poems . . . that speak, on the whole, with piercing clarity of the pathos, beauty, pride, and anger in Negro lives. The format is dignified, and notes on the artists (some of whose work is reproduced in full color) are appended. The author, young and black, has interpreted some of the paintings rather narrowly so that the poems cannot quite stand alone, but these are in the minority." Chicago. Children's Bk Center

Among the prominent American artists, both Black and white, whose paintings are represented are: Charles Alston, Thomas Eakins, Romare Bearden, John Wilson, Ben Shahn, and Andrew Wyeth

Kennedy, X. J.

The phantom ice cream man; more nonsense verse; illus by David McPhail. Atheneum Pubs. 1979 56p illus $6.95 (3-6)   811

1 Nonsense verses
ISBN 0-689-50132-3   LC 78-23681

"A Margaret K. McElderry book"

In this "collection of imaginary beasts and far out situations (plus seven limericks), [the author] interests kids in tyrannosaurus rex's teeth, the Nineteenth-Moon-of-Neptune Beasts who devour human rockets like eggs with funny bugs inside, and a vampire bat that attacks the umpire for his call." Sch Library J

"Recalling the dexterous rhythms and unexpected rhymes of such masters of nonsense as Lear and Carroll, the poet has successfully blended contemporary references with traditional verse forms to produce a fresh, original celebration of absurdity. . . . Yet frequently, as in the best of humorous writing, the light-hearted tone coexists with a more serious note, as demonstrated by the wolf who chooses not to devour the human questioner because he's 'into natural foods/That nothing has been done to.' . . . The decorative drawings show skillful juxtapositions of fantasy and reality." Horn Bk

Krauss, Ruth

Somebody spilled the sky; illus. by Eleanor Hazard. Greenwillow Bks. 1979 32p illus $6.95, lib. bdg. $6.67 (k-3)   811

ISBN 0-688-80186-2; 0-688-84186-4   LC 78-14306

Children "are bound to read and reread [the author's] opus, a must-have like 'A Hole Is to Dig,' 'The Carrot Seed' et al. Abetting her unparalleled amphigories are Hazard's crazy drawings in blue and white, pictures that the poet's lines sometimes swirl around, chase or embrace. What makes Krauss's inventions irresistible is her genius for echoing the daft but unassailable logic of children." Pub W

Kuskin, Karla

Any me I want to be; poems. Harper 1972 unp illus lib. bdg. $8.79 (1-4)   811

ISBN 0-06-023616-7   LC 77-105485

Illustrated by the author

These thirty poems "do not describe; instead, the poet has tried—and, with refreshing, edged but gentle humor and not an ounce of condescension, succeeded—'to get inside each subject and briefly be it.' . . . The subjects—and moods and pacing, too—range from a mirror to the moon. . . . There is more than a touch of A. A. Milne here, and a bit of Edward Lear, and a bit of Ogden Nash. But mostly it is Karla, Kuskin, who, as any you might like to be, is fun, funny, and therefore wise." Sat Rev

Near the window tree; poems and notes. Harper 1975 63p illus lib. bdg. $8.79 (2-5)   811

ISBN 0-06-023540-3   LC 74-20394

"An Ursula Nordstrom book"

In the notes preceding each of her thirty-two verses, Mrs. Kuskin describes how she "felt when she was making her poems. . . . [Some of her poems focus on] words like bug, moustache, worm, cat, and family." Christian Sci Monitor

"Not only can one enjoy the poetry, but the [author's] drawings and the accompanying notes give a sense of conversing with the author and understanding what goes on before, during, and after a poem. This combination is very useful to a classroom teacher who is interested in stirring children to write." Rdng Teacher

Lawrence, Jacob

Harriet and the promised land. Windmill/Simon & Schuster 1968 unp illus lib. bdg. $6.73 (2-5)   811

1 Tubman, Harriet (Ross)—Poetry 2 Underground railroad—Poetry
ISBN 0-671-65027-0   LC 68-25752

Illustrated by the author

"Simple rhymes tell the story of Harriet Tubman, the slave who led many of her people North to freedom." Adventuring With Bks. 2d edition

"The strength of this volume is in the forceful, stylized paintings by the famous black artist, which capture the degradation of slavery." Brooklyn Art Bks for Children

Lee, Dennis

Alligator pie; the poems were written by Dennis Lee; the pictures were drawn by Frank Newfeld. Houghton 1975 [c1974] 64p illus $6.95 (k-3)   811

1 Nonsense verses
ISBN 0-395-21596-X   LC 75-332788

First published 1974 in Canada

Contains "nonsensical narrative poems, rhymes for games, humorous and rhythmic four-liners, tongue-twisters, and verses based on Peter Rabbit and Winnie-the-Pooh. Jingly, sunny, silly poems." Chicago. Children's Bk Center

A slender volume which "introduces American children to a fresh, new voice from Canada. Percussive rhythms, an acrobatic use of language, and a fine variety of form, meter, and subject matter distinguish the verses. . . . Although the overall design of the colorful book is original and attractive, the humor in the exaggerated, somewhat mannered pictures is not nearly as spontanous as that in the verses." Horn Bk

Lee, Dennis—*Continued*

Garbage delight; the poems were written by Dennis Lee; the pictures were drawn by Frank Newfeld. Houghton [1978 c1977] 64p illus $6.95 (3-6)   811

1 Nonsense verses
ISBN 0-395-27201-7   LC 78-14836

This is an illustrated collection of more than fifty humorous poems

"Junk food is the subject of 'Garbage Delight,' an assortment about to be gobbled up by an avid monster. This is a bouncy, wild piece of foolishness like many of the other entries. Some are gentler adventures, such as 'The Operation' where a rueful child waits for mom to mend the teddy bear he has mangled. What readers will probably fancy most in a splendid book is Lee's prod to the imagination, 'The Big Molice Pan and the Bertie Dumb,' word twisters that could lead to contests by kids trying to decipher their meaning." Pub W

Livingston, Myra Cohn

A lollygag of limericks; with drawings by Joseph Low. Atheneum Pubs. 1978 44p illus $6.95 (5 and up)   811

1 Limericks
ISBN 0-689-50104-8   LC 77-18060

"A Margaret K. McElderry book"

"Livingston's limericks people sonorous English locales with 32 ridiculous adult and animal figures and their paraphernalia, caricatured in Low's droll line scratchings. There are none you'd care to meet in the flesh; they're an arrogant, crusty, greedy, lazy bunch of complaining snobs and fools. Meter and rhyme fit with gymnastic grace and tongue-twisters stay within defined bounds. . . . This gallery of misfits—week-old babies who make erudite speeches, hens who try to lay half an egg by standing on one leg—is amusing." Sch Library J

The Malibu, and other poems; illus. by James J. Spanfeller. Atheneum Pubs. 1972 44p illus $4.25 (4 and up)   811

ISBN 0-689-30308-4   LC 72-190557

"A Margaret K. McElderry book"

"Most of the [40] poems are observations on everyday life, nature, pollution, peace, people, animals, books. The young person's viewpoint is well maintained throughout." Sch Library J

The author "writes with a free-flowing rhythm and an effect of spontaneity. Themes and mood vary, some of the selections light and humorous, others throughtful. . . . Many of the poems reflect the child's view of self. Although this book is recommended for a particular reading-level span, there are no boundaries for good poetry—adults may enjoy this, and it can be read aloud to younger children." Chicago. Children's Bk Center

O sliver of liver; together with other triolets, cinquains, haiku, verses and a dash of poems; drawings by Iris Van Rynbach. Atheneum Pubs. 1979 42p illus $7.95 (3 and up)   811

ISBN 0-689-50133-1   LC 78-21190

"A Margaret K. McElderry book"

"Over 40 poems in this slim anthology speak simply and feelingly about a variety of things: T-shirts, liver, lunch and umbrellas, seasons and holidays, triolets, haiku, cinquains, and concrete. The moods vary from funny to sad. Fine black-and-white drawings decorate the text. The poetry is pleasing if not great, and in its deceptive easiness, will stretch young imaginations to see with more perception and read with more pleasure." Sch Library J

Longfellow, Henry Wadsworth

The children's own Longfellow. Houghton 1920 103p illus $7.95 (5 and up)   811

ISBN 0-395-06889-4

First published 1908

Includes 8 colored illustrations by various artists

Contents: The wreck of the Hesperus; The village blacksmith; Evangeline [selection]; The song of Hiawatha [selection]; The building of the ship; The castle-builder; Paul Revere's ride; The building of the Long Serpent

McCord, David

All day long; fifty rhymes of the never was and always is; drawings by Henry B. Kane. Little 1966 104p illus $6.95 (4-6)   811

ISBN 0-316-55508-8   LC 66-17688

Poems about the haunting delights, surprises and wit of childhood

"The topics are simple but intriguing, the writing has rhythm, humor, and imaginative zest; the black and white illustrations are attractive, many of them also humorous." Chicago. Children's Bk Center

Away and ago; rhymes of the never was and always is; illus. by Leslie Morrill. Little 1975 96p illus $5.95 (4-6)   811

ISBN 0-316-55513-4

"Fun with words, language, and drawings in a small, but well-filled book of over fifty poems by [the author], who has always brought together enjoyment and poetry for children. Includes poetry for certain holidays and occasions, but this book will be off the shelf all around the year." Adventuring with Bks

Every time I climb a tree; illus. by Marc Simont. Little 1967 unp illus lib. bdg. $8.95 (1-3)   811

ISBN 0-316-55514-2   LC 67-25611

Twenty-five poems selected from the author's collections: Far and few, Take sky and All day long, all entered separately

"All the Simont drawings coincide happily with the McCord mentality: sassy, inventive, fresh." Bk World

Far and few; rhymes of the never was and always is; drawings by Henry B. Kane. Little 1952 99p illus $6.95   811

ISBN 0-316-55502-9   LC 52-8336

These sixty poems show the author's "skill as a poet and his understanding of youngsters' moods and interest. The moods range from pure nonsense to quiet reflection. The lilt of the verses is varied and musical. . . . This book is one of the choicest additions to the children's poetry shelf in many years." Children's Bks Too Good to Miss

For me to say; rhymes of the never was and always is; drawings by Henry B. Kane. Little 1970 100p illus $5.95 (4-6)   811

ISBN 0-316-55511-8   LC 76-122534

A "collection that is with few exceptions, light in topic and tone, with breezy humor and relish of word play, and with small, neat illustrations that often implement the poems. Some of the selections are, indeed, word games as well as poetry. . . . The author shows, in a final section . . . [how to write] verse forms. Included here are the ballade, the tercet, the villanelle, the clerihew, the cinquain and haiku." Sutherland. The Best in Children's Bks

One at a time; his collected poems for the young; with full subject index as well as an index of first lines. With illustrations by Henry B. Kane. Little [1977] 494p illus $10.95 (4-6)   811

ISBN 0-316-55516-9   LC 77-21792

This book "is a collection of the poems previously published in 'Far and Few,'—'Take Sky,' 'All Day Long,' 'For Me to Say' and 'Away and Ago' [all entered separately]. . . . This one-volume edition, with a short introduction by the poet . . . is likely to be most useful to teachers and school resource persons: children's collections that already hold the five individual titles should find those sufficient for use by young readers." Sch Library J

The star in the pail; illus. by Marc Simont. Little 1975 unp illus lib. bdg. $6.95 (k-3)   811

ISBN 0-316-55515-0   LC 75-15605

"A selection of poems for younger children comprises some chosen from earlier volumes of McCord poetry and some that have been previously published in magazines or newspapers." Chicago. Children's Bk Center

McCord, David—*Continued*

"From the simplest of objects—a pail, a clock, an animal cracker—and from the commonest of creatures—a starfish, a daddy longlegs, a dog—the poet, as always, extracts wit and imagery, yoking the simplest of words to shapely rhymes and verses. . . . Always ingenious, but never marred by sophistication, the transparent verses have been stripped down to essentials to show and accept things as they are and—at the same time—to show the poet as he is: 'Of all the stars in heaven there was one to spare,/And he silvered in the water and I left him there.' The watercolor paintings form visual epigrams in which composition and space catch the essence of each poem." Horn Bk

Take sky; more rhymes of the never was and always is; drawings by Henry B. Kane. Little 1962 107p illus $6.95 (4-6)   811

ISBN 0-316-55509-6   LC 62-12392

A collection of forty-eight humorous poems on various subjects ranging in form from short verses to longer narrative poetry
"Diversity of imagination and humor makes a volume that bears dipping into again and again for quiet enjoyment and for reading aloud. Henry Kane's pencil drawings make beautiful pages, with great variety in layout." Horn Bk
"Adult help may be needed for understanding the verse-lessons part 'by Professor Swigley Brown' about couplet, triolet, quatrain, and limerick." Sch Library J

McGinley, Phyllis

A wreath of Christmas legends; illus. by Leonard Weisgard. Macmillan Pub. Co. 1967 62p illus $5.95, pa 95¢ (5 and up)   811

1 Christmas—Poetry 2 Jesus Christ—Nativity—Poetry
ISBN 0-02-765410-9; 0-02-044450-8   LC 67-19676
A collection of 15 poems based on medieval legends of the first Christmas
"The black and white illustrations of birds and beasts have a precise grace, and the page layout is dignified. The poems have the felicitous phrasing, the polished simplicity, and the quick shafts of humor that distinguish Miss McGinley's work." Chicago. Children's Bk Center

The year without a Santa Claus; pictures by Kurt Werth. Lippincott 1947 unp illus $8.95 (k-3)   811

1 Christmas—Poetry
ISBN 0-397-30399-8   LC 57-10332

The author's verse and "the illustrator's agreeable pictures give new life to an old theme. When Santa Claus announces that he is much too tired for Christmas capers and is going to take his first vacation, the weeping children of the world . . . decide to give Santa a Merry Christmas. What happens when Santa receives his gifts climaxes a story-poem which will be enjoyed by the whole family." Booklist

Merriam, Eve

It doesn't always have to rhyme; drawings by Malcolm Spooner. Atheneum Pubs. 1964 83p illus lib. bdg. $5.95 (4 and up)   811

ISBN 0-689-20671-2   LC 64-11893

Here is a collection of over 50 humorous poems on a variety of subjects including vocabulary and "the very fun of poetry and its infinite possibilities." Horn Bk

Rainbow writing. Atheneum Pubs. 1976 51p $6.95 (4 and up)   811

ISBN 0-689-30527-3   LC 76-4468

This is a collection of poems exploring words, poetics, emotions and contemporary life
"In her latest poetry collection Merriam once again demonstrates her ability to capture vivid images and moods with an economy of words. . . . Containing both simple and complex poems, this collection offers something for everyone and can be used successfully in poetry workshops." Sch Library J

There is no rhyme for silver; drawings by Joseph Schindelman. Atheneum Pubs. 1962 70p illus lib. bdg. $3.07 (2-5)   811

ISBN 0-689-20272-5   LC 62-10254

A mostly humorous collection of poems for children dealing with such things as kittens, space, flying, asking questions, wishing, summer rain, the Optileast and the Pessimost (imaginery beasts), and exploring
"Joseph Schindelman's drawings are good complements to the poetry." Bookmark

Millay, Edna St Vincent

Edna St Vincent Millay's Poems selected for young people; woodcuts by Ronald Keller. Harper 1979 115p illus $8.95, lib. bdg. $8.79 (4 and up)   811

ISBN 0-06-024218-3; 0-06-024219-1   LC 77-25671
First published 1929
"The beauty of this book lies not in its format (which is ordinary, save for the charmingly innocent woodcuts by Ronald Keller), nor in its novelty (all of the poems have been published before), but in the fine, enduring quality of the poet's verse. There are short, simple rhymes about flowers and trees and burdocks stuck in socks to captivate the youngest readers, as well as longer, symbolic pieces for the more seasoned audience. This is a book one can treasure as a child, then revisit without disappointment as an adult. Many poetry books for young people insist on presenting only poems which deal with description, or bright, happy emotions. This excludes fully half of what poetry is all about. In contrast, the reader of 'Poems' will also find pieces dealing gently with poverty, disappointment, and the death of loved ones." Best Sellers

Mizumura, Kazue

Flower, moon, snow; a book of haiku; illus. with woodcuts by the author. Crowell 1977 unp illus $7.95, lib. bdg. $7.89 (2-4)   811

1 Nature in poetry 2 Haiku
ISBN 0-690-01291-8; 0-690-01290-X   LC 76-41180
Thirty brief poems about nature in the Japanese haiku style
"Exhibiting the sensitivity to nature which is apparent in her earlier works, the author has created a book which is at once more sophisticated and more naive. Strikingly simple woodcut illustrations in brown, black, and gray blend harmoniously with the text and reflect the themes of the title. . . . Although the traditional haiku form is not strictly adhered to, the spirit of the art is present throughout." Horn Bk
"A short introduction, explaining the technique of haiku writing and some of the differences between Japanese and English poetry, is suitable for classroom use." Sch Library J

If I were a cricket. . . . Crowell 1973 unp illus $7.95, lib. bdg. $7.89 (k-2)   811

1 Love poetry 2 Animals—Poetry
ISBN 0-690-00075-8; 0-690-00076-6   LC 73-3495
"Small creatures such as a spider, firefly, snail, etc. are used to pronounce tender messages of love. . . . The appealing word images and mosaic-like drawings—pastels alternating with spreads done in black, white, and gray—; will provide many opportunities for sharing warm feelings with very young children." Sch Library J

Moore, Clement C.

The night before Christmas (k-3)   811

1 Christmas—Poetry
Some editions are:
Grosset $4.95 Illustrated by Leonard Weisgard (ISBN 0-448-02935-9; LC 49-11041)
Houghton $6.95 With pictures by Jessie Wilcox Smith. Has title: 'Twas the night before Christmas (ISBN 0-395-06952-1; LC 12-28683)
Lippincott $5.95 Illustrated by Arthur Rackham (ISBN 0-397-30276-2; LC 54-12759)
McGraw $5.95 Paul Galdone drew the pictures. Has title: A visit from St Nicholas (ISBN 0-07-042900-6; LC 68-24348)
Rand McNally $6.95, lib. bdg. $4.97 Illustrated by Tasha Tudor (ISBN 0-528-82181-4; 0-528-80144-9; LC 75-8858)

First published 1823
This popular Christmas poem has been a favorite with American children ever since the author wrote it for his children in 1822. It is from this poem that we get the names for the Christmas reindeer

Moore, Lilian

Little raccoon and poems from the woods; drawings by Gioia Fiammenghi. McGraw 1975 40p illus $5.95, lib. bdg. $6.95 (k-3) **811**
1 Nature in poetry
ISBN 0-07-042913-8; 0-07-042914-6   LC 75-14303

"Little raccoon wanders through the woods and in poetic verse sees, feels, and hears 'Big burly bumblebee buzzing through the grass,' 'Spider's spinning her silver lace,' and 'dry leaves, talking in hoarse whispers.' Moore captures the voices and silences of the forest, the comings and goings of the animals, the feelings and moods of the woodland in her short, simple poems. . . . Drawings in shades of green, brown, blue, and gold match the naturalistic scenes." Booklist

See my lovely poison ivy, and other verses about witches, ghosts and things; pictures by Diane Dawson. Atheneum Pubs. 1975 40p illus $7.95 (1-4)   **811**
1 Halloween—Poetry
ISBN 0-689-30468-4   LC 75-8581

"A ghostly celebration of Halloween in light verse. Poems about ghouls who might wear ghoul-oshes, skeletons afraid of bone-loving dogs, witches shopping in the supermarket for preserved worms, a monster with an aching fang, and a lost and hungry dragon will make amusing and sprightly additions to the Halloween story hour." Horn Bk

"There is no great depth to the poetry, but some of the poems are quite amusing. This will help to fill the requests for Halloween material. The black and white drawings humorously compliment the poetry." Children's Bk Rev Serv

Morrison, Bill

Squeeze a sneeze. Houghton 1977 32p illus lib. bdg. $6.95 (k-3)   **811**
1 Nonsense verses
ISBN 0-395-25151-6   LC 76-62503
Illustrated by the author

The author "uses nonsense rhyming to teach creative word association as well as word enjoyment. Readers are invited to follow the author's examples of word play such as 'share a pear with a hungry bear' or 'make sure it's dark if you bark at a shark.'" Sch Library J

"The rhymes are nonsensical, but the illustrations make the word plays work. Young children will delight in hearing, repeating, and seeing this book. It is a book that a child would return to, time and time again." Children's Bk Rev Serv

Morrison, Lillian

The sidewalk racer, and other poems of sports and motion. Lothrop 1977 62p illus $7.25, lib. bdg. $6.96 (5 and up)   **811**
1 Sports—Poetry
ISBN 0-688-41805-8; 0-688-51805-2   LC 77-907

"This is a collection of poems about one of childhood's favorite pastimes. There are poems representing most of the popular sports: football, boxing, track, jumprope and baseball. Some of the thirty-eight poems are accompanied by fuzzy black-and-white photographs that convey a feeling of motion." Children's Bk Rev Serv

"The poems are written from the viewpoint of the participant or of the spectator; all are crisp, sharp, brief impressions of a memory, a mood, or a high moment, and most of the poems have a fluidity that are admirably suited to their subjects." Chicago. Children's Bk Center

Who would marry a mineral? Riddles, runes, and love tunes; decorations and renderings by Rita Flodén Leydon. Lothrop 1978 61p illus $6.95, lib. bdg. $6.67 (5 and up)   **811**
ISBN 0-688-41846-5; 0-688-51846-X   LC 78-2494

"Best known as the popular compiler of funny, tender, and gently insulting autograph verse, Morrison collects her own playful poems here with a bravado that will appeal to young [preteens and] teens. Love tunes and charms are interspersed with riddles and slender concrete poems. She offers lines to say aloud, fresh images and unforced rhymes. . . . A spare type-face and the delicate lilt of Leydon's line drawings keep the mood of light romance." Sch Library J

Nash, Ogden

The cruise of the Aardvark; pictures by Wendy Watson. Evans, M.&Co. 1967 unp illus $3.95 (3-5)   **811**
1 Aardvark—Poetry 2 Animals—Poetry 3 Noah's Ark—Poetry
ISBN 0-87131-019-8   LC 67-27296

Aardvark, thoroughly disgruntled when the weather turned rainy, decided to go on a cruise. His fellow passengers were travelling two by two, and Noah was the captain of the ship. This story in verse recounts the events of this remarkable voyage

"The inventive verse and humorous drawings of this sprightly tale will please young and old alike. . . . The aardvark of this story is an impertinent snob, a gourmet (ants preferred), and a horrendous portrait painter." Sch Library J

O'Neill, Mary

Hailstones and halibut bones; adventures in color; illus. by Leonard Weisgard. Doubleday 1961 59p illus $5.95, lib. bdg. $6.90, pa $1.95 (k-4)   **811**
1 Color—Poetry
ISBN 0-385-07911-7; 0-385-07912-5; 0-385-05374-6
LC 60-7138

"Stimulating to the imagination and pleasing to the eye is this unusual introduction to color. Twelve simple poems relate thoughts, moods, and images to the colors of the spectrum." Chicago

"The book will be useful to those teaching little children to identify colors." Pub W

Orgel, Doris

Merry merry FIBruary; illus. by Arnold Lobel. Parents Mag. Press [distributed by Four Winds] 1977 unp illus $6.25, lib. bdg. $5.71 (k-3)   **811**
1 Nonsense verses
ISBN 0-8193-0900-1; 0-8193-0901-X   LC 77-650

"The traditional calendar is augmented by an entirely original extra month—FIBruary. After a rhymed introduction twenty-eight verses are arranged in four weekly groups, each one separated by a calendar page which pictorially sums up the madcap proceedings of the previous seven days. The buffoonery is undeniably childlike: 'Every FIBruary Zoo Day,/All the animals must wear/ Shoes and socks and pants and dresses— You and me, though, we go bare.' Other quatrains deal with such incongruities as a centipede with only ninety-nine galoshes, a leopard with flowery spots, and an agile nonagenarian who turns cartwheels on his window sill. Soft-hued watercolor illustrations expand the preposterous nonsense in every verse." Horn Bk

A **Peaceable** kingdom; the Shaker abecedarius; illus. by Alice and Martin Provensen; afterword by Richard Meran Barsam. Viking 1978 unp illus $8.95 (k-3)   **811**
1 Alphabet 2 Animals—Poetry
ISBN 0-670-54500-7   LC 78-125
Published in Shaker Manifesto of July, 1882 under title: Animal rhymes

"Combining familiar home and barnyard creatures with those found only in whimsy, the Shakers taught their children the alphabet through this 26-line rhymed verse, which uses a successive letter at the beginning of each line." Booklist

"The artists . . . made the 'abecedarius' into a rather handsome, authentic-looking picture book printed on carefully antiqued paper. Done in muted color, the illustrations are full of straight-faced humor; too skillfully composed and executed to look quite like primitives, they display, nevertheless, a winsome naiveté. Printed beneath the horizontal pictures, the words are separated by beckoning commas, thus drawing the eye from left to right and on to the turning of the page." Horn Bk

Prelutsky, Jack

Circus; pictures by Arnold Lobel. Macmillan Pub. Co. 1974 unp illus $5.95, pa $2.50 (k-3)   **811**
1 Circus—Poetry
ISBN 0-02-775060-4; 0-02-044760-4   LC 73-6055

Prelutsky "presents the attractions of the big top in verses and they are made visible in Lobel's witty color pictures. . . . For children who haven't experienced the thrills of the greatest show on earth,

Prelutsky, Jack—*Continued*

this book tells about the performing seals, the acrobats, sword-swallowers, fire eaters, human cannonballs and more." Pub W

"Best for reading aloud, the alliterative poems which move in a fast, bouncing rhythm require a nimble-tongued storyteller. Although the book may be overly long to hold the attention of youngest listeners, Lobel's detailed, full-color drawings add humor and interest to this ode to the big top." Sch Library J

It's Halloween; pictures by Marylin Hafner. Greenwillow Bks. 1977 56p illus $5.95, lib. bdg. $5.71 (1-3)   811

1 Halloween—Poetry
ISBN 0-688-80102-1; 0-688-84102-3   LC 77-2141

"Greenwillow Read-alone"
"A gathering of thirteen light-hearted verses celebrates for beginning readers the deliciously frightening aspects of Halloween. Although a few seem constrained by the format, the majority demonstrate the inventive use of words and agile rhythms characteristic of the poet's style. . . . The illustrations, most of them in four colors, highlight the contrast between the real and the imagined, thus providing an appropriate visual extension for the simple text." Horn Bk

Nightmares; poems to trouble your sleep; illus. by Arnold Lobel. Greenwillow Bks. 1976 38p illus $7.95, lib. bdg. $7.63 (2-5)   811

1 Monsters—Poetry
ISBN 0-688-80053-X; 0-688-84053-1   LC 76-4820

"Deliciously awful, a collection of poems [that] is calculated to evoke icy apprehension, and the poems about wizards, bogeymen, ghouls, ogres (well, one poem apiece to each or to others of their ilk) are exaggerated just enough to bring simultaneous grins and shudders. Prelutsky uses words with relish and his rhyme and rhythm are, as usual, deft." Chicago. Children's Bk Center

"The magnificent black-and-white illustrations which depict the monsters and the horrors are rich in cross-hatching and in chiaroscuro effects; and consistent with the poet's intention, the artist —for the purpose of dramatic contrast—occasionally introduces into some of his pictures the miniature figures of naïvely unsuspecting children." Horn Bk

The Queen of Eene; poems. Pictures by Victoria Chess. Greenwillow Bks. 1978 32p illus $7.50, lib. bdg. $7.20 (k-3)   811

1 Nonsense verses
ISBN 0-688-80144-7; 0-688-84144-9   LC 77-17311

"Fourteen original poems are presented in . . . picture-book format. Humorous, nonsensical, the verses mostly concern foolish characters like 'The Pancake Collector' who explains, 'I have pancakes in most of my pockets,/and concealed in the linings of suits./There are tiny ones stuffed in my mittens/and larger ones packed in my boots,' or 'Poor old Penelope/great are her woes,/a pumpkin has started/to grow from her nose.' Most of the poems are given a double-page spread and all are accompanied by detailed, appropriately droll black-and-white illustrations. It's an attractive package, and most children will enjoy the contents whether they are reading or listening." Sch Library J

The snopp on the sidewalk, and other poems; pictures by Byron Barton. Greenwillow Bks. 1977 unp illus $6.25, lib. bdg. $6.48 (k-4)   811

1 Nonsense verses
ISBN 0-688-80084-X; 0-688-84084-1   LC 76-46323

"Employing alliteration, metaphor, repetition, and portmanteau words within the framework of traditional rhymed verse forms, the poet has conjured into reality a menagerie of imaginary beings. . . . Despite the pseudo-macabre situations, the tone of the twelve poems is gleefully ghoulish without being gruesome, a mood complemented by the modulating grays and curvilinear patterns of the stylized, cartoonlike illustrations. A delectably bizarre gathering of marvelously outrageous nonsense." Horn Bk

Richards, Laura E.

Tirra lirra; rhymes old and new; foreword by May Hill Arbuthnot; with illus. by Marguerite Davis. Little 1955 194p illus $5.95 (3-5)   811

1 Nonsense verses
ISBN 0-316-74415-8   LC 55-3066

"These nonsense verses have been selected from the author's early books and from pages of 'St. Nicholas.' " Booklist

This "is still in demand in children's libraries, and treasured in homes. . . . For no one who has ever known the frog who 'lived in a bog, on the banks of Lake Okeefinokee'; the 'elephant who tried to use the telephant'; the owl, the eel and the warming pan who 'went to call on the soap-fat man'; and the other members of the gay Tirra Lirra company is ever likely to forget them." Horn Bk

Riley, James Whitcomb

The gobble-uns'll git you ef you don't watch out! James Whitcomb Riley's "Little Orphant Annie;" illus. by Joel Schick. Lippincott 1975 unp illus $8.95 (1-4)   811

1 Monsters—Poetry
ISBN 0-397-31621-6   LC 74-23110

This is the classic story poem of ill-mannered children spirited away by the ferocious Gobble-uns, as told by Little Orphant Annie

"This 1885 poem in Midwest dialect has always given a few chills to those with vivid imaginations. Now the 'Gobble-uns' have been sketched in all their sinister glory—and they look a lot like your average, mean-eyed, snaggle-toothed heavy. Gruesome enough for those who like that sort of thing, but don't offer this book to the timid. The black and white drawings of rotund Annie and the characters in her stories help clarify obscurities in the verse for youngsters." Children's Bk Rev Serv

Sandburg, Carl

Wind song; illus. by William A. Smith. Harcourt 1960 127p illus $5.95, pa $1.50 (4 and up)   811

ISBN 0-15-297497-0; 0-15-697096-1   LC 60-10248

A collection of poems for children and young people chosen from the poet's published works plus sixteen new poems. The poems are grouped under the following headings: New poems; Little people; Little album; Corn belt; Night; Blossom themes; Wind, sea, and sky

"Selected by Carl Sandburg himself for 'young folks.' Well-printed and designed with a black and white drawing for each one of the seven groupings. An original and distinctive book of poems that will be enjoyed by all ages." Ontario Library Rev

Silverstein, Shel

Where the sidewalk ends; the poems & drawings of Shel Silverstein. Harper 1974 166p illus $9.95, lib. bdg. $9.89 (3 and up)   811

1 Humorous poetry 2 Nonsense verses
ISBN 0-06-025667-3; 0-06-025668-0   LC 73-105486

"There are skillful, sometimes grotesque line drawings with each of the 127 poems, which run in length from a few lines to a couple of pages. The poems are tender, funny, sentimental, philosophical, and ridiculous in turn, and they're for all ages. . . . [Subjects include] an anti-nose-picking poem and one about belching—but that's life." Sat Rev

The author "has an excellent sense of rhythm and rhyme and a good ear for alliteration and assonance . . . that make these poems a pleasure to read aloud. The author's equally distinctive pen drawings which are scattered throughout will also draw fans." Sch Library J

Smith, William Jay

Laughing time; nonsense poems; illus. by Fernando Krahn. Delacorte Press/Seymour Lawrence 1980 116p $9.95   811

1 Nonsense verses
ISBN 0-440-05534-2   LC 80-65839

"A Merloyd Lawrence book"
"Some of the poems in this collection first appeared in the following books by William Jay Smith: Laughing time [1955], Boy Blue's book of beasts [1957], Puptents and pebbles [1959], Mr. Smith and other nonsense [1968], and also in Cricket Magazine." Verso of title page

Smith, William J.—*Continued*

This selection from the author's nonsense verse includes poems about everyday objects and events, numerous animals (both familiar and exotic), limericks and a nonsense ABC

Starbird, Kaye

The covered bridge house, and other poems; illus. by Jim Arnosky. Four Winds 1979 53p illus $6.95 (3-6) **811**

ISBN 0-590-07544-6   LC 79-11418

The author "translates impressions of emotions, personalities, and events into imaginative verse. The focus sharpens when she gives her attention to children's capricious capers such as Heather's nasty disposition in 'Jump Rope Song,' Ruth's altercation with a dentist in 'Ruth,' Hugh's problem of spelling 'kangaroo' in 'The Spelling Test,' a young boy's active imagination in 'Artie,' and Beverley's antics at camp in 'Watch Out!' " Booklist

"These 35 poems, while not of a moving, or introspective, or lyrical character, and not always observant of measures, are consistently great fun to read, and that's not saying little. . . . Young readers will be easily captivated by the gentle humor, the easy musicality of the rhymes, and the upbeat windup of each poem. . . . The small black-and-white scratchboard illustrations punctuating several pages are as unobtrusive as they are attractive." Sch Library J

Thayer, Ernest Lawrence

Casey at the bat; illus. by Paul Frame. Prentice-Hall 1964 unp illus lib. bdg. $4.95, pa $1.50 **811**

1 Baseball—Poetry
ISBN 0-13-120410-6; 0-13-120402-5   LC 64-13248

"The classic poem that relates how the fate of the Mudville nine came to rest on that paragon hitter, Casey, and then to the disbelief of all that 'mighty Casey' had struck out is here presented in picture book form." Pub W

"The well-known narrative poem is here interpreted with broad humor in comical pictures in orange and black. . . . The illustrations . . . convey a feeling of the period of the poem." Booklist

Thurman, Judith

Flashlight, and other poems; illus. by Regina Rubel. Atheneum Pubs. 1976 34p illus $6.95 (2-5) **811**

ISBN 0-689-30515-X   LC 75-29442

"These twenty-five short poems use words to display in a warm new light such common things as soap, closets, rags, and kisses." LC. Children's Bks 1976

"Images are fresh and observations penetrating, although never beyond a child's comprehension. Engagingly illustrated with simple sketches highlighted with cross-hatching, the collection should stimulate imaginative perception." Horn Bk

Updike, John

A child's calendar; illus. by Nancy Ekholm Burkert. Knopf 1965 unp illus $3.25, lib. bdg. $4.99 (k-3) **811**

1 Seasons—Poetry
ISBN 0-394-81059-7; 0-394-91059-1   LC 65-21555

"A poem for each month, a picture for each poem; the poetry has simplicity of style and familiarity of subject that are appealing, and has, here and there, a freshly imaginative image. The illustrations are delicate and precise in detail." Chicago. Children's Bk Center

Watson, Clyde

Catch me & kiss me & say it again; rhymes. Pictures by Wendy Watson. Collins [distributed by Philomel Bks.] 1978 64p illus $7.95, lib. bdg. $7.99 (k-1) **811**

ISBN 0-529-05436-1; 0-529-05438-8   LC 78-17644

A collection of rhymes "for brushing teeth, learning how to walk, playing finger games, grabbing a diaper, clipping fingernails, dividing things fairly, getting fed, undergoing thunderstorms, bathing, going to bed, and having fun in all kinds of everyday ways." Booklist

"Alternatives to Ms. Goose, these Mother Watson rhymes flow through human family activities with soft humor, natural as unprocessed honey. . . . Words are juicy and rhythm of the shorter verse ingenuous. Some adopt traditional phrases or follow traditional form with sprightly new steps and the rhymes sound like they have always been a part of our folklore. Wendy Watson works her grease pencil and water colors into larger, rounder shapes than the pointed little animal illustrations of 'Father Fox's Pennyrhymes [entered below] There is less mischief here. . . . But there is warmth and whimsy, immediacy and laughter in the pictured doings of a family of four inhabiting a New England farmhouse; and the pages are filled with gentle tones of primary color." Sch Library J

Father Fox's pennyrhymes; illus. by Wendy Watson. Crowell 1971 56p illus $8.95, lib. bdg. $8.79 (k-3) **811**

1 Nonsense verses
ISBN 0-690-29213-9; 0-690-29214-7   LC 71-146291

"A collection of short, original nonsense rhymes, illustrated with a bounty of high-spirited pictures. Some of the verses are impish or boisterous or just plain silly; some are similar to counting-out rhymes and jump-rope jingles; a few are as gentle as lullabies. All are highly rhythmic and reminiscent of the traditional rhymes of folklore. The water-color-and-ink illustrations are somewhat whimsical in their busyness; tiny pictures printed in sequence—like comic strips—as well as single, full-page pictures are brimming with minute detail and activity." Horn Bk

Watson, Nancy Dingman

Blueberries lavender; songs of the farmer's children; poems. Drawings by Erik Blegvad. Addison-Wesley 1977 unp illus lib. bdg. $5.95 (3-5) **811**

1 Country life—Poetry 2 Nature in poetry
ISBN 0-201-08568-2   LC 76-18226

"A collection of poems that celebrate the small events of the seasons in a rural setting." Chicago. Children's Bk Center

"The honest unforced images—of bringing home cats, hiding away from everyone after a spanking, building a snow woman—and easygoing rhythms can be shared even by those who are far removed from churning butter, tapping sugar maples, and washing hair in rainwater. Blegvad's detailed ink drawings of New England country life have the same quiet, down-home appeal." Sch Library J

Whitman, Walt

Overhead the sun; lines from Walt Whitman; woodcuts by Antonio Frasconi. Farrar, Straus 1969 unp illus $4.95 (5 and up) **811**

ISBN 0-374-35676-9   LC 69-20284

"A strikingly beautiful book with full-page, multi-colored sensitive woodcuts by Antonio Frasconi accompanying 16 of his selections from 'Leaves of Grass.' This brilliant artist captures the mood and dignity of the text and gives an imposing interpretation to it." Top of the News

Worth, Valerie

More Small poems; pictures by Natalie Babbitt. Farrar, Straus 1976 41p illus $5.95 (3-5) **811**

ISBN 0-374-35022-1   LC 76-28323

Companion volume to the author's Small poems, entered below

"The author and the illustrator . . . have created [a] miniature treasury of spontaneous, expressive verse. Homely, everyday items are endowed with unexpected new life. . . . With economy of phrase, deceptive simplicity, and artless skill the poet celebrates, among other things, a pumpkin, a toad, a safety pin, a kitten, weeds, earthworms, and sidewalks." Horn Bk

Small poems; pictures by Natalie Babbitt. Farrar, Straus 1972 41p illus $4.95 (3-5) **811**

ISBN 0-374-37072-9   LC 72-81488

"In twenty-four poems about such topics as raw carrots, cows, jewels, grasses, and crickets, the author gives added dimensions to the object by a suggestive turn of phrase or an unusual perspective. . . . The illustrations, in perfect harmony

Worth, Valerie—*Continued*

with the poems, suggest the possibilities of the items but are never so precise as to limit their potential scope. Both text and illustrations have been housed in a book in which the texture of the pages, the typography, the layout, and even the color of the binding are as understated, but as beautiful, as the text and illustrations." Horn Bk

Still More Small poems; pictures by Natalie Babbitt. Farrar, Straus 1978 41p illus $5.95 (3-5)　　　　　　　　　　　　　　　811

ISBN 0-374-37258-6　　　　　　LC 78-11739
Companion volume to: Small poems, and More Small poems, both entered above
"Sketches, in free verse, of everyday objects, animals, places, sensations, and situations, from sounds a bell makes . . . to a drowsy turtle's speculations . . . to the miraculous ability of a hen, 'all quirk/And freak and whim' to produce so pure and calm an item as an egg." Sch Library J
"Small is beautiful. The collaborators always prove that economy can result in images rich as Croesus. . . . Ink drawings as understated yet infused with mystery as the lines . . . amplify mood and meaning." Pub W

811.08　American poetry— Collections

Adoff, Arnold

(ed.) Black out loud; an anthology of modern poems by black Americans; drawings by Alvin Hollingsworth. Macmillan Pub. Co. 1970 86p illus lib. bdg. $5.95 (5 and up)
　　　　　　　　　　　　　　　　811.08

1 American poetry—Black authors—Collections
ISBN 0-02-700100-8　　　　　　LC 74-99117
This anthology includes "poems by established writers like Gwendolyn Brooks, LeRoi Jones and Langston Hughes, but many are by gifted younger writers. Topically grouped in six sections." Chicago. Children's Bk Center
"Pride dominates the collection—pride in being blacks and pride in being poets. . . . The sixty-seven poems are blunt and vital. . . . The poets try to relate the pain of the black experience, they tell of their heroes, of their encounters with white America, and of their dreams." Horn Bk
Biographical notes: p77-81. Includes an Index to authors, titles, and first lines

(ed.) Celebrations; a new anthology of black American poetry; comp. and ed. by Arnold Adoff; introduced by Quincy Troupe. Follett 1977 285p $5.96, lib. bdg. $7.98 (5 and up)
　　　　　　　　　　　　　　　　811.08

1 American poetry—Black authors—Collections
ISBN 0-695-80699-8; 0-695-40699-X　　LC 76-19888
Sequel to the editor's: I am the darker brother, entered below
This anthology "is arranged chronologically in twelve sections with headings like "The Idea of Ancestry' and 'Young Soul' and includes poets like Gwendolyn Brooks, Lucille Clifton, and Julian Bond." Children's Bk Rev Serv
"Most of the 85 Black American writers represented are currently active and a preponderance of the 240 poems date from the 1970s, with most of the remaining from the 60s. Biographical notes on the poets are included, as is a complete index. A valuable resource because it contains many poems not previously published, or published by small presses, this collection is also a fine introduction to some important contemporary poets and poetry for today's young people." Sch Library J

(ed.) I am the darker brother; an anthology of modern poems by Negro Americans; drawings by Benny Andrews; foreword by Charlemae Rollins. Macmillan Pub. Co. 1968 128p illus lib. bdg. $8.50, pa $1.95 (5 and up)
　　　　　　　　　　　　　　　　811.08

1 American poetry—Black authors—Collections
ISBN 0-02-700080-X; 0-02-041120-0　　LC 68-12077

"Selections by 28 American Negro poets who reflect on the past, the current social scene, and the hope for the future. . . . In a brief foreword, Charlemae Rollins discusses creativity, poetry, and the Negro." Sch Library J
"A most interesting anthology, with many contributions from such well-known poets as Brooks, Dunbar, Hayden, Hughes, and McKay, and a broad representation of selections from the work of some two dozen other modern authors. The format is dignified and spacious." Chicago. Children's Bk Center
Includes notes, biographies, and indexes to authors and first lines

(ed.) My black me; a beginning book of poetry. Dutton 1974 83p lib. bdg. $6.50 (5 and up)　　　　　　　　　　　　　811.08

1 American poetry—Black authors—Collections
ISBN 0-525-35460-3　　　　　　LC 73-16445
This collection of fifty poems contains works by Langston Hughes, Don L. Lee, Nikki Giovanni and others. The book's "six sections are untitled and loosely grouped thematically. . . . Topics covered are pride in Blackness, modern heroes and martyrs (e.g., Malcolm X and Dr. King), ghetto life, as well as the struggles and mistreatment of Blacks in this country. The focus [is] on Black awareness and helping one another." Library J
"There are poems that speak in protest, but as a collection the poems are a positive affirmation of blackness, and they have been wisely chosen for younger readers." Chicago. Children's Bk Center
Biographical notes and indexes to authors and to first lines are included

The **Dog** writes on the window with his nose, and other poems; collected by David Kherdian; pictures by Nonny Hogrogian. Four Winds 1977 31p illus lib. bdg. $5.95 (k-3)　　　　　　　　　　　　811.08

1 American poetry—Collections　2 Nature in poetry
ISBN 0-590-07448-2　　　　　　LC 76-26516
"Kherdian believes that the best poems for children are not those written for them, but those chosen wisely from the whole body of poetry. Some of his own work is included, as are selections from Kerouac, Brautigan, Roethke, Corso, Ferlinghetti and others, including one by Ruth Krauss that was designed for children." Chicago. Children's Bk Center
This collection of twenty-two haiku-type poems "is lyrical and should be shared with all ages. The free-verse poems tell of animals and poetry and are delightfully illustrated. Pictures and poems go so well together that it is difficult to imagine one without the other. A book to be savored." Children's Bk Rev Serv

Easter buds are springing; poems for Easter; selected by Lee Bennett Hopkins; illus. by Tomie de Paola. Harcourt 1979 30p illus $5.95 (2-4)　　　　　　　　　　811.08

1 Easter—Poetry　2 American poetry—Collections
ISBN 0-15-224705-X　　　　　　LC 78-10888
The poems "move through Easter morning greetings, speculations about the Easter rabbit, celebrations of Christ risen, flowers, colors, and egg hunts. Drawings are gay enough in jelly bean purple, but aside from one March Hare in mask, cape, and 'Try and Egg Me On' shirt, they are expected de Paola, and demure. The 19 poems are pleasant, useful to satisfy school assignments and build some anticipation for the season." Sch Library J

Emrich, Duncan

(comp.) American folk poetry: an anthology. Little 1974 xxxi, 831p illus $24.95　811.08

1 Ballads, American　2 Folk songs—U.S.
ISBN 0-316-23722-1　　　　　　LC 74-3499
This volume includes "songs, poems, and ballads arranged under the broad headings: children's ballads; hymns, religious pieces, and carols; wars and other disasters; songs of occupations and sea, forest, mines; songs of cowboys, Mormons, outlaws." Library J
"The annotated selections, often familiar but sometimes exceedingly quaint . . . show a distinct English, Irish, and Scotch heritage modified by American taste. Texts are given without music but Library of Congress archive numbers are noted for items recorded in its folklore series. Extensive bibliography and indexes by title and first line." Booklist

Ghost poems; ed. by Daisy Wallace; illus. by Tomie de Paola. Holiday House 1979 30p illus lib. bdg. $5.95 (k-3)　　811.08

1 Ghosts—Poetry 2 American poetry—Collections 3 English poetry—Collections
ISBN 0-8234-0344-0　　　　　　LC 78-11028

"Mostly inducing titters rather than terrors—is this collection by rhymsters with an active sense of the absurd. . . . Among the 17 entertainers are the old Scottish prayers ('Ghosties and Ghoulies'), two American Indian songs and contributions from conjurers of the past and present: Nancy Willard, Lilian Moore, X. J. Kennedy, Jack Prelutsky, et al., as well as anonymous selections from legends." Pub W

"De Paola moves away from his usual cheerful and bucolic style in illustrating a pleasantly varied, but not outstanding book of ghostly poems for reading aloud. Some are quasi-humorous, not always with total success, but some of the selections (Nancy Willard's 'The Games of Night,' William Mayne's 'Haunted') have both an eerie quality and a polished simplicity." Chicago. Children's Bk Center

Giant poems; ed. by Daisy Wallace; illus. by Margot Tomes. Holiday House 1978 32p illus lib. bdg. $5.95 (2-4)　　811.08

1 Giants—Poetry 2 American poetry—Collections 3 English poetry—Collections
ISBN 0-8234-0326-2　　　　　　LC 77-21038

"Opening with the oft-chanted 'Fe, Fi, Fo, Fum!' Wallace's collection of verses about giants goes on to feature 16 more. Michael Patrick Hearn moans about 'a kid of my size,' suffering the gentle name of Stanley. Why, complains Stanley, couldn't a huge fellow like him have been dubbed Thunderoar or Blunderbore or Asundertore! Lilian Moore gives us Dinosaur Rex; Shel Silverstein sings of a boy with a giant for an imaginary friend; Jack Prelutsky describes the fight between 'Huffer and Cuffer,' two thumping fellows who beat each other short; and Dennis Lee soothes little readers with a lullabye. Glad to be cozy in bed, his child thinks of the gale outside, 'Like a Giant in a Towel.' " Pub W

"Tomes' strong-lined pen-and-ink drawings surround the poetry with scenes carefully matching the words but original in their own graphic extension. Her giants are individualized, too, from fierce to fatuous to downright friendly." Booklist

Go with the poem; a new collection; chosen by Lilian Moore. McGraw 1979 125p $7.95 (4 and up)　　811.08

1 American poetry—Collections
ISBN 0-07-042880-8　　　　　　LC 78-8393

"Mostly unrhymed, this book emphasizes good poetry by contemporary Americans, including Denise Levertov, William Carlos Williams, William Stafford, Lucille Clifton, David Budbill and Charles Reznikoff." NY Times Bk Rev

This collection "has been wisely selected—both for its levels of complexity in vocabulary and concept, and in the subjects of the poems—for the intended audience. . . . Selections are grouped by such subjects as seasons, sports, or the city; a combined author-title index is included." Chicago. Children's Bk Center

Golden slippers; an anthology of Negro poetry for young readers; comp. by Arna Bontemps; with drawings by Henrietta Bruce Sharon. Harper 1941 220p illus $10, lib. bdg. $8.97 (5 and up)　　811.08

1 American poetry—Black authors—Collections
ISBN 0-06-010395-7; 0-06-010404-X　　LC 41-22155

"Containing a representative collection of Negro verse, by such poets as Langston Hughes, Claude McKay, Countee Cullen, Paul Laurence Dunbar, and James Weldon Johnson [this] is not limited in appeal to the young people for whom it was compiled." Wis Library Bul

"Mr. Bontemps' preference for the short lyric with a strong rhythmic pattern makes . . this anthology a selection young people should enjoy." L. C. Children & Poetry

Hine, Al
(ed.) This land is mine; an anthology of American verse; illus. by Leonard Vosburgh. Lippincott 1965 244p illus $8.95 (5 and up)　　811.08

1 American poetry—Collections 2 U.S.—History—Poetry
ISBN 0-397-30840-X　　　　　　LC 65-13437

"A collection of over 100 poems, with comments by the compiler tracing the history of the United States from Indian days to the present." Adventuring With Bks. 2d edition

"The selections are varied in quality and in kind. . . . An index of first lines and an author index are appended; there is no alphabetical listing of titles." Chicago. Children's Bk Center

Hopkins, Lee Bennett
(comp.) Girls can too! A book of poems; illus. by Emily McCully. Watts, F. 1972 45p illus lib. bdg. $4.90 (k-3)　　811.08

1 Girls—Poetry 2 Sex role—Poetry 3 American poetry—Collections
ISBN 0-531-02587-X　　　　　　LC 72-887

The compiler has selected 19 poems by such poets as Dorothy Aldis, Myra Cohn Livingston, David McCord and Aileen Fisher illustrating various activities typical in a young girl's life

"Delightful collection of poems depicting many of the activities and feelings of children with emphasis on what little girls can experience. The pen and ink illustrations are perfectly charming." Notable Children's Trade Bks (Social Studies)

(comp.) On our way: poems of pride and love; photographs by David Parks. Knopf 1974 63p illus lib. bdg. $5.99 (3-6)　　811.08

1 American poetry—Black authors—Collections
ISBN 0-394-92773-7　　　　　　LC 73-15112

"A good anthology . . . [this] speaks clearly about the joy and challenge of being young and Black in America. The poems, some of which are in Black English, are simple and powerful." Christian Sci Monitor

The book "includes some lesser known works and has the added bonus of David Parks's photographs —one for each poem—featuring black children and adults in a variety of moods and settings." NY Times Bk Rev

I'm mad at you; verses selected by William Cole; illus. by George MacClain. Collins [distributed by Philomel Bks.] 1978 62p illus lib. bdg. $6.95 (2-4)　　811.08

1 Anger—Poetry 2 American poetry—Collections
ISBN 0-529-05363-2　　　　　　LC 77-25497

In this collection of poems "humor seems to be Cole's prescribed antidote for anger, which isn't taken very seriously here—none of it is of the truly fierce variety but runs more to irritation or tantrums." Booklist

"The lead poem, by Mr. Cole, and others by such poets as Shel Silverstein, X. J. Kennedy and John Ciardi, are classic examples of humorous verse for children. . . . The illustrations . . . are just as wacky as the writing they depict." NY Times Bk Rev

Larrick, Nancy
(comp.) I heard a scream in the street; poems by young people in the city; illus. with photographs by students. Evans, M.&Co. 1970 141p illus $5.95 (5 and up)　　811.08

1 American poetry—Collections 2 Cities and towns—Poetry 3 Children as authors
ISBN 0-87131-064-3　　　　　　LC 79-122820

"From class magazines, workshops and community centers, student newspapers and college poetry projects, from young people in twenty-three cities, Nancy Larrick has chosen almost eighty poems that testify to the perception, vision, and candor of the young. There is little humor or gentleness: the poems are fierce in statement of condemnation or pride, sometimes rough in structure but often impressive. The authors' names are given but not their ages (the range was fourth grade through high school at the time of writing)." Chicago. Children's Bk Center

Includes an Index of poets and titles and an Index of first lines

Larrick, Nancy—*Continued*

(comp.) Poetry for holidays; drawings by Kelly Oechsli. Garrard 1966 64p illus lib. bdg. $5.49 (1-4)   **811.08**

1 Holidays—Poetry 2 American poetry—Collections

ISBN 0-8116-4100-7   LC 66-10724

Poems for Halloween, Christmas, Saint Valentine's Day, Easter, and other holidays, by such authors as Harry Behn, Marchette Chute, Aileen Fisher, Langston Hughes, Henry Wadsworth Longfellow, and Ruth Sawyer

"The more than 50 poems covering 10 holidays and special days are tried and true, the drawings are enjoyable, and the collection is of a length to appeal to and be easily handled by children." Booklist

Includes an index of authors

Monster poems; ed. by Daisy Wallace; illus. by Kay Chorao. Holiday House 1976 29p illus lib. bdg. $6.95 (2-4)   **811.08**

1 Monsters—Poetry 2 American poetry—Collections

ISBN 0-8234-0268-1   LC 75-17680

"These poems, collected from several sources, feature a Griggle who giggles while eating lunch, a nine-foot Ugstabuggle with hairy, grasping hands, a spangled pandemonium who is missing from the zoo, an Ambley-Gombley who sits upon a train track, and a Slithergadee who crawls out of the sea. Chorao's orange-and-blue creatures swarm over and around the rhymes, which are set off in white blocks, and lurk in corners and margins to add humor and eye-catching novelty for the reader." Booklist

The Moon's the North Wind's cooky: night poems; selected and illus. by Susan Russo. Lothrop 1979 36p illus $5.95, lib. bdg. $5.71 (k-3)   **811.08**

1 American poetry—Collections 2 English poetry—Collections 3 Night—Poetry

ISBN 0-688-41879-1; 0-688-51879-6   LC 78-32178

"Fourteen poems celebrate the mysteries and delights of nighttime: shadows, the moon, and creatures that sing and fly. Tidily presented in a small volume, the verses are illustrated with fanciful drawings. The artist achieves various effects in soft grays accented with black. She has chosen chiefly modern poetry, opening with Nikki Giovanni's 'Goodnight' and an anonymous tonguetwister. . . . Such contemporary poets as Joan Aiken, Felice Holman, and Karla Kuskin are represented along with earlier writers like Robert Louis Stevenson and Vachel Lindsay." Horn Bk

Oh, such foolishness! Poems selected by William Cole; pictures by Tomie de Paola. Lothrop 1979 36p illus $5.95, lib. bdg. $5.71   **811.08**

1 Nonsense verses 2 American poetry—Collections 3 English poetry—Collections

ISBN 0-397-31807-3   LC 78-1622

"Cole has trained a new gallery of sillies (in properly rhyming verse) into sitting still one to a page above de Paola's black-and-white drawings in a format which invites browsing. He culled these characters and impossible situations from titles by contemporary poets and from traditional folk rhymes." Sch Library J

"Children, loving corn, will sprout these verses without fear; and if such food for fun takes the intimidation out of poetry books, so much the better, especially for reluctant readers who will find this one easy to manage." Booklist

On city streets; an anthology of poetry, selected by Nancy Larrick; illus. with photographs by David Sagarin. Evans, M.&Co. 1968 158p illus $6.95 (5 and up)   **811.08**

1 American poetry—Collections 2 Cities and towns—Poetry

ISBN 0-87131-080-5   LC 68-30505

"This anthology of poems compiled by Nancy Larrick, with the help of more than 100 city children, has the perfect, the perfectly exact title. Country and suburban children who read the poems (and look at the photographs) will know what life is like on city streets; children who live on city streets will feel the elation of recognition." Pub W

"Sharp, immediate, full of evocative music . . . the book has poems whose sequences arrive thrilling and smiting at one's life. . . . The short ones, the loving ones, the mysterious ones, the shouting ones, the ones with animals, the ones from other cultures, the ones perhaps most like children—very frail and very strong, like bubbles. . . . [This book] opens up a great landscape of poems that children want." NY Times Bk Rev

Includes an Index of poets and titles and an Index of first lines

A **Paper** zoo; a collection of animal poems by modern American poets; selected by Renée Karol Weiss; pictures by Ellen Raskin. Macmillan Pub. Co. 1968 38p illus $5.95 (1-4)   **811.08**

1 Animals—Poetry 2 American poetry—Collections

ISBN 0-02-792580-3   LC 68-10124

"Presented in a picture book given an almost psychedelic look by Ellen Raskin's brilliant designs of paper-cut creatures, this small collection invites an audience of very young listeners, to whom its poems about animals will certainly appeal, while at the same time its selections from writing by the first rank of modern American poets is for any age." L.C. Children & Poetry

Poems here and now; ed. by David Kherdian; linoleum cuts by Nonny Hogrogian. Greenwillow Bks. 1976 64p illus $7.25, lib. bdg. $6.96 (4 and up)   **811.08**

1 American poetry—Collections

ISBN 0-688-80024-6; 0-688-84024-8   LC 75-37586

"Whether eliciting excitement, a chuckle, or serious thinking, these poems strike sparks and collectively leave a warm afterglow. All are economical, brief, their razor-sharp images and well-turned phrases memorable. . . . Authors include Ruth Krauss, William Carlos Williams, Jack Kerouac, James Wright, A. R. Ammons, and Robert Creeley; editor Kherdian's taste is pleasing; he's right: the poems do indeed prompt surprise, delight, and wonder. And curious readers will appreciate appended sections explaining unfamiliar terms and giving background notes on the many authors." Booklist

Postcard poems; a collection of poetry for sharing; ed. by Paul B. Janeczko. Bradbury Press 1979 105p $8.95 (4 and up)   **811.08**

1 American poetry—Collections

ISBN 0-87888-155-7   LC 79-14192

"This volume of short poems is shaped like a large postcard and filled with verses to be savored, jotted down and sent to a friend because as editor Janeczko states, 'The poems in this collection are gifts from the poets, meant to be shared.' The very brief poems by mostly 20th century authors contain common themes of the cycles of life and the gamut of human emotions. Because of the appealing format and simple brevity of the poetry . . . [readers] will let the book do as Judith Hemschemeyer's opening poem suggests. 'Let me wrap a poem around you.'" VOYA

Reflections on a gift of watermelon pickle . . . and other modern verse [comp. by] Stephen Dunning, Edward Lueders [and] Hugh Smith. Lothrop [1967 c1966] 139p illus $7.50, lib. bdg. $7.20 (5 and up)   **811.08**

1 American poetry—Collections

ISBN 0-688-41231-9; 0-688-51231-3   LC 67-29527

Text edition of this title first published 1966 by Scott

"Although some of the [114] selections are by recognized modern writers, many are by minor or unknown poets, and few will be familiar to the reader. Nearly all are fresh in approach and contemporary in expression. . . . Striking photographs complementing or illuminating many of the poems enhance the attractiveness of the volumes." Booklist

"This compact, handsome anthology . . . should do at least two things for the young reader: help train his ear away from the iambic stress of traditional verse and teach him that subjects for poetry need not be 'poetic.' . . . There is a solidity to the poetry that is bound to leave a mark on the reader's mind." NY Times Bk Rev

Author-title index

Some haystacks don't even have any needle, and other complete modern poems; comp. by Stephen Dunning, Edward Lueders [and] Hugh Smith. . . . Lothrop 1969 192p illus $9.50 (6 and up) **811.08**

1 American poetry—Collections
ISBN 0-688-41445-1   LC 75-5424

"Editorial direction: Leo Kneer; development: Nora Rotzoll, Philip Brantingham, Ronald Mochel; design: Don Marvine." Title page

"The book contains more than 125 modern poems from magazines including the 'New Yorker', 'Harpers', and the 'little' magazines. . . . Tasteful, ingenious, the varied, relevant poems . . . will turn on even confirmed poetry haters. The coy title and the lack of a first-line index are small faults in a book as praiseworthy as this one—the poems about trivia and tragedy, garbage and glory, intriguingly patterned on the pages and complemented by scattered color reproductions of modern art, constitute a happening for today and a lasting delight." Library J

Indexes of titles and authors are included

The **Whispering** wind; poetry by young American Indians; ed. by Terry Allen; with an introduction by Mae J. Durham. Doubleday 1972 128p lib. bdg. $5.90, pa $1.95 (5 and up) **811.08**

1 American poetry—American Indian authors—Collections
ISBN 0-385-07405-0; 0-385-01032-X LC 78-157572

This "is a sampling of the work of students at the Institute of American Indian Arts in Santa Fe. All poems are of high quality, the techniques ranging from lyrical metaphors of nature to intricate abstractions, from primitive drumbeat rhythms to the idiom of today's urban youth." NY Times Bk Rev

The **Wind** has wings; poems from Canada; comp. by Mary Alice Downie & Barbara Robertson; illus. by Elizabeth Cleaver. Oxford 1978 [c1968] 95p illus pa $7.95 (5 and up) **811.08**

1 Canadian poetry—Collections
ISBN 0-19-540287-1   LC 79-308081

Frst published 1968 by Henry Z. Walck, Inc.

"An absolutely delightful anthology, some of the selections about things peculiarly Canadian, some on topics of a serious nature, and some of deft absurdity. There are folk-like poems translated from the French, some particularly nice animal poems, and some very conventional selections. The illustrations have a great deal of vitality and are as varied as is the poetry." Chicago. Children's Bk Center

Witch poems; ed. by Daisy Wallace; illus. by Trina Schart Hyman. Holiday House 1976 30p illus lib. bdg. $6.95 (2-5) **811.08**

1 Witches—Poetry 2 American poetry—Collections 3 English poetry—Collections
ISBN 0-8234-0281-9   LC 76-9036

These poems "will give nobody nightmares, only a lot of fun. Along with the comic poems about contemporary witches (even darkness has its lighter side), [Wallace] includes incantations by Shakespeare and L. Frank Baum, and a few anonymous spells not written to please children at all but to raise a fair wind and make enchanted horses fly. All the poems are rich in the rhymes, refrains and wordplay of which good incantations are made, from E. E. Cummings's 'Hist Whist' to Sonja Nikolay's 'Witches' Menu.'" NY Times Bk Rev

"A collection of 20 short witch poems, most by contemporary authors (X. J. Kennedy, Karla Kuskin, and company) but also including four traditional chants." Sch Library J

812 American drama

Bennett, Rowena

Creative plays and programs for holidays. . . . Plays, Inc. 1966 448p illus $9.95 (3-6) **812**

1 Holidays—Drama 2 Seasons—Drama 3 Holidays—Poetry 4 Seasons—Poetry
ISBN 0-8238-0005-9   LC 66-16448

"Royalty-free plays, playlets, group readings, and poems for holiday and seasonal programs for boys and girls." Subtitle

"The short plays composed of simple sentences lend themselves to easy memorization by lower and middle grades. There is a great deal of variety in the subject matter as well as the genre." Sch Library J

Production notes: p439-48

Boiko, Claire

Children's plays for creative actors; a collection of royalty-free plays for boys and girls. Plays, Inc. 1967 368p $9.95 (3-6) **812**

1 One act plays
ISBN 0-8238-0006-7   LC 67-21413

Here are thirty-five one-act plays, playlets, comedies, fantasies, holiday plays, and fairy tales. Some of the plays feature choral speaking. Included are plays for Christmas, New Years, Washington's and Lincoln's birthdays, Thanksgiving, Halloween, Book Week, Arbor Day, and other special occasions

Carlson, Bernice Wells

Funny-bone dramatics; illus. by Charles Cox. Abingdon 1974 96p illus lib. bdg. $4.95 (k-3) **812**

ISBN 0-687-13867-1   LC 73-21515

"The selection of speak-up riddles, jokes for enactment with puppets, skits and plays (many based on the familiar droll or simpleton motifs of folk tradition) will be a convenient resource for creative dramatics programs. The book progresses from short riddles to multicharacter plays, and the tone is predominantly slapstick." Horn Bk

This book is "designed to polish clarity, timing, acting, and reaction, and other comic acting techniques. . . . With a glossary of acting terms and a short reading list, this . . . will provide good routines for young entertainers." Sch Library J

Childress, Alice

When the rattlesnake sounds; a play; drawings by Charles Lilly. Coward, McCann & Geoghegan 1975 32p illus $6.95 (5 and up) **812**

1 Tubman, Harriet Ross—Drama 2 Abolitionists—Drama
ISBN 0-698-20342-9   LC 75-10456

"This three chapter, one-act play is set in the hotel laundry where Harriet Tubman worked for several months in order to raise money for the abolitionist movement. Recounting her efforts to encourage a young co-worker, it is an inspirational dramatization of the faith, courage, and determination which helped Tubman overcome fears for her own safety while freeing slaves via the Underground Railroad." Sch Library J

"Handsomely produced with evocative, representational black-and-white illustrations, the book offers the young reader a rare opportunity for an aesthetic experience while becoming aware of the techniques used by the dramatist to develop situation and characters." Horn Bk

Davis, Ossie

Escape to freedom; a play about young Frederick Douglass. Viking [1978 c1976] 89p $7.95 (5 and up) **812**

1 Douglass, Frederick—Drama 2 Slavery in the U.S.—Drama
ISBN 0-670-29775-5   LC 77-25346

"First performed in 1976, the five scenes and the prologue present episodes from the life of Frederick Douglass: his childhood in a slave cabin, his zeal in learning how to read, his treatment on a slave-breaking plantation, his experiences in Baltimore, and his escape to New York. The directions for the stage production are informal and improvisational. For example, the various parts in the play, except for the role of Fred Douglass, are taken by six actors listed as Black Woman, Black Man, Black Boy, White Woman, White Man, White Boy; and the cast is responsible for rearranging the sets. To accompany the mood of the action, the scenes are interspersed with such well-known spirituals and folk songs as 'Give Me That Old-Time Religion,' 'Go Tell It on the Mountain,' and 'Blue-Tail Fly.'" Horn Bk

"Dramatically, this is the most challenging, interesting, and entertaining play for young people to appear in a long time." Sch Library J

Selected bibliography: p89

Fisher, Aileen

Holiday programs for boys and girls. New, rev. ed. Plays, Inc. 1980 393p $10.95 (4 and up)　　**812**

1 Holidays—Drama　2 One act plays
ISBN 0-8238-0244-2　　LC 80-18642
First published 1953
"A collection of easily produced, nonroyalty plays—some of them in verse—poems, group readings, and recitations for holidays and special occasions observed in schools. . . . [It] will probably be helpful for teachers planning classroom or assembly programs. Production notes are given." Booklist [review of the 1953 edition]

Henderson, Nancy

Celebrate America; a baker's dozen of plays; illus. by Paul Frame. Messner 1978 128p illus lib. bdg. $7.79 (5 and up)　　**812**

1 One act plays
ISBN 0-671-32907-3　　LC 78-15169
Eleven of these thirteen one act plays are original works by the author, one is a pantomime of Ernest Thayer's poem Casey at the bat, and another is a Christmas scene adapted from Louisa May Alcott's novel Little women
"Though the quality of individual plays varies, from the strong and moving 'Soul Force' (highlighting incidents in the life of Martin Luther King) to the strained humor of 'Legend for Our Time' (about the energy crisis), this collection as a whole demonstrates a sure dramatic sense and command of dialogue and employs a variety of techniques (pantomime, flashbacks, parody) to illustrate aspects of American life. There is always a message, but rarely does it overwhelm the play itself. Written for school and community group productions, the stagings are kept simple and flexible." Sch Library J

Korty, Carol

Plays from African folktales; with ideas for acting, dance, costumes and music; illus. by Sandra Cain; music by Saka Acquaye and Afolabi Ajayi. Scribner 1975 128p illus music lib. bdg. $7.95 (4-6)　　**812**

1 Folk drama 2 One act plays 3 Folklore—Africa
ISBN 0-684-14199-X　　LC 74-24418
"Four plays based on African folklore—two of them taken from Ananse stories—are the basis for a useful introduction to methods of dramatizing folktales." Horn Bk
"The dialogue is crisp, and the tales have action and humor. The author . . . gives useful suggestions for scenery, costumes and masks, rehearsing, and performing. All the tales have to do with animals, although there are some human characters, and the author gives advice on ways to use the scripts and on incorporating music and dance. Entertaining, not too long or difficult, and flexible, the plays are easy to mount. A glossary of terms precedes the plays; they are followed by an excellent divided bibliography." Chicago. Children's Bk Center

Silly soup; ten zany plays, with songs and ideas for making them your own; photographs by Jamie Cope; music by Mary Lynn Solot. Scribner 1977 148p illus music lib. bdg. $7.95 (3-6)　　**812**

1 Folk drama 2 One act plays
ISBN 0-684-15171-5　　LC 77-32102
A collection of ten short plays based on traditional noodlehead folktales, particularly the Jewish Chelm tales of Poland and the medieval English Gotham tales. "Various situations find the simpleton characters selling a bag of gold for a bag of air, taking down the walls of a house to let in the sunshine, and exchanging two mismatched shoes for the others of the same pairs. All the plays are adaptable and can be presented in five to ten characters, as well as a minimum of scenery and props. Five songs, to be used as fillers, and helpful production notes are included, along with hints for improvisation, creating comic characters, and general performance. . . . Annotated bibliography appended." Booklist
"The vitality of the scripts, the recommendations on techniques, and the open improvisational quality which leaves room for individual creativity

make this the best play book to come out in years. Black-and-white photographs of kids having a good time indicate possible classroom use but are otherwise not helpful." Sch Library J
Theater terms: p4-6

Preston, Carol

A trilogy of Christmas plays for children; music selected by John Langstaff; illus. with music, photographs, and diagrams. Harcourt 1967 135p illus music $5.95 (5 and up)　　**812**

1 Christmas—Drama
ISBN 0-15-290450-6　　LC 67-17157
The three plays "are variations on the Nativity theme. One is contemporary (with Nativity scenes in a play-within-the-play) and one adapted rfom Medieval folk and miracle plays; the third is based on English miracle plays and old carols. The dialogue is flavored with appropriate idiom and vocabulary without being too quaint, indeed the plays are in the best of taste. Sources are discussed and quite complete instructions given for staging, lighting, simple choreography, et cetera. An appendix gives information about sources for obtaining appropriate music." Sutherland. The Best in Children's Bks

Thane, Adele

Plays from famous stories and fairy tales; royalty-free dramatizations of favorite children's stories. Plays, Inc. 1967 463p $9.95 (4-6)　　**812**

1 One act plays 2 Folk drama
ISBN 0-8238-0060-1　　LC 67-16952
"Twenty-eight royalty-free, one act plays are included in this collection of adaptations from well-known folktales, fairy tales, children's classics and old favorites. The dramatizations are simple, often compressing into a scene or two several incidents from a book; they are adequately written and some are moderately funny. Because of the appeal of the sources, a useful collection. Brief notes on costumes, props, lights, setting, et cetera, are appended." Chicago. Children's Bk Center

812.08　American drama—Collections

Dramatized folk tales of the world; a collection of 50 one-act plays—royalty-free adaptations of stories from many lands; ed. by Sylvia E. Kamerman. Plays, Inc. 1971 575p $9.95 (3 and up)　　**812.08**

1 Folk drama—Collections 2 One act plays
ISBN 0-8238-004-0　　LC 72-142792
These "one-act plays, royalty free, include some about folk heroes, some that are based on books . . . and such old favorites as 'Stone soup.' The sources are not given, but the plays are based on tales from twenty-six countries, some being prefaced by an author's note. The dramatization is of variable quality, but the book is useful both as a source for short plays and as a compilation with an international and literary flavor. Production notes are provided." Chicago. Children's Bk Center
"This book is a must, especially for school libraries." Library J

Fifty plays for junior actors; a collection of royalty-free, one-act plays for young people; ed. by Sylvia E. Kamerman. Plays, Inc. 1966 676p $9.95 (4 and up)　　**812.08**

1 American drama—Collections 2 One act plays
ISBN 0-8238-0034-2　　LC 66-17944
Here are "plays for children in the middle and upper grades which can be performed with simple settings and properties and can be adapted for large or small casts. Comedies, fairy tales, mysteries, science fiction, and dramatizations for special occasions and on various subjects are contained in the serviceable collection of entertaining plays. Helpful production notes are provided at the end of the book." Booklist

Little plays for little players; fifty non-royalty plays for children; ed. by Sylvia E. Kamerman. Plays, Inc. 1969 335p $8.95   **812.08**

1 American drama—Collections 2 One act plays
ISBN 0-8238-0035-0   LC 75-97943

First published 1952. Contains plays originally published in Plays, the Drama Magazine for Young People

Here are simple-to-produce plays for the primary grades. "To meet the demands for plays the year round, there is a wide variety of material covering all the important holidays, as well as dramatizations of legends and fantasies which young children love. Often, intangible ideas such as the importance of good health, safety, voting, etc., can be effectively taught through dramatic means, and this book therefore contains plays on these subjects." Preface

On stage for Christmas; a collection of royalty-free, one-act Christmas plays for young people; ed. by Sylvia E. Kamerman. Plays, Inc. 1978 488p $10.95   **812.08**

1 Christmas—Drama 2 One act plays
ISBN 0-8238-0226-X   LC 78-15517

"An anthology that can be used independently by older readers and by adults working with younger children contains ten plays for junior and senior high, ten for the middle grades, eight for the lower grades, and four dramatizations of Christmas classics, adapted from 'Little Women,' 'A Christmas Carol,' 'The Christmas Nutcracker,' and a medieval mystery play." Chicago. Children's Bk Center

"While some of the selections have contrived plots, stiff dialogue, and artificial characters, others offer more artistic and certainly practical possibilities for school productions, facilitated by brief notes on playing time, costumes, properties, setting, lighting, and sound effects at the end of the book. Most of the plays have a large enough cast to involve a class in either acting or stage work, and where students are not up to writing their own material, this will prove useful." Booklist

A Treasury of Christmas plays; one-act royalty-free plays for stage or microphone performance and round-the-table reading; ed. by Sylvia E. Kamerman. Plays, Inc. 1975 509p $9.95   **812.08**

1 Christmas—Drama 2 One act plays
ISBN 0-8238-0203-5   LC 76-350906

First published 1958

"Included in this volume are [forty] traditional and modern one-act plays for young people—contemporary comedies, dramatizations of the Christmas Story, plays with flexible casts, musical backgrounds—all revealing the true spirit of Christmas." Preface

817.08 American satire and humor—Collections

Clark, David Allen

Jokes, puns, and riddles; illus. by Lionel Kalish. Doubleday 1968 288p illus $4.95, lib. bdg. $5.90 (4-6)   **817.08**

1 American wit and humor 2 Jokes 3 Riddles
ISBN 0-385-09018-8; 0-385-09019-6   LC 67-19070

Partial contents: Brain teasers; Daffinitions; Insults and wisecracks; Hippies, hairdos, and hermits; Done with a pun; World-wide whimsey; Silly dillies; Historical howlers; Elephants, elephants, elephants

"The happy feature of [this collection] is not only that it's a good reference book but that it's inoffensive in content. A nice, innocuous, funny slice of comedy, for any youngster." NY Times Bk Rev

De Regniers, Beatrice Schenk

The Abraham Lincoln joke book; illus. by William Lahey Cummings. Random House 1965 92p illus lib. bdg. $4.69 (4-6)   **817.08**

1 Lincoln, Abraham, President U.S. 2 American wit and humor 3 Jokes
ISBN 0-394-91079-6   LC 65-18162

"Here are the wit and wisdom of a great American—more than sixty jokes and humorous stories told by and about Abraham Lincoln. He used humor to prove a point, to help answer questions, or to cheer up people around him." p 1

818 American miscellany

Sandburg, Carl

The Sandburg treasury; prose and poetry for young people. . . . Introduction by Paula Sandburg; illus. by Paul Bacon. Harcourt 1970 480p illus $8.95 (5 and up)   **818**

ISBN 0-15-270180-X   LC 79-120818

"Including 'Rootabaga stories,' 'Early moon,' 'Wind song,' 'Abe Lincoln grows up,' 'Prairietown boy.' " Title page

This volume brings together all of Sandburg's books for young people: his whimsical stories, two books of poetry, a version of his biography of Abraham Lincoln, and portions of his autobiography specially edited for children

Index of titles for stories and poems: p478-80

820.8 English literature—Collections

Lewis, Richard

(ed.) Journeys; prose by children of the English-speaking world. Simon & Schuster 1969 215p illus $4.95   **820.8**

1 Children as authors 2 English literature—Collections
ISBN 0-671-20364-9   LC 70-87882

Companion volume to: Miracles, entered in class 821.08

"To show the entire scope of children's capacity to create literature Lewis has compiled a delightful collection of prose. . . . The more than 150 short pieces—descriptions, essays, stories, fantasies—written by children from age four to fourteen from nine English-speaking countries reveal the perceptiveness and candor of children and demonstrate the ability of children to express their thoughts and feelings freely and with imagination." Booklist

"The best use of the collection will probably be to inspire adults to encourage and allow children to express themselves as freely and as fully in prose as in poetry." Horn Bk

Mayne, William

(ed.) Ghosts; an anthology. Elsevier/Nelson Bks. 1971 187p $7.95 (6 and up)   **820.8**

1 Ghosts 2 English literature—Collections
ISBN 0-525-66112-3   LC 72-140081

First published by Thomas Nelson

The editor has compiled an "anthology of stories, poems and factual accounts of ghosts, goblins, trolls, [and] 'poltergeists.' " Pub W

Although the selections "may be read satisfactorily in any order, it is worth noting the excellent organization of the material. In a brief preface, the editor discusses the arrangement, indicating the stories that are pure fiction, those that are based on legend, and those that are true accounts. Each story is also prefaced by an imaginative paragraph that sets the tone for . . . the selections [which] have a wide range of settings—from England and Scotland, Norway and Sweden, India and China—indicating that ghosts and the belief in them are respecters of no time or place. A substantial, imaginative, and suitably shivery anthology." Horn Bk

821 English poetry

Aiken, Joan

The skin spinners; poems; drawings by Ken Rinciari. Viking 1976 83p illus $7.95 (5 and up)   **821**

ISBN 0-670-64950-3   LC 75-29306

This writer "has gathered together more than fifty of her poems, varied in meter and form and unified only by the fecundity of her imagination. Joan Aiken's poetry is as multifaceted as her

Aiken, Joan—*Continued*

short stories—eerie, dreamlike, impish, whimsical, enigmatic—and always the precise words are summoned to illuminate the idea, to vitalize the image." Horn Bk

This is a "fine sampling from Aiken. Accompanied by attractive black pen drawings on nearly every spread, the collection contains poems suited to the interests and abilities of middle-grade readers although most are better aimed toward junior and senior high school students who will understand references to Mozart, Daphne and Apollo, the Loreleis, and the like." Sch Library J

Index of first lines: p81-83

Belloc, Hilaire

The bad child's book of beasts, and More beasts for worse children, and A moral alphabet; with pictures by B. T. B. Dover 1961 157p illus pa $2.50 (1-4)   821

1 Animals—Poetry 2 Nonsense verses
ISBN 0-486-20749-8   LC 61-2226

Also available in hardcover from Peter Smith for $4.25 (ISBN 0-8446-1627-3)

The bad child's book of beasts was first published 1896 in England, 1923 in the United States; More beasts for worse children was first published 1897 in England, 1923 in the United States; A moral alphabet was first published 1899 in England

The bad child's book of beasts and More beasts for worse children combine "absurd verses and line drawings presenting the idiosyncracies of such beasts as the Yak, the Dodo and the Camelopard." Bks for Boys and Girls

Browning, Robert

The Pied Piper of Hamelin; illus. by Kate Greenaway. Warne 1899 48p illus $9.95 (3 and up)   821

ISBN 0-7232-0586-8

This long nineteenth century poem tells of the piper who, employed to rid the town of rats, also pipes the children of the town into the mountain

"With Kate Greenaway's inimitable illustrations, it is a 'must have' for every library. . . . It deserves a place in every children's room, so that the illustrations as well as the poem may become a part of each child's heritage." Library J

Carroll, Lewis

The hunting of the snark; an agony in eight fits; illus. by Mervyn Peake. Chatto & Windus [distributed by Merrimack Bk. Service] 1953 44p illus $4.95 (4 and up)   821

1 Nonsense verses
ISBN 0-7011-0605-0

Text first published 1876. First published with these illustrations 1941

A long nonsense poem, parodying heroic ballads, which describes the adventures of the Bellman and his oddly assorted crew who hunt the mysterious snark

Lewis Carroll's Jabberwocky; illus. by Jane Breskin Zalben; with annotations by Humpty Dumpty. Warne 1977 unp illus lib. bdg. $8.95 (1-3)   821

1 Nonsense verses
ISBN 0-7232-6145-8   LC 77-75040

"In Zalben's intricate double-page watercolor illustrations interpreting Lewis Carroll's nonsense poem 'Jabberwocky,' Humpty Dumpty takes readers through a fantasy world in which trees grow candy and cakes, a raccoon-like creature has three tails and an eye patch, and green pigs shed green tears. Zalben uses color well and the nonsense is visualized in a style rich in detail without appearing cluttered. An annotation of the poem, in the form of a discussion between Alice and Humpty Dumpty, appears as a natural extension at the end of this book which could be useful as a handsome starting point for teaching creative poetry or language development." Sch Library J

De La Mare, Walter

Peacock pie; a book of rhymes; with drawings by Edward Ardizzone. Faber & Faber 1980 121p illus pa $3.25 (4 and up)   821

ISBN 0-571-18014-0

Text first published 1913. This is a reprint of the edition published 1958 in England

"Illustrations that perfectly echo the moods of the poems help to make this collection of children's verse, by one of England's best loved poets, a favourite possession of those children who long to venture into the realms of Earth and Air, Witches and Fairies, Places and People, Boys and Girls, and Beasts of all descriptions." Ontario Library Rev

Rhymes and verses; collected poems for children; with drawings by Elinore Blaisdell. Holt 1947 344p illus $8.95 (4 and up)   821

ISBN 0-03-031710-X   LC 47-30200

This volume contains selections from the published works of this English poet. The poems are arranged under such headings as: Green grow the rashes, O; All round about the town; All creatures great and small; Fairies—witches—phantoms, etc. Indexed by title and first line

Greenaway, Kate

Marigold garden; pictures and rhymes by Kate Greenaway. Warne [1910] 56p illus $7.95 (k-2)   821

1 Flowers—Poetry
ISBN 0-7232-0588-4

First published 1885 by Routledge and Sons

"Flower verses written in simple rhyme for very young children. The floral theme is well developed in the design, colour, and arrangement of the pictures." Toronto

Under the window; pictures & rhymes; engraved & printed by Edmund Evans. Warne [n.d.] 56p illus $7.95 (k-2)   821

ISBN 0-7232-0587-6

First published 1878 by Routledge and Sons

This is "a collection of simple rhymes on subjects of childhood. The block prints illustrating the verses have gaily solemn figures dressed in large bonnets, slim gowns and smocks, pictured with a delicacy of colour which makes this book precious among picture books." Toronto

Hughes, Ted

Moon-whales, and other Moon poems; drawings by Leonard Baskin. Viking 1976 86p illus $7.95 (6 and up)   821

1 Moon—Poetry
ISBN 0-670-48864-X   LC 76-6168

"The poet has chosen the moon as a base for grossly exaggerated earthly forms, which he imagines living there. . . . Similar in theme or atmosphere, the poems, with their wit, fantasy, and richness of words and images, should be taken in small doses to permit the full savoring of the author's brilliance. The ink-line drawings of the specters and the monsters are completely in tune with the poetic conceptions." Horn Bk

Season songs; pictures by Leonard Baskin. Viking 1975 77p illus $10 (6 and up)   821

1 Seasons—Poetry 2 Nature in poetry
ISBN 0-670-62725-9   LC 74-18280

"The poems included here are . . . distilled from the Devon countryside, a region of unique charm and natural beauty. They are more than image, color, sound: they are alive with whatever it is that vibrates on the downs of Devon. Hughes does not describe; he evokes and enchants. . . . Metrically they owe somewhat to Old English verse. There are even echoes of nursery rhymes. The book has delightful illustrations in color and in black and white by the distinguished American artist, Leonard Baskin." Choice

Lear, Edward

The complete nonsense of Edward Lear; ed. and introduced by Holbrook Jackson. Dover [1951] 288p illus pa $3   821

1 Nonsense verses
ISBN 0-486-20167-8   LC 51-14566

Lear, Edward—*Continued*

Available in a hardcover edition from Peter Smith for $6.75 (ISBN 0-8446-0722-3)

Reprint of the 1947 Faber edition published in England

"This is a choice contribution to the literature of laughter. Limericks, verses of all kinds, alphabets and botanics are as daft and amusing as the pictures [by the author]." Adventuring With Bks

Edward Lear's The Scroobious Pip; completed by Ogden Nash; illus. by Nancy Ekholm Burkert. Harper 1968 unp illus $8.95, lib. bdg. $8.79 (2-6)   821

1 Animals—Poetry 2 Nonsense verses
ISBN 0-06-023764-3; 0-06-023765-1   LC 68-10373

The original unfinished text was first published 1953 in the U.S. by the Harvard University Press in the author's: Teapots and quails

"A beautiful book, its large pages filled with pictures of birds, beasts, fish, and insects; handsome in format and design, the book is distinguished by the delicate charm of the illustrations. The Lear verses, left incomplete at his death, have been filled in by Nash; his additions are in brackets. The nonsense poetry bears a subtle message of acceptance, as all the creatures challenge the Pip (a bit of every species, class, genus etc. in one appealing package) to explain what he is; his firm and only response is that he is himself, the Scroobious Pip." Chicago. Children's Bk Center

The Jumblies, and other nonsense verses; with drawings by L. Leslie Brooke. Warne [1954] unp illus $4.95 (2-6)   821

1 Nonsense verses
ISBN 0-7232-0583-3   LC 54-11480
First published 1900

Here is a selection of rhymes, including The Owl and the Pussy Cat, taken from the author's nonsense books

"Superbly funny pictures, some in colour." Four to Fourteen

The owl and the pussy-cat; illus. by Barbara Cooney. Little 1969 26p illus $6.95 (k-3)   821

1 Nonsense verses
ISBN 0-316-51840-9   LC 69-15759

This book "features the original English version of Lear's rhyme. Yellow, turquoise, and green drawings capture the nautical setting of this tale about that amorous pair, a jaunty, Don Juan owl and a coquettish cat. In the illustrations, both sport distinctly modern, human trappings—Pussycat, for example, wears a great big beach hat while owl strums his guitar with true aplomb. Time doesn't diminish the appeal of Lear's version, and this book will delight both ear and eye." Sch Library J

The owl and the pussy-cat; illus. by Gwen Fulton. Atheneum Pubs. 1977 unp illus $6.95 (k-3)   821

1 Nonsense verses
ISBN 0-689-30609-1   LC 77-77869
"A Jonathan Cape book"

"Full-page illustrations executed in elegant colored wash perpetuate the whimsical fantasy of Lear's oft-quoted poem. Fulton features a sad-eyed owl, a saucy tabby cat, a plump pig, and a green and russet turkey against a glacé background of idyllic peacefulness." Booklist

The pelican chorus & other nonsense verses; with drawings by L. Leslie Brooke. Warne [1954] unp illus $4.95 (2-6)   821

1 Nonsense verses
ISBN 0-7232-0584-1   LC 54-11481
First published 1900

This is a selection of rhymes from the author's nonsense books

Milne, A. A.

Now we are six; with decorations by Ernest H. Shepard. Dutton [1961 c1927] 104p illus $6.95 (k-3)   821

ISBN 0-525-36126-X   LC 61-16258

First published 1927. "Reprinted September 1961 in this completely new format designed by Warren Chappell." Verso of title page

Companion volume to: When we were very young, listed below

"The boy or girl who has liked 'When we were very young' and 'Winnie-the-Pooh' will enjoy reading about Alexander Beetle who was mistaken for a match, the knight whose armor didn't squeak, and the old sailor who had so many things which he wanted to do. There are other entertaining poems, also, and many pictures as delightful as the verses." Pittsburgh

When we were very young; with decorations by Ernest H. Shepard. Dutton [1961 c1924] 102p illus $6.95 (k-3)   821

ISBN 0-525-42580-2   LC 61-16259

First published 1924. "Reprinted September 1961 in this completely new format designed by Warren Chappell." Verso of title page

Companion volume to: Now we are six, entered above

Verse "written for Milne's small son, Christopher Robin, which for its bubbling nonsense, its whimsy, and the unexpected surprises of its rhymes and rhythms, furnishes immeasurable joy to children." Right Bk for the Right Child

It is for "very small children (and for their elders who get a surreptitious joy from what is meant for their little ones). . . . Mr. Milne's gay jingles have found a worthy accompaniment in the charming illustrations of Mr. Shepard." Sat Rev

The world of Christopher Robin; the complete When we were very young and Now we are six; with decorations and new illus. in full color, by E. H. Shepard. Dutton 1958 234p illus $9.95 (k-3)   821

ISBN 0-525-43292-2   LC 58-9571

Also available as part of a boxed set together with: The world of Pooh, entered separately in the Fiction section, for $18.50 (ISBN 0-525-43348-1)

In this combined edition of the two titles entered separately above "the black-and-white illustrations of the original book have been retained and in addition the artist has created end papers and eight full-page illustrations in color. While libraries undoubtedly prefer the separate books many will also want this appealing combination volume." Booklist

Raskin, Ellen

Goblin market [by] Christina Rossetti; illus. and adapted by Ellen Raskin. Dutton 1970 30p illus lib. bdg. $7.95 (3-6)   821

1 Fairies—Poetry
ISBN 0-525-30744-3   LC 76-115984

"The poem, which the artist notes is a favorite of hers, is certainly suited to her style—here sort of 'mod Pre-Raphaelite'. . . . Her goblins attractively evil, appear in the quasi-animal forms the text implies; her imaginative costuming of them from many periods suggests a timeless Evil that has taken random, whimsical form. . . . The excesses of language are partially pared (197 lines cut), and though still 'old fashioned,' the story line is tightened." Library J

Rossetti, Christina G.

Sing-song; a nursery rhyme book; illus. by Arthur Hughes. Dover 1968 129p illus pa $2 (k-2)   821

ISBN 0-486-22107-5   LC 68-55822

A reprint of the title first published 1872 in England

"Christina Rossetti provides the young child with an ideal introduction to lyric poetry in the verses of Sing Song. . . . Many of the verses have homely, familiar subjects, but they are written with lyric grace and with a subtle simplicity in the choice of words." Children and Bks

Stevenson, Robert Louis

A child's garden of verses (k-4)   821

Some editions are:

Dent, J.M. (The Children's illustrated classics) $5.50 With drawings in colour by Mary Shillabeer and wood engravings by the author (ISBN 0-460-05047-8; LC 60-52206)

Golden Press lib. bdg. $7.62 Illustrated by Alice and Martin Provensen (ISBN 0-307-65557-1; LC 65-7407)

Stevenson, Robert L.—*Continued*

Grosset $4.95, lib. bdg. $10.15 Illustrated by Gyo Fujikawa (ISBN 0-448-02878-6; 0-448-032-1; LC 57-13979)

Scribner (Scribner Illustrated classics) lib. bdg. $12.50 Illustrated by Jessie Wilcox Smith (ISBN 0-684-20949-7)

First published 1885 in England with title: Penny whistles

"Verses known and loved by one generation after another. Among the simpler ones for pre-school children are: Rain; At the Seaside; and Singing." Right Bk for the Right Child

"Poems full of music and rhythm, by a poet who always kept his ability to live in a child's world." A. T. Eaton's Treasure for the Taking

821.08   English poetry— Collections

Amelia mixed the mustard, and other poems; selected and illus. by Evaline Ness. Scribner 1975 47p illus lib. bdg. $7.95 (2-5)   **821.08**

1 Women—Poetry   2 English poetry—Collections 3 American poetry—Collections
ISBN 0-648-14271-6   LC 74-14077

"All the poems collected here star girls; the pictures for the title poem suggest that the artist's muse has been working overtime. Instead of an obvious scene, such as a daughter and mother at a table, we find Amelia holding onto the reins of her horse and doubled up in glee as her mother is perched backward on her mount, in a state of collapse from eating the custard in which Amelia has 'mixed the mustard.' The idea is all the funnier in comparison with the rigidly correct riding habits of mother and child and the unfussed dignity of the equines. Among the poets represented here are A. E. Housman, Edna St. Vincent Millay, Hilaire Belloc, John Keats and others, including some moderns." Pub W

As I walked out one evening; a book of ballads; selected by Helen Plotz. Greenwillow Bks. 1976 265p $9.25, lib. bdg. $8.88 (5 and up)   **821.08**

1 Ballads, English   2 Ballads, American   3 Folk songs
ISBN 0-688-80054-8; 0-688-84054-X   LC 76-10306

An "informative introduction discusses the form, appeal, and origins of the ballad, and the book is divided into six areas: Magic and Miracles, Narratives, Broadsides and Satires, War, Work, and Love. This is an anthology with breadth and discrimination, including among its selections some of the traditional ballads, story songs of the Depression Era, cowboy songs, political ballads, songs of tall tale heroes, and others. Separate author, title, and first line indexes are included." Chicago. Children's Bk Center

"Impressive in scope, the book encompasses not only traditional ballads from the British Isles and from America but selections by fifty poets—from Shakespeare, Keats, and Byron to Edith Sitwell, Langston Hughes, and John Betjeman." Horn Bk

The **Birds** and the beasts were there; animal poems selected by William Cole; woodcuts by Helen Siegl. Collins [distributed by Philomel Bks.] 1963 320p illus lib. bdg. $7.99 (5 and up)   **821.08**

1 Animals—Poetry   2 English poetry—Collections 3 American poetry—Collections
ISBN 0-529-03742-4   LC 63-18467

These are poems about small animals of the woods and fields, dogs, cats, horses, donkeys, big beasts, wild beasts, leapers and flyers and impossible animals. Some of the poets included are Peggy Bennett, William Blake, Elizabeth Coatsworth, Rachel Field, Arthur Guiterman, Don Marquis, Ogden Nash, James Reeves and Shakespeare

"Funny poems, sad poems, exhilarating flagwaving kinds of poems, all of them about animals, should make poetry-lovers, admiring animals as they do already, fill find unending delight in this splendid, solid volume with its attractive woodcut illustrations." Christian Sci Monitor

Indexed by author and title

Cole, William

(comp.) Humorous poetry for children; illus. by Ervine Metzl. Collins [distributed by Philomel Bks.] 1955 124p illus lib. bdg. $6.99 (5 and up)   **821.08**

1 Humorous poetry   2 English poetry—Collections 3 American poetry—Collections
ISBN 0-529-03480-8   LC 55-5283

First published by World Publishing Company

Here is "a collection of humorous poems, some by well-known and others by obscure poets. Some of the well-known poets have a reputation for light verse; others are better known for their serious verse. The quality varies from slightly better than doggerel to quite good poetry, and there is something here for every taste in humor from the most obvious to quite subtle." Chicago. Children's Bk Center

"Well arranged and indexed." NY Pub Library

(comp.) Poems for seasons and celebrations; illus. by Johannes Troyer. Collins [distributed by Philomel Bks.] 1961 191p illus lib. bdg. $6.99 (5 and up)   **821.08**

1 Holidays—Poetry   2 Seasons—Poetry   3 English poetry—Collections   4 American poetry— Collections
ISBN 0-529-03660-6   LC 61-12012

First published by World Publishing Company

Arranged chronologically beginning with the New Year, this is a collection of over 140 poems, traditional and modern, English and American, celebrating various holidays and the four seasons. Both an author and title index are included

"Poetry for special occasions is always in demand, but the variety of both mood and form in the poems of this book will make it a delight for any time of the year, in homes as well as libraries. Ranging from the Bible, Shakespeare, and Robert Herrick down to the present, with several poems by two new poets written especially for this book, the collection is fresh and unhackneyed, excellent for reading aloud, and wholly inviting. Charming line drawings." Horn Bk

(comp.) Poems of magic and spells; illus. by Peggy Bacon. Collins [distributed by Philomel Bks.] 1960 224p illus lib. bdg. $6.99 (4 and up)   **821.08**

1 Fairies—Poetry   2 English poetry—Collections 3 American poetry—Collections
ISBN 0-529-03587-1   LC 60-5802

First published by World Publishing Company

"In handsome format, a fine collection of ninety poems, about strange people and magical events. From Jonson and Shakespeare, Blake and Coleridge, to contemporary authors, there is a good range of . . . poets. Of the sixty poets whose work is included, most are represented by one selection; eight anonymous poems are included. . . . The illustrations are perfectly suited to the theme of the book. Separate title and first line indexes are appended. . . . Suitable for reading aloud." Chicago. Children's Bk Center

(comp.) Rough men, tough men; poems of action and adventure; illus. by Enrico Arno. Viking 1969 225p illus $5.95 (5 and up)   **821.08**

1 Adventure and adventurers—Poetry   2 English poetry—Collections   3 American poetry—Collections
ISBN 0-670-60863-7   LC 78-85871

"Represented are 72 different authors, not including the prolific 'Anonymous' author of 32 items. The rough and tough men are cowboys and prospectors, pirates and outlaws, soldiers and sailors, knights of old, railroaders and robbers. It is a treasury that . . . [demonstrates] that poetry is not all soft sighs and swoonings." Best Sellers

Includes indexes of authors and titles

De La Mare, Walter

(ed.) Come hither; a collection of rhymes & poems for the young of all ages; decorations by Warren Chappell. Knopf 1957 xxxi, 777, xxi p illus $25   **821.08**

1 English poetry—Collections   2 American poetry —Collections
ISBN 0-394-40336-3   LC 57-8123

De La Mare, Walter—*Continued*

First published 1923

"Nearly five hundred selections representing a poet's choice, and including a number from modern writers. There is an introduction, in the form of a story, which shows the development of Mr. De La Mare's own love of poetry from the days of his early boyhood. The many notes 'written about and roundabout the poems' are also of unusual interest." Pittsburgh

It serves as an "outstanding anthology of English poetry." Ontario Library Rev

Author index, title and first line index, and an index of notes

Eaton, Anne Thaxter

(comp.) Welcome Christmas! A garland of poems; decorated by Valenti Angelo. Viking 1955 128p illus lib. bdg. $5.95 (4 and up)

821.08

1 Christmas—Poetry 2 English poetry—Collections 3 American poetry—Collections
ISBN 0-670-12800-7   LC 55-14954

"This useful anthology of [about fifty] Christmas poems and carols includes selections from ancient broadsides and from less familiar verses such as those of William Morris. Modern poets whose verse expresses 'the inner meaning of Christmas' are represented by Walter de la Mare, Katharine Tynan, Dorothy Sayers and others." Bks for Boys and Girls, Supplement to 3d edition

Contains Index of titles and first lines and Alphabetical list of authors

For a child; great poems old and new; collected by Wilma McFarland; illus. by Ninon. Westminster Press 1947 96p illus $4.50 (k-3)

821.08

1 English poetry—Collections 2 American poetry—Collections
ISBN 0-664-32001-5   LC 47-2711

Here are poems of nature and the seasons, songs of home, family, and childhood pets, verses reflecting the everyday life of a child. Represented are R. L. Stevenson, Lois Lenski, Eleanor Farjeon, Robert Browning, Christopher Morley, Swinburne and many others

"Format and gay, colored illustrations give it the appearance of a picture book." Booklist

From morn to midnight; [illus. by] Satomi Ichikawa; children's verses chosen by Elaine Moss. Crowell 1977 unp illus $8.95, lib. bdg. $8.79 (k-3)

821.08

1 English poetry—Collections
ISBN 0-690-01393-0; 0-690-01394-0   LC 77-2548

A "combination of soft watercolor illustrations with poems of well-known and contemporary authors. The poems are chronologically ordered to describe the day of a child from dawn until bedtime." Children's Bk Rev Serv

"Both the art and poetry have that elusive quality known as charm, supported by considerable traditional skill. . . . The full-page watercolor paintings into which the lines are set reflect a Greenaway spirit, with children larking about in old-fashioned clothes and unalloyed glee. The settings are irresistibly idyllic; abandon cynicism, all ye who enter here. Poems and pictures will ring in the head." Booklist

Gaily we parade; a collection of poems about people, here, there & everywhere; selected by John E. Brewton; illus. by Robert Lawson. Macmillan Pub. Co. 1940 218p illus $4.95 (3-6)

821.08

1 English poetry—Collections 2 American poetry—Collections
ISBN 0-02-712340-5   LC 40-27636

The collection is divided into groups as follows: Come buy; To the shops we go; These make a town; Relatives all; At our house; Neighbors of ours; Willingly to school; Sing ho! Ye sailormen; Beyond far blue hills; Out in the country; We are the music makers; Ring-a-ring o'fairies; Some see this and some see that; At the royal court; Ring around the world; Bells for Christmas ring; Funny folk; Dustman comes; Vespers

"Mr. Brewton has specialized in poems about people. The title is well chosen, for a livelier, more spirited collection could scarcely have been assembled. The authors range from Blake and Keats to Rachel Field and Elizabeth Madox Roberts." Library J

A **Galaxy** of verse; selected and with a commentary by Louis Untermeyer; with editorial assistance by Bryna Ivens Untermeyer. Evans, M.&Co. 1978 224p illus $6.95 (5 and up)

821.08

1 English poetry—Collections 2 American poetry—Collections
ISBN 0-87131-258-1   LC 78-1255

"Untermeyer groups poems into traditional story, limerick, nonsense, and people and animal portraits, plus serious verse on beauty and the 'ways of the world.' " Sch Library J

Includes indexes of poets and titles, and of first lines

The **Golden** journey; poems for young people; comp. by Louise Bogan and William Jay Smith; woodcuts by Fritz Kredel. Regnery [1976 c1965] 275p illus pa $3.95 (4 and up)

821.08

1 English poetry—Collections 2 American poetry—Collections
ISBN 0-8092-7963-0

First published 1965 by Reilly & Lee

The poems are "grouped in sections by subject: love poems, animal poems, country poems, etc. . . . The illustrations preceding each section are attractive woodcuts in a dark green. The selections are varied, the poems ranging from amusing jingles to classics, and the poets ranging from Skelton and Herrick (clearly a favorite of the compilers) to Walt Kelly. . . . The anthology is nicely balanced in every sense; sources are cited; author and title indexes are appended." Chicago. Children's Bk Center

The **Golden** Treasury of poetry; selected and with a commentary by Louis Untermeyer; illus. by Joan Walsh Anglund. Golden Press 1959 324p illus $9.95, lib. bdg. $16.85 **821.08**

1 English poetry—Collections 2 American poetry—Collection
ISBN 0-307-16852-2; 0-307-60852-2   LC 59-4473

"Mr Untermeyer has collected here [in twelve categories] over 400 poems to enjoy, ranging from Chaucer to Ogden Nash, and including the familiar and the unfamiliar, nonsense lyrics, limericks, and a fine selection of ballads. Brief comments on particular poems, poets, forms of poetry, or subjects are unobtrusive and interesting. The illustrations, on every page, give the book such a lively appearance that confirmed haters of poetry will be irresistibly drawn into reading." Horn Bk

Separate indexes of authors, titles, and first lines

A **Great** big ugly man came up and tied his horse to me; a book of nonsense verse; [comp. and] illus. by Wallace Tripp. Little 1973 46p illus $6.95 (k-3)

821.08

1 Nonsense verses
ISBN 0-316-85280-5   LC 74-189265

This book is "a case of an imaginative illustrator taking a new look at some old words—nursery rhymes, oral chants, verse and occasional doggerel, and coming up with some zany interpretations. Assorted animals and humans frolic through the pages in a lively series of 41 bits of verse spanning several centuries. . . . About half the verses are nursery rhymes; the rest run to oral verse, some limericks and one parody." NY Times Bk Rev

The **Home** book of verse for young folks; selected and arranged by Burton Egbert Stevenson; decorations by Willy Pogány. [Rev. and enl. ed] Holt 1958 xxii, 676p $8.95

821.08

1 English poetry—Collections 2 American poetry—Collections
ISBN 0-03-032645-1

First published 1915

A poetry anthology divided into the following sections: In the nursery, The duty of children, Rhymes of childhood, Just nonsense, Fairyland, The glad evangel, This wonderful world, Stories in rhyme, My country, The happy warrior, Life lessons, A garland of gold

"A delightful collection including old favorites and new poems for children of all ages. . . . Indexes of authors, titles and first lines. Twelve decorated pages and end-papers." Booklist

How to eat a poem & other morsels; food poems for children; selected by Rose H. Agrie; illus. by Peggy Wilson. Pantheon Bks. 1967 87p illus lib. bdg. $5.99 (3-5)
821.08

1 Food—Poetry   2 English poetry—Collections
3 American poetry—Collections
ISBN 0-394-916220　　　　LC 67-14230

"A collection of poems about food, employing delightful uses of rhymes, rhythms, words and ideas. Sources range from fragments of prose works or longer poems, to nonsense verses of writers now out of print." Bruno. Bks for Sch Libraries, 1968

"Some of the contributors are Ciardi, Merriam, McGinley, McCord, Sendak, Farjeon, and Coatsworth; a few short rhymes from Mother Goose are tucked in here and there." Chicago. Children's Bk Center

"Sprightly drawings accentuated with pink and yellow add to the jovial atmosphere. Delicious fare for browsing and to enliven curriculum units on food and health." Booklist

Includes indexes of authors and first lines

An **Inheritance** of poetry; collected and arranged by Gladys L. Adshead and Annis Duff; with decorations by Nora S. Unwin. Houghton 1948 415p illus $14.95 (5 and up)
821.08

1 English poetry—Collections   2 American poetry —Collections
ISBN 0-395-06537-2　　　　LC 48-4023

A collection of poetry, mainly English and American, by poets famous and little known, gathered from a great variety of sources. Sonnets, ballads, and hero poems, gay rhymes, songs, and deeply spiritual verses are here

The "selection is fresh but includes both the expected and the unexpected. Divisions are indicated only by a full-page drawing at the beginning of each one, and by the poems in the division. Nora Unwin's illustrations are in the exact mood of the poems. An admirable book—one that will certainly instill in a child a love of poetry. For all ages, from earliest childhood through the teens and beyond." Library J

"It is a fat, sturdy book, pleasing in appearance with large print and the authors have been inspired to compile not only the usual author, title and first line indices but also a source index and an index of musical settings." Ontario Library Rev

Larrick, Nancy
(ed.) Piper, pipe that song again! Poems for boys and girls; illus. by Kelly Oechsli. Random House 1965 85p illus lib. bdg. $4.99 (2-5)
821.08

1 English poetry—Collections   2 American poetry —Collections
ISBN 0-394-91508-9　　　　LC 65-10494

A poetry collection "appropriate for reading aloud to younger children. Most of the selections are the work of contemporary writers; much of the material is humorous, many of the poems are about nature or about animals. The black and white illustrations are attractive; there is no table of contents; separate author and title indexes are appended." Chicago. Children's Bk Center

Laughable limericks; comp. by Sara and John E. Brewton; illus. by Ingrid Fetz. Crowell 1965 147p illus music $8.95 (4 and up)
821.08

1 Limericks   2 English poetry—Collections
3 American poetry—Collections
ISBN 0-690-48667-7　　　　LC 65-16179

A collection of limericks old and new by such poets as Gelett Burgess, John Ciardi, Lewis Carroll, Robert Louis Stevenson, Ogden Nash, and Edward Lear

The verses are "arranged in groups under such headings as 'Bugs, Bees, and Birds,' 'Crawlers, Croakers, and Creepers,' 'Behavior—Scroobious and Strange,' 'Laughs Anatomical,' and 'School and College.' . . . David McCord concludes the fun with some limericks which give advice on how to write more limericks." Horn Bk

"Black and white line drawings match the fun in this delightful collection of nonsense verses on a multitude of subjects which children of all ages will enjoy." Ontario Library Rev

Index of authors: p140-41. Index of first lines p142-47

Lewis, Richard
(ed.) Miracles; poems by children of the English-speaking world. Simon & Schuster 1966 215p illus $8.95
821.08

1 English poetry—Collections   2 Children as authors
ISBN 0-671-47540-1　　　　LC 66-20248

Companion volume to: Journeys, entered in class 820.8

Poems on a variety of subjects by children between the ages of 4 and 13. The authors come from such varied backgrounds as the United States, England, Ireland, New Zealand, Kenya, Uganda, and Australia

"Poems chosen with a keen appreciation of the spontaneity of children's creative expression." Children's Bks. 1966

Livingston, Myra Cohn
(ed.) Listen, children, listen; an anthology of poems for the very young; illus. by Trina Schart Hyman. Harcourt 1972 96p illus $5.95 (k-4)
821.08

1 English poetry—Collections   2 American poetry —Collections
ISBN 0-15-245570-1　　　　LC 70-167836

"Sophisticated verses as well as simple ones (but not less effective) are well represented. The poems range from the nonsense of Belloc and Lear to the sensitivity of Emily Dickinson, T. S. Eliot, e.e. cummings, William Butler Yeats and other poets, old and new." Pub W

"The black-and-white drawings on almost every page are remarkably fine visual extensions of the imagery of the poems. And the pictures of the children, the animals and the birds, and the delightfully hairy uglies should invite repeated viewings as the poems should invite repeated readings." Horn Bk

Love, Katherine
(comp.) A little laughter; illus. by Walter H. Lorraine. Crowell 1957 114p illus $6.95 (3-6)
821.08

1 Humorous poetry   2 English poetry—Collections   3 American poetry—Collections
ISBN 0-690-49804-7　　　　LC 57-10283

"An anthology of light-hearted poetry that one would be glad to have at hand for many an occasion. . . . The selections happily include favorites from Lear, Richards, Belloc, and Eliot, Kenneth Grahame and Walter de la Mare, interspersed with just as happy but less easily found choices from such modern poets as Harry Behn, Palmer Brown, and J. R. R. Tolkien. The pen-and-ink sketches introduce a giddiness of their own, occasionally suggesting Lear's graphic humor." Horn Bk

Indexes of authors, titles and first lines: p109-14

The **Man** in the Moon as he sails the sky, and other Moon verse; collected and illus. by Ann Schweninger. Dodd 1979 48p illus $7.95 (k-3)
821.08

1 Moon—Poetry   2 English poetry—Collections
ISBN 0-396-07741-2　　　　LC 79-52051

"Twenty-one poems express a quiet joy about the world of night and the moon which presides over it. Delicately painted pictures in soft muted colors accompany each poem. The selections range from such traditional or well-known verse as 'Hey diddle, diddle' and 'The Moon's the North Wind's Cooky' to less familiar but equally appropriate lines as Kathryn Maxwell Smith's 'Tonight the color/Of the moon/Is amber tea/In a silver spoon.' The latter is illustrated by a fox and a raccoon sitting down to tea beneath a full amber-colored moon. Many of the pieces are from Mother Goose, but Vachel Lindsay, Edward Lear, William Wordsworth, and others are represented. The illustrations are framed against a white background, and credit for the sources of the poems appears in the back, giving the volume a clean, uncluttered appearance —elegant in its simplicity." Horn Bk

My poetry book; an anthology of modern verse for boys and girls. Rev. ed. Selected and arranged by Grace Thompson Huffard and Laura Mae Carlisle in collaboration with Helen Ferris; introduction by Marguerite de Angeli; illus. by Willy Pogány. Holt 1956 504p illus lib. bdg. $7.95 (5 and up) **821.08**

1 English poetry—Collections 2 American poetry
—Collections
ISBN 0-03-033630-9 LC 56-10924

First published 1934

Over "five hundred poems are included in this interesting anthology. . . . They are arranged under broad subject headings indicative of children's interest. . . . Author, title, and first-line indexes, and a glossary of unusual and difficult words." Booklist

The reader "will notice two salient features. The first is the open-mindedness with which its choice of poems has been made; the second is the way in which they all fit somehow into the active or contemplative life of children." NY Her Trib Bks

My tang's tungled and other ridiculous situations; humorous poems collected by Sara and John E. Brewton and G. Meredith Blackburn III; illus. by Graham Booth. Crowell 1973 111p illus $8.95 (3-6) **821.08**

1 Humorous poetry 2 English poetry—Collections 3 American poetry—Collections
ISBN 0-690-57223-9 LC 73-254

This collection "includes tongue tanglers, topsy-turvies, poems about the vexations of family life, the peculiarities of animal life, and the contradictions of school life—as well as a liberal sprinkling of just plain nonsense." Horn Bk

"The assortment of authors is impressive: T. S. Eliot, Elizabeth Coatsworth, Theodore Roethke, Hilaire Belloc, Shel Silverstein and John Ciardi are a few. . . . Small chuckles and big laughs abound here. The illustrations are ridiculously funny." Pub W

Includes title, author and first line indexes

Of quarks, quasars, and other quirks; quizzical poems for the supersonic age; collected by Sara and John E. Brewton and John Brewton Blackburn; illus. by Quentin Blake. Crowell 1977 114p illus $8.95 (5 and up) **821.08**

1 English poetry—Collections 2 American poetry
—Collections 3 Civilization, Modern—Poetry
ISBN 0-690-01286-8 LC 76-54747

"An anthology of children's poetry spoofing modern life and scientific progress. Credit card overuse, TV mania, computer craziness, transplants, and atomic bombs are parodied in original and outrageous verse with serious undertones. . . . With such contributors as Eve Merriam, Ogden Nash, and John Updike." Sch Library J

The humorous mood is "ably abetted by Quentin Blake's wacky sketches. This is quite a collection for a subject that isn't supposed to lend itself to poetry; it should find a ready audience in anyone who wants to have a little fun or who has ever had a run-in with our machine-oriented world. It's also something to hand a reader who 'doesn't like poetry.'" Appraisal

Oh, how silly! Poems selected by William Cole; drawings by Tomi Ungerer. Viking 1970 94p illus lib. bdg. $3.95 (3-6) **821.08**

1 Nonsense verses 2 English poetry—Collections
3 American poetry—Collections
ISBN 0-670-52095 LC 74-123020

A collection of humorous verse by both English and American poets, past and present. Along with the familiar names of Ogden Nash and Hilaire Belloc, the editor has included such poets as Shel Silverstein, Jack Prelutsky and Alexander Resnikoff

It "is sure to be popular with readers who enjoy the absurd." Booklist

Author index: p91-92. Title index. p93-94

Oh, that's ridiculous! Poems selected by William Cole; drawings by Tomi Ungerer. Viking 1972 80p illus lib. bdg. $6.95 (3-6) **821.08**

1 Nonsense verses 2 English poetry—Collections
3 American poetry—Collections
ISBN 0-670-52107-8 LC 70-183934

Here are limericks and nonsense rhymes by various authors, including Gelett Burgess, Ogden Nash, Theodore Roethke, A. E. Housman, and others

"There are a few rhymes that have the tinge of children's doggerel, but most of them are delightfully silly. . . . The illustrations are divinely, fittingly mad." Chicago. Children's Bk Center

Author index: p78. Title index: p79-80

Oh, what nonsense! Poems selected by William Cole; drawings by Tomi Ungerer. Viking 1966 80p illus lib. bdg. $6.95 (3-6) **821.08**

1 Nonsense verses 2 English poetry—Collections
3 American poetry—Collections
ISBN 0-670-52117-5 LC 66-6763

"Nonsense verses, both naughty and nice, cavort across the pages in company with comical poker-faced characters. Because many of the verses are those of modern poets (Mr. Lear and Mr. Carroll are conspicuous in their absence), the anthology is as fresh as it is gleeful. Also included among the fifty selections are anonymous pieces—words to songs, counting rhymes, jump-rope rhymes. The illustrations are peculiarly amusing, a few of them positively unnerving." Horn Bk

Author index: p77-78. Title index: p79-80

One thousand poems for children; based on the selections of Roger Ingpen; selected and arranged by Elizabeth Hough Sechrist; with decorative drawings by Henry C. Pitz. Macrae Smith Co. 1946 601p illus $9.75
821.08

1 English poetry—Collections 2 American poetry
—Collections
ISBN 0-8255-8146-X LC 46-4924

First published 1903 with Roger Ingpen as the compiler

Part I includes selections, grouped by subject for children from nursery age to sixth grade; part II, for seventh to tenth grades. . . . [There are] decorated end papers and black and white drawings. Indexes of authors, first lines and titles." Bookmark

The **Oxford** Book of children's verse; chosen and ed. with notes, by Iona and Peter Opie. Oxford 1973 407p illus $15.95 **821.08**

1 English poetry—Collections 2 American poetry
—Collections
ISBN 0-19-812140-7 LC 73-76871

Arranged chronologically, these 332 selections from British and American children's poetry include works by such poets as Chaucer, Charles and Mary Lamb, Kipling, Farjeon, Milne, Eliot and Nash. Poets still living are not included

This "volume serves as a solid base for a logical presentation of the historical development of children's verse. . . . Although few child readers will find the collection especially exciting because of the clear connections of the verses with the historical periods that produced them, scholars at last have an intelligent, comprehensive anthology of verse for children or about children that clearly demonstrate changing attitudes and values. An excellent chronological collection that should be in every library." Choice

Includes sources and biographical notes and indexes of authors, first lines and familiar titles

Parker, Elinor

(ed.) 100 more story poems; illus. by Peter Spier. Crowell 1960 374p illus $8.95 (6 and up) **821.08**

1 English poetry—Collections 2 American poetry
—Collections
ISBN 0-690-59690-1 LC 60-11543

"The collection is well rounded, containing favorites like 'The Jumblies,' 'The Listeners,' 'The Vision of Sir Launfal' and a wide representation of poets such as Poe, Yeats, Thackeray, and Browning and a good portion of English and Scottish ballads. The section on Christmastide is noteworthy, being devoted almost exclusively to lovely poems about the Christ Child." Library J

Includes indexes of authors, titles, and first lines

The **Poetry** troupe; an anthology of poems to read aloud; comp. by Isabel Wilner; decoration by Isabel Wilner. Scribner 1977 223p lib. bdg. $9.95   **821.08**

1 English poetry—Collections 2 American poetry —Collections

ISBN 0-684-15198-7   LC 77-9439

"During her years as a librarian in an elementary laboratory school on a college campus, the compiler has worked with childen in 'poetry troupes' that invite both active participation and passive listening. The groups vary in age, taste, and sophistication; girls and boys help to hunt down the poems to be shared and present them in an assortment of ways to classes of college students as well as of children. The collection represents poetry that has brought great pleasure to readers and to audiences; and while most of the authors are familiar enough, the poems themselves are buoyant and unhackneyed. . . . With indexes of authors, titles, and first lines." Horn Bk

Rainbow in the sky; collected and ed. by Louis Untermeyer; illus. by Reginald Birch. Harcourt 1935 xxvii, 498p illus $12.95 (k-4)   **821.08**

1 English poetry—Collections 2 American poetry —Collections 3 Nursery rhymes

ISBN 0-15-265477-1   LC 35-27286

"More than five hundred poems from Mother Goose to modern times are included in this anthology for younger children. Mr. Birch's drawings in black and white are lively and . . . amusing." NY Pub Library

"This is a grand, large collection that is a necessity for the young child's library." Sat Rev

Author, title and first line indexes

Roofs of gold; poems to read aloud; ed. and with an introduction by Padraic Colum. Macmillan Pub. Co. 1964 179p illus $7.95 (6 and up)   **821.08**

1 English poetry—Collections 2 American poetry —Collections

ISBN 0-02-722920-3   LC 64-23076

"For this anthology of poems intended for reading aloud a noted Irish storyteller and poet has selected more than 80 poems outstanding for their visualness, striking imagery, picturesqueness, action and humor, and lack of subjectiveness. . . . Supplemented with notes illuminating the historical background of 14 of the poems and illustrated with a few decorative wood engravings." Booklist

"An anthology that contains very few unusual selections; the poems are chiefly . . . old favorites. . . . A few newer poets are represented—including Mr. Colum. Arrangement is fairly random." Chicago. Children's Bk Center

Sechrist, Elizabeth Hough

(comp.) Poems for red letter days; illus. by Guy Fry. Macrae Smith Co. 1951 349p illus lib. bdg. $5.97   **821.08**

1 Holidays—Poetry 2 English poetry—Collections 3 American poetry—Collections

ISBN 0-8255-8155-9   LC 51-14010

"A poetry anthology ranging from Shakespeare to Edgar Guest and provided with good indexes [of authors, titles, first lines] and the happy arrangement by season, holiday, and to-be-celebrated-in-the-schools weeks should by all means be recommended. This one is further enhanced by an attractive format." Library J

Shrieks at midnight; macabre poems, eerie and humorous; selected by Sara and John E. Brewton; drawings by Ellen Raskin. Crowell 1969 177p illus $8.95 (4 and up)   **821.08**

1 English poetry—Collections 2 American poetry —Collections

ISBN 0-690-73518-9   LC 69-11824

A "collection of spooky, weird, extremely humorous poems, including funny bits of terror by such poets as Lewis Carroll, Ogden Nash, Hilaire Belloc, Langston Hughes, Dorothy Parker, James Reeves, and a few good old 'Author Unknowns.' Puns, epitaphs, and old ballads are represented." Sch Library J

The illustrations "are full of verve and splendid visual puns. . . . Miss Raskin is inventive, amusing, happily horrifying." NY Times Bk Rev

Index of authors: p167-68. Index of titles: p169-72. Index of first lines: p173-77

Straight on till morning; poems of the imaginary world; selected by Helen Hill, Agnes Perkins, and Alethea Helbig; illus. by Ted Lewin. Crowell 1977 150p illus $9.95 (4 and up)   **821.08**

1 English poetry—Collections 2 American poetry —Collections

ISBN 0-690-01303-5   LC 76-55414

"This is a collection of modern poems for children that really defies strict categorization. It includes nonsense rhymes and serious verse, rat riddles, ghost poems, and songs. Many well-known writers are represented: Eve Merriam, Mark Van Doren, May Swenson, and Langston Hughes to name a few." Children's Bk Rev Serv

"The unhackneyed choices, the realistic shaded pencil drawings, and the pleasing format invite browsing as well as rereading; and the anthology is full of poems that take an imaginative plunge in the opening lines." Horn Bk

Sung under the silver umbrella; poems for young children; selected by the Literature Committee of the Association for Childhood Education; illus. by Dorothy Lathrop. Macmillan Pub. Co. 1935 xxiii, 211p illus $4.95 (k-2)   **821.08**

1 English poetry—Collections 2 American poetry —Collections

ISBN 0-02-706180-9   LC 35-7155

"A subject grouping of about 200 tried and true poems for young children, with an introduction about poetry by Padraic Colum. Author and first line index." Hodges. Bks for Elem Sch Libraries

"An anthology of authentic poetry for children from four to eight years old, which contains a varied and distinguished selection. Each group begins with the simplest poems for the youngest and progresses to more difficult examples. The collection includes nonsense verse, fine lyric poetry, free verse, Japanese haiku, and several Psalms. Dorothy Lathrop's delicate pictures add to the charm of this unusual anthology." Children's Bks Too Good To Miss

They've discovered a head in the box for the bread, and other laughable limericks, by John E. Brewton and Lorraine A. Blackburn; illus. by Fernando Krahn. Crowell 1978 129p illus $7.95, lib. bdg. $7.95   **821.08**

1 Limericks 2 English poetry—Collections 3 American poetry—Collections

ISBN 0-690-01388-4; 0-690-03883-6   LC 77-26598

"A grab bag of more than 200 limericks. . . . Loosely grouped by topic—animals, music, love, silly mistakes . . . etc.—the verses vary in their level of sophistication but strike a mean of easy, literal humor. Krahn's doughy cartoons are on hand to generate additional amusement; useful as a broad sampler, with indexes of authors, titles, and first lines appended." Booklist

This way, delight; a book of poetry for the young; ed. by Herbert Read; illus. by Juliet Kepes. Pantheon Bks. 1956 155p illus lib. bdg. $5.69 (5 and up)   **821.08**

1 English poetry—Collections 2 American poetry —Collections

ISBN 0-394-91741-3   LC 56-6014

"The distinguished poet and writer has compiled an anthology of some one hundred and twenty-five poems chosen from among great writers and each can be understood within the range of children's experience." Commonweal

"Imaginatively illustrated, it is rounded out with the essay 'What is poetry,' which points to 'deep delight' as the best introduction to the world of poetry." L.C. Children & Poetry

The table of contents is at the back of the book, preceding the indices of first lines and authors

Thompson, Blanche Jennings

(ed.) All the Silver pennies; combining Silver pennies and More Silver pennies; decorations by Ursula Arndt. Macmillan Pub. Co. 1967 224p illus $7.95 (3-6)   **821.08**

1 English poetry—Collections 2 American poetry —Collections

ISBN 0-02-789330-8   LC 67-4508

Thompson, Blanche J.—*Continued*

This is a reissue in one volume of two anthologies of modern verse for children: Silver pennies (1925) and More Silver pennies (1938)

"Time-tested poems for children, organized into Part I for the young child and Part II for older children. Includes an introduction, notes for individual poems, and author, title, and first-line indexes." Hodges. Bks for Elem Sch Libraries

Among the important poets of the early twentieth century whose works are included are Sara Teasdale, James Stephens, William Butler Yeats, James Joyce, Edna St. Vincent Millay, Robert Frost and Carl Sandburg

Tom Tiddler's ground; a book of poetry for children, chosen and annotated by Walter De La Mare; with a foreword by Leonard Clark and drawings by Margery Gill. Knopf [1962 c1961] 253p illus lib. bdg. $5.39 **821.08**

1 English poetry—Collections
ISBN 0-394-91757-X   LC 62-9471

First published 1931 in England. This 1962 American edition was copyrighted 1961 in England

More than 225 "game rhymes and nursery rhymes, lyrics, storytelling poems—poems of all kinds by many different poets are included here. Only a few are so-called poems for children, but the selection was made with children in mind. There are no specific divisions, but often one poem suggests another, and they read pleasantly in sequence. Most of the longer poems have been placed toward the end of the book." Horn Bk

"It is a handsome book, a delight to handle. . . . There are many comments by Mr. de la Mare at the end of the book, quiet seemingly casual remarks as if he were talking to each individual reader trying to show him how added understanding brings increased delight." NY Her Trib Bks

Includes indexes of authors and first lines

Very young verses; comp. by Barbara Peck Geismer and Antoinette B. Suter; illus. by Mildred Bronson. Houghton 1945 210p illus $7.95 (k-1)   **821.08**

1 English poetry—Collections 2 American poetry
—Collections
ISBN 0-395-06779-0   LC 45-2306

The poems are arranged under subjects: Birds, beasts, and bugs; About me; About other people and things; About going places; About the seasons; About the weather; Just pretend; Just for fun; Prayers

"An anthology of poems chosen for their appeal to children, 'either for their content, rhythm, words, sound or humor.' Intended for children under six; a good selection for reading aloud. Should become a permanent feature in every poetry collection." Wis Library Bul

Wings from the wind; an anthology of poems selected and illus. by Tasha Tudor. Lippincott 1964 119p illus lib. bdg. $7.89 (3-6)   **821.08**

1 English poetry—Collections 2 American poetry
—Collections
ISBN 0-397-30789-6   LC 64-19059

"Mother Goose, Wordsworth, Longfellow, Mary Webb, Shakespeare, Robert Frost are among those represented [in this collection of 65 poems]. Each poem is embellished with soft black-and-white illustrations . . . . Each section has a full-page color plate. This is a handsome book." Sch Library J

822 English drama

Bradley, Alfred

Paddington on stage; adapted by Alfred Bradley and Michael Bond; with drawings by Peggy Fortnum. Houghton 1977 [c1974] 112p illus $6.95 (2-5)   **822**

1 Bears—Drama
ISBN 0-395-25155-9   LC 76-62497

First published 1974 in England

"Based on the play 'The Adventures of Paddington Bear,' this has seven short playlets, each with two or three scenes that focus on one ploy of the bear from Peru who lives with a London family. Each play is preceded by a list of properties, and the dialogue and humor retain much of the flavor of the original Paddington stories [by Michael Bond, entered in the Fiction section] although no visual medium can retain the ingenuous quality of the original. Nevertheless, the adventures of the small creature who always manages to get out of the trouble he's gotten into are good material and provide good theatrical fodder, and the brevity and simplicity of the plays make them useful for children's productions." Chicago. Children's Bk Center

Langstaff, John

Saint George and the dragon; a mummer's play; with woodcuts by David Gentleman. Atheneum Pubs. 1973 47p illus music lib. bdg. $4.95 (4-6)   **822**

1 Christmas—Drama 2 Folk drama 3 George, Saint—Drama
ISBN 0-689-30421-8   LC 73-75437

"A Margaret K. McElderry book"

This dramatic production version of an old folk play includes music of the traditional songs, instructions for performing the sword dance, stage directions, and costume suggestions

The play "offers an original approach to the traditional holiday pageantry. This version with glowing woodcuts is meant to be performed, not just read. There's everything to delight both audience and young actors: a dragon, a comic hobby horse, dancers, a noble knight, and a magical fool. The mixture of ritual and good-natured buffoonery makes this ancient mummer's play very appealing." Christian Sci Monitor

822.3 William Shakespeare

Lamb, Charles

Tales from Shakespeare, by Charles & Mary Lamb; with 8 colour plates and line drawings in the text by Arthur Rackham. Dent 1957 304p illus (The Children's illustrated classics) $6.50   **822.3**

1 Shakespeare, William—Adaptations
ISBN 0-460-05039-7   LC 58-860

First published in 1807, these twenty plays of Shakespeare transposed into prose—the comedies by Mary Lamb, the tragedies by Charles Lamb—have taken their place as an English classic

Presented "with the object of making children familiar with the plots of Shakespeare's plays, these [are] beautifully written stories." Four to Fourteen

Shakespeare's England, by the editors of Horizon Magazine, in consultation with Louis B. Wright; illus. with paintings, drawings, and engravings of the period. Am. Heritage [distributed by Harper] 1964 153p illus maps lib. bdg. $12.89 (6 and up) **822.3**

1 Shakespeare, William—Contemporary England
2 Theater—Great Britain 3 Great Britain—History—Tudors, 1485-1603
ISBN 0-06-922591-2

"A Horizon Caravel book"

A portrayal of Shakespeare as a man of his time against the background of England under Elizabeth I and James I

"A book that should enthrall the student of English history as much as it does the reader interested in the theatre. The illustrations [many from European sources] are handsome, varied, and carefully placed and captioned. . . . It gives, especially, interesting material about touring companies, patronage, literary criticism, and the intrigue and competition in the world of Elizabethan actors and playwrights." Chicago. Children's Bk Center

Further reference: p151

827   English satire and humor

Blake, Quentin
The improbable book of records; comp. by
Quentin Blake and John Yeoman and illus.
by Quentin Blake. Atheneum Pubs. 1976
[c1975] unp illus $6.95 (3-6)   **827**

1 Curiosities and wonders—Anecdotes, facetiae,
satire, etc.
ISBN 0-689-30535-4   LC 76-4466

First published 1975 in England with title: The
Puffin Book of improbable records
"This spoof of the 'Guinness Book of World
Records' requires no familiarity with the original;
it should amuse even the uninitiated. From the
first piece of information—that the book 'is the
only one to be issued to all the U.S. Marines as
part of their survival kit on account of the high
nutritional value of its paper and printing ink'—
and from the accompanying illustration of the
compilers measuring an octopus's tentacle, it becomes clear that the author-artist team has produced another zany creation. The inventiveness
of the records is almost less brilliant than the
way they are visually depicted; the artist has
worked out all the intricacies of a man balancing
twenty-eight bananas on his nose and the subtle
qualities of a potato bearing a striking resemblance to Queen Victoria. . . . Every improbable
record is wonderfully absurd; each picture, even
more madcap; and the entire creation, delightful."
Horn Bk

828   English miscellany

Carroll, Lewis
The complete works of Lewis Carroll; with
an introduction by Alexander Woollcott and
illus. by John Tenniel. Vintage 1976 1293p
illus pa $5.95   **828**

ISBN 0-394-71661-2   LC 75-28505

Reprint of the Modern Library edition published
1936
In addition to Alice's adventures in Wonderland,
Through the looking glass, Sylvie and Bruno,
Sylvie and Bruno concluded, The hunting of the
snark, Phantasmagoria and other poems, and
Three sunsets and other poems, this volume col-
lects Carroll's shorter prose, verse, stories, games,
puzzles, problems, acrostics and a selection from
Symbolic logic

Greenaway, Kate
The Kate Greenaway treasury; introduction
by Ruth Hill Viguers; an anthology of the
illustrations and writings of Kate Greenaway;
ed. and selected by Edward Ernest, assisted
by Patricia Tracy Lowe. Collins [distributed
by Philomel Bks] 1967 319p illus $14.95   **828**

ISBN 0-529-00313-9   LC 67-23363

First published by World Publishing Company
This collection contains the complete text and
pictures for A Apple pie, The Pied Piper of
Hamelin, by Robert Browning. A day in a child's
life, by M.B. Foster, and the Alphabet, with selections from Mother Goose, Little Ann, and others.
A biography of Kate Greenaway, a selection of
her letters to and from John Ruskin, excerpts from
Anne Carroll Moore's A century of Kate Greenaway, and a bibliography are included
"A valuable insight into the life and work of a
truly creative artist whose vision of childhood
was translated into gay and tender picture books."
Library J

Milne, A. A.
The Christopher Robin story book. . . .
Decorations by Ernest H. Shepard. Dutton
[1966 c1957] 171p illus $6.95 (k-3)   **828**

ISBN 0-525-27933-4   LC 66-12251

A reissue in new format of the title first pub-
lished 1929
"Introduced and selected by the author from
When we were very young; Now we are six;
Winnie-the-Pooh; The house at Pooh Corner."
Title page
"You will find here a collection of verses and
stories, mostly about a little boy called Christopher
Robin." Author's note

Descriptions of the titles listed above can be
found entered separately. Winnie-the-Pooh and
The house at Pooh Corner are entered under Fiction, while the other two titles are entered in
class 821

831   German poetry

Koenig, Alma Johanna
Gudrun: tr. from the German by Anthea
Bell. Lothrop 1979 187p illus $8.50, lib.
bdg. $8.16 (6 and up)   **831**

ISBN 0-688-41899-6; 0-688-51899-0   LC 79-917

This "13th-Century heroic poem composed in
Middle High German, concerns the adventures,
sufferings, and triumph of a Baltic princess captured by the Normans. The story, filled with kidnappings, gory battles, and various treacheries,
moves swiftly with a large cast of superb heroes
and equally determined heroines, especially Gudrun
and her ferocious mother Hilde." Sch Library J
"The translator has admirably preserved the tone
of heroic romance in a modern prose style. . . .
Today's readers may find the medieval elements
of courtly chivalry and Christian pietism quite a
change from their usual fare, but those who succumb to the adventure of the story will enjoy
a narrative that blends the flavors of Chrétien de
Troyes and Beowulf.' Horn Bk

873   Latin epic poetry
and fiction

Church, Alfred J.
The Aeneid for boys and girls, retold by
Alfred J. Church; illus. by Eugene Karlin;
afterword by Clifton Fadiman. Macmillan
Pub. Co. 1962 172p illus $6.95 (6 and up)
                                          873

1 Aeneas
ISBN 0-02-718400-5   LC 62-19424

"The Macmillan classics"
"This is the story of the sack of Troy and of the
wanderings of King Aeneas until he establishes a
new kingdom in Italy." Bks for Boys & Girls
"A simple and dignified prose rendering of the
Aeneid. The monologues and conversations are
translated almost literally, and the whole version
keeps close to the original in spirit and atmosphere.
There are . . . attractive illustrations in delicate
colors, and the binding is artistic and serviceable."
Booklist

883   Classical Greek epic poetry
and fiction

Picard, Barbara Leonie
The Iliad of Homer; retold by Barbara
Leonie Picard; illus. by Joan Kiddell-Monroe.
Oxford 1960 208p illus $14.95 (6 and up) **883**

1 Trojan War
ISBN 0-19-274517-4

"Relates the incidents which took place in the
ninth year of the Trojan War, centering around
Achilles' quarrel with Agamemnon and the death
of Patrocius. Includes a prologue and an epilogue
and a list of names, with identifications." Hodges.
Bks for Elem Sch Libraries

The Odyssey of Homer; retold by Barbara
Leonie Picard; illus. by Joan Kiddell-Monroe.
Oxford 1952 271p illus $12.95 (6 and up) **883**

1 Ulysses
ISBN 0-19-274508-5   LC 52-11464

Homer's epic poem tells of the strange and
terrible adventures Odysseus must endure as he
makes his way home to Ithaca after the Trojan
War. Together with his crew, Odysseus meets the
one-eyed Cyclops; the giant, Polyphemus; the
enchantress, Circe; and Scylla, the hideous creature
of six heads
Map on lining-papers

891.7 Russian literature

A **Harvest** of Russian children's literature; ed. with introduction and commentary, by Miriam Morton; foreword by Ruth Hill Viguers. Univ. of Calif. Press 1967 474p illus $22.95, pa $5.95 **891.7**

1 Russian literature—Collections
ISBN 0-520-00886-3; 0-520-01745-5 LC 67-21384

This is "a superb anthology for any collection, useful for a number of diverse purposes and, better still, a source of pleasure in its variety, scope, and quality. All of the material included is in print in Russia today; the selections range from classic writers like Tolstoy and Gorky to contemporary authors, some of whose work has already been published in English—Chukovsky and Sholokhov, for example. The book's contents are divided both by age groups and by genre or type of literature; the illustrations are also from Russian children's books. Many of the selections are preceded by notes about the author. The editor has provided a long, thoughtful, and informative introduction. Separate author and title indexes are appended." Sutherland. The Best in Children's Bks

The **Moon** is like a silver sickle; a celebration of poetry by Russian children; collected and tr. by Miriam Morton; illus. by Eros Keith. Simon & Schuster 1972 93p illus $4.95 (4 and up) **891.7**

1 Russian poetry—Collections 2 Children as authors
ISBN 0-671-65198-6 LC 72-77768

Ninety-two poems, selected and "translated from poetry composed by young Russians, bring glimpses into sentiments, expressions, and experiences of children in a foreign land. Both boys and girls from the ages of four to fifteen wrote poems which are about themselves and the world around them." Top of the News

"Many of the poems are charming; however, some have been damaged by the attempt to preserve the rhyme in translation. Dreamy, delicate monochrome illustrations add much to the book's appeal." Sch Library J

895.6 Japanese literature

Baron, Virginia Olsen
(ed.) The seasons of time; tanka poetry of ancient Japan; illus. by Yasuhide Kobashi. Dial Press 1968 63p illus $4.95 (6 and up) **895.6**

1 Japanese poetry—Collections 2 Nature in poetry
ISBN 0-8037-7785-X LC 68-15254

This anthology opens with poems about spring, then moves "into summer, autumn and winter. Tanka poetry, which the introduction translates as 'short song,' is an ancient form. Most of the poems here were first collected between 759 and 905." Pub W

The poems "together with interpretive wash-and-ink drawings in black and white comprise a book that is distinctive in design as well as in pictorial and poetic content. . . . An understanding of the poems is greatly aided by the editor's brief introduction describing the source and traditional symbolism of the poems and tanka." Booklist

Cricket songs; Japanese haiku; tr. by Harry Behn; with pictures selected from Sesshu and other Japanese masters. Harcourt 1964 unp illus $4.95 (4 and up) **895.6**

1 Haiku 2 Japanese poetry—Collections 3 Nature in poetry
ISBN 0-15-220890-9 LC 64-11489

"A collection of Japanese 'haiku'—nonrhyming, three-line, seventeen-syllable nature poems suggesting the seasons of the year—selected and translated by an American poet. The 'haiku' presented here speak of chirping frogs, the moon, rain, fog, a sleeping butterfly, cicadas buzzing in the sun, and other aspects of nature." Booklist

"A small, exquisite book . . . perfect for reading aloud or to inspire creative writing of poetry." Hodges. Bks for Elem Sch Libraries

Lewis, Richard
(ed.) In a spring garden; pictures by Ezra Jack Keats. Dial Press 1965 unp illus $6.95, lib. bdg. $6.46, pa $1.75 (k-3) **895.6**

1 Haiku 2 Japanese poetry—Collections 3 Nature in poetry
ISBN 0-8037-4024-7; 0-8037-4025-5; 0-8037-4033-6 LC 65-23965

An "introductory collection of twenty-eight haiku which follow a day in spring from a red morning sky to the passing of a giant firefly." Children's Bks Too Good to Miss

"The universal quality of childhood is exemplified by the haiku, e.g. 'Just simply alive/Both of us, I/And the poppy' is complemented by the brilliant collage and water color illustrations. This beautiful, creative blend of poetry and illustrations is most wecome to the poetry collection for young children." Sch Library J

More Cricket songs; Japanese haiku; tr. by Harry Behn; illus. with pictures by Japanese masters. Harcourt 1971 64p illus $4.50 (4 and up) **895.6**

1 Haiku 2 Japanese poetry—Collections 3 Nature in poetry
ISBN 0-15-25540-8 LC 77-137755

Companion volume to: Cricket songs, entered above

"The haiku here are drawn from the work of twenty-nine poets, the selections varied in mood and subject, deceptively simple in their miniature perfection, and translated with that sensitivity and authority that indicate the poet's vision." Chicago. Children's Bk Center

897 Literatures of North American native languages

Belting, Natalia
(comp.) Our fathers had powerful songs; illus. by Laszlo Kubinyi. Dutton 1974 unp illus map lib. bdg. $7.95 (3-6) **897**

1 American poetry—American Indian authors—Collections
ISBN 0-525-36485-4 LC 73-13968

"Selected and translated into English, poems from one Canadian Indian and several American Indian tribes are illustrated by softly drawn, imaginative pictures in black and white. Like other Indian poetry, these reflect a closeness to and reverence for nature and a quiet joy in the dignity of men and the power of the gods. The collection comprises nine poems, one each from the Apache, Cochiti, Diegueno, Kwakiutl, Luiseno, Mandan, Navaho, Papago, and Wintu cultures." Chicago. Children's Bk Center

"An interesting addition to poetry shelves as well as to North American Indian collections. . . .; The poetry expresses an understated intensity." Sch Library J

In the trail of the wind; American Indian poems and ritual orations; ed. by John Bierhorst. Farrar, Straus 1971 201p illus $6.95, pa $4.95 (6 and up) **897**

1 American poetry—American Indian authors—Collections
ISBN 0-374-33640-7; 0-374-50901-8 LC 71-144822

This "collection of poetry, taken from the oral literature of more than 30 tribes of Indians of North, Central, and South America and the Eskimos, is arranged topically under such headings as The beginning, Of rain and birth, The words of war, and Death. . . . Background information on certain aspects of Indian thought and the problems of translation are discussed in the introduction. Appended are notes on each poem including translator and source; a glossary of tribes, cultures, and languages; and suggestions for further reading." Booklist

"A fascinating book to read, and to reread. . . . Its illustrations, selected from period engravings, makes it a distinguished book to look at as well." Pub W

Jones, Hettie
(comp.) The trees stand shining; poetry of the North American Indians; paintings by Robert Andrew Parker. Dial Press 1971 unp illus $7.95, lib. bdg. $7.45 (3-6)   **897**

1 American poetry—American Indian authors—Collections
ISBN 0-8037-9083-X; 0-8037-9084-8   LC 79-142452

"The poems are grouped by subject, with sources given, most of them reflecting the love and respect for natural things that are part of the great heritage of the Indian cultures of North America; They were originally songs, many of them brief fragments that seem almost chants or lamentations." Chicago. Children's Bk Center
"Fourteen large full-color paintings are provided for this handsome picture book. . . . Some are like rich impressionistic backdrops and illuminate the intense, haikulike word images. . . . Others portray animal or human figures against sweeping brush strokes of color." Horn Bk

Rasmussen, Knud
(comp.) Beyond the high hills; a book of Eskimo poems; photos by Guy Mary-Rousselière. Collins [distributed by Philomel Bks] 1961 32p illus $6.95 (4 and up)   **897**

1 Eskimo poetry—Collections
ISBN 0-529-03690-8   LC 61-14072

First published by World Publishing Company
"Poems collected by a Danish explorer among the Eskimos of the Hudson Bay region and the Musk Ox people of the Copper Country. Remarkably clear in expression and in imagery these poems are, as explained by the foreword 'really songs, chanted spontaneously to celebrate the hunt or other adventures, great sorrow or great happiness, or merely the joy of being alive.' The text and striking complementary color photographs taken in the same area by an Oblate priest make an unusual and beautiful book of value in connection with social studies as well as literature." Booklist

Songs of the dream people; chants and images from the Indians and Eskimos of North America; ed. and illus. by James Houston. Atheneum Pubs. 1972 83p illus $5.95 (4 and up)   **897**

1 American poetry—American Indian authors—Collections
ISBN 0-689-30306-8   LC 72-77130

"A Margaret K. McElderry book"
This book contains "Indian and Eskimo songs and chants gathered from many North American tribes." Booklist
"The verses, many short and haiku-like, are rich with the magic of words and ritual. . . . Distinctive, two-color drawings of Eskimo and Indian artifacts, labeled with tribal designations, illuminate the text. A Foreword notes the significance of dreams and the employment of secret terms in the songs." Horn Bk
Suggestions for further reading: p[86]

900   GEOGRAPHY AND HISTORY

909   General world history

Foster, Genevieve
Birthdays of freedom; from early man to July 4, 1776. Scribner 1973 128p illus maps lib. bdg. $6.95 (5 and up)   **909**

1 Civilization—History 2 Freedom
ISBN 0-684-13496-9   LC 73-5183

Originally published separately in two volumes, 1952 and 1957 respectively. Book I: The ancient world; Book II: From the fall of Rome to July 4, 1776
Includes information on the early Egyptians, democracy in Athens, the Magna Carta, and other high points or setbacks in the struggle for freedom

909.08   Modern history, 1450/1500-

Foster, Genevieve
The world of William Penn; illus. by the author. Scribner [n.d.] 192p illus maps $15 (5 and up)   **909.08**

1 Seventeenth century 2 Penn, William
ISBN 0-684-15725-X

"Hudson River edition"
Reprint of the title first published 1973
The author looks at the whole world as it existed during the time of William Penn, and how it affected the direction of his life
"The clear textual treatment brings to life the backgrounds and activities of the second half of the seventeenth and the first quarter of the eighteenth century—in the arts and sciences, and in war and peace. Portraits, scenes, diagrams, and pictorial maps clarify and enliven the text. The broad compass of the book permits paths to cross, as when William Penn meets with Peter the Great. An enlightened approach to the study of world history." Horn Bk

Year of Columbus, 1492. Scribner 1969 64p illus maps lib. bdg. $5.95 (3-6)   **909.08**

1 Fifteenth century 2 Columbus, Christopher 3 America—Exploration
ISBN 0-684-16573-2   LC 77-85268

This book, illustrated by the author, gives "younger children a world-wide perspective on historic events. About half of the . . . book is devoted to Columbus and half to the concurrent activities of Copernicus, Leonardo da Vinci, and Michelangelo and events in Ethiopia, China, Japan, Peru, and Mexico." Booklist
The author writes "in a manner calculated to whet the reading appetites of middle graders. . . . Illustrations are plentiful, and include carefully researched maps and charts. Wider in scope than most books bearing on the subject for this age group." Sch Library J

909.7   World history, 1700-1799

Foster, Genevieve
Year of independence, 1776. Scribner 1970 64p illus maps lib. bdg. $5.95 (3-6)   **909.7**

1 Eighteenth century 2 U.S.—History—Revolution, 1775-1783 3 U.S. Declaration of Independence
ISBN 0-684-12689-3   LC 75-106531

"This book consists of three parts. First, the author describes political events in the United States from 1776 to 1783. Parts two and three present some of the artistic and scientific developments in other parts of the world during the same period." Commonweal
"Copiously illustrated with [the author's] two-color pictures and maps." Booklist

909.81   World history, 1800-1899

Foster, Genevieve
Year of Lincoln, 1861. Scribner 1970 64p illus maps lib. bdg. $5.95 (3-6)   **909.81**

1 Nineteenth century 2 Lincoln, Abraham, President U.S. 3 U.S.—History—Civil War, 1861-1865
ISBN 0-684-20823-7   LC 76-121746

"The author uses 1861 and the start of the American Civil War as her base and gives a brief historical perspective of the importance during that period of Lincoln, Darwin, Mark Twain, Dickens, Frederick Douglass, Queen Victoria, Empress Tzu Hsi, and Prince (later Emperor) Mutsuhito, who followed up Commodore Perry's introduction of Western culture to Japan with 'enlightened' economic reform." Horn Bk
The survey "moves from 1830 to 1865. . . . Useful but not unusual in the coverage of American history; the second half of the book has some interesting material, but each section seems isolated. An index is appended." Chicago. Children's Bk Center

Foster, Genevieve—*Continued*

The year of the horseless carriage, 1801; illus. by the author. Scribner 1975 95p illus lib. bdg. $6.95 (3-6) **909.81**

1 Nineteenth century
ISBN 0-684-14198-1 LC 74-29161
"This book pertains to the period from 1801 to 1821. During this time, Napoleon Bonaparte was influencing the course of Europe, Thomas Jefferson was President of the United States, Ludwig van Beethoven was composing 'Eroica,' and Richard Trevithick was working on an invention that ultimately would replace the horse as a primary means of transportation." Cur Ref Bks
"This across-the-board approach to history is, as it is in other Foster books, a stimulating one; the writing is direct and brisk, the illustrations interesting if not always informative." Chicago. Children's Bk Center

909.82 World history, 1900-1999

Foster, Genevieve

The year of the flying machine, 1903; illus. by the author. Scribner 1977 96p illus lib. bdg. $6.95 (3-6) **909.82**

1 Twentieth century
ISBN 0-684-15182-0 LC 77-9074
"Foster relates and discusses outstanding events of the first decade of the 20th Century in three sections, each of which starts with the exploits of Wilbur and Orville Wright and their heavier-than-air manned flights. Other events and personages described are: Theodore Roosevelt, 'the youngest man to assume the Presidency of the U.S.'; Marconi and his wireless telegraph; Marie and Pierre Curie and their experiments with radium; Ford and his motor car; Lenin and the Russian Revolution of 1905; Einstein and his theory of relativity; Freud's 'The Interpretation of Dreams'; Admiral Perry at the North Pole; and, as climax, the U.S. War Department accepting the plane of the Wright Brothers. The bold black-and-white illustrations add to the text which is as well written and informative as the author's biographies for children." Sch Library J

910 General geography. Travel

Yolen, Jane

The wizard islands; illus. by Robert Quackenbush; includes photographs, old documents, and maps. Crowell 1973 115p illus maps $3.95 (5 and up) **910**

1 Islands
ISBN 0-690-89671-9 LC 73-4474
"Some fact and some fiction are included in eleven stories about islands, ranging from a completely factual description of Surtsey to discussions of islands whose existence has been claimed but is doubtful, from the mystifying art of Easter Island to stories of island-based events that have had ghostly legends added to fact." Chicago. Children's Bk Center
The book "is informative . . . generally thought provoking. The colorful jacket and black and white book illustrations are excellent and very appropriate to the storytelling mood that the author establishes." Rdng Teacher
For further reading: p110-11

910.3 Geography—Dictionaries, encyclopedias, gazetteers

Webster's New geographical dictionary. Merriam maps $14.95 **910.3**

1 Geography—Dictionaries 2 Gazetteers
First published 1949 with title: Webster's Geographical dictionary. Periodically revised
This dictionary includes "some 47,000 geographical names from biblical times, ancient Greece and Rome, medieval Europe, and today's world. Entries provide gazetteer-type information, geographical features, monuments, and a brief history. Pronunciation is marked and cross references are given

for alternative spellings. There are 217 inset maps included in the text. Additional features include a list of geographical terms, signs and symbols, and information on maps and map projections." Wynar. Guide to Ref Bks for Sch Media Centers [review of the 1972 edition]
"A very useful, standard ready reference tool." Cur Ref Bks [review of the 1972 edition]

Worldmark Encyclopedia of the nations. . . . Worldmark Press, distributed by Wiley 5v illus maps $99.50 **910.3**

1 Geography—Encyclopedias 2 World history—Encyclopedias 3 World politics—Encyclopedias 4 United Nations
First published 1960 in one volume, arranged in one alphabet. Periodically revised to bring material up to date
"A practical guide to the geographic, historical, political, social & economic status of all nations, their international relationships, and the United Nations system." Title page [fifth edition]
Contents: v 1 United Nations; v2 Africa; v3 Americas; v4 Asia & Australasia; v5 Europe
Includes bibliographic references

910.4 Accounts of travel. Seafaring life

Graham, Robin Lee

The boy who sailed around the world alone, by Robin Lee Graham with Derek L. T. Gill; editor: Frances Giannoni. Golden Press 1973 140p illus maps $6.95, lib. bdg. $12.23 (5 and up) **910.4**

1 Dove (Sloop) 2 Voyages around the world
ISBN 0-307-16510-8; 0-307-66510-0 LC 73-85652
Robin Graham is a Californian who set out on a solo round-the-world voyage in 1967 on a 24-foot sloop. This book recounts that journey which lasted nearly five years
"Robin, sailed around the world in 'Dove' when he was only 16, with no companions except for a couple of pet cats. The writing reveals Robin as a modest, wholly likable boy. Clearly mature for his age, he took time out to get married to Patti, a girl he met on one of his island stops, and to start a family. . . . Illustrated with color photos from various sources, including the National Geographic Society." Pub W

Heyerdahl, Thor

Kon-Tiki; a special Rand McNally color edition for young people. Rand McNally 1960 165p illus maps pa $4.95 (4 and up) **910.4**

1 Kon-Tiki Expedition, 1947 2 Pacific Ocean 3 Ethnology—Polynesia
ISBN 0-528-87175-7 LC 60-14279
Adapted from the author's: Kon-Tiki: across the Pacific by raft, published 1948 in Norway, 1950 in the U.S.
An account of the author's adventures as he sailed across the Pacific from Peru to Polynesia on a primitive raft attempting to establish the route of the pre-Inca Indians
"The text has been cut moderately to eliminate portions merely obstacles to young readers. The book's size and typography seem perfect for a youngster's hands and eyes." Chicago Sunday Trib

McClung, Robert M.

Treasures in the sea. Natl. Geographic Soc. 1972 29p illus map (k-3) **910.4**

1 Buried treasure 2 Diving, Submarine
ISBN 0-87044-122-1 LC 72-91421
Obtainable only as part of a set for $9.95 with: Dinosaurs, by Kathryn Jackson, class 567.9 Dogs working for people, by Joanna Foster, class 636.7; and Lion cubs, by the National Geographic Society, class 599.74
"Books for young explorers"
Prepared by the Special Publications Division of the National Geographic Society
Following a description of the sinking of a Spanish treasure ship and the struggles of pirates for booty, this book describes how modern divers search for sunken treasure and the living treasure of the sea life they encounter
"Here are excellent color photos to complement the text. . . . A lovely introductory book." Appraisal

Murphy, Barbara Beasley

Thor Heyerdahl and the reed boat Ra [by] Barbara Beasley Murphy and Norman Baker; foreword by Thor Heyerdahl. Lippincott 1974 64p illus map $7.95 (4 and up)   **910.4**

1 Ra (Boat)   2 Voyages and travels   3 Heyerdahl, Thor
ISBN 0-397-31503-1   LC 73-20260

"Convinced that the similarity between some cultural aspects of life in the ancient Middle East and among ancient Indians of the New World meant some communication, Heyerdahl had a papyrus boat built that duplicated those pictured in Egyptian carvings. He proposed to sail to America, and he used the trip also as an opportunity to demonstrate that men from different cultures could live in amity. The first voyage was unsuccessful, the second brought the Ra triumphantly into Barbados; the details of the provision, the accidents and dangers, the way the crew lived and coped with emergencies is engrossing." Chicago. Children's Bk Center

"The author's ability to transport the reader into the feeling of 'being there' should appeal to the reader. The many photographs taken along the way highlight this book, and help make this an interesting, informative . . . historical event." Best Sellers

Stockton, Frank R.

Buccaneers & pirates of our coasts. Macmillan Pub. Co. 1967 248p illus $6.95, pa 79¢ (5 and up)   **910.4**

1 Pirates
ISBN 0-02-788520-8; 0-02-045310-8   LC 67-2393

First published 1898

Here are true accounts of such sea-going scoundrels, who plundered North America from the sixteenth through the nineteenth century, as Jean Lafitte, Henry Morgan, Blackbeard, Captain Kidd, and others

"In this reissue of a classic favorite, the grim and precarious calling of piracy is treated with romance and excitement. . . . This book continues to provide good escape reading for those who would dream of the derring-do of bygone times." Adventuring with Bks. 2nd edition

"Illustrated with old prints and engravings." Hodges. Bks for Elem Sch Libraries

Whipple, Addison Beecher Colvin

Famous pirates of the New World; illus. by Robert Pious. Random House 1958 184p illus maps lib. bdg. $4.39 (5 and up)   **910.4**

1 Pirates
ISBN 0-394-90535-0   LC 58-6189

"World Landmark books"

"Blackbeard, Captain Flood, Dixey Bull, women pirates who wore men's clothes, prayer-saying pirates out to bring order out of lawlessness and chaos, pirates who retired and lived their lives out as respectable citizens are all here. Planks are walked, ships are sunk, treasures are buried and dug up." Christian Sci Monitor

910.5   Geography—Periodicals

National Geographic World. National Geographic Soc. $5.85 per year (3-6)   **910.5**

1 Geography—Periodicals   2 Voyages and travels —Periodicals
ISSN 0361-5499

Monthly. First published 1975

This magazine "is intended for children ages 8-12, and is produced with the same concern for accuracy and quality as its parent magazine. The emphasis is on the pictorial—splendid full-color photographs and drawings in an 8½ by 10¾-inch format. It contains articles and features on a variety of subjects, intriguing games, puzzles, supersize posters, punch-out-projects, and contributions from readers. There is no advertising, and the subscription rate is unusually low. A must for all libraries!" Katz. Magazines for Libraries. 3d edition

Underhill, Charles S.

(comp.) Handy key to your "National Geographics"; subject and picture locater. The author pa $5.25   **910.5**

1 National Geographic Magazine—Indexes 2 Geography—Periodicals—Indexes 3 Pictures—Indexes

Biennial. First published 1954. Since 1962, all issues have been cumulative from 1915

An index to subjects and pictures, including art work, maps and other illustrations, of the National Geographic magazines. Arrangement is alphabetical citing issues, though not specific page references, published in the preceding year. "The arrangement of citations under headings and subheadings is seldom alphabetical. Under certain headings the order is geographical, from north to south, from the Western Hemisphere to the Eastern; under others, such as historical, it is chronological; under others, like Aviation or Birds, it is by types, which may be combined with the other methods. In short, related subjects will usually be found in close proximity, even if the relationship is not stated. As with any reference tool, it takes a little familiarity to use it best. The basic treatment of the 'Geographic' is by region. References here are usually to entire articles. In other headings such as Industry or Sports, citations are usually to parts of articles only and may require some searching in the issues named." Foreword [to the 1974 edition]

912   Atlases

Cartwright, Sally

What's in a map? Illus. by Dick Gackenbach. Coward, McCann & Geoghegan 1976 31p illus map lib. bdg. $5.29 (k-2)   **912**

1 Maps   2 Map drawing
ISBN 0-698-30635-X   LC 76-10694

The author "approaches the concept of what a map is by relating the drawing of things and places to related positions in space in a way that small children can easily grasp. A science teacher, she invites children to orient themselves in familiar situations . . . and explains how that is translated to a piece of paper." Chicago. Children's Bk Center

"This excellent book can well be used as a basis for a social studies unit in early-childhood classrooms. It suggests a variety of first-hand experiences that would lead any child or adult to a better understanding of maps and their uses. Adults will realize that reading this book without providing for the experiences discussed is quite pointless. Every page says: 'learn by doing,' and every activity is an invitation for the child to personalize and concretize general concepts." Children's Bk Rev Serv

Fuchs, Erich

Looking at maps; illus. by Erich Fuchs; editorial direction: Barbara Fenton. Abelard-Schuman 1976 unp illus lib. bdg. $9.79 (2-4)   **912**

1 Maps
ISBN 0-200-00167-1   LC 75-42554

The author "offers a clear and concise explanation of numerous kinds of maps and the ways they can be used. The handsome full-color illustrations lend a great deal of understanding to the text, and librarians will find this an excellent addition to geographical resources." Sch Library J

Goode's World atlas. Rand McNally illus maps $12.95, pa $10.95   **912**

1 Atlases   2 Geography, Commercial—Maps

All editions from the first in 1922 to 1949, published with title: Goode's School atlas. Through the 8th edition compiled by John Paul Goode thereafter edited by Edward B. Espenshade, Jr. Periodically revised

This "is an excellent school atlas. . . . [It] is a physical, political, and economic atlas, with worldwide informaiton in the first section. Following this, the maps are arranged sequentially by continent and regions within the continents. . . . The introduction contains useful information on map reading, including how to understand scales and projections. . . . The atlas contains beautifully executed physiographic maps. . . . Small

Goode's World atlas—*Continued*

inset maps of some of the world's principal cities are included, but this coverage, as in most atlases, is far from complete. The atlas is sturdily bound. . . . Recommended as a 'first purchase' for all school libraries." Wynar. Guide to Ref Bks for Sch Media Centers [review of the 1970 edition]

Includes glossary

Hammond Citation world atlas. Hammond illus maps $17.95   912

1 Atlases

First published 1966. Periodically revised to bring material up-to-date

Each section concerning a state or country has an index that lists the cities in that area, the population, the map coordinates, and for the United States ZIP code numbers are given. Topographic maps which indicate valleys and mountains of each section are given along with resource area maps indicating dominant land use, minerals and manufacturing assets of the area. Inset maps of major cities are included plus the national flags for foreign countries

National Geographic Society

National Geographic Picture atlas of our fifty states; [Margaret Seeden, editor.] The Society 1978 304p illus maps $16.95, lib. bdg. $16.95 (4-6)   912

1 U.S.—Maps 2 Atlases
ISBN 0-87044-216-3; 0-87044-213-9   LC 78-10385

"Prefaced by a short explanation about atlases and a pictorial survey of America's many faces, the text is divided into 10 geographic areas for detailed attention by state. Information includes a comprehensive map indicating major cities, physical features, and state resources; major statistics; state bird, tree, and flag pictures; a brief commentary; and a two-page spread of representative photographs. Interspersed are special sections on energy in the home, agriculture wonders, and natural forces that shape weather. 'Facts at Your Fingertips,' a bibliography, and list of abbreviations used are appended as well as a plastic-coated, two-by-three-foot Landsat map taken by satellite (political map on verso), placed in a pocket on the back cover." Booklist

National Geographic Picture atlas of our world [Ross S. Bennett, editor] The Society 1979 312p illus maps $14.95, lib. bdg. $16.95 (4 and up)   912

1 Atlases
ISBN 0-87044-311-9; 0-87044-312-7   LC 79-17204

This atlas focuses on more than 160 countries on six continents, the Arctic and Antarctic and the oceans. For each country the reader will encounter a map, a descriptive text and a fact box which includes information on its size, population, capital, economy, etc. An index of 5,000 place names, a glossary of unfamiliar words and a poster size wall map of the world are also included

"Like the Rand McNally atlas by Ogilvie and Waitley, reviewed below, this is an oversize book that contains general material about the earth and mapping it. . . . Here, however, the pages are better deesigned and the illustrations of better quality, and there are more (and clearer) maps." Chicago. Children's Bk Center

Ogilvie, Bruce

Rand McNally Picture atlas of the world, by Bruce Ogilvie and Douglas Waitley. Rand McNally 1979 96p illus maps $7.95, lib. bdg. $7.97 (3-6)   912

1 Atlases
ISBN 0-528-82043-5; 0-528-80015-9   LC 79-13842

This "book is intended to introduce the young reader to the atlas. It contains information about how the earth was formed, space, the weather, the history of maps, and the future of the earth. There is an index and a glossary (but no pronunciations are given). For each continent, there is a map of the terrain, a political map, an animal map, and a 'life of the land' map." Children's Bk Rev Serv.

"The pages have a fragmented, cluttered appearance. Drawings and photographs are fully captioned, but in very small print. The book gives a great deal of information, and the maps are good, but the format is unattractive." Chicago. Children's Bk Center

Rand McNally Cosmopolitan world atlas. Rand McNally illus maps $35   912

1 Atlases

First published 1949. Periodically revised. 1965-1967 volumes appeared with title: Rand McNally New Cosmopolitan world atlas

"Map types include physical, political, metropolitan area, and oceanographic. Cartographic information is as . . . complete as practicable. All the maps are well executed, pleasing to the eye, and uncluttered, thus lending themselves to facile reading. . . . There are also lavishly illustrated, informative articles on the atmosphere, geology, and the ocean world. A superior general atlas, with exceptionally comprehensive coverage." Library J [review of the 1971 edition]

The **Whole** earth atlas. Hammond 1978 256p illus maps pa $6.95   912

1 Atlases
ISBN 0-8437-2500-1   LC 77-91610

This atlas includes U.S. Zip codes; a word gazetteer index; world, continent, country and state maps; resource, topographic, population and vegetation maps; flags of nations. Photographs are included with the maps of states

The **World** book atlas. Field Enterprises illus maps $19.95   912

1 Atlases

First published 1963. Frequently revised

"Map types include general reference, historic, physiographic and thematic (i.e., demographic, economic, political, social, etc.) Arrangement is by continent or major geographical region with separate section on the United States, Canada, and the moon. Many graphs and attractive color photos combine effectively with the text to complement the maps (most of which were adapted from Rand McNally's Cosmo series, long popular with school teachers). Population figures for major cities are shown along with a pronouncing gazetteer. Well-constructed, though far from comprehensive." American Ref Bks Annual, 1972 [review of the 1970 edition]

List of abbreviations and glossary included

For a fuller review see: The Booklist and Subscription Books Bulletin, January 15, 1965

914.1   Geography of and travel in the British Isles

Sasek, M.

This is historic Britain. Macmillan Pub. Co. 1974 60p illus map $6.95 (3-6)   914.1

1 Great Britain—Description and travel
ISBN 02-778200-X   LC 73-18345

In pictures and text, the author/illustrator presents a tour of famous and historic places, buildings and monuments in England, Wales and Scotland, with brief comments on the events and personalities associated with these sites

"The book can serve as an adjunct to a historical unit of the curriculum, but the primary appeal is visual: carefully detailed and accurate paintings in restrained color of the period architecture found in castles, cathedrals, and historic buildings." Chicago. Children's Bk Center

914.11   Geography of and travel in Scotland

Sasek, M.

This is Edinburgh. Macmillan Pub. Co. 1961 59p illus $5.95 (3-6)   914.11

1 Edinburgh—Description
ISBN 0-02-778180-1   LC 61-3676

This book depicts in "paintings and brief captions, some of the sights and famous landmarks of Edinburgh." Booklist

The author/illustrator "has caught the greyness of the city, the misty, romantic aura surrounding Castle Rock and the bustle of Princes Street perfectly. He seems to have enjoyed painting an enormous variety of tartans, and they give the book a special charm." Pub W

914.15   Geography of and travel in Ireland

Sasek, M.
This is Ireland. Macmillan Pub. Co. [1965 c1964] 59p illus map $4.95 (3-6)   **914.15**

1 Ireland—Description and travel
ISBN 0-02-778350-2
First published 1964 in England
In this pictorial tour of Ireland, the author-artist describes the country's history, geography, cathedrals, colleges and universities, landmarks of Irish history and civilization, and people. "Shamrocks, shillelaghs and sheep, bathed in all-pervading green and accompanied by harps, jaunting carts and a leprecaun or two, enliven this gay, bright and pleasantly conventional book." Bk Week
The text "consists chiefly of brief captions (a phrase, a sentence, or at most a few paragraphs) for utterly charming [watercolor] pictures. The book has a little less cohesion than do the books about individual cities, but it does convey atmosphere and give information. . . . It is delightful for browsing." Chicago. Children's Bk Center

914.2   Geography of and travel in England

Streatfeild, Noel
The Thames; London's river; illus. by Kurt Wiese; maps by Fred Kliem. Garrard 1964 96p illus map (Rivers of the world) lib. bdg. $3.68 (4-6)   **914.2**

1 Thames River   2 Great Britain
ISBN 0-8116-6362-0   LC 64-12628
"Describes the Thames from its source, and how it becomes a great river by the time it empties into the North Sea. Its history includes peoples, buildings and river traffic." Sch Library J
"A book that gives a great deal of specific detail and that has some vivid passages of writing, but is weakened by the loose organization of material and by digressions into ancillary subject matter. . . . Interesting but spotty." Chicago. Children's Bk Center

914.21   Geography of and travel in London

Sasek, M.
This is London. Macmillan Pub. Co. 1959 60p illus $4.95 (3-6)   **914.21**

1 London—Description
ISBN 0-02-778510-6
This picture travel book "describes in sprightly text and handsome, vividly colored illustrations [by the author] the delights of London. [Sasek] has included such points of interest as St. Paul's Cathedral and the British Museum, but he has given almost equal importance to such everyday sights as the mail boxes and Smith's bookstalls. He has not neglected any of the things with special appeal for the young, the various kinds of guards' uniforms, for example, and the double decker buses." Pub W

914.5   Geography of and travel in Italy

Sasek, M.
This is Rome. Macmillan Pub. Co. 1960 60p illus $5.95 (3-6)   **914.5**

1 Rome (City)—Description
ISBN 0-02-780390-2   LC 60-2678
The author-artist provides a "panoramic view of Rome with many interesting close-ups of her people, buildings and great art." Library J
This volume "is oversize and is filled with beautiful and humorous paintings of both famous landmarks and typical local touches. It is informational, it is evocative and nostalgic." Chicago. Children's Bk Center

This is Venice. Macmillan Pub. Co. 1961 56p illus $4.95 (3-6)   **914.5**

1 Venice—Description
ISBN 0-02-781050-X   LC 61-65479

"Mr. Sasek's text combines history, description, special tips to travelers, and statistics—such as the dimensions of a gondola. His illustrations . . . are the key to the city, and take one up and down the waterway and alleyways, showing the pigeons, palaces and piazzas." NY Times Bk Rev
"The romantic background of Venice, both historical and present-day, naturally makes this . . . an especially fascinating volume. His paintings have their usual brilliance and flavor and, accompanied by humorous text, ensure a wide range of interest again." Horn Bk

914.94   Geography of and travel in Switzerland. Alps

National Geographic Society
The Alps; prepared by the Special Publications Division. The Society 1973 207p illus maps $6.95 (6 and up)   **914.94**

1 Alps
ISBN 0-87044-109-4   LC 72-75384
"An attractive, personal account of the widely diverse experiences to be found in the Alps of the countries sharing this mountain range (Switzerland, France, Liechtenstein, Germany, Italy, Austria, Yugoslavia). . . . The tone throughout is enthusiastic; and the first-person narrations should have avid travelers phoning the airlines as they read. Scenes range from the cultivated formality of Lake Como to the traditional transhumance (migration of herds to summer pasturage). Maps and historical information are supplied; and the photographs are very appealing." Library J
Additional reading: p207

914.95   Geography of and travel in Greece

Sasek, M.
This is Greece. Macmillan Pub. Co. 1966 60p illus maps $3.95 (3-6)   **914.95**

1 Greece, Modern—Description and travel
ISBN 0-02-778260-3   LC 66-10844
Illustrated by the author, this is an introduction to the Mediterranean country through a tour of ancient landmarks and modern everyday scenes
"Though the layout is sometimes confusing, the poster pictures of ancient and modern Greece have a pleasing sense of vista, and the reader leaves the book with a definite idea of the country and its significance." NY Times Bk Rev

915.1   Geography of and travel in China and adjacent areas

Sasek, M.
This is Hong Kong. Macmillan Pub. Co. 1965 60p illus maps lib. bdg. $5.95 (3-6)   **915.1**

1 Hongkong
ISBN 0-02-778190-9   LC 65-19787
In this pictorial tour the author-illustrator describes Hong Kong's geography, transportation, harbors, cities, peoples, homes, religions, farm and factory products, and language
Here "the astounding beauty and variety of Hong Kong are captured in brilliant scenic spreads. Concise, lively text." Horn Bk

917.3   Geography of and travel in the United States

Arnold, Pauline
How we named our states, by Pauline Arnold and Percival White. Criterion Bks [1966 c1965] 192p illus maps $7.95 (5 and up)   **917.3**

1 Names, Geographical—U.S.   2 U.S.—History
ISBN 0-200-71911-4   LC 65-24208

Arnold, Pauline—*Continued*

The authors trace the reasons for the names of the states and their capitals, often including historical anecdotes through which the panorama of America's early history emerges

"There are interesting bits of historical information and, although the book doesn't have reference use, it is useful for the information it gives and enjoyable for browsing. An index is appended." Chicago. Children's Bk Center

Goetz, Delia

State capital cities; illus. with 92 photographs. Morrow 1971 159p illus lib. bdg. $7.92 (4-6)   **917.3**

1 Capitals (Cities)   2 Cities and towns—U.S.
ISBN 0-688-31955-6   LC 70-155991

This book consists of "brief sketches of each of the state capitals and Washington, D.C., covering the founding of the city, the derivation of the name, the design of the capitol building, and some of the activities presently carried on there." Sch Library J

National Geographic Society

The new America's wonderlands; our national parks; [prepared by National Geographic Book Service; Ross Bennett, editor] The Society 1980 463p illus maps (World in color lib) $12.95   **917.3**

1 National parks and reserves—U.S.   2 Natural monuments—U.S.
ISBN 0-87044-004-7   LC 80-12579

First published 1959 with title: America's wonderlands

More than 300 national parks are described in text and color photographs along with efforts to preserve the natural beauty of these areas

Folded map in end-paper pocket

Visiting our past: America's historylands. The Society 1977 400p illus maps (World in color lib) $12.95 (5 and up)   **917.3**

1 U.S.—History—Pictorial works   2 U.S.—Description and travel 3 Historical sites
ISBN 0-87044-003-9   LC 77-21828

More than 400 color illustrations and the writings of Daniel J. Boorstin and seven other author-historians focus on representative sites, from border to border, that portray America's history

Pizer, Vernon

Ink, Ark., and all that; how American places got their names; illus. by Tom Huffman. Putnam 1976 122p illus $8.95 (5 and up)   **917.3**

1 Names, Geographical—U.S.   2 U.S.—History, Local
ISBN 0-399-20532-2   LC 76-13176

This book discusses "the hows and whys and whens of the names of American places." Pub W

This is a "fascinating survey, which is also a kind of social history. In general, the chapters parallel the chronology of United States history, focusing first on early periods and then on naming the new country and the individual states; later the author discusses the problems which surfaced in the 1800's when enthusiasm, rather than logic, dictated geographic designation." Horn Bk

917.47   Geography of and travel in New York

Sasek, M.

This is New York. Macmillan Pub. Co. 1960 60p illus $5.95 (3-6)   **917.47**

1 New York (City)—Description
ISBN 0-02-779530-6   LC 60-16324

Beginning with the purchase of Manhattan Island from the Indians in 1626, the author-artist presents the pageant of New York City and its skyscrapers, subways, boats, bridges, parks, and people

"An impressionistic tour of New York City in brief text and the author's gay, colorful pictures." Hodges. Bks for Elem Sch Libraries

917.53   Geography of and travel in the District of Columbia (Washington)

Sasek, M.

This is Washington, D.C. Macmillan Pub. Co. 1969 60p illus maps $4.95 (3-6)   **917.53**

1 Washington, D.C.—Description
ISBN 0-02-778240-9   LC 69-13394

The reader is taken on a guided tour of Washington, D.C. and is shown the interesting places in the nation's capital. Historical facts and views of the national government at work are also included

"The chief lure, as always, is in [the author-artist's] illustrations. The buildings are drawn with photographic precision, and the page layout and use of color are skilled." Sat Rev

Shaw, Ray

Washington for children; a comprehensive guide to the unusual, offbeat, and exciting in and around Washington, for young people, families and teachers. Scribner 1975 196p illus maps pa $3.95   **917.53**

1 Washington, D.C.—Description
ISBN 0-684-14023-3   LC 74-16357

This guidebook provides information on over 300 activities in the Washington, D.C. area, including tours of government agencies and buildings, historical areas, museums, parks, and amusements

"The volume lists the activities by subject or function. Within chapters labeled 'Government,' 'American Life and History,' 'On the Job,' 'Sea and Sky,' etc., the guide leads readers to such diverse and offbeat places as a working grist mill, a bagel bakery, an exhibit featuring the largest African bush elephant ever shot, or a fox hunt. . . . Each entry gives, where appropriate, addresses, telephone numbers, age groups, days and hours of admission, cost, and availability of guided tours, along with a brief description. Maps showing the relative location of places mentioned are included at the beginning of each chapter. However, they are not drawn to scale and should only be used in conjunction with a good city map. The reader must search for information, for the index is of little value." Ref & Subscription Bks Revs

917.64   Geography of and travel in Texas

Sasek, M.

This is Texas. Macmillan Pub. Co. 1967 60p illus map $5.95 (3-6)   **917.64**

1 Texas—Description and travel
ISBN 0-02-780740-1   LC 66-18204

The author-illustrator gives his "impressions of such diversities as grain elevators in the Panhandle, prairie dogs in Lubbock . . . the King Ranch and such modern attractions as the Houston Astrodome . . . [and] Dallas's Neiman-Marcus Specialty Store." NY Times Bk Rev

"An entertaining and fun-poking hodgepodge of places and faces, bits of historical information, oddities, and statistics." Sat Rev

917.94   Geography of and travel in California

Sasek, M.

This is San Francisco. Macmillan Pub. Co. 1962 60p illus $5.95 (3-6)   **917.94**

1 San Francisco—Description
ISBN 0-02-780830-0   LC 62-3936

The author-artist presents his views of San Francisco including such sights as the Golden Gate Bridge, Stow Lake, the zoo's koala bears, Chinatown, the cable cars, Union Square with its underground garage, and a machine that washes your money

"The casual text, the format, and the humor in both text and delightful illustrations give the flavor and individual quality of the city rather than giving information of a guidebook variety." Chicago. Children's Bk Center

919.4   Geography of and travel in Australia

Sasek, M.
This is Australia. Macmillan Pub. Co. [1971 c1970] 60p illus map $4.95 (3-6)   **919.4**
1 Australia—Description and travel
ISBN 0-02-778160-7   LC 79-117960
First published 1970 in England
Illustrated by the author, "the book focuses on major cities, historical sites and new architecture, and on the plants and animals that are so intriguing to non-Australians, giving tangentially some impressions of the atmosphere and character of the country." Chicago. Children's Bk Center
"This is another informative and diverting pictorial introduction to a region. The architectural precision of the street scenes and buildings is impressive, and the humor of the text (more captions than running commentary) is reflected in the witty touches of caricature in the drawings of people." Sat Rev

920   BIOGRAPHY

Books of biography are arranged as follows: 1 Biographical collections (920)   2 Biographies of individuals alphabetically by names of biographees (92)

920   Collective biography

Alexander, Rae Pace
(comp.) Young and black in America; introductory notes by Julius Lester. Random House 1970 139p illus $3.95, lib. bdg. $4.99, pa $1.95 (6 and up)   **920**
1 Blacks—Biography   2 Autobiographies
ISBN 0-394-80482-1; 0-394-90482-6; 0-394-70804-0
LC 70-117005
Episodes from the autobiographies "of eight black men and women (Frederick Douglass, Richard Wright, Daisy Bates, Malcolm X, Jimmy Brown, Anne Moody, Harry Edwards, and David Parks) describe the stark discrimination and despair of their youthful experiences. This is not new material, but the excerpts in toto have a bleak power that is impressive. Each selection is preceded by an editorial comment that gives biographical information and some background for the excerpt. An appended bibliography gives information about hardcover and paperback editions of the books from which the selections were made." Chicago. Children's Bk Center

Burt, Olive W.
Negroes in the early West; illus. by Lorence F. Bjorklund. Messner 1969 96p illus lib. bdg. $6.64 (4-6)   **920**
1 Blacks—Biography   2 Frontier and pioneer life —The West (U.S.)
ISBN 0-671-32146-3   LC 74-81390
Biographies of black soldiers, explorers, businessmen, cowboys and mountain men who contributed to the development of the West. A chapter on black women pioneers is also included
"Although somewhat pedestrian in treatment, the book provides useful material on the role played by several little-known Negroes in the westward expansion of the U.S. Appropriately illustrated with fine drawings." Booklist
Suggestions for further reading: p91-92

Captains of industry, by the editors of American Heritage, The Magazine of History. Author: Bernard A. Weisberger; consultant: Allan Nevins. Am. Heritage [distributed by Harper] 1966 153p illus lib. bdg. $9.89 (5 and up)   **920**
1 Capitalists and financiers   2 U.S.—Industries—History
ISBN 0-06-026379-2   LC 66-17232
"American Heritage Junior library"
"Brief biographies of ten industrial giants of the late nineteenth and early twentieth centuries, emphasizing their personalities and accomplishments and touching lightly on their personal lives. Excellent contemporary photographs and prints and a list for further reading." Hodges. Bks for Elem Sch Libraries

Chittenden, Elizabeth F.
Profiles in black and white; stories of men and women who fought against slavery; illus. with photographs and engravings. Scribner 1973 182p illus $6.95 (5 and up)   **920**
1 Abolitionists   2 Blacks—Biography
ISBN 0-684-13387-3   LC 73-2929
"A well-written, interesting portrayal of the sometimes unsuccessful but nonetheless courageous effort of lesser-known individual to improve the lot of Black Americans before and after the Civil War. [Among the 12 persons] covered are: Theodore Parker, an activist minister; Elijah Lovejoy, a crusading newspaper editor; P.B.S. Pinchback, a Black politician endeavoring to work within the system; and educators like Prudence Crandall, Charlotte Forten, and Sarah Dickey, who extended educational opportunities for Blacks. Despite frequent fictionizing of feelings and dialogue, this collection can serve as a useful introduction to more detailed and scholarly accounts of abolitionist and civil rights activists. Most other books on the topic in this grade range focus on the more famous historical figures." Sch Library J
Bibliography: p176-79

Cone, Molly
The Ringling Brothers; illus. by James and Ruth McCrea. Crowell 1971 40p illus (Crowell biographies) $6.95, lib. bdg. $6.89 (2-4)   **920**
1 Ringling Brothers   2 Circus—Biography
ISBN 0-690-70287-6; 0-690-70288-4   LC 70-132295
"An entertaining account of how five brothers were captivated by the circus and eventually owned the 'Greatest Show on Earth.'" Chicago
"The style is simple, the print large, and the subject is alluring." Sat Rev

Cottler, Joseph
Heroes of civilization, by Joseph Cottler and Haym Jaffe. Rev. ed. Little 1969 393p $7.50 (5 and up)   **920**
1 Scientists   2 Explorers   3 Inventors
ISBN 0-316-15790-2   LC 69-10655
First published 1931
"Brief story-essays about the lives of 36 'heroes of civilization' are presented. These include eight explorers . . . nine physical scientists . . . [eight] inventors . . . and ten biological scientists. . . . Each biography recreates the youth and active years of accomplishment of the individual showing how determination, courage, hard work, and new ideas enabled him to achieve his goal The factual content is reasonably accurate, within the limitations of brevity and the intended audience." Sci Bks

Coy, Harold
Presidents. Watts, F. illus lib. bdg. $5.90, pa $1.25 (4-6)   **920**
1 Presidents—U.S.
ISBN 0-531-00615-8; 0-531-02316-8
"A First book"
First published 1952 with title: The first book of Presidents. Periodically revised to keep material up to date
"A discussion of the Presidency—the qualifications and duties required by the office; the process of election; the President's salary, household, and social life; the Cabinet; and the traditional two-party system—is followed by brief biographical sketches of each U.S. President." Sch Library J

Davis, Burke
Heroes of the American Revolution; illus. with photographs, prints and maps. Random House 1971 146p illus maps $4.95, lib. bdg. $6.99 (5 and up)   **920**
1 U.S.—History—Revolution, 1775-1783—Biography
ISBN 0-394-82152-1; 0-394-92152-6   LC 79-136578
A "treatment of eleven men who contributed in various ways to the success of our War of Independence. In a few pages one meets first the major war-related activity of the men and then a brief general biography. The book is copiously illustrated with copies of famous paintings of the men and events. An index increases its reference value." Best Sellers
"Davis's book is vividly written, has judicious and relevant quotes from the sources, contains wholesome good humor—and a properly highminded appraisal of Washington himself." NY Times Bk Rev

Emberlin, Diane

Contributions of women: science. Dillon Press 1977 158p illus lib. bdg. $7.95 (5 and up)
920

1 Women scientists
ISBN 0-87518-136-8   LC 76-30621

Short profiles of women who have made outstanding contributions to science: Annie Cannon, Lillian Gilbreth, Margaret Mead, Rachel Carson, Ruth Patrick, and Eugenie Clark

"The accounts happily avoid fictionalization and are even-toned rather than adulatory; the whole is geared to researching students—a final section briefly summarizes the lives of other women achievers in science." Booklist
Suggested reading: p159

Facklam, Margery

Wild animals, gentle women; illus. with line drawings by Paul Facklam and with photographs. Harcourt 1978 139p illus $5.95 (5 and up)
920

1 Zoologists 2 Women—Biography 3 Animals—Habits and behavior
ISBN 0-15-296987-X   LC 77-88961

These are portraits of eleven women involved with ethology, the study of animal behavior, including Eugenie Clark, Dian Fossey, Jane Goodall and Ruth Harkness. The animals these women have worked with are also discussed: sharks, gorillas, chimpanzees, giant pandas, apes, beavers, owls, porpoises, and whales

"Some of the biographies, such as that of Jane Goodall, are already fairly familiar. Others, however, although unfailingly fascinating, will constitute new encounters for young readers. A fine example of the latter is Belle Benchley, who, with no formal zoological background, devoted a brilliant twenty-eight year career to developing the once-struggling San Diego Zoo into an international showplace. . . . Written in a highly entertaining, richly anecdotal style, [this book] deserves abundant success." Best Sellers
Bibliography: p129-31. Organizations to help you learn about animal watching: p133

Feerick, John D.

The first book of Vice-Presidents of the United States, by John D. and Emalie P. Feerick. Watts, F. illus lib. bdg. $5.90 (4-6)
920

1 Vice-Presidents—U.S.
"A First book"
First published 1967 with title: The Vice-Presidents of the United States. Periodically revised to keep material up to date
"Brief, factual descriptions of the office and duties of the Vice-President are coupled with interesting sketches of the life of each man who has held that office from John Adams to the present." Sch Library J

Greenfield, Eloise

Childtimes; a three-generation memoir, by Eloise Greenfield and Lessie Jones Little; with material by Pattie Ridley Jones. Drawings by Jerry Pinkney and photographs from the authors' family albums. Crowell 1979 175p illus $8.95, lib. bdg. $8.89 (4 and up)
920

1 Black women
ISBN 0-690-03874-7; 0-690-03875-5   LC 77-26581

The authors "offer a remarkable human history, with material adapted from records (oral and written) left by Little's mother, the late Pattie Ridley Jones. The 'childtimes' of the three women stretch back to the 1880s in North Carolina where Jones was born, grandchild of freed slaves. The recollections of the writers engross readers who follow changes in the lives of each through the years, in this legacy from people Greenfield calls 'just three marchers in a procession that stretches across the ocean to Africa. . . .' The book's immediacy is heightened by photos from family albums and Pinkney's drawings." Pub W

Gridley, Marion E.

American Indian women. Hawthorn Bks. 1974 178p illus $6.95 (5 and up)
920

1 Indians of North America—Biography 2 Women—U.S.—Biography
ISBN 0-8015-0234-9   LC 73-362

The author sketches the lives of nineteen historical and contemporary Indian women, including Pocahontas, Mary Musgrove, Sacajawea, Susan La Flesche Picotte, Pablita Velarde, and Maria and Marjorie Tallchief

"The profiles are packed with information regarding cultures and beliefs of American Indians. . . . The material on the lesser known women is especially valuable, and an eight-page photo insert, an index, and a useable, updated bibliography complete the coverage." Library J

Gurney, Gene

Flying aces of World War I; illus. with photographs. Random House 1965 185p illus map lib. bdg. $5.99 (4-6)
920

1 World War, 1914-1918—Aerial operations 2 Air pilots
ISBN 0-394-90560-1   LC 65-10489

"World Landmark books"
"Recounts the exploits of the famed Flying Aces of World War I, who, in their frail single-seated planes, made aviation history. American, British, French, and German fliers are included, with a list of 58 high-scoring pilots." Hodges. Bks for Elem Sch Libraries

Hayden, Robert C.

Eight black American inventors. Addison-Wesley 1972 142p illus lib. bdg. $6.95 (5 and up)
920

1 Black inventors
ISBN 0-201-02823-9   LC 78-164402

"An Addisonian Press book"
This book "is a useful addition to the biographies of black Americans of the nineteenth and early twentieth centuries [including G. A. Morgan, F. M. Jones, L. H. Latimer, and G. T. Woods]. The men selected all invented devices or machines which markedly improved industrial processes. Brief descriptions of their lives and accomplishments, emphasizing their outstanding intelligence, aptitude, and persistence in the face of definite discrimination, bring their contributions to the reader's attention in a sincere but uninspired manner. Illustrations of inventions as drawn by their creators add interest to the text as do photographs of the inventors." Appraisal

Seven black American scientists. Addison-Wesley 1970 172p illus lib. bdg. $6.95 (5 and up)
920

1 Black scientists
ISBN 0-201-02828-X   LC 77-118997

"An Addisonian Press book"
The seven biographical sketches presented here "are representative rather than exhaustive: Charles Drew, Dr. Daniel Hall Williams, Benjamin Banneker, Charles H. Turner, Ernest E. Just, Matthew Henson, George W. Carver. The contribution of each to his scientific field is described without technical jargon, and the question of racial barriers is treated without bias or emotion." Sci Bks
Glossary: p163-65

Hirsch, S. Carl

Guardians of tomorrow; pioneers in ecology; illus. by William Steinel. Viking 1971 192p illus lib. bdg. $5.95 (5 and up)
920

1 Naturalists 2 Ecology—Biography 3 Conservation of natural resources
ISBN 0-670-35646-8   LC 76-136818

"The philosophy and accomplishments of seven men and one woman who were concerned with protecting the natural resources and environment of the U.S. are presented in an account which is useful for both its brief biographical information on the early ecologists and its history of the conservation movement. Included are Thoreau, Marsh, Olmsted, Muir, Pinchot, Norris, Leopold, and Carson. Hirsch concludes the account with an examination of the challenges facing today's guardians of the environment." Booklist
Suggestions for further reading: p179-82

Johnston, Johanna

The Indians and the strangers; illus. with woodcuts by Rocco Negri. Dodd 1972 109p illus lib. bdg. $5.95 (2-5)
920

1 Indians of North America—Biography
ISBN 0-396-06610-0   LC 72-1447

Johnston, Johanna—*Continued*

"Not full biographies, but short sketches that describe the confrontations between some major figures in American Indian history and the white men with whom they warred or planned for peace, this gives an excellent overview of the remorseless manipulation and persecution of Indians. It does so particularly effectively because the text, very simply written, is so restrained and objective, including some instances of amicable relationships; it is in the mounting evidence that the impact is made. The stories are chronologically arranged." Chicago. Children's Bk Center

A special bravery; illus. by Ann Grifalconi. Dodd 1967 94p illus lib. bdg. $5.95 (2-5)   920

1 Blacks—Biography
ISBN 0-396-06728-X   LC 67-20777
"The lives of 15 American Negroes from Crispus Attucks to Martin Luther King, Jr. are presented briefly in a book designed and written for easy reading. . . . Printed in short lines that give the appearance of blank verse, almost every biographical sketch is accompanied by a full-page action drawing of the subject." Booklist
"Miss Johnston's own special bravery is in her frank, didactic treatment of prejudice and discrimination." NY Times Bk Rev

Jones, Hettie

Big star fallin' mama; five women in black music. Viking 1974 150p illus $7.95 (5 and up)
                                               920

1 Black singers 2 Women singers
ISBN 0-670-16408-9   LC 73-5152
"Ma Rainey, Bessie Smith, Mahalia Jackson, Billie Holiday, and Aretha Franklin are portrayed in their life situations: on the stage, in theatres, at night clubs, performing at special shows, playing and singing ragtime, recording and/or singing at Gospel gatherings. Hettie Jones gives an insight into black music from the 1920's to 1967. She tries to preserve the cultural value of black music which tends to be the basis for our rock music—of the 1970's. Blues, jazz, ragtime, spirituals, rock music —each has its distinctive way of conveying to the reader the feelings of these black women." Best Sellers
The biographies "are written with candor and sensitivity, objective in viewpoint and vigorous in style." Chicago. Children's Bk Center
Bibliography: p137-38. Discography: p139-40

McNeer, May

Armed with courage, by May McNeer and Lynd Ward. Abingdon 1957 112p illus $6.95 (4-6)   920

1 Biography 2 Courage
ISBN 0-687-01740-8   LC 57-13739
This book contains "biographical sketches of seven great humanitarians: Gandhi, Schweitzer, Nightingale, Grenfell, Carver, Addams, and Father Damien." Adventuring with Bks. 2d edition
"The biographies are vividly written and with the attractive format and illustrations make this a good book for school and public libraries, personal ownership and Sunday schools." Horn Bk

Nathan, Dorothy

Women of courage; illus. by Carolyn Cather. Random House 1964 188p illus lib. bdg. $5.99, pa 75¢ (4-6)   920

1 Woman—U.S.—Biography
ISBN 0-394-90407-9; 0-394-82186-6   LC 63-7827
This book contains short biographies of Susan B. Anthony, Jane Addams, Mary McLeod Bethune, Amelia Earhart and Margaret Mead
"Although the choice of subjects seems random and although much of the material is familiar, the biographies should serve to encourage a reader's interest in full-length biographies." Chicago. Children's Bk Center
Bibliography: p178-81

Noble, Iris

Contemporary women scientists of America; photographs. Messner 1979 153p illus lib. bdg. $7.29 (5 and up)   920

1 Women scientists
ISBN 0-671-32920-0   LC 78-21292

"Nine women scientists working successfully in the U.S. are portrayed in brief individual biographical sketches. Noble explains the research and achievements of women such as Margaret Mead (whose recent death is noted), Joanne Simpson, Estelle Ramey, Dixie Lee Ray, and Isabella Karle, stressing the odds (poverty, juggling work and family, sexual discrimination, nepotism) that they overcame to gain their noteworthy positions." Booklist

Posell, Elsa Z.

Russian composers; illus. with photographs. Houghton 1967 181p illus $4.25 (5 and up) 920

1 Composers, Russian 2 Music, Russian
ISBN 0-395-07034-1   LC 67-22172
"Brief biographies of 17 composers arranged chronologically from Glinka to Shostakovich describe each composer's family background, education, personality, and musical works. Separate discussions of music under the czars and under the Soviets stress the importance of the fine arts throughout Russian history and the privileges accorded talented musicians and composers since the Revolution. . . . Illustrated with full-page portraits of the composers." Booklist
"The biographies are necessarily brief, consisting of fact after fact presented at almost breathtaking speed." Christian Sci Monitor
Suggested reading on Russian music and musicians: p[182]

Rollins, Charlemae Hill

Famous American Negro poets. Dodd 1965 95p illus (Famous biographies for young people) $5.95 (5 and up)   920

1 Poets, American 2 Black authors
ISBN 0-396-05129-4   LC 65-11811
This is a "collective biography of a dozen Negro poets, with the material chronologically arranged and with a section of portraits (some drawings, some photographs) inserted. . . . Each of the biographical sketches is a few pages long, gives some facts about the subject's personal life and more about his writing, and quotes a poem or poems. A bibliography of books by the poets or anthologies in which their works appear is included." Chicago. Children's Bk Center
"The book is useful for reference as well as for enjoyable reading." Wis Library Bul

They showed the way; forty American Negro leaders. Crowell 1964 165p lib. bdg. $8.95 (5 and up)   920

1 Blacks—Biography
ISBN 0-690-81612-X   LC 64-20692
The forty "brief biological sketches represent a great variety of occupations and professions in which Negroes have made a great contribution to American life." Adventuring With Bks. 2d edition
"Although the individual factual accounts are almost too brief . . . the book is worthwhile because it contains a number of persons not found in other collective biographies." Booklist

Rudström, Lennart

A family; with paintings by Carl Larsson and a text by Lennart Rudström. Putnam 1980 unp illus $7.95   920

1 Larsson family 2 Painters, Swedish
ISBN 0-399-20700-7   LC 79-14291
Original Swedish edition 1979
"The family is Larsson's, brilliantly portrayed in the domestic scenes he so delighted in painting. Rudstrom's chatty text affects a disarming tone, telling readers about the poverty of Larsson's early life and the great pride he took in establishing a comfortable home for his large family. The text offers little analytical commentary; rather, it directs readers to family members, backgrounds, and the artist's activities at the time of various paintings [from the mid-1880's to 1918]." Booklist
"Two parallel texts appear on left-hand pages facing the paintings on the right. Since the pictures are arranged chronologically, the major text is roughly biographical. . . . The minor texts, decorated with tiny sketches or reproductions in black and white, are printed in columns of small type and offer information which can be anecdotal or technical but is often disjointed and irrelevant. The luminous beauty of the paintings, however, remains unmarred by the author's

Rudström, Lennart—*Continued*

ineptitude; recreating family life of a vanished era, they lovingly depict the artist's wife and his numerous children and variously recall the spirit of Boutet de Monvel, Whistler, and Mary Cassatt." Horn Bk

Silverman, Judith

Index to collective biographies for young readers; elementary and junior high school level. 3d ed. Bowker 1979 xxxii, 405p $19.95 **920**

1 Biography—Indexes 2 Biography—Bibliography
ISBN 0-8352-1132-0 LC 79-472

First published 1970 with title: An index to young readers' collective biographies

This volume lists about 7,245 people, representing the contents of 942 collective biographies which "are considered those most suitable for elementary and junior high school-level reading although a number of them also can be found in high school libraries. The index aims to be inclusive rather than selective. . . . [An alphabetical listing of biographies] contains pertinent data about the birth, death, nationality, and field of activity, followed by symbols referring to titles where the individual's biography appears. The second major section—'Subject Listing of Biographies'—lists individuals under appropriate fields of activity and under nationalities. . . . The next section is 'Indexed Books by Title' in which the biographies covered in each book are noted. This is followed by 'Key to Publishers' and by the 'Index to Subject Headings.' " Ref & Subscription Bks Revs

Steele, William O.

Westward adventure; the true stories of six pioneers; maps by Kathleen Voute. Harcourt 1962 188p maps $5.95 (5 and up) **920**

1 Adventure and adventurers 2 Frontier and pioneer life
ISBN 0-15-294999-2 LC 62-9479

"Utilizing little-known sources, the author tells the true stories of six people—an Indian trader, a writer, a farmer's wife, an explorer, a colonizer, and a Moravian brother—who ventured into the American wilderness west and south of the 13 colonies during the eighteenth century. Recounting the experience of each he shows the reasons for their hazardous journeys, depicts their characters and personalities, and vivifies life on the frontier." Booklist

Bibliography: p185-88

Sterling, Philip

Four took freedom; the lives of Harriet Tubman, Frederick Douglass, Robert Smalls, and Blanche K. Bruce [by] Philip Sterling and Rayford Logan; illus. by Charles White. Doubleday 1967 116p illus pa $2.50 (4-6) **920**

1 Blacks—Biography
ISBN 0-385-03844-5 LC 65-17229

"Zenith books"
"Succinct accounts of the lives of four American blacks and their escape from slavery. The drama, pathos, and great excitement of these biographies will cause children to be interested in learning more about Harriet Tubman, Frederick Douglass, Robert Small, and Blanche K. Bruce. Well-selected and well-told incidents from these lives give the reader an understanding of some social issues facing us today." Rdng Ladders

Young and female; turning points in the lives of eight American women: personal accounts comp. with introductory notes by Pat Ross. Random House 1972 107p illus lib. bdg. $4.99, pa $2.95 (6 and up) **920**

1 Women—U.S.—Biography 2 Autobiographies
ISBN 0-394-92392-8; 0-394-70808-3 LC 76-37417

"Selections from eight autobiographies of modern women, each showing a turning point in the author's life and each prefaced by an editorial note that gives some biographical information and facts about the biographee's careers. The women who write of being young and female are Margaret Bourke-White, Shirley Chisholm, Dorothy Day, Edna Ferber, Althea Gibson, Emily Hahn, Shirley MacLaine, and Margaret Sanger." Chicago. Children's Bk Center

920.03 Biography—Dictionaries

Current biography: cumulated index, 1940-1970. Wilson, H.W. 1973 113p $6 **920.03**

1 Biography—Dictionaries—Indexes
ISBN 0-8242-0520 LC 40-27432

An index to Current biography yearbook, entered below

"Reference libraries will welcome this handy volume since it will replace the three decennial indexes that they have had to search up to now to cover the first thirty years of this very useful series. There are cross-references from variants of names and pseudonyms. Not only is the place of the original biography for each name shown, but the obituaries and updated sketches are noted also." Cur Ref Bks

Current biography yearbook. Wilson, H.W. illus $24 **920.03**

1 Biography—Dictionaries
ISSN 0084-9499 LC 40-27432

Annual. First published 1940 with title: Current biography

Also issued monthly except August with the subscription price of $12

Fourth book of junior authors & illustrators; ed. By Doris de Montreville and Elizabeth D. Crawford. Wilson, H.W. 1978 370p illus (Junior authors ser) $17 **920.03**

1 Authors—Dictionaries 2 Illustrators—Dictionaries 3 Children's literature—Bio-bibliography
ISBN 0-8242-0568-5 LC 78-115

Companion volume to: The Junior book of authors, 2d ed. edited by Stanley J. Kunitz, More junior authors, edited by Muriel Fuller, and Third book of junior authors, edited by Doris de Montreville and Donna Hill, all entered below

"Biographies of some 250 authors, selected for inclusion by a committee of specialists, are accompanied by photographs of the authors and their signatures (where approved). Many of the sketches were written by the authors themselves, so that the volume is a delight to browse in as well as a useful storehouse of information. Sources of further biographical facts are indicated for each writer. A cumulative index to the whole 'Junior Author' series completes the volume. An obvious purchase for collections on children's literature." Cur Ref Bks

The Junior book of authors; ed. by Stanley J. Kunitz and Howard Haycraft. 2d ed. rev. Illus. with 232 photographs and drawings. Wilson, H.W. 1951 309p illus (The Authors ser) $12 **920.03**

1 Authors—Dictionaries 2 Illustrators—Dictionaries 3 Children's literature—Bio-bibliography
ISBN 0-8242-0028-4 LC 51-13057

First published 1934

Biographical and autobiographical sketches of 289 authors and illustrators of books for children and young people are presented. Generally informal in style, the book gives vital statistics and short lists of representative titles for each of the subjects. There are 232 portraits and a necrology. Each account gives birth date, death date—if subject is deceased—author's background, mention of his work, and a photograph, or drawing

Followed by: More junior authors, edited by Muriel Fuller, and Third book of junior authors, edited by Doris de Montreville and Donna Hill, both entered below, and Fourth book of junior authors, edited by Doris de Montreville and Elizabeth D. Crawford, entered above

More junior authors; ed. by Muriel Fuller. Wilson, H.W. 1963 235p illus (The Authors ser) $10 **920.03**

1 Authors—Dictionaries 2 Illustrators—Dictionaries 3 Children's literature—Bio-bibliography
ISBN 0-8242-0036-5 LC 63-11816

Companion volume to: The Junior book of authors, 2d ed, edited by Stanley J. Kunitz and Howard Haycraft, and Fourth book of junior authors and illustrators, ed. by Doris de Montreville and Elizabeth D. Crawford, entered above, and Third book of junior authors, edited by Doris de Montreville and Donna Hill, entered below

More junior authors—*Continued*
"Includes biographical or autobiographical sketches [arranged alphabetically] of 268 authors and illustrators of books for children and young people. The great majority are authors and illustrators who have become prominent since the publication of the second edition." Preface
"Selected from a preliminary list of almost 1,200 names, by a distinguished group of librarians working with children and young people in school and public libraries, the sketches represent only the most familiar and popular names. Photographs of many of the writers accompany the well-written accounts which should appeal to young people because of their personal flavor. Only partial lists of works by, and none about, the authors are given." Cur Ref Bks

Third book of junior authors; ed. by Doris de Montreville and Donna Hill. Wilson, H.W. 1972 320p illus (The Authors ser) $12   **920.03**
1 Authors—Dictionaries   2 Illustrators—Dictionaries   3 Children's literature—Bio-bibliography
ISBN 0-8242-0408-5   LC 75-149381
Companion volume to: The Junior book of authors, 2d ed. edited by Stanley Kunitz and Howard Haycraft. More junior authors, edited by Muriel Fuller, and Fourth book of junior authors, ed. by Doris de Montreville and Elizabeth D. Crawford, all entered above
Contains 255 sketches, both biographical and autobiographical, with 249 portraits, of authors and illustrators of books for children and young people. New to this volume in the series are the lists of selected works and of biographical references. An index of authors and illustrators is included which covers this volume and, in addition, its two predecessors
"An important purchase for libraries serving children." Cur Ref Bks

Twentieth-Century children's writers; with a preface by Naomi Lewis; editor: D. L. Kirkpatrick. St Martins 1978 1507p $40   **920.03**
1 Authors—Dictionaries   2 Children's literature—Bio-bibliography   3 Children's literature—History and criticism
ISBN 0-321-82413-0   LC 79-110314
This volume contains the "biographies of some 60 English-language authors, [accompanied by] bibliographies of their books for both children and adults and a signed critical essay on each by one of 160 contributors. The book is prefaced with an essay by Naomi Lewis which gives an overall view of the literature of the century . . . [and offers] observations on the nature of children's reading and the motives which prompt authors to direct their efforts towards young readers. There is an appendix which includes . . . representative writers of the late nineteenth century, and a supplementary essay by Anthea Bell on children's books in translation [with a] . . . select list of foreign authors whose works have appeared in English." Times (London) Lit Sup
"In most cases a statement or reflection by the author on his own writing is presented as well. As might be expected, the essays are uneven in quality: Some are appreciative in nature, focusing on the best book or books an author has written, while others give more thorough consideration to an entire body of work." Horn Bk

Ward, Martha E.
Authors of books for young people. 2d ed by Martha E. Ward and Dorothy A. Marquardt. Scarecrow 1971 579p $19   **920.03**
1 Authors—Dictionaries   2 Children's literature—Bio-bibliography
ISBN 0-8108-0404-2   LC 70-157057
First published 1964
This volume contains "brief biographical entries for some 2,100 writers of juvenile books. . . . The entries, arranged alphabetically by name, give dates, profession, place of birth, education and degrees, family and residence, career, interests, and a partial list of writings. The entries vary in fullness. . . . [The book] identifies publisher and year for each title listed and provides cross references for pseudonyms. . . . The Preface indicates three factors for inclusion. The biographies were taken from an 'author file' compiled in the Children's Department of the Free Public Library of Quincy, Illinois. Secondly, 'a contemporary author whose biography proved difficult to locate was given preference' over a well-known author. Thirdly, all Newbery and Caldecott winners are included." Am Ref Bks Annual, 1972

Authors of books for young people; supplement to the 2d ed. by Martha E. Ward and Dorothy A. Marquardt. Scarecrow 1979 302p $12   **920.03**
1 Authors—Dictionaries   2 Children's literature—Bio-bibliography
ISBN 0-8108-1159-6   LC 78-16011
"This supplement adds brief biographical sketches for 1,250 authors to those in the basic volume [entered above]. The sketches vary greatly in the amount of information presented and in their completeness in listing the authors' publications. Some of the entries provide details of the author's birth, education, and career, but others consist of only a sentence or two." Cur Ref Bks

Illustrators of books for young people. 2d ed. by Martha E. Ward and Dorothy A. Marquardt. Scarecrow 1975 223p lib. bdg. $9   **920.03**
1 Illustrators—Dictionaries   2 Children's literature—Bio-bibliography
ISBN 0-8108-0819-6   LC 75-9880
First published 1970
This book provides brief biographical information for 750 illustrators of books for children. References to works where additional information about an illustrator can be found follow many of the entries. A list of Caldecott Medal winners and a title index have been provided
"The Preface to the first edition states, 'Any contemporary illustrator whose biography proved difficult to locate was given preference for inclusion over a well-known illustrator whose biographical information was more readily available.' This criterion, although not restated in the Preface to the second edition, still governs the coverage. . . . And because of this criterion, many important illustrators are left out of this edition." Ref. & Subscription Bks Revs

Webster's Biographical dictionary; a dictionary of names of noteworthy persons with pronunciations and concise biographies. Merriam $15   **920.03**
1 Biography—Dictionaries
William Allan Neilson, editor in chief
First published 1943 and frequently reprinted with slight revisions
"Forty thousand people of historical importance from all countries . . . are given brief concise factual treatment. The work treats fully persons prominent in all fields except sports, motion pictures, contemporary theater, and radio, entries for which were cut to the minimum. Syllabication and pronunciation is given for surnames. American and British subjects receive the fullest treatment. . . . 'Webster's' has lost much of its value as a contemporary source, because of the slight revisions since the first 1943 edition." Booklist [review of the 1972 edition]
The entries "vary from a few lines to a full page. Concise and clearly written, the sketches are unsigned but considered trustworthy and adequate. Liberal cross references aid the user in locating information. Also included are tables of popes, American government officials, and rulers of various countries." Peterson. Ref Bks for Elem and Jr High Sch Libraries [review of the 1968 edition]

92   Individual biography

Lives of individuals are arranged alphabetically under the names of the persons written about. A number of subjects have been added to the titles in this section to aid in curriculum work. It is not necessarily recommended that these subjects be used in the library catalog

Abzug, Bella S.
Faber, Doris. Bella Abzug; illus. with photographs. Lothrop 1976 162p illus $8.25, lib. bdg. $7.92 (5 and up)   **92**
1 Politicians, American   2 Women politicians   3 U.S. Congress. House
ISBN 0-688-41776-0; 0-688-51776-5   LC 76-21869
"The first half of the book chronicles Abzug's early political activism—as a student leader at Hunter College, as a lawyer defending those charged with subversion during the McCarthy era and later defending civil rights workers, and as an unpaid lobbyist for Women Strike for Peace.

Abzug, Bella S.—*Continued*

The rest of the coverage centers on Abzug's radical and increasingly effective congressional career and her hard fought re-election campaign when her district was gerrymandered in 1972. . . . Although many of the photographs are disappointingly fuzzy, this is an enthusiastic and candid biography in a conversational style that makes lively, informative reading." Sch Library J
Suggestions for further reading: p157-58

Adams, Samuel

Chidsey, Donald Barr. The world of Samuel Adams. Elsevier/Nelson Bks. 1974 192p front $7.95 (5 and up) **92**

1 U.S.—History—Revolution, 1775-1783—Biography
ISBN 0-525-66383-5   LC 74-698

First published by Thomas Nelson

"Beginning with a characterization of Adams, Chidsey explains the need for the taxes levied on the American colonies by England and the intimidating tactics used by the Sons of Liberty to prevent the enforcement of the tax laws. Emphasizing the lack of competent leadership in England and the British failure to realize that the colonies could unite, he shows how Adams used events like the Boston Massacre to stir the people to resistance to British rule." Booklist

"Though Adams is the central character, Chidsey is more effective relaying the 'world' than the man. The best descriptions are of the city and countryside. The people and their habits bring life to the narrative. . . . [Thus] this is an entertaining book." Choice
For further reading: p183-89

Fritz, Jean. Why don't you get a horse, Sam Adams? Illus. by Trina Schart Hyman. Coward, McCann & Geoghegan 1974 47p illus $6.95 (3-5) **92**

1 U.S.—History—Revolution, 1775-1783—Biography
ISBN 0-698-20292-9   LC 73-88023

Sam Adams "wears his soles thin treading the cobblestones and wharves of Boston while agitating against the King. Although reasonable in most respects—he knows when to hold his rebellious tongue and when to unleash it—Sam stubbornly refuses to ride a horse. Despite goading from cousin John Adams and an 'unheroic' escape from the Redcoats via horse drawn carriage, Sam persists in his pedestrian preferences until an appeal to his patriotism finally convinces him to get a horse." Sch Library J

"Hyman's seemingly effortless, deft lines and the engaging drollery reflected in her details amply extend Fritz' bridled humor. An afterword attests to the historical facts behind the amusing perspective, and the novel approach . . . works well to raise this above the crowd of Bicentennial-related publications." Booklist

Addams, Jane

Keller, Gail Faithfull. Jane Addams; illus. by Frank Aloise. Crowell 1971 41p illus (Crowell biographies) $6.95 (1-3) **92**

1 Hull House, Chicago 2 Social work—Biography
ISBN 0-690-45791-X   LC 71-139098

In 1889 Jane Addams founded Hull House, a settlement house in a poor section of Chicago. It became a center for community activity where people of all ages and nationalities came seeking advice, recreation, meals and company. The author depicts the forty-five-year career of this pioneer in social work who in 1931 was awarded the Nobel Peace Prize

Allen, Ethan

Brown, Slater. Ethan Allen and the Green Mountain Boys; illus. by William Moyers. Random House 1956 184p illus map lib. bdg. $5.99 (5 and up) **92**

1 U.S.—History—Revolution, 1775-1783—Biography
2 Green Mountain Boys
ISBN 0-394-90366-8   LC 56-5457

"Landmark books"

As a young man Ethan Allen championed the cause of his fellow Vermonters when the governor of New York tried to impose on them the ancient feudal system of landowning. This led to the formation of the Green Mountain Boys who, under Ethan's leadership, captured Fort Ticonderoga from the British in the Revolutionary War. These and other events in the life of this great American are related in this biography

"A simply written, perceptive account. . . . Allen emerges as a vigorous character, not always a wise leader, but a dedicated man whose basic motives were honest and worth while, and who was not afraid to fight against any odds for what he thought was right." Chicago. Children's Bk Center

Holbrook, Stewart Hall. America's Ethan Allen; pictures by Lynd Ward. Houghton 1949 95p illus lib. bdg. $8.95 pa $3.95 (5 and up) **92**

1 U.S.—History—Revolution, 1775-1783—Biography
2 Green Mountain Boys
ISBN 0-395-24449-8; 0-395-24908-2   LC 49-10780

This is the story of a great and fearless American figure, Ethan Allen, hero of Fort Ticonderoga and one of the first men who saw America's destiny and rebelled against authority from England

"Told with spirit and pace, this story of the Green Mountain Boys and the founding of Vermont gives fresh interest to a segment of American history. The illustrations in full color accentuate the stature of the hero and evoke the rugged frontier." NY Pub Library

Anderson, Marian

Newman, Shirlee P. Marian Anderson: lady from Philadelphia. Westminster Press 1966 175p illus $5.50 (5 and up) **92**

1 Black singers 2 Women singers
ISBN 0-664-32370-7   LC 66-10933

"From early childhood Marian Anderson embraced music for which she had great talent; she endured indignities and succeeded somewhat in alleviating prejudices by her regal appearance and ladylike conduct. In . . . [this biography] Miss Newman traces the life of this great singer from her high school days . . . to her final concert at Carnegie Hall." Best Sellers

"A warm, readable biography about a great black artist and humanitarian which shows her struggle to achieve." NY Public Library. The Black Experience in Children's Bks
Selected bibliography: p163-65

Tobias, Tobi. Marian Anderson; illus. by Symeon Shimin. Crowell 1972 40p illus (A Crowell biography) lib. bdg. $6.89 (2-4) **92**

1 Black singers 2 Women singers
ISBN 0-690-51847-1   LC 79-139101

"Beautifully illustrated with the soft and gentle faces that are [the ilustrator's] distinctive style, a biography of the great singer is simply written, dispassionate in tone, and balanced in treatment. The text describes the now-familiar (but never before so competently written for very young readers) story of the small girl in Philadelphia whose big, golden voice was so appreciated by the members of her church that they financed her first professional training. The rest is musical history." Chicago. Children's Bk Center

Anthony, Susan Brownell

Noble, Iris. Susan B. Anthony. Messner 1975 189p lib. bdg. $5.29 (5 and up) **92**

1 Women—Civil rights
ISBN 0-671-32715-1   LC 74-30230

This is a biography of the nineteenth century crusader for women's rights who also contributed her talents to the antislavery movement
Bibliography: p181-82

Peterson, Helen Stone. Susan B. Anthony, pioneer in woman's rights; illus. by Paul Frame. Garrard [1971] 96p illus (Americans all) lib. bdg. $5.88 (3-5) **92**

1 Women—Civil rights
ISBN 0-8116-4570-3   LC 76-151991

"This sympathetic biography covers the career of Susan B. Anthony from age 12 until her death. with emphasis on her involvement with women's rights and brief mention of her work for black emancipation. Miss Anthony is not presented as a superwoman, nor does the author make comparisons between her and like-minded ladies today. There is too much fictionized dialogue and attributed emotion in the childhood section, but the account of her later life is more accurate and the writing is clear and generally factual throughout. [It is] illustrated with photographs, engravings, and less effective two-color pen-and-ink sketches." Library J

Archibald, Nate

Devaney, John. Tiny! The story of Nate Archibald. Putnam 1977 159p illus (Putnam Sports shelf) lib. bdg. $6.29 (4 and up)   92

1 Basketball—Biography 2 Black athletes
ISBN 0-399-61098-7   LC 77-3214

"In the South Bronx area of New York City, drugs flow freely, luring youngsters into a state of limbo where they can temporarily escape the deprivations of poverty. Preferring to find his highs on the basketball court, Nathaniel ('Nate the Skate,' 'Tiny') Archibald, with the guidance of a concerned coach, was encouraged to stay in school and develop his athletic talent. His perseverance paid off: now a professional basketball star, Tiny is determined to help other ghetto youths avoid drugs and has funded a basketball tournament in the South Bronx. Tiny also returns to the neighborhood to work with the youngsters as much as possible during the off-season. Just as Tiny has made his way in professional sports without detaching himself from his roots, so this biography chronicles his life and vividly describes the slum conditions from which he grew, thus fostering social awareness as it relates fascinating anecdotes in an involving, not overly fictionalized book. With black-and-white game shots." Booklist

Armstrong, Louis

Cornell, Jean Gay. Louis Armstrong, Ambassador Satchmo; illus. by Victor Mays. Garrard [1972] 96p illus (Americans all) lib. bdg. $5.88 (4-6)   92

1 Black musicians
ISBN 0-8116-4576-2   LC 75-188567

This is the story of Louis Armstrong, who began his musical career on New Orleans street corners and later became a world-famous jazz trumpeter and ambassador of good will

Iverson, Genie. Louis Armstrong; illus. by Kevin Brooks. Crowell 1976 33p illus (Crowell biographies) lib. bdg. $6.89 (2-4)   92

1 Black musicians
ISBN 0-690-01127-X   LC 76-4975

The text begins "with details of Louis's childhood, five years after his birth in 1900 in New Orleans. The author traces Satchmo's astonishing career through his arrest and confinement in a home for waifs at age 12 (a disaster which had its bright side, since Louis learned to play the cornet in the institution) and on to his final days. Nearly all the facts are here, except that strangely, Iverson mentions only one of Armstrong's wives, Lucille." Pub W

"A straightforward, accurate presentation of Armstrong's life with a minimum of fictionizing and sentimentality. A simple explanation of jazz is woven smoothly into the text and the illustrations evoke the vitality of Armstrong's music." Sch Library J

Arnold, Benedict

Alderman, Clifford Lindsey. The dark eagle: the story of Benedict Arnold. Macmillan Pub. Co. 1976 136p map $7.95 (4 and up)   92

1 Generals 2 U.S.—History—Revolution, 1775-1783—Biography
ISBN 0-02-700210-1   LC 75-40087

"A biography of the American traitor from his Connecticut boyhood and early business concerns to his disgrace and death in London. The emphasis is on Arnold's military career; the leadership and determination he displayed during the ill-fated expedition to Quebec as well as the successful campaigns and personal grievances associated with his roles in the capture of Ticonderoga and the battle of Saratoga." Sch Library J

"While neither personalized nor intimate, the account will help bring the man and his time to life for readers." Booklist

Banneker, Benjamin

Patterson, Lillie. Benjamin Banneker, genius of early America; illus. by David Scott Brown. Abingdon 1978 142p illus $6.95 (3-6)   92

1 Black scientists
ISBN 0-687-02900-7   LC 77-13216

A "biography of the distinguished free Black mathematician, astronomer, and surveyor (1731-1806). Banneker fashioned the first American-made clock, aided in surveying the site of our nation's capitol, and published several popular almanacs." Sch Library J

"This book is slow reading, but it is thorough, the information itself fascinating, and the illustrations true to the era." Children's Bk Rev Serv
Bibliography: p141-42

Barton, Clara Harlowe

Boylston, Helen Dore. Clara Barton, founder of the American Red Cross; illus. by Paula Hutchison. Random House 1955 182p illus. lib. bdg $5.99 (4 and up)   92

1 Nurses 2 Red Cross
ISBN 0-394-90358-7   LC 55-5824

The story of the shy young school teacher who started the first public school in New Jersey and whose Civil War nursing service grew into the foundation of the American Red Cross with its peacetime as well as wartime services

"An interesting and well-paced . . . biography of Clara Barton, emphasizing her work as an army nurse during the Civil War rather than her work as the founder of the American Red Cross." Chicago. Children's Bk Center

Beard, Daniel Carter

Blassingame, Wyatt. Dan Beard, scoutmaster of America; illus. by Dom Lupo. Garrard [1972] 80p illus lib. bdg $3.68 (3-5)   92

1 Boy Scouts 2 Naturalists
ISBN 0-8116-6754-5   LC 72-76325

This is the story of Daniel Carter Beard, the writer, artist, and naturalist whose love of young people and of nature led him to start a boys' club called the Sons of Daniel Boone. He later helped Sir Robert Baden-Powell to organize the Boy Scouts of America

Bear's Heart

Supree, Burton. Bear's Heart; scenes from the life of a Cheyenne artist of one hundred years ago with pictures by himself; text by Burton Supree, with Ann Ross; afterword by Jamake Highwater. Lippincott 1977 63p illus $8.95 (4 and up)   92

1 Cheyenne Indians—Biography
ISBN 0-397-31746-8   LC 76-48952

"Bear's Heart was a Cheyenne who rode with a group of Oklahoma Reservation deserters accused of killing a settler family. He and other prisoners were shipped east to a Florida prison where they were kept for three years. While there, Bear's Heart kept a journal he illustrated with colored pencil drawings; these artfully composed, softly stylized pictures are what illustrate this account of his time with the white man. An afterword . . . interprets Bear's Heart's experience in terms of today's ethnic consciousness. Highwater points out how the drawings reflect the prisoner's assimilation into white culture and how Bear's Heart's appreciation for white power blinded him to its effects on his people. . . . A generous format—large print, liberal amounts of white space, and a drawing facing each page of text—makes an attractive package; in all, a quietly incisive look at an unhappier segment of our past." Booklist

Beaumont, William

Epstein, Sam. Dr Beaumont and the man with the hole in his stomach, by Sam and Beryl Epstein; illus. by Joseph Scrofani. Coward, McCann & Geoghegan 1978 57p illus map lib. bdg. $5.99 (4-6)   92

1 St Martin, Alexis 2 Digestion 3 Physicians
ISBN 0-698-30680-5   LC 77-7236

"This is the account of a pioneer researcher and the man upon whom he based his discoveries. Egotistical, ambitious Dr. Beaumont happens to save the life of Alexis St. Martin after a shooting accident leaves the voyageur's stomach exposed. In spite of a mutual dislike, the two men use each other the rest of their lives, Beaumont for purposes of experimenting on the digestive system and St. Martin for supporting himself and his family. The situation reveals much about earlier medicine, frontier life, class distinctions, and the conceits of human nature." Booklist

"The personalities of the two men are especially well delineated, both in the text and in Scrofani's rugged black-and-white line drawings." Sch Library J
Selected bibliography: [p60-61]

Beebe, Charles William

Blassingame, Wyatt. William Beebe: underwater explorer; illus. by Victor Mays. Garrard 1976 96p illus (Americans all) lib. bdg. $5.88 (3-6)   92

1 Naturalists 2 Underwater exploration
ISBN 0-8116-4584-3   LC 75-29069

"Blassingame covers the undersea exploits and adventures of the scientist and author William Beebe—his experiments with diving helmets to test the depths to which men could descend; his role in shooting the first underwater film footage of sea life; his dives in the bathysphere with its inventor, Otis Barton, where he observed firsthand the mysterious and fascinating forms of life 1,400 feet underwater. Written in simple understandable language, this is a good addition to the very popular topic of undersea exploration." Sch Library J

Bell, Alexander Graham

Shippen, Katherine B. Mr. Bell invents the telephone; illus. by Richard Floethe. Random House 1952 183p illus lib. bdg. $5.99 (4 and up)   92

1 Inventors 2 Telephone
ISBN 0-394-90330-7   LC 52-7227

"Landmark books"
"Bell's work with the deaf, his invention of the telephone, and his difficulties in getting it accepted are the highlights of a readable biography." Hodges. Bks for Elem Sch Libraries

Berig, Karen

Faulkner, Margaret. I skate! Little 1979 154p illus $8.95 (5 and up)   92

1 Ice skating—Biography
ISBN 0-316-26002-9   LC 79-15932

The author's "photographs and text are the result of time spent closely watching 11-year-old Karen Berig, a Boston figure skater preparing for the New England Figure Skating Championships. The picture has a human slant too often missed in athlete or artist profiles. Karen's insecurity and negative experiences are as much a part of the story as her successes; even these are tempered by the realization that luck plays a greater part than one would like to think. The photographs are generally clear and well chosen and the text flows smoothly." Booklist
A glossary and end papers with diagrams illustrating skating figures are included

Bernstein, Leonard

Cone, Molly. Leonard Bernstein; illus. by Robert Galster. Crowell 1970 30p illus (Crowell biographies) pa $1.45 (3-5)   92

1 Conductors (Music) 2 Composers, American
ISBN 0-690-00209-2   LC 79-94792

This biography tells the story of Leonard Bernstein's life, from the time he was ten and received an old piano from his Aunt Clara to his adult success as composer and conductor
"The warm, off-beat illustrations, many in blue and gold, are done in a flat, child-like style and are most appropriate to the story." Sch Library J

Berry, Martha McChesney

Phelan, Mary Kay. Martha Berry; illus. by Charles W. Walker. Crowell 1972 41p illus (A Crowell biography) lib. bdg. $6.89 (2-4)   92

1 Berry Schools, Mount Berry, Ga. 2 Educators
ISBN 0-690-52113-8   LC 77-158699

This is the story of a Georgia plantation owner's daughter whose desire to help the poor children in the Appalachian Mountains near her home led to the establishment of Sunday schools which evolved into innovative boarding schools combining work and study. Today a high school, Berry Academy, and Berry College remain as testaments to her work
The story "is told in a straightforward manner with little fictionalization." Sch Library J

Bethune, Mary (McLeod)

Greenfield, Eloise. Mary McLeod Bethune; illus. by Jerry Pinkney. Crowell 1977 32p illus (A Crowell biography) lib. bdg. $6.49 (3-5) 92

1 Educators 2 Black women
ISBN 0-690-01129-6   LC 76-11522

"Details the life of Mary McLeod Bethune from her childhood in South Carolina to the founding of her school and her active role in the National Youth Administration under Franklin D. Roosevelt." Horn Bk
"Written with a simple, natural flow, this biography for younger readers does not have all the fascinating details of the life of the great educator, but it gives salient facts and is nicely balanced in treatment. The illustrations, rather scribbly pencil drawings, do not do justice to a woman who grew beautiful as she grew old, but they are adequate. The story of Mary McLeod, the only child in a poor family (seventeen children) who could go to school and who through her devotion and courage, became a figure of national importance as an educator and a black leader, is always thrilling; Greenfield has wisely chosen not to laud, but to let the facts speak for themselves." Chicago. Children's Bk Center

Blackwell, Elizabeth

Clapp, Patricia. Dr Elizabeth; the story of the first woman doctor. Lothrop 1974 156p lib. bdg. $6.96 (4 and up)   92

1 Women physicians
ISBN 0-688-51581-9   LC 73-17702

An "account written in journal form as though by its subject. The author has kept close to important realities in relating Blackwell's struggles to open the medical profession to women in 1847 and to raise its educational and hygienic standards." Booklist
"By writing in first person, Ms. Clapp helps the reader live through the many highs and lows of Dr. Blackwell's life. Although the book does have the power to create deep interest and feeling within the reader, the theme of rights for women is almost overdone." Cath Library World

Blegvad, Erik

Self portrait: Erik Blegvad; written and illus. by Erik Blegvad; with pictures also by Harold Blegvad [and others]. Addison-Wesley 1979 27p illus lib. bdg. $7.95 (4-6)   92

1 Illustrators
ISBN 0-201-00498-4   LC 78-23765

"This book is a portfolio of [the artist's] life seen through his work. There are bright landscapes and seascapes of his native Denmark, some charming loose drawings of Paris in the late 1940's, when he lived and worked there, views of America, where he moved with his American wife in the early 50's, book and magazine illustration. To both this art and the concise narration that accompanies it Mr. Blegvad brings quiet humor, a gifted hand and a generous spirit." NY Times Bk Rev

Bonheur, Rosa

Price, Olive. Rosa Bonheur, painter of animals; illus. by Cary. Garrard 1972 144p illus lib. bdg. $3.94 (4-6)   92

1 Painters, French 2 Women artists
ISBN 0-8116-4515-0   LC 71-190739

The author describes her subject's special love of nature and animals, which, combined with the talent for painting inherited from her artist-father, established Rosa Bonheur as much acclaimed artist of the nineteenth century. The French art world and her many famous fellow painters provide a backdrop for the story of the first woman to win the Legion of Honor medal

Boone, Daniel

Averill, Esther. Daniel Boone; illus. by Feodor Rojankovsky. Harper 1945 56p illus maps lib. bdg. $9.89 (3-6)   92

1 Frontier and pioneer life
ISBN 0-06-020181-9   LC 46-1265

A life of Daniel Boone, relating his adventures as a hunter and scout, his capture and adoption by the Cherokee Indians, and his escape from them to warn Boonesborough of the attack planned by the Indians
"Miss Averill quotes freely from Boone's own words. Her book has drama and strength." NY Her Trib Bks

Bradford, William

Jacobs, W. J. William Bradford of Plymouth Colony: illus. with authentic prints, documents, and maps. Watts, F. 1974 57p illus maps (A Visual biography) lib. bdg. $4.90 (4-6)   **92**

1 Massachusetts—History—Colonial period, 1600-1775 2 Pilgrims (New England colonists)
ISBN 0-531-02724-4   LC 74-870

"Original maps and drawings by William K. Plummer." Verso of title page
This biography of the first governor of the Plymouth Colony examines the idealistic motives and practical capabilities of the Pilgrims that made the colony an early model of self-government at work
A note on sources: p53

Braille, Louis

Davidson, Margaret. Louis Braille; the boy who invented books for the blind; illus. by Janet Compere. Hastings House [1972 c1971] 80p illus $5.95 (3-5)   **92**

1 Blind
ISBN 0-8038-4281-3
First published 1971 by Scholastic Book Services in a paperback edition
"The little French boy was only three when he blinded himself in his father's workshop. . . . By the age of 12, he had begun devising his raised-dot system. Sightless students were enormously excited by his invention, but Louis had a hard time convincing administrators of its value. Fortunately, before his death at age 43, he saw his Braille win acceptance. Children will be intrigued by the 'feelable' alphabet and will enjoy this warm biography." Pub W

Neimark, Anne E. Touch of light; the story of Louis Braille; illus. by Robert Parker. Harcourt 1970 186p illus $5.95 (4 and up)   **92**

1 Blind
ISBN 0-15-289605-8   LC 75-96319

This book "traces Braille's life and accomplishment from the age of three when he was blinded by an accident and conveys his obsession to learn to read and to make books available to the blind." Booklist
The author "tells Louis Braille's story with simplicity—it is a touching and compassionate story, in no way melodramatic—but all the way through it remains a dramatic story." Pub W
Bibliography: p185-86

Bridgman, Laura Dewey

Hunter, Edith Fisher. Child of the silent night; illus. by Bea Holmes. Houghton 1963 124p illus $7.95 (3-5)   **92**

1 Blind 2 Deaf
ISBN 0-395-06835-5   LC 63-14523

"Biographies of persons who have overcome physical handicaps can often reassure and inspire. This is the story of Laura Bridgman, a blind-deaf child whose successful attempts at communication paved the way for Helen Keller." Cincinnati

Cabot, John

Kurtz, Henry Ira. John and Sebastian Cabot; illus. with authentic prints and maps. Watts, F. 1973 58p illus maps (A Visual biography) pa $1.95 (4-6)   **92**

1 Cabot, Sebastian 2 Explorers 3 America—Exploration
ISBN 0-531-02364-8   LC 72-12796

John Cabot was responsible for the British claims in North America, but he is often overshadowed by his son Sebastian. This book highlights the importance of John Cabot's accomplishments and paints a picture of the commercial trade interests of Venice and England that set him on his way
"Based on accurate and extensive research in which sources are noted, Kurtz does an excellent job of showing how events in the East affected Europe. . . . The clear and interesting text is accompanied by black-and-white illustrations as well as contemporary prints and maps which provide a wealth of detail about life at sea." Sch Library J

Syme, Ronald. John Cabot and his son Sebastian; illus. by William Stobbs. Morrow 1972 96p illus map lib. bdg. $6.48 (3-5)   **92**

1 Cabot, Sebastian 2 Explorers 3 America—Exploration
ISBN 0-688-31816-9   LC 70-168477

"This briskly written account traces what is known of the life of John Cabot and his explorations of the coast of North America. In the final section, Syme focuses on John Cabot's boastful son, Sebastian, pointing out that Sebastian's many confusing and contradictory claims make it difficult to ascertain the truth about his activities. Illustrated with numerous black-and-white drawings and a map showing the route of John Cabot's two voyages." Booklist

Cabot, Sebastian

Kurtz, Henry Ira. John and Sebastian Cabot. See entry under Cabot, John   **92**

Syme, Ronald. John Cabot and his son Sebastian. See entry under Cabot, John   **92**

Carnegie, Andrew

Shippen, Katherine B. Andrew Carnegie and the age of steel; illus. with photographs and with drawings by Ernest Kurt Barth. Random House 1958 183p illus lib. bdg. $5.99 (4 and up)   **92**

1 Capitalists and financiers 2 Steel industry and trade
ISBN 0-394-90380-3   LC 58-6179

"Landmark books"
"The poor Scottish boy who rose to be a steel magnate and one of the world's great philanthropists is the subect of a sympathetic biography. A success story emphasizing the importance of ambition and hard work and including much information about the development of the steel industry." Hodges. Bks for Elem Sch Libraries

Carson, Rachel Louise

Latham, Jean Lee. Rachel Carson: who loved the sea; illus. by Victor Mays. Garrard 1973 80p illus lib. bdg. $5.49 (3-5)   **92**

1 Biologists 2 Women scientists
ISBN 0-8116-6312-4   LC 72-11475

"A Discovery book"
"This short career-biography tells about scientist Rachel Carson's girlhood and . . . explains the difficulties of entering a field dominated by men. Because her knowledge of marine biology was coupled with an ability to write well, she was assigned to prepare scripts for a radio program, 'Romance under the Waters;' these articles became the nucleus for her notable books about the sea." Sch Library J
"The personal material tends to be superficial, so that the reader learns how Rachel Carson took care of young relatives rather than what sort of person she was; however, the book does give the most pertinent facts about a subject who is important because of what she accomplished, and it touches on the topical issue of pollution." Chicago. Children's Bk Center

Sterling, Philip. Sea and earth; the life of Rachel Carson; illus. with photographs. Crowell 1970 213p illus (Women of America) $7.95 (6 and up)   **92**

1 Biologists 2 Women scientists
ISBN 0-690-72288-5   LC 70-87157

In this account of the marine biologist, author and conservationist, Sterling tells of Miss Carson's "childhood, young womanhood, the years of work and the later years of success marred by sickness. The smear campaign against her is described . . . [her] fight against it, and her . . . vindication." Christian Sci Monitor
This "biography is objective in tone, smoothly and seriously written, and thoroughly documented with an impressive list of sources." Sat Rev

Cartier, Jacques

Syme, Ronald. Cartier, finder of the St Lawrence; illus. by William Stobbs. Morrow 1958 95p illus map lib. bdg. $5.71 (4-6)   **92**

1 Explorers 2 America—Exploration 3 St Lawrence River
ISBN 0-688-31146-6   LC 57-9023

Cartier, Jacques—*Continued*

"An account of the French explorer's voyages to the New World in search of a waterway to the Pacific Ocean, his meetings with Indians and the building of two forts on the St. Lawrence River." Pub W

"A map shows the routes of Cartier's first two voyages (the later ones are only briefly covered in the text) while doublespread and other black-and-white drawings reconstruct realistically scenes of the voyaging, meetings with Indians, and wilderness life." Horn Bk

Carver, George Washington

Aliki. A weed is a flower: the life of George Washington Carver; written and illus. by Aliki. Prentice-Hall 1965 unp illus lib. bdg. $5.95, pa $1.50 (k-3)　　92

1 Black scientists
ISBN 0-13-947861-2; 0-13-947879-5　　LC 65-25223

A read-aloud picturebook biography which "gives a fairly balanced picture of Dr. Carver as a person and of his research and teaching. The illustrations are most attractive in their composition and use of color." We Build Together

Towne, Peter. George Washington Carver; illus. by Elzia Moon. Crowell 1975 32p illus lib. bdg. $6.79 (3-5)　　92

1 Black scientists
ISBN 0-690-00777-9　　LC 74-34296

"This biography provides younger readers with a broad perspective of Carver's attempts to teach his people to help themselves. Although the author is succinct in detailing biographical information about his subject from his birth on the farm of a white man to his teaching positions at Ames, Iowa and Tuskegee, Alabama, the text reads well without any noticeable gaps. Carver's concern with discovering new ways of utilizing plants and his methods of spreading his knowledge throughout the South are the key threads in the well-documented account." Sch Library J

Chamberlain, Wilton Norman

Rudeen, Kenneth. Wilt Chamberlain; illus. by Frank Mullins. Crowell 1970 32p illus (Crowell biographies) $5.95, lib. bdg. $6.89 (2-5)　　92

1 Basketball—Biography　2 Black athletes
ISBN 0-690-89458-9; 0-690-01134-2　　LC 74-94800

This biography "describes Wilt's boyhood, the difficulties of growing up both black and extra-tall, and the young athlete's prowess and progress at school, at college, with the Harlem Globetrotters, and . . . with the Lakers. Then to his nightclub in his beloved Harlem, and his present prosperity." Christian Sci Monitor

This book has "good, easy reading type and . . . [is] most attractively designed and illustrated. . . . [The story emphasizes] the dedication and hard work necessary for black Americans to make their way [and] should fill an immediate need." Commonweal

Champlain, Samuel de

Jacobs, W. J. Samuel de Champlain; illus. with authentic prints, documents, and maps. Watts, F. 1974 58p illus maps (A Visual biography) lib. bdg. $4.90 (4-6)　　92

1 Explorers　2 Canada—History—To 1763 (New France)　3 America—Exploration
ISBN 0-531-01275-1　　LC 73-14554

"Original maps by William K. Plummer." Verso of title page

Biography of the French explorer who founded Quebec City and Montreal and was responsible for the exploration and settlement of Canada in the 1600's

Chaplin, Charles

Jacobs, David. Chaplin, the movies, & Charlie; illus. with picture portfolios. Harper 1975 143p illus $8.95, lib. bdg. $8.79 (5 and up)　　92

1 Motion pictures—Biography
ISBN 0-06-022782-6; 0-06-022783-4　　LC 75-6291

This is a biography "of the silent film's great clown, serious actor, and devoted director. In this book of the famous funny man the author tells of his early life, his career in vaudeville, and his Keystone Comedy days. . . . The serious side of Charles Chaplin, the perfectionist actor and director, is also always present." Children's Bk Rev Serv

"This excellent introduction to the career of the famous happy-sad comedian and creative filmmaker is the first to be written for children. Jacobs dwells at length on the content and artistry of Chaplin's films, pointing out the difference between Charlie the Tramp, and Charles the Director. During the course of his research, the author obviously became 'hooked' on Chaplin. So will the reader of this book. Thirty-two pages of photographs are included as well as a dated listing of all of his films and an index." Instructor

Chapman, John

Aliki. The story of Johnny Appleseed; written and illus. by Aliki. Prentice-Hall 1963 unp illus lib. bdg. $5.95, pa $1.50 (k-3)　　92

1 Frontier and pioneer life
ISBN 0-13-850800-3; 0-13-850818-6　　LC 63-8507

This is a picture-story of "Johnny Appleseed, the New Englander who wandered through the Middle West in the early days distributing seeds of apple trees for planting, and remaining to share his love for wild creatures, pioneer folk, and nature." Christian Sci Monitor

Charles, Ray

Mathis, Sharon Bell. Ray Charles; illus. by George Ford. Crowell 1973 31p illus (A Crowell biography) $6.95, lib. bdg. $6.89 (2-5)　　92

1 Black musicians
ISBN 0-690-67065-6; 0-690-67066-4　　LC 72-7552

This is a biography of the popular black singer who overcame his blindness to achieve renown in the music world

"Enhanced by Ford's two-color charcoal drawings, this will broaden Black biography collections." Sch Library J

Chavez, César Estrada

Franchere, Ruth. Cesar Chavez; illus. by Earl Thollander. Crowell 1970 42p illus (Crowell biographies) pa $2.95 (2-5)　　92

1 Migrant labor　2 Mexican Americans—Biography
ISBN 0-690-18385-2　　LC 78-101927

Coming from a Mexican-American family of migrant workers, César Chavez has experienced first hand the miserable conditions under which the migrant worker lives and works. This is a biography of Chavez—unionizer of the grape pickers of California and leader of a nationwide grape boycott to get decent wages for migrant workers

"The type is large, and the illustrations, line drawings with orange and gold overlays, give a feeling for the vast, dry setting. In spite of its picture-book format, this could be useful with older, reluctant readers." Sch Library J

Chisholm, Shirley (St Hill)

Haskins, James. Fighting Shirley Chisholm. Dial Press 1975 211p illus $7.95 (6 and up)　　92

1 U.S. Congress. House　2 Black women　3 Women politicians
ISBN 0-8037-4835-3　　LC 74-20384

"A biography of the first black woman to serve in the United States Congress gives a good balance of personal and professional material, is written with vigorous admiration, and is candid about incidents not included in other Chisholm biographies written for young people. All her biographers have made it clear that Shirley Chisholm is honest, courageous, and forthright; Haskins stresses the decisions she has had to make about paramount causes: would she take a stand on an issue as a black or as a woman when the stands conflicted, for example. . . . This is a lesson in political structure and in the necessity for practical compromise to achieve idealistic goals." Chicago. Children's Bk Center

Bibliography: p201-05

Chukovsky, Kornei

The silver crest; my Russian boyhood; tr. from the Russian by Beatrice Stillman. Holt 1976 182p $6.95 (6 and up)　　92

1 Authors, Russian
ISBN 0-03-014241-5　　LC 75-32248

Chukovsky, Kornei—*Continued*

Original Russian edition published 1963

"Kornei Chukovsky was both an authority on the language of childhood and a children's author. This account of his late childhood has the same qualities of candor and humor that have made his poetry popular. Son of an unwed mother, the eleven-year-old Kornei was evicted from school on a slim pretext because he was socially undesirable. The ploys he tries in order to stay in school and keep his friends, the misery he feels when he fails in the former and is little more successful in the latter, are as touching as they are comical." Chicago. Children's Bk Center

Churchill, Sir Winston Leonard Spencer

Reynolds, Quentin. Winston Churchill; illus. with photographs. Random House 1963 183p illus maps lib. bdg. $5.99 (4 and up)   92

1 Politicians, British 2 Great Britain—History—20th century
ISBN 0-394-90556-3   LC 63-7831

"World Landmark books"

"The many facets of Sir Winston's personality and career are brought out in a smoothly written biography, ending with his resignation as prime minister in 1955. Photographs include pictures of his funeral." Hodges. Bks for Elem Sch Libraries
Other books of interest: p178-79

Clark, Eugenie

McGovern, Ann. Shark lady; true adventures of Eugenie Clark; illus. by Ruth Chew. Four Winds [1979 c1978] 83p illus $6.95 (3-5)   92

1 Sharks 2 Zoologists 3 Women scientists
ISBN 0-590-07604-3   LC 78-22126

"Fascinated by the aquarium when she was a child, Eugenie Clark never wavered in her desire to become an ichthyologist, and after obtaining her doctorate, she became director of a marine laboratory, a noted author, and a professor of zoology. While her biography is written simply, it describes a rewarding career, and it should appeal to readers because of the exciting underwater research Clark has done, particularly in investigating the habits of sharks." Chicago. Children's Bk Center

Bibliography of adult books and articles by Eugenie Clark: p83

Clemens, Samuel Langhorne

McNeer, May. America's Mark Twain; with illus. by Lynd Ward. Houghton 1962 159p illus lib. bdg. $6.95 (5 and up)   92

1 Authors, American
ISBN 0-395-19842-9   LC 60-9097

This book tells about Mark Twain's life of adventure on the Mississippi River, his success as a humorist, his escapades that entertained America and most of Europe, and the tragedies that befell him in later life

"This version is a joy to read and to look at. . . . The Wards have worked together with genuine affection and respect for their subject—and for their readers. As a supplement to Mark Twain's life, they have added at the end of each chapter a sort of preview of the particular book which was related to that part of his life. These little previews, each consisting of several pages with text and pictures illustrating sample episodes, are designed to interest the reader in exploring the books themselves." Horn Bk

Clemente, Roberto Walker

Rudeen, Kenneth. Roberto Clemente; illus. by Frank Mullins. Crowell 1974 32p illus (A Crowell biography) lib. bdg. $6.89 (2-4)   92

1 Baseball—Biography
ISBN 0-690-0032-6   LC 73-12794

A biography of the Puerto Rican who began to train himself as a baseball player in his youth, became an outstanding member of the Pittsburgh Pirates baseball club, and died tragically in a plane crash while on a good will mission to earthquake-damaged Nicaragua

The book is "simply written, straightforward in tone, and well-organized." Chicago. Children's Bk Center

Cody, William Frederick

Aulaire, Ingri d'. Buffalo Bill, by Ingri & Edgar Parin d'Aulaire. Doubleday 1952 unp illus lib. bdg. $8.95 (1-4)   92

1 Frontier and pioneer life—The West (U.S.)
ISBN 0-385-07605-3   LC 52-10232

Youngsters "will be enthusiastic about this recreation of the life of one of their heroes. Beginning with his boyhood in Kansas Territory and his friendship with the Kickapoo Indians, the biography authentically pictures the outstanding events of his long and exciting life against the background of our western frontier. The illustrations, in the d'Aulaire manner, are bright and filled with interesting details." Library J

"The text is factual, with no talking down, and the many big pictures a pleasant introduction to the old west." NY Her Trib Bks

Map on lining-papers

Columbus, Christopher

Aulaire, Ingri d'. Columbus [by] Ingri & Edgar Parin d'Aulaire. Doubleday 1955 56p illus $7.95 (1-4)   92

1 Explorers 2 America—Exploration
ISBN 0-385-07606-1   LC 55-9011

"This is an account of Columbus' four voyages to the New World. . . . The authors have a lively enthusiasm for their subject, and have imbued this biography with the excitement of exploring the unknown, and they have successfully brought to life the restless ambitious spirit, which sent Columbus out into the 'trackless waste of the sea.' The illustrations are striking full-page lithographs, some in colour and some in black and white, and imaginative marginal drawings." Ontario Library Rev

This book "is perhaps better suited to a child who has already heard the story and who has begun to want more information. . . . The portrait of the aging, disappointed man who 'wanted too much and so did not get enough' in no way detracts from the reader's sense of his greatness. Rather it adds to our understanding." NY Times Bk Rev

Sperry, Armstrong. The voyages of Christopher Columbus; written and illus. by Armstrong Sperry. Random House 1950 186p illus lib. bdg. $5.99 (5 and up)   92

1 Explorers 2 America—Exploration
ISBN 0-394-90301-3   LC 50-11712

"Landmark books"

An account of the four voyages of Columbus, relating the oft-told incidents as well as the seldom-heard accounts of his sea voyages, the mutinies of his crews, and land colonization

"Mr. Sperry brings all his feeling for the sea and his ability to tell a brisk adventure story to his tale of Columbus; his hero is appealingly real and his fine pictures a moving dramatic unit." NY Her Trib Bks

Ventura, Piero. Christopher Columbus; based on the text by Gian Paolo Ceserani. Random House [1979 c1978] unp illus $3.95, lib. bdg. $4.99 (4-6)   92

1 America—Exploration 2 Explorers
ISBN 0-394-83907-2; 0-394-93907-7   LC 77-86146

"This begins with a brief outline of Christopher Columbus' life and an explanation of the explorations of the period and the search for a route to the Indies. The story is told in brief sections: the departure, the three ships, the crew, the Sargasso Sea life on board, a new world, et cetera; some sections have a page of print, some only a sentence or two. The information given is accurate but sketchy, the illustrations often giving more facts than the text." Chicago. Children's Bk Center

"Ventura's hand shows a steadfast penchant for detail, bright color, and good humor. Panoramic scenes, gay-looking and astutely composed against large expanses of white space, overflow with eye-tickling line and animation. Even instructional illustrations like the cross-sectional view of one of Columbus' loaded ships, have a humor that belies the book's non-fictional label. . . . Columbus is portrayed as an explorer rather than the 'discoverer' of America, and the account limits itself largely to his first voyage." Booklist

Corbett, James John

Hoff, Syd. Gentleman Jim and the great John L.; story and pictures by Syd Hoff. Coward, McCann & Geoghegan 1977 47p illus lib. bdg. $6.59 (1-3)   **92**

1 Sullivan, John Lawrence 2 Boxing—Biography
ISBN 0-698-30669-4   LC 77-175

"A Break-of-day book"

The author recounts the 1892 heavyweight boxing championship match between John L. Sullivan and "Gentleman Jim" Corbett

"This adds a new note to the material available for young independent readers, and Hoff's turn-of-the-century cartoon-style pictures have a bouncy humor." Chicago. Children's Bk Center

Cortés, Hernando

Jacobs, W. J. Hernando Cortes; illus. with authentic prints, documents, and maps. Watts, F. 1974 58p illus maps (A Visual biography) lib. bdg. $4.90 (4-6)   **92**

1 Explorers 2 Mexico—History
ISBN 0-531-00974-2   LC 73-9509

"A brief but vivid record of the epic battles led by Hernando Cortes in 1519-21 that destroyed the Mexican Aztec civilization. The text has been carefully researched and two events—the defeat of 'La Noche Triste' and the battle at Atumbo—are especially well detailed. Illustrated with fascinating prints and maps." Sch Library J

Cousteau, Jacques Yves

Iverson, Genie. Jacques Cousteau; illus. by Hal Ashmead. Putnam 1976 62p illus lib. bdg. $5.99 (3-5)   **92**

1 Underwater exploration 2 Oceanography—Research
ISBN 0-399-60987-3   LC 75-25822

"This brief account of the life of Cousteau covers his early boyhood through the projects he currently involves himself in to understand and protect the sea. The famed oceanographer's early interest in the ocean led to the invention of the aqualung, which subsequently allowed him to film the water's depths. Work by Cousteau and his crew aboard the Calypso is explained, and incidents of feeding and studying fish are included. Although print size indicates a younger reading level than the vocabulary requires, children whose only exposure to Cousteau has been via television will find a short, readable introduction here. Black-and-white drawings accompany the text." Booklist

Craft, Ellen

Freedman, Florence B. Two tickets to freedom; the true story of Ellen and William Craft, fugitive slaves. See entry under Craft, William   **92**

Craft, William

Freedman, Florence B. Two tickets to freedom; the true story of Ellen and William Craft, fugitive slaves; illus. by Ezra Jack Keats. Simon & Schuster 1971 96p illus lib. bdg. $5.95 (4-6)   **92**

1 Craft, Ellen 2 Slavery in the U.S. 3 Blacks—Biography
ISBN 0-671-65169-2   LC 71-162713

"Based on contemporary documents and on William Craft's 'Running a Thousand Miles for Freedom,' published in 1861, this is the . . . true story of how Craft and his wife escaped slavery [in Georgia] in 1848. Ellen Craft, a light-skinned woman, dressed as a man and her husband posed as her servant . . . [After their arrival in the North] friends helped the Crafts escape to England, where they lived prosperously until after the Civil War, when they came back to Georgia to open a school." Chicago Children's Bk Center

"The story is not well known, so children may need some introduction to it. But once begun, it is hard to put down. . . . Ezra Jack Keats' charcoal drawings effectively decorate the text. An excellent selection for history buffs and those who enjoy warm human interest stories." Sch Library J

Sources: p96

Crazy Horse, Oglala Indian

Meadowcroft, Enid La Monte. Crazy Horse, Sioux warrior; illus. by Cary. Garrard 1965 80p illus lib. bdg. $5.49 (2-5)   **92**

1 Oglala Indians—Biography
ISBN 0-8116-6600-X   LC 65-10090

"This life of the great Sioux warrior [of the Oglala tribe] tells not only of the white men's injustices but also of the unreasoning warfare of the Indians among themselves." Adventuring With Bks

"A sympathetic and interesting account. . . . The illustrations, by Cary, are excellent." NY Times Bk Rev

Curie, Marie (Sklodowska)

Veglahn, Nancy. The mysterious rays: Marie Curie's world; illus. by Victor Juhasz. Coward, McCann & Geoghegan 1977 63p illus lib bdg. $5.99 (3-6)   **92**

1 Chemists 2 Women scientists
ISBN 0-698-30681-3   LC 77-8361

This "introduction to the Polish scientist who discovered radium focuses on her years spent trying to isolate the element, a process made more difficult by the Curies' lack of money and good laboratory facilities. But what could have been a tidily crafted biography falls prey to stilted fictionalization. . . . With charcoal drawings that have a sketch-book appearance." Booklist

Curtis, Edward S.

Boesen, Victor. Edward S. Curtis, photographer of the North American Indian [by] Victor Boesen and Florence Curtis Graybill. Dodd 1977 191p illus $6.95 (5 and up)   **92**

1 Photographers 2 Indians of North America
ISBN 0-396-07430-8   LC 76-53435

"Co-written by one of Edward Curtis's daughters, the book is the highly readable story of an excellent photographer who, in 1899, realized that the culture of western American Indians would soon be wiped out. He resolved to make a permanent record of the Indians, a project which took him thirty years to complete. . . . His travels were financed by his own work and by J. Pierpont Morgan, who wanted to see the photographs ' "In books—the most beautiful set . . . ever published." ' The account of Curtis's exciting travels as the twenty volumes take form is interspersed with laudatory newspaper and magazine criticism of his photography. Information on the life of the Indians themselves is the most fascinating aspect of the biography; in coastal California and Oregon, for example, Curtis and his assistants discovered '75 languages and more than 10,000 songs' and took '40,000 pictures—covering 80 tribes. . . .' A handsome book, generously filled with the photographer's haunting portraits and landscapes." Horn Bk

Custer, George Armstrong

Reynolds, Quentin. Custer's last stand; illus. by Frederick T. Chapman. Random House 1951 185p illus lib. bdg. $5.99 (5 and up)   **92**

1 Generals 2 Little Big Horn, Battle of the, 1876
ISBN 0-394-90320-X   LC 51-14189

"Landmark books"

"The life story of the famous U.S. cavalry officer —boyhood, preparation for and training at West Point, Civil War experiences, Indian fighting, and the disastrous battle at Little Big Horn. The courageous, headstrong soldier is animatedly portrayed in this exciting and well-written book." Booklist

"The realistic portrayal of the relations between the Indians and white men make this an important addition to the books on the making of America." Library J

Dickinson, Emily

Barth, Edna. I'm nobody! Who are you? The story of Emily Dickinson; drawings by Richard Cuffari. Seabury [distributed by Houghton] 1971 128p illus $6.95 (5 and up)   **92**

1 Poets, American 2 Women authors
ISBN 0-395-28843-6   LC 72-129211

"A Clarion book"

This is "a very good biography that begins with the nine-year-old Emily, smoothly incorporates passages of her writing within the context of the

Dickinson, Emily—*Continued*

text, and includes selected poems at the conclusion of the biographical material. The writing style is direct and informal, all of the dialogue based on research, and the tone is objective. A bibliography, a list of sources, an index of poems by first lines, and a general index are appended." Sutherland. The Best in Children's Bks

Disney, Walt

Montgomery, Elizabeth Rider. Walt Disney: master of make-believe; illus. by Vic Mays. Garrard 1971 96p illus (Americans all) lib. bdg. $5.88 (3-5)   92

1 Motion pictures—Biography 2 Motion picture cartoons
ISBN 0-8116-4568-1   LC 71-146705

This "interesting, simply written narrative biography . . . covers Disney's life from his harsh, unhappy childhood to his death in 1966. [The author] relates some of the problems Disney encountered during his early years in Hollywood, describes the origin of Mickey Mouse and other well-known Disney cartoon characters, and tells how Disney's dream of a clean imaginative amusement park led to the development of Disneyland." Booklist

Douglass, Frederick

Bontemps, Arna. Frederick Douglass: slave-fighter-freeman; illus. by Harper Johnson. Knopf 1959 177p illus lib. bdg. $5.99 (4 and up)   92

1 Abolitionists 2 Slavery in the U.S. 3 Blacks—Biography
ISBN 0-394-91168-7   LC 59-6410

Frederick Douglass was born a slave. When he got his hard-won freedom, he dedicated his life to the cause of freedom for all men. From a lowly slave boy, he forged ahead to become a great statesman, newsman, orator, and writer. The path was rough but the goal worth winning

"Mr. Bontemps has used great restraint in this account of the sufferings of those early years, but even so this is an exciting story of struggle against almost insurmountable odds, and of the triumph of human greatness. Direct style, large type and good illustrations make this an appealing book." Horn Bk

Drew, Charles Richard

Bertol, Roland. Charles Drew; illus. by Jo Polseno. Crowell 1970 31p illus (Crowell biographies) lib. bdg. $7.89 (3-5)   92

1 Physicians 2 Black scientists 3 Medicine—Biography
ISBN 0-690-18598-7   LC 77-94789

This is "a fictionalized biography of the Negro doctor who discovered how to make blood transfusions and how to preserve blood. . . . [The author] traces Drew's life: his childhood desire to be a jockey, the discrimination he encountered while an athlete at Amherst College, his blood research at McGill University, and the controversy he generated during World War II when he insisted that black and white blood could be used interchangeably in transfusions." Sch Library J

"The account also contains some interesting sidelights on scientific research. Designed for young readers, the book is printed in large type with pictures on almost every page." Booklist

Du Bois, William Edward Burghardt

Hamilton, Virginia. W. E. B. Du Bois; a biography; illus. with photographs. Crowell 1972 218p illus $8.95 (6 and up)   92

1 Blacks—Biography
ISBN 0-690-87256-9   LC 70-175106

This is an account of the life and career of W.E.B. Du Bois who "struggled for ninety-five years as educator, writer, intellectual, and poet against prejudice and fear. . . . [The author describes Du Bois'] life from his birth in 1868 as a free man in Great Barrington, Massachusetts, to his death in 1963 in Ghana, a Ghanian citizen. . . . The book is an affirmation of Du Bois' life, and a fascinating historical document of the Black Movement in America." Horn Bk

This "work is meticulously annotated, comprehensive, and generally objective—too detailed for pre-teens, perhaps, but extremely good for slightly older readers." Christian Sci Monitor
Bibliography: p204-08

Dunbar, Paul Laurence

Schultz, Pearle Henriksen. Paul Laurence Dunbar: black poet laureate; illus. by William Hutchinson. Garrard 1974 143p illus lib. bdg. $5.88 (4 and up)   92

1 Poets, American 2 Black authors
ISBN 0-8116-4516-9   LC 73-22071

The author shows "what it was like for Dunbar to grow up in the Midwest of the late 1800's, and a good selection of photographs from the period are included. Although some dialogue is fictionalized, there is also a healthy sampling of Dunbar's better-known dialect poems, which have particular appeal to children, as well as verse in his classical style." Sch Library J

Duniway, Abigail Scott

Morrison, Dorothy Nafus. Ladies were not expected; Abigail Scott Duniway and women's rights; illus. with prints, photographs and a map. Atheneum Pubs. 1977 146p illus map $6.95 (5 and up)   92

1 Women—Suffrage
ISBN 0-689-30599-0   LC 77-2969

"Morrison has kept to rich original sources in her biography of Abigail Scott Duniway, an Oregon crusader for women's rights. Duniway was a writer and news editor during her varied career and left the kind of material that could supply occasional verbatim dialogue. . . . She went west with her family at 17, saw her mother, sweetheart, and baby brother die on the trail, and found hard work waiting for her and her sisters on arriving at their new home. She soon married Ben Duniway, whose crippling accident pushed her into the role of primary breadwinner. Duniway supported his wife's independent ways and in later years approved of her campaigns for women's suffrage; Abigail lived to see her home state pass such a bill in 1912. Photographs and reproductions of old documents illustrate the fast-moving text." Booklist

"It is a welcome addition to any biography shelf. . . . Readers will enjoy the debates of the day on women's rights and will feel rewarded by their acquaintance with the spunky Abigail. The book is a pleasant way to introduce children to the struggle for suffrage." Interracial Bks for Children Bul
Bibliography: p137-40

Earhart, Amelia

Mann, Peggy. Amelia Earhart: first lady of flight; illus. by Kiyo Komoda. Coward-McCann & Geoghegan 1970 126p illus lib. bdg. $6.29 (3-5)   92

1 Women air pilots
ISBN 0-698-30008-4   LC 71-106932

This is "a fictionalized biography of Amelia Earhart which stresses her personal courage and her belief that women should have the same opportunities to develop and use their abilities as men. The book covers Earhart's tomboy childhood, her growing preoccupation with airplanes, her record-breaking flights, and her ill-fated attempt to fly around the world." Booklist

Edison, Thomas Alva

Cousins, Margaret. The story of Thomas Alva Edison; illus. with photographs and map. Random House 1965 175p illus map lib. bdg. $5.99 (4-6)   92

1 Inventors
ISBN 0-394-90410-9   LC 65-22652

"Landmark books"
"A readable biography of one of America's greatest inventors, with emphasis on his part in the development of the photograph, the incandescent light, and motion pictures." Hodges. Bks for Elem Sch Libraries
Includes bibliography

North, Sterling. Young Thomas Edison; illus. with photographs, decorations, diagrams, and maps by William Barss. Houghton 1958 182p illus maps $2.95 (5 and up)   92

1 Inventors
ISBN 0-395-07252-2   LC 58-9637

Edison, Thomas A.—*Continued*

"North star books"
"A biography of Thomas A. Edison, stressing his inventions and the fact that his life was fruitful despite many vicissitudes and disappointments." Pub W
"A well-written, authentic biography which reveals the human qualities of the inventor as well as his genius." Booklist

Eisenhower, Dwight David, President U. S.

Faber, Doris. Dwight Eisenhower. Abelard-Schuman 1977 116p illus lib. bdg. $6.79 (5 and up)   92

1 Generals 2 Presidents—U.S.
ISBN 0-200-00172-8   LC 76-44001

"A biography of Dwight D. Eisenhower, commander of American forces in Europe during World War II and last military hero to reach the White House. Eisenhower's education at West Point, rise in the military, successful leadership during World War II, short stay as president of Columbia University, and two terms as President are chronicled in a clear, readable style. Faber's coverage is accurate and objective, making this a good choice if additional material about Eisenhower is needed." Sch Library J
Bibliography: p113

Ellington, Duke

Montgomery, Elizabeth Rider. Duke Ellington: king of jazz; illus. by Paul Frame. Garrard 1972 96p illus lib. bdg. $5.88 (3-5)   92

1 Black musicians 2 Jazz musicians
ISBN 0-8116-4573-8   LC 70-179401

"A few photographs add interest to a biography of the eminent jazz musician who has slowly been recognized by musicologists as a serious composer. Most of the material here is concerned with Duke Ellington's career; exciting as is his music, his progress as a performer-composer has been too steady to be very dramatic, and the tepid style in which the book is written adds little excitement to the story. An index is appended." Chicago. Children's Bk Center

Ericsson, John

Latham, Jean Lee. Man of the Monitor; the story of John Ericsson; pictures by Leonard Everett Fisher. Harper 1962 231p illus lib. bdg. $8.79 (5 and up)   92

1 U.S.—History—Civil War, 1861-1865—Naval operations 2 Monitor (Ironclad) 3 Inventors
ISBN 0-06-023711-2   LC 62-8037

The author "presents a lively sketch of John Ericsson, Swedish-born engineer and inventor . . . best remembered for designing and supervising the construction of the 'Monitor.' She takes up his story in a somewhat sentimental vein when he is nine and his family is on the verge of ruin. About half the book covers his life from child genius in Sweden to modest success in England; the remaining part describes his frustrated early days in America to final triumph at the close of the Civil War. . . . Miss Latham's story moves at a good pace, uncluttered by dates and details. Its main difficulty is with the dialogue, which seems to fall short in its attempt to reach the young teenager because of its artificiality." Best Sellers
This book "has value not only as a biography but also as a good book of the Civil War period." Chicago. Children's Bk Center

Faraday, Michael

Veglahn, Nancy. Coils, magnets and rings; Michael Faraday's world; illus. by Christopher Spollen. Coward, McCann & Geoghegan 1976 59p illus $5.95 (3-5)   92

1 Scientists
ISBN 0-698-20384-4   LC 76-14385

"Against a backdrop of nineteenth-century England, an engaging portrait emerges of the man who discovered electromagnetism, made other scientific breakthroughs, and still had time to enjoy life and people." LC. Children's Bks 1976
"This biography is tailored to the young reader; written in language and terms easy for a child to understand. . . . Although Veglahn covers Faraday's experiments, she does not attempt to explain them in detail, which makes this book quite readable. The outstanding black-and-white charcoal drawings help to produce a fine book." AAAS Sci Bks & Films
Includes glossary and bibliography

Farragut, David Glasgow

Latham, Jean Lee. Anchor's aweigh; the story of David Glasgow Farragut; illus. by Eros Keith. Harper 1968 273p illus maps lib. bdg. $8.79 (5 and up)   92

1 Admirals 2 U.S.—History—Civil War, 1861-1865 —Naval operations 3 U.S.—History, Naval
ISBN 0-06-023703-1   LC 68-24319

The author "skillfully re-creates the character and personality of a famed American naval hero in a lively narrative account replete with authentically drawn scenes of marine warfare and life aboard sailing vessels. Incidents of Farragut's personal life are included but major focus is on his service with the U.S. Navy which began during the War of 1812 at age ten and was climaxed by his action in Mobile Bay as admiral in the Union Navy. The book is illustrated with small drawings of ships and maps." Booklist

Feelings, Tom

Black pilgrimage. Lothrop 1972 72p illus lib. bdg. $7.92 (5 and up)   92

1 Black artists 2 Illustrators
ISBN 0-688-51630-0   LC 70-177328

This black "children's book illustrator describes his life and work, particularly his decision to leave the United States and live in Africa. Tom Feelings grew up in Bedford-Stuyvesant, served in the army, and went to art school. He drew and painted the life he knew, but it was not until he worked for a time in Ghana that Feelings saw how much the oppression suffered by his people was evident in his pictures. [His illustrations supplement the text throughout]." Sat Rev
"His statement is honest, often bitter, and always sensitive, particularly interesting for the insight his own work gave Tom Feelings into the attitudes of black Americans after he had been in Africa and returned. The illustrations, some in color and some in black and white, are stunning." Sutherland. The Best in Children's Bks

Ford, Henry, 1863-1947

Quackenbush, Robert. Along came the Model T! How Henry Ford put the world on wheels. Parents Mag. Press [distributed by Four Winds] 1978 unp illus $6.50, lib. bdg. $6.19 (2-4)   92

1 Automobile industry and trade 2 Inventors
ISBN 0-8193-0952-4; 0-8193-0953-2   LC 77-10057

"Henry Ford's obsession with building a 'smaller, lightweight horseless carriage' is traced from his childhood delight in fixing watches and repairing toys through his early experimentation to his success with the Model T. Emphasis is on the inventor's dedication to his work and the frustrations encountered. . . . A few perfunctory paragraphs on the final pages mention the problems created by the automotive assembly line and the energy crisis to which automobiles have contributed all over the world. . . . Diagrams for 'how to build a model "Tin Lizzie"' and 'how a car works' are appended." Booklist
"This author-illustrator has written an absorbing biography of the automotive pioneer. The text is spiced by brashly colored, full-page paintings of Henry as a boy and by small drawings, on alternate pages, of a boy and girl hearing all about the mechanical genius from a gas-station attendant." Pub W

Forten, Charlotte L.

Longsworth, Polly. I, Charlotte Forten, black and free. Crowell 1970 248p $6.95 (6 and up)   92

1 Black women 2 Teachers
ISBN 0-690-42869-3   LC 79-109901

"Civil war movements and black-American history form the major part of the account, its framework based on a journal kept by the granddaughter of James Forten, well-to-do black sailmaker of Philadelphia. More intimate and lively portions of the writing . . . describe Charlotte's teen-age life in Salem, Massachusetts, where she came in 1854 to study and then to teach. . . . Charlotte seemed always to meet the great leaders, both black and white. . . . Case histories of individual slaves and eyewitness accounts of historic meetings and trials further enrich the biographical history." Horn Bk
Biography: p234-37

Fortune, Amos

Yates, Elizabeth. Amos Fortune, free man; illus. by Nora S. Unwin. Dutton 1950 181p illus lib. bdg. $8.95 (4 and up)   **92**

1 Blacks—Biography 2 Slavery in the U.S.
ISBN 0-525-25570-2   LC 50-7154

Awarded the Newbery Medal, 1951

"Born free in Africa, Amos Fortune was sold into slavery in America in 1725. After more than 40 years of servitude Amos was able to purchase his freedom and in time, that of several others. He died a tanner of enviable reputation, a landowner, and a respected citizen of his community. Based on fact, this is a . . . story of a life dedicated to the fight for freedom and service to others. Large print." Booklist

"It is a moving story, underlaid with deep religious feeling, which thoughtful young people will find absorbing." NY Times Bk Rev

Frank, Anne

Anne Frank: the diary of a young girl; tr. from the Dutch by B. M. Mooyaart-Doubleday; with an introduction by Eleanor Roosevelt (6 and up)   **92**

1 World War, 1939-1945—Jews 2 Netherlands—History—German occupation, 1940-1945 3 Jews in the Netherlands

Some editions are:
Doubleday $8.95; lib. bdg. $9.90 (ISBN 0-385-04019-9; 0-385-09190-7; LC 67-66285)
Modern Lib. $3.95 (ISBN 0-394-60298-6; LC 58-11474)

Original Dutch edition 1947; this translation first published 1952 by Doubleday

Two Jewish "families went into hiding in the abandoned half of a warehouse in Amsterdam during the Nazi occupation. Anne, the thirteen-year-old, recorded what she saw and felt about the relationships of eight people living under the strain of hunger, of crowded housing, and fear of discovery and death. . . . [This story tells of Anne's] shifting relationship to her parents and sister, and her growing self-awareness." Rdng Ladders

"A book that derives its lasting interest less from its war background . . . than as an unaffected, often moving account of the dreams and soul searchings of an adolescent." Ontario Library Rev

Franklin, Benjamin

Aliki. The many lives of Benjamin Franklin; written down and illus. by Aliki. Prentice-Hall 1977 32p illus lib. bdg. $6.95 (1-3)   **92**

ISBN 0-13-556019-5   LC 77-5508

"Aliki's captioned cartoons—lightly lined and washed—expand or punctuate her easy text, which sketches Franklin's life from childhood on. His inventiveness and multifaceted career as a writer, printer, politician, and diplomat are all touched on to comprise an efficient, lightweight introduction for picturebook readers." Booklist

Aulaire, Ingri d'. Benjamin Franklin [by] Ingri & Edgar Parin d'Aulaire. Doubleday 1950 48p illus $8.95, lib. bdg. $9.90 (2-4)   **92**

ISBN 0-385-07219-8; 0-385-07603-7   LC 66-4602

"There is vigour and simplicity in the telling of this story of Benjamin Franklin for young children, and wisdom in the choice of incidents from his varied and active career [from printer and inventor to author and statesman]. The full-page lithographs in colour and in sepia are effectively designed and not only portray Franklin's story but give an expansive picture of the time. The marginal drawings, which include Poor Richard's sayings add to the general attractiveness of the book as well as providing further details of the life and customs of pre-revolutionary America." Ontario Library Rev

Daugherty, James. Poor Richard; illus. with lithographs in two colors by the author. Viking 1941 158p illus lib. bdg. $6.50 (6 and up)   **92**

ISBN 0-670-56450-8   LC 41-52011

"Benjamin Franklin's charm, intellectual curiosity, humor, practicality, and wisdom are displayed in a vigorous portrait. Well-chosen quotations give flavor to the text, and sparing use is made of fictionalization in conversation and in the handling of incidents. The pace is swift, the chapter headings intriguing. The author's lithographs have a robust spirit suitable to the times." Coughlan. Creating Independence, 1763-1789

Fritz, Jean. What's the big idea, Ben Franklin? Illus. by Margot Tomes. Coward, McCann & Geoghegan 1976 46p illus $6.95 (3-5)   **92**

ISBN 0-698-20365-8   LC 75-25902

The text "focuses on Franklin's multifaceted career but also gives personal details and quotes some of his pithy sayings. Enough background information about colonial affairs is given to enable readers to understand the importance of Franklin's contributions to the public good but not so much that it obtrudes on his life story. Although the text is not punctuated by references or footnotes, a page of notes (with numbers for pages referred to) is appended." Chicago. Children's Bk Center

This "well-researched and documented narrative reflects the humor, virtues, flaws, and zest for living characteristic of the subject. As in her earlier studies . . . the author successfully emphasizes and enlarges upon a particular trait—in this instance, the zeal for translating ideas into action—not to the point of caricature but rather as a child might instinctively distill the essence of a fascinating adult from close observation. . . . The illustrations suggest the sturdy and ingenious charm of colonial art. A balanced and vigorous biographical portrait." Horn Bk

Freeman, Elizabeth

Felton, Harold W. Mumbet: the story of Elizabeth Freeman; illus. by Donn Albright. Dodd 1970 63p illus lib. bdg. $6.95 (4-6)   **92**

1 Black women 2 Slavery in the U.S.
ISBN 0-396-06558-9   LC 74-108785

This "fictionalized biography of the first slave to achieve freedom through the courts portrays Elizabeth Freeman as a quiet woman heroically determined to force a literal interpretation of the Massachusetts constitution's provision that all men are created equal. In his introduction Felton cites some of the few sources of information about Mrs. Freeman before telling her story, which . . . makes interesting reading." Booklist

Frémont, John Charles

Syme, Ronald. John Charles Frémont; the last American explorer; illus. by Richard Cuffari. Morrow 1974 190p illus map $6.50, lib. bdg. $6.24 (5 and up)   **92**

1 Explorers 2 The West (U.S.)—Exploration
ISBN 0-688-20120-2; 0-688-30120-7   LC 74-4198

The explorer and pathfinder whose expeditions into the American West made viable a route for travelers to Oregon and California is the subject of this biography

The writing "is generally clear, and nicely done black-and-white line drawings illustrate prominent persons or scenes mentioned in the text." Sch Library J

Bibliography: p189-90

Fulton, Robert

Judson, Clara Ingram. Boat builder; the story of Robert Fulton; illus. by Armstrong Sperry. Scribner 1940 121p illus lib. bdg. $5.95 (4-6)   **92**

1 Inventors 2 Steamboats
ISBN 0-684-13469-1   LC 40-32220

"The first half deals with the inventor's boyhood, beginning with his first day of school at the age of eight, and is more fictionalized than the latter half. The story of the 'Clermont's' voyage is told in detail. Fulton's interest in submarines and torpedoes is attributed . . . to a desire 'to make weapons so powerful that war and piracy would be impossible.' . . . There is some sentimentality, but it is, on the whole, a very usable and simple biography. Excellent format." Library J

Galilei, Galileo

Cobb, Vicki. Truth on trial: the story of Galileo Galilei; illus. by George Ulrich. Coward, McCann & Geoghegan 1979 63p illus lib. bdg. $5.99 (3-5)   92

1 Astronomers
ISBN 0-698-30709-7   LC 79-237

"While Cobb introduces invented dialogue, most of her text is authoritative in a biography that focuses on Galileo's ideas rather than his personal life. She makes the question of conflicting theories the center of the book, explaining lucidly the differences between Ptolemaic and Copernican theories of the structure of the universe; equally vivid is her presentation of Galileo's persecution by the Church of Rome, with his capitulation to the demands of the court of the Inquisition that he renounce his support of the Copernican theory that the sun was the center of the system, a fact that Galileo had corroborated through the use of the telescope he had perfected. . . . A brief bibliography is appended." Chicago. Children's Bk Center

Gama, Vasco da

Syme, Ronald. Vasco da Gama; sailor toward the sunrise; illus. by William Stobbs. Morrow 1959 95p illus map lib. bdg. $6 (4-6)   92

1 Explorers
ISBN 0-688-31588-7   LC 59-5018

The author "gives a straightforward but compelling account of the Portuguese navigator who discovered the sea-route to India. He describes Vasco da Gama's voyage around Cape Horn, recounts his experiences in east Africa and in India, and portrays him as an honest and fearless but violent-tempered, ruthless man who brought new wealth to Portugal but also made countless enemies for his country. Forceful illustrations in black and white." Booklist

Gandhi, Mohandas Karamchand

Coolidge, Olivia. Gandhi. Houghton 1971 278p illus $7.95 (5 and up)   92

ISBN 0-395-12573-1   LC 71-161645

Using photographs, newspaper articles, pamphlets, and personal letters, the author presents a biography of India's spiritual leader Mahatma Gandhi

"This is certainly one of the most astute and objective biographies of Gandhi that have been published for young people, giving an unusually balanced picture of his strengths and weaknesses. In an excellent preface, the author discusses Gandhi's inconsistencies, his mistakes in judgment, his proclivity for giving advice on subjects (like medical treatment) on which he was uninformed. The book substantiates and illustrates these failings, but it is equally forthright about Gandhi's dedication, his integrity, his charismatic personality—and it gives a coherent picture of Gandhi's role in India's struggle for Independence, and of his place in the movement for peaceful resistance. A glossary of Indian terms and an index are appended." Chicago. Children's Bk Center

Gannett, Deborah Sampson

McGovern, Ann. The secret soldier; the story of Deborah Sampson; illus. by Ann Grifalconi. Four Winds 1975 62p illus lib. bdg. $5.95 (3-5)   92

1 U.S.—History—Revolution, 1775-1783—Biography 2 Soldiers—U.S. 3 Women soldiers
ISBN 0-590-07432-6   LC 75-15819

A "biography of Deborah Sampson who, disguised as a boy, fought for one and a half years in the Continental army until her true identity was discovered (Deborah then became a wife and mother but still continued to defy convention by traveling and lecturing). History and biography from childhood to young adulthood, paralleling the young nation's fight for freedom with Deborah's own desire for independence and selfhood." Sch Library J

Gautama Buddha

Serage, Nancy. The prince who gave up a throne; a story of the Buddha; illus. by Kazue Mizumura. Crowell 1966 62p illus $7.95 (4-6)   92

1 Buddhism
ISBN 0-690-65566-5   LC 66-7076

"Historical fact and legend are interwoven in a simple retelling of the real and mystical experiences which reveal the intense religious faith and great human compassion of Prince Siddhartha who became the Buddha. Basing her interpretation on authentic sources but changing the emphasis of the story 'from a desire to escape pain to a desire to find eternal joy,' the author presents the life and precepts of the founder of Buddhism with sensitivity and understanding. Black-and-white drawings reflect the Oriental origin of the story." Booklist

Gehrig, Lou

Rubin, Robert. Lou Gehrig: courageous star. Putnam 1979 160p illus (Putnam Sports shelf) lib. bdg. $6.29 (5 and up)   92

1 Baseball—Biography
ISBN 0-399-61135-5   LC 78-31604

"Lou Gehrig, son of impoverished German immigrants and embodiment of the American dream, manifested his industriousness on the baseball diamond, where he became a legend of the New York Yankees. Tragically, his baseball career and his life met an untimely end through a form of chronic poliomyelitis commonly referred to as 'Lou Gehrig's disease.' Robert Rubin recaps Gehrig's dramatic life with honesty built from a wealth of anecdotes and warm reminiscences by Gehrig's wife and teammates. Reconstructed dialogue and thoughts ring true, while game analyses and statistics are never oppressive. Though Gehrig lived in a different era, the values of his life will always be relevant, especially as recounted in this engaging fictionalized biography." Booklist

George III, King of Great Britain

Fritz, Jean. Can't you make them behave, King George? Pictures by Tomie de Paola. Coward, McCann & Geoghegan 1977 45p illus $6.95 (3-5)   92

1 Great Britain—Kings and rulers
ISBN 0-698-20315-1   LC 75-33722

In this biography, "as the title indicates, George's relationship with the American colonies is seen as that of a father whose harsh ways of dealing with his children eventually results in their rebellion and his loss. . . . Fritz tells readers that the King made buttons, loved sauerkraut and fruit, and had his queen's hairdresser serve meals to cut down on the number of servants. She also adds a note about the King's afliction with porphyria, a disease now believed to be the cause of his bizarre behavior in later life." Sch Library J

"Another of Fritz's witty, warts-and-all portraits of Revolutionary War leaders. . . . [She] uses reverse strategy showing that George III, although obstinate and short-sighted, really wasn't such a bad fellow. As usual there are many humanizing tidbits (a reluctant Latin scholar, young George wrote, 'Mr. Caesar, I wish you would go to the devil!') And Tomie de Paola supplies comic caricatures of the pasty-faced monarch who, as pictured on the front cover, looks as if he'd just been hit with a king-size migraine." NY Times Bk Rev

Geronimo, Apache chief

Syme, Ronald. Geronimo, the fighting Apache; illus. by Ben F. Stahl. Morrow 1975 95p illus map $7.25, lib. bdg. $6.96 (3-5)   92

1 Apache Indians—Biography
ISBN 0-688-22013-4; O-688-32013-9   LC 74-16337

"This biography spans the Apache chieftain's life from childhood until death, emphasizing his battles against the 'White Eyes.' " Sch Library J
Bibliography: p95

Goddard, Robert Hutchings

Quackenbush, Robert M. The boy who dreamed of rockets; how Robert H. Goddard became the father of the space age. Parents Mag. Press 1978 unp illus lib. bdg. $6.95 (2-5)   92

1 Physicists 2 Rocketry
ISBN 0-590-07724-4   LC 78-21882

"Goddard's lifetime interests in science, engineering and rockets are interestingly outlined for upper elementary readers. Significant highlights from his boyhood experiences to posthumous honors are included in this compact biography. In addition to the biographical material, there is a

Goddard, Robert H.—*Continued*
prologue setting the stage for Goddard's entry into the field of rocketry, instructions for making a simple, rubber band launched model rocket, and a brief explanation of how a rocket works. The latter, unfortunately, gives the erroneous impression that spent rocket stages normally are exploded into small pieces before they return to earth. This is the only real blemish in an otherwise well done work. There are no page numbers, index, glossary or notes about the author, just interesting reading." AAAS Sci Bks & Films

Gordy, Berry
Movin' up; Pop Gordy tells his story. Harper 1979 144p illus $7.95, lib. bdg. $7.89 (5 and up)   92
  1 Blacks—Biography
  ISBN 0-06-022053-8; 0-06-022054-6   LC 78-22493
"Just before his death in 1978 at age 90, the author completed the tape-recorded sessions of oral history which resulted in this autobiographical memoir. 'Pop' Gordy . . . tells of his childhood in the South and his business experience there and in Detroit where he raised a family (his son is the founder and president of Motown Records). In the cadence of Black English, this easy-to-read and entertaining document shows the perseverance of a strong and confident man overcoming the social and political obstacles many Blacks had to face in a hostile society. It also shows a unique ability to maintain a sense of humor, and balance amidst hardships. . . . Alex Haley provides a short, meaningful introduction which helps to put Pop Gordy's life in a historical perspective." Sch Library J
"While he describes how he found that blacks had to endure prejudice in the North as in the South, Gordy expresses no rancor in his autobiography. It's a buoyant story of a man who saw clearly, 'Life is really somethin'. You just got to know how to live it. There's lots to learn." Pub W

Graham, Martha
Terry, Walter. Frontiers of dance; the life of Martha Graham; illus. with photographs. Crowell 1975 177p illus (Women of America ser) $10.95 (5 and up)   92
  1 Dancers 2 Modern dance—Biography
  ISBN 0-690-00920-8   LC 75-9871
This "biography skillfully combines a sense of the artist's innovative powers with a feeling for her personality and temperament. Early in life, she learned from her father, a doctor, that the movements of the body tell the truth about emotions; and when, as a teenager, she saw a performance by Ruth St. Denis, she knew she would devote her life to dancing. The book follows her development from the time of her association with Ruth St. Denis and Ted Shawn to the present, and—best of all—explains carefully what makes her contemporary dance forms different from those of classical ballet." Horn Bk
  Bibliography: p169-70

Guthrie, Janet
Olney, Ross R. Janet Guthrie: first woman at Indy. Harvey House 1978 54p illus lib. bdg. $5.79 (4 and up)   92
  1 Automobile racing—Biography 2 Women athletes 3 Indianapolis Speedway Race
  ISBN 0-8178-5882-2   LC 78-111983
"Sharing his impressions of Guthrie the person as well as facts on her background and incredible career as a race car driver, Olney has written an appealing book about an unusual woman. A graduate physicist working for an aviation firm, Guthrie applied to NASA for a spot as a woman astronaut before she indulged her racing hobby to the point that it became the focus of her life. Relating the sacrifices Guthrie made prior to earning her starting position at the Indianapolis 500, this thoughtfully written minibiography is a worthwhile addition to collections on women's opportunities and sports." Booklist

Hamer, Fannie Lou
Jordon, June. Fannie Lou Hamer; illus. by Albert Williams. Crowell 1972 39p illus (A Crowell biography) lib. bdg. $7.89, pa. $1.45 (2-4)   92
  1 Black women 2 Blacks—Civil rights
  ISBN 0-690-2889418; 0-690-00634-9   LC 70-184982

Fannie Lou Hamer "had worked in the cotton fields since she was six-years-old. Her independence and impatience with racial hatred encouraged her to be among the first to sign up during voter registration drives in the summer of 1962. She lived through violence to tell her story to the American public, became active in the fight for political reform and established the Freedom Farm Cooperative, a self-help project to provide food for poor families." Elem English
"Using a starkly simple prose style, the author has achieved maximum effect with a minimum of detail. She creates for younger readers a true people's heroine in a chronicle of the triumph of one woman's confidence in herself and in her race." Horn Bk

Hancock, John
Fritz, Jean. Will you sign here, John Hancock? Pictures by Trina Schart Hyman. Coward, McCann & Geoghegan 1976 47p illus $6.95 (3-5)   92
  1 U.S.—History—Revolution, 1775-1783—Biography
  ISBN 0-698-20308-9   LC 75-33243
"A straightforward biography of the rich Boston dandy with the gigantic signature. When he signed the Declaration of Independence he quipped, 'There! George the Third can read "that" without his spectacles. Now he can double his reward for my head.' " Sat Rev
"An affectionate look at a flamboyant, egocentric, but kindly, patriot, the book is a most enjoyable view of history. John Hancock had almost everything—wealth, good looks, winning ways—but he yearned for universal popularity. . . . He was governor of Massachusetts eleven times . . . Hancock tried being a military hero [during the Revolutionary War] but he was an utter failure. . . . The delightful illustrations exactly suit the times and the extraordinary character of John Hancock." Horn Bk

Handy, William Christopher
Montgomery, Elizabeth Rider. William C. Handy: father of the blues; illus. by David Hodges. Garrard 1968 95p illus (Americans all) lib. bdg. $5.88 (3-4)   92
  1 Black musicians 2 Blues (Songs, etc.)
  ISBN 0-8116-4551-7   LC 68-22639
"An interesting and authentic account of the great originator of Negro blues. The biography starts with Handy as a 12-year-old boy and continues through his life realistically depicting the biases, prejudices, and problems he encountered." Adventuring With Bks. 2d edition

Haydn, Franz Joseph
Lasker, David. The boy who loved music; illus. by Joe Lasker. Viking 1979 unp illus lib. bdg. $9.95 (2-5)   92
  1 Composers, Austrian
  ISBN 0-670-18385-7   LC 79-14651
"Based on historical fact, this is the story of the composition of Franz Joseph Haydn's 'Farewell Symphony.' Prince Nicolaus Esterhazy loves his summer castle so much that he stays there well into autumn, keeping his musicians away from their families and friends. Karl, a horn player in the royal orchestra, loves music but he loves his family too, and like the other musicians, is quite unhappy about his lengthy sojourn away from home. No one can persuade the Prince to leave until Haydn composes a new symphony with an unusual ending." Sch Library J
"Rich full-color pictures accompany a running text to illuminate brilliantly the various forms of courtly entertainment, such as a lively country fair with sideshows, a masked ball, and a hunting party." Horn Bk

Henry, Patrick
Campion, Nardi Reeder. Patrick Henry, firebrand of the Revolution; illus. by Victor Mays. Little 1961 261p illus $6.95 (5 and up)   92
  1 U.S.—History—Colonial period, 1600-1775—Biography
  ISBN 0-316-12765-5   LC 61-5329
"Lawyer, soldier, legislator, five times governor of Virginia, the greatest orator of his times . . . Patrick Henry had 'a consummate knowledge of

Henry, Patrick—*Continued*

the human heart, which directed his eloquence and enabled him to gain a popularity with the people at large perhaps never equaled.' His easy friendliness, ability to enjoy life fully, and pleasure in his family, along with his deep convictions regarding the dignity and rights of man and the excitement of his power with words make Patrick Henry a hero especially congenial to young people. This is a vivid presentation of that hero, of the times, and of the great men who made possible a new country and a new government." Horn Bk
"This competent and well-documented biography presents a three-dimensional portrait of its somewhat flamboyant protagonist. Virtues are stressed, but shortcomings are acknowledged." Sat Rev
Biography of principal sources: p253

Fritz, Jean. Where was Patrick Henry on the 29th of May? Illus. by Margot Tomes. Coward, McCann & Geoghegan 1975 47p illus $6.95 (3-5)   92
    1 U.S.—History—Colonial period, 1600-1775—Biography
    ISBN 0-698-20307-0   LC 74-83014
A "portrait of a founding father. Patrick Henry was born on May 29, and the author uses this date to focus on significant periods in his life. Henry's skill at oratory is shown in development as well as his anger at English laws, until they peak in his famous speech—described with a restraint which lets the natural drama emerge." Children's Bk Rev Serv
"The color pictures are artful evocations of the 17th century in America and the text presents Patrick Henry as a human being—not a sterilized historic 'figure.' . . . [The author] describes his most famous speech (and the events which led to it) so vividly that readers can virtually see and hear him. She is no less compelling as she describes the glories of the country during those times—before the axe and technology defaced them." Pub W

Henry The Navigator, Prince of Portugal
Jacobs, W. J. Prince Henry, the Navigator; with authentic prints, documents, and maps. Watts, F. 1973 53p illus maps (A Visual biography) pa $1.95 (5-6)   92
    1 Explorers
    ISBN 0-531-02367-2   LC 72-11511
This is "a dry but informative non-fictionalized report on Portuguese maritime exploration and trade expansion under Henry's brilliant, dedicated guidance and patronage. The illustrations—old prints, maps, and portraits—amplify the brief account, which notes the cruelties of early explorers like Da Gama as well as the significance of their achievements in terms of the 'progress' of western civilization." Booklist
Bibliography: p53

Heyerdahl, Thor
Blassingame, Wyatt. Thor Heyerdahl: Viking scientist. Elsevier/Nelson Bks. 1979 100p illus maps $7.95 (5 and up)   92
    1 Explorers 2 Anthropologists
    ISBN 0-525-66626-5   LC 79-1002
First published by Thomas Nelson
"Anthropologist, explorer, and adventurer Heyerdahl developed theories about the role of the sea in the movements of population and dramatized and recorded them in three best sellers. Thor's childhood and early scientific leanings are . . . [covered in this] biography, the bulk of which retells the highlights of the preparations for and voyages of the Kon Tiki, Ra I and II, and his expedition to Easter Island (Aku Aku)." Sch Library J

Hickok, James Butler
Holbrook, Stewart. Wild Bill Hickok tames the West; illus. by Ernest Richardson. Random House 1952 179p illus lib. bdg. $5.99 (4-6)   92
    1 Frontier and pioneer life—The West (U.S.)
    ISBN 0-394-90325-0   LC 52-7224

"Landmark books"
An account of "the man who was a member of the Underground Railroad, a Union spy during the Civil War, a stage driver and plainsman, and finally, one of the greatest single forces in the bringing of order to the lawless western frontier." Pub W
"A readable [biography]. . . . The author justifies Hickok's many slayings in terms of the lack of laws and legally appointed law enforcement 'offices and of the general code of the period in which Hickok lived." Chicago. Childen's Bk Center
Bibliography: p179

Homer, Winslow
Hyman, Linda. Winslow Homer: America's old master. Doubleday 1973 95p illus lib. bdg. $5.90 (5 and up)   92
    1 Artists, American
    ISBN 0-385-07823-4   LC 72-92225
Illustrated with black and white and color reproductions of Winslow Homer's paintings
The author "traces Homer's life and work from his early years as an apprentice in a print shop, through the years he spent as an illustrator during the Civil War, up to the end of his life as a well-known and successful painter of the sea and other aspects of nature and wildlife." Best Sellers
"The generous sampling of pictures enables the reader to observe for himself the sensitive qualities of the artist which the author so deftly describes." Babbling Bookworm

Houdini, Harry
Ernst, John. Escape king: the story of Harry Houdini; illus. by Ray Abel. Prentice-Hall 1975 unp illus $5.95, pa $1.50 (4 and up)   92
    1 Magicians
    ISBN 0-13-283416-2; 0-13-283424-3   LC 73-15696
"In this portrait of a man who was determined to be great, Mr. Ernst shows the discipline and drive that made the difference in Houdini's career. Through careful research from original and published sources, Mr. Ernst gives an accurate picture of Houdini the man and Houdini the artist." Adventuring with Bks. 2d ed.

Kendall, Lace. Houdini: master of escape. Macrae Smith Co. 1960 187p front $6.50 (6 and up)   92
    1 Magicians
    ISBN 0-8255-5075-0   LC 60-14035
"A biography of the man who began his career as a magician at the age of nine and by hard work, self-mastery, and unswerving purpose rose to fame as the greatest escape artist of all time." Bks for Children, 1960-1965

Hughes, Langston
Myers, Elisabeth P. Langston Hughes: poet of his people; illus. by Russell Hoover. Garrard 1970 144p illus (Creative people in the arts and sciences ser) lib. bdg. $3.94 (4-6)   92
    1 Poets, American 2 Black authors
    ISBN 0-8116-4507-X   LC 76-94412
"Poet, novelist, playwright and lyricist—Langston Hughes was all these. From his earliest childhood days as a writer, he believed he could write best from his own experience. It was this belief that led him to become, for over thirty years, one of black America's loudest and most illustrious spokesmen. Here is an uncomplicated, sympathetic yet factual account of Hughes' life that devotes equal space to his early years and career. . . . A combination of good black-and-white photos and adequate drawings enhance the text, which is also indexed." Sch Library J

Walker, Alice. Langston Hughes, American poet; illus. by Don Miller. Crowell 1974 33p illus (A Crowell biography) lib. bdg. $7.89 (2-4)   92
    1 Poets, American 2 Black authors
    ISBN 0-690-00219-X   LC 73-9565
In this biography of the beloved black writer, the author traces Langston Hughes' childhood in Kansas, the discovery of his poems by Vachel Lindsay, his later fame as a writer, and his efforts to bring his work directly to the people

Hughes, Langston—*Continued*

The author "includes a candid assessment of the poet's bitter, biased father that is not usually found in books about Hughes written for children. The illustrations are adequate, the biography as substantial as one for the primary grades reader can be." Chicago. Children's Bk Center

Inouye, Daniel Ken

Goodsell, Jane. Daniel Inouye; illus. by Haru Wells. Crowell 1977 32p illus (A Crowell biography) lib. bdg. $7.89 (3-5)   92

1 Politicians, American 2 U.S. Congress. Senate
ISBN 0-690-01358-2   LC 77-1405

"Inouye's accomplishments as a U.S. Senator and a war hero (he lost his right arm during W.W.II) are stressed in the context of Hawaiian events and attitudes. The issue of Hawaiian statehood and the conflict between the islands' Japanese American ('nisei') and white ('haoles') populations are clearly explained. Simply written and illustrated with sketches, this biography is useful for its skillful mirroring of the problems of a multicultural society through the life of a man who had to overcome a handicap." Sch Library J

Ishi

Kroeber, Theodora. Ishi; last of his tribe; drawings by Ruth Robbins. Parnassus Press 1964 209p illus maps $7.95 (5 and up)   92

1 Yana Indians
ISBN 0-87466-049-1   LC 64-19401

"The true story of a California Yahi Indian [discovered in 1911 by anthropologists] who survives the invasion by the white man, while the rest of his tribe die off." A L A Notable Bks, 1964

Written "with a grave simplicity . . . utterly right for the subject. The cultural details are quite unobtrusive: they are simply there, an evidence of the author's knowledge and empathy." Chicago. Children's Bk Center

Glossary of Yahi words: p[211]

Jackson, Andrew, President U.S.

De Kay, Ormonde. Meet Andrew Jackson, by Ormonde De Kay, Jr. Illus. by Isa Barnett. Random House 1967 87p illus $2.95 (2-4)   92

1 Presidents—U.S. 2 U.S.—History—1815-1861—Biography
ISBN 0-394-80066-4   LC 67-19495

"Step-up books"
"In this high-interest low vocabulary book is a story of one of America's most famous heroes and presidents. Although in easy vocabulary and large print, it loses none of the excitement and adventure of this great president who as a boy fought in the American Revolution, became a judge, a soldier, an Indian fighter and a great general in the War of 1812." Bruno. Bks for Sch Libraries, 1968

Jackson, Mahalia

Jackson, Jesse. Make a joyful noise unto the Lord! The life of Mahalia Jackson, queen of gospel singers; illus. with photographs. Crowell 1974 160p illus (Women of America) $8.95 (5 and up)   92

1 Black singers 2 Women singers
ISBN 0-690-43344-1   LC 72-7549

"An often moving portrait of 'Sister Haley.' From choir girl in New Orleans to world-renowned artist, she never let European music destroy her Afro-American roots. . . . Parallel to the story of her rise to fame are the accounts of major developments in the civil rights movements of the 1950's and 1960's and her increasing support of them up to her death in 1972." Horn Bk
Bibliography included in Acknowledgments

Jackson, Reggie

Libby, Bill. The Reggie Jackson story. Lothrop 1979 224p illus $7.95, lib. bdg. $7.63 (5 and up)   92

1 Baseball—Biography 2 Black athletes
ISBN 0-688-41889-9; 0-688-51889-3   LC 79-684

"The standard Libby formula format—a sympathetic personal profile backed with quotes from [the baseball star] and associates and combined

with an almost documentary survey of Jackson's professional career, statistics, controversies, et al. Along the way, Libby includes glimpses of the lives and personalities of Charles Finley, George Steinbrenner, Billy Martin, and Thurman Munson. Well stocked with black-and-white photos, this should be a mover among Jackson fans." Sch Library J

Jackson, Thomas Jonathan

Fritz, Jean. Stonewall; with drawings by Stephen Gammell. Putnam 1979 152p illus map $7.95, pa $2.50 (4 and up)   92

1 Generals 2 U.S.—History—Civil War, 1861-1865—Biography
ISBN 0-399-20698-1; 0-399-20699-X   LC 79-12506

"Fritz's trenchant, compassionate life of General Thomas Jonathan Jackson grips the reader and makes one understand why Stonewall is an honored legend in American history. Gammell's dramatic drawings of great personages and grave events illustrate the biography of the Confederate leader, as unlikely a hero as General Grant. Most of his life Jackson endured as a loser, like Grant, at almost everything he tried. Seeing him in that light, the reader is impressed by the man's determination to hone skills that made him a military genius, loved by his troops. The tragic irony of his death at age 39 is movingly described." Pub W
A bibliography is appended

Jefferson, Thomas, President U.S.

Barrett, Marvin. Meet Thomas Jefferson; illus. by Angelo Torres. Random House 1967 86p illus map $3.95, lib. bdg. $4.99 (2-4)   92

1 Presidents—U.S. 2 U.S.—History—1783-1809—Biography
ISBN 0-394-80067-2; 0-394-90067-7   LC 67-19496

"Step-up books"
This book describes the man who was a friend to the Indians and to the British governors. He wrote the Declaration of Independence, and as third President of the United States, purchased Louisiana and doubled his country's size without any bloodshed

Jemison, Mary

Gardner, Jeanne LeMonnier. Mary Jemison: Seneca captive; illus. by Robert Parker. Harcourt 1966 128p illus map $5.50 (4-6)   92

1 Indians of North America—Captivities 2 Seneca Indians
ISBN 0-15-252190-9   LC 66-23287

This book encompasses "the years from Mary Jemison's capture by Indians in 1758 to her death in 1833. . . . The account describes Mary's gradual change in attitude from hatred and distrust of the Indians to understanding and acceptance of their culture and way of life." Booklist
This "biography focuses on the close family relationships and the culture of the Senecas. . . . Useful as background for a study of the French and Indian wars and to show how the culture of the Indians changed with the encroachment of the white man and his civilization." Sch Library J
Bibliography: p127-28

Lenski, Lois. Indian captive; the story of Mary Jemison; written and illus. by Lois Lenski. Lippincott 1941 269p illus $9.95 (5 and up)   92

1 Indians of North America—Captivities 2 Seneca Indians
ISBN 0-397-30072-7   LC 41-51956

First published by Stokes
Mary Jemison, a white child of Scotch-Irish parentage was captured by the Indians in 1758, and taken from her Pennsylvania home to a Seneca village in New York State. This story is based on records and recounts for young readers her experiences in the early years of her captivity

"The ways of living followed by the Seneca Indians in the Eighteenth Century have been carefully studied as background for this book and the drawings are not only attractive, but exact and authentic." Horn Bk
Bibliography: p[273]. Map on lining-papers

Johnson, James Weldon

Egypt, Ophelia Settle. James Weldon Johnson; illus. by Moneta Barnett. Crowell 1974 40p illus (A Crowell biography) lib. bdg. $7.89 (2-4)   92

1 Authors, American 2 Black authors
ISBN 0-690-00215-7   LC 73-9521

The author "covers Johnson's childhood in Jacksonville, Florida during the late 19th Century and his adult accomplishments as an editor; author and poet; teacher; lyric composer and musician; lawyer; foreign service officer; and Administrative Secretary of the NAACP." Sch Library J

"The text is simply written, most of it devoted to Johnson's childhood and the early part of his career, but it touches on his major contributions and it avoids the adulatory tone that would be so easy to adopt with a subject so deserving." Chicago. Children's Bk Center

Jones, Mary Harris

Atkinson, Linda. Mother Jones; the most dangerous woman in America. Crown 1978 246p illus $7.95 (6 and up)   92

1 Labor unions—U.S.—Biography
ISBN 0-517-53201-8   LC 77-15863

"The author outlines the life and times of Irish-born labor organizer Mary Harris Jones, affectionately called 'Mother Jones' by the laborers to whom she dedicated herself. Brief facts of Jones' early life—arrival in America, education, marriage—give way to a broad picture of labor struggles in the late eighteenth and early nineteenth century, Jones' involvement with such organizations as the Knights of Labor and the UMW, and her organizing activities across the country. A liberal sprinkling of quotes from Jones' speeches, etc. adds some sense of her vitality, but Atkinson fails to close in on the charismatic effectiveness and unique personality that identified Jones as one of history's first women activists and made her successful in defying manipulative employers. A good overall perspective nonetheless." Booklist
Bibliography: p238-40

Joplin, Scott

Evans, Mark. Scott Joplin and the ragtime years; illus. with photographs. Dodd 1976 120p illus $5.95 (5 and up)   92

1 Composers, American 2 Black musicians
ISBN 0-396-07308-5   LC 75-38362

A biography of the black musician who at the turn of the century composed The Maple Leaf Rag and other piano ragtime pieces as well as the opera Treemonisha

"A slightly dry but still palatable treatment of the Ragtime King's life and contemporary climate of popular music. Joplin is not painted—only sketched—but enough of his character is evident to make the work readable. In spite of irritatingly frequent lapses into imagined dialogue, the story seems essentially authentic, and a fair notion of the musical times can be gleaned from it. With black-and-white historical photos." Booklist

Joseph, Nez Percé Chief

Davis, Russell. Chief Joseph: war chief of the Nez Percé, by Russell Davis and Brent Ashabranner. McGraw 1962 190p illus map lib. bdg. $7.95 (5 and up)   92

1 Nez Percé Indians—Biography 2 Indians of North America—Wars
ISBN 0-07-015926-2   LC 62-12779

A "biography of the Indian leader who wanted peace but instead became the greatest fighting chief of the Nez Percé. His slogan was 'Whenever white man treats Indians as they treat each other, then we shall have no more wars.'" Adventuring With Bks. 2d edition

"It would be easy to turn so much grief into sentimentality, so much action into mere blood and thunder. With restraint, the authors avoid both pitfalls. They vary the pace with interesting Indian lore." NY Times Bk Rev

Keller, Helen Adams

Peare, Catherine Owens. The Helen Keller story. Crowell 1959 183p illus $8.95 (5 and up)   92

1 Blind 2 Deaf
ISBN 0-690-37520-4   LC 59-10979

This is a "biography of Helen Keller, the child who was deaf and blind, and therefore mute, who became, with the loving, intelligent guidance of Anne Sullivan Macy, a graduate of Radcliffe College, a most potent force in coordinating the work with the blind as both writer and lecturer and an outstanding woman of the world." Bookmark
Selected bibliography: p176-79

Kemble, Frances Anne

Scott, John Anthony. Fanny Kemble's America; illus. with photographs. Crowell 1973 146p illus map (Women of America) $8.95 (5 and up)   92

1 Abolitionists 2 Actors and actresses
ISBN 0-690-28911-1   LC 72-7557

The author "brings to life the celebrated English Shakespearean actress who married Pierce Butler, a wealthy young slaveowner, in 1834 while on tour in America. Quoting extensively from Fanny Kemble's journals and letters the author follows the course of her life focusing on the stormy years of her marriage and showing how her independence of mind, belief in equality of the sexes, and strong antislavery views were prime factors in the conflict between her and her husband." Booklist

"The book is a pronounced success, giving both a perceptive picture of a courageous woman and a vivid picture of the historical period." Chicago. Children's Bk Center
Bibliography: p138-40

Kennedy, John Fitzgerald, President U.S.

Four days: the historical record of the death of President Kennedy; comp. by United Press International and American Heritage Magazine. Am. Heritage [distributed by Simon & Schuster] 1964 143p illus $2.95   92

1 Kennedy, John Fitzgerald, President U.S.—Assassination 2 Kennedy, John Fitzgerald, President U.S.—Funeral and memorial services
ISBN 0-671-26870-8   LC 64-16872

Introduction by Bruce Catton

This record of the four days from November 22 to November 25, 1963 includes the report by United Press reporter Merriman Smith of the assassination of President Kennedy, eulogies, and comments from the world press. Photographs record the death of the President, the funeral, and the shooting of Lee Harvey Oswald in the police station at Dallas

"A restrained, well-designed, very moving record." Atlantic

Kherdian, Veron

Kherdian, David. The road from home; the story of an Armenian girl. Greenwillow Bks. 1979 238p map $8.95, lib. bdg. $8.59 (6 and up)   92

1 Armenians in Turkey 2 Armenian massacres, 1915-1923
ISBN 0-688-80205-2; 0-688-84205-4   LC 78-72511

The author presents a "biography of his mother's early life as a young Armenian girl. Veron Dumehjian was part of a prosperous Armenian family in Turkey, but the Armenian minority undergoes a holocaust when the Turkish government persecutes its Christian minorities. In 1915 Veron and her family are deported and, as refugees, live through hardships of disease, starvation, bombing, and fire until, at sixteen, Veron is able to go to America as a 'mail-order' bride." Babbling Bookworm

"The Armenian massacres of the late 1800s and early 1900s have not been the object of as much attention as the annihilation of the Jews during World War II, but they were no less horrifying. In his dedication the author quotes Adolf Hitler's remark of 1939 [regarding plans to exterminate the Polish peoples:] . . . 'After all who remembers today the extermination of the Armenians?' . . . Veron moves from family to orphanage to refugee camp, honestly recording the pain of loss and the exhilaration of making new friends. . . . Her relationships sustain her always, particularly those with her father, grandmother, and aunt. The book is a portrait of an individual who retains an appreciation for the small things of life in the midst of gross inhumanity." Horn Bk

King, Billie Jean

Burchard, Marshall. Sports hero: Billie Jean King, by Marshall and Sue Burchard. Putnam 1975 93p illus (The Sports hero biographies) lib. bdg. $6.29 (2-4)   **92**

1 Tennis—Biography   2 Women athletes
ISBN 0-399-60907-5   LC 74-16623

"Using an easy-to-read format with large print and a liberal sprinkling of photographs (inexplicably interrupted by several stilted pencil sketches), the Burchards lightly chronicle Billie Jean King's rise from a beginning tennis player in Long Beach, California, to a high-ranking professional. Also included are King's activities toward equalizing the sport by demanding top money prizes for women contenders and advocating that the major amateur tournaments be opened to pro competitors." Booklist

Glossary: p[94-95]

King, Martin Luther

Clayton, Ed. Martin Luther King: the peaceful warrior; illus. by David Hodges. 3d ed. Prentice-Hall 1968 95p illus lib. bdg. $5.95 (5 and up)   **92**

1 Blacks—Biography   2 Blacks—Civil rights
ISBN 0-13-559765-X   LC 68-57178

First published 1964

Biography of the black leader who tried to achieve equality for his race through nonviolent methods

"An amazing amount of drama and material is packed into this short, clear, moving biography." Commonweal

De Kay, James T. Meet Martin Luther King, Jr. Illus. with photographs and drawings by Ted Burwell. Random House 1969 89p illus $3.95 lib. bdg. $4.99 (2-5)   **92**

1 Blacks—Biography   2 Blacks—Civil rights
ISBN 0-394-80055-9; 0-394-90055-3   LC 73-79789

"Step-up books"

"The major concern of this useful biography for reluctant readers is with Dr. King's philosophy of civil disobedience and with his leadership of the civil rights movement. The writing is simple, clear and objective though pedestrian. The print is large and readable; the photographs are good and give the book a sense of immediacy." Library J

Faber, Doris. The assassination of Martin Luther King, Jr. by Doris and Harold Faber. Watts, F. 1978 85p illus lib. bdg. $6.45 (5 and up)   **92**

1 King, Martin Luther—Assassination   2 Blacks—Biography   3 Ray, James Earl
ISBN 0-531-02465-2   LC 78-1726

"A Focus book"

"King's background and schooling are briefly recapped; his growing involvement with civil rights issues is highlighted, with special attention to the escalating controversy that surrounded his activism. More to the point, however, is the Fabers' evaluation of the conspiracy theories that blossomed before and after James Earl Ray's guilty plea and sentencing: they conclude, on the basis of a lack of credible evidence, that Ray acted alone, though their final words admit that loose ends and unanswered questions still keep the conspiracy notion alive." Booklist

A selected bibliography: p77

Haskins, James. The life and death of Martin Luther King, Jr. Lothrop 1977 176p illus lib. bdg. $6.96 (5 and up)   **92**

1 Blacks—Biography   2 Blacks—Civil rights
ISBN 0-688-51802-3   LC 77-3157

The author "writes about the civil rights leader in a simple, readable manner. Part one describes the development of the civil rights movement; part two describes the assassination, and an inordinate amount of space is given to James Earl Ray and the theory of a conspiracy behind the murder. The FBI's and the CIA's harrassment of King is wisely included, for no biography of the man would be honest if it did not acknowledge that information about Dr. King's personal life was used in an attempt to blackmail him." Horn Bk

Young, Margaret B. The picture life of Martin Luther King, Jr. Illus. with photographs. Watts, F. 1968 45p illus lib. bdg. $6.45 (1-3)   **92**

1 Blacks—Biography   2 Blacks—Civil rights
ISBN 0-531-00981-5   LC 67-20866

"A very good selection of photographs accompanies a very simple but quite adequate outline of Martin Luther King's life, the book having been published before his assassination. The vocabulary is simple, the print large, and the writing style straightforward." Chicago. Children's Bk Center

Koehn, Ilse

Mischling, second degree; my childhood in Nazi Germany; with a foreword by Harrison E. Salisbury. Greenwillow Bks. 1977 240p $8.95, lib. bdg. $8.59 (6 and up)   **92**

1 World War, 1939-1945—Jews   2 Germany—History—1933-1945   3 Jews in Germany
ISBN 0-688-80110-2; 0-688-84110-4   LC 77-6189

This story "is told in retrospect by an author who did not know why her loving parents separated until after the war, when she learned that it had helped her and her mother avoid the consequences of the fact that her father had one Jewish parent. Liberals and intellectuals, the Koehns coped, as many did, with a government and a philosophy they detested. And Ilse, a young adolescent, was drafted into the Hitler Youth, forced to go through the motions of devotion. Like Anne Frank, she had youth's resilience; she accepted what she could not change and found moments of excitement or pleasure despite fear, loneliness, and the harsh regime of the Hitler Youth camps." Chicago. Children's Bk Center

"Appealing Ilse is a survivor, and her book is a powerful human document." Babbling Bookworm

Lafitte, Jean

Tallant, Robert. Pirate Lafitte and the Battle of New Orleans; illus. by John Chase. Random House 1951 186p illus lib. bdg. $4.39 (5 and up)   **92**

1 Pirates   2 New Orleans, Battle of, 1815
ISBN 0-394-90319-6   LC 51-13894

"Landmark books"

A biography of the slave smuggler and privateer who, because of his aid to the Americans in the battle of New Orleans, was acclaimed a patriot

"A carefully written, exciting account of a mysterious and controversial figure. His bold undertakings are evaluated in the light of the customs of the times and places in which he lived. Emphasis is on background material and events in his career that explain why he was on the American side in the Battle of New Orleans. . . . Excellent format." Library J

Map on lining papers

La Salle, Robert Cavelier, sieur de

Syme, Ronald. La Salle of the Mississippi; illus. by William Stobbs. Morrow 1953 184p illus lib. bdg. $6.95 (4 and up)   **92**

1 Explorers   2 America—Exploration
ISBN 0-688-21591-2   LC 52-12119

An account of the French navigator and colonizer. It describes his first voyages, efforts to find sites for settlement and trade, the founding of Quebec, experiences with the Indians and finally his death at the hands of a treacherous follower

"Gives a picture which is authentic in its interpretation of La Salle's character, and dramatic in the telling of his accomplishments." Ontario Library Rev

Map on lining-papers

Lawick-Goodall, Jane, Barones van

Coerr, Eleanor. Jane Goodall; drawings by Kees de Kiefte. Putnam 1976 61p illus lib. bdg. $5.99 (2-4)   **92**

1 Zoologists   2 Women scientists
ISBN 0-399-60994-6   LC 75-32503

"Here's an attractive and appealing biography of the well-known scientist and author Jane Goodall. The print is large and soft pencil illustrations complement almost every page. The reader will learn of Jane's childhood fascination with animals, how she got her start as secretary to Dr. Louis Leakey, and of her fascinating life among the

Lawick-Goodall, J. Barones van—*Continued*
chimpanzees on the shores of Lake Tanganyika in Tanzania. Later Jane divided her time between her own education, her research on chimpanzee behavior, and her husband's work filming and writing about lions, cheetahs, hyenas, leopards, jackals and wild dogs." Appraisal
"Teachers and librarians should find this book useful for introducing children to careers in ethnology or related fields; this is an especially good source for stimulating an awareness of nontraditional careers for women." AAAS Sci Bks & Films

Lawrence, Thomas Edward
MacLean, Alistair. Lawrence of Arabia; illus. by Gil Walker. Random House 1962 177p illus maps lib. bdg. $4.39 (6 and up)   92
1 World War, 1914-1918—Middle East
ISBN 0-394-90552-0   LC 62-7878
"World Landmark books"
This book "deals almost entirely with Lawrence's exploits as leader of the Arabs in their rebellion against the Turks during World War I. . . . The book ends, not with Lawrence's death in 1935, but in 1922 when at last he had seen his Arab friends freed in part from foreign rule." Chicago Sunday Trib
"This is no attempt to write a complete biography, or even to try to give any idea of Lawrence's complex character. Rather it is a war story and a very good one, based on Lawrence's own writings and on writings about him. . . . It is a stirring story of desert warfare with fine glimpses of young Lawrence." NY Her Trib Bks
Other [adult] books about T. E. Lawrence: p173

Lee, Ann
Campion, Nardi Reeder. Ann the Word; the life of Mother Ann Lee, founder of the Shakers. Little 1976 208p illus map lib. bdg. $7.95 (5 and up)   92
1 Shakers—History
ISBN 0-316-12767-1   LC 76-6568
Campion "has written an impeccably documented biography of the extraordinary religious leader who was called the 'female Christ.' Surviving indignities in the slums of Manchester, England, Ann Lee developed a revulsion to sex. After becoming a preacher for a group of religious reformers, she faced new problems in New York City, where she went in 1774 with a few faithful Shakers and where, near Albany, she succeeded in establishing the first Shaker colony in 1776. . . . Tenets of the faith are illustrated by a number of Shaker hymns, composed for work, prayer, and dancing. The author describes the spread of Shaker colonies—until there were about six thousand members—and their subsequent decline." Horn Bk
Bibliography: p197-200

Lee, Robert Edward
Commager, Henry Steele. America's Robert E. Lee [by] Henry Steele Commager & Lynd Ward. Houghton 1951 111p illus $10.95 (5 and up)   92
1 Generals 2 U.S.—History—Civil War, 1861-1865
—Biography
ISBN 0-395-06707-3   LC 51-6327
An account of the great Confederate general's life and military career from his childhood to the surrender at Appomattox
"The progress of the war is described vividly and impartially. There could be no more moving account of a surrender than the one on the closing pages taken from a Union officer's diary." Chicago Sunday Trib
"The illustrations, in color and black and white, half page, full page, and double page, are superb. Mr. Ward has caught the spirit as well as the substance of events and of the people." Sat Rev

Leif Ericsson
Janeway, Elizabeth. The Vikings; illus. by Henry C. Pitz. Random House 1951 175p illus lib. bdg. $5.99 (4-6)   92
1 Explorers 2 Eric the Red 3 Vikings
ISBN 0-394-90312-9   LC 51-13561
"Landmark books"
The story of Leif the Lucky and his father Eric the Red in Iceland, Greenland and Vinland

For this readable history, the author has partially "chosen the medium of fiction to tell her story, but in the interest of historical accuracy she has explained, in her foreword, which parts of her story are fact and which are fiction." NY Times Bk Rev

Jensen, Malcolm C. Leif Erikson, the Lucky; illus. with authentic prints and documents. Watts, F. 1979 57p illus maps (A Visual biography) lib. bdg. $5.45 (4-6)   92
1 America—Exploration 2 Vikings 3 Explorers
ISBN 0-531-02297-8   LC 78-11181
"Jensen not only presents a portrait of Erikson the shrewd opportunist, leader of men and consummate sailor, but also examines the curiously civilized aspects of Viking culture which shaped the man, and which sharply contrast with the Vikings' image as fierce marauders. Drawing on old Norse sagas, traditional myths, and recent archaeological discoveries, he plots the voyages of Leif, his father and brothers, and details their probable discoveries of Vinland—what is today Atlantic Canada'. . . . A lucid treatment of Leif and good introduction to Viking culture, highlighted by numerous well-chosen illustrations and maps." Sch Library J
A note on sources: p55

Lincoln, Abraham, President U.S.
Aulaire, Ingri d'. Abraham Lincoln, by Ingri & Edgar Parin d'Aulaire. Doubleday 1957 unp illus $8.95, lib. bdg. $9.90 (2-4)   92
1 Presidents—U.S.
ISBN 0-385-07669-X; 0-385-07674-6   LC 57-2502
Awarded the Caldecott Medal, 1940
First published 1939
"The story devotes itself more to pioneer phases than to darker scenes of Lincoln's later life, and it closes before he has started for Ford's Theater." NY Her Trib Bks
Presented "in a brief, direct, semiwhimsical text and in notable lithographic drawings by the authors, some of which have soft rich color, others being reproduced in black and white. The illustrations, detailed and faithful to the atmosphere of the various settings are both tender and humorous in their interpretation. . . . A distinguished piece of bookmaking." Bookmark
Map on lining-papers

McNeer, May. America's Abraham Lincoln; illus. by Lynd Ward. Houghton 1957 119p illus lib. bdg. $3.57 (5 and up)   92
1 Presidents—U.S. 2 U.S.—History—Civil War, 1861-1865—Biography
ISBN 0-395-06917-3
"This is not merely a recounting of the events of his life but a really perceptive picture of the man himself. . . . One can trace his development from the boy who, in spite of his love of fun, is already a serious thinker to the man whose strength and determination are softened by compassion, particularly as he visits the soldiers on the battlefield or in the hospitals." Horn Bk
"This biography is outstanding for its simple, yet dignified, language and, though comparatively short, the background and important events of Lincoln's life are made very real. Beautiful illustrations in color and black and white by Lynd Ward are perfectly suited to the story and in themselves tell a memorable tale." Library J

Phelan, Mary Kay. Mr Lincoln's inaugural journey; drawings by Richard Cuffari. Crowell 1972 211p illus map $8.95 (5 and up)   92
1 Presidents—U.S. 2 U.S.—History—Civil War, 1861-1865—Biography
ISBN 0-690-54562-6   LC 76-175110
"A detailed, carefully documented account of Abraham Lincoln's departure from Springfield and his journey to Washington to take the oath of office as President. The trip, a rambling tour through seven states, is given immediacy by the use of present tense and is given suspense by the foreknowledge of an assassination plot uncovered by the Pinkerton agency and kept secret even from Lincoln until he was close to the Baltimore engagement during which the plotters hoped to kill him." Chicago Children's Bk Center
"Based on firsthand sources the story includes no imagined conversations and is skillfully written and suspenseful." Booklist
Bibliography: p199-203

Lindbergh, Charles Augustus, 1902-1974

Grierson, John. I remember Lindbergh; with an introduction by Anne Morrow Lindbergh. Harcourt 1977 192p illus $8.95 (6 and up)   **92**

1 Air pilots
ISBN 0-15-238895-8   LC 77-76436

"In this vivid, sympathetic account of Charles Lindbergh, Grierson warmly extols the flying career and heroism of his personal friend and aviator colleague. Though his concentration is clearly on Lindbergh the pilot—with detailed, statistics-filled accounts of Lindbergh's early interest in airplanes, his participation in the first air mail deliveries, an hour-by-hour recapitulation of his solo flight across the Atlantic, and his 30,000-mile air route survey venture with his wife Anne—Grierson does not neglect the man. The stubbornness, obsession with privacy, and prejudice against the press merge with the gentleness, courage, and concern for all living beings. . . . The oft-found glamour surrounding Lindbergh is swept away, leaving a realistic portrayal of the man and the flier." Booklist

Mackenzie, Sir Alexander

Syme, Ronald. Alexander Mackenzie, Canadian explorer; illus. by William Stobbs. Morrow 1964 96p illus map lib. bdg. $6.96 (3-5)   **92**

1 Explorers 2 Canada—Exploring expeditions
ISBN 0-688-31010-9   LC 64-10133

An "account of the voyages of discovery of the young Scotsman who was sent to take charge of the Northwest Fur Company at Fort Chipewyan in 1788. The hardships, disappointments, and reverses of his struggle to reach the Pacific along the Mackenzie and Peace Rivers through the rugged mountains and forests of western Canada are [described]. . . . Excerpts from Mackenzie's journals add interest and authenticity. His stubborn, canny Scottish character comes through the text, and William Stobbs' vigorous illustrations give some idea of the forbidding terrain." Sch Library J

McLoughlin, John

Morrison, Dorothy Nafus. The eagle & the fort; the story of John McLoughlin; illus. with old prints, photographs, & maps. Atheneum Pubs. 1979 178p illus $7.95 (6 and up)   **92**

1 Northwest, Pacific—History 2 Hudson's Bay Company
ISBN 0-689-30691-1   LC 78-12911

"The Eagle, John McLoughlin, was an eighteenth-century Canadian physician who left his Quebec home for the Northwest, where he became a key figure in its development. . . . In time he rose to become . . . chief factor [of the Hudson's Bay Company] for the entire Northwest. While in the position, he built a string of forts, advised on settlement strategies, and worked to keep peace between conflicting Indian, American, and British interests. Morrison narrates her account straightforwardly and relies on letters, papers, and accounts by contemporaries for emphatic description and character shaping. Not a commonly known name but a formidable character, one worth knowing by this account." Booklist
Bibliography: p163-73

Macy, Anne (Sullivan)

Brown, Marion Marsh. The silent storm [by] Marion Marsh Brown [and] Ruth Crone; illus. by Fritz Kredel. Abingdon 1963 250p illus $7.95 (5 and up)   **92**

1 Women teachers 2 Blind 3 Deaf 4 Keller, Helen Adams
ISBN 0-687-38453-2   LC 63-10807

This biography of Annie Sullivan reveals that "the famous teacher of Helen Keller had a grim childhood scarred with anger, fear, and partial blindness. This book flashes back to those early years as Annie travels to the Keller's household and then tells of the valiant efforts that led to a Radcliffe degree for Helen and marriage for Annie." Pub W
"The characters of both Annie Sullivan and Helen Keller are vividly life-like and the [somewhat fictionalized] dialogue has a wonderful naturalness about it." Best Sellers

Malone, Mary. Annie Sullivan; illus. by Lydia Rosier. Putnam 1971 61p illus (A See and read Beginning to read biography) lib. bdg. $5.99 (2-4)   **92**

1 Women teachers 2 Blind 3 Deaf 4 Keller, Helen Adams
ISBN 0-399-60031-0   LC 71-121943

The story "begins when ten-year-old Annie Sullivan arrives with her little brother at the Massachusetts state poor house. The last two-thirds of the book treat her association with Helen Keller, but still it is Annie's—not Helen's—story." Elementary English
Illustrated by "simple sepia and turquoise line drawings in cross-hatch style that convey the appearance of blind eyes without making them look grotesque. . . . It is forthright, honest and factual." Sch Library J
Key words: p[62]

Magellan, Ferdinand

Syme, Ronald. Magellan, first around the world; illus. by William Stobbs. Morrow 1953 71p illus maps lib. bdg. $6.24 (4-6)   **92**

1 Explorers 2 Voyages around the world
ISBN 0-688-31594-1   LC 53-7102

An "account of Magellan's voyages and discoveries from the time back in 1504 when he set out as an ordinary seaman with Vasco da Gama's fleet." Christian Sci Monitor
"Striking storytelling illustrations, including six doublespreads, are an important part of the book's portrayal of history." Horn Bk

Malcolm X

Adoff, Arnold. Malcolm X; illus. by John Wilson. Crowell 1970 41p illus (Crowell biographies) $6.95, pa $1.95 (2-5)   **92**

1 Blacks—Biography
ISBN 0-690-51413-1; 0-690-51415-8   LC 70-94787

"This short forthright biography vividly outlines the events, both tragic and rewarding, which influenced the life and thought of Malcolm X from childhood to death and clearly evinces his significance as a black leader. The account describes the adverse effects of Malcolm's bitter childhood experiences, the changes which began during his incarceration in the Norfolk Prison Colony, his association with the Black Muslims and his later break with them, and the hostility of both black and white groups toward his Organization of Afro-American Unity." Booklist
"Deceptively simple text and illustrations help to produce the picture of a vigorous character, without sensationalism." Top of the News

Marquette, Jacques

Kjelgaard, Jim. Explorations of Père Marquette; illus. by Stephen J. Voorhies. Random House 1951 181p illus maps lib. bdg. $5.99 (4-6)   **92**

1 Joliet, Louis 2 Explorers 3 America—Exploration 4 Mississippi River
ISBN 0-394-90317-X   LC 51-13563

"Landmark books"
A simply told account of the Jesuit priest and Louis Joliet, who opened the Great Lakes and Mississippi regions. The information is based on Père Marquette's journals
"In addition to being a good story of a real hero, this addition to the 'Landmark' series will be useful for supplementary reading on exploration." Library J

Martin de Porres, Saint

Bishop, Claire Huchet. Martin de Porres, hero; illus. by Jean Charlot. Houghton 1954 120p illus $4.25, pa 95¢ (5 and up)   **92**

1 Saints 2 Blacks—Biography
ISBN 0-395-06634-4; 0-395-17704-9   LC 53-10992

"Martin de Porres, a Negro-Spanish child born in poverty and subject to prejudice and mistreatment, devoted his life to work with the underprivileged in sixteenth-century Peru. An inspiring story of dedication and self-sacrifice." Hodges. Bks for Elem Sch Libraries

Mayo, Charles Horace

Goodsell, Jane. The Mayo brothers; illus. by Louis S. Glanzman. Crowell 1972 41p illus (A Crowell biography) lib. bdg. $6.49, pa $1.45 (2-4)   92

1 Mayo, William James 2 Physicians
ISBN 0-690-52751-7; 0-690-00639-X   LC 70-139104

In boyhood, both William and Charles Mayo helped their doctor-father in his office and often went with him when he visited his sick patients. When they became old enough each in turn went to medical school. This biography tells the story of their lives and careers bound up with the development of the now world-famous Mayo Clinic from a small hospital opened by their father in Rochester, Minnesota, in 1889

"This is an interesting biography of the Mayo brothers and their achievement in the world of medicine, written in an easy style—interesting to the young child, as it points out facts which he can readily understand and relate to, and in no way appears to be teaching him. At the same time there is a great deal of information imparted." Appraisal

Mayo, William James

Goodsell, Jane. The Mayo brothers. See entry under Mayo, Charles Horace   92

Mays, Willie Howard

Sullivan, George. Willie Mays; illus. by David Brown. Putnam 1973 64p illus (A See and read Beginning to read biography) lib. bdg. $5.99 (1-3)   92

1 Baseball—Biography 2 Black athletes
ISBN 0-399-60824-9   LC 72-97227

Childhood anecdotes and career highlights round out this presentation of the life story of baseball star Willie Mays

Mead, Margaret

Epstein, Sam. She never looked back; Margaret Mead in Samoa, by Sam and Beryl Epstein; illus. by Victor Juhasz. Coward, McCann & Geoghegan 1980 64p illus lib. bdg. $5.99 (4-6)   92

1 Anthropologists 2 Ethnology—Samoan Islands 3 Women scientists
ISBN 0-698-30715-1   LC 78-31821

"Although this [book] focuses on Mead's life and work in Samoa, gathering material for 'The Coming of Age in Samoa,' it also gives biographical information that covers the whole span of her life and her distinguished career. This covers an interesting period in Mead's life, and although the writing is rather dry, the book has good balance and reflects the scientific attitudes and the research mehods used by anthropologists in the field. The illustrations are adequate, more decorative than informative and, in two instances, seem in conflict with the text about a minor detail of dress." Chicago. Children's Bk Center

Includes a glossary of 17 Samoan words used in the text. Selected bibliography: p64

Meir, Golda

Davidson, Margaret. The Golda Meir story. Rev. ed. Scribner 1981 228p illus $9.95   92

ISBN 0-684-16877-4   LC 80-26970

First published 1976

Concentrating on the early life of the Israeli prime minister, "the story begins when Golda is five, in 1903. Her family live in Kiev where they are constantly threatened by pogroms. Finally, they come to the United States where life is hard for immigrants but where no Cossacks threaten. As the narrative builds, we follow Golda's growing up, quitting school, marrying and bearing children. But we also find how destiny found larger roles for her to play." Pub W [review of 1976 edition]

"An attractively produced work which is aptly titled, for it is a heavily fictionalized account with a sometimes ecstatic tone and liberal exclamation points. The proportion of space devoted to Golda Meir's growing up and preparing for a career is generous. . . . Her personality and ardent Jewishness come through vividly in the recounting of both early incidents and later Middle Eastern experiences." Horn Bk [review of 1976 edition]

Bibliography: p222-23

Dobrin, Arnold. A life for Israel; the story of Golda Meir; illus. with photographs. Dial Press 1974 98p illus $4.95, lib. bdg. $4.58 (4-6)   92

1 Israel—History
ISBN 0-8037-4816-7; 0-8037-4817-5   LC 73-15442

Golda's life makes a story inherently inspiring and fast-paced; this brief, forthright report, together with early and recent black-and-white photographs, lets her light shine through without neglecting some of the shadows over her personal life as work took precedence over family. There is some tendency to misrepresent the Middle Eastern conflict in giving Golda her due, and the bias is of course purely Zionist." Booklist

Miller, Bertha E. (Mahony)

Ross, Eulalie Steinmetz. The spirited life: Bertha Mahony Miller and children's books. Selected bibliography comp. by Virginia Haviland. Horn Bk. 1973 274p illus $12   92

1 Children's literature—History and criticism
ISBN 0-87675-057-9   LC 73-84132

This is "a stately, detailed, and sometimes nostalgic trip into early crusading for children's literature. Bertha Mahony Miller's intense creative energy, her feminine independence and her optimistic sense of wonder are highlighted throughout the account of her childhood, her founding of the successful Bookshop for Boys and Girls in Boston, the launching and long, fruitful editorship of 'The Horn Book,' and her contribution to publications on children's literature. Her close association with such pioneers in the field as Alice Jordan and Anne Carroll Moore and her enormous correspondence, including exchanges with Beatrix Potter, will bring contemporary professionals in touch with earlier developments. [The] comprehensive bibliography points to directions for further pursuit of the subject." Booklist

Mitchell, Arthur

Tobias, Tobi. Arthur Mitchell; illus. by Carole Byard. Crowell 1975 32p illus lib. bdg. $7.89 (3-5)   92

1 Ballet dancers 2 Blacks—Biography 3 Dance Theatre of Harlem
ISBN 0-690-00662-4   LC 74-13730

"Arthur Mitchell had always wanted to be a dancer, but he had not considered ballet until one of the founders of the New York City Ballet invited him (Mitchell had just graduated from High School of Performing Arts) to study at the company's training school. Black ballet dancers were rare, but Mitchell was determined and dedicated, and his later success was a testament to his tenacity as well as to his ability. Known internationally as the director of the Dance Theatre of Harlem, Mitchell . . . devotes his time to helping and teaching young aspirants." Chicago. Children's Bk Center

"An attractive format—large, clean type and sepia pastel drawings overlayed with yellow and blue—enhances this fine biography." Sch Library J

Muhammad Ali

Lipsyte, Robert. Free to be Muhammad Ali. Harper 1978 124p $7.95, lib. bdg. $7.89 (5 and up)   92

1 Boxing—Biography 2 Black athletes
ISBN 0-06-023901-8; 0-06-023902-6 LC 77-25640

"An Ursula Nordstrom book"

"While highlighting the champion's extraordinary career and charisma, Lipsyte doesn't neglect mention of his human failings, contradictions in Ali's character that make him one of the most controversial public figures of his time. The text covers events in the life of Muhammad Ali from his boyhood through all his trials and triumphs, except for the latest. It's too bad that it was written before the aging gladiator's second match with Spinks." Pub W

"What one . . . derives from this slim biography is a sense not only of Ali's mercurial personality, but also of the affection and respect the author feels for him as an ahlee and as a man. . . . [The auhor writes] with taste and an honest resolve to delve beyond the usual level of puffery and jock hype, which in his own field makes him almost as unique as Ali." NY Times Bk Rev

Nascimento, Edson Arantes do

Haskins, James S. Pelé; a biography. Doubleday 1976 185p illus $6.95 (6 and up)
92

1 Soccer—Biography
ISBN 0-385-11565   LC 75-39123

The author "prefaces the biography of the renowned soccer player with an explanation of the game and a brief history of its origin and development into the world's most popular sport. The story of Pelé's life is balanced in coverage, has a consistently admiring tone, and is inherently dramatic (rather than being dramatized by the author) because of the special abilities that Pelé has as an athlete and because of the exciting record he has made as a sports star and as an idolized hero of fans the world over. A glossary of soccer terms, some statistical tables, and a selective bibliography are appended." Chicago. Children's Bk Center

Noguchi, Isamu

Tobias, Tobi. Isamu Noguchi: the life of a sculptor; a biography for young people; illus with photographs. Crowell 1974 42p illus lib. bdg. $7.89 (3-6)
92

1 Sculptors, American
ISBN 0-690-45014-1   LC 72-7560

The author tells "of the Japanese-American sculptor's troubled youth, his search for a unique mode of expression, and the artistry of his creations." Booklist

This work "written in a grave, direct style is illustrated with many photographs of the sculptor's work, and a few of his studios. . . . An interesting and unusual biography, this should be of special concern to readers who are students of any art form." Chicago. Children's Bk Center

Oakley, Annie

Alderman, Clifford Lindsey. Annie Oakley and the world of her time. Macmillan Pub. Co. 1979 91p illus $8.95 (5 and up)
92

ISBN 0-02-700270-5   LC 78-31838

This is an account of the life of the famous sharpshooter from her childhood in the 1860's to her death in 1926, featuring her role as entertainer in Buffalo Bill's Wild West Show and other shows of the time

"This is a good biography to balance out collections which feature mostly males. It should be introduced to those who might not consider picking up a biography of a woman, but will be interested in this account because of the nature of Annie's talents." Sch Library J
Bibliography: p85-86

Ortiz, Juan

Steele, William O. The wilderness tattoo; a narrative of Juan Ortiz; illus. with old prints. Harcourt 1972 184p illus map $5.95 (5 and up)
92

1 Indians of North American—Captivities 2 Soto, Hernando de 3 Explorers 4 America—Exploration
ISBN 0-15-297325-7   LC 77-167838

When Pánfilo de Narváez sailed from Spain in 1527 to explore Florida, seventeen-year-old Juan Ortiz was a member of his expedition. One year later, he was captured by Indians on the shores of Tampa Bay. This is an account of his life with the Indians and of his later participation in Hernando de Soto's expedition through what became the southeastern United States

"A well-written and researched narrative biography interlaced with 'interludes' giving historical background and enhanced by an eight-page section of appropriate prints and woodcuts." Booklist
Selected bibliography: p183-84

Osceola, Seminole chief

Syme, Ronald. Osceola, Seminole leader; illus. by Ben F. Stahl. Morrow 1976 96p illus map $6.75, lib. bdg. $6.48 (4-6)
92

1 Seminole Indians—Biography 2 Indians of North America—Government relations
ISBN 0-688-22054-1; 0-688-32054-6   LC 75-22373

"This short book is as much an explication of the three Seminole wars and the perfidy of the U.S. government in its relationship with the Seminoles as it is a biography of Osceola, about whose personal life few facts are known. Born in 1804, he was the son of William Powell, an English trader who abandoned his family in 1815, and Polly Copinger, a Creek Indian. Fleeing north Georgia, where the U.S. militia was engaged in a war with the Creek Nation, Asi-Yahola and his mother went south and found refuge in a small Seminole village near the Tampa Bay. The government's efforts to establish a reservation between Leesburg and Ocala and then to deport the Seminoles to Oaklahoma were met at first with grudging acceptance, followed by growing resistance as U.S. promises were broken. Osceola (as he came to be known through military reports) led the ultimately successful guerrilla-type resistance until his capture under a flag of truce by General T. S. Jesup in 1837. A clear and direct text set in good-sized type distinguishes this simple, but not oversimplified, sympathetic presentation of a complex series of tragic events." Booklist
Bibliography: p94

Parks, Rosa Lee

Greenfield, Eloise. Rosa Parks; illus. by Eric Marlow. Crowell 1973 32p illus (A Crowell biography) $7.95, lib. bdg. $7.89 (2-4)
92

1 Blacks—Civil rights 2 Black women
ISBN 0-690-71210-3; 0-690-71211-1

"Effective balance between dialogue and narrative relates facts about Rosa Parks' life and about segregated southern society. The engaging text, illustrated with expressive line drawings, builds quickly to the climax—the Montgomery, Alabama bus boycott precipitated by the arrest and jailing of Rosa Parks who refused to give up her bus seat to a white rider. This is a valuable addition for elementary school and public libraries needing supplementary material on the Civil Rights Movement." Sch Library J

Pocahontas

Aulaire, Ingri d'. Pocahontas, by Ingri & Edgar Parin d'Aulaire. Doubleday 1946 unp illus $7.95, lib. bdg. $8.90 (2-4)
92

1 Indians of North America—Biography
ISBN 0-385-07454-9; 0-385-07650-9   LC 46-11835

With "simplicity and dignity, the . . . authors have told the story of Pocahontas and Captain John Smith, bringing in the romantic and courageous elements as well as authentic historical fact. The lithographs are colourful, primitive in design and picture the story of Pocahontas from her childhood [in the Virginia wilderness] to her reception as a princess in England." Ontario Library Rev

Polo, Marco

Marco Polo's adventures in China, by the editors of Horizon Magazine. Author: Milton Rugoff; consultant: L. Carrington Goodrich. . . . Am. Heritage [distributed by Harper] 1964 153p illus maps lib. bdg. $12.89 (5 and up)
92

1 China—Social life and customs 2 Voyages and travels 3 Explorers
ISBN 0-06-024960-9   LC 64-14324

"A Horizon Caravel book"

"Illustrated with paintings, maps, and illuminations, many of the period." Title page

The author describes Marco Polo's four-year overland journey to China and the seventeen years he spent in the service of Kublai Khan

"A competently written account . . . the restrained prose sets off admirably the exotic and romantic facts. The book gives very good background material about the known world of the thirteenth century. Illustrations in this volume are reproductions of Oriental and Occidental scenes, or artifacts, or maps not necessarily associated with Marco Polo but typical of the period, or of places; there are many examples of Venetian art, for example." Chicago. Children's Bk Center
Further reference: p151

Potter, Beatrix

Aldis, Dorothy. Nothing is impossible; the story of Beatrix Potter; drawings by Richard Cuffari. Atheneum Pubs. 1969 156p illus $7.95 (4-6)
92

1 Authors, English 2 Illustrators, English 3 Women authors 4 Women artists
ISBN 0-689-20618-6   LC 69-13528

Potter, Beatrix—*Continued*

"Adhering to fact with regard to characters and incidents but using imagined conversations, Aldis . . . re-creates Beatrix Potter's life focusing on her lonely but not unhappy Victorian childhood and young womanhood and showing how her genius developed." Booklist

"The narrative makes use of extracts from Beatrix Potter's letters and journal. . . . The simple style makes available to the middle reader the events in the life of a Beatrix Potter and at the same time conveys the atmosphere of her life wih her parents and her enchantment with nature and with country life. The pencil drawings are in keeping with the unglamorized events of the story and wisely avoid any suggestions of Beatrix Potter's own style." Horn Bk

A list of Beatrix Potter's books: p155-56

Lane, Margaret. The magic years of Beatrix Potter. Warne 1978 216p illus $25   92

1 Authors, English 2 Illustrators, English 3 Women authors 4 Women artists
ISBN 0-7232-2108-1   LC 78-52636

The author "expands on her earlier biography 'The Tale of Beatrix Potter' [entered below] to include heretofore unpublished drawings, recently discovered photographs taken by the artist's father, and an entrancing array of reproductions from the famous books. Glimpses of Potter's personal life, beginnings of her publishing career, and growth of her artistic talents unfold through the revealing narrative but more strikingly through the inclusion of rough sketches, unfinished drawings, and variant pictures that she made prior to publication. A fascinating opportunity to become reacquainted with Peter Rabbit, Mrs. Tiggywinkle, Jeremy Fischer, Jemima Puddleduck, and other Potter creations." Booklist
Bibliography: p211-12

Lane, Margaret. The tale of Beatrix Potter; a biography. Rev. ed. Warne 1968 173p illus $20   92

1 Authors, English 2 Illustrators, English 3 Women authors 4 Women artists
ISBN 0-7232-0138-2   LC 68-22444

First published 1946
This biography of the English author of Peter Rabbit and other famous children's stories, covers her girlhood as the only daughter in a wealthy home and her happy years of farming and raising sheep as "Mrs. Heelis of Sawrey." Includes material on 15 years in her early life about which little was known until her journal was decoded and published in 1966

"Closing The Tale of Beatrix Potter and thinking back over it, one is conscious of the great debt we owe Margaret Lane, both for her choice of material and her treatment of it. It is a fully rounded picture she has given us of an original personality, and there is in it not one trace of the sentimentality which would have so irked the creator of all those salty little characters who live between the covers of these twentieth century classics. Their enduring charm and fidelity to the English countryside defy time and imitation." Horn Bk [review of 1946 edition]
The Beatrix Potter books: p167-68

Reiss, Johanna

The journey back. Crowell 1976 212p $8.95 (4 and up)   92

1 Netherlands—History 2 Jews in the Netherlands
ISBN 0-690-01252-7   LC 76-12615

Sequel to: The upstairs room, entered below
The author "describes the aftermath of war: the broken or alienated families, the scarcity of food and clothing, the ruptured relationships with friends and neighbors, the people still weak or ill. Or missing. For Annie, there is the tragedy of parting from the beloved Oosterveld family who had sheltered her, the pain of seeing her older sisters leave home, the problems of adjusting to a new stepmother whom she cannot seem to please. . . . A vivid evocation of the bittersweet lot of survivors in wartime, and a poignant, trenchant picture of a young adolescent in a fragmented Jewish family in Holland." Chicago. Children's Bk Center

The upstairs room. Crowell 1972 273p $8.95 (4 and up)   92

1 World War, 1939-1945—Jews 2 Netherlands—History—German occupation, 1940-1945 3 Jews in the Netherlands
ISBN 0-690-85127-8   LC 77-187940

"The author recalls her experiences as a Jewish child hiding from the Germans occupying her native Holland during World War II. When German pressure on Dutch Jews is stepped up ten-year-old Annie and her twenty-year-old sister Sini, separated from their father and eldest sister who hide elsewhere and from their mother dying in a hospital, are taken in by a Dutch farmer, his wife and mother who hide the girls in an upstairs room of the farm house." Booklist

In relating her experiences "the author has skillfully captured, in a first person narrative, the tone, impressions, and expressions of the eight-year-old girl telling the story. Excellent characterization of real people reinforces a stirring and absorbing story which is filled with moments that are tense, frightening, sad, and humorous but never melodramatic. It is a story that is timeless though it is set in a specific period in history." Top of the News
Followed by: The journey back, entered above

Revere, Paul

Fritz, Jean. And then what happened, Paul Revere? Pictures by Margot Tomes. Coward, McCann & Geoghegan 1973 45p illus $6.95 (2-4)   92

1 U.S.—History—Revolution, 1775-1783—Biography
ISBN 0-698-20274-0   LC 73-77423

This "description of Paul Revere's ride to Lexington is funny, fast-paced, and historically accurate; it is given added interest by the establishment of Revere's character: busy, bustling, versatile, and patriotic, a man who loved people and excitement. The account of his ride is preceded by a description of his life and the political situation in Boston, and it concludes with Revere's adventures after reaching Lexington." Chicago. Children's Bk Center

This "slightly unfamiliar and entertaining version of [Revere's] 'Big Ride' is documented in the informal and readable notes at the end of the book. The light-hearted humor in the illustrations—like that in the writing—proves that historical accuracy need not be solemn." Horn Bk

Richards, Linda Ann Judson

Collins, David R. Linda Richards: first American trained nurse; illus. by Cary. Garrard 1973 80p illus lib. bdg. $5.49 (3-6)   92

1 Nurses
ISBN 0-8116-6312-2   LC 73-5889

"A Discovery book"
"This interesting biography of Linda Richards . . . America's first graduate nurse, covers her childhood, her struggle to obtain adequate education, and her work to set up training programs for women in this country as well as in Japan where she lived for five years. The emphasis is on the difficulties that serious, capable women of that era encountered in entering the medical field." Sch Library J

Richter, Hans Peter

I was there; tr. from the German by Edite Kroll. Holt 1972 204p lib. bdg. $5.95 (6 and up)   92

1 National socialism 2 Youth—Germany 3 Germany—Social conditions
ISBN 0-03-088372-5   LC 72-76581

Original German edition, 1962
"This narrative recreates the atmosphere of Nazi Germany, the day-to-day life and attitudes, from a young boy's perspective." Chicago

"It is the author's intent to explore the diversity of reasons which compelled youngsters to join the Hitler youth movement and to delineate the extent to which that movement both dictated and reflected the life style of the Third Reich. Historical events are frequently handled as staccato preludes to the personal agonies they induced." Horn Bk

Richthofen, Manfred Albrecht, Freiherr von

Wright, Nicolas. The Red Baron. McGraw [1977 c1976] 116p illus map lib. bdg. $6.95 (5 and up)   92

1 World War, 1914-1918—Germany 2 World War, 1914-1918—Aerial operations 3 Air pilots
ISBN 0-07-072040-1   LC 77-78759

First published 1976 in England
"Young readers who know only of Snoopy's unseen adversary should find this admiring account of the real Red Baron of interest. Manfred von Richthofen's competitive childhood training and discipline is described, but, as he lived only 26 years, the focus is on the World War I air battles in which he demonstrated the flying skills that made him a pilot renowned and respected by all factions. His final battle (it is uncertain who actually fired the fatal shot) is recounted in great detail. The readable biography is accompanied by many contemporary photographs which capture well the nationalistic pride of the period." Sch Library J

Robeson, Paul

Greenfield, Eloise. Paul Robeson; illus. by George Ford. Crowell 1975 32p illus (Crowell biographies) lib. bdg. $7.89 (2-5)   92

1 Blacks—Biography
ISBN 0-690-00660-8   LC 74-13663

"Born in 1898 the son of a runaway slave, Paul suffered the tragic loss of his mother; she died in a fire. His courageous father was an inspiration to the boy, who grew up to become in college a debating champion, a winner in four sports, twice an All-American football end, a member of Phi Beta Kappa, valedictorian of his graduating class. He studied law but became famous as an actor and concert singer. His travails during the 1940s and 1950s are recorded: accused of Communist sympathies, he was blacklisted and refused a passport." Pub W
"This format and style are appealing to the beginning reader and useful for the high-interest-low-reading level that many teachers and librarians encounter. This is a clearly written account of Robeson's life and work. . . . It is not meant to be an in-depth study but a good introduction to the life and contributions of a fine musician and a man of conviction." Children's Bk Rev Serv

Hamilton, Virginia. Paul Robeson; the life and times of a free black man; illus. with photographs. Harper 1974 217p illus lib. bdg. $8.79 (6 and up)   92

1 Blacks—Biography
ISBN 0-06-022189-5   LC 72-82892

"Drawing information from an impressive list of sources, [the author] painstakingly tells the story of Robeson's life: his academic, athletic, musical, and theatrical accomplishments, and his long struggle—not for personal success but for the freedom of his people and their right to decent, dignified lives. . . . Virginia Hamilton deals objectively and skillfully with the tangled complexities of Robeson's beliefs and with the American political climate of the Cold War period. . . . An important book for readers of all ages." Horn Bk
Bibliography: p205-09

Robinson, John Roosevelt

Breakthrough to the big league; the story of Jackie Robinson, by Jackie Robinson and Alfred Duckett; illus. with 21 photographs. Harper 1965 178p illus lib. bdg. $7.89 (5 and up)   92

1 Baseball—Biography 2 Black athletes
ISBN 0-06-025046-1   LC 64-19719

"A Breakthrough book"
"Jackie Robinson describes his impoverished childhood and early racial degradation, a stay at a college in Los Angeles where he began a career in sports, and even greater racial problems when he became the first Negro in the major leagues. The chatty text becomes vivid because it is so clearly drawn from Robinson's own speech. As a plain-speaking, highly personal sharing of experience, the book is a forceful picture of the challenge of crossing barriers." Rdng Ladders for Human Relations. 5th edition

Rudeen, Kenneth. Jackie Robinson; illus. by Richard Cuffari. Crowell 1971 40p illus (A Crowell biography) lib. bdg. $7.89, pa $2.95 (2-4)   92

1 Baseball—Biography 2 Black athletes
ISBN 0-690-45650-6; 0-690-00208-4   LC 75-139100

"A very good biography for young readers, with balanced treatment of Robinson's childhood, his years as a college athlete, and his career in professional baseball. The writing is matter-of-fact, brisk, and candid. . . . The problems Robinson encountered as the first black player in major league baseball are [also] described." Chicago. Children's Bk Center

Rogers, Robert

Gauch, Patricia Lee. The impossible Major Rogers; drawings by Robert Andrew Parker. Putnam 1977 61p illus map $5.95 (4-6)   92

1 U.S.—History—French and Indian War, 1755-1763—Biography
ISBN 0-399-20593-4   LC 76-51233

"During England's wars with France that raged throughout the late 18th Century, the American frontier 'hung like a juicy plum' between these two European powers. Major Robert Rogers, ex-smuggler and counterfeiter, became a military leader at this time, exhibiting traits of ingenuity, determination, and daring that made him one of the real heroes of the frontier. Borrowing tactics, equipment, and weapons from the Indians, he captured their villages and he and his men obtained the information that made possible England's victory over France and control of the Lake Champlain region." Sch Library J
"The circumstances of his triumphs and the reasons for his downfall are skillfully woven into the narrative; thus balance is preserved while an encyclopedic tone is avoided. The informal style permits explanatory asides without condescension; invented dialogue is kept to a minimum, so that authenticity is maintained. An excellent choice for reading aloud, the text is not difficult but sophisticated enough for a slightly older audience than the format might suggest." Horn Bk

Roosevelt, Eleanor (Roosevelt)

Goodsell, Jane. Eleanor Roosevelt; illus. by Wendell Minor. Crowell 1979 38p illus (A Crowell biography) lib. bdg. $7.89, pa $1.45 (2-4)   92

1 Presidents—U.S.—Wives
ISBN 0-690-25626-4; 0-690-25627-2   LC 71-106573

Once a shy and awkward young girl, Eleanor Roosevelt grew up to become the wife of the thirty-second President of the United States. This biography pictures her as a child, as a wife and mother, as a First Lady helping the underprivileged of all nations and, in her later years, as a worker for the cause of making a better world for all people

Roosevelt, Franklin Delano, President U.S.

Franklin Delano Roosevelt, by the editors of American Heritage, The Magazine of History. Author: Wilson Sullivan; consultant: Frank Freidel. Am. Heritage [distributed by Harper] 1970 153p illus $9.95, lib. bdg. $12.89 (5 and up)   92

1 Presidents—U.S. 2 U.S.—Politics and government—1933-1945—Biography
ISBN 0-06-026086-6; 0-06-026087-4   LC 73-105906

"American Heritage Junior library"
"An excellent biography, broad in coverage and profusely illustrated with good photographs, the writing mature and straightforward, the attitude admiring but discerning. The author gives a vivid picture of the depression era, recovery measures, political campaigns and the 'diplomatic minuet' that preceded World War II concluding with a resume of the war and a brief, poignant account of Roosevelt's death." Chicago. Children's Bk Center
Further reference: p149

Roosevelt, Franklin Delano, President U.S.
—Continued

Johnson, Gerald W. Franklin D. Roosevelt; portrait of a great man; illus. with 30 photographs; decorations by Leonard Everett Fisher. Morrow 1967 192p illus $7.75, lib. bdg. $7.44 (5 and up) **92**

1 Presidents—U.S.
ISBN 0-688-21314-6; 0-688-31314-0

"In this book no attempt will be made to tell the whole story. Much of it does not help us to understand. Roosevelt, for usually he did what he had to do, what any other man in his high office would have had to do. But there were a few instances in which the kind of man he was decided the kind of thing he did, and those events are are ones I have tried to select for this biography." Author's note

The author's "thesis is that Roosevelt was just another bright and capable young man in politics until his illness, and that the crippling effects of polio brought out the courage and determination that made him a statesman. Perhaps the most interesting aspect of the book is in the picture it gives of the political struggles of the beginner." Sat Rev

Rose, Edward, fl. 1811-1834

Felton, Harold W. Edward Rose: Negro trail blazer; illus. with photographs, prints of the period, and maps. Dodd 1967 111p maps $5.95 (5 and up) **92**

1 Blacks—Biography 2 Frontier and pioneer life —The West (U.S.)
ISBN 0-396-05597-4   LC 67-21521

"This is a readable account of the life and times of Edward Rose, a fearless Negro mountain man who, since he knew the ways of the Indians, served as an able guide and interpreter for trappers who sought to establish a fur trade with the Indians of the West during the early part of the 19th century. Written in simple language in a documentary style, the book presents a clear picture of the lives of the trappers during the period, interspersed with occasional moments of excitement and adventure." Sch Library J

Selected bibliography: p106-08

Ruth, George Herman

Verral, Charles Spain. Babe Ruth, Sultan of Swat. Garrard 1976 95p illus lib. bdg. $5.88 (3-6) **92**

1 Baseball—Biography
ISBN 0-8116-6679-4   LC 75-38825

"Always in trouble as a young boy, George Herman Ruth was sent to a Catholic school for instruction and discipline. It was there that he learned to play baseball, a game that led him to a career of records. His ability to hit home runs made him a hero to sports enthusiasts though he was originally signed as a pitcher. In his lifetime he set or equaled more than fifty official major league records." Adventuring with Bks

The author "writes a candid biography, noting Ruth's temper tantrums and wild living as well as his charitable acts and legendary playing." Booklist

Salomon, Haym

Milgrim, Shirley. Haym Salomon, liberty's son; illus. by Richard Fish. Jewish Publication Society of America 1975 119p illus $4.50 (5 and up) **92**

1 United States—History—Revolution, 1775-1783 —Biography 2 Jews—Biography
ISBN 0-8276-0073-9   LC 75-17349

A "portrait of the Jewish broker who was primarily responsible for financing the American Revolution. Milgrim begins with Salomon's activities with the Sons of Liberty, and through . . . dialogue and details about Salomon's background and family, vividly describes his eventual emergence as Revolutionary financier in Philadelphia. Her pertinent remarks on Salomon's Judaism, his active involvement in Jewish causes, and his philosophical attitude toward the relationship of Jews and revolution are intriguing and meaningful." Sch Library J

Sasaki, Sadako

Coerr, Eleanor. Sadako and the thousand paper cranes; paintings by Ronald Himler. Putnam 1977 64p illus $7.95 (3-6) **92**

1 Leukemia 2 Atomic bomb—Physiological effect
ISBN 0-399-20520-9   LC 76-9872

"A story about a young girl of Hiroshima who died from leukemia ten years after the dropping of the atom bomb. Her dreams of being an outstanding runner are dimmed when she learns she has the fatal disease. But her spunk and bravery, symbolized in her efforts to have faith in the story of the golden crane, are beautifully portrayed by the author. Sadako was a real person for whom a statue has been erected in the Hiroshima Peace Park. Her legend has been alive to the Japanese for many years and this sensitive book now enables young Americans to share her story." Babbling Bookworm

"The story is told tenderly but with neither a morbid nor a sentimental tone; it is direct and touching. Himler's black and white drawings capture both the vitality that is Sadako's outstanding quality, and, later in the story, the poignancy of the loving family's efforts to make her last days as happy as they can." Chicago. Children's Bk Center

Seattle, Chief of the Suquamish and allied tribes

Boring, Mel. Sealth. Dillon Press 1978 58p illus (The Story of an American Indian) lib. bdg. $5.95 (5 and up) **92**

1 Suquamish Indians—Biography
ISBN 0-87518-155-4   LC 77-25470

" 'Sealth,' who became chief of the Suquamish Indians in the closing years of the 18th Century, witnessed the disintegration of his people's culture during the first half of the 19th Century, when the Pacific Northwest became a mecca for white homesteaders and businessmen. A man of peace, Sealth (known among whites as Chief Seattle) refused to take up arms and tried, tragically, to act as a mediator." Sch Library J

Singer, Isaac Bashevis

A day of pleasure; stories of a boy growing up in Warsaw; with photographs by Roman Vishniac. Farrar, Straus 1969 227p illus $8.95, pa $5.95 (4 and up) **92**

1 Jews in Poland
ISBN 0-374-31749-6; 0-374-13217-8   LC 70-95461

Translated from the original Yiddish. Fourteen of these episodes previously appeared in somewhat different form in the author's book: In my father's court

An autobiographical collection of stories in which the author writes of his boyhood, as a rabbi's son, in Warsaw, from 1908 to 1918

The stories "present a well-rounded picture of Jewish ghetto life—religion, schooling, family life, friendships, relationships with neighbors, and the richness of the Jewish experience." Wolfe. About 100 Bks

Sitting Bull, Dakota chief

O'Connor, Richard. Sitting Bull: war chief of the Sioux; illus. by Eric von Schmidt. McGraw 1968 144p illus lib. bdg. $7.95 (4-6) **92**

1 Dakota Indians—Biography
ISBN 0-07-047582-2   LC 68-13523

"A thought-provoking account of the white man's treatment of the Indians and of a great Sioux chief whose overriding concern was the welfare of his people. Realizing that with the encroachment of the white man the free-roaming life of the Plains Indians was coming to an end, Sitting Bull believed he could help his people most through diplomacy and courage. This attractive, enjoyable detailed biography treats Sitting Bull as a poet, diplomat, and man of mercy, as well as a man of war." Library J

"The treachery of the white Americans as depicted here is beyond belief. One feels that it must be possible to say something in their favour, but the author does not say it. Nevertheless he gives a fascinating account of Sitting Bull and his world." Times (London) Lit Sup

Smith, John, 1580-1631

Syme, Ronald. John Smith of Virginia; illus. by William Stobbs. Morrow 1954 192p illus $6.95 (5 and up) 92

1 U.S.—History—Colonial period, 1600-1775—Biography
ISBN 0-688-21597-1 LC 54-5521

This biography emphasizes John Smith's leadership of the struggling English colonists in seventeenth century Virginia. It tells of his legendary rescue by Pocahontas, and also his work as explorer and map maker

"It makes good reading for those who like quick blood-and-thunder action. At the same time it gives a real impression of the early colony at Jamestown. William Stobbs' drawings as usual add strength to the historical picture." Horn Bk

Map on lining-papers

Soto, Hernando de

Syme, Ronald. De Soto, finder of the Mississippi; illus. by William Stobbs. Morrow 1957 96p illus map lib. bdg. $6.96 (4-6) 92

1 Explorers 2 Mississippi River 3 America—Exploration
ISBN 0-688-31224-1 LC 57-5061

A story of Hernando de Soto's great adventures in the New World. He and his followers were the first Europeans to see the Mississippi. With Pizarro he made the journey to Peru; he also led his own expedition through Florida

"The story, one of almost constant hardship, is well told, and its attractive illustrations will help interest younger readers. Older slow readers, or those who want a quick review, will also find it useful." Horn Bk

Spallanzani, Lazzaro

Epstein, Sam. Secret in a sealed bottle; Lazzaro Spallanzani's work with microbes, by Sam and Beryl Epstein; illus. by Jane Sterrett. Coward, McCann & Geoghegan 1979 63p illus (Science discovery bks) lib. bdg. $5.49 (4-6) 92

1 Biologists
ISBN 0-698-30700-3 LC 78-1494

A biography of the 18th century Italian whose experiments with microbes disproved the theory of spontaneous generation and provided a base for the work of future scientists

"A comparison of the book with an encyclopedia article revealed no essential facts to be missing. It is hard to say with certainty, however, which parts of the book are factual and which are fictionalized. Obviously, the authors intended readers to absorb the essence rather than the detail of carefully worked out descriptions and conversations. The book is worthwhile for its setting, for its demonstration of Spallanzani's reasoning, and for giving a sense of how a prodigious scientist worked." Horn Bk

Glossary: p60. Some people to know about: p61-62. Selected bibliography: p63

Squanto, Wampanoag Indian

Bulla, Clyde Robert. Squanto, friend of the Pilgrims; illus. by Peter Burchard. Crowell 1954 106p illus $8.95 (2-4) 92

1 Wampanoag Indians—Biography
ISBN 0-690-76642-4 LC 54-9145

The "story of a Pawtuxet Indian boy [who became associated with the Wampanoag tribe after plague decimated his people and] who made friends with some early English voyagers to the new world, went back to England with them for a visit and returned to these shores in time to welcome the Pilgrims." Pub W

"A highly fictionalized account. . . . The author gives no authority for his version of Squanto's first meeting with white men and it is not one of the more generally accepted versions. Aside from this point the book gives an interestingly new and different approach to the subject of the first settlement in New England." Chicago. Children's Bk Center

Stowe, Harriet Elizabeth (Beecher)

Johnston, Johanna. Harriet and the runaway book; the story of Harriet Beecher Stowe and Uncle Tom's cabin; illus. by Ronald Himler. Harper 1977 80p illus lib. bdg. $7.89 (3-5) 92

1 Women authors 2 Slavery in the U.S.
ISBN 0-06-022840-7 LC 76-24308

The author "presents the rebellious child Harriet and the grown woman full of a passion to make known the horrors of slavery. The author also delivers a statement for women's liberation and conveys the atmosphere of the pre-Civil War period. Two brief final chapters summarize the years from the beginning of the war to the Emancipation Proclamation and the years following the publication of 'Uncle Tom's Cabin.' " Horn Bk

"A smoothly fictionalized biography is printed in large type on spacious pages, illustrated by softly drawn black and white pictures, and written in a direct, informal style. While the book's emphasis is on the writing of 'Uncle Tom's Cabin,' it gives balanced treatment to other aspects and periods of Stowe's life." Chicago. Children's Bk Center

Sullivan, John Lawrence

Hoff, Syd. Gentleman Jim and the great John L. See entry under Corbett, James John 92

Takashima

A child in prison camp. Morrow 197_ [c1971] 63p illus $9.25, lib. bdg. $8.88 (6 and up) 92

1 World War, 1939-1945—Canada 2 Japanese in Canada 3 Concentration camps
ISBN 0-688-20113-X; 0-688-30113-4 LC 74-1268

First published 1971 in Canada

"Takashima tells of her childhood experiences in an internment camp during World War II. In March, 1942, Japanese-Canadians were ordered to evacuate the west coast of Canada, and author Shichan's father and older brother were separated from the rest of the family. Six months later father rejoins Shichan, her older sister and their mother at a newly built camp in the Rockies. For the next 3 years, Shichan faces the difficulties of living under constant surveillance and attending a make-shift school, and witnesses conflicts within the Japanese community. Conditions slowly improve as it becomes clear that Japan will lose the war but then all must decide whether to rebuild a life in Canada or return to defeated Japan." Sch Library J

Tallchief, Maria

Tobias, Tobi. Maria Tallchief; illus. by Michael Hampshire. Crowell 1970 32p illus (A Crowell biography) lib. bdg. $7.89 pa $1.95 (2-4) 92

1 Ballet dancers 2 Osage Indians—Biography
ISBN 0-690-51829-3; 0-690-51830-7 LC 77-87159

"Elizabeth Marie Tallchief's father was Osage her mother Scots-Irish, and the family well able to afford both dancing and piano lessons for their daughters. But when the family moved to California, a ballet teacher said that Betty Marie had been taught wrong and would have to start over. At seventeen she came to New York, joining the Ballet Russe company, where her dancing earned her solo parts. Wed to the choreographer George Ballanchine, she rose to prima ballerina after divorce, she remarried. At the age of forty-one, America's most famous ballet dancer retired to devote herself to her daughter and husband The writing style is dry, simple, and factual but the ethnic and cultural appeals are strong and the soft almost photographic illustrations are most attractive." Chicago. Children's Bk Center

Tecumseh, Shawnee chief

Schraff, Anne. Tecumseh. Dillon Press 1979 56p illus map (The Story of an American Indian) lib. bdg. $5.95 (5 and up) 92

1 Shawnee Indians—Biography
ISBN 0-87518-166-X LC 78-13956

A biography of the Shawnee chief who united a confederacy of Indians to save their land from the advance of the white settlers and soldiers

Thoreau, Henry David

Stern, Philip Van Doren. Henry David Thoreau: writer and rebel. Crowell 1972 183p $8.95 (5 and up)   92

1 Authors, American
ISBN 0-690-37715-0   LC 74-139108

This biography follows the growth of Thoreau as thinker and writer, placing him within the distinguished intellectual circle of early nineteenth century America

This book "is clearly and succinctly written and supported by well selected incidents and quotations. [The author's] balanced discussion of both Thoreau's life and his works convincingly portrays a man whose thoughts are relevant to all ages." Library J

Bibliography: p175-76

Thorpe, James Francis

Fall, Thomas. Jim Thorpe; illus. by John Gretzer. Crowell 1970 33p illus. (A Crowell biography) lib. bdg. $7.89, pa $2.95 (2-5)   92

1 Athletes 2 Sauk Indians—Biography
ISBN 0-690-46218-0; 0-690-46219-0   LC 72-94793

From his boyhood at Indian boarding schools in Oklahoma Territory to his reward of a gold medal for the decathlon in the 1912 Olympic Games, this biography examines the abilities of Jim Thorpe, one of the world's finest all-around athletes

This biography has "social relevance. . . . Jim Thorpe, lonely and often troubled as a boy, endured hardships common to Indians in the Oklahoma Territory. The author portrays convincingly how, out of his early experience came the skills which later made him famous." NY Times Bk Rev

Toussaint Louverture, Pierre Dominique

Syme, Ronald. Toussaint: the black liberator; illus. by William Stobbs. Morrow 1971 191p illus map $6.50, lib. bdg. $6.24 (5 and up)   92

1 Blacks—Biography 2 Haiti—History
ISBN 0-688-21806-7; 0-688-31806-1   LC 72-152072

Born a slave in 1743, Toussaint, the man who started the island of Haiti on the path toward freedom, did not become free himself until 1777. In this biography, the author traces Toussaint's career from his humble beginnings as a plantation overseer to his tragic end in a French prison

"Objective in tone, candid in approach, and written with authoritative informality, Syme's biography of the Haitian leader is both informative and interesting reading." Chicago. Children's Bk Center

Bibliography: p[192]

Truth, Sojourner

Ortiz, Victoria. Sojourner Truth, a self-made woman. Lippincott 1974 157p illus $7.95 (6 and up)   92

1 Black women 2 Women—Civil rights 3 Abolitionists
ISBN 0-397-31504-X   LC 73-22290

This biography traces Sojourner Truth's rise from slavery to national prominence as a speaker against social injustices against blacks and women

The author "goes far beyond the well-known 'Ain't I a Woman?' speech to present evidence of this woman's understanding of people and institutions and her uncanny ability to transmit that understanding to others. Unfortunately there is no bibliography, but the fine writing style and insightful portrayal make this valuable for Black studies and women's rights collections." Sch Library J

Tubman, Harriet (Ross)

Epstein, Sam. Harriet Tubman: guide to freedom, by Sam and Beryl Epstein; illus. by Paul Frame. Garrard 1968 96p illus (Americans all) lib. bdg. $5.58 (3-5)   92

1 Black women 2 Underground railroad
ISBN 0-8116-4550-9   LC 68-22638

This is "an episodic narrative biography of the heroic slave who freed and helped hundreds of her fellow Negroes. Illustrated with two-color drawings and photographs, the brief account is easy to read and inspiring." Booklist

Sterling, Dorothy. Freedom train: the story of Harriet Tubman; illus. by Ernest Crichlow. Doubleday 1954 191p illus lib. bdg. $5.95 (5 and up)   92

1 Black women 2 Underground railroad
ISBN 0-385-07111-6   LC 54-5181

This is "an excellent portrait of Harriet Tubman, the resourceful and fearless escaped slave who led over 300 Negroes out of bondage. Beginning with her miserable existence as a slave field hand and her own escape, this engrossing account follows Harriet Tubman's hazardous adventures and almost incredible feats as she shuttled up and down the land transporting parties of fugitive slaves to freedom, her amazing war activities as nurse, scout, and spy for the Union army, and her last years working for the advancement of her race." Booklist

Includes bibliography

Tudor, Tasha

Tudor, Bethany. Drawn from New England: Tasha Tudor; a portrait in words and pictures. Collins [distributed by Philomel Bks] 1979 95p illus $10.95 (5 and up)   92

1 Illustrators, American 2 Women artists
ISBN 0-529-05531-7   LC 79-14230

The author, "oldest daughter of well-loved illustrator Tasha Tudor, relates the story of her mother's life through smooth-flowing narrative, old and contemporary photographs, and samples of the artist's work. The rural New England scenes, Corgi-filled pictures, and homespun details that individualize Tudor's illustrations are all a reflection of the simple, old-fashioned life-style she lives and believes in. . . . [This book] serves not only as a biographical portrait of a woman following her own dream and a commentary on a contemporary artist, but also as a glimpse into a world people lived in a hundred years ago." Booklist

Tutenkhamûn, King of Egypt

Schlein, Miriam. I, Tut: the boy who became pharaoh; illus. by Erik Hilgerdt. Four Winds 1979 unp illus lib. bdg. $7.95 (3-5)   92

1 Egypt—Kings and rulers
ISBN 0-590-07571-3   LC 78-15603

This is a "first-person narrative biography of the ancient Egyptian boy king, Tutankhamun. In the course of the story, Tut matures from a young prince whose father is the revered pharaoh Amenhotep the Magnificent to [his own reign]. . . . As pharaoh Tut is revered by his people as the head of government and religion. On land he rides in a golden chariot and on water is a bejewelled barge of gold. But at home in his palace, he is powerless to prevent famines, the greed of his generals or his own sudden death at the age of 18, after only a nine-year reign." NY Times Bk Rev

"Simple and dignified, the story should appeal to the many children who know of the tomb and its treasures; the writing is carefully factual, the illustrations faithful to the known art and decorative motifs of ancient Egypt. The author's notes, a glossary, and bibliography of sources are appended." Chicago. Children's Bk Center

Verne, Jules

Born, Franz. Jules Verne; the man who invented the future; tr. from the German by Juliana Biro; illus. by Peter P. Plasencia. Prentice-Hall 1964 102p illus lib. bdg. $5.95 (5 and up)   92

1 Authors, French
ISBN 0-13-512228-7   LC 64-11463

Original German edition published 1960

"Two-thirds of the book reviews plots or exciting events of Verne's outstanding novels and relates them to later real-life expeditions, discoveries and inventions. Only one chapter concentrates on Verne's life, providing the background of childhood and early struggles before fame touched him." NY Times Bk Rev

"Juliana Biro's translation of this book from the German makes a swift, absorbing biography. Verne's fertile imagination, his scientific accuracy, and his careful documentation and research set good standards for children. The fact that some of his fantastic ideas of so long ago have now come true will make this book very much alive to young readers . . . steeped in events of the space age." Christian Sci Monitor

Verrazano, Giovanni da

Syme, Ronald. Verrazano: explorer of the Atlantic Coast; illus. by William Stobbs. Morrow 1973 95p illus map lib. bdg. $6.96 (4-6)   92

1 Explorers 2 America—Exploration
ISBN 0-688-31771-5   LC 72-7130

A "biography of the Florentine explorer who sailed up the coast of North America searching for a passage to the Pacific in 1524. Sent by the French king, Verrazano was hunting a trade route; his hopes, based on erroneous information about the continent, were not fulfilled but he did find New York Bay and was treated with great courtesy by the Indians of the region." Chicago. Children's Bk Center

"Excerpts from his journal, including some vivid descriptions of Indians, add interest to this readable book and Stobbs' strong, black-and-white illustrations capture the spirit of the text." Sch Library J
Bibliography: p[96]

Washington, Booker Taliaferro

Graham, Shirley. Booker T. Washington: educator of hand, head, and heart; frontispiece and jacket by Donald W. Lambo. Messner 1955 192p front lib. bdg. $5.29 (5 and up)   92

1 Educators 2 Blacks—Biography 3 Tuskegee Institute
ISBN 0-671-32562-0   LC 55-9855

"A sympathetic story of the slave who overcame tremendous difficulties to establish the Tuskegee Normal and Industrial School for the education of his people." Hodges. Bks for Elem Sch Libraries
Bibliography: p185

Washington, George, President U.S.

Aulaire, Ingri d'. George Washington, by Ingri & Edgar Parin d'Aulaire. Doubleday 1936 unp illus $8.95, lib. bdg. $9.90 (2-4)   92

1 Presidents—U.S.
ISBN 0-385-07306-2; 0-385-07611-8   LC 36-27417

"Using their usual technique of lithographing on stone the d'Aulaires have done a gay, stylized picture book in five colors showing Washington's life. Familiar incidents have been chosen. The most appealing small animals find their way into many of the pictures. The text is a simple recounting of his life." Booklist

"The D'Aulaires have given our newest generation material for true and joyous hero-worship." NY Her Trib Bks

West, Benjamin

Henry, Marguerite. Benjamin West and his cat Grimalkin, by Marguerite Henry and Wesley Dennis. Bobbs 1947 147p illus $6.95 (4-6)   92

1 Painters, American 2 Cat 3 Friends, Society of
ISBN 0-672-50220-8   LC 47-3820

"As a small boy, Quaker-born Benjamin West, known as the 'father of American painting,' wanted so much to paint that he made his own brushes from his cat's tail, made his colors from earth and clay, and used boards for paper. This is a well-written story, touched with humor and tenderness, of Benjamin's boyhood at his father's inn near Philadelphia, of his early experiences and training in painting, and of his adventures with his remarkable cat, Grimalkin." Booklist

"The happy way in which Benjamin West's biography is combined with a real cat story gives this book an unusually friendly appeal. . . . A delightful picture of American Quaker life before the Revolution. . . . [Drawings] are admirably suited to it." Horn Bk

Wheatley, Phillis

Fuller, Miriam Morris. Phillis Wheatley, America's first black poetess; illus. by Victor Mays. Garrard 1971 94p illus (Americans all) lib. bdg. $5.88 (3-6)   92

1 Poets, American 2 Black authors 3 Women authors
ISBN 0-8116-4569-X   LC 77-154858

This book traces the life of one of America's first black poets from her sale as a child slave to her death as a freedwoman in 1784

Wiesenthal, Simon

Noble, Iris. Nazi hunter: Simon Wiesenthal. Messner 1979 158p lib. bdg. $7.29 (5 and up)   92

1 Jews—Biography 2 Holocaust, Jewish (1939-1945) 3 War crime trials
ISBN 0-671-32964-2   LC 79-15783

"Nazi hunter Simon Wiesenthal emerges from Noble's admiring biography as a man driven—driven in the beginning by thoughts of revenge for the treatment that he and his family received at the hands of the Nazi S.S., then by desire for justice and to see 'that the madness of the Holocaust could not happen again.' Dogged persistance in the face of public apathy, governmental resistance, open hostility, and the efforts of ODESSA has paid off for Wiesenthal in the exposure and apprehension of such Nazi war criminals as Adolf Eichmann and Franz Murer. . . . It should be noted that the author has drawn heavily upon Wiesenthal's book, 'The Murderers Among Us.' " Sch Library J

"Wiesenthal's own experiences in concentration camps, his close encounters with imminent execution, and his struggles for survival are vividly portrayed, capturing all the horror of the Nazi regime. His postwar investigations into the whereabouts of former Nazi leaders make exciting reading, and the search process as described here rivals any fiction for breathtaking suspense." Booklist

Wilder, Laura Ingalls

West from home; letters of Laura Ingalls Wilder to Almanzo Wilder, San Francisco, 1915. Ed. by Roger Lea MacBride; historical setting by Margot Patterson Doss. Harper 1974 124p illus $7.95, lib. bdg. $7.89, pa $1.95 (6 and up)   92

1 San Francisco—Description
ISBN 0-06-024110-1; 0-06-024111-X; 0-06-440081-6
LC 73-14342

This collection is "edited from letters sent to her beloved husband while Laura spent two months in late 1915 visiting their daughter and immersing herself in the sights of bustling San Francisco and the exciting Panama-Pacific Exposition. Wilder readers of all ages will lose themselves in this trip—the adults with nostalgia and wholesome pleasure, the youth with wonder and awe over the sights vividly described in her inimitable combination of homespun literary and journalistic styles." Children's Bk Rev Serv

"One of the most noteworthy aspects of her letters is that they reveal her budding interest in writing. . . . The book is prefaced with two competent essays that provide historical background." Horn Bk

Wright, Orville

Reynolds, Quentin. The Wright brothers; pioneers of American aviation; illus. by Jacob Landau. Random House 1950 183p illus lib. bdg. $5.99 (3-6)   92

1 Wright, Wilbur 2 Aeronautics—History
ISBN 0-394-90310-2   LC 50-11766

This is the story of how these two Americans—who made their living running a bicycle shop—invented, built, and flew the first airplane

Readers "will eagerly seize upon this book which portrays simply but vividly the story of two boys who flew the first heavier-than-air machine. Very well written, with excellent characterizations, good print, wide margins, and delightful illustrations." Library J

Wright, Wilbur

Reynolds, Quentin. The Wright brothers. See entry under Wright, Orville   92

Zemach, Margot

Self portrait: Margot Zemach: written and illus. by Margot Zemach. Addison-Wesley 1978 31p illus lib. bdg. $7.95 (3-6)   92

1 Illustrators, American 2 Women artists
ISBN 0-201-09096-1   LC 78-17140

"Zemach chooses some details she thinks will interest children and outlines the rest of her picture book autobiography. . . . She writes mostly

Zemach, Margot—Continued

flat prose, turned into dry humor through understatement and contrary pictures. Of her relationship with husband/collaborator Harve, she says, 'because we were best friends, we worked well together'; then she draws a two-room flat in total chaos—cat, dishes, hanging cloths and diapers, etc.—and adds a warmth, that never leaves the pages. Interwoven . . . are characters from the Zemachs' award-winning books, identified by notes at the end. The text is episodic but the pictures, colorful and calamitous, bring the whole to life." Sch Library J

929   Genealogy

Gilfond, Henry

Genealogy: how to find your roots. Watts, F. 1978 80p illus lib. bdg. $6.90 (6 and up)   **929**

1 Genealogy
ISBN 0-531-01455-X   LC 77-14989
"An Impact book"
"Gilfond presents a short and very simplified approach for beginning genealogists to follow as well as more typical research tips. One of the most satisfactory features is the section on the techniques of interviewing, both oral and written, in which Gilfond makes suggestions of people to question and methods of analyzing the information obtained. The clearly printed illustrations include family group pictures and reproductions of old documents as well as several different kinds of work sheets." Sch Library J
Bibliography p75-76

929.4   Personal names

Lambert, Eloise

Our names; where they came from and what they mean, by Eloise Lambert and Mario Pei. Lothrop 1960 192p lib. bdg. $7.92 (5 and up)   **929.4**

1 Names, Personal 2 Names
ISBN 0-688-51378-6   LC 60-12019
The authors present "little-known facts about first, last, and brand names." Sat Rev
"The study is rather inclusive and mature in approach and treatment for young readers but offers much fascinating information for the interested." Booklist

Shankle, George Earlie

American nicknames; their origin and significance. 2d ed. Wilson, H.W. 1955 524p $15   **929.4**

1 Nicknames 2 Names, Personal—U.S. 3 Names. Geographical—U.S.
ISBN 0-8242-0004-7   LC 55-5038
First published 1937
"More than 4000 nicknames, belonging to famous Americans, cities and states, political organizations, and military regiments, arranged in dictionary form with cross references, with sources given in footnotes." Booklist
"What makes the book so authoritative is the citation to sources of information, which cover newspapers, biographical directories, interviews, and other varied sources. . . . It should be remembered that not only persons and places but things and events are included, e.g. William Jennings Bryan's 'Grape-juice Diplomacy,' or Harvard's 'Great Butter Rebellion'. . . . Because of Mr. Shankle's interesting style, this makes good reading as well as good reference." Cur Ref Bks

929.9   Flags

Crouthers, David D.

Flags of American history; flag illustrations by Nicholas Zarrelli. Hammond 1973 93p illus (Profile ser) $4.95, lib. bdg. $4.39 (6 and up)   **929.9**

1 Flags—U.S.
ISBN 0-8437-3080-3; 8437-3965-7   LC 73-8607

First published 1962
Eighty-nine flags which figured in American history are pictured in this book. The author identifies the importance of the flags in our nation's history

Eggenberger, David

Flags of the U.S.A. Enl. ed. Crowell 1964 222p illus $9.95 (6 and up)   **929.9**

1 Flags—U.S.
ISBN 0-690-30491-9   LC 64-12115
First published 1959
"Describing first the flags of the countries that colonized the New World, the author traces the history of the flags in our country up to the evolution of the fifty-star flag of the United States today. Many drawings are included in addition to the color plates illustrating national, naval, army, and regimental flags as well as the national flag as it evolved. The text is solid with information about the flags themselves and about the historical background to which they are related. . . . Chief use of the book will probably be as a reference source, especially since the closing section is a compilation of facts about the flag code and tradition, and since the index is thorough." Chicago. Children's Bk Center

Evans, I. O.

The observer's book of flags; fully illus. with 74 plates in colour and approximately 60 line drawings. [Rev. ed] Warne [distributed by Scribner] 1975 191p illus $4.95   **929.9**

1 Flags
ISBN 0-684-14941-9   LC 75-331780
"The Observer's pocket series"
Title on spine: Flags
First published 1959 in England
The aim of this pocket-sized "book is not only to help the observer to recognise the most important of the world's flags but to increase his knowledge of flag-lore. These emblems, which we all know so well, form part of Heraldry, 'the shorthand of history'; they are at once practical, as signs of national identity, and charged with emotional significance, as symbols of national loyalty." Preface

Freeman, Mae Blacker

Stars and stripes; the story of the American flag; illus. by Lorence Bjorklund. Random House 1964 57p illus music lib. bdg. $5.99 (2-5) •   **929.9**

1 Flags—U.S.
ISBN 0-394-90134-7   LC 64-11173
Here is the story of the first American flag, how it changed as the United States grew, and events in which the flag played an important part. Also included are rules about the flag; the Pledge of Allegiance: words and melody for "The Star-Spangled Banner"; how flags are made; dates when each of the 50 states joined the Union
"The blue-printed text with red topic headings is appropriate for the subject, but a bit distracting; illustrations are good." Chicago. Children's Bk Center

Parrish, Thomas

The American flag; illus. with photographs, prints and drawings. Simon & Schuster 1973 101p illus lib. bdg. $7.95 (4 and up)   **929.9**

1 Flags—U.S.
ISBN 0-671-65204-4   LC 72-92156
"This well-written account traces the evolution of the present-day flag from its British origins. Beginning with the historic placing of the American flag on the moon in 1969, Parrish interestingly describes the incidents and legends related to the changes in our flag. The idea that the flag does not stand for American perfection but rather represents our highest goals is carefully pointed out. The illustrations and photographs are well placed in the clear text." Sch Library J
Flag talk: Important words and their meanings: p96-99

930-999 HISTORY

930 The ancient world to ca. 499

Goode, Ruth

People of the first cities; illus. by Richard Cuffari. Macmillan Pub. Co. 1977 166p illus map lib. bdg. $7.95 (5 and up)   930

1 Civilization, Ancient 2 Cities and towns—History
ISBN 0-02-736430-5   LC 77-6279

In a continuation of People of the Ice Age [entered in class 573.3] the author traces "the story of various peoples who lived 5,000 years ago. Discussion of the Sumerians, Egyptians, Mesopotamians, Phoenicians, Cretans, and early Greeks combines a look at their achievements (calendar, alphabet) and daily life-styles (homes, clothing, burial customs) with a broad archaeological overview. Specific details on pyramids, tombs of the pharaohs and palaces of the Cretan kings make this valuable for research. . . . Full-page illustrations dividing each chapter evoke a general feeling for the period." Booklist

Unstead, R. J.

Looking at ancient history. Macmillan Pub. Co. [1960] 112p illus maps $8.95 (4-6)   930

1 History, Ancient 2 Civilization, Ancient
ISBN 0-02-790650-7   LC 60-16223

"A history of the ancient world—Egypt, Mesopotamia, Greece, and Rome—presented in brief text and many drawings and photographs. While it is mainly a social history, other aspects such as political events and outstanding men of the times are not neglected; a separate chapter is devoted to Alexander the Great. The wide spacing between paragraphs and the topical arrangement of the text give the book the appearance of an outline. Packed with information and easy to read." Booklist

930.1 Archeology

Baumann, Hans

The caves of the great hunters. Newly illus. and rev. ed. Pantheon Bks. 1962 183p illus maps lib. bdg. $6.99 (5 and up)   930.1

1 Lascaux Cave, France 2 Art, Ancient 3 Man, Prehistoric
ISBN 0-394-91006-0   LC 62-15414

Originally published 1953 in Germany
"The story of the discovery and paintings of the prehistoric caves of Europe, many of which were found by children." The AAAS Sci Bk List for Children. 3d edition
"Children will read this book as a good adventure story and will get at the same time a lively introduction to art and archeology." Sat Rev

Freeman, Mae Blacker

Finding out about the past; illus. with photographs. Random House 1967 79p illus lib. bdg. $5.99 (3-5)   930.1

1 Archeology
ISBN 0-394-90144-4   LC 67-14439

"The author gives a step-by-step description of the work of archaeologists, expanded to show the development of early civilizations through the discovery of the Dead Sea Scrolls, Swiss lake houses, Lascaux Cave, Machu Picchu, Pompeii and others." Bruno. Bks for Sch Libraries, 1968
"A welcome addition to the social studies curriculum. . . . A topical index and encompassing table of contents augment the excellent text. A good beginning book which will prepare young children for the many books on archaeology which start at slightly higher grade levels." Sch Library J

Hall, Jennie

Buried cities. Rev. under the editorship of Lily Poritz; introduction by Katharine Taylor. Macmillan Pub. Co. 1964 116p illus lib. bdg. $4.95 (5 and up)   930.1

1 Excavations (Archeology) 2 Cities and towns, Ruined, extinct, etc.
ISBN 0-02-741940-1   LC 64-20737

First published 1922
Description of the archeological rediscovery of riches found in four lost cities: Pompeii, Herculaneum, Olympia and Mycenae
"Here is a book that will lead children not only to a better understanding of material seen in museums but also to a further interest in reading about ancient times in the world's history. Especially interesting and valuable is the text descriptive of the illustrations." Literary Rev

932 Egypt to 640

Fairservis, Walter A.

Egypt, gift of the Nile [by] Walter A. Fairservis, Jr. Illus. with photographs, and with drawings by Jan Fairservis. Macmillan Pub. Co. 1963 146p illus map $4.95 (6 and up)   932

1 Egypt—Antiquities 2 Egypt—Civilization
ISBN 0-02-734360-X   LC 63-16102

"Civilization is outlined in picture and essay in this pictorial survey of Egypt's history, art, and architecture from prehistoric times to the fall of the New Kingdom. . . . [There is] a section of photographs with captions giving a survey of Egypt's tombs and its art. The rest of the book includes chapters on the political history, crafts, e.g. metalwork, pottery, papyrus paper, and how to write hieroglyphics, and an account of what is known about the daily life of the people. The appendix includes a . . . two-page 'chronicle of Egypt's history,' a list of important dates, and a list of archaeological discoveries since World War II." Library J
"The abundant photographs, the fresh pattern of organization, the swift interpretations of the archeologist-author, who is a professor of anthropology and is familiar with 'digs' and museum treasures, together with the beautiful typography of this book make it a choice gift for young people attracted to scholarly adventure and discovery." Christian Sci Monitor
Glossary: p133-36. Suggestions for further reading: p137

Glubok, Shirley

Discovering Tut-ankh-Amen's tomb. . . . Foreword by Eric Young; designed by Gerard Nook. Macmillan Pub. Co. 1968 143p illus $12.95, pa $5.95 (4 and up)   932

1 Tutenkhamûn, King of Egypt 2 Egypt—Antiquities
ISBN 0-02-736030-X; 0-02-043320-4   LC 68-12069

"Abridged and adapted from 'The tomb of Tut-ankh-Amen' by Howard Carter and A. C. Mace." Title page
This "firsthand account of one of the most exciting and important archaeological discoveries of the twentieth century combines the immediacy of discovery with scholarship. . . . The first chapters give the information necessary for a full appreciation of the historical setting of The Valley of the Tombs of the Kings and the significance of a burial tomb relatively unmarred by looting. The remainder of the book tells in increasingly suspense-filled chapters of the discovery of the tomb, the survey and clearing of the antechamber, the opening of the sealed door, the clearing of the burial chamber and opening of the sarcophagus, the opening of the three coffins, and finally the examination of the royal mummy." Horn Bk
This "is a dramatic story. The suspense of the adventure into the unknown mounts with each new clue disclosed. . . . Shirley Glubok's abridgment and adaptation . . . is excellent, and the photographs are informative and beautiful." NY Times Bk Rev

Payne, Elizabeth

The pharaohs of ancient Egypt; illus. with photographs. Random House 1964 191p illus maps lib. bdg. $5.99 (5 and up)   932

1 Egypt—Kings and rulers 2 Egypt—History
ISBN 0-394-90559-8   LC 64-21857

"The entire history of the Pharaohs is covered in this . . . account which begins with the discovery and deciphering of the Rosetta Stone—the key to knowledge of ancient Egypt. Early chapters deal with the unification of the country under Menes (shortly before 3200 B.C.). . . . Later chapters depict the reigns of queen Hatshepsut, Thutmose III, and Akhnaton. A closing chapter deals with

Payne, Elizabeth—*Continued*

Rameses II and the aftermath. The author is particularly lucid in describing the character of the Pharaohs; their foibles and faults. The book has good photographs, two excellent maps, a selected bibliography and is indexed." Sci Bks

Robinson, Charles Alexander

The first book of ancient Egypt, by Charles Alexander Robinson, Jr. Pictures by Lili Rethi. Watts, F. 1961 61p illus lib. bdg. $5.90 (4 and up)   932

1 Egypt—Antiquities 2 Egypt—Civilization
ISBN 0-531-00462-7   LC 61-5201

The author "gives an outline of Egyptian history from its beginning to its fall, 1085 B.C., showing Egyptian daily life, religion, science and art. The book is unusually well illustrated with pencil drawings in colour." Ontario Library Rev

Swinburne, Irene

Behind the sealed door; the discovery of the tomb and treasures of Tutankhamun [by] Irene and Laurence Swinburne. Sniffen Court Bks. [distributed by Atheneum Pubs] 1977 96p illus $12.95 (5 and up)   932

1 Egypt—Antiquities 2 Tutenkhamûn, King of Egypt 3 Carter, Howard
ISBN 0-930790-01-4   LC 77-88476

"Published in cooperation with the Metropolitan Museum of Art"

"In 1922, after years of search, Howard Carter discovered the tomb of 'King Tut' and, unlike most of the pharaohs' burial sites, it had not been stripped of its treasures over the centuries (he was buried around 1344 B.C.) by grave robbers. The Swinburnes have written . . . [an] account of Carter's search and the painstakingly slow procedures used once the tomb was unearthed." Children's Bk Rev Serv

"The Swinburne's simplified text tells of the momentous event in an exciting, straightforward narrative. The photographs, many of which were taken on the scene by Harry Burton, are skillfully integrated into the text and are dramatically laid out to lead the reader through each successive discovery. . . . The photographs in color reveal a sampling of the priceless treasures unearthed by Carter, and a transparent insert shows the three coffins and the mummy of 'the boy king.'" Horn Bk

935 Mesopotamia and the Iranian Plateau to 637

Baumann, Hans

In the land of Ur; the discovery of ancient Mesopotamia; tr. by Stella Humphries. Pantheon Bks. 1969 166p illus map lib. bdg. $6.39 (6 and up)   935

1 Mesopotamia—Antiquities 2 Mesopotamia—Civilization
ISBN 0-394-90807-4   LC 77-77434

Original German edition, 1968

This "introduction to the early history of the 'land between the two rivers,' Mesopotamia, recounts the archaeological discoveries of the ruins of ziggurats and palaces and whole cities long buried under the shifting sands. . . . There are also: a glossary of the words, places, and people; a list of the more famous explorers of Mesopotamia; a listing of the major excavations; a chronological table with the names of the kings, and a map of the area." Best Sellers

It "is necessarily a fragmentary account. Still, it is somewhat redeemed . . . by Mr. Baumann's apt use of quotations from the cuneiform records, so many of which were found in the Assyria Library of Ashurbanipal, and by the similarly apt choice of color photos and line drawings." NY Times Bk Rev

Gregor, Arthur S.

How the world's first cities began; illus. by W. T. Mars. Dutton 1967 64p illus map lib. bdg. $6.50 (4-6)   935

1 Mesopotamia—Civilization 2 Cities and towns—History
ISBN 0-525-32417-8   LC 67-4594

In this book which focuses on the Mesopotamian civilization, the author unfolds the story of the long and gradual development of the first cities. Here also is the story of the emergence of civilization

"The illustrations are adequate, the book is written in an easy, conversational style." Chicago. Children's Bk Center

936.1 British Isles

Branley, Franklyn M.

The mystery of Stonehenge; illus. by Victor G. Ambrus. Crowell 1969 51p illus maps lib. bdg. $8.79 (4 and up)   936.1

1 Stonehenge 2 Great Britain—Antiquities
ISBN 0-690-57046-5   LC 69-11823

"How long did men toil to build the still-impressive ring of massive stones on the Salisbury plain? How did they do it, and what was it for? Scientists can only conjecture, save for the time of building, now determined by carbon-14 dating to have been approximately 1800 B.C. The author discusses the various theories about the ways in which primitive men might have made the stone pillars, brought them to the site, and erected them. He describes the tentative answers as to the reason for its existence: the possibility that it had religious significance or was used for astronomical observation. Fascinating material in a lucid, measured book, the handsome illustrations and diagrams making vivid the massive effort that went into the building of Stonehenge." Chicago. Children's Bk Center

Thwaite, Anthony

Beyond the inhabited world; Roman Britain. Seabury [distributed by Houghton] [1977 c1976] 125p illus $8.95 (6 and up)   936.1

1 Great Britain—History—To 1066 2 Great Britain—Antiquities
ISBN 0-395-28928-9   LC 76-17526

"A Clarion book"

First published 1976 in England

"For almost 400 years there were Roman troops in Britain: that is as long a period as from the time of Queen Elizabeth I to the present day. And the influence of Roman government and Roman habits lasted much longer than that, among the ordinary people of Britain—those people we call 'Romano-British'. This book tells you about the life of those people; their houses, farms, shops, temples, roads; how they fitted into the rest of the great Roman Empire, how they were ruled and how they sometimes rebelled against that rule; how they worked, what things they used, what they believed in." Introduction

This book "is primarily directed at a school-age audience and is well designed for its purpose with large clear print and numerous well reproduced photographs. . . . Anthony Thwaite has used some of the more accessible literature to provide a picture of Roman Britain which, if traditional, succeeds in being lively and imaginative, and is one which children will certainly find interesting reading." Times (London) Lit Sup

Bibliography: p119-21

937 Roman Empire

Brooks, Polly Schoyer

When the world was Rome, 753 B.C. to A.D. 476, by Polly Schoyer Brooks and Nancy Zinsser Walworth. Lippincott 1972 235p illus maps $9.95 (6 and up)   937

1 Rome—History
ISBN 0-397-31214-8   LC 76-179345

"An accurate, well-researched introduction to ancient Rome, enlivened with excerpts from writings of men of the various periods. Military expansion and political institutions are covered, along with interesting portraits of such men who wielded power as Gaius and Tiberius Gracchus, Pompey, Caesar, Octavius, Pliny the Younger and Pliny the Elder, Galen, and Constantine. Clear maps and reproductions lend authenticity to the text." School Library J

"Illustrated with many photographic reproductions; an extensive bibliography of ancient and modern sources, including books especially recommended for young readers, is appended." Booklist

[Fagg, Christopher]
Ancient Rome. Warwick Press [1979 c1978] 44p illus maps (Modern Knowledge lib) lib. bdg. $6.90 (4-6)   **937**

1 Rome—Civilization
ISBN 0-531-09110-4   LC 78-63100

First published 1978 in England
"Illustrators: Nigel Chamberlain, Brian and Constance Dear." Verso of title page
This book describes various aspects of the civilization of ancient Rome. A chronology of major events between 735 B.C. and 476 B.C. is included
Glossary: p42-43

Robinson, Charles Alexander
The first book of ancient Rome [by] Charles Alexander Robinson, Jr. [Rev. ed] Watts, F. [1965 c1964] 66p illus maps lib. bdg. $5.90 (4-6)   **937**

1 Rome—History 2 Rome—Civilization
ISBN 0-531-00466-X   LC 64-1774

First published 1959
Contents: The founding of Rome; The Roman Republic; Hannibal; Trouble in the State; Daily life in Rome; Julius Caesar; Cicero; Augustus and the Roman Empire; Literature and art in the Augustan Age; After Augustus; Constantine and Christianity; Rome's legacy; Words inherited from the Romans
"Keeping in mind that this is a 'first' book, with no pretensions of being comprehensive, much ground is covered in brief span. . . . This fills a definite need on this lower grade level." Library J

938   Greece to 323

Asimov, Isaac
The Greeks: a great adventure. Houghton 1965 326p illus maps $9.95 (6 and up)   **938**

1 Greece—History 2 Civilization, Greek
ISBN 0-395-06574-7   LC 65-12174

"A long, detailed, and lively history of ancient Greece from the first infiltration by southward-wandering tribes in 2000 B.C. through the centuries of warfare, the Golden Age, the decline of power, and—with the fall of Constantinople—the end of Greek influence. The last pages of the book bring the history of Greece up to date succinctly and competently. Despite the distracting use of parenthetical guides to pronunciation, the informally written text is enjoyable because of the conversational quality of the writing. The material is well-organized, divided into topics within chapters. A table of dates and an index, both lengthy, are appended." Chicago. Children's Bk Center

Coolidge, Olivia
The golden days of Greece; illus. by Enrico Arno. Crowell 1968 211p illus $9.95 (4-6)   **938**

1 Greece—History 2 Civilization, Greek
ISBN 0-690-33473-7   LC 68-21599

"Highlights of Greek history combined with anecdotes depicting the exploits of gods and men and accounts describing the lives and accomplishments of Greek philosophers, artists, poets, and playwrights provide a lively, illuminating introduction to ancient Greek civilition." Booklist
"The author draws parallels with contemporary situations and events and gives special attention to the everyday life of ancient Athenian and Spartan boys. The black-and-white Greek-style illustrations are usually good and there is a useful glossary." Sch Library J
"It is largely through the lives and exploits of notable personalities that the author presents her skillfully unified view of ancient Greece. Although the style is instructive and at times almost condescending the book provides a valuable basis for further study." Horn Bk

Robinson, Charles Alexander
The first book of ancient Greece, by Charles Alexander Robinson, Jr. Pictures by Lili Rethi. Watts, F. 1960 61p illus maps lib. bdg. $5.90 (4-6)   **938**

1 Civilization, Greek 2 Greece—Antiquities
ISBN 0-531-00463-5   LC 60-5570

"Robinson points out succinctly contributions of his ancient subject to life today, its role as creator 'of what we call Western civilization.' His survey of mythology, historical events, daily life, art, drama, and philosophy is brief, but of interest and value for first reading on the subject. Maps, index, lively and informative two-color sketches, and a glossary of words inherited from the Greeks [are included]." Horn Bk

[Rutland, Jonathan]
See inside an ancient Greek town [author: Jonathan Rutland; editor, Adrian Sington; illustrations: Bill Stallion, Linden Artists, Tudor Art] Warwick Press 1979 29p illus map lib. bdg. $6.90 (4 and up)   **938**

1 Greece—History 2 Civilization, Greek
ISBN 0-531-09159-7   LC 79-63368

"Elements of life in ancient Greece are reconstructed through clear, color photographs of artifacts, statuary, and present-day sites of historic ruins, along with diagrams and artists' renditions that show buildings as they looked 4,000 years ago. . . . [The book details] the agora (market-place), temples, gymnasium, homes, defenses, and occupations of the people. Especially worthwhile are the charts of the Greek alphabet, illustration of the Acropolis in its original state, list of festivals and their English equivalents, and cross section of a Greek home." Booklist
Glossary of terms: p28

Van Duyn, Janet
The Greeks; their legacy; illus. in black and white and full color. McGraw [1972] 192p illus maps (Early culture ser) lib. bdg. $8.50 (5 and up)   **938**

1 Civilization, Greek 2 Greece—Antiquities
ISBN 0-07-067038-2   LC 70-170885

The author traces the cultural heritage of ancient Greece, including the growth of democracy, the evolution of the theatre, the beginnings of scientific and philosophical investigation, and the start of the Olympic games
Suggested reading: p187-88

940.1   Europe—Middle Ages, 476-1453

Buehr, Walter
Knights and castles, and feudal life. Putnam 1957 72p illus lib. bdg. $5.29 (4 and up)   **940.1**

1 Knights and knighthood 2 Castles
ISBN 0-399-603417   LC 56-10267

"This book describes many aspects of life in feudal times, does not over-romanticize the glamour of knights and castles and shows something of the hard life led by peasants. It covers the daily life and household tasks in a castle as well as its layout and the ways by which it was defended against attack. It shows the different classes of society in the feudal system, the training of a knight, his arms and armour and describes a tourney and a typical siege." Ontario Library Rev

Uden, Grant
A dictionary of chivalry; illus. by Pauline Baynes. Crowell [1969 c1968] 352p illus $25 (6 and up)   **940.1**

1 Chivalry—Encyclopedias 2 Knights and knighthood—Encyclopedias 3 Civilization, Medieval
ISBN 0-690-23815-0   LC 67-10477

"A handsome, lively, and informative reference book on the Age of Chivalry. The alphabetically arranged entries range in length from one sentence to several paragraphs and cover such topics as people, events, places, accoutrements, clothing, and weapons, at times incorporating quotations from literature and early chronicles. Sharply drawn illustrations, some in full color, border each page of easy-to-read single-column type. Numerous cross-references throughout the text and an appended subject index add to the usefulness of the book." Booklist

Unstead, R. J.

Living in a castle; illus. by Victor Ambrus. Addison-Wesley 1971 43p illus (The 'Living in' ser) lib. bdg. $5.95 (4-6) **940.1**

1 Feudalism 2 Castles
ISBN 0-201-08495-3

A fictional account of daily life in a feudal castle in southern England in the year 1250. The author describes the various occupants of the castle and their traditional duties, and details the events of a single day, from the business problems of the lord and his steward to the menu of the evening meal. Included also is an analysis of the architectural plan of the castle

940.3 World War I, 1914-1918

Hoobler, Dorothy

An album of World War I, by Dorothy and Thomas Hoobler. Watts, F. 1976 96p illus maps lib. bdg. $7.90 (5 and up) **940.3**

1 World War, 1914-1918
ISBN 0-531-01169-0   LC 75-44281

An "overview of World War I that charts its progression by briefly describing major battles. The prologue scans contemporary European politics, listing key nations and their relationship with each other. The remainder of the presentation considers the important military maneuvers of each consecutive year till the war's end. There is no overt editorializing; statistics are left to speak for themselves. Photographs, at least one per page, show political leaders, battle maps, and troops of both sides." Booklist
"Thankfully, the Hooblers have selected many photos which have not appeared in other similar accounts." Sch Library J

Snyder, Louis L.

The first book of World War I; maps by Leonard Derwinski. Watts, F. 1958 94p illus maps lib. bdg. $6.45 (5 and up) **940.3**

1 World War, 1914-1918
ISBN 0-531-00675-1   LC 58-5813

Companion volume to the author's: The first book of World War II, class 940.53
"An interesting and informative overview of the first World War. The author has, by presenting the events that set the stage for the conflict and by making clear the relationship between the harsh treaty of World War I and the inevitability of World War II, given more than a record of one war. The book shows as well the confusion and complication of political and economic relationships between countries." Chicago. Children's Bk Center
"Like the other volume this is profusely illustrated with well-chosen photographs." Booklist
World War I words: p94

940.4 World War I, 1914-1918 (Military conduct of the war)

Hoobler, Dorothy

The trenches; fighting on the Western Front in World War I, by Dorothy and Thomas Hoobler. Putnam 1978 191p illus maps $9.95 **940.4**

1 World War, 1914-1918—Campaigns and battles
ISBN 0-399-20640-X   LC 78-2698

"The horrific warfare of the trenches is the focus of this history of the first World War. Using personal narratives from participants on both sides, the authors describe the bloody, futile struggles that followed the fortification of the western front. Sacrificing some clarity by interspersing the descriptions of trench life with the narrative of the military campaigns, the Hooblers still achieve . . . [an] image of the reality of war and its stunning impact on the individual soldier." Horn Bk
For further reading: p180-85

940.53 World War 2, 1939-1945

Leckie, Robert

The story of World War II; illus. with photographs & maps. Random House 1964 193p illus maps $4.95, lib. bdg. $5.99 (5 and up) **940.53**

1 World War, 1939-1945
ISBN 0-394-80295-0; 0-394-90295-5   LC 64-21721

"Landmarks books"
"Designed for 'reading' rather than reference. This account . . . gives more space to the war in the Pacific than other areas. The struggle in Finland, in Norway and the Balkans; the fall of France; the Battle of Britain; the campaigns in North Africa and Italy; all these are described in readable but not overly dramatised chapters which would give the young reader a fair picture of the events of those days." Toronto

Snyder, Louis L.

The first book of World War II. Watts, F. 1958 94p illus maps lib. bdg. $6.45, pa $1.25 (5 and up) **940.53**

1 World War, 1939-1945
ISBN 0-531-00676-X; 0-531-023-02319-2 LC 58-5167

Companion volume to the author's: The first book of World War I, class 940.3
"Here in brief are causes, occasion, the 'phony' war, Dunkirk, 'Hitler master of Europe' after the fall of France, and the Battle of Britain. Then the various theaters of war are mentioned, the Balkans, North Africa, and the Pacific after the Japanese attack on Pearl Harbor. Finally there is the closing in on the Germans in Europe and the A-Bomb victory over Japan. Some suggestions of the problems of peace are made with hope for victory over war itself." NY Her Trib Bks
"The writing is lively, maps are good, and the book [is] . . . profusely illustrated with photographs." Chicago. Children's Bk Center
World War II words: p93

940.54 World War 2, 1939-1945 (Military conduct of the war)

Bliven, Bruce

The story of D-Day: June 6, 1944; illus. by Albert Orbaan. Random House 1956 180p illus map $2.95, lib. bdg. $5.99 (5 and up) **940.54**

1 Normandy, Attack on, 1944
ISBN 0-394-80362-0; 0-394-90362-5   LC 56-5458

"Landmark books"
An account of the planning and resources of the Allied invasion of Normandy which was the turning point of the Second World War, and of the brave men who implemented it
"A brief, dramatic account . . . recommended for reluctant older readers." Hodges. Bks for Elem Sch Libraries

Carter, Hodding

The Commandos of World War II; illus. with photographs and maps. Random House 1966 168p illus maps $2.95, lib. bdg. $5.99 (5 and up) **940.54**

1 Great Britain. Combined Operations Command
2 World War, 1939-1945
ISBN 0-394-80561-5; 0-394-90561-X   LC 66-15407

"World Landmark books"
"The Commandos (first formed to hit Germany through France in World War II) were highly skilled as a hit-and-run force of guerilla fighters, specializing in speed and surprise. Based on actual British war records, the origin, training, and operations of these skilled volunteer soldiers are reported in a straightforward narrative. A brief picture of their wartime activity in England and elsewhere is given along with character portrayals of a few of the leaders. The author achieves dramatic impact as he portrays the heroism and the dangers endured by this group. The illustrations enhance and clarify the text." Sch Library J
Bibliography: p161-62

Graff, Stewart

The story of World War II; illus. with photographs. Dutton 1978 88p illus maps lib. bdg. $7.95 (4-6)   **940.54**

1 World War, 1939-1945
ISBN 0-525-40355-8   LC 77-7522

This book describes "Hitler's invasion of Poland, his march on Russia, the opening of the Pacific theater with Japan's attack on Pearl Harbor, the North Atlantic sea battles, the North African front, etc.—without getting bogged down in sideline detail. With black-and-white war photographs and an index for easy access." Booklist

Hough, Richard

The Battle of Britain; the triumph of R.A.F. fighter pilots. Macmillan Pub. Co. 1971 88p illus maps $5.95 (5 and up)   **940.54**

1 Britain, Battle of, 1940   2 World War, 1939-1945
—Aerial operations
ISBN 0-02-744590-9   LC 73-138029

An account of the Luftwaffe's air invasion of England and the struggle of the Royal Air Force to bring about the defeat of the Germans in the Battle of Britain

"Hough's book is a well-written, well-organized account of the battle. While never neglecting the human interest aspect, Hough concentrates on presenting readers with a very clear picture of why the Battle of Britain was important, and why and how it was won by the British and lost by Germany. . . . The photographs are plentiful and well selected." Library J

For further reading: p86

Reynolds, Quentin

The Battle of Britain; illus. by Clayton Knight. Random House 1953 182p illus lib. bdg. $5.99 (6 and up)   **940.54**

1 Britain, Battle of, 1940   2 World War, 1939-1945
—Personal narratives   3 World War, 1939-1945—
Aerial operations
ISBN 0-394-90510-5   LC 53-6267

"World Landmark books"

"An account of the 83 days it took to defeat the German Luftwaffe's air invasion of England told very simply by a newspaper correspondent who was there to observe it. Because of the successful transmittal of British understatement, the book provides an objective appraisal of the action without an emotional involvement on the part of the reader." Booklist

Shirer, William L.

The sinking of the Bismarck; illus. with photographs & maps. Random House 1962 178p illus maps lib. bdg. $5.99 (5 and up)   **940.54**

1 Bismarck (Battleship)   2 World War, 1939-1945
—Naval operations
ISBN 0-394-90551-2   LC 62-7877

"World landmark books"

A "reconstruction of the sinking of the German battleship 'Bismarck' by Great Britain in 1941. The suspenseful account begins with the British Admiralty's receipt of a report that the 'Bismarck' had been sighted heading for the North Atlantic, follows the more than 2,000-mile chase of the elusive ship through heavy seas, and closes with the cornering and sinking of the battleship." Booklist

"Maps help make even clearer this unforgettable story of courage and dogged determination." NY Her Trib Bks

A note on sources: p171-72

Taylor, Theodore

Air raid—Pearl Harbor! The story of December 7, 1941; illus. by W. T. Mars. Crowell 1971 185p illus maps $8.95 (5 and up)   **940.54**

1 Pearl Harbor, Attack on, 1941
ISBN 0-690-05373-8   LC 76-132303

"Well-documented and written with all the suspense of a mystery story, this is a detailed account of the events that led up to the disaster of Pearl Harbor. The story is told both from the American and the Japanese viewpoints, with all of the errors in planning, the gaps in communication, the secrecy of tactics and strategy; the text moves from the flurries of activity in Washington, the veiled manoeuvres of the fleet that had sailed from Japan in November, to the pre-Christmas relaxation of Pearl Harbor, the diplomatic backing and the filling gaining impetus as December 7 approaches." Sutherland. The Best in Children's Bks

Bibliography: p177-78

Battle in the Arctic seas; the story of convoy PQ 17; illus. by Robert Andrew Parker. Crowell 1976 151p illus $8.95 (6 and up)   **940.54**

1 World War, 1939-1945—Naval operations
2 World War, 1939-1945—Arctic Ocean
ISBN 0-690-01084-2   LC 75-33655

"A Guild book"

"World War II's Convoy PQ 17 was slated to carry much-needed military supplies to Russians engaged in holding back German forces. The convoy's course took it through Arctic waters patrolled by German air and sea craft. Using diary excerpts and present-tense narrative, Taylor sets the scene and charts the converging events that influenced Allied commanders in their decision to abandon protective measures for the convoy. The order for them to 'scatter' ensured German attack, and when it came the results were disastrous: Taylor records that never in contemporary military history did a convoy lose as many ships as PQ 17. Reportage of this 'bitter military lesson' is succinct yet many-sided; an instructive close-up for the World War II section of your history shelf." Booklist

Bibliography: p143-44

Tregaskis, Richard

John F. Kennedy and PT-109. Random House 1962 192p illus lib. bdg. $5.99 (5 and up)   **940.54**

1 Kennedy, John Fitzgerald, President U.S.
2 PT-109 (Boat)   3 World War, 1939-1945—Naval operations
ISBN 0-394-90399-4   LC 62-9009

"Landmark books"

"A good book about operations in the Solomon Islands during World War II, with the story of Kennedy's shipwreck while in command of Torpedo Patrol-109. The material is dramatic, some of the battle scenes are vividly described, and there is no adulatory note in any of the author's references to Lt. Kennedy." Chicago. Children's Bk Center

"The book is best through the graphic descriptions of the disaster when PT-109 was struck by the Japanese destroyer and the excitement surrounding the efforts of Kennedy to save his crew. . . . Young readers will find this an attractive and inspiring offering." Best Sellers

941   British Isles

Hinds, Lorna

Looking at Great Britain. Lippincott 1973 64p illus maps (Looking at other countries) $8.95 (4-6)   **941**

1 Great Britain
ISBN 0-397-31335-7   LC 73-5947

This is an introduction to the history, geography, people, customs, and industries of Great Britain

"The attractive format—photographs, half in color, appear on every page—is the outstanding feature of this supplemental book. The pictures are well synchronized with the text which combines geography with a short travelogue on England, Wales, and Scotland. . . . British terms are used in the text; however, there is no glossary to explain 'firth,' 'moor,' etc." Sch Library J

941.1   Scotland

Campbell, Donald Grant

Scotland in pictures; prepared by Donald Grant Campbell, Irving Nach and others. Sterling 1979 64p illus map (Visual geography ser) lib. bdg. $4.99, pa $2.95 (4 and up)   **941.1**

1 Scotland
ISBN 0-8069-1051-8; 0-8069-1050-X   LC 79-106472

First published 1963

The book describes the land, history, government, people, and economy of Scotland

941.5 Ireland

Ireland in pictures; prepared by Rhoda Fagen and others. Sterling 1978 64p illus map (Visual geography ser) lib. bdg. $4.99, pa $2.95 (4 and up) **941.5**

1 Ireland
ISBN 0-8069-1025-9; 0-8069-1024-0 LC 62-12600
First published 1962
Ireland's geography, history, government, people, and economy are the topics covered

O'Brien, Elinor
The land and people of Ireland. Rev. ed. Lippincott 1972 159p illus map (Portraits of the nations ser) $8.95 (5 and up) **941.5**

1 Ireland
ISBN 0-397-31299-7 LC 76-38335
First published 1953
This is an introduction to the history, geography, culture and people of Ireland

942 England and Wales

Goodall, John S.
The story of an English village. Atheneum Pubs. 1979 unp illus $7.95 (3-6) **942**

1 Cities and towns—England—Pictorial works
ISBN 0-689-50125-0 LC 78-56242
"A Margaret K. McElderry book"
First published 1978 in England
"Beginning with a fourteenth-century rural site that includes a wayside cross, a church, and a thatched cottage—all dominated by a castle stronghold—the wordless illustrations show the same place and the same house, both interior and exterior, over a period of six hundred years. Gradually the peaceful crossroads change into the center of a country village, which later becomes a thriving town, then a prosperous city, and finally a scene of traffic-jammed urban sprawl. Not only the inanimate objects but the people as well—their activities, costumes, and general demeanor—reflect the shifting pattern of life over the centuries." Horn Bk
"The details are interesting, and the book gives a good picture of the growth and change in an English village, but the appeal may be limited, for some readers, by a static quality and by unfamiliarity of some of the details." Chicago. Children's Bk Center

Street, Alicia
The land and people of England. Rev. ed. Lippincott 1969 155p illus map (Portraits of the nations ser) $8.95 (5 and up) **942**

1 Great Britain
ISBN 0-397-31373-X LC 68-10769
First published 1946 with title: The land of the English people
The book discusses England's history, geographical area, social life and customs, natural resources, agriculture and industry

942.01 England—Early history to 1066

Crossley-Holland, Kevin
Green blades rising; the Anglo-Saxons. Seabury [distributed by Houghton] 1976 [c1975] 143p illus maps $8.95 (6 and up) **942.01**

1 Anglo-Saxons 2 Great Britain—History—To 1066
ISBN 0-8164-3154-X LC 75-4576
"A Clarion book"
First published 1975 in England
"This book describes in detail the cultural achievements and the daily life of the Anglo-Saxons. . . . The author explores poetry, sculpture, architecture, jewelry, the manuscripts which

were copied by the Anglo-Saxon monks and artistic productions. . . . Later, King Alfred was a powerful promoter of education. He reestablished monasteries and monastic schools, he urged bishops to start cathedral schools, he learned Latin himself and translated five great Anglo-Saxon books. He set out to make his court a center of education. . . . The twelfth century saw the development of religious literature and literary and scholarly achievements. The book gives a remarkable picture of the Anglo-Saxon life and its contributions to our own. There are excellent black-and-white illustrations and maps and the colored plates." Best Sellers
Bibliography: p137-39

942.02 England—Norman period, 1066-1154

Duggan, Alfred
Growing up with the Norman Conquest; illus. by C. Walter Hodges. Pantheon Bks. [1966 c1965] 217p illus lib. bdg. $5.99 (6 and up) **942.02**

1 Great Britain—History—Norman period, 1066-1154 2 Great Britain—Social life and customs
ISBN 0-394-91206-3 LC 65-20654
First published 1955 in England
This book describes the daily life of children during the reign of William the Conqueror at various economic levels "in a Norman castle, a Saxon hall, a London house, an abbey, a peasant village. Food, clothing, recreation, education, and daily work routines are all shown . . . also, the growing complexity of the lives of these people, as language, law, and age-old custom felt the breath of change." Christian Sci Monitor
Mr. Duggan's writing displays "delightful wit, and the easy familiarity with detail that is born only of deep knowledge." Chicago. Children's Bk Center

942.05 England—Tudor period, 1485-1603

Hodges, C. Walter
The battlement garden; Britain from the Wars of the Roses to the Age of Shakespeare. Houghton/Clarion [1980 c1979] 144p illus map $10.95 (6 and up) **942.05**

1 Great Britain—History—Tudors, 1485-1603 2 Great Britain—Civilization
ISBN 0-395-29184-4 LC 79-15849
First published 1979 in England
"A descriptive account and appreciation of the age of the Tudors. Although the great historical events of the era are not neglected, the course of life in sixteenth-century England is made vivid essentially by its association with personalities. . . . Royalty and commoners, country life and London life, entertainment and the arts, education and the theater are all evoked. . . . The book admirably exercises skillful control over its rich and complex subject matter." Horn Bk

943 Germany

Wohlrabe, Raymond A.
The land and people of Germany, by Raymond A. Wohlrabe and Werner E. Krusch. Rev. ed. Lippincott 1972 159p illus map (Portraits of the nations ser) $8.95 (5 and up) **943**

1 Germany
ISBN 0-397-31261-X LC 75-37248
First published 1957
This introduction to Germany, past and present, describes the history, geography, economy, culture and people of the Federal Republic of Germany as well as the German Democratic Republic

943.085　Germany—Weimar Republic, 1918-1933

Switzer, Ellen

How democracy failed. Atheneum Pubs. 1975 176p illus $7.95 (4 and up)　　**943.085**

1 Germany—History—1918-1933 2 Germany—History—1933-1945
ISBN 0-689-30459-5　　　　　　LC 74-19461

"The author, who lived through the decline of the Weimar Republic, decided to interview those who, like herself, had been teenagers in the 1930's. 'Looking back, might they be able to shed some light on what had happened in their country and why? And might their insights perhaps provide a useful lesson to us in the United States?' As a result of her travels in Germany in 1972 and 1973, she has created a unique kind of history-as-reminiscence. Present-day German artists, politicians, teachers, or journalists could recall exactly when the Nazi era began for them; for one boy, it began when he saw uniformed men 'heaving bricks, bottles and boulders' through the glass display cases of Berlin's largest department store. A personal account rather than a documented study, the narrative has an easy, conversational tone." Horn Bk

943.086　Germany—Third Reich, 1933-1945

Goldston, Robert C.

The life and death of Nazi Germany; illus. with photographs and drawings by Donald Carrick. Bobbs 1967 224p illus maps $7.95 (5 and up)　　**943.086**

1 Germany—Politics and government—1933-1945
2 Hitler, Adolf 3 National socialism
ISBN 0-672-50354-9　　　　　　LC 66-29906

"The history of Germany is covered in enough detail to give the reader an understanding of the forces and factors that made possible the emergence of a Hitler and the subservience of a people whose cultural achievements and heritage should have made them impervious to demagoguery. The author's contempt for Hitler and his followers . . . [is evident]. The rise of the Nazi party and the course of events that led to the war are described in great detail. . . . The author gives a broad picture of the roles of other nations and of the forces and important figures within the country. Intelligent, lucid, and dramatic—an absorbing and important book." Chicago. Children's Bk Center
Bibliography: p213-16

943.087　Germany—Later 20th century, 1945-

Dornberg, John

The two Germanys. Dial Press 1974 215p illus maps $8.95 (5 and up)　　**943.087**

1 Germany, East 2 Germany, West
ISBN 0-8037-8757-X　　　　　　LC 73-15446

The author "discusses the events leading up to the division of Germany and then gives an objective overview of East and West German national development, including short biographies of influential leaders, the industrial boom after World War II, the role of women, and the future of youth. Interesting anecdotes provide insight into the differences between the people of both nations. This concise, well-written account . . . is mostly free of the biases which mar many other books on the subject." Sch Library J
Recommended readings: p207-09

943.1　East Germany

Fles, Barthold

East Germany. Watts, F. 1973 64p illus map lib. bdg. $4.90 (4 and up)　　**943.1**

1 Germany, East
ISBN 0-531-00807-X　　　　　　LC 73-5816

"A First book"
Illustrated with photographs
"After a brief summary of events, post World War II, that led to the growth of the GDR (Communist German Democratic Republic), the author . . . traces 'political, industrial, social, and cultural development of East Germany.' The Berlin Wall, labor troubles, rebuilding industries and homes, commodity shortages, educational restructuring, cultural changes based on a government-centered atmosphere rather than on individual-oriented goals [are all described]." Best Sellers
Bibliography: p62

Singer, Julia

Impressions; a trip to the German Democratic Republic; text and pictures by Julia Singer. Atheneum Pubs. 1979 172p illus $8.95 (4-6)　　**943.1**

1 Germany, East
ISBN 0-689-30696-2　　　　　　LC 78-11299

"A six-week trip to East Germany in 1977, in which Singer visited children and their parents in homes and schools, provides focus for the author's comments and reflections on life in the German Democratic Republic. Young American readers will find commonalities of life-style and interests as the author describes daily events, family celebrations, and school festivities; however, Singer's efforts result in a near-paradisiacal picture of children who are always happy, healthy, well behaved, and highly motivated. Middle-grade children are featured and seem to be the book's target audience as well; yet background knowledge of East Germany's political situation, of terms such as cooperative farming, fascism, apprenticeships, and a socialist state is necessary. The text, arranged by places visited, would benefit from maps, and the lack of an index deters research; nevertheless, the warm personal feelings emerging from Singer's journeys overflow the pages and can provide new insights for children who share this with an adult commentator." Booklist

943.6　Austria

Rothkopf, Carol Zeman

Austria. Watts, F. 1976 68p illus maps lib. bdg. $4.90 (4 and up)　　**943.6**

1 Austria
ISBN 0-531-00842-8　　　　　　LC 75-38675

"A First book"
"An introduction to the history, people, customs, and culture of Austria through descriptions of the nine provinces. In discussing each one, the author relates its geography, economic resources, tourist attractions, food specialties, and famous citizens, resulting in a distinct feeling for the country and people. A brief historical review traces the rise of the empire through the rule of the Habsburgs to the emergence of the republic after World War I. A special summary features essential facts about geography, economy, and government. Black-and-white photographs accompany the text." Booklist

Wohlrabe, Raymond A.

The land and people of Austria, by Raymond A. Wohlrabe and Werner E. Krusch. Rev. ed. Lippincott 1972 159p illus map (Portraits of the nations ser) $8.95 (5 and up)　　**943.6**

1 Austria
ISBN 0-397-31395-0　　　　　　LC 72-5518

First published 1956
An introduction to the people, history, geography, and culture of the European country known for its famous composers and scenic beauty, particularly the Alps, and the Danube region

943.7　Czechoslovakia

Hall, Elvajean

The land and people of Czechoslovakia. [Rev] Lippincott [1972 c1966] 154p illus map (Portraits of the nations ser) $8.95 (5 and up)　　**943.7**

1 Czechoslovakia
ISBN 0-397-31601-1　　　　　　LC 79-37762

Hall, Elvajean—*Continued*

First published 1966
This "account describes the geographic features and complex history of Czechoslovakia and the varied cultural heritage of the people. The book also describes the formation of the nation following World War I, the tragic events leading to and during the German occupation of the country under Hitler, the establishment of a communist government after World War II, and the effect of communism on present-day Czechoslovakian life and customs." Booklist [review of the 1966 edition]

943.8 Poland

Kelly, Eric Philbrook

The land and people of Poland; rev. by Dragos D. Kostich. Rev. ed. Lippincott 1972 143p illus map (Portraits of the nations ser) $7.95 (5 and up)   943.8

1 Poland
ISBN 0-397-31313-6   LC 73-37924

First published 1943 with title: The land of the Polish people
This book covers Poland's history, the cities of Krakow and Warsaw as they were before the past war and as they are today, people of the past and the present, folklore, and social life and customs. Includes keys to pronunciation

943.9 Hungary

Gidal, Sonia

My village in Hungary. Pantheon Bks. 1974 86p illus maps lib. bdg. $5.69 (3-6)   943.9

1 Hungary—Social life and customs
ISBN 0-394-92127-5   LC 74-152

"Zoltán Sardi, a Hungarian farmer's son, describes his family, village, and country. Gidal follows him to school, to the commune where he is researching a homework assignment, and to the homes of friends. An excellent addition to the series, this boasts exceptional black-and-white photographs, a glossary of Hungarian words used; and maps of Hungary as well as Zoltán's village." Sch Library J

944 France

Bragdon, Lillian J.

The land and people of France. Rev. ed. Lippincott 1972 157p illus map (Portraits of the nations ser) lib. bdg. $8.95 (5 and up)   944

1 France
ISBN 0-397-31190-7   LC 78-37605

First published 1939 with title: The land of Joan of Arc
The author describes the geography of France from the metropolitan centers to the famous resort areas and provinces. Also provided is a discussion of France's complex history

945 Italy

Epstein, Sam

The first book of Italy. Rev. ed. by Sam and Beryl Epstein; illus. with photographs. Watts, F. 1972 90p illus map lib. bdg. $4.90 (4 and up)   945

1 Italy
ISBN 0-531-00562-3   LC 72-257

First published 1958
The book provides a "description of the religion, art, education, crafts, living conditions, and politics of the Italian people, with geographical and historical facts interwoven throughout." Sch Library J

Winwar, Frances

The land and people of Italy. Rev. ed. Lippincott 1972 159p illus map (Portraits of the nations ser) $8.95 (5 and up)   945

1 Italy
ISBN 0-397-31300-4   LC 79-38309

First published 1951 with title: The land of the Italian people
This survey of Italian geography, culture and history offers information on the Renaissance, industry, literature, art, and notable Italians, including Marco Polo, Columbus, Michelangelo, and Mussolini

946 Spain

Goldston, Robert

Spain. Watts, F. 1972 88p illus maps lib. bdg. $4.90 (4 and up)   946

1 Spain
ISBN 0-531-00781-2   LC 72-3717

"A First book"
The author describes the geography, history, industry, people, culture and projected future of Spain
He "emphasizes the many changes which have taken place in Spain and tells how the tourist boom has influenced the country's economy in recent years. Well illustrated with black-and-white photographs and three maps." Booklist

Loder, Dorothy

The land and people of Spain. Rev. ed. Lippincott 1972 157p illus map (Portraits of the nations ser) $8.95 (5 and up)   946

1 Spain
ISBN 0-397-31303-9   LC 72-1368

First published 1955
This book describes the history and civilization of Spain, with accounts of its foreign domination, influences, religion, and political conflicts from the times of the Romans, through the Moors and Napoleon to the Civil War and contemporary factions. Places of note are described, and attention is given to the country's commerce, industry and natural resources, and the life of the people
"An especially interesting aspect of the account is the introduction of outstanding writers and artists, with a discussion of how their work reflects the section of the country in which each lived or the temper of the times in which each one worked." Chicago. Children's Bk Center [review of the 1955 edition]

947 Russia

Almedingen, E. M.

Land of Muscovy; the history of early Russia; illus. by Michael Charlton. Farrar, Straus [1972 c1971] 147p illus map lib. bdg. $4.95 (5 and up)   947

1 Russia—History
ISBN 0-374-34310-1   LC 72-79864

First published 1971 in England with title: Rus into Muscovy
This work deals with "the early history of Russia, primarily the reign of Ivan IV, known as Ivan the Terrible, and his successors up to the start of a new dynasty with Michael Romanov. In addition to tracing political events Almedingen details the daily life and customs of city and country folk in a briskly written account that will interest history buff or student." Booklist

Hewitt, Philip

Looking at Russia. Lippincott 1977 64p illus (Looking at other countries) $8.95 (4-6)   947

1 Russia
ISBN 0-397-31747-6   LC 76-41169

"Photographs, some black and white, some in sharp, clear color, emphasize the 'looking at' aspect of the title. The accompanying commentary briefly sketches history, government, and daily life before proceeding to a systematic introduction of major regions; Moscow and Leningrad are especially highlighted. The tone is cooly nonpartisan, though little feel of the people themselves comes through—a flaw considering today's availability of information. . . . Useful for classroom assignments and browsing." Booklist

Morton, Miriam

Pleasures and palaces; the after-school activities of Russian children. Atheneum Pubs 1972 136p illus map $5.25 (4 and up)   **947**

1 Children in Russia 2 Russia—Social life and customs
ISBN 0-689-30057-3   LC 72-76477

This is an account of the activity circles or kruzhki, sponsored by the Young Pioneers to help Soviet children decide on future careers. These meetings are held in pioneer palaces, hence the title, and serve as an after-school activity for children to enjoy

"Motivated Soviet students are described in the various career activities that are offered—not unlike the current emphasis on career education courses in the United States. An interesting aspect is the apparent lack of stereotyped sex roles in career orientation." Notable Children's Trade Bks (Social Studies)

Nazaroff, Alexander

The land and people of Russia. [Rev] Lippincott [1972 c1966] 190p illus maps (Portraits of the nations ser) lib. bdg. $8.95 (5 and up)   **947**

1 Russia
ISBN 0-397-30706-3   LC 70-37860

First published 1944 with title: The land of the Russian people

A survey of Russia's history from the earliest times through rule by the czars and emperors to the present Soviets. It describes also the country's vast and varied terrain, including Siberia, Moscow, Leningrad and western Russia

Rice, Tamara Talbot

Finding out about the early Russians; introduction by Harrison E. Salisbury. Lothrop [1964 c1962] 168p illus maps $6.75 (6 and up)   **947**

1 Russia—History 2 Russia—Civilization 3 Russia—Antiquities
ISBN 0-688-41233-5   LC 64-14442

First published 1963 in England. Line drawings by Margaret Scott, maps by Ursula Suess

"Russian history from 3000 B.C. to the time of Peter the Great is surveyed with special attention to the Russian influence on world art, architecture, and religion. Maps and numerous photographs and paintings illustrate the text." Hodges. Bks for Elem Sch Libraries

Snyder, Louis L.

The first book of the Soviet Union. Rev. ed. Watts, F. 1972 84p illus map lib. bdg. $4.90 (4 and up)   **947**

1 Russia
ISBN 0-531-00638-7   LC 78-4842

First published 1959

The author traces the life of the Soviet Uion from czarist rule through the revolution of 1917 to the modern Communist state. Also detailed are the stages in Soviet space exploration. Facts about geography, education, and activities of the people complete this presentation

948 Scandinavia

Carter, Samuel

Vikings bold: their voyages & adventures, by Samuel Carter III; illus. by Ted Burwell. Crowell 1972 195p illus maps $8.95 (5 and up)   **948**

1 Vikings
ISBN 0-690-86191-5   LC 70-127602

The author describes the life of the Vikings on land and sea, including their advanced form of democracy, their great leaders, their military triumphs and rare defeats, and their westward journeys which brought them to Iceland, Greenland, and eventually the coast of North America

Selected further reading: p189-90

Rich, Louise Dickinson

The first book of the Vikings; pictures by Lili Réthi. Watts, F. 1962 66p illus map lib. bdg. $4.90 (4 and up)   **948**

1 Vikings
ISBN 0-531-00660-3   LC 62-7390

Here is "the life of the Vikings at home and abroad: their democratic organization, laws, games, their ships, their love of the sea and the feeling of brotherhood expressed in their sagas, all told in a manner that stirs the imagination and conveys the author's own interest in her subject. Illustrations are black-and-white pen drawings, and are useful for school projects." Ontario Library Rev

"Much more information about the Vikings than is usually found in books for elementary schools. . . . No bibliography, unfortunately." Horn Bk

The **Vikings**, by the editors of Horizon Magazine. Author: Frank R. Donovan; consultant: Sir Thomas D. Kendrick. Illus. with drawings, illuminations, carvings, and maps, many of the period. Am. Heritage [distributed by Harper] 1964 153p illus maps $9.95, lib. bdg. $12.89 (6 and up)   **948**

1 Vikings
ISBN 0-06-021715-4; 0-06-021716-2   LC 64-17106

"A Horizon Caravel book"

An account of the Scandinavians of 800-1100 B.C. who raided and plundered, then settled the lands of Europe, and also discovered Greenland

"A profusely illustrated and immensely detailed book about the Vikings, well-organized and written in a style that is slightly ponderous. Mr Donovan gives good general background material about the Northmen, then follows with accounts of their raids and explorations in different parts of the world. In discussing the Vikings in the New World, the author is most careful to distinguish between fact and conjecture. In addition to the index there is appended a list of suggestions for further reading, the list being accompanied by a useful note on museums and libraries in the United States that contain Viking art or artifacts." Chicago. Children's Bk Center

948.1 Norway

Hall, Elvajean

The land and people of Norway. Rev. ed. Lippincott 1973 159p illus map (Portraits of the nations ser) $8.95 (5 and up)   **948.1**

1 Norway
ISBN 0-397-31408-6   LC 72-10777

First published 1963

This is a survey of the history, geography, social life and customs, and the politics and government of Norway. The author also describes Norway's status as an industrial nation and as a participant in international trade

948.5 Sweden

Arbman, Maj

Looking at Sweden. Lippincott 1971 64p illus (Looking at other countries) lib. bdg. $8.95 (4-6)   **948.5**

1 Sweden
ISBN 0-397-31362-4   LC 78-128403

"The book gives a fairly revealing if sketchy view of Sweden describing the people and their homes, the country's history, cities and regions, industry, education, and recreation. Less tourist-oriented than some of the other titles in the series but, like them, of particular interest and value for its good color and black-and-white photographs. Maps, facts, and figures on the endpapers." Booklist

948.9 Denmark

Wohlrabe, Raymond A.
The land and people of Denmark, by
Raymond A. Wohlrabe and Werner E.
Krusch. Rev. ed. Lippincott 1972 160p illus
map (Portraits of the nations ser) $8.95 (5
and up)   **948.9**
1 Denmark
ISBN 0-397-31296-2   LC 70-37942
First published 1961
"This profile of Denmark traces its history from
prehistoric times to the present, takes the reader
on a tour of the country, discusses the art, music,
literature and men of science, and describes life,
customs, agriculture, and industry in present-day
Denmark. . . . Illustrated with a few photographs
and a map." Booklist
"Naturally there is a chapter on Hans Christian
Andersen. This is a worthwhile addition to any
library." Best Sellers

948.97 Finland

Berry, Erick
The land and people of Finland. Rev. ed.
Lippincott 1972 159p illus map (Portraits of
the nations ser) $8.95 (5 and up)   **948.97**
1 Finland
ISBN 0-397-31255-5   LC 78-37246
First published 1959
This study of Finnish people traces the history
of Finland from its nomadic origins through
centuries of Swedish and Russian domination to
the present. Also included is a description of the
country's geographical features. Descriptions of
the Finnish cultural heritage, of mythology and
folk literature, and the social and economic life
styles complete the presentation

949.1 Iceland

Berry, Erick
The land and people of Iceland. Rev. ed.
Lippincott 1972 158p illus map (Portraits of
the nations ser) $8.95 (5 and up)   **949.1**
1 Iceland
ISBN 0-397-31401-9   LC 72-1569
First published 1959
This is an introduction to Iceland, describing the
history, geography, economy, culture and people of
the island republic

949.2 Netherlands

Barnouw, Adriaan J.
The land and people of Holland, by Adriaan
J. Barnouw and Raymond A. Wohlrabe. Rev.
ed. Lippincott 1972 159p illus map (Portraits
of the nations ser) $8.95 (5 and up)   **949.2**
1 Netherlands
ISBN 0-397-31254-7   LC 79-37249
First published 1961
This is an introduction to the history, geography,
people and culture of Holland

Cohn, Angelo
The first book of the Netherlands. Rev.
ed. Illus. with photographs. Watts, F. 1971
80p illus map lib. bdg. $4.90 (4 and up) **949.2**
1 Netherlands
ISBN 0-531-00593-3   LC 73-189995
First published 1962
The author explains the important role geography
has played in the history and development of the
Netherlands. Information about the government,
cities, industries, culture and unique qualities of
the country is included
Other books to read: p77

949.3 Belgium

Loder, Dorothy
The land and people of Belgium. Rev. ed.
Lippincott 1973 143p illus maps (Portraits of
the nations ser) $8.95 (5 and up)   **949.3**
1 Belgium
ISBN 0-397-31462-0   LC 72-13301
First published 1957
The author surveys Belgium's history and cities,
as well as the way of life of the Flemish-speaking
people and the Walloons, or French-speaking
people

949.5 Greece

Gianakoulis, Theodore
The land and people of Greece. [Rev] Lippincott [1972 c1965] 160p illus map (Portraits
of the nations ser) $8.95 (5 and up)   **949.5**
1 Greece, Modern 2 Greece
ISBN 0-397-31523-6   LC 75-37745
First published 1952
Against a detailed background of Greek history
from earliest to modern times, this book surveys
Greece's physical geography, culture, government,
and social and economic conditions

Warren, Ruth
Modern Greece. Rev. ed. Watts, F. 1979
64p illus lib. bdg. $5.90 (4-6)   **949.5**
1 Greece, Modern
ISBN 0-531-02934   LC 79-13465
"A First book"
First published 1966 with title: The first book
of modern Greece
This book provides an introduction to life in
modern Greece. The government, capital, villages,
islands, economy, educational system, religion,
festivals, and sports are explained briefly

949.6 Balkan Peninsula

Kostich, Dragoš D.
The land and people of the Balkans;
Albania, Bulgaria, Yugoslavia. Rev. ed.
Lippincott 1973 159p illus map (Portraits of
the nations ser) lib. bdg. $8.95 (5 and up) **949.6**
1 Balkan Peninsula
ISBN 0-397-31398-5   LC 73-7709
First published 1962
An introduction to the geography, history, politics,
social life and culture of the Balkan area which
contains the three modern nations of Albania,
Bulgaria, and Yugoslavia

949.8 Romania

Hale, Julian
The land and people of Romania. Lippincott 1972 143p illus map (Portraits of the
nations ser) $8.95 (5 and up)   **949.8**
1 Romania
ISBN 0-397-31288-1   LC 78-151481
The book provides a brief survey of the history,
geography, economic and social life of the people
of Romania

951 China and adjacent areas

Gray, Noel
Looking at China. Lippincott [1975 c1974]
64p illus maps (Looking at other countries)
$8.95 (4-6)   **951**
1 China
ISBN 0-397-31584-8   LC 74-7046
"A concise, lively, and colorful look at modern-
day mainland China. Gray covers history, geography, industry, science, and transportation but
concentrates on the seven major cities and the
daily lives of the people. The arrangement is sometimes illogical . . . and Gray glosses over the
negative aspects of Chinese life. . . . However,
the text reads smoothly and numerous color photographs provide a clear, well-balanced picture of
Chinese life." Sch Library J

Rau, Margaret

The Yangtze River; illus. with photos. Messner 1970 96p illus map lib. bdg. $3.64 (4-6)   **951**

1 Yangtze River
ISBN 0-671-32336-9   LC 76-123558

"The Yangtze River is followed from source to mouth in this book. The text integrates the geography, history, and political background of China. . . . Many black and white photos amplify the reading." Adventuring with Bks

951.05 China—Period of People's Republic, 1949-

Rau, Margaret

Our world: the People's Republic of China. [Rev. ed.] Messner 1978 127p illus map lib. bdg. $7.79 (6 and up)   **951.05**

1 China
ISBN 0-1671-32870-0   LC 78-960

First published 1974

"The first half of the book is a capsule history emphasizing recent times, the development of Communism and the contributions of Mao Tsetung. The remainder describes China as it is today—education, industry, and agriculture—and ends with a few questions about the future." Best Sellers [review of first edition]

The author has written "a brisk and objective overview." Chicago. Children's Bk Center [review of first edition]

The people of new China; with photographs by the author. Messner 1978 128p illus lib. bdg. $7.79 (4-6)   **951.05**

1 China
ISBN 0-671-32870-0   LC 78-960

"The focus is on contemporary life, with chapters devoted either to life in a town or a village, or to life in such a major city as Peking or Shanghai. In discussing the living patterns of residents, Rau covers such aspects of modern life as education, industry, familial relationships, and the arts. The tone is not laudatory, but it is sympathetic; the writing style is direct and the material well-organized. A pronunciation guide and an index are appended." Chicago. Children's Bk Center

Sidel, Ruth

Revolutionary China: people, politics, and ping-pong. Delacorte Press 1974 178p illus map $6.95 (6 and up)   **951.05**

1 China
ISBN 0-440-07410-X   LC 73-15396

The author, who visited China in 1971-1972, gives a brief history of China from early times to the end of the cultural Revolution. She then discusses Communist China today: the communes, social and economic achievements and conditions, education and language reform, life in Peking and other major cities, and China's renewed importance in world affairs

This book is "largely informational rather than interpretive. . . . Still, Sidel is careful to present life-styles of the Chinese on their own terms, fairly and favorably comparing them to prerevolutionary days." Booklist

Bibliography: p173-74

951.9 Korea

Gurney, Gene

North & South Korea, by Gene and Clare Gurney. Watts, F. 1973 87p illus map lib. bdg. $4.47 (4 and up)   **951.9**

1 Korea
ISBN 0-531-00804-5   LC 73-4278

"A First book"

The authors discuss the history, geography, customs, industries and cities of one of the oldest countries in the world, now divided by war and political philosophy

"A concise history of North and South Korea . . . albeit from a pro-South Korean point of view." Sch Library J

Solberg, S. E.

The land and people of Korea. Rev. ed. Lippincott 1973 159p illus maps (Portraits of the nations ser) $8.95 (5 and up)   **951.9**

1 Korea
ISBN 0-397-31405-1   LC 73-602

First published 1966

"The first part of the book highlights the major conflict of Korea's long, turbulent history including the causes of the late Korean War and the present, unsolved problems of unification. The latter part of the book discusses Korean art, literature, education, and religion and describes the daily life and customs of the people and the planting and harvesting of rice, and contrasts village and city life in South Korea." Booklist [review of the 1966 edition]

"A very good book for its coverage and the detailed and extensive historical section." Chicago. Children's Bk Center [review of the 1966 edition]

952 Japan

Masters, Robert V.

Japan in pictures. [Rev. ed] Sterling 1978 64p illus (Visual geography ser) lib. bdg. $4.99, pa $2.95 (4 and up)   **952**

1 Japan
ISBN 0-8069-1011-9; 0-8069-1010-0   LC 60-14338

First published 1961

Japan's history, geography, people, art and literature, economy, and government are discussed

Vaughan, Josephine Budd

The land and people of Japan. Rev. ed. Lippincott 1972 158p illus map (Portraits of the nations ser) $8.95 (5 and up)   **952**

1 Japan
ISBN 0-397-31301-2   LC 72-38543

First published 1952

This introduction to Japan describes its history, geography, people and culture

Yashima, Taro

The village tree. Viking [1972 c1953] unp illus pa $1.25 (k-3)   **952**

1 Japan 2 Children in Japan
ISBN 0-670-05072-5   LC 73-160555

"Viking Seafarer books"

First published 1953

A "beautiful interpretation in poetic prose and picture of the author's childhood portrayed as he recalls the fun he enjoyed with other boys by the river where a great tree still stretches its branches. The brief text and full-color sketches illustrate, in an atmosphere of great peace and happiness, the kind of tree-play, diving and underwater fun that boys anywhere might invent." Horn Bk

953 Arabian Peninsula and adjacent areas

Berger, Gilda

Kuwait and the rim of Arabia; Kuwait, Bahrain, Qatar, Oman, United Arab Emirates, Yemen, People's Democratic Republic of Yemen. Watts, F. 1978 64p illus maps lib. bdg. $4.90 (4 and up)   **953**

1 Arab countries 2 Persion Gulf States
ISBN 0-531-02235-8   LC 78-18759

"A First book"

This book looks at the Persian Gulf States with coverage of their geography, their history, people, culture and language. Discussion of their recently achieved wealth, the position they hold in the Middle East and in relation to the world economy is also included

For further reading: p61

Clifford, Mary Louise

The land and people of the Arabian Peninsula. Lippincott 1977 191p illus map (Portraits of the nations ser) $8.95 (5 and up)   **953**

1 Arab countries 2 Persian Gulf States
ISBN 0-397-31685-2   LC 76-49576

Clifford, Mary L.—*Continued*

"Examining the eight nations of the Arabian Peninsula in relation to one another, this overview provides a perspective not found in single books on Arab countries. Capsule descriptions of the political relation among countries within and outside the Peninsula are useful; the chapters on Islam, Arab culture, customs, language, and life styles are lively; and, the information on the small countries of the Peninsula (Yemen Arab Republic, People's Democratic Republic of Yemen, Oman, Bahrein, Qatar, and the United Arab Emirates) is not easily found elsewhere. In approaching OPEC and the Arab oil embargo, however, the author is excruciatingly fair to the Arabs, slighting their actions against Israel and Jews in general." Sch Library J

Lancaster, Fidelity

The Bedouin; William Lancaster, consultant; illus. by Maurice Wilson. Gloucester Press [distributed by Watts, F.] 1978 31p illus map (The Civilization library) lib. bdg. $6.90 (4 and up)   **953**

1 Bedouins
ISBN 0-531-01447-9   LC 78-2679
The brief text, accompanied by many illustrations, describes the history, social life and customs, and culture of the Arabic-speaking nomads in Syria, Iraq, Jordan, other countries of the Arabian Peninsula, and in North Africa

Woods, Geraldine

Saudi Arabia. Watts, F. 1978 63p illus lib. bdg. $6.45 (4-6)   **953**

1 Saudi Arabia
ISBN 0-531-02234-X   LC 78-9517
"A First book"
A discussion of the history, geography, people and culture of a country that during the past 50 years has grown from poverty and obscurity to become one of the world's wealthiest countries
Books for further reading: p59

954 India

Bergman Sucksdorff, Astrid

Chendru: the boy and the tiger; English version by William Sansom. Harcourt 1960 [c1959] unp illus $6.50 (3-6)   **954**

1 India—Social life and customs   2 Muria
3 Tigers
ISBN 0-15-216431-6   LC 60-3281
First published 1959 in France
Illustrated with photographs by the author
Colored photographs and text tell the story of Chendru, a young boy of India, and his pet tiger. This book also pictures the everyday life and activities of the Murias, a primitive tribe living in the jungle village of Gahr-Bengal, India
"Excellent for social studies in that it shows India is not all maharajahs, precious jewels, and Taj Mahals!" Library J

Bothwell, Jean

The first book of India; rev. by Jane Whipple. [3d] rev. ed. Watts, F. 1978 64p illus lib. bdg. $4.90 (4-6)   **954**

1 India
ISBN 0-531-02229-3   LC 78-2511
"A First book"
First published 1966
"An introduction to India . . . [which discusses] geography and climate, history and government, the economy, and village life. Many of the black-and-white photos show works of art . . . those sections which treat language, arts, and the caste system, are especially thorough." Sch Library J [review of 1971 edition]
Glossary: p59-60. Some other books to read: p61

954.9 Pakistan. Sri Lanka

Lang, Robert

The land and people of Pakistan. Rev. ed. Lippincott 1974 159p illus map (Portraits of the nations ser) lib. bdg. $8.95 (5 and up)   **954.9**

1 Pakistan
ISBN 0-397-31551-1   LC 74-792

First published 1968
Partial contents: The land of the great river Indus; Ancient cities and Buddhist ruins; Muslims and Moghuls; British rule and the struggle for independence; Pakistan becomes a nation; An historic city; Lahore; Life in a mud-walled village in the Punjab; Feasts, fasts, and festivals; Troubled Kashmir
"Well written and readable, this portrait of Pakistan . . . [includes the] changes caused by the . . . civil war and separation of East Pakistan (Bangladesh). Lang has also included material on the emerging role of women and changes in education. The complicated history is well explained as are social customs. A thoughtful appraisal of how Pakistan will fare in the future concludes this overview which has many excellent new photographs." Sch Library J

Wilber, Donald N.

The land and people of Ceylon. Rev. ed. Lippincott 1972 156p illus map (Portraits of the nations ser) lib. bdg. $8.95 (5 and up)   **954.9**

1 Sri Lanka
ISBN 0-397-31399-3   LC 72-15668
This introduction to the island nation of Ceylon discusses its history and geography, as well as its industries, its political life, and the customs of its people

956.1 Turkey

Constantinople; city on the Golden Horn, by the editors of Horizon Magazine. Author: David Jacobs; consultant: Cyril A. Mango. Am. Heritage [distributed by Harper] 1969 153p illus maps lib. bdg. $12.89 (6 and up)   **956.1**

1 Istanbul—History
ISBN 0-06-022799-0   LC 78-81403
"A Horizon Caravel book"
The author "traces the history of Constantinople from its founding by Greek settlers in the seventh century B.C. to the 1920's, with major emphasis on the period during which it became, successively, the capital of the East Roman, the Byzantine, and the Ottoman Turk Empires. He describes the personalities and events that dominated the city's development, discusses Constantinople's role as a bridge between Eastern and Western culture, and comments on the sack of Constantinople by Crusaders in 1204 and its conquest by Turks in 1453. The text, maps, contemporary art and modern photographs ably portray the city's historic importance and rich, diverse heritage." Booklist
Further reading: p149

Spencer, Willian

The land and people of Turkey. Rev. ed. Lippincott 1972 158p illus map (Portraits of the nations ser) $8.95 (5 and up)   **956.1**

1 Turkey
ISBN 0-397-31328-4   LC 72-6041
An introduction to the history, social conditons and geography of Turkey as the author guides the reader through modern Ankara, Asia Minor, the cities of the Hittites and the Turkish riviera, ending in Istanbul

956.7 Iraq

Fichter, George S.

Iraq. Watts, F. 1978 57p illus lib. bdg. $4.90 (4 and up)   **956.7**

1 Iraq
ISBN 0-531-02236-6   LC 78-8707
"A First book"
Discusses Iraq's history, geography, government, economy, people, culture and contemporary politics
Bibliography: p53

956.91 Syria

Copeland, Paul W.

The land and people of Syria. [Rev] Lippincott [1972 c1964] 160p illus map (Portraits of the nations ser) $8.95 (5 and up)   **956.91**

1 Syria
ISBN 0-397-31537-6   LC 77-37732

Copeland, Paul W.—*Continued*
First published 1964
This book "explores Syria's location, its strange customs, and her people who are Arabs of Semitic stock, all of which give to this country in the Near East an aura of fantasy and the enchantment of Aladdin and his magic lamp. Paul Copeland explains Muslim holy days and holidays, famous old towns where early Christians had built monastic retreat houses, and the various types of architecture. Pictures of every phase of Syria's culture show great diversity of development. Short index." Best Sellers
The book "is simple enough for a child of 11 to get an excellent idea of the nation and its people, yet so comprehensive that we wish we had read it before we visited the country." Bk Week

Gilfond, Henry
Syria. Watts, F. 1978 60p illus map lib. bdg. $6.45 (4 and up)   **956.91**
1 Syria
ISBN 0-531-02238-2   LC 78-9304
"A First book"
This book discusses Syria's history, geography, people, culture and current political situation, emphasizing conflicts with neighboring Israel
For further reading: p57

956.92   Lebanon

Newman, Gerald
Lebanon. Watts, F. 1978 66p illus maps lib. bdg. $4.90 (4 and up)   **956.92**
1 Lebanon
ISBN 0-531-02237-4   LC 78-16590
"A First book"
The reader is introduced to the history, geography, economy, religion, customs and traditions of the smallest country in the Middle East
For further reading: p63

956.94   Israel

Ellis, Harry B.
Israel: one land, two peoples. Crowell 1972 183p illus maps $8.95 (6 and up)   **956.94**
1 Israel—History 2 Israeli-Arab relations
ISBN 0-690-45028-1   LC 73-175104
This book tells the story of the Jews and their "promised land" from the time of Abraham through the periods of exile and return and the development of modern Israel. It describes current political and social conditions in Israel and traces the roots of conflicting Arab and Jewish claims to the land from ancient times to the present
"This is distinguished for its impartiality and its clear perception of the complexities of relationships, needs, obligations, and loyalties of the two groups that share an ancestry, each having a firm conviction that the land must be their own. Harry Ellis gives excellent historical background for the problem that seems insoluble yet has, in some small areas, already seen some amelioration. A thoughtful and informative book." Chicago. Children's Bk Center
Books for further reading: p174-76

Kubie, Nora Benjamin
Israel. [3d] rev. ed. Watts, F. 1978 66p illus maps lib. bdg. $4.90 (4 and up)   **956.94**
1 Israel
ISBN 0-531-02239-0   LC 78-17524
"A First book"
First published 1953 with title: The first book of Israel
An introduction to the modern state. The author discusses the social, political and cultural institutions as well as daily life in Israel. She also discusses the Palestinian movement and the Yom Kippur War
"It is valuable and informative so long as one remembers that it presents only one side of the matter." Christian Sci Monitor [review of 1968 edition]
Selected reading: p63-64

956.95   Jordan

Poole, Frederick King
Jordan; rev. by Linda O'Brien. Rev. ed. Watts, F. 1978 62p illus maps lib. bdg. $4.90 (4 and up)   **956.95**
1 Jordan
ISBN 0-531-02241-2   LC 78-16652
First published 1974
"A First book"
"This presentation acknowledges the strife that has ripped much of Jordan's recent history, but analysis is peripheral and the thrust of the book is toward describing the geographical and cultural factors that shape the country. Poole introduces the people, mainly the Bedouin of the east, along with the role they have come to play in the national military, and the displaced Palestinians of the west, who form nearly 40 percent of the population and who opposed Hussein in the 1970 civil war. A perspective on the Moslem tradition of Hashemite rule, personified by King Hussein, and on today's Jordan, its progress, and its future round out this introductory survey." Booklist [review of 1974 edition]
The book includes a discussion of Jordan's position in events of the Arab-Israeli crisis through 1977
For further reading: p57

957   Siberia

Lengyel, Emil
Siberia. Watts, F. 1974 65p illus map lib. bdg. $4.90 (4 and up)   **957**
1 Siberia
ISBN 0-531-00821-5   LC 73-14873
"A First book"
This book surveys Siberia's weather, geography, natural resources, cities, population, religion, history, industries and future, as well as the Trans-Siberian Railroad
"A concise, accurate overview." Sch Library J
Books for further reading: p63

959.5   Malaysia. Singapore

Poole, Frederick King
Malaysia & Singapore. Watts, F. 1975 59p illus map lib. bdg. $3.90 (4 and up)   **959.5**
1 Malaysia 2 Singapore
ISBN 0-531-02778-3   LC 74-13439
"A First book"
"This competently written description of two adjacent Asian nations covers their geography, natural resources, racial and cultural composition, recent history, and modern social and economic advancements. The writing is clear, and black-and-white photographs are additionally informative. Suggested titles for further reading are appended." Booklist

959.704   Vietnam—Independence, 1949-

Lifton, Betty Jean
Children of Vietnam [by] Betty Jean Lifton and Thomas C. Fox. Illus. with photographs by Thomas C. Fox. Atheneum Pubs. 1972 111p illus map $5.95 (6 and up)   **959.704**
1 Vietnamese Conflict, 1961-1975—Children
ISBN 0-689-30056-5   LC 72-75274

"A moving portrayal of the anguish suffered by the young victims of the war. Interviews with the children are interspersed with songs, poetry, prose, and photographs." Chicago
"The book ends with a sad account of the My Lai tragedy by some of the young survivors. In no other book on Vietnam is the plight of these children so personally and movingly depicted." Sch Library J

959.8 Indonesia

Smith, Datus C.
The land and people of Indonesia, by Datus
C. Smith, Jr. [Rev] Lippincott [1972 c1968]
158p illus map (Portraits of the nations ser)
$8.95 (5 and up)   959.8
> 1 Indonesia
> ISBN 0-397-31533-3   LC 73-37731
> First published 1961
> "The author surveys Indonesia's geography, natu-
> ral resources, religions, languages, education, arts,
> the people and their way of life. He also details
> the country's complex history as it emerged from
> colonial status to independence

Weatherbee, Donald E.
Ancient Indonesia and its influence in
modern times. Watts, F. 1974 84p illus maps
lib. bdg. $4.90 (4 and up)   959.8
> 1 Indonesia—History
> ISBN 0-531-02732-5   LC 74-3004
> "A First book"
> "The author demonstrates the closeness of
> Indonesia to its history by tracing the develop-
> ment of the island from prehistoric man, through
> the Indonesian empires and foreign conquests, to
> today's independence. At each step, the practices
> of the past are related to the current way of life
> in the island nation." Adventuring with Bks

959.9 Philippines

Nance, John
The land and people of the Philippines.
Lippincott 1977 192p illus (Portraits of the
nations ser) $8.95 (5 and up)   959.9
> 1 Philippine Islands
> ISBN 0-397-31656-9   LC 76-30543
> The author discusses the history, geography,
> culture, government, industry, natural resources
> and people of this nation of islands
> "Nance has devoted about half of his book to
> the period before . . . [the U.S.] became involved
> in the Philippines. . . . Many photographs are re-
> produced, and the book contains a good index. It
> deserves many readers." Best Sellers

960 Africa

Bernheim, Marc
In Africa [by] Marc & Evelyne Bernheim.
Atheneum Pubs. 1973 unp illus $8.95 (k-3)
                                               960
> 1 Africa
> ISBN 0-689-30315-7   LC 72-85913
> "A Margaret K. McElderry book"
> "A picture book of ninety-one highly effective
> photographs has sequences that illustrate varied
> types of African houses, costumes, occupations,
> and activities in the forest, on the desert, or on
> the coast. From these well-reproduced pictures,
> aspects of geography and culture are made vivid—
> so lively are the people and scenes of action. Cap-
> tions provide simple but adequate identifications
> in a word, a phrase, or a short sentence." Horn
> Bk

Murphy, E. Jefferson
Understanding Africa; illus. by Louise E.
Jefferson. Rev. ed. Crowell 1978 208p illus
maps $8.95, lib. bdg. $9.79 (6 and up)   960
> 1 Africa
> ISBN 0-690-03834-8; 0-690-03846-1   LC 77-11560
> First published 1969
> "Chapters on geography, peoples and nations,
> on the European discovery of and colonization
> of much of Africa, the subsequent (recent) inde-
> pendence of these colonies, with the chapter 'Africa
> Faces the Future,' all provide the reader with a
> realistic grasp of African anthropology, ancient
> traditions, the coming of Arab and European
> slave-traders, missionaries, explorers and, most
> important of all, African nationalism with its

complex problems; all written with a simplicity
recommending it to educated young people. . . .
The book is worth its price for the outstanding
illustrations and maps done by Louise Jefferson,
illustrations which confirm the saying that one picture is worth a thousand words. With the fine
maps one is brought up to date about the location
and names of the new nations, identifying them
with former colonies from which they emerged.
A book to dispel previous haziness and prejudice
about a burgeoning continent." Best Sellers
> Suggested reading list: p187-83

Musgrove, Margaret
Ashanti to Zulu: African traditions; pictures by Leo and Diane Dillon. Dial Press
1976 unp illus $8.95, lib. bdg. $8.44 (3-6)   960
> 1 Africa—Social life and customs 2 Ethnology—
> Africa
> ISBN 0-8037-0357-0; 0-8037-0358-9   LC 76-6610
> Awarded the Caldecott Medal, 1977
> "In brief texts arranged in alphabetical order,
> each accompanied by a large framed illustration,
> the author introduces 'the reader to twenty-six
> African peoples by depicting a custom important
> to each.' Her purpose is to 'give the reader not
> only a feeling for the vastness of the African
> continent and the variety of her peoples but for
> the place that tradition holds at the very heart
> of African life.' In fulfilling her purpose, she has
> been aided immeasurably by the illustrators;
> and the pictures, which admirably embody the
> subject matter of the book, are worthy of inde-
> pendent discussion as works of art. In most
> of the paintings the artists 'have included a man,
> a woman, a child, their living quarters, an artifact,
> and a local animal' and have, in this way, stressed
> the human and the natural ambience of the vari-
> ous peoples depicted. . . . The clearly limned fig-
> ures often recall the contours of African wood
> sculpture but are subordinated to the carefully
> composed placement of diagonals and parallels.
> . . . The controlled, rich art successfully glorifies
> the great variety of folkways found among the
> Black peoples of Africa." Horn Bk

961 Tunisia and Libya

Lawson, Don
Morocco, Algeria, Tunisia, and Libya.
Watts, F. 1978 66p illus map lib. bdg. $6.45
(4 and up)   961
> 1 Africa, North
> ISBN 0-531-02233-1   LC 78-17770
> "A First book"
> The author describes the history, geography,
> economic and social conditions, and the culture
> of the four North African states
> For further reading: p63

962 Egypt

Lengyel, Emil
Modern Egypt. [2d] rev. ed. Watts, F.
1978 66p illus map lib. bdg. $5.90 (5 and
up)   962
> 1 Egypt
> ISBN 0-531-02240-4   LC 78-17769
> "A First book"
> First published 1973
> The author surveys Egypt's geography, history,
> cities, religions, culture and politics. Information
> on Sadat's visit to Jerusalem in 1977 is included
> Includes bibliography

Mahmoud, Zaki Naguib
The land and people of Egypt. Rev. ed.
Lippincott 1972 159p illus map (Portraits of
the nations ser) $8.95 (5 and up)   962
> 1 Egypt
> ISBN 0-397-31259-8   LC 71-37247
> First published 1959
> "Describes the geography of Egypt and its effect
> on the character of the people and traces the his-
> tory and the social, economic, and political de-
> velopment of the country." Booklist
> The Egyptian author presents the material
> 'clearly and concisely. . . . Good format, index,
> table of contents, first-class photographs, good
> map." Library J

964   Morocco

Spencer, William

The land and people of Morocco. Rev. ed.
Lippincott 1973 160p illus map (Portraits of
the nations ser) $8.95 (5 and up)   964

1 Morocco
ISBN 0-397-31481-7   LC 73-4906

First published 1965
An introduction to the geography, people, history,
social life, and cities of the North African country
which is separated from Europe by the strait of
Gibraltar

966   West Africa

Bernheim, Marc

The drums speak; the story of Kofi, a boy
of West Africa [by] Marc & Evelyne Bernheim. Harcourt [1972 c1971] unp illus $6.50
(3-5)   966

1 Children in West Africa   2 Africa, West
ISBN 0-15-224233-3   LC 70-137761

"A brief story in a large format about a West
African village boy. By passing an exam, Kofi wins
the chance to become the first of his village to go
to high school; then, by conquering his fear of
heights and climbing a coconut tree in the coming-
of-age ceremony, he wins the chief's endorsement
of him as eventual successor." Sch Library J
"Brilliant, large, color photographs give importance to a slender volume with a forced sociological narrative. The rich tones of printed
costumes and jungle verdure are remarkably sharp
in detail; the boy's activities in the cocoa grove,
in canoe-building, and with animals are vivid."
Horn Bk

Clifford, Mary Louise

The land and people of Sierra Leone.
Lippincott 1974 159p illus map (Portraits of
the nations ser) $8.95 (5 and up)   966

1 Sierra Leone
ISBN 0-397-31490-6   LC 73-20317

The author discusses the geography, history,
economy, government, culture and people of this
West African country
"Clifford provides a straightforward overview of
the West African nation that in the eighteenth
century was viewed as a refuge for freed slaves
from the U.S. and continental Europe. Description
of historical and political events outweighs social
and cultural examination, but this still works
well as useful introductory fare." Booklist

Perl, Lila

Ghana and Ivory Coast: spotlight on West
Africa; illus. with 74 photographs. Morrow
1975 160p illus maps $5.95, lib. bdg. $7.92
(6 and up)   966

1 Ghana   2 Ivory Coast
ISBN 0-688-31833-9   LC 74-23106

The author discusses "the terrain and the people
of the fifteen countries of West Africa. Dealing
with the politics and economics of the Ivory Coast
and of modern Ghana—the first independent, ex-
colonial nation in black Africa—and with the
future of West Africa, the author effectively projects the similarities and differences between
Ghana and the Ivory Coast, comparing the
former's 'hopes and shattered dreams of the
Nkrumah years' with the economic growth of the
Ivory Coast. She also considers issues of democratic principles, military regimes, links with
former colonial masters . . . possibilities for economic cooperation and for the fifteen-nation
Organization of African Unity." Horn Bk
"In this personalized survey . . . Perl strikes
a nice balance between examining the past and
present as well as the social and political, . . .
Informative and well illustrated with many of the
author's own photographs, this is a preferred choice
over standard series treatments." Booklist
Bibliography: p155-56

Watson, Jane

The Niger: Africa's river of mystery. Maps
by Henri Fluchere. Garrard 1971 96p illus
maps (Rivers of the world) lib. bdg. $3.68
(4-6)   966

1 Niger River
ISBN 0-8116-6374-4   LC 76-135581

The text "traces the history of the Niger River
from the time of the Mali and Songhai empires
to the present. The author describes the efforts of
such European explorers as Mungo Park and Richard Lander to map the course of the river from its
source to the sea, discusses briefly the period of
European colonization of the region, and concludes
with a look at present-day life along the river."
Booklist

966.7   Ghana

Bleeker, Sonia

The Ashanti of Ghana; illus. by Edith G.
Singer. Morrow 1966 160p illus map lib.
bdg. $6.67 (4-7)   966.7

1 Ashantis   2 Ghana
ISBN 0-688-31052-4   LC 66-14751

The author "describes, in a semifictionalized
style, the culture, daily life, customs and government of the Ashanti, a tribal group living in the
central region of the land now called Ghana.
Of particular interest is the account of their religion based on ancestor worship. The last three
chapters trace the history of the Ashanti from
the time when the Europeans established a profitable gold and slave trade with the West Coast
natives, up to the present, when Ghana has become an independent nation. The material is well
presented and will be useful in the classroom as
well as for general reading. There are detailed
and informative line drawings, and an excellent
index." Sch Library J

Sale, J. Kirk

The land and people of Ghana. Rev. ed.
Lippincott 1972 159p illus map (Portraits of
the nations ser) $8.95 (5 and up)   966.7

1 Ghana
ISBN 0-397-31298-9   LC 74-377734

First published 1963
This introduction to Ghana, the first black
African country to achieve independence in the
twentieth century, describes its history, social
and cultural life, geography and economy

966.9   Nigeria

Forman, Brenda

The land and people of Nigeria, by Brenda
Forman and Harrison Forman. [Rev] Lippincott [1972 c1964] 160p illus map (Portraits
of the nations ser) $8.95 (5 and up)   966.9

1 Nigeria
ISBN 0-397-31205-9   LC 77-37925

First published 1964
This book introduces the history, religion, political, social and economic conditions, and regions
of the African land that became an independent
nation in 1960

Jenness, Aylette

Along the Niger River; an African way of
life; text and photographs by Aylette Jenness.
Crowell 1974 135p illus map $8.95 (5 and
up)   966.9

1 Nigeria—Social life and customs
ISBN 0-690-00514-8   LC 73-20061

The author describes life in the town of Yelwa,
Nigeria—its inhabitants, their customs, their culture, and their adaptations to western technology
"This is not just a travelogue: the book is sympathetic, thoughtful, and objective. Well-written,
well-organized, and informative, it gives historical
background for a discussion of the life styles of
tribes that are fishers or herders or farmers or
town dwellers, commenting perceptively on cultural integration, mores, and patterns of individual
and group life. A bibliography and a relative index
are appended." Chicago. Children's Bk Center

967 Central Africa

Bleeker, Sonia
The Pygmies; Africans of the Congo forest;
illus. by Edith G. Singer. Morrow 1968 143p
illus map lib. bdg. $6.67 (4-7) **967**

1 Pygmies
ISBN 0-688-31462-7 LC 68-25481

"An excellent study of the diminutive Pygmy
tribe, a formerly great nation shrouded in legend
and mystery, now dwelling in the jungles of Central Africa. Dealing with the everyday lives of the
Mbuti Pygmies, Miss Bleeker describes in detail
their religion, history, family structure, hunting
techniques, and manhood rites. The accompanying
black-and-white drawings lack detail and realism." Sch Library J

"The text conveys the author's admiration for
as well as her knowledge of the tribe." Horn Bk

Carpenter, Allan
Gabon, by Allan Carpenter and James
Hughes; consulting editor, Robert Hamilton.
Childrens Press 1976 96p illus (Enchantment
of Africa) lib. bdg. $10 (4 and up) **967**

1 Gabon
ISBN 0-516-04563-6 LC 76-6465

An introduction to the people, history, culture,
government, geography, resources and major cities
of Gabon

967.6 East Africa

Bleeker, Sonia
The Masai; herders of East Africa; illus.
by Kisa N. Sasaki. Morrow 1963 155p illus
maps lib. bdg. $6.67 (4 and up) **967.6**

1 Masai
ISBN 0-688-31460-0 LC 63-12632

This is a "description of the history, customs,
ceremonies, religion, and daily life of the nomadic
Masai herders of eastern Africa. Included is a
vivid account of the training of boys for warfare
and girls for homemaking. . . . Very little information exists for children on this group." Sch Library J

"Here is a concise, scholarly, yet thoroughly interesting and enjoyable narrative of the Masai.
. . . [It] should capture the interest of most
young readers by its style and sketches." Best
Sellers

Perl, Lila
East Africa; Kenya, Tanzania, Uganda;
illus. with 58 photographs. Morrow 1973 160p
illus map lib. bdg. $6.96 (4-6) **967.6**

1 Africa, East
ISBN 0-688-30088-X LC 73-4927

This book offers background on the geography,
people and history of East Africa. The first chapter
looks at the area as a whole and the following
chapters examine individual present-day conditions
of Tanzania, Uganda, and Kenya
Bibliography: p154-55

967.8 Tanzania

Kaula, Edna Mason
The land and people of Tanzania. Lippincott 1972 139p illus map (Portraits of the
nations ser) $8.95 (5 and up) **967.8**

1 Tanzania
ISBN 0-397-31544-9 LC 72-5660

An "account of the growth of and the progress
being made in Tanzania since independence in
1964. Kaula briefly but adequately covers geography, the people, and history and outlines the
rise of President Nyerere and the Tanganyika
African National Union (the TANU party). The
rest of the book treats the effects on the people
of government programs to improve agriculture,
education, medicine, transportation, industry, and
urban conditions. Accompanied by good black-
and-white photographs, this provides new material
which will be valuable where African studies are
taught." Sch Library J

968 Southern Africa

Bleeker, Sonia
The Zulu of South Africa; cattlemen,
farmers, and warriors; illus. by Kisa N.
Sasaki. Morrow 1970 160p illus maps lib.
bdg. $6.24 (4 and up) **968**

1 Zulus
ISBN 0-688-21451-7 LC 71-118059

An "account of the Zulu people, this book includes a historical narrative; a full picture of Zulu
customs concerning daily life, marriage, and cattle
raising; and a description of life in modern South
Africa. The author uses fictional characters in
episodes to tell about customs, but she tells the
life of historically known leaders as well. This
is a sympathetic study of the Zulu told without
polemic. Line drawings illustrate many parts of the
book showing details of life and custom that are
difficult to comprehend without pictures." Sci Bks

"Dependably comprehensive and authentic. . . .
The material is well-organized, the writing
straightforward and objective." Chicago. Children's
Bk Center

Newlon, Clarke
Southern Africa: the critical land. Dodd
1978 22p illus maps $6.95 (6 and up) **968**

1 Africa, Southern
ISBN 0-396-07589-4 LC 78-7724

"Southern African nations, deemed critical in
the opening chapter because of their potential
strategic and economic leverage, come under crisp
review here, though with U.S. and western interests in mind. That coloring doesn't diminish the
factual solidity of the account, which delves into
colonial histories and doesn't hesitate to sketch the
dimensions of current political unrest. Separate
chapters consider diamonds and gold, describing
their empire-building developers as well as the
minerals themselves. Newlon is firmly critical of
apartheid policies, giving voice to white supremacy
arguments and the truths contained in them
(South African blacks are the best educated and
best fed on the continent) and then refuting them.
Although some cited developments are presently
outdated by recent events, this survey remains
meatier than most—current and incisive, even with
its imperfections." Booklist

970.004 North American native races

Baker, Betty
Settlers and strangers; native Americans of
the desert Southwest and history as they saw
it. Macmillan Pub. Co. 1977 88p illus map
$7.95 (4 and up) **970.004**

1 Indians of North America—Southwest, New
ISBN 0-02-708220-2 LC 77-4925

"A history of the native Americans of the Southwest, whose lives and religion were shaped by
the desert. Migrating in prehistoric times over the
land bridge from Siberia southward to warmer
lands, the itinerant hunters settled down to become corn growers, basket weavers, and makers
of pottery—the Pueblo Indians, Hopi, Pima, and
Papago. In the sixteenth century cruelty entered
their lives with the arrival of the Spaniards, who
forced the Indians to become slaves; then the
tribes contended with raiding Apaches and Nava-
hos and later with land-taking ranchers. Native
Americans of the Southwest have kept many of
the old ways, and the tribes have remained separate from one another." Horn Bk

"Unpleasant facts are not glossed over. Black-
and-white illustrations from various sources have
been used to illustrate the volume. Anthropologists
specializing in southwestern Native Americans
might quibble over a few of Baker's conclusions;
however, this is a useful addition to southwestern
and other libraries. A map of the tribes and areas
discussed is included." Children's Bk Rev Serv

Baldwin, Gordon C.

The Apache Indians; raiders of the Southwest. Four Winds 1978 221p illus map $9.95 (6 and up)   **970.004**

1 Apache Indians
ISBN 0-590-07321-4   LC 77-21439

"The author sets out to trace the evolution of the complex social and economic structure of Apache life. The Apaches are not a single tribe but a group of seven distinct territorial and cultural groups. Their early history is very much the same as that of the tribes upon whose lands they encroached. Descriptions of the Apache wars —at first intertribal, later with the Spanish and the Americans—place warfare and raiding within a social context and deal with the stereotypes which came to be associated with the Apaches. Regional variations in family structure and education, housing and clothing, arts and rituals—before contact with Europeans—are described in detail, and a picture emerges very different from that of life on the reservation. A final chapter details economic enterprises undertaken by tribal units and the contemporary resurgence of ethnic identity." Horn Bk

"This book is a well-written and researched scholarly study, a combination of Apache culture and history. Excellent map, drawings, and photographs, bibliography, and index. Recommended for classroom use and for general reading." Babbling Bookworm

How Indians really lived. Putnam 1967 223p illus maps (A Science survey bk) lib. bdg. $5.49 (5 and up)   **970.004**

1 Indians of North America—History
ISBN 0-399-60268-2   LC 67-14801

"Generally concentrating on major tribes, but including many of the smaller ones as well, [the author] presents a detailed and easily comprehensible picture of how the Indians lived and thought, with a great deal of specific information about types and construction of homes, gathering and preparation of food, also clothing, cosmetics, and hairstyles, social units and kinship structures, recreation, politics, warfare, and religion. . . . The writing is smooth and consistently interesting, and the book never gets bogged down in details. The photographs—mostly of museum exhibits and 19th century location shots—are adequate but not distinguished." Sch Library J

Bibliography: p216-17. Glossary: p218-20

Baylor, Byrd

When clay sings; illus. by Tom Bahti. Scribner 1972 unp illus lib. bdg. $8.95 (1-4)   **970.004**

1 Indians of North America—Art   2 Indians of North America—Southwest, New   3 Pottery
ISBN 0-684-12807-1   LC 70-180758

By putting together pieces of pottery, the reader can reconstruct what the Indian way of life might have been like in the times when the pottery was made

"'Every piece of clay, Indian parents tell children who find shards, should be treated with respect, since it was a part of somebody's life. They even say it has its own small voice and sings in its own way.' The pages, handsome in earth colors and black and white, show designs derived from prehistoric Indian pottery of the Southwest, and the text consists of what the children of today imagine about the four cultures (Anasazi, Mogollon, Hohokam, and Mimres) from which the clay pottery came. The book is dignified in format, the illustrations and text beautifully united, and the text both reveals the richness of the ancient cultures and hints, to the reader, the ways in which one learns about prehistory from artifacts." Chicago. Children's Bk Center

Bealer, Alex W.

Only the names remain; the Cherokees and the Trail of Tears; illus. by William Sauts Bock. Little 1972 88p illus $5.95 (4-6)   **970.004**

1 Cherokee Indians
ISBN 0-316-08520-0   LC 71-169008

The author describes "the rise of the Cherokee Nation, with its written language, constitution, and republican form of government, and its tragic betrayal in the 1830s." Chicago

"The author's narrative style, which is dramatic and immediate, is intensified by the illustrator's meticulous and evocative black-and-white illustrations. A helpful index is appended." Horn Bk

Deloria, Vine

Indians of the Pacific Northwest; from the coming of the white man to the present day [by] Vine Deloria, Jr. Doubleday 1977 207p illus maps $6.95, lib. bdg. $7.90 (6 and up)   **970.004**

1 Indians of North America—Northwest, Pacific   2 Indians of North America—Government relations
ISBN 0-385-09790-5; 0-385-09791-3   LC 74-18789

"This book covers the history of the Indians who live in the state of Washington between the Pacific Ocean and the Cascade Mountains right down to the 1970's and their current litigation over the salmon fishing rights." Children's Bk Rev Serv

"In what is essentially a legal and political history, Deloria introduces the tribes of the Puget Sound region with an eye toward their historic and current victimization and their efforts at fighting back. . . . A feisty, forthright account; sympathetic, thorough, and never dull. With black-and-white photographs." Booklist

Ehrlich, Amy

Wounded Knee: an Indian history of the American West; adapted for young readers by Amy Ehrlich from Dee Brown's Bury my heart at Wounded Knee. Holt 1974 202p illus maps $6.95 (6 and up)   **970.004**

1 Indians of North America—The West (U.S.)   2 Indians of North America—Wars   3 The West (U.S.)—History
ISBN 0-03-091559-7   LC 73-21821

This book traces the plight of the Navaho, Apache, Cheyenne and Sioux Indians in their struggles against the white man in the West between 1860 and 1890. It recounts battles and their causes, participants, and consequences during this era

"Some chapters [of the original] have been deleted, others condensed, and in some instances sentence structure and language have been simplified. The editing is good, and this version is interesting, readable, and smooth. A good choice for junior high students who may find the 470-page original tough going." Sch Library J

Includes bibliographies

Elliott, Paul Michael

Eskimos of the world; illus. with drawings and photographs. Messner 1976 128p illus maps lib. bdg. $7.29 (4-6)   **970.004**

1 Eskimos
ISBN 0-671-32767-4   LC 76-25964

"After briefly introducing four contemporary Eskimo children whose lives are a mix of old and new, Elliott looks back at traditional Eskimo ways with an eye to how they ensured the people's survival in an inhospitable climate. Much of the recounting is by season, and along the way some of the grimmer aspects of Eskimo life are taken into account: starvation was always the worst fear, and in a famine, cannibalism was not unknown; loyalties were to the band; stealing from strangers was accepted; murder and kidnapping of women also occurred. Practical matters of food, housing, and means of hunting also receive their due, and the final two chapters follow the uneven fortunes of modern Eskimos. Straightforward, more explicit than many other cultural portraits, and plentifully illustrated with black-and-white photographs." Booklist

Elting, Mary

The Hopi way; illus. by Louis Mofsie. Evans, M.&Co. 1969 63p illus $3.95 (2-4)   **970.004**

1 Hopi Indians
ISBN 0-87131-097-X   LC 72-88692

This story "tells how Louis Mofsie, a Hopi Indian who was born and raised in New York City, spends a summer in his ancestral Hopi village in Arizona." Cooperative Children's Bk. Center. Materials on Indians of North Am

"While the matter-of-fact style tends to make the book more informational than entertaining, Mofsie's account of what it meant to him to share in daily activities and celebration with his Hopi relatives and . . . [the] clear, simple drawings of events effectively interpret the Hopi way of life for young readers." Booklist

Hopi words in this book: p63

Erdoes, Richard

The native Americans: Navajos; text and photographs by Richard Erdoes; ed. by Marvin L. Reiter. Sterling 1978 84p illus $12.95, lib. bdg. $11.69 (4 and up)   970.004

1 Navaho Indians
ISBN 0-8069-2740-2; 0-8069-2741-0   LC 78-57885

"An oversize book, profusely illustrated with color photographs, gives the history of the Navajos, describes the beauty and the harshness of the land in which they live, the 'Four Corners,' and devotes separate chapters to discussions of traditional and modern ways of life—living patterns which are at times in conflict. Erdoes, who has written many books about native Americans, is knowledgeable, sympathetic, and lucid. . . . The photograph-and-caption pages are used effectively (as with pictures of the natural beauty of the reservation) instead of text, in some page sequences. The author is candid about Navajo problems, respectful toward Navajo traditions, and objective in assessing the dignity and resilience in which the Navajos are coping as they have in the past—with change. An index is appended." Chicago. Children's Bk Center

The rain dance people; the Pueblo Indians, their past and present. Knopf 1976 280p illus $7.95 (5 and up)   970.004

1 Pueblo Indians
ISBN 0-394-82394-X   LC 75-157

"The durability of ancient southwestern cultures is the major theme of this book. Journalist-photographer-artist Erdoes relates the story of the survival of Pueblo peoples and their ancestors through prehistoric climatic-environmental changes, Spanish conquistadores, Christian missionaries, mountain men, Anglo settlers, modern business interests, and the U.S. Bureau of Indian Affairs and Bureau of Land Management. The perseverance of these people in the face of continuing challenges is explained in terms of cultural values expressed through their world view, religion, social structure, and childrearing practices. The lengthy narration necessarily and generously dips into the data of archeologists, historians, ethnologists and journalists." AAAS Sci Bks & Films

"Erdoes's book is a pleasure to read. His descriptions of Pueblo life and crafts are a treasure for any bookshelf, and the accompanying photographs and illustrations, though black-and-white, serve to enhance rather than distract from the reading." Best Sellers

The sun dance people; the Plains Indians, their past and present; written and photographed by Richard Erdoes. Knopf 1972 218p illus map $5.95, lib. bdg. $6.99, pa $2.45 (5 and up)   970.004

1 Indians of North America—Great Plains
ISBN 0-394-82316-8 0-394-92316-2; 0-394-70803-2
LC 77-155812

In this book the lives of the Plains Indians are examined in both historical and contemporary contexts. The author describes the era when the Indians lived in tepees, hunted buffalo, counted coups, and fought against the U.S. Cavalry. He then tells of today's Indian, living on reservations in tarpaper shacks, trying to farm infertile land, having their children taken to government boarding schools, and dealing with the U.S. Bureau of Indian Affairs

"The book is well done, and filled with . . . fascinating information. . . . [It] is liberally illustrated with reproductions of old prints and paintings and photographs by the author. . . . Erdoes's versions [of some of the battles] are not the same as those in most textbooks. Chivington and Custer both wear the black hats of the villain, and high time." NY Times Bk Rev

Folsom, Franklin

Red power on the Rio Grande; the native American revolution of 1680. Introduction by Alfonso Ortiz; jacket and symbol illus. by J. D. Roybal. Follett 1973 144p illus $5.95, lib. bdg. $5.97 (5 and up)   970.004

1 Pueblo Revolt, 1680 2 Pueblo Indians
ISBN 0-695-80374-3; 0-695-40374-5   LC 72-85581

This is an "account of the Pueblo Native American uprising of 1680 against Spanish control in the Southwest, which was one of the few Indian victories in the history of white-Indian contact in America. Superbly organized by Popé and other Pueblo leaders, the rebellion represented the efforts of a people humiliated, oppressed, and exploited by the ruling class." Sch Library J

"The author presents the Indian's view of the battle for repossession of the American Southwest. Only the records of Spanish conquerors remain, painting the Indian in the colors of 'savage.' Franklin Folsom has attempted to end this neglect of an intricately planned and successfully executed revolution. The reader, quite sensibly, is on the side of the Red Man. . . . Additional tabulated information enriches an already excellent book." Best Sellers

Sources: p137-40

Gridley, Marion E.

Indian tribes of America; illus. by Lone Wolf. Hubbard Press 1973 63p illus lib. bdg. $4.95 (4-6)   970.004

1 Indians of North America
ISBN 0-528-82816-X   LC 76-24843

The author discusses the major Indian tribes of the Northeast, Southeast, Plains, and Northwest coast, emphasizing the unique life style of each group

Hofsinde, Robert

The Indian and his horse; written and illus. by Robert Hofsinde (Gray-Wolf) Morrow 1960 96p illus lib. bdg. $6.48 (4-6)   970.004

1 Indians of North America 2 Horses
ISBN 0-688-31421-X   LC 60-5243

"Mr. Hofsinde discusses the coming of the horse and the first uses of the animal; the catching, raiding, trading and training of horses; and the breeds of horses used by Indians. He describes the buffalo horse, the war horse, and the medicine horse; he traces the development of increasingly complex equipment: he closes with a brief description of the horse by contemporary American Indians." Chicago. Children's Bk Center

The author "investigates [his subject] thoroughly and presents his findings simply and well." NY Her Trib Bks

The Indian medicine man; written and illus. by Robert Hofsinde (Gray-Wolf) Morrow 1966 94p illus lib. bdg. $6.48 (4-7)   970.004

1 Indians of North America 2 Medicine man
ISBN 0-688-31618-2   LC 66-11594

Discussed are "the importance and training of the Indian medicine man; the specific curative practices of the Sioux, Iroquois, Apache, Navaho, Ojibwa, and Northwest Indian tribes; and the status of the medicine man today." Booklist

A "concise and interesting book. . . . The black and white drawings are excellent in giving details of costumes, buildings, and artifacts but are awkward in depicting people." Chicago. Children's Bk Center

Indian warriors and their weapons; written and illus. by Robert Hofsinde (Gray-Wolf) Morrow 1965 96p illus lib. bdg. $6 (3-6)
970.004

1 Indians of North America 2 Arms and armor
ISBN 0-688-31613-1   LC 65-11041

"A brief account of the weapons and war tactics of seven famous American Indian tribes." Horn Bk

"Hofsinde's discussion is both authoritative and sympathetic. . . . Good illustrations." Sci Bks

Kirk, Ruth

Hunters of the whale; an adventure in Northwest Coast archaeology, by Ruth Kirk with Richard D. Daugherty; photographs by Ruth and Louis Kirk. Morrow 1974 160p illus map $8.25, lib. bdg. $7.92 (5 and up) 970.004

1 Ozette Indian Village 2 Makah Indians—Antiquities
ISBN 0-688-20109-1; 0-688-30109-6   LC 73-17317

This is a description of "the natives of the Makah Indian village of Ozette, Washington, as they strive to dig up and preserve records of their past. With the help of archaeologist, Richard Daugherty, and a crew of 25 college students from across the country, the Indians unearthed, preserved and catalogued over 20,000 artifacts, some as old as 6000 years." Babbling Bookworm

Kirk, Ruth—*Continued*

"The text and the photographs offer all the excitement and suspense of a superior detective story which should appeal to all readers, whether or not they are interested in archeology, anthropology and related subjects." Pub W

Lyons, Grant

The Creek Indians; illus. by David Kingham. Messner 1978 96p illus maps lib. bdg. $7.29 (4-6)   **970.004**

1 Creek Indians
ISBN 0-671-32985-6   LC 77-29255

"This history of the Creek Confederacy begins with the Creek emergence myth, describes their way of life prior to contact with whites, continues through the periods of white exploration and settlement, the wars, the removal to Indian Territory (Oklahoma), to the present-day situation." Sch Library J

"The story is a sad one that Lyons relates dispassionately. Pen-and-ink drawings provide illustration." Booklist

Marriott, Alice

Indians on horseback; drawings by Margaret Lefranc. Crowell [1968 c1948] 136p illus $8.95 (4-6)   **970.004**

1 Indians of North America—Great Plains
ISBN 0-690-43768-4   LC 48-8606

Reprint of a book first published 1948
Contents: Who the Plains Indians are; What the Great Plains are; When the white men came; One man's life on the plains; How the tribes governed themselves; The Sun Dance ceremony; Indian doctors and medicines; A Plains Indian cookbook; How the Plains Indians made things; What the Plains Indians are doing now; Bibliography

"The author, an experienced ethnologist who has lived with descendants of the original inhabitants of this area, writes about her subject with sympathetic understanding." Sat Rev

Newman, Gerald

The changing Eskimos. Watts, F. 1979 48p illus map lib. bdg. $5.90 (2-4)   **970.004**

1 Eskimos
ISBN 0-531-02271-4   LC 78-15956

"An Easy-read fact book"

"This overview with numerous full-color photos focuses on how past generations of this sturdy people adapted their clothing, housing, and diet to the physical environment and how present-day Eskimos cope with the effects of American culture and technological progress. Preserving the traditions of their arts and crafts, conserving their wildlife and natural resources, and educating their young are shown as areas of concern for Eskimos today." Sch Library J

"While the coverage has little depth, the book can serve well as an introduction to the changing culture of the Eskimo peoples; clearly and simply written. . . . Phonetic spellings are given for words deemed difficult for the primary grades reader." Chicago. Children's Bk Center

Pitseolak, Peter

Peter Pitseolak's Escape from death; drawings and story by Peter Pitseolak; introduced and ed. by Dorothy Eber. Delacorte Press/Seymour Lawrence [1978 c1977] unp illus $7.95, lib. bdg. $7.45 (3-5)   **970.004**

1 Eskimos 2 Wilderness survival
ISBN 0-440-06894-0; 0-440-06896-7   LC 77-83236

"A Merloyd Lawrence book"

The author, an Eskimo, relates the "account of a hunting trip with his son, which nearly ended in disaster after the engine failed and his open boat, trapped in an ice field, was carried into the Hudson Strait. After two days on the ice, the man dreamed that they would be saved; indeed, a path in the ice opened, and they returned safely." Horn Bk

The book is "illustrated by Pitseolak with bold, clean, primitive paintings. The writing is direct and simple, a moving narrative that reveals the author's courage, piety, and modesty. It is contemporary (Pitseolak died in 1973) but the story has a timeless quality in its evocation of the isolated wastes, and the stoic and dignified Eskimo acceptance of Arctic life." Chicago. Children's Bk Center

Reit, Seymour

Child of the Navajos; photographs by Paul Conklin. Dodd 1971 64p illus lib. bdg. $5.95 (2-4)   **970.004**

1 Navaho Indians
ISBN 0-396-06414-0   LC 74-162608

This is the story of Jerry Begay, a nine-year-old Navajo boy living on the tribe's reservation in Arizona. The reader follows Jerry through his third-grade school activities, sees him at home helping with family chores, and joins him in exploring Black Mesa, the harsh terrain that is his home

Sheppard, Sally

Indians of the eastern woodlands. Watts, F. 1975 88p illus lib. bdg. $6.45 (5 and up)   **970.004**

1 Indians of North America   2 Iroquois Indians 3 Algonquian Indians
ISBN 0-531-00825-8   LC 74-13609

"A First book"

This book touches "on prehistory, sociological order of tribes, wampum, government, spirits, shamans, legends, heroes, music and art, arrival of the white man, treaties, reservation life today, and the future. Readers will have trouble sorting out the portions pertaining to the Iroquois from those about the Algonquians; however, Indians of the Eastern U.S. have regretfully been largely ignored in children's books. . . . Thus despite Sheppard's occasionally dull and confusing style, some libraries may want this as an additional reference source." Sch Library J

Steele, William O.

Talking bones; secrets of Indian burial mounds; drawings by Carlos Llerena-Aguirre. Harper 1978 63p illus $6.95, lib. bdg. $6.79 (3-5)   **970.004**

1 Mounds and mound builders   2 Indians of North America—Antiquities
ISBN 0-06-025768-7; 0-06-025769-5   LC 76-58687

This book "describes the burial practices of four prehistoric mound-building cultures of the Ohio region. The discovery by archeologists of each of the ancient sites is described, followed by the author's re-creation of probable funeral practices. The huge mounds of the 'Adena' people and the shell mounds of an earlier and even simpler culture are contrasted to the more elaborate death-cults of the Bone House and Hopewell Indians. The focus of the book is specialized and seems to capitalize on current curiosity about death, but within the limits he has set himself, Steele elucidates a small slice of history." Sch Library J

"Periodic ink drawings are usually dramatic—perhaps overly so—in their depiction of textual topics." Booklist

Selected bibliography: p57-59. Chronology: p60

Tamarin, Alfred

Ancient Indians of the Southwest [by] Alfred Tamarin and Shirley Glubok. Doubleday 1975 96p illus $5.95, lib. bdg. $6.90 (5 and up)   **970.004**

1 Indians of North America—Southwest, New 2 Southwest, New—Antiquities
ISBN 0-385-09247-4; 0-385-09252-0   LC 74-33984

"The origins of these ancient peoples and their accomplishments are skillfully presented in a lucid, fascinating narrative which begins at the end of the ice age when big game hunters migrated from Asia across the land bridge to Alaska and continues until the early farmers appeared. Gradually, as in the development of all civilizations, the leisure time provided by settlement as opposed to continual migration created an environment in which art could flourish; and it is through their art and architecture that much of these ancient life-styles can be reconstructed. Although the Spanish dominance of the Southwest put an end to the unwritten history of these early tribes, 'links with the past endure.' A complementary study to Shirley Glubok's 'The Art of the Southwest Indians' (Macmillan) [entered in class 709.01] the book may also be used as a reference work by those interested in exploring the archaeological background of the stylized kivas, kachinas, and other motifs." Horn Bk

Map on lining-papers

Tamarin, Alfred—*Continued*

We have not vanished; Eastern Indians of the United States. Follett 1974 160p illus lib. bdg. $5.97 (6 and up)   970.004

1 Indians of North America
ISBN 0-695-40332-X   LC 73-90052

"There are more questions raised here than are answered, and the dry prose and repetitive organizational structure make it seem as if the book could have been reduced to one large chart. . . . Aside from these disappointments, Tamarin's point that Eastern U.S. native Americans have not vanished and indeed are increasing is well taken, especially in view of the predominance of juvenile publishing on the historical aspects of Western tribes. This provides a demographic picture, state by state, of present-day Eastern tribes with up-to-date information useful for school work." Booklist

Bibliography: p152-54

Tunis, Edwin

Indians. Rev. ed. Written and illus. by Edwin Tunis. Crowell 1979 157p illus $12.95, lib. bdg. $12.89 (5-7)   970.004

1 Indians of North America
ISBN 0-690-03806-2; 0-690-01283-7   LC 79-84950

First published 1959 by World Publishing Company

A "survey of nine major groups of North American Indians before their first encounters with white settlers. . . . For the crafts of the Indians and their ingenuity in meeting the challenges of their varying environments . . . Tunis shows a genuine respect, and there seems to be no substitute for his contribution in this area." Sch Library J

970.01   North America—Period of prehistory, discovery, exploration

Asimov, Isaac

The shaping of North America, from earliest times to 1763. Houghton 1973 261p illus maps $5.95 (6 and up)   970.01

1 America—Exploration   2 North America—History
ISBN 0-395-15493-6   LC 72-7931

"The discovery and settlement of North America are surveyed at a fast pace beginning with the legendary transatlantic voyages of the Phoenicians and the Irish and concluding with the withdrawal of the French in 1763. Considering the amount of space and time covered in a little over 200 pages, a surprising number of factual details are included. . . . Maps and a table of dates are included." Booklist

Buehr, Walter

The French explorers in America; written and illus. by Walter Buehr. Putnam 1961 93p illus lib. bdg. $5.29 (4-6)   970.01

1 America—Exploration 2 Explorers 3 French in North America
ISBN 0-399-60189-9   LC 61-11941

The author "briefly describes the explorations of such men as Cartier, Champlain, and La Salle and discusses their influence on the settlement of America. Illustrated with maps and drawings." Hodges. Bks for Elem Sch Libraries

Discoverers of the New World, by the editors of American Heritage, The Magazine of History; narrative by Josef Berger in consultation with Lawrence C. Wroth. Am. Heritage [distributed by Harper] 1960 153p illus maps, lib. bdg. $9.89 (5 and up) 970.01

1 America—Exploration 2 Explorers
ISBN 0-06-020486-9   LC 60-10300

"American Heritage Junior library"

"Illustrated with maps, paintings, prints, and drawings of the period." Half title page

"Three hundred years of exploration by daring men of many countries, all seeking a short route to the Indies, are depicted with an authenticity we have come to expect in the series. Tales of accomplishment and avarice, of the familiar as well as lesser-known adventures unfold in smooth sequence. Illustrations, many in color, include reproductions of rare manuscript maps, paintings, prints, etc., from national museums. Useful in curriculum for both elementary and junior high, but fascinating reading for everyone." Library J

For further reading [and] Bibliography: p151

Golding, Morton J.

The mystery of the Vikings in America. Lippincott 1973 159p illus maps $8.95 (6 and up)   970.01

1 America—Exploration 2 Vikings
ISBN 0-397-31247-4   LC 73-4541

The author discusses the various controversies concerning the Vikings. He also covers their background and way of life, their unique ships, and the navigational expertise which enabled them to explore and settle Viking Iceland, Greenland, and finally Vinland (i.e. America)

"Well illustrated with medieval and specially drawn maps of Viking explorations, this is both an excellent introduction to a fascinating part of European and American history and a wonderful tool in helping a young student understand historical problems. Author Golding is scrupulous in presenting both sides of all possible disputed questions—and with the Vikings there are many—asking the young reader to decide which evidence is strongest. He also adds intelligent bibliography notes for further research. Good pictures and outline drawings of Viking boats, implements, etc. A beautiful book." Best Sellers

Lauber, Patricia

Who discovered America? Settlers and explorers of the New World before the time of Columbus; illus. with photographs, prints, and maps. Random House 1970 128p illus map lib. bdg. $6.39 (4 and up)   970.01

1 America—Antiquities 2 America—Exploration
ISBN 0-394-91855-X   LC 71-99431

The author gives an "account of the known and speculative evidence in the New World's beginnings and re-beginnings, discoveries and rediscoveries. . . . A long-view examination of human and animal migrations and development during and after the Ice Age flows . . . into a discussion of pre-Columbian outside influences and their possible origins." NY Times Bk Rev

Selected bibliography: p124-25

May, Julian

Before the Indians; illus. by Symeon Shimin. Holiday House 1969 unp illus map lib. bdg. $7.95 (2-4)   970.01

1 North America—Antiquities 2 Man, Prehistoric
ISBN 0-8234-0005-0   LC 73-5236

An account of "the world of prehistoric America as far back as that of the Paleo-Indians, who inhabited our continent forty thousand years ago. The brief text—easy for young readers—and the picture details, which amplify the story of how archeologists derive their knowledge, make an inviting introduction to early cultures—from those of the Ancient Hunters and Big Game Hunters to the Old Desert Culture people, Archaic people, and the Burial Mound people." Horn Bk

"Although primarily chronological, this is a rather haphazard presentation of facts. . . . The text is continuous, the pages not numbered, and there is no index. The writing is direct and simple, so that the book is good for browsing or as an introduction either to archeology or to a study of American Indians." Chicago. Children's Bk Center

971.27   Manitoba

Kurelek, William

A prairie boy's summer; paintings and story by William Kurelek. Houghton 1975 unp illus $7.95 (3-5)   971.27

1 Children in Canada 2 Farm life—Canada
3 Summer
ISBN 0-395-20280-9   LC 74-32137

Kurelek, William—*Continued*

A companion volume to the author's: A prairie boy's winter, entered below

This book shows "many details of the artist's life when he was a boy growing up on a farm in western Canada. . . . Summer brought a great variety of experiences, including such regular, homely chores as milking and such demanding ones as driving the tractor that pulled the huge mowing machines. There was also the fun of skinny dipping, the excitement of great thunderstorms that swept across the prairie, and the drudgery of 'stooking,' when grain had to be bundled by hand during wet spells." Horn Bk

"It is, of course, the pictures by this distinguished Canadian artist that give the book its distinction; each full-color page glows with life and vigor, and the paintings have both a felicity of small details and a remarkable evocation of the breadth and sweep of the Manitoba prairie." Chicago. Children's Bk Center

A prairie boy's winter; paintings and story by William Kurelek. Houghton 1973 unp illus $7.95 (3-5)   971.27

1 Children in Canada   2 Winter   3 Farm life—Canada
ISBN 0-395-17708-1   LC 73-8913

Based on his own experiences, the author depicts the rigors and pleasures of boyhood winters on a Manitoba farm in the 1930's including hauling hay, playing hockey, and surviving a blizzard

"Kurelek's 20 full-page paintings combine a child's directness of expression with a technique subtle enough to make absolute distinctions in tone and texture between newly fallen snow and the waterlogged blanket of slush that characterizes the landscape of early spring. He captures the color of cold, the weight of a late autumn sky heavy with pending precipitation." NY Times Bk Rev

971.4   Quebec

Tanobe, Miyuki

Québec: Je t'aime; I love you. Tundra Bks. 1976 unp illus lib. bdg. $12.95 (4-6)   971.4

1 Quebec (Province)—Social life and customs 2 Bilingual books—French-English
ISBN 0-912766-42-5   LC 76-23273

"The text of this volume is arranged in parallel columns of French and English. To describe the working class neighborhoods of Montreal and Quebec the author/artist presents her paintings of 'the corner grocery store, the poultry market, election time, carnival time, a wedding party, boys playing hockey . . . icefishing and maple sugaring." Horn Bk

"While a few of the twenty-two full color paintings show scenes in the countryside outside Montreal, most of the pictures show the color and vigor of the cosmopolitan city and the vitality of its ethnic neighborhoods. Tanobe's text—partly descriptive and partly biographical—extends the information given by the paintings. . . . It is a bit too florid and too personal to make interesting reading, but it can be browsed through fairly painlessly. The painting, however, is wonderfully robust." Chicago. Children's Bk Center

971.9   Northern territories

Harrison, Ted

Children of the Yukon. Tundra Bks. 1977 unp illus $9.95 (2-4)   971.9

1 Children in Canada
ISBN 0-912766-83-2   LC 77-79543

"A teacher and an artist, Harrison illustrates his descriptions of life in the Yukon with poster-simple paintings that have clean, solid shapes usually heavily outlined; the colors are clear and strong, the people's faces without feature. The text gives some historical material about the Yukon and the gold rush, but most of it is devoted to description of everyday life or special events of the year. There are also facts about the region and its peoples, and a brief comment on the conflict between the native peoples' traditional way of life and the demands imposed on them by . . . pressure for oil and minerals." Chicago. Children's Bk Center

972   Middle America. Mexico

Beck, Barbara L.

The first book of the ancient Maya; pictures by Page Cary. Watts, F. 1965 87p illus maps lib. bdg. $6.45 (4 and up)   972

1 Mayas
ISBN 0-531-00464-3   LC 65-11746

"This social history of the Mayans gives brief attention to their religion, trade, communications, sculpture, painting, crafts, and architecture of the period of the flowering of their civilization. One chapter affords an overview of the major classical cities, the revolt of the peasants, migration and Toltec assimilation, important post-classical cities, and the Spanish conquest. Many illustrations show the art, temples, plans of cities, artifacts, and writing. This introductory book packs a great many facts concisely into its few pages." Sch Library J

The first book of the Aztecs; pictures by Page Cary. Watts, F. 1966 72p illus maps lib. bdg. $6.45 (4 and up)   972

1 Aztecs
ISBN 0-531-00476-7   LC 66-18671

"This introductory account succinctly highlights the historical background, daily life, religious and social structure, and major achievements of the Aztec nation and explains the probable cause of its overwhelming defeat by the Spaniards in 1521. Numerous detailed drawings, some reproduced from native codices, authentically depict Aztecan architecture, customs, and life." Booklist

Karen, Ruth

Feathered serpent; the rise and fall of the Aztecs. Four Winds 1979 184p illus lib. bdg. $9.95 (6 and up)   972

1 Aztecs
ISBN 0-590-07413-X   LC 78-22129

"The author surveys the brief flourishing of the Aztec civilization, emphasizing the 'cataclysmic vision of the universe' which resulted in its enigmatic and sometimes brutal culture. . . . The book examines the possible reasons for the Aztec's pessimistic outlook on life and its connection to their ritualistic practice of human sacrifice. The text is enlivened by numerous excerpts from the diaries of Spanish soldiers, who described in detail their impressions of the civilization that both dazzled and terrified them. The author delineates the tragic misunderstandings that led to the Spanish conquest of the Aztecs and its continuing effect on present-day Mexico. Included at the end is a fictional story of a young Aztec warrior. With suggested readings, a glossary, and an index." Horn Bk

Perl, Lila

Mexico, crucible of Americas; illus. with photographs. Morrow 1978 159p illus $8.95, lib. bdg. $8.59 (6 and up)   972

1 Mexico
ISBN 0-688-22148-3; 0-688-32148-8   LC 77-20203

"A broad survey of Mexican history and contemporary life. . . . Perl describes the country geographically, and discusses the struggle for independence in the nineteenth century. . . . Later chapters describe foods, entertainment, the class structure, Spanish and Indian heritage, education, and many of the problems of daily life as well as those of the larger political, industrial, and economic scenes. Perl also discusses the influence of the United States on Mexican life, and Mexico's role in relation to other countries of Latin America and the world." Chicago. Children's Bk Center

Bibliography: p156

972.81   Guatemala

Jenness, Aylette

A life of their own; an Indian family in Latin America; text and photographs by Aylette Jenness and Lisa W. Kroeber; drawings by Susan Votaw. Crowell 1975 133p illus map $8.95 (5 and up)   972.81

1 Indians of Central America—Guatemala 2 Guatemala—Social conditions
ISBN 0-690-00572-5   LC 75-15964

Jenness, Aylette—*Continued*

"A documentary based on personal and sympathetic observation of a way of life. The authors spent a great deal of time with one family but also explored the health clinic, the school, the market, and the government of a Guatemalan town. Although the native language of the Hernandez family was Cakchiquel, they spoke some Spanish, as did the authors, and were able to communicate without too much difficulty. . . . The last section of the book is called a 'Workshop' and gives instructions for weaving, cooking, making festival figures, running a market (with Spanish words for numbers and often-used phrases) and other projects that can enable the reader to learn exactly how the Hernandez family and their neighbors live. A vocabulary and a relative index are appended." Chicago. Children's Bk Center

"It's easy to get involved in this expository look at how a relatively prosperous Guatemalan Indian family lives; the authors obviously loved putting their book together and care as much about their readers as they do their subject. That concern adds a personal dimension that is evident throughout the photojournalistic presentation." Booklist

972.87 Panama

Markun, Patricia Maloney

The Panama Canal. Rev. ed. Watts, F. 1979 66p illus map lib. bdg. $5.90 (5 and up)   972.87

1 Panama Canal
ISBN 0-531-04075-5   LC 79-14510

"A First book"
First published 1958 with title: The first book of the Panama Canal

This book traces the development of the Panama Canal from its planning stage and its construction to the present day

"Brief comments about the 1978 treaty and its future implications appear, yet omit mention of the accompanying controversy. . . . The fictionalized introductory chapter . . . describes a canal pilot's day of maneuvering a vessel through the waters." Booklist

Other books to read: p64

972.91 Cuba

Ortiz, Victoria

The land and people of Cuba. Lippincott 1973 157p illus map (Portraits of the nations ser) $8.95 (5 and up)   972.91

1 Cuba
ISBN 0-397-31382-9   LC 72-11878

"Highlighting individuals important in Cuba's history Ortiz surveys the island's past—its discovery and colonization, the decimation of the native population, the influx of different ethnic groups including African slaves, the struggle for independence, U.S. intervention and the Spanish-American War, and life under the Batista regime. In the second half of the book she describes the Cuban revolution and, emphasizing achievements rather than problems, gives a basically optimistic overview of social, economic, and cultural progress in Cuba under Castro. A map and numerous photographs complement the briskly written text." Booklist

972.95 Puerto Rico

Colorado, Antonio J.

The first book of Puerto Rico. [3d] rev. ed. Watts, F. 1978 66p illus map lib. bdg. $5.90 (5 and up)   972.95

1 Puerto Rico
ISBN 0-531-01292-1   LC 77-17520

First published 1965
This book discusses Puerto Rico's history, geography, economics, people, cities and towns, education, art, sports, historic buildings, the capital city of San Juan, politics and elections (through 1976), and relations with the United States

Glossary: p62-63

Perl, Lila

Puerto Rico; island between two worlds. Morrow 1979 159p illus $9.50, lib. bdg. $9.12 (6 and up)   972.95

1 Puerto Rico
ISBN 0-688-22181-5; 0-688-32181-X   LC 79-1130

"Perl painstakingly and accurately surveys the island in all its aspects: geography, ethnic composition, religion, economics, local costume, folklore, political history, and the diverse influences which, for good or bad, have shaped it. Two-thirds of the book is devoted to the condition of Puerto Rico today—the agriculture, the government and its efforts and policies, the contrasting life styles, education, tourism, the new look imparted by modern architecture, etc. In the last chapter, the pros and cons of commonwealth status vs. statehood vs. total independence are examined with lucid objectivity." Sch Library J

Bibliography: p156

Singer, Julia

We all come from someplace: children of Puerto Rico; text and photographs by Julia Singer. Atheneum Pubs. 1976 88p illus $6.95 (4-6)   972.95

1 Puerto Rico 2 Children in Puerto Rico
ISBN 0-689-30531-1   LC 75-46577

"This photographic picture-study gives many views of the island [of Puerto Rico] and of the people who live there. Children and young people describe their way of life in short, simple statements, each one illustrated by an informative, black-and-white photograph. Through their eyes we glimpse historical sites remaining from the days of the Indians and the Spaniards and contrasting ways of modern life in the mountain village, in a fishing village, and in a town where life revolves around the sugar industry. Children describe the happiness of the Christmas holidays and give an appreciation of the large city of Mayaguez." Horn Bk

"Many, many small—but on the whole interesting and well-printed—black-and-white photographs accompany a brief text. . . . Although the book is not colorful, the reader does get a good feeling for the several different Puerto Rican life styles described in the words of the children [and] in the pictures." Children's Bk Rev Serv

973 United States

As I saw it: women who lived the American adventure; collected by Cheryl G. Hoople. Dial Press 1978 187p illus $8.95 (6 and up)   973

1 Women—U.S. 2 U.S.—History—Personal narratives
ISBN 0-8037-0339-2   LC 78-51324

"A series of letters, journal and diary excerpts, and other historical documents gives varied and absorbing accounts of some of the adventures and accomplishments in the lives of women in American history. A few are well known—such people as Narcissa Whitman, Abigail Adams, or Clara Barton—and in the statements by them and others (slaves, doctors, spies, pioneers, early colonists in California or New England) there are both personal troubles and triumphs, and a broad view of American history. Each excerpt is prefaced by the compiler's introduction." Chicago. Children's Bk Center

"The outstanding characteristics of the women are their bravery and fortitude; no doubt many readers will be inspired to investigate further their lives and final achievements." Horn Bk

Selected bibliography: p186-87

Brandt, Sue R.

Facts about the 50 states. Rev. ed Watts, F. 1979 66p illus maps lib. bdg. $5.90 (4-6)   973

1 United States
ISBN 0-531-02899-2   LC 79-13261

"A First book"
First published 1970
This book supplies basic information on the fifty states, such as state capitals, size, population, nicknames, emblems, etc. Organization is by subject rather than by state

Commager, Henry Steele
The first book of American history; pictures by Leonard Everett Fisher. Watts, F. 1957 62p illus lib. bdg. $6.45 (4-6)   973

1 U.S.—History
ISBN 0-531-00458-9   LC 57-7537
A "readable overview of United States history from early colonial days to the present time. Because of the brevity of the text the author has had to resort to some rather sweeping generalizations, but he has, for the most part, avoided misleading oversimplifications. The text will probably have more meaning for readers with some familiarity with the subject than for younger readers who are approaching American history for the first time." Chicago. Children's Bk Center

Johnson, Gerald W.
America grows up; a history for Peter; illus. by Leonard Everett Fisher. Morrow 1960 223p illus $8.75 (5 and up)   973

1 U.S.—History
ISBN 0-688-21015-5   LC 60-5206
Second book in a trilogy, begun in: America is born
"This has a sweep, a scope, and a fresh approach that make it a joy to read. Mr. Johnson is both objective and sensitive; he explores the larger issues of United States history and the forces that move toward events. . . . The book begins with the formation of the thirteen colonies into one union of states, and ends with the United States about to engage in World War I. Again, in this volume the illustrations by Mr. Fisher are dramatic and powerful. An excellent and comprehensive index is appended." Chicago. Children's Bk Center
Followed by: America moves forward o.p. 1981

America is born; a history for Peter; illus. by Leonard Everett Fisher. Morrow 1959 254p illus $8.75 (5 and up)   973

1 U.S.—History
ISBN 0-688-21071-1   LC 59-7405
The first title of a "three-volume history of the U.S., this covers the period from Columbus' discovery of America through the Revolution to the Constitutional Convention of 1787. . . . [The] person-to-person style and the keenness and remarkable clarity with which the author explores and evaluates motives, causes, and effects make this a meaningful and exciting book. Illustrated with many bold, dramatic drawings." Booklist
Followed by: America grows up

Lawson, Robert
Watchwords of liberty; a pageant of American quotations. New ed. with text and illus. by Robert Lawson. Little 1957 115p illus $7.95 (3-6)   973

1 U.S.—History 2 Quotations
ISBN 0-316-51742-9   LC 57-4017
First published 1943
Here are the words of great Americans in war and in peace—more than fifty of the famous quotations which highlight memorable moments in American history from the time of the Pilgrims
"Intended to give youngsters . . . a more vivid sense of the great hours in our history, but a great many grownups will enjoy and profit by it also." Spring'd Republican
"Illustrated with full page drawings in black and white." Cleveland

Tunis, Edwin
The young United States, 1783 to 1830; a time of change and growth; a time of learning democracy; a time of new ways of living, thinking and doing; written and illus. by Edwin Tunis. Crowell [1976 c1969] 159p illus $12.95 (6 and up)   973

1 U.S.—Social life and customs 2 U.S.—History —1783-1865
ISBN 0-690-01065-6   LC 75-29613
A reprint of the title first published 1969 by World
"Topically organized, the text describes the different kinds of communities of the period, factories and inventions, schools and colleges, the growth of the west, travel, the arts, et cetera. There is a minimal amount of invention; the author explains in a prefatory note that occasionally a family or a town is meant to serve as an amalgam and example of the type. The index is extensive." Sutherland. The Best in Children's Bks

Weitzman, David
My backyard history book; illus. by James Robertson. Little 1975 128p illus $8.95, pa $5.95 (4 and up)   973

1 U.S.—History—Miscellanea 2 U.S.—History, Local
ISBN 0-316-92901-8; 0-316-92902-6   LC 75-6577
"The Brown paper school series"
"Backyard history means delving into a past that's close to home; building family archives by figuring out family trees or interviewing parents and elderly relatives about their younger days; developing a feel for their life-style by noticing old appliances and gadgets that might be around the house; and checking out immediate neighborhoods or older sections of town for evidence of bygone days. Related activities include examining old Sears, Roebuck catalogs, making rubbings of picturesque tombstones, manhole covers, or decorative stone facings, photographing old buildings, and becoming an amateur student of architecture." Booklist
"Full of fascinating social studies activities to be pursued 'scientifically' by elementary children. The clever, down-to-earth tasks will not only keep children happy and busy for weeks, but will give them a taste of historical research techniques. The illustrations are clear and concise. The humor injected into every page is the kind of slap-stick hilarity kids love. 'I hate history' is doomed to extinction by this book. In sharp contrast to the action-packed text, the outside of the book is a study in bland anonymity." AAAS Sci Bks & Films

973.1 U.S.—Period of prehistory, discovery, exploration to 1607

Campbell, Elizabeth A.
The carving on the tree; illus. by William Bock. Little 1968 88p illus $7.95 (3-5)   973.1

1 Roanoke Island—History
ISBN 0-316-12564-4   LC 67-21180
An "account of the brief life of the lost colony of Roanoke. The story offers vivid portraits of men such as Governor John White, who tried to get expeditions organized to save the small colony, and Simon Fernando, the captain who left the colonists on Roanoke Island against their own wishes." Adventuring with Bks. 2d edition
"Although the size of type and format of the book are suitable for a younger reader, events have not been over-simplified. The story is powerful and moving and should be read more than once. Effective illustration in gold, black, and white." Horn Bk

Duvoisin, Roger
And there was America; written and illus. by Roger Duvoisin. Knopf 1938 75p illus lib. bdg. $6.99 (3-5)   973.1

1 America—Exploration 2 U.S.—History
ISBN 0-394-90910-0   LC 38-27992
A narrative for young readers relating the early discoveries and settlements of North America made by peoples of many lands. It includes stories of Leif Ericsson, Columbus, Ponce de Leon, Hudson, the Pilgrims, Roger Williams, and others
"This account of finding America . . . is full of signs and wonders and yet of facts which give a true picture of this great adventure. The brilliant, glowing, illustrations and the short sentences add to the dramatic appeal and bring the story to the level of the young child's interest." Wis Library Bul

973.2 U.S.—Colonial period, 1607-1775

Alderman, Clifford Lindsey
The story of the thirteen colonies; illus. by
Leonard Everett Fisher. Random House 1966
187p illus lib. bdg. $5.99 (5 and up)   **973.2**
1 U.S.—History—Colonial period, 1600-1775
ISBN 0-394-90415-X   LC 67-641
"Landmark books"
The author "describes the events leading up to
the establishment of the colonies, including the
lives and characters of the men most important
in each colony's history." Library J
"Mr Alderman writes smoothly, and the book
will (hopefully) stimulate young Americans to discover more about the lively, complex world that
existed here before 1776." NY Times Bk Rev
Bibliography: p176-80

Siegel, Beatrice
A new look at the Pilgrims; why they
came to America; illus. by Douglas Morris.
Walker & Co. 1977 82p illus. lib. bdg. $5.85
(4-6)   **973.2**
1 Pilgrims (New England colonists)
ISBN 0-8027-6292-1   LC 76-57060
In a question-and-answer format "the author
traces the separatist movement that led people
from England to Holland to America. Background
information on seventeenth-century England and
Holland sets the scene for the future pilgrims'
discontent and tells why they felt forced to emi-
grate and seek a new land where they were free
to worship and live as thy chose. How they
organized, financed, and finally completed their
voyage are concisely chronicled." Children's Bk
Rev Serv
"A handy, workable introduction, with a descriptive table of contents rather than an index, and
softened, articulate black-and-white illustrations."
Booklist
Suggested further reading: p81-82. Map on lining-papers

Sloane, Eric
ABC book of early Americana; a sketch-
book of antiquities and American firsts.
Doubleday 1963 unp illus $4.95, lib. bdg. $5.90
(4 and up)   **973.2**
1 U.S.—Social life and customs—Colonial period,
1600-1775 2 Alphabet
ISBN 0-385-04663-4; 0-385-05169-7   LC 63-18657
Pencil sketches accompany descriptions of early
American objects from the almanack, hex sign, and
johnny-cake to the niddy noddy, quill pen, and
zig-zag fence. Includes a section on the alphabet
"Mr. Sloane has hand-lettered his alphabet and
the names of articles so that his pages are not only
informative but extremely pleasant to look at.
Particularly engaging is the artist's admiration for
the work of skilled craftsmen." Bk Week

Tunis, Edwin
Colonial living; written and illus. by Edwin
Tunis. Crowell [1976 c1957] 155p illus $12.95
(6 and up)   **973.2**
1 U.S.—Social life and customs—Colonial period,
1600-1775
ISBN 0-690-01063-X   LC 75-29611
A reprint of the title first published 1957 by
World
"A comprehensive portrayal of the details of
life in the United States in the 17th and 18th
centuries. Over 200 detailed drawings supplement
and amplify the text. Among the aspects of colonial
life described in the book are food and dress,
architecture and industries, tools and utensils, communications and customs. An excellent reference
book; the smooth writing and occasional bits of
humor provide reading that is enjoyable as well as
informative." Chicago. Children's Bk Center

The tavern at the ferry; illus. by the author.
Crowell 1973 109p illus $9.95 (5 and up)
        973.2
1 U.S.—Social life and customs—Colonial period
1600-1775 2 U.S.—History—Colonial period, 1600-
1775
ISBN 0-690-00099-5   LC 73-4488

"Tracing the development of the taverns and
ferry-crossings along the Pennsylvania and New
Jersey sides of the Delaware River, [the author]
perforce traces the growth of transportation of
commerce, and—finally—of rebellion in the colonies. . . . The main characters in the story are
the family and descendants of Henry Baker, a
Quaker who came to the New World in 1684 and
settled in what became Makefield Township, Bucks
County, Pennsylvania. The account of how the
Baker house became first a convenient place for
the occasional wayfarer to get help in crossing the
river, then an 'ordinary,' or ordinary household,
whose master sold food and drink, and finally a
full-fledged tavern is intermittently interrupted by
chapters of a more general nature: Expansion,
Enterprise and Taverns in Country and Town.
. . . The final section describes Washington's crossing of the Delaware and the battle of Trenton,
events which make an appropriately grand finale
for a book on ferry crossings." Horn Bk
This book "is profusely illustrated with pictures
that give, in their meticulous detail, authoritative
information about clothing, buildings, weapons,
vehicles, and other artifacts of the period. . . .
Useful for social studies, fascinating for the
history buff or the reader interested in Americana,
well organized and written, this is a handsome
book." Chicago. Children's Bk Center

973.3 U.S.—Revolution and confederation, 1775-1789

Bliven, Bruce
The American Revolution, 1760-1783; illus.
by Albert Orbaan. Random House 1958 182p
illus maps $2.95, lib. bdg. $5.99 (5 and up)
        973.3
1 U.S.—History—Revolution, 1775-1783
ISBN 0-394-80383-3; 0-394-90383-8   LC 58-6183
"Landmark books"
An "overview of the causes, battles, and results
of the Revolution." Hodges. Bks for Elem Sch
Libraries
"This very readable account . . . may well serve
as introductory material for a more detailed study.
. . . Events are viewed within the larger framework of European history. [Illustrated with]
drawings and a section of infrequently seen photographs." Library J

Colby, Jean Poindexter
Lexington and Concord, 1775: what really
happened; illus. with photographs by Barbara
Cooney [and] old prints and maps. Hastings
House 1975 128p illus maps lib. bdg. $7.95
(5 and up)   **973.3**
1 Lexington, Battle of, 1775 2 Concord, Battle
of, 1775 3 U.S.—History—Revolution, 1775-
1783
ISBN 0-8038-4292-9   LC 74-11466
The author provides an account of the events
"at Lexington and Concord in 1775 and also a
record of the sources behind the account. . . .
In addition, the book includes a summary of
events leading to the war, an annotated list of
prominent men on both sides, [and] a tour of
Lexington and Concord." NY Times Bk Rev
"The volume does not include any unusual information or historical material not easily available
elsewhere; but the writing is brisk and light, and
the book has been enhanced with prolific illustrations, which show everything from quaint drawings of cows grazing on Boston Common to
present-day photographs of historic buildings."
Horn Bk
Bibliography: p122-25

Commager, Henry Steele
The great Declaration; a book for young
Americans; written and ed. by Henry Steele
Commager. Drawings by Donald Bolognese.
Bobbs 1958 112p illus $6.95 (6 and up)   **973.3**
1 U.S. Declaration of Independence
ISBN 0-672-50301-8   LC 58-12915
"A distinguished historian, using excerpts from
official documents, letters, and diaries, skillfully
weaves together the story of the Declaration of
Independence, explaining how it came into being
and describing the men who discussed, debated,
and finally drafted it. The text is complemented
with pen sketches and reproductions of contemporary paintings and woodcuts." Wis Library Bul

Commager, Henry S.—*Continued*
"The narrative passages by the author (through which the quoted material is unified) are as moving and vivid as the proclamations and letters themselves." Chicago. Children's Bk Center
Bibliography included in Notes: p109-10

Dalgliesh, Alice
The Fourth of July story; illus. by Marie Nonnast. Scribner 1956 unp illus $8.95 (2-4)　　973.3
1 Fourth of July 2 U.S. Declaration of Independence
ISBN 0-684-13164-1　　　　LC 56-6138
The author tells "of the events that led up to the decision of the colonies to break with England, of the actual writing of the Declaration of Independence, and of its reception by the people of the colonies." Chicago. Children's Bk Center
"For the sake of clarity [the author] has deliberately chosen not to indicate the exact chronology of the signing of the Declaration. . . . [An account] notable for its compactness, its readability and its sense of history in the making." NY Times Bk Rev
"The many full-page colored illustrations will help the young child to understand the meaning of this, one of the most colorful and dramatic of our American holidays." Sat Rev

Davis, Burke
Black heroes of the American Revolution; foreword by Edward W. Brooke; with prints and portraits of the period. Harcourt 1976 80p illus $6.95 (5 and up)　　973.3
1 U.S.—History—Revolution, 1775-1783—Blacks
ISBN 0-15-208560-2　　　　LC 75-42218
The author "focuses his attention on a group of American patriots whose contributions in the flight for independence have been widely over-looked because, for the most part, they went unrecorded. In a very readable style, the author relates the stories of a few of the approximtely 5000 Black soldiers who participated in the Revolution, emphasizing their unselfishness fighting a war from which few of them would substantially benefit. In addition, there is an excellent chapter on the exploits of several predominantly Black infantry companies." Sch Library J
"The illustrations are appropriate being prints and portraits of the period." Children's Bk Rev Serv
For further reading: p78

Griffin, Judith Berry
Phoebe and the General; illus. by Margot Tomes. Coward, McCann & Geoghegan 1977 47p illus $7.95 (2-5)　　973.3
1 Washington, George, President U.S. 2 Fraunces, Phoebe 3 U.S.—History—Revolution, 1775-1783
ISBN 0-698-29377-1　　　　LC 76-8921
"Phoebe Fraunces is persuaded by her father, who keeps the famous New York tavern, to become General George Washington's housekeeper. When a plot against Washington's life is coming to a climax, Phoebe is asked to watch for a man whose name begins with T and to report daily to her father. At a dinner party Phoebe clearly emerges as the heroine when she acts with marked presence of mind to save the General." Horn Bk
"Margot Tomes's pen and ink illustrations have the drawing and muted color of hand-tinted prints. Her final delicate portrait of Washington thanking Phoebe and Fraunces strikes a balance of design and emotion that is warm yet restrained. It almost speaks." NY Times Bk Rev

Loeper, John J.
Going to school in 1776; illus. with old woodcuts. Atheneum Pubs. 1973 79p illus lib. bdg. $6.95 (3-6)　　973.3
1 U.S.—Social life and customs 2 Education—U.S.—History 3 Children in the U.S.
ISBN 0-689-30089-1　　　　LC 72-86949
The author tells what it was like to be a child and to go to school in America in 1776. He describes children's dress, schools, teachers, school books, lessons, discipline and after-school recreation
Bibliography: p[83-84]

Lomask, Milton
The first American Revolution. Farrar, Straus 1974 280p maps $7.95 (6 and up)　973.3
1 U.S.—History—Revolution, 1775-1783
ISBN 0-374-32337-2　　　　LC 73-90972
This is an "account of all of the ramifications concerned with the American Revolution—the military, political, economic and social. The book is divided into three sections—the revolution, the war and the peace." Children's Bk Rev Serv
"This book about the turbulent years from 1763-1784 steers a clear course between over-romanticizing and over-denigrating the American Revolution. The author admits that the Revolution was not fought against royal tyranny and also counters Beardian arguments that it was mainly fought for economic reasons; he points to the propagandistic nature of the Declaration of Independence as well as to the sincerity of some of the colonists' actions. And he accurately records a number of points much confused by legend." Horn Bk
Bibliography: p267-71

Mason, F. Van Wyck
The winter at Valley Forge; illus. by Harper Johnson. Random House 1953 180p illus lib. bdg. $5.99 (5 and up)　　973.3
1 U.S.—History—Revolution, 1775-1783 2 Valley Forge, Pa.—History
ISBN 0-394-90333-1　　　　LC 53-6258
"Landmark books"
"The six long months of hunger, killing cold, and disease, the heartaches and despair suffered by General Washington's 'ragtag and bobtail' army in the winter encampment at Valley Forge are vividly reconstructed in this semi-factual, semi-narrative account." Booklist

Phelan, Mary Kay
Four days in Philadelphia, 1776; illus. by Charles Walker. Crowell 1967 189p illus $8.95 (5 and up)　　973.3
1 U.S. Declaration of Independence
ISBN 0-690-31485-X　　　　LC 67-18521
The author reconstructs "the four July days of debate that preceded the adoption of the Declaration of Independence by the Continental Congress. . . . [She 'cuts'] from actor to actor—Thomas Jefferson, John Adams and many less familiar signers. Using original journals and letters, she describes what each man was like, his thoughts and problems, how he behaved from hour to hour in the taverns, lodgings, and meeting halls of Philadelphia." Bk World
Bibliography: p179-83

Midnight alarm; the story of Paul Revere's ride; illus. by Leonard Weisgard. Crowell 1968 131p illus maps $8.95 (3-6)　　973.3
1 Revere, Paul 2 U.S.—History—Revolution, 1775-1783
ISBN 0-690-53638　　　　LC 68-17080
"A vivid present-tense narrative evokes the uneasy atmosphere of a city occupied by enemy troops and reconstructs the preparations for and details of Paul Revere's dramatic ride to warn Lexington patriots of a British attack." Booklist
"The historic ride is presented in a straightforward manner. . . . Satisfactory as curriculum-oriented background in history and supplementary information to accompany Longfellow's poem [entered in class 811]." Sch Library J
Bibliography: p121-23

The story of the Boston Massacre; illus. by Allan Eitzen. Crowell 1976 146p illus $8.95 (6 and up)　　973.3
1 Boston Massacre, 1770
ISBN 0-690-00716　　　　LC 75-25961
"In a present-tense narrative that evokes the tense mood of Boston in the months before the Massacre, the author objectively portrays the underlying causes and graphically describes the event. Also included is the town's angry reaction and details of the soldiers' trial. Generous use of primary sources and colorful descriptions of the famous patriots involved make this a very appealing account of one of the more significant chapters in American history." Sch Library J
Bibliography: p137-40

Phelan, Mary K.—*Continued*

The story of the Boston Tea Party; drawings by Frank Aloise. Crowell 1973 113p illus $8.95 (4-6)   973.3

1 Boston Tea Party, 1773
ISBN 0-690-77653-5   LC 72-7554

This is "a detailed treatment of the causes and events of the Boston Tea Party on December 16, 1773. Phelan describes the town meetings and secret sessions in Boston, Whigs versus Tories, and the influence of such colonists as Sam Adams, John Hancock, and Paul Revere. The participants are pictured not as fanatics but as patriots who tried to find a peaceful way to resolve the issue of unfair taxation and turned to the tea party raid only as a last resort. Written in the present-tense, the mood of the period is evoked with striking immediacy. Frank Aloise's line drawings re-create the incidents with an exciting, on-the-spot quality. Quotations are documented, conversations have not been fictionalized, and an index and lengthy bibliography are included. For reference or read in its entirety, this is an important addition to accounts of the Revolutionary War period." Sch Library J

Taylor, Theodore

Rebellion town, Williamsburg, 1776; drawings by Richard Cuffari. Crowell 1973 212p illus $8.95 (5 and up)   973.3

1 U.S.—History—Revolution, 1775-1783—Causes
2 Virginia—History—Colonial period, 1600-1775
ISBN 0-690-00019-7   LC 73-10187

Emphasizing events in Williamsburg, Virginia, this account of the colonial independence movement begins with Patrick Henry's speech in 1763 against the British Crown

"While the text is not cohesive, there are some moments of drama and a vivid picture of Patrick Henry as he develops from a rustic figure with a gift for oratory to a seasoned legislator who becomes the first governor of the state of Virginia. The book also makes clear how much of our Declaration of Independence (and other, similar documents in other countries) was based on the work of George Mason, whose Declaration of Rights for the Virginia colony was adapted by Thomas Jefferson." Chicago. Children's Bk Center
Bibliography: p202-05

973.4 U.S.—Constitutional period, 1789-1809

Neuberger, Richard L.

The Lewis and Clark Expedition; illus. by Winold Reiss. Random House 1951 180p illus map lib. bdg. $5.99 (4 and up)   973.4

1 Lewis and Clark Expedition 2 Clark, William, 1770-1838 3 Lewis, Meriwether
ISBN 0-394-90315-3   LC 51-14181

"Landmark books"
"This brisk retelling of a much chronicled event makes the 33 men and their amazing undertaking seem very real." Booklist
"The last chapter telling what happened later to the leaders is a satisfactory conclusion, leaving no loose ends. References to contemporary figures should lead to further reading. Format is excellent and double-page spread map showing the route is easy to follow and clarifies the material." Library J

Phelan, Mary Kay

The story of the Louisiana Purchase; illus. by Frank Aloise. Crowell 1979 149p illus map $7.95, lib. bdg. $7.89 (5 and up)   973.4

1 Louisiana Purchase 2 U.S.—History—1783-1809
ISBN 0-690-03955-7; 0-690-03956-5   LC 78-22505

"The political maneuvering and delicate diplomacy which led to the purchase of the land are shown through conversations—which the author based on reports by the participants—and excerpts from letters, diaries, and newspapers of the era. The writing style of the present-tense narrative is unexceptional, but the dialogue is smooth and believable and gives enticing glimpses into the personalities of such men as Thomas Jefferson, James Monroe, and Napoleon Bonaparte. Bibliography and index." Horn Bk

Tallant, Robert

The Louisiana Purchase; illus. by Warren Chappell. Random House 1952 183p illus lib. bdg. $4.99 (5 and up)   973.4

1 Louisiana Purchase 2 U.S.—History—1783-1809
ISBN 0-394-90324-2   LC 52-7229

"Landmark books"
The book "reviews the world situation which influenced Napoleon to sell the vast Louisiana territory to the United States and describes the negotiations which preceded the sale." Hodges. Bks for Elem Sch Libraries
"Altogether this makes a colorful and exciting chapter in American history." Library J

973.6 U.S.—Middle 19th century, 1845-1861

Baker, Betty

The Pig War; pictures by Robert Lopshire. Harper 1969 64p illus map (An I can read History bk) lib. bdg. $6.89 (k-2)   973.6

1 Northwest, Pacific—History 2 U.S.—History—1815-1861
ISBN 0-06-020333-1   LC 69-10212

It is the year 1859, and on a tiny island between the United States and British Canada, "a war almost begins when British pigs raid an American garden. All ends well when the islanders unite to get rid of the soldiers of both sides." Minnesota

973.7 U.S.—Administration of Abraham Lincoln, 1861-1865 (Civil War)

Davis, Burke

Appomattox; closing struggle of the Civil War; ed. by Walter Lord; illus. with 29 Civil War photographs and drawings. Harper 1963 167p illus maps lib. bdg. $8.79 (6 and up)   973.7

1 Appomattox Campaign, 1865
ISBN 0-06-021401-5   LC 63-17280

"A Breakthrough book"
Based on the author's Gray Fox: Robert E. Lee and the Civil War, published 1956 by Rinehart
This is an "account of the few days before, during and after the surrender of Lee to Grant at the home of Maj. Wilmer McLean on Palm Sunday, 1865." America
"Contemporary photographs of people and places are captioned in an informative and incisive way." Toronto Boys and Girls House

Reit, Seymour

Ironclad! A true story of the Civil War; illus. with old prints and drawings by the author. Dodd 1977 92p illus map $5.95 (4-6)   973.7

1 Hampton Roads, Battle of, 1862 2 Monitor (Ironclad) 3 Merrimac (Frigate)
ISBN 0-396-07403-0   LC 76-50649

In this "reconstruction of the historic Civil War sea battle between the Northern 'Monitor' and Southern 'Merrimac', Reit delineates some behind-the-scenes tensions that deepen the picture of battle: there was, for example, widespread lack of faith in the 'Monitor' and friction between Secretary of Navy Gideon Welles and Secretary of War Edwin Stanton, an avowed skeptic of the vessel's abilities; the near sinking of the ship during a storm as it was being escorted to active duty lends truth to Stanton's sentiments. But the 'tin-can-on-a-raft,' as its detractors called it, did withstand battle conditions and blocked the heretofore lethal progress of the 'Merrimac' through the Northern fleet of wooden ships. The story unfolds from several viewpoints, including that of a young crew member who provides the central focus; in an epilogue Reit places the battle in historical context and lists the fates of the ship's commander and focal crewmen." Booklist

973.8 U.S.—Later 19th century, 1865-1901 (Period of reconstruction)

Goble, Paul
Red Hawk's account of Custer's last battle; the Battle of the Little Bighorn, 25 June 1876 [by] Paul and Dorothy Goble. Pantheon Bks. [1970 c1969] 59p illus map lib. bdg. $5.99 (4 and up)   973.8
1 Little Big Horn, Battle of the, 1876 2 Custer, George Armstrong 3 Dakota Indians 4 Cheyenne Indians
  ISBN 0-394-90158-4   LC 76-77415
First published 1969 in England
"Drawing from the accounts of actual Indian warriors who participated in the Battle of the Little Big Horn, the authors have created the character Red Hawk, a young Oglala Sioux, to tell the Indian version of Custer's Last Stand. Red Hawk's moving account of the warriors' efforts to fend off the attacking horse soldiers is contrasted and accentuated by the cold, factual passages, drawn from military records, which detail the movements of the cavalry." Sch Library J
"The illustrations, filled with drama, movement and occasional moments of stilness, are based on the work of Plains Indians of the period." New Statesman
Bibliography: p[62-63]

Hilton, Suzanne
The way it was—1876. Westminster Press 1975 216p illus $6.95 (6 and up)   973.8
1 U.S.—Social life and customs 2 U.S.—History—1865-1898
  ISBN 0-664-32558-0   LC 74-20665
"A detailed discussion of what life was like in the year the United States became one hundred years old ought to be informative and dull; it has no right to be as entertaining as Suzanne Hilton makes it as she describes clothing, education (the incident in which an elocution teacher trains her class to lilt is hilarious), sports, medicine, clothing, home manufacture (one concoction for soft skin sent a girl to bed, the author says, 'smelling like a macaroon') and travel. . . . Based on thorough research but written with spontaneity, the book is both amusing and useul." Chicago. Children's Bk Center
Bibliography: p205-10

973.91 U.S.—Early 20th century, 1901-1953

Cook, Ann
What was it like? When your grandparents were your age, by Ann Cook, Herb Mack, and Marilyn Gittell. Pantheon Bks. 1976 94p illus lib. bdg. $4.99, pa $3.95 (3-6)   973.91
1 U.S.—Social life and customs
  ISBN 0-394-92993-4; 0-394-82993-X   LC 75-35893
"A credible attempt to communicate the fact that history is people from the past linked to us by basic experiences but separated by the development of different social circumstances. Descriptions of life in the first part of the twentieth century are accompanied by antique-brown photographs of everything from beaches to baby care, fashions, and the price of groceries. The book will require special teacher guidance for relating such human-interest materials to history texts and following up on the suggestion that students put together a 'time capsule' album of their own." Booklist

974 Northeastern United States

Loeb, Robert H.
New England village; everyday life in 1810, by Robert H. Loeb, Jr. Doubleday 1976 98p illus $6.95, lib. bdg. $7.90 (4-6)   974
1 New England—Social life and customs 2 Old Sturbridge Village, Sturbridge, Mass. 3 Pawtucket, R. I. Old Slater Mill
  ISBN 0-385-11488-5; 0-385-11489-3   LC 76-2791

An "account of everyday life in New England during the early 19th Century. Through a tour of a typical village (Old Sturbridge is the model) with stops at the reconstructed farmhouse, village shops, school, and a nearby textile mill (Old Slater Mill in Rhode Island), farming methods, home life, and local industry are given full and detailed coverage. Illustrated with period engravings and black-and-white photographs from Old Sturbridge Village." Sch Library J

974.4 Massachusetts

Beck, Barbara L.
The Pilgrims of Plymouth; illus. with photographs. Watts, F. 1972 89p illus map lib. bdg. $4.47 (5 and up)   974.4
1 Pilgrims (New England Colonists)
  ISBN 0-531-00776-6   LC 79-187970
"A First book"
This book traces the story of the Pilgrims and Plymouth Colony from the early days in Scrooby and the years in Holland until Plymouth joined with the Massachusetts Bay Colony in 1691. It treats their economy, relationship with the Indians, daily life and customs, government, law and religion
A selected bibliography: p84

Bowen, Gary
My village, Sturbridge; wood engravings designed by Gary Bowen and engraved by Randy Miller. Farrar, Straus 1977 57p illus $6.95 (4-6)   974.4
1 Old Sturbridge Village, Sturbridge, Mass.
  ISBN 0-374-35110-4   LC 77-10059
"Old Sturbridge Village in Massachusetts is actually a museum consisting of eighteenth- and early nineteenth-century buildings and artifacts. Among other items it includes Isaiah Thomas's Worcester printing office originally built in 1783. In the present volume the village is envisioned as a real historical community by a fictitious young engraver, True Mason, who has been apprenticed to the famous printer and has worked in the Sturbridge printing shop for three years. Cast in the form of a letter to Isaiah Thomas, the book consists of alternating pages of text and wood engravings which give verisimilitude to the occupations and activities of the imagined inhabitants. The elegant illustrations create precise vignettes of life as it might have been lived in an American village during the early 1800s." Horn Bk

Daugherty, James
The landing of the Pilgrims; written and illus. by James Daugherty. Random House 1950 186p illus lib. bdg. $5.99 (5 and up)   974.4
1 Pilgrims (New England Colonists) 2 Massachusetts—History—Colonial period, 1600-1775 3 Bradford, William
  ISBN 0-394-90302-1   LC 50-10542
Only slightly fictionized, this is the story of William Bradford based on his own writings. Beginning with the young Will's decision to join the Separatists in Scrooby, England, the narrative tells of the travels of the Pilgrims to Holland and then to the New World, and of their adventures and hardships during the early years of their life there
"Humor enters into the story . . . dry, delightful humor. . . . [The account] is curiously timely." Sat Rev

Fritz, Jean
Who's that stepping on Plymouth Rock? Illus. by J. B. Handelsman. Coward, McCann & Geoghegan 1975 30p illus $6.95 (3-5) 974.4
1 Plymouth Rock
  ISBN 0-698-20325-9   LC 74-30593
An "account of the Rock which is visited yearly by about one and a half million people. It stands now under a monument on the waterfront of Plymouth, Massachusetts, sacred to the memory of the First Comers (Pilgrims) but it has figured in many adventures since the Pilgrims did—or did not—step upon it in 1620." Pub W

Fritz, Jean—Continued

The author's "true history of that chunk of New England granite should go far toward dispelling forever from young minds the vision of Pilgrim footsteps upon it. . . . Its peregrinations, as told in this charmingly illustrated, gentle debunking of its legend, make both a delightful story and a perceptive commentary on how the myth-making process works in American history." NY Times Bk Rev

Loeb, Robert H.

Meet the real Pilgrims; everyday life on Plimoth plantation in 1627, by Robert H. Loeb, Jr. in consultation with Plimoth Plantation. Doubleday 1979 101p illus $6.95, lib. bdg. $7.90 (4-6)   **974.4**

1 Pilgrims (New England Colonists) 2 Massachusetts—History—Colonial period, 1600-1775
ISBN 0-385-14152-1; 0-385-14153-X   LC 78-1208

The author "takes 'you' on a visit to Plimoth and introduces you . . . to various members of the community, who describe their roles in the colony's life." Chicago. Children's Bk Center

Smith, E. Brooks

(ed.) Pilgrim courage; from a firsthand account by William Bradford, Governor of Plymouth Colony. . . . Adapted and ed. by E. Brooks Smith [and] Robert Meredith and illus. by Leonard Everett Fisher. Little 1962 108p illus maps $6.95 (5 and up)   **974.4**

1 Pilgrims (New England Colonists) 2 Massachusetts—History—Colonial period, 1600-1775
ISBN 0-316-80045-7   LC 62-8314

"Selected episodes from his original history of Plimoth Plantation and passages from the journals of William Bradford and Edward Winslow." Title page

"The selections have been judiciously abridged and edited, with early syntax untangled, archaic words modernized, and bracketed statements covering omissions supplied to give continuity." Horn Bk

Weisgard, Leonard

The Plymouth Thanksgiving; written and illus. by Leonard Weisgard. Doubleday 1967 unp illus $6.95, lib. bdg. $7.90 (3-5)   **974.4**

1 Pilgrims (New England Colonists) 2 Massacusetts—History—Colonial period, 1600-1775
ISBN 0-385-07312-7; 0-385-08297-5   LC 67-15379

"The text is based on events cited in William Bradford's diary and the dates used are those of the old-style calendar; a list of the Mayflower's passengers is included. The story of the first Thanksgiving is told in a businesslike, crisp style and includes the usual essentials of religous persecution, pilgrimage, the death of half the small company in that first grim winter, the help of the Indians, the harvest and the rejoicing, and the praise to God." Chicago. Children's Bk Center

"Comprehensive [and] carefully researched. . . . The many illustrations (some in color, and some in black and white) are handsome indeed, adding informational details to those given by the text." Sat Rev

Wood, James Playsted

Colonial Massachusetts. Elsevier/Nelson Bks. 1969 176p illus maps (Colonial histories) lib. bdg. $6.75 (5 and up)   **974.4**

1 Massachusetts—History—Colonial period, 1600-1775
ISBN 0-525-67101-3   LC 71-82917

First published by Thomas Nelson

In ths book the author "includes both the Plymouth and Massachusetts Bay settlements, pointing out differences and similarities in their backgrounds, development and way of life. . . . [He gives] information on the character and personality of eminent Colonial leaders and clergymen, and vitalizes his account with quotations from Colonial records and writings. [The book] covers the major facets of Massachusetts life and history up to 1776." Booklist

"The text is greatly enriched by the use of letters, eyewitness accounts, documents, maps, photographs . . . [and] a guide to historic sites." Social Studies

Bibliography: p167-68

974.5 Rhode Island

Webb, Robert N.

The Colony of Rhode Island; illus. with contemporary prints and maps. Watts, F. 1972 89p illus map lib. bdg. $6.45 (5 and up) **974.5**

1 Rhode Island—History
ISBN 0-531-00778-2   LC 70-189517

"A First book"

"Covers the period from the arrival of the first settler, a recluse who is not credited with founding the colony, through 1790 when Rhode Island became a state after holding out for two years. There are also sections on historical sights in modern Rhode Island, a chronology, a selective bibliography and an index." Sch Library J

974.7 New York

The **Erie** Canal, by the editors of American Heritage, The Magazine of History. Author: Ralph K. Andrist; consultant: Carter Goodrich. Am. Heritage [distributed by Harper] 1964 153p illus maps lib. bdg. $12.89 (5 and up)   **974.7**

1 Erie Canal
ISBN 0-06-020101-0   LC 64-13898

"American Heritage Junior library"

"The problems in constructing the Erie Canal and the place in United States history of the short-lived canal era are made vivid with primitive paintings, early photographs and brisk text." Horn Bk

"A close historical and geographical examination. . . . The young readers will enjoy the story and the usual good illustrations." Best Sellers

For further reading: p149

Spier, Peter

The legend of New Amsterdam; written and illus. by Peter Spier. Doubleday 1979 unp illus $6.95, lib. bdg. $7.90 (1-4)   **974.7**

1 New York (City)—History 2 New York (City)—Social life and customs 3 Bogardus, Annetje Jans
ISBN 0-385-13979-9; 0-385-13180-1   LC 78-6032

A "history of Manhattan Island, a Dutch settlement in the 1600s. . . . We share life as experienced by the children of the times. When not in Meester Roelantsen's Trivial School (tuition, two beaver skins per year), they helped with chores and then visited exciting places: the gristmill, Fort Amsterdam, the shipyard; they watched the glassblower and the smithy, the carpenter and even sometimes Pieter Stuyvesant himself. Mostly, the tykes relished teasing poor 'Crazy Annie Bogardus,' even when they were severely punished. Annie amused them by her visions of today's metropolis, which turned out to be far from crazy." Pub W

"Wonderfully detailed paintings of the buildings and the people of the bustling town of New Amsterdam have fine perspective, use of color, vitality, and humor. . . . [The book ends] with a surprise on the last page, a picture of the stone towers that today buttress the tip of the island. A map of the town in 1600 and a list of the occupants of each house or business enterprise are appended to a book that has a palatable text that complements the visual and historical interest of the illustrations." Chicago. Children's Bk Center

974.8 Pennsylvania

Lengyel, Emil

The colony of Pennsylvania; illus. with contemporary prints and photographs. Watts, F. 1974 86p illus maps lib. bdg. $6.45 (5 and up)   **974.8**

1 Pennsylvania—History
ISBN 0-531-02721-X   LC 74-846

"This history of the Pennsylvania colony focuses on William Penn's founding of his 'holy experiment' and also discusses the Quakers, the Indians, and Benjamin Franklin's part in the Revolution. The events are portrayed clearly and accurately." Sch Library J

For further reading: p81-82

Milhous, Katherine

Through these arches; the story of Independence Hall. Lippincott 1964 96p illus $6.50
(5 and up)   **974.8**

1 Philadelphia. Independence Hall 2 U.S.—History—Colonial period, 1600-1775
ISBN 0-397-307583   LC 64-13810

Illustrated by the author

The reader is taken on a visit to Philadelphia's Independence Hall as it is today, while the author recounts the history and events it has seen

"While it is a picture book in form, with color on many of its ninety-six pages, it is not for young children, but excellent as a family book in which even adults may find interesting facts." Sat Rev

Miller, Natalie

The story of the Liberty Bell; illus. by Betsy Warren. Childrens Press 1965 30p illus pa $1.95 (2-4)   **974.8**

1 Liberty Bell 2 Philadelphia—History
ISBN 0-516-04622-3   LC 65-12215

"Cornerstones of freedom"

In 1752 the Liberty Bell was first cast for the Pennsylvania State House in Philadelphia. Gradually the bell became a symbol of America's fight for independence. The author tells how Philadelphia's inhabitants gathered when the bell rang to discuss tax laws and freedom

975.3   Washington, D.C.

Phelan, Mary Kay

The burning of Washington: August 1814; illus. by John Gretzer. Crowell 1975 179p illus $8.95 (5 and up)   **975.3**

1 Washington, D. C.—History 2 U.S.—History—War of 1812
ISBN 0-690-00486-9   LC 74-30025

A "narrative and steady rein on converging events make a cohesive hour-by-hour account of the 1814 burning of Washington federal buildings. Focus shifts between the opposing forces in the drama: opening chapters describe a tense capital with citizens abandoning the city and key government officials scrambling unsuccessfully to meet the impending crisis. The view soon shifts to describe movements of the British forces and the motivations of the commanders. Personalities—President and Mrs. Madison, British commanders Cockburn and Ross, and various U.S. cabinet officials—are deftly sketched." Booklist

"An extensive bibliography and index are included. Historical writing at its finest, with carefully chosen quotations and an abundance of interesting anecdotes and facts, this is a useful reference source as well as an enjoyable read." Sch Library J

975.5   Virginia

Lacy, Dan

The colony of Virginia. Watts, F. 1973 85p illus lib. bdg. $6.45 (6 and up)   **975.5**

1 Virginia—History—Colonial period, 1600-1775
ISBN 0-531-00784-7   LC 72-10780

"A First book"

"A simple, well-written, compact history of colonial Virginia, from the establishment of Jamestown to the ratification of the Constitution [in 1788]. The format is attractive and the illustrations appropriate." Sch Library J
Books for further reading: p81

Tunis, Edwin

Shaw's Fortune; the picture story of a Colonial plantation; drawn and written by Edwin Tunis. Crowell [1976 c1966] 63p illus $12.95 (3-6)   **975.5**

1 Plantation life 2 Virginia—Social life and customs
ISBN 0-690-01066-4   LC 75-29640

A reprint of the title first published 1966 by World

"If this book had no text, only captions to the illustrations, it would be enjoyable and informative; the pencil drawings are meticulous in detail, clearly based on authoritative familiarity with plantation life. Shaw's Fortune is described as it evolved from a cabin in a clearing to the almost self-sufficient establishment of 1752. Mr. Tunis discusses the clothing, education, recreation, and family patterns of the Shaw family. Even more interesting are the descriptions of the home industries and crafts of the plantation: spinning and weaving, growing tobacco, gathering and packing tobacco, hewing and sawing timber. . . . The illustrations are useful for an older audience as well." Chicago. Children's Bk Center

975.6   North Carolina

Lacy, Dan

The colony of North Carolina; illus. with photographs and contemporary prints. Watts, F. 1975 86p illus maps lib. bdg. $6.45 (4 and up)   **975.6**

1 North Carolina—History
ISBN 0-531-00830-4   LC 74-22217

"A First book"

The book traces the history of North Carolina from its founding in 1587 as the Lost Colony on Roanoke Island to the ratification of its constitution in 1789
For further reading: p81

Roberts, Bruce

Where time stood still; a portrait of Appalachia [by] Bruce and Nancy Roberts. Crowell-Collier Press 1970 114p illus map $6.95 (5 and up)   **975.6**

1 Appalachian region—Social conditions 2 North Carolina—Social conditions 3 Appalachian region—Social life and customs 4 North Carolina—Social life and customs
ISBN 0-02-777440-6   LC 77-96452

Focusing on Madison county in North Carolina, the authors describe in photographs and text the life and customs of the people of Appalachia, as well as the various problems they face—poverty, poor education, lack of industry, disease, inadequate transportation, a landscape blighted by strip mining and a prevailing sense of despair

"The straightforward, unsentimental writing creates a clear picture of poverty, suffering, ignorance and stubborness contrasted with beauty, loyalty and hope. The history, people, crafts, livelihoods, education, politics, customs and welfare of the area are all treated with knowledge and concern. The oversize format makes effective use of the photographic essay which elucidates the text. . . . It stimulates concern for all humanity and leaves the challenge to help combat poverty and hopelessness." Sch Library J
Bibliography: p[115]

975.8   Georgia

Vaughan, Harold Cecil

The colony of Georgia. Watts, F. 1975 88p illus maps lib. bdg. $6.45 (4 and up)   **975.8**

1 Georgia—History
ISBN 0-531-02774-0   LC 74-8790

The author "traces the history of the 13th colony from De Soto's search for gold in 1540 to the end of the Revolutionary War. Vaughan also ascribes proper importance to James Oglethorpe who founded the colony as a refuge for the poor, debtors, etc." Sch Library J
Bibliography: p83

977   North central states

Ault, Phil

These are the Great Lakes; illus. with photographs and a map. Dodd 1972 174p illus map $5.95 (5 and up)   **977**

1 Great Lakes 2 Great Lakes region
ISBN 0-396-06607-0   LC 72-1533

A description of the Great Lakes area and 350 years of its history: from Indians and French explorers, steamboats and the growth of cities to the locks at Sault Ste Marie, water pollution, the St Lawrence Seaway, and atomic power plants
Bibliography: p171-72

Barry, James P.
The Great Lakes; illus. with photographs by the author. Watts, F. 1976 62p illus maps lib. bdg. $6.45 (4-6) **977**
1 Great Lakes 2 Great Lakes region
ISBN 0-531-00337-X   LC 76-15641
"A First book"
"An initial chapter traces the route of the 'Red Wing,' a freighter filled with grain, as it moves from Duluth through the waterways, canals, and locks of the Great Lakes to Port Cartier on the Atlantic Ocean. Following this glimpse of the modern scene, Barry backtracks, giving brief information on the area's geologic beginnings, Indian tribes, and early French and British explorations. Returning to contemporary times, the author generalizes on tourist attractions, summarizes the lakes' shipping industry, and describes pollution problems." Booklist
"The text includes clear definitions of unusual or unfamiliar terms, and despite the prosaic photos, there are many helpful drawings describing the workings of a lock, illustrating relative depth of the lakes, etc." Sch Library J

977.3   Illinois

Phelan, Mary Kay
The story of the great Chicago fire, 1871; illus. by William Plummer. Crowell 1971 191p illus map $8.95 (5 and up) **977.3**
1 Chicago—Fire, 1871
ISBN 0-690-77671-3   LC 72-109910
This is an account of the famous Chicago fire of October 1871 which raged through the city for thirty hours leaving an area one mile wide and five miles long in ashes. It is also the story of how outstanding businessmen and ordinary citizens of Chicago joined forces to rebuild their city
"Regional or general interest in the Chicago fire . . . may be served by this book. Events are presented with a sense of their importance, and, in some cases, human interest; background of the city before the fire is fairly well handled. The book is written in the present tense, evidently in an effort to add drama or immediacy." Sch Library J
Bibliography: p180-84

978   Western states

Adams, Samuel Hopkins
The Santa Fe Trail; illus. by Lee J. Ames. Random House 1951 181p illus lib. bdg. $5.99 (5 and up) **978**
1 Santa Fé Trail 2 The West (U.S.)—History
ISBN 0-394-90313-7   LC 51-14138
"Landmark books"
"Partially fictionized account of the daring men, Spaniards first and later Americans, who laid the trail which opened up and developed the great Southwest. In particular it follows Captain William Becknell's wagon expedition, the first to make the journey, recounting succinctly and engrossingly, the hardships, discipline problems, and narrow escapes encountered on the trail. Throughout, the author . . . points to savagery by the whites matching that of the Indians." Booklist

Cowboys and cattle country, by the editors of American Heritage, The Magazine of History; narrative by Don Ward; in consultation with J. C. Dykes. Am. Heritage 1961 153p illus map $7.95 (5 and up) **978**
1 Cowhands 2 The West (U.S.)—History
ISBN 0-8281-0389-5   LC 61-18251
"American Heritage Junior library"
"Covers the cowboy and his job from the earliest Spanish vaqueros to TV's Richard Boone. . . . The illustrations [include] paintings by famous western artists such as Frederic Remington and Charles Russell, maps, posters, daguerreotypes, and photographs collected from . . . historical sources." Chicago Sunday Trib
"Don Ward throws a lasso around the Old West and ropes in a kicking, bawling account of trail-driving days and the rugged breed of men that herded the longhorns to market. Here is what life was really like. . . . And at the end there's a showdown with hard words for movie and TV versions of the West and the American cowboy." NY Times Bk Rev
For further reading: p151

Rounds, Glen
The cowboy trade; written and illus. by Glen Rounds. Holiday House 1972 95p illus $8.95 (4 and up) **978**
1 Cowhands 2 The West (U.S.)—History
ISBN 0-8234-0206-1   LC 73-119804
A "picture of how cowboys lived and worked in the Old West, carefully pointing out that the demanding, monotonous, and frequently unpleasant life that cowboys actually led bears little resemblance to what is portrayed on television and in the movies. Enlivened by frequent humor in both the text and the drawings, the book covers such topics as the cowboy's duties, equipment, dress, behavior in town, and life during the winter." Booklist
"Narrated with zest and affection, the book offers an honest, incisive look at the life style of the American cowboy. . . . Unpretentious but interpretive sketches reflect the gusto of the text." Horn Bk

The prairie schooners. Holiday House 1968 95p illus map $8.95 (4-6) **978**
1 Overland journeys to the Pacific (U.S.)
2 Oregon Trail
ISBN 0-8234-0088-3   LC 68-31936
Illustrated by the author, this book tells what it was like to make the grueling trek west from the Missouri River during the years of the Oregon migration between 1843 and 1868
"By vivid description and focus on minor incidents, the author recreates the lumbering prairie schooner and its occupants. Will be valuable for 'Northwest' history study and for entertaining reading." Bruno. Bks for Sch Libraries, 1968
"Lit with humor and gusto, both in the succinct prose and simple sketches." Horn Bk

The treeless plains; written and illus. by Glen Rounds. Holiday House 1967 95p illus $8.95 (4-6) **978**
1 Frontier and pioneer life—The West (U.S.)
2 Sod houses
ISBN 0-8234-0122-7   LC 67-4999
A "lively but fully authentic account of sod houses of early settlers on the Great Plains. Full of wry humor as it tells of their peculiar housekeeping problems, fun and 'fraid holes.' Line drawings add greatly to the immediacy and realism of this memorable book." Bruno. Bks for Sch Libraries, 1968

Tunis, Edwin
Frontier living; written and illus. by Edwin Tunis. Crowell [1976 c1961] 165p illus maps $12.95 (6 and up) **978**
1 Frontier and pioneer life—The West (U.S.)
2 The West (U.S.)—History
ISBN 0-690-01064-8   LC 75-29639
A reprint of the title first published 1961 by World
In this book "we shall talk about the conditions of daily living, changing materially as men and women moved the frontier westward, met new conditions, and at the same time, settled new bases behind it and gradually improved communication with them and with the old ones." Foreword

978.7   Wyoming

Kirk, Ruth
Yellowstone; the first national park; photographs by Ruth and Louis Kirk. Atheneum Pubs. 1974 103p illus maps lib. bdg. $6.25 (5 and up) **978.7**
1 Yellowstone National Park
ISBN 0-689-50006-8   LC 74-76273
"A Margaret K. McElderry book"
The author describes the plant and animal life of the park, as well as its famous geysers. She also discusses wildlife policies, and provides a travel guide for those planning to visit Yellowstone
"The book is well organized and has excellent graphic support. The writing style is readable and interesting." Sci and Children

979.8   Alaska

Stefansson, Evelyn
Here is Alaska. New rev. ed. Scribner 1973
178p illus maps lib. bdg. $6.95 (6 and up)
           979.8

1 Alaska
ISBN 0-684-13253-2   LC 72-11228

First published 1943
"The book explores all aspects of Alaskan life,
agricultural and urban, geographic and historical,
and industrial; it discusses the Eskimos, the Indians, the oil rush and the struggle between indus-
trialists and environmentalists. Useful, well-organized and well-written." Chicago. Children's Bk
Center

981   Brazil

Brown, Rose
The land and people of Brazil; rev. by
Leslie F. Warren. Rev. ed. Lippincott 1972
158p illus map (Portraits of the nations ser)
$8.95 (5 and up)   **981**

1 Brazil
ISBN 0-397-31342-X   LC 79-38952

First published 1946
A description of Brazil which covers the country's history and geography as well as its people
—their lives, customs, and occupations. Illustrated
with photographs

Kendall, Sarita
Looking at Brazil. Lippincott [1975 c1974]
64p illus maps (Looking at other countries)
$8.95 (4-6)   **981**

1 Brazil
ISBN 0-387-31527-9   LC 73-19605

First published 1974 in England
"Excellent photographs and maps detail the
sharp contrasts in the economy, geography, and
climate of this South American nation. [The
author] clearly explains why, despite its vast size
and rich natural resources, Brazil is still relatively
poor and backward. She pulls no punches in relating the hardships and poverty that have resulted from government mismanagement (e.g.
native Indians and immigrants endure poor education, unemployment, disease, and substandard living conditions) and explains why plans for the
new capital of Brasilia have failed. [This is]
an objective, well-illustrated account." Sch Library J

982   Argentina

Hall, Elvajean
The land and people of Argentina. Rev.
ed. Lippincott 1972 159p illus map (Portraits
of the nations ser) $8.95 (5 and up)   **982**

1 Argentine Republic
ISBN 0-397-31257-1   LC 77-37251

First published 1960
In this introduction to Argentina, the author
surveys its history and the varied life of its
peoples, past and present

984   Bolivia

Warren, Leslie F.
The land and people of Bolivia. Lippincott
1974 156p illus map (Portraits of the nations
ser) $8.95 (5 and up)   **984**

1 Bolivia
ISBN 0-397-31578-3   LC 74-8911

The book provides a survey of the history, geography, major cities, natural resources, and social
customs of Bolivia

985   Peru

Beals, Carleton
The incredible Incas: yesterday and today
illus. with photographs by Marianne Greenwood. Abelard-Schuman [1974 c1973] 191p
illus $8.95 (5 and up)   **985**

1 Incas
ISBN 0-200-71901-7   LC 72-207

This is "a factually accurate account of the history of the Inca people. [There is] detailed information of everyday life. Information is interjected
by tales and anecdotes of the people and relevant
comments on change from past days of Inca
supremacy to the position of the people today."
New Bks for Young Readers
   Bibliography: p179-80

Beck, Barbara L.
The first book of the Incas; pictures by
Page Cary. Watts, F. 1966 78p illus maps
lib. bdg. $6.45 (4 and up)   **985**

1 Incas
ISBN 0-531-00558-5   LC 66-10579

"A serious and informative text, the plentiful
illustrations giving many details of buildings, costumes, and artifacts. The author describes the
pre-Inca cultures, the early history of the highland
people whose record begins in approximately 1250
A.D., and the years of the great Inca empire
from the advent of the first strong ruler—Pacha-
cuti—in 1438 to the time of the Spanish conquest
in 1532. The book gives, in addition to the historical material, many facts about daily life, religion, mores, medicine, class and caste, engineering, et cetera. A list of rulers and of important
dates and an index are appended." Chicago. Children's Bk Center

Gemming, Elizabeth
Lost city in the clouds; the discovery of
Machu Picchu; illus. by Michael Eagle
Coward, McCann & Geoghegan 1980 75p illus
lib. bdg. $5.99 (5 and up)   **985**

1 Machu Picchu, Peru   2 Peru—Antiquities
3 Bingham, Hiram   4 Incas
ISBN 0-698-30698-8   LC 78-31877

"High in the Peruvian mountains a lost, almost
perfectly preserved Inca city lay buried beneath
jungle growth for 400 years. In 1911 a Yale professor, Hiram Bingham, found the city, opening
the way for excavation and research. Use of dialogue to tell the story of Bingham's search and
discovery lends a fictional tone, but balance is
provided with the inclusion of facts, statistics,
and material from his own descriptions. Information on the Inca people and speculation on why
they left the area is coupled with remarks about
the difficulties of reaching the remote jungle citadel and with descriptions of the archaeologists'
work. Arguments about the significance of Machu
Picchu and theories of various scholars are noted
in the final chapters." Booklist
"Immaculate use is made of difficult Spanish and
Quechua words. Glossary, bibliography, chronology of important dates, and a list of museums
having Peruvian collections are all helpful. The
only flaw is the lack of color photographs that
would show the remarkable stairways, masonry,
height, etc. of the ruins." Sch Library J

Mangurian, David
Children of the Incas. Four Winds 1979
73p illus $8.95 (4-6)   **985**

1 Quechua Indians   2 Peru—Social life and customs
ISBN 0-590-07500-4   LC 79-12186

"The author's words and those of the thirteen-
year-old boy Modesta tell about Quechua Indian
life high in the Peruvian Andes. The descriptions
are detailed, and the language is often informal.
. . . The superb photography remarkably reveals
the life of the people: sheepherding, handicrafts,
market days, school activities, and the problems
of health and disease." Horn Bk

989.5 Uruguay

Dobler, Lavinia
The land and people of Uruguay. Rev. ed. Lippincott 1972 160p illus map (Portraits of the nations ser) $8.95 (5 and up) **989.5**
1 Uruguay
ISBN 0-397-31391-8   LC 72-3741
First published 1965
The author discusses the history, geography, government, economy, people and customs of the smallest country in South America

990 Pacific Ocean islands (Oceania)

Captain Cook and the South Pacific, by the editors of Horizon Magazine. Author: Oliver Warner; consultant: J. C. Beaglehole. Am. Heritage [distributed by Harper] 1963 153p illus maps $9.95, lib. bdg. $12.89 (5 and up) **990**
1 Islands of the Pacific 2 Discoveries (in geography) 3 Cook, James
ISBN 0-06-026355-5; 0-06-026356-3   LC 63-19987
"A Horizon Caravel book"
"The great and popular explorer is revealed as zealous, determined, precise, cool. For him, exploration was a quest based on intelligence, and discipline was an art rooted in planning. . . . [The book includes a] section dealing with the impact of Cook's discoveries on Western civilization, especially on the arts." Horn Bk
"Technical aspects and the scientific procedures of the day are explained. But more than that the young reader is given a fair picture of the personality of Cook. . . . The book is replete with the usual handsome illustrations." Best Sellers
Further reference: p151

May, Charles Paul
Oceania: Polynesia, Melanesia, Micronesia. Elsevier/Nelson Bks. 1973 224p illus map (World neighbors) $7.95 (5 and up) **990**
1 Islands of the Pacific
ISBN 0-525-67068-8; 0-525-67069-6   LC 72-13152
First published by Thomas Nelson
"An overall view of the islands of the Pacific Ocean which includes their possible origins, the sources of plants, animals, and insects, and the coming of human inhabitants as well as their history and present development. The author devotes considerable space to a description of everyday life covering clothing, food, sports, education, handicrafts, religion, dances, crops, and business and mentions foreign artists and writers who have used the South Seas as subject material." Booklist
"The many photographs accompanying the text aid understanding, and this will be a useful supplementary title where courses are given in world geography and the culture of other lands." Sch Library J
Other books of interest: p217-18

993 New Zealand

Kaula, Edna Mason
The land and people of New Zealand. [Rev.] Lippincott [1972 c1964] 160p illus maps (Portraits of the nations ser) $8.95 (5 and up) **993**
1 New Zealand
ISBN 0-397-30748-9   LC 76-37764
First published 1964
A "short history, from 14th-century Polynesian settlement to the present decade. Interwoven are descriptions of the natural scene, social life, economics and politics, also the spectacular scenery, strange wildlife, the remarkable Maoris and their past and present relationships to the white settlers." Sch Library J [review of the 1964 edition]
"Photographs, engravings, and maps enhance this book." Best Sellers [review of the 1964 edition]

994 Australia

Blunden, Godfrey
The land and people of Australia. Rev. ed. Lippincott 1972 144p illus map (Portraits of the nations ser) $8.95 (5 and up) **994**
1 Australia
ISBN 0-397-31256-3   LC 73-37234
First published 1954
After a description of the geography and geological history of the continent of Australia and an account of its aboriginal people, plants and animals, the author discusses the country's cities and states, language and customs, government and food supply as these have developed over the years

Henderson, W. F.
Looking at Australia [by] W. F. and R. A. Henderson. Lippincott 1977 64p illus (Looking at other countries) $8.95 (4-6) **994**
1 Australia
ISBN 0-397-31703-4   LC 76-29054
This book supplies "brief information about . . . [Australia's] history, geography, people, cities culture, and industries. Satisfactory writing is supplemented by a mixture of black-and-white and sharp color photographs. Attempts to include personal insights into leisure activities, daily life, homes, sports, and schools unfortunately result in innocuous generalizations. . . . Although little attempt is made to discuss the economic or political problems of [Australia] . . . the descriptive material will be helpful for research reports." Booklist

996 Polynesia

Mann, Peggy
Easter Island; land of mysteries; illus. with photographs. Holt 1976 224p illus map $6.95 (6 and up) **996**
1 Easter Island
ISBN 0-03-014056-0   LC 75-32247
The author "evokes a sense of history and mystery in her synthesis of what is known about Easter Island and its inhabitants, past and present. She traces the arrivals and reactions of the various discoverers over the years and the work of modern-day archaeologists attempting to unravel the many mysteries of the island—particularly the unique giant statues and the inscribed wooden tablets which so far remain undeciphered. A fascinating part of her account is the discussion of the Stone Age people themselves—how they lived during the Golden Age when the statues were carved, during the 200-year 'Statue-over-throwing Time,' and after the arrival of missionaries and other foreigners—including the tourists of today." Booklist
"Archaeological evidence which appears to confirm many legends is . . . cited (particularly those findings of the Heyerdahl expedition in 1955), and interesting quotes from explorers, missionaries, and archaeologists (e.g., Cook, Brother Eugene, Loti, Englert, Heverdahl, Mulloy, etc.) enhance the narrative." Sch Library J
Bibliography: p213-15

Pine, Tillie S.
The Polynesians knew, by Tillie S. Pine and Joseph Levine; pictures by Marilyn Hirsh. McGraw 1974 unp illus map lib. bdg. $7.95 (4-6) **996**
1 Polynesia 2 Science—Experiments
ISBN 0-07-050090-8   LC 73-13972
This book tells how the early Polynesians mastered navigation, printing, and the manufacture of many useful objects. The authors present simple experiments so that the reader can explore modern-day applications of the same principles
Among the projects "included are boat construction and navigation, weaving, fire-making, cooking, lamp-making, carving, music and the use of coconuts. On each page are simple two-color drawings of the Polynesians and the project and its relationship to our culture. . . . The projects are intended to demonstrate, at an attainable level of understanding for children in middle grades, scientific principles which are known and used by peoples all over the world." Sci Bks

998 Arctic islands and Antarctica

Asimov, Isaac

How did we find out about Antartica? Illus. by David Wool. Walker & Co. 1979 64p illus $6.95, lib. bdg. $6.89   998

1 Antarctic regions
ISBN 0-8027-6370-7; 0-8027-6371-5   LC 79-2199

"Asimov reviews ideas, names, and events that have shaped the path of Antarctic exploration. He starts with the notion that the earth is round, an idea that once spurred far-reaching sea voyages culminaing in mid-nineteenth-century certitude that an Antarctic continent actually existed. Later portions review the Antarctic's overland explores, while a concluding chapter looks at some of the life forms that weather the continent's extremes. With utilitarian black-and-white illustrations of explorers, plus maps and diagrams." Booklist

Harrington, Lyn

The polar regions; earth's frontiers. Elsevier/Nelson Bks. 1973 192p illus maps (World neighbors) $7.95 (5 and up)   998

1 Polar regions
ISBN 0-525-66338-X   LC 73-10191

First published by Thomas Nelson
This "information source on both the Arctic and Antarctic regions describes natural phenomena, native cultures, explorations, and research and development. Valuable for its scope, which is broader both geographically and topically than most books on the subject, and illustrated with black-and-white photographs and maps. A chronology and suggestions for further reading are included." Booklist

Laycock, George

Beyond the Arctic Circle. Four Winds 1978 116p illus map $7.95 (5 and up)   998

1 Arctic regions
ISBN 0-590-07481-4   LC 77-15844

The author covers "geological, biological, sociological, and historical aspects of the arctic region. He describes the traditional lifestyle of the Eskimo peoples and the ways in which it has changed with the advent of white settlers and their technology and industries; he gives the historical background of European exploration; he describes the plants and animals of the region and the impact of industrial development and the changes in hunting patterns on the wildlife. Throughout the text, the author emphasizes the need for conservation and for preservation of ecological balance. Several personal anecdotes are included, and the photographs are of good quality and well placed." Chicago. Children's Bk Center
Glossary: p109. Bibliography: p111-12

Orlob, Helen

The Northeast Passage; black water, white ice. Elsevier/Nelson Bks. 1977 141p maps $6.95 (5 and up)   998

1 Northeast Passage
ISBN 0-525-66564-1   LC 77-9064

First published by Thomas Nelson
The author "records with precision the history of Siberian Arctic marine exploration since the 16th Century. The exploits of English, Swedish, Norwegian, American, and Russian explorers seeking a maritime passage across the top of the Eurasian land mass are detailed with judicious use made of actual journal accounts. Not written about as much as its Northwest counterpart, the story of the search for the Northeast Passage has elements of courage and stamina, disaster and triumph that will surely appeal to readers seeking adventure." Sch Library J
Bibliography: p123-27

Scarf, Maggie

Antarctica: exploring the frozen continent; illus. with photographs and maps. Random House 1970 82p illus maps lib. bdg. $4.39 (3-6)   998

1 Antarctic regions
ISBN 0-394-90799-X   LC 78-109227

"The story of the discovery and exploration of a continent which is dedicated as a base station for scientific studies introduces the young reader to geographic and meteorological information in a pleasant, informal manner. The continent is described as a huge natural laboratory, ideal for the study of weather, gravity, and the upper atmosphere of the earth." The AAAS Sci Bk List for Children

FICTION

A number of subjects have been added to the books in this section to aid in curriculum work. It is not necessarily recommended that these subjects be used in the library catalog

Achebe, Chinua

How the leopard got his claws, by Chinua Achebe and John Iroaganachi; with The lament of the deer, by Christopher Okigbo; illus. by Per Christiansen. Third Press 1973 35p illus $4.95 (4-6)   Fic

1 Fables 2 Animals—Fiction
ISBN 0-89388-056-6   LC 72-93382

"An Odarkai book"
First published 1972 in Nigeria
This fable tells how the jungle animals forfeited their formerly peaceful cooperative existence by cowardly acceptance of a tyrant's rule. Guided by the wise and gentle King Leopard, they had built a village hall to protect them in the rainy season. The dog, laughed at as ugly because he was the only animal with sharp teeth, had refused to help. But when his cave was flooded he came to the hall and drove out the other animals with his biting. They then accepted the dog as king and stoned King Leopard when he refused to join them. King Leopard had a blacksmith forge terrible new teeth and claws for him and his vengeance left the animals homeless and at war with each other. The dog became the human hunter's slave in return for protection. The tale concludes that if some day the animals can make peace among themselves, they can join together to keep away their common enemy, the hunter

Adams, Richard

Watership Down. Macmillan Pub. Co. [1974 c1972] 429p illus $10.95 (5 and up)   Fic

1 Rabbits—Fiction 2 Allegories
ISBN 0-02-700030-3   LC 73-6044

First published 1972 in England
"A small number of male rabbits, frightened by the imminent destruction of their warren, embark upon a hazardous exodus across the English downs in search of a new home. . . . These refugees are constantly beset by dangers and temptations, but fortunately they share among them the qualities of bravery, endurance and resourcefulness required for survival. In the course of their wanderings, these rabbits learn to care for each other, learn to work together. In time they find another warren, but the new community, lacking female company, faces the prospect of extinction. The search for female rabbits draws our heroes to a distant rabbit fortress ruled by a Fascist general of military genius. In two great battles our friends' outnumbered troops must prove their cleverness and courage." Newsweek
"An adventure tale about rabbits that has overtones of social comment, distinctive characterization, an intricate but sturdy plot, and a wonderfully flowing style. . . . The descriptions of the Berkshire countryside are poetic, but the most enthralling aspect of the story is surely the magnitude of the rabbit world, with its cultural patterns, tradition, folklore, language, and vigor." Chicago. Children's Bk Center
Lapine glossary: p427-29

Adkins, Jan

Luther Tarbox. Scribner 1977 32p illus lib. bdg. $5.95 (2-4)   Fic

1 Boats and boating—Fiction 2 Fisheries—Fiction
ISBN 0-684-14931-1   LC 77-6711

Illustrated by the author
"Luther is a happy man; he loves his boat, he loves his wife, he has a superb compass, and he sings in a clear, sweet tenor. Caught in a fog while pulling lobster traps, Luther . . . [meets boats full] of people who can't find their way back to harbor. Luther makes them wait while he gets around to all his traps; he sings as he works;

Adkins, Jan—*Continued*

his retinue dutifully follows him: a motorboat, a cabin cruiser, and Coast Guard vessel, and more. Fortunately his wife has made enough chowder for everybody, so they are all happy, almost as happy as Luther." Chicago. Children's Bk Center

"Luther's salty conversation is as canny as his navigation, and the exchanges among his fellow sailors characterize each of them with economy and humor. The language of the book is rich and rhythmic; some of the detailed black-and-white pictures are drawn from unexpected angles." Horn Bk

Adler, C. S.

The magic of the Glits; illus. by Ati Forberg. Macmillan Pub. Co. 1979 112p illus $7.95 (5 and up)   **Fic**

1 Friendship—Fiction
ISBN 0-02-700120-2   LC 78-12149

"Jeremy, 12, feels that the summer he is spending with his mother on Cape Cod has been ruined by his broken leg. To add to his annoyance, withdrawn, fearful 7-year-old Lynette, a friend of the family's daughter who is still grieving for her drowned mother, comes for a visit. Pressured into befriending her, Jeremy invests the 'Glits,' imaginary little creatures. Their shared fantasy forms a bond and Jeremy finds a real attachment and sense of companionship growing between them." Sch Library J

"Scene and characters are quickly and firmly set, the game is imaginative, and the personality changes are satisfying. Readers caught up by this will probably overlook the sudden, pat resolution of Lynette's future (as well as her overage wisdom) for the sake of the underlying friendship." Booklist

The silver coach. Coward, McCann & Geoghegan 1979 122p $7.95 (4-6)   **Fic**

1 Divorce—Fiction 2 Grandmothers—Fiction
ISBN 0-698-20504-9   LC 79-10430

"Twelve-year-old Chris and her younger sister resent having to spend the summer following their parents' separation in their grandmother's remote woodland home. Chris is surprised, however, to discover a different kind of grandmother than she expected and becomes fascinated with a tiny silver coach on the bedroom shelf. The miniature, her grandmother tells her, works magic; and in the course of a surprising summer, Chris realizes the truth in her grandmother's words. She also grows, . . . reconciling herself at last to the inevitable divorce." Booklist

"Adler tells an absorbing story skillfully, investing the fabulous coach with as much credibility as she puts into the empathetic characters." Pub W

Aiken, Joan

Arabel's raven; illus. by Quentin Blake. Doubleday 1974 118p illus $5.95, lib. bdg. $6.90 (4-6)   **Fic**

1 Ravens—Fiction
ISBN 0-385-07493-X; 0-385-08675-X   LC 73-81120

"Arabel's father rescues a raven while driving home his taxi one evening. Mortimer, the raven, soon becomes a prized pet that causes untold problems. It eats stairs, sleeps in Arabel's refrigerator, is flyjacked, and often says 'Nevermore,' especially when it answers the telephone. A delightfully funny book of three adventures for children who can appreciate British humor." Adventuring with Bks

Midnight is a place. Viking 1974 287p $7.95 (5 and up)   **Fic**

1 Great Britain—Fiction 2 Orphans—Fiction
ISBN 0-670-47483-5   LC 74-760

"A boy and girl, Lucas Bell and Anna-Marie Murgatroyd, are homeless and penniless when Midnight Court burns to the ground. They had been living with a guardian, Mr. Randolph, who had won the estate and the town mill through chicanery from Mr. Murgatroyd. The children's only friend, their tutor, is Mr. Oakapple, who is burned badly and has to be hospitalized after the blaze which kills Randolph. The children earn their living at dangerous jobs but are lucky to find Lady Murgatroyd, the girl's grandmother." Pub W

"With her customary vivacity and inventiveness, the author has created another novel steeped in nineteenth-century literary traditions and devices. . . . The melodrama, which manages to avoid even a hint of sentimentality, never flags as it goes from incident to incident and reaches a happy ending." Horn Bk

The wolves of Willoughby Chase; illus. by Pat Marriott. Doubleday [1963 c1962] 168p illus $5.95, lib. bdg. $6.90 (5 and up)   **Fic**

1 Great Britain—Fiction
ISBN 0-385-03594-2; 0-385-06398-9   LC 63-18034

First published 1962 in England

"Set in a country house in nineteenth-century England and related in the style of a Victorian melodrama, this story follows the adventures of two little cousins who are left in the care of an evil governess. The children are chased by wolves, and their parents are lost at sea. The wicked Miss Slighcarp sends them to an orphanage from which they escape and travel four hundred miles to London with their friend Simon and his geese. With the help of the family lawyer and the police constables from Bow Street Miss Slighcarp and her accomplice are outwitted." NY Times Bk Rev

"The title is musical and intriguing; the story, an excellent spoof on Victorian books, will make adults laugh. . . . Young readers will probably take it seriously as an adventure story and not know it is tongue-in-cheek; a family might have a good time reading it aloud." Sat Rev

Followed by: Black hearts in Battersea. Doubleday lib. bdg. $4.50 (ISBN 0-385-07781-5; LC 64-20376)

Alcott, Louisa May

Eight cousins (5 and up)   **Fic**

1 Family life—Fiction 2 New England—Fiction
Some editions are:

Grosset (Louisa May Alcott lib) $4.95 (ISBN 0-448-02359-8)

Little $8.95 Illustrated by Hattie Longstreet Price (ISBN 0-316-03091-0; LC 34-27189)

First published 1875

Set in New England, here are the "scrapes, mischief and fun of one girl and her seven boy cousins." Pittsburgh

"Filled with exciting and valorous action, humor, and truth the fantasy is completely convincing and has some of the appeal of the Narnia books." Booklist

Followed by: Rose in bloom, first published 1876, available from:

Grosset (Louisa May Alcott lib) $4.95 (ISBN 0-448-02366-0)

Little $8.95 With illustrations in color by Hattie Longstreet Price (ISBN 0-316-03098-8)

Little women; or Meg, Jo, Beth and Amy (5 and up)   **Fic**

1 Family life—Fiction 2 New England—Fiction
Some editions are:

Collins [distributed by Philomel Bks] $15 Illustrated by Tasha Tudor (ISBN 0-529-00529-8; LC 75-82776)

Dent (Children's illustrated classics) $9 Illustrated with 8 drawings & 8 colour plates by S. Van Abbé (ISBN 0-460-05002-8)

Grosset (Illustrated junior lib) $6.95 Illustrated by Louis Jambor (ISBN 0-448-05819-7)

Grosset (Louisa May Alcott lib) $4.95 (ISBN 0-448-02364-4)

Little $9.95 With illustrations in color by Jessie Wilcox Smith (ISBN 0-316-03095-3)

Little (Centennial ed) $10.95 With a new introduction by Cornelia Meigs; illustrated in color by Jessie Wilcox Smith (ISBN 0-316-03090-2)

Macmillan Pub. Co. (The Macmillan classics) $6.95, pa $1.95 Illustrated by Betty Fraser; afterword by Clifton Fadiman. (ISBN 0-02-700180-6; 0-02-041230-4; LC 62-18384)

Raintree (Raintree's illustrated classics) lib. bdg. $7.99 (ISBN 0-8393-6210-2; LC 78-2919)

First published 1868

The story of the New England home life of the four March sisters. Each "little woman's" personality differs: Jo's quick temper and restless desire for the freedom of a boy's life; Meg's hatred of poverty and her longing for pretty clothes; Amy's all-engulfing self-interest; and gentle Beth's love of home and family

The tale is "related with sympathy, humour, and sincerity. This lively natural narrative of family experience is as well-loved today as when it first appeared." Bks for Boys & Girls. 3d edition

Followed by these books:

Little men. First published 1871, available from:

Grosset (Illustrated junior lib) $5.95 Illustrated by Douglas W. Gorsline (ISBN 0-448-05818-9; LC 47-1200)

Grosset (Louisa May Alcott lib) $4.95 (ISBN 0-448-02363-6)

Little $8.95 With illustrations by Reginald Birch (ISBN 0-316-03094-5)

Macmillan Pub. Co. $4.95, pa $1.95 Illustrated by Paul Hogarth; afterword by Clifton Fadiman (ISBN 0-02-700150-4; 0-02-041150-2; LC 63-14828)

Alcott, Louisa M.—*Continued*

Jo's boys. first published 1886, available from:
Dent (Children's illustrated classics) $9 Illustrated with 4 colour plates and line drawings in the text by Harry Toothills (ISBN 0-460-05044-3)
Grosset (Illustrated junior library) $5.95 Illustrated by Louis Jambor (ISBN 0-448-05813-8; LC 49-48971)
Grosset (Louisa May Alcott lib) $4.95 ISBN 0-448-02362-8
Little $8.95 With illustrations in color by Clara M. Burd (ISBN 0-316-03093-7)

Alexander, Lloyd

The book of three. Holt 1964 217p illus lib. bdg. $7.95 (4 and up)   **Fic**

1 Fantastic fiction
ISBN 0-03-089821-8   LC 64-18250

"The first of five books about the mythical land of Prydain finds Taran, an assistant pig keeper, fighting with Prince Gwydion against the evil which threatens the kingdom. Elements of Welsh mythology are incorporated in a stirring tale, told in literate style and teeming with unusual characters." Hodges. Bks for Elem Sch Libraries
"Related in a simple, direct style, this fast-paced tale of high adventure has a well-balanced blend of fantasy, realism, and humor. Although the Welsh Mabinogion is the inspiration for the story and some of the characters, the incidents, mood, and characterizations are more reminiscent of Tolkien's trilogy." Sch Library J
Followed by these books, also available from Holt:
The black cauldron lib. bdg. $7.95 (ISBN 0-03-089687-8; LC 65-13868)
The castle of Llyr lib. bdg. $7.95 (ISBN 0-03-019066-5; LC 66-13461)
Taran Wanderer lib. bdg. $7.95 (ISBN 0-03-089732-7; LC 67-10230)
The High King lib. bdg. $7.95 Awarded the Newbery Medal, 1969 (ISBN 0-03-089504-9; LC 68-11833)

The cat who wished to be a man. Dutton 1973 107p lib. bdg. $7.95, pa $1.95 (4-6)   **Fic**

1 Cats—Fiction   2 Fairy tales
ISBN 0-525-27545-2; 0-525-45034-3   LC 73-77447

"When his cat Lionel begged to be turned into a man for just a little while, the old magician relented, but exacted a promise that Lionel would return home without delay. Alas. neither foresaw that Lionel (a Billy Budd among thieves) would fall in love, would resent and fight against injustice, would rid the town of Brightford of its mercenary mayor. Nor did they know that the magician's spell-making would break down and Lionel remain a man." Chicago. Children's Bk Center
This is "a comic and ebullient fantasy; just right for reading aloud." Horn Bk

The first two lives of Lukas-Kasha. Dutton 1978 213p lib. bdg. $8.50 (4 and up)   **Fic**

1 Fairy tales
ISBN 0-525-29748-0   LC 77-26699

"Lukas-Kasha . . . in submitting to a showman's bid to aid in a magic act, is thrust into another world. The land is Abadan, and there Lukas is forthwith declared King, a delightful state of affairs to begin with, but one that grows ever more hazardous as Lukas begins to exercise his royal prerogative. An oily Grand Vizier is his archenemy; a forthright captive girl from the neighboring, gem-rich kingdom of Bishangari is a regal benefactor, as Lukas, who was a resourceful layabout in his old world, puts his wits to full use in outfoxing the murderous Vizier bent on conquering the Bishagaris." Booklist
"What gives the story its final high gloss are the depth and nuance of the serious conversation and the transfusion of pithy ideas into the derring-do setting, ideas that are universally applicable. That's the frosting: it crowns a confection of polished style, well-paced plot, and engaging wit." Chicago. Children's Bk Center

The marvelous misadventures of Sebastian; grand extravaganza, including a performance by the entire cast of the Gallimaufry-Theatricus. Dutton 1970 204p lib. bdg. $9.95, pa $1.95 (4 and up)   **Fic**

1 Adventure and adventurers—Fiction 2 Musicians—Fiction
ISBN 0-525-34739-9; 0-525-45009-2   LC 70-166879

National Book Award, 1970
"Steeped in an eighteenth century atmosphere, the fanciful story of a young musician who, having lost his position because of the harshness of the Royal Treasurer of Hamelin-Loring, goes off to seek his fortune. Sebastian meets a princess in disguise and devotes himself to saving her from a fate worse than death; he is aided by a mysteriously omniscient people's hero; he acquires a perceptive cat, becomes a clown, is given a violin with magical powers; he is imprisoned and saves his own life and the throne of the princess by playing the violin until the villainous Regent dances to his death." Sutherland. The Best in Children's Bks

The book "is all very eloquent, action-packed and ridiculous; but hybrids are the author's special talent. His prose is a disarming mixture of Regency grandeur and Medieval robustness. His plot uses and discards a dozen clichés of children's books without batting an eye. Most important, he knows how to write character in a way that can touch the heart." NY Times Bk Rev

The wizard in the tree; illus. by Laszlo Kubinyi. Dutton 1975 137p illus lib. bdg. $7.95 (4-6)   **Fic**

1 Fairy tales
ISBN 0-525-43128-4   LC 74-23760

"When an overworked, orphaned servant girl with a firm faith in magic releases a displaced, crotchety enchanter from his centuries-long imprisonment in an oak, the impact on an eighteenth-century rural English village is at once chaotic and comic. Mallory, a determined, self-reliant female, is an apt choice as foil for acid-tongued Arbican whose wit is sharper than his wizardry, for he is out of practice because of long confinement. Arbican intends only to transport himself to Vale Innis, the Land of Heart's Desire, to which his peers have long since journeyed. But his inability to control his magical powers inevitably brings him and Mallory into confrontation with the villainous Squire Scrupnor. . . . The meticulously detailed, black-and-white illustrations effectively complement the story through their resemblance to eighteenth-century engravings." Horn Bk

Ames, Mildred

Is there life on a plastic planet? Dutton 1975 134p lib. bdg. $7.95 (4 and up)   **Fic**

1 Science fiction
ISBN 0-525-32594-8   LC 75-6746

"Hollis is an overweight misfit whose every waking hour seems to be structured by her mother. In an effort to regain the freedom that her mother had programmed out of her life, she accepts the offer of Ms. Eudora. manager of the Living Doll Store, to let a robot replace her at school, at afterschool lessons, and gradually everywhere. Her hateful cousin, Addison, accepts the same offer for opposite reasons—he has too much freedom. They both become unhappier still when robot twins take over their lives in the real world. Of course a small war between robots and children is the climax, with humans winning because only they can regret and feel sorry. In between such heavy messages on the meaning of being human, Ames manages to tell an appealing story. In addition to kids' liking it, it may also teach any parents who read it a lesson in not turning their children into automatons." Sch Library J

Anckarsvärd, Karin

The mysterious schoolmaster; tr. from the Swedish by Annabelle MacMillan; illus. by Paul Galdone. Harcourt 1959 190p illus $6.50, pa $1.35 (5 and up)   **Fic**

1 Sweden—Fiction   2 Mystery and detective stories
ISBN 0-15-256527-2; 0-15-663971-8   LC 59-10170

First published 1955 in Sweden
"Two [Swedish] youngsters in secondary school, Cecilia and Michael, stumble upon the fact that there is something very peculiar about the new physics teacher. By the time the teacher and his accomplice have been caught in their plan to map fortifications, Cecilia and Michael have been involved in dangerous incidents, but have been instrumental in foiling espionage in a manner that is dashing, foolhardy, and not completely believable." Chicago. Children's Bk Center

Anckarsvärd, Karin—*Continued*

"This far-better-than-average mystery story . . . has dramatic incidents, a continuously fast pace, and novelty of background. . . . The Swedish school life will strike American children as being interestingly like their own." Horn Bk

Followed by these books, also available from Harcourt:

The robber ghost $6.50, pa $1.50 (ISBN 0-15-267804-2; 0-15-678350-9; LC 61-6307)

Madcap mystery $5.95, pa $2.75 (ISBN 0-15-250175-4; 0-15-655108-X; LC 62-8343)

Andersen, Hans Christian

The emperor's new clothes (2-5)   **Fic**

1 Fairy tales

Some editions are:
Houghton lib. bdg. $7.95, pa $2.50 Designed and illustrated by Virginia Lee Burton (ISBN 0-395-18415-0; 0-395-28594-1; LC 49-10479)

Troll Assocs. lib. bdg. $5.21 Illustrated by Pamela Baldwin Ford (ISBN 0-89375-132-4; LC 78-18063)

A tale about the vain emperor whose only concern was his wardrobe. It tells of the clever rascals who pocketed the money given them to weave beautiful cloth for the emperor but did not weave any, his flattering courtiers who dared not voice their own opinions, and the child who pointed out the deceit as the emperor paraded proudly with nothing on

This favorite fairy tale "is really a gentle satire, but as usual, Andersen does not let the satire spoil the story. One thing which adds interest is the fact that it was a little boy who not only saw the truth but spoke it; a little child led them. Though this may be the point of most interest to children, to the adult the emperor's reaction to the child's revelation is a never-ending source of glee." Johnson, E. Anthology of Children's Lit

Hans Christian Andersen's The fir tree; illus. by Nancy Ekholm Burkert. Harper 1970 34p illus $8.95, lib. bdg. $8.79 (2-5)   **Fic**

1 Christmas—Fiction 2 Fairy tales
ISBN 0-06-020077-4; 0-06-020078-2   LC 73-121800

This translation of the fairy tale is by H. W. Dulcken

Surrounded by the beauties of the forest, the little fir tree was unhappy and longed for its moment of glory. It came one Christmas Eve but it was neither what the tree expected nor wanted

"The delicacy and meticulousness of the illustrative details of this edition, beautiful in soft colors or in black and white, should please old fans and the felicity of mood should attract new ones." Chicago. Children's Bk Center

The little match girl; illus. by Blair Lent. Houghton 1968 43p illus lib. bdg. $7.95 (2-5)   **Fic**

ISBN 0-395-21625-7   LC 68-28050

This is the "touching story of the lonely, shivering child who sees visions in the flames of the matches she cannot sell, and whose last vision is the loving grandmother who is dead and who comes to take the child. The illustrations are tremendously effective, the tiny figure lost and lorn against towering grey buildings and driving snow; even the glorious warmth and comfort of the hallucinations are pictured in muted tones." Sutherland. The Best in Children's Bks

The nightingale (3-5)   **Fic**

1 Nightingales—Fiction 2 Fairy tales

Some editions are:
Harper $8.95, lib. bdg. $7.79 Translated by Eva Le Gallienne; designed and illustrated by Nancy Ekholm Burkert. Has title: Hans Christian Andersen's The nightingale (ISBN 0-06-023780-5; 0-06-023781-3; LC 64-18574)

Troll Assocs. lib. bdg. $5.21, pa $1.50 Illustrated by James Watling. Has title: The emperor and the nightingale (ISBN 0-89375-134-0; 0-89375-112-X; LC 78-18065)

This is the "story of the Emperor's nightingale which entertained him with exquisite song. Replaced by a gorgeous jewel-encrusted artificial bird, the nightingale is banished from the empire, only to return later to save the Emperor from sure death." Pub W

The princess and the pea; illus. by Paul Galdone. Seabury [distributed by Houghton] 1978 unp illus lib. bdg. $8.95 (1-4)   **Fic**

1 Fairy tales
ISBN 0-395-28807-X   LC 77-12707

"A Clarion book"

"Veteran artist Galdone gives a new and sprightly look to the classic tale of the superfastidious princess. Bright hues contrast with pale shades in arresting paintings of the locale and Andersen's characters. The telling is brisk as the well-known prince seeks in vain for a bride but finds no princess who seems real in all the world. When the pretty unknown girl shows up at the royal castle and asks for shelter from a storm, it's great fun to see the calculating expression on the queen's face as she plans to test the princess for sensitivity. Of course, the stranger becomes the prince's bride when she passed a sleepless night because of the pea under the 20 mattresses and 20 featherbeds towering over her four-poster." Pub W

The Snow Queen; with illus. by Marcia Brown. Scribner 1972 95p illus lib. bdg. $6.95 (4-6)   **Fic**

1 Fairy tales
ISBN 0-684-12611-7   LC 72-168499

This translation of the fairy tale is by R. P. Keigwin

The classic story of young Kay's capture by the Snow Queen, and of his friend Gerda who rescues him

The artist "selected pen and ink as the medium for this distinguished new edition of a classic tale. The black-and-white drawings have flexibility, delicacy, and strength, and are admirably suited to the poignant text. The innocence of the two children, the cold beauty of the Snow Queen, the mystic, far-seeing eyes of the Finnish woman, the good-natured rowdiness of the little robber girl— these are among the striking characterizations achieved in the many fine drawings that interpret mood and character." Horn Bk

The steadfast tin soldier (1-4)   **Fic**

1 Toys—Fiction 2 Fairy tales

Some editions are:
Houghton $8.95 Illustrated by Paul Galdone (ISBN 0-395-28964-5; LC 79-4325)

Scribner lib. bdg. $8.95 Translated by M. R. James; illustrated by Marcia Brown (ISBN 0-684-12507-2; LC 53-11744)

A favorite among Hans Christian Andersen's stories, this tells of the adventures of a tin soldier and his love for a little toy dancer

Thumbelina (1-4)   **Fic**

1 Fairy tales

Some editions are:
Morrow $8.95, lib. bdg. $8.59 Translated by Richard Winston and Clara Winston; illustrated by Lisbeth Zwerger. Has title: Thumbeline (ISBN 0-688-22235-8; 0-688-32235-2; LC 80-13012)

Troll Assocs. lib. bdg. $5.21, pa $1.50 Illustrated by Christine Willis Nigognossian (ISBN 0-89375-141-3; 0-89375-119-7; LC 78-18080)

After some frightening adventures, a little girl only one inch high "finally flies with a swallow to the land of sun, flowers, and fairies." Adventuring with Bks. 2d edition

"Here we find the feminine counterpart of Tom Thumb. . . . In this story we see how deftly Andersen intermingles fantasy with folklore. He has taken the theme of an old tale and touched it with the magic of imagination." Johnson, E. Anthology of Children's Lit

The ugly duckling (1-4)   **Fic**

1 Swans—Fiction 2 Fairy tales

Some editions are:
Scribner lib. bdg. $8.95, pa $1.25 Translated by R. P. Keigwin; illustrated by Adrienne Adams (ISBN 0-684-12646-X; 0-684-13037-8; LC 65-21364)

Scroll Press $5.50 Translated by R. P. Keigwin; illustrated by Toma Bogdanovic (ISBN 0-87592-055-1; LC 75-143207)

Troll Assocs. lib. bdg. $5.21, pa $1.50 Illustrated by Jennie Williams (ISBN 0-89375-128-6; 0-89375-106-5; LC 78-18059)

A story about an ugly "duckling" who led an unhappy life until he grew into a beautiful swan

Andersen, Hans C.—*Continued*

The wild swans; tr. by M. R. James; illus. by Marcia Brown. Scribner [1963] 80p illus lib. bdg. $6.95 (3-6)   **Fic**

1 Fairy tales
ISBN 0-684-12978-7   LC 63-18748

Text from Hans Andersen's: Forty-two stories, published 1959 by A. S. Barnes

This is "the tale of the princess seeking to break the spell that turned her 11 brothers into swans." Booklist

"The softness of swans-down, the steady sound of surf, the solitude of a great wood, the elegance of a King's palace, the purity of heart of a gentle princess—all these qualities have been caught to perfection in Marcia Brown's gray and rose pictures." Pub W

Anderson, C. W.

The blind Connemara. Macmillan Pub. Co. 1971 80p illus $4.95 (3-5)   **Fic**

1 Horses—Fiction
ISBN 0-02-70500-9   LC 76-158172

The "plot involves Rhonda, a youngster who loves horses but cannot afford one, and the horse who needs the love and patience only she can give him. Rhonda proves that even a supposedly worthless blind pony will respond to affection and careful training." Library J

"Although the outcome may be anticipated early in the book by most readers, it will probably satisfy all who dote on horse stories. The soft black and white illustrations are attractive, and the message of kindness to animals is worthy." Chicago. Children's Bk Center

Anderson, Margaret J.

Searching for Shona. Knopf 1978 159p $6.95, lib. bdg. $6.99 (5 and up)   **Fic**

1 World War, 1939-1945—Fiction 2 Scotland—Fiction 3 Orphans—Fiction
ISBN 0-394-83724-X; 0-394-93724-4   LC 77-17056

"It was not surprising that Marjorie Malcolm-Scott impulsively changed identities with orphaned Shona McInnes and was thus evacuated to Scotland during World War II and not sent to unknown relatives in Canada. Shy, friendless Marjorie was also an orphan, and she was being brought up by well-off but uninterested relatives. In the confusion of wartime the deception was successful, and Marjorie found herself for the first time in a happy home. She and Anna Ray, another orphan, were sent to live with unmarried twin sisters, who gave them comforting care. Years later, when the war was over and Marjorie was starting medical studies in Edinburgh, she found Shona but was actually relieved when the girl refused to resume her own identity." Horn Bk

"The war is well integrated into the story (the plot would be totally incredible in any but that chaotic time) and the author's treatment of the theme of switched identities is sensitive. The characters have depth and behave believably. Anderson's simple, almost stark prose is most expressive." Sch Library J

Angell, Judie

Tina Gogo. Bradbury Press 1978 196p $7.95 (6 and up)   **Fic**

1 Friendship—Fiction 2 Foster home care—Fiction
ISBN 0-87888-132-8   LC 77-16439

The story revolves around eleven-year-old Tina Gogolavsky, who is "a problem foster child and her giant leap into maturity one summer when she befriends another girl and her 'typical' family in a small community around a lake resort." Children's Bk Rev Serv

"In a well-paced plot that is never melodramatic, Angell gingerly peels away the layers of hurt and mistrust beneath which Tina . . . has buried herself revealing a miraculously resilient and sturdy core. . . . Relationships between the characters are skillfully drawn and this is, altogether, nicely done." Sch Library J

Arkin, Alan

The lemming condition; illus. by Joan Sandin. Harper 1976 57p illus $4.95, lib. bdg. $6.89 (5 and up)   **Fic**

1 Lemmings—Fiction
ISBN 0-06-020133-9; 0-06-020134-7   LC 75-6296

"Disturbed that no other lemming can answer his question of whether or not lemmings can swim, Bubber decides to find out himself. Two feet stuck uncomfortably into a nearby pond tell him all he needs to know, and now he anxiously ponders the fate of his family and friends—indeed all the lemmings who feel moved to travel west to the sea that afternoon. A crotchety old recluse lemming who disdains his own species counsels Bubber that he must not give in to such craziness if he doesn't feel like it. Ultimately Bubber doesn't, though he does succumb to their mechanical frenzy for a few breathless minutes. . . . Facile, upbeat dialogue among Bubber's family and friends serves to quickly delineate common attitudes, and Arkin manages to mesh the biological habits of lemmings with the human characteristics he imposes upon them. The resulting contemporary parable is arch but solid enough to provoke its share of discussion." Booklist

Armer, Laura Adams

Waterless Mountain; illus. by Sidney Armer and Laura Adams Armer. McKay 1931 212p illus $8.95 (5 and up)   **Fic**

1 Navaho Indians—Fiction 2 Arizona—Fiction
ISBN 0-679-20233-1   LC 31-28005

A reprint of the title first published by Longmans, Green and Company

Awarded the Newbery Medal, 1932

This is "an unusual story of Navaho Indian life as seen through the eyes of Younger Brother, who learns the songs of the medicine men and makes new songs for himself. The customs and tribal beliefs are skillfully woven into the narrative. The author is noted for her copies of sand paintings." Pittsburgh

"Written with sympathy and understanding, it reveals the mysticism and love of beauty which is innate in the Indian of the highest type. All children who like poetry and who care for the Indian will enjoy it. The illustrations in aquatone by the author and Sidney Armer reflect the beauty of the story and its setting in the deserts and canyons of northern Arizona." Cleveland

Armstrong, William H.

Sounder; illus. by James Barkley. Harper 1969 116p illus $6.95, lib. bdg. $6.89, pa $1.50 (5 and up)   **Fic**

1 Blacks—Fiction 2 Dogs—Fiction 3 Poverty—Fiction 4 Family life—Fiction
ISBN 0-06-020143-6; 0-06-020144-4; 0-06-080379-7   LC 70-85030

Awarded the Newbery Medal, 1970

Set in the South, at one level this "is the story of the coon dog, Sounder, and his devotion to his master. It is also a story of humans: the father, a black sharecropper, who must steal to feed his children, the timid mother fighting for survival, and the son who grows to maturity through his father's prison term and the devotion of Sounder." Best Sellers

"There is an epic quality in the deeply moving, long-ago story of cruelty, loneliness, and silent suffering. The power of the writing lies in its combination of subtlety and strength. Four characters are unforgettable: the mother, with her inscrutable fortitude and dignity; the crushed and beaten father; the indomitable boy; and the 'human animal,' Sounder." Horn Bk

Arthur, Ruth M.

A candle in her room; illus. by Margery Gill. Atheneum Pubs 1966 212p illus pa $1.95 (5 and up)   **Fic**

1 Dolls—Fiction
ISBN 0-689-70315-5   LC 66-12854

"An old house in Wales and a malevolent witch doll, Dido, dominate this story of three generations of the Mansell girls, all of whom come under Dido's spell. Excellent characterization, strong sense of place, and a haunting story of lives lived in an atmosphere of mystery and evil." Hodges. Bks for Elem Sch Libraries

Requiem for a princess; illus. by Margery Gill. Atheneum Pubs. 1967 182p illus pa $1.95 (6 and up)   **Fic**

1 Great Britain—Fiction 2 Adoption—Fiction
ISBN 0-689-70419-4   LC 67-2667

"Fifteen-year-old Willow Forrester, bickering with one of her classmates, is told contemptuously that she is an adopted child. Heartsick, Willow worries herself into physical debility and

Arthur, Ruth M.—*Continued*

is sent to recuperate at a private house that has become a guest home. Here she has a mystical experience; having seen the portrait of a Spanish girl who had lived in the house as the adopted child of the Cornish owners, Willow identifies with the long-dead Isabel, and her nights are spent in dream-sequences in which she lives the life that Isabel lived in the sixteenth century." Chicago. Children's Bk Center

"This is a smoothly written, first-person narrative with intriguing plot development and well-drawn characterization, sure to capture young readers from its beginning." Wis Library Bul

Atwater, Richard

Mr Popper's penguins, by Richard and Florence Atwater; illus. by Robert Lawson. Little 1938 138p illus $6.95 (3-5)   **Fic**

1 Penguins—Fiction
ISBN 0-316-05842-4   LC 38-27840

When Mr Popper, a mild little painter and decorator with a taste for books and movies on polar explorations, was presented with a penguin, he named it Captain Cook. Mr Popper and his family exerted themselves to make the new pet happy, but the poor bird grew so lonely that they appealed to an aquarium and got another penguin named Greta. From that moment on life was changed for the Popper family

"To the depiction of the penguins in all conceivable moods Robert Lawson [the] artist has brought not only his skill but his individual humor, and his portrayal of the wistful Mr. Popper is memorable." NY Times Bk Rev

"Here is a find, a book not only funny, but universally funny. Children will cherish it; so will anybody with a love of joy." NY Her Trib Bks

Aulaire, Ingri d'

Children of the Northlights; by Ingri & Edgar Parin d'Aulaire. Viking 1935 unp illus lib. bdg. $6.50 (2-4)   **Fic**

1 Lapland—Fiction
ISBN 0-670-21741-7   LC 35-27299

"A notable picture story book which spans a year in the life of Lise and Lasse, two little children of Lapland. It is the result of the D'Aulaires' long journey by boat and sled into the north of Norway, and contains much interesting information concerning the customs of the Lapps." Booklist

"A distinguished book full of color, fun and the charm of ways that are just different enough to be fascinating." Horn Bk

Avi

Emily Upham's revenge; or, How Deadwood Dick saved the banker's niece; a Massachusetts adventure; pictures by Paul O. Zelinsky. Pantheon Bks. 1978 172p illus $6.95, lib. bdg. $6.99 (4-6)   **Fic**

1 Robbers and outlaws—Fiction 2 Massachusetts —Fiction
ISBN 0-394-83506-9; 0-394-93506-3   LC 77-13739

"In Massachusetts in 1875 Emily's father leaves home in a desperate mood in order to 'get money, "dignity be damned!" ' This crass aim and the 'awful word' her father used shock Emily to the core, for although she is only seven, she is a proper young lady who views money and lying as the sources of all evil. Her mother sends her off to North Brookfield to stay with her uncle. There she meets Seth Marple, a reader of dime novels about 'Deadwood Dick.' Seth, who is not too careful about telling the straight truth, is hiding out after destroying some U.S. mail. The prim Emily and the canny Seth are a juvenile Bonnie-and-Clyde. Living in Seth's forest hideout, witnessing a bank robbery, disposing of stolen money, and holding up trains to ask the fare are only a few of their capers." Children's Bk Rev Serv

"Everything about Avi's new novel is a brilliant spoof on 19th-century morality tales. The author is abetted in the creation of absurdity by Zelinsky, whose mannered, expertly exaggerated drawings are as funny as the story." Pub W

Night journeys. Pantheon Bks. 1979 143p $6.95, lib. bdg. $6.99 (5 and up)   **Fic**

1 Pennsylvania—Fiction 2 Friends, Society of— Fiction 3 Orphans—Fiction 4 Indentured servants—Fiction
ISBN 0-394-84116-6   LC 78-10151

"Looking back on his youth, the narrator, Peter York, tells of an episode during his adolescence in colonial Pennsylvania which proved to be a turning point in his life. Orphaned, he had been sent to live with a family of kindly but undemonstrative Quakers whose ways he did not understand and whom he consequently resented, thinking that they did not care for him. When two children who had been indentured servants to a harsh master in a nearby county make a bid for freedom, both Peter and his foster father are called upon to help capture them. Though at first they cooperate, each for very different reasons, they both soon come to realize that no matter what the cost they must heed their consciences rather than uphold the law. As each becomes aware of the other's faltering but persistent struggle toward integrity, the distance between them closes and they begin a new warm and supportive relationship." Sch Library J

"Both the description and the dialogue provide a suitable historical accent and the suspense keeps the book moving as briskly as the Delaware River, which figures importantly in the story." Christian Sci Monitor

Babbitt, Natalie

The eyes of the Amaryllis. Farrar, Straus 1977 127p lib. bdg. $7.95 (5 and up)   **Fic**

1 Sea stories 2 Grandmothers—Fiction
ISBN 0-374-32241-4   LC 77-11862

"Set in the late 19th century, this is a story in which the sea sets the mood, not an ocean of, sparkling waves but an ocean of fog and storm, an enemy. It has taken the ship 'Amaryllis,' and for three decades Geneva Reade, the captain's widow, has waited for some sign, some message. When her grandchild Jenny comes to visit, she too is drawn into Gran's obsessive searching for the sign. . . . The sign, the figurehead of the 'Amaryllis,' is washed up but Gran returns it during a hurricane that she interprets as a wrathful demand for a return of the 'eyes,' the eyes of the figurehead that can see and guard the wrecked ship." Chicago. Children's Bk Center

The story "has as its central theme the idea that love can be mistaken or misunderstood but that it can never be fully satisfied or completely destroyed. . . . An intricate combination of patterns, like a jacquard weave, the book succeeds as a well-wrought narrative in which a complex philosophic theme is developed through the balanced, subtle use of symbol and imagery. It is a rare story, accessible to the discriminating pre-adolescent; because of its perfect scale and transcendent style, it neither diminishes the subject nor the audience." Horn Bk

Goody Hall; story and pictures by Natalie Babbitt. Farrar, Straus 1971 176p illus $8.95 (4-6)   **Fic**

1 Mystery and detective stories
ISBN 0-374-32745-9   LC 73-149221

In this Gothic mystery "Hercules Feltwright, a would-be actor, comes to a magnificent house— Goody Hall—to tutor the young master, Willet Goody. The boy soon announces his firm conviction that his father is not dead and interred in the family tomb. In trying to find an answer for Willet, Hercules' way is marked by chilling events, including a gypsy seance on a rainy night and a thrilling descent into Mr. Goody's burial vault." Wis Library Bul

"Lightened by humor and colored by suspense, the story whirls its delightfully just-short-of-burlesqued characters in a triumphant gavotte of melodrama." Sat Rev

Kneeknock Rise; story and pictures by Natalie Babbitt. Farrar, Straus 1970 117p illus $6.95 (3-5)   **Fic**

1 Allegories 2 Superstition—Fiction
ISBN 0-374-34257-1   LC 79-105622

"It was firmly understood by all those who lived near the Mammoth Mountains that any peculiar circumstance was due to the malevolent influence of a mysterious creature on the bleak and rocky heights of Kneeknock Rise. Egan, visiting Uncle Anson in the little village at the foot of the terrible cliff, hears the strange wail of the Megrimum during a storm. Taunted by his cousin Ada, he climbs up, and finds that the Megrimum's 'voice' is caused by a hot spring in a cave, but when he tries to explain this to the villagers, they will have none of it." Sat Rev

"An enchanting tale imbued with a folk flavor, enlivened with piquant imagery and satiric wit, and enhanced by an inviting format and amusing black-and-white drawings." Booklist

Babbitt, Natalie—Continued

The search for delicious. Farrar, Straus 1969 167p illus $8.95 (5 and up)   **Fic**

ISBN 0-374-36534-2   LC 69-20374

"An Ariel book"
The Prime Minister is compiling a dictionary and when no one at court can agree on the meaning of delicious, the King sends his twelve-year-old messenger to poll the country
"The characters' names fit their roles. The theme, foolish arguments can lead to great conflict, may not be clear to all children who will enjoy this fantasy." Best Sellers

Tuck everlasting. Farrar, Straus 1975 139p $7.95 (4 and up)   **Fic**

1 Fantastic fiction
ISBN 0-374-37848-7   LC 75-33306

"The Tuck family have unwittingly drunk from a spring of life and suffer a sort of eternal youth that keeps them apart from the changes that occur naturally in time. Eleven-year-old Winnie Foster stumbles on their secret just about the same time as does a stranger with devilish intentions, and she must assume some burdensome decisions about life and death, which she does with grace. Winnie intuits the Tucks' basic goodness, rescues them when they are charged with kidnapping and murder, and neither divulges their secret nor shares the water." Booklist
"The story is macabre and moral, exciting and excellently written. It has no absolute end, because Time hasn't." NY Times Bk Rev

Bacon, Martha

Sophia Scrooby preserved; illus. by David Omar White. Little 1968 227p illus $6.95 (5 and up)   **Fic**

1 Slavery in the U.S.—Fiction 2 Blacks—Fiction
ISBN 0-316-07508-6   LC 68-21167

"An Atlantic Monthly Press book"
"Born in 1768, the small daughter of an African chieftain is taken into slavery and lives with a Connecticut family that fosters her natural bent for education and musical training. Sophia and the Scroobys are separated, and she falls into the clutches of pirates, is the captive of a voodoo queen, the companion to an English lady of means, and a performer at Drury Lane before her reunion with the Scroobys in Canada." Sutherland. The Best in Children's Bks
"Martha Bacon has a lively style and when she is sure of her scene, writes with wit and perception. . . . But her story is too thin: the themes obtrude." NY Times Bk Rev

Bagnold, Enid

"National Velvet"; illus. by Paul Brown. Morrow 1949 306p illus $9.50, lib. bdg. $9.12 (6 and up)   **Fic**

1 Horses—Fiction 2 Great Britain—Fiction
ISBN 0-688-21422-3; 0-688-31422-8   LC 49-10997

First published 1935
An English girl, Velvet Brown, wins a magnificent piebald horse in a lottery and determines to enter and win the Grand National Steeplechase even though girls are not allowed to ride in that race
"The atmosphere, characters, setting, and situations are natural and fresh, the values wholesome. Unlike stories of a similar genre, this goes beyond the winning of the big race and includes the aftermath." Booklist
"Admittedly improbable in plot but unforgettably whimsical, racy and jolly in its very British humor, this book is made uncommon by its understanding of and delight in youngsters." Lenrow. Reader's Guide to Prose Fic

Bailey, Carolyn Sherwin

Miss Hickory; with lithographs by Ruth Gannett. Viking 1946 120p illus $7.95, Penguin pa $1.50 (3-5)   **Fic**

1 Dolls—Fiction 2 New Hampshire—Fiction
ISBN 0-670-47940-3; 0-14-030956-X   LC 46-7275

Awarded the Newbery Medal, 1947
"With her hickory nut head glued to a body made of an apple-wood twig, Miss Hickory may have seemed to be merely a country doll—but actually, she was a real person, who had all sorts of exciting adventures after Great-Granny Brown closed her New Hampshire home for the winter." Bookmark

"Fascinating and harmonious lithographs adorn this imaginative and delightful story. . . . A refreshingly original story, full of the love of the countryside and its outdoor residents. There is a lovely Christmas chapter in the book." Horn Bk

Baker, Betty

The spirit is willing. Macmillan Pub. Co. 1974 135p $6.95 (5 and up)   **Fic**

1 Arizona—Fiction
ISBN 0-02-708270-9   LC 73-8576

"Young Carrie Thatcher is the heroine in this light novel of the newly civilized American West. Under the hot Arizona sun, Carrie and her theatrical companion Portia set out to find summer excitement. When the girls sneak into the Rough-n-Ready Saloon to observe an Indian mummy on display, they are discovered and forthwith dragged, not without feeling self-important, into the center of the news-hungry town's attention. . . . Aside from a weak and hasty resolution to both the plot and to Carrie's personal worries, the book provides satisfying entertainment." Booklist

Walk the world's rim. Harper 1965 168p illus lib. bdg. $8.79, pa $1.25 (5 and up)   **Fic**

1 Estévan—Fiction 2 Núñez Cabeza de Vaca, Alvar—Fiction 3 America—Exploration—Fiction
ISBN 0-06-020381-1; 0-06-440026-3   LC 65-11458

Chakho, an Indian boy, travels from Texas to Mexico City with the black slave Esteban, Cabeza de Vaca, and two other Spanish explorers in the 16th century
"Told against an authentic background, the story has much to say about freedom and human dignity." Hodges. Bks for Elem Sch Libraries
"The book is written with an economy of construction that enhances the richness of its emotional impact." Chicago. Children's Bk Center
Bibliography: p169

Baker, Charlotte

Cockleburr Quarters; illus. by Robert Owens. Prentice-Hall 1972 176p illus $4.95 (4-6)   **Fic**

1 Blacks—Fiction 2 Dogs—Fiction
ISBN 0-13-139485-1   LC 78-37960

A story about Dolph, a black boy, and his friends who find a homeless dog and her eight puppies. To Dolph and his sister, the puppies are the beginning of a new awareness
"Although weakened by an all-problems-solved pat ending, the story of the black neighborhood community of Cockleburr Quarters is lively and believable, permeated with the belief in humane treatment for animals. . . . The dialogue is realistic, the home setting one in which it is accepted that there is an 'uncle' in the house, that two of Dolph's sisters have illegitimate babies, and that one of them goes off with Uncle, leaving her child for her mother to bring up, but this is emphasized less than the industry and ambition of other members of the family." Chicago. Children's Bk Center

Baldwin, Anne Norris

A little time. Viking 1978 119p $6.95 (4-6)   **Fic**

1 Mongolism—Fiction 2 Mentally retarded children—Fiction 3 Family life—Fiction
ISBN 0-670-43392-6   LC 77-27764

"Ten-year-old Sarah is one of five children, and the story she tells is primarily about her brother Matt, a four-year-old who's mongoloid. That's what she explains to Ginny, the new classmate she hopes will become a friend—but Ginny seems horrified and ends the promising relationship. So, torn between her love for Mattie and her resentment toward him, Sarah is miserable. Cumulating difficulties convince the children's parents to try custodial care for Matt, but they miss him and bring him home—and everybody's happier." Chicago. Children's Bk Center
"All aspects of having a retarded child at home with the family are explored in this well-told story. The characters are sympathetic, the plot is believable and the difficulties and joys of having a mongoloid child are realistically portrayed. This is a good book for those children who have had experiences with a retarded child, as well as an introduction to the problem for those who have not." Children's Bk Rev Serv

Ball, Zachary

Bristle Face. Holiday House 1962 206p $7.95 (5 and up)   **Fic**

1 Dogs—Fiction 2 Mississippi—Fiction
ISBN 0-8234-0013-1   LC 62-2219

"In the fox-hunting back country of Mississippi in 1900, fourteen-year-old orphaned Jase Landers and his newly adopted dog Bristle Face are befriended by Lute Swank, a lazy but kind and understanding storekeeper. Told by Jase, the perceptive narrative tells how turtle-chasing dog develops into a keen-nosed trail dog, how Lute wins the Widow Jarkey and his campaign for sheriff, and how Jase finds a permanent home. . . . The local idiom in the dialog may cause some reading difficulty but it adds much to the atmosphere of the tale." Booklist

"As Jase tells the story, quoting all the pithy comments of Lute, his friends and the widow Jarkey, it is side-splittingly funny . . . and exciting, poignant and satisfying with tragedy tempered by hope. . . . An excellent tale of the enduring friendship of a boy and a dog." NY Her Trib Bks
Followed by: Sputters (o.p. 1981)

Barret, Leighton

The adventures of Don Quixote de la Mancha; adapted from the Motteux translation by Leighton Barret, and illus. with drawings by Warren Chappell. Knopf 1960 307p illus lib. bdg. $5.99 (5 and up)   **Fic**

1 Adventure and adventurers—Fiction 2 Spain—Fiction 3 Knights and knighthood—Fiction
ISBN 0-394-90892-9   LC 60-9442

Adapted for younger readers from the work by Miguel de Cervantes
Original Spanish edition published in two parts, 1605 and 1615
"Treats of the pleasant manner of the knighting of that famous gentleman, Don Quixote, of the dreadful and never-to-be imagined adventure of the windmills, of the extraordinary battle he waged with what he took to be a giant, and of divers other rare and notable adventures and strange enchantments which befell this valorous and witty knight-errant." Pittsburgh
"A flavorful version of the addled knight's adventures, amusingly illustrated." Hodges, Bks for Elem Sch Libraries

Barrie, J. M.

Peter Pan (3-5)   **Fic**

1 Fairy tales
Some editions are:
Scribner $14.95 Illustrations by Trina Schart Hyman (ISBN 0-684-16611-9; LC 80-14510)
Scribner lib. bdg. $7.95 Illustrated by Nora S. Unwin (ISBN 0-684-13214-1; LC 50-9328)
First published 1911 by Scribner with title: Peter and Wendy
This is the story of "how Wendy, John, and Michael flew with Peter Pan, the boy who never grows up, to adventures in the Never-Never Land with pirates, redskins, and the fairy Tinker Bell. [It is] in Barrie's inimitable style, pleasing the child with delightful absurdities and the adult with good-humored satire." Right Bk for the Right Child

Baudouy, Michel-Aimé

Old One-Toe; tr. by Marie Ponsot; illus. by Johannes Troyer. Harcourt 1959 190p illus $6.50 (5 and up)   **Fic**

1 Foxes—Fiction 2 France—Fiction
ISBN 0-15-257780-7   LC 59-10944

First published 1957 in France
A "story set in the woods and fields around an old mill house where four children from Paris are visiting their aunt. The central characters are One-Toe, a cunning, marauding red fox tracked by hunters and championed by the children, the boy Piet, who discovers the joy in learning the ways of the forest creatures, particularly One-Toe, and the Commandant, an elderly and skillful hunter who shares his love and knowledge of the forest with Piet and matches wits with One-Toe." Booklist
"Superb characterization of children and adults, and of two special dogs. A prose style that is freshly poetic and evocative heightens feelings, relationships, and unusual scenes, and makes the book (a French prize-winner) one worth sharing aloud." Horn Bk

Bauer, Marion Dane

Shelter from the wind. Seabury [distributed by Houghton] 1976 108p $6.95 (5 and up)   **Fic**

1 Runaways—Fiction 2 Oklahoma—Fiction
ISBN 0-395-28890-8   LC 75-28184

"A Clarion book"
This story is about "a girl, two dogs, and a crotchety, but canny, old lady. Stacy hates Barbara, hates her shrill voice screaming at her, hates the baby inside Barbara's stomach, so she runs away. Barbara is her stepmother, the woman Stacy's father married five years after Stacy's mother ran off with another man. Off in the desert of the Oklahoma Panhandle, Stacy quickly realizes her grave error in starting out without any water or supplies. Fortunately, she is rescued, and the rescuers help to give her a new outlook on life." Babbling Bookworm
"The powerful concrete imagery and strong realistic characterization allow the author to explore such subjects as alcoholism and childbirth with rare sensitivity and unflinching avoidance of sentimentality. Although this book is not for all children, it will have an important place in most library collections." Sch Library J

Baum, L. Frank

The Wizard of Oz (3-6)   **Fic**

1 Fantastic fiction
Some editions are:
Dent (Children's illustrated classics ser) $5.60 Illustrated with four colour plates and line drawings in the text by Biro (ISBN 0-460-02726-3)
Grosset (Illustrated junior lib) $5.95 Illustrated by Evelyn Copelman; adapted from the famous pictures by W. W. Denslow (ISBN 0-448-05826-X; LC 56-14198)
Macmillan Pub. Co. (The Macmillan classics) $5.95 Illustrated by W. W. Denslow (ISBN 0-02-708520-1; LC 62-18836)
Random House $4.95, lib. bdg. $5.99 Edited by Allen Chaffer (ISBN 0-394-80689-1; 0-394-90689-6; LC 50-10602)
First published 1900 with title: The wonderful Wizard of Oz
Here are the adventures of Dorothy who, in her dreams, escapes from her bed in Kansas to visit the Emerald City and to meet the wonderful Wizard of Oz, the Scarecrow, the Tin Woodman, and the Cowardly Lion
Some other books about Oz are:
The marvelous land of Oz. Dent $11 (ISBN 0-460-02750-6)
The patchwork girl of Oz. Contemporary Bks. $7.95 (ISBN 0-8092-8565-7)

Bawden, Nina

Carrie's war. Lippincott 1973 159p illus $8.95 (4 and up)   **Fic**

1 Wales—Fiction 2 World War, 1939-1945—Fiction
ISBN 0-397-31450-7   LC 72-13253

"Carrie, recently widowed, takes her children to the small Welsh mining town where she and her younger brother, Nick, had been evacuated during World War II. Carrie is tormented by her mistaken belief that she caused a fire at the time which may have killed people she loved. For the most part, the story revolves around Carrie and Nick's days spent in the home of rigid, strict Mr. Evans and his kindly sister, their friendship with Hepzibah Green, who may have been a witch, and Albert Sandwich, another evacuee." Library J
"The pace and the dialogue and the characterisation all add up to a whole which could be read with interest and pleasure by any age, and in which the lessons are implied, delicately, in the behaviour and relationships of the principal actors, never rammed home. . . . Beautifully told, perceptive, tough and at the same time tender, this is the sort of book from which I believe children learn about other people and about themselves." New Statesman

The peppermint pig; frontispiece by Charles Lilly. Lippincott 1975 191p front $8.95 (5 and up)   **Fic**

1 Pigs—Fiction 2 Family life—Fiction 3 Great Britain—Fiction
ISBN 0-397-31618-6   LC 74-26922

"Just after the turn of the century, the Greengrass family left their comfortable London home because of financial problems and settled in a Norfolk country town. Father was going off to try his fortune in America, so Mother and the four

Bawden, Nina—*Continued*

children would be dependent upon the good grace and the generosity of two relatives, the schoolmistresses Aunt Sarah and Aunt Harriet. The story unfolds from the viewpoint of nine-year-old Poll, the youngest and naughtiest of the children, who frequently locks horns with her brother Theo. . . . Into their lives comes Johnnie, a remarkable runt pig who grows into a beloved family pet. . . . Representing a departure for the author, the story is historical rather than contemporary, subtle rather than mysterious; and its plot is more relaxed than suspenseful. Time and setting come sharply through the writing, which is typically graceful, witty, clear, and fluid." Horn Bk

Rebel on a rock. Lippincott 1978 158p $9.95 (5 and up)   **Fic**

1 Spies—Fiction
ISBN 0-397-31772-7   LC 77-10686

"Twelve-year-old Jo, the narrator, her mother, older brother, and small adopted brother and sister (who are Black) are taken on what Albert, her charming, mild-mannered stepfather, calls a 'vacation.' At first, being in an exotic country is fun—but soon Jo has reason to believe that Albert is a spy involved in a plot to overthrow the tyrannical dictator and restore the President to his rightful place. In a remote village dominated by an ancient fortification on a rock, Jo meets a young boy who tells her he is the son of the President-in-exile, and dreams of the rebellion to come." Sch Library J

This "book is in a sense a sequel to Carrie's War [entered above, which deals with Jo's mother, Carrie]. . . . It is an easy book to read, accessible to many children who find some other highly praised writers too 'literary', too slow. But it is also honest and thought-provoking. It faces up to many unpalatable facts and will certainly give its readers some idea of what it means to live in a police state and also how easy it was for tourists in Franco's Spain or the Colonel's Greece to lick their ice creams and return home (as the American ladies so nearly do in Rebel on a Rock) thinking all was well." Times (London) Lit Sup

The robbers. Lothrop 1979 155p $7.50, lib. bdg. $7.20 (5 and up)   **Fic**

1 Grandmothers—Fiction   2 Family life—Fiction
3 London—Fiction   4 Friendship—Fiction
ISBN 0-688-41902-X   LC 79-4152

"Solitary and happy, nine-year-old Philip lived with his grandmother in an apartment in a seaside castle; his mother was dead, his father a peripatetic television reporter. When his father married an American, Philip went to London for what he thought was a visit; it proved to be a long stay. Precocious and articulate, Philip made only one friend, Darcy, a street-wise boy whose family (an arthritic father, brother Bing who was a street peddler, Bing's black wife Addie, a beautiful and sensitive woman) made Philip welcome. It is when Bing is sentenced for selling stolen goods that the two boys, desperate, plan their robbery of a rich neighbor's home." Chicago. Children's Bk Center

"It is always character that counts with Nina Bawden. Motive, action, setting—everything is simple, clear-cut and selective, and totally adequate for the task of creating a particular corner of London in which believable people speak, act, suffer and learn from their mistakes." Growing Point

The runaway summer. Lippincott 1969 185p $9.95 (4-6)   **Fic**

1 Great Britain—Fiction
ISBN 0-397-31102-8   LC 77-82408

This is "the story of two children's efforts to hide a Kenyan boy who, they believe, has entered England illegally. . . . The feeling that her parents do not want her has made [eleven-year-old Mary] cherish her unhappiness so stubbornly that she will not respond to the kindness of her aunt and her grandfather, with whom she has come to live. Her discovery of Krishna Patel and her determination to save him from the authorities lead her to seek help from a neighbor boy, Simon. He is just the friend Mary needs, and she begins to emerge from her unpleasant shell." Horn Bk

The author "writes so well. Not for her the adult-oriented view of the child. She is there with the child describing the adults—and filling the pages with action. This being a Nina Bawden book, the ending is both happy and realistic." Christian Sci Monitor

The witch's daughter. Lippincott 1966 181p $8.95 (4 and up)   **Fic**

1 Blind—Fiction 2 Scotland—Fiction
ISBN 0-397-30922-8   LC 66-7115

This story, set on the Scottish island of Skua, involves "much more than the capture of jewel thieves. Perdita, a lonely orphan, is rejected by the other children because of her unusual power to see into the future. Through the arrival of a blind girl, Janey, and Janey's brother Tim, Perdita comes to realize that her powers are not a sign of witchcraft, but a special talent." Rdng Ladders. 5th edition

"A credible suspense story, with a likeable and resourceful cast. A plausible plot, superior dialogue and an appropriate setting." NY Times Bk Rev

Beatty, John

Holdfast [by] John and Patricia Beatty. Morrow 1972 222p lib. bdg. $7.92 (6 and up)   **Fic**

1 Great Britain—History—Tudors, 1485-1603—Fiction 2 Dogs—Fiction
ISBN 0-688-31434-1   LC 75-187902

"This is steeped in the lore of a well-realized Elizabethan England and peopled with convincing historical as well as fictional characters. Motherless twelve-year-old Catriona Burke, daughter of the Earl of Kilrain who is killed fighting with the British against rebel Irish lords, is taken against her will to England where as a ward of Queen Elizabeth I she is placed with a titled English family. Her friend and companion, an Irish wolfhound, is separated from her and later becomes known as Holdfast, London's best known bear and bull baiter. The plot follows the separate experiences of girl and dog until the two come together again in a dramatic climax in the sports arena. The appended notes give background information and sources." Booklist

Who comes to King's Mountain? [By] John and Patricia Beatty. Morrow 1975 287p lib. bdg. $6.96 (6 and up)   **Fic**

1 U.S.—History—Revolution, 1775-1783—Fiction 2 South Carolina—Fiction
ISBN 0-688-32041-4   LC 75-11997

"Living in a Scottish settlement in South Carolina during the revolutionary hostilities of 1780, young Alec MacLeod is forced to choose between conflicting family loyalties. A scout to Francis Marion, he is caught, tried as a spy after a battle on King's Mountain, and surprisingly rescued by his courageous grandmother." LC. Children's Bks 1975

"By exploring the diverse forces involved in defining one's convictions as well as by providing concrete examples of the disparate political issues underlying the American Revolution, the authors graphically counter the over-simplified interpretations of history all too frequently perpetuated in the past. Extensive explanatory notes and a list of sources are appended." Horn Bk

Beatty, Patricia

By crumbs, it's mine! Frontispiece by Loring Eutemey. Morrow 1976 254p front lib. bdg. $7.92 (5 and up)   **Fic**

1 Southwest, New—Fiction
ISBN 0-688-32062-7   LC 75-31574

"Set in the Arizona Territory during the late 19th century, the story stars a shrewd young lady, Damaris Boyd, and her family. When father loses all their money in a poker game and is lured into the gold rush, he leaves all his responsibilities on the 14-year-old girl's shoulders. She lambastes the winner of her father's money and stirs his conscience so that he deeds her his traveling hotel. Soon Damaris has involved her mother, brother and sister (plus others she can inveigle) in the running of the Nomad." Pub W

"There are many amusing incidents, treats, and frustrations but the story is almost incidental to the tremendous amount of information on early days in the southwest that one absorbs in a pleasant and effortless way. Ms. Beatty is noted for authenticity and it is obvious she has done her homework well on this." Children's Bk Rev Serv

Sources included in Author's notes

Beatty, Patricia—*Continued*

Hail Columbia; illus. by Liz Dauber. Morrow 1970 251p illus lib. bdg. $8.40 (5 and up) **Fic**

1 Women—Civil rights—Fiction 2 Oregon—Fiction
ISBN 0-688-31371-X   LC 72-105319

"After an absence of 19 years, Louisa's Aunt Columbia returns to Astoria, Oregon in 1893 for a year's visit. She is not the 'sainted maiden aunt' the family expected but an active suffragette accompanied by her two children. Neither Captain Baines, Louisa's vociferous, autocratic father, nor the town can abide emancipated women so the year that follows is one of upheaval and surprises as spirited, civic-minded Aunt Columbia embarks on one cause after another, doing good and winning friends and supporters. Narrated by thirteen-year-old Louisa, this zestful story with a memorable and likable adult heroine is fast-paced and eventful." Booklist

How many miles to sundown; frontispiece by Robert Quackenbush. Morrow 1974 222p front lib. bdg. $7.92 (5 and up) **Fic**

1 The West (U.S.)—Fiction
ISBN 0-688-30102-9   LC 73-14583

This story "introduces thirteen-year-old Beulah Land (Beeler) Quiney, who demonstrates . . . that 'nineteenth-century Texas women were every bit as strong as their men.' The saga begins when Nate Graber, searching for his missing father, accepts help from eleven-year-old Leo Quiney. . . . Leo had helped himself to Beeler's horse, and the determined young woman set forth after her property with her pet steer Travis. In spite of the boys' protestations against her joining them, the duo becomes a trio—trekking through Texas, New Mexico, and Arizona Territories in search of Mr. Graber. In the course of the search, Beeler conclusively proves that she is the equal of any Quiney man." Horn Bk

"Humorous and suspenseful episodes throughout the story will be enjoyed by the many children who love tales of the Old West. Girls especially will enjoy meeting Beeler . . . who won't let Nate, Leo or any other male put her down." Cath Library World

Just some weeds from the wilderness. Morrow 1978 254p $8.95, lib. bdg. $8.59 (5 and up) **Fic**

1 Oregon—Fiction
ISBN 0-688-22137-8; 0-688-32137-2   LC 77-28433

"Set in a small Oregon town in 1874, this story told by thirteen-year-old Lucinda describes the way in which her family was affected by the financial depression of that year. Lucinda and her mother live with Aunt Adelina and Uncle Silas, and they face the prospect, because Silas is almost bankrupt, of having to ask the charity of other kin. But Aunt Adelina saves the day; trying one recipe after another for growing hair or making face powder, Adelina comes up with a tonic. Her husband is so horrified when she permits her picture to be put on the label (distinct shades of Lydia Pinkham) that he leaves home to board with the local saloonkeeper." Chicago. Children's Bk Center

"A strong cast of secondary characters embellishes the plot, and, as always, there is plenty of history—particularly pertaining to the status of women—woven between the lines. Some of the latter is handled too deliberately, and Lucinda's forthright, upstanding ways are ever so reminiscent of preceding Beatty protagonists. The writer's hand is practiced, however, and her fans won't mind these mild deficiencies, especially in view of the humor, good pacing, and strong personalities." Booklist

Lacy makes a match. Morrow 1979 222p $7.95, lib. bdg. $7.63 (5 and up) **Fic**

1 California—Fiction
ISBN 0-688-22183-1; 0-688-32183-6   LC 79-9813

"Lacy Bingham, thirteen, describes her efforts to marry off her older brothers; her adoptive mother is dead and Lacy, although she loves Pa Bingham and the boys, dislikes housework and cleaning. When her oldest brother suddenly marries, Lacy takes on the job (secretly) of finding wives for the other two. The story is set in California in 1893, and Lacy is as lively and unconventional as a girl of that period could be convincingly. There's an abundance of action and humor in the writing, and the plot is credible and credibly told as the work of an adolescent. A sub-plot that has to do with Lacy's efforts to gain information about her natural parents is nicely handled, and the period details are smoothly incorporated." Chicago. Children's Bk Center

Bellairs, John

The house with a clock in its walls; pictures by Edward Gorey. Dial Press 1973 179p illus $6.95, lib. bdg. $6.46 (5 and up) **Fic**

1 Witchcraft—Fiction
ISBN 0-8037-3821-8; 0-8037-3823-4   LC 72-7600

In 1948, Lewis, a ten-year-old orphan, goes to New Zebedee, Michigan with his warlock Uncle Jonathan, who lives in a big mysterious house and practices white magic. Together with their neighbor, Mrs. Zimmerman, a witch, they search to find a clock that is programmed to end the world and has been hidden in the walls of the house by the evil Isaac Izard

"Bellairs's story and Edward Gorey's pictures are satisfyingly frightening." Pub W

Followed by these books, also available from Dial Press:

The figure in the shadows $6.95, lib. bdg. $6.46 (ISBN 0-8037-4916-3; 0-8037-4917-1; LC 74-2885)
The letter, the witch, and the ring $7.95, lib. bdg. $7.45 (ISBN 0-8037-4740-3; 0-8037-4741-1; LC 75-28968)

The treasure of Alpheus Winterborn; illus. by Judith Gwyn Brown. Harcourt 1978 180p illus $6.95 (5 and up) **Fic**

1 Buried treasure—Fiction
ISBN 0-15-289936-7   LC 77-88959

"His parents' continual quarrels and his father's subsequent heart attack trigger Anthony's determination to find the eccentric Alpheus Winterborn's legacy, supposedly hidden within the town. While working with his good friend Miss Eells, the local librarian, he finds clues pointing first to the old Winterborn mansion and then to the library itself. Anthony's attempts to play detective boomerang, however, until the night when he is inadvertently trapped in the library with Hugo Philpotts, the sneaky bank vice-president who thinks himself to be the rightful heir." Booklist

"The story is rather overburdened with melodramatic incident toward its end, and the characterization of the banker (and, to a lesser extent, of Miss Eells) seems overdrawn, but the book has pace and suspense, and the ending should satisfy readers, for Anthony does find the treasure and gains a great deal of money." Chicago. Children's Bk Center

Benary-Isbert, Margot

The Ark; tr. by Richard and Clara Winston. Harcourt 1953 246p $6.50, pa $1.95 (5 and up) **Fic**

1 Germany—Fiction 2 Family life—Fiction
ISBN 0-15-203901-5; 0-15-607921-6   LC 52-13677

Original German edition, 1948

"The Lechow family, after nine months of moving from refugee camp to refugee camp following World War II, finally settles in Western Germany. The happiness of being together means so much to the family that the oldest boy, Matthias, does work which he dislikes until he and Margret, his sister, find satisfactory employment on a farm and are able to make a home for the family in an old street car. There is a climate of warmth and tenderness within the family which encompasses their lonely landlady, and a small playmate who proceeds to make his home with them." Rdng Ladders. 2d edition

"This rare and perceptive book, reflecting something of the author's own experience, contains much of importance to reach the hearts and minds of young Americans. [Written] with an acute awareness of the effect of war on children and adolescents; with a consciousness of homely details that interest them; and with a wonderful depth of feeling for country things." Horn Bk

Benchley, Nathaniel

Feldman Fieldmouse; a fable; drawings by Hilary Knight. Harper 1971 96p illus lib. bdg. $6.89, pa $1.50 (3-5)   **Fic**

1 Mice—Fiction
ISBN 0-06-020484-2; 0-06-440032-8   LC 72-135773

Fendall Fieldmouse is befriended by Lonny, a boy who knows how to talk to mice. As a pet, Fendall leads a lazy, contented life. This story tells what happens when Fendall's uncle, Feldman Fieldmouse, appears to take over his nephew's education

An engaging fanciful tale. . . . The style is delightful, the animal characters amusing, and the dialogue witty." Chicago. Children's Bk Center

Bennett, Anna Elizabeth

Little witch; illus. by Helen Stone. Lippincott 1953 127p illus $7.89 (3-5)   **Fic**

1 Witchcraft—Fiction
ISBN 0-397-30240-1   LC 52-13721

"Miniken Snickasee was the daughter of a witch. She could ride on a broom; she could brew magic spells; she didn't have to go to school at all; and yet she wasn't happy. She wanted to be just an ordinary child. In a fresh and imaginative story, full of humor, Miss Bennett tells what happened when Miniken stole away from her mother and set out for school all by herself. Helen Stone's pictures of the 'little witch' and her adventures are exactly right too. Fun to read aloud to both boys and girls in October—or in any other month." Horn Bk

Berends, Polly Berrien

The case of the elevator duck; illus. by James K. Washburn. Random House 1973 54p illus lib. bdg. $5.99 (3-5)   **Fic**

1 Ducks—Fiction 2 Apartment houses—Fiction
3 Mystery and detective stories
ISBN 0-394-92115-1   LC 72-158380

Gilbert finds a lost duck in the elevator of his apartment building, and must do some secret detective work to find its owner, since no pets are allowed in the housing project

A "light mystery for beginning readers. The action is humorously illustrated by Washburn's line sketches; and Berends' first-person, short-sentence story is personable, plausible, and useful for librarians needing simple, satisfying material for their easy mystery shelves." Booklist

Bianco, Margery Williams

The little wooden doll; with pictures by Pamela Bianco. Macmillan Pub. Co. 1925 65p illus $3.50 (2-4)   **Fic**

1 Dolls—Fiction
ISBN 0-02-710110-X   LC 25-18186

"An old-fashioned wooden doll has spent many days in the attic with only the mice and the spiders for company. But they are good friends and, with their aid, she becomes the treasure of a poor little girl. The drawings [in color and black and white] were done by the author's daughter when she was a little girl." Providence

It is "a slight but tender little story." Bookshelf

Blades, Ann

Mary of Mile 18; story and pictures by Ann Blades. Tundra Bks. 1971 unp illus $10.95, pa $4.95 (2-4)   **Fic**

1 Canada—Fiction 2 Farm life—Fiction
3 Wolves—Fiction 4 Mennonites—Fiction
ISBN 0-912766-44-1; 0-912766-34-4   LC 79-179430

"In the simple story Mary Fehr finds a wolf pup which her father doesn't want her to keep until it alerts him to a chicken-thieving coyote. Blades' appreciation of the Canadian wilderness and of those who eke out a living there is apparent in her richly colored and textured primitive watercolors. Providing a breathtaking backdrop to the story, they contrast the stark frozen landscape with the cozy warmth of the seven-member Fehr family inside their rustic farmhouse." Sch Library J

"Mile 18 is in reality a Mennonite community in Canada and Mary was a student in the school where the author taught. The picture of the frigid country and the hardworking people who endure the hardships of this isolated community is well portrayed." Best Bks for Children

Blaine, Marge

Dvora's journey; illus. by Gabriel Lisowski. Holt 1979 126p illus $6.95 (3-5)   **Fic**

1 Refugees, Jewish—Fiction 2 Family life—Fiction
ISBN 0-03-048306-9   LC 78-26349

"It is turn-of-the-century, prerevolutionary Russia, a time when barely grown sons are being drafted and anti-Semitism is more than simmering. Twelve-year-old Dvora learns that her parents have decided to move the family to America. . . . The long, sometimes harrowing trip to Hamburg comprises most of the book; and an interesting, though not uncommon twist, finds the family at the seaport with money enough to send only two of them across the ocean. Readers will be exposed to many of the realities of the times and, in spite of some oversimplification in characterization and the absence of a few important scenes, will feel satisfied and entertained." Booklist

Blegvad, Lenore

The great hamster hunt, by Lenore and Erik Blegvad. Harcourt 1969 32p illus $5.95 (1-3)   **Fic**

1 Hamsters—Fiction
ISBN 0-15-232500-X   LC 69-13780

Illustrated by Erik Blegvad

Nicholas wanted to own a hamster but his mother refused all his requests. When his friend Tony went away, Nicholas was allowed to look after Tony's hamster. But the day before Tony was expected to return, the hamster escaped. The search taught Nicholas and his family a great deal about hamsters and Nicholas was at last allowed to have a hamster of his own

"The perky drawings add to the pleasure of a realistic and satisfying story that is written with grace and humor." Sat Rev

Blos, Joan W.

A gathering of days; a New England girl's journal, 1830-32; a novel. Scribner 1979 144p $7.95 (6 and up)   **Fic**

1 New Hampshire—Fiction
ISBN 0-684-16340-3   LC 79-16898

Awarded the Newbery Medal, 1980

"Her 14th is a pivotal year for 19th-Century New Englander Catherine Cabot Hall—one of change, loss, and leave taking. It's allowed to unfold slowly, as it was lived, in spare, pithy journal entries. In the course of it, her widowed father weds; her bookish stepmother unbends; and Catherine lets down her own reserve, notch by reluctant notch. . . . Blos adroitly sidesteps the worst sin historical fiction for this age is heir to: her characters are truly of their times, not 1970s sensibilities masquerading in 1830s homespun, and old-fashioned in the best sense of the word—principled. The 'simple' life on the farm is well-nigh idealized, the larger issues of the day are felt . . . but it is the small moments between parent and child, friend and friend that are at the fore, and the core, of this low-key, intense, and reflective book." Sch Library J

Blue, Rose

Grandma didn't wave back; illus. by Ted Lewin. Watts, F. 1972 62p illus lib. bdg. $6.90 (3-5)   **Fic**

1 Grandmothers—Fiction 2 Old age—Fiction
ISBN 0-531-02557-8   LC 79-189568

A ten-year-old girl learns to accept the fact that her grandmother is growing senile and must be sent to a nursing home

"The problems of senility and its effect on the family, especially children, are treated with warmth and understanding. The soft gray-and-white illustrations are excellent and add much to the appealing book." Sch Library J

Blue, Rose—*Continued*

A month of Sundays; illus. by Ted Lewin. Watts, F. 1972 59p illus lib. bdg. $6.90 (3-5)
Fic

1 Divorce—Fiction 2 New York (City)—Fiction
ISBN 0-531-02037-1   LC 72-182293

"This story gives a credible portrayal of a ten-year-old boy's reaction to his parents' divorce. Unhappy over the divorce and at having to leave his friends, school, and home in the suburbs, Jeffrey finds it difficult at first to make friends in the city, misses his father, and discovers that having a working mother is not always easy for either of them. Time, new friends, and a conversation with his father about their activities together on Sundays help Jeffrey to adjust to and accept his new life." Booklist

"Adequately written, sensible and realistic in its evaluation of adjustment to change, casually interracial, the story has an added asset: its positive attitude toward change from suburban to urban life." Chicago. Children's Bk Center

Blume, Judy

Are you there God? It's me, Margaret. Dell [1974 c1970] pa $1.50 (5 and up) **Fic**

1 Adolescence—Fiction 2 Religions—Fiction
ISBN 0-440-90419-6

"Laurel Leaf Library"
First published 1970 by Bradbury Press
"A perceptive story about the emotional, physical, and spiritual ups and downs experienced by 12-year-old Margaret, child of a Jewish-Protestant union." Adventuring with Bks. 2d edition
"The writing style is lively, the concerns natural, and the problems are treated with both humor and sympathy, but the story is intense in its emphasis on the four girls' absorption in, and discussions of, menstruation and brassieres." Chicago. Children's Bk Center

Freckle juice; illus. by Sonia O. Lisker. Four Winds 1971 40p illus lib. bdg. $5.95 (2-4)

ISBN 0-590-07242-0   LC 74-161016

"A gullible second-grader pays 50¢ for a recipe to grow freckles." Best Bks for Children
"Spontaneous humor, sure to appeal to the youngest reader." Horn Bk

It's not the end of the world. Bradbury Press 1972 169p $7.95 (4-6) **Fic**

1 Divorce—Fiction 2 Parent and child—Fiction
ISBN 0-87888-042-9   LC 70-181739

Unwilling to adjust to her parents' impending divorce, twelve-year-old Karen Newman attempts a last ditch effort at arranging a reconciliation. This story tells how her scheme goes awry when an unplanned confrontation between her parents sharply illuminates for Karen the reality of the situation
"Eventually Karen comes to accept her parents' divorce and recognizes that it is not the end of the world for any of them. A believable first-person story with good characterization, particularly of twelve-year-old Karen, and realistic treatment of the situation." Booklist

Otherwise known as Sheila the Great. Dell [1976 c1972] 118p pa $1.50 (4-6) **Fic**

1 Fear—Fiction
ISBN 0-440-46701-2

"A Yearling book"
First published 1972 by Dutton
Ten-year-old Sheila is secretly afraid of dogs, spiders, bees, ghosts and the dark. When she and her family leave New York for their summer home, she has to face up to her problems
"An unusual and merry treatment of the fears of a young girl. . . . This is a truly appealing book in which the author makes her points without a single preachy word." Pub W

Tales of a fourth grade nothing; illus. by Roy Doty. Dutton 1972 120p illus lib. bdg. $7.95 (3-6) **Fic**

1 Brothers—Fiction 2 Family life—Fiction
ISBN 0-525-40720-0   LC 70-179050

This story describes the trials and tribulations of nine-year-old Peter Hatcher who is saddled with a pesky two-year-old brother named Fudge who is constantly creating trouble, messing things up, and monopolizing their parents' attention. Things come to a climax when Fudge gets at Peter's pet turtle
"Illustrations that are reminiscent of the cartoons of Gluyas Williams capture the humor. . . . The episode structure makes the book a good choice for reading aloud." Sat Rev

Then again, maybe I won't; a novel. Bradbury Press 1971 164p $6.95 (5 and up) **Fic**

1 Adolescence—Fiction
ISBN 0-87888-035-6   LC 77-156548

"Thirteen-year-old Tony is not as thrilled as his parents are when the family's finances improve and they move to affluent suburbia. The 'nice' boy next door (of whom Tony's mother heartily approves) proves to be an inveterate shoplifter. Tony is, in fact, bothered by the eagerness of his parents to live up to their surroundings. He's also just discovered how he reacts to sexual provocation—and he worries about that, too. . . . Deftly handled, Tony's dilemma is really that he has become mature enough to see the conflicts and imperfections in his own life and in those around him, and he is sensitive enough to accept compromise." Chicago. Children's Bk Center

Bodecker, N. M.

The Mushroom Center disaster; pictures by Erik Blegvad. Atheneum Pubs. 1974 48p illus $6.95, pa $1.95 (2-4) **Fic**

1 Insects—Fiction 2 Ecology—Fiction
ISBN 0-689-30424-2   LC 73-85317

"A Margaret K. McElderry book"
"An assortment of insects living in a quaint and tidy community of mushroom houses becomes the victim of littering humans. Under the guidance of an enterprising beetle, the little village recycles a huge pile of refuse into usable items." Booklist
"The finely detailed, black-and-white drawings in a small (7" × 6") format extend the expressiveness of this imaginative nature fantasy." Sch Library J

Bødker, Cecil

The leopard; tr. by Gunnar Poulsen. Atheneum Pubs. 1975 186p lib. bdg. $7.95 (4 and up) **Fic**

1 Ethiopia—Fiction
ISBN 0-689-30444-7   LC 74-19314

Mildred L. Batchelder Award, 1977
Original Danish edition published 1970
"Tibeso's chance discovery that the blacksmith of a neighboring village is in fact the scar-footed cattle thief who has been raiding local herds sets in motion an eventful journey for the boy. After the pursuing blacksmith abandons him for dead in a deserted village, Tibeso falls in with some traders who see in his story the proof they need to bring about the smith's downfall. Their aim is eventually achieved, but not before Tibeso, caught at cross-purposes, flees to secure his own safety but is singularly unlucky in his attempts to evade the treacherous blacksmith. The chain of events that terminate a tumultuous conclusion may provoke incredulous reactions but does ultimately stay within the realm of possibility, determinedly pushing the reader on through this Ethiopian adventure story." Booklist

Silas and the black mare; tr. from the Danish by Sheila La Farge. Delacorte Press/Seymour Lawrence 1978 153p $6.95, lib. bdg. $6.46 (5 and up) **Fic**

1 Horses—Fiction 2 Denmark—Fiction
ISBN 0-440-07921-7; 0-440-07922-5   LC 77-86303

"A Merloyd Lawrence book"
Original Danish edition published 1967
"Silas appears in dramatic fashion, drifting aimlessly in a small boat, and the horsetrader Bartolin first thinks the boy is dead; but Silas is hale enough to work a shrewd bargain and win the black mare, Bartolin's horse. A series of adventures culminates in a long and stirring episode in which all the characters of previous incidents are brought together: Bartolin, the small band of performers from whom Silas had run away, the crippled boy who has helped him, the peddler who has thrashed him, and even the black mare which had been stolen from him." Chicago. Children's Bk Center

Bødker, Cecil—*Continued*

"Bødker's writing, even in translation, is spare and clean, harshly appropriate to the country and people described. It is a bizarre and hostile story illuminated only rarely by glimmers of love or caring, but readers who felt an affinity with Julia Cunningham's 'Dorp Dead' [entered below] will recognize and appreciate this novel's bleak power." Sch Library J

Followed by these books, also available from Delacorte Press/Seymour Lawrence:

Silas and Ben-Godik $7.95; lib. bdg. $7.45 (ISBN 0-440-07923-3; 0-440-07924-1; LC 78-50459)

Silas and the runaway coach $7.95, lib. bdg. $7.45 (ISBN 0-440-07953-5; 0-440-07954-3; LC 78-50465)

Bond, Michael

A bear called Paddington; with drawings by Peggy Fortnum. Houghton 1960 [c1958] 128p illus $6.95 (2-5)   **Fic**

1 Bears—Fiction 2 Great Britain—Fiction

ISBN 0-395-06636-0   LC 60-9096

First published 1958 in England

"Mr. and Mrs. Brown first met Paddington on a railway platform in London. Noticing the sign on his neck reading 'Please look after this bear. Thank you,' they decided to do just that. From there on home was never the same though the Brown children were delighted." Pub W

"Listeners devoted to another small bear will most certainly like him, although he is no Pooh. . . . Peggy Fortnum's pen-and-ink sketches present a winsome little bear in bewitching poses and costume. Fun for reading aloud to devotees of this style of fantasy." Horn Bk

Some other books about Paddington are also available from Houghton:

More about Paddington $7.95 (ISBN 0-395-06640-9; LC 62-12247)

Paddington abroad $6.95 (ISBN 0-395-14331-4; LC 72-2753)

Paddington at large $6.95 (ISBN 0-395-96641-7; LC 63-14525)

Paddington at work $6.95 (ISBN 0-395-06637-9; LC 67-20372)

Paddington goes to town $6.95 (ISBN 0-395-06635-2; LC 68-28054)

Paddington helps out $7.95 (ISBN 0-395-06639-5; LC 61-10633)

Paddington marches on $6.95 (ISBN 0-395-06642-5; LC 65-14925)

Paddington on top $5.95 (ISBN 0-395-21897-7; LC 75-17026)

Paddington takes the air $7.95 (ISBN 0-395-10909-4; LC 78-147902)

Paddington takes the test $6.95 (ISBN 0-395-2951-X; LC 80-16972)

Paddington takes to TV $6.95 (ISBN 0-395-19881-X; LC 74-8202)

The tales of Olga da Polga; illus. by Hans Helweg. Macmillan Pub. Co. [1973 c1971] 113p $4.95 (2-5)   **Fic**

1 Guinea pigs—Fiction

ISBN 0-02-711730-8   LC 72-89048

First published 1971 in England

The adventures of Olga da Polga, a vain and talented guinea pig, as she leaves the pet shop to enter the world of the Sawdust People (guinea pigs' name for humans)

"The book will delight . . . [children] who like to imagine that their pets have their own lives and personalities. The style is easy and the characters flow from the author's pen, but he sketches his animal friends with a much surer stroke than the humans." Jr Bookshelf

Followed by these books, available from Hastings House:

Olga meets her match $6.95 (ISBN 0-8038-5377-7; LC 75-9627)

Olga carries on $6.95 (ISBN 0-8038-5380-7; LC 77-8710)

Bond, Nancy

A string in the harp. Atheneum Pubs. 1976 370p illus $9.95 (6 and up)   **Fic**

1 Fantastic fiction 2 Taliesin—Fiction 3 Wales —Fiction

ISBN 0-689-50036-X   LC 75-28181

"A Margaret K. McElderry book"

"Set in the hills of Northern Wales, this masterfully integrates a Welsh legend into the story of young Peter Morgan. Brought to Wales against his wishes when his recently widowed father accepts a University post at Aberystwyth, Peter feels hostile and lonely. His relationships with his family and surroundings begin subtly changing after he discovers a harp tuning key which shows him events in the life of the centuries old bard, Taliesin. Peter comes to believe that the key has been urging him toward some unknown duty which he alone can perform; ultimately, he succeeds in bringing about a proper ending for the tale of Taliesin." Sch Library J

"The interweaving of Welsh background, the intermittently-told story of Taliesin, and the problems of family adjustments is adroit. The characters are drawn with depth, changing and growing in their maturity and in their understanding of each other." Chicago. Children's Bk Center

Bonham, Frank

Durango Street. Dutton 1965 190p $7.95 (6 and up)   **Fic**

1 Juvenile delinquency—Fiction

ISBN 0-525-28950-X   LC 65-21273

"On probation after leaving the Pine Valley Honor Camp, Rufus Henry finds himself once more engaged in gang activities as a matter of self-defense. . . . City worker Alex Robbins takes the [gangs] under his wing and through him they gradually change to more wholesome recreation." Best Sellers

A "powerful novel about teen-age gangs and the tortuous protocol of intramural gang fights. . . . The boys are neither overdrawn nor sugar-coated; the attitudes of parents, neighbors, and police are utterly convincing." Chicago. Children's Bk Center

The forever formula. Dutton 1979 181p $8.50 (5 and up)   **Fic**

1 Science fiction

ISBN 0-525-30025-2   LC 79-11381

In the twenty-second century, "it's a dire world that teenaged Evan Clark awakens in, having been cryonized in 1984. The rulers are ancient creatures kept alive by a drug that makes them resemble guppies. Although rich and privileged at the expense of others, the selfish minority are bored and eager to regain youth as well as ensure eternal life. Locked in young Evan's brain is the formula invented by his father who had destroyed the secret, and now scientists are bent on scanning the youth's memory. But Evan and a brave nurse escape and join an underground group to do battle with the overlords." Pub W

"Bonham treats readers to a fast-paced plot, some vivid images, and a clear, though simplistic, view of the future where the refusal to use pesticides results in a marked increase of rats and lice; where advanced age is disparaged; where nuclear wastes are indiscriminately rocketed into outer space; and where faith is invested in computers and clones." Sch Library J

Mystery of the fat cat; illus. by Alvin Smith. Dutton 1968 160p illus lib. bdg. $7.95 (5 and up)   **Fic**

1 Boys' clubs—Fiction 2 Mystery and detective stories

ISBN 0-525-35588-X   LC 68-18348

"A cat who inherited a fortune, Buzzer Atkins, is the center of attention in this action-filled adventure. The Boys Club is to receive the remainder of the inheritance when Buzzer dies, and many suspect that the cat thought to be Buzzer is an imposter. Boys Club members [who are mostly Black and Mexican-Americans] take drastic measures to secure the inheritance and save their club. Ralphie, a mentally retarded boy, provides the information needed to solve the mystery. Peer-group pressures, conflicts, and rivalry figure in the plot. Dialogue patterns fit the life-styles of the characters, although they may seem a bit startling to sheltered children from affluent neighborhoods." Keating. Building Bridges of Understanding Between Cultures

"Their unraveling of the mystery is believable and exciting. The characters are lively, the dialogue natural, and the inclusion of a backward child as a sympathetic—and contributing—character adds to the book's appeal." Chicago. Children's Bk Center

Bontemps, Arna

The fast Sooner hound, by Arna Bontemps and Jack Conroy; illus. by Virginia Lee Burton. Houghton 1942 28p illus lib. bdg. $7.95 (2-5)   **Fic**

1 Dogs—Fiction 2 Railroads—Fiction
ISBN 0-395-18657-9   LC 42-21755
A "tall tale of railroad days in the far west." Horn Bk
"He would sooner run than eat and so got his name, and was he fast! As he could not be parted from his master, a railroad fireman, and could not ride in the cab, he ran beside the train. In a race with the Cannon Ball, a crack train, of course he won in spite of a detour to play with a rabbit. The excitement and hilarity of the race are the climax of a fresh picture book." Bookmark
The "drawings have a beautiful rhythm and a fine sense of motion. . . . The countryside is made vivid in beautiful greens and browns, and the locomotives convey the thrill and excitement which real locomotives have for children." NY Times Bk Rev

Bosse, Malcolm J.

The 79 squares. Crowell 1979 185p $7.95, lib. bdg. $7.89 (6 and up)   **Fic**

1 Friendship—Fiction   2 Old age—Fiction 3 Gardens—Fiction
ISBN 0-690-03999-9   LC 79-7591
"A young man on the outs with his family, school and the law experiences love and trust for the first time when he meets and eventually befriends an 82-year-old ex-convict. Using his garden as a subtle metaphoric teaching device, the rather strange yet extremely wise old man teaches Eric how to see the world and his place in it by first studying a microscopic part of it. Only after acquiring a new vision does Eric find the courage to cope with peer pressure." VOYA
The book "is valuable particularly for its depiction of a friendship between an old person and a young one. The story is so compelling and the imagery so visual that the reader seems to see it all happening. This is only appropriate because the story is about learning to see." Interracial Bks for Children

Boston, L. M.

The children of Green Knowe; with illus. by Peter Boston. Harcourt 1955 157p illus $5.95, pa $1.95 (4-6)   **Fic**

1 Fantastic fiction 2 Great Britain—Fiction
ISBN 0-15-217147-9; 0-15-616870-7   LC 55-7608
First published 1954 in England
"In the big ancestral house at Green Knowe [in England] to which a little boy comes to stay with his great-grandmother, hangs a portrait of three children who generations before had grown up there. As Tolly uses their room and playthings and listens to Granny's stories about them, the children become as real to him as they are to his great-grandmother—so real that Tolly thinks he hears and sees them. A special book for the imaginative child, in which mood predominates and fantasy and realism are skillfully blended; not the least of the book's charm is the rapport that exists between the lonely little boy and the understanding old woman who lives with her memories." Booklist

Several other books about Green Knowe are also available from Harcourt (unless otherwise noted):
An enemy at Green Knowe pa $1.95 (ISBN 0-15-628792-7)
The river at Green Knowe $5.95, pa $1.95 (ISBN 0-15-267446-2; 0-15-677701-0; LC 59-8950)
The stones of Green Knowe $6.95 (Atheneum Pub. ISBN 0-689-50058-0; LC 75-44143)
A stranger at Green Knowe $5.75, pa $1.95 (ISBN 0-15-281752-2; 0-15-685657-3; LC 61-10108)
Treasure of Green Knowe $6.95, pa $1.95 (ISBN 0-15-289979-0; 0-15-691302-X; LC 58-8731)

The fossil snake; illus. by Peter Boston. Atheneum Pubs. 1976 [c1975] 53p illus $5.95 (4-6)   **Fic**

1 Snakes—Fiction
ISBN 0-689-50037-8   LC 75-26997
"A Margaret K. McElderry book"
First published 1975 in England
"Rob discovers a fossil snake which is over a million years old but perfectly preserved. The local museum is eager to have the treasure but Rob is passionately determined to keep it. He puts the petrified artifact near the radiator in his room and lo! finds that heat has brought it back to life. The action gets fast and funny thereafter, as thugs are frightened off the property by the rearing, hissing monster. . . . The day comes when Ra, as Rob has named his serpent, grows much too huge to be domesticated. In a touching finale, the boy takes the ancient creature to the top of a mountain in the wilderness and sets it free." Pub W
"Boston's writing style and her establishment of mood are as deft and polished as ever, and she captures the fierce, protective love Rob has for his pet most beautifully, but the fantasy element doesn't quite convince." Chicago. Children's Bk Center

The sea egg; illus. by Peter Boston. Harcourt 1967 94p illus $4.95 (3-5)   **Fic**

1 Fantastic fiction 2 Seashore—Fiction
ISBN 0-15-271050-7   LC 67-3334
"This exquisitely written little fantasy is woven around an episode in the lives of two boys. While on a seaside vacation Toby and Joe purchase an egg-shaped stone which they put in a deep tide pool in the hope that it will hatch a rare sea creature. The egg disappears and two days later the boys see a child merman or triton living with the seals. Mood rather than action dominates the description of their play in the sea and the special night swim which the boys share with their unusual companion. Probably limited in appeal to the highly imaginative reader." Booklist

Bottner, Barbara

Dumb old Casey is a fat tree. Harper 1979 42p illus $6.95, lib. bdg. $6.89 (2-4)   **Fic**

1 Ballet—Fiction
ISBN 0-06-020616-0; 0-06-020617-9   LC 78-19474
"Casey has always wanted to be a ballet dancer, despite being fat, despite Patrick's teasing, despite being worst in her class for a while, despite being cast as a tree in the recital when she'd hoped to be the wicked prince." Sch Library J
Casey eventually "realizes—after all the envious heartache about how much better the other girls are—that what she loves best is not being best but the joy of dancing. Blithe, occasionally touching, and always realistic, the story Casey tells is both pithy and appealing." Chicago. Children's Bk Center

Bradbury, Bianca

Two on an island; illus. by Robert MacLean. Houghton 1965 139p illus $6.95 (4-6)   **Fic**

1 Survival (after airplane accidents, shipwrecks, etc.)—Fiction 2 Maine—Fiction
ISBN 0-395-06651-4   LC 65-12175
"Two children are marooned on a tiny island just off shore from a large city on the Atlantic Coast. Hunger, thirst, exposure, fright, and courage are all ingredients of a three-day ordeal during which Trudy and Jeff learn much about themselves and each other." Rdng Ladders. 5th edition
"The plausible framework for this unusual test of endurance has more than mere detail of dealing with [hardship]. . . . Miss Bradbury skillfully develops the heightened clash of different personalities." Horn Bk

Brady, Esther Wood

The toad on Capitol Hill. Crown 1978 139p $6.95 (4-6)   **Fic**

1 Family life—Fiction 2 U.S.—History—War of 1812—Fiction 3 Washington, D.C.—Fiction
ISBN 0-517-53319-7   LC 77-15861
"Dorsy McCurdy has loved the Washington City of 1812 and enjoyed the freedom her father allowed while they lived at Mrs. Pringle's Boarding House. Now, however, her father has married a woman (mother of obnoxious sons Tyler and Brandon) who plans to refashion Dorsy into a young lady. Unhappy over the situation, Dorsy superstitiously wishes on a white toad for the quick removal of her new family; but when arriving British troops turn the capital into a turmoil, Dorsy finds herself fearfully alone with an ill Brandon. Later when Tyler shows up, the three join forces in the barricaded house, and a new family spirit is founded upon Mama and Papa's return." Booklist

Brady, Esther W.—*Continued*

"Besides learning about the War of 1812, children will gain a sense of how much we've changed, as a country and a culture, in some ways, and how little in others. The universality of family interactions and human feelings are well portrayed. Dorsy, at eleven, is a realistic focal character—she is brave, impulsive, self-centered, concerned, furious—all in turn and all appropriately." Children's Bk Rev Serv

Toliver's secret; illus. by Richard Cuffari. Crown 1976 166p illus $6.95 (4-6)   **Fic**

1 U.S.—History—Revolution, 1775-1783—Fiction
ISBN 0-517-52621-2   LC 76-15997

"Ellen overhears her grandfather planning to carry a message through British lines to General Washington. A broken ankle causes him to enlist Ellen's aid, though she is only ten and not particularly willing or daring. Carrying a message concealed in a loaf of bread and disguised as a boy, she risks her life many times as all the well-laid plans go awry." Adventuring with Bks. 2d edition

"Brady's characters have depth e.g., a British soldier is realistically conveyed as being homesick for his family and country, and the growth of Ellen's confidence in herself is convincing. Events develop naturally and the author's research doesn't overpower the story. In all, this is brisk and engaging." Sch Library J

Brenner, Barbara

On the frontier with Mr Audubon. Coward, McCann & Geoghegan 1977 96p illus $6.95 (4 and up)   **Fic**

1 Mason, Joseph—Fiction 2 Audubon, John James—Fiction
ISBN 0-698-20385-2   LC 76-41601

"Thirteen-year-old Joseph Mason describes his travels down the Mississippi River and in the Southern swamps and forests and cities. As pupil-assistant, Joseph helped shoot specimens of birds never before pictured in guide books, helped paint some of the details or background, and suffered with Audubon through poverty, illness, and homesickness. Whether describing life on a flatboat or on the crowded docks of New Orleans, the narrative (based on thorough research) is lively and natural, and through Joseph's eyes Brenner draws a perceptive, candid picture of the great artist who had been jailed for debt, branded a wastrel, and gone from a pampered childhood in France to near penury in America. Joseph's journal is a fictional device, but the facts it records are documented, and it gives a memorable picture of the artist and his work." Chicago. Children's Bk Center

"Brenner's notes give the background details that started her research about this little-known apprentice, and historical photographs and Audubon reproductions add authenticity." Sch Library J

Wagon wheels; pictures by Don Bolognese. Harper 1978 64p illus (An I can read history bk) $6.95, lib. bdg. $7.89 (2-4)   **Fic**

1 Frontier and pioneer life—Fiction 2 Blacks—Fiction
ISBN 0-06-020668-3; 0-06-020669-1   LC 76-21391

A "frontier story for beginning independent readers describes the experiences of a black family which comes from Kentucky to Kansas in the 1870's. The story is told by one of the three boys; the writing is simple and direct, yet it has a narrative flow and gives a vivid picture of both the hardships of pioneer life and of the love and courage of the family. The book is based on fact: Nicodemus, Kansas, was a black community and there really was an Ed Muldie who journeyed there and who left the younger boys in the hands of eleven-year-old Johnny while he went ahead to find better land; there really was a famine in Nicodemus that ended because of the kindness of some Osage Indians, and the three boys really did strike out alone to join their father, following his directions and having a happy reunion." Chicago. Children's Bk Center

"The heroes that history books forget are the subject of [this book]. . . . Don Bolognese's sketches show [the boy's] hardships with an economy of line and a commendable lack of melodrama." NY Times Bk Rev

A year in the life of Rosie Bernard; illus. by Joan Sandin. Harper 1971 179p illus lib. bdg. $7.89 (4-6)   **Fic**

1 Family life—Fiction 2 Brooklyn—Fiction
ISBN 0-06-020657-8   LC 70-157902

Motherless, Rosie Bernard comes to Brooklyn in 1932 to live with her three cousins, two aunts, two uncles and grandparents while her actor-father travels. How she adjusts to her new life, wrestles with the problem of being half Jewish and half Christian, as well as winning a bout with pneumonia is portrayed

"When Daddy appears with a fiancee, Rosie runs away, but she is too sensible and pliant to maintain her resentment long, and her year ends with acceptance of the new situation. The story has an easy flow and humor, a delightful protagonist, and an understanding portrayal of an only child learning to love and be loved by her grandparents." Sutherland. The Best in Children's Bks

Bridgers, Sue Ellen

All together now; a novel. Knopf 1979 238p $7.95, lib. bdg. $7.99 (6 and up)   **Fic**

1 Grandparents—Fiction 2 Mentally retarded—Fiction 3 Friendship—Fiction
ISBN 0-394-84098-4; 0-394-94098-9   LC 78-12244

"Because her father is a pilot serving in the Korean War and her mother is busy holding down two jobs, twelve year old Casey Flanagan spends the summer vacation with her grandparents in a small southern town. Shy, lonely and somewhat resentful, the youngster slowly begins to respond to her environment and to become involved in the lives of those around her. Among the people who contribute to Casey's emotional growth are her devoted grandparents, her fun-loving uncle and his earthy girl friend, a warm-hearted spinster, a middle-aged 'dancin man', and, most important of all, Dwayne, a thirty-three year old man with the mind of a child." Best Sellers

"It is the delicacy with which Bridgers weaves together the various strains of her story that creates the beauty of the book. There are no caricatures among the people and nothing artificial in the telling. Dwayne's mental recreation of a live baseball game, youngsters learning to fish on an open pier, and Casey's onset of possible polio are thoroughly convincing miniatures within the larger creation. And the whole is a smooth rendition of emotions captured by just the right phrase, or revealed through a single important observation. The commingling of love at all levels of life stands out as the lesson Casey learns. . . . [This novel] is the deceivingly effortless writing of an artist at work." Christian Sci Monitor

Home before dark. Knopf 1976 176p $6.95 (6 and up)   **Fic**

1 Family life—Fiction 2 Migrant labor—Fiction
ISBN 0-394-83299-X   LC 76-8661

"After years as a migrant laborer, James Earl brings his family to settle down and work on the tobacco farm inherited by his younger brother Newt. Fourteen-year-old Stella is particularly pleased; she's anxious to have a better life, to make something more of herself than her timid, fearful mother has. Stella admires Newt's brisk wife, is admired by two boys and learns to care for one of them, and resists (eventually succumbing) the genuinely affectionate overtures made by her stepmother after her mother's death and James Earl's rather hasty second marriage." Chicago. Children's Bk Center

"No summary can convey the tremendous integrity of a book like 'Home Before Dark.' The author speaks with a voice that is intensely lyrical yet wholly un-selfconscious. Character and theme have been developed with such painstaking attention that each episode seems inevitable and right." NY Times Bk Rev

Briggs, K. M.

Hobberdy Dick. Greenwillow Bks. [1977 c1975] 239p illus $8.25, lib. bdg. $7.92 (5 and up)   **Fic**

1 Fairies—Fiction
ISBN 0-688-80079-3; 0-688-84079-5   LC 76-39896

First published 1955 in England

"Hobberdy Dick, an English hobgoblin who has guarded the Cotswold manor house for centuries, is apprehensive about the new owners, a city merchant and his family, until Joel, the eldest son,

Briggs, K. M.—*Continued*

shows true feeling for the old country ways. Hobberdy connives to keep Joel at Widford and plays a prominent hand in the winning of his lady love, Anne Seckar. With subtle magic and impish tricks, Dick sees to a peaceful death for old Mrs. Dimbleby, secret celebrations for the children at Christmas and May Day (forbidden in their Puritan household), Martha's release from the village witch, and discovery of lost gold hidden in the stables. Set in the 1700s, the . . . tale is hampered by a slow beginning and overly long descriptions but offers a clear picture of country life of the day and an appealing portrayal of a fairy creature at work." Booklist

Brink, Carol Ryrie

The bad times of Irma Baumlein; pictures by Trina Schart Hyman. Macmillan Pub. Co. 1972 134p illus $7.95, pa $1.95 (4-6)   **Fic**

1 Dolls—Fiction 2 Truthfulness and falsehood—Fiction
ISBN 0-02-714220-5; 0-02-041900-7   LC 76-182018

"Irma's bad times begin when she tries to impress her classmates in a new school by claiming to own the biggest doll in the world. When she's asked to exhibit it at the school fair, she panics and 'borrows' a dummy from her family's store." Pub W

"The characterization is adequate, the plot farfetched here and there, but the story has plenty of action, humor, and the perennial appeal of a protagonist in a predicament with which readers can identify." Chicago. Children's Bk Center

Caddie Woodlawn; illus. by Trina Schart Hyman. [New ed] Macmillan Pub. Co. 1973 275p illus $7.95, pa $1.95 (4-6)   **Fic**

1 Frontier and pioneer life—Fiction 2 Wisconsin—Fiction
ISBN 0-02-713670-1; 0-02-041880-9   LC 73-588

Awarded the Newbery Medal, 1936
First published 1935
Caddie Woodlawn was eleven in 1864. Because she was frail, she had been allowed to grow up a tomboy. Her capacity for adventure was practically limitless, and there was plenty of adventure on the Wisconsin frontier in those days. The story covers one year of life on the pioneer farm, closing with the news that Mr Woodlawn had inherited an estate in England, and the unanimous decision of the family to stay in Wisconsin. Based upon the reminiscences of the author's grandmother
The typeface "is eminently clear and readable, and the illustrations in black and white . . . are attractive and expressive." Wis Library Bul

Brookins, Dana

Alone in Wolf Hollow. Seabury [distributed by Houghton] 1978 137p $6.95 (5 and up)   **Fic**

1 Orphans—Fiction 2 Mystery and detective stories
ISBN 0-395-28849-5   LC 77-13118

"A Clarion book"
"Orphans Bart Cadle and his younger brother Arnie are sent to live with their Uncle Charlie in an isolated house in the woods. Since the death of his wife, Uncle Charlie has become an alcoholic and appears on the brink of insanity. He eventually sends the boys away before disappearing himself, but gutsy Bart and Arnie manage to stay on 'Alone in Wolf Hollow' . . . where they find the body of a murdered waitress and sense that they are being watched. As the plot unfolds, Bart slowly realizes who the murderer is." Sch Library J
"Though the secondary characters remain tantalizingly shadowy, the boys are well developed and their relationship perceptive; subtly planted clues maintain suspense to the conclusion." Booklist

Brooks, Walter R.

Freddy, the detective; with illus. by Kurt Wiese. Knopf 1932 263p illus lib. bdg. $6.39 (3-5)   **Fic**

1 Pigs—Fiction 2 Domestic animals—Fiction 3 Mystery and detective stories
ISBN 0-394-90827-9   LC 32-17150

This is a story about the animals on Mr Bean's farm. Freddy, the pig, sets up in business as a detective, after reading the stories of Sherlock Holmes. He then solves a number of very mysterious cases

"This book will be great fun for all who have not outgrown the gift of fitting becoming personalities to our animal friends." NY Her Trib Bks
Another book about Freddy is also available from Knopf: Freddy and the baseball team from Mars lib. bdg. $5.99 (ISBN 0-394-90810-4; LC 55-8948)

Brown, Jeff

Flat Stanley; pictures by Tomi Ungerer. Harper 1964 unp illus lib. bdg. $7.89 (1-3)   **Fic**

ISBN 0-06-020681-0   LC 63-1725

"When an enormous bulletin board fell on him as he lay in bed Stanley Lambchop emerged as flat as a pancake. Once he got used to his half-inch thickness Stanley came to enjoy it and so did his parents—he could be lowered through sidewalk gratings, mailed to California, rolled up like wallpaper and tied with a string for carrying, and disguised as a framed picture to help catch art thieves in the museum. Comical colored pictures accentuate the humor of this rib-tickling story." Booklist

Brown, Palmer

Hickory. Harper 1978 42p illus $6.95, lib. bdg. $7.49 (2-4)   **Fic**

1 Mice—Fiction 2 Friendship—Fiction
ISBN 0-06-020887-2; 0-06-02088-0   LC 77-11849

Illustrated by the author
"Hickory, a field mouse, lives with his family in a grandfather clock case. They spend their days in warm companionship, outwitting the farmer's wife as the hours and seasons tick contentedly by. But Hickory is enchanted by the stories other field-mice have told him: life in the fields where the air is more 'salubrious,' and where it is possible to eat 'wheat . . . from the husk' and a 'sunlit blackberry bursting on the bramble.' One spring, off he goes, with the blessings of his mother, to make it on his own. He does, too, but the loneliness grows and grows until he makes a friend—a grasshopper. At the end of summer, a distraught Hickory makes a decision to forsake his home and family and to save the life of his friend by heading for warmer climes." Sch Library J
"A profusion of colored illustrations embellishes every page; both story and pictures are executed with elegance, restraint, and meticulous care, creating a precise, convincing world." Horn Bk

Buck, Pearl S.

The big wave; illus. with prints by Hiroshige and Hokusai. Day [1973 c1948] 78p illus lib. bdg. $7.89 (4 and up)   **Fic**

1 Japan—Fiction
ISBN 0-381-99923-8   LC 73-168129

A reissue of the volume first published 1948
"The Japanese boys, Kino, son of a mountainside farmer, and Jiya, son of a fisherman, are only friends until the day a tidal wave sweeps away Jiya's family and village, and Jiya is alone. Kino's family helps Jiya through his grief, and the boys grow up as brothers. The lure of the sea is stronger for Jiya, and when grown, he returns to build again on the ocean's shore." Rdng Ladders. 5th edition
"A gem of a story telling something about the eternal truths of life and death—and helping us to understand the Japanese heart." Asia

Buff, Mary

Magic maize, by Mary and Conrad Buff. Houghton 1953 76p illus $3.57 (3-6)   **Fic**

1 Corn—Fiction 2 Mayas—Fiction 3 Guatamala—Fiction
ISBN 0-395-06666-2   LC 53-6212

"An Indian boy of Guatemala becomes friends with the 'gringos' who have developed a new kind of maize and who are doing research in the Mayan ruins. As he learns to trust the foreigners, so too, but reluctantly, does his father who has clung to the ancient religion and customs of his [Mayan] forefathers." Pub W
"The story is conventional, but the pictures [by Conrad Buff] have great value. They will give the children a vivid sense of Central American Guatemala and its people." Sat Rev

Bulla, Clyde Robert

The best of Lor; illus. by Ruth Sanderson. Crowell 1977 54p illus $7.95 (3-5) **Fic**

1 Great Britain—Fiction 2 Elephants—Fiction
ISBN 0-690-01377-9   LC 77-6751

This is a story "about a boy and a beast. The beast is an elephant, brought to England as part of Julius Ceasar's invading troops. The elephant escapes from the Roman army. The boy befriends the beast. To people who have never before seen an elephant, the beast and his young master present an imposing sight." West Coast Rev of Bks

"This is an excellent story to read aloud to a class of children. There is adventure and excitement that will cause youngsters to want to hear more." Children's Bk Rev Serv

Conquista! [By] Clyde Robert Bulla & Michael Syson; illus. by Ronald Himler. Crowell 1978 33p illus $7.95, lib. bdg. $7.89 (3-5) **Fic**

1 Indians of North America—Fiction 2 Horses—Fiction
ISBN 0-690-03870-4; 0-690-03871-2   LC 77-26585

"A story that tells how the Indians might have acquired their first horse. In 1541, on Coronado's expedition into North America, one of his soldiers loses his horse. At the same time, an Indian youth, Little Wolf, is waiting in the desert for a sign from the sun-god that will give him his adult name. Suddenly, the horse appears. Little Wolf, fearing it is a devil, tries to kill it. . . . By great will power, Little Wolf conquers his fright and manages to ride the animal, and is finally convinced it is a gift from the sun-god, especially when it follows him home. . . . The authors state in a preface that the book is not actual history, only conjecture; and, in the last chapter, they explain the impact horses made on the Indians' life. Though very short (with large print) the book is well written, with great emotional impact. Readers will empathize with both boy and horse." Sch Library J

Ghost of Windy Hill; illus. by Don Bolognese. Crowell 1968 84p illus $6.95, lib. bdg. $7.89 (2-5) **Fic**

1 Orphans—Fiction 2 New England—Fiction
ISBN 0-690-32763-3; 0-690-32764-1   LC 68-11059

"When the Carver family, who do not believe in ghosts, move to a farmhouse near Boston for a month to prove that it is not haunted, twelve-year-old Jamie and ten-year-old Lorna soon discover that there are more strange things going on outside than inside the house. Their friendly interest in a supposedly disabled beggar boy eventually leads to the discovery that he is not really a cripple but an unfortunate orphan being exploited by a villainous reprobate. While not outstanding, the simply written story set in mid-nineteenth-century New England is a diverting tale of popular appeal." Booklist

Shoeshine girl; illus. by Leigh Grant. Crowell 1975 84p illus $7.95 (3-5) **Fic**

ISBN 0-690-00758-2   LC 75-8516

"When ten-and-a-half Sara Ida, a spirited defiant youngster, becomes involved with a friend who steals for kicks, her parents send her to an aunt for the summer. Denied an allowance (for discipline), Sara Ida finds a job as a shoeshine girl and discovers the satisfaction of earning her own pocket money and becomes less self-centered." Children's Bk Rev Serv

"This is a quiet story with little drama but it's psychologically sound, well-structured, and satisfying in its realistic development of the changes in its protagonist." Chicago. Children's Bk Center

The sword in the tree; illus. by Paul Galdone. Crowell 1956 113p illus $8.95 (2-5) **Fic**

1 Arthur, King—Fiction 2 Knights and knighthood—Fiction
ISBN 0-690-79908-X   LC 56-5699

A story of England in King Arthur's days. Shan, the son of Lord Weldon, took on the duties of a knight and sought redress against his uncle, who had usurped his father's rights. A picture of the Knights of the Round Table and King Arthur develops

"A good story for beginning readers, this is also excellent for the older child who is a slow reader, because of the stimulating combination of exciting adventure, short sentences, and easy vocabulary." NY Times Bk Rev

"This book itself is most inviting with many decorative black and white sketches by Paul Galdone showing scenes of knights and castles." NY Her Trib Bks

Viking adventure; illus. by Douglas Gorsline. Crowell 1963 117p illus lib. bdg. $7.89 (3-5) **Fic**

1 Vikings—Fiction
ISBN 0-690-86015-3   LC 63-7208

"Once again Mr. Bulla writes a good story, with strong plot interest, which is also very easy to read. This one will be particularly welcome because its subject is perennially interesting to young readers. . . . [The story] tells of young Sigurd and his rigorous training in strength and courage under the firm but affectionate guidance of his father. This training is put to severe test during a long voyage in a great Viking ship to Wineland [America]." Horn Bk

Bunting, Eve

Ghost of summer. Warne 1977 192p $7.95 (6 and up) **Fic**

1 Northern Ireland—Fiction 2 Buried treasure—Fiction
ISBN 0-7232-6141-5   LC 76-45310

"Fifteen-year-old Kevin's introduction to northern Ireland is a hollow voice speaking to him from the graveyard he must cross to get to his clergyman-grandfather's house. Not only is his grandfather in danger of having his house taken away because of government plans to build a new motorway, but strange lights and figures are seen at night in the nearby graveyard. Are they people who have come to hunt for the buried, secret treasure of the highwayman, Smiling Matt McGuire, who is buried in the graveyard? Kevin finds himself thrust into the enmity of the warring political groups in Northern Ireland, relating the problem to the school bussing clashes in his own home in Boston." West Coast Rev of Bks

"Set against the backdrop of social and religious unrest near Ulster, this well constructed novel, which skillfully mixes mystery, fantasy, and politics, can keep readers going from the first page until the last." Sch Library J

Burch, Robert

D. J.'s worst enemy; illus. by Emil Weiss. Viking 1965 142p illus $6.50 (4-6) **Fic**

1 Farm life—Fiction 2 Georgia—Fiction
ISBN 0-670-27456-9   LC 65-13356

A first-person story. "In the peach county of Georgia, D. J. Madison lives the joys of boyhood with his sidekick, Nutty, and the neighboring Castor boys. He teases his younger brother, Renfroe, and his older sister, Clara May, until they share a secret and he feels left out. The reformation which occurs leads to D.J.'s greater appreciation of his family." Wis Library Bul

Queenie Peavy; illus. by Jerry Lazare. Viking 1966 159p illus $7.95 (5 and up) **Fic**

1 Parent and child—Fiction 2 Georgia—Fiction
ISBN 0-670-58422-3   LC 66-15649

"Defiant, independent and intelligent, 13-year-old Queenie idolized her father who was in jail and was neglected by her mother who had to work all the time. Growing up in the 1930's in Georgia, Queenie eventually understands her father's real character, herself and her relationships to those about her." Wis Library Bul

"There is no straining here to formulate a story about a problem child. On the surface the account is as dispassionate as a case study, but considerably more convincing, and Queenie is so real that the reader becomes deeply involved in everything that concerns her." Horn Bk

Skinny; illus. by Don Sibley. Viking 1964 127p illus lib. bdg. $6.95 (4-6) **Fic**

1 Hotels, motels, etc.—Fiction 2 Orphans—Fiction 3 Georgia—Fiction
ISBN 0-670-64999-6   LC 64-12638

Burch, Robert—*Continued*

"A sociable 12-year-old orphan boy, taken in by the proprietor of a small town hotel in Georgia, wins the affection of everyone through his sincerity and innocently humorous outlook on life." Bks on Exhibit

"Life in a small southern town during the 1930s is well described as Skinny tries various ruses in order to stay with Miss Bessie." Rdng Ladders for Human Relations. 5th ed.

Wilkin's ghost; illus. by Lloyd Bloom. Viking 1978 152p illus $7.95 (5 and up)   Fic

1 Friendship—Fiction 2 Georgia—Fiction
ISBN 0-670-76897-9   LC 78-6293

Wilkin Coley, a thirteen-year-old living in rural Georgia during the 1930's, "was somewhat superstitious and believed a local legend that the tree from which a man had been hanged was haunted. To his relief he discovered that the white object he saw during a thunderstorm was only the shirt of Alex Folsom, a boy of about fifteen, who had just returned from Atlanta after an absence of two years. Alex had been accused of stealing but denied his guilt. Wilkin generously befriended the older boy, helped him when he was sick, and found work for him. Tired of his humdrum life, the farm boy, who was actually on the best of terms with his parents and brothers, decided to run away to Atlanta with Alex but was deterred at the last moment when Alex proved after all to be a liar and a thief." Horn Bk

"Throughout the book there is a warm, realistic family feeling. Each character is an individual. Wilkin develops responsibility and determination in his actions. Even though the setting is in the past, the plot is contemporary." Children's Bk Rev Serv

Burchard, Peter

Bimby. Coward-McCann 1968 91p illus $5.95 (4-6)   Fic

1 Slavery in the U.S.—Fiction 2 Blacks—Fiction
3 Georgia—Fiction
ISBN 0-698-20012-8   LC 68-23866

Set on the Georgia coast shortly before the Civil War, this is the "story of one crucial day in the life of a young American slave—the day in which he decides to risk his life to reach freedom." Best Bks of the Year, 1968

"Simply written and illustrated by the author, 'Bimby' is a moving tribute to the human spirit and a valuable insight into a past that still haunts us." NY Times Bk Rev

Burnett, Frances Hodgson

A little princess; pictures by Tasha Tudor. Lippincott 1963 240p illus $10, lib. bdg. $9.79 (4-6)   Fic

1 School stories 2 Great Britain—Fiction
ISBN 0-397-30693-8; 0-397-31339-X   LC 63-15435

First American edition published 1892 by Scribner in shorter form with title: Sara Crewe
The story of Sara Crewe, a girl who is sent from India to a boarding school in London, left in poverty by her father's death, and rescued by a mysterious benefactor

"For three generations Mrs. Burnett has lured little girls . . . to slip into the person of Sara Crewe and try as she does to act as a princess despite the malicious people who surround her. The story is inevitably adorned with sentimental curlicues but the reader will hardly notice them since the story itself is such a satisfying one." Pub W

The secret garden (4-6)   Fic

Some editions are:
Dent $11 Illustrated by Jenny Williams (ISBN 0-460-05101-6)
Lippincott $10 Pictures by Tasha Tudor (ISBN 0-397-30632-6 LC 62-17457)

First published 1909 by Stokes
"Neglected by his father because of his mother's death at his birth, Colin lives the life of a spoilt and incurable invalid until, on the arrival of an orphaned cousin, the two children secretly combine to restore his mother's locked garden and Colin to health and his father's affection." Four to Fourteen

Burnford, Sheila

The incredible journey; with illus. by Carl Burger. Little 1961 145p illus $8.95 (4 and up)   Fic

1 Animals—Fiction 2 Cats—Fiction 3 Dogs—Fiction 4 Ontario—Fiction
ISBN 0-316-11714-5   LC 61-5313

"An Atlantic Monthly Press book"
"The loyalty of animals to home and master is a familiar theme. But for sheer inventiveness, this story of a young Labrador retriever, an old bullterrier, and a Siamese cat on a 250-mile trek through the Canadian wilderness [in Ontario] is exceptional. These pampered house pets, each in his own way, share the hazards of the journey. Even the aloof and independent cat brings her kill to the old bullterrier after he is injured in a battle with a bear, and each resists the human beings who try to detain them from reaching their former home. The author's intimate knowledge of the ways of these animals gives credibility to a tale of intense drama and suspense." Children's Bks Too Good to Miss

Burstein, Chaya M.

Rifka bangs the teakettle; written and illus. by Chaya M. Burstein. Harcourt 1970 191p illus $4.95 (5 and up)   Fic

1 Russia—Fiction 2 Jews in Russia—Fiction
ISBN 0-15-266944-2   LC 79-91068

"Jewish Rifka, ten, who lives in a small town in Czarist Russia in 1904, is happy helping her mother, yet finds it hard to see her five-year-old brother starting school, knowing that she, being a girl, will not receive an education. She is delighted therefore when her older brother offers to teach her to read and write—and sorely disappointed when she learns he will soon marry and go away. Based on the recollections of the author's mother who grew up in a Russian village, this is a warm and animated episodic story, richly illuminating in its portrayal of a Jewish family, village life, and Jewish mores and customs." Booklist

Followed by: Rifka grows up. Hebrew Pub. $6.95 (ISBN 0-88482-906-5 LC 76-41412)

Butterworth, Oliver

The enormous egg; illus. by Louis Darling. Little 1956 187p illus $7.95 (4 and up)   Fic

1 Dinosaurs—Fiction
ISBN 0-316-11904-0   LC 56-5622

"Up in Freedom, New Hampshire, one of the Twitchell's hens laid a remarkable egg—long, leathery-shelled, and so enormous that she could neither cover it nor turn it. Six weeks later when a live dinosaur hatched from the egg, the hen was dazed and upset, the Twitchells dumbfounded, and the scientific world went crazy. Twelve-year-old Nate who had taken care of the egg and made a pet out of the Triceratops tells of the hullabaloo, both local and national, resulting from the freak biological mix-up. Good fun; the many pictures are as amusing as the story." Booklist

The trouble with Jenny's ear; illus. by Julian de Miskey. Little 1960 275p illus $6.95 (4 and up)   Fic

1 Brothers and sisters—Fiction 2 Mind reading—Fiction
ISBN 0-316-11907-5   LC 60-5874

"The trouble with Jenny's ear was that she could hear people's unspoken thoughts. This remarkable ability resulted from her brothers' interest in electronics; with loud-speakers, tape recorders, intercom, and closed-circuit television all over the house Jenny's ear became oversensitive to sound. How the two enterprising boys capitalized on six-year-old Jenny's telepathic ear to try to make a needed $50,000 and what developed from their scheme are recounted in a laughable, preposterous story—and a satire on television quiz shows." Booklist

Byars, Betsy

After the Goat Man; illus by Ronald Himler. Viking 1974 126p illus $7.95 (5 and up)   Fic

ISBN 0-670-10908-8   LC 74-8200

Byars, Betsy—*Continued*

Figgy's "grandfather, the town's oddball nicknamed the Goat Man, has barricaded himself with his shotgun in their old cabin in a last ditch attempt to halt the wrecking crew from flattening their home for a superhighway. In a crisis which develops when they set out to talk the old man away from the cabin, Ada, Figgy, [overweight] Harold and the Goat Man become linked by their mutual caring, generosity and gentleness." NY Times Bk Rev

"The restrained plot, developed through spare, unsentimental prose, effectively and clearly delineates the need to recognize individual dignity and the pangs of adolescence. A compassionate and artistic treatment of human problems." Horn Bk

The cartoonist; illus. by Richard Cuffari. Viking 1978 119p illus $7.95 (4 and up)   **Fic**

1 Family life—Fiction
ISBN 0-670-20556-7   LC 77-12782

"Everybody needs his own private space and Alfie has his in the attic. . . . That's where he goes to draw cartoons he thinks are touched with genius. But his mother doesn't like him to be up there so much. . . . It's annoying but it's nothing to worry about until she announces that his brother has lost his job and he and his wife are coming home to live in the attic. Alfie's world is threatened and he protects it the only way he knows how. He goes up the ladder, locks the trap door and doesn't come down or talk to anybody no matter how much they plead with him. During the twenty-four hours he's locked away, he does a lot of growing up while he hears the problem that drove him up being resolved below him." West Coast Rev of Bks

"Alfie's ultimate reconciliation of his real and imaginary worlds is conveyed with extraordinary sensitivity to the thoughts and emotions of a child. Yet the tone of the book is neither serious nor somber; humorous dialogue is used throughout both to characterize and to narrate." Horn Bk

The 18th emergency; illus. by Robert Grossman. Viking 1973 126p illus $7.95 (4-6)   **Fic**

1 Fear—Fiction
ISBN 0-670-29055-6   LC 72-91399

"You can tell quite a bit about a boy when his nickname is 'Mouse.' And when Mouse incites the vengefulness of the school's bully, you know he is petrified with apprehension. Mouse's friend Ezzie has survival plans for emergency situations (being bitten by a tarantula, or being threatened by an octopus) but none for Imminent Beating by Large Boy. Most of the story is concerned with Mouse's fear of this eighteenth emergency, his efforts to avoid it, his feeble attempts to get adult sympathy; when he comes to the inevitable, Mouse surprises himself by his stalwart acceptance of the fight." Chicago. Children's Bk Center

"For its skillful portrayal of the loneliness of fear as well as a boy's emotional battle with himself—his frantic thoughts, his fantasies of escape, his gradual awakening to the way things are as against the way he wishes they were—'The 18th Emergency' weighs in . . . as a bantam champion." NY Times Bk Rev

The house of wings; illus. by Daniel Schwartz. Viking 1972 142p illus $8.95 (4-6)   **Fic**

1 Cranes (Birds)—Fiction   2 Grandfathers—Fiction
ISBN 0-670-38025-3   LC 77-183933

"A young boy reeling from the pain of temporary parental abandonment forges a relationship with an eccentric grandfather whom he despises. In attempting to rescue and mend a wounded crane, they come to respect each other for what they are, and as men." Bk World

This story "has an unsentimental and potent message about wildlife and draws a telling portrait of a human relationship. Save for the brief appearance of the parents, Sammy and his grandfather are the only characters. The book's spare construction makes it strong." Sat Rev

The midnight fox; illus. by Ann Grifalconi. Viking 1968 157p illus $7.95 (4-6)   **Fic**

1 Foxes—Fiction
ISBN 0-670-47473-8   LC 68-27566

"City-bred Tommy hates the idea of spending the summer on Aunt Millie's farm while his parents bicycle through Europe. Once he is there, however, a black fox shatters his conviction that he and animals share a mutual antipathy; fascinated, he stalks and watches the wild creature for two months—until it steals some of Aunt Millie's poultry and has to be hunted down." Booklist

"What distinguishes the story from many others on the same theme is the simplicity and beauty of the writing and the depth of the characterization." Horn Bk

The pinballs. Harper 1977 136p $7.95, lib. bdg. $7.89 (5 and up)   **Fic**

1 Foster home care—Fiction   2 Friendship—Fiction
ISBN 0-06-020917-8; 0-06-020918-6   LC 76-41518

"Of the three children in a foster home, Carlie is the oldest, an adolescent whose brittle and sophisticated toughness hides an aching need for love. She's been brutally treated by a hostile stepfather; Harvey is thirteen, confined to a wheelchair because both legs were broken when his father (alcoholic, missing the wife who had run off to join a commune) accidentally ran over him; eight-year-old Thomas J is lonesome for the octogenarian twins (hospitalized) who have taken care of him since he was abandoned at the age of two. It's Carlie who has called them all pinballs, people who just get sent somewhere to be out of the way. No choice about their lives. But, with loving patience on the part of their foster parents and with a growing affection for each other, the three children gain security and enough assurance to feel that they do have some control about the direction of their lives." Chicago. Children's Bk Center

"The stark facts about three ill-matched, abused children living in a foster home could have made an almost unbearably bitter novel; but the economically told story, liberally spiced with humor, is something of a tour de force. . . . A deceptively simple, eloquent story, its pain and acrimony constantly mitigated by the author's light, offhand style and by Carlie's wryly comic view of life." Horn Bk

The summer of the swans; illus. by Ted CoConis. Viking 1970 142p illus $7.95 (5 and up)   **Fic**

1 Mentally retarded children—Fiction   2 Brothers and sisters—Fiction
ISBN 0-670-68190-3   LC 72-106919

Awarded the Newbery Medal, 1970

"The thoughts and feelings of a young girl troubled by a sense of inner discontent which she cannot explain are tellingly portrayed in the story of two summer days in the life of fourteen-year-old Sara Godfrey. Sara is jolted out of her self-pitying absorption with her own inadequacies by the disappearance of her ten-year-old retarded brother who gets lost while trying to find the swans he had previously seen on a nearby lake. Her agonizing, albeit ultimately successful, search for Charlie and the reactions of others to this traumatic event help Sara gain a new perspective on herself and life." Booklist

"Seldom are the pain of adolescence and the tragedy of mental retardation presented as sensitively and as unpretentiously as in the story of Sara and Charlie. . . . [This is] a subtly told story, echoing the spoken and unspoken thoughts of young people." Horn Bk

The TV kid; illus. by Richard Cuffari. Viking 1976 123p illus $7.95 (4-6)   **Fic**

1 Television and children—Fiction
ISBN 0-670-73331-8   LC 75-37944

"TV addict Lennie scores low on his school tests, but in his fantasies he's big winner of every sort of giveaway quiz show. He lives with his mother in a decrepit summer motel and his lonely hobby is breaking into nearby summer cottages. Bitten by a rattler while hiding under a cottage during a neighborhood police check, Lennie is rescued barely in time for the anti-venom shots to save him, after many a miraculous rescue adventure show and selling jingles have flashed past in his fevered memory. The long and painful recovery is Lennie's reality cure. He leaves the hospital determinedly working on a science report about his dalliance with death, never to be tempted again from his homework by sitcoms, commercials, or prize shows." Sch Library J

Byars, Betsy—*Continued*

"Byars avoids what could be a melodramatic ending for Lennie-the-TV-star with well-developed characters, splurges of humor, and a suspenseful but believable plot. She also successfully uses satire that children can relate to, which is rarely found in a children's book." Booklist

Trouble River; illus. by Rocco Negri. Viking 1969 158p illus $7.95 (4-6)   **Fic**

1 Frontier and pioneer life—Fiction   2 Rivers—Fiction
ISBN 0-670-73257-5   LC 69-18260

Dewey Martin and his grandmother must make their way down the Trouble River on a home-made raft to escape the danger of hostile Indians. They find the raft hard to navigate on the river, but they persevere and eventually reach Hunter City and safety

"A philosophy of not giving up amid hardships and a sense of real love and family solidarity predominate." Rdng Ladders. 5th edition

Byfield, Barbara Ninde

Andrew and the alchemist; illus. by Deanne Hollinger. Doubleday 1977 102p illus $5.95, lib. bdg. $6.90 (4-6)   **Fic**

1 Alchemy—Fiction   2 Fantastic fiction
ISBN 0-385-12233-0; 0-385-12234-9   LC 76-7694

"In the kingdom of Oliver XI, Andrew, son of a traveling tinker, is apprenticed to P. C. Delver, an eccentric alchemist who performs his art in the cellar of a bakery run by agreeable Mrs. Strawspinner and daughter Sassie. When a frozen lake outside the town wall rises mysteriously and the royal treasury disappears, Delver is imprisoned. His innocence is proven by Sassie and Andrew who discover that the prime minister is the thief, and Mrs. Strawspinner eventually reveals why the lake is rising. The evil prime minister is turned to stone, and happiness reigns once more. Despite lapses into modern slang ('gee,' 'wow,' 'yep') inappropriate to the Medieval setting, Byfield spins an entertaining tale of alchemy, evil-eyed basilisks, secret tunnels, and palace intrigue." Sch Library J

Calhoun, Mary

Katie John; pictures by Paul Frame. Harper 1960 134p illus lib. bdg. $8.79, pa $1.95 (4-6)   **Fic**

1 Houses—Fiction
ISBN 0-06-020951-8; 0-06-440028-X   LC 60-5775

"When the Tuckers inherited an old house in a Missouri town, they decided to live in it until they could get it ready to sell. Ten-year-old Katie John was gloomy at the prospect—until she made a new friend, helped to solve a mystery, and learned to love the house." Hodges. Bks for Elem Sch Libraries

A "story with a likable heroine, lively doings, and a credible ending." Booklist

Some other books about Katie John are also available from Harper:

Depend on Katie John lib. bdg. $8.79, pa $1.95 (ISBN 0-06-020926-7; 0-06-440029-8; LC 61-7328)
Honestly, Katie John lib. bdg. $8.79, pa $1.95 (ISBN 0-06-020936-4; 0-06-440030-1; LC 68-8473)
Katie John and Heathcliff $8.95, lib. bdg. $8.79 (ISBN 0-06-020931-3; 0-06-020932-1; LC 80-7770)

Callen, Larry

Pinch; illus. by Marvin Friedman. Little 1975 179p illus $6.95 (5 and up)   **Fic**

1 Country life—Fiction   2 Pigs—Fiction
ISBN 0-316-12495-8   LC 75-25618

"An Atlantic Monthly Press book"

A story of Pinch's adolescent "admiration for Paw and how it leads him to be a pig trainer, of all things. Set in bayou country." Children's Bk Rev Serv

"Most of the male population seems to spend most of its time, in the story, swapping and lying, so that the book verges on tall tale, but remains realistic if exaggerated. It's an amusing, rambling tale of one crafty character pitted against another. . . . There's little variation in the tale and little to balance the folksy, loquacious characterization and dialogue, but for the lovers of homespun humor or regional fiction, this should have strong appeal." Chicago. Children's Bk Center

Followed by these books, also available from Little:

The deadly mandrake $6.95 (ISBN 0-316-12496-6; LC 77-28448)
Sorrow's song $7.95 (ISBN 0-316-12497-4; LC 78-31789)
Muskrat war $8.95 (ISBN 0-316-12498-2; LC 80-36700)

Cameron, Eleanor

The court of the stone children. Dutton 1973 191p $8.95, lib. bdg. $8.95 (5 and up)   **Fic**

1 Museums—Fiction   2 Mystery and detective stories   3 Ghosts—Fiction
ISBN 0-525-28350-1   LC 73-77451

In a San Francisco museum of French art and furniture, Nina encounters the ghost of Dominique, a girl who lived in the nineteenth-century. Spurred on by the appearance of the ghost, Nina sets out to untangle a murder mystery which has remained unsolved since Napoleon's day

"A nice concoction of mystery, fantasy, and realism adroitly blended in a contemporary story. . . . The characters are interesting, the plot threads nicely integrated." Chicago. Children's Bk center

A room made of windows; illus. by Trina Schart Hyman. Little 1971 271p $9.95 (5 and up)   **Fic**

ISBN 0-316-12523-7   LC 77-140479

"An Atlantic Monthly Press book"

"This is the tale of Julia, an aspiring young author, who is highly intelligent but emotionally immature. Although she revels in the satisfactions of good friends and progress in her writing, she is troubled by her mother's desire to remarry, the death of a much-loved elderly friend, and problems of those around her." Wis Lib Bul

"The portrayal and interaction of interesting and diverse characters are given unity and meaning by the genius of a fine storyteller." Top of the News

Followed by a book dealing with Julia's childhood: Julia and the hand of God. Dutton lib. bdg. $8.95 (ISBN 0-525-32910-2; LC 77-4507)

The terrible churnadryne; illus. by Beth and Joe Krush. Little 1959 125p illus $6.95 (4-6)   **Fic**

1 California—Fiction   2 Mystery and detective stories
ISBN 0-316-12535-0   LC 59-7339

"An Atlantic Monthly Press book"

"Tom and Jennifer see a huge and mysterious monster roaming about in the fog and mist in a California coastal town. Few people believe them, but they eventually organize to trap the monster." Adventuring with Bks. 2d edition

"The story skirts the edge of fantasy while it tells [of events] with humor and good characterization. . . . A different kind of mystery with a great deal of atmosphere." Horn Bk

To the green mountains. Dutton 1975 180p $8.95 (5 and up)   **Fic**

1 Ohio—Fiction
ISBN 0-525-41355-3   LC 75-6758

"This story of Kath Rule, who is growing up during World War I, evokes the past in Midwest America artfully. Kath's mother, estranged from her husband, manages a hotel in Columbus, Ohio, and Kath is tenderly treated by the staff, especially Grant and his wife, Tissy, a black couple. Mrs. Rule gets law books into Grant's hands and encourages him to study. She endures pangs of conscience when her help leads to a crisis and tragedy. The story brings all the people in the girl's circle to brilliant life and it is through her eyes and ears that we know them, and her with her longings for a 'proper' home, far away in the hills where her grandmother lives." Pub W

"This is surely the best of Eleanor Cameron's realistic fiction; her characters are vivid, they are affected by—and affect—each other and the course of the story; relationships are intricate but not confusing; the dialogue is smooth, the story line both fluid and cohesive." Chicago. Children's Bk Center

Cameron, Eleanor—*Continued*

The wonderful flight to the Mushroom Planet; with illus. by Robert Henneberger. Little 1954 214p illus $9.95 (4-6)   **Fic**

1 Science fiction
ISBN 0-316-12537-7   LC 54-8310

"An Atlantic Monthly Press book"

Two boys help a neighbor build a space ship in answer to an ad and take off for the dying planet of Basidium. There they help the inhabitants to restore an essential food to their diets and thereby save the life of the planet

"Scientific facts are emphasized in this well-built story. Since they are necessary to the development of the story the reader absorbs them naturally as he soars with the boys on the mission." NY Times Bk Rev

Some other books about the Mushroom Planet, the boys and Mr Bass are also available from Little:

Mr Bass's planetoid $7.95 (ISBN 0-316-12525-3; LC 58-5174)
A mystery for Mr Bass $7.95 (ISBN 0-316-12531-8; LC 60-9344)
Stowaway to the Mushroom Planet $7.95 (ISBN 0-316-12534-2; LC 56-8461)
Time and Mr Bass $7.95 (ISBN 0-316-12536-9; LC 67-2905)

Carew, Jan

The third gift; illus. by Leo and Diane Dillon. Little 1974 32p illus $7.95 (3-5)   **Fic**

1 Africa—Fiction
ISBN 0-316-12847-3   LC 73-12061

Set in Africa in the far past and drawing on folkloric themes, this tale "has a rich, poetic quality that is echoed in the brilliant colors and intricate patterns of the handsome illustrations. A prophet who had led his people from famine to a land of plenty decrees that when he dies, the tribe's young men must climb the Nameless Mountain, and that he who climbs the highest shall bring a gift to his people. Three times in the tribe's history, a gift is brought to the people; first they are given the gift of work, then the gift of beauty, then the gift of fantasy, of imagination and faith. 'So,' the story ends, 'with the gifts of Work and Beauty and Imagination, the Jubas became poets and bards and creators, and they live at the foot of Nameless Mountain to this day.' The writing style is rather grave and ornate, not as direct as most traditional folklore is, which may limit its appeal to some readers and be an added attraction for those who enjoy poetic prose." Chicago. Children's Bk Center

Carlson, Natalie Savage

Ann Aurelia and Dorothy; pictures by Dale Payson. Harper 1968 130p illus lib. bdg. $8.79 (4-6)   **Fic**

1 Foster home care—Fiction 2 Blacks—Fiction
ISBN 0-06-020959-3   LC 68-10781

"Ann Aurelia, living in a foster home because her mother has remarried and can't have her, makes friends with Dorothy, another fifth grader with whom she shares pranks and good times. When her mother reappears, Ann must decide whether to stay with her foster mother or rejoin her real one." Bruno. Bks for Sch Libraries, 1968

The author "isn't peddling any clichés like 'poor, oppressed white girl finds love and comfort and goodness in black home.' All the people in this story . . . black and white, are normal, decent people. The black girl is no miracle of maturity. If she is the natural leader of the two, this is because she knows the district better and for the moment has the more stable background. And what is exceptionally well-realized is the girls' enjoyment of each other. This is no forced friendship for the sake of a 'mixed' story." Christian Sci Monitor

The empty schoolhouse; pictures by John Kaufmann. Harper 1965 119p illus lib. bdg. $8.79 (3-5)   **Fic**

1 School integration—Fiction 2 School stories
ISBN 0-06-020981-X   LC 65-11452

"Ten-year-old Lullah Royall was overjoyed when they desegregated St. Joseph's parochial school for it meant she could go to school with her best friend, Oralee Fleury. In the ensuing atmosphere of hatred and fear, however, Lullah finds her joy short-lived and Oralee no longer a friend. Told by Lullah's older sister Emma, the story describes the turbulent emotions aroused by integration in a small Louisiana community." Booklist

"When the subject is integration and the audience is young children, there is danger in talking too much. Labeling children Negro and white and airing their racial feelings can be as divisive in print as it is in real life. Mrs. Carlson makes no such mistake. . . . It takes skill and restraint to keep a story simple and the relationships warm against such a background; Mrs. Carlson succeeds admirably." NY Times Bk Rev

The family under the bridge; pictures by Garth Williams. Harper 1958 99p illus lib. bdg. $8.79 (3-5)   **Fic**

1 Tramps—Fiction 2 Paris—Fiction 3 Christmas —Fiction
ISBN 0-06-020991-7   LC 58-5292

"Old Armand, a Parisian hobo, enjoyed his solitary, carefree life working only when he felt like it and moving about from one hidey-hole to another with his belongings in a topless baby buggy. Then came a day just before Christmas when Armand, who wanted nothing to do with children because they spelled homes, responsibility, and regular work, found that three homeless children and their working mother had claimed his shelter under the bridge. How the hobo's heart and life become more and more deeply entangled with the little family and their quest for a home is told with warmth and humor in a charming and memorable story." Booklist

"Garth Williams' illustrations are perfect for this thoroughly delightful story of humor and sentiment which includes a Christmas Eve party given by the ladies of Notre Dame for the homeless of Paris and an inside view of a gypsy encampment." Library J

The happy orpheline; pictures by Garth Williams. Harper 1957 96p illus lib. bdg. $9.89 (2-4)   **Fic**

1 Orphans—Fiction 2 France—Fiction
ISBN 0-06-21007-9   LC 57-9260

"Twenty orphan girls dread adoption because it will mean separation. One gets lost and involved in adventures with the 'queen of France' who threatens to adopt her. Enough French words to spark the interest of a beginning French student." Sch Library J

Some other books about the orphelines are also available from Harper:

A brother for the orphelines lib. bdg $9.89 (ISBN 0-06-020961-5; LC 59-5315)
A grandmother for the orphelines $8.95, lib bdg. $8.79 (ISBN 0-06-020993-3; 0-06-020994-1; LC 80-7769)
The orphelines in the enchanted castle lib. bdg. $9.89 (ISBN 0-06-021046-X; LC 63-14368)
A pet for the orphelines lib. bdg. $9.89 (ISBN 0-06-021056-7; LC 62-7947)

Carner, Chas

Tawny; illus. by Donald Carrick. Macmillan Pub. Co. 1978 152p illus $7.95 (5 and up)   **Fic**

1 Death—Fiction 2 Farm life—Fiction 3 Deer—Fiction 4 New Hampshire—Fiction
ISBN 0-02-716700-3   LC 77-17411

The "story of a boy's painful adjustment to the recent death of his twin brother in a hunting accident and his relationship with an injured doe which he nurses back to health. But when 'Tawny' creates havoc one night in the farmhouse kitchen, Trey comes to the realization that he must 'let go' of the doe, allowing her to return to the freedom of her natural life in the wild. Simultaneously, he realizes he must 'let go' of his deceased brother and summon up 'the courage to be himself.' " Sch Library J

"This realistic story of life on a New Hampshire farm will hold interest for animal lovers. . . . The ending is particularly well done—not trite as it might have been." Children's Bk Rev Serv

Carr, Mary Jane

Children of the covered wagon; a story of the old Oregon Trail; illus. by Bob Kuhn. Crowell 1957 [c1943] 318p illus $9.95 (4-6)   **Fic**

1 Oregon Trail—Fiction 2 Overland journeys to the Pacific (U.S.)—Fiction
ISBN 0-690-18987-7   LC 56-13460

Carr, Mary J.—*Continued*

First published 1934 with illustrations by Esther Brann

Recounts the dangers and experiences of a covered wagon trip from Missouri to the Willamette Valley, Oregon, in 1844. The story is told from the viewpoint of young Jerry Stephen who, with his cousin Jim and small Myra Dean, the doctor's daughter, went through their share of the perils of the journey bravely

"The thrills and hardships . . . are well depicted. . . . There is heroism and humor in the telling." Wis Library Bul

Carrick, Carol

Some friend! Pictures by Donald Carrick. Houghton 1979 112p illus $6.95 (3-6)   **Fic**

1 Friendship—Fiction
ISBN 0-395-28966-1   LC 79-11490

"Clarion books"

"Rob and Mike have been good buddies for a long time, but Mike is becoming dissatisfied with the nature of the friendship. Rob is the 'leader' and tends to be thoughtless and authoritarian; Mike won't challenge Rob's notions for fear of destroying the relationship. When Mike finally attempts to assert himself, there's a big fight. Eventually Mike realizes that Rob won't ever really change, and that if the friendship is to continue, Mike will simply have to accept Rob the way he is. The conclusion makes a good point, and although the story doesn't explore the personalities beyond just what is revealed in their relationship, it contains sufficient characterization to make both boys interesting." Booklist

Carroll, Lewis

Alice's adventures in Wonderland (4 and up)   **Fic**

1 Fantastic fiction

Some editions are:
Delacorte Press/Seymour Lawrence (A Merloyd Lawrence bk) $7.95, lib. bdg. $7.45 Illustrated by Tove Jansson. (ISBN 0-440-00069-6; 0-440-00075-0; LC 77-72625)
Potter, C.N. $7.95, pa $3.95 Illustrated by Ralph Steadman. Has title: Alice in Wonderland (ISBN 0-517-50135-X; LC 73-82899)
St Martins $7.95 Illustrated by Sir John Tenniel (ISBN 0-312-01821-5; LC 77-77324)

"First told in 1862 to the little Liddell girls. Written out for Alice Liddell, published, and first copy given to her in 1865." Arnold

"A rabbit who took a watch out of his waistcoat pocket seemed well-worth following to Alice so she hurried after him across the field, down the rabbit hole, and into a series of adventures with a group of famous and most unusual characters." Let's Read Together

This fantasy "is one of the most quoted books in the English language. Every child should be introduced to Alice, though its appeal will not be universal." Adventuring With Bks. 2d edition

Followed by: Through the looking glass, and what Alice found there, entered below

Alice's adventures in Wonderland, and Through the looking glass (4 and up)   **Fic**

1 Fantastic fiction

Some editions are:
Dent (Children's illustrated classics) $9 with the original engravings by John Tenniel, of which 8 have been redrawn in colour by Diana Stanley (ISBN 0-460-05029-X)
Dutton (Everyman's lib) $7.50, pa $2.95 Actual illustrations by the author. Prefatory note by Roger Lancelyn Greene (ISBN 0-460-00836-6; 0-460-01836-1)
Grosset (Illustrated junior lib) $5.95 Illustrated by John Tenniel. Has title: Alice in Wonderland and Through the looking glass (ISBN 0-448-05804-9)
Hall, G.K.&Co. (Classics in large print) $10.95 (ISBN 0-8161-3070-1; LC 80-13451)
Macmillan Pub. Co. (The Macmillan classics) lib. bdg. $6.95, pa $1.95. With illustrations by John Tenniel. Afterword by Clifton Fadiman (ISBN 0-02-717410-7; 0-02-042350-0 LC 63-14836)
Schocken lib. bdg. $9.95. With sixty six illustrations by Mervyn Peake (ISBN 0-8052-3716-X; LC 79-64115)

An omnibus edition of the two titles listed separately

Through the looking glass, and what Alice found there; illus by Sir John Tenniel. St Martins 1977 235p illus. $7.95 (4 and up)   **Fic**

1 Fantastic fiction
ISBN 0-312-80374-5   LC 77-77325

First published 1872

In this sequel to Alice's adventures in Wonderland, entered above, Alice climbs through a looking glass into a country where "everything is reversed, just as reflections are reversed in a mirror. Brooks and hedges divide the land into a checkerboard and Alice finds herself a white pawn in the whimsical and fantastic game of chess that constitutes the bulk of the story. . . . The ballad 'Jabberwocky' is found in the tale." Reader's Ency

"Besides kings, knights, pawns, and the other pieces of the game, there are more eccentric animals and people who have something to say. The careless White Queen and the fiery-tempered Red Queen are very amusing, and Tweedledum and Tweedledee are responsible for the song of 'The Walrus and the Carpenter.' " Keller's Reader's Digest of Bks

Caudill, Rebecca

A certain small shepherd; with illus. by William Pène Du Bois. Holt 1965 48p illus lib. bdg. $6.95, pa $1.95 (4-6)   **Fic**

1 Physically handicapped children—Fiction
2 Appalachian Mountains—Fiction 3 Christmas—Fiction
ISBN 0-03-089755-6; 0-03-080107-9   LC 65-17604

The author tells of "the singlemindeded enthusiasm of [Jamie], a little mute boy, who is given the part of one of the shepherds in a church celebration. . . . The pageant never takes place as a blizzard immobilizes the poor mountain community where the child lives, but the small shepherd is so deeply committed to his part that he acts it out impulsively [and speaks] when a baby is born to a family of travelers, caught by the storm and obliged to take refuge in the church." Bk Week

"There is a terrible poignancy in the episodes . . . of the cruel sting of laughter from other children over Jamie's grunts as he counts for hide-and-seek; of Jamie's knowing the answers in school but not being able to utter them. . . . [A story] that renews and revitalizes the meaning of love and joy." NY Times Bk Rev

Did you carry the flag today, Charley? Illus. by Nancy Grossman. Holt 1966 94p illus lib. bdg. $6.95, pa $1.65 (2-4)   **Fic**

1 Appalachian Mountains—Fiction 2 School stories
ISBN 0-03-089753-X; 0-03-086620-0   LC 66-11422

A "story about a small and lively boy, just turned five, who has his first encounter with the necessary strictures of the classroom at a summer school in Appalachia. Charley, obstreperous youngest in a family of ten, is given a full picture of the joys and the responsibilities he will encounter; his brothers and sisters tell him that one child 'who has been specially good that day' has the honor of carrying the flag at the head of the line to the bus. They ask every day, but they hardly expect Charley to carry the flag, since he has an affinity for trouble, usually emanating from curiosity. He does, of course, carry the flag in the last episode. This is a realistic and low-keyed story with good dialogue, although Charley seems precocious, and excellent classroom scenes." Chicago. Children's Bk Center

Chaikin, Miriam

I should worry, I should care; drawings by Richard Egielski. Harper 1979 103p illus $7.95, lib. bdg. $7.89 (3-5)   **Fic**

1 Jews in New York (City)—Fiction 2 Brooklyn—Fiction 3 Family life—Fiction
ISBN 0-06-021174-1; 0-06-021175-X   LC 78-19480

"Molly and her family had just moved to a new apartment in Brooklyn, and Molly faced the usual hurdles of making new friends and starting classes in a new school. The story of a Jewish family in the period of Nazi atrocities is anecdotal and humorous; Molly knows how upset her parents get when they listen to news on the radio, but she can't help feeling happy about her new friends, and her days are filled with small but exciting adventures." Chicago. Children's Bk Center

Chaikin, Miriam—*Continued*

"Chaikin's picture of a young girl in 1930's New York is unassuming but on target. Family interactions are well drawn: her brother, along with scattered friends, neighbors, and more troubles on the horizon as European news grows more disturbing, are all smoothly shown. The milieu is strong, the story easygoing—a nice contribution in a range where successful fiction is hard to find." Booklist

Chambers, John W.

Fritzi's winter; drawings by Carole Kowalchuk Odell. Atheneum Pubs. 1979 116p illus $8.95 (4-6)   **Fic**

1 Cats—Fiction 2 Fire Island, N.Y.—Fiction
ISBN 0-689-30727-6   LC 79-14672

"The Arnold family canot find their Siamese cat, Fritzi, when it is time to leave their house on Fire Island for the winter, so she is left to cope with the unfamiliar problems of finding food, shelter, and safety. Fritzi does survive, and does find her way back to the Arnolds the next summer after her last benefactor packs up and leaves her." Sch Library J

"With Odell's fine and realistic views of the area and its wildlife, Chambers's story amounts to a dramatic adventure in survival. Readers will be pulling for the wily cat all the way." Pub W

Childress, Alice

A hero ain't nothin' but a sandwich. Coward, McCann & Geoghegan 1973 126p $7.95 (6 and up)   **Fic**

1 Narcotic habit—Fiction 2 Blacks—Fiction 3 Harlem, New York (City)—Fiction
ISBN 0-698-20278-3   LC 73-82035

Set in Harlem, this is the story of thirteen-year-old Benjie Johnson, a heroin addict, who "gives his pathetically defensive version of his state in various chapters which are interspersed by the views of his mother, stepfather, grandmother, two of his teachers and others, including Walter the Pusher." Pub W

The author's "incisive examination is heightened by her skilled use of the vernacular, and she packs honesty, immediacy, and humor into an exceptionally compelling story with a difficult, realistic non-resolution. Despite its potential for ruffling conservative communities, librarians are urged to consider purchasing this book because of its artistic integrity." Booklist

Christopher, John

Empty world. Dutton [1978 c1977] 134p $8.50 (5 and up)   **Fic**

1 Science fiction 2 Plague—Fiction
ISBN 0-525-29250-0   LC 77-18917

First published 1977 in England

"The world is afflicted by the Calcutta Plague, a blight which kills by aging people prematurely. In quiet Winchelsea Neil Miller watches helplessly as his familiar world disintegrates. He is fortunate enough to be immune from the disease but he is powerless to help his friends, teachers and family as they wither and die around him. He leaves Winchelsea for London to search for other survivors and finds there two girls who have also escaped the plague. Despite the tensions that erupt in their relationship, Neil and the girls face the task of surviving the destruction of society." Times (London) Lit Sup

The novel "involved me immediately, held me throughout. . . . Developments are simple and deftly handled. The author's risk in allowing events to seem random, unplotted, to emerge out of the main character's needs and reactions, works for plausibility. . . . Issues are raised—of values, of morality, of hope or the loss of hope. Neil himself never seems childish; his feelings are those we all might experience in an empty world. In fact, one does not feel that Mr. Christopher has written this book for children—but rather that he has written a superb book that happens to be good reading for the young." NY Times Bk Rev

Prince in waiting. Macmillan Pub Co. 1970 182p $4.95, pa 95¢ (6 and up)   **Fic**

1 Science fiction
ISBN 0-02-718410-2; 0-02-022400-0   LC 70-119838

This first book of a trilogy takes place around the year 2000 after a volcanic disaster. It presents a circumscribed world which has reverted to a feudal, anti-technical society "located in

the general area of Winchester and Salisbury, England. . . . The powerful, vivid story is told by Luke Perry, who at thirteen was chosen Prince in Waiting, when his father was proclaimed the new Prince of Winchester in the Seance Hall by Ezzard, the local Seer. . . . After a series of harrowing events, including conflagration, battle, and treachery, Luke is compelled to flee along with Ezzard to the seer's stronghold near Salisbury—obviously Stonehenge." Horn Bk

"A book that stands alone but whets the reader's appetite for volume two. . . . Style, dialogue, and characterization are good although not outstanding; the strongest qualities of the book are the wholly conceived setting and the well-paced and well-constructed plot." Chicago. Children's Bk Center

Followed by these books, also available from Macmillan Pub. Co:
Beyond the burning lands $7.95, pa $1.95 (ISBN 0-02-718420-X; 0-02-042380-2; LC 78-152288)
The Sword of the Spirits $4.95, pa $1.95 (ISBN 0-02-718340-8; 0-02-042640-2; LC 74-20762)

The White Mountains. Macmillan Pub. Co. 1967 184p $6.95, pa $2.75 (5 and up)   **Fic**

1 Science fiction
ISBN 0-02-718360-2; 0-02-042710-7   LC 67-1262

"The world of the future is ruled by huge and powerful machine-creatures, the Tripods, who control mankind by implanting metal caps in their skulls when they reach the age of fourteen. Three boys [Will, Henry, and Beanpole] . . . see that the people about them are mindless conformists [and] decide to flee to the White Mountains (Switzerland), where there is a colony of free men. Their journey is hazardous, bringing them at one time into an almost medieval French household and another into the ruins of a deserted and crumbling Paris." Sat Rev

"A remarkable story . . . it belongs to the school of science-fiction which puts philosophy before technology and is not afraid of telling an exciting story." Times (London) Lit Sup

Followed by these books, also available from Macmillan Pub. Co:
The city of gold and lead $7.95, pa $1.95 (ISBN 0-02-718380-7; 0-02-042700-X; LC 67-21245)
The pool of fire $7.95, pa $1.95 (ISBN 0-02-718350-5; 0-02-042720-4; LC 68-23062)

Church, Richard

Five boys in a cave. Day [1951 c1950] 180p $6.95 (6 and up)   **Fic**

1 Adventure and adventurers—Fiction 2 Caves—Fiction
ISBN 0-381-99854-1   LC 51-10431

First published 1950 in England with title: The cave

Five English boys go to explore a cave, the entrance to which had been discovered by accident. Two of the boys are stranded beside an underground river, but the other three manage a rescue

"These dangerous adventures are told with masterly suspense and tension; Mr. Church, who is a poet, has used all his senses to give the beautiful and terrifying details of the story. In a formal, almost old-fashioned way, he shows the characters of the five boys and their changing relations under the press of circumstance. This is a first-rate adventure story, informed with wit and human warmth and understanding: a distinguished book for parents as well as their children." NY Times Bk Rev

Clapp, Patricia

Constance; a story of early Plymouth. Lothrop 1968 255p illus lib. bdg. $7.44 (5 and up)   **Fic**

1 Pilgrims (New England colonists)—Fiction 2 Massachusetts—History—Colonial period, 1600-1775—Fiction
ISBN 0-688-51127-9   LC 68-14064

The imaginary "journal kept by Constance Hopkins, daughter of Stephen Hopkins and ancestress of Patricia Clapp. Constance began jotting down her impressions and intimate thoughts at the age of fifteen on the eve of the 'Mayflower's' arrival and continued up to the day of her wedding five years later. With disarming candor, quick wit, and sprightliness she tells of her despair at leaving London, the discomforts of the voyage, her instant hatred of the wilderness and fear of the native savages, her gradual awareness of growing up during the agonies of the dreadful Sickness and

Clapp, Patricia—*Continued*

the famine, her new understanding of her step-mother, her awareness of the political and economic issues of the settlement, her friends and flirtations, her often immodest impulses, and her narrow escape from marrying the wrong man." Horn Bk

"The characters come alive, the writing style is excellent, and the historical background is smoothly integrated." Chicago. Children's Bk Center

I'm Deborah Sampson; a soldier in the War of the Revolution. Lothrop 1977 176p lib. bdg. $7.44 (5 and up) **Fic**

1 Gannett, Deborah Sampson—Fiction 2 U.S.—History—Revolution, 1775-1783—Fiction
ISBN 0-688-51799-4 LC 76-51770

This is a fictional "treatment of the known facts (not substantiated by a bibliography) about a descendant of famous New England Puritans. Born in 1760, the great-great-granddaughter of Governor Bradford—one of a large family of children—lived up to her mother's challenge to be strong, free, and loyal. Parceled out by her mother to work for people who would feed her, she was finally indentured until she was eighteen. In an appreciative household she and Robbie, the most sensitive son, fell in love on the eve of the Revolution. When he died on sentry duty, Debbie could not rest until she was accepted as a private—well-disguised as a young man; when her sex was discovered she was discharged but contrived to re-enlist. For over a year she managed to survive brutal trials and to escape detection until she was hospitalized." Horn Bk

"The writing style is vigorous, the historical details accurate and unobtrusive, and the language and concepts consistently appropriate for the period." Chicago. Children's Bk Center

Jane-Emily. Lothrop 1969 160p lib. bdg. $6.96 (5 and up) **Fic**

1 Ghosts—Fiction
ISBN 0-688-51019-1 LC 69-14326

"While visiting her grandmother, young Jane finds a crystal ball which reflects the image of Emily, a dead girl. Jane is soon possessed by the ghost of Emily, and the events which follow are chilling." Cincinnati

"Well written and with a convincing strong Gothic strain, the story is spellbinding, building up to an exciting climax." Horn Bk

Clark, Ann Nolan

Secret of the Andes; with drawings by Jean Charlot. Viking 1952 130p illus $7.95, Penguin pa $1.25 (4 and up) **Fic**

1 Incas—Fiction 2 Peru—Fiction
ISBN 0-670-62975-8; 0-14-030926-8 LC 52-8075

Awarded the Newbery Medal, 1953

"A young South American Indian boy searches for his destiny, eventually realizing that he wants to be a llama herder just as he has been trained to do. Interwoven into the story is the history of the Spanish conquerors and the value of continuing the ancient Incan traditions." Rdng Ladders. 5th edition

It is a "rarely beautiful and subtle story. . . . Perceptive young readers will respond to the beauty of the telling, with mysticism in Incan songs and vivid description of wild and unvisited grandeur in the high Andes. It has a distinguished format, with richly toned lithograph frontispiece, end papers and jacket." Horn Bk

Clark, Mavis Thorpe

The min-min. Macmillan Pub. Co. 1969 216p $7.95, pa $1.95 (5 and up) **Fic**

1 Runaways—Fiction 2 Australia—Fiction
ISBN 0-02-718960-0; 0-02-042280-6 LC 79-78086

First published 1967 in England

"In this novel set in Australia, Reg has vandalized the schoolhouse, so the 'coppers' will surely send him away; his sister, Sylvie, is trapped by unending household tasks, helped not at all by an ailing mother and drinking father. Like the aborigines' min-min, an elusive light which beckons but remains unreachable, Sylvie's dream of further education seems futile. So the two run away deep into the Australian outback. . . . Their destination is the sheep-station of Gulla Tank and the sympathetic ear of a friend, Mrs. Tucker." NY Times Bk Rev

"A story of adolescent growth and family relationships with perceptive characterization and a novel locale." Horn Bk

Cleary, Beverly

Beezus and Ramona; illus. by Louis Darling. Morrow 1955 159p illus $7.25, lib. bdg. $6.96, pa $1.50 (3-5) **Fic**

ISBN 0-688-21076-7; 0-688-31076-1; 0-688-25078-5
LC 55-7623

Ramona Quimby, a strong-willed four-year-old who first appeared as a minor character in the author's Henry Huggins books, entered below, has a whole book in which to try the patience of well-behaved big sister Beezus. Wearing the rabbit ears she constructed at nursery school, Ramona moves purposefully through her world, leaving destruction and distraction in her wake. This is a very funny book; its situations are credible, and it has a perceptive handling of family relationships that is unfortunately rare in easily read books." Horn Bk

"Young readers who have small brothers and sisters will understand Beezus' perplexity about her relationship with four-year-old Ramona and will be interested in the conclusion that you don't have to love them all the time." Wis Library Bul

Followed by these books, also available from Morrow:

Ramona the grace $7.25, lib. bdg. $6.96 (ISBN 0-688-21721-4; 0-688-31721-9; LC 68-12981)
Ramona the brave $7.25, lib. bdg. $6.96 (ISBN 0-688-22015-0; 0-688-32015-5; LC 74-164968)
Ramona and her father $7.25, lib. bdg. $6.96 (ISBN 0-688-22114-9; 0-688-32113-3; LC 77-1614)
Ramona and her mother $6.75, lib. bdg. $6.48 (ISBN 0-688-22195-5; 0-688-32195-X; LC 79-10323)

Ellen Tebbits; illus. by Louis Darling. Morrow 1951 160p illus $7.25, lib. bdg. $6.96 (3-5) **Fic**

1 School stories
ISBN 0-688-21264-6; 0-688-31264-0 LC 51-11430

"Ellen Tebbits is eight years old, takes ballet lessons, wears bands on her teeth, and has a secret—she wears woolen underwear. But she finds a friend in Austine, a new girl in school, who also wears woolen underwear. They have the usual troubles that beset 'best friends' in grade school plus some that are unusual." Pittsburgh

"Their experiences in the third grade are comical and very appealing to children in the middle grades." Hodges. Bks for Elem Sch Libraries

Henry Huggins; illus. by Louis Darling. Morrow 1950 155p illus $6.25, lib. bdg. $6.96 (3-5) **Fic**

ISBN 0-688-25385-7; 0-688-31385-X LC 50-8615

"Henry Huggins is a typical small boy who, quite innocently, gets himself into all sorts of predicaments—often with the very apt thought, 'Won't Mom be surprised.' There is not a dull moment but some hilariously funny ones in the telling of Henry's adventures at home and at school." Booklist

Some other books about Henry Huggins are also available from Morrow:

Henry and Beezus $7.44, lib. bdg. $6.96 (ISBN 0-688-21383-9; 0-688-31383-3; LC 52-5930)
Henry and Ribsy $7.75, lib. bdg. $7.44, pa $1.50 (ISBN 0-688-21383-0; 0-688-31382-5; 0-688-25382-2; LC 54-6402)
Henry and the clubhouse $7.25, lib. bdg. $6.96 (ISBN 0-688-21381-2; 0-688-31381-7; LC 62-8161)
Henry and the paper route $7.75, lib. bdg. $7.44 (ISBN 0-688-21380-4; 0-688-31380-9; LC 57-8562)
Ribsy $7.25, lib. bdg. $6.96 (ISBN 0-688-21662-5; 0-688-31662-X; LC 64-13263)

Mitch and Amy; illus. by George Porter. Morrow 1967 222p illus $7.75, lib. bdg. $7.44 (3-5) **Fic**

1 Twins—Fiction 2 School stories
ISBN 0-688-21688-9; 0-688-31688-3 LC 67-1293

"The twins Mitch and Amy are in the fourth grade. Mitch is plagued by a bully and by reading difficulties. Amy struggles with multiplication tables, and their patient mother mediates their squabbles." Sch Library J

"The writing style and dialogue, the familial and peer group relationships, the motivations and characterizations all have the ring of truth. Written with ease and vitality, lightened with humor, the story is perhaps most appealing because it is clear that the author respects children." Chicago. Children's Bk Center

Cleary, Beverly—*Continued*

The mouse and the motorcycle; illus. by
Louis Darling. Morrow 1965 158p illus $7.25,
lib. bdg. $6.96 (3-5)   **Fic**

1 Mice—Fiction
ISBN 0-688-21698-6; 0-688-31698-0   LC 65-20956

"A fantasy about Ralph, a mouse, who learns
to ride a toy motorcycle and goes on wild rides
through the corridors of the hotel were he lives.
Keith, the boy to whom the motorcycle belongs,
becomes fast friends with Ralph and defends
him when danger threatens." Hodges. Bks for
Elem Sch Libraries

"The author shows much insight into the
thoughts of children. She carries the reader into
an imaginative world that contains many realistic
emotions." Wis Library Bul

Followed by: Runaway Ralph. Morrow $7.95, lib.
bdg. $7.44 (ISBN 0-688-21701-X; 0-688-31701-4; LC
77-95786)

Otis Spofford; illus. by Louis Darling.
Morrow 1953 191p illus $7.25, lib. bdg. $6.96,
pa $1.50 (3-5)   **Fic**

1 School stories
ISBN 0-688-21720-6; 0-688-31720-0; 0-688-26720-3
LC 53-6660

"Otis, a mischievous, fun loving boy, is always
getting in and out of trouble. His mother, a dancing teacher, is busy earning their living and often
leaves Otis on his own. This book tells of several
episodes in Otis's life—from his sneaking vitamins
to a white rat to 'disprove' a diet experiment, to
getting his final 'come-uppance' when a trick on
Ellen Tebbits [heroine of the book entered above]
backfires." Rdng Ladders. 5th edition

"This writer has her elementary school down
pat, and manages to report her growing boys,
teachers, and P.T.A. meetings so that parents
chuckle and boys laugh out loud." NY Her Trib
Bks

Socks; illus. by Beatrice Darwin. Morrow
1973 156p illus $7.25, lib. bdg. $6.96 (3-5)
Fic

1 Cats—Fiction 2 Infants—Fiction
ISBN 0-688-20067-2; 0-688-30067-7   LC 72-10298

"The Brickers' kitten, Socks, is jealous when
they bring a baby home from the hospital. How
he copes with this rivalry makes an amusing story
true to cat nature." Cleveland Pub Library

"Not being child-centered, this may have a
smaller audience than earlier Cleary books, but it
is written with the same easy grace, the same
felicitous humor and sharply observant eye." Chicago. Children's Bk Center

Cleaver, Vera

Ellen Grae [by] Vera and Bill Cleaver;
illus. by Ellen Raskin. Lippincott 1967 89p
illus $8.95 (4-6)   **Fic**

1 Truthfulness and falsehood—Fiction   2 Mentally handicapped—Fiction
ISBN 0-397-30938-4   LC 67-10623

"Eleven-year-old Ellen Grae is an imaginative
and original girl and an inventor of tall tales. She
is also the only one in whom simple-minded Ira
confides the horrible facts of an attempted euthanasia, of death by rattlesnake venom, and the burial
of his parents in a nearby swamp. Caught in the
responsibility of knowing, she is confronted with
the realities of conformity and life as it is; she
must choose between asserting her own integrity
or resigning to the status quo. Her choice may
confuse some; to others it may appear as a comment upon adult values and their effect upon the
young." Wis Library Bul

Followed by: Lady Ellen Grae. Lippincott $8.95
(ISBN 0-397-31012-9; LC 68-10981)

Grover [by] Vera and Bill Cleaver; illus.
by Frederic Marvin. Lippincott 1970 125p
illus $8.95 (4-6)   **Fic**

1 Death—Fiction
ISBN 0-397-31118-4   LC 69-12001

Companion volume to the authors': Ellen Grae,
and: Lady Ellen Grae, entered above

Ten-year-old Grover "goes through an agonizing
period of adjustment beginning with his mother's
sudden departure to the hospital and ending with
his eventual acceptance of her death. The strain

is increased by adult attempts to 'protect' him
from the truth during her illness and by his father's
withdrawal into grief after her suicide." Booklist

Although the elements of the story "may sound
grim, there's nothing depressing about this book—
it seems very real, with its most deeply touching
or dramatic moments heightened by superbly
comic incidents or dialogue." Sch Library J

Me too [by] Vera and Bill Cleaver.
Lippincott 1973 158p $8.95 (5 and up)   **Fic**

1 Mentally handicapped children—Fiction
2 Twins—Fiction
ISBN 0-397-31485-X   LC 73-7631

"The story concerns two girls, twins, 12 years
old. Lydia is bright and intelligent; Lorna is an
exceptional child with a mental age of about 5.
During the summer in which the father deserts
the family, Lydia takes on the care and education
of Lornie. Her dream is that she will make Lornie
so much like herself that no one will be able to
tell the difference." NY Times Bk Rev

"The contrast between the twins is dramatic,
the interplay fascinating, and Lydia's efforts
and self-searching moving. But her failure is
neither pathetic nor sad; for she has grown during
her trials and frustrations, has learned to accept
the reality of her father's desertion, and has come
to an understanding of the 'exceptional' status
of her sister." Horn Bk

Queen of hearts [by] Vera and Bill
Cleaver. Lippincott 1978 158p $8.95 (6 and
up)   **Fic**

1 Grandmothers—Fiction   2 Old age—Fiction
3 Family life—Fiction
ISBN 0-397-31771-9   LC 77-18252

"Wilma and her grandmother had never had a
loving relationship, so it was with dismay that
Wilma learned that taking care of Granny, who
had had a slight stroke, was up to her. Wilma's
parents worked, and the attempts they made to
have someone else stay with Granny had failed.
Hostile, critical, and obstinate, Granny drove them
all away. Wilma didn't really enjoy her responsibility, but she recognized it as a responsibility,
and somehow she and Granny achieved a modus
vivendi." Chicago. Children's Bk Center

"Young readers will find this a quick-flowing
novel covering the multiple harassments that many
old come to face, along with the unique humor
with which they view so many of their experiences. . . . The Cleavers present a realistic view
of what it means to grow old and not be fully
understood or appreciated for the wealth of experience that often comes from a long life." Best
Sellers

Where the lilies bloom [by] Vera & Bill
Cleaver; illus. by Jim Spanfeller. Lippincott
1969 174p illus $8.95 (5 and up)   **Fic**

1 Orphans—Fiction   2 Appalachian Mountains—
Fiction   3 Brothers and sisters—Fiction
ISBN 0-397-31111-7   LC 75-82402

"Mary Call Luther [is] fourteen years old and
made of granite. When her sharecropper father
dies, Mary Call becomes head of the household,
responsible for a boy of ten and a retarded, gentle
older sister. Mary and her brother secretly bury
their father so they can retain their home; tenaciously she fights to keep the family afloat by selling medicinal plants and to keep them together by
fending off [Kiser Pease, their landlord], who
wants to marry her sister." Sat Rev

"The setting is fascinating, the characterization
good, and the style of the first-person story distinctive." Chicago. Children's Bk Center

Followed by: Trial Valley. Lippincott $8.95
(ISBN 0-397-31722-0; LC 76-54303)

Clements, Bruce

I tell a lie every so often. Farrar, Straus
1974 149p illus $5.95 (6 and up)   **Fic**

1 Truthfulness and falsehood—Fiction   2 Frontier and pioneer life—Fiction
ISBN 0-374-33619-9   LC 73-22356

"Our hero, 14-year-old Henry Desant, keeps the
laughs coming in his account of what happens
when he tells a couple of lies (in a worthy cause)
to his older brother, Clayton. Fifteen years earlier,
in 1833, their cousin, Hanna, had been taken by
the Indians. Henry tells Clayton that a young
white girl has been reported living in an Indian
settlement 500 miles north of their home in St.
Louis. This fib sets the two on a boat journey

Clements, Bruce—*Continued*

up the Missouri River . . . into and out of wild adventures including . . . a game of wits with the Indians and a stunning encounter with the girl who may or may not be lost Hanna." Pub W

Clifford, Eth

The curse of the moonraker; a tale of survival. Houghton 1977 188p $6.95 (5 and up)
Fic

1 Survival (after airplane accidents, shipwrecks, etc.)—Fiction
ISBN 0-395-25837-5   LC 77-24431

"Shortly after leaving Australia, the square-rigged 'Moonraker' is dashed to pieces in treacherous waters, leaving only eight crew members, one woman passenger, and Cat, the young cabin boy, as survivors. The story, tautly told by Cat, is one of perseverance and determination against great odds and one in which survival is continuously endangered by the eruption of human emotions as they all struggle to stay alive. Finally reaching the Auckland Islands, the group ekes out a frugal existence for more than a year, in which time they fight illness, bad weather, and despair, bury one man, see four leave to find help (never to return), and eventually are rescued by a seal-hunting ship. Cat's development from boy to man is well handled, and his observations of the relationships and reactions of the survivors add a perceptive note to a story based on an actual incident." Booklist

The rocking chair rebellion. Houghton 1978 147p $6.95 (6 and up)
Fic

1 Old age—Fiction 2 Volunteer workers—Fiction
ISBN 0-395-27163-0   LC 78-14834

"Opie (short for Penelope) has no intention of becoming involved with the residents of the Maple Ridge Home for the Aged, but an unexpected turn of events leads her to become a volunteer worker. Her sympathies are engaged; and, encouraged by her father, who wants her to be a social worker, she assists with some of the projects—organizing a raffle and setting up a block party. Several of the more hale and hearty of the inmates buy a house on her street, intending to establish an arrangement for communal living. Bitter opposition arises among the neighbors, but the sale is successfully defended in court by Opie's father." Horn Bk

"Using Opie as narrator allows the author to reveal events and issues through the eyes of a bright, articulate adolescent. The treatment of the familiar theme is thoughtful, and Clifford successfully avoids stereotypes in either people or institutions." Sch Library J

Clifton, Lucille

The lucky stone; illus. by Dale Payson. Delacorte Press 1979 64p illus $6.95, lib. bdg. $6.46 (3-5)
Fic

1 Blacks—Fiction 2 Charms—Fiction
ISBN 0-440-05121-5; 0-440-05122-3   LC 78-72862

"Four short stories about four generations of Black women and their dealings with a lucky stone. . . . Clifton uses as a frame device a grandmother telling the history of the stone to her granddaughter; by the end the granddaughter has inherited the stone herself. The plot is necessarily episodic, spanning the period from just before the Emancipation Proclamation to the present, so that we see slavery, a revival meeting, and a traveling circus. . . . The story is written in Black dialect, but the language is . . . understandable from the context. The pencil drawings give a sort of indefinite hazy quality appropriate to the magic." Sch Library J

"This book contains information on various aspects of Black culture—slavery, religion and extended family—all conveyed in a way that is both positive and accurate." Interracial Bks for Children Bul

Clymer, Eleanor

Luke was there; illus. by Diane de Groat. Holt 1973 74p illus lib. bdg. $5.95 (3-6)
Fic

1 Runaways—Fiction 2 New York (City)—Fiction
ISBN 0-03-011161-7   LC 73-7170

Set in New York City, this is the story of Julius and his brother Danny, who "are committed to a children's shelter where Luke, a young Black conscientious objector, becomes the focus of Julius' respect and affection. When Luke must leave to serve his military time in a federal hospital, Julius reacts to his departure by running away . . . but he can't run from heartache or fast enough to avoid the danger and treachery that awaits on New York City's streets." Sch Library J

"Told in the first person, the story shows credible and moving insight concerning a child's response to difficult problems. Brown-and-white drawings effectively interpret both the personalities and the city scenes." Horn Bk

Me and the Eggman; illus. by David K. Stone. Dutton 1972 56p illus lib. bdg. $6.95 (3-6)
Fic

1 Farm life—Fiction 2 Runaways—Fiction
ISBN 0-525-34775-5   LC 75-179054

"Running away from responsibilities at home, Donald finds himself involved in even greater ones with an old, lonely farmer." NY Pub Library Children's Bks & Recordings, 1972

"Neither the relationship between the man and the boy nor the picture given of farm life moves beyond the boundaries of realism, and the story is told convincingly as a first-person narrative." Chicago. Children's Bk Center

My brother Stevie. Holt 1967 76p front lib. bdg. $5.95 (4-6)
Fic

1 Brothers and sisters—Fiction 2 Teachers—Fiction
ISBN 0-03-089508-1   LC 67-10231

Annie Jenner, a twelve-year-old living with her harsh but well-meaning grandmother, is overwhelmed by the responsibility of caring for her difficult younger brother, Stevie. When she is befriended by an understanding teacher, however, she gains new strength to cope with her dilemma

"Miss Clymer opens a world which many youthful readers may have little contact with. She depicts it skillfully and sympathetically, so that Annie, Stevie, and their grandmother emerge as vivid personalities. And if that pretty and kindly school teacher, Miss Stover, who sets everything right, may seem a little too good to be true, at least she's the kind of teacher every slum child (and some non-slum children, too) dreams of coming across some day. This is a warm and sentimental, as well as an adventuresome, little book." Bk Week

Coatsworth, Elizabeth

The cat who went to heaven; illus. by Lynd Ward. Macmillan Pub. Co. 1958 62p illus $7.95 (4 and up)
Fic

1 Cats—Fiction 2 Japan—Fiction
ISBN 0-02-719710-7   LC 58-10917

First published 1930. The 1958 edition is a reprint with new illustrations of the book which won the Newbery Medal award in 1931

"Watched by his little cat, Good Fortune, a Japanese artist paints a picture of the Buddha receiving homage from the animals. By tradition the cat should not be among them, but the artist risks his reputation by adding Good Fortune and is vindicated by a miracle." Hodges. Bks for Elem Sch Libraries

"Into this lovely and imaginative story the author has put something of the serenity and beauty of the East and of the gentleness of a religion that has a place even for the humblest of living creatures." NY Times Bk Rev

Marra's world; illus. by Krystyna Turska. Greenwillow Bks. 1975 83p illus lib. bdg. $6.48 (2-5)
Fic

1 Maine—Fiction 2 Seals (Animals)—Fiction
ISBN 0-688-84007-8   LC 75-9520

"Marra has lived her life in a small Maine fishing village under the shadow of her grandmother's hatred, her father's neglect, and her peers' ridicule. After a prestigious new doctor's daughter befriends her, she begins to change her self-image and discover the source of her strangeness—her mother, who long ago loved and mysteriously left her, is a selkie, the very seal that guides Marra and her friend through a sudden heavy fog to safety." Booklist

Coatsworth, Elizabeth—*Continued*

"Reworking the old legend of the seal-people into a poetic, original story, the distinguished and prolific writer proves that she has lost none of her sensitivity and skill. Line drawings capture and extend the mood of the book with sympathetic interpretations of characters and events." Horn Bk

Cohen, Barbara

Benny. Lothrop 1977 154p $7.25, lib. bdg. $6.96 (4-6) **Fic**

1 Jews in the U.S.—Fiction 2 Family life—Fiction

ISBN 0-688-41804-X; 0-688-51804-4   LC 77-242

"Set in New Jersey in 1939, this is both a nicely honed period piece and a warm family story. Benny is twelve, and he loves playing baseball. But his sister is doing her mother's work while Ma recuperates from a hysterectomy, and older brother Sheldon studies constantly for a scholarship exam, so it's Benny who has to work in the family store. Pa just can't see that playing ball is important, although he eventually relents—and even comes to a ball game. Benny stops feeling sorry for himself when he realizes how unhappy Arnulf, a German refugee, is. It isn't just that he's homesick, but that his Jewish mother is dead—and his father and stepmother, neither of them Jewish, don't want the stigma of having a Jew in their home. It's Benny who finds Arnulf when he runs away; for once, even Sheldon stops sneering and appreciates the fact that Benny has compassion and commonsense." Chicago. Children's Bk Center

The author "has a deft touch with family dynamics. Benny's self-assertion is healthy as well as satisfying, and the story's late thirties setting generates an unobtrusive history lesson." Booklist

The carp in the bathtub; illus. by Joan Halpern. Lothrop 1972 48p illus lib. bdg. $6.96 (2-4) **Fic**

1 Jews in New York (City)—Fiction 2 Carp—Fiction

ISBN 0-688-51627-0   LC 72-1079

Set in New York City. "Leah and Harry have made friends of Joe, the appealing carp their mother has swimming in the bathtub, awaiting its execution on the Feast of Seder. Joe will make marvelous 'gefilte' fish but the children are determined to save him. They sneak him into the tub of a neighbor, but alas; his change of scene is only a reprieve, not a pardon. A delightfully warm book with pictures equally appealing." Pub W

The innkeeper's daughter. Lothrop 1979 159p $7.50, lib. bdg. $7.20 (6 and up) **Fic**

1 Hotels, motels, etc.—Fiction

ISBN 0-688-41906-2; 0-688-51906-7   LC 79-2421

Sequel to: R, my name is Rosie

"A sensitive and satisfying semi-autobiographical novel of a young girl growing up in the late 1940s. Rachel Gold, 16, believes herself to be fat and ugly and often resents the demands on her as the oldest child. Her understanding mother, Bea, a Jewish widow raising three children and running a small hotel in New Jersey, seems to share none of Rachel's doubts and insecurities; she tackles life with determination and common sense. Then, on New Year's Eve, the hotel burns down. Mrs. Gold contemplates marriage to one of the regular hotel customers with whom she has developed a rapport; Rachel must cope with the departure of a handsome young man who lives at the hotel and shares her intellectual concerns. Finally an old painting, saved coincidentally from the fire, is discovered to be extremely valuable and the family faces a new beginning. The mother-daughter relationship is well drawn; the era and place are nicely evoked, as is the supporting cast of characters." Sch Library J

Thank you, Jackie Robinson; drawings by Richard Cuffari. Lothrop 1974 125p illus lib. bdg. $6.96 (4-6) **Fic**

1 Baseball—Fiction   2 Friendship—Fiction 3 Blacks—Fiction

ISBN 0-688-51580-0   LC 73-17703

"Fatherless, Sam had never seen a baseball game until he met Davy. Davy was sixty, black, and the cook in Sam's mother's restaurant. Sam describes the trips to Ebbets Field with Davy, and sometimes with Davy's daughter and son-in-law; he is casual and candid about their discussions of race and the problems created when they travel together to other ball parks. The book ends on a poignant note, with Davy in the hospital after a heart attack and Sam bringing him a baseball (procured after considerable effort) signed by Jackie Robinson." Chicago. Children's Bk Center

"Cohen's characters have unusual depth and her story succeeds as a warm, understanding consideration of friendship and, finally, death." Booklist

Cohen, Peter Zachary

Deadly game at Stony Creek; pictures by Michael J. Deas. Dial Press 1978 107p illus $6.95, lib. bdg. $6.46 (5 and up) **Fic**

1 Dogs—Fiction

ISBN 0-8037-1816-0; 0-8037-1817-9   LC 78-51772

"Baseball is the most important thing in Cliff's life, and he is terrified that the pack of wild dogs loose in the countryside near his family's farm will maim him as they did young Karla Dobley. Cliff is forced to join the hunt for the dogs when some of the family's sheep are destroyed. In a suspenseful story that shifts perspective back and forth from the dogs to Cliff and his friend Eddie, the author spins an exciting adventure that will make a super read-aloud for teachers. Reluctant readers (especially boys) will enjoy this on their own." Children's Bk Rev Serv

Collier, James Lincoln

The bloody country, by James Lincoln Collier and Christopher Collier. Four Winds 1976 183p $7.95 (6 and up) **Fic**

1 Pennsylvania—History—Fiction 2 Frontier and pioneer life—Fiction

ISBN 0-590-07411-3   LC 75-34461

"An engrossing story which is based on historical facts of a Connecticut man, Daniel Buck and his family, who settled [in Pennsylvania] near the banks of the Susquehanna in Wyoming Valley in the 1750's, survived the Wyoming Massacre, suffered disastrous losses in a flood, and struggled against the injustice of the Pennamites' legal maneuvers to wrest their land from them. Told by young Ben in a breezy conversational style, he is first seen as a youngster of seven though we share his thoughts and actions as he matures to a boy of fifteen." Children's Bk Rev Serv

"A gripping and dramatic presentation of the personal problems, attitudes, emotions, and controversies underlying political events, the novel breathes life into textbook history and permits young people to realize that unknown citizens were as much a part of the past as their more celebrated contemporaries." Horn Bk

My brother Sam is dead, by James Lincoln Collier and Christopher Collier. Four Winds 1974 216p illus $7.95, pa $1.95 (6 and up) **Fic**

1 U.S.—History—Revolution, 1775-1783—Fiction

ISBN 0-590-07339-7; 0-590-10279-6   LC 74-8350

To Tim Meeker, in the Tory village of Redding Ridge, Connecticut, the rebellion against England was an event that had nothing to do with him. Then his older brother Sam joined the Minutemen. The story shows how Sam's decision affected his family and what happened when the town became caught up in the Revolution

"A fast-moving tale of adventure and tragedy. The complex factors which influenced the political choices of everyday citizens and soldiers are skillfully developed and add significantly to the book's strength." Babbling Bookworm

Collodi, Carlo

The adventures of Pinocchio (3-6) **Fic**

1 Puppets and puppet plays—Fiction 2 Fairy tales

Some editions are:

Grosset (Illustrated junior library) $5.95 (ISBN 0-448-05801-4; LC 46-22697)

Macmillan Pub. Co. $17.50, pa $9.95 Translated by Carol della Chiesa; illustrated by Attilio Mussino (ISBN 0-02-722820-7; 0-02-042780-8; LC 25-26908)

An Italian classic for children, written late in the 19th century

"When Geppetto discovered a piece of wood which talked, he carved it into a marionette and named him Pinocchio. Although he is a wooden boy, Pinocchio has a lively and nimble mind and an ardent curiosity which lead to unexpected and

Collodi, Carlo—*Continued*

extraordinary results. A lighthearted and original fantasy in which children can identify themselves with Pinocchio and grasp the simple and practical morality which underlies the story." Bks for Boys and Girls

Colman, Hila

Diary of a frantic kid sister. Crown 1973 119p $4.95 (4 and up) **Fic**
1 Family life—Fiction 2 Brothers and sisters—Fiction
ISBN 0-517-50262-3   LC 72-92388

"To an eleven-year-old with a glamorous sister life in general and parents in particular often seem unfair. Fortunately Sarah Grinnell is a resilient girl, a quality reflected in her diary as it chronicles her reactions during the year she begins to realize her personal dependence. As her mother, hoping to resolve her middle-aged frustrations, enters therapy and her glamorous sister is jilted by her boyfriend, Sara recognizes that each age has its own difficulties, and that much of growing up is learning to adapt and cope. Written with humor and verve despite the polly-anna-ish ending, the book should appeal greatly to those pre-adolescents who feel that they will never emerge from their personal limbo." Booklist

Cone, Molly

Mishmash; illus. by Leonard Shortall. Houghton 1962 114p illus $7.95 (3-5) **Fic**
1 Dogs—Fiction
ISBN 0-395-06711-1   LC 62-10316

The dog Mishmash moved like a cyclone into Pete's heart, his family's new house, the neighbor's gardens and life was never the same again! Pete, who was new in town, found that suddenly good old Mish had introduced him to practically everybody. But Pete had to solve the problem of troublesome Mish, also the problem of what to give his teacher

"Sprightly and enjoyable [the book's] charm [is] enhanced by Leonard Shortall's lively pictures." NY Her Trib Bks

Some other books about Mishmash are also available from Houghton:
Mishmash and the sauerkraut mystery $6.95, pa 95¢ (ISBN 0-395-06702-2; 0-395-18556-4; LC 65-14923)
Mishmash and the substitute teacher $6.95 (ISBN 0-395-06709-X; LC 63-18441)
Mishmash and the Venus flytrap $6.95 (ISBN 0-395-24376-9; LC 75-44380)

Conford, Ellen

And this is Laura. Little 1977 179p $6.95 (4 and up) **Fic**
1 Extrasensory perception—Fiction 2 Family life—Fiction
ISBN 0-316-15300-1   LC 76-53583

"Preadolescent Laura Hoffman is convinced that she is an ordinary run-of-the-mill person in a family of super-achievers. . . . Only Laura, who relates the story, has no special talent until she accidentally discovers her psychic powers and becomes an instant celebrity among her classmates. At first her ability to predict the future seems only a harmless divertissement, but when that future portends possible disaster, she wonders if this newly emerged gift is as much a liability as it is an asset. She finally resolves the problem and, at the same time, realizes that parental love is more than mere pride in the accomplishments of one's children." Horn Bk

"The validity of ESP is not questioned (it's just a trendy peg on which to hang a familiar message), but the story is lively, fast-paced, and written in natural dialogue (including an occasional 'hell' or 'dammit')." Sch Library J

Dear Lovey Hart, I am desperate. Little 1975 170p $6.95 (6 and up) **Fic**
1 Journalism—Fiction 2 School stories
ISBN 0-316-15306-0   LC 75-16238

"Carrie Wasserman, freshman reporter on the school newspaper, is assigned the secret identity of Lovey Hart, columnist and expert on love and the opposite sex. Obviously, writing an advice column is not an easy job and, of course, her neat solutions to difficult problems get her into serious trouble thus dooming her early success." Children's Bk Rev Serv

"The action and the story culminate in an unexpected confrontation, with all concerned learning some hard lessons." Pub W

Followed by: We interrupt this semester for an important bulletin. Little $7.95 (ISBN 0-316-15309-5; LC 79-9133)

Dreams of Victory; illus by Gail Rockwell. Little 1973 121p illus $6.95 (4-6) **Fic**
ISBN 0-316-15294-3   LC 72-8437

"Victory Benneker couldn't dance; she couldn't skate; she got only six votes in an election for class president; and she was a miserable failure in an unimportant role in the class play. Despite the optimistic name her mother had given her, nothing came out to her satisfaction. But Vicky had a wonderful safeguard. She could daydream. And so fertile was her imagination that she became—in turn—the first woman President, winner of the Miss Galaxy Beauty Contest, recipient of an Oscar for her acting." Horn Bk

"The fiasco episodes are ruefully funny, the classroom scenes amusing, and the conversations between Vicky and her parents especially deft; while the focus is on the situation rather than the plot, there is enough action in the catalog of small failures to sustain interest, and many children can empathize with Vicky as a character." Chicago. Children's Bk Center

Felicia the critic; illus. by Arvis Stewart. Little 1973 145p illus $6.95 (4-6) **Fic**
ISBN 0-316-15295-1   LC 73-7831

"When her negative communications meet with looks of loathing, Felicia, mostly undaunted and with good intentions, embarks on a career as a constructive critic, hoping that she will be valued for her talent. She systematizes her job by compiling lists of suggestions for the local traffic cop, her children's-book-author aunt, and a restaurant owner, to name a few. Felicia's audacity continues to be regarded with coldness by her family, her friends, and many of her victims. Nevertheless, she is so often on target that some people find themselves taking up her advice in spite of themselves." Booklist

"Fresh, entertaining, and percipient. . . . It all adds up to a deft, sympathetic portrait of a real child—a loner aware of the obtuseness and supercritical responses of other people." Horn Bk

The luck of Pokey Bloom; illus. by Bernice Loewenstein. Little 1975 135p illus $6.95 (3-6) **Fic**
1 Family life—Fiction
ISBN 0-316-15305-2   LC 74-26556

"Pre-adolescent Pokey Bloom is a contest addict with a deplorable rate of return on her investment in time, stamps, and boxtops. But her notable lack of success is not Pokey's principal concern—she's certain to win if only she sends in more entries and increases her effort. What does concern her, however, is her deteriorating relationship with older brother Gordon. He has changed from a protective, sympathetic, and amusing companion into a grouchy health-food advocate with a strange penchant for mumbling mysteriously into the telephone while crouching in the hall closet. Fortunately for family harmony, Gordon's behavior is diagnosed." Horn Bk

"The threads of the plot are Pokey's luck (she wins fourth prize in one contest) and Gordon's peculiar behavior (first love) but the story is told in such a blithe style no stronger plot is really needed; the several episodes involving Pokey's friends are amusing, but this is above all a warm family story, with good parent-child relationships, firm characterization, and smooth dialogue." Chicago. Children's Bk Center

Me and the terrible two; illus. by Charles Carroll. Little 1974 117p illus $7.95 (3-6) **Fic**
1 Friendship—Fiction 2 Twins—Fiction
ISBN 0-316-15303-6   LC 73-18393

"Dorrie, a sixth-grader . . . not only loses her best friend when the family next door moves to Australia, but must be plagued by the new incumbents—a pair of zany, prankish, totally self-sufficient, identical-twin boys. Dorrie, predictably, not only manages to survive, but ultimately settles into a three-way friendship with her tormentors." Horn Bk

"A witty, brisk and altogether effective story." Pub W

Coolidge, Olivia

Come by here; illus. by Milton Johnson. Houghton 1970 239p illus $5.95 (5 and up)
Fic

1 Orphans—Fiction 2 Blacks—Fiction
ISBN 0-395-10912-4 LC 72-115451

Minty Lou's warm, secure world is shattered when her parents are accidentally killed. She becomes an unwelcomed burden in homes where both money and hope are in short supply. Set in Baltimore in 1900, this book is based on an actual life story of a Black girl who struggled to regain the security she once had known
"Minty Lou's is not a cheering story, but it should be read, not only for its insights into black history but for its realistic depiction of conditions which too often apply, in some measure, to human beings of any color." Sch Library J

Cooper, Susan

Dawn of fear; illus. by Margery Gill. Harcourt 1970 157p illus $5.95 (5 and up)
Fic

1 Great Britain—Fiction 2 World War, 1939-1945 —Fiction
ISBN 0-15-266201-4 LC 71-115755

During World War II, three English boys' fearless unconcern with the enemy planes that flew daily on their way to bomb London, gradually underwent a change as the night raids grew more severe. This is the story of how, through the destruction—not by bombs—of the secret camp they were building, the boys came face-to-face with grown-up hatred, and then they knew the meaning of fear
"The characterization [is] deft and the dialogue natural [and] the relationship between the boys and a young man who is about to enter the Merchant Navy [is] particularly perceptive." Sutherland. The Best in Children's Bks

Jethro and the jumbie; illus. by Ashley Bryan. Atheneum Pubs. 1979 28p illus lib. bdg. $6.95 (2-4)
Fic

1 Caribbean area—Fiction 2 Brothers—Fiction 3 Ghosts—Fiction
ISBN 0-689-50140-4 LC 79-14667

"A Margaret K. McElderry Book"
"The boy Jethro was furious with his ' "mean self-ish promise-breakin' brother," ' who had agreed to take him fishing on his eighth birthday. Jethro stomped off, so angry he shed his fear of the 'jumbie,' the ghostlike creature traditionally said to inhabit the bush outside the village. As in the manner of folk tales, realism is sprinkled with magical adventures, and Jethro cheerfully observed at the conclusion, ' "Sometimes . . . things that ain't real can be a whole big help to people that are." ' Horn Bk
The author "has created a warm and amusing tale that picks up the cadence of Caribbean dialogue and integrates it well, lending a distinct island flavor to the narrative. The soft gray pencil drawings with their deceptively simple shadings hint of lush, tropical countrysides while subtly expanding the humor. An imaginative rendering to read aloud or alone." Booklist

Over sea, under stone; illus. by Margery Gill. Harcourt [1966 c1965] 252p illus $6.25, pa $2.95 (5 and up)
Fic

1 Good and evil—Fiction 2 Fantastic fiction 3 Great Britain—Fiction
ISBN 0-15-259034-X; 0-15-670542-7 LC 66-11199

First published 1965 in England
"Three children—Barney, Jane, and Simon—spending a summer holiday in a seaside village in Cornwall find a crumbling parchment map in an attic. Unwittingly they have stumbled upon the clues to a long-sought relic of Arthurian days, a relic which is not merely of antiquarian interest but which also holds some secret source of strength and goodness. Protected and aided by enigmatic, scholarly Great-Uncle Merry, the children struggle to decipher the clues and plot their quest, until at last, against a . . . gay holiday background, the ancient battle of good against evil is fought once more." Horn Bk
"This is one of the best mysteries we have had in some time. The air of mysticism and the allegorical quality of the continual contest between good and evil add much value to a fine plot, setting, and characterization." Library J

Followed by these books, available from Atheneum Pubs.:
The dark is rising $8.95, pa $2.95 (ISBN 0-689-30317-3; 0-689-70420-8; LC 72-85916)
Greenwitch $8.95, pa $2.50 (ISBN 0-689-30426-9; 0-689-70431-3; LC 73-85319)
The grey king $8.95, pa $2.95 (ISBN 0-689-50029-7; 0-689-70448-8; LC 75-8526) Awarded the Newbery Medal, 1976
Silver on the tree $9.95, pa $2.95 (ISBN 0-689-50088-2; 0-689-70467-4; LC 77-5361)

Corbett, Scott

The discontented ghost. Dutton 1978 180p $7.95 (6 and up)
Fic

1 Ghosts—Fiction 2 Great Britain—Fiction
ISBN 0-525-28775-2 LC 78-18013

"A Unicorn book"
A "retelling of Oscar Wilde's 'The Canterville Ghost'—from the ghost's point of view. Sir Simon de Canterville is the resident haunt, having stayed on at his ancestral home some 300 years after his death, and by 1884 quite proud of his record. His wife (whom he is said to have murdered but did not) has performed the services of an assistant, playing the housekeeper. Though somewhat weary of his role, Sir Simon has little doubt that he will roust out the new American family who buys his home and is stunned to find that one set of twins, Yankee common sense, and 'Pinkerton's Champion Stain Remover and Paragon Detergent' prove more than a self-respecting ghost can handle. In a complete turnabout, Sir Simon finds it easier to join 'em than haunt 'em and helps young lovers unite, unearths an ancient treasure, and eventually goes off to Italy for a change of pace." Sch Library J
"This is the most sophisticated of Corbett's ghost stories, a well-written comedy with carefully developed characters and a beguiling plot that doesn't lose out by having its ends tied up neatly." Booklist

The lemonade trick; illus. by Paul Galdone. Little 1960 103p illus lib. bdg. $6.95 (3-5)
Fic

1 Fantastic fiction
ISBN 0-316-15694-9 LC 59-7361

"An Atlantic Monthly Press book"
A brew from his Feats O'Magic chemistry set, given to him by the mysterious Mrs Graymalkin, changes Kerby into a perfect gentleman; unfortunately, it has the opposite effect on good boys
"An ingenious bit of magic has been mixed by [the author] and dashingly illustrated . . . to please eight-year-old readers . . . and even some a bit older who like a fairly simple story that doesn't take too long to read." NY Her Trib Bks
Some other books in the "Trick" series are also available from Little:
The baseball trick lib. bdg. $6.95 (ISBN 0-316-15708-2; LC 65-18360)
The black mask trick lib. bdg. $6.95 (ISBN 0-316-15656-6; LC 75-28405)
The disappearing dog trick lib. bdg. $6.95 (ISBN 0-316-15706-6; LC 63-7314)
The hairy horror trick lib. bdg. $6.95 (ISBN 0-316-15702-3; LC 70-77443)
The hangman's ghost trick lib. bdg. $6.95 (ISBN 0-316-15728-7; LC 77-23021)
The hockey trick lib. bdg. $6.95 (ISBN 0-316-15716-3; LC 74-5022)
The home run trick lib. bdg $6.95 (ISBN 0-316-15693-0; LC 72-3478)
The turnabout trick lib. bdg. $6.95 (ISBN 0-316-15700-7; LC 67-3009)

Corbin, William

Golden mare; illus. by Pers Crowell. Coward-McCann 1955 122p illus $5.95 (4-6)
Fic

1 Horses—Fiction 2 Physically handicapped children—Fiction
ISBN 0-698-20054-3 LC 55-6891

A "story of a handicapped boy [with a rheumatic heart condition] whose affection for an old mare brings him to a complete realization of his unique capabilities." Cincinnati
"This is an unusual horse story, sensitive without being sentimental, and so simply written that many fourth-graders will join older children in reading it." Horn Bk

Corcoran, Barbara

A dance to still music; illus. by Charles Robinson. Atheneum Pubs. 1974 180p illus $8.95, pa $1.95 (5 and up)   Fic

1 Deaf—Fiction 2 Florida—Fiction 3 Runaways—Fiction
ISBN 0-689-30406-4; 0-689-70440-2   LC 74-75558

"As fourteen-year-old Margaret struggles to cope with deafness caused by a recent illness, her misery is compounded by the loneliness of strange surroundings; for her mother has moved from Maine to Florida in search of a better job. When her mother decides to marry, Margaret knows that she will be sent away to a special school. . . . Flight back to Maine and the security of her grandfather's house seem the only solution, but she never actually leaves Florida. In her efforts to help a Key West fawn that is hit by a truck, she is joined by a middle-aged woman. Josie, who accepts Margaret's deafness and self-imposed silence without surprise or comment and takes the girl and the wounded deer to the refuge of her small houseboat at the edge of the Gulf. Matter-of-fact Josie . . . not only helps return the fawn to health but also helps Margaret come to terms with her deafness and family relationships." Horn Bk

"The major characters are convincing, especially the protagonist and her mother—not a bad woman, but lacking in understanding." Chicago. Children's Bk Center

Sasha, my friend; drawings by Richard L. Shell. Atheneum Pubs. 1969 203p illus $7.95, pa 95¢ (5 and up)   Fic

1 Wolves—Fiction 2 Montana—Fiction
ISBN 0-689-20582-1; 0-689-70358-9   LC 69-18968

"After her mother's death teen-age Hallie and her father move from Los Angeles to northwestern Montana for his health. Living in a trailer on a Christmas tree farm and isolated from school, Hallie is homesick, desolate, and unprepared for wilderness living but, as she learns to cope, acquires an orphaned wolf cub for company, and experiences the friendship and helpfulness of neighbors, she begins to regard the place as home." Booklist

"The themes are not new to children's books: a girl's painful adjustment to wilderness living and a fierce attachment to an unconventional pet. But the author, who lives in Montana by preference, writes with conviction as she tells an absorbing story set against the austere beauty of her adopted state." Horn Bk

Coren, Alan

Arthur the Kid; illus. by John Astrop. Little [1978 c1977] 73p illus $6.95 (3-5)   Fic

1 The West (U.S.)—Fiction 2 Robbers and outlaws—Fiction
ISBN 0-316-15734-1   LC 77-26989

First published 1976 in England

"Derby-sporting [ten-year-old] Arthur responds to a newspaper ad from the bungling Black Hand Gang. . . . With Arthur in charge, instead of robbing a Wells Fargo office, the gang members, dressed as women, hand over one hundred thousand dollars to Wells Fargo officials, collect a big reward, and ultimately turn away from criminal pursuits." Sch Library J

"Coren's funny situations, broadened by comical drawings and heightened by clever dialogue, entertain from start to finish." Booklist

Some other books about Arthur are also available from Little:

Arthur and the great detective $7.95 (ISBN 0-316-15736-8; LC 79-23511)
Arthur's last stand $6.95 (ISBN 0-316-15742-2; LC 79-14052)
Buffalo Arthur $6.95 (ISBN 0-316-15738-4; LC 78-6398)
Klondike Arthur $6.95 (ISBN 0-316-15733-3; LC 78-23176)
The Lone Arthur $6.95 (ISBN 0-316-15739-2; LC 78-6459)
Railroad Arthur $6.95 (ISBN 0-316-15737-6; LC 77-28419)

Coutant, Helen

First snow; pictures by Vo-Dinh. Knopf 1974 30p illus lib. bdg. $5.69 (2-4)   Fic

1 Death—Fiction 2 Vietnamese in the U.S.—Fiction
ISBN 0-394-92831-8   LC 74-1187

This is the "story of a Vietnamese family's first winter in New England. The excitement and happiness of the impending first snow is mingled with the uncertainty and sadness of Grandmother's dying. Young Lien soon sees dying as a natural process: a change—just as in the life of a snowflake." Children's Bk Rev Serv

"So 'that' was dying, something disappeared and in its place came something else! This is the Buddhist view, the oneness of life and death. . . . The story has a quiet serenity and delivers effectively its message of the continuity of the life-death cycle." Chicago. Children's Bk Center

Crayder, Dorothy

She, the adventuress; illus. by Velma Ilsley. Atheneum Pubs. 1973 188p illus $5.95, pa $1.95 (5 and up)   Fic

1 Ocean travel—Fiction
ISBN 0-689-30082-4; 0-689-70457-7   LC 72-86931

"Since pre-teen Maggie has to travel alone from Iowa to Italy, she decides to pretend it's a glamorous adventure. But the shipboard stowaway, an international art thief, and a man from Interpol are no daydream." Chicago

"Reduced to simple plot summary, the story would sound contrived and heavily dependent on an unlikely combination of possible occurrences, but it succeeds admirably as an entertainment because of the adolescent heroine's believable reactions and the evocation of the momentous minutiae of shipboard existence." Horn Bk

Cresswell, Helen

A game of catch; illus. by Ati Forberg. Macmillan Pub. Co. 1977 43p illus $5.95 (3-6)   Fic

1 Space and time—Fiction 2 Fantastic fiction
ISBN 0-02-725440-2   LC 76-46991

First published 1969 in England

This is a "story of two children who are spending a few days with an aunt before leaving England for Canada. Kate and Hugh walk through a deserted museum and Kate is sure that she hears other children's laughter. Nobody else sees the two children from an 18th century painting who later play a game of ball with Kate on the skating pond—but when Kate sees the painting a second time, the girl is holding the ball Kate had thrown her at the end of the game. When she'd first seen the picture, the boy was holding the ball." Chicago. Children's Bk Center

"The economy of the style and the precision of the diction evoke equally well the winter season and the lingering overtones of time associated with the castle and the painting. Kate's sensitivity and credulity . . . are skillfully set off by Hugh's innate skepticism, while the flow of the narrative has a feeling of inevitability. Black-and-white drawings correspond with the mood and the imagery of the story without approximating its sculptured, deliberate elegance." Horn Bk

Ordinary Jack; being the first part of the Bagthorpe saga. Macmillan Pub. Co. 1977 195p $6.95 (5 and up)   Fic

1 Family life—Fiction
ISBN 0-02-725540-9   LC 77-5146

In this first volume of a series, the author introduces the Bagthorpe family. "The leading player in the first comedy is 11-year-old Jack. Every one of the Bagthorpes is a genius in several areas, except Jack. He has no talents at all. His irreverent Uncle Parker, seeing the boy's need to be special in some way rather than tolerated, devises The Campaign. The two soon have their relatives flummoxed with 'proofs' that Jack is clairvoyant." Pub W

"In the great tradition of English humor and logical nonsense, the author presents as penetrating a family portrait as can be found in a book for children. . . . [She] writes with a marvelous sense of the comic and of dramatic timing: since the book, as the subtitle indicates, is only the beginning of a major family chronicle, there are limitless possibilities in what is yet to come." Horn Bk

Followed by these books, also available from Macmillan Pub. Co:

Absolute zero $6.95 (ISBN 0-02-725550-6; LC 77-12675)
Bagthorpes unlimited $6.95 (ISBN 0-02-725430-5; LC 78-3561)
Bagthorpes v. the world $6.95 (ISBN 0-02-725420-8; LC 79-13260)

Cresswell, Helen—*Continued*

The winter of the birds. Macmillan Pub. Co. 1975 244p $8.95 (6 and up) **Fic**

ISBN 0-02-725510-7 LC 75-34278

"The story tells of a boy who is in training to be a hero. He goes about it in the typically practical British way . . . and really overlooks the fact that in his own small fashion, he is already quite heroic. He befriends an elderly recluse, finds a lost uncle, learns of his true relationship to his adopted parents through a kind and gentle giant of an Irishman, whom he believes to be a true hero." Babbling Bookworm

"The narrative, as well as the subtleties of the style, makes unusual demands on young readers, who will be rewarded for their efforts by the remarkable imaginative elements, the humor, and the distinctive individuality of the characters." Horn Bk

Cummings, Betty Sue

Hew against the grain. Atheneum Pubs. 1977 174p $6.95 (6 and up) **Fic**

1 U.S.—History—Civil War, 1861-1865—Fiction 2 Family life—Fiction
ISBN 0-689-30551-6 LC 76-25593

This is an "account of the impact of the Civil War on one Virginia family. Mattilda's home and crops are destroyed by soldiers, and her father succumbs to insanity as his family crumbles. Her own 'war wound' is the loss of her virginity at 15 when she is raped by a man whom she subsequently shoots. With the aid of her friend Docia, a slave, Mattilda fights against what Grandpa Hume calls 'dwindling'—losing the resources, courage, or spirit to face life." Sch Library J

"The story gives a grim and convincing picture of the wartime difficulties of civilians and of the burdens assumed by those women forced to do work to which they were unaccustomed. The writing style of this first novel is highly competent, with a smooth narrative flow and believable characters and dialogue; the plot is rather turgid with dramatic incidents, however, for in addition to the two rapes there are murders [and] family feuds." Chicago. Children's Bk Center

Cunningham, Julia

Burnish me bright; pictures by Don Freeman. Pantheon Bks. 1970 78p illus lib. bdg. $6.99 (4-6) **Fic**

1 Physically handicapped children—Fiction 2 Pantomimes—Fiction 3 France—Fiction
ISBN 0-394-90851-1 LC 71-101183

A mute orphan boy's "friendship with a dying mime helps him to learn a skill which incidentally strengthens the inner resources he needs for survival and for his relationships with others." Top of the News

"Two underlying themes—the perils of being different and death—are handled with poignant directness." Adventuring With Bks. 2d edition

Come to the edge. Pantheon Bks. 1977 79p $4.95, lib. bdg. $6.99 (5 and up) **Fic**

1 Runaways—Fiction 2 Foster home care—Fiction
ISBN 0-394-83432-1; 0-394-93432-6 LC 76-44017

Fourteen-year-old "Gravel Winter escapes from a foster [home] farm. In a nearby town he lends his eyes, his strength, and the sound of his voice to three lonely and mysterious inhabitants. And he almost loses himself." West Coast Rev of Bks

"What Miss Cunningham has created—despite a few Gothic twists—is a parable about love and man's inability to accept it in the face of his own unworthiness. The fact that Gravel does eventually learn to love and be loved, makes a moving ending; but even if the resolution had been different, I would have been shaken by this story. Miss Cunningham tells the truth about life and tells it in ways that are completely her own. In other words, she is an artist." NY Times Bk Rev

Dorp dead; illus. by James Spanfeller. Pantheon Bks. 1965 88p illus $3.95, lib. bdg. $6.99 (5 and up) **Fic**

1 Orphans—Fiction
ISBN 0-394-81089-9; 0-394-91089-3 LC 65-11441

"In this highly symbolic story orphan Gilly Ground describes his deliberately lonely life. He shuns friendships, disguises his intelligence, is glad to leave the orphanage to be the solitary apprentice of Kobalt the laddermaker. The security of

Kobalt's routine soon becomes stifling, however, and Gilly discovers that he is, in fact, to become a prisoner. Helped by the dog Mash, with whom he has shared affection, Gilly escapes to the promise of freedom." Rdng Ladders. 5th edition

"In fine clean line James Spanfeller's illustrations bring out the sensitive character of a frightened child who awakens from an ugly dream to a smiling world." NY Times Bk Rev

Curry, Jane Louise

The Bassumtyte treasure. Atheneum Pubs. 1978 129p $7.95 (5 and up) **Fic**

1 Buried treasure—Fiction 2 Great Britain—Fiction 3 Mystery and detective stories
ISBN 0-689-50100-5 LC 77-14381

"A Margaret K. McElderry book"
"When orphaned Tommy Bassumtyte goes to England to live with his distant cousin Thomas in Boxleton House, he carries with him his grandfather's curiously engraved medallion and has memorized the secret rhyme which is supposed to be the key to finding the family treasure. The treasure is sorely needed, as Thomas is no longer able to maintain the beautiful ancient mansion and may be forced to sell it. But at Boxleton House the boy finds everything necessary for complete happiness: Cousin Thomas is warm and welcoming; the house has a secret room and a mysterious history; young Tommy closely resembles an Elizabethan portrait of the first Small Thomas; and he even meets the ghost of Lady Margaret, Small Thomas's grandmother." Horn Bk

"This adroitly conceived mystery—with only a touch of (perhaps unnecessary) time fantasy—has a strong, readable line, with time for the characters and a clever integration of historical incident." Booklist

The daybreakers; illus. by Charles Robinson. Harcourt 1970 191p illus $5.95 (4 and up) **Fic**

1 Blacks—Fiction 2 West Virginia—Fiction 3 Fantastic fiction
ISBN 0-15-222853-5 LC 72-94332

In a milltown in West Virginia "two black children and one white . . . achieve the impossible: they live in two worlds, in the ugly milltown and in an ancient, beautiful world they discover for themselves. They are able to live in both reality and fantasy, because their story is told by a writer who is magnificently at ease in both worlds." Pub W

Ghost Lane. Atheneum Pubs. 1979 158p illus $6.95 (5 and up) **Fic**

1 Mystery and detective stories 2 Great Britain—Fiction
ISBN 0-689-50129-3 LC 78-73399

"A Margaret K. McElderry book"
"While vacationing with his father in a small English village, 11-year-old Richard Morgan makes friends with elderly Mr. Drew who lives in the Goslings manor house, target of several mysterious robberies. Evidence points to the Ghost Mob, a clever gang of thieves, but Richard fears that someone on the inside is collaborating with the robbers. With his new friends Fan and her strangely silent brother Nolly, Richard sets out to solve the mystery by delving into the shady history of the Goslings. Curry has crafted a likeable group of characters and an amiable portrait of village life." Sch Library J

The ice ghosts mystery. Atheneum Pubs. 1972 215p $7.95, pa $1.95 (4 and up) **Fic**

1 Austria—Fiction 2 Mystery and detective stories
ISBN 0-689-30302-5; 0-689-70421-6 LC 74-190552

"A Margaret K. McElderry book"
"The mystery is threefold. First, Mrs. Bird and her three children attempt to learn whether Professor Bird, a California seismologist, is missing or dead after his disappearance during a ski trip in Austria. Secondly, they try to find an explanation for the ghosts who keep superstitious people away from a vast mountain cave. Finally, they ferret out the origin of elusive, illegal underground detonations that cause earthquakes and avalanches. The complex plot is ingeniously woven and sustained in a beautifully vivid setting." Horn Bk

Curry, Jane L.—*Continued*

Poor Tom's ghost. Atheneum Pubs. 1977 178p map $8.95 (5 and up) **Fic**

1 London—Fiction 2 Fantastic fiction
ISBN 0-689-50072-6
LC 76-28468

"A Margaret K. McElderry book"
"Thirteen-year-old Roger Nicholas, intelligent, introspective, and burdened with unnecessary worries, has never had what he considers a real home. When his father, a talented actor now married to an actress with a daughter of her own, inherits an old house on the Thames outside London, Roger hopes they'll put down roots and become a proper family. But the house comes equipped with a restless, heart-broken ghost of an Elizabethan actor—'Poor Tom' Garland—and his tragedy reaches out to subtly influence the lives of the Nicholas family. Roger hears, sees, and then enters 16th-Century London where betrayal and plague have nearly finished Garland. Only with great perseverance does Roger manage to change the past, in the process changing himself and learning that people rather than places provide security." Sch Library J
"The writing style is nicely honed, the characters and dialogue convincing, and the relationships effective; it is pleasant, too, to encounter a second-marriage family with no adjustment problems." Chicago. Children's Bk Center

The watchers. Atheneum Pubs. 1975 235p illus $6.95 (5 and up) **Fic**

1 West Virginia—Fiction 2 Fantastic fiction
ISBN 0-689-50030-0
LC 75-8582

"A Margaret K. McElderry book"
"When thirteen-year-old Ray can't get along with his stepmother, he is sent off to his mother's kinfolk in a remote section of southern West Virginia. As he settles in with his mysterious kin, Ray is drawn into an ancient struggle with a nameless evil represented by a stone snake in an old coal mine. This is the old Pendragon legend deftly transported to the West Virginia hills and interpreted as a struggle against an evil, insatiable hunger. Ms. Curry relates this hunger to the destruction of the land." Children's Bk Rev Serv
"This is a two-level story: the family fights against the depredation of the land and, like their ancestral Watchers, who are incorporated as a fantasy element, they fight as guardians of a sacred site. The two themes are adroitly meshed, and the author has created a colorful set of characters, a well-constructed story, and a vivid setting." Chicago. Children's Bk Center

Dahl, Roald

James and the giant peach; a children's story; illus. by Nancy Ekholm Burkert. Knopf 1961 118p illus $6.95, lib. bdg. $6.99 (4-6) **Fic**

1 Peach—Fiction
ISBN 0-394-81282-4; 0-394-91282-9
LC 61-8127

After the death of his parents, little James is forced to live with Aunt Sponge and Aunt Spike, two cruel old harpies. A magic potion causes the growing of a giant-sized peach on a puny peach tree. James sneaks inside the peach and finds a new world of insects. With his new family, James heads for many adventures
"A 'juicy' fantasy, 'dripping' with humor and imagination." Commonweal

Dalgliesh, Alice

The bears on Hemlock Mountain; illus. by Helen Sewell. Scribner 1952 unp illus lib. bdg. $7.95 (1-4) **Fic**

1 Bears—Fiction
ISBN 0-684-12654-0
LC 52-11023

"This is the story of a little boy sent by his mother to borrow an iron pot from an aunt who lived on the other side of Hemlock Mountain—really only a hill. Jonathan's mother did not believe that there were bears on Hemlock Mountain but Jonathan did. . . . The two-color, somewhat stylized illustrations seem right for the story." Booklist
"Jonathan's adventure is a tall tale passed down in Pennsylvania, which might have happened to a pioneer boy almost anywhere. Full of suspense and humor, it will make good reading aloud." NY Her Trib Bks

The courage of Sarah Noble; illus. by Leonard Weisgard. Scribner 1954 52p illus lib. bdg. $6.95 (2-4) **Fic**

1 Frontier and pioneer life—Fiction 2 Indians of North America—Fiction 3 Connecticut—Fiction
ISBN 0-684-12795-4
LC 54-5922

"Here is a remarkable book for younger readers —a true pioneer adventure, written for easy reading but without any sacrifice of literary quality or depth of feeling. . . . Sarah, though only eight, was her father's companion on a grueling and dangerous journey to build a new home in the Connecticut wilderness of 1707, and she succeeded well in following her mother's advice to 'keep up your courage, Sarah Noble.' When, however, the log house was finished and her father was leaving her with the Indians while he went back alone to get the rest of the family, Sarah, who had been very brave, confessed that she had lost her courage. To this her father made the discerning and heartening reply, 'To be afraid, and to be brave is the best courage of all.' " Horn Bk
"Based on a true incident in Connecticut history —the founding of New Milford—this story is one to be long remembered for its beautiful simplicity and dignity. Leonard Weisgard's pictures add just the right sense of background." NY Times Bk Rev

Danziger, Paula

The cat ate my gymsuit. Delacorte Press 1974 147p $6.95, lib. bdg. $6.46 (5 and up) **Fic**

1 School stories 2 Teachers—Fiction
ISBN 0-440-01612-6; 0-440-01696-7
LC 74-8898

Marcy Lewis is bored by school and tyrannized by her father. With the help of an unconventional teacher, she conquers many of her feelings of insecurity and, in turn, rallies the student body in support of the teacher who was fired because of her behavior

The pistachio prescription; novel. Delacorte Press 1978 154p $6.95 (5 and up) **Fic**

1 Family life—Fiction 2 School stories
ISBN 0-440-06936-X
LC 77-86330

"Thirteen-year-old Cassie, who tells the story, has asthma, is a hypochondriac, and eats pistachio nuts compulsively when anything goes wrong. And almost everything does, she thinks. But Cassie's elected president of the freshman class, she acquires Bernie, she has the stalwart support of her friend Vickie, who won't let Cassie retreat into coddling fears, and she manages to cope with a nagging mother, parental quarrels, and a hostile, competitive sister. When Mom and Dad separate, the sisters unite protectively against Mom's sniping; Cassie begins to understand that the situation is irrevocable, that she can live through the years before she is able to leave home, and that she can even abjure pistachio nuts. Not unusual in theme, this is unusually well done: the characterization and dialogue are strong, the relationships depicted with perception, and the writing style vigorous." Chicago. Children's Bk Center

Daringer, Helen F.

Adopted Jane; illus. by Kate Seredy. Harcourt 1947 225p illus pa $1.25 (4-6) **Fic**

1 Orphans—Fiction
ISBN 0-15-602950-2
LC 47-30260

Jane was a plain little girl with beautiful eyes and a large fund of integrity. Ever since she could remember Jane had lived in an orphanage, and she longed for a family and a dog of her own. There came a summer when she had the blissful experience of having two visits to real homes, and at the end she has acquired both a home and a dog. The time of the story is about 1900
"This is a refreshing story, told skillfully and with a flair for creating amusing and interesting people. Kate Seredy's drawings make the period around 1900. But wherever and whenever Jane lived, she would be well worth knowing." Sat Rev

Davies, Andrew

Conrad's war. Crown [1980 c1978] 120p $7.95 (5 and up) **Fic**

1 War—Fiction 2 Fantasy—Fiction
ISBN 0-517-54007-X
LC 79-28289

First published 1978 in England
"The story of a Mittyish boy, Conrad Pike. Furious at his father, Great Writer of soppy plays about kissing, Conrad dreams of heroic themes:

Davies, Andrew—Continued

how he would have whipped the Nazis single-handedly, back during World War II. Then the war 'leaks' into his quiet English suburb, via Conrad's fantasies. At times he's driving an invincible tank straight at a group of enemy soldiers. Then he's piloting a mighty Lancaster over bombing targets in Germany. But when our hero suddenly finds he's Kolonel Konrad von Pikehofen, with orders to machine-gun a French ambulance, and later is switched into a British POW, Conrad begins to fall out of love with war." Pub W

"Skillfully the author winds down the story and finishes it off with a superb ending. The writing is terse and pointed, the conversations witty and unrestrained, and the fantasy artlessly woven into the fabric of the tale." Horn Bk

Davis, Burke

Mr Lincoln's whiskers; illus. by Douglas Gorsline. Coward, McCann & Geoghegan [1979 c1978] 33p illus $6.95 (4-6) **Fic**

1 Lincoln, Abraham, President U.S.—Fiction
ISBN 0-698-20455-7 LC 77-29208

"On October 15, 1860, 12-year-old Grace Bedell wrote a letter to Presidential candidate Abraham Lincoln suggesting that if Mr. Lincoln were to grow whiskers, she might be able to get all of her brothers to vote for him in the upcoming election. Grace's now historical suggestion led to Lincoln's growing his famous beard and serves as the premise for this fictional glimpse at Lincoln the man—his background, his character, his family, his sense of humor." Sch Library J

"The blend of history and storytelling is tight, with an author's note offering additional background, plus a reprint of the full text of Bedell's and Lincoln's letters. Gorsline's precise drawings of Lincoln fit perfectly. They're softly realistic, right in line with the text." Booklist

De Angeli, Marguerite

The door in the wall. Doubleday [1964 c1949] 120p illus $6.95, lib. bdg. $7.90, pa $1.95 (4-6) **Fic**

1 Physically handicapped children — Fiction 2 Great Britain—History—Plantagenets, 1154-1399 —Fiction
ISBN 0-385-07283-X; 0-385-05743-1; 0-385-07909-5 LC 64-7025

Awarded the Newbery Medal, 1950
First published 1949

"Thirteenth-century England with its castles and churches and traveling folk is evident in the adventures of Robin, crippled son in a noble family. Wartime conditions and the great London plague combine to take Robin away from his castle home. He meets Brother Luke who teaches him wood carving; he falls in with the minstrel, John-in-the-Wynd, who journeys with him from London through Oxford and farther north to rejoin his parents and serve his King." Horn Bk

"An enthralling and inspiring tale of triumph over handicap. [The author-artist's] unusually beautiful illustrations, full of authentic detail, combine with the text to make life in England during the Middle Ages come alive." NY Times Bk Rev

Degens, T.

Transport 7-41-R. Viking 1974 171p $7.95 (6 and up) **Fic**

1 World War, 1939-1945—Fiction 2 Refugees—Fiction
ISBN 0-670-72429-7 LC 74-10930

A thirteen-year-old girl describes her trip to Cologne from the Russian sector of occupied Germany as she travels aboard a refugee transport. Her relationships with other passengers in the boxcar bring her into contact with a wide range of human behavior, from intense greed and pettiness to loyalty and staunch idealism

"A powerful and unforgettable novel, taut and dramatic, which succeeds both as a suspense-filled adventure tale and as an evocative study of the psychological and emotional effects of war on its most innocent victims—children." Horn Bk

DeJong, Meindert

The house of sixty fathers; pictures by Maurice Sendak. Harper 1956 189p illus lib. bdg. $8.79 (4-6) **Fic**

1 China—Fiction 2 World War, 1939-1945—Fiction
ISBN 0-06-021481-3 LC 56-8148

"A vividly realistic story of China during the early days of the Japanese invasion. Tien Pao, a small Chinese boy, and his family fled inland on a sampan when the Japanese attacked their coastal village, but Tien Pao was separated from his parents during a storm and swept back down the river on the sampan. . . . Once again the author has shown his ability to paint starkly realistic word pictures that give the reader the full impact of the terror, pain, hunger and finally the joy that Tien Pao knew during his search for his family." Chicago. Children's Bk Center

"The hero is a very engaging character, the kind who makes young readers feel sure that they, too, would be brave and clever if left to their own devices in a situation like this." Pub W

Journey from Peppermint Street; pictures by Emily Arnold McCully. Harper 1968 242p illus $7.95, pa $2.95 (4-6) **Fic**

1 Netherlands—Fiction
ISBN 0-06-021488-0; 0-06-0440011-5 LC 68-27870

"Siebren's first journey away from his Dutch village by the sea begins with small incidents, exciting only for a boy who has had to spend all his free time at home caring for a troublesome baby brother. By the end of three days, however, he has caught a gigantic pike in the marsh, survived a tornado, and discovered a secret passageway in the ancient monastery where his aunt lives. Through these adventures Siebren has also learned to love and understand his gruff old grandfather, his deaf-and-dumb uncle, and his courageous little aunt." Booklist

It is "beautifully written, with vivid characterization. . . . The relationships between Siebren and the members of his family are particularly good; they have a universality that is compelling." Chicago. Children's Bk Center

The wheel on the school; pictures by Maurice Sendak. Harper 1954 298p illus $10, lib. bdg. $9.89, pa $2.95 (4-6) **Fic**

1 Storks—Fiction 2 School stories 3 Netherlands—Fiction
ISBN 0-06-021585-2; 0-06-021586-0; 0-06-44021-2 LC 54-8945

Awarded the Newbery Medal, 1955

"Long ago, there had been storks on the roofs of the Dutch village of Shora, but when the storm came and the great waves sent salt spray flying over the dikes, the storks had gone away and never returned. The six school children of Shora are determined that the storks shall come back. Their enthusiasm arouses the whole village, and the story of the coming of the storks is a tale of faith and ingenuity, and even of physical endurance and courage when the great storms and crashing seas threaten their plans." Ontario Library Rev

"This unusual tale is told with much lively, colloquial children's talk, and plenty of humor. . . . Few writers of today offer this sort of realism to the young, with its insight that stimulates imagination and its clear beauty, like that of a Vermeer painting." NY Her Trib Bks

"It is difficult to imagine drawings more in time with the text than these unforgettable ones by Maurice Sendak." NY Times Bk Rev

Delton, Judy

Kitty in the middle; illus. by Charles Robinson. Houghton 1979 135p illus $6.95 (2-5) **Fic**

1 Catholics in the U.S.—Fiction 2 Friendship—Fiction 3 School stories
ISBN 0-395-28004-4 LC 78-31434

"Delton, in her first longer juvenile work, has gone beyond remembering her childhood; she seems to have crawled inside the skin of a nine-year-old girl, taking all her writing skills with her. Beside the alternately funny and thought-provoking episodes, the book will be remembered for Kitty and her friends . . . who attend Saint Anthony's Parochial School in St. Paul in 1942. For the most part, the details of being nine and in a Catholic school are timeless. No less amusing, though, are such scenes as Eileen's leading the trio to attend the wedding and feast of an unknown couple, or the three girls' meeting the resident of the neighborhood haunted house. Without doubt, there is a lasting place for such honest, deftly done work." Booklist

Followed by: Kitty in the summer $6.95 (ISBN 0-395-29456-8; LC 80-17665)

Dickens, Charles

A Christmas carol in prose (4 and up) **Fic**

1 Christmas—Fiction 2 Ghosts—Fiction 3 Great Britain—Fiction

Some editions are:
Lippincott $8.95 Illustrated by Arthur Rackham. Has title: A Christmas carol (ISBN 0-397-00033-2; LC 52-13330)
Macmillan Pub. Co. (The Macmillan classics) $3.95 Illustrated by John Groth. Afterword by Clifton Fadiman (ISBN 0-02-730300-4; LC 63-14837)
St Martins $9.95 With illustrations by Peter Fluck and Roger Law; photographed by John Lawrence Jones (ISBN 0-312-13403-7; LC 79-65390)
Written in 1843
"This Christmas story of nineteenth century England has delighted young and old for generations. In it, a miser, Scrooge, through a series of dreams, finds the true Christmas spirit. . . . The story ends with the much-quoted cry of Tiny Tim, the crippled son of Bob Cratchit, whom Scrooge now aids: 'God bless us, every one!'" Haydn. Thesaurus of Bk Digests
"There is perhaps no story in English literature better known . . . or one that carries a more potent appeal to the Christmas sentiment." Spring'd Republican

The magic fishbone (3-5) **Fic**

1 Fairy tales

Some editions are:
Harvey House lib. bdg. $5.29 Illustrated by Faith Jaques (ISBN 0-08178-4612-3; LC 69-17741)
Vanguard $5.95 Illustrated by Louis Slobodkin (ISBN 0-8149-0296-0; LC 53-10806)
Taken from: A holiday romance, first published 1868
"A practical little princess and her peppery fairy godmother solve the problems of the royal family with nonsensical charm." Cincinnati
"This little masterpiece bubbles with fun and humor and is especially recommended for the storyteller." Library J

Dickinson, Peter

Annerton Pit. Little 1977 175p $6.95 (6 and up) **Fic**

1 Ghosts—Fiction 2 Blind—Fiction 3 Great Britain—Fiction
ISBN 0-316-18430-6 LC 77-9885

"An Atlantic Monthly Press book"
"It is blind, thirteen-year-old Jake who manages to free his elder brother, his ghost-hunting grandfather, and himself from haunted Annerton Pit and the revolutionaries who hold them prisoners." LC Children's Bks 1977
"A powerful, wholly original novel is constructed with enormous skill and written with rare perception and intuition. . . . The story of the [boys] incarceration and of their attempts to escape from the chill, slimy, terrifying underground labyrinth, the horror of the deliberate, detailed writing approaches that of Poe. But there are also intimations of Dostoevsky for the greatest impact of the novel is psychological. . . . [Jake] is the real hero of the book." Horn Bk

The gift. Little [1974 c1973] 188p $6.95 (5 and up) **Fic**

1 Clairvoyance—Fiction
ISBN 0-316-18427-6 LC 73-21980

"An Atlantic Monthly Press book"
"Davy Price has inherited The Gift of clairvoyance from a legendary Welsh ancestor. Sometimes entertaining (at church Davy tunes into the sex fantasies of parishioners) and sometimes embarrassing (he unintentionally eavesdrops on the millionaire pipedreams of his down-and-out father), the gift becomes a terrifying burden when Davy's mind is flooded with the mad imaginings of a half-wit [named Wolf] out to destroy the Prices. From Wolf's distorted visions . . . Davy discovers and helps foil a robbery scheme involving his father." Library J
"The author has avoided sensationalism by consistently retaining the perspective of his adolescent protagonist both in dialogue and in narration. Superb touches of humor, contrasting sharply with the gravity of the situations, give depth to the characterizations and balance to the structure without destroying the feeling of thrill and suspense." Horn Bk

Dicks, Terrance

The Baker Street Irregulars in the case of the missing masterpiece. Elsevier/Nelson Bks. [1979 c1978] 141p $6.95 (5 and up) **Fic**

1 Mystery and detective stories
ISBN 0-525-6656-7 LC 79-18861

First published 1978 in England with title: The case of the missing masterpiece
"It's because of a challenge from a hostile bully that Dan, a Conan Doyle fan, announces that he will solve the mystery of a stolen painting by the time school resumes after a half-term holiday. With the help of three friends, all of whom expose themselves to danger, he and they find clues that lead Dan to deduce the villain, understand how the crime took place, and prevent a murder." Chicago. Children's Bk Center
"While the mystery itself is not overly original, the abundance of action, the determination of Dan and his friends, and the fast plotting will leave young readers hoping for a sequel." Sch Library J

Dixon, Paige

Lion on the mountain; illus. by J. H. Breslow. Atheneum Pubs. 1972 118p illus $6.95 (5 and up) **Fic**

1 Hunting—Fiction
ISBN 0-689-30050-6 LC 72-75268

Animal-loving Jamie and his father, who hunt only for the meat they need, become unwilling guides for a Hemingway-inspired city hunter who kills for the pleasure of killing and to obtain trophies. When he is asked to track a rare mountain lion to obtain photographs, Jamie is almost certain that the man intends to kill it
"A fast-paced outdoor adventure which explores man's relationship with nature." Minnesota

Doty, Jean Slaughter

The crumb. Greenwillow Bks. 1976 122p lib. bdg. $6.48 (6 and up) **Fic**

1 Ponies—Fiction
ISBN 0-688-84035-3 LC 75-33648

"Cindy, who works at a stable and owns her own pony (The Crumb), dreams of being an accomplished rider. When given the opportunity to compete in a show, Cindy and The Crumb walk away with a trophy and a blue ribbon for a big jumping class. However, she later discovers that her pony has been accidentally electrocuted in another horse's stall. . . . Cindy finally pieces together what has happened in this well-written story that leaves the heroine still enthusiastic about horses but much wiser to the ins and outs of riding competitions." Sch Library J

Drury, Roger W.

The champion of Merrimack County; illus. by Fritz Wegner. Little 1976 198p illus $7.95 (4-6) **Fic**

1 Mice—Fiction
ISBN 0-316-19349-6 LC 76-6453

"Janet Berryfield and her mother discover O Crispin the mouse on his racing bicycle speeding around the rim of Mr. Berryfield's prized antique bathtub. They don't know it but the mouse is practicing to be 'The Champion of Merrimack County'—that is until a carelessly placed piece of soap spells disaster in the form of one ruined bathtub, one smashed up bicycle, and one dislocated mouse tail. Chapters alternate between Mrs. Berryfield's hilarious efforts at the hospital to get O Crispin X-rayed and Janet's lamer attempts to get the mouse's bicycle fixed before Mr Berryfield, the 'ogre,' comes home with his fierce band of pet store cats and cheese-baited mousetraps. The light and zany plot is nicely tied together, the characters are adequately developed, and the fantastic bike racing mouse is a very intriguing little fellow." Sch Library J

Du Bois, William Pène

The alligator case; story and pictures by William Pène Du Bois. Harper 1965 63p illus lib. bdg. $8.79 (3-5) **Fic**

1 Circus—Fiction 2 Mystery and detective stories
ISBN 0-06-021746-4 LC 65-11446

"This is the tallish tale of three dastardly thieves who use a small-town circus as cover for their crime. Using an amazing series of disguises, the boy detective tenaciously follows clues, suspecting

Du Bois, William P.—*Continued*

that the criminals have used alligator costumes to merge with those of the performers. (The cashier, of course, is a real alligator.) The author has immense fun with plot and word-plays." Chicago. Children's Bk Center

The twenty-one balloons; written and illus. by William Pène Du Bois. Viking 1947 179p illus $8.95 (5 and up)   **Fic**

1 Balloons—Fiction
ISBN 0-670-73441-1   LC 47-2533

Awarded the Newbery Medal, 1948
"Professor Sherman set off on a flight across the Pacific in a giant balloon, but three weeks later the headlines read 'Professor Sherman in wrong ocean with too many balloons.' This book is concerned with the professor's explanation of this phenomenon. His account of his one stopover on the island of Krakatoa which blew up with barely a minute to spare to allow time for his escape, is the highlight of this hilarious narrative." Ontario Library Rev
"There is a twinkling humor underneath every word of the story that leaves the reader wondering. . . . The drawings are in keeping with the period and show great strength and originality. An exciting book that will be claimed by every member of the family." Sat Rev

Dunlop, Eileen

Elizabeth, Elizabeth; illus. by Peter Farmer. Holt [1977 c1975] 185p illus $6.95 (6 and up)   **Fic**

1 Space and time—Fiction   2 Scotland—Fiction 3 Fantastic fiction
ISBN 0-03-019311-7   LC 76-46758

First published 1975 in England with title: Robinsheugh
"Elizabeth Martin must spend the summer in Scotland with her aunt Kate, an Oxford scholar who is absorbed in researching the Melville family at their estate Robinsheugh. Her relationship with her preoccupied aunt deteriorating, Elizabeth, resentful and bewildered, finds an old hand mirror with the power to transport her to 17th Century Robinsheugh. She begins spending more and more time in the past where she is accepted by the Melville family as their daughter Elizabeth and becomes increasingly more fascinated by and devoted to her brother Robin. What begins as an adventure within her control gradually turns into an obsessive nightmare, in which Robin becomes an evil force and her own identity almost disappears. Action is carefully paced and tension skillfully built in this well-crafted tale of suspense." Sch Library J

Fox farm. Holt [1979 c1978] 149p illus $7.95 (5 and up)   **Fic**

1 Foster home care—Fiction   2 Dogs—Fiction 3 Scotland—Fiction
ISBN 0-03-049051-0   LC 78-14091

First published 1978 in England
"Living on a farm in the Scottish Lowlands, Adam is a foster child in a warm and welcoming household. Motherless and abandoned by his father, the boy is aloof, indifferent, and suspicious. . . . He is especially frustrating to Richard, a loyal, generous, and tolerant boy, who longs for Adam to accept him as a brother and as a friend. When Richard's father is forced to shoot a dangerous marauding fox, Adam is furious . . . and finding what he assumes to be the vixen's starving cub, he lavishes his pent-up affection on the tiny animal and determines to keep it as a secret pet. To his astonishment Richard offers to cooperate, and the two boys share the heavy responsibility for the clandestine care of Foxy—whose real identity comes as a complete surprise." Horn Bk
"The adventures of the two lads trying to keep a secret sustain a high level of suspense. The denouement falls flat though, when Foxy turns out to be an abandoned dog. Despite the weak ending, the tale is engagingly told and the characterizations well-done." Sch Library J

Eager, Edward

Half magic; drawings by N. M. Bodecker. Harcourt 1954 217p illus $6.95, pa $2.95 (4-6)   **Fic**

ISBN 0-15-233078-X; 0-15-637990-2   LC 54-5153

"Three sisters, a brother and a widowed mother made up the family. Jane, the eldest, found a magic charm [an ancient coin] which granted half of any

wish; after finding that out, and barring accidents, the children wished for twice as much as they wanted. The charm made for a week of adventures including Katharine's defeat of Sir Launcelot in a thoroughly unfair tourney and ending with mother's acquisition of a new husband amid a burst of what Mark called 'love blah.'" NY Times Bk Rev
"The chief effect of such a book is humor, arising from the ridiculous yet logical situations. . . . [It is] a book whose total contribution is one of fun and relaxation." Sat Rev

Several other books in this series are also available from Harcourt:
Knight's castle $6.75, pa $1.65 (ISBN 0-15-243102-0; LC 56-5234)
Magic by the lake $7.95 (ISBN 0-15-250441-9; LC 57-5267)
Magic or not? pa $1.95 (ISBN 0-15-655121-7; LC 78-71152)
Seven day magic $5.95 (ISBN 0-15-272919-4; LC 62-17040)

Eckert, Allan W.

Incident at Hawk's Hill; with illus. by John Schoenherr. Little 1971 137p illus $7.95 (6 and up)   **Fic**

1 Badgers—Fiction   2 Saskatchewan—Fiction
ISBN 0-316-20866-3   LC 77-143718

This account of an actual incident in Saskatchewan at the turn of the century tells of six-year-old Ben Macdonald, more attuned to animals than to people, who gets lost on the prairie and is nurtured by a female badger for two months before being found. Although a strange bond continues between the boy and the badger, the parents' understanding of their son and his communication with them improve as a result of the bizarre experience
"A really beautiful, simple book. . . . The descriptions of life in the wild are magnificent, the dignity of the animal against the greed and foolishness of man is illuminating. It is simply a very deeply moving, well written book which readers of every age will appreciate." Jr Bookshelf

Edmonds, Walter D.

Bert Breen's barn. Little 1975 270p illus $8.95 (6 and up)   **Fic**

1 Farm life—Fiction   2 New York (State)—Fiction
ISBN 0-316-21166-4   LC 75-2157

"The entire plot of this lengthy novel revolves around young Tom Dolan's acquisition of a sturdy barn and the treasure rumored to be hidden in it. Tom, his mother, and his two sisters live in turn-of-the-century upstate New York, and are very poor, a condition which Tom resolutely plans to change, beginning with buying and moving the barn on the old Breen place." Children's Bk Rev Serv
"This is a long, quiet story with strong characters and a well-knit plot, its strength lying in the felicity of details, the full picture it gives of a bygone way of life. . . . There's no preaching of virtue here, but the story is permeated with the homely virtues of industry and honesty, although Edmonds invests them with neither sentimentality nor glamor. Sedate, but a good, solid read." Chicago. Children's Bk Center

The matchlock gun; illus. by Paul Lantz. Dodd 1941 50p illus lib. bdg. $5.95 (4-6)   **Fic**

1 New York (State)—Fiction   2 U.S.—History—French and Indian War, 1755-1763—Fiction
ISBN 0-396-06369-1   LC 41-17547

Awarded the Newbery Medal, 1942
"New York State during the French and Indian War is the setting for this story of a boy's courage and resourcefulness. In his father's absence, ten-year-old Edward Alstine helps his mother fight off an Indian attack by firing an old Spanish musket." Hodges. Bks for Elem Sch Libraries
"As literature, this story for ten-year-olds ranks with anything Mr. Edmonds has written for adults. The words are within their vocabulary—save for a few Dutch phrases they will find interesting—and though the tale is one of suspense, mounting terror and a climax of heroism what happens is no more than many a ten-year-old in our early history went through." NY Her Trib Bks
"The dramatic telling of a tragic incident in the life of a colonial family . . . is heightened by lithographs of unusual quality. An authentic story." NY Pub Library

Ellis, Mel

The wild horse killers. Holt 1976 191p $6.95 (6 and up) **Fic**

1 Horses—Fiction 2 Montana—Fiction
ISBN 0-03-014866-9 LC 75-22156

"Although this book is fiction, it's rooted in realities. Sandra Bradford lives on a ranch with her father. He is determined that her favorite stallion, Rimrock Red, shall be gelded to make him manageable. But Red escapes the vet and careens off, to join a herd of wild horses. Following the horse, Sandra witnesses the slaughter of the glorious, free creatures. They are hunted down by men greedy for profits to be collected when the horses are sold to pet-food companies, etc. The story of the girl's fight for the lives of the endangered horses is convincing and suspenseful." Pub W

Embry, Margaret

The blue-nosed witch; pictures by Carl Rose. Holiday House 1956 [c1955] 45p illus $6.95 (1-4) **Fic**

1 Witches—Fiction 2 Halloween—Fiction
ISBN 0-8234-0011-5 LC 56-14143

Blanche, a real witch, though a young one, had a nose that glowed a marvelous blue in the dark. One Halloween, cruising on her broom with black cat, Brockett, she found a band of children and joined them on their trick-or-treat forage

Engdahl, Sylvia Louise

Enchantress from the stars; drawings by Rodney Shackell. Atheneum Pubs. 1970 275p illus lib. bdg. $8.69, pa 95¢ (6 and up) **Fic**

1 Science fiction
ISBN 0-689-20508-2; 0-689-70309-0 LC 74-98609

This science fiction story "examines the relationship between peoples of three different levels of cultural advancement. Action takes place on the planet Andrecia whose medieval culture is in danger of being destroyed by invading colonizers with an advanced technology but no regard for the natives or their civilization. Elana, narrator of the story, her father, and her betrothed, members of a highly advanced society with command of psychic powers as well as technology, are sent to Andrecia to help the natives repel the invaders but must do so without revealing their true identity or interfering with the natural cultural progression of either the Andrecians or the invaders." Booklist

"Emphasis is on the intricate pattern of events rather than on characterization, and readers will find fascinating symbolism—and philosophical parallels to what they may have observed or thought. The book is completely absorbing and should have a wider appeal than much science fiction." Horn Bk

Followed by: The far side of evil. Atheneum Pubs. lib. bdg $6.50, pa 95¢ (ISBN 0-689-20649-6; 0-689-70357-0; LC 77-134808)

This star shall abide; drawings by Richard Cuffari. Atheneum Pubs. 1972 247p front $6.95, pa $2.50 (6 and up) **Fic**

1 Science fiction
ISBN 0-689-30026-3; 0-689-70458-5 LC 79-175553

"Set on a distant planet settled many years earlier by the only survivors of a doomed solar system this is the story of Noren, an intelligent young villager who resents the religious taboos that keep knowledge from him. The devout rural civilization is ruled by Scholars, who live in the Inner City, which is closed to Villagers, and the Technicians who serve the Scholars. Heretical in outlook and actions Noren makes his way to the gates of the Inner City where he is captured, taken inside, and given a chance to recant and join the ranks of the Scholars. Individual characters and the society as a whole are credibly developed and suspense is well maintained in an above average science fiction tale." Booklist

Followed by: Beyond the Tomorrow Mountains, o.p. 1981

Enright, Elizabeth

Gone-Away Lake; illus. by Beth and Joe Krush. Harcourt 1957 192p illus pa $1.95 (4-6) **Fic**

ISBN 0-15-636460-3 LC 57-5172

A novel of "childlike summer fun; the exploring of unfamiliar woods and swampland—Lake Tarrigo had disappeared and become a swamp called Gone-Away; the establishing of a club and a clubhouse; little girls dressing up in old costumes and little boys planning space travel. The eleven- and twelve-year-old cousins, Portia and Julian, are children one would like to meet. Orange-haired 'Jule' is on the way to becoming an entomologist; 'Porsh,' whose new tooth braces, he says, make her look 'just like the front of a Buick,' is with him in every venture. Their exploits are forwarded by helpful Mrs. Minnie Cheever and her brother, still living in turn-of-the-century style in derelict summer homes beside the varnished lake. Excellent writing, clear in setting of scene and details of nature, and strong in appeal for children." Horn Bk

Followed by: Return to Gone-Away Lake. Harcourt pa $1.15 (ISBN 0-15-676900-X; LC 61-6113)

Thimble summer; written and illus. by Elizabeth Enright. Rinehart 1938 124p illus lib. bdg. $5.95 (4-6) **Fic**

1 Farm life—Fiction 2 Wisconsin—Fiction
ISBN 0-03-015686-8 LC 38-27586

"Awarded the Newbery Medal, 1939

A story about life on a Wisconsin farm. When "Garnet finds a silver thimble near the river just before a much needed rain, she thinks the thimble is an omen of a happy summer. Exciting things do happen: Garnet and a friend are accidentally locked in at the library; she hitchhikes to a town eighteen miles away; and she is trapped on a ferris wheel at the moment she is supposed to be showing her pig at the fair." Rdng Ladders

"There is swift keen characterization, natural conversation, and almost inspired selection of incident and detail, and rare humor and skill in the telling. Bright full-page illustrations in color, line drawings and lovely end papers will make it attractive to the girls from nine to twelve who will find Garnet Linden and her experiences absorbing." Library J

Erickson, Russell E.

A toad for Tuesday; pictures by Lawrence Di Fiori. Lothrop 1974 63p illus lib. bdg. $6.48 (2-4) **Fic**

1 Toads—Fiction 2 Owls—Fiction 3 Mice—Fiction 4 Friendship—Fiction
ISBN 0-688-51569-X LC 73-19900

"Warton and Morton, toad brothers, are enjoying Morton's delicious beetle brittle and Warton decides to take some to an elderly aunt despite the wintry weather. He makes skis and sets off, stopping to rescue a mouse who tells him that there is a dangerous owl in the wood. And Warton is indeed caught by the owl, who says he will save this tasty morsel until Tuesday, his birthday. By that time Warton has so endeared himself to the owl by his friendly ways that plans have changed—but Warton doesn't know it. He escapes with the help of a troop of skiing mice, relatives of the one he'd saved, and they go off to safety, but risk their lives to rescue the owl from a fox." Chicago. Children's Bk Center

The book "stresses friendship, caring for and helping others without motivational self-gain. . . . Real feelings are expressed in this story. Fine illustrations." Children's Bk Rev Serv

Some other books about Warton and Morton are also available from Lothrop:

Warton and Morton $6.25, lib. bdg. $6 (ISBN 0-688-41771-X; 0-688-51771-4; LC 76-9017)

Warton and the king of the skies $6.95, lib. bdg. $6.67 (ISBN 0-688-41852-X; 0-688-51852-4; LC 78-4919)

Warton and the traders $6.50, lib. bdg. $6.24 (ISBN 0-688-41886-4; 0-688-51886-9; LC 78-25689)

Warton's Christmas Eve adventure lib. bdg. $6.96 (ISBN 0-688-51822-2; LC 77-4847)

Erwin, Betty K.

Go to the room of the eyes; illus. by Irene Burns. Little 1969 180p illus $6.95 (4-6) **Fic**

1 Seattle—Fiction 2 Mystery and detective stories
ISBN 0-316-24946-7 LC 71-77446

The Evans family, with their six children "move into an old mansion on Seattle's Capitol Hill and immediately become involved in tracking down clues in a treasure hunt left by children who lived in the house 30 years before." Booklist

The book "includes themes other than the mystery (an interracial friendship, adjustment to a new school) and . . . the writing style is adequate, with some humor and with realistic family relationships." Chicago. Children's Bk Center

Estes, Eleanor

Ginger Pye. Harcourt 1951 250p illus $6.95, pa $2.95 (4-6)   **Fic**

1 Dogs—Fiction
ISBN 0-15-237374-8; 0-15-634750-4   LC 44-8963

Awarded the Newbery Medal, 1952

The Pyes lived in the little New England town of Cranbury. There was Mr. Pye, a famous ornithologist, his pretty young wife, their two children Jerry and Rachel, and Gracie the cat. Later there was the dog Ginger. The story is about the loss of Ginger, and his return to his beloved family, through the cleverness of Uncle Benny, aged three

"Not many writers can give us the mind and heart of a child as Eleanor Estes can. . . . [She] has illustrated [the book] with her own drawings —vivid, amusing sketches that point up and confirm the atmosphere of the story. It is a book to read and reread." Sat Rev

Followed by: Pinky Pye. Harcourt $7.95, pa $1.75 (ISBN 0-15-262076-1; 0-15-671840-5; LC 58-5708)

The hundred dresses; illus. by Louis Slobodkin. Harcourt 1944 80p illus $6.95, pa $2.50 (4-6)   **Fic**

ISBN 0-15-237374-8; 0-15-642350-2   LC 44-8963

"The 100 dresses are just dream dresses, pictures Wanda Petronski has drawn, but she describes them in self-defense as she appears daily in the same faded blue dress. Not until Wanda, snubbed and unhappy, moves away leaving her pictures at school for an art contest, do her classmates realize their cruelty." Bks for Deaf Children

"Written with great simplicity it reveals, in a measure, the pathos of human relationships and the suffering of those who are different. Mr. Slobodkin's water-colors interpret the mood of the story and fulfill the quality of the text." NY Pub Library

The lost umbrella of Kim Chu; illus. by Jacqueline Ayer. Atheneum Pubs. 1978 85p illus $7.95 (3-5)   **Fic**

1 Chinese Americans—Fiction   2 New York (City) —Fiction
ISBN 0-689-50111-0   LC 78-59156

"A Margaret K. McElderry book"

"Kim forgets her father's umbrella at the library in her New York City neighborhood, Chinatown. At home, a look at her stern grandmother sends the little girl flying back to the library but the umbrella is gone. She has to find it. Inside its bamboo handle is a scroll, honoring Kim's father for the dragon he fashioned to usher in The Year of the Dragon. With her best friend, Mae Lee, Kim embarks on the frantic quest. It culminates in a triumphant retrieval of the precious umbrella, after many wild surprises, on a Staten Island ferry boat." Pub W

"Spirited, sketchy illustrations and an attractive grown-up style layout mark this for young, but good readers." Sch Library J

The Moffats; illus. by Louis Slobodkin. Harcourt 1941 290p illus $6.50, pa $2.25 (4-6)   **Fic**

1 Family life—Fiction
ISBN 0-15-255095-X; 0-15-661850-8   LC 41-51893

"The story of a family, not poverty-stricken but just poor, never strikes a false note: no sentimentality. . . . There are four young Moffats, from five and a half to fifteen, and Mama. Mostly we see things through the eyes of nine-year-old Janey, and her viewpoint is seldom commonplace. . . . The author has succeeded in conveying the large significance of small events is children's lives." Library J

Some other books about the Moffats are also available from Harcourt:

The middle Moffat $8.95, pa $2.95 (ISBN 0-15-253663-9; 0-15-659536-2; LC 42-36272)

Rufus M. $8.95 (ISBN 0-15-269415-3; LC 43-51239)

The witch family; illus. by Edward Ardizzone. Harcourt 1960 186p illus $7.50, pa $1.95 (1-4)   **Fic**

1 Witches—Fiction   2 Halloween—Fiction
ISBN 0-15-298571-9; 0-15-697645-5   LC 60-11250

"The Old Witch, the Little Witch Girl and Witch Baby are all the creations of crayons wielded by Amy and Clarissa, two little girls almost seven who sit drawing at home in Washington. As their imaginations run riot, the witches take on an independent life of their own, and the two groups mix and mingle in a series of adventures that reach a climax on Halloween. Ardizzone's pictures add the perfect illustration to a book full of wonderful fun." Library J

Certain to give pleasure "to children who are not afraid of venturing beyond vocabulary levels, who enjoy play with words, and who like their reality and fantasy mixed; and especially if it is read aloud by adults who are able 'to give themselves up' to the childlike nonsense and fancy of the story." Horn Bk

Ewing, Kathryn

A private matter; illus. by Joan Sandin. Harcourt 1975 88p illus $5.95 (4-6)   **Fic**

1 Parent and child—Fiction
ISBN 0-15-263576-9   LC 74-23673

"Marcy hasn't seen her father since she was little, so when an elderly couple moves next door, she gradually adopts Mr. Endicott as her new father. Suddenly Mrs. Endicott dies, and the lonely Mr. Endicott tells Marcy he is going to return to his hometown. Marcy is deeply hurt but, after he leaves, she realizes how much he must have missed his wife and can accept her mother's pending remarriage and moving to a new house. Marcy, her parents, and the Endicotts are realistic characters with their own strong points and shortcomings; the story develops quickly and naturally to a moving, satisfying conclusion; and, Joan Sandin's appealing illustrations make the characters even more human and likeable." Sch Library J

Farley, Carol

The garden is doing fine; illus. by Lynn Sweat. Atheneum Pubs. 1975 185p illus $7.95 (6 and up)   **Fic**

1 Death—Fiction
ISBN 0-689-30475-7   L C75-9516

"This examines the impact of parental death on a young child. Corrie's father is dying of cancer, which Corrie and her mother refuse to accept. . . . Corrie recalls former happier times and is outraged at the injustice of his suffering. She prays for him and thinks of him often but another part of her is also aware of boys, games, and school activities. Finally, when she can no longer deny the imminence of his death, she is consoled by the realization that his kindness and love will live on through her." Sch Library J

The author shows "skill in evoking a powerful emotional response to the situation and . . . facility in re-creating the dying father's personality through the reminiscences of those who loved him." Horn Bk

Farley, Walter

The Black Stallion; illus. by Keith Ward. Random House 1941 275p illus $3.95 lib. bdg. $5.99, pa $1.95 (4 and up)   **Fic**

1 Horses—Fiction
ISBN 0-394-80601-8; 0-394-90601-2; 0-394-83609-X   LC 41-21882

A boy and a wild black stallion, the only survivors from a shipwreck, live for a time on an uninhabited island, and somehow manage to exist until they are rescued. Back in the United States the boy and a retired jockey tame the horse and race him to the entire satisfaction of all concerned

Some other books about the Black Stallion are also available from Random House:

The Black Stallion and Flame $3.95, lib. bdg. $5.99, pa $1.95 (ISBN 0-394-80605-0; 0-394-90605-5; 0-394-84372-X; LC 60-10029)

The Black Stallion and Satan $3.95, lib. bdg. $5.99, pa $1.95 (ISBN 0-394-80605-0; 0-394-90605-5; 0-394-83914-5; LC 49-6117)

The Black Stallion and the girl $3.95, lib. bdg. $5.99, pa $1.75 (ISBN 0-394-82145-9; 0-394-92145-3; 0-394-83614-6; LC 75-147884)

The Black Stallion challenged! $3.95, lib. bdg. $5.99, pa $1.95 (ISBN 0-394-80617-4; 0-394-90617-9; 0-394-84371-1; LC 64-15094)

The Black Stallion mystery $3.95, lib. bdg. $5.99, pa $1.95 (ISBN 0-394-80613-1; 0-394-90613-6; 0-394-83611-1; LC 57-7527)

The Black Stallion picture book $4.95, lib. bdg. 5.99 (ISBN 0-394-84174-3; 0-394-94174-8; LC 78-20653)

The Black Stallion returns $3.95, lib. bdg. $5.99, pa $1.95 (ISBN 0-394-80602-6; 0-394-90602-0; 0-394-836103; LC 45-8763)

The Black Stallion revolts $3.95, lib. bdg. $5.99, pa $1.95 (ISBN 0-394-80609-3; 0-394-90609-8; 0-394-83613-8; LC 49-6117)

Farley, Walter—*Continued*

The Black Stallion's courage $3.95, lib. bdg. $5.99, pa $1.95 (ISBN 0-394-80612-3; 0-394-90612-8; 0-394-83918-8; LC 56-5471)
The Black Stallion's filly $3.95, lib. bdg. $5.99, pa $1.95 (ISBN 0-394-80608-5; 0-394-90608-X; 0-394-83916-1; LC 52-7216)
The Black Stallion's ghost $3.95, lib. bdg. $5.99, pa $1.95 (ISBN 0-394-80618-2; 0-394-90618-7; 0-394-83919-6; LC 77-81313)
The Black Stallion's sulky colt $3.95, lib. bdg. $5.99, pa $1.95 (ISBN 0-394-80610-7; 0-394-90610-1; 0-394-83917-X; LC 54-7011)
Son of the Black Stallion $3.95, lib. bdg. $5.99, pa $1.95 (ISBN 0-394-80603-4; 0-394-90603-9; 0-394-83612-X; LC 47-3369)

Fenner, Carol

The skates of Uncle Richard; illus. by Ati Forberg. Random House 1978 46p illus $4.95, lib. bdg. $5.99 (2-4) **Fic**

1 Ice skating—Fiction 2 Blacks—Fiction
ISBN 0-394-83553-0; 0-394-93553-5   LC 78-55910

This book "tunes in on the fantasies of nine-year-old Marsha, plump and awkward but yearning to become a champion like the only black figure skater she's ever seen—the one in her head. An actual Christmas gift of her uncle's childhood skates seems to ruin her dream, however; they are ugly and, worse still, don't seem to hold her up. Then her dashing but unpredictable uncle himself appears and Marsha, with some help and some hard work, begins to find her own place on real ice." Booklist

"An unpretentious story that echoes the hopes of many little girls, told and pictured with sensitivity and care." Horn Bk

Field, Rachel

Calico bush; engravings on wood by Allen Lewis. Macmillan Pub. Co. 1931 213p illus $8.95 (4 and up) **Fic**

1 Frontier and pioneer life—Fiction 2 U.S.—History—French and Indian War, 1755-1763—Fiction 3 Maine—Fiction
ISBN 0-02-734620-X   LC 31-32338

This is the story of Marguerite, called Maggie, a brave little French girl 'bound out' to a family of American pioneers in the days of the French and Indian War

"Colonial Maine in its days of first settlement is the background for this story. The hardships of pioneer life and the dangers from hostile Indians make it a very exciting tale of adventure." Wis Library Bul

Hitty: her first hundred years; with illus. by Dorothy P. Lathrop. Macmillan Pub. Co. 1929 207p illus $7.95 (4 and up) **Fic**

1 Dolls—Fiction
ISBN 0-02-734840-7   LC 29-22704

Awarded the Newbery Medal, 1930

"Hitty, a doll of real character carved from a block of mountain ash, writes the story of her eventful life from the security of an antique-shop window which she shares with Theobold, a rather over-bearing cat. Her career, begun in a quiet Maine village, is crowded with adventures and she gives lively doll's-eye glimpses of the widely differing places and people that she encounters during her hundred years, and of the manners and modes of her times. The illustrations by Dorothy P. Lathrop are the happiest extension of the text. Will be enjoyed by both grown-ups and children." Cleveland

It is the author's "careful yet unlabored re-creation of the [1800's] period that adds to the value of the book and heightens the effect of Miss Field's keen characterization." NY Her Trib Bks

Fife, Dale

North of danger; map and decorations by Haakon Saether. Dutton 1978 72p illus lib. bdg. $7.95 (5 and up) **Fic**

1 World War, 1939-1945—Fiction 2 Norway—Fiction
ISBN 0-525-36035-2   LC 77-26199

"A Unicorn book"

"Arne Kristiansen set out by himself to warn his father, a glacialist in Spitsbergen, that the Nazi invaders of Norway were about to take possession of the northern archipelago. The twelve-year-old boy managed to remain in the area when British warships were evacuating the population of the capital city. Armed with supplies and a map, Arne braved the coming winter darkness until he was able to reach and warn his father. Not the least of his concerns was a hermit, a German trapper whom he first mistrusted but who ultimately helped him reach his goal." Horn Bk

"The author shows a respect for people and an openness to understanding and accepting them. 'North of danger' is excellent as a counterpoint to the vast majority of war-related books which cannot recognize any humanity in those on the other side. This story will appeal to reluctant readers as well as enthusiastic ones; it is short and filled with adventure. Middle school readers will find satisfaction in reading about how a twelve-year-old is confronted by a major crisis, and how he handles it." Children's Bk Rev Serv

Who's in charge of Lincoln? Illus. by Paul Galdone. Coward, McCann & Geoghegan 1965 61p illus lib. bdg. $5.59 (2-4) **Fic**

1 Blacks—Fiction 2 Washington, D.C.—Fiction
ISBN 0-698-30406-3   LC 65-13286

"A resourceful little New York boy thwarts some bank robbers, goes by train to Washington, D.C., visits his namesake's Memorial statue, and returns safely, with no one realizing that he has had an extraordinary experience. It happens when his mother goes to the hospital for a new baby and he is left alone despite careful plans. This is a funny, believable story about an engaging Negro child whose security is firmly based on warm family relationships." Moorachian. What is a City?

Some other books about Lincoln are also available from Coward, McCann & Geoghegan

What's the prize, Lincoln? lib. bdg. $5.59 (ISBN 0-698-30396-2; LC 76-152231)
Who goes there, Lincoln? lib. bdg. $5.59 (ISBN 0-698-30565-5; LC 74-83016)
Who'll vote for Lincoln? lib. bdg. $5.59 (ISBN 0-698-30665-1; LC 76-57127)

Finlayson, Ann

Rebecca's war; illus. by Sherry Streeter. Warne 1972 280p illus $5.95 (5 and up) **Fic**

1 U.S.—History—Revolution, 1775-1783—Fiction 2 Philadelphia—Fiction
ISBN 0-7232-6090-7   LC 78-183735

While her father and brothers are fighting the British, fourteen-year-old Rebecca Ransome is left in charge of the family house and her small brother and sister. This story, set in Philadelphia during the American Revolution, tells of Rebecca's resourcefulness in helping the rebel cause in the face of the enemy occupation of the city and even her own house

"While Rebecca at times seems larger than life, her courage is infused with enough humor and recklessness to make her a believable and likeable heroine." Sch Library J

Fisher, Leonard Everett

The death of Evening Star; the diary of a young New England whaler; written and illus. by Leonard Everett Fisher. Doubleday 1972 125p illus $6.95, lib. bdg. $7.90 (5 and up) **Fic**

1 Sea stories 2 Whaling—Fiction
ISBN 0-385-07649-5; 0-385-08631-8   LC 75-164719

New England whaling of the 1840's is observed through the secret diary kept by a young cabin boy throughout the ill-fated voyage of the whaler Evening Star. The boy's story is revealed in this fictionalized account by a narrator who mysteriously acquires the rain-soaked diary on a stormy night in the not-so-distant past

"The whaling jargon is accurate; the handsome black-and-white scratchboard illustrations are detailed and graphic; but the author' research has produced more than a historical documentary. . . . Rather, by judicious use of the story-within-a-story technique, he adds further dimension to his tale by suggesting a sense of the past, the possible influence of supernatural forces, and the conflict between good and evil. . . . An engrossing combination of social history and the occult." Horn Bk

The warlock of Westfall; written and illus. by Leonard Everett Fisher. Doubleday 1974 119p illus lib. bdg. $5.95 (5 and up) **Fic**

1 Witchcraft—Fiction 2 Massachusetts—History—Colonial period, 1600-1775—Fiction
ISBN 0-385-04476-3   LC 73-82625

Fisher, Leonard E.—*Continued*

In seventeenth-century Massachusetts "a senile old man invents a family out of loneliness, and at night he puts markers on their imaginary graves. When some cocky boys spy on him and tell the townspeople, witchcraft hysteria and tragedy result." Chicago

"Somber yet dramatic, the stark black and white illustrations in Fisher's distinctive style are particularly well suited to the taut and brooding atmosphere evoked in this tale of witch-hunting in colonial America. . . . Both the mood of the times and the physical atmosphere are skillfully evoked in a stirring and convincing story." Chicago. Children's Bk Center

Fitzgerald, John D.

The Great Brain; illus. by Mercer Mayer. Dial Press 1967 175p illus $6.95, lib. bdg. $6.46 (4 and up)   **Fic**

1 Utah—Fiction
ISBN 0-8037-3074-8; 0-8037-3076-4   LC 67-22252

"The Great Brain was Tom Dennis ('T.D.') Fitzgerald, age ten, of Adenville, Utah; the time, 1896. . . . This autobiographical yarn is spun by his brother John Dennis ('J.D.'), age seven . . . who can tell stories about himself and his family with enough tall-tale exaggeration to catch the imagination." Horn Bk

Some other books about the Great Brain are also available from Dial Press:
The Great Brain at the academy $6.95, lib. bdg. $6.46 (ISBN 0-8037-3039-X; 0-8037-3040-3; LC 72-712)
The Great Brain does it again $6.95, lib. bdg. $6.46 (ISBN 0-8037-3065-X; 0-8037-3066-8; LC 74-18600)
The Great Brain reforms $6.95, lib. bdg. $6.46 (ISBN 0-8037-3067-5; 0-8037-3068-3; LC 72-7601)
Me and my little brain $6.95, lib. bdg. $6.46 (ISBN 0-8037-5531-7; 0-8037-5532-5; LC 71-153732)
More adventures of the Great Brain $6.95, lib. bdg. $6.46 (ISBN 0-8037-5819-7; 0-8037-5821-9; LC 73-85547)
The return of the Great Brain $5.95, lib. bdg. $5.47 (ISBN 0-8037-7403-6; 0-8037-7413-3; LC 73-15443)

Fitzhugh, Louise

Harriet the spy; written and illus. by Louise Fitzhugh. Harper 1964 298p illus $7.95, lib. bdg. $8.79 (4 and up)   **Fic**

1 School stories
ISBN 0-06-021910-6; 0-06-021911-4   LC 64-19711

"A marvelous and terrifying child, Harriet. An imaginative and intelligent sixth grader, she has two preoccupations: she writes and she spies. Harriet writes honestly and caustically her opinions of her peers and of adults, and she spies in an organized and industrious way. When her classmates find Harriet's notebook, war ensues and Harriet finds she is an outcast. Having just been separated from the one adult with whom she was in rapport, Harriet becomes very upset and is taken to a psychiatrist. His suggestions are sensible, and Harriet, too bright to be anything but bored at home, goes back to school and a more constructive channeling of her rampaging abilities." Chicago. Children's Bk Center

"Children will love everything about the book and probably accept without question the rather too neatly contrived happy ending and the remote, ineffectual parents. Their elders will admire the book's vigor and originality and the essential truth of the children's thoughts and actions." Bk Week

Another book about Harriet is also available from Harper: The long secret $8.95, lib. bdg. $8.79 (ISBN 0-06-021410-4; 0-06-021411-2; LC 65-23370)

Nobody's family is going to change. Farrar, Straus 1974 221p illus $9.95 (5 and up)   **Fic**

1 Family life—Fiction 2 Blacks—Fiction
ISBN 0-374-35539-8   LC 74-19152

This story about a conventional middle class black family focuses on the ambition of eleven-year-old Emma to be a lawyer, and her brother Willie's desire to become a dancer despite strong parental disapproval

"Beneath the surface layer of plot and of characters that suggest stereotypes but take on a life of their own is a probe of the intense, destructive Sheridan family relationships. Emma, from whose viewpoint the story is told, comes to confront her father's distaste and indifference toward her as a person and to perceive her mother's determination to ignore the unpleasant undercurrents in their family. With surprising but believable acumen she figures out that she herself must change . . . must realize that her parents are not going to transform their attitudes. . . . The only shaky ground is the difficulty of a white author's depicting a black family accurately and intimately." Booklist

Flack, Marjorie

Walter the lazy mouse; illus. by Cyndy Szekeres. Doubleday 1963 95p illus $5.95, lib. bdg. $6.90, pa $1.95 (2-4)   **Fic**

1 Mice—Fiction 2 Frogs—Fiction
ISBN 0-385-02772-9; 0-385-03771-6; 0-385-01078-8
                                              LC 62-16500

A reissue of a title first published 1937

Walter, a mouse, was so lazy he never went anywhere on time. His seven brothers and sisters, as well as his father and mother, were accustomed to seeing him so rarely that they moved one day and forgot to tell him. That's when Walter's adventure began. While searching for his family he met three very backward frogs, whom he tried to teach, so that there just wasn't time to be lazy

This is a "whimsical . . . classic. The unforgettable scenes of Walter's ingenious mouse house and games of real live leap frog are captured in [new] illustrations." Growing Up With Bks

Fleischman, Paul

The birthday tree; pictures by Marcia Sewall. Harper 1979 unp illus $6.95, lib. bdg. $6.89 (2-4)   **Fic**

1 Trees—Fiction
ISBN 0-06-021915-7; 0-06-021916-5   LC 78-22155

"After losing three sons to the sea, a sailor and his wife pack their meager belongings and head inland. Soon a son, Jack, is born and they attempt to root him to the land via a seedling planted to celebrate the event. 'The Birthday Tree' and Jack flourish until the boy runs off to sea and is wrecked upon a desert island. . . . The style is fine for independent reading but the imagery would find its due in the hands of a good storyteller. Marcia Sewall's blunt-faced characters and sparse illustrations evoke and rustic spirit of the words. The pencil sketches and subdued backgrounds are simple reinforcements for a well-told tale." Sch Library J

Fleischman, Sid

By the Great Horn Spoon! Illus. by Eric von Schmidt. Little 1963 193p illus $7.95 (4-6)   **Fic**

1 California—Gold discoveries—Fiction
ISBN 0-316-28577-3   LC 63-13459

"An Atlantic Monthly Press book"

"Jack and his aunt's butler, Praiseworthy, stow away on a ship bound for California. Here are their adventures aboard ship and in the Gold Rush of '49." Pub W

"This whimsical situation-adventure promises only fun. . . . Pen-and-ink drawings." Chicago. Sch J

Chancy and the grand rascal; illus. by Eric von Schmidt. Little 1966 179p illus $7.95 (4-6)   **Fic**

1 Frontier and pioneer life—Fiction
ISBN 0-316-28575-7   LC 66-14903

"An Atlantic Monthly Press book"

"A young boy sets out to find his brothers and sisters, separated by the death of their parents in the Civil War, and meets a 'Grand Rascal' who leads him through many adventures in the battle of wits and colorful tall-talking." Bruno. Bks for Sch Libraries, 1968

"This is one of those rare children's books where language and story are one. It is a world of hyperbole and homely detail, an ebullient, frontier, Bunyanesque world, coarse, new and incurably optimistic." Christian Sci Monitor

The ghost in the noonday sun; illus. by Warren Chappell. Little 1965 173p illus $7.95 (4-6)   **Fic**

1 Pirates—Fiction 2 Buried treasure—Fiction
ISBN 0-316-28576-5   LC 65-10794

"An Atlantic Monthly Press book"

"A real pirate story unfolds when twelve-year-old Oliver Finch is shanghaied aboard the 'Bloody Molly' and made to search for buried treasure—all because the villainous captain thinks that a

Fleischman, Sid—*Continued*

boy born at the stroke of midnight ought to have the power to see the ghost of Gentleman Jack dancing on the treasure that fills his grave. Told with humor, color, and plenty of salty language." Wis Library Bul

The ghost on Saturday night; illus. by Eric von Schmidt. Little 1974 57p illus $6.95 (3-5)   **Fic**

1 Robbers and outlaws—Fiction
ISBN 0-316-28583-8   LC 73-14751

"Opie makes a career of guiding folk through dense fog [in a California town] and saves up the coins he earns to buy a saddle; his great-aunt Etta will buy him a horse to go with it when he has done his share of the purchase. So the boy is disappointed when a visitor, Professor Pepper, gives him two tickets to a ghost-raising instead of a nickel. Opie and his aunt go to the performance at which Crookneck John, a long-dead bandit, is supposed to appear. But the Professor and his henchman use the act as a coverup for a bank robbery, a theft that's thwarted by the resourcefulness of our boy, Opie." Pub W

"The short scenario, illustrated with figures as overstated and caricatured as those in the text, is filled with the same kind of hyperbole, piquant phrasing, and bravura that have made the author's other books so delightful and so much fun to read." Horn Bk

The Hey Hey Man; illus. by Nadine Bernard Westcott. Little 1979 31p illus $7.95 (2-4)   **Fic**

1 Robbers and outlaws—Fiction
ISBN 0-316-26001-0   LC 78-31702

"An Atlantic Monthly Press book"

"When a sly thief absconds with the farmer's gold buried beneath the Hey Hey Tree for protection, the evil act is seen by the Hey Hey Man. This feisty little wood spirit . . . confounds the thief by lengthening his nose, widening his ears to cabbage size, and finally changing the stolen gold pieces into vermin. Beaten, the thief sinks away, but the surprised farmer later finds his scratching dogs 'shedding coins as if they were fleas' while the Hey Hey Man chortles in the background." Booklist

"As in the marvelous chronicles of the McBroom family, the style and rhythm of American tall tales dominate the story. . . . Artfully composed, the tale would be a natural vehicle for storytellers. The illustrations are caricatures using elongated figures, which have an appropriate homespun appearance." Horn Bk

Humbug Mountain; illus. by Eric von Schmidt. Little 1978 149p illus $7.95 (4 and up)   **Fic**

1 The West (U.S.)—Fiction   2 Frontier and pioneer life—Fiction
ISBN 0-316-28569-2   LC 78-9419

"An Atlantic Monthly Press book"

"Dime novels are Wiley's oases of fantasy wherein he dreams of becoming a hero like Quickshot Billy Bodeen. Moving from place to place with his family at the turn of the century (his printer father is looking for just the right site for a shop), life begins to imitate art. Wiley finds himself in the midst of outlaws and con-men in what his grandfather has said is a prosperous city on the Missouri River but which turns out to be empty of any amenities—as well as of Grandpa who has disappeared leaving only a disheveled steamboat in the weeds. False rumors of gold and business and building boom abound and the rascals almost win—but Grandpa shows up just in time, bringing riches and rescue." Sch Library J

"There's a lot going on here. Twists, turns, unexpected surprises. The style is straightforward and the spoken language is Twainish. Things are 'perishing' this or 'infernally' that. Which is what Eric von Schmidt's illustrations are also—perishing good and infernally effective." NY Times Bk Rev

Jingo Django; illus. by Eric von Schmidt. Little 1971 172p illus $6.95 (4-6)   **Fic**

1 Orphans—Fiction   2 Buried treasure—Fiction
ISBN 0-316-28580-3   LC 75-140481

"An Atlantic Monthly Press book"

"Jingo Hawks, of Mrs. Daggatt's Beneficent Orphan House in Boston, is hired out to General Dirty-Face Jim Scurlock as a chimney sweep. A

mysterious Mr. Peacock 'buys' Jingo and, financed by Peacock's highly saleable artistic talent, they set out on a treasure hunt pursued by Daggatt and Scurlock. Hilarious scenes follow involving highwaymen, gypsies and a block of ice which becomes a rapidly melting life raft. Readers are clued in early to the fact that Mr. Peacock is really Jingo's father and that his mother was a beautiful gypsy girl who died when Jingo (Django is his gypsy name) was little." Sch Library J

"The story is a vitally told, just-plain-fun tale to read. The broadly farcical caricaturing of the line drawings perfectly complements the burlesque mood of the story." Horn Bk

McBroom tells a lie; illus. by Walter Lorraine. Little 1976 46p illus $5.95 (3-5)   **Fic**

ISBN 0-316-28572-2   LC 76-8396

"An Atlantic Monthly Press book"

"To old admirers of the Tall Tale Teller Extraordinary, McBroom, even the admission of a lie, with which he begins this story, should be amusing. Well, he admits he told a lie once, but not until the end of another tale full of whoppers does he say what the lie was. By that time McBroom's children have saved the marvelously fertile farm from going to a demanding neighbor by producing a crop of tomatoes as he'd required. Overnight, and in a dust storm. How? Wellll . . . seems that the children built a machine powered by popcorn exploding from the heat of some sunlight that had once frozen in a sudden cold snap, and they gathered fire flies and the firefly-light made the tomatoes grow. The lie? Well, McBroom said the neighbor's cow had mistaken the popcorn for snow and had frozen to death. Not true. All she did was catch a terrible cold." Chicago. Children's Bk Center

Walter Lorraine "uses black-and-white pen and wash drawings . . . the pictures have a comfortably haphazard quality which successfully reflects the outrageous humor of the story." Sch Library J

Some other books about McBroom are also available from Little:

McBroom and the beanstalk $5.95 (ISBN 0-316-28570-6; LC 77-22177)
McBroom and the great race $7.95 (ISBN 0-316-28568-4; LC 79-22609)

Mr Mysterious & Company; illus. by Eric von Schmidt. Little 1962 151p illus $7.95 (4-6)   **Fic**

1 Magic—Fiction   2 Frontier and pioneer life—Fiction
ISBN 0-316-28578-1   LC 62-7105

"An Atlantic Monthly Press book"

"An engaging story of a traveling magic show during the 1880's in which Pa is Mr. Mysterious and the whole family performs. A sound philosophy of good will and common sense underlies their sheer, happy bravado as they play the frontier towns westward to California." Chicago

Fleming, Ian

Chitty-Chitty-Bang-Bang; the magical car; illus. by John Burningham. Random House 1964 111p illus $4.95 (4-6)   **Fic**

1 Automobiles—Fiction
ISBN 0-394-81021-X   LC 64-21282

Commander Caractacus Pott rescues a racing car "from junk-heap oblivion and names it after the two sneezes and two explosions with which it starts. . . . 'Ch-Ch-B-B' flies, floats, and has a talent for getting the Pott family out of trouble." Library J

"This is fine fun, and the pictures of the family, the villains, French villages and Chitty are marvelous. The first third of the book is excitingly fresh and convincing, full of accurate and humorous details that make the magic absolutely believable. Then the [author] began to pile up the thrilling moments too fast in a Perils-of-Pauline or Hardy-Boys fashion. Had the author sustained the imaginative mood throughout, this story might have been one of the really distinctive children's fantasies." Bk Week

Foley, Louise Munro

Tackle 22; illus. by John Heinly. Delacorte Press 1978 unp illus $6.95, lib. bdg. $6.46 (2-4)   **Fic**

1 Football—Fiction
ISBN 0-440-08461-4; 0-440-08465-2   LC 78-50425

Foley, Louise M.—*Continued*

"With their quarterback downed by mumps, the empty-lot Wildcats are faced with canceling Saturday's deciding ball game with their rivals until archetypal younger brother Herbie shows up. Herbie throws a mean tackle, and there seems hope for the team until it turns out Herbie tackles anything—dogs, garbage cans, and trees, as well as opponents. Then an archetypal older brother gives coach Lenny some advice, which Herbie uses to win the game. The outcome is pretty predictable, but meanwhile there's sympathy for the eternal plight of the youngest wanting to be included and for the kind of raggedy neighborhood sports devotion that still evades Little League supervision. All timing is done by alarm clocks. With slapstick pen-and-ink drawings." Booklist

Forbes, Esther

Johnny Tremain; a novel for old & young; with illus. by Lynd Ward. Houghton 1943 256p front $8.95 (5 and up)   **Fic**

1   U.S.—History—Revolution,   1775-1783—Fiction 2 Boston—Fiction
ISBN 0-395-06766-9   LC 43-16483

Awarded the Newbery Medal, 1944
This story of a young Boston apprentice during the exciting year of the Tea Party, culminates in the Battle of Lexington. It is a story of Boston in revolt—and a very young man in love—as seen through the experiences of a courier for the revolutionary Committee of Public Safety
"This is Esther Forbes at her brilliant best. She has drawn the character of Johnny Tremain with such sympathy and insight that he may well take his place with Jim Hawkins, Huck Finn and other young immortals. . . . Youth, particularly, will get from it [a] live and clear and significant picture of a great period in American history." Bk Week

Fox, Paula

How many miles to Babylon? A novel; illus. by Paul Giovanopoulos. White 1967 117p illus lib. bdg. $5.95 (4-6)   **Fic**

1 Blacks—Fiction 2 Brooklyn—Fiction
ISBN 0-87250-415-8   LC 67-19301

Ten-year-old James Douglas, a black boy who lives in Brooklyn, knows his mother is in the hospital but fantasizes that she has gone to Africa, home of his ancestors. He runs away from his aunts to find his mother. After a harrowing encounter with three dog thieves, he returns home to find his mother back in their room
"Against the background, suggested rather than described, Jimmy is a small bewildered victim of an almost overwhelming situation. . . . [The story] is far more important for young people who have no knowledge of Negro ghettos than it is for children to whom the setting may be all too familiar." Horn Bk

The slave dancer; a novel. With illus. by Eros Keith. Bradbury Press 1973 176p illus $8.95 (6 and up)   **Fic**

1 Slave trade—Fiction 2 Sea stories
ISBN 0-87888-062-3   LC 73-80642

Awarded the Newbery Medal, 1974
Set in 1840, this "is the story of fourteen-year-old Jessie, impressed into service on a slave ship so that he can play his fife. To his horror, Jessie discovers that he is a slave dancer, his piping meant to keep the wretched black captives jigging in order to maintain their health—the motive mercenary rather than humanitarian. Jessie and a slave his age escape after a shipwreck and are taken in by a black man who sends each of them safely on his way—but this is after a four-month voyage on which Jessie has learned the horrors of the slave trade and the depravity and avarice of the crew." Chicago. Children's Bk Center
"Hunger and thirst, hazardous voyaging under sail, a degraded crew's callousness, calculated torture, and greed are not minimized but have the veracity of the retelling in a journal. Jessie is a fully realized figure, whose perceptions and agonies are presented in depth." Horn Bk

The stone-faced boy; illus. by Donald A. Mackay. Bradbury Press 1968 106p illus $7.95 (4-6)   **Fic**

1 Brothers and sisters—Fiction   2 Family life—Fiction
ISBN 0-87888-000-3   LC 68-9053

"The story is a perceptive character study of a lonely, timid middle child in a family of five self-possessed, individualistic children. To save himself from teasing by classmates and siblings, Gus Oliver has learned to mask his feelings so well that he has lost all ability to show emotion. Even the startling and unexpected arrival of an eccentric, outspoken great-aunt appears to leave Gus unmoved but the night his sister inveigles him into going out in the dark and the cold to rescue a stray dog, he gains a new-found confidence in himself." Booklist

Franzen, Nils-Olof

Agaton Sax and Lispington's grandfather clock; illus. by Quentin Blake. Deutsch [1979 c1978] 127p illus $6.95 (4-6)   **Fic**

1 Mystery and detective stories
ISBN 0-233-96964-0   LC 78-74456

First published 1978 in England
"The unflappable international detective from Bykoping solves his ninth mystery . . . matching wits with his archrivals, the dangerous Herr Gustafson and the treacherous Mosca. The two villains are out to steal the latest invention of Andreas Kark—an engine that runs on light. Kidnappings, escapes, chases, and double-crossings abound before Agaton finally brings his enemies to justice and recovers the machine. [The author] has his tongue as firmly in cheek as ever, and there's plenty of humor and action in the small-print text and in Quentin Blake's illustrations to keep attentions on target." Sch Library J
Another book about Agaton Sax is also available from Deutsch: Agaton Sax and the diamond thieves $6.50 (ISBN 0-233-95724-3; LC 79-64183)

Frazier, Neta Lohnes

Stout-hearted seven. Harcourt 1973 174p $5.95 (5 and up)   **Fic**

1 Sager family—Fiction 2 Frontier and pioneer life—Fiction 3 Oregon Trail—Fiction
ISBN 0-15-281450-7   LC 73-5240

"Using diaries, letters, manuscripts, and interviews the author has adhered to witnesses' accounts of the actual events in her fictionalized account of the seven Sager children whose real parents died on the Oregon Trail and whose adopted parents, Marcus and Narcissa Whitman, were killed by Indians three years later, along with two Sager boys and a girl. The hardships that the children, newborn to fourteen years old, endure include starvation, illness, accidents, exhaustion, filth, fear, and abandonment; and their continued adjustment, courageous acceptance, and mutual loyalty are a greater tribute to American history than any glorified Western myth. Care has been taken to present the Indians' motivation for the massacre as well as the Whitmans' sometimes misplaced religious zeal. The account is occasionally slow but combines accurate history with adventure appeal." Booklist

Friis, Babbis

Kristy's courage; tr. from the Norwegian by Lise Somme McKinnon; illus. by Charles Geer. Harcourt 1965 159p illus $5.95 (3-6)   **Fic**

1 Speech disorders—Fiction
ISBN 0-15-243371-6   LC 65-18728

"Seven-year-old Kristy is handicapped by a speech defect and finds the world unsympathetic to her problems." Best Bks for Children

Fritz, Jean

Brady; illus. by Lynd Ward. Coward, McCann & Geoghegan 1960 223p illus $7.95 (4 and up)   **Fic**

1 Slavery in the U.S.—Fiction 2 Underground railroad—Fiction 3 Pennsylvania—Fiction
ISBN 0-698-20014-4   LC 60-12488

"In 1836, after Brady, a Pennsylvania preacher's son, discovered [an Underground railroad] station near his family's farm and knew his father did not trust him with that secret, he wished he had never heard of slavery because it had got him into such trouble; but in a time of great need he was able to prove that he was becoming a man. The writing of this story is unhurried and vivid. Brady is entirely believable—both he and his father are drawn with particular skill—and the incidents of controversy centered in Abolitionism and church division are made exciting. The background of farm and family activity has colorful period flavor." Horn Bk

Fritz, Jean—Continued

The cabin faced west; illus. by Feodor Rojankovsky. Coward, McCann, and Geoghegan 1958 124p illus $7.95 (3-6)　　　**Fic**

1 Scott, Ann (Hamilton)—Fiction 2 Frontier and pioneer life—Fiction 3 Pennsylvania—Fiction
ISBN 0-698-20016-0　　　LC 57-10714

"Ann is unhappy when her family moves from Gettysburg to the Pennsylvania frontier, but she soon finds friends and begins to see that there is much to enjoy about her new home—including a visit from General Washington." Hodges. Bks for Elem Sch Libraries

"Ann is a very real little heroine, demure and appealing in Mr. Rojankovsky's pencil sketches." NY Her Trib Bks

Early thunder; illus. by Lynd Ward. Coward, McCann & Geoghegan 1967 255p illus $7.95 (6 and up)　　　**Fic**

1 U.S.—History—Colonial period, 1600-1775—Fiction 2 Salem, Mass.—Fiction
ISBN 0-698-20036-5　　　LC 67-24217

"The political conflict in Salem, Mass., 1774-75, is realized in the agony of David, the 14-year-old son of a Tory doctor, who struggles to determine where his own allegiance lies." Coughlan. Creating Independence, 1763-1789

"The period details and the historical background are excellent, both in themselves and in the easy way they are incorporated into the story. The characters are believable, but are less interesting as people than as examples of people's attitudes. The plot, based on some facts . . . is less interesting in itself than it is as a means of showing the general pattern and movement of events and morale." Chicago. Children's Bk Center
Map on lining-papers

George Washington's breakfast; Paul Galdone drew the pictures. Coward, McCann, & Geoghegan 1969 unp illus lib. bdg. $5.99 (2-4)　　　**Fic**

1 Washington, George, President U.S.—Fiction
ISBN 0-698-30099-8　　　LC 69-11475

George W. Allen "was named for George Washington and he had the same birthday. It made him feel almost related. So related he wanted to know everything he could about George Washington. . . . [He especially wanted to] know what George Washington ate for breakfast. He got his grandmother to promise she'd cook George Washington's breakfast if he found out what it was, and he was going to find out—no matter what." About the Bk

"Paul Galdone's red, white, and blue illustrations don't equal many of his earlier ones, but they are appropriate to the story and, like it, are not overstated. Younger and reluctant readers may enjoy this, as it offers a painless way of picking up information." Sch Library J

Gage, Wilson

The ghost of Five Owl Farm; illus. by Paul Galdone. Collins [distributed by Philomel Bks] 1966 127p illus lib. bdg. $5.99 (4-6)　**Fic**

1 Twins—Fiction 2 Mystery and detective stories
ISBN 0-529-03889-7　　　LC 75-20088

"Ted, who has a rather scornful opinion of his ten-year-old twin cousins, is disgusted to discover they are arriving for a visit during his spring vacation. A scheme to keep them busy investigating planted clues indicating mysterious activity around the barn takes an unexpected turn when the twins convince Ted that there really are weird things going on in the old barn at night. The story gains originality and freshness through the deft blending of eeriness and humor with delightful characters [and] . . . bits of nature lore." Booklist

Gannett, Ruth Stiles

My father's dragon; illus. by Ruth Chrisman Gannett. Random House 1948 86p illus lib. bdg. $5.99 (1-4)　　　**Fic**

1 Dragons—Fiction 2 Fantastic fiction 3 Animals —Fiction
ISBN 0-394-91438-4　　　LC 48-6521

This is a combination of fantasy, sense, and nonsense. It describes the adventures of a small boy, Elmer Elevator, who befriended an old alley cat and in return heard the story of the captive baby dragon on Wild Island. Right away Elmer decided to free the dragon. The tale of Elmer's voyage to Tangerina and his arrival on Wild Island, his encounters with various wild animals, and his subsequent rescue of the dragon follows

"This is without question, the funniest book that we have seen for a month of Sundays. It is also an exciting adventure story that will please small boys and girls, and their elders, from Maine to Florida and from Canada to Mexico. As a book to share with children it is a treasure, and storytellers will read it with a solemn joy, hearing in imagination the delighted chuckles of their listeners." Sat Rev

Followed by: Elmer and the dragon and The dragons of Blueland

Gardam, Jane

A long way from Verona. Macmillan Pub. Co. 1971 190p $4.95, pa $1.25 (6 and up)　**Fic**

1 Great Britain—Fiction
ISBN 0-02-735780-5; 0-02-043220-8　　LC 76-171923

"In England during World War II this engaging, often amusing first-person narrative views everyday life through the eyes of an introspective, outspoken thirteen-year-old aspiring writer, Jessica Vye, whose father gave up teaching for the ministry and moved his family to a country village from which Jessica travels 10 miles by train to school each day. . . . Although there is not much action in the story, it successfully mirrors typical, and sometimes not so typical, adolescence as Jessica describes with great felicity experiences in school and out, her insecurities, and her ambitions." Booklist

The summer after the funeral. Macmillan Pub. Co. 1973 151p $5.95 (6 and up)　**Fic**

1 Great Britain—Fiction
ISBN 0-02-735880-1　　　LC 73-4058

A sensitive 16-year-old girl, whose clergymanfather has recently died, runs away from home in search of "a Heathcliff to fulfill her image of herself as a reincarnated Emily Brontë. . . . [Following adventures with a middle-aged artist and with] the teacher, Mr. Bell . . . Athene's summer of divine discontent ends where it began—at the parsonage which was once her home." Horn Bk

The author "is very good on young grief, desperation, elation, first love . . . very good on settings . . . very good on subsidiary characters, mostly English spinsters, auntlike if not actually aunts. . . . Generally the tone is discreet, contained. . . . A definite if muted element of wishfulfillment is one reason her books are so readable." NY Times Bk Rev

Garfield, James B.

Follow my Leader; illus. by Robert Greiner. Viking 1957 191p illus lib. bdg. $8.95 (4 and up)　　　**Fic**

1 Blind—Fiction 2 Guide dogs—Fiction
ISBN 0-670-32332-3　　　LC 57-1611

"An 11-year-old blind boy gradually resumes his normal life with the aid of loyal friends and his guide dog, Leader." Hodges. Bks for Elem Sch Libraries

Garfield, Leon

Mister Corbett's ghost; illus. by Alan E. Cober. Pantheon Bks. 1968 87p illus lib. bdg. $5.99 (5 and up)　　　**Fic**

1 Ghosts—Fiction 2 London—Fiction
ISBN 0-394-91601-8　　　LC 68-12653

In this story set in London, "young Benjamin Partridge is apprentice to a harsh, relentless apothecary. On a black and windy New Year's Eve —when he should have been merrymaking at home—Benjamin is sent to deliver some medicine to a mysterious, black-cloth customer. In fury and despair the boy sets forth, willing the death of his detested master with every step he trudges. But long before the night is over, his . . . errand has turned into an . . . adventure with the Devil himself." Horn Bk

"Garfield's writing is always evocative, his dialogue period-perfect, and his characters vivid." Chicago. Children's Bk Center

Garfield, Leon—*Continued*

The night of the comet; a comedy of courtship featuring Bostock and Harris. Delacorte Press 1979 149p $7.95, lib. bdg. $7.45 (5 and up) **Fic**

1 Love—Fiction 2 Friendship—Fiction 3 Great Britain—Fiction
ISBN 0-440-06656-5; 0-440-06657-5 LC 79-50670

English edition has title: Bostock and Harris
Sequel to: The strange affair of Adelaide Harris
One of the two main characters, Bostock, age "thirteen and a half, stood 'on the threshold of manhood.' In fact, he'd knocked on the door but as yet had received no definite answer.' Nevertheless, he was smitten with [his friend] Harris's sister—who loathed him. But Harris, with his calculating intelligence, had read a learned article on the courtship of animals and undertook to guide his oafish friend through the course of true love in exchange for his own heart's desire—a brass telescope belonging to Bostock's father, which he particularly coveted for the imminent appearance of a comet. To carry the farce and to resolve the plot—almost mathematical in its intricacy and symmetry—other more or less lovelorn characters are important links in a long chain of mistaken identities. . . . A delicious literary concoction bubbling along with the author's perfect sense of dramatic timing and with his mixture of earthy humor and effervescent wit." Horn Bk

Smith; illus. by Antony Maitland. Pantheon Bks. 1967 218p illus lib. bdg. $5.69 (5 and up) **Fic**

1 Juvenile delinquency—Fiction 2 London—Fiction
ISBN 0-394-91641-7 LC 67-20223

"A 12-year-old pickpocket pursued by other thieves, leads a swift-paced descent into 18th century London's underground peopled with timeless personalities cleverly self-revealed through dialogue passages that echo Dickens." Best Bks for Children, 1968

Garner, Alan

Elidor. Collins [distributed by Philomel Bks. 1979 c1965] 148p $7.95 (5 and up) **Fic**

1 Fantastic fiction
ISBN 0-529-05417-5 LC 78-8379

First published 1965 in England: 1967 in U.S. by Walck
"A city wasteland, with its half-ruined church and houses awaiting the demolition gang, is the threshold between the real and the magical world. . . . Abruptly, Malebron (a vaguely Arthurian figure disguised as a lame fiddler) transports young Roland, his sister Helen and his two older brothers to Elidor, a once-golden land of four castles, three of which are already in the hands of 'the enemy.' . . . Responding to Malebron's plea, [Roland] and the others take the four treasures of Elidor back to their own world (suburban Manchester) for safety. The result is a series of glorious battles as 'the enemy' battles at the children's doors." Bk Week

"Ambitiously imagined and worked out with a hard economical tension: the reader is kept—except for some dazzling visionary moments—well on the present-day human side of the arena. . . . The climax, a peak after chapters of mounting terror, is brilliant. The threads of myth make a nice unraveling." New Statesman

The owl service. Collins [distributed by Philomel Bks. 1979 c1967] 156p $7.95 (5 and up) **Fic**

1 Wales—Fiction
ISBN 0-529-05520-1 LC 79-10140

First published 1967 in England and in the U.S. by Walck
A "tale of three children who are fated to replay the hostilities which have long stalked the valley where Alison, her stepbrother Roger, and their parents come to spend vacation. The two children and Gwyn, the housekeeper's son, find an unusual dinner service in the loft above Alison's room. When the girl shows a sample plate to Gwyn's mother, she is startled to see that the composite owl design has disappeared. Gwyn is puzzled by his mother's vehement reaction to Alison's presumed insolence and decides to remain silent about the strange events which have been taking place. . . . None of those involved can flee the spell cast by the unleashed forces." Best Sellers
"This is not a story which 'uses' supernatural aids to induce effects of brooding uneasiness and fear. . . . [It] is a complex of attractions and hostilities between persons, classes, myth and modern day reality." Times (London) Lit Sup

The stone book; etchings by Michael Foreman. Collins [distributed by Philomel Bks 1978 c1976] 63p illus $6.95 (4 and up) **Fic**

1 Great Britain—Fiction
ISBN 0-529-05503-1 LC 78-7965

First published 1976 in England
"The young daughter of a stonemason wants to learn to read, but yearns—even if she can't read it—for a prayerbook to carry to Chapel, as the other girls do. Instead, her father takes her deep into a cleft in the hill, where she can read the record of the rocks: figures, and marks of the tide, and a handprint just the size of her own. And footprints. The handprint proves to be one her father made when he was her size, and she feels the joy of knowing that past generations have been in the same place. The other girls press flowers in their prayerbooks but what Father makes Mary is a stone book that's even more wonderful, for the split stone shows the marks of an ancient fern." Chicago. Children's Bk Center
"Though elegantly crafted, the [book] will pose a challenge to American children: language will be an immediate problem, since Briticisms . . . usually left unexplained, will take a while to decipher from context. More important, the book's subtleties and abstractness will demand sophisticated readers." Booklist

Followed by these books also available from Philomel:
Granny reardun $6.95 (ISBN 0-529-05505-8; LC 78-8141)
The Aimer Gate $6.95 (ISBN 0-529-05506-6; LC 78-20964)
Tom Fobble's day $6.95 (ISBN 0-529-05507-4; LC 78-26927)

The weirdstone of Brisingamen; a tale of Alderly. Collins [distributed by Philomel Bks 1979 c1960] 224p $7.95 (6 and up) **Fic**

1 Good and evil—Fiction 2 Fantastic fiction
ISBN 0-529-05519-8 LC 78-24635

First published 1960 in England
"Weirdstone is the story of two children, Colin and Susan, who find themselves caught up in conflict between ancient champions of good and evil. It is Susan's crystal teardrop bracelet that sparks their involvement; it seems this heirloom is really Firefrost, the all-important magical stone long lost by the benevolent wizard Cadellin and long coveted by Nastrond, the Great Spirit of Darkness. The tale is complex and thoroughly involving despite slower final portions when journeys play out a bit too long and several new faces appear fortuitously." Booklist

Followed by: The moon of Gomrath. Collins [distributed by Philomel Bks] $7.95 (ISBN 0-529-05416-7; LC 77-16425)

Garrigue, Sheila

Between friends. Bradbury Press 1978 160p $7.95 (5 and up) **Fic**

1 Moving, Household—Fiction 2 Friendship—Fiction 3 Mongolism—Fiction
ISBN 0-87888-133-6 LC 77-90952

"Jill is 12 and [has moved] from California to Massachusetts. Her first and most loyal caring friend is Dede, who is mentally and physically retarded because of Down's syndrome. Jill's loyalties are tangled between Dede and her friends, Marla, Karen, and Connie, who find 'retards gross and creepy,' and her pregnant mother, who has lost a retarded child and fears Dede may be a 'jinx.' With courage and through her friendship with Dede, Jill begins to understand both retarded children and the meaning of friendship." Babbling Bookworm
"Garrigue's exploration of a complex social and ethical issue is well done. The characterization of Jill is especially good, and the depiction of Dede's mother, who is desperate for some acceptance of her daughter, provides some unusual and valuable insights." Sch Library J

Gates, Doris

Blue willow; illus. by Paul Lantz. Viking 1940 172p illus $8.95, Penguin pa $1.50 (4 and up) **Fic**

1 Migrant labor—Fiction 2 California—Fiction
ISBN 0-670-17557-9; 0-14-030924-1 LC 40-32435

Gates, Doris—*Continued*

"Janey was so tired of always moving on to another place so that Father would have work. She longed for a home, friends and school-days like the other children had. Her only possession was a blue willow plate, which she prized above everything in the world. Then she met Lupe and knew what it was to have a friend, and after many adventures in which the blue willow plate played no small part, Janey learned at last what it was to have a settled home, as well." Ontario Library Rev

"This book may be used to consider the differences between the family patterns of old stock Americans and those of Mexican-Americans, and also the poignant longing for security that grows out of the disorganized family life of many migratory workers." Rdng Ladders

Gauch, Patricia Lee

This time, Tempe Wick? Illus. by Margot Tomes. Coward, McCann & Geoghegan 1974 43p illus $6.95 (3-5) **Fic**

1 U.S.—History—Revolution, 1775-1783—Fiction 2 Wick, Temperance—Fiction
ISBN 0-698-20300-3 LC 74-79706

Based on a Revolutionary War legend about a real girl, this story tells how Tempe Wick helped feed and clothe the thousands of American soldiers who spent the winters of 1780 and 1781 in Jockey Hollow, New Jersey. When the soldiers mutinied, Tempe had to use her wits and courage to prevent two of them from stealing her horse

"The book presents a realistic and humane view of the war and of the people who fought it. . . . The writing is the perfect vehicle for the illustrations—in the artist's inimitable style—which capture the down-to-earth, unpretentious, and humorous quality of the storytelling." Horn Bk

Thunder at Gettysburg; drawings by Stephen Gammell. Coward, McCann & Geoghegan 1975 46p illus $6.95 (3-5) **Fic**

1 Gettysburg, Battle of, 1863—Fiction
ISBN 0-698-20329-1 LC 75-7561

"The immediacy of war, the sense of loss, and the pervading feeling of death all become close companions of Tillie Pierce, as well as the other residents of Gettysburg, Pennsylvania on July 1, 1863 when an almost accidental battle between Union and Confederate forces becomes a turning point in the Civil War. Separated from her family by a neighbor in an attempt to keep her out of the battle, Tillie is swept right into its midst, and for the next three days before she eventually rejoins her family, she becomes very much acquainted with the realities of life and death." Sch Library J

"Gauch has drawn on the experiences of a real person, in this case Tillie Pierce Alleman, whose 1889 book 'At Gettysburg' provided the basis of the story. Gammell's thorough pencilled scenes are full of atmosphere and acute emotion, their escalating drama effectively congruent with that of the story." Booklist

George, Jean Craighead

Julie of the wolves; pictures by John Schoenherr. Harper 1972 170p illus $7.95, lib. bdg. $7.89, pa $1.25 (6 and up) **Fic**

1 Eskimos—Fiction 2 Wolves—Fiction 3 Arctic regions—Fiction
ISBN 0-06-021943-2; 0-06-021944-0; 0-06-44058-1 LC 72-76509

Awarded the Newbery Medal, 1973
"Lost in the Alaskan wilderness thirteen-year-old Miyax [Julie in English] an Eskimo girl, is gradually accepted by a pack of Arctic wolves that she comes to love." Booklist

"The superb narration includes authentic descriptions and details of the Eskimo way-of-life and of Eskimo rituals. . . . The story graphically pictures the seasonal changes of the vast trackless tundra and reveals Miyax's awakening to the falseness of the white man's world. Through the eyes of Julie, who survives for months in the wilderness with the wolves, the author lovingly describes the wildlife: the golden plover, the snow buntings, the snowshoe rabbits, as well as the wolves. She evokes in full measure the terrors of losing directions and facing storms in abysmal temperatures. The whole book has a rare, intense reality which the artist enhances beautifully with animated drawings." Horn Bk

My side of the mountain; written and illus. by Jean George. Dutton 1959 178p illus lib. bdg. $7.95, pa $2.95 (5 and up) **Fic**

1 Outdoor life—Fiction 2 Catskill Mountains—Fiction
ISBN 0-525-35530-8; 0-525-45030-0 LC 59-7799

"A New York City boy determines to run away from home and to live alone and be completely self-sufficient. This, his diary, tells about his adventures during the year he spent in the Catskills—his struggle for survival, his dependence on nature, his animal friends, and his ultimate realization that he needs human companionship." Pub W

"The book is all the more convincing for the excellence of style, the subtlety of humor, aptness of phrases, and touches of poetry. Sam's descriptions . . . have the fascination of detail that children appreciate in 'Robinson Crusoe.' Sam's own personality emerges clearly. . . . This book brings a great deal to children; emphasis on the rewards of courage and determination and an abundance of scientific knowledge, certainly, but, far more important, unforgettable experiences in the heart of nature." Horn Bk

"The black-and-white drawings of the things Sam made—fish hooks, animal snares, willow whistles—and how he did things—cooked and ate and washed and slept—should prove useful perhaps even a challenge to boy and girl scouts aike." Best Sellers

The summer of the falcon. Crowell 1962 153p illus $6.95 (6 and up) **Fic**

1 Falcons—Fiction
ISBN 0-690-79269-7 LC 62-16543

June has been given a falcon by her family. She tends her pet and trains it toward its eventual independence. At the same time, June resents growing up. The story covers three years in her life, from thirteen to sixteen, and shows how, as she trains her falcon, she herself learns to accept adulthood." Library J

"The nature lore is beautifully handled, but the special emphasis is on the tensions in the family which are most convincingly depicted." NY Her Trib Bks

Who really killed Cock Robin? An ecological mystery. Dutton 1971 149p illus lib. bdg. $8.95, pa $1.95 (4-6) **Fic**

1 Ecology—Fiction
ISBN 0-525-42700-7; 0-525-45001-4 LC 76-157944

"The residents of Saddleboro were ecology conscious, and none more so than the mayor, whose particular pride was the robins nesting in a hat on his front porch. Nevertheless, despite the carefulness of its citizens, the town is subject to some undetected pollutant, for one day the father robin is found dead. Young Tony Isidoro, assisted by his friend Mary Alice, decides to investigate the cause." Sat Rev

"A great deal of sound ecological information is presented, and the story is timely and entertaining. Above all, the message is clear: 'The Earth is one ecosystem.' " Horn Bk

The wounded wolf; pictures by John Schoenherr. Harper 1978 32p illus $6.95, lib. bdg. $6.89 (2-4) **Fic**

1 Wolves—Fiction 2 Arctic regions—Fiction
ISBN 0-06-021949-1; 0-06-021950-5 LC 76-58711

"On an Arctic ridge, crippled [wolf] Roko is at the mercy of predators—ravens, a fox, a herd of muskoxen and others—and separated from his pack. Far away, the leader, Kiglo, calls the roll and realizes that Roko is missing. Hearing the shrieks of the animals who hold the wounded wolf at bay, Kiglo runs to rout them and feed Roko until he recovers." Pub W

"This is a powerfully written account of a wounded wolf. . . . Black-and-white illustrations cover the pages and convey the feeling of the snow-covered barren wilderness and the cold. A beautiful book that will be appreciated best by a special child." Children's Bk Rev Serv

Geras, Adele

The girls in the velvet frame. Atheneum Pubs. 1978 149p $6.95 (4 and up) **Fic**

1 Family life—Fiction 2 Jews in Palestine—Fiction 3 Jerusalem—Fiction
ISBN 0-689-30729-2 LC 79-12352

Geras, Adele—*Continued*

First published 1978 in England

This "is the story about widowed Sarah Bernstein and her five young daughters, set in Jerusalem just before World War I. The . . . plot centers on attempts to make contact with the oldest child Isaac, who has emigrated to America and has not been heard from. . . . The girls, especially the three older ones, are interested in everything—from the flirtations of their middle-aged, vivacious Aunt Mimi to having their photographs taken. Woven into the narrative is the . . . story of the arranged courtship of Rifka, the oldest daughter, and David—which proves surprisingly happy for both of them." Horn Bk

"The details of family life among five charming sisters are vividly depicted in this novel for young readers. . . . Interaction among family members, customs, and dialogue overshadow the story but in no way lessen the quality of this work, which is sure to be enjoyed by middle-grade readers." Children's Bk Rev Serv

Gipson, Fred

Curly and the wild boar; illus. by Ronald Himler. Harper 1979 88p illus $5.95, lib. bdg. $6.49 (5 and up)   **Fic**

1 Boars—Fiction 2 Country life—Fiction
ISBN 0-06-022014-7; 0-06-022015-5   LC 77-25644

"Although his father, Catfish, and his brother, Shinnery Red, have warned Curly that a wild boar is dangerous, Curly is determined to catch the boar that ruined his melon patch and spoiled his chance of winning a prize at the county fair. Curly has three fights with the boar, fights in which dogs, a horse, and a catamount participate." Chicago. Children's Bk Center

"Suspenseful, vivid, about real people no better than they should be, this is the kind of yarn cowpokes used to exchange as they sat around at night—maybe some still do. Young readers . . . might not understand some of Catfish Waggoner's (Curly's father) country comparisons, but they'll enjoy him and Shinnery Red . . . as colorful characters. Less polished than 'Old Yeller' (maybe because Gipson died in 1973 without having got around to a final rewrite), Curley's story is nevertheless fine fare for young and old, and well structured for reading aloud to a class." Sch Library J

Old Yeller; drawings by Carl Burger. Harper 1956 158p illus $9.95, lib. bdg. $9.89, pa $1.50 (6 and up)   **Fic**

1 Dogs—Fiction 2 Texas—Fiction 3 Frontier and pioneer life—Fiction
ISBN 0-06-11545-9; 0-06-011546-7; 0-06-08002-X
LC 56-8780

"Travis at fourteen was the man of the family during the hard summer of 1860 when his father drove his herd of cattle from Texas to the Kansas market. It was the summer when an old yellow dog attached himself to the family and won Travis' reluctant friendship. Before the summer was over, Old Yeller proved more than a match for thieving raccoons, fighting bulls, grizzly bears, and mad wolves. This is a skillful tale of a boy's love for a dog as well as a description of a pioneer boyhood and it can't miss with any dog lover." Horn Bk

Girion, Barbara

Misty and me. Scribner 1979 139p $7.95 (4-6)   **Fic**

1 Dogs—Fiction
ISBN 0-684-16227-X   LC 79-15925

"When her mother goes to work sixth-grader Kim schemes to demonstrate her sense of responsibility (and thus eligibility for dog ownership). Using money earned for babysitting her brother (Willie the Whiner), Kim buys a puppy from the local shelter and hires Mrs. Mac (struggling to live on Social Security) to feed and care for Misty until the secret can be revealed. Meanwhile, Kim contends with best friend Lisa's sudden interest in boys and clothes; after-school co-ed disco classes; and fears that Misty is growing to love Mrs. Mac. When the latter has a heart attack, the game is up. Kim's folks admire her resourcefulness (but not her dishonesty); Willie stops whining; Lisa and Kim are reunited." Sch Library J

"Kim's narration reveals Girion's real knack for articulating a character through dialogue. Kim is lovable and thoroughly appealing in her desire to take responsibility and in her reluctance to become as boy-crazy as her friends. . . . A terrific tear-jerker ending has Kim giving her

beloved Misty to Mrs. Mac, who is moving away. This selfless act may seem a little corny but it's thoroughly satisfying. The story is appealing, with light humor, mild pathos, and a captivating plot." Booklist

Goble, Paul

Lone Bull's horse raid [by] Paul and Dorothy Goble; pictures by Paul Goble. Bradbury Press 1973 unp illus $8.95 (3-6) **Fic**

1 Dakota Indians—Fiction
ISBN 0-87888-059-3   LC 73-76546

"This story tells of Lone Bull's first horse raid and the battle it led to, which enabled Lone Bull to stand before his people as a warrior. In addition to factual material about how an Indian horse-raiding party operated, insight is provided into the values and culture of a society that idealized the warrior." Sch Library J

"Based on the art of the Plains Indians, the detailed panoramic spreads and smaller scenes of horsemen and tipis are full of rhythmic design and driving movement." Horn Bk

Includes bibliography

Godden, Rumer

The dolls' house; illus. by Tasha Tudor. Puffin Bks. [1976 c1947] 126p illus pa $1.25 (2-4)   **Fic**

1 Dollhouses—Fiction 2 Dolls—Fiction
ISBN 0-14-030942-X   LC 62-18693

First published 1947 in England; 1948 by Viking in the U.S. Copyright renewed 1962

Adventures of a brave little hundred-year-old Dutch farthing doll, her family, their Victorian dollhouse home and the two little English girls to whom they all belonged. Tottie's great adventure was when she went to the exhibition. Dolls through the ages, and was singled out for notice by The Queen who opened the exhibition

"Each doll has a firmly drawn, recognizably true character; the children think and behave convincingly; only the grown-ups are remote and Olympian, as grown-ups must be. The story is enthralling, and complete in every detail. . . . This is an exceptionally good book." Spectator

Mouse house; illus. by Adrienne Adams. Viking 1957 63p illus $5.95, Penguin pa $1.95 (2-4)   **Fic**

1 Mice—Fiction
ISBN 0-670-49147-0; 0-14-050170-3   LC 57-13962

"Upstairs in Mary's room was Mouse House, a little jewelry box in the shape of a furnished house inhabited by two cloth mice; down in the cellar lived a family of real mice crowded into a broken flower pot with not an eighth of an inch to spare. The enchanting story tells how, through the adventures of Bonnie, the little mouse that was crowded out of the nest and found her way upstairs, Mouse House became the comfortable new home of a family of real mice." Booklist

"Rumer Godden offers both quality in her writing and delightful fantasy in her story pattern. Children will be captivated by the illustrations so perfectly suited in every smallest detail to this Mouse family story." Top of the News

Godolphin, Mary

Pilgrim's progress; drawings by Robert Lawson; retold and shortened for modern readers, by Mary Godolphin. Lippincott 1976 119p illus pa $2.95 (4-6)   **Fic**

ISBN 0-397-31705-0   LC 39-23070

"The text is that of the 1884 edition of The pilgrim's progress in words of one syllable, by Mary Godolpin, published by McLoughlin. This edition first published by Stokes in 1939

"Without omitting any of the better known incidents, she has yet managed to shorten Bunyan's extremely wordy and repetitious story to less than one-fifth its original length." Foreword

"The excellent illustrations will do much in introducing the classic to boys and girls of today. An outstanding addition to fine children's editions." Booklist [review of 1939 edition]

Goffstein, M. B.

Goldie the dollmaker. Farrar, Straus 1969 55p illus $7.95 (3-5)   **Fic**

1 Dolls—Fiction 2 Lamps—Fiction
ISBN 0-374-32739-4   LC 79-85369

Goffstein, M. B.—*Continued*

"An Ariel book"
"Goldie is an orphan who lives alone in the woods and makes dolls with heartbreaking smiles that are irresistible to children. When Goldie buys a Chinese lamp that costs many more dolls than she can afford, her friend Omus calls her crazy. The joy of owning the lamp gives way to regret and loneliness until the maker of the lamp appears in her dream and she understands that she has a friend in this lamp-maker as she is a friend to the children who own her dolls." Library J
At the end "Goldie Rosenzweig realizes that she is not alone. Children, too, will realize that they are not alone—for once again, M. B. Goffstein has spoken to them in their language. With the simplest of words and the plainest of illustrations, she manages to transform Goldie—an ageless creature—into the essence of childhood solitude; and if there is an elusive quality to the book, all the better. An artist as gentle and serious as Miss Goffstein needs little definition." NY Times Bk Rev

Two piano tuners. Farrar, Straus 1970 65p illus $5.95 (3-5)   **Fic**
1 Piano—Fiction
ISBN 0-374-38019-8   LC 71-106399
"Little orphaned Debbie Weinstock comes to live with her Grandpa Reuben, the world's best piano tuner, who wants her to become a concert pianist like the famous Isaac Lipman with whom he used to travel. Debbie dutifully practices her piano lessons but is interested only in becoming a piano tuner like her grandfather. After Grandpa Reuben takes her to hear the great artist play and finds that Debbie is impressed only by the fact that the piano stays in tune no matter how hard Mr. Lipman plays, he relents and agrees to teach her piano tuning. The understated humor and warmth of the story are enhanced by the author's spare line drawings." Booklist

Grahame, Kenneth

The open road; from The wind in the willows; illus. by Beverly Gooding. Scribner 1979 32p illus $9.95 (2-5)   **Fic**
1 Animals—Fiction 2 Friendship—Fiction
ISBN 0-684-16471-X   LC 79-22614
"In this second chapter of Kenneth Grahame's 'Wind in the Willows,' Rat, Mole and Toad of Toad Hall wander off in a gypsy caravan which is eventually replaced by a motorcar." Library J
"Though similar in spirit to Adrienne Adams' illustrations for 'The River Bank,' another picture book made from a chapter of 'Wind in the Willows' and [entered below] these pictures have quite a different artistic tone. They are focused much more sharply than Adams' soft lines and diffused colors and catch the countryside with almost botanical precision. Still, there is the same coziness reflecting the animals' world; and where picture book audiences are old enough to enjoy Grahame's sophisticated tongue, there will be the same reaction of welcome." Booklist

The reluctant dragon; illus. by Ernest H. Shepard. Holiday House 1953 [c1938] unp illus $4.95 (3-5)   **Fic**
1 Dragons—Fiction 2 Fairy tales
ISBN 0-8234-0093-X   LC 38-28954
A reissue of the 1938 book which is a chapter from: Dream days
A story of the boy who made friends with a dragon and arranged a match for him with St George
"When considered for its excellent bookmaking and for its enduring humor and charm heightened by the Ernest Shepard illustrations, it is a title for every child's library. And a good many adults, if they do not already know him, will be delighted with this delectable dragon who had a kind heart. . . . The book belongs wherever it finds a kindred spirit." Library J

The river bank; from The wind in the willows; illus. by Adrienne Adams. Scribner 1977 30p illus. lib. bdg. $7.95 (2-5)   **Fic**
1 Animals—Fiction 2 Friendship—Fiction
ISBN 0-684-15046-8   LC 77-3167
A picture book version of the first chapter of Grahame's classic work, which is entered below. The chapter forms a complete story in itself

"Adams' arresting paintings are full of the lovely gifts of springtime: the many colors and shapes of buds and blossoms, the blue of the river and the pervasive shades of green that enhance the various hues. She quickens the pastoral settings with life and invests them with humor, just as surely as Grahame did. . . . Fed up with spring-cleaning his underground home, Mole goes off for his first sight of the river. . . . Mole meets the friendly Rat, at home by the waters, and experiences the joys of a wholly new way of living." Pub W
"While Grahame's classic, because of format and long expository passages, usually appeals only to older children who are good readers, this introduction in picture book format will perhaps induce younger children to seek out the rest of the classic story." Booklist

The wind in the willows (4-6)   **Fic**
1 Animals—Fiction
Some editions are:
Ariel Bks. [distributed by Holt] $16.95 Illustrated by Michael Hague (ISBN 0-03-056294-5; LC 80-12509)
Collins [distributed by Philomel Bks] $8.95 Illustrated by Tasha Tudor (ISBN 0-529-00119-5; LC 66-14847)
Scribner (Golden anniversary edition) $8.95, lib. bdg. $12.50, pa $3.95 Illustrated in color and black and white by Ernest H. Shepard (ISBN 0-684-12819-5; 0-684-20838-5; 0-684-71788-3; LC 60-5241)
First published 1908 by Scribner
"The simple joys of life——Water Rat's pleasure in messing about in boats, Toad's enthusiasm for caravans and motor cars, the embracing light and warmth of kindly Badger's home, the brave boyish impulse that sent Mole into the winter wildwood—are expressed in terms of the familiar and universal values that lie close to the human heart, yet placed in a world where instinct is the predominating factor. Humour, perception, and poetic feeling are written into a story which is an imaginative springboard for any reader." Bks for Boys & Girls
This is a "choice book for reading aloud. . . . [The] dignified discourse [of the animals] is very amusing. . . . And the exquisite descriptions of the woods and riverbanks take on fresh color and depth. Although many children will not start this book by themselves, almost every youngster gets a glow of pleasure from listening." A Parent's Guide to Children's Rdng. 4th edition

Gray, Elizabeth Janet

Adam of the road; illus. by Robert Lawson. Viking 1942 317p illus $10 (5 and up)   **Fic**
1 Great Britain—Fiction 2 Middle Ages—Fiction 3 Minstrels—Fiction
ISBN 0-670-10435-3   LC 42-10681
Awarded the Newbery Medal, 1943
Tale of a minstrel and his son Adam, who wandered through southeastern England in the thirteenth century. Adam's adventures in search of his lost dog and his beloved father led him from St Alban's Abbey to London, and thence to Winchester, back to London, and then to Oxford where the three were at last reunited
"Without display of erudition, the framework of history is sound and the sense of place as strong as if written on the spot. The appearance of this book, from type to Mr. Lawson's many drawings, is so right it falls upon the eye like music on the ear." NY Her Trib Bks
Map on lining-papers

Greaves, Margaret

A net to catch the wind; drawings by Stephen Gammell. Harper 1979 40p illus $6.95, lib. bdg. $6.89 (2-4)   **Fic**
1 Princes and princesses—Fiction 2 Unicorns—Fiction 3 Fairy tales
ISBN 0-06-022104-6; 0-06-022105-4   LC 78-20265
This is an "original fairy tale about a king who tricks his gentle daughter into helping him capture a beautiful wild colt. Both girl and horse escape, and when they return a year later to the now-penitent king, the horse has turned into a unicorn." Children's Bk Rev Serv
"This is not a book for readers who can overdose on words like 'gossamer' and 'thistledown,' yet the old King grieving for his lost horses is quite touching, really. Margaret Greaves manages this tissue-thin fantasy with dexterity, and youngsters of Mirabelle's age and condition are sure to be captivated." NY Times Bk Rev

Green, Melinda

Rachel's recital; written and illus. by Melinda Green. Little 1979 47p illus $6.95 (2-4)   **Fic**

1 Pianists—Fiction
ISBN 0-316-32634-8   LC 79-1510

"An Atlantic Monthly Press book"
"Rachel is a spunky little girl who, for awhile, is the victim of her mother's musical aspirations. She is made to take piano lessons from Mr. Gratz (who has hairy ears) and practice in his apartment everyday while he is out. But there is too much going on in Rachel's mind and out in the street for her to concentrate. The day of reckoning comes when she is supposed to play in a recital with three other piano students. . . . The author/artist has a good sense of comedy; her streetscenes teem with life, showing the city at a time when it was more hospitable to people—pushcarts, kids playing marbles and jump rope, neighbors leaning out of windows watching and calling to each other." Sch Library J

Greene, Bette

Philip Hall likes me. I reckon maybe. Pictures by Charles Lilly. Dial Press 1974 135p illus $6.95, lib. bdg. $6.46 (4-6)   **Fic**

1 Friendship—Fiction 2 Blacks—Fiction 3 Arkansas—Fiction
ISBN 0-8037-6098-1; 0-8037-6096-5   LC 74-2887

This "story tells of a year in the life of a bright and lively black girl whose only real problems resulted from her infatuation with the boy from the next farm. . . . The book . . . deals chiefly with Beth's minor trials and triumphs: She tracks down a pair of turkey thieves, discovers that she is allergic to dogs, embarks on a vegetable-selling business venture, rescues Philip when he injures his leg on a mountaintop, and, finally, wins first prize in a calf-raising contest." Horn Bk
"The action is sustained; the narration, in first person Black dialect, is good or bad, depending on your linguistic stance; the illustrations are excellent black-and-white pencil sketches. This is a pleasant, undemanding little tale, good for a rainy afternoon." Rdng Teacher

Summer of my German soldier. Dial Press 1973 230p $7.95 (6 and up)   **Fic**

1 World War, 1939-1945—Fiction 2 Prisoners of war—Fiction
ISBN 0-8037-8321-3   LC 73-6025

"Patty Bergen, daughter of the shopkeeper in Jenkinsville, Arkansas, is a lonely, misunderstood 12-year-old during a crucial summer. When German prisoners of war are encamped outside the town, at the height of World War II hostilities, Patty secretly makes friends with Anton and helps him hide out when he escapes. The FBI track down the prisoners and shoot him dead; Patty's family are vilified as 'Jew-Nazi' and forced to give up their home and business. Patty, too young to be tried for treason, goes to a reform school." Pub W
"Patty's story . . . is more than a mirror of reality. It offers no panaceas for loneliness, no easy solutions for problems; and this verisimilitude extends to the depiction of the minor characters as well. Although they seem types at first, they become individuals because of the particular details Patty chooses to recall. . . . A moving first novel, unforgettable because of the genuine emotion it evokes." Horn Bk

Greene, Constance C.

Beat the turtle drum; illus. by Donna Diamond. Viking 1976 119p illus $7.50 (5 and up)   **Fic**

1 Sisters—Fiction 2 Death—Fiction
ISBN 0-670-15241-2   LC 76-14772

"Joss saves money for her 11th birthday so that she can rent a horse for a week. She and her older sister, who narrates the story, have the happiest week of their lives until Joss falls from the apple tree and breaks her neck. Joss's death stuns the family. Mother lies in bed sedated by tranquilizers, Dad takes to drink, and 13-year-old Kate is left to her own resources. Slowly she gathers strength from her older cousin Mona, the wife of the man who rented the horse and a former teacher." Sch Library J
"In this sensitive and realistic story the author examines one family's handling of what may well be the ultimate family crisis—the death of one [of] the children. Both the narrator, Kate, and the younger sister, Joss, are believable girls who quickly gain the reader's empathy. Joss's

absorption in horses will attract many children to this book. Kate's reactions to Joss's death and to the family's dealing with it are likely to be touching and fascinating to the middle-school-age children." Children's Bk Rev Serv

The ears of Louis; illus. by Nola Langner. Viking 1974 90p illus lib. bdg. $7.95 (4-6)   **Fic**

1 Prejudices and antipathies—Fiction
ISBN 0-670-28718-0   LC 74-8694

His big ears are Louis' special problem, but the support of an elderly neighbor and an unexpected talent help the small boy handle the teasing and bullying of his classmates
"This has none of the gritty kind of realism used so often in today's 'character molding' books. Rather, its strength lies in a low-key approach, complete with unique but understated characters and a great deal of humor and empathy. The black-and-white drawings, of which there are a few, charmingly reflect the story." Booklist

A girl called Al; illus. by Byron Barton. Viking 1969 127p illus $6.95 (5 and up)   **Fic**

1 Friendship—Fiction
ISBN 0-670-34153-3   LC 69-18255

"Told in the first person in a disarmingly casual, amusing style, the story deals with a few months in the lives of the two seventh-grade girls. The narrator (never actually named) is a forthright, good-humored child whose family life is stable and secure. Her best friend Al (short for Alexandra), whose parents are divorced, lives in an apartment down the hall with her busy, distracted working mother. Al—a bright, over-fat girl—proudly tries to be a 'non-conformist' to hide the hurt and loneliness. Their unconventional friendship with Mr Richards, an elderly ex-bartender who works as assistant superintendent of the building, draws the girls together." Horn Bk
"Both the pre-teen protagonists and the minor performers—sketched with admirable economy—are accurately and affectionately drawn." NY Times Bk Rev

Followed by these books, also available from Viking:
I know you, Al $7.95 (ISBN 0-670-39048-8; LC 75-9741)
Your old pal, Al $7.95 (ISBN 0-670-79575-5; LC 79-12350)

I and Sproggy; illus. by Emily McCully. Viking 1978 155p illus $8.95 (5 and up)   **Fic**

1 Brothers and sisters—Fiction 2 New York (City)—Fiction
ISBN 0-670-38980-3   LC 78-6096

"Adam is almost 11, living with his divorced mother near Gracie Mansion (home of New York City's mayor) and fostering two major ambitions. He wants to be the mayor's honored guest and to get rid of a new stepsister, Sproggy. She has come from England with Adam's father and second wife and the girl has many sins. She is closer to 11 than Adam, she has a crazy accent and Adam's dog likes her. Sproggy tags after her stepbrother and crowns her offenses when his best friends invite her to join their boys' club." Pub W
"Especially notable are the understated description of Adam's relationship with his parents and friends; the realistic, pleasant picture of one aspect of life in New York City; and the many natural, humorous episodes characteristic of the author's work." Horn Bk

Isabelle the itch; illus. by Emily A. McCully. Viking 1973 126p illus lib. bdg. $7.95 (4-6)   **Fic**

ISBN 0-670-40177-3   LC 72-91404

Isabelle, a hyperactive fifth grader, spends a great deal of time getting nowhere, until she realizes that she must channel her energy in order to reach her goals, which include taking over her brother's paper route and winning the fifty-yard dash at school
"A refreshing book in many ways: it's good clean fun with no redeeming social value; the ten-year-old heroine is in perpetual motion, running, fighting, and talking, while her father bakes bread on Saturdays—both break a mold without being 'counter-culture.' Isabelle's mother is an honestly normal blend of impatience and loving warmth. None of the children are brooding introverts but react to each other with natural spontaneity ranging from mean teasing to kindness. Low-key and somewhat episodic . . . this is fun to read alone or aloud." Booklist

Greene, Constance C.—*Continued*

Leo the lioness. Viking 1970 118p lib. bdg. $6.95 (6 and up) **Fic**

ISBN 0-670-42456-0   LC 71-123022

"Thirteen can be a very bad age, especially when your sister is fifteen, attractive to boys, and the owner of a bikini. Tibb consoles herself by remembering that she is a Leo, which she firmly believes is the best sign in the zodiac. Leos are strong and steadfast and practically everything good. The year brings disappointments: the babysitter whom she still reveres marries out of necessity, Tibb's best friend becomes boy-crazy, and the moods of her sister are a real burden." Sat Rev

"Not an unusual theme, the adolescent girl who grows into a more mature person, but is handled unusually well here. The writing is convincingly that of a teen-ager, the problems are universal and imbued with a humor that does not lessen their importance; the dialogue is excellent and the relationships are drawn with sympathetic understanding." Sutherland. The Best in Children's Bks

The unmaking of Rabbit. Viking 1972 125p lib. bdg. $6.95 (5 and up) **Fic**

ISBN 0-670-74136-1   LC 72-80519

"Paul has been shunted off to live with his grandmother in a small town because his flighty and divorced mother is living it up in New York and can't be tied down by her 11-year-old son. Known as Rabbit because his ears stick out, the boy is miserable, living in the hope that his mother will get the promised bigger apartment with room for him. A crisis arises when some of his classmates involve Paul in breaking and entering; he goes along, for a while, because he yearns to be accepted but surprises the bullies and himself by changing his mind in time. There is a bittersweet resolution as Paul realizes that a future with his mother is a pipe-dream but a hint of future happiness as he makes a new friend. A solid plot and well-defined characterizations." Pub W

Greenfield, Eloise

Sister; drawings by Moneta Barnett. Crowell 1974 83p illus $6.95 (4 and up) **Fic**

1 Family life—Fiction   2 Blacks—Fiction
ISBN 0-690-00497-4   LC 73-22182

A 13-year-old black girl whose father is dead watches her 16-year-old sister drifting away from her and her mother and fears she may fall into the same self-destructive behavior herself. While waiting for her sister's return home, she leafs through her diary, reliving both happy and unhappy experiences while gradually recognizing her own individuality

"The book is strong . . . strong in perception, in its sensitivity, in its realism." Chicago. Children's Bk Center

Talk about a family; illus. by James Calvin. Lippincott 1978 60p illus lib. bdg. $8.95 (3-5) **Fic**

1 Family life—Fiction   2 Blacks—Fiction
ISBN 0-397-31789-1   LC 77-16423

"Genny's parents haven't been getting along well for months. But she's certain all of that will change as soon as brother Larry gets home from the service. And things do change for the James family, though not the way Genny expects them to." Children's Bk Rev Serv

This book "portrays a middle-income Black family facing change. Without denying the pain and hurt that divorce causes, it shows the warmth of family ties, the bond of friendships, and a strong sense of neighborhood. Moralizing is kept to a minimum, and the characters are remarkably well developed." Sch Library J

Greenwald, Sheila

All the way to wits' end. Little 1979 138p illus $6.95 (4-6) **Fic**

1 Family life—Fiction
ISBN 0-316-3270-4   LC 79-15936

"An Atlantic Monthly Press book"

"When her debt-ridden family moves into a small development house, away from the large place in the enclave of their ancestor-proud relatives, Drucilla fosters secret notions of improving their lot. If her parents would sell some of their priceless antiques, she and her sister and brother could wear modern outfits instead of the 'good clothes' handed down by generations of cousins.

Drucilla could rein in her teeth with braces and no longer be known by her peers as Bugs Bunny. With Machiavellian schemes, she induces her parents to part with their treasures but then sees that they are all going too far. Just in time, she calls a halt when she realizes that some things are precious, not to be traded for blue jeans and wall-to-wall carpet." Pub W

"There are some lively episodes, good dialogue, and adequate characterization; while Greenwald sees perceptively the ambivalence of a child's need to conform and her need to feel the security of permanence, she is less convincing in depicting the rather abrupt conversion of Drucilla's mother." Chicago. Children's Bk Center

Griese, Arnold A.

At the mouth of the luckiest river; illus. by Glo Coalson. Crowell 1973 64p illus $8.95, lib. bdg. $8.79 (4-6) **Fic**

1 Athabascan Indians—Fiction
ISBN 0-690-10786-2; 0-690-10787-0   LC 72-7548

"The story of an Athabascan Indian boy of a century ago is effectively illustrated with black and white pictures that reflect the isolation of the setting and the drama of the plot. Tatlek, who uses sled dogs to help in his hunting, is crippled and fatherless, axious to prove that he is a man, puzzled by the animosity of the medicine man who says that using the dogs (a practice Tatlek has learned from Eskimo traders) will provoke the anger of the spirits, the yegas. When the medicine man warns that he has been told by an owl that the Eskimos are coming to kill the tribe, Tatlek and his friend go off by dogsled to spy on the Eskimo camp and so learn that the medicine man has lied to both sides. He races back to tell his people: will they believe him or the medicine man they fear? And if they do not believe him, Tatlek knows he will be reviled. The story is told in a rather heavy writing style, but it has suspense enough to compensate for this, and it is very successful in creating mood and atmosphere and in incorporating cultural details unobtrusively." Sutherland. The Best in Children's Bks

Griffiths, Helen

The last summer; Spain 1936; illus. by Victor Ambrus. Holiday House 1979 151p illus $7.95 (5 and up) **Fic**

1 Spain—History—Civil War, 1936-1939—Fiction
2 Horses—Fiction
ISBN 0-8234-0361-0   LC 79-10469

"Having failed two school subjects, young Eduardo languishes at his stern father's country estate where he's forced to apply himself to his studies. The only break in the boy's day is time he spends listening to old Baltasar's tales about the wonder mare, Gaviota, beloved of Eduardo's deceased aunt. The child's father, away from home, is murdered by revolutionary soldiers as Spain's Civil War breaks out. Baltasar and others are also victims of the war, leaving Eduardo and the horse to try to slip through opposing armies on a long, tense hegira during which they are sometimes helped, sometimes betrayed. Griffiths, well known for many novels based on her love for animals, tells a rousing and moving story here, an evocation of sad history as well as an engrossing adventure." Pub W

Gripe, Maria

The glassblower's children; with drawings by Harald Gripe; tr. from the Swedish by Sheila La Farge. Delacorte Press 1973 170p illus $6.95, lib. bdg. $6.46 (4-6) **Fic**

1 Fairy tales
ISBN 0-440-03051-X; 0-440-03065-X   LC 73-949
Original Swedish edition 1964

This is a "story about the kidnapping of a glassblower's two children by a wealthy lord who hopes to alleviate his wife's ennui by giving her something she does not already have. Once added to her collection, however, the children pall on her quickly, and a sinister governess takes over their care, terrifying both the children and everyone in the castle before the good wizard Flutter Mildweather comes to the rescue along with her raven Wise Wit." Booklist

"Set in the Gothic mood, the tale of the struggle between the sisters is a saga of good and evil. Style, mood, and tempo are adroitly integrated, and the illustrations—reminiscent of Leonard Everett Fisher's scratch-board work—effectively support the story." Chicago. Children's Bk Center

Gripe, Maria—*Continued*

Hugo and Josephine; with drawings by Harald Gripe; tr. from the Swedish by Paul Britten Austin. Delacorte Press 1969 168p illus lib. bdg. $4.58 (3-5) **Fic**

1 Friendship—Fiction 2 School stories 3 Sweden —Fiction
ISBN 0-440-03930-4   LC 69-18438

"A Seymour Lawrence book"
Original Swedish edition, 1962
Sequel to: Josephine
"Josephine hated her real name so much that she refused to answer to it in school, where her classmates teased her and the teacher tried to smooth over an awkward situation; but it was Hugo who defended her and became her staunch friend. Hugo, very much his own man, is the most convincing example of self-possession to come along in many years of children's books, and the quiet, episodic story of his and Josephine's friendship has an innocent charm. There's a Swedish flavor, but the apppeal is universal, with thanks to the translator who preserved the artless, direct style of the author." Sat Rev
Followed by: Hugo

In the time of the bells; with drawings by Harald Gripe; tr. from the Swedish by Sheila La Farge. Delacorte Press/Seymour Lawrence 1976 208p illus $6.95, lib. bdg. $6.46 (5 and up) **Fic**

1 Kings and rulers—Fiction 2 Fairy tales
ISBN 0-440-04012-3; 0-440-04014-0   LC 76-5594

"A Merloyd Lawrence book"
Original Swedish edition, 1965
"The strange, haunting-toned story of adolescent King Arvid, who is more suited to scholarship than to ruling, and his 'whipping boy,' Helge, who turns out to be his illegitimate brother and—by temperament—the rightful heir to the throne. The two boys, after becoming involved with sisters who reflect their respective differences, eventually exchanged destinies." Booklist
"The author's latest story offers sharp characterization in a philosophical fairy tale full of discussion of determinism and free will. . . . The exploration of distinctive secondary characters, such as the sharp-witted dwarf and the ethereal queen-to-be, add to the richness of the tale; and when the author strays from the main plot, she does so to enlarge upon her philosophical theme." Horn Bk

The night daddy; with drawings by Harald Gripe; tr. from the Swedish by Gerry Bothmer. Delacorte Press 1971 150p illus lib. bdg. $4.58 (4-6) **Fic**

1 Baby sitters—Fiction
ISBN 0-440-06391-4   LC 77-132365

"A Seymour Lawrence book"
Original Swedish edition, 1968
This story deals with "the developing friendship between an adult and a child. . . . The night daddy, a young writer hired as babysitter for precocious, fatherless Julia, [and Julia herself] describe their relationship in a series of alternating journal entries." Pub W
"The story has a direct, ingenuous style and a warmth and affection that are truly touching." Sat Rev
Followed by Julia's house. Delacorte Press $5.95. lib. bdg. $5.47 (ISBN 0-440-04413-8; 0-440-04476-6; LC 74-22632)

Haar, Jaap ter

Boris; tr. from the Dutch by Martha Mearns; illus. by Rien Poortvliet. Delacorte Press [1970 c1969] 152p illus $4.50 (5 and up) **Fic**

1 Leningrad—Siege, 1941-1944—Fiction
ISBN 0-440-00747-X   LC 77-122770

"A Seymour Lawrence book"
Original Dutch edition, 1966. This translation first published 1969 in England
"The siege of Leningrad is vividly depicted in a moving, grimly realistic story of a twelve-year-old Russian boy who learns to forgive during the hostilities of war. Foraging for buried potatoes in Noman's-land, Boris and his friend Nadia are captured by a group of German soldiers who share their food with the starving children and risk their own lives to return Boris and Nadia safely to the Russian lines." Booklist

Hale, Lucretia P.

The complete Peterkin papers; with the original illus. Introduction by Nancy Hale. Houghton 1960 302p illus $5.95 (5 and up) **Fic**

1 Family life—Fiction
ISBN 0-395-06792-8   LC 60-9095

The first of the Peterkin papers appeared in: Our Young Folks, in 1867 and continued in its successor: Saint Nicholas, until 1879. First published in book form 1880. This is the first one volume edition of the tales. Included are four stories that have not been in print since the 1886 edition, and the complete text of: The last of the Peterkins
"Such a resourceful and ingenuous family as the Peterkins is seldom beheld. Undaunted by the little difficulties of everyday life, they meet every crisis with spirit [and the help of the Lady from Philadelphia]. Like all good nonsense stories, it is told with a very straight face." Bks for Boys & Girls. 3d edition
"Here are all that gaiety and absurdity—the absurdity of the familiar and the commonplace that give these stories their special character." NY Times Bk Rev

Hall, Lynn

Riff, remember. Follett 1973 107p $4.95, lib. bdg. $5.97 (4 and up) **Fic**

1 Dogs—Fiction
ISBN 0-695-80413-8; 0-695-40413-X   LC 73-81998

"Riff's life changes dramatically after his first owner's death; from a luxurious, well-regulated household, the elegant borzoi is transplanted into the rough world of a hunting camp, where he becomes the special pet of a gentle young boy who is also something of a misfit. When the boy is killed in a hunting accident, Riff proves himself by tracking down the man who is responsible, and thus wins the love of the boy's father." Booklist

Hamilton, Virginia

Arilla Sun Down. Greenwillow Bks. 1976 248p $8.79, lib. bdg. $8.40 (6 and up) **Fic**

1 Indians of North America—Fiction 2 Blacks—Fiction
ISBN 0-688-80058-0; 0-688-84058-2   LC 76-13180

"Arilla Adams is of a mixed black and Indian family. Each member is unique—her mother, a creative dancer; her father, an intuitive strider of old and new ways, her brother, Sun Run, possessed with a kind of heroic charisma. In the course of the book Arilla finds her own importance as one who has confronted illusions and fear with courage and curiosity. She has stepped down the path to becoming a writer." Booklist
"In an unusual, colorful, and sometimes confusing combination of Black, Indian and teenage parlance, 12-year-old Arilla Adams tells of coming to terms with her strange and unpredictable family. . . . Aside from the structural and language complexity (stream-of-consciousness prose mixing verbless sentences and participial phrases), Arilla's feelings and thoughts are not at all typical of most 12-year-olds. Nonetheless, very memorable and moving scenes from the story lodge in readers' minds." Sch Library J

The house of Dies Drear; illus. by Eros Keith. Macmillan Pub. Co. 1968 246p lib. bdg. $7.95 (5 and up) **Fic**

1 Ohio—Fiction 2 Mystery and detective stories 3 Blacks—Fiction
ISBN 0-02-742500-2   LC 68-23059

Thirteen-year-old Thomas Small moves with his family from North Carolina to a house in Ohio which is reputed to be haunted because of its connection with run-away slaves and murders of the past. In his search to answer the secrets of the past, Thomas also finds a deeper sense of his own connection with that past
"The answer to the mystery comes in a startling dramatic dénouement that is pure theater. This is gifted writing; the characterization is unforgettable, the plot imbued with mounting tension. It is in a way irrelevant that the principals are black, for the haunting story and the author's craftsmanship are paramount, but, in a deeper sense, that this kind of book has been written about Negroes is of tremendous importance. Not a problem novel, [this] is memorable literature that gives dignity to black heritage." Sat Rev

Hamilton, Virginia—*Continued*

Justice and her brothers. Greenwillow Bks. 1978 217p $8.50, lib. bdg. $8.16 (6 and up) **Fic**

1 Brothers and sisters—Fiction 2 Twins—Fiction 3 Thought transference—Fiction
ISBN 0-688-80182-X; 0-688-84182-1 LC 78-54684

"With school out for the summer and her parents gone for most of the day, 11-year-old Justice is left in the company of her twin brothers, Thomas and Levi, two years older and as different in personality as they are identical in appearance. Thomas, the aggressive dominating twin, has a bad stutter and a highly developed talent as a drummer; he is often cruel and Justice is afraid of him. Levi, a gentle, articulate music lover who enjoys cooking, tries to protect Justice but he is completely under his twin's mental control much of the time." Sch Library J

"Here is Miss Hamilton at her best, plunging her characters into unique situations in order to work out the ambivalence and antagonisms of family relationships which she understands so well. She . . . risks even more than usual when she gives the identical twins the power of telepathic communication with each other." NY Times Bk Rev

M. C. Higgins, the great (6 and up) **Fic**

1 Blacks—Fiction 2 Family life—Fiction 3 Appalachian region—Fiction

Some editions are:
Hall, G.K.&Co. lib. bdg. $9.95 Large type edition (ISBN 0-8161-6356-1; LC 76-1002)
Macmillan Pub Co. $7.95 (ISBN 0-02-742480-4; LC 72-92439)

First published 1974 by Macmillan Publishing Company
Awarded the Newbery Medal, 1975

"The oldest son of a poor Black family whose roots are in the hills [of Appalachia] May Cornelius Higgins tends his younger brothers and sisters while his father and mother work long, hard hours. Into M. C.'s lonely life come two strangers—the 'dude' who wants to tape his mother's beautiful singing voice, and a Black teenage girl traveling cross-country for the summer who shows M.C. there is a world beyond his mountain. M.C.'s relationships with these two strangers and with his proud, stubborn father break down the boy's adolescent illusions and fantasies and permit him to become an adult with the power and responsibility to lead a life of his own choosing." Sch Library J

"Visual images are strong and vivid; and many passages are poetic in their beauty. . . . All of the themes are handled contrapuntally to create a memorable picture of a young boy's growing awareness of himself and of his surroundings." Horn Bk

Zeely; illus. by Symeon Shimin. Macmillan Pub. Co. 1967 122p illus $7.95, pa $1.50 (4 and up) **Fic**

1 Blacks—Fiction
ISBN 0-02-742470-7; 0-02-043510-X LC 66-31616

"Imaginative eleven-year-old Geeder is stirred when she sees Zeely Tayber, who is dignified, stately, and six-and-a-half feet tall. Geeder thinks Zeely looks like the magazine picture of the Watusi queen. Through meeting Zeely personally and getting to know her, Geeder finally returns to reality." Rdng Ladders for Human Relations. 5th ed.

"A carefully constructed mood narrative with a little bit of mystery and a great deal of understanding for girls going through the hero-worshiping phase." Wis Library Bul

Hámori, László

Dangerous journey; tr. from the Swedish by Annabelle MacMillan; illus. by W. T. Mars. Harcourt 1962 190p illus $5.95, pa $1.75 (5 and up) **Fic**

1 Refugees, Hungarian—Fiction
ISBN 0-15-221790-8; 0-15-023821-7 LC 62-8742

Original Swedish edition, 1959

During the Russian occupation of Hungary, twelve-year-old Latsi and his friend Pishta flee from Budapest in a freight car. This is only the beginning of a dangerous journey for Latsi who seeks freedom and hopes to join his parents who had fled earlier to Sweden

"In addition to his youth and inexperience [Latsi] has the problems of refugees everywhere with language barriers, unscrupulous 'helpers,' red tape homesickness and confusion. . . . Enlightening reading for American boys and girls." Pub W

Hanlon, Emily

The swing. Bradbury Press 1979 209p $7.95 (5 and up) **Fic**

1 Deaf—Fiction 2 Stepchildren—Fiction
ISBN 0-87888-146-8 LC 78-26400

"Beth is eleven and deaf. She feels that the swing near her family's summer home is a dear and private possession, although she'd found it already put up in a tree that is not on her parents' property. Danny, three years older, resents Beth's preempting the swing; he too thinks of it as his private place, and he needs a private place because he so desperately is fighting the stepfather who keeps trying to be a real father to him. The twined plots have to do with Danny's being persecuted by some bullies and Beth's anguished concern for some wild bears; at the close of the story the two become friends." Chicago. Children's Bk Center

This story "manages to depict the disparate feelings of the adults in coping with the problems of their children and at the same time accurately portrays the anguish and joys of two young people in the throes of growing up." VOYA

Härtling, Peter

Oma; illus. by Jutta Ash; tr. by Anthea Bell. Harper 1977 96p illus $6.95 (3-5) **Fic**

1 Grandmothers—Fiction 2 Old age—Fiction
ISBN 0-06-022237 LC 76-58719

Original German edition published 1975

"The story of an elderly German woman and her relationship with a small grandson, who comes to live with her when his parents are killed. The two cope with the differences and conflicts imposed by poverty as well as by a situation that has brought striking changes in the lifestyles of each." Chicago. Children's Bk Center

"This warm, often humorous story of mutual love and respect is most notable for the picture it gives of Oma, a self-reliant, individualistic woman. She tries not only to provide for Kalle's physical needs, but also to understand the boy and the ways and pressures of his generation, as well as to help him to become independent and develop a good sense of values. Sincere, honest, and plain in style, this open-ended story of a strong, older woman and her grandson should appeal to young readers." Children's Bk Rev Serv

Haugaard, Erik Christian

Hakon of Rogen's saga; illus. by Leo and Diane Dillon. Houghton 1963 132p illus $6.95, pa 95¢ (6 and up) **Fic**

1 Vikings—Fiction
ISBN 0-395-06803-7; 0-395-16037-5 LC 63-10901

"Hakon, living at the end of the Viking period, is the rightful heir to the island of Rogen. Because of Hakon's youth, his uncle tries to take possession of Rogen. As he deals with treachery, vengeance, and dishonesty, Hakon develops from a boy into a man." Rdng Ladders. 5th edition

"Hakon of Rogen's Saga, though not drawn from legend, is so infused with the feeling of the Norse sagas, and the author is so steeped in them and so completely at home in their settings, that the story has the atmosphere and conviction of a northern epic." Horn Bk

Followed by: A slave's tale. Houghton $7.95 (ISBN 0-395-06804-5; LC 65-12171)

The little fishes; illus. by Milton Johnson. Houghton 1967 214p illus $6.95 (6 and up) **Fic**

1 Orphans—Fiction 2 World War, 1939-1945—Fiction 3 Italy—Fiction
ISBN 0-395-06802-9 LC 67-14701

"Twelve-year-old Guido is one of the orphans who lived by their wits in the streets of Naples during World War II. His remarkable spirit . . . enables him to keep himself and two of the other street-children alive and hopeful of the future. With Anna and her little brother Mario, Guido makes his way to Cassino where Mario, never as strong as the other children, dies. After the Allied victory at Cassino, Guido and Anna decide to stay together and continue their journey still hopeful of finding a new home." Library J

"Whatever happened to Guido, the story of his struggle to escape the bitterness and hatred and degradation of the unclean waters of war is much more than the lesson in history Erik Haugaard calls it in his preface. It is a lesson in life, written in a bare, simple prose which vibrates with love and understanding. The Little Fishes is a deeply moving and beautiful testimonial to the triumph of the human spirit." Bk Week

Haugaard, Erik C.—*Continued*

Orphans of the wind; illus. by Milton Johnson. Houghton 1966 186p illus $7.95 (6 and up)   **Fic**

1 Sea stories 2 U.S.—History—Civil War, 1861-1865—Fiction
ISBN 0-395-06805-3   LC 66-17172

"At twelve, Jim is signed on as a deckboy for the Civil War blockade runner 'Four Winds' by his selfish uncle. Leaving Bristol and sailing to Charleston, his life is changed by the people he meets and the things that happen. Many crewmen are concerned about slavery and question the ship's cargo of guns and powder. When the ship is burned Jim and three of his fellow crewmen row to shore. In order to travel North to join what they feel is the right cause, they travel with the Confederate Army. Their feelings as men in battle as well as their desire to do the right thing are well described." Rdng Ladders. 5th edition

Hays, Wilma Pitchford

Pilgrim Thanksgiving; illus. by Leonard Weisgard. Coward-McCann 1955 unp illus lib. bdg. $4.99 (3-5)   **Fic**

1 Thanksgiving Day—Fiction 2 Pilgrims (New England colonists)—Fiction
ISBN 0-698-30281-8   LC 55-10791

"Damaris Hopkins finds that the best thing about the first Thanksgiving feast is making friends with the dreaded Indians." Hodges. Bks for Elem Sch Libraries
"The true meaning of Thanksgiving is here brought out in an authentic and personal narrative of a real Pilgrim family, and in the beautiful saffron, brown and black illustrations." NY Times Bk Rev

Haywood, Carolyn

"B" is for Betsy; written and illus. by Carolyn Haywood. Harcourt 1939 159p illus $6.95, pa $2.50 (2-4)   **Fic**

1 School stories
ISBN 0-15-204975-4; 0-15-611695-2   LC 39-6264

"The first day of school is a momentous one. For Betsy it would have been overwhelming but for the comforting knowledge of the presence of Koala bear in her schoolbag and the new friendship with Ellen. A simple, direct story of a six-year-old girl's first year in school; the incidents chosen are the commonplace ones which loom large in a child's life. . . . Appealing black-and-white illustrations; large type, well leaded." Booklist

Some other books about Betsy are available from Morrow (unless otherwise noted):
Back to school with Betsy $7.95, pa $1.95 (Harcourt ISBN 0-15-205512-6; 0-15-610200-5; LC 43-51225)
Betsy and Billy $6.95, pa $2.50 (Harcourt ISBN 0-15-206765-5; 0-15-611868-8; LC 41-51926)
Betsy and Mr Kilpatrick lib. bdg. $7.92 (ISBN 0-688-31085-0; LC 76-20747)
Betsy and the boys $6.95, pa $1.95 (Harcourt ISBN 0-15-206944-5; 0-15-011688-X; LC 45-35133)
Betsy and the circus lib. bdg. $7.92 (ISBN 0-688-31086-9; LC 54-7623)
Betsy's busy summer lib. bdg. $8.40 (ISBN 0-688-31087-7; LC 56-7894)
Betsy's little star lib. bdg. $7.92 (ISBN 0-688-31088-5; LC 50-8510)
Betsy's play school $8.25, lib. bdg. $7.95 (ISBN 0-688-22115-7; 0-688-32115-1; LC 77-1615)
Betsy's winterhouse lib. bdg. $7.92 (ISBN 0-688-31090-7; LC 58-8374)
Merry Christmas from Betsy lib. bdg. $7.92 (ISBN 0-688-31695-6; LC 72-119844)
Snowbound with Betsy lib. bdg. $7.92 (ISBN 0-688-31684-0; LC 62-10656)

Little Eddie; written and illus. by Carolyn Haywood. Morrow 1971 190p illus lib. bdg. $7.92 (2-4)   **Fic**

ISBN 0-688-31682-4   LC 47-30839

Seven-year-old Eddie Wilson is a little boy who knows what he wants and goes after it. Collecting —stray animals and junk—is his favorite activity. His projects, which sometimes inconvenience his parents, are graphically told. Betsy and some of the other playmates from the author's series entered above reappear here

Some other books about Eddie are also available from Morrow:
Annie Pat and Eddie lib. bdg. $7.92 (ISBN 0-688-31045-1; LC 60-11077)
Eddie and Gardenia lib. bdg. $7.92 (ISBN 0-688-31255-1; LC 51-11435)
Eddie and his big deals, lib. bdg. $7.92 (ISBN 0-688-31251-9; LC 55-8453)
Eddie and Louella, lib. bdg. $7.92 (ISBN 0-688-31254-3; LC 59-10547)
Eddie and the fire engine, lib. bdg. $7.92 (ISBN 0-688-31252-7; LC 49-9783)
Eddie makes music lib. bdg. $8.40 (ISBN 0-688-21256-X; LC 57-9111)
Eddie, the dog holder, lib. bdg. $7.92 (ISBN 0-688-31253-5; LC 66-6357)
Eddie's green thumb lib. bdg. $7.92 (ISBN 0-688-31257-8; LC 64-18998)
Eddie's happenings lib. bdg. $7.92 (ISBN 0-688-31258-6; LC 79-154975)
Eddie's menagerie $8.95, lib. bdg. $8.59 (ISBN 0-688-22158-0; 0-688-32158-5; LC 78-6519)
Eddie's pay dirt lib. bdg. $7.92 (ISBN 0-688-31259-4; LC 53-7101)
Eddie's valuable property $8.25, lib. bdg. $7.92 (ISBN 0-688-22014-2; 0-688-32014-7; LC 74-17499)
Ever-ready Eddie lib. bdg. $7.92 (ISBN 0-688-31277-2; LC 68-27687)

Heide, Florence Parry

Banana twist. Holiday House 1978 111p $7.95 (4-6)   **Fic**

ISBN 0-8234-0334-3   LC 78-6818

"Hooked by a prep school rep who promises a fridge and TV in every dorm room, Jonah D. Krock is gung-ho to file his application. You'd expect Jonah, an habitual liar himself, to see through that claim but he's focused on flimflamming the Fairlee Admissions Board with sanctimonious answers to their questionnaire. That is, when he isn't plotting to dodge neighbor Goober Grube, a walking psychology textbook who's taken it into his head that Jonah has a 'thing' for bananas. Hypocrisy pays off as Jonah gets into Fairlee, but he doesn't get rid of Goober, his boarding school roomie-to-be." Sch Library J
"Told with sparkling ease, this whacky story oozes funny situations at every turn of the page." Booklist

Growing anyway up. Lippincott 1976 128p $7.95 (6 and up)   **Fic**

1 Mentally ill children—Fiction
ISBN 0-397-31657-7   LC 75-40033

"Florence Stirkel, who tells the story, is a withdrawn and disturbed child whose undemonstrative mother, a widow, decides to move to Pennsylvania to be near her sister-in-law, Nina. Florence dislikes the private school in which she has been enrolled, and she dislikes the man who courts and later marries her mother. Only Aunt Nina, volatile and affectionate, awakens Florence's interest and gives her self-confidence. Nina, in fact, is Florence's bridge to a stability that is only beginning to be evident by the end of the book. The adult characters are convincing enough but not explored in depth; Florence is. Her fears, her compulsive patterns of behavior (saying words backwards, feeling unsafe unless she looks in certain directions in a certain way a certain number of times) her self-denigration, are depicted with sharp perception." Sutherland. The Best in Children's Bks

Henry, Marguerite

Black Gold; illus. by Wesley Dennis. Rand McNally 1957 172p illus $5.95, pa $2.95 (4-6)   **Fic**

1 Black Gold (Race horse)—Fiction 2 Horse racing—Fiction
ISBN 0-528-82130-X; 0-528-87688-0   LC 57-14557

The story "of a black stallion, [a Kentucky Derby winner] whose splendid turf record put him in the front rank of champions. Black Gold's courage and will to win were strengthened by the faith which two people, his trainer and his rider, held in him. Marguerite Henry tells their story with conviction, and with a sympathetic knowledge of horses and the people who care for them. Black and white illustrations by Wesley Dennis are full of action." Ontario Library Rev

Henry, Marguerite—*Continued*

Brighty of the Grand Canyon; illus. by Wesley Dennis. Rand McNally 1953 222p illus $6.95, lib. bdg. $4.79, pa $2.95 (4 and up)   **Fic**

1 Donkeys—Fiction 2 Grand Canyon—Fiction
ISBN 0-528-82150-4; 0-528-80163-5; 0-528-87689-9
LC 53-7233

Drawn from a real-life incident, this is the story of "Brighty, the shaggy little burro who roamed the canyons of the Colorado River [and] had a will of his own. He liked the old prospector and Uncle Jim and he helped solve a mystery, but chiefly he was the freedom loving burro." Chicago
"Only those who are unfamiliar with the West would say it is too packed with drama to be true. And the author's understanding warmth for all of God's creatures still shines through her superb ability as a story teller making this a vivid tale." Christian Sci Monitor

Justin Morgan had a horse; illus. by Wesley Dennis. Rand McNally 1954 169p illus $6.95, pa $2.95 (4 and up)   **Fic**

1 Morgan horse—Fiction 2 Vermont—Fiction
ISBN 0-528-82255-1; 0-528-87682-1   LC 54-8903

An expanded version of the book first published 1945 by Wilcox & Follett
Story of the brave little Vermont work horse from which came the famous American breed of Morgan horses. Justin Morgan first owned the horse, but it was the boy Joel Goss who loved "Litte Bub", later called "Justin Morgan", followed him through his career, rescued him from a cruel master, and finally had the pleasure of having him ridden by James Monroe when he was President of the United States
A horse story "in a book that is rich in human values—the sort of book that makes you proud and sometimes brings a lump to your throat." Bk Week
Books consulted: p[174-75]

King of the Wind; illus. by Wesley Dennis. Rand McNally 1948 172p illus $5.95, lib. bdg. $5.97, pa $2.95 (4 and up)   **Fic**

1 Horses—Fiction
ISBN 0-528-82265-9; 0-528-80174-0; 0-528-87686-4
LC 48-8773

Awarded the Newbery Medal, 1949
"A beautiful, sympathetic story of the famous [ancestor of a line of great thoroughbred horses] . . . and the little mute Arabian stable boy who accompanies him on his journey across the seas to France and England [in the eighteenth century]. The lad's fierce devotion to his horse and his great faith and loyalty are skillfully woven into an enthralling tale which children will long remember. The moving quality of the writing is reflected in the handsome illustrations." Wis Library Bul
Books consulted: p[174]

Mustang, wild spirit of the West; illus. by Robert Lougheed. Rand McNally 1966 222p illus $5.95, lib. bdg. $5.97, pa $2.95 (5 and up)   **Fic**

1 Johnston, Annie (Bronn)—Fiction 2 Mustang—Fiction
ISBN 0-528-82327-2; 0-528-80176-7; 0-528-87683-X
LC 66-8847

The "story of how Wild Horse Annie Johnston successfully led the . . . fight to save the mustangs from virtual extinction. Tells of her lifelong fight, first in Nevada and then on a national level, against the cruel practices of mustangers who hunt their prey in planes and trucks." Adventuring with Bks. 2d edition

San Domingo: the medicine hat stallion; illus. by Robert Lougheed. Rand McNally 1972 230p illus $4.95 (4-6)   **Fic**

1 Horses—Fiction 2 Frontier and pioneer life—Fiction
ISBN 0-528-87687-2   LC 72-7416

The author "traces twelve-year-old Peter's coming of age in the rough Nebraska Territory of the mid 1800's. In spite of his father's cruelty, which never basically changes, Peter finds staunch allies in his sympathetic mother, a lively old surveyor named Brislawn, and a faithful Dalmation. But Peter's first love and constant companion is an Indian pony, San Domingo, who shared his boyhood adventures and dies carrying him to safety as a Pony Express rider. Robert Lougheed's vivid drawings and paintings add to the historical setting." Booklist

White stallion of Lipizza; illus. by Wesley Dennis. Rand McNally 1964 116p illus pa $2.95 (5 and up)   **Fic**

1 Lippizaner horse—Fiction 2 Vienna. Spanish Riding School—Fiction 3 Horseback riding—Fiction
ISBN 0-528-87050-5   LC 64-17445

The "story of a young boy and his [Lipizzaner] show stallion in the Spanish Court Riding School of Vienna. The book [also] relates factual history of horsemanship and a rider's devotion to the art of classical riding." Pub W
"The book seems over-extended, however, with many incidents that do not contribute to the story line; the writing style is pedestrian, the authenticity of detail about the horses giving the book its chief value." Chicago. Children's Bk Center

Misty of Chincoteague; illus. by Wesley Dennis. Rand McNally 1947 173p illus $6.95, pa $2.95 (4 and up)   **Fic**

1 Chincoteague pony—Fiction 2 Chincoteague Island—Fiction 3 Assateague Island—Fiction
ISBN 0-528-82315-9; 0-528-87685-6   LC 47-11404

"Each year the wild ponies of Assateague, a small island in Chesapeake Bay, are driven to the neighboring island of Chincoteague to be sold as children's pets. This is the story of one pony, Misty, and the two Chincoteague children who owned her. The atmosphere of the islands and an understanding of the freedom-loving ponies pervade the story and illustrations." Hodges. Bks for Elem Sch Libraries
Two other books about the ponies of Chincoteague Islands are available from Rand McNally:
Sea Star, orphan of Chincoteague $6.95, pa $2.95 (ISBN 0-528-82370-1; 0-528-87687-2; LC 49-11474)
Stormy, Misty's foal $5.95, pa $2.95 (ISBN 0-528-82083-4; 0-528-87690-2; LC 63-13334)

Herman, Charlotte

Our snowman had olive eyes. Dutton 1977 103p lib. bdg. $7.95 (4-6)   **Fic**

1 Grandmothers—Fiction 2 Family life—Fiction
ISBN 0-525-34690-0   LC 77-7143

"At first reluctant to share her room with her 79-year-old Bubbie (Yiddish for grandmother), ten-year-old Sheila soon realizes how lucky she is. Bubbie makes Sheila cookies without a recipe, teaches her how to make a plant cutting, and cures her cough. Her well-meaning ideas to keep Bubbie busy (Sheila seems to be the only one who understands that Bubbie needs to feel useful) often get her in trouble, but when Bubbie decides to live with her other son, Sheila is left with her fond memories." Sch Library J
"Told in the first person, Sheila's reminiscences of her special relationship with her grandmother evoke genuine emotion and suggest the loneliness of aging as well as the concept that growing old does not necessarily mean growing disagreeable. An unpretentious, haunting novel which handles a difficult topic with delicacy and humor." Horn Bk

Heyman, Anita

Exit from home. Crown 1977 277p $7.50 (6 and up)   **Fic**

1 Jews in Russia—Fiction 2 Russia—Fiction
ISBN 0-517-52903-3   LC 77-23323

The author "brings the crisis-ridden days of Russia at the turn of the century into focus through her hero, Samuel, a Jewish boy. A family tragedy harrows him with guilt and forces him to buckle down to his studies at the religious school. But the youth's immersion in books has another result. Samuel learns about the oppressions suffered by his people and becomes one of a group of secret revolutionaries. . . . He loses hopes and illusions, especially after an aborted uprising in 1905. Finally, Samuel is on his way to what he believes will be a new, better life in America." Pub W
"While the message is somber, the writing is not; it is enlivened by good dialogue and by the vivid picture it gives of the Russian Jewish community and its reaction to the first stirrings of rebellion." Chicago. Children's Bk Center

Hickman, Janet

The stones; illus. by Richard Cuffari. Macmillan Pub. Co. 1976 116p illus $7.95 (6 and up)   Fic

ISBN 0-02-743760-4   LC 76-11037

"An elderly man with a German name becomes the target of harassment by a group of boys in a small midwestern town. Among them is 11-year-old Garrett McKay, who acutely misses his soldiering father and chafes at looking after his younger sister. When the recluse, nicknamed Jack Tramp, reacts to their pranks by brnging out his shotgun and wildly discharging it, parental concern brings out a county social worker whose visit implies relegating Jack to the county home. Garrett, in the meantime, is forced to see Jack in human terms. . . . Hickman's story is a quiet examination of behavior and consequences. Her "villains" are boys-next-door whose mischief arises out of boredom rather than any inherent meanness on their part; yet in fact they set into motion the destruction of Jack's spirit. Nicely done—the kind of thoughtful probing that will make for good book discussion." Booklist

Hightower, Florence

The ghost of Follonsbee's Folly; illus. by Ati Forberg. Houghton 1958 218p illus $5.95 (5 and up)   Fic

1 Mystery and detective stories
ISBN 0-395-06814-2   LC 57-12091

"Follonsbee's Folly, an old house of pre-Civil War vintage in the country, is the new home of the Stackpole family, individuals all, and their Negro housekeeper, Angela, who rules them with a firm but loving hand. The mansion's intriguing history unearthed by Elsie, twelve, and the identity of the vagabond young Negro man with whom Tom, eleven, secretly spends idyllic days on the river, provide the mystery for this thoroughly enjoyable story. . . . Situations are lively, the humor unforced, and, except for one occasion when memorable Angela steps out of character, the characters are remarkably believable." Booklist

Hildick, E. W.

Louie's lot. White, David [1968 c1965] 146p $3.95 (6 and up)   Fic

1 Great Britain—Fiction
ISBN 0-87250-220-1   LC 68-10662

First published 1965 in England

Louie is "a milk delivery man . . . in a small English town. Fourteen-year-old Tim Shaw passes the arduous tests to fill a vacancy in Louie's squad but finds that succeeding on the job is even more difficult. . . . An explanatory preface . . . of English slang expressions [is included]." Library J

This "lively adventure story is written with adult humor that doesn't condescend to youth, yet makes clear that no matter how momentous troubles seem, the world is not really coming to an end." NY Times Bk Rev

Another book about Louie is: Louie's ransom. Knopf $6.95, lib. bdg. $6.99 (ISBN 0-394-83458-5; 0-394-93458-X; LC 77-212140)

Manhattan is missing; illus. by Jan Palmer. Avon [1970 c1969] 189p illus pa $1.25 (4-6)   Fic

1 Cats—Fiction 2 New York (City)—Fiction 3 British in the U.S.—Fiction 4 Mystery and detective stories
ISBN 0-380-01488-2

"Camelot books"

First published 1969 by Doubleday

"An English family sublets a New York apartment and assumes responsibility for Manhattan, the owner's precious Siamese cat. But Manhattan is kidnapped and held for ransom. In tracking down the culprit, the children, with the help of new American friends, learn something of Central Park, the subway, and other aspects of New York City." Moorachian. What is a City?

"This is a lively, very funny story. Mr Hildick's keen awareness of human nature, his good ear for conversation, and his obvious enjoyment of his subject make for delightful reading." Bk World

Hilgartner, Beth

A necklace of fallen stars; illus. by Michael R. Hague. Little 1979 209p illus $8.95 (4-6)   Fic

1 Fairy tales
ISBN 0-316-36236-0   LC 79-14916

"The King of Visin has three daughters, the youngest of whom "should have been born a boy.' To punish her, he arranges a marriage to a political ally. She runs away, supporting herself along the way by telling . . . minstrel tales. . . . She is pursued by magicians with crystal balls, soldiers, spirits, and all manner of Celtic demons, but in the end, is . . . won back to the fold by grief at her father's death. The language, especially the made-up Celtic names, is appropriate and interesting." Sch Library J

"With many serpentine twists and surprises, the story is refreshingly different and a natural attraction, of course, for youthful feminists." Pub W

Hinton, S. E.

The outsiders. Viking 1967 188p lib. bdg. $7.95 (5 and up)   Fic

1 Juvenile delinquency—Fiction
ISBN 0-670-53257-6   LC 67-13606

In a small Oklahoma city, "the outsiders are the tough, lower class boys who have a running feud with a middle class gang. . . .Ponyboy [an outsider] is witness to a murder by one of his pals; the two boys go to a hideaway, decide to give themselves up, and stop to help rescue some small children from a fire. Ponyboy's partner dies in the hospital, and out of his grief and despair come some insight." Chicago. Children's Bk Center

"This remarkable novel by a seventeen-year-old girl gives a moving, credible view of the outsiders from the inside—their loyalty to each other, their sensitivity under tough crusts, their understanding of self and society." Horn Bk

Hoban, Russell

The mouse and his child; pictures by Lillian Hoban. Harper 1967 181p illus $7.95, lib. bdg. $7.89 (4-6)   Fic

1 Fantastic fiction
ISBN 0-06-022377-4; 0-06-022378-2   LC 67-19624

A fantasy "that chronicles the hazardous and heroic adventures of a broken windup mouse child and his father in search of happiness and security. Love and valor ultimately triumph over violence and evil in a realistically created world of humanly characterized windup toys and real animals including a malevolent rat, a fortune-telling frog, a scholarly snapping turtle, and a play-producing crow. Limited in appeal but for the special reader a rare treat and for the perceptive adult a delight to share. Small black-and-white drawings fittingly complement the spirit of the story." Booklist

Hodges, Margaret

The freewheeling Joshua Cobb; illus. by Richard Cuffari. Farrar, Straus 1974 108p illus $5.95 (4 and up)   Fic

1 Bicycles and bicycling—Fiction 2 Camping—Fiction
ISBN 0-374-32464-6   LC 74-11456

Sequel to: The hatching of Joshua Cobb, o.p. 1981

"It is the first bicycle camping trip for Josh. He and four others pedal through New England, stopping at youth hostels. The group's excitement and adventures make an interesting story. The trials with one member and Josh's growth in independence provide some good thought-provoking situations for the reader." Adventuring With Bks

Hoff, Syd

Irving and me. Harper 1967 226p $8.95 (5 and up)   Fic

1 Jews in the U.S.—Fiction 2 Florida—Fiction
ISBN 0-06-022498-3   LC 67-7749

"Poor Artie, he wanted to live in Brooklyn forever, but a thirteen-year-old has little choice. His parents wanted to move to Florida, and that was how Artie met Irving. He had a few problems: girls, bullies, the youth director of the Community Center, and no dog; and his life was not eased by the determined companionship of Irving, a boy

Hoff, Syd—*Continued*

with a real flair for doing the wrong thing. Once Artie resigned himself to the fact that his girl had given her heart to another, and decided to keep a stray dog, he was willing to admit that Florida wasn't so bad. The story has a zestful, zany, sometimes sophisticated humor; told by Artie, it is spontaneous and colloquial; and it is refreshingly casual about being Jewish and about being an only child." Sutherland. The Best in Children's Bks

Holland, Barbara

Prisoners at the kitchen table. Houghton 1979 122p front $8.95 (4-6)   **Fic**

1 Kidnapping—Fiction
ISBN 0-395-28969-6   LC 79-11730

"Clarion books"
"The kidnapping of two children unfolds from the point of view of Josh, a quiet, cautious child who admires the gutsy, daredevil nature of his friend Polly. In the course of the abduction, their roles are reversed: Polly becomes frightened and helpless while Josh, although just as frightened, thinks clearly and carefully and eventually engineers their escape." Booklist
"It is Josh who realizes that [the kidnappers] Bill and Verna are as much prisoners of their situation as he is. . . . The focus here is on feelings, not plot. The author could have embellished the escape with more suspense, but she keeps it well within the realm of realism. Readers never learn whether Bill and Verna are captured, a plus since by novel's end it is apparent that the couple are pathetic losers." Sch Library J

Holland, Isabelle

Alan and the animal kingdom. Lippincott 1977 191p $8.95 (4-6)   **Fic**

1 Orphans—Fiction 2 Animals—Fiction
ISBN 0-397-31745-X   LC 76-55371

"An orphan, the [hero] has lived with several relatives and is heartbroken when the animals he loves are destroyed by the authorities at the breakup of his home when his uncle dies. Alan is sent to live with his great-aunt Jessie and is consoled when she allows him to keep strays he collects. Life is good until Jessie succumbs to a heart attack. Determined to keep her death a secret and save his pets, Alan finds it increasingly difficult to cope with reality and deceive teachers, among other interested adults." Pub W
"This is an absorbing and skillfully written book with excellent character development of Alan, a twelve-year-old. . . . Ms. Holland does well in helping us to understand what is behind Alan's actions, and what kinds of feelings he is experiencing. This is a sympathetic book—sometimes sad, sometimes funny, sometimes joyful. Life doesn't work out for Alan exactly the way he would like; it never has, and maybe never will. But we are left with an end that is realistic and, most likely, positive." Children's Bk Rev Serv

Dinah and the Green Fat Kingdom. Lippincott 1978 189p $7.95 (5 and up)   **Fic**

1 Family life—Fiction 2 Obesity—Fiction
ISBN 0-397-31818-9   LC 78-8612

12-year-old Dinah Randall is overweight and miserable but resents her family's nagging her to lose weight. "Mother bribes, bargains, and threatens; older brother Tony teases; and perfect-in-every-way cousin Brenda (who lives with the Randalls) poses a constant threat by smugly existing in a thin state. Dinah's only solace is dreaming and writing about the Green Fat Kingdom where fat is beautiful. While pressure on the home front mounts, Dinah receives some badly needed support from surprising sources: an 'ugly' puppy she buys, the understanding nutritionist her mother sends her to, and a cerebral palsy victim who has learned to deal with his problem." Sch Library J
"The author's storytelling skill, sensitivity, and psychological acumen raise the book above the level of its own topicality." Horn Bk

Holling, Holling Clancy

Minn of the Mississippi; written and illus. by Holling Clancy Holling. Houghton 1951 85p illus lib. bdg. $9.95, pa $3.95 (4-6)   **Fic**

1 Turtles—Fiction 2 Mississippi River—Fiction
ISBN 0-395-17578-X; 0-395-27399-4   LC 51-6290

Minn of the Mississippi is a tough snapping turtle. The story of the Mississippi River is here told in text and pictures as Minn is carried from the Minnesota headwaters of the Mississippi to the Gulf of Mexico. The time required in Minn's life is twenty-five years but the story reaches back into history to make the tale complete
"In telling the story of Minn, a snapping turtle, the author touches on the geography, history, geology and climate of the Mississippi River. . . . Illustrated with full page pictures in color and many marginal pencil drawings." Los Angeles. Sch Libraries

Paddle-to-the-sea; written and illus. by Holling Clancy Holling. Houghton 1941 unp illus lib. bdg. $9.95, pa $2.95 (4-6)   **Fic**

1 Great Lakes—Fiction
ISBN 0-395-15082-5; 0-395-29203-4   LC 41-13399

A toy canoe with a seated Indian figure is launched in Lake Nipigon by the Indian boy who carved it and in four years travels thru all the Great Lakes and the St Lawrence River to the Atlantic. An interesting picture of the shore life of the lakes and the river with striking full page pictures in bright colors and marginal pencil drawings
"The canoe's journey is used to show the flow of currents and of traffic, and each occurrence is made to seem plausible. . . . There are also diagrams of a sawmill, a freighter, the canal locks at the Soo, and Niagara Falls." Library J
"This is geography of the best kind made vivid by the power of imagination." Horn Bk

Seabird; written and illus. by Holling Clancy Holling. Houghton 1948 58p illus lib. bdg. $8.95, pa $3.95 (4-6)   **Fic**

1 Whaling—Fiction 2 Sea stories
ISBN 0-395-18230-1; 0-395-26681-5   LC 48-7832

Seabird is an ivory gull carved by Ezra Brown when he was just a boy while on a whaler in 1832. It brought luck and good sailing to him and to his descendants on all the seven seas, and through many years of thrilling sea adventures
"Through four generations of seamen Seabird saw the whaler give way to the clipper, the clipper yield to steam, the airplane succeed both. The subject takes the reader over the globe and provides room for imagination to aid history in vitalizing the period. The beauty of the illustrations [full-page color pictures and decorative sketches] gives the book distinction." Horn Bk

Tree in the trail; written and illus. by Holling Clancy Holling. Houghton 1942 unp illus lib. bdg. $8.95 (4 and up)   **Fic**

1 Trees—Fiction 2 Sante Fé Trail—Fiction
ISBN 0-395-18228-X   LC 42-25811

"The story of a cottonwood tree that watched the pageant of history on the Santa Fe trail where it stood, a landmark to travelers and a peace-medicine tree to Indians, for over 200 years." Booklist
"The care with which this [book] is documented by pictures makes it exceptional usefulness. Besides the large color plates, every important detail in the story appears in small pencil studies on the wide margins of facing pages." NY Her Trib Bks

Holm, Anne

North to freedom; tr. from the Danish by L. W. Kingsland. Harcourt 1965 190p $5.95 (6 and up)   **Fic**

1 Refugees—Fiction
ISBN 0-15-257550-2   LC 65-12612

"Twelve-year-old David, whose only memory is of life in a prison camp, escapes and makes his way across Europe alone. Before he is reunited with his mother, his prison-bred fear of people has gradually faded, and he has learned that goodness as well as evil exists in the world." Hodges. Bks for Elem Sch Libraries
First published 1963 in Denmark. Winner of the 1963 Gyldendal Prize for the best Scandinavian children's book
"The writing style is good, the psychological insight into David's changing reactions is perceptive: as the boy meets people, he slowly loses the suspicion and hostility engendered by past life. . . . The story is somewhat weakened by the pat ending." Chicago. Children's Bk Center

Holman, Felice

The murderer. Scribner 1978 151p lib. bdg. $7.95 (5 and up) **Fic**

1 Jews in the U.S.—Fiction 2 Pennsylvania—Fiction

ISBN 0-684-15904-X   LC 78-14266

"Set in a coal mining town in Pennsylvania in the depths of the Depression, [this story] follows one Hershy Marks, age 12—bright, curious store-keeper's son and Jew in a sea of prejudiced Polish miners in Ashlymine, Pennsylvania." Sch Library J

"A broad world found in a small town, a large vista in a brief novel, Hershy's progress toward his Bar Mitzvah and the decline of his father's hardware store are the motivating forces of this novel. Each leads to an unlikely conclusion, both allow much to be explored, allow the story to include the feeling of business and family life, a sense of what the depression was like in a daily way, and the personal side of a distinctly American conflict of cultures." Christian Sci Monitor

Slake's limbo. Scribner 1974 117p $7.95 (6 and up) **Fic**

1 Runaways—Fiction 2 Subways—Fiction 3 New York (City)—Fiction

ISBN 0-684-13926-X   LC 74-11675

Aremis Slake, at the age of thirteen, takes to the New York City subways as a refuge from an abusive home life and oppressive school system

"The economically told chronicle of Slake's adventures is more than a survival saga; it is also an eloquent study of poverty, of fear, and finally of hope." Horn Bk

Hoover, H. M.

The Delikon. Viking 1977 148p $9.95 (5 and up) **Fic**

1 Science fiction

ISBN 0-670-26681-7   LC 76-54271

In this novel "the young Delikon teacher Varina (aged 307) and the two human children she is training as future leaders are caught up in the violent revolution which will end the centuries-long colonial rule of Earth by the Delikon. In a series of harrowing and often nightmarish adventures, the children escape human captors, face Delikon weapons, lose their dearest friend, and finally reach safety." Sch Library J

"A gracefully written novel of the future which can be read on two levels: as an exciting adventure story and as a novel—beyond the scope of much science fiction—with implications on the nature of human beings." Horn Bk

Treasures of Morrow. Four Winds 1976 171p $6.95 (5 and up) **Fic**

1 Science fiction

ISBN 0-590-07420-2   LC 75-28098

Sequel to: Children of Morrow, o.p. 1981

"The adventures of a girl and boy involved with two future societies. After the Death of the Seas when 93 percent of all living creatures die due to human carelessness, only two groups survive. Tia and Rabbit escape from the primitive, repressive society of Base, located northeast of San Francisco, and are rescued by explorers from Morrow, who fix their location by telepathic communication. Although at first the children are overjoyed with the advanced utopian society at Morrow . . . their delight is mixed with dread after they promise to accompany the curious Elite back to Base in order to investigate the other human survivors. There is plenty of excitement and danger as well as truths which apply to all societies." Sch Library J

Household, Geoffrey

Escape into daylight. Little 1976 138p illus lib. bdg. $6.95 (6 and up) **Fic**

1 Kidnapping—Fiction 2 Great Britain—Fiction

ISBN 0-316-37436-9   LC 76-10162

"An Atlantic Monthly Press book"

"Carrie Falconer, young daughter of a British movie star, is kidnapped and held for ransom. When Mike Browse, son of a local farmer, unwittingly sees too much, he too is kidnapped and locked up with Carrie in the pitch black cellar of an old abbey. The self-reliant children manage to escape and are chased through surrounding fields and woods. The villains are ruthless. The children are terrified but enterprising, and the suspense is terrific." Sch Library J

Both Mike "and Carrie are intelligent and inventive within the bounds of credibility in a story that has firm structure, action and suspense, and an ingenious setting." Chicago. Children's Bk Center

Houston, James

Frozen fire; a tale of courage; drawings by the author. Atheneum Pubs. 1977 149p $8.95 (6 and up) **Fic**

1 Wilderness survival—Fiction 2 Arctic regions—Fiction

ISBN 0-689-50083-1   LC 77-6366

"A Margaret K. McElderry book"

"Based on the true and dramatic ordeal of an Eskimo boy in the 1960's, this adventure story is set . . . in the far north. Kayak, a classmate of Matthew Morgan's in their Baffin Island school, suggests to his new friend Mattoosie (Matthew) that they take a snowmobile and go to the rescue of Mattoosie's father when the latter, a prospector, disappears. The spare can of gasoline leaks, and the two boys face a homeward trek through seventy-five miles of whirling snow and bitter cold." Chicago. Children's Bk Center

"Convincing dialogue, good pace, and lean style mark this as first-class adventure with a partial basis in fact." Sch Library J

Ghost paddle; a northwest coast Indian tale; written and illus. by James Houston. Harcourt 1972 55p illus $5.50 (4-6) **Fic**

1 Indians of North America—Fiction

ISBN 0-15-230760-5   LC 72-72364

"In a tale of the Northwest Canadian Indian, the author tells of an island clan tired of warfare with the Inland River people and determined to make a peace-seeking expedition to these Indians. Two canoes set forth, led by brave young Hooits and his father, the famous chieftain Wasco, who has carved for his son a 'ghost' paddle with magical powers. Hooits wields this implement against a gigantic slave of the Inland Warriors, defeats the giant, and thus secures an opportunity to talk about deceptions of the past and make the way clear to the resumption of friendship." Horn Bk

The author's "writing, like his illustrations, has a stark and dramatic simplicity that is eminently right for the dignity of the Indian peoples he describes. . . . The story is so deftly imbued with the spirit and the cultural details of Hooits' people that the incorporation seems effortless, and the theme has a pertinence for today." Chicago. Children's Bk Center

Howe, Deborah

Bunnicula; a rabbit-tale of mystery, by Deborah and James Howe; illus. by Alan Daniel. Atheneum Pubs. 1979 98p illus $8.95 (3-5) **Fic**

1 Animals—Fiction 2 Mystery and detective stories

ISBN 0-689-30700-4   LC 78-11472

"When the Monroes add a new pet to their household and vegetables are drained of their juices and turn white overnight, all the clues point to the little bunny they found in the theater the night they went to see a Dracula movie. The Monroes do not suspect Bunnicula, but their bookish cat, Chester, does. He sits up late reading Edgar Allan Poe and 'The Mark of the Vampire,' and he enlists the help of Harold, the dog, in getting to the bottom of the mystery." Children's Bk Rev Serv

"The plot is less important in the story than the style: blithe, sophisticated, and distinguished for the wit and humor of the dialogue. If readers like shaggy dog stories at all, they'd have to search hard for a funnier one." Chicago. Children's Bk Center

Huddy, Delia

Time piper. Greenwillow Bks. [1979 c1976] 247p $7.95, lib. bdg. $7.63 (5 and up) **Fic**

1 Science fiction

ISBN 0-688-80212-5; 0-688-84212-7   LC 78-24339

"First published 1976 in England

"Luke Crantock accepts a job at Tom Humboldt's lab in London, where Humboldt hopes to reverse the flow of time by means of tachyons, recently discovered subatomic particles. Luke has been followed to London by cold, strangely silent

Huddy, Delia—*Continued*

Griselda—or 'Hare' as she calls herself—a girl he rescued from a gang of boys at home. . . . The completion of Humboldt's experiment—a moment of past time momentarily alive in the present—finally links and resolves Luke's concerns. Griselda and other children who have been gravitating toward the lab, appear at the moment of time reversal. The scene revealed on the time frame shows what turns out to be the original followers of the Pied Piper of Hamelin. The denouement explains how Humboldt's machine had to have been the original Pied Piper and has now re-united the 800-year-old children with their souls, making them whole at last." Sch Library J

"The plot is incidental compared to the theme of a gifted young man's relationship to his family, neighbors, and peers. Before going to London to work on the time machine, eighteen-year-old Luke is at odds with his family and the village, none of whom considers him 'normal' because of his exceptional intelligence. Nor do they understand the strange, silent girl, Hare, to whom Luke feels an emotional pull. . . . A strange yet satisfying book showing how society alienates people it doesn't understand. A good book for intelligent, perceptive young people, but not for everyone." Children's Bk Rev Serv

Hunt, Irene

Across five Aprils; jacket and endsheets by Albert John Pucci. Follett 1964 223p illus $4.95, lib. bdg. $4.98 (6 and up) **Fic**

1 U.S.—History—Civil War, 1861-1865—Fiction 2 Illinois—Fiction 3 Farm life—Fiction
ISBN 0-695-80100-7; 0-695-40100-9   LC 64-17209

"It was April 1861 when the Civil War became a reality for the Creighton family on their farm in southern Illinois. One by one the war pulled the able-bodied men away leaving only the youngest, Jethro, to keep the farm going. This great war that ran across five Aprils is here chronicled by means of what happened to the various members of Jethro's family." Pub W

"In handling her characters the author is particularly skillful. . . . Young readers will appreciate this story more for its warmth of character study than for the action involved, although there is action and the reader is made anxious to see how the family finally makes out at the end of the war." Best Sellers

Up a road slowly; cover painting by Don Bolognese. Follett 1966 192p $4.95, lib. bdg. $4.98 (6 and up) **Fic**

ISBN 0-695-89009-3; 0-695-49009-5   LC 66-16937

Awarded the Newbery Medal, 1967
"Julie Trelling describes her life from the time her mother dies until her high school graduation: ten years. Aunt Cordelia's ramrod soul seems hard to live with, but Julie finds, to her surprise, when her father remarries and wants his daughter at home again, that she has become used to Aunt Cordelia and loves her dearly. The problems of jealousy, first love, parental relations, and snobbishness are handled with ease and honesty; the more serious problems of alcoholism and of emotional disturbance in adult characters are handled with dignity. A moving and beautifully written book." Sutherland. The Best in Children's Bks

William; a novel. Scribner 1977 188p lib. bdg. $7.95 (5 and up) **Fic**

1 Family life—Fiction 2 Unmarried mothers—Fiction
ISBN 0-684-14902-8   LC 76-52455

"Mama keeps her family going with increasing difficulty as the cancer that is killing her brings more pain. Then Sarah, a 16-year-old runaway hiding out to have her baby, moves in next door. The two women help each other out until their families are absorbed into one—responsible William, flighty Amy, blind Carla, and baby Elizabeth, born at home during a hurricane shortly before Mama's death. . . . Memorable personalities and relationships completely overshadow the mention that Sarah and her child are white, Mamma and her children black. In fact, any messages in the book are absorbed through the well-crafted development of the story. Sweet but strong." Booklist

Hunter, Kristin

Soul Brothers & sister Lou. Scribner 1968 248p $8.95 (6 and up) **Fic**

1 Blacks—Fiction
ISBN 0-684-12661-3   LC 68-29365

"An idealistic fourteen-year-old Negro girl grows up trying to maintain some kind of honest perspective in a tough world of ghetto poverty, violence, meaningless white values, and extremes of black bitterness. Louretta Hawkins' efforts to form a social club and singing group in her brother's print shop are jeopardized by misguided destructiveness on the part of both her friends and the police, who gun to death an innocent boy during their raid on a gang dance. Through difficult, disillusioning experiences Louretta discovers what 'soul' is, puts it into her music, and makes a hit record." Booklist

The author "packs a wallop in her first book for young people, which has won the 1968 award of the Council on Interracial Books for Children for the best book by a Negro for older children. . . . Her story is taut, fast moving, absorbing and believable as it probes with honest realism the problems of a wide range of unforgettable characters. . . . This powerful book deserves wide reading." Bk World

Hunter, Mollie

The haunted mountain; a story of suspense; illus. by Laszlo Kubinyi. Harper 1972 125p illus lib. bdg. $8.97, pa $1.95 (5 and up) **Fic**

1 Scotland—Fiction 2 Fantastic fiction
ISBN 0-06-022667-6; 0-06-440041-7   LC 77-183164

"MacAllister defies tradition and plows the Goodman's Croft, a small portion of land that all Scottish Highlanders once set aside for the sidhe, the small shadowy people who have an ancient magic at their command. Although MacAllister wins his initial confrontations with the angered sidhe, they eventually capture and enslave him; only the courage and loyalty of his son saves MacAllister from certain death." Booklist

"Written in bleak, spare prose [this novel] makes good use of its highland setting, where such things seem more possible anyhow, even down to the local names given to certain lakes and mountains. It all happens at no particular time in the past, and has the atmosphere of a real legend. That it is in fact an original work is a tribute to the sustained imagination that went into the gripping mini-epic." New Statesman

The kelpie's pearls; drawings by Stephen Gammell. Harper 1976 134p illus $5.95, lib. bdg. $6.89 (4-6) **Fic**

1 Fantastic fiction 2 Scotland—Fiction
ISBN 0-06-022656-0; 0-06-022659-5   LC 75-25404

First published 1964 in England. Published 1966 in U.S. by Funk
"A kelpie who can change into a black horse with flaming eyes, the Loch Ness monster, a good witch . . . and Tirnan-Og (the land of eternal youth) are woven into [this] . . . fantasy. Morag MacLeod, a lonely old woman, befriends a kelpie and Torquil, a boy who understands animals so well he can almost talk to them, but she makes an enemy of wicked Alasdair, the trapper, because she will not help him steal the kelpie treasure horde of pearls." Sch Library J

"This is so enchantingly told in the gentle dialect of the Highlands that it is a spellbinder from first to last. Read it aloud—in school, home or library." Horn Bk

A sound of chariots. Harper 1972 242p lib. bdg. $8.79 (5 and up) **Fic**

1 Death—Fiction 2 Scotland—Fiction
ISBN 0-06-022669-2   LC 72-76523

A story set in post World War I Scotland. Bridie McShane's happy early childhood is interrupted by the death of her beloved father whose favorite child she was. Her sorrow colors her life as she matures, leading her to morbid reflections on time and death which she finally learns to deal with through her desire to write poetry

"The rich flavor of time and place, the details of poverty, hard work, and religious and political fervor add strength to the story." Horn Bk

Hunter, Mollie

A stranger came ashore; a story of suspense. Harper 1975 163p lib. bdg. $8.79, pa $1.50 (6 and up) **Fic**

1 Shetland Islands—Fiction 2 Animals, Mythical —Fiction
ISBN 0-06-440082-4; 0-06-022652-8 LC 75-10814

"'It was a while ago, in the days when they used to tell stories about creatures called the Selkie Folk,' that on a fiercely stormy night a mysterious stranger appeared from the wild waters off the Shetland Islands. Sheltered by the Hendersons, an island family, the handsome, amiable young foreigner, who called himself Finn Learson, soon won the favor of the crofters and of beautiful Elspeth Henderson. But her twelve-year-old brother Robbie had been nurtured on their grandfather's old tales; the boy suspected that Finn was really the legendary Great Selkie, who could shed his seal skin to walk the earth as a man and who carried off young girls to his crystal palace at the bottom of the sea. For Robbie, the old stories, the omens, and the warning his grandfather had whispered on the eve of his death gradually shifted into focus like the bits of a kaleidoscope, and the boy sought help from the only person who would listen—the inscrutable, raven-like wizard, Yarl Corbie. On a festival night filled with ancient ritual and primitive traditions, Robbie faced a double terror as the struggle between earth magic and sea magic was joined. The author has written another suspense story finely laced with folklore; her storytelling is as spontaneous as it is irresistible." Horn Bk

The stronghold. Harper 1974 259p $8.95, lib. bdg. $8.79 (6 and up) **Fic**

1 Druids and Druidism—Fiction 2 Scotland—Fiction
ISBN 0-06-022653-6; 0-06-022654-4 LC 73-14340

Set during the days when Druids were the priests in Scotland and the Romans raided the Scottish coasts for slaves, this is the story of Coll, a youth crippled as a result of such a raid, who designs fortresses to turn back the Roman invaders

The author "takes an enormous leap back in time, to the origins of the brochs—mysterious circular Bronze Age fortresses found only in the Highlands and islands of Scotland. . . . The force of Druidical magic, and the mercilessness of tribal ritual, are effectively shown without sadistic overemphasis on detail. And the story of Coll's generation coming of age entwines neatly with the building of the first broch and the rejection of an ambitious traitor. This . . . is a good book well-written, original and convincing." Christian Sci Monitor

The third eye. Harper 1979 276p $7.95, lib. bdg. $8.79 (6 and up) **Fic**

1 Scotland—Fiction
ISBN 0-06-022676-5; 0-06-022677-3 LC 78-22159

"The locale [of this novel] is the Scottish Highlands of the early 1900s, where young Jinty (Janet) tries valiantly to keep faith with the Earl of Ballinford after his death. Jinty has 'the third eye,' the sensitivity that pierces the facades of family and others in her village. It is this insight that has attracted the 'bad old Earl' (as he is known by most) to Jinty and elicited his confidence. Jinty knows that the Earl has taken his life, in a seeming accident, to spare his only son, doomed by an ancient curse. The child has to face a grilling by the implacable Procurator Fiscal, investigating the death, since she was the last to speak to the Earl." Pub W

The "strength of the novel lies in the characterization of the mother and of the three daughters; they are powerfully differentiated: determined, emotional Mrs. Morrison; passionate Meg, who in defiance of her mother's wishes marries at seventeen; cool, calculating Linda, who conspires to make the most of herself in the hotel business; and fey, observant, sympathetic Jinty, whose point of view gives the novel its ultimate meaning and mood." Horn Bk

The walking stones; a story of suspense; illus. by Trina Schart Hyman. Harper 1970 143p illus pa $1.25 (5 and up) **Fic**

1 Scotland—Fiction 2 Fantastic fiction
ISBN 0-06-440034-4 LC 79-121807

"Circles of huge standing stones are familiar in Celtic countries, but it is seldom that anyone expects them to move. The stones in young Donald's highland glen were due to walk down to the river for a centennial ceremony very soon after the completion of a dam that would drown the glen. The Bodach, an old man with mystical powers, was determined to delay the flooding until after the stones had walked. He succeeded, with the help of Donald, who would one day inherit the Bodach's powers." America

This is "a smooth blending of realism and fantasy, a story that reflects Celtic folklore. . . . The story has pace and suspense, and the writing has an authentic cadence that adds to the flavor of the Scottish setting." Chicago. Children's Bk Center

The wicked one; a story of suspense. Harper 1977 136p lib. bdg. $7.89, pa $1.95 (4 and up) **Fic**

1 Scotland—Fiction 2 Fairy tales
ISBN 0-06-022648-X; 0-06-440117-0 LC 76-41515

"In a story set in the Scottish Highlands, Colin Grant lives with his wife and three sons; a forester, he also has a small croft that supports his family nicely. But Colin has a terrible temper, and when he loses it and strikes at a supernatural creature, the Grollican, his troubles begin. His outbuildings are torn down, his haystacks ripped apart, and—worst of all—he falls in love with a beautiful, mischievous fairy. But there's a truce between the fairy folk and human beings, and his enchantress helps Colin by giving him an enchanted horse that never tires, a horse that later proves to be a bewitched girl who is loved by the youngest son. Seeing no way to escape the Grollican, Colin goes to America. And guess who's come over on another boat? And is tricked into serving the Grant family for all time?" Chicago. Children's Bk Center

"Somewhat reminiscent of the author's earlier work 'The Kelpie's Pearl's,' [entered above] the book exudes a fine Highland flavor and is an excellent example of the author's ability to interplay strong, solid characters with creatures from the Otherworld in tales of excitement and humor." Horn Bk

Hurmence, Belinda

Tough Tiffany. Doubleday 1980 166p $7.95, lib. bdg. $8.90 (5 and up) **Fic**

1 Family life—Fiction 2 Poverty—Fiction
ISBN 0-385-15082-2; 0-385-15083-0 LC 79-6979

"Tiffany is eleven, a sensitive, curious child who likes to think she's tough; she is tough in the sense of having courage and stamina, but she's also charitable and loving. Youngest child of a large family, she is fascinated by the stories her grandmother tells of slave ancestors and local lore; she's worried about her mother's extravagance and eternal indebtedness; she's upset because an older sister is pregnant. Hurmence uses enough dialect to flavor the dialogue without burdening it; her characterizations are sharply drawn, and she has—in a fine first novel—used every situation in the book to develop and extend her characters, particularly the redoubtable Tiffany." Chicago. Children's Bk Center

Hurwitz, Johanna

Busybody Nora; illus. by Susan Jeschke. Morrow 1976 64p illus lib. bdg. $6 (2-4) **Fic**

1 Apartment houses—Fiction 2 City life—Fiction
ISBN 0-688-32057-0 LC 75-25921

"To five-year-old Nora and her little brother Teddy, their large apartment building in New York City is an exciting place to be. After learning there are as many as 200 people living 'in the same house,' Nora resolves to learn all their names and bring everyone together like one big happy family. Readers view big and little episodes in Nora and Teddy's lives through a nearly unblemished window on childhood. . . . Susan Jeschke's penciled sketches show rare sensitivity in awakening the tenement's personalities." Booklist

Some other books about Nora are also available from Morrow:

New neighbors for Nora $6.50, lib. bdg. $6.25 (ISBN 0-688-22173-4; 0-688-32173-7; LC 78-12631)

Nora and Mrs Mind-Your-Own Business, lib. bdg. $6 (ISBN 0-688-32097-X; LC 76-54283)

Hurwitz, Johanna—*Continued*

The law of gravity; illus. by Ingrid Fetz. Morrow 1978 192p illus. $7.50, lib. bdg. $6.67 (4-6) **Fic**

1 Fear—Fiction 2 Mothers—Fiction 3 Parent and Child—Fiction 4 New York (City)—Fiction
ISBN 0-688-22142-4; 0-688-32142-9 LC 77-13656

"Eleven-year-old Margot, whose mother has not descended from their fourth floor walk-up on N.Y.'s Upper West Side since the family moved there nine years before, decided to spend the summer persuading her to come downstairs. Content with homemaking and rooftop gardening . . . [her mother] resists the campaign. In a final effort, Margot, believing she has Newton's law on her side (what goes up must come down), hides out overnight in one of her favorite haunts, the library. Her friend, Bernie, finds her and takes her home before bedtime but not before Mom, in a panic, has made it to the stoop." Sch Library J

"There's gentleness running through the story in the mother-daughter relationshp, in the affably drawn summer friendship shared by Margot and Bernie, and in Margot's father's tolerance. Moreover, the posed questions of love and acceptance, only partly answered, are good ones to ponder." Booklist

Much ado about Aldo; pictures by John Wallner. Morrow 1978 95p illus $7.95, lib. bdg. $7.63 (3-5) **Fic**

1 Vegetarianism—Fiction
ISBN 0-688-22160-2; 0-688-32160-7 LC 78-5434

Eight-year-old Aldo "was interested in everything, and especially animals. He looked upon his two cats, Poughkeepsie and Peabody, as his brothers, and when his teacher set up terrariums containing crickets and chameleons, he was appalled to realize that some creatures actually ate others. Although blessed with a hearty appetite, he became a vegetarian instantly and got himself into trouble with the principal by trying to save the crickets from the chameleons. Aldo is an earnest and likable character in a convincing family story with a pleasant urban setting. The author has a remarkable ability to project the amusements and worries of childhood, conveying them in a deceptively simple style." Horn Bk

Followed by: Aldo Applesauce. Morrow $7.50, lib. bdg. $7.20 (ISBN 0-688-22199-8; 0-688-32199-2; LC 79-16200)

Irving, Washington

Rip Van Winkle; with drawings by Arthur Rackham. Lippincott 1967 64p illus $10 (5 and up) **Fic**

1 New York (State)—Fiction
ISBN 0-397-30981-3 LC 67-19272

First appeared 1819-1820 in Irving's: The sketch book of Geoffrey Crayon, Gent.

"Rip Van Winkle was a lazy, good-natured ne'er-do-well. He had an impatient wife who scolded constantly. On one of his hunting trips Rip met an odd crew of Dutchmen in the forests of the Catskill Mountains. They were playing nine-pins. Rip was ordered to serve them liquor, of which he also drank. As a result, he fell into a sleep which lasted twenty years. . . . The story emphasizes changes in American political life during the twenty years he slept." World Bk

Irwin, Hadley

The Lilith summer. Feminist Press 1979 109p $7.95 (5 and up) **Fic**

1 Elderly—Fiction 2 Friendship—Fiction
ISBN 0-912670-51-7 LC 78-24379

"Twelve-year-old Ellen is spending the summer as a paid companion to 77-year-old Lilith, who in turn is being compensated for staying with Ellen. When the two discover that their well-meaning relatives have conned them into watching each other, they form an uneasy alliance, which eventually leads to a warm and caring relationship." Booklist

"Lee Hadley and Annabelle Irwin have collaborated under the name 'Hadley Irwin' in this well-written, sympathetic but not sentimental story. . . . Ellen seems a little young for 12, but Lilith and her friends are original and well-developed characters, having interesting nooks and crannies, and pockets of memories, that many years of living bring. Honest things are said about getting old . . . and some musty bugaboos get an airing

(senility, loneliness, suicide). But there's plenty of sunshine and flowers, poems and adventures, with even some romance at 77 to balance out the somber side. All in all, an enjoyable, worthwhile book." Sch Library J

Ish-Kishor, Sulamith

A boy of old Prague; drawings by Ben Shahn. Pantheon Bks. 1963 90p illus lib. bdg. $5.99 (5 and up) **Fic**

1 Jews in Bohemia—Fiction 2 Prague—Fiction
ISBN 0-394-90978-X LC 63-15482

"Tomás, a peasant boy, lives on the domains of the young Bohemian lord near the city of Prague in the sixteenth century, experiencing the harsh life of the serf and sharing the Christians' superstitious hatred of the Jews. As part payment of a debt he is given by his lord to an old Jew of the ghetto to be his bond servant. The succinct, sharply felt first-person narrative describes sensitively and with realism Tomás' reaction to the first kindness and respect he has ever known and the effect on him of witnessing a pogrom instigated by his once-admired lord." Booklist

"Important in subject, dramatic in incident, and sensitive in characterization, it is highly recommended. Ben Shahn's deft character sketches and darkly atmospheric ghetto scenes add enormously to the effectiveness of the book." Horn Bk

The Master of Miracle; a new novel of the Golem; pictures by Arnold Lobel. Harper 1971 108p illus lib. bdg. $7.89 (5 and up) **Fic**

1 Golem—Fiction 2 Jews in Bohemia—Fiction 3 Prague—Fiction
ISBN 0-06-026089-0 LC 77-160644

This "beautifully written fantasy based on the Jewish golem legend is set in the 16th century Prague ghetto. . . . Gideon, a lonely orphan of uncertain parentage, is entrusted with controlling the golem, a huge clay humanoid fashioned by 'the master of miracle,' the venerated High Priest of Prague, in order to save the ghetto population from a pogrom. In his excitement, Gideon forgets to deactivate the golem when the task is completed and so faces punishment. The background is skillfully done and Gideon is a well-developed character." Rdng Ladders. 5th edition

Our Eddie. Pantheon Bks. 1969 183p $4.95, lib. bdg. $5.99 (6 and up) **Fic**

1 Jews—Fiction
ISBN 0-394-81455-X; 0-394-91455-4 LC 69-13456

"The moving story of a Jewish family whose stern, zealous father is so immersed in his own activities as Hebrew teacher and Zionist that he is indifferent to the personal problems of his wife and children and the illness which is gradually crippling his son Eddie. The story is told in part by an American boy who becomes friendly with the family in London and in part by the youngest daughter Sybil who describes the family's experiences after moving to America and Eddie's subsequent death. A realistic story imbued with warmth and tenderness." Booklist

James, Will

Smoky, the cow horse; illus. by the author. Scribner 1929 263p illus $8.95 (6 and up) **Fic**

1 Cowhands—Fiction 2 Horses—Fiction
ISBN 0-684-12875-6 LC 29-19426

"Scribner Illustrated classics"

First published 1926

Awarded the Newbery Medal, 1927

"The story of a cowpony from his wild colthood on the range through varied incidents of his life. . . . Told in Will James' graphic cowboy language and fully illustrated with pencil sketches." Wis Library Bul

"Smoky's career is told in a breezy, consciously uncultured but nevertheless rather attractive, often really charming, manner. Throughout the book one finds a good-humored, simple, wide-hearted spirit—which is a thing so rare that one always looks forward to meeting it again." New Repub

Jansson, Tove

Comet in Moominland; written and illus. by Tove Jansson; tr. by Elizabeth Portch. Avon [1976 c1959] 192p illus pa $1.25 (4-6)   **Fic**

1 Comets—Fiction
ISBN 0-380-00436-4

"An Avon Camelot book"
Original Swedish edition, 1946. First published in this translation 1951 in England, 1967 in the United States by H.Z. Walck

"Jansson won the 1966 Hans Christian Andersen Medal for the . . . Moomin books. . . . [This] adventure begins] when an ominous star appears over Moominvalley. Moomintroll sets forth on a journey to the observatory, gathering friends [and adventures] along the way." Sat Rev

"Plot? Irrelevant. Characters? Moomins, Sniff, Hemulens, Snorks, a Muskrat Philosopher (who sits and thinks about how unnecessary everything is), Hattifatteners, Snufkin, tree-spirits, water spooks. . . . But it's no use. . . . Why do children and other enlightened people love this? As Louis Armstrong said of another great art: if you got to ask, lady, you'll never know." Bk World

Some other books in this series are also available from Avon:

Finn Family Moomintroll pa $1.25 (ISBN 0-380-00350-3)

Moominland midwinter pa $1.25 (ISBN 0-380-00748-7)

Moominpappa at sea pa $1.25 (ISBN 0-380-01726-1)

Moominsummer madness pa $1.25 (ISBN 0-380-00633-2)

Moominvalley in November pa $1.25 (ISBN 0-380-00765-7)

Tales from Moominvalley pa $1.25 (ISBN 0-380-00911-0)

Jarrell, Randall

The animal family; decorations by Maurice Sendak. Pantheon Bks. 1965 179p illus $6.95 (4 and up)   **Fic**

1 Animals—Fiction
ISBN 0-394-81043-0   LC 65-20659

A "tale about a lonely hunter who acquires an amazing family. One by one, he takes into his log cabin by the sea a mermaid, a bear cub, a lynx, and a small boy washed ashore from a shipwreck. The arrival and adjustment of each new member to this extraordinary family circle are sensitively related with touches of humor and wisdom." Booklist

"Simple enough to read aloud to children too young to read the book by themselves, the story probably best suited to the sensitive reader who can appreciate the perceptive writing." Chicago. Children's Bk Center

The bat-poet; pictures by Maurice Sendak. Macmillan Pub. Co. 1964 42p illus $3.95, pa $1.95 (2-4)   **Fic**

1 Bats—Fiction 2 Poets—Fiction
ISBN 0-02-747640-5; 0-02-043910-5   LC 76-17823

The bat-poet, a little brown bat, "opened his eyes to the daytime and began to see the world in another light. . . . He made up poems about the daytime world's sights and sounds, and recited them to the unappreciative ears of his fellow bats and then hunted around for more receptive listeners, (other small animals and birds in his environment). Hidden in his 'discourse' are explanations of iambic pentameter and iambic trimeter." Toronto

"Fortunately, the book does not come right out and baldly make its points about poetry, one, two, three. But like a good poem, it uses words, to make the reader think and feel the ideas, rather than just hear them. A lovely book, perfectly illustrated —one well worth a child's attention and affection." Pub W

Johnson, Annabel

The grizzly, by Annabel and Edgar Johnson; pictures by Gilbert Riswold. Harper 1964 160p illus lib. bdg. $7.89 (5 and up)   **Fic**

1 Bears—Fiction 2 Camping—Fiction 3 Parent and child—Fiction
ISBN 0-06-22871-7   LC 64-11931

"Eleven-year-old David, living with his divorced mother, is doubtful about going on a camping trip with his father. When a grizzly injures the father and disables the truck, David surprises both himself and his father by his resourcefulness." Hodges. Bks for Elem Sch Libraries

Jones, Diana Wynne

Charmed life. Greenwillow Bks. 1977 218p $7.50, lib. bdg. $7.20 (5 and up)   **Fic**

1 Witches—Fiction 2 Fantastic fiction
ISBN 0-688-80138-2; 0-688-84138-4   LC 77-18414

"Gwendolen Chant is . . . absolutely sure that her magic powers will make her ruler of the world. When she and her brother Eric (Cat) become orphans, the renowned necromancer, Chrestomanci, takes them to live at his castle. Gwendolen immediately begins queening it over the household and playing shabby tricks on the family. Chrestomanci divests her of her witch's gifts, whereupon Gwendolen conjures a spell that puts her into the body of a girl named Janet, and Janet is bewildered to find herself in Gwendolen's body. Meantime, Cat sticks to his role as a quite normal boy until the day when his mean sister gathers an army of wicked sorcerers to attack Chrestomanci Castle. Then he finds he's more powerful than Gwendolen and saves the day." Pub W

'Set in a time vaguely reminiscent of Edwardian England, the novel presumes the existence of numerous worlds—past, present, and future—each with its own history. The concept is ingenious— if complicated—yet the plot is not difficult to follow, and shy small Cat, intimidated by his selfish sister, is a particularly appealing character." Horn Bk

Dogsbody. Greenwillow Bks. [1977 c1975] 242p $7.75, lib. bdg. $7.44 (6 and up)   **Fic**

1 Dogs—Fiction 2 Fantastic fiction
ISBN 0-688-80074-2; 0-688-84074-4   LC 76-28715

First published 1975 in England
"Sirius, the Dog Star, falsely accused in the heavens of losing the Zoi, is sentenced to earth as a pup in order to search for this sacred object, which has fallen as a meteorite. Rescued from drowning by Kathleen, an Irish waif abused by her uncle's family, Sirius develops a close bond of affection with the girl. However, it is the search for the Zoi that compels Sirius, a quest that seems futile until help comes from Sol, Earth, and Moon. [The author] . . . intricately weaves contemporary family tensions with the evil powers' struggle to gain control of the Zoi and incidentally portrays a touching child-dog relationship. Her ability to tell the story through a dog's eyes in a believable way is to her credit." Booklist

Jones, Weyman

Edge of two worlds; illus. by J. C. Kocsis. Dial Press 1968 143p illus $5.95 (5 and up)   **Fic**

1 Sequoya, Cherokee Indian—Fiction 2 Texas—Fiction 3 Frontier and pioneer life—Fiction
ISBN 0-440-2211-7   LC 68-15256

Based on incidents in the life of Sequoyah, creator of the Cherokee's written language. "This is a story of a young Missouri boy and an old Cherokee Indian [Sequoyah] who face a long and difficult journey across the plains together; first as enemies, then as comrades in peril." Pub W

"The writing is taut and sustained and will especially be enjoyed by better readers." Wis Library Bul

Jordan, June

New life: new room; illus. by Ray Cruz. Crowell 1975 52p illus lib. bdg. $7.89 (2-4)   **Fic**

1 Family life—Fiction 2 Brothers and sisters—Fiction 3 Blacks—Fiction
ISBN 0-690-00212-2   LC 73-9755

"A Black family with three children is faced with the problem of rearranging their small apartment in a housing project to accommodate a new baby. Rudy and Tyrone are informed that, henceforth, they must share their bedroom (for 'men only') with sister Linda. Uncomfortable with this disruption of their lives, the three children are helped through the transition by a loving and sensitive father who has a great knack for turning adversity into adventure. On the day their mother goes to the hospital, the children, encouraged by their dad to be independent, self-reliant and considerate of one another, plunge into setting their new room." Interracial Bks For Children Bul

Juster, Norton

The phantom tollbooth; illus. by Jules Feiffer. Epstein & Carroll [distributed by Random House] 1961 255p illus $7.95, pa $1.95 (4-6)   **Fic**

1 Fantastic fiction
ISBN 0-394-81500-9; 0-394-82199-8   LC 61-13202

"Milo thinks 'almost everything is a waste of time' until he drives through the toy toll-booth in his room and finds himself in the Kingdom of Wisdom. . . . From Faintly Macabre, the not-so-wicked Which he learns of the feud between King Azaz the Unabridged of Dictionopolis, city of words, and the Mathemagician who rules Digitopolis, city of numbers. Accompanied by the ticking watchdog, Tock, and the foolish loveable Humbug, Milo sets out on a hazardous journey through the Mountains of Ignorance to rescue the princesses, Sweet Rhyme and Pure Reason." NY Times Bk Rev
"It's all very clever. The author plays most ingeniously on words and phrases . . . and on concepts of averages and infinity and such . . . while the pictures are even more diverting than the text, for they add interesting details. . . . Any one fascinated by language and capable of appreciating the implications of the allegory will grin delightedly at the witty comments on wisdom and the verbal cleverness." NY Her Trib Bks

Kaplan, Bess

The empty chair. Harper [1978 c1975] 243p lib. bdg. $8.79 (6 and up)   **Fic**

1 Jews in Canada—Fiction 2 Death—Fiction 3 Family life—Fiction 4 Canada—Fiction
ISBN 0-06-023093-2   LC 77-11852

First published 1975 in Canada with title: Corner store
Set in Canada in the 1930's this "is a story of Jewish family life, having Becky Devine as its central character. Life, as she knows it, is basically good. She secretly yearns for luxuries beyond her reach and escapades enjoyed by her friends, but she manages to accept her lot and tries to find daily pleasure with her brother Saul, her father, Papa, and, of course, Mama! Their . . . existence is sparked with joy and anticipation when Mama announces that she is pregnant. Unfortunately, this happiness is cruelly snatched away when Mama and the baby die at childbirth. The enthralling part of the story involves how Becky and her family, with their meddling relatives and well-meaning friends, survive with the emptiness in both their hearts and the house. Papa must be married again because they need a housekeeper and a mother. Becky must therefore cope with Mama's haunting 'ghost' and the struggle to accept a replacement for Mama." Best Sellers
This "is a notable evocation of a child's naïveté and perplexity when confronted with matters beyond her experience—birth, death, sex, love. The book is also remarkable for its integration of Jewish traditions with universal concerns of childhood. A glossary of Yiddish words is appended." Horn Bk

Karl, Jean E.

Beloved Benjamin is waiting. Dutton 1978 150p lib. bdg. $7.95 (4-6)   **Fic**

1 Family life—Fiction 2 Life on other planets—Fiction 3 Science fiction
ISBN 0-525-26372-1   LC 77-25286

"As the last of four siblings left at home, Lucinda Gratz has to find a way to avoid getting caught in the crossfire of her parents' violent fights. She discovers a secret entrance to the deserted old caretaker's house in the cemetery across the street and, when she's threatened by a local gang after her parents' desertion, begins to live there. In the midst of all these problems, she is contacted by intelligent life from outer space through the medium of a broken iron statue of a young boy who died in 1889." Booklist
"Karl's new novel successfully combines space fantasy of the alien-contact variety with a suspenseful adventure of the grimly down-to-earth sort. . . . Lucinda is an appealing character, and her successful coping with an unusual survival situation will hold young readers' interest. The tension created by the lurking gang members is well maintained, and the alien-contact aspect is handled lightly enough (eventually fading due to

atmospheric conditions) to be considered finally as a product of Lucinda's imagination if the determinedly literal-minded wish to do so." Sch Library J

Kästner, Erich

Emil and the detectives; a story for children; tr. by May Massee; illus. by Walter Trier. Doubleday 1930 224p illus $5.95 (4-6)   **Fic**

1 Berlin—Fiction 2 Mystery and detective stories
ISBN 0-385-07289-9   LC 30-24339

Original German edition published 1928 in Switzerland
On his way to Berlin to visit his grandmother, Emil fell asleep and had his money stolen by the man who shared his compartment. Although he came from the country Emil was not stupid, and he determined to get that money back. He followed the man, met the boy with the auto horn, who summoned his friends, and among them all they caught a very clever thief
"The satisfying adventures will please young readers while many older ones will delight in the revealing glimpse of boyhood in a book refreshingly objective rather than analytic." Booklist

The little man; pictures by Rick Schreiter; tr. from the German by James Kirkup. Knopf 1966 183p illus lib. bdg. $5.69 (4-6)   **Fic**

1 Circus—Fiction
ISBN 0-394-91402-3   LC 67-2072

Mildred L. Batchelder Award, 1968
Original German edition published 1963 in Switzerland
"Maxie, who is two inches tall, has been left an orphan by the tiny parents who came from a Bohemian village of tiny people. A protégé of the famous conjuror, Professor Hokus von Pokus, Maxie becomes a famous circus and television star; among his ancillary activities, he rescues himself from his own kidnapping." Chicago. Children's Bk Center
"It is also a story that almost stands up and begs to be read out loud, for it is rich with the ingredient that warrants calling it a 'good' children's book; its appeal is both to the adult who reads it and to the child who listens to it." Pub W

Kay, Mara

In face of danger. Crown [1977 c1976] 210p $6.95 (6 and up)   **Fic**

1 Jews in Germany—Fiction 2 National socialism—Fiction 3 Germany—Fiction
ISBN 0-517-53119-4   LC 77-21949

First published 1976 in England with title: Storm warning
"Touring pre-W.W. II Germany with her journalist uncle Dick, Ann begins to understand the terrible changes that are taking place in the country. When an auto accident puts her uncle in the hospital and prevents their safe return to England, Ann becomes a boarder in a small German household. There, she discovers that two Jewish girls are being hidden in the attic and becomes involved in locating their parents and helping them family escape the imminent Nazi roundups." Sch Library J
"This is a haunting story, a thriller, which vividly conveys the mood of Germany preparing for war while persecuting Jews and non-Nazis. Although it lacks the quality and reality of an autobiographical account, it does bring the terror alive for young readers." Babbling Bookworm

Keith, Harold

Rifles for Watie. Crowell 1957 332p $8.95 (6 and up)   **Fic**

1 Watie, Stand—Fiction 2 U.S.—History—Civil War, 1861-1865—Fiction
ISBN 0-690-70181-0   LC 57-10280

Awarded the Newbery Medal, 1958
"Young Jeff Bussey longs for the life of a Union soldier during the Civil War, but before long he realizes the cruelty and savagery of some men in the army situation. The war loses its glamor as he sees his very young friends die. When he is made a scout, his duties take him into the ranks of Stand Watie, leader of the rebel troops of the Cherokee Indian Nation, as a spy. He makes good friends among the enemy troops and falls in love with Lucy Washbourne, beautiful part-Cherokee girl and rebel sympathizer." Stensland. Lit By and About the Am Indian

Keith, Harold—*Continued*

"An exceptionally well-written story of the Civil War as it was fought in the western states. . . . Jeff's change from a somewhat carefree boy who saw only one side of the war and was eager to get into a real battle to a mature young man capable of understanding, even though he did not agree with, the beliefs of the enemy, gives the story added depth and reality of characterizations." Chicago. Children's Bk Center

Kelly, Eric P.

The trumpeter of Krakow; decorations by Janina Domanska; foreword by Louise Seaman Bechtel. Macmillan Pub. Co. 1966 208p illus $7.95, pa $1.95 (5 and up)   **Fic**

1 Poland—Fiction
ISBN 0-02-750140-X; 0-02-044150-9   LC 66-16712
Awarded the Newbery Medal, 1929
"A reissue of a book first published 1928, in a new handsomely designed and illustrated format." Booklist
"How the commemoration of an act of bravery and self-sacrifice in ancient Krakow saved the lives of a family two centuries later. In this story of Poland, there is adventure and mystery aplenty." St Louis [review of the 1928 edition]

Kendall, Carol

The Gammage Cup; illus. by Erik Blegvad. Harcourt 1959 221p illus $6.50, pa $1.95 (4-6)   **Fic**

1 Fantastic fiction
ISBN 0-15-230572-6; 0-15-634277-4   LC 59-8953
"In the Land between the Mountains live a lost people, The Minnipins, who faithfully preserve their ancient customs until challenged by a few nonconformists. When they are attacked by an enemy race, it is the banished rebels who save the Minnipins from destruction." Hodges. Bks for Elem Sch Libraries
"This highly creative fantasy [offers] . . . an almost inexhaustible variety of reading pleasures: plot surprises, humor, fascinating characters, richness of ideas, and delight in words. . . . The story, generous in length, rises to a wonderfully dramatic climax in the final out-and-out battle." Horn Bk
Followed by: The whisper of Glocken. Harcourt $5.95 (ISBN 0-15-295697-2; LC 65-21698)

Kennedy, Richard

The blue stone; drawings by Ronald Himler. Holiday House 1976 93p illus $7.95 (3-5)   **Fic**

1 Fairy tales
ISBN 0-8234-0283-5   LC 76-9035
"Jack sees a blue stone fall from heaven. His wife, Bertie, thinks it is a soup stone, promptly swallows it, and turns into a chicken. Mishaps arise out of a classic mini-battle between good and evil which centers upon the mystery stone: Jack becomes a rooster, pigs turn into bread, and loaves revert to pigs until a troubador's musical riddle provides Jack with the clues needed to control the stone." Sch Library J
"A good read-aloud with plenty of action and humor, both of which get a boost from Himler's robust pencil drawings." Booklist

Kerr, Judith

When Hitler stole Pink Rabbit; illus. by the author. Coward, McCann & Geoghegan [1972 c1971] 191p illus $6.95 (4 and up)   **Fic**

1 Refugees, Jewish—Fiction
ISBN 0-698-20182-5   LC 71-185765
First published 1971 in England
"Anna, aged nine, finds that her family suddenly has to leave Berlin for Switzerland because the Nazis have won an election. In packing, she has to choose between two stuffed animals—an old beloved pink rabbit and a new dog. She chooses the dog, assuming that their exile will be temporary. Only gradually as her family moves from Switzerland to France to England in search of a meagre living does she realize that she will never return to Germany and that she will never see the rabbit again." Economist
"This tale of a refugee family is based on the author's childhood experiences and, although anti-Semitism in Germany and financial depression

everywhere are a somber backdrop, the book is warm and cozy, filled with the small, homely details of events that are important in a child's life." Sat Rev
Followed by: The other way round. Coward, McCann & Geoghegan $7.95 (ISBN 0-638-20335-6)

Kerr, M. E.

Dinky Hocker shoots smack. Harper 1972 198p $8.95, lib. bdg. $7.79 (6 and up)   **Fic**

1 Obesity—Fiction
ISBN 0-06-023150-5; 0-06-023151-3   LC 72-80366
"Susan 'Dinky' Hocker is overweight; when an overweight boy becomes interested in her and encourages her to reveal the person hidden beneath the protective 'layer' of fat, her family mocks the two youngsters. Dinky screams for attention by smearing 'Dinky Hocker Shoots Smack' all over town on the night when her mother is receiving an award for fighting drug addiction. Then her family turns from public charity to the home." Best Sellers
"The writer is sensitive not only to the dialogue, but to the themes of today's preoccupations. . . . This is a brilantly funny book that will make you cry. It is full of wit and wisdom and an astonishing immediacy that comes from spare, honest writing." NY Times Bk Rev

Kesteven, G. R.

The awakening water. Hastings House [1979 c1977] 160p $6.95 (5 and up)   **Fic**

1 Science fiction
ISBN 0-8038-0471-7   LC 78-27186
First published 1977 in England
"In the early years of the 21st-Century, after the 'devastation' of 1997, a 13-year-old boy tastes fresh water for the first time. He then begins to question his life and runs away to join others who have previously escaped the 'Party.' The story of how this resourceful group of youngsters survive is enjoyable, and the contrast between the 'doped' masses and the group of 'lost ones' is well drawn. . . . Kesteven's latest has well-developed characters and plot and an unexpected, but plausible and optimistic, ending." Sch Library J

Key, Alexander

Escape to Witch Mountain; illus. by Leon B. Wisdom, Jr. Westminster Press 1968 172p illus $7.50 (5 and up)   **Fic**

1 Science fiction
ISBN 0-664-32417-7   LC 68-11206
Orphaned "Tony and his sister Tia, who is mute to others but able to communicate with him . . . [are] menaced by a thug with a custody order. They flee to the town shown on their map, which is located deep in the Great Smokies. Closely pursued, their need for sanctuary prompts them to piece together out of deeply repressed memories the story of a trip . . . from a disintegrating planet to a carefully prepared new home on earth." Sch Library J
Followed by: Return from Witch Mountain. Westminster Press $8.50 (ISBN 0-664-32630-7; LC 77-26992)

The forgotten door. Westminster Press 1965 126p $7.95 (6 and up)   **Fic**

1 Science fiction
ISBN 0-664-32342-1   LC 65-10170
"A strange child falls—from another planet—through a doorway onto a Southern Appalachian landing place. People, both evil in intent and good, wonder at Jon's differences: his mind reading, his capacity to communicate with animals, his ability to make his feet 'light' so that he can move as quickly as a deer. A rock hound and his family, who run a gem shop for tourists, accept the boy. Defending him against suspicious neighbors, they come under the spell of Jon's revelation of another way of life." Horn Bk
"Call it adventure, mystery, or science fiction, this deceptively simple story is tension-packed, thought-provoking, and oddly disturbing." Library J

Kimmel, Margaret Mary

Magic in the mist; illus. by Trina Schart Hyman. Atheneum Pubs. 1975 unp illus lib. bdg. $5.95 (1-4)   Fic

1 Witches—Fiction 2 Wales—Fiction
ISBN 0-689-50026-2   LC 74-18186

"A Margaret K. McElderry book"

A "tale of a young Welsh lad, Thomas. Thomas lives alone, except for his pet toad, Jeremy, at the end of a damp, uncomfortable bog. He's studying to be a wizard but the poor boy can't conjure up enough spells even to keep the fire going in his little cottage. But life becomes brighter on a strange day when Thomas and Jeremy find a baby dragon out near the fen. They take the infant indoors and feed him. In gratitude, the dragon breathes fire on the sticks in Thomas's fireplace and soon has a cheerful blaze going." Pub W

King, Clive

Me and my million. Crowell [1979 c1976] 180p $7.95, lib. bdg. $7.89 (5 and up)   Fic

1 Crime—Fiction 2 London—Fiction
ISBN 0-690-03971-9; 0-690-03972-7   LC 78-22501

First published 1976 in England by Penguin Books

"Ringo, a young lad, wanders all over London with a stolen painting worth a million pounds in a laundry sack. His brother and a pal had stolen the painting and given it to Ringo to deliver across town. Ringo's problem begins as soon as he has to transfer to a number 41 bus. He has 'reading difficulties' and boards a 14 bus. Soon he is in difficulties of all kinds." Best Sellers

"Ringo's mishaps with the painting . . . make for a thoroughly unbelievable but hilarious story; and the breezy boy, who had neither a sense of grammar nor of manners and was insensitive to the refinements of religion and of art, was actually a keen observer of human weaknesses and responses. At the end, having rescued the painting from threatened destruction, he was able to say, 'When they'd got it all sorted out they decided I was a little hero, not a villain.' " Horn Bk

Kingman, Lee

The year of the raccoon. Houghton 1966 246p front $8.95 (6 and up)   Fic

1 Raccoons—Fiction
ISBN 0-395-06865-7   LC 66-8341

"Fifteen-year-old Joey, the middle son in a brilliant family, considers himself a disappointment to his parents. A pet raccoon helps to tide him over a difficult period in which he proves himself a person of worth and impotrance." Hodges. Bks for Elem Sch Libraries

This book "is perhaps closer to everyday reality, less an idealized, isolated instance than most child-animal stories. Its hero . . . is also a lover of nature and a keen-eyed observer of the world around him. But he is more accident-prone, more boy, less a wish fulfillment figure." Bk Week

"The many-faceted story has humor, excellent characterization, and problems that build up to a dramatic but convincing climax." Horn Bk

Kipling, Rudyard

The elephant's child; illus. by Leonard Weisgard. Walker & Co. 1971 32p illus $7.95, lib. bdg. $7.85 (1-4)   Fic

1 Elephants—Fiction
ISBN 0-8027-6020-1; 0-8027-6021-X   LC 73-104661

"This well-known whimsical fantasy that explains how the insatiably curious elephant child got his trunk is a fine example of one of Kipling's greatest classics. Weisgard's use of bold color and form makes one feel that he is in the jungle." Adventuring with Bks, 1977

How the leopard got his spots; illus. by Leonard Weisgard. Walker & Co. [1973 c1972] unp illus $7.95, lib. bdg. $7.85 (1-4)   Fic

1 Leopards—Fiction
ISBN 0-8027-6111-9; 0-8027-61112-7   LC 72-81373

First published 1972 in England

"Kipling's tale from the 'Just so stories' telling how the Ethiopian and the leopard changed color is strikingly illustrated by Weisgard's paintings, which project the atmosphere of hot plains or shadowy forest with a skillful contrast of colors." Booklist

How the rhinoceros got his skin; illus. by Leonard Weisgard. Walker & Co. 1974 unp illus $7.95, lib. bdg. $7.85 (1-4)   Fic

1 Rhinoceros—Fiction
ISBN 0-8027-6149-6; 0-8027-6150-X   LC 73-76356

"This is about a Parsee whose freshly baked cake is eaten by a Rhinoceros. For revenge the Parsee puts itchy cake crumbs inside the Rhino's skin while the beast is bathing. The animal rubs its hide so much that its skin falls into the folds that are the trademark of the rhino." Sch Library J

"The soft, slightly stylized plane figures of Weisgard's Parsee and Rhinoceros go well with Kipling's quaint, witty text." Booklist

Kjelgaard, Jim

Big Red. . . . Illus. by Bob Kuhn [New ed] Holiday House 1956 [c1945] 254p illus $8.95 (4 and up)   Fic

1 Dogs—Fiction
ISBN 0-8234-0007-7   LC 66-2767

First published 1945

"The story of a champion Irish setter and a trapper's son who grew up together, roaming the wilderness." Title page

Together they conquered blizzards and varmints, and eventually tracked down Old Majesty, the great outlaw bear. In the process boy and dog grew to real maturity, and found a place for themselves

"A tale which paints the stern life of the Wintapi wilderness in strong, clear strokes." NY Times Bk Rev

Some books about Big Red's offspring are also available from Holiday House:

Irish Red $8.95 (ISBN 0-8234-0060-3; LC 51-3090)
Outlaw Red $8.95 (ISBN 0-8234-0084-0; LC 53-12624)

Knight, Eric

Lassie come-home; illus. by Marguerite Kirmse. Holt [1978 c1940] 248p illus $6.95 (4 and up)   Fic

1 Dogs—Fiction 2 Great Britain—Fiction
ISBN 0-03-044101-3   LC 78-3570

Reissue of the title first published 1940

Story of a prize collie belonging to a Yorkshire boy from a humble home. When the family went on the dole, Lassie was sold to a wealthy man and taken hundreds of miles away to Scotland. But Lassie had still kept her loyalty to a boy in England. She escaped from the kennels in Scotland and after gruelling hardships, made her way back to her first home

Konigsburg, E. L.

About the B'nai Bagels; written & illus. by E. L. Konigsburg. Atheneum Pubs. 1969 172p illus lib. bdg. $8.95, pa $1.95 (4-6)   Fic

1 Jews in the U.S.—Fiction 2 Little league baseball—Fiction
ISBN 0-689-20631-3; 0-689-70348-1   LC 69-13529

"A warm and humorous story of a Jewish Little League team. Twelve-year-old Mark Stezer has problems: his mother is manager of the team; his brother is coach. This makes some sticky situations and 'overlaps' in his life. And he has worries about losing his best friend. Mark matures, having to make some difficult decisions on his own." Rdng Ladders. 5th edition

"Continuing to explore aspects of suburban life, the author has written a Little League baseball story, featuring, as chief character, a delightful example of that increasingly familiar literary heroine, the Jewish Mother. . . . Penetrating characterizations emerge by implication; and the author's unfailing humor and her deep understanding of human nature are as noticeable as ever." Horn Bk

From the mixed-up files of Mrs Basil E. Frankweiler; written and illus. by E. L. Konigsburg. Atheneum Pubs. 1967 162p illus $7.95, pa $1.95 (4 and up)   Fic

1 New York (City) Metropolitan Museum of Art—Fiction
ISBN 0-689-20586-4; 0-689-70308-2   LC 67-18988

Konigsburg, E. L.—*Continued*
Awarded the Newbery Medal, 1968
"Claudia, feeling misunderstood at home, takes her younger brother and runs away to New York where she sets up housekeeping in the Metropolitan Museum of Art, making ingenius arrangements for sleeping, bathing, and laundering. She and James also look for clues to the authenticity of an alleged Michelangelo statue, the true story of which is locked in the files of Mrs. Krankweiler, its former owner. Claudia's progress toward maturity is also a unique introduction to the Metropolitan Museum." Moorachian. What is a City?

Jennifer, Hecate, Macbeth, William McKinley, and me, Elizabeth; written and illus. by E. L. Konigsburg. Atheneum Pubs. 1967 117p illus lib. bdg. $6.95, pa $1.95 (4-6) **Fic**

1 Friendship—Fiction 2 Witchcraft—Fiction 3 Blacks—Fiction
ISBN 0-689-30007-7; 0-689-70296-5 LC 67-10458

"Jennifer, who claims to be a witch, at first overwhelms and dominates her new classmate Elizabeth, who is convinced by coincidences that Jennifer really has magic powers. Eizabeth's gradual self assertion leads to a fight and real friendship. Incidental and inconspicuously woven in is the fact that Jennifer is Negro and Elizabeth is white." Bruno. Bks for Sch Libraries. 1968
"A brillant engrossing, funny, sad, and touching book. . . . Mrs. Konigsburg draws children as they are, rather than as adults would like them to be. Jennifer is not at all polite; Elizabeth is not above lying to her elders; and the one child thought perfect by 'every grown-up in the whole of U. S. of A.' is known by Elizabeth for what she really is: two faced and mean. . . . All in all, Mrs. Konigsburg has stirred realism and humor into a triumphant brew." Bk Week

A proud taste for scarlet and miniver; written and illus. by E. L. Konigsburg. Atheneum Pubs. 1973 201p illus $9.95, pa $1.95 (5 and up) **Fic**

1 Eleanor of Aquitaine, consort of Henry II—Fiction
ISBN 0-689-30111-1; 0-689-70429-1 LC 73-76320

This is an historical novel about the 12th century queen, Eleanor of Aquitaine, wife of kings of France and England and mother of King Richard the Lion Heart and King John. Impatiently awaiting the arrival of her second husband, King Henry II, in heaven, she recalls her life with the aid of some contemporaries
The author "has succeeded in making history amusing as well as interesting. . . . The characterization is superb—not only of Eleanor, who dominates the Tales, but of aesthetic Abbot Suger, who was responsible for the invention of Gothic architecture, and of William the Marshal, who always backed the winning Plantagenet. . . . The black-and-white drawings are skillfully as well as appropriately modeled upon medieval manuscript illuminations and add their share of joy to the book." Horn Bk

Krumgold, Joseph
. . . and now Miguel; illus. by Jean Charlot. Crowell 1953 245p illus $8.95 (6 and up) **Fic**

1 Shepherds—Fiction 2 Sheep—Fiction 3 New Mexico—Fiction
ISBN 0-690-09118-4 LC 53-8415

Awarded the Newbery Medal, 1954
A memorable and deeply moving story of a family of New Mexican sheepherders, in which Miguel, neither child nor man, tells of his great longing to accompany men and sheep to summer pasture, and expresses his need to be recognized as a maturing individual. Harmonious illustrations." Cincinnati
The "seasonal life of the shepherds is realistically and sensitively drawn. Nevertheless the book's appeal is likely to be limited because of the introspective character that the author has given to Miguel and because of the stylized form in which the tale is told." Ontario Library Rev

Onion John; illus. by Symeon Shimin. Crowell 1959 248p illus $8.95 (5 and up) **Fic**

1 Friendship—Fiction
ISBN 0-690-59957-9 LC 59-11395

Awarded the Newbery Medal, 1960
The story, "at once humorous and compassionate, of Andy Rusch, twelve, and European-born Onion John, the town's odd-jobs man and vegetable peddler who lives in a stone hut and frequents the dump. Andy . . . tells of their wonderful friendship and of how he and his father, as well as Onioin John, are affected when the Rotary Club, at his father's instigation, attempts to transform Onion John's way of life." Booklist
"This is certainly one of the distinguished books of our time with all the literary finesse and perceptiveness of 'Miguel' [entered above] and stronger story appeal. The problems it deals with are basic: how understanding can we be of the bits of alien culture and superstition an immigrant clings to? . . . How does a 12-year-old boy meet his father on a man-to-man basis after a conscientious struggle inside? . . . The writing has dignity and strength. There is conflict, drama, and excellent character portrayal. There should be more of this kind of realism in children's books." Library J

Lamorisse, Albert
The red balloon. Doubleday 1957 [c1956] unp illus $7.95, pa $1.95 (1-4) **Fic**

1 Balloons—Fiction 2 Paris—Fiction
ISBN 0-385-00343-9; 0-385-14297-8 LC 57-9229

Original French edition published 1956
"The chief feature of this book is the stunning photographs, many in color, which were taken during the filming of the French movie of the same name. A little French schoolboy Pascal catches a red balloon which turns out to be magic. The streets of Paris form a backdrop for a charming story and superb photographs. . . . The photographs will interest any age." Library J

Lampman, Evelyn Sibley
The shy stegosaurus of Cricket Creek illus. by Hubert Buel. Doubleday 1955 218p illus $6.95 (5 and up) **Fic**

1 Dinosaurs—Fiction
ISBN 0-385-07490-5 LC 55-9233

Joan and Joey Brown and their widowed mother were trying to make a go of a newly acquired ranch but were having a hard time until Joan and Joey found a real dinosaur, genus stegosaurus, who proved to be a loyal friend
"To an adult it is far-fetched imagining, but Mrs. Lampman's vigorous, humorous style makes it good reading nevertheless. There are delightful line cuts." NY Her Trib Bks

Squaw Man's son. Atheneum Pubs. 1978 172p illus $6.95 (5 and up) **Fic**

1 Indians of North America—Fiction 2 Modoc Indians—Wars, 1873—Fiction 3 Prejudices and antipathies—Fiction
ISBN 0-689-50102-1 LC 77-17503

"A Margaret K. McElderry book"
"An historical novel about the Modoc war of 1872-1873. It is written from the viewpoint of a thirteen-year-old boy who leaves his home when his father's new wife objects to having a half-Indian in the house. He joins his mother and her people on the land that the government has assigned to them, which they must share with the Klamaths, a tribe that resents their presence. Billy, the protagonist, is the helpless observer of the insensitivity of white officials to the tribe's problems, of the growing fury of the cheated Indians, and of the hopeless and horrible war waged between a thousand white soldiers and fifty Indian warriors. Billy's white father saves him from being sent to a reservation, but he is still unacceptable to his stepmother and the townspeople, and the book ends with Billy leaving for San Francisco, hopeful that his uncle will take him in." Best Sellers
"Lampman carefully presents both sides of the uprising, integrating Billy's dilemmas, which could easily belong to anyone born of a mixed heritage with the historical background." Booklist

White captives. Atheneum Pubs. 1975 181p $6.95 (5 and up) **Fic**

1 Oatman, Olive Ann—Fiction 2 Indians of North America—Fiction
ISBN 0-689-50023-8 LC 74-18187

"A Margaret K. McElderry book"
"The story of Olive Oatman's five years of slavery among the Apache and Mohave Indians was first recorded in 1857, a year after her return

Lampman, Evelyn S.—*Continued*

to white society. At that time, the account became a relative best-seller and fanned the flames of anti-Indian feeling. Lampman's current version, told mainly from Olive's viewpoint but shifting at times to those of a few of the Indian characters, affords readers a degree of insight into the world of the two tribes, depicting the Apaches and Mohave as neither heartless nor holy. The narrative itself is well paced, though often depressing, and the characters are convincing enough to sustain reader involvement." Booklist

Langton, Jane

Her Majesty, Grace Jones; formerly The majesty of Grace; pictures by Emily Arnold McCully. Harper [1974 c1961] 189p illus lib. bdg. $8.79, pa $2.95 (4 and up)   **Fic**

1 Depressions, Economic—Fiction
ISBN 0-06-023691-4; 0-06-440027-1   LC 74-2616

Reissue of a title first published 1961, with illustrations by the author, under title: The majesty of Grace

"The story of the Jones family during the Depression, particularly of Grace who, a plain, ordinary girl with six faults, imagines herself the rightful heir to the British throne. During the worrisome, penny-pinching time when Pop is jobless and family treasures, including the car Petunia, are converted into cash, Grace finds it hard to believe that prosperity is just around the corner and writes to her 'real' father, King George, for help. She finally realizes that her escape into pretense is not only foolish but selfish and is relieved to learn that she has virtues that offset her faults." Booklist [review of 1961 edition]

Followed by: The boyhood of Grace Jones. Harper lib. bdg. $8.75, pa $1.50 (ISBN 0-06-023687-6; 0-06-440065-4; LC 72-80364)

Lawrence, Mildred

Touchmark; illus. by Deanne Hollinger. Harcourt 1975 184p illus $7.50 (5 and up)   **Fic**

1 Orphans—Fiction 2 U.S.—History—Revolution, 1775-1783—Fiction
ISBN 0-15-289603-1   LC 75-11579

"Abigail (Nabby) Jones' ambition to apprentice herself to a pewterer seems out of the question; such a role is unsuitable for a Boston girl of 1776. Her oft-voiced frustration at such taboos and at the general edge men and boys have in life echoes some very vogue sentiments; and so Lawrence's energetic portrayal of the ever-striving Nabby seems consciously styled to get a message across as well as maintain reader interest. If Nabby's benevolent personality and Lawrence's mile-a-minute plot don't set you blinking, then the story of how Nabby works her way into an apprentice-ship, betters the life of her master's crippled daughter, and involves herself in patriot activities of revolutionary Boston will be entertaining." Bookilst

Lawson, Robert

Ben and me; a new and astonishing life of Benjamin Franklin, as written by his good mouse Amos; lately discovered, ed. & illus. by Robert Lawson. Little 1939 113p illus $6.95 (5 and up)   **Fic**

1 Franklin, Benjamin—Fiction 2 Mice—Fiction
ISBN 0-316-51732-1   LC 39-24448

This "diary" of Amos the mouse provides a mouse-eye view of the major incidents in Ben Franklin's life

"How Amos, a poor church mouse, oldest son of a large family, went forth into the world to make his living, and established himself in Benjamin Franklin's old fur cap, 'a rough frontier-cabin type of residence,' and made himself indispensable to Ben with his advice and information, and incidentally let himself in for some very strange experiences is related here in a merry compound of fact and fancy." Bookmark

"The sophisticated and clever story is illustrated by even more sophisticated and clever line drawings." Roundabout of Bks

Mr Revere and I . . . Set down and embellished with numerous drawings by Robert Lawson. Little 1953 152p illus $7.95 (5 and up)   **Fic**

1 Revere, Paul—Fiction 2 Horses—Fiction 3 U.S.—History—Revolution, 1775-1783—Fiction
ISBN 0-316-51739-9   LC 52-10952

"Being an account of certain episodes in the career of Paul Revere, Esq., as recently revealed by his horse, Scheherazade, late pride of His Royal Majesty's 14th Regiment of Foot." Subtitle

"A delightful tale which is perfect for reading aloud to the whole family. The make-up is excellent, illustrations are wonderful, and the reader will get a very interesting picture of the American Revolution." Library J

Rabbit Hill. Viking 1944 127p illus lib. bdg. $8.50, Penguin pa $1.50 (3-6)   **Fic**

1 Animals—Fiction
ISBN 0-670-58675-7; 0-14-031010-X   LC 44-8234

Awarded the Newbery Medal, 1945

"The small animals living at Rabbit Hill were excited and concerned about the new folks who were moving into the Big House. Shiftless folk without a garden meant hard times for the animals, planting folks meant good times. The story centres around the Rabbit family—Father, a southern gentleman from Kentucky; Mother, a born worrier; little Georgie, their son, and the pride and joy of the whole community; and the gruff old rabbit, Uncle Analdos." Ontario Library Rev

"Robert Lawson, because he loves the Connecticut country and the little animals of field and wood and looks at them with the eye of an artist, a poet and a child, has created for the sensitive reader of any age, a whole, fresh, lively, amusing world." NY Times Bk Rev.

Followed by: The tough winter. Viking $6.95, Penguin pa $1.95 (ISBN 0-670-72208-1; 0-14-031215-3; LC 54-4416)

Lee, Mildred

The rock and the willow. Lothrop 1963 223p $7.75 (6 and up)   **Fic**

1 Depressions, Economic—Fiction 2 Alabama—Fiction
ISBN 0-688-41424-9   LC 63-19689

A story about "Enie, one of many children in a large and very poor family. Set in the farm land of Alabama in the 1930's. It covers four years in the life of the Singleton family. . . . Ernie, just going into high school, is the one who is different, who longs for [education and for] something better and, deep down, knows that she will find it." Library J

"A tremendously moving story. . . . Candid and perceptive, the starkness of the story is never stark for effect; the bleakness of the depression years and the grim burdens of Enie's life are natural and real." Chicago. Children's Bk Center

Sycamore year. Lothrop 1974 191p $8.25, lib. bdg. $7.92 (6 and up)   **Fic**

1 Unmarried mothers—Fiction 2 Friendship—Fiction
ISBN 0-688-41643-8; 0-688-51643-2   LC 74-6409

"This is the story told by Wren Fairchild of her first year in the small town of Sycamore, the year in which she turns fourteen. Wren is just, but just, beginning to be aware of boys and is resentful when her best friend Anna secretly begins to date Tony. Anna, a year older, has been dedicated only to her goal of becoming a singer, her mother—about to marry again after years of bitterness about her husband's desertion—thinks her too young to date, and Tony is a sly and undependable person in Wren's opinion. Tony has indeed dropped Anna by the time she learns that she is pregnant . . . and Anna shares her burden only with Wren. The truth comes out, of course, and Wren learns how much compassion and wisdom her parents have, since they learn of it before Anna's mother does. And Anna learns how much she had underestimated both her mother and her new stepfather." Chicago. Children's Bk Center

"Skillful handling of various complex relation-ships makes this one of the better reflections of teenage trials and pleasures, picturing with understanding Wren's loyalty and efforts to protect Anna." Horn Bk

LeGuin, Ursula K.

Very far away from anywhere else. Atheneum Pubs. 1976 89p $6.95 (6 and up) **Fic**

1 Friendship—Fiction
ISBN 0-689-30525-7   LC 76-4472

"Owen Thomas Griffiths is a loner. His brilliance sets him apart at school; his failure to conform dismays his parents. Owen yearns to study at M.I.T. but his father and mother insist that he go to a state college, enjoy the car they have given him and live what they call a normal life. The youth finds what he has always sought, someone to talk to and share his feelings with. She is Natalie Field, a girl who is absolutely dedicated to her goal. She will succeed where women seldom have, as a composer of serious music. Their friendship is the theme of a superb novel which entertains as it teaches the need for priorities." Pub W

A wizard of Earthsea; drawings by Ruth Robbins. Parnassus Press 1968 205p illus $7.95 (6 and up) **Fic**

1 Fantastic fiction
ISBN 0-87466-057-2   LC 68-21992

"An imaginary archipelago is the setting for . . . [this] fantasy about a talented but proud, overzealous student of wizardry. In a willful misuse of his limited powers, the novice wizard unleashes a shadowy, malevolent creature that endangers his life and the world of Earthsea. To atone for his misdeed, Ged goes on a perilous journey through the island kingdom to find the baleful beast and destroy its evil influence." Booklist

A "powerful fantasy-allegory. Though set as prose, the rhythms of the language are truly and consistently poetical." Rdng Ladders. 5th edition

Followed by these titles available from Atheneum Pubs:

The Tombs of Atuan lib. bdg. $6.95 (ISBN 0-689-20680-1; LC 70-154753)
The farthest shore lib. bdg. $9.95 (ISBN 0-689-30054-9; LC 72-75273)

L'Engle, Madeleine

Meet the Austins. Vanguard 1960 191p $6.95 (5 and up) **Fic**

1 Family life—Fiction 2 Orphans—Fiction
ISBN 0-8149-0552-5   LC 60-9726

"A present-day story of the family of a country doctor, told by the twelve-year-old daughter, during a year in which a spoiled young orphan, Maggy, comes to live with them. . . . [This is an] account of the family's adjustment to Maggy and hers to them." Horn Bk

"It is an unusual book, far better than most in style and in sensitivity, yet sufferng from an overly weak story line. There are intimate details of home life which everyone will recognize with pleasure; there is great warmth in the family relationship, and it is movingly communuicated to the reader. There are also, unfortunately, moments when the Austins become just a little too good to be true, and the going gets a wee bit sticky." NY Times Bk Rev

A wrinkle in time. Farrar, Straus 1962 211p $4.50 (6 and up) **Fic**

1 Fantastic fiction
ISBN 0-374-38613-7   LC 62-7203

Awarded the Newbery Medal, 1963

"A brother and sister, together with a friend, go in search of their scientist father who was lost while engaged in secret work for the government on the tesseract problem. A tesseract is a wrinkle in time. The father is a prisoner on a forbidding planet, and after awesome and terrifying experiences, he is rescued, and the little group returns safely to Earth and home." Children's Bks Too Good to Miss

"Truth would make one add that the book is a generous sprinkling of aphoristic quotations in at least seven languages, and that it considers quite seriously the philosophic problems of good and evil." Library J

"It makes unusual demands on the imagination and consequently gives great rewards." Horn Bk

Followed by these books also available from Farrar, Straus:

A swiftly tilting planet $7.95 (ISBN 0-374-37362-0; LC 78-9648)
A wind in the door $7.95 (ISBN 0-374-38443-6; LC 73-75176)

Lenski, Lois

Strawberry girl; written and illus. by Lois Lenski. Lippincott 1945 193p illus $8.95 (4-6) **Fic**

1 Florida—Fiction
ISBN 0-397-30109-X   LC 45-7609

Awarded the Newbery Medal, 1946

"A strong sense of place pervades this story of Birdie Boyer, a little Cracker girl who helps her Florida family to raise strawberries and to cope with the shiftless Slaters next door." Hodges. Bks for Elem Sch Libraries

"An authentic regional tale told with humor and vigor." Children's Bks Too Good to Miss

LeRoy, Gen

Emma's dilemma. Harper 1975 123p lib. bdg. $6.89, pa $1.50 (4-6) **Fic**

1 Family life—Fiction
ISBN 0-06-023789-9; 0-06-440078-6   LC 75-6293

"Emma Williams' symptoms of stodginess include getting her homework done early and walking her sheep dog Pearl on time each morning. In her own mind she concedes that she hates change and takes life seriously. A best friend's comment that she is uptight evokes an angry reaction, but privately Emma mulls over the criticism. Coincident with her deepening malaise is a crisis precipitated when Emma's grandmother, who has come to live with the family, turns out to be allergic to dogs. Pearl must go to 'the country' . . . to live with cousins, and Emma comes to grips with the loss through some helpful remarks by young Herbie Johnson, an attention-starved child for whom she dutifully babysits. Her sudden insight into her behavior results in a turnabout of attitudes toward Herbie, her grandmother, and change in general—not unlike the tidy resolution of a TV situation drama. But like the latter, this will have its appeal." Booklist

Levitin, Sonia

The mark of Conte; illus. by Bill Negron. Atheneum Pubs. 1976 226p illus $8.95, pa $1.95 (6 and up) **Fic**

1 School stories
ISBN 0-689-30506-0; 0-689-70462-3   LC 75-23041

"Conte Mark, a High Intelligence Child (HIC) in a Southern California high school, discovers that the computer has him registered as Mark Conte as well. Frustrated in his attempts to explain the error to Mr. Rhinefinger, his counselor . . . Conte declares war on the computer and Vista Mar High School. He devises an intricate scheme that will have him remain registered under both names and graduate in two years. How he manages to keep the scheme afloat . . . is the plot in toto." Sch Library J

"This is a spoof, of course, but it's a spoof just this side of reality, because all of the daft, hilarious things that happen and the people in Conte's life could be true. The author writes with zest and vitality, poking fun at everything in sight, but doing it with affection." Chicago. Children's Bk Center

Levoy, Myron

Alan and Naomi. Harper 1977 192p $7.95, lib. bdg. $7.89 (6 and up) **Fic**

1 Friendship—Fiction 2 Jews in New York (City)—Fiction 3 Mentally ill—Fiction 3 World War, 1939-1945—Fiction
ISBN 0-06-023799-6; 0-06-023800-3   LC 76-41522

"Alan Silverman is a Jewish boy, living in New York during World War II. His chief joy in life stems from his friendship with Shaun Kelly and playing stickball, after school, outside their apartment building. Alan's parents persuade him to spend his afternoons instead with Naomi, a 'crazy' girl from France. She's a refugee, a Jewish girl whose father has been murdered before her eyes by the Gestapo. Alan resents the takeover of his time until he begins to see Naomi coming out of her catatonic state, thanks to his companionship. She gradually becomes well enough to go to school and it looks as if the story will have a happy ending. But another violent act throws Naomi back into her withdrawn state and she is institutionalized." Pub W

"This warming story with its ethnic humor, its compassionate families, and its heart-wrenching ending is one of the more honest approaches to the repercussions of W.W.II." Sch Library J

Lewis, C. S.
The lion, the witch and the wardrobe; a story for children; illus. by Pauline Baynes. Macmillan Pub. Co. 1950 154p illus $7.95, pa $1.95 (4 and up) **Fic**

1 Fantastic fiction
ISBN 0-02-758110-1; 0-02-044220-3 LC 50-10611

This begins "the 'Narnia' stories, outstanding modern fairy tales with an underlying theme of good overcoming evil. In this first title, four English children walk through the wardrobe in a strange home they are visiting and enter the cold, wintry land of Narnia, which is suffering under the spell of the White Witch. They are guided to the noble lion Aslan and loyally aid him in freeing Narnia and its inhabitants from their unhappy fate." Children's Bks Too Good To Miss

Followed by these books, also available from Macmillan Pub. Co:
Prince Caspian $7.95, pa $1.95 (ISBN 0-02-758550-6; 0-02-044240-8; LC 51-12799)
The voyage of the Dawn Treader $7.95, pa $1.95 (ISBN 0-02-758800-9; 0-02-044260-2; LC 52-4219)
The silver chair $7.95, pa $1.95 (ISBN 0-02-758770-3; 0-02-044250-5; LC 53-12553)
The horse and his boy $7.95, pa $1.95 (ISBN 0-02-757670-1; 0-02-044200-9; LC 54-12817)
The magician's nephew, pa $1.95 (ISBN 0-02-044230-0; LC 55-14869)
The last battle 07.95, pa $1.95 (ISBN 0-02-757890-9; 0-02-044210-6; LC 56-9362)

Lewis, Elizabeth Foreman
Young Fu of the upper Yangtze; illus. by Ed Young; introduction by Pearl S. Buck. [Rev. ed] Holt 1973 267p illus lib. bdg. $7.95 (5 and up) **Fic**

1 China—Fiction
ISBN 0-03-007471-1 LC 72-91654

First published 1932. Awarded the Newbery Medal, 1933
Set in China in the 1920's, this story describes the adventures of Young Fu, a country boy, who goes with his widowed mother to live in the city of Chungking, and is apprenticed to a master coppersmith

"This handsome fortieth-anniversary edition ... has subtle pen-and-ink drawings, a brief historical introduction by Pearl Buck, and concluding background notes enlarged to contrast facts about old and new China." Booklist
Glossary of Chinese words: p253-55

Lewis, Naomi
The Snow Queen [by] Hans Christian Andersen; a new adapted version by Naomi Lewis; illus. by Errol Le Cain. Viking 1979 unp illus $10 (3-5) **Fic**

1 Fairy tales
ISBN 0-670-65378-0 LC 78-10462

After a long and difficult quest which takes her through a cycle of the seasons, a girl finds her friend, who has been enchanted by the Snow Queen and left, frozen, in her icy palace in the far North. As the girl repeats a song about the Christ-child which she used to sing to him, her tears of love and grief melt the ice and free the boy

"For modern children whose attention spans are tuned to a quicker-paced life than Andersen's leisurely style can entertain, a shortened adaptation is probably appropriate in picture-book format. It is a shame to sacrifice the grace, logic, and quirky detail of the original, however. ... As it stands, Lewis' version will require some acceptance of arbitrary fairy-tale conventions strung together." Booklist
"Le Cain is a master in the tradition of the great fantasy illustrators—Walter Crane, Kay Nielsen, Edmund Dulac, to name only a few. ... Alternating between rectangular and circular frames, the illustrations decorating this beautifully designed book (lacking only in the crowding of the front matter) are highly stylized, exquisitely detailed, and brightly colored. The artist's style is varied and engaging; he delights in filling his art with flowers and figures that hold the eye after the focal point of the action is apprehended." Sch Library J

Lexau, Joan M.
Striped ice cream; illus. by John Wilson. Lippincott 1968 95p illus $6.95 (2-4) **Fic**

1 Birthdays—Fiction 2 Blacks—Fiction 3 Family life—Fiction
ISBN 0-397-31046-3 LC 68-10774

"Mama had refused to go on welfare. She worked in a button factory and tried to augment a scanty income by outside cleaning. The older children helped with housework and odd jobs, but Becky, the youngest, feared that with Mama worrying about new school shoes for five children she might not have chicken-spaghetti and striped ice cream (vanilla, strawberry and chocolate) for her eighth birthday." Bk World
"Despite the upright tone and somber notes of realism that creep in, Miss Lexau has achieved an exceedingly warm and satisfying story of a [black] city family that is true to childhood." NY Times Bk Rev

Lindgren, Astrid
Pippi Longstocking; tr. from the Swedish by Florence Lamborn; illus. by Louis S. Glanzman. Viking 1950 158p illus $5.95, Penguin pa $1.95 (3-6) **Fic**

1 Sweden—Fiction
ISBN 0-670-55745-5; 0-14-030957-8 LC 50-10396

Original Swedish edition, 1945
Nine-year-old Pippi is a little Swedish girl who "lives alone with her horse and monkey, and foils all attempts of police, schools, and polite neighbors to make her conform to the accepted social pattern. Her wild doings are shared by a very 'nice,' normal little boy and girl who live next door. Her rare conversation includes tall tales of her life in many lands, with her father, a ship's captain. Sometimes Pippi admits she invents, but her hoards of gifts and of gold pieces are real. ... It is ably, vivaciously translated by Florence Lamborn, and most amusingly illustrated." NY Her Trib Bks
"Pippi's fantastic stories and humorous escapades exemplify many of the frustrations of normal children. They will, therefore, delight young readers." NY Times Bk Rev

Some other books about Pippi are also available from Viking:
Pippi goes on board $7.95, Penguin pa $1.95 (ISBN 0-670-55677-7; 0-14-030959-4; LC 57-4316)
Pippi in the South Seas $6.95, Penguin pa $1.95 (ISBN 0-670-55711-0; 0-14-030958-6; LC 59-4758)
Pippi on the run $8.50 (ISBN 0-670-55751-X; LC 75-31944)

Lindquist, Jennie D.
The golden name day; pictures by Garth Williams. Harper 1955 247p illus lib. bdg. $7.89, pa $1.50 (3-5) **Fic**

1 Swedish Americans—Fiction 2 Country life—Fiction 3 New England—Fiction
ISBN 0-06-023881-X; 0-06-440024-7 LC 55-8823

"A summer with Swedish friends on a New England farm was full of delights for nine-year-old Nancy, except for one thing—the Swedish calendar did not include her name day. When a way was found to allow her to share the Swedish custom of celebrating a name day, all was perfect." Hodges. Bks for Elem Sch Libraries
Followed by: The little silver house

Lippincott, Joseph Wharton
The Wahoo bobcat; illus. by Paul Branson. Lippincott 1950 207p illus $10 (5 and up) **Fic**

1 Bobcats—Fiction 2 Florida—Fiction
ISBN 0-397-30198-7 LC 50-14557

"A great bobcat roamed the swamps of Florida and was hunted by all except Sammy, a boy who became his friend and protector. A dramatic story with vivid background and colorful characters, useful to encourage conservation." Hodges. Bks for Elem Sch Libraries

Wilderness champion; the story of a great hound; illus. by Paul Bransom. Lippincott 1944 $6.95, lib. bdg. $4.82 (5 and up) **Fic**

1 Dogs—Fiction 2 Wolves—Fiction 3 Canada—Fiction
ISBN 0-397-30099-9; 0-397-31320-9 LC 44-9586

Lippincott, Joseph W.—*Continued*

"On the way to his ranger cabin in the Alberta mountains, Johnny loses his favorite pup, Reddy, and this exciting, colorful story tells how Reddy becomes the running mate of King, an old black wolf, how he returns to Johnny, wins fame as a hunter and then goes back to stay with King, his 'first loyalty,' until the old wolf's death." Bookmark

The author's "style is forthright, unpretentious, but he can make you remember the wilderness and the suspense of the chase, the savagery of titanic battles, almost as clearly as if you had seen them first hand." NY Times Bk Rev

Lipsyte, Robert

One fat summer. Harper 1977 152p $8.95, lib. bdg. $8.79 (6 and up)   **Fic**

1 Obesity—Fiction
ISBN 0-06-023895-X; 0-06-023896-8   LC 76-49746

"An Ursula Nordstrom book"

"Bobby Marks is 14 and fat. How fat, he doesn't know because he jumps off the scale when it hits 200 pounds. In one action-packed summer Bobby learns that altered physical appearance can bolster self-esteem. He's not sure he likes his friend Joanie's new nose and new ego, but he's certainly pleased with his own svelte new image. The slimming is a result of his summer job; tending the grounds of the town miser." West Coast Rev of Bks

"This is far superior to most of the summer-of-change stories: any change that takes place is logical and the protagonist learns by action and reaction to be both self-reliant and compassionate, understanding [his tormentor] Pete's weakness as well as the bullying persecutor's motivation. The plot elements are nicely balanced and paced, the characterization is developed with insight, and the writing style is deft and polished." Chicago. Children's Bk Center

Little, Jean

From Anna; pictures by Joan Sandin. Harper 1972 201p illus $8.79, pa $1.95 (4 and up)   **Fic**

1 Blind—Fiction 2 Germans in Canada—Fiction
3 Family life—Fiction
ISBN 0-06-023912-3; 0-06-440044-1   LC 72-76505

"Often ridiculed by her older brothers and sisters and chided by her mother for her awkwardness and lack of ability nine-year-old Anna is prickly and uncommunicative, but when her family moves to Canada in 1933 to get away from the growing oppression in their native Germany a doctor discovers that Anna has an acute vision problem. Fitted with glasses and sent to a special school for visually handicapped children Anna is slowly drawn out of her shell by an understanding teacher and new friends. Despite the implausibility of Anna's parents' never even suspecting her difficulty in seeing and the borderline sentimentality of the climax this is an engaging story of Anna's adjustment to life and her family's to a new homeland." Booklist

Followed by: Listen for the singing. Dutton lib. bdg. $7.95 (ISBN 0-525-33705-9; LC 76-58323)

Look through my window; pictures by Joan Sandin. Harper 1970 258p illus lib. bdg. $8.79, pa $2.95 (4-6)   **Fic**

1 Family life—Fiction 2 Friendship—Fiction
ISBN 0-06-023924-7; 0-06-440010-7   LC 71-105470

Emily's very predictable life as an only child suddenly changes when her family moves into an eighteen-room house and her cousins—those wild Sutherland kids—come to stay with them. She discovers that life in a big family can be rewarding if sometimes exasperating and after meeting Kate she discovers both the hurts and the joys of true friendship

"The small but absorbing crises of famly life are described with vitality, and the book is garlanded with Emily's and Kate's rapt discussions of books and their candid exploration of what it means to be Jewish (as Kate is)." Sat Rev

Followed by: Kate. Harper $8.79, pa $2.95 (ISBN 0-06-023914-X; 0-06-440037-9; LC 70-148419)

Mine for keeps; with illus. by Lewis Parker. Little 1962 186p illus $7.95 (4-6) **Fic**

1 Cerebral palsy—Fiction 2 Physically handicapped—Fiction
ISBN 0-316-52793-9   LC 62-12381

"Sarah Jane Copeland, home from a cerebral palsy center, is unhappy not to get the pampering she had expected from her parents. In caring for a timid puppy and helping a sick boy, Sarah Jane forgets her self-pity and begins to lead a normal life. An interesting story with insight into the problems of rehabilitating the handicapped." Hodges. Bks for Elem Sch Libraries

"One of the most valuable aspects of the book is in the depiction of Sally's family; they are real people, who try to help, but who make mistakes and lose their tempers." Chicago. Children's Bk Center

One to grow on; illus. by Jerry Lazare. Little 1969 140p illus $6.95 (4-6)   **Fic**

1 Truthfulness and falsehood—Fiction 2 Family life—Fiction
ISBN 0-316-52796-3   LC 69-11784

This story "focuses on a twelve-year-old middle child who, wanting attention, lies to such an extent that her family distrusts her. Through a hurtful experience with a schoolmate, Lisa, who is a malicious liar, and the help of a discerning and sympathetic godmother who gives her a vacation away from her family, Janie comes to understand her own problem and Lisa's and is able to be herself and to accept Lisa as she is." Booklist

"The story flows easily, and the characterization and relationships are especially vivid in the depiction of shifting allegiance in Janie's circle of friends and in the warm realistic family scenes." Sat Rev

Take wing; illus. by Jerry Lazare. Little 1968 176p illus $7.95 (4-6)   **Fic**

1 Mentally retarded children—Fiction
ISBN 0-316-52795-5   LC 68-14748

"Although her parents refuse to admit it, Laurel knows that there's something wrong with her younger brother. When her mother is hospitalized, Laurel's aunt comes to take over the household—and the family is forced to acknowledge the fact that seven-year-old James is retarded." Library J

"The author has written an absorbing story that is a thoroughly realistic treatment of a too common situation in which parents ignore reality to the detriment of the whole family. Recommended reading for parents and teachers as well as for young people." Horn Bk

Lively, Penelope

The ghost of Thomas Kempe; illus. by Antony Maitland. Dutton 1973 186p illus lib. bdg. $7.95 (4-6)   **Fic**

1 Ghosts—Fiction 2 Great Britain—Fiction
ISBN 0-525-30495-9   LC 73-77456

"Workmen getting an English cottage ready for its new tenants break an old bottle and let loose the spirit of Thomas Kempe, a sorcerer whose mortal remains have been buried since 1639. Thus begin the persecutions and perils of young James Harrison, a prankish boy who moves into the house and is blamed for the high jinks of the ghost. Aware that he can't convince his pragmatic parents that the house is haunted and that he is not to blame for the tricks played when the vicar comes to call, as well as other disasters, Jim seeks out an exorcist." Pub W

"Although the British vocabulary and spelling may seem strange at times to middle graders, they are sure to enjoy this exciting and involving tale of the supernatural." Sch Library J

A stitch in time. Dutton 1976 140p lib. bdg. $7.95 (4-6)   **Fic**

1 Space and time—Fiction
ISBN 0-525-40040-0   LC 76-23118

"Maria is an only child. Her parents are quiet people, and Maria, accustomed to being on her own, prefers to hold conversations in her head rather than talk to people who do not understand. Perhaps that is why she notices so many strange things about the Victorian house they rent for the summer holidays by the sea. To begin with, there are the unexplained noises. . . . Then there is the sampler stitched in 1865 by a little girl named Harriet, and the discovery that Harriet lived in this very house. It is clear that something odd happened to Harriet—but what?" Sch Library J

"Any suspicion of narrative inertia is masked . . . by descriptive energy. The pages sparkle with jokes, perceptions and neat felicities. Maria herself, a sophisticated child with a well-nigh Murdochian concern for contingency, is a little triumph." New Statesman

Lively, Penelope—*Continued*

The voyage of QV 66; illus. by Harold Jones. Dutton [1979 c1978] 172p illus $7.95 (4-6)   **Fic**

1 Animals—Fiction   2 Great Britain—Fiction
ISBN 0-525-42120-3   LC 78-12098

First published 1978 in England
The author "has written an anthropomorphic animal story. Combining ancient fables with contemporary science fiction, she imagines that the world has been overwhelmed by floods and that human beings have been evacuated to Mars, leaving the animals to inherit the earth with its gradually receding waters. Pal, the dog, relates the events. Along with the horse Ned, the cow Freda, the cat Pansy, the pigeon called Offa, and Stanley —who is obviously a monkey and doesn't know it— Pal sets sail in an abandoned boat in an attempt to find the London Zoo, where Stanley hopes to discover his identity." Horn Bk

"The adventures provide action, but the joy of this deftly written tale is in the humor of its dialogue, its sly satirizing of human beings and its warmth and consistency of characterization." Chicago. Children's Bk Center

London, Jack

Call of the wild (5 and up)   **Fic**

1 Dogs—Fiction   2 Alaska—Fiction
Some editions are:
Dent (Children's illustrated classics) $9 With two colour plates and line drawings in the text by Charles Pickard (ISBN 0-460-05077-X; LC 68-114638
Macmillan Pub. Co. (Macmillan Classics) $5.95 Illustrated by Karvel Kezer; afterword by Clifton Fadiman (ISBN 0-02-759510-2; LC 63-14831)

First published 1903 by Macmillan Pub Co.
"The dog hero, Buck, is stolen from his comfortable home and pressed into service as a sledge dog in the Klondike. At first he is abused by both men and dogs, but he learns to fight ruthlessly and finally finds in John Thornton a master whom he can respect and love. When Thornton is murdered, he breaks away to the wilds and becomes the leader of a pack of wolves." Reader's Ency

"London works out in the course of the story his ideas on the need for adaptation to survive and on the influence of heredity. The book is at once sentimental and poetic." Herzberg. The Reader's Ency of Am Lit

White Fang (5 and up)   **Fic**

1 Dogs—Fiction   2 Alaska—Fiction
Some editions are:
Dent (Children's illustrated classics) $9 With four colour plates and line drawings in the text by Charles Pickard (ISBN 0-460-05077-X; LC 68-86113)
Macmillan Pub. Co. $7.95 (ISBN 0-02-574750-9)

First published 1905 by Macmillan Pub. Co.
White Fang "is about a dog, a cross-breed, sold to Beauty Smith. This owner tortures the dog to increase his ferocity and value as a fighter. A new owner, Weedon Scott, brings the dog to California, and, by kind treatment, domesticates him. White Fang later sacrifices his life to save Scott." Haydn. Thesaurus of Bk Digests

"The subject is one which fits the author's peculiar gifts admirably and gives him full scope." NY Times Bk Rev

Lovelace, Maud Hart

Betsy-Tacy; illus. by Lois Lenski. Crowell 1940 112p illus lib. bdg. $8.79 (2-4)   **Fic**

1 Friendship—Fiction   2 Minnesota—Fiction
ISBN 0-690-13805-9   LC 40-30965

Betsy and Tacy (short for Anastacia) were two little five-year-olds, such inseparable friends that they were regarded almost as one person. This is the story of their friendship in a little Minnesota town in the early 1900's

The author "has written a story about two very natural, very appealing little girls. More than this, she has written a story of real literary merit as well as one with good story interest." Library J

Followed by these books, also available from Crowell:

Betsy-Tacy and Tib lib. bdg. $8.79 (ISBN 0-690-13876-8; LC 41-18714)
Over the big hill, a Betsy-Tacy story $9.95, lib. bdg. $8.79 (ISBN 0-690-13521-1; 0-690-13520-3; LC 42-23557)

Down town, a Betsy-Tacy story lib. bdg. $8.79 (ISBN 0-690-13450-9; LC 43-51264)
Heaven to Betsy, a Betsy-Tacy high school story $9.95 (ISBN 0-690-13733-8; LC 45-9806)
Betsy in spite of herself $9.95 (ISBN 0-690-13662-5; LC 46-11995)
Betsy was a junior, a Betsy-Tacy high school story $9.95 (ISBN 0-690-13946-2; LC 47-11043)
Betsy and Joe, a Betsy-Tacy high school story $9.95 (ISBN 0-690-13378-2; LC 48-8096)
Betsy and the great world $9.95 (ISBN 0-690-13591-2; LC 52-8657)
Betsy's wedding $9.95 (ISBN 0-690-13733-8; LC 55-11108)

Lowry, Lois

Anastasia Krupnik. Houghton 1979 113p illus $6.95 (4-6)   **Fic**

1 Family life—Fiction
ISBN 0-395-28629-3   LC 79-18625

This book describes the tenth year in the life of fourth-grader Anastasia. As she "experiences rejection of a long labored-over poem, fights acceptance of the coming arrival of a baby sibling, deliberates about becoming Catholic (in order to change her name), has a crush on Washburn Cummings who constantly dribbles an imaginary basketball, and learns to understand her senile grandmother's inward eye, she grows and matures." Booklist

"Although the episodic story is somewhat slight, Anastasia's father and mother—an English professor and an artist—are among the most humorous, sensible, and understanding parents to be found in recent children's fiction, and Anastasia herself is an amusing and engaging heroine." Horn Bk

A summer to die; illus. by Jenni Oliver. Houghton 1977 illus 154p $6.95 (5 and up)   **Fic**

1 Sisters—Fiction   2 Death—Fiction
ISBN 0-395-25338-1   LC 77-83

"Themes on birth and death are juxtaposed. . . . Thirteen-year-old Meg, her pretty 15-year-old sister Molly, and their parents move to the country so that their father can write a book. Lonely at first and slightly jealous of popular, vivacious Molly, Meg befriends an elderly neighbor and a young couple living nearby; she also begins to recognize and develop her own talents. The sense of family security and the tranquility of surroundings, however, is shattered when Molly becomes terminally ill. As she weakens, her overwhelming interest becomes the baby expected by the young neighbors, and it is through the drama of their baby's birth at home, with Meg sharing in the experience, that the poignant link between birth and death is made." Sch Library J

"As told by Meg, the chronicle of this experience is a sensitive exploration of the complex emotions underlying the adolescent's first confrontation with human mortality; the author suggests nuances of contemporary conversation and situations without sacrificing the finesse with which she limits her characters. Not simply another story on a subject currently in vogue, the book is memorable as a well-crafted reaffirmation of universal values. A remarkable first novel." Horn Bk

McCaffrey, Anne

Dragonsong. Atheneum Pubs. 1976 202p $9.95 (6 and up)   **Fic**

1 Fantastic fiction
ISBN 0-689-30507-9   LC 75-30530

A fantasy story, set on the imaginary planet of Pern. "Menolly, a young Pernese girl, is a gifted musician trained by the dying Harper. Harpers are keepers of the valued Teaching Songs. In Menolly's community it is forbidden for a woman to become a Harper. After the Harper dies, Menolly's father forbids her to practice or perform any of her music. In despair she runs away and discovers a group of elusive and valued fire lizards. Menolly protects the lizards and teaches her music to them. . . . She and the lizards are rescued by the dragonriders and taken to another part of Pern. There she finds acceptance for her musical talents and respect for her ability to befriend the fire lizards. Although the text is sometimes confusing, the bizarre setting and Menolly's adventures and frustrations make exciting reading." Best Sellers

Followed by these books, also available from Atheneum Pubs:

Dragonsinger $8.95 (ISBN 0-689-30570-2; LC 76-40988)
Dragondrums $8.95 (ISBN 0-689-30685-7; LC 78-11318)

McCloskey, Robert

Homer Price. Viking 1943 149p illus $8.95,
Penguin pa $1.95 (4 and up)   **Fic**

ISBN 0-670-37729-5; 0-14-030927-6   LC 43-16001

Six blithe stories about the adventures of an
American boy, Middlewestern variety. Homer is
a poker-faced youth to whom almost anything
might happen, and usually does. Sometimes he is
catching burglars with the aid of his pet skunk,
Aroma, or making non-stop doughnuts in his uncle's
lunchroom; or else he is discovering that Super-
Duper, the comic strip hero, has feet of clay

"This boy is a real boy, thinking out loud and
living out these rich and hilarious dilemmas with
solemn and devastating humor." Horn Bk

Another book about Homer Price is also avail-
able from Viking: The Centerberg tales $8.95,
Penguin pa $2.50 (ISBN 0-670-20977-5; 0-14-031072-X;
LC 51-10675)

McCord, Jean

Turkeylegs Thompson. Atheneum Pubs. 1979
242p $8.95 (5 and up)   **Fic**

1 Brothers and sisters—Fiction
ISBN 0-689-30686-5   LC 78-12174

"To her mother and teachers she was Betty
Ann, a gawky, rebellious adolescent who skipped
school and daydreamed; to her schoolmates she
was Turkeylegs Thompson, whose pugilistic career
began when the boys taunted her for trying to
play on the school's basketball team. But the real
source of Turkey's anger was the sense of hopelessness caused by her family problems and by
the feeling that 'all adults were recognized as
people, but kids were frequently ignored.' Forced
by her parents' separation to assume responsibility
for the whining, pants-wetting seven-year-old
brother whom she disliked and for Laura, the
three-year-old sister whom she loved and mothered,
Turkeylegs was left with no one who understood
her. As a consequence, the tragic events of the
summer she was twelve, particularly the sudden
death of her sister, threatened to curb her courage
and independence." Horn Bk

"Jean McCord has not only told a compelling
story, she has, with infinite finesse and compassion, followed an adolescent's experiments in
survival through to her tentative acceptance of
the idea of restitution. The reader, moreover, has
no doubt that in her own deliberate way Turkeylegs will eventually find out how to be happy."
NY Times Bk Rev

MacDonald, Betty

Mrs Piggle-Wiggle; illus. by Hilary
Knight. Lippincott 1957 118p illus $6.95,
pa $2.50 (2-4)   **Fic**

ISBN 0-397-30380-7; 0-397-31710-7   LC 47-1876

Chapters follow "the amazing versatility of Mrs
Piggle-Wiggle who loves children good or bad, who
never scolds but who has positive cures for 'Answer-
Backers,' 'Never-Want-To-Go-To-Bedders,' and
other children with special problems." Bks for Deaf
Children

"Mrs. Piggle-Wiggle, the widow of a pirate,
has a cure for every childish bad habit imaginable.
In this volume she cures Melody Foxglove of being
a crybaby, Nicholas Semicolon of being a bully,
Harbin Quadrangle of being a slowpoke—and reforms other assorted offspring who had annoying
habits. . . . [The author] mixes a little psychology
with a lot of common sense, and seasons with
nonsense, to produce the most palatable type of
lecture on good behavior. Hilary Knight's illustrations catch the mood of the whole delightful
business." Chicago Sunday Trib

Some other books about Mrs Piggle-Wiggle are
also available from Lippincott:

Hello, Mrs Piggle-Wiggle $6.95, pa $2.50 (ISBN
0-397-30364-5; 0-397-31708-5; LC 57-5613)
Mrs Piggle-Wiggle's farm $6.95, pa $2.50 (ISBN
0-397-30273-8; 0-397-31711-5; LC 54-7299)
Mrs Piggle-Wiggle's magic $6.95, pa $2.50 (ISBN
0-397-30384-X; 0-397-31709-3; LC 49-11124)

Macdonald, George

At the back of the North Wind; with 8
colour plates and line drawings by E. H.
Shepard. Dent [1956] 325p illus $9 (4-6)
Fic

1 Fairy tales
ISBN 0-460-05036-2   LC 57-610

First published 1871

"There is a rare quality in Macdonald's lovely fairy
tales which relates spiritual ideals with the everyday things of life. This one tells of Diamond, the
little son of a coachman, and his friendship with
the North Wind who appears to him in various
guises." Bks for Boys & Girls

The light princess; with pictures by Maurice
Sendak. Farrar, Straus [1977 c1969] 110p
illus $5.95 (3-6)   **Fic**

1 Fairy tales
ISBN 0-374-34455-8   LC 69-14981

"An Ariel book"
Text first published 1926 by Macmillan. First
published with these illustrations 1969

"The problems of the princess who had been
deprived, as an infant, of her gravity and whose
life hung in the balance when she grew up are
amusing as ever and the sweet capitulation to
love that brings her (literally) to her feet, just
as touching. All of the best of MacDonald is
reflected in the Sendak illustrations: the humor
and wit, the sweetness and tenderness, and the
sophistication—and they are beautiful." Sutherland.
The Best in Childrens Bks

The Princess and the goblin (3-6)   **Fic**

1 Fairy tales

Some editions are:
Airmont (Classics ser) pa $1.25 (ISBN 0-8049-0156-2)
Cook (Macdonald fairy tale ser) pa $1.95 (ISBN
0-89191-164-2)
Penguin Bks. pa $1.50 With the original illustra-
tions by Arthur Hughes (ISBN 0-14-030220-4)

First published 1872
"Living in a great house on the side of a mountain in a country where hideous spiteful goblins
inhabit the dark caverns below the mines, little
Princess Irene and Curdie the miner's son have
many strange adventures. . . . To adults Macdonald's stories have an allegorical significance, to
each succeeding generation of children they are
wonderful fairytale adventures." Four to Fourteen

Followed by: The princess and Curdie, some editions of which are:
Cook (Macdonald fairy tale ser) pa $1.95 (ISBN
0-89191-165-0)
Penguin Bks. pa $1.50 (ISBN 0-14-030260-3)

McGinley, Phyllis

The plain princess; with pictures by Helen
Stone. Lippincott 1945 62p illus $8.95 (2-4)
Fic

1 Fairy tales
ISBN 0-397-30107-3   LC 45-9782

"Rich and spoiled Princess Esmeralda has everything her heart desires except good looks. In this
charming, whimsical fairy tale sensible Dame Goodwit, knowing how to change 'a Plain Young Lady
into a Beautiful Young Lady,' takes Esmeralda to
live in her shabby but cheerful, busy cottage where,
during months of work and play with Dame
Goodwit's five lovely daughters, the Princess,
little by little, acquires a down-tilted nose, a
dimply smile and a twinkle in her eye." Bookmark

"Charm, wit and common sense are deftly combined in this endearing story. The gaiety of the
text is sustained in the illustrations." NY Pub
Library

McGraw, Eloise Jarvis

Mara, daughter of the Nile. Coward,
McCann & Geoghegan 1953 279p $7.95 (5
and up)   **Fic**

1 Egypt—Fiction
ISBN 0-698-20087-X   LC 53-9564

Set in ancient Egypt, when the court was torn
by a rivalry between Queen Hatshepsut and her
young half-brother, this novel concerns the dangerous and romantic role played by Mara, a slave
girl, on both sides of the royal intrigue

"The book contains many details about Egyptian
life. The characters are solid flesh and blood beneath their ancient costumes and the vigor of
their thoughts, emotions and actions lend an
appeal beyond that of historical fiction. This is
a good full bodied story." NY Times Bk Rev

MacGregor, Ellen

Miss Pickerell goes to Mars; illus. by Paul
Galdone. McGraw 1951 128p illus $6.95 (4-6)
Fic

1 Space flight to Mars—Fiction   2 Science fiction
ISBN 0-07-044560-5   LC 51-13241

MacGregor, Ellen—*Continued*

"Whittlesey House publications"

When Miss Pickerell returned from her month's vacation she was very surprised to find someone had been living in her house and that a large rocket ship was in her pasture. How Miss Pickerell took off with the rocket ship crew, and what she found on Mars are told here

"This mixture of humor and scientific fact will please nine to eleven year olds, with its many funny pictures and large type. Miss Pickerell is a happily drawn character, a most welcome intruder into the cold world of interstellar space." NY Her Trib Bks

Some other books about Miss Pickerell written by Ellen MacGregor are also available from McGraw:

Miss Pickerell and the Geiger counter lib. bdg. $6.95 (ISBN 0-07-044554-0; LC 53-5758)

Miss Pickerell goes undersea lib. bdg. $6.95 (ISBN 0-07-044558-3; LC 53-9890)

Some other books about Miss Pickerell written by Dora Pantell after Ellen MacGregor's death, but published as being authored by Ellen Mac-Gregor and Dora Pantell, are also available from McGraw:

Miss Pickerell and the supertanker $7.95 (ISBN 0-07-044588-5; LC 78-8241)

Miss Pickerell meets Mr H.U.M. $5.95, lib. bdg. $6.95 (ISBN 0-07-044577-X; 0-07-044578-8; LC 74-2126)

Miss Pickerel on the Moon, lib. bdg. $6.95 (ISBN 0-07-044551-6; LC 64-66411)

Miss Pickerell tackles the energy crisis $7.95 (ISBN 0-07-044589-3; LC 79-24149)

Miss Pickerell takes the bull by the horns $6.95 (ISBN 0-07-044582-6; LC 75-41454)

Miss Pickerell to the earthquake rescue $6.95 (ISBN 0-07-044586-9; LC 76-52447)

McHargue, Georgess

Stoneflight; drawings by Arvis Stewart. Avon [1976 c1975] 223p illus pa $1.25 (5 and up)   Fic

1 New York (City)—Fiction 2 Family life—Fiction 3 Fantastic fiction
ISBN 0-380-00632-4

"A Camelot book"
First published 1975 by Viking

"A contemporary New York City story—a fantasy which draws upon ancient beliefs and motifs of the supernatural. [The author] has interwoven the magic with the realism of a child deeply troubled by the constant bickering of her parents. Janie Harris has refused to go to summer camp; her friends have vanished; and both mother and father are trapped in unrewarding professional pursuits. The story develops out of Janie's conversations with a stone griffin on the cornice of her apartment-house roof, for she discovers how to quicken him and other statues of animals and birds that decorate the city. When brought to life, Griff takes her on nighttime flights over the 'black silk scarf' of a city below and to a climactic gathering in Central Park of all the figures she has sketched during her jaunts around the city—including the two New York Public Library lions." Horn Bk

"The fantasy is sharpened because the people are real. The illustrations help to show Janie's real as well as her imagined life." Children's Bk Rev Serv

MacKellar, William

The witch of Glen Gowrie; illus. by Ted Lewin. Dodd 1978 144p illus $5.95 (5 and up)   Fic

1 Witches—Fiction 2 Scotland—Fiction
ISBN 0-396-07531-2   LC 77-16864

"A strange and unlikely friendship comes about between Gavin Fraser and Meg Leckie after the boy rescues the witch's dog from a steel trap. Gavin's love of animals is nurtured as he spends time at Meg's helping to care for the wounded wildlife she lovingly nurses. Shortly before Meg mysteriously disappears the night her home is devastated by fire, she hints of a great treasure. The mercenary Mr. Cuthbertson, town councilor determined to gain possession of it, is continually thwarted, seemingly by the ghostly and humorous tricks of old Meg herself. Gavin finally realizes that the treasure is meant for him—and that it is other than gold." Booklist

"MacKellar has an ear for Scottish dialogue; his characters are well drawn; and he has captured the harsh yet beautiful qualities of this rugged landscape." Sch Library J

Macken, Walter

The flight of the Doves. Macmillan Pub. Co. 1968 200p lib. bdg. $5.95, pa $1.95 (4-6)   Fic

1 Orphans—Fiction 2 Runaways—Fiction 3 Ireland—Fiction
ISBN 0-02-762060-3; 0-02-044400-1   LC 68-12083

"Orphaned Finn and his younger sister Derval, brutally mistreated by Uncle Toby, their legal guardian, run away from their English home. Concentrating upon a vague memory of a visit long ago to Granny O'Flaherty in the west of Ireland, Finn carefully plots their escape. Walking, hiding, begging rides, sometimes sustained by beneficent strangers, or hindered by unscrupulous ones, the children—a brave and believable pair—cross the Irish sea and begin their journey toward freedom." Horn Bk

"The sights and sounds of Ireland are in this book, the seedy streets and the pinched urban existence as well as the blue mountains in the distance. The impetus, however, lies in the characters of Finn and Derval. They shine out like two good little deeds in a naughty world." NY Times Bk Rev

McKillip, Patricia A.

The house on Parchment Street; drawings by Charles Robinson. Atheneum Pubs. [1978 c1973] 190p illus pa $1.95 (5 and up)   Fic

1 Ghosts—Fiction 2 Great Britain—Fiction
ISBN 0-689-70451-8   LC 72-86941

"An Aladdin book"
First published 1973

"An American teenager comes to England for a month's stay with relatives. Carol finds her cousin Bruce hostile and she herself is ill-at-ease; however, when Bruce realizes that Carol too has seen the cellar ghosts that intrigue him, he changes his attitude. The ghosts—a beckoning girl who speaks, and a man who fades into the wall, cannot be seen by adults. The mystery of the ghosts' behavior is ferreted out, and they are appeased and vanish after some detective work by the cousins." Chicago. Children's Bk Center

This is "a thoroughly satisfying tale of mystery and secret adventure, much wider in appeal than the usual ghost story." Sch Library J

The riddle-master of Hed. Atheneum Pubs. 1976 228p illus $8.95 (5 and up)   Fic

1 Fantastic fiction
ISBN 0-689-30545-1   LC 76-5492

The author "has created an intricate and varied world in this first book of a . . . trilogy; the protagonist is Prince of Hed, a small and peaceful island. A former student at the College of Riddle-Masters on the mainland, Morgon has, in a riddle contest, won the hand of a princess, but he learns from a harpist called Deth, a man who has lived for centuries. Together they go to claim the princess, but they never reach her father's palace, for Morgon has the mark of three stars on his face, and there are similar marks on an unusual harp and sword. He must fulfill his role but does not want to be the Star-Bearer, who has an important and mysterious destiny, but Morgon finds, in a series of fantastic adventures, that he has friends to protect him and teach him new magic powers, as well as enemies who try several times to kill him on a tortuous journey to the domain of the High One." Chicago. Children's Bk Center

"Many of the elements and the names appear to be drawn from Welsh mythology, but the author has the ability to deal with familiar themes in a fresh manner and a poetic facility in description. The book . . . leaves the story at an outrageously suspenseful point. Morgon is an appealing hero, and although the fantasy is complex, the further untangling of the story of his quest should be anticipated with interest. A map and a list of people and places is included." Horn Bk

Followed by these books, also available from Atheneum Pubs:

Heir of sea & fire $7.95 (ISBN 0-689-30606-7; LC 77-4650)

Harpist in the wind $8.95 (ISBN 0-689-30687-3; LC 78-11410)

McKinley, Robin

Beauty: a retelling of the story of Beauty and the beast. Harper 1978 247p $7.95, lib. bdg. $8.79 (5 and up)   Fic

1 Fairy tales
ISBN 0-06-024149-7; 0-06-024150-0   LC 77-25636

McKinley, Robin—*Continued*

"McKinley has shorn away the didacticism and made significant changes in plot, characters, and tone in the literary fairy tale of Madame de Beaumont to produce an enthralling, full-length novel set years ago, perhaps in Britain, in the days of merchant sailing ships. The youngest in a close-knit, warm family, much loved by her practical, homebody sisters, Beauty is plain, hardworking, intelligent, and a reader of the classics. Her devoted sisters are extremely reluctant to allow her to satisfy the Beast's requirement of a life in exchange for his rose. The Beast is a wealthy prince from an overly pious family, placed under a spell by an offended witch until a virtuous maiden should love him for himself alone." Children's Bk Rev Serv

"The author has fun with the magic: plates and chairs run to serve the guest; the bed makes itself; the library contains books not yet written (Beauty likes Browning but can't understand A.C. Doyle); and whenever she's lost in the castle, her room is always around the next turn. Except for the jarring 'okay' and 'uh,' this reads like a fantasy-gothic." Sch Library J

McSwigan, Marie

Snow treasure; illus. by Mary Reardon. Dutton 1942 178p illus lib. bdg. $9.95 (4-6)   **Fic**

1 World War, 1939-1945—Fiction   2 Norway—Fiction
ISBN 0-525-39556-3   LC 42-2896

Set in the early days of the Nazi occupation, this is the story of how a group of Norwegian children managed to get blocks of gold out of Norway by fastening them to their sleds and coasting through the German camps

"A dramatic reconstruction of an actual happening. . . . Well written and superior to previous books about the war in that the actions of the children are planned and controlled by their elders. Striking black and white illustrations." Booklist

Mann, Peggy

My dad lives in a downtown hotel; illus. by Richard Cuffari. Doubleday 1973 92p illus $6.95 (3-5)   **Fic**

1 Divorce—Fiction
ISBN 0-385-07080-2   LC 72-90049

This is the story of 10-year-old Joey and his reactions and gradual adjustment to his parents' divorce

"A realistic story of a child's reaction to his parents' separation. . . . The ending is hopeful: Joey's mother spends more time with him, and his father is relaxed and able to spend at least a day with him each week. Cuffari's sensitive, full-page, black-and-white illustrations help to create an accurate portrayal of a troubled middle-class family." Sch Library J

There are two kinds of terrible. Doubleday 1977 132p $6.95, lib. bdg. $7.90 (5 and up)   **Fic**

1 Death—Fiction   2 Parent and child—Fiction
ISBN 0-385-09588-0; 0-385-08185-5   LC 76-42372

"It's one kind of terrible to break your arm just as summer vacation starts, Rob finds. But the other kind of terrible is immeasurably worse: having your mother die. Although Rob loves his father, he hardly knows the man he thinks of as a 'cold fish,' while he has been, as an only child, very close to his mother. Mom goes to the hospital for tests—and she never comes back. Cancer. The author . . . describes, through Rob's telling, the stages of anguish: waiting, fearing, knowing, and facing the fact, and the reactions of fear, anger, and grief. Rob tells of the separate burdens of the service, the funeral, the gathering after the funeral, and the utter loneliness after all these. The story ends on a note of encouragement, as Rob and his father move toward a new closeness, a change that is attained gradually and believably." Chicago. Children's Bk Center

"This is a sensitive and perceptive treatment of a subject where more books are still needed for young readers. It might well be too tough—as perhaps any high quality fiction book would be—for a child to read when directly involved in this situation. However, it could be useful to such a child afterwards, and certainly would be excellent for peer age friends, as well as adults, in helping a child cope with a parental death. The reader can gain insights into the feelings of the grieving child and the surviving grieving parent." Children's Bk Rev Serv

Mark, Jan

Thunder and Lightnings; illus. by Jim Russell. Crowell [1979 c1976] 181p illus $7.95, lib. bdg. $7.89 (5 and up)   **Fic**

1 Airplanes—Fiction   2 Great Britain—Fiction   3 Friendship—Fiction
ISBN 0-690-03901-8; 0-690-03902-6   LC 78-4778

First published 1976 in England

Set in Norfolk, this is a "perceptive story of an unusual friendship between two boys of unlike backgrounds and personalities. . . . Victor, the more unusual character, is slow in school but sophisticated in his ability to identify airplanes. He is friendly to the newcomer Andrew, a racing-car devotee, and they become companions in plane-watching. Little details sharply define their different home backgrounds—Victor's so sterile with cleanliness and order, Andrew's so welcoming and comfortable. Humorous conversations lighten the pictures of domestic life and reveal the boys' attitudes toward their contrasting lifestyles, but their passionate interest in aircraft is the focus of the story." Horn Bk

Under the autumn garden; illus. by Judith Gwyn Brown. Crowell [1979 c1977] 211p illus $8.95 (4-6)   **Fic**

1 Excavations (Archeology)—Fiction   2 Great Britain—Fiction
ISBN 0-690-03903-4; 0-690-03904-2   LC 78-4779

First published 1977 in England

"Ten-year-old Matthew lives in a Norfolk village, and for an assigned class project he must do research on some aspect of local history. The boy is aware that remnants of a thirteenth-century priory still stand near his house, and he is also acquainted with a legend about the ghost of Sir Oliver, the medieval knight who had built the priory. With only vague notions of method or purpose, he decides to do archaeological digging. But his inept efforts prove unproductive, and since Matthew has nothing on paper to show that he has done any homework, the boy must endure scoldings at school and at home. When the deadline has passed, he does discover something exciting and important, but by this time he has learned much more than bits of regional history." Horn Bk

This book "is rich in characterization, sensitive to relationships among children, lightened by the humor of the dialogue and colored by local idiom. [The] gentle and perceptive story is distinctively English in flavor but its differences should present no barrier to enjoyment by children elsewhere." Chicago. Children's Bk Center

Mason, Miriam E.

Caroline and her kettle named Maud; with illus. by Kathleen Voute. Macmillan Pub. Co. 1951 134p illus $3.95 (2-4)   **Fic**

1 Frontier and pioneer life—Fiction   2 Kettles—Fiction   3 Michigan—Fiction
ISBN 0-02-763280-6   LC 51-13835

Caroline was "going on eight" when her family moved to frontier Michigan. She had hoped for a gun for a farewell present, but instead she was given a shiny copper kettle. To add to her woe, Old Witch, the cow Caroline hated, went along. But in the wilds of Michigan Caroline's kettle and Old Witch proved just as useful as the gun she did not possess

In large print for "early readers, this offers a very real small girl, plenty of action, and a good honest look at pioneer America." NY Her Trib Bks

Masterman-Smith, Virginia

The treasure trap; illus. by Roseanne Litzinger. Four Winds 1979 200p illus $7.95 (4-6)   **Fic**

1 Mystery and detective stories
ISBN 0-590-07615-9   LC 79-11722

"A lively but controlled zaniness permeates this mystery/adventure concerning the disappearance of a despised old miser and the rumors of a buried treasure in or about his mansion. Billy Beak meets Angel Wilson, the current resident of the mansion, and the two join forces to investigate the fate of the old man and find the treasure. . . . Dialogue is pleasantly exuberant and a buoyant, cheerful tone is evident throughout the work. As a mystery, this is not particularly well crafted, but it is nice light reading." Booklist

Mathis, Sharon Bell

Teacup full of roses. Viking 1972 125p $7.95 (6 and up) **Fic**

1 Blacks—Fiction 2 Family life—Fiction 3 Narcotic habit—Fiction
ISBN 0-670-69434-7   LC 74-162675

A "story of the tragedy haunting a black ghetto family. Their lives are dominated by Paul, the oldest boy, a gifted artist who is hooked on heroin. Joe is the hard-working and dependable son, determined that David, the youngest, shall have a chance at college. When Paul steals the money Joe has saved for David—the younger boy tries to get it back from the pusher, with terrible results." Pub W

"Stark and uncompromising, the brief, episodic novel explores the many facets of love and loyalty as it concentrates on a single tragic week in the lives of a black, inner-city family. . . . But the author's skillful blending of dialogue and description and her superb characterization of the mother as a purposeful, devoted woman caught in a bewildering and difficult situation add strength and credibility to the story. The book represents a further development in the growing collection of literature dealing with the black experience." Horn Bk

Matthews, Ellen

The trouble with Leslie; illus. by Unada Gliewe. Westminster Press 1979 109p illus $7.95 (4-6) **Fic**

1 Family life—Fiction
ISBN 0-664-32653-6   LC 79-12348

"The trouble with Leslie is that she is three years old, and her brother Eric has been put in charge of her and the house while their mother goes to library school and their father works. Filled with amusing incidents, it is a lively story with a non-traditional look at family roles. Children with younger brothers and sisters will find lots to identify with here." Children's Bk Rev Serv

Mayne, William

Earthfasts. Dutton [1967 c1966] 154p lib. bdg. $7.95 (5 and up) **Fic**

1 Fantastic fiction 2 Great Britain—Fiction
ISBN 0-525-29008-7   LC 67-16464

First published 1966 in England

Two twentieth century English boys become involved in unusual adventures when "an eighteenth-century English drummer boy returns to earth carrying a candle which causes the past to become confused with the present and sets off a series of fantastic events involving King Arthur, a boggart, and other legendary characters. For the imaginative reader with sufficient background to appreciate the historical allusions." Hodges. Bks for Elem Sch Libraries

"Original and brilliant in conception, the intricate story demands one's full attention and even some suspension of incredulity for the less imaginative reader." Horn Bk

A year and a day. Dutton 1976 86p lib. bdg. $6.95 (4-6) **Fic**

1 Fairy tales 2 Great Britain—Fiction
ISBN 0-525-43450-X   LC 75-34160

"In the Cornwall of a bygone time, Becca and Sara Polwarne and their parents discover a 'fairy child,' a young boy sitting naked in a nest of grass on Midsummer's Eve. Unable to communicate with them in their own language, Adam—as they christen the child—does convey his special understanding of animals and nature. The prediction of the village witch (that Adam will disappear in 'A Year and a Day') comes true, but Becca and Sara's loss is softened by the birth of a baby brother." Sch Library J

"The story is direct and luminously clear; the narrative, though not at all complex, is unmistakably William Mayne's. Less allusive than usual, his style remains, nevertheless, somewhat elliptical but so metaphoric and beautifully cadenced, one almost instinctively wants to read the book aloud." Horn Bk

Mazer, Norma Fox

A figure of speech. Delacorte Press 1973 197p $7.95, pa $1.50 (6 and up) **Fic**

1 Grandfathers—Fiction 2 Old age—Fiction
ISBN 0-440-02638-5; 0-440-94374-4   LC 73-6239

"Jenny has always felt alienated from her short-sighted, thoroughly middle-class family. Her one bulwark is her grandfather, who came to live with the family the year Jenny was born and, feeling as unwanted as she, virtually raised her to adolescence. Shifting the focus between Jenny and her grandfather the narrative chronicles the climactic weeks in the crowded Pennoyer household following the elder son's arrival with his new bride. His indulgent parents plan to move the old man into a nursing home so that the young couple can have the basement apartment. The denouement is tragic, not simply because the old man dies but because Jenny cannot reconcile her family's post-mortem commentaries with their actions toward the man who had once lived with them. The subordinate characters are seen primarily from Jenny's and the grandfather's points of view; they are one-dimensional types, hypocritical and unlikeable. . . . Yet, the tendency toward melodramatic oversimplification is offset by the significance of the situation and by the crusty personality of grandfather, who refuses to 'go gentle into that good night.'" Horn Bk

Menotti, Gian Carlo

Gian-Carlo Menotti's Amahl and the night visitors; this narrative adaptation by Frances Frost preserves the exact dialog of the opera; illus. by Roger Duvoisin. McGraw 1952 86p illus lib. bdg. $6.95 (4 and up) **Fic**

1 Christmas—Fiction 2 Magi—Fiction
ISBN 0-07-041484-X   LC 52-10343

"Whittlesey House publications"

The story of a crippled shepherd boy who entertained the Wise Men on their way to Bethlehem, of the simple gift he gave them for the Christ Child, and of the miraculous gift he received in return

"A sentimental tale, like many Christmas stories, and moving if not read too close to the Biblical story. . . . For me, Roger Duvoisin's drawings are the best part of the book, beautiful, glowing, warm and humorous." NY Times Bk Rev

Merrill, Jean

The pushcart war; with illus. by Ronni Solbert. Young Scott Bks. 1964 222p illus lib. bdg. $7.95 (5 and up) **Fic**

1 New York (City)—Fiction 2 Trucks—Fiction
ISBN 0-201-09313-8   64-13581

"By 1976 arrogant, mammoth trucks threaten to crowd people, small cars, pushcarts, and peddlers off the streets of New York. When a truck contemptuously runs down a pushcart, the peddlers rebel and wage a guerrilla war against the trucks, using a primitive, but effective, secret weapon. Funny, dramatic, tongue-in-cheek satire on the sheer bigness which is overwhelming urban life but which is here, for once, defeated by the little people who 'are' the city." Moorachian. What is a City?

The superlative horse; illus. by Ronni Solbert. Young Scott Bks. 1961 79p illus lib. bdg. $5.95 (4-6) **Fic**

1 Horses—Fiction 2 China—Fiction
ISBN 0-201-09357-9   LC 61-16201

"This story was suggested by a Taoist tale in the Book of Lieh Tzu, c. 350 B.C. The illustrations were suggested by scenes in the frescoes of the Tun-huang caves in Western China." Half-title page

"The son of a lowly fuel hawker wins the post of High Groom after proving his ability to distinguish between the superior and the inferior in horses. Because his talent has wider application, he later becomes the Chief Minister too." Asia: a Guide to Bks for Children

"An unusual story about ancient China . . . illustrated beautifully in appropriate technique that resembles the art of early China. . . . Although the writing style has a quiet dignity, it does not lack momentum and seems particularly well suited to the period and place." Chicago. Children's Bk Center

The toothpaste millionaire; prepared by the Bank Street College of Education. Houghton [1974 c1972] 90p illus lib. bdg. $6.95 (4-6) **Fic**

1 Business—Fiction
ISBN 0-395-18511-4   LC 73-22055

First copyright 1972
Illustrated by Jan Palmer

"The teller of the tale is a classmate of brilliantly inventive sixth-grade Rufus Mayflower, who 'doesn't seem to mind that I'm white and he's

Merrill, Jean—*Continued*

black.' Rufus makes and markets an extraordinarily inexpensive toothpaste—which still sells at a low price even when stockholders, promotion, and all the necessary apparatus of a growing business introduce expenses." Horn Bk

The story "is laden rather heavily with arithmetic and business details, but rises above it. . . . The illustrations are engaging, the style is light, the project interesting (with more than a few swipes taken at advertising and business practices in our society) and Rufus a believable genius." Chicago. Children's Bk Center

Miles, Betty

Just the beginning. Knopf 1976 143p $5.95 lib. bdg. $6.99 (4-6)   Fic

1 Family life—Fiction
ISBN 0-394-83226-4; 0-394-93226-4   LC 75-28545

"Living in 'one of the ten richest towns in the whole United States,' 13-year-old Catherine is mortified when her mother goes to work as a cleaning lady. Add an older sister who excels at everything and find Catherine having real trouble feeling a part of things. Cathy and the story move smoothly through several crises, including her mother's work, her suspension from school for cutting class, and the accidental death of a classmate. Only when she becomes involved in tutoring, babysitting, and working on the school yearbook does Cathy begin to realize her own possibilities. Cathy, as well as the supporting characters emerge as well rounded, with diverse views and reactions. . . . The action is low-key as a whole, with no dramatic climax, but interest never lags." Sch Library J

The trouble with thirteen. Knopf 1979 108p $6.95. lib. bdg. $6.99 (5 and up)   Fic

1 Friendship—Fiction
ISBN 0-394-83930-7; 0-394-93930-1   LC 78-31678

"Best friends Rachel and Annie have always shared everything—books, friends, likes, dislikes, and a fear of becoming teenagers. Then, suddenly, Rachel's parents separate, and she and her mother must move to New York City. For Annie, the narrator of the story, it is the first of many events which disrupt her life. Struggling with the imminent separation from Rachel, she is heartbroken when her pet dog dies and wonders 'when the sadness would fade.' As the two friends enjoy their last days together, Annie gradually comes to accept the changes in her life—even the ones yet to come." Horn Bk

"Annie and Rachel are distinct, fully drawn characters, not meant to stand for Everygirl nor needlessly quirky. They are authentic, the plot is balanced and believable, the pace is sure, and the book is a winner." Sch Library J

Miles, Miska

Annie and the Old One; illus. by Peter Parnall. Little 1971 44p illus $6.95 (1-4)   Fic

1 Navaho Indians—Fiction 2 Death—Fiction
ISBN 0-316-57117-2   LC 79-129900

"An Atlantic Monthly Press book"

"Annie, a young Navajo girl, struggles with the realization that her grandmother, the Old One, must die. Slowly and painfully, she accepts the fact that she cannot change the cyclic rhythms of the earth to which the Old One has been so sensitively attuned." Wis Library Bul

This is "a poignant, understated, rather brave story of a very real child, set against a background of Navajo traditions and contemporary Indian life. Fine expressive drawings match the simplicity of the story." Horn Bk

Jenny's cat; illus. by Wendy Watson. Dutton 1979 39p illus $6.95 (2-4)   Fic

1 Cats—Fiction 2 Family life—Fiction
ISBN 0-525-32746-0   LC 79-11501

"A Unicorn book"

Jenny's unhappiness about moving to a new town and the frequent absence of her father, a train conductor, is eased when her mother lets her keep a stray cat. Jenny has assured her nervous mother that the cat is a male and will be no problem to care for. When the cat turns out to be pregnant, Jenny's parents decide it must go. Jenny runs away with the cat and is given shelter by her new friend, Doris, but quickly reveals herself when she overhears her worried parents telling Doris they will let Jenny keep her pet. Papa arranges for the cat to be spayed, a cat-loving neighbor and Doris are glad

to take two of the kittens, and Papa indicates that he will convince Mama to let Jenny keep the third

"The story has an old-fashioned feel, both in setting and exposition. Jenny is a well-intentioned, determined sort, in contrast to her mother who is a loving but curiously fearful and naive woman. What end this latter characterization serves isn't clear, but it is offset by the sharpness of Jenny's character and a storyline that will set sympathetic response. The charcoal-sketched illustrations are proficient but bland." Booklist

Nobody's cat; illus. by John Schoenherr. Little 1969 43p illus $6.95 (2-4)   Fic

1 Cats—Fiction
ISBN 0-316-56969-0   LC 68-12351

"An Atlantic Monthly Press book"

"Here are city sights and sounds from the point of view of a tough, resourceful alley cat. Independent rather than homeless, he survives because he knows the ways of the city. Striking, full-page illustrations show him responding to many challenges and encounters, including a brief stay at a school where he accepts attention but does not sacrifice his independence. This convincing, sensitive presentation is written and illustrated with fidelity to the nature of the cat." Moorachian. What is a City?

Miles, Patricia

The gods in winter. Dutton 1978 140p lib. bdg. $7.50 (5 and up)   Fic

1 Demeter—Fiction 2 Fantastic fiction 3 Great Britain—Fiction
ISBN 0-525-30748-6   LC 77-16704

"A story that blends fantasy and reality most effectively is based on the idea that Demeter still roams the earth mourning her lost daughter and rejoicing when she finds her child. Thus the cold, dreary winter; thus the effulgence of spring. Here the goddess comes in the guise of a housekeeper to the Bramble family, who have just moved to a new home in the English countryside. The story is told by Adam, one of the three Bramble children, and he is relieved when he learns that his sister (and later his mother) have also begun to suspect that Mrs. Korngold has supernatural powers and that there is a connection between her and the unusually raw winter they've had." Chicago. Children's Bk Center

"An entertaining and undemanding family fantasy. . . . It is eminently readable. Patricia Miles has shown in her earlier books how well she can handle narrative, moving her stories along swiftly and with a good measure of humour. In this she is as skilled as ever, but at the expense here of that sense of threat and danger which the story demands, and which is frequently promised, but seldom materializes." Times (London) Lit Sup

Millstead, Thomas

Cave of the moving shadows. Dial Press 1979 217p illus $7.95, lib. bdg. $7.45 (5 and up)   Fic

1 Man, Prehistoric—Fiction
ISBN 0-8037-1388-6; 0-8037-1387-8   LC 79-10890

This is the "story of an adolescent artist struggling to find his place in Cro-Magnon society. . . . Young Kimba, sole survivor of his parents' tribe, is adopted as an infant. His new parents are kind, and because he has power over animals as well as natural artistic talent, he is chosen by the aging shaman to be his successor, even though Kimba's dream is to be a hunter like his beloved foster father. In the course of the story Kimba becomes the first in his tribe to tame an animal and proves that he is indeed a capable hunter when he and his dog save the old shaman from a cave bear. He comes to realize, however, that his tribe will need his mental and spiritual leadership even more than his spear, and finally can accent with pride his role as shaman-to-be. The author's descriptions of Cro-Magnon life are vivid, exciting, and often fascinating." Sch Library J

Milne, A. A.

The house at Pooh Corner; with decorations by Ernest H. Shepard. Dutton [1961 c1928] 180p illus $6.95 (1-4)   Fic

1 Bears—Fiction 2 Animals—Fiction 3 Toys—Fiction
ISBN 0-525-32302-3   LC 61-16260

Milne, A. A.—*Continued*

Sequel to: Winnie-the-pooh
First published 1928
"Pooh and Piglet built a house for Eeyore at Pooh Corner. They called it that because it was shorter and sounded better than did Pooh-anpiglet Corner. Christopher Robin, Rabbit, and other old acquaintances of 'Winnie-the-Pooh' appear, and a new friend, Tigger, is introduced." Pittsburgh
"It is hard to tell what Pooh Bear and his friends would have been without the able assistance of Ernest H. Shepard to see them and picture them so cleverly. . . . They are, and should be, classics." NY Times Bk Rev

The Pooh story book; with decorations and illus. in full color E. H. Shepard. Dutton 1965 77p illus $7.95 (1-4)   Fic
1 Bears—Fiction 2 Animals—Fiction 3 Toys—Fiction
ISBN 0-525-37546-5   LC 65-19580
Excerpts from: The house at Pooh Corner and Winnie-the-Pooh
Contents: In which a house is built at Pooh Corner for Eeyore; In which Piglet is entirely surrounded by water; In which Pooh invents a new game and Eeyore joins in
This compilation is "illustrated with new pictures by Mr. Shepard very much like those drawings he did for the original Milne editions. An attractive book with some pictures in color." Sch Library J

Winnie-the-Pooh; illus. by Ernest H. Shepard, colored by Hilda Scott. Dutton [1974 c1926] 161p illus lib. bdg. $6.95 (1-4)   Fic
1 Bears—Fiction 2 Animals—Fiction 3 Toys—Fiction
ISBN 0-525-43034-2   LC 74-7215
First published 1926
"To Christopher Robin his toys are real people who talk and play with him in his games of make-believe." Hodges. Bks for Elem Sch Libraries
"'Winnie-the-Pooh' is a joy; full of solemn idiocies and the sort of jokes one weeps over helplessly, not even knowing why they are so funny, and with it all the real wit and tenderness which alone could create such a priceless little masterpiece. [Toy] Kanga and baby Roo, Piglet, and above all Pooh and Christopher Robin himself, are characters no one can afford to miss. . . . The drawings by E. H. Shepard which accompany the story are thoroughly delightful." Sat Rev
Map on lining-papers
Followed by: The house at Pooh Corner, entered above

The world of Pooh; the complete Winnie-the-Pooh and The House at Pooh Corner; with decorations and new illus. in full color by E. H. Shepard. Dutton 1957 314p illus $9.95 (1-4)   Fic
1 Bears—Fiction 2 Animals—Fiction 3 Toys—Fiction
ISBN 0-525-43320-1   LC 57-8986
Also available as part of a boxed set together with: The world of Christopher Robin, entered separately in class 821, for $18.50 (ISBN 0-525-43348-1)
This combined edition of the two titles entered separately above contains the original black and white "illustrations and eight delightful new full-page pictures printed in lovely soft colors." Pub W
"Despite the fact that separate volumes are usually preferable, many libraries will want this pleasing combination volume." Booklist

Mohr, Nicholasa

Felita; pictures by Ray Cruz. Dial Press 1979 112p illus $6.95, lib. bdg. $6.46 (3-5)   Fic
1 City life—Fiction 2 Puerto Ricans in the United States—Fiction
ISBN 0-8037-3143-4;; 0-8037-3144-2   LC 79-50151
"When nine-year-old Felita's Puerto Rican family moves to a better neighborhood, she is sad about leaving old friends. Their new neighbors are hate-filled, prejudiced people. The family returns to the old area. Throughout their ordeal, Felita's grandmother helps her understand her problems." Children's Bk Rev Serv

"The candid message is practical: 'You must feel strength inside.' A few words in Spanish and Ray Cruz's art work fit in perfectly. Mohr scores with her first story for younger readers, capturing the spirit of family and neighborhood." Sch Library J

Nilda; a novel; with pictures by the author. Harper 1973 292p illus $8.95, lib. bdg. $8.79 (6 and up)   Fic
1 Puerto Ricans in New York (City)—Fiction
ISBN 0-06-024331-7; 0-06-024332-5   LC 73-8046
"Nilda's chronicle of barrio life has an unmistakable ring of authenticity. . . . She is ten years old at the outset, and her observations of people, places, kindness, cruelty, prejudice, and friendships are piercingly real. Over the four-year time span Nilda experiences the gradual dissolution of her family: her leftist, anti Catholic stepfather dies slowly of heart disease; her eldest brother Jimmy becomes a criminal and drug addict; the onset of World War II calls away Victor and Paul, her two favorite brothers; and Frankie the disliked youngest brother begins running with a gang and threatens to follow Jimmy's footsteps. Through one crisis after another her mother has been Nilda's only bastion of security, but finally she too becomes ill, and before dying, powerfully confronts her daughter with the ultimate emptiness of her life, spent entirely for her children. . . . A book with language and scenes that may offend various groups, but the author's honesty and skill in telling her story make the book entirely defensible." Booklist

Monjo, F. N.

King George's head was made of lead; illus. by Margot Tomes. Coward, McCann & Geoghegan 1974 47p illus $5.95 (2-4)   Fic
1 U.S.—History—Revolution, 1775-1783—Fiction 2 George III, King of Great Britain—Fiction
ISBN 0-698-20298-8   LC 74-79705
Events leading to the outbreak of the American Revolution are told "by a statue of King George III which was sent to the colonies in 1770. The figure was toppled by irate patriots; its body was used to make ammunition for the Revolutionary Cause." Pub W
"Bold illustrations in gold, orange, and rust and the use of cartoon bubbles to enclose dialogue underscore the rollicking wit of the text." Sch Library J

Letters to Horseface; being the story of Wolfgang Amadeus Mozart's journey to Italy, 1769-1770, when he was a boy of fourteen; illus. & designed by Don Bolognese & Elaine Raphael. Viking 1975 91p illus $8.95 (4 and up)   Fic
1 Mozart, Johann Chrysostom Wolfgang Amadeus —Fiction
ISBN 0-670-42738-1   LC 74-23766
A "portrayal of the 14-year-old Mozart's journey through the major cities of Italy in the late 18th Century. In his letters to his sister Nannerl, affectionately known as 'Horseface,' Mozart describes the gaiety of the society and culture in those cities as he views it. During this trip to demonstrate his musical abilites, Mozart amasses many observations and memories which will serve as the inspiration for future compositions. It is on this trip that he receives his first 'scrittura' to compose an opera for the city of Milan. Illustrated with handsome sepia drawings in the manner of an 18th-Century sketch-book. . . . Good reading even for children not familiar with Mozart's life and music." Sch Library J

Moore, Lilian

The snake that went to school; illus. by Mary Stevens. Random House 1957 114p illus lib. bdg. $5.99 (2-4)   Fic
1 Snakes—Fiction
ISBN 0-394-90101-0   LC 57-10204
"Hank's most cherished memento from summer camp was a pet snake, but his mother said he had to get rid of it before school started. The pet shop wouldn't take it, and his friends' mothers would have none of it. The fourth-grade teacher let Hank keep the snake in the science room, but in some mysterious way it got out. Story is humorous and true to life." Sch Library J

Morey, Walt

Gentle Ben; illus. by John Schoenherr. Dutton 1965 191p illus lib. bdg. $8.95 (5 and up)   Fic

1 Bears—Fiction 2 Alaska—Fiction
ISBN 0-525-30429-0   LC 65-21290

Set in Alaska before statehood, this is the story of 13-year-old Mark Anderson who befriends a huge brown bear which has been chained in a shed since it was a cub. Finally Mark's father buys the bear, but Orca City's inhabitants eventually insist that the animal, named Ben, be shipped to an uninhabited island. However, the friendship of Mark and Ben endures

The author "has written a vivid chronicle of Alaska, its people and places, challenges and beauties. Told with simplicity and dignity which befits its characters, human and animal, [it] is a memorable reading experience." Sch Library J

Year of the black pony. Dutton 1976 152p lib. bdg. $8.95 (5 and up)   Fic

1 Family life—Fiction 2 Ponies—Fiction
ISBN 0-525-43455-0   LC 75-33805

"Set in Oregon at the turn of the century, the story of a boy's love for a pony is smoothly meshed with a family story. Chris had yearned for the wild, beautiful pony in a neighbor's herd, but he had never expected his stepfather to buy the animal. Chris's father had died, and his doughty mother had proposed a marriage of convenience to Frank Chase, a proposal instigated by her fear that she would not be able to support her children. The children become fond of Frank, and Frank becomes fond of Ma—but to Ma it remains a business deal. Or it does until a crisis (the pony's severe illness) follows several episodes in which Ma has learned that Frank really cares for Chris and his sister and that the pony she so disapproved of because he was dangerous fills a real need in Chris's life." Chicago. Children's Bk Center

"The distinctive characterization, especially of Chris's mother, and the unusual plot element represented by her daring decision blend nicely with the local color of the story and with the theme of a boy's devotion to an animal." Horn Bk

Morgan, Alison

A boy called Fish; illus. by Joan Sandin. Harper 1973 201p illus pa $1.25 (5 and up)   Fic

1 Dogs—Fiction 2 Wales—Fiction
ISBN 0-06-440051-4   LC 72-9859

First published 1971 in England
A Welsh boy nicknamed Fish who lives unhappily with his father and stepmother adopts an abandoned mongrel dog. When the animal is suspected of killing sheep, the boy's father immediately orders it destroyed and Fish runs away with it. The story tells of his adventures with his friend Jimmy, who sets out during a snowstorm to bring him supplies

"Although the background of the narrative is Welsh farm country, it sets up no barrier to enjoyment by American readers; and the characterization and narration are those of a first-rate story teller." Horn Bk

Moskin, Marietta

Lysbet and the fire kittens; illus. by Margot Tomes. Coward, McCann & Geoghegan 1973 46p illus lib. bdg. $6.59 (2-4)   Fic

1 New York (City)—History—Fiction
ISBN 0-698-30522-1   LC 73-97315

"A Break-of-day book"
" 'Ma always said only stupid, lazy housewives let their fires die at night!' but that's just what happened to nine-year-old Lysbet, unexpectedly on her own overnight. In the morning Lysbet not only sets a roaring new fire but flies through other necessary chores as well—everything except feeding Stuyver, her cat, ready to have kittens any time. Then it's off to skate during First Skating Day—a holiday in 1662 New Amsterdam. Lysbet belatedly remembers Stuyver and hurries home, only to smell smoke and find Stuyver gone. She sounds the alarm, finds Stuyver with five new kittens, and when her father arrives, receives praise for sounding the warning so soon. Margot Tomes' pictures are delightful interpretation of the easy-to-read story." Booklist

Waiting for mama; illus. by Richard Lebenson. Coward, McCann & Geoghegan 1975 91p $6.95 (3-5)   Fic

1 Jews in New York (City)—Fiction 2 New York (City)—Fiction
ISBN 0-698-20319-4   LC 74-21068

"For two years, small Becky had dreamed of being reunited with her mother, left behind with an ailing baby when the rest of the family emigrated from Czarist Russia to the United States. During that time, while her father and older brother and sister saved money for the tickets which would make that reunion possible, she attended school, learned to speak English, and discovered how to find her way among the crowded tenements of New York's Lower East Side. Indeed, the changes in her short life had been so abrupt and so numerous that the memories of her former home—a quiet farm village—were virtually eclipsed by the noise and bustle of city life. But with the imminent arrival of her mother, she began to wish that she too could contribute in a tangible way to the family's efforts." Horn Bk

"The turn-of-the-century setting is well drawn though not overcolored, and Becky's need to be mothered and to contribute to the family fund for Mama's overseas passage are simply expressed. Lebenson's black-and-white watercolors add a fine touch of realism." Booklist

Mukerji, Dhan Gopal

Gay-Neck; The story of a pigeon; illus. by Boris Artzybasheff. Dutton [1968 c1927] 191p illus lib. bdg. $7.95 (6 and up)   Fic

1 Pigeons—Fiction 2 India—Fiction
ISBN 0-525-30400-2   LC 68-13419

Awarded the Newbery Medal 1928
First published 1927
This is the story of a carrier pigeon that was born in India. The first part of the book tells of his training and adventures in India; the second tells of his part in the World war, where he served with honor

"It is packed with a philosophy and beauty which in no way impedes the moving quality of the story itself. Any child would be the richer for having this book put into his hands, while the decorations by Boris Artzybasheff have a beauty of design completely in harmony with the text." NY Evening Post

Myers, Steven J.

The enchanted sticks; illus. by Donna Diamond. Coward, McCann & Geoghegan 1979 unp illus $6.95 (3-5)   Fic

1 Japan—Fiction 2 Fairy tales
ISBN 0-698-20483-2   LC 78-27725

In this original tale set in ancient Japan "an old man gathers wood in a forest near Kyoto. Cut from a tree by a robber chief, the sticks form into words begging the old man not to burn them as he prepares his supper. Amazed, the man releases the things and they dance gleefully, then arrange themselves into happy faces. The sticks and human pass contented days as good companions—conversing and playing games. But the bandits, growing bolder, become a menace to the country. They kidnap the emperor's daughter and keep her in a cage high in a tree. The old man and the sticks attack and win a ferocious battle at the stirring climax of an unusual story." Pub W

"Donna Diamond's framed line drawings on alternate pages are lively and appropriate, reminiscent in style of the drawings in Hokusai's famous 'Sketchbooks'. The book is well designed and well printed, with a delicately drawn forest landscape frieze at the head of each page." Sch Library J

Myers, Walter Dean

Fast Sam, Cool Clyde & Stuff. Viking 1975 190p (6 and up)   Fic

1 Harlem, New York (City)—Fiction 2 Blacks—Fiction 3 Friendship—Fiction
ISBN 0-670-30874-9   LC 74-32383

"When Stuff moves to 116th Street in Harlem, his first problem is appearing extra cool so he can make new friends. He soon meets Sam and Clyde, and the three share sad times, adventures, and friendship." Cincinnati

"The episodic narrative contains much more than lively accounts of basketball games. Such likely elements as police encounters, death, drugs, and sex are introduced as part of the background

Myers, Walter D.—*Continued*

of Harlem teenagers—balanced, however, by normal concerns with school, parents, eating, and dancing. In their adventures and experiences—some of them comic, some of them saddening—Stuff and his friends feel very close to each other." Horn Bk

Mojo and the Russians. Viking 1977 151p $7.95 (6 and up) **Fic**

1 Harlem, New York (City)—Fiction 2 Voodooism—Fiction 3 Blacks—Fiction
ISBN 0-670-48437-7 LC 77-23454

"When Dean, streaking around a corner in a bicycle race with his friend Kitty, accidentally knocked a woman down, he set off a chain of ludicrous events that led him and his gang all the way from the streets of Harlem to the Russian Consulate, the New York City police, and the FBI. Dean's furious victim was Drusilla, a neighborhood character—a Voodoo practitioner, who terrified the boy when she threatened to 'fix him good' by making 'his tongue split like a lizard's and his eyes to cross.' At the same time Dean's friends noticed that Drusilla's amiable friend Willie seemed to be involved in some sort of intrigue with a couple of suspicious Russians who drove about in a limousine. The children plotted an elaborate investigation, hoping to blackmail Willie into convincing the 'Mojo lady' to call off her magic spell. . . . [The author] takes a sympathetic but absolutely unsentimental approach to his characters; with an accurate feeling for the thoughts and folkways of children, he sets down their spontaneous conversation as the perfect extension of the lively farce." Horn Bk

The young landlords. Viking 1979 197p $8.95 (6 and up) **Fic**

1 New York (City)—Fiction 2 Landlord and tenant—Fiction
ISBN 0-670-79454-6 LC 79-13264

"This is the story of a group of black teenagers living in New York City who become the owners of a run-down slum building. Led by Paul (the narrator) and his soon-to-be girl friend Gloria, they try to cope with the day-to-day (and night-to-night) pressures of running the building." Sch Library J

"The story is presented with a masterful blend of humor and realism; dialogue is lively and authentic, and the many characters are drawn with compassion. The author has once again demonstrated his keen sensitivity to the joys and frustrations of adolescence as well as his thorough knowledge of the New York City street scene." Horn Bk

Neufeld, John

Edgar Allan. Phillips 1968 95p $8.95 (5 and up) **Fic**

1 Adoption—Fiction 2 Race relations—Fiction 3 Family life—Fiction
ISBN 0-87599-149-1 LC 68-31175

Set in a southern California town and "narrated by Michael the twelve-year-old son in Rev. Fickett's family, this records the arrival and adoption of a tiny Negro boy [Edgar Allan] into the well-to-do white family. Mary Nell, the eldest, is . . . bitterly opposed to this manifestation of her parents' sense of righteousness. . . . Nevertheless, Edgar Allan becomes a happy alert child and member of the family until he is enrolled in nursery school. Anger and disapproval from schoolmates and church members, threatening phone calls and division of the once close family circle are the result. After much soul-searching by the members of the Fickett family, they realize that their community is not yet mature enough to accept this source of conflict in its midst." Best Sellers

"There is no melodrama [here], no stunning climax: people of good will have made a gesture and have not been strong enough to withstand pressure. The story is told with thoughtful simplicity, and the reactions and interactions of the family members are perceptive and convincingly drawn." Sat Rev

Neville, Emily Cheney

Berries Goodman. Harper 1965 178p lib. bdg. $9.89, pa $1.50 (5 and up) **Fic**

1 Jews and Gentiles—Fiction 2 Jews in the U.S. —Fiction
ISBN 0-06-024384-8; 0-06-440072-7 LC 65-14485

When his family moves from New York City to the suburbs, Berries Goodman feels uprooted and lonely—an outsider—until he meets another outsider in his class, Sidney Fine. Sidney is Jewish. The situation that develops after Sidney suffers a near-fatal accident forces Berries to recognize the power of prejudice. He does not understand the reason for it; all he understands is that he has lost his best friend

"The book is told in appropriate teen idiom by Berries six years later when he and Sidney find each other again. For more than a 'problem' story, this is a wonderful chunk of life with good family feeling, outstanding characters and rare understanding." Sch Library J

It's like this, Cat; pictures by Emil Weiss. Harper 1963 180p illus $7.95, lib. bdg. $7.89, pa $1.95 (5 and up) **Fic**

1 Cats—Fiction 2 New York (City)—Fiction
ISBN 0-06-024390-2; 0-06-024391-0; 0-06-440073-5
LC 62-21292

Awarded the Newbery Medal, 1964

"Written in the first person, present tense in a style . . . [that is] humorous and easy, this is an outstanding story of a fourteen-year-old growing up in the neighborhood of Gramercy Park in New York City. He tells of life in the city and his relationships with his parents, neighbors, and friends. It is his pet, a stray tom cat whom he adopts, that brings him two new friends, one a troubled boy and the other his first girl." Wis Library Bul

"A story told with a great amount of insight into human relationships and in words that easily match the current speech of the hero's contemporaries. . . . This all provides a wonderfully real picture of a city boy's outlets and of one likeable adolescent's inner feelings. An exceedingly fresh, honest, and well-rounded piece of writing." Horn Bk

Newfield, Marcia

A book for Jodan; illus. by Diane De Groat. Atheneum Pubs. 1975 unp illus lib. bdg. $8.95 (3-5) **Fic**

1 Divorce—Fiction
ISBN 0-689-50010-6 LC 74-18192

"A Margaret K. McElderry book"

"Jodan, a nine-year-old saddened by her parents' divorce, learns that she is still loved by her mother with whom she lives on the West Coast as well as her father who lives on the East Coast. The message is repeatedly stressed in this loosely constructed story which centers on Jodan's feelings of anger and loss." Sch Library J

"Jodan's story is warmly and sensitively told. The portrayal of her pain and self-doubts are clearly shown without being maudlin. Any child going through the same experience would identify with Jodan and maybe understand his or her own feelings better. The book would also be good for parents to see how divorce affects a child." Children's Bk Rev Serv

Newman, Robert

The case of the Baker Street Irregular; a Sherlock Holmes story. Atheneum Pubs. 1978 216p illus $8.95 (5 and up) **Fic**

1 London—Fiction 2 Mystery and detective stories
ISBN 0-689-30641-5 LC 77-15463

"London is a strange and terrifying city to young Andrew, who has just arrived from Cornwall with his tutor, Mr. Dennison. Matters are made worse when he witnesses Mr. Dennison's kidnapping and is himself pursued by the same cabbie. Sanctuary is provided by the Wigginses family, and it is through Sam that Andrew becomes a Baker Street Irregular (one of the street urchins who occasionally work for Sherlock Holmes). In the process of helping Mr. Holmes, Andrew learns the truth about his own origins." Children's Bk Rev Serv

"The author is as urbane and fluent as the legendary Mr. Holmes; he seems thoroughly comfortable with the characters, the atmosphere, and the turn-of-the-century London setting; and the story moves along with unflagging energy." Horn Bk

Night spell; illus. by Peter Burchard. Atheneum Pubs. 1977 189p illus $8.95 (5 and up) **Fic**

1 Orphans—Fiction 2 Supernatural—Fiction 3 New England—Fiction
ISBN 0-689-30559-1 LC 76-25207

Newman, Robert—*Continued*

"Tad is surprised to learn that Martin Gorham, a one-time friend of his grandfather, has been his benefactor since the death of his parents. But even more puzzling is why Mr. Gorham wants him to spend the summer in the isolated Victorian mansion where he lives with his two mute servants. Ignored and lonely, Tad gradually becomes friends with Karen, only to find himself drawn into a mystery concerning a missing painting, Mr. Gorham's lost daughter, and the accidental death of Karen's friend, Nonny. Tad learns that Nonny is communicating with Karen to complete an unfinished task, and his involvement deepens when strange dreams haunt his nights." Booklist

"What begins as a subdued suspense story acquires overtones of psychic phenomena and winds up dramatically with a hurricane and solutions for everyone's problems. . . . Terse dialogue, some sympathetic insights into loneliness and the need to belong, and good characterizations make this a satisfying story, but no thriller." Children's Bk Rev Serv

Nichols, Ruth

The marrow of the world; illus. by Trina Schart Hyman. Atheneum Pubs. 1972 168p illus lib. bdg. $6.95 (5 and up)   **Fic**

1 Fantastic fiction   2 Witches—Fiction
ISBN 0-689-30309-2   LC 76-190558

"A Margaret K. McElderry book"

"Philip and his cousin Linda, adopted as a foundling by Philip's aunt and uncle, are drawn by a powerful force into an alternate magical world in which lies the secret of Linda's true identity. They have been summoned by an evil witch to descend through the caverns of the dwarfs to buy a portion of the marrow of the world with which the witch can prolong her now fading life. Having little choice, the pair set out on their mission with Philip determined to save Linda who has two natures—witch and human—each struggling for dominance." Booklist

A walk out of the world; illus. by Trina Schart Hyman. Harcourt 1969 192p illus $6.95 (4-6)   **Fic**

1 Fantastic fiction
ISBN 0-15-294514-8   LC 68-13777

"A walk in a forest on an eerie day leads Judith and Tobit into another world, where they find that Judith . . . is the one who must right an ancient wrong. It's been 500 years since a usurper seized the throne in the White City and sent the queen and her family into exile; a restlessness in the earth hints the time is near for his comeuppance." Bk World

"The writing is disciplined and beautiful; the story exciting and triumphant; there is a youthfulness about it that gives it unusual quality. That the moving between the two worlds [fantasy and reality] is accomplished not with the ease of most fantasies but with deep sorrow seems to stem from the intuition of a young writer." Horn Bk

Nordstrom, Ursula

The secret language; pictures by Mary Chalmers. Harper 1960 167p illus lib. bdg. $7.89, pa $2.95 (3-5)   **Fic**

1 School stories
ISBN 0-06-024576-X; 0-06-440022-0   LC 60-7701

A "story about two eight-year-old girls at boarding school. None of the experiences that Vicky and Martha have are unusual; none dramatic; yet all of the details of their year make absorbing reading. Vicky is homesick and Martha is a rebel; as they adjust to each other and as they adapt themselves to the pattern of school life, both girls find satisfactions and both grow up a little. The writing style has a gentle humor, a warm understanding, and an easy narrative flow that seems effortless." Chicago. Children's Bk Center

Norton, Andre

Dragon magic; illus. by Robin Jacques. Crowell 1972 213p illus $8.95 (4 and up)   **Fic**

1 Fantastic fiction   2 Space and time—Fiction
3 Dragons—Fiction
ISBN 0-690-24489-1   LC 70-158697

"Four stories that are fanciful as episodes lived by each of four boys, the whole set within a realistic framework. In a dusty abandoned house Sig finds a box that has on its cover four dragons, each in a different color. One by one, he and the other three put together the pieces, each working separately and with a different color, and each boy slips back in time to an adventure: Sig, who is of German descent, lives an episode in ancient times and fights the dragon Fafnir, a black boy becomes a Nubian slave of princely blood in Babylon, a boy of Chinese descent goes back in time to China; Artie Jones becomes Artos Pendragon. When the four boys meet and talk about their experiences, they become friends." Chicago. Children's Bk Center

"Legend, fantasy, and historical and contemporary situations are interwoven in an absorbing story. Despite the wealth and range of dragon lore and legendry, the story has clarity and immediacy; and the values of courage, loyalty, and strength met in the past help each boy meet problems of the present." Horn Bk

Norton, Mary

Bed-knob and broomstick; illus. by Erik Blegvad. Harcourt 1957 189p illus $5.95, pa $1.65 (3-5)   **Fic**

1 Fantastic fiction   2 Witches—Fiction
ISBN 0-15-206228-9; 0-15-611500-X   LC 57-11341

A combined edition of: The magic bed-knob, first published 1943 by Putnam and Bonfires and broomsticks, first published 1947 in England

"In the first book, Carey, Charles, and Paul Wilson, visiting their aunt one summer, meet the very proper Miss Price, who is somewhat embarrassed when the children discover that she is studying to become a witch. Modest as she is about her prowess, Miss Price does succeed in giving to a bed-knob the power of transporting passengers. After some exciting adventures, the children return to London. Two years and one book later, they read an ad inserted by Miss Price for summer boarders. They convince Mrs. Wilson to send them to Miss Price and are dismayed to find that she has given up witchcraft. Urging one last ploy, they negotiate a trip to the past: from the 17th century they return with a necromancer who eventually takes Miss Price back to his own time as his wife. While there is one unpleasant note in text and illustration of Negroid cannibals, the story has the same quiet humor and calm acceptance of the fantastic as does 'The Borrowers' . . . [listed below]." Chicago. Children's Bk Center

The Borrowers; illus. by Beth and Joe Krush. Harcourt 1953 180p illus $5.50, pa $1.50 (3-6)   **Fic**

1 Fairy tales
ISBN 0-15-209987-5; 0-15-613600-7   LC 53-7870

First published 1952 in England

A "fascinating fantasy about a tiny family that lived beneath the kitchen floor of an old English country house and 'borrowed' from the larger human residents to fill their modest needs. Their sudden discovery by a small boy visitor almost proves to be their undoing. The imaginative details about the activities of the miniature people have tremendous appeal for children." Children's Bks Too Good to Miss

Some other books about the Borrowers are also available from Harcourt:

The Borrowers afield $6.95, pa $1.95 (ISBN 0-15-210166-7; 0-15-613601-5; LC 55-11011)
The Borrowers afloat $5.95, pa $1.95 (ISBN 0-15-210345-7; 0-15-613603-1; LC 59-5630)
The Borrowers aloft $5.50, pa $1.50 (ISBN 0-15-210524-7; 0-15-613604-X; LC 61-11751)
The complete adventures of the Borrowers. A combined edition of: The Borrowers; The Borrowers afield; The Borrowers afloat; The Borrowers aloft, pa $7.95 (ISBN 0-15-613605-8)
Poor Stainless $4.95 (ISBN 0-15-263221-2; LC 70-140781)

Nostlinger, Christine

Konrad; tr. by Anthea Bell; illus. by Carol Nicklaus. Watts, F. 1977 135p illus lib. bdg. $7.90 (4-6)   **Fic**

1 Parent and child—Fiction
ISBN 0-531-01341-3   LC 77-7489

Original German edition, 1975. This translation first published 1976 in England with title: Conrad

The author "tells the story of a factory-made child of seven who is delivered by mistake to a scatter-brained but delightful woman, Mrs. Bartolotti is a free-wheeling eccentric, and she becomes fond of Konrad, but she can't adjust to his perfection. Konrad is always truthful, helpful, polite, industrious, and sensible. He's been programmed that way. Konrad is not a success with

Nostlinger, Christine—*Continued*

his classmates, if the teacher asks who knows who broke the window, Konrad tells her, of course. He always tells the truth. . . . So—when the factory catches up with its error and comes to reclaim Konrad, the only way for Mrs B. to keep him is to reprogram him until he's such a scamp that the factory will reject him as not being their product." Chicago. Children's Bk Center

"The children in the story act more like kindergarteners than third graders, but the battle for Konrad against the forces of conformity represented by his original programmers is zany. Amusing on several levels, this will be most enjoyed by children for its slapstick portrayal of Konrad's behavior modification from goody-goody to regular kid." Sch Library J

O'Brien, Robert C.

Mrs Frisby and the rats of NIMH; illus. by Zena Bernstein. Atheneum Pubs. 1971 223p illus lib. bdg. $8.95, pa $1.95 (4 and up)
Fic

1 Mice—Fiction 2 Rats—Fiction
ISBN 0-689-20651-8; 0-689-70413-5   LC 74-134818

Awarded the Newbery Medal, 1972

"Mrs. Frisby, a widowed mouse, is directed by an owl to consult with the rats that live under the rosebush about her problem of moving her sick son from the family's endangered home. Upon entering the rats' quarters, Mrs. Frisby discovers to her astonishment that the rats are not ordinary rodents, but highly intelligent creatures that escaped from an NIMH laboratory after being taught to read. How the rats help Mrs. Frisby and she, in turn, helps them from being captured, is told in a thoroughly enjoyable animal fantasy." Booklist

"The story is fresh and ingenious, the style witty, and the plot both hilarious and convincing." Sat Rev

O'Connell, Jean S.

The dollhouse caper; with illus. by Erik Blegvad. Crowell [1976 c1975] 82p illus $6.95 (4-6)
Fic

1 Dolls—Fiction
ISBN 0-690-01024-7   LC 75-25501

"Dollhouses and their families really can come alive—but not all the time. In this story the dolls come to life at night, which is only fair, since 'The humans only come to life in the daytime.' Of course, even dollhouse families have their problems. . . . They are the only witnesses when a pair of burglars break into their owner's home one night. The dolls attempt to warn the household of the impending danger and finally foil the robbery themselves; they never again fear banishment to the attic." NY Times Bk Rev

"This book has it all: humor in dialogue, a convincing blend of realism and fantasy, good characterization, smooth writing style, a sturdy plot and satisfying ending, and the merest touch of sentiment. 'And' Blegvad's wonderfully detailed, brisk drawings." Chicago. Children's Bk Center

O'Connor, Jane

Yours till Niagara falls, Abby; illus. by Margot Apple. Hastings House 1979 128p illus lib. bdg. $7.95 (4-6)
Fic

1 Camps—Fiction 2 Friendship—Fiction
ISBN 0-8038-8601-2   LC 79-19782

"Abby's best friend, Merle, balks at going away to summer camp but decides it will be okay if Abby goes, too. Abby engineers parental approval (with some difficulty) and is set for a 'super fantabulous, perfectly perfect summer'—until Merle breaks her ankle in dance class. O'Connor builds the rest of her story out of Abby's reluctant solo venture into everyday camp experiences, which include coming to terms with some diverse cabin mates. . . . The story is nicely put together and has moments of genuine humor: it is light, satisfying fare for middle graders, especially the camp veterans among them." Booklist

O'Dell, Scott

The black pearl; illus. by Milton Johnson. Houghton 1967 140p illus $5.95 (6 and up)
Fic

1 Pearl fisheries—Fiction 2 Rays (Fishes)—Fiction 3 Baja California—Fiction
ISBN 0-395-06961-0   LC 67-23311

"The people of Baja California feared a demon creature, a giant ray—El Manta Diablo. He was believed to live in a cave at the end of a lagoon, and though a few Indians who 'had a pact with El Manta Diablo' dared to dive for pearls, no one had searched in the cave. A pearl taken from the Manta would bring only ill fortune. Yet Ramón Salazar, goaded by the taunts of the greatest pearl diver of his father's fleet, dared to enter the cave to dive for a pearl even more wonderful than the one El Sevillano had boasted of. And he found it—the Paragon of Pearls, the Pearl of Heaven. Then came the encounter with the Manta." Horn Bk

"The stark simplicity of the story and the deeper significance it holds in the triumph of good over evil add importance to the book, but even without that the book would be enjoyable as a rousing adventure tale with supernatural overtones and beautifully maintained tempo and suspense." Chicago. Children's Bk Center

The captive. Houghton 1979 210p $8.95 (6 and up)
Fic

1 Mayas—Fiction 2 Mexico—Fiction
ISBN 0-395-27811-2   LC 79-15809

This is the first volume of a projected series to be called: City of the seven serpents

This story set in the 16th century, "centers on the adventures of a young Jesuit seminarian who goes to the New World as part of a Spanish expedition. Full of Christian idealism, Julián Escobar believes his role is to convert the savages. Instead, he succumbs to the temptation to pose as the reincarnated Mayan deity [Kukulcán]." Children's Bk Rev Serv

"Characterizations are all finely drawn, and Julián's transformation from insecure, humane seminarian to pretend god is remarkable in its honest development." Sch Library J

Island of the Blue Dolphins. Houghton 1960 184p $6.95 (5 and up)
Fic

1 Wilderness survival—Fiction 2 San Nicolas Island, Calif.—Fiction 3 Indians of North America—Fiction
ISBN 0-395-06962-9   LC 60-5213

Awarded the Newbery Medal, 1961

"Because her brother had missed the ship that was taking their tribe to the mainland, Karana, a young Indian girl, remains with him. After her brother's death she lives alone for eighteen years on this wildly beautiful, treeless island off the coast of California. The struggle for survival is told in grim, realistic detail, alleviated by Karana's ability to find some comfort, beauty, and a measure of happiness in her solitary life. Based on the few facts known about an actual experience, the story is told with stark simplicity beautifully fitted to such a deeply moving experience." Children's Bks Too Good to Miss

"Years of research must have gone into this book to turn historical fact into so moving and lasting an experience." Horn Bk

Followed by: Zia. Houghton $7.95 (ISBN 0-395-24393-9; LC 75-44156)

The King's fifth; decorations and maps by Samuel Bryant. Houghton 1966 264p illus $5.95 (6 and up)
Fic

1 Estévan—Fiction 2 Mexico—History—Fiction
ISBN 0-395-06963-7   LC 66-7763

"Writing at night in his cell between sessions of his 20-day trial for withholding the King's Fifth or royal share of treasure, Estéban de Sandoval, young cartographer with Coronado, recalls all that happened on the hazardous, inglorious journey he made with Captain Mendoza and five others to the Seven Cities of Cibola to find gold. The low-keyed, powerful writing and the first-person narration, which skillfully interweaves Estéban's chronicle of the past with his report of the ongoing trial, give a strong sense of reality and immediacy to this compelling, deeply felt story of a boy who, almost too late, comes to realize the awful cost of the lust for gold in honor and human life." ALA Bks for Children, 1966-67

Sing down the moon. Houghton 1970 137p $7.95 (5 and up)
Fic

1 Navaho Indians—Fiction
ISBN 0-395-10919-1   LC 71-98513

A "story based on the white and Navajo conflict of the Civil War period. The United States Government, provoked by the raiding of some Navajos, appointed Kit Carson to drive them out of their traditional home place, the Canyon de

O'Dell, Scott—*Continued*

Chelly in Arizona. The story is told in the first person by a young Navajo girl who is kidnapped and enslaved by Spaniards, then rescued by her husband-to-be. She and her clan are forced out of the Canyon by white soldiers (who burned their peach trees, killed their sheep and destroyed their hogans) and are marched 400 miles, under tragic hardships, to Fort Sumner where they are to make a new life." Library J

"There is a poetic sonority of style, a sense of identification, and a note of indomitable courage and stoicism that is touching and impressive." Sat Rev

Oppenheim, Shulamith

The selchie's seed; illus. by Diane Goode. Bradbury Press 1975 82p illus $7.95 (4-6)   **Fic**

1 Shetland Islands—Fiction. 2 Seals (Animals)—Fiction 3 Mermaids—Fiction 4 Fantastic fiction
ISBN 0-87888-076-3   LC 74-22854

This "novel is based on the North Sea islanders' legend that seals (selchies) can shed their skin, and take on human form. . . . Marian Sinclare falls under the spell of an injured white whale which refuses to leave the voe near her home. Eventually, Marian is drawn back to the sea—one of her ancestors was a selchie who mated with a human—and is transformed into a full-fledged mermaid." Sch Library J

The author "has fashioned elements from the Scottish legend . . . into a vividly inscribed, bittersweet fantasy. The story's remote, wintry setting and strong-willed characters gain an appropriate moody romanticism in Goode's soft scenes of windswept sea cliffs and hearty figures in flowing garb." Booklist

Orgel, Doris

A certain magic. Dial Press 1976 176p $7.95 (5 and up)   **Fic**

ISBN 0-8037-5405-1   LC 75-9204

"Eleven-year-old Jenny accidentally finds her Aunt Trudi's diary 'copybook.' Jenny is so fascinated with it that when her family goes to England on vacation, Jenny finds the now grown-up children her aunt lived with. Jenny brings back her aunt's childhood doll with an emerald hidden inside. Naturally, Aunt Trudi gives Jenny her very own 'copybook.' Some mystery is involved in tracking down the emerald. Diary entries give clues and are the highlight of the book." Children's Bk Rev Serv

"The book keeps a nice pace as it moves from present to past in Trudi's diary, building suspense along the way. The characters—Jenny's artist mother and lawyer father; Trudi, a successful translator now in her 50's—are individual and believable. But most interesting are the themes of guilt and evil that motivate the story in terms that children can well understand." Sch Library J

The devil in Vienna. Dial Press 1978 246p $7.95 (6 and up)   **Fic**

1 Austria—Fiction   2 Jews in Austria—Fiction   3 Holocaust, Jewish (1939 - 1945) — Fiction   4 Friendship—Fiction
ISBN 0-8037-1920-5   LC 78-51319

"Although fictional, the events in this story about the Nazi occupation of Austria are based on the author's experiences as a child in Vienna. Inge is Jewish, her best friend Lieselotte is the daughter of a Nazi officer so devoted to Hitler that he had moved his family to Germany, returning only after the Anschluss. Although the girls have been forbidden to meet by both sets of parents, Inge knows her friend is loyal; when her parents are having difficulty in leaving the country, Inge turns to Lieselotte's uncle, a Catholic priest, for help. The story ends with the refugees' safe arrival in Yugoslavia." Chicago. Children's Bk Center

"The book arouses in its readers anguish, fury, admiration, scorn—it couldn't be a more effective story or a more powerful illustration of the reason 'never to forget.'" Pub W

The mulberry music; pictures by Dale Payson. Harper 1971 130p illus lib. bdg. $7.89, pa $1.95 (4 and up)   **Fic**

1 Death—Fiction 2 Grandmothers—Fiction
ISBN 0-06-024612-X; 0-06-440104-9   LC 70-159040

This is the story of eleven-year old Liza's gradual acceptance of her grandmother's illness and death

"An extremely perceptive novel that tells what happens to a sensitive child when her favorite person becomes seriously ill. . . . In a straight-forward manner [the author] deals with Libby's emotions, which range from anger to fear and panic." Adventuring with Bks. 2d edition

Ormondroyd, Edward

Time at the top; illus. by Peggie Bach. Parnassus Press 1963 176p illus $6.50 (5 and up)   **Fic**

1 Fantastic fiction
ISBN 0-87466-029-7   LC 63-10140

"The elevator in her apartment house traveled past the top floor one day, and carried Susan Shaw to a Victorian mansion that had stood on the same site in 1881. With Robert and Victoria Walker, Susan unearthed a buried hoard of gold and rescued Mrs. Walker from a fortune hunter. This appealing combination of mystery and fantasy contrasts noisy, hectic, twentieth century city life with quiet, leisurely country life in the same area a hundred years previously, and ends with an original surprise." Moorachian. What is a City?

"The plot is sturdy and well-paced, the writing style lively and easy; the conversation is especially good, with some of the adult characters being etched with mild acidity in some monologues." Chicago. Children's Bk Center

Followed by: All in good time. Parnassus Press $7.95 (ISBN 0-87466-072-6; LC 75-1688)

Otis, James

Toby Tyler; or, Ten weeks with a circus; illus. by George Wilson. Grosset 1967 183p illus $2.95 (4-6)   **Fic**

1 Circus—Fiction 2 Monkeys—Fiction
ISBN 0-448-05483-3   LC 67-24233

"Companion library"
First published 1880

"Little Toby ran away from home with the lemonade man to join the circus, and then worked very hard to run away from the circus and go home again. In the meantime he had made several good friends, including the Living Skeleton and Mr. Stubbs, the monkey." Bks for Boys & Girls

Ottley, Reginald

Boy alone; illus. by Clyde Pearson. Harcourt [1966 c1965] 191p illus $6.95 (5 and up)   **Fic**

1 Ranch life—Fiction 2 Dogs—Fiction 3 Australia—Fiction
ISBN 0-15-267700-3   LC 66-11204

First published 1965 in England with title: By the sandhills of Yamboorah

"On an isolated cattle ranch in Australia a nameless boy works as a 'wood and water joey.' His aloneness, his longing for a dog to call his own, and his relationships with other workers on the ranch are understandingly depicted." Hodges. Bks for Elem Sch Libraries

This book "conveys powerfully the feel of Australia and the feeling of adolescence." Times (London) Lit Sup

Followed by: The roan colt. Harcourt $5.50 (ISBN 0-15-267700-3; LC 67-348)

Pascal, Francine

Hangin' out with Cici. Viking 1977 152p $6.95 (5 and up)   **Fic**

1 Parent and child—Fiction 2 Space and time—Fiction
ISBN 0-670-36045-7   LC 76-57700

"Victoria, a 14-year-old with an unfortunate penchant for trouble, bumps her head while riding on a train and travels back in time to 1944, where she meets Cici. After several hilarious escapades, Victoria realizes that Cici is her own mother, and the discovery gives her a new perspective on her own problems." Sch Library J

"Here is a humorous and touching story that deals head on with a painful conflict between an adolescent girl and her mother. The author has contrived an ingenious plot, cleverly maneuvered with exquisite detail and realism." Children's Bk Rev Serv

Paterson, Katherine

Bridge to Terabithia; illus. by Donna Diamond. Crowell 1977 128p illus $7.95 (4-6) **Fic**

1 Friendship—Fiction 2 Death—Fiction
ISBN 0-690-01359-0   LC 77-2221

Awarded the Newbery Medal, 1978

"Ten-year-old Jess Aarons is a loner, far too talented and sensitive to fit easily into a traditional, isolated, rural Virginia lifestyle. The Burke family moves into the community to escape the rigors of city life, and Jess and Leslie become best friends. Leslie appreciates Jess's art and teaches him that imagination and caring, and love for learning are nothing to be ashamed of. They create Terabithia, a private secret kingdom in the woods where their imaginations rule them and set their limits. The joy turns to tragedy as Leslie is killed in an accident on her way through the woods. Jess's subsequent dealing with her death is [developed]." Children's Bk Rev Serv

"Jess and his family are magnificently characterized; the book abounds in descriptive vignettes, humorous sidelights on the clash of cultures, and realistic depictions of rural school life. The symbolism of falling and of building bridges forms a theme throughout the story, which is one of remarkable richness and depth, beautifully written." Horn Bk

The great Gilly Hopkins. Crowell 1978 148p $7.95, lib. bdg. $7.89 (5 and up) **Fic**

1 Foster home care—Fiction
ISBN 0-690-03837-2; 0-690-03838-0   LC 77-27075

"Cool, scheming, and deliberately obstreperous, 11-year-old Gilly is ready to be her usual obnoxious self when she arrives at her new foster home. Dreaming of the day her own beautiful mother will arrive to take her away, Gilly plots to use William Ernest, paranoid seven-year-old; the blind, poetry loving black man who lives next door; and sniffling, friend-starved Agnes Stokes, a sixth-grade classmate. But Gilly's old tricks don't work against the all-encompassing love of the huge, half-illiterate Mrs. Trotter, and subsequently she finds herself unwillingly pulled into all their lives. Determined not to care, she writes a letter full of wild exaggerations to her real mother that brings, in return, a surprising visit from an unknown grandmother. What she also discovers is the necessity for being responsible for one's actions and a sense of what love really is." Booklist

The master puppeteer; illus. by Haru Wells. Crowell [1976 c1975] 179p illus $8.95 (6 and up) **Fic**

1 Japan—Fiction 2 Puppets and puppet plays—Fiction
ISBN 0-690-00913-5   LC 75-8614

"In 18th-Century Osaka, Japan, Jiro, son of a starving puppetmaker, runs away from home to apprentice himself to Yoshida, the ill-tempered master of the Hanaza puppet theater. As Jiro works to learn the art of the puppeteer and travels among the savage, hunger-crazed bands of night rovers in search of his parents, he becomes aware of a mysterious connection between Saboro, a Robin Hood-like figure, and the Hanaza theater itself." Sch Library J

"The make-believe world of the Japanese puppet theatre merges excitingly with the hungry, desperate realities of 18th century Osaka in this better-than-average junior novel. Although the ending is abrupt and the character motivation sometimes vague, the work maintains a successful degree of suspense as apprentice puppeteer Jiro seeks to uncover the true identity of a mysterious Robin Hood figure. Paterson's details of the unrest of the poor and the arrogance of the wealthy merchants in feudal Japan ring true. Special treats are the black and white illustrations and the author's descriptions of the exacting art of the Bunraku theatre." Children's Bk Rev Serv

Of nightingales that weep; illus. by Haru Wells. Crowell 1974 170p illus $8.95 (6 and up) **Fic**

1 Japan—Fiction
ISBN 0-690-00485-0   LC 74-8294

"Takiko, daughter of a famous samurai killed in the wars, is taken into the court of the boy emperor Antoku as a musician and personal servant. Takiko's conflicting loyalties to the Heike-supported court, a dashing Genji warrior, and her physically grotesque but goodhearted peasant stepfather form the impetus for her internal development while the war rages around her." Booklist

"The period in Japanese history (1180-85) is recreated well; however, Takiko's reformation (apparently due to disfigurement and rejection) is unbelievable." Sch Library J

Pearce, Philippa

The battle of Bubble and Squeak; illus. by Alan Baker. Deutsch [1979 c1978] 88p illus $5.95 (3-6) **Fic**

1 Gerbils—Fiction 2 Family life—Fiction
ISBN 0-233-96986-1   LC 78-74460

First published 1978 in England

"When two gerbils—Bubble and Squeak—come to live at the Parkers, the reaction is mixed. Sid's mum hates them 'like rats!'; Sid's stepfather is understanding of Mum but remembers the white mice he had as a boy; Sid's small sisters adore them; and Sid himself, well, the gerbils are the most special thing that's ever happened to him." Sch Library J

The "question of whether the gerbils are kept or not is—while appealing in itself—not the core of the story. The core is really in the delicate balance of the parent-child relationship, and the facets here are explored with sympathy and percipience, especially in the characterization of the children's stepfather, who valiantly supports the children and sees their need for pets yet doesn't want to antagonize his wife and make it even harder for the children." Chicago. Children's Bk Center

Tom's midnight garden; illus. by Susan Einzig. Lippincott 1959 [c1958] 229p illus $7.95 (4 and up) **Fic**

1 Fantastic fiction 2 Space and time—Fiction
ISBN 0-397-30475-7

First published 1958 in England, where it was awarded the Carnegie Medal as the outstanding English children's book of that year

"Tom would rather have stayed home at the risk of catching measles from his brother than spend the holidays with his unimaginative uncle and aunt in their pokey flat with its chilling and unwelcome atmosphere. But one night, when the old grandfather clock struck thirteen, and Tom crept downstairs to investigate, he discovered a wonderful garden with well laid out flower beds and, best of all, very climbable trees. In daylight the garden vanished and only in his nocturnal visits did he find it waiting for him. Here he met Hatty, a little girl of the late Victorian era. The secret of his garden and his passage back into time continued to puzzle Tom, until he and Hatty found a clue in the grandfather clock. In the end Tom was able to provide his own theory of Time." Ontario

"The author claims as her readers those of '9 up': rightly so, for this brilliant fantasy on the theme of time has a quality capable of capturing all ages. . . . A work of the greatest distinction." New Statesman

Peck, Richard

The ghost belonged to me; a novel. Viking 1975 $7.95 (5 and up) **Fic**

1 Ghosts—Fiction
ISBN 0-670-33767-6   LC 74-34218

"Apprised of his ability to see 'the Unseen,' 13-year-old Alexander Armsworth is at first skeptical. But when he encounters the ghost of a young Creole by the name of Inez Dumaine in his barnloft, Alexander is impelled by her warning to stop a trolley before it plunges its occupants to a watery death. Discovering that Inez has been the victim of a similar tragedy, Alexander, with the help of his friend/enemy, Blossom Culp, and his 85-year-old great-uncle, finally brings peace to Inez' unquiet spirit." Sch Library J

"This tale is truly humorous, even witty at times. The story holds together with no lapses into contrivance. Set in 1900 in the area from the upper Mississippi Valley to New Orleans, it satisfies requests for mystery and adventure." Rdng Teacher

Followed by: Ghosts I have been. Viking $7.95 (ISBN 0-670-33813-3; LC 77-9469)

Peck, Robert Newton

A day no pigs would die. Knopf [1973 c1972] 150p $7.95 (6 and up) **Fic**

1 Shakers—Fiction 2 Farm life—Fiction 3 Vermont—Fiction
ISBN 0-394-48235-2   LC 72-259

Peck, Robert N.—*Continued*

This story deals with "coming of age on a Shaker farm in Vermont in the 1920s. . . . [It] concerns young Rob's pig—his growth, his Rutland Fair blue ribbon, and his inevitable slaughter. Surrounding this are details of farm life." Sat Rev Educ

This "book gives a vivid picture of the simplicity and goodness of the Shaker Way, but its real strength is in the depth of family love." Chicago. Children's Bk Center

Mr Little; illus. by Ben Stahl. Doubleday 1979 87p illus $6.95, lib. bdg. $7.90 (3-5)   **Fic**

1 Teachers—Fiction
ISBN 0-385-13657-9; 0-385-13658-7   LC 78-22347

"Drag and Finley are disappointed when their new teacher is not the pretty Miss Kellogg but a rather stuffy young man named Mr. Little. The name seems to fit him, but Mr. Little turns out to be 'bigger' than the two tricksters believed." Children's Bk Rev Serv

"The slight story is well paced and told almost entirely through dialogue and short sentences, which makes this accessible to reluctant and slow readers." Booklist

Soup; illus. by Charles C. Gehm. Knopf 1974 96p illus $4.95, lib. bdg. $5.99 (5 and up)   **Fic**

1 Friendship—Fiction 2 Vermont—Fiction
ISBN 0-394-82700-7; 0-394-92700-1   LC 73-15117

"Peck strings together a series of . . . autobiographical recollections centered around boyhood good times with his friend Soup. . . . Peck tells of their throwing apples from sticks and inevitably breaking a window, rolling down a hill inside a barrel, or sneaking a smoke from cornsilk 'tobacco' in an acorn pipe. Neighborhood characters add color to the tellings. Janice Riker, the only person Soup is afraid of, is expert at captive and torture games; Aunt Carrie constantly wishes thrashings on Peck, but we are treated to her comic downfall as a trussed-up captive in a downpour." Booklist

"Rural Vermont during the 1920's is the setting for this nostalgic account. . . . In a laconic and wryly humorous style, the author relates the activities of the mischievous twosome. . . . The black-and-white pencil drawings, artistically executed in the manner of Norman Rockwell, reflect the understated story." Library J

Followed by these books, also available from Knopf:
Soup & me $4.95, lib. bdg. $5.99 (ISBN 0-394-83157-8; 0-394-93157-2; LC 75-9514)
Soup for president $5.95, lib. bdg. $5.99 (ISBN 0-394-83675-8; 0-394-936752-2; LC 77-13522)
Soup's drum $6.95, lib. bdg. $6.99 (ISBN 0-394-84251-1; 0-394-94251-5; LC 79-17982)

Perl, Lila

Dumb like me, Olivia Potts. Seabury [distributed by Houghton] 1976 181p illus $7.95 (4-6)   **Fic**

1 Brothers and sisters—Fiction 2 Mystery and detective stories
ISBN 0-395-28870-3   LC 76-7986

"A Clarion book"
The heroine of this novel "dislikes school and hates her old-maid teacher who expects her to be as smart as her siblings. Olivia proves that she is not so dumb when she solves a neighborhood mystery by seeing the connection between one neighbor's stolen license plates, another's stolen TV set, and the strange goings-on in the backyard next door. In the end Olivia gets transferred to a homeroom with a more understanding teacher." Sch Library J

"Olivia and [her friend] Anita are likeable youngsters whose adventures make a suspenseful story the younger set is sure to enjoy." Adventuring with Bks

That crazy April. Seabury [distributed by Houghton] 1974 188p front $6.95 (5 and up)   **Fic**

1 Family life—Fiction 2 Women's liberation movement—Fiction
ISBN 0-395-28869-X   LC 73-14812

"A Clarion book"
"Eleven-year-old Cress Richardson is caught in an identity crisis between her ardent 'women's rights' mother and her 'male chauvinistic' teacher and friends. . . . While she is working it out, her beautiful model friend, Monique, gets Cress a job in a department store bridal show as a 'boy' page. Further complications in Cress' dilemma arise when her brilliant and beloved cousin, Xandra, decides to quit college to get married, much to Cress' mother's disapproval." Babbling Bookworm

"One of the best feminist stories to appear so far. . . . Although her mother wants to make a crusading issue out of Cress's exclusion from metal-working club, Cress is adamantly non-crusading. The gamut of feminist issues is dealt with, often humorously, but with clarity and suspense. Not at all didactic, the story has humor, tension, sound character development, and a loving but liberated family." Children's Bk Rev Serv

Petry, Ann

Tituba of Salem Village. Crowell 1964 254p $8.95 (6 and up)   **Fic**

1 Tituba—Fiction 2 Salem, Mass.—Fiction 3 Witchcraft—Fiction 4 Blacks—Fiction
ISBN 0-690-82677-X   LC 64-20691

This is the "story of Tituba, one of the trio of women convicted at the beginning of the Salem witch trials. Sold in Barbados to a preacher bound for Boston, this capable slave-woman left the warmth of the islands for the cold of New England, and an easy-going community for one threaded with meanness, suspicion and fear. . . . Miss Petry's controlled style heightens the suspense as the reader watches Tituba step by step become caught in the events that precipitated the nightmarish trials." Pub W

"The restrained but dramatic narrative recreates with telling effect the climate of superstition and intolerance which prevailed in seventeenth-century Salem, [and] brings to life not only Tituba but also the people around her." Booklist

Pevsner, Stella

And you give me a pain, Elaine. Seabury [distributed by Houghton] 1978 182p $7.50 (5 and up)   **Fic**

1 Brothers and sisters—Fiction 2 Family life—Fiction
ISBN 0-395-28877-0   LC 78-5857

"A Clarion book"
"Thirteen-year-old Andrea, who tells the story, is the youngest of three; her adored brother Joe is away at college and her sister Elaine, sixteen, is the bane of Andrea's life, a sulky and rebellious adolescent who can't get along with Andrea or with their parents. Depressed by her own plodding personality and resentful of the attention Elaine gets when she defies her parents, Andrea is jolted into despair when Joe is killed in a motorcycle accident. This isn't a book with a strong story line, but it is strong in every other way: it is convincing as a first-person record, it is perceptive in establishing the fluctuations in personal relationships, it has excellent dialogue, and it balances nicely the several aspects of Andrea's life." Chicago. Children's Bk Center

Keep stompin' till the music stops. Seabury [distributed by Houghton] 1977 136p front $6.95 (3-6)   **Fic**

1 Learning disabilities—Fiction 2 Family life—Fiction
ISBN 0-395-28875-4   LC 76-27845

"A Clarion book"
"Richard is 12 and painfully coming to grips with his dyslexia. His great-grandfather—a sympathetic character—is about to be shipped off to a retirement trailer-village in Florida. Four generations gather for several days in his Galena, Illinois home where bossy Aunt Violet will break the news to the old man. But Grandpa rebels and solves the problem by making arrangements of his own to preserve his home and his independence. Richard also seems to accept his learning disability and gain some confidence." Sch Library J

The author "peppers her perceptive story with witty dialogue as she successfully reaches into the head of a young boy grappling with a problem." Booklist

Pevsner, Stella—*Continued*

A smart kid like you. Seabury [distributed by Houghton] 1975 216p front $7.50 (4 and up) **Fic**

1 Divorce—Fiction
ISBN 0-395-28876-2   LC 74-19320

"A Clarion book"

"After her parents' divorce Nina finds herself in conflict with her mother, who tries to 'baby' her. When she discovers her seventh grade math teacher is her father's new wife, life becomes even more complicated. The adjustments Nina makes and the new understanding she reaches about herself and her parents make this a warm and sensitive novel. [The author] handles Nina's 'growing pains' with humor and compassion." Adventuring with Bks

Phipson, Joan

The cats. Atheneum Pubs. 1976 168p $6.95 (6 and up) **Fic**

1 Kidnapping—Fiction   2 Australia—Fiction
ISBN 0-689-50061-0   LC 75-43608

"A Margaret K. McElderry book"

"Two brothers are kidnapped for ransom and held in the inaccessible wilds of the Australian bush. As things begin to go wrong for the kidnappers, with their plans deteriorating and with the experience of being attacked by a band of huge wild cats, the roles of the kidnappers and their victims are curiously reversed. The brothers must take charge and rescue the group." Children's Bk Rev Serv

"The story is told chiefly from the point of view of straightforward, extroverted Jim, who is a foil for his brother, while Willy, an animal lover, enjoys an almost mystical feeling for the solitude of the wilderness. Brash Socker and pusillanimous Kevin are well-contrasted, too; and the narrative about the quartet of four skillfully individualized youths is effective for its combination of character portrayal, suspense, and irony." Horn Bk

The family conspiracy; illus. by Margaret Horder. Harcourt [1964 c1962] 224p illus $5.95 (5 and up) **Fic**

1 Australia—Fiction   2 Family life—Fiction
ISBN 0-15-227110-4   LC 64-11494

First published 1962 in England

"The resourceful children in this Australian family conspire to earn money themselves when they believe there are no family funds to pay for their mother's necessary operation. Mrs Barker is a believable character who demonstrates the firm and selfless nature of many a mother." Cincinnati

Followed by: Threat to the Barkers. Harcourt $4.95 (ISBN 0-15-286310-9; LC 63-59169)

When the city stopped. Atheneum Pubs. 1978 181p $8.95 (5 and up) **Fic**

1 Strikes and lockouts—Fiction   2 Australia—Fiction
ISBN 0-689-50121-8   LC 78-6930

"A Margaret K. McElderry book"

"Nick Lorimer, 13, and his 11-year-old sister Binkie are alone in their Sydney apartment when a nationwide strike shuts down all services. The children don't know their mother is unconscious, after an auto accident, in a hospital. Their father is away, also, unable to get home. With other refugees, Nick and Binkie trudge out of the dead city. The little group includes Mrs. Piggott, their maid, and her crippled husband Jo, as well as an abandoned boy and girl. They encounter kindness from some, but danger from looters and other thugs who are liberated when all the rules are broken." Pub W

"Phipson has captured the tension and fear of Nick and his sister Binkie most vividly. . . . The book shows in credible fashion how such a situation brings out the best in some people, the worst in others, and it's a cracking good read." Chicago. Children's Bk Center

Pinkwater, Daniel Manus

Alan Mendelsohn, the boy from Mars. Dutton 1979 248p $8.95 (5 and up) **Fic**

1 Science fiction
ISBN 0-525-25360-2   LC 78-12052

"The author introduces Leonard Neeble and Alan Mendelsohn, both new to Bat Masterson Junior High School. The boys, looking for additions to Alan's massive collection of comic books,

discover a shop which deals in occult materials. Pooling their resources, they purchase a portable Omega Meter and the first volume of the Klugarsh Mind Control Course. . . . Using the incredible new power they gain, they succeed in achieving an adventure on the lost continent of Waka-Waka." Horn Bk

"In this exaggerated, tongue-in-cheek story of time-slips and thought control, Pinkwater lampoons con men and dupes, psychic powers, quack medicos, natural food faddists and assorted weird characters with great humor if, occasionally, at great length. Leonard and Alan repeatedly fall for confidence tricks and repeatedly profit from them, as when they buy a Mind Control Omega Meter and find that, for them, it works. If nothing succeeds like excess, the author has achieved a triumph of improbable folderol." Chicago. Children's Bk Center

Blue moose; written and illus. by Manus Pinkwater. Dodd 1975 47p illus lib. bdg. $5.25 (1-3) **Fic**

1 Moose—Fiction   2 Restaurants, bars, etc.—Fiction
ISBN 0-396-07151-1   LC 75-12575

"Mr. Breton owns a restaurant and is a very good cook who feels he's not appreciated by his customers. He hates the cold, snowy winters—until the day he meets a talking blue moose who comes in to warm himself, tries the clam chowder, and finds it so delectable that he stays on as headwaiter (and star attraction) at the restaurant." Adventuring with Bks

"Serio-comic narration is perfectly complemented by black-and-white line drawings of a very professional moose—mittens drying on his antlers, serving bowls line up properly between the antler tips, etc. A quietly pleasing and most rewarding book." Sch Library J

Fat men from space; written and illus. by Daniel Manus Pinkwater. Dodd 1977 57p illus lib. bdg. $5.50 (3-5) **Fic**

1 Food—Fiction   2 Science fiction
ISBN 0-396-07461-8   LC 77-6091

"Young William goes to the dentist and comes out with a filling that receives radio programs. Exploring the infinite possibilities of a tooth radio, he attaches a wire to a chainlink fence, touches it to his molar, and tunes in on an invading 'spaceburger' from the planet Spiegel. Before he can warn anyone of earth's peril, he is captured and 'floated' up to the spaceburger where he meets the invaders—fat men with glasses, wearing plaid sport jackets. Their raid is successful—Earth is stripped of all its junk food. The fat men leave to pursue a giant potato pancake in another galaxy and release William who floats back down to find everyone at home going on an enforced health diet." Sch Library J

"Message books aren't usually this much fun, but Pinkwater makes his a polished romp." Chicago. Children's Bk Center

The Hoboken chicken emergency. Prentice-Hall 1977 83p illus $7.95 (3-6) **Fic**

1 Chickens—Fiction
ISBN 0-13-392514-5   LC 76-41910

"Young Arthur Bobowicz happens to acquire Henrietta [a 266-pound chicken] by a strange twist of fate during his fruitless search for a turkey Thanksgiving morning. Boy and giant chicken become attached, father rejects giant chicken as unrealistic family pet, giant chicken runs wild and turns mean, town panics, boy grieves. Finally, after wasting $60,000 and a new semi-official limousine on a fake chicken hunter, the mayor is persuaded to reverse his own and the town's attitude to one of loving acceptance, offered in the form of Henrietta's favorite food, potatoes. Boy and giant chicken are reunited. A contemporary tall tale that will stretch middle graders' imagination, sense of humor, and enthusiasm for reading. For absurdity with perfect timing, not many can match the author." Booklist

Lizard music; written and illus. by D. Manus Pinkwater. Dodd 1976 157p illus $5.95 (4 and up) **Fic**

1 Science fiction
ISBN 0-396-07357-3   LC 76-12508

"The story tells of a boy named Victor, left in the care of his teenage sister, Leslie, while his parents are on vacation. No sooner do they leave than Leslie defects; she's off on a trip with friends,

Pinkwater, Daniel M.—*Continued*

a situation which Victor doesn't mind at all. Pleased at being his own boss, he eats what he likes and stays up to watch TV at all hours. Victor is bemused by a program of music presented by a group of lizards, all talented and apparently highly intelligent. The next day, he meets a strange, enigmatic fellow, Chicken Man, who leads the boy into fabulous adventures, culminating on the island inhabited by the civilized lizards." Pub W

"A marvelous sense of humor and a strong feeling of morality pervade this intriguing science fiction story. Some of the dialogue, in its attempt to be mysterious, becomes a bit difficult to follow at times, but all the loose ends and subplots reach a satisfying conclusion." Children's Bk Rev Serv

[Politzer, Anie]

My journals and sketchbooks [by] Robinson Crusoe. Harcourt 1974 78p illus $6.95 (4 and up)   Fic

1 Survival (after airplane accidents, shipwrecks, etc.)—Fiction
ISBN 0-15-267836-0   LC 74-2240

Text by Anie Politzer. Drawings by Michel Politzer

Original French edition published 1972

Based on Daniel Defoe's novel Robinson Crusoe, this work is presented as a newly-discovered journal and sketchbook in which the "real" Robinson Crusoe describes his experiences after being shipwrecked and the items he constructed in order to survive

"The drawings are handsome, meticulously detailed and spirited; we feel the artist, Michel Politzer, deserves special credit. The reader is given graphic examples of the animal and plant life of Crusoe's island, of how he learned to make baskets and tools, of his home and ingenious ways of coping with his lonely, exiled years." Pub W

Poole, Josephine

Catch as catch can; a story of suspense; illus. by Kiyo Komoda. Harper 1970 163p illus pa $2.95 (5 and up)   Fic

1 Mystery and detective stories   2 Great Britain —Fiction
ISBN 0-06-440014-X   LC 78-105461

"Traveling from London to the country, fourteen-year-old Piers and his cousin Virginia witness a man's fatal leap from their moving train. The cousins are questioned sharply by a strangely inquisitive woman passenger, but it is not until Piers discovers a paper with a cryptic message in his pocket that their curiosity is aroused. Their attempts to decipher the message become increasingly dangerous as they are pursued by a gang of smugglers who finally kidnap Piers to get the information they need. An above-average mystery with well-sustained suspense." Booklist

Pope, Elizabeth Marie

The Perilous Gard; illus. by Richard Cuffari. Houghton 1974 280p illus $5.95 (6 and up)   Fic

1 Great Britain—Fiction   2 Druids and Druidism —Fiction
ISBN 0-395-18512-2   LC 73-21648

"Kate Sutton, lady-in-waiting to Princess Elizabeth, is exiled because her . . . sister, Alicia, has dispatched a critical letter to Queen Mary Tudor. Sent to Perilous Gard, an old castle in Derbyshire surrounded by many odd legends, Kate meets Randal, an old half-witted minstrel; Sir Geoffrey Heron, master of the castle; and Sir Geoffrey's younger brother Christopher. Through clues in Randal's songs, Kate stumbles on the secret of the castle: it is the last stronghold of the Fairy Folk (or People of the Hill). Discovering his long-believed dead niece is held by the Fairies as their next sacrifice, Christopher exchanges himself for the child and Kate, witnessing the agreement, is also taken captive." Sch Library J

"Pope blends a scholar's knowledge of Tudor England with a liberating dash of fantasy. [Her story] borders on the ridiculous, but [she] has crafted all these complicated ingredients into an exciting adventure. Never suggesting that her Fairy Folk are anything more than human, she makes the fanatic [Druid] priestesses completely credible. And Kate—brave, down to earth, self-effacing—is a noble foil to the fantastic doings above and below ground. But best of all is the author's use of old English ballads and riddle songs as keys that unlock the mystery of the Gard." Christian Sci Monitor

The Sherwood ring; illus. by Evaline Ness. Houghton 1958 266p illus $7.95 (6 and up)   Fic

1 Ghosts—Fiction   2 U.S.—History—Revolution, 1775-1783—Fiction   3 New York (State)—Fiction
ISBN 0-395-07033-3   LC 57-12085

"Peggy Grahame, newcomer to her American family estate near the Hudson, becomes attached to a young British scholar who arrives to study its history [and the part one of his ancestors played in the Revolutionary War]. In backward-in-time episodes . . . Peggy meets ghosts from the past and sees her ancestor Barbara Grahame falling in love with a clever British officer." Horn Bk

"The transitions from modern life to the thrilling happenings of the eighteenth century are simply and deftly handled, and the events of Revolutionary days have a quiet accuracy of detail, suggesting far more than is said. . . . This has the excellence and naturalness of fine English historical stories." NY Her Trib Bks

Preussler, Otfried

The Satanic mill; tr. by Anthea Bell. Macmillan Pub. Co. 1973 250p lib. bdg. $5.95, pa $1.95 (6 and up)   Fic

1 Witchcraft—Fiction   2 Germany—Fiction
ISBN 0-02-775170-8; 0-02-044770-1   LC 72-90992

Original German edition 1971. This translation first published 1972 in England

A 14-year-old beggar boy becomes a virtual prisoner in a mill in Germany which is actually a school for black magic. He becomes his master's star pupil, but the more he learns of the mill's dark secrets, the more determined he becomes to escape from the master's bondage

"Although the book fails symbolically to indicate anything more than a romantic cliché about the world, in sheer storytelling it succeeds remarkably well in its evocation of the seventeenth-century atmosphere, in its development of characters, and in its building of tension and drama." Horn Bk

Pyle, Howard

Men of iron. Harper 1891 328p illus lib. bdg. $9.89 (5 and up)   Fic

1 Knights and knighthood—Fiction   2 Great Britain—History—Lancaster and York, 1399-1485 —Fiction   3 Henry IV, King of England—Fiction
ISBN 0-06-024801-7   LC 4-35677

In this novel a young nobleman receives his spurs, is knighted, "and vanquishes his own and his father's enemies in the days of Henry IV when chivalry was in full flower." Cincinnati

A "portrayal of life in the great castles and of the training of young nobles for knighthood." Toronto

Rabe, Berniece

The girl who had no name. Dutton 1977 149p lib. bdg. $7.95 (5 and up)   Fic

1 Family life—Fiction   2 Missouri—Fiction
ISBN 0-525-30660-9   LC 76-56768

"The scene is the mid-1930's in Missouri. The only identity Girlie has the 'Baby Girl Webster' on her birth certificate. One of 10 girls, the 12-year-old, is motherless and sent to live with her poorest married sister, Lil, by her father. By eavesdropping, Girlie has learned that her father had convinced himself that she was the child of another man. He couldn't bear the guilt of acknowledging that having too many children had killed his wife. In her new, temporary home Girlie and her cat (Clark Gable) survive as she gets to know gentle Lil and works out her destiny." Pub W

"Abundant details of domestic economy of the depression period—involving babies, husbands, food, and other daily problems—are discussed naturally as are biological questions related to Girlie's parentage. . . . What might seem depressing is relieved by Girlie's lively spunkiness, honesty, and courage along with her understandable tearfulness in facing the almost endless changes in her life. The many adult characters as well as Girlie herself are well rounded." Horn Bk

Naomi. Elsevier/Norton Bks. 1979 192p $7.95 (6 and up)   Fic

1 Farm life — Fiction   2 Missouri — Fiction 3 Family life—Fiction
ISBN 0-525-66444-0   LC 75-4599

Rabe, Berniece—*Continued*
First published by Thomas Nelson
"Naomi is 10 at the outset of the story; by the conclusion she is 14 and has come to a hard-won understanding of herself, as well as taken the first step toward her goal of becoming a nurse —or better yet—a doctor. These years show Naomi struggling to maintain her identity in a large farm family of southeastern Missouri." Booklist
"This is a discerning portrait of a young adolescent who is beginning to come to terms with her individuality and to gain perspective about her family; it's also a vivid portrait of a place and a time and a way of life." Chicago. Children's Bk Center

The orphans. Dutton 1978 184p $7.95 (5 and up)   Fic
1 Orphans—Fiction 2 Twins—Fiction 3 Missouri—Fiction
ISBN 0-525-36450-1   LC 78-9418
"Ten-year-old twins Little Adam and Eva, are left homeless for a second time when their uncles try to race a train in their Ford pick-up—and lose. . . . After a stint in a St. Louis orphanage [they] wind up in backwoods Missouri with G-Mama, their earthy 75-year-old step-grand-mother. Adam, who takes it upon himself to find a secure home for his fearful, mistreated sister, has his work cut out for him when the pair find G-Mama with a broken hip and the town's female sheriff, 'Ericky' Wheeler, on their case. G-Mama's deteriorating condition can't be hidden and, over the old lady's protests, Erica takes all three into custody (her own)." Sch Library J
"Rabe's strong female duo plays a telling counterpoint to Little Adam's private notions of being a man to his family. It's good, too, to see little Eva, though worried over spiders and seemingly the weaker twin, show hearty spunk where it counts. . . . Characters stay well in mind, as does the Depression-wracked Missouri country setting." Booklist

Raskin, Ellen
Figgs & phantoms. Dutton 1974 152p illus lib. bdg. $9.95, pa $1.95 (5 and up)   Fic
1 Family life—Fiction
ISBN 0-525-29680-8; 0-525-45035-1   LC 73-17309
Illustrated by the author
"This concerns Mona Lisa Newton, fat and frustrated member of the Figg Newton family in the town of Pineapple. Of the Figg Newton family, which includes ex-variety show stars Truman the Human Pretzel and uncles Romulus and Remus, Mona loves only Uncle Florence Italy Figg—a book dealer who dreams of dying and going to Capri, the Figg fantasy heaven. When Florence dies, Mona embarks on a clue-solving search for Capri, takes a wild mind trip, and returns a wiser and happier person." Booklist
"It's a mad, mad, mad, mad book. . . . Yeasty style and high humor should appeal to all readers except those who like their fiction served up with sobriety." Chicago. Children's Bk Center

The mysterious disappearance of Leon (I mean Noel). Dutton 1971 149p illus lib. bdg. $8.95, pa $1.95 (4 and up)   Fic
1 New York (City)—Fiction 2 Mystery and detective stories
ISBN 0-525-35540-5; 0-525-45010-6   LC 70-157953
"Wed at the age of five to a seven-year-old husband (it solved a business difficulty for their two families), the very young Mrs. Leon Carillon immediately loses her spouse, who is sent off to boarding school. This is the hilarious account of her search for Leon, aided by adopted twins, when she is older. With clever clues to stimulate the reader's participation, the story is a bouquet of wordplay garnished with jokes, sly pokes at our society, daft characters, and soupçon of slapstick. Fresh and funny, it's the kind of book that passes from child to child." Sat Rev
The author "has ingeniously incorporated a word puzzle, a game about names and turns of mind and phrase in her first full-length novel (a mystery). The result is a highly original romp into comedy and absurdity in both text and illustrations." Pub W

The tattooed potato and other clues. Dutton 1975 170p $8.95 (5 and up)   Fic
1 Mystery and detective stories
ISBN 0-525-40805-3   LC 74-23764

"A baffled Chief of Detectives in New York City turns repeatedly to the painter Garson, who uses brilliant deductive powers to solve a series of crimes (all ridiculous) while apparently oblivious to the menacing tenants who frighten his assistant, Dickery Dock (she's seventeen and the protagonist) and who bear such names as Shrimps Marinara and Manny Mallomar. And there's a mystery about Garson himself." Chicago. Children's Bk Center
"Raskin has come up with another intricate, one-of-a-kind comedy. . . . At her zany best [the author] consciously copies Marx Brother routines . . . but the preposterous plot, mad-cap characters, and comic shticks never conceal the home truths about dreams and disguises, artists and con artists." Sch Library J

The Westing game. Dutton 1978 185p lib. bdg. $9.95 (5 and up)   Fic
1 Mystery and detective stories
ISBN 0-525-42320-6   LC 77-18866
Awarded the Newbery Medal, 1979
"Another mystery puzzle for fans of Raskin's earlier novels. This one centers on the challenge set forth in the will of eccentric multimillionaire Samuel Westing. Sixteen heirs of diverse backgrounds and ages are assembled in the old 'Westing house,' paired off, and given clues to a puzzle they must solve—apparently in order to inherit. . . . So the race is on, intensified by shifting identities and the suspicion that Westing was murdered by one of the heirs." Sch Library J
"The author's whodunits, in all their complex subtleties, have the same relation to run-of-the-mill mystery books that chess—which has an important role in this book—has to a child's game of luck. . . . The rules of the game make eight pairs of the players; each oddly matched couple is given a ten thousand dollar check and a set of clues. The result is a fascinating medley of word games, disguises, multiple aliases and subterfuges—in a demanding but rewarding book." Horn Bk

Rawlings, Marjorie Kinnan
The yearling; with pictures by N. C. Wyeth. Scribner 1939 400p illus $20, pa $4.95 (6 and up)   Fic
1 Florida—Fiction 2 Deer—Fiction
ISBN 0-684-20922-5; 0-684-71878-2   LC 39-27939
"Pulitzer prize edition"
First published 1938; Awarded Pulitzer Prize, 1939
"Young Jody Baxter lives a lonely life in the scrub forest of Florida until his parents unwillingly consent to his adopting an orphan fawn. The two become inseparable until the fawn destroys the meager crops. Then Jody realizes that this situation offers no compromise. In the sacrifice of what he loves best, he leaves his own yearling days behind." Rdng Ladders
"With its excellent descriptions of Florida scrub landscapes, its skillful use of native vernacular, its tender relation between Jody and his pet fawn, The Yearling is a simply written, picturesque story of boyhood." Time

Rawls, Wilson
Where the red fern grows; the story of two dogs and a boy. Doubleday 1961 212p $6.95, lib. bdg. $7.90 (6 and up)   Fic
1 Dogs—Fiction 2 Ozark Mountains—Fiction
ISBN 0-385-02059-7; 0-385-05619-2   LC 61-9201
"Looking back more than 50 years to his boyhood in the Ozarks, the narrator recalls how he achieved his heart's desire in the ownership of two redbone hounds, how he taught them all the tricks of hunting, and how they won the championship coon hunt before Old Dan was killed by a mountain lion and Little Ann died of grief. Although some readers may find this novel hackneyed and entirely too sentimental, others will enjoy the fine coon-hunting episodes and appreciate the author's feeling for nature." Booklist

Rice, Eve
The remarkable return of Winston Potter Crisply; a novel. Greenwillow Bks. 1978 212p illus $7.50, lib. bdg. $7.20 (5 and up)   Fic
1 New York (City)—Fiction 2 Mystery and detective stories
ISBN 0-688-80145-5; 0-688-84145-7   LC 77-28101

Rice, Eve—*Continued*

"Becky and Max see their brother on the streets of New York when he is supposed to be at Harvard studying. They follow him, and his actions seem highly suspicious. Maybe he is a spy, they think. They have a series of unusual misadventures while trying to track their brother who is really a busy artist trying to prove he can make a living as a painter. Their parents know about this all the time and are helping him to arrange a showing of his paintings, unbeknownst to Becky and Max." Babbling Bookworm

"Becky, the narrator, is an intelligent blithe spirit, and despite the menacing elements, her story is a brisk, good-humored whodunit, with the city and the delightfully eccentric characters coming vividly to life." Horn Bk

Richter, Conrad

Light in the forest; illus. by Warren Chappell. Knopf 1966 176p illus $4.95, lib. bdg. $5.99 (6 and up)   **Fic**

1 Delaware Indians—Fiction
ISBN 0-394-81404-5; 0-394-91404-X   LC 67-146

A reset and newly illustrated edition for young people of a title first published 1953

"A boy stolen in early childhood and brought up by the Delawares is at fifteen suddenly returned to the family he has forgotten. He resents his loss of independence, hates the brutality of the white man's civilization, and longs only for a return to the Indians whom he remembers as peace-loving and kind. His return to the Delawares does not, however, bring him peace; rather, he must make a bitter choice between helping his Indian brothers kill a group of unsuspecting white men or helping the white men escape. This is both vivid re-creation of outdoor life and a provocative study in conflicting loyalties." Horn Bk

Richter, Hans Peter

Friedrich; tr. from the German by Edite Kroll. Holt 1970 149p lib. bdg. $5.95 (5 and up)   **Fic**

1 Jews in Germany—Fiction 2 Germany—Fiction
ISBN 0-03-012721-1   LC 78-119098

Mildred L. Batchelder Award, 1972
Original German edition, 1961

In Germany in 1929 two-4-year-old boys, one a Jew named Friedrich, become friends. History envelops them, and through a series of tragic events the reader sees how this friendship is affected. The story ends with Friedrich's death in 1942 during an air raid

"The tragedy and terror suffered by German Jews are made more vivid by the simplicity and candor of a child's viewpoint and by the focus on one small, obscure family." Sat Rev

"Episodes are closely correlated with actual events, laws, decrees, and regulations which are listed in a chronology." Booklist

Roach, Marilynne K.

Presto: or, The adventures of a turnspit dog; written and illus. by Marilynne K. Roach. Houghton 1979 148p illus $7.95 (4 and up)   **Fic**

1 Dogs—Fiction 2 London—Fiction
ISBN 0-395-28269-1   LC 79-11746

"The narrative is centered on the protagonist—the dog Presto. Managing to escape a turnspit wheel in an inn, he experienced the ups and downs of [18th century] London street life. Terrorized by the leader of a canine pack, he was befriended by Dick Oates, owner of a Punch and Judy show, and by Margery Daw, a street waif: and the haps and mishaps of these human beings are woven into Presto's adventures. The animals—chiefly cats, dogs, cows, and horses—are presented anthropomorphically, but never do they converse with the human characters. Yet their commentaries on the failings and weaknesses of mankind are humorously satirical, in keeping with the boisterous eighteenth-century manner of the story. . . . The black-and-white oval-shaped line drawings at the head of each chapter are entirely compatible with the lively comic atmosphere of the story." Horn Bk

Roberts, Charles G. D.

Red Fox; illus. by John Schoenherr; introduction by David McCord. Houghton 1972 187p illus $4.95 (4 and up)   **Fic**

1 Foxes—Fiction 2 Canada—Fiction
ISBN 0-395-13735-7   LC 77-187419

First published 1905 by Page with illustrations by Charles Livingston Bull

"Here is a biography of a superbly clever fox in Eastern Canada, from his birth to his masterpiece of trickery which saves his life for the last time." Appraisal

"Children today will find this account of the wily fox and his relationships with the other animals in the New Brunswick woods both moving and informative. The dramatic story, one of the best of its type, is supported by striking black-and-white pen-and-ink drawings by John Schoenherr and there is also an excellent introduction by David McCord." Sch Library J

Roberts, Willo Davis

The view from the cherry tree. Atheneum Pubs. 1975 181p $8.95, pa $1.95 (5 and up)   **Fic**

1 Mystery and detective stories
ISBN 0-689-30483-8; 0-689-70464-X   LC 75-6759

"Thoroughly disgruntled by the furor which accompanies his sister's wedding, eleven-year-old Rob Mallory retires to his favorite perch in the cherry tree. There, he is a horrified witness to the murder of an unpleasant neighborhood recluse. Because of the wedding preparations and the arrival of hordes of relatives, no adult will believe Rob's story. Soon, he finds that someone knows—and is trying to kill him, too." Children's Bk Rev Serv

"Although written in a direct and unpretentious style, this is essentially a sophisticated story, solidly constructed, imbued with suspense, evenly paced, and effective in conveying the atmosphere of a household coping with the last-minute problems and pressure of a family wedding." Chicago. Children's Bk Center

Robertson, Keith

Henry Reed, Inc. Illus. by Robert McCloskey. Viking 1958 239p illus lib. bdg. $8.95 (5 and up)   **Fic**

ISBN 0-670-36796-6   LC 58-4758

"Henry Reed, on vacation from the American School in Naples, keeps a record of his research into the American free-enterprise system, to be used as a school report on his return. With a neighbor, Midge Glass, he starts a business in pure and applied research, which results in some very free and widely enterprising experiences, all recorded deadpan in his journal. Very funny and original escapades." Hodges. Bks for Elem Sch Libraries

Some other books about Henry Reed are also available from Viking:

Henry Reed's babysitting service, lib. bdg. $8.95 (ISBN 0-670-36825-3; LC 66-11908)
Henry Reed's big show, lib. bdg. $5.50 (ISBN 0-670-36839-3; LC 76-123026)
Henry Reed's journey, lib. bdg. $7.95 (ISBN 0-670-36854-7; LC 68-8522)

In search of a sandhill crane; illus. by Richard Cuffari. Viking 1973 201p illus $8.95, Penguin Bks. pa $2.25 (5 and up)   **Fic**

1 Wilderness areas—Fiction 2 Cranes (Birds)—Fiction 3 Michigan—Fiction
ISBN 0-670-39662-1; 0-14-031259-5   LC 72-9910

"Fifteen-year-old Link Keller did not believe that any place could be so lonely and isolated as his Aunt Harriet's cabin on Michigan's Upper Peninsula, but he knew that to be polite he had to endure two weeks cheerfully. Besides he had promised to take some photographs of a sandhill crane for his uncle in New York. In the occasional company of a Chippewa Indian, Link gradually develops an interest in the wilderness and with a little encouragement from his aunt has some exciting and amusing experiences." Booklist

"While there is a small element of suspense in Link's search for the sandhill crane, the story as a whole is quiet and contained, its strength in the economy of structure, the convincing characterization, the wealth of natural lore, and the evocation of the setting of the beautiful North Woods." Chicago. Children's Bk Center

Robinson, Barbara

The best Christmas pageant ever; pictures by Judith Gwyn Brown. Harper 1972 80p illus $6.95, lib. bdg. $6.89 (4-6)   **Fic**

1 Christmas—Fiction 2 Pageants—Fiction
ISBN 0-06-025043-7; 0-06-025044-5   LC 72-76501

Robinson, Barbara—*Continued*

In this story the Herdmans, "absolutely the worst kids in the history of the world," discover the meaning of Christmas when they bully their way into the leading roles of the local church nativity play

"Although there is a touch of sentiment at the end (Imogene has tears in her eyes, the Wise Men produce not the usual gift but the Christmas ham that had been in their charity basket) the story otherwise romps through the festive preparations with comic relish, and if the Herdmans are so gauche as to seem exaggerated, they are still enjoyable, as are the not-so-subtle pokes at pageant-planning in general." Chicago. Children's Bk Center

Robinson, Joan G.

The dark house of the sea witch. Coward, McCann & Geoghegan 1979 128p $7.50 (5 and up)   Fic

1 Brothers and sisters—Fiction 2 Great Britain—Fiction
ISBN 0-698-20494-8   LC 79-10845

"When the Bennetts decided to leave Meg and Maxie with the 'au pair' girl Hannah at their summer cottage for a day and a half, they had no way of knowing that Meg was worried by their departure for London. Meg was also fearful of their neighbor—tall, dark Mrs. Jarvis—who wore long raggedy skirts made of patchwork; and the girl tried to convince her young brother that the strange woman was a witch. Ambivalent in her feelings towards Maxie, Meg became terrified when she couldn't find him after Hannah had suddenly departed to attend a wedding in Germany. Befriended by Mrs. Jarvis, who actually was an eccentric artist, Maxie was happy to pose for a portrait; and before the Bennetts returned, Meg learned how to discount her dire prognostications and even how to love her brother." Horn Bk

"Robinson carefully builds suspense, creating a scary story that grows to wider dimensions as she subtly shows that people are not always what they seem. The theme is not new, but the characterizations bring fresh insights to this readable and flavorful British story." Booklist

Robinson, Veronica

David in silence; illus. by Victor Ambrus. Lippincott 1966 [c1965] 126p illus $8.50, (4-6)   Fic

1 Deaf—Fiction
ISBN 0-397-30867-1   LC 66-10900

First published 1965 in England

"The story is set in a small English town, where the neighborhood children are interested but uncomfortable with the new boy, David. David has always been deaf, and his older brother tries to explain to Michael, who is David's age and has made friendly overtures, what the problems of communication are. David is chased by a gang of boys playing a game, gets lost and frightened in an abandoned tunnel, and finds Michael and safety. At the close of the story there has been some change in the attitude of the other boys, but nothing melodramatic or unrealistic." Chicago. Children's Bk Center

"As a documentary study [this book] is excellent, precisely yet imaginatively conveying the difficulty of crossing that baffling wall over which the deaf regard the land of sound, the ordinary hearing crowd regard the deaf. . . . The splendid chapters of climax (the lost boy's journey) compellingly lift the story out of the merely informational field." Times (London) Lit Sup

Rockwell, Thomas

How to eat fried worms; pictures by Emily McCully. Watts, F. 1973 115p illus lib. bdg. $7.90 (3-6)   Fic

1 Worms—Fiction
ISBN 0-531-02631-0   LC 73-4262

"The stakes are high when Alan bets $50 that his friend Billy can't eat 15 worms (one per day). . . . Billy's mother, instead of upchucking, comes to her son's aid by devising gourmet recipes like Alsatian Smothered Worm. Alan wants to win as desperately as Billy, who is itching to buy a used minibike, and few holds are barred in the contest." Sch Library J

"A hilarious story that will revolt and delight bumptious, unreachable, intermediate-grade boys and any other less particular mortals that read or listen to it. . . . The characters and their families and activities are natural to a T, and this juxtaposed against the uncommon plot, makes for some colorful, original writing in a much-needed comic vein." Booklist

Rockwood, Joyce

Groundhog's horse; drawings by Victor Kalin. Holt 1978 115p illus lib. bdg. $6.95 (4-6)   Fic

1 Cherokee Indians—Fiction 2 Horses—Fiction
ISBN 0-03-021526-9   LC 77-22676

"Groundhog is eleven, a Cherokee living in Appalachia in the mid-eighteenth century. Proud of his horse Midnight, Groundhog can't understand why others can't appreciate her rare qualities. When Midnight is stolen by the Creeks as a taunting gesture (they have taken no other horses) and his tribe's warriors refuse to risk battle just to recapture one horse, Groundhog runs off to do it on his own. His successful adventure brings him kudos when he returns with his horse; Midnight, he say, was the one who knew the way home, and Groundhog at last feels that his family and friends recognize how unusual his beloved pet is." Chicago. Children's Bk Center

This "is an engaging, understated story. . . . Groundhog is a believable and ingratiating young man, and his growing courage, compassion and self-confidence are presented with grace and subtlety. . . . The characters exercise intelligence, imagination and creativity in pursuing their goals. Capture by an opposing side does not imply death, but rather affectionate adoption, for the protagonist. All Cherokees speak grammatically and in full sentences. They possess humor, complex emotions and appear genuinely human. . . . Against the surefire background of a solid boy-loves-horse story, a fragment of traditional culture illuminated and vitalized. Without being preachy or affected, 'Groundhog's Horse' is a worthwhile contribution and thoroughly recommended." Interracial Bks For Children Bul

To spoil the sun. Holt 1976 180p illus $6.95 (6 and up)   Fic

1 Cherokee Indians—Fiction
ISBN 0-06-018066-X   LC 76-10568

"There are, understandably, no first-hand written accounts of American Indian life during the 16th Century. However, this story of the Cherokee people of the southern Appalachians shortly after the first voyage of Columbus seems remarkably authentic. Rain Dove, a young Cherokee girl, tells about daily Indian life as well as war games, marriage customs, hunts, and societal living. Also included are accounts, based on fact, of the first visits of Spanish explorers, and the appearance of smallpox, the devastating 'invisible fire,' which wiped out more than half of entire villages. A fascinating picture of American Indian life which brings a clearer understanding of the effect of the White Man's coming." Sch Library J

"An afterword provides necessary historical background which might have been more helpful as a foreword. For the mature reader." Horn Bk

Rodgers, Mary

Freaky Friday. Harper 1972 145p $6.95, lib. bdg. $6.89, pa $1.95 (4 and up)   Fic

1 Mothers—Fiction
ISBN 0-06-025048-8; 0-06-025049-6; 0-06-080392-4
LC 74-183158

" 'When I woke up this morning, I found I'd turned into my mother.' So begins the most bizarre day in the life of 13-year-old Annabel Andrews, who discovers one Friday morning she has taken on her mother's physical characteristics while retaining her own personality. Readers will giggle in anticipation as Anabel plunges madly from one disaster to another trying to cope with various adult situations." Pub W

"There's nothing didactic here; the story bubbles along in fine style as Annabel sees herself as others see her (a more complimentary set of attitudes than she might have anticipated) and adjusts to the rigors of her mother's problems and the inevitable complications of changed roles. A fresh, imaginative, and entertaining story." Chicago. Children's Bk Center

Another book about Annabel Andrews is also available from Harper: A billion for Boris $6.95, lib. bdg. $5.79, pa $1.95 (ISBN 0-06-025047-X; 0-06-025054-2; 0-06-440075-1; LC 74-3586)

Rodowsky, Colby

Evy-ivy-over. Watts, F. 1978 153p lib.
bdg. $7.90 (5 and up)   **Fic**

1 Extrasensory perception—Fiction   2 Grandmothers—Fiction
ISBN 0-531-02245-5   LC 78-6989

"Until she entered sixth grade, Slug enjoyed
the freedom of living with her grandmother
Gussie, who had earned a unique place in their
small community because of the ability to see
things 'from the edges of time not yet happened.'
It was Gussie who had taught Slug to transform
ordinary events into adventures and who had
shaped the course of her granddaughter's life—
first, by nicknaming her Slug-a-bed and secondly,
by giving her a home when the child's indifferent
mother vanished. . . . The two felt a special bond
between them until the world outside began to
interject doubts and fears. Slug [was] suddenly
aware of her secondhand clothes and shabby environment . . . since she vacillated between loyalty
to her grandmother and a desire to be accepted by
her schoolmates. Not until a near tragedy occurred
did she acknowledge that they were different from
other people, at the same time recognizing that
they need not stand apart." Horn Bk
"Tension is carefully controlled, characters are
well drawn, and the maturation of Slug is credibly
handled." Sch Library J

Roth, Arthur

The iceberg hermit. Four Winds 1974 201p
$7.96, pa $1.95 (6 and up)   **Fic**

1 Survival (after airplane accidents, shipwrecks,
etc.)—Fiction   2 Arctic regions—Fiction
ISBN 0-590-07301-X; 0-590-01582-6   LC 74-7435

This book "describes the loneliness and immense
courage of a seventeen-year-old Scottish boy, the
sole survivor of a whaling ship which sinks in
the Arctic Seas north of Greenland in the mid-
1800's. Marooned on an iceberg and totally dependent on his own resources, Allan wages an
incredible battle against the cold, snowstorms,
gloomy sunless days, and despair from lack of
human contact. The story is based on an actual
historical incident." Babbling Bookworm
"Roth's book "represents the ultimate adventure
novel: one man, alone, struggling to survive in
a dangerous environment. This kind of yarn must
be told in a series of exciting and suspenseful
scenes. The hero must be tough, skillful and lucky,
characteristics possessed by Allan Gordon in lusty
degree. . . . It is an incredible story, a legend
ideal for the adventure novel. Arthur Roth tells the
story so well that it doesn't matter whether it's
historically true." NY Times Bk Rev

Rounds, Glen

The blind colt; written & illus. by Glen
Rounds. Holiday House 1960 unp illus $8.95
(4-6)   **Fic**

1 Ponies—Fiction   2 South Dakota—Fiction
ISBN 0-8234-0010-7   LC 60-2171

First published 1941
Set in the South Dakota Badlands, this is the
story of a pony colt that was born blind. It tells
of his experiences growing up with a mustang
band, and of his eventual adoption and training
by ten-year-old Whitey
"The story has stood the test of time and is well
worth continued replacement. The courage of the
horse in spite of his handicap, the feeling of apprehension throughout the story lest Whitey have to
give up the colt, the authentic feeling of cowboy life
pervading all the stories of this author have just
as much impact on the present-day reader as they
did when the book first appeared." Library J
Some other books in this series are also available from Holiday House:
Stolen pony $8.95 (ISBN 0-8234-0110-3; LC 71-3445)
Whitey and the wild horse $3.95 (ISBN 0-8234-
0138-3; LC 58-14735)
Whitey ropes & rides $3.95 (ISBN 0-8234-0139-1;
LC 56-14274)

Mr Yowder and the giant bull snake;
written and illus. by Glen Rounds. Holiday
House 1978 unp illus lib. bdg. $6.95 (2-5)
                                           Fic

1 Snakes—Fiction   2 The West (U.S.)—Fiction
ISBN 0-8234-0311-4   LC 77-24136

"Old man Yowder is painting 'Pike's Peak or
Bust' on covered wagons out on the prairie in
return for coffee, flour, or other supplies when a
young bull snake slithers up to his bedroll. Yowder
scolds the reptile who asks, logically enough,
'Where did you learn to talk snake?' thus beginning a beautiful friendship. Before you can count
to ten, Yowder and the bull snake (who does
bodybuilding exercises) are helping the U.S. Army
capture buffalo. And before you finish swallowing
that, they're ruining a perfectly good day for Mr.
Buffalo Bill and the President of the United States.
A master of the American tall tale, Rounds is at
his best in this side-slapping story. His dead-pan
country dialogue is so authentic that readers are
completely taken in by all the foolishness. His
quirky black-and-white line drawings show the
hilarity of a situation which the text treats with
mock gravity." Sch Library J
Another book about Mr Yowder is also available
from Holiday House: Mr Yowder and the steamboat. lib bdg. $5.95 (ISBN 0-8234-0294-0;
LC 76-43089)

Rutgers van der Loeff, Anna

Avalanche! Illus. by Gustav Schrotter.
Morrow 1958 [c1957] 219p illus $7.25 (6 and
up)   **Fic**

1 Switzerland—Fiction   2 Disasters—Fiction
ISBN 0-688-21055-4   LC 58-5253

Original Dutch edition published 1955. This translation first published 1957 in England
"Story of a Swiss boy's experience when he, the
people of his village, and a group of war orphans
from an international Children's Village are caught
in an avalanche." Pub W
"The author has written with great understanding of the effect that tension and tragedy have on
human beings and their relationships with each
other. Awarded the prize for the best children's
book [of the year, when it was first] published in
Holland." Chicago. Children's Bk Center

Sachs, Marilyn

Amy and Laura; illus. by Tracy Sugarman.
Doubleday 1966 189p illus lib. bdg. $6.95
(4-6)   **Fic**

1 Sisters—Fiction
ISBN 0-385-06984-7   LC 66-10724

Two "sisters face the family problem of a con-
valescent mother as well as their own individual
problems at school." LC. Children's Bks. 1966
"Natural conversations and a lively pace well
within the grasp of average readers assure popular
reception of a story that is as realistic as it is
readable." Horn Bk

Dorrie's book; drawings by Anne Sachs.
Doubleday 1975 136p illus $5.95, lib. bdg. $6.90
(4-6)   **Fic**

1 Family life—Fiction
ISBN 0-385-03350-8; 0-385-03213-7   LC 74-33688

"Dorrie O'Brien, an only child, was taken everywhere by her doting parents, and the three of
them were the best of friends. She lived in an
apartment overlooking San Francisco Bay. Then
when she was eleven years old, this blessed situation was changed; Dorrie's mother discovered that
she was pregnant. After triplets were born, Dorrie's
self-pity turned to misery, and life became one
long session with bottles, diapers, and screaming
babies. To make matters worse, they had to move
to an ugly old house in the suburbs, and the two
neglected children next door more or less moved
in with them. Told as though it had been written
by Dorrie for a school assignment, the story of
her reluctant adjustment to her large and unwanted family is extremely funny." Horn Bk
"A truly unique and charming story, illustrated
with child-like sketches by the author's daughter."
Children's Bk Rev Serv

Marv; illus. by Louis Glanzman. Doubleday 1970 160p illus lib. bdg. $4.95 (4-6) **Fic**

1 Brothers and sisters—Fiction
ISBN 0-385-00009-X   LC 73-116250

This is the "story of a boy who is considered a
failure by his much admired older sister. Marv is a
day-dreamer, a doodler, and a prolific builder,
marvelously inventive but impractical. He dreams
of such elaborate schemes as automating the
butcher's shop and kidnapping Hitler, and he builds
revolving doors that lead nowhere and other
useless contraptions. No matter how he tries Marv

Sachs, Marilyn—*Continued*
cannot, in the eyes of his brilliant sister, create anything of benefit to anyone. Marv does not change but his ill-fated attempts to impress his sister keep the reader's fullest sympathies with the well-meaning dreamer." Booklist

A pocket full of seeds; illus. by Ben Stahl. Doubleday 1973 137p illus $6.95, lib. bdg. $7.90 (5 and up) **Fic**

1 World War, 1939-1945—Fiction 2 France—History—German occupation, 1940-1945—Fiction 3 Jews in France—Fiction
ISBN 0-385-06091-2; 0-385-06092-0   LC 73-79708

"Nicole Nieman is eight when she leaves the foster home in which she and her small sister have been living, and rejoins the parents who had not until then been able to afford a home big enough for four. Self-assured and rather self-satisfied, Nicole is baffled by the hostility of some of her classmates, a hostility that presages the persecution that French Jews suffered during World War II. When her parents are taken by the Nazis, Nicole goes to her foster parents; since it is unsafe there, she goes to school, where the teacher, who Nicole has disliked, shows unexpected compassion and takes Nicole in as a boarding pupil. A touching story, realistic in the way Nicole adjusts to the drastic changes of war and changes from a blithe eight-year-old to a mature adolescent. Style and characterization are deft, and the atmosphere of the place and period are convincingly recreated." Chicago. Children's Bk Center

A summer's lease. Dutton 1979 124p $7.95 (5 and up) **Fic**

1 Authors—Fiction 2 Teachers—Fiction
ISBN 0-525-40480-5   LC 78-12486

"Gloria was determined to get to college [and become a writer] despite her widowed mother's insistence that she take a secretarial course and start earning money. She had the backing of her beloved English teacher, Mrs. Horne, and she was sure that Mrs. Horne would select her as assistant editor of the high school literary magazine—and that would be her passport to continuing education. Gloria, who tells, the story, is arrogant, conceited about her literary prowess, jealous of and harsh toward those she considers her rivals. . . . Gloria changes during a summer [in 1943] in which Mrs. Horne invites her and her rival, Jerry, to the Horne summer home to help take care of a group of younger children. Gloria resents Jerry's appointment (with her) as co-assistant editor, she despises his kind and charitable manner, and she is jealous because her adored Mrs. Horne so clearly finds Jerry a nicer person, although she's fond of both students. It is in the observation of Jerry's behavior and her own, in the reactions of the children to both of them, and the sobering realization (when the youngest child, who adored Jerry, dies) that one cannot always go back and make amends, that Gloria learns charity." Chicago. Children's Bk Center

"Maybe a handful of authors can compete with Sachs in creating unaffected, literate prose about fully individualized characters in memorable stories. . . . The summer teaches Gloria something about herself. . . . But there is no phony reformation or any bathos to mar this wonderful novel." Pub W

The truth about Mary Rose; illus. by Louis Glanzman. Doubleday 1973 159p illus $5.95, lib. bdg. $6.90 (4 and up) **Fic**

1 Family life—Fiction
ISBN 0-385-09448-5; 0-385-09449-3   LC 72-89128

"Fans of 'Veronica Ganz' [entered below] will be pleased to learn that Sach's highly individual heroine now has children of her own, one of whom narrates this story. Eleven-year-old Mary Rose Ramirez is named for her aunt, Veronica's sister, who was killed in a fire at age 11. The central question: was Mary Rose Ganz an angelic child who died a heroine (as grandmother says)? Was she the selfish, bitchy terror that Uncle Stanley remembers? Or was she a 'poor, little thing' as Veronica remembers? The question arises when Mary Rose's artist father wins a competition that lands him a job in New York, and the family moves to Veronica's mother's house in the Bronx." Sch Library J

"Woven through and around the story of Mary Rose is a rich and perceptive picture of the intricacies of family relationships, a picture peopled with vivid characters. Particularly telling: the obdurately prejudiced grandmother." Chicago. Children's Bk Center

Veronica Ganz; illus. by Louis Glanzman. Doubleday 1968 156p illus lib. bdg. $6.95 (4 and up) **Fic**

1 School stories
ISBN 0-385-01436-8   LC 68-11813

"At thirteen Veronica, the bully of her school in the Bronx, hasn't got a friend. Afraid of being made fun of because she's so big, she has long since beaten (boys) or slapped (girls) her classmates into subservience. (She also enjoys making sport of teachers and a librarian.) Then a new boy arrives. Although small, Peter is smart and he side-steps Veronica's persistent attempts to pulverize him. At last the big girl and the undersized boy have a confrontation, which brings some pleasant surprises for the belligerent Veronica." Bk World

Followed by: Peter and Veronica. Doubleday lib. bdg. $7.95 (ISBN 0-385-06639-2; LC 69-12226)

Saint-Exupéry, Antoine de
The little prince; written and drawn by Antoine de Saint-Exupéry; tr. from the French by Katherine Woods. Harcourt 1943 91p illus $5.95, pa $1.50 **Fic**

ISBN 0-15-246503-0; 0-15-652820-7   LC 67-1144

Also available from Harcourt in French language edition for $7.95, pa $1.95 (ISBN 0-15-243818-1; 0-15-650300-X; LC 43-5812); German pa $1.95 (ISBN 0-15-625285-6; LC 73-4886); Spanish pa $1.75 (ISBN 0-15-628450-2; LC 73-5511)

"A flier has [a] forced landing in the Sahara. He is met by the little Prince of Asteroid B612. The Prince tells the flier of his experiences on many planets with men, flowers, and animals." Library J

"Only time and use will determine whether adults or children will enjoy this book more, or whether both will enjoy it equally. A great many children will treasure it without necessarily grasping its full significance." Booklist

St George, Judith
Mystery at St Martin's. Putnam 1979 151p $7.95 (5 and up) **Fic**

1 Mystery and detective stories 2 Counterfeits and counterfeiting—Fiction
ISBN 0-399-20702-3   LC 79-17547

"After Ruth is called in to the school office for making a ski trip payment with a bad ten-dollar bill, she begins to suspect that the counterfeiting operation originates in her father's church. Though she fears that knowing her father is rector of St. Martin's will dim classmate Kenny's interest in her, she can't allow her father to be implicated by the surfacing rumors and decides to act. In the midst of her sister's wedding reception when everyone is occupied, Ruth takes matters into her own hands and goes exploring in the dim, rarely used reaches of the church basement. Not only does she discover a printing press but also finds herself in danger from a man whom she least suspected. The crisp style and brisk pace, accompanied by a rounded characterization of Ruth and a well-developed plot, mix well in this exciting, readable mystery." Booklist

St John, Wylly Folk
The ghost next door; illus. by Trina Schart Hyman. Harper 1971 178p illus lib. bdg. $7.89 (4 and up) **Fic**

1 Ghosts—Fiction 2 Spiritualism—Fiction 3 Mystery and detective stories
ISBN 0-06-026628-7   LC 71-157896

"Lindsey and Tammy, twelve-year-old neighbors of Miss Judith, are determined to discover how Miss Judith's niece, Sherry, knows so much about the activities of her dead half sister, Miranda, since Sherry has never been told of Miranda's existence. Before the question of whether Sherry is in contact with Miranda's ghost is satisfactorily, if not completely answered, Lindsey and Tammy help to expose a fraudulent medium and use some amateur psychology to obtain clues. While not entirely convincing, it is a fast-paced first-person story for mystery lovers." Booklist

Salten, Felix

Bambi (4-6)   Fic

1 Deer—Fiction

Some editions are:

Grosset (Thrushwood bks) $3.95 Illustrated by Kurt Wiese (ISBN 0-448-02518-3)

Simon & Schuster $5.95 Illustrated by Barbara Cooney (ISBN 0-671-65136-6; LC 74-124383)

Original German edition published 1923. First American edition published 1928 by Simon & Schuster

"Bambi is a young deer, growing up in a forest, at first a curious child playing about his mother in glade and meadow, conversing with grasshoppers, squirrels and his own little cousins, Faline and Gobo."

"Felix Salten's story of deer life in the woods that fringe the Danube is neither sentimental nor used to point a moral. It derives its dramatic value, legitimately, from the animals' fear and terror of their historic enemy—man. . . . In his absorption with details that author has brought his whole forest to life, yet these details are selected with a poet's intuition for delicacy of effect." NY Her Trib Bks

Say, Allen

The ink-keeper's apprentice. Harper 1979 185p $7.95, lib. bdg. $7.89 (6 and up)   Fic

1 Japan—Fiction 2 Artists—Fiction

ISBN 0-06-025208-1; 0-06-025209-X   LC 78-20264

"The setting is Tokyo, the time is five years after World War II, and thirteen-year-old Kiyoi tells the story. His parents are divorced and the grandmother with whom he has lived has given him an allowance so that he can live alone, visiting her weekly. Kiyoi's ambition to be a cartoonist so impresses Noro Shinpei, Japan's greatest cartoonist, that he takes the boy on as appentice. As Kiyoi describes the small events of the next few years, he gives a good picture of an adolescent growing toward maturity: gaining independence, gaining proficiency as an artist, adapting to changing circumstances, and making the decision to accept his father's offer to move (as Say did when he was sixteen) to the United States." Chicago. Children's Bk Center

"Written in a frank but nonsensational style, the narrative juxtaposes the American and Western influences on modern Japanese living with the persisting ancient ways: Kiyoi was as familiar with Michelangelo's 'David' and Van Gogh's paintings as he was with comic strips, and he referred to his growing awareness of sex and love without prurience. The dialogue is lively, the characters are sharply drawn, and the episodes of the loose, realistic narrative are significant events in the maturing of a self-reliant Japanese adolescent." Horn Bk

Schaefer, Jack

Old Ramon; illus. by Harold West. Houghton 1960 102p illus $7.95, pa $2.95 (5 and up)   Fic

1 Shepherds—Fiction 2 Sheep—Fiction 3 Southwest, New—Fiction

ISBN 0-395-07087-2; 0-395-15056-6   LC 60-5211

"In this brief story about sheepherding in the Southwest, Old Ramon takes the son of his patron out for a season to teach him the way of the sheep. As they move the flock toward the mountains with their two dogs—encountering river crossings, desert heat, rattlesnakes, sandstorms, and wolves—the boy learns not only how to handle the sheep but also something about responsibility, bravery, and the difficult business of becoming a man. . . . The book is written with a simplicity, humor, and depth which will appeal to readers of all ages." Booklist

Schoenherr, John

The barn; written and illus. by John Schoenherr. Little 1968 40p illus lib. bdg. $4.95 (2-4)   Fic

1 Skunks—Fiction 2 Animals—Fiction

ISBN 0-316-77421-9   LC 68-26992

"An Atlantic Monthly Press book"

"Strong pictures in black and white combine meticulously realistic drawings of animals with delicate background details. The drama of the illustrations is tempered by the quiet writing, which describes the predatory excursions of a hungry skunk, himself preyed upon by an owl who must fed three owlets. Low-keyed, the text is less a story than a revealing vignette of the constant struggle for survival in the animal world." Sutherland. The Best in Children's Bks

Schulman, Janet

The nutcracker, by E. T. A. Hoffmann; adapted by Janet Schulman; illus. by Kay Chorao. Dutton 1979 62p illus $6.95 (3-5)   Fic

1 Fairy tales 2 Christmas—Fiction

ISBN 0-525-36245-2   LC 79-11223

"Schulman has gone to Hoffmann's original story, 'The Nutcracker and the King of Mice,' published in Germany in 1816, rather than to the more familiar ballet version on which most adaptations for children are based; her one addition from the ballet is the Sugar Plum Fairy." Chicago. Children's Bk Center

"The story-within-a-story is handled in a graceful, neatly composed fashion, and the text has a slightly formal, old-fashioned sound, that sets the stage for the reveries and romance. . . . Chorao's black-and-white illustrations have their usual charm: they are gentle and sentimental with small, delicate details under a filmy haze. Her faces tend to be weak and lacking in expression, but the dreamy quality of the gray tones sets an appropriate mood." Booklist

Sebestyen, Ouida

Words by heart. Little 1979 162p $7.95 (5 and up)   Fic

1 Blacks—Fiction 2 Race relations—Fiction 3 Family life—Fiction

ISBN 0-316-77931-8   LC 78-27847

"An Atlantic Monthly Press book"

"The year is 1910; Ben Sills, ambitious for his children, has bravely moved his family from the comparative security of an all-Black Southern town to take up life as American citizens in a white community further west. Ben is hard-working and dependable and soon incurs the enmity of the Haneys, a family of shiftless, ignorant sharecroppers. Moreover, Ben's oldest child, twelve-year-old Lena, hungry for book-reading and learning and almost always at the head of the class, is making the townspeople uneasy; the old Southern fear and animosity are ignited anew. When Ben is hired by wealthy old Mrs. Chism to do Mr. Haney's neglected work, he is doomed by the tenant farmer's vengeance." Horn Bk

"This is an impressive first novel about race relationships and nonviolence, written in an easy, vigorous style and candid in its depiction of discrimination. . . . Shot by Haney's son, Lena's dying father urges her to take no revenge, but to save the boy if she can. Thus Lena learns, as she has learned so much from her father, to forgive. A most moving story about a black family strong in their love and pride." Chicago. Children's Bk Center

Seed, David

Stream runner. Four Winds 1979 185p lib. bdg. $7.95 (5 and up)   Fic

1 Fishing—Fiction 2 California—Fiction

ISBN 0-590-07568-3   LC 78-21769

"On his way to the local swimming pool one morning, fourteen-year-old Leif Collins encounters a number of 'remembering spots'—places which spark a series of recollections spanning the four years he has lived in Dunsmuir, a railroad town in northern California. Leif is an introspective boy who is aware of his appreciation of each moment. He recalls family scenes and days spent swimming and frolicking with his friends, but most of his reminiscences center on his experiences while fishing for trout. . . . The boy spends many happy hours with only his thoughts for company, sharpening his fishing skills and learning the ways of the trout. The book ends at the close of the day as Leif and his friends go for a moonlight swim and talk and joke and wonder about the future." Horn Bk

"Sometimes [Leif] seems a bit too wise and heroic for his age, and sometimes his time shifts are confusing because they have a nostalgic reminiscent quality that belongs to an older person. But dialogue is natural when it happens, the setting clean and country-fresh." Booklist

Selden, George

The cricket in Times Square; illus. by Garth Williams. Farrar, Straus 1960 151p illus $7.95 (3-6) **Fic**

1 Cats—Fiction 2 Crickets—Fiction 3 Mice—Fiction 4 New York (City)—Fiction
ISBN 0-374-31650-3   LC 60-12640

"An Ariel book"

"A touch of magic comes to Times Square subway station with Chester, a cricket from rural Connecticut. He is introduced to the distinctive character of city life by three friends: Mario Bellini, whose parents operate a newsstand; Tucker, a glib Broadway mouse; and Harry, a sagacious cat. Chester saves the Bellinis' business by giving concerts from the newsstand, bringing to rushing commuters moments of beauty and repose. This modern fantasy shows that, in New York, anything can happen." Moorachian. What is a City?

Followed by these books, also available from Farrar, Straus:

Tucker's countryside $9.95 (ISBN 0-374-37854-1; LC 69-14975)

Harry Cat's pet puppy $8.95 (ISBN 0-374-32856-0; LC 74-12436)

The genie of Sutton Place. Farrar, Straus 1973 175p $8.95 (4 and up) **Fic**

ISBN 0-374-32527-8   LC 72-90531

Adapted from the television play written by the author and Kenneth Heuer

"A large brown genie is evoked by a boy in trouble, in a sophisticated but somewhat low-comedy story set in New York City. Tim's father has just died, and he is not enthralled to hear that he must live with his wealthy Aunt Lucy in Sutton Place. Tim prefers the comfortable milieu of Greenwich Village and the companionship of his friend Madame Sosostris—Antiques and Seances. The crux of the problem: Aunt Lucy is allergic to dogs. The genie turns Tim's dog into a man, one that Aunt Lucy finds not unattractive, and there's a French farce atmosphere as the uncomfortable dog repeatedly makes woofy noises and is nearly discovered. There's also a romance between Aunt Lucy's intellectual maid and the genie, who happily becomes mortal at the end of the story. There's a good bit of wit in the writing, exaggeration of characters, overstimulated plot albeit original in concept." Chicago. Children's Bk Center

Sendak, Maurice

Higglety pigglety pop! or, There must be more to life; story and pictures by Maurice Sendak. Harper 1967 69p illus $7.95, lib. bdg. $7.89 (2-4) **Fic**

1 Dogs—Fiction
ISBN 0-06-025487-4; 0-06-025488-2   LC 67-18553

In this modern fairy tale "Jennie, the Sealyham terrier, leaves home because 'there must be more to life than having everything.' When she applies for a job as the leading lady of the World Mother Goose Theater, she discovers that what she lacks is experience. What follows are her adventures and her gaining of experience; finally Jennie becomes the leading lady of the play." Wis Library Bul

"The story has elements of tenderness and humor; it also has . . . typically macabre Sendak touches. . . . The illustrations are beautiful, amusing, and distinctive." Sutherland. The Best in Children's Bks

Seredy, Kate

The Good Master; written and illus. by Kate Seredy. Viking 1935 210p illus $5.95 (4-6) **Fic**

1 Farm life—Fiction 2 Hungary—Fiction
ISBN 0-670-34592-X   LC 35-17487

Into this story of Jancsi, a ten-year-old Hungarian farm boy and his little hoyden of a cousin Kate from Budapest, is woven a description of Hungarian farm life, fairs, festivals, and folk tales. Under the tutelage of Jancsi's kind father, called by the neighbors The Good Master, Kate calms down and becomes a more docile young person

"The steady warm understanding of the wise father, the Good Master, is a shining quality throughout." Horn Bk

Followed by: The singing tree. o.p. 1981

The white stag; written and illus. by Kate Seredy. Viking 1937 94p illus $8.95 (4-6) **Fic**

1 Hungary—Fiction
ISBN 0-670-76375-6   LC 37-37800

Awarded the Newbery Medal, 1938

"Striking illustrations interpret this hero tale of the legendary founding of Hungary, when a white stag and a red eagle led the people to their promised land." Hodges. Bks for Elem Sch Libraries

Serraillier, Ian

The silver sword; illus. by C. Walter Hodges. Phillips [1959 c1956] 187p illus $8.95 (5 and up) **Fic**

1 World War, 1939-1945—Fiction 2 Refugees, Polish—Fiction
ISBN 0-87599-104-1   LC 59-6556

First published 1956 in England, and 1959 in the United States by Criterion Books

"Three Polish children struggle to find their parents after the family becomes separated following the Nazi invasion in 1940. In late August, 1945, they reach their goal in Switzerland, after wanderings and 'ordeals before which the bravest spirit might quail.' For over two-and-a-half years the two girls are without Edek, their brother and lifeline who was imprisoned for smuggling food. Jan, a homeless boy who met their father while he was searching for them, becomes the fourth in the group, a talisman figure like the silver sword he treasures, now aiding, now endangering them with his unpredictable exploits and irrepressible love of animals. Jan remains—with Ruth, the eldest—the most memorable and sympathetic character, and his charm lingers long after the book is closed. English critics said this book is 'touched with greatness.' A powerful story-idea transcends unexceptional writing, and there is no tinge of condemnation of any nation involved." Horn Bk

Sewell, Anna

Black Beauty (4-6) **Fic**

1 Horses—Fiction 2 Great Britain—Fiction
Some editions are:
Dent(Children's illustrated classics) Illustrated by Lucy Kemp-Welch $9 (ISBN 0-460-05012-5)
Macmillan Pub. Co. (Macmillan classics) $3.95 Illustrated by John Groth. Afterword by Clifton Fadiman (ISBN 0-02-070-X; LC 62-18395)
Raintree Childrens Bks. (Raintree's illustrated classics) lib. bdg. $7.99 (ISBN 0-8393-6209-9; LC 78-3823)

First published 1877

"As Black Beauty, a fine horse, goes from one master to another, readers learn the story of his life in nineteenth century England." Gateways to Readable Bks

The book has "enjoyed tremendous popularity for many years. Some childen wept over Beauty's sufferings. . . . 'Black Beauty' was written as a protest against the tight checkrein and other more serious cruelties to horses. It relates, in the first person, a good story. . . . Black Beauty, while presumably a real horse thinks and talks out of horse character. He is humanly sensitive to the social and moral tone of the people with whom he lives." Arbuthnot. Children & Bks. 3d edition

Sharmat, Marjorie Weinman

Getting something on Maggie Marmelstein: pictures by Ben Shecter. Harper 1971 101p illus lib. bdg. $7.89 (3-5) **Fic**

1 School stories
ISBN 0-06-025552-8   LC 78-157895

"Crisply told by Thad Smith, this story of boy/girl rivalry involves the trouble that develops when Thad calls Maggie Marmelstein a mouse. She retaliates by threatening to tell that she has seen him helping her mother cook. His desperate search for something on Maggie leads to his discovery that she writes mushy fan letters to movie stars. Rehearsals for a dramatization of 'The Frog Prince' provide an entertaining backdrop for their competition, the means of ending it, and much of the humor in the well-executed story." Sch Library J

"Simple black-and-white illustrations provide a natural extension of the text which combines genuine character and plot development with amusing dialog." Pub W

Followed by: Maggie Marmelstein for president. Harper $7.95, lib. bdg. $7.89, pa $1.95 (ISBN 0-06-025542-0; 0-06-025555-2; 0-06-440079-4; LC 75-6300)

Sharp, Margery

The rescuers; with illus. by Garth Williams
Little 1959 149p illus $7.95 (3-6)   **Fic**

1 Mice—Fiction
ISBN 0-316-78314-5   LC 59-6477

This is "a story featuring animals. The Prisoners'
Aid Society of mice [one of whose members is
Miss Bianca, the pampered pet of an ambassador's
son] want to free a Norwegian poet held captive
in the Black Castle in a barbarous country. The
difficulties and intrigues of the sleek, sophisticated
spy and her helpers who are chosen for the task
by the Society, and their eventual triumph, provide
the adventure and suspense in this liberally illustrated tale." Pub W

"Many line drawings in the artist's best style,
giving individuality to a great number of small
animals, make this volume look like a children's
book; the text, which is a 'heroic tale' in talking-
animal fantasy, has no audience limitations. . . .
Delightful family fare, with some humorous allusions and overtones to enrich the story for older
listeners and, for all, the most charming deft
details of characterization, scene, and incident."
Horn Bk

Some other books about Miss Bianca and her
friends are also available from Little:
Bernard into battle $7.95 (ISBN 0-316-78326-9;
LC 78-11332)
Bernard the Brave $8.95 (ISBN 0-316-78292-0; LC
76-53829)
Miss Bianca $7.95 (ISBN 0-316-78310-2; LC 62-9556)
Miss Bianca and the bridesmaid $6.95 (ISBN 0-316-
78299-8; LC 73-160352)
Miss Bianca in the Antarctic $8.95 ISBN 0-316-
78294-7; LC 75-158484)
Miss Bianca in the Orient $6.95 (ISBN 0-316-
78319-6; LC 79-119110)
Miss Bianca in the salt mines $6.95 (ISBN 0-316-
78311-0; LC 66-14901)

Shotwell, Louisa R.

Roosevelt Grady; illus. by Peter Burchard.
Collins [distributed by Philomel Bks.] 1963
151p illus $5.95 (4-6)   **Fic**

1 Migrant labor—Fiction 2 Blacks—Fiction
ISBN 0-529-03780-7   LC 63-14778

First published by World Publishing Company
The story of Roosevelt Grady, "a boy in a lively
[black] family, migrant crop-workers of the Eastern seaboard, and his problems moving from one
school to another and trying to make friends."
Pub W

"Written with candor and simplicity, a convincing story that has good characterization and a
setting described with sympathy but no sentimentality. There is no reference in the text to the
fact that the characters are [black]; this is shown
in the illustrations. Several of the characters have
names like Pearly Ann, Bethalene, Lulubelle,
Princess Anne; this seems unfortunate, since it
may type the characters for readers who are not
aware that this is a custom of a regional and
economic level rather than a racial idiosyncrasy."
Chicago. Children's Bk Center

Shura, Mary Francis

The gray ghosts of Taylor Ridge; illus.
by Michael Hampshire. Dodd 1978 128p
$5.95 (5 and up)   **Fic**

1 Ghosts—Fiction
ISBN 0-396-07526-6   LC 77-16861

"A search for their father's compass . . . takes
13-year-old Nat and his sister to an old Civil
War homestead on Taylor Ridge. Unexpectedly,
they meet old Boomer, a blind recluse who tells
them tales of gray ghosts, invisible horses that
roam the hills at dusk, and treasure lost more
'than 100 years ago. . . . When a call for help
from Boomer brings them again to the ridge, the
two play a vital role in righting some old wrongs,
finding the lost treasure, and eventually discovering the whereabouts of the lost compass." Booklist

"The story has pace, the writing style is fairly
fluent if uneven, and the element of suspense
should appeal to readers. Too, Shura makes Nat's
changing opinion of his doughty little sister both
gradual and believable." Chicago. Children's Bk
Center

Shyer, Marlene Fanta

Welcome home, Jellybean. Scribner 1978
152p lib. bdg. $7.95 (5 and up)   **Fic**

1 Mentally handicapped children—Fiction 2 Brothers and sisters—Fiction
ISBN 0-684-15519-2   LC 77-17970

"'When my sister turned thirteen the school
where she lived got her toilet-trained and my
mother decided she ought to come home to live,
once and for all.' So begins Neil Oxley's story
of how it was to have his profoundly retarded
sister re-enter the family circle. Mr. Oxley's
prophecy, 'It's not going to be easy,' is more than
borne out as Gerri's unintended mischief (pulling
down curtains, removing labels from cans) increases family tensions, and her persistent nighttime head-banging alienates apartment neighbors.
In the end, Mr. Oxley is the casualty, opting to
move out rather than accede to the engulfing demands Gerri's presence makes." Booklist

"Painful, honest, and convincing, this is quietly
written and very effective in evoking sympathy
and understanding for retarded children and for
their families." Chicago. Children's Bk Center

Simon, Marcia L.

A special gift. Harcourt 1978 132p $5.95
(5 and up)   **Fic**

1 Ballet dancers—Fiction 2 Sex role—Fiction
ISBN 0-15-277865-9   LC 78-4329

"Peter, a popular basketball player, also excels
at ballet studies with his sister, Elizabeth. But
he keeps his dance lessons a secret, for fear of
sharing the fate of ostracized fat Malcolm and
other classmates who don't conform. When Peter
wrenches a muscle and is on crutches, a nasty
bunch of kids corner him and Elizabeth and add
physical abuse to jeers of 'faggot' and other epi-
thets. But the gang is surprised when brother
and sister hold fast. Although the confrontation
hurts, it steels Peter's resolution to play a role
in 'The Nutcracker.'" Pub W

"The plot is interesting, the characters well
developed and three dimensional, and the writing,
good. . . . [This book] is just what . . . [boys
taking ballet] need to understand that they are
not alone, and that it's possible to survive growing up, even if their choice is the road less
taken." Sch Library J

Simon, Norma

We remember Philip; pictures by Ruth
Sanderson. Whitman, A. 1979 unp illus $3.94,
lib. bdg. $5.25 (2-4)   **Fic**

1 Death—Fiction 2 School stories
ISBN 0-8075-8709-5   LC 78-11691

"Concept books"
"After the accidental death of their teacher's
son, Sam and his classmates discuss their thoughts
with understanding parents and their principal.
During the rest of the year, the children find
ways to help their teacher. Though they never met
Philip, the children decide to plant a tree as a
special way of remembering him." Children's Bk
Rev Serv

"The pictures are softly drawn and realistic,
appropriate for the quiet and warmth of the
story, which makes a clear but not didactic statement about sharing grief." Chicago. Children's Bk
Center

Singer, Isaac Bashevis

The fools of Chelm and their history;
pictures by Uri Shulevitz; tr. by the author
and Elizabeth Shub. Farrar, Straus 1973 57p
illus $4.95 (3-6)   **Fic**

1 Jews—Fiction
ISBN 0-374-32444-1   LC 73-81500

The "town of Chelm is just like every place else,
only worse, as numerous shortages, foolish citizens,
and inept leaders combine to make life thoroughly
miserable. . . . Singer mocks the 'advantages'—
such as war, crime, and revolution—that civilization brings to Chelm, as the leadership changes
but never improves, passing from Gronam Ox to
Bunem Pokraka to Feitel Thief and, finally, to the
women of the town." Booklist

"Drawing loosely—very loosely—on [Jewish]
Chelm legendry, the author satirizes government,
politics, and human foibles in a story that should
have different meanings to readers of different ages
but that emerges for all readers as a smooth,
humorous narrative—an amusing story, well-told.
The pen-and-ink illustrations embellish the text,
adding droll touches of their own." Horn Bk

Singer, Marilyn

It can't hurt forever; illus. by Leigh Grant. Harper 1978 186p illus $7.95, lib. bdg. $8.79 (4 and up)   Fic

1 Hospitals—Fiction 2 Heart—Surgery—Fiction
ISBN 0-06-025681-8; 0-06-025682-6   LC 77-25657

"Ellie Simon enters the hospital for corrective heart surgery. Despite her parents' intelligent efforts to comfort her, she is afraid of the pain she anticipates and also of dying. She does find support from some of the nurses and from other young patients, but others exacerbate her fears either through lack of sensitivity or, in one instance, deliberately." Sch Library J

This first-person account "is strictly bibliotherapy but interesting enough nonetheless. Personality types are instantly recognizable—nice doctors, nurses, patients, and parents are offset by their mean or problematic counterparts. Emotional seesawing is correctly sketched, and the problems of befriended fellow patients introduce holding secondary story lines. Medical information generously sandwiched between story lines is interesting in its own right but will be especially relevant to youngsters themselves facing surgery for Ellie's 'pretty common' [condition] 'patent ductus arteriosus.' Effectively supportive." Booklist

Skurzynski, Gloria

What happened in Hamelin. Four Winds 1979 177p illus $7.95 (5 and up)   Fic

1 Thirteenth century—Fiction
ISBN 0-590-07625-6   LC 79-12814

"An adroitly crafted, believable story about the happenings in Hamelin, Germany, in 1284. Told through the eyes of Geist, an orphaned baker's apprentice, the narrative encompasses the 22 days of the stranger Gast's stay in the village. . . . Geist becomes the Piper's admirer and follower—and thus his conspirator in luring first the rats and then the children from the city. . . . Factual evidence, elaborated upon in an appended author's note, extends the authenticity yet never intrudes on the plot line. It is Skurzynski's attention to consistently and fully developed characters that adds the human complexity and gives a dimension that breathes life into this age-old legend." Booklist

Sleator, William

Into the dream; illus. by Ruth Sanderson. Dutton 1979 137p illus $7.50 (5 and up)   Fic

1 Extrasensory perception—Fiction 2 Psychokinesis—Fiction 3 Flying saucers—Fiction
ISBN 0-525-32583-2   LC 78-11825

The story "begins with Paul's recurring dream and his surprise when he finds that Francine, one of his classmates but not a friend, has been having the same dream. In their frightening dream, they are trying to reach a small child who is happily going toward a bright and curiously dangerous light. The two children discover that they can, to a limited extent, read each other's minds, and they agree that the child in their dream must also be telepathic; if they can find a common experience in their own lives, perhaps they can find who and where the child is. And that's the beginning of the final adventure, dangerous but successful." Chicago. Children's Bk Center

"Tightly woven suspense and an ingenious, totally involving plot line . . . make this a thriller of top-notch quality." Booklist

Slobodkin, Louis

The space ship under the apple tree. Macmillan Pub. Co. 1952 114p illus $6.95, pa $1.95 (3-5)   Fic

1 Science fiction
ISBN 0-02-785340-3; 0-02-045000-1   LC 52-14184

Illustrated by the author

"An ordinary summer vacation turns into high adventure when Eddie tracks what looks like a falling star to the old apple tree and finds a strange little man standing upside down on one of the branches." Bks for Deaf Children

"An entertaining blend of Boy Scout activities, pseudo science, and country fun." Hodges. Bks for Elem Sch Libraries

Some other books about Eddie and his friend Marty from the planet Martinea are also available from Macmillan Pub. Co.:

Round trip space ship $4.95 (ISBN 0-02-785400-0; LC 68-11007)

The space ship in the park $5.95 (ISBN 0-02-784700-4; LC 70-187799)
The space ship returns to the apple tree, pa $1.95 (ISBN 0-02-045010-9; LC 58-11080)
The three-seated space ship $5.95, pa $1.95 (ISBN 0-02-785480-9; 0-02-045020-6; LC 62-11357)

Slote, Alfred

Hang tough, Paul Mather. Lippincott 1973 156p $7.95 (4 and up)   Fic

1 Leukemia—Fiction 2 Little league baseball—Fiction
ISBN 0-397-31451-5   LC 72-11531

"When Paul begins his story, he is in the hospital and talking to his doctor. Very deftly the author makes it clear that Paul's prime interest in life is baseball; he's been a star [pitcher] on two Little League teams, and has just moved to town. Paul's retrospective account is without sentimentality or self-pity, but the tragic fact is that he has leukemia and knows it. He has, against orders, seized a chance to play baseball and it has exhausted him. There are some baseball scenes, but these are balanced by the family sequences and the conversations between Paul and Dr. Kinsella. Both the doctor-patient relationship and the bond between Paul and his younger brother are beautifully developed, and the story of Paul's candor and courage is convincing, sad but never morbid, in a book that has depth and integrity." Chicago. Children's Bk Center

Jake. Lippincott 1971 155p $4.95, pa $2.50 (4-6)   Fic

1 Little league baseball—Fiction 2 Blacks—Fiction
ISBN 0-397-31414-0; 0-397-31327-6   LC 72-151469

"An above-average sports story with a well-developed plot, nonstereotyped characterizations, and fast-paced baseball action. Jake is a self-reliant eleven-year-old [black boy] who lives with his young rock musician uncle, comes and goes when he wants, and virtually runs his Little League team, the Print-Alls. Jake's difficulties begin when the league president warns that the Print-Alls will be disbanded unless they have a male coach at each game and Jake's principal threatens to send him to a foster home. Both problems are eventually solved, but not without further complications for Jake and the team." Booklist

Matt Gargan's boy. Lippincott 1975 159p $6.95 (4 and up)   Fic

1 Baseball—Fiction 2 Divorce—Fiction
ISBN 0-397-31617-8   LC 74-26669

"Baseball-playing Danny Gargan's chief concern is keeping his divorced mother from dating other men so that when his father retires from major league baseball the two can get back together again. His plans begin to go awry with the appearance of the Warren family; not only does his mother obviously like Mr. Warren, a widower, but one of his daughters is a competent ballplayer who wants to try out for Danny's team. Danny's eventual coming to terms with situations that he cannot change is well handled; and Slote's able use of first-person narrative fosters some apt characterizations as well as added insight into the mechanics of Danny's diminishing egotistical and male chauvinistic streaks." Booklist

Smith, Alison

Reserved for Mark Anthony Crowder. Dutton 1978 123p lib. bdg. $7.95 (5 and up)   Fic

1 Family life—Fiction 2 Gardening—Fiction
ISBN 0-525-38199-6   LC 78-6460

"Mark, a very tall, smart, awkward, introspective scapegoated sixth grader, cannot seem to find a comfortable place for himself among his peers. His father, a local college coach, is very disappointed in his son's athletic ability, and although his mother is supportive, his real ally is Uncle Edward, who lives with the family. Mark gets into trouble both at home and at school, and his misery is very moving. As a punishment, he is directed to plant the family summer vegetable garden. With the help of Uncle Edward and the library, Mark makes a success of the garden, both personally and financially." Children's Bk Rev Serv

"A work of marked perception in character relationships. . . . Boyish responses with a certain humor add credibility and lighten the psychological overtones of the book." Horn Bk

Smith, Doris Buchanan

Kelly's creek; illus. by Alan Tiegreen. Crowell 1975 69p illus $7.95 (4-6)   **Fic**

1 Learning disabilities—Fiction 2 Marshes—Fiction
ISBN 0-690-00731-0   LC 75-6761

"A learning disability blocks Kelly's progress at school. His worried parents insist that he try harder to do his exercises and improve, and until he does, they make his daily sojourns to the nearby marsh off limits. Kelly finds the curb intolerable, for the marsh is the one place where he doesn't feel 'dumb.' He knows the terrain and with the help of Phillip, a marine biology student who is conducting a study there, has begun to learn about the wildlife surrounding him. Kelly's unique knowledge proves to be his saving grace: at Phillip's suggestion he displays his specimens and lectures to his class, achieving the success he needs to bolster his self-confidence and work to a break-through in his perception exercises. A simple story, perhaps resolved a little too easily, but instructive in its portrayal of a boy with learning problems and appealing enough to keep readers along for the story alone." Booklist

Kick a stone home. Crowell 1974 152p $6.95 (5 and up)   **Fic**

ISBN 0-690-00535-0   LC 74-4209

This book "brings to life Sara Jane Chambers, who at 15 struggles through and emerges triumphant from the early phases of sexuality and adulthood. Not an ordinary tomboy-turns-feminine story, this has real characters who develop believably in the current age, when it is not masculine for a girl like Sara to love sports and want to become a veterinarian, nor feminine for a close male friend to sympathize with her about a sadistic instructor. Satisfyingly romantic, yet closely concerned with the formation of Sara's new self-image." Booklist

A taste of blackberries; illus. by Charles Robinson. Crowell 1973 58p illus $7.95, lib. bdg. $7.89 (3-6)   **Fic**

1 Death—Fiction 2 Friendship—Fiction
ISBN 0-690-80511-X; 0-690-80512-8   LC 72-7558

A "portrayal of the death of a close friend. While gathering Japanese beetles to help a neighbor, Jamie is stung by a bee and falls screaming and writhing to the ground. His best friend (never named) disgustedly stalks off, only to find later that Jamie is dead of the bee sting. The boy feels guilty because he thought Jamie was clowning and didn't try to help. The boy is very withdrawn the week of the funeral, but comes to grips with the tragedy and learns to manage his grief." Sch Library J

"A difficult and sensitive subject, treated with taste and honesty, is woven into a moving story about a believable little boy. The black-and-white illustrations are honest, effective, and sensitive." Horn Bk

Snyder, Carol

Ike and Mama and the once-a-year suit; drawings by Charles Robinson. Coward, McCann & Geoghegan 1978 47p illus $5.95 (2-4)   **Fic**

1 Parent and child—Fiction 2 Shopping—Fiction
3 New York (City)—Fiction
ISBN 0-698-20436-0   LC 77-21429

"Ike and 13 other neighborhood boys troop down to Stanton Street for the dress suits that must last all year, Mama being recognized as the local clothing maven who can get the best outfit for the least money. Sure enough, she maneuvers her way around the shopkeeper, after threatening a walk-out, and gets each boy what he wants as well—even Ike's midnight-blue mohair." Booklist

"Set in the Bronx (N.Y.) in 1918, this charming and humorous little story, with its muted pencil drawings, will appeal to the young reader. The book's brevity and large-print text make this [suitable as] an 'early reader.'" Children's Bk Rev Serv

Followed by: Ike and Mama and the block wedding. Coward, McCann & Geoghegan $6.95 (ISBN 0-698-20461-1; LC 78-11702)

Snyder, Zilpha Keatley

Below the root; illus. by Alton Raible. Atheneum Pubs. 1975 231p illus $8.95 (5 and up)   **Fic**

1 Fantastic fiction
ISBN 0-689-30457-9   LC 74-19489

"The Kindar, who long ago came to their lush planet from devastated Earth, live in the peaceful, controlled world of Green Sky, a vertical world of cities and roadways made of the vines, branches, and treetrunks of a tall forest. The forest floor is forbidden territory for under it, held down by vine roots, live the dreaded Pash-Shan. Raamo, a curious 13-year-old boy, is selected with Genaa, a highly intelligent girl, to become an Ol-zhaan or priest. During his year of training Raamo begins to doubt the skills and wisdom of the Ol-zhaan, and when he, Genaa, and a young priest make the forbidden journey down to the earth, they come to realize the conformity and ignorance by which they are ruled. By story's end, however, Raamo has only just begun to trust his own judgment and visions and to understand that the evil he faces is complex and institutionalized." Sch Library J

"What may have extra appeal for today's readers is the philosophy with which the story is imbued: the detestation of war, the disapproval of killing animals for food, the belief that children can be brought up to develop their talents and to become men and women to whom brotherhood is not a word but a way of life." Chicago. Children's Bk Center

Followed by these books, also available from Atheneum Pubs.:
And all between $8.95 (ISBN 0-689-30514-1; LC 75-29315)
Until the celebration $7.95 (ISBN 0-689-30572-9; LC 76-40984)

The changeling; illus. by Alton Raible. Atheneum Pubs. 1970 220p illus $7.95, pa 95¢ (4 and up)   **Fic**

1 Friendship—Fiction
ISBN 0-689-20610-0; 0-689-70351-1   LC 79-11575

Martha was a shy seven-year-old when she met Ivy, the daughter of a disreputable, vagabond family. This story, told partly in flashbacks, tells about their "long friendship in which Ivy, wildly imaginative and firmly insisting she was a changeling, led in fanciful play—interspersed with some mischief. A natural dancer, Ivy was given the lead in a junior high play, and a jealous competitor made it appear that Ivy was the perpetrator of an act of vandalism. Although Martha's brother confessed that he and two others had been the culprits, Ivy left town. Only when she was a high school sophomore did Martha learn that Ivy was dancing in New York, and she became sharply aware that her own poise and popularity were due in large measure to the salubrious influence of Ivy's personality." Sutherland. The Best in Children's Bks

"Though the finale is weak, the story is distinguished by its vivid characterization and sensitive writing." Sat Rev

The Egypt game; drawings by Alton Raible. Atheneum Pubs. 1967 215p illus lib. bdg. $8.95, pa $2.95 (4 and up)   **Fic**

ISBN 0-689-30006-9; 0-689-70297-3   LC 67-2717

"Six children of different ethnic backgrounds secretly play a game invented by a white girl and a [black] girl who are fascinated by their own imaginations and by ancient Egypt. The Egypt game helps solve one girl's personal problems and it leads to the capture of a mentally ill murderer who attacks one of the girls." Wis Library Bul

"This may prove to be one of the controversial books of the decade: it is strong in characterization, the dialogue is superb, the plot is original, and the sequences in which the children are engaged in sustained imaginative play are fascinating, and often very funny. On the other hand, the murder scare and the taciturn, gloomy Professor seem grim notes. In this story, the fact that the children are white, [black], and Oriental seems not a device but a natural consequence of grouping in a heterogeneous community. [This] is a distinguished book." Sat Rev

Snyder, Zilpha K.—*Continued*

The headless cupid; illus. by Alton Raible. Atheneum Pubs. 1971 203p illus $8.95, pa $1.95 (4 and up)   **Fic**

1 Occult sciences—Fiction
ISBN 0-689-20687-9; 0-689-70414-3   LC 78-154763

"Amanda the 12-year-old daughter of their new stepmother, proclaims herself an expert in the occult and puts the Stanley children, 11-year-old David and his three younger siblings, through an initiation, a series of ritual ordeals, and a seance. The children learn that in 1896 their house had been the scene of poltergeist activity which culminated in the beheading of a carved cupid figure on the stairway. Thereafter it seems that the poltergeist has returned, but David proves that the manifestations are being caused by Amanda. However, in a final plot twist, the cupid's head is recovered through a genuine ESP experience. This is believable fiction—with a touch of fantasy—supported throughout by solid, three-dimensional characterizations." Sch Library J

Followed by: The famous Stanley kidnapping case. Atheneum Pubs. $8.95 (ISBN 0-689-30728-4; LC 79-12308)

The velvet room; drawings by Alton Raible. Atheneum Pubs. 1965 216p illus lib. bdg. $7.95, pa $1.95 (4-6)   **Fic**

1 Migrant labor—Fiction 2 Depressions, Economic—Fiction 3 California—Fiction
ISBN 0-689-30040-9; 0-689-70430-5   LC 65-10474

"Beset by the problems of growing up [in California during the Depression] in a migrant worker's family, Robin finds refuge from the real world in a deserted mansion with a book-lined room and a mysterious past." Adventuring With Bks. 2d edition

"Robin's character has far more facets than the usual sensitive child of fiction who needs a private place for dreaming. She is normally selfish and has a tough resilience behind her sensitivity. Her brothers and sisters are real children too. The reader, however, remembers not the realism of the rather stark tale of a migratory worker's family, but the magical aura through which an imaginative child sees the world. Illustrations characteristic of the artist reflect atmosphere and mood." Horn Bk

The witches of Worm; illus. by Alton Raible. Atheneum Pubs. 1972 183p illus $8.95, pa $2.95 (4 and up)   **Fic**

1 Witchcraft—Fiction 2 Cats—Fiction
ISBN 0-689-30066-2; 0-689-70426-7   LC 72-75283

Jessica, the neglected child of a swinging divorcee, "finds a deserted, new-born kitten which she calls 'Worm' since it is virtually hairless and blind. When this Worm turns—daily becoming more dominant over its mistress—Jessica is convinced she is in the grip of a hellish force that makes her play harmful tricks on her mother and on her few friends." Pub W

"This is a haunting story of the power of mind and ritual, as well as of misunderstanding, anger, loneliness and friendship. It is written with humor, pace, a sure feeling for conversation and a warm understanding of human nature." Commonweal

Sobol, Donald J.

Encyclopedia Brown, boy detective; illus. by Leonard Shortall. Elsevier/Nelson Bks. 1963 88p illus $5.95, pa $2.98 (3-5)   **Fic**

1 Mystery and detective stories
ISBN 0-525-67200-1; 0-525-67800-X   LC 63-9632

First published by Thomas Nelson
"Leroy Brown earns his nickname by applying his encyclopedic learning to community mysteries. The reader is asked to anticipate solutions before checking them in the back of the book." Adventuring With Bks. 2d edition

"The answers are logical; some are tricky, but there are no trick questions, and readers who like puzzles should enjoy the . . . challenge. The episodes are lightly humorous, brief, and simply written." Chicago. Children's Bk Center

Some other titles featuring Encyclopedia Brown are also available from Elsevier/Nelson Bks.:

Encyclopedia Brown and the case of the dead eagles $5.95, pa $2.98 (ISBN 0-525-67220-6; 0-525-67801-8; LC 75-15911)

Encyclopedia Brown and the case of the midnight visitor $5.95, pa $2.98 (ISBN 0-525-67221-4; 0-525-67806-9; LC 77-22159)

Encyclopedia Brown and the case of the secret pitch $5.95, pa $2.98 (ISBN 0-525-67202-8; 0-525-67808-5; LC 65-19640)

Encyclopedia Brown finds the clues $5.95, pa $2.98 (ISBN 0-525-67204-4; 0-525-67802-6; LC 66-10230)

Encyclopedia Brown gets his man $5.95, pa $2.98 (ISBN 0-525-67206-0; 0-525-67803-4; LC 67-24666)

Encyclopedia Brown keeps the peace $5.95, pa $2.98 (ISBN 0-525-67208-7; 0-525-67804-2; LC 73-82912)

Encyclopedia Brown lends a hand $5.95, pa $2.98 (ISBN 0-525-67218-4; 0-525-67805-0; LC 74-10281)

Encyclopedia Brown saves the day $5.95, pa $2.98 (ISBN 0-525-67210-9; 0-525-67807-7; LC 71-117149)

Encyclopedia Brown shows the way $5.95, pa $2.98 (ISBN 0-525-67216-8; 0-525-67809-3; LC 72-2911)

Encyclopedia Brown solves them all $5.95, pa $2.98 (ISBN 0-525-67212-5; 0-525-67810-7; LC 68-22746)

Encyclopedia Brown takes the case $5.95, pa $2.98 (ISBN 0-525-66818-5; 0-525-67811-5; LC 73-6443)

Encyclopedia Brown tracks them down $5.95, pa $2.98 (ISBN 0-525-67214-1; 0-525-67812-3; LC 77-160147)

Sorensen, Virginia

Miracles on Maple Hill; illus. by Beth and Joe Krush. Harcourt 1956 180p illus $5.95, pa $1.95 (4 and up)   **Fic**

1 Family life—Fiction
ISBN 0-15-254558-1; 0-15-660440-X   LC 56-8358

Awarded the Newbery Medal, 1957
"Ever since Father had returned from a [war] prison camp, weary, hurt and discouraged, home had been an unhappy place with everyone irritable and worried. Hoping that the outdoor life would help Father, ten-year-old Marly, who believed in miracles, and her family moved from the city to Maple Hill to open and live in Grandmother's old Pennsylvania farmhouse. This heartwarming, memorable family story tells of the miracles that happened during a year from one sugaring time to the next—the miracles of nature and the changing seasons, wonderful neighbors, and, best of all, Father's steady improvement and the family's drawing together again in understanding and happiness." Booklist

Southall, Ivan

Ash Road. Greenwillow Bks. [1978 c1965] 184p $7.50, lib. bdg. $7.20 (5 and up)   **Fic**

1 Forest fires—Fiction 2 Australia—Fiction
ISBN 0-688-80135-8; 0-688-84135-X   LC 77-15063

First published 1965 in Australia. First American edition published 1966 by St Martin's Press

"On a hot gusty summer Saturday a bushfire brings death, destruction and near despair to the families living on Ash Road in the Australian foothills. It is an unforgettable day of crisis for a group of children who find themselves alone at home in the fire's path. Mr. Southall traces the inexorable spread of the fire by constantly shifting focus from the older boys who carelessly started it to the children and to the worried adults. . . . Miraculously, the children—and the others—survive, tempered and matured by their ordeal." NY Times Bk Rev

"The reader is swept up in the panic and despair of a world on fire, a world in which humans clutching for survival display their best and worst traits. The mounting dramatic suspense holds interest until the last page. There is little character development, and the conversations are sometimes stilted. Despite this, the author is a master in pacing a story which grips the reader." Library J

Hills End. Macmillan Pub. Co. [1974 c1962] 215p $5.95 (6 and up)   **Fic**

1 Australia—Fiction
ISBN 0-02-786120-1   LC 63-15002

First published 1962 in Australia. This is a reissue of the first American edition published 1963 by St Martins

"Few ever missed the annual picnic of Hills End. This year, because of a fabricated tale of prehistoric drawings, seven children are not going. Instead they find themselves climbing up to the caves high above the town, led by their teacher, Miss Godwin, who had planned to explore alone. These events, however, combine to save the lives of the people of Hills End when a sudden, violent storm threatens to devastate the town, maroon their families, and trap the children in the caves." Rdng Ladders. 5th edition

Southall, Ivan—*Continued*

"Australian adventure with a difference. . . . In plot, a cross between 'Robinson Crusoe' and a happy-ending 'Lord of the Flies.' The background and touches of dialect set the scene adequately. . . . The handling of pace and incident is excellent." Library J

Speare, Elizabeth George

The bronze bow. Houghton 1961 255p $7.95, pa $2.45 (6 and up)   **Fic**

1 Jesus Christ—Fiction 2 Palestine—Fiction
3 Christianity—Fiction
ISBN 0-395-07113-5; 0-395-13719-5   LC 61-10640

Awarded the Newbery Medal, 1962
"A book about the days of the early Christians. A vividly written story of a young Jewish rebel who was won over to the gentle teachings of Jesus. Daniel had sworn vengeance against the Romans who had killed his parents, and he had become one of a band of outlaws. Forced to return to the village to care for his sister, Daniel found ways—dangerous ways—to work against the Roman soldiers. Each time he saw the Rabbi Jesus, the youth was drawn to his cause; at last he resolved his own conflict by giving up his hatred and, as a follower of the Master, accepting his enemies. The story has drama and pace, fine characterization, and colorful background detail; the theme of conflict and conversion is handled with restraint and perception." Chicago. Children's Bk Center

"While the figure of Jesus remains in the background, with some free quotation of scripture, he is also the catalyst in this moving, vivid, and well-written picture of the spiritual vs. the material, vengeance vs. love." Library J

The witch of Blackbird Pond. Houghton 1958 249p $6.95 (6 and up)   **Fic**

1 Wichcraft—Fiction 2 Puritans—Fiction 3 Connecticut—Fiction
ISBN 0-395-07114-3   LC.58-11063

Awarded the Newbery Medal, 1959
"Headstrong and undisciplined, Barbados-bred Kit Tyler is an embarrassment to her Puritan relatives, and her sincere attempts to aid a reputed witch soons bring her to trial as a suspect." Children's Bks Too Good to Miss

"Three satisfactorily concluded romances run through this absorbing story [set in Connecticut]. The New England of colonial times—of candle-dipping, soap-boiling, and corn-husking bees—is realistically drawn as background for a solidly written character study." Horn Bk

Sperry, Armstrong

Call it courage; illus. by the author. Macmillan Pub. Co. 1940 95p illus lib. bdg. $4.95, pa 95¢ (5 and up)   **Fic**

1 Polynesia—Fiction
ISBN 0-02-786030-2; 0-02-045060-5   LC 40-4229

Awarded the Newbery Medal, 1941
"Because he fears the ocean, a Polynesian boy is scorned by his people and must redeem himself by an act of courage. His lone journey to a sacred island and the dangers he faces there earn him the name Mafatu, 'Stout Heart.' Dramatic illustrations add atmosphere and mystery." Hodges. Bks for Elem Sch Libraries

Spykman, E. C.

A lemon and a star. Harcourt 1955 214p $5.95 (5 and up)   **Fic**

1 Family life—Fiction
ISBN 0-15-244713-X   LC 55-7614

"An understanding and honest portrayal of childhood in the story of four motherless children who live with their father and servants in a country home near Charlottesville in the early 1900's. Theodore, thirteen, the tyrannical older brother, Hubert who is only eight but knows a thing or two, Edie the spoiled little sister, and sensitive ten-year-old Jane who is the main character, are living, memorable children; their day-to-day lives are as full and adventurous as their energies and imaginations can make them. The thoroughly satisfying story ends with the father's remarriage and the children's reactions to the warm, wise stepmother." Booklist

Followed by these books, also available from Harcourt:

Terrible, horrible Edie $6.50, pa $2.95 (ISBN 0-15-284788-X; 0-15-688650-2; LC 60-8412)
Edie on the warpath pa $2.50 (ISBN 0-15-627650-X; LC 66-14797)

Spyri, Johanna

Heidi (4-6)   **Fic**

1 Alps—Fiction 2 Switzerland—Fiction

Some editions are:
Dent (Children's illustrated classics) Illustrated with 8 colour plates and line drawings by Vincent O. Cohen $9 (ISBN 0-460-05013-3; LC 52-8405)
Grosset (Illustrated junior lib.) $5.95 (ISBN 0-448-05812-X)
Macmillan Pub. Co. (The Macmillan classics) $4.95 Afterword by Clifton Fadiman; illustrated by Greta Elgaard (ISBN 0-02-786550-9; LC 62-18396)
Raintree Childrens Bks. (Raintree's Illustrated classics) lib. bdg. $7.99 (ISBN 0-8393-6206-4; LC 78-5489)
First published 1880
"The story of Heidi is the story of the greatness of her affection for her pet goats, for Peter and her grandfather, and for her mountain home. Permeating the whole tale is the play of sunshine and shadow on the slopes of the jagged peaks of the great, glittering, snow-capped mountains of Heidi's [Swiss] Alpine home. A book which finds a responsive chord in every young heart." Toronto

Stearns, Pamela

The mechanical doll; illus. by Trina Schart Hyman. Houghton 1979 45p illus $6.95 (4-6)   **Fic**

1 Dolls—Fiction 2 Middle East—Fiction 3 Fairy tales
ISBN 0-395-27809-0   LC 78-24351

"King Kultan-dai cherishes his life-sized mechanical doll, Tariim, more than all the treasures in his kingdom. Wicked Prince Boan twits Hulun the musician for losing his favored place to the dancing toy, and Hulun breaks Tariim in a jealous fit. Banished by the king, the musician wanders contrite and disconsolate until chance brings him Tariim's fragments. Carefully, he reconstructs the doll but Boan kills Hulun, steals the new creation and presents it to Kultan-dai. The truth, however, comes out and the story . . . ends with a scene of retribution and a miracle." Pub W

The author "brings a folkloric mood to this original telling of a thought-provoking yet exciting story. Hyman's sensitive brown line drawings add depth." Booklist

Steele, William O.

The lone hunt; illus. by Paul Galdone. Harcourt 1956 176p illus $6.75, pa $1.75 (5 and up)   **Fic**

1 Frontier and pioneer life—Fiction 2 Tennessee—Fiction
ISBN 0-15-248293-8; 0-15-652983-1   LC 56-10074

"Smarting at being forever tied down at home by what he considered girls' chores, Yance Caywood, eleven, was overjoyed to be allowed to join the hunt organized to track down a buffalo, the first one seen in Tennessee for 30 years. When one by one the men turned back, Yance slipped off alone into the frozen wilderness determined to bring in the buffalo or die trying. The story of the boy's lone hunt and his yearning for independence is . . . sharply real and . . . gripping." Booklist

The magic amulet. Harcourt 1979 114p $6.95 (4-6)   **Fic**

1 Man, Prehistoric—Fiction
ISBN 0-15-250427-3   LC 78-20573

This "is the story of young Tragg. Following its tribal code, Tragg's nomadic family abandons him to die when he is severely wounded by a saber-toothed tiger. They leave him with only a spear and his uncle's carved-bone bracelet or amulet. Tragg is determined to live, and we follow him as he regains strength, finds another tribe and a life of continuing danger and survival—perhaps due to the powers of the amulet. . . . The book is set in prehistoric times in southeastern North America." Babbling Bookworm

"The story, which conveys a strong sense of primitive life, is filled with turbulent episodes: encounters with animals, the antagonism of ill-disposed human beings, and a stampede of mammoths. At the same time, the protagonist's thoughts and feelings contribute considerably to the intensity of the narrative." Horn Bk

Steele, William O.—*Continued*

The perilous road; illus. by Paul Galdone. Harcourt 1958 191p illus $6.25, pa $1.95 (5 and up) **Fic**

1 U.S.—History—Civil War, 1861-1865—Fiction
2 Tennessee—Fiction
ISBN 0-15-260644-0; 0-15-671696-8   LC 58-6820

"Ten-year-old Chris, enraged when the Yankees raid his father's farm and baffled when his older brother joins the Northern Army, tries to aid the Confederacy in every possible way. Only when his spy report threatens his brother's life and he himself is caught in a cavalry raid does he realize the meaning of his father's words, 'war is the worst thing that can happen to folks.'" Library J

"Mr. Steele makes the tensions and excitements of the Brothers' War very real, and the customs of the mountain people, the speech and setting are well integrated into the narrative." NY Times Bk Rev

Wilderness journey; illus. by Paul Galdone. Harcourt 1953 209p illus $6.75 (4-6) **Fic**

1 Frontier and pioneer life—Fiction
ISBN 0-15-297318-4   LC 55-9006

A "lively picture of frontier days in the story of a boy who journeys over the Wilderness Trail to the French Salt Lick in the company of a Long Hunter. Small for his age and as 'unhandy as all git,' ten-year-old Flan agreed with the general opinion that he was not much account. On the dangerous trek through the wilderness Flan discovered that size was often less important than quick wit and endurance and that what mattered most was knowing you could do what you had to do." Booklist

Steig, William

Abel's island. Farrar, Straus 1976 117p illus $5.95 (3-6) **Fic**

1 Mice—Fiction 2 Survival (after airplane accidents, shipwrecks, etc.)—Fiction
ISBN 0-374-30010-0   LC 75-35918

"Abel is a mouse who lives in cultured comfort on an inherited income and dotes on his bride Amanda. Ever gentlemanly, Abel leaves the safety of a cave (they've taken shelter while on a picnic) to rescue Amanda's gauzy scarf. He is swept off by wind and rain, catapulted into a torrent of water, and lands on an island. This is really sort of a Robinson Crusoe Tale, as the heretofore pampered and indolent Abel learns to cope with solitude, find food and shelter, avoid a predatory owl, and eventually find his way back—a year later—to his loving wife and luxurious home." Chicago. Children's Bk Center

"Over and above the imperturbable dignity of the style, there are moments of compensating wit, as when we are told that Abel 'had studied mushrooms in Souris's "Botany" at home' or that he 'estimated the island to be about 12,000 tails long, 5,000 wide.' The line drawings washed with gray faithfully and delightfully record not only the rigors of Abel's experiences but the refinement of his domestic existence." Horn Bk

Dominic; story and pictures by William Steig. Farrar, Straus 1972 145p illus $6.95 (4-6) **Fic**

1 Dogs—Fiction
ISBN 0-374-31822-0   LC 70-188272

Dominic, a gregarious dog, sets out on the high road one day, going no place in particular, but moving along to find whatever he can. And that turns out to be plenty, including an invalid pig who leaves Dominic his fortune; a variety of friends and adventures; and even—in the end—his life's companion

"A singular blend of naïveté and sophistication, comic commentary and philosophizing, the narrative handles situation clichés with humor and flair—perhaps because of the author's felicitous turn of phrase, his verbal cartooning, and his integration of text and illustrations. A chivalrous and optimistic tribute to gallantry and romance." Horn Bk

The real thief; story and pictures by William Steig. Farrar, Straus 1973 58p illus $4.95 (2-5) **Fic**

1 Animals—Fiction 2 Robbers and outlaws—Fiction
ISBN 0-374-36217-3   LC 73-77910

"Proud of his job as guard to the Royal Treasury, loyal to his king (Basil the bear) Gawain the goose is baffled by the repeated theft of gold and jewels from the massive building to which only Gawain and Basil have keys. He is heartsick when the king dismisses him publicly and calls him a disgrace to the kingdom. Sentenced to prison, the goose flies off to isolation. The true thief, a mouse, is penitent and decides that he will go on stealing so that the king will know Gawain is innocent; still suffering guilt, he takes back the loot piece by piece, searches for Gawain, and confesses. They decide to keep it secret, but Gawain goes back to accept royal apologies and greater status than before." Chicago. Children's Bk Center

"For young readers or listeners, it's an involving story with animal characters displaying more real emotions than many supposedly human characters. Steig's gray line-and-wash drawings provide a charming accompaniment to a wholly winning story." Sch Library J

Steptoe, John

Train ride. Harper 1971 unp illus $8.95, lib. bdg. $8.79 (3-6) **Fic**

1 New York (City)—Fiction 2 Blacks—Fiction
ISBN 0-06-025773-3; 0-06-025774-1   LC 70-146001

Illustrated by the author

"Having boasted about his familiarity with New York City transport, Charlie can hardly refuse when some of his friends suggest going to Times Square. The boys enjoy the sights, see more white people than they ever did in Brooklyn, enjoy the brightness and the penny arcade. Their money gone, they wheedle free rides and get home to the beatings they had realized were coming. Next day, they decide they won't go again—but it was worth it. . . . The illustrations are stunning, vibrant with color and effective in composition. The story has an all-boy quality: contempt for girls, the relish of a ploy, the fellowship and resourcefulness that emerge particularly when children function as a group. The writing style is adequate, livened only by the cadence of black idiom, a fact that will make the book welcome to some and anathema to others." Chicago. Children's Bk Center

Stevenson, Robert Louis

Treasure Island (6 and up) **Fic**

1 Buried treasure—Fiction 2 Pirates—Fiction
Some editions are:
Dent (Children's illustrated classics) $11 Illustrated by S. Van Abbé (ISBN 0-460-05001-X)
Raintree Childrens Bks. (Raintree's illustrated classics) lib. bdg. $7.99 (ISBN 0-8393-6211-0; LC 78-3553)
Schocken lib. bdg. $9.95, pa $4.95 Drawings by Mervyn Peake (ISBN 0-8052-3707-0; 0-8052-0620-5; LC 78-74610)

First published 1882

Young Jim Hawkins discovers a treasure map in the chest of an old sailor who dies under mysterious circumstances at his mother's inn. He shows it to Dr. Livesey and Squire Trelawney who agree to outfit a ship and sail to Treasure Island. Among the crew are the pirate Long John Silver and his followers who are in pursuit of the treasure. After dangerous encounters, their mutiny is thwarted and the treasure is recovered with the aid of Ben Gunn, a sailor marooned by the pirates long ago and believed dead

"A masterpiece among romances. . . . Pew, Black Dog, and Long John Silver are a villainous trio, strongly individualized, shedding an atmosphere of malignancy and terror. The scenery of isle and ocean contrasts vividly with the savagery of the action." Baker's Best

Stevenson, William

The bushbabies; illus. by Victor Ambrus. Houghton 1965 278p illus $8.95 (4 and up) **Fic**

1 Kenya—Fiction
ISBN 0-395-07116-X   LC 65-22509

"Jackie, the daughter of an English game warden, discovers she has lost the permit necessary to take her pet tarsier or bushbaby out of Africa. Enlisting the help of Tembo, an African headman, she leaves the ship to return her pet to his native Kenya. A hazardous and suspenseful journey follows." Wis Library Bul

This is "a most unusual story, both in the setting and in the beautifully built-up relationship between two people disparate in age, sex, race, and station." Chicago. Children's Bk Center

Stewart, A. C.

Silas and Con. Atheneum Pubs. 1977 119p
$5.95 (5 and up)   **Fic**

1 Scotland—Fiction
ISBN 0-689-50086-6   LC 77-23318

"A Margaret K. McElderry book"

"Ten-year-old Silas, abandoned by his uncaring
mother and cruel stepfather, sets off across the
Scottish plains with Con, a scruffy stray dog, and
Tip, a toy monkey. . . . After experiencing life in
a town and on a farm, Silas takes off again,
rescuing a heifer (the mother of a stillborn calf)
from the market wagon and, as a gesture that
marks a turning point, leaving the toy monkey in
her place. His next destination is an island owned
by a legless one-eyed man who calls Silas 'little
Moses' and treats the boy with patience and generosity." Sch Library J

"A haunting, multidimensional story which, because of its allusive style and subtle symbolism,
can be introduced to older as well as to intermediate readers." Horn Bk

Stewart, Mary

The little broomstick; illus. by Shirley
Hughes. Morrow 1972 [c1971] 192p illus lib.
bdg. $6.96 (3-6)   **Fic**

1 Witches—Fiction   2 Great Britain—Fiction
ISBN 0-688-31507-0   LC 77-168476

First published 1971 in England

"Ten-year-old Mary is bored and lonely during
her holiday at her great-aunt's house in Shrop-
shire, England, until she befriends a black cat,
discovers a rare flower in the woods, and accidentally rubs the handle of a small birch broomstick with the flower. The broom springs to life,
carrying Mary and her cat to a mysterious school
for witches where the cat is borrowed for transformation experiments and Mary has to become a
practitioner of magic and spells to rescue him."
Booklist

Stolz, Mary

Belling the tiger; pictures by Beni
Montresor. Harper 1961 64p illus lib.
bdg. $6.89 (1-3)   **Fic**

1 Mice—Fiction
ISBN 0-06-025811-X   LC 61-5776

"Asa and Rambo, the two youngest and least
important mice of a waterfront house, are assigned
the job of belling the cat. They have just obtained,
with great difficulty, a belled collar when they are
chased onto a ship by a cat and sail off to a
strange land. The diverting tale, effectively illustrated with charming black-and-white drawings,
tells how the timid mice bell not a cat but a tiger,
frighten an elephant, and, back home, demand that
they be elevated to pantry mice." Booklist

By the highway home. Harper 1971 194p
$8.95, lib. bdg. $8.79 (6 and up)   **Fic**

1 Family life—Fiction
ISBN 0-06-025830-6; 0-06-025831-4   LC 71-159406

"Thirteen-year-old Catty Reed's world is upset:
her beloved older brother Beau has been killed in
Vietnam and no one talks about him or is happy
anymore; her father, a chemical engineer, loses
his job and cannot find work; and the family must
sell the house and move to Vermont where they
will help Catty's uncle run his inn. Characters—
particularly Catty, her beautiful, self-centered
older sister, her lovable little brother, her parents,
and Beau—and family relationships are uncommonly
well drawn in the perceptive and refreshing story
of the Reed family's individual adjustments to the
changing situation and new life." Booklist

Cat in the mirror. Harper 1975 199p $8.95,
lib. bdg. $8.79 (5 and up)   **Fic**

1 Fantastic fiction   2 Space and time—Fiction
3 Egypt—Fiction
ISBN 0-06-025832-2; 0-06-025833-0   LC 75-6307

"An Ursula Nordstrom book"

"Teen-aged Erin is scorned by her classmates,
dubbed 'Blowfish Gandy,' because of her habit
of filling her cheeks with air, a nervous reaction
to tension. At home, Erin is miserable because
her chic mother has no time for her. In fact, the
girl has only one friend, her father, until she meets
in school Seti, an Egyptian youth. Later, she is
visiting the Egyptian room of the Metropolitan
Museum when she hears her classmates saying

cruel things about her. In despair, Erin runs and
hits her head against a mastaba (the covering of
a burial pit) and is instantly in ancient Egypt.
Known there as Irun, the girl is among counterparts of her modern contemporaries." Pub W

"There is impressive realism in the tightly constructed story, in which the details complete the
symmetry, speech anachronisms help to unite the
two parts of the story, and analogies and transitions are apt and smooth. Erin-Irun is a lovable,
eager, and interesting child; however, it is the
human relationships so sharply drawn and continued across time that make the story unique."
Horn Bk

A dog on Barkham Street; pictures by
Leonard Shortall. Harper 1960 184p illus lib.
bdg. $7.89 (4-6)   **Fic**

1 Dogs—Fiction
ISBN 0-06-025841-1   LC 60-5787

"Fifth-grader Edward Frost has two seemingly
insurmountable problems—to rid himself of the
constant tormenting by the bully who lives next
door and to convince his parents that he is responsible enough to have a dog. It is the coming of
his irresponsible vagabond uncle with a beautiful
young collie that precipitates the solution of Edward's problems." Booklist

"Simple, everyday events and very familiar
people make up this story, but there is nothing
ordinary about the way those ingredients are
assembled. . . . This author has a remarkable
ability to get inside her characters, whether they
are young boys, adolescent girls, parents or hobos,
and the result in this book is a reading experience
as sharp as reality." Horn Bk

Followed by: The bully of Barkham Street.
Harper lib. bdg. $8.79 (ISBN 0-06-025821-7; LC 63-
9090). Also available in a large print edition for
$7.50 (ISBN 0-06-025823-3)

The edge of next year. Harper 1974 195p
lib. bdg. $8.79 (6 and up)   **Fic**

1 Death—Fiction   2 Family life—Fiction   3 Alcoholics—Fiction
ISBN 0-06-025858-6   LC 74-3587

"An Ursula Nordstrom book"

"The Woodwards were a happy family. Orin
was fourteen and Victor ten the October day the
car skidded after avoiding a driver in the wrong
lane, the day that their mother was killed. And
after that, their father slowly, steadily immersed
himself in drinking until he knew that he might
lose his job, knew that he must get help. The
story ends on a realistically hopeful note, but for
all three Woodwards it has been a slow, painful
adjustment—not only to bereavement but to the
ways in which each of them reacted." Chicago.
Children's Bk Center

Ferris wheel. Harper 1977 131p $7.95 lib.
bdg. $7.89, pa $1.95 (4-6)   **Fic**

1 Family life—Fiction   2 Vermont—Fiction
ISBN 0-06-025859-4; 0-06-025860-8; 0-06-440112-X
     LC 76-41511

"An Ursula Nordstrom book"

This book is "about a Vermont nine-year-old
whose best friend moves to California and whose
strong temper puts her at constant odds with a
younger brother. Her family is loving and supportive, however, and in the end Polly has the
maturity to reach out to an unhappy neighbor her
own age. There is more theme than plot, but the
characters and relationships are well drawn, the
dialogue runs smoothly, and the setting is comfortably deep-rooted." Booklist

Go and catch a flying fish. Harper 1979
213p $7.95, lib. bdg. $7.89 (5 and up)   **Fic**

1 Family life—Fiction
ISBN 0-06-025867-5; 0-06-025868-3   LC 78-21785

"An Ursula Nordstrom book"

This "novel reveals the intensities of feeling of
the thirteen-year-old girl Taylor, her younger
brother Jem, and little B.J. as they view their
parents' disintegrating marriage. Taylor's consuming interest in birds and Jem's equally intense
devotion to marine creatures do not compensate
for missing their mother when she leaves their
Florida home 'to get away and have some space
and think things over'; but B.J. is inconsolable,
and the older children attempt with supreme sensitivity to fill his needs. The picture of their
courageous and sensible reliance on each other
and their intelligent interest in ecology (they deplore ' "the murdered body of Florida" ') make the
story remarkable." Horn Bk

Stolz, Mary—*Continued*

The noonday friends. Harper 1965 182p illus lib. bdg. $7.89, pa $1.95 (4-6)   Fic
1 Family life—Fiction 2 Friendship—Fiction 3 New York (City)—Fiction
ISBN 0-06-025946-9; 0-06-440009-3   LC 65-20257
Illustrated by Louis S. Glanzman
"Franny hated qualifying for a free school lunch ticket, never having enough to wear, having to hurry home to care for her little brother; but nothing seemed to bother her twin brother Jim. Their father had trouble keeping a job, their mother had to work, and Franny's home duties meant that the desired friendship with a classmate became largely a noonday affair shared over lunch. This memorable story of children in Greenwich Village illustrates their reactions to problems, families, and each other." Moorachian. What is a City?
This is "a realistic story of the family relationship and school life of a little girl in a lower middle-class urban family." Univ. of Chicago. Reading

A wonderful, terrible time; pictures by Louis S. Glanzman. Harper 1967 182p illus lib. bdg. $7.89 (4-6)   Fic
1 Camps—Fiction 2 Blacks—Fiction 3 New York (City)—Fiction
ISBN 0-06-026064-5   LC 67-21573
"Sue Ellen and Mady are enjoying a comfortable summer with doll parties, walks through the dimestore, and cooling half hours at the open fire hydrant when they receive the unexpected gift of two weeks away at camp." Booklist
"A good book as a camp story or as a picture of friendship values, but the most striking aspect is the fact that both at home and at camp, the girls are in a racially mixed community where integration is not The Issue of the book. Mady and Sue Ellen are both [black]; while this is a fact that enters naturally into the dialogue, it is a minor fact compared to the importance of personalities and familial relationships." Chicago. Children's Bk Center

Storr, Catherine

Clever Polly and the stupid wolf with illus. by Marjorie-Ann Watts. [2d ed] Faber & Faber 1979 95p illus $7.95 (2-4)   Fic
1 Wolves—Fiction
ISBN 0-571-18011-6

First published 1955 in England
"Tongue-in-cheek adventures of Polly and a pursuing wolf who wants to eat her in the manner of the best-known wolves of folklore. As he imitates the methods of one after another, Polly continues to outwit him until, in the end, it appears he will be picking daisies forever in an effort to get them to 'tell him he can have her.' . . . This is old-fashioned and British in tone but very funny for reading aloud and enhanced with perky black-and-white pencil sketches." Sch Library J

Streatfeild, Noel

Ballet shoes; illus. by Richard Floethe. Random House 1937 249p illus lib. bdg. $6.99 (4-6)   Fic
1 Ballet—Fiction 2 Theater—Fiction 3 London—Fiction
ISBN 0-394-90875-9   LC 37-4081

First published 1936 in England
Three little girls attend the Children's Academy of Dancing in London to train for the professional stage. Petrova prefers the mechanics of automobiles and airplanes, but Pauline becomes a promising young actress and Posy shows great skill as a dancer
"The author has made real a section of life too often distorted by fiction. By pointing out some of the things which make up stage magic, she has done a real service to the theater for its young audience." NY Her Trib Bks

Thursday's child; illus. by Peggy Fortnum. Random House [1971 c1970] 275p illus $4.50 lib. bdg. $5.99 (4 and up)   Fic
1 Orphans—Fiction 2 Great Britain—Fiction
ISBN 0-394-82096-7; 0-394-92096-1   LC 71-123073

First published 1970 in England
Ten-year-old Margaret Thursday, an "orphan of turn-of-the-century England refuses to be subdued by anybody—or anything. For openers, she becomes the first runaway from St. Luke's orphanage [taking two little orphan boys with her;] the first girl to work as a 'legger' on the canals; and as the story ends she has started a career as actress (playing Little Lord Fauntleroy) . . . with a repertory theater group." Best Sellers
"Although the setting and situations are in the turn-of-the-century tradition of 'orphan stories,' the heroine is a remarkably contemporary character whose final decision to remain independent of her would-be benefactors is logical and consistent with a fully realized personality. A fresh and sprightly addition to a perennially popular genre." Horn Bk

When the sirens wailed; illus. by Judith Gwyn Brown. Random House 1976 176p illus $5.95, lib. bdg. $6.99 (4 and up)   Fic
1 World War, 1939-1945—Fiction 2 Great Britain—Fiction
ISBN 0-394-82096-7; 0-394-93147-5   LC 75-38326
First published 1974 in England with title: When the siren wailed
"With the onset of World War II, London's schoolchildren are evacuated to 'safe' areas in the country; Streatfeild's story follows the fortunes of the [three] Clark children, . . . poor but spirited south Londoners who find themselves in Dorset under the guardianship of a Colonel Stranger Stranger, an upright country squire. Initially there is a clash of life-styles but also a mutual respect of sorts. . . . When the squire's death threatens to land the children with Miss Justworthy, the disliked local billeting officer, they determinedly make their way home to a besieged London, only to find their home gone and their mother missing. . . . The happy ending Streatfeild fashions could be called contrived, but it's satisfying—enough within the realm of possibility to be believed and certainly fitting Streatfeild's well-developed sense of the storytelling craft." Booklist

Street, James H.

Good-bye, my Lady. Lippincott 1954 222p $9.95 (5 and up)   Fic
1 Dogs—Fiction 2 Mississippi—Fiction
ISBN 0-397-00049-9   LC 54-9416
"Skeeter, a swamp boy who lives with his Uncle Jess in Mississippi, finds a rare breed of hunting dog lost in the swamps, trains it, and grows to love it. Through his own desire to keep the dog, he comes to see and understand the hidden desires in the lives of those around him. With the help of his uncle, he decides that he must return Lady to her rightful owner. Thus he crosses the first hurdle in the maturing process and the search for values." Rdng Ladders

Strete, Craig Kee

When grandfather journeys into winter; illus by Hal Frenck. Greenwillow Bks. 1979 86p illus $6.95, lib. bdg. $6.67 (3-6)   Fic
1 Indians of North America—Fiction 2 Grandfathers—Fiction 3 Death—Fiction
ISBN 0-688-80193-5; 0-688-84193-7   LC 78-14830
"The story of a native American child, Little Thunder, and the old man Tayhua, who is his grandfather and who has also served as father and teacher to the boy. Tayhua, with his caustic wit and wry humor, scorns the white man but concedes that Little Thunder must learn what he can in the white man's school. Tayhua watches other men, white and Indian, try for five hundred dollars as a reward for riding a dangerous, untamed horse; he tells the white owner that he will ride the horse if he can have the animal [for Little Thunder] rather than the money. In a magnificent display of courage and tenacity, he breaks the horse, but the ride is difficult and Tayhua old and frail—and he dies. . . . Little Thunder tearfully sits by his dying grandfather's bedside to have a last talk and to understand that death is a part of life." Chicago. Children's Bk Center
The author "writes in dramatic scenes that could almost be played on stage. . . . Each of these scenes will raise thought and discussion concerning the cultural differences between native American and white. A kind of broad-joke humor is threaded in with the sadness here; neither dominates the ultimate dignity of the old man's spirit." Booklist

Suhl, Yuri

Uncle Misha's partisans. Four Winds 1973
221p $6.95 (5 and up)   **Fic**

1 World War, 1939-1945—Fiction   2 Jews in the
Ukraine—Fiction   3 Ukraine—Fiction
ISBN 0-590-07295-1   LC 73-76459

"The exploits of a twelve-year-old Ukrainian
boy, Motele, are modeled from an actual group of
resistance fighters during the Second World War.
Orphaned by the Nazis, Motele is harbored in the
forest of the partisans. As he joins their perilous
missions, his skill in playing the violin causes him
to be sent on a dangerous assignment which involves striking a blow at the Nazis and thus
avenging the death of his family." Top of the
News

"Richly detailed, convincing, and consistently
told from a twelve-year-old's point of view, the
account has immediacy, poignancy, strong character interest, and suspense." Horn Bk

Sunderlin, Sylvia

Antrim's orange; illus. by Diane de Groat.
Scribner 1976 57p illus lib. bdg. $6.95 (3-5)
     Fic

1 Orange—Fiction
ISBN 0-684-14497-2   LC 75-21636

"The gift of an orange is a rare event in Antrim's life because fruit is scarce in war-torn England. His grandmother from London brings the
treat, and Antrim is so overwhelmed he cannot
eat it. Showing it to his friends, to the gardener,
and to his teacher, he glories in their admiration.
Then while playing, Antrim accidentally drops the
fruit, but his despair turns into expectation as he
realizes that the time has come to peel and
share it; in doing so, he finds a new dimension to
giving. [The] drawings—all in soft gray, black,
and white except the stand-out orange, which is
shown in its own color—lend graphic strength to
the story." Booklist

Sutcliff, Rosemary

Blood feud. Dutton [1977 c1976] 144p lib.
bdg. $7.50 (5 and up)   **Fic**

1 Vikings—Fiction   2 Istanbul—Fiction
ISBN 0-525-26730-1   LC 76-58502

First published 1976 in England

"Young Viking Thormod's purchase of Jestyn,
who was captured on the coast of Britain, leads to
their becoming 'shoulder-to-shoulder' men, when
Jestyn came to Thormod's aid in a street fight. He
joins a blood feud to avenge the murder of Thormod's father by two Herulfson brothers of his valley in Jutland. Two against two, they make a trek
to Miklagard (Constantinople) toward which the
Herulfsons have already departed. After a winter
in Kiev, six thousand Russians and Vikings journey to Miklagard to support Emperor Basil II in
his troubles at home and on the Turkish frontiers.
The blood feud never forgotten, three of the four
sworn foes die. Injured Jestyn, now a physician's
helper and too young at twenty 'to find himself on
the garbage heap,' cares for the last, dying Herulfson." Horn Bk

"The chasm between children's and adults' literature narrows to a crack in historical fiction. In
'Blood Feud' it is scarcely visible at all and not
only because the hero is no longer a child (nor
even that stereotype of history-for-children, a
child by our century's reckoning but an adult
in his own). The issues Rosemary Sutcliff weaves
into her narrative, with the skill one would expect
from her, are not at all childish." Economist

Glossary: [p145]

Song for a dark queen. Crowell [1979 c1978]
181p illus $7.95, lib. bdg. $7.89 (6 and up)
     Fic

1 Boadicea, Queen—Fiction   2 Great Britain—
History—To 1066—Fiction
ISBN 0-690-03911-5; 0-690-03912-3   LC 78-19514

First published 1978 in England

"Boudicca, Queen of the Iceni, a hill tribe of
Roman Britain, finds when her husband dies in
A.D. 61, that the 'protection' of the Roman emperor
is truly confiscation of property and oppression.
Avenging the rape of her daughters, she leads a
revolt, sacking three cities before her forces are
crushed. Defeated, she kills herself by taking poison.
Cadwan, Harper to the Queen, is narrator, revealing, with the affectionate superiority of an
elder and with the awed respect of a subject, her
complexities as Royal Princess, Queen wife, and

mother. The story is a grisly one, from the brutal
beating of the Queen that begins the uprising to
the slaughter that ends it." Sch Library J

"Her history is given striking immediacy in
vivid scenes and dramatic action through the
author's insight, poetic gifts, and formidable ability to supply detail." Horn Bk

Author's glossary: p177-81

Sun horse, moon horse; decorations by
Shirley Felts. Dutton [1978 c1977] 111p illus
lib. bdg. $7.95 (5 and up)   **Fic**

1 Great Britain—History—To 1066—Fiction
ISBN 0-525-40495-3   LC 77-25440

First published 1977 in England

"Lubrin Dhu is the small dark son of an Iron
Age chieftain who dies defending the clan against
a tribe retreating before the Roman menace.
Lubrin frees his clan by creating for his captors a
vast horse image on the side of the chalk hills,
knowing as he does so that only his death will
breathe true life into the horse." Times (London)
Lit Sup

Sutcliff country is austere and ennobling; her
characters are dwarfed by a sense of their historical and mythical significance. But as always, the
story is fast-moving and brilliantly vivid, and
Lubrin Dhu is a likeable hero." Christian Sci Monitor

Swahn, Sven Christer

The island through the gate; tr. from the
Swedish by Patricia Crampton. Macmillan
Pub. Co. [1974, c1973] 183p illus $4.95 (5
and up)   **Fic**

1 Islands—Fiction   2 Fantastic fiction
ISBN 0-02-788760-X   LC 73-14012

"A summer of mystery and unquiet begins for
Michael Saltash when his rubber raft carries him
from off the coast of a French seaside resort to the
island of Oberour. Stranded and unable to communicate with his parents or the police, Michael
has only two friends on the island, Jannie and
Katie. He soon realizes that his companions and
the other inhabitants of Oberour are spellbound by
a force—real or imagined—which seems to rule their
every action and to thwart Michael's attempts to
leave. He does finally escape, but the looming
question of a magical presence is never answered.
An assortment of odd personalities and an ancient
book of spells add color to an artfully woven suspense story." Booklist

Swayne, Sam

Great- grandfather in the honey tree; written
and illus. by Sam and Zoa Swayne. Viking
1949 53p illus lib. bdg. $3.95 (2-4)   **Fic**

ISBN 0-670-34932-1   LC 49-11494

This story tells how great-grandfather went out
to net some geese and came home with a barrel of
honey, a bear, a fish, a partridge, a deer and seven
wild turkeys, as well as the net of geese

"This book absolutely crackles with action and
humor. It leaves a grown-up breathless with
laughter and envy." Sat Rev

Sypher, Lucy Johnston

The edge of nowhere; illus. by Ray Abel.
Atheneum Pubs. 1972 211p illus $6.95 (4-6)
     Fic

1 North Dakota—Fiction
ISBN 0-689-30069-7   LC 72-75285

"An engaging story, old-fashioned in tone, set
in 1916 and based on the author's childhood in
Wales, North Dakota, on 'the edge of nowhere.'
Before six months are up sixth grader Lucy Johnston's New Year wishes for a dog, a friend her
age, and some excitement are all fulfilled. On that
New Year's night half the stores on Main Street
burn down and other buildings, including the John-
stons' home, are threatened. Later a blizzard traps
Lucy and her slightly older brother in the house
alone for several days, Lucy gets her dog, a new
preacher with three daughters moves to town, and
Lucy takes charge of two small children and an
old Woman during a tornado. Although the dialog
is occasionally stilted, the characterizations are
credible and the story conveys a sense of the
times." Booklist

Talbot, Charlene Joy

An orphan for Nebraska. Atheneum Pubs. 1979 208p $7.95 (4-6) **Fic**

1 Orphans—Fiction 2 Nebraska—Fiction 3 Frontier and pioneer life—Fiction
ISBN 0-689-30698-9   LC 78-12179

"Orphaned by the death of his mother on the way from Ireland to New York City in the 1870's, Kevin O'Rourke lives a newsboy's street life until he and others like him are sent out West by the Children's Aid Society. The smallest of the lot, Kevin is the last to be chosen for work; instead of going to a farming homestead, he ends up with the editor-printer of a small newspaper. The account of his progress toward a career makes good reading, with original elements as well as the usual ones found in pioneer stories—problems, disasters, and festivities. Kevin is a believable character, and his situation introduces the exciting as well as the dreary aspects of life in a frontier community." Horn Bk

Taylor, Mildred D.

Song of the trees; pictures by Jerry Pinkney. Dial Press 1975 48p illus $5.95, lib. bdg. $5.47 (4-6) **Fic**

1 Trees—Fiction 2 Depressions, Economic—Fiction 3 Blacks—Fiction 4 Mississippi—Fiction
ISBN 0-8037-5452-3; 0-8037-5453-1   LC 74-18598

"During the depression, David Logan had to go to Louisiana for work, leaving Grandmother, Mother, and four children to shift for themselves in Mississippi. Told from the point of view of eight-year-old Cassie, the story relates how white men force a deal with the impoverished family for the right to cut down the beautiful forest behind their home; for three days Cassie listened to 'the foreign sounds of steel against the trees and the thunderous roar of those ancient loved ones as they crashed upon the earth.' But the father returned with a box of explosives, willing to destroy the entire forest—as well as himself—if the white men did not leave his land." Horn Bk

"The writing style, although at times self-conscious, smoothly backs up the element of dignity in the story's message and in its well-drawn black characters. The fine black-and-white pictures are a little stiff but relay the setting and human dynamics well." Booklist

Followed by: Roll of thunder, hear my cry. Dial Press $7.95 Awarded the Newbery Medal, 1977 (ISBN 0-8037-7473-7; LC 76-2287)

Taylor, Sydney

All-of-a-kind family; illus. by Helen John. Follett 1951 192p illus $4.95, lib. bdg. $5.97 (4-6) **Fic**

1 Jews in New York (City)—Fiction 2 New York (City)—Fiction
ISBN 0-695-80280-1; 0-695-40280-3   LC 51-13398

"Five little Jewish girls grow up in New York's lower East side in a happy home atmosphere before the first World War." Pittsburgh

"A genuine and delightful picture of a Jewish family . . . with an understanding mother and father, rich in kindness and fun though poor in money. The important part the public library played in the lives of these children is happily evident; and the Jewish holiday celebrations are particularly well described." Horn Bk

Some other books about this family are also available from Follett (unless otherwise noted):

All-of-a-kind family downtown $4.95, lib. bdg. $6.99 (ISBN 0-695-80308-5; 0-695-40308-7; LC 70-184789)
Ella of all of a kind family lib. bdg. $7.95 (Dutton ISBN 0-525-29238-1; LC 77-26991)
More All-of-a-kind family $4.95, lib. bdg. $4.98 (ISBN 0-695-85880-7; 0-695-45880-9; LC 54-10104)

Taylor, Theodore

The cay. Doubleday 1969 137p $6.95, lib. bdg. $7.90 (5 and up) **Fic**

1 Race relations—Fiction 2 Caribbean area—Fiction 3 Survival (after airplane accidents, shipwrecks, etc.)—Fiction 4 Blind—Fiction
ISBN 0-385-07906-0; 0-385-08152-9   LC 69-15161

"Phillip, a resident of the war-torn Caribbean island of Curacao, is forced to leave his home. As he is being evacuated, the ship on which he is being transported is sunk. With only an old West Indian man as a companion and guide, he ekes out a precarious existence on a tiny island. Burdened with blindness, caused by a head injury around the time of the shipwreck, the boy [overcomes his racial prejudice and] grows in understanding and maturity as he faces ever increasing challenges." Wis Library Bul

"World War II provides the background for this sensitive tale of two survivors of a torpedoed ship, a blind white boy and a black seaman. . . . An absorbing story about the color of friendship and human dignity." Top of the News

Teetoncey; illus. by Richard Cuffari. Doubleday 1974 153p illus $4.95, lib. bdg. $5.90 (6 and up) **Fic**

1 Amnesia—Fiction 2 North Carolina—Fiction
ISBN 0-385-09584-8; 0-385-09587-2   LC 73-13097)

This first novel in the Hatteras Banks trilogy is about eleven-year-old Ben O'Neal, who lives "with his mother on the Outer Banks of North Carolina in 1898. After a storm, he rescues a young girl, victim of a shipwreck, who is washed up on the beach. The girl eventually recovers physically but remains [amnesiac] mute and unresponsive. In the process of helping Teetoncey recover, Ben comes to terms with his manhood, his mother, and his image of his dead father." Children's Bk Rev Serv

"The novel is rich with details of local geography, history, and folklore; but they are kept subordinate to the presentation of the dramatic tension between [Ben and his mother] and to the unfolding of Ben's growing awareness of his feelings for Teetoncey. Although the story is sympathetically and realistically told from the boy's point of view, the best-realized character in the book is the boy's mother." Horn Bk

Followed by these books, also available from Doubleday:

Teetoncey and Ben O'Neal $5.95, lib. bdg. $6.90 (ISBN 0-385-06688-0; 0-385-04504-2; LC 74-4875)
The odyssey of Ben O'Neal $5.95, lib. bdg. $6.90 (ISBN 0-385-00166-5; 0-385-00289-0; LC 76-23800)

Tennant, Veronica

On stage, please; a story; illus. by Rita Briansky. Holt 1979 176p illus $7.95 (4-6) **Fic**

1 Ballet—Fiction
ISBN 0-03-049306-4   LC 79-4819

First published 1977 in Canada

"Jennifer Allen, aged 10, auditions and is accepted for study at the Professional School of Ballet in Toronto. She works hard through her first year, survives jealousies, and makes some friends. She suffers a sprained ligament but recovers in time to make her first appearance with the professional company as an attendant in 'Cinderella.' The characters aren't fully developed, and the plot offers nothing unusual; but the integration of the factual material with the ballet school setting is well realized." Sch Library J

Thiele, Colin

Blue Fin; pictures by Roger Haldane. Harper 1974 243p illus lib. bdg. $8.79, pa $2.95 (6 and up) **Fic**

1 Sea stories 2 Fisheries—Fiction
ISBN 0-06-026105-6; 0-06-440077-8   LC 73-14328

First published 1969 in Australia

"'Blue Fin' is Snook Pascoe's father's tuna fishing boat, but the hero of the book . . . is homely, ungainly, and shy Snook himself, who, although blamed and disparaged as a jinx by his scornful father, saves both of their lives when a disaster hits their boat." Babbling Bookworm

"A gripping good story, masterfully woven around a trite theme, is made exciting by vivid words, clear characterization, beautiful language, sound information, and an unusual revelation of outcome of incidents often before completion of events creating the climax. About Australian off-shore tuna fishing, the wealth of information may deter an immature or casual reader, but once begun, the story itself takes over and the information becomes incidental." Children's Bk Rev Serv

Fight against Albatross Two. Harper [1976 c1974] 243p lib. bdg. $7.89 (6 and up) **Fic**

1 Petroleum pollution of water—Fiction 2 Australia—Fiction
ISBN 0-06-026099-8   LC 75-37104

Thiele, Colin—*Continued*

First published 1974 in Australia with title: Albatross Two

"The explosion of an offshore oil rig brings to a head the townspeople's resentment to the rig's presence, as the escaping oil imperils the crayfish beds and shoreline of the small Australian village." LC. Children's Bks 1976

"The characters are varied and convincing, the conflict between two concepts of the public good presented quite objectively, and the setting and pace of the story provide color and excitement." Chicago. Children's Bk Center

The shadow on the hills. Harper [1978 c1977] 216p lib. bdg. $8.95 (6 and up) **Fic**

1 Australia—Fiction 2 Farm life—Fiction 3 Friendship—Fiction
ISBN 0-06-026126-9   LC 77-11829

First published 1977 in Australia

"Bodo Schneider is an Australian Tom Sawyer, sometimes the unwitting victim of schoolboy pranks but more often the instigator of outlandish schemes. With the impending Depression, however, Bodo quickly learns the grim realities of survival on a farm. His encounters [and friendship] with an old half-crazed hermit also become part of his rites of passage to manhood." Children's Bk Rev Serv

"The tension and pace of the story combined with a lively humor make it an exceptional choice for reading aloud." Horn Bk

Storm Boy; pictures by John Schoenherr. Harper [1978 c1963] 61p illus $7.95, lib. bdg. $7.89 (3-5) **Fic**

1 Pelicans—Fiction 2 Australia—Fiction
ISBN 0-06-026133-1; 0-06-026134-X   LC 77-25675

Text first published 1963 in Australia

In this story, "Storm Boy, who lives with his father on a wild, lonely coast, rescues three storm-battered baby pelicans, one of which becomes his constant companion. Calling the bird Mr. Percival, he trains it as a retriever, and after a shipwreck the bird carries a line and manages to drop it to the beleaguered crew so that the men are pulled ashore. The pelican has a way of warning ducks when hunters are near, and he ultimately falls victim to the cruel men who kill for sport." Horn Bk

The author creates "a vivid picture of the wild South Australian coast. . . . Young readers who would appreciate the length might find unfamiliar words and expressions difficult, but this would be a pleasant enough short book for middle graders." Sch Library J

Thomas, Ianthe

Hi, Mrs Mallory! Pictures by Ann Toulmin-Rothe. Harper 1979 48p illus $7.95, lib. bdg. $7.89 (2-5) **Fic**

1 Friendship—Fiction 2 Blacks—Fiction 3 Elderly—Fiction
ISBN 0-06-026128-5; 0-06-026129-3   LC 78-3013

"Li'l Bits is the teller of the story about her friendship with old Mrs. Mallory; every day after school the young black girl and her white friend would talk, draw, have delicious snacks, and tell stories. Li'l Bits' mother thought the old woman's house a shambles (dirt floor, cardboard windows) and Mrs. Mallory a foolish old woman who told her daughter silly tales, but she was gentle and understanding when she had to tel Li'l Bits that her friend had died." Chicago. Children's Bk Center

"The sadness of the sudden death of the old lady and the void it leaves in Li'l Bits' life is mitigated when Mrs. Mallory's dog, Lazlo, moves in with Li'l Bits—a poignant reminder, or a legacy, of a relationship built on the sharing of selves that Li'l Bits can never forget nor negate. Full page pencil [and wash] sketches set the scene of rural isolation and lives of bare necessity. It 'looks' easy enough for reluctant readers, but Li'l Bits narrative is in a vernacular that may confuse, though most children will not be hampered by it. It's fine for reading aloud and an excellent opener to talk about love, death, poverty, friendship, and age." Sch Library J

Thrasher, Crystal

The dark didn't catch me. Atheneum Pubs. 1975 182p $7.95, pa $1.95 (5 and up) **Fic**

1 Indiana—Fiction 2 Depressions, Economic—Fiction 3 Family life—Fiction
ISBN 0-689-50025-4; 0-689-70465-8   LC 74-18193

"A Margaret K. McElderry book"

"Seely, a second of four children, describes her family's move [during the Depression] into the southern Indiana hills where her father mistakenly counts on finding work. Her twelfth year was a time of personal, family, and school developments, all reported with frank detail. Domestic relationships twisted by pain and hardship, deaths, and economic austerity are not softened but are related as a slice of life." Horn Bk

This "is by no means a sentimental remembrance. It is a tough, funny, tragic splendid first novel filled with vivid characters." NY Times Bk Rev

Followed by: Between dark and daylight. Atheneum Pubs. $9.95 (ISBN 0-689-50150-1; LC 79-12423)

Thurber, James

The great Quillow; illus. by Doris Lee. Harcourt 1975 c1944 54p illus pa $1.95 (3-5) **Fic**

1 Fairy tales
ISBN 0-15-636490-5   LC 75-6613

"A Voyager book"

First published 1944 in hardcover

"He was called the Great Quillow in derision, for he was only the village toy maker and so regarded by the truly important people, the baker, the butcher, the tailor and others, as a person of little consequence. But when the giant Hunder appears on the scene, threatening to wipe out the village, it is the ingenious toy maker who gets the better of him." Wis Library Bul

"It is the old folk-theme—as old as the Panchatantra—of intelligence and courage against brute force. Mr. Thurber has brought to it grace and humor and a phrasing that is an unending delight. The drawings are a delight, too. It is a book for everyone." Sat Rev

Many moons; illus. by Louis Slobodkin. Harcourt 1943 unp illus $5.95, pa $2.25 (1-4) **Fic**

1 Fairy tales
ISBN 0-15-251873-8; 0-15-656980-9   LC 43-51250

Awarded the Caldecott Medal, 1944

This is "the story of a little princess who fell ill of a surfeit of raspberry tarts and would get well only if she could have the moon. The solving of this baffling court problem, how to get the moon, results in an original and entertaining picture-storybook." Booklist

"Louis Slobodkin's pictures float on the pages in four colors: black and white cannot represent them. They are the substance of dreams . . . the long thoughts little children, and some adults wise as they, have about life." NY Her Trib Bks

The 13 clocks; illus. by Marc Simont. Simon & Schuster 1950 124p illus $8.95, pa $3.95 (6 and up) **Fic**

1 Fairy tales
ISBN 0-671-72100-3; 0-671-22944-3   LC 50-11076

This is "a fairy tale not for [younger] children about a duke, so cold and cruel that time has frozen around him, who has imprisoned a beautiful princess in his castle, and about a prince who rescues her by performing a seemingly impossible task." New Yorker

"Mr. Thurber has done it again, though I don't know just what it is he has done this time—a fairy tale, a comment on human cruelty and human sweetness or a spell, an incantation compounded of poetry and logic and wit." NY Her Trib Bks

Titus, Eve

Basil of Baker Street; illus. by Paul Galdone. McGraw 1958 96p illus lib. bdg. $8.95 (3-5) **Fic**

1 Mice—Fiction 2 Mystery and detective stories 3 Doyle, Sir Arthur Conan—Parodies, travesties, etc.
ISBN 0-07-064907-3   LC 58-8050

"Whittlesey House publications"

"Basil of Baker Street is the Sherlock Holmes of the mouse world, having studied scientific sleuthing at the feet of the famous English detective. Here in an entertaining, delightfully illustrated story Basil's assistant, Dr. Dawson, tells how the great Basil solves a baffling kidnapping case, restores the children to their parents, and brings the dangerous kidnappers to justice. Acquaintance with Sherlock Holmes and Dr. Watson is not essential to the enjoyment of this small-scale detective story." Booklist

Another book about Basil is also available from McGraw: Basil in Mexico $7.95, lib. bdg. $7.95 (ISBN 0-07-064898-0; 0-07-064900-6; LC 75-10827)

Tolan, Stephanie S.

Grandpa—and me. Scribner 1978 120p lib. bdg. $6.95 (5 and up)   Fic

1 Grandfathers—Fiction   2 Old age—Fiction 3 Family life—Fiction 4 Suicide—Fiction
ISBN 0-684-15339-4   LC 77-18254

"Speaking into a tape recorder, 11-year-old Kerry keeps a journal of the summer when her grandfather becomes senile and, faced with a future in a nursing home, drowns himself." Sch Library J

"This is a realistic and sympathetic depiction of one pattern of old age, convincing save for Kerry's tenacity in hiding from her parents that she's seen Grandpa do such things as urinate outdoors, wear his pants inside-out, and mistake her for his dead sister. The writing style is smooth, the dialogue well-written." Chicago. Children's Bk Center

Tolkien, J. R. R.

Farmer Giles of Ham; embellished by Pauline Baynes. Houghton 1978 [c1976] 63p illus $6.95, pa $4.95 (5 and up)   Fic

1 Fairy tales
ISBN 0-395-07121-6; 0-395-26799-4

First published 1949 in England; first U.S. edition 1950

Farmer Giles accidentally fires his blunderbuss at a giant and becomes a national hero. It is a situation Farmer Giles finds quite appealing until a dragon appears and people turn to their national hero for protection

The Father Christmas letters; ed. by Baillie Tolkien. Houghton 1976 unp illus $8.95, pa $4.95   Fic

1 Santa Claus—Fiction
ISBN 0-395-24981-3; 0-395-28262-4   LC 77-362616

"J. R. R. Tolkien's children were, for twenty years, the fortunate recipients of an annual letter from Father Christmas, the British equivalent of Santa Claus. They even included envelopes with carefully simulated North Pole stamps, and they describe the tribulation of preparing for Christmas when your chief assistant is a bumbling polar bear. Tolkien's daughter-in-law has selected some of the letters and most of Toikien's pictures; the stories can be read by independent readers, but they can also be used for reading aloud to younger children, and many of the author's adult or young adult fans will probably enjoy the recitals of amusing woes. . . . Inventive, amusing, and—because each letter can be read separately—excellent for installment reading." Chicago. Children's Bk Center

The hobbit; or, There and back again; illus. by the author. Houghton 1938 310p illus $6.95 (4 and up)   Fic

1 Fairy tales
ISBN 0-395-07122-4   LC 38-5859

First published 1937 in England

A tale of the adventures of Bilbo Baggins, the hobbit, in a land inhabited by dwarfs, elves, goblins, dragons, and humans—although the last named play only a small part in the story. Bilbo's adventures begin when he is persuaded to join a band of dwarfs, led by Gandalf, the Wizard, who are off on an expedition to recover the treasure stolen by Smaug, the Dragon, and hidden in the depths of the Lonely Mountain

"The background of the story is full of authentic bits of mythology and magic and the book has the rare quality of style. It is written with a quiet humor and the logical detail in which children take delight. Nine- and ten-year-olds who discovered the book in the English edition have greeted it with keen enthusiasm, but this is a book with no age limits." Horn Bk

Smith of Wooton Major; with illus. by Pauline Baynes. Houghton 1978 [c1975] 61p illus $5.95, pa $4.95 (5 and up)   Fic

1 Fairy tales
ISBN 0-395-08259-5; 0-395-26800-1

First published 1967

"Every 24 years, the Master Cook of Wootton Major bakes a great cake for the Feast of the Good Children. . . . A certain piece of the cake contains a tiny, magic star. It is swallowed by Smith, perhaps the least remarkable child in the village, and from that day on . . . his life becomes privileged. He travels deep into the world of Faery. . . . Then one day the time comes when Smith, now a grandfather, must give up his star and allow it to pass to another chosen child." NY Times Bk Rev

"The more closely [this book] is examined, the more it reveals the grandeur of its conception. . . . Its parts are tightly yet discreetly interlinked and there is not one thing superfluous. . . . This astonishing little book . . . [has] a certain justice, a ring of truth. . . . [It] is a book for anyone over the age of eight. And whoever reads it at eight, will no doubt still be going back to it at eighty." New Statesman

Tolle, Jean Bashor

The great Pete Penney. Atheneum Pubs. 1979 90p $7.95 (3-6)   Fic

1 Little league baseball—Fiction
ISBN 0-689-50145-5   LC 79-14603

"A Margaret K. McElderry book"

"Eleven-year-old Pete (Priscilla) Penney, baseball player and tomboy, meets a tiny invisible man who gives her a perfect pitch. Before her team can win the championship, she insults the man, Mike McGlory, who departs with his gift. Pete now must rely on her own talents and she finds that they are good." Children's Bk Rev Serv

"This is an amusing if mildly didactic story stressing self reliance. Especially notable is the author's matter-of-fact handling of girls in Little League baseball." Sch Library J

Towne, Mary

Goldenrod. Atheneum Pubs. 1977 180p $6.95 (4-6)   Fic

1 Baby sitters—Fiction
ISBN 0-689-30597-4   LC 77-1578

"Goldenrod came from her job as a supermarket checker to baby-sit with the five Madder children. On her very first day at the Madder's she catapulted herself and the children into another place, Gorseville. . . . They soon learned that each person could pick a place that began with the first letter of one's first name, and with all of them concentrating, Val could take them to Venice, Heath to the Himalayas, and so on. Most of the book is, therefore, a series of lightly related episodes; the internal action of these seems a bit contrived. However, there's adventure and variety, the writing style is adequate, Goldenrod herself is a refreshing character." Chicago. Children's Bk Center

Townsend, John Rowe

Good-bye to the jungle. Lippincott [1967 c1965] 184p illus lib. bdg. $5.53 (6 and up)   Fic

1 Great Britain—Fiction 2 Family life—Fiction
ISBN 0-397-31426-4   LC 67-2765

First published 1965 in England with title: Widdershins Crescent

"The jungle is a slum [in Cobchester, England] scheduled for demolition, and most of the members of the Thompson family are delighted at the prospect of moving to a new housing development. Walter Thompson is a shiftless, irresponsible braggart whose two children are being brought up less by the mistress who lives with them than by the adolescent cousins, Sandra and Kevin, whose parents are dead. Kevin tells the story of the family's struggle to achieve a modicum of respectability." Sat Rev

"Both the characters and the events are presented as mixtures, hateful and sympathetic, sad and funny, potentially both evil and good. There is injustice, Mr. Townsend says to his readers; the innocent suffers with the guilty, there is squalor and poverty and misery. But, he says, there is hope, there is courage and there is love. Besides making these unusual statements Mr. Townsend has written an excellent story with lively and credible characters." Times (London) Lit Sup

Followed by two books dealing with earlier events in 'the jungle' also available from Lippincott:

Pirate's Island lib. bdg. $5.53 (ISBN 0-397-31425-6; LC 68-14619)
Trouble in the jungle (published in England as: Gumble's Yard) $8.95, lib. bdg. $8.79 (ISBN 0-397-31108-7; 0-397-31109-5; LC 69-12003)

The intruder. Lippincott [1970 c1969] 220p $8.95 (6 and up)   Fic

1 Great Britain—Fiction
ISBN 0-397-31126-5   LC 79-101903

First published 1969 in England

"Set in a village in England, on the coast of the Irish Sea, a dramatic and compelling story with the fine characterization, and imaginative plot, and a remarkable evocation of atmosphere and mood. Sixteen-year-old Arnold Haithwaite has

Townsend, John R.—*Continued*

never been told who he really is; he lives with his 'dad' (he is the old man's illegitimate grandson but has not been told that) and he sees his dad fall more and more under the spell of the stranger, who claims his name is also Arnold Haithwaite, and who moves in and takes command of the household, his goal being to commercialize the town, once thriving and now moribund. The intruder is so plausible that none of the adults to whom Arnold turns for help take him seriously, although it is clear to the reader that the man is not only evil but criminal. The solution is unexpected but plausible, the exciting ending a fitting one to a tale pregnant with suspense." Chicago. Children's Bk Center

Noah's castle. Lippincott [1976 c1975] 256p $7.95 (6 and up) **Fic**

1 Great Britain—Fiction 2 Parent and child—Fiction 3 Fathers—Fiction
ISBN 0-397-31654-2   LC 75-30709

First published 1975 in England
This novel is set in England in the not too distant future, when runaway inflation threatens most of the population with starvation. "Barry, the middle boy in a large family, tells of how his father moves wife and children into a fortress-like suburban home which he crams with food and clothing. Hoarding, of course, is illegal; no one is to know of the family cache. But the father's providence backfires as his children register their disapproval of what they see as selfishness. Mr. Townsend has invigorated these pages with lots of haunting scenes as outsiders (for good reasons and bad) fight for the supplies. And he poses a basic moral question: How far does one go to protect one's own?" Pub W

The visitors. Lippincott 1977 221p $7.95 (6 and up) **Fic**

1 Science fiction 2 Great Britain—Fiction
ISBN 0-397-51752-2   LC 77-7197

First published in England with title: The Xanadu Manuscript
"John Dunham, teen-age narrator, and his family become involved with the Wyatts, parents and daughter who have time-traveled from the year 2149 to present-day Cambridge, England." Children's Bk Rev Serv
"A fantasy firmly rooted in the reality of contemporary England displays the author's ability to design a substantial plot, his skill in portraying major and minor characters and dramatizing their interrelationships, and his crisp, confident storytelling. . . . Enriching the story are the author's fine instinct for elaborate, almost cinematic detail, his sensitivity to the range of human emotions, and his communication of a real sense of place." Horn Bk

Travers, P. L.

Mary Poppins; illus. by Mary Shepard. Harcourt 1962 206p illus $6.95, pa $2.25 (4-6) **Fic**

1 Fantastic fiction
ISBN 0-15-252410-X; 0-15-657680-5   LC 34-28306

First published 1934
"Here are related the remarkable things that transpired during the time Mary Poppins served as nursemaid for the [British] Banks family. This astonishing person blew in with an east wind and stayed as she had agreed until it changed, and after that, life was never the same for Jane and Michael. Delightful nonsense that defies an age boundary of appreciation. Amusing line drawings." Booklist
"The Poppins books are extremely British, with cooks, gardeners, maids, nanas, nurseries, and teas. . . . But children who like these books like them enormously and wear them to shreds with rereadings." Children and Bks
Some other books about Mary Poppins are also available from Harcourt:
Mary Poppins comes back $5.95, pa $2.45 (ISBN 0-15-252589-0; 0-15-657683-X; LC 36-27038)
Mary Poppins from A to Z $4.50, lib. bdg. $4.50 (ISBN 0-15-252590-4; 0-15-252591-2; LC 62-15629)
Mary Poppins in the park $5.95, pa $2.45 (ISBN 0-15-252947-0; 0-15-657690-2; LC 52-10066)
Mary Poppins opens the door $5.95, pa $2.45 (ISBN 0-15-252768-0; 0-15-657690-2; LC 43-17570)

Tregarthen, Enys

The doll who came alive; ed. by Elizabeth Yates; illus. by Nora S. Unwin. Day 1972 75p illus $6.95 (3-5) **Fic**

1 Dolls—Fiction 2 Fairy tales
ISBN 0-381-99683-2   LC 70-179780

First published 1942
These are the adventures of a young English girl named Jyd with her wooden Dutch doll named Jane that comes to life because it is loved so much
"Very romantic and somewhat moralistic, the story's appeal—in addition to the ever-entrancing lure of dolls for some children—is in the unusual setting and in the vigorous imagination of Jyd." Chicago. Children's Bk Center

Treviño, Elizabeth Borton de

I, Juan De Pareja. Bell Bks. 1965 180p $6.95 (6 and up) **Fic**

1 Pareja, Juan de—Fiction 2 Velázquez, Diego Rodríguez de Silva y—Fiction
ISBN 0-374-33531   LC 65-19330

"Bell books"
Awarded the Newbery Medal, 1966
The black slave boy, Juan de Pareja, "began a new life when he was taken into the household of the Spanish painter, Velázquez. As he worked beside the great artist learning how to grind and mix colors and prepare canvases, there grew between them a warm friendship based on mutual respect and love of art. Created from meager but authentic facts, the story, told by Juan, depicts the life and character of Velázquez and the loyalty of the talented seventeenth-century slave who eventually won his freedom and the right to be an artist. The author's sensitive treatment of the affectionate relationship between these two men results in a beautiful story of the brotherhood of man." Booklist

Twain, Mark

The adventures of Huckleberry Finn (5 and up) **Fic**

1 Mississippi River—Fiction 2 Missouri—Fiction

Some editions are:
Dent (The Children's illustrated classics) $9 Illustrated with colour plates and drawings in the text by C. Walter Hodges (ISBN 0-460-055031-1; LC 55-1997)
Dodd (Great illustrated classics) $8.95 With sixteen full-page illustrations, descriptive captions and introductory remarks by Stanley T. Williams (ISBN 0-396-07742-0)
Grosset (Illustrated junior lib) $5.95 Illustrated by Donald McKay (ISBN 0-448-05800-6; LC 48-6226)
Hall, G.K.&Co. $13.95 Large print book (ISBN 0-8161-3079-5)
Harper (A Holiday ed) $9.95, lib. bdg. $9.87 (ISBN 0-06-014376-2; 0-06-014377-0)
Macmillan Pub. Co. (The Macmillan classics) $5.95, pa $1.95 Illustrated by John Falter; afterword by Clifton Fadiman (ISBN 0-02-789550-5; 0-02-045550-X; LC 62-19421)
Companion volume to: The adventures of Tom Sawyer, entered below
First published 1885
"Huck, escaping from his blackguardly father, who had imprisoned him in a lonely cabin, meets Jim, a runaway slave, on Jackson's Island in the Mississippi River. Together they float on a raft down the mighty stream. . . . Two confidence men join them and they drift into many extraordinary adventures, in the course of which Tom Sawyer reappears. Tom's Aunt Sally wants to adopt Huck, who decides he had better disappear again, lest he be 'sivilized.' . . . The struggle in Huck's soul between his 'respectable' Southern prejudices and his growing appreciation of Jim's value and dignity as a human being is an ironic and powerful indictment of the moral blindness of a slave-holding society." The Reader's Ency of Am Lit
"'Huckleberry Finn' is a more complex book than 'Tom Sawyer.' It is written in Huck's own fluent, colloquial speech and suffused with the humour of Mark Twain." Bks for Boys & Girls

The adventures of Tom Sawyer (5 and up) **Fic**

1 Mississippi River—Fiction 2 Missouri—Fiction

Some editions are:
Dent (Children's illustrated classics) $9 Illustrated with colour plates and drawings in the text by C. Walter Hodges (ISBN 0-460-05030-3; LC 55-14558)

Twain, Mark—*Continued*

Dodd (Great illustrated classics) $8.95 With biographical illustrations and drawings from early editions of the book, together with an introduction by Louis B. Salomon (ISBN 0-396-07742-0; LC 58-13029)
Grosset (Illustrated junior lib) $5.95 Illustrated by Donald McKay (ISBN 0-448-05802-2; LC 46-22588)
Harper (A Holiday ed) $10 (ISBN 0-06-014465-3)
Macmillan Pub. Co. (The Macmillan classics) $3.95 Illustrated by John Falter; afterword by Clifton Fadiman (ISBN 0-02-789630-7; LC 62-19420)

Companion volume to: The adventures of Huckleberry Finn, entered below
First published 1876
The plot "is episodic, dealing in part with Tom's pranks in school, Sunday school, and the respectable world of his Aunt Polly, and in part with his adventures with Huck Finn, the outcaste son of the local ne'er-do-well. . . . Tom and Huck witness a murder and, in terror of the murderer, Injun Joe, secretly flee to Jackson's Island. They are searched for, are finally mourned for dead, and return to town in time to attend their own funeral. Tom and his sweetheart, Becky Thatcher, get lost in a cave in which Injun Joe is hiding. . . . The story closely follows incidents involving Twain and his friends that occurred in Hannibal, Mo." The Reader's Ency of Am Lit
"Tom is undoubtedly an idle, thoughtless, and mischievous boy, but his escapades are related with equally undoubted humour and in vigorous and original style." Bks for Boys & Girls

12 adventures of the celebrated Baron Munchausen; selected and illus. by Brian Robb. Deutsch [1979 c1978] 105p illus lib. bdg. $6.95 (3-5)   **Fic**

1 Adventure and adventurers—Fiction
ISBN 0-233-97019-3   LC 80-455986
First published 1947 in England; this reissue first published 1978 in England. The original collection of tall tales narrated by Baron Munchausen was first published anonymously in England in 1785 and has been attributed to Rudolph Erich Raspe
"Robb's treatment is graphically comic from cover to cover, with cartoons on nearly every page. This, plus the shortened, slightly adapted single adventures makes an appealing and useful introduction to the notorious baron. . . . The straightfaced telling is matched by the master art teacher's illustrations that capture the outlandish aplomb with which the Baron flattens himself when swallowed by the fish or whips the wolf devouring his horse into its victim's harness." Sch Library J

Uchida, Yoshiko

Journey home; illus. by Charles Robinson. Atheneum Pubs. 1978 131p illus $7.95 (4 and up)   **Fic**

1 Japanese Americans—Fiction 2 Family life—Fiction
ISBN 0-689-50126-9   LC 78-8792
"A Margaret K. McElderry book"
Sequel to: Journey to Topaz, o.p. 1981
"The bittersweet story of a Japanese-American family's struggle to return to a normal life after their relocation camp experience in Utah. . . . Seen through the eyes of twelve-year-old Yuki, the plight of her parents, who want to return to California, the disillusionment of her brother, who returns from the war with shattered dreams, and the despair of her friends, who want to rebuild their lives in spite of the hostility outside the camp, take on a special poignancy." Children's Bk Rev Serv
"This book fills a great need in describing the cruel treatment inflicted upon Japanese-Americans during World War II by their fellow Americans." Sch Library J

The promised year; illus. by William M. Hutchinson. Harcourt 1959 192p illus $6.50 (4-6)   **Fic**

1 Japanese in California—Fiction 2 California—Fiction 3 Cats—Fiction 3 Flower gardening—Fiction
ISBN 0-15-263866-0   LC 59-9270
"Story of a 10-year-old girl who comes from Japan to California to spend a year with her aunt and uncle. Because her uncle has no use for her cat Tama, to which he is allergic, and seems stern and interested only in his carnation-growing business, Keiko thinks he does not like her and

even blames him for Tama's disappearance. It is by her actions when her aunt is in the hospital and the carnation crop is imperiled by smog that Keiko and Uncle Henry come to understand and love each other." Booklist
"Adjustment to the life of a Japanese-American household and to an American community, interesting sidelights on the carnation industry, unusually real characters—all these are part of a story that only someone completely at home in the two cultures could have written with so much humor and verve." Horn Bk
Glossary: p191. Pronunciation of proper names: p191-92

Ullman, James Ramsey

Banner in the sky. Lippincott 1954 252p $8.95 (6 and up)   **Fic**

1 Mountaineering—Fiction 2 Alps—Fiction
ISBN 0-397-30264-9   LC 54-7296
"Those in the little Swiss village think no one can climb the Citadel. Rudi, whose father had lost his life trying, joins the party of Captain Winter who believes the mountain can be conquered. The story shows a boy's struggle to develop independence and become a man." Rdng Ladders. 5th edition
"Based upon the author's personal experiences . . . with some details from the original ascent of the Matterhorn, the story has authenticity, atmosphere, and excitement which for the most part disguise a spectacular, patterned plot." Booklist

Underwood, Betty

The tamarack tree; illus. by Bea Holmes. Houghton 1971 230p illus $5.95 (6 and up)   **Fic**

1 Philleo, Prudence (Crandall)—Fiction 2 Discrimination in education—Fiction 3 Connecticut—Fiction
ISBN 0-395-12761-0   LC 76-161649
"A story built on the case of Prudence Crandall's persecution by the townspeople who resented the inclusion of black students in her seminary. Canterbury, Connecticut was not ready, in 1833, to accept this, and its reaction precluded the attendance of a white girl who had come there and expected to attend. Bernadette had come to stay with the Fry family preparatory to attending Oberlin College, and her sympathy for Miss Crandall and her pupils was awakened by indignation when she learned that a sick girl had been refused medicine by a storekeeper. . . . The story moves with good pace, the characters are convincing, the historical material accurate and the fictional material realistic; the book gives, within its small frame of locale, a clear and vivid picture of the conflicting attitudes of the times." Chicago. Children's Bk Center

Van Leeuwen, Jean

The great Christmas kidnapping caper; pictures by Steven Kellogg. Dial Press 1975 133p illus $7.95, lib. bdg. $7.45 (3-5)   **Fic**

1 Mice—Fiction 2 Christmas—Fiction
ISBN 0-8037-5415-9   LC 75-9201
Sequel to: The great cheese conspiracy
"The toy shop at Macy's department store is a perfect winter home for Marvin the Magnificent mouse and his gang. During after-store hours they bounce on waterbeds, eat cheese, caviar, and pickles from the delicatessen, and ride the electric trains. The only one who notices them is the store's Santa Claus, who, in true Santa fashion, leaves them cookies and candy. When Santa fails to appear one morning and the newspaper announces his disappearance, the mouse gang resolve to locate the kidnapper and rescue Santa. . . . Kellogg's expressive drawings add to the fun." Booklist

I was a 98-pound duckling. Dial Press 1972 102p $5.95 (6 and up)   **Fic**

1 Self perception—Fiction
ISBN 0-8037-4139-1   LC 72-714
"Kathy McGruder tells how her life changed overnight and she became a new person just as the 'Allure' magazine article said was possible. As the story opens Kathy is bemoaning her hair, and other beauty problems as well as her lack of dates. Then at the Saturday night square dance which she attends with reluctance she is approached by a dashing stranger and her brief idyllic encounter with this handsome junior counselor from a camp not only enhances her own self-image but launches her social life. Frothy, amusing fare with bright characterizations." Booklist

Van Stockum, Hilda

The borrowed house. Farrar, Straus 1975
215p $6.95 (5 and up)   **Fic**

1 World War, 1939-1945—Fiction 2 Netherlands—
History—German occupation, 1940-1945—Fiction
3 Jews in the Netherlands—Fiction 4 National
socialism—Fiction
ISBN 0-374-30888-8   LC 75-8853

"Janna goes from Germany to Amsterdam during World War II to join her parents, a famous
acting couple. The girl, aged 12, has been in-
doctrinated satisfactorily by her Hitler Youth
Group: the Aryans are a master race; Jews are
inferior; Germans are destined to rule the world.
But in the house from which the Dutch owners
have been evicted so that Janna and her parents
can take it over, she meets a Jewish boy, Sef,
who is hidden (in a secret room) by the servants
of the Dutch family. As the friendship between
boy and girl grows, Janna becomes disillusioned
about the 'glorious' Third Reich." Pub W

"This World War II story is not only a good
presentation of an important historical period but
provides material for discussions concerning courage, prejudice and the danger of unquestioning
acceptance of an ideology. The adventure and
mystery interwoven with serious themes will lure
even reluctant readers to this book." Rdng Teacher

The winged watchman; written and illus.
by Hilda Van Stockum. Farrar, Straus 1962
204p illus lib. bdg. $6.95 (4 and up)   **Fic**

1 World War, 1939-1945—Fiction 2 Netherlands—
History—German occupation, 1940-1945—Fiction
ISBN 0-374-38448-7   LC 62-16280

"A Bell book"

A "story about a Dutch family in the time of
German occupation during [World War II]. The
winged watchman is a windmill, one of those used
by the Dutch underground to send messages by
positioning the vanes of the mill. The two boys
of the Verhagen family become involved in the
resistance movement, and their parents help Dirk
Jan and Joris conceal a British flyer. Excellent
family relationships, and good pace in plot development. The Verhagen family is impressive in its
courage, patriotism, and calm faith, but it is the
whole Dutch people who are the heroes of this
moving book." Chicago. Children's Bk Center

Verne, Jules

Twenty thousand leagues under the sea (5
and up)   **Fic**

1 Submarines—Fiction 2 Sea stories

Some editions are:
Dent (Children's illustrated classics) $9 With four
colour plates and line drawings in the text by
William McLaren (ISBN 0-460-05071-0; LC 66-
66050)
Macmillan Pub. Co. $4.95 Illustrated by Charles
Molina; afterword by Clifton Fadiman (ISBN 0-
02-791640-5; LC 62-18394)

First published 1869

"In 1867, an unknown monster is roaming the
seas. A U.S. Navy ship, commanded by Captain
Farragut, is sent to find it, carrying as passengers
French scientist, P. Aronnax (the narrator), his
servant, Conseil, and a famous harpooner, Ned
Land. One night the monster is sighted, but Captain Farragut comes off badly in the encounter.
During the fight, Arronax, faithful Conseil and
Ned Land go overboard. They find refuge on the
back of the monster, which turns out to be a
submarine propelled by electricity and working
along principles very similar to those of the modern submarine. The three men are taken into the
'Nautilus' and become the prisoners of Captain
Nemo, who gives them the liberty of the ship,
but declares his intention of keeping them forever." Haydn. Thesaurus of Bk Digests

"Anticipating submarine construction, the author
describes the wondrous voyages, piracies, and disasters of a submarine ship. The Byronic Captain
Nemo is not a bad specimen of Verne's intrepid
leaders." Baker's Best

Followed by: The mysterious island

Vestly, Anne-Cath.

Aurora and Socrates; tr. from the Norwegian
by Eileen Amos; illus. by Leonard Kessler.
Crowell [1977 c1975] 143p illus $7.95 (3-5)
     Fic

1 Family life—Fiction 2 Baby sitters—Fiction
3 Norway—Fiction
ISBN 0-690-01293-4   LC 76-43038

Original Norwegian edition, 1969. This translation
first published 1975 in England

Continues the adventures of the Norwegian family
begun in: Hello Aurora, o.p. 1981

"The smooth sailing of a . . . family featuring a
house-person father, working on his dissertation
in Greek history, and a lawyer mother, away long
hours each day, hits some ripples when the two
children, 'Aurora and Socrates', face their father's
absence during the final stages of defending his
thesis. Being cared for by neighbor Gran, who lives
a more rural, secluded life, and by Uncle Brande
teaches the youngsters to adapt to unfamiliar ways
of doing everyday things." Sch Library J

"With perceptive characterization, the writing
intimately conveys childish feelings about small
and necessary details of family life and playing
with friends. Despite the Scandinavian background,
the reader feels a universality in the characters
and their relationships. Ideal for reading aloud to
younger children." Horn Bk

Vining, Elizabeth

The taken girl. Viking 1972 190p lib.
bdg. $7.95 (5 and up)   **Fic**

1 Orphans—Fiction 2 Philadelphia—Fiction
3 Whittier, John Greenleaf—Fiction 4 Abolitionists—Fiction
ISBN 0-670-69099-6   LC 79-185349

Set in 1837, this is the story of Veer Schuyler,
a fourteen-year-old orphan who, after an unhappy
experience with a New Jersey family, is delighted
when a "Philadelphia woman who keeps a boarding house offers to take her. Although the Quaker
residents, among them John Greenleaf Whittier,
are all older they treat her as an equal and include
her in their activities, mostly antislavery. Veer
blossoms under responsibility and proves to be
an asset especially in a crisis brought on by mounting opposition to the abolitionists." Booklist

"The book has historical interest and an attractive protagonist; it is capably written and has no
lack of action; it is weakened somewhat by the
fact that the material about the anti-slavery movement almost overwhelms the story." Chicago.
Children's Bk Center

Wagner, Jane

J. T. With pictures by Gordon Parks, Jr.
Dell [1971 c1969] 124p illus pa $1.25 (3-6)
     Fic

1 Cats—Fiction 2 Harlem, New York (City)—
Fiction 3 Blacks—Fiction
ISBN 0-440-44275-3

"A Yearling book"

First published 1969 by Van Nostrand-Reinhold

"J. T., a constant worry to his anxious mother
since his father has left, is running from neighborhood toughs [who are] after the radio he has
stolen, when he finds a badly wounded one-eyed
alley cat. Secretly and ingeniously J. T. builds a
shelter for the cat in an abandoned stove and feeds
and nurses it until it is killed by a car. His brief
association with the cat and the resultant understanding of the adults in his life are sharply felt."
Booklist

"This appealing story about a little Harlem boy
. . . is based on a film shown on the CBS [tele-
vision] Children's Hour. The illustrations are excellent photographs of the cast." NY Pub Library.
The Black Experience in Children's Bks

Waldron, Ann

The integration of Mary-Larkin Thornhill.
Dutton 1975 137p lib. bdg. $7.95 (6 and up)
     Fic

1 School integration—Fiction 2 School stories
ISBN 0-525-32580-8   LC 75-15505

"The travails and triumphs of Mary-Larkin.
Integration comes to her town, Stonewall. Virtually
all her friends and their families move, to avoid a
transfer to a black junior high school. Mary-
Larkin's father is a minister and at war with
discrimination; her mother is equally determined
that integration shall work. The girl finds herself
with only one white friend at school, 'Critter,' a
boy she despises but learns to respect. She also
makes friends with the blacks after some trying
experiences." Pub W

"Because of the absence of any element of violence, the author was able to develop the story
in a somewhat comic vein. Die-hard adults are
contrasted with the earnest yet good-humored
evangelical Thornhills, while emotional and even
bitter outbursts on the part of both black and
white young people are balanced by the account
of how they finally learned to live together." Horn
Bk

Walker, David

Big Ben; illus. by Victor Ambrus. Houghton 1969 134p $5.95 (3-5) **Fic**

1 Dogs—Fiction
ISBN 0-395-07167-4   LC 74-82477

An automobile accident on the highway that ran past the Bruce farm was responsible for the fact that Big Ben, a bumbling St Bernard pup, became the Bruces' dog. However, although Big Ben was gentle, a bad-tempered neighboring farmer and his miserable dog caused him and his young owners, Tim and Jinny Bruce many problems

"With simplicity, [the author] tells a good story featuring very real people and a very lovable dog." Sch Library J

Walsh, Jill Paton

A chance child. Farrar, Straus 1978 185p $8.95 (5 and up) **Fic**

1 Fantastic fiction   2 Great Britain—Fiction
3 Child labor—Fiction
ISBN 0-374-31236-2   LC 78-21521

An illegitimate child "raised in a locked closet chances out of his prison when it is knocked open by a wrecking ball. Accepting the only name he's heard, Creep wanders down a river, through a lock, and into the past, where he finds children of the English Industrial Revolution just as mistreated as he. Joining forces with two of them, he establishes a place for himself, grows up, and leaves a message to be discovered by his brother, the only person who ever fed or cared for him." Booklist

The story provides the author "with a fictional peg upon which to hang well-researched and blood chilling accounts of the blighting labor conditions youngsters withstood in the 'bad old days.' Detailed descriptions of the workings of giant machines, the dreary and crippling tasks required to keep them going, and the transformation of green lands into grim pits and slashes in the earth are raw, precise, and memorable. Clipped dialogue including dialect and period idioms is pungent and, despite some unusual vocabulary, will not be a problem to good readers. . . . The dramatic tension is sustained throughout by the artful handling of the time travel theme and the deft juxtaposition in alternate chapters of a parallel plot: Creep's half brother searches for the missing boy, tracking him, finally, to a capsule farewell in an obscure volume of Parliamentary Papers." Sch Library J

Fireweed. Avon 1973 141p pa $1.75 (5 and up) **Fic**

1 London—Bombardment, 1940—Fiction 2 World War, 1939-1945—Fiction
ISBN 0-380-01185-9

First published 1969 in England; 1970 in U.S. by Farrar, Straus

A "first-person story about two lonely young English teen-agers of differing backgrounds who meet by chance and join forces for protection and companionship during the bombing raids on London in 1940. Despite the hardships and heartaches of everyday life in the wartorn city, fifteen-year-old Bill, the narrator, and Julie, who is slightly younger, enjoy their free, unsupervised existence. . . . [The] dependent relationship which develops between them, and which ends abruptly when Julie is hospitalized after being rescued from a collapsed building and her family appears on the scene, reveals the naivete and vulnerability as well as the self-reliance of youth." Booklist

"The end is as poignant, as bitter, and as inevitable as a classic tragedy. The setting is at once theatrical and realistic, the theme touching, the plot simple and effective. Moreover, the writing has an effortless, colloquial flow." Sat Rev

Goldengrove. Farrar, Straus 1972 130p $4.50 (6 and up) **Fic**

1 Great Britain—Fiction   2 Brothers and sisters —Fiction
ISBN 0-374-32696-7   LC 72-81484

"At their grandmother's seaside home in Cornwall cousins Madge and Paul discover this vacation is different. Paul is still a child, while Madge, about to leave childhood behind, is drawn to the blind professor who rents Gran's cottage and is content to sit reading to him. When the children learn that they are really brother and sister separated years earlier by their parents' divorce Paul is young enough to relish the idea, but Madge feeling rejected by her father offers her love to the professor who also rejects her. Set in

a richly evoked seascape and peopled with believable characters sympathetically portrayed the quiet, gentle story . . . reflects with sensitivity and immediacy the bittersweetness of growing up." Booklist

Followed by: Unleaving. Farrar, Straus $5.95 (ISBN 0- 374-38042-2; LC 76-8857)

Ward, Lynd

The silver pony; a story in pictures. Houghton 1973 174p illus $10.95 (2-4) **Fic**

1 Horses—Fiction   2 Stories without words
ISBN 0-395-14753-0   LC 72-5402

"Eighty pictures in shades of gray, black, and white tell the story of a lonely farm boy whose dreams of his adventures on a winged horse become confused with reality. One night the boy leans out his window fantasizing that the horse is carrying him to the moon; but the dream turns into a nightmare as rockets and missiles fill the air around them, then explode, killing the horse and sending the boy hurtling through space—really out the window to his own yard below. The boy recovers physically and, with the help of his parents, doctor, and a real colt, emotionally. This is a complex story subtly conveyed without words —a unique experience for readers and nonreaders alike." Booklist

Weik, Mary Hays

The Jazz Man; woodcuts by Ann Grifalconi. Atheneum Pubs. 1966 42p illus lib. bdg. $6.95, pa $1.95 (3-5) **Fic**

1 Jazz music—Fiction   2 Blacks—Fiction   3 Harlem, New York (City)—Fiction
ISBNN 0-689-30021-2; 0-689-30098-0   LC 66-5715

"Lame and lonely, isolated because he lives on the top floor of a large Harlem building, young Zeke finds comfort and pleasure listening to the jazz pianist in a neighboring apartment. But his mother, defeated by poverty, leaves home. Then his father disappears and, finally, even the jazz man moves away. For a brief time, Zeke is truly abandoned." Moorachian. What is a City?

"Illustrated with expressive woodcuts, an honest picture of a child with real problems." Notable Children's Bks. 1966

Westall, Robert

The machine gunners. Greenwillow Bks. [1976 c1975] 186p $7.75, lib. bdg. $7.44 (6 and up) **Fic**

1 World War, 1939-1945—Fiction   2 Great Britain —Fiction
ISBN 0-688-80055-6; 0-688-84055-8   LC 76-13630

First published 1975 in England

"This story of World War II recreates vividly the drama and terror of a small town [in northern England] that is strafed daily by German planes and that expects invasion. One of the children, Chas, has stumbled on a machine gun in a downed plane; with the help of four other youngsters and a retarded adult, the gun is hidden (in an underground shelter which the children equip and man) and used. Military authorities suspect the group, but cannot find the shelter. And they never suspect that a German soldier is also there; Rudi has stumbled in, tired and ill, been taken prisoner and become a friend, exchanging his knowledge of gunnery for a promised escape boat. The final episode is taut with suspense; the entire story is fast-paced and convincing, with strong characterization and dialogue. The writing style is competent and even, its sober realism given variety by moments of pathos or humor." Chicago. Children's Bk Center

The Watch House. Greenwillow Bks. 1977 218p $7.50, lib. bdg. $7.20 (5 and up) **Fic**

1 Ghosts—Fiction   2 Great Britain—Fiction
ISBN 0-688-80149-8; 0-688-84149-X   LC 77-19088

"Miserable, almost desperate, over her parents' disintegrating marriage, Anne is brought by her nagging, insensitive mother to stay with two elderly people in Garmouth, the North Sea town of 'The Machine Gunners' [entered above]. Fascinated by the Watch House, a decaying museum filled with the relics of disasters at sea, the lonely girl becomes aware of extraordinary occurrences: Urgent pleas for help appear in writing on a dusty shelf, a human skull suddenly adopts the violent behavior of a poltergeist, and messages in Morse code are dispatched by a disembodied force. Aided by two new friends . . . Anne ferrets out evidence about historic local shipwrecks, information made

Westall, Robert—*Continued*

meaningful by her mesmeric visions of the past; and it becomes clear that the importunate ghost is, in turn, haunted by an even more compelling specter." Horn Bk

"The price of admission to 'The Watch House' is high in terms of effort and patience demanded, but for those readers who can manage the challenging vocabulary and major doses of British slang and dialect, the rewards are numerous and varied. Westall is a wordsmith of consummate skill . . . his characters are believable, unique, and multi-dimensional; and he has important things to say about values, responsibility, and relationships." Sch Library J

The wind eye. Greenwillow Bks. [1977 c1976] 213p illus $7.75, lib. bdg. $7.44 (5 and up)   **Fic**

1 Great Britain—Fiction 2 Cuthbert, Saint—Fiction 3 Space and time—Fiction 4 Fantastic fiction
ISBN 0-688-80114-5; 0-688-84114-1   LC 77-5162
First published 1976 in England
Set on the Northumbrian coast, this story centers on a contemporary English family. "The Studdards have come there for a holiday in an old house willed to Bertrand by his recently deceased uncle. The children soon discover a very old boat of unusual design which turns out to be a kind of time machine that takes them back to St. Cuthbert's period and for Beth and Sally, to the saint himself." Sch Library J

This "intriguing time-shift story has a solid contemporary base and is at the same time a perceptive story of the adjustment to stepparents of three children who have an affinity that transcends their divided loyalties. . . . Westall's characterization is firm, particularly astute in drawing the petulant, egocentric Madeleine and her relationships with other family members. The plot is tightly constructed and nicely meshes realistic and fantastic aspects, and the story has good pace and a compelling narrative flow." Chicago. Children's Bk Center

White, E. B.

Charlotte's web; pictures by Garth Williams. Harper 1952 184p illus $5.95, lib. bdg. $6.49, pa $1.95 (3-6)   **Fic**

1 Pigs—Fiction 2 Spiders—Fiction
ISBN 0-06-026385-7; 0-06-026386-5;   LC 52-9760
Also available in a large type edition for $10 (ISBN 0-06-026387-3; LC 77-3886)
The story of a little girl who could talk to animals, but especially the story of the pig, Wilbur, and his friendship with Charlotte, the spider, who could not only talk but write as well

"Illustrated with amusing sketches . . . [this] story is a fable for adults as well as children and can be recommended to older children and parents as an amusing story and a gentle essay on friendship." Library J

Stuart Little; illus. by Garth Williams. Harper 1945 131p illus $5.95, lib. bdg. $6.49, pa $1.95 (3-6)   **Fic**

1 Mice—Fiction
ISBN 0-06-026395-4; 0-06-026396-2; 0-02-440056-5   LC 45-9585
Into a normal American family there was born a second son whom everybody noticed was no bigger than a mouse. It was no time at all until everybody knew that he was a mouse. This is the story of the life and adventures of this unusual person, named Stuart by his parents

"Although 'Stuart Little' may be listed as a children's book, and children will undoubtedly be the excuse for getting it into the house, it is for all ages, all shapes and sizes of readers who like the light fantastic tone." Sat Rev

The trumpet of the swan; pictures by Edward Frascino. Harper 1970 210p illus $6.95, lib. bdg. $6.89, pa $1.95 (3-6)   **Fic**

1 Swans—Fiction
ISBN 0-06-026397-0; 0-06-026398-9; 0-06-44048-4   LC 72-112484
"The focus of this book is Louis, a trumpeter swan who was born mute. Unable to court a lovely swan, Serena, Louis is saved from a lonely fate by his father, who steals a trumpet so that his son may communicate better. Because he is talented and resourceful, Louis is able to earn enough money

as a professional musician to pay for the instrument, and most importantly, to win Serena." Wis Library Bul

The author "deftly blends true birdlore with fanciful adventures in a witty, captivating fantasy." Booklist

White, Robb

Fire storm; a novel. Doubleday 1979 111p $6.95, lib. bdg. $7.90 (4 and up)   **Fic**

1 Forest fires—Fiction
ISBN 0-385-14630-2; 0-385-14631-0   LC 78-72186
"A forest ranger, full of righteous indignation, hunts for a boy who he is sure set a forest fire. In doing this, he puts himself and the boy in the middle of a 'fire storm.' But the boy is wise in the ways of the woods and fires, and he saves both himself and the ranger. The ending is a surprise both to the reader and to the forest ranger." Babbling Bookworm

"Emphasis on dialogue interspersed with terse descriptive passages suggest a play rather than a fully developed novel. Fast-moving and spare, the narrative maintains suspense as the protagonists rapidly establish and intensify the conflict. Because of its brevity, pace, and uncomplicated structure, the book could serve as bait for the reluctant reader and also appeal to aficionados of the survival story." Horn Bk

Wibberley, Leonard

John Treegate's musket. Farrar, Straus 1959 188p $6.95 (6 and up)   **Fic**

1 U.S.—History—Revolution, 1775-1783—Fiction 2 Boston—Fiction
ISBN 0-374-33762-4   LC 59-10188
"An Ariel book"
The first of a series of books about the Treegate family, this begins a trilogy set during the Revolutionary War. A second trilogy set during the War of 1812 begins with: Leonard's prey, entered below
In 1769, just after his pro-Royalist father has sailed for England on business, 11-year-old Peter Treegate of Boston unwittingly becomes involved in a dock murder. Fleeing arrest, he takes refuge on an American cargo ship which is subsequently wrecked off the South Carolina coast. Peter is rescued by a Scotsman who, in 1775, helps him rejoin his father, now an embattled American patriot, ready to fight at Bunker Hill

An "unusually clear presentation of the political and military mind of the period." Bookmark

Followed by: Peter Treegate's war and Treegate's raiders, both o.p. 1980

Leopard's prey. Farrar, Straus 1971 183p $4.50 (6 and up)   **Fic**

1 U.S.—History—War of 1812—Fiction 2 Sea stories
ISBN 0-374-34378-0   LC 78-149225
"An Ariel book"
This is the first novel in a trilogy about events connected with the War of 1812. It continues the chronicles of the Treegate family begun in: Johnny Treegate's musket, entered above

Manley Treegate "becomes involved in an incident that was one of the provocative causes of the War of 1812: the firing of the British frigate 'Leopard' on the American frigate 'Chesapeake,' and the impressment of several of its seamen. Young Manley Treegate is accused of helping a deserter and impressed as a powder boy, escapes and is picked up by a Haitian pirate and returned home when a large reward is offered." Chicago. Children's Bk Center

Followed by these books, also available from Farrar, Straus:
Red pawns $5.95 (ISBN 0-374-36240-8; LC 73-82695)
The last battle $7.95 (ISBN 0-374-34349-7; LC 75-42104)

Wier, Ester

The loner; illus. by Christine Price. McKay 1963 153p illus $5.95 (5 and up)   **Fic**

1 Shepherds—Fiction 2 Migrant labor—Fiction 3 Montana—Fiction
ISBN 0-679-20097-5   LC 63-9334
"A juvenile migratory worker, who knows neither his name nor his age, searches for identity. . . . After his only friend is killed by a farm machine, the rootless waif winds up with a Montana sheep herder, a lonely old woman. Living with her, he adjusts painfully at first, to a new life, earns the name David, slays his Goliath (a grizzly bear) and best of all, overcomes his self-doubt." NY Times Bk Rev

Wier, Ester—*Continued*

"Unusually well developed characterization of both people and animals. The shocking death . . . is realistically but not morbidly treated. Many values for a young adolescent, especially one who is himself a 'loner' or who has sustained a sudden personal tragedy. A sensitive [tale]." Sch Library J

Wiggin, Kate Douglas

The Birds' Christmas Carol; illus. by Jessie Gillespie. Memorial ed. Houghton 1941 84p illus $9.95 (3-5) **Fic**

1 Christmas—Fiction
ISBN 0-395-07204-2   LC 41-52029

"How Carol Bird made a merry Christmas for the 'Ruggleses in the rear.'" Prentice and Power
A well-known Christmas story, first published 1888, which has both humor and pathos. Nearly every page of this edition is illustrated in color or in black and white

Rebecca of Sunnybrook farm (4 and up) **Fic**

1 New England—Fiction

Some editions are:
Houghton (Riverside bookshelf) $5.95 With illustrations by Helen Mason Grose (ISBN 0-395-07074-0; LC 25-18699)
Macmillan Pub. Co. (The Macmillan classics) $6.95 Illustrated by Lawrence Beall Smith (ISBN 0-02-792660-5; LC 62-18397)
First published 1903
"A child character that will be loved as long as there are girls and sympathetic grown-ups to read the book. Rebecca, high-spirited and loving, comes to live with her two austere old-maid aunts. The effect of that sunny personality in the hitherto gloomy house is touchingly shown in the course of the story." Bookshelf for Boys and Girls

Wilder, Laura Ingalls

Farmer boy; illus. by Garth Williams. Newly illustrated, uniform ed. Harper 1953 371p illus $8.95, lib. bdg. $8.79, pa $2.95 (4-6) **Fic**

1 Farm life—Fiction 2 New York (State)—Fiction
ISBN 0-06-026425-X; 0-06-026421-7; 0-06-440003-4
LC 52-7527
First published 1933
"This story takes the reader to New York State in the 1860's, when Almanzo Wilder, later to appear in the 'Little House' stories [entered below], is nine years old. His life on a farm is described in humorous, realistic detail." Hodges. Bks for Elem Sch Libraries
"Not only is the story of Almanzo a delightful tale, but we have never read a more faithful account of life on a farm in the days before good farms and farm-houses became mechanized and electrified." Boston Transcript

Little house in the big woods; illus. by Garth Williams. Newly illustrated, uniform ed. Harper 1953 237p illus (4-6) **Fic**

1 Frontier and pioneer life—Fiction 2 Wisconsin—Fiction
ISBN 0-06-026430-6; 0-06-026431-4; 0-06-440001-8
LC 527525
First published 1932
This book, the first in a series, "has a refreshingly genuine and lifelike quality. . . . [and takes place] on the edge of the Big Woods of Wisconsin. . . . The story of Laura, and Mary and their parents, who lived in a log cabin, miles from neighbors and a settlement, is full of incidents and accounts of daily doings that boys and girls will enjoy." NY Times Bk Rev
Followed by these books, also available from Harper:
Little house on the prairie $8.95, lib. bdg. $8.79, pa $1.25 (ISBN 0-06-026445-4; 0-06-026446-2; 0-06-080357-6; LC 52-7526)
On the banks of Plum Creek $8.95, lib. bdg. $8.79, pa $2.95 (ISBN 0-06-026470-5; 0-06-026471-3; 0-06-440004-2; LC 52-7528)
By the shores of Silver Lake $8.95, lib. bdg. $8.79, pa $2.95 (ISBN 0-06-026416-0; 0-06-026417-9; 0-06-440005-0; LC 52-7529)

The long winter $8.95, lib. bdg. $8.79, pa $2.95 (ISBN 0-06-026460-8; 0-06-026461-6; 0-06-440006-9; LC 52-7530)
Little town on the prairie $8.95, lib. bdg. $8.79, pa $2.95 (ISBN 0-06-026450-0; 0-06-026451-0; 0-06-440007-7; LC 52-7531)
These happy golden years $8.95, lib. bdg $8.79, pa $2.95 (ISBN 0-06-026480-2; 0-06-026481-0; 0-06-440008-5; LC 52-7532)
The first four years $8.95, lib. bdg. $8.79, pa $1.95 (ISBN 0-06-026426-8; 0-06-026427-6; 0-06-440031-X; LC 76-135774)

Wilkinson, Brenda

Ludell. Harper 1975 170p $7.95, lib. bdg. $8.79 (6 and up) **Fic**

1 Blacks—Fiction 2 Georgia—Fiction
ISBN 006-026491-8; 0-06-026492-6   LC 75-9390

"Ludell Wilson lives with her grandmother in a small Georgia town. Her unmarried mother works in New York. Ludell is in fifth grade in a segregated school, presided over by a teacher who is unfeeling about any special problems her students might have. Most of the book centers on that period and on Ludell's relationship with her friends and the church-going grandmother who cares for her. However, the last few chapters pass swiftly through the next two years, when Ludell falls in love and decides to become a writer." Adventuring with Bks
The author "has worked her own Southern childhood background into a vividly atmospheric story." Booklist
Followed by these books, also available from Harper:
Ludell and Willie $7.95, lib. bdg. $8.79 (ISBN 0-06-026487-X; 0-06-026488-8; LC 76-18402)
Ludell's New York time $8.95, lib. bdg. $8.79 (ISBN 0-06-02648606; 0-06-026498-5; LC 79-3173)

Willard, Barbara

The lark and the laurel. Harcourt 1970 207p $5.95 (6 and up) **Fic**

1 Great Britain—History—Tudors, 1485-1603—Fiction

"Cecily Jolland's father is a turncoat Lancastrian and as Richard III's supporter can expect no mercy from the victorious party he deserted. Only his own danger would have made him consent to leave Cecily, so delicately brought up . . . at Mantlemass Manor with her mannish aunt, the sister whom he had wronged. . . . Her father's expected return gradually becomes a threat as Cecily learns to love country life, the forest, her aunt and above all their neighbour Lewis Mallory." Best Sellers
"From the very first sentence it is obvious just how practiced a storyteller Miss Willard is. 'Cecily has been brought to Mantlemass at dusk.' . . . At once we feel Cecily's helplessness. Mantlemass has a properly medieval taste, and dusk is the right time for shady goings-on. And never does Miss Willard fall below the standard of that opening as she unravels an entrancing tale of cruel fathers, arranged marriages, sensible aunts, and a true love." Christian Sci Monitor
Followed by:
The sprig of broom o.p. 1981
A cold wind blowing o.p. 1981
The iron lily. Dutton $5.95 (ISBN 0-525-32592-1; LC 74-7195)
Harrow and harvest o.p. 1981

Storm from the west; illus. by Douglas Hall. Harcourt [1964 c1963] 189p illus $5.95 (6 and up) **Fic**

1 Scotland—Fiction 2 Family life—Fiction
ISBN 0-15-280480-3   LC 64-17089

First published 1963 in England with title: The battle of Wednesday week
This is a thoroughly entertaining story of family relationships and conflicts. Two sets of children, two of them English and four Americans, are brought together through the marriage of their widowed parents. When their prejudices and jealousies become too much, the parents leave the children, ranging in age from ten to sixteen, at the mother's cottage in Kilmorah, Scotland, and go off together. Forced to work out their problems alone, the children do so in ways that are both realistic and, often, humorous. Good characterization and excellent sibling relationships." Eakin. Good Bks for Children

Willard, Nancy

The Island of the Grass King; the further adventures of Anatole; illus. by David McPhail; decorative letters by John O'Connor. Harcourt 1979 120p illus $7.95 (4 and up)   Fic

1 Fantastic fiction
ISBN 0-15-239082-0   LC 78-20574

Sequel to: Sailing to Cythera, published as part of Sailing to Cythera, and other Anatole stories

"Anatole is concerned because his grandmother needs fennel to cure her asthma, and none grows in her garden. So he goes off to look for some, accompanied by his cat, Plumpet, and his silver teapot, Quicksilver, riding on a winged rainbow horse. He reaches the 'Island of the Grass King' where, after several adventures, he meets the Grass King, who wears a crown of fennel. Because Anatole has brought the King's daughter back to him from her captivity as a glass statute, the King gives him fennel for his grandmother's garden." Babbling Bookworm

"This is a book for those who revel in the unexpected, in wonderful invention, in powerful and vivid and even mystical fancy. It is fluent, graceful, full of details that surprise yet rub together comfortably with a kind of kaleidoscopic consistency. There are snatches and echoes of poetry . . . flashes of humor and of insight into children, and no sentimentality (the pet cat talks, but also likes a little mole for supper). McPhail's fine line illustrations are as lively, detailed, and well-realized as the book itself." Sch Library J

Williams, Jay

Danny Dunn and the homework machine, by Jay Williams and Raymond Abrashkin; illus by Ezra Jack Keats. McGraw 1958 141p illus $5.95 (3-6)   Fic

1 Computers—Fiction
ISBN 0-07-070519-4   LC 58-10015

"Whittlesey House publications"
"Professor Bullfinch leaves Danny in charge of his miniature automatic computer while he goes to Washington. Danny and two friends work out a scheme using the computer to do their homework. Complications develop when a jealous boy tells their teacher and sabotages the machine." Library J
"Amusing and ingenious." Hodges. Bks for Elem Sch Libraries

Some other books about Danny Dunn also available from McGraw are:
Danny Dunn and the anti-gravity paint lib. bdg. $6.95 (ISBN 0-07-070531-3; LC 67-2719)
Danny Dunn and the automatic house lib. bdg. $6.95 (ISBN 0-07-070533-X; LC 65-22111)
Danny Dunn and the fossil cave lib. bdg. $6.95 (ISBN 0-07-070526-7; LC 61-13173)
Danny Dunn and the smalliflying machine lib. bdg. $6.95 (ISBN 0-07-070537-2; LC 73-7563)
Danny Dunn and the swamp monster lib. bdg. $6.95 (ISBN 0-07-070539-9; LC 77-165257)
Danny Dunn and the universal glue lib. bdg. $6.95 (ISBN 0-07-070550-X; LC 77-78764)
Danny Dunn and the voice from space lib. bdg. $6.95 (ISBN 0-07-070535-6; LC 67-22974)
Danny Dunn and the weather machine $5.95 (ISBN 0-07-070521-6; LC 59-9995)
Danny Dunn, invisible boy $5.95, lib. bdg. $6.95 (ISBN 0-07-070546-1; 0-07-070547-X; LC 73-17415)
Danny Dunn on a desert island lib. bdg. $6.95 (ISBN 0-07-070517-8; LC 57-10924)
Danny Dunn on the ocean floor lib. bdg. $6.95 (ISBN 0-07-070524-0; LC 67-2720)
Danny Dunn, scientific detective lib. bdg. $6.95 (ISBN 0-07-070549-6; LC 75-10826)
Danny Dunn, time traveler lib. bdg. $6.95 (ISBN 0-07-070530-5; LC 63-18545)

The magic grandfather; illus. by Gail Owens. Four Winds 1979 149p illus $7.95 (4-6)   Fic

1 Witchcraft—Fiction 2 Grandfathers—Fiction
ISBN 0-590-07588-8   LC 78-22285

"A super grandpa, humorous, loving, and understanding, is secretly following his own hobby, magic. His grandson Sam is a TV addict who unwittingly moves him into one of Grandpa's spells and zaps Grandpa right out of this world. It's up to Sam to learn enough of the occult from Grandpa's books to get Grandpa back again. And Sam does, and for him TV is replaced by magic!" Babbling Bookworm

"Sam enlists the aid of his cousin Sarah. The two experiment with various spells, encountering some amusing situations before they finally accomplish their goal. Williams, author of the Danny Dunn series, uses the same lighthearted style, lacing it well with doses of magic that offset the unbelievable aspects of the plot. Owens' full-page line and wash drawings add their own touch of reality." Booklist

Williams, Margery

The velveteen rabbit; or, How toys become real; with illus. by William Nicholson. Doubleday illus $4.95, lib. bdg. $5.90 (2-4)   Fic

1 Toys—Fiction 2 Rabbits—Fiction 3 Fairy tales
ISBN 0-385-07725-4; 0-385-07748-3
First published 1922 by Doran
"About the adventures of a rabbit, velveteen at first, and finally, through the agency of the 'Fairy of old toys,' a real rabbit, of whom we catch a last glimpse in William Nicholson's lifelike pictures as he twinkles off into a real wood." Bks for Boys & Girls

Winterfeld, Henry

Casaways in Lilliput; tr. from the German by Kyrill Schabert; illus. by William M. Hutchinson. Harcourt 1960 [c1958] 188p illus $5.95 (4-6)   Fic

1 Fantastic fiction
ISBN 0-15-214820-5   LC 60-8413
Original German edition 1958
"A drifting raft brings three children to an island visible only in a mirage—it is the land of Lilliput, surrounded by a 'layer of air which makes it vanish.' The two boys and a girl . . . meet miniature people speaking English taught by the giant Gulliver who had visited their land 250 years ago. Innocently terrifying them into flight, the three young giants manage, through discovery of a streamlined train, to get a town and convince the residents that they are harmless." Horn Bk
"A lively and ingenious book, well-written, and with the perennial appeal of the combination of the familiar and fantastic." Chicago. Children's Bk Center

Detectives in togas; tr. from the German by Richard and Clara Winston; illus. by Charlotte Kleinert. Harcourt [1966 c1956] 205p illus pa $1.43 (5 and up)   Fic

1 Mystery and detective stories 2 Rome—Fiction
ISBN 0-15-625315-1   LC 56-6922
"Voyager books"
First published 1956 in hardcover
"A rollicking mystery story set in ancient Rome. A group of school boys become involved in the mystery when one of their members is accused of having defaced the wall of a temple by scrawling the words 'Caius is a dumbell' on it in red paint. The other boys rally round to save him and in proving his innocence uncover a political plot. . . . The solving of the mystery is well-handled and plausible." Chicago. Children's Bk Center
"The author's merry style and his ability to draw flesh-and-blood boys and the amusing line drawings of Charlotte Kleinert make this an attractive volume." Sat Rev
Followed by: Mystery of the Roman ransom. Harcourt pa $1.75 (ISBN 0-15-662340-4; LC 77-3673)

Wojciechowska, Maia

Shadow of a bull; drawings by Alvin Smith. Atheneum Pubs. 1964 165p illus $7.95 (6 and up)   Fic

1 Bullfights—Fiction 2 Spain—Fiction
ISBN 0-689-30042-5   LC 64-12563
Awarded the Newbery Medal, 1965
"Manolo was the son of the great bullfighter Juan Olivar. Ever since his father's death the town of Arcangel [Spain] has waited for [the time] when Manolo would be twelve and face his first bull. From the time he was nine and felt in his heart that he was a coward, Manolo worked and prayed that he might at least face this moment with honor, knowing it could well bring his death." Pub W
"In spare, economical prose [the author] makes one feel, see, smell the heat, endure the hot Andalusian sun and shows one the sand and glare of the bullring. Above all, she lifts the veil and gives glimpses of the terrible loneliness in the soul of a boy. Perhaps the ending was ever so slightly contrived. But the whole is so good it does not detract from an eloquent, moving book, superbly illustrated." NY Times Bk Rev
Glossary of bullfighting terms: p157-65

Wolitzer, Hilma

Toby lived here. Farrar, Straus 1978 147p
$6.95 (5 and up)   **Fic**

1 Foster home care—Fiction 2 Single parent
family—Fiction 3 Mental illness—Fiction
ISBN 0-374-37625-5   LC 78-4550

"The story of a twelve-year-old girl's adjustment to her young mother's nervous breakdown is
told with emotional sincerity and perceptiveness.
At the outset Toby and her younger sister Anne
are sent to a foster home while their mother is
recovering. The book focuses on Toby's unwilling-
ness and inability to express her feelings of guilt
and resentment as well as on her discomfort in
finding herself with a set of foster parents. . . .
Her loneliness and fear are often compounded by
the lies which she tells to 'cover her mother's
situation; yet her foster parents are amazingly
understanding. Though the author's style lacks
smoothness in parts, she approaches a sensitive
subject with honesty and care. The open-ended
conclusion to the book seems both appropriate and
inevitable." Horn Bk

Wormser, Richard

The black mustanger; illus by Don
Bolognese. Morrow 1971 190p illus $6.75, lib.
bdg. $6.48 (5 and up)   **Fic**

1 Horses—Fiction 2 The West (U.S.)—Fiction
3 Blacks—Fiction
ISBN 0-688-21104-6; 0-688-31104-0   LC 79-142992

In post-Civil War days the Riker family moved
from Tennessee to Texas where they hoped to
escape from the problems and hatreds of the
past. But they found life just as difficult there
and it was not until Mesteño Will, a half black-
half Apache mustanger appeared that things
began to improve

"The setting is colorful, the construction of the
story taut and economical, the plot well-paced
and convincing." Sutherland. The Best in Children's Bks

Wrightson, Patricia

The ice is coming. Atheneum Pubs. 1977
222p illus $5.95 (5 and up)   **Fic**

1 Fantastic fiction 2 Australia—Fiction
ISBN 0-689-50081-5   LC 76-45438

"A Margaret K. McElderry book"
"Only Wirrun, a young Aboriginal man living
among the white inhabitants of an Australian
coastal town, recognizes that something strange
and sinister is happening. . . . It is the beginning of an attempt by the Ninya, ancient
ice creatures, to overwhelm the land. . . . The
Ninya must first capture the eldest Nargun,
an age-old monster with the power of fire.
Wirrun, accompanied by one of the Mimi, rock
spirits of the north, attempts to find the eldest
Nargun first. Helped by other spirits and by
other Aborigines, he confronts the Ninya." Sch
Library J
This "story begins slowly, gathers momentum
like a boulder, and pounds to a smashing finish
in which all the scattered forces of the landscape, spirit and mortal, are mustered to turn
back the deadly cold. Few books for young
readers, East or West, convey so grand and
sweeping a sense of the land, or are written
with such majestic grace." NY Times Bk Rev

Followed by these books, also available from
Atheneum Pubs:
The dark bright water $7.95 (ISBN 0-689-50122-6;
LC 78-8793)
Journey behind the wind $8.95 (ISBN 0-689-50198-
6; LC 80-25005)

The Nargun and the stars. Atheneum Pubs.
1974 184p illus $6.95 (5 and up)   **Fic**

1 Fantastic fiction 2 Australia—Fiction
ISBN 0-689-30432-3   LC 73-85323

"A Margaret K. McElderry book"
First published 1973 in England
This is a fantasy set in Northern Australia.
An ancient stone monster called the Nargun
"threatens to crush the home of orphaned
Simon's middle-aged cousins, Charlie and Edie.
To rid themselves of the Nargun they seek help
from other supernatural beings . . . [the] swamp
creatures called the Potkoorok, and . . . tree
inhabitants (the Turongs) who are large black
shadows with long wispy beards. The three
humans must also cope with Nyols . . . spirits
who live deep in the heart of the mountain

itself, but through chicanery and quick-witted-
ness, Charlie, Edie, and Simon finally are free
from the Nargun's power." Library J
"The characters, seemingly plain and uncomplicated people, subtly come to life as complex
human beings; and the essentially simple plot
is worked into the rich fabric of a story that
begins serenely, arches up to a great crescendo
of suspense, and then falls away at the end to
'a whisper in the dark.' " Horn Bk

A racecourse for Andy; illus. by Margaret
Horder. Harcourt 1968 156p illus $5.95 (5
and up)   **Fic**

1 Australia—Fiction 2 Mentally retarded children—Fiction 3 Horse racing—Fiction
ISBN 0-15-265080-6   LC 68-11507

Sydney, Australia is the setting of this story
about "mentally retarded Andy [who] 'buys'
the local racetrack from a bottlepicker. Convinced that he is the owner, no amount of logic
can persuade Andy that he isn't." Sch Library J
"This outstanding story . . . has no aura of
sentimentality, no obtrusive message; it is
poignant just because of the simple acceptance
of Andy by both adults and children. They do
not tolerate him, they like and protect him. A
distinguished book." Sat Rev

Wyss, Johann David

The Swiss family Robinson; ed. by William
H. G. Kingston, illus. by Lynd Ward.
Grosset 1949 388p illus $5.95 (5 and up)   **Fic**

1 Survival (after airplane accidents, shipwrecks, etc.)—Fiction
ISBN 0-448-05822-7   LC 49-49096

"Illustrated junior library"
Originally published 1813 in Switzerland
Tale of a Swiss family shipwrecked on a
desert island, and of their adventures there
"The very improbability of this tale makes it
delightful. 'They did sail in the tubs,' says the
Spectator, 'and train zebras and ostriches for
riding, and grow pines and apples in the same
garden,' and why shouldn't they?" Olcott

Yates, Elizabeth

Carolina's courage; illus. by Nora S.
Unwin. Dutton 1964 94p illus lib. bdg. $7.50
(3-5)   **Fic**

1 Frontier and pioneer life—Fiction 2 Dolls—
Fiction
ISBN 0-525-27480-4   LC 64-10697

"Carolina, her family, and her beloved china
doll Lydia-Lou leave their New Hampshire home
and make a long journey in an ox-drawn covered
wagon to their new home in the Nebraska wilderness. Carolina proves that she is a real pioneer
when she makes the costly sacrifice of trading
her Lydia-Lou for the wagon train's safe passage
through Indian country. A warm, sensitive story
of a close-knit family whose mutual love and
steadfast courage enable them to face the
sorrows, the hardships, and the dangers of
pioneer life." Booklist
"The authoritative writing is that of a poet.
. . . Illustrations are as rich and simple as
these innocent [characters'] lives." NY Times
Bk Rev

Yep, Laurence

Child of the owl. Harper 1977 217 $7.95,
lib. bdg. $8.79 (5 and up)   **Fic**

1 Chinese Americans—Fiction 2 Grandmothers—
Fiction 3 San Francisco—Fiction
ISBN 0-06-026739-9; 0-06-026743-7   LC 76-24314

The story is set in "San Francisco's Chinatown
in the early '60s. . . . Casey, a young Chinese
girl whose father [Barney] is a compulsive
gambler, must live for a time with [Paw-Paw,
her grandmother, whom] she has never seen.
Casey has never thought of herself as Chinese
but life in Chinatown forces her to decide who
she really is. Grandmother is the one who tells
Casey the legend of the owl spirit, and who
helps her realize that she is a child of the
owl—that she may never feel completely at ease
as a Chinese or as an American, but that she
cannot completely cut herself off from her Chinese
heritage." Christian Sci Monitor

Yep, Laurence—*Continued*

"The author is well-qualified to write fiction portraying life in San Francisco's Chinatown before immigration rules were relaxed in 1965—a part of the city he regards as 'not so much a place as a state of mind . . . and of heart.' . . . [The book] is a haunting piece of fiction in which the many elements are masterfully blended." Horn Bk

Dragonwings. Harper 248p $8.95, lib. bdg. $8.79, pa $2.95 (5 and up)   **Fic**

1 Chinese Americans—Fiction   2 San Francisco —Fiction
ISBN 0-06-026737-2; 0-06-026738-0; 0-06-440085-9
LC 74-2625

This is "the story of a talented Chinese immigrant (Windrider) and his son (Moonshadow) who, in the early 1900's, dream of building a flying machine and succeed in making their dream come true. Along with the dream they must contend with the realities of the new land. . . . The story is told in the first person with delightful humor, as young Moonshadow reacts to the strange ways of the White 'demons.' Through his vision the reader learns many authentic details of life in China, where Moonshadow lived with his mother and grandmother, and of life in San Francisco's early Chinatown where Moonshadow has joined his father." Interracial Bks for Children Bul

"The plot seems occasionally forced, and at times the language seems more ornate than that which a young immigrant would be likely to use; but never mind. If it were only a fantastic story of high adventure, 'Dragonwings' would be a success, but as an exquisitely written poem of praise to the courage and industry of the Chinese-American people, it is a triumph." NY Times Bk Rev

Sea glass. Harper 1979 213p $8.95, lib. bdg. $8.79 (6 and up)   **Fic**

1 Chinese Americans—Fiction   2 Parent and child—Fiction   3 California—Fiction   4 Sports—Fiction
ISBN 0-06-026744-5; 0-06-026745-3   LC 78-22487

"Being Chinese-American in a little town like Concepcion has its drawbacks for Craig Chin. His father wants him to 'try twice as hard as any Western person,' and the other kids call him the 'Buddha Man.' He gets help in his struggle just to be himself from an unexpected source, when old Uncle Quail invites Craig to share the wonders of his seaside recluse with him." Children's Bk Rev Serv

The author "skillfully packs a host of important themes (ethnicity, self-worth, family expectations, social status, etc.) into a winning, often moving story. He also makes distinct and complex characters out of stock types (wise old uncle, rebellious soulmate, hard-driving Dad.)" Sch Library J

Sweetwater; pictures by Julia Noonan. Harper 1973 201p illus $8.95 (6 and up)   **Fic**

1 Science fiction
ISBN 0-06-026735-6   LC 72-9867

"In a science fantasy set on the planet Harmony, the descendants of stranded starship crews live in the half-submerged city of Old Sion. Tyree, who tells the story, belongs to the Silky colony of Old Sion and loves the simple life they lead. A musician, the boy studies with Amadeus, the great alien teacher (and one of the most sympathetic alien characters of science fiction). The city's existence is threatened by a faction that wants to modernize Old Sion, and the Silkies must also combat the sea creatures, the Hydra, which invade the colony. The final sequence is fast-paced and has well-maintained suspense, and the plot—although ornate and diffuse—is imaginative. The characterization is good, but the strongest aspect of the story is in the vivid evocation of setting." Chicago. Children's Bk Center

Yolen, Jane

The boy who had wings; pictures in wax-crayon by Helga Aichinger. Crowell 1974 unp illus lib. bdg. $8.79 (3-5)   **Fic**

1 Greece—Fiction
ISBN 0-690-15900-5   LC 73-17010

"Cast in the general style of a legend, the story tells of Aetos, a Greek boy who was born with a pair of soft, 'golden-white' wings. His family was uneasy and ashamed, and his mother made him a black goat-hair cape to cover his shoulders, admonishing him never to show his wings. Forgotten and lonely, Aetos played by himself. . . . Not until his father was lost in a mountain storm did Aetos discover the great joy of flying; for when he set forth in search of his father, the icy mountain winds tore the cape from his shoulders and the great golden wings were freed. But after the rescue of his father, the beautiful wings, frozen by the bitter cold, dropped from his shoulders." Horn Bk

"An original tale with allegorical overtones distinguished by dazzling art work. . . . The simple story is set off to best advantage by the impressive full-page wax-crayon paintings. Aichinger achieves myriad effects and textures—from sea foam to a spinner's yarn—to convey a timeless Aegean scene." Sch Library J

The seeing stick; pictures by Remy Charlip and Demetra Maraslis. Crowell 1977 unp illus $6.95, lib. bdg. $6.79 (2-4)   **Fic**

1 Blind—Fiction   2 China—Fiction
ISBN 0-690-00455-9; 0-690-00596-2   LC 75-6946

"Yolen tells a sensitive and graceful story of a small, blind [Chinese] princess whose rich, powerful father, the Emperor, cannot give her the most precious gift of all—her sight. A tattered, old wood carver brings her the wide world, however, by telling stories of wonders he has seen on his travels and carving them into the golden wood of a stick. As he invites her to feel not only the cane but objects surrounding her, she begins to see with 'eyes on the tips of her fingers.'" Sch Library J

Yolen and Charlip "are at their best here. So is their collaborator Maraslis, in her first appearance in a book. The illustrators worked in concert to create pencil drawings and misty pastel-crayon scenes that look like watercolors. . . . Yolen doesn't falsify her touching tale but proves that the princess and others have ways of seeing that don't need eyes." Pub W

Zei, Alki

Petros' war; tr. from the Greek by Edward Fenton. Dutton 1972 236p lib. bdg. $8.79 (5 and up)   **Fic**

1 World War, 1939-1945—Fiction   2 Greece, Modern—Fiction
ISBN 0-525-36962-7   LC 73-179059
Mildred L. Batchelder Award, 1974
Original Greek edition, 1971

When World War II came to Greece, 10-year-old Petros found his dreams of heroism shattered by the grim reality of endurance under the Fascist occupation. He painted slogans on walls for the Resistance but when his best friend was shot in an Athens demonstration he realized that there would be no liberation for the dead

"Here are pleasure and sorrow, courage and cowardice, grandeur and pettiness, all shown with a Chaucerian humor, through the lively family and friends of one sublimely ordinary boy. . . . This is a book which every child should read." Times (London) Lit Sup

The sound of the dragon's feet; tr. from the Greek by Edward Fenton. Dutton 1979 113p $8.50 (5-6)   **Fic**

1 Parent and child—Fiction   2 Russia—Fiction
ISBN 0-525-39712-4   LC 79-14917
Original Greek edition, 1977

In this "story, set in 1894 in a Russian town near the Polish-Lithuanian border, 10-year-old Sasha opens her eyes to the great differences between the rich and the poor around her and begins to question the injustices she observes. She seeks answers from her adored father, an apolitical doctor who treats the sick whether or not they can pay, and from her tutor, a young revolutionary in exile in her town. She obtains help from both of them for a poor girl her own age whom she has found ill in a dark cellar." Sch Library J

"Never didactic or doctrinaire, the story, with its episodic but subtly woven plot, is filled with the faint, distant rumblings of the Russian Revolution, while the richly varied characters are refracted through the momentary but urgent experiences—pleasurable as well as thought-provoking—of an alert young child." Horn Bk

Zhitkov, Boris

How I hunted the little fellows; tr. from the Russian by Djemma Bider; illus. by Paul O. Zelinsky. Dodd 1979 unp illus $6.95 (2-4) **Fic**

1 Ships—Models—Fiction 2 Russia—Fiction
ISBN 0-396-07692-0   LC 79-11738

The story is set in "a long-gone Russian town where little Boria (the narrator) visits his grandmother. Generous and loving, the woman nevertheless forbids Boria to touch her treasure, a marvelously complete miniature steamship—her 'dear memory.' But the boy is obsessed by finding tiny sailors he envisions inside the ship. When he's alone, he pulls the graceful thing apart and can't put it together again." Pub W

"In addition to skillfully suggesting the motif of little people frequently found in children's books, Boria's story astutely reveals the intenseness of the child's experiences and his emotional relationship with his grandmother. The narrative, however, ends abruptly and somewhat inconclusively. . . . The carefully detailed and shaded hatched drawings on practically every page evoke a mood of late nineteenth-century domesticity and successfully portray the steamship and its imaginary little crew." Horn Bk

Zimnik, Reiner

The bear and the people; written and illus. by Reiner Zimnik; tr. from the German by Nina Ignatowicz. Harper 1971 78p illus lib. bdg. $8.79 (3-6) **Fic**

1 Bears—Fiction
ISBN 0-06-026818-2   LC 76-105474

Original German edition, 1956

"A bear and his master travel round the fairs of Central Europe, the man a juggler and the bear dancing. Rivals threaten, using the arts of the devil . . . with the help of God are defeated. The years pass, the coming of the motor drives the devoted pair off the highways, and eventually the man dies. After further mishaps and adventures the bear finally achieves happiness in a life half wild, half tamed." Jr Bookshelf

"A beautiful, unusual, deceptively simple tale. . . . Early in the tale, the Bearman, bear and a friend, the Henman, confront the Dudas, a lying, thieving lot, at the big Fair (topless dancers and a bit of swearing add to the realism of this encounter). . . . Pen-and-ink illustrations are in harmony with the text and children of almost any age should be caught up in this deeply moving story." Library J

S C STORY COLLECTIONS

Books in this class contain both collections of short stories by one author and collections by more than one author. Folk tales are entered in class 398.2. Collections of general literature, American literature, English literature, etc.—which may include but are not limited to short stories—are entered in classes 808.8, 810.8, 820.8, etc.

A-haunting we will go; ghostly stories and poems; selected by Lee Bennett Hopkins and illus. by Vera Rosenberry. Whitman, A. 1977 127p illus $7.75 (3-6) **S C**

1 Ghosts—Fiction 2 Short stories
ISBN 0-8075-0006-2   LC 76-45449

Stories included are: How Horace learned to moan, by E. Ireland; Jimmy takes vanishing lessons, by W. R. Brooks; The ninety-sixth ghost, by L. B. Hopkins; The ghost in the orchard, by A. Fisher; Mrs Alcott's visitor, by M. Arenstein; Gray man's warning, by B. and N. Roberts; The friendly ghost, by E. Yates; Here we go! by M. Leach; The house that lacked a bogie, by S. Nic Leodhas; The stubbornest man in Maine, by M. Jagendorf; The dancing jug, by L. De Osma; The ghost catcher, by L. De; A box on the ear, by R. Manning-Sanders

"A collection of 13 short ghostly tales [and 3 poems] sure to appeal to young readers intrigued with 'things that go bump in the night.' Stories included . . . vary from puzzling mysteries ('The Ghost in the Orchard') and funny encounters ('The House that Lacked a Bogie') to troubling experiences ('Gray Man's Warning'). Gray-shaded drawings, more amusing than scary, illustrate the text." Booklist

Aiken, Joan

The faithless lollybird; illus. by Eros Keith. Doubleday [1978 c1977] 255p illus $6.95, lib. bdg. $7.90 (6 and up) **S C**

1 Short stories
ISBN 0-385-13073-2; 0-385-13074-0   LC 77-72999

First published 1977 in England

"Most of the 13 selections (one is in verse) are modern fairy tales: a witch inadvertently steals a young king's Sunday memories; a lost football team hides in a haunted tower; a plump and freckled mermaid plays cat's cradle with sea foam; and, the faithless lollybird of the title weaves beautiful tapestries out of bus tickets, milk bottle caps, tails of police horses, and orange peels. All are touched with mystery of magic and enlivened by Aiken's inventiveness, wit, and skill with words." Sch Library J

Alden, Raymond M.

Why the chimes rang, and other stories; with illus. by Evelyn Copelman. Bobbs 1945 146p illus. pa $6.95 (3-5) **S C**

1 Fairy tales 2 Short stories
ISBN 0-672-50582-7   LC 45-10261

First published 1908

A collection of eleven "unusually successful modern fairy tales each with its allegory and not too obtrusive moral." NY State Lib

Aleichem, Sholom

Holiday tales of Sholom Aleichem; selected and tr. by Aliza Shevrin; illus. by Thomas di Grazia. Scribner 1979 145p illus $8.95 (5 and up) **S C**

1 Jews—Fiction 2 Fasts and feasts—Judaism—Fiction 3 Short stories
ISBN 0-684-16118-4   LC 79-753

The "translator has chosen seven [stories] for young readers, partly because she considers them to be among [the author's] finest work and also becau▢e they show how Jews celebrated holidays—not only as religious observances but as family festivals. Six of them are first-person narratives presented from a boy's point of view; all seven deal not with solemn holy days but with joyous holidays—three center on Passover, two on Sukkos, one on Chanukah, and one on Purim. . . . One finds many of the famous hallmarks of Sholom Aleichem's writing: the mischief of boys, touches of melodrama and pathos, bits of folksy superstition and philosophy, and above all an innate understanding of human nature, shown in the humor, often ironic, of the character portrayals." Horn Book

Alexander, Lloyd

The town cats, and other tales; illus. by Laszlo Kubinyi. Dutton 1977 126p illus lib. bdg. $8.50 (3-5) **S C**

1 Cats—Fiction 2 Fairy tales 3 Short stories
ISBN 0-525-41430-4   LC 76-13647

"The author presents a collection of eight original stories about outstanding felines. The stories appear to be set in various countries and resemble European folk tales; each one shows a cat as a devoted, loyal, but independent creature—and wiser than human beings. 'The Cat-King's Daughter' tells of true love assisted by a sagacious puss named Margot. The wryly humorous story 'The Cat Who Said No' is about a fearless bazaar tomcat who dared to checkmate the royal Shira-Zar the Mighty in a game of chess. And in 'The Apprentice Cat,' Witling's affectionate owners try him at various trades before realizing that 'he was a master at being a cat; which, in itself, was already a quite remarkable achievement.'" Horn Bk

"There's great style to these cat stories in the fairy tale mode. Alexander is a master of the form and his language flows easily, effortlessly." Booklist

Alfred Hitchcock's Supernatural tales of terror and suspense; illus by Robert Shore. Random House 1973 172p illus $5.95, lib. bdg. $6.99 (5 and up) **S C**

1 Horror—Fiction 2 Short stories
ISBN 0-394-82676-0; 0-394-92676-5   LC 73-3694

Alfred Hitchcock's Supernatural tales of terror and suspense—*Continued*

Contents: The triumph of death, by H. R. Wakefield; The strange valley, by T. V. Olsen; The Christmas spirit, by D. B. Bennett; The bronze door, by R. Chandler; Slip stream, by S. Hodgson; The quest for "Blank Claveringi," by P. Highsmith; Miss Pinkerton's apocalypse, by M. Spark; The reunion after three hundred years, by A. Tolstoy; The attic express, by A. Hamilton; The pram, by A. W. Bennett; Mr. Ash's studio, by H. R. Wakefield

"Eleven spine-tingling stories have been taken from adult collections and compiled for children." Booklist

Andersen, Hans Christian

Ardizzone's Hans Andersen: fourteen classic tales; selected and illus. by Edward Ardizzone; tr. by Stephen Corrin. Atheneum Pubs. 1979 [c1978] 191p illus $10.95 (3-6)   **SC**

1 Fairy tales 2 Short stories
ISBN 0-689-40128-5   LC 78-18908

"A Margaret K. McElderry book"

The translator "tells that he has 'made slight cuts in certain descriptive passages . . . taking liberties with the original Danish'; the reader, however, is not aware of these modifications for the narratives flow smoothly and convey the familiar force of the original storyteller . . . Most of the tales are old favorites and represent Andersen's originality as well as his indebtedness to folklore; for example, in addition to 'The Emperor's New Clothes,' 'The Ugly Duckling,' 'The Little Mermaid,' and 'The Snow Queen' . . . 'there are such derivative stories as 'Big Claus and Little Claus,' 'The Wild Swans,' and 'The Tinder Box.' Since the selection was made by the illustrator, his pictures doubtless represent a labor of love; and nowhere does his affinity for the stories show better than in his black-and-white hatched drawings. The expressively realistic vignettes suggest etchings and are economical in style, capturing the simple but dramatic moments that make the stories memorable. On the other hand, the full-page watercolor paintings—despite their careful composition— are not the equal of the drawings. The artist's pastel tones may be justified in terms of the streak of idealistic fantasy present in the tales, but they fail to incorporate the bittersweet yet astringent element in Andersen's style." Horn Bk

The complete fairy tales and stories; tr. from the Danish by Erik Christian Haugaard; forword by Virginia Haviland. Doubleday 1974 xxiv, 1101p $17.95, lib. bdg. $18.90 (4 and up)   **SC**

1 Fairy tales 2 Short stories
ISBN 0-385-01901-7; 0-385-05867-5   LC 73-83583

This translation "follows the text and the order of the stories in the Danish edition of 1874 which Andersen edited." Foreword

"In its completeness this collection of Andersen's 156 stories reveals his genius for preserving human character and folk culture. Haugaard's translation is eloquent, elegantly formal and aesthetically sensitive to fine gradations of tone and color, which doubtless belong to the original as well. These qualities will make the volume a lasting fireside reader while the tales plus the author's preface and notes on his stories will serve the Andersen student admirably." Booklist

"Not all of the fairy tales will appeal to young readers, and many of the stories were intended for adults. In addition the lack of illustrations and the length of the book make it more of a resource book . . . than a children's anthology." Sch Library J

Dulac's The Snow Queen, and other stories from Hans Andersen. Doubleday [1976 c1975] 143p illus $7.95, lib. bdg. $8.90 (3-6)   **SC**

1 Fairy tales 2 Short stories
ISBN 0-385-11677-2; 0-385-11678-0   LC 76-7308

First published 1975 in England

"This collection of five Andersen tales includes 'The Snow Queen,' 'The Nightingale,' 'The Emperor's New Clothes,' 'The Little Mermaid,' and 'The Wind's Tale.' Fifteen magnificent watercolors from Dulac's original 1911 volume have been included to illustrate the stories in the rich colors and intricate detail for which the early-twentieth-century painter is famous. Paper, print, and reproductions add up here to fine bookmaking. A literary and artistic experience to share with children." Booklist

Hans Andersen: his classic fairy tales; from the new translation by Erik Haugaard; illus. by Michael Foreman. Doubleday [1978 c1976] 185p illus $8.95 (3-6)   **SC**

1 Fairy tales 2 Short stories
ISBN 0-385-13364-2   LC 78-107654

First published 1976 in England

"An attractive format and the freshness of Haugaard's translation of these 18 tales selected from 'The Complete Fairy Tales and Stories' [entered above] make this Andersen a good choice for today's readers. The stories are some of the best known and most asked for . . . plus a few less familiar, like the humorous satire, 'The Dung Beetle.'" Sch Library J

Illustrated "with 18 full-color and 21 black-and-white drawings. The enchantment of Andersen's fairy world reverberates through Foreman's interpretations: the limpid blues and greens of 'The Snow Queen,' 'The Red Shoes,' and 'The Little Match Girl'; the rich, earthy tones of 'The Steadfast Tin Soldier,' 'The Dung Beetle,' 'The Swineherd,' and 'The Tinderbox'; the light airiness found in 'The Nightingale' and 'Inchelina'; the mystic lavenders that permeate 'The Wild Swans,' and 'The Ugly Duckling'; and the understated humor of the shaded line drawings for 'The Princess and the Pea' and 'The Emperor's New Clothes.' Delicately drawn pencil vignettes—many caricatured—head each story to draw children into the waiting magic." Booklist

Seven tales; tr. from the Danish by Eva Le Gallienne; pictures by Maurice Sendak. Harper 1959 127p illus lib. bdg. $8.79 (2-5)   **SC**

1 Fairy tales 2 Short stories
ISBN 0-06-023791-0   LC 59-16151

"Translator and artist show understanding and appreciation of Andersen's poignant stories. Charming illustrations, large print, and open page invite independent reading." Hodges. Bks for Elem Sch Libraries

Averill, Esther

Jenny and the Cat Club; a collection of favorite stories about Jenny Linsky; written and illus. by Esther Averill. Harper 1973 5v in 1 illus lib. bdg. $6.89 (k-2)   **SC**

1 Cats—Fiction
ISBN 0-06-020223-8   LC 72-9862

Includes the following previously published titles, all of which are o.p. 1981: The Cat Club (1944); Jenny's first party (1948); When Jenny lost her scarf (1951); Jenny's adopted brothers (1952); How the brothers joined the Cat Club (1953)

These stories tell "about Jenny Linsky, the little black cat who overcame her shyness and joined that organization of the elite of feline society, the Cat Club. The gentle heroine and the ingenious dialogue are as charming as ever, and Jenny's small adventures have a timeless appeal." Chicago. Children's Bk Center

Several other books about Jenny are listed under Averill, Esther. The school for cats, in the Easy books section

Babbitt, Natalie

The Devil's storybook; stories and pictures by Natalie Babbitt. Farrar, Straus 1974 101p illus $7.95 (4-6)   **SC**

1 Devil—Fiction 2 Short stories
ISBN 0-374-31770-4   LC 74-5488

Ten "stories about the machinations of the Devil to increase the population of his realm. He is not always successful and, despite his clever ruses, meets frustration as often as his intended victims do." Horn Bk

"Twists of plot within traditional themes and a briskly witty style distinguish this book, illustrated amusingly with black-and-white line drawings." Booklist

Carlson, Natalie Savage

The talking cat, and other stories of French Canada; retold by Natalie Savage Carlson; pictures by Roger Duvoisin. Harper 1952 87p illus lib. bdg. $8.79 (3-6)   **SC**

1 French Canadians—Fiction 2 Canada—Fiction
3 Short stories
ISBN 0-06-021081-8   LC 52-5429

Carlson, Natalie S.—*Continued*

"These seven once-in-another-time tales of French Canada were told first by the author's great-great uncle, . . . handed down in her family and now retold in an enchanting manner that will appeal to today's storytellers." Wis Library Bul

"They are not, I am glad to say, written in dialect. Easy for the children to read themselves and perfect for the story hour." Horn Bk

These tales "are not folklore, but their unexpected turn of events and the slyness of their humor give them something of the quality of the 'tall tale.' " Ontario Lobrary Rev

A **Chilling** collection; tales of wit and intrigue; an anthology chosen by Helen Hoke. Dent [distributed by Elsevier/Nelson Bks] 1980 140p $6.95 (5 and up)   **S C**

1 Short stories
ISBN 0-525-66662-1   LC 79-18864

"This collection of stories and poems includes science fiction, fantasy, and ghost stories. Despite 'chilling' in the title, the stories are more amusing than scary. Several are taken from well known authors (Ray Bradbury's 'The Invisible Boy,' Arthur C. Clarke's 'An Ape About the House,' Joan Aiken's 'Bad Dream'), and all are well written. For the age group, the inclusion of Tennyson's 'The Kraken' seems questionable, but overall, the book provides entertaining reading for middle school students." Sch Library J

Chrisman, Arthur Bowie

Shen of the sea; Chinese stories for children; illus. by Else Hasselriis. Dutton [1968 c1953] 221p illus $9.95 (5 and up)   **S C**

1 China—Fiction 2 Fairy tales 3 Short stories
ISBN 0-525-38244-0   LC 68-13420

First published 1925; copyright renewed 1953
Awarded the Newbery Medal, 1926

Here are "original tales of China told with humor and illustrated with distinctive silhouettes. [These] stories reveal Chinese philosophy and way of life." Asia. A Guide to Bks for Children

The stories' "charm lies in the brisk directness of the telling and in the very serious face with which Mr Chrisman conceals his bubbling glee over the utterly subversive conduct of his characters." Boston Transcript

Christmas stories round the world; ed. and with introductions by Lois S. Johnson; illus. by D. K. Stone. Rand McNally 1970 103p illus pa $2.95 (3-5)   **S C**

1 Christmas—Fiction 2 Short stories
ISBN 0-528-87032-7   LC 71-110365

First published 1960

Each of these twelve stories is prefaced with a few paragraphs about the observance of Christmas in the country of the story following

Illustrated "with 12 large, full-color pictures and a number of small, black-and-white spot drawings." Sch Library J

Dalgliesh, Alice

(comp.) Christmas; a book of stories old and new; illus. by Hildegard Woodward. [Rev. ed] Scribner 1950 244p illus lib. bdg. $6.95 (4 and up)   **S C**

1 Christmas—Fiction 2 Short stories
ISBN 0-684-12667-2   LC 50-9804

First published 1934

"The stories and poems which are included in this Christmas anthology are those which have been enjoyed by children. The Christmas legend has given way to realistic or slightly fanciful tales. The four divisions of the material is into the headings: Christmas stories and wonder tales, The first Christmas, Christmas in old time America, Christmas in other lands." Wis Library Bul

An "excellent collection. . . . The illustrations are particularly childlike, appropriate and charming." NY Times Bk Rev

Farjeon, Eleanor

The little bookroom; Eleanor Farjeon's short stories for children, chosen by herself; illus. by Edward Ardizzone. Oxford 1955 302p illus $4.95 (1-4)   **S C**

1 Fairy tales 2 Short stories
ISBN 0-19-277099-3   LC 56-28856

Received the Hans Christian Andersen award, 1956

"Fantasy, realism, humor, and wisdom are to be found in this collection of 27 delightful stories selected by the author from her own writings and characterized by her inventiveness and her charm and beauty of expression. The book takes its title from a dusty little room crammed with a motley assortment of overflow books in which the author browsed as a child. A book to be savored and treasured; a perfect choice for reading aloud. Harmonious illustrations." Booklist

Fleischman, Sid

Jim Bridger's alarm clock, and other tall tales; illus. by Eric von Schmidt. Dutton 1978 56p illus $7.95 (2-4)   **S C**

1 The West (U.S.)—Fiction 2 Bridger, James—Fiction 3 Short stories
ISBN 0-525-32795-9   LC 78-5854

"A Unicorn book"

" 'Jim Bridger' was a ramshackle, sharp-eyed army scout' who from time to time came wandering out of the mountains with strange and wonderf'l tales. One has to do with a flat-topped mountain whose slab sides are so perfect that echoes bounced off them can be heard for miles. This comes in mighty handy when Jim works to outwit Buryin' John the fiddler, who refuses to play for the local barn dance, or when some bank robbers ride into town just after all the gunpowder is used up celebrating the Fourth of July. Fleichman cleverly weaves incidents such as these into three tales that are well matched in exaggeration and hilarity." Booklist

"Fleischman is among the few bona fide humorists who write for young readers and they're sure to make his new book warmly welcome. . . . Von Schmidt scores as an illustrator who portrays the author's nutty inventions with vivid drawings in black and white, overlaid with ruddy tones." Pub W

Fox, Paula

The little swineherd, and other tales; illus. by Leonard Lubin. Dutton 1978 114p illus $7.95 (4 and up)   **S C**

1 Short stories
ISBN 0-525-14750-0   LC 78-5435

"A Henry Robbins book"

Fox's book includes "five fairytale-fables: a young swineherd learns to use opportunity when it comes his way; a vain rooster is intimidated by a rooster vane and is taught by an understanding hen that beauty must come from within; a donkey who has spent his life going in circles making a mill grind finds that straight lines are hardly different than circles; an alligator's 'wisdom' is threatened by two human researchers; a small raccoon finds self-confidence when she learns to play magnificent music on a flute. The stories are strung together with a running dialogue between an entrepreneur duck and a goose who tells stories to frogs." Sch Library J

"Beautifully simple in language, cadence in storytelling style, replete with dialogue, the narratives are full of concrete detail and humor; but it will take more than a superficial reader to understand why they end as they do. In each of the unconventional black-and-white illustrations elaborately modeled figures or faces are set against a background of unshaded linear drawing." Horn Bk

Friends are like that! Stories to read to yourself; selected by the Child Study Children's Book Committee at Bank Street; illus. by Leigh Grant. Crowell 1979 114p illus $7.95, lib. bdg. $7.89 (2-4)   **S C**

1 Friendship—Fiction 2 Short stories
ISBN 0-690-03979-4; 0-690-03980-8   LC 78-22513

"These 10 humorous and heartwarming selections, all centering on friendship, include two poems by Zolotow and [Sherry] Kafka and eight stories by familiar authors such as Steptoe, Greenfield, and

Friends are like that!—*Continued*

Carlson. Chosen for readability and appeal, the collection is attractively set in an inviting format accompanied by expressive, black line drawings. Though mostly excerpted from longer works . . . the stories stand by themselves and provide springboards for reluctant readers as well as accessible lures for those not willing or able to tackle a long book." Booklist

Hamilton, Virginia

Time-ago lost: more tales of Jahdu; illus. by Ray Prather. Macmillan Pub. Co. 1973 85p illus $4.95 (3-5)   S C

1 Blacks—Fiction   2 Short stories
ISBN 0-02-742450-2   LC 72-85187

Companion volume to the author's: The time-ago tales of Jahdu, entered below
"This second installment of Jahdu Tales begins . . . in a 'tight little room in a fine, good place called Harlem' where Mama Luka tells stories about a 'strong black boy' named Jahdu. In the first two stories Jahdu is running east through a dark world to his birthplace for rebirth. The third story, the freest, most imaginative one, tells how Jahdu discovered light and is an expansion of Far Eastern philosophy in its contrasts of yin and yang, hot and cold, night and day. The last story melds Jahdu's magic into Lee Edward's urban life, showing how much you must let the imagination soar even in the face of Trouble. The stories here require close reading plus an extremely relaxed and fluid imagination. Vigorous illustrations." NY Times Bk Rev

The time-ago tales of Jahdu; illus. by Nonny Hogrogian. Macmillan Pub. Co. 1969 61p illus $5.95 (3-5)   S C

1 Blacks—Fiction   2 Short stories
ISBN 0-02-742460-X   LC 70-78089

"After school each day, [in Harlem] Lee Edward stayed with Mama Luke until his mother came home from work. Each day, she told a story of Jahdu. . . . Breathless, Lee Edward listens to the stories of long ago, stories of the crafty boy who grew wiser and more powerful, and he knows that when he grows up he will be, like Jahdu, strong and proud." Chicago. Children's Book Center
"The four stories are nothing less than a history of the black man's changing role in American society. First, Jahdu must awaken to his own powers: then come two stories in which he uses this power with enthusiasm if not wisdom. Finally, Jahdu discovers happiness in being 'a strong, black boy.'" NY Times Bk Rev

Hardendorff, Jeanne B.

Witches, wit, and a werewolf; retold by Jeanne B. Hardendorff; illus. by Laszlo Kubinyi. Lippincott 1971 124p illus $7.95, pa $2.50 (5 and up)

1 Short stories
ISBN 0-397-31542-2; 0-397-31251-2   LC 75-153516

In this collection of humorous and scary stories, the author retells fifteen folk, ghost and witchcraft tales from Maupassant, Wiggin, Aesop and others. Three tales by Bierce, Dickens and Richard Hughes are also included
"Several of the stories may require adult interpretation of such terms as corpse candle . . . but there is enough variety in the selections to interest both readers and storytellers." Booklist

Harper, Wilhelmina

(comp.) Easter chimes; stories for Easter and the spring season; illus. by Hoot von Zitzewitz. New, rev. ed. Dutton 1965 253p illus $7.95   S C

1 Easter—Fiction   2 Short stories
ISBN 0-525-21037-0   LC 64-10688

First published 1942
"A collection of stories [legends] and a few poems for Easter, with emphasis on seasonal rather than religious stories. . . . The book will undoubtedly fill a need in libraries for holiday material." Booklist

(comp.) The harvest feast; stories of Thanksgiving, yesterday and today; illus. by W. T. Mars. New, rev. ed. Dutton 1965 256p illus $7.95   S C

1 Thanksgiving Day—Fiction   2 Short stories
ISBN 0-525-31510-1   LC 65-21282

First published 1938
This anthology includes "poems and stories by many well known authors on the theme of Thanksgiving. The first part contains stories of long-ago Thanksgivings; the second part is made up of Thanksgiving stories of today. The collection is suitable for reading aloud or for story telling." Wis Library Bul

(comp.) Merry Christmas to you; stories for Christmas; illus. by Fermin Rocker. New, rev. ed. Dutton 1965 254p illus $7.95   S C

1 Christmas—Fiction   2 Short stories
ISBN 0-525-34852-2   LC 65-21283

First published 1935
An anthology "of Christmas stories and poems, many old favorites, for telling and reading aloud. The wide variety includes miracle, fairy, and modern tales written by many distinguished authors." Adventuring with Bks. 2d edition
It is noted when a story is suitable "for younger readers or listeners. Contains a two-page list of Christmas books for boys and girls." Wis Library Bul

Harter, Walter

Osceola's head, and other American ghost stories; illus. by Neil Waldman. Prentice-Hall 1974 71p illus $4.95 (4-6)   S C

1 Ghosts—Fiction   2   U.S.—History—Fiction
3 Short stories
ISBN 0-13-642991-2   LC 73-13892

"A description of witches, poltergeists, and warlocks introduces ten ghost stories based on incidents in American history. The stories are short, interesting to read, and feature ghosts from various eras—for example, 'The Ghost at Valley Forge' visited George Washington; 'The Actor Who Wouldn't Stay Dead' concerns the ghost of John Wilkes Booth; and 'Osceola's Head' is about the spirit of the Indian leader. Neil Waldman's gray-and-white sketches of the ghostly characters complement these stories about the preternatural." Sch Library J

Haunting tales; ed. by Barbara Ireson; illus. by Freda Woolf. Dutton [1974 c1973] 279p illus $7.95 (5 and up)   S C

1 Ghosts—Fiction   2 Short stories
ISBN 0-525-31533-0   LC 74-7222

First published 1973 in England
Contents: Huw, by G. Palmer; The man who didn't believe in ghosts, by S. Nic Leodhas; Hans and his master, by R. Manning-Sanders; The haunted trailer, by R. Arthur; The magic shop, by H. G. Wells; John Charrington's wedding, by E. Nesbit; The ghostly earl, by R. Chetwynd-Hayes; Through the veil, by Sir A. C. Doyle; The doll's ghost, by M. Crawford; A long day without water, by J. Aiken; The demon king, by J. B. Priestley; Faithful Jenny Dove, by E. Farjeon; The twilight road, by H. F. Brinsmead; Fiddler, play fast, play faster, by R. Sawyer; Uncle Einar, by R. Bradbury; The ghost ship, by R. Middleton; Jimmy takes vanishing lessons, by W. R. Brooks; The crossways, by L. P. Hartley; Master ghost and I, by B. Softly
"All kinds of ghosts, differing in form, personality, and intent, flit through these nineteen stories—hobo spooks who frequent trailers; rum-drinking spirits sailing on a ship; and apparitions who fall in love with each other. In fact, the collection tends to accentuate the humorousness of haunting rather than the terror." Horn Bk

Haunts, haunts, haunts; selected by Helen Hoke; illus. by Charles Keeping. Watts, F. 1977 191p illus. lib. bdg. $7.90 (5 and up)   S C

1 Ghosts—Fiction   2 Horror—Fiction   3 Short stories
ISBN 0-531-00098-2   LC 76-56146

Contents: Close behind him, by J. Wyndham; The house surgeon, by R. Kipling; The helmsman, by F. Kafka; Me and my shadow, by E. F. Russell; The waxfork, by A. M. Burrage; The inn, by

Haunts, haunts, haunts—*Continued*

A. M. Burrage; The cloak, by R. Bloch; The soul cages, by T. C. Croker; The whistling room, by W. H. Hodgson; The music of Erich Zann, by H. P. Lovecraft; Deadline, by R. Matheson; Don't look behind you, by F. Brown

Ths book contains "old-fashioned horror tales in the Gothic tradition of werewolves, haunted rooms, the blood-oozing footprints, and . . . lighter stories. . . . Authors range from Kipling . . . to Kafka . . . with lesser lights in between. Young people . . . will devour this." Sch Library J

Hautzig, Esther

The case against the wind, and other stories, by I. L. Peretz; tr. and adapted by Esther Hautzig; drawings by Leon Shtainmets. Macmillan Pub. Co. 1975 96p illus $6.95 (4 and up) **S C**

1 Jews—Fiction 2 Short stories
ISBN 0-02-770990-6   LC 75-14193

"Ten wise, gently humorous tales by one of the first Jewish writers to publish in demotic Yiddish rather than scholarly Hebrew. These short moralities, set in villages, in the court of Solomon, and in heaven, are designed to teach articles of Jewish faith. Despite occasional melodrama, they are entertaining tales of human comedy. Noteworthy additions include a foreword on the life of Peretz in 19th-Century Europe and an alphabetical glossary of Jewish traditions." Sch Library J

Housman, Laurence

The rat-catcher's daughter; a collection of stories; selected and with an afterword by Ellin Greene; illus. by Julia Noonan. Atheneum Pubs. 1974 169p illus $6.95 (4 and up) **S C**

1 Fairy tales 2 Short stories
ISBN 0-689-30420-X   LC 73-75436

"A Margaret K. McElderry book"

"Here are [twelve tales of] princesses both sweet and selfish, magic toys, crafty gnomes, brave boys and foolhardy ones, and . . . an appreciation of old age and death as part of nature. Not all of the tales are from the English tradition—one is Oriental, one American Indian." Pub W

"With their lovely imagery, their lilting use of language, their skillful twists of plot, these tales, drawn from a number of Housman's collections now out of print, are a delight to read or tell. Beautifully illustrated by Julia Noonan's sensitive pencil drawings." Babbling Bookworm

Hunter, Mollie

A furl of fairy wind; four stories; drawings by Stephen Gammell. Harper 1977 58p illus $7.95, lib. bdg. $7.89 (2-5) **S C**

1 Fairy tales 2 Short stories
ISBN 0-06-022674-9; 0-06-022675-7   LC 76-58732

The first of these four stories "introduces a genuine Scottish Brownie who must receive his bowl of hot porridge every night—and wreaks havoc in the household if not so indulged. In the second story a boy foolishly enters the fairy world on Midsummer's Eve, when the little people do not like to have strangers among them. The third story tells of a peddler who receives from a fairy woman an extravagant reward for one of his ordinary pots; and in the last tale, an orphan girl has forgotten how to smile, until a 'furl of fairy wind' blows around the house." Horn Bk

"No stranger to lovers of fantasy, Hunter offers four stories here that insure readers a refreshing escape from mundane reality. She writes entrancingly, as expected, infusing the tales with warmth and gentle humor. And Gammell graces the collection with wonderful scenes of people and places in the dream landscapes." Pub W

Irving, Washington

Rip Van Winkle, The legend of Sleepy Hollow, and other tales; illus. by Roberta Carter Clark. Grosset 1967 158p illus $2.95 (4-6) **S C**

1 Short stories
ISBN 0-448-05482-5   LC 67-24232

"Companion library"

The first story is entered separately in the Fiction section

Other tales included in this collection are: The spectre bridegroom and The Moor's legacy

Just for fun; a collection of original humorous stories; ed. by Ann Durell. Dutton 1977 84p $5.95 (4-6) **S C**

1 Short stories
ISBN 0-525-32950-1   LC 77-7497

This collection "includes seven short, lively yarns by Lloyd Alexander, Scott Corbett, Sidney Offit, Alfa-Betty Olsen and Marshall Efron, Marilyn Sachs, Marjorie Sharmat, and Bob Stine. Some make use of fantasy or nonsense, others strive for comedy in realistic situations, and there's a sassy spoof of 'Jack and the Beanstalk.'" Children's Bk Rev Serv

The book offers "young readers breezy amusement in short doses. . . . Though the authors vary from fantasy to reality in their approach, the accent is on humor, and the length makes these particularly appropriate for reading aloud." Booklist

Karl, Jean E.

The turning place: stories of a future past. Dutton 1976 213p $8.95 (6 and up) **S C**

1 Science fiction 2 Short stories
ISBN 0-525-41573-4   LC 75-33669

"Following an alien-designed holocaust, Earth's inhabitants start over from scratch and eventually expand to reach the limits—and the core—of our galaxy. With such a monumental history to tell, the author has chosen a short-story form, providing important glimpses into a multicenturial panorama through the explorations of various young protagonists. Despite a rather painful artificiality and lack of momentum in early stories, the book picks up rapidly and blossoms finally in a fascinating exploration of human emotion and scientific bystery. A flawed but rewarding mind expander." Booklist

Kipling, Rudyard

The jungle book; illus. by Fritz Eichenberg. Grosset 1950 244p illus (Illustrated junior library) $5.95 (4 and up) **S C**

1 Animals—Fiction 2 India—Fiction 3 Short stories
ISBN 0-448-05814-6   LC 50-12311

First published 1894

These are stories of India and "the jungle life of Mowgli who was adopted by the wolf pack and taught the laws of the jungle by Bagheera the panther and Baloo the bear. Also unconnected stories of such animal personalities as Rikki Tikki the mongoose and Kotic the white seal." Toronto

The second jungle book; with illus. by J. Lockwood Kipling. Doubleday 1923 [c1895] 238p illus $4.50 (4 and up) **S C**

1 Animals—Fiction 2 India—Fiction 3 Short stories
ISBN 0-385-07483-2; 0-385-08708-X

First published 1895

"Stories of animal life in the East Indian forest, where the animals talk together and tell the secrets of the jungle." Pittsburgh

The animals in these eight tales "are not men in hides and on all fours discussing human problems. Kipling's genius represents them thinking and behaving, each according to his own peculiar beastly habit and experience, with such dramatic skill that one is almost forced to believe that he has intimately dwelt among them." Keller's Reader's Digest of Bks

Just so stories (3-6) **S C**

1 Animals—Fiction 2 India—Fiction 3 Short stories

Some editions are:
Doubleday $3.50 Black and white illustrations throughout by the author (ISBN 0-385-07351-8)
Doubleday $8.95, lib bdg. $9.90 Pictures by Joseph M. Gleeson (ISBN 0-385-07352-6; 0-385-07110-8; LC 46-20643)
Doubleday $8.95, lib bdg. $13.90 (Anniversary edition) Illustrated by Etienne Delessert; foreword by Nelson Doubleday (ISBN 0-385-07225-2; 0-385-07443-3 LC 79-170932)

The book consists of twelve animal fables

"While Kipling's original and humorous elucidation of how the elephant got his trunk and the leopard his spots are barely believable, he has nevertheless drawn animal characteristics and habits 'just so.' First published in 1902." Bks for Boys & Girls. 3d edition

Konigsburg, E. L.

Altogether, one at a time; illus. by Gail E. Haley [and others] Atheneum Pubs. 1971 79p illus lib. bdg. $7.95, pa $1.25 (4-6)   S C

1 Short stories
ISBN 0-689-20638-0; 0-689-70415-1   LC 70-134814

Compelled to invite a child he doesn't want to his birthday party in 'Inviting Jason,' Stanley likes the boy even less afterwards, but for a different reason. A 10-year-old boy learns something about old age in 'The Night of the Leonids' when he realizes his grandmother has lost her last chance to see a shower of stars that occurs only once every 33½ years. The spirit of a long dead camp counsellor helps an obese girl make up her mind that she will never have to attend Camp Fat again. In 'Momma at the Pearly Gates,' Momma tells the story of how, as a girl, she was called a 'dirty nigger' by a white classmate." Library J

"Not all of the stories in this book are equally successful. . . . But even the weaker items in the collection have the virtue of respecting their audience enough to demand some mental work in the midst of the fun. Assistance is given by the illustrations of the four artists, whose various styles underline the individuality of the stories." NY Times Bk Rev

Throwing shadows. Atheneum Pubs. 1979 151p $8.95 (5 and up)   S C

1 Individuality—Fiction   2 Short stories
ISBN 0-689-30714-4   LC 79-10422

"This is a collection of five original short stories. Each of the stories is told in the first person and concerns a pre-adolescent boy as he learns a little about his identity. The boys come from a variety of geographical backgrounds, races, and cultures. . . . As each boy discovers a new facet of his personality or accepts an old one, he throws a shadow that is uniquely his own." Children's Bk Rev Serv

"There is a wealth of information on a variety of subjects: hunting fossilized shark teeth; life in an Equadorian weaving village; Hungary during World War II and the Communist takeover; antiques; etc. The stories are equally valuable on the personal level as all the characters—young and old—struggle and grow, try to understand themselves and each other. . . . The stories each occupy about 30 pages but have the spacious quality of a novel; characters and events have a chance to develop naturally rather than seeming pushed along." Sch Library J

Leach, Maria

The thing at the foot of the bed, and other scary tales; illus. by Kurt Werth. Collins [distributed by Philomel Bks] 1959 126p illus lib. bdg. $5.99 (3-6)   S C

1 Ghosts—Fiction   2 Short stories
ISBN 0-529-03545-6   LC 59-6658

First published by World Publishing Company

This is an eerie collection of twenty-three short tales and two poems which include funny stories and scary ones, and shivery witch stories; also a section entitled "Do's and don'ts about ghosts"

"There is also information about legends and folklore concerning ghosts. A very amusing book, it is also a well-illustrated attractive package." Pub W

Includes: Author's notes and bibliography

Levoy, Myron

The witch of Fourth Street, and other stories; pictures of Gabriel Lisowski. Harper 1972 110p illus pa $1.95 (4-6)   S C

1 New York (City)—Fiction   2 Short stories
ISBN 0-06-440059-X   LC 74-183174

"The eight stories [set on the Lower East Side of New York in the 1920's] tell about a group of neighbors, young and old: little Cathy Dunn, terrified of the old woman who sold pencils at the corner; the old-clothesman and his horse called Socrates; Vincent DeMarco, whose father longed for a set of electric trains; Mrs. Dunn, with her kitchen hencoop and fire-escape farm; and Aaron Kandel, whose grandmother on her sixtieth birthday expunged the bitter childhood memory of a Russian program. Tales and characters are highly original, sometimes humorous, sometimes poignant, and often profound. The art of the short story is not always one that children recognize; one would serve the book well by introducing it, or better still, reading it aloud. The soft drawings are exactly right." Horn Bk

Macdonald, George

The complete fairy tales of George Macdonald; with original illus. by Arthur Hughes; introduction by Roger Lancelyn Green. Schocken Bks. [1977 c1961] 288p illus lib. bdg. $8.95, pa $4.95 (4 and up)   S C

1 Fairy tales   2 Short stories
ISBN 0-8052-3700-3; 0-8052-0579-9   LC 77-80272

First published 1961 in England with title: The light princess, and other tales

"A collection of eight short original fairy tales by the nineteenth-century Scottish writer turned English professor includes the original woodcuts, intricately executed by the painter Arthur Hughes. A short introduction traces Macdonald's life and work, commenting briefly on the backgrounds of the included selections. . . . Format makes this more a candidate for adults wanting tales to tell or read aloud." Booklist

Newell, Hope

The little old woman who used her head, and other stories; pictures by Margaret Ruse and Ann Merriman Peck. Elsevier/Nelson Bks. [1973] 127p illus $6.95 (1-3)   S C

1 Short stories
ISBN 0-525-66328-2   LC 73-17036

An expanded version of the book first published 1935 by Thomas Nelson with title: The little old woman who used her head

Here are nineteen short episodes about an old woman who solved her many problems by an ingenious and amusing manner of using her head

"Sufficiently simple for children of eight to read and useful for story telling and reading aloud to younger children. Amusing illustrations." Booklist [review of the 1935 edition]

Paterson, Katherine

Angels & other strangers; family Christmas stories. Crowell 1979 118p $7.95 (5 and up)   S C

1 Christmas—Fiction   2 Short stories
ISBN 0-690-03992-1   LC 79-63797

"The author weaves stories about miracles of the Christmas season—miracles that take place on a truly human level. Each story is based on the Christian message of the birth of Christ and the significance that message takes on for the characters. She writes of the poor, the desolate, and the lonely as well as of the arrogant, the complacent, and the proud." Horn Bk

Picard, Barbara Leonie

The faun and the woodcutter's daughter; illus. by Charles Stewart. Criterion Bks. 1964 255p illus $6.95 (4 and up)   S C

1 Fairy tales   2 Short stories
ISBN 0-200-71999-8   LC 63-19081

First published 1951 in England

"Fourteen original allegorical fairy tales. . . . Although the central theme, the triumph of love and selfless courage, dominates all the stories, each one is remarkably different from the others. They are written in the smooth prose of the traditional tale and would be delightful for reading aloud. As stories for telling they will have a wide audience." Horn Bk

Ritchie, Alice

The treasure of Li-Po; with illus. by T. Ritchie. Harcourt 1949 154p illus $4.50 (3-6)   S C

1 China—Fiction   2 Fairy tales   3 Short stories
ISBN 0-15-290158-2   LC 49-10204

"While the six charming tales in this book are not traditional, they have an authentic Chinese flavor and the quality of the true fairy tale. The title story has to do with a humble basket-maker and his generosity, and into the others, enter such characters as a faithful lantern-bearer, a fox's child who becomes human, and a devoted son who travels through strange lands to the country of sleep to find a cure for his ailing father. The illustrations by T. Ritchie are drawn with humor and repose." Horn Bk

Roach, Marilynne K.

Encounters with the invisible world; being ten tales of ghosts, witches, & the devil himself in New England; written and illus. by Marilynne K. Roach. Crowell 1977 131p illus $7.95 (5 and up) **S C**

1 Ghosts—Fiction   2 New England—Fiction
3 Short stories
ISBN 0-690-01277-2   LC 76-22186

"These ten whimsical and fastpaced tales of ghosts, witches, and demons comprise one of the few collections of the supernatural focusing on a particular area of the U.S. Adapted from New England legends, the colloquial narration, simple dialogue, and old Yankee settings give . . . [a] regional backdrop to universal motifs like a bargain struck with the devil, a ghostly peddler's tragic end, and a witch spinning the fates of men." Sch Library J

The stories "have the flavor of country store tale swapping and should prove good read-aloud material. Author notes indicate sources. A few literal pen-and-ink drawings [by the author] decorate the text." Booklist

Sandburg, Carl

Rootabaga stories; illus. and decorations by Maud and Miska Petersham. Harcourt 1936 2v in 1 illus $12.95 (5 and up) **S C**

1 Short stories 2 Fairy tales
ISBN 0-15-29057-3   LC 36-27138

This edition contains: Rootabaga stories (1922) and Rootabaga pigeons (1923) reprinted in one volume. They are also available in a two volume paperback edition: Rootabaga stories $2.25 (ISBN 0-15-678900-0); Rootabaga pigeons $2.50 (ISBN 0-15-678901-9)

"A collection of unique nonsense stories combining the realism of the American middle West with a great deal of fancy and symbolism. A certain amount of repetition and the use of mouth-filling words create a rhythm and a singing quality which make the stories particularly suitable for reading aloud." Right Bk for the Right Child

Sechrist, Elizabeth Hough

(ed.) 13 ghostly yarns. Newly illus. rev. ed. Illus. by Albert Michini. Macrae Smith Co. 1963 211p illus lib. bdg. $7.97 (5 and up) **S C**

1 Ghosts—Fiction 2 Short stories
ISBN 0-8255-8171-0   LC 63-20357

First published 1932 by R. Swain in a somewhat different version; this version first published 1942 by Macrae Smith Company

Contains the following stories: A ghost story, by M. Twain; The soul of the great bell, by L. Hearn; My grandfather, Hendry Watty, by Sir A. Quiller-Couch; The water ghost of Harrowby Hall, by J. K. Bangs; The bold dragoon, by W. Irving; Peter Rugg, the missing man, by W. Austin; The Devil in the belfry, by E. A. Poe; The Spectre Bridegroom, by W. Irving; Haunted Subalterns, by R. Kipling; The gray champion, by N. Hawthorne; Marley's ghost, by C. Dickens; My own true ghost story, by R. Kipling. A play, Hamlet's ghost, by W. Shakespeare, is also included

Shreve, Susan

Family secrets; five very important stories; illus. by Richard Cuffari. Knopf 1979 56p illus $5.95, lib. bdg. $5.99 (3-5) **S C**

1 Family life—Fiction 2 Short stories
ISBN 0-394-83896-3; 0-394-93896-8   LC 78-12471

"An intriguing collection of short vignettes whose protagonist, 10-year-old Sammy, is troubled by the death of his pet, the suicide of the boy across the street, fear of his parents' hypothetical divorce, friction when senile Gradma Welty moves in, and guilt over having cheated on a math test. Family relationships form the basis for each story and are handled with warmth tempered by humanity. The emphasis throughout is not on unrealistic solutions to life's dilemmas but on the attempts of a young boy to cope with dignity. Shreve tells these tales in appropriately muted tones. They are heavy on substance yet marked by simplicity which now and then comes very close to being elegant." Sch Library J

Singer, Isaac Bashevis

Naftali the story teller and his horse, Sus, and other stories; pictures by Margot Zemach. Farrar, Straus 1976 129p illus $6.95 (4-6) **S C**

1 Poland—Fiction 2 Jews in Poland—Fiction
3 Short stories
ISBN 0-374-35490-1   LC 76-26917

Three of the stories "continue the adventures of the fools of Chelm, characters whose zaniness has tickled readers of all ages in earlier collections by the author [including The fools of Chelm and their history, entered in the Fiction section]. The title story, however, is a moving account of Naftali who lived long ago in Poland, of his inordinate love of stories (deplored by his family). When he grew up, the young man was full of wisdom and wondrous tales. With his faithful horse, Sus, he spent his life traveling and passing on to little children the books he had collected over the years." Pub W

Soyer, Abraham

The adventures of Yemima, and other stories; tr. by Rebecca S. Beagle and Rebecca Soyer; introduction by Peter S. Beagle; illus. by Raphael Soyer. Viking 1979 70p illus $7.95 (4-6) **S C**

1 Fables 2 Short stories
ISBN 0-670-10616-X   LC 78-26017

"Abraham Soyer was a writer and a Hebrew teacher. His original stories for children, first published in Palestine 40 years ago, have been lovingly translated by his daughter and daughter-in-law. They are written with the flowing cadences and rich imagery of the true storyteller and an underlying loveliness that comes from a firm belief in the ultimate triumph of goodness. The six stories are wise, magical, lively, and humorous. A brave little girl outwits a fox and a wolf; two sly and greedy animals get their just deserts; a devout woman receives the gift of flying money. Sensitive, poignant pencil sketches by acclaimed artist Raphael Soyer are an evocative accompaniment to these gentle tales." Sch Library J

Time to laugh; funny tales from here and there, selected by Phyllis R. Fenner; illus. by Henry C. Pitz. Knopf 1942 illus lib. bdg. $5.99 (4 and up) **S C**

1 Short stories
ISBN 0-394-91752-9   LC 42-19684

Contents: How Pat got good sense, by C. J. Finger; Devil's hide, by P. Fillmore; Mr A and Mr P. by M. Bianco; The simpleton and his little black hen, by H. Pyle; Conal and Donal and Taig, by S. MacManus; The drawbridge, by L. Frost; Baby rainstorm, by G. Rounds; Laughing Prince, by P. Fillmore; Emperor's new clothes, by H. C. Andersen; Ah Mee's invention, by A. B. Chrisman; Ghost's ghost, by W. C. White; Three innkeepers, by R. Hughes; About Elizabeth Eliza's piano, by L. P. Hale; Peterkins try to become wise, by L. P. Hale; Gudbrand on the Hillside, by G. W. Dasent; Rats, by J. B. S. Haldane; Palace on the rock, by R. Hughes; Juan Cigarron, by R. Sawyer; Ebenezer Never-Could-Sneezer, by G. S. Pattillo; Wee Red Man, by S. MacManus

"Most are unusually good storytelling material. . . . Highly recommended." Library J

Told under the magic umbrella; modern tales of fancy and humor; selected by the Literature Committee of the Association for Childhood Education International; illus. by Elizabeth Orton Jones. Macmillan Pub. Co. 1939 242p illus $12.95 (k-4) **S C**

1 Fairy tales 2 Short stories 3 Storytelling—Collections
ISBN 0-02-707050-6   LC 39-8355

"The Umbrella books"

"This volume is devoted to 33 modern fanciful tales, arranged from the more elementary ones on, the majority appealing to the imaginative interests of children in the second, third and fourth grades. There is Marjorie Flack's nursery story, 'Ask Mr. Bear'; Emma L. Brock's 'Gingham Lena,' about 'the smudgy, carefree adventurous rag doll'; Caroline D. Emerson's 'Merry-go-round and the Griggses,' an irresistible humorous tale. Edith Rickert's 'Bojabi tree,' an adapted folk tale, and others by Margery Bianco, Carl Sandburg, Eleanor Farjeon, Clare Leighton and so on." Bookmark

Universe ahead: stories of the future; selected and introduced by Sylvia Engdahl and Rick Roberson; illus. by Richard Cuffari. Atheneum Pubs. 1975 336p illus $8.95 (6 and up)   S C

1 Science fiction   2 Short stories
ISBN 0-689-30474-9   LC 75-8849

Contents: The animal, by R. Stephens; It's such a beautiful day, by I. Asimov; Ararat, by Z. Henderson; The wilderness, by R. Bradbury; Cloudlab, by R. Roberson; Old Man Henderson, by K. Neville; Nightmare brother, by A. E. Nourse; The samaritan, by R. Harper; Lower than angels, by A. Budrys; Kyrie, by P. Anderson; The Christmas present, by G. R. Dickson; Ranging, by J. Jakes; The beckoning trail, by S. Engdahl and R. Roberson

"According to the editors, this collection of stories is not intended as an introduction to SF but to be enjoyed by teen-aged readers interested in the future. The stories come from Seventeen and Boys' Life as well as more traditional SF publications. Two of the stories were written by the editors especially for the anthology. . . . The stories by Asimov, Dickson, and Nourse can be found in collections of each author's stories, but, on the whole, this offering is fresh and fulfills the purposes of the editors admirably." Sch Library J

Walsh, Jill Paton

Children of the fox; pictures by Robin Eaton. Farrar, Straus 1978 115p illus $7.95 (5 and up)   S C

1 Themistokles—Fiction   2 Greece—Fiction   3 Short stories
ISBN 0-374-31242-7   LC 78-8138

"Three stories that are linked by their association with the Athenian hero. Themistokles, are told by three young people who lived during the time of the Persian Wars and the shifting relationship between Athens and Sparta. Aster, the first narrator, helps Themistokles when the Athenians have fled to Salamis; the second tale is told by Demeas, who makes a long run to Sparta to bring a message to the leader; in the third story, Themistokles is a fugitive whose live is saved by a young princess who helps him reach Persia and safety from the Spartans and Athenians who have accused him of bribery." Chicago. Children's Bk Center

"Well integrated, clear explanations of the historical events allow young readers to sense the atmosphere of the past, while the lively characterizations bring a contemporary ambience to the tales." Booklist

Wilde, Oscar

The Happy Prince, and other stories; illus. with four colour plates and line drawings in the text by Peggy Fortnum. Dent 1968 154p illus $11 (3-6)   S C

1 Fairy tales   2 Short stories
ISBN 0-460-05075-3   LC 68-95987

"Children's illustrated classics"

A combined edition, first published 1952 in England, of The Happy Prince, and other stories (1888) and A house of pomegranates (1891)

"Writing his [nine] fairy tales to express his ideas and feelings about the world and the people in it, Oscar Wilde has imbued them with a beauty and charm of his own that appeals to grown-ups and boys and girls alike." Bks for Boys & Girls

Williams, Jay

The practical princess, and other liberating fairy tales; illus. by Rick Schreiter. Parents Mag. Press [distributed by Four Winds] 1978 99p illus lib. bdg. $8.95 (2-6)   S C

1 Fairy tales   2 Short stories
ISBN 0-590-07725-2   LC 78-6998

"A collection to elate feminists. . . . Tales of six smart girls who outthink and outdo lolly-gagging males. 'Petronella' goes off on a knightly errand, to rescue a prince rumored under the spell of necromancer Albion. She does but the prince is a jerk so she weds Albion instead. On the other hand, Sylvia takes 'Stupid Marco' in hand when he's utterly at a loss, sent to prove himself by rescuing a princess." Pub W

"Five of the six inverted tales in this book have been previously published in picture book format. Thus, the ever practical Bedelia and adventurous Petronella may already be old friends. However, the sly humor of the inversions and the sophisticated approach of these stories has appeal for older children, who will find the present format more acceptable. The silhouettes, reminiscent of Rackham, are beautiful and add interest to the text. This is a good collection of original stories and offers promise of fun for story hours." Children's Bk Rev Serv

Yolen, Jane

The girl who cried flowers, and other tales; illus. by David Palladini. Crowell 1974 55p illus $9.95, lib. bdg. $8.79 (4-6)   S C

1 Fairy tale   2 Short stories
ISBN 0-690-00216-5; 0-690-00217-3   LC 73-8903

"The five stories are original but have a flavor of long ago. Each is memorable and stays with you. The unifying factor in this book is the ability of the protagonist in each story to do something very unusual. Naturally, the special trait offers disadvantages as well as advantages. Included are a boy who can stare everyone down, a girl whose tears are flower petals, and a girl who has an obsession to know the future. Each tale can be listened to (or read) for several purposes; each can be attended to on several levels. The plots themselves are good, as each individual copes with the straits caused by his or her trait. In addition, each story offers symbolic discussion about something very important in life. . . . Finally, there is the beauty of Yolen's language, which instantly sucks you into the story and glues you there." Rdng Teacher

E   EASY BOOKS

This section consists mostly of fiction books which would interest children from pre-school through second grade. For the most part, those easy books which have a definite nonfiction subject content are classified with other nonfiction books. Easy books listed here include:

1 All picture books whether fiction or nonfiction which the young child can use independently

2 Fiction books with very little text, widely spaced or scattered, with large print, and with vocabulary suitable for children with reading levels of grades 1-2

3 Picture storybooks with a larger amount of text to be used primarily by or with children in pre-school through grade 2

Adams, Adrienne

The Easter egg artists. Scribner 1976 unp illus lib. bdg. $8.95   E

1 Rabbits—Fiction   2 Egg decoration—Fiction
ISBN 0-684-14652-5   LC 75-39301

"A rabbit family of three paint designs on Easter eggs, or at least Mother and Father do. Their son Orson is lackadaisical about the family calling. But on their winter vacation, Orson helps with big projects: painting designs on a house, a bridge, and an airplane. When they return home and start the big project of the year (100 dozen eggs), Orson's enthusiasm leads to a new product, comic ostrich eggs; these are so successful that his parents have to help him fill orders. The story ends with Easter over, parents relaxing in their garden chairs, and Orson painting a flagpole." Chicago. Children's Bk Center

"Delectable pastel illustrations enhance a good story about personal identity that makes a splendid Easter offering." Sch Library J

A woggle of witches. Scribner 1971 unp illus lib. bdg. $8.95, pa $2.95   E

1 Witches—Fiction   2 Halloween—Fiction
ISBN 0-684-12506-4; 0-684-15331-9   LC 70-161536

Illustrated by the author, here are the adventures of a woggle of witches on Halloween night as they wake up the forest to feast on bat stew, circle the moon on their brooms, and descend on a corn field only to be frightened away by a group of trick-or-treaters

"This book is just right for storytelling to pre-school and primary groups: the minimal text is greatly expanded by lovely, dusky double-page spreads which humorously highlight the airborne antics." Sch Library J

Adoff, Arnold

Black is brown is tan; pictures by Emily Arnold McCully. Harper 1973 31p illus lib. bdg. $8.79   **E**

1 Stories in rhyme 2 Family life—Fiction
3 Color of people—Fiction
ISBN 0-06-020084-7   LC 72-9855

This story in rhyme describes "a warm, racially-mixed family who reads, cuts wood, plays, and eats together." Booklist

"The illustrations appear rough, and the text reads better if done aloud. Although this title is not the best, it deals fairly with the subject and serves as an important beginning in the field of easy books for children about different kinds of families." Children's Bk Rev Serv

MA nDA LA; pictures by Emily McCully. Harper 1971 unp illus $6.95, lib. bdg. $7.89 **E**

ISBN 0-06-020085-5; 0-06-020086-3   LC 76-146000

The text of this chant celebrating an African family's cultivation and harvest of a corn crop "consists entirely of syllables from the word mandala, the name of a Hindu or Buddhist symbol of the universe, rearranged to tell a simple story in which MA stands for mother, DA for father, LA for singing, and HA for laughing, RA for cheering, NA for sighing, and AH for feeling good." Booklist

"It must be read aloud to get the full effect of a child's blithe crooning, it must be seen for the full effect of the dark figures . . . against the colors of the tropical foliage. Not suitable for group use, but right for reading aloud to an individual child." Chicago. Children's Bk Center

Where wild Willie, by Arnold Adoff; pictures by Emily Arnold McCully. Harper 1978 31p illus $6.95, lib. bdg. $6.79   **E**

1 Stories in rhyme
ISBN 0-06-020092-8; 0-06-020093-6   LC 76-21390

"Willie is young, a child who stays out late and joyously explores the neighborhood, a child whose parents are concerned but not frantic. The poem describes . . . Willie's rambles and then the voices from home speak for themselves, an antiphonal arrangement in which the two draw closer until Willie comes home." Chicago. Children's Bk Center

"One and two syllable words drop in impressionistic patterns of rhyms and alliteration. Specific are left to McCully's soft orange, green, and blue wash over black lines. A poem of reassurance, for reading aloud to the very young." Sch Library J

Ahlberg, Janet

Each peach pear plum; an 'I spy' story [by] Janet and Allan Ahlberg. Viking [1979 c1978] unp illus $8.95   **E**

1 Stories in rhyme
ISBN 0-670-28705-9   LC 78-16726

First published 1978 in England

This book "invites children to play 'I spy' and point out nursery rhyme and story characters such as Jack and Jill, the Three Bears, Cinderella, etc. who are semi-hidden within . . . [the] illustrations." Sch Library J

The characters hide "in a pleasant, rural, watercolor world that's decorative but never precious or self-regarding. This is a lovely small book, well-conceived and very well drawn, gentle, humorous, unsentimental." NY Times Bk Rev

Alexander, Lloyd

The king's fountain; illus. by Ezra Jack Keats. Dutton 1971 unp illus lib. bdg. $7.95
E

ISBN 0-525-33240-5   LC 72-133109

A "king decides to build a fountain in his garden for 'the glory of his name.' Unfortunately for the city, it would eliminate the water supply. A poor man tries to find someone with wisdom, courage and persuasive speech to point out to the king the disastrous consequences of the plan. Everyone lets him down. . . . The despairing poor man realizes he must go himself." NY Times Bk Rev

"Stunningly beautiful full-page paintings, among the artists' finest, greatly expand this short, trenchant parable. . . . Keats's acrylics on canvas

effectively evoke the Near Eastern setting; Alexander's theme—that the buck must stop with Everyman, that each person's conscience must form a continuum with constructive action—has obvious relevance for readers of any time or place." Library J

Alexander, Martha

Blackboard bear; story and pictures by Martha Alexander. Dial Press 1969 unp illus $5.95, lib. bdg. $5.47, pa $1.50   **E**

1 Bears—Fiction
ISBN 0-8037-0651-0; 0-8037-0652-9; 0-8037-0126-8
                                      LC 69-17975

This small, "sparely worded, fantastical picture-book stars a little boy who is spurned when he attempts to play with the bigger boys. Told to go play with his teddy bear, he defiantly tosses teddy out the window and, on his blackboard, draws a big bear, which then steps right down to become his friend and playmate. . . . The softly-hued illustrations will carry the story for sensitive, imaginative children, and capture childhood feelings of solitude and revenge." Sch Library J

Followed by: And my mean old mother will be sorry, blackboard bear. Dial $6.95, lib. bdg. $6.46, pa $1.50 (ISBN 0-8037-0592-1; 0-8037-0593-X; 0-8037-0126-8)

Bobo's dream. Dial Press 1970 unp illus $4.95, lib. bdg. $4.58, pa $1.75   **E**

1 Dogs—Fiction 2 Blacks—Fiction 3 Stories without words
ISBN 0-8037-0686-3; 0-8037-0687-1;
0-8037-09471-4   LC 73-102825

This story without words tells "how a black boy and his dachshund feel about each other. Boy and dog settle under a shady tree to enjoy a book, a bone, and companionship. A large dog tries to steal the dachshund's bone, but the boy retrieves the bone. The grateful dog dreams of daring exploits in which he comes to the rescue of his master." Keating. Building Bridges of Understanding Between Cultures

"Unpretentious three-color drawings, childlike and humorous, show that might does not make right." Horn Bk

Nobody asked me if I wanted a baby sister; story and pictures by Martha Alexander. Dial Press 1971 unp illus $5.95, lib. bdg. $5.47, pa $1.75   **E**

1 Brothers and sisters—Fiction 2 Infants—Fiction
ISBN 0-8037-6401-4; 0-8037-6402-2; 0-8037-6410-3
                                      LC 78-153731

"Jealous of the fuss made over his baby sister, Oliver bundles Bonnie into his wagon and, wheeling her around the neighborhood, tries to give her away. He changes his mind, however, and decides to keep her when the baby, unhappy at being held by strangers, cries until he takes her." Booklist

"Not a brand-new theme, but pictures and text together make a charming variation, the precise little drawings affectionate and humorous, the writing ingenious and direct." Chicago. Children's Bk Center

Another book about Oliver is also available from Dial Press: When the new baby comes, I'm moving out $5.95, lib. bdg. $5.47 (ISBN 0-8037-9557-2; 0-8037-9558-0; LC 79-4275)

Sabrina; story and pictures by Martha Alexander. Dial Press 1971 unp illus $5.95, lib. bdg. $5.47   **E**

1 Names, Personal—Fiction
ISBN 0-8037-7547-4; 0-8037-7546-6   LC 72-134855

"Sabrina had never thought that her name was the least peculiar until the day she started nursery school. Then mistaking the other children's whispered admiration for scorn, she tried to escape from her name and become a Lisa or a Susan—until she realized that she actually had an enviable 'princess' name. . . . Diminutive boys and girls, busy with nursery-school activities, are shown on clean, uncluttered, small-sized pages." Horn Bk

Alexander, Martha—*Continued*

We never get to do anything; story and pictures by Martha Alexander. Dial Press 1970 unp illus $4.95, lib. bdg. $4.58, pa $1.75

E

ISBN 0-8037-9415-0; 0-8037-9416-9; 0-8037-9781-8
LC 78-121575

The ingredients of this story are a "small boy, large dog, busy mother, hot summer day. Adam wants to go swimming, but his mother is hanging out laundry. He disappears, is hauled back and tied to the clothesline. 'We never get to do anything,' Adam grumbles, as he slips out of his sunsuit and bares off 'au naturel.' He looks enviously at a dog under a hydrant, at birds in a fountain, at an overflowing drainpipe. Then—o joy! Rain falls, Adam shoves his empty sand box under the drain, and on the last page he is blissfully relaxing in a do-it-yourself pool." Sat Rev

"The text is slight but more than adequate, since the pictures almost tell the story. The tidy, brisk little drawings have affection and humor; the ending sheer triumph." Chicago. Children's Bk Center

Aliki

At Mary Bloom's; written and illus. by Aliki. Greenwillow Bks. 1976 unp illus lib. bdg. $7.44

E

1 Animals—Fiction
ISBN 0-688-84048-5
LC 75-45482

"A girl's pet mouse has babies, and she is anxious to share this news with her neighbor, Mary Bloom. Hesitant about disturbing Mary, her baby, and her many pets, the girl calls before dropping in and is later welcomed by calm pets and a friendly Mary, who sees that the event calls for a celebration." Children's Bk Rev Serv

"The unrelieved pandemonium feared by the heroine of Aliki's new book is graphically presented in riotous pictures and a few well-chosen words." Pub W

June 7! Macmillan Pub. Co. 1972 unp illus lib. bdg. $4.95

E

1 Family life—Fiction 2 Birthdays—Fiction
ISBN 0-02-700400-7
LC 72-75347

Illustrated by the author
"On that memorable date, the doorbell rings at the home of the narrator; she lives with her mother and father and her brother. In come her mother's parents and- her father's parents and their son and daughter-in-law, and so on until the house is bursting with people, all related in a variety of bewildering degrees. These are all identified as the story progresses to its climax, when everybody sings 'Happy Birthday' to the narrator. An engaging story and pictures and a painless way of learning how to keep track of relationships." Pub W

The two of them; written and illus. by Aliki. Greenwillow Bks. 1979 unp illus $8.50, lib. bdg. $8.16

E

1 Grandfathers—Fiction 2 Death—Fiction
ISBN 0-688-80225-7; 0-688-84225-9
LC 79-10161

This is a book "about the love between a child and her grandparent. All through her infancy he makes her things to use and play with, tells her stories and sings to her; when she is a little older he gladly accepts her help with his work, 'and every year she loved him even more than the things he made for her.' Then her grandfather becomes bedridden, and she brings him food, and sings to him, and tells him stories just as he did when she was a baby. She knows he will die, but is not aware of how deep her grief will be. When he dies, she sits in the orchard he loves and thinks of how the blossoms come each year and are followed by the fruit, and, the story ends, 'She would be there to watch it grow, and pick the fruit, and to remember.'" Chicago. Children's Bk Center

"The eloquent illustrations in muted full color and the smaller soft-pencil drawings show the life the two shared as well as the tenderness and pure pleasure implicit in their relationship. . . . The book transcends the labored introductions to geriatrics which have proliferated in contemporary children's literature and describes with sensitivity and truth the changing seasons of human life." Horn Bk

Allard, Harry

Bumps in the night; pictures by James Marshall. Doubleday 1979 32p illus $6.95, lib bdg. $7.90

E

1 Ghosts—Fiction 2 Animals—Fiction
ISBN 0-385-12942-4; 0-385-12943-2
LC 78-22301

"Marshall's chunky, silly animal figures add humor to a friendly-ghost story for the read-aloud audience. Dudley the stork is terrified by a bumping noise and something wet touching his cheek; his best friend Trevor Hog advises having a medium preside at a séance. Madame Kreep comes, goes into a trance, and the ghost appears; he's a horse named Donald who used to live in the house and is now lonely. Donald soon becomes a friend to all helping Trevor with his arithmetic, telling Dudley funny stories when he can't sleep, showing Dagmar the Baboon how to dance a jig, etc." Chicago Children's Bk Center

I will not go to market today; pictures by James Marshall. Dial Press 1979 unp illus $6.95, lib. bdg. $6.46

E

1 Shopping—Fiction 2 Chickens—Fiction
ISBN 0-8037-4019-0; 0-8037-4020-4
LC 78-7247

"Fenimore B. Buttercrunch, a not-so-intrepid rooster, is deterred day after day from going to the market to buy some strawberry jam. Blizzards, earthquakes, and hurricans send him scurrying back to his cozy home. The perfect day comes at last, and he gets jam." Children's Bk Rev Serv

"Marshall adds his own touches to this gloriously light and simple tale: eggs fry on the sidewalk while beasts' tongues loll during a heat wave; the frothy effects of a bubblebath are blown away in a stylized hurricane of wind curlicues and bending tulips; and the venerable tomes, Julia Chicken and Craig Cluckborn, are shaken from their shelf during an earthquake." Sch Library J

It's so nice to have a wolf around the house; illus. by James Marshall. Doubleday 1977 unp illus $6.95, lib. bdg. $7.90, pa $2.95

E

1 Wolves—Fiction
ISBN 0-385-11300-5; 0-385-11301-3; 0-385-15188-8
LC 76-4883

"An elderly man and his elderly pets decide they need a fresh face about the place. Cuthbert Devine wolf and bank robber, pretends to be a dog when he applies for the post, and the old man is too near-sighted to spot the deception. Cuthbert proves to be a treasure, hardworking and cheerful and devoted; when the old man sees an article about the bank robbery, he realizes he's been duped Cuthbert faints and goes into a decline; sobbing he says that he's always wanted to be good but never had a chance because everyone expected wolves to be bad. Supported by the old man, Cuthbert confesses to the police, is let off because he is reformed, and the story ends with all hands (and paws and fins) enjoying life in Arizona whither they've moved because of Cuthbert's health." Chicago. Children's Bk Center

"Marshall's illustrations feature more of his chubby, tiny-eyed characters, whose poses further the story's droll humor. Moreover, the plot is well defined and moves quickly; a jolly, happy-ever after ending fits just right with the prevailing nonsense." Booklist

Miss Nelson is missing! [By] Harry Allard [and] James Marshall. Houghton 1977 32p illus lib. bdg. $7.95

E

1 School stories
ISBN 0-395-25296-2
LC 76-5591

Illustrated by James Marshall
"The kids in room 207 were so fresh and naughty that they lost their sweet-natured teacher, the blonde Miss Nelson, and got in her place the sour souled Miss Swamp." NY Times Bk Rev

"Humor and suspense fill the pages of [this book]. . . . On one page I found the drawings a treat and the text great. Then I turned the page to find the drawings great, and the text a treat Appreciation of teachers shines through it all with imagination and great humor." Christian Sci Monitor

Allen, Jeffrey

Mary Alice, operator number 9; pictures by James Marshall. Little 1975 unp illus $6.95 **E**

1 Telephone—Fiction 2 Animals—Fiction
ISBN 0-316-03425-8   LC 75-12513

"Humorously expressive characters and situations drawn in pastel watercolors reflect the wit of this appealing story about the familiar fear of being dispensable. When Mary Alice Duck, the telephone company's indefatigable time operator, is put out of commission by a bad cold, each of her substitutes proves inappropriate. Eric Snake's hiss is too sinister, Jake Dog is imprecise, Charlie Armadillo's eyes can't locate the clock, and so on. In desperation Boss Chicken decides to take over, only to be corrected by Mary Alice at the other end of the phone. Upon returning to work, Mary Alice is relieved to learn that she is truly unique, a feeling that can be related to at any level." Sch Library J

Anderson, C. W.

Billy and Blaze. Macmillan Pub. Co. 1962 [c1936] 48p illus $5.95, pa $1.95   **E**

1 Ponies—Fiction
ISBN 0-02-701880-6; 0-02-041420-X   LC 62-14797

"The Billy and Blaze books"
First published 1936. Reissued 1962 in a new format

A picture-story book about Billy, "a little boy who loved horses more than anything else in the world," and his pony Blaze. There is a picture for each sentence of text

"The book has the convincing quality of actual experience, for the artist-author understands horses and knows how to make them come to life on the printed page." NY Times Bk Rev

Some other books about Billy and Blaze are also available from Macmillan:

Blaze and the forest fire $5.95, pa $1.95 (ISBN 0-02-702080-0; 0-02-041420-X; LC 62-14796)
Blaze and the gray spotted pony $5.95, pa $1.95 (ISBN 0-02-701150-X; 0-02-041480-3; LC 68-10997)
Blaze and the Indian cave $6.95 (ISBN 0-02-702470-9; LC 64-14529)
Blaze and the lost quarry $4.95, pa $2.25 (ISBN 0-02-702490-3; 0-02-041440-4; LC 66-10356)
Blaze and the mountain lion $6.95 (ISBN 0-02-702630-2; LC 59-11293)
Blaze and Thunderbolt $5.95 (ISBN 0-02-702870-4; LC 55-14874)
Blaze finds forgotten roads $5.95 (ISBN 0-02-701340-5; LC 76-117970)
Blaze finds the trail $5.50; pa $1.95 (ISBN 0-02-703130-6; 0-02-041430-7; LC 50-10357)
Blaze shows the way $5.95 (ISBN 701990-X; LC 74-78090)

Anderson, Lonzo

The day the hurricane happened; illus by Ann Grifalconi. Scribner 1974 39p illus lib. bdg. $6.95   **E**

1 Hurricanes—Fiction 2 Virgin Islands of the U.S.—Fiction
ISBN 0-684-13495-0   LC 73-1382

Set on St John, in the Virgin Islands, this is the story of a family coping with a hurricane. "Two small children, Eldra and Albie, tell their father of the strange flags (warning flags) they have seen on a flagpole. Father, a constable, goes off to warn others while Grandfather tells the children and their mother what to do. Their house is destroyed, too—during the lull of the storm's eye—each ties himself to a tree to wait out the buffeting of the hurricane." Chicago. Children's Bk Center

"Family solidarity and a by-product of information on hurricanes make this interesting, even adventuresome material for the beginning-to-read group. Grifalconi's broad watercolors capture the tension engendered by the storm and its aftermath." Booklist

The Halloween party; illus. by Adrienne Adams. Scribner 1974 unp illus lib. bdg. $8.95. pa $2.95   **E**

1 Halloween—Fiction
ISBN 0-684-14002-0; 0-684-16004-8   LC 74-8193

"Colorful, spooky illustrations complement this account of a Halloween party attended by real ogres, witches, gremlins and one human—namely young Faraday Folsum. Faraday, going to a costume party, almost becomes the flavor in the stew. The illustrations (as of little gremlins flying on a broomstick) are particularly delightful and provide true Halloween atmosphere." Adventuring with Bks

Izzard; illus. by Adrienne Adams. Scribner 1973 unp illus lib. bdg. $8.95   **E**

1 Lizards—Fiction 2 Virgin Islands of the U.S.—Fiction
ISBN 0-684-13247-8   LC 72-9032

"Jamie of St. John in the Virgin Islands finds a lizard egg and it hatches in his hand. The little anole thinks that he's her mother! But, the time comes when Izzard realizes she's really a lizard, and Jamie learns with difficulty to let her go, physically and emotionally." Babbling Bookworm

This is "not an unusual boy-animal plot, but [it is] given freshness here by the fact that the pet is unusual, the telling is deft, and the illustrations are handsome in the carefree detail with which they are drawn." Chicago. Children's Bk Center

Anglund, Joan Walsh

In a pumpkin shell, a Mother Goose ABC. Harcourt 1960 unp illus $5.95, pa $1.95   **E**

1 Nursery rhymes 2 Alphabet
ISBN 0-15-238269-0; 0-15-644425-9   LC 60-10243

This is "a combination alphabet and nursery rhyme book. Each letter of the alphabet and the word for which it stands is followed by a nursery rhyme in which the word beginning with that letter appears—for instance, D stands for dog and the nursery rhyme is 'Old Mother Hubbard,' S stands for shoe and the nursery rhyme is 'The old woman who lived in a shoe.' Each rhyme is charmingly illustrated in a colored or pen-and-ink drawing. A lovely book for young children. "Booklist"

Anno, Mitsumasa

Anno's alphabet; an adventure in imagination. Crowell [1975 c1974] unp illus $8.95, lib. bdg. $8.79   **E**

1 Alphabet
ISBN 0-690-00540-7; 0-690-00541-5   LC 73-21652

The artist "has produced another exercise in optical delusion featuring more of his technical virtuosity and visual witticisms. Each alphabetic character is cleanly painted as though fashioned of wood; but a searching look reveals the subtle deception which turns the realistic letters into three-dimensional surrealistic forms. Lines and textures are sharply communicated, but shapes are convoluted, angled, or inverted to produce an uncanny effect of motion. Facing each letter is an object, appropriately chosen but unconventionally illustrated; while the page borders are embellished with intertwining pen-and-ink drawings that conceal pictures of plants, animals, and objects, most of which are identified at the end of the book." Horn Bk

Anno's Counting book. Crowell 1977 c1975 unp illus $7.95, lib. bdg. $8.79   **E**

1 Counting
ISBN 0-680-01287-X; 0-690-01288-8   LC 76-28977

First published 1975 in Japan

"From zero (just the barren, snow-covered valley), each double-page spread from one through 12 expands to include another horse, adult, child, tree, etc. Over the course of a year (each picture represents a different month and time of day as recorded by the clock on the church steeple) a little town grows up with viewers witnessing the building of bridges, streets, and railroads. Stacked colored blocks on each left-hand margin correspond to the number represented and are an easy way of teaching the basic principles of the decimal system (for 12, there is a pile of 10 blocks with two more stacked beside)." Sch Library J

"Carefully outlined drawings and the soft watercolor tones of the pictures produce a delightfully idyllic effect and suggest arrangement of stylized toys, but only careful searching and enumerating will reveal all of the series of objects specified by a particular number. A counting book devised to encourage the observation of arithmetical subtleties and not merely based on simple concepts calculated to inform beginners." Horn Bk

Anno's journey. Collins [distributed by Philomel Bks 1978 c1977] unp illus $7.95 lib. bdg. $7.99   **E**

1 Europe—Pictorial works 2 Stories without words
ISBN 0-529-05418-3; 0-529-05419-1   LC 77-16336

Original Japanese edition, 1977

"In a panorama which unrolls wordlessly, a traveler rides horseback over a landscape that seems distinctly European, shown in meticulously detailed illustrations of everyday life, artifacts, and

Anno, Mitsumasa—*Continued*

architecture. Hints and fragments of stories abound, carried from scene to scene; one sees anachronisms and visual jokes, children and grown-ups at games and sports, and characters from classics like 'Red Riding Hood' and 'The Pied Piper of Hamelin' all the way to 'Sesame Street.' Suggestions of famous paintings are casually inserted into natural settings. . . . Although the observer's omnipotent viewpoint engenders a certain remoteness, the magnificent architectural renderings of cathedrals, farmhouses, castles, and towns; the pleasure of identifying and unraveling the many puzzles, visual puns, and tricks; and the fascinating yet enigmatic purpose behind the book all make the artwork worth repeated examination. A page of description and explanatory notes is appended." Horn Bk

"Most children will need the help of informed adults to decipher the puzzles. But even beginners should enjoy turning the pages of an exceptional book and responding to the beauties depicted." Pub W

The King's flower. Collins [distributed by Philomel Bks.] 1979 c1976 29p illus $7.95, lib. bdg. $7.91   E

1 Kings and rulers—Fiction 2 Size and shape—Fiction
ISBN 0-529-05458-2; 0-529-05459-9   LC 78-9596

Original Japanese edition, 1976
Size is the "focus of a story about a foolish king who wants everything he possesses to be the biggest in the world. It's true that his huge crown is uncomfortable, that he has trouble using a knife and fork bigger than he is, and that he has to go outdoors to nibble on the biggest chocolate bar in existence—but he's undaunted in his idiocy until he has tried and failed to grow the world's biggest flower in the world's biggest pot. The pot is huge, but the tulip that grows there is just a tulip; however, it is beautiful, and the king bows to nature and admits that he can't do everything and that perhaps it's just as well he can't." Chicago. Children's Bk Center

"The series of amplifications provides the kind of humor readily appreciated by small children, while some details may only be perceived by those more sophisticated. . . . With clarity and a brilliant use of color Anno presents his story in a medieval setting. The originality of his graphics serves a tale for which an afterword underscores the message: 'We must be content, and recognize that each flower, each worm, is something natural and indispensable.'" Horn Bk

Topsy-turvies; pictures to stretch the imagination. Weatherhill [distributed by Lippincott] 1970 27p illus $6.50   E

1 Puzzles
ISBN 0-8348-2004-8   LC 71-96054

This book consists of illustrations featuring the activities of some elves. Each picture "features little men with pointed hats in unlikely situations involving matching staircases that don't, level platforms that aren't, walls and ceilings that are floors, and mazes that turn upside down." Library J

"In a constant flow of motion through the ensuing pages, the elves march or run or dive—may even rest—but are never static figures. Both in their faces and in their bodies they express individual and very human moods; tired, mischievous, or speculative, they are always alive. Although younger children may not be able to discover the 'real' solutions to the puzzles the elves demonstrate, they will be captivated by the little figures as they progress through their elaborately conceived world of building blocks, bottles, and playing cards. Older children, too, will be fascinated by the sophisticated perspective puzzles presented in sharply detailed line and watercolor drawings subtly vibrant with color." Horn Bk

Upside-downers; more pictures to stretch the imagination. Weatherhill [distributed by Lippincott] 1971 27p illus $6.50   E

1 Puzzles
ISBN 0-8348-2005-6   LC 71-157269

"Awakened from their sleep, the kings' own soldiers in the land of playing cards resume their age-old quarreling over what is up and what is down until an old king with a new idea proclaims that since the world is round, up and down are all in the point of view. The reader is encouraged

to examine the picture book from various angles both by the many optical illusions in the gaily colored illustrations and by the fact that part o the text is printed upside down." Booklist

"In a companion volume to Topsy-Turvies [entered above] the artist performs further feats of optical ingenuity with the same joyous dexterity that characterized the earlier book. . . . A kind of mad logic runs through the book." Horn Bk

Ardizzone, Edward

Little Tim and the brave sea captain. [2 ed. completely redrawn and with additiona text]. Oxford 1955 unp illus $8.95   E

1 Sea stories
ISBN 0-19-27954-22   LC 55-1363

First published 1936
The story "tells how Tim stowed away on a ship learned to be useful, and showed his courage when the ship was wrecked." Horn Bk

"The pictures [by the author] are rapid wash drawings full of swing, salt and slap, the sea scenes especially good, full of action." NY Her Trib Bks

Some other books about Tim are also available from Oxford (unless otherwise noted):
Tim in danger pa $3.95 (ISBN 0-19-272106-2)
Tim to the lighthouse pa $3.95 (ISBN 0-19-272107-0)
Ship's cook Ginger $7.95 Macmillan Pub. Co
ISBN 0-02-705680-5; LC 78-7518)

Armitage, Ronda

The lighthouse keeper's lunch [by] Ronda and David Armitage. Deutsch [distributed by Elsevier-Dutton] 1979 c1977 unp illus $5.95   E

1 Lighthouses—Fiction 2 Gulls—Fiction
ISBN 0-233-96868-7   LC 78-74457

First published 1977 in England
"Each day Mrs Gringing prepares hearty lunches for her husband, the lighthouse keeper, and shoots the basket of viands via a long cable, stretching from the couple's cliffside cottage, to the beacon But then avid seagulls take to feasting on the goodies. The Gringings try various schemes to outwit the scavengers, all in vain, until the smart lady packs a lunch of mustard sandwiches. . . . The Armitages' fanciful comedy boasts Ronda's light touch in the telling (notably in the jaunty comments of the thieving birds), plus David's grand seascapes and his inspired two-page spread—pictures of the hijacked gustatory triumphs." Pub W

Aruego, Jose

Look what I can do. Scribner 1971 unp illus lib. bdg. $6.95, pa $2.95   E

1 Water buffalo—Fiction
ISBN 0-684-12493-9; 0-684-16215-6   LC 73-15888 0

The story of two carabaos who get carried away trying to outdo each other and almost come to a sad end." Booklist

"There are just fifteen words in this story . . . whose valuable message should be intelligible to the young non-reader. . . . Sprightly, cartoon-like drawings [by the author] are the focal point." Bk World

We hide, you seek, by Jose Aruego and Ariane Dewey. Greenwillow Bks. 1979 unp illus $7.95, lib. bdg. $7.63   E

1 Camouflage (Biology)—Fiction
ISBN 0-688-80201-X; 0-688-84201-1   LC 78-13638

"An oafishly good-natured rhino, invited into a jungle-wide game of hide and seek, bumbles from one scene to the next, accidentally exposing would-be hiders (leopards, crocodiles, lions) at every stop; then, turning the tables on his playmates, cleverly hides himself. Readers are served up a wealth of information in 27 words (plus end-papers that give a page-by-page identification of the species pictured) and droll scenes drenched in the vibrant tones of an East African palette." Sch Library J

Asch, Frank

Moon Bear. Scribner 1978 unp illus lib. bdg. $8.95   E

1 Bears—Fiction 2 Moon—Fiction
ISBN 0-684-15810-8   LC 78-9444

Asch, Frank—*Continued*

"A bear who admires the moon is dismayed to see it becoming smaller each night. He theorizes that it may be undernourished and so sets out honey for it. He doesn't know that birds are eating the honey, and just about starves himself to feed the moon until one of the birds sets him straight." Sch Library J

Asch's illustrations "in brown and glittering gold contrast with sober shades to give elfin appeal to the ludicrous story about Bear's misconception." Pub W

Sand cake; A Frank Asch bear story. Parents Mag. Press [1979 c1978] unp illus $4.95, lib. bdg. $4.99   **E**

1 Bears—Fiction 2 Beaches—Fiction
ISBN 0-8193-0985-0; 0-8193-0986-9   LC 78-11183

"Bright, solid colors are used to illustrate a story in which a small bear matches his father's imaginative play. Restless while his parents are sunning at the beach, Baby Bear offers to make a cake if his father will eat it. Yes, he will, if his offspring will use milk, eggs, and flour. No way. Yes, there is, says Papa Bear, and he draws eggs, wheat, and a cow in the sand. Baby Bear looks at the resultant sand cake with no appetite, then draws a picture of himself around it. 'Here I am, and I have eaten the cake. See it in my stomach.' Happy to be outwitted, Papa Bear hugs his child, and they both move with alacrity to the real cake that Mama Bear brings out of the picnic basket. The pictures can help the small child understand the joke, and the book has a cozy happy-family feeling." Chicago. Children's Bk Center

Turtle tale. Dial Press 1978 unp illus $6.50 lib. bdg. $6.29, pa $2.75   **E**

1 Turtles—Fiction
ISBN 0-8037-8782-0; 0-8037-8783-9; 0-8037-8785-5
       LC 78-51328

"The turtle, having been bonked by a falling apple, decides to keep his head pulled in, stating that's what a wise turtle would do.' He is wonderfully ridiculous as he proceeds towards the pond, a green hemisphere with yellow tail and feet below, bumping and falling because he can't see. Frustration and hunger and a tearful night lead him to take the opposite extreme: he decides to keep his head out, which is fine until it rains and a passing fox starts to leap on him. At that moment the turtle sees that wisdom may lie in sometimes keeping his head out and sometimes pulling it in. It's not long before the fox is gone and the sun is once more shining." Sch Library J

"Large print, a simple text, and colorful illustrations [by the author] that enhance the story make this a very desirable book. It will appeal to both listeners and readers. It is ideal for a small group at storytime and would adapt well to a flanne board." Children's Bk Rev Serv

Aulaire, Ingri d'

Animals everywhere, by Ingri and Edgar Parin. d'Aulaire. Doubleday 1954 unp illus $4.50, lib. bdg. $5.40   **E**

1 Animals—Pictorial works
ISBN 0-385-07216-3; 0-385-07703-3   LC 54-5904

This book introduces very young children to animals from the tropics to the arctic regions. The authors picture animals in their natural habitats

"The generous doublespread pictures in color provide hours of entertainment for a small child. The brief text when read aloud will give him the fun of hunting for each animal mentioned, and he will surely want to imitate the cries the authors have so thoughtfully included." Horn Bk

Don't count your chicks [by] Ingri & Edgar Parin d'Aulaire. Doubleday 1943 unp illus $7.95, lib. bdg. $8.90, pa $1.95   **E**

1 Chickens—Fiction 2 Farm life—Fiction
ISBN 0-385-07282-1; 0-385-07609-6; 0-385-05233-2
       LC 43-51293

The story "tells of the laughable schemes of the old woman who counted too much on her eggs before they were hatched and found herself left with only her little red house, her dog and cat, and her cock and hen." Ontario Library Rev

"A humorous story illustrated [by the authors] with large lithographs showing colorful country scenes." Hodges. Bks for Elem Sch Libraries

Ola, by Ingri & Edgar Parin d'Aulaire. Doubleday 1932 unp illus $6.95   **E**

1 Norway—Fiction
ISBN 0-385-07670-3   LC 32-28980

The adventures of Ola, a little Norwegian boy, who went out on his skis one wintry day. He got lost in a snowdrift and was dug out by Per the peddler with whom he went to visit the Lapps, then a fishing village on the coast, and finally the bird rocks where he collected down from the birds' nest

"A beautiful and entirely childlike large picture book of Norway which is authentic in spirit and in every detail. The artists have provided an appealing story as accompaniment to lithographic drawings in full color and in black and white which record the adventures of Ola and serve also as a pictorial background for future reading of Norse literature." NY Pub Library

Averill, Esther

The school for cats; written and illus. by Esther Averill. Harper 1947 31p illus lib. bdg. $6.89   **E**

1 Cats—Fiction
ISBN 0-06-020281-5   LC 47-30683

This is the story of Jenny Linsky, a timid little cat sent to a school for cats while her master was at sea. At first she was terrified of a tough firehouse cat, and ran away. But later she was sorry, returned to school, and made a place for herself

"Deftly handled, nicely proportioned, this story has the sense of reality which is the earmark of good fantasy. Five to 8-year-olds who have their own problems of adjustment in school will rejoice in Jenny's moral triumph. The pictures, drawn with a sophisticated simplicity, are a perfect complement to the text." NY Times Bk Rev

Some other books about Jenny and her friends are also available from Harper:
Captains of the city streets $5.95. lib. bdg. $7.89, pa 95¢ (ISBN 0-06-020176-2; 0-06-020177-0; 0-06-440070-0; LC 72-76500)
The fire cat lib. bdg. $7.89 (ISBN 0-02-020196-7; LC 60-10234)
The hotel cat pa $1.95 (ISBN 0-06-440057-3; LC 74-77941)
Jenny's bedside book lib. bdg. $7.89 (ISBN 0-02-020241-6; LC 59-8963)
Jenny's birthday book lib. bdg. $7.89 (ISBN 0-02-020251-3; LC 54-6589)
Jenny goes to sea lib. bdg. $6.89 (ISBN 0-02-020220-3; LC 57-9261)
Jenny's moonlight adventure lib. bdg. $6.89 (ISBN 0-06-020266-1; LC 49-8288)
Another book, Jenny and the Cat Club; a collection of favorite stories about Jenny Linsky, is entered in the Story Collection section

Babbitt, Natalie

The something; story and pictures by Natalie Babbitt. Farrar, Straus 1970 unp illus $2.95   **E**

1 Night—Fiction
ISBN 0-374-37137-7   LC 70-125143

"Mylo is an ugly, hair-covered, bucktoothed little boy who is afraid of an indefinable Something coming in through his window at night. Given some modeling clay by his concerned mother, Mylo finally succeeds in making a statue of the Something but it is not until he meets the Something—an attractive little girl—in a dream that he discovers he is no longer afraid. Illustrated with drawings that endow the grotesque Mylo and his mother with endearing charm and printed on soft yellow pages except for the dream sequence which appears on gray pages, the clever, ironic story interprets common childhood fears of the dark in a way that should prove highly amusing to many small children." Booklist

Balian, Lorna

Humbug witch. Abingdon 1965 unp illus $5.95   **E**

1 Witches—Fiction
ISBN 0-687-18023-6   LC 65-14089

Illustrations by the author accompany this story of "a little witch and her unsuccessful attempts at witchcraft. One evening she wearily takes off piece after piece of comical attire—the last of which proves to be a mask, revealing a hilarious little girl underneath! Too good to miss." Adventuring With Bks. 2d edition

Balian, Lorna—*Continued*

Where in the world is Henry? [Story and pictures by Lorna Balian] Abingdon Press [1980 c1972] unp illus $5.95   **E**

ISBN 0-687-45092-6   LC 79-10391

First published 1972 by Bradbury Press

The innocent question in the title leads a sister to answer a younger brother about Henry's relative whereabouts under a quilt (in a room, in a house, in a town/state/country, on a continent, on a planet, in the universe). Who Henry is will surprise everyone, except the two kids talking

"Although the general theme (finding someone lost) is a familiar one, youngsters should enjoy this journey of discovery. . . . With its judicious use of red and appealingly open format, this title would be an attractive addition to the read-aloud shelf." Wis Library Bul

Barrett, Judi

Animals should definitely not wear clothing; written by Judi Barrett and drawn by Ron Barrett. Atheneum Pubs. 1970 unp illus lib. bdg. $8.95, pa $2.95   **E**

1 Animals 2 Clothing and dress
ISBN 0-689-20592-9; 0-689-70412-7   LC 70-115078

"The pitfalls of clothing for animals are humorously described in this unusual picture book. A minimum of words in oversized letters illuminate pictures such as a snake slithering out of his trousers or a walrus in a sopping wet sports jackets." Wis Library Bul

Benjamin's 365 birthdays; written by Judi Barrett and drawn by Ron Barrett. Atheneum Pubs. 1974 unp illus lib. bdg. $7.95, pa $1.95   **E**

1 Birthdays—Fiction
ISBN 0-689-30130-8; 0-689-70443-7   LC 72-86926

"Benjamin loves birthdays so much that the thought of waiting a whole year after his ninth till his next one makes him weep and then inspires him to rewrap his presents, one each day, and go on to wrap everything in his house." Booklist

Benjamin's "solution to prolonging pleasure will amuse preschoolers familiar with post-party blues. . . . The theme is familiar, but its execution both in text and humorously detailed illustrations is fresh and spontaneous." Horn Bk

Bartoli, Jennifer

Nonna; illus. by Joan Drescher. Harvey House 1975 unp illus lib. bdg. $5.99   **E**

1 Grandmothers—Fiction 2 Death—Fiction
ISBN 0-8178-5212-3   LC 74-25423

This story "treats the subject of death in an understanding, natural manner. The story depicts a young child's internalization of the external events surrounding the death of a beloved grandmother. Eventually things return to normal, new people move into grandma's house, and family life continues with sad-sweet memories of Nonna." Rdng Teacher

"Although there have been many recent books about losing a beloved grandparent, this is the first that very calmly and naturally discusses burial and the disposal of property. Nothing macabre here, the emphasis being on how loved Nonna was and how much the memories of her are treasured. Primarily for reading aloud, the book may also be enjoyed by independent readers." Chicago. Children's Bk Center

Barton, Byron

Wheels. Crowell 1979 unp illus $6.95, lib. bdg. $6.89   **E**

1 Wheels
ISBN 0-690-03951-4 0-690-03952-2   LC 78-20541

"Bright pictures in tidy rectangles have big blocks of color and some resemblance to the awkward drawing of young children; each picture takes up most of a page, and a line or two beneath each tells a running story of the development of the wheel, the kinds of vehicles wheels have been used for (from prehistoric times to today) and the broad variety of wheels today." Chicago. Children's Bk Center

Battles, Edith

What does the rooster say, Yoshio? Pictures by Toni Hormann. Whitman, A. 1978 unp illus lib. bdg. $5.50   **E**

1 Animal communication—Fiction 2 Japanese language—Fiction
ISBN 0-8075-3628-8   LC 78-12824

"Visiting a play farm, Yoshio meets Lynn. She can't understand him, nor can he understand her—but as they go about seeing the animals, each imitates the sounds of animals as they are conventionally reproduced in their own languages; for example they see a dog (He says 'Wan, wan,' and she says 'Bowwow') and a duck ('Quack, quack' and 'Ga ga') and so on, until they see a cow and they both say 'Moo moo.' Happy, they run back to their mothers, mooing in unison." Chicago. Children's Bk Center

"This very simple story is illustrated with gaily painted pictures of children. An excellent beginning reader to use in multi-racial schools and for story-telling: the Katakana symbols for the Japanese sounds are added to the text and are a good way of introducing the idea of languages being written with different symbols." Sch Library J

Baylor, Byrd

Everybody needs a rock; with pictures by Peter Parnall. Scribner 1974 unp illus lib. bdg. $7.95, pa $2.95   **E**

1 Rocks
ISBN 0-684-13899-9; 0-684-16011-0   LC 74-9163

The free verse of this book speaks "to the spiritual-sensual affinity that can spring up between a living being and an inanimate object, specifically in this case, a rock. Not just any rock, Baylor is careful to note, but 'a special rock that you find yourself and keep as long as you can—maybe forever.' To this end she unaffectedly sets out her own 10 rules for discovering that special rock." Booklist

"Parnall's striking pictures combine mysticism and a splendid sense of dignity. The lines of his drawings (which combine black-and-white with earthen shades) soar and suggest rather than depict the text, a quality which enhances Ms. Baylor's inspired and economical message." Pub W

Guess who my favorite person is; illus. by Robert Andrew Parker. Scribner 1977 unp illus lib. bdg. $7.95   **E**

ISBN 0-684-15197-9   LC 77-7151

A "book celebrating the pleasures of favorite things. A young man and a little girl who chance to meet in an alfalfa field take turns choosing sounds, places to live, dreams, colors, and smells—'We must have named a hundred favorite things that afternoon.' The combination of thoughtfulness, friendliness, and sensitivity in the text with the peaceful, subtle watercolors—including a magnificent illustration of falling stars—makes the book a unique experience." Horn Bk

Hawk, I'm your brother; illus. by Peter Parnall. Scribner 1976 unp illus lib. bdg. $7.95, pa $2.95   **E**

1 Hawks—Fiction
ISBN 0-684-14571-5; 0-684-16218-0   LC 75-39296

"Driven by the desire to fly, Rudy Soto steals a baby hawk from its nest in the hope that having a hawk as his 'brother' will somehow enable him to take flight. Seeing the hawk's frustration in confinement, the boy finally releases it. But the hawk remembers Rudy and the two call back and forth to each other across the mountains. Through their communication, Rudy begins to experience flying vicariously—the pull of the wind, the sense of open space. In giving the hawk its freedom he has found a new power. Now the hawk is truly his brother." Interracial Bks For Children Bul

"In the poetic simplicity of the writing, Baylor echoes the quietness of the desert and she captures the essence of the desert people's affinity for natural things. Both are reflected in Parnall's spacious illustrations, as clean and poetic as is the writing." Chicago. Children's Bk Center

The other way to listen, by Byrd Baylor and Peter Parnall. Scribner 1978 unp illus lib. bdg. $7.95   **E**

ISBN 0-684-15651-2   LC 78-23430

Baylor, Byrd—*Continued*

Illustrated by Peter Parnall

The text is "spoken by a child, who remembers . . . conversations with the old man who could hear the cactus flowers blooming or the rock murmuring to the lizard perching on it. There was no way, he said, to teach such listening, but one must feel that each object or creature is important, and one must be silent and patient. The child tried and tried to no avail, and then one morning, singing to the hills, heard the hills sing too. And, as the old man had said, it wasn't surprising at all, but seemed the most natural thing in the world." Chicago. Children's Bk Center

"Set in pages of varied design, the book is a tribute to the idea that spareness is effective. The flowing sketches with minimal lines are brightened by the addition of yellowish orange; the short text does not have an unnecessary word." Horn Bk

Your own best secret place, by Byrd Baylor and Peter Parnall. Scribner 1979 unp illus $9.95   E

ISBN 0-684-16111-7   LC 78-21243

Illustrated by Peter Parnall

"In the hollow at the foot of a cottonwood tree, a girl finds notes left by a boy who once claimed the hollow as his special place. The girl remembers her own secret place and those of friends—a barn, a sand dune, a pear tree—and in a wistful, gentle tone, expresses the significance of these private dwellings." Booklist

Belpré, Pura

Santiago; illus. by Symeon Shimin. Warne 1969 31p illus lib. bdg. $7.95   E

1 Puerto Ricans in New York (City)—Fiction 2 Chickens—Fiction
ISBN 0-7232-6019-2   LC 70-85218

Also available in a Spanish language edition, lib. bdg. $7.95 (ISBN 0-7232-6020-6)

Selina, Santiago's pet hen had been left behind in Puerto Rico when the family had moved to New York, yet Santiago talked about her incessantly. Everyone believed him except Ernie whom he wanted to impress most. But one day Santiago had an opportunity to convince Ernie

"The story is not strong, but it is modest, and realistic, and the illustrations are lovely, those of the two boys (Ernie is black) being especially sensitive in the capture of fleeting moods." Chicago. Children's Bk Center

Bemelmans, Ludwig

Madeline's rescue; story and pictures by Ludwig Bemelmans. Puffin Bks. 1978 c1953 unp illus pa $2.50   E

1 Dogs—Fiction 2 Paris—Fiction 3 Stories in rhyme
ISBN 0-14-050207-6   LC 77-2573

First published 1953 by Viking
Awarded the Caldecott Medal, 1954
Sequel to: Madeline, o.p. 1981

A picture-story book with rhymed text about little Madeline in Paris. This time she falls into the Seine and is rescued by "a dog that kept its head." The dog, named Genevieve, was promptly adopted by Madeline's boarding school mistress and her twelve pupils. When Genevieve was turned out by snobbish trustees the little girls were inconsolable, until Genevieve solved their problem

"This sort of tale will amuse and delight children. For grown-ups, the joy will be in the Bemelmans views of Paris." N Y Her Trib Bks

Benchley, Nathaniel

George, the drummer boy; pictures by Don Bolognese. Harper 1977 61p illus (An I can read history bk) $6.95, lib. bdg. $7.89   E

1 Lexington, Battle of, 1775—Fiction 2 Concord, Battle of, 1775—Fiction
ISBN 0-06-020500-8; 0-06-020501-6   LC 76-18398

The author presents the beginning of the American Revolution as seen through the eyes of a young drummer for those British troops that faced the Minutemen at Lexington and Concord. Viewing history from this angle the author makes a quiet point: allies and enemies were very much alike. George is not a demon but a friendly, frightened boy." NY Times Bk Rev

"To George, Boston is home turf and the idea that the common people would be hostile to him is confusing and disheartening. . . . Despite a easing lightheartedness in the dialogue, the story

offers rudimentary consideration of the several sides of war and could spark introductory American history discussions. With spacious print and over-colored but not unappealing red, white, and blue illustrations." Booklist

A ghost named Fred; pictures by Ben Shecter. Harper 1968 unp illus (An I can read mystery) $6.95, lib. bdg. $7.89, pa $1.95   E

1 Ghosts—Fiction
ISBN 0-06-020473-7; 0-06-020474-5; 0-06-444022-8   LC 68-24322

"George, an imaginative child used to playing alone, went into an empty house to get out of the rain; there he met an absent-minded ghost named Fred, who knew there was a treasure but had forgotten where. Only when Fred opened an umbrella for George's homeward journey did the treasure materialize." Chicago. Children's Bk Center

"More humorous than scary . . . this is a pleasing and acceptable ghost story for beginning readers." Booklist

Sam the Minuteman; pictures by Arnold Lobel. Harper 1969 62p illus (An I can read history bk) $6.95, lib. bdg. $7.89   E

1 Lexington, Battle of, 1775—Fiction
ISBN 0-06-020473-7; 0-06-020480-X   LC 68-10211

In this book about the Minutemen and the "Lobster Backs," the British soldiers, the author describes what it must have been like for a young boy to fight in the Battle of Lexington, which marked the beginning of the American Revolution

"The story, told from a boy's viewpoint, conveys a sense of immediacy. . . .Excellent drawings faithfully re-create the people, the time, and the place; [set] against soft pencil-gray and mustard brown [are] the scarlet-coated British troops." Horn Bk

The strange disappearance of Arthur Cluck; pictures by Arnold Lobel. Harper 1967 64p illus (An I can read mystery) $6.95, lib. bdg. $7.89, pa $1.95   E

1 Owls—Fiction 2 Chickens—Fiction
ISBN 0-06-020477-X; 0-06-020478-8; 0-06-440024-4   LC 67-4151

"An amusing nonsense story in which a wise old bird with detective instincts solves the mystery of the disappearance of a baby chick." Chicago. Children's Bk Center

"Not much of a mystery but entertaining." Sch Library J

Berenstain, Stan

Bears on wheels, by Stan and Jan Berenstain. Random House 1969 unp illus $3.95, lib. bdg. $4.99   E

1 Bears—Fiction 2 Counting
ISBN 0-394-80967-X; 0-394-90967-4   LC 72-77840

"A Bright & early book"

The authors' illustrations are used with numbers in this counting book which tells the story of a small bear who goes out for a ride on one small wheel. As the bear rides on, traffic and unwanted passengers accumulate

Berson, Harold

Balarin's goat; story and pictures by Harold Berson. Crown 1972 unp illus $3.95   E

1 Goats—Fiction
ISBN 0-517-50105-8   LC 72-79795

"To his goat Fleurette, Balarin gives hugs and flower wreaths and the finest delicacies, but to his wife Marinette, he shows only bad temper. At last Marinette rebels and answers Balarin's snarl with a baa. She puts Fleurette in the bed and spends the night in the goat house, while Balarin dreams that his wife has really turned into a goat. Awakened by a lick from Fleurette, he rushes out and begs Marinette to return, promising to be kind, patient, and cheerful. The author's modest drawings invest the homely threesome, drawn from an old folktale, with ironic humor." Booklist

Joseph and the snake. Macmillan Pub. Co. 1979 unp illus $6.95   E

1 Foxes—Fiction 2 Snakes—Fiction
ISBN 0-02-709200-3   LC 78-12317

Illustrated by the author

"Fleeing from a hard taskmaster, Joseph encounters a ravenous snake and frees it from the rock it is pinned under, only to have it threaten

Berson, Harold—*Continued*

to devour him. . . . A sly fox saves him by tricking the snake into reenacting the original situation. . . . Joseph rewards the fox by showing him his master's larder only to be captured by the vigilant master who threatens to do away with him. . . . Joseph placates the master by promising to show him where a treasure is hidden. Of course, the treasure is under a rock, which the foolish master raises, only to be devoured by the even-more ravenous snake." Sch Library J

"This is a lively tale which will appeal to children and be useful at story hours. . . . Easy-to-read, nicely illustrated, and evoking the traditional French setting of many folktales, readers will enjoy the sense of adventure and the satisfying conclusion." Children's Bk Rev Serv

Beskow, Elsa

Pelle's new suit; picture book by Elsa Beskow; tr. by Marion Letcher Woodburn. Harper 1929 unp illus lib. bdg. $8.89   **E**

1 Sweden—Fiction
ISBN 0-06-020496-6

"Charming pictures tell the story of how Pelle earned his new suit. He is shown raking hay, bringing in wood, feeding pigs, going on errands and at the same time, each process in the making of the suit is followed, beginning with the shearing of the lamb. The coloring of the pictures (which show both Swedish peasant house interiors and out-of-door scenes) is quite lovely." NY Libraries

Birnbaum, A.

Green Eyes; story and pictures by A. Birnbaum. Golden Press 1973 c1953 lib. bdg. $9.15   **E**

1 Cats—Fiction
ISBN 0-307-60182-X   LC 53-12576

"Told in the first person, this picture storybook . . . gives the high spots in the first year of a cat—from the time he first climbs out of his box to explore to the time when he is quite willing to curl up in his snug box by the fire on a cold winter's night." Library J

The story "is simple enough for the smallest child. The pictures are subtle and amusing enough to charm adults." Pub W

Bishop, Bonnie

No one noticed Ralph; illus. by Jack Kent. Doubleday 1979 unp illus $4.95, lib. bdg. $5.90   **E**

1 Parrots—Fiction
ISBN 0-385-12158-X; 0-385-12159-8   LC 78-18555

"A Reading on my own book"

"Children who like to court attention will understand why a parrot sulks one day [when he remains unnoticed]. Ralph eventually becomes a feathered hero in this lively tale of the joys and tribulations of parrothood. Bonnie Bishop's winged wit deserves Jack Kent's sprightly illustrations." Sch Library J

Another book about Ralph is: Ralph rides away. Doubleday $4.95, lib. bdg. $5.90 (ISBN 0-385-14213-7; 0-385-14214-5; LC 78-20710)

Bishop, Claire Huchet

The man who lost his head; illus. by Robert McCloskey. Viking 1942 unp illus lib. bdg. $7.95   **E**

ISBN 0-670-45349-8   LC 42-25584

"A man without a head tries several substitutes but finds none satisfactory. Droll illustrations match the absurdity of the story." Hodges. Bks for Elem Sch Libraries

Twenty-two bears; illus. by Kurt Wiese. Viking 1964 31p illus lib. bdg. $6.95   **E**

1 Bears—Fiction 2 Counting
ISBN 0-670-73507-8   LC 64-12636

"This picture [counting] book describes the antics of a large family of bears in the wild woods of Wyoming." Library J

"Kurt Wiese's bears have individuality and lively humor. His sure, soft line is a lasting pleasure." Commonweal

Blaine, Marge

The terrible thing that happened at our house; story by Marge Blaine; pictures by John C. Wallner. Four Winds [1980 c1975] unp illus lib. bdg. $8.95   **E**

1 Family life—Fiction 2 Mothers—Fiction
ISBN 0-590-07780-5

A reprint of the 1975 edition published by Parents Magazine Press

A story "about the plaint of a young girl who longs for life as it used to be before her mother returned to work. Before that 'terrible thing' happened, life was calm and orderly. . . . After Mother goes back to teaching science . . . the chaos of rushed breakfasts and lost sneakers ensues. But Mother doesn't quit her job. Instead they work out cooperative compromises in which the children share some chores and the story ends with the family spending leisure time together again." Sch Library J

"Both the text and the full-color, full-of-motion pop art make a fresh, up-front approach to a realistically phrased common problem." Booklist

Blood, Charles L.

The goat in the rug; as told to Charles L. Blood & Martin Link by Geraldine; illus. by Nancy Winslow Parker. Four Winds [1980 c1976] unp illus lib. bdg. $8.95   **E**

1 Goats—Fiction 2 Navaho Indians—Fiction 3 Rugs—Fiction
ISBN 0-590-07763-5

A reprint of the 1976 edition published by Parents Magazine Press

"A goat's-eye view of how a Navajo rug is made, from the shearing of our supposed narrator ('Geraldine') to the dyeing and weaving. By the time the rug is finished, Geraldine has grown enough wool to start another one." Sat Rev

"Parker's vivid primary colored illustrations are as enjoyable and humorous as the instructive text." Sch Library J

Blue, Rose

I am here: yo estoy aqui; pictures by Moneta Barnett. Watts, F. 1971 unp illus lib. bdg. $4.33   **E**

1 Puerto Ricans in the U.S.—Fiction 2 School stories
ISBN 0-531-01943-8   LC 79-117183

"Luz, who speaks no English, is lonely and frightened in kindergarten, until a Spanish speaking aide and her teacher help her to understand how to exchange words with the other children." Rdng Ladders. 5th edition

This is "a warm and agreeable story of a minority child, illustrated with unpretentious, expressive two-color drawings on every page." Booklist

Bonsall, Crosby

And I mean it, Stanley. Harper 1974 32p illus $6.95, lib. bdg. $7.89   **E**

ISBN 0-06-020570-9; 0-06-020568-7   LC 73-14324

"An Early I can read book"

This story "depicts a small scamp playing with neighborhood discards near a high board fence. As she constructs a junkyard sculpture, she conducts a one-sided conversation with the invisible Stanley, who is presumably behind the fence. Although she insists over and over 'I don't want to play with you,' it's a classic case of protesting too much. When Stanley finally makes his grand entrance, he surprises readers as well as the scruffy heroine." Library J

"A childlike and genuinely humorous creation, the book is also a positive portrayal of a girl in a non-stereotyped role." Horn Bk

The case of the hungry stranger. Harper 1963 64p illus (An I can read mystery) lib. bdg. $6.89, pa $2.95   **E**

1 Mystery and detective stories
ISBN 0-06-020571-7; 0-06-444026-5   LC 63-17947

Also available from Harper in a Spanish language edition, lib. bdg. $6.89 (ISBN 0-06-020574-1)

Illustrated by the author

"Wizard, Skinny, Tubby, and Snitch are four sturdy little boys who share a no-girls-allowed clubhouse. Wizard pronounces himself a private

Bonsall, Crosby—*Continued*

eye, and soon Mrs Meech, the lady next door, commissions him to discover who has stolen her blueberry pie. One scarcely resents the vocabulary limitations, for the author has combined real humor, suspense and even definite characterization." Horn Bk

Some other books in this series are also available from Harper:

The case of the cat's meow lib. bdg. $7.89, pa $1.95 (ISBN 0-06-020561-X; 0-06-4440107-6; LC 65-11451)
The case of the double cross $6.95, lib. bdg. $7.89 (ISBN 0-06-020602-0; 0-06-020603-9; LC 80-7768)
The case of the dumb bells $6.95, lib. bdg. $7.89 (ISBN 0-06-020623-3; 0-06-020624-1; LC 66-8267)
The case of the scaredy cats $6.95, lib. bdg. $7.89 (ISBN 0-06-020565-2; 0-06-020566-0; LC 75-159039)

The day I had to play with my sister. Harper 1972 32p illus $6.95, lib. bdg. $7.89 **E**

1 Brothers and sisters—Fiction
ISBN 0-06-020575-X; 0-06-020576-8   LC 72-76507

"An early I can read book"
Illustrated by the author, this story tells of an impatient boy who tries to teach his younger sister to play hide and seek
"The extremely simple text, written from the boy's point of view, is one with which children can readily identify. Pastel illustrations on every page add touches of humor to the text, which is divided into chapters. The realistic atmosphere makes Bonsall's book an excellent addition to the very early reading shelves." Sch Library J

Mine's the best. Harper 1973 32p illus lib. bdg. $7.89 **E**

ISBN 0-06-020578-4   LC 72-9863

"An Early I can read book"
"Two boys meet by the seashore and create a fracas over whose inflated rubber sea monster is the 'best'—they are identical. During the arguments about whose is bigger, has more spots, can be ridden more easily and so forth, the toys take such a pummeling that they deflate. This signals the appearance of a little girl; her toy is still new and whole, clearly 'the best.'" Pub W
"The humorous illustrations [by the author] add immeasurably to the simple text, which even earliest readers can enjoy." Sch Library J

Tell me some more; pictures by Fritz Siebel. Harper 1961 64p illus lib. bdg. $7.89 **E**

1 Libraries—Fiction
ISBN 0-06-020601-2   LC 61-5773

"An I can read book"
"A fresh and original introduction to the public library, a special place where one can hold an elephant, pat a lion on the nose, tickle a seal, and do all sorts of unusual things. At least that's what Andrew told Tim, and Tim always answered 'Tell me some more.' The artist has caught the small boys' delight in books." Chicago
"Highly original and full of fun. . . . Humorous sketches in which the children appear in black line only, although bright color is added for backgrounds and animals." Horn Bk

Who's a pest? Harper 1962 64p illus lib. bdg. $7.89 **E**

ISBN 0-06-020621-7   LC 62-13310

"An I can read book"
"In this truly funny . . . book a small boy named Homer proves that he is not a pest as his four sisters, a rabbit, chipmunk, and lizard claim. The drawings [by the author] are as laughable as the text and the tongue-twisting dialog begs to be read aloud." Booklist
Followed by: Piggle. Harper $6.95, lib. bdg. $7.89 (ISBN 0-06-020579-2; 0-06-020580-6 LC 73-5478)

Brandenberg, Franz

I wish I was sick, too! Illus. by Aliki. Greenwillow Bks. 1976 32p illus $7.75, lib. bdg. $7.44 **E**

1 Sick—Fiction 2 Cats—Fiction
ISBN 0-688-80047-5; 0-688-84047-7   LC 75-46610

Edward and Elizabeth, feline siblings "turn up sick here. First it's Edward, feeling miserable, receiving meals in bed, and listening to stories from grandmother. But all that attention seems great to Elizabeth, and she grouches. . . . Soon, however, it's her turn to take to bed, and despite the special considerations now coming her way, she envies Edward his health; when she's better, both cat children agree, 'The best part of being sick is getting well.' The untidy linework is accented with patches of color and the children's facial expressions are especially funny—don't miss Elizabeth's fuming or her sick-bed stupor." Booklist

Some other books about Edward and Elizabeth are also available from Greenwillow Bks. (unless otherwise noted):

No school today! $7.95 (Macmillan Pub. Co. ISBN 0-02-711930-0; LC 74-13186)
A picnic, hurrah! $5.95, lib. bdg. $5.71 (ISBN 0-688-80115-3; 0-688-84115-3; LC 77-3950)
A robber! A robber! lib. bdg. $7.92 (ISBN 0-688-84027-2; LC 75-26999)
A secret for grandmother's birthday lib. bdg. $7.92 (ISBN 0-688-84012-4; LC 75-10606)

Nice new neighbors; illus. by Aliki. Greenwillow Bks. 1977 56p illus $5.95, lib. bdg. $5.71 **E**

1 Mice—Fiction 2 Friendship—Fiction
ISBN 0-688-80105-6; 0-688-84105-8   LC 77-1651

"Greenwillow Read-alone"
"A newly moved-in family of fieldmice children makes vain attempts to join other youngsters in game playing. After being rebuffed by juvenile representatives of each nearby household, the resourceful mouse children decide to create their own play, based on the old favorite 'Three Blind Mice.' Suddenly, they become very popular and end up with a grand production in which all the neighborhood children take part." Booklist
"Aliki uses pale pinks and greens in combination with black and white for her lively, scrawly drawings of small animals; her illustrations have some touches (balloon captions, framed sequence drawings for a play) that will be familiar to cartoon-conscious beginning independent readers." Chicago. Children's Bk Center

Some other books about the Fieldmouse family are also available from Greenwillow Bks.:
Everyone ready? $5.95, lib. bdg. $5.71 (ISBN 0-688-80198-6; 0-688-84198-8; LC 78-13744)
Six new students $5.95, lib. bdg. $5.71 (ISBN 0-688-80124-2; 0-688-84124-4; LC 77-24883)
What can you make of it? lib. bdg. $5.71 (ISBN 0-688-80083-3; LC 76-44406)

Brian Wildsmith's The twelve days of Christmas. Watts, F. 1972 unp illus $3.95, lib. bdg. $4.99, pa $2.95 **E**

1 Carols
ISBN 0-531-01555-6; 0-531-01554-8; 0-531-02386-9   LC 71-182554

"The text of the traditional English Christmas song surrounded by [Wildsmith's] small but clear drawings in black and white appears on the left-hand page opposite full-page, stylized paintings in glowing colors. Oversize in format and distinctive in presentation, the book will be especially useful for story hour showing and for display." Booklist

Briggs, Raymond

Father Christmas. Coward, McCann & Geoghegan 1973 unp illus $7.50 **E**

1 Santa Claus—Fiction 2 Christmas—Fiction
ISBN 0-698-20272-4   LC 73-77885

Illustrated by the author in cartoon format, this book "portrays Christmas Eve as Santa sees it. Dreaming of tropic weather, he grumbles his way through the preparations for a long, cold night of work: feeding the animals, loading the sleigh, packing a snack. He grumbles at chimneys, catches cold, wearily distributes gifts, and rides home to a steaming bath and a solitary Christmas dinner." Chicago. Children's Bk Center
"A Christmas book with tremendous appeal for a wide age range: very young children will enjoy the homely, intimate details of this individualistic Santa . . . older ones will appreciate the gently satirical humor in his reluctance to go to work and his gruff, monosyllabic comments throughout. . . . Each small picture is precisely detailed, convincingly well-drawn, and alive with action; the longer and larger frames—including some full-page spreads—offer a lot of visual contrast in size, color, and contents." Booklist

Briggs, Raymond—*Continued*

Jim and the beanstalk; written and illus. by Raymond Briggs. Coward, McCann 1970 unp illus lib. bdg. $5.89   **E**

1 Fairy tales
ISBN 0-698-30203-6   LC 77-111062

"A sprightly sequel to the original tale, illustrated alternately in black and white and in melting color. Jim sees a tall plant outside his window, an invitation to climbing. He goes up, meets a sad and aging giant who complains that some boy once came up and robbed his father. Ruthfully, Jim arranges to improve the giant's lot by getting him false teeth and spectacles. The delighted giant, now able to read the poetry he had missed . . . suggests Jim cut down the beanstalk (now that he can chew again) lest he be tempted to indulge once more in fried boys on toast. Silly and engaging, the story is enhanced by the humorous details of the illustrations." Sutherland. The Best in Children's Bks

The snowman. Random House 1978 unp illus $4.95, lib. bdg. $5.99   **E**

1 Stories without words 2 Dreams—Fiction
3 Snow—Fiction
ISBN 0-394-83973-0; 0-394-93973-5   LC 78-55904

A "wordless picture book about a small boy who expertly fashions a snowman and then dreams that his splendid creation comes alive. Affably greeting the child, the snowman enters the house and is introduced to the delights and dangers of gadgetry. . . . Finally, no longer earthbound, the two friends go soaring over city and countryside, magical in their snowy beauty." Horn Bk

"The pastel-toned pencil-and-crayon pictures in their neat rectangular frames will hold the attention of primary 'readers.' Their older siblings, sneaking a peek, are likely to find them irresistible, too." Sch Library J

Bright, Robert

Georgie. Doubleday 1944 unp illus $5.95, lib. bdg. $6.90, pa $1.95   **E**

1 Ghosts—Fiction
ISBN 0-385-07307-0; 0-385-0761216; 0-385-08030-1
                                             LC 44-7589

Also available from Doubleday in a Spanish language edition. lib. bdg. $6.90 (ISBN 0-385-12005-2; LC 76-23789)

"Georgie is an extremely personable little ghost who lives with the Whittakers and haunts their house. Trouble begins for Georgie when he feels it necessary to find another house to haunt. Every house already has a ghost. The friendliness of little Georgie and the [author's] just pleasantly spooky-looking pictures make this the perfect Halloween picture storybook for little children." Booklist

Some other books about George are also available from Doubleday:
Georgie and the buried treasure $6.95, lib. bdg. $7.90 (ISBN 0-385-14626-4; 0-385-14627-2; LC 78-22305)
Georgie and the magician $6.95, lib. bdg. $7.90, pa $1.95 (ISBN 0-385-04824-6; 0-385-05948-5; 0-385-01021-4; LC 66-10822)
Georgie and the noisy ghost $6.95, lib. bdg. $7.90 (ISBN 0-385-03103-3; 0-385-05336-3; LC 77-139453)
Georgie and the robbers $5.95 lib. bdg. $6.90 pa $1.95 (ISBN 0-385-01470-8; 0-385-14483-6; 0-385-13341-3; LC 63-11384)
Georgie goes West $5.95, lib. bdg. $6.90 (ISBN 0-385-05271-5; 0-385-05277-4; LC 73-79650)
Georgie to the rescue $5.95, lib. bdg. $6.90, pa $1.95 (ISBN 0-385-07308-9; 0-385-07613-4; 0-385-08067-0; LC 56-5582)
Georgie's Christmas carol $6.95, lib. bdg. $7.90 (ISBN 0-385-02344-8; 0-385-02410-X; LC 74-4832)
Georgie's Halloween $6.95, lib. bdg. $7.90, pa $1.95 (ISBN 0-385-07773-4; 0-385-07778-5; 0-385-01017-6; LC 58-7154)

My red umbrella. Morrow 1959 unp illus lib. bdg. $6   **E**

1 Umbrellas and parasols—Fiction 2 Counting
ISBN 0-688-31619-0   LC 59-7928

Also available in the Spanish language edition lib. bdg. $5.52 (ISBN 0-688-31788-X)

"A good read-aloud story for very young listeners, about a little girl whose red umbrella grew to accommodate all the creatures who sought shelter under it. Cheerful colored pictures by the author." Hodges. Bks for Elem Sch Libraries

"It can be used as a counting book." Booklist

Brooke, L. Leslie

Johnny Crow's garden; a picture book drawn by L. Leslie Brooke. Warne 1903 unp illus $6.95   **E**

1 Animals—Fiction 2 Stories in rhyme
ISBN 0-7232-0567-1

"The animal friends who come to Johnny Crow's garden are amazing personalities, introduced to little children in a simple and memorable fashion through a nonsense rhyme with its perfect, accompanying illustrations." Bks for Boys and Girls

Followed by: Johnny Crow's party. Warne $6.95 (ISBN 0-7232-0566-3)

Brooks, Gregory

Monroe's island; story and pictures by Gregory Brooks. Bradbury Press 1979 unp illus $7.95   **E**

1 Imagination—Fiction
ISBN 0-87888-140-9   LC 78-25719

One day while Monroe is taking a bath, his imagination, a blue beast, runs away with him to a desert island where chocolate chip cookies grow on trees. Brightly colored full-page illustrations accompany the brief text

Brooks, Ron

Timothy and Gramps. Bradbury Press 1978 unp illus $6.95   **E**

1 Grandfathers—Fiction 2 School stories
ISBN 0-87888-139-5   LC 78-17389

Gramps and Timmy "are two loners whose favorite pasttime is exchanging heroic stories they invent. At school, though, shy Timmy is unhappy. He has nothing to regale the kids with at show-and-tell time and is too timid to join them at play during recess. But one day, he gets a great idea. Timmy invites Gramps to school and the intuitive old gentleman responds by narrating one of his most enthralling tales. Thereafter, all the boys and girls want to hear more about Gramps, and Timmy obliges. Soon he is one of the gang and decides school isnt so bad, after all." Pub W

The book's "distinction lies in the handsome pen-and-ink illustrations warmed with the soft colors of the English countryside." Sch Library J

Brown, Marc

Arthur's nose. Little 1976 32p illus lib. bdg. $7.95   **E**

1 Nose—Fiction 2 Animals—Fiction
ISBN 0-316-1193-7   LC 75-30610

"An Atlantic Monthly Press book"

"Arthur the aardvark is unhappy with his long nose. When he finally decides to visit a rhinologist to have it changed, he discovers that he can't come up with a different kind of nose that suits him. No alterations are done, for Arthur comes to realize that 'I'm just not me without my nose.' The overworked lesson is pleasantly conveyed with surprisingly little text and large and colorful illustrations [by the author] so that independent readers may be tempted to pick this up." Sch Library J

Some other books about Arthur are also available from Little:
Arthur's eyes, lib. bdg. $7.95 (ISBN 0-316-11063-9; LC 79-11734)
Arthur's valentine $7.95 (ISBN 0-316-11062-0; LC 80-14001)

Brown, Marcia

All butterflies; an ABC, cut by Marcia Brown. Scribner 1974 unp illus lib. bdg. $9.95   **E**

1 Alphabet
ISBN 0-684-13771-2   LC 73-19364

"Handsome woodcuts in muted colors show creatures of all kinds in realistic or fanciful situations, save for a few pictures in which they would be inappropriate (the Arctic, the ocean depths) butterflies of varied shapes and colors appear on all the pages. Each of the double-page spreads uses words for two letters of the alphabet: 'All Butterflies, Cat Dance, Elephant Fly? Giraffes High.' Some of the pictures have a grave serenity, others are vigorous or humorous. Moderately useful as an alphabet book, graphically delightful." Chicago. Children's Bk Center

Brown, Marcia—*Continued*

How, Hippo! Scribner 1969 unp illus $6.95

E

1 Hippopotamus—Fiction
ISBN 0-684-12543-9   LC 69-17059

Little Hippo has stayed close to his mother ever since the night he was born. This story, illustrated by the author, tells what happened to him the very first time he wandered too far away from his mother

The woodcuts, which "are primarily in shades of blue, green, and pink, capture the various expressions of the hippo pair and the mean crocodile." Sch Library J

Brown, Margaret Wise

A child's good night book; illus. by Jean Charlot. Young Scott Bks. 1950 unp illus lib. bdg. $7.95

E

Night—Fiction

ISBN 0-201-09155-0   LC 43-15137

As an invitation to sleepiness the author writes of birds and animals, sailboats, automobiles and little children as they settle down for the night

The brief text is accompanied by full-page softly colored lithographs

Goodnight moon; pictures by Clement Hurd. Harper 1947 unp illus $5.95, lib. bdg. $6.89, pa $1.95

E

Rabbits—Fiction 2 Stories in rhyme 3 Night—Fiction
ISBN 0-06-020705-1; 0-06-020706-X; 0-06-443017-0
LC 47-30762

Written in rhymed verse

"The coming of night is shown in pictures which change from bright to dark as a small rabbit says good night to the familiar things in his nest." Hodges. Bks for Elem Sch Libraries

"A clever goodnight book in which pages are progressively darker as the leaves are turned. There are many objects to identify and children enjoy picking out familiar words." Bks for Deaf Children

The runaway bunny; pictures by Clement Hurd. Harper 1972 c1942 unp illus $5.95, lib. bdg. $6.89, pa $1.95

E

1 Rabbits—Fiction
ISBN 0-06-020765-5; 0-06-020766-3; 0-06-443018-9
LC 71-183168

Reissue, with some illustrations redrawn, of the title first published 1942

"Within a framework of mutual love, a bunny tells his mother how he will run away and she answers his challenge by indicating how she will catch him." Sch Library J

"The text has the simplicity of a folk tale and the illustrations are black and white or double page drawings in startling colour effects to illustrate the more imaginative parts of the theory." Ontario Library Rev

Wait till the moon is full; pictures by Garth Williams. Harper 1948 unp illus $7.95, lib. bdg. $7.89

E

Raccoons—Fiction 2 Night—Fiction
ISBN 0-06-020800-7; 0-06-020801-5   LC 48-9278

"The mystery and wonder of nighttime is presented here in a way to sharpen the awareness of the very young child and to dispel any fears of it which the more timorous may have. . . . This is very slight, but the words, the rhythm and the mood have a great deal of charm and humor, which is matched by Garth Williams' pictures of a cozy, well-furnished raccoon home and the moonlit world waiting outside." NY Times Bk Rev

Wheel on the chimney, by Margaret Wise Brown and Tibor Gergely. Lippincott 1954 unp illus $8.95

E

1 Storks—Fiction
ISBN 0-397-30288-6   LC 54-8486

"First there was one stork, then there were two. They built their nest on a wheel on the chimney of a little Hungarian house, thus promising good luck to the family. This annual ritual inspired Gergely's tracing of the stork's migration from their summer European habitat to their winter sojourn in Africa." Secondary Educ Brd

"The simple text tells of the ways of storks and of the hazards of their long flight south, while the illustrations [by Tibor Gergely] in strong contrasting colours show much of the beauty and interest of the seas and continents the great birds cross in their journey." Ontario Library Rev

Brunhoff, Jean de

The story of Babar, the little elephant; tr. from the French by Merle S. Haas. Random House 1933 47p illus $4.95, lib. bdg. $5.99

E

1 Elephants—Fiction
ISBN 0-394-80575-5; 0-394-90575-X   LC 33-30566

Original French edition published 1931

"Babar runs away from the jungle and goes to live with an old lady in Paris, where he adapts quickly to French amenities. Later he returns to the jungle and becomes king. Much of the charm of the story is contributed by the author's gay pictures." Hodges. Bks for Elem Sch Libraries

Some other books about Babar by Jean de Brunhoff are also available from Random House:

Babar and Father Christmas $4.95, lib. bdg. $5.99 (ISBN 0-394-80578-X; 0-394-90578-4; LC 40-31350)

Babar and his children $4.95, lib. bdg. $5.99 (ISBN 0-394-80577-1; 0-394-90577-6; LC 38-32022)

Babar and Zephir $4.95, lib. bdg. $5.99 (ISBN 0-394-80579-8; 0-394-90579-2; LC 42-36269)

Babar the king $4.95, lib. bdg. $5.99 (ISBN 0-394-80580-1; 0-394-90580-6; LC 35-20680)

The travels of Babar $4.95, lib. bdg. $5.99 (ISBN 0-394-80576-3; 0-394-90576-8; LC 34-31074)

Some other books about Babar by Laurent de Brunhoff are also available from Random House:

Babar and the professor $4.95, lib. bdg. $5.99 (ISBN 0-394-80590-0; 0-394-90590-3; LC 57-11753)

Babar and the Wully-Wully $4.95, lib. bdg. $5.99 (ISBN 0-394-83077-6; 0-394-93077-0; LC 75-8069)

Babar comes to America $4.95, lib. bdg. $5.99 (ISBN 0-394-80588-7; 0-394-90588-1; LC 65-18163)

Babar learns to cook $3.99, lib. bdg. $4.99 (ISBN 0-394-94108-X; 0-394-84108-5; LC 78-11769)

Babar loses his crown $3.95, lib. bdg. $4.99 (ISBN 0-394-80045-1; 0-394-90045-6; LC 67-21918)

Babar saves the day pa $1.25 (ISBN 0-394-83341-4; LC 76-11684)

Babar the magician $2.50 (ISBN 0-394-84360-6; LC 79-65799)

Babar visits another planet $4.95, lib. bdg. $5.99 (ISBN 0-394-82429-6; 0-394-92429-0; LC 72-1584)

Babar's birthday surprise $4.95, lib. bdg. $5.99 (ISBN 0-394-80591-7; 0-394-90591-1; LC 74-123071)

Babar's castle $4.95, lib. bdg. $5.99 (ISBN 0-394-80586-0; 0-394-90586-5; LC 62-8994)

Babar's cousin $4.95, lib. bdg. $5.99 (ISBN 0-394-80581-X; 0-394-90581-4; LC 48-8143)

Babar's fair $4.95, lib. bdg. $5.99 (ISBN 0-394-80584-4; 0-394-90584-9; LC 55-8963)

Babar's mystery $4.95, lib. bdg. $5.99 (ISBN 0-394-83920-X; 0-394-93920-4; LC 78-55912)

Buckley, Helen E.

Grandfather and I; pictures by Paul Galdone. Lothrop 1959 unp illus lib. bdg. $7.92

E

1 Grandfathers—Fiction
ISBN 0-688-51211-9   LC 58-10716

"Unlike mothers, fathers, brothers, sisters, cars and buses, Grandfather does not hurry but has time to play with the little boy, walk slowly with him, sit and rock, sing and talk as long as they wish." Wis Library Bul

"The repetitive text, the uncluttered colored pictures, and the amusing surprise ending will please young children." Booklist

Grandmother and I; pictures by Paul Galdone. Lothrop 1961 unp illus lib. bdg. $7.92

E

1 Grandmothers—Fiction
ISBN 0-688-51204-6   LC 60-12031

"Brief text and full-page pictures in bright colors show how just right Grandmother's lap is for many things: for sitting and thinking; for when you have measles, or when lightning flashes, or 'when you don't want to do anything but sit in the big chair, and rock back and forth, and back and forth.'" Horn Bk

"The illustrations are pleasant, realistic and sympathetic but not sentimental." Chicago. Children's Bk Center

Budney, Blossom

A kiss is round; verses; pictures by Vladimir Bobri. Lothrop 1954 unp illus lib. bdg. $7.92 **E**

1 Size and shape
ISBN 0-688-51177-5 LC 54-7884

A picture book intended to teach the concept of roundness, with the aid of brief verses

"This is a book to stimulate and sharpen a child's perception of forms, but first of all it is great fun. It is good to look at, for Bobri has illustrated it with an originality to match the author's. His color is bright but soft, his line is witty and his humor genial." NY Times Bk Rev

Bulla, Clyde Robert

Daniel's duck; pictures by Joan Sandin. Harper 1979 60p illus $6.95, lib. bdg. $7.89 **E**

1 Wood carving—Fiction
ISBN 0-06-02908-9; 0-06-020909-7 LC 77-25647

"An I can read book"

"Daniel, who lived in 'a cabin on a mountain in Tennessee,' wanted 'to make something for the spring fair,' as the rest of his family were doing. Using the block of wood and the knife his father gave him, the boy carved a duck with its head looking backward. At the fair, people laughed when they saw the carving, and Daniel thought his work was being ridiculed: but he was more than consoled by a famous local wood-carver, who not only praised Daniel's duck but offered to buy it. The easy-to-read story and the simple format are excellently served by the subdued three-color illustrations, which round out the account of a traditional Appalachian family." Horn Bk

Keep running, Allen! Pictures by Satomi Ichikawa. Crowell 1978 unp illus $6.95, lib. bdg. $6.79 **E**

1 Brothers and sisters—Fiction
ISBN 0-690-01374-4; 0-690-01375-2 LC 77-23311

"Allen is the youngest of four, and in order to keep up with his sister and brothers as they dash about investigating neighborhood phenomena he's always on the run. He trips on a shoelace just as the others race over the brow of a hill, and discovers how pleasant it is to lie in the sun and watch small creatures. His siblings retrace their steps to urge him on, but they succumb too." Chicago. Children's Bk Center

"Ichikawa has dressed the children in old-fashioned knickers, pinafores, and suspendered pants and set them into a spring green landscape. The lines are delicate, the colors fresh pastel. Visually it's a celebration of innocence; storywise, a comfortable parable on the benefits of self-assertion." Booklist

The poppy seeds; illus. by Jean Charlot. Crowell 1955 unp illus $7.50 **E**

1 Mexico—Fiction
ISBN 0-690-64856-1 LC 55-5835

"A small boy's sharing of his precious gift of seeds with neighbors in a dry Mexican village makes a story that has meaning and interest for young children and gives a strong impression of [the] Mexican scene. Its theme is the old one of a little child showing the way and accomplishing what grown people cannot, for it was Pablo's impulse to share his seeds and the brilliant flowers resulting that melted the heart of crotchety Old Anthony and brought to the whole village the long-needed gift of water from his selfishly guarded spring. The text has a simplicity that makes good reading aloud." Horn Bk

"The Charlot pictures as, always, are superb in their strength, clarity and dramatic simplicity." NY Her Trib Bks

Bunting, Eve

Winter's coming; pictures by Howard Knotts. Harcourt 1977 unp illus $4.95, pa. $1.65 **E**

1 Winter—Fiction 2 Family life—Fiction
ISBN 0-15-298036-9; 0-15-298037-7 LC 76-28321

"A Let me read book"

An "account of the natural signs of the advent of a hard winter and the preparations made by a family. Mother preserves food. Grandma knits scarves and mittens. Grandpa makes new sleds. Dad repairs the roof and replenishes the woodpile." Chicago. Children's Bk Center

The illustrator's "lovely, gentle grey-and-white charcoal sketches of a farm family help make this beginning reader special. The illustrations . . . dominate nearly each page while the few lines of text flow smoothly with a child narrator describing the signs of winter that his parents and grandparents have pointed out. The story avoids the beginning reader trap of starting each sentence in the same way, and the specific signals of a hard winter ahead will be enlightening to many urban and suburban children. . . . A cozy, pleasant choice." Sch Library J

Burningham, John

Come away from the water, Shirley. Crowell 1977 unp illus $7.95, lib. bdg. $7.89 **E**

1 Pirates—Fiction 2 Beaches—Fiction
ISBN 0-690-01360-4; 0-690-01361-2 LC 77-483

"Shirley and her parents come to the beach: her mother gives periodic instructions, such as, 'Don't stroke the dog, Shirley, you don't know where he's been,' or, 'You won't bring any of that smelly seaweed home, will you Shirley.' The parents sit in folding chairs, with no sign of Shirley. She is on the facing pages, rowing a dog out to a pirate ship, battling the crew, escaping with a map, digging for treasure, standing triumphant and jewel-draped—in her vessel. Then a meek little Shirley goes as she has come, along the beach with her parents." Chicago. Children's Bk Center

"While the dull parent/imaginative child theme is hardly new, Burningham's view of it is fresh and fun. Shirley's parents appear on the left of each pair of pages, virtually immobile in pale pastels; facing them on the opposite page, Shirley goes adevnturing in action-packed and richly colored tableaux." Sch Library J

Another book about Shirley is: Time to get out of the bath, Shirley. Crowell $6.95, lib. bdg $7.89 (ISBN 0-690-01378-7; 0-690-01379; LC 76-58503)

Mr Gumpy's outing. Holt [1971 c1970] unp illus lib. bdg. $6.95 **E**

1 Animals—Fiction
ISBN 0-03-089733-5 LC 77-159507

First published 1970 in England

"Mr. Gumpy is about to go off for a boat ride and is asked by two children, a rabbit, a cat, a dog, and other animals if they may come. To each Mr. Gumpy says yes, if—if the children don't squabble, if the rabbit won't hop, if the cat won't chase the rabbit or the dog tease the cat, and so on. Of course each does exactly what Mr. Gumpy forbade, the boat ips over, and they all slog home for tea in friendly fashion." Sutherland. The Best in Children's Bks

The illustrations, skillfully drawn cross-hatched brown ink drawings alternating with full-page impressionistic paintings dominantly in muted greens and browns, are outstanding for their very expressive animals and numerous warm, humorous touches. . . . And, the simple, cumulative text and easy, natural attitudes of Gumpy and company are sure to please the picture-book audience." Sch Library J

Followed by: Mr Gumpy's motor car. Crowell $7.95, lib bdg. $7.89 (ISBN 0-690-00798-1; 0-690-00799-X; LC 75-4582)

Burton, Virginia Lee

Katy and the big snow; story and pictures by Virginia Lee Burton. Houghton 1943 32p illus lib. bdg. $10.95, pa $2.50 **E**

1 Tractors—Fiction 2 Snow—Fiction
ISBN 0-395-18155-0; 0-395-18562-9 LC 43-18856

"Katy is a crawler tractor who saves the city when it is snowed in by a blizzard. Though personified, Katy is presented accurately in the author's colored illustrations." Hodges. Bks for Elem Sch Libraries

"Anyone who has ever watched a small [child's] intense interest in one of these monsters of iron and steel that roll the roads or plow the fields will rejoise that this artist and author has made it possible for children to follow the fortunes of Katy." NY Times Bk Rev

The little house; story and pictures by Virginia Lee Burton. Houghton 1942 40p illus lib. bdg. $8.95, pa $2.95 **E**

1 Houses—Fiction 2 Cities and towns—Fiction
ISBN 0-395-18156-9; 0-395-25938-X LC 42-24744

Awarded the Caldecott Medal, 1943

"The little house was very happy as she sat on the quiet hillside watching the changing seasons. As the years passed, however, tall buildings grew

Burton, Virginia L.—_Continued_

up around her, and the noise of city traffic disturbed her. She became sad and lonely until one day someone who understood her need for twinkling stars overhead and dancing apple blossoms moved her back to just the right little hill." Children's Bks Too Good To Miss

"This story is important in showing changes in a neighborhood and in telling what happens as cities grow larger and swallow up more and more fields and orchards." Rdng Ladders

"An original and charming picture book. . . . The colors are clear and beautiful and effectively suggest day and night in both country and city, and the aspects of the seasons." NY Times Bk Rev

Mike Mulligan and his steam shovel; story and pictures by Virginia Lee Burton. Houghton 1939 unp illus lib. bdg. $7.95, pa $2.95 **E**

1 Steam shovel—Fiction
ISBN 0-395-06681-6; 0-395-25939-8   LC 39-30335

"This is fun both in its text and gay crayon drawings. Mike Mulligan remains faithful to his steam shovel, Mary Anne, against the threat of the new gas and Diesel-engine contraptions and digs his way to a surprising and happy ending." New Yorker

Byars, Betsy

Go and hush the baby; illus. by Emily A. McCully. Viking 1971 unp illus lib. bdg. $6.95
E

1 Infants—Fiction   2 Brothers—Fiction
ISBN 0-670-34270-X   LC 72-136825

"Just as he is about to leave the house, bat in hand, Will is asked by his mother to pacify the baby. He performs and the baby smiles, but as soon as Will leaves the crying resumes. Play a game, mother suggests. Finally Will launches on a story that quiets the baby and so intrigues the storyteller that he is surprised when he loses his audience to a nursing bottle. 'Well, I have to play this game of baseball anyway,' he announces as he goes off." Chicago. Children's Bk Center

"A charming little picture book, told with simplicity and illustrated with appealing two-color drawings." Booklist

Caines, Jeannette

Abby; pictures by Steven Kellogg. Harper 1973 32p illus $7.95, lib. bdg. $7.89   **E**

1 Adoption—Fiction   2 Brothers and sisters—Fiction   3 Blacks—Fiction
ISBN 0-06-020921-6; 0-06-020922-4   LC 73-5480

Abby, an adopted pre-schooler, "loves to look at her baby book, even more, to listen to stories told by her mother and by her brother, Kevin, about the day she became part of the family. . . . A crisis arises when Kevin announces he can't be bothered with her because she's a girl. But the clouds roll by when big brother says he was only fooling and that he loves her. In fact, he will even take her to school with him and feature Abby at show-and-tell time." Pub W

This "story of a warm and loving black family living in a city apartment could be used to introduce the subject of adoption. . . . Shaded drawings showing the family at home perfectly complement the story: theres a shaggy dog underfoot, a child's picture of a monster on the wall, an overstuffed chair with sagging springs, and a mom wearing slacks and glasses who gives big hugs to her very believable kids." Sch Library J

Daddy; pictures by Ronald Himler. Harper 1977 32p illus $7.95, lib. bdg. $7.89   **E**

1 Parent and child—Fiction   2 Divorce—Fiction
ISBN 0-06-020923-2; 0-06-020924-0   LC 76-21388

"Even though Windy and her father live apart, they have a special relationship. Every Saturday, her father comes to visit, and . . . share happy experiences. They play hide and seek, make funny faces with shaving cream, go to the supermarket, make chocolate pudding, color in coloring books." Interracial Bks for Children Bul

"The warm text and sensitive drawings will give children of divorced parents a strong sense of identity and a positive perspective from which to review their own family situations. Easy reading, 'Daddy' is an important book." Children's Bk Rev Serv

Calhoun, Mary

Cross-country cat; illus. by Erick Ingraham. Morrow 1979 unp illus $6.95, lib. bdg. $6.67
E

1 Cats—Fiction
ISBN 0-688-22186-6; 0-688-32186-0   LC 78-31718

"With his family—The Kid, The Woman and The Man—Henry is at a ski lodge but yowls his Siamese cat's disdain at using the tiny skis and pole The Kid makes for him. Then the pet leaps unnoticed from the family car when they leave for home, to retrieve a prized possession. Now the smart cat is deserted. The only way to catch up with the humans is to dare the skis. His adventures multiply on the slope and come to an abrupt but gratifying stop when Henry is reunited with his people after escaping from a pursuing coyote." Pub W

"Only the careful blending of skills by a talented author and illustrator could turn such a farfetched plot into a warm, rich, and rewarding story. The realistic illustrations seem to be enveloped in a glowing light and invite the reader to step right into the story." Children's Bk Rev Serv

Cameron, Polly

I can't said the ant; a second book of nonsense; words and pictures by Polly Cameron. Coward, McCann & Geoghegan 1961 unp illus lib. bdg. $5.29   **E**

1 Nonsense verses
ISBN 0-698-30197-8   LC 61-13400

"Nonsense rhymes tell how the ants, the spiders, and the kitchen utensils help to put poor broken Miss Teapot back on the shelf. Each helper is shown in an amusing picture." Hodges. Bks for Elem Sch Libraries

"Fun with rhyming, and an unobtrusive moral that dates back to [Robert] Bruce and the spider." Sat Rev

Carle, Eric

Do you want to be my friend? Crowell 1971 unp illus $8.95   **E**

1 Mice—Fiction   2 Stories without words
ISBN 0-690-24276-X   LC 70-140643

"The only text is the title question at the start and a shy 'Yes' at the close. The pictures do the rest, as the hopeful mouse overtakes one large creature after another. With each encounter, the mouse sees (on the right-hand page) an interesting tail. Turn the page, and there is a huge lion, or a malevolent fox, or a peacock, and then, at last, another wee mouse." Sat Rev

"Good material for discussion and guessing games. . . . The pictures tell an amusing story and they are good to look at as well." Times (London) Lit Sup

The grouchy ladybug. Crowell 1977 unp illus $8.95, lib. bdg. $8.79   **E**

1 Ladybugs—Fiction
ISBN 0-690-01391-4; 0-690-01392-2   LC 77-3170

Illustrated by the author

"Hour by hour, a hungry, irritable ladybug challenges everyone she meets to a fight. As the creatures encountered by the ladybug become larger, so do the pages and the accompanying print. The climax is reached on the tail of a Blue Whale. The story is resolved with the ladybug returning to her starting point, contrite and pleasant at last." Children's Bk Rev Serv

"The finger paint and collage illustrations— as bold as the feisty hero—are satisfyingly placed on pages sized to suit the successive animals that appear (one is cut in the fan shape of the whale's tail). Tiny clocks show the time of each enjoyable encounter, with the sun rising and setting as the action proceeds." Sch Library J

1, 2, 3 to the zoo. Collins [distributed by Philomel Bks.] 1968 unp illus $7.95, lib. bdg. $7.99   **E**

1 Counting   2 Animals—Pictorial works
ISBN 0-529-00479-8; 0-529-00480-1   LC 68-26967

First published by World Publishing Company
Illustrated by the author

After a lone elephant on a flatcar, for number one, this counting book gives groups of "animals in ascending numbers on their way to the zoo in open box cars." NY Times Bk Rev

Carle, Eric—*Continued*

"Superb paintings of animals, bold, lively, handsome, spreading over big double-spread pages. . . . This is a book to grow with its owner. They tiny mouse lurking in every picture may remain invisible to the smallest reader and, as the title implies, the book is waiting to teach the art of counting." Christian Sci Monitor

The very hungry caterpillar. Collins [distributed by Philomel Bks.] 1970 unp illus $8.95, lib. bdg. $8.99   **E**

1 Caterpillars—Fiction
ISBN 0-529-00775-4; 0-529-00776-2   LC 70-82764
First published by World Publishing Company
Illustrated by the author
"This caterpillar is so hungry he eats right through the pictures on the pages of the book—and after leaving many holes emerges as a beautiful butterfly on the last page." Best Bks for Children, 1972

Carrick, Carol

The highest balloon on the common; pictures by Donald Carrick. Greenwillow Bks. 1977 unp illus $8.75, ilb. bdg. $7.92   **E**

1 Balloons—Fiction 2 Fairs—Fiction
ISBN 0-688-80100-5; 0-688-84100-7   LC 77-23309
The story describes "the activities of Old Home Day on a village common where a small wandering boy becomes frightened by the unfamiliar appearance of his familiar surroundings. Because the balloon tied to his wrist can be seen above the crowd, his father is able to find him. The muted paintings in light brown and red show children enjoying rides on an old fire truck, getting balloons from a man on stilts, feasting on cotton candy and hot dogs, and watching teams of ponies in a weight-pulling contest." Horn Bk

Paul's Christmas birthday; pictures by Donald Carrick. Greenwillow Bks. 1978 unp illus $7.90, lib. bdg. $7.63   **E**

1 Birthdays—Fiction 2 Christmas—Fiction
ISBN 0-688-80159-5; 0-688-84159-7   LC 77-28408
"When Paul comes home from school complaining that nobody talks about anything but Christmas, and he wishes that the day before Christmas weren't his birthday, his mother comes up with a plan. All his friends get invitations to a birthday party where they will 'meet someone from outer space,' and that someone turns out to be Santa Claus. . . . Paul is happy, and Paul's father (bearing a marked resemblance to Santa) agrees that Santa will probably come again for Paul's birthday next year, now that he knows the way." Chicago. Children's Bk Center
"The watercolor and charcoal scenes are full and happy, showing wintry small-towns landscapes and snug American interiors. The family cat, perched above Paul as he reads a book or looking on as he blows his birthday candles out is an especially homey, humorous inclusion." Booklist

Carrick, Donald

The deer in the pasture. Greenwillow Bks. 1976 unp illus lib. bdg. $7.92   **E**

1 Deer—Fiction
ISBN 0-688-84023-X   LC 75-23193
"Farmer Wakeman's herd of cows accept a lonely deer who follows them into the barn each evening. When deer season approaches, Mr. Wakeman and the warden drive the animal to a place in the woods where, to prevent the deer from following them back, the warden fires his gun and frightens the deer. The realistic double-page illustrations are nicely done in muted hues of brown and green; the brief large-print text is carefully placed within each picture; and the pacific choices of farmer and game warden should appeal to naturalists." Sch Library J

Caudill, Rebecca

Contrary Jenkins, by Rebecca Caudill and James Ayars; illus. by Glen Rounds. Holt 1969 unp illus lib. bdg. $5.95   **E**

1 Tennessee—Fiction
ISBN 0-03-015046-9   LC 69-11345
"In the tradition of the Tennessee tale come the exploits of one of the most stubborn individuals that anyone could possibly want to meet. As soon as a person said 'yes,' Contrary Jenkins would say 'no.' Several episodes in this hill character's life are recounted in appropriate dialect." Wis Library Bul
"Vigorous, comic illustrations capture the obdurate bravado of Ebenezer Jenkins, called Contrary, in a charming tale for the readaloud audience. . . . His various adventures are hilarious, and the writing style has the true storyteller's cadence and rhythm." Chicago. Children's Bk Center

A pocketful of cricket; illus. by Evaline Ness. Holt 1964 unp illus lib. bdg. $5.95, pa $1.95   **E**

1 Crickets—Fiction 2 Farm life—Fiction
ISBN 0-03-089752-1; 0-03-086619-7   LC 64-12617
"A six-year-old Kentucky farm boy on his way home with the cows one afternoon catches a cricket, makes a pet and friend of it, and on the first day of school takes it along in his pocket. Happily the teacher understands about friends and instead of putting Cricket out lets Jay introduce Cricket in the first 'Show and tell.'" Booklist
"A perceptive nature story with distinctively designed pictures of farm life. Excellent for reading aloud." Hodges. Bks for Elem Sch Libraries

Cauley, Lorinda Bryan

The animal kids. Putnam 1979 unp illus $8.95   **E**

1 Parties—Fiction 2 Animals—Fiction
ISBN 0-0399-20677-9   LC 78-23632
"Three girls and a boy, in a sunny suburban world without grownups, crash a party strictly for animals by disguising themselves as a toddler-shaped lion, tiger, rabbit and dog. The animals—bear, lion, giraffe, assorted rodents—are dressed in human clothes. The kids mistakenly think they've fooled their hosts, and the animals (like parents) indulge their young guests' self-delight. In the end, the children leave, elated at their success, and the animals take off 'their' disguises: the lion's a bear, the bear's a lion, the raccoon's a dog." NY Times Bk Rev
"Cauley's exuberant, nonstop, full-color paintings need only a few words to tell the tale." Pub W

Charlip, Remy

Thirteen [by] Remy Charlip & Jerry Joyner. Parents Mag. Press [distributed by Four Winds] 1975 unp illus $7.95, lib. bdg. $7.95   **E**

1 Stories without words
ISBN 0-590-17712-5; 0-590-07712-0   LC 75-8875
This book "is not only original in its use of imagery, but it also suggests an entirely different approach to picture books from the one recognized in the United States and in Europe. The pictures do not illustrate a story, nor are they simply drawn as works of art; the images respond to each other—not to any verbal concept. Each double-page spread contains thirteen different illustrations that are part of thirteen graphic sequences. Some of these are narrative, but most of them are concerned with changing and evolving visual forms. . . . All of these images, beautifully executed in pastels, have been carefully arranged on the pages. The book may have to be introduced to children because it is not immediately obvious." Horn Bk

Chenery, Janet

The toad hunt; pictures by Ben Shecter. Harper 1967 64p illus (A Science I can read bk) $6.95 lib. bdg. $7.89   **E**

1 Amphibians—Fiction
ISBN 0-06-021262-4; 0-06-021263-2   LC 66-18653
"While hunting for a toad, Teddy and Peter find a turtle, salamander, polliwogs and frogs." Best Bks for Children, 1968
"This story, though it is not likely to keep readers glued to their chairs, is pleasantly told. Several of Ben Shecter's illustrations are particularly amusing." NY Times Bk Rev

Chess, Victoria

Alfred's alphabet walk. Greenwillow Bks. 1979 unp illus $8.50 lib. bdg. $8.16   **E**

1 Alphabet 2 Animals—Fiction
ISBN 0-688-80223-0; 0-688-84223-2   LC 79-1185
"On Saturday morning, Alfred's mother told him to stay in the front yard and learn all the letters

Chess, Victoria—*Continued*

from A to Z. But Alfred hid the alphabet book in a tree trunk and ran right out of the yard. He kept on going all day from encounters with two Ancient Alligators through (in strict alphabetical order) a final fright from a Zebra and a Zoril. Now able to recite the alphabet (from experience rather than study), Alfred collects a hug from his mother. Capitals are used to emphasize each letter, which is employed a number of times in an alliterative sentence under the full-color, Gorey-esque illustrations on every page. Alfred and his mother are mystery mammals—maybe possums. They are appealingly ugly, as is the whole fiercely smiling pack of wildlife presented. This is an amusing change from splashy decorator/designer efforts to showcase their art via the alphabet. It's acutely uncute." Sch Library J

Chorao, Kay

Molly's Moe; stories and pictures by Kay Chorao. Seabury [distributed by Houghton] 1976 unp illus $7.50   E

1 Toys—Fiction
ISBN 0-395-28784-7   LC 76-3526

"A Clarion book"
"Molly loses things all the time. Mother is discouraged and angry. She promises Molly a treat of her choosing if she can make it through a shopping trip without losing anything. The shopping trip is successful and both Molly and Mother are proud until they get home and Molly realizes she's lost Moe, her beloved and irreplaceable stuffed stegosaurus. There is no cheering her up now—not until she remembers where she put Moe for safe-keeping." Children's Bk Rev Serv
"Completely tuned in to a young child's meandering attention span and a young mother's thinning patience with it, Chorao lives up to her potential here both as artist and writer. . . . The pencil drawings have a wonderful lived-in look, and the characters' expressions are variously rich." Booklist
Followed by: Molly's lies. Seabury [distributed by Houghton] $7.50 (ISBN 0-395-28784-7 LC 78-12383)

Christian, Mary Blount

The lucky man; illus. by Glen Rounds. Macmillan Pub. Co. 1979 63p illus $6.95   E

1 Justice—Fiction
ISBN 0-02-718270-3   LC 79-11024

"Ready-to-read"
"Poor Felix gets into one jam after another. His rich brother evicts [his] family from their shack so Felix sets off for town to plead his case in court. On the way, he makes enemies of all he tries to befriend and an angry mob follows him into the courtroom to demand his hanging. The judge, however, listens patiently to the stories and delivers a verdict which proves that the meek can inherit the earth, on occasion." Pub W
The author's "crisp writing, an intelligent plot and Glen Rounds' country-style illustrations combine to make [this book] a lucky choice." Sch Library J

Clark, Margery

The poppy seed cakes; illus by Maud and Miska Petersham. Doubleday 1924 unp illus $6.95, lib. bdg. $7.90   E

1 Russians in the U.S. 2 Russia—Fiction
ISBN 0-385-07457-3; 0-385-03834-8   LC 24-27351

"Auntie Katushka came from the old country with a bag full of presents, a featherbed, a shawl and five pounds of poppy seeds. She came to visit Andrewshek who was four years old. The story tells about the fun and pranks of Andrewshek and his little friend Erminka." St Louis Monthly Bul
"A nursery book of some novelty, beautifully decorated; dog, ducks, goat, and red-topped boots enter into its simple but springhtly annals. We have seen few books for [young] children . . . that are more thoroughly artistic in appearance, pictorially vivid, or jollier in simple narrative. The setting is, of course, Russian—which, however, lends the book a flavor of its own." Sat Rev
"A read-aloud story for kindergarten and early primary pupils, telling of Auntie Katushka who came from Russia and told wonderful stories to four-year-old Andrewshek." Hodges. Bks for Elem Sch Libraries

Cleary, Beverly

The real hole; pictures by Mary Stevens. Morrow 1960 unp illus lib. bdg. $6.96
ISBN 0-688-31655-7   LC 60-5797

Four-year-old "Jimmy's twin sister liked to pretend things but Jimmy liked real things. If he played with hammer and nails he wanted them to be real grown-up hammer and nails, and when he dug a hole he wanted to use a real shovel and dig a real grown-up hole. This is the story, illustrated with likable drawings in color and in black and white, of the hole that four-year-old Jimmy dug and the satisfying use to which it was put." Booklist

Clifton, Lucille

Amifika; illus. by Thomas DiGrazia. Dutton 1977 unp illus lib. bdg. $7.95   E

1 Parent and child—Fiction 2 Blacks—Fiction
ISBN 0-525-25548-6   LC 77-5887

"Mama and Cousin Katy are talking about Daddy's coming home after a long time away in the service, but there's no room in their tiny boarding house space: 'We'll just get rid of something he won't miss. Lot of stuff around here he won't even remember.' And Amifika assumes he's what will be gotten rid of, interpreting everything accordingly from then on. Finally he 'runs away,' falls asleep, and awakens in his father's arms—they both remember each other joyously." Booklist
"Clifton's perceptive prose, written in the Black vernacular, will appeal to any youngster afraid they may be expendable. The dreamy illustrations in soft brown crayon are also pleasing and warm." Sch Library J

The boy who didn't believe in spring; pictures by Brinton Turkle. Dutton 1973 unp illus lib. bdg. $7.95, pa $1.95   E

1 Spring—Fiction 2 City life—Fiction 3—Blacks—Fiction
ISBN 0-525-27145-7; 0-525-45038-6   LC 72-89844

Also available in a Spanish language edition $6.95 (ISBN 0-525-59170-9; LC 75-34070)
"The days are getting longer and everybody's talking about spring, but tough little King Shabazz whispers 'No such thing' at school and hollers 'Where is it at?' to his mother. Finally he and his friend Tony set out to get some spring and, after tripping over flowers in a vacant lot, find on the seat of an abandoned car a nest with four eggs. 'Man, it's Spring,' realizes King Shabazz. The boys' relationship and conversations are natural and spiced with humor while the full-color illustrations express a child's eye view of city streets." Booklist

Three wishes; illus. by Stephanie Douglas. Viking 1976 unp illus lib. bdg. $6.95   E

1 Friendship—Fiction 2 Blacks—Fiction
ISBN 0-670-71063-6   LC 75-5579

"Nobie and her friend Victor are taking a walk when Nobie finds a penny with her birth year on it, which is of course lucky, since one has three wishes. Noble wishes it weren't so cold—and the sun comes out; when they're back in Nobie's kitchen, the two quarrel. 'Man, I wish you would get out of here.' Inadvertently, wish #2, and Victor leaves. Nobie's Mama tells her the best thing to wish for is good friends. 'Usually when I hear the grown people talkin bout different things they want, they be talking bout money . . .' Nobie goes outdoors, thinking of what a good friend Victor has been, and there he is, grinning at her. So Nobie knows that penny-luck is real, her third wish has come true. This is a realistic story of friendship; the lucky penny is an embellishment to a theme that has been used in other books, but this is a nice variant. The pictures, some in grey and black, and some in color, use mixed media; they are bold and uncluttered but page-filling and heavy." Chicago. Children's Bk Center

Clymer, Eleanor

Horatio; drawings by Robert Quackenbush. Atheneum Pubs. [1974 c1968] 63p illus pa $1.25   E

1 Cats—Fiction
ISBN 0-689-70403-8   LC 67-18999

First published 1968
Horatio, a portly, middle-aged cat, runs away from home because he feels he is being put upon

Clymer, Eleanor—*Continued*

by two neighborhood children and the numerous stray beasts his mistress is too kind to turn away. He quickly discovers, however, that his dignity suffers even more out in the world, particularly when two lost kittens follow him around with expectations of being cared for. Horatio returns to his old hearth with a new appreciation for its warmth. The cat's plump figure and disgusted expressions are amusingly portrayed in bright orange and green drawings." Booklist

Some other books about Horatio are also available from Atheneum Pubs.:

Horatio goes to the country lib. bdg. $7.95 (ISBN 0-689-30734-9; LC 78-5137)
Horatio solves a mystery lib. bdg. $8.95 (ISBN 0-689-30734-9; LC 79-22590)
Horatio's birthday lib. bdg $6.95 (ISBN 0-689-30520-6; LC 76-89)
Leave Horatio alone lib. bdg. $6.95 (ISBN 0-689-30405-6; LC 74-75557)

Cohen, Miriam

Will I have a friend? Pictures by Lillian Hoban. Macmillan Pub. Co. 1967 unp illus $6.95, pa $2.50   E

1 School stories 2 Friendship—Fiction
ISBN 0-02-722790-1; 0-02-042620-8   LC 67-5219

"As Jim approaches nursery school, his chief concern is whether he will have a friend there. For most of his first day he moves around on the edge of things, until someone speaks to him, and they play together. Colored wash drawings show pleasantly recognizable toys, equipment, and activities of a typical nursery school." Moorachian. What is a City?

"The setting is an urban neighborhood, the children a racially mixed group, and the story—simply told—should encourage the child anticipating the start of school." Sat Rev

Some other books about Jim and his classmates in kindergarten and first grade are available from Greenwillow Bks. (unless otherwise note):
"Bee my valentine!" $7.95, lib. bdg. $7.63 (ISBN 0-688-80129-3; 0-688-84129-5; LC 77-21950)
Best friends $5.95, pa $2.50 (Macmillan Pub. Co. ISBN 0-02-722800-2; 0-02-042610-0; LC 70-146620)
First grade takes a test $7.95, lib. bdg. $7.63 (ISBN 0-688-80265-6; 0-688-84265-8; LC 80-10316)
Lost in the museum $7.25, lib. bdg. $6.96 (ISBN 0-688-80187-0; 0-688-84187-2; LC 78-16765)
The new teacher, pa $1.25 (Collier Bks. ISBN 0-02-042390-X; LC 78-165239)
No good in art $7.95, lib. bdg. $7.63 (ISBN 0-688-80234-6; 0-688-84234-8; LC 79-16566)
Tough Jim $4.95 (Macmillan Pub. Co. ISBN 0-02-722760-X; LC 73-19065)
When will I read? $8.25, lib. bdg. $7.92 (ISBN 0-688-80073-4; 0-688-84073-6; LC 76-28320)

Cole, Brock

The King at the door; words and pictures by Brock Cole. Doubleday 1979 unp illus $7.95, lib. bdg. $8.90   E

1 Kings and rulers—Fiction
ISBN 0-385-14718-X; 0-385-14719-8   LC 78-20064

"Little Baggit would seem to play the fool as he gives up his ale, supper, wraps, and donkey to a weary stranger who says he's the king but has no crown or bags of gold. Certainly the innkeeper, who offers a mug of dishwater . . . and the dog's dinner . . . in mocking response to the king, thinks so. But morning shows Baggit to be quite right after all when a coach rolls up and the king collects him to come live at the castle." Booklist
The tale "is illustrated by comic drawings in line and in watercolor, with a rough use of line that is reminiscent of Margot Zemach's work. . . . The humor, the vivacity of the illustrations, the theme of kindness rewarded, and the repeating pattern of the way in which each kind act is performed make the story appealing." Chicago. Children's Bk Center

Coletta, Irene

From A to Z; the collected letters of Irene and Hallie Coletta. Prentice-Hall 1979 unp illus $7.95   E

1 Alphabet 2 Riddles
ISBN 0-13-331678-5   LC 78-21263

"Twenty-six clever rhymes . . . are set forth in full-page rebuses, each one framed by a border

which depicts a variety of objects representing the appropriate letter. Only the right-hand pages are printed; curiously, all of the left-hand ones remain blank. Executed in black line, the drawings look pleasantly old-fashioned—quite in keeping with a fresh and diverting presentation of a long-popular form of visual riddle." Horn Bk

Conford, Ellen

Impossible, possum; illus. by Rosemary Wells. Little 1971 32p illus lib. bdg. $6.95   E

1 Opossums—Fiction
ISBN 0-316-15297-8   LC 77-150047

"All possums hang by their tails—all except Randolph, a young possum with an embarrassing problem. But clever sister Geraldine comes up with a solution to dispel Randolph's fears and to give him confidence in himself." Pub W
"Droll illustrations add to the humor of the easily read story." Booklist
Some other books in this series are also available from Little:
Eugene the brave lib. bdg. $6.95 (ISBN 0-316-15292-7; LC 77-24241)
Just the thing for Geraldine lib. bdg. $6.95 (ISBN 0-316-15304-4; LC 74-7193)

Cooney, Barbara

Chanticleer and the fox; adapted and illus. by Barbara Cooney. Crowell 1958 unp illus $6.95, lib. bdg. $7.89   E

1 Fables 2 Foxes—Fiction 3 Roosters—Fiction
ISBN 0-690-18561-8; 0-690-18562-6   LC 58-10449
Awarded the Caldecott Medal, 1959
"Adaptation of the 'Nun's Priest's Tale' from the Canterbury Tales." Verso of title page
"The familiar fable of the vain cock and the shrewd fox from Chaucer's 'Canterbury tales' has been skillfully adapted for children and presented in picturebook form. The excellent storytelling, the beautiful pictures with their rich, sparkling colors and authentically detailed, medieval background, and the clean-looking, handsomely designed format make this a truly distinguished book." Booklist
"This handsome picture book with its rather lengthy text will be excellent for reading aloud to children." Library J

Craft, Ruth

Carrie Hepple's garden; illus. by Irene Haas. Atheneum Pubs. 1979 unp illus lib. bdg. $9.95   E

1 Stories in rhyme 2 Gardens—Fiction
ISBN 0-689-50099-8   LC 78-397
"A Margaret K. McElderry book"
"The neighborhood children are afraid of Carrie Hepple, but when three of them finally venture onto her property to retrieve a lost ball they discover an entrancing secret garden, complete with lush midsummer greenery, neatly particularized flowers, and the orangey aroma of fresh-based hermit buns. . . . Carrie Hepple, imagined by the children as a witchy lady with 'whiskery' hair turns out to be a sweet old body. . . . And her supposed 'familiar,' Old Sausage, is none other than a resident hedgehog, for whom she leaves a nightly saucer of milk." NY Times Bk Rev
"The pictures have a ghostly beauty highlighted by patches of lively color, and the story has the misty charm of half-remembered childhood adventure. Although marred somewhat by the awkward internal rhyme scheme that slows the text with clumsy phrasing, the extra-large type and skillful artwork make up for it." Sch Library J

The winter bear; illus. by Erik Blegvad. Atheneum Pubs. 1975 [c1974] 25p illus lib. bdg. $5.95, pa $2.50   E

1 Toys—Fiction 2 Winter—Fiction 3 Stories in rhyme
ISBN 0-689-50017-3; 0-689-70456-9   LC 74-18178
"A Margaret K. McElderry book"
First published 1974 in England
This is a simple "telling of the afternoon of a young girl and her brothers. On a cold day, they set off on a walk: 'One gathered together a jaunty bouquet./ A bouquet? On a bleak winter's day?/ But look . . . seeds, dried weeds./ Bryony wine and old man's beard. . . .' And they meet birds, a cow and other creatures, then, near the end of their exploring, a wonderful find, a brown knitted bear, stuck high in a tree. This treasure they carry home; they mend him and dress him and put him in a warm, friendly place." Pub W

Credle, Ellis

Down, down the mountain. Elsevier/Nelson
Bks. 1961 unp illus $6.95   E

1 Mountain life—Southern States—Fiction 2 Blue
Ridge Mountains—Fiction
ISBN 0-525-66020-8

First published 1934 by Thomas Nelson
The story of Hetty and her brother Hank who
lived in a log cabin in the Blue Ridge mountain
country. They longed for new creaky shoes and the
only way to get them seemed to be to raise a crop
of turnips and sell them. This they did and the
very next day after their trip to town to sell their
turnips, they wore their beautiful new squeaky
shoes to church
"The drawings [by the author] have zest and
humor and a sympathetic understanding of the
mountain country; they are attractively reproduced
in two colors, and the result is a genuinely American picture book with freshness, strength and
imagination." NY Times Bk Rev

Crews, Donald

Freight train. Greenwillow Bks. 1978 unp
illus $7.95, lib. bdg. $7.63   E

1 Railroads 2 Color
ISBN 0-688-80165-X; 0-688-84165-1   LC 78-2303
"Crews, with a minimum of descriptive words,
has drawn a stylized freight train passing by,
slowly at first, then in a blur of black and bright
color." Babbling Bookworm
"This is a beautifully executed colorful picture
book with extra large letters for the beginning
reader." Children's Bk Rev Serv
"The young child can learn to identify the engine,
the caboose and the different cars. . . . A delightful introduction to railroad transportation and to
the colors in the spectrum." America

Croll, Carolyn

Too many Babas. Harper 1979 63p illus.
$5.95, lib. bdg. $6.89   E

1 Cookery—Fiction
ISBN 0-06-021383-3; 0-06-021384-1   LC 78-22474
"An I can read book"
Baba Edis' soup is ruined when, quite literally,
too many cooks spoil her broth: Baba Basha added
too much salt, Baba Yetta too much pepper and
Baba Molka too much garlic. They resolve to start
again but this time only Baba Edis may add the
salt, pepper and garlic
The author's illustrations of the "plump peasants are appealing and when their second batch
of soup turns out well, real warmth, sharing and
satisfaction make a hearty meal." Sch Library J

Crowe, Robert L.

Clyde monster; illus. by Kay Chorao. Dutton 1976 unp illus lib. bdg. $6.95   E

1 Monsters—Fiction 2 Night—Fiction 3 Fear—
Fiction
ISBN 0-525-28025-1   LC 76-10733
The monster child "is happy in the forest during the day but hates to go to bed at night—for
fear of humans springing on him as he sleeps. His
understanding parents convince him that humans
and monsters, long ago, had agreed not to scare
each other. So Clyde goes peacefully to bed. Just
in case, though, he asks that they leave the rock
entrance to his cave open a bit, so the moon will
be his comforting night light." Pub W
"The now familiar table-turning theme for children afraid of monsters takes on effective, rational
proportions in a very amusing tale. . . . Chorao's
softly grotesque portraits add character without
chill, though the use of blue skyground and glaring
yellow moon seems gratuitous among the figura-
tively colorful black-and-white drawings." Booklist

Dana, Doris

The elephant and his secret; based on a
fable by Gabriela Mistral; in Spanish and
English; illus. by Antonio Frasconi. Atheneum
Pubs. 1974 unp illus $5.95   E

1 Elephants—Fiction 2 Fables 3 Bilingual books
—Spanish-English
ISBN 0-689-30430-7   LC 73-75432
"A Margaret K. McElderry book"
This story "concerns a time, long ago, when the
elephant did not yet exist but yearned to be the
biggest creature on earth. He covers himself with
the shadow of a mountain which gives him his
great, gray shape and the fable goes on to tell
how he got his tusks and his comparatively small
eyes." Pub W
"The well-designed title page, the uncrowded bilingual text, and the nine doublespread woodcuts
in effective black, white, orange, and purple are a
graphic delight. The text is . . . embellished with
poetic details." Horn Bk

Dauer, Rosamond

Bullfrog grows up; illus. by Byron Barton.
Greenwillow Bks. 1976 56p illus lib. bdg. $5.71
E

1 Frogs—Fiction 2 Mice—Fiction
ISBN 0-688-84020-5   LC 75-19097
"Greenwillow Read-alone"
This title "deals amusingly with the metamorphosis of a frog which Chris and Matt, two mice,
bring home from a pond. The story of Bullfrog's
developing unusually big feet after he loses his
tail turns from fact to humorous fantasy as he
learns to play cards, eat hamburgers, and indulge
in pillow fights." Horn Bk
"Byron Barton's spry pictures of the unusual
household will attract beginning readers, and the
natural dialog is definitely above primer quality."
Sch Library J
Some other books about Bullfrog are also available from Greenwillow Bks:
Bullfrog and Gertrude go camping $5.95, lib. bdg.
$5.71 (ISBN 0-688-80207-9; 0-688-84207-0; LC
78-13740)
Bullfrog builds a house $5.95, lib. bdg. $5.71 (ISBN
0-688-80090-4; 0-688-84090-6; LC 76-54820)

Daugherty, James

Andy and the lion. Viking 1938 unp illus
lib. bdg. $8.95   E

1 Lions—Fiction
ISBN 0-670-12433-8   LC 38-27390
A modern picture story of Androcles and the
lion in which Andy, who read a book about lions,
was almost immediately plunged into action. The
next day he met a circus lion with a thorn in his
paw. Andy removed the thorn and earned the lion's
undying gratitude
"This is a tall tale for little children. It is typically American in its setting and its fun. . . .
"[Daugherty's] large full page illustrations are in
yellow, black and white and the brief, hand-lettered
text on the opposite page is clear and readable."
Library J

Davis, Alice Vaught

Timothy Turtle; illus. by Guy Brown Wiser.
Harcourt 1940 unp illus $5.95, pa $1.35   E

1 Turtles—Fiction 2 Animals—Fiction
ISBN 0-15-288368-1; 0-15-690450-0   LC 40-32634
"The comic predicament of a turtle who falls on
his back and cannot turn over with the help of
by his animal friends. A colorful picture story for
little children." Cleveland

De Groat, Diane

Alligator's toothache. Crown 1977 unp illus
$4.95   E

1 Alligators—Fiction 2 Teeth—Fiction 3 Stories
without words
ISBN 0-517-52805-3   LC 76-22780
Illustrated by the author
"Alligator is afraid of the dentist and her party
plans are delayed for a time. But her helpful
friends trick her into seeing the dentist and soon
she is relieved of her misery. The party is resumed
and even the dentist joins in the fun." Children's
Bk Rev Serv
"Although the story will not lessen children's
fear of the dentist, the plot is easy to follow, and
the different moods of comic fear, despair, and
disappointment come across through the colorful
illustrations very well." Sch Library J

Delton, Judy

The new girl at school; illus. by Lillian
Hoban. Dutton 1979 unp illus $7.95   E

1 School stories
ISBN 0-525-35780-7   LC 79-11409
"When Mother gets a new job, Marcia gets a
new school. No one notices her octopus dress and
she sits alone in the bus seats for two. She

Delton, Judy—*Continued*

threatens to run away and get the mumps, but gradually she makes friends, learns subtraction, and life is again good. The sparse dialogue works well; the illustrations are weakened by the lack of full color but Hoban's familiar droll characters are still effective." Sch Library J

Two good friends; pictures by Giulio Maestro. Crown 1974 132p illus lib. bdg. $5.50   E

1 Friendship—Fiction 2 Bears—Fiction 3 Ducks —Fiction
ISBN 0-517-51401-X   LC 73-88181

"Duck and Bear have different ways of keeping house, but each sees the virtues of the other's ways, and each knows that friendship means toleration of differences. Duck is a tidy housekeeper, but no cook; Bear is a dab hand at baking, but creates havoc in the kitchen." Chicago. Children's Bk Center

"The charming crayon-like pictures and the equally attractive text blend into a book that is outstanding. A good choice for reading aloud but also an excellent book for the novice reader. Without moralizing, the story shows the wisdom of sharing talents." Children's Bk Rev Serv

Some other books about Duck and Bear and their friends are also available from Crown:
Rabbit finds a way lib. bdg. $4.95 (ISBN 0-517-52030-3; LC 74-23102)
Three friends find spring lib. bdg. $6.95 (ISBN 0-517-52888-6; LC 76-46294)
Two is company lib. bdg. $4.95 (ISBN 0-517-52601-8; LC 75-45180)

De Paola, Tomie

Andy (that's my name). Prentice-Hall 1973 unp illus $4.95, pa $1.25   E

1 Word games—Fiction
ISBN 0-13-036731-1; 0-13-036749-4   LC 73-4583

"A group of costumed children spurn the advances of a smaller boy who comes on the scene pulling a wagon with large letters: A.N.D.Y. They seize on this, and remove the last two, add another letter, and make 'can,' then 'fan,' and by shifting letters, words like 'hand' and 'dandy.' Finally Andy tumbles everything off and moves away with the original letters, murmuring that he may be little but he's important." Chicago. Children's Bk Center

"The text (all in the form of conversation balloons) is humorously extended by Tomie de Paola's soft, expressive, pastel wash illustrations. . . . 'Andy' should meet the need for preschool material on human relationships (sharing) as well as on spelling and word composition." Sch Library J

Big Anthony and the magic ring; story and pictures by Tomie de Paola. Harcourt 1979 unp illus $7.95, pa $3.95   E

1 Witches—Fiction 2 Italy—Fiction
ISBN 0-15-207124-5; 0-15-611907-2   LC 78-23631

"In a sequel to 'Strega Nona' [entered in class 398.2], Big Anthony once more tampers with his employer's magic and runs afoul of it. One spring night he observes the old woman slip a tiny gold ring on . . . and turning into a beautiful lady with elegant clothes, she goes to the village square and dances the tarantella all night long. The next day, when Strega Nona goes to visit her godchildren, Big Anthony finds the ring and is transformed into Handsome Big Anthony in splendid attire. After a night of dancing with the ladies, Anthony becomes weary of their adulation, but—unlike Strega Nona—he cannot disencumber himself from the ring and return to his own humble self." Horn Bk

"De Paola shades his illustrations with earthy spring tones that reflect the Italian village atmosphere and provide a contrasting backdrop to the bright humor that reverberates across the pages, culminating in a clever ending that snugly completes this magical story." Booklist

"Charlie needs a cloak." Story and pictures by Tomie de Paola. Prentice Hall [1974 c1973] $4.95   E

1 Wool—Fiction 2 Shepherds—Fiction
ISBN 0-13-128355-3   LC 73-16365

"Charlie the shepherd, a black faced sheep, and a filching mouse combine skills and pranks to create a beautiful new red cloak. The facts of clothmaking are amusingly presented." Brooklyn. Art Bks for Children

Helga's dowry; a troll love story; story and pictures by Tomie de Paola. Harcourt 1977 unp illus $8.95, pa $2.95   E

1 Fairy tales
ISBN 0-15-233701-6; 0-15-640010-3   LC 76-54953

"The tale tells of the lovely 'Troll Maiden,' Helga, who was orphaned as a child and is therefore poor and without a dowry. Handsome Lars asks Helga for her hand, but when Plain Inge offers a rich dowry, he cannot resist her. Odin has supposedly decreed that unmarried Troll Maidens must wander the earth forever; to forestall fate, Helga performs sorcery and earns a rich fortune in the Land of People. By a magical transformation, she outwits Inge on the day before the wedding. Fickle Lars now admires Helga's dowry, but the story shows him getting his comeuppance." Horn Bk

"Humor bubbles through text and pictures with squatty, buck-toothed, detailed trolls and bemused bystanders cavorting across richly colored paintings trimmed with hearts-and-flowers. An amusing tale from an accomplished hand." Booklist

Nana Upstairs & Nana Downstairs; story and pictures by Tomie de Paola. Putnam 1973 unp illus lib. bdg. $5.89   E

1 Grandmothers—Fiction 2 Death—Fiction
ISBN 0-399-60787-0   LC 72-77965

"A tender, unpretentious story describing four-year-old Tommy's Sunday visits with his grandmother, Nana Downstairs, and his invalid great-grandmother, Nana Upstairs. When Nana Upstairs is tied into her chair so she won't fall out, Tommy demands to be tied also, and the two sit side by side companionably eating candy and discussing the Little People. Then Tommy experiences his first contact with death when Mother tells him simply and honestly that Nana Upstairs has died, comforting him first when he grasps her absence, and again in the middle of the night. De Paola's illustrations in pink and beige softly complement the text." Booklist

Watch out for the chicken feet in your soup; story and pictures by Tomie de Paola. Prentice-Hall, 1974 unp illus lib. bdg. $6.95, pa $1.50   E

1 Grandmothers—Fiction 2 Italian Americans— Fiction
ISBN 0-13-945782-8; 0-13-945766-6   LC 74-8201

"Joey brings his friend Eugene over to visit his Old World Italian grandmother and through Eugene's eyes gains a new appreciation of his grandmother." Children's Bk Rev Serv

"Nice in itself, and attractively illustrated, the story's bonus is that it can help a child adjust to the ideas that there's nothing wrong (far from it) with people who have a foreign accent and that differences (in manners, in food, in home decorations) are interesting rather than peculiar." Chicago. Children's Bk Center

De Regniers, Beatrice Schenk

Laura's story; illus. by Jack Kent. Atheneum Pubs. 1979 unp illus $7.95   E

1 Mothers—Fiction
ISBN 0-689-30677-6   LC 78-12623

"Laura tells her mother a 'true' story in which she imagines herself to be very large and her mother quite small. Mother promptly gets lost and is swallowed by a fish, which is ingested in turn by a dog, and so on through several larger creatures. A series of timely sneezes aids Mother's escape to home where Laura can take care of her until she is ready to tuck Laura into bed." Sch Library J

"Kent's slightly dizzy-looking cartoons keep to simple lines and strong, flat color. The book has distilled a behavioral pattern exactly—without losing its audience in the process." Booklist

A little house of your own; drawings by Irene Haas. Harcourt 1954 unp illus $5.25   E

ISBN 0-15-245787-9   55-5236

"This is a delightful book by an author who obviously understands children well and has observed them very carefully. Her descriptions of little 'houses,' the places to which one can retire for a few moments of peace and privacy will instantly strike a chord in little boys and girls and give them a few new ideas as well. Among these make believe 'houses' are, for example, the space under

De Regniers, Beatrice S.—*Continued*
the dining room table and a corner, behind a large chair. . . . The illustrations are perfectly matched to the text." Pub W

May I bring a friend? Illus. by Beni Montresor. Atheneum Pubs. 1964 unp illus lib. bdg. $7.95, pa $2.95 **E**

1 Animals—Fiction
ISBN 0-689-20615-1 0-689-70405-4   LC 64-19562

Awarded the Caldecott Medal, 1965
"Each time the little boy in this picture book is invited to take tea or dine with the King and Queen, he brings along a somewhat difficult animal friend. Their Highnesses always cope and are wonderfully rewarded in the end." Pub W

"The pictures are simpler, with a more direct story quality, than some of Montresor's previous work. . . . The technique, particularly of the more elaborate illustrations, is interesting. The pictures, suggesting the kind of sketches made for stage scenery, have an unusual texture and a three dimensional quality." Toronto

"Rich color and profuse embellishment adorn an opulent setting. Absurdities and contrasts are so imaginatively combined in a hilarious comedy of manners that the merriment can be enjoyed on several levels." Horn Bk

The shadow book; photographs by Isabel Gordon. Harcourt 1960 unp illus $5.95 **E**

1 Shades and shadows
ISBN 0-15-272991-7   LC 60-10244

A "picture book which traces a day in the life of a child from the time he wakes in the morning to see shadows on his bedroom wall until the time when the shadows lengthen as evening comes. It is illustrated with photographs of children and their shadows." Pub W

"This beautiful book . . . has the validity of a fine poem on a small but exciting topic." Sat Rev

Din dan don, it's Christmas; pictures by Janina Domanska. Greenwillow Bks. 1975 unp illus $8.25, lib. bdg. $7.92 **E**

1 Carols
ISBN 0-688-80003-3; 0-688-84003-5   LC 75-8509

Based on an old Polish carol
"The brief text features the duck, the gander, the turkey, a rooster, a sparrow and others as they play bagpipes, beat the drums, blow the trumpet and march to Bethlehem, along with the shepherds, the Magi and others, to meet the baby Jesus." Pub W

"The pictures are alive with the brilliance and the translucence of stained-glass windows, but the glowing figures, peasant designs, and onion-domed towers on a scratchboard base suggest needlework with Eastern European motifs. The book is a triumph of artwork and printing, but the inclusion of the music would have made the work complete." Horn Bk

Dolbier, Maurice
Torten's Christmas secret; illus. by Robert Henneberger. Little 1951 61p illus lib. bdg. $5.95 **E**

1 Christmas—Fiction 2 Fairy tales
ISBN 0-316-18914-6   LC 51-12428

"How Santa and one of his helpers, Torten, managed to take care of all the bad little boys and girls at Christmas as well as the good ones." Library J

"An imaginative tale of the things that happened at the North Pole when the gnome, Torten, and his good friend Drusus, the polar bear, set out to do something about the bad children whose stockings might not be filled at Christmas. The liveliness of the story and of the many colored pictures makes it one of the gayest Christmas books we have had for a long time. Storytellers and the children themselves will welcome it." Horn Bk

Domanska, Janina
What do you see? Pictures by Janina Domanska. Macmillan Pub. Co. 1974 unp illus lib. bdg. $6.95 **E**

1 Animals—Fiction 2 Stories in rhyme
ISBN 0-02-732830-9   LC 73-6052

The frog, the fly, the bat and the fern all see the world differently, but it takes the soaring lark to show them that they are all correct

The author-illustrator "uses what appears to be scratch painting and collage technique to create a most inviting, imaginative world. With each turn of the page, the reader is delighted by a new creation of color and contrast. The body shapes are anatomically correct but filled with designs and colors that challenge the imagination of the reader. The visual intensity of these illustrations makes the book appealing to even very young children. It would also be effective to read to early and pre-readers. The text uses simple language, with much repetition and rhyming. The print is large. It would be fairly easy for youngsters to begin to recognize some of the words and begin to 'read' the story themselves." Rdng Teacher

Du Bois, William Pène
Bear Circus. Viking 1971 48p illus lib. bdg. $4.95, Penguin pa $1.50 **E**

1 Koalas—Fiction 2 Circus—Fiction
ISBN 0-670-15073-8; 0-670-05085-7   LC 76-153665

A companion volume to: Bear party, o.p. 1981
The koala bears lose "their food supply (the leaves of the gum trees) to a horde of grasshoppers, but some kindly kangaroos appear and carry the bears to new territory. To show their gratitude, the slow-moving koalas spend seven long years mounting a great circus; but the first performance is scarcely ended when the grasshoppers return and the kangaroos must effect a second mass rescue." Horn Bk

"This tale of friendship-extraordinary is delightful nonsense sedately told, with [the author-illustrator's] pictures as amusing as they are lovely. . . . A completely engaging, joyous book." Sat Rev

Duncan, Jane
Brave Janet Reachfar; pictures by Mairi Hedderwick. Seabury [distributed by Houghton] 1975 unp illus $7.95 **E**

1 Scotland—Fiction 2 Farm life—Fiction 3 Snow—Fiction
ISBN 0-395-28737-1   LC 74-8693

"A Clarion book"
Published in England with title: Herself and Janet Reachfar

A "satisfying tale of a little girl who is brave and resourceful; of all of Janet Reachfar's family, Grandmother is the most respected and feared: when 'Herself' gets 'on about' things, Janet clears out. During an unexpected spring snow in the Scottish Highlands Janet disobeys Grandmother's orders and goes alone to East Hill to bring in the sheep. Mairi Hedderwick's pastel color wash illustrations faithfully depict the rolling hills and far vistas of Northern Scotland." Sch Library J

Some other titles about Janet Reachfar are also available from Houghton:

Janet Reachfar and Chickabird $7.95 (ISBN 0-395-28788-X; LC 77-12709)
Janet Reachfar and the Kelpie $7.50 (ISBN 0-395-28789-8; LC 75-44166)

Duvoisin, Roger
A for the Ark. Lothrop 1952 unp illus lib. bdg. $8.40 **E**

1 Alphabet 2 Noah's Ark
ISBN 0-688-50985-1   LC 52-12846

God commanded Noah to take two of every kind of animal into the Ark, so he went straight through the alphabet to be sure to include them all! This is the introduction to Roger Duvoisin's presentation of the Old Testament story of the flood

'[In a brilliant charming, colorful book, rather nonsensical as to drawings [made by the author] very realistic in its dramatic, simple text, Mr. Duvoisin plays on a familiar theme in a new way." NY Her Trib Bks

Petunia; written and illus. by Roger Duvoisin. Knopf 1950 unp illus lib. bdg. $6.99 **E**

1 Geese—Fiction
ISBN 0-394-90865-1   LC 50-10286

A picture story book about Petunia, the silly goose, who found a book and carried it around because she thought it would make her wise. After a catastrophe brought on by Petunia's silliness she suddenly discovered that it's what is inside the book that counts

Duvoisin, Roger—*Continued*

"Not since 'The Little Red Hen' has there been written such an engaging story of a poultry heroine. . . . Delightfully illustrated by the author in black-and-white and color wash." Library J

Some other books about Petunia are also available from Knopf:

Petunia, beware! lib. bdg. $6.99 (ISBN 0-394-90867-8; LC 58-9938)

Petunia, I love you lib. bdg. $6.99 (ISBN 0-394-90870-8; LC 65-21559)

Petunia takes a trip lib. bdg. $6.99 (ISBN 0-394-90869-4; LC 53-7632)

Petunia's Christmas lib. bdg. $6.99 (ISBN 0-394-90868-6; LC 52-6391)

Petunia's treasure $5.50, lib. bdg. $6.99 (ISBN 0-394-83155-1; 0-394-93155-6; LC 75-2540)

Two lonely ducks; a counting book. Knopf 1955 unp illus lib. bdg. $6.99   **E**

1 Ducks—Fiction 2 Counting
ISBN 0-394-91783-9   LC 55-7087

A counting book that describes in pictures and brief text how a pair of ducks raised a large family of ten ducklings

"Valuable as an introduction to the sequence of numbers 1 to 10, set in bold type and large figures (with the ducklings to count as evidence), this book also offers a limited acquaintance with nature study. The repetition of phrases and numerals gives the very young some of the advantages of a first reader." NY Times Bk Rev

Veronica; written and illus. by Roger Duvoisin. Knopf 1961 unp illus lib. bdg. $6.99   **E**

1 Hippopotamus—Fiction
ISBN 0-394-91792-8   LC 61-6051

"Longing to be different, a hippopotamus named Veronica left the herd where nobody noticed her and walked until she reached a city. There she was not just different, she was gloriously conspicuous, so conspicuous in fact that she ended in jail. Veronica's misadventures in the city and her return to the mudbank and the acclaim of the herd are recounted in a diverting picture book illustrated with laughable drawings in color and in black and white." Booklist

Some other books about Veronica are olso available from Knopf:

Lonely Veronica lib. bdg. $6.99 (ISBN 0-394-31364-7; LC 63-14603)

Our Veronica goes to Petunia's farm lib. bdg. $6.99 (ISBN 0-394-91469-4; LC 62-14767)

Veronica and the birthday present $4.95, lib. bdg. $6.99 (ISBN 0-394-82282-X; 0-394-92282-4; LC 71-154547)

Eastman, P. D.

Are you my mother? Written and illus. by P. D. Eastman. Beginner Bks. 1960 63p illus $3.95, lib. bdg. $4.99   **E**

1 Birds—Fiction
ISBN 0-394-80018-4; 0-394-90018-9   LC 60-13495

Also available in a bilingual Spanish-English edition for $4.95, lib. bdg. $4.99 (ISBN 0-394-81596-3; 0-394-91596-8; LC 67-3636)

"A small bird falls from his nest and searches for his mother. He asks a kitten, a hen, a dog, a cow, a boat, [and] a plane . . . 'Are you my mother?' Repetition of words and phrases and funny pictures are just right for beginning readers." Chicago

Ehrlich, Amy

Thumbelina [by] Hans Christian Andersen; pictures by Susan Jeffers; retold by Amy Ehrlich. Dial Press 1979 unp illus $9.95   **E**

1 Fairy tales
ISBN 0-8037-8815-0; 0-8037-8814-2   LC 79-50146

"This sumptuous picture-book version of the classic Andersen story [entered in the Fiction section] has an adapted text that shows some softening of the tale's harsher edges but keeps to the primary story line fairly well. The subtle changes in mood and flavor will bother purists, but children won't notice them; they'll be caught up in the action as depicted in Jeffers' striking, pastel-dominated pictures. These are great, showy spreads that have powerful presence and reinforce the story's tempered tone. Refined, intricate hatching lines gracefully shape and give dimension in a way reminiscent of Nancy Burkert." Booklist

Eichenberg, Fritz

Ape in a cape; an alphabet of odd animals. Harcourt 1952 unp illus $6.95, pa $1.35   **E**

1 Animals—Pictorial works 2 Alphabet
ISBN 0-15-203722-5; 0-15-607830-9   LC 52-6908

"Each letter of the alphabet from A for ape to Z for zoo is represented by a full-page picture of an animal with a brief nonsense rhyme caption explaining it. For example: mouse in a blouse, pig in a wig, toad on the road, whale in a gale." Pub W

"The skill of a craftsman distinguishes this picture book illustrated [by the author] with hold and lively drawings printed in three colors." NY Pub Library

Dancing in the moon; counting rhymes. Harcourt 1955 20p illus $7.95, pa $1.85   **E**

1 Animals—Pictorial works 2 Counting
ISBN 0-15-221443-7; 0-15-623811-X   LC 55-8674

This book "introduces numbers up to twenty, from '1 raccoon dancing in the moon' to '20 fishes juggling dishes.' The three-color wonderfully detailed and humorous drawings [by the author] show gay and serious animals and birds who can be examined with fun again and again. . . . And the irresistible rhyming lines are likely to be chanted over and over." Horn Bk

Emberley, Ed

A birthday wish. Little 1977 unp lib. bdg. $5.95   **E**

1 Birthdays—Fiction 2 Animals—Fiction 3 Stories without words
ISBN 0-316-23409-5   LC 77-5147

Illustrated by the author, this is a "wordless picture book featuring a young mouse who makes a silent birthday wish for ice cream. Thorugh an unlikely and humorous chain of events, the wish comes true." Sch Library J

"From the decorative endpapers in pretty colors at the front to their match at the back, the picture story is a lark, a joyous adventure. . . . Emberley has never been more imaginative or more amusing." Pub W

Ed Emberley's ABC. Little 1978 unp illus lib. bdg. $6.95   **E**

1 Alphabet
ISBN 0-316-23408-7   LC 77-28099

Animals "fashion the initial letters of their names. The exhaust from a racing car driven by an ant produces 'A.' A benign bear persuades a ladybug to make a 'B' from blueberries. An imposing elephant daintily picks eggs from a basket and arranges them into an 'E.' And we laugh out loud at the yak who plies knitting needles industriously to give us 'Y.'" Pub W

Emberley's "pictures are filled with enough goings-on and detail to invite concentrated examination; indeed, a few of them are almost too jammed with energetic business. But the pages show great ingenuity of conception and design, the color work is strikingly beautiful and subtle, and the whole book—including jacket, binding, end papers, and hand-lettered text—constitutes a handsome, unified production." Horn Bk

The wing on a flea; a book about shapes; written and illus. by Ed Emberley. Little 1961 48p illus $6.95   **E**

1 Size and shape
ISBN 0-316-23600-4   LC 61-6570

"Gay rhymes and lively green-and-blue drawings show children how to identify triangles, circles, and rectangles in the everyday objects around them. Though some of the examples are a little far-fetched, this should prove effective in nudging boys and girls toward more intelligent observation." Library J

The Wizard of Op. Little 1975 unp illus lib. bdg. $5.95   **E**

1 Witchcraft—Fiction
ISBN 0-316-23610-1   LC 75-20345

Illustrated by the author

"After a young prince is turned into a frog, he first tries the conventional kiss from a princess, but that fails, so he visits several wizards. When their spells also flop, the frog prince travels to the

Emberley, Ed—*Continued*

Wizard of Op, who turns the prince into one animal after another until at last he is successful. The wizard himself disappears at the end, although clues are given as to where and what he is now." Sch Library J

"Would you like to have spots appear before your eyes? How about swirling lines or twirling circles? An intriguing and amusingly disturbing collection of optical illusions, this book a good children's version of a 'coffee table' book. . . . This story is well told with entertaining cartoons and imaginative vocabulary. However, the illustrations, each of which is spread over two pages, are the true highlight. This book is sure to appeal to adults, as well as to 'selected children." Children's Bk Rev Serv

Erskine, Jim

The snowman. Crown 1978 unp illus lib. bdg. $5.95

E

1 Snow—Fiction   2 Bears—Fiction
ISBN 0-517-53202-6   LC 77-19348

"Two active bear boys with the imposing names of Berkley and Calvin rush gleefully out to play in the first snowfall. Snug and warm in their bright mittens, boots and jackets the pals make a big snowman, then get into a fierce fight over whose it is. Too tired and wet to battle any longer, they go home, where Berkley's mother gives him hot soup and dries his clothes. The boy revives and goes out again. He meets Calvin, they glower at each other and are about to redeclare war until they see that their attacks have ruined their joint creation. Friends again, they make a bunch of little snowmen to share." Pub W

Eskine's "firm line drawings overlaid with blue, orange, brown, and green stand sharp against snow-white backgrounds. . . . Diminutive in format as well as in narrative content, the book presents an inviting appearance to very young children." Horn Bk

Ets, Marie Hall

Gilberto and the Wind. . . . Viking 1963 32p illus lib. bdg. $7.95, Penguin pa $2.50   E

1 Winds—Fiction
ISBN 0-670-34025-1; 0-14-050276   LC 63-8527

"I am Gilberto and this is the story of me and the Wind." Title page

"A little Mexican boy thinks aloud about all the things his playmate the wind does with him, for him, and against him. The wind calls him to play, floats his balloon, refuses to fly his kite, blows his soap bubbles into the air, races with him, and rests with him under a tree." Sch Library J

"In brown, black, and white against soft gray pages, this author-artist has caught in a very appealing book . . . the emotions and attitudes of childhood." Horn Bk

In the forest; story and pictures by Marie Hall Ets. Viking 1944 unp illus lib. bdg. $6.95 Penguin pa $1.95   E

1 Animals—Fiction
ISBN 0-670-39687-7; 0-14-050180-0   LC 44-7727

"A delightful, oblong book, with an amusing black and white picture to each page and a sentence or two about a very small boy with a new horn and paper hat who goes for a walk in a great big forest. Along with him go a wild lion, two elephant babies, two brown bears, three kangaroos, two little monkeys, a stork and a rabbit, making quite a parade. But strangely enough, when Dad comes hunting for him and he opens his eyes, there are no animals at all!" Bookmark

"The drawings are soft and lovely. There is a strange impression conveyed, as if one really moved through a great, dim forest." Library J

Just me; written and illus by Marie Hall Ets. Viking 1965 32p illus $6.95 Penguin pa $1.95   E

ISBN 0-670-41109-4; 0-14-050325-0   LC 65-13349

"A little boy plays a game commonly enjoyed by small children for its imaginative as well as muscular demands. He goes from one animal to another, mimicking its ambulation, moving 'just like' it. When there is a chance to take a boat ride with Dad, the game ends abruptly, and another kind of imitation begins—emulation of father." Horn Bk

"Strong, simply designed illustrations and brief, rhythmic text." LC. Children's Bks, 1965

Nine days to Christmas, by Marie Hall Ets and Aurora Labastida; illus. by Marie Hall Ets. Viking 1959 48p illus lib. bdg. $9.95

E

1 Mexico—Fiction   2 Christmas—Fiction
ISBN 0-670-51350-4   LC 59-16438

Awarded the Caldecott Medal, 1960

This "is the story of Ceci, a little girl of Mexico City, just five, and now old enough to have her own posada, the gay parties held on the nine days preceding Christmas. She may also choose her own pinata. . . . The pictures capture all the gaiety, excitement and anticipation preparatory to the Christmas season. With simple lines, a few colors, and a soft gray background that deepens in intensity as the day comes to a close, Marie Ets has caught the brilliant richness of color, the movement and vibrant life that are so much a part of this handsome city." Top of the News

Play with me; story and pictures by Marie Hall Ets. Viking 1955 31p illus lib. bdg. $7.95 Penguin pa $2.50   E

1 Animals—Fiction
ISBN 0-670-55977-6; 0-14-050178-9   LC 55-14845

On a sunny morning in the meadow an excited little girl tries to catch the meadow creatures and play with them. But, one by one, they all run away. Finally, when she learns to sit quietly and wait, there is a happy ending

The "pictures done in muted tones of brown, gray and yellow . . . accurately reflect the little girl's rapidly changing moods of eagerness, bafflement, disappointment and final happiness." NY Times Bk Rev

"Simplicity of text and freshness of drawing make this ideal fare for the very youngest." Library J

Evans, Mari

Jim flying high; illus. by Ashley Bryan. Doubleday 1979 unp illus $7.95, lib. bdg. $8.90

E

1 Fishes—Fiction
ISBN 0-385-14129-7; 0-385-14130-0   LC 78-22628

"Bryan uses strong but muted colors in paintings that are intricate and stylized to illustrate [this] story in Black idiom by Evans, and there's a matching in text and pictures of cheerfulness and humor. The commentator is one of the boys who sees Jim, a flying fish, get stuck in a tree. Jim gasps as he dries out, but he refuses to acknowledge that he needs help, even when his parents swim up ('Boy, you better get down outa that tree,' his mother says) and even when Olukun, Ruler-of-the-Water, urges him to come down. He isn't tired, says Jim, he likes it. When everybody takes pity on the stubborn fish and tosses water at him, Jim recuperates, takes off, and executes some fancy flying before returning to the water. The writing is poetic and also has a fine storytelling quality." Chicago. Children's Bk Center

Falls, Charles Buckles

The A B C book. Doubleday 1923 unp illus $6.95, lib. bdg. $7.90, pa $1.49   E

1 Animals—Pictorial works   2 Alphabet
ISBN 0-385-07663-0; 0-385-07698-3; 0-385-08097-2
                                     LC 23-2228

"'A is for Antelope, Z is for Zebra.' An animal A B C with fine decorative wood blocks in colour illustrating each animal." Bks for Boys & Girls

The **Farmer** in the dell; illus. by Diane Zuromskis. Little 1978 unp illus lib. bdg. $6.95   E

1 Singing games
ISBN 0-316-98889-8   LC 77-17074

"You already know the text; the pictures that accompany it here are clean and cozy, each circle bound and center-set opposite a line or verse of text. There's lots of creamy white space to be seen, and it contrasts nicely with the brown-toned, green-blue-yellow-highlighted drawings. The figures are cheerful—a boyish-looking farmer, his golden-haired wife, their cuddly but not too sweet animals—and the look is fancifully pristine. A pleasant enough confection for picturebook browsers drawn to the familiar lines they can 'read' to themselves." Booklist

E

Fatio, Louise

The happy lion; pictures by Roger Duvoisin. McGraw 1954 unp illus lib. bdg. $7.95   **E**

1 Lions—Fiction 2 France—Fiction
ISBN 0-07-020044-0   LC 54-6732

"Whittlesey House publications"

"A lion in a zoo in France is everybody's favorite—until he escapes. Then his only friend is a little boy who leads him back to his cage." Hodges. Bks for Elem Sch Libraries

"Children will chuckle over a little boy's success in settling a problem that perplexed all the grown-ups." Horn Bk

"A merry nonsense story, whose pictures have captured an air of irresponsible gaiety." Ontario Library Rev

Some other books about the happy lion are also available from McGraw:

The happy lion and the bear lib. bdg. $7.95 (ISBN 0-07-020060-2; LC 64-19504)

The happy lion in Africa lib. bdg. $7.95 (ISBN 0-07-020043-2; LC 55-8896)

The happy lion roars lib. bdg $7.95 (ISBN 007-020048-3; LC 56-12263)

The happy lion's quest lib. bdg. $7.95 (ISBN 0-07-020054-8; LC 61-13428)

The happy lion's vacation lib. bdg. $7.95 (ISBN 0-07-020062-9; LC 67-5705)

The three happy lions lib. bdg. $7.95 (ISBN 0-07-020050-5; LC 59-10706)

Feder, Jane

Beany; pictures by Karen Gundersheimer. Pantheon Bks. 1979 unp illus $4.95, lib. bdg. $4.99   **E**

1 Cats—Fiction
ISBN 0-394-83734-7; 0-394-93734-1   LC 78-10416

"Through small, detailed, colorful drawings we meet a young boy and his cat, Beany, who grow up together and are 'almost best friends.' We enjoy joining them while they are painting, playing hide-and-seek, eating, and sleeping. Warmth and love comes through the short, easy text, which will be liked by young people with pets." Children's Bk Rev Serv

Feder, Paula Kurzband

Where does the teacher live? Pictures by Lillian Hoban. Dutton 1979 48p illus $5.95   **E**

1 Teachers—Fiction 2 School stories
ISBN 0-525-42586-1   LC 78-13157

"A Fat cat book"

"Three enterprising members of Class 2-3, arguing about where Mrs. Greengrass, their teacher, lives, decide to play detective and watch her. One day she walks, another one takes a bus, once she hails a cab, one day a friend picks her up. They are baffled, and ask here; she tells them she lives on the West Side and gives the three a ride home in her uncle's ice cream truck. Each lives in a different kind of building, but none of them sees Mrs. Greengrass reach home. Last picture: Mrs. Greengrass reading contentedly on the deck of her houseboat." Chicago. Children's Bk Center

"The easy-to-read text is sometimes simplified to the point of choppiness, but the story is engaging and suspenseful. The illustrations are rendered in the artist's characteristic poster-paint colors and sketchy outlines, giving the brick buildings and wrought-iron fences of the New York City neighborhood a friendly appearance." Horn Bk

Feelings, Muriel

Jambo means hello; Swahili alphabet book; pictures by Tom Feelings. Dial Press 1974 $5.95, lib. bdg. $5.47   **E**

1 Alphabet 2 Swahili language 3 Africa, East
ISBN 0-8037-4346-7; 0-8037-4350-5   LC 73-15441

Companion volume to: Moja means one, entered below

This book "gives a word for each letter of the alphabet (the Swahili alphabet has 24 letters) save for 'q' and 'x', and a sentence or two provides additional information. A double-page spread of soft black and white drawings illustrates each word; for example: 'V, vyombo are utensils (vee-cam-bow). A craftsman makes utensils for the village. Carved wooden bowls and ladles and pitchers made from gourds are useful and decorative objects for the home.' The picture shows such a craftsman making one object and surrounded by others. The text gives a considerable amount of information about traditional East African life as well as some acquaintance with the language that is used by approximately 45 million people." Chicago. Children's Bk Center

"By using tissue paper to create the final art, the illustrator has shaped doublespreads that almost appear to be frescoes, with lines and cracks as much a part of their essence as the painted area itself. . . . Integrated totally in feeling and mood, the book has been engendered by an intense, personal vision of Africa—one that is warm, all-enveloping, quietly strong and filled with love." Horn Bk

Moja means one; Swahili counting book; pictures by Tom Feelings. Dial Press 1971 unp illus $7.95, lib. bdg. $7.45, pa $1.75   **E**

1 Counting 2 Swahili language 3 Africa, East
ISBN 0-8037-5776-X; 0-8037-5777-8; 0-8037-5711-5   LC 76-134856

The book "uses double-page spreads for each number, one to ten, with beautiful illustrations that depict aspects of East African culture as well as numbers of objects in relation to the various numbers." Pub W

"A short introduction explaining the importance of Swahili and providing a map of the areas in which it is spoken expands the book's use beyond the preschool level of the text into the first three school grades." Sch Library J

Zamani goes to market; illus. by Tom Feelings. Seabury [distributed by Houghton] 1970 unp illus $6.95   **E**

1 Africa, East
ISBN 0-395-28791-X   LC 70-97032

"A Clarion book"

"Zamani, an East African boy, accompanies his father to market for the first time and decides to spend the shilling his father gives him on a necklace for his mother." Adventuring With Bks. 2d edition

"A harmonious and unified picture storybook. The soft browns and golds of the pencil drawings convey a gentle, pleasant atmosphere of African village life, with its spirit of family closeness." Horn Bk

Felt, Sue

Rosa-too-little; story and pictures by Sue Felt. Doubleday 1950 unp illus lib. bdg. $7.95   **E**

1 Libraries—Fiction
ISBN 0-385-07654-1   LC 50-9505

Rosa was too little for this, too little for that, and it made her sad. But her main heartache was the fact that she could not join the library and take out books because she was too little to write her name

"It is a very touching yet quite unsentimental tale, with realistic pictures in two colors. It brings the branch library and Rosa's neighborhood alive for the happy recognition of all city children." NY Her Trib Bks

Fisher, Aileen

Going barefoot; illus. by Adrienne Adams. Crowell 1960 unp illus lib. bdg. $8.79   **E**

1 Animals—Fiction 2 Stories in rhyme
ISBN 0-690-33331-5   LC 60-6238

A picture book of poetry "describing the joys of going barefoot and a child's envy of the many little animals and birds who are not required to wear shoes." Pub W

The "spontaneous rhyming text and pleasing drawings in color and in black and white create a happy mood of anticipation and discovery." Booklist

I like weather; illus. by Janina Domanska. Crowell 1963 unp illus lib. bdg. $8.79   **E**

1 Seasons—Fiction 2 Weather—Fiction 3 Stories in rhyme
ISBN 0-690-43130-9   LC 62-16541

A story in verse about a boy and his dog who seek the pleasures of the four seasons of the year with their different kinds of weather

Listen, rabbit; illus. by Symeon Shimin. Crowell 1964 unp illus lib. bdg. $8.79   **E**

1 Rabbits—Fiction 2 Stories in rhyme
ISBN 0-690-49592-7   LC 64-10860

In this rhyming narrative "a little boy tells the story of how he wanted a pet. When he saw a

Fisher, Aileen—*Continued*

wild rabbit, he hoped it might be his pet; but if the rabbit didn't want to leave the fields, just to be friends would be enough. It is difficult, though, to get to be friends with a rabbit. There are too many things to frighten it away. However, patience and love are rewarded." Christian Sci Monitor

"Sunset, rainy, snowy, moonlit, and pale-green spring scenes have a maximum of atmosphere and lovely color with the jumping or hiding rabbit always an appealing focus." Horn Bk

Flack, Marjorie

Angus and the ducks; told and pictured by Marjorie Flack. Doubleday 1930 unp illus $4.95, lib. bdg. $5.90, pa $1.95   **E**

1 Dogs—Fiction   2 Ducks—Fiction
ISBN 0-385-07213-9; 0-385-07600-2; 0-385-01026-5
                        LC 30-26829

A "picture book describing the amusing experiences of Angus, a Scotch terrier puppy, when curiosity led him to slip under the hedge." Cleveland

This book "stands out for good and sufficient reasons. It is good to look at, it is delightful to read aloud, it is a convenient size for small hands to hold, and above all it has an inner and outer harmony." NY Her Trib Bks

Some other titles about Angus are also available from Doubleday:

Angus and the cat $5.95, lib. bdg. $6.90, pa $1.49 (ISBN 0-385-07212-0; 0-385-07599-5; 0-385-08822-1; LC 31-32343)
Angus lost $5.95, lib. bdg. $6.90, pa $1.49 (ISBN 0-385-07214-7; 0-385-07601-0; 0-385-08009-3; LC 32-21558)

Ask Mr. Bear. Macmillan Pub. Co. 1932 unp illus $4.95, pa $2.95   **E**

1 Animals—Fiction   2 Birthdays—Fiction
ISBN 0-02-735390-7; 0-02-043090-6   LC 58-8370
First published 1932

Danny did not know what to give his mother for a birthday present, so he set out to ask various animals—the hen, the duck, the goose, the lamb, the cow and others, but he met with very little success until he met Mr Bear

This "will have a strong appeal to very young children because of its repetition, its use of the most familiar animals, its gay pictures and the cumulative effect of the story." NY Times Bk Rev

The story about Ping, by Marjorie Flack and Kurt Wiese. Viking 1933 unp illus lib. bdg. $7.95, Penguin pa $1.95   **E**

1 Ducks—Fiction   2 China—Fiction
ISBN 0-670-67223-8; 0-14-050241-6   LC 33-29356

The story of Ping, a duck who lived on a houseboat in the Yangtze River

"An irresistible picture book with so much atmosphere and kindly humor that its readers of any age will unconsciously add to their understanding and appreciation of a far distant country. . . . Few books for little children have the genuinely artistic quality of this one." NY Times Bk Rev

"Colorful illustrations by Kurt Wiese and a humorous text make this a good animal story and a delightful introduction to Chinese life." Children's Bks Too Good to Miss

Flora, James

The great green Turkey Creek monster; story and pictures by James Flora. Atheneum Pubs. 1976 unp illus $7.95, pa $1.95   **E**

ISBN 0-689-50060-2; 0-689-70459-3   LC 75-43894

"A Margaret K. McElderry book"

"Ernie Bogwater's store in Turkey Creek is invaded by a monster vine which snakes out of all the emporium's apertures and into further mischief. It drops a skunk into Mrs. Grogan's bath water; it glues a boy to the seat of his bike, puts ice cream down people's backs, and so on. . . . Finally a trombone-playing boy stops the growth but the local children persuade the authorities to spare the vine's life and let it out, each year, to help celebrate the Fourth of July." Pub W

"Like his vine, Flora's tall tale grows at a rapid good-humored rate, and the ink-and-wash illustrations are cleverly matched to the text (readers are guided along by the ever-growing vine which acts as a framing device and visual focal point)." Sch Library J

Foster, Doris Van Liew

A pocketful of seasons; illus. by Talivaldis Stubis. Lothrop [1961] unp illus lib. bdg. $7.92   **E**

1 Seasons—Fiction
ISBN 0-688-51600-9   LC 60-53422

"The changing seasons bring different reactions to a farmer and a little boy. Illustrations effectively show changing moods and colors." Hodges. Bks for Elem Sch Libraries

Françoise

Jeanne-Marie counts her sheep. Scribner 1951 unp illus lib. bdg. $9.95   **E**

1 Counting   2 Sheep—Fiction   3 France—Fiction
ISBN 0-684-13175-7   LC 51-9415

"A little French girl counts the number of lambs her sheep may have and plans what she will buy with the money from their wool. . . . Designed to help the child . . . in learning his numbers." Pub W

"Another gay, colorful, and delightful picture book by a famous author-illustrator. . . . A natural for the nursery group." Library J

Some other books about Jeanne-Marie are also available from Scribner:

Noël for Jeanne-Marie lib. bdg. $7.95 [ISBN 0-684-13165-X; LC 53-12093]
Springtime for Jeanne-Marie lib. bdg $8.95 (ISBN 0-684-12719-9; LC 55-14216)
What time is it, Jeanne-Marie? lib. bdg. $6.95 (ISBN 0-684-12457-2; LC 63-21302)

Freeman, Don

Beady Bear; story and pictures by Don Freeman. Viking 1954 48p illus lib. bdg. $6.95, Penguin pa $1.95   **E**

1 Teddy bears—Fiction
ISBN 0-670-15056-8; 0-14-050197-5   LC 54-12295

A picture-story book about a toy Teddy bear who tried living in a cave, but found it not to his liking. Beady Bear was glad to be rescued by the little boy who had the much-needed key

"There is wholesome emotional satisfaction here for those pre-schoolers who have similar toy attachments. With simple page-by-page black and white scratchboard illustrations for each rhythmic sentence, this is the kind of book small children will delight in 'reading' to themselves after a couple of out-loud readings by mother." NY Times Bk Rev

Corduroy; story and pictures by Don Freeman. Viking 1968 32p illus lib. bdg. $6.95, Penguin pa $2.25   **E**

1 Teddy bears—Fiction   2 Blacks—Fiction
ISBN 0-670-24133-4; 0-14-050173-8   LC 68-16068

"One day Corduroy, a toy bear who lives in a big department store, discovers he has lost a button. That night he goes to look for it and in his search he sees many strange and wonderful things. He does not find his button, but the following morning he finds what he has always wanted—a friend, Lisa. Love and affection prevail through the friendship of Corduroy and Lisa, a pretty black girl." Rdng Ladders, 5th ed.

"The art and story are direct and just right for the very young who like bears and escalators." Bk World

Dandelion; story and pictures by Don Freeman. Viking 1964 48p illus lib. bdg. $7.95, Penguin pa $2.50   **E**

1 Lions—Fiction
ISBN 0-670-25532-7; 0-14-050218-1   LC 64-21472

"Dandelion, properly invited by note to Jennifer Giraffe's tea-and-taffy party, pays no heed to the words, 'Come as you are.' At his regular haircut appointment he allows Lou Kangaroo and helper to do him up properly, according to the new fashions for lions. But pride goeth before a fall—and it is not surprising that Jennifer's tall door is closed on the unrecognizable stranger; nor that after being restored by a heavy rainfall to something nearer his usual state, he makes the party, after all. Mr. Freeman cleverly depicts an assortment of personalities in his many animal characters. The party scenes and the barber shop are wonderfully amusing." Horn Bk

Freeman, Don—*Continued*

Fly high, fly low. Viking 1957 58p illus lib. bdg. $6.95 E

1 Pigeons—Fiction 2 San Francisco—Fiction
ISBN 0-670-32218-0 LC 57-13961

"The picture book story of a pigeon that made his home in the lower loop of the letter 'B' in an electric-light sign on top of a tall San Francisco hotel. On a morning when Sid had flown off to the park, disaster struck—the sign was moved and his mate, the net, and the two precious eggs with it. Sid's search for home and mate is excitingly told in a lively narrative and handsome colored pictures with sweeping views of San Francisco." Booklist

The guard mouse; story and pictures by Don Freeman. Viking 1967 47p illus lib. bdg. $6.95 E

1 Mice—Fiction 2 London—Fiction
ISBN 0-670-35639-5 LC 67-2452

Grenadier Guard Mouse Clyde at Buckingham Palace, while off duty "settles the tired children of his visiting New York cousins in his bearskin hat, places it gently alongside his sentry box, and takes off with the parents on a whirlwind tour of London. . . . [When he rushes] back for the Changing of the Guard, [he] discovers [his] fur hat has disappeared. The commotion brings the Queen, who calls Scotland Yard, [to] find the hat." Horn Bk

"The illustrations are awash with color, movement, humorous details, and a splendid feeling of amused affection for Londoners." Sat Rev

Norman the doorman. Viking 1959 64p illus lib. bdg. $7.95, Penguin pa $2.95 E

1 Mice—Fiction 2 Museums—Fiction
ISBN 0-670-51515-9; 0-14-050288-2 LC 59-16171

"Norman, the mouse doorman at the basement of the museum, wins an award with a 'sculpture' made from mousetrap parts. Full-color lithographs by the author are as full of fun as the imaginative text." Hodges. Bks for Elem Sch Libraries

Freeman, Lydia

Pet of the Met, by Lydia and Don Freeman. Viking 1953 63p illus $5.95 E

1 Mice—Fiction 2 Cats—Fiction 3 Opera—Fiction
ISBN 0-670-54875-8 LC 53-8719

"It is an exciting day when the Met offers The Magic Flute at the children's matinee. Down from his cosy attic harp case comes Maestro Petrini, a mouse who earns his daily cheese as the prompter's page-turner; and up from his fiddle case in the basement creeps Mephisto, a cat whose appearance fits his name. What happens when each is bewitched by the Magic Flute music is sheer fun." Horn Bk

"The economical prose (scarcely more than captions) is perfectly integrated with the pictures. In the latter the intensity of color, the vigor of line heighten the theatrical effect of both setting and plot." NY Times Bk Rev

Freschet, Berniece

Elephant & friends; illus. by Glen Rounds. Scribner [1978 c1977] 48p illus lib. bdg. $6.95 E

1 Elephants—Fiction 2 Friendship—Fiction
3 Animals—Fiction
ISBN 0-684-15530-3 LC 77-13868

"Something must be done, Elephant decides. There is a drought on the land, he is thin and tired and hungry, and he's worried about the plight of his friends as well as his own hapless state. One by one the animals agree to join Elephant in his march across the long desert to the cool forest. Some of the smaller creatures collapse and Elephant carries them—until he, too, sinks to the ground, overcome by fatigue, hunger, and heat. Crisis! They see men! Hunters, like those who had once driven Elephant's family away from the forest. It is Leopard who comes forth with a plan to save them all by frightening the hunters, who spread such tales after they have run away that the animals are left in peace for a hundred years in the beautiful, cool forest." Chicago. Children's Bk Center

"An original talking-beast tale judiciously borrows folklore motifs to create a suspenseful, fluidly

told mini-drama with a comic climax. Expressive line drawings interpret the various moods of the protagonists and complement the action of the story." Horn Bk

The happy dromedary; illus. by Glen Rounds. Scribner 1977 32p illus lib. bdg. $6.95 E

1 Camels—Fiction
ISBN 0-684-14853-6 LC 76-1323

"When the King of the Animals allows each beast to choose his own home, the dromedary picks the flat, quiet desert. Before long she returns to the Animal King, however, asking first for large, floppy feet to walk in sand and then for a hump to store food and water. For a while the dromedary is happy, until the others begin ridiculing her looks. Once again she returns to the king, this time asking to be returned to her former self, but the king refuses. Instead he lengthens the dromedary's neck and pushes back her nose, creating such a proud look that the other animals are respectfully impressed." Booklist

"The narrative is original and told in a good, direct storytelling style. The line drawings of the animals and birds and of their environments, colored with purple and light brown crayon, are in keeping with the simplicity of the story and quietly emphasize its implicit humor." Horn Bk

The web in the grass; illus. by Roger Duvoisin. Scribner 1972 unp illus lib. bdg. $8.95 E

1 Spiders—Fiction
ISBN 0-684-12956-6 LC 72-1165

This is the story of a little spider as she carries on her daily activities—spinning a web to trap insects for food, hiding from her enemies, and forming a sac where she lays her eggs which soon hatch into hundreds of spiderlings

"This book is delightful because it presents spiders as neutral animals who have specific life functions, but who are inherently neither good nor bad. The life cycle of the spider is presented in story form with excellent color drawings." AAAS Sci Bk List for Children

Froman, Robert

Bigger and smaller; illus. by Gioia Fiammenghi. Crowell 1971 33p illus (Young math bks) pa $1.45 E

1 Size and shape
ISBN 0-690-14197-1 LC 78-132297

"One can tell whether an object is big or small by comparing it with another object. So begins the general theme of this . . . book, which asks young readers to make their own decisions. They also learn that it is possible for the same object to be big in relation to a second object and small in relation to a third (an elephant is big compared to a man but small compared to a dinosaur). The child will be stimulated to undertake endless comparisons, as to size, of the objects around him, and of the unfamiliar in the illustrations." Sci Bks

"The concept of relative size is presented here with a good deal of imagination and liveliness. . . . Throughout this stimulating introduction the reader is asked to make decisions and at the end is encouraged to explore the concept further. Humorous colored or black-and-white drawings on every page." Booklist

Gackenbach, Dick

Harry and the terrible Whatzit. Seabury [distributed by Houghton] 1977 unp illus $7.95 E

1 Fear—Fiction
ISBN 0-395-28795-2 LC 76-40205

"A Clarion book"
Illustrated by the author

The author "tells of timid Harry, a boy who is convinced that something horrible lurks in the cellar of his house. Harry has never ventured below stairs. When his mother goes down to the basement to get a jar of pickles, he tries to stop her, in vain. Waiting in trepidation for her return, the boy suspects that the Whatzit has grabbed her. In spite of his terror, Harry goes downstairs and confronts the ogre. He is surprised and pleased when his bravery diminishes the huge demon and glad to find his mother outside where she's picking flowers." Pub W

Gackenback, Dick—*Continued*

"The drawings have clean lines and earth colors, the writing style is pared down to smooth simplicity; the message is not highly original, nor is the method of conveying it, but this is an acceptable and amiable statement about conquering fear by facing it." Chicago. Children's Bk Center

Hound and Bear; story and pictures by Dick Gackenbach. Seabury [distributed by Houghton] 1976 unp illus lib. bdg. $7.95 **E**

1 Friendship—Fiction 2 Dogs—Fiction 3 Bears—Fiction
ISBN 0-395-28796-0 LC 76-3525

"A Clarion book"
The author "tells three stories about Hound who indulges his penchant for practical jokes at the risk of a sound friendship. In 'The Long Night,' Hound paints his pal Bear's windows black. Bear oversleeps until Hound wakes him with howling laughter. In the second, the friends trade places, Bear stays at Hound's place and handles some necessary chores; Hound, on the other hand, eats everything in sight at Bear's house and refuses a package that arrives. Maybe because both jokes backfire, Hound reforms in the third story or maybe his redemption arises from Bear's threat to break up the relationship in the event of another trick." Pub W

"The contrast between the anthropomorphized duo is effectively captured in energetic vignettes executed in pen and ink with added tones of brown and gray." Horn Bk

Gaeddert, LouAnn

Noisy Nancy Norris; illus. by Gioia Fiammenghi. Doubleday 1965 63p illus lib. bdg. $6.95 **E**

1 Apartment houses—Fiction 2 City life—Fiction
ISBN 0-385-04749-5 LC 65-10180

"Nancy loved to bang, jump, rattle, run, shout and laugh. She never kept still until the landlady threatened eviction, and then she became such a sad, quiet little girl that the landlady baked her some favorite cookies and asked her please to make just a little noise." Moorachian. What is a City?

This is "an unpretentious, thoroughly engaging picture-story book. The diverting colored illustrations are most expressive." Booklist
Followed by: Noisy Nancy and Nick. Doubleday lib. bdg. $6.95 (ISBN 0-385-01542-9; LC 70-79385)

Gág, Wanda

The A B C bunny; hand lettered by Howard Gág. Coward-McCann 1933 unp illus $6.29, lib. bdg. $5.49, pa $2.50 **E**

1 Rabbits—Fiction 2 Alphabet 3 Stories in rhyme
ISBN 0-698-20000-4; 0-698-30000-9; LC 0-698-20465-4

An alphabet book which tells in verse and pictures the story of a little rabbit's adventures. The verse has been set to music by the author's sister
"The book has the freshness of invention, and the drawings, the beauty, humor and originality characteristic of this artist's work. The illustrations are original lithographs." NY Times Bk Rev
Music on endpapers

Millions of cats. Coward-McCann 1928 unp illus $7.95, lib. bdg. $6.29, pa $2.50 **E**

1 Cats—Fiction
ISBN 0-698-20091-8; 0-698-30236-2; 0-698-20434-4 LC 28-21571

"An unusual story-picture book [illustrated by the author] about a very old man and very old woman who wanted one little cat and who found themselves with 'millions and billions and trillions of cats.'" St Louis

It is "a perennial favorite among children and takes a place of its own, both for the originality and strength of its pictures and the living folktale quality of its text." N Y Her Trib Bks

Nothing At All. Coward-McCann 1941 unp illus lib. bdg. $4.49 **E**

1 Dogs—Fiction
ISBN 0-698-30264-8 LC 41-19723

Nothing At All was an invisible orphan puppy, with two visible and loving brother puppies. With the help of a jackdaw, some magic, and a great deal of strenuous effort, little Nothing At All achieved visibility and all three were adopted by two kindly children. And the other puppies remarked how nice it was to see Something-after-all

"In a series of lithographic drawings in colors, Wanda Gag has invested the unseen with a reality that goes straight to the heart of child or grownup. Here are humor, beauty, strength of draughtsmanship and a fresh child-like conception of life most reassuring in a world even more upset for animals than for human beings." Horn Bk

Snippy and Snappy. Coward-McCann 1931 unp illus lib. bdg. $4.49 **E**

1 Mice—Fiction
ISBN 0-698-30319-9 LC 31-28018

This story tells how Snippy, and Snappy, two little field mice, ventured forth one day in search of cheese, and were rescued by their father just as they were about to investigate a mouse trap

"The text is fuller than in 'Millions of cats' [entered above]. . . . The drawings have Wanda Gág's distinctive power, sweep and rhythm." NY Libraries

Gage, Wilson

Down in the boondocks; pictures by Glen Rounds. Greenwillow Bks. 1977 32p illus $5.95, lib. bdg. $5.71 **E**

1 Deaf—Fiction 2 Stories in rhyme
ISBN 0-688-80085-8; 0-688-84085-X LC 76-45380

"Greenwillow Read-alone"
Story in rhyme about a deaf farmer who lives in the boondocks. "A hollering wife, crowing rooster, cackling hen, roaring bulldog, squeaking wagon, and braying mule do little to mar the farmer's sense of calm. Luckily for him, a hen-poaching thief who arrives at dawn has very good ears; he is scared silly and turns tail on the boondocks for good. The hop-along verse propels readers through a cacophonous tale that finds harmonious visualization in Rounds' every-funny illustrations." Booklist

Mrs Gaddy and the ghost; pictures by Marylin Hafner. Greenwillow Bks. 1979 55p illus $5.95, lib. bdg. $5.71 **E**

1 Ghosts—Fiction
ISBN 0-688-80179-X; 0-688-84179-1 LC 78-16366

"Greenwillow Read-alone"
"Plump Mrs. Gaddy is very happy living on her farm; she has fields and a meadow, chickens and a mule. . . . But she also has an unwanted boarder —a hungry ghost who keeps her awake with its nocturnal feasting. Mrs. Gaddy tries many ploys to rid her house of 'the ghostly thing,' including bug spray and a trap baited with gingerbread. Finally she writes a polite letter asking it to haunt another house in the neighborhood. But the ghost—who is really a benign creature—bursts into tears upon reading the letter, and Mrs. Gaddy allows it to stay. . . . The simple text is spiced with such colorful expression as 'bless my big toe!' and 'tarnation.' The illustrations in warm tones of pink and sepia ink are full of witty and imaginative detail." Horn Bk

Squash pie; pictures by Glen Rounds. Greenwillow Bks. 1976 56p illus $5.95, lib. bdg. $5.71 **E**

1 Farm life—Fiction
ISBN 0-688-80031-9; 0-688-84031-0 LC 75-29157

"Greenwillow read-alone"
"Because he liked squash pie, farmer wanted to grow it, but every time he planted, someone stole the crop. In desperation, he planted potatoes —their eyes could see the thief; corn—the ears could hear him; and a dogwood tree—the bark would scare him. Nothing worked, so his good wife, feeling he deserved the pie, threw peaches in the air and when they fell with a squash, made him his pie. Glen Rounds' illustrations, as usual, capture the tongue-in-cheek humor of this easy-to-read tall tale." Children's Bk Rev Serv

Gantos, Jack

Rotten Ralph; illus. by Nicole Rubel. Houghton 1976 unp illus lib. bdg. $6.95, pa $2.95 **E**

1 Cats—Fiction
ISBN 0-395-24276-2; 0-395-29202-6 LC 75-34101

"The protagonist of this story is a mean and nasty cat, Ralph. As his young owner, Sarah,

Gantos, Jack—*Continued*

and her family say, he is very difficult to love. Finally on a trip to the circus his behavior becomes unforgivable and they leave him. There he is treated as miserably as he has treated everyone else and he comes home a week later a wiser, more benevolent cat—well, almost." Children's Bk Rev Serv

The "bright watercolor scenes . . . capturing Ralph's demonic meanness and his family's chagrin are a perfect complement to the text." Sch Library J

Garelick, May

Where does the butterfly go when it rains; with pictures by Leonard Weisgard. Young Scott Bks. 1961 unp illus lib. bdg. $6.95   **E**

1 Animals 2 Rain and rainfall
ISBN 0-201-09401-0   LC 61-2006

"Pictures of flowers and animals . . . adorn this simple picture book which shows children how various creatures protect themselves from the rain. The question about the butterfly however, is never answered." Pub W

"The soft blue misty pictures and the lilting poetic style create a mood of mystery and a real appreciation of nature. Excellent for discussion and pondering." Adventuring With Bks. 2d edition

Gauch, Patricia Lee

Aaron and the Green Mountain Boys; pictures by Margot Tomes. Coward, McCann & Geoghegan 1972 62p illus lib. bdg. $6.29   **E**

1 Vermont—History—Fiction 2 U.S.—History—Revolution, 1775-1783—Fiction
ISBN 0-698-30423-3   LC 70-169246

"A Break-of-day book"

"Based on a true Revolutionary War incident, this simply written, attractively illustrated story has action, excitement, and a very believable nine-year-old central character. When the Redcoats capture Fort Ticonderoga and head toward Bennington, Vermont, where supplies are stored, Aaron longs to deliver messages to the general or ride with his father and the Green Mountain Boys, but he is relegated to staying home and helping his grandfather bake bread for the army. Not until his father and the Green Mountain Boys arrive home exhausted and hungry from a long march does Aaron recognize the importance of bread to the war effort." Booklist

Gilchrist, Theo E.

Halfway up the mountain; pictures by Glen Rounds. Lippincott 1978 46p illus lib. bdg. $4.95   **E**

1 Robbers and outlaws—Fiction 2 Cookery—Fiction
ISBN 0-397-31805-7   LC 77-29020

"A Lippincott I-like-to read book"

"A slow-moving old man and a half-blind old woman drive a dread bandit from their mountainside shack. The couple are happy together except for one thing—they have boiled beef for dinner every day. In vain, the old man asks for pork or chicken. But the spirit who lives in the oldest aspen tree gives him no consolation: ' "There are worse things than beef." ' Then the bandit drives them out of the cabin and sleeps on the stove to keep warm. In the morning the old woman comes into the kitchen as usual, and her lifelong habit serves them well. Recognizing the condiments by touch, she salts and peppers what she assumes is a slab of beef on the stove and begins to insert slivers of garlic. Blinded by the seasonings, [bandit] Bloodcoe runs down the mountain and leaves his sacks of gold behind." Horn Bk

"This tall tale . . . is ably spun and stands out among beginning readers for its flowing style, clever plot, and subtle wisdom. Glen Rounds' country-style illustrations are another asset." Sch Library J

Ginsburg, Mirra

The chick and the duckling; tr. [and adapted] from the Russian of V. Suteyev; pictures by Jose & Ariane Aruego. Macmillan Pub. Co. 1972 unp illus lib. bdg. $5.95   **E**

1 Ducks—Fiction 2 Chickens—Fiction
ISBN 0-02-735940-9   LC 74-188773

"The adventures of a duckling who is a leader and a chick who follows suit. When the chick

decides that an aquatic life is not for him, this brief selection for reading aloud comes to a humorous conclusion." Wis Library Bul

"The sunny simplicity of the illustrations is just right for a slight but engaging text, and they add a note of humor that is a nice foil for the bland directness of the story. . . . Easy enough to be read by a beginning reader, but too right (by length, subject, and level of concept) for the lap audience not to be directed primarily at them." Chicago. Children's Bk Center

Mushroom in the rain; adapted from the Russian of V. Suteyev; pictures by Jose Aruego & Ariane Dewey. Collier Bks. [1978 c1974] unp illus pa $2.50   **E**

1 Animals—Fiction 2 Mushrooms—Fiction
ISBN 0-02-043270-4   LC 77-17222

First published 1974 in hardcover by Macmillan

An ant, a butterfly, a mouse, a sparrow and a rabbit take shelter under a mushroom during a rainstorm. The other animals convince a fox who is hunting the rabbit that the rabbit couldn't possibly fit under a mushroom with all of them, and they themselves don't know how it was possible until a wise frog explains

"An intriguing variation on a somewhat familiar theme springs to life with irresistible pictures; subdued and rain-drenched at first, they fairly burst—after the storm—into a riot of joyous colors." Horn Bk

Three kittens; tr. [and adapted] from the Russian of V. Suteyev; pictures by Giulio Maestro. Crown 1973 unp illus lib. bdg. $6.95   **E**

1 Cats—Fiction
ISBN 0-517-50328-X   LC 72-96414

Three kittens "chase a mouse into flour and all turn white, chase a toad through an old stovepipe and all turn black, dive into a pond after fish and come home as before: black, gray, white." Top of the News

"Economically told with a maximum of nine words on a page, this is a charming story. . . . The simple, expressive pictures in soft yellow and beige match the playful mood of the story." Sch Library J

Goble, Paul

The friendly wolf [by] Paul and Dorothy Goble; pictures by Paul Goble. Bradbury Press [1975 c1974] unp illus $7.95   **E**

1 Indians of North America—Fiction 2 Wolves—Fiction
ISBN 0-87888-104-2   LC 76-353731

First published 1974 in England

This "is the story of two Indian children who are separated from their family while berry hunting. A wolf befriends them and leads them home, where it [the wolf] is honored by the tribe. The artwork by Paul Goble is especially noteworthy for its sharpness; the colorful tiny details of buds, animals, and flowers will delight all readers." Chidren's Bk Rev Serv

The girl who loved wild horses; story and illus. by Paul Goble. Bradbury Press 1978 unp illus $8.95   **E**

1 Indians of North America—Fiction 2 Horses—Fiction
ISBN 0-87888-121-2   LC 77-20500

Awarded the Caldecott Medal, 1979

An Indian "girl living with her people attracts the devotion of wild horses in their territory. When she is separated from her family by a fearful storm, the noble stallion—king of the herd—leads the girl and his charges to safety. Later, she returns to her people but they understand that she feels the wild horses are now her family. With the tribe's permission, she goes off with the horses but return to the Indian village on a visit, each year. At a time when she does not return, hunters see a ghostly mare floating beside the mighty stallion as he gallops at the head of his herd." Pub W

"Elaborate double-page spreads burst with life, revealing details of flowers and insects, animals and birds. . . . The concluding scene shows two wild horses magnificently framed against a burning red sun. The story is told in simple language, and the author has included verses of a Navaho and a Sioux song about horses. Both storytelling and art express the harmony with and the love of nature which characterize Native American culture." Horn Bk

Goffstein, M. B.

Fish for supper. Dial Press 1976 unp illus
$4.95, lib. bdg. $4.58   **E**

1 Grandmothers—Fiction 2 Fishing—Fiction
ISBN 0-8037-2571-X; 0-8037-2572-8   LC 75-27598

"Grandmother's routine, beginning at five A.M.,
involves getting ready to go fishing, rowing her
boat, catching some fish, cleaning, cooking and
eating the fish and then going to bed to rest up
for the next day's fishing. Grandmother is a
happy loner who will bring smiles to young and
old alike." Interracial Bks for Children Bul
"With her economy of line and of words, the
author-artist is a mistress of understatement. The
tidy drawings, without a single superfluous stroke
of the pen, balance perfectly with the reticent
storytelling." Horn Bk

My Noah's ark; story and pictures by M. B.
Goffstein. Harper 1978 unp illus $6.95, lib.
bdg. $6.49   **E**

1 Toys—Fiction
ISBN 0-06-022022-8; 0-06-022023-6   LC 77-25666

During her childhood the narrator "received a
wooden ark and tiny animals, which her father
had carved. 'Two spotted leopards, two meek
sheep, two gray horses, and two white doves'
were joined by other creatures over the years.
She kept them through marriage and motherhood,
sharing the story—both of Noah's ark and of her
tiny one—with children and grandchildren. Then
as an old woman in her nineties, she reflects,
'[E]veryone is gone, and the ark holds their
memories'. . . . The author's rich imagination
endows inanimate objects with a life all their own.
Typically restrained, naive drawings share in telling the quiet story which manages to capture deep
emotion." Horn Bk

Natural history. Farrar, Straus 1979 unp
illus $7.95   **E**

ISBN 0-374-35498-7   LC 79-7318

The text and illustrations describe the riches
of the earth and how people can promote peace
and goodwill by sharing equitably with each other
and their fellow creatures
"With a respect for life as profound as that of
St. Francis or Albert Schweitzer, M. B. Goffstein
is neither bombastic nor self-righteous. 'Homeless
dogs and cats are scared and lonely. Old people
look in garbage hopefully, though we have riches
we are born to share. . . . Every living creature
is our brother and our sister.' Although her line
is as simple and as definitive as ever, the artist
has used water-color, thus adding to her pictures
another kind of delicacy and a new warmth of
feeling." Horn Bk

Neighbors. Harper 1979 unp illus $5.95, lib.
bdg. $6.89   **E**

1 Friendship—Fiction
ISBN 0-06-022018-X; 0-06-022019-8   LC 78-19491

"Sincere but misguided attempts to make friends
with a new neighbor takes the narrator of this
story through a year of pie-baking, shoveling snow,
cleaning house, and, finally, striking just the right
note of friendly curiosity that leads to a getting-
acquainted breakfast." Sch Library J
"Scores a hit with inimitably precise drawings
and a story utterly simple and incredibly touching." Pub W

Goodall, John S.

The adventures of Paddy Pork. Harcourt
1968 unp illus $5.95   **E**

1 Pigs—Fiction 2 Stories without words
ISBN 0-15-201589-2   LC 68-26425

"While his mother is shopping, Paddy darts away
to find a traveling circus that had caught his eye.
The amusing story depicts how Paddy becomes lost
in the woods and nearly [becomes] a wolf's dinner,
his disastrous attempts to join the bears' act when
he does find the circus, and his eventual happy
reunion with his mother." Sch Library J
"There is no text to this picture book: detailed
black-and-white drawings tell the whole story.
. . . The insertion of half-width pages between
the full-width pages gives the delightful effect of
opening doors, peering around corners, and uncovering surprises." Booklist
Some other books about Paddy Pork are also
available from Atheneum Pubs. (unless otherwise
noted):
The ballooning adventures of Paddy Pork $5.95
(Harcourt ISBN 0-15-205693-9; LC 69-18625)

Paddy Pork's holiday $6.95 (ISBN 0-689-50043-2;
LC 75-28278)
Paddy's evening out $4.95 (ISBN 0-689-30412-9;
LC 72-98006)
Paddy's new hat $6.95 (ISBN 0-689-50172-2; LC 80-
80129)

Creepy castle. Atheneum Pubs. 1975 unp
illus $4.95   **E**

1 Mice—Fiction 2 Castles—Fiction 3 Stories
without words
ISBN 0-689-50027-0   LC 74-16836

"A Margaret K. McElderry book"
"A medieval adventure is portrayed in a book
without words, with alternate half and full pages
used to change the scene economically and cleverly.
Two mice approach the castle, followed by a
stealthy, evil figure (another mouse) who locks
them in. Our hero thwarts bats and a menacing
dragon, pushes his fair lady out of a window
and into the moat. He follows her; they are
rescued by a frog, who ferries them to safety
on his lily pad. They creep up on the villain,
dump him into the pond just as he is about to
shoot an arrow at a placid fowl, and caper
estatically home. The story is clear, the plot
sturdy, the pictures exciting and romantic. Great
fun." Chicago. Children's Bk Center

Shrewbettina's birthday. Harcourt 1971 c1970
unp illus $4.95   **E**

1 Shrews—Fiction 2 Mice—Fiction 3 Birthdays
—Fiction 4 Stories without words
ISBN 0-15-274080-5   LC 71-162303

First published 1970 in England
"As Shrewbettina goes marketing for her birthday party, her purse is snatched by a [mouse]
thief. A dashing young friend apprehends the
villain and restores her money; and the day ends
happily with a gala evening of feasting and dancing." Horn Bk
"John Goodall has used half-page insertions between the pages to add an extra bit of action to
a story without text. The Victorian dress and
the English village setting give a quaint and
pastoral flavor to the story. . . . Soft, sentimental
drawings have a pastel charm, telling the tale
very clearly." Chicago. Children's Bk Center

The surprise picnic. Atheneum Pubs. 1977
unp illus $6.95   **E**

1 Cats—Fiction 2 Stories without words
ISBN 0-689-50074-2   LC 76-28455

"A Margaret K. McElderry book"
This story without words follows the adventures
of a cat family "who set out in their rowboat for
a picnic on an island. While mother sets the food
on a big rock, brother gambols and sister starts
a fire. The little family turns away from the feast
long enough for the 'rock' to walk away with the
food. It's a formidable turtle which the cats can't
cope with. They start for home, only to find that
their boat has broken loose and, to add to their
woes, a thunderstorm strikes. After much suspense,
the cats wind up with a surprise picnic and are
safe at home when we leave them." Pub W
"The momentum of the plot is heightened by the
use of half-page inserts, which provide a quick
change of action. . . . [This technique] has not always been compatible with the difficulties inherent
in color printing. Thus, despite the beguiling sweetness of the feline protagonists, the frequent dis-
parities in color from full- to half-page are obvious." Horn Bk

Goudey, Alice E.

The day we saw the sun come up; illus.
by Adrienne Adams. Scribner 1961 unp illus
lib. bdg. $8.95   **E**

1 Sun
ISBN 0-684-12365-7   LC 61-5787

"Two children rise before dawn and see the sun
come up for the first time in their lives . . . then
they note through the day how their shadows
change as the sun moves. At dusk their mother
explains night and day, and the movement of the
earth. The prose is simple and childlike, the
explanations are lucid and accurate, yet there is
a lyric quality to the writing. The illustrations are
soft in color and quality, the scenes at sunrise
and sunset are especially lovely, with delicate
nuances of tone." Chicago. Children's Bk Center
"This little book edges toward the thin lines that
divide poetry from science and entertainment from
instruction. Beginning as a summer holiday romp,
complete with picnic lunch, the story gradually
turns an analytical eye toward the sun overhead."
Christian Sci Monitor

Graham, Lorenz

Song of the boat; pictures by Leo and Diane Dillon. Crowell 1975 unp illus $7.95, lib. bdg. $7.89   **E**

1 Africa—Fiction
ISBN 0-690-75231-8; 0-690-75232-6   LC 74-5183

"Graham draws on the idiomatic English of West Africa to tell of Flumbo, who goes with his son Momolu to search for a tree he can fashion into a new canoe. The quest is realized through a dream of Momolu's in which the spirit people reveal to him 'one fine tree, fine past all he ever see before.' Out of it Flumbo makes a magnificent canoe, and after crediting Momolu, takes his family for a ride down the river." Booklist

"The woodcuts—some black and white and some colored with magenta and orange—present solid, often massive, figures against settings articulated with bold line. Like the text, the woodcuts feel indigenous to Africa, but, at the same time, both text and pictures retain a universal element." Horn Bk

Graham, Margaret Bloy

Be nice to spiders. Harper 1967 unp illus $8.95, lib. bdg. $8.79   **E**

1 Spiders—Fiction 2 Animals—Fiction 3 Zoological gardens—Fiction
ISBN 0-06-022072-4; 0-06-022073-2   LC 67-17101

"The story of Helen, Billy's pet spider, who weaves her webs in the local zoo and thus helps keep the flies off the backs of the animals. The title comes from an order issued by the zoo superintendent to his cleaning staff to leave spider webs alone." Christian Sci Monitor

The "slight humor and fitting cartoon illustrations [by the author] will appeal to young children." Bruno Bks for School Libraries, 1968

Gramatky, Hardie

Hercules; the story of an old-fashioned fire engine; written and illus. by Hardie Gramatky. Putnam 1940 unp illus lib. bdg. $5.99, pa $3.50   **E**

1 Fire engines—Fiction
ISBN 0-399-60240-2; 0-399-20728-7   LC 40-34108

"A dramatic picture storybook in brilliant colors in which [Hercules] the old horse-drawn fire engine becomes a hero and saves the City Hall. Children will delight in the gusto and fun." NY Pub Library

Little Toot; pictures and story by Hardie Gramatky. Putnam 1939 unp illus $7.95, lib. bdg. $5.99, pa $2.95   **E**

1 Tugboats—Fiction
ISBN 0-399-20144-0; 0-399-60422-7; 0-399-20649-3
LC 39-24222

Story and pictures describe the early career of a saucy little tug-boat too pleased with himself to do any real work until one day when he found himself out on the ocean in a storm. Then Little Toot earned the right to be called a hero

The illustrations are "mobile, exciting affairs in nautical blues and greens and stormy blacks, painted in a dashing offhand manner which exactly matches the bravado of Little Toot." NY Times Bk Rev

"Mr. Gramatky tells his story with humor and enjoyment, giving, too, a genuine sense of the water front in both pictures and story." Horn Bk

Several other books about Little Toot are also available from Putnam:
Little Toot on the Mississippi $6.95 (ISBN 0-399-20364; LC 73-76717)
Little Toot on the Thames lib. bdg. $5.79 (ISBN 0-399-20483-0; LC 75-10450)
Little Toot through the Golden Gate $6.95 (ISBN 0-399-20483-0; LC 75-10450)

Gray, Nigel

It'll all come out in the wash; pictures by Edward Frascino. Harper 1979 32p illus $7.95, lib. bdg. $7.89   **E**

1 Parent and child—Fiction
ISBN 0-06-022067-8; 0-06-022074-0   LC 78-22482

"Like every mother's nightmare this small heroine goes from one mess to another as she tries out grown-up tasks. Each time her father comes to her rescue chanting. 'It'll all come out in the wash.'" Children's Bk Rev Serv

"Frascino's quick cartoon-like illustrations further the good humor by exaggerating the disorder." Sch Library J

Green, Norma

The hole in the dike; retold by Norma Green; pictures by Eric Carle. Crowell 1975 [c1974] unp illus $8.95, lib. bdg. $8.79   **E**

1 Netherlands—Fiction
ISBN 0-690-00734-5; 0-690-00676-4   LC 74-23562

Adapted from a story which was first published in Hans Brinker; or, The siver skates, by M. M. Dodge

The "tale of the brave lad who saved Holland from disaster by using his finger to plug a leak in the dike." Children's Bk Rev Serv

"Almost all of the full-color collage and paint illustrations are doublespreads with bold, angular forms and with profusely brush-stroked patterns. They add a strong element of visual drama to the simple, traditional story." Horn Bk

Greenaway, Kate

A Apple pie. Warne n.d. unp illus $7.95   **E**

1 Alphabet
ISBN 0-7232-0590-6

A reprint of the Greenaway A B C book, with the original illustrations in color, which first appeared in 1886, published by Routledge and Sons

A picture "book in which little girls in quaint frilled dresses with flowing sashes, and little boys in long breeches, merrily demolish A—apple pie." Toronto

Greenfield, Eloise

Me and Neesie; illus. by Moneta Barnett. Crowell 1975 unp illus lib. bdg. $6.49   **E**

1 Blacks—Fiction
ISBN 0-690-00715-9   LC 74-23078

"A familiar situation is depicted in this picture book—the relationship between an only child and her imaginary frend. Janell's atler ego, Neesie, is a happy-go-lucky free spirit who defies all parental authority in an amusing and delightful way. When Aunt Bea arrives to visit the family, Janell is asked by her mother to refrain from her make-believe play. But Neesie, being irrepressible, intrudes herself upon the scene, creating a delicate situation for all. When Janell's first day at school leads to the formation of new and real friendships, she returns home to find that Neesie has mysteriously disappeared—the need for her existence having faded away." Interracial Bks for Children Bul

"It is a warm, delightful family story. The children and Aunt Bea speak comfortably in rich and lively conversation which reflects shades of the Black vernacular English. This gives the book a special flavor. Illustrations of the children with corn-rowed hair, Mama's afro, and Aunt Bea's hair pulled back into a bun with hat atop reveal a cultural difference—a truth supporting integration in books, and foster honest equality in writing. The rhythm of sentence structure should make for easy and fun reading." Rdng Teacher

She come bringing me that little baby girl; illus. by John Steptoe. Lippincott 1974 unp illus $8.95   **E**

1 Brothers and sisters—Fiction 2 Infants—Fiction 3 Blacks—Fiction
ISBN 0-397-31586-4   LC 74-8104

"For Kevin, who had wanted a baby brother, the arrival of his pink-shawled baby sister proved a bitter disappointment. Not only was she the wrong sex, she also cried too much, had too many wrinkles to look new, and most provoking of all she occupied everyone's attention. How he changed his opinion about his sister is developed in a sensitive first-person text, complemented and extended by the poignant, darkly brilliant, three-color illustrations. A familiar situation handled with rare charm, culminating in a visual and verbal paean to familial love." Horn Bk

Gretz, Susanna

Teddy bears 1 to 10; written and illus. by Susanna Gretz. Follett 1969 unp illus $5.95, lib. bdg. $5.97   **E**

1 Counting 2 Teddy bears—Fiction
ISBN 0-695-88460-3; 0-695-48460-5   LC 68-9563

This book is "simple, and childlike. Each pair of pages has a readily evocative phrase and a teddy-bear picture, beginning with 'I teddy bear' and the

Gretz, Susanna—*Continued*

furry toy pictured on the opposite page. And then,
'2 old teddy bears,' '3 dirty old teddy bears,' '4
teddy bears in the wash.' A restful, unpretentious
counting book in soft warm colors." Horn Bk
   Several other books about these teddy bears are
also available from Follett:
The bears who stayed indoors $5.95, lib. bdg. $5.97
(ISBN 0-695-80178-3; 0-695-40178-5; LC 76-118919)
The bears who went to the seaside $4.95, lib. bdg.
$5.97 (ISBN 0-695-80375-1; 0-695-40375-3; LC 72-
86763)
Teddybears abc $6.95, lib. bdg. $6.99 (ISBN 0-695-
80540-1; 0-695-40540-3; LC 74-15416)

Gurney, Nancy

   The king, the mice and the cheese, by
Nancy and Eric Gurney. Beginner Bks. 1965
63p illus $3.95, lib. bdg. $4.99   E

   1 Mice—Fiction 2 Animals—Fiction
   ISBN 0-394-80039-7; 0-394-90039-1   LC 65-21212

   "I can read it all myself"
   Also available in a bilingual Spanish-English edition, ilb. bdg. $5.99 (ISBN 0-394-91600-X and in a
bilingual French-English edition for $3.50, lib. bdg.
$5.99 (ISBN 0-394-80172-3; 0-394-90173-8)
   The king loves to eat cheese, but unfortunately
so do the mice. When the royal food supply is
raided by the mice, the king calls on his wise men
and on the animals of the kingdom for a solution
to the problem

Haas, Irene

   The Maggie B. Atheneum Pubs. 1975 unp
illus lib. bdg. $9.95   E

   1 Boats and boating—Fiction
   ISBN 0-689-50021-1   LC 74-18183

   "A Margaret K. McElderry book"
   "Maggie wishes for a boat which she could captain, 'with someone nice for company,' and since
she wishes on the North Star, of course her wish
is granted. For company, she has her baby brother,
James, a tidy farm on deck, a snug cabin and a
whole day of sailing, singing sea chanteys, playing
with James and keeping everything ship-shape."
Pub W
   "Irene Haas's illustrations elevate this simple
story into a fanciful adventure. The flavorful text
suffers from an occasional rhythmic jolt, though
never a serious enough one to shatter the reverie.
Black and white brush drawings alternate with full
color paintings, which, like a homespun patchwork quilt, are handsome rather than exquisite,
cluttered with intriguing patterns and details." NY
Times Bk Rev

Hader, Berta

   The big snow, by Berta and Elmer Hader.
Macmillan Pub. Co. 1948 unp illus $6.95,
pa $2.50   E

   1 Animals—Pictorial works 2 Winter
   ISBN 0-02-737910-8; 0-02-043300-X   LC 48-10240

   Awarded the Caldecott Medal, 1949
   This book shows "the birds and animals which
come for the food put out by an old couple after a
big snow." Hodges. Bks for Elem Sch Libraries
   "There is no real story but children will enjoy
the animals' busy preparation for winter and the
book catches some of the excitement of the first
snowfall." Christian Sci Monitor
   "Both the coloured and black and white pictures
are descriptive. . . . They carry through the feeling
of the story in a dignified and enjoyable way."
Ontario Library Rev

Hall, Donald

   Ox-cart man; pictures by Barbara Cooney.
Viking 1979 unp illus $8.95   E

   1 New England—Fiction
   ISBN 0-670-53328-9   LC 79-14466

   Awarded the Caldecott Medal, 1980
   "It is fall and a farmer loads a cart with the
year's produce, journeys to market, sells, buys,
and returns to his family to begin the year's work
anew. The journey, and the ensuing year, unfold
at a stately pace against the rich 19th-century
New England backdrop alive with the subtly changing colors and activities of the succeeding seasons."
Sch Library J

   "The stunning combination of text and illustrations, suggesting early American paintings on wood,
depict the countryside through which [the farmer]
travels, the jostle of the marketplace, and the
homely warmth of family life." Horn Bk

Hamilton, Morse

   My name is Emily [by] Morse and Emily
Hamilton; pictures by Jenni Oliver. Greenwillow Bks. 1979 unp illus $6.95, lib.
bdg. $6.67   E

   1 Runaways—Fiction 2 Sisters—Fiction 3 Fath-
     ers—Fiction
   ISBN 0-688-80181-1; 0-688-84181-3   LC 78-4537

   "Emily has run away—but not very far—and as
the story opens, she's back in her front yard again.
The man in the yard is kind and friendly, but he's
not at all sure that Emily really is his little girl.
In the course of the tongue-in-cheek questioning
which follows, Emily's father reveals that he understands her feelings about her demanding baby
sister. At that point, Mother appears on the porch
with baby Kate. Emily's identity is confirmed,
and everyone happily enters the house for dinner."
Sch Library J
   "Warmth and empathy permeate this comfortably told tale, reflected in the autumn-soft illustrations that add touches of humor." Booklist

Handforth, Thomas

   Mei Li. Doubleday 1938 unp illus $6.95, lib.
bdg. $7.90   E

   1 China—Fiction 2 Fairs—Fiction
   ISBN 0-385-07401-8; 0-385-07639-8   LC 38-27994
   Awarded the Caldecott Medal, 1939
   The story "tells of Mei Li, a little girl of North
China, and her day at the Fair in the town and of
her part in all the doings along with her brother
San Yu, his kitten Igo and her thrush, until at the
end of a long day she goes riding home on a camel
just in time to greet the Kitchen God at midnight
on New Year's Eve." Horn Bk
   "This gay, brief story, with its really wonderful
big black and white drawings, illustrated by [the
author] will give children a wealth of clear, simple
impressions of traditional Chinese life. . . . [It is
an] original and artistic picture book." Sat Rev

Hautzig, Deborah

   The handsomest father; pictures by Muriel
Batherman. Greenwillow Bks. 1979 47p illus
$5.95, lib. bdg. $5.71   E

   1 Parent and child—Fiction 2 School stories
   ISBN 0-688-80214-1; 0-688-84214-3   LC 78-21277

   " Greenwillow Read-alone book"
   The author "broaches a subject which has surely
concerned some apprehensive children: 'Will "my"
dad measure up at the school day for fathers?'
Although Marsha expects to be embarrassed by
her dad's manners or appearance (she even plays
sick on the big day), she is helped by a friend's
uncritical acceptance of her own parent. By the
end of the day, Marsha concludes that her dad is
truly 'The Handsomest Father.'" Sch Library J
   "The illustrations are simple, subdued and
lightly colored line drawings . . . the story is
direct, ingenuous without being too cute, and
lightly amusing." Chicago. Children's Bk Center

Hazen, Barbara Shook

   The gorilla did it; illus. by Ray Cruz.
Atheneum Pubs. 1974 unp illus $6.95, pa $1.95   E

   1 Gorillas—Fiction
   ISBN 0-689-30138-3; 0-689-70438-0   LC 73-84828

   "An imaginary ape interrupts the boy's nap, and
together they make a wreck of his room, to his
mother's annoyance. She can hardly believe him
when he lays the blame on a gorilla she can't see."
Sat Rev
   "The absolute pitch of familiarity in the dialog
and line drawings, which contrast the huge, inno-
cent-but-destructive gorilla in blue with everything
unimagined in black and white, makes a picture
book humorously tuned into a child's fantasy friend
without making fun of it. The child could pass for
boy or girl, and the mommy is archetypal: plenty
of room for identification here." Booklist
   Another book about the imaginary gorilla is:
Gorilla wants to be the baby. Atheneum Pubs.
$6.95 (ISBN 0-689-30654-7; LC 78-5972)

Hazen, Barbara S.—*Continued*

Where do bears sleep? Illus. by Ian E. Staunton. Addison-Wesley 1970 42p illus lib. bdg. $7.95 **E**

1 Sleep—Poetry
ISBN 0-201-02801-8   LC 70-88686

"A charming 'good-night' picture book tells where different animals take their rest and, at the end, where a child sleeps." Booklist
"The print is large, with the animal's name in a contrasting color, so that the book is visually dramatic as well as informative." Sat Rev

Why couldn't I be an only kid like you, Wigger; pictures by Leigh Grant. Atheneum Pubs. 1975 unp illus $7.95, pa $1.95 **E**

1 Family life—Fiction
ISBN 0-689-30488-9; 0-689-70460-7   LC 75-8973

"Lucky Wigger, an only child, never has to give way to the demands of brothers and sisters, accept hand-me-downs, or stay at home when his parents go out because taking him along is 'cheaper than getting a sitter.' As these advantages are enumerated by an envious friend who envisions such a life as a perpetual delight, Wigger's impressions of the same situations are depicted as somewhat less ideal. The two differing views are presented in a brisk, running commentary complemented by expressive pen-and-ink drawings." Horn Bk

Heide, Florence Parry

The shrinking of Treehorn; drawings by Edward Gorey. Holiday House 1971 unp illus lib. bdg. $6.95 **E**

ISBN 0-8234-0189-8   LC 78-151753

Treehorn spends an unhappy day and night shrinking. Yet when he tells his mother, father, teacher and principal of his problem they're all too busy to do anything about it. To Treehorn's great relief he finally discovers a magical game that restores him to his natural size, but then he starts turning green!
This "is an imaginative little whimsy, whose sly humor and macabre touches are perfectly matched in Edward Gorey's illustrations." Bk World

Heilbroner, Joan

This is the house where Jack lives; illus. by Aliki. Harper 1962 62p illus lib. bdg. $7.89 **E**

1 Nonsense verses
ISBN 0-06-022286-7   LC 62-7311

"An I can read book"
"A city apartment building is the setting for this modern version of the old cumulative nonsense rhyme about Jack and his house." Cincinnati
"The illustrations are gay and humorous, echoing in the drawings the cumulative parts of the rhyme." Chicago. Children's Bk Center

Heyward, Du Bose

The country bunny and the little gold shoes; as told to Jenifer; pictures by Marjorie Flack. Houghton 1939 unp illus lib. bdg. $7.95, pa $2.95 **E**

1 Rabbits—Fiction 2 Easter—Fiction
ISBN 0-395-15990-3; 0-395-18557-2   LC 39-8350

This is an Easter story for young readers which grew out of a story the author has told and retold to his young daughter. It is of the little country rabbit who wanted to become one of the five Easter bunnies, and how she managed to realize her ambition
"It is really imaginative and well written. It ought to be read to little children. . . . The colored pictures are just right too." New Yorker

Hill, Elizabeth Starr

Evan's corner; illus. by Nancy Grossman. Holt 1967 unp illus lib. bdg. $6.95, pa $1.45 **E**

1 Blacks—Fiction 2 Family life—Fiction
ISBN 0-03-015056-6; 0-03-080123-0   LC 66-10110

"Creating a haven in a corner of [his family's] . . . crowded apartment brought real satisfaction to Evan only after he shared his talent for decoration with brother Adam." Top of the News

"Despite the author's purposeful earnestness, an appealing little [black] boy emerges in the simple, sensitive storytelling. Abundant illustrations—done in soft water colors—present vivid, warmly sympathetic views of Evan and his life at home and in the city's restless, kaleidoscopic streets." Horn Bk

Himler, Ronald

Wake up, Jeremiah. Harper 1979 unp illus $7.95, lib. bdg. $7.89 **E**

1 Sun—Fiction
ISBN 0-06-022323-5; 0-06-022324-3   LC 77-25679

"Jeremiah senses something urging him to wake up. . . . Leaping into his clothes, he tumbles downstairs, outside, across the dewy grass, over a wall, to the top of a hill. He arrives just in time. Jeremiah stands still, reveling in the miracle as he watches the sun rise. Then he runs home, up the stairs again and nito his parents' bedroom to report the exciting news; It is the beginning of a new day." Pub W
day." Pub W
"All of the paintings are in full color, an impressionistic sort of realism reminiscent of Andrew Wyeth. The pictures and words combine to portray simply and joyfully the wonder of a common miracle." Sch Library J

Hirsh, Marilyn

Potato pancakes all around; a Hanukkah tale; written and illus. by Marilyn Hirsh. Bonim Bks. 1978 unp illus $6.95 **E**

1 Hanukkah (Feast of Lights)—Fiction
ISBN 0-88482-762-3   LC 78-17927

"A combination of joke, recipe, and traditional Hanukkah scenario, this tells of peddler Samuel's arrival in a village on the first night of the holiday. For the family who receives him as a guest, he makes potato pancakes 'from a crust of bread,' with appropriate additions suggested by various household members. The drawings in yellow and brown are clumsier than Hirsh's usual work, particularly in facial expressions, but there is humor in the dialogue and libraries needing Hanukkah material . . . will use this." Booklist

Hoban, Lillian

Arthur's Christmas cookies; words and pictures by Lillian Hoban. Harper 1972 63p illus $6.95, lib. bdg. $7.89 **E**

1 Chimpanzees—Fiction 2 Christmas—Fiction
3 Baking—Fiction
ISBN 0-06-022367-7; 0-06-022368-5   LC 72-76496

"An I can read book"
When Arthur decides to make Christmas cookies for his parents, a "disastrous mistake in the ingredients makes the cookies inedible but the story ends happily when Arthur turns them into holiday decorations." Pub W
The characters are chimpanzees but "are endearingly like human children. Their conversation is realistically childlike, as are their actions. The Christmas setting is appealing, the plot has problem, conflict, and solution yet is not too complex for the beginning independent reader, and the simplicity and humor make the book an appropriate one for reading aloud to preschool children also." Chicago. Children's Bk Center
Some other books about Arthur are also available from Harper:
Arthur's honey bear $6.95, lib. bdg. $7.89 (ISBN 0-06-022369-3; 0-06-022370-7; LC 73-14325)
Arthur's pen pal $6.95, lib. bdg. $7.89 (ISBN 0-06-022371-5; 0-06-022372-3; LC 75-6289)
Arthur's prize reader $6.95, lib. bdg. $7.89 (ISBN 0-06-022379-0; 0-06-022380-4; LC 77-25637)

The sugar snow spring; words and pictures by Lillian Hoban. Harper 1973 39p illus $5.95, lib. bdg. $6.89 **E**

1 Mice—Fiction 2 Easter—Fiction
ISBN 0-06-022333-2; 0-06-022334-0   LC 72-9866

"Everett Mouse didn't come back from a food-hunting expedition, so son Oscar must try to get grain and straw for the expected new baby's bed. When things look their grimmest, an Easter Rabbit rescues and reunites the family." Chicago
"Pale blue, green, and yellow drawings complement the appealing story which will be enjoyed by young animal lovers." Sch Library J

Hoban, Russell

Bedtime for Frances; illus. by Garth Williams. Harper 1960 unp illus $6.95, lib. bdg. $7.89, pa $1.95   E

1 Badgers—Fiction
ISBN 0-06-0223502; 0-06-022351-0; 0-06-44305-7
                                     LC 60-8347

"A little badger with a lively imagination comes up with one scheme after another to put off going to sleep but father badger proves himself as smart as his daughter." Bookmark

"Nothing at all unusual in this story—but Mr. Williams was inspired to make Frances a small round appealing badger, with kindly badger parents, although badgers are not mentioned in the text. The soft humorous pictures of these lovable animals in human predicaments are delightful." Horn Bk

Some other books about Frances are also available from Harper:

A baby sister for Frances $6.95, lib. bdg. $7.95 pa $1.95 (ISBN 0-06-022335-9; 0-06-022336-7; 0-06-443006-5; LC 64-15154)

A bargain for Frances $6.95, lib. bdg. $7.89, pa $1.95 (ISBN 0-06-022329-4; 0-06-022330-8; 0-06-444001-X; LC 70-80533)

Best friends for Frances $6.95, lib. bdg. $7.89, pa $1.95 (ISBN 0-06-022327-8; 0-06-022328-6; 0-06-443008-1; LC 71-77935)

A birthday for Frances $6.95, lib. bdg. $7.89, pa $1.95 (ISBN 0-06-022338-3; 0-06-022339-1; 0-06-443007-3; LC 64-24321)

Bread and jam for Frances $6.95, lib. bdg. $7.89 (ISBN 0-06-022359-6; 0-06-022360-X; LC 64-19605)

Dinner at Alberta's; pictures by James Marshall. Crowell 1975 unp illus $6.95, lib. bdg. $6.89   E

1 Crocodiles—Fiction 2 Etiquette—Fiction
ISBN 0-690-23992-0; 0-690-23993-9   LC 73-94796

"Arthur, the smallest member of the crocodile family, has atrocious table manners. Badgering by the family doesn't help until he is invited to Alberta's house for dinner. How Arthur is helped to learn appropriate social graces is exceedingly funny and will delight all who urge children to reform their manners." Children's Bk Rev Serv

"Other illustrators have worked successfully with Russell Hoban, but it would be hard to envision a better matching of text and illustration than he and James Marshall achieve here. The pictures have a rakish flair that fits the sensible nonsense of the story admirably; the crocodile characters have a seriocomic blandness. . . . Arthur's week of practicing table manners is hilarious, and if he's meant to teach a lesson to the audience, they won't mind knowing about it." Chicago. Children's Bk Center

Another book about Arthur is: Arthur's new power. Crowell $6.95, lib. bdg. $6.89 (ISBN 0-690-01370-1; 0-690-01371-X; LC 77-11550)

Emmet Otter's Jug-Band Christmas; pictures by Lillian Hoban. Parents Mag. Press [dist. by Four Winds] 1971 unp illus $3.95, lib. bdg. $3.99   E

1 Otters—Fiction 2 Christmas—Fiction
ISBN 0-590-17707-9; 0-590-07707-4   LC 76-117560

A "story of a poor Otter family, young Emmet and his widowed mother, and of their determination to give each other a very special present for Christmas. Although their plans don't quite turn out as expected, they are rewarded with something more special than any present." Pub W

"A warm, unsentimental story with expressive, old-fashioned colored illustrations." Booklist

How Tom beat Captain Najork and his hired sportsmen; illus. by Quentin Blake. Atheneum Pubs. 1974 unp illus $7.95, pa $1.95   E

ISBN 0-689-30441-2; 0-689-70444-5   LC 74-75573

Tom's aunt, Miss Fidget Wonkham-Strong, disapproves of his constant fooling around and calls in Captain Najork and his hired sportsmen to teach Tom a lesson. But Tom beats them at their own games

"The story and Quentin Blake's pictures are a combination of originality and hilarity, from start to quirky close." Pub W

Another book about Tom and Captain Najork is: A near thing for Captain Najork. Atheneum Pubs. lib. bdg. $7.95 (ISBN 0-689-30503-6; LC 75-29464)

The little Brute family; pictures by Lillian Hoban. Macmillan Pub. Co. 1966 unp illus $5.95, pa $1.95   E

1 Family life—Fiction
ISBN 0-02-744110-5; 0-02-043650-5   LC 66-16102

"A family of five disagreeable Brutes and their unpleasant home life are happily transformed when Baby Brute brings home a little lost good feeling which he finds wandering around in a field of daisies. The beguiling story and pictures present a lesson in human relationships which is both funny and meaningful to small children." Booklist

Another book about the Brute family is: The stone doll of Sister Brute. Macmillan Pub. Co. $3.50 (ISBN 0-02-744080-X; LC 68-12089)

The Mole family's Christmas; pictures by Lillian Hoban. Four Winds 1980 unp illus lib. bdg. $8.95   E

1 Moles (Animals)—Fiction 2 Christmas—Fiction
ISBN 0-590-07774-0   LC 72-77788

A reprint of the 1969 edition published by Parents Mag. Press

"An amusing story of a mole family who, through the efforts of their enterprising son, receive the gift of a telescope from the fat man in the red suit which enables them to see the stars. Engaging illustrations add to the charm and appeal of the book." Booklist

Nothing to do; pictures by Lillian Hoban. Harper 1964 32p illus lib. bdg. $7.89   E

1 Opossums—Fiction
ISBN 0-06-022390-1   LC 64-18575

"Walter Possum, like most other young children, can never think of anything to do until his father gives him a magic something-to-do stone. A useful lesson is lightly veiled in this slight but pleasing story that second-graders can read for themselves." Sch Library J

"Walter Possum and his little sister Charlotte have those human qualities that make the behavior of Frances the badger child [in Bedtime for Frances, entered above] so engaging and self-reflecting for young listeners." Horn Bk

The sorely trying day; pictures by Lillian Hoban. Harper 1964 unp illus lib. bdg. $7.89   E

1 Family life—Fiction
ISBN 0-06-022421-5   LC 64-11836

"Poor, weary father, after 'a sorely trying day,' came home to a commotion of brawling children, misbehaving pets, and a distraught mother. One by one the guilty characters repented, confessed, and submitted to a week's punishment . . . and peace and contentment were restored." Horn Bk

A "burlesque of the Victorian moral tale. . . . Delightfully illustrated." Chicago. Children's Bk Center

Hoban, Tana

Big ones, little ones. Greenwillow Bks. 1976 unp illus $6.75, lib. bdg. $6.48   E

1 Animals—Pictorial works
ISBN 0-688-80040-8; 0-688-84040-X   LC 75-34440

"There is no text in this picture book, just two black-and-white photographs facing each other of a parent and offspring (sometimes both parents) of polar bear, hippo, sheep, baboon, zebra, elephant, horse, giraffe, pig, elk and camel families, as well as the peahen and peachick, duck and duckling. A final page does have small pictures of each with printed identification above; otherwise, the appealing pictures speak for themselves." Appraisal

"On the whole, children will find the pictures engrossing and the book a good starter toward identifying fellow creatures." Booklist

Circles, triangles and squares. Macmillan Pub. Co. 1974 unp illus $6.95   E

1 Size and shape
ISBN 0-02-744830-4   LC 72-93305

"There is no division of the material into sections and no text here, simply a series of photographs in which the three most familiar geometric

Hoban, Tana—*Continued*

forms occur. Often more than one shape appears in the photograph." Chicago. Children's Bk Center
"An imaginative exercise for the development of visual awareness." Horn Bk

Count and see. Macmillan Pub Co. 1972 unp illus $6.95, pa. $2.25   **E**

1 Counting
ISBN 0-02-744800-2; 0-02-043640-8   LC 72-175597
"A counting book that moves from 1 to 15, then —in tens—to 50, and then to 100. The left hand pages are black, with large numerals and the number-word in white, and with large white dots to corroborate the counting. The right hand pages are clear photographs in black and white, all objects that are easy to recognize: 4 children, 8 windows, 12 eggs in a carton, 15 cookies on a baking sheet, 40 peanuts, 100 peas in their pods, ten per pod." Chicago. Children's Bk Center
"The texture of the photographs, the vivid capturing of small objects, and the graphic excellence of its design make the book outstanding in comparison with the many dismal, unattractive counting books in print." Horn Bk

Is it red? Is it yellow? Is it blue? An adventure in color. Greenwillow Bks. 1978 unp illus $7.95, lib. bdg. $7.63 (k-2)   **E**

1 Color 2 Size and shape
ISBN 0-688-80171-4; 0-688-84171-6   LC 78-2549
"The author-photographer captures scenes from everyday life in vibrant hues. On the first page the six basic colors are identified in circles—red, yellow, blue, orange, green, and purple. The wordless book is simply designed and opens the eye to the marvelous world of color; each stark-white page contains one photograph which nearly fills it. In the bottom margin the predominant colors in the photograph are indicated by a row of corresponding circles; for instance beneath a picture of a cut watermelon are circles of red and green. The circles not only emphasize the color but make the viewer aware of the varied textures and shapes in the photographs; thus, a close-up of a grinning jack-o'-lantern becomes also an abstract composition of curves, triangles, and squares. The book is not a random hodgepodge of photographs—color, movement, and theme are subtly controlled." Horn Bk

Look again! Macmillan Pub. Co. 1971 unp illus $6.95   **E**

1 Nature photography
ISBN 0-02-744050-8   LC 72-127469
"This captivating book of photographs invites the reader to look once through a two-inch cut-out square at a pattern or portion of something larger. On the next page, the complete picture of the object is revealed. On the verso of the second page is another view of the object. And so, as each set is displayed, one is impelled to look again and again and again. This unusual and exciting book is one that should not be missed." Wis Library Bul

One little kitten. Greenwillow Bks. 1979 unp illus $7.50, lib. bdg. $7.20   **E**

1 Cats—Fiction 2 Stories in rhyme
ISBN 0-688-80222-2; 0-688-84222-4   LC 78-31862
This is a "picture book that has a rhyming text and that presents some concepts of position (inside, behind, through). . . . [A] kitten wakes and plays, hides, pounces on string, investigates some shoes, and decides it's time to retire; '. . . It's getting late. Will they wait? Hug me tight. Good-night-goodnight,' the book ends as the kitten and its siblings snuggle up to a mother cat. Not substantial, but appealing." Chicago. Children's Bk Center

Over, under & through, and other spatial concepts. Macmillan Pub. Co. 1973 unp illus $6.95   **E**

1 Vocabulary
ISBN 0-02-744820-7   LC 72-81055
In brief text and photographs, the author depicts several spatial concepts—over, under, through, on, in, around, across, between, beside, below, against, and behind
"Children who are confused by these concepts may need help understanding that many of the pictures illustrate more than one concept. However,

both the photographs and the format, with the words printed large on broad yellow bands at the beginning of each section, are uncluttered and appealing." Booklist

Push pull, empty full; a book of opposites. Macmillan Pub. Co. 1972 unp illus $6.95, pa $1.95   **E**

1 English language—Synonyms and antonyms
ISBN 0-02-744810-X; 0-02-043600-9   LC 72-175597
Brief text and black and white photographs illustrate fifteen pairs of opposites—push pull, empty full, wet dry, in out, up down, thick thin, whole broken, front back, big little, first last, many few, heavy light, together apart, left right, and day night
"Most of the meanings are immediately apparent from the pictures although some children may have difficulty with thick (elephants) and thin (flamingos)." Booklist

Shapes and things. Macmillan Pub. Co. 1970 unp illus $6.95   **E**

1 Size and shape
ISBN 0-02-744060-5   LC 70-102965
This book, without text, contains photograms—photographs made without a camera by placing an object in direct contact with light-sensitive photographic paper. The author's purpose is to introduce new ways of seeing and to present the understated beauty of pure shape
"It is a book through which a small child may wish to browse, alone or with a friend to share the pleasure of recognizing simple things by their shapes. . . . The objects, white on black, are almost wholly in silhouette, although there are hints of shadow. Some of the pages are almost blunt: a single apple. Some are arranged in patterns on a theme: tools, sewing things, kitchen utensils. Very attractive, useful for discussion, good for stirring perceptual acuteness." Sat Rev

Where is it? Macmillan Pub. Co. 1974 unp illus $5.95   **E**

1 Rabbits—Fiction 2 Easter—Fiction 3 Stories in rhyme
ISBN 0-02-744070-2   LC 73-8573
In this story in rhyme, illustrated with photographs, a rabbit searches for its own Easter basket full of garden vegetables
The author's "photography here is outstanding. . . . The type is large and the scanning lines short while some end words rhyme—all factors considered helpful to the decoding practice of the youngest readers as well as older reluctants." Sch Library J

Hoff, Syd

Barkley. Harper 1975 32p illus $6.95, lib. bdg. $7.89   **E**

1 Dogs—Fiction 2 Circus—Fiction
ISBN 0-06-022447-9; 0-06-022448-7   LC 75-6290
"An Early I can read book"
"Barkley, an aging circus dog, has had a long career doing tricks—until one day the four dogs on his back become a painful load. His owner retires him and Barkley walks away from the circus. But he is missed and reinstated, because he is needed to teach tricks to young dogs." Horn Bk
"The story is a pleasant diversion on an ever-popular subject and Hoff's familiar cartoon-like characters will entice children to read the simple text." Sch Library J

Danny and the dinosaur; story and pictures by Syd Hoff. Harper 1958 64p illus $6.95, lib. bdg. $7.89, pa $1.95   **E**

1 Dinosaurs—Fiction
ISBN 0-06-022465-7; 0-06-022466-5; 0-06-444002-8   LC 58-7754

Also available in a Spanish language edition lib. bdg. $7.89 (ISBN 0-06-022469-X; LC 69-14450)
"An I can read book"
The story is "about an amiable dinosaur who leaves his home in the museum to stroll about town and play with Danny, a small boy who loves dinosaurs. The dinosaur talks (of course) to Danny's friends and plays games with them, visits the zoo, goes to a baseball game and enjoys, with a beatific smile, an ice cream cone." Chicago. Children's Bk Center

Hoff, Syd—*Continued*

"The bold, humorous, colored pictures convey the imaginative story of the wonderful day the dinosaur steps out of the museum to play with Danny [and share his exploits around town]. Because of the simple vocabulary and sentence structure, first-graders can actually read this story." Library J

Hogrogian, Nonny

Apples. Macmillan Pub. Co. 1972 unp illus $4.95

E

1 Stories without words
ISBN 0-02-744010-9   LC 71-146626

A "picture book without words, the plot slight but clear. Two children and some animals cross, in turn, a green and sunny landscape, discarding their apple cores. One by one, apple trees spring up until the pages are filled with trees bearing ripe fruit. . . . In the end the apple vendor (who was seen at the beginning) is picking apples and filling his cart." Chicago. Children's Bk Center

"The tender greens and blues make a charming background for the steady progression of characters that move with the rhythm of a piece of music. One must not look too closely for a story line because the story is not so important as is the experience of viewing the book." Horn Bk

Carrot cake. Greenwillow Bks. 1977 unp illus $7.25, lib. bdg. $7.20

E

1 Rabbits—Fiction 2 Marriage—Fiction
ISBN 0-688-80061-0; 0-688-84061-2   LC 76-17628

Illustrated by the author
"A rabbit and his bride are presented as ecstatic honeymooners, at first. But when the excitement of the wedding and setting up their new home abates, the couple find it hard to communicate. Mr. Rabbit gets very chatty and bossy while the lady gives her husband confused answers to all his remarks. Finally, she has had enough of his arrogance. . . . Their first quarrel has salubrious results. The ending of the delightful book shows the pair sharing a treat, carrot cake, and arriving at decisions based on mutual respect as well as love." Pub W

"Although the story has the repetition and the incongruous humor of a folk tale, the conclusion seems a bit limp. The modest, soft-colored illustrations, however, strike a delicate balance with the text; and the result is a nicely integrated picture book." Horn Bk

Holland, Viki

We are having a baby; photographs by the author. Scribner 1972 unp illus lib. bdg. $7.95, pa $2.95

E

1 Brothers and sisters—Fiction 2 Infants—Fiction
ISBN 0-684-12809-8; 0-684-16012-9   LC 70-179441

"A warm, gently reassuring photo-story narrated by four-year-old Dana chronicles her reactions to the birth of her brother from her curiosity about the baby before he is born to her moments of jealousy, uncertainty, and pride after Mother and the baby return home from the hospital. Except for a rather superfluous dream sequence, the photographs of Dana, her parents, the hospital, and the baby seem completely natural. No pictures of the actual birth are included though one lovely photograph shows Dana's mother breast-feeding the baby while Dana watches intently at her shoulder." Booklist

Hosie's alphabet; pictures by Leonard Baskin; words by Hosea, Tobias & Lisa Baskin. Viking 1972 unp illus lib. bdg. $6.95

E

1 Alphabet
ISBN 0-670-37958-1   LC 76-190716

Hosie was three when he asked his father to draw this alphabet for him. He, his mother and his brother have chosen such unusual phrases as: G, a ghastly, garrulous gargoyle, to go along with the pictures

"A stunning book that is definitely not the pedantic and traditional alphabet book. The ear will enjoy the unusual tongue-tantalizing words and the eye will delight in the beauty and variety of illustrations. The graphic design in the painting and in the printing is dramatic and in complete harmony with the short text consisting of words that, though they are out of the ordinary and not in the day to day vocabulary of small children, will tickle their senses and pique their curiosity." Top of the News

Hughes, Shirley

David and Dog. Prentice-Hall [1978 c1977] unp illus lib. bdg. $7.95

E

1 Toys—Fiction 2 Brothers and sisters—Fiction
ISBN 0-13-197301-0   LC 77-27070

First published 1977 in England with title: Dogger

"David's stuffed toy, Dog, is his favorite companion and accompanies him wherever he goes. On one family outing, 'David and Dog' become separated and Dog winds up for sale at a booth at the school fair. David finds Dog, but too late—a little girl has just purchased him and refuses to relinquish him. David's sister Bella comes to the rescue by trading a newly-won teddy bear for Dog, and all ends happily." Sch Library J

"Dramatic intensity is scaled to a preschooler's emotions; the backdrop of the story's climax is a busy panorama of side shows, costume parades, and amateur athletic events. As the economical text develops the relationship between the central characters, the detailed full-color illustrations delineate the urban English setting and complement the homely plot. A subtle, balanced, and loving portrayal which touches the core of family relationships without sounding forced or contrived." Horn Bk

George the babysitter. Prentice-Hall [1977 c1975] unp illus lib. bdg. $6.95

E

1 Baby sitters—Fiction
ISBN 0-13-352682-8   LC 77-4833

First published 1975 in England with title: Helpers

"George comes to babysit for a mother of three who works afternoons in this engaging picture book by one of England's most eminent children's book illustrators. The deft, realistic paintings have fine use of line and color, and the simple story describes, with understated humor, the vicissitudes of the daily round, as George copes with a disorderly kitchen and bedroom, three lively children, and a procession of chores. The children help, but when Mother comes home and wonders how George could have managed without them, Hughes pictures an exhausted George slumped in an armchair, hand pressed to harried brow." Chicago. Children's Bk Center

Moving Molly. Prentice-Hall [1979 c1978] unp illus lib. bdg. $7.95

E

1 Moving, Household—Fiction
ISBN 0-13-604587-1   LC 78-16732

First published 1978 in England
"Molly is too little for school when her family moves from the city to a new house in the country. Mum is busy painting and papering. When Dad's at home, he's working hard on the garden. Molly's brother Patrick and sister Joanie are engaged in various pursuits also, so the youngest child is alone, mostly, and wistful. She ventures into the yard next door, through a break in the fence, and finds deserted plants to care for, a pride of cats to watch in a jungly place and other interests. Best of all, Molly finds friends next door, when twins her age move into the empty house." Pub W

"The illustrations showing comfortable family life are very English in appearance but universal in appeal and add immeasurably to the warm, simple story." Horn Bk

Hurd, Edith Thacher

Johnny Lion's book; pictures by Clement Hurd. Harper 1965 63p illus lib. bdg. $7.89

E

1 Lions—Fiction
ISBN 0-06-022706-0   LC 65-14490

"An I can read book"
"A small lion, told to stay home and read his new book while his parents are out hunting, reads about another small lion. Less dutiful than the reader, the lion cub in the book wanders off and is later put to bed early. Johnny Lion pretends to his parents that he has strayed, but quickly informs them that he has really stayed home and read his book." Chicago. Children's Bk Center

The "book-within-a-book technique is admirably handled, though it may be a bit sophisticated for the youngest readers without some guidance. More experienced readers . . . will enjoy the gay pictures and understand the central idea that adventures in a book are almost as exciting and interesting as real ones." NY Times Bk Rev

Some other books about Johnny Lion are also available from Harper:

Johnny Lion's bad day lib. bdg. $7.89 (ISBN 0-06-022708-7; LC 78-85035)
Johnny Lion's rubber boots lib. bdg. $7.89 (ISBN 0-06-022710-9; LC 70-183165)

Hurd, Edith T.—*Continued*

Last one home is a green pig; pictures by Clement Hurd. Harper 1959 63p illus lib. bdg. $7.89 **E**

1 Ducks—Fiction 2 Monkeys—Fiction
ISBN 0-06-022716-8   LC 59-8972

"An I can read book"
"A duck and a monkey use many ingenious means of transportation when they race each other home." Hodges. Bks for Elem Sch Libraries
An "excellent use of green and tan watercolor wash and bold black figures on white background plus well spaced type make a most attractive format." Library J

Hutchins, Pat

Changes, changes. Macmillan Pub. Co. 1971 unp illus $5.95, pa 95¢ **E**

1 Toys—Fiction 2 Dolls—Fiction 3 Stories without words
ISBN 0-02-745870-9; 0-02-043770-6   LC 70-123133

"Bright colored building blocks and wooden dolls create their own adventures and solve their own problems as they progress from house to fire engine, to barge, to truck, to locomotive, and back home." Top of the News
"Another book for the very young child who delights in 'reading' by himself, the lack of text amply compensated for by the bright, bold pictures and the imaginative use of blocks and two stiff little dolls." Chicago. Children's Bk Center

Clocks and more clocks. Macmillan Pub. Co. 1970 unp illus $6.95 **E**

1 Clocks and watches—Fiction 2 Time—Fiction
ISBN 0-02-745860-1   LC 74-102966

"A quaint old gentleman, Mr. Higgins, in a neat little cutaway house, is shown in simple drawings with elaborate detail. To check his grandfather clock, he buys another; there is a discrepancy, so he buys a third and a fourth. Still they disagree. He calls in a specialist, who goes from clock to clock, watch in hand, and pronounces them all correct. Mr. Higgins promptly buys a watch . . . 'And since he bought his watch all his clocks have been right,' the story ends. Children who are ready—or just beginning—to tell time will enjoy the fact that Mr. Higgins never sees the very obvious answer. Simply told, nicely conceived." Sutherland. The Best in Children's Bks

Don't forget the bacon! Greenwillow Bks. 1976 unp illus $7.75, lib. bdg. $7.44 **E**

1 Shopping—Fiction
ISBN 0-688-80019-X; 0-688-84019-1   LC 75-17935

The story tells of "an absent-minded child repeatedly revising a shopping list as he passes interesting objects. One item, for example, is a 'cake for tea,' but he sees, in turn, a bicyclist's cape and a man raking leaves, and the item becomes a 'cape for me,' and a 'rake for leaves.' Saying the four items over, the boy remembers the last ('. . . and don't forget the bacon') correctly—but it's the one thing he doesn't bring home. Sheer nonsense, of course." Chicago. Children's Bk Center
"A good part of this story's charm lies in its color pictures, especially shots of the child's companion, a pet dog which is shown bemused by various creatures and things it encounters on the trip." Pub W

Good-night, Owl! Macmillan Pub. Co. 1972 unp illus $7.95, pa $1.95 **E**

1 Owls—Fiction
ISBN 0-02-745900-4; 0-02-043730-7   LC 72-186355

Illustrated by the author
Owl takes revenge on the birds and the animals who have not let him sleep during the day
"The ending is perky, the pictures funny, and the simplicity and repetition of pattern in the text are encouraging for the pre-reader." Chicago. Children's Bk Center

Happy birthday, Sam. Greenwillow Bks. 1978 unp illus $7.50, lib. bdg. $7.20 **E**

1 Birthdays—Fiction
ISBN 0-688-80160-9; 0-688-84160-0   LC 78-1295

Illustrated by the author
Sam "wakes to find that being a year older hasn't changed the fact that he can't reach a light switch, or the clothes in his closet, or the tap above the sink where he'd like to play with the boat he's received as a present from his parents. Then Grandpa's present arrives; it's a small, sturdy chair, and it enables Sam to reach everything." Chicago. Children's Bk Center
"Sunny yellow and bright green predominate in this cheerfully stylized, full-color picture books, sure to be appreciated by those wishing birthdays would bring a few extra inches." Booklist

One-eyed Jake. Greenwillow Bks. 1979 unp illus $7.95, lib. bdg. $7.63 **E**

1 Pirates—Fiction
ISBN 0-688-80183-8; 0-688-84183-X   LC 78-18346

"A pirate as mean as they come, One-Eyed Jake loads his ship so full of stolen loot that to avoid sinking he tosses his cook onto a passenger ship, his bosun onto a cargo boat, and Jim the cabin boy onto a fishing boat—places, as it happened, they preferred to be anyway. The key to the cabin that Jim tosses to Jake is the scoundrel's final undoing." Children's Bk Rev Serv
"The clear, repetitious text should present no problems for early readers, and the double-page spreads done in flamboyant full color are brimming with activity and incidental details." Horn Bk

Rosie's walk. Macmillan Pub. Co. 1968 unp illus $6.95, pa $2.25 **E**

1 Chickens—Fiction 2 Foxes—Fiction
ISBN 0-02-745850-4; 0-02-043750-1   LC 68-12090

"In this diverting picture book only 33 words are used to guide the way through the [author-illustrator's] doublespread stylized pictures aglow with sunshiny colors, and even those few words are not actually needed. Rosie the hen goes for a walk around the farm and gets home in time for dinner, completely unaware that a fox has been hot on her heels every step of the way. The viewer knows, however, and is not only held in suspense but tickled by the ways in which the fox is foiled at every turn by the unwitting hen. A perfect choice for the youngest." Booklist

The surprise party. Macmillan Pub. Co. 1969 unp illus $6.95, pa 95¢ **E**

1 Animals—Fiction
ISBN 0-02-745830-X; 0-02-043760-9   LC 69-18239

Illustrated by the author
Rabbit whispers to Owl, "I'm having a party tomorrow. It's a surprise." But Owl passes the news along to Squirrel as "Rabbit is hoeing the parsley tomorrow. It's a surprise." And by the time the word has spread to each of Rabbit's friends, there are conflicting opinions as to what Rabbit is really planning to do
"Full-page, ultra-cheerful pictures in yellow, orange, and green carry this story." Sch Library J

Titch. Macmillan Pub. Co. 1971 unp illus $5.95, pa 95¢ **E**

1 Brothers and sisters—Fiction
ISBN 0-02-745880-6; 0-02-043780-3   LC 77-146622

"How does it feel to be the youngest child in the family? To have an older brother and sister who lead a more exciting life? . . . [The author] has, with a minimum of well-chosen words and bright, engaging illustrations, triumphantly related the story of a small boy who surpasses his brother and sister with one simple action." Pub W
"The amazing growth of Titch's tiny seed, planted as his share of a family project, is a satisfying conclusion to the story as well as a logical symbol of human potentiality for the many small persons who will sympathize with his position and delight in his success. Imaginative realism for preschoolers which is reassuring, but never condescending." Horn Bk

The wind blew. Macmillan Pub. Co. 1974 unp illus $6.95 **E**

1 Winds—Fiction 2 Stories in rhyme
ISBN 0-02-745910-1   LC 73-11691

"Full-color paintings illustrate a rhymed cumulative text depicting the frantic efforts of unwary pedestrians to recover possessions snatched away by a mischievous and unpredictable wind. . . . Although the brief text is a pleasant, rhythmic accompaniment to the pictures, the story can be 'read' from the doublespread illustrations. A humorous and imaginative treatment of a familiar situation." Horn Bk

Isadora, Rachel

Ben's trumpet. Greenwillow Bks. 1979 unp illus $6.95 **E**

ISBN 0-688-80194-3   LC 78-12885
1 Jazz music—Fiction 2 Black musicians—Fiction 3 Trumpet—Fiction
Illustrated by the author

"Ben, a black child, sits on the fire escape and listens to the great music from a Harlem nightclub. Coming home from school, he steps inside the Zig Zag Jazz Club to watch the musicians pratice. ... Ben admires all the players but most of all the trumpeter, 'the cat's meow.' The boy pretends he's playing, and becomes disconsolate when other kids taunt him because he has no trumpet. But the musician from the Zig Zag takes an interest in Ben and we leave him as he's learning to blow sweet music." Pub W

"The art is astonishingly varied in its brilliant re-creation—in the margins, in the urban backgrounds—of the commercial art of the 20's and 30's: silhouettes, black and white keyboards, dominos and zig-zags, Art Deco razzmatazz. The author succeeds in her evident ambition to make us see the music of a jazz trumpet, but she accomplishes this while capturing the realistic tenement world and family friends of a black city child in a checked poor-boy cap. A first-rate picture book." NY Times Bk Rev

Max; story & pictures by Rachel Isadora. Macmillan Pub. Co. 1976 unp illus $5.95 **E**

1 Baseball—Fiction 2 Ballet—Fiction
ISBN 0-02-747450-7   LC 76-9088

Max "is the star of his baseball team. On a Saturday morning, he has time to spare before his game and accepts (with some hidden disdain) the invitation of his sister, Lisa, to watch her ballet class in action. Max is surprised to find himself interested and happy to join the students at their teacher's suggestion. ... The experience pays off at the ball park where Max hits a home run. Now he warms up for the game each week at Lisa's dancing class. The pictures are an ebullient combination of grace and comedy, with the leggy students dipping and soaring, in contrast to Max in his uniform." Pub W

Willaby. Macmillan Pub. Co. 1977 unp illus $6.95 **E**

1 School stories 2 Drawing—Fiction
ISBN 0-02-747460-7   LC 77-4469
Illustrated by the author

This is the "story of a first grader who likes to draw. Her understanding teacher recognizes her talent in this area and silently encourages her interest even though she would rather draw than play or do her math. When the teacher is absent due to illness, Willaby says 'get well' by drawing a picture of a fire truck on her card and then forgets to sign her name on the drawing. Willaby is embarrassed and makes other get well cards for Miss Finney, but when she arrives at school on Monday, she finds a thank you note on her desk." Children's Bk Rev Serv

"Lighthearted charcoal sketches portray Willaby's predicament—of having a gift that is sometimes a blessing and sometimes an embarrassment—with humor and tenderness and provide an engaging view of a happy classroom setting." Sch Library J

Iwasaki, Chihiro

A new baby is coming to my house. McGraw [1972 c1970] unp illus lib. bdg. $5.95 **E**

1 Brothers and sisters—Fiction 2 Infants—Fiction
ISBN 0-07-032075-6   LC 70-39317
First published 1970 in Japan

"A gentle story about a little girl awaiting the arrival of her new baby brother and her mother home from the hospital. She plans many things to do with him and is surprised to find he is so tiny. Instead of the usual disappointment, she only cries. 'I want to hold him.He is my very own brother.' The delicate watercolors match the gentle nature of the story." Adventuring With Bks

Jaques, Faith

Tilly's house; written and illus. by Faith Jaques. Atheneum Pubs. 1979 unp illus lib. bdg. $9.95 **E**

1 Dolls—Fiction
ISBN 0-689-50138-2   LC 78-31105

"A Margaret K. McElderry book"

"Tilly, the dollhouse's long-suffering kitchen maid, endures endless drudgery and constant nagging from Cook. Fed up, she walks out, determined to find a place of her own. With the help of her umbrella she rappels down the side of the chest and negotiates each stair until she reaches the lower floor. There she meets Edward, the teddy bear, who, after a number of unworkable suggestions, locates the perfect place for Tilly to set up housekeeping and helps her renovate an old box on the greenhouse shelf into her own cheerful home." Booklist

"The enticing watercolors that show every step in Tilly's emancipation are half the joys in a remarkable fantasy." Pub W

Jeffers, Susan

Wild Robin; retold and illus. by Susan Jeffers. Dutton 1976 unp illus lib. bdg. $8.95 **E**

1 Fairy tales
ISBN 0-525-42787-2   LC 76-21343

"The artist has retold a story from 'Little Prudy's Fairy Book' by Sophie May [pseudonym of Rebecca Sophia Clarke], a story which was loosely based on the well-known folk tale 'Tamlane.' A sly, disobedient boy ran away from home when even his loving sister Janet lost patience with his wild ways. He was captured by the fairies and, although he led a carefree life, he became lonely and homesick. Finally, from an elf whose 'little stone heart was touched,' Janet learned the spell which would free him, and she bravely rescued him." Horn Bk

"The text is short. The story is stated and not over-explained. The illustrations are big, graphically rendered, beautifully colored double-page spreads that catch, hold, and bring the eyes back to discover small details and to re-examine and interpret facial expressions." Sch Library J

Jensen, Virginia Allen

What's that? [By] Virginia Allen Jensen [and] Dorcas Woodbury Haller. Collins [distributed by Philomel Bks.] [1979 c1977] 23p illus pa $9.95 **E**

1 Blind, Books for the 2 Size and shape—Fiction
ISBN 0-399-20760-0   LC 78-8613
Original Danish edition, 1977. This translation first published 1978 in England

"While someone reads, the child with his fingertips explores the raised surfaces on each set of facing pages. ... Little Rough, who 'lives on a straight path in a circle with Long Rough and Wide Rough' looks for his friend, Little Shaggy, who lives in a triangle with Big Shaggy. Little Shaggy has run off, and in his search Little Rough is joined by friends of other textures—the Littles, Spot, Stripe and Smooth." NY Times Bk Rev

"A 'picture' book designed for blind and partially sighted children who are not old enough to read braille. Printed in black on bright yellow (the best combination for partially sighted children), with all the pictures feelable, blind children finally have a book that they can share with sighted children and with their parents. It is a marvelous idea, one that is executed with a great deal of care and skill. ... It is spiral-bound." Children's Bk Rev Serv

Jewell, Nancy

Bus ride; pictures by Ronald Himler. Harper 1978 32p illus lib. bdg. $7.89 **E**

1 Buses—Ficton 2 Travel—Fiction
ISBN 0-06-022842-3   LC 76-58689

"Janie goes by bus at night to visit her grandfather who, she knows, will be waiting at the depot near his country home. Her parents see her safely on the bus, but the child is apprehensive at traveling alone, in spite of their attentions and knowing her grandfather will meet her at the end of the journey. Fortunately, motherly Mrs. Rivers senses Janie's fears and sits beside the girl. The trip becomes an adventure, with Mrs. Rivers sharing treats of food and pointing out fascinations in the changing landscape." Pub W

"Ms. Jewell gets right inside this child and makes you go back into your own childhood to remember one of those lonesome journeys of your own. The black-and-white illustrations by Himler depict real people and real feelings in a quiet and honest way that encourages you to pause and to look, as well as to read this well-put-together book." Babbling Bookworm

Johnson, Crockett

Harold and the purple crayon. Harper 1955 unp illus $5.95, lib. bdg. $6.89   **E**

ISBN 0-06-022935-7; 0-06-022936-5   LC 55-7683

Illustrated by the author

This story describes the "fantasy of a small boy who decides to go for a walk one night. He uses his purple crayon to draw all the things necessary for a successful walk—a moon, a path, houses, the ocean, a boat, a mountain, a balloon, and finally his own room again. Imaginative children (the book is not for the literal-minded child, or adult) can appreciate Harold's adventures, and they may even be tempted to imitate his drawings on the nearest flat surface. . . . Nursery school teachers and parents should find this a book that is fun to use with children to stimulate them in their own imaginative adventures." Chicago. Children's Bk Center

Some other books about Harold are also available from Harper:

Harold's ABC lib. bdg. $6.89 (ISBN 0-06-022956-X; LC 63-14444)

Harold's circus lib. bdg. $6.89 (ISBN 0-06-022966-7; LC 59-5318)

Harold's trip to the sky lib. bdg. $6.89 (ISBN 0-06-022986-1; LC 57-9262)

A picture for Harold's room $6.95, lib. bdg. $7.89 (ISBN 0-06-023005-3; 0-06-023006-1; LC 60-6372)

Johnston, Tony

Night noises, and other Mole and Troll stories; pictures by Cyndy Szekeres. Putnam 1977 63p illus lib. bdg. $6.29   **E**

1 Friendship—Fiction   2 Moles (Animals)—Fiction   3 Fairies—Fiction

ISBN 0-399-61016-2   LC 76-3553

"A See and read book"

The four "stories are about Mole's wishes which his friend Troll promises to fulfill, a rainy ending to a happy visit, a loose tooth, and mysterious night noises. Cyndy Szekeres' soft, amusing, and expressive sketches blend in nicely with the text." Sch Library J

Joslin, Sesyle

Brave Baby Elephant; pictures by Leonard Weisgard. Harcourt 1960 unp illus $4.95   **E**

1 Elephants—Fiction

ISBN 0-15-211598-6   LC 60-10245

The author "tells a story of a baby elephant who makes all kinds of preparations for a journey which turns out to be simply a trip upstairs at bedtime." Pub W

"Small children will be beguiled by the stylized colored pictures and by the suspense engendered as Baby Elephant readies himself . . . for his big adventure, the nature of which is not revealed until the end of the story. The animals are tenderly humanized in both the story and illustrations." Booklist

Another book about Baby Elephant is: Baby Elephant and the secret wishes. Harcourt $6.50 (ISBN 0-15-205156-2; LC 62-14244)

Kahl, Virginia

The Duchess bakes a cake; written and illus. by Virginia Kahl. Scribner 1955 unp illus lib. bdg. $7.95   **E**

1 Cake—Fiction   2 Stories in rhyme

ISBN 0-684-12313-4   LC 55-14215

"The Duchess lived happily with her Duke and thirteen daughters until one day she became bored and decided to bake a 'lovely light luscious delectable cake.' It was light, all right—so light that it rose almost to the sky and took the Duchess up with it. After vainly trying to bring her down with cannon shot and arrows, the people gave up and decided she would simply have to remain on top of the cake. Then the baby Gunhilde began crying for her supper—and there was the solution." Chicago. Children's Bk Center

"A fine nonsense story, told in lively rhymes and illustrated with bright pictures." Hodges. Bks for Elem Sch Libraries

Another book about the Duchess is: Plum Pudding for Christmas. Scribner lib. bdg. $8.95 (ISBN 0-684-12427-0; LC 56-9283)

How do you hide a monster? Scribner 1971 unp illus lib. bdg. $8.95   **E**

1 Sea monsters—Fiction   2 Stories in rhyme

ISBN 0-684-12318-5   LC 73-143926

Illustrated by the author and written in rhymed verse, this is a story about Phinney, a friendly sea serpent, who almost lost his life when he was mistaken for a frightful monster

"Offers spontaneous, amusing rhymes in an original plot." Horn Bk

Kalan, Robert

Blue sea; illus. by Donald Crews. Greenwillow Bks. 1979 unp illus $6.95, lib. bdg. $6.67   **E**

1 Size and shape—Fiction   2 Fishes—Fiction

ISBN 0-688-80184-6; 0-688-84184-6   LC 78-18396

"On a deep-blue background, the words 'blue sea' appear in a paler shade and then the first of Crew's eye-filling paintings, 'little fish,' in bright yellow. While Kalan keeps his text to an irreducible minimum, the pictures increase in color and complexity. Big green fish takes out after the wee swimmer. Bigger magenta fish chases both. Biggest orange fish follows, with jaws agape to swallow the first three. But biggest, bigger and big can't get through holes in a series of snares that the tiny yellow hero slips into and out of. So the final page of this cheerful charmer is the same as the first: 'blue sea,' 'little fish.' " Pub W

Rain; illus. by Donald Crews. Greenwillow Bks. 1978 unp illus $7.95, lib. bdg. $7.63   **E**

1 Rain and rainfall

ISBN 0-688-80139-0; 0-688-84139-2   LC 77-25312

Brief text and illustrations describe a rainstorm, beginning with a blue sky, yellow sun and white clouds being replaced by gray sky and rain and ending with a bright rainbow-spanned scene

Kantrowitz, Mildred

Willy Bear; illus. by Nancy Winslow Parker. Parents Mag. Press [distributed by Four Winds] 1976 unp illus lib. bdg. $7.89   **E**

1 Teddy bears—Fiction   2 School stories

ISBN 0-590-07781-3   LC 76-2744

"A monologue by a little boy to his teddy bear on the night before their first day of school. The boy is afraid, but pretends that it is the bear who is afraid, and talks himself out of his own misgivings." NY Times Bk Rev

"The monologue reads aloud extremely well, especially on a one-to-one basis; spare line drawings with few details in appropriate pastel shades set the mood to a tee. Bibliotherapy with bounce." Sch Library J

Kay, Helen

One mitten Lewis; illus. by Kurt Werth. Lothrop 1955 unp illus lib. bdg. $7.44   **E**

ISBN 0-688-51082-5   LC 54-7883

Lewis was the losingest little boy in town—and mostly he lost mittens. Not both mittens, of course, never a pair of them—Oh no, only one! This little story explains the solution adopted by Lewis' mother

"Entertaining could-be-true story. . . . Surprise ending." Bks for Deaf Children

Keats, Ezra Jack

Apt. 3. Macmillan Pub. Co. 1971 unp illus $8.95   **E**

1 City life—Fiction   2 Blind—Fiction

ISBN 0-02-749510-8   LC 78-123135

Set in a dingy tenement house, this book describes "the encounter of two young and lonely boys with a blind musician whose beautiful music helps them learn that communication is possible through ways other than words." Wolfe. About 100 Bks

"The subtle colors of Keats's paintings and his restrained use of detail to establish atmosphere make Apt. 3 a pleasure to look at, but it is less a story than a situation picture book." Sat Rev

Dreams. Macmillan Pub. Co. 1974 unp illus $6.95, pa $2.50   **E**

1 City life—Fiction

ISBN 0-02-749610-4; 0-02-044060-X   LC 73-15857

A "city story of a Puerto Rican boy Roberto whose paper mouse saves Archie's cat from a dog in the night when everyone else is dreaming." Children's Bk Rev Serv

Keats, Ezra J.—*Continued*

"Keats captures in brilliant oranges, blues, reds, and greens the sense of a hot, steamy summer night in a densely packed big city. Children will love this book, and it will provide them with opportunity after opportunity for recounting their own experiences with the shadow world that reigns at night." Rdng Teacher

Jennie's hat. Harper 1966 unp illus $8.95, lib. bdg. $8.79   E

1 Hats—Fiction
ISBN 0-06-023113-0; 0-06-023114-9   LC 66-15683
"Jennie is counting on a new hat from her aunt—and dreaming of its beauty. A very plain hat comes, and after unsuccessful attempts to make herself a hat, Jennie goes to church in the drab one. In the interval she has fed her friends the birds, and they save the day by flying down and trimming the hat for her." Sat Rev

This fantasy "has a sense of freshness, of spring, about it. Attractive, colorful pictures [by the author] make most telling use of collage." Christian Sci Monitor

The snowy day. Viking 1962 32p illus lib. bdg. $7.95, Penguin pa $2.25   E

1 Snow—Fiction
ISBN 0-670-65400-0; 0-14-050182-7   LC 62-15441
Awarded the Caldecott Medal, 1963
A small "boy's ecstatic enjoyment of snow in the city is shown in vibrant pictures. Peter listens to the snow crunch under his feet, makes the first tracks in a clean patch of snow, makes angels and a snowman. At night in his warm bed he thinks over his adventures, and in the morning wakens to the promise of another lovely snowy day." Moorachian. What is a City?

"It is refreshing to have a natural story in which only the illustrations show that Peter is a Negro child." Library J

A mood "picture book which is outstanding for [the author-illustrator's] adroit use of vivid colors and interesting 'cutpaper' shapes. . . . These [are] bold drawings. This is a perfect book for the nursery school age as well as for those in kindergarten and first grade." Pub W

Some other books about Peter and his friends are:
Goggles! Macmillan Pub. Co. $6.95, pa $2.25 (ISBN 0-02-749590-6; 0-02-044100-2; LC 70-78081)
Hi, cat! Macmillan Pub. Co. $6.95, pa $1.95 (ISBN 0-02-749600-7; 0-02-044120-7; LC 71-102968)
A letter to Amy. Harper $8.95, lib. bdg. $8.79 (ISBN 0-06-023108-4; 0-06-023109-2; LC 68-24329)
Pet show! Macmillan Pub. Co. $5.95, pa $2.25 (ISBN 0-02-749620-1; 0-02-044070-1; LC 73-156843)
Peter's chair. Harper $8.95, lib. bdg. $8.79 (ISBN 0-06-023111-4; 0-06-023112-2; LC 67-4816)
Whistle for Willie. Viking lib. bdg. $7.95, Penguin pa $2.25 (ISBN 0-670-76240-7; 0-14-050202-5; LC 64-13595)

Kellogg, Steven

Can I keep him? Story and pictures by Steven Kellogg. Dial Press 1971 unp illus $7.50, lib. bdg. $6.46, pa $1.95   E

1 Pets—Fiction
ISBN 0-8037-0988-9; 0-8037-0989-7; 0-8037-1305-3   LC 72-142453
"Lonely Arnold wants a playmate but his mother objects to every one he suggests—grandma is allergic to cat fur, bears have a disagreeable odor, pythons shed their skins which clog the vacuum cleaner, and so on." Booklist

"Finely detailed pictures of Arnold's real and imagined pets and an amusing, cumulative storyline." Library J

Much bigger than Martin; story and pictures by Steven Kellogg. Dial Press 1976 unp illus $5.95, lib. bdg. $5.47, pa $1.95   E

1 Brothers—Fiction
ISBN 0-8037-5809-X; 0-8037-5810-3; 0-8037-5811-1   LC 75-27599
"All the frustrations of being younger and smaller than an older sibling come pouring out in this humorous treatment of a very real problem. Henry doesn't like being Martin's little brother when he's victim in games, gets the smallest piece of cake, or finds the basketball loop too high for his shots. Stretching and watering himself doesn't help, while eating a lot of apples only makes him sick; there seems to be no remedy. . . . [The author] adds an ingenious twist to his

ending—Henry makes stilts! The imagination scenes, where Henry perceives himself as a giant towering over Martin, are where Kellogg's touches of subtle humor and whimsical detail are most effective. The black line drawings are washed in hues of gold, green, and blue." Booklist

The mysterious tadpole. Dial Press 1977 unp illus $6.95, lib. bdg. $6.46, pa $2.50   E

1 Pets—Fiction
ISBN 0-8037-6245-3; 0-8037-6246-1; 0-8037-6244-5   LC 77-71517
The author "describes the problems Louis has in finding accommodations for his tadpole Alphonse. Sent by Uncle McAlister, Alphonse has grown gargantuan. Not until he uses his ability as a retriever (Louis has shown him a picture of a pirate treasure ship) and dives for loot in a sunken ship, can Alphonse have a suitable home; Louise builds him a large swimming pool. . . . Alphonse, by the way, has been caught by Uncle McAlister in Loch Ness." Chicago. Children's Bk Center

"Humor, emphasized by an understated text, vibrates through Kellogg's expressively detailed black line drawings awash in mellow colors. The cohesively integrated text and illustrations will lead to a thoroughly enjoyable picture book experience." Booklist

The mystery of the missing red mitten; story and pictures by Steven Kellogg. Dial Press 1974 unp illus $4.95, lib. bdg. $4.58, pa $1.50   E

ISBN 0-8037-6195-3; 0-8037-6194-5; 0-8037-5749-2   LC 73-15439
"Annie loses a red mitten and sets out to search for it with her dog, Oscar. She fantasizes about the mitten's possible fate (e.g., 'Do you think that the mouse and his family are using my mitten for a sleeping bag?' and imagins planting her remaining mitten and reaping a multitude from the resultant mitten tree. Annie's search ends when what appears to be the heart of a snowman is revealed to be the missing mitten." Sch Library J

"Kellogg's imagination extends from a clever story to captivating black-and-white drawings with accents of red. His use of a bubble to show the little girl's thoughts is perfect. And this is a perfect book for a winter day." Babbling Bookworm

Pinkerton, behave! Story and pictures by Steven Kellogg. Dial Press 1979 unp illus $7.95, lib. bdg. $7.45   E

1 Dogs—Fiction
ISBN 0-8037-6573-8; 0-8037-6575-4   LC 78-31794
"Pinkerton is a large dog modeled after the author-artist's harlequin Great Dane. He appears to be untrainable, both at home and at obedience school. Actually, he responds consistently to commands, but when he is told to fetch, he tears the newspaper to shreds; and when he is told to get the burglar, he licks the face of the dummy he is expected to destroy. One day, when a real burglar appears, Binkerton's small owner remembers the dog's idiosyncracies, commands him to fetch, and all ends well." Sch Library J

"Kellogg wittily captures expressions and movements of animal and human, wisely allowing the focal humor to emanate through the faces and action and forgoing the background detail usually found in his work. In addition, bright, lively colors and spare use of narrative blend to help make this a splendid comedic success." Booklist

Kennedy, Richard

The leprechaun's story; illus. by Marcia Sewell. Dutton 1979 unp illus $8.95   E

1 Fairy tales   2 Ireland—Fiction
ISBN 0-525-33472-6   LC 79-11410
"A Unicorn book"
"When a jaunty tradesman caught a leprechaun at his cobbling, he demanded his reward of a pot of gold, which would be his as long as he did not take his eyes off the leprechaun. The creature tried to distract him by warning him of imaginary impending disasters and leading him over obstacles which demanded attention—all to no avail, however. The leprechaun then told a long, circumstantial, progressively more and more woeful story of a poor widow with five starving children, finally reducing the tradesman to closing his eyes in tears." Horn Bk

"The lilting prose of this picture book fits in nicely with its Irish setting and theme. . . . The drawings are charming, but the predominant color

Kennedy, Richard—*Continued*

is an unfortunate shade of lime-green. The story
is a typical one of Irish lore. . . . It is none the
less appealing for its familiar theme." Children's
Bk Rev Serv

Kepes, Juliet

Five little monkeys; story and illus. by
Juliet Kepes. Houghton 1952 32p illus lib.
bdg. $6.95, pa $2.25   **E**

1 Monkeys—Fiction
ISBN 0-395-19112-2; 0-395-26688-2   LC 52-6898

Picture story book about five little monkeys
living in the jungle who learn a valuable lesson
through their capture of Terrible, the Tiger

The author's "prose is uneven, sometimes stilted,
sometimes every expressive but it is her pictures
which carry the fun and suspense of the story.
Hers is a never-never jungle, as imaginative as
Rousseau's, where lion and tiger and African tiger and
Indian nilgai meet and all of them are portrayed
with a brilliant handling of design and color." NY
Times Bk Rev

Kessler, Leonard

Here comes the strikeout. Harper 1965 64p
illus (A Sports I can read bk) $6.95, lib.
bdg. $7.89, pa $1.95   **E**

1 Baseball—Fiction
ISBN 0-06-023155-6;0-06-023156-4;0-06-444011-7
         LC 65-10728

Also available in a Spanish language edition, lib.
bdg. $7.89 (ISBN 0-06-023154-8)

"A delightful book for beginning independent
readers, the engaging illustrations showing Willie,
the friend and mentor of the strikeout king
(Bobby, a white boy), to be Negro. Bobby, in
despair because his batting is weak, tries Willie's
lucky hat. No luck! Then Willie coaches Bobby,
who practices and practices and finally gets a hit
—no instant success, but a combination of hard
work and encouragement from Willie. The home
attitude is good, too." We Build Together

Another book about Willie and Bobby, in which
they help another child overcome swimming problems. is: Last one in is a rotten egg. Harper lib.
bdg. $7.89 (ISBN 0-06-023158-0; LC 69-10209)

Kick, pass, and run. Harper 1966 64p illus
(A Sports I can read bk) $6.95, lib. bdg. $7.89,
pa $1.95   **E**

1 Football-Fiction
ISBN 0-06-023159-9; 0-06-023160-2; 0-06-444012-5
         LC 66-18656

"Football rules and terms are tackled in easy-to-
read, easy-to-remember terms and reinforced by
the illustrated glossary that follows the comic
story of animal teams imitating the Giants and the
Jets." Best Bks for Children, 1968

"May [also] appeal to the older reluctant reader."
Hodges. Bks for Elem Sch Libraries

Another book about the animals, in which they
hold their own Olympic games, is: On your mark,
get set, go! Harper $6.95, lib. bdg. $7.89 (ISBN
0-06-023152-1; 0-06-023153-X; LC 72-76516)

Kingman, Lee

Peter's long walk; pictures by Barbara
Cooney. Doubleday 1953 47p illus lib.
bdg. $4.95   **E**

ISBN 0-385-07747-5   LC 52-11010

"Because he had been assured that when he was
five and went to school in the village he would
have someone to play with, lonely Peter was off
to the village the morning after his fifth birthday
before his mother was even awake. Small children who share Peter's eagerness to start school
will be captivated by the little boy's surprising
experiences from farm to village and home again.
The story is told with appealing repetition and
rhythm and the pictures capture the feeling of
spring in the country and the essence of childhood." Booklist

Klein, Norma

Girls can be anything; illus by Roy Doty.
Dutton 1973 unp illus. lib. bdg. $7.95, pa $2.50
     E

1 Women—Employment—Fiction   2 Sex role—
Fiction
ISBN 0-525-30662-5; 0-525-45029-7   LC 72-85258

"Marina and Adam are best friends but the little
girl rebels at always performing traditional female
roles in their games. She has to be a nurse while
Adam plays doctor, stewardess while he pilots a
jet, and first lady when he's president. With the
encouragement of her parents, Marina convinces
Adam that she too could be a doctor (after all,
her own aunt is a famous surgeon), a pilot, and
even, some day, president." Pub W

"The cartoon-like illustrations in red, white, and
blue make the point with a smile, and the dialog
could be heard anywhere around the block." Booklist

Knight, Hilary

Where's Wallace? Story and panoramas by
Hilary Knight. Harper 1964 40p illus $8.95,
lib. bdg. $8.79   **E**

1 Orangutans—Fiction
ISBN 0-06-023170-X; 0-06-023171-8   LC 64-19717

"A kindly zookeeper cooperates with Wallace, a
little orangutan who likes to explore the city
occasionally. Detailed color spreads invite readers
and listeners to find Wallace in unlikely places."
Hodges. Bks for Elem Sch Libraries

Knotts, Howard

Great-Grandfather, the baby and me; a
story and pictures by Howard Knotts.
Atheneum Pubs. 1978 30p illus lib. bdg. $6.95
     E

1 Infants—Fiction   2 Brothers and sisters—Fiction   3 Grandfathers—Fiction
ISBN 0-689-30656-3   LC 78-2940

"When Daddy goes away to bring Mommy and
the new baby home, the boy is upset. So, he goes
to Great-Grandfather for comfort and solace. Great-
Grandfather tells the boy a story of his own youth
when he once rode many miles just to see a new
baby. As the story ends, Daddy, Mommy, and the
new baby have arrived, and the boy has decided
that he is happy to see all of them." Sch Library J

"The exchange is full of warmth, and Grandfather's reminiscences constitute a most interesting story within a story. Most pleasurable, though,
is the sense of love between the two and how it
works to cure some very real feelings. Illustrated
with black-and-white pencil sketches that are full
of light hatching for a soft, somewhat delicate
look that matches the story well." Booklist

The winter cat; story and pictures by
Howard Knotts. Harper 1972 32p illus $6.95,
lib. bdg. $6.89   **E**

1 Cats—Fiction   2 Winter—Fiction
ISBN 0-06-023166-1; 0-06-023167-X   LC 72-26525

"A winsome, wild gray cat is homeless and nameless but enjoying his freedom until he sees a
strange new sight: snow. Though he grows daily
colder and more hungry, he still refuses the neighborhood children's offers of food and friendship.
They leave him scraps of food and, after a while,
he begins to trust them. At last, the children coax
him into their house and 'Homer' gets a name
and a home after all." Pub W

"Illustrations of small, precise figures in black,
white, and grey convey the snow-wrapped stillness
of winter in a simply written book that has a
sedate and gentle text." Chicago. Children's Bk
Center

Krahn, Fernando

The biggest Christmas tree on earth. Little
1978 unp illus lib. bdg. $5.95   **E**

1 Christmas—Fiction   2 Stories without words
ISBN 0-316-50309-6   LC 78-9824

"An Atlantic Monthly Press book"

"A story told in pictures alone shows a girl
whose ball rolls into the hollow of a tree. She
follows it and is hoisted up to a work chamber,
fitted out with an artificial tail like the squirrels
who are decorating the tree; she helps pull out
birds' tail feathers to decorate the branches while
spiders hang balls on the tree. An eagle carries
her home, and all the townspeople join her in
gazing with admiration at the biggest tree in the
world." Chicago. Children's Bk Center

"A simple joyousness marks . . . [the] last
scene; readers in warm climes might also appreciate the snowless landscape." Booklist

Krahn, Fernando—*Continued*

Who's seen the scissors? Dutton 1975 unp illus lib. bdg. $5.95   **E**

1 Stories without words
ISBN 0-525-42710-4   LC 74-26857

"A rotund tailor stands tacking a lapel. His red shears rest on the cutting table beside pins and bolt. But not for long. Before the startled eyes of the tailor the scissors embark on a comically destructive flight, snipping right through anything that invites such action: the harness reins linking a horse and wagon-driver, a newspaper in the hands of its reader, a little girl's long braid, a dog's leash, and on and on until their capricious will is spent and they dutifully return to the tailor, who quickly cages the delinquent cutters. Soft pencil drawings provide a muted backdrop for the bright red scissors, whose path is made clear for the youngest followers by tiny red dots. Wordless slapstick sure to evoke some hearty chuckles." Booklist

Krasilovsky, Phyllis

The cow who fell in the canal; illus. by Peter Spier. Doubleday 1957 unp illus $6.95, lib. bdg. $7.90, pa $1.49   **E**

1 Cows—Fiction 2 Netherlands—Fiction
ISBN 0-385-07585-5; 0-385-07740-8; 0-385-08096-4
LC 56-8236

Picture story about Hendrika, a fat cow living in Holland. Hendrika loved her master and was usually content to eat a great deal and produce rich creamy milk—though she sometimes got bored. But after she fell into the canal and floated down to the distant city on a raft she was never bored again, because she had so much to think about

The artist's "watercolor illustrations are remarkable for details lovingly recalled, panoramic scenes of town and country, and colors as fresh and clean as a newly scrubbed Dutch floor." Cincinnati

The man who didn't wash his dishes; illus. by Barbara Cooney. Doubleday 1950 unp illus $6.95, lib. bdg. $7.90, pa $1.95   **E**

ISBN 0-385-07735-1; 0-385-06353-9; 0-385-13343-X
LC 50-8726

"When there were so many dirty dishes that there was no place to sit, the man set them out for the rain to wash, but thereafter he washed his dishes right after each meal." ALA Children's Service Division. Selected Lists of Children's Bks and Recordings

The man who tried to save time; pictures by Marcia Sewall. Doubleday 1979 unp illus $4.95, lib. bdg. $5.90   **E**

1 Time—Fiction
ISBN 0-385-12998-X; 0-385-12999-8   LC 77-74304

"A Reading on my own book"
"Beginners will find Krasilovsky's spacey comedy and Sewall's colorful illustrations more than worth the time spent on this Reading-On-My-Own item. Life is happy for 'the man' and his white cat who live in a cozy house. He's well liked at the office where he works, a neat and reliable employee. Then our hero gets an idea, unfortunately. To save time, he begins eating breakfast at night and sleeping in his clothes on top of his bed, buying tons of food to save extra shopping trips, overwatering his plants so they won't need attention for a spell, etc. It's not long before everything gets out of hand at home—to the dismay of his cat—and at work—to the despair of his boss. Luckily, the man sees the folly of his ways which he changes—just in time." Pub W

Kraus, Robert

Whose mouse are you? Pictures by Jose Aruego. Macmillan Pub. Co. 1970 unp illus $7.95, pa $2.25   **E**

1 Mice—Fiction 2 Stories in rhyme
ISBN 0-02-751190-1; 0-02-044160-6   LC 70-89931

In this story in rhyme, "a little mouse feeling unloved and therefore hostile toward members of his family mentally places each in a hazardous situation, heroically rescues them, and so restores himself in their affection." Booklist

"Bold drawings in pink and grey add sparkle to this simple question-and-answer text." Children's Bks, 1970

Krauss, Ruth

The carrot seed; pictures by Crockett Johnson. Harper 1945 unp illus $5.95, lib. bdg. $6.89   **E**

ISBN 0-06-023350-8; 0-06-023351-6   LC 45-4530

Simple text and pictures show how the faith of a small boy, who planted a carrot seed, was rewarded

"One of the most satisfying picture books of the year. Satisfying, that is, from the youthful viewpoint. Grownups may not understand—but that doesn't matter. . . . Crockett Johnson's pictures are perfect and the brief text is just right." Bk Week

The growing story; pictures by Phyllis Rowand. Harper 1947 unp illus $8.95, lib. bdg. $8.79   **E**

1 Growth—Fiction
ISBN 0-06-023380-X; 0-06-023381-8   LC 47-30688

"Watching the animals and plants growing through the seasons, a little boy worries considerably about his own seeming lack of growth—until he puts on last year's clothes and sees actual proof that he too has grown. The subject, the simply written text, and the detailed, stylized pictures should prove satisfying fare for little children." Booklist

A hole is to dig; a first book of first definitions; pictures by Maurice Sendak. Harper 1952 unp illus $5.95, lib. bdg. $6.89   **E**

ISBN 0-06-023405-9; 0-06-023425-3   LC 52-7731

Humorous, unexpected definitions of things and actions which have a place in the child's world. Samples: A hole is to plant a flower; A hole is to sit in; A mountain is to climb to the top; Dishes are to do; A nose is to blow; Steps are to sit on

"A revelation to grownups as to children's impressions, this could also be the basis of a wonderful game of questions and answers which would set children thinking. Maurice Sendak has illustrated it with drawings bouncing with action and good humor." NY Times Bk Rev

A very special house; pictures by Maurice Sendak. Harper 1953 unp illus $7.95, lib. bdg. $8.79   **E**

ISBN 0-06-023455-5; 0-06-023456-3   LC 53-7115

"The very special house is a house which exists in the imagination of a small boy—a house where the chairs are for climbing, the walls for writing on, and the beds for jumping on; a house where a lion, a giant, or a dead mouse is welcome, and where nobody ever says stop. Told in a chanting rhythm that demands participation by the reader; the imaginary characters, objects, and doings are pictured in line drawings almost as a child would scribble them while the real little boy stands out boldly in bright blue overalls." Booklist

Kroll, Steve

Santa's crash-bang Christmas; illus. by Tomie de Paola. Holiday House 1978 unp illus lib. bdg. $6.95   **E**

1 Christmas—Fiction 2 Santa Claus—Fiction
ISBN 0-8234-0302-5   LC 77-3025

"As if Santa Claus wasn't having a hard enough time on Christmas Eve with falling out of the sleigh, on top of the fireplace ashes, into the Christmas tree, and against the hanging chandelier, he finds a misplaced polar bear in his pack and Gerald, a stowaway elf, in his sleigh. To make matters worse, the bear charges around the house, with Santa and Gerald in pursuit, leaving chaos in their wake. Eventually, all three arrive back on the roof; with the polar bear at the reins and Santa clinging to the side, clutching Gerald's hand, they ride off across the sky. The sleeping household, however, awakes to everything in order and a houseful of presents. De Paola extracts full measure from this amusing tale with a clumsy Santa, wide-eyed elf,

Kroll, Steve—*Continued*

and lovable polar bear. The three characters are done in red, brown, and white against gray wash until the present-strewn Christmas morning scene splashes forth in full color." Booklist

Kruss, James

3x3: three by three; a picturebook for all children who can count to three; pictures by Strachan. Macmillan Pub. Co. 1965 unp illus $4.75   E

ISBN 0-02-751210-X   LC 65-10302

Original German edition published 1963

In this book animals and hunters march "smartly across the page. Three cocks crow, three cats dance, three mice look on; foxes chase chickens, cats chase mice, dogs chase foxes, and so on." Times (London) Lit Sup

"Eva J. Rubin's pictures in pseudo-old-fashioned technique scamper across the pages, adding hilarity to an already 'three times' cheery book." America

Kuskin, Karla

Roar and more. Harper 1956 unp illus $6.95, pa $1.95   E

1 Animals
ISBN 0-06-023620-5; 0-06-443019-7   LC 56-8138

A picture book showing various animals and indicating in its brief text the kind of sounds each makes

"The author-artist is well aware of the cast of humor in the youngest, and one should be warned that this could be a very noisy book at times. . . . However, purring like the cat and making bubbly sounds like the fish give balance and relief. The illustrations are simple, clear, and clever." Sat Rev

Langner, Nola

Freddy, my grandfather. Four Winds 1979 unp illus $6.95   E

1 Grandfathers—Fiction
ISBN 0-590-07577-2   LC 79-9926

"Freddy is a fiercely independent old man, a colorful character seen through the eyes of an adoring grandchild in a series of word-pictures which introduce Freddy's Hungarian roots; his talents in drawing and sewing; his best friend, Jerome, with whom he enjoys violent name-calling arguments; his lady friend, Mrs. Klug, who owns a Girdle Shop; the way he eats ('shlurping') and the way he smells ('half cigars and half lemons'); and how he gets dressed up to go out and 'combs his three long side hairs over his bald head.' Freddy, like many other grandparents, is an expert at reassuring a frightened child during a thunderstorm, and his love and affection are clearly shown in the child's glowing if jumbled description." Sch Library J

"A small girl's affection for Freddy, her grandfather, becomes apparent in her descriptions of his habits, speech, and behavior. The narrative has an ingenuous simplicity that gives a clear picture of the grandfather's personality. The black-and-white illustrations are soft and a little smudgy, but faces have character, and the softness of pencil lines emphasizes the nature of the story as a memory. Told in loving tones, this tribute leaves the reader with a warm, tender feeling." Booklist

Lapsley, Susan

I am adopted; pictures by Michael Charlton. Bradbury Press 1975 [c1974] unp illus $4.95
                                                         E

1 Adoption—Fiction
ISBN 0-87888-075-5   LC 74-22852

First published 1974 in England

"The adopted child speaks: 'My name is Charles. I am adopted. So is my sister, Sophie. She is only little. I have a tractor. It was a birthday present,' and he goes on to speak of family affairs and his friend and his rabbit and, incidentally, being adopted. That means, he ends, belonging. What emerges is an impression of a happy child who knows he is adopted, finds it mildly interesting, but is so busy with other concerns and so secure that the adoption is presented casually as one of the facts of life, not as a problem." Chicago. Children's Bk Center

"Charlton's realistic watercolour illustrations convey very nicely the warmth and security of family life." Times (London) Lit Sup

Lasker, Joe

He's my brother; story and illus. by Joe Lasker. Whitman, A. 1974 unp illus lib. bdg. $6.50   E

1 Slow learning children—Fiction
ISBN 0-8075-3218-5   LC 73-7318

A young boy describes the various experiences his slow-learning younger brother has at home and in school

"Written for youngest readers, this is humorously illustrated in alternating watercolor and black-and-white spreads. Young children will sympathize with Jamie's story even though they may not realize that the boy suffers from learning disabilities or an 'invisible handicap' as described in the author's note addressed to parents at the end of the book." Sch Library J

Lasky, Kathryn

My island grandma; pictures by Emily McCully. Warne 1979 unp illus lib. bdg. $7.95
                                                         E

1 Grandmothers—Fiction 2 Islands—Fiction
ISBN 0-7232-6159-8   LC 78-12489

"A young girl named Abbey reminisces about the fun she has with her grandmother when her family summers on a Maine island. There is no plot per se; merely a listing of activities the two share. But the character of the incidents points ·to a bond that's deep and special. . . . This is low-key, but the feeling of warmth is steady, the mood tender." Booklist

Lawrence, James

Binky brothers, detectives; pictures by Leonard Kessler. Harper 1968 60p illus (An I can read mystery) lib. bdg. $7.89, pa $1.95
                                                         E

1 Mystery and detective stories
ISBN 0-06-023759-7; 0-06-444003-6   LC 68-10374

"Although the detective business in which he and his older brother Pinky are engaged was his idea, Dinky is treated as a helper, not a partner, until he solves the mystery of the missing catcher's mitt and outsmarts Pinky as well. An agreeable story with amusing illustrations." Booklist

Followed by Binky brothers and the Fearless Four. Harper lib. bdg. $6.89 (ISBN 0-06-023761-9; LC 75-77936)

Leaf, Munro

The story of Ferdinand; illus. by Robert Lawson. Viking 1936 unp illus. lib. bdg. $6.95, Penguin pa $1.95   E

1 Bulls—Fiction 2 Bullfights—Fiction 3 Spain—Fiction
ISBN 0-670-67424-9; 0-14-050234-3   LC 36-19452

"Ferdinand was a peace-loving little bull who preferred smelling flowers to making a reputation for himself in the bull ring. His story is told irresistibly in pictures and few words." Wis Library Bul

"The drawings picture not only Ferdinand but Spanish scenes and characters as well." NY Libraries

Wee Gillis; illus. by Robert Lawson. Viking 1938 unp illus lib. bdg. $5.95   E

1 Scotland—Fiction
ISBN 0-670-75608-3   LC 38-27807

"Faced with two loyalties—to live in the Highlands and stalk stags with his father's people, or go down into the Lowlands and raise long-haired cows with his mother's people—Wee Gillis solves the problem in his sturdy Scottish way." Booklist

This "is not quite so subtle a fable as Ferdinand's but perhaps an even better story to read aloud." Sat Rev

"The drawings of Robert Lawson combine beauty and humor with a reality that makes the reader feel he has taken a trip to Scotland. With its gray plaid cover, beautifully reproduced illustrations and fine design, this is a distinguished volume." NY Times Bk Rev

Leech, Jay

Bright Fawn and me, by Jay Leech and Zana Spencer; illus. by Glo Coalson. Crowell 1979 unp illus $6.95, lib. bdg. $6.89   E

1 Cheyenne Indians—Fiction 2 Sisters—Fiction
ISBN 0-690-03937-9; 0-690-03938-7   LC 78-19215

Leech, Jay—*Continued*

"Set a century ago, the story is told by a Cheyenne child whose family is participating in an inter-tribal fair, and whose pleasure is dimmed by the fact that she is in charge of her small sister, Bright Fawn. Bright Fawn, plump and cheerful, draws fond comments from passersby, but her sister is not enchanted by the repeated remark, 'You have a fine little sister,' while she's coping with a clinging little hand, a dirty and sticky face that Bright Fawn refuses to have cleaned, and the slow, stumbling walk that's all Bright Fawn can manage. Still, when another girl echoes her comment that her little sister is a pest, she becomes irritated, and offers a protective, loving hand. Told with a sweet simplicity, the story shows the eternal and universal qualities of a sibling relationship, and it's enhanced by the illustrations, in soft earth colors, of two attractive children in varied scenes of the cheerful bustle of the fair." Chicago. Children's Bk Center

Levitin, Sonia

A sound to remember; pictures by Gabriel Lisowski. Harcourt 1979 unp illus $6.95 **E**

1 Jews—Fiction
ISBN 0-15-277248-0   LC 79-87522

"The young boy, Jacov, the butt of whispering and teasing, was a bit clumsy and slow of speech. Nevertheless, the rabbi chose to give him the hono of blowing the ram's horn on Rosh Hashanah. Jacov had imagined the notes would sound 'almost like living things, with bodies and spirits of their own,' but when the day arrived, he first brought forth only a faint crackling tone, then only a weak and trembling one, and after that, nothing. But on Yom Kippur, the rabbi himself played a shofar along with Jacov, and the two together achieved a beautiful harmony." Horn Bk
"The tone of this simple story is graceful and sedate, appropriate for the religious setting. Extensive cross-hatching gives soft texture to the black-and-white illustrations; subdued and decorous, they suit the story nicely. There's little action here, and not much in the way of characterization, but a warm sincerity pervades the slight plot and gives it strength." Booklist

Who owns the moon? Illus. by John Larrecq. Parnassus Press 1973 unp illus $6.95, lib. bdg. $5.38   **E**

1 Moon—Fiction
ISBN 0-87466-066-1; 0-87466-005-X   LC 73-77124

This is the story of three argumentative farmers, each of whom claims to own the moon, and of how the wise teacher in the valley resolves their quarrel
"The simple story basically provides a background for the illustrations, which portray boldly-shaped, blustering men, furrowed and cultivated fields, and beautiful night skies dominated by lunar light. Bright yellow and blue endpapers depicting the moon in different stages, the varied layout of pictures and text, and the composition of each illustration to fill an arch-shaped form enhance the physical appearance of the book; the rustic tones and the earthiness of the illustrations convey the comic, peasant coarseness of the story." Horn Bk
Another book about the farmers and their wives is: A single speckled egg. Parnassus Press $6.95 (ISBN 0-87466-074-2; LC 75-4189)

Levy, Elizabeth

Something queer is going on (a mystery); illus. by Mordicai Gerstein. Delacorte Press 1973 unp illus $6.95, lib. bdg. $6.46, pa $2.75   **E**

1 Mystery and detective stories
ISBN 0-40-08121-; 0-440-08122-X; 0-440-08141-6
                                     LC 72-1385

"Jill arrives home to find her dog Fletcher missing; armed with sets of identifying pictures of Fletcher from all angles, she and friend Gwen conduct a house-to-house search. The finger of guilt points to television commercial producer Fiedler Fernback, who denies knowing Fletcher before he has even seen the dog's picture. The next day the girls, accompanied by Jill's mother, follow Fernback to his television studio where they find Fletcher on camera for a dog food commercial. For the youngest mystery fans a patly plausible story with zany illustrations a la 'Mad' magazine." Booklist

Several other books in this mystery series are also available from Delacorte:
Something queer at the ballpark $6.95, lib. bdg. $6.46, pa $2.75 (ISBN 0-440-05992-5; 0-440-05993-3; 0-440-08287-0; LC 74-16332)
Something queer at the library $6.95, lib. bdg. $6.46, pa $2.75 (ISBN 0-440-08127-0; 0-440-08128-9; 0-440-08288-9; LC 76-49906)
Something queer on vacation $6.95, lib. bdg. $6.46 (ISBN 0-440-08346-X; 0-440-008347-8; LC 78-72858)

Lewis, Thomas P.

Hill of fire; pictures by Joan Sandin. Harper 1971 63p illus (An I can read history bk) $6.95, lib. bdg. $7.89   **E**

1 Mexico—Fiction 2 Paricutin (Volcano)—Fiction
ISBN 0-06-023803-8; 0-06-023804-6   LC 70-121802

"The hill of fire is Paricutin and the story . . . is about the way this volcanic eruption changes the lives of the people who lived near it, in particular the man in whose field the hill of fire began." Top of the News
"Here is basically a human story, sympathetically and expressively illustrated with simple lines and warm colors, that will give readers understanding of a people, as well as a good story based on fact." Sch Library J

Lexau, Joan M.

Benjie; illus. by Don Bolognese. Dial Press 1964 unp illus $6.95, lib. bdg. $6.46   **E**

1 Blacks—Fiction 2 Bashfulness—Fiction
ISBN 0-8037-0537-9; 0-8037-0536-0   LC 64-12294

"Benjie, a small Negro boy who lives with his grandmother in a one-room city apartment, is so painfully shy that he cannot talk to anyone, even the neighbors. But when Granny loses a favorite earring, he tries to find it, and in doing so, overcomes his shyness. The loving relationship between the child and his grandmother gives warmth and credibility to a charming, picture book." Moorachian. What is a City?
Followed by: Benjie on his own. Dial Press $6.95, lib. bdg. $6.46 (ISBN 0-8037-0712-6; 0-8037-0713-4; LC 72-102830)

Emily and the klunky baby and the next-door dog; pictures by Martha Alexander. Dial Press 1972 unp illus $5.95, lib. bdg. $5.47   **E**

1 Divorce—Fiction 2 Parent and child—Fiction
ISBN 0-8037-2309-1; 0-8037-2310-5   LC 77-181789

On a sunny winter day, when her divorced mother is too preoccupied with tax forms to notice the little girl, frustrated Emily decides to run away. She takes her baby brother and her sled, but has to contend with the next-door dog and getting lost which complicates her resolution to reach Daddy
"Joan Lexau has captured the lonely, puzzled, angry feelings of a little girl in crisis. . . . This book may be almost too real in its treatment of a whole family's frustration. The mother looks absolutely frazzled and the house seems cold, as if the heat had been turned back." Christian Sci Monitor

The homework caper; pictures by Syd Hoff. Harper 1966 64p illus (An I can read mystery) lib. bdg. $7.89   **E**

1 Mystery and detective stories
ISBN 0-06-023856-9   LC 66-11493

"The strange disappearance of Bill's missing arithmetic homework is resolved through true detective methods." Best Bks for Children, 1968
"An entertaining book for the beginning reader, illustrated with cartoon-style pictures that are very simply drawn and very funny. . . . The scenes between [Bill's friend] Ken and his baby sister are amusing . . . and the book has a happy balance of home and school episodes." Chicago. Children's Bk Center

I hate Red Rover; pictures by Gail Owens. Dutton 1979 55p illus $5.95   **E**

1 School stories 2 Grandfathers—Fiction 3 Games—Fiction
ISBN 0-525-32527-1   LC 78-12873

"A Fat cat book"
"Realistic drawings, softly shaded but precise in detail, illustrate a story for beginning independent readers. Jill, smaller than the others in her class, never is able to break through the locked hands

Lexau, Joan M.—*Continued*

of her classmates (or keep them from breaking through) and so she hates the playground game of Red Rover, hates being laughed at. Grampa, her comforter, confesses he dreads being laughed at, because he's going to get false teeth and knows he'll look ludicrous. Jill is determined to play Red Rover the right way and succeeds; when she comes to tell Grampa of her triumph, laughing, he takes his teeth out and they both laugh at that." Chicago. Children's Bk Center

I should have stayed in bed; pictures by Syd Hoff. Harper 1965 48p illus lib. bdg. $6.89
E

1 Blacks—Fiction
ISBN 0-06-023861-5   LC 65-10726

"Everything goes wrong for Sam—one day—shoes on the wrong feet, late for school, trouble with teacher—until he starts all over at lunch time. Easy and humorous, with inter-racial friendships unobtrusively portrayed." ALA Children's Serv. Div. Selected Lists of Children's Bks and Recordings

Me day; pictures by Robert Weaver. Dial Press 1971 unp illus $4.95, lib. bdg. $5.47
E

1 Birthdays—Fiction 2 Blacks—Fiction 3 Divorce—Fiction
ISBN 0-8037-5572-4; 0-8037-5573-2   LC 76-153736

"What begins as a particularly good day for Rafer quickly turns into disappointment when there is no birthday letter from his [divorced] father. But then a mysterious errand to the local store reveals a surprise that turns an ordinary birthday into a very special 'me day.'" Pub W

"Lifting the book out of the ordinary as a portrayal of a black family are the positive tone, lack of moralizing, and the heads-up attitude of the family members as they cope with the problems of a broken home. . . . The cadence of black speech is effectively incorporated in the natural-sounding dialogue, and softly shaded black-and-white illustrations skillfully depict facial expressions and reinforce the mood of the text." Sch Library J

The rooftop mystery; pictures by Syd Hoff. Harper 1968 64p illus (An I can read mystery) lib. bdg. $7.80
E

1 Mystery and detective stories 2 Blacks—Fiction
ISBN 0-06-023865-8   LC 68-16821

"A humorous mystery for beginning readers that features a Negro boy, Sam, and his well-intentioned friends, Albert and Amy Lou. Sam searches frantically for his sister's favorite doll when it is lost on moving day. Albert and Amy Lou try to help. Comical illustrations add chuckles." Keating. Building Bridges of Understanding Between Cultures

"The cartoon illustrations show the children to be both blacks and whites." NY Pub Library. The Black Experience in Children's Bks

Lindgren, Astrid

The Tomten; adapted by Astrid Lindgren from a poem by Viktor Rydberg; illus. by Harald Wiberg. Coward-McCann 1961 unp illus $6.50, lib. bdg. $5.99, pa $2.50
E

1 Winter—Fiction 2 Fairy tales
ISBN 0-698-20147-7; 0-698-30370-9;   0-698-20487-5
LC 61-1065

"Snowy farm pictures and warm scenes inside barn, sheds, and house show the Tomten, a little Swedish troll, going quietly about to the animals on cold winter nights comforting them with the promise that spring will come. The text was adapted from a nineteenth-century poem by Viktor Rydberg, and the pictures are by an outstanding Swedish painter of animals and nature. An unusual and beautiful picture book." Horn Bk

The Tomten and the fox; adapted by Astrid Lindgren from a poem by Karl-Erik Forsslund; illus. by Harald Wiberg. Coward-McCann 1966 unp illus lib. bdg. $5.89, pa $2.50
E

1 Foxes—Fiction 2 Winter—Fiction 3 Fairy tales
ISBN 0-698-30371-7; 0-698-20488-3   LC 65-25501

A story taken from an old Swedish poem

"Inside, the family celebrates around a candle-lit tree before going to bed. Outside, the snow glistens in the moonlight, and Reynard the fox creeps toward the hen house. But Tomten [the troll] guardian of all life on the farm, admonishes Reynard, satisfies his hunger with a bowl of porridge, and sends him back to his den in the forest just as the morning star brightens the sky." Horn Bk

This picture book "is set at Christmastime, although it is not a Christmas story. The text is slight but it is gently appealing. . . . The illustrations are quite lovely: soft in technique, subdued in color and mood, perfectly catching the feeling of the hushed and blue-white quiet of the countryside on a snowy night." Chicago. Children's Bk Center

Lionni, Leo

Alexander and the wind-up mouse. Pantheon Bks. [1970] c1969 unp illus lib. bdg. $6.99, pa $1.45
E

1 Mice—Fiction
ISBN 0-399-90914-3; 0-394-82911-5   LC 76-77423

Illustrated by the author

"Alexander wants to be a wind-up mouse like Willie, who is the little girl's favorite toy. A magic lizard can change him, but then he learns that Willie's key is broken and decides to turn Willie into a real mouse like himself." Adventuring With Bks. 2d edition

"The illustrations employ the same imaginative collage techniques [as the author's Frederick entered below]—less subtly perhaps, but with even richer and more spectacular effects. Tissue-paper, marbleized and patterned papers, newspaper, Japanese rice paper are some of the surfaces used to provide a brilliant background for the endearing little grey mouse who looks a lot like Frederick but has a personality all his own." Sch Library J

The biggest house in the world. Pantheon Bks. 1968 unp illus lib. bdg. $6.99
E

1 Snails—Fiction
ISBN 0-394-90944-5   LC 68-12646

"In this picture book [illustrated by the author] a small snail has a very large wish. He wants the largest house in the world. But by telling the youngster a story, his wise father helps him to see the impracticality of being encased in a magnificent monstrosity too big to move." Bk Week

Fish is fish. Pantheon Bks. 1970 unp illus lib. bdg. $6.99, pa $1.45
E

1 Fishes—Fiction 2 Frogs—Fiction
ISBN 0-394-80440-0; 0-394-82799-6   LC 78-117452

Illustrated by the author

The frog tells the fish all about the world above the sea. The fish, however, can only visualize it in terms of fish-people, fish-birds and fish-cows

"The story is slight but pleasantly and simply told, the illustrations are page-filling, deft, colorful, and amusing." Chicago. Children's Bk Center

Frederick. Pantheon Bks. 1967 unp illus lib. bdg. $6.99, pa $1.95
E

1 Mice—Fiction
ISBN 0-394-91040-0; 0-394-82614-0   LC 67-6482

"While other mice are gathering food for the winter, Frederick seems to daydream the summer away. When dreary winter comes, it is Frederick the poet-mouse who warms his friends and cheers them with his words." Wis Library Bul

"This captivating book is about a field mouse, but it sings a hymn of praise to poets in a gentle story that is illustrated [by the author] with gaiety and charm. The mice are plump little creatures with round, wondering eyes and the backgrounds of the pages echo in soft tones the appropriate colors of the seasons Frederick enjoys." Sat Rev

Inch by inch. Obolensky 1960 unp illus $7.95
E

1 Worms—Fiction 2 Birds—Fiction
ISBN 0-8392-3010-9   LC 60-14899

Also available in a French language edition (ISBN 0-8392-3028-1) and a Spanish language edition (ISBN 0-8392-3030-3) for $7.95 each

"An Astor book"

Illustrated by the author, this is a "small tale about an inchworm who liked to measure the robin's tail, the flamingo's neck, the whole of a hummingbird but not a nightingale's song." Christian Sci Monitor

Lionni, Leo—*Continued*

"This is a book to look at again and again. The semi-abstract forms are sharply defined, clean and strong, the colors subtle and glowing, and the grassy world of the inchworm is a special place of enchantment." NY Times Bk Rev

Little blue and little yellow; a story for Pippo and Ann and other children. Obolensky 1959 unp illus $7.95   **E**

1 Color—Fiction
ISBN 0-8392-3018-4   LC 59-12398
"An Astor book"
The author uses "splashes of color and abstract forms to tell the story of little blue and his friend little yellow who hugged and hugged each other until they were green—and unrecognizable to their parents." Booklist
"So well are the dots handled on the pages that little blue and little yellow and their parents seem to have real personalities. It should inspire interesting color play and is a very original picture book by an artist." NY Her Trib Bks

Swimmy. Pantheon Bks. 1963 unp illus lib. bdg. $6.99, pa $1.25   **E**

1 Fishes—Fiction
ISBN 0-394-91713-8; 0-394-82620-5   LC 63-8504
Also available in a French language edition for $3.50 (ISBN 0-394-81715-X) and a Spanish language edition, $3.50, lib. bdg. $5.69 (ISBN 0-394-81709-5; 0-394-91709-X)
"Swimmy, an insignificant fish, escapes when a whole school of small fish are swallowed by a larger one. As he swims away from danger he meets many wonderful, colourful creatures and later saves another school of fish from the jaws of the enemy." Ontario Library Rev
"To illustrate his clever, but very brief story, Leo Lionni has made a book of astonishingly beautiful pictures, full of undulating, watery nuances of shape, pattern, and color." Horn Bk

Lipkind, William

Nubber Bear; illus. by Roger Duvoisin. Harcourt 1966 unp illus $5.50   **E**

1 Bears—Fiction 2 Stories in rhyme
ISBN 0-15-257590-1   LC 66-6187
"Some of Duvoisin's most agreeable pictures grace a winning story of a little bear who creeps out of the family cave at night and ventures into the forbidden Middle Wood in search of honey. With the help of several night creatures Nubber Bear gets his honey; he also gets a spanking on his return home. Nubber is an engaging character who habitually speaks in rhyme—'If only I could be always good and still get to the Middle Wood'—and his story will arouse a sympathetic response in children. The colored illustrations mirror the action, humor, and suspense of the tale." Booklist

Little, Lessie Jones

I can do it by myself, by Lessie Jones Little and Eloise Greenfield; illus. by Carole Byard. Crowell 1978 unp illus $7.95, lib. bdg. $7.89   **E**

1 Birthdays—Fiction 2 Blacks—Fiction
ISBN 0-690-01369-8; 0-690-01375-2   LC 77-11554
"It's Mama's birthday, and Donny knows just the right plant he can get for his precious dollar. His older brother teases and offers to come with him, his mother is a bit apprehensive about his going off alone, and the assistant in the flower shop is rude. The owner of the shop, however, treats his small customer with grave courtesy, and Donny goes off to face the biggest obstacle of all, a barking dog that frightens him. When he gets home—what satisfaction he feels at Mama's joy and what pride, as he says to his brother, 'See? I told you I could do it by myself.'" Chicago. Children's Bk Center
"The story is well and simply told with enough interesting incidental detail—'[The wagon] had belonged to his father when he was a little boy, and his father had left it for him when he moved away.'—to erase a slight tendency toward wordiness. The drawings using soft pencil and charcoal lines enlivened by pale green washes are especially good at portraying emotion." Sch Library J

Lobel, Anita

The troll music; story and pictures by Anita Lobel. Harper 1966 unp illus lib. bdg. $7.89   **E**

1 Musicians—Fiction 2 Fairy tales
ISBN 0-06-023930-1   LC 66-7117
"This beautifully illustrated story involves a group of travelling musicians who played lovely music until a mischievous troll cast a spell over them while they were sleeping; then only animal sounds come from their instruments. The people run them out, but the animals like their music. Together the musicians and animals work out a plan to charm the troll, but it takes Mrs. Troll to set him straight." Bruno. Bks for Sch Libraries, 1968

Lobel, Arnold

Frog and Toad are friends. Harper 1970 64p illus $6.95, lib. bdg. $7.89, pa $1.95   **E**

1 Frogs—Fiction
ISBN 0-06-023957-3; 0-06-023958-1; 0-06-44020-6   LC 73-105492
"An I can read book"
Here are five stories, illustrated by the author, which recount the adventures of two best friends—Toad and Frog. The stories are: Spring; The story; A lost button; A swim; The letter
"Five very short stories in a direct and ingenuous style, appealing because of their ease and the familiarity of the situations, translated into animal terms. The mild humor that permeates the tales . . . adds to the value of some of the concepts obliquely presented (differences in shape and size in 'A Lost Button'; time concepts in 'Spring') and the give-and-take of a fast friendship is gently affectionate." Chicago. Children's Bk Center
Several other books about Frog and Toad are available from Harper:
Days with Frog and Toad $6.95, lib. bdg. $7.89 (ISBN 0-06-023963; 0-06-023964-6; LC 78-21786)
Frog and Toad all year $6.95, lib. bdg. $7.89 (ISBN 0-06-023950-6; 0-06-023951-4; LC 76-2343)
Frog and Toad together $6.95, lib. bdg. $7.95, pa $1.95 (ISBN 0-06-023959-X; 0-06-023960-3; 0-06-444021-4; LC 73-183163)

Grasshopper on the road; Harper 1978 62p illus $6.95, lib. bdg. $7.89   **E**

1 Locusts—Fiction 2 Animals—Fiction
ISBN 0-06-023961-1; 0-06-023962-X   LC 77-25653
"An I can read book"
"Grasshopper's journey is divided into six chapters. In each chapter he meets a different animal or animals attending to a spectrum of tasks. The chapters weave a tale of habit—doing without questioning. Grasshopper gives his need-for-change reaction to each one, but only a worm in his apple home is open to change." Children's Bk Rev Serv
"The contemporary version of the fable of the ant and the grasshopper is told in a repetitive I-Can-Read text and extended in three-color illustrations which delicately capture the grasshopper's microcosmic world view." Horn Bk

How the rooster saved the day; pictures by Anita Lobel. Greenwillow Bks. 1977 unp illus $7.50, lib. bdg. $7.44   **E**

1 Roosters—Fiction
ISBN 0-688-80063-7; 0-688-84063-9   LC 76-17602
"The story of a clever rooster who outwits a thief. Captured by a robber who plans to kill him so that, without the crowing that starts the day, there will be no light (and better working conditions for the robber), the cock protests that he is deaf. His reasons are so ludicrous that the robber is overcome with laughter; the cock cannot crow because he moos or quacks (he says) having been so much with cows or ducks. To show what he means, the robber loudly imitates a cock-crow . . . and the sun comes up." Chicago. Children's Bk Center
The author "retains the economy and pace of a well-polished traditional tale. The illustrations, brilliantly executed in tones of yellow, orange, and gray, are framed as stage settings." Horn Bk

Mouse soup. Harper 1977 63p illus $6.95, lib. bdg. $7.89   **E**

1 Mice—Fiction
ISBN 0-06-023967-0; 0-06-023968-9   LC 76-41517
"An I can read book"
Illustrated by the author

Lobel, Arnold—*Continued*

"In an effort to save himself from a weasel's stew pot, a little mouse tells the weasel four separate stories." West Coast Rev of Bks

"An artistic triumph with enough suspense, humor and wisdom to hold any reader who has a trace of curiosity and compassion. . . . The little one triumphs over the big one, and every child will rejoice. The exquisite wash drawings in mousey shades of grays, blues, greens and golds, have enough humor and pathos to exact repeated scrutiny. Like the stories, they improve with each reading." NY Times Bk Rev

Mouse tales. Harper 1972 61p illus $6.95 lib. bdg. $7.89, pa $1.95   E

1 Mice—Fiction
ISBN 0-06-023941-7; 0-06-023942-5; 0-06-444013-3
LC 72-76511

"An I can read book"
Papa Mouse tells seven bedtime stories, one for each of his sons
Contents: The wishing well; Clouds; Very tall mouse and very short mouse; The mouse and the winds; The journey; The odd mouse; The bath

"The illustrations [by the author] have soft colors and precise, lively little drawings of the imaginative and humorous events in the stories. The themes are familiar to children: cloud shapes, wishing, a tall and a short friend who observe—and greet—natural phenomena on a walk, taking a bath, et cetera." Chicago. Children's Bk Center

On the day Peter Stuyvesant sailed into town. Harper 1971 unp illus lib. bdg. $9.89   E

1 Stuyvesant, Peter—Fiction 2 New York (City)—History—Fiction 3 Stories in rhyme
ISBN 0-06-023972-7   LC 75-148420

Illustrated by the author, this is the "story of Peter Stuyvesant who, arriving in New Amsterdam in 1647, found the whole dirty place a total disgrace, and angrily set the Dutchmen to work transforming the village into a pleasant place in which to live." Booklist

"The illustrations, many framed like Dutch tiles, are done in yellow and blue and have a rhythm and humor that complement the verses exactly. The double-page spread at the end of the book—showing the future of Peter's tidy city—provides an unexpected shock of recognition." Horn Bk

Owl at home. Harper 1975 64p illus $6.95 lib. bdg. $7.89   E

1 Owls—Fiction
ISBN 0-06-023948-4; 0-06-023949-2   LC 74-2630

"An I can read book"
Five stories, illustrated by the author, describe the adventures of a lovably foolish owl

"A child reader or listener in a kind of one-upmanship over wide-eyed tufted Owl will bristle with anxiety to have him perceive what causes two bewildering bumps under the blanket at the foot of his bed. The best scope for Lobel's inventiveness in drawing is, however, the opening episode where 'poor old' Winter makes a pushy entry into Owl's home. Muted browns and greys are countered by an animation that fully reveals Owl's distresses and contentments." Washington Post Children's Bk World

Small pig; story and pictures by Arnold Lobel. Harper 1969 63p illus lib. bdg. $7.89   E

1 Pigs—Fiction
ISBN 0-06-023932-8   LC 69-10213

"An I can read book"
This "is the story of a pig who, finding the clean farm unbearable, runs away to look for mud—and ends up stuck in cement. His facial expressions alone are worth the price of the book; the illustrations, in blue, green, and gold, are a perfect complement to the story. Humor, adventure, and short, simple sentences provide a real treat for beginning readers." Sch Library J

A treeful of pigs; pictures by Anita Lobel. Greenwillow Bks. 1979 unp illus $7.95, lib. bdg. $7.63   E

1 Laziness—Fiction 2 Pigs—Fiction 3 Farm life—Fiction
ISBN 0-688-80177-3; 0-688-84177-5   LC 78-1810

"At market one day, a farmer sees a dozen little pigs for sale. To his wife's objection that raising them would mean a lot of work, the farmer replies that 'It would not be hard. We will do it together.' When the time comes to plant the corn for feeding the pigs, or to dig them a mud hole, or to carry their water, or to harvest the corn, the farmer lies in bed and promises to help when the pigs bloom in the garden, or grow on trees. Even when the farmer's wife engineers these improbable events, the farmer refuses to bestir himself until one day the pigs are gone. This loss jolts the farmer out of his lazy ways and when he vows never to return to them, his wife releases the pigs from the cellar. . . . The pictures are infused with the spirit of peasant art and the Slavic tradition." Sch Library J

"This is clearly a tale of a marriage saved by the last-minute reform of a male chauvinist pig! It has some of the best drawings I've seen from Anita Lobel . . . and the text, while not so aphoristic and subtle as that of Arnold Lobel's brilliant Frog and Toad books [entered above], is full of piggy energy and fun." NY Times Bk Rev

Lord, John Vernon

The giant jam sandwich; story and pictures by John Vernon Lord; with verses by Janet Burroway. Houghton 1973 [1972] 32p illus lib. bdg. $8.95   E

1 Wasps—Fiction 2 Stories in rhyme
ISBN 0-395-16033-2   LC 72-13578

First published 1972 in England
This is a story in rhymed verse "about the citizens of Itching Down, who, attacked by four million wasps, make a giant jam sandwich to attract and trap the insects. With dump truck, spades, and hoes the people spread butter and strawberry jam across an enormous slice of bread; then, when the wasps settle, they drop the other slice from five helicopters and a flying tractor." Booklist

"Highly amusing in the details of John Vernon Lord's illustrations. . . . The figures are deliciously grotesque their expressions wickedly accurate and the colours cheerfully vivid." Jr Bookshelf

Lowrey, Janette Sebring

Six silver spoons; pictures by Robert Quackenbush. Harper 1971 63p illus (An I can read history bk) lib. bdg. $6.89   E

1 U.S.—History—Revolution, 1775-1783—Fiction
ISBN 0-06-024037-7   LC 77-105469

This is the "story of two Colonial children who, on the eve of the Revolution, are attempting to get their Revere silver spoons through the British lines to their mother for her birthday." Pub W

"The credible plot and effectively portrayed setting make this an excellent historical story for beginning readers. Illustrated with colored drawings on almost every page." Booklist

McClenathan, Louise

My mother sends her wisdom; illus. by Rosekrans Hoffman. Morrow 1979 unp illus $7.95, lib. bdg. $7.63   E

1 Russia—Fiction
ISBN 0-688-22193-9; 0-688-32193-3   LC 79-164

"Set in old Russia, this is an original story in folk tradition. The cleverness of a peasant woman frustrates the greediness of a moneylender who refuses to accept her words of wisdom and suffers financially as a result. . . . While many books of this genre emphasize cunning and trickery, this one celebrates wisdom and ingenuity." Booklist

"The animated pictures (some pencil drawings, some full color) are realistically drawn but arranged in a fantastical way on the page, with elements spilling over or leaning against the picture frames. They have a well-ordered elaborateness and display a filigree of detail—clocks, costumes, and painted Easter eggs; samovars and domes; flora and fauna—that demands close and repeated scrutinizing." Sch Library J.

McCloskey, Robert

Blueberries for Sal. Viking 1948 54p illus lib. bdg. $7.95   E

1 Bears—Fiction 2 Maine—Fiction
ISBN 0-670-17591-9   LC 48-4955

"The author-artist tells what happens on a summer day in Maine when a little girl and a bear cub, wandering away from their blueberry-picking mothers, each mistakes the other's mother for its

McCloskey, Robert—*Continued*

own. The Maine hill-side and meadows are real and lovely, the quiet humor is entirely childlike, and there is just exactly the right amount of suspense for small children." Wis Library Bul

Another book about Sal is: One morning in Maine. Viking lib. bdg. $8.95 (ISBN 0-670-52627-4; LC 52-6983)

Burt Dow, deep-water man; a tale of the sea in the classic tradition. Viking 1963 61p illus lib. bdg. $8.95   E

1 Whales—Fiction 2 Sea stories
ISBN 0-670-19748-3   LC 62-15446

The "adventure of an old Maine fisherman, who puts to sea in a leaky dory accompanied by his giggling pet gull and who almost meets disaster in the belly of a huge whale." Atlantic

"The enchanting scenes of Durt Dow making off with his multi-colored dory into the wild, purple sea and meeting pink-mouthed whales really needs no text at all. It's a deep water voyage into art." Christian Sci Monitor

Lentil. Viking 1940 unp illus lib. bdg. $8.95   E

1 Mouth-organ—Fiction 2 Ohio—Fiction
ISBN 0-670-42357-2   LC 40-8617

Picture-story book about a small boy who could not sing, but who could work wonders on a simple harmonica, especially on the day when the great Colonel Carter returned to his home town

"Big, vigorous, amusing pictures [by the author] in black-and-white, with an Ohio small-town background." New Yorker

Make way for ducklings. Viking 1941 unp illus lib. bdg. $8.95   E

1 Ducks—Fiction 2 Boston—Fiction
ISBN 0-670-45149-5   LC 41-51868

Awarded the Caldecott Medal, 1942

"A family of baby ducks was born on the Charles River near Boston. When they were old enough to follow, Mother Duck, with some help from a friendly policeman, trailed them through Boston traffic to the pond in the Public Garden. . . . This large picture book . . . is both picturesque and amusing." Bookmark

"In a series of large lithographs [the author-illustrator] reveals his instinct for the beauty of wild life and that of the city [of Boston] and a sure knowledge of ducks and their ways. . . . There are some very beautiful drawings in this book." Horn Bk

Time of wonder. Viking 1957 63p illus lib. bdg. $8.95   E

1 Maine—Description and travel
ISBN 0-670-71512-3   LC 57-14197

Awarded the Caldecott Medal, 1958

"A summer on an island in Maine is described through the simple everyday experiences of children, but also reveals the author's deep awareness of an attachment to all the shifting moods of season and weather, and the salty, downright character of the New England people. Written in rhythmic style and occasionally rhyme, this is a fine example of illustrating and writing." Top of the News

Robert McCloskey "has succeeded in transferring his love for the island to the printed page and as you listen to his words and look at his pictures you feel that every day and every season is a 'time of wonder.' This is entirely different from any book he has done before, and he has made it a thing of great beauty." Horn Bk

MacDonald, Golden

Red light, green light; illus. by Leonard Weisgard. Doubleday 1944 unp illus $5.95   E

1 Traffic regulations
ISBN 0-385-07651-7   LC 44-8554

"The Red Light says they can't go, the Green Light says they can, as the truck and the jeep, the horse, the boy and dog, the cat and mouse go through the day, obeying signals. Even when all things are asleep, the Red Light and Green Light wink good night. Echoing the rhythm of the text are the striking oblong book's bold vivid [lithograph] drawings in sepia, red and green." Bookmark

MacGregor, Ellen

Theodore Turtle; pictures by Paul Galdone. McGraw 1955 32p illus lib. bdg. $6.95   E

1 Turtles—Fiction
ISBN 0-07-044567-2   LC 55-8289

"Whittlesey House publications"

"The story of turtle with a one-track mind. Theodore just wanted to go down town, but he couldn't seem to get ready. Every time he found one thing he needed, he mislaid another! The highly detailed drawings are cheerful in yellow and red and help make this especially nice for reading to young children." Horn Bk

Mack, Stan

10 bears in my bed; a goodnight countdown. Pantheon Bks. 1974 unp illus $2.95, lib. bdg. $3.99   E

1 Counting 2 Bears—Fiction
ISBN 0-394-82902-6; 0-394-92902-0   LC 74-151

"A small boy finds 10 bears in his bed (count 'em, 10). He demands that they 'Roll over, roll over.' The company of the bears diminishes, one by one. One 'flew out,' one 'skated out,' one 'roared out' (on a motorcycle), one 'chugged out' (on a train). All this nonsense is drolly pictured and the bemused reader gets an idea not only of subtraction but of some intriguing word usage." Pub W

McLeod, Emilie Warren

The bear's bicycle; illus. by David McPhail. Little 1975 31p illus lib. bdg. $6.95   E

1 Bears—Fiction 2 Bicycles and bicycling—Fiction
ISBN 0-316-56203-3   LC 74-28282

"An Atlantic Monthly Press book"

"Bicycle safety is demonstrated through colorful pictures leavened by a parallel set of humorous pictures of a teddy-bear-turned-real who takes the hazardous consequences of ignoring the safety rules." Rdng Teacher

McPhail, David

The bear's toothache; written and illus. by David McPhail. Little 1972 31p illus lib. bdg. $7.95   E

1 Bears—Fiction 2 Teeth—Fiction
ISBN 0-316-56312-9   LC 79-140482

"An Atlantic Monthly Press book"

"In this delightful fantasy, a small boy receives a nocturnal visit from a bear with a sore tooth. Pulling on the tooth doesn't work, eating fails to loosen it, and hitting it with a pillow breaks a lamp and wakes up father. The boy's cowboy rope is securely fastened to tooth and bedpost and, as the bear jumps out the window, the tooth finally pops out. The grateful bear then gives it to the boy to put under his pillow. The simple text is accompanied by full-page pastel pictures which are filled with action and detail and are superbly suited to this imaginative bedtime tale." Sch Library J

The train. Little 1977 32p illus $5.95   E

1 Railroads—Fiction
ISBN 0-316-56316-1   LC 76-45791

"An Atlantic Monthly Press book"
Illustrated by the author

"Just before bedtime Matthew's baby brother played with—and broke—the older boy's electric train. Matthew was certain that he could mend it; but it was late, and after listening to their father read a book about trains, both boys were tucked into bed. However, Matthew 'wasn't tired so he decided to get up and work on the train.' With a smooth transition the story slides into a dream fantasy: The conductor explained that the train was broken down; Mathew repaired and refurbished it, helped to load baggage and to punch tickets for the passengers (among whom was his own family), and assisted the fireman and the engineer. Drowsy at last, he was carried to a sleeping car—the top bunk of his own bed." Horn Bk

"The pen-and-ink illustrations, warmed with color pencil, support the text to perfection, presenting Matthew, train, and passengers with just the right mix of concrete detail and dream world alchemy." Sch Library J

Maestro, Betsy

Busy day: a book of action words, by Betsy and Giulio Maestro. Crown 1978 unp illus lib. bdg. $5.95 **E**

1 Vocabulary 2 Circus—Fiction
ISBN 0-517-53288-3 LC 77-15635

Illustrated by Giulio Maestro

"This portrays activities which might be performed during a day at the circus. Each page contains an action word with an 'ing' ending (29 in all) and an accompanying illustration which depicts circus characters or animals engaged in waking, washing, dressing, eating, working, resting, playing, sleeping, etc." Sch Library J

"The Maestros' new book is uncommonly imaginative and a source of fun for toddlers as well as an artful introduction to verbs. An amiable elephant stretches luxuriously after a good night's sleep in the first of many amusing color pictures. The kicker is that the elephant is in the top half of a pair of bunk beds. In the lower is his co-worker a mustachioed human. . . . The last picture, 'sleeping,' shows the friends snuggled in their bunks after an honest day's work." Pub W

Another book involving the clown and the elephant is: On the go: a book of adjectives. Crown lib. bdg. $5.95 (ISBN 0-517-53596-3; LC 78-25774)

Harriet goes to the circus, by Betsy and Giulio Maestro. Crown 1977 unp illus (A Number concept bk) lib. bdg. $6.95 **E**

1 Counting 2 Circus—Fiction 3 Elephants—Fiction
ISBN 0-517-52844-4 LC 76-40204

Illustrated by Giulio Maestro

"Harriet, an elephant, makes an effort to be early and is first in line, anxious to have a good seat at a circus performance. Mouse is second. Duck is third, et cetera. Owl is tenth and last, but somebody opens a door near Owl—so Owl is first and Harriet is tenth in line. But all is well: ten chairs are arranged in a circle around the ring, so everybody has a front seat." Chicago. Children's Bk Center

"This book would not be one you could read again and again to the same children. However, it accomplishes its purpose nicely by clearly defining ordinal numbers in a graphic way. The large print and superb illustrations make the book irresistible for 'picture readers.'" Children's Bk Rev Serv

Another book about Harriet is: Harriet reads signs and more signs. Crown lib. bdg. $7.95 (ISBN 0-517-54167-X)

Mahy, Margaret

The boy who was followed home; pictures by Steven Kellogg. Watts, F. 1975 unp illus lib. bdg. $5.90 **E**

1 Hippopotamus—Fiction 2 Witches—Fiction
ISBN 0-531-02834-8 LC 75-4866

In this "humorous story, Robert, for some unexplained reason, is adopted by a growing number of hippopotami. His parents are most patient with the situation until the number of hippos reaches twenty-seven. Robert's father calls in the services of a local witch to rid the boy of his rapidly growing horde of friends. The witch solves the problem in an unexpected and delightful (and not totally successful) way." Children's Bk Rev Serv

"Kellogg is in his element, drawing the perfect details and more; each picture tells a tale of its own while sweeping the story right along. Swathes of lemon yellow and pinkish lavender are balanced with lots of clean white space and fine line work. The artist's sense of the absurd has made connections with an author's experience in what appeals to children." Booklist

Maiorano, Robert

Francisco; illus. by Rachel Isadora. Macmillan Pub. Co. 1978 unp illus $7.95 **E**

1 Dominican Republic—Fiction
ISBN 0-02-762170-7 LC 78-4574

This is the "story of Francisco, whose home is in the Dominican Republic. The present-tense narrative introduces Francisco riding his donkey Duarté by the sea. After Francisco's fisherman father leaves to tend the family's sick grandmother and Francisco fails at fishing and beach-combing efforts to provide food for the family, Duarté becomes a lifesaver; by offering rides to beach-lolling tourists, Francisco will have the means to feed his family." Booklist

"Francisco's ingenuity will amuse and impress readers of this tale. The black-on-beige illustrations intrigue us, conveying a sense of the Dominican Republic—the tropical climate, foaming sea, busy markets, and economic contrasts." Children's Bk Rev Serv

Mari, Iela

The apple and the moth, by Iela and Enzo Mari. Pantheon Bks. [1970] c1969 unp illus lib. bdg. $5.99 **E**

1 Moths
ISBN 0-394-90857-0 LC 70-101180

Original Italian edition published 1969

"In an eye-catching, wordless picture book, the life cycle of a moth is clearly and simply depicted in the brightly colored, graphic illustrations. A caterpillar bores from the core of an apple through the skin, forms a cocoon on a branch, emerges in the spring as a moth, flies to a blossoming tree, and deposits another egg among the petals to begin the cycle anew." Booklist

The chicken and the egg, by Iela and Enzo Mari. Pantheon Bks. [1970] c1969 unp illus lib. bdg. $5.99 **E**

1 Chickens
ISBN 0-394-90858-9 LC 74-101181

Original Italian edition published 1969

"A book without words. The pictures, colorful and captivating, tell the story of the chicken life cycle, and they are bound to get the child to talk about them. . . . [The book] encourages the child to supply the words himself. The book will intrigue and excite most youngsters (and even some not-so-youngsters as well)." The AAAS Science Bk List for Children

Marshall, James, 1942-

George and Martha; written and illus. by James Marshall. Houghton 1972 46p illus lib. bdg. $7.95, pa $2.25 **E**

1 Hippopotamus—Fiction 2 Friendship—Fiction
ISBN 0-395-16619-5; 0-395-19972-7 LC 74-184250

In these five short episodes which include a misunderstanding about split pea soup, invasion of privacy and a crisis over a missing tooth, two not very delicate hippopotamuses reveal various aspects of friendship

"The pale pictures of these creatures and their adventures—in yellows, pinks, greens, and grays—capture the directness and humor of the stories." Horn Bk

Some other books about George and Martha are also available from Houghton:

George and Martha, encore lib. bdg. $7.95; pa $2.95 (ISBN 0-395-17512-7; 0-395-25379-9; LC 73-5845)
George and Martha, one fine day lib. bdg. $5.95 (ISBN 0-395-27154-1; LC 78-60494)
George and Martha rise and shine lib. bdg. $6.95, pa $2.25 (ISBN 0-395-24738-1; 0-395-28006-0; LC 76-14350)
George and Martha, tons of fun $6.95 (ISBN 0-395-29524-6; LC 80-13592)

The guest. Houghton 1975 38p illus lib. bdg. $5.95 **E**

1 Friendship—Fiction 2 Snails—Fiction 3 Animals—Fiction
ISBN 0-395-20277-9 LC 74-29445

"Marshall's latest heroine, Mona, is a bit difficult to classify biologically—a moose, perhaps?—but she is certainly another of his wonderfully understanding, sensitive and sophisticated creatures. One day while Mona is practicing her piano scales we meet Maurice, the snail, who is climbing up her back. Invited to stay, Maurice loves Mona's french toast, answers the phone for her, and together they play hide-and-seek. All goes well, until Maurice disappears. Mona is despondent and worried for her friend, but the story ends happily when he returns with his whole family." Children's Bk Rev Serv

"Not as hilarious as other Marshalls—more of a smile than a laugh. But the illustrations [by the author] of huge Mona in assorted smart skirts and dainty pumps and Maurice carrying his house on his back like a piece of pink bubble gum are delicious." Sch Library J

Marshall, James, 1942- —*Continued*

Yummers! Houghton 1973 30p illus lib. bdg. $6.95
E

1 Pigs—Fiction 2 Turtles—Fiction 3 Reducing—Fiction
ISBN 0-395-14757-3 LC 72-5400

Illustrated by the author

Worried about her weight, Emily Pig "jumps rope; her friend Eugene [Turtle] suggests a walk as better exercise, but the walk is interrupted by a series of snacks. Emily, who has said 'Yummers,' to everything, finally has a tummy ache. She thinks it must have been due to all the walking, and agrees with Eugene when he suggests that she stay in bed and eat plenty of good food." Chicago. Children's Bk Center

"Corpulent, amiable Emily moves with monumental charm in the humorous, bright pastel pictures." Horn Bk

Martin, Patricia Miles

The little brown hen; illus. by Harper Johnson. Crowell 1960 23p illus $6.95
E

1 Blacks—Fiction 2 Chickens—Fiction
ISBN 0-690-49733-4 LC 60-6240

A young black boy's "search for his missing brown hen and his desire to give his mother some ducks for her birthday come to a happy conclusion when he finds the little brown hen in the woods brooding a nestful of ducklings." Booklist

"An attractive picture-book story about black Americans in a rural setting." Keating. Building Bridges of Understanding Between Cultures

The rice bowl pet; illus. by Ezra Jack Keats. Crowell 1962 unp illus lib. bdg. $7.89
E

1 Chinese Americans—Fiction 2 Pets—Fiction 3 San Francisco—Fiction
ISBN 0-690-69969-7 LC 62-7744

A picture-story book with a "background of San Francisco, especially of Chinatown and Fisherman's Wharf. The story is about Ah Jim's efforts to find a pet which is small enough to fit into his rice bowl (his mother's stipulation) and yet which is alive and warm and pleasant to hold (his own requirements)." Horn Bk

"An appealing story that points up, without preaching, courtesy and consideration for others." NY Times Bk Rev

Marzollo, Jean

Close your eyes; pictures by Susan Jeffers. Dial Press 1978 unp illus $7.95, lib. bdg. $7.45
E

1 Lullabies
ISBN 0-8037-1609-5; 0-8037-1610-9 LC 76-42935

"There are two stories going on here, one the sleepy visions of a small child [evoked by the lullaby rhyme text], the other, the comic efforts by the father to put the child to sleep." Babbling Bookworm

"The text is interpreted in magnificent full-color pastel-toned illustrations, remarkable for their clarity, meticulous detail, and delicate line. Another dimension is added through the artist's juxtaposition of two interpretations—one delineating dream fantasies in lush oversized images, the other depicting a weary father cajoling his child into bed in a contrapuntal series of smaller vignettes. . . . The book is a charming production in the old-fashioned tradition of a warm and reassuring bed-time story." Horn Bk

Massie, Diane Redfield

Chameleon was a spy; story and pictures by Diane Redfield Massie. Crowell 1979 unp illus $6.95, lib. bdg. $6.89
E

1 Spies—Fiction 2 Chameleons—Fiction 3 Pickles—Fiction
ISBN 0-690-03909-3; 0-690-03910-7 LC 78-19510

"Since he was so good at concealing himself by changing colors, Chameleon was prepared to take on the job of being an industrial spy; his mission was to retrieve the secret formula that the Perfect Pickle Company had stolen from the Pleasant Pickle Company. Caught in the act, chased around the pickling plant, and carrying the formula, Chameleon fell into a bottle and was trapped when it was capped. His bottle was sold, the customer was horrified, and the thieving company was closed for selling contaminated food. Rescued, Chameleon was feted by his employers, especially when he was able to reconstruct the words (damaged by immersion) to complete the formula." Chicago. Children's Bk Center

"The story is imaginative and the illustrations—several to a page alternating between black-and-white and color—are delicately drawn and full of humor." Sch Library J

Mathis, Sharon Bell

The hundred penny box; illus. by Leo and Diane Dillon. Viking 1975 47p illus lib. bdg. $6.95
E

1 Family life—Fiction 2 Elderly—Fiction
ISBN 0-670-38787-8 LC 74-23744

A "portrayal of the conflict between Michael's one-hundred-year-old great-great-aunt Dew and his mother, who hopes to help the old woman live in the present by disposing of reminders of the past. Aunt Dew lives largely through memories of each year of her life as Mike counts the one hundred pennies she keeps in an 'old cracked-up wacky-dacky box with a broken top.' Michael understands that Aunt Dew cannot live with his mother's reality, and he fights to save the hundred penny box." Rdng Teacher

"Soft, misty pictures in brown and white reflect the tenderness that is the prevailing note of a touching story about a child and a very old woman. . . . Most of the story consists of dialogue, much of it between aunt Dew and Michael, and while the author gives a strong picture of family relationships and family continuity, it is the love and trust between the two protagonists that is the dominant theme. Beautifully written, the restraint of the style makes the book's message of the love the more effective." Chicago. Children's Bk Center

Matthiesen, Thomas

ABC; an alphabet book; photographed in color by Thomas Matthiesen. Platt 1966 unp illus $3.50
E

1 Alphabet
ISBN 0-448-41050-8 LC 66-13382

"Familiar objects—shoes, a clock, a balloon—represent the 26 letters of the alphabet." Hodges. Bks for Elem Sch Libraries

"The forthright, three-dimensional photography is colorful in more than the literal sense. Each letter is given in upper and lower case, and the simplest things used to illustrate them are photographed with great imagination. You can hear a child's questions and sense his concentration as he pores over these pictures." Bk Week

Things to see; a child's world of familiar objects; photographed in color by Thomas Matthiesen. Platt 1966 unp illus $3.50
E

ISBN 0-448-41051-6 LC 66-13381

"A compilation of color photographs, each full page and each faced by a page that has a few lines of text and—in heavy type face—the name of the pictured object. The arrangement is random; the pictures are excellent both in the choices of subjects and in the quality of reproductions. The text verges on cuteness here and there, but is for the most part rather simple, almost naive in style; the short sentences and large print could be read by beginning readers, but probably won't be because of the format." Chicago. Children's Bk Center

Mayer, Mercer

A boy, a dog, and a frog. Dial Press 1967 unp illus $4.95, lib. bdg. $4.58, pa $1.75
E

1 Frogs—Fiction 2 Stories without words
ISBN 0-8037-0763-0; 0-8037-0767-3; 0-8037-0769-X
LC 67-22254

"Without the need for a single word, humorous, very engaging pictures [by the author] tell the story of a little boy who sets forth with his dog and a net on a summer day to catch an enterprising and personable frog. Even very young preschoolers will 'read' the tiny book with the greatest satisfaction and pleasure." Horn Bk

Mayer, Mercer—*Continued*

Some other books in this series are also available from Dial Press:

A boy, a dog, a frog, and a friend $4.50, lib. bdg. $4.17, pa $1.75 (ISBN 0-8037-0754-1; 0-8037-0755-X; 0-8037-0804-1; LC 70-134857)

Frog goes to dinner $4.50, lib. bdg. $4.17, pa $1.75 (ISBN 0-8037-3386-0; 0-8037-3381-X; 0-8037-2733-X; LC 74-2881)

'Frog on his own $3.95, lib. bdg. $3.69, pa $1.95 (ISBN 0-8037-2701-1; 0-8037-2695-3; 0-8037-2716-X; LC 73-6018)

Frog, where are you? $3.95, lib. bdg. $3.69, pa $1.75 (ISBN 0-8037-2737-2; 0-8037-2732-1; 0-8037-2729-1; LC 72-85544)

One frog too many $3.50, lib. bdg. $3.39 (ISBN 0-8037-4838-8; 0-8037-4858-2; LC 75-6325)

There's a nightmare in my closet. Dial Press 1968 unp illus $6.95, lib. bdg. $6.46, pa $1.95   E

1 Fear—Fiction
ISBN 0-8037-8682-4; 0-8037-8683-2; 0-8037-8574-7
                                              LC 68-15250

"Childhood fear of the dark and the resulting exercise in imaginative exaggeration are given that special Mercer Mayer treatment in this dryly humorous fantasy. Young children will easily empathize with the boy and can be comforted by his experience. The boy decides to rid himself of his particular fear, a buck-toothed, cross-eyed, polka-dotted creature lurking in his closet. As it approaches in the dark, he quickly turns on the light and shoots, only to have it cry hysterically in horror. So he soothes it by gently tucking it in his bed. When that ordeal is over, the boy realizes another nightmare might be in the closet, but it will have to stay there, since his bed is already beast-filled." Sch Library J

What do you do with a kangaroo? Four Winds [1974, c1973] unp illus $6.95, pa $1.95   E

1 Animals—Fiction 2 Stories in rhyme
ISBN 0-590-07286-2; 0-590-10007-6   LC 72-87073

The author's "energetic verse tells how his plucky heroine deals with a menagerie of persnickety beasts that delight in making nuisances of themselves. The problems begin with a fussy kangaroo that jumps in the window, sits on the bed, sniffs disdainfully at the wrinkled sheets and demands, 'Change them now and make them smooth and fluff up the pillows if you please.' She swiftly dispatches him ('Get out of my bed, you kangaroo') only to find harassing her in turn an opossum, a llama, a raccoon, a moose, a tiger, and a camel. She effectively copes by day but at night the animals group on her bed en masse, refusing to be moved. So, as Mayer's humorous, earthy-colored scenes show, she lets them stay while she snuggles down for the night. Good fantasy fun." Booklist

You're the scaredy-cat. Four Winds [1980 c1974] unp illus lib. bdg. $7.95   E

1 Camping—Fiction
ISBN 0-590-07783-X   LC 79-22185

A reprint of the 1974 edition published by Parents Magazine Press

This is "a largely visual comedy featuring two would-be campers who begin their out-door venture equipped with blankets, food, and one over-active imagination. As the nameless instigator of the project begins the night with a scarey story, his sleepy companion dozes, leaving the talker, disgusted, to fall asleep on his own and dream of the garbage can monster he has conjured up. Though the dream dissipates, a large dog raiding a nearby garbage can brings the whole vivid creation to life for the talker, who summarily joins his departed companion back at the house and nervily asserts, '"You" came in first, so "you're" the scaredy-cat.' An entertaining, easy-to-read jest that satisfactorily supports Mayer's penchant for dreaming up creepy creatures." Booklist

Miles, Miska

Apricot ABC; illus. by Peter Parnall. Little 1969 unp illus $6.95   E

1 Alphabet 2 Stories in rhyme
ISBN 0-316-57030-3   LC 68-22072

"An Atlantic Monthly Press book"
"The artist's clean, sharply detailed drawings for a fauna-and-flora ABC give lively action as well as identifiable form to a sequence of natural subjects—from 'A' for 'An apricot tree grew knobby and tall' to 'Yellow sun shines' and 'Rains

zig and zag.' Locating the large capital letters could be made a kind of game, for these are interwoven into green, leafy sketches. The even rhyming lines tell of the insects and plants among which an apricot falls, and of a hen with feathers fluffed —a monster to the frightened frog—that finds the fruit a 'magnificent meal' and leaves only a seed. . . . Artistically the author-artist collaboration is successful; the combination of life-cycle and ecological concepts with ABC rhymes raises the level of interest above the usual ABC audience." Horn Bk

Swim, Little Duck; illus. by Jim Arnosky. Little 1976 30p illus $6.95   E

1 Ducks—Fiction
ISBN 0-316-57033-8   LC 75-30700

"An Atlantic Monthly Press book"
"A little duck goes out to see the world and is joined by a frog, a pig, and a rabbit, but fin is that his own pond is the best after all." Best Bks for Children

"A gentle, innocent story, simply told, with descriptions such as 'a redwing went sliding away on a breeze' sure to frame a picture in a child's mind. Arnosky's black line drawngs washed with brown lend the homely adventurers great appeal." Booklist

Milhous, Katherine

The egg tree; story and pictures by Katherine Milhous. Scribner 1950 unp illus lib. bdg. $8.95   E

1 Pennsylvania Dutch—Fiction 2 Easter—Fiction 3 Egg decoration—Fiction
ISBN 0-684-12716-4   LC 50-6017

Awarded the Caldecott Medal, 1951
"A seasonal book with the illustrations and 'things to do' aspect of more value than the actual story. A group of children taking part in a Pennsylvania Dutch Easter have an Easter egg hunt and learn how to decorate eggs and hang them on an Easter egg tree. The full page coloured illustration sare Pennsylvania Dutch in character and the smaller ones are decorative Easter egg designs." Ontario Library Rev

There "are lovely illustrations and decorations . . . plus directions for making an egg tree." NY Times Bk Rev

Miller, Edna

Mousekin's golden house; story and pictures by Edna Miller. Prentice-Hall 1964 32p illus lib. bdg. $6.95, pa $1.50   E

1 Mice—Fiction 2 Halloween—Fiction
ISBN 0-13-604421-2; 0-13-604439-5   LC 64-16429

"A wood mouse, coming upon an abandoned jack-o-lantern, discovers it can be converted into a cozy nest for the winter. An eye which sees and loves each detail of woodland life illuminates the artist-author's lovely water-colors. The story is neither anthropomorphic nor sentimental." Sch Library J

Some other books about Mousekin are also available from Prentice-Hall:

Mousekin finds a friend lib. bdg. $5.95, pa $1.50 (ISBN 0-13-604413-1; 0-13-604397-6; LC 67-18924)

Mousekin takes a trip lib. bdg. $5.95, pa $1.50 (ISBN 0-13-604363-1; 0-13-604348-8; LC 75-35922)

Mousekin's ABC lib. bdg. $5.95, pa $1.50 (ISBN 0-13-604389-5; 0-13-604371-2; LC 79-176159)

Mousekin's Christmas Eve lib. bdg. $6.95, pa $1.50 (ISBN 0-13-604454-9; 0-13-604447-6; LC 65-25244)

Mousekin's close call lib. bdg. $6.95 (ISBN 0-13-604207-4; LC 77-27571)

Mousekin's family lib. bdg. $5.95, pa $1.50 (ISBN 0-13-604462-X; 0-13-604157-4; LC 69-12673)

Mousekin's woodland birthday lib. bdg. $6.95 (ISBN 0-13-604405-0; LC 74-4210)

Mousekin's woodland sleepers lib. bdg. $5.95, pa $1.50 (ISBN 0-13-604470-0; 0-13-604561-8; LC 70-107961)

Minarik, Else Holmelund

Little Bear; pictures by Maurice Sendak. Harper 1957 63p illus $6.95, lib. bdg. $7.89, pa $1.95   E

1 Bears—Fiction
ISBN 0-06-024240-X; 0-06-024241-8; 0-06-444004-4
                                              LC 57-9263

Also available in a Spanish language edition, lib. bdg. $7.89 (ISBN 0-06-024244-2; LC 69-14452)

"An I can read book"
Four episodes "about Little Bear, a charming creature who will delight young readers [and

Minarik, Else H.—*Continued*

listeners] as he persuades his mother to make him a winter outfit—only to discover his fur coat is all he needs; makes himself some birthday soup—and then is surprised with a birthday cake; takes an imaginary trip to the moon, and finally goes happily off to sleep as his mother tells him a story about 'Little Bear.'" Chicago. Children's Bk Center

The pictures "depict all the warmth of feeling and the special companionship that exists between a small child and his mother." Pub W

Some other books about Little Bear are also available from Harper:

Father Bear comes home $6.95, lib. bdg. $7.89, pa| $1.95 (ISBN 0-06-02423-2; 0-06-024231-0; 0-06-444014-1; LC 59-5794)

A kiss for Little Bear $6.95, lib. bdg. $7.89 (ISBN 0-06-024298-1; 0-06-024299-X; LC 68-16820)

Little Bear's friend $6.95, lib. bdg. $7.89 (ISBN 0-06-024255-8; 0-06-024256-6; LC 60-6370)

Little Bear's visit $6.95, lib. bdg. $7.89, pa $1.95 (ISBN 0-06-024265-5; 0-06-024266-3; 0-06-444023-0; LC 61-11451)

No fighting, no biting! Pictures by Maurice Sendak. Harper 1958 62p illus $6.95, lib. bdg. $7.89, pa $1.95

E

1 Alligators—Fiction
ISBN 0-06-024290-6; 0-06-024291-4; 0-06-444015-X
LC 58-5293

"An I can read book"
"A young lady who is unable to read in peace because of two children squabbling beside her tells them a story about two little alligators whose fighting and biting almost lead to disastrous consequences with a big hungry alligator. Children are sure to accept and enjoy the lesson in| this little adventure tale and be amused by the expressive old-fashioned drawings." Booklist

Mizumura, Kazue

If I built a village. Crowell 1971 unp illus $7.95, lib. bdg. $7.89

E

ISBN 0-690-42903-7; 0-690-42904-5   LC 77-140645

"A child playing with building blocks muses about what he would have in his world if he built a village, a town, or a city." Booklist
"An entirely childlike book with a simple but poetic statement on ecology. . . . The [author-] illustrator's bright, energetic designs of leaping rabbits and trout, owls, mice, geese, and moles—all in their respective habitats—are pictured in alternating black and white, and sunny full-color wash-spreads. The theme is effectively expressed without becoming burdensome for the small child." Horn Bk

If I were a mother . . . Crowell [1968] unp illus lib. bdg. $7.89

E

1 Mothers—Fiction   2 Animals—Fiction
ISBN 0-690-42917-7   LC 67-23688

Illustrated by the author
"A little girl dreams of being a mother—in terms of the mothers she knows. She thinks of the mother cat keeping her kittens neat and clean, the bear teaching her cubs what and how to eat (not all sweets), and the mare letting her foal stand on his own feet as soon as he is ready. At last she decides that of all the mothers she knows, she would most want to be like her own." Booklist
"A combination of simplicity and sentimentality with colorful wash drawings." Bruno. Bks for Sch Libraries, 1968

The way of an ant. Crowell 1970 unp illus $7.95, lib. bdg. $7.89

E

1 Ants—Fiction
ISBN 0-690-87044-2; 0-690-87045-0   LC 72-87155

"An ant wants to climb to the sky—to the highest point that he can reach. He first tries a tall blade of grass, then moves on to a dandelion, rose, sunflower, apple tree, etc. Each time he reaches a pinnacle, he spots some point higher, hurries down to the ground, and begins a new climb. Finally, old, proud of his past accomplishments, but unable to climb anymore, he realizes that 'As long as he kept on climbing, The blue sky grew higher and higher.'" Library J

"The visual lesson of the value of striving depicts a sunnily beautiful, growing world; the alternating black-and-white and predominantly green-and-yellow pictures on tall pages are striking." Horn Bk

Modell, Frank

Tooley! Tooley! Greenwillow Bks. 1979 unp illus $6.95, lib. bdg. $6.67

E

1 Dogs—Fiction
ISBN 0-688-80092-0; 0-688-84092-2   LC 76-49645

"Two boys who wish they had money to see a movie see a notice that money is being offered for the retrieval of a lost dog. Milton, who constantly disparages his friend Marvin's ideas as silly, collects every brown and white dog he sees; Marvin uses his head and goes to a butcher's shop, thinking that if he were a dog he'd be lured by the smell. There is a dog there, and he jumps up eagerly when Marvin calls, 'Tooley,' and Marvin wins the reward, and he doesn't even point out to Milton that his ideas aren't always silly." Chicago. Children's Bk Center
"The color-cartoon illustrations are even more animated than the swift text." Pub W

Moeri, Louise

Star Mother's youngest child; illus. by Trina Schart Hyman. Houghton 1975 unp illus $3.95, pa $2.50

E

1 Christmas—Fiction
ISBN 0-395-21406-8; 0-395-29929-2   LC 75-9743

"On earth a crotchety Old Woman laments her loneliness with, 'Just once! I'd like to celebrate a Christmas! Is that too much to ask?' In the heavens Star Mother's Youngest Child pleads, 'just once I want to celebrate Christmas like they do down there!' On Christmas morning the Old Woman answers a knock and finds an ugly child with spiky yellow hair on the doorstep. Complaining every step of the way, she invites him in and together they decorate a tree with colored yarn, old beads, and thimbles. They feast on fresh bread and ham bone soup and enjoy the sound of village church bells. From meager offerings they even devise presents for each other. Brown-and-white line drawings keep the warm mood of the book, and Hyman's details reflect the changes in the characters as the Old Woman and the Ugly Child experience Christmas together. Word- and picture-perfect." Booklist

Monjo, F. N.

The drinking gourd; pictures by Fred Brenner. Harper 1970 62p illus (An I can read history bk) lib. bdg. $7.89

E

1 Underground railroad—Fiction
ISBN 0-06-024330-9   LC 68-10782

Set in New England in the decade before the Civil War. For mischievous behavior in church, Tommy is sent home to his room, but wanders instead into the barn. There he discovers that his father is helping runaway slaves escape to Canada
"The simplicity of dialogue and exposition, the level of concepts, and the length of the story [makes] it most suitable for the primary grades reader. The illustrations are deftly representational, the whole a fine addition to the needed body of historical books for the very young." Chicago. Children's Bk Center

The one bad thing about father; pictures by Rocco Negri. Harper 1970 62p illus (An I can read history bk) $6.95

E

1 Roosevelt family—Fiction   2 Roosevelt, Theodore, President U.S.—Fiction
ISBN 0-06-024333-3   LC 71-85036

The author ascribes this childhood diary to Quentin Roosevelt, youngest son of President Theodore Roosevelt. It is a fictitious memoir of family life at the White House and at the summer home at Oyster Bay, New York which provides glimpses into the history of the period as well as the vigorous activities of our twenty-sixth President
"This is harder than many books in the series, with more sophisticated humor; but it's a very amusing account of life in the White House from a child's viewpoint. Rocco Negri's pen-and-ink drawings in color are a fine, funny complement to the text." Sch Library J

Moore, Lilian

Little raccoon and the thing in the pool; pictures by Gioia Fiammenghi. McGraw 1963 44p illus lib. bdg. $5.95   E

1 Raccoons—Fiction
ISBN 0-07-042892-1   LC 62-16274

"Whittlesey House publications"
"Little Raccoon meets several animal friends on the way to the pool to catch crayfish for supper. He is apprehensive on the first trip without his mother and becomes frightened of his reflection in the water. After several unsuccessful attempts, he succeeds in overcoming his fear and brings home the crayfish. Children will enjoy the humor of Little Raccoon's fear of his own reflection." Sch Library J
"The ink line drawings (half of them with blue added) amplify the playful spirit of the words." Horn Bk

Munari, Bruno

ABC. Collins [distributed by Philomel Bks.] 1960 unp illus $8.95, lib. bdg. $8.99   E

1 Alphabet
ISBN 0-529-03620-7; 0-529-03621-5   LC 60-11461

First published by World Publishing Company
Title on spine: Bruno Munari's ABC
Illustrated by the author, the pictures "are handsome and original, but every object is clear and simple enough for even a very small child to identify. The objects are familiar ones, and there are two or more words, adjectives as well as nouns, for many of the letters. For example. 'U' is represented by an umbrella that is up and 'L' by a long leaf and a little leaf." Pub W
"With clean lines and brilliant full-color work, Bruno Munari's 'ABC' is at once unconventional, yet childlike, modern, yet timeless. A bold and refreshing kind of ABC book, its great simplicity almost conceals its art." Sch Library J

Bruno Munari's zoo. Collins [distributed by Philomel Bks.] 1963 unp illus $8.95, lib. bdg. $8.91   E

1 Animals—Pictorial works
ISBN 0-529-03799-8; 0-529-03800-5   LC 63-14773

First published by World Publishing Company
"A stunning picture book of birds and beasts original in design, brilliant with color, and touched with humor. The pictures are all doublespreads and the text is merely an identifying line or two to the page." Booklist

The circus in the mist. Collins [distributed by Philomel Bks.] [1969 c1968] unp illus $6.95   E

1 Circus
ISBN 0-529-00756-8   LC 78-2766

Originally published 1968 in Italy. First published in the United States by World Publishing Company
"Ingeniously using semitranslucent pages, pages of different colors, peepholes, and design to good effect a well-known Italian artist and designer has created a unique and diverting picture book with surprises on every page. There is no real story line but interest is captured and sustained by changing mood and pace as the viewer is led through fog-dimmed city streets, into the brightness, movement, and excitement of a circus, and then home again across a misty park. While the book may seem too experimental and gimmicky to many adults, children will undoubtedly find it great fun." Booklist

Myers, Walter Dean

The dragon takes a wife; illus. by Ann Grifalconi. Bobbs 1972 unp illus $7.95   E

1 Dragons—Fiction 2 Fairy tales
ISBN 0-672-51586-5   LC 71-172340

"A jazzed-up version of the dragon who wants a wife and must fight for her. Harry was not a good fighter, so he went for help to the kingdom where all the good fairies lived. Mabel Mae asked, 'What's buggin you, baby?' and after she heard, 'I can dig where you're coming from.' Mabel Mae gave Harry five good suggestions with magic power for each one and every time he blew the chance to win. When Mabel Mae

turned herself into a dragon, Harry found her really worth fighting for, and he won. Reportedly, the first black fairy tale. It's really tongue in cheek." Adventuring with Bks

Myrick, Mildred

The Secret Three; drawings by Arnold Lobel. Harper 1963 64p illus $7.89   E

1 Clubs—Fiction 2 Ciphers—Fiction 3 Seashore—Fiction
ISBN 0-06-024355-4   LC 63-13323

"An I can read book"
"Three boys, two on the mainland and one on an island lighthouse, exchange messages in a bottle carried by the tide. They organize a club with a secret code, handshake, and name. On a trip to the island the boys explore the lighthouse and camp out overnight." Sch Library J
"The cryptography is elementary enough for the age of the readers, and should delight girls as well as boys. The illustrations are charming." Chicago. Children's Bk Center

Nakatani, Chiyoko

My teddy bear; story and pictures by Chiyoko Nakatani. Crowell 1976 29p illus $4.50, lib. bdg. $7.89   E

1 Teddy bears—Fiction
ISBN 0-690-01077-X   LC 75-34110

Original Japanese edition published 1975
"Like most children, the small boy in this tale considers his teddy bear his best friend. The boy takes readers through a day as the pals play together, go for walks, protect each other from the tough dog next door and (in short) stick together through thick and thin, even when they fight. Naturally, evening finds boy and teddy settled down in mutually comforting slumber." Pub W
"Imbued with guileless warmth, simplicity, and love, the bright, expressive paintings and the few essential, well-chosen words are wholly right for a fledgling audience." Horn Bk

Ness, Evaline

Do you have the time Lydia? Written and illus. by Evaline Ness. Dutton 1971 unp illus $7.95, pa $1.25   E

1 Brothers and sisters—Fiction
ISBN 0-525-28790-6; 0-525-45024-6   LC 79-157950

Spanish language edition available for $7.95 (ISBN 0-525-41325-1)
Lydia, who lived with her family on a tropical island, was always so busy painting pictures, reading books, hammering nails, sewing clothes, and baking cakes that she never had time to finish anything. But it wasn't until she disappointed her younger brother that she finally learned the true significance of time
"Many familiar details drawn from daily child life contribute to the believability of the characters and situations. . . . The personalities of the children emerge from the expressive ink drawings shaded with pencil and highlighted in sunny shades of pink, orange, and yellow." Sch Library J

Sam, Bangs & Moonshine; written and illus. by Evaline Ness. Holt 1966 unp illus lib. bdg. $6.95, pa $1.95   E

1 Fantasy—Fiction
ISBN 0-03-012716-5; 0-03-080111-7   LC 66-10113

Awarded the Caldecott Medal, 1967
"Motherless Samantha (called Sam), living on an island, had the lonely child's predilection for daydreams: her mother was not dead—but a mermaid, and Sam had at home not only Bangs, her wise old cat (who would talk), but a fierce lion and a baby kangaroo! Her practical fisherman-father was worried' . . . for a change, talk "Real" not "Moonshine." "Moonshine" spells trouble.' Not until her wildly exaggerated 'Moonshine' talk sent her only friend [Thomas] with her beloved cat to near destruction did Sam realize the grown-up differences between true imagination and uncontrolled flights of fancy." Horn Bk
"In this unusually creative story the fantasy in which many, many children indulge is presented in a realistic and sympathetic context. The illustrations in ink and pale color wash (mustard, grayishaqua) have a touching realism, too. This is an outstanding book and one that no library will want to miss." Sch Library J

Newberry, Clare Turlay

The kittens' ABC; verse and pictures by Clare Turlay Newberry. New ed. completely redrawn. Harper [1965 c1946] unp illus $9.95, lib. bdg. $9.79 **E**

1 Alphabet 2 Cats—Poetry
ISBN 0-06-024450-X; 0-06-024451-8   LC 64-19712

A reissue of the title published 1946

Each letter of the alphabet is represented by a picture of a kitten or cat, accompanied by a brief verse

The illustrations of "the animals are so appealingly furry that small children will want to pat and stroke them. This is a book to share with children for the pleasure of the pictures and mildly amusing verse rather than for its alphabet instruction." Booklist

Marshmallow; story and pictures by Clare Turlay Newberry. Harper 1942 unp illus $8.95, lib. bdg. $8.79 **E**

1 Rabbits—Fiction 2 Cats—Fiction
ISBN 0-06-024460-7; 0-06-024461-5   LC 42-22858

"A little white bunny, looking as soft as a marshmallow, comes to live in the house with a pampered bachelor cat who at first does not know whether or not to accept so strange a thing. But before long the big black cat and the little white bunny are such friends that, cuddled up together, asleep, and playing, they give the artist an excuse for some of her best work." Bookmark

It is a delightful combination of beauty, understanding of children and animals, and droll humor." NY Times Bk Rev

Nicholson, William

Clever Bill. Farrar, Straus 1977 22p illus $5.95 **E**

1 Toys—Fiction
ISBN 0-374-31363-6   LC 72-81331

Illustrated by the author

Reissue of the title first published 1926 by Doubleday

"It is always a joy to find outstanding old children's books rising from obscurity.... The colors of [toy soldier Bill Davis'] brave British Guardsman's uniform are as bright as the day they were painted ... and so are all the enchanting scenes in the nonstop fantasy. Mary gets a letter from her aunt, inviting her to come for a visit. She has a tense time, packing all her necessities: her gloves with the thumbs, Apple Grey (her horse on wheels), blue teapot and lots of other things. Cramming her suitcase full and rushing to the train, Mary forgets [her toy soldier] Clever Bill Davis. So he leaps up and runs, and runs, and runs. He runs so fast that he is just in time to meet Mary when her train stops at Dover." Pub W

Noah's Ark; illus. by Peter Spier. Doubleday 1977 unp illus $7.95, lib. bdg. $8.90 **E**

1 Noah's Ark 2 Bible stories 3 Stories in rhyme
ISBN 0-385-09473-6; 0-385-12730-8   LC 76-43630

Awarded the Caldecott Medal, 1978

"A seventeenth-century Dutch poem, 'The Flood' by Jacobus Revius, opens the otherwise almost wordless book. Skillfully translated by the artist and set in a readable, appropriately archaic type, the artlessly reverent verses add an unexpected dimension to the full-color pictures. Peter Spier's characteristic panoramas are marvels of minute detail, activity, vitality, and humor; a few of the scenes are quiescent and serenely beautiful. The artwork is presented on single pages and in double-page spreads as well as in small vertical and horizontal panels, and even the handsome endpapers, title page, and half-title page add to the dramatic narrative. Another outstanding work by an artist whose picture books are notable for their aesthetic quality, integrity, and engaging wholesomeness." Horn Bk

Nødset, Joan L.

Come here, cat; pictures by Steven Kellogg. Harper 1973 unp illus lib. bdg. $7.89 **E**

1 Cats—Fiction
ISBN 0-06-024558-1   LC 72-9858

"A young girl chases a cat through the halls, up the stairs to the roof of her apartment house, and back down again coaxing and cajoling it to be her friend." Elementary English

"The ingenuousness of the girl ... [is] well served by the artist's line drawings in shades of brown and orange on tan. Having appropriately simplified his style to picture a simple story, he squanders his inventive ingenuity in occasional corners only and sets up a happy contrast between the single-minded little girl and the bustling, exuberant urban community in which she lives." Horn Bk

Go away, dog; pictures by Crosby Bonsall. Harper 1963 unp illus lib. bdg. $7.89 **E**

1 Dogs—Fiction
ISBN 0-06-024556-5   LC 63-11162

"In a brief volume with expressive pictures touched with red, an important, complete tale develops as a little boy who doesn't like dogs becomes irresistibly drawn to an importunate puppy brimming with playfulness and affection. The drawings captivate as fully as do the words, each so rightly expressing the feelings of boy and dog." Horn Bk

Who took the farmer's [hat]? Pictures by Fritz Siebel. Harper 1963 unp illus lib. bdg. $7.89 **E**

1 Animals—Fiction
ISBN 0-06-024566-2   LC 62-17964

"Away flew the farmer's hat. In his search for it he found that his hat could be many things to many animals including, most permanently, a bird's nest." Pub W

Norris, Louanne

An oak tree dies and a journey begins, by Louanne Norris & Howard E. Smith, Jr. Illus. by Allen Davis. Crown 1979 unp illus $6.95 **E**

1 Trees—Fiction 2 Natural history—Fiction
ISBN 0-517-53723-0   LC 79-14061

"The authors recount the death of an old forest giant and the slow journey down rivers to its final resting place on an ocean beach. The process of natural forces—that death means not an end of existence but a changing of state or condition and a continuation of usefulness to nature—is the dominant theme. This sets a mood of quiet transition, and the strength of the old oak never ceases, even as it is carried down currents, sat upon by children, frogs, raccoons, snakes and gulls, and lived on by barnacles, mussels, oysters, and seaweed. The black-and-white, pen-and-ink illustrations on every page portray the weathering of the oak in an appropriately blurry style." Sch Library J

Oakley, Graham

The church mouse. Atheneum Pubs. 1972 unp illus $9.95, pa $2.95 **E**

1 Mice—Fiction 2 Cats—Fiction
ISBN 0-689-30058-1; 0-689-70475-5   LC 72-75276

Illustrated by the author

"Arthur, the church mouse, had a happy and peaceful life.... However, Arthur was lonely, so he invited the town mice to live with him and they made a pact with the parson—a weekly cheesefest in return for odd jobs. All went well until Sampson [the church cat], dreaming, chased some mice and disrupted a service. The congregation was irate, the parson sadly announced a general eviction. The situation was saved when the combined efforts of Sampson and the mice foiled a burglar, and they all were invited to stay on." Chicago. Children's Bk Center

"Full-color paintings with an abundance of activity and detail contribute much to the telling of the story.... Very British allusions give the fulsome text a certain sophistication; but the action and the clever illustrations are wholly childlike in their fun." Horn Bk

Some other books about the church mice and Sampson, the church cat, are also available from Atheneum Pubs.:

The church cat abroad lib. bdg. $6.95, pa $2.95 (ISBN 0-689-30124-3; 0-689-70472-0; LC 73-76327)
The church mice adrift lib. bdg. $7.95, pa $2.95 (ISBN 0-689-30562-1; 0-689-70473-9; LC 76 25705)
(ISBN 0-689-30562-1; 0-689-70473-9; LC 76-25705)
The church mice and the moon lib. bdg. $7.95, 74-75569)
The church mice at bay, lib. bdg. $8.95 (ISBN 0-689-30629-6; LC 78-62260)
The church mice at Christmas $10.95 (ISBN 0-689-30797-7; LC 80-14518)
The church mice spread their wings lib. bdg. $7.95 (ISBN 0-689-30496-X; LC 75-15102)

Ormondroyd, Edward

Broderick; illus. by John Larrecq. Parnassus Press 1969 unp illus $6.95, lib. bdg. $4.77   E

1 Mice—Fiction 2 Surfing—Fiction
ISBN 0-87466-041-6; 0-87466-009-2   LC 77-83752

"A young mouse with a fondness for chewing the covers of books becomes an avid reader through the accidental discovery of a book about mice. Inspired by the exploits of such literary mouse personalities as Anatole and Miss Bianca, Broderick determines to make his own mark in the world and by diligent practice wins fame and fortune as a surfer. The author and the illustrator . . . have created a very real and endearing mouse hero to delight small children." Booklist

"This gay story is told with a straight face in polished style, the illustrations matching the deftness and humor of the writing. Appended is a brief list of other books about famous mice." Chicago. Children's Bk Center

Theodore; illus. by John M. Larrecq. Parnassus Press 1966 unp illus $5.95   E

1 Teddy bears—Fiction
ISBN 0-87466-056-4   LC 66-10352

"Because Lucy was careless, her poor bear Theodore got mixed up with the clothes in the laundry basket and was taken to the self-service laundry. When he emerged he was so clean that Lucy did not recognize him. But a friendly dog and two disputing cats remedied that situation, and Lucy and Theodore were happily reunited. The simple story, engaging line drawings washed with blue and yellow, and the well-designed format make a book for the youngest children that is all of a piece—unpretentious and charming." Horn Bk

Followed by: Theodore's rival. Parnassus Press $5.95 (ISBN 087466-035-1; LC 76-156876)

Over in the meadow; illus. by Ezra Jack Keats. Four Winds [1972 c1971] unp illus $8.95   E

1 Counting 2 Stories in rhyme
ISBN 0-590-17197-6   LC 79-182111

Text based on the original version by Olive A. Wadsworth. This counting rhyme tells about the animals in the meadow and their young, describing where they live, what noises they make and what their favorite activities are

"Children can enjoy both the counting and the animals, whose prompt obedience is more cheery compliance than a lesson. ('Buzz!' said the mother. 'We buzz,' said the five. So they buzzed and they hummed, near the snug behive.') The illustrations are colorful and lively, and the little creatures are easy to see for the counting." Sat Rev

Oxenbury, Helen

Pig tale. Morrow 1973 unp illus lib. bdg. $7.92   E

1 Pigs—Fiction 2 Stories in rhyme
ISBN 0-688-30092-8   LC 73-6357

Illustrated by the author

This is the "story of what happened to two little pigs who are discontented with their simple life. They suddenly find themselves overburdened with the luxurious life they thought they wanted and, in the end, choose the carefree, simple life that they had to begin with." Top of the News

"A unified, hilarious picture book with crisp, concise verses and absurd, full-color illustrations that emphasize the blithe innocence of the massive porkers." Horn Bk

Parish, Peggy

Amelia Bedelia; pictures by Fritz Siebel. Harper 1963 unp illus $5.95, lib. bdg. $6.89   E

ISBN 0-06-024640-5; 0-06-024641-3   LC 63-14367

"Amelia Bedelia is a maid whose talent for interpreting instructions literally results in comical situations, such as dressing the chicken in fine clothes." Hodges. Bks for Elem Sch Libraries

Some other books about Amelia Bedelia are available from Harper (unless otherwise noted):

Amelia Bedelia and the surprise shower $6.95, lib. bdg. $7.89, pa $1.95 (ISBN 0-06-024642-1; 0-06-024643-X; 0-06-444019-2; LC 66-18655)

Amelia Bedelia helps out $5.95, lib. bdg. $5.71 (Greenwillow Bks. ISBN 0-688-80231-1; 0-688-84231-3; LC 79-11729)

Come back, Amelia Bedelia $6.95, lib bdg. $7.89, pa $1.95 (ISBN 0-06-024667-7; 0-06-024668-5; 0-06-444016-8; LC 73-121799)

Good work, Amelia Bedelia $5.95. lib. bdg. $5.71 (Greenwillow Bks. ISBN 0-688-80022-X; 0-688-84022-1; LC 75-20360)

Play ball, Amelia Bedelia $6.95, lib. bdg. $7.89, pa $1.95 (ISBN 0-06-024655-3; 0-06-024656-1; 0-06-444005-2; LC 71-85028)

Teach us, Amelia Bedelia $5.95, lib. bdg. $5.71 (Greenwillow Bks. ISBN 0-688-80069-6; 0-688-84069-8; LC 72-22663)

Thank you, Amelia Bedelia $4.95, lib. bdg. $6.89 ISBN 0-06-024665-0; 0-06-024652-9; LC 64-11835)

Parker, Nancy Winslow

Poofy loves company; written and illus. by Nancy Winslow Parker. Dodd 1980 unp illus lib. bdg. $7.95   E

1 Dogs—Fiction
ISBN 0-396-00783-8   LC 79-20095

"Neatly dressed and carrying her teddy bear and balloon, Sally goes with her mother to visit a woman who owns a large, shaggy-haired dog named Poofy. Sally, overwhelmed by the rambunctious pet, soon finds her balloon stolen, her teddy bear turned into a cushion, her cookie snatched away, and her clothes in disarray. As the disgruntled mother plucks her frazzled daughter from the chaos, the hostess says demurely, 'Do come again.' Poofy just loves company." Booklist

"The humor is as dry and crisp as the drawings and the effect as buoyant as the bright colors. Neatly scrubbed Sally comes on a bit too placid, so the humor of her gradual reduction to sockless rubble—and the underlying inference that Poofy is behaving exactly as Sally would 'like' to behave—will surely not be lost on any preschooler who has ever been dragged along on a visit to 'one of Mother's friends.'" Sch Library J

Parkin, Rex

The red carpet; story and pictures by Rex Parkin. Macmillan Pub. Co. 1948 unp illus $5.95   E

1 Carpets—Fiction 2 Stories in rhyme
ISBN 0-02-770020   LC 48-6703

A tale in rhyme and colorful pictures about a runaway carpet. When it was rolled out of the hotel to receive a visiting duke, it rolled on and on, down the street, along the highway and over the country roads, bringing excitement wherever it went

Parnall, Peter

The mountain; written and illus. by Peter Parnall. Doubleday 1971 unp illus $6.95   E

1 Natural resources—U.S. 2 Pollution
ISBN 0-385-05800-4   LC 72-14575

This "picture book on the ecology theme . . . tells of a mountain in the West on which flowers grow and animals live. It is a beautiful place which some people want to preserve, so the mountain is made into a national park. But then trees are cut down, roads are built, tourists flock, etc. Refuse grows but the flowers don't and the animals can't." Sch Library J

"An unusually good book on preserving ecological balance, lucid enough in its message to be understood by preschool children, sophisticated enough in its treatment to be appreciated by the reader in primary grades. The illustrations are spare in composition and beautifully detailed." Chicago. Children's Bk Center

Payne, Emmy

Katy No-Pocket; pictures by H. A. Rey. Houghton 1944 unp illus lib. bdg. $8.95, pa $2.95   E

1 Kangaroos—Fiction 2 Animals—Fiction
ISBN 0-395-06996-3; 0-395-13717-9   LC 44-8099

Katy Kangaroo was most unfortunately unprovided with a pocket in which to carry her son Freddy. She asked other animals with no pockets how they carried their children but none of their answers seemed satisfactory. Finally a wise old owl advised her to try to find a pocket in the City, and so off she went and in the City she found just what she and Freddy needed

"Truly amusing pictures by Rey make this worth the . . . price." Library J

Pearson, Susan

Izzie; paintings by Robert Andrew Parker. Dial Press 1975 unp illus $6.95, lib. bdg. $6.46

E

1 Toys—Fiction
ISBN 0-8037-4094-X 0-8037-4905-8   LC 74-18597
"When Cary's favorite stuffed cat Izzie is cleaned up, he looks like new, but by that time Cary is off to school and although she misses Izzie, she no longer needs him." Best Bks for Children

Peet, Bill

Big bad Bruce. Houghton 1977 38p illus $7.95

E

1 Bears—Fiction 2 Witches—Fiction
ISBN 0-395-25150-8   LC 76-62502
Illustrated by the author
"A clowning bully, Bruce is a bear whose idea of fun is watching other animals scamper away when he rolls huge boulders down a hill. Almost hit, an angry witch shrinks Bruce to a wee creature; the forest animals recognize and chase him, and the witch takes him home for a pet. The story ends with a tiny bear who hasn't changed at all; when last seen, he is gleefully rolling small stones at helpless insects." Chicago. Children's Bk Center
"The best elements of a Saturday-morning cartoon show are delivered in this picture-book story which will satisfy young readers and listeners as well as the adults who share it with them. The language of the text is almost musical, with lots of words used for the sheer pleasure or appropriateness of their sounds. The illustrations are colorful and amusing. Sure to be enjoyed by slightly older readers for its humor and language, this is also a winner for story-telling." Children's Bk Rev Serv

Cowardly Clyde. Houghton 1979 38p illus lib. bdg. $8.95

E

1 Horses—Fiction 2 Courage—Fiction 3 Knights and knighthood—Fiction
ISBN 0-395-27802-3   LC 78-24343
"The brave Sir Galavant and his cowardly steed Clyde are introduced [in this book]. A 'giant owl-eyed ox-footed ogre, nearly as big as a barn' has been menacing the countryside. Sir Galavant and Clyde take up the challenge to rid the farmers of the terror. Setting off into the woods, horse and rider are eventually separated, and Clyde overcomes hs cowardliness in a heroic effort to save Galavant; the faithful steed also manages to lead the ogre to doom, making Galavant 'an instant hero.' The exploit is entertainingly described with the exaggerations of a tall tale and with such mouthfilling words as 'whuffling and gruffling' and 'huffling snuffling'. The text and the full-color drawings perfectly complement each other in the hyperbolic drama." Horn Bk

Eli. Houghton 1978 38p illus lib. bdg. $7.95

E

1 Lions—Fiction 2 Vultures—Fiction 3 Friendship—Fiction
ISBN 0-395-26454-5   LC 77-17500
"The story of pathetic Eli, a 'king of the jungle' who's too old to fight. Feeding on leftovers one day, Eli is disgusted by hovering vultures, but 'noblesse oblige' compels him to rescue one bird, Vera, from a jackal who snatches her. Eli routs the jackal and earns the unwelcome friendship of the birds. Not even his most outrageous insults rid the lion of his faithful companions. And a good thing, too. Comes the day when the hunters are closing in on him; Vera and the flock persuade Eli to play dead, and swoop down on him. The hunters see no glory in hauling off a dead body, apparently the feast of vultures, and the old cat is saved." Pub W
"A too-obvious ending is countered by the author-artist's flair for exaggerated expressions, plentiful action, and bold use of color as Peet creates another worthy member for his popular menagerie." Booklist

Huge Harold; written and illus. by Bill Peet. Houghton 1961 45p illus lib. bdg. $9.95

E

1 Rabbits—Fiction 2 Stories in rhyme
ISBN 0-395-18225-5   LC 61-5131
"Harold the rabbit grows and grows—to dimensions which deprive him of normal hiding places

but help him, after a bizarre chase, to an astonishing and wonderful achievement." Horn Bk
This story, "told in rhyming couplets and colored drawings, is action filled and laughable." Booklist

The whingdingdilly; written and illus. by Bill Peet. Houghton 1970 60p illus lib. bdg. $8.95

E

1 Dogs—Fiction 2 Witches—Fiction
ISBN 0-395-24729-2   LC 71-98521
"Scamp, the dog, wants to be a horse, but a well-meaning witch turns him into a Whingdingdilly with the hump of a camel, zebra's tail, giraffe's neck, elephant's front legs and ears, rhinoceros' nose, and reindeer's horns." Adventuring With Bks. 2d edition
"While not the most original of the author-illustrator's work, the lively, amusing picture-book tale is good fun and will please Peet fans." Booklist

Peppé, Rodney

Circus numbers; a counting book. Delacorte Press 1969 unp illus $5.95, lib. bdg. $5.47

E

1 Counting 2 Circus—Pictorial works
ISBN 0-440-01288-0; 0-440-01289-9   LC 75-86381
In this book readers encounter 1 ringmaster, 2 horses etc. up to 10 clowns, 20 doves and then "100 elephants, divided according to units of 10 (9 to a cage drawn by the 10th). . . . Sets of bright blue stars are sprinkled through the book, providing a second chance to count each number. Minimum text in large, clear upper- and lower-case type together with the impact of the [author's] jolly, poster-like illustrations set a smart tempo." Sch Library J

Odd one out. Viking 1974 unp illus lib. bdg. $7.95, pa $1.25

E

1 Puzzles
ISBN 0-670-52029-2; 0-670-05097-0   LC 73-17298
"An adventure that will tickle little readers by an appeal to their sense of the absurd. Combining collage and gouache, the colorful pictures are not only decorative but puzzles to be solved. Little Peter has a strange day. At breakfast, the table offers the usual fare plus a frog. Walking through his garden, he finds flowers, trees, a wheelbarrow . . . plus a traffic light. In school . . . a monkey sits among the students." Pub W
"On each colorful double-spread, Peppe deliberately includes an animal or object that belongs in the next spread. In addition to these 'mistakes' the pre-school and primary age children will also enjoy discovering an alphabet running across the side of a bus, a van, and blackboard in the middle of a city street; consecutive numbers from one to nine on objects in the toyshop, and a series of clocks that keep track of time as Peter's day progresses from breakfast to bedtime." Sch Library J

Perry, Patricia

Mommy and Daddy are divorced, by Patricia Perry & Marietta Lynch. Dial Press 1978 unp illus $6.95, lib. bdg. $6.46

E

1 Divorce—Fiction
ISBN 0-8037-5770-0; 0-8037-5771-9   LC 77-86268
"The younger of two small boys, Ned, tells about good times he and his older brother Joey enjoy when Daddy comes to play with them on his day off. Then he describes the children's hurt and anger when the father leaves and later, their reaction to a talk with their mother." Pub W
"The photographs record so many interactions and pairings (mother alone with children, children together, father with children, parents together pleasantly and in anger) as to almost certainly invite identification and useful comment by young listeners. A tactful and knowing book by authors whose training and experience with young children inform nearly every page." Sch Library J

Petersham, Maud

The box with red wheels; a picture book by Maud and Miska Petersham. Macmillan Pub. Co. 1949 unp illus $7.95, pa 95¢

E

1 Animals—Fiction
ISBN 0-02-771340-7; 0-02-044830-9   LC 49-11325
Picture book in which curious animals investigate a box with red wheels and find a new playmate inside—a baby

Petersham, Maud—*Continued*

"The story is flat and probably intentionally so to set off the inherent vitality of pictures and format. . . . These two well known author-illustrators have made a charming picture book out of interests consistently appealing to very small children." NY Times Bk Rev

The circus baby; a picture book by Maud and Miska Petersham. Macmillan Pub. Co. 1950 unp illus $4.95 **E**

1 Elephants—Fiction 2 Clowns—Fiction 3 Circus —Fiction
ISBN 0-02-771670-8 LC 50-9295

A picture book all about the circus elephant and her baby, and the circus clown family. When the mother elephant tried to train her child to eat at table, like the clown baby, the results were disastrous

"It is a simple tale, whose joy is mostly in the lovely pictures, the wonderful poses and expressions of the two elephants, the charming colors. Little children all love baby animals, and the troubles of this irresistible small elephant will give them great joy." NY Her Trib Bks

Peterson, Esther Allen

Frederick's alligator; illus. by Susanna Natti. Crown 1979 unp illus lib. bdg. $6.95 **E**

1 Alligators—Fiction 2 Imagination—Fiction
ISBN 0-517-53597-1 LC 78-15597

"A small boy regales everyone he meets—his mother and the mailman as well as his teacher and classmates—with tales of imaginary pets: a lion in the closet, a timber wolf in the basement, and a grizzly bear in the attic. His listeners naturally greet the news with stolid disbelief. Then Frederick claims to have a baby alligator under his bed; and when he actually reveals the creature at home and produces it for show-and-tell at school, his skeptical audience suddenly becomes respectful. . . . [The book has] humorous, relaxed colored illustrations, which reflect the little boy's bouncy enthusiasm and accompany him through his moment of triumph." Horn Bk

Piatti, Celestino

Celestino Piatti's Animal ABC; English text by Jon Reid. Atheneum Pubs. 1966 [c1965] unp illus $4.95 **E**

1 Alphabet 2 Animals—Poetry
ISBN 0-689-20335-7 LC 66-12851

Original German edition published 1965 in Switzerland

This alphabet book shows "animals from alligator to zebra, with a witty four-line rhyme for each." Hodges. Bks for Elem Sch Libraries

In this "brilliantly handsome alphabet book . . . the artist has made remarkable expressionistic pictures full of contrasting colors and startling patterns, shapes, and textures. . . . The book is full of controlled humor and fantasy." Horn Bk

The happy owls. Atheneum Pubs. 1964 [c1963] unp illus $7.95 **E**

1 Owls—Fiction
ISBN 0-689-20337-3 LC 64-3620

Original German edition published 1963 in Switzerland

A picture book illustrated by the author. "Originally a Dutch story, this version has been translated from the German." Top of the News

"The other fowl, always quarreling, ask the two happy owls how they live together so peacefully. The owls describe their contentment in the phenomena of the seasons, but the other birds cannot understand this and they go back to living and squabbling as before." Chicago. Children's Bk Center

"Beautiful designs and rich colours carry the mood and narrative of . . . [this legendary tale] through the four seasons of the year." Toronto

Pienkowski, Jan

Colors. Harvey House 1975 [c1974] unp lib. bdg. $5.29 **E**

1 Color
ISBN 0-8178-5232-8 LC 74-83404

First published 1974 in England

In this concept book, the author uses 10 easily recognizable objects as examples of colors, each preceded by the name of the color. The illustrations are "most striking. The electrifying black cat and the grinning green frog almost leap off the page." Sch Library J

Piper, Watty

The little engine that could; retold by Watty Piper [from The pony engine, by Mabel C. Bragg] Golden anniversary ed. Illus. by Ruth Sanderson. Platt 1976 unp illus $5.95 **E**

1 Locomotives—Fiction
ISBN 0-448-47373-9 LC 75-24534

First published 1930 with different illustrations

"When a train carrying good things to children breaks down, the little blue engine proves his courage and determination. The rhythmic, repetitive text encourages children to help tell the story." Hodges. Bks for Elem Sch Libraries

Platt, Kin

Big Max; with pictures by Robert Lopshire. Harper 1965 64p illus (An I can read mystery) lib. bdg. $7.89, pa $1.95 **E**

1 Elephants—Fiction 2 Mystery and detective stories
ISBN 0-06-024751-7; 0-06-444006-0 LC 65-14488

"Big Max, the world's greatest detective, travels by umbrella to help the king find Jumbo, his prize elephant, who has mysteriously disappeared." Library J

"The answer to the riddle of Jumbo's escape over the wall of the castle courtyard comes step by step through the dead-pan deductions of Big Max's professionally conducted sleuthing. The spontaneous fun of the text . . . has a happy complement in the pictures." Horn Bk

Another book about Big Max is: Big Max in the mystery of the missing moose. Harper $6.95, lib. bdg. $7.89 (ISBN 0-06-024756-8; 0-06-024757-6; LC 76-58727)

Politi, Leo

The butterflies come. Scribner [1972 c1957] unp illus lib. bdg. $8.95 **E**

1 Butterflies
ISBN 0-684-12348-7 LC 57-6848

A reissue of the title first published 1957

Illustrated by the author

The "story of the Monarch butterflies coming to the Monterey Peninsula. . . . The chalk-like illustrations help the reader visualize swarms of beautiful orange butterflies filling the sky and settling in trees. All the facts of nature used in the story are true. The occasion of the return of the butterflies is viewed from the perspective of two children." Adventuring with Bks

Moy Moy. Scribner 1960 unp illus lib. bdg. $7.95 **E**

1 Chinese Americans—Fiction 2 New Year— Fiction 3 Los Angeles—Fiction
ISBN 0-684-13178-1 LC 60-6413

Illustrated by the author

"Moy Moy, who lives on Chanking Street in Los Angeles, experiences the first Chinese New Year she is old enough to appreciate. Through her wondering eyes, in simple words, and pictures reminiscent of Chinese lacquer work, are depicted the children's lion dance, the dragon parade, firecrackers, goodies, toys—all the brilliant splendor of the festival." Moorachian. What is a City?

Pedro, the angel of Olvera Street. Scribner 1946 unp illus music lib. bdg. $8.95, pa $2.95 **E**

1 Mexican Americans—Fiction 2 Los Angeles— Fiction 3 Christmas—Fiction
ISBN 0-684-12628-1; 0-684-16003-X LC 46-11872

"Beguiling both in text and in the pictures with their soft, rich colors, this is the story of Mexican Olvera Street, little and lost in the heart of the great city of Los Angeles, but loved by young Pedro because of the shops and good Mexican foods, the music, the friendly people and the artisans at work at their interesting crafts. How Pedro, who sings like an angel, is chosen at Christmastime to lead La Posada is a happy introduction to a traditional Mexican custom. The words and music of two carols are included." Bookmark

Politi, Leo—*Continued*

Song of the swallows. Scribner 1949 unp illus music lib. bdg. $7.95   E

1 Swallows—Fiction 2 California—Fiction 3 San Juan Capistrano Mission (California)--Fiction
ISBN 0-684-92309-2   LC 49-8215

Awarded the Caldecott Medal, 1950
"The swallows always appeared at the old Mission of Capistrano on St Joseph's Day and Juan who lived nearby wondered how they could tell that from all others. This tender poetic story of the coming of springtime is touched by the kindliness of the good Fathers of the Mission as a little boy knew it. Lovely pictures [by the author] in soft colors bring out the charm of the southern California landscape and the melody of the swallow song adds to the feeling of Spring." Horn Bk
"There are three double-page paintings of the mission. ... . Two songs are given in full, with the music." Sat Rev

Polushkin, Maria

The little hen and the giant; pictures by Yuri Salzman. Harper 1977 31p illus $7.95, lib. bdg. $7.89   E

1 Chickens—Fiction 2 Giants—Fiction 3 Fairy tales
ISBN 0-06-024782-7; 0-06-024783-5   LC 76-58712

"The Russian ambience of both narrative and illustrations adds to the appeal of this tale of a small, determined hen with strong maternal instincts who resists oppression and destroys a wicked egg thief-giant. While accomplishing her task she encounters (and swallows) a fox, a wolf, a bear, and a lake, all drawn with skill. The story has both suspense and humor, and the image of the plump fowl on the last page, protectively clucking to her newly hatched chicks, can only be warmly reassuring in the nursery. Large, lively, three-color illustrations are perfect for showing to small story hour groups." Sch Library J

Pomerantz, Charlotte

The piggy in the puddle; pictures by James Marshall. Macmillan Pub. Co. 1974 unp illus $6.95   E

1 Pigs—Fiction 2 Stories in rhyme
ISBN 0-02-774900-2   LC 73-6047

"The squishy-squashy, mooshy-squooshy, oofy-poofy joy of mud is celebrated in this rhythmic tale of a small pig that scorns soap and refuses to leave her puddle. Her pleasure is infectious and finally mother, father, and brother join her in 'the very merry middle' of the 'muddy little puddle.'" Booklist
"The soft pastel drawings add just the right touch to the humorous bedtime story which demands to be read aloud." Children's Bk Rev Serv

Potter, Beatrix

The pie and the patty-pan. Warne illus lib. bdg. $3.50   E

1 Cats—Fiction 2 Dogs—Fiction
ISBN 0-7232-0608-2

Illustrated by the author
First published 1905 with title: A tale of the pie and the patty-pan
"Ribby, a pussy cat, invites a little dog named Duchess to tea." Bks for Boys and Girls

The sly old cat; written and illus. by Beatrix Potter. Warne [1972 c1971] 34p illus $5.95   E

1 Cats—Fiction 2 Rats—Fiction
ISBN 0-7232-1420-4   LC 73-163984

"Written in 1906, this is the tale of "an unusual tea party at [Cat's house in] which a rat saves himself from being the dessert." NY Pub Library. Children's Bks & Recordings, 1972
"Appearing now for the first time, the book is simple, slight, and ingenious, but amiable in its good-versus-evil appeal." Sat Rev

The story of Miss Moppet. Warne illus lib. bdg. $3.50   E

1 Cats—Fiction 2 Mice—Fiction
ISBN 0-7232-0612-0

Also available in a French language edition $4 (ISBN 0-7232-0635-X)
Illustrated by the author
First published 1906
Miss Moppet is a kitten who uses her wiles to capture a curious mouse. But her trickery amounts to naught when she herself is outwitted
Some other books about Moppet's brother Tom and sister Mittens are also available from Warne:
The roly-poly pudding lib. bdg. $3.50 (ISBN 0-7232-0607-4) Also available in a French language edition $4 (ISBN 0-7232-0657-0)
The tale of Tom Kitten lib. bdg. $3.50 (ISBN 0-7232-0599-X) Also available in a French language edition $4 (ISBN 0-7232-0657-0)

The tailor of Gloucester. Warne illus $6.95   E

1 Tailors—Fiction 2 Mice—Fiction 3 Christmas —Fiction
ISBN 0-7232-0594-9

Also available in a French language edition for $4 (ISBN 0-7232-0658-9)
First published 1903
"The cat Simpkin looked after his master when he was ill, but it was the nimble-fingered mice who used snippets of cherry-coloured twist and so finished the embroidered waist coat for the worried tailor. A Christmas-time story set in old Gloucester." Four to Fourteen
"A readaloud classic in polished style, perfectly complemented by the author's exquisite watercolor illustrations." Hodges. Bks for Elem Sch Libraries

The tale of Jemima Puddle-duck. Warne illus lib. bdg. $3.50   E

1 Ducks—Fiction
ISBN 0-7232-0600-7

Also available in a French language edition for $4 (ISBN 0-7232-0653-8)
Illustrated by the author
First published 1908
"Jemima Puddle-duck's obstinate determination to hatch her own eggs, makes a story of suspense and sly humor." Bks for Boys and Girls

The tale of Mr Jeremy Fisher. Warne illus lib. bdg. $3.50   E

1 Frogs—Fiction
ISBN 0-7232-0598-1

Also available in a French language edition (ISBN 0-7232-0656-2) and a Latin language edition (ISBN 0-7232-2104-9) for $4 each
Illustrated by the author
First published 1906
Mr Jeremy Fisher, a frog, encounters some problems when he goes fishing
The author's "paintings of lily pads and green marshes are cool and lovely." Bks for Boys and Girls

The tale of Mrs Tiggy-Winkle. Warne illus lib. bdg. $3.50   E

1 Hedgehogs—Fiction
ISBN 0-7232-0597-3

Also available in a French language edition for $4 (ISBN 0-7232-0652-X)
Illustrated by the author
First published 1905
"Little Lucy loses her pocket-handkin, and finds Mrs. Tiggy-Winkle, a hedgehog washer-woman." Bks for Boys and Girls

The tale of Mrs Tittlemouse. Warne illus lib. bdg. $3.50   E

1 Mice—Fiction
ISBN 0-7232-0602-3

First published 1910
The now classic story of Mrs Tittlemouse, a very tidy, particular woodmouse, illustrated with the author's delicate water colors

The tale of Peter Rabbit. Warne illus lib. bdg. $3.50   E

1 Rabbits—Fiction
ISBN 0-7232-0592-2

Also available in the following foreign language editions: French (ISBN 0-7232-0650-3); Latin (ISBN 0-7232-0648-1); Spanish (ISBN 0-7232-0671-6) for $4 each
First published 1901
All about the famous rabbit family consisting of Flopsy, Mopsy, Cotton-tail and especially Peter

Potter, Beatrix—*Continued*

Rabbit who disobeys Mother Rabbit's admonishment not to go into Mr McGregor's garden

"Distinctive writing and a strong appeal to a small child's sense of justice and his sympathies make this an outstanding story. The water color illustrations [by the author] add charm to the narrative by their simplicity of detail and delicacy of color." Children's Bks Too Good to Miss

Some other books about Peter Rabbit and his family are also available from Warne:

The tale of Benjamin Bunny lib. bdg. $3.50 (ISBN 0-7232-0595-7) Also available in a French language edition $4 (ISBN 0-7232-0651-1)
The tale of Mr Tod lib. bdg. $3.50 (ISBN 0-7232-0605-8)
The tale of the flopsy bunnies lib. bdg. $3.50 (ISBN 0-7232-0601-5) Also available in a French language edition $4 (ISBN 0-7232-0655-4)

The tale of Pigling Bland. Warne illus lib. bdg. $3.50   E

1 Pigs—Fiction
ISBN 0-7232-0606-6
Illustrated by the author
First published 1913
"Pigling's story ends happily with a perfectly lovely little black Berkshire pig called Pigwig." Bks for Boys and Girls

The tale of Squirrel Nutkin. Warne illus lib. bdg. $3.50   E

1 Squirrels—Fiction
ISBN 0-7232-0593-0
Also available in a French language edition for $4 (ISBN 0-7232-0654-6)
Illustrated by the author
First published 1903
Each day the squirrels gather nuts, Nutkin propounds a riddle to Mr Brown, the owl, until impertinent Nutkin, over-estimating Mr Brown's patience, gets his due

The tale of the faithful dove; illus. by Marie Angel. 2d ed. Warne 1970 unp illus lib. bdg. $3.95   E

1 Pigeons—Fiction
ISBN 0-7232-1336-4   LC 75-109403
Written in 1907. First published 1956
"A gentle story of a little pigeon who was chased into a chimney by a hawk. An unillustrated, posthumous manuscript by the author which is illustrated [by Marie Angel] and printed in the style and format of the other Potter books." Best Bks for Children, 1972

The tale of Tuppenny; illus. by Marie Angel. Warne [1973 c1971] 39p illus lib. bdg. $3.95 E

1 Guinea pigs—Fiction
ISBN 0-7232-6097-4   LC 72-89477
Text written 1903. This version first published 1971 in England in Leslie Linder's: A history of the writings of Beatrix Potter, including unpublished work

"In a town inhabited by guinea pigs, a quack medication was touted, guaranteed to grow hair. ... After using several bottles of this, poor Tuppenny began to grow hair—but at a fantastic rate. The surprised concocter, beleaguered, vanished; Tuppenny had to spend all his time getting his hair cut until he finally gave up and joined a circus as Tuppenny the Hairy Guinea Pig." Chicago. Children's Bk Center
For its first publication the text "was reworked by the author for use as the first chapter of the 1929 Fairy Caravan.... Presented here in its original form, it is better written.... The book has been issued in the small format of the 'Peter Rabbit' series. While the artist's style is appropriately reminiscent of Potter, her skillfully detailed, softly colored illustrations would be more effective in a larger book. Nevertheless, the tale retains the charm, directness, and lack of sentimentality for which Beatrix Potter is so highly regarded." Sch Library J

The tale of two bad mice. Warne illus lib. bdg. $3.50   E

1 Mice—Fiction
ISBN 0-7232-0596-5
Also available in a French language edition $4 (ISBN 0-7232-0596-5)
Illustrated by the author
First published 1904
"Two mischievous little mice pilfer a doll's house to equip their own. They are caught and finally make amends for what they have done. Perfectly charming illustrations and a most enticing tale." Adventuring With Bks. 2d edition

Prelutsky, Jack

The mean old mean hyena; illus. by Arnold Lobel. Greenwillow Bks. 1978 unp illus $7.95, lib. bdg. $7.63   E

1 Hyenas—Fiction 2 Stories in rhyme
ISBN 0-688-80163-3; 0-688-84163-5   LC 78-2300
The hyena "paints a sleeping zebra plaid, stuffs tufts of sneezy snuff into a snoozing elephant's trunk, ties a napping ostrich's neck in a knot, snips off a dozing lion's mane—and finally gets caught, whereupon he pulls Brer Rabbit's briar patch trick, begging just please not to be tickled, which is of course what the animals do. After this harmless punishment, the mean hyena runs off scott free—surely a wish fulfillment if ever there was one. Lobel's gray-and-gold wash drawings on almost every page are clean, mean, and to the point." Booklist

"Prelutsky's trickster tale is witty and alive with wonderfully onomatopoetic words and lilting rhythm. It makes a fine read-aloud book, especially for anyone who likes to ham it up. Prelutsky reminds us how dynamic poetry can be. A tour de force." Children's Bk Rev Serv

Preston, Edna Mitchell

Squawk to the moon, Little Goose; illus. by Barbara Cooney. Viking 1974 unp illus lib. bdg. $6.95   E

1 Geese—Fiction 2 Moon—Fiction
ISBN 0-670-66609-2   LC 72-91394
This is the "story of a gosling that is both silly and resourceful. . . . Tucked in for the night, Little Goose steals out for a night ramble; she sees the moon covered by a cloud and wakes the farmer with her squawking; it happens again when she sees the moon reflected in the pond and decides it has fallen. When she's caught by a fox, Little Goose squawks, but the disgruntled farmer won't get up a third time. However, Little Goose uses her wits and outfoxes the fox, going home to a maternal spank and cuddle." Chicago. Children's Bk Center

"Ms. Cooney has infused her watercolor illustrations with so much personality, drollery and beauty that fortunate owners of this book will find themselves gazing at the pictures again and again, finding new aspects at which to marvel each time. And Ms. Preston's fable is equally enchanting." Pub W

Provensen, Alice

A book of seasons [by] Alice and Martin Provensen. Random House 1976 unp illus lib. bdg. $3.99, pa 95¢   E

1 Seasons
ISBN 0-394-93242-0; 0-394-83242-6   LC 75-36470
"A Random House picturebook"
Color pictures of the year-round activities of children provide the focus for this book about the changing seasons

The year at Maple Hill Farm [by] Alice and Martin Provensen. Atheneum Pubs. 1978 unp illus $5.95, lib. bdg. $5.69   E

1 Seasons—Fiction 2 Farm life—Fiction 3 Animals—Fiction
ISBN 0-689-30642-3; 0-689-20494-9   LC 77-18518
"A Jonathan Cape book"
An "exploration of the varied monthly activities of the animals that dwell at Maple Hill Farm. To start the year, a two-page spread captures the wintry feel of January, where bundled farmers feed the waiting animals as twilight falls. February finds goat, cat, and pony mothers busily attending their babies; . . . during the hot, lazy August days only the dog's tail stirs; in October restless birds and busy squirrels herald autumn's arrival; and finally in December barn companions huddle sleepily together out of the snow. Sharp-eyed children will see many other happenings in their seasonal journey around the calendar and will discover new meanings in the familiar habits of their animal friends." Booklist

"Each of the twelve double-page spreads has a running line of general comment across the tops of the pages . . . and captions for the other pictures, of which there may be one or several. The

Provensen, Alice—*Continued*

text is direct, mildly humorous, and informative; the illustrations are perky and amusing, with soft, bright colors and the appeal of animals, animals, animals." Chicago. Children's Bk Center

Quackenbush, Robert

Detective Mole; written and illus. by Robert Quackenbush. Lothrop 1976 63p illus (A Fun to read bk) $6.95, lib. bdg. $6.67 **E**

1 Moles (Animals)—Fiction 2 Mystery and detective stories
ISBN 0-688-41726-4; 0-688-51726-9   LC 75-25806

"A nearsighted but stalwart private eye solves half-a-dozen mysteries for his animal neighbors. The mysteries are none too clever, and as on television, the plots seem like formula creations. But there are some laughs to be gotten out of the brief tales, and they'll probably make readers feel smart. The author's crowded, green-and-white drawings are mostly funny, too." Booklist

Some other books about Detective Mole are also available from Lothrop:

Detective Mole and the circus mystery $6.95, lib. bdg. $6.67 (ISBN 0-688-41936-4; 0-688-51936-9; LC 79-20083)

Detective Mole and the seashore mystery $6.95, lib. bdg. $6.67 (ISBN 0-688-41917-8; 0-688-51917-2; LC 79-14431)

Detective Mole and the secret clues $6.95, lib. bdg. $6.67 (ISBN 0-688-41783-3; 0-688-51783-8; LC 76-39895)

Detective Mole and the tip-top mystery $6.95, lib. bdg. $6.67 (ISBN 0-688-41858-3; 0-688-51858-3; LC 78-6082)

Quin-Harkin, Janet

Peter Penny's dance; pictures by Anita Lobel. Dial Press 1976 unp illus $7.95, lib. bdg. $7.47, pa $2.50 **E**

1 Voyages around the world—Fiction
ISBN 0-8037-7183-5; 0-8037-7184-3; 0-8037-7180-0
LC 75-27600

"Peter, a 19th-century English sailor, is a dancin' fool, and he's challenged to dance his way around the world in five years, the reward to be the beautiful Lavinia. So of course he does it, with many adventures en route: bullfights, feasting with the Masai, dancing over the Great Wall." Sat Rev

"The story is carefully written; the illustrations, beautifully executed; and the format, stunningly presented. . . . Each country visited by Peter is artistically conveyed in characteristic tones and style." Babbling Bookworm

Raskin, Ellen

And it rained. Atheneum Pubs. 1969 unp illus lib. bdg. $6.95 **E**

1 Rain and rainfall—Fiction 2 Animals—Fiction
ISBN 0-689-20587-2   LC 69-18967

Illustrated by the author
"Ellen Raskin presents the pig, the parrot, the potto, and an all-star cast of characters in And it rained." Title page

A tale of what happens "when a group of animals are frustrated [by recurring rain] in their attempts to have a proper four o'clock tea." Wis Library Bul

"The wisdom contained in this deceptively simple story may be lost on some small children, but all youngsters will be charmed by the [author's] finely detailed pictures, which alternate yellow and blue backgrounds with the green foregrounds. In the backgrounds, among exotic trees, other animals—which are identified at the back of the book—frolic. A fun, witty achievement." Sch Library J

Ghost in a four-room apartment. Atheneum Pubs. 1969 unp illus lib. bdg. $8.29, pa $1.95 **E**

1 Ghosts—Fiction
ISBN 0-689-20354-3; 0-689-70446-1   LC 69-13521

This story, illustrated by the author, is about a poltergeist who haunts a four-room apartment and creates havoc there. The narrative is divided between the ghost, who recounts his activities, and a narrator who describes in verse the members of the haunted family and their relatives

"The illustrations are a series of stained-glass showcases for Miss Raskin's considerable talents.

Bright blocks of colorfully detailed line drawings exploit the hilarity of bewildered guests trying to dodge objects flying about everywhere." NY Times Bk Rev

Nothing ever happens on my block. Atheneum Pubs. 1966 unp illus lib. bdg. $6.95, pa $1.95 **E**

ISBN 0-689-20588-0; 0-689-70436-4   LC 66-12853

Illustrated by the author
"Chester Filbert, the personification of the 'grass is greener,' sits on the curb longing to see fierce lions, monsters, or other fantastic sights. Meanwhile he misses all the fantastic events, including robberies and fires transpiring around him. Much of the fun is in combing the [author's] illustrations for all the things Chester is missing." Minnesota

"In all fairness to Chester all those thefts and parachute jumps never happened on my block either. This in no way detracts from the inventive excellence of the book, which is a delight." NY Times Bk Rev

Spectacles. Atheneum Pubs. 1968 unp illus lib. bdg. $5.93, pa $1.95 **E**

1 Eyeglasses—Fiction
ISBN 0-689-20352-7; 0-689-70317-1   LC 68-12234

Illustrated by the author
Even though nearsighted "Iris swears that there's a fire-breathing dragon at the door, a giant pygmy nuthatch on the lawn, a chestnut mare in the parlor, her readers will see, by flipping the page each time, that it's only Great-aunt Fanny, her friend Chester, and the baby sitter respectively. Iris detests specs but gets them, anyway." Sch Library J

"Laughable picture book, conceived and illustrated with imagination and humor. May be useful with children resisting needed glasses." Booklist

Who, said Sue, said whoo? Atheneum Pubs. 1973 unp illus $8.95, pa $1.95 **E**

1 Animals—Fiction 2 Stories in rhyme
ISBN 0-689-30096-4; 0-689-70425-9   LC 72-86947

Illustrated by the author, this "cumulative rhyming tongue-twister with a surprise ending . . . will provide both aural and visual fun for children. Driving her car through a jungle of fantastical vegetation, Sue collects a menagerie of beasts by asking which one is making whatever noise she hears. Her car quickly unloads, however, when the one animal she has not been able to identify throughout the book finally appears—a skunk, who drives away with a chimpanzee unable to smell because of a cold. The brightly colored pictures, splashed liberally with lime green, are nicely nonsensical." Booklist

Rayner, Mary

Mr and Mrs Pig's evening out. Atheneum Pubs. 1976 unp illus $8.95, pa $2.50 **E**

1 Pigs—Fiction
ISBN 0-689-30530-3; 0-689-70463-1   LC 76-4476

"Even though Mrs. Pig assures them she has hired a very nice lady from the babysitting agency, her 10 piglets moan and groan in protest. She goes to the door and ushers in a cloaked, sinister figure, the babysitter who answers to the name of Mrs. Wolf. Tension mounts as Mrs. Wolf turns on the oven and makes for the piglets' bedroom, where she grabs one brother and heads back to the preheated oven. The piglets rally round to rescue their brother for an exciting and victorious ending." NY Times Bk Rev

"If humour and terror (resolved) are the ingredients of treasured nursery-stories, Mary Rayner's [book] will be loved till its sturdy binding falls off. Mary Rayner is a born storyteller . . . and now she proves herself also to be a superb illustrator. . . . [The] book has style, wit, excitement, high drama, and pathos." Times (London) Lit Sup

Followed by: Garth Pig and the icecream lady. Atheneum Pubs. $8.95 (ISBN 0-689-30598-2; LC 77-1647)

Reiss, John J.

Colors; a book by John J. Reiss. Bradbury Press 1969 unp illus $7.95 **E**

1 Color
ISBN 0-87888-008-9   LC 69-13653

Things to eat and wear and animals to chase appear in this introduction to the primary and secondary colors

"The simplest of formats and a sophisticated use of color and design combine to make a big and

Reiss, John J.—*Continued*
beautiful first book for the child learning to distinguish colors. The text consists entirely of the names of colors and the names of objects pictured. . . . The shades are vibrant, the layout stunning." Sat Rev

Numbers; a book. Bradbury Press 1971 unp illus $7.95   E

1 Counting
ISBN 0-87888-029-1   LC 76-151313

"This is a big, brilliantly colored picture book which first counts from one to ten and then by tens to one hundred and ends with the number one thousand (raindrops). It enumerates such things as shoes, starfish arms, baseball players, kites, radishes, crayons, beads, gumballs, and centipede legs. The colorful pages and clear drawings invite viewer participation both in identifying objects and counting them." Booklist

Shapes; a book. Bradbury Press 1974 unp illus $7.95   E

1 Size and shape
ISBN 0-87888-053-4   LC 73-76545

"Absolutely luscious in its spectrum of vivid colors . . . [this book presents] examples of such shapes as oval, circle, triangle, rectangle, and square. Reiss carries it a bit farther, showing how squares form a cube, or circles a sphere, and he tosses in a few more complex shapes at the close of the book to intrigue the audience: a hexagon, an octagon, a pentagon. Examples of each shape are included; for rectangles, for example, there are doors, wooden planks, and sticks of gum. Animals cavort among the shapes, adding interest to the visual appeal and the clearly presented concepts." Chicago. Children's Bk Center

Rey, H. A.
Cecily G. and the 9 monkeys. Houghton 1942 31p illus lib. bdg. $7.95, pa pa $1.95   E

1 Giraffes—Fiction 2 Monkeys—Fiction
ISBN 0-395-18430-4; 0-395-25380-2   LC 42-20276

A nonsense book describing in prose and picture the adventures of a lonely giraffe, and some homeless little monkeys
"Mr. Rey's big, colored pictures of Cecily Giraffe are unexpected and laughable, and it's remarkable to how many surprising uses his nine young monkeys can put one obliging giraffe." NY Libraries

Curious George. Houghton 1941 unp illus lib. bdg. $7.95, pa $1.95   E

1 Monkeys—Fiction
ISBN 0-395-17075-3; 0-395-15023-X   LC 41-16054

Also available in a Spanish language edition: lib. bdg. $7.95, pa $2.95 (ISBN 0-395-17075-3; 0-395-24909)
Illustrated by the author
Colored picture book, with simple text, describing the adventures of a curious small monkey, and the difficulties he had in getting used to city life, before he went to live in the zoo
"The bright lithographs in red, yellow, and blue, are gay and lighthearted, following the story closely with the same speed and animated humour." Ontario Library Rev

Some other books about Curious George are also available from Houghton:
Curious George flies a kite, lib. bdg. $7.95, pa $2.95 (ISBN 0-395-16965-8; 0395-25937-1; LC 58-8163)
Curious George gets a medal lib. bdg. $7.95, pa $1.95 (ISBN 0-395-16973-9; 0-395-18559-9; LC 57-7206)
Curious George goes to the hospital, by Margaret & H. A. Rey in collaboration with the Children's Hopistal Medical Center lib. bdg. $7.95, pa $1.95 (ISBN 0-395-18158-5; 0-395-07062-7; LC 65-19301)
Curious George learns the alphabet lib. bdg. $7.95, pa $2.45 (ISBN 0-395-16031-6; 0-395-18559-9; LC 62-12261)
Curious George rides a bike lib. bdg. $6.95, pa $1.95 (ISBN 0-305-16964-X; 0-395-17444-9; LC 52-8728)
Curious George takes a job lib. bdg. $6.95, pa $1.95 (ISBN 0-395-15086-8; 0-395-18649-8; LC 47-5527)

Rice, Eve
New blue shoes; story and pictures by Eve Rice. Macmillan Pub. Co. 1975 unp illus lib. bdg. $7.95   E

1 Shoes and shoe industry—Fiction 2 Shopping—Fiction
ISBN 0-02-775960-1   LC 74-13259

"Shoe shopping is a special treat for most children and often an occasion for lively debate; Rice zeroes in on the process, picturing Mama going out with Rebecca, who is adamant about acquiring a pair of blue shoes. 'Blue?' says Mama. 'I think brown would be much nicer.' Rebecca is stubborn. 'I want "nice" shoes . . . nice new blue shoes!' She gets them and on the way home has second thoughts, though Mama is happy enough to soothe Rebecca's doubts and assure her that her choice is respectable. The plain, three-color line drawings proceed in framed scenes that are literal and easy to follow." Booklist

Papa's lemonade, and other stories. Greenwillow Bks. 1976 56p illus $5.95, lib. bdg. $5.71   E

1 Family life—Fiction 2 Dogs—Fiction
ISBN 0-688-80041-6; 0-68884041-8   LC 75-38754

"Greenwillow Read-alone"
"Five loosely connected episodes deal with the everyday problems of an appealing dog family—from a shattered piggy bank to making 'lemonade' with oranges." Sch Library J
"The book has mild humor, good family relationships, and a writing style that is nicely gauged for the audience." Chicago. Children's Bk Center

Sam who never forgets. Greenwillow Bks. 1977 unp illus $7.50, lib. bdg. $7.20   E

1 Zoological gardens—Fiction 2 Animals—Fiction
ISBN 0-688-80088-2; 0-688-84088-4   LC 76-30370

Sam is "a zoo keeper who 'never, never forgets' to feed the animals promptly at three o'clock. The beasts have their doubts when it looks like Sam has neglected to feed poor Elephant who is both hungry and crestfallen. Happily, Sam returns with a whole wagon of hay." Sch Library J
"A simple, unpretentious story with child appeal that lies in the naive, straightforward telling and elemental emotional interactions of the characters. . . . Rice has forsaken her pen drawings for bright, unlined colored shapes. The figures are pleasantly stylized, the scenes evenly composed; it's all precisely tuned to the younger picture-book audience." Booklist

Roche, P. K.
Good-bye, Arnold! Story and pictures by P. K. Roche. Dial Press 1979 unp illus $6.95, lib. bdg. $6.46   E

1 Brothers—Fiction 2 Mice—Fiction
ISBN 0-8037-3031-4; 0-8037-3032-2   LC 79-50750

"When Webster's big brother Arnold (both 'boys' pictured as mouse children) goes away for a week's visit to grandma's, Webster is glad for the breather. He promptly tries out all Arnold's heretofore forbidden toys, gets a bigger piece of pie at dinner, and sleeps in his brother's coveted top bunk, among other things. As the week wears on, though, Webster begins to recollect some of the fun times he had with Arnold. And in the middle of one night he awakens to yell worriedly, 'I hear too much quiet!' When Saturday brings Arnold's return, both children are happy to see each other. The framed illustrations project a benevolent mood. Interiors are softly colored and country cozy with wide board floors, flower-sprigged walls, and fat stuffed chairs. Low key and good humored, both visually and psychologically." Booklist
Followed by: Webster and Arnold. Dial Press lib. bdg. $5.89, pa $2.25 (ISBN 0-8037-9436-3; 0-8037-9432-0; LC 80-11595)

Rockwell, Anne
Albert B. Cub & Zebra; an alphabet storybook. Crowell 1977 unp illus $7.95, lib. bdg. $8.49   E

1 Alphabet 2 Stories without words
ISBN 0-690-01350-7; 0-690-01351-5   LC 76-54224

"The wordless story of Albert B. Cub's search for his missing friend, Zebra, combines with an alphabet-puzzle format and the result functions well on all levels. The alphabet is clearly and

Rockwell, Anne—*Continued*

attractively represented in large upper and lower case letters. The picture puzzles are crammed with fascinating objects and actions from apes under arches and artists painting angels to zebras eating zinnias in zoos. A more complicated story in words at the back of the book (suitable for reading aloud) supplements and explicates Rockwell's clear, bright, and amusing watercolors. There is a lot here to muse over, laugh at, and come back to over and over again." Sch Library J

Blackout, by Anne & Harlow Rockwell. Macmillan Pub. Co. 1979 63p illus $6.95 **E**

1 Storms—Fiction 2 Electric power failures—Fiction
ISBN 0-02-777610-7 LC 78-12185

"Ready-to-read"
"Grey tones used with black and white make the simple, almost bland pictures appropriately shadowed for a simplified account of a power failure due to an ice storm. The members of the family notice a live wire emitting sparks, and Father calls the power company. With no lights and no heat, everybody puts on extra clothing and sleeps in front of the fireplace. Mother and Father turn off the water so the pipes won't freeze, they shop in a dark store, they manage to get a small supply of wood and candles. The power company fixes the dangerous wire, goes off to cope with other emergencies, and then—at last—electrical power is restored and the house gets warm again. The text is carefully gauged for a primary grades audience, it's painlessly informative about safety measures, and it conveys quite vividly the tension and suspense of living through a blackout." Chicago. Children's Bk Center

Rockwell, Harlow

My nursery school. Greenwillow Bks. 1976 unp illus $7.50, lib. bdg. $7.20 **E**

1 Nursery school
ISBN 0-688-80025-4; 0-688-84025-6 LC 75-25871

"Clear, simple pictures with no clutter and plenty of white space illustrate the activities described by a small girl who, delivered by father and picked up by mother, spends a happy morning. She speaks of her teachers and of the other nine children in the class, what she and they best like to do, of the plants and pets, playground activities, classroom equipment, marching and singing." Chicago. Children's Bk Center
"The author-artist is particularly skillful at speaking directly through words and pictures to the feelings and interests of very young children. What could so easily be banal and commonplace—a picture book about a child's daily activities—is utterly simple yet aesthetically satisfying. . . . The brief, carefully enunciated text is stated in the first person." Horn Bk

Rojankovsky, Feodor

Animals in the zoo; illus. by Feodor Rojankovsky. Knopf 1962 unp illus lib. bdg. $6.99 **E**

1 Animals 2 Alphabet
ISBN 0-394-90706-X LC 61-6052

The author has written an alphabet book in which the alligator, the baboon, cheetah, dromedary, elephant, fennec, and giraffe through the yak and the zebra illustrate letters
"Worth lingering over are the appealing soft-eyed fennec, the huge, open-mouthed hippo, the Dürer-like jackrabbit, the leaping kangaroos, the quetzal's realistic feathers, and the velvety seals." Horn Bk

Animals on the farm. Knopf 1967 unp illus lib. bdg. $6.99 **E**

1 Domestic animals
ISBN 0-394-91875-4 LC 67-18586

Illustrated by the author
This picture book identifies 19 farm animals, including goats, cats, horses, donkeys, cows, pigs, sheep, rabbits, and turkeys
"A pleasant helpful books with large softly coloured pictures." Ontario Library Rev

F. Rojankovsky's ABC; an alphabet of many things. Golden Press [1971 c1970] unp illus lib. bdg. $9.15 **E**

1 Alphabet
ISBN 0-307-65529-6 LC 71-112690

"A Big Golden book"
Each letter of the alphabet is illustrated on a separate page with pictures of familiar objects such as airplane, button, clown, etc.

Rose, Gerald

The tiger-skin rug. Prentice-Hall 1979 unp illus lib. bdg. $6.95 **E**

1 Tigers—Fiction 2 India—Fiction
ISBN 0-13-921585-9 LC 78-18395

"Children will love this clever story about a real tiger who pretends to be a tiger-skin rug in the Rajah's palace. The brightly colored illustrations are vividly expressive. One almost feels it as the tiger is washed, hung to dry, and dragged up the stairs. He eventually saves the Rajah from three robbers and becomes a family pet." Children's Bk Rev Serv

Rosen, Winifred

Henrietta and the day of the iguana; illus. by Kay Chorao. Four Winds 1978 unp illus lib. bdg. $6.95 **E**

1 Shopping—Fiction 2 Department stores—Fiction
3 Iguanas—Fiction
ISBN 0-590-07471-7 LC 77-19047

"Henrietta hates shopping. So, what does she do when her mother and her older sister Evelyn—who love to shop—drag her along? She thinks of buying herself an iguana, that's what. She even gets her dad to take her iguana-shopping on a Saturday in the rain—for a lizard she finally decides she doesn't want after all." Children's Bk Rev Serv
"Another entertaining story about doughty little Henrietta (the erstwhile wild woman of Borneo, self-styled) is illustrated by nicely textured black and white drawings that echo the humor of the text. Henrietta tells the story, sometimes with a trace of the Plaza's Eloise. . . . The father-child relationship is warm and candid, the dialogue is natural, and the story has a deftly humorous treatment of a not uncommon childhood reaction." Chicago. Children's Bk Center

Roy, Ron

Three ducks went wandering; pictures by Paul Galdone. Seabury [distributed by Houghton] 1979 unp illus $8.95 **E**

1 Ducks—Fiction
ISBN 0-395-28954-8 LC 78-12629

"A Clarion book"
"Three bright-looking ducklings pass from one diversion to the next, oblivious of the various dangers that stalk them along the way. These—a charging bull, a family of foxes, a hawk, and a snake—find their predatory inclinations stymied by the ducklings' successive moves. Galdone's exuberant, astutely composed drawings magnify the drama and the humor to good effect." Booklist

Ryan, Cheli D.

Hildilid's night; illus. by Arnold Lobel. Macmillan Pub. Co 1971 unp illus lib. bdg. $4.50, pa 95¢ **E**

1 Night—Fiction
ISBN 0-02-777990-4; 0-02-044810-4 LC 75-146627

"An old woman who hates the night tries to sweep it out, tie it up, feed it to her hound, burn it, and drown it; she stamps on it, spanks it, and even spits on it, but the night takes no notice. She decides she will not notice the night and settles down to sleep to be fresh and ready to turn her back on it when it returns." Booklist
"A streak of ochre lights up the last few pages, underscoring the joke [on Hildilid]. . . . A curious, furious tale told in rich considered language that begs to be read aloud." NY Times Bk Rev

Sandburg, Carl

The wedding procession of the Rag Doll and the Broom Handle and who was in it; pictures by Harriet Pincus. Harcourt [1967 c1950] unp illus $6.50, pa $2.25 **E**

1 Dolls—Fiction 2 Marriage customs and rites—Fiction
ISBN 0-15-294930-5; 0-15-695487-7 LC 67-2763

A picture book version of a tale from: Rootabaga stories, entered in the story collections section, first published 1922 and recopyrighted 1950
"A splendid procession at the rag doll's wedding is led by the nuptial pair, who are followed by limp

Sandburg, Carl—*Continued*

and lumpy fun babies. Dolled up in birthday-party colors and quaintly modern costumes, they parade in a line—laughing, licking, tickling, wiggling, chuzzling, snozzling, clear to the 'last of all,' the staggering Sleepy heads." Horn Bk

"Small children (and the parents who read it with them) will be very grateful, as they giggle over this antic picture book story, that no one told Harriet Pincus that Carl Sandburg . . . [was] high man on the Legend In His Time totem pole. . . . For she has illustrated this story . . . not with the solemn reverence due the work of a Living Legend, but with the earthy exuberance that Sandburg had when he wrote it, way back in 1922." Pub W

Sauer, Julia L.

Mike's house; illus. by Don Freeman. Viking 1954 31p illus lib. bdg. $3.50   E

1 Libraries—Fiction 2 Snow—Fiction
ISBN 0-670-47573-4   LC 54-8562

"Because 'Mike Mulligan' is his favorite book, four-year-old Robert loves the public library—'Mike's House'—and never misses a story hour there. One day he gets lost in a snowstorm and is helped by many kindly people before arriving at the library." Hodges. Bks for Elem Sch Libraries

"The humor and understanding of the text are perfectly complemented by Don Freeman's vigorous illustrations." NY Times Bk Rev

Scheer, Julian

Rain makes applesauce [by] Julian Scheer & Marvin Bileck. Holiday House 1964 unp illus $8.95   E

ISBN 0-8234-0091-3   LC 64-56216
Illustrated by Marvin Bileck

"A book of original nonsense, illustrated with intricate drawings. Small children love the refrains, 'Rain makes applesauce' and 'You're just talking silly talk,' and enjoy the fantastic details in the pictures." Hodges. Bks for Elem Sch Libraries

Schick, Eleanor

One summer night. Greenwillow Bks. 1977 unp illus lib. bdg. $7.44   E

1 City life—Fiction
ISBN 0-688-84072-8   LC 76-25199
Illustrated by the author

"Stirred by a warm summer breeze, Laura takes to dancing in her room, spreading a contagion of joy and mirth throughout her block. Two little girls across the street catch it first, then Mr. Stein next door and Mrs. Cameron across the courtyard—until finally the whole block on which Laura lives is teeming with people dancing, singing, and playing music. Evoking warmth and good feelings, this unique picture story takes a rare look at the positive interrelationships among people of diverse ethnic backgrounds living together in an urban setting. The illustrations are earthy, rhythmical, and splendidly detailed." Children's Bk Rev Serv

Peggy's new brother. Macmillan Pub. Co. 1970 unp illus lib. bdg. $4.95   E

1 Infants—Fiction 2 Brothers and sisters—Fiction
ISBN 0-02-781140-9   LC 70-99124

The author's "clean-lined and simply-drawn pictures show a small girl and a pregnant mother; grandmother's appearance heralds the arrival of the new baby. Peggy, who has had the usual doubts about the value of babies versus that of cats, finds that her new brother is a scene-stealer. Disgruntled but anxious to participate, Peggy tries to help but finds that she is not deft enough; but—only Peggy can make the baby laugh when he is cranky. Not innovative, but so natural and realistic a picture book that it can be very effective in preparing the small child for a new baby." Chicago. Children's Bk Center

Summer at the sea. Greenwillow Bks. 1979 56p illus $5.95, lib. bdg. $5.71   E

1 Seashore—Fiction 2 Summer—Fiction
ISBN 0-688-80116-1; 0-688-84116-3   LC 77-3026

"Greenwillow Read-alone"

"Schick brings to mind the warm, nostalgic flavors of a seaside summer and does so by tuning in carefully to a child's perceptions. The loose

structure of sketches is well chosen for capturing a meandering, pleasant time as the girl narrator describes her neighbor Loretta ('She never got married, not even when she was young') or the garden she makes with her father, who brings pansies from the city. Poetic mood-touches are memorable for their color and simplicity. . . . The trip back to the city rounds out an experience. 'Summers can't last forever,' the girl's father tells her—but memories last a long time. Schick uses her own subtle crosshatched shadings and soft-sculptured figures to catch her characters' feelings as well as the lights and hues of the setting. A refreshing break from more standard plotline realizations of childhood experiences." Booklist

Schlein, Miriam

Fast is not a ladybug; a book about fast and slow things; illus. by Leonard Kessler. Young Scott Bks. 1953 unp illus lib. bdg. $5.95   E

1 Speed
ISBN 0-201-09181-X   LC 53-7805

A book about slow things and fast things and the relations between slow and faster, slow and slower —a ladybug, a little boy running, a fire engine, a train on a track, a cloud on a lazy day, and a seed slowly growing

"Amusing illustrations and simple text present the concept that speed is relative." Hodges. Bks for Elem Sch Libraries

Heavy is a hippopotamus; pictures by Leonard Kessler. Young Scott Bks. 1954 unp illus lib. bdg. $5.95   E

1 Weights and measures
ISBN 0-201-09217-4   LC 54-9913

Ounces, pounds, tons—what do they mean? In this elementary book the author develops an understanding of weights and measures by showing different ways of thinking about heaviness or lightness in relation to some familiar objects

The author "is ably assisted by illustrator Leonard Kessler, who can make something as prosaic as a weighing machine almost as funny and attractive as a very heavy hippopotamus." NY Times Bk Rev

Shapes; pictures by Sam Berman. Young Scott Bks. 1952 unp illus lib. bdg. $5.95   E

1 Size and shape
ISBN 0-201-09343-X   LC 52-8836

"Familiar objects help develop geometric concepts of round, square, line, straight line, curve, long, and tall." Hardgrove. Math Library—Elem and Jr High Sch

"This is a brilliant little book which will help to train a youngster's eye and make him sharply aware of form and design." NY Times Bk Rev

Schulman, Janet

Camp KeeWee's secret weapon; pictures by Marylin Hafner. Greenwillow Bks 1979 63p illus $5.95, lib. bdg. $5.71   E

1 Camps—Fiction 2 Softball—Fiction
ISBN 0-688-80185-4; 0-688-84185-6   LC 78-16742

"Greenwillow Read-alone"

"Although readers may be briefly disheartened by long time gaps between some chapters and a too-sudden ending, they will find here a warmly told story about a common experience. Schulman writes clearly from the child's point of view as her protagonist, Jill, looks with foreboding at seemingly insurmountable obstacles of adjusting to summer camp. Jill does find her niche—friends and a respected position on the softball team—in quite plausible ways. . . . Hafner's color illustrations are as contemporary and easy to enjoy as ever." Booklist

Schweitzer, Byrd Baylor

Amigo; illus. by Garth Williams. Macmillan Pub. Co. 1963 41p illus lib. bdg. $5.95, pa $2.95   E

1 Mexico—Fiction 2 Prairie dogs 3 Stories in rhyme
ISBN 0-02-781300-2; 0-02-044950-X   LC 63-18124

"This story in verse about a little Mexican boy who longs for a dog, but is satisfied by making friends with a prairie dog, is a charming one, told with sympathetic understanding and pictures in

Schweitzer, Byrd B.—*Continued*

soft desert colors. The amusing and touching feature of it is that boy and prairie dog think they are taming each other. 'Now/Francisco thought/ "I've tamed me a prairie dog. He's my greatest joy."/And/Amigo thought/"Mine is the best pet. I've tamed me a boy." ' " Sat Rev

Scott, Ann Herbert

On mother's lap; drawings by Glo Coalson. McGraw 1972 unp illus lib. bdg. $7.95   E

1 Eskimos—Fiction   2 Parent and child—Fiction
ISBN 0-07-055897-3   LC 76-39726

"While rocking back and forth on his mother's lap, Michael suggests adding, one by one, his dolly, boat, reindeer blanket, and puppy. Michael is dubious when his baby sister cries and mother suggests holding her also but he discovers the truth in mother's words that 'there is always room on Mother's lap.' The slight story . . . is told with minimal words and is beautifully illustrated with softly expressive pictures depicting an Eskimo mother and her children." Booklist

Sam; drawings by Symeon Shimin. McGraw 1967 unp illus $5.95   E

1 Blacks—Fiction   2 Family life—Fiction
ISBN 0-07-055803-5   LC 67-22968

"Sam is an engaging Negro child trying desparately to get his busy family to notice him. Not until he bursts into tears of frustration do his parents and brother and sister realize his need to be part of the group. A simple story with warm, attractive illustrations." Hodges. Bks for Elem Sch Libraries

Segal, Lore

Tell me a Mitzi; pictures by Harriet Pincus. Farrar, Straus 1970 unp illus $4.95   E

1 Family life—Fiction
ISBN 0-374-37392-2   LC 69-14980

The author injects an element of fantasy into these three stories of family life, the first of which deals with Mitzi's safari to grandma's and grandpa's house, the second with a confrontation with the common cold, and the third with her brother Jacob's encounter with a Presidential motorcade

"The illustrations, while they do not boast attractive children, are full of vitality and humor, the busy urban neighborhood and homely people having a rueful charm." Sutherland. The Best in Children's Bks

Tell me a Trudy; pictures by Rosemary Wells. Farrar, Straus 1977 unp illus $8.95   E

1 Family life—Fiction
ISBN 0-374-37395-7   LC 77-24123

"Following the same format as 'Tell Me a Mitzi,' [entered above] a little girl named Martha cajoles her mother and her father into telling stories. Each tale features Trudy, her younger brother Jacob, and her parents and gently satirizes a common family situation. In the first story Trudy's grandma lures stubborn children to bed; in the second, parents are found squabbling over toys; the third story deals with Trudy's fear of robbers in the bathroom. . . . Flamboyant color and caricatured figures heighten the humor of a straightfaced text." Horn Bk

Sendak, Maurice

In the night kitchen. Harper 1970 unp illus $8.95, lib. bdg. $8.79   E

1 Dreams—Fiction
ISBN 0-06-25489-0; 0-06-025490-4   LC 70-105483

"In a highly original dream fantasy a small boy falls through the dark, out of his clothes, and into the bright night kitchen where he is stirred into the cake batter and almost baked, jumps into the bread dough, kneads and shapes it into an airplane, and flies up over the top of the Milky Way to get milk for the bakers." Booklist

The author-illustrator "abandons his recent subtle, evocative black-and-white echoes of the 19th-Century English illustrators for a bold, graphic style that evokes a more recent past—the comic books and movies of his own childhood in the 1930's. Both story and pictures combine the timeless themes of childhood fantasy with concrete images of food products (favorite pop art subjects)

and the wild illogic of the animated cartoons familiar to today's children through TV." Sch Library J

Nutshell library. Harper 1962 4v illus $7.95   E

ISBN 0-06-025500-5   LC 62-13315

Each of these volumes is also available separately in larger format, lib. bdg. each $7.89

Contents v 1 Alligators all around; an alphabet (ISBN 0-06-025530-7); v2 Chicken soup with rice; a book of months (ISBN 0-06-025535-8); v3 One was Johnny; a counting book (ISBN 0-06-025540-4); v4 Pierre; a cautionary tale in five chapters and a prologue (ISBN 0-06-025965-5)

"A box of four delights, tiny enough for a child to hide away and keep. All the stories are both written and illustrated by Sendak, who is the Picasso of children's books, and each of them has a function." Time

This boxed set of pocket-size books is suitable for gifts or display. However, for circulation or classroom use the larger editions are recommended

Where the wild things are; story and pictures by Maurice Sendak. Harper 1963 unp illus $7.95, lib. bdg. $7.89   E

ISBN 0-06-025520-X; 0-06-025521-8   LC 63-21253

Awarded the Caldecott Medal, 1964

"A tale of very few words about Max, sent to his room for cavorting around in his wolf suit, who dreamed of going where the wild things are, to rule them and share their rumpus. Then a longing to be 'where someone loved him best of all' swept over him." Bk Week

"This vibrant picture book in luminous, understated full color has proved utterly engrossing to children with whom it has been shared. . . . A sincere, perceptive contribution which bears repeated examination." Horn Bk

Serraillier, Ian

Suppose you met a witch; illus. by Ed Emberley. Little 1973 unp illus lib. bdg. $6.95   E

1 Witches—Fiction   2 Stories in rhyme
ISBN 0-316-78125-8   LC 75-105731

Told in verse, this is the story of Roland and Miranda who, "popped and tied into the sack of an evil crone, are whisked off to her traditional candy house, there to be devoured. But the resourceful children outwit the hag as enchanted readers will find to their satisfaction. . . . [The illustrator] has created an unsurpassably horrible witch but his scenes of violence are tempered by gentle scenes of swans on a lake and a rose garden as the hero and heroine take on other guises to escape their captor." Pub W

Seuss, Dr

And to think that I saw it on Mulberry Street. Vanguard 1937 unp illus $5.95   E

1 Nonsense verses   2 Stories in rhyme
ISBN 0-8149-0387-8   LC 37-8873

This book tells in rhyme accompanied by pictures how little Marco saw a horse and wagon on Mulberry Street. Then "how that horse became a zebra, then a reindeer, then an elephant, and how the cart turned into a band wagon with a retinue of police to guide it through the traffic on Mulberry Street, only the book can properly explain." Christian Sci Monitor

"A fresh, inspiring picture-story book [illustrated by the author] in bright colors. . . . As convincing to a child as to the psychologist in quest of a book with an appeal to the child's imagination." Horn Bk

Another book about Marco is: McElligot's pool. Random House $4.95, lib. bdg. $5.99 (ISBN 0-394-80083-4; 0-394-90083-9; LC 47-4895)

The cat in the hat. Random House 1957 61p illus $3.95, lib. bdg. $4.99   E

1 Cats—Fiction   2 Nonsense verses   3 Stories in rhyme
ISBN 0-394-80001-X; 0-394-90001-4   LC 57-1811

Also available in a bilingual Spanish-English edition for $3.95, lib. bdg. $5.99 (ISBN 0-394-81626-9; 0-394-91626-3) and a bilingual French-English edition for $3.50, lib. bdg. $5.99 (ISBN 0-394-80171-1; 0-394-90171-1)

Seuss, Dr—*Continued*

A nonsense story in verse illustrated by the author about an unusual cat and his tricks which he displayed for the children on rainy day

"Using simple vocabulary and verse form, the author, with fertile imagination, has produced a beginning reader that avoids the usual dullness of limited vocabulary and frequent word repetition." Top of the News

Followed by The cat in the hat comes back! Beginner Bks $3.95, lib. bdg. $4.39 (ISBN 0-394-80002-8; 0-394-90002-2; LC 58-9017)

The 500 hats of Bartholomew Cubbins. Vanguard 1938 unp illus $5.95   **E**

1 Hats—Fiction
ISBN 0-8149-0388-6   LC 38-30610

"A read-aloud story telling what happened to Bartholomew Cubbins when he couldn't take his hat off before the King." Hodges. Bks for Elem Sch Libraries

"It is a lovely bit of tomfoolery which keeps up the suspense and surprise until the last page, and of the same ingenious and humorous imagination are the author's black and white illustrations in which a red cap and then an infinite number of red caps titillate the eye." NY Times Bk Rev

Followed by Bartholomew and the oobleck. Random House $4.95, lib. bdg. $5.99 (ISBN 0-394-80075-3; 0-394-90075-8; LC 49-11423)

Horton hatches the egg. Random House 1940 unp illus $4.95, lib. bdg. $5.99   **E**

1 Elephants—Fiction 2 Nonsense verses 3 Stories in rhyme
ISBN 0-394-80077-X; 0-394-90077-4   LC 40-27753

"Left in charge of a bird's egg, Horton the elephant [faithful one hundred per cent] guards it through so many trials that his final triumph is most gratifying. Rollicking verse and the illustrations make Horton an endearing figure." Let's Read Together

"A moral is a new thing to find in a Dr. Seuss book, but it doesn't interfere much with the hilarity with which he juggles an elephant up a tree. . . . Neither young nor old are going to quibble with the fantastic comedy of his pictures." NY Times Bk Rev

Followed by Horton hears a Who! Random House $4.95, lib. bdg. $5.99 (ISBN 0-394-80078-8; 0-394-90078-2; LC 54-7012)

How the Grinch stole Christmas. Random House 1957 unp illus $4.95, lib. bdg. $5.99   **E**

1 Christmas—Fiction 2 Nonsense verses 3 Stories in rhyme
ISBN 0-394-80079-6; 0-394-90079-0   LC 57-7526

Illustrated by the author

"The Grinch lived on a mountain where it was able to ignore the people of the valley except at Christmas time when it had to endure the sound of their singing. One year it decided to steal all the presents so there would be no Christmas, but much to its amazement discovered that people did not need presents to enjoy Christmas. It thereupon reformed, returned the presents and joined in the festivities." Chicago. Children's Bk Center

"The verse is as lively and the pages are as bright and colorful as anyone could wish. Reading the book aloud will be a fascinating exercise." Sat Rev

If I ran the circus. Random House 1956 unp illus lib. bdg. $5.99   **E**

1 Circus—Fiction 2 Nonsense verses 3 Stories in rhyme
ISBN 0-394-80080-X; 0-394-90080-4   LC 56-9469

The author-illustrator "presents the fabulous Circus McGurkus with its highly imaginative young owner, Morris McGurk and its intrepid performer, Sneelock, behind whose store the circus is to be housed. There are the expected number of strange creatures with nonsensical names, but the real humor lies in the situations, and especially those involving Mr. Sneelock. There is fun for the entire family here." Chicago. Children's Bk Center

If I ran the zoo. Random House 1950 unp illus $4.95, lib. bdg. $5.99   **E**

1 Zoological gardens—Fiction 2 Nonsense verses 3 Stories in rhyme
ISBN 0-394-80081-8; 0-394-90081-2   LC 50-10185

"This rhyming tale [illustrated by the author] of young Gerald McGrew who thought of all sorts of unusual animals he'd have in a zoo is Dr. Seuss at his best. It will be a treasure for the storyteller if she learns the verses by heart and holds the book up so that the children may see the pictures of the ten-footed lion, the hen 'who roosts in another hen's top-knot,' the bustard 'who only eats custard with sauce made of mustard' and all the others." Horn Bk

"As you turn the pages, the imaginings get wilder and funnier, the rhymes more hilarious. There will be no age limits for this book, because families will be forced to share rereading and quotation, for a long, long time." NY Her Trib Bks

Sharmat, Marjorie Weinman

Burton and Dudley; illus. by Barbara Cooney. Holiday House 1975 unp illus lib. bdg. $5.95   **E**

1 Opossums—Fiction   2 Walking—Fiction
3 Friendship—Fiction
ISBN 0-8234-0260-6   LC 75-1091

"Dudley Possum goes to visit his friend, Burton Possum. Dudley is an outdoor type who loves long walks, but Burton likes nothing so much as sitting quietly at home. The two pals agree to try each other's way and the complications that result give each a new understanding and a warmer relationship." Pub W

"Barbara Cooney's pen-and-ink illustrations, while not up to her best, are still pleasant, and the text is well written with touches of mild humor." Sch Library J

Edgemont; illus. by Cyndy Szekeres. Coward, McCann & Geoghegan [1977 c1976] unp illus $6.95, pa $2.95   **E**

1 Old age—Fiction 2 Turtles—Fiction
ISBN 0-698-20375-5; 0-698-20523-5   LC 76-113

"Edgemont, a 101-year-old turtle who sits around in a frayed sweater and slippers reading books with yellowed pages, realizes that he is not as happy as he could be. Crawling out for some adventure, he meets Blanche, a faded 99-year-old turtle beauty in a red feathered dress who spends much of her time reminiscing in a hammock. She and Edgemont do the 'turtle trot', make beautiful gingerbread together, tell stories, and befriend lonely Rupert Mouse and the other neighborhood youngsters." Sch Library J

"A delightful, droll depiction of how it feels to be old, to be relegated to the sidelines by others in society. . . . In these days of longevity and the 'senior citizen' classification, children need help in understanding old age. Edgemont evokes a warmth and caring in the reader. The book is well written, with vocabulary the young reader can handle and illustrations that make you smile affectionately." Children's Bk Rev Serv

Goodnight, Andrew; goodnight, Craig. Pictures by Mary Chalmers. Harper 1969 32p illus lib. bdg. $7.89   **E**

1 Sleep—Fiction 2 Brothers—Fiction
ISBN 0-06-025548-X   LC 69-10205

A "picture book of special interest to small boys describes the bedtime antics of two brothers. Andrew refuses to settle down to sleep until he obtains from his older brother Craig a promise to play ball with him the next day." Booklist

"The pale, demure illustrations have a note of humor, and the young listener should relish the fun and the typical bedtime pranks." Sat Rev

Griselda's new year; pictures by Normand Chartier. Macmillan Pub. Co. 1979 63p illus $6.95   **E**

1 Geese—Fiction 2 New Year—Fiction
ISBN 0-02-782420-9   LC 79-11375

"A Ready-to-read"

"Griselda, a silly goose, blows her Happy New Year Horn and wishes herself the best year yet. She resolves to be good, brave and kind—to make someone happy. The way fair Griselda goes about keeping her vows is related in six chapters, the fun escalating in each." Pub W

This text for beginning readers is "illustrated by humorous animal pictures, softly-tinted line drawings. . . . The read-aloud audience should enjoy the comic miscarriage of her good intentions; there are verve and wit in the style and in the development of Griselda's good deeds, unappreciated by the recipients but completely satisfying to the silly goose." Chicago. Children's Bk Center

Sharmat, Marjorie W.—*Continued*

I'm not Oscar's friend anymore; illus. by Tony DeLuna. Dutton 1975 32p illus lib. bdg. $6.95   E

1 Friendship—Fiction
ISBN 0-525-32537-9   LC 74-23767

"A small boy mulls over the fight he's had with his ex-best friend Oscar. He envisions Oscar moping, Oscar penitent, Oscar bored, finding the humor has gone out of television and the joy out of life. In fact, all the feelings he's having himself. He decides to give Oscar one more chance, and walks by his house. No result. He gives him still one more chance and telephones; Oscar doesn't even remember the fight they had—but that's immaterial, Oscar is going to come over and life is back to happy normal." Chicago. Children's Bk Center

"All children can identify with this well conceived book. The teacher can lead into discussions of interpersonal relationships, anger, sensitivity, and friendship. The boy who is imagining Oscar's misery is sketched in ink; what he imagines is shown in a large three-color illustration. A little dachshund reflects the emotions the boy is feeling. A very good addition to the classroom library." Rdng Teacher

Mooch the messy; pictures by Ben Shecter. Harper 1976 61p illus $6.95, lib. bdg. $7.89   E

1 Rats—Fiction
ISBN 0-06-025531-5; 0-06-025532-3   LC 76-3842

"An I can read book"
"Mooch the rat likes to live in a mess: shoes on the table, candy under the bed, clothing draped over every piece of furniture. He is delighted when his father comes to visit, and shows off the glories of his tunnels; his father, however, thinks Mooch's hole is in dreadful condition and does not approve, when they go on a picnic, of his son's practice of leaving jam jars open for the ants to get into. So Mooch tidies his hole and pleases Father; he is sorry to see Father leave but immediately, happily, scatters things about in comfortable chaos. The plot is slight, but it has amusing details." Chicago. Children's Bk Center

"Ben Shecter's brown-and-gold drawings are suitably homey, with just the right amount of expression and detail." Booklist

Nate the Great; illus. by Marc Simont. Coward, McCann & Geoghegan 1972 60p illus lib. bdg. $6.59   E

1 Mystery and detective stories
ISBN 0-698-30444-6   LC 75-183552

"A Break-of-day book"
Nate the Great, a junior detective who has found missing balloons, books, slippers, chickens and even a goldfish, is now in search of a painting of a dog by Annie, the girl down the street

"The illustrations capture the exaggerated, tongue-in-cheek humor of the story." Booklist

Some other books about Nate the Great are also available from Coward, McCann & Geoghegan:
Nate the Great and the lost list lib. bdg. $6.59
  (ISBN 0-698-30593-0; LC 76-350105)
Nate the Great and the phony clue lib. bdg. $6.59
  (ISBN 0-698-30650-3; LC 76-42461)
Nate the Great and the sticky case lib. bdg. $6.59
  (ISBN 0-698-30697-X; LC 77-17011)
Nat the Great goes undercover lib. bdg. $6.59
  (ISBN 30547-7; LC 74-79700)

The 329th friend; illus. by Cyndy Szekeres. Four Winds 1979 unp illus $8.95   E

1 Friendship—Fiction   2 Raccoons—Fiction
3 Animals—Fiction
ISBN 0-590-07558-6   LC 78-21770

"Cyndy Szekeres has a field day drawing 329 more or less cuddly animals of all sorts, some au naturel and some brightly clad, as they gather to share the feast laid on by Emery Racoon. Emery, bored by his solitude and his own dullness, has invited 328 guests, hoping that one of them will become his friend. 329 forks, 329 glasses, 329 eggs, 329 napkins (he had to cut up a dozen sheets for those), 329 tarts, and so on. Everyone comes, nobody talks to him; Emery picks up his food and goes into the house for a solitary picnic, where he tells himself jokes and stories and decides that he's his own best friend. His guests clamor for him, praise his hospitality, and take off; Emery begins the long clean-up, but he's happy at the knowledge that 'Today I found a good friend I never noticed before,' he's found himself. The exaggeration (lunch for 329) will appeal to children, as will the animals, but it's Sharmat's style that puts this not-too-substantial tale across." Chicago. Children's Bk Center

Shaw, Charles G.

It looked like spilt milk. Harper 1947 unp illus lib. bdg. $7.89   E

ISBN 0-06-025565-X   LC 47-30767

White silhouettes on a blue background with simple captions: "sometimes it looked like a tree," "sometimes it looked like a bird," etc. lead to a surprise ending "sometimes it looked like spilt milk, but what it was was—"

"What one thing could look like all of these? On the last page you are told, and I could no more tell you now than I could spoil an adult mystery by a review that gives away its solution." NY Her Trib Bks

Shecter, Ben

Molly Patch and her animal friends. Harper 1975 59p illus lib. bdg. $6.89   E

1 Animals—Fiction   2 Friendship—Fiction
ISBN 0-06-025589-7   LC 75-6304

"Tired of the noisy city, Molly Patch moves to the country where she learns from Bear, Snake, Frog, Crow, Mouse, etc., the ways of human nature and shares her sensibleness and sensitivity in return. Each of the tiny tales about a different animal friend ends with a graceful short verse by Molly." Sch Library J

"Although clearly moralistic, this is a charming set of stories with certain appeal for young children. The personality quirks of the animals, and their relations with each other, can well remind readers of themselves and their friends. However, here, justice always triumphs. The soft-tone brown illustrations [by the author] are slightly fanciful, homelike, and well in keeping with the story's style. This is an especially suitable book for reading aloud to individual children or to small, friendly groups." Children's Bk Rev Serv

Showers, Paul

The listening walk; illus. by Aliki. Crowell 1961 unp illus $6.89   E

1 Sounds
ISBN 0-690-49663-X   LC 61-10495

"Let's-read-and-find-out-books"
In pictures and text this book shows many of the sights and sounds a boy may see on a walk down the street and through the park. Among them are such sounds as those of his father's shoes on the sidewalk, a power lawn mower, the brakes of a car stopping quickly, a jet plane flying over the park, ducks quacking, and pigeons flying down to be fed by people in the park

Shulevitz, Uri

Dawn; words and pictures by Uri Shulevitz. Farrar, Straus 1974 unp illus $6.95   E

ISBN 0-374-31707-0   LC 74-9761

"Drawn from a Chinese poem, the spare text tells of an old man and his grandson asleep by the shore of a mountain lake. With the approach of daylight, the watercolor illustrations, which start out small, dark, and blurred, slowly become more focused and detailed: the moon casts a soft glow; a breeze riffles the water; mists rise. As the old man and the boy push out on to the lake in their boat, a hint of color suffuses the scene; and finally, in a visual tour-de-force, the sun rises over the mountain and they are bathed in full color." Sch Library J

"The purity of the hues, well-produced on ample spreads, the subtle graphic development from scene to scene, and the sharply focused simplicity of the few words make this a true art experience." Horn Bk

Hanukah money, by Sholem Aleichem; tr. and adapted by Uri Shulevitz and Elizabeth Shub; illus. by Uri Shulevitz. Greenwillow Bks. 1978 30p illus $7.50, lib. bdg. $7.20   E

1 Jews—Fiction   2 Hanukkah (Feast of Lights)—Fiction
ISBN 0-688-80120-X; 0-688-83120-1   LC 77-26693

"A vignette of pre-World War I Eastern European Jewish life, in which the home ritual of

Shulevitz, Uri—*Continued*

lighting Hanukah candles and the traditional practice of frying potato pancakes becomes intertwined with the holiday custom of giving money to children as a gift for a joyous season. Told in the first person, the story not only reflects the exuberance of two young boys but . . . humorously portrays the idiosyncracies of the grownups. . . . Appropriately colored in somber tones of brown, green, mauve, and yellow, the fine-line drawings are crystal clear. Beautifully composed, filled with picturesque detail, and genially depicting the absurdness of the human comedy, the illustrations are a perfect and loving accompaniment for the classic short story." Horn Bk

"Some passages seem to echo chanted prayer rhythms. Beginning, middle, and end, however, are a bit vague in direction, as are transitions, particularly into a last dream. . . . Still, such an atmospheric piece will evoke nostalgia in adults reading aloud and will further acculturate children involved in their own traditional celebrations." Booklist

One Monday morning. Scribner 1967 unp illus $8.95, pa $2.95   **E**

1 Fantasy—Fiction
ISBN 0-684-13195-1; 0-684-16009-9   LC 66-24483
Illustrated by the author
" 'One Monday morning, the king, the queen, and the little prince came to visit me. But I wasn't home. . . .' So goes the daydream of a small child in a drab tenement. As the week progresses, the royal entourage, in the panoply of playing card figures, increases. Their pageantry blots out the grey background while commonplace activities play counterpoint to the fantasy theme." Moorachian. What is a City?

"Humor, dignity, imagination, and a remarkable interplay between text and illustration make . . . [this] a beautiful book that is easy and fun to read. . . . Children will be able to identify, understand, and enjoy both worlds of [the book's] imaginative child." Wis Library Bul

Rain, rain, rivers; words and pictures by Uri Shulevitz. Farrar, Straus 1969 unp illus $8.95   **E**

1 Rain and rainfall—Fiction
ISBN 0-374-36171-1   LC 73-85370
"In her attic room a little girl hears the rain. Outside her window the gutters are rain-swollen, the rain beats down on the city streets and the few scurrying people, cold and wet. The rain pours into country streams, the brooks feed the rivers, the rain-lashed rivers pour into the frothing sea. Only at the end is their a change of mood, as a pale, watery sun shines on delightful puddles and the joyful children reappear. The little girl feels the urgent freshening and sees her tiny potted plant begin to grow." Chicago. Children's Bk Center

"Even more distinguished than [the illustrations for] his earlier Caldecott winning book, [The Fool of the World and the flying ship by Arthur, Ransome, entered in class 398.2] is this lovely bouyant hymn to the wonders of rain on cities, mountains, meadows, and sea. This lovely book brings a renewal of life and spirit—even as the rain itself." Commonweal

Simon, Norma

I was so mad! Illus. by Dora Leder. Whitman 1974 unp illus lib. bdg. $5.95   **E**

1 Anger
ISBN 0-8075-3520-6   LC 73-22425
In this book "children catalog the things that make them mad and learn that adults get angry, too. They are helped to realize why they get angry and how to handle their frustrations." Best Bks for Children

Skorpen, Liesel Moak

His mother's dog; pictures by M. E. Mullin. Harper 1978 46p illus $6.95, lib. bdg. $6.79   **E**

1 Dogs—Fiction
ISBN 0-06-025722-9; 0-06-025723-7   LC 76-58707
"The boy gets the first of many blows when his parents give him not the dog he always wanted, a lusty Newfoundland, but a wee cocker spaniel. The next blow falls when the pet snubs his owner and favors the child's mother. Worst of all, a baby sister invades . . . [his] home and

takes most of his mother's attention. The future brightens considerably, however, thanks to an unexpected switch in the attitude of the family pet." Pub W

"Jealousy, rejection, and love intertwine in this almost-real tale. Lifelike illustrations in three colors capture the nuances of a story that could happen to any one of its young listeners." Children's Bk Rev Serv

Mandy's grandmother; pictures by Martha Alexander. Dial Press 1975 unp illus $4.95, lib. bdg. $4.58   **E**

1 Grandmothers—Fiction
ISBN 0-8037-4962-7; 0-8037-4963-5   LC 74-20383
This book "deals with the relationship between Mandy, a jean-wearing, pony-riding preschooler; her mother, a frantic domestic type; and her grandmother, a grey-hair-in-a-bun knitter who is paying her very first visit to Mandy's home. Grandmother and granddaughter do not meet each other's expectations. But their loneliness and need for affection result happily in mutual compromise. Grandmother becomes more accepting of Mandy as she is, and the two enjoy one another's company —Mandy learning to knit and Grandmother learning to whistle." Interracial Bks for Children Bul

"Alexander's muted watercolors reinforce the sense of security by focusing on familiar details in tidy, little frames. Excessive sentimentality is held in check by characters who are pictured as pleasantly ordinary, realistically imperfect." Sch Library J

Old Arthur; pictures by Wallace Tripp. Harper 1972 46p illus lib. bdg. $8.79   **E**

1 Dogs—Fiction
ISBN 0-06-025715-6   LC 72-76515
This is the story of a special friendship which develops between a young boy and an old dog who is forced to leave a farm when he can no longer work effectively

"Sweet but not saccharine, both the story and illustrations offer young readers a quiet blend of reality and security." Booklist

Skurzynski, Gloria

Martin by himself; illus. by Lynn Munsinger. Houghton 1979 36p illus lib. bdg. $6.95   **E**

1 Mothers—Employment—Fiction
ISBN 0-395-28271-3   LC 79-11748
"On mother's first day of work Martin returns home, sadly leaving a trail of mud across the empty house. He strews his clothes about and while making a sandwich discovers that peanut butter is great for drawing on the refrigerator. Bored again, Martin invites the dog inside but Gus promptly urinates on the rug. A disgusted Martin cleans up, putting Mother's best, but now smelly, towels in a bubble bath (which overflows) and finally uses meatloaf to coax Gus out of the door. When mother arrives, she momentarily views the mess in alarm but sees Martin's woebegone face and sits down patiently to discuss the situation with him. . . . Pale blues and yellows over thin brown line work provide a homey backdrop for Martin's loneliness and resulting shenanigans, which are amusingly portrayed in this contemporary tale." Booklist

Sleator, William

Once, said Darlene; pictures by Steven Kellogg. Dutton 1979 55p illus $5.95   **E**

1 Fantastic fiction
ISBN 0-525-36410-2   LC 78-12643
"A Fat cat book"
"At age five or so, Darlene has had a checkered past, according to her. She relates endless stories about when she was a princess, living in a glittering palace and entertained often by a magician. Darlene always ends by saying sadly that she can't tell what happened then. The neighborhood kids get fed up with the girl's whoppers and declare she can't play with them any more unless she confesses to lying. But one boy, Peter, believes Darlene and is amazed to find himself transported to the palace of Princess Darlene where he finds out what happened because of the magician. . . . Each incident is enhanced by Kellogg's charming pictures of real, appealing children and the contrasting scenes in fantasy land." Pub W

Slobodkin, Louis
Magic Michael. Macmillan Pub. Co. 1944 unp
illus lib. bdg. $4.95, pa 95¢   E

1 Imagination—Fiction
ISBN 0-02-784680-6; 0-02-045040-0   LC 44-6840

This is a picture story book about an imaginative small boy who liked to pretend he was some
kind of bird or animal. Then one day his father
bought him a bicycle and Michael decided to give
up his idle fancies and become just a boy
"In this first book, entirely his own, Mr. Slobodkin has evidently enjoyed picturing his son's
lively imagination, and he again shows understanding and humorous tolerance of children. Result is a book of animated, playful, clever drawings in color." Library J

Slobodkina, Esphyr
Caps for sale; a tale of a peddler, some
monkeys & their monkey business; told and
illus by Esphyr Slobodkina. Young Scott Bks
1947 unp illus lib. bdg. $6.95   E

1 Monkeys—Fiction   2 Peddlers and peddling—
Fiction
ISBN 0-201-09147-X   LC 47-29233

A picture book story which "provides hilarious
confusion. A cap peddler takes a nap under a tree.
When he wakes up, his caps have disappeared. He
looks up in the tree and sees countless monkeys,
each wearing a cap and grinning." A Parent's
Guide To Children's Rdng

Smith, Jim
The Frog Band and the onion seller. Little
1976 unp illus $7.95   E

1 Frogs—Fiction   2 Mystery and detective stories
ISBN 0-316-80005-8   LC 76-27177

Illustrated by the author
"This is the first in a series promised by Smith.
If the succeeding volumes are as much fun, he
will have many loyal fans. The story, pure tomfoolery, sports brilliant paintings, humorously detailed.
The famous Alphonse le Flic, detective, heads the
frog cast. He's hired by the poor French Duke de
Buffo Buffo to locate a treasure pinpointed on a
map the nobleman finds in his shabby chateau.
Disguised as an onion seller, Alphonse crossed the
channel and lands, to run afoul of the Frog Band,
whose lorry he causes to crash. With them on his
heels, the sleuth goes through mad adventures, recovers the treasure chest and brings it to the Duke.
Alas, it contains trash, so the nobleman throws
it out—along with Alphonse. To the joy of both
the box breaks and disgorges hidden gold pieces."
Pub W
Some other books about the Frog Band and
Alphonse are also available from Little:
Alphonse and the Stonehenge mystery $7.95 (ISBN
0-316-80162-3; LC 79-89060)
The Frog Band and Durrington Dormouse $7.95,
pa $3.95 (ISBN 0-316-80155-0; 0-316-80159-3; LC
77-10549)
The Frog Band and the mystery of Lion Castle
$7.95, pa $3.95 (ISBN 0-316-80161-5; 0-316-
80160-7; LC 78-61426)

Smith, Lucia B.
My mom got a job; illus. by C. Christina
Johanson. Holt 1979 unp illus lib. bdg. $5.95
          E

1 Mothers—Employment—Fiction   2 Family life
—Fiction
ISBN 0-03-048321-2   LC 79-1494

"Smith's child narrator reflects on and recites
the pluses and minuses in her days, changes occurring when her mother goes to work outside the
home. The little girl misses cozy hours after
school when she and her mother traded confidences
over milk and cookies. But now, says the child,
staying with a neighbor in the afternoons and helping care for her baby is 'an important job and I
like that.' Going through the week with the girl
and sharing her thoughts can be a reassuring experience for other kids in her situation. Adding
to the book's points are Johanson's illustrations,
trim ink sketches with rosy touches, depicting
slightly exaggerated characters in recognizable
areas: the schoolroom, supermarket, home, etc."
Pub W

Solot, Mary Lynn
100 hamburgers; the getting thin book;
Paul Galdone drew the pictures. Lothrop 1972
unp illus lib. bdg. $6.96   E

1 Reducing—Fiction
ISBN 0-688-51247-X   LC 72-75016

"If it is possible for the fat child to approach
the subject of his fatness cheerfully, he can with
this little book. It is written in the first person: the
little boy soliloquizing on the woes of being fat;
his pleasure in eating; and then, his understanding and acceptance of the doctor's advice about
getting thin. The accompanying pictures illustrate
the mood splendidly; the information and advice
given is sound but not too severe, and the tone is
always sympathetic." Appraisal

Sonneborn, Ruth A.
Friday night is Papa night; illus. by Emily
A. McCully. Viking 1970 unp illus lib.
bdg. $6.95   E

1 Puerto Ricans in the U.S.—Fiction   2 Family
life—Fiction
ISBN 0-670-32938-X   LC 75-102918

Because Pedro's father is unable to come home
during the week, each Friday night is a special
occasion. One evening Papa doesn't come, and the
children are brokenhearted. But when a weary
Papa finally does arrive in the middle of the
night, with popsicles and presents for everyone,
they all agree it is time for a celebration
"The structure is slight, but the story conveys a
real feeling of family love, echoed in the illustrations of an attractive Puerto Rican family." Chicago. Children's Bk Center

Spier, Peter
Bored—nothing to do! Doubleday 1978 unp
illus $6.95, lib. bdg. $7.90   E

1 Airplanes—Fiction
ISBN 0-385-13177-1; 0-385-13178-X   LC 77-20726

"A mother orders her young sons to 'do' something: 'I was never bored at your age!' So they
do. Guided by a handbook, the boys misappropriate
the wheels from a baby carriage, bed sheets, wire
from a fence and every essential requirement to
construct an airplane—Including the engine from
the family car. Wheeling the impressive flyer out
of the garage, the boys take off and soar over the
countryside until their parents espy them and
screech them down. The enterprising brothers
then take their craft apart and return each borrowed bit." Pub W
"The text is almost superfluous, but the colorful, detailed drawings offer great scope for discussion, poring over, and enjoying. A fantasy to
which young children will relate." Children's Bk
Rev Serv

Crash!. Bang! Boom! Doubleday 1972 unp
illus $6.95, lib. bdg. $7.90, pa $2.95   E

1 Sounds
ISBN 0-385-06780-1; 0-385-02496-7; 0-385-15240-X
                                       LC 70-157625

"In a colorful cacophony of precise sound —
[the author-illustrator] sets out to capture visually the audible quality of inanimate objects: the
BLUBBA-LUBBA-LUBBA of a pot of boiling
potatoes and the PFF PFF PFF of a bicycle tire
being pumped up. Clean white pages are filled
with detailed, bright-colored pictures of objects
grouped according to use, relationship, or activity." Horn Bk

Fast-slow, high-low; a book of opposites.
Doubleday 1972 unp illus $7.95, lib. bdg. $8.90,
pa $2.95   E

1 English language—Synonyms and antonyms
ISBN 0-385-06781-X; 0-385-02876-8; 0-385-15241-8
                                       LC 72-76207

"Pages filled with delightful drawings, in pairs,
that illustrate objects or concepts like fast or
slow, young or old, over or under, heavy or light,
dark or light, and so on. There is no print on the
pages save the headings. The book may require
adult interpretation in many instances, since some
of the pictures may need translations. . . . Useful for development of awareness of differences,
yet limited by the subtlety of some examples, the
book is not the best choice for learning opposites
but it is probably the most attractive." Chicago.
Children's Bk Center

Spier, Peter—*Continued*

Gobble, growl, grunt. Doubleday 1971 unp illus $7.95, lib. bdg. $8.90, pa $2.95   **E**

1 Animals—Pictorial works   2 Animal communication
ISBN 0-385-06779-8; 0-385-00681-0; 0-385-15242-6
LC 79-144300

"Over 600 animals parade across double-page spreads, identified by name and the sound each animal makes. There is no need for any other text; the illustrations speak for themselves in a humorous and lighthearted fashion." Pub W

"Children who enjoy pictures of animals will have hours of fun poring over the lively illustrations while parents can use the book with young children to identify animals and their sounds." Booklist

Oh, were they ever happy! Doubleday 1978 unp illus $6.95, lib. bdg. $7.90   **E**

1 House painting—Fiction
ISBN 0-385-13175-5; 0-385-13176-3   LC 77-78144

"Having heard their parents talk about how much the house (large, three-storied) needs painting, three children take it on themselves to surprise their parents, who have gone off to do a day of errands. The babysitter, who was to be there 'in a few minutes,' hasn't shown up. Hauling out a ladder and all the paint of the garage, the children proceed to produce a rainbow patchwork on house, garage, fence, themselves, and the bathroom where they clean up. The children preen themselves on how delighted their parents will be when they see the finished job." Chicago. Children's Bk Center

"While the text relates a straight-faced narrative of the escapade, Spier's colorful illustrations depict the comedy as many-hued dollops of paint haphazardly appear. . . . The final scene—a full view of the house-of-many-colors—is sure to induce giggles from children and sympathetic groans from adults reading the story aloud." Booklist

Tin Lizzie; written and illus. by Peter Spier. Doubleday 1975 unp illus. $7.95, lib. bdg. $8.90, pa $1.95   **E**

1 Automobiles—Fiction
ISBN 0-385-09470-1; 0-385-07069-1; 0-385-13342-1
LC 74-1510

A story of one Model T Ford, "The Tin Lizzie was a sight to behold and wonder at when it arrived in a small American town back in 1903. The car's first owner kept it for over 10 years, then sold it to a newly married couple. Lizzie continued to function well, serving her growing family, until 1929 when the car was picked up by a farmer and demoted to toting hay, then retired to a pasture where little children used it as a toy. But in the 1970s, the Model T was bought by an antique car fancier and now enjoys its celebrity status." Pub W

"Spier's drawings are invariably pleasing, detailed-filled panoramas that capture the changing face of changing times; the full-color paintings are suffused with the rumpled comfort of an unstarched cotton shirt. What might, in different hands, have made us carsick becomes, under Spier's direction, an enjoyable piece of Americana." NY Times Bk Rev

Steig, William

The amazing bone. Farrar, Straus 1976 unp illus $7.95   **E**

1 Pigs—Fiction   2 Bones—Fiction
ISBN 0-374-30248-0   LC 76-26479

Illustrated by the author

A pretty pig called "Pearl dawdles on her way home from school on a spring day and happens upon a magic bone; it can speak in any language. The two become friends and the bone agrees to live with Pearl and her family. They are attacked by muggers in the forest but the bone scares them off. They're not so lucky, however, when a fox which can't be intimidated grabs them and drags them to his house where he plans to roast Pearl for dinner. The story sizzles with suspense until an unexpected twist and a happy end." Pub W

"Steig's marvelously straightfaced telling comes with a panoply of ultra-spring landscapes for pink-dressed Pearl to tiptoe through. And there's no holding back the chortles at the wonderfully expressive faces the artist delights in. This is a tight mesh of witty storytelling and art bound to please any audience." Booklist

Amos & Boris. Farrar, Straus 1971 unp illus $6.95   **E**

1 Mice—Fiction   2 Whales—Fiction
ISBN 0-374-30278-2   LC 72-165403

Illustrated by the author, this story "has two heroes, Amos the mouse and Boris the whale, 'a devoted pair of friends with nothing at all in common, except good hearts and a willingness to help their fellow mammal.' And help each other they do indeed, in a most uncommon way." Pub W

"The water-color paintings deftly convey changing qualities of light—day and night, sunshine and rain—and a realistic flowing and heaving of seawater. . . . [The] genuine story builds its atmosphere and mood with freshness, compassion, and child interest, and is enhanced by the illustrations." Horn Bk

Caleb & Kate. Farrar, Strauss 1977 unp illus $7.95   **E**

1 Dogs—Fiction   2 Witches—Fiction
ISBN 0-374-31016-5   LC 77-4947

"Though Caleb the carpenter loves Kate the weaver very much, he leaves her one day because of a quarrel. In the deep woods where he is resting Yedida the witch turns him into a dog. The tale of his faithfulness and love for his wife, even though he is a dog, is . . . told. Their love is shared to the end, when a remarkable turn of events enables him to return to his former self." Children's Bk Rev Serv

"The well-cadenced storytelling has a certain old-fashioned elegance of language, and the humor is emphasized by an atmosphere of mock-pathos. William Steig is a superb artist with the literary ingenuity to produce durable, energetic stories; the result is another unified picture book in which text and illustrations are fully worthy of each other." Horn Bk

Farmer Palmer's wagon ride; story and pictures by William Steig. Farrar, Straus 1974 unp illus $6.95   **E**

1 Pigs—Fiction   2 Donkeys—Fiction
ISBN 0-374-32288-0   LC 74-9949

Farmer Palmer, a pig and his hired hand Ebenezer, an ass, manage an unusually hazardous trip home from the market by putting to use the presents they had bought for the family

"The text, longer than that of most picture books, boasts some captivating and original onomatopoeia, lending itself to reading aloud. Full-color illustrations add action, expression, and countryside colors appropriate to the story." Booklist

Sylvester and the magic pebble. Windmill Bks. [distributed by] Simon & Schuster 1969 unp illus $6.95, lib. bdg. $6.70   **E**

1 Donkeys—Fiction
ISBN 0-671-66511-1; 0-671-66512-X   LC 69-14484

Awarded the Caldecott Medal, 1970

"Sylvester the young donkey was a pebble collector; one day he found a flaming red stone, shiny and round—and quite unaccountably able to grant wishes. Overjoyed, Sylvester was planning to share his magic with his family when 'a mean, hungry lion' appeared. Startled and panicky, Sylvester wished himself transformed into a rock. In vain his grieving parents searched for their beloved child; all the worried animals took up the hunt. Then, after months of sorrow and mourning, poor Sylvester was fortuitously but logically restored. A remarkable atmosphere of childlike innocence pervades the book; the [author's] beautiful pictures in full, natural color show daily and seasonal changes in the lush countryside and greatly extend the kindly humor and the warm, unselfconscious tenderness." Horn Bk

Steptoe, John

Stevie. Harper 1969 unp illus $8.95, lib. bdg. $8.79   **E**

1 Blacks—Fiction
ISBN 0-06-025763-6; 0-06-025764-4   LC 69-16700

Illustrated by the author

A small Black boy, Robert "tells the story of the intruder, Stevie, who comes to stay at his house because both parents are working. Stevie is a pest. He tags along after Robert, he messes up toys, he

Steptoe, John—*Continued*

wants everything he sees. Worst of all, 'my momma never said nothin' to him.' But Robert is an only child, and after Stevie goes, the house is still. He remembers the games they played, the way Stevie looked up to him." Sat Rev

"While characters in this picture-story are black, the theme of childhood jealousy and rivalry for Mother's attention is universal. The story evokes a warm response and the bold pastel paintings are notable." Top of the News

Stevenson, James

"Could be worse!" Greenwillow Bks. 1977 unp illus $7.75, lib. bdg. $7.44   E

1 Grandfathers—Fiction   2 Dreams—Fiction
ISBN 0-688-80075-0; 0-688-84075-2   LC 76-28534

"Two children comment on the fact that their grandfather, a quiet, harassed-looking gentleman, goes through the same routine every morning. Same food. Same reactions to any reports of trouble by the children: 'Could be worse.' But one day Grandpa fools them and tells a long, involved story of a dream-fantasy in which he went from one peril to another. 'What do you think of that?' And the children gleefully shout, 'Could be worse!' " Chicago. Children's Bk Center

"Stevenson's sketchy watercolors, arranged in panels, trace Grandpa's adventures as he wanders precipitously through air, over land, and under sea, into and out of danger. A read-aloud picture story guaranteed to tickle young funny bones and, without prompting, to elicit a chorus of 'could be worse' before the last page is turned." Booklist

Fast friends; two stories. Greenwillow Bks. 1979 64p illus $5.95, lib. bdg. $5.71   E

1 Friendship—Fiction   2 Animals—Fiction
ISBN 0-688-80197-8; 0-688-84197-X   LC 78-14828

"Greenwillow Read-alone"

" 'Fast Friends' is an apt pun for [these] two stories. In the first, the better tale, a snail and a turtle discover the speedy joys of skateboarding. In the second, a mouse and a turtle learn about the reciprocity of friendship. James Stevenson's loose jointed illustrations keep things moving." Sch Library J

Howard. Greenwillow Bks. 1980 32p illus $7.95, lib. bdg. $7.63   E

1 Ducks—Fiction   2 New York (City)—Fiction
ISBN 0-688-80255-9; 0-688-84255-0   LC 79-16562

"Line and watercolor drawings, softly colored and filled with wonderfully detailed scenes of New York City, illustrate a story that is told with verve and humor, and that has a surprise ending the lap audience (and their readers-aloud) should enjoy. A duck, Howard, misses his group's take-off for the south and then loses his way when he tries to catch up. Landing on a New York rooftop in a snowstorm, he flies down to investigate and makes some new friends, a frog and three mice, with whom he has a series of winter adventures. And then comes spring, and Howard hears his group overhead and flies off to join them. Then, the surprise. The illustrations are Stevenson at his best." Chicago. Children's Bk Center

Monty. Greenwillow Bks. 1979 unp illus $7.95, lib. bdg. $7.63   E

1 Alligators—Fiction   2 Animals—Fiction
ISBN 0-688-80209-5; 0-688-84209-7   LC 78-11409

Illustrated by the author

"Tom, Doris, and Arthur (a rabbit, a duck, and a frog) always call for their alligator friend Monty when it's time to cross the river to get to school. One day Monty decides he's had enough of being taken for granted, enough of listening to his three friends order him about with 'Don't wobble so much,' 'Let's see some more speed,' and 'More to the right!' He announces he's taking a vacation. The efforts the three students make to find another way to cross the river are hilarious." Chicago. Children's Bk Center

"Monty returns to duty in time to save the day —this time with more appreciative riders. Though inquisitive children may wonder why the duck and frog don't ford the stream themselves, the funnily conceived scenes compensate, fitting nicely into Stevenson's cartoon-style format. Pale, soft colors match the low-key message of a tale sure to elicit a long smile." Booklist

The Sea View Hotel. Greenwillow Bks. 1978 unp illus $7.50, lib. bdg. $7.20   E

1 Summer resorts—Fiction   2 Vacations—Fiction
3 Animals—Fiction
ISBN 0-688-80168-4; 0-688-84168-6   LC 78-2749

"Back in the days of buggies and potted ferns, a family of three (animals, Edwardian vintage) go for a vacation. Hubert's parents sink happily into the plush gentility of the resort hotel, but [mouse-child] Hubert is bored to death. He can't swim (annual invasion by stinging jelly-fish) and he can't play (not another child there) and the other guests are annoyed by his noise. Then Hubert finds Alf, the handyman. Alf shows him natural wonders, skips stones with him, and reveals his hobby: a home-made flying machine.... The machine—and Hubert—have a marvelous, dangerous, unplanned ride. So, when they leave, Hubert is already hoping that for their next vacation his parents will choose the Sea View Hotel." Chicago. Children's Bk Center

"A story with simplicity, harmony, and ease in the the telling plus pictures that have joy and warmth, all fused into the form of a comic book taken beyond its limits.... The characters, whose bodies in their turn-of-the-century clothing seem human, have heads of birds, turtles, dogs, or whatever suits their personality or Stevenson's whimsy. The relaxed cartoon drawings, black-and-white pen-and-ink with a wash, may come one to a double page, or four to a page, but usually somewhere in between." Sch Library J

Wilfred the rat. Greenwillow Bks. 1977 unp illus $6.75, lib. bdg. $6.48   E

1 Animals—Fiction   2 Friendship—Fiction
ISBN 0-688-80103-X; 0-688-84103-1   LC 77-1091

"A rather depressed-looking rat, Wilfred was a loner with no friends and no place to go until he happened upon a closed amusement park. There he made two congenial new acquaintances, Dwayne, a squirrel, and Ruppert, a chipmunk. With pleasure they showed him around, and they all had a wonderful time together until the amusement park reopened. Although the owner and his ferocious dog disliked animals, Wilfred decided to stay with his friends—who retreated to the safety of a nearby pizza shop—and observed the excitement. But when he was offered a job for a daredevil performace, he felt the pleasures of friendship and loyalty were more important and rejoined Ruppert and Dwayne." Horn Bk

"Stevenson is one of the best cartoonists on the scene; his drawings are lively and funny and deft. The story is told in direct, unembellished style and, while the basic plot is not highly original, the setting and the denouement's drama make it a more palatable variant." Chicago. Children's Bk Center

The worst person in the world. Greenwillow Bks. 1978 unp illus $7.50, lib. bdg. $7.20   E

1 Friendship—Fiction
ISBN 0-688-80127-7; 0-688-84127-9   LC 77-22141

Illustrated by the author

"When the worst person in the world (who's also one of the meanest) meets the ugliest creature in the world (who's also one of the nicest), we all know what happens. Ugly plans a party, hats, balloons and all, for the neighborhood, in Worst's house, cleaned and polished for the occasion. Worst hates it all, of course, and Ugly leaves in distress to play ball with the kids and drown his sorrows in friendliness. But Worst finds a stray party hat, likes the way he looks in it, and suddenly finds his own meanness offensive. Going outside, he displays his good intentions by retrieving a lost ball. Then he invites everyone back for a party, and Ugly comes too." Sch Library J

"A blithe if predictable story illustrated by cartoon-style drawings.... Not the sturdiest of plots or the most original concept, but the style is jaunty and the pictures amusing." Chicago. Children's Bk Center

Stolz, Mary

Emmett's pig; pictures by Garth Williams. Harper 1959 61p illus lib. bdg. $7.89   E

1 Pigs—Fiction
ISBN 0-06-02586-X   LC 58-7763

"An I can read book"

"Although Emmett lives in a city apartment and is surrounded by toy pigs, pictures and books about pigs, his great desire for a real live pig is finally

Stolz, Mary—*Continued*
granted as a birthday present—a pig to be his own, but to be boarded on a farm outside the city." Wis Library Bul
This book is "far above the average in both interest and illustration." Bookmark

Suhl, Yuri
Simon Boom gives a wedding; illus. by Margot Zemach. Four Winds 1972 unp illus lib. bdg. $6.72   **E**

1 ISBN 0-590-07209-9   LC 70-16105
"No illustrator but Margot Zemach could create such whimsical illustrations to match this funny, preposterous tale about braggart Simon Boom, who always had to buy the best, even if 'sometimes the best happens to be a size too short, or too long, or absurdly out of season.' When Simon's daughter is to be married, he is determined to serve only the best food at the wedding party—and the incredulous wedding guests are astounded when only pure spring water is served." Pub W

Swift, Hildegarde H.
The little red lighthouse and the great gray bridge, by Hildegarde H. Swift and Lynd Ward. Harcourt 1942 unp illus $6.95, pa $1.95   **E**

1 Lighthouses—Fiction   2 George Washington Bridge—Fiction
ISBN 0-15-247040-9; 0-15-652840-1   LC 73-12861
"After the great beacon atop the . . . George Washington Bridge was installed, the little red lighthouse feared he would no longer be useful, but when an emergency arose, the little lighthouse proved that he was still important." Hodges. Bks for Elem Sch Libraries
"The story is written with imagination and a gift for bringing alive this little lighthouse and its troubles. . . . [Lynd Ward's] illustrations have some distinction and one in particular, the fog creeping over the river clutching at the river boats, has atmosphere, rhythm and good colour." Ontario Library Rev

Talbot, Toby
A bucketful of moon; pictures by Imero Gobbato. Lothrop 1976 47p illus lib. bdg. $6.96   **E**

1 Moon—Fiction
ISBN 0-688-51727-7   LC 75-26818
"Sure that the reflection in her water bucket is the moon itself, a foolish old woman sets off to retrieve the orb when it spills out with the water after her bucket breaks. Though she spies it in a number of places—first the sky, then twinned in a billy goat's eyes, and later at a disgruntled miller's window—her chase proves futile until she winds up in the stream beneath the bridge where she first lost the moon. There she sees the reflection once again and this time successfully captures it in a new bucket supplied by the bucket-maker she had earlier shown her treasure to." Booklist
"Fast-paced text just right for reading aloud, is full of delicious language and imagery and Gobbato's blue-tinged drawings add a gentle slapstick mood to the good-natured folk humor of the story." Sch Library J

Taylor, Mark
Henry the explorer; illus. by Graham Booth. Atheneum Pubs. [1976 c1966] unp illus pa $1.95   **E**

ISBN 0-689-70427-5   LC 66-10416
First published 1966 in hardcover
"One morning after breakfast Henry packed his explorer's kit and, with his dog, set out to explore the world. By nightfall he had made several important discoveries—including the fact that he was far from home and unsure of the way. Henry's safe return ahead of the search party and his anticipation of his next exploring expedition climax . . . [a] mildly suspenseful picture-book story." Booklist
"This appealing picture-tale adventure has a storyteller's concise narrative that should make it one of those books which stand up under repeated sharing." Horn Bk
Some other books about Henry are also available from Atheneum Pubs.:
Henry the castaway pa $1.95 (ISBN 0-689-70442-9)
Henry explores the mountains lib. bdg. $9.95 (ISBN 0-689-30461-7; LC 74-19315)

Thomas, Ianthe
Walk home tired, Billy Jenkins; pictures by Thomas di Grazia. Harper 1974 unp illus lib. bdg. $6.89   **E**

1 Blacks—Fiction
ISBN 0-06-026109-9   LC 73-5497
Nina, a young black girl, walks home pretending that she is being transported by a silver sailboat, a plane, and a train. City blocks seem to fly by as she and her skeptical little friend Billy Jenkins take imaginary flight
The illustrator's "antique brown-and-white city street scenes have an air-brushed, dreamland atmosphere out of which the expressive features of the girl and boy emerge like familiar faces in a crowd. A brief, gratifying journey through one beguiling girl's imagination." Booklist

Titus, Eve
Anatole; pictures by Paul Galdone. McGraw 1956 32p illus lib. bdg. $6.95   **E**

1 Mice—Fiction   2 France—Fiction
ISBN 0-07-064908-1   LC 56-10333
"Whittlesey House publications"
"Anatole is a French mouse who was made quite unhappy one day by hearing some people saying rude and unpleasant things about mice. He resolved never to go hunting for food in a house again, and turned his attention to the Duval Cheese Factory. There he spent every evening tasting the cheeses and leaving notes on them, rating them as to quality and indicating where improvements could be made. The owners were delighted and made him their official taster." Chicago. Children's Bk Center
"A very original story. . . . Anatole [is] wearing a beret at a rakish angle, and Paul Galdone's pictures of the typically French town in which he lives are gay and lively." Pub W
Some other books about Anatole are also available from McGraw:
Anatole and the cat lib. bdg. $6.95 (ISBN 0-07-064910-3; LC 57-10229)
Anatole and the piano lib. bdg. $6.95 (ISBN 0-07-064892-1; LC 66-8728)
Anatole and the Pied Piper $7.95 (ISBN 0-07-064897-2; LC 78-23513)
Anatole and the thirty thieves lib. bdg. $5.72 (ISBN 0-07-064888-3; LC 70-77562)

Tobias, Tobi
Moving day; pictures by William Pène du Bois. Knopf 1976 unp illus $4.95, lib. bdg. $5.99   **E**

1 Moving, Household—Fiction
ISBN 0-394-93115-7; 0-394-83115-2   LC 75-22275
"The artist's impeccable draughtsmanship and the clear colors of his uncluttered pictures echo the simple precision of the text, which is a small girl's running commentary. 'We're moving soon,' she begins, and lists all the tasks, the decisions, the final emptiness of the old house, and the farewells to familiar surroundings. After the move, there's the first meal and first night in the new home. Throughout the book, the confidant and alter ego is the stuffed bear who is the child's constant companion and her solace. It is Bear who is nervous, not she; it is Bear who must learn to like the new home, not she. The experience of moving as well as the relegation of reactions to a toy have been described in other picture books for the very young; this is not highly original, but it's nicely done." Chicago. Children's Bk Center

Petey; paintings by Symeon Shimin. Putnam 1978 30p illus lib. bdg. $6.95   **E**

1 Gerbils—Fiction   2 Death—Fiction
ISBN 0-399-20555-1   LC 76-25515
"Emily describes her apprehension on finding her gerbil Petey unresponsive one afternoon; her father gently tells her that Petey is old for a gerbil, that he's had a happy life due to Emily's loving care, that the pet book states there is nothing that can be done. Petey dies and is buried; when offered new gerbils, Emily decides she isn't ready. Maybe later." Chicago. Children's Bk Center
"Illustrated in soft pastel, this is one of the more thoughtful books about death for this age level. It is easy to empathize with Emily and the parents deal with her problem matter-of-factly without sugarcoating or sentimentalizing." Sch Library J

Tompert, Ann

Charlotte & Charles; illus. by John Wallner. Crown 1979 unp illus lib. bdg. $8.95   E

1 Giants—Fiction
ISBN 0-517-53660-9   LC 78-26363

"Charlotte and Charles, two giants, welcome humans who sail into their harbor although Charles warns his optimistic wife that 'people turn against you, sooner or later.' He's right. At first, the settlers thank the hospitable couple for help in building houses, roads, etc. Then greed tempts the newcomers to plot against their friends. Since loud bell ringing turns giants to stone, the humans set the clamor going continually but Charlotte and Charles save themselves by plugging their ears. The bell causes an earthquake that destroys the island, leaving the humans destitute, while the giants swim off to settle elsewhere." Pub W

"The striking full-color illustrations (executed in watercolors, then camera separated and printed in four colors) are richly hued and dexterously shaded to add dimension. . . . Wallner's careful attention to detail and discerning use of perspective add visual interest as he brings this thought-provoking but (for the average child) somewhat abstract tale into the realm of understanding by extracting its inherent emotions and individualizing them in the characters' faces and actions. A story with undercurrents to be shared with perceptive children." Booklist

Little fox goes to the end of the world; a story with pictures by John Wallner. Crown 1976 unp illus lib. bdg. $6.95   E

1 Foxes—Fiction
ISBN 0-517-52600-X   LC 75-44381

"A wily little fox tells mother of her plans to travel to the end of the world. Mother is afraid for her, but Little Fox is prepared for all contingencies. With childlike bravado the young vixen describes how she would fend off bears, elephants and crocodiles on her voyage." NY Times Bk Rev

"The brief story is related in the style of a child's exuberant prattle, with the setting rapidly switching from forest to mountains to sea. Wallner's bold, colorful crayon illustrations are so full of action that they seem to leap off the oversized pages." Sch Library J

Torgersen, Don Arthur

The girl who tricked the troll; illus. by Tom Dunnington. Childrens Press 1978 31p illus lib. bdg. $7.35   E

1 Fairy tales
ISBN 0-516-03465-0   LC 77-17198

"When Karin eats some troll berries, against her father's expressed warning, Trumble Town farm suffers. The tractor won't steer, the cows stop milking, eggs disappear, and the crops wither. Confronting the angry troll, Karin learns that she must ask him a question he can't answer to make him go away. Her books don't help, but a hint from her Uncle Hans, who is knowledgeable in the ways of trolls, helps her come up with the right query. Torgersen's tale is laced with bits of troll lore and hints of traditional tales that even very young readers will recognize (e.g., the troll stamps himself into the ground in much the same way Rumplestiltskin did). Dunnington's watercolor illustrations are bright and lively . . . the print is large and clear, and the pages uncluttered. With a little assistance, the book is accessible to early readers, but it really demands to be read aloud to a group." Sch Library J

Tresselt, Alvin

Autumn harvest; illus. by Roger Duvoisin. Lothrop 1951 unp illus lib. bdg. $7.44   E

1 Autumn
ISBN 0-688-51155-4   LC 51-8824

The author and artist "describe in bright, appropriately colored pictures and rhythmic text, the changes that take place in the countryside in the season between late summer and Thanksgiving." Booklist

"There is a subtle interplay between text and pictures, which makes one sharply aware of the mellow light of Indian summer, the sharpness of first frost, the smell of bonfires. In a few instances the borders surrounding the pages of text distract the eye from the facing illustrations, but as a whole this book is lovely to look at and to listen to." NY Times Bk Rev

Follow the wind; pictures by Roger Duvoisin. Lothrop 1950 unp illus lib. bdg. $7.44   E

1 Winds
ISBN 0-688-51156-2   LC 50-10974

"Rhythmic text and pictures in splashy colors tell about the wind that blew for days and days, dancing with the dandelions, tossing the kite, blowing off hats, turning the windmill, sometimes a gale, now a breeze, until finally it quietly rocked itself to sleep." Booklist

"Excellent not only as a picture book but also for use in the younger children's nature classes." Horn Bk

"Hi, Mister Robin!" Pictures by Roger Duvoisin. Lothrop 1950 unp illus lib. bdg. $7.44   E

1 Spring
ISBN 0-688-51168-6   LC 50-7904

After a "little boy who is tired of winter sees the first robin, he watches the changes in the landscape from bare branches to blossoms on the peach tree. Then, he is told, the spring has come." Horn Bk

"This very tenuous little story, of watching and waiting, is retold with a enrichment of 'looking' in the big color pictures. Mr. Duvoisin combines a love of the atmospheric with ability to make details clear and dramatic for the child. . . . For anyone not in the country, the pages offer fields, brooks, trees and the drama of a cold world changing to the warmth of spring." NY Her Trib Bks

Hide and seek fog; illus by Roger Duvoisin. Lothrop 1965 unp illus lib. bdg. $6.96   E

1 Fog
ISBN 0-688-51169-X   LC 65-14087

"This is not a plotted story but rather a mood picture book . . . describing a fog which rolls in from the sea to veil an Atlantic seacoast village for three days. The beautiful paintings, most of them double-spreads, and the brief, poetic text sensitively and effectively evoke the atmosphere of 'the worst fog in twenty years' and depict the reactions of children and grown-ups to it." Booklist

Rain drop splash; pictures by Leonard Wiesgard. Lothrop 1946 unp illus lib. bdg. $7.44   E

1 Rain and rainfall
ISBN 0-688-51165-1   LC 46-11878

"The brief, poetic text follows the falling raindrops as they form first a puddle and then a pond, spilling over into a brook, tumbling into a lake, overflowing into a river until, just before the sun comes out, the river flows into the sea." Bookmark

"Striking pictures in tones of yellow and brown . . . describe a rainstorm in terms a small child can understand." Booklist

White snow, bright snow; illus. by Roger Duvoisin. Lothrop 1947 33p illus $8.25, lib. bdg. $7.92   E

1 Snow
ISBN 0-688-41161-4; 0-688-51161-9   LC 47-11601
Awarded the Caldecott Medal, 1948

"The approach of the first snowfall of winter is forecast by the postman, the policeman, the farmer, and the rabbit—all friends of the young child. The description of winter activities and the changes brought about by the coming of spring are told in rhythmic prose that is not only beautiful and vivid but also childlike in its simplicity. . . . Clear-colored pictures add to the charm of this book." Children's Bks Too Good To Miss

The world in the candy egg; illus. by Roger Duvoisin. Lothrop 1967 unp illus lib. bdg. $7.92   E

1 Easter—Fiction
ISBN 0-688-51160-0   LC 67-3799

"Each of the toys in a toyshop peeks into a spun-sugar Easter egg and sees the things that please him most, and a little girl sees the whole 'magic world, little world, made for a child's delight.'" Hodges. Bks for Elem Sch Libraries

Tresselt, Alvin—*Continued*
"The magical world of a candy egg comes alive in this gentle picture book-fantasy. . . . The text, combining prose and poetry, and the lovely springtime color illustrations make an appealing book." Sch Library J

Tudor, Tasha
The dolls' Christmas. Walck, H. Z. 1950 unp illus $5.95, pa $2.50 **E**
1 Dolls—Fiction 2 Christmas—Fiction
ISBN 0-8098-1026-3; 0-8098-2912-6 LC 59-12744
"Story of two dolls who live in a large-size dollhouse and of the party, consisting of a dinner and a marionette show of 'Little Red Riding Hood,' that was given for them and their doll and toy friends at Christmas. Slight, written from the outside looking in, with sweet pictures by the author, of the dolls and their owners." Library J

1 is one. Walck, H. Z. [distributed by Rand McNally] 1956 unp illus pa $2.95 **E**
1 Counting
ISBN 0-528-87679-1 LC 56-11381
First published by Oxford
"The author-artist has with characteristic charming quaintness written and illustrated a counting book. Delicately tinted, decoratively bordered pictures and rhyming lines of text count from one to twenty. The fact that some of the objects are pictured too indistinctly for easy counting should not lessen the over-all enjoyment of the book." Booklist

Turkle, Brinton
Deep in the forest. Dutton 1976 unp illus lib. bdg. $7.95 **E**
1 Bears—Fiction 2 Stories without words
ISBN 0-525-28617-9 LC 76-21691
"Published almost twenty years ago, [Janice Brustlein's] 'Little Bear's Sunday Breakfast' (Lothrop) was an ingenious reversal of the story of Goldilocks and the three bears. Essentially the same idea is now treated in an entirely different way in an equally delightful book. An inquisitive bear cub wanders away from his mother and discovers an attractive, well-kept log cabin in the forest. Like Goldilocks in the fairy tale, he samples food, chairs, and beds, and the havoc he raises is discovered by the little girl and her parents upon their return from a walk. Except for the names on the porridge bowls, the book is wordless. The gray, yellow, and white illustrations [by the author] not only give a rustic early American charm to the interior scenes but graphically portray the emotions of the bears and of the human beings." Horn Bk

Obadiah the Bold; story and pictures by Brinton Turkle. Viking 1965 unp illus lib. bdg. $4.95 **E**
1 Friends, Society of—Fiction 2 Nantucket, Mass.—Fiction
ISBN 0-670-52001-2; 0-14-050233-5 LC 65-13350
"This story, with its setting in Nantucket about one hundred years ago, shows young Obadiah in the midst of a happy Quaker family. Brothers will tease, however, and when Obadiah wants to 'play pirate' (in hopes of someday being one), he is not spared a little fright. An understanding father helps his son think about following in the footsteps of another kind of seafarer, his grandfather, Captain Obadiah Starbuck." Rdng Ladders. 5th edition
The story "is told in clear, clean prose; its pictures, bright with color and humor, reflect the story's mood with a mirror's exactness." Pub W
Some other books about Obadiah are also available from Viking (unless otherwise noted):
The adventures of Obadiah lib. bdg. $4.50, pa $1.50 (ISBN 0-670-10614-3; 0-670-05091-1; LC 75-190713)
Rachel and Obadiah lib. bdg. $7.95 (Dutton ISBN 0-525-28020-5; LC 77-15661)
Thy friend, Obadiah lib. bdg. $6.95 (ISBN 0-670-71229-9; LC 69-18861)

Tworkov, Jack
The camel who took a walk; pictures by Roger Duvoisin. Dutton 1951 unp illus lib. bdg. $7.95, pa $2.95 **E**
1 Camels—Fiction
ISBN 0-525-27393-X; 0-525-45021-1

First published by Aladdin Books
A nonsense picture-story book about a beautiful young camel who took an early morning walk, about a terrible tiger that planned to pounce on her, and the plans of the monkey, the squirrel, and the bird—all of which came to naught
"Excitement rises to a surprise ending, which will be a relief to young children and a merry joke to slightly older ones. . . . The pictures are full of imagination and humor." NY Times Bk Rev

Uchida, Yoshiko
The birthday visitor; illus. by Charles Robinson. Scribner 1975 unp illus $5.95 **E**
1 Japanese Americans—Fiction 2 Birthdays—Fiction
ISBN 0-684-14229-5 LC 74-14076
"Emi, who lives in California and is periodically bored by eminent visitors from Japan, is just a little sulky because one man, a minister, is going to stay with her family on the night of her birthday dinner. She complains to the elderly Wadas (who function as grandparents) and is told she may be pleasantly surprised. Emi doubts it. But the lively young minister turns out to be very understanding, and he helps with a bird's funeral so that it's the best service Emi's ever held. In fact, she decides, her seventh birthday is nice in every way." Chicago. Children's Bk Center
"The ingenuous narrative is a successful blend of American and Japanese elements. . . . The pencil drawings discreetly embellished with watercolor tones of blue and brown and with touches of black embody perfectly the simple everyday realism of the story and convey with dignity and charm the Japanese quality of the telling." Horn Bk

The rooster who understood Japanese; illus. by Charles Robinson. Scribner 1976 unp illus lib. bdg. $8.95 **E**
1 Japanese Americans—Fiction 2 Roosters—Fiction
ISBN 0-684-14672-X LC 76-13450
Mrs. Kitamura, a babysitter, is fond of animals and maintains a bilingual menagerie named for heroes of American history. When Mrs. K. must give up her rooster, Mr. Lincoln (an unfriendly neighbor has been complaining), little third grader Miyo finds a new home for her babysitter's pet. And, unlike many elderly characters in children's fiction, Mrs. K is a strong individual and a free spirit by her own admission." Sch Library J
"Robinson's soft, serene watercolors in shades of aqua and salmon expand the story's mood; the varied Japanese-American family situations are nicely portrayed. It's a relaxing, satisfying story all around." Booklist

Udry, Janice May
Let's be enemies; pictures by Maurice Sendak. Harper 1961 unp illus $4.95, lib. bdg. $5.79 **E**
1 Friendship—Fiction
ISBN 0-06-026130-7; 0-06-026131-5 LC 61-5777
"John, annoyed because James is entirely too bossy, decides that he no longer wants him for a friend and goes to tell him so. Instead of becoming enemies, they agree that it would be more fun to go skating. An artless little treatise on childhood friendships, with illustrations that exactly suit the story." Hodges. Bks for Elem Sch Libraries

The moon jumpers; pictures by Maurice Sendak. Harper 1959 unp illus $8.95, lib. bdg. $8.79 **E**
ISBN 0-06-026145-5; 0-06-026146-3 LC 58-7757
"Here is a child's exhilaration and enchantment with the liveliness of summer nights, with the magic of moonlight and the downy warmth of the night wind. The goldfish play with the moonfish in the lily pond, the fireflies come from the woods, and a giant moth flies by on his search for moon flowers. At this time the call of 'Children, oh, children' from the house is meaningless, for there are no children present, only Moon Jumpers." Lutheran Educ
"There are black-and-white drawings and brief text in between double-page spreads in full luminous color. The pictures are the kind that children can enter directly 'into' and feel . . . the exhilaration of just being alive and full of motion." Horn Bk

Udry, Janice M.—*Continued*

A tree is nice; pictures by Marc Simont. Harper 1956 unp illus $6.95, lib. bdg. $7.89　**E**

1 Trees
ISBN 0-06-026155-2; 0-06-026156-0　　LC 56-5153
Awarded the Caldecott Medal, 1957
In childlike terms and in enticing pictures, colored and black and white, author and artist set forth reasons why trees are nice to have around—trees fill up the sky, they make everything beautiful, cats get away from dogs in them, leaves come down and can be played in, and trees are nice to climb in, to hang a swing in, or to plant. A picture book sure to please young children." Booklist

What Mary Jo shared; pictures: Eleanor Mill. Whitman, A. 1966 unp illus $5.95　**E**

1 Blacks—Fiction 2 School stories
ISBN 0-8075-8842-3　　　LC 66-16082
"Whenever Mary Jo [a little black girl] selected something to 'show and tell', her classmates had already chosen it. Finally she brought a very special person to share with the class—her [physician] father." NY Pub Library. The Black Experience in Children's Bks
"The writing is smooth and natural, and the illustrations, done in soft colors and black and white, are charming." We Build Together
Some other books about Mary Jo are also available from Whitman, A.:
Mary Jo's grandmother $5.95 (ISBN 0-8075-4984-3; LC 78-126433)
What Mary Jo wanted $5.95 (ISBN 0-8075-8848-2; LC 68-9123)

Ungerer, Tomi

Crictor. Harper 1958 32p illus $7.95, lib. bdg. $7.89　**E**

1 Snakes—Fiction
ISBN 0-06-026180-3; 0-06-026181-1　　LC 58-5288
"An entertaining bit of nonsense about the boa constrictor that was sent to Madame Bodot, who lived and taught school in a little French town. She called the snake Crictor and he became a great pet, learned, debonair and brave. The boys used him for a slide and the girls for a jump-rope. When Crictor captured a burglar by coiling around him until the police came, he was awarded impressive tokens of esteem and affection of the townspeople. Engaging line drawings [by the author] echo the restrained and elegant absurdities of the text." Chicago. Children's Bk Center

Emile. Harper 1960 32p illus lib. bdg. $8.79　**E**

1 Octopus—Fiction
ISBN 0-06-026191-9　　　LC 60-5788
"Emile is an octopus who lives for a while with Captain Samofar, a deep sea diver whom Emile rescued from a shark. Children who enjoyed the author's Crictor [entered above] will be equally delighted with this diverting picture-book tale of the eight-legged hero who is a gifted musician, works as a lifeguard, sometimes saving four people at one time, entertains the bathers by forming himself into different shapes such as a chair, a car, and a bird, and helps capture a gang of smugglers." Booklist

Moon Man. Harper [1967] 40p illus $8.95, lib. bdg. $9.79　**E**

1 Science fiction
ISBN 0-06-026234-6; 0-06-026235-4　　LC 66-12135
Descending to Earth on the fiery tail of a comet Moon Man is captured and thrown into jail by panicky officials as a suspected invader. He escapes by means of unique lunar powers, has a gay time until the police begin pursuit and then, realizing that he can never live peacefully on this planet, returns to the moon via a spacecraft built by a long-forgotten scientist. The cleverly imaginative tale and the boldly drawn illustrations filled with strong colors, action, and humor make the over-size picture book a natural for small [children.]" Booklist

One, two, where's my shoe? Harper 1964 unp illus lib. bdg. $7.89　**E**

1 Puzzles
ISBN 0-06-026241-9　　　LC 64-12811
A picture puzzle book concealing "pumps, oxfords, boots, mocassins! Fnd them in the shoulders, snouts, beards, and beaks of a virtually textless shape-identification book, where familiar forms hide in bold, vividly colored pictures [by the author]." Horn Bk

Zeralda's ogre. Harper 1967 unp illus lib. bdg. $9.89　**E**

1 Fairy tales 2 Cookery—Fiction
ISBN 0-06-026259-1　　　LC 67-14069
Humorous, grotesque illustrations in vivid colors effectively capture the droll quality of a picture-book tale about a child-eating ogre whose dietary habits are changed by the culinary art of a very young cook. . . . [Small children] will find the artless Zeralda's conversion of the horrendous ogre with scrumptious creations of roast turkey á la Cinderella and chocolate sauce Rasputin both satisfying and amusing." Booklist

Van Allsburg, Chris

The garden of Abdul Gasazi, written and illus. by Chris Van Allsburg. Houghton 1979 unp illus lib. bdg. $8.95　**E**

1 Magic—Fiction 2 Dogs—Fiction
ISBN 0-395-27804-X　　　LC 016844
"When Fritz, the naughty dog, ran into the garden of Abdul Gasazi, a retired magician, Alan was terrified, for he knew that dogs were not allowed beyond the vine-covered wall. Fritz eluded Alan, who ultimately came to the magician's imposing house and politely requested the return of the dog. His request was granted, but Fritz, who had been turned into a duck, compounded his original naughtiness by flying away with Alan's cap." Horn Bk
The full page "lithographlike drawings are astonishing—eerie, monumental, surreal and witty all at once—and the effect of the whole is original and unforgettable." Bks of the Times

Van Leeuwen, Jean

Tales of Oliver Pig; pictures by Arnold Lobel. Dial Press 1979 64p illus lib. bdg. $5.89, pa $1.95　**E**

1 Pigs—Fiction 2 Family life—Fiction
ISBN 0-8037-8736-7; 0-8037-8737-5　　LC 79-4276
"Dial Easy-to-read"
"Oliver encounters many true-to-life situations and decides how to cope with them: what to do on a rainy day, how to make a bad day into a good one, what to do when Grandma comes, how to dress for the snow, and most confusing, what to do when Mother cries. . . . The uncrowded pages have type big enough for children to read easily. The story is equally effective as a read-aloud or as a motivation for beginning readers." Children's Bk Rev Serv
The book is "filled with the warmth of the commonplace, the jostling joys and sorrows of siblings and the love of a pig family. . . . Arnold Lobel's illustrations, often in miniature, carry on the tender, yet never sentimental tone." Sch Library J

Van Woerkom, Dorothy O.

Donkey Ysabel; pictures by Normand Chartier. Macmillan Pub. Co. 1978 47p illus $6.95　**E**

1 Donkeys—Fiction 2 Farm life—Fiction
ISBN 0-02-791280-9　　　LC 78-5140
"Ready-to-read"
"Jealous at being replaced by a car, 'Donkey Ysabel' doesn't try to outsmart the auto or use any other means to re-establish her preeminence. . . . It is the car's ailments (flat tires and engine trouble) that cause the farm family once more to rely on animal over machine." Sch Library J
"An amusing and suspenseful tale, hard to beat as a way to draw beginners into reading on their own. Chartier's scenes of a Mexican farm dance with color and life. . . . Experiencing the battles for supremacy between car and donkey is great fun, especially when Pig, Rooster and Goat kibbitz on the sidelines." Pub W

Harry and Shellburt; pictures by Erick Ingraham. Macmillan Pub. Co. 1977 47p illus $6.95　**E**

1 Rabbits—Fiction 2 Turtles—Fiction 3 Friendship—Fiction
ISBN 0-02-791290-6　　　LC 77-5352
"Ready-to-read"
"Harry the Hare is Shellburt the Tortoise's dinner guest, and during the meal, Shellburt remarks

Van Woerkom, Dorothy O.—*Continued*

that the hare and the tortoise were once foes, not friends like them. Then Shellburt tells the story of the famous race. Harry simply can't believe that his ancestor was so stupid as to let a slowpoke beat him and challenges his pal to a repeat of the contest." Pub W

"The emphasis is on the enduring nature of true friendships and on winning graciously. Erick Ingraham's detailed pencil and charcoal drawings with olive-and-gold overtones reinforce the story which is suitable for both reading independently and aloud." Sch Library J

Meat pies & sausage; three tales of Fox and Wolf; retold by Dorothy O. Van Woerkom; illus. by Joseph Low. Greenwillow Bks. 1976 56p illus lib. bdg. $5.71 **E**

1 Foxes—Fiction 2 Wolves—Fiction
ISBN 0-688-84034-5 LC 75-33160

"A Greenwillow read-alone book"
Three tales in which Fox matches wits with Wolf and wins have a Slavic flavor and evidence the author's keen sense of humor. This volume [is] full of action and familiar forest creatures." Booklist

"In the genre of Br'er Rabbit, Ms. Woerkom writes for the beginning reader with charm and wit. Three-color illustrations by Joseph Low underscore the humor of the situations." Adventuring with Bks

Viorst, Judith

Alexander and the terrible, horrible, no good, very bad day; illus. by Ray Cruz. Atheneum Pubs. 1972 unp illus $7.95, pa $1.95 **E**

ISBN 0-689-30072-7; 0-689-70428-3 LC 72-75289

The author "describes the plight of a boy for whom everything goes wrong from the moment he steps out of bed and discovers he has gum stuck in his hair to his return to bed that night when he has to wear his hated railroad-train pajamas and the cat decides to sleep with one of his brothers instead of with him. His mother consoles him by remarking that some days are like that." Booklist

"The humor and truthfulness of the text combined with Ray Cruz's expressive black-and-white illustrations should make this story a favorite." Wis Library Bul

Another book about Alexander is: Alexander, who used to be rich last Sunday. Atheneum Pubs. $7.95, pa $1.95 (ISBN 0-689-30602-4; 0-689-70476-3; LC 77-1579)

My mama says there aren't any zombies, ghost, vampires, creatures, demons, monsters, fiends, goblins, or things; drawings by Kay Chorao. Atheneum Pubs. 1973 unp illus $7.95, pa $1.95 **E**

1 Monsters—Fiction 2 Mothers—Fiction
ISBN 0-689-30102-2; 0-689-70439-9 LC 73-76331

This book deals humorously with the childhood sense of being threatened by "imaginary monsters and a mother's reassurances that they don't exist. While wanting to believe her mother, Nick is also aware that she often makes mistakes . . . like the time she made Nick wear his boots on a sunny day." Sch Library J

"Ms. Chorao's drawings accent the spirit of Ms. Viorst's latest set piece, an amiable expression of human experiences." Pub W

Rosie and Michael; illus. by Lorna Tomei. Atheneum Pubs. 1974 unp illus $7.95, pa $1.95 **E**

1 Friendship—Fiction
ISBN 0-689-30439-0; 0-689-70466-6 LC 74-75571

"Rosie and Michael catalog the humorous, sometimes elaborate particulars of their eventful friendship: she likes him even when he's dopey and he likes her even when she's grouchy. . . . In the same vein further testimonials reflecting magnanimity and loyal support dispatch any chagrin that either buddy might harbor. Though repetition begins to weigh heavily, the serio-comic message is buoyed by Tomei's detailed, grotesquely interpretive pen-and-ink caricatures that lend a 'Mad' magazine touch to the whole panoply." Booklist

The tenth good thing about Barney; illus. by Erik Blegvad. Atheneum Pubs. 1971 25p illus $8.95, pa $1.95 **E**

1 Death—Fiction 2 Cats—Fiction
ISBN 0-689-20688-7; 0-689-70416-X LC 71-154764

"A little boy saddened by the death of his cat thinks of nine good things about Barney to say at his funeral. Later his father helps him discover a tenth good thing: Barney is in the ground helping grow flowers and trees and grass and 'that's a pretty nice job for a cat.' " Booklist

"The author succinctly and honestly handles both the emotions stemming from the loss of a beloved pet and the questions about the finality of death which naturally arise in such a situation. . . . An unusually good book that handles a difficult subject straightforwardly and with no trace of the macabre." Horn Bk

Waber, Bernard

An anteater named Arthur. Houghton 1967 46p illus lib. bdg. $7.95, pa $2.45 **E**

1 Anteaters—Fiction
ISBN 0-395-20336-8; 0-395-25936-3 LC 67-20374

Illustrated by the author
"Although Arthur is an anteater, he embodies the exasperating, if lovable, ways of all little boys from the moment he declines the red ants his mother offers him for breakfast, wanting brown ones instead, until he dashes back to the house to kiss his mother goodby before going off to school." Bruno. Bks for Sch Libraries, 1968

"Children and mothers will recognize themselves in this book, which casually pokes fun at the way things are but also suggests, in the easy and good-humored relationship that exists between mother and son . . . that they really aren't so bad." New Yorker

A firefly named Torchy. Houghton 1970 29p illus lib. bdg. $5.95 **E**

1 Fireflies—Fiction
ISBN 0-395-18656-0 LC 74-122906

"So zealous was Torchy in his light-producing activities that he greatly upset many nocturnal animals with his blazing show. After a refreshing evening flashing among the many lights of a city, however, the firefly returns home, tired, happy and still twinkling." Wis Library Bul

"This daft little tale has a modicum of message and a maximum of fun. The pert writing is outshone by the brilliant arabesques of color and movement in the [author's] illustrations." Sat Rev

Good-bye, funny dumpy-lumpy. Houghton 1977 64p illus lib. bdg. $6.95 **E**

1 Family life—Fiction 2 Cats—Fiction
ISBN 0-395-24735-7 LC 76-14349

"The era is Edwardian and the family feline, but the home truths easily transfer to their modern human counterparts. In the title story the family pays its last respects to a sofa on its last legs and learns to make do with a less 'lived-in' model. 'Everybody,' as in 'Everybody is outside without a jacket and a hat,' plays on that most commonly marshalled childhood defense. The humor in 'Great Grandfather' isn't at the expense of the senile centenarian but in the children's guileless interest in his second childhood. Her 'Picnic' spoiled by a soused spouse, tearful ex-teacher Aunt Effie conducts an unplanned lesson in grown-up vulnerability. On an upbeat note, 'The Outdoor Concert' turns into a round of musical laps as siblings compete for parental affection." Sch Library J

"The gray wash drawings supply nostalgic details of family life and Waber . . . catches the spirit of real children by artless anthropomorphism in every spontaneous move, in animated, harmless bickering, and in humorous responses to adults." Horn Bk

The house on East 88th Street. Houghton 1962 48p illus lib. bdg. $7.95, pa $2.95 **E**

1 Crocodiles—Fiction 2 New York (City)—Fiction
ISBN 0-395-18157-7; 0-395-19970-0 LC 62-8144

"In an amusing fantasy, Mr. and Mrs. Joseph F. Primm and their young son Joshua move into a new home in New York City and discover a crocodile [named Lyle] in the bathtub. The illustrations [by the author] detail the wrought iron railings, the graceful doorway with its fanlight, the sweeping staircase, elaborate fireplaces, and ornate

Waber, Bernard—*Continued*

chandeliers, characteristic of a comfortable old brownstone dwelling." Moorachian. What is a City?

Some other books about Lyle are also available from Houghton:

Lovable Lyle lib. bdg. $8.95, pa $1.95 (ISBN 0-395-19858-5; 0-395-25378-0; LC 69-14728)

Lyle and the birthday party lib. bdg. $7.95, pa $2.45 (ISBN 0-395-15080-9; 0-395-17451-1; LC 66-8646)

Lyle finds his mother lib. bdg. $7.95, pa $2.25 ISBN 0-395-19489-X; 0-395-27398-6; LC 74-5336)

Lyle, Lyle, crocodile lib. bdg. $8.95, pa $2.45 (ISBN 0-395-16995-X; 0-395-13720-9; LC 65-19305)

I was all thumbs. Houghton 1978 48p illus lib. bdg. $6.95   E

1 Octopus—Fiction
ISBN 0-395-21404-1   LC 75-11689

Illustrated by the author

"Legs is an octopus who has always lived in Captain Pierre's shipboard laboratory. (The mollusk explains that he had protested the name; after all, his appendages are arms, not legs.) But laboratory life is good to Legs; he has plenty of hearty meals and time for long naps. Then one day, the captain decides to set the octopus free. Legs is not amused. His glass case is the only home he's ever known. How will he cope with sea life? Nevertheless into the water he goes, set loose in a swoosh of waves. After an exciting comedy in which Legs is 'all thumbs,' he settles comfortably into briny life. The pictures are vibrant; the story is great fun and includes bits of lore on octopus life. Children will laugh at the captain's puns, although Legs never did." Pub W

Ira sleeps over. Houghton 1972 48p illus lib. bdg. $7.95, pa $2.95   E

ISBN 0-395-13893-0; 0-395-20503-4   LC 72-75605

"A small boy's joy in being asked to spend the night with a friend who lives next door is unrestrained until his sister raises the question of whether or not he should take his teddy bear. Torn between fear of being considered babyish and fear of what it may be like to sleep without his bear, Ira has a hard time deciding what to do. His dilemma is resolved happily, however, when he discovers that his friend Reggie also has a nighttime bear companion. An appealing picture book which depicts common childhood qualms with empathy and humor in brief text and colorful illustrations [by the author]." Booklist

Wagner, Jenny

The Bunyip of Berkeley's Creek; pictures by Ron Brooks. Puffin Bks. in association with Childerset [1977 c1973] unp illus pa $2.95   E

1 Animals, Mythical—Fiction
ISBN 0-14-050126-6

First published 1973 in Australia; 1977 in the United States by Bradbury Press

The Bunyip is "an Australian folk-monster who lives at the bottom of deep water holes. . . . Having crawled out of Berkeley's Creek, the Bunyip seeks to know his nature; he asks a platypus, a wallaby, and an emu what he looks like. 'Horrible' is the universal unsettling response. To compound his problems, a scientist informs him that Bunyip do not exist. Retreating to a quiet 'billabong' to rest, the Bunyip is delighted when a dark, muddy shape—like himself but female—crawls out of the water inquiring, 'What am I?'" Horn Bk

The author's "tersely mythic tale finds haunting realization in Brooks' color with pen-and-ink illustrations. The pictures, while not sinister, have a dark, almost vibrating clarity, suggesting the half-light visualization of dream. Both texture and characterization are vaguely Wild-Thing-like, though broader in actual view as a rule and clearly original. The Bunyip's countenance is at first horrific, then pathetically oafish and mismatched, and finally endearingly homely. Designed with care for a caring audience." Booklist

Ward, Lynd

The biggest bear. Houghton 1952 84p illus lib. bdg. $7.95, pa $1.95   E

1 Bears—Fiction
ISBN 0-395-14806-5; 0-395-15024-8   LC 52-8730

Awarded the Caldecott Medal, 1953

"Johnny Orchard never did acquire the bearskin for which he boldly went hunting. Instead, he brought home a cuddly bear cub, which grew in size and appetite to mammoth proportions and worried his family and neighbors half to death!" Children's Bks Too Good to Miss

"A perfect collaboration between Lynd Ward, distinguished artist, and Lynd Ward, writer, this first story written for small children has everything they will love—imagination, humor, excitement, and beautiful and dramatic full-page illustrations." Chicago Sunday Trib

Wasson, Valentina P.

The chosen baby; illus. by Glo Coalson. [Rev. ed] Lippincott 1977 unp illus $6.95   E

1 Adoption—Fiction
ISBN 0-397-31738-7   LC 76-41391

First published 1939

"The story describes a couple who have not had children although they wanted them: the Browns go to an adoption agency, and then wait. And wait. When they are telephoned, they rush over and are instantly captivated by a baby boy whom they name Peter. There are some reassuring incidents about the welcome given by the extended family, and then about the adoption of a second child and Peter's reaction to a baby sister. . . . This won't answer every question, but it's a fine first book for very young adopted children, and it can foster understanding in the child who is not adopted." Chicago. Children's Bk Center

Watanabe, Shigeo

How do I put it on? Getting dressed; pictures by Yasuo Ohtomo. Collins [distributed by Philomel Bks] 1979 28p illus $6.95, lib. bdg. $6.99   E

1 Clothing and dress—Fiction 2 Bears—Fiction
ISBN 0-529-05555-4; 0-529-05557-0   LC 79-12714

"An I can do it all by myself book"
Original Japanese edition, 1977

A young bear demonstrates the wrong and right way to put on a shirt, pants, a cap, and shoes

"The single-mindedness of this most elementary of how-to's, and its ingenuous protagonist, combine to appeal to the very youngest of book lovers. . . . [The text asks] 'Do I put it on like this?' Children will chime in with the bear's answers; soon second-guessing the bruin becomes a rewarding game during inevitably requested rereadings. Illustrations, large and in color, are uncluttered." Booklist

Watson, Clyde

Tom Fox and the apple pie; illus. by Wendy Watson. Crowell 1972 unp illus $3.95, lib. bdg. $4.79   E

1 Foxes—Fiction
ISBN 0-690-82783-0; 0-690-82784-9   LC 74-171010

Tom Fox was the laziest, greediest, sweetest and youngest of all the Fox children. Unable to resist the apple pie sold at the Fair, he dashed off before finishing his chores. How he gets the apple pie and what he does with it is told here

Watson, Nancy Dingman

The birthday goat; pictures by Wendy Watson. Crowell 1974 unp illus $5.95, lib. bdg. $6.79, pa $2.95   E

1 Goats—Fiction
ISBN 0-690-00145-2; 0-690-00146-0; 0-690-03811-9   LC 73-3389

"Warned of a kidnapper at loose, yet wanting to celebrate Paulette's birthday, the goat family, including baby Souci, sets off for the carnival, where the mean Pig abducts Souci. Eventually, after seizing the kidnapper, visiting Pickpocket Place (where napped babes are auctioned), and consulting a hesitatingly inept policeman, baby Souci turns up. She had hidden from the mean Pig under Mother's hat." Rdng Teacher

"In cartoon strip style, a series of lively pictures almost tell the tale of an exciting day by themselves, each frame filled with color, action and humor. There is also dialogue (in balloons) and it is amusing dialogue to read aloud. . . . This is humor at the child's level, it's a good picture of family affection, and it has the carnival background for added interest." Chicago. Children's Bk Center

Welber, Robert

The winter picnic; pictures by Deborah Ray. Pantheon Bks. 1970 unp illus lib. bdg. $5.99, pa 95¢   **E**

1 Winter—Fiction
ISBN 0-394-90444-3; 0-394-82621-3   LC 77-77418

"A small boy who is unconvinced that one must wait for summer to have a picnic, makes some dishes out of snow, fixes and carries out a lunch of peanut-butter-and-jelly sandwiches, potato chips, and lemonade, and prevails upon his busy mother to have a picnic with him in the snow. A winning picture book with a simple, natural story and paintings in bright colors against snow-white backgrounds." Booklist

Wells, Rosemary

Benjamin & Tulip. Dial Press 1973 unp illus $6.95, lib. bdg. $6.46, pa $1.50   **E**

1 Raccoons—Fiction
ISBN 0-8037-1808-X; 0-8037-2057-2; 0-8037-0545-X   LC 73-6018

"This is the story of two raccoons with a problem: Tulip wants to fight Benjamin, but Benjamin isn't the fighting type. However, enough is enough, and Benjamin gets . . . [even] when he and his huge watermelon accidentally fall from a tree and land right smack on top of Tulip." Babbling Bookworm

"The brief text, interpreted in delicately amusing pastel and pen-and-ink drawings [by the author] is appropriate to the size of the book, comfortably scaled for small hands." Horn Bk

Max's first word. Dial Press 1979 unp illus $2.95   **E**

1 Vocabulary—Fiction 2 Brothers and sisters—Fiction
ISBN 0-8037-6066-3   LC 78-59745

"Very first books"

The book depicts "the trials of put-upon Ruby and her infant brother, Max. The cute, cuddly anthropomorphs are portrayed in brightly colored pictures, their . . . adventures related in a minimal text. Ruby puts a cup on Max's high-chair tray and orders him to say 'cup.' Slamming the cup firmly down, Max shouts 'Bang!' And 'Bang!' is what he responds to all Ruby's teaching as she points out things in the kitchen: pot, broom, egg, etc. When she hands Max an apple, she says 'yum-yum,' whereupon the tricky baby hollers 'Delicious!' " Pub W

"In a very small book with heavy board pages. Wells has created an engaging character, a very young rabbit called Max, and has managed to make a brief but nicely structured story that is deft and humorous. It's the sort of book that very young children ask for repeatedly and are soon 'reading' themselves." Chicago. Children's Bk Center

Some other books about Max and Ruby are also available from Dial Press:

Max's new suit $2.95 (ISBN 0-8037-6065-5; LC 79-50747)
Max's ride $2.95 (ISBN 0-8037-6069-8; LC 79-50746)
Max's toys; a counting book $2.95 (ISBN 0-8037-6068-X; LC 79-50748)

Morris's disappearing bag; a Christmas story. Dial Press 1975 unp illus $5.95, lib. bdg. $5.47, pa $1.95   **E**

1 Rabbits—Fiction 2 Christmas—Fiction
ISBN 0-8037-5441-8; 0-8037-5510-4; 0-8037-5509-0   LC 75-9202

"Christmas day can be full of disappointments, especially if you only get a teddy bear, and your older brother and sisters get nifty gifts like a hockey stick, a beauty kit, and a chemistry set. . . . Morris is so frustrated with his gift that he invents a disappearing bag, one that becomes an instant hit with his brother and sisters. With new bargaining power due to his bag, Morris finally gets his chance to share the older children's gifts." Babbling Bookworm

"Christmas, magic, and getting the family temporarily to disappear add up to three irresistible themes, and Wells treats them imaginatively. The author-artist does, along with careful color and line work, some wonderful things with Morris' ears and eyes, expressing exactly the sentiments of a putout preschool rabbit." Booklist

Noisy Nora; story and pictures by Rosemary Wells. Dial Press 1973 unp illus $4.95, lib. bdg. $4.58, pa $2.25   **E**

1 Mice—Fiction 2 Family life—Fiction 3 Stories in rhyme
ISBN 0-8037-6638-6; 0-8037-6639-4; 0-8037-6193-7   LC 72-6068

Little Nora, tired of being ignored, tries to gain her family's attention by being noisy. When this doesn't work Nora disappears but returns when she is sure she has been missed

"A small book with rhymed verses and anthropomorphic mice has been illustrated with buoyant pastel drawings that add humorous details to the story. . . . The universal emotion of a child's feeling slighted because of its siblings has been given life in a simple book." Horn Bk

Wildsmith, Brian

ABC. Watts, F. [1963 c1962] unp illus lib. bdg. $5.95   **E**

1 Alphabet
ISBN 0-531-01525-4   LC 63-7131

First published 1962 in England
Illustrated by the author

An alphabet book which illustrates animals and objects, identifying each on a facing page in capital and lower case letters, setting off the first letter with special emphasis." NY Times Bk Rev

"Bold, original pictures drawn in the individual style of an artist provide an excellent beginning for a child's education. Children should have a variety of books with this sort of picture, pictures that are paintings and not merely illustrations." NY Her Trib Bks

Brian Wildsmith's Birds. Oxford [1980 c1967] unp illus pa $3.95   **E**

1 Birds—Pictorial works
ISBN 0-19-272117-8

First published 1967 by Franklin Watts

"Mr. Wildsmith has tied a series of pictures of birds . . . to their group names: a watch of nightingales, a nye of pheasants, a congregation of plover, et cetera. There is no other text." Sat Rev

"Birds—how well the subject lends itself to this artist's exquisite use of color! . . . The child will have fun with the terms while absorbing truly beautiful illustrations." Horn Bk

Brian Wildsmith's Fishes. Watts, F. 1968 unp illus lib. bdg. $5.95   **E**

1 Fishes—Pictorial works
ISBN 0-531-01528-9   LC 68-12046

The author explains in his foreword the origins of the various names that have been given to groups of fishes by fishermen, zoologists and poets. The main part of the book consists of illustrations of fishes

"The colors are no less magnificent, though the page designs perhaps less striking, than in the artist's earlier zoological sequences—and the total richness is still a reward. To the fortunate small child who may have peered at the near-fantasies of the aquarium, these creatures may seem no more bizarre: the 'herd' of rainbow-wrapped sea horses, the 'hoves' of radiantly spotted trout, the 'flotilla' of spear-headed swordfish, the 'stream' of irridescent minnows." Horn Bk

Brian Wildsmith's 1, 2, 3's. Watts, F. 1965 unp illus lib. bdg. $5.95   **E**

1 Counting 2 Size and shape
ISBN 0-531-01527-0   LC 65-10782

"Taking the basic shapes—the rectangle, the triangle, and the circle—Wildsmith relates them to numbers. The geometric shapes illustrate the numbers one through ten. The higher the number the more complex the figure becomes—7 makes a house; 8 a man; 10 a locomotive. The author's intent is to help children appreciate the role of these three shapes in building more complex figures." Wis Library Bul

The author-illustrator gives "kaleidoscopic presentation of counting for the beginner. . . . The closing pages contain exercises for picking out designated shapes. Although it may not be possible to predict the importance of the book as an introduction to mathematics, it can stand alone as an introduction to form and color." Horn Bk

Wildsmith, Brian—*Continued*

Brian Wildsmith's Puzzles. Watts, F. 1971
c1970 unp illus lib. bdg. $5.95   E

1 Puzzles
ISBN 0-531-01550-5   LC 75-125533
First published 1970 in England
Illustrated by the author
"The puzzles range from pictures in which there
are hidden details to those that require comparison
or deduction to find the answer." Chicago. Children's Bk Center
"Brilliant colors that almost leap from the page
are often used as clues to very simple puzzles that
can help sharpen a child's powers of observation
while he enjoys the fun of finding answers." Sat
Rev

The circus. Oxford [1979 c1970] unp illus
pa $3.95   E

1 Circus—Pictorial works
ISBN 0-19-272102-X
First published 1970 in England; in the United
States by Watts with title: Brian Wildsmith's
Circus
"Enclosed between a notice that the circus is
coming to town and an announcement of its move
to the next place is a series of pictures with no
text. In double-page spreads Brian Wildsmith has
painted vibrant, beautiful illustrations of animals
and acrobats, clowns and jugglers, birds on a
seesaw, and the full panoply of a circus parade.
The pictures have action and humor and . . . are
remarkable for the quality of the colors." Sat Rev

The little wood duck. Watts, F. 1973
[c1972] unp illus lib. bdg. $5.95   E

1 Ducks—Fiction
ISBN 0-531-02593-4   LC 72-3828
First published 1972 in England
"Unlike his brothers and sisters, the youngest
duckling couldn't swim properly but only in circles,
because one of his feet was larger than the other.
This peculiarity brought him nothing but scolding
and teasing, until the day he saved the others by
swimming round and round in front of a fox who
was waiting to pounce upon them. Giddy from
watching, the fox collapsed, and the little wood
ducks raced for safety." Horn Bk
"Mr Wildsmith illustrates his brief narrative with
all the gorgeous colour and minute attention to
detail that we have come to expect of him."
Times (London) Lit Sup

Wild animals. Oxford [1979 c1967] unp
illus pa $3.95   E

1 Mammals—Pictorial works
ISBN 0-19-272103-8
First published 1967 in England; in the United
States by Watts with title: Brian Wildsmith's
Wild animals
Illustrated by the author
"A pride of lions, a lepe of leopards, a skulk of
foxes, and a cete of badgers are among the cleverly
captured groups of wild beasts that stalk the vivid,
glowing pages of this fascinating picture book. A
splendid, eyecatching . . . volume." Booklist

Will

Finders keepers, by Will and Nicolas.
Harcourt 1951 unp illus $6.50, pa $2.50   E

1 Dogs—Fiction
ISBN 0-15-227529-0; 0-15-630950-5   LC 51-12326
Awarded the Caldecott Medal, 1952
"Nap and Winkle, two dogs, find a bone while
digging. Says Nap, 'I saw it first.' Says Winkle, 'I
touched it first.' In turn they ask a farmer, a goat,
an apprentice barber and a big dog. 'Whose bone
is it, Nap's or mine?' When the big dog starts
away with that bone, Nap and Winkle fight the
big dog to regain their prize—and then both chew
away at it together. Story and pictures will appeal
to children." Pittsburgh
"There is a touch of folk-lore or the fable in this
story. . . . The illustrations [by Nicolas] have
many humorous touches and achieve a highly
dramatic effect by the artist's use of red, gold and
black." Ontario Library Rev

The two Reds, by Will and Nicolas.
Harcourt 1950 unp illus $6.50   E

1 Cats—Fiction 2 New York (City)—Fiction
ISBN 0-15-292127-3   LC 50-13863

This book tells how Red, the cat, saved Red, the
boy, and how the two became firm friends from
that time
"The drawing is highly sophisticated, yet it has
the forthrightness and humor of a child's viewpoint. The economical text and the vigor of the
illustrations make this a notable picture book."
NY Times Bk Rev

Willard, Nancy

Papa's panda; illus. by Lillian Hoban.
Harcourt 1979 unp illus lib. bdg. $5.95   E

1 Giant panda—Fiction
ISBN 0-15-259462-0   LC 78-31787
"James wants a teddy bear for his birthday.
Nothing else will do. Papa has bought him a toy
panda. Ingeniously, he distracts his son by fabricating a tale of a 'real' panda who comes to visit.
. . . [He] is so big he eats the family out of house
and home, he takes up all the beds, and he even
spanks Papa (depicted in one of Lillian Hoban's
illustrations). What a relief it is to James to open
a box with a small, stuffed panda inside." Sch Library J
"Children will scarcely pause for breath during
Willard's swift telling, except to enjoy Hoban's
larky drawings—black-and-white, real and imaginary views, with flashes of rosy red." Pub W

Simple pictures are best; story by Nancy
Willard; pictures by Tomie De Paola.
Harcourt 1977 unp illus $7.95, pa $2.95   E

1 Photography—Fiction
ISBN 0-15-274958-6; 0-15-682625-9   LC 76-4923
"To celebrate their wedding aniversary, a country
shoemaker and his wife, who 'lived in a small
house so far from other houses that their road
seemed the last road in the world,' arrange to have
their picture taken. Despite the frustrated photographer's insistent refrain that '[s]imple pictures
are best,' the two obstinately persist in demonstrating their success and versatility by adding to the
composition a substantial sampling of their possessions, including prize vegetables, ornate hats, musical instruments, a freshly baked pie, and the one-
eyed family cat." Horn Bk
"The surprise ending will delight young readers
and the bouncy, funny illustrations prove again
that de Paola's pictures are best." West Coast Rev
of Bks

Williams, Barbara

Albert's toothache; illus. by Kay Chorao.
Dutton 1974 unp illus lib. bdg. $6.95, pa $1.95
E

1 Turtles—Fiction
ISBN 0-525-25368-8; 0-525-45037-8   LC 74-4040
This is the "story of a small turtle, toothless as
are all of his kind, who takes to his bed with an
announced toothache. His mother worries; his
father thunders incredulous impatience; his siblings
cast scorn. So it goes until grandmother investigates and discovers 'where' he has a toothache."
Library J
"The humor of the concise dialogue and of the
stylized repetitions of the narrative is carefully reflected in the sepia-line and half-tone drawings
that reveal the anthropomorphically domestic life
of the turtles." Horn Bk

Jeremy isn't hungry; pictures by Martha
Alexander. Dutton 1978 unp illus lib. bdg. $5.95
E

1 Infants—Fiction 2 Brothers—Fiction
ISBN 0-525-32760-6   LC 78-4924
"Mama's taking a shower and rushing to get
dressed while preschooler Davey tries to help by
caring for his younger brother, Jeremy. Jeremy
is crying, probably from hunger, and Mama says
feed him. Davey's problems (from getting Jeremy
into his chair to deciphering contents of a baby
food bottle when he can't read) are hilariously
understated in a running conversation between
him and his mother." Booklist
"Probably nobody but Alexander could have
matched the harrowing goings on as perfectly as
she does with her spirited scenes. . . . Every move
the willing little boy makes creates a crisis that
propels mum out of the bath to the kitchen.
Jeremy throws the kind of nonstop tantrums that
every infant seems born knowing exactly how to
stage at the precise wrong moments. Each page
is crazy fun and the story as a whole is as suspenseful as a novel." Pub W

Williams, Barbara—*Continued*

Kevin's grandma; illus. by Kay Chorao. Dutton 1975 unp illus lib. bdg. $7.95, pa $1.95

E

1 Grandmothers—Fiction
ISBN 0-525-33115-8; 0-525-45039-4 LC 74-23713

"The small storyteller's much loved grandma does all the things a grandma is expected to do. But Kevin tells him how his grandmother is different. She's into Yoga and Judo and brings Kevin peanut butter soup on her Honda and sky dives." Children's Bk Rev Serv

"Whether or not readers can identify with the gentle, loving grandma or the equally loving, madcap one, they will be delighted by the black-and-white line drawings by Kay Chorao and will sympathize with Kevin, who can't help making the truth a little more interesting." Babbling Bookworm

Williams, Garth

The chicken book. Delacorte Press 1970 31p illus $5.95, lib. bdg. $5.47

E

1 Counting 2 Chickens—Poetry
ISBN 0-440-01202-3; 0-440-01203-1 LC 69-12504

"An attractive picture book for the very young, originally published in 1946 by Howell, Soskind." Booklist

"There no-nonsense mother informs five hungry chicks that the way to a full gizzard is through arduous scratching. This old, brief counting rhyme is greatly expanded by [the author's] bright, full-page, beautifully drawn, very funny pictures." Library J

Williams, Jay

Everyone knows what a dragon looks like; illus. by Mercer Mayer. Four Winds 1976 unp illus $9.95, pa $5.95

E

1 Dragons—Fiction 2 China—Fiction
ISBN 0-590-07284-6; 0-590-07751-1 LC 74-13121

"In a city on the Chinese border, long ago, the gatekeeper was a small, cheerful boy named Han. He was the only person who was courteous to the fat, bald, old man who appeared one day announcing that he was a dragon and that he could save the city of Wu. For Wu was threatened by invasion. The Mandarin's advisers had agreed that prayer was the one thing that might stop the Wild Horsemen of the north—but it didn't. And the old man was scoffed at, for although each of the ruler's advisers had a different idea of what a dragon looked like, they all agreed he didn't look old and shabby. However, for Han's sake, the old man saved the city; he became a mighty wind and drove off the invaders, and then he changed his shape and sprang into the sky, a glorious and terrible dragon. He was never seen again, but Han was heaped with honors and riches for his part in saving the city, and from then on everybody knew what a dragon looked like, '. . . a small, fat, bald old man,' the story ends." Chicago. Children's Bk Center

"The theme of this story is that appearances can be deceiving. Mercer Mayer provides a series of emotionally expressive illustrations scaled down to a child's eye level. The humanized characters realistically portray fear, anger or joy. . . . Now we see exotic Mayer, recalling Chinese scroll paintings. Careful attention has been paid to background detail, perspective and layout, drawing the eye into each superb illustration and creating a three-dimensional effect." NY Times Bk Rev

Wittman, Sally

A special trade; pictures by Karen Gundersheimer. Harper 1978 unp illus $7.95, lib. bdg. $7.89

E

1 Friendship—Fiction 2 Old age—Fiction
ISBN 0-06-026553-1; 0-06-026554-X LC 77-25673

"Old Bartholomew used to take Nelly, a little girl, for walks in her stroller. Now she takes him for walks in his wheelchair. Karen Gundersheimer's illustrations . . . show the pleasures of a special friendship between Nelly as she is growing up and the grandfatherly Bartholomew." Babbling Bookworm

"A heartwarming story. . . . Small, detailed illustrations in color perfectly convey the special feeling of friendship and love." Horn Bk

Yarbrough, Camille

Cornrows; illus. by Carole Byard. Coward, McCann & Geoghegan 1979 unp illus $7.95 E

1 Blacks—Fiction 2 Hair—Fiction
ISBN 0-698-20462-X LC 78-24010

"Mama's and Great Grammaw's stories are something Sister and the brother she calls MeToo look forward to. 'Storytellin time' is a daily affair, and this time, as the children sit to have their hair braided, they hear the regal history of cornrowing. Grammaw and Mama describe it as ancient and symbolic, a sign of clan, religion, or social status, and come slavery times, a sign of disgrace. After that most celebratory history Mama draws the children into a 'hair name game.' Clapping, Sister and MeToo listen to Mama's long chant of styles and names: 'Name it Robeson/name it Malcolm/you can name it Dr. King./Name it DuBois,/name it Garvey./name it something you can sing.'" Booklist

"Dialect is used but not overused. Byard's black-and-white drawings . . . are attractive and welcome." Sch Library J

Yashima, Taro

Crow Boy. Viking 1955 37p illus lib. bdg. $7.95, Penguin pa $2.25 E

1 School stories 2 Japan—Fiction
ISBN 0-670-24931-9; 0-14-050172-X LC 55-13626

"A young boy from the mountain area of Japan goes to school in a nearby village, where he is taunted by his classmates and feels rejected and isolated. Finally an understanding teacher helps the boy gain acceptance. The other students recognize how wrong they have been and nickname him 'Crow Boy' because he can imitate the crow's calls with such perfection." Adventuring With Bks. 2d edition

"A moving story interpreted by the author's distinctive illustrations, valuable for human relations and for its picture of Japanese school life." Hodges. Bks for Elem Sch Libraries

Seashore story. Viking 1967 unp illus $4.95

E

1 Japan—Fiction 2 Folklore—Japan
ISBN 0-670-62710-0 LC 66-11914

An ancient Japanese tale "with a Rip Van Winkle motif is told to young ballet-school campers on a Japanese beach. This mysterious tale of Urashima . . . follows the adventures of a fisherman who is carried on a turtle's back to a palace under the sea, where he becomes unconscious of time. On his return home, he is suddenly transformed into an old man." Horn Bk

"The author's misty illustrations have the same haunting quality as the story." Hodges. Bks for Elem Sch Libraries

Umbrella. Viking 1958 30p illus lib. bdg. $7.95, Penguin pa $2.75 E

1 Umbrellas and parasols—Fiction
ISBN 0-670-73858-1; 0-14-050240-8 LC 58-14714

Illustrated by the author

"Momo, given an umbrella and a pair of red boots on her third birthday, is overjoyed when at last it rains and she can wear her new rain togs." Hodges. Bks for Elem Sch Libraries

In this simple tale, young children "will be carried along by their identification with the actions of this very real little girl. . . . The beauty of the book makes this worthwhile." Horn Bk

Followed by: Momo's kitten. o.p. 1981

Ylla

Two little bears. Harper 1954 unp illus lib. bdg. $8.79, pa $1.95 E

1 Bears—Fiction
ISBN 0-06-026811-5; 0-06-443016-2 LC 54-8963

The author "a photographer of distinction, has written and pictured a tale of her own pet bear cubs playing with spontaneous abandon, and looking out on a strange and puzzling world with grave innocence." Sat Rev

Yolen, Jane

The girl who loved the wind; pictures by Ed Young. Crowell 1972 unp illus $9.95, lib. bdg. $9.89 E

1 Winds—Fiction
ISBN 0-690-33100-2; 0-690-33101-0 LC 71-171012

"Wanting his beautiful daughter Danina to have no unhappiness in her life, her father—a wealthy

Yolen, Jane—*Continued*

Eastern merchant of long ago—builds a house walled on three sides and open to the sea on the fourth. Danina grows up surrounded by kindness, supplied with flowers and music, and she knows only smiles and happiness until she hears the wind moaning its description of the world outside and its mixture of pleasure and sorrow. Troubled and restless, Danina spreads her cape and sails off on the wind, over the sea, to learn what goes on in the 'ever-changing world.'" Chicago. Children's Bk Center

"The striking illustrations, combining watercolor and collage, are stylized and oriental. The story unfolds at a measured pace, with a subtly implied message that life must be a mixture of happiness and sadness." Booklist

Zacharias, Thomas

But where is the green parrot? A picture book by Thomas and Wander Zacharias. Delacorte Press 1968 unp illus $4.95, lib. bdg. $4.58, pa $2.75
E

ISBN 0-440-0141-2; 0-440-0872-7; 0-440-0142-0
LC 67-24090

"A Seymour Lawrence book"
Originally published 1965 in Germany
Illustrated by Wanda Zacharias

"This picture book is an amusing game rather than a story. A green parrot is to be found somewhere in each of nine full-color double-spreads, more carefully hidden in some than in others. The illustrations showing among other things a toy chest, a house, a train, and a garden are large, clearly drawn, and pleasingly detailed while the text merely describes the scene and asks the question: But where is the green parrot?" Booklist

Zemach, Harve

The judge; an untrue tale; with pictures by Margot Zemach. Farrar, Straus 1969 unp illus $7.95
E

1 Judges—Fiction 2 Stories in rhyme 3 Nonsense verses
ISBN 0-374-33960-0
LC 79-87209

"An engaging and humorous nonsense story told in rhyme and illustrated with raffish deftness. Enthroned on his bench, a curmudgeon of a judge hears a prisoner plead that he didn't know that what he did was against the law, but that he had seen a horrible beast. 'This man has told an untrue tale. Throw him in jail!' Each additional prisoner adds to the story; each infuriates the judge." Sutherland. Best in Children's Bks

"In a perfect, wordless conclusion, a splendidly ludicrous monster is pictured devouring the doubting magistrate, while the five freed prisoners walk happily away. The illustrations, featuring absurd, somewhat Hogarthian caricatures, make a cosmic, thoroughly unified picture book." Horn Bk

Mommy, buy me a china doll; adapted from an Ozark children's song; pictures by Margot Zemach. Farrar, Straus [1975 c1966] unp illus $5.95
E

1 Folk songs—Ozark Mountains
ISBN 0-374-35005-1
LC 66-16943

A reprint of the title first published 1966 by Follett

A "picture book version of the cumulative folk song that has the appeals of repetition, of a chain of mildly nonsensical actions, and of a warmly satisfying ending. Eliza Lou's request for a china doll leads to proposals that it be bought with Daddy's feather bed, so Daddy would have to sleep in the horsey's bed, and the horsey would have to sleep in Sister's bed, and so on, and so on. Each page of print is faced by a full-page illustration in color, humorous in mood." Chicago. Children's Bk Center

The princess and Froggie; stories by Harve and Kaethe Zemach; pictures by Margot Zemach. Farrar, Straus 1975 unp illus $5.95
E

1 Frogs—Fiction 2 Friendship—Fiction
ISBN 0-374-36116-9
LC 75-697

"Three disarming vignettes starring 'the princess' and her friend Froggie, who is adept at easing crisis situations. . . . Coupled with Margot Zemach's unconventional graphic interpretation, the stories become droll farce. The frumpy princess in a shapeless Sunday dress with a bedraggled ribbon in her hair is a merry departure from the usual type; and Mama doesn't recall any royal matrons on the scene lately. Blithe tongue-in-cheek comedy for the very young." Booklist

Zimelman, Nathan

The lives of my cat Alfred; pictures by Evaline Ness. Dutton 1976 unp illus lib. bdg. $6.95
E

1 Cats—Fiction
ISBN 0-525-33942-6
LC 75-35514

Alfred "is remarkable even for a feline. His human friend, a small boy, tells us that Alfred appreciates learning and is welcome at the local school because of his decorous behavior. We learn other facts about Alfred and come to share his friend's belief that the cat might have been around to teach the Mona Lisa her smile; he might have sailed with Columbus and played a part in other significant events. The boy concludes that he's lucky Alfred has chosen to spend one of his lives with him." Pub W

"Only committed cat lovers could produce a picture book that celebrates both the obvious virtues and the less conventional characteristics of cats. . . . The self-possessed feline hero dominates most of the pictures, which are printed on well-designed pages in warm tones of chocolate and rusty brown." Horn Bk

Zion, Gene

Dear garbage man; pictures by Margaret Bloy Graham. Harper 1957 unp illus lib. bdg. $7.89
E

1 Refuse and refuse disposal—Fiction
ISBN 0-06-026841-7
LC 57-5355

Stan, the new garbage man, cannot bear to throw away anything that might possibly be useful. . . . Then he realizes that trash can still be useful if he will only grind it up so that it can be used as fill to make new land for playgrounds and parks." Good Bks for Children

"Stan's gigantic junk swap is hilarious. Pictures and text poke fun at human nature, while they show the workings of the sanitation department of a bustling metropolis." Moorachian. What is a City?

Harry the dirty dog; pictures by Margaret Bloy Graham. Harper 1956 unp illus $6.95, lib. bdg. $7.89, pa $1.95
E

1 Dogs—Fiction
ISBN 0-06-026865-4; 0-06-026866-2; 0-06-443009-X
LC 56-8137

"A runaway dog becomes so dirty his family almost doesn't recognize him. Harry's flight from scrubbing brush and bath water takes him on a tour of the city. Road repairs, railroad yards, construction sites, and coal deliveries contribute to his grimy appearance and show aspects of city life that contrast with the tidy suburb that is 'home.'" Moorachian. What is a City?

"Harry's fun and troubles are told simply, and the drawings are full of action and humor. The combination will have great appeal for the very young." Horn Bk

Some other books about Harry are also available from Harper:

Harry and the lady next door $6.95, lib. bdg. $7.89, pa $1.95 (ISBN 0-06-26851-4; 0-06-026852-2; 0-06-44008-7; LC 60-9452)
Harry by the sea $7.95, lib. bdg. $7.89, pa $1.95 (ISBN 0-06-026855-7; 0-06-026856-5; 0-06-443010-3; LC 65-21302)
No roses for Harry $7.95, lib. bdg. $7.89, pa $1.95 (ISBN 0-06-026890-5; 0-06-026891-3; 0-06-443011-1; LC 58-7752)

The plant sitter; pictures by Margaret Bloy Graham. Harper 1959 unp illus lib. bdg. $8.79, pa $1.95
E

1 Plants—Fiction
ISBN 0-06-026901-4; 0-06-443012-X
LC 59-5842

"Tommy's father and mother were surprised when their house became filled with plants, and Tommy explained that he was caring for the plants for all the neighbors who had gone on vacation. Tommy enjoyed having the house crowded with plants, but his father was rather irritated. The plants had such good care that they became overgrown, so Tommy found out about trimming them

Zion, Gene—*Continued*

and making cuttings. When the neighbors came home, they were very pleased with Tommy's work." Chicago. Children's Bk Center

"Wonderful fun, and a bit of science, too, for the kindergarten age, with . . . blue, green, and yellow drawings giving bright impressions of luxurious plant life." Horn Bk

Zolotow, Charlotte

The hating book; pictures by Ben Shecter. Harper 1969 32p illus $4.95, lib. bdg. $5.89 **E**

1 Friendship—Fiction
ISBN 0-06-026923-5; 0-06-026924-3   LC 69-14444

"A little girl tells of several instances of being rebuffed by her friend, ending with the comment, 'I hated my friend.' Finally, at the urging of her mother, she goes to see the friend and asks her why she's been so 'rotten.' The answer is that 'Sue said Jane said you said I looked like a freak.' The actual remark had been that she looked 'neat.' The point of the book is clear as the two friends make plans to play together the following day." Rdng Ladders. 5th edition

Mr Rabbit and the lovely presents; pictures by Maurice Sendak. Harper 1962 unp illus $8.95, lib. bdg. $8.79, pa $1.95 **E**

1 Birthdays—Fiction 2 Color—Fiction 3 Rabbits —Fiction
ISBN 0-06-026945-6; 0-06-026946-4; 0-06-443020-0
LC 62-7590

"A serious little girl and a tall, otherworldly white rabbit converse about a present for her mother. '"But what?" said the little girl. "Yes, what?" said Mr. Rabbit.' It requires a day of searching—for red, yellow, green, and blue, all things the mother likes, to make a basket of fruit for the present." Horn Bk

"The quiet story, told in dialogue, is illustrated in richly colored pictures which exactly fit the fanciful mood." Hodges. Bks for Elem Sch Libraries

My friend John; pictures by Ben Shecter. Harper 1968 32p illus $5.95, lib. bdg. $6.89 **E**

1 Friendship—Fiction
ISBN 0-06-026947-2; 0-06-026948-0   LC 68-10209

A picture book about "two small boys who are best friends, carrying on their routine activities. Particularly interesting is the author's implication that the minor differences which exist between the two are not a deterrent to the formation of a valid friendship." Sch Library J

"The drawings in this warm and engaging picture book are uncluttered, expressive, and altogether likable." Booklist

My grandson Lew; pictures by William Pene du Bois. Harper 1974 30p illus $5.95, lib. bdg. $6.89 **E**

1 Death—Fiction 2 Grandfathers—Fiction
ISBN 0-06-026961-8; 0-06-026962-6   LC 73-66336

"An Ursula Nordstrom book"

"Warm, rich, and beautiful, a comforting consideration of death. Lew, now six, awakes and remembers back to when he was two and his grandfather came to him in the night when he called. . . . Lew recounts the images he has retained and then his mother tells of her remembrances, concluding, 'We will remember him together and neither of us will be so lonely as we would be if we had to remember him alone.' Pène du Bois' finely washed illustrations exude a serenity and understanding perfectly in tune with the story." Booklist

The quarreling book; pictures by Arnold Lobel. Harper 1963 unp illus $4.95, lib. bdg. $5.89 **E**

ISBN 0-06-026975-8; 0-06-026976-6   LC 63-14445

"Father forgets to kiss Mother goodbye when starting to work one morning, so Mother is unhappy and becomes cross with Jonathan James who takes out his feelings on his sister, and the chain continues until reversed by the dog who thinks being shoved off the bed is just a game and lots of fun. The sequence, then starts in happy reverse until at five, with the rain ending, Mr. James comes home and kisses Mrs. James." Sch Library J

It is "a worthwhile book which clearly demonstrates the far-reaching effects one's actions have on others. Even the youngest child will grasp its lesson easily. The illustrations are whimsical, detailed and expressive." NY Times Bk Rev

A tiger called Thomas; pictures by Kurt Werth. Lothrop 1963 unp illus lib. bdg. $7.44 **E**

1 Halloween—Fiction
ISBN 0-688-51623-8   LC 63-16777

"Fall colors and fanciful costumes make this Halloween story attractive to children. Shy Thomas, new to the neighborhood, goes out in his tiger suit and finds that he already has many friends." Hodges. Bks for Elem Sch Libraries

"Pleasantly illustrated, the story has a simple but satisfying plot, light writing style, and a gentle message." Chicago. Children's Bk Center

William's doll; pictures by William Pène Du Bois. Harper 1972 30p illus $6.95, lib. bdg. $7.89 **E**

1 Dolls—Fiction 2 Sex role—Fiction
ISBN 0-06-027047-0; 0-06-027048-9   LC 70-183173

When little William asks for a doll, the other boys scorn him and his father tries to interest him in conventional boys' playthings such as a basketball and a train. His sympathetic grandmother buys him the doll, explaining his need to have it to love and care for so that he can practice being a father

"Very, very special. The strong, yet delicate pictures . . . convey a gentleness of spirit and longing most effectively, as William pantomimes his craving." NY Times Bk Rev

AUTHOR, TITLE, SUBJECT, AND ANALYTICAL INDEX

This Index to the books in the Classified Catalog includes author, title, subject and analytical entries, arranged in one alphabet. Added entries for illustrators and joint authors are also included.

For further directions for use of this index, see page viii.

A for the Ark. Duvoisin, R.   **E**

AAAS Science film catalog   016.5

A **Apple** pie. Greenaway, K.   **E**
> *also in* Greenaway, K. The Kate Greenaway treasury p228-48   828

ABC. See Alphabet

ABC. Matthiesen, T.   **E**

ABC. Munari, B.   **E**

ABC. Wildsmith, B.   **E**

The **A B C** book. Falls, C. B.   **E**

ABC book of early Americana. Sloane, E.   973.2

ABC books. See Alphabet

The **A B C** bunny. Gág, W.   **E**
> *also in* The Arbuthnot Anthology of children's literature p63   808.8

ABC, Ed Emberley's. Emberley, E.   **E**

ABC of ecology. Milgrom, H.   363.7

The **ABC's** of origami. Sarasas, C.   736

A.D. 123: Rome builds a wall. Sutcliff, R.
> *In* The Arbuthnot Anthology of children's literature p738-42   808.8

ALA Filing rules   025.3

APC. See All People's Congress

Aardema, Verna
> Behind the back of the mountain (4-6)   398.2
>> Contents: Little hen eagle; The trick on the trek; Tshinyama's heavenly maidens; How Blue Crane taught Jackal to fly; The winning of Kwelanga; Sebgugugu the glutton; This for that; Tusi and the great beast; Saso and Gogwana the witch; The house in the middle of the road
> Half-a-ball-of-kenki (k-2)   398.2
> The riddle of the drum (k-2)   398.2
> The Sloogeh Dog and the stolen aroma
>> *In* The Arbuthnot Anthology of children's literature p323-25   808.8
>> *In* Time for old magic p200-02   398.2
> Tales from the story hat (3-6)   398.2
>> Contents: Tricksy Rabbit; Wikki, the weaver; The Sloogeh Dog and the stolen aroma; Madame Giraffe; Monkeys in the sausage tree; Nansii and the eagle; How Dog outwitted Leopard; Koi and the kola nuts; The prince who wanted the moon
> Who's in Rabbit's house? (k-3)   398.2
> Why mosquitoes buzz in people's ears (k-3)   398.2

Aardvark
> **Poetry**
> Nash, O. The cruise of the Aardvark (3-5)   811

Aaron, Hank. See Aaron, Henry Louis

Aaron, Henry Louis
> *See pages in the following book:*
> Sullivan, G. Baseball's art of hitting p107-15 (5 and up)   796.357

Aaron and the Green Mountain Boys. Gauch, P. L.   **E**

Aaron's gift. Levoy, M.
> *In* Levoy, M. The witch of Fourth Street, and other stories p84-98   **S C**

Abacus
> Dilson, J. The abacus: a pocket computer (5 and up)   513.028

The **abacus:** a pocket computer. Dilson, J.   513.028

Abbott, Jacob
> *See pages in the following books:*
> Andrews, S. ed. The Hewins lectures, 1947-1962 p129-49   028.5
> Jordan, A. M. From Rollo to Tom Sawyer, and other papers p72-81   028.5
> Yankee Doodle's literary sampler of prose, poetry, and pictures p89-92   028.5

Abbott, R. Tucker
> Sea shells of the world (5 and up)   594

Abbott, Robert Sengstacke
> *See pages in the following book:*
> Rollins, C. H. They showed the way p 1-5 (5 and up)   920

Abbreviations
> *See also* Signs and symbols

Abby. Caines, J.   **E**

Abdul-Jabbar, Kareem
> *See pages in the following book:*
> Devaney, J. The story of basketball p103-08 (5 and up)   796.32

Abe buys a barrel. Peterson, M. N.
> *In* Fifty plays for junior actors p460-70   812.08

Abe Lincoln grows up. Sandburg, C.
> *In* Sandburg, C. The Sandburg treasury p383-477   818

Abe Lincoln grows up; excerpt. Sandburg, C.
> *In* Holiday ring p34-39   394.2

Abe Lincoln's other mother; excerpt. Bailey, B.
> *In* Stories to dramatize p265-70   372.6

Abecassis, Andrée
> (illus.) Brown, L. C. Elephant seals   599.74

Abel, Ray
> (illus.) Ernst, J. Escape king: the story of Harry Houdini   92
> (illus.) Garrison, W. Why didn't I think of that?   608
> (illus.) Sypher, L. J. The edge of nowhere   **Fic**

Abel's island. Steig, W.   **Fic**

Abenaki Indians. See Abnaki Indians

Abe's winkin' eye. Fisher, A.
> *In* Fisher, A. Holiday programs for boys and girls p172-88   812

Adler, Peggy
Geography puzzles (4-6)   **793.7**
Math puzzles (4-6)   **793.7**
Metric puzzles (4-6)   **389**
(illus.) Adler, I. Hot and cold   **536**
(illus.) Adler, I. Magic house of numbers   **793.7**

Adler, Ruth
(jt. auth.) Adler, I. The calendar   **529**
(illus.) Adler, I. Color in your life   **535.6**
(illus.) Adler, I. Magic house of numbers   **793.7**
(jt. auth.) Adler, I. Taste, touch and smell   **612**
(jt. auth.) Adler, I. Your eyes   **612**

Adler, Susan
(jt. auth.) Kipnis, L. You can't catch diabetes from a friend   **616.4**

Admetus
See pages in the following book:
Gates, D. The golden god: Apollo p54-76 (4 and up)   **292**

Admirals
Latham, J. L. Anchor's aweigh; the story of David Glasgow Farragut (5 and up)   **92**

Adobe Christmas. Peterson, M. N.
In A Treasury of Christmas plays p254-62   **812.08**

Adoff, Arnold
Big sister tells me that I'm black (1-3)   **811**
Black is brown is tan   **E**
(ed.) Black out loud (5 and up)   **811.08**
(ed.) Celebrations (5 and up)   **811.08**
(ed.) I am the darker brother (5 and up)   **811.08**
I am the running girl (3-5)   **811**
Malcolm X (2-5)   **92**
MA nDA LA   **E**
(ed.) My black me (5 and up)   **811.08**
Under the early morning trees (4-6)   **811**
Where wild Willie   **E**

Adolescence
See pages in the following book:
Johnson, C. B. Love and sex and growing up p37-44 (4 and up)   **613.9**

Fiction
Blume, J. Are you there God? It's me, Margaret (5 and up)   **Fic**
Blume, J. Then again, maybe I won't (5 and up)   **Fic**

Adolescent psychology
LeShan, E. You and your feelings (6 and up)   **155.5**

Adopted Jane. Daringer, H. F.   **Fic**

Adoption
Bunin, C. Is that your sister? (k-3)   **362.7**

Bibliography
See pages in the following book:
Fassler, J. Helping children cope p100-14   **016.3627**

Fiction
Arthur, R. M. Requiem for a princess (6 and up)   **Fic**
Caines, J. Abby   **E**
Lapsley, S. I am adopted   **E**
Neufeld, J. Edgar Allan (5 and up)   **Fic**
Wasson, V. P. The chosen baby   **E**

Adriatic Sea
See pages in the following book:
Kostich, D. D. The land and people of the Balkans p35-46 (5 and up)   **949.6**

Adshead, Gladys L.
(comp.) An Inheritance of poetry. See An Inheritance of poetry   **821.08**

Advent
See also Christmas

Adventure. Camp Fire Girls, Inc.   **369.47**

Adventure and adventurers
Steele, W. O. Westward adventure (5 and up)   **920**
See also Explorers; Frontier and pioneer life; Heroes and heroines; Sea stories; Voyages and travels

Fiction
Alexander, L. The marvelous misadventures of Sebastian (4 and up)   **Fic**
Barret, L. The adventures of Don Quixote de la Mancha (5 and up)   **Fic**
Church, R. Five boys in a cave (6 and up)   **Fic**
12 adventures of the celebrated Baron Munchausen (3-5)   **Fic**

Poetry
Cole, W. comp. Rough men, tough men (5 and up)   **821.08**

The **adventure** book of weather. See Milgrom, H. Understanding weather   **551.6**

The **adventure** of three little rabbits
In Stories to dramatize p25-27   **372.6**

The **adventures** of a thistle. Andersen, H. C.
In Andersen, H. C. The complete fairy tales and stories p967-70

The **adventures** of Aku. Bryan, A.   **398.2**
See also Anansi the spider-man

The **adventures** of Ciad. MacManus, S.
In MacManus, S. Hibernian nights p60-73   **398.2**

Adventures of Ciad, son of the King of Norway
MacManus, S. The adventure of Ciad
In MacManus, S. Hibernian nights p60-73   **398.2**

The **adventures** of Don Quixote de la Mancha. Barret, L.   **Fic**

The **Adventures** of Haroun-al-Raschid, Caliph of Bagdad
In The Arabian nights entertainments p316-19   **398.2**

The **adventures** of Huckleberry Finn. Twain, M.   **Fic**

The **adventures** of Little Peachling. Redesdale, Lord
In Fairy tales from many lands p84-86   **398.2**
See also Momotaro

The **adventures** of Magboloto. Sechrist, E. H.
In Sechrist, E. H. Once in the first times p67-75   **398.2**

The **adventures** of Obadiah. Turkle, B. See note under Turkle, B. Obadiah the Bold   **E**

The **adventures** of Paddington bear. See Bradley, A. Paddington on stage   **822**

The **adventures** of Paddy Pork. Goodall, J. S.   **E**

The **adventures** of Pinocchio. Collodi, C.   **Fic**

The **adventures** of Pinocchio; excerpt. Collodi, C.
  In The Arbuthnot Anthology of children's literature p496-98 **808.8**
The **Adventures** of Prince Camaralzaman and the Princess Badoura
  In The Arabian nights entertainments p216-66 **398.2**
The **adventures** of Spider. Arkhurst, J. C. **398.2**
  See also Anansi the spider-man
The **adventures** of the Countess Jeanne. Uden, G.
  In The Arbuthnot Anthology of children's literature p471-74 **808.8**
The **adventures** of Tom Sawyer. Twain, M. **Fic**
The **adventures** of Yemima. Soyer, A.
  In Soyer, A. The adventures of Yemima, and other stories p 1-13 **S C**
The **adventures** of Yemima, and other stories. Soyer, A. **S C**
Adventures with a cardboard tube. Milgrom, H. **507**
Adventures with a straw. Milgrom, H. **507**
Adventuring with books. National Council of Teachers of English. Committee on the Elementary School Booklist **011**
Aeneas
  Church, A. J. The Aeneid for boys and girls (6 and up) **873**
  See also pages in the following book:
  Hamilton, E. Mythology p319-42 (6 and up) **292**
The **Aeneid** for boys and girls. Church, A. J. **873**
Aerial apes. Teleki, G. **599.88**
Aerodynamics
  Barnaby, R. S. How to make & fly paper airplanes (5 and up) **629.133**
  Corbett, S. What makes a plane fly? (3-6) **629.132**
  Kaufmann, J. Streamlined (2-4) **531**
  Simon, S. The paper airplane book (3-5) **629.133**
  See also Aeronautics; Balloons
Aeronautics
  Bendick, J. The first book of airplanes (3-5) **629.13**
  See also Aerodynamics; Airplanes; Balloons; Flight; Flying saucers; Helicopters; Kites; Rockets (Aeronautics)
  Flights
  Foster, J. T. The flight of the Lone Eagle (5 and up) **629.13**
  See also pages in the following book:
  Wilson, M. Jet journey p22-47 (3 and up) **387.7**
  History
  See pages in the following book:
  Reynolds, Q. The Wright brothers (3-6) **92**
Aeronautics, Commercial
  Wilson, M. Jet journey (3 and up) **387.7**
  See also Air lines
Aesop
  Aesop's fables; selections
  In The Arbuthnot Anthology of children's literature p415-20 **808.8**
  In Darrell, M. ed. Once upon a time p235-47 **808.8**
  In Time for old magic p277-84 **398.2**

The **Hare** and the tortoise. See The Hare and the tortoise **398.2**
The **north** wind and the sun; adaptation. See Siks, G. B. The wind and the sun
The **shepherd** boy and the wolf
  In Stories to dramatize p119 **372.6**
The **thief** and the innkeeper; adaptation. See Hardendorff, J. B. A werewolf or a thief?
The **town** mouse and the country mouse
  In Stories to dramatize p103-04 **372.6**
  In Told under the green umbrella p74-77 **398.2**
  Galdone, P. Three Aesop fox fables **398.2**
  Jacobs, J. The fables of Aesop **398.2**
  Rice, E. Once in a wood; ten tales from Aesop **398.2**
Aesop (as subject)
  Drama
  See pages in the following book:
  Fifty plays for junior actors p481-97 **812.08**
Aesop, man of fables. Phillips, E.
  In Fifty plays for junior actors p481-97 **812.08**
Aesop's fables; selections. Aesop
  In The Arbuthnot Anthology of children's literature p415-20 **808.8**
  In Time for old magic p277-84 **398.2**
Afanas'ev, Alexsandr Nikolaevich
  The death of Koshchei the Deathless
  In Red fairy book p14-26 **398.2**
  The flying ship
  In Yellow fairy book p180-87 **398.2**
  The Norka
  In Red fairy book p99-106 **398.2**
  Russian fairy tales **398.2**
    Contents: The wondrous wonder, the marvelous marvel; The fox physician; The death of the cock; Misery; The castle of the fly; The turnip; Riddles; The enchanted ring; The just reward; Salt; The golden slipper; Emelya the simpleton; The three kingdoms; The pike with the long teeth; The bad wife; The miser; The nobleman and the peasant; Ivanushka the Little Fool; The crane and the heron; Alioslia Popovich; The fox confessor; The bear; The spider; Baba Yaga and the brave youth; Prince Ivan and Princess Martha; The cat, the cock, and the fox; Baldak Borisievich; Know Not; The magic shirt; The three pennies; The princess who wanted to solve riddles; A soldier's riddle; The dead body; The frog princess; The speedy messenger; Vasilisa, the priest's daughter; The wise maiden and the seven robbers; The mayoress; Ivan the Simpleton; Father Nicholas and the thief; Burenushka, the little red cow; The jester; The precious hide; The cross is pledged as security; The daydreamer; The taming of the shrew; Quarrelsome Demyan; The magic box; Bukhtan Bukhtanovich; The fox and the woodcock; The fox and the crane; The two rivers; Nodey, the priest's grandson; The poor wretch; The fiddler in hell; The old woman who ran away; The singing tree and the talking bird; The ram who lost half his skin; The fox as midwife; The fox, the hare, and the cock; Baba Yaga; The ram, the cat, and the twelve wolves; The fox and the woodpecker; The snotty goat; Right and wrong; The potter; The self-playing gusla; Marco the Rich and Vasily the Luckless; Ivanko the bear's son; The secret ball; The indiscreet wife; The cheater cheated; The Maiden Tsar; Ivan the Cow's Son; The wolf and the goat; The wise little girl; Danilo the Luckless; Ivan the peasant's son and the thumb-sized man; Death of a miser; The footless champion and the handless champion; Old favors are soon forgotten; The sheep, the fox, and the wolf; The brave laborer; Daughter and stepdaughter; The stubborn wife; Snow White and the fox; Foma Berennikov; The peasant, the bear, and the fox; Good advice; Horns; The armless maiden; Frolka Stay-at-Home; The milk of wild beasts; How a husband weaned his wife from fairy tales; The cock and the hen; The fox and the lobster; Nikita the Tanner; The wolf; The goat shedding on one side; The bold knight, the apples of youth, and the water

Afanas'ev, Alexsandr N.—*Continued*

of life; Two out of the sack; The man who did not know fear; The merchant's daughter and the maidservant; The priest's laborer; The peasant and the corpse; The arrant fool; Lutoniushka; Barter; The grumbling old woman; The white duck; If you don't like it, don't listen; The magic swan geese; Prince Danila Govorila; The wicked sisters; The princess who never smiled; Baba Yaga; Jack Frost; Husband and wife; Little Sister Fox and the wolf; The three kingdoms, copper, silver, and golden; The cock and the hand mill; Tereshichka; King Bear; Magic; The one-eyed evil; Sister Alionushka, brother Ivanushka; The seven Semyons; The merchant's daughter and the slanderer; The robbers; The lazy maiden; The miraculous pipe; The Sea King and Vasilisa the Wise; The fox as mourner; Vasilisa the Beautiful; The bun; The foolish wolf; The bear, the dog, and the cat; The bear and the cock; Dawn, Evening, and Midnight; Two Ivans, soldier's sons; Prince Ivan and Byely Polyanin; The crystal mountain; Koshchev the Deathless; The Firebird and Princess Vasilisa; Beasts in a pit; The dog and the woodpecker; Two kinds of luck; Go I know not whither, bring back I know not what; The wise wife; The goldfish; The golden-bristled pig, the golden-feathered duck, and the golden-maned mare; The duck with golden eggs; Elena the Wise; Treasure-trove; Maria Morevna; The soldier and the king; The sorceress; Ilya Muromets and the dragon; The devil who was a potter; Clever answers; Dividing the goose; The feather of Finist, the Bright Falcon; The Sun, the Moon, and the Raven; The bladder, the straw, and the shoe; The thief; The vampire; The beggar's plan; Woman's way; The foolish German; The enchanted princess; The raven and the lobster; Prince Ivan, the firebird, and the gray wolf; Shemiaka the judge

Vasilisa the beautiful. See Vasilisa the beautiful   **398.2**

The white duck
In Yellow fairy book p133-38   **398.2**

Affection. See Friendship; Love

Africa

Bernheim, M. In Africa (k-3)   **960**
Murphy, E. J. Understanding Africa (6 and up)   **960**

Art

See Art, African

Fiction

Carew, J. The third gift (3-5)   **Fic**
Graham, L. Song of the boat   **E**

Folklore

See Folklore—Africa

Legends

See Legends—Africa

Social life and customs

Musgrove, M. Ashanti to Zulu: African traditions (3-6)   **960**

Africa, East

Feelings, M. Jambo means hello   **E**
Feelings, M. Moja means one   **E**
Perl, L. East Africa (4-6)   **967.6**

Fiction

Feelings, M. Zamani goes to market   **E**

Africa, North

Lawson, D. Morocco, Algeria, Tunisia, and Libya (4 and up)   **961**

Africa, South. See South Africa

Africa, Southern

Newlon, C. Southern Africa: the critical land (6 and up)   **968**

Folklore

See Folklore—Africa, Southern

Africa, West

Bernheim, M. The drums speak (3-5)   **966**

Folklore

See Folklore—Africa, West

Social life and customs

Price, C. Dancing masks of Africa (2-6)   **732**

African-Americans. See Blacks

African art. See Art, African

African civilization. See Civilization, African

African crafts. Kerina, J.   **745.5**

African crafts for you to make. D'Amato, J.   **745.5**

African folktales, Plays from. Korty, C.   **812**

African myths and legends. Arnott, K.   **398.2**

African songs. See Songs, African

African trio: The fierce creature. Winther, B.
In Dramatized folk tales of the world p3-6   **812.08**

African trio: The princess who was hidden from the world. Winther, B.
In Dramatized folk tales of the world p10-14   **812.08**

African trio: When the hare brought the sun. Winther, B.
In Dramatized folk tales of the world p6-9   **812.08**

Africanders. See Boers

Afro-Americans. See Blacks

After the Goat Man. Byars, B.   **Fic**

After the great fire. Baumann, H.
In Baumann, H. The stolen fire p149-50   **398.2**

An afternoon with the oldest inhabitant. Estes, E.
In The Arbuthnot Anthology of children's literature p627-33   **808.8**

Agaton Sax and Lispington's grandfather clock. Franzen, N.   **Fic**

Agaton Sax and the diamond thieves. Franzen, N. See note under Franzen, N. Agaton Sax and Lispington's grandfather clock   **Fic**

Agayk and the strangest spear. Edmonds, I. G.
In Time for old magic p261-63   **398.2**

Age

Physiological effect

See pages in the following book:
Silverstein, A. Aging p17-31, 55-66 (5 and up)   **305.2**

The age of chivalry. Bulfinch, T.
In Bulfinch, T. Bulfinch's Mythology   **291**

The age of fable. Bulfinch, T.
In Bulfinch, T. Bulfinch's Mythology   **291**

Aged. See Elderly

The aged mother. Grimm, J.
In Grimm, J. The complete Grimm's fairy tales p826-27   **398.2**

Aggregates. See Set theory

Aging

Silverstein, A. Aging (5 and up)   **305.2**

Aglauros

See pages in the following book:
Gates, D. The warrior goddess: Athena p18-23 (4 and up)   **292**

Agre, Patricia

(illus.) Sobol, H. L. Cosmo's restaurant   **647**
(illus.) Sobol, H. L. Jeff's hospital book   **362.1**

Agre, Patricia—*Continued*

(illus.) Sobol, H. L. My brother Steve is retarded   **362.3**

(illus.) Sobol, H. L. My other-mother, my other-father   **306.8**

(illus.) Sobol, H. L. Pete's house   **690**

Agree, Rose H.

(comp.) How to eat a poem & other morsels. See How to eat a poem & other morsels.   **821.08**

Agricultural chemistry

See also Soils

Agricultural laborers. See Migrant labor

Agricultural pests

See pages in the following book:

Mintz, L. M. Vegetables in patches and pots p53-56 (3-6)   **635**

Biological control

See Pests—Biological control

Agriculture

Hays, W. P. Foods the Indians gave us (5 and up)   **641.3**

Lavine, S. A. Indian corn and other gifts (4 and up)   **641.3**

See also pages in the following books:

Goode, R. People of the Ice Age p107-43 (5 and up)   **573.3**

Pringle, L. Our hungry Earth p43-63 (5 and up)   **338.1**

See also Botany, Economic; Gardening; Organiculture; also names of agricultural products, e.g. Corn, and headings beginning with the words Agricultural and Farm

Denmark

See pages in the following book:

Wohlrabe, R. A. The land and people of Denmark p145-48 (5 and up)   **948.9**

Egypt

See pages in the following book:

Mahmoud, Z. N. The land and people of Egypt p117-27 (5 and up)   **962**

Ghana

See pages in the following book:

Sale, J. K. The land and people of Ghana p21-26 (5 and up)   **966.7**

Great Britain

See pages in the following books:

Hodges, C. W. The battlement garden p28-32 (6 and up)   **942.05**

Street, A. The land and people of England p57-65 (5 and up)   **942**

History

See pages in the following book:

Gregor, A. S. Man's mark on the land p10-20 (4 and up)   **304.2**

Indonesia

See pages in the following book:

Smith, D. C. The land and people of Indonesia p60-69, 110-14 (5 and up)   **959.8**

Ireland

See pages in the following book:

O'Brien, E. The land and people of Ireland p15-17, 85-86 (5 and up)   **941.5**

Italy

See pages in the following book:

Epstein, S. The first book of Italy p11-16 (4 and up)   **945**

Japan

See pages in the following book:

Vaughan, J. B. The land and people of Japan p19-26 (5 and up)   **952**

Morocco

See pages in the following book:

Spencer, W. The land and people of Morocco p16-19 (5 and up)   **964**

Nigeria

See pages in the following books:

Forman, B. The land and people of Nigeria p113-21 (5 and up)   **966.9**

Jenness, A. Along the Niger River p18-28 (5 and up)   **966.9**

Norway

See pages in the following book:

Hall, E. The land and people of Norway p98-108 (5 and up)   **948.1**

Research

See pages in the following book:

Archer, J. Hunger on planet Earth p52-64 (6 and up)   **338.1**

Romania

See pages in the following book:

Hale, J. The land and people of Romania p14-16, 132-33 (5 and up)   **949.8**

Sri Lanka

See pages in the following book:

Wilber, D. N. The land and people of Ceylon p91-94, 137-41 (5 and up)   **954.9**

United States

See pages in the following book:

Sandler, M. W. The way we lived p8-18 (4 and up)   **331.09**

Uruguay

See pages in the following book:

Dobler, L. The land and people of Uruguay p82-88 (5 and up)   **989.5**

Agriculture, Soilless. See Plants—Soilless culture

Agrippa von Nettesheim, Heinrich Cornelius

See pages in the following book:

Aylesworth, T. G. The alchemists: magic into science p85-91 (6 and up)   **540.1**

Ah-dunno Ben. Jagendorf, M. A.

In Jagendorf, M. A. Folk stories of the South p216-18   **398.2**

Ah Mee's invention. Chrisman, A. B.

In Chrisman, A. B. Shen of the sea p17-28   **S C**

In Time to laugh p116-26   **S C**

Ah Tcha the sleeper

In Chrisman, A. B. Shen of the sea p146-57   **S C**

In Gruenberg, S. M. ed. Favorite stories old and new p388-93   **808.8**

In Harper, W. comp. Ghosts and goblins p141-49   **398.2**

In Witches, witches, witches p5-14   **808.8**

A-haunting we will go   **S C**

Ahlberg, Allan
  (jt. auth.) Ahlberg, J. Each peach pear plum
                               E

Ahlberg, Janet
  Each peach pear plum   **E**

A-hunting we will go. See Langstaff, J. Oh,
  a-hunting we will go   **784.4**

Aichinger, Helga
  The shepherd (k-3)   **232.9**
  (illus.) Bolliger, M. Noah and the rainbow
                                 221.9
  (illus.) Bulla, C. R. Jonah and the great fish
                                 221.9
  (illus.) Yolen, J. The boy who had wings
                                 Fic

Aiken, Conrad
  Cats and bats and things with wings (k-4)
                                   811

Aiken, Joan
  Arabel's raven (4-6)   **Fic**
  Black hearts in Battersea. See note under
    Aiken, J. The wolves of Willoughby Chase
                                 Fic
  The faithless lollybird (6 and up) **S C**
    Contents: The faithless lollybird; The rain
    child; The man who pinched God's letter; Kiss
    your hand to the magpie; A handful of dark
    blue fur; The night the stars were gone; The
    cat who lived in a drainpipe; Moonshine in the
    mustard pot; Memory; Cat's cradle; The looking-
    glass tree; Crusader's Toby
  A long day without water
    In Haunting tales p132-55 (5 and up) **S C**
  Midnight is a place (5 and up)   **Fic**
  The skin spinners: poems (5 and up) **821**
  The wolves of Willoughby Chase (5 and up)
                                   Fic

Aiken, Lucy. See Godolphin, Mary

Aikido
  See pages in the following books:
  Reisberg, K. The martial arts p57-64 (4 and
  up)   **796.8**
  Ribner, S. The martial arts p121-24, 139-52
  (5 and up)   **796.8**

Aili's quilt. Jagendorf, M. A.
  In Jagendorf, M. A. Noodlehead stories
    from around the world p196-201 **398.2**

The **Aimer** Gate. Garner, A. See note under
  Garner, A. The stone book   **Fic**

Air
  See pages in the following book:
  Wyler, R. Prove it! p25-40 (1-3) **507**
  See also Atmosphere

Pollution
  See pages in the following books:
  Miles, B. Save the earth! p33-53 (4 and up)
                                   363.7
  Weiss, M. E. What's happening to our cli-
  mate p62-73? (5 and up)   **551.6**

Pollution—Law and legislation
  Stevens, L. A. How a law is made (5 and up)
                                 328.73

Quality
  See also Air—Pollution

Air conditioning
  See pages in the following book:
  Harman, C. Skyscraper goes up p106-12
  (5 and up)   **690**

Air lines
  See pages in the following book:
  Bendick, J. The first book of airplanes p36-41
  (3-5)   **629.13**

Air pilots
  Grierson, J. I remember Lindbergh (6 and
  up)   **92**
  Gurney, G. Flying aces of World War I (4-6)
                                   920
  Wright, N. The Red Baron [biography of
  Richthofen, Manfred Albrecht, Freiherr
  von] (5 and up)   **92**
  See also Women air pilots

Air planes. See Airplanes

Air pollution. See Air—Pollution

Air ports. See Airports

Air raid—Pearl Harbor! Taylor, T. **940.54**

Air terminals. See Airports

Air traffic control
  See pages in the following book:
  Bendick, J. The first book of airplanes p26-32
  (3-5)   **629.13**

Air transport. See Aeronautics, Commercial

Air warfare. See names of wars with the subdivision Aerial operations, e.g. World War,
  1914-1918—Aerial operations

Aircraft. See Airplanes; Helicopters

Airlines. See Air lines

Airplane Andy. Tousey, S.
  In Gruenberg, S. M. ed. Favorite stories
  old and new p123-30   **808.8**

Airplane engines. See Airplanes—Engines

Airplanes
  Ames, L. J. Draw 50 airplanes, aircraft &
  spacecraft (4 and up)   **743**
  Navarra, J. G. Superplanes (5 and up)
                                   629.133
  See also types of airplanes, e.g. Bombers

Design and construction
  See pages in the following book:
  Hellman, H. Transportation in the world of
  the future p146-70 (5 and up) **380.5**

Engines
  See pages in the following book:
  Bendick, J. The first book of airplanes p10-14
  (3-5)   **629.13**

Fiction
  Mark, J. Thunder and Lightnings (5 and up)
                                   Fic
  Spier, P. Bored—nothing to do!   **E**

Models
  Barnaby, R. S. How to make & fly paper air-
  planes (5 and up)   **629.133**
  Curry, B. Model aircraft (4-6) **629.133**
  Lopshire, R. A beginner's guide to building
  and flying model airplanes (5 and up)
                                   629.133
  Ross, F. Flying paper airplane models (5 and
  up)   **629.133**
  Ross, F. Historic plane models (5 and up)
                                   629.133
  Simon, S. The paper airplane book (3-5)
                                   629.133
  Weiss, H. Model airplanes and how to build
  them (5 and up)   **629.133**

Pilots
  See Air pilots

Airplanes, Jet propelled. See Jet planes

Airplanes, Military
    Delear, F. J. Helicopters and airplanes of the U.S. Army (5 and up)   **623.74**
    See also pages in the following book:
    Navarra, J. G. Superplanes p39-56 (5 and up)   **629.133**
    See also Bombers; Fighter planes

Airports
    Wilson, M. Jet journey (3 and up)   **387.7**
    See also pages in the following book:
    Bendick, J. The first book of airplanes p22-25 (3-5)   **629.13**
            Traffic control
    See Air traffic control

Airships
    See also Balloons

Airways
    See also Air lines

Airy-go-round. Du Bois, W. P.
    In The Arbuthnot Anthology of children's literature p583-88   **808.8**

Akers, Susan Grey
    Akers' Simple library cataloging   **025.3**

Akhnaton. See Amenhetep IV, King of Egypt

Akkadians (Sumerians) See Sumerians

Aktaion. See Actaeon

Alabama
            Fiction
    Lee, M. The rock and the willow (6 and up)   **Fic**

Aladdin
    Aladdin and the wonderful lamp
    In The Arabian nights entertainments p295-315   **398.2**
    In The Arbuthnot Anthology of children's literature p302-09   **808.8**
    In The Golden Treasury of children's literature p378-88   **808.8**
    In Time for old magic p181-88   **398.2**
    Dawood, N. J. Aladdin and the enchanted lamp
    In Dawood, N. J. Tales from the Arabian nights p39-114   **398.2**
    Hunt, V. Aladdin and the wonderful lamp
    In Blue fairy book p75-91   **398.2**
    Story of Aladdin
    In The Arabian nights p97-189   **398.2**
    In The Arthur Rackham Fairy book p153-81   **398.2**
    Thane, A. Aladdin and his wonderful lamp
    In Thane, A. Plays from famous stories and fairy tales p38-57   **812**

Aladdin and his wonderful lamp. Thane, A.
    In Thane, A. Plays from famous stories and fairy tales p38-57   **812**
    See also Aladdin

Aladdin and the enchanted lamp. Dawood, N. J.
    In Dawood, N. J. Tales from the Arabian nights p39-114   **398.2**
    See also Aladdin

Aladdin and the wonderful lamp
    In The Arabian nights entertainments p295-315   **398.2**
    In The Arbuthnot Anthology of children's literature p302-09   **808.8**

    In The Golden Treasury of children's literature p378-88   **808.8**
    In Time for old magic p181-88   **398.2**
    See also Aladdin

Aladdin and the wonderful lamp. Hunt, V.
    In Blue fairy book p75-91   **398.2**
    See also Aladdin

Alakai Swamp
    See pages in the following book:
    Laycock, G. Exploring the great swamp p35-40 (4-6)   **574.5**

Alan and Naomi. Levoy, M.   **Fic**

Alan and the animal kingdom. Holland, I.   **Fic**

Alan Mendelsohn, the boy from Mars. Pinkwater, D. M.   **Fic**

Alaska
    Stefansson, E. Here is Alaska (6 and up)   **979.8**
            Earthquake, 1964
    See pages in the following book:
    Lauber, P. Earthquakes p3-9, 71-72 (4-6)   **551.2**
            Fiction
    London, J. Call of the wild (5 and up)   **Fic**
    London, J. White Fang (5 and up)   **Fic**
    Morey, W. Gentle Ben (5 and up)   **Fic**

Alaska pipeline
    Shumaker, V. O. The Alaska pipeline (4-6)   **388.5**

Albania
    See also Balkan Peninsula

Albatross Two. See Thiele, C. Fight against Albatross Two   **Fic**

Albatrosses
    Fisher, H. I. Wonders of the world of the albatross (4 and up)   **598**

Albert, Burton
    Codes for kids (3-6)   **652**
    More Codes for kids (3-6)   **652**

Albert, Rollin'
    A new angle on Christmas
    In On stage for Christmas p262-71   **812.08**

Albert B. Cub & Zebra. Rockwell, A.   **E**

Alberto and the monsters. Sechrist, E. H.
    In Sechrist, E. H. Once in the first times p204-13   **398.2**

Alberts, Edith
    (illus.) Marks, M. K. Op-tricks   **702.8**

Albert's toothache. Williams, B.   **E**

Albertus Magnus, Saint, Bp. of Ratisbon
    See pages in the following book:
    Aylesworth, T. G. The alchemists: magic into science p64-73 (6 and up)   **540.1**

Albright, Donn
    (illus.) Felton, H. W. Mumbet: the story of Elizabeth Freeman   **92**

Album of astronomy. McGowen, T.   **523**

Album of dinosaurs. McGowen, T.   **567.9**
    also in McGowen, T. Dinosaurs & other prehistoric animals   **567.9**

Album of horses. Henry, M.   **636.1**

Album of North American birds. Dugdale, V.   **598**

Album of prehistoric animals. McGowen, T.
    In McGowen, T. Dinosaurs & other prehistoric animals   **567.9**

Album of reptiles. McGowen, T.   **597.9**

Aldis, Dorothy—*Continued*

William and Jane
In Gruenberg, S. M. ed. Favorite stories old and new p23-28 **808.8**

Aldo Applesauce. Hurwitz, J. See note under Hurwitz, J. Much ado about Aldo **Fic**

Aldridge, Ira Frederick
See pages in the following book:
Rollins, C. H. They showed the way p6-11 (5 and up) **920**

Aldrin, Edwin Eugene
See pages in the following book:
Branley, F. M. Pieces of another world p 1-11 (5 and up) **552**

Aleichem, Sholom
Holiday tales of Sholom Aleichem (5 and up) **S C**
Contents: Really a sukkah; Benny's luck; A ruined Passover; The esrog; The goldspinners; The Passover exiles; The first commune
Shulevitz, U. Hanukah money **E**

Aleppo, Syria
See pages in the following book:
Copeland, P. W. The land and people of Syria p103-11 (5 and up) **956.91**

Aleutian Islands
See pages in the following book:
Stefansson, E. Here is Alaska p127-35 (6 and up) **979.8**

Natural history
See Natural history—Aleutian Islands

Alexander, Lloyd
The black cauldron. See note under Alexander, L. The book of three **Fic**
The book of three (4 and up) **Fic**
The book of three; excerpt
In The Arbuthnot Anthology of children's literature p514-18 **808.8**
The castle of Llyr. See note under Alexander, L. The book of three **Fic**
The cat who wished to be a man (4-6) **Fic**
The first two lives of Lukas-Kasha (4 and up) **Fic**
Gurgi
In The Arbuthnot Anthology of children's literature p514-18 **808.8**
The High King. See note under Alexander, L. The book of three **Fic**
How the cat swallowed thunder
In Just for fun p3-12 (4-6) **S C**
The king's fountain **E**
The marvelous misadventures of Sebastian (4 and up) **Fic**
Newbery Medal acceptance paper
In Newbery and Caldecott Medal books: 1966-1975 p48-52 **028.5**
Taran Wanderer. See note under Alexander, L. The book of three **Fic**
The town cats, and other tales (3-5) **S C**
Contents: The town cats; The Cat-King's daughter; The cat who said no; The cat and the golden egg; The cobbler and his cat; The painter's cat; The cat and the fiddler; The apprentice cat
The wizard in the tree (4-6) **Fic**

About
See pages in the following book:
Newbery and Caldecott Medal books: 1966-1975 p53-55 **028.5**

Alexander, Martha
And my mean old mother will be sorry, blackboard bear. See note under Alexander, M. Blackboard bear **E**
Blackboard bear **E**
Bobo's dream **E**
Nobody asked me if I wanted a baby sister **E**
Sabrina **E**
We never get to do anything **E**
When the new baby comes, I'm moving out. See note under Alexander, M. Nobody asked me if I wanted a baby sister **E**
(illus.) Lexau, J. M. Emily and the klunky baby and the next-door dog **E**
(illus.) Skorpen, L. M. Mandy's grandmother **E**
(illus.) Williams, B. Jeremy isn't hungry **E**

Alexander, Rae Pace
(comp.) Young and black in America (6 and up) **920**

Alexander and the terrible, horrible, no good, very bad day. Viorst, J. **E**

Alexander and the wind-up mouse. Lionni, L. **E**

Alexander Mackenzie, Canadian explorer. Syme, R. **92**

Alexander the Great
See pages in the following books:
Coolidge, O. The golden days of Greece p178-95 (4-6) **938**
Mahmoud, Z. N. The land and people of Egypt p21-23, 34-35 (5 and up) **962**
Unstead, R. J. Looking at ancient history p74-78 (4-6) **930**
Van Duyn, J. The Greeks p167-86 (5 and up) **938**

Alexander, who used to be rich last Sunday. Viorst, J. See note under Viorst, J. Alexander and the terrible, horrible, no good, very bad day **E**

Alexandria, Egypt
See pages in the following book:
Mahmoud, Z. N. The land and people of Egypt p34-38, 102-06 (5 and up) **962**

Alexeieff, Alexander
(illus.) Afanas'ev, A. Russian fairy tales **398.2**

Alfalfa, beans, & clover. Rahn, J. E. **583**

Alfred Hitchcock's Supernatural tales of terror and suspense **S C**

Alfred's alphabet walk. Chess, V. **E**

Algae
See pages in the following books:
Cooper, E. K. Science on the shores and banks p46-47, 153-65 (5 and up) **574.92**
Hutchins, R. E. Plants without leaves p11-35 (5 and up) **586**
Silverstein, A. A world in a drop of water p25-30 (3-5) **576**
Zim, H. S. Seashores p18-35 (5 and up) **574.92**

Algebra
Weiss, M. E. 666 jellybeans! All that (3-5) **512**
See also Probabilities

Alger, Leclaire. See Nic Leodhas, Sorche

Algeria
See pages in the following book:
Lawson, D. Morocco, Algeria, Tunisia, and Libya p18-33 (4 and up) **961**

American periodicals

Indexes

Abridged Readers' guide to periodical literature 051
Readers' guide to periodical literature 051
Subject index to children's magazines 051

American poetry 811

American Indian authors

Belting, N. Whirlwind is a ghost dancing (3-6) 398.2

American Indian authors—Collections

Belting, N. comp. Our fathers had powerful songs (3-6) 897
In the trail of the wind (6 and up) 897
Jones, H. comp. The trees stand shining (3-6) 897
Songs of the dream people (4 and up) 897
The Whispering wind (5 and up) 811.08

Black authors—Collections

Adoff, A. Black out loud (5 and up) 811.08
Adoff, A. ed. Celebrations (5 and up) 811.08
Adoff, A. ed. I am the darker brother (5 and up) 811.08
Adoff, A. ed. My black me (5 and up) 811.08
Golden slippers (5 and up) 811.08
Hopkins, L. B. comp. On our way (3-6) 811.08

See also pages in the following book:
Rollins, C. comp. Christmas gif' p20-21, 58-102 (4 and up) 394.2

Collections

Amelia mixed the mustard, and other poems (2-5) 821.08
The Birds and the beasts were there (5 and up) 821.08
Cole, W. comp. Humorous poetry for children (5 and up) 821.08
Cole, W. comp. Poems for seasons and celebrations (5 and up) 821.08
Cole, W. comp. Poems of magic and spells (4 and up) 821.08
Cole, W. comp. Rough men, tough men (5 and up) 821.08
De La Mare, W. ed. Come hither 821.08
The Dog writes on the window with his nose, and other poems (k-3) 811.08
Easter buds are springing (2-4) 811.08
Eaton, A. T. comp. Welcome Christmas! (4 and up) 821.08
For a child (k-3) 821.08
Gaily we parade (3-6) 821.08
A Galaxy of verse (5 and up) 821.08
Ghost poems (k-3) 811.08
Giant poems (2-4) 811.08
Go with the poem (4 and up) 811.08
The Golden journey (4 and up) 821.08
The Golden Treasury of poetry 821.08
Hine, A. ed. This land is mine (5 and up) 811.08
The Home book of verse for young folks 821.08
Hopkins, L. B. comp. Girls can too! (k-3) 811.08
How to eat a poem & other morsels (3-5) 821.08
I'm mad at you (2-4) 811.08
An Inheritance of poetry (5 and up) 821.08
Larrick, N. comp. I heard a scream in the street (5 and up) 811.08

Larrick, N. ed. Piper, pipe that song again! (2-5) 821.08
Larrick, N. comp. Poetry for holidays (1-4) 811.08
Laughable limericks (4 and up) 821.08
Livingston, M. C. ed. Listen, children, listen (k-4) 821.08
Love, K. comp. A little laughter (3-6) 821.08
Monster poems (2-4) 811.08
The Moon's the North Wind's cooky (k-3) 811.08
My poetry book (5 and up) 821.08
My tang's tungled and other ridiculous situations (3-6) 821.08
Of quarks, quasars, and other quirks (5 and up) 821.08
Oh, how silly! (3-6) 821.08
Oh, such foolishness! (3 and up) 811.08
Oh, that's ridiculous! (3-6) 821.08
Oh, what nonsense! (3-6) 821.08
On city streets (5 and up) 811.08
One thousand poems for children 821.08
The Oxford Book of children's verse 821.08
A Paper zoo (1-4) 811.08
Parker, E. ed. 100 more story poems (6 and up) 821.08
Poems here and now (4 and up) 811.08
The Poetry troupe 821.08
Postcard poems (4 and up) 811.08
Rainbow in the sky (k-4) 821.08
Reflections on a gift of watermelon pickle . . . and other modern verse (5 and up) 811.08
Roofs of gold (6 and up) 821.08
Sechrist, E. H. comp. Poems for red letter days 821.08
Shrieks at midnight (4 and up) 821.08
Some haystacks don't even have any needle, and other complete modern poems (6 and up) 811.08
Straight on till morning 821.08
Sung under the silver umbrella (k-2) 821.08
They've discovered a head in the box for the bread, and other laughable limericks (5 and up) 821.08
This way, delight (5 and up) 821.08
Thompson, B. J. ed. All the Silver pennies (3-6) 821.08
Very young verses (k-1) 821.08
Wings from the wind (3-6) 821.08
Witch poems (2-5) 811.08

American poets. See Poets, American

American politicians. See Politicians, American

American Revolution. See United States—History—Revolution, 1775-1783

The **American** Revolution, 1760-1783. Bliven, M. 973.3

The **American** riddle book 398

American sculpture. See Sculpture, American

The **American** songbag. Sandburg, C. ed. 784.7

American songs. See Songs, American

American-Spanish War, 1898. See United States—History—War of 1898

American tall-tale animals. Stoutenburg, A. 398.2

American wit and humor

Clark, D. A. Jokes, puns, and riddles (4-6) 817.08
De Regniers, B. S. The Abraham Lincoln joke book (4-6) 817.08

Anansi and Snake the postman. Sherlock, P.
In Sherlock, P. West Indian folk-tales p71-76 **398.2**

Anasi and the alligator eggs. Sherlock, P. M.
In Sherlock, P. M. Anansi, the spider man p84-93 **398.2**

Anansi and the crabs. Sherlock, P. M.
In Sherlock, P. M. Anansi, the spider man p95-103 **398.2**

Anansi and the elephant exchange knocks. Courlander, H.
In Courlander, H. The hat-shaking dance, and other tales from the Gold Coast p63-69 **398.2**

Anansi and the elephant go hunting. Courlander, H.
In Courlander, H. The hat-shaking dance, and other tales from the Gold Coast p38-45 **398.2**

Anansi and the fish country. Sherlock, P. M.
In Sherlock, P. M. Anani, the spider man p70-75 **398.2**

Anansi and the Old Hag. Sherlock, P. M.
In Sherlock, P. M. Anansi, the spider man p20-29 **398.2**

Anansi and the plantains. Sherlock, P. M.
In Sherlock, P. M. Anansi, the spider man p64-69 **398.2**

Anansi and Turtle and Pigeon. Sherlock, P. M.
In Sherlock, P. M. Anansi, the spider man p31-34 **398.2**

Anansi borrows money. Courlander, H.
In Courlander, H. The hat-shaking dance, and other tales from the Gold Coast p55-58 **398.2**

Anansi hunts with Tiger. Sherlock, P.
In Sherlock, P. West Indian folk-tales p118-24 **398.2**

Anansi plays dead. Courlander, H.
In Courlander, H. The hat-shaking dance, and other tales from the Gold Coast p20-24 **398.2**

Anansi steals the palm wine. Courlander, H.
In Courlander, H. The hat-shaking dance, and other tales from the Gold Coast p77-79 **398.2**

Anansi, the oldest of animals. Courlander, H.
In Courlander, H. The hat-shaking dance, and other tales from the Gold Coast p9-12 **398.2**

Anansi the spider. McDermott, G. **398.2**

Anansi the spider-man
Arkhurst, J. C. The adventures of Spider **398.2**
Bryan, A. The adventures of Aku **398.2**
Bryan, A. The dancing granny **398.2**
Courlander, H. Anansi's hat-shaking dance
In The Arbuthnot Anthology of children's literature p321-23 **808.8**
In Time for old magic p198-200 **398.2**
Courlander, H. The hat-shaking dance, and other tales from the Gold Coast **398.2**
Droog, J. Compa Nanzi and the spotted cow
In Laughing together p67-70 **808.87**
Haley, G. E. A story, a story **398.2**
Korty, C. Ananse's trick does double work
In Korty, C. Plays from African folktales p53-77 **812**
McDermott, G. Anansi the spider **398.2**
Sherlock, P. Anansi and Candlefly
In Sherlock, P. West Indian folk-tales p97-102 **398.2**

Sherlock, P. Anansi and Snake the postman
In Sherlock, P. West Indian folk-tales p71-76 **398.2**
Sherlock, P. Anansi hunts with Tiger
In Sherlock, P. West Indian folk-tales p118-24 **398.2**
Sherlock, P. M. Anansi, the spider man **398.2**
Sherlock, P. Anansi's old riding-horse
In Sherlock, P. West Indian folk-tales p105-11 **398.2**
Sherlock, P. M. Bandaloo
In The Arbuthnot Anthology of children's literature p396-99 **808.8**
Sherlock, P. Born a monkey, live a monkey
In Sherlock, P. West Indian folk-tales p135-43 **398.2**
Sherlock, P. Dry-Bone and Anansi
In Sherlock, P. West Indian folk-tales p77-85 **398.2**
Sherlock, P. From tiger to Anansi
In The Fairy tale treasury p86-91 **398.2**
Sherlock, P. Mancrow, bird of darkness
In Sherlock, P. West Indian folk-tales p65-70 **398.2**
Sherlock, P. Mr Wheeler
In Sherlock, P. West Indian folk-tales p144-51 **398.2**
Sherlock, P. Tiger story, Anansi story
In Sherlock, P. West Indian folk-tales p45-58 **398.2**
Sherlock, P. Why women won't listen
In Sherlock, P. West Indian folk-tales p112-17 **398.2**
Sherlock, P. Work-let-me-see
In Sherlock, P. West Indian folk-tales p125-29 **398.2**

Anansi's hat-shaking dance. Courlander, H.
In The Arbuthnot Anthology of children's literature p321-23 **808.8**
In Courlander, H. The hat-shaking dance, and other tales from the Gold Coast p13-17 **398.2**
In Time for old magic p198-200 **398.2**

Anansi's old riding-horse. Sherlock, P.
In Sherlock, P. West Indian folk-tales p105-11 **398.2**

Anansi's rescue from the river. Courlander, H.
In Courlander, H. The hat-shaking dance, and other tales from the Gold Coast p59-62 **398.2**

Anastasia Krupnik. Lowry, L. **Fic**

Anatomy
Patent, D. H. Sizes and shapes in nature—what they mean (5 and up) **574.4**
See also Anatomy, Comparative; Anatomy, Human; Bones; Nervous system; Physiology

Anatomy, Artistic
Slobodkin, L. The first book of drawing (5 and up) **741.2**
See also Figure drawing

Anatomy, Comparative
Cooper, G. Inside animals (4-6) **591.4**
Lovaudais, M. The skeleton book (3-6) **596**
Zim, H. S. What's inside of animals? (2-5) **591.4**

See also pages in the following book:
Silverstein, A. The skeletal system p49-55 (4 and up) **612**

Anatomy, Dental. See Teeth

Anatomy, Human
Brenner, B. Bodies (k-2) 612
Wilson, R. How the body works (4 and up) 612

See also names of organs, e.g. Heart

Anatomy of plants. See Botany—Anatomy

Anatole. Titus, E. **E**

Anatole and the cat. Titus, E. See note under Titus, E. Anatole **E**

Anatole and the piano. Titus, E. See note under Titus, E. Anatole **E**

Anatole and the Pied Piper. Titus, E. See note under Titus, E. Anatole **E**

Anatole and the thirty thieves. Titus, E. See note under Titus, E. Anatole **E**

Ancestry. See Genealogy; Heredity

Anchor's aweigh; the story of David Glasgow Farragut. Latham, J. L. 92

Ancient architecture. See Architecture, Ancient

Ancient art. See Art, Ancient

Ancient civilization. See Civilization, Ancient

Ancient history. See History, Ancient

Ancient Indians of the Southwest. Tamarin, A. 970.004

Ancient Indonesia and its influence in modern times. Weatherbee, D. E. 959.8

Ancient Rome. Fagg, C. 937

The ancient visitors. Cohen, D. 001.9

Anckarsvärd, Karin
Madcap mystery. See note under Anckarsvärd, K. The mysterious schoolmaster **Fic**
The mysterious schoolmaster (5 and up) **Fic**
The robber ghost. See note under Anckarsvärd, K. The mysterious schoolmaster **Fic**

Ancona, George
And what do you do? (3-6) 331.7
Growing older (3-6) 305.2
It's a baby (k-2) 612
Monsters on wheels (3-6) 629.2
(illus.) Brenner, B. Bodies 612
(illus.) Brenner, B. Faces 152.1
(jt. auth.) Charlip, R. Handtalk 419
(illus.) Jackson, L. A. Grandpa had a windmill, Grandma had a churn 630.1

And all between. Snyder, Z. K. See note under Snyder, Z. K. Below the root **Fic**

And I dance mine own child. Farjeon, E.
In Farjeon, E. The little bookroom p216-43 **S C**

And I mean it, Stanley. Bonsall, C. **E**

And it came to pass 783.6

And it rained. Raskin, E. **E**

And my mean old mother will be sorry, blackboard bear. Alexander, M. See note under Alexander, M. Blackboard bear **E**

... and now Miguel. Krumgold, J. **Fic**

And so my garden grows 398

And then what happened, Paul Revere? Fritz, J. 92

And there was America. Duvoisin, R. 973.1

And this is Laura. Conford, E. **Fic**

And to think that I saw it on Mulberry Street. Seuss, Dr **E**
also in Gruenberg, S. M. ed. Favorite stories old and new p217-21 808.8

And what do you do? Ancona, G. 331.7

And you give me a pain, Elaine. Pevsner, S. **Fic**

Anders, Hanns-Jörg
(illus.) Isenbart, H. H. A foal is born 636.1

Ander's new cap
The Cap that mother made
In Gruenberg, S. M. ed. Favorite stories old and new p68-71 808.8
In Holiday ring p98-101 394.2

Andersen, Hans Christian
Ardizzone's Hans Andersen: fourteen classic tales (3-6) **S C**
Contents: The steadfast tin soldier; The emperor's new clothes; The little mermaid; The flying trunk; The shirt collar; The princess and the pea; Big Claus and Little Claus; The wild swans; The ugly duckling; The tinder box; Thumbelina; The snow queen; The darning needle; The nightingale

Big Claus and Little Claus
In Yellow fairy book p210-23 398.2
Blockhead-Hans
In Yellow fairy book p309-13 398.2
[The complete fairy tales and stories (4 and up) **S C**
Contents: The tinderbox; Little Claus and Big Claus; The princess and the pea; Little Ida's flowers; Inchelina; The naughty boy; The traveling companion; The little mermaid; The emperor's new clothes; The magic galoshes; The daisy; The steadfast tin soldier; The wild swans; The garden of Eden; The flying trunk; The storks; The bronze pig; The pact of friendship; A rose from Homer's grave; The sandman; The rose elf; The swineherd; The buckwheat; The angel; The nightingale; The sweethearts; The ugly duckling; The pine tree; The Snow Queen; Mother Elderberry; The darning needle; The bell; Grandmother; The hill of the elves; The red shoes; The jumping competition; The shepherdess and the chimney sweep; Holger the Dane; The little match girl; From the ramparts of the citadel; From a window in Vartov; The old street lamp; The neighbors; Little Tuck; The shadow; The old house; A drop of water; A happy family; The story of a mother; The collar; The flax; The bird Phoenix; A story; The silent album; The old gravestone; There is a difference; The world's most beautiful rose; The year's story; On the last day; It is perfectly true; The swan's nest; A happy disposition; Grief; Everything in its right place; The pixy and the grocer; The millennium; Under the willow tree; Five peas from the same pod; A leaf from heaven; She was no good; The last pearl; The two maidens; The uttermost parts of the sea; The piggy bank; Ib and little Christina; Clod Hans; The thorny path; The servant; The bottle; The philosopher's stone; How to cook soup upon a sausage pin; The pepperman's nightcap; "Something"; The old oak tree's last dream; The talisman; The bog king's daughter; The winners; The bell deep; The evil king; What the wind told about Valdemare Daae and his daughters; The girl who stepped on bread; The watchman of the tower; Ann Lisbeth; Children's prattle; A string of pearls; The pen and the inkwell; The dead child; The cock and the weathercock; "Lovely"; A story from the dunes; The puppeteer; The two brothers; The old church bell; The twelve passengers; The dung beetle; What father does is always right; The snowman; In the duckyard; The muse of the twentieth century; The ice maiden; The butterfly; Psyche; The snail and the rosebush; "The will-o'-the-wisps are in town," said the bog witch; The windmill; The silver shilling; The Bishop of Børglum Cloister and his kinsmen; In the children's room; The golden treasure; How the storm changed the signs; The teapot; The songbird of the people; The little green ones; The pixy and the gardener's wife; Peiter, Peter, and Peer; Hidden but not forgotten; The janitor's son; Moving day; The snowdrop; Auntie; The toad; Godfather's picture book; The rags; The two islands; Who was the happiest; The wood nymph; The family of Hen-Grethe; The adventures of a thistle; A question of imagination; Luck can be found in a stick; The comet; The days of the week; The sunshine's story; Great-grandfather; The candles; The most incredible; What the whole family said; "Dance, dance, dolly mine"; "It is you the fable is about"; The great sea serpent; The gardener and his master; The professor and the flea; The story old Johanna told; The front door key; The cripple; Auntie Toothache

Angles are easy as pie. Froman, R.   **516**

Anglo-American cataloging rules   **025.3**

Anglo-Saxons
Crossley-Holland, K. Green blades rising (6 and up)   **942.01**

Anglo-Spanish War, 1739-1748
See pages in the following book:
Vaughan, H. C. The colony of Georgia p51-57 (4 and up)   **975.8**

Anglund, Joan Walsh
(illus.) The Golden Treasury of poetry. See The Golden Treasury of poetry   **821.08**
In a pumpkin shell   **E**

About
See pages in the following book:
Lanes, S. G. Down the rabbit hole p31-43   **028.5**

Angola
See pages in the following book:
Newlon, C. Southern Africa: the critical land p160-69 (5 and up)   **968**

The **angry** moon. Sleator, W.   **398.2**

Angus and the cat. Flack, M. See note under Flack, M. Angus and the ducks   **E**

Angus and the ducks. Flack, M.   **E**

Angus lost. Flack, M. See note under Flack, M. Angus and the ducks   **E**

The **animal**. Stephens, R.
In Universe ahead: stories of the future p11-28   **S C**

Animal ABC, Celestine Piatti's. Piatti, C.   **E**

Animal atlas of the world. Jordan, E. L.   **599**

Animal babies. See Animals—Infancy

Animal babies. Ylla   **591.3**

Animal behavior. See Animals—Habits and behavior

Animal camouflage. See Camouflage (Biology)

Animal communication
Amon, A. Reading, writing, chattering chimps (5 and up)   **599.88**
Dean, A. How animals communicate (4-6)   **591.5**
Jacobs, F. Sounds in the sea (4-6)   **591.92**
Ricciuti, E. R. Sounds of animals at night (3-5)   **591.5**
Selsam, M. E. The language of animals (5 and up)   **591.5**
Spier, P. Gobble, growl, grunt   **E**
Van Woerkom, D. Hidden messages (2-4)   **595.7**
See also pages in the following book:
Patent, D. H. Reptiles and how they reproduce p33-40 (5 and up)   **597.9**

Fiction
Battles, E. What does the rooster say, Yoshio?   **E**

Animal doctors. Curtis, P.   **636.089**

Animal drawing. See Animal painting and illustration

Animal fact/animal fable. Simon, S.   **591**

The **animal** family. Jarrell, R.   **Fic**

Animal friendship
In One trick too many p29-30   **398.2**

Animal games. Freedman, R.   **591.5**

Animal homes. See Animals—Habitations

Animal homes. Cartwright, S.   **591.5**

Animal hospital. Berger, M.   **636.089**

Animal intelligence
Freedman, R. How animals learn (5 and up)   **591.5**
See also Animals—Habits and behavior

Animal invaders. Silverstein, A.   **591.5**

The **animal** kids. Cauley, L. B.   **E**

Animal kingdom. See Zoology

Animal language. See Animal communication

Animal locomotion
Silverstein, A. The muscular system (4-6)   **574.1**
See also pages in the following book:
Patent, D. H. Sizes and shapes in nature—what they mean p61-74 (5 and up)   **574.4**

Animal lore. See Animals, Mythical; Animals in literature

Animal migration. See Animals—Migration

Animal painting and illustration
Ames, L. J. Draw 50 dinosaurs and other prehistoric animals (5 and up)   **743**
Bolognese, D. Drawing horses and foals (4-6)   **743**
Emberley, E. Ed Emberley's Drawing book of animals   **743**
Frame, P. Drawing cats and kittens (5 and up)   **743**
See also pages in the following book:
Weiss, H. Pencil, pen and brush p6-13   **741.2**
See also Animals—Pictorial works

Animal physiology. See Zoology

Animal pictures. See Animals—Pictorial works

Animal populations
McClung, R. M. Mice, moose, and men (4 and up)   **591.5**

Animal products. See names of special products, e.g. Wool

Animal psychology. See Animal intelligence

Animal rhymes. See A Peaceable kingdom   **811**

Animal riddles, Bennett Cerf's Book of. Cerf, B.   **793.7**

Animal signs. See Animal tracks

Animal stories. See Animals—Fiction

Animal tracks
Arnosky, J. Crinkleroot's book of animal tracks and wildlife signs (2-4)   **591.5**
Baylor, B. We walk in sandy places (k-2)   **591.5**
Branley, F. M. Big tracks, little tracks (k-2)   **591.5**
Mason, G. F. Animal tracks (4 and up)   **591.5**
Murie, O. J. A field guide to animal tracks   **591.5**

Animal training. See Animals—Training

Animal travelers. Swift, D.   **591.5**

Animals
Barrett, J. Animals should definitely not wear clothing   **E**
Clemens, V. P. Super animals and their unusual careers (4 and up)   **636.08**
Garelick, M. Where does the butterfly go when it rains   **E**
Kuskin, K. Roar and more   **E**
Rojankovsky, F. Animals in the zoo   **E**
Simon, S. Animal fact/animal fable (1-4)   **591**
See also pages in the following books:
The Arbuthnot Anthology of children's literature p855-59   **808.8**

Animals—Poetry—*Continued*

Fisher, A. Do bears have mothers, too? (k-2) **811**

Gardner, J. A child's bestiary (4-6) **811**

I went to the animal fair (k-3) **808.81**

Lear, E. Edward Lear's The Scroobious Pip (2-6) **821**

Mayer, M. What do you do with a kangaroo? **E**

Mizumura, Kazue. If I were a cricket (k-2) **811**

Nash, O. The cruise of the Aardvark (3-5) **811**

A Paper zoo (1-4) **811.08**

A Peaceable kingdom (k-3) **811**

Piatti, C. Celestino Piatti's Animal ABC **E**

Under the tent of the sky (3-6) **808.81**

See also pages in the following books:

The Arbuthnot Anthology of children's literature p34-49 **808.8**

Favorite poems, old and new p153-79 (4-6) **808.81**

Field, R. Poems p63-72 (2-5) **811**

The Golden Treasury of poetry p27-81 **821.08**

My poetry book p184-210 (5 and up) **821.08**

One thousand poems for children p105-24, 403-34 **821.08**

Parker, E. ed. 100 more story poems p307-43 (6 and up) **821.08**

Piping down the valleys wild p105-26, 139-60 **808.81**

Rainbow in the sky p229-48 (k-4) **821.08**

Sung under the silver umbrella p59-74 (k-2) **821.08**

Very young verses p 1-42 (k-1) **821.08**

Protection
See Animals—Treatment

Research
See pages in the following book:
Berger, M. Animal hospital p96-104 (4 and up) **636.089**

Sexual behavior
See pages in the following book:
Patent, D. H. Sizes and shapes in nature—what they mean p128-34 (5 and up) **574.4**

Songs and music
The Fireside song book of birds and beasts **784.4**

Sweetly sings the donkey (2-5) **784.1**

South America
Shuttlesworth, D. E. The wildlife of South America (5 and up) **591.9**

Sri Lanka
See pages in the following book:
Wilber, D. N. The land and people of Ceylon p24-27 (5 and up) **954.9**

Stories
See Animals—Fiction; Fables

Tanzania
See pages in the following book:
Kaula, E. M. The land and people of Tanzania p107-15 (5 and up) **967.8**

Training
See pages in the following book:
Freedman, R. How animals learn p109-27 (5 and up) **591.5**

See also names of animals with the subdivision Training, e.g. Dogs—Training

Transportation
See pages in the following book:
McCoy, J. J. In defense of animals p113-27 (5 and up) **179**

Treatment
McCoy, J. J. In defense of animals (5 and up) **179**

Wyoming
See pages in the following book:
Kirk, R. Yellowstone p49-57 (5 and up) **978.7**

Animals, Aquatic. See Fresh water animals

Animals, Cruelty to. See Animals—Treatment

Animals, Domestic. See Domestic animals

Animals, Extinct. See Extinct animals

Animals, Fictitious. See Animals, Mythical

Animals, Fossil. See Fossils

Animals, Fresh water. See Fresh water animals

Animals, Imaginary. See Animals, Mythical

Animals, Marine. See Marine animals

Animals, Mythical

McHargue, G. The beasts of never (5 and up) **398**

McHargue, G. Meet the werewolf (4 and up) **398**

Schwartz, A. comp. Kickle snifters and other fearsome critters (2-5) **398**

Dictionaries
Sedwick, P. Mythological creatures (5 and up) **291.03**

Fiction
Hunter, M. A stranger came ashore (6 and up) **Fic**

Wagner, J. The Bunyip of Berkeley's Creek **E**

Animals, Predatory. See Predatory animals

Animals, Prehistoric. See Fossils

Animals, Rare. See Rare animals

Animals, Sea. See Marine animals

Animals, War use of
See also Dogs, War use of

Animals and their niches. Pringle, L. **591.5**

The **Animals'** Christmas **394.2**

Animals come to my house. Kellner, E. **639**

Animals everywhere. Aulaire, I. d' **E**

The **animals** go on trial. Sechrist. E. H.
In Sechrist, E. H. Once in the first times p64-66 **398.2**

Animals in danger **591.5**

Animals in literature
See pages in the following books:
Jan, I. On children's literature p82-89 **028.5**
Townsend, J. R. Written for children p120-30 **028.5**

See also Animals—Fiction; Animals—Poetry; Bible—Natural history

Animals in motion pictures
See pages in the following book:
Clemens, V. P. Super animals and their unusual careers p108-27 (4 and up)   **636.08**

Animals in television
See pages in the following book:
Clemens, V. P. Super animals and their unusual careers p64-80 (4 and up)   **636.08**

Animals in the pit
Afanas'ev, A. Beasts in a pit
In Afanas'ev, A. Russian fairy tales p498   **398.2**

Animals in the zoo. Rojankovsky, F.   **E**

The **animals** in winter. Riordan, J.
In Riordan, J. Tales from Central Russia p222-26   **398.2**

Animals of the Bible. Asimov, I.   **220.8**

Animals of the Bible. Bible. Selections   **220.8**

Animals on the farm. Rojankovsky, F.   **E**

Animals should definitely not wear clothing. Barrett, J.   **E**

Animals that build their homes. McClung, R. M.   **591.5**

Animals that frighten people. Shuttlesworth, D. E.   **591.5**

Animals that live in the sea. Straker, J. A.   **591.92**

Animals' winter quarters
Riordan, J. The animals in winter
In Riordan, J. Tales from Central Russia p222-26   **398.2**

Animals with backbones, A first look at. Selsam, M. E.   **596**

Animated cartoons. See Motion picture cartoons

Ankara
See pages in the following book:
Spencer, W. The land and people of Turkey p83-95 (5 and up)   **956.1**

Ann Aurelia and Dorothy. Carlson, N. S.   **Fic**
also in Friends are like that! p81-109   **S C**

Ann the Word; the life of Mother Ann Lee, founder of the Shakers. Campion, N. R.   **92**

Anna's silent world. Wolf, B.   **362.4**

Anne Boleyn. Leach, M.
In Leach, M. Whistle in the graveyard p22-23   **398.2**

Anne Frank: the diary of a young girl. Frank, A.   **92**

Anne Lisbeth. Andersen, H. C.
In Andersen, H. C. The complete fairy tales and stories p620-29   **S C**

Annerton Pit. Dickinson, P.   **Fic**

Annie and the Old One. Miles, M.   **Fic**

Annie Oakley and the world of her time. Alderman, C. L.   **92**

Annie Pat and Eddie. Haywood, C. See note under Haywood, C. Little Eddie   **Fic**

Annie Sullivan [biography of Anne Sullivan Macy] Malone, M.   **92**

Anniversaries and holidays. Gregory, R. W.   **394.2**

Anniversary. Sangster, M. E.
In It's time for Christmas p204-13   **394.2**

Annixter, Jane
The year of the she-grizzly (4-6)   **599.74**

Annixter, Paul
(jt. auth.) Annixter, J. The year of the she-grizzly   **599.74**

Anno, Mitsumasa
Anno's alphabet   **E**
Anno's Counting book   **E**
Anno's journey   **E**
The King's flower   **E**
Topsy-turvies   **E**
Upside-downers   **E**

Anno's alphabet. Anno, M.   **E**

Anno's Counting book. Anno, M.   **E**

Anno's journey. Anno, M.   **E**

The **Annotated** Mother Goose, nursery rhymes old and new   **398**

Annuals. See Almanacs; and general subjects with the subdivision Yearbooks, e.g. Statistics—Yearbooks

Another way to weigh an elephant. Blumengeld, L.
In Popular plays for classroom reading p94-99   **808.82**

Ant. See Ants

Antarctic expeditions. See Antarctic regions

Antarctic Regions
Asimov, I. How did we find out about Antarctica?   **998**
Scarf, M. Antarctica: exploring the frozen continent (3-6)   **998**
See also pages in the following book:
Harrington, L. The polar regions p143-81 (5 and up)   **998**

Antarctica: exploring the frozen continent. Scarf, M.   **998**

An **anteater** named Arthur. Waber, B.   **E**

Anteaters
Fiction
Waber, B. An anteater named Arthur   **E**

The **antelope** skin. Courlander, H.
In Courlander, H. Olode the hunter, and other tales from Nigeria p29-31   **398.2**

Antelope's mother: The woman in the moon. Courlander, H.
In Courlander, H. Olode the hunter, and other tales from Nigeria p72-76   **398.2**

Anthology of children's literature, The Arbuthnot   **808.8**

Anthony, Susan Brownell
Noble, I. Susan B. Anthony (5 and up)   **92**
Peterson, H. S. Susan B. Anthony, pioneer in woman's rights (3-5)   **92**
See also pages in the following book:
Nathan, D. Women of courage p3-39 (4-6)   **920**

Anthropologists
Blassingame, W. Thor Heyerdahl: Viking scientist (5 and up)   **92**
Epstein, S. She never looked back; Margaret Mead in Samoa (4-6)   **92**

Anthropology
McKern, S. S. The many faces of man (5 and up)   **572**

Antibiotics
See pages in the following book:
Selsam, M. E. Plants that heal p82-88 (4-6)   **581.6**

Antin, Mary
See pages in the following book:
As I saw it; women who lived the American adventure p183-85 (6 and up)   **973**

Antique car models. Ross, F.   **629.2**

Architecture, Chinese
See pages in the following book:
Paine, R. M. Looking at architecture p50-57
(4 and up)   **720.9**

Architecture, Domestic
Hoag, E. American houses: colonial, classic,
and contemporary (6 and up)   **728**
Huntington, L. P. Simple shelters (3-5)   **728**
Leacroft, H. The buildings of ancient man
(5 and up)   **722**
Siberell, A. Houses (2-4)   **728**
See also Houses

Designs and plans
Myller, R. From idea into house (5 and up)
     728

Architecture, Egyptian
Leacroft, H. The buildings of ancient Egypt
(5 and up)   **722**
See also pages in the following books:
Mahmoud, Z. N. The land and people of
Egypt p20-32 (5 and up)   **962**
Paine, R. M. Looking at architecture p14-19
(4 and up)   **720.9**

Architecture, French
See pages in the following book:
Paine, R. M. Looking at architecture p58-
64, 84-89 (4 and up)   **720.9**

Architecture, Gothic
Grant, N. Cathedrals (4-6)   **726**
Macaulay, D. Cathedral: the story of its
construction (4 and up)   **726**
See also pages in the following book:
Paine, R. M. Looking at architecture p58-64
(4 and up)   **720.9**

Architecture, Greek
Leacroft, H. The buildings of ancient Greece
(5 and up)   **722**

Architecture, Indonesian
See pages in the following book:
Smith, D. C. The land and people of Indo-
nesia p102-06 (5 and up)   **959.8**

Architecture, Islamic
Leacroft, H. Buildings of early Islam (5 and
up)   **722**

Architecture, Italian
See pages in the following book:
Paine, R. M. Looking at architecture p66-73
(4 and up)   **720.9**

Architecture, Medieval
See also Castles

Architecture, Mesopotamian
See pages in the following book:
Paine, R. M. Looking at architecture p20-25
(4 and up)   **720.9**

Architecture, Mexican
See pages in the following book:
Paine, R. M. Looking at architecture p42-49
(4 and up)   **720.9**

Architecture, Modern

20th century
See pages in the following book:
Paine, R. M. Looking at architecture p98-113
(4 and up)   **720.9**

Architecture, Naval. See Shipbuilding

Architecture, Renaissance
See pages in the following book:
Paine, R. M. Looking at architecture p66-73
(4 and up)   **720.9**

Architecture, Roman
Leacroft, H. The buildings of ancient Rome
(5 and up)   **722**
Macaulay, D. City (4 and up)   **711**

Architecture, Romanesque
Grant, N. Cathedrals (4-6)   **726**

Arctic expeditions. See Arctic regions

Arctic regions
Laycock, G. Beyond the Arctic Circle (5 and
up)   **998**
See also pages in the following books:
Harrington, L. The polar regions p71-141 (5
and up)   **998**
National Geographic Society. The new Amer-
ica's wonderlands   **917.3**
See also Northeast Passage

Fiction
George, J. C. Julie of the wolves (6 and
up)   **Fic**
George, J. C. The wounded wolf (2-4)   **Fic**
Houston, J. Frozen fire (6 and up)   **Fic**
Roth, A. The iceberg hermit (6 and up)   **Fic**

Ardizzone, Edward
Little Tim and the brave sea captain   **E**
Ship's cook Ginger. See note under Ardizzone, E. Little Tim and the brave sea
captain   **E**
Tim in danger. See note under Ardizzone, E.
Little Tim and the brave sea captain   **E**
Tim to the lighthouse. See note under Ardizzone, E. Little Tim and the brave sea captain   **E**
(illus.) Andersen, H. C. Ardizzone's Hans
Andersen: fourteen classic tales   **S C**
(illus.) De La Mare, W. Peacock pie   **821**
(illus.) De La Mare, W. Stories from the
Bible   **221.9**
(illus.) Estes, E. The witch family   **Fic**
(illus.) Farjeon, E. The little bookroom   **S C**

About
See pages in the following book:
Authors and illustrators of children's books
p 1-5   **028.5**

Ardizzone's Hans Andersen: fourteen classic
tales. Andersen, H. C.   **S C**

Are you my mother? Eastman, P. D.   **E**

Are you there God? It's me, Margaret.
Blume, J.   **Fic**

Area. Srivastava, J. J.   **516**

Arenstein, Misha
Mrs Alcott's visitor
In A-haunting we will go p65-72   **S C**

Argentina. See Argentine Republic

Argentine Republic
Hall, E. The land and people of Argentina
(5 and up)   **982**

Social conditions
See pages in the following book:
Meltzer, M. The human rights book p23-30
(6 and up)   **323.4**

Arndt, Ursula—*Continued*
(illus.) Barth, E. Witches, pumpkins, and grinning ghosts **394.2**
(illus.) Cantwell, M. St Patrick's Day **394.2**
(illus.) A Christmas feast. See A Christmas feast **808.81**
(illus.) Thompson, B. J. ed. All the Silver pennies **821.08**

Arno, Enrico
(illus.) Charosh, M. Straight lines, parallel lines, perpendicular lines **516**
(illus.) Cole, W. comp. Rough men, tough men **821.08**
(illus.) Coolidge, O. The golden days of Greece **938**
(illus.) Courlander, H. The hat-shaking dance, and other tales from the Gold Coast **398.2**
(illus.) Courlander, H. The king's drum, and other African stories **398.2**
(illus.) Courlander, H. Olode the hunter, and other tales from Nigeria **398.2**
(illus.) Courlander, H. The tiger's whisker, and other tales and legends from Asia and the Pacific **398.2**
(illus.) Fritz, J. Brendan the Navigator **398.2**
(illus.) Ross, E. S. ed. The lost half-hour **372.6**

Arnold, Benedict
Alderman, C. L. The dark eagle: the story of Benedict Arnold (4 and up) **92**

Arnold, E. W.
Make him smile
In One hundred plays for children p 1-9 **808.82**

Arnold, Lois
(jt. auth.) Arnold, N. The great science magic show **793.8**

Arnold, Ned
The great science magic show (5 and up) **793.8**

Arnold, Pauline
How we named our states (5 and up) **917.3**

Arnosky, Jim
Crinkleroot's book of animal tracks and wildlife signs (2-4) **591.5**
A kettle of hawks and other wildlife groups (2-4) **591.5**
(illus.) Freschet, B. Porcupine baby **599.32**
(illus.) Freschet, B. Possum baby **599.2**
(illus.) Miles, M. Swim, Little Duck **E**
(illus.) Starbord, K. The covered bridge house, and other poems **811**

Arnott, Kathleen
African myths and legends (4 and up) **398.2**
Contents: Why the dog is the friend of man; The man who learned the language of the animals; Tortoise and the lizard; The rubber man; Tortoise and the baboon; Spider and the lion; Thunder and Lightning; Why the crab has no head, or, How the first river was made; A test of skill; The tale of the Superman; Why the bushfowl calls at dawn and why flies buzz; Spider and Squirrel; Unanana and the elephant; Spider's web; The magic horns; Snake magic; Hare and the corn bins; What the squirrel saw; Hare and the Hyena; The calabash children; The blacksmith's dilemma; The magic drum; Why the sun and the moon live in the sky; The monkey's heart; The children who lived in a tree-house; Why the bat flies at night; Tug of war; The discontented fish; Hallabau's jealousy; Goto, king of the land and the water; The singing drum and the mysterious pumpkin; The snake chief; Fereyel and Debbo Engal the witch

Around and around—love. Miles, B. **152.4**

Around the world in 80 dishes. Van der Linde, P. **641.5**

Arrant fool
Afanas'ev, A. The arrant fool
In Afanas'ev, A. Russian fairy tales p334-36 **398.2**

The **arrival** of Paddington. Bradley, A.
In Bradley, A. Paddington on stage p13-29 **822**

Arrow to the sun. McDermott, G. **398.2**

Arrowood, Clinton
(illus.) Elliott, D. Frogs and the ballet **792.8**

Art
Chase, A. E. Looking at art (5 and up) **701**
Grigson, G. Shapes and stories (5 and up) **701**

See also Architecture; Arts and crafts; Collage; Drawing; Graphic arts; Illustration of books; Painting; Photography, Artistic; Sculpture

Analysis, interpretation, appreciation
See Art appreciation

Galleries and museums
Weisgard, L. Treasures to see (1-4) **708**

History
Batterberry, A. R. The Pantheon Story of art for young people (5 and up) **709**

Art, Abstract
See pages in the following book:
Batterberry, A. R. The Pantheon Story of American art for young people p132-35 (5 and up) **709.73**
See also Kinetic art

Art, African
Glubok, S. The art of Africa (4 and up) **709.6**
Price, C. Made in West Africa (5 and up) **709.6**

Art, American
Batterberry, A. R. The Pantheon Story of American art for young people (5 and up) **709.73**
Glubok, S. The art of America from Jackson to Lincoln (4 and up) **709.73**
Glubok, S. The art of America in the early twentieth century (4 and up) **709.73**
Glubok, S. The art of America in the gilded age (4 and up) **709.73**
Glubok, S. The art of America since World War II (4 and up) **709.73**
Glubok, S. The art of colonial America (4 and up) **709.73**
Glubok, S. The art of the new American nation (4 and up) **709.73**
See also pages in the following books:
Batterberry, A. R. The Pantheon Story of art for young people p125-31 (5 and up) **709**
Caney, S. Steven Caney's Kids' America p202-35 (4 and up) **790.1**

Art, Ancient
Baumann, H. The caves of the great hunters (5 and up) **930.1**

Art, Asian
See pages in the following book:
Batterberry, A. R. The Pantheon Story of art for young people p148-55 (5 and up) **709**

The **art** and industry of sandcastles. Adkins, J. **728.8**

Art appreciation
Chase, A. E. Looking at art (5 and up) **701**
Grigson, G. Shapes and stories (5 and up) **701**
Art from found objects. Comins, J. **745.5**
Art galleries. See Art—Galleries and museums
Art industries and trade

United States
Colby, C. B. Early American crafts (4 and up) **670**
Fisher, L. E. The homemakers (4 and up) **670**
Tunis, E. Colonial craftsmen and the beginnings of American industry (5 and up) **670**
Art museums. See Art—Galleries and museums
The **art** of Africa. Glubok, S. **709.6**
The **art** of America from Jackson to Lincoln. Glubok, S. **709.73**
The **art** of America in the early twentieth century. Glubok, S. **709.73**
The **art** of America in the gilded age. Glubok, S. **709.73**
The **art** of America since World War II. Glubok, S. **709.73**
The **art** of ancient Mexico. Glubok, S. **709.01**
The **art** of ancient Rome. Glubok, S. **709.37**
The **art** of Beatrix Potter. Potter, B. **741.64**
The **art** of China. Glubok, S. **709.51**
The **art** of colonial America. Glubok, S. **709.73**
The **art** of India. Glubok, S. **709.54**
The **art** of Japan. Glubok, S. **709.52**
The **art** of Nancy Ekholm Burkert. Burkert, N. E. **741.64**
The **art** of photography. Glubok, S. **770.9**
The **art** of the comic strip. Glubok, S. **741.5**
The **art** of the Eskimo. Glubok, S. **709.98**
The **art** of the Etruscans. Glubok, S. **709.37**
The **art** of the new American nation. Glubok, S. **709.73**
The **art** of the North American Indian. Glubok, S. **709.01**
The **art** of the Northwest coast Indians. Glubok, S. **709.01**
The **art** of the Plains Indians. Glubok, S. **709.01**
The **art** of the Southeastern Indians. Glubok, S. **709.01**
The **art** of the Southwest Indians. Glubok, S. **709.01**
The **art** of the Spanish in the United States and Puerto Rico. Glubok, S. **709.73**
The **art** of the story-teller. Shedlock, M. L. **372.6**
The **art** of the Vikings. Glubok, S. **709.02**
The **art** of the Woodland Indians. Glubok, S. **709.01**
The **art** of Walt Disney. Finch, C. **791.43**
Artemis
See pages in the following book:
Gates, D. The golden god: Apollo p58-60 (4 and up) **292**
Arthur, King
Bulfinch, T. Bulfinch's Mythology (6 and up) **291**
Hieatt, C. The Castle of Ladies (4 and up) **398.5**

Hieatt, C. The knight of the cart (4 and up) **398.2**
Picard, B. L. Stories of King Arthur and his knights (5 and up) **398.2**
Robbins, R. Taliesin and King Arthur (3-5) **398.2**
See also pages in the following books:
Reeves, J. The shadow of the hawk, and other stories p49-83, 129-53 (5 and up) **398.2**
Shedlock, M. L. The art of the story-teller p173-78 **372.6**

Drama
See pages in the following book:
Dramatized folk tales of the world p106-27 (5 and up) **812.08**

Fiction
Bulla, C. R. The sword in the tree (2-5) **Fic**
Arthur, Lee
Sportsmath: how it works (4-6) **796**
Arthur Robert
The haunted trailer
In Haunting tales p40-62 **S C**
Arthur, Ruth M.
A candle in her room (5 and up) **Fic**
Requiem for a princess (6 and up) **Fic**
Arthur and the great detective. Coren, A. See note under Coren, A. Arthur the Kid **Fic**
Arthur in the cave. Thomas, W. J.
In Shedlock, M. L. The art of the story-teller p173-78 **372.6**
Arthur Mitchell. Tobias, T. **92**
The **Arthur** Rackham Fairy book (3-6) **398.2**
Arthur the Kid. Coren, A. **Fic**
Arthurian romances. See Arthur, King
Arthur's Christmas cookies. Hoban, L. **E**
Arthur's eyes. Brown, M. See note under Brown, M. Arthur's nose **E**
Arthur's honey bear. Hoban, L. See note under Hoban, L. Arthur's Christmas cookies **E**
Arthur's last stand. Coren, A. See note under Coren, A. Arthur the Kid **Fic**
Arthur's new power. Hoban, R. See note under Hoban, R. Dinner at Alberta's **E**
Arthur's nose. Brown, M. **E**
Arthur's pen pal. Hoban, L. See note under Hoban, L. Arthur's Christmas cookies **E**
Arthur's prize reader. Hoban, L. See note under Hoban, L. Arthur's Christmas cookies **E**
Arthur's valentine. Brown, M. See note under Brown, M. Arthur's nose **E**
The **artificial** earthquake. Sechrist, E. H.
In Sechrist, E. H. Once in the first times p91-93 **398.2**
Artificial intelligence
See pages in the following book:
Berger, M. Bionics p55-63 (6 and up) **617**
Artificial islands
See pages in the following book:
Rutland, J. See inside an oil rig and tanker (5 and up) **338.2**
Artificial organs
Berger, M. Bionics (6 and up) **617**
Artificial respiration
See pages in the following book:
Vandenburg, M. L. Help! Emergencies that could happen to you, and how to handle them p39-41 (2-5) **616.02**

Artificial satellites

See pages in the following books:

Asimov, I. How did we find out about outer space p49-59 (5 and up) **629.4**

Shuttlesworth, D. E. The moon p93-100 (5 and up) **523.3**

Artificial satellites in telecommunication

See pages in the following book:

Neal H. E. Communication p171-78 (5 and up) **001.51**

Artigas, José Gervasio

See pages in the following book:

Dobler, L. The land and people of Uruguay p33-46 (5 and up) **989.5**

Artistic anatomy. See Anatomy, Artistic

Artists

Fiction

Say, A. The inn-keeper's apprentice (6 and up) **Fic**

Artists, American

Hyman, L. Winslow Homer: America's old master (5 and up) **92**

Artists' materials

Sattler, H. R. Recipes for art and craft materials (4 and up) **745.5**

Arts

Polette, N. E is for everybody: a manual for bringing fine picture books into the hands and hearts for children **028.5**

See also pages in the following book:

Neal, H. E. Communication p162-70 (5 and up) **001.51**

Bibliography

See pages in the following book:

Sutherland, Z. Children & books p494-96 **028.5**

Arts, American

See pages in the following book:

Tunis, E. The young United States, 1783 to 1830 p123-28 (6 and up) **973**

Arts, British

See pages in the following book:

Hodges, C. W. The battlement garden p100-07 (6 and up) **942.05**

Arts, English. See Arts, British

Arts, Graphic. See Graphic arts

Arts, Icelandic

See pages in the following book:

Berry, E. The land and people of Iceland p122-31 (5 and up) **949.1**

Arts, Nigerian

See pages in the following book:

Forman, B. The land and people of Nigeria p85-96 (5 and up) **966.9**

Arts, Spanish

See pages in the following book:

Loder, D. The land and the people of Spain p66-72 (5 and up) **946**

Arts and crafts

See pages in the following book:

Erdoes, R. The rain dance people p240-57 (5 and up) **970.004**

See also Basket making; Beadwork; Design, Decorative; Handicraft; Modeling; Needlework; Pottery; Stencil work; Weaving; Wood carving

Arts and crafts you can eat. Cobb, V. **745.5**

Arts of clay. Price, C. **738.3**

Arts of wood. Price, C. **736**

Artzybasheff, Boris

Seven Simeons (3-6) **398.2**

(illus.) Mukerji, D. G. Gay-Neck: the story of a pigeon **Fic**

Aruego, Ariane

(jt. auth.) Aruego, J. A crocodile's tale **398.2**

(illus.) Ginsburg, M. The chick and the duckling **E**

Aruego, Jose

A crocodile's tales (k-3) **398.2**

Look what I can do **E**

We hide, you seek **E**

(illus.) Duff, M. Rum pum pum **398.2**

(illus.) Ginsburg, M. The chick and the duckling **E**

(illus.) Ginsburg, M. How the sun was brought back to the sky **398.2**

(illus.) Ginsburg, M. Mushroom in the rain **E**

(illus.) Ginsburg, M. The strongest one of all **398.2**

(illus.) Kraus, R. Whose mouse are you? **E**

Arunta tribe. See Aranda tribe

Arwin, Melanie Gaines

(illus.) Meyer, C. Mask magic **391**

(illus.) Ribner, S. The martial arts **796.8**

Aryeh-Ben-Gadi and Fox-of-the-Burnt-Tail. Soyer, A.

In Soyer, A. The adventures of Yemima, and other stories p21-36 **S C**

As Hai Low kept house. Chrisman, A. B.

In Chrisman, A. B. Shen of the sea p208-21 **S C**

As I saw it: women who lived the American adventure (6 and up) **973**

As I walked out one evening **821.08**

As I went over the water. See Sendak, M. Hector Protector, and As I went over the water **398**

As long as this. Leach, M.

In Leach, M. The thing at the foot of the bed, and other scary tales p44-45 **S C**

Asbjørnsen, Peter Christen

Boots and his brothers

In Time for old magic p120-22 **398.2**

In Told under the green umbrella p146-55 **398.2**

Bushy bride

In Red fairy book p317-23 **398.2**

Buttercup

In Giants & Witches and a dragon or two p108-14 (4-6) **398.2**

The cat on the Dovrefell. See The Cat on the Dovrefell **398.2**

Dapplegrim

In Red fairy book p235-46 **398.2**

East o' the sun and west o' the moon

In The Arbuthnot Anthology of children's literature p252-57 **808.8**

In Blue fairy book p 1-13 **398.2**

In Time for old magic p135-40 **398.2**

East of the sun and west of the moon (3-6) **398.2**

Contents: East of the sun and west of the moon: The blue belt; The lassie and her godmother; The three princesses of Whiteland; The widow's son; The three princesses in the mountain

Farmer Weathersky

In Red fairy book p286-95 **398.2**

Baba Yaga and the brave youth
Afanas'ev, A. Baba Yaga and the brave youth
In Afanas'ev, A. Russian fairy tales p76-79
398.2

Baba Yaga and the little girl with the kind heart. Ransome, A.
In Ross, E. S. ed. The lost half-hour p61-74
372.6
In Witches, witches, witches p19-30 **808.8**
See also Vasilisa the beauty

Babar and Father Christmas. Brunhoff, J. de. See note under Brunhoff, J. de. The story of Babar, the little elephant **E**
Babar and his children. Brunhoff, J. de. See note under Brunhoff, J. de. The story of Babar, the little elephant **E**
Babar and the professor. Brunhoff, L. de. See note under Brunhoff, J. de. The story of Babar, the little elephant **E**
Babar and the Wully-Wully. Brunhoff, L. de. See note under Brunhoff, J. de. The story of Babar, the little elephant **E**
Babar and Zephir. Brunhoff, J. de. See note under Brunhoff, J. de. The story of Babar, the little elephant **E**
Babar comes to America. Brunhoff, L. de. See note under Brunhoff, J. de. The story of Babar, the little elephant **E**
Babar learns to cook. Brunhoff, L. de. See note under Brunhoff, J. de. The story of Babar, the little elephant **E**
Babar loses his crown. Brunhoff, L. de. See note under Brunhoff, J. de. The story of Babar, the little elephant **E**
Babar saves the day. Brunhoff, L. de. See note under Brunhoff, J. de. The story of Babar, the little elephant **E**
Babar the king. Brunhoff, J. de. See note under Brunhoff, J. de. The story of Babar, the little elephant **E**
Babar the magician. Brunhoff, L. de. See note under Brunhoff, J. de. The story of Babar, the little elephant **E**
Babar visits another planet. Brunhoff, J. de. See note under Brunhoff, J. de. The story of Babar, the little elephant **E**
Babar's birthday surprise. Brunhoff, L. de. See note under Brunhoff, J. de. The story of Babar, the little elephant **E**
Babar's castle. Brunhoff, J. de. See note under Brunhoff, J. de. The story of Babar, the little elephant **E**
Babar's cousin. Brunhoff, L. de. See note under Brunhoff, J. de. The story of Babar, the little elephant **E**
Babar's fair. Brunhoff, L. de. See note under Brunhoff, J. de. The story of Babar, the little elephant **E**
Babar's French lessons. Brunhoff, L. de **448**
Babar's mystery. Brunhoff, L. de. See note under Brunhoff, J. de. The story of Babar, the little elephant **E**
Babbitt, Bradford
(illus.) Morgan, A. First chemistry book for boys and girls **540**
Babbitt, Ellen C.
The Banyan Deer
In The Arbuthnot Anthology of children's literature p349-50 **808.8**
In Time for old magic p228-29 **398.2**

Granny's Blackie
In The Arbuthnot Anthology of children's literature p348-49 **808.8**
In Time for old magic p227-28 **398.2**
Jataka tales (1-3) **398.2**
Contents: The monkey and the crocodile; How the turtle saved his own life; The merchant of Seri; The turtle who couldn't stop talking; The ox who won the forfeit; The sandy road; The quarrel of the quails; The measure of rice; The foolish, timid rabbit; The wise and the foolish merchant; The elephant Girly-Face; The banyan deer; The princes and the watersprite; The king's white elephant; The ox who envied the pig; Granny's Blackie; The crab and the crane; Why the owl is not king of the birds
The monkey and the crocodile
In Gruenberg, S. M. ed. Favorite stories old and new p472-73 **808.8**
The turtle who couldn't stop talking
In Gruenberg, S. M. ed. Favorite stories old and new p222 **808.8**
Babbitt, Natalie
The Devil's storybook (4-6) **S C**
Contents: Wishes; The very pretty lady; The harps of Heaven; The imp in the basket; Nuts; A palindrome; Ashes; Perfection; The rose and the minor demon; The power of speech
The eyes of the Amaryllis (5 and up) **Fic**
Goody Hall (4-6) **Fic**
Kneeknock Rise (3-5) **Fic**
The search for delicious (5 and up) **Fic**
The something **E**
Tuck everlasting (4 and up) **Fic**
(illus.) Worth, V. More Small poems **811**
(illus.) Worth, V. Small poems **811**
(illus.) Worth, V. Still More Small poems **811**
Babe Ruth. See Ruth, George Herman
Babe Ruth, Sultan of Swat. Verral, C. S. **92**
Babe the Blue Ox. Shephard, E.
In North American legends p175-83 **398.2**
Babies. See Infants
Baboon-skins
Berger, T. Baboon-skins
In Berger, T. Black fairy tales p124-34 **398.2**
Baboushka and the three kings. Robbins, R. **398.2**
Babson, Walt
All kinds of codes (5 and up) **652**
Baby animals. See Animals—Infancy
Baby Elephant and the secret wishes. Joslin, S. See note under Joslin, S. Brave Baby Elephant **E**
Baby rainstorm. Rounds, G.
In Time to laugh p74-84 **S C**
A **baby** sister for Frances. Hoban, R. See note under Hoban, R. Bedtime for Frances **E**
Baby sitters
Saunders, R. The Franklin Watts Concise guide to babysitting (5 and up) **649**
Fiction
Gripe, M. The night daddy (4-6) **Fic**
Hughes, S. George the babysitter **E**
Towne, M. Goldenrod (4-6) **Fic**
Vestly, A. C. Aurora and Socrates (3-5) **Fic**
A **baby** starts to grow. Showers, P. **612**
The **baby** water buffalo. Cheney, C.
In Cheney, C. Tales from a Taiwan kitchen p133-36 **398.2**
The **baby's** lap book. Chorao, K **398**
Bacchus. See Dionysus

Bailey, Carolyn Sherwin
A basket for Thanksgiving
In Harper, W. comp. The harvest feast p137-47　**S C**
A bow to Thanksgiving
In Thanksgiving p163-74　**394.2**
How ice cream came
In Gruenberg, S. M. ed. Favorite stories old and new p223-25　**808.8**
Miss Hickory (3-5)　**Fic**
Mr Easter Rabbit
In Harper, W. comp. Easter chimes p219-23　**S C**
Newbery Medal acceptance paper
In Newbery Medal books: 1922-1955 p296-99　**028.5**
The sugar egg
In Harper, W. comp. Easter chimes p69-74　**S C**
The tree that trimmed itself
In Association for Childhood Education International. Told under the Christmas tree p41-44　**808.8**
About
See pages in the following book:
Newbery Medal books: 1922-1955 p290-95　**028.5**

Bailey, Joseph H.
(Illus.) Cortesi, W. W. Explore a spooky swamp　**574.92**

Bailey, Margery
Bergamot
In Witches, witches, witches p221-30 **808.8**
The brownie in the house
In Told under the magic umbrella p172-79　**S C**

Baja California
Fiction
O'Dell, S. The black pearl (6 and up)　**Fic**
Natural history
See Natural history—Baja California

Bakacs, George
(illus.) Silverstein, A. Cells: building blocks of life　**574.8**
(illus.) Silverstein, A. The respiratory system　**574.1**

Bake bread! Solomon, H.　**641.8**

Baker, Alan
(illus.) Pearce, P. The battle of Bubble and Squeak　**Fic**

Baker, Augusta
The horned woman
In Witches, witches, witches p 1-4　**808.8**
Storytelling: art and technique　**372.6**

Baker, Betty
At the center of the world (4-6)　**398.2**
Contents: Earth magician; Coyote drowns the world; The killing pot; The monster eagle; The killing of Eetoi; The first war
The Pig War (k-2)　**973.6**
Settlers and strangers (4 and up)　**970.004**
The spirit is willing (5 and up)　**Fic**
Walk the world's rim (5 and up)　**Fic**

Baker, Charlotte
Cockleburr Quarters (4-6)　**Fic**

Baker, Henry
See pages in the following book:
Tunis, E. The Tavern at the ferry p 1-8, 11-14 (5 and up)　**973.2**

Baker, Laura Nelson
The friendly beasts (k-3)　**783.6**

Baker, Margaret
The lost merbaby
In Told under the magic umbrella p133-44　**S C**
Rhyming ink
In Gruenberg, S. M. ed. Favorite stories old and new p478-83　**808.8**
Tomson's Halloween
In Harper, W. comp. Ghosts and goblins p124-40　**398.2**
A week of Sundays
In Gruenberg, S. M. ed. Favorite stories old and new p359-63　**808.8**

Baker, Norman
(jt. auth.) Murphy, B. B. Thor Heyerdahl and the reed boat Ra　**910.4**

Baker, Richard
(jt. comp.) Keller, C. comp. The star spangled banana, and other revolutionary riddles　**793.7**

Baker, Robert H.
(jt. auth.) Zim, H. S. Stars　**523**

Baker, Samm Sinclair
The indoor and outdoor grow-it book (1-6)　**635**

The Baker Street Irregulars in the case of the missing masterpiece. Dicks, T.　**Fic**

The bakers. Adkins, J.　**641.8**

Bakers and bakeries
Jenness, A. The bakery factory: who puts the bread on your table (4 and up)　**664**

Baker's clay craft. See Bread dough craft

Baker's daughter
Bianco, M. W. The baker's daughter
In It's time for story hour p29-35　**372.6**

The Baker's new coat. Self, M. C.
In It's time for story hour p51-59　**372.6**

The bakery factory: who puts the bread on your table. Jenness, A.　**644**

Baking
See pages in the following books:
Coskey, E. Christmas crafts for everyone p35-110 (5 and up)　**745.59**
Girl Scouts of the United States of America. Cooking out-of-doors p99-122 (4 and up)　**641.5**
Girl Scouts of the United States of America. Girl Scout cookbook p108-39 (4 and up)　**641.5**
Kohn, B. The organic living book p62-69 (4 and up)　**635**
See also names of baked products, e.g. Bread
Fiction
Hoban, L. Arthur's Christmas cookies　**E**
The baking contest. Simon, S.
In Fifty plays for junior actors p554-63　**812.08**

Balance of nature. See Ecology

Balarin's goat. Berson, H.　**E**

Balch, Glenn
The book of horses (4 and up)　**636.1**

Baldak Borisievich
Afans'ev, A. Baldak Borisievich
In Afanas'ev, A. Russian fairy tales p90-96　**398.2**

Balder
Barth, E. Balder and the mistletoe (3-5)　**293**
Hodges, M. Baldur and the mistletoe (4-6)　**293**

Bang, Molly Garrett
Wiley and the Hairy Man (1-4)   398.2
(illus.) Bang, B. The old woman and the rice thief   398.2

Bangladesh
See pages in the following book:
Lang, R. The land and people of Pakistan p73-88 (5 and up)   954.9

Bangs, Edward
Steven Kellogg's Yankee Doodle (k-3)   784.7

Bangs, John Kendrick
The water ghost of Harrowby Hall
In Sechrist, E. H. ed. 13 ghostly yarns p45-59   S C

Bank Street College of Education, New York
Merrill, J. The toothpaste millionaire (4-6)   Fic

Banneker, Benjamin
Patterson, L. Benjamin Banneker, genius of early America (3-5)   92
See also pages in the following books:
Hayden, R. C. Seven black American scientists p44-67 (5 and up)   920
Johnson, J. A special bravery p25-29 (2-5)   920
Rollins, C. H. They showed the way p20-23 (5 and up)   920

Banner in the sky. Ullman, J. R.   Fic

Bannerman, Helen
Little Black Sambo
In Stories to dramatize p28-40   372.6

Bannon, Laura
(illus.) Bowman, J. C. Tales from a Finnish tupa   398.2

Bantus
See pages in the following books:
Kaula, E. M. The land and people of Tanzania p24-27 (5 and up)   967.8
Perl, L. East Africa p39-45 (4-6)   967.6

The Banyan Deer. Babbitt, E. C.
In The Arbuthnot Anthology of children's literature p349-50   808.8
In Babbitt, E. C. Jataka tales p58-62   398.2
In Time for old magic p 228-29   398.2

The Banyan Deer. Haviland, V.
In Haviland, V. Favorite fairy tales told in India p91-95   398.2

Barbecue cooking. See Outdoor cookery

Barbee, Lindsey
Columbus sails the sea
In One hundred plays for children p375-81   880.82
The flag of the United States
In One hundred plays for children p796-802   808.82
A guide for George Washington
In One hundred plays for children p297-311   808.82
The holly hangs high
In One hundred plays for children p482-91   808.82
A letter to Lincoln
In One hundred plays for children p268-76   808.82

Barber, Richard
A companion to world mythology (5 and up)   291.03

Barber's clever wife
Kamala and the seven thieves
In Tatterhood, and other tales p55-60   398.2

Barefoot in bed. Jagendorf, M. A.
In Jagendorf, M. A. Noodlehead stories from around the world p43-44   398.2

A bargain for Frances. Hoban, R. See note under Hoban, R. Bedtime for Frances   E

A bargain's a bargain; play. Carlson, B. W.
In Carlson, B. W. The right play for you p32-37   792

Baring, Maurice
The blue rose
In Shedlock, M. L. The art of the storyteller p204-12   372.6

Baring-Gould, Ceil
(ed.) The Annotated Mother Goose, nursery rhymes old and new. See The Annotated Mother Goose, nursery rhymes old and new   398

Baring-Gould, William S.
(ed.) The Annotated Mother Goose, nursery rhymes old and new. See The Annotated Mother Goose, nursery rhymes old and new   398

Barker, Albert
Black on white and read all over (4-6)   686.2

Barkin, Carol
(jt. auth.) James, E. How to keep a secret   652
(jt. auth.) James, E. What do you mean by "average"?   519.5

Barkley, James
(illus.) Armstrong, W. H. Sounder   Fic

Barkley. Hoff, S.   E

Barksdale, Lena
The first Thanksgiving (3-5)   394.2

Barley
See pages in the following book:
Goldin, A. Grass p50-55 (5 and up)   584

Barlowe, Dorothea
(illus.) Zim, H. S. The big cats   599.74
(illus.) Zim, H. S. Seashores   574.92
(illus.) Zim, H. S. Trees   582.16

Barlowe, Sy
(illus.) Zim, H. S. Seashores   574.92
(illus.) Zim, H. S. Trees   582.16

Barmecide's feast
In The Arthur Rackham Fairy book p190-95   398.2

The barn. Schoenherr, J.   Fic

Barnaby, Ralph S.
How to make & fly paper airplanes (5 and up)   629.133

Barnes, Harold
The proud cock
In Shedlock, M. L. The art of the storyteller p191-94   372.6

Barnett, Grace T.
Treasure in the Smith house
In Fifty plays for junior actors p3-18   812.08

Barnett, Ida B. Wells
See pages in the following books:
As I saw it: women who lived the American adventure p178-81 (6 and up)   973
Rollins, C. H. They showed the way p24-26 (5 and up)   920

Barnett, Isa
(illus.) De Kay, O. Meet Andrew Jackson   92

Barth, Edna—*Continued*
Lilies rabbits, and painted eggs (3-6)   394.2
Shamrocks, harps, and shillelaghs (3-6)   394.2
Turkeys Pilgrims, and Indian corn (3-6)   394.2
Witches, pumpkins, and grinning ghosts (3-6)   394.2

Bartholomew and the oobleck. Seuss, Dr. See note under Seuss, Dr. The 500 hats of Bartholomew Cubbins   E

Bartlett, John
(comp.) Familiar quotations   808.88

Bartlett, Robert Merrill
Thanksgiving Day (1-3)   394.2

Bartoli, Jennifer
Nonna   E

Barton, Byron
Wheels   E
(illus.) Adler, D. A. Roman numerals   513
(illus.) Berger, M. The new food book   641
(illus.) Branley, F. M. How little and how much   389
(illus.) Dauer, R. Bullfrog grows up   E
(illus.) Froman, R. Angles are easy as pie   516
(illus.) Greene, C. C. A girl called Al   Fic
(illus.) Prelutsky, J. The snopp on the sidewalk, and other poems   811
(illus.) Schwartz, P. D. You can cook   641.5
(illus.) Simon, S. The paper airplane book   629.133

Barton, Clara Harlowe
Boylston, H. D. Clara Barton, founder of the American Red Cross (4 and up)   92

Barton, Harriett
(illus.) Busch, P. S. Cactus in the desert   583

Bartram, Robert
(illus.) Helfman, H. Tricks with your fingers   793.8

Baruch, Dorothy Walter
Big Fellow's first job
In Gruenberg, S. M. ed. Favorite stories old and new p78-82   808.8

Barwell, Eve
Disguises you can make (4-6)   391

Bascove, Barbara
(illus.) Evslin, B. The green hero   398.2

Baseball
Antonacci, R. J. Baseball for young champions (4 and up)   796.357
Brewster, B. Baseball (3-5)   796.357
Kalb, J. The easy baseball book (1-3)   796.357
Sullivan, G. Baseball's art of hitting (5 and up)   796.357
Sullivan, G. The catcher, baseball's man in charge (5 and up)   796.357
Sullivan, G. Home run! (4 and up)   796.357
Sullivan, G. Pitchers and pitching (5 and up)   796.357

See also pages in the following books:
The Junior illustrated encyclopedia of sports p31-147 (5 and up)   796.03
Keith, H. Sports and games p16-38 (5 and up)   796

See also Little league baseball; Softball; T-Ball

Biography
Libby, B. The Reggie Jackson story (5 and up)   92
Robinson, J. Breakthrough to the big league (5 and up)   92

Rubin, R. Lou Gehrig: courageous star (5 and up)   92
Rudeen, K. Jackie Robinson (2-4)   92
Rudeen, K. Roberto Clemente (2-4)   92
Sullivan, G. Willie Mays (1-3)   92
Verral, C. S. Babe Ruth, Sultan of Swat (3-6)   92

Encyclopedias
Turkin, H. The official encyclopedia of baseball   796.357

Fiction
Cohen, B. Thank you, Jackie Robinson (4-6)   Fic
Isadora, R. Max   E
Kessler, L. Here comes the strikeout   E
Slote, A. Matt Gargan's boy (4 and up)   Fic

Poetry
Thayer, E. L. Casey at the bat   811

Statistics
See pages in the following book:
Arthur, L. Sportsmath: how it works p30-48 (4-6)   796

Baseball for young champions. Antonacci, R. J.   796.357

The **baseball** trick. Corbett, S. See note under Corbett, S. The lemonade trick   Fic

Baseball's art of hitting. Sullivan, G.   796.357

Bashfulness
Fiction
Lexau, J. M. Benjie   E

Basic basketball strategy. Knosher, H.   796.32
Basic football strategy. Dolan, E. F.   796.332
Basic media skills through games. Bell, I. W.   371.3

Basil in Mexico. Titus, E. See note under Titus, E. Basil of Baker Street   Fic
Basil of Baker Street. Titus, E.   Fic

A **basket** for Thanksgiving. Bailey, C. S.
In Harper, W. comp. The harvest feast p137-47   S C

Basket making
See pages in the following books:
Gilbreath, A. Fun with weaving p72-94 (4-6)   746.1
Hofsinde, R. Indian arts p48-54 (4-6)   709.01

Basketball
Antonacci, R. J. Basketball for young champions (5 and up)   796.32
Coombs, C. Be a winner in basketball (5 and up)   796.32
Gault, C. The Harlem Globetrotters and basketball's funniest games (3-6)   796.32
Knosher, H. Basic basketball strategy (4 and up)   796.32
Monroe, E. The basketball skill book (4 and up)   796.32
Sullivan, G. Better basketball for girls (5 and up)   796.32
Sullivan, G. This is pro basketball (5 and up)   796.32

See also pages in the following books:
The Junior illustrated encyclopedia of sports p149-96 (5 and up)   796.03
Keith, H. Sports and games p39-66 (5 and up)   796

Basketball—*Continued*

Biography

Devaney, J. The story of basketball (5 and up) **796.32**

Devaney, J. Tiny! The story of Nate Archibald (4 and up) **92**

Rudeen, K. Wilt Chamberlain (2-5) **92**

Dictionaries

Clark, S. Illustrated basketball dictionary for young people (3-6) **796.32**

Liss, H. Basketball talk for beginners (4 and up) **796.32**

History

Devaney, J. The story of basketball (5 and up) **796.32**

Statistics

See pages in the following book:

Arthur, L. Sportsmath: how it works p49-63 (4-6) **796**

Basketball for young champions. Antonacci, R. J. **796.32**

The **basketball** skill book. Monroe, E. **796.32**

Basketball talk for beginners. Liss, H. **796.32**

Baskets in a little cart. Manning-Sanders, R. *In* Manning-Sanders, R. A book of dragons p95-102 **398.2**

Baskin, Barbara Holland

Notes from a different drummer **016.8**

(ed.) The Special child in the library. See The Special child in the library **027.62**

Baskin, Hosea

Hosie's alphabet. See Hosie's alphabet **E**

Baskin, Leonard

(illus.) Hosie's alphabet. See Hosie's alphabet **E**

(illus.) Hosie's aviary. See Hosie's aviary **598**

(illus.) Hughes, T. Moon-whales, and other Moon poems **821**

(illus.) Hughes, T. Season songs **821**

Baskin, Tobias

Hosie's aviary. See Hosie's aviary **598**

Bason, Lillian

Spiders (k-3) **595.4**

The **Bassumtyte** treasure. Curry, J. L. **Fic**

Bastianelo. Haviland, V. *In* Haviland, V. Favorite fairy tales told in Italy p55-66 **398.2**

Bat. See Bats

The **bat.** Leen, N. **599.4**

The **bat-poet.** Jarrell, R. **Fic**

Bates, Mrs D. B.

See pages in the following book:

As I saw it: women who lived the American adventure p65-75 (6 and up) **973**

Bates, Daisy (Gatson)

See pages in the following book:

Alexander, R. P. comp. Young and black in America p39-56 (6 and up) **920**

Bates, Katharine Lee

See pages in the following book:

Browne, C. A. The story of our national ballads p230-37 (5 and up) **784.7**

Bathyscaphe

See pages in the following book:

Berger, M. Oceanography lab p48-57 (4-6) **551.46**

Batlle y Ordóñez, José

See pages in the following book:

Dobler, L. The land and people of Uruguay p58-62 (5 and up) **989.5**

Batrachia. See Amphibians

Bats

Kaufmann, J. Bats in the dark (1-3) **599.4**

Lauber, P. Bats (4-6) **599.4**

Lavine, S. A. Wonders of the bat world (4 and up) **599.4**

Leen, N. The bat (4 and up) **599.4**

See also pages in the following books:

Batten, M. The tropical forest p97-102 (5 and up) **574.5**

Brady, I. Wild babies p16-23 (4-6) **591.3**

Cohen, D. Night animals p52-58 (4-6) **591.5**

National Geographic Society. Wild animals of North America p47-75 **599**

Shuttlesworth, D. E. Animals that frighten people p51-61 (5 and up) **591.5**

Fiction

Jarrell, R. The bat-poet (2-4) **Fic**

Bats in the dark. Kaufmann, J. **599.4**

Battaglia, Aurelius

(illus.) The Fireside book of favorite American songs. See The Fireside book of favorite American songs **784.7**

Batten, John D.

(illus.) Indian fairy tales. See Indian fairy tales **398.2**

(illus.) Jacobs, J. English fairy tales **398.2**

Batten, Mary

The tropical forest (5 and up) **574.5**

Batterberry, Ariane Ruskin

The Pantheon Story of American art for young people (5 and up) **709.73**

The Pantheon Story of art for young people (5 and up) **709**

Batterberry, Michael

(jt. auth.) Batterberry, A. R. The Pantheon Story of American art for young people **709.73**

Batteries, Electric. See Electric batteries

Battle in the Arctic seas. Taylor, T. **940.54**

A **battle** nobody won. Thompson, V. L. *In* Thompson, V. L. Hawaiian myths of earth p15-19 **398.2**

The **battle** of Bay Minette. Jagendorf, M. A. *In* Jagendorf, M. A. Folk stories of the South p19-22 **398.2**

The **Battle** of Britain. Hough, R. **940.54**

The **Battle** of Britain. Reynolds, Q. **940.54**

The **battle** of Bubble and Squeak. Pearce, B. **Fic**

Battle of New Orleans, 1815. See New Orleans, Battle of, 1815

Battle of the birds

Campbell, J. F. The battle of the birds *In* Fairy tales from many lands p15-27 **398.2**

The **battle** of Wednesday week. See Willard, B. Storm from the west **Fic**

The **battlement** garden. Hodges, C. W. **942.05**

Battles, Edith

What does the rooster say, Yoshio? **E**

Battles

Poetry

See pages in the following book:

Parker, E. ed. 100 more story poems p145-85 (6 and up) **821.08**

Baucis
See pages in the following book:
Gates, D. Lord of the sky: Zeus p37-42 (4 and up) 292

Baudouy, Michel-Aimé
Old One-Toe (5 and up) Fic

Bauer, Caroline Feller
Handbook for storytellers 372.6

Bauer, John
(illus.) Olenius, E. comp. Great Swedish fairy tales 398.2

Bauer, Marion Dane
Shelter from the wind (5 and up) Fic

Bauernschmidt, Marjorie
(illus.) Morrison, L. comp. A diller, a dollar 808.88
(illus.) Morrison, L. comp. Remember me when this you see 808.88

Baum, L. Frank
Dorothy meets the Wizard
In The Golden Treasury of children's literature p256-70 808.8
The marvelous land of Oz. See note under Baum, L. F. The Wizard of Oz Fic
The patchwork girl of Oz. See note under Baum, L. F. The Wizard of Oz Fic
The Wizard of Oz (3-6) Fic
The Wizard of Oz; dramatization. See Schwartz, L. S. The Wizard of Oz

About
See pages in the following book:
Only connect p156-69 028.5

Baum, Willi
(illus.) Fletcher, A. M. Fishes dangerous to man 597

Bauman, A. F.
Santa's alphabet
In On stage for Christmas p374-82 812.08

Baumann, Elwood D.
The Devil's Triangle (6 and up) 001.9

Baumann, Hans
The caves of the great hunters (5 and up) 930.1
In the land of Ur (6 and up) 935
The stolen fire (4-6) 398.2
Contents: Staver and Vassilissa; Dobrinya at the Saracens' Mount; Urismag; George in the realm of darkness; Tardanak; Kara Khan's daughter; The herald of war; Big Kihuo and Little Kihuo; Nana Miriam; Mbega the kigego; The leopard; The stolen fire; Etana's flight to Heaven; Muchukunda and Krishna; Kutune Shirka and the golden otter; Isanagi and Isanami; Kesar of Ling and the giant of the north; Girrowin; The Prince of the House of Liu; Prince Five-Weapons; One-Two-Man and Stone-shirt; The flute player; Smoking Star; Vitziton and the first quarrel; The seven deeds of Onkoito; Norwan; After the great fire

Bavaria
See pages in the following book:
National Geographic Society. The Alps p100-19 (6 and up) 914.94

Bavosi, John
(illus.) Parker, S. Life before birth: the first nine months 612

Bawden, Nina
Carrie's war (4 and up) Fic
The peppermint pig (5 and up) Fic
Rebel on a rock (5 and up) Fic
The robbers (5 and up) Fic
The runaway summer (4-6) Fic
The witch's daughter (4 and up) Fic

About
See pages in the following book:
Townsend, J. R. A sounding of storytellers p18-29 028.5

Bay, J. C.
Hatch, M. C. 13 Danish tales 398.2

Bayless, Roger
(illus.) Kohl, J. The view from the oak 591.5

Bayley, Nicola
Nicola Bayley's Book of nursery rhymes. See Nicola Bayley's Book of nursery rhymes 398

Baylor, Byrd
Before you came this way (1-4) 709.01
The desert is theirs (1-4) 574.5
Everybody needs a rock E
Guess who my favorite person is E
Hawk, I'm your brother E
The other way to listen E
Sometimes I dance mountains (k-3) 792.8
They put on masks (1-4) 391
The way to start a day (1-3) 291.4
We walk in sandy places (k-2) 591.5
When clay sings (1-4) 970.004
Your own best secret place E
For another title by this author see Schweitzer, Byrd Baylor

Baynes, Pauline
(illus.) Barber, R. A companion to world mythology 291.03
(illus.) Lewis, C. S. The lion, the witch and the wardrobe Fic
(illus.) The Puffin Book of nursery rhymes. See The Puffin Book of nursery rhymes 398
(illus.) Tolkien, J. R. R. Farmer Giles of Ham Fic
(illus.) Tolkien, J. R. R. Smith of Wooton Major Fic
(illus.) Uden, G. A dictionary of chivalry 940.1

Be a frog, a bird, or a tree. Carr, R. 613.7
Be a rockhound. Keen, M. L. 549
Be a smart shopper. Gay, K. 640.73
Be a winner in basketball. Coombs, C. 796.32
Be a winner in football. Coombs, C. 796.332
Be a winner in ice hockey. Coombs, C. 796.96
Be a winner in soccer. Coombs, C. 796.334
Be a winner in tennis. Coombs, C. 796.342
Be a winner in track and field. Coombs, C. 796.4

Be nice to spiders. Graham, M. B. E

Beach, Marcia Moray
On the fence
In Fifty plays for junior actors p19-34 812.08

The **beachcomber's** book. Kohn, B. 745.5

Beaches
See also Seashore

Fiction
Asch, F. Sand cake E
Burningham, J. Come away from the water, Shirley E

The **beaded** moccasins. Bennett, R.
In Bennett, R. Creative plays and programs for holidays p202-09 812

Beadwork
Hofsinde, R. Indian beadwork (5 and up)
746.5
See also pages in the following book:
D'Amato, J. American Indian craft inspirations p14-34 (5 and up)
745.5

Beady Bear. Freeman, D.   **E**

Beale Street folks. Jagendorf, M. A.
In Jagendorf, M. A. Folk stories of the South p260-65   398.2

Bealer, Alex W.
Only the names remain (4-6)   970.004

Bealmear, J. H.
The covetous Councilman
In Dramatized folk tales of the world p504-13   812.08

Beals, Carleton
The incredible Incas: yesterday and today (5 and up)   985

The **beam.** Grimm, J.
In Grimm, J. The complete Grimm's fairy tales p645   398.2

Beam of straw
Grimm, J. The beam
In Grimm, J. The complete Grimm's fairy tales p645   398.2

Beame, Rona
Emergency! (3-6)   362.1
Ladder Company 108 (3-5)   363.3

The **bean** boy. Bowden, J. C.   398.2

The **bean** Boy. Shannon, M.
In It's time for story hour p46-50   372.6
In Told under the magic umbrella p165-71   **S C**

Beans
See pages in the following books:
Hays, W. P. Foods the Indians gave us p26-52 (5 and up)   641.3
Lavine, S. A. Indian corn and other gifts p37-46 (4 and up)   641.3

Beany. Feder, J.   **E**

The **bear.** Afanas'ev, A.
In Afanas'ev, A. Russian fairy tales p74-75   398.2

Bear and skrattel
The Cat on the Dovrefell   398.2
Grimm, J. The bear and the skrattel
In Mayne, W. ed. Ghosts p87-97   820.8

Bear and the cock
Afanas'ev, A. The bear and the cock
In Afanas'ev, A. Russian fairy tales p455-56   398.2

The **bear** and the kingbird. Grimm, J.   398.2
See also Wren and the bear

The **bear** and the people. Zimnik, R.   **Fic**

The **bear** and the skrattel. Grimm, J.
In Mayne, W. ed. Ghosts p87-97   820.8
See also Bear and skrattel

Bear and the wildcat. Credle, E.
In Credle, E. Tall tales from the high hills, and other stories p27-29   398.2

A **bear** as big as a cloud. Stoutenburg, A.
In Stoutenburg, A. American tall-tale animals p34-44   398.2

A **bear** called Paddington. Bond, M.   **Fic**

Bear Circus. Du Bois, W. P.   **E**

Bear Cub Scout book. Boys Scouts of America   369.43

Bear goes fishing. Bowman, J. C.
In Bowman, J. C. Tales from a Finnish tupa p263   398.2
See also Why the bear has a stumpy tail

Bear in the black hat. Credle, E.
In Credle, E. Tall tales from the high hills, and other stories p55-63   398.2

Bear mouse. Freschet, B.   599.32

Bear says, North
Bowman, J. C. Stupid bear
In Bowman, J. C. Tales from a Finnish tupa p257   398.2

Bear, the dog, and the cat
Afanas'ev, A. The bear, the dog, and the cat
In Afanas'ev, A. Russian fairy tales p453-55   398.2

Beard, Daniel Carter
Blassingame, W. Dan Beard, scoutmaster of America (3-5)   92

Bears
Morey, W. Operation blue bear (4-6)   599.74
See also pages in the following books:
Brady, I. Wild babies p42-50 (4-6)   591.3
Clemens, V. P. Super animals and their unusual careers p181-90 (4 and up)   636.08
Shuttlesworth, D. E. Animals that frighten people p30-40 (5 and up)   591.5
See also Grizzly bear; Polar bears

Drama
Bradley, A. Paddington on stage (2-5)   822

Fiction
Alexander, M. Blackboard bear   **E**
Asch, F. Moon Bear   **E**
Asch, F. Sand cake   **E**
Berenstain, S. Bears on wheels   **E**
Bishop, C. H. Twenty-two bears   **E**
Bond, M. A bear called Paddington (2-5)   **Fic**
Dalgliesh, A. The bears on Hemlock Mountain (1-4)   **Fic**
Delton, J. Two good friends   **E**
Erskine, J. The snowman   **E**
Gackenbach, D. Hound and Bear   **E**
Galdone, P. The three bears (k-2)   398.2
Johnson, A. The grizzly (5 and up)   **Fic**
Lipkind, W. Nubber Bear   **E**
McCloskey, R. Blueberries for Sal   **E**
Mack, S. 10 bears in my bed   **E**
McLeod, E. W. The bear's bicycle   **E**
McPhail, D. The bear's toothache   **E**
Milne, A. A. The house at Pooh Corner (1-4)   **Fic**
Milne, A. A. The Pooh story book (1-4)   **Fic**
Milne, A. A. Winnie-the-Pooh (1-4)   **Fic**
Milne, A. A. The world of Pooh (1-4)   **Fic**
Minarik, E. H. Little Bear   **E**
Morey, W. Gentle Ben (5 and up)   **Fic**
Peet, B. Big bad Bruce   **E**
Turkle, B. Deep in the forest   **E**
Ward, L. The biggest bear   **E**
Watanabe, Shigeo. How do I put it on? Getting dressed   **E**
Ylla. Two little bears   **E**
Zimnik, R. The bear and the people (3-6)   **Fic**

The **bear's** bicycle. McLeod, E. W.   **E**

Beginning stamp collecting. Olcheski, B. **769.56**

Beginning-to-read riddles and jokes. Gilbreath, A. T. **793.7**

Behavior. See Human behavior

Behind the back of the mountain. Aardema, V. **398.2**

Behind the scenes at the aquarium. Paige, D. **639.3**

Behind the sealed door. Swinburne, I. **932**

Behn, Harry
The little hill (1-4) **811**
(comp.) Cricket songs. See Cricket songs **895.6**
(comp.) More Cricket songs. See More Cricket songs **895.6**

Behr, Joyce
(illus.) Rosenbloom, J. Twist these on your tongue **808.88**

Behr, Marion
(illus.) Lazar, W. The Jewish holiday book **394.2**

Belgium
Loder, D. The land and people of Belgium (5 and up) **949.3**

Social life and customs
Sechrist, E. H. Christmas everywhere p100-06 **394.2**

Belgrade
See also pages in the following books:
Kostich, D. D. The land and people of the Balkans p21-24 (5 and up) **949.6**

Belief and doubt
See also Truth

Bell, Alexander Graham
Shippen, K. B. Mr Bell invents the telephone (4 and up) **92**
See also pages in the following book:
Cottler, J. Heroes of civilization p239-48 (5 and up) **920**

Bell, Corydon
(illus.) Diggins, J. E. String, straightedge, and shadow **516**

Bell, Giorgetta
(illus.) Coskey, E. Easter eggs for everyone **745.594**

Bell, Irene Wood
Basic media skills through games **371.3**

Bell, Thelma Harrington
Black Face
In Gruenberg, S. M. ed. Favorite stories old and new p169-76 **808.8**

Bell
Andersen, H. C. The bell
In Andersen, H. C. The complete fairy tales and stories p275-79 **S C**

Bell-deep
Andersen, H. C. The bell deep
In Andersen, H. C. The complete fairy tales and stories p588-91 **S C**

The bell ringer of Pinsk. Kelly, E. P.
In Christmas stories round the world p61-71 **S C**
In Harper, W. comp. Merry Christmas to you p68-86 **S C**

Bellairs, John
The figure in the shadows. See note under Bellairs, J. The house with the clock in its walls **Fic**
The house with a clock in its walls (5 and up) **Fic**

The letter, the witch, and the ring. See note under Bellairs, J. The house with the clock in its walls **Fic**
The treasure of Alpheus Winterborn (5 and up) **Fic**

Bellamy, Charles
See pages in the following book:
Whipple, A. B. C. Famous pirates of the New World p128-30 (5 and up) **910.4**

Bellerophon
See pages in the following book:
Gates, D. The warrior goddess: Athena p50-61 (4 and up) **292**

Belling the tiger. Stolz, M. **Fic**

Belloc, Hilaire
The bad child's book of beasts
In Belloc, H. The bad child's book of beasts, and More beasts for worse children, and A moral alphabet **821**
The bad child's book of beasts, and More beasts for worse children, and A moral alphabet (1-4) **821**
A moral alphabet
In Belloc, H. The bad child's book of beasts, and More beasts for worse children, and A moral alphabet **821**
More beasts for worse children
In Belloc, H. The bad child's book of beasts, and More beasts for worse children, and A moral alphabet **821**

Bells
Bailey, B. Bells, bells, bells (4 and up) **789**
Yolen, J. Ring out! (5 and up) **789**

Poetry
See pages in the following book:
Yolen, J. Ring out! p113-22 (5 and up) **789**

Bells, bells, bells. Bailey, B. **789**

Belmont antics. Jagendorf, M. A.
In Jagendorf, M. A. Noodlehead stories from around the world p229-33 **398.2**

Beloved Benjamin is waiting. Karl, J. E. **Fic**

Below the root. Snyder, Z. K. **Fic**

Belpré, Pura
Dance of the animals (k-2) **398.2**
Once in Puerto Rico (3-6) **398.2**
Contents: The land of brave men; The legend of the Royal Palm; Guaní; The legend of the hummingbird; Amapola and the butterfly; Iviahoca; Yuisa and Pedro Mexías; The legend of Ceiba of Ponce; The little blue light; The chapel on Cristo Street; The cistern of San Cristobal; The Rogativa; The miracle of Hormigueros; Pedro Animala and the carrao bird; The stone dog; The parrot who wouldn't say Cataño; Pablo and the pirate's ghost
Perez and Martina (2-4) **398.2**
Santiago **E**
The three Magi
In The Animals' Christmas p62-71 **394.2**
In Holiday ring p247-52 **394.2**

Belting, Natalia
(comp.) Our fathers had powerful songs (3-6) **897**
Whirlwind is a ghost dancing (3-6) **398.2**

Belton, John
Card games (4 and up) **795.4**
Dice games (4 and up) **795.1**
Domino games (4 and up) **795.3**
Solitaire games (4 and up) **795.4**

Beltrán, Alberto
(illus.) Traven, B. The creation of the sun and the moon **398.2**

Benny. Cohen, B.   Fic

Benny's animals, and how he put them in order. Selsam, M. E.   591

Benny's flag. Krasilovsky, P.
In Holiday ring p115-18   394.2

Benny's luck. Aleichem, S.
In Aleichem, S. Holiday tales of Sholom Aleichem p17-44   S C

Ben's trumpet. Isadora, R.   E

Benson, Sally
Stories of the gods and heroes (5 and up)
292

Bensurdatu
Haviland, V. The story of Bensurdatu
In Haviland, V. Favorite fairy tales told in Italy p20-41   398.2

Bentley, Carolyn
(illus.) Brandt, S. R. How to improve your written English   808
(illus.) Eisner, V. Quick and easy holiday costumes   391

Benvenuti
(illus.) The Three little pigs. See The Three little pigs   398.2

Berbers
See pages in the following book:
Spencer, W. The land and people of Morocco p23-27, 36-40 (5 and up)   964

Bereavement
Bernstein, J. E. Loss and how to cope with it (5 and up)   155.9
LeShan, E. Learning to say good-by (4 and up)   155.9

Bibliography
Bernstein, J. E. Books to help children cope with separation and loss   016.3627

Berelson, Howard
(illus) Asimov, I. Animals of the Bible
220.8
(illus.) Fenten, D. X. Gardening . . . naturally   635
(illus.) Fenten, B. Natural foods   641.3

Berends, Polly Berrien
The case of the elevator duck (3-5)   Fic

Berenstain, Jan
(jt. auth.) Berenstain, S. Bears on wheels
E

Berenstain, Michael
The lighthouse book (2-4)   387.1
The ship book (k-3)   387.2

Berenstain, Stan
Bears on wheels   E

Bergamot. Bailey, M.
In Witches, witches, witches p221-30
808.8

Bergaust, Erik
Colonizing space (5 and up)   629.44

Berger, Gilda
Kuwait and the rim of Arabia (4 and up)
953
Physical disabilities (6 and up)   362.4
(jt. auth.) Berger, M. The new food book
641

Berger, Josef
Discoverers of the New World. See Discoverers of the New World   970.01

Berger, Melvin
Animal hospital (4 and up)   636.089
Bionics (6 and up)   617
Building construction (4 and up)   690
Disease detectives (5 and up)   614.4

Energy from the sun (1-3)   621.47
Enzymes in action (6 and up)   574.19
The new food book (4 and up)   641
The new water book (4-6)   553.7
Oceanography lab (4-6)   551.46
Printing plant (4 and up)   686.2
Quasars, pulsars and black holes in space (4 and up)   523
The story of folk music (5 and up)   781.7
The trumpet book (4 and up)   788

Berger, Terry
Black fairy tales (4 and up)   398.2
Contents: The moss-green princess; The serpent's bride; The fairy frog; The enchanted buck; The beauty & the beast; The story of the shining princess; The three little eggs; The rabbit prince; The fairy bird; Baboon-skins
How does it feel when your parents get divorced? (3-6)   306.8
Special friends (1-3)   305.2

Bergman Sucksdorff, Astrid
Chendru: the boy and the tiger (3-6)   954

Berig, Karen
Faulkner, M. I Skate! (5 and up)   92

Bering, Vitus Jonassen
See pages in the following book:
Orlob, H. The Northeast Passage p43-56 (5 and up)   998

Berlin, Irving
See pages in the following books:
Browne, C. A. The story of our national ballads p267-72 (5 and up)   784.7

Berlin
See pages in the following books:
Dornberg, J. The two Germanys p13-30 (5 and up)   943.087
Wohlrabe, R. A. The land and people of Germany p106-13 (5 and up)   943

Fiction
Kästner, E. Emil and the detectives (4-6)
Fic

Berman, Sam
(illus.) Schlein, M. Shapes   E

Bermuda Triangle
Bauman, E. D. The Devil's Triangle (6 and up)   001.9
Cusack, M. J. Is there a Bermuda Triangle? (5 and up)   001.9

Bernard, George
(illus.) The Chicken and the egg. See The Chicken and the egg   636.5
(illus.) Common frog. See Common frog
597.8

Bernard into battle. Sharp, M. See note under Sharp, M. The rescuers   Fic

Bernard the Brave. Sharp, M. See note under Sharp, M. The rescuers   Fic

Bernath, Stefen
(illus.) Huntington, L. P. Simple shelters
728

Bernhard, Josephine B.
Lullaby
In Association for Childhood Education International. Told under the Christmas tree p4-7   808.8

Bernheim, Evelyne
(jt. auth.) Bernheim, M. The drums speak
966
(jt. auth.) Bernheim, M. In Africa   960

Bernheim, Marc
The drums speak (3-5)   966
In Africa (k-3)   960

Birds—*Continued*
Uruguay
See pages in the following book:
Dobler, L. The land and people of Uruguay
p20-25 (5 and up)   **989.5**

The West (U.S.)
Peterson, R. T. A field guide to Western
birds   **598**
The **Birds** and the beasts were there   **821.08**
Birds and their nests. Earle, O. L.   **598**
Birds and their nests. Vevers, G.   **598**
Birds are flying. Kaufmann, J.   **598**
Birds as pets. Villiard, P.   **636.6**
Birds at night. Gans, R.   **598**
The **Birds'** Christmas carol. Olfson, L.
In A Treasury of Christmas plays p483-95
                                               812.08
The **birds'** Christmas Carol. Wiggin, K. D.
                                               Fic
Birds eat and eat and eat. Gans, R.   **598**
Birds' eggs. See Birds—Eggs and nests
Birds in flight. Kaufmann, J.   **598**
Birds' nests. See Birds—Eggs and nests
The **birds** of America. Audubon, J. J.   **598**
Birds of prey
Hogner, D. C. Birds of prey (4-6)   **598**
National Geographic Society. Water, prey,
and game birds of North America   **598**
See also names of birds of prey, e.g.
Falcons
Birmingham, Lloyd
(Illus.) Milgrom, H. Understanding weather
                                               551.6
(illus.) Weiss, M. E. Storms—from the in-
side out   **551.5**
Birnbaum, A.
Green eyes   **E**
Biro
(illus.) Baum, L. F. The Wizard of Oz **Fic**
Birth, Multiple
See pages in the following book:
Williams, G. Twins p51-59 (5 and up) **155.4**
See also Twins
Birth control
See pages in the following book:
Johnson, E. W. Love and sex in plain lan-
guage p91-105 (6 and up)   **613.9**
Birth of a foal. Miller, J.   **636.1**
Birth of a forest. Selsam, M. E.   **581.5**
The **birth** of Bran. Stephens, J.
In Stephens, J. Irish fairy tales p91-108
                                               398.2
The **birth** of Simnel cake. Farjeon, E.
In Greene, E. comp. Clever cooks p130-33
                                               398.2
The **birth** of Sunset's kittens. Stevens, C.
                                               636.8
Birth rate
See also Population
A **birthday** for Frances. Hoban, R. See note
under Hoban, R. Bedtime for Frances   **E**
The **birthday** goat. Watson, N. D.   **E**
The **birthday** of the Infanta. Wilde, O.
In Wilde, O. The Happy Prince, and
other stories p70-92   **S C**

The **birthday** tree. Fleischman, P.   **Fic**
The **birthday** visitor. Uchida, Yoshiko   **E**
A **birthday** wish. Emberley, E.   **E**
Birthdays
Price, C. Happy days (4-6)   **392**
Bibliography
Gregory, R. W. Anniversaries and holidays
                                               394.2
Fiction
Aliki. June 7!   **E**
Barrett, J. Benjamin's 365 birthdays   **E**
Carrick, C. Paul's Christmas birthday   **E**
Emberley, E. A birthday wish   **E**
Flack, M. Ask Mr Bear   **E**
Goodall, J. S. Shrewbettina's birthday   **E**
Hutchins, P. Happy birthday, Sam   **E**
Lexau, J. M. Me day   **E**
Lexau, J. M. Striped ice cream (2-4)   **Fic**
Little, L. J. I can do it by myself   **E**
Uchida, Yoshiko. The birthday visitor   **E**
Zolotow, C. Mr Rabbit and the lovely pres-
ents   **E**
Birthdays of freedom. Foster, G.   **909**
Bishop, Bonnie
No one noticed Ralph   **E**
Ralph rides away. See note under Bishop, B.
No one noticed Ralph   **E**
Bishop, Claire Huchet
The ferryman
In With a deep sea smile p42-55   **372.6**
The five Chinese brothers (1-3)   **398.2**
The man who lost his head   **E**
Martin de Porres, hero (5 and up)   **92**
Twenty-two bears   **E**
Bishop, Isabella Lucy (Bird)
See pages in the following book:
As I saw it: women who lived the American
adventure p77-79 (6 and up)   **973**
Bishop of Börglum and his kindred
Andersen, H. C. The Bishop of Börglum
Cloister and his kinsmen
In Andersen, H. C. The complete fairy
tales and stories p820-26   **S C**
The **Bishop** of Börglum Cloister and his kins-
men. Andersen, H. C.
In Andersen, H. C. The complete fairy
tales and stories p820-26   **S C**
The **bishop's** candlesticks. Hugo, V.
In Stories to dramatize p323-29   **372.6**
Bismarck (Battleship)
Shirer, W. L. The sinking of the Bismarck
(5 and up)   **940.54**
Biter bit
The Biter bit
In Green fairy book p198-206   **398.2**
Biters, hoppers, and feathered floppers. Stout-
enburg, A.
In Stoutenburg, A. American tall-tale ani-
mals p118-28   **398.2**
Bitter, Gary G.
Exploring with metrics (3-5)   **389**
Exploring with pocket calculators (3-6)
                                               510.28
Bittern and the hoopoe
Grimm, J. The bittern and the hoopoe
In Grimm, J. The complete Grimm's fairy
tales p710-11   **398.2**

Bjorklund, Lorence F.
  (illus.) Burt, O. W. Negroes in the early West   **920**
  (illus.) Freedman, R. How birds fly   **598**
  (illus.) Freeman, M. B. Stars and stripes   **929.9**
  (illus.) May, J. How the animals came to North America   **591.5**
  (illus.) Showers, P. Indian festivals **394.2**

Black, Irma Simonton
  Spoodles: the puppy who learned
    In Gruenberg, S. M. comp. Let's hear a story p62-67   **808.8**
  The Black American in books for children: readings in racism   **028.5**

Black Americans. See Blacks

Black artists
  Feelings, T. Black pilgrimage (5 and up)   **92**

Black athletes
  Devaney, J. Tiny! The story of Nate Archibald (4 and up)   **92**
  Libby, B. The Reggie Jackson story (5 and up)   **92**
  Lipsyte, R. Free to be Muhammad Ali (5 and up)   **92**
  Robinson, J. Breakthrough to the big league (5 and up)   **92**
  Rudeen, K. Jackie Robinson (2-4)   **92**
  Rudeen, K. Wilt Chamberlain (2-5)   **92**
  Sullivan, G. Willie Mays (1-3)   **92**

Black authors
  Egypt, O. S. James Weldon Johnson (2-4)   **92**
  Myers, E. P. Langston Hughes: poet of his people (4-6)   **92**
  Rollins, C. Famous American Negro poets (5 and up)   **920**
  Schultz, P. H. Paul Laurence Dunbar: black poet laureate (4 and up)   **92**
  Walker, A. Langston Hughes, American poet (2-4)   **92**

The **Black B C's.** Clifton, L.   **305.8**

Black Beauty. Sewell, A.   **Fic**

Black Bull of Norroway
  The Black Bull of Norroway
    In Blue fairy book p344-48   **398.2**
    In Tatterhood, and other tales p49-54   **398.2**
  Steel, F. A. The Black Bull of Norroway
    In The Arbuthnot Anthology of children's literature p162-66   **808.8**
    In Time for old magic p21-25   **398.2**
    See also Whitebear Whittington

Black cat of the witch-dance-place
  Olcott, F. J. The Black cat of the Witch-Dance-Place
    In Witches, witches, witches p194-96   **808.8**

The **black cat's eyes.** Leach, M.
  In Leach, M. Whistle in the graveyard p95-97   **398.2**

The **black cauldron.** Alexander, L. See note under Alexander, L. The book of three   **Fic**

The **Black experience in children's audiovisual materials**   **016.3058**

The **Black experience in children's books**   **016.3058**

Black Face. Bell, T. H.
  In Gruenberg, S. M. ed. Favorite stories old and new p169-76   **808.8**

Black fairy tales. Berger, T.   **398.2**

Black fighting men in U.S. history. Wakin, E.   **355**

Black folklore. See Folklore, Black

The **black ghost dog.** Jagendorf, M. A.
  In Jagendorf, M. A. Folk stories of the South p308-12   **398.2**

Black Gold. Henry, M.   **Fic**

Black Gold (Race horse)

Fiction

  Henry, M. Black Gold (4-6)   **Fic**

Black Hawk, Sauk chief
  See pages in the following book:
    In Johnston, J. The Indians and the strangers p83-88 (2-5)   **920**

Black hearts in Battersea. Aiken, J. See note under Aiken, J. The wolves of Willoughby Chase   **Fic**

Black heroes of the American Revolution. Davis, B.   **973.3**

Black holes (Astronomy)
  Asimov, I. How did we find out about black holes? (5 and up)   **523.8**
    See also pages in the following book:
  Berger, M. Quasars, pulsars and black holes in space p45-49 (4 and up)   **523**

Black in America. Jackson, J.   **305.8**

Black inventors
  Hayden, R. C. Eight black American inventors (5 and up)   **920**

Black is brown is tan. Adoff, A.   **E**

Black literature (American) See American literature—Black authors

Black magic (Witchcraft) See Witchcraft

The **black mask trick.** Corbett, S. See note under Corbett, S. The lemonade trick   **Fic**

Black musicians
  Cornell, J. G. Louis Armstrong, Ambassador Satchmo (4-6)   **92**
  Evans, M. Scott Joplin and the ragtime years (5 and up)   **92**
  Iverson, G. Louis Armstrong (2-4)   **92**
  Mathis, S. B. Ray Charles (2-5)   **92**
  Montgomery, E. R. Duke Ellington: king of jazz (3-5)   **92**
  Montgomery, E. R. William C. Handy: father of the blues (3-4)   **92**

Fiction

  Isadora, R. Ben's trumpet   **E**

The **black mustanger.** Wormser, R.   **Fic**

Black on white and read all over. Barker, A.   **686.2**

Black out loud. Adoff, A. ed.   **811.08**

The **black pearl.** O'Dell, S.   **Fic**

Black pilgrimage. Feelings, T.   **92**

Black poetry. See American poetry—Black authors

Black politicians. See Politicians, British

Black, red, and gold. Manning-Sanders, R.
  In Manning-Sanders, R. A book of enchantments and curses p82-93   **398.2**

Black scientists
  Aliki. A weed is a flower: the life of George Washington Carver (k-3)   **92**
  Bertol, R. Charles Drew (3-5)   **92**
  Hayden, R. C. Seven Black American scientists (5 and up)   **920**

Blackfoot Indians. See Siksika Indians

Blackmail

In Jataka tales p16-19   398.2

Blackout. Rockwell, A.   E

Blackouts. See Electric power failures

Blacks

Clifton, L. The Black B C's (k-2)   305.8

See also Slavery in the United States

Bibliography

The Black experience in children's books
    016.3058

See also pages in the following book:

Meacham, M. Information sources in children's literature p108-17   011

Biography

Adoff, A. Malcolm X (2-5)   92

Alexander, R. P. comp. Young and black in America (6 and up)   920

Bishop, C. H. Martin de Porres, hero (5 and up)   92

Bontemps, A. Frederick Douglass: slave-fighter-freeman (4 and up)   92

Burt, O. W. Negroes in the early West (4-6)   920

Chittenden, E. F. Profiles in black and white (5 and up)   920

Clayton, E. Martin Luther King: the peaceful warrior (5 and up)   92

DeKay, J. T. Meet Martin Luther King, Jr. (2-5)   92

Faber, D. The assassination of Martin Luther King, Jr. (5 and up)   92

Felton, H. W. Edward Rose: Negro trail blazer (5 and up)   92

Freedman, F. B. Two tickets to freedom; the true story of Ellen and William Craft, fugitive slaves (4-6)   92

Gordy, B. Movin' up (5 and up)   92

Graham, S. Booker T. Washington: educator of hand, head, and heart (5 and up)   92

Greenfield, E. Paul Robeson (2-5)   92

Hamilton, V. Paul Robeson (6 and up)   92

Hamilton, V. W. E. B. Du Bois (6 and up)   92

Haskins, J. The life and death of Martin Luther King, Jr. (5 and up)   92

Johnston, J. A special bravery (2-5)   920

Rollins, C. H. They showed the way (5 and up)   920

Sterling, P. Four took freedom (4-6)   920

Syme, R. Toussaint: the black liberator (5 and up)   92

Tobias, T. Arthur Mitchell (3-5)   92

Yates, E. Amos Fortune, free man (4 and up)   92

Young, M. B. The picture life of Martin Luther King, Jr. (1-3)   92

Civil rights

Clayton, E. Martin Luther King: the peaceful warrior (5 and up)   92

DeKay, J. T. Meet Martin Luther King, Jr. (2-5)   92

Greenfield, E. Rosa Parks (2-4)   92

Griffin, J. H. A time to be human (5 and up)   305.8

Haskins, J. The life and death of Martin Luther King, Jr. (5 and up)   92

Jackson, J. Black in America (6 and up)   305.8

Jordan, J. Fannie Lou Hamer (2-4)   92

Sterling, D. Tear down the walls! (6 and up)   323.4

Young, M. B. The picture life of Martin Luther King, Jr. (1-3)   92

See also pages in the following books:

The Arbuthnot Anthology of children's literature p882-86   808.8

Kohn, B. The spirit and the letter p105-18 (5 and up)   323.4

Sechrist, E. H. It's time for brotherhood p85-109 (5 and up)   361

Fiction

Alexander, M. Bobo's dream   E

Armstrong, W. H. Sounder (5 and up)   Fic

Bacon, M. Sophia Scrooby preserved (5 and up)   Fic

Baker, C. Cockleburr Quarters (4-6)   Fic

Brenner, B. Wagon wheels (2-4)   Fic

Burchard, P. Bimby (4-6)   Fic

Caines, J. Abby   E

Carlson, N. S. Ann Aurelia and Dorothy (4-6)   Fic

Childress, A. A hero ain't nothin' but a sandwich (6 and up)   Fic

Clifton, L. Amifika   E

Clifton, L. The boy who didn't believe in spring   E

Clifton, L. The lucky stone (3-5)   Fic

Clifton, L. Three wishes   E

Cohen, B. Thank you, Jackie Robinson (4-6)   Fic

Coolidge, O. Come by here (5 and up)   Fic

Curry, J. L. The daybreakers (4 and up)   Fic

Fenner, C. The skates of Uncle Richard (2-4)   Fic

Fife, D. Who's in charge of Lincoln? (2-4)   Fic

Fitzhugh, L. Nobody's family is going to change (5 and up)   Fic

Fox, P. How many miles to Babylon? (4-6)   Fic

Freeman, D. Corduroy   E

Greene, B. Philip Hall likes me. I reckon maybe (4-6)   Fic

Greenfield, E. Me and Neesie   E

Greenfield, E. She come bringing me that little baby girl   E

Greenfield, E. Sister (4 and up)   Fic

Greenfield, E. Talk about a family (3-5)   Fic

Hamilton, V. Arilla Sun Down (6 and up)   Fic

Hamilton, V. The house of Dies Drear (5 and up)   Fic

Hamilton, V. M. C. Higgins, the great (6 and up)   Fic

Hamilton, V. Time-ago lost: more tales of Jahdu (3-5)   S C

Hamilton, V. The time-ago tales of Jahdu (3-5)   S C

Hamilton, V. Zeely (4 and up)   Fic

Hill, E. S. Evan's corner   E

Hunter, K. Soul Brothers & sister Lou (6 and up)   Fic

Jordan, J. New life: new room (2-4)   Fic

Konigsburg, E. L. Jennifer, Hecate, Macbeth, William McKinley, and me, Elizabeth (4-6)   Fic

Lexau, J. M. Benjie   E

Lexau, J. M. I should have stayed in bed   E

Blake, Quentin—*Continued*
(illus.) Franze, N. Agaton Sax and Lispington's grandfather clock **Fic**
(illus.) Hoban, R. How Tom beat Captain Najork and his hired sportsmen **E**
(illus.) Rees, E. Riddles, riddles everywhere **398**

Blanchard, Marjorie Page
The outdoor cookbook (6 and up) **641.5**
Blanche's high-flying Halloween. Embry, M.
In Witches, witches, witches p45-55 **808.8**

Blanco, Tomás
The Child's gifts (5 and up) **232.9**

Bland, Edith (Nesbit)
See pages in the following books:
Horn Book Reflections on children's books and reading p211-17 **028.5**
Townsend, J. R. Written for children p102-06 **028.5**

For another title by this author see Nesbit, E.

Bland, Joellen
Oliver Twist
In Popular plays for classroom reading p266-83 **808.82**

Blanton, Catherine
The dulce man
In One hundred plays for children p23-30 **808.82**

Blass, Jacqueline
(illus.) Weber, A. Elizabeth gets well **362.1**

Blassingame, Wyatt
Dan Beard, scoutmaster of America (3-5) **92**
Story of the Boy Scouts (4 and up) **369.43**
Thor Heyerdahl: Viking scientist (5 and up) **92**
William Beebe: underwater explorer (3-6) **92**
Wonders of crows (5 and up) **598**
Wonders of raccoons (4-6) **599.74**

Blatt, Joseph
(jt. auth.)) Sullivan, M. B. Feeling free **362.4**

Blaze and the forest fire. Anderson, C. W. See note under Anderson, C. W. Billy and Blaze **E**

Blaze and the gray spotted pony. Anderson, C. W. See note under Anderson, C. W. Billy and Blaze **E**

Blaze and the Indian cave. Anderson, C. W. See note under Anderson, C. W. Billy and Blaze **E**

Blaze and the lost quarry. Anderson, C. W. See note under Anderson, C. W. Billy and Blaze **E**

Blaze and the mountain lion. Anderson, C. W. See note under Anderson, C. W. Billy and Blaze **E**

Blaze and Thunderbolt. Anderson, C. W. See note under Anderson, C. W. Billy and Blaze **E**

Blaze finds forgotten roads. Anderson, C. W. See note under Anderson, C. W. Billy and Blaze **E**

Blaze finds the trail. Anderson, C. W. See note under Anderson, C. W. Billy and Blaze **E**

Blaze shows the way. Anderson, C. W. See note under Anderson, C. W. Billy and Blaze **E**

Bleaching
See also Dyes and dyeing

Blechman, R. O.
(illus.) Kohn, B. What a funny thing to say! **422**

Bleeker, Sonia
The Ashanti of Ghana (4 and up) **966.7**
The Masai (4 and up) **967.6**
The Pygmies (4 and up) **967**
The Zulu of South Africa (4 and up) **968**
(jt. auth.) Zim, H. S. Life and death **128**

Blegvad, Erik
(illus.) Hark! Hark! The dogs do bark, and other rhymes about dogs. See Hark! Hark! The dogs do bark, and other rhymes about dogs **398**
(illus.) Mittens for kittens, and other rhymes about cats. See Mittens for kittens, and other rhymes about cats **398**
Self portrait; Erik Blegvad (4-6) **92**
(illus.) This little pig-a-wig, and other rhymes about pigs. See This little pig-a-wig, and other rhymes about pigs **398**
(illus.) Yellow fairy book. See Yellow fairy book **398.2**
(jt. auth.) Blegvad, L. The great hamster hunt **Fic**
(illus.) Bodecker, N. M. The Mushroom Center disaster **Fic**
(illus.) Craft, R. The winter bear **E**
(illus.) Kendall, C. The Gammage Cup **Fic**
(illus.) Norton, M. Bed-knob and broomstick **Fic**
(illus.) O'Connell, J. S. The dollhouse caper **Fic**
(illus.) Selsam, M. E. Plenty of fish **639.3**
(illus.) Viorst, J. The tenth good thing about Barney **E**
(illus.) Watson, N. D. Blueberries lavender **811**

Blegvad, Lenore
The great hamster hunt (1-3) **Fic**
(comp.) Hark! Hark! The dogs do bark, and other rhymes about dogs. See Hark! Hark! The dogs do bark, and other rhymes about dogs **398**
(comp.) Mittens for kittens, and other rhymes about cats. See Mittens for kittens, and other rhymes about cats **398**
(comp.) This little pig-a-wig, and other rhymes about pigs. See This little pig-a-wig, and other rhymes about pigs **398**

Blériot, Louis
See pages in the following book:
Ross, F. Historic plane models p47-51 (5 and up) **629.133**

The **blessed** gift of joy is bestowed upon man. Rasmussen, K.
In North American legends p101-06 **398.2**

Bley, Edgar S.
The best singing games for children of all ages **796.1**

Blind
Brown, M. M. The silent storm [biography of Anne Sullivan Macy] (5 and up) **92**
Davidson, M. Louis Braille (3-5) **92**
Hunter, E. F. Child of the silent night [biography of Laura Dewey Bridgman] (3-5) **92**
Malone, M. Annie Sullivan [biography of Anne Sullivan Macy] (2-4) **92**
Neimark, A. E. Touch of light; the story of Louis Braille (4 and up) **92**

Blue moose. Pinkwater, M.   **Fic**

Blue Mountains
  The Blue Mountains
    In Yellow fairy book p244-54   **398.2**
The blue-nosed witch. Embry, M.   **Fic**

Blue Ridge Mountains
              Fiction
  Credle, E. Down, down the mountain   **E**
The blue rose. Baring, M.
    In Shedlock, M. L. The art of the story-
        teller p204-12   **372.6**
Blue sea. Kalan, R.   **E**

Blue silver. Sandburg, C.
    In Gruenberg, S. M. ed. Favorite stories
        old and new p234-35   **808.8**
    In Sandburg, C. Rootabaga stories v2
        p215-18   **S C**
    In Sandburg, C. The Sandburg treasury
        p159-60   **818**
The blue stone. Kennedy, R.   **Fic**
Blue whale. Cook, J. J.   **599.5**
The blue whale. Grosvenor, D. K.   **599.5**
The blue whale. Mizumura, K.   **599.5**
Blue willow. Gates, D.   **Fic**

Bluebeard
  Perrault, C. Blue Beard
    In The Andrew Lang Fairy tale treasury
        p110-15   **398.2**
    In The Arthur Rackham Fairy book p143-
        52   **398.2**
    In Blue fairy book p290-96   **398.2**
    In The Classic fairy tales p106-09   **398.2**
    In The Golden Treasury of children's lit-
        erature p106-16   **808.8**
    In Perrault, C. Perrault's Complete fairy
        tales p78-88   **398.2**
Blueberries for Sal. McCloskey, R.   **E**
Blueberries lavender. Watson, N. D.   **811**
Blueprints for better reading. Cleary, F. D.
              028.5

Blues (Songs, etc.)
  Montgomery, E. R. William C. Handy: fa-
    ther of the blues (3-4)   **92**

Blumberg, Rhoda
  Sharks (4-6)   **597**
  UFO (5 and up)   **001.9**

Blume, Judy
  Are you there God? It's me, Margaret (5
    and up)   **Fic**
  Freckle juice (2-4)   **Fic**
  It's not the end of the world (4-6)   **Fic**
  Otherwise known as Sheila the Great (4-6)
              Fic
  Tales of a fourth grade nothing (3-6)   **Fic**
  Then again, maybe I won't (5 and up)   **Fic**

Blumengeld, Lenore
  Another way to weigh an elephant
    In Popular plays for classroom reading
        p94-99   **808.82**

Blunden, Godfrey
  The land and people of Australia (5 and up)
              994

Boadicea, Queen
              Fiction
  Sutcliff, R. Song for a dark queen (6 and up)
              Fic

Boars
              Fiction
  Gipson, F. Curly and the wild boar (5 and
    up)   **Fic**

The **boaster** no man could kill. Thompson,
  V. L.
    In Thompson, V. L. Hawaiian tales of
        heroes and champions p66-71   **398.2**
Boat builder; the story of Robert Fulton.
  Judson, C. I.   **92**

Boatbuilding
  See also Shipbuilding
Boating. See Boats and boating
Boats, Submarine. See Submarines

Boats and boating
  Corbett, S. What makes a boat float? (3-5)
              532

  See also pages in the following book:
  Boy Scouts of America. Fieldbook p218-39
              369.43

  See also Sailing; Ships; Steamboats

              Fiction
  Adkins, J. Luther Tarbox (2-4)   **Fic**
  Haas, I. The Maggie B   **E**
Bob o' the Carn. Colwell, E.
    In Colwell, E. Round about and long ago
        p117-21   **398.2**
Bobby's best Hanukkah. Binstock, R. A.
    In Association for Childhood Education
        International. Told under the Christ-
        mas tree p241-53   **808.8**

Bobcat
    See pages in the following books:
  Brady, I. Wild babies p 1-8 (4-6)   **591.3**
  Harris, J. Endangered predators p51-65 (5
    and up)   **599.74**
Bobo's dream. Alexander, M.   **E**

Bobri, Vladimir
  (illus.) Budney, B. A kiss is round   **E**
  (illus.) Gans, R. Icebergs   **551.3**

Bobrizky, George
  (illus.) Mara, T. First steps in ballet   **792.8**
The **Bobtail** monkey
    In Sakade, F. ed. Japanese children's fa-
        vorite stories p113-20   **398.2**

Boccaccio, Tony
  Racquetball basics (4 and up)   **796.34**

Bock, Vera
  (illus.) Bridled with rainbows. See Bridled
    with rainbows   **808.81**

Bock, William
  (illus.) Campbell, E. A. The carving on
    the tree   **973.1**

Bock, William Sauts
  (illus.) Bealer, A. W. Only the names re-
    main   **970.004**

Bodecker, N. M.
  Hurry, hurry, Mary dear! And other non-
    sense poems (2-5)   **811**
  Let's marry said the cherry, and other non-
    sense poems (2-5)   **811**
  The Mushroom Center disaster (2-4)   **Fic**
  (illus.) Eager, E. Half magic   **Fic**
Bodies. Brenner, B.   **612**

Bødker, Cecil
  The leopard (4 and up)   **Fic**
  Silas and Ben-Godik. See note under Bød-
    ker, C. Silas and the black mare   **Fic**
  Silas and the black mare (5 and up)   **Fic**
  Silas and the runaway coach. See note un-
    der Bødker, C. Silas and the black mare
              Fic

Body, Human. See Physiology

Body and mind. See Mind and body

Body language
Castle, S. Face talk, hand talk, body talk (k-2) **153.6**

Body weight control. See Reducing

Bodybuilding, Weight training and. Columbu, F. **796.4**

Boehm, Linda
(illus.) Barnett, N. I know a dentist **617.6**

Boers
See pages in the following book:
Bleeker, S. The Zulu of South Africa p138-43 (4 and up) **968**

Boesen, Victor
Edward S. Curtis, photographer of the North American Indian (5 and up) **92**

The bog king's daughter. Andersen, H. C.
In Andersen, H. C. The complete fairy tales and stories p553-84 **S C**

Bogan, Louise
(comp.) The Golden journey. See The Golden journey **821.08**

Bogardus, Annetje Jans
Spier, P. The legend of New Amsterdam (1-4) **974.7**

Bogart, Gary L.
(ed.) Junior high school library catalog. See Junior high school library catalog **011**

Bogdanovic, Toma
(illus.) Andersen, H. C. The ugly duckling **Fic**

The boggart and the farmer. Colwell, E.
In Colwell, E. Round about and long ago p57-60 **398.2**
See also Farmer Grigg's boggart

Bogle, Kate Cutler
(jt. auth.) Cutler, K. N. Crafts for Christmas **745.59**

Bogs. See Marshes

Bohemia

Folklore
See Folklore—Bohemia

Boiko, Claire
All hands on deck
In Popular plays for classroom reading p206-17 **808.82**
Children's plays for creative actors (3-6) **812**

Contents: Small crimson parasol; Peter, Peter, Peter; Anywhere and everywhere; The wonderful circus of words; The big shoo; Spaceship Santa Maria; Penny wise; Scaredy cat; The wayward witch; The runaway bookmobile; The insatiable dragon; Meet the pilgrims; The Christmas revel; Star bright; Mother Goose's Christmas surprise; A clean sweep; The marvelous Time Machine; Young Abe's destiny; The "T" party; Cupivac; A tale of two drummers; The exterior decorator; Lion to lamb; Cinder-Riley; The snowman who overstayed; All hands on deck; The crocus who couldn't bloom; Sun up; The punctuation proclamation; Terrible Terry's surprise; Trouble in Tree-Land; All about mothers; Operation litterbug; The Franklin reversal; All points West

Cinder-Riley
In Fifty plays for junior actors p54-63 **812.08**

Lady Moon and the thief
In Dramatized folk tales of the world p23-31 **812.08**

Pepe and the cornfield bandit
In Dramatized folk tales of the world p324-33 **812.08**

Take me to your Marshal
In Popular plays for classroom reading p22-31 **808.82**
We interrupt this program
In On stage for Christmas p285-97 **812.08**

Bois, William Pène du. See Du Bois, William Pène

Bojabi tree
Rickert, E. The Bojabi tree
In Told under the magic umbrella p101-12 **S C**

The bold dragoon. Irving, W.
In Sechrist, E. H. ed. 13 ghostly yarns p61-74 **S C**

The bold heroes of Hungry Hill. McManus, S.
In MacManus, S. Hibernian nights p212-23 **398.2**

Bold knight, the apples of youth, and the water of life
Afanas'ev, A. The bold knight, the apples of youth, and the water of life
In Afanas'ev, A. Russian fairy tales p314-20 **398.2**

Bolivia
Warren, L. The land and people of Bolivia (5 and up) **984**

Bolliger, Max
Noah and the rainbow (k-3) **221.9**

Bolognese, Don
Drawing horses and foals (4-6) **743**
(illus.) Balestrino, P. The skeleton inside you **612**
(illus.) Benchley, N. George, the drummer boy **E**
(illus.) Brenner, B. Wagon wheels **Fic**
(illus.) Bulla, C. R. Ghost of Windy Hill **Fic**
(illus.) Commager, H. S. The great Declaration **973.3**
(illus.) Gates, D. The warrior goddess: Athena **292**
(illus.) George, J. C. All upon a sidewalk **595.7**
(illus.) George, J. C. All upon a stone **595.7**
(illus.) Lexau, J. M. Benjie **E**
(illus.) Monjo, F. N. Letters to Horseface **Fic**
(illus.) Ryder, J. Fireflies **595.7**
(illus.) Wormser, R. The black mustanger **Fic**

Bolton, Ivy
The golden egg
In Harper, W. comp. Easter chimes p195-207 **S C**

Bolts and nuts
See pages in the following book:
Weiss, H. What holds it together? p15-18 (3-5) **621.8**

Bombers
Cooke, D. C. Famous U.S. Air Force bombers (5 and up) **623.74**

Bonaparte, Napoleon. See Napoleon I, Emperor of the French

Bond, Michael
A bear called Paddington (2-5) **Fic**
More about Paddington. See note under Bond, M. A bear called Paddington **Fic**
Olga carries on. See note under Bond, M. The tales of Olga da Polga **Fic**
Olga meets her match. See note under Bond, M. The tales of Olga da Polga **Fic**

Boots of buffalo leather. Grimm, J.
  In Grimm, J. The Brothers Grimm: popular folk tales p166-69   **398.2**
  In Grimm, J. The complete Grimm's fairy tales p808-11   **398.2**
Border life. See Frontier and pioneer life
Bordier, Georgette
  (illus.) Streatfeild, N. A young person's guide to ballet   **792.8**
Bored—nothing to do! Spier, P.   **E**
Borghese, Anita
  The down to earth cookbook (4-6)   **641.5**
  The international cookie jar cookbook (4 and up)   **641.8**
Boring, Mel
  Sealth [biography of Seattle, Chief of the Suquamish and allied tribes]   **92**
Boris, Georgette
  (illus.) Carlson, B. W. The right play for you   **792**
Boris. Haar, J. ter   **Fic**
Born, Franz
  Jules Verne (5 and up)   **92**
Born a monkey, live a monkey. Sherlock, P.
  In Sherlock, P. West Indian folk-tales p135-43   **398.2**
Born in a stable. Preston, C.
  In Preston, C. A trilogy of Christmas plays for children p65-93   **812**
Born on the circus. Powledge, F.   **791.3**
The **borrowed** house. Van Stockum, H.   **Fic**
The **Borrowers.** Norton, M.   **Fic**
The **Borrowers**; excerpt. Norton, M.
  In The Arbuthnot Anthology of children's literature p510-12   **808.8**
The **Borrowers** afield. Norton, M. See note under Norton, M. The Borrowers   **Fic**
The **Borrowers** afloat. Norton, M. See note under Norton, M. The Borrowers   **Fic**
The **Borrowers** aloft. Norton, M. See note under Norton, M. The Borrowers   **Fic**
The **borrowing** of 100,000 arrows. Wyndham, R.
  In Wyndham, R. Tales the people tell in China p40-47   **398.2**
Borrowing the enemies' arrows
  Wyndham, R. The borrowing of 100,000 arrows
  In Wyndham, R. Tales the people tell in China p40-47   **398.2**
Borski, Lucia Merecka
  King Bartek
  In The Arbuthnot Anthology of children's literature p274-76   **808.8**
  In Time for old magic p157-59   **398.2**
Borten, Helen
  Halloween (1-3)   **394.2**
  (illus.) Branley, F. M. Rain and hail   **551.57**
  (illus.) Cone, M. Purim   **296.4**
  (illus.) Goldin, A. Where does your garden grow?   **631.4**
Bosomworth, Mary Musgrove Matthews. See Musgrove, Mary
Bosse, Malcolm J.
  The 79 squares (6 and up)   **Fic**
Bostock and Harris. See Garfield, L. The night of the comet   **Fic**
Boston, L. M.
  The children of Green Knowe (4-6)   **Fic**
  The children of Green Knowe; excerpt
  In The Arbuthnot Anthology of children's literature p535-39   **808.8**

An enemy at Green Knowe. See note under Boston, L. M. The children of Green Knowe   **Fic**
The fossil snake (4-6)   **Fic**
The river at Green Knowe. See note under Boston, L. M. The children of Green Knowe   **Fic**
The sea egg (3-5)   **Fic**
The stones of Green Knowe. See note under Boston, L. M. The children of Green Knowe   **Fic**
A stranger at Green Knowe. See note under Boston, L. M. The children of Green Knowe   **Fic**
Tolly's new home
  In The Arbuthnot Anthology of children's literature p535-39   **808.8**
Treasure of Green Knowe. See note under Boston, L. M. The children of Green Knowe   **Fic**
Boston, Lucy Maria. See Boston, L. M.
Boston, Peter
  (illus.) Boston, L. M. The children of Green Knowe   **Fic**
  (illus.) Boston, L. M. The fossil snake   **Fic**
  (illus.) Boston, L. M. The sea egg   **Fic**
Boston
Fiction
Forbes, E. Johnny Tremain (5 and up)   **Fic**
McCloskey, R. Make way for ducklings   **E**
Wibberley, L. John Treegate's musket (6 and up)   **Fic**
Boston. Committee of Correspondence
  See pages in the following book:
Phelan, M. K. The story of the Boston Tea Party p53-57, 69-84 (4-6)   **973.3**
Boston Massacre, 1770
Phelan, M. K. The story of the Boston Massacre (6 and up)   **973.3**
  See also pages in the following book:
Davis, B. Black heroes of the American Revolution p33-40 (5 and up)   **973.3**
Boston Tea Party, 1773
Phelan, M. K. The story of the Boston Tea Party (4-6)   **973.3**
Botany
Dowden, A. O. Look at a flower (6 and up)   **582.13**
Stonehouse, B. A closer look at plant life (5 and up)   **581**
  See also pages in the following book:
Cooper, E. K. Science in your own back yard p68-99 (5 and up)   **507**
  See also Bulbs; Flowers; Fruit; Gardening; Plants; Seeds; Shrubs; Trees; Weeds
Anatomy
Zim, H. S. What's inside of plants? (2-4)   **581.4**
  See also pages in the following book:
Selsam, M. E. How to grow house plants p10-14 (4-6)   **635.9**
Ecology
Milne, L. J. Because of a flower (5 and up)   **582.13**
Selsam, M. E. Birth of a forest (4-6)   **581.5**
  See also pages in the following book:
Batten, M. The tropical forest p18-27 (5 and up)   **574.5**

Botany—*Continued*

Experiments

Rahn, J. E. More about what plants do (5 and up) **581.3**

Rahn, J. E. Seeing what plants do (3-5) **581**

Selsam, M. E. Play with plants (3-6) **581**

Nomenclature

See Plant names, Popular

Physiology

See Plant physiology

Terminology

See also Plant names, Popular

Botany, Economic

Schaeffer, E. Dandelion, pokeweed, and goosefoot (4 and up) **581.6**

See also Plants, Edible

Botany, Medical

Schaeffer, E. Dandelion, pokeweed, and goosefoot (4 and up) **581.6**

Selsam, M. E. Plants that heal (4-6) **581.6**

See also pages in the following book:

Kettelkamp, L. The healing arts p13-18 (5 and up) **615.5**

Botany of the Bible. See Bible—Natural history

Both ends of the leash. Unkelbach, K. **636.7**

Bothwell, Jean

The first book of India (4-6) **954**

Botswana

See pages in the following book:

Newlon, C. Southern Africa: the critical land p185-92 (5 and up) **968**

Böttger, Johann Friedrich

See pages in the following book:

Aylesworth, T. G. The alchemists: magic into science p103-08 (6 and up) **540.1**

Böttiger, Johann Friedrich. See Böttger Johann Friedrich

The bottle. Andersen, H. C.

In Andersen, H. C. The complete fairy tales and stories p492-500 **S C**

Bottle neck

Andersen, H. C. The bottle

In Andersen, H. C. The complete fairy tales and stories p492-500 **S C**

Bottner, Barbara

Dumb old Casey is a fat tree (2-4) **Fic**

Boudicca. See Boadicea, Queen

Bouki and Ti Bef. Courlander, H.

In Courlander, H. The piece of fire, and other Haitian tales p94-96 **398.2**

Bouki buys a burro. Courlander, H.

In Courlander, H. The piece of fire, and other Haitian tales p55-57 **398.2**

Bouki cuts wood. Courlander, H.

In Courlander, H. The piece of fire, and other Haitian tales p76-80 **398.2**

Bouki gets whee-ai. Courlander, H.

In Courlander, H. The piece of fire, and other Haitian tales p20-22 **398.2**

Bouki rents a horse. Courlander, H.

In Courlander, H. The piece of fire, and other Haitian tales p25-28 **398.2**

Bouki's glasses. Courlander, H.

In Courlander, H. The piece of fire, and other Haitian tales p89-90 **398.2**

Bourbon, House of

See pages in the following book:

Loder, D. The land and the people of Spain p77-85 (5 and up) **946**

Bourhill, E. J.

Fairy tales from South Africa; adaptation. See Berger, T. Black fairy tales **398.2**

Bourke, Linda

(illus.) Sullivan, M. B. Feeling free **362.4**

Bourke-White, Margaret

See pages in the following book:

Young and female p91-104 (6 and up) **920**

Bova, Ben

The weather changes man (5 and up) **551.6**

Bow and arrow

See also Archery

A **bow** to Thanksgiving. Bailey, C. S.

In Thanksgiving p163-74 **394.2**

Bowden, Charlotte Edmands

(illus.) Foley, D. J. Christmas the world over **394.2**

Bowden, Joan Chase

The bean boy (1-3) **398.2**

Why the tides ebb and flow (k-2) **398.2**

Bowen, Gary

My village, Sturbridge (4-6) **974.4**

Bowker (R. R. Company)

Educational film locator of the Consortium of University Film Centers and R. R. Bowker Company. See Educational Film locator of the Consortium of University Film Centers and R. R. Bowker Company **016.3713**

Bowling

Dolan, E. F. The complete beginner's guide to bowling (5 and up) **794.6**

Ravielli, A. What is bowling? (3-5) **794.6**

See also pages in the following books:

The Junior illustrated encyclopedia of sports p197-230 (5 and up) **796.03**

Keith, H. Sports and games p67-79 (5 and up) **796**

Bowman, James Cloyd

Hidden Laiva

In Time for old magic p143-47 **398.2**

Pecos Bill becomes a coyote

In North American legends p169-74 **398.2**

The pig-headed wife

In The Arbuthnot Anthology of children's literature p261-62 **808.8**

Tales from a Finnish tupa (4 and up) **398.2**

Contents: Ship that sailed by land and sea; Men of the wallet; Mouse bride; Vaino and the swan princess; Hidden Laiva; Antti and the wizard's prophecy; Lippo and Tapio; Wooing of Seppo Ilmarinen; Jurma and the sea god; Timo and the Princess Vendla; Severi and Vappu; Ei-Niin-Mita, or No-So-What; Girl who sought her nine brothers; Two pine cones; Kalle and the wood grouse; Niilo and the wizard; Urho and Marja; Mielikki and her nine sons; Leppä Pölkky and the blue cross; Liisa and the prince; Pig-headed wife; Finland's greatest fisherman; Stupid Peikko; Wise men of Holmola; Pekka and the rogues; End of the world; Mouse that turned tailor; The feast; Farmers three; Stupid wolf; Wily fox; Song of the fox; Wolf and the fox; Fox as a judge; Rooster and the hen; Why the squirrel lives in trees; Vain bear; Wisdom of the rabbit; Fox and the rabbit; Stupid bear; Song of the wolf; Bear goes fishing; Rabbit's self-respect

Timo and the Princess Vendla

In The Arbuthnot Anthology of children's literature p262-64 **808.8**

Bowman, Phila B.
The Christmas tree
In Harper, W. comp. Merry Christmas to
you p38-43 **S C**
The Easter Bunnies and the Lily
In Harper, W. comp. Easter chimes p189-
94 **S C**
A **box** on the ear. Manning-Sanders, R.
In A-haunting we will go p123-27 **S C**
In Manning-Sanders, R. A book of ghosts
& goblins p9-13 **398.2**
The **box** with red wheels. Petersham, M. **E**
Boxing
See pages in the following books:
The Junior illustrated encyclopedia of sports
p231-70 (5 and up) **796.03**
Keith, H. Sports and games p80-104 (5 and
up) **796**

Biography
Hoff, S. Gentleman Jim [Corbett] and the
great John L. (1-3) **92**
Lipsyte, R. Free to be Muhammad Ali (5
and up) **92**
A **boy**, a dog, a frog, and a friend. Mayer, M.
See note under Mayer, M. A boy, a
dog, and a frog **E**
A **boy**, a dog, and a frog. Mayer, M. **E**
Boy alone. Ottley, R. **Fic**
Boy alone; excerpt. Ottley, R.
In The Arbuthnot Anthology of children's
literature p725-29 **808.8**
A **boy** and his pa. Rawlings, M. K.
In Holiday ring p122-30 **394.2**
The **boy** and the cloth. Courlander, H.
In Courlander, H. The tiger's whisker,
and other tales and legends from
Asia and the Pacific p80-82 **398.2**
The **boy** and the trolls, or the adventure. Sten-
ström, W.
In Olenius, E. comp. Great Swedish fairy
tales p203-20 **398.2**
The **boy** and the water-sprite. Haviland, V.
In Haviland, V. Favorite fairy tales told
in Sweden p3-13 **398.2**
The **Boy** and the wolves
In Yellow fairy book p123-25 **398.2**
A **boy** called Fish. Morgan, A. **Fic**
The **boy** drummer of Vincennes. Carmer, C.
811
Boy friends, girl friends, just friends. Richards,
A. K. **158**
The **Boy** in Nazareth. King. E. E.
In It's time for Christmas p198-203 **394.2**
The **boy** knight of Reims; excerpt. Lowns-
bery, E.
In Stories to dramatize p214-18 **372.6**
Boy meets girl [play] Stone, P.
In Free to be . . . you and me p24-31
810.8
A **boy** of old Prague. Ish-Kishor S. **Fic**
Boy Scout handbook. See Boy Scouts of
America. The official Boy Scout handbook
369.43
Boy Scouts
Blassingame, W. Dan Beard, scoutmaster of
America (3-5) **92**
Handbooks, manuals, etc.
Boy Scouts of America. Bear Cub Scout
book (3-4) **369.43**
Boy Scouts of America. The official Boy
Scout handbook **369.43**

Boy Scouts of America. Webelos Scout
book (4-5) **369.43**
Boy Scouts of America. Wolf Cub Scout
book **369.43**
History
Blassingame, W. Story of the Boy Scouts
(4 and up) **369.43**
Boy Scouts of America
Bear Cub Scout book (3-4) **369.43**
Fieldbook **369.43**
The official Boy Scout handbook **369.43**
Reading **028.5**
Webelos Scout book (4-5) **369.43**
Wolf Cub Scout book (2-3) **369.43**
Blassingame, W. Story of the Boy Scouts
(4 and up) **369.43**
Boy who cried "Wolf"
Wolf! Wolf!
In The Tall book of nursery tales p74-76
398.2
The **boy** who didn't believe in spring. Clif-
ton, L. **E**
Boy who discovered the spring. Alden, R. M.
In Alden, R. M. Why the chimes rang,
and other stories p41-52 **S C**
In It's time for Easter p176-83 **394.2**
The **boy** who dreamed of rockets; how Rob-
ert H. Goddard became the father of the
space age. Quackenbush, R. M. **92**
The **boy** who drew cats. Hearn, L.
In A chilling collection p63-66 **S C**
In The Golden Treasury of children's lit-
erature p525-27 **808.8**
In Gruenberg, S. M. ed. Favorite stories
old and new p373-76 **808.8**
**Boy who had a moon on his forehead and a
star on his chin**
The Boy who had a moon on his forehead
and a star on his chin
In Indian fairy tales p156-78 **398.2**
The **boy** who had wings. Yolen J. **Fic**
The **boy** who kept his finger in the dike.
Lewis, M.
In The Golden Treasury of children's lit-
erature p522-23 **808.8**
Boy who killed the Dif
Wheeler, P. The boy who killed the Dif
In Giants & witches and a dragon or two
p189-208 **398.2**
The **boy** who loved music [biography of Franz
Joseph Haydn] Lasker, D. **92**
The **boy** who sailed around the world alone.
Graham, R. L. **910.4**
The **boy** who was followed home. Mahy, M.
E
The **boy** who was never afraid. Smedberg, A.
In Olenius, E. comp. Great Swedish fairy
tales p143-52 **398.2**
See also Youth who could not shiver
and shake
Boy who went out of the world. Alden, R. M.
In Alden, R. M. Why the chimes rang,
and other stories p66-79 **S C**
The **boy** who wore turtle shell moccasins. Yel-
low Robe, R.
In Yellow Robe, R. Tonweya and the
eagles, and other Lakota Indian tales
p59-65 **398.2**
The **boy** with the golden knucklebones. Rior-
dan J.
In Riordan, J. Tales from Tartary p70-78
398.2

Brandenberg, Franz
Everyone ready? See note under Brandenberg, F. Nice new neighbors **E**
I wish I was sick, too! **E**
Nice new neighbors **E**
No school today! See note under Brandenberg, F. I wish I was sick, too! **E**
A picnic, hurrah! See note under Brandenberg, F. I wish I was sick, too! **E**
A robber! A robber! See note under Brandenberg, F. I wish I was sick, too! **E**
A secret for grandmother's birthday. See note under Brandenberg, F. I wish I was sick, too! **E**
Six new students. See note under Brandenberg, F. Nice new neighbors **E**
What can you make of it? See note under Brandenberg, F. Nice new neighbors **E**

Brandreth, Gyles
The biggest tongue twister book in the world (4 and up) **808.88**

Brandt, Sue R.
Facts about the 50 states (4-6) **973**
How to improve your written English (4-6) **808**
How to write a report (6 and up) **808**

Brandt, Willy
See pages in the following book:
Dornberg, J. The two Germanys p93-101, 114-22 (5 and up) **943.087**

Branley, Franklyn M.
The beginning of the earth (1-3) **551**
The Big Dipper (k-2) **523.8**
Big tracks, little tracks (k-2) **591.5**
A book of flying saucers for you (2-4) **001.9**
A book of Mars for you (2-4) **523.4**
A book of moon rockets for you (1-3) **629.4**
A book of stars for you (2-4) **523.8**
Color, from rainbows to lasers (6 and up) **535.6**
Columbia and beyond (4-6) **629.44**
Comets, meteoroids, and asteroids (6 and up) **523.2**
Eclipse (2-4) **523.7**
The end of the world (5 and up) **525**
Experiments in the principles of space travel (5 and up) **629.4**
Flash, crash, rumble, and roll (k-3) **551.5**
Floating and sinking (1-3) **532**
Gravity is a mystery (1-3) **531**
High sounds, low sounds (1-3) **534**
Light and darkness (1-3) **535**
Measure with metric (2-4) **389**
The mystery of Stonehenge (4 and up) **936.1**
The nine planets (6 and up) **523.4**
North, south, east, and west (1-3) **526**
Oxygen keeps you alive (1-3) **574.1**
Pieces of another world (5 and up) **552**
Rain and hail (k-3) **551.57**
Roots are food finders (2-4) **581.1**
Shakes, quakes, and shifts: earth tectonics (5 and up) **551.1**
Snow is falling (k-3) **551.57**

Solar energy (5 and up) **621.47**
Sunshine makes the seasons (2-4) **525**
Think metric! (3-6) **389**
Weight and weightlessness (1-3) **531**

Bransom, Paul
(illus.) Lippincott, J. W. The Wahoo bobcat **Fic**
(illus.) Lippincott, J. W. Wilderness champion **Fic**

Brant, Joseph, Mohawk chief
See pages in the following book:
Johnston, J. The Indians and the strangers p59-66 (2-5) **920**

Brasília
See pages in the following books:
Brown, R. The land and people of Brazil p104-08 (5 and up) **981**
Kendall, S. Looking at Brazil p58-61 (4-6) **981**

Brate, Charlotte
The pony tree
In Told under the magic umbrella p59-63 **S C**

Brave against his will
Hatch, M. C. Brave in spite himself
In Hatch, M. C. 13 Danish tales p122-38 **398.2**

Brave Baby Elephant. Joslin, S. **E**

The Brave beetle
In Jataka tales p12-13 **398.2**

Brave in spite of himself. Hatch, M. C.
In Hatch, M. C. 13 Danish tales p122-38 **398.2**

Brave Janet Reachfar. Duncan, J. **E**

Brave laborer
Afanas'ev, A. The brave laborer
In Afanas'ev, A. Russian fairy tales p276-77 **398.2**

Brave little tailor
Grimm, J. The brave little tailor
In The Andrew Lang Fairy tale treasury p64-72 **398.2**
In Blue fairy book p306-16 **398.2**
Grimm, J. The gallant tailor
In Grimm, J. Household stories p109-17 **398.2**
Grimm, J. The valiant little tailor
In Grimm, J. The complete Grimm's fairy tales p112-20 **398.2**
In Grimm, J. Fairy tales of the Brothers Grimm p71-80 **398.2**
Grimm, J. The valiant tailor
In Grimm, J. Grimm's Fairy tales p44-53 **398.2**
Thane, A. The brave little tailor
In Thane, A. Plays from famous stories and fairy tales p397-413 **812**
See also Jack and the varmints; Johnny Gloke

The brave little tailor [play]. Thane, A.
In Thane, A. Plays from famous stories and fairy tales p397-413 **812**

The brave man of Golo. Courlander, H.
In Courlander, H. The king's drum, and other African stories p51-55 **398.2**

The brave men of Austwick. Jagendorf, M. A.
In Jagendorf, M. A. Noodlehead stories from around the world p119-21 **398.2**

Brave tin soldier
Andersen, H. C. The steadfast tin soldier
Fic
also in Andersen, H. C. Ardizzone's Hans Andersen: fourteen classic tales p9-14
S C
also in Andersen, H. C. The complete fairy tales and stories p112-17 **S C**
also in Andersen, H. Hans Andersen: his classic fairy tales p98-102 **S C**
also in Andersen, H. C. Seven tales p114-28 **S C**
also in The Arbuthnot Anthology of children's literature p501-04 **808.8**
also in Gruenberg, S. M. ed. Favorite stories old and new p314-17 **808.8**
also in Yellow fairy book p303-08 **398.2**

Brazil
Brown, R. The land and people of Brazil (5 and up) **981**
Kendall, S. Looking at Brazil (4-6) **981**

Exploring expeditions
See pages in the following book:
Kendall, S. Looking at Brazil p23-25 (4-6) **981**

Bread
Adkins, J. The bakers (4-6) **641.8**
Johnson, H. L. Let's bake bread (2-5) **641.8**
Meyer, C. The bread book (3-6) **641.8**
Solomon, H. Bake bread! (4 and up) **641.8**
See also pages in the following books:
Berger, M. Enzymes in action p54-60 (6 and up) **574.19**
Girl Scouts of the United States of America. Girl Scout cookbook p108-19 (4 and up) **641.5**
Kohn, B. The organic living book p62-69 (4 and up) **635**
Penner, L. R. The colonial cookbook p87-92 (5 and up) **641.5**
Rockwell, H. I did it p45-56 (1-3) **745.5**
Bread and jam for Frances. Hoban, R. See note under Hoban, R. Bedtime for Frances
E
The **bread** book. Meyer, C. **641.8**
Bread dough craft
Chernoff, G. T. Clay-dough play-dough (1-4) **745.5**
Sommer, E. The bread dough craft book (3-6) **745.5**
The **bread** dough craft book. Sommer, E. **745.5**
Break Mountains. Courlander, H.
In Courlander, H. The piece of fire, and other Haitian tales p23-24 **398.2**
Breakthrough to the big leagues. Robinson, J. **92**
A **breath** of air. Leach, M.
In Leach, M. Whistle in the graveyard p105 **398.2**
Breathing. See Respiration
Breda, Frederick J.
(illus.) Silverstein, A. Cats: all about them **636.8**
(illus.) Silverstein, A. Hamsters: all about them **599.32**
Breeden, Paul
(illus.) Pringle, L. Wild foods **581.6**
Breeder reactors. See Nuclear reactors

Bremen town musicians
Grimm, J. The Bremen town musicians **398.2**
also in The Fairy tale treasury p110-13 **398.2**
also in Grimm, J. About wise men and simpletons p111-15 **398.2**
also in Grimm, J. The Brothers Grimm: popular folk tales p23-26 **398.2**
also in Grimm, J. The complete Grimm's fairy tales p144-48 **398.2**
also in Grimm, J. Grimm's Fairy tales p114-18 **398.2**
also in Grimm, J. Household stories p136-39 **398.2**
Grimm, J. The four musicians
In The Arbuthnot Anthology of children's literature p200-02 **808.8**
In Time for old magic p48-50 **398.2**
Grimm, J. The musicians of Bremen
In Grimm, J. The best of Grimm's fairy tales **398.2**
In Grimm, J. Tales from Grimm p87-100 **398.2**
In Stories to dramatize p43-46 **372.6**
McMurray, L. B. The street musicians
In Told under the green umbrella p67-73 **398.2**
Roberts, W. The musicians of Bremen town
In Dramatized folk tales of the world p155-61 **812.08**
Rockwell, A. The Bremen town musicians
In Rockwell, A. The old woman and her pig, & 10 other stories p52-61 **398.2**
See also Jack and the robbers
Brendan, Saint
Legends
Fritz, J. Brendan the Navigator (3-5) **398.2**
Brendan the Navigator. Fritz, J. **398.2**
Brenggen field
Duvoisin, R. "Brenggen" field
In Duvoisin, R. The three sneezes, and other Swiss tales p230-33 **398.2**
Brennan, M. Beth
(illus.) Benjamin, C. L. Running basics **796.4**
Brenner, Barbara
Baltimore orioles (k-2) **598**
Beware! These animals are poison (3-5) **591.6**
Bodies (k-2) **612**
Faces (k-2) **152.1**
Lizard tails and cactus spines (4-6) **597.9**
On the frontier with Mr Audubon (4 and up) **Fic**
A snake-lover's diary (5 and up) **597.9**
Wagon wheels (2-4) **Fic**
A year in the life of Rosie Bernard (4-6) **Fic**
(illus.) Monjo, F. N. The drinking gourd **E**
Brer Bear gets a taste of man. Faulkner, W. J.
In Faulkner, W. J. The days when the animals talked p85-88 **398.2**
Brer Fox meets Mister Trouble. Faulkner, W. J.
In Faulkner, W. J. The days when the animals talked p137-38 **398.2**
Brer Fox tries farming, too. Faulkner, W. J.
In Faulkner, W. J. The days when the animals talked p110-14 **398.2**

Brison-Stack, Guy
(illus.) Hokus pokus: with wands, water & glasses   793.8

Bristle Face. Ball, Z.   Fic

Britain, Battle of, 1940
Hough, R. The Battle of Britain (5 and up)   940.54
Reynolds, Q. The Battle of Britain (6 and up)   940.54

Britannica Junior encyclopedia for boys and girls   031

British Americans
Cates, E. H. The English in America (5 and up)   305.8

British art. See Art, British

British arts. See Arts, British

British castles. Unstead, R. J.   728.8

British in Africa
See pages in the following book:
Bleeker, S. The Ashanti of Ghana p21-31 (4 and up)   966.7

British in India
See pages in the following book:
Bothwell, J. The first book of India p42-44 (4-6)   954

British in Sierra Leone
See pages in the following book:
Clifford, M. L. The land and people of Sierra Leone p38-85 (5 and up)   966

British in the United States
Fiction
Hildick, E. W. Manhattan is missing (4-6)   Fic

British Museum (Natural History)
Nature at work. See Nature at work   574.5
Parker, S. Life before birth: the story of the first nine months (3-6)   612

Brittany
See pages in the following book:
Bragdon, L. J. The land and people of France p83-88 (5 and up)   944

Broadcasting
See also Television broadcasting

Brock, Betty
I can fly!
In The Arbuthnot Anthology of children's literature p523-26   808.8
No flying in the house; excerpt
In The Arbuthnot Anthology of children's literature p523-26   808.8

Brock, Emma L.
Ballet
In Gruenberg, S. M. ed. Favorite stories old and new p63-68   808.8
Gingham Lena
In Told under the magic umbrella p12-17   S C
(illus.) Jacobs, J. Johnny-cake   398.2

Brock, Virginia
Piñatas (4 and up)   745.59

Broderick, Dorothy M.
Image of the black in children's fiction   028.5
An introduction to children's work in public libraries   027.62
Library work with children   027.62
Training a companion dog (4 and up)   636.7

Broderick. Ormondroyd, E.   E

Brodsky, Beverly
Jonah (k-3)   221.9
For another title by this author see McDermott, Beverly Brodsky

Broekel, Ray
Stadler, V. Even the devil is afraid of a shrew   398.2

Broido, Arnold
Davis, M. K. Music dictionary   780.3

The Broken pot
In Indian fairy tales p38-39   398.2

Broken windows. Paterson, K.
In Paterson, K. Angels & other strangers p105-18   S C

Bronowski, J.
Biography of an atom (4 and up)   539

Bronson, Clark
(illus.) Dugdale, V. Album of North American birds   598

Bronson, Mildred
(illus.) Very young verses. See Very young verses   821.08

Bronson, Wilfrid S.
Beetles (4 and up)   595.7
Dogs (3 and up)   636.7

Bronx Zoo. See New York (City). Zoological Park

Bronze boar
Andersen, H. C. The bronze pig
In Andersen, H. C. The complete fairy tales and stories p156-66   S C

The bronze bow. Speare, E. G.   Fic

The bronze door. Chandler, R.
In Alfred Hitchcock's Supernatural tales of terror and suspense p38-67   S C

The bronze pig. Andersen, H. C.
In Andersen, H. C. The complete fairy tales and stories p156-66   S C

Bronze ring
The Bronze ring
In Blue fairy book p14-26   398.2

Bronzeville boys and girls. Brooks, G.   811

Brook in the king's garden. Alden, R. M.
In Alden, R. M. Why the chimes rang, and other stories p41-52   S C

Brooke, L. Leslie
Johnny Crow's garden   E
Johnny Crow's party. See note under Brooke, L. L. Johnny Crow's garden   E
(illus.) Lear, E. The Jumblies, and other nonsense verses   821
(illus.) Lear, E. The pelican chorus & other nonsense verses   821
About
See pages in the following book:
A Horn Book Sampler on children's books and reading p60-69, 224-27   028.5

Brookins, Dana
Alone in Wolf Hollow (5 and up)   Fic

Brooklyn
Fiction
Brenner, B. A year in the life of Rosie Bernard (4-6)   Fic
Chaikin, M. I should worry, I should care (3-5)   Fic
Fox, P. How many miles to Babylon? (4-6)   Fic

Brooks, Barbara
(illus.) Schnurnberger, L. E. Kings, queens, knights & jesters: making medieval costumes   391.09

Brooks, Gregory
Monroe's island   **E**
Brooks, Gwendolyn
Bronzeville boys and girls (2-5)   **811**

About
See pages in the following book:
Rollins, C. Famous American Negro poets
p87-91 (5 and up)   **920**
Brooks, Polly Schoyer
When the world was Rome (6 and up)   **937**
Brooks, Ron
Timothy and Gramps   **E**
(illus.) Wagner, J. The Bunyip of Berkeley's
Creek   **E**
Brooks, Walter R.
Freddy and the baseball team from Mars.
See note under Brooks, W. R. Freddy,
the detective   **Fic**
Freddy, the detective (3-5)   **Fic**
Henry and his dog Henry
In Gruenberg, S. M. ed. Favorite stories
old and new p257-63   **808.8**
Jimmy takes vanishing lessons
In A-haunting we will go p28-41   **S C**
In Haunting tales p235-45   **S C**
Broom and brush industry
See pages in the following book:
Fisher, L. E. The homemakers p29-35 (4
and up)   **670**
Broom market day. Molloy, L. L.
In One hundred plays for children p656-65
    808.82
Brooms and brushes
See also Broom and brush industry
Brother and sister
Afanas'ev, A. Sister Alionushka, brother
Ivanushka
In Afanas'ev, A. Russian fairy tales p406-
10   **398.2**
Grimm, J. Brother and sister
In Grimm, J. The complete Grimm's fairy
tales p67-73   **398.2**
In Grimm, J. Household stories p65-71
    398.2
In Grimm, J. The juniper tree, and other
tales from Grimm v 1 p42-54   **398.2**
In Red fairy book p120-28   **398.2**
Grimm, J. Little Brother and Little Sister
In Grimm, J. The Brothers Grimm:
popular folk tales p47-54   **398.2**
Riordan, J. Sister Alyonushka and Brother
Ivanushka
In Riordan, J. Tales from Central Russia
p107-11   **398.2**
**Brother Annancy fools Brother Fire. Carter,
D. S.**
In Carter, D. S. Greedy Mariani, and other
folktales of the Antilles p68-72   **398.2**
**Brother Breeze and the pear tree. Sherlock,
P. M.**
In Sherlock, P. M. Anansi, the spider
man p13-19   **398.2**
A **brother** for the orphelines. Carlson, N. S.
See note under Carlson, N. S. The happy
orpheline   **Fic**
Brother Gaily. Grimm, J.
In Grimm, J. The juniper tree, and other
tales from Grimm v 1 p129-49   **398.2**
See also Brother Lustig

Brother Lustig
Grimm, J. Brother Gaily
In Grimm, J. The juniper tree, and other
tales from Grimm v 1 p129-49   **398.2**
Grimm, J. Brother Lustig
In Grimm, J. The complete Grimm's fairy
tales p367-77   **398.2**
Brother Mike. Colwell, E.
In Colwell, E. Round about and long ago
p68-69   **398.2**
Brother Rabbit and Brother Bear. See Mr
Rabbit and Mr Bear
Brother Rabbit and Brother Bull-Frog
Jagendorf, M. A. The smartest one in the
woods
In Jagendorf, M. A. Folk stories of the
South p22-24   **398.2**
Brother Rabbit's riding-horse
Faulkner, W. J. Brer Rabbit and his riding
horse
In Faulkner, W. J. The days when the
animals talked p146-51   **398.2**
Brotherhood, It's time for. Sechrist, E. H.
    361
Brothers
Fiction
Blume, J. Tales of a fourth grade nothing
(3-6)   **Fic**
Byars, B. Go and hush the baby   **E**
Cooper, S. Jethro and the jumbie (2-4)   **Fic**
Kellogg, S. Much bigger than Martin   **E**
Roche, P. K. Good-bye, Arnold!   **E**
Sharmat, M. W. Goodnight, Andrew; good-
night, Craig   **E**
Williams, B. Jeremy isn't hungry   **E**
Brothers and sisters
Fiction
Alexander, M. Nobody asked me if I
wanted a baby sister   **E**
Bonsall, C. The day I had to play with
my sister   **E**
Bulla, C. R. Keep running, Allen!   **E**
Butterworth, O. The trouble with Jenny's
ear (4 and up)   **Fic**
Byars, B. The summer of the swans (5
and up)   **Fic**
Caines, J. Abby   **E**
Cleaver, V. Where the lilies bloom (5 and
up)   **Fic**
Clymer, E. My brother Stevie (4-6)   **Fic**
Colman, H. Diary of a frantic kid sister
(4 and up)   **Fic**
Fox, P. The stone-faced boy (4-6)   **Fic**
Greene, C. C. I and Sproggy (5 and up)
    Fic
Greenfield, E. She come bringing me that
little baby girl   **E**
Hamilton, V. Justice and her brothers (6
and up)   **Fic**
Holland, V. We are having a baby   **E**
Hughes, S. David and Dog   **E**
Hutchins, P. Titch   **E**
Iwasaki, Chihiro. A new baby is coming
to my house   **E**
Jordan, J. New life: new room (2-4)   **Fic**
Knotts, H. Great-Grandfather, the baby
and me   **E**
McCord, J. Turkeylegs Thompson (5 and
up)   **Fic**
Ness, E. Do you have the time, Lydia?   **E**
Perl, L. Dumb like me, Olivia Potts (4-6)
    Fic

Bulla, Clyde R.—*Continued*

The poppy seeds	E
St Valentine's Day (1-3)	394.2
Shoeshine girl (3-5)	Fic
Squanto, friend of the Pilgrims (2-4)	92
The sword in the tree (2-5)	Fic
A tree is a plant (k-2)	582.16
Viking adventure (3-5)	Fic

About
See pages in the following book:
Authors and illustrators of children's books
p28-40   028.5

Bullard, Brian
I can dance (4-6)   792.8

Bulletin boards
Nardini, M. L. Fundamentals of bulletin
board design   371.3

Bulletin of the Center for Children's Books.
Chicago. University. Graduate Library
School   028.1

Bullfights

Fiction
Leaf, M. The story of Ferdinand   E
Wojciechowska, W. Shadow of a bull (6
and up)   Fic

Bullfrog and Gertrude go camping. Dauer, R.
See note under Dauer, R. Bullfrog grows
up   E

Bullfrog builds a house. Dauer, R. See note
under Dauer, R. Bullfrog grows up   E

Bullfrog grows up. Dauer, R.   E

Bulls

Fiction
Leaf, M. The story of Ferdinand   E

Bully learns a lesson
Davis, R. Bully learns a lesson
In Davis, R. Padre Porko, the gentle-
manly pig p75-86   398.2

The **bully** of Barkham Street. Stolz, M. See
note under Stolz, M. A dog on Barkham
Street   Fic

Bumps in the night. Allard, H.   E

Bun
Afanas'ev, A. The bun
In Afanas'ev, A. Russian fairy tales
p447-49   398.2
Brown, M. The bun   398.2
Riordan, J. The bun
In Riordan, J. Tales from Central Russia
p31-33   398.2
See also Pancake

Bunche, Ralph Johnson
See pages in the following books:
Johnston, J. A special bravery p81-85 (2-5)
920
Sechrist, E. H. It's time for brotherhood
p245-50 (5 and up)   361

Bunin, Catherine
Is that your sister? (k-3)   362.7

Bunin, Sherry
(jt. auth.) Bunin, C. Is that your sister?
362.7

Bunnicula. Howe, D.   Fic

Bunting, Eve
Ghost of summer (6 and up)   Fic
Winter's coming   E

Bunyan, John
Godolphin, M. Pilgrim's progress (4-6) Fic

Bunyan, Paul
McCormick, D. J. Paul Bunyan swings his
axe (4-6)   398.2
Rounds, G. Ol' Paul, the mighty logger
(3-6)   398.2
See also pages in the following books:
The Arbuthnot Anthology of children's
literature p373-74   808.8
Gruenberg, S. M. ed. Favorite stories old
and new p491-94   808.8
Malcolmson, A. Yankee Doodle's cousins
p229-60 (4 and up)   398.2
North American legends p175-83 (5 and up)
398.2
Time for old magic p249-50   398.2

Drama
See pages in the following book:
Dramatized folk tales of the world p514-25
812.08

The **bunyip** lives again; play. Carlson, B. W.
In Carlson, B. W. The right play for
you p61-68   792

The **Bunyip** of Berkeley's Creek. Wagner, J.
E

Buon Natale. Cama, A.
In Christmas stories round the world
p73-78   S C

Buoniconti, Nick
(jt. auth.) Anderson, D. Defensive football   796.332

Burack, A. S.
(ed.) One hundred plays for children. See
One hundred plays for children   808.82
(ed.) Popular plays for classroom reading.
See Popular plays for classroom reading
808.82

Burch, Robert
D. J.'s worst enemy (4-6)   Fic
The pride of the county
In The Arbuthnot Anthology of children's
literature p666-69   808.8
Queenie Peavy (5 and up)   Fic
Queenie Peavy; excerpt
In The Arbuthnot Anthology of children's
literature p666-69   808.8
Skinny (4-6)   Fic
Wilkin's ghost (5 and up)   Fic

Burchard, Marshall
Sports hero: Billie Jean King (2-4)   92

Burchard, Peter
Balloons (3-6)   629.133
Bimby (4-6)   Fic
Jed; excerpt
In The Arbuthnot Anthology of children's
literature p761-63   808.8
A Yankee meets a young Confederate
In The Arbuthnot Anthology of children's
literature p761-63   808.8
(illus.) Bulla, C. R. Squanto, friend of the
Pilgrims   92
(illus.) Newman, R. Night spell   Fic
(illus.) Shotwell, L. R. Roosevelt Grady
Fic

Burchard, Sue
(jt. auth.) Burchard, M. Sports hero: Billie
Jean King   92

Burenushka, the little red cow. Afanas'ev, A.
In Afanas'ev, A. Russian fairy tales p146-50
398.2

Burger, Carl
All about cats (5 and up) 636.8
(illus.) Burnford, S. The incredible journey Fic
(illus.) Gipson, F. Old Yeller Fic
(illus.) North, S. Little Rascal 599.74

Burgess, Gelett
The three elevators
In Told under the magic umbrella p64-67 S C

Burgess, Robert F.
Exploring a coral reef (4-6) 574.92

Burglon, Nora
Christmas coin
In Dalgliesh, A. comp. Christmas p168-79 S C
In The joy! p23-29 394.2

Burgoyne, John
See pages in the following book:
Lomask, M. The first American Revolution p198-208 (6 and up) 973.3

Buried cities. See Cities and towns, Ruined, extinct, etc.

Buried cities. Hall, J. 930.1

Buried treasure
McClung, R. M. Treasures in the sea (k-3) 910.4

Fiction
Bellairs, J. The treasure of Alpheus Winterborn (5 and up) Fic
Bunting, E. Ghost of summer (6 and up) Fic
Curry, J. L. The Bassumtyte treasure (5 and up) Fic
Fleischman, S. The ghost in the noonday sun (4-6) Fic
Fleischman, S. Jingo Django (4-6) Fic
Stevenson, R. L. Treasure Island (6 and up) Fic

Burkert, Nancy Ekholm
The art of Nancy Ekholm Burkert 741.64
(illus.) Andersen, H. C. Hans Christian Andersen's The fir tree Fic
(illus.) Andersen, H. C. The nightingale Fic
(illus.) Dahl, R. James and the giant peach Fic
(illus.) Grimm, J. Snow-White and the seven dwarfs 398.2
(illus.) Lear, E. Edward Lear's The Scroobious Pip 821
(illus.) Updike, J. A child's calendar 811

Burlingame, Cora
The three wishes
In One hundred plays for children p609-17 808.82

Burnett, Bernice
The first book of holidays (4 and up) 394.2

Burnett, Frances Hodgson
A little princess (4-6) Fic
A little princess; dramatization. See Thane, A. The little princess
The secret garden (4-6) Fic

Burnford, Sheila
The beginning of the journey
In The Arbuthnot Anthology of children's literature p729-32 808.8
The incredible journey (4 and up) Fic

Burning of the rice fields
Hodges, M. The wave 398.2

The burning of Washington: August 1814. Phelan, M. K. 975.3

Burningham, John
Come away from the water, Shirley E
Mr Gumpy's motor car. See note under Burningham, J. Mr Gumpy's outing E
Mr Gumpy's outing E
Time to get out of the bath Shirley. See note under Burningham, J. Come away from the water, Shirley E
(illus.) Fleming, I. Chitty-Chitty-Bang-Bang Fic

Burnish me bright. Cunningham, J. Fic

Burns, Irene
(illus.) Erwin, B. K. Go to the room of the eyes Fic

Burns, Marilyn
The book of think (4 and up) 153.4
I am not a short adult! (3-6) 305.2
The I hate mathematics! book (5 and up) 793.7
This book is about time (5 and up) 529

Burrage, A. M.
The inn
In Haunts, haunts, haunts p88-103 S C

Burris, Burmah
(illus.) Carlson, B. W. Listen! And help tell the story 372.6

Burros. See Donkeys

Burroway, Janet
Lord, J. V. The giant jam sandwich E

Burrows, Bill
(illus.) Wheat, J. K. Let's go to the moon 629.45

Burstein, Chaya M.
Rifka bangs the teakettle (5 and up) Fic
Rifka grows up. See note under Burstein, C. M. Rifka bangs the teakettle Fic

Burt, DeVere E.
(illus.) Laycock, G. Caves (5 and up) 551.4

Burt, Olive W.
The horse in America (5 and up) 636.1
Negroes in the early West (4-6) 920

Burt, William Henry
A field guide to the mammals 599

Burt Dow, deep-water man. McCloskey, R. E

Burtle, Gerry Lynn
The mystery of the Gumdrop Dragon
In Fifty plays for junior actors p86-107 812.08

Burton, Sir Richard Francis
See pages in the following book:
Cottler, J. Heroes of civilization p67-79 (5 and up) 920

Burton, Virginia Lee
Caldecott Medal acceptance paper
In Caldecott Medal books: 1938-1957 p88-92 028.5
Choo Choo: the story of a little engine who ran away
In Gruenberg, S. M. comp. Let's hear a story p88-96 808.8
Katy and the big snow E
The little house E
Mike Mulligan and his steam shovel E
(illus.) Andersen, H. C. The emperor's new clothes Fic
(illus.) Bontemps, A. The fast Sooner hound Fic

About
See pages in the following books:
Authors and illustrators of children's books p41-55 028.5
Caldecott Medal books: 1938-1957 p93-97 028.5

Burton, Virginia L.—*Continued*
The Illustrator's notebook p45-49   **741.64**

Burton, W. F. P.
The honey gatherer's three sons
In The Arbuthnot Anthology of children's
literature p325-26   **808.8**
In Time for old magic p202-03   **398.2**
Look behind as well as before
In The Arbuthnot Anthology of children's
literature p326   **808.8**
In Time for old magic p203   **398.2**

Burton and Dudley. Sharmat, M. W.   **E**

Burwell, Ted
(illus.) Carter, S. Vikings bold: their
voyages & adventures   **948**
(illus.) De Kay, J. T. Meet Martin Luther
King, Jr.   **92**

Bus ride. Jewell, N.   **E**

Busch, Phyllis S.
Cactus in the desert (1-3)   **583**
A walk in the snow (1-4)   **551.57**
Wildflowers and the stories behind their
names (4-6)   **582.13**

Buses
Fiction
Jewell, N. Bus ride   **E**

Bush, Chan
(jt. auth.) Olney, R. R. Better skate-board-
ing for boys and girls   **796.2**
(jt. auth.) Olney, R. R. Roller skating!
796.2

Bush, George W.
See pages in the following book:
Burt, O. W. Negroes in the early West
p41-46 (4-6)   **920**

The bushbabies. Stevenson, W.   **Fic**

The bushbabies; excerpt. Stevenson, W.
In The Arbuthnot Anthology of children's
literature p719-24   **808.8**

Bushmen
Marcus, R. B. Survivors of the stone age
(5 and up)   **306**

Bushy bride
Asbjörnsen, P. C. Bushy bride
In Red fairy book p317-23   **398.2**

Busia, Kofi Abrefa
See pages in the following book:
Sale, J. K. The land and people of Ghana
p120-25 (5 and up)   **966.7**

Business
Amazing Life Games Company. Good cents
(4 and up)   **658**
See also pages in the following book:
Caney, S. Steven Caney's Kids' America
p386-401 (4 and up)   **790.1**

Fiction
Merrill, J. The toothpaste millionaire (4-6)
Fic

Business cycles. See Depressions, Economic

Business depressions. See Depressions, Economic

Buslow, Robert Michael
(illus.) Asch, F. Running with Rachel   **796.4**

Busoni, Rafaello
(illus.) A Treasury of Christmas songs and
carols. See A Treasury of Christmas songs
and carols   **783.6**

Busy day: a book of action words. Maestro, B.
E

The busy farmer's wife
In Juba this and Juba that p60-61   **372.6**

Busybody Nora. Hurwitz, J.   **Fic**

But where is the green parrot? Zacharias, T.
E

Butcher. baker, cabinetmaker. Saul, W.   **331.4**

Butter
See pages in the following book:
Meyer, C. Milk, butter, and cheese p47-54
(5 and up)   **641.3**

Buttercup. Asbjörnsen, P. C.
In Giants & witches and a dragon or two
p108-14   **398.2**

Buttercup. Undset, S.
In Witches, witches, witches p32-36   **808.8**

Butterfield, John
Pinkerton, R. The first overland mail (5
and up)   **383**

Butterflies
The Butterfly cycle (3-6)   **595.7**
Klots, A. B. A field guide to the butter-
flies of North America, east of the Great
Plains   **595.7**
Mitchell, R. T. Butterflies and moths (4
and up)   **595.7**
Patent, D. H. Butterflies and moths (5 and
up)   **595.7**
Politi, L. The butterflies come   **E**
See also pages in the following books:
Ewbank, C. Insect zoo p61-81 (4 and up)
595.7
Simon, S. Pets in a jar p73-77 (4 and up)
639
Teale, E. W. The junior book of insects
p55-71 (6 and up)   **595.7**
Zim, H. S. Insects p58-82 (4 and up)   **595.7**
See also Caterpillars; Moths

Habits and behavior
See pages in the following book:
Hopf, A. L. Nature's pretenders p13-18 (6
and up)   **591.5**

Migration
See pages in the following book:
Swift, D. Animal travelers p33-43 (1-3)
591.5

Butterflies and moths. Mitchell, R. T.   **595.7**

Butterflies and moths. Patent, D. H.   **595.7**

The butterflies come. Politi, L.   **E**

Butterfly
Andersen, H. C. The butterfly
In Andersen, H. C. The complete fairy
tales and stories p782-84   **S C**

The Butterfly cycle (3-6)   **595.7**

The butterfly that stamped. Kipling, R.
In Kipling, R. Just so stories   **S C**

Butterworth, Hezekiah
A Thanksgiving dinner that flew away
In Harper, W. comp. The harvest feast
p148-58   **S C**

Butterworth, Oliver
The enormous egg (4 and up)   **Fic**
The trouble with Jenny's ear (4 and up)   **Fic**

C

Cameron, Eleanor—*Continued*

Julia and the hand of God. See note under Cameron, E. A room made of windows   **Fic**

Mr Bass's planetoid. See note under Cameron, E. The wonderful flight to the Mushroom Planet   **Fic**

A mystery for Mr Bass. See note under Cameron, E. The wonderful flight to the Mushroom Planet   **Fic**

A room made of windows (5 and up)   **Fic**

Stowaway to the Mushroom Planet. See note under Cameron, E. The wonderful flight to the Mushroom Planet   **Fic**

The terrible churnadryne (4-6)   **Fic**

Time and Mr Bass. See note under Cameron, E. The wonderful flight to the Mushroom Planet   **Fic**

To the green mountains (5 and up)   **Fic**

The wonderful flight to the Mushroom Planet (4-6)   **Fic**

Cameron, Polly

I can't said the ant   **E**

Camouflage (Biology)

Cole, J. Find the hidden insect (k-3)   **595.7**

Hopf, A. L. Nature's pretenders (6 and up)   **591.5**

McClung, R. M. How animals hide (k-3)   **591.5**

Selsam, M. E. Hidden animals (k-3)   **591.5**

See also pages in the following books:

Fegely, T. D. The world of freshwater fish p37-42 (5 and up)   **597**

Freedman, R. How animals defend their young p43-53 (5 and up)   **591.5**

Kettelkamp, L. Tricks of eye and mind p94-101 (4 and up)   **535**

Fiction

Aruego, J. We hide, you seek   **E**

Camp cooking. See Cookery, Outdoor

Camp Fat. Konigsburg, E. L.
In Konigsburg, E. L. Altogether, one at a time p29-54   **S C**

The **Camp** Fire Blue Bird Series. Camp Fire Girls, Inc.   **369.47**

Camp Fire Girls

Handbooks, manuals, etc.

Camp Fire Girls, Inc. Adventure (4-6)   **369.47**

Camp Fire Firls, Inc. The Blue Bird wish (1-3)   **369.47**

Camp Fire Girls, Inc. The Camp Fire Blue Bird Series (1-3)   **369.47**

Camp Fire Girls, Inc. Discovery (6 and up)   **369.47**

Camp Fire Girls, Inc.

Adventure (4-6)   **369.47**
The Blue Bird wish (1-3)   **369.47**
The Camp Fire Blue Bird Series (1-3)   **369.47**
Discovery (6 and up)   **369.47**

Camp followers

See pages in the following book:

DePauw, L. G. Founding mothers p179-89 (6 and up)   **305.4**

Camp KeeWee's secret weapon. Schulman, J.   **E**

The **camp** on the Big Onion. Shephard, E.
In The Arbuthnot Anthology of children's literature p373-74   **808.8**

Campaign funds

United States

Gray, L. L. How we choose a president p103-08 (5 and up)   **324.6**

Campaigns, Presidential

United States

See Presidents—United States—Election

Campbell, Donald Grant

Scotland in pictures (4 and up)   **941.1**

Campbell, Elizabeth A.

The carving on the tree (3-5)   **973.1**

Campbell, J. F.

The battle of the birds
In Fairy tales from many lands p15-27   **398.2**

Campbell, Marie

A stepchild that was treated mighty bad
In North American legends p147-54   **398.2**

Camping

Gray, W. R. Camping adventure (k-3)   **796.54**

Janes, E. C. The first book of camping (3-6)   **796.54**

See also pages in the following books:

Boy Scouts of America. Fieldbook p32-65   **369.43**

Frankel, L. Bike-ways (101 things to do with a bike) p68-80 (4-6)   **796.6**

See also Backpacking

Fiction

Hodges, M. The freewheeling Joshua Cobb (4 and up)   **Fic**

Johnson, A. The grizzly (5 and up)   **Fic**

Mayer, M. You're the scaredy-cat   **E**

Camping adventure. Gray, W. R.   **796.54**

Campion, Nardi Reeder

Ann the Word; the life of Mother Ann Lee, founder of the Shakers (5 and up)   **92**

Patrick Henry, firebrand of the Revolution (5 and up)   **92**

Camps

Fiction

O'Connor, J. Yours till Niagara falls, Abby (4-6)   **Fic**

Schulman, J. Camp KeeWee's secret weapon   **E**

Stolz, M. A wonderful, terrible time (4-6)   **Fic**

Can I keep him? Kellogg, S.   **E**

Canada

See pages in the following book:

Discoverers of the New World p112-25 (5 and up)   **907.01**

Biography—Bibliography

See pages in the following book:

Egoff, S. The republic of childhood p204-38   **028.5**

Exploration

See America—Exploration

Exploring expeditions

Syme, R. Alexander Mackenzie, Canadian explorer (3-5)   **92**

Fiction

Blades, A. Mary of Mile 18 (2-4)   **Fic**

Carlson, N. S. The talking cat, and other stories (3-6)   **S C**

Kaplan, B. The empty chair (6 and up)   **Fic**

Castles

Adkins, J. The art and industry of sand-castles (4 and up) **728.8**

Buehr, W. Knights and castles, and feudal life (4 and up) **940.1**

Duggan, A. The castle book (4 and up) **728.8**

Macaulay, D. Castle (5 and up) **728.8**

Unstead, R. J. British castles (5 and up) **728.8**

Unstead, R. J. Living in a castle (4-6) **940.1**

Unstead, R. J. See inside a castle (5 and up) **728.8**

Fiction

Goodall, J. S. Creepy castle **E**

Models

Cummings, R. Make your own model forts & castles (5 and up) **623**

Castro, Fidel

See pages in the following book:

Ortiz, V. The land and people of Cuba p77-83 (5 and up) **972.91**

Cat. See Cats

Cat and Dog. Sherlock, P.

In Sherlock, P. West Indian folk-tales p93-96 **398.2**

The **cat** and Mahadeo. Leach, M.

In Leach, M. The lion sneezed p11 **398.2**

Cat and mouse in partnership. Grimm, J.

In Grimm, J. The complete Grimm's fairy tales p21-23 **398.2**

In Grimm, J. Household stories p37-39 **398.2**

In Yellow fairy book p 1-4 **398.2**

See also Cat and the mouse in partnership

Cat and mouse keep house. Grimm, J.

In Grimm, J. Tales from Grimm p27-38 **398.2**

See also Cat and the mouse in partnership

The **cat** and Nirantali. Leach, M.

In Leach, M. The lion sneezed p10 **398.2**

Cat and the dream man

Finger, C. Cat and the dream man

In Finger, C. Tales from silver lands p197-225 **398.2**

The **cat** and the fiddler. Alexander, L.

In Alexander, L. The town cats, and other tales p95-111 **S C**

The **cat** and the fox. Grimm, J.

In Grimm, J. More Tales from Grimm p61-62 **398.2**

See also Fox and the cat

The **cat** and the golden egg. Alexander, L.

In Alexander, L. The town cats, and other tales p49-61 **S C**

Cat and the mouse

Jacobs, J. Cat and the mouse

In Jacobs, J. English fairy tales p188-89 **398.2**

Cat and the mouse in partnership

Grimm, J. Cat and mouse in partnership

In Grimm, J. The complete Grimm's fairy tales p21-23 **398.2**

In Grimm, J. Household stories p37-39 **398.2**

In Yellow fairy book p 1-4 **398.2**

Grimm, J. Cat and mouse keep house

In Grimm, J. Tales from Grimm p27-38 **398.2**

Cat and the parrot

Bryant, S. C. The cat and the parrot

In It's time for story hour p81-84 **372.6**

In Ross, E. S. ed. The lost half-hour p101-05 **372.6**

Haviland, V. The cat and the parrot

In Haviland, V. Favorite fairy tales told in India p27-34 **398.2**

The **cat** ate my gymsuit. Danziger, P. **Fic**

The **Cat** Club. Averill, E.

In Averill, E. Jenny and the Cat Club **S C**

The **cat** in the hat. Seuss, Dr **E**

The **Cat** in the hat Beginner book dictionary **423**

The **Cat** in the hat Beginner book dictionary in French. See The Cat in the hat Beginner book dictionary **423**

The **Cat** in the hat Beginner book dictionary in Spanish. See The Cat in the hat Beginner book dictionary **423**

The **cat** in the hat comes back! Seuss, Dr. See note under Seuss, Dr. The cat in the hat **E**

Cat in the mirror. Stolz, M. **Fic**

Cat Inspector. Jagendorf, M. A.

In Jagendorf, M. A. New England bean-pot p226-30 **398.2**

The **Cat**-King's daughter. Alexander, L.

In Alexander, L. The town cats, and other tales p19-33 **S C**

Cat 'n mouse

Cat 'n mouse

In The Jack tales p127-34 **398.2**

The **Cat** on the Dovrefell **398.2**

See also Bear and skrattel

The **cat** that walked by himself. Kipling, R.

In Kipling, R. Just so stories **S C**

Cat, the cock and the fox

Afanas'ev, A. The cat, the cock, and the fox

In Afanas'ev, A. Russian fairy tales p86-88 **398.2**

The **cat**, the dog, and death. Courlander, H.

In Courlander, H. The piece of fire, and other Haitian tales p24-36 **398.2**

The **cat** who lived in a drainpipe. Aiken, J.

In Aiken, J. The faithless lollybird p111-48 **S C**

The **cat** who said no. Alexander, L.

In Alexander, L. The town cats, and other tales p35-48 **S C**

The **cat** who thought she was a dog and the dog who thought he was a cat. Singer, I. B.

In Singer, I. B. Naftali the storyteller and his horse, Sus, and other stories p103-08 **S C**

The **cat** who went to heaven. Coatsworth, E. **Fic**

The **cat** who wished to be a man. Alexander, L. **Fic**

Catabilid conquest. Karl, J. E.

In Karl, J. E. The turning place: stories of a future past p85-121 **S C**

Cataloging

Akers, S. G. Akers' Simple library cataloging **025.3**

Anglo-American cataloging rules **025.3**

Piercy, E. J. Commonsense cataloging **025.3**

See also Subject headings

Cataloging—*Continued*

Audio-visual materials

Weihs, J. Nonbook materials: the organization of integrated collections   025.3

Catalogs, Card
ALA Filing rules   025.3

Catalogs, Classified
Books for children, 1960-1965   011
The Elementary school library collection   011
Junior high school library catalog   011

Catalogs, Library. See Library catalogs

Catalogs, Subject
Subject guide to Children's books in print   015.73

See also Subject headings

Catch as catch can. Poole, J.   **Fic**

Catch me & kiss me & say it again. Watson, C.   811

Catch the wind. Dennis, L.   621.4

The **catchee**. Konigsburg, E. L.
In Konigsburg, E. L. Throwing shadows p29-45   **S C**

The **catcher**, baseball's man in charge. Sullivan, G.   796.357

Caterpillars
McClung, R. M. Caterpillars and how they live (2-4)   595.7
Selsam, M. E. Terry and the caterpillars (k-2)   595.7

See also pages in the following book:
Anderson, M. J. Exploring the insect world p71-76 (5 and up)   595.7

Fiction

Carle, E. The very hungry caterpillar   **E**

Caterpillars and how they live. McClung, R. M.   595.7

Cates, Edwin H.
The English in America (5 and up)   305.8

Catfishes
See pages in the following book:
Silverstein, A. Animal invaders p72-77 (5 and up)   591.5

Cathedral: the story of its construction. Macaulay, D.   726

Cathedrals
Grant, N. Cathedrals (4-6)   726
See also Architecture, Gothic

Europe

Macaulay, D. Cathedral: the story of its construction (4 and up)   726

Cather, Carolyn
(illus.) Nathan, D. Women of courage   920

Cather, Katharine Dunlap
The Easter eggs
In Harper, W. comp. Easter chimes p173-86   **S C**

Catherine of Aragon, consort of Henry VIII, King of England
See pages in the following book:
Aymar, B. Laws and trials that created history p24-31 (6 and up)   345

Catholic Church
See pages in the following book:
Hall, E. The land and people of Argentina p47-50, 132-34 (5 and up)   982

Catholics in the United States
Fiction
Delton, J. Kitty in the middle (2-5)   **Fic**

Catlin, George
(illus.) Fronval, G. Indian signs and signals   001.56

Catrinella, come up higher! Manning-Sanders, R.
In Manning-Sanders, R. A book of enchantments and curses p120-28   398.2

Cats
Burger, C. All about cats (5 and up)   636.8
De Paola, T. The kids' cat book (2-4)   636.8
Fichter, G. S. Cats (5 and up)   599.74
Leen, N. Cats (3-5)   636.8
Rockwell, J. Cats and kittens (4 and up)   636.8
Silverstein, A. Cats: all about them (4 and up)   636.8
Stevens, C. The birth of Sunset's kittens (k-4)   636.8
Zim, H. S. The big cats (3-6)   599.74
Zim, H. S. Little cats (3-5)   599.74

See also pages in the following books:
Chrystie, F. N. Pets p26-39 (4 and up)   636.08
Stevens, C. Your first pet p83-93 (2-4)   636.08

Fiction

Alexander, L. The cat who wished to be a man (4-6)   **Fic**
Alexander, L. The town cats, and other tales (3-5)   **S C**
Averill, E. Jenny and the Cat Club (k-2)   **S C**
Averill, E. The school for cats   **E**
Birnbaum, A. Green eyes   **E**
Brandenberg, F. I wish I was sick, too!   **E**
Burnford, S. The incredible journey (4 and up)   **Fic**
Calhoun, M. Cross-country cat   **E**
Chambers, J. W. Fritzi's winter (4-6)   **Fic**
Cleary, B. Socks (3-5)   **Fic**
Clymer, E. Horatio   **E**
Coatsworth, E. The cat who went to heaven (4 and up)   **Fic**
Feder, J. Beany   **E**
Freeman, L. Pet of the Met   **E**
Gág, W. Millions of cats   **E**
Gantos, J. Rotten Ralph   **E**
Ginsburg, M. Three kittens   **E**
Goodall, J. S. The surprise picnic   **E**
Hildick, E. W. Manhattan is missing (4-6)   **Fic**
Hürlimann, R. The proud white cat (k-3)   398.2
Hoban, T. One little kitten   **E**
Knotts, H. The winter cat   **E**
Leach, M. The lion sneezed (4-6)   398.2
Miles, M. Jenny's cat (2-4)   **Fic**
Miles, M. Nobody's cat (2-4)   **Fic**
Neville, E. It's like this, Cat (5 and up)   **Fic**
Newberry, C. T. Marshmallow   **E**
Nodset, J. L. Come here, cat   **E**
Oakley, G. The church mouse   **E**
Potter, B. The pie and the patty-pan   **E**
Potter, B. The sly old cat   **E**
Potter, B. The story of Miss Moppet   **E**
Selden, G. The cricket in Times Square (3-6)   **Fic**
Seuss, Dr. The cat in the hat   **E**

Chamberlain, Wilton Norman
Rudeen, K. Wilt Chamberlain (2-5)   92
See also pages in the following book:
Devaney, J. The story of basketball p76-78
(5 and up)   796.32
Chambers, Aidan
Introducing books to children   028.5
Chambers, John W.
Fritzi's winter (4-6)   Fic
Chameleon was a spy. Massie, D. R.   E
Chameleons
White, W. The American chameleon (4-6)
597.9

Fiction

Massie, D. R. Chameleon was a spy   E
The **champion** of Merrimack County. Drury,
R. W.   Fic
The **champion** spearsman. Thompson, V. L.
In Thompson, V. L. Hawaiian tales of
heroes and champions p58-65   398.2
The **championship** of Ireland. Sutcliff, R.
In The Arbuthnot Anthology of children's
literature p465-71   808.8
In Time for old magic p329-35   398.2
Champlain, Samuel de
Jacobs, W. J. Samuel de Champlain (4-6)
92
See also pages in the following book:
Discoverers of the New World p118-25 (5
and up)   970.01
A **chance** child. Walsh, J. P.   Fic
Chancy and the grand rascal. Fleischman, S.
Fic
Chandler, Anna Curtis
A Chinese Rip Van Winkle
In One hundred plays for children p37-44
808.82
Chandler, Raymond
The bronze door
In Alfred Hitchcock's Supernatural tales
of terror and suspense p38-67   S C
Changeling
Grimm, J. The elves: third story
In Grimm, J. The complete Grimm's fairy
tales p200   398.2
In Grimm, J. Household stories p175
398.2
Grimm, J. The goblins
In Grimm, J. The juniper tree, and other
tales from Grimm v 1 p150-51 398.2
Grimm, J. The woman and the changeling
elf
In Grimm, J. About wise men and simple-
tons p34   398.2
The **changeling**. Snyder, Z. K.   Fic
The **changelings**. Nyblom, H.
In Olenius, E. comp. Great Swedish fairy
tales p153-69   398.2
Changes, changes. Hutchins, P.   E
The **changing** city. Müller, J.   307.7
The **changing** countryside. Müller, J.   307.7
The **changing** Eskimos. Newman, G.   970.004
Chano. Yellow Robe, R.
In Yellow Robe, R. Tonweya and the
eagles, and other Lakota Indian
tales p21-23   398.2
Chano's first buffalo hunt. Yellow Robe, R.
In Yellow Robe, R. Tonweya and the
eagles, and other Lakota Indian
tales p31-41   398.2

Chanticleer and Partlett
Grimm, J. The death of the hen
In Grimm, J. Household stories p12-13
398.2
Grimm, J. The death of the little hen
In Grimm, J. The complete Grimm's fairy
tales p365-67   398.2
Chanticleer and the fox. Cooney, B.   E
Chanukah. See Hanukkah (Feast of Lights)
Chanukah. Greenfeld, H.   296.4
The **chapel** on Cristo Street. Belpré, P.
In Belpré, P. Once in Puerto Rico p60-63
398.2
Chaplin, Charles
Jacobs, D. Chaplin, the movies, & Charlie
(5 and up)   92
See also pages in the following book:
Edelson, E. Funny men of the movies p21-31
(6 and up)   791.43
Chaplin, the movies, & Charlie. Jacobs, D. 92
Chapman, Eunice
See pages in the following book:
Faber, D. The perfect life p68-74 (6 and up)
289
Chapman, Frederick T.
(illus.) Reynolds, Q. Custer's last stand   92
Chapman, John
Aliki. The story of Johnny Appleseed (k-3)
92
See also pages in the following books:
Malcolmson, A. Yankee Doodle's cousins
p119-28 (4 and up)   398.2
North American legends p196-203 (5 and up)
398.2

Drama

See pages in the following book:
Dramatized folk tales of the world p537-48
812.08

Fiction

See pages in the following book:
Stories to dramatize p207-10   372.6
Chappell, Warren
The Nutcracker (2-5)   792.8
(illus.) Barret, L. The adventures of Don
Quixote de la Mancha   Fic
(illus.) De La Mare, W. Come hither   821.08
(illus.) Grimm, W. Hansel and Gretel   782.1
(illus.) Richter, C. Light in the forest   Fic
(illus.) Updike, J. The Ring   782.1
Characters and characteristics in literature

Dictionaries

Fisher, M. Who's who in children's books
028.5
Charades
Howard, V. Pantomimes, charades & skits
(4-6)   792.3
Charlemagne

Romances

Baldwin, J. The story of Roland (6 and up)
398.2
Bulfinch, T. Bulfinch's Mythology (6 and up)
291
Charles, Ray
Mathis, S. B. Ray Charles (2-5)   92
**Charles V, Emperor of the Holy Roman Em-
pire**
See pages in the following book:
Loder, D. The land and the people of Spain
p50-54 (5 and up)   946

Chendru: the boy and the tiger. Bergman Sucksdorff, A.   954
Chenery, Janet
   The toad hunt   **E**
   Wolfie (k-3)   595.4
Cheney, Cora
   Tales from a Taiwan kitchen (4-6)   398.2
   Contents: How the dragon lost his tail; A New Year's story; The lantern baby; The man who loved tiny creatures; Good neighbors come in all sizes; The reward; Curious Taro; How to become a dragon; The clam girl; Sister Na-Tao; The happy ghost; The story of the Weaving Maid; The wicked stone horse of Shilin; Waiting for rabbits; Winter bamboo; The Tiger Witch; The baby water buffalo; Wu-Feng; The mud-baked hen; Lin Tachian; A story of poets
Cheng, Hou-tien
   The Chinese New Year (1-4)   394.2
   Scissor cutting for beginners (1-3)   736
   Six Chinese brothers (k-3)   398.2
Chen, Tony
   (illus.) Cooper, T. T. Many hands cooking   641.5
Cheng's fighting cricket
   Carpenter, F. Cheng's fighting cricket
   In Carpenter, F. Tales of a Chinese grandmother p217-25   398.2
Cheops, King of Egypt
   See pages in the following book:
   Payne, E. The pharaohs of ancient Egypt p43-67 (5 and up)   932
Chermak, Sylvia
   Peter and the wolf
   In Dramatized folk tales of the world p375-80   812.08
   A visit from St Nicholas
   In On stage for Christmas p357-62   812.08
Chernoff, Goldie Taub
   Clay-dough play-dough (1-4)   745.5
   Easy costumes you don't have to sew (3-5)   391
Cherokee Indians
   Bealer, A. W. Only the names remain (4-6)   970.004
Fiction
   Rockwood, J. Groundhog's horse (4-6)   **Fic**
   Rockwood, J. To spoil the sun (6 and up)   **Fic**
Cherry, Lynne
   (illus.) Van Woerkom, D. Hidden messages   595.7
Cherry, or The frog bride. Grimm, J.
   In Grimm, J. Fairy tales of the Brothers Grimm p29-35   398.2
Cherry the frog bride
   Grimm, J. Cherry, or The frog bride
   In Grimm, J. Fairy tales of the Brothers Grimm p29-35   398.2
Chess, Victoria
   Alfred's alphabet walk   **E**
   (illus.) Prelutsky, J. The Queen of Eene   811
Chess
   Kidder, H. Illustrated chess for children (4-6)   794.1
   Leeming, J. The first book of chess (4-6)   794.1
   Lombardy, W. Chess for children, step by step (4-6)   794.1
   Reinfeld, F. Chess for children (5 and up)   794.1
   Sarnoff, J. The chess book (4-6)   794.1
The chess book. Sarnoff, J.   794.1
Chess for children. Reinfeld, F.   794.1

Chess for children, step by step. Lombardy, W.   794.1
Chesterman, Charles W.
   The Audubon Society Field guide to North American rocks and minerals (2-4)   549
Chestnut Grey. Riordan, J.
   In Riordan, J. Tales from Central Russia p184-89   398.2
Chetwynd-Hayes, R.
   The ghostly earl
   In Haunting tales p88-109   **S C**
Chew, Ruth
   (illus.) McGovern, A. Shark lady; true adventures of Eugenie Clark   92
Cheyenne Indians
   Goble, P. Red Hawk's account of Custer's last battle (4 and up)   973.8
   See also pages in the following book:
   Ehrlich, A. Wounded Knee: an Indian history of the American West p53-75, 105-21, 150-61 (6 and up)   970.004
Biography
   Supree, B. Bear's Heart   92
Fiction
   Leech, J. Bright Fawn and me   **E**
Chiang, Kai-Shek
   See pages in the following book:
   Rau, M. Our world: the People's Republic of China p27-42 (6 and up)   951.05
Chicago
Fire, 1871
   Phelan, M. K. The story of the great Chicago fire, 1871 (5 and up)   977.3
Riot, August 1968
   See pages in the following books:
   Aymar, B. Laws and trials that created history p181-92 (6 and up)   345
   David, A. Famous criminal trials p83-98 (5 and up)   345
Chicago. University. Graduate Library School
   Bulletin of the Center for Children's Books   028.1
   A critical approach to children's literature   028.5
Chicago Eight. See Chicago—Riot, August, 1968
Chicanos. See Mexican Americans
The chick and the duckling. Ginsburg, M.   **E**
A chick hatches. Cole, J.   636.5
The Chicken and the egg (3-6)   636.5
The chicken and the egg. Mari, I.   **E**
The chicken book. Williams, G.   **E**
Chicken Licken
   In The Tall book of nursery tales p55-61   398.2
   See also Chicken-Little
Chicken-Little
   Chicken Licken
   In The Tall book of nursery tales p55-61   398.2
   Galdone, P. Henny Penny   398.2
   Henny-Penny
   In The Arbuthnot Anthology of children's literature p154-55   808.8
   In The Arthur Rackham Fairy book p66-70   398.2

Chicken-Little—*Continued*

Jacobs, J. Henny-Penny
In The Fairy tale treasury p12-15   **398.2**
In Jacobs, J. English fairy tales p113-16   **398.2**
In Time for old magic p9-10   **398.2**
Rockwell, A. Henny-Penny
In Rockwell, A. The three bears & 15 other stories p63-70   **398.2**

Chicken soup with rice. Sendak, M.
In Sendak, M. Nutshell library v2   **E**

Chickens
The Chicken and the egg (3-6)   **636.5**
Cole, J. A chick hatches (k-3)   **636.5**
Flanagan, G. L. Window into an egg (4-6)   **636.5**
Mari, I. The chicken and the egg   **E**
Selsam, M. E. Egg to chick (k-3)   **636.5**
See also pages in the following book:
Weber, W. J. Care of uncommon pets p93-109 (5 and up)   **636.08**

Fiction
Allard, H. I will not go to market today   **E**
Aulaire, I. d'. Don't count your chicks   **E**
Belpré, P. Santiago   **E**
Benchley, N. The strange disappearance of Arthur Cluck   **E**
Galdone, P. The little red hen (k-1)   **398.2**
Ginsburg, M. The chick and the duckling   **E**
Hutchins, P. Rosie's walk   **E**
Little Red Hen; illus. by J. Domanska (k-1)   **398.2**
Martin, P. M. The little brown hen   **E**
Pinkwater, D. M. The Hoboken chicken emergency (3-6)   **Fic**
Polushkin, M. The little hen and the giant   **E**

Poetry
Williams, G. The chicken book   **E**

Chickens come home to roost. Jagendorf, M. A.
In Jagendorf, M. A. Folk stories of the South p213-15   **398.2**

Ch'ien Lung, Emperor of China
See pages in the following book:
The Arbuthnot Anthology of children's literature p877-79   **808.8**

Chidsey, Donald Barr
The world of Samuel Adams (5 and up)   **92**

Chief Joseph: war chief of the Nez Percé. Davis, R.   **92**

The **Chief** of the Gurensi. Courlander, H.
In Courlander, H. The king's drum, and other African stories p13-16   **398.2**

The chief of the well. Courlander, H.
In Courlander, H. The piece of fire, and other Haitian tales p15-19   **398.2**

The **chief's** knife. Courlander, H.
In Courlander, H. Olode the hunter, and other tales from Nigeria p50-53   **398.2**

Chien-Nang. Manning-Sanders, R.
In Manning-Sanders, R. A book of charms and changelings p16-20   **398.2**

Chien Tang. Manning-Sanders, R.
In Manning-Sanders, R. A book of dragons p20-24   **398.2**

Chilbik and the greedy Czar. Titiev, E.
In Titiev, E. How the Moolah was taught a lesson & other tales from Russia p9-26   **398.2**

Child, Charles
(illus.) Benét, R. A book of Americans   **811**

Child, Lydia Maria
Over the river and through the wood (1-3)   **784.6**

Child and parent. See Parent and child

Child authors. See Children as authors

Child development
Harris, R. H. Before you were there   **155.4**
Samson, J. Watching the new baby (3-5)   **649**
See also Child psychology

A **child** in prison camp. Takashima   **92**

Child in the grave
Andersen, H. C. The dead child
In Andersen, H. C. The complete fairy tales and stories p642-46   **S C**

Child labor
Fiction
Walsh, J. P. A chance child (5 and up)   **Fic**

United States
See pages in the following books:
Meltzer, M. Taking root p115-28 (6 and up)   **305.8**
Sandler, M. W. The way we lived p76-81 (4 and up)   **331.09**

Child of the Navajos. Reit, S.   **970.004**

Child of the owl. Yep, L.   **Fic**

Child of the silent night [biography of Laura Dewey Bridgman]. Hunter, E. F.   **92**

Child psychology
Stein, S. B. About phobias (k-3)   **155.4**
Bibliography
Bernstein, J. E. Books to help children cope with separation and loss   **016.3627**
Dreyer, S. S. The bookfinder   **011**
Fassler, J. Helping children cope   **016.3627**
Gillis, R. J. Children's books for time of stress   **016.3627**

Child study. See Child development; Child psychology

Child Study Children's Book Committee at Bank Street
Friends are like that! See Friends are like that! (2-4)   **S C**

The **child** who was made of snow. Bennett, R.
In Bennett, R. Creative plays and programs for holidays p283-87   **812**

Childe Rowland
Jacobs, J. Childe Rowland
In Jacobs, J. English fairy tales p117-24   **398.2**

Childhood Education: a journal for teachers, administrators, church-school workers, librarians, pediatricians   **372.05**

Children
Burns, M. I am not a short adult! (3-6)   **305.2**
See also Exceptional children; Infants

Adoption
See Adoption

Care and hygiene
Hautzig, E. Life with working parents: practical hints for everyday situations (5 and up)   **649**
Saunders, R. The Franklin Watts Concise guide to babysitting (5 and up)   **649**

Children's literature—History and criticism
—*Continued*

Children and literature	028.5
Children's Literature	028.505
Children's Literature in Education	028.505
Children's literature review	028.5
Chosen for children	028.5
Cook, E. The ordinary and the fabulous	028.5

Council on Interracial Books for Children. Racism and Sexism Resource Center for Educators. Human — and anti-human — values in children's books **028.5**

A Critical history of children's literature **028.5**

Egoff, S. The republic of childhood **028.5**

Fisher, M. Who's who in children's books **028.5**

Halsey, R. V. Forgotten books of the American nursery **028.5**

Hazard, P. Books, children & men **028.5**

Horn Book Reflections on Children's books and reading **028.5**

A Horn Book Sampler on children's books and reading **028.5**

Huck, C. S. Children's literature in the elementary school **028.5**

The Illustrator's notebook **741.64**

Illustrators of children's books: 1744-1945 **741.64**

Illustrators of children's books: 1946-1956 **741.64**

Illustrators of children's books: 1957-1966 **741.64**

Illustrators of children's books: 1967-1976 **741.64**

Issues in children's book selection **028.5**

Jan, I. On children's literature **028.5**

Jordan, A. M. Children's classics **011**

Jordan, A. M. From Rollo to Tom Sawyer, and other papers **028.5**

Karl, J. From childhood to childhood **028.5**

Lanes, S. G. Down the rabbit hole **028.5**

Larrick, N. A parent's guide to children's reading **028.5**

Literature and young children **028.5**

Lukens, R. A critical handbook of children's literature **028.5**

MacCann, D. The child's first books **028.5**

Newbery and Caldecott Medal books: 1956-1965 **028.5**

Newbery and Caldecott Medal books: 1966-1975 **028.5**

Newbery Medal books: 1922-1955 **028.5**

Only connect **028.5**

Phaedrus **028.505**

Pierpont Morgan Library, New York. Early children's books and their illustration **028.5**

Ross, E. S. The spirited life: Bertha Mahony Miller and children's books **92**

Sadker, M. P. Now upon a time **028.5**

Signal **028.505**

Smith, L. H. The unreluctant years **028.5**

Suitable for children? **028.5**

Sutherland, Z. Children & books **028.5**

Thwaite, M. F. From primer to pleasure in reading **028.5**

Townsend, J. R. A sounding of storytellers **028.5**

Townsend, J. R. Written for children **028.5**

Twentieth-Century children's writers **920.03**

Whalley, J. I. Cobwebs to catch flies **028.5**

Wilkin, B. T. Survival themes in fiction for children and young people **016.8**

Yankee Doodle's literary sampler of prose, poetry, and pictures **028.5**

Periodicals

Bookbird	028.505

Chicago. University. Graduate Library School. Bulletin of the Center for Children's Books **028.1**

Children's Literature	028.505
Children's Literature in Education	028.505
Ebony Jr.	051
Growing Point	028.505
The Horn Book Magazine	028.505
Interracial Books for Children Bulletin	028.505
The Junior Bookshelf	028.1
Phaedrus	028.505
Signal	028.505

Periodicals—Indexes

Subject index to children's magazines **051**

Reviews—Indexes

Children's book review index **028.1**

Technique

Hunter, M. Talent is not enough **808.06**

Yolen, J. Writing books for children **808.06**

Children's Literature **028.505**

Children's literature; a guide to reference sources **011**

Children's literature; a guide to reference sources; first supplement **011**

Children's literature; a guide to reference sources; second supplement **011**

Children's Literature Association

Children's Literature. See Children's Literature **028.505**

Children's Literature in Education **028.505**

Children's literature in the elementary school. Huck, C. S. **028.5**

Children's literature review **028.5**

Children's mathematics books. Matthias, M. **016.51**

Children's media market place **070.5025**

The **children's** own Longfellow. Longfellow, H. W. **811**

Children's plays for creative actors. Boiko, C. **812**

Children's poetry

See also Nursery rhymes

Bibliography

Children & poetry: a selective, annotated bibliography **016.8**

See also pages in the following books:

Bauer, C. F. Handbook for storytellers p137-57 **372.6**

Sutherland, Z. Children & books p301-07 **028.5**

History and criticism

See pages in the following books:

Chicago. University. Graduate Library School. A critical approach to children's literature p53-66 **028.5**

Children and literature p263-71 **028.5**

Egoff, S. The republic of childhood p239-54 **028.5**

Huck, C. S. Children's literature in the elementary school p305-75 **028.5**

Coatsworth, Elizabeth—*Continued*

About

See pages in the following books:

Authors and illustrators of children's books
p84-107   028.5

Newbery Medal books: 1922-1955 p94-98
                                                       028.5

Cobb, Vicki

Arts and crafts you can eat (4 and up)
                                                       745.5

How the doctor knows you're fine (2-4)
                                                       616

Magic . . . naturally! Science entertainments
& amusements (4 and up)   793.8

More Science experiments you can eat (5
and up)   507

Science experiments you can eat (5 and
up)   507

Supersuits (3-6)   613

Truth on trial: the story of Galileo Galilei
(3-5)   92

The **cobbler** and his cat. Alexander, L.
In Alexander, L. The town cats, and
other tales p63-77   S C

The **cobbler's** tale. Jones, E. O.
In Told under the magic umbrella p27-29
                                                     S C

Cober, Alan E.
(illus.) Garfield, L. Mister Corbett's ghost
                                                       Fic

Coblentz, Catherine Cate

Andrew Brewster's own secret
In Thanksgiving p65-73   394.2

Leyden's day of thanksgiving
In Thanksgiving p74-83   394.2

Martin and Abraham Lincoln; excerpt
In The Arbuthnot Anthology of children's
literature p756-61   808.8

The secret in the Brewsters' attic in Leyden
In Thanksgiving p59-64   394.2

Coburn, Doris

A spit is a piece of land (4-6)   551.4

Cobwebs to catch flies. Whalley, J. I.   028.5

Cochise, Apache chief

See pages in the following book:

Ehrlich, A. Wounded Knee: an Indian history of the American West p19-35 (6 and
up)   970.004

Cochrane, Louise

Shadow puppets in color (2-5)   791.5

Cock-a-doodle-doo! Cock-a-doodle-dandy! Kapp,
P.   784.6

Cock and the bean

Afanas'ev, A. The death of the cock
In Afanas'ev, A. Russian fairy tales p17-19
                                                       398.2

Cock and the hand mill

Afanas'ev, A. The cock and the hand mill
In Afanas'ev, A. Russian fairy tales p387-
89   398.2

The **cock** and the hen. Afanas'ev, A.
In Afanas'ev, A. Russian fairy tales p309
                                                       398.2

The **cock** and the mouse and the little red hen.
Rockwell, A.
In Rockwell, A. The three bears & 15
other stories p17-32   398.2
See also Cock, the mouse and the little
red hen

The **cock** and the sparrow-hawk. Sechrist,
E. H.
In Sechrist, E. H. Once in the first times
p25-27   398.2

The **cock** and the weathercock. Andersen,
H. C.
In Andersen, H. C. The complete fairy
tales and stories p647-49   S C

The **cock, the mouse, and the little red hen**

Lefèvre, F. The cock, the mouse, and the
little red hen
In The Arbuthnot Anthology of children's
literature p155-57   808.8
In Time for old magic p10-12   398.2

Rockwell, A. The cock and the mouse and
the little red hen
In Rockwell, A. The three bears & 15
other stories p17-32   398.2

The **cock** who wanted to be shah. Riordan, J.
In Riordan, J. Tales from Tartary p50-53
                                                       398.2

Cockleburr Quarters. Baker, C.   Fic

Cockroaches

Cole, J. Cockroaches (3-6)   595.7

Pringle, L. Cockroaches: here, there, and
everywhere (k-3)   595.7

See also pages in the following book:

Simon, S. The secret clocks p30-34 (5 and
up)   574.1

Fiction

Belpré, P. Perez and Martina (2-4)   398.2

Cockroaches: here, there, and everywhere.
Pringle, L.   595.7

Cocoa

See also Chocolate

CoConis, Constantinos
(illus.) Gates, D. The golden god: Apollo
                                                       292

CoConis, Ted
(illus.) Byars, B. The summer of the swans
                                                       Fic

Cocoons. See Butterflies; Caterpillars; Moths

The **code** & cipher book. Sarnoff, J.   652

The **code** of life. Silverstein, A.   575.1

Codes, ciphers and secret writing. Gardner, M.
                                                       652

Codes for kids. Albert, B.   652

Cody, William Frederick

Aulaire, I. d'. Buffalo Bill (1-4)   92

Coelacanth

Aliki. The long lost coelacanth: and other
living fossils (1-3)   597

Coerr, Eleanor

Jane Goodall [biography of Jane Lawick-
Goodall] (2-4)   92

Sadako and the thousand paper cranes [a
biography of Sadako Sasaki] (3-6)   92

Coffee

See pages in the following book:

Brown, R. The land and people of Brazil
p28-30, 71-75 (5 and up)   981

Coffin cash. Kendall, C.
In Kendall, C. Sweet and sour p108-[12]
                                                       398.2

Coffin lid

Afanas'ev, A. The peasant and the corpse
In Afanas'ev, A. Russian fairy tales p333-
34   398.2

Cognition. See Knowledge, Theory of

Cohen, Barbara
Benny (4-6)   Fic
The carp in the bathtub (2-4)   Fic
The innkeeper's daughter (6 and up)   Fic
Thank you, Jackie Robinson (4-6)   Fic

Cohen, Daniel
The ancient visitors (6 and up)   001.9
In search of ghosts (6 and up)   133
Night animals (4-6)   591.5
Real ghosts (4-6)   133.1
What really happened to the dinosaurs?
(4-6)   567.9
The world of UFOs (6 and up)   001.9
The world's most famous ghosts (4 and up)
                                               133.1

Cohen, David
(illus.) Etkin, R. The rhythm band book
                                               785.06

Cohen, David, 1909-
Multi-ethnic media. See Multi-ethnic media
                                               016.3058

Cohan, George Michael
See pages in the following book:
Browne, C. A. The story of our national
ballads p257-59 (5 and up)   784.7

Cohen, Miriam
"Bee my valentine!" See Cohen, M. Will I
have a friend?   E
Best friends. See note under Cohen, M.
Will I have a friend?   E
First grade takes a test. See Cohen, M.
Will I have a friend?   E
Lost in the museum. See Cohen, M. Will I
have a friend?   E
The new teacher. See Cohen, M. Will I
have a friend?   E
No good in art. See Cohen, M. Will I have
a friend?   E
Tough Jim. See Cohen, M. Will I have a
friend?   E
When will I read? See Cohen, M. Will I
have a friend?   E
Will I have a friend?   E

Cohen, Peter Zachary
Deadly game at Stony Creek (5 and up)
                                               Fic

Cohen, Robert
The color of man (5 and up)   572

Cohen, Vincent O.
(illus.) Spyri, J. Heidi   Fic

Cohn, Alfred A.
(illus.) Clark, A. N. Along sandy trails
                                               574.9

Cohn, Angelo
The first book of the Netherlands (4 and
up)   949.2

Coils, magnets and rings. Veglahn, N.   92

Coin collecting. See Coins

Coin collectors' handbook. Reinfeld, F.   737.4

Coins
Andrews, C. J. Fell's International coin book
                                               737.4
Andrews, C. J. Fell's United States coin
book   737.4
Reinfeld, F. Coin collectors' handbook 737.4
Reinfeld, F. How to build a coin collection
                                               737.4

Rosenfeld, S. The story of coins (5 and up)
                                               737.4
Severn, B. Magic with coins and bills (6 and
up)   793.8
See also pages in the following book:
Caney, S. Steven Caney's Kids' America
p376-82 (4 and up)   790.1

Coker, Paul
(illus.) Riedel, M. Winning with numbers
                                               310

Colbert, Anthony
(illus.) Colwell, E. Round about and long
ago   398.2
(illus.) Riordan, J. Tales from Tartary 398.2

Colbert, Mildred
The salt in the sea
In One hundred plays for children p618-32
                                               808.82

Colbo, Ella Stratton
The first New England Christmas tree
In One hundred plays for children p507-17
                                               808.82
The heroine of Wren
In One hundred plays for children p813-20
                                               808.82

Colby, C. B.
Arms of our fighting men (4 and up)   623.4
Early American crafts (4 and up)   670
Fighting gear of World War II (4 and up)
                                               355.8
Revolutionary War weapons (4 and up)
                                               623.4
Sailing ships (3-6)   387.2
Space age fire fighters (3-6)   628.9

Colby, Jean Poindexter
Lexington and Concord, 1775: what really
happened (5 and up)   973.3

Cold
Adler, I. Hot and cold (4-6)   536

Cole, Ann
I saw a purple cow, and 100 other recipes
for learning. See I saw a purple cow, and
100 other recipes for learning   372.1
A Pumpkin in a pear tree. See A Pumpkin
in a pear tree   745.59

Cole, Brock
The King at the door   E

Cole, Joanna
A calf is born (k-2)   636.2
A chick hatches (k-3)   636.5
Cockroaches (3-6)   595.7
Dinosaur story (k-3)   567.9
Find the hidden insect (k-3)   595.7
Fleas (3-6)   595.7
My puppy is born (k-3)   636.7
Plants in winter (1-3)   581
Twins (3-6)   612

Cole, Leonard
(illus.) Liss, H. Fishing talk for beginners
                                               799.1

Cole, William
(comp.) Beastly boys and ghastly girls. See
Beastly boys and ghastly girls   808.81
(comp.) The Birds and the beasts were
there. See The Birds and the beasts were
there   821.08
(ed.) Dinosaurs and beasts of yore. See
Dinosaurs and beasts of yore   808.81
(comp.) Humorous poetry for children (5
and up)   821.08

Cole, William—*Continued*

(comp.) I went to the animal fair. See I went to the animal fair   808.81

(comp.) I'm mad at you. See I'm mad at you   811.08

(comp.) Oh, how silly! See Oh, how silly!   821.08

(comp.) Oh, such foolishness! See Oh, such foolishness!   811.08

(comp.) Oh, that's ridiculous! See Oh, that's ridiculous!   821.08

(comp.) Oh, what nonsense! See Oh, what nonsense!   821.08

(comp.) Poems for seasons and celebrations (5 and up)   821.08

(comp.) Poems of magic and spells (4 and up)   821.08

(comp.) Rough men, tough men (5 and up)   821.08

Coletta, Hallie
(jt. auth.) Coletta, I. From A to Z   E

Coletta, Irene
From A to Z   E

Collage
See pages in the following books:
Comins, J. Art from found objects p69-94   745.5
The Illustrator's notebook p90-92   741.64

The collar. Andersen, H. C.
In Andersen, H. C. The complete fairy tales and stories p366-68   S C
See also Shirt collar

Collect, print and paint from nature. Hawkinson, J.   751.42

Collecting. See Collectors and collecting

Collecting cocoons. Hussey, L. J.   595.7

Collecting small fossils. Hussey, L. J.   560

Collecting stamps. Villiard, P.   769.56

Collection development (Libraries) See Libraries—Collection development

Collections of literature. See names of literatures and literary forms with the subdivision Collections, e.g. English literature—Collections; Poetry—Collections

Collections of natural specimens. See names of specimens with the subdivision Collection and preservation, e.g. Shells—Collection and preservation

Collections of objects. See Collectors and collecting; and names of objects with the subdivision Collectors and collecting, e.g. Postage stamps—Collectors and collecting

Collective settlements

China
See pages in the following books:
Rau, M. Our world: the People's Republic of China p99-107 (6 and up)   951.05
Sidel, R. Revolutionary China: people, politics, and ping-pong p3-12, 59-78 (6 and up)   951.05

Israel
See pages in the following books:
Dobrin, A. A life for Israel; the story of Golda Meir p30-37 (4-6)   92
Kubie, N. B. Israel p36-39 (4 and up)   956.94

Collectors and collecting
See pages in the following book:
Thomson, P. Museum people p197-219 (5 and up)   069
See also names of objects collected with the subdivision Collectors and collecting, e.g. Postage stamps—Collectors and collecting; and names of natural specimens with the subdivision Collection and preservation, e.g. Shells—Collection and preservation

College and school drama

Collections
One hundred plays for children   808.82
Popular plays for classroom reading (4-6)   808.82

Collections—Periodicals
Plays, the Drama Magazine for Young People   808.82

Collier, Christopher
(jt. auth.) Collier, J. L. The blood country   Fic
(jt. auth.) Collier, J. L. My brother Sam is dead   Fic

Collier, James Lincoln
The bloody country (6 and up)   Fic
My brother Sam is dead (6 and up)   Fic

Collier's encyclopedia   031

Collier's Encyclopedia yearbook. See Collier's encyclopedia   031

Collingwood, G. H.
Knowing your trees   582.16

Collins, David R.
Linda Richards: first American trained nurse (3-6)   92

Collins, Michael
Flying to the moon and other strange places (5 and up)   629.45

Collins, Patricia
(illus.) Hopf, A. L. Biography of a giraffe   599.73

Collodi, Carlo
The adventures of Pinocchio (3-6)   Fic
The adventures of Pinocchio; criticism
In Children and literature p71-77   028.5
The adventures of Pinocchio; excerpt
In The Arbuthnot Anthology of children's literature p496-98   808.8
The adventures of Pinocchio; dramatization. See Thane, A. Pinocchio goes to school
Pinocchio's ears become like those of a donkey
In The Arbuthnot Anthology of children's literature p496-98   808.8
A stick of wood that talked
In The Golden Treasury of children's literature p229-34   808.8

Colman, Hila
Diary of a frantic kid sister (4 and up)   Fic

Coloma, Louis de
Perez the Mouse
In Harper, W. comp. Merry Christmas to you p230-40   S C

The colonel teaches the judge a lesson in good manners. Jagendorf, M. A.
In Jagendorf, M. A. Folk stories of the South p59-61   398.2

Colonial America, The art of. Glubok, S.   709.73

Columbus Day—*Continued*
Poetry
See pages in the following book:
Sechrist, E. H. comp. Poems for red letter
days p179-83   821.08
Columbus sails the sea. Barbee, L.
In One hundred plays for children p375-
81   808.82
Colwell, Eileen
Round about and long ago (3-6)   398.2
Contents: The wizard of Alderley Edge; The enchanted fisherman; The Devil's bridge; The wizard
of Long Sleddale; The cuckoo of Borrowdale; The
enchanted princess; The fairies of Midridge; The
mysterious traveller; The fish and the ring; The
tailor and the fairies; The boggart and the farmer;
The pedlar of Swaffham; The giant of the fens;
Brother Mike; The green children; The king and
the witch; The little man in green; The farmer
and the cheeses; Jack Buttermilk; The little red
hairy man; The giant and the Wrekin; Jack and
the white cap; The great bell of Bosham; The piglet and the fairy; The dragon of Shervage Wood;
The pixy visitors; Bob o' the Carn; Skillywidden
Combs, Bob
(illus.) Ford, B. How birds learn to sing
598
Combustion
See also Fire
Come and laugh with Bobby Gum. Jagendorf,
M. A.
In Jagendorf, M. A. Folk stories of the
South p242-44   398.2
Come away from the water, Shirley. Burning-
ham, J.   E
Come back, Amelia Bedelia. Parish, P. See
note under Parish, P. Amelia Bedelia   E
Come by here. Coolidge, O.   Fic
Come here, cat. Nodset, J. L.   E
Come hither. De La Mare, W. ed.   821.08
Come to the edge. Cunningham, J.   Fic
Come to the fair. Henderson, N.
In Henderson, N. Celebrate America p76-
85   812
Come visit a prairie dog town. Alston, E.
599.32
Comedians
Edelson, E. Funny men of the movies (6
and up)   791.43
Comet
Andersen, H. C. The comet
In Andersen, H. C. The complete fairy
tales and stories p978-81   S C
Comet in Moominland. Jansson, T.   Fic
Comets
See pages in the following books:
Branley, F. M. Comets, meteoroids, and
asteroids p61-76 (6 and up)   523.2
Simon, S. Look to the night sky p50-56
(4 and up)   523
Fiction
Jansson, T. Comet in Moominland (4-6)
Fic
Comets, meteoroids, and asteroids. Branley,
F. M.   523.2
Comic books, strips, etc.
Cummings, R. Make your own comics for
fun and profit (5 and up)   741.5
Glubok, S. The art of the comic strip (4-6)
741.5
Comic strips. See Comic books, strips, etc.

The **coming** of buffalo. Marriott, A.
In Marriott, A. American Indian mythol-
ogy   398.2
The **coming** of corn (Cheyenne). Marriott, A.
In Marriott, A. American Indian mythol-
ogy   398.2
The **coming** of corn (Mikasuki). Marriott, A.
In Marriott, A. American Indian mythol-
ogy   398.2
The **coming** of corn (Zuni). Marriott, A.
In Marriott, A. American Indian mythol-
ogy   398.2
The **coming** of Max. St Clair, M. H.
In Gruenberg, S. M. ed. Favorite stories
old and new p149-52   808.8
The **coming** of the Prince. McGowan, J.
In A Treasury of Christmas plays p438-49
812.08
The **coming** of the Spaniards. Sechrist, E. H.
In Sechrist, E. H. Once in the first times
p107-09   398.2
Coming of the yams. Courlander, H.
In Courlander, H. The hat-shaking dance,
and other tales from the Gold Coast
p96-100   398.2
The **Coming** of Wasicun
In The Sound of flutes, and other Indian
legends p74-81   398.2
Comins, Jeremy
Art from found objects (5 and up)   745.5
Eskimo crafts, and their cultural back-
grounds (3-6)   745.5
Latin American crafts, and their cultural
backgrounds (4 and up)   745.5
Commager, Henry Steele
America's Robert E. Lee (5 and up)   92
The first book of American history (4-6)
973
The great Constitution (5 and up)   342
The great Declaration (6 and up)   973.3
The great Proclamation (6 and up)   326
The **Commandos** of World War II. Carter, H.
940.54
Commencements
Drama
See pages in the following book:
Fisher, A. Holiday programs for boys and
girls p347-68 (4 and up)   812
Commerce
See also Business; Retail trade; Trans-
portation
Commercial aeronautics. See Aeronautics,
Commercial
Commercial aviation. See Aeronautics, Com-
mercial
Commercial fishing. Zim, H. S.   639
Common frog (3-6)   597.8
Common market. See European Economic
Community
The **common** market. Rothkopf, C. Z.   382.9
Commonsense cataloging. Piercy, E. J.   025.3
Communes. See Collective settlements
Communicable diseases
Nourse, A. E. Lumps, bumps, and rashes
(5 and up)   616.9
See also Bacteriology; Germ theory of
disease

AUTHOR, TITLE, SUBJECT, AND ANALYTICAL INDEX
FOURTEENTH EDITION, 1981

Communication

Stewig, J. W. Sending messages (2-4)
001.51

See also pages in the following book:

Burns, M. I am not a short adult! p109-24 (3-6)
305.2

See also Language and languages; Telecommunication

History

Neal, H. E. Communication (5 and up)
001.51

Communication among animals. See Animal communication

Communications relay satellites. See Artificial satellites in telecommunication

Communism

See pages in the following book:

Kostich, D. D. The land and people of the Balkans p99-121 (5 and up)
949.6

China

See pages in the following book:

Rau, M. Our world: the People's Republic of China p42-58 (6 and up)
951.05

Czechoslovakia

See pages in the following book:

Hall, E. The land and people of Czechoslovakia p106-14, 146-50 (5 and up)
943.7

Indonesia

See pages in the following book:

Smith, D. C. The land and people of Indonesia p73-75, 139-43 (5 and up)
959.8

Romania

See pages in the following book:

Hale, J. The land and people of Romania p92-101 (5 and up)
949.8

Communities, Space. See Space colonies

Community and libraries. See Libraries and community

Compae Rabbit's ride. Carter, D. S.
In Carter, D. S. Greedy Mariani, and other folktales of the Antilles p41-45
398.2

A **companion** to world mythology. Barber, R.
291.03

Companions of the forest

Macdonnell, A. Companions of the forest
In It's time for story hour p206-12   372.6

The **Company** you keep
In Jataka tales p45-47   398.2

Comparative anatomy. See Anatomy, Comparative

Comparative physiology. See Physiology, Comparative

Comparative religion. See Religions

Compass

Branley, F. M. North, south, east, and west (1-3)
526

See also pages in the following book:

Boy Scouts of America. Fieldbook p20-27
369.43

Compere, Janet

(illus.) Davidson, M. Louis Braille   92

The **complete** beginner's guide to backpacking. Lyttle, R. B.
796.5

The **complete** beginner's guide to bowling. Dolan, E. F.
794.6

The **complete** beginner's guide to gymnastics. Dolan, E. F.
796.4

The **complete** beginner's guide to making and flying kites. Dolan, E. F.
796.1

The **complete** beginner's guide to photography. Laycock, G.
770.28

Complete book of horses and horsemanship, C. W. Anderson's. Anderson, C. W. 636.1

Complete dog book. American Kennel Club
636.7

Complete fairy tales, Perrault's. Perrault, C.
398.2

The **complete** fairy tales and stories. Andersen, H. C.   S C

The **complete** fairy tales of George MacDonald. MacDonald, G.   S C

The **complete** Grimm's fairy tales. Grimm, J.
398.2

The **complete** nonsense of Edward Lear. Lear, E.
821

The **complete** Peterkin papers. Hale, L. P.   Fic

Complete version of Ye three blind mice. Ivimey, J. W.
398

The **complete** works of Lewis Carroll. Carroll, L.
828

Composers, American

Cone, M. Leonard Bernstein (3-5)   92
Evans, M. Scott Joplin and the ragtime years (5 and up)   92

Composers, Austrian

Lasker, D. The boy who loved music [biography of Franz Joseph Haydn] (2-5)   92

Composers, Russian

Posell, E. Z. Russian composers (5 and up)
920

Composition (Rhetoric) See English language—Composition and exercises

Compost

Rockwell, H. The compost heap (k-1) 631.8

The **compost** heap. Rockwell, H.   631.8

Compton yearbook. See Compton's Encyclopedia and fact-index   031

Compton's Encyclopedia and fact-index   031

Compton's Pictured encyclopedia. See Compton's Encyclopedia and fact-index   031

Computers

Halacy, D. S. What makes a computer work? (2-4)   001.64
Lewis, B. Meet the computer (3-5)   001.64
Srivastava, J. J. Computers (2-4)   001.64

See also pages in the following book:

Bendick, J. Electronics for young people p108-14 (5 and up)
621.381

See also Calculating machines

Fiction

Williams, J. Danny Dunn and the homework machine (3-6)   Fic

Conal and Donal and Taig. MacManus, S.
In Time to laugh p58-66   S C

Conant, Isabelle Hunt

(illus.) Conant, R. A field guide to reptiles and amphibians of Eastern and Central North America   597.6

Conant, Roger

A field guide to reptiles and amphibians of Eastern and Central North America   597.6

Conceited apple branch

Andersen, H. C. There is a difference
In Andersen, H. C. The complete fairy tales and stories p386-89   S C

Conservation of forests. See Forests and forestry

Conservation of natural resources
Asimov, I. Earth: our crowded spaceship (5 and up)   **304.6**
Hirsch, S. C. Guardians of tomorrow (5 and up)   **920**
Miles, B. Save the earth! (4 and up)   **363.7**

Conservation of the soil. See Soil conservation

Conservation of wildlife. See Wildlife—Conservation

Consortium of University Film Centers
Educational film locator of the Consortium of University Film Centers and R. R. Bowker Company. See Educational Film locator of the Consortium of University Film Centers and R. R. Bowker Company   **016.3713**

Constance. Clapp, P.   **Fic**

Constantes and the Dhrako
Haviland, V. Constantes and the dragon
In Haviland, V. Favorite fairy tales told in Greece p3-19   **398.2**
Manning-Sanders, R. Constantantes and the dragon
In Manning-Sanders, A. A book of dragons p9-19   **398.2**

Constantes and the dragon. Haviland, V.
In Haviland, V. Favorite fairy tales told in Greece p3-19   **398.2**

Constantes and the dragon. Manning-Sanders, R.
In Manning-Sanders, R. A book of dragons p9-19   **398.2**

Constantine I, the Great
See pages in the following book:
Brooks, P. S. When the world was Rome, 753 B.C. to A.D. 476 p199-223 (6 and up)   **937**

Constantinople. See Istanbul

Constantinople   **956.1**

Constellations. See Astronomy; Stars

The **constellations.** Gallant, R. A.   **523.8**

Constitutional amendments

United States
See United States. Constitution—Amendments

The **Constitutional** amendments. Katz, W. L.   **342**

Constitutional history
See also names of countries with the subdivision Constitutional history, e.g. United States—Constitutional history

Constitutional law
See also Civil rights

Construction. See Building

Construction of roads. See Roads

Consumer education
Gay, K. Be a smart shopper (4-6)   **640.73**
See also pages in the following book:
Issues in children's book selection p125-35   **028.5**

Consumer protection
See pages in the following books:
The Arbuthnot Anthology of children's literature p886-90   **808.8**
Gay, K. Be a smart shopper p49-62 (4-6)   **640.73**

Consumption of energy. See Energy consumption

Contact lenses
Kelley, A. Lenses, spectacles, eyeglasses, and contacts (5-7)   **617.7**

Contagious diseases. See Communicable diseases

Contaminated food. See Food contamination

Contamination of the environment. See Pollution

Contemporary art. See Art, Modern—20th century

Contemporary women scientists of America. Noble, I.   **920**

The **contest.** Hogrogian, N.   **398.2**

Continental drift
Branley, F. M. Shakes, quakes, and shifts: earth tectonics (5 and up)   **551.1**
Fodor, R. V. Earth in motion (5 and up)   **551.1**
Kiefer, I. Global jigsaw puzzle (6 and up)   **551.1**

See also pages in the following books:
Asimov, I. How did we find out about earthquakes? p35-40 (5 and up)   **551.2**
Jenkins, M. M. Kangaroos, opossums, and other marsupials p50-58 (5 and up)   **599.2**
Lauber, P. Earthquakes p34-36, 41-44 (4-6)   **551.2**
Wyckoff, J. The story of geology p158-63 (5 and up)   **551**

Contrary. Caudill, R.   **E**

Contrary Chueh Chun. Chrisman, A. B.
In Chrisman, A. B. Shen of the sea p185-95   **S C**

Contributions of women: science. Emberlin, D.   **920**

Conundrums. See Riddles

Conversion of waste products. See Recycling (Waste, etc.)

Conveying machinery
See also Hoisting machinery

Cook, Ann
What was it like? When your grandparents were your age (3-6)   **973.91**

Cook, Elizabeth
The ordinary and the fabulous   **028.5**

Cook, Fred J.
The rise of American political parties (5 and up)   **324.273**

Cook, James
Captain Cook and the South Pacific   **990**
See also pages in the following books:
Cottler, J. Heroes of civilization p37-50 (5 and up)   **920**
Kaula, E. M. The land and people of New Zealand, 1728-1799 p56-62 (5 and up)   **993**
Mann, P. Easter Island p31-38 (6 and up)   **996**

Cook, Jan
(illus.) Cook, J. J. Blue whale   **599.5**
(illus.) Cook, J. J. The nocturnal world of the lobster   **595.3**

Cook, Joseph J.
Blue whale (4 and up)   **599.5**
The nightmare world of the shark (4 and up)   **597**
The nocturnal world of the lobster (4-6)   **595.3**
Wonders of the pelican world (4 and up)   **598**

The **cook** and the house goblin. Manning-Sanders, R.
In Manning-Sanders, R. A book of ghosts & goblins p30-37   **398.2**

Cook book for boys and girls, The Seabury. Moore, E.   **641.5**

Cookbook for boys & girls, Betty Crocker's   **641.5**

A **cookbook** for girls and boys. Rombauer, I. S.   **641.5**

Cooke, Ann
Giraffes at home (1-3)   **599.73**

Cooke, David C.
Famous U.S. Air Force bombers (5 and up)   **623.74**
Famous U.S. Navy fighter planes (5 and up)   **623.74**
Inventions that made history (5 and up)   **609**

Cooke, Flora J.
How the robin's breast became red
In Stories to dramatize p77-78   **372.6**
The maid who defied Minerva
In Stories to dramatize p119-21   **372.6**

Cooke, John
(illus.) The Butterfly cycle. See The Butterfly cycle   **595.7**
(illus.) The Spider's web. See The Spider's web   **595.4**

Cookery
Barta, G. Metric cooking for beginners (4 and up)   **641.5**
Better Homes and Gardens New Junior cook book (3-6)   **641.5**
Betty Crocker's Cookbook for boys & girls (3-6)   **641.5**
Cobb, V. Arts and crafts you can eat (4 and up)   **745.5**
Cobb, V. Science experiments you can eat (5 and up)   **507**
Cooper, T. T. Many hands cooking (4 and up)   **641.5**
De Paola, T. Things to make and do for Valentine's Day (1-3)   **394.2**
Ellison, V. H. The Pooh cook book (4 and up)   **641.5**
Gaeddert, L. Your night to make dinner (6 and up)   **641.5**
Girl Scouts of the United States of America. Girl Scout cookbook (4 and up)   **641.5**
Greene, E. comp. Clever cooks (3-6)   **398.2**
Hautzig, E. Cool cooking (2-5)   **641.5**
MacGregor, C. The storybook cookbook (3-6)   **641.5**
Meyer, C. Christmas crafts (5 and up)   **745.59**
Moore, E. The Seabury Cook book for boys and girls (1-3)   **641.5**
Paul, A. Kids cooking (3-6)   **641.5**
Paul, A. Kids cooking without a stove (1-3)   **641.5**
Penner, L. R. The colonial cookbook (5 and up)   **641.5**
Perl, L. Hunter's stew and Hangtown fry (4 and up)   **641.5**
Perl, L. Slumps, grunts, and snickerdoodles (4 and up)   **641.5**
Pringle, L. Wild foods (5 and up)   **581.6**
A Pumpkin in a pear tree (1-4)   **745.59**

Purdy, S. Christmas cookbook (4 and up)   **641.5**
Purdy, S. Halloween cookbook (4 and up)   **641.5**
Rombauer, I. S. A cookbook for girls and boys (4 and up)   **641.5**
Schwartz, P. D. You can cook (5 and up)   **641.5**
Shapiro, R. Wide world cookbook (5 and up)   **641.5**
Van der Linde, P. Around the world in 80 dishes (3-6)   **641.5**
Walker, B. M. The Little House cookbook (5 and up)   **641.5**
See also pages in the following books:
Caney, S. Steven Caney's kids' America p148-79 (4 and up)   **790.1**
Cassell, S. Indoor games and activities p33-45 (3-6)   **793**
Cutler, K. N. Crafts for Christmas p82-93 (3 and up)   **745.59**
Hays, W. P. Foods the Indians gave us p102-13 (5 and up)   **641.3**
Hoople, C. G. The heritage sampler p3-11 (5 and up)   **745.5**
It's time for Christmas p92-101 (4 and up)   **394.2**
It's time for Thanksgiving p234-49 (4 and up)   **394.2**
Jenness, A. A life of their own p30-35 (5 and up)   **972.81**
Kohn, B. The beachcomber's book p68-76 (3-6)   **745.5**
Kohn, B. The organic living book p70-75 (4 and up)   **635**
Rollins, C. comp. Christmas gif' p110-18 (4 and up)   **394.2**
See also Baking; Bread; Cake; Confectionery; Cookies; Salads

Dairy products
Meyer, C. Milk, butter, and cheese (5 and up)   **641.3**

Fiction
Croll, C. Too many Babas   **E**
Gilchrist, T. E. Halfway up the mountain   **E**
Ungerer, T. Zeralda's ogre   **E**

Food, Natural
Borghese, A. The down to earth cookbook (4-6)   **641.5**
Calvin, R. 1 pinch of sunshine, ½ cup of rain (4-6)   **641.5**
Cooper, J. Love at first bite (4 and up)   **641.5**
Dobrin, A. Peter Rabbit's natural foods cookbook (3-5)   **641.5**
Parents' Nursery School. Kids are natural cooks (3-6)   **641.5**

Herbs
See pages in the following book:
Dowden, A. O. This noble harvest p65-74 (4 and up)   **635**

Meat
Perl, L. The hamburger book (5 and up)   **641.6**

New England
See pages in the following book:
Loeb, R. H. New England village p86-89 (4-6)   **974**

Coren, Alan—*Continued*
Klondike Arthur. See note under Coren, A. Arthur the Kid **Fic**
The Lone Arthur. See note under Coren, A. Arthur the Kid **Fic**
Railroad Arthur. See note under Coren, A. Arthur the Kid **Fic**

Corfe, Tom
St Patrick and Irish Christianity (5 and up) **274.15**

Cormorants
Scott, J. D. The submarine bird (4 and up) **598**

Corn
Aliki. Corn is maize (1-3) **633.1**
See also pages in the following books:
Barth, E. Turkeys, Pilgrims, and Indian corn p79-83 (3-6) **394.2**
Fenton, C. L. Plants we live on p11-21 (4-6) **581.6**
Goldin, A. Grass p36-49 (5 and up) **584**
Hays, W. P. Foods the Indians gave us p68-87 (5 and up) **641.3**
Hoople, C. G. The heritage sampler p31-37 (5 and up) **745.5**
Lavine, S. A. Indian corn and other gifts p7-28 (4 and up) **641.3**

Fiction
Buff, M. Magic maize (3-6) **Fic**
Corn is maize. Aliki **633.1**
The **Corn** Maiden. Picard, B. L.
In Picard, B. L. The faun and the woodcutter's daughter p47-56 **S C**

Cornell, Jean Gay
Louis Armstrong, Ambassador Satchmo (4-6) **92**

Cornrows. Yarbrough, C. **E**

Cornwallis, Charles Cornwallis, 1st Marquis of
See pages in the following book:
Lomask, M. The first American Revolution p231-49 (6 and up) **973.3**

Coronado, Francisco Vasquez de. See Vasquez de Coronado, Francisco

Coronis
See pages in the following book:
Gates, D. The golden god: Apollo p49-54 (4 and up) **292**

Corporations, Multinational. See International business enterprises

Corpulence. See Obesity

Corrigan, Adeline
(ed.) Holiday ring. See Holiday ring **394.2**

Corrigan, Barbara
I love to sew (4-6) **646.2**
Of course you can sew! (5 and up) **646.4**

Corsair of Spouting Horn. Jagendorf, M. A.
In Jagendorf, M. A. New England beanpot p21-25 **398.2**

Corsairs. See Pirates

Corson, Hazel W.
Fish in the forest
In Dramatized folk tales of the world p388-99 **812.08**
In Popular plays for classroom reading p45-55 **808.82**
Triumph for two
In Dramatized folk tales of the world p47-60 **812.08**

Cortés, Hernando
Jacobs, W. J. Hernando Cortes (4-6) **92**
See also pages in the following books:
Discoverers of the New World p72-77 (5 and up) **970.01**
Karen, R. Feathered serpent p119-29 (6 and up) **972**

Cortesi, Wendy W.
Explore a spooky swamp (k-3) **574.5**

Cortez, Hernando. See Cortés, Hernando

Corwin, Judith Hoffman
(illus.) Gilbreath, A. Fun with weaving **746.1**
(illus.) Weiss, M. E. 666 jellybeans! All that? **512**
(illus.) Zim, H. S. Medicine **615**

Cosgrove, Margaret
Eggs—and what happens inside them (3-6) **591.3**

Coskey, Evelyn
Christmas crafts for everyone (5 and up) **745.59**
Easter eggs for everyone (5 and up) **745.594**

Cosman, Anna
How to read and write poetry (5 and up) **808.1**

Cosmogony. See Universe

Cosmology, Biblical. See Creation

Cosmopolitan world atlas, Rand McNally **912**

Cosmo's restaurant. Sobol, H. L. **647**

Cosner, Shaaron
Masks around the world, and how to make them (5 and up) **391**

Costantino, Joan
Secrets at the Mardi Gras
In It's time for Easter p227-38 **394.2**

The **costly** feast. Jagendorf, M. A.
In Jagendorf, M. A. Noodlehead stories from around the world p105-10 **398.2**

Costume
Barwell, E. Disguises you can make (4-6) **391**
Chernoff, G. T. Easy costumes you don't have to sew (3-5) **391**
Eisner, V. Quick and easy holiday costumes (3-6) **391**
Gilbreath, A. Making costumes for parties, plays, and holidays (4-6) **391**
Leeming, J. The costume book **391**
Parish, P. Costumes to make (4-6) **391**
Parish, P. Let's be early settlers with Daniel Boone (2-5) **745.5**
Purdy, S. Costumes for you to make (4 and up) **391**
See also pages in the following book:
Caney, S. Steven Caney's Kids' America p130-45 (4 and up) **790.1**
See also Indians of North America—Costume and adornment

History
Fox, L. M. Folk costume of Southern Europe (4 and up) **391.09**
Fox, L. M. Folk costume of Western Europe (4 and up) **391.09**
Schnurnberger, L. E. Kings, queens, knights and jesters: making medieval costumes (4 and up) **391.09**
The **costume** book. Leeming, J. **391**

County government

See pages in the following book:

Eichner, J. A. The first book of local government p5-10 (4 and up)   352

County officers. See County government

Couper, Heather

Space frontiers (3 and up)   500.5

Courage

McNeer, M. Armed with courage (4-6)   920
   See also Fear

Fiction

Peet, B. Cowardly Clyde   **E**

The **courage** of Sarah Noble. Dalgliesh, A.   **Fic**

The **Courage** Piece. Leuser, E.
   In Fifty plays for junior actors p280-92   812.08

Courlander, Harold

Anansi's hat-shaking dance
   In The Arbuthnot Anthology of children's literature p321-23   808.8
   In Time for old magic p198-200   398.2

The fire on the mountain
   In The Arbuthnot Anthology of children's literature p312-14   808.8
   In Time for old magic p191-93   398.2

The hat-shaking dance, and other tales from the Gold Coast (3-6)   398.2

Contents: All stories are Anansi's;; Anansi, the oldest of animals; Anansi's hat-shaking dance; Two feasts for Anansi; Anansi plays dead; Liar's contest; Why wisdom is found everywhere; Osebo's drum; Anansi and the elephant go hunting; Planting party; Okraman's medicine; Anansi borrows money; Anansi's rescue from the river; Anansi and the elephant exchange knocks; How the lizard lost and regained his farm; Anansi steals the palm wine; Elephant's tail; Porcupine's hoe; Sword that fought by itself; Nyame's well; Coming of the yams

The king's drum, and other African stories (4-6)   398.2

Contents: The song of Gimmile; The chief of the Gurensi; Three fast men; The King of Sedo; The fisherman; A song for the new chief; The search: who gets the chief's daughter; The king's drum; The Sky God's daughter; The wedding of the hawk; How poverty was revealed to the king of Adja; Three sons of a chief; The brave man of Golo; The feast; Frog's wives make ndiba pudding; Two friends: how they parted; The hunter and his talking leopard; The past and the future; The elephant hunters; A father-in-law and his son-in-law; The donkeys ask for justice; The lion's share; Nawasi goes to war; Ruda, the quick thinker; The giraffe hunters; The stone lute; Why the chameleon shakes his head; The hemp smoker and the hemp grower; The message from the moon

The leopard's daughter
   In With a deep sea smile p56-60   372.6

Olode the hunter, and other tales from Nigeria (4-6)   398.2

Contents: Olomu's bush rat; The man who looked for death; Ekun and Opolo go looking for wives; The lizard's lost meat; The antelope skin; Olode the hunter becomes an Oba; How Kjapa, who was short, became long; Ijapa cries for his horse; Kigbo and the bush spirits; The chief's knife; Why the lion, the vulture, and the hyena do not live together; Ijapa and the Oba repair a roof; Sofo's escape from the leopard; How Ologbon-Ori sought wisdom; Ijapa and Yanrinbo swear an oath; Antelope's mother; The woman in the moon; The Oba asks for a mountain; The journey to Lagos; Ijapa goes to the Osanyin shrine; Ijapa and the hot-water test; Ogungbemi and the battle in the bush; The quarrel between Ile and Orun; Ijapa demands corn fufu; The wrestlers; How the people of Ife become scattered; How Moremi saved the town of Ife; The staff of Ornamiyan; The first woman to say "dim"; Why no one lends his beauty

The piece of fire, and other Haitian tales (4-6)   398.2

Contents: Merisier, stronger than the elephants; The chief of the well; Bouki gets whee-ai; Break Mountains; Bouki rents a horse;; Pierre Jean's tortoise; The cat, the dog, and death; Sweet misery; The gun, the pot, and the hat; The lizard's big dance; Bouki buys a burro; Ticoumba and the President; Nananbouclou and the piece of fire; The fisherman; Who is the older; The voyage below the water; Bouki cuts wood; The donkey driver; The blacksmiths; Bouki's glasses; Charles Legoun and his friend; Bouki and Ti Bef; The King of the animals; Janot cooks for the Emperor; Jean Britisse, the champion; Waiting for a turkey

The search: who gets the chief's daughter
   In With a deep sea smile p70-74   372.6

Talk
   In Gruenberg, S. M. ed. Favorite stories old and new p354-57   808.8

The tiger's tail
   In Gruenberg, S. M. ed. Favorite stories old and new p396-97   808.8

The tiger's whisker, and other tales and legends from Asia and the Pacific (4-6)   398.2

Contents: The scholar of Kosei; The tiger's whisker; The tiger's minister of state; The trial of the stone; The hidden treasure of Khin; The king who ate chaff; The musician of Tagaung; The rice puller of Chaohwa; The spear and shield of Huan-tan; The ambassador from Chi; The king of the forest; The trial of Avichára-pura; The prince of the six weapons; The man from Kailasa; Krishna the cowherd; The scholars and the lion; The traveler and the nut tree;; The debt; The boy and the cloth; The wrestler of Kyushu; The counting of the crocodiles; Abunuwas the trickster; The spotted rug; The philosophers of King Darius; Dinner for the monk; The well diggers; Guno and Koyo and the Kris; The learned men; The war of the plants; Maui the great; The great lizard of Nimple

Uncle Bouqui and Godfather Malice
   In The Arbuthnot Anthology of children's literature p39-401   808.8
   In Time for old magic p268-70   398.2

The **court** of King Arithmetic. Chaloner, G.
   In Fifty plays for junior actors p118-27   812.08

The **court** of the stone children. Cameron, E.   **Fic**

Courtesy

   See also Etiquette

Cousin Greylegs, the great red fox and Grandfather Mole

Pyle, H. Cousin Greylegs, the great red fox and Grandfather Mole
   In Pyle, H. The wonder clock p77-88   398.2

Cousins, Margaret

The story of Thomas Alva Edison (4-6)   92
The story of Thomas Alva Edison; excerpt
   In Holiday ring p172-75   394.2

Cousteau, Jacques-Ives

Dolphins (5 and up)   599.5

About

Iverson, G. Jacques Costeau (3-5)   92

Coutant, Helen

First snow (2-4)   **Fic**

The **covered** bridge house, and other poems. Starbird, K.   811

Coverlets. See Quilts

The **covetous** Councilman. Bealmear, J. H.
   In Dramatized folk tales of the world p504-13   812.08

The **cow** and the thread. Jagendorf, M. A.
   In Jagendorf, M. A. Noodlehead stories from around the world p68-72   398.2

Cow Bu-cola. Manning-Sanders, R.
In Manning-Sanders, R. A book of ogres and trolls p75-79   398.2

Cow ghost
Du Bois, W. P. Elizabeth—the cow ghost
In Gruenberg, S. M. ed. Favorite stories old and new p487-90   808.8

The **cow** who fell in the canal. Krasilovsky, P.   E

Cowardly Clyde. Peet, B.   E

The **cowboy** trade. Rounds, G.   978

Cowboys. See Cowhands

Cowboys and cattle country (5 and up)   978

Cowgirls. See Cowhands

Cowhands
Cowboys and cattle country (5 and up)   978
Rounds, G. The cowboy trade (4 and up)   978

See also pages in the following books:
Burt, O. W. The horse in America p128-36 (5 and up)   636.1
Dobler, L. The land and people of Uruguay p104-10 (5 and up)   989.5
Hall, E. The land and people of Argentina p90-105 (5 and up)   982

See also Rodeos

Fiction
James, W. Smoky, the cow horse (6 and up)   Fic

Cowper, William
The diverting history of Jack Gilpin
In Caldecott, R. The Randolph Caldecott treasury p205-35   741.9
The diverting history of John Gilpin
In Randolph Caldecott's John Gilpin and other stories   398

Cows
Fiction
Krasilovsky, P. The cow who fell in the canal   E
Sewell, M. The wee, wee mannie and the big, big coo (k-2)   398.2
Infancy
Cole, J. A calf is born (k-2)   636.2

Cox, Charles
(illus.) Carlson, B. W. Funny-bone dramatics   812

Coy, Harold
Presidents (4-6)   920

Coyote and the fox
De Huff, E. W. The coyote and the fox
In Gruenberg, S. M. ed. Favorite stories old and new p338-40   808.8

Coyote drowns the world. Baker, B.
In Baker, B. At the center of the world p8-15   398.2

Coyotes
See pages in the following book:
Harris, J. Endangered predators p37-50 (5 and up)   599.74
Fiction
Hodges, M. The Fire Bringer (2-4)   398.2

The **crab** and the crane. Babbitt, E. C.
In Babbitt, E. C. Jataka tales p84-89   398.2

Crab and the monkey
The Crab and the monkey
In Sakade, F. ed. Japanese children's favorite stories p94-96   398.2

The **crab** that played with the sea. Kipling, R.
In Kipling, R. Just so stories   S C

Crabs
Holling, H. C. Pagoo (4 and up)   595.3
Zim, H. S. Crabs (3-5)   595.3

Cradle songs. See Lullabies

The **cradle** that rocked by itself. Leach, M.
In Leach, M. The thing at the foot of the bed, and other scary tales p75-76   S C

Craft, Ellen
Freedman, F. B. Two tickets to freedom; the true story of Ellen and William Craft, fugitive slaves (4-6)   92
See pages in the following book:
Chittenden, E. F. Profiles in black and white p68-87 (5 and up)   920

Craft, Ruth
Carrie Hepple's garden   E
Pieter Brueghel's The fair (2-4)   759.9493
The winter bear   E

Craft, William
Freedman, F. B. Two tickets to freedom (4-6)   92
See also pages in the following book:
Chittenden, E. F. Profiles in black and white p68-87 (5 and up)   920

The **craft** of sail. Adkins, J.   623.88

Crafts for Christmas. Cutler, K. N.   745.59

Craig, M. Jean
The donkey prince (k-3)   398.2

Cramblit, Joella
Flowers are for keeping (5 and up)   745.92
(jt. auth.) Belton, J. Card games   795.4
(jt. auth.) Belton, J. Dice games   795.1
(jt. auth.) Belton, J. Domino games   795.3
(jt. auth.) Belton, J. Solitaire games   795.4

Crane, Walter
(illus.) The Anotated Mother Goose, nursery rhymes old and new. See The Annotated Mother Goose, nursery rhymes old and new   398
(illus.) Grimm, J. Household stories   398.2

Crane and the crab
Babbitt, E. C. The crab and the crane
In Babbitt, E .C. Jataka tales p84-89   398.2

Crane and the heron
Afanas'ev, A. The crane and the heron
In Afanas'ev, A. Russian fairy tales p66   398.2
Riordan, J. The crane woos the heron
In Riordan, J. Tales from Central Russia p144-45   398.2

The **crane** woos the heron. Riordan, J.
In Riordan, J. Tales from Central Russia p144-45   398.2
See also Crane and the heron

Cranes (Birds)
Fiction
Byars, B. The house of wings (4-6)   Fic
Robertson, K. In search of a sandhill crane (5 and up)   Fic

Cranes, derricks, etc.
Zim, H. S. Hoists, cranes, and derricks (3-6)   621.8
See also pages in the following book:
Harman, C. Skyscraper goes up p49-57 (5 and up)   690

Cranes, Whooping. See Whooping cranes

Cricket songs   **895.6**
Crickets
  George, J. C. All upon a stone (1-3)   **595.7**
  Hogner, D. C. Grasshoppers and crickets (2-5)   **595.7**
  See also pages in the following books:
  Ricciuti, E. R. Shelf pets p92-97 (5 and up)   **639**
  Ricciuti, E. R. Sounds of animals at night p31-39 (3-5)   **591.5**
Fiction
  Caudill, R. A pocketful of cricket   **E**
  Seldon, G. The cricket in Times Square (3-6)   **Fic**
Cricket's Jokes, riddles and other stuff   **793.7**
Crictor. Ungerer, T.   **E**
Crime
  See also Trials
Fiction
  King, C. Me and my million (5 and up)   **Fic**
Criminal investigation
  See also Fingerprints
Criminal law
  See also Trials
The **Crimson** feather. Watts, F. B.
  In Fifty plays for junior actors p627-34   **812.08**
Crinkleroot's book of animal tracks and wildlife signs. Arnosky, J.   **591.9**
The **cripple.** Andersen, H. C.
  In Andersen, H. C. The complete fairy tales and stories p1045-57   **S C**
Crippled children. See Physically handicapped children
Crippled people. See Physically handicapped
Critchlow, Dennis
  (illus.) Reinfeld, F. Chess for children **794.1**
A **critical** approach to children's literature. Chicago. University. Graduate Library School   **028.5**
A **critical** handbook of children's literature. Lukens, R.   **028.5**
A **critical** history of children's literature   **028.5**
Criticism
  See pages in the following book:
  Children and literature p391-414   **028.5**
  See also Books—Reviews; also literature, film, and music subjects with the subdivision History and criticism, e.g. American literature—History and criticism
Crochet for beginners. Rubenstone, J.   **746.43**
Crocheting
  Parker, X. L. A beginner's book of knitting and crocheting (5 and up)   **746.43**
  Rubenstone, J. Crochet for beginners (3-5)   **746.43**
  See also pages in the following book:
  Meyer, C. Yarn—the things it makes and how to make them p11-42 (4 and up)   **746.4**
Crocker, Betty
  Betty Crocker's Cookbook for boys & girls. See Betty Crocker's Cookbook for boys & girls   **641.5**
Crockery. See Pottery

Crockett, David
  See pages in the following books:
  Gruenberg, S. M. ed. Favorite stories old and new p398-402   **808.8**
  Malcolmson, A. Yankee Doodle's cousins p149-55 (4 and up)   **398.2**
  North American legends p192-95 (5 and up)   **398.2**
Crocodile and Hen. Lexau, J. M.   **398.2**
Crocodiles
  Gross, R. B. Alligators and other crocodilians (2-5)   **597.9**
  Zim, H. S. Alligators and crocodiles (4-6)   **597.9**
  See also pages in the following books:
  Huntington, H. E. Let's look at reptiles p50-57 (4-6)   **597.9**
  Patent, D. H. Reptiles and how they reproduce p107-14 (5 and up)   **597.9**
  Shuttlesworth, D. E. Animals that frighten people p80-88 (5 and up)   **591.5**
Fiction
  Aruego, J. A crocodile's tale (k-3)   **398.2**
  Galdone, P. The monkey and the crocodile (k-2)   **398.2**
  Hoban, R. Dinner at Alberta's   **E**
  Waber, B. The house on East 88th Street   **E**
A **crocodile's** tales. Aruego, J.   **398.2**
The **crocus** who couldn't bloom. Boiko, C.
  In Boiko, C. Children's plays for creative actors p272-81   **812**
Crofut, Susan
  (illus.) Crofut, W. The moon on the one hand   **784.6**
Crofut, William
  The moon on the one hand (3-6)   **784.6**
Croker, T. Crofton
  The soul cages
  In Haunts, haunts, haunts p124-39   **S C**
Croll, Carolyn
  Too many Babas   **E**
Crompton, Anne Eliot
  The winter wife (1-3)   **398.2**
Crone, Ruth
  (jt. auth.) Brown, M. M. The silent storm [biography of Anne Sullivan Macy]   **92**
Crook, Beverly Courtney
  Invite a bird to dinner (4-6)   **745.59**
Crook, George
  See pages in the following book:
  Ehrlich, A. Wounded Knee: an Indian history of the American West p42-50, 145-52 (6 and up)   **970.004**
The **crooked** pine. Ginsburg, M.
  In Ginsburg, M. The twelve clever brothers, and other fools p44-47   **398.2**
Crosher, G. R. See Kesteven, G. R.
Cross, Helen Reeder
  Christmas without Kriss Kringle
  In Christmas stories round the world p95-100   **S C**
Cross-country cat. Calhoun, M.   **E**
Cross country running. See Track athletics
The **cross** is pledged as security. Afanas'ev, A.
  In Afanas'ev, A. Russian fairy tales p159-60   **398.2**

The **cross** princess. MacLellan, E.
    In Fifty plays for junior actors p322-32
        812.08

Cross purposes. MacDonald, G.
    In MacDonald, G. The complete fairy tales
    of George MacDonald p187-209 **S C**

Cross-surety
    Afanas'ev, A. The cross is pledged as secu-
    rity
    In Afanas'ev, A. Russian fairy tales p159-60
        398.2

Cross your fingers, spit in your hat. Schwartz,
    A. comp.   **398**

Crossing the bridge. Leach, M.
    In Leach, M. Whistle in the graveyard
    p75   **398.2**

Crossing to Salamis. Walsh, J. P.
    In Walsh, J. P. Children of the fox **S C**

Crossley, B. Alice
    (ed.) Popular plays for classroom reading.
    See Popular plays for classroom reading
        808.82

Crossley-Holland, Kevin
    Green blades rising (6 and up)   **942.01**

The **crossways**. Hartley, L. P.
    In Haunting tales p246-55   **S C**

Crouch, Marcus
    (ed.) Chosen for children. See Chosen for
    children   **028.5**

Crouthers, David D.
    Flags of American history (6 and up) **929.9**

Crow
    Wojcicki, K. W. The crow
    In Yellow fairy book p92-94   **398.2**

Crow and the lobster
    Afanas'ev, A. The raven and the lobster
    In Afanas'ev, A. Russian fairy tales p612
        398.2

Crow Boy. Yashima, T.   **E**

Crow Indians
    See pages in the following books:
    Hofsinde, R. Indian costumes p33-39 (3-6)
        391
    Hofsinde, R. Indian warriors and their
    weapons p68-76 (3-6)   **970.004**

Crowe, Robert L.
    Clyde monster   **E**

Crowell, Pers
    (illus.) Corbin, W. Golden mare   **Fic**

Crowell's Handbook of classical mythology.
    Tripp, E.   **292.03**

Crowninshield, Ethel
    Surprise for Sally
    In Gruenberg, S. M. comp. Let's hear a
    story p139-43   **808.8**

Crows
    Blassingame, W. Wonders of crows (5 and
    up)   **598**
    Pringle, L. Listen to the crows (3-6) **598**

Crude oil. See Petroleum

The **Cruel** crane outwitted
    In Indian fairy tales p46-50   **398.2**

Cruelty to animals. See Animals—Treatment

The **cruise** of the Aardvark. Nash, O.   **811**

The **crumb**. Doty, J. S.   **Fic**

Crumbs on the table
    Grimm, J. The crumbs on the table
    In Grimm, J. The complete Grimm's fairy
    tales p768-69   **398.2**

Crusader's Toby. Aiken, J.
    In Aiken, J. The faithless lollybird p236-55
        S C

The **cruse** of oil—165 B.C. Levinger, E. E.
    In Association for Childhood Education
    International. Told under the Christ-
    mas tree p290-95   **808.8**

Crusoe, Robinson
    (illus.) [Politzer, A.] My journals and sketch-
    books   **Fic**

Crustacea
    See pages in the following books:
    Cooper, E. K. Science on the shores and
    banks p104-18 (5 and up)   **574.92**
    Zim, H. S. Commercial fishing p47-52 (3-6)
        639
    Zim, H. S. Seashores p68-79 (5 and up)
        574.92
    See also names of shellfish, e.g. Crabs;
    Lobsters

Cruz, Ray
    (illus.) Borghese, A. The down to earth
    cookbook   **641.5**
    (illus.) Hazen, B. S. The gorilla did it **E**
    (illus.) Jordan, J. New life: new room **Fic**
    (illus.) MacGregor, C. The storybook cook-
    book   **641.5**
    (illus.) Mohr, N. Felita   **Fic**
    (illus.) Schlein, M. What's wrong with being
    a skunk   **599.74**
    (illus.) Titiev, E. How the Moolah was
    taught a lesson & other tales from Russia
        398.2
    (illus.) Viorst, J. Alexander and the terrible,
    horrible, no good, very bad day   **E**

A **cry** from the earth: music of the North
    American Indians. Bierhorst, J.   **781.7**

Cryptography
    Albert, B. Codes for kids (3-6)   **652**
    Albert, B. More Codes for kids (3-6)   **652**
    Babson, W. All kinds of codes (5 and up)
        652
    Gardner, M. Codes, ciphers and secret writ-
    ing (5 and up)   **652**
    James, E. How to keep a secret (4-6) **652**
    Kohn, B. Secret codes and ciphers (4 and up)
        652
    Lamb, G. Secret writing tricks (5 and up)
        652
    Peterson, J. How to write codes and send
    secret messages (2-4)   **652**
    Sarnoff, J. The code & cipher book (3-6)
        652

Crystal ball
    Grimm, J. The crystal ball
    In Grimm, J. The complete Grimm's fairy
    tales p798-801   **398.2**

Crystal coffin
    Grimm, J. The crystal coffin
    In Green fairy book p333-40   **398.2**
    Grimm, J. The glass coffin
    In Grimm, J. The complete Grimm's fairy
    tales p672-78   **398.2**

The **crystal** flask. Asbrand, K.
    In One hundred plays for children p570-76
        808.82

Crystal mountain
    Afanas'ev, A. The crystal mountain
    In Afanas'ev, A. Russian fairy tales p482-
    84   **398.2**

Crystalline rocks. See Rocks

D

D Day. See Normandy, Attack on, 1944

DDT (Insecticide)
> *See pages in the following book:*
Graham, A. Bug hunters p33-50 (5 and up)
632

D. J.'s worst enemy. Burch, R.   **Fic**

DNA
Silverstein, A. The code of life (6 and up)
575.1
> *See also pages in the following book:*
Nourse, A. E. Viruses p53-60 (5 and up)
576

D'Adamo, Anthony
(illus.) Barker, A. Black on white and read all over   **686.2**

Daddy. Caines, J.   **E**

Daddy longlegs
Hawes, J. My daddy longlegs (1-3)   **595.4**

Daddy Mention and Sourdough Gus. Jagendorf, M. A.
> *In* Jagendorf, M. A. Folk stories of the South p87-89   **398.2**

Daedalus
Serraillier, I. A fall from the sky (4-6)
292
> *See also pages in the following book:*
Gates, D. Lord of the sky: Zeus p98-106 (4 and up)   **292**

Dag and Daga, and the flying troll of Sky Mountain. Östenson, H.
> *In* Olenius, E. comp. Great Swedish fairy tales p185-94   **398.2**

Da Gama, Vasco. See Gama, Vasco da

Dahl, Roald
James and the giant peach (4-6)   **Fic**

Dahnsen, Alan
Bicycles (2-4)   **629.2**

Dairy products
Meyer, C. Milk, butter, and cheese (5 and up)   **641.3**

Daisy
Andersen, H. C. The daisy
> *In* Andersen, H. C. The complete fairy tales and stories p108-111   **S C**

Dakota Indians
Goble, P. Red Hawk's account of Custer's last battle (4 and up)   **973.8**
> *See also pages in the following books:*
Ehrlich, A. Wounded Knee: an Indian history of the American West p76-105, 130-45, 162-86 (6 and up)   **970.004**
Hofsinde, R. Indian costumes p86-91 (3-6)
391
Hofsinde, R. The Indian medicine man p21-32 (4-7)   **970.004**
Hofsinde, R. Indian warriors and their weapons p35-56 (3-6)   **970.004**

Biography
O'Connor, R. Sitting Bull: war chief of the Sioux (4-6)   **92**

Fiction
Goble, P. Lone Bull's horse raid (3-6)
Fic

Dalfunka where the rich live forever. Singer, I. B.
> *In* Singer, I. B. Naftali the storyteller and his horse, Sus, and other stories p29-35   **S C**

Dalgliesh, Alice
The bears on Hemlock Mountain (1-4)   **Fic**
(comp.) Christmas (4 and up)   **S C**
Christmas in Provence
> *In* Association for Childhood Education International. Told under the Christmas tree p173-83   **808.8**
> *In* Dalgliesh, A. comp. Christmas p147-58   **S C**
The courage of Sarah Noble (2-4)   **Fic**
The Fourth of July story (2-4)   **973.3**
The kitten on the canal boat
> *In* The Arbuthnot Anthology of children's literature p754-56   **808.8**
The Thanksgiving story (k-2)   **394.2**
White Christmas
> *In* Dalgliesh, A. comp. Christmas p180-88   **S C**

Dalphin, Marcia
(comp.) Illustrators of children's books: 1946-1956. See Illustrators of children's books: 1946-1956   **741.64**

Dalton, Ann
(illus.) Waters, J. F. Hungry sharks   **597**

Dalton, Anne
(illus.) Reeves, J. The shadow of the hawk, and other stories   **398.2**

The dam builders. Kelly, J. E.   **627**

Damascus
> *See pages in the following book:*
Copeland, P. W. The land and people of Syria p84-93 (5 and up)   **956.91**

D'Amato, Alex
(jt. auth.) D'Amato, J. African crafts for you to make   **745.5**
(jt. auth.) D'Amato, J. Algonquian and Iroquois crafts for you to make   **745.5**
(jt. auth.) D'Amato, J. American Indian craft inspirations   **745.5**
(jt. auth.) D'Amato, J. Colonial crafts for you to make   **745.5**
(jt. auth.) D'Amato, J. More Colonial crafts for you to make   **745.5**
(illus.) Ruchlis, H. Your changing earth
551

D'Amato, Janet
African crafts for you to make (4 and up)
745.5
Algonquian and Iroquois crafts for you to make (4-6)   **745.5**
American Indian craft inspirations (5 and up)   **745.5**
Colonial crafts for you to make (4 and up)
745.5
Indian crafts (4 and up)   **745.5**
More Colonial crafts for you to make (4 and up)   **745.5**
(illus.) Ruchlis, H. Your changing earth
551

Dame Gudbrand
Ashbjörnsen, P. C. Gudbrand on the hillside
> *In* The Arbuthnot Anthology of children's literature p244-46   **808.8**

De Kiefte, Kees
(illus.) Coerr, E. Jane Goodall [biography of Jane Lawick-Goodall] 92

De la Fontaine, Jean. See La Fontaine, Jean de

De la Mare, Walter
Clever Grethel
In Greene, E. comp. Clever cooks p109-14 398.2
(ed.) Come hither 821.08
Peacock pie (4 and up) 821
Rhymes and verses (4 and up) 821
Stories from the Bible (5 and up) 221.9
(ed.) Tom Tiddler's ground. See Tom Tiddler's ground 821.08

About
See pages in the following book:
Horn Book Reflections on children's books and reading p265-79 028.5

Delano, Irene
(illus.) Blanco, T. The Child's gifts 232.9

De la Ramée, Louise. See Ramée, Louise de la

De Larrea, Victoria
(illus.) Juba this and Juba that. See Juba this and Juba that 372.6

Delaware Indians
Fiction
Richter, C. Light in the forest (6 and up) Fic

Delear, Frank J.
Helicopters and airplanes of the U.S. Army (5 and up) 623.74

De Leeuw, Adèle
The Girl Scout story (2-5) 369.463

Delessert, Etienne
(illus.) Kipling, R. Just so stories S C

The Delikon. Hoover, H. M. Fic

Del Monte, Jacques
Andrews, C. J. Fell's International coin book 737.4
Andrews, C. J. Fell's United States coin book 737.4

De Long, George Washington
See pages in the following book:
Orlob, H. The Northeast Passage p73-81 (5 and up) 998

Deloria, Vine
Indians of the Pacific Northwest (6 and up) 970.004

Delta Plan, Netherlands
See pages in the following book:
Cohn, A. The first book of the Netherlands p13-17 (4 and up) 949.2

Deltaplan. See Delta Plan, Netherlands

Delton, Judy
Kitty in the middle (2-5) Fic
Kitty in the summer. See note under Delton, J. Kitty in the middle Fic
The new girl at school E
Rabbit finds a way. See Delton, J. Two good friends E
Three friends find spring. See Delton, J. Two good friends E
Two good friends E
Two is company. See note under Delton, J. Two good friends E

Delulio, John
(illus.) Paul, A. Kids outdoor gardening 635

DeLuna, Tony
(illus.) Sharmat, M. W. I'm not Oscar's friend anymore E

Demeter
Farmer, P. The story of Persephone (3-5) 292
Gates, D. Two queens of heaven: Aphrodite [and] Demeter (4 and up) 292

Fiction
Miles, P. The gods in winter (5 and up) Fic

Deming, Dorothy
Grey ghosts
In One hundred plays for children p45-52 808.82
Old man river
In One hundred plays for children p53-60 808.82

De Miskey, Julian. See Miskey, Julian de

The demon king. Priestley, J. B.
In Haunting tales p156-73 S C

The Demon with the matted hair
In Indian fairy tales p194-98 398.2

Demonology
See also Witchcraft

Demonstrations for black civil rights. See Blacks—Civil rights

De Montreville, Doris
(ed.) Fourth book of junior authors & illustrators. See Fourth book of junior authors & illustrators 920.03
(ed.) Third book of junior authors. See Third book of junior authors 920.03

Demuth, Jack
City horse (3-6) 363.2

Demuth, Patricia
(jt. auth.) Demuth, J. City horse 363.2

Denmark
Wohlrabe, R. A. The land and people of Denmark (5 and up) 948.9

Antiquities
See pages in the following book:
Wohlrabe, R. A. The land and people of Denmark p15-20 (5 and up) 948.9

Fiction
Bødker, C. Silas and the black mare (5 and up) Fic

Folklore
See Folklore—Denmark

Dennis, J. Richard
Fractions are parts of things (2-4) 513

Dennis, Landt
Catch the wind (5 and up) 621.4

Dennis, Lisl
(illus.) Dennis, L. Catch the wind 621.4

Dennis, Wesley
(illus.) Henry, M. Album of horses 636.1
(illus.) Henry, M. Black Gold Fic
(illus.) Henry, M. Brighty of the Grand Canyon Fic
(illus.) Henry, M. Justin Morgan had a horse Fic
(illus.) Henry, M. Misty of Chincoteague Fic
(illus.) Henry, M. White stallion of Lipizza Fic

Denslow, W. W.
(illus.) Baum, L. F. The Wizard of Oz Fic

Densmore, Frances
Bierhorst, J. comp. Songs of Chippewa 781.7

Dentistry
Barnett, N. I know a dentist (1-3)   **617.6**
Rockwell, H. My dentist (k-2)   **617.6**
  See also pages in the following book:
Nourse, A. E. The tooth book p41-64 (5 and up)   **617.6**
  See also Orthodontics

De Osma, Lupe
The dancing jug
  In A-haunting we will go p111-17   **S C**
The witches' ride
  In The Arbuthnot Anthology of children's literature p407-08   **808.8**
  In Harper, W. comp. Ghosts and goblins p228-33   **398.2**
  In Time for old magic p273-74   **398.2**

Deoxyribonucleic acid. See DNA

De Paola, Tomie
Andy (that's my name)   **E**
Big Anthony and the magic ring   **E**
Charlie needs a cloak   **E**
The cloud book (k-3)   **551.57**
The clown of God (k-3)   **398.2**
Helga's dowry   **E**
The kids' cat book (2-4)   **636.8**
The Lady of Guadalupe (k-3)   **232.9**
Nana Upstairs & Nana Downstairs   **E**
The popcorn book (k-3)   **641.6**
The quicksand book (k-3)   **552**
Strega Nona (k-3)   **398.2**
Things to make and do for Valentine's Day (1-3)   **394.2**
Watch out for the chicken feet in your soup   **E**
(illus.) Balestrino, P. Hot as an ice cube   **536**
(illus.) The Cat on the Dovrefell. See The Cat on the Dovrefell   **398.2**
(illus.) Easter buds are springing. See Easter buds are springing   **811.08**
(illus.) Fritz, J. Can't you make them behave, King George? [biography of George III, King of Great Britain]   **92**
(illus.) Ghost poems. See Ghost poems)   **811.08**
(illus.) Keller, C. comp. The star spangled banana, and other revolutionary riddles   **793.7**
(illus.) Kroll, S. Santa's crash-bang Christmas   **E**
(illus.) Oh, such foolishness! See Oh, such foolishness!   **811.08**
(illus.) Saunders, R. The Franklin Watts Concise guide to babysitting   **649**
(illus.) Willard, N. Simple pictures are best   **E**

Department stores
Fiction
Rosen, W. Henrietta and the day of the iguana   **E**

The departure. Daringer, H. F.
  In Thanksgiving p49-58   **394.2**

DePauw, Linda Grant
Founding mothers (6 and up)   **305.4**

Depend on Katie John. Calhoun, M. See note under Calhoun, M. Katie John   **Fic**

Depressions, Economic
Katz, W. L. An album of the Great Depression (5 and up)   **330.973**
Fiction
Langton, J. Her Majesty, Grace Jones (4 and up)   **Fic**
Lee, M. The rock and the willow (6 and up)   **Fic**

Snyder, Z. K. The velvet room (4-6)   **Fic**
Taylor, M. D. Song of the trees (4-6)   **Fic**
Thrasher, C. The dark didn't catch me (5 and up)   **Fic**

De Prieto, Mariana Beeching. See Prieto, Mariana Beeching de

De Regniers, Beatrice Schenk
The Abraham Lincoln joke book (4-6)   **817.08**
Circus (k-3)   **791.3**
It does not say meow, and other animal riddle rhymes (k-1)   **793.7**
Laura's story   **E**
A little house of your own   **E**
Little Sister and the Month Brothers (k-3)   **398.2**
May I bring a friend?   **E**
Red Riding Hood (1-3)   **398.2**
The shadow book   **E**
Something special (k-2)   **811**

Dermatitis. See Skin—Diseases

DeRoin, Nancy
(ed.) Jataka tales. See Jataka tales   **398.2**

Derricks. See Cranes, derricks, etc.

De Sable, Jean Baptiste Pointe. See Pointe de Sable, Jean Baptiste

Descent. See Heredity

De Schweinitz, Karl
Growing up (2-5)   **612**

Desegregation in education. See School integration

Desert animals
Baylor, B. We walk in sandy places (k-2)   **591.5**
Brenner, B. Lizard tails and cactus spines (4-6)   **597.9**
Rinard, J. E. Wonders of the desert world (k-3)   **574.9**
  See also names of desert animals, e.g. Camels

Desert ecology
Baylor, B. The desert is theirs (1-4)   **574.5**
Pringle, L. The gentle desert (4-6)   **574.5**

The desert is theirs. Baylor, B.   **574.5**

Desert plants
Brenner, B. Lizard tails and cactus spines (4-6)   **597.9**
Rinard, J. E. Wonders of the desert world (k-3)   **574.9**
  See also pages in the following book:
Patent, D. H. Sizes and shapes in nature—what they mean p103-09 (5 and up)   **574.4**
  See also names of desert plants, e.g. Cactus

The deserted children. Curtis, E. S.
  In Curtis, E. S. The girl who married a ghost, and other tales from the North American Indian p45-51   **398.2**

Deserted mine
Sawyer, R. The deserted mine
  In Sawyer, R. The way of the storyteller   **372.6**

Deserts
Atwood, A. The wild young desert (4 and up)   **551.4**
Clark, A. N. Along sandy trails (2-5)   **574.9**
Rinard, J. E. Wonders of the desert world (k-3)   **574.9**
  See also pages in the following books:
Clifford, M. L. The land and people of the Arabian Peninsula p17-27 (5 and up)   **953**

Deserts—*Continued*

Coburn, D. A spit is a piece of land p109-16 (4-6) **551.4**

Gallant, R. A. Earth's changing climate p175-79 (6 and up) **551.6**

See also Desert animals; Desert plants

Poetry

Caudill, R. Wind, sand and sky (1-4) **811**

Design

See pages in the following book:

Pettit, F. H. How to make whirligigs and whimmy diddles, and other American folkcraft objects p305-14 (5 and up) **745.5**

Design, Decorative

Ellison, E. C. Fun with lines and curves (4 and up) **745.4**

Designs, Floral. See Flower arrangement

De Soto, Hernando de. See Soto, Hernando de

De Soto, finder of the Mississippi. Syme, R. **92**

Desoxyribonucleic acid. See DNA

Dessable Jean Baptiste. See Pointe de Sable, Jean Baptiste

Desserts

See pages in the following books:

Better Homes and Gardens New Junior cook book p52-63 (3-6) **641.5**

Betty Crocker's Cookbook for boys & girls p123-40 (3-6) **641.5**

Girl Scouts of the United States of America. Girl Scout cookbook p120-39 (4 and up) **641.5**

Paul, A. Kids cooking without a stove p11-22 (1-3) **641.5**

Penner, L. R. The colonial cookbook p97-110 (5 and up) **641.5**

Schwartz, P. D. You can cook p147-70 (5 and up) **641.5**

Detective Mole. Quackenbush, R. **E**

Detective Mole and the circus mystery. Quackenbush, R. See note under Quackenbush, R. Detective Mole **E**

Detective Mole and the seashore mystery. Quackenbush, R. See note under Quackenbush, R. Detective Mole **E**

Detective Mole and the secret clues. Quackenbush, R. See note under Quackenbush, R. Detective Mole **E**

Detective Mole and the tip-top mystery. Quackenbush, R. See note under Quackenbush, R. Detective Mole **E**

Detectives in togas. Winterfeld, H. **Fic**

De Treviño, Elizabeth (Borton) See Treviño, Elizabeth (Borton) de

Deulin, Charles

The enchanted canary
In Red fairy book p247-64 **398.2**

The enchanted watch
In Green fairy book p55-61 **398.2**

The little soldier
In The Andrew Lang Fairy tale treasury p243-59 **398.2**
In Green fairy book p166-87 **398.2**

The nettle spinner
In Red fairy book p278-85 **398.2**

Deutsch, Babette

The clever judge
In The Arbuthnot Anthology of children's literature p299-300 **808.8**
In Time for old magic p178-79 **398.2**

Devaney, John

The story of basketball (5 and up) **796.32**

Tiny! The story of Nate Archibald (4 and up) **92**

De Veaux, Diane

(comp.) The Black experience in children's audiovisual materials. See The Black experience in children's audiovisual materials **016.3058**

Development. See Embryology; Evolution

Devereux, Frederick L.

Horseback riding (4-6) **798.2**

Devil

Fiction

Babbitt, N. The Devil's storybook (4-6) **S C**

Scribner, C. The devil's bridge (2-4) **398.2**

Stadler, V. Even the devil is afraid of a shrew (k-3) **398.2**

Turska, K. The magician of Cracow (k-3) **398.2**

Valen, N. The Devil's tail (2-4) **398.2**

The **Devil** and his grandmother. Grimm, J.
In Grimm, J. The complete Grimm's fairy tales p563-66 **398.2**
In Yellow fairy book p46-49 **398.2**
See also Dragon and his grandmother

The **devil** and his three golden hairs. Grimm, J.
In Grimm, J. The juniper tree, and other tales from Grimm v 1 p80-93 **398.2**
See also Giant with the golden hair

Devil and the wind. Hooke, H. M.
In Hooke, H. M. Thunder in the mountains p211-17 **398.2**

Devil in red flannel. Jagendorf, M. A.
In Jagendorf, M. A. New England bean-pot p231-35 **398.2**

Devil in the barrel. Jagendorf, M. A.
In Jagendorf, M. A. New England bean-pot p84-88 **398.2**

The **devil** in the belfry. Poe, E. A.
In Sechrist, E. H. ed. 13 ghostly yarns p95-108 **S C**

Devil in the steeple. Jagendorf, M. A.
In Jagendorf, M. A. New England bean-pot p153-57 **398.2**

The **devil** in Vienna. Orgel, D. **Fic**

Devil who was a potter

Afanas'ev, A. The devil who was a potter
In Afanas'ev, A. Russian fairy tales p576-77 **398.2**

The **Devil** with the three golden hairs. Grimm, J.
In Grimm, J. The complete Grimm's fairy tales p151-58 **398.2**
See also Giant with the golden hair

Devil's hide. Fillmore, P.
In Time to laugh p17-35 **S C**

The **Devil's** storybook. Babbitt, N. **S C**

De Villeneuve, Madame. See Villeneuve, Madame de

Devil's bride

Durham, M. J. The Devil's bride
In The Arbuthnot Anthology of children's literature p289-90 **808.8**
In Time for old magic p168-69 **398.2**

The **Devil's** bridge. Colwell, E.
In Colwell, E. Round about and long ago p23-26 **398.2**

The **devil's** bridge. Scribner, C. **398.2**

The **Devil's** Field. Holman, F.
In Holman, F. The Drac p19-39   398.2
Devil's sooty brother
Grimm, J. The Devil's sooty brother
In Grimm, J. The complete Grimm's fairy
tales p463-66   398.2
The **Devil's tail.** Valen, N.   398.2
Devil's Triangle. See Bermuda Triangle
The **Devil's** Triangle. Baumann, E. D.   001.9
The **Devil's trick.** Singer, I. B.
In Singer, I. B. Zlateh the goat, and other
stories p71-73   398.2
The **devoted** friend. Wilde, O.
In Wilde, O. The Happy Prince, and other
stories p27-39   S C
Devotion. See Worship
De Waard, E. John
Electric cars (5 and up)   629.2
Dewey, Ariane
(jt. auth.) Aruego, J. We hide, you seek   E
(illus.) Duff, M. Rum pum pum   398.2
(illus.) Ginsburg, M. How the sun was
brought back to the sky   398.2
(illus.) Ginsburg, M. Mushroom in the rain
E
(illus.) Ginsburg, M. The strongest one of
all   398.2
Dewey, Melvil
Abridged Dewey Decimal classification and
relative index   025.4
Dewey Decimal classification. See Classification,
Dewey Decimal
De Wit, Dorothy
Children's faces looking up   372.6
Diabetes
Kipnis, L. You can't catch diabetes from a
friend (2-5)   616.4
Silverstein, A. The sugar disease: diabetes
(5 and up)   616.4
Dialects. See names of languages with the
subdivision Dialects, e.g. English language
—Dialects
Diamond, Donna
(illus.) Greene, C. C. Beat the turtle drum
Fic
(illus.) Myers, S. J. The enchanted sticks
Fic
(illus.) Paterson, K. Bridge to Terabithia
Fic
The **diamond.** Soyer, A.
In Soyer, A. The adventures of Yemima,
and other stories p37-41   S C
Diamond Jim and Big Bill. Jagendorf, M. A.
In Jagendorf, M. A. New England bean-pot
p212-15   398.2
Diamonds
See pages in the following book:
Newlon, C. Southern Africa: the critical land
p56-75 (6 and up)   968
Diamonds and toads
Perrault, C. The fairies
In Perrault, C. Perrault's Complete fairy
tales p42-46   398.2
Perrault, C. The fairy
In The Classic fairy tales p100-02   398.2
Perrault, C. Toads and diamonds
In The Andrew Lang Fairy tale treasury
p106-09   398.2
In The Arthur Rackham Fairy book p196-98
398.2
In Blue fairy book p286-89   398.2
Diana. See Artemis

Diary of a frantic kid sister. Colman, H.   Fic
Dias, Earl J.
The Christmas starlet
In On stage for Christmas p107-27   812.08
Dias, Earl S.
Christmas spirit
In A Treasury of Christmas plays p79-94
812.08
Disasters
Fiction
Rutgers van der Loeff, A. Avalanche! (6 and
up)   Fic
Diccon and Elfrida
In Midsummer magic p91-116   398.2
Dice
Belton, J. Dice games (4 and up)   795.1
Dice games. Belton, J.   795.1
Dick Whittington
In The Arthur Rackham Fairy book p30-40
398.2
See also Dick Whittington and his cat
Dick Whittington and his cat
Brown, M. Dick Whittington and his cat
398.2
Dick Whittington
In The Arthur Rackham Fairy book p30-40
398.2
The History of Whittington
In Blue fairy book p217-26   398.2
Jacobs, J. Whittington and his cat
In Jacobs, J. English fairy tales p167-78
398.2
In Time for old magic p25-29   398.2
Reeves, J. Dick Whittington and his cat
In Reeves, J. English fables and fairy
stories p221-34   398.2
Thane, A. Dick Whittington and his cat
In Thane, A. Plays from famous stories
and fairy tales p414-29   812
Dickens, Charles
Captain Murderer
In Hardendorff, J. B. Witches, wit, and a
werewolf p97-101   S C
A Christmas carol
In Darrell, M. ed. Once upon a time
p171-234   808.8
A Christmas carol; abridged
In Stories to dramatize p329-39   372.6
A Christmas carol; dramatization. See
Hackett, W. A Christmas carol
A Christmas carol; dramatization. See Olfson, L. A Christmas carol
A Christmas carol; dramatization. See Thane,
A. A Christmas carol
A Christmas carol in prose (4 and up)   Fic
Cratchits' Christmas dinner
In Dalgliesh, A. comp. Christmas p205-11
S C
In Take joy! p30-31   394.2
The magic fishbone (3-5)   Fic
also in The Golden Treasury of children's
literature p349-54   808.8
also in Gruenberg, S. M. ed. Favorite stories
old and new p299-309   808.8
also in It's time for story hour p194-205
372.6
The magic fishbone; dramatization. See
Peterson, M. N. The magic fishbone
Marley's ghost
In Sechrist, E. H. ed. 13 ghostly yarns
p177-97   S C
Oliver Twist; dramatization. See Bland, J.
Oliver Twist

Dickey, Sarah
See pages in the following book:
Chittenden, E. F. Profiles in black and white p125-41 (5 and up)   920
Dickinson, Emily
Barth, E. I'm nobody! Who are you? The story of Emily Dickinson (5 and up) 92
I'm nobody! Who are you? (3-6)   811
Poems for youth (5 and up)   811
Dickinson, Peter
Annerton Pit (6 and up)   Fic
The gift (5 and up)   Fic
See also pages in the following book:
Townsend, J. R. A sounding of storytellers p41-54   028.5
Dicks, Terrance
The Baker Street Irregulars in the case of the missing masterpiece (5 and up) Fic
Dickson, Gordon R.
The Christmas present
In Universe ahead: stories of the future p268-80 (6 and up)   S C
Dictionaries
See pages in the following book:
Larrick, N. A parent's guide to children's reading p165-73   028.5
See also names of languages with the subdivision Dictionaries, e.g. English language—Dictionaries
Dictionary buying guide. Kister, K. F. 016.423
Dictionary for children, Macmillan   423
Dictionary for large print users, The Merriam-Webster   423
A **dictionary** of chivalry. Uden, G.   940.1
A **dictionary** of fairies. See Briggs, K. An encyclopedia of fairies: hobgoblins, brownies, bogies, and other supernatural creatures   398.03
The **dictionary** of Greek & Roman mythology. See Kravitz, D. Who's who in Greek and Roman mythology   292.03
A **dictionary** of mythical places. Palmer, R.   398.03
Dictionary of nursery rhymes, The Oxford   398
Did you carry the flag today, Charley? Caudill, R.   Fic
Did you carry the flag today, Charley? excerpt. Caudill, R.
In The Arbuthnot Anthology of children's literature p605-08   808.8
Diet
Gilbert, S. You are what you eat (5 and up)   641.1
Riedman, S. R. Food for people (6 and up)   641.1
See also Nutrition
Dieting. See Reducing
Dietz, Betty Warner
Musical instruments of Africa (6 and up)   781.91
Di Fiori, Lawrence
(illus.) Erickson, R. E. A toad for Tuesday   Fic
Dig, drill, dump, fill. Hoban, T.   621.8
Digestion
Elgin, K. The human body: the digestive system (4 and up)   612
Epstein, S. Dr. Beaumont and the man with the hole in his stomach (4-6)   92

Showers, P. What happens to a hamburger (1-3)   612
Silverstein, A. The digestive system (4 and up)   612
Zim, H. S. Your stomach and digestive tract (3-6)   612
See also pages in the following books:
Berger, M. The new food book p62-71 (4 and up)   641
Riedman, S. R. Food for people p105-13 (6 and up)   641.1
The **digestive** system. Silverstein, A.   612
Diggins, Julia E.
String, straightedge, and shadow (6 and up)   516
Di Grazia, Thomas
(illus.) Aleichem, S. Holiday tales of Sholom Aleichem   S C
(illus.) Clifton, L. Amifika   E
(illus.) Thomas, I. Walk home tired, Billy Jenkins   E
A **diller,** a dollar. Morrison, L.   808.88
Dillon, Diane
(illus.) Aardema, V. Behind the back of the mountain   398.2
(illus.) Aardema, V. Who's in Rabbit's house?   398.2
(illus.) Aardema, V. Why mosquitoes buzz in people's ears   398.2
(illus.) Belting, N. Whirlwind is a ghost dancing   398.2
(illus.) Carew, J. The third gift   Fic
(illus.) Graham, L. Song of the boat   E
(illus.) Greenfield, E. Honey, I love, and other love poems   811
(illus.) Haugaard, E. C. Hakon of Rogen's saga   Fic
(illus.) Mathis, S. B. The hundred penny box   E
(illus.) Musgrove, M. Ashanti to Zulu: African traditions   960
(illus.) Serwadda, W. M. Songs and stories from Uganda   784.4
Dillon, Leo
(illus.) Aardema, V. Behind the back of the mountain   398.2
(illus.) Aardema, V. Who's in Rabbit's house?   398.2
(illus.) Aardema, V. Why mosquitoes buzz in people's ears   398.2
(illus.) Belting, N. Whirlwind is a ghost dancing   398.2
(illus.) Carew, J. The third gift   Fic
(illus.) Graham, L. Song of the boa   E
(illus.) Greenfield, E. Honey, I love, and other love poems   811
(illus.) Haugaard, E. C. Hakon of Rogen's saga   Fic
(illus.) Mathis, S. B. The hundred penny box   E
(illus.) Musgrove, M. Ashanti to Zulu: African traditions   960
(illus.) Serwadda, W. M. Songs and stories from Uganda   784.4
Dilly-dilly-doh! Manning-Sanders, R.
In Manning-Sanders, R. A book of spooks and spectres p36-38   398.2
Dilson, Jesse
The abacus: a pocket computer (5 and up)   513.028
Dimensions
Adler, D. A. 3D, 2D, 1D (2-4)   530.8
Din dan don, it's Christmas   E

Dinah and the Green Fat Kingdom. Holland, I.
Fic

Diners. See Restaurants, bars, etc.

Dinky Hocker shoots smack. Kerr, M. E. **Fic**

Dinner at Alberta's. Hoban, R. **E**

Dinner for the monk. Courlander, H.
In Courlander, H. The tiger's whisker, and other tales and legends from Asia and the Pacific p111-13 **398.2**

Dinnerstein, Harvey
(illus.) Meltzer, M. Remember the days **305.8**

Dinosaur days. Knight, D. C. **567.9**

Dinosaur National Monument
See pages in the following book:
National Geographic Society. The new America's wonderlands **917.3**

Dinosaur story. Cole, J. **567.9**

Dinosaur time. Parish, P. **567.9**

Dinosaurs
Aliki. My visit to the dinosaurs (k-3) **567.9**
Ames, L. J. Draw 50 dinosaurs and other prehistoric animals (5 and up) **743**
Cohen, D. What really happened to the dinosaurs? (4-6) **567.9**
Cole, J. Dinosaur story (k-3) **567.9**
Halstead, B. A closer look at prehistoric reptiles (4-6) **567.9**
Jackson, K. Dinosaurs (k-3) **567.9**
Knight, D. C. Dinosaur days (k-3) **567.9**
McGowen, T. Album of dinosaurs (3-5) **567.9**
McGowen, T. Dinosaurs & other prehistoric animals (3-6) **567.9**
Parish, P. Dinosaur time (k-2) **567.9**
Pringle, L. Dinosaurs and people (4 and up) **567.9**
Pringle, L. Dinosaurs and their world (3-5) **567.9**
Shuttlesworth, D. E. Dodos and dinosaurs (4-6) **567.9**
Shuttlesworth, D. E. To find a dinosaur (5 and up) **567.9**
See also Tyrannosaurus rex

Fiction
Butterworth, O. The enormous egg (4 and up) **Fic**
Hoff, S. Danny and the dinosaur **E**
Lampman, E. S. The shy stegosaurus of Cricket Creek (5 and up) **Fic**

Poetry
Dinosaurs and beasts of yore **808.81**

Dinosaurs and beasts of yore **808.81**

Dinosaurs & other prehistoric animals. McGowen, T. **567.9**

Dinosaurs and people. Pringle, L. **567.9**

Dinosaurs and their world. Pringle, L. **567.9**

Diolé, Philippe
(jt. auth.) Cousteau, J. I. Dolphins **599.5**

Dionysos. See Dionysus

Dionysus
See pages in the following books:
Coolidge, O. The golden days of Greece p98-112 (4-6) **938**
Gates, D. Lord of the sky: Zeus p110-24 (4 and up) **292**

Diptera. See Mosquitoes

Direct taxation. See Income tax

The **dirty** bride. Curtis, E. S.
In Curtis, E. S. The girl who married a ghost, and other tales from the North American Indian p73-80 **398.2**

Dirty shepherdess
Sébillot, P. The old flea-bag
In Green fairy book p160-65 **398.2**

Disabled. See Handicapped; Physically handicapped

Disadvantaged children. See Socially handicapped children

The **disappearing** dog trick. Corbett, S. See note under Corbett, S. The lemonade trick
Fic

The **disappearance** of Peter Rugg. Roach, M. K.
In Roach, M. K. Encounters with the invisible world p116-25 **S C**

Disappearing energy. Shuttlesworth, D. E.
333.79

Disasters
See also names of particular disasters, e.g. San Francisco—Earthquake and fire, 1906

Discography. See Sound recordings

The **discontented** fish. Arnott, K.
In Arnott, K. African myths and legends p156-59 **398.2**

The **discontented** ghost. Corbett, S. **Fic**

Discoverers. See Explorers

Discoverers of the New World **970.01**

Discoveries (in geography)
Captain Cook and the South Pacific (5 and up) **990**
See also America—Exploration; Antarctic regions; Arctic regions; Explorers; Northeast passage; Voyages and travels

Discoveries (in science) See Inventions

Discovering books and libraries. Cleary, F. D. **028.7**

Discovering nature indoors **591**

Discovering the mysterious egret. Scott, J. D. **598**

Discovering Tut-ankh-Amen's tomb. Glubok, S. **932**

Discovering what earthworms do. Simon, S. **595.1**

Discovering what frogs do. Simon, S. **597.8**

Discovering what gerbils do. Simon, S. **636.08**

Discovering what puppies do. Simon, S. **636.7**

Discovery. Camp Fire Girls, Inc. **369.47**

Discovery of salt. Wyndham, R.
In Wyndham, R. Tales the people tell in China p9-13 **398.2**

Discrimination
See pages in the following books:
Sung, B. L. The Chinese in America p90-96 (5 and up) **305.8**
See also Minorities

Discrimination in education

Fiction
Underwood, B. The tamarack tree (6 and up) **Fic**

Discussion groups
See pages in the following books:
The Arbuthnot Anthology of children's literature p958-65 **808.8**

Disease detectives. Berger, M.   614.4
Disease detectives. Wolfe, L.   614.4
Disease germs. See Bacteriology; Germ theory
of disease
Diseases
    See pages in the following book:
Berger, M. Enzymes in action p77-86 (6 and
up)   574.19
    See also names of diseases and groups of
diseases, e.g. Epilepsy; communicable
diseases; and subjects with the subdivision
Diseases, e.g. Skin—Diseases
Diseases, Communicable. See Communicable
diseases
Diseases, Contagious. See Communicable dis-
eases
Diseases, Infectious. See Communicable dis-
eases
Diseases and pests. See Insects, Injurious and
beneficial
Diseases of plants. See Plants—Diseases
Disguises you can make. Barwell, E.   391
Diskin, Eve
Yoga for children (4 and up)   613.7
Dislocations
Nourse, A. E. Fractures, dislocations, and
sprains (4-6)   617
Dismal Swamp
    See pages in the following book:
Laycock, G. Exploring the great swamp p27-
34 (4-6)   574.5
Disney, Walt
Finch, C. The art of Walt Disney   791.43
Montgomery, E. R. Walt Disney: master of
make-believe (3-5)   92
    See also pages in the following book:
Children and literature p116-25   028.5
Disney (Walt) Productions
Finch, C. The art of Walt Disney   791.43
The disowned student. Kim, So-un
    In Kim, So-un. The story bag p166-71
                                             398.2
Displaced persons. See Refugees
Disposal of refuse. See Refuse and refuse dis-
posal
Distler, Pamela Sweet
(illus.) Scott, J. D. Discovering the mysteri-
ous egret   598
The Ditmars tale of wonders. Grimm, J.
    In Grimm, J. The complete Grimm's fairy
tales p662   398.2
Ditmarsch tale of wonders
Grimm, J. The Ditmars tale of wonders
    In Grimm, J. The complete Grimm's fairy
tales p662   398.2
Divali
    See pages in the following book:
More Festivals in Asia p47-54 (2-5)   394.2
The diverting history of Jack Gilpin. Cowper, W.
    In Caldecott, R. The Randolph Caldecott
treasury p205-35   741.9
    See also John Gilpin
The diverting history of John Gilpin. Cow-
per, W.
    In Randolph Caldecott's John Gilpin, and
other stories   398
    See also John Gilpin

Dividing the axe. Ginsburg, M.
    In Ginsburg, M. The twelve clever broth-
ers, and other fools p60-63   398.2
Dividing the goose
Afanas'ev, A. Dividing the goose
    In Afanas'ev, A. Russian fairy tales p579-
80   398.2
Divination
    See also Fortune telling
Diving
Sullivan, G. Better swimming and diving for
boys and girls (5 and up)   797.2
    See also pages in the following book:
Keith, H. Sports and games p210-21 (5 and
up)   796
Diving, Submarine
McClung, R. M. Treasures in the sea (k-3)
                                            910.4
Divorce
Berger, T. How does it feel when your par-
ents get divorced? (3-6)   306.8
Gardner, R. The boys and girls book about
divorce (4 and up)   306.8
LeShan, E. What's going to happen to me?
(4-6)   306.8
Richards, A. How to get it together when
your parents are coming apart (5 and up)
                                            306.8
Stein, S. B. On divorce (k-3)   306.8
White, A. S. Divorce (3-6)   306.8
    See also pages in the following book:
Kalb, J. What every kid should know p108-
[28] (5 and up)   158

Bibliography
    See pages in the following book:
Fassler, J. Helping children cope p114-27
                                          016.3627

Fiction
Adler, C. S. The silver coach (4-6)   Fic
Blue, R. A month of Sundays (3-5)   Fic
Blume, J. It's not the end of the world (4-6)
                                            Fic
Caines, J. Daddy   E
Lexau, J. M. Emily and the klunky baby and
the next door dog   E
Lexau, J. M. Me day   E
Mann, P. My dad lives in a downtown hotel
(3-5)   Fic
Newfield, M. A book for Jodan (3-5)   Fic
Perry, P. Mommy and Daddy are divorced
                                             E
Pevsner, S. A smart kid like you (4 and up)
                                            Fic
Slote, A. Matt Gargan's boy (4 and up)   Fic
Diwali. See Divali
Dixie, the Knight of the Silver Spurs. Jagen-
dorf, M. A.
    In Jagendorf, M. A. Folk stories of the
South p77-78   398.2
Dixon, Paige
Lion on the mountain (5 and up)   Fic
Silver Wolf (4 and up)   599.74
The young grizzly (4-6)   599.74
Djakarta
    See pages in the following book:
Smith, D. C. The land and people of Indo-
nesia p45-52 (5 and up)   959.8

Dogs

American Kennel Club. Complete dog book **636.7**
Bronson, W. S. Dogs (3 and up) **636.7**
Fichter, G. S. Working dogs (4-6) **636.7**
Foster, J. Dogs working for people (k-3) **636.7**
Hess, L. A dog by your side (3-6) **636.7**
Hess, L. A puppy for you (3-5) **636.7**
McCloy, J. Dogs at work (4-6) **636.7**
Pinkwater, J. Superpuppy (5 and up) **636.7**
Unkelbach, K. Both ends of the leash (3-6) **636.7**
Unkelbach, K. How to bring up your pet dog (4 and up) **636.7**

See also pages in the following books:
Chrystie, F. N. Pets p3-25 (4 and up) **636.08**
Stevens, C. Your first pet p95-109 (2-4) **636.08**
See also classes of dogs, e.g. Guide dogs

Fiction

Alexander, M. Bobo's dream **E**
Armstrong, W. H. Sounder (5 and up) **Fic**
Baker, C. Cockleburr Quarters (4-6) **Fic**
Ball, Z. Bristle Face (5 and up) **Fic**
Beatty, J. Holdfast (6 and up) **Fic**
Bemelman, L. Madeline's rescue **E**
Bontemps, A. The fast Sooner hound (2-5) **Fic**
Burnford, S. The incredible journey (4 and up) **Fic**
Cohen, P. Z. Deadly game at Stony Creek (5 and up) **Fic**
Cone, M. Mishmash (3-5) **Fic**
Dunlop, E. Fox farm (5 and up) **Fic**
Estes, E. Ginger Pye (4-6) **Fic**
Flack, M. Angus and the ducks **E**
Gackenbach, D. Hound and Bear **E**
Gág, W. Nothing At All **E**
Gipson, F. Old Yeller (6 and up) **Fic**
Girion, B. Misty and me (4-6) **Fic**
Hall, L. Riff, remember (4 and up) **Fic**
Hoff, S. Barkley **E**
Jones, D. W. Dogsbody (6 and up) **Fic**
Kellogg, S. Pinkerton, behave! **E**
Kjelgaard, J. Big Red (4 and up) **Fic**
Knight, E. Lassie come-home (4 and up) **Fic**
Lippincott, J. W. Wilderness champion (5 and up) **Fic**
London, J. Call of the wild (5 and up) **Fic**
London, J. White Fang (5 and up) **Fic**
Modell, F. Tooley! Tooley! **E**
Morgan, A. A boy called Fish (5 and up) **Fic**
Nodset, J. L. Go away, dog **E**
Ottley, R. Boy alone (5 and up) **Fic**
Parker, N. W. Poofy loves company **E**
Peet, B. The whingdingdilly **E**
Potter, B. The pie and the patty-pan **E**
Rawls, W. Where the red fern grows (6 and up) **Fic**
Rice, E. Papa's lemonade, and other stories **E**
Roach, M. K. Presto: or, The adventures of a turnspit dog (4 and up) **Fic**
Sendak, M. Higglety pigglety pop! (2-4) **Fic**
Skorpen, L. M. His mother's dog **E**
Skorpen, L. M. Old Arthur **E**
Steig, W. Caleb & Kate **E**
Steig, W. Dominic (4-6) **Fic**
Stolz, M. A dog on Barkham Street (4-6) **Fic**

Street, J. H. Good-bye, my Lady (5 and up) **Fic**
Van Allsburg, C. The garden of Abdul Gasazi **E**
Walker, D. Big Ben (3-5) **Fic**
Will. Finders keepers **E**
Zion, G. Harry the dirty dog **E**

Infancy
Cole, J. My puppy is born (k-3) **636.7**
Hess, L. Life begins for puppies (4-6) **636.7**
Selsam, M. E. How puppies grow (k-3) **636.7**
Simon, S. Discovering what puppies do (3-5) **636.7**

Poetry
Hark! Hark! The dogs do bark, and other rhymes about dogs (k-2) **398**

Training
Broderick, D. M. Training a companion dog (4 and up) **636.7**
Landshoff, U. Okay, good dog (1-3) **636.7**
Unkelbach, K. Both ends of the leash (3-6) **636.7**

See also pages in the following book:
Pinkwater, J. Superpuppy p144-87 (5 and up) **636.7**

Dogs, War use of
See pages in the following book:
Fichter, G. S. Working dogs p20-26 (4-6) **636.7**

The **Dogs** are having an election
In The Sound of flutes, and other Indian legends p23-24 **398.2**
Dogs at work. McCloy, J. **636.7**
Dogs for the blind. See Guide dogs
The **dog's** nose is cold. Sherlock, P.
In Sherlock, P. West Indian folk-tales p34-38 **398.2**
Dogs of America. Sabin, F. **636.7**
Dogs working for people. Foster, J. **636.7**
Dogsbody. Jones, D. W. **Fic**
Doing a trick with eyeballs
In The Sound of flutes, and other Indian legends p86-89 **398.2**
Doing the media. Center for Understanding Media **371.3**

Dolan, Edward F.
Basic football strategy (4 and up) **796.332**
The complete beginner's guide to bowling (5 and up) **794.6**
The complete beginner's guide to gymnastics (5 and up) **796.4**
The complete beginner's guide to making and flying kites (5 and up) **796.1**
Starting soccer (5 and up) **796.334**

Dolan, Tom
(illus.) Reid, G. K. Pond life **574.92**

Dolbier, Maurice
Torten's Christmas secret **E**

Doll. See Dolls
Doll making. See Dollmaking
The **doll** who came alive. Tregarthen, E. **Fic**
Dollar watch and the five jack rabbits. Sandburg, C.
In Sandburg, C. Rootabaga stories v 1 p141-50 **S C**
In Sandburg, C. The Sandburg treasury p57-61 **818**
The **dollhouse** caper. O'Connell, J. S. **Fic**

Douglass, Frederick

Bontemps, A. Frederick Douglass: slave-fighter-freeman (4 and up) **92**

See also pages in the following books:

Alexander, R. P. comp. Young and black in America p5-16 (6 and up) **920**

Johnston, J. A special bravery p40-44 (2-5) **920**

Rollins, C. H. They showed the way p46-52 (5 and up) **920**

Sterling, P. Four took freedom p34-65 (4-6) **920**

Drama

Davis, O. Escape to freedom (5 and up) **812**

Dove (Sloop)

Graham, R. L. The boy who sailed around the world alone (5 and up) **910.4**

Dowden, Anne Ophelia

The blossom on the bough (5 and up) **582.16**

Look at a flower (6 and up) **582.13**

State flowers (5 and up) **582.13**

This noble harvest (4 and up) **635**

Wild green things in the city (4 and up) **582.13**

(illus.) Busch, P. S. Wildflowers and the stories behind their names **582.13**

Down, down the mountain. Credle, E. **E**

also in It's time for story hour p14-22 **372.6**

Down in the boondocks. Gage, W. **E**

Down the rabbit hole. Lanes, S. G. **028.5**

Down the well

Duvoisin, R. Down the well

In Duvoisin, R. The three sneezes, and other Swiss tales p67-88 **398.2**

Down to earth; excerpt. Wrightson, R.

In The Arbuthnot Anthology of children's literature p579-82 **808.8**

The **down** to earth cookbook. Borghese, A. **641.5**

Down town, a Betsy-Tacy story. Lovelace, M. H. See note under Lovelace, M. H. Betsy-Tacy **Fic**

Downer, Marion

Kites (4-6) **796.1**

Downey, William R.

(illus.) Simon, S. Deadly ants **595.7**

Downhill racers. See Coaster cars

Downie, Mary Alice

(comp.) The Wind has wings. See The Wind has wings **811.08**

Downing, Charles

Russian tales and legends (4 and up) **398.2**

Down's syndrome. See Mongolism

Doyle, Sir Arthur Conan

Sherlock Holmes and the Red-headed League; dramatization. See Olfson, L. Sherlock Holmes and the Red-headed League

Through the veil

In Haunting tales p110-16 **S C**

Parodies, travesties, etc.

Titus, E. Basil of Baker Street (3-5) **Fic**

The **Drac.** Holman, F. **398.2**

The **Drac;** tale. Holman, F.

In Holman, F. The Drac p 1-17 **398.2**

Dracula, Prince of Wallachia. See Vlad the Impaler, Dracula, Prince of Wallachia

Dragon and his grandmother

The dragon and his grandmother

In Giants & witches and a dragon or two p155-61 **398.2**

Grimm, J. The Devil and his grandmother

In Grimm, J. The complete Grimm's fairy tales p563-66 **398.2**

In Yellow fairy book p46-49 **398.2**

Grimm, J. The dragon and his grandmother

In Grimm, J. Tales from Grimm p225-34 **398.2**

Manning-Sanders, R. The dragon and his grandmother

In Manning-Sanders, R. A book of dragons p79-86 **398.2**

Dragon magic. Norton, A. **Fic**

The **dragon** of Shervage Wood. Colwell, E.

In Colwell, E. Round about and long ago p110-13 **398.2**

Dragon of the North

The Dragon of the North

In The Andrew Lang Fairy tale treasury p285-98 **398.2**

In Yellow fairy book p12-26 **398.2**

The **dragon** of the well. Manning-Sanders, R.

In Manning-Sanders, R. A book of dragons p123-28 **398.2**

The **dragon** takes a wife. Myers, W. D. **E**

Dragondrums. McCaffrey, A. See note under McCaffrey, A. Dragonsong **Fic**

Dragonflies

Hutchins, R. E. The world of dragonflies and damselflies (5 and up) **595.7**

Simon, H. Dragonflies (5 and up) **595.7**

See also pages in the following books:

Anderson, M. J. Exploring the insect world p121-30 (5 and up) **595.7**

Teale, E. W. The junior book of insects p140-48 (6 and up) **595.7**

Dragons

See pages in the following book:

McHargue, G. The beasts of never p13-35 (5 and up) **398**

Fiction

Domanska, J. King Krakus and the dragon (k-2) **398.2**

Gannett, R. S. My father's dragon (1-4) **Fic**

Grahame, K. The reluctant dragon (3-5) **Fic**

Manning-Sanders, R. A book of dragons (3-6) **398.2**

Myers, W. D. The dragon takes a wife **E**

Norton, A. Dragon magic (4 and up) **Fic**

Williams, J. Everyone knows what a dragon looks like **E**

Dragonsinger. McCaffrey, A. See note under McCaffrey, A. Dragonsong **Fic**

Dragonsong. McCaffrey, A. **Fic**

Dragonwings. Yep, L. **Fic**

Drainage

See also Sewerage

Drakesbill and his friends

Drakestail

In The Golden Treasury of children's literature p88-95 **808.8**

Haviland, V. Drakestail

In Haviland, V. Favorite fairy tales told in France p76-91 **398.2**

Marelle, C. Drakestail

In Red fairy book p220-27 **398.2**

See also Valiant blackbird

Drakestail. See Drakesbill and his friends

Drama

See also Ballet; One act plays; Opera; Pantomimes; Puppets and puppet plays; Theater; also American drama; English drama; etc. and names of special subjects and historical events with the subdivision Drama, e.g. Holidays—Drama

Collections

Carlson, B. W. The right play for you (4 and up)   **792**

See also American drama—Collections; College and school drama—Collections

Collections—Periodicals

Plays, the Drama Magazine for Young People   **808.82**

Indexes

Kreider, B. A. comp. Index to children's plays in collections   **808.82**

Play index   **808.82**

Drama in education

Siks, G. B. Drama with children   **372.6**

Stories to dramatize   **372.6**

See also pages in the following book:

The Arbuthnot Anthology of children's literature p965-71   **808.8**

Drama with children. Siks, G. B.   **372.6**

Dramatized folk tales of the world (3 and up)   **812.08**

Draper, Nancy

Ballet for beginners (5 and up)   **792.8**

Draw 50 airplanes, aircraft & spacecraft. Ames, L. J.   **743**

Draw 50 boats, ships, trucks & trains. Ames, L. J.   **743**

Draw 50 buildings and other structures. Ames, L. J.   **743**

Draw 50 dinosaurs and other prehistoric animals. Ames, L. J.   **743**

Draw 50 famous cartoons. Ames, L. J.   **741.5**

The **drawbridge.** Frost, L.

In Time to laugh p67-73   **S C**

Drawing

Ames, L. J. Draw 50 airplanes, aircraft & spacecraft (4 and up)   **743**

Ames, L. J. Draw 50 boats, ships, trucks & trains (4-6)   **743**

Ames, L. J. Draw 50 buildings and other structures (5 and up)   **743**

Ames, L. J. Draw 50 dinosaurs and other prehistoric animals (5 and up)   **743**

Ames, L. J. Draw 50 famous cartoons (4-6)   **741.5**

Bolognese, D. Drawing horses and foals (4-6)   **743**

Emberley, E. Ed Emberley's Big green drawing book (2-6)   **741.2**

Emberley, E. Ed Emberley's Drawing book: make a world (2-6)   **743**

Emberley, E. Ed Emberley's Drawing book of animals   **743**

Emberley, E. Ed Emberley's Drawing book of faces (2-6)   **743**

Emberley, E. Ed Emberley's Great thumbprint drawing book (2-6)   **743**

Frame, P. Drawing cats and kittens (5 and up)   **743**

Slobodkin, L. The first book of drawing (5 and up)   **741.2**

Weiss, H. Pencil, pen and brush (5 and up)   **741.2**

Zaidenberg, A. How to draw with pen & brush (3 and up)   **741.2**

See also Figure drawing; Geometrical drawing; Illustration of books; Pastel drawing; Pen drawing

Fiction

Isadora, R. Willaby   **E**

Drawing book: make a world, Ed Emberley's. Emberley, E.   **743**

Drawing book of animals, Ed Emberley's. Emberley, E.   **743**

Drawing book of faces, Ed Emberley's. Emberley, E.   **743**

Drawing cats and kittens. Frame, P.   **743**

Drawing horses and foals. Bolognese, D.   **743**

Drawn from New England: Tasha Tudor. Tudor, B.   **92**

The **dreaded** black dog. Yolen, J.

In Yolen, J. The wizard islands p20-25   **551.4**

The **dreadful** dragon. Brydon, M. W.

In Fifty plays for junior actors p64-85   **812.08**

The **dream.** Dawood, N. J.

In Dawood, N. J. Tales from the Arabian nights p229-30   **398.2**

Dream days. See Grahame, K. The reluctant dragon   **Fic**

The **dream** keeper, and other poems. Hughes, L.   **811**

Dreams

Kettelkamp, L. Dreams (5 and up)   **154.6**

See also pages in the following books:

Hall, E. Possible impossibilities p120-30 (6 and up)   **133.8**

Silverstein, A. Sleep and dreams p69-94 (6 and up)   **154.6**

See also Fantasy; Sleep

Fiction

Briggs, R. The snowman   **E**

Sendak, M. In the night kitchen   **E**

Stevenson, J. "Could be worse!"   **E**

Poetry

Fox, S. C. The blue horse, and other night poems (k-3)   **811**

Dreams. Keats, E. J.   **E**

Dreams of Victory. Conford, E.   **Fic**

Drescher, Joan

(illus.) Bartoli, J. Nonna   **E**

(illus.) Zubrowski, B. Bubbles   **541.3**

Dresselhaus, Mildred

See pages in the following book:

Noble, I. Contemporary women scientists of America p138-51 (5 and up)   **920**

Dresser, Paul

See pages in the following book:

Browne, C. A. The story of our national ballads p241-43 (5 and up)   **784.7**

Dressmaking

Corrigan, B. Of course you can sew! (5 and up)   **646.4**

Dune fox. Roach, M. K.   574.5

The **dung** beetle. Andersen, H. C.
In Andersen, H. C. The complete fairy
  tales and stories p705-12   S C
In Andersen, H. Hans Andersen: his
  classic fairy tales p48-56   S C

Duniway, Abigail Scott
Morrison, D. N. Ladies were not expected;
  Abigail Scott Duniway and women's rights
  (5 and up)   92

Dunlop, Eileen
Elizabeth, Elizabeth (6 and up)   Fic
Fox farm (5 and up)   Fic

Dunne, Robert
(jt. auth.) Livaudais, M. The skeleton book
                                                  596

Dunne, Robert L.
(illus.) Miller, D. Egg carton critters 745.54

Dunning, Stephen
(comp.) Reflections on a gift of watermelon
  pickle . . . and other modern verse. See
  Reflections on a gift of watermelon pickle
  . . . and other modern verse   811.08
(comp.) Some haystacks don't even have any
  needle, and other complete modern poems.
  See Some haystacks don't even have any
  needle, and other complete modern poems
                                               811.08

Dunnington, Tom
(illus.) Torgersen, D. A. The girl who tricked
  the troll   E

Duplicating processes. See Copying processes
and machines

Duran, Daniel Flores
Latino materials   016.3058

Durango Street. Bonham, F.   Fic

Duration of life
Grimm, J. The duration of life
In Grimm, J. The complete Grimm's fairy
  tales p716-18   398.2

Durell, Ann
(ed.) Just for fun. See Just for fun   S C

Durenceau, Andre
(illus.) Mitchell, R. T. Butterflies and moths
                                               595.7

Durham, Mae J.
The Devil's bride
In The Arbuthnot Anthology of children's
  literature p289-90   808.8
In Time for old magic p168-69   398.2

Duroska, Lud
Tennis for beginners (3 and up)   796.342

Du Sable, Jean Baptiste. See Pointe de Sable,
Jean Baptiste

Dutch Americans
TenZythoff, G. J. The Dutch in America (5
  and up)   305.8

The **Dutch** boy and the dike
In Gruenberg, S. M. ed. Favorite stories
  old and new p363-66   808.8
See also Leak in the dike

The **Dutch** in America. TenZythoff, G. J.
                                               305.8

Dutton, Maude Barrows
The partridge and the crow
In The Arbuthnot Anthology of children's
  literature p420   808.8
In Time for old magic p284   398.2
The tyrant who became a just ruler
In The Arbuthnot Anthology of children's
  literature p420-21   808.8
In Time for old magic p284-85   398.2

Duvall, Lucille M.
The chosen one
In A Treasury of Christmas plays p313-29
                                               812.08
Little Chip's Christmas tree
In A Treasury of Christmas plays p383-89
                                               812.08
Valentine's Day
In Fifty plays for junior actors p178-88
                                               812.08

Duvoisin, Roger
A for the Ark   E
And there was America (3-5)   973.1
The bad joke that ended well
In Stories to dramatize p150-52   372.6
Caldecott Medal acceptance paper
In Caldecott Medal books: 1938-1957 p166-
  74   028.5
Lonely Veronica. See note under Duvoisin,
  R. Veronica   E
Our Veronica goes to Petunia's farm. See
  note under Duvoisin, R. Veronica   E
Petunia   E
Petunia, beware! See note under Duvoisin, R.
  Petunia   E
Petunia, I love you. See note under Duvoisin,
  R. Petunia   E
Petunia takes a trip. See note under Duvoisin,
  R. Petunia   E
Petunia's Christmas. See note under Duvoisin,
  R. Petunia   E
Petunia's treasure. See note under Duvoisin,
  R. Petunia   E
The three sneezes, and other Swiss tales (4-6)
                                               398.2
Contents: The three sneezes; Green Pea John;
Absent-minded farmer; Pig music; Bad joke that
ended well; It all came out of an egg; Silly Jean;
For lack of a thread; Wolf and the fox; Red-
chicken; Private La Ramée; Down the well; Herds-
man of Lona; Stubborn man; Herdsman's choice;
Vaudai; Four towers of Vufflens; Hole of the
Burgundians; For an oven full of bread; Bad old
woman; Pontius Pilate; Foolish folks; Grateful
Bergmännlein; Baltzli; Hans Kuhschwanz; Flaxen
thread; Fritz and Franz; Secret of the rock; Old
Man of the Mountains; Haunted Alp; Vengeance
of the dwarf; Knight with the stone heart; Schoch,
d'Altschmidja Spinnt Noch; The alphorn; How
the robber band was tricked; "Brenggen" field;
Wise Alois
Two lonely ducks   E
Veronica   E
Veronica and the birthday present. See note
  under Duvoisin, R. Veronica   E
(illus.) Carlson, N. S. The talking cat, and
  other stories of French Canada   S C
(illus.) Fatio, L. The happy lion   E
(illus.) Freschet, B. The web in the grass   E
(illus.) Haviland, V. Favorite fairy tales told
  in France   398.2
(illus.) Lipkind, W. Nubber Bear   E
(illus.) Menotti, G. C. Gian-Carlo Menotti's
  Amahl and the night visitors   Fic
(illus.) Ross, P. What ever happened to the
  Baxter place?   307.7
(illus.) Tresselt, A. Autumn harvest   E
(illus.) Tresselt, A. The beaver pond   574.92
(illus.) Tresselt, A. Follow the wind   E
(illus.) Tresselt, A. "Hi, Mister Robin!"   E
(illus.) Tresselt, A. Hide and seek fog   E
(illus.) Tresselt, A. It's time now!   525
(illus.) Tresselt, A. White snow, bright snow
                                                E
(illus.) Tresselt, A. The world in the candy
  egg   E
(illus.) Tworkov, J. The camel who took a
  walk   E

Duvoisin, Roger—*Continued*

About

See pages in the following books:

Authors and illustrators of children's books p125-34 **028.5**

Caldecott Medal books: 1938-1957 p175-83 **028.5**

Dvora's journey. Blaine, M. **Fic**

Dwarf and the cobbler's sons

Pulver, M. B. The dwarf and the cobbler's sons

In Harper, W. comp. Merry Christmas to you p94-101 **S C**

Pulver, M. B. The dwarf and the cobbler's sons; adaptation

In Stories to dramatize p87-90 **372.6**

Dwarf Long Nose

In Greene, E. comp. Clever cooks p56-86 **398.2**

See also Longnose, the dwarf

Dwarf with the long beard

Manning-Sanders, R. The dwarf with the long beard

In Manning-Sanders, R. A book of charms and changelings p40-50 **398.2**

Dwellings. See Architecture, Domestic; Houses; and classes of people with the subdivision Housing, e.g. Indians of North America—Housing

Dyer, Esther R.

Cooperation in library service to children **027.62**

(comp.) Cultural pluralism & children's media. See Cultural pluralism & children's media **027.8**

Dyes and dyeing

See pages in the following books:

Houck, C. Warm as wool, cool as cotton p64-76 (3-6) **677**

Raben, M. Textile mill p42-49 (4 and up) **677**

Dyspepsia. See Indigestion

E

E is for everybody: a manual for bringing fine picture books into the hands and hearts for children. Polette, N. **028.5**

ESP. See Extrasensory perception

Ea and Eo

In The Lazies p56-58 **398.2**

Each peach pear plum. Ahlberg, J. **E**

Eager, Edward

Half magic (4-6) **Fic**

Knight's castle. See note under Eager, E. Half magic **Fic**

Magic by the lake. See note under Eager, E. Half magic **Fic**

Magic or not? See note under Eager, E. Half magic **Fic**

Seven day magic. See note under Eager, E. Half magic **Fic**

Eager, Fred

Italic handwriting for young people **745.6**

Eagle, Michael

(illus.) Gemming, E. Lost city in the clouds **985**

The Eagle and the bat

In The Sound of flutes, and other Indian legends p90 **398.2**

The **eagle** and the fort; the story of John McLoughlin. Morrison, D. N. **92**

Eagles

Lavine, S. A. Wonders of the eagle world (4 and up) **598**

Ear

See also Hearing

Ear of corn

Grimm, J. The ear of corn

In Grimm, J. The complete Grimm's fairy tales p791-92 **398.2**

Earhart, Amelia

Mann, P. Amelia Earhart: first lady of flight (3-5) **92**

See also pages in the following books:

Nathan, D. Women of courage p117-46 (4-6) **920**

Ross, F. Historic plane models p167-70 (5 and up) **629.133**

Earl Gerald. Leach, M.

In Leach, M. Whistle in the graveyard p20-21 **398.2**

Earl Mar's daughter

Jacobs, J. Earl Mar's daughter

In Jacobs, J. English fairy tales p159-63 **398.2**

Earle, Olive L.

Birds and their nests (3-6) **598**

Nuts (3-6) **582.16**

Peas, beans, and licorice (4-6) **583**

Pond and marsh plants (3-6) **581.92**

The rose family (4-6) **583**

State birds and flowers **598**

State trees (4 and up) **582.16**

Early American children's books. Rosenbach, A. S. W. **011**

Early American crafts. Colby, C. B. **670**

Early children's books and their illustration. Pierpont Morgan Library, New York **028.5**

Early moon. Sandburg, C.

In Sandburg, C. The Sandburg treasury p161-207 **818**

Early thunder. Fritz, J. **Fic**

Early Years **372.05**

The **ears** of Louis. Greene, C. C. **Fic**

Earth

Asimov, I. How did we find out the earth is round? (4-6) **525**

Branley, F. M. The beginning of the earth (1-3) **551**

Branley, F. M. The end of the world (5 and up) **525**

Polgreen, J. Sunlight and shadows (1-3) **525**

See also pages in the following books:

Branley, F. M. The nine planets p44-51 (6 and up) **523.4**

Freeman, M. The sun, the moon, and the stars p3-13 (2-4) **523**

See also Creation; Geography; Geology; Universe

Crust

See pages in the following book:

Wyckoff, J. The story of geology p18-23, 114-38 (5 and up) **551**

Internal structure

See pages in the following book:

McNulty, F. How to dig a hole to the other side of the world (2-4) **551.1**

Earth, Effect of man on. See Man—Influence on nature

Earth Day

Drama
See pages in the following book:

Fisher, A. Holiday programs for boys and girls p261-310 (4 and up)   **812**

Earth gnome

Grimm, J. The earth gnome
In Grimm, J. More Tales from Grimm p171-87   **398.2**

Grimm, J. The gnome
In Grimm, J. The complete Grimm's fairy tales p420-24   **398.2**

Earth in motion. Fodor, R. V.   **551.1**

Earth magician. Baker, B.
In Baker, B. At the center of the world p 1-6   **398.2**

Earth: our crowded spaceship. Asimov, I. **304.6**

Earth sciences
See also Geology

Earthenware. See Pottery

Earthfasts. Mayne, W.   **Fic**

Earthquakes

Asimov, I. How did we find out about earthquakes? (5 and up)   **551.2**

Brown, B. W. Historical catastrophes: earthquakes (5 and up)   **551.2**

Lauber, P. Earthquakes (4-6)   **551.2**

Marcus, R. B. The first book of volcanoes & earthquakes (5 and up)   **551.2**

Mercer, C. Monsters in the earth (5 and up)   **551.2**

Simon, S. Danger from below: earthquakes, past, present, and future (4 and up) **551.2**

See also pages in the following books:

Kiefer, I. Global jigsaw puzzle p71-73 (6 and up)   **551.1**

Lauber, P. This restless earth p21-42 (5 and up)   **551**

Wyckoff, J. The story of geology p132-38 (5 and up)   **551**

See also Volcanoes

United States
See pages in the following book:

Mercer, C. Monsters in the earth p79-104 (5 and up)   **551.2**

Earth's changing climate. Gallant, R. A. **551.6**

The **earth's** story. Ames, G.   **551**

Earthworms

Darling, L. Worms (1-3)   **595.1**

Hess, L. The amazing earthworms (3-5)   **595.1**

Lauber, P. Earthworms, underground farmers (3-5)   **595.1**

Pringle, L. Twist, wiggle, and squirm (1-3)   **595.1**

Simon, S. Discovering what earthworms do (3-5)   **595.1**

See also pages in the following books:

Cooper, E. K. Science in your own back yard p100-05 (5 and up)   **507**

Rhine, R. Life in a bucket of soil p23-30 (5 and up)   **595**

Simon, S. Pets in a jar p53-57 (4 and up)   **639**

Earthworms, underground farmers. Lauber, P.   **595.1**

East Africa. Perl, L.   **967.6**

East and West
See also Acculturation

East Germany. See Germany, East

East Germany. Fles, B.   **943.1**

East Indian Americans

Bagai, L. B. The East Indians and the Pakistanis in America (5 and up)   **305.8**

The **East** Indians and the Pakistanis in America. Bagai, L. B.   **305.8**

East o' the sun and west o' the moon

Asbjörnsen, P. C. East o' the sun and west o' the moon
In The Arbuthnot Anthology of children's literature p252-57   **808.8**

In Asbjörnsen, P. C. East of the sun and west of the moon p19-34   **398.2**

In Blue fairy book p 1-13   **398.2**

In Time for old magic p135-40   **398.2**

East of the sun and west of the moon. Asbjörnsen, P. C.   **398.2**

Easter

Barth, E. Lilies, rabbits, and painted eggs (3-6)   **394.2**

Fisher, A. Easter (1-3)   **394.2**

It's time for Easter (4 and up)   **394.2**

See also pages in the following books:

Araki, C. Origami in the classroom: Book II p21-25 (4 and up)   **736**

Cutler, K. N. From petals to pinecones p78-81 (4 and up)   **745.58**

Sechrist, E. H. Red letter days p67-78 **394.2**

Drama
See pages in the following book:

Fisher, A. Holiday programs for boys and girls p257-60 (4 and up)   **812**

Fiction

Harper, W. comp. Easter chimes   **S C**

Heyward, D. B. The country bunny and the little gold shoes   **E**

Hoban, L. The sugar snow spring   **E**

Hoban, T. Where is it?   **E**

Milhous, K. The egg tree   **E**

Tresselt, A. The world in the candy egg   **E**

Poetry

Easter buds are springing (2-4)   **811.08**

See also pages in the following books:

It's time for Easter p141-55 (4 and up) **394.2**

O frabjous day! p131-47 (5 and up)   **808.81**

Sechrist, E. H. comp. Poems for red letter days p75-78   **821.08**

Easter buds are springing   **811.08**

Easter bunnies and the lily

Bowman, P. B. The Easter Bunnies and the Lily
In Harper, W. comp. Easter chimes p189-94   **S C**

Easter Bunny's breakfast

Potter, M. C. Easter Bunny's breakfast
In Harper, W. comp. Easter chimes p85-91   **S C**

Easter chimes. Harper, W. comp.   **S C**

The **Easter** egg artists. Adams, A.   **E**

The **Easter** eggs. Cather, K. D.
In Harper, W. comp. Easter chimes p173-86   **S C**

Easter eggs for everyone. Coskey, E. **745.594**

Eddie goes to dancing school. Haywood, C.
In The Arbuthnot Anthology of children's literature p608-11   **808.8**

Eddie makes music. Haywood, C. See note under Haywood, C. Little Eddie   **Fic**

Eddie, the dog holder. Haywood, C. See note under Haywood, C. Little Eddie   **Fic**

Eddie's green thumb. Haywood, C. See note under Haywood, C. Little Eddie   **Fic**

Eddie's happenings. Haywood, C. See note under Haywood, C. Little Eddie   **Fic**

Eddie's menagerie. Haywood, C. See note under Haywood, C. Little Eddie   **Fic**

Eddie's pay dirt. Haywood, C. See note under Haywood, C. Little Eddie   **Fic**

Eddie's valuable property. Haywood, C. See note under Haywood, C. Little Eddie **Fic**

Edelson, Edward
Funny men of the movies (6 and up)   **791.43**
Great monsters of the movies (4-6)   **791.43**
Great movie spectaculars   **791.43**

Edgar Allan. Neufeld, J.   **Fic**

The **edge** of next year. Stolz, M.   **Fic**

The **edge** of nowhere. Sypher, L. J.   **Fic**

Edge of two worlds. Jones, W.   **Fic**

Edgemont. Sharmat, M. W.   **E**

Edgun
(illus.) Hatch, M. C. 13 Danish tales   **398.2**

Edie on the warpath. Spykman, E. C. See note under Spykman, E. C. A lemon and a star   **Fic**

Edinburgh
Description
Sasek, M. This is Edinburgh (3-6)   **914.11**

Edison, Thomas Alva
Cousins, M. The story of Thomas Alva Edison (4-6)   **92**
North, S. Young Thomas Edison (5 and up)   **92**

See also pages in the following books:
Cottler, J. Heroes of civilization p249-59 (5 and up)   **920**
Holiday ring p172-75 (4 and up)   **394.2**

Editors and editing. See Publishers and publishing

Edmonds, Emma
See pages in the following book:
As I saw it: women who lived the American adventure p89-97 (6 and up)   **973**

Edmonds, I. G.
Agayk and the strangest spear
In Time for old magic p261-63   **398.2**
BMX! Bicycle motocross for beginners (5 and up)   **796.6**
Buddhism (4 and up)   **294.3**
Islam (5 and up)   **297**

Edmonds, Walter D.
Bert Breen's barn (6 and up)   **Fic**
The matchlock gun (4-6)   **Fic**
Newbery Medal acceptance paper
In Newbery Medal books: 1922-1955 p212-24   **028.5**
About
See pages in the following book:
Newbery Medal books: 1922-1955 p210-11 **028.5**

Edmondson, Madeleine
(jt. auth.) Cole, J. Twins   **612**

Education
See also Audio-visual education; Books and reading; Educators; Teachers; Teaching

Argentine Republic
See pages in the following book:
Hall, E. The land and people of Argentina p77-82, 126-31 (5 and up)   **982**

Belgium
See pages in the following book:
Loder, D. The land and people of Belgium p92-94, 100-03 (5 and up)   **949.3**

China
See pages in the following books:
Rau, M. Our world: the People's Republic of China p81-92 (6 and up)   **951.05**
Sidel, R. Revolutionary China: people, politics, and ping-pong p125-36 (6 and up) **951.05**

Cuba
See pages in the following book:
Ortiz, V. The land and people of Cuba p118-26 (5 and up)   **972.91**

Denmark
See pages in the following book:
Wohlrabe, R. A. The land and people of Denmark p60-63, 140-42 (5 and up)   **948.9**

Egypt
See pages in the following book:
Mahmoud, Z. N. The land and people of Egypt p135-44 (5 and up)   **962**

Great Britain
See pages in the following books:
Hodges, C. W. The battlement garden p67-73 (6 and up)   **942.05**
Street, A. The land and people of England p46-51 (5 and up)   **942**

Indonesia
See pages in the following book:
Smith, D. C. The land and people of Indonesia p129-37 (5 and up)   **959.8**

Islands of the Pacific
See pages in the following book:
May, C. P. Oceania: Polynesia, Melanesia, Micronesia p155-62 (5 and up)   **990**

Japan
See pages in the following book:
Vaughan, J. B. The land and people of Japan p89-93 (5 and up)   **952**

Nigeria
See pages in the following book:
Forman, B. The land and people of Nigeria p63-74 (5 and up)   **966.9**

Norway
Hall, E. The land and people of Norway p126-32 (5 and up)   **948.1**

Periodicals
Learning   **370.5**
Teacher   **370.5**

Sri Lanka
See pages in the following book:
Wilber, D. N. The land and people of Ceylon p128-32 (5 and up)   **954.9**

Elliott, Sarah M.
Our dirty water (4-6)   363.7
The **ellipse.** Charosh, M.   516
Ellis, Alec
(ed.) Chosen for children. See Chosen for children   028.5
Ellis, Harry B.
Israel: one land, two peoples (6 and up)   956.94
Ellis, Mel
The wild horse killers (6 and up)   Fic
Ellison, Elsie C.
Fun with lines and curves (4 and up)   745.4
Ellison, Virginia H.
The Pooh cook book (4 and up)   641.5
Elsa. Adamson, J.   599.74
Elsie Piddock skips in her sleep. Farjeon, E.
In Told under the magic umbrella p217-37   S C
Elting, Mary
The Hopi way (2-4)   970.004
Elves. See Fairies
Elves and the shoemaker
Grimm, J. The elves and the shoemaker
In The Arbuthnot Anthology of children's literature p199-200   808.8
In The Fairy tale treasury p118-21   398.2
In Stories to dramatize p49-50   372.6
In Time for old magic p47-48   398.2
Grimm, J. The elves and the shoemaker whose work they did
In Grimm, J. About wise men and simpletons p31-32   398.2
Grimm, J. The elves: first story
In Grimm, J. The complete Grimm's fairy tales p197-98   398.2
In Grimm, J. Household stories p171-72   398.2
Grimm, J. The shoemaker and the elves
In Grimm, J. More tales from Grimm p251-57   398.2
Littledale, F. The elves and the shoemaker   398.2
Rockwell, A. The shoemaker and the elves
In Rockwell, A. The three bears & 15 other stories p71-77   398.2
Scudder, H. E. The elves and the shoemaker
In Told under the green umbrella p47-51   398.2
Thane, A. The elves and the shoemaker
In Thane, A. Plays from famous stories and fairy tales p90-104   812
Very, A. The Shoemaker and the elves
In On stage for Christmas p391-402   812.08
The **elves** and the shoemaker whose work they did. Grimm, J.
In Grimm, J. About wise men and simpletons p31-32   398.2
See also Elves and the shoemaker
The **elves** ask a servant girl to be godmother. Grimm, J.
In Grimm, J. About wise men and simpletons p33   398.2
See also Maiden's visit
The **elves:** first story. Grimm, J.
In Grimm, J. The complete Grimm's fairy tales p197-98   398.2
In Grimm, J. Household stories p171-72   398.2
See also Elves and the shoemaker

The **elves:** second story. Grimm, J.
In Grimm, J. The complete Grimm's fairy tales p199   398.2
In Grimm, J. Household stories p173   398.2
See also Maiden's visit
The **elves:** third story. Grimm, J.
In Grimm, J. The complete Grimm's fairy tales p200   398.2
In Grimm, J. Household stories p175   398.2
See also Changeling
Emancipation of slaves. See Slavery in the United States
Emancipation of women. See Women—Civil rights
Emancipation Proclamation
Commager, H. S. The great Proclamation (6 and up)   326
Emberley, Barbara
Drummer Hoff (k-3)   398
One wide river to cross (k-3)   784.4
(illus.) Schackburg, R. Yankee Doodle   784.7
Emberley, Ed
A birthday wish   E
Caldecott Medal acceptance paper
In Newbery and Caldecott Medal books: 1966-1975 p199-204   028.5
Ed Emberley's ABC   E
Ed Emberley's Big green drawing book (2-6)   741.2
Ed Emberley's Drawing book: make a world (2-6)   743
Ed Emberley's Drawing book of animals (2-6)   743
Ed Emberley's Drawing book of faces (2-6)   743
Ed Emberley's Great thumbprint drawing book (2-6)   743
Green says go (k-3)   535.6
The wing on a flea   E
The wizard of Op   E
(illus.) Branley, F. M. The Big Dipper   523.8
(illus.) Emberley, B. Drummer Hoff   398
(illus.) Emberley, B. One wide river to cross   784.4
(illus.) Gans, R. Birds eat and eat and eat   598
(illus.) Goldin, A. Straight hair, curly hair   612
(illus.) Hawes, J. Ladybug, ladybug, fly away home   595.7
(illus.) Schackburg, R. Yankee Doodle   784.7
(illus.) Serraillier, I. Suppose you met a witch   E
(illus.) Sitomer, M. What is symmetry?   516
About
See pages in the following books:
Authors and illustrators of children's books p135-40   028.5
Newbery and Caldecott Medal books: 1966-1975 p205-07   028.5
Emberlin, Diane
Contributions of women: science (5 and up)   920

Embroidery

Miller, I. P. The stitchery book (5 and up)
746.44

See also pages in the following book:

Hoople, C. G. The heritage sampler p39-45 (5 and up) **745.5**

See also types of embroidery, e.g. Crewelwork

Embry, Margaret

Blanche's high-flying Halloween
In Witches, witches, witches p45-55 **808.8**

The blue-nosed witch (1-4) **Fic**

Embryology

Cosgrove, M. Eggs—and what happens inside them (3-6) **574.3**

Day, B. The secret world of the baby **612**

Flanagan, G. L. Window into an egg (4-6)
636.5

May, J. A new baby comes (1-4) **612**

Nilsson, L. How was I born? (3-6) **612**

Parker, S. Life before birth: the story of the first nine months (3-6) **612**

Portal, C. The beauty of birth (3-6) **612**

Selsam, M. E. Egg to chick (k-3) **574.3**

Showers, P. A baby starts to grow (k-2)
612

Showers, P. Before you were a baby (1-3)
612

Zappler, G. From one cell to many cells (2-4) **574.3**

See also Reproduction

Emelya the simpleton. Afanas'ev, A.
In Afanas'ev, A. Russian fairy tales p46-48
398.2

Emergencies. See Accidents; First aid

Emergency! Beame, R. **362.1**

Emerson, Caroline Dwight

The merry-go-round and the Griggses
In Gruenberg, S. M. ed. Favorite stories old and new p463-66 **808.8**
In Told under the magic umbrella p18-22
S C

Emil and the detectives. Kästner, E. **Fic**

Emily and the klunky baby and the next door dog. Lexau, J. M. **E**

Emily Upham's revenge. Avi **Fic**

Emily's famous meal. Jagendorf, M. A.
In Jagendorf, M. A. Folk stories of the South p210-13 **398.2**

Emile. Ungerer, T. **E**

Emma's dilemma. LeRoy, G. **Fic**

Emmet Otter's Jug-Band Christmas. Hoban R. **E**

Emmett, Daniel Decatur

See pages in the following book:

Browne, C. A. The story of our national ballads p124-34 (5 and up) **784.7**

Emmett's pig. Stolz, M. **E**

Emotional stress. See Stress (Psychology)

Emotionally disturbed children. See Mentally ill children

Emotions

LeShan, E. What makes me feel this way? (3-6) **152.4**

LeShan, E. You and your feelings (6 and up)
155.5

Stein, M. L. Good and bad feelings (3-6)
152.4

See also pages in the following books:

Adams, B. Like it is: facts and feelings about handicaps from kids who know p69-91 (4-6) **362.4**

Kalb, J. What every kid should know p10-27 (5 and up) **158**

See also names of emotions, e.g. Anger

Bibliography

See pages in the following book:

Gillis, R. J. Children's books for times of stress p77-117 **016.3627**

The **emperor** and the kite. Yolen, J. **398.2**

The **Emperor** and the nightingale. See Andersen, H. C. The nightingale **Fic**

The **emperor** penguins. Mizumura, K. **598**

Emperor's new clothes

Andersen, H. C. The emperor's new clothes
Fic

also in Andersen, H. C. Ardizzone's Hans Andersen: fourteen classic tales p15-22 **S C**

also in Andersen, H. C. The complete fairy tales and stories p77-81 **S C**

also in Andersen, H. Dulac's The Snow Queen, and other stories from Hans Andersen p66-72 **S C**

also in Andersen, H. Hans Andersen: his classic fairy tales p119-24 **S C**

also in The Arbuthnot Anthology of children's literature p565-68 **808.8**

also in The Arthur Rackham Fairy book p240-45 **398.2**

also in The Fairy tale treasury p174-79 **398.2**

also in The Golden Treasury of children's literature p214-19 **808.8**

also in Gruenberg, S. M. ed. Favorite stories old and new p317-21 **808.8**

also in Stories to dramatize p210-14 **372.6**

also in Time to laugh p108-15 **S C**

also in Yellow fairy book p27-32 **398.2**

Foley, M. A. The Emperor's new robes
In Fifty plays for junior actors p203-21
812.08

The **Emperor's** new robes. Foley, M. A.
In Fifty plays for junior actors p203-21
812.08

See also Emperor's new clothes

The **Emperor's** Nightingale. Thane, A.
In Thane, A. Plays from famous stories and fairy tales p3-19 **812**
See also Nightingale

Employment of women. See Women—Employment

The **empty** chair. Kaplan, B. **Fic**

The **empty** schoolhouse. Carlson, N. S. **Fic**

The **empty** schoolroom. Johnson, P. H.
In A Chilling collection p103-18 **S C**

The **empty** sea. Thompson, V. L.
In Thompson, V. L. Hawaiian tales of heroes and champions p93-102 **398.2**

Empty world. Christopher, J. **Fic**

Emrich, Duncan
(comp.) American folk poetry: an anthology
811.08
(comp.) The hodgepodge book **398**
(comp.) The nonsense book of riddles, rhymes, tongue twisters, puzzles and jokes from American folklore (3 and up) **398**
(ed.) The Whim-wham book. See The Whim-wham book **398**

Enano
Finger, C. El Enano
In Finger, C. Tales from silver lands p59-68 **398.2**

The **enchanted** boy. Hunter, M.
In Hunter, M. A furl of fairy wind p17-29
S C

Enchanted buck
Berger, T. The enchanted buck
In Berger, T. Black fairy tales p43-54
398.2

The Enchanted buck
In Tatterhood, and other tales p143-48
398.2

Enchanted canary
Deulin, C. The enchanted canary
In Red fairy book p247-64 **398.2**

The **enchanted** candle. Manning-Sanders, R.
In Manning-Sanders, R. A book of enchantments and curses p28-35 **398.2**

Enchanted cave of Cesh Corran
Stephens, J. The enchanted cave of Cesh Corran
In Stephens, J. Irish fairy tales p201-18
398.2

Enchanted cow
Davis, M. G. The enchanted cow
In Harper, W. comp. Ghosts and goblins p60-66 **398.2**
In Witches, witches, witches p37-44 **808.8**

The **enchanted** fisherman. Colwell, E.
In Colwell, E. Round about and long ago p19-22 **398.2**

Enchanted grouse
Bowman, J. C. Kalle and the wood grouse
In Bowman, J. C. Tales from a Finnish tupa p129-40 **398.2**

Enchanted horse
The Enchanted horse
In The Arabian nights entertainments p358-89 **398.2**

The Story of the enchanted horse
In The Golden Treasury of children's literature p356-64 **808.8**

Enchanted mule
Haviland, V. The enchanted mule
In Haviland, V. Favorite fairy tales told in Spain p70-87 **398.2**

Enchanted pig
The Enchanted pig
In Red fairy book p84-98 **398.2**

The **enchanted** princess. Afanas'ev, A.
In Afanas'ev, A. Russian fairy tales p600-11 **398.2**

The **enchanted** princess. Colwell, E.
In Colwell, E. Round about and long ago p34-39 **398.2**

The **enchanted** ring. Afanas'ev, A.
In Afanas'ev, A. Russian fairy tales p31-37
398.2

The **enchanted** ring. Fénelon, F. de S. de la Mothe
In The Andrew Lang Fairy tale treasury p220-27 **398.2**
In Green fairy book p62-71 **398.2**

Enchanted snake
The Enchanted snake
In Green fairy book p188-97 **398.2**

The **enchanted** sticks. Myers, S. J. **Fic**

Enchanted watch
Deulin, C. The enchanted watch
In Green fairy book p55-61 **398.2**

The **Enchanted** wine jug. Manning-Sanders, R.
In Manning-Sanders, R. A book of charms and changelings p21-33 **398.2**
See also Why the dog and cat are enemies

Enchantments and curses, A book of. Manning-Sanders, R. **398.2**

Enchantress from the stars. Engdahl, S. L.
Fic

Encounters with the invisible world. Roach, M. K. **S C**

Encyclopedia and fact-index, Compton's **031**

Encyclopedia Brown and the case of the dead eagles. Sobol, D. J. See note under Sobol, D. J. Encyclopedia Brown, boy detective
Fic

Encyclopedia Brown and the case of the midnight visitor. Sobol, D. J. See note under Sobol, D. J. Encyclopedia Brown, boy detective **Fic**

Encyclopedia Brown and the case of the secret pitch. See note under Sobol, D. J. Encyclopedia Brown, boy detective **Fic**

Encyclopedia Brown, boy detective. Sobol, D. J. **Fic**

Encyclopedia Brown finds the clues. Sobol, D. J. See note under Sobol, D. J. Encyclopedia Brown, boy detective **Fic**

Encyclopedia Brown gets his man. Sobol, D. J. See note under Sobol, D. J. Encyclopedia Brown, boy detective **Fic**

Encyclopedia Brown keeps the peace. Sobol, D. J. See note under Sobol, D. J. Encyclopedia Brown, boy detective **Fic**

Encyclopedia Brown lends a hand. Sobol, D. J. See note under Sobol, D. J. Encyclopedia Brown, boy detective **Fic**

Encyclopedia Brown saves the day. Sobol, D. J. See note under Sobol, D. J. Encyclopedia Brown, boy detective **Fic**

Encyclopedia Brown shows the way. Sobol, D. J. See note under Sobol, D. J. Encyclopedia Brown, boy detective **Fic**

Encyclopedia Brown solves them all. Sobol, D. J. See note under Sobol, D. J. Encyclopedia Brown, boy detective **Fic**

Encyclopedia Brown takes the case. Sobol, D. J. See note under Sobol, D. J. Encyclopedia Brown, boy detective **Fic**

Encyclopedia Brown tracks them down. Sobol, D. J. See note under Sobol, D. J. Encyclopedia Brown, boy detective **Fic**

Encyclopedia buying guide **016**

An **encyclopedia** of fairies: hobgoblins, brownies, bogies, and other supernatural creatures. Briggs, K. **398.03**

The **encyclopedia** of sports. Menke, F. G.
796.03

Encyclopedia of sports, The Junior illustrated 796.03

Encyclopedias
Britannica Junior encyclopaedia for boys and girls 031
Collier's encyclopedia 031
Compton's Encyclopedia and fact-index 031
Guinness Book of world records 032
Kane, J. N. Famous first facts 031
Merit students encyclopedia 031
The New Book of knowledge 031
The New Lincoln Library encyclopedia 031
The Statesman's year-book 310.5
The World Book encyclopedia 031

See also pages in the following book:
Larrick, N. A parent's guide to children's reading p175-83 028.5

See also subjects with the subdivision Encyclopedias, e.g. Sports—Encyclopedias

Bibliography
Encyclopedia buying guide 016

End of the world
Branley, F. M. The end of the world (5 and up) 525

The **End** of the world
In The Sound of flutes, and other Indian legends p124-25 398.2

End of the world. Bowman, J. C.
In Bowman, J. C. Tales from a Finnish tupa p239-41 398.2

The **end** of the world: the buffalo go. Marriott, A.
In Marriott, A. American Indian mythology 398.2

Endangered animals. See Rare animals
Endangered plants. See Rare plants
Endangered predators. Harris, J. 599.74
Endings. Bradley, B. 155.9
The **endocrine** system. Silverstein, A. 612

Endocrinology
See also Glands, Ductless; Hormones

Endowed charities. See Endowments

Endowments
See pages in the following book:
Sechrist, E. H. It's time for brotherhood p184-93 (5 and up) 361

Endurance, Physical. See Physical fitness

An **Enemy** at Green Knowe. Boston, L. M.
See note under Boston, L. M. The children of Green Knowe Fic

Energy. See Force and energy; Power resources

Energy. Adler, I. 531

Energy conservation
Shuttlesworth, D. E. Disappearing energy (5 and up) 333.79

See also pages in the following book:
Kiefer, I. Energy for America p153-84 (6 and up) 333.79

See also Energy consumption; Recycling (Waste, etc.)

Energy consumption
See pages in the following book:
Branley, F. M. Solar energy p 1-12 (5 and up) 621.47

Energy for America. Kiefer, I. 333.79
Energy from the sun. Berger, M. 621.47

Energy policy
Kiefer, I. Energy for America (6 and up) 333.97

Energy resources. See Power resources

Engdahl, Sylvia
The beckoning trail
In Universe ahead: stories of the future p301-36 S C
Enchantress from the stars (6 and up) Fic
The far side of evil. See note under Engdahl, S. L. Enchantress from the stars Fic
This star shall abide (6 and up) Fic
(ed.) Universe ahead: stories of the future. See Universe ahead: stories of the future S C

Engineering
See also types of engineering, e.g. Civil engineering

Engines
Weiss, H. Motors and engines and how they work (5 and up) 621.4
See also Airplanes—Engines; Automobiles—Engines; Solar engines; Steam engines

England
See also Great Britain

Description and travel
Street, A. The land and people of England (5 and up) 942

Folklore
See Folklore—Great Britain

History
See Great Britain—History

Engle, Eloise
The Finns in America (5 and up) 305.8

Englebardt, Leland S.
You have a right (6 and up) 346

Englefield, Cicely
George and Angela
In Told under the magic umbrella p50-54 S C

Engler, Larry
Making puppets come alive 791.5

English art. See Art, British
English ballads. See Ballads, English
English composition. See English language—Composition and exercises
English drama 822
English fables and fairy stories. Reeves, J. 398.2
English fairy tales. Jacobs, J. 398.2
English folk and fairy tales. See Jacobs, J. English fairy tales 398.2
English folk songs. See Folk songs, English
English grammar. See English language—Grammar
English in Africa. See British in Africa
The **English** in America. Cates, E. H. 305.8
English in India. See British in India
English in Sierra Leone. See British in Sierra Leone
English in the United States. See British in the United States

English language

Antonyms
See English language—Synonyms and antonyms

English language—*Continued*

Composition and exercises
Brandt, S. R. How to improve your written English (4-6) **808**
Cassedy, S. In your own words (6 and up) **808**
Jackson, J. Turn not pale, beloved snail **808**

Dialects
See pages in the following book:
Issues in children's book selection p81-89 **028.5**

Dictionaries
The American Heritage School dictionary (4 and up) **423**
The Cat in the hat Beginner book dictionary (k-3) **423**
Children's dictionary (3-6) **423**
Macmillan Dictionary for children (3-6) **423**
The Magic world of words (1-3) **423**
The Merriam-Webster Dictionary for large print users **423**
The Random House School dictionary (4 and up) **423**
Schulz, C. M. The Charlie Brown dictionary (k-3) **423**
Scott, Foresman Beginning dictionary (3-5) **423**
Scott, Foresman Intermediate dictionary (5 and up) **423**
6,000 words: a supplement to Webster's Third New International dictionary **423**
Webster's Intermediate dictionary (5 and up) **423**
Webster's New Elementary dictionary (4 and up) **423**
Webster's New Students dictionary (5 and up) **423**
Webster's New World dictionary for young readers (4 and up) **423**
Webster's Third New International dictionary of the English language **423**
Wright, W. W. The rainbow dictionary (1-4) **423**

Dictionaries—Bibliography
Kister, K. F. Dictionary buying guide **016.423**

Dictionaries—History
Kraske, R. The story of the dictionary (5 and up) **413**

Etymology
Asimov, I. More Words of science (6 and up) **503**
Asimov, I. Words from the Exodus (6 and up) **222**
Asimov, I. Words from the myths (6 and up) **292**
Asimov, I. Words of science and the history behind them (6 and up) **503**
Kohn, B. What a funny thing to say! (5 and up) **422**

Grammar
Brandt, S. R. How to improve your written English (4-6) **808**

History
See pages in the following book:
Kohn, B. What a funny thing to say! p11-22 (5 and up) **422**

Periodicals
Language Arts **420.5**

Reading materials
See Reading materials

Slang
See pages in the following book:
Kohn, B. What a funny thing to say! p43-50 (5 and up) **422**

Study and teaching—Periodicals
Language Arts **420.5**

Synonyms and antonyms
Hoban, T. Push pull, empty full **E**
Schiller, A. In other words (3-5) **423**
Schiller, A. Junior thesaurus (5 and up) **423**
Spier, P. Fast-slow, high-low **E**

English literature
See also Ballads, English

Collections
Lewis, R. ed. Journeys **820.8**
Mayne, W. ed. Ghosts (6 and up) **820.8**

English poetry **821**

Collections
Amelia mixed the mustard, and other poems (2-5) **821.08**
The Birds and the beasts were there (5 and up) **821.08**
Cole, W. comp. Humorous poetry for children (5 and up) **821.08**
Cole, W. comp. Poems for seasons and celebrations (5 and up) **821.08**
Cole, W. comp. Poems of magic and spells (4 and up) **821.08**
Cole, W. comp. Rough men, tough men, (5 and up) **821.08**
De La Mare, W. ed. Come hither **821.08**
Eaton, A. T. comp. Welcome Christmas! (4 and up) **821.08**
For a child (k-3) **821.08**
From morn to midnight (k-3) **821.08**
Gaily we parade (3-6) **821.08**
A Galaxy of verse (5 and up) **821.08**
Ghost poems (k-3) **811.08**
Giant poems (2-4) **811.08**
The Golden journey (4 and up) **821.08**
The Golden Treasury of poetry **821.08**
The Home book of verse for young folks **821.08**
How to eat a poem & other morsels (3-5) **821.08**
An Inheritance of poetry (5 and up) **821.08**
Larrick, N. ed. Piper, pipe that song again! (2-5) **821.08**
Laughable limericks (4 and up) **821.08**
Lewis, R. ed. Miracles **821.08**
Livingston, M. C. ed. Listen, children, listen (k-4) **821.08**
Love, K. comp. A little laughter (3-6) **821.08**
The Man in the Moon as he sails the sky, and other Moon verse (k-3) **821.08**
The Moon's the North Wind's cooky (k-3) **811.08**
My poetry book (5 and up) **821.08**
My tang's tungled and other ridiculous situations (3-6) **821.08**
Of quarks, quasars, and other quirks (5 and up) **821.08**
Oh, how silly! (3-6) **821.08**
Oh, such foolishness! (3 and up) **811.08**

Europe

Animals
See Animals—Europe

Biography—Bibliography
Hotchkiss, J. European historical fiction and biography for children and young people 016.8

Folklore
See Folklore—Europe

History—Fiction-Bibliography
Hotchkiss, J. European historical fiction and biography for children and young people 016.8

Pictorial works
Anno, M. Anno's journey **E**

European common market. See European Economic Community

European Economic Community
Rothkopf, C. Z. The common market **382.9**

European historical fiction and biography for children and young people. Hotchkiss, J. **016.8**

European historical fiction for children and young people. See Hotchkiss, J. European historical fiction and biography for children and young people **016.8**

European War, 1914-1918. See World War, 1914-1918

Europeans in Africa
See pages in the following book:
Bleeker, S. The Ashanti of Ghana p107-24 (4 and up) **966.7**

Europeans in Ghana
See pages in the following book:
Sale, J. K. The land and people of Ghana p58-73 (5 and up) **966.7**

Eutemey, Loring
(illus.) Gould, M. Skateboards, scooterboards & seatboards you can make **688.6**

Evaluation of literature. See Books—Reviews; Books and reading; Books and reading—Best books; Criticism

Evans C. S.
Cinderella (3-5) **398.2**
The sleeping beauty (3-5) **398.2**

Evans, Edmund
(illus.) Greenaway, K. Under the window **821**

Evans, Eva Knox
Goat comes to the Christmas party
In Association for Childhood Education International. Told under the Christmas tree p132-36 **808.8**
In Rollins, C. comp. Christmas gif' p45-50 **394.2**

Evans, George K.
Ehret, W. The international book of Christmas carols **783.6**

Evans, I. O.
The observer's book of flags **929.9**

Evans, Ivor H.
(ed.) Brewer's Dictionary of phrase and fable. See Brewer's Dictionary of phrase and fable **803**

Evans, Katherine
(illus.) Elkin, B. Six foolish fishermen **398.2**

Evans, Mari
Jim flying high **E**

Evans, Mark
Scott Joplin and the ragtime years (5 and up) **92**

Evans, Timothy
(illus.) Gilbreath, A. Making costumes for parties, plays, and holidays **391**
(illus.) Zim, H. S. Metric measure **389**

Evans' corner. Hill, E. S. **E**

Even the devil is afraid of a shrew. Stadler, V. **398.2**

Even unto the end of the world. Jewett, E. M.
In It's time for Easter p159-69 **394.2**

Ever-ready Eddie. Haywood, C. See note under Haywood, C. Little Eddie **Fic**

Everett Anderson's Christmas coming. Clifton, L. **811**

Everett Anderson's friend. Clifton, L. **811**

Everett Anderson's nine month long. Clifton, L. **811**

Everett Anderson's 1 2 3. Clifton, L. **811**

Everett Anderson's year. Clifton, L. **811**

Everglades National Park
See pages in the following book:
National Geographic Society. The new America's wonderlands **917.3**

Evergreens
See also Redwood

Every man heart lay down. Graham, L. **232.9**

Every time I climb a tree. McCord, D. **811**

Everybody needs a rock. Baylor, B. **E**

Everyone knows what a dragon looks like. Williams, J. **E**

Everyone ready? Brandenberg, F. See note under Brandenberg, F. Nice new neighbors **E**

Everyone's trash problem: nuclear wastes. Hyde, M. O. **621.48**

Everything in its right place
Andersen, H. C. Everything in its right place
In Andersen, H. C. The complete fairy tales and stories p416-23 **S C**

Eve's various children
Grimm, J. Eve's various children
In Grimm, J. The complete Grimm's fairy tales p734-36 **398.2**

The **evil** king. Andersen, H. C.
In Andersen, H. C. The complete fairy tales and stories p592-94 **S C**

The **evil** weed. Holman, F.
In Holman, F. The Drac p57-71 **398.2**

Evolution
Asimov, I. How did we find out about our human roots? (4 and up) **573.2**
May, J. How the animals came to North America (2-4) **591.5**
Merrill, M. W. Skeletons that fit (4-6) **575**
See also Biology; Color of animals; Color of people; Creation; Embryology; Heredity; Man—Influence of environment; Mendel's law

Evslin, Bernard
The green hero (5 and up) **398.2**

Evy-ivy-over. Rodowsky, C. **Fic**

Ewbank, Constance
Insect zoo (4 and up) **595.7**

Ewing, Juliana H.
The hillman and the housewife
In Stories to dramatize p102-03 **372.6**
Murdoch's Rath
In It's time for story hour p180-86 **372.6**

Extinct animals
McClung, R. M. Lost wild worlds (6 and up) 591.9

See also pages in the following books:
Merrill, M. W. Skeletons that fit p46-55 (4-6) 575

Pringle, L. Death is natural p37-46 (4 and up) 574.2
See also names of extinct animals, e.g. Mastodon

Poetry
Dinosaurs and beasts of yore 808.81

Extinct cities. See Cities and towns, Ruined, extinct, etc.

Extrasensory perception
Kettelkamp, L. Investigating psychics (5 and up) 133.8
Kettlekamp, L. Sixth sense (5 and up) 133.8

Fiction
Conford, E. And this is Laura (4 and up) Fic
Rodowsky, C. Evy-icy-over (5 and up) Fic
Sleator, W. Into the dream (5 and up) Fic

Extraterrestrial life. See Life on other planets

Eye
Adler, I. Your eyes (3-5) 612
Showers, P. Look at your eyes (k-2) 612
Ylla. Whose eye am I? (k-3) 591
See also pages in the following books:
Brindze, R. Look how many people wear glasses p21-40 (6 and up) 617.7
Kettelkamp, L. Tricks of eye and mind p17-28 (4 and up) 535
See also Vision

Surgery
Sobol, H. L. Jeff's hospital book (k-3) 362.1

Eye winker, Tom Tinker, chin chopper. Glazer, T. 796.1

Eyeglasses
Brindze, R. Look how many people wear glasses (6 and up) 617.7
Kelley, A. Lenses, spectacles, eyeglasses, and contacts (5 and up) 617.7

Fiction
Raskin E. Spectacles E

The **eyes** of the Amaryllis. Babbitt, N. Fic

Ezra's Thanksgivin' out West. Field, E.
In Harper, W. comp. The harvest feast p226-38 S C

F

Faber, Doris
The assassination of Martin Luther King, Jr. (5 and up) 92
Bella Abzug (5 and up) 92
Dwight Eisenhower (5 and up) 92
The perfect life (6 and up) 289

Faber, Harold
(jt. auth.) Faber, D. The assassination of Martin Luther King, Jr. 92

Fables
Achebe, C. How the leopard got his claws (4-6) Fic
Babbitt, E. C. Jataka tales (1-3) 398.2

Brown, M. Once a mouse (k-3) 398.2
Cooney, B. Chanticleer and the fox E
Dana, D. The elephant and his secret E
The Frogs who wanted a king and other songs from La Fontaine 784.7
Gaer, J. The fables of India (5 and up) 398.2
Galdone, P. The monkey and the crocodile (k-2) 398.2
Galdone, P. Three Aesop fox fables (k-3) 398.2
The Hare and the tortoise (k-3) 398.2
Jacobs, J. The fables of Aesop (4 and up) 398.2
Jataka tales (3-5) 398.2
Lexau, J. M. Crocodile and Hen (k-1) 398.2
Quigley, L. The blind men and the elephant (k-3) 398.2
Rice, E. Once in a wood: ten tales from Aesop (1-3) 398.2
Soyer, A. The adventures of Yemima, and other stories (4-6) S C
Wildsmith, B. The miller, the boy and the donkey (k-2) 398.2
Wildsmith, B. The rich man and the shoemaker (k-2) 398.2

See also pages in the following books:
The Arbuthnot Anthology of children's literature p414-23 808.8
Darrell, M. (ed.) Once upon a time p235-47 808.8
Gruenberg, S. M. ed. Favorite stories old and new p403-21 808.8
Sutherland, Z. Children & books p193-97 028.5
Time for old magic p277-81 398.2
See also Animals—Fiction; Folklore

Bibliography
See pages in the following book:
Bauer, C. F. Handbook for storytellers p121-24 372.6

Fables; selections. Aesop
In Darrell, M. ed. Once upon a time p235-47 808.8
The **fables** of Aesop. Jacobs, J. 398.2
The **fables** of India. Gaer, J. 398.2
Fables of La Fontaine; selections. La Fontaine, J. de
In The Arbuthnot Anthology of children's literature p422-23 808.8
In Time for old magic p286-87 398.2

Fabrics
Buehr, W. Cloth from fiber to fabric (5 and up) 677
See also pages in the following book:
Corrigan, B. Of course you can sew! p15-19 (5 and up) 646.4
See also names and types of fabrics; e.g. Wool

Face
Emberley, E. Ed Emberley's Drawing book of faces (2-6) 743
The **face** in the courthouse window. Jagendorf, M. A.
In Jagendorf, M. A. Folk stories of the South p16-17 398.2
Face talk, hand talk, body talk. Castle, S. 153.6

Fairy tales—*Continued*

Gripe, M. The glassblower's children (4-6) **Fic**

Gripe, M. In the time of the bells (5 and up) **Fic**

Harris, R. Beauty and the beast (2-4) **398.2**

Hatch, M. C. 13 Danish tales (3-5) **398.2**

Haviland, V. Favorite fairy tales told in Czechoslovakia (2-5) **398.2**

Haviland, V. Favorite fairy tales told in Denmark (3-5) **398.2**

Haviland, V. Favorite fairy tales told in France (2-5) **398.2**

Haviland, V. Favorite fairy tales told in Greece (2-5) **398.2**

Haviland, V. Favorite fairy tales told in India (2-5) **398.2**

Haviland, V. Favorite fairy tales told in Ireland (2-5) **398.2**

Haviland, V. Favorite fairy tales told in Italy (2-5) **398.2**

Haviland, V. Favorite fairy tales told in Japan (2-5) **398.2**

Haviland, V. Favorite fairy tales told in Norway (2-5) **398.2**

Haviland, V. Favorite fairy tales told in Scotland (2-5) **398.2**

Haviland, V. Favorite fairy tales told in Spain (2-5) **398.2**

Haviland, V. Favorite fairy tales told in Sweden (2-5) **398.2**

Hilgartner, B. A necklace of fallen stars (4-6) **Fic**

Housman, L. The rat-catcher's daughter (6 and up) **S C**

Hunter, M. A furl of fairy wind (2-5) **S C**

Hunter M. The wicked one (4 and up) **Fic**

Hutton W. The sleeping beauty (1-4) **398.2**

Indian fairy tales (4-6) **398.2**

Jacobs, J. English fairy tales (4-6) **398.2**

Jeffers, S. Wild Robin **E**

Kennedy R. The blue stone (3-5) **Fic**

Kennedy, R. The leprechaun's story **E**

Le Prince de Beaumont, M. Beauty and the beast **398.2**

Lewis, N. The Snow Queen (3-5) **Fic**

Lindgren, A. The Tomten **E**

Lindgren A. The Tomten and the fox **E**

Littledale, F. The elves and the shoemaker (k-3) **398.2**

Lobel, A. The troll music **E**

Lowe, P. T. The tale of Czar Saltan (3-5) **398.2**

Lowe, P. T. The tale of the golden cockerel (3-5) **398.2**

Lubin, L. B. The white cat (1-3) **398.2**

MacDonald, G. At the back of the North Wind (4-6) **Fic**

MacDonald, G. The complete fairy tales of George MacDonald (4 and up) **S C**

Macdonald, G. The light princess (3-6) **Fic**

Macdonald, G. The Princess and the goblin (3-6) **Fic**

McGinley, P. The plain princess (2-4) **Fic**

McKinley, R. Beauty: a retelling of the story of Beauty and the beast (5 and up) **Fic**

MacManus, S. Hibernian nights (4 and up) **398.2**

Manning-Sanders, R. A book of charms and changelings (3-6) **398.2**

Manning-Sanders, R. A book of dragons (3-6) **398.2**

Manning-Sanders, R. A book of ogres and trolls (3-6) **398.2**

Manning-Sanders, R. A book of witches (3-6) **398.2**

Mayer, M. Beauty and the beast **398.2**

Mayne, W. A year and a day (4-6) **Fic**

Myers, S. J. The enchanted sticks (3-5) **Fic**

Myers, W. D. The dragon takes a wife **E**

Norton, M. The Borrowers (3-6) **Fic**

Olenius, E. comp. Great Swedish fairy tales (4 and up) **398.2**

Perrault, C. Cinderella (k-3) **398.2**

Perrault, C. Perrault's Complete fairy tales (4-6) **398.2**

Perrault, C. Puss in boots (k-3) **398.2**

Picard, B. L. The faun and the woodcutter's daughter (4 and up) **S C**

Pollushkin, M. The little hen and the giant **E**

Pyle, H. King Stork (k-3) **398.2**

Pyle, H. Pepper & salt (4-6) **398.2**

Pyle, H. The wonder clock (4-6) **398.2**

Red fairy book (4-6) **398.2**

Reeves, J. English fables and fairy stories (4-6) **398.2**

Riordan, J. Tales from Central Russia (5 and up) **398.2**

Riordan, J. Tales from Tartary (5 and up) **398.2**

Ritchie, A. The treasure of Li-Po (3-6) **S C**

Rockwell, A. The three bears & 15 other stories (k-3) **398.2**

Sandburg, C. Rootabaga stories (5 and up) **S C**

Schulman, J. The nutcracker (3-5) **Fic**

Stearns, P. The mechanical doll (4-6) **Fic**

Steel, F. A. Tattercoats (k-3) **398.2**

Stephens, J. Irish fairy tales (6 and up) **398.2**

Stern, S. The Hobyahs (k-2) **398.2**

The Tall book of nursery tales (k-2) **398.2**

Tatterhood, and other tales (3-6) **398.2**

The Three wishes (k-2) **398.2**

Thurber, J. The great Quillow (3-5) **Fic**

Thurber, J. Many moons (1-4) **Fic**

Thurber, J. The 13 clocks (6 and up) **Fic**

Told under the green umbrella (1-4) **398.2**

Told under the magic umbrella (k-4) **S C**

Tolkien, J. R. R. Farmer Giles of Ham (5 and up) **Fic**

Tolkien, J. R. R. The hobbit (4 and up) **Fic**

Tolkien, J. R. R. Smith of Wooton Major (5 and up) **Fic**

Torgersen, D. A. The girl who tricked the troll **E**

Tregarthen, E. The doll who came alive (3-5) **Fic**

The Twelve dancing princesses (k-3) **398.2**

Uchida, Y. The magic listening cap (3-6) **398.2**

Ungerer, T. Zeralda's ogre **E**

Van Woerkom, D. O. The queen who couldn't bake gingerbread (k-3) **398.2**

Wiesner, W. Hansel and Gretel: a shadow puppet picture book (1-4) **791.5**

Wilde, O. The Happy Prince, and other stories (3-6) **S C**

Family life—Fiction—*Continued*

Bawden, N. The robbers (6 and up)   **Fic**
Benary-Isbert, M. The Ark (5 and up)   **Fic**
Blaine, M. Dvora's journey (3-5)   **Fic**
Blaine, M. The terrible thing that happened at our house   **E**
Blume, J. Tales of a fourth grade nothing (3-6)   **Fic**
Brady, E. W. The toad on Capitol Hill (4-6)   **Fic**
Brenner, B. A year in the life of Rosie Bernard (4-6)   **Fic**
Bridgers, S. E. Home before dark (6 and up)   **Fic**
Byars, B. The cartoonist (4 and up)   **Fic**
Chaikin, M. I should worry, I should care (3-5)   **Fic**
Cleaver, V. Queen of hearts (6 and up)   **Fic**
Cohen, B. Benny (4-6)   **Fic**
Colman, H. Diary of a frantic kid sister (4 and up)   **Fic**
Conford, E. And this is Laura (4 and up)   **Fic**
Conford, E. The luck of Pokey Bloom (3-6)   **Fic**
Cresswell, H. Ordinary Jack (5 and up)   **Fic**
Cummings, B. S. Hew against the grain (6 and up)   **Fic**
Danziger, P. The pistachio prescription (5 and up)   **Fic**
Estes, E. The Moffats (4-6)   **Fic**
Fitzhugh, L. Nobody's family is going to change (5 and up)   **Fic**
Fox, P. The stone-faced boy (4-6)   **Fic**
Geras, A. The girls in the velvet frame (4 and up)   **Fic**
Greenfield, E. Sister (4 and up)   **Fic**
Greenfield, E. Talk about a family (3-5)   **Fic**
Greenwald, S. All the way to wits' end (4-6)   **Fic**
Hale, L. P. The complete Peterkin papers (5 and up)   **Fic**
Hamilton, V. M. C. Higgins, the great (6 and up)   **Fic**
Hazen, B. S. Why couldn't I be an only kid like you, Wigger   **E**
Herman, C. Our snowman had olive eyes (4-6)   **Fic**
Hill, E. S. Evan's corner   **E**
Hoban, R. The little Brute family   **E**
Hoban, R. The sorely trying day   **E**
Holland, I. Dinah and the Green Fat Kingdom (5 and up)   **Fic**
Hunt, I. William (5 and up)   **Fic**
Hurmence, B. Tough Tiffany (5 and up)   **Fic**
Jordan, J. New life: New Room (2-4)   **Fic**
Kaplan, B. The empty chair (6 and up)   **Fic**
Karl, J. E. Beloved Benjamin is waiting (4-6)   **Fic**
L'Engle, M. Meet the Austins (5 and up)   **Fic**
LeRoy, G. Emma's dilemma (4-6)   **Fic**
Lexau, J. M. Striped ice cream (2-4)   **Fic**
Little, J. From Anna (4 and up)   **Fic**
Little, J. Look through my window (4-6)   **Fic**
Little, J. One to grow on (4-6)   **Fic**
Lowry, L. Anastasia Krupnik (4-6)   **Fic**
MacHargue, G. Stoneflight (5 and up)   **Fic**
Mathis, S. B. The hundred penny box   **E**

Mathis, S. B. Teacup full of roses (6 and up)   **Fic**
Matthews, E. The trouble with Leslie (4-6)   **Fic**
Miles, B. Just the beginning (4-6)   **Fic**
Miles, M. Jenny's cat (2-4)   **Fic**
Morey, W. Year of the black pony (5 and up)   **Fic**
Neufeld, J. Edgar Allan (5 and up)   **Fic**
Pearce, P. The battle of Bubble and Squeak (3-6)   **Fic**
Perl, L. That crazy April (5 and up)   **Fic**
Pevsner, S. And you give me a pain, Elaine (5 and up)   **Fic**
Pevsner, S. Keep stompin' till the music stops (3-6)   **Fic**
Phipson, J. The family conspiracy (5 and up)   **Fic**
Rabe, B. The girl who had no name (5 and up)   **Fic**
Rabe, B. Naomi (6 and up)   **Fic**
Raskin, E. Figgs & phantoms (5 and up)   **Fic**
Rice, E. Papa's lemonade, and other stories   **E**
Sachs, M. Dorrie's book (4-6)   **Fic**
Sachs, M. The truth about Mary Rose (4 and up)   **Fic**
Scott, A. H. Sam   **E**
Sebestyen, O. Words by heart (5 and up)   **Fic**
Segal, L. Tell me a Mitzi   **E**
Segal, L. Tell me a Trudy   **E**
Shreve, S. Family secrets (3-5)   **S C**
Smith, A. Reserved for Mark Anthony Crowder (5 and up)   **Fic**
Smith, L. B. My mom got a job   **E**
Sonneborn, R. A. Friday night is Papa night   **E**
Sorensen, V. Miracles on Maple Hill (4 and up)   **Fic**
Spykman, E. C. A lemon and a star (5 and up)   **Fic**
Stolz, M. By the highway home (6 and up)   **Fic**
Stolz, M. The edge of next year (6 and up)   **Fic**
Stolz, M. Ferris wheel (4-6)   **Fic**
Stolz, M. Go and catch a flying fish (5 and up)   **Fic**
Stolz, M. The noonday friends (4-6)   **Fic**
Thrasher, C. The dark didn't catch me (5 and up)   **Fic**
Tolan, S. S. Grandpa—and me (5 and up)   **Fic**
Townsend, J. R. Good-bye to the jungle (6 and up)   **Fic**
Uchida, Y. Journey home (4 and up)   **Fic**
Van Leeuwen, J. Tales of Oliver Pig   **E**
Vestly, A. C. Aurora and Socrates (3-5)   **Fic**
Waber, B. Goodbye, funny dumpy-lumpy   **E**
Wells, R. Noisy Nora   **E**
Willard, B. Storm from the west (6 and up)   **Fic**

Family life education
  See also Sex education

Family names. See Names, Personal

The **family** of Hen-Grethe. Andersen, H. C.
  In Andersen, H. C. The complete fairy tales and stories p954-66   **S C**

Family relations. See Family life

Family secrets. Shreve, S.   **S C**

Family trees. See Genealogy

The family under the bridge. Carlson, N. S.   **Fic**

Famines
> Archer, J. Hunger on planet Earth (6 and up)   **338.1**

Famous American Negro poets. Rollins, C.   **920**

Famous criminal trials. David, A.   **345**

Famous first facts. Kane, J. N.   **031**

Famous pirates of the New World. Whipple, A. B. C.   **910.4**

The famous Stanley kidnapping case. Snyder, Z. K. See note under Snyder, Z. K. The headless cupid   **Fic**

Famous U.S. Air Force bombers. Cooke, D. C.   **623.74**

Famous U.S. Navy fighter planes. Cooke, D. C.   **623.74**

Fanny Kemble's America. Scott, J. A.   **92**

The fantastic bicycles look. Lindblom, S.   **629.2**

Fantastic fiction
> Alexander, L. The book of three (4 and up)   **Fic**
> Babbitt, N. Tuck everlasting (4 and up)   **Fic**
> Baum, L. F. The Wizard of Oz (3-6)   **Fic**
> Bond, N. A string in the harp (6 and up)   **Fic**
> Boston, L. M. The children of Green Knowe (4-6)   **Fic**
> Boston, L. M. The sea egg (3-5)   **Fic**
> Byfield, B. N. Andrew and the alchemist (4-6)   **Fic**
> Carroll, L. Alice's adventures in Wonderland (4 and up)   **Fic**
> Carroll, L. Alice's adventures in Wonderland, and Through the looking glass (4 and up)   **Fic**
> Carroll, L. Through the looking glass, and what Alice found there (4 and up)   **Fic**
> Cooper, S. Over sea, under stone (5 and up)   **Fic**
> Corbett, S. The lemonade trick (3-5)   **Fic**
> Cresswell, H. A game of catch (3-6)   **Fic**
> Curry, J. L. The daybreakers (4 and up)   **Fic**
> Curry, J. L. Poor Tom's ghost (5 and up)   **Fic**
> Curry, J. L. The watchers (5 and up)   **Fic**
> Dunlop, E. Elizabeth, Elizabeth (6 and up)   **Fic**
> Gannett, R. S. My father's dragon (1-4)   **Fic**
> Garner, A. Elidor (5 and up)   **Fic**
> Garner, A. The weirdstone of Brisingamen (6 and up)   **Fic**
> Hoban, R. The mouse and his child (4-6)   **Fic**
> Hunter, M. The haunted mountain (5 and up)   **Fic**
> Hunter, M. The kelpie's pearls (4-6)   **Fic**
> Hunter, M. The walking stones (5 and up)   **Fic**
> Jones, D. W. Charmed life (5 and up)   **Fic**
> Jones, D. W. Dogsbody (6 and up)   **Fic**
> Juster, N. The phantom tollbooth (4-6)   **Fic**
> Kendall, C. The Gammage Cup (4-6)   **Fic**
> LeGuin, U. K. A wizard of Earthsea (6 and up)   **Fic**
> L'Engle, M. A wrinkle in time (6 and up)   **Fic**
> Lewis, C. S. The lion, the witch and the wardrobe   **Fic**
> McCaffrey, A. Dragonsong (6 and up)   **Fic**
> MacHargue, G. Stoneflight (5 and up)   **Fic**
> McKillip, P. A. The riddle-master of Hed (5 and up)   **Fic**
> Mayne, W. Earthfasts (5 and up)   **Fic**
> Miles, P. The gods in winter (5 and up)   **Fic**
> Nichols, R. The marrow of the world (5 and up)   **Fic**
> Nichols, R. A walk out of the world (4-6)   **Fic**
> Norton, M. Bed-knob and broomstick (3-5)   **Fic**
> Norton, A. Dragon magic (4 and up)   **Fic**
> Oppenheim, S. The selchie's seed (4-6)   **Fic**
> Ormondroyd, E. Time at the top (5 and up)   **Fic**
> Pearce, A. P. Tom's midnight garden (4 and up)   **Fic**
> Sleator, W. Once, said Darlene   **E**
> Snyder, Z. K. Below the root (5 and up)   **Fic**
> Stolz, M. Cat in the mirror (5 and up)   **Fic**
> Swahn, S. C. The island through the gate (5 and up)   **Fic**
> Travers, P. L. Mary Poppins (4-6)   **Fic**
> Walsh, J. P. A chance child (5 and up)   **Fic**
> Westall, R. The wind eye (5 and up)   **Fic**
> Willard, N. The Island of the Grass King (4 and up)   **Fic**
> Winterfeld, H. Castaways in Lilliput (4-6)   **Fic**
> Wrightson, P. The ice is coming (5 and up)   **Fic**
> Wrightson, P. The Nargun and the stars (5 and up)   **Fic**

See also pages in the following book:

The Arbuthnot Anthology of children's literature p476-599   **808.8**

Bibliography
Lynn, R. N. Fantasy for children   **016.8**

See also pages in the following book:

Sutherland, Z. Children & books p247-54   **028.5**

History and criticism
See pages in the following books:

Children and literature p231-49   **028.5**

Huck, C. S. Children's literature in the elementary school p255-90   **028.5**

Sutherland, Z. Children & books p213-46   **028.5**

Fantasy

Fiction
Davies, A. Conrad's war (5 and up)   **Fic**

Ness, E. Sam, Bangs & Moonshine   **E**

Shulevitz, U. One Monday morning   **E**

Fantasy for children. Lynn, R. N.   **016.8**

Far and few. McCord, D.   **811**

Far East

Folklore
See Folklore—Far East

The far side of evil. Engdahl, S. L. See note under Engdahl, S. L. Enchantress from the stars   **Fic**

Faraday, Michael
Veglahn, N. Coils, magnets and rings (3-5)
92

Farb, Peter
The land, wildlife, and peoples of the Bible (5 and up)   220.8
The story of dams (5 and up)   627

Farber, Norma
How does it feel to be old? (2-4)   811
Small wonders (2-5)   811

Farjeon, Eleanor
The birth of Simnel cake
  In Greene, E. comp. Clever cooks p130-33
     398.2

Faithful Jenny Dove
  In Haunting tales p 174-94   S C
The lady's room
  In With a deep sea smile p82-85   372.6
The little bookroom (1-4)   S C
Contents: King and the corn; King's daughter cries for the moon; Young Kate; Flower without a name; The goldfish; Clumber Pup; Miracle of the poor island; Girl who kissed the peachtree; Westwoods; The barrel-organ; Giant and the mite; Little dressmaker; Lady's room; Seventh princess; Leaving paradise; Little lady's roses; In those days; Connemara donkey; The Tims; Pennyworth; And I dance mine own child; The lovebirds; San Fairy Ann; Glass peacock; Kind farmer; Old surly and the boy; Pannychis

Little Boy Pie
  In Gruenberg, S. M. ed. Favorite stories old and new p244-49   808.8
Elsie Piddock skips in her sleep
  In Told under the magic umbrella p205-16
     S C

About
See pages in the following book:
A Horn Book Sampler on children's books and reading p255-58   028.5

Farley, Carol
The garden is doing fine (6 and up)   Fic

Farley, Walter
The Black Stallion (4 and up)   Fic
The Black Stallion and Flame. See note under Farley, W. The Black Stallion   Fic
The Black Stallion and Satan. See note under Farley, W. The Black Stallion   Fic
The Black Stallion and the girl. See note under Farley, W. The Black Stallion   Fic
The Black Stallion challenged! See note under Farley, W. The Black Stallion   Fic
The Black Stallion mystery. See note under Farley, W. The Black Stallion   Fic
The Black Stallion picture book. See note under Farley, W. The Black Stallion   Fic
The Black Stallion returns. See note under Farley, W. The Black Stallion   Fic
The Black Stallion revolts. See note under Farley, W. The Black Stallion   Fic
The Black Stallion's courage. See note under Farley, W. The Black Stallion   Fic
The Black Stallion's filly. See note under Farley, W. The Black Stallion   Fic
The Black Stallion's ghost. See note under Farley, W. The Black Stallion   Fic
The Black Stallion's sulky colt. See note under Farley, W. The Black Stallion   Fic
Son of the Black Stallion. See note under Farley, W. The Black Stallion   Fic

A **farm**. Larsson, C.   759.85

Farm animals. See Domestic animals

Farm buildings
  See also names of specific farm buildings, e.g. Barns

Farm life
Ross, P. What ever happened to the Baxter place? (2-4)   307.7

Canada
Kurelek, W. A prairie boy's summer (3-5)
     971.27
Kurelek, W. A prairie boy's winter (3-5)
     971.27

Fiction
Aulaire, I. d'. Don't count your chicks   E
Blades, A. Mary of Mile 18 (2-4)   Fic
Burch, R. D. J.'s worst enemy (4-6)   Fic
Carner, C. Tawny (5 and up)   Fic
Caudill, R. A pocketfull of cricket   E
Clymer, E. Me and the Eggman (3-6)   Fic
Duncan, J. Brave Janet Reachfar   E
Edmonds, W. D. Bert Breen's barn (6 and up)   Fic
Enright, E. Thimble summer (4-6)   Fic
Gage, W. Squash pie   E
Hunt, I. Across five Aprils (6 and up)   Fic
Lobel, A. A treeful of pigs   E
Peck, R. N. A day no pigs would die (6 and up)   Fic
Provensen, A. The year at Maple Hill Farm   E
Rabe, B. Naomi (6 and up)   Fic
Seredy, K. The Good Master (4-6)   Fic
Thiele, C. The shadow on the hills (6 and up)   Fic
Van Woerkóm, D. O. Donkey Ysabel   E
Wilder, L. I. Farmer boy (4-6)   Fic

New England
See pages in the following book:
Loeb, R. H. New England village p35-43 (4-6)   974

Sweden
Larsson, C. .A. A farm (4-6)   759.85

United States
Jackson, L. A. Grandpa had a windmill, Grandma had a churn (2-4)   630.1
See also pages in the following books:
Sandler, M. W. The way we lived p8-18 (4 and up)   331.09
Tunis, E. The young United States, 1783 to 1830 p15-27 (6 and up)   973

Farm produce

Marketing
See pages in the following book:
Jenness, A. A life of their own p59-75 (5 and up)   972.81

Farmer boy. Wilder, L. I.   Fic
Farmer boy; excerpt. Wilder, L. I.
  In The Arbuthnot Anthology of children's literature p763-67   808.8

Farmer Grigg's boggart
Colwell, E. The boggart and the farmer
  In Colwell, E. Round about and long ago p57-60   398.2
Pyle, H. Farmer Grigg's boggart
  In It's time for story hour p69-76   372.6
  In Pyle, H. Pepper & salt p69-81   398.2

Farmer Palmer's wagon ride. Steig, W.   E

Farmer, Penelope

Charlotte sometimes; excerpt

In The Arbuthnot Anthology of children's literature p562-65 **808.8**

The story of Persephone (3-5) **292**

When in the world am I?

In The Arbuthnot Anthology of children's literature p562-65 **808.8**

Farmer, Peter

(illus.) Dunlop, E. Elizabeth, Elizabeth **Fic**

The **farmer** and the cheeses. Colwell, E.

In Colwell, E. Round about and long ago p85-86 **398.2**

The **farmer** and the demon. Sechrist, E. H.

In Sechrist, E. H. Once in the first times p119-25 **398.2**

Farmer and the money lender

Steel, F. A. The farmer and the money-lender

In Indian fairy tales p152-55 **398.2**

The **farmer** and the snake. Lester, J.

In Lester, J. The knee-high man, and other tales p24-26 **398.2**

Farmer Giles of Ham. Tolkien, J. R. R. **Fic**

The **Farmer** in the dell **E**

Farmer Weatherbread

Asbjørnsen, P. C. Farmer Weathersky

In Red fairy book p286-95 **398.2**

Farmer Weathersky. Asbjørnsen, P. C.

In Red fairy book p286-95 **398.2**

The **farmer's** secret. Jagendorf, M. A.

In Jagendorf, M. A. Noodlehead stories from around the world p100-01 **398.2**

Farmers three. Bowman, J. C.

In Bowman, J. C. Tales from a Finnish tuba p247-48 **398.2**

Farming. See Agriculture

Farming on shares

How Bobtail beat the Devil

In Grandfather tales p88-98 **398.2**

Farragut, David Glasgow

Latham, J. L. Anchor's aweigh (5 and up) **92**

The **farthest** shore. LeGuin, U. K. See note under LeGuin, U. K. A wizard of Earthsea **Fic**

Fascism

See pages in the following book:

Hale, J. The land and people of Romania p83-90 (5 and up) **949.8**

See also National socialism

Italy

See pages in the following book:

Winwar, F. The land and people of Italy p143-48 (5 and up) **945**

Fashion

See pages in the following book:

Hilton, S. The way it was—1876 p112-29 (6 and up) **973.8**

See also Costume

Fassler, Joan

Helping children cope **016.3627**

The **fast**. Hautzig, E.

In Hautzig, E. The case against the wind, and other stories p39-43 **S C**

Fast and easy needlepoint. Hodgson, M. A. **746.44**

Fast breeder reactors. See Nuclear reactors

Fast friends. Stevenson, J. **E**

Fast is not a ladybug. Schlein, M. **E**

Fast Sam, Cool Clyde & Stuff. Myers, W. D. **Fic**

Fast-slow, high-low. Spier, P. **E**

The **fast** Sooner hound. Bontemps, A. **Fic**

Fasteners

Weiss, H. What holds it together? (3-5) **621.8**

The **Fastest** animal, the fastest man, the fastest story

In The Sound of flutes, and other Indian legends p71 **398.2**

Fasts and feasts

Judaism

Becker, J. Jewish holiday crafts (4 and up) **745.5**

Cuyler, M. Jewish holidays (2-6) **394.2**

Epstein, M. All about Jewish holidays and customs (4-6) **296.4**

Lazar, W. The Jewish holiday book (3-6) **394.2**

Purdy, S. G. Jewish holiday cookbook (4-6) **641.5**

Purdy, S. G. Jewish holidays (4 and up) **394.2**

See pages in the following book:

Rossel, S. Judaism p28-44 (4 and up) **296**

See also names of individual fasts and feasts, e.g. Yom Kippur

Judaism—Fiction

Aleichem, S. Holiday tales of Sholom Aleichem (5 and up) **S C**

Fat men from space. Pinkwater, D. M. **Fic**

Father Bear comes home. Minarik, E. H. See note under Minarik, E. H. Little Bear **E**

Father Christmas. See Santa Claus

Father Christmas. Briggs, R. **E**

The **Father** Christmas letters. Tolkien, J. R. R. **Fic**

Father Fox's pennyrhymes. Watson, C. **811**

Father hits the jackpot. Garver, J.

In Fifty plays for junior actors p222-35 **812.08**

A **father**-in-law and his son-in-law. Courlander, H.

In Courlander, H. The king's drum, and other African stories p71-73 **398.2**

Father in the laundry room. Vestly, A. C.

In The Arbuthnot Anthology of children's literature p701-05 **808.8**

Father Nicholas and the thief. Afanas'ev, A.

In Afanas'ev, A. Russian fairy tales p145-46 **398.2**

Fathers

Fiction

Hamilton, M. My name is Emily **E**

Townsend, J. R. Noah's castle (6 and up) **Fic**

Father's Day

Poetry

See pages in the following book:

Sechrist, E. H. comp. Poems for red letter days p151-54 **821.08**

The **father's** legacy. Kim, So-un

In Kim, So-un. The story bag p186-98 **398.2**

Fertilization of plants
Rahn, J. E. How plants are pollinated (5 and up)   581.1
See also pages in the following books:
Anderson, M. J. Exploring the insect world p38-46 (5 and up)   595.7
Patent, D. H. Sizes and shapes in nature—what they mean p123-28 (5 and up)   574.4
Riedman, S. R. Trees alive p88-96 (5 and up)   582.16

Fertilizers and manures
Rockwell, H. The compost heap (k-1)   631.8
See also pages in the following book:
Pringle, L. Our hungry Earth p81-86 (5 and up)   338.1

Fes, Morocco. See Fez, Morocco

Festival of fire
See pages in the following book:
Festivals In Asia p17-22 (2-5)   394.2

Festival of lights. Foster, G.
In Association for Childhood Education International. Told under the Christmas tree p285-88   808.8

Festival of Saint Nicholas. Dodge, M. M.
In Dalgliesh, A. comp. Christmas p159-67   S C

Festivals
Festivals (3-6)   394.2
Temko, F. Folk crafts for world friendship   745.59

See also Holidays

Asia
Festivals in Asia (2-5)   394.2
More Festivals in Asia (2-5)   394.2

Bangladesh
See also Bengali New Year

Burma
See also Thingyan

Cambodia
See also New Year—Cambodia

China
See also Ko Nien

India
See also Divali

Indonesia
See also Lebaran

Iran
See also Festival of fire

Japan
Epstein, S. A year of Japanese festivals (4-6)   394.2
See also pages in the following book:
Vaughan, J. B. The land and people of Japan p62-75 (5 and up)   952
See also Boys' Day; Hinamatsuri

Jews
See Fasts and feasts—Judaism

Korea
See also Tan-O Day

Laos
See also Pimai

Malaysia
See also Hari Raya

Nepal
See also Dasain

North America
Showers, P. Indian festivals (1-3)   394.2

Pakistan
See also Eid-ul-Fitr

Philippine Islands
See also Santacruzan

Sri Lanka
See pages in the following book:
Wilber, D. N. The land and people of Ceylon p103-09 (5 and up)   954.9
See also New Year—Sri Lanka

Syria
Copeland, P. W. The land and people of Syria p47-53 (5 and up)   956.91

Taiwan
Cheney, C. Tales from a Taiwan kitchen (4-6)   398.2

Thailand
See also Loy Krathong

Vietnam
See also Mid-autumn Festival

Festivals [title]   394.2
Festivals in Asia   394.2
Festivals in Asia, More   394.2

Fetus
Parker, S. Life before birth: the story of the first nine months (3-6)   612

Fetz, Ingrid
(illus.) Hurwitz, J. The law of gravity   Fic
(illus.) Laughable limericks. See Laughable limericks   821.08
(illus.) Showers, P. Before you were a baby   612

Feudalism
Buehr, W. Knights and castles, and feudal life (4 and up)   940.1
Unstead, R. J. Living in a castle (4-6)   940.1

See also pages in the following books:
The Arbuthnot Anthology of children's literature p864-66   808.8
Duggan, A. Growing up with the Norman Conquest p3-50 (6 and up)   942.2

Fever
Berry, J. R. Why you feel hot, why you feel cold (2-4)   612
See also names of fevers, e.g. Malaria

Fez, Morocco
See pages in the following book:
Spencer, W. The land and people of Morocco p42-47, 120-31 (5 and up)   964

Fiammenghi, Gioia
(illus.) Froman, R. Bigger and smaller   E
(illus.) Froman, R. The greatest guessing game   513
(illus.) Gaeddert, L. Noisy Nancy Norris   E
(illus.) Moore, L. Little raccoon and poems from the woods   811
(illus.) Moore, L. Little raccoon and the thing in the pool   E

Financiers. See Capitalists and financiers

Finch, Christopher
The art of Walt Disney   **791.43**

Fincher, E. B.
The Bill of rights (5 and up)   **342**

Finches
See pages in the following book:
Villiards, P. Birds as pets p39-74 (5 and up)
    636.6

Find the constellations. Rey, H. A.   **523.8**

Find the hidden insect. Cole, J.   **595.7**

Finders keepers. Will   **E**

Finding out about the early Russians.
Rice, T.   **947**

Finding out about the past. Freeman, M. B.
    930.1

Fine, Joan
I carve stone (5 and up)   **731.4**

Finestkind o'day. McMillan, B.   **639**

Finger, Charles J.
How Pat got good sense
In Time to laugh p3-16   **S C**
The hungry old witch
In A Chilling collection p84-92   **S C**
In Giants & witches and a dragon or two
p50-63   **398.2**
In Harper, W. comp. Ghosts and goblins
p30-43   **398.2**
In Witches, witches, witches p90-100 **808.8**
If you had a wish?
In Told under the magic umbrella p189-96
    S C
The magic ball
In Witches, witches, witches p56-64 **808.8**
Tales from silver lands (5 and up)   **398.2**
Contents: Tale of three tails; Magic dog; Calabash
man; Na-Ha the fighter; Humming-bird and the
flower; Magic ball; El Enano; Hero twins; Four
hundred; Killing of Cabrakan; Tale of the Gentle
Folk; Tale that cost a dollar; Magic knot; Bad
wishers; Hungry old witch; Wonderful mirror; Tale
of the lazy people; Rairu and the Star Maiden; Cat
and the dream man

About
See pages in the following book:
Newbery Medal books: 1922-1955 p37-38
    028.5

Finger alphabet. See Deaf—Means of communication

Finger games. See Finger play

Finger marks. See Fingerprints

Finger play
Glazer T. Do your ears hang low? (k-3)
    796.1
Glazer, T. Eye Winker, Tom Tinker, chin
chopper (k-3)   **796.1**
Grayson, M. Let's do fingerplays (k-2)
    796.1
Nelson, E. L. Singing and dancing games
for the very young   **796.1**
See also pages in the following books:
Carlson, B. W. Listen! And tell the story
p15-40   **372.6**
With a deep sea smile p93-100   **372.6**

Finger prints. See Fingerprints

Finger puppets. Ross, L.   **791.5**

Fingerprint detective. Millimaki, R. H.   **363.2**

Fingerprints
Millimaki, R. H. Fingerprint detective (5
and up)   **363.2**

Fink, Mike
See pages in the following book:
Malcolmson, A. Yankee Doodle's cousins
p129-37 (4 and up)   **398.2**

Finland
Berry E. The land and people of Finland
(5 and up)   **948.97**

Finland's greatest fisherman. Bowman, J. C.
In Bowman, J. C. Tales from a Finnish
tupa p205-06   **398.2**

Finlay, Jeremy
(illus.) Peter, D. Claire and Emma   **362.4**
(illus.) White, P. Janet at school   **362.4**

Finlay, Winifred
The White Lady of Blenkinsopp
In A Chilling collection p95-102   **S C**

Finlayson, Ann
Rebecca's war (5 and up)   **Fic**

Finn Family Moomintroll. Jansson, T. See note
under Jansson, T. Comet in Moominland
    Fic

Finn MacCool. See Finn Mac Cumaill

Finn McCool. Lynch, M.
In Dramatized folk tales of the world p218-
26   **812.08**

Finn Mac Cumaill
Evslin, B. The green hero (5 and up)   **398.2**
See also pages in the following book:
Stephens, J. Irish fairy tales p35-108 (6 and
up)   **398.2**

Drama
See pages in the following book:
Dramatized folk tales of the world p218-26
    812.08

Finnish Americans
Engle, E. The Finns in America (5 and up)
    305.8

The **Finns** in America. Engle, E.   **305.8**

Fir Tree
Andersen, H. C. The Fir tree
In Andersen, H. C. Seven tales p19-45
    S C
In Dalgliesh, A. comp. Christmas p6-18 **S C**
In Harper, W. comp. Merry Christmas to
you p194-207   **S C**
In It's time for Christmas p229-37   **394.2**
In Take joy! p14-22   **394.2**
Andersen, H. C. Hans Christian Andersen's
The fir tree   **Fic**
Andersen, H. C. The pine tree
In Andersen, H. C. The complete fairy
tales and stories p225-33   **S C**

Fire
Haines, G. K. Fire (1-3)   **541.3**
See also pages in the following book:
Allison, L. The wild inside p84-92 (5 and up)
    500
See also Fires

Fiction
Hodges, M. The Fire Bringer (2-4)   **398.2**

Fire balls. See Meteors

**Fire-bird, the horse of power, and Princess
Vasilissa**
Afanas'ev A. The Firebird and Princess
Vasilisa
In Afanas'ev, A. Russian fairy tales p494-97
    398.2

The **first** book of the ancient Maya. Beck, B. L. **972**

The **first** book of the Aztecs. Beck, B. L. **972**

The **first** book of the Incas. Beck, B. L. **985**

The **first** book of the Netherlands. Cohn, A. **949.2**

The **first** book of the opera. Streatfeild, N. **782.1**

The **first** book of the Panama Canal. See Markun, P. M. The Panama Canal **972.87**

The **first** book of the Soviet Union. Snyder, L. L. **947**

The **first** book of the Vikings. Rich, L. D. **948**

The **first** book of Vice-presidents of the United States. Feerick, J. D. **920**

The **first** book of volcanoes & earthquakes. Marcus, R. B. **551.2**

The **first** book of World War I. Snyder, L. L. **940.3**

The **first** book of World War II. Snyder, L. L. **940.53**

First chemistry book for boys and girls. Morgan, A. **540**

The **first** Christmas. Bible. New Testament. Selections
In Told under the green umbrella p175-78 **398.2**

The **first** Christmas tree. Capell, L. C.
In A Treasury of Christmas plays p279-87 **812.08**

The **first** commune. Aleichem, S.
In Aleichem, S. Holiday tales of Sholom Aleichem p122-41 **S C**

The **first** Easter eggs. Bennett, R.
In Bennett, R. Creative plays and programs for holidays p71-79 **812**

First emperor's magic whip
Carpenter, F. First emperor's magic whip
In Carpenter, F. Tales of a Chinese grandmother p134-41 **398.2**

First facts, Famous. Kane, J. N. **031**

The **first** flute. Carter, D. S
In The Arbuthnot Anthology of children's literature p409-11 **808.8**

The **first** four years. Wilder, L. I. See note under Wilder, L. I. Little house in the big woods **Fic**

First graces **242**

First grade takes a test. Cohen, M. See note under Cohen, M. Will I have a friend? **E**

First humming bird
Belpré, P. The legend of the hummingbird
In Belpré, P. Once in Puerto Rico p25-28 **398.2**

First ladies
United States
See Presidents—United States—Wives

A **first** look at animals with backbones. Selsam, M. E. **596**

A **first** look at animals without backbones. Selsam, M. E. **592**

A **first** look at birds. Selsam, M. E. **598**

A **first** look at flowers. Selsam, M. E. **582.13**

A **first** look at insects. Selsam, M. E. **595.7**

A **first** look at monkeys and apes. Selsam, M. E. **599.8**

A **first** look at sharks. Selsam, M. E. **597**

A **first** look at the world of plants. Selsam, M. E **581**

The **first** New England Christmas tree. Colbo, E. S.
In One hundred plays for children p507-17 **808.82**

The **first** New England dinner. Warren, M. R.
In Harper, W. comp. The harvest feast p27-36 **S C**

The **first** of May. Haviland, V.
In Haviland, V. Favorite fairy tales told in Greece p71-81 **398.2**

The **first** overland mail. Pinkerton, R. **383**

First prayers **242**

The **first** schlemiel. Singer, I. B.
In Singer, I. B. Zlateh the goat, and other stories p55-65 **398.2**

First snow. Coutant, H. **Fic**

First steps in ballet. Mara, T. **792.8**

The **first** tale of Alabama. Jagendorf, M. A.
In Jagendorf, M. A. Folk stories of the South p3-4 **398.2**

The **first** Thanksgiving. Barksdale, L. **394.2**

The **first** transatlantic cable. Nathan, A. G. **621.382**

The **first** two lives of Lukas-Kasha. Alexander, L. **Fic**

The **first** war. Baker, B.
In Baker, B. At the center of the world p43-49 **398.2**

The **first** woman to say "dim". Courlander, H.
In Courlander, H. Olode the hunters, and other tales from Nigeria p121-23 **398.2**

Fischstrom, Margot (Zemach)
See pages in the following book:
Newbery and Caldecott Medal books: 1966-1975 p260-64 **028.5**

Fish, Helen Dean
(ed.) Bible. Selections. Animals of the Bible **220.8**

Fish. See Fishes

Fish and how they reproduce. Patent, D. H. **597**

Fish and the ring
Colwell, E. The fish and the ring
In Colwell, E. Round about and long ago p46-50 **398.2**
Jacobs, J. Fish and the ring
In Jacobs, J. English fairy tales p190-94 **398.2**
Reeves, J. The fish and the ring
In Reeves, J. English fables and fairy stories p35-48 **398.2**

The **Fish** angel
In Levoy, M. The witch of Fourth Street, and other stories p75-83 **S C**

Fish as food. See Sea food

Fish for supper. Goffstein, M. B. **E**

Fish friends. Stoutenburg, A.
In Stoutenburg, A. American tall-tale animals p54-67 **398.2**

Fish in the forest. Corson, H. W.
In Dramatized folk tales of the world p388-99 **812.08**
In Popular plays for classroom reading p45-55 **808.82**

Fish is fish. Lionni, L. **E**

The **fish** tale. Carrick, M.
In Carrick, M. The wise men of Gotham **398.2**

The **fish** with the deep sea smile. Brown, M. W.
In Gruenberg, S. M. ed. Favorite stories
old and new p503-04   **808.8**

Fisher, Aileen
Cricket in a thicket (k-3)   **811**
Do bears have mothers, too? (k-2)   **811**
Easter (1-3)   **394.2**
The ghost in the orchard
  In A-haunting we will go p54-64   **S C**
Going barefoot   **E**
Holiday programs for boys and girls (4 and
up)   **812**
Contains the following plays: The weaver's son;
Day of destiny; Ghosts on guard; The voice of
liberty; Once upon a time; Treasure hunt; Mother
of Thanksgiving; Unexpected guests; Angel in the
looking glass; Time out for Christmas; A Christmas
tree for Kitty; The spirit of Christmas; The Christ-
mas cake; Abe's winkin' eye; New hearts for old;
Hearts, tarts and valentines; Washington marches
on; What now, planet Earth; Trouble in the air;
On strike; Mother's day off and on; Look to a new
day
I like weather   **E**
I stood upon a mountain (k-3)   **113**
In one door and out the other (1-3)   **811**
Listen, rabbit   **E**
My cat has eyes of sapphire blue (2-4)   **811**
Nine cheers for Christmas
  In A Treasury of Christmas plays p330-38
    812.08
One-ring circus
  In One hundred plays for children p61-68
    808.82
Sing the songs of Christmas
  In A Treasury of Christmas plays p222-40
    812.08
Special edition
  In One hundred plays for children p69-79
    808.82
Thanksgiving blues
  In It's time for Thanksgiving p82-88
    394.2
Thanksgiving came on Wednesday
  In Thanksgiving p293-301   **394.2**
Up a Christmas tree
  In On stage for Christmas p403-07   **812.08**
The way to Norwich
  In One hundred plays for children p80-86
    808.82

Fisher, Anne B.
Stories California Indians told (3-5)   **398.2**
Contents: How California was made; How Coyote
helped to light the world; Why grizzly bears walk
on all fours; How Coyote got his voice; How animals brought fire to man; What happened to six
wives who ate onions; How the first rainbow was
made; How Coyote became a friend to man; How
Coyote put fish in Clear Lake; How the great rocks
grew; How Coyote put salmon in the Klamath
River; Why women talk more than men

Fisher, Dorothy Canfield
A new pioneer
  In Harper, W. comp. The harvest feast
  p182-91   **S C**
  In It's time for Thanksgiving p42-47   **394.2**

Fisher, Harvey I.
Wonders of the world of the albatross (4
and up)   **598**

Fisher, Leonard Everett
Alphabet art (4-7)   **411**
The blacksmiths (4 and up)   **682**
The cabinetmakers (4 and up)   **684.1**
The death of Evening Star (5 and up)   **Fic**
The factories (5 and up)   **338.09**
The glassmakers (4 and up)   **666**
The homemakers (4 and up)   **670**
The papermakers (4 and up)   **676**

The peddlers (4 and up)   **658.85**
The potters (4 and up)   **666**
The printers (4 and up)   **686.2**
The railroads (5 and up)   **385.09**
The shipbuilders (4 and up)   **623.8**
The shoemakers (4 and up)   **685**
The silversmiths (4-6)   **739.2**
The tanners (4 and up)   **675**
The warlock of Westfall (5 and up)   **Fic**
The weavers (4 and up)   **746.1**
The wigmakers (4 and up)   **679**
(illus.) Alderman, C. L. The story of the
thirteen colonies   **973.2**
(illus.) Commager, H. S. The first book of
American history   **973**
(illus.) Johnson, G. W. America grows up
    973
(illus.) Johnson, G. America is born   **973**
(illus.) Johnson, G. W. The Congress
    328.73
(illus) Johnson, G. W. Franklin Roosevelt
    92
(illus.) Latham, J. L. Man of the Monitor;
the story of John Ericsson (5 and up)   **92**
(illus.) Scheffer, V. B. Little Calf   **599.5**
(illus.) Singer, I. B The wicked ciy   **221.9**

Fisher, Margery
Growing Point. See Growing Point   **028.505**
Who's who in children's books   **028.5**

Fisher, Mildred L.
(jt. auth.) Fisher, H. I. Wonders of the
world of the albatross   **598**

Fisher, R. M.
Namu: making friends with a killer whale
(k-3)   **599.5**

Fisheries
Zim, H. S. Commercial fishing (3-6)   **639**
  See also Pearlfisheries; Whaling

Fiction
Adkins, J. Luther Tarbox (2-4)   **Fic**
Thiele, C. Blue Fin (6 and up)   **Fic**

Maine
McMillan, B. Finestkind o'day (2-4)   **639**

Nigeria
See pages in the following book:
Jenness, A. Along the Niger River p56-71
(5 and up)   **966.9**

Norway
See pages in the following book:
Hall, E. The land and people of Norway p88-
97 (5 and up)   **948.1**

Puerto Rico
See pages in the following book:
Singer, J. We all come from someplace:
Children of Puerto Rico p62-70 (4-6)
    972.95

The **fisherman**. Courlander, H.
  In Courlander, H. The king's drum, and
other African stories p22-24   **398.2**

Fisherman and his soul
Wilde, O. The fisherman and his soul
  In Wilde, O. The Happy Prince, and other
stories p93-134   **S C**
  In Witches, witches, witches p125-68
    808.8

Fisherman and his wife
Grimm, J. About a fisherman and his wife
  In Grimm, J. About wise men and simple-
tons p5-14   **398.2**

Fleischman, Sid
  By the Great Horn Spoon! (4-6)   **Fic**
  Chancy and the grand rascal (4-6)   **Fic**
  The ghost in the noonday sun (4-6)   **Fic**
  The ghost on Saturday night (3-5)   **Fic**
  The Hey Hey Man (2-4)   **Fic**
  Humbug Mountain (4 and up)   **Fic**
  Jim Bridger's alarm clock, and other tall tales (2-4)   **S C**
  Contents: Jim Bridger's alarm clock; The fiddler who wouldn't fiddle; The fifth of July
  Jing Django (4-6)   **Fic**
  McBroom and the beanstalk. See note under Fleischman, S. McBroom tells a lie   **Fic**
  McBroom and the great race. See note under Fleischman, S. McBroom tells a lie   **Fic**
  McBroom tells a lie (3-5)   **Fic**
  Mr Mysterious & Company (4-6)   **Fic**
  Mr Mysterious's secrets of magic (3-6) **793.8**

Fleishman, Seymour
  (illus.) Carmer, C. The boy drummer of Vincennes   **811**

Fleming, Ian
  Chitty-Chitty-Bang-Bang (4-6)   **Fic**

Fles, Barthold
  East Germany (4 and up)   **943.1**

Fletcher, Alan Mark
  Fishes dangerous to man (4-6)   **597**

Flies
  See pages in the following book:
  Teale, E. W. The junior book of insects p210-16 (6 and up)   **595.7**

Flight
  Corbett, S. What makes a plane fly? (3-6)   **629.132**
  See also pages in the following books:
  Asimov, I. How did we find out about outer space? p9-17 (5 and up)   **629.4**
  Yolen, J. World on a string p44-61 (4 and up)   **629.133**
  See also Aeronautics

The **flight** of the Doves. Macken, W.   **Fic**
The **flight** of the Lone Eagle. Foster, J. T.   **629.13**
Flight to freedom. Buckmaster, H.   **326**
Flight to Mars. See Space flight to Mars
Flight to the moon. See Space flight to the moon
Flippy's flashlight. Marsh, C.
  In Gruenberg, S. M. comp. Let's hear a story p44-51   **808.8**
Floating and sinking. Branley, F. M.   **532**
The **floating** stone. Foulk, C. W.
  In One hundred plays for children p643-48   **808.82**

Floethe, Richard
  (illus.) Shippen, K. B. Mr Bell invents the telephone [biography of Alexander Graham Bell]   **92**
  (illus.) Streatfeild, N. Ballet shoes   **Fic**

Flood, James
  See pages in the following book:
  Whipple, A. B. C. Famous pirates of the New World p12-38 (5 and up)   **910.4**

Floods
Control
  See also Dams
Fiction
  See pages in the following book:
  Gates, D. Lord of the sky: Zeus p27-34 (4 and up)   **292**

Flora, James
  The great green Turkey Creek monster   **E**
  Why I like Charlie
  In Friends are like that! p 1-4   **S C**

Flora. See Botany; Plants
Floral decoration. See Flower arrangement
Florence
Description
  See pages in the following book:
  Winwar, F. The land and people of Italy p114-18 (5 and up)   **945**

Florian, Douglas
  (illus.) Van Woerkom, D. O. Tit for tat   **398.2**

Floriculture. See Flower gardening
Florida
Fiction
  Corcoran, B. A dance to still music (5 and up)   **Fic**
  Hoff, S. Irving and me (5 and up)   **Fic**
  Lenski, L. Strawberry girl (4-6)   **Fic**
  Lippincott, J. W. The Wahoo bobcat (5 and up)   **Fic**
  Rawlings, M. K. The yearling (6 and up)   **Fic**
Natural history
  See Natural history—Florida

Flower arrangement
  Cramblit, J. Flowers are for keeping (5 and up)   **745.92**
  Munari, B. A flower with love (4 and up)   **745.92**

Flower gardening
  See pages in the following books:
  Cutler, K. N. Growing a garden, indoors or out p32-39 (4 and up)   **635**
  Fenten, D. X. Gardening . . . naturally p35-48 (4 and up)   **635**
  See also Bulbs; House plants
Fiction
  Uchida, Y. The promised year (4-6)   **Fic**

Flower, moon, snow. Mizumura, Kazue   **811**
The **flower** of happiness on Sunnymount Crest. Smedberg, A.
  In Olenius, E. comp. Great Swedish fairy tales p175-84   **398.2**
Flower queen's daughter
  The Flower queen's daughter
  In Yellow fairy book p173-79   **398.2**
A **flower** with love. Munari, B.   **745.92**
Flower without a name. Farjeon, E.
  In Farjeon, E. The little bookroom p36-39   **S C**

Flowers
  Dowden, A. O. Look at a flower (6 and up)   **582.13**
  Milne, L. J. Because of a flower (5 and up)   **582.13**
  Rahn, J. E. How plants are pollinated (5 and up)   **581.1**
  Selsam, M. E. A first look at flowers (1-3)   **582.13**
  See also pages in the following book:
  Cooper, E. K. Science in your own back yard p68-78 (5 and up)   **507**
  See also Flower arrangement; Flower gardening; Plants; State flowers; Wild flowers; and names of flowers; e.g. Lilacs

Folklore—*Continued*

The Three little pigs (k-1)	398.2
Time for old magic	398.2
Told under the green umbrella (1-4)	398.2
Van Woerkom, D. O. Tit for tat (1-3)	398.2
Wolkstein, D. Lazy stories (3-5)	398.2
Yellow fairy book (4-6)	398.2
Zemach, H. A penny a look (k-3)	398.2

See also pages in the following books:

The Arbuthnot Anthology of children's literature p148-413	808.8
Children and literature p206-12	028.5
Egoff, S. The republic of childhood p56-94	028.5
Huck, C. S. Children's literature in the elementary school p157-210	028.5
Jan, I. On children's literature p30-41	028.5
Sutherland, Z. Children & books p156-83	028.5
With a deep sea smile p41-92	372.6

See also Fairies; Fairy tales; Geographical myths; Halloween; Plant lore; Superstition; Weather lore

Africa

Aardema, V. Tales from the story hat (3-6)	398.2
Arnott, K. African myths and legends (4 and up)	398.2
Bryan, A. The adventures of Aku (3-5)	398.2
Courlander, H. The king's drum, and other African stories (4-6)	398.2
Haley, G. E. A story, a story (k-3)	398.2
Korty, C. Plays from African folktales (4-6)	812
Robinson, A. Singing tales of Africa (3-5)	398.2

See also pages in the following books:

Bleeker, S. The Masai p118-23 (4 and up)	967.6
Bleeker, S. The Zulu of South Africa p22-25 (4 and up)	968

Africa—Bibliography

Folklore from Africa to the United States	016.398

See also pages in the following book:

Issues in children's book selection p136-41	028.5

Africa, Southern

Aardema, V. Behind the back of the mountain (4-6)	398.2
Berger, T. Black fairy tales (4 and up)	398.2

Africa, West

Aardema, V. Why mosquitoes buzz in people's ears (k-3)	398.2
Arkhurst, J. C. The adventures of Spider (2-5)	398.2

Appalachian region

Still, J. Way down yonder on Troublesome Creek (3-6)	398

Armenia

Hogrogian, N. The contest (1-3)	398.2
Hogrogian, N. One fine day (k-3)	398.2

Asia

Courlander, H. The tiger's whisker, and other tales and legends from Asia and the Pacific (4-6)	398.2

Bibliography

See pages in the following books:

Bauer, C. F. Handbook for storytellers p104-15, 157-80	372.6
Sutherland, Z. Children & books p184-92	028.5

Blue Ridge Mountains

Credle, E. Tall tales from the high hills, and other stories (4 and up)	398.2

Bohemia

Gag, W. Gone is gone (k-3)	398.2

Caucasus

Ginsburg, M. The strongest one of all (k-3)	398.2

China

Bishop, C. H. The five Chinese brothers (1-3)	398.2
Carpenter, F. Tales of a Chinese grandmother (4 and up)	398.2
Cheng, Hou-tien. Six Chinese brothers (k-3)	398.2
Hume, L. C. Favorite children's stories from China and Tibet (3-6)	398.2
Kendall, C. Sweet and sour (4-6)	398.2
Mosel, A. Tikki Tikki Tembo (k-2)	398.2
Wyndham, R. Tales the people tell in China (3-6)	398.2
Yolen, J. The emperor and the kite (k-3)	398.2
Young, E. The terrible Nung Gwama (k-3)	398.2

Congo (Brazzaville)

Lexau, J. M. Crocodile and Hen (k-1)	398.2

Cornwall

See Folklore—Great Britain

Czechoslovakia

Haviland, V. Favorite fairy tales told in Czechoslovakia (2-5)	398.2

Denmark

Coombs, P. The magic pot (k-3)	398.2
Hatch, M. C. 13 Danish tales (3-5)	398.2
Haviland, V. Favorite fairy tales told in Denmark (3-5)	398.2
Lobel, A. King Rooster, Queen Hen (1-3)	398.2

Egypt

How Djadja-em-ankh saved the day (4 and up)	398.2

See also pages in the following book:

Mahmoud, Z. N. The land and people of Egypt p66-71 (5 and up)	962

England

See Folklore—Great Britain

Europe

Bulfinch, T. Bulfinch's Mythology (6 and up)	291

Far East

Kirkup, J. The magic drum (3-5)	398.2

Finland

Bowman, J. C. Tales from a Finnish tupa (4 and up)	398.2

France

Brown, M. Stone soup (k-3)	398.2
Galdone, P. Cinderella (k-2)	398.2
Galdone, P. Puss in Boots (k-2)	398.2

Folklore—France—*Continued*

Harris, R. Beauty and the beast (2-4)   **398.2**
Haviland, V. Favorite fairy tales told in France (2-5)   **398.2**
Holman, F. The Drac (5 and up)   **398.2**
Le Prince de Beaumont, M. Beauty and the beast   **398.2**
Lubin, L. B. The white cat (1-3)   **398.2**
Mayer, M. Beauty and the beast   **398.2**
Perrault, C. Cinderella (k-3)   **398.2**
Perrault, C. Perrault's Complete fairy tales (4-6)   **398.2**
Perrault, C. Puss in boots (k-3)   **398.2**
Rockwell, A. Poor Goose: a French folktale (1-3)   **398.2**
The Twelve dancing princesses (k-3)   **398.2**

Germany

Craig, M. J. The donkey prince (k-3)   **398.2**
De Regniers, B. S. Red Riding Hood (1-3)   **398.2**
Gág, W. Wanda Gág's The sorcerer's apprentice (k-3)   **398.2**
Galdone, P. Little Red Riding Hood (k-2)   **398.2**
Galdone, P. The table, the donkey and the stick (k-3)   **398.2**
Grimm, J. About wise men and simpletons (3-6)   **398.2**
Grimm, J. The bear and the kingbird (k-3)   **398.2**
Grimm, J. The best of Grimm's fairy tales (1-4)   **398.2**
Grimm, J. The Bremen town musicians (k-3)   **398.2**
Grimm, J. The Brothers Grimm: popular folk tales (4 and up)   **398.2**
Grimm, J. Cinderella (1-3)   **398.2**
Grimm, J. The complete Grimm's fairy tales (4 and up)   **398.2**
Grimm, J. Fairy tales of the Brothers Grimm (4 and up)   **398.2**
Grimm, J. The fisherman and his wife (1-4)   **398.2**
Grimm, J. The goose girl (2-4)   **398.2**
Grimm, J. Grimm's Fairy tales (3-6)   **398.2**
Grimm, J. Hans in luck (k-2)   **398.2**
Grimm, J. Hansel and Gretel; illus. by A. Adams (k-3)   **398.2**
Grimm, J. Hansel and Gretel; illus. by A. Lobel (1-3)   **398.2**
Grimm, J. Hansel and Gretel; illus. by L. Zwerger (k-3)   **398.2**
Grimm, J. Household stories (4-6)   **398.2**
Grimm, J. The juniper tree, and other tales from Grimm (4 and up)   **398.2**
Grimm, J. King Grisly-Beard (k-3)   **398.2**
Grimm, J. King Thrushbeard (1-3)   **398.2**
Grimm, J. Little Red Riding Hood (k-3)   **398.2**
Grimm, J. More Tales from Grimm (4-6)   **398.2**
Grimm, J. Rapunzel (1-4)   **398.2**
Grimm, J. The seven ravens (k-3)   **398.2**
Grimm, J. Snow White (k-3)   **398.2**
Grimm, J. Snow White and Rose Red (1-3)   **398.2**
Grimm, J. Snow-White and the seven dwarfs; illus. by N. E. Burkert (k-3)   **398.2**
Grimm, J. Snow White and the seven dwarfs; illus. by Wanda Gág (1-4)   **398.2**
Grimm, J. Tales from Grimm (4-6)   **398.2**

Grimm, J. Tom Thumb (k-3)   **398.2**
Grimm, J. The twelve dancing princesses (k-3)   **398.2**
Grimm, J. Wanda Gág's Jorinda and Joringel (k-3)   **398.2**
Grimm, J. The wolf and the seven little kids (k-3)   **398.2**
Hürlimann, R. The proud white cat (k-3)   **398.2**
Hutton, W. The sleeping beauty (1-4)   **398.2**
Littledale, F. The elves and the shoemaker (k-3)   **398.2**
Shub, E. Clever Kate (1-3)   **398.2**
Van Woerkom, D. O. The queen who couldn't bake gingerbread (k-3)   **398.2**

Ghana

Courlander, H. The hat-shaking dance, and other tales from the Gold Coast (3-6)   **398.2**
McDermott, G. Anansi the spider (k-3)   **398.2**

Great Britain

Calhoun, M. The witch's pig (k-3)   **398.2**
Carrick, M. The wise men of Gotham (3-5)   **398.2**
Colwell, E. Round about and long ago (3-6)   **398.2**
Galdone, P. The three little pigs (k-2)   **398.2**
Gauch, P. L. On to Widecombe Fair (k-3)   **398.2**
Jacobs, J. English fairy tales (4-6)   **398.2**
Jacobs, J. Johnny-cake (k-3)   **398.2**
Opie, I. The lore and language of schoolchildren   **398**
Reeves, J. English fables and fairy stories (4-6)   **398.2**
Seuling, B. The teeny tiny woman (k-2)   **398.2**
Steel, F. A. Tattercoats (k-3)   **398.2**
Stern, S. The Hobyahs (k-2)   **398.2**
The Three wishes (k-2)   **398.2**
Zemach, H. Duffy and the devil (k-3)   **398.2**

Great Britain—Encyclopedias

Briggs, K. An encyclopedia of fairies: hobgoblins, brownies, bogies, and other supernatural creatures   **398.03**

Greece

Aliki. The twelve months (k-2)   **398.2**

Greece, Modern

Aliki. Three gold pieces (k-2)   **398.2**
Haviland, V. Favorite fairy tales told in Greece (2-5)   **398.2**

Haiti

Courlander, H. The piece of fire, and other Haitian tales (4-6)   **398.2**
Thompson, V. L. Hawaiian myths of earth, sea, and sky (3-6)   **398.2**
Thompson, V. L. Hawaiian tales of heroes and champions (4-6)   **398.2**

Indexes

Index to fairy tales, myths and legends   **398.2**
Index to fairy tales, myths and legends; supplement   **398.2**
Index to fairy tales, myths and legends; second supplement   **398.2**
Index to fairy tales, 1949-1972   **398.2**
Index to fairy tales, 1973-1977   **398.2**

Folklore—*Continued*

India

Babbitt, E. C. Jataka tales (1-3) 398.2
Bang, B. The old woman and the rice thief (k-2) 398.2
Brown, M. Once a mouse (k-3) 398.2
Duff, M. Rum pum pum (k-3) 398.2
Gaer, J. The fables of India (5 and up) 398.2
Galdone, P. The monkey and the crocodile (k-2) 398.2
Haviland, V. Favorite fairy tales told in India (2-5) 398.2
Indian fairy tales (4-6) 398.2
Jataka tales (3-5) 398.2
Price, C. The valiant chattee-maker (k-3) 398.2
Quigley, L. The blind men and the elephant (k-3) 398.2

Iran

Mehdevi, A. S. Persian folk and fairy tales (4-6) 398.2

Ireland

Evslin, B. The green hero (5 and up) 398.2
Haviland, V. Favorite fairy tales told in Ireland (2-5) 398.2
MacManus, S. Hibernian nights (4-7) 398.2
Stephens, J. Irish fairy tales (6 and up) 398.2
What do you feed your donkey on? (k-3) 398

Italy

Bowden, J. C. The bean boy (1-3) 398.2
De Paola, T. Strega Nona (k-3) 398.2
Haviland, V. Favorite fairy tales told in Italy (2-5) 398.2

Jamaica

Sherlock, P. M. Anansi, the spider man (4-6) 398.2

Japan

Haviland, V. Favorite fairy tales told in Japan (2-5) 398.2
Hodges, M. The wave (3-5) 398.2
McDermott, G. The stonecutter (k-3) 398.2
Mosel, A. The funny little woman (k-2) 398.2
Sakade, F. ed. Japanese children's favorite stories (2-4) 398.2
Say, A. Once under the cherry blossom tree (1-3) 398.2
Uchida, Y. The magic listening cap (3-6) 398.2
Winthrop, E. Journey to the bright kingdom (2-4) 398.2
Yashima, T. Seashore story E
Zemach, K. The beautiful rat (k-3) 398.2

Kenya

Robinson, A. Three African tales (3-6) 398.2

Korea

Kim, So-un. The story bag (4 and up) 398.2

Lapland

Stadler, V. Even the devil is afraid of a shrew (k-3) 398.2

Latin America

The Snow and the sun (1-4) 398

Mexico

Aardema, V. The riddle of the drum (k-2) 398.2

Morocco

Berson, H. Kassim's shoes (k-3) 398.2

New England

Jagendorf, M. A. New England bean-pot (5 and up) 398.2

See also pages in the following book:

Andrews, S. ed. The Hewins lectures, 1947-1962 p321-41 028.5

Nigeria

Courlander, H. Olode the hunter, and other tales from Nigeria (4-6) 398.2
Dayrell, E. Why the sun and the moon live in the sky (k-2) 398.2
Gerson, M. J. Why the sky is far away (1-3) 398.2

Norway

Asbjörnsen, P. C. East of the sun and west of the moon (3-6) 398.2
Asbjörnsen, P. C. The squire's bride (1-4) 398.2
Asbjörnsen, P. C. The three Billy Goats Gruff (k-3) 398.2
Aulaire, I. d' D'Aulaires' Trolls (3-6) 398
The Cat on the Dovrefell (k-2) 398.2
Galdone, P. The three Billy Goats Gruff (k-2) 398.2
Haviland, V. Favorite fairy tales told in Norway (2-5) 398.2
Lobel, A. The pancake (1-3) 398.2
Wiesner, W. Turnabout (k-3) 398.2

See also pages in the following book:

Hall, E. The land and people of Norway p55-61 (5 and up) 948.1

Persia

See Folklore—Iran

Philippine Islands

Aruego, J. A crocodile's tale (k-3) 398.2
Sechrist, E. H. Once in the first times (4-6) 398.2

Poland

Domanska, J. The best of the bargain (k-2) 398.2
Domanska, J. King Krakus and the dragon (k-2) 398.2
Turska, K. The magician of Cracow (k-3) 398.2

Puerto Rico

Belpré, P. Dance of the animals (k-2) 398.2
Belpré, P. Once in Puerto Rico (3-6) 398.2
Belpré, P. Perez and Martina (2-4) 398.2

Romania

See pages in the following book:

Hale, J. The land and people of Romania p122-30 (5 and up) 949.8

Russia

Afanas'ev, A. Russian fairy tales 398.2
Artzybasheff, B. Seven Simeons (3-6) 398.2
Brown, M. The bun (k-2) 398.2
Downing, C. Russian tales and legends (4 and up) 398.2
The Firebird, and other Russian fairy tales (5 and up) 398.2
Ginsburg, M. The proud maiden, Tungak, and the Sun (1-3) 398.2

Folklore—Russia—*Continued*

Ginsburg, M. Striding slippers (k-3)   398.2
Ginsburg, M. The twelve clever brothers, and other fools (3-5)   398.2
Grasshopper to the rescue (k-3)   398.2
Jameson, C. The clay pot boy (k-2)   398.2
The Lazies (3-5)   398.2
Lowe, P. T. The tale of Czar Saltan (3-5)   398.2
Lowe, P. T. The tale of the golden cockerel (3-5)   398.2
One trick too many (1-3)   398.2
The Peasant's pea patch (k-3)   398.2
Ransome, A. The Fool of the World and the flying ship (k-3)   398.2
Reyher, B. My mother is the most beautiful woman in the world (1-4)   398.2
Riordan, J. Tales from Central Russia (5 and up)   398.2
Riordan, J. Tales from Tartary (5 and up)   398.2
Small, E. Baba Yaga (k-3)   398.2
Titiev, E. How the Moolah was taught a lesson & other tales from Russia (2-4)   398.2
Vasilisa the beautiful (k-3)   398.2
See also pages in the following book:
A Harvest of Russian children's literature p123-83 (4 and up)   891.7

Scotland
Haviland, V. Favorite fairy tales told in Scotland (2-5)   398.2
Sewall, M. The wee, wee mannie and the big, big coo (k-2)   398.2

Sierra Leone
Robinson, A. Three African tales (3-6)   398.2

South America
Finger, C. Tales from silver lands (5 and up)   398.2

Southern States
Bang, M. G. Wiley and the Hairy Man (1-4)   398.2
Grandfather tales (4 and up)   398.2
The Jack tales (4-6)   398.2
Jagendorf, M. A. Folk stories of the South (4 and up)   398.2

Spain
Davis, R. Padre Porko, the gentlemanly pig (4-6)   398.2
Haviland, V. Favorite fairy tales told in Spain (2-5)   398.2

Sweden
Haviland, V. Favorite fairy tales told in Sweden (2-5)   398.2
Olenius, E. comp. Great Swedish fairy tales (4 and up)   398.2

Switzerland
Duvoisin, R. The three sneezes, and other Swiss tales (4-6)   398.2

Taiwan
Cheney, C. Tales from a Taiwan kitchen (4-6)   398.2

Tibet
Hume, L. C. Favorite children's stories from China and Tibet (3-6)   398.2

Turkey
Van Woerkom D. O. The friends of Abu Ali (k-3)   398.2
Walker, B. Teeny-Tiny and the witch-woman (k-3)   398.2

Uganda
Serwadda, W. M. Songs and stories from Uganda   784.4

Ukraine
Tresselt, A. The mitten (k-2)   398.2

United States
Emrich, D. comp. The hodgepodge book   398
Emrich, D. comp. The nonsense book of riddles, rhymes, tongue twisters, puzzles and jokes from American folklore (3 and up)   398
Galdone, J. The tailypo (k-3)   398.2
Lester, J. The knee-high man, and other tales (k-3)   398.2
North American legends (5 and up)   398.2
Schwartz, A. comp. Kickle snifters and other fearsome critters (2-5)   398
Schwartz, A. comp. Tomfoolery (4 and up)   398
Schwartz, A. ed. Whoppers (4 and up)   398.2
Schwartz, A. comp. Witcracks (4 and up)   398
Stoutenburg, A. American tall-tale animals (4-6)   398.2
The Whim-wham book   398

United States—Bibliography
See pages in the following book:
Folklore from Africa to the United States p123-52   016.398

Vietnam
Clark, A. N. In the Land of Small Dragon (2-4)   398.2

West Indies
Bryan, A. The dancing granny (1-4)   398.2
Carter, D. S. Greedy Mariani, and other folktales of the Antilles (3 and up)   398.2
Sherlock, P. West Indian folk-tales (4-6)   398.2

West Indies—Bibliography
See pages in the following book:
Folklore from Africa to the United States p103-21   016.398

Zaïre
McDermott, G. The magic tree (k-3)   398.2

Folklore, Arabic
The Arabian nights (5 and up)   398.2
The Arabian nights entertainments (5 and up)   398.2
Dawood, N. J. Tales from the Arabian nights (5 and up)   398.2

Folklore, Ashanti
Aardema, V. Half-a-ball-of-kenki (k-2)   398.2
Courlander, H. The hat-shaking dance, and other tales from the Gold Coast (3-6)   398.2
McDermott, G. Anansi the spider (k-3)   398.2

Folklore, Black
Faulkner, W. J. The days when the animals talked (5 and up)   398.2
Lester, J. The knee-high man, and other tales (k-3)   398.2

Folklore, Black—*Continued*
Bibliography
Folklore from Africa to the United States
016.398

Folklore, Eskimo
Eskimo songs and stories (3 and up)   398.2
Ginsburg, M. The proud maiden, Tungak, and the Sun (1-3)   398.2
See also pages in the following book:
Egoff, S. The republic of childhood p20-55
028.5

Folklore, Gypsy
Jagendorf, M. A. The gypsies' fiddle, and other gypsy tales (5 and up)   398.2

Folklore, Indian
See pages in the following book:
Egoff, S. The republic of childhood p20-55
028.5
See also Indians of North America— Legends
Bibliography
Folklore of the North American Indians
016.398

Folklore, Jewish
Hirsch, M. Could anything be worse? (k-3)   398.2
Singer, I. B. Mazel and Shlimazel (2-5)   398.2
Singer, I.B. When Shlemiel went to Warsaw & other stories (4 and up)   398.2
Singer, I. B. Zlateh the goat, and other stories (4 and up)   398.2
Zemach, M. It could always be worse (k-3)   398.2

Folklore, Masai
Aardema, V. Who's in Rabbit's house? (k-3)   398.2

Folklore, Medical. See Folk medicine
Folklore, Slavic
De Regniers, B. S. Little Sister and the Month Brothers (k-3)   398.2

Folklore, Slovenian
Ginsburg, M. How the sun was brought back to the sky (k-2)   398.2

Folklore, Yoruba
Courlander, H. Olode the hunter, and other tales from Nigeria (4-6)   398.2

Folklore from Africa to the United States
016.398
Folklore of plants. See Plant lore
Folklore of the North American Indians
016.398

Follow my Leader. Garfield, J. B.   Fic
Follow the wind. Tresselt, A.   E
The folly of panic. Shedlock, M. L.
In Shedlock, M. L. The art of the story-teller p222-24   372.6
See also Timid hare

Folmsbee, Beulah
Goblin parade
In One hundred plays for children p390-98
808.82
\(comp.) Illustrators of children's books: 1744-1945. See Illustrators of children's books: 1744-1945   741.64

Folsom, Franklin
Red power on the Rio Grande (5 and up)
970.004

Foma Berennikov. Afanas'ev, A.
In Afanas'ev, A. Russian fairy tales p284-87
398.2

Fontaine, Jean de la. See La Fontaine
Fonteneau, M.
Mon premier Larousse en couleurs   443
Food
Berger, M. The new food book (4 and up)
641
Cobb, V. Science experiments you can eat (5 and up)   507
Cobb, V. More Science experiments you can eat (5 and up)   507
Gilbert, S. You are what you eat (5 and up)
641.1
Hays, W. P. Foods the Indians gave us (5 and up)   641.3
Lavine, S. A. Indian corn and other gifts (4 and up)   641.3
Riedman, S. R. Food for people (6 and up)
641.1
See also pages in the following book:
Silverstein, A. Allergies p60-68 (5 and up)
616.97
See also Cookery; Vitamins; also names of foods, e.g. Fruit; and types of foods, e.g. Food, Natural

Contamination
See Food contamination
Control
See Food supply
Fiction
Pinkwater, D. M. Fat men from space (3-5)
Fic
Poetry
How to eat a poem & other morsels (3-5)
821.08
Preservation
See also pages in the following book:
Berger, M. The new food book p106-23 (4 and up)   641
See also Food, Dried

Food, Dried
See pages in the following book:
Hoople, C. G. The heritage sampler p23-29 (5 and up)   745.5

Food, Natural
Fenten, B. Natural foods (5 and up)   641.3
See also pages in the following book:
Kohn, B. The organic living book p56-61 (4 and up)   635
See also Cookery—Food, Natural

Food additives
See pages in the following books:
Berger, M. The new food book p113-23 (4 and up)   641
Riedman, S. R. Food for people p145-62 (6 and up)   641.1

Food adulteration and inspection
See also Meat inspection
Food chains (Ecology)
Pringle, L. Chains, webs & pyramids (4-6)
574.5
Pictorial works
Van Soelen, P. Cricket in the grass (1-5)
574.5

Food contamination
See pages in the following book:
Kozuszek, J. H. Hygiene p45-52 (4-6)   613

Food for people. Riedman, S. R.   **641.1**

Food plants. See Plants, Edible

Food supply

Archer, J. Hunger on planet Earth (6 and up)   **338.1**

Perl, L. The global food shortage (6 and up)   **338.1**

Pringle, L. Our hungry Earth (5 and up)   **338.1**

See also pages in the following book:

Berger, M. The new food book p124-31 (4 and up)   **641**

Foods the Indians gave us. Hays, W. P.   **641.3**

The **fool** and the birch. Ginsburg, M.

In Ginsburg, M. The twelve clever brothers, and other fools p24-31   **398.2**

Fool and the birch tree

Ginsburg, M. The fool and the birch

In Ginsburg, M. The twelve clever brothers, and other fools p24-31   **398.2**

The **Fool** and the magic fish. Riordan, J.

In Riordan, J. Tales from Central Russia p165-74   **398.2**

The **Fool** of the World and the flying ship. Ransome, A.   **398.2**

See also Flying ship

Fooling around with words. Tremain, R.   **793.7**

Foolish Fishermen

Elkin, B. Six foolish fishermen   **398.2**

Foolish folks. Duvoisin, R.

In Duvoisin, R. The three sneezes, and other Swiss tales p146-51   **398.2**

The **foolish** frog. Seeger, P.   **784.4**

Foolish German

Afanas'ev, A. The foolish German

In Afanas'ev, A. Russian fairy tales p600   **398.2**

Foolish lad

Hatch, M. C. Foolish lad

In Hatch, M. C. 13 Danish tales p37-45   **398.2**

The **foolish** lion and the silly rooster. Jagendorf, M. A.

In Jagendorf, M. A. Noodlehead stories from around the world p89-92   **398.2**

Foolish man

Tashijian, V. The foolish man

In The Arbuthnot Anthology of children's literature p283-85   **808.8**

In Time for old magic p166-68   **398.2**

Foolish milkmaid

In The Tall book of nursery tales p23-24   **398.2**

The **"Foolish People".** Jagendorf, M. A.

In Jagendorf, M. A. Noodlehead stories from around the world p271-73   **398.2**

The **foolish,** timid little hare. De Huff, E. W.

In Gruenberg, S. M. ed. Favorite stories old and new p341-43   **808.8**

See also Timid hare

The **foolish,** timid rabbit. Babbitt, E. C.

In Babbitt, E. C. Jataka tales p39-43   **398.2**

See also Timid hare

The **foolish** wife and her three foolish daughters. Haviland, V.

In Haviland, V. Favorite fairy tales told in Greece p29-37   **398.2**

Foolish wolf

Afanas'ev, A. The foolish wolf

In Afanas'ev, A. Russian fairy tales p450-52   **398.2**

Riordan, J. The foolish wolf

In Riordan, J. Tales from Central Russia p207-10   **398.2**

Fools' bells ring in every town. Jagendorf, M. A.

In Jagendorf, M. A. Noodlehead stories from around the world p164-72   **398.2**

The **fools** of Chelm and the stupid carp. Singer, I. B.

In Singer, I. B. Naftali the storyteller and his horse, Sus, and other stories p75-81   **S C**

The **fools** of Chelm and their history. Singer, I. B.

The **fools** of Gotham. See Wise men of Gotham

Fool's paradise. Singer, I. B.

In Singer, I. B. Zlateh the goat, and other stories p5-16   **398.2**

Football

Anderson, D. Defensive football (3-6)   **796.332**

Antonacci, R. J. Football for young champions (4 and up)   **796.332**

Coombs, C. Be a winner in football (5 and up)   **796.332**

Dolan, E. F. Basic football strategy (4 and up)   **796.332**

Jackson, C. P. How to play better football (4 and up)   **796.332**

See also pages in the following books:

The Junior illustrated encyclopedia of sports p271-381 (5 and up)   **796.03**

Keith, H. Sports and games p105-35 (5 and up)   **796**

Fiction

Foley, L. M. Tackle 22 (2-4)   **Fic**

Kessler, L. Kick, pass, and run   **E**

Statistics

See pages in the following book:

Arthur, L. Sportsmath: how it works p11-29 (4-6)   **796**

Football for young champions. Antonacci, R. J.   **796.332**

Football on a lake. Manning-Sanders, R.

In Manning-Sanders, R. A book of spooks and spectres p17-21   **398.2**

Footless and blind champions

Afanas'ev, A. The footless champion and the handless champion

In Afanas'ev, A. Russian fairy tales p269-73   **398.2**

The **footless** champion and the handless champion. Afanas'ev, A.

In Afanas'ev, A. Russian fairy tales p269-73   **398.2**

For a child (k-3)   **821.08**

For an oven full of bread

Duvoisin, R. For an oven full of bread

In Duvoisin, R. The three sneezes, and other Swiss tales p126-29   **398.2**

For lack of a thread

Duvoisin, R. For lack of a thread

In Duvoisin, R. The three sneezes, and other Swiss tales p44-47   **398.2**

For me to say. McCord, D.   **811**

For soldiers everywhere; play. Carlson, B. W.

In Carlson, B. W. The right play for you p142-45   **792**

For younger readers: braille and talking books
011

Forage plants
See pages in the following book:
Goldin, A. Grass p75-88 (5 and up)   584
See also names of forage plants, e.g. Legumes

Forberg, Ati
(illus.) Adler, C. S. The magic of the Glits   Fic
(illus.) Cresswell, H. A game of catch   Fic
(illus.) Fenner, C. The skates of Uncle Richard   Fic
(illus.) Fisher, A. Easter   394.2
(illus.) Hightower, F. The ghost of Follonsbee's Folly   Fic

Forbes, Esther
Johnny Tremain (5 and up)   Fic
Newbery Medal acceptance paper
In Newbery Medal books: 1922-1955 p248-54   028.5
"That a man can stand up"
In The Arbuthnot Anthology of children's literature p748-53   808.8

About
See pages in the following book:
Newbery Medal books: 1922-1955 p245-47   028.5

Forbes, Robin
Click: a first camera book (3-5)   770.28

Forbidden room
Grimm, J. Fitcher's bird
In Grimm, J. The Brothers Grimm: popular folk tales p72-76   398.2
In Grimm, J. The complete Grimm's fairy tales p216-20   398.2
Grimm, J. Fitcher's feathered bird
In Grimm, J. The juniper tree, and other tales from Grimm v 1 p71-79   398.2

Force and energy
Adler, I. Energy (3-5)   531
See also Mechanics

Ford, Barbara
How birds learn to sing (4 and up)   598

Ford, George
(illus.) Greenfield, E. Paul Robeson   92
(illus.) Mathis, S. B. Ray Charles   92

Ford, H. J.
(illus.) The Andrew Lang Fairy tale treasury. See The Andrew Lang Fairy tale treasury   398.2
(illus.) The Arabian nights entertainments. See The Arabian nights entertainments   398.2

Ford, Henry, 1863-1947
Quackenbush, R. Along came the Model T! (2-4)   92
See also pages in the following book:
Captains of industry p127-45 (5 and up)   920

Ford, Pamela Baldwin
(illus.) Andersen, H. C. The emperor's new clothes   Fic
(illus.) Tatterhood, and other tales. See Tatterhood, and other tales   398.2

Fording the river in a copper cauldron. Jagendorf, M. A.
In Jagendorf, M. A. The gypsies' fiddle, and other gypsy tales p170-76   398.2

Forecasting, Weather. See Weather forecasting

Foreman, Michael
(illus.) Andersen, H. Hans Andersen: his classic fairy tales   S C
(illus.) Garner, A. The stone book   Fic
(illus.) Grimm, J. The Brothers Grimm: popular folk tales   398.2
(illus.) Walker, B. Teeny-Tiny and the witch-woman   398.2

Forenames. See Names, Personal

Forest bride
Bowman, J. C. Mouse bride
In Bowman, J. C. Tales from a Finnish tupa p25-33   398.2

Forest conservation. See Forests and forestry

Forest ecology
Batten, M. The tropical forest (5 and up)   574.5
Lerner, C. On the forest edge (3-5)   574.5
List, A. A walk in the forest (5 and up)   574.5
Pringle, L. Into the woods (4-6)   574.5
Pringle, L. Natural fire (5 and up)   574.5
Selsam, M. E. Birth of a forest (4-6)   581.5

Forest fires
Pringle, L. Natural fire (5 and up)   574.5

Fiction
Southall, I. Ash Road (5 and up)   Fic
White, R. Fire storm (4 and up)   Fic

Forest full of friends. Alden, R. M.
In Alden, R. M. Why the chimes rang, and other stories p92-105   S C

Forest influences
See pages in the following book:
Kirk, R. Yellowstone p38-48 (5 and up)   978.7
See also Botany—Ecology

Forester, C. S.
Horatio enjoys his punishment
In The Golden Treasury of children's literature p32-39   808.8
Poo-Poo brings the dragon home
In The Golden Treasury of children's literature p29-31   808.8
Poo-Poo finds a dragon
In The Golden Treasury of children's literature p25-28   808.8

Forestry. See Forests and forestry

Forests and climate. See Forest influences

Forests and forestry
Dowden, A. O. The blossom on the bough (5 and up)   582.16
Lerner, C. On the forest edge (3-5)   574.5
Pringle, L. Into the woods (4-6)   574.5
Pringle, L. Natural fire (5 and up)   574.5
Selsam, M. E. Birth of a forest (4-6)   581.5
See also pages in the following book:
Riedman, S. R. Trees alive p102-24 (5 and up)   582.16
See also Lumber and lumbering; Trees

New Zealand
See pages in the following book:
Kaula, E. M. The land and people of New Zealand p116-22 (5 and up)   993

North America
List, A. A walk in the forest (5 and up)   574.5

The **forever** formula. Bonham, F.   Fic

Freedom of worship. See Religious freedom

Freedom train: the story of Harriet Tubman. Sterling, D.   92

Freeman, Don
  Beady Bear   E
  Corduroy   E
  Dandelion   E
  Fly high, fly low   E
  The guard mouse   E
  Norman the doorman   E
  (illus.) Cunningham, J. Burnish me bright   Fic
  (jt. auth.) Freeman, L. Pet of the Met   E
  (illus.) Sauer, J. L. Mike's house   E

Freeman, Elizabeth
  (Felton, H. W. Mumbet: the story of Elizabeth Freeman (4-6)   92

Freeman, Ira
  (jt. auth.) Freeman, M. The sun, the moon, and the stars   523

Freeman, Lydia
  Pet of the Met   E

Freeman, Mae Blacker
  Finding out about the past (3-5)   930.1
  Stars and stripes (2-5)   929.9
  The sun, the moon, and the stars (2-4)   523

Freeman, Margaret
  (illus.) Aldis, D. All together   811

Freeman, Mary Wilkins
  The pumpkin giant
  In Harper, W. comp. The harvest feast p159-72   S C

Freer Gallery of Art, Washington, D.C.
  See pages in the following book:
  Thomson, P. Museum people p162-69 (5 and up)   069

Freetown, Sierra Leone
Description
  See pages in the following book:
  Clifford, M. L. The land and people of Sierra Leone p43-63, 110-17 (5 and up)   966

The **freewheeling** Joshua Cobb. Hodges, M.   Fic

Freezing. See Ice

Freight train. Crews, D.   E

Frémont, John Charles
  Syme, R. John Charles Frémont (5 and up)   92

French, Callic
  See pages in the following book:
  As I saw it: women who lived the American adventure p156-59 (6 and up)   973

French Americans
  The French in America (5 and up)   305.8

French architecture. See Architecture, French

French art. See Art, French

French Canadian literature
Bibliography
  Canadian books for young people [and] Livres canadiens pour la jeunesse   015.71

French Canadians
Fiction
  Carlson, N. S. The talking cat, and other stories of French Canada (3-6)   S C

The **French** doll's surprise. Bennett, R.
  In Bennett, R. Creative plays and programs for holidays p363-66   812

The **French** explorers in America. Buehr, W.   973.1

French in North America
  Buehr, W. The French explorers in America (4-6)   970.01

French language
  Cooper, L. Fun with French (4 and up)   448

Dictionaries
  Fonteneau, M. Mon premier Larousse en couleurs   443

French language editions
  The Cat in the hat Beginner book dictionary   423
  Lionni, L. Inch by inch   E
  Lionni, L. Swimmy   E
  Potter, B. The story of Miss Moppet   E
  Potter, B. The tailor of Gloucester   E
  Potter, B. The tale of Jemima Puddle-duck   E
  Potter, B. The tale of Mr Jeremy Fisher   E
  Potter, B. The tale of Mrs Tiggy-Winkle   E
  Potter, B. The tale of Mrs Tittlemouse   E
  (Potter, B. The tale of Peter Rabbit   E
  Potter, B. The tale of Squirrel Nutkin   E
  Potter, B. The tale of two bad mice   E
  Saint-Exupéry, A. de. The little prince   Fic

The **French** in America. Kunz, V. B.   305.8

Frenck, Hal
  (illus.) Strete, C. K. When grandfather journeys into winter   Fic

Freschet, Berniece
  Bear mouse (2-4)   599.32
  Elephant & friends   E
  Grizzly bear (2-4)   599.74
  The happy dromedary   E
  Lizard lying in the sun (1-3)   597.9
  The owl and the prairie dog (k-4)   598
  Porcupine baby (k-3)   599.32
  Possum baby (k-3)   599.2
  Skunk baby (2-4)   599.74
  Turtle pond (k-3)   597.9
  The web in the grass   E

Fresh water animals
  Fegely, T. D. The world of freshwater fish (5 and up)   597
  Reid, G. K. Pond life (6 and up)   574.92
  See also pages in the following book:
  Shuttlesworth, D. E. The wildlife of South America p67-77 (5 and up)   591.9
  See also Aquariums; and names of fresh water animals, e.g. Beavers

Fresh water biology
  Cooper, E. K. Science on the shores and banks (5 and up)   574.92
  Kane, H. B. The tale of a pond (4 and up)   574.5
  See also Aquariums; Fresh water animals; Fresh water plants; Marine biology

Fresh water ecology
  See also Marsh ecology; Pond ecology

Fresh water plants
Earle, O. L. Pond and marsh plants (3-6) **581.92**
Pringle, L. Water plants (1-3) **581.92**
Reid, G. K. Pond life (6 and up) **574.92**
See also pages in the following books:
Cooper, E. K. Science on the shores and banks p165-72 (5 and up) **574.92**
Pels, G. The care of water pets p44-48 (4-6) **639.3**
See also Aquariums

Freshman, Esther
The heavenly jam
In Thanksgiving p311-17 **394.2**

Freshman, Shelley
(illus.) Branley, F. M. Sunshine makes the seasons **525**
(illus.) Srivastava, J. J. Area **516**

Freud, Sigmund
See pages in the following book:
Foster, G. The year of the flying machine, 1903 p79-83 (3-6) **909.82**

Freudenberger, Helen L.
Jack and Jill
In One hundred plays for children p649-55 **808.82**

Freund, Rudolf
(illus.) Zim, H. S. Flowers **582.13**

Friday night is Papa night. Sonneborn, R. A. **E**

Friedman, Marvin
(illus.) Callen, L. Pinch **Fic**

Friedrich. Richter, H. P. **Fic**

Friedrichsen, Carol S.
The Pooh craft book (3-6) **745.592**

Friend, Charlotte
See pages in the following book:
Noble, I. Contemporary women scientists of America p64-78 (5 and up) **920**

The **friendly** beasts. Baker, L. N. **783.6**

The **friendly** frog. Aulnoy, Mme d'
In Perrault, C. Perrault's Complete fairy tales p135-62 **398.2**

The **friendly** ghost. Yates, E.
In A-haunting we will go p79-88 **S C**

The **friendly** wolf. Goble, P. **E**

Friends, Society of
Henry, M. Benjamin West and his cat Grimalkin (4-6) **92**
See also pages in the following books:
Lengyel, E. The colony of Pennsylvania p48-55 (5 and up) **974.4**
Tunis, E. The tavern at the ferry p 1-10 (5 and up) **973.2**
Fiction
Avi. Night journeys (5 and up) **Fic**
Turkle, B. Obadiah the Bold **E**

Friends and neighbors
In Jataka tales p22-26 **398.2**

Friends are like that! **S C**

The **friends** of Abu Ali. Van Woerkom, D. O. **398.2**

Friendship
Berger, H. Special friends (1-3) **305.2**
Richards, A. K. Boy friends, girl friends, just friends (6 and up) **158**
See also pages in the following books:
Kalb, J. What every kid should know p52-73 (5 and up) **158**
LeShan, E. You and your feelings p60-74 (6 and up) **155.5**
Bibliography
See pages in the following book:
Gillis, R. J. Children's books for times of stress p173-87 **016.3627**
Fiction
Adler, C. S. The magic of the Glits (5 and up) **Fic**
Angell, J. Tina Gogo (6 and up) **Fic**
Bawden, N. The robbers (5 and up) **Fic**
Bosse, M. J. The 79 squares (6 and up) **Fic**
Brandenberg, F. Nice new neighbors **E**
Bridgers, S. E. All together now (6 and up) **Fic**
Brown, P. Hickory (2-4) **Fic**
Burch, R. Wilkin's ghost (5 and up) **Fic**
Byars, B. The pinballs (5 and up) **Fic**
Carrick, C. Some friend! (3-6) **Fic**
Clifton, L. Three wishes **E**
Cohen, B. Thank you, Jackie Robinson (4-6) **Fic**
Conford, E. Me and the terrible two (3-6) **Fic**
Delton, J. Kitty in the middle (2-5) **Fic**
Delton, J. Two good friends **E**
Erickson, R. E. A toad for Tuesday (2-4) **Fic**
Freschet, B. Elephant & Friends **E**
Friends are like that! (2-4) **S C**
Gackenbach, D. Hound and Bear **E**
Garfield, L. The night of the comet (5 and up) **Fic**
Garrigue, S. Between friends (5 and up) **Fic**
Goffstein, M. B. Neighbors **E**
Grahame, K. The open road (2-5) **Fic**
Grahame, K. The river bank (2-5) **Fic**
Greene, B. Philip Hall likes me. I reckon maybe (4-6) **Fic**
Greene, C. C. A girl called Al (5 and up) **Fic**
Gripe, M. Hugo and Josephine (3-5) **Fic**
Irwin, H. The Lilith summer (5 and up) **Fic**
Johnston, T. Night noises, and other Mole and Troll stories **E**
Konigsburg, E. L. Jennifer, Hecate, Macbeth, William McKinley, and me (4-6) **Fic**
Krumgold, J. Onion John (5 and up) **Fic**
Lee, M. Sycamore year (6 and up) **Fic**
LeGuin, U. K. Very far away from anywhere else (6 and up) **Fic**
Levoy, M. Alan and Naomi (6 and up) **Fic**
Little, J. Look through my window (4-6) **Fic**
Lovelace, M. H. Betsy-Tacy (2-4) **Fic**
Mark, J. Thunder and Lightnings (5 and up) **Fic**
Marshall, J. George and Martha **E**
Marshall, J. The guest **E**

Frog queen
Afanas'ev, A. The frog princess
In Afanas'ev, A. Russian fairy tales p119-23
Riordan, J. The Frog Princess
In Riordan, J. Tales from Central Russia
p129-37 **398.2**

Frog travelers
The two frogs
In The Lazies p26-27 **398.2**
In Shedlock, M. L. The art of the story-
teller p213-15 **372.6**
Frog went a-courtin'. Langstaff, J. **784.4**
Frog, where are you? Mayer, M. See note un-
der Mayer, M. A boy, a dog, and a frog
E

Froghoppers
See pages in the following book:
Hutchins, R. E. The bug clan p17-20 (5
and up) **595.7**

Frogs
Common frog (3-6) **597.8**
Hawes, J. Why frogs are wet (k-3) **597.8**
McClung, R. M. Peeper, first voice of spring
(2-4) **597.8**
Ommanney, F. D. Frogs, toads & newts
(4-6) **597.6**
Simon, D. Discovering what frogs do (2-4)
597.8
Simon, H. Frogs and toads of the world
(5 and up) **597.8**
Zim, H. S. Frogs and toads (2-5) **597.8**
See also pages in the following books:
Conant, R. A field guide to reptiles and
amphibians of Eastern and Central North
America p297-350 **597.6**
Cooper, E. K. Science on the shores and
banks p119-29 (5 and up) **574.92**
Fichter, G. S. Keeping amphibians and rep-
tiles as pets p6-20 (4 and up) **639**
Pels, G. The care of water pets p27-30 (4-6)
639.3
Ricciuti, E. R. Shelf pets p13-27 (5 and up)
639
Ricciuti, E. R. Sounds of animals at night
p5-18 (3-5) **591.5**
Selsam, M. E. The language of animals p33-
40 (5 and up) **591.5**
Simon, S. Pets in a jar p39-43, 48-52 (4 and
up) **639**
Zappler, G. Amphibians as pets p44-50, 59-72
(5 and up) **639**
See also Toads

Fiction
Dauer, R. Bullfrog grows up **E**
Flack, M. Walter the lazy mouse (2-4) **Fic**
Lionni, L. Fish is fish **E**
Lobel, A. Frog and Toad are friends **E**
Mayer, M. A boy, a dog, and a frog **E**
Potter, B. The tale of Mr Jeremy Fisher **E**
Smith, J. The Frog Band and the onion
seller **E**
Zemach, H. The princess and Froggie **E**
Frogs and the ballet. Elliott, D. **792.8**
Frogs and Toads. Zim, H. S. **597.8**
Frogs and toads of the world. Simon, H.
597.8
Frogs of Windham Town. Jagendorf, M. A.
In Jagendorf, M. A. New England bean-
pot p202-05 **398.2**
Frogs, toads & newts. Ommanney, F. D.
597.6

Frogs, toads, salamanders, and how they re-
produce. Patent, D. H. **597.6**
The **Frogs** who wanted a king and other
songs from La Fontaine **784.7**
Frog's wives make ndiba pudding. Cour-
lander, H.
In Courlander, H. The king's drum, and
other African stories p58-59 **398.2**
Frolka Stay-at-Home
Afanas'ev, A. Frolka Stay-at-Home
In Afanas'ev, A. Russian fairy tales p299-
302 **398.2**
From A to Z. Coletta, I. **E**
From a window in Vartov. Andersen, H. C.
In Andersen, H. C. The complete fairy
tales and stories p311-12 **S C**
From Anna. Little, J. **Fic**
From apple seed to applesauce. Johnson, H. L.
634
From bad to good to bad to good. Kendall, C.
In Kendall, C. Sweet and sour p39-41
398.2
From cell to clone. Facklam, M. **575.1**
From childhood to childhood. Karl, J. **028.5**
From idea into house. Myller, R. **728**
From morn to midnight (k-3) **821.08**
From one cell to many cells. Zappler, G.
574.3
From petals to pinecones. Cutler, K. N.
745.58
**From primer to pleasure in reading. Thwaite,
M. F.** **028.5**
**From Rollo to Tom Sawyer, and other papers.
Jordan, A. M.** **028.5**
From seed to jack-o'-lantern. Johnson, H. L.
635
From seed to salad. Johnson, H. L. **635**
From the loom of the dead. Hardendorff, J. B.
In Hardendorff, J. B. Witches, wit, and a
werewolf p13-21 **S C**
**From the mixed-up files of Mrs Basil E.
Frankweiler. Konigsburg, E. L.** **Fic**
**From the mixed-up files of Mrs Basil E.
Frankweiler; excerpt. Konigsburg, E. L.**
In The Arbuthnot Anthology of children's
literature p655-60 **398.2**
**From the ramparts of the citadel. Andersen,
H. C.**
In Andersen, H. C. The complete fairy
tales and stories p309-10 **S C**
From tiger to Anansi. Sherlock, P. M.
In The Fairy tale treasury p86-91 **398.2**
In Sherlock, P. M. Anansi, the spider
man p3-12 **398.2**
See also Anansi the spider-man
From trails to superhighways. Paradis, A. A.
625.7
Froman, Robert
Angles are easy as pie (2-4) **516**
Bigger and smaller **E**
The greatest guessing game (2-4) **513**
Mushrooms and molds (1-3) **589.2**
Rubber bands, baseballs and doughnuts (2-4)
514
Frondizi, Arturo
See pages in the following book:
Hall, E. The land and people of Argentina
p144-48 (5 and up) **982**

The **front** door key. Andersen, H. C.
  In Andersen, H. C. The complete fairy tales and stories p1039-48 **S C**

Frontier and pioneer life
  Aliki. The story of Johnny Appleseed [biography of John Chapman] (k-3) **92**
  Averill, E. Daniel Boone (3-6) **92**
  Parish, P. Let's be early settlers with Daniel Boone (2-5) **745.5**
  Steele, W. O. Westward adventure (5 and up) **920**
  Walker, B. M. The Little House cookbook (5 and up) **641.5**
    See also pages in the following book:
  Burt, O. W. The horse in America p77-84 (5 and up) **636.1**
    See also Cowhands; Indians of North America—Captivities; Overland journeys to the Pacific (U.S.)

Fiction
  Brenner, B. Wagon wheels (2-4) **Fic**
  Brink, C. R. Caddie Woodlawn (4-6) **Fic**
  Byars, B. Trouble River (4-6) **Fic**
  Clements, B. I tell a lie every so often (6 and up) **Fic**
  Collier, J. L. The bloody country (6 and up) **Fic**
  Dalgliesh, A. The courage of Sarah Noble (2-4) **Fic**
  Field, R. Calico bush (4 and up) **Fic**
  Fleischman, S. Chancy and the grand rascal (4-6) **Fic**
  Fleischman, S. Humbug Mountain (4 and up) **Fic**
  Fleischman, S. Mr Mysterious & Company (4-6) **Fic**
  Frazier, N. L. Stout-hearted seven (5 and up) **Fic**
  Fritz, J. The cabin faced west (3-6) **Fic**
  Gipson, F. Old Yeller (6 and up) **Fic**
  Henry, M. San Domingo: the medicine hat stallion (4-6) **Fic**
  Jones, W. Edge of two worlds (5 and up) **Fic**
  Mason, M. E. Caroline and her kettle named Maud (2-4) **Fic**
  Steele, W. O. The lone hunt (5 and up) **Fic**
  Steele, W. O. Wilderness journey (4-6) **Fic**
  Talbot, C. J. An orphan for Nebraska (4-6) **Fic**
  Wilder, L. I. Little house in the big woods (4-6) **Fic**
  Yates, E. Carolina's courage (3-5) **Fic**

The West (U.S.)
  Aulaire, I. d'. Buffalo Bill [biography of William Frederick Cody] (1-4) **92**
  Burt, O. W. Negroes in the early West (4-6) **920**
  Felton, H. W. Edward Rose: Negro trail blazer (5 and up) **92**
  Holbrook, S. Wild Bill Hickok tames the West (4-6) **92**
  Levenson, D. Women of the West (4 and up) **305.4**
  Rounds, G. The treeless plains (4-6) **978**
  Tunis, E. Frontier living (6 and up) **978**
Frontier living. Tunis, E. **978**
Frontiers of dance; the life of Martha Graham. Terry, W. **92**

Fronval, George
  Indian signs and signals (4-6) **001.56**
Frost, Frances
  Menotti, G. C. Gian-Carlo Menotti's Amahl and the night visitors **Fic**
Frost, Lesley
  The drawbridge
    In Time to laugh p67-73 **S C**
Frost, Robert
  Stopping by woods on a snowy evening (k-3) **811**
  You come too (5 and up) **811**
The **Frost**, the Sun and the Wind. Riordan, J.
  In Riordan, J. Tales from Central Russia p106 **398.2**
Frozen fire. Houston, J. **Fic**
Fruit
  Day, J. W. What is a fruit? (1-3) **582**
  Selsam, M. E. The apple and other fruits (3-5) **583**
    See also pages in the following book:
  Shuttlesworth, D. E. The hidden magic of seeds p26-29 (2-4) **582**
    See also names of fruits, e.g. Apple
Frustration. See Emotions
Fry, Guy
  (illus.) It's time for Thanksgiving. See It's time for Thanksgiving **394.2**
  (illus.) Sechrist, E. H. comp. Poems for red letter days **821.08**
Fry, Rosalind
  (illus.) Showers, P. A baby starts to grow **612**
  (illus.) Showers, P. Use your brain **612**
Fryatt, Norma R.
  (ed.) A Horn Book Sampler on children's books and reading. See A Horn Book Sampler on children's books and reading **028.5**
Ftera, Constance
  (illus.) Simon, S. The optical illusion book **152.1**
Fuchs, Erich
  Journey to the moon (4 and up) **629.45**
  Looking at maps (2-4) **912**
Fuel
    See also names of fuel, e.g. Coal
Fujikawa, Gyo
  (illus.) Mother Goose. See Mother Goose **398**
  (illus.) Stevenson, R. L. A child's garden of verses **821**
Fulahs
    See pages in the following books:
  Forman, B. The land and people of Nigeria p30-36 (5 and up) **966.9**
  Jenness, A. Along the Niger River p42-55 (5 and up) **966.9**
Fulani. See Fulahs
Fulford, Deborah
  (illus.) Ommanney, F. D. Frogs, toads & newts **597.6**
Fuller, Miriam Morris
  Phillis Wheatley, America's first black poetess (3-6) **92**
Fuller, Muriel
  (ed.) More junior authors. See More junior authors **920.03**
Fulton, Gwen
  (illus.) Lear, E. The owl and the pussy-cat **821**

The **garden** is doing fine. Farley, C. **Fic**

The **garden** of Abdul Gasazi. Van Allsburg, C. **E**

The **garden** of Eden. Andersen, H. C.
In Andersen, H. C. The complete fairy tales and stories p132-44 **S C**

Garden of paradise
Andersen, H. C. The garden of Eden
In Andersen, H. C. The complete fairy tales and stories p132-44 **S C**

Garden pests. See Agricultural pests; Insects, Injurious and beneficial; Plants—Diseases

Gardener
Andersen, H. C. The gardener and his master
In Andersen, H. C. The complete fairy tales and stories .p1015-21 **S C**

The **gardener** and his master. Andersen, H. C.
In Andersen, H. C. The complete fairy tales and stories p1015-21 **S C**

Gardening
Baker, S. S. The indoor and outdoor grow-it book (1-6) **635**
Cutler, K. N. Growing a garden, indoors or out (4 and up) **635**
Lavine, S. A. Wonders of herbs (5 and up) **635**
Paul, A. Kids outdoor gardening (3-6) **635**
Walsh, A. B. A gardening book: indoors and outdoors (4-6) **635**
See also pages in the following books:
Caney, S. Steven Caney's Kids' America p96-106 (4 and up) **790.1**
Shuttlesworth, D. E. The hidden magic of seeds p36-41 (2-4) **582**
See also Organiculture; Vegetable gardening; Window gardening

Fiction
Smith, A. Reserved for Mark Anthony Crowder (5 and up) **Fic**

A **gardening** book: indoors and outdoors. Walsh, A. B. **635**

Gardening . . . naturally. Fenten, D. X. **635**

Gardening without soil. Riedman, S. R. **635**

Gardens
Fiction
Bosse, M. J. The 79 squares (6 and up) **Fic**
Craft, R. Carrie Happle's garden **E**

Gardens, Miniature
See pages in the following book:
Selsam, M. E. How to grow house plants p19-21, 50-62 (4-6) **635.9**

Gardner, Herb
How I crossed the street for the first time all by myself; short story
In Free to be . . . you and me p100-11 **810.8**

Gardner, James B.
Illustrated soccer dictionary for young people (5 and up) **796.334**

Gardner, Jeanne LeMonnier
Mary Jemison: Seneca captive (4-6) **92**

Gardner, John
A child's bestiary (4-6) **811**

Gardner, Martin
Codes, ciphers and secret writing (5 and up) **652**

Gardner, Mercedes
King Midas
In Dramatized folk tales of the world p177-90 **812.08**

Gardner, Richard
The boys and girls book about divorce (4 and up) **306.8**

Gardner, Richard M. See Cummings, Richard

Gardner, Robert
Shadow science (4-6) **535**

Garelick, May
About owls (1-3) **598**
Where does the butterfly go when it rains **E**

Garfield, James B.
Follow my Leader (4 and up) **Fic**

Garfield, Leon
Mister Corbett's ghost (5 and up) **Fic**
The night of the comet (5 and up) **Fic**
Smith (5 and up) **Fic**
About
See pages in the following book:
Townsend, J. R. A sounding of storytellers p66-80 **028.5**

Garner, Alan
The Aimer Gate. See note under Garner, A. The stone book **Fic**
Elidor (5 and up) **Fic**
Granny reardun. See note under Garner, A. The stone book **Fic**
The moon of Gomrath. See note under Garner, A. The weirdstone of Brisingamen **Fic**
The owl service (5 and up) **Fic**
The stone book (4 and up) **Fic**
Tom Fobble's day. See note under Garner, A. The stone book **Fic**
The weirdstone of Brisingamen (6 and up) **Fic**
About
See pages in the following book:
Townsend, J. R. A sounding of storytellers p81-96 **028.5**

Garnet, Henry Highland
See pages in the following book:
Rollins, C. H. They showed the way p70-71 (5 and up) **920**

Garrigue, Sheila
Between friends (5 and up) **Fic**

Garrison, Webb
Why didn't I think of that? (4 and up) **608**

Garson, Eugenia
(ed.) The Laura Ingalls Wilder songbook. See The Laura Ingalls Wilder songbook **784**

Garth Pig and the icecream lady. Rayner, M. See note under Rayner, M. Mr and Mrs Pig's evening out **E**

Garver, Juliet
Father hits the jackpot
In Fifty plays for junior actors p222-35 **812.08**
A howling success
In Popular plays for classroom reading p56-68 **808.82**

Gas
See also Gases

Gas, Natural
See pages in the following books:
Kiefer, I. Energy for America p36-41 (6 and up) **333.79**
Macaulay, D. Underground p85-87 (5 and up) **624**

Gas and oil engines
See also subjects with the subdivision Engines, e.g. Automobile—Engines

Gas companies. See Public utilities

Gases

    See pages in the following books:

    The Arbuthnot Anthology of children's literature p892-94   **808.8**

    Gallant, R. A. Fires in the sky p52-58 (5 and up)   **523.8**

Gates, Doris

    Blue willow (4 and up)   **Fic**

    A fair wind for Troy (4 and up)   **292**

    The golden god: Apollo (4 and up)   **292**

    Lord of the sky: Zeus (4 and up)   **292**

    Mightiest of mortals: Heracles (4 and up)   **292**

    Two queens of heaven: Aphrodite [and] Demeter (4 and up)   **292**

    The warrior goddess: Athena (4 and up)   **292**

    About

    See pages in the following book:

    Authors and illustrators of children's books p157-64   **028.5**

Gates, Frieda

    Easy to make monster masks and disguises (1-3)   **745.59**

Gates, Horatio

    See pages in the following book:

    Lomask, M. The first American Revolution p199-206 (6 and up)   **973.3**

Gateways to readable books. Withrow, D. E.   **011**

A gathering of days. Blos, J. W.   **Fic**

Gauch, Patricia Lee

    Aaron and the Green Mountain Boys   **E**

    The impossible Major Rogers (4-6)   **92**

    On to Widecombe Fair (k-3)   **398.2**

    This time, Tempe Wicke? (3-5)   **Fic**

    Thunder at Gettysburg (3-5)   **Fic**

Gauchos. See Cowhands

Gaughran, Bernard

    (jt. auth.) Katz, W. L. The Constitutional amendments   **342**

Gault, Clare

    The Harlem Globetrotters and basketball's funniest games (3-6)   **796.32**

Gault, Frank

    (jt. auth.) Gault, C. The Harlem Globetrotters and basketball's funniest games   **796.32**

Gautama Buddha

    Edmonds, I. G. Buddhism (4 and up)   **294.3**

    Rawding, F. W. The Buddha (5 and up)   **294.3**

    Serage, N. The prince who gave up a throne (4-6)   **92**

    See also pages in the following book:

    Kettelkamp, L. Religions, East and West p37-45 (5 and up)   **291**

Gaver, Mary V.

    (ed.) The Elementary school library collection. See The Elementary school library collection   **011**

Gawain

    Hieatt, C. The Castle of Ladies (4 and up)   **398.2**

Gay, Kathlyn

    Be a smart shopper (4-6)   **640.73**

Gay, Zhenya

    The Shire colt

    In Gruenberg, S. M. ed. Favorite stories old and new p176-82   **808.8**

Gay-Neck: the story of a pigeon. Mukerji, D. G.   **Fic**

Gazetteers

    Webster's New geographical dictionary   **910.3**

Geber. See Jabir ibn Haiyān

Geer, Charles

    (illus.) Friis, B. Kristy's courage   **Fic**

Geese

    Scott, J. D. Canada geese (4 and up)   **598**

    Fiction

    Duvoisin, R. Petunia   **E**

    Preston, E. M. Squawk to the moon, Little Goose   **E**

    Sharmat, M. W. Griselda's new year   **E**

Gehm, Charles C.

    (illus.) Peck, R. N. Soup   **Fic**

Gehrig, Lou

    Rubin, R. Lou Gehrig: courageous star (5 and up)   **92**

Geisel, Theodor Seuss

    See pages in the following books:

    Authors and illustrators of children's books p165-71   **028.5**

    Lanes, S. G. Down the rabbit hole p79-89   **028.5**

    Only connect p316-22   **028.5**

    For works by this author see Seuss, Dr

Geismer, Barbara Peck

    (comp.) Very young verses. See Very young verses   **821.08**

Geller, Uri

    See pages in the following book:

    Hall, E. Possible impossibilities p144-57 (6 and up)   **133.8**

Gemme, Leila Boyle

    Soccer is our game (k-2)   **796.334**

    T-ball is our game (k-2)   **796.357**

Gemming, Elizabeth

    Lost city in the clouds (5 and up)   **985**

    Maple harvest (4-6)   **633.6**

    Wool gathering (4-6)   **338.1**

Genealogy

    Gilfond, H. Genealogy: how to find your roots (6 and up)   **929**

    See also pages in the following book:

    Caney, S. Steven Caney's Kids' America p26-37 (4 and up)   **790.1**

Genealogy: how to find your roots. Gilfond, H.   **929**

General encyclopedias in print. See Encyclopedia buying guide   **016**

General Moulton strikes a bargain. Roach, M. K.

    In Roach, M. K. Encounters with the invisible world p84-95   **S C**

Generals

    Alderman, C. L. The dark eagle: the story of Benedict Arnold (4 and up)   **92**

    Commager, H. S. America's Robert E. Lee (5 and up)   **92**

    Faber, D. Dwight Eisenhower (5 and up)   **92**

    Fritz, J. Stonewall [biography of Thomas Jonathan Jackson] (4 and up)   **92**

    Reynolds, Q. Custer's last stand (5 and up)   **92**

George and Angela. Englefield, C.
In Told under the magic umbrella p50-54
S C

George and Martha. Marshall, J. **E**

George and Martha encore. Marshall, J. See note under Marshall, J. George and Martha **E**

George and Martha, one fine day. Marshall, J. See note under Marshall, J. George and Martha **E**

George and Martha rise and shine. Marshall, J. See note under Marshall, J. George and Martha **E**

George and Martha, tons of fun. Marshall, J. See note under Marshall, J. George and Martha **E**

George in the realm of darkness. Baumann, H.
In Baumann, H. The stolen fire p26-28
398.2

George Peabody College for Teachers, Nashville, Tenn.
Free and inexpensive learning materials
016.3713

George the babysitter. Hughes, S. **E**
George, the drummer boy. Benchley, N. **E**
George Washington Bridge
Fiction
Swift, H. H. The little red lighthouse and the great gray bridge **E**
George Washington's breakfast. Fritz, J. **Fic**
Georgia, Lowell
(illus.) Bridge, L. M. The playful dolphins
599.5
Georgia
Fiction
Burch, R. D. J.'s worst enemy (4-6) **Fic**
Burch, R. Queenie Peavy (5 and up) **Fic**
Burch, R. Skinny (4-6) **Fic**
Burch, R. Wilkin's ghost (5 and up) **Fic**
Burchard, P. Bimby (4-6) **Fic**
Wilkinson, B. Ludell (6 and up) **Fic**

History
Vaughan, H. C. The colony of Georgia (4 and up) **975.8**
Georgie. Bright R.
Georgie and the buried treasure. Bright, R. See note under Bright, R. Georgie **E**
Georgie and the magician. Bright, R. See note under Bright, R. Georgie **E**
Georgie and the noisy ghost. Bright, R. See note under Bright, R. Georgie **E**
Georgie and the robbers. Bright, R. See note under Bright, R. Georgie **E**
Georgie finds a grandpa. Young, M.
In Gruenberg, S. M. comp. Let's hear a story p97-101 **808.8**
Georgie goes West. Bright, R. See note under Bright, R. Georgie **E**
Georgie to the rescue. Bright, R. See note under Bright, R. Georgie **E**
Georgie's Christmas carol. Bright, R. See note under Bright, R. Georgie **E**
Georgie's Halloween. Bright, R. See note under Bright, R. Georgie **E**
Georgy Piney-Woods Peddler. Jagendorf, M. A.
In Jagendorf, M. A. Folk stories of the South p99-105 **398.2**

Geoscience. See Geology
Geothermal resources
See pages in the following book:
Kiefer, I. Energy for America p117-26 (6 and up) **333.79**
Geras, Adele
The girls in the velvet frame (4 and up) **Fic**
Gerbils
Dobrin, A. Gerbils (3-6) **636.08**
Silverstein, A. Gerbils: all about them (4 and up) **599.32**
Simon, S. Discovering what gerbils do (2-5) **636.08**
See also pages in the following books:
Stevens, C. Your first pet p7-17 (2-4) **636.08**
Weber, W. J. Care of uncommon pets p82-92 (5 and up) **636.08**
Fiction
Pearce, P. The battle of Bubble and Squeak (3-6) **Fic**
Tobias, T. Petey **E**
Gerbils: all about them. Silverstein, A. **599.32**
Gerbils, and other small pets. Shuttlesworth, D. E. **636.08**
Gergely, Tibor
(jt. auth.) Brown, M. W. Wheel on the chimney **E**
Germ theory of disease
See pages in the following book:
Asimov, I. How did we find out about germs? p43-55 (5 and up) **616**
German Americans
Kunz, V. B. The Germans in America (5 and up) **305.8**
German language
Cooper, L. Fun with German (4 and up) **438**
See also pages in the following book:
Wohlrabe, R. A. The land and people of Germany p127-33 (5 and up) **943**
German language editions
Saint-Exupéry, A. de. The little prince **Fic**
German literature
See pages in the following book:
Wohlrabe, R. A. The land and people of Germany p127-33 (5 and up) **943**
Germanic art. See Art, Germanic
Germanic legends. See Legends, Germanic
The **Germans** in America. Kunz, V. B. **305.8**
Germans in Canada
Fiction
Little, J. From Anna (4 and up) **Fic**
Germany
Wohlrabe, R. A. The land and people of Germany (5 and up) **943**
Fiction
Benary-Isbert, M. The Ark (5 and up) **Fic**
Kay, M. In face of danger (6 and up) **Fic**
Preussler, O. The Satanic mill (6 and up) **Fic**
Richter, H. P. Friedrich (5 and up) **Fic**
Folklore
See Folklore—Germany
History—1918-1933
Switzer, E. How democracy failed (4 and up) **943.085**

Germany—*Continued*
History—1933-1945
Koehn, I. Mischling, second degree (6 and up) **92**
Switzer, E. How democracy failed (4 and up) **943.085**
Industries
See pages in the following book:
Dornberg, J. The two Germanys p123-42 (5 and up) **943.087**
Politics and government—1933-1945
Goldston, R. The life and death of Nazi Germany (5 and up) **943.086**
Social conditions
Richter, H. P. I was there (6 and up) **92**
Social life and customs
See pages in the following book:
Sechrist, E. H. Christmas everywhere p111-17 **394.2**

Germany (Democratic Republic) See Germany, East
Germany (Federal Republic) See Germany, West
Germany, East
Dornberg, J. The two Germanys (5 and up) **943.087**
Fles, B. East Germany (4 and up) **943.1**
Singer, J. Impressions (4-6) **943.1**
Germany, West
Dornberg, J. The two Germanys (5 and up) **943.087**
Germination
Rahn, J. E. Watch it grow, watch it change (5 and up) **581.3**
See also pages in the following book:
Mintz, L. M. Vegetables in patches and pots p31-38 (3-6) **635**
Germs. See Bacteriology; Germ theory of disease
Geronimo, Apache chief
Syme, R. Geronimo, the fighting Apache (3-5) **92**
See also pages in the following book:
Ehrlich, A. Wounded Knee: an Indian history of the American West p36-50 (6 and up) **970.004**
Geronimo, the fighting Apache. Syme, R. **92**
Gerontology
Research
See pages in the following book:
Silverstein, A. Aging p55-66 (5 and up) **305.2**
Gerson, Mary-Joan
Why the sky is far away (1-3) **398.2**
Gerstein, Mordicai
(illus.) Levy, E. Something queer is going on (a mystery) **E**
Gesture. See Nonverbal communication
Getting along in your family. Naylor, P. R. **306.8**
Getting born. Freeman, R. **591.1**
Getting something on Maggie Marmelstein. Sharmat, M. W. **Fic**
Getting started in calligraphy. Baron, N. **745.6**
The **Gettysburg** Address. Lincoln, A. President U.S.
In Foster, G. Year of Lincoln, 1861 p28-29 **909.81**

Gettysburg, Battle of, 1863
Fiction
Gauch, P. L. Thunder at Gettysburg (3-5) **Fic**
Geysers
See pages in the following book:
Kirk, R. Yellowstone p21-56 (5 and up) **978.7**
Ghana
Bleeker, S. The Ashanti of Ghana (4 and up) **966.7**
Perl, L. Ghana and Ivory Coast: spotlight on West Africa (6 and up) **966**
Folklore
See Folklore—Ghana
Ghana and Ivory Coast: spotlight on West Africa. Perl, L. **966**
Ghent
See pages in the following book:
Loder, D. The land and people of Belgium p95-101 (5 and up) **949.3**
The **ghost** at Valley Forge. Harter, W.
In Harter, W. Osceola's head, and other American ghost stories p7-11 **S C**
The **ghost** belonged to me. Peck, R. **Fic**
The **ghost** catcher. De, L.
In A-haunting we will go p118-22 **S C**
Ghost dance
See pages in the following book:
Ehrlich, A. Wounded Knee: an Indian history of the American West p170-78 (6 and up) **970.004**
Ghost in a four-room apartment. Raskin, E. **E**
Ghost in the house. Miller, H. L.
In Popular plays for classroom reading p3-21 **808.82**
The **ghost** in the noonday sun. Fleischman, S. **Fic**
The **ghost** in the orchard. Fisher, A.
In A-haunting we will go p54-64 **S C**
The **ghost** in the shed. Roach, M. K.
In Roach, M. K. Encounters with the invisible world p 1-8 **S C**
Ghost Lane. Curry, J. L. **Fic**
A **ghost** named Fred. Benchley, N. **E**
The **ghost** next door. St John, W. F. **Fic**
The **ghost** of Blackbeards wife. Yolen, J.
In Yolen, J. The wizard islands p32-35 **551.4**
The **ghost** of Dark Hollow Run. Malcolmson, A.
In Malcolmson, A. Yankee Doodle's cousin p37-44 **398.2**
The **ghost** of Dorothy Dingley. Mayne, W.
In Mayne, W. ed. Ghosts p118-23 **820.8**
The **ghost** of Five Owl Farm. Gage, W. **Fic**
The **ghost** of Follonsbee's Folly. Hightower, F. **Fic**
Ghost of summer. Bunting, E. **Fic**
Ghost of the spring and the shrew
Afanas'ev, A. The bad wife
In Afanas'ev. A. Russian fairy tales p56-57 **398.2**
The **ghost** of Thomas Kempe. Lively, P. **Fic**
The **ghost** of Thomas Kempe; excerpt. Lively, P.
In The Arbuthnot Anthology of children's literature p557-62 **808.8**

The **gift** of the magi. Henry, O.
  In Take joy! p47-51   **394.2**
The **gift** of the old pine tree. Simon, C. M.
  In Christmas stories round the world
    p33-38   **S C**
A **gift** of the unicorn. Wyndham, R.
  In Wyndham, R. Tales the people tell in
    China p34-37   **398.2**
Gift wrapping
      See pages in the following book:
  Hautzig, E. Let's make more presents p139-43
    (4 and up)   **745.5**
Gifts
  Cutler, K. N. Crafts for Christmas (3 and
    up)   **745.59**
  Hautzig, E. Let's make gifts (3 and up)
                                                               745.5
  Hautzig, E. Let's make more presents (4 and
    up)   **745.5**
  Purdy, S. Christmas gifts for you to make
    (4-6)   **745.59**
Gifts for the first birthday. Sawyer, R.
  In It's time for Christmas p194-97   **394.2**
Gifts for the harvest festival. Marson, U.
  In Thanksgiving p281-89   **394.2**
Gilbert, Christine B.
  (ed.) Best books for children. See Best books
    for children   **011**
Gilbert, Helen Earle
  Mrs Mallaby's birthday
  In Stories to dramatize p62-68   **372.6**
Gilbert, Sara
  You are what you eat (5 and up)   **641.1**
Gilbert, William P.
  (illus.) Sabin, F. Dogs of America   **636.7**
Gilberto and the wind. Ets, M. H.   **E**
Gilbreath, Alice Thompson
  Beginning-to-read riddles and jokes (1-3)
                                                               793.7
  Fun with weaving (4-6)   **746.1**
  Making costumes for parties, plays, and holi-
    days (4-6)   **391**
  More beginning crafts for beginning readers
    (k-3)   **745.5**
Gilbreth, Lillian Evelyn (Moller)
      See pages in the following book:
  Emberlin, D. Contributions of women: science
    p29-53 (5 and up)   **920**
Gilchrist, Theo E.
  Halfway up the mountain   **E**
Gilfond, Henry
  Genealogy: how to find your roots (6 and
    up)   **929**
  Syria (4 and up)   **956.91**
Gilgamesh
      See pages in the following books:
  The Arbuthnot Anthology of children's liter-
    ature p455-58   **808.8**
  Baumann, H. In the land of Ur p57-69 (5 and
    up)   **935**
  Time for old magic p319-22   **398.2**
Gilkison, Grace
  (illus.) Told under the green umbrella. See
    Told under the green umbrella   **398.2**
Gill, Derek L. T.
  Graham, R. L. The boy who sailed around
    the world alone   **910.4**
Gill, Margery
  (illus.) Arthur, R. M. A candle in her room
                                                               Fic
  (illus.) Arthur, R. M. Requiem for a prin-
    cess   **Fic**

(illus.) Cooper, S. Dawn of fear   **Fic**
(illus.) Cooper, S. Over sea, under stone **Fic**
(illus.) Tom Tiddler's ground. See Tom Tid-
  dler's ground   **821.08**
Gillen, Denver
  (illus.) Nathan, A. G. The first transatlantic
    cable   **621.382**
Gillespie, Jessie
  (illus.) Wiggin, K. D. The Birds' Christmas
    Carol   **Fic**
Gillespie, John T.
  (ed.) Best books for children. See Best books
    for children   **011**
  Creating a school media program   **027.8**
  Introducing books   **028.1**
  Juniorplots   **028.1**
  More Juniorplots   **028.1**
  Paperback books for young people   **070.5025**
  The young phenomenon: paperbacks in our
    schools   **027.8**
Gillham, Charles
  How the little owl's name was changed
  In The Arbuthnot Anthology of children's
    literature p394-96   **808.8**
  In Time for old magic p263-65   **398.2**
Gillis, Ruth J.
  Children's books for time of stress   **016.3627**
Gillum, Helen L.
  Veterinary medicine (6 and up)   **636.089**
Gilmore, H. H.
  Model boats for beginners (5 and up)   **623.8**
  Model submarines for beginners (5 and up)
                                                               623.8
Gilstrap, Robert
  Allah will provide
  In The Arbuthnot Anthology of children's
    literature p310-12   **808.8**
  In Time for old magic p189-91   **398.2**
Gimpel's golden broth. Simon, S.
  In Simon, S. The wisemen of Helm and
    their merry tales p77-88   **398.2**
Gin rummy. See Rummy (game)
Ginger Pye. Estes, E.   **Fic**
Gingerbread Boy
  Bryant, S. C. The Gingerbread Boy
  In The Fairy tale treasury p7-11   **398.2**
  Galdone, P. The gingerbread boy   **398.2**
  Gingerbread boy
  In The Tall book of nursery tales p16-22
                                                               398.2
  Rockwell, A. The gingerbread man
  In Rockwell, A. The three bears & 15
    other stories p33-44   **398.2**
      See also The bun; Johnny-cake; Pancake;
    Wee bannock
Gingerbread houses
      See pages in the following book:
  Williams, V. B. It's a gingerbread house
    (2-4)   **641.8**
The **gingerbread** man. Rockwell, A.
  In Rockwell, A. The three bears & 15 other
    stories p33-44   **398.2**
      See also Gingerbread boy
Gingham Lena. Brock, E. L.
  In Told under the magic umbrella p12-17
                                                               S C
Ginsburg, Mirra
  The chick and the duckling   **E**
  How the sun was brought back to the sky
    (k-2)   **398.2**
  (ed.) The Lazies. See The Lazies   **398.2**

Glubok, Shirley—*Continued*

The art of America since World War II (4 and up)   709.73

The art of ancient Mexico (4 and up)   709.01

The art of ancient Rome (4 and up)   709.37

The art of China (4 and up)   709.51

The art of colonial America (4 and up)   709.73

The art of India (4 and up)   709.54

The art of Japan (4 and up)   709.52

The art of photography (4 and up)   770.9

The art of the comic strip (4-6)   741.5

The art of the Eskimo (4 and up)   709.98

The art of the Etruscans (4 and up)   709.37

The art of the new American nation (4 and up)   709.73

The art of the North American Indian (4 and up)   709.01

The art of the Northwest coast Indians (4 and up)   709.01

The art of the Plains Indians (5 and up)   709.01

The art of the Southeastern Indians (4 and up)   709.01

The art of the Southwest Indians (4 and up)   709.01

The art of the Spanish in the United States and Puerto Rico (4 and up)   709.73

The art of the Vikings (4 and up)   709.02

The art of the Woodland Indians (4 and up)   709.01

Discovering Tut-ankh-Amen's tomb (4 and up)   932

Dolls, dolls, dolls (3-6)   688.7

Knights in armor (4 and up)   623.4

The mummy of Ramose (5 and up)   393

Olympic games in ancient Greece (5 and up)   796.4

(jt. auth.) Tamarin, A. Ancient Indians of the Southwest   970.004

(jt. auth.) Tamarin, A. Voyaging to Cathay   382.09

Glue

See pages in the following books:

Sattler, H. R. Recipes for art and craft materials p23-27 (4 and up)   745.5

Weiss, H. What holds it together? p25-30 (3-5)   621.8

The **gnome**. Grimm, J.

In Grimm, J. The complete Grimm's fairy tales p420-24   398.2

See also Earth gnome

Gnomes. See Fairies

Go and catch a flying fish. Stolz, M.   Fic

Go and hush the baby. Byars, B.   E

Go away, dog. Nodset, J. L.   E

Go I know not whither, bring back I know not what. Afanas'ev, A.

In Afanas'ev, A. Russian fairy tales p504-20   398.2

See also Go I know not whither—fetch I know not what

Go I know not whither—fetch I know not what

Afanas'ev, A. Go I know not whither, bring back I know not what

In Afanas'ev, A. Russian fairy tales p504-20   398.2

Bowman, J. C. Ei-Niin-Mita, or No-So-What

In Bowman, J. C. Tales from a Finnish tupa p105-15   398.2

Go tell Aunt Rhody. Quackenbush, R.   784.4

Go to the room of the eyes. Erwin, B. K.   Fic

Go with the poem (4 and up)   811.08

The **goat** and the tiger. Carter, D. S.

In Carter, D. S. Greedy Mariani, and other folktales of the Antilles p35-40   398.2

Goat comes to the Christmas party. Evans, E. K.

In Association for Childhood Education International. Told under the Christmas tree p132-36   808.8

In Rollins, C. comp. Christmas 'gif p45-50   394.2

Goat girl

Manning-Sanders, R. Tatterhood

In Manning-Sanders, R. A book of witches p94-103   398.2

Tatterhood

In Tatterhood, and other tales p 1-6   398.2

The **goat** in the rug. Blood, C. L.   E

The **goat** shedding on one side. Afanas'ev, A.

In Afanas'ev, A. Russian fairy tales p312-13   398.2

Goat that went to school. Credle, E.

In Credle, E. Tall tales from the high hills, and other stories p133-44   398.2

Goats

Jenkins, M. M. Goats, sheep, and how they live (5 and up)   599.73

Scott, J. D. The book of the goat (4-6)   636.3

Fiction

Asbjörnsen, P. C. The three Billy Goats Gruff (k-3)   398.2

Berson, H. Balarin's goat   E

Blood, C. L. The goat in the rug   E

Galdone, P. The three Billy Goats Gruff (k-2)   398.2

Grimm, J. The wolf and the seven little kids (k-3)   398.2

Watson, N. D. The birthday goat   E

The **goat's** funeral. Riordan, J.

In Riordan, J. Tales from Central Russia p73-75   398.2

Goats in the turnip field

Poulsson, E. The three goats

In Told under the green umbrella p78-80   398.2

Goats, sheep, and how they live. Jenkins, M. M.   599.73

Gobbato, Imero

(illus.) Colum, P. The girl who sat by the ashes   398.2

(illus.) Talbot, T. A bucketful of moon   E

Gobble, growl, grunt. Spier, P.   E

The **Gobble**-uns'll git you ef you don't watch out! Riley, J. W.   811

Goble, Dorothy

(jt. auth.) Goble, P. The friendly wolf   E

(jt. auth.) Goble, P. Lone Bull's horse raid   Fic

Goble, Paul

The friendly wolf   E

The girl who loved wild horses   E

Lone Bull's horse raid (3-6)   Fic

Red Hawk's account of Custer's last battle (4 and up)   973.8

(illus.) The Sound of flutes, and other Indian legends. See The Sound of flutes, and other Indian legends   398.2

Goblin, a wild chimpanzee. Teleki, G.   599.88

Goldengrove. Walsh, J. P.   **Fic**

Goldfish

Cooper, K. All about goldfish as pets (3 and up)   **639.3**

Selsam, M. E. Plenty of fish (k-3)   **639.3**

Wong, H. H. My goldfish (k-2)   **597**

Zim, H. S. Goldfish (2-5)   **639.3**

See also pages in the following book:

Stevens, C. Your first pet p49-63 (2-4)   **636.08**

The goldfish. Afanas'ev, A.

In Afanas'ev, A. Russian fairy tales p528-32   **398.2**

The goldfish. Farjeon, E.

In Farjeon, E. The little bookroom p40-46   **S C**

The goldfish. Street, J.

In Told under the magic umbrella p154-64   **S C**

Goldie the dollmaker. Goffstein, M. B.   **Fic**

Goldilocks and the three bears

In Stories to dramatize p23-25   **372.6**

See also Three bears

Goldin, Augusta

Grass (5 and up)   **584**

Salt (1-3)   **553.6**

Spider silk (1-3)   **595.4**

Straight hair, curly hair (k-2)   **612**

The sunlit sea (1-3)   **574.92**

Where does your garden grow? (1-3)   **631.4**

Golding, Morton J.

The mystery of the Vikings in America (6 and up)   **970.01**

Goldner, Jameson C.

(illus.) Dolan, E. F. Starting soccer   **796.334**

Goldsmith, Sophie L.

Louisa Alcott's wish

In One hundred plays for children p87-94   **808.82**

The goldspinners. Aleichem, S.

In Aleichem, S. Holiday tales of Sholom Aleichem p86-108   **S C**

Goldstein, Nathan

(illus.) Halacy, D. S. What makes a computer work?   **001.64**

(illus.) Johnson, C. What makes a clock tick?   **681.1**

Goldston, Robert

The life and death of Nazi Germany (5 and up)   **943.086**

Spain (4 and up)   **946**

Golem

Fiction

Ish-Kishor, S. The Master of Miracle (5 and up)   **Fic**

The Golem. McDermott, B. B.   **398.2**

Golf

Ravielli, A. What is golf? (3-6)   **796.352**

Smith, P. Golf techniques: how to improve your game (5 and up)   **796.352**

See also pages in the following books:

The Junior illustrated encyclopedia of sports p383-449 (5 and up)   **796.03**

Keith, H. Sports and games p136-55 (5 and up)   **796**

Golf techniques: how to improve your game. Smith, P.   **796.352**

Goloshes of fortune

Andersen, H. C. The magic galoshes

In Andersen, H. C. The complete fairy tales and stories p82-107   **S C**

Golovikka

Afanas'ev, A. The mayoress

In Afanas'ev, A. Russian fairy tales p141   **398.2**

Gone-Away Lake. Enright, E.   **Fic**

Gone is gone. Gág, W.   **398.2**

also in The Fairy tale treasury p48-55   **398.2**

See also Man who was going to mind the house

Gonorrhea

See pages in the following book:

Johnson, E. W. V.D.: venereal disease and what you should do about it p39-48 (5 and up)   **616.95**

Good advice

Afanas'ev, A. Good advice

In Afanas'ev, A. Russian fairy tales p289-91   **398.2**

Good and bad feelings. Stein, M. L.   **152.4**

Good and evil

Fiction

Cooper, S. Over sea, under stone (5 and up)   **Fic**

Garner, A. The weirdstone of Brisingamen (6 and up)   **Fic**

Good and evil. Riordan, J.

In Riordan, J. Tales from Central Russia p45-52   **398.2**

Good bargain

Grimm, J. The good bargain

In Grimm, J. The complete Grimm's fairy tales p51-55   **398.2**

Good bugs and bad bugs in your garden. Hogner, D. C.   **632**

Good-bye, Arnold! Roche, P. K.   **E**

Good-bye, funny dumpy-lumpy. Waber, B.   **E**

Good-bye, my Lady. Street, J. H.   **Fic**

Good-bye to the jungle. Townsend, J. R.   **Fic**

Good cents. Amazing Life Games Company   **658**

The good child and the bad child, and Gatto-mammone, and what the kittens said. Leach, M.

In Leach, M. The lion sneezed p43-51 **398.2**

The good-for-nothings. Grimm, J.

In Grimm, J. More Tales from Grimm p77-83   **398.2**

See also Vagabonds

The good fortune kettle. Haviland, V.

In Haviland, V. Favorite fairy tales told in Japan p23-29   **398.2**

See also Accomplished and lucky tea kettle

Good housewife and her night labors

Haviland, V. The good housewife and her night labors

In Haviland, V. Favorite fairy tales told in Scotland p59-70   **398.2**

In Time for old magic p29-31   **398.2**

The good knight ghost. Bendick, J.

In A Chilling collection p29-44   **S C**

The good little bad little pig. Brown, M. W.
  In Gruenberg, S. M. ed. Favorite stories
    old and new p36-40   **808.8**

Good little mouse
  Aulnoy, Comtesse d'. The good little mouse
  In Aulnoy, Comtesse d'. The White Cat,
    and other old French fairy tales
    p129-50   **398.2**
  Aulnoy, Comtesse d'. The little good mouse
  In The Andrew Lang Fairy tale treasury
    p116-27   **398.2**
  In Red fairy book p159-72   **398.2**

The **Good** Master. Seredy, K.   **Fic**

Good morning, Mr Rabbit. Bennett, R.
  In Bennett, R. Creative plays and programs
    for holidays p80-85   **812**

Good neighbors come in all sizes. Cheney, C.
  In Cheney, C. Tales from a Taiwan kitchen
    p53-55   **398.2**

Good-night, Owl! Hutchins, P.   **E**

The **good** ogre. Manning-Sanders, R.
  In Manning-Sanders, R. A book of ogres
    and trolls p9-19   **398.2**

    See also Three copecks

Good reading for the disadvantaged reader.
  Spache, G. D.   **011**

The **good** sons. Soyer, A.
  In Soyer, A. The adventures of Yemima,
    and other stories p42-46   **S C**

The **good** woman. Manning-Sanders, R.
  In Manning-Sanders, R. A book of ghosts
    & goblins p119-23   **398.2**

Good work, Amelia Bedelia. Parish, P. See
  note under Parish, P. Amelia Bedelia   **E**

Goodall, Jane, Barones van Lawick- See Lawick-Goodall, Jane, Barones van

Goodall, John S.
  The adventures of Paddy Pork   **E**
  The ballooning adventures of Paddy Pork.
    See note under Goodall, J. S. The adven-
    tures of Paddy Pork   **E**
  Creepy castle   **E**
  Paddy Pork's holiday. See note under Good-
    all, J. S. The adventures of Paddy Pork   **E**
  Paddy's evening out. See note under Goodall,
    J. S. The adventures of Paddy Pork   **E**
  Paddy's new hat. See note under Goodall,
    J. S. The adventures of Paddy Pork   **E**
  Shrewbettina's birthday   **E**
  The story of an English village (3-6)   **942**
  The surprise picnic   **E**

Goode, Diane
  (illus.) Le Prince de Beaumont, M. Beauty
    and the beast   **398.2**
  (illus.) Oppenheim, S. The selchie's seed   **Fic**
  (illus.) Steel, F. A. Tattercoats   **398.2**

Goode, John Paul
  Goode's World atlas. See Goode's World
    atlas   **912**

Goode, Ruth
  People of the first cities (5 and up)   **930**
  People of the Ice Age (5 and up)   **573.3**

Goodenow, Girard
  ((illus.) Conklin, G. The bug club book   **595.7**

Goode's School atlas. See Goode's World atlas   **912**

Goode's World atlas   **912**

Gooding, Beverley
  (illus.) Grahame, K. The open road   **Fic**

Goodnight, Andrew; goodnight, Craig. Sharmat,
  M. W.   **E**

Goodnight moon. Brown, M. W.   **E**

Goodrich, Samuel Griswold
  See pages in the following book:
  Jordan, A. M. From Rollo to Tom Sawyer,
    and other papers p61-71   **028.5**

Goodsell, Jane
  Daniel Inouye (3-5)   **92**
  Eleanor Roosevelt (2-4)   **92**
  The Mayo brothers (2-4)   **92**

Goody Hall. Babbitt, N.   **Fic**

Goose. See Geese

Goose girl
  Grimm, J. The goose girl   **398.2**
  also in Blue fairy book p278-85   **398.2**
  also in Grimm, J. The Brothers Grimm:
    popular folk tales p158-65   **398.2**
  also in Grimm, J. The complete Grimm's
    fairy tales p404-11   **398.2**
  also in Grimm, J. Fairy tales of the
    Brothers Grimm p51-58   **398.2**
  also in Grimm, J. Grimm's Fairy tales
    p32-38   **398.2**
  also in Grimm, J. Household stories p20-25   **398.2**
  also in Time for old magic p78-81   **398.2**

Goose-girl at the well
  Grimm, J. The goose-girl at the well
  In Grimm, J. The complete Grimm's fairy
    tales p725-34   **398.2**

Goose that laid the golden eggs
  In The Tall book of nursery tales p120   **398.2**

Gooseberry Garden. Lenski, L.
  In Told under the magic umbrella p23-26   **S C**

Goralasi and the spectres. Manning-Sanders, R.
  In Manning-Sanders, R. A book of spooks
    and spectres p107-11   **398.2**

Gorbaty, Norman
  (illus.) Riedman, S. R. Hormones: how they
    work   **612**

Gordillo, Henry E. F.
  (illus.) Harris, R. H. Before you were three   **155.4**

Gordon, Isabel
  (illus.) De Regniers, B. S. The shadow book   **E**

Gordon, Margaret
  (illus.) Horder, M. On Christmas day   **783.6**

Gordy, Berry
  Movin' up (5 and up)   **92**

Gore, Harriet Margolis
  What to do when there's no one but you
    (2-5)   **616.02**

Gore Gorinskoe
  Afanas'ev, A. Misery
  In Afanas'ev, A. Russian fairy tales p20-24   **398.2**

Gorey, Edward
  (illus.) Bellairs, J. The house with a clock
    in its walls   **Fic**
  (illus.) Ciardi, J. The man who sang the
    sillies   **811**
  (illus.) Ciardi, J. You read to me, I'll read
    to you   **811**
  (illus.) De Regniers, B. S. Red Riding Hood   **398.2**
  (illus.) Heide, F. P. The shrinking of Tree-
    horn   **E**

Great Britain—Fiction—*Continued*

Garfield, L. The night of the comet (5 and up) **Fic**

Garner, A. The stone book (4 and up) **Fic**

Gray, E. J. Adam of the road (5 and up) **Fic**

Hildick, E. W. Louie's lot (6 and up) **Fic**

Household, G. Escape into daylight (6 and up) **Fic**

Knight, E. Lassie come-home (4 and up) **Fic**

Lively, P. The ghost of Thomas Kempe (4-6) **Fic**

Lively, P. The voyage of QV 66 (4-6) **Fic**

McKillip, P. A. The house on Parchment Street (5 and up) **Fic**

Mark, J. Thunder and lightnings (5 and up) **Fic**

Mark, J. Under the autumn garden (4-6) **Fic**

Mayne, W. Earthfasts (5 and up) **Fic**

Mayne, W. A year and a day (4-6) **Fic**

Miles, P. The gods in winter (5 and up) **Fic**

Poole, J. Catch as catch can (5 and up) **Fic**

Pope, E. M. The Perilous Gard (6 and up) **Fic**

Robinson, J. G. The dark house of the sea witch (5 and up) **Fic**

Sewell, A. Black Beauty **Fic**

Stewart, M. The little broomstick (3-6) **Fic**

Streatfeild, N. Thursday's child (4 and up) **Fic**

Streatfeild, N. When the sirens wailed (4 and up) **Fic**

Townsend, J. R. Good-bye to the jungle (6 and up) **Fic**

Townsend, J. R. The intruder (6 and up) **Fic**

Townsend, J. R. Noah's castle (6 and up) **Fic**

Townsend, J. R. The visitors (6 and up) **Fic**

Walsh, J. P. A chance child (5 and up) **Fic**

Walsh, J. P. Goldengrove (6 and up) **Fic**

Westall, R. The machine gunners (6 and up) **Fic**

Westall, R. The Watch House (5 and up) **Fic**

Westall, R. The wind eye (5 and up) **Fic**

Folklore

See Folklore—Great Britain

History

Street, A. The land and people of England (5 and up) **942**

History—To 1066

Crossley-Holland, K. Green blades rising (6 and up) **942.01**

Thwaite, A. Beyond the inhabited world (6 and up) **936.1**

See also pages in the following book:

Carter, S. Vikings bold: their voyages & adventures p79-89 (5 and up) **948**

History—To 1066—Fiction

Sutcliff, R. Song for a dark queen (6 and up) **Fic**

Sutcliff, R. Sun horse, moon horse (5 and up) **Fic**

History—Norman period, 1066-1154

Duggan, A. Growing up with the Norman Conquest (6 and up) **942.02**

History—Plantagenets, 1154-1399—Fiction

De Angeli, M. The door in the wall (4-6) **Fic**

History—Lancaster and York, 1399-1485—Fiction

Pyle, H. Men of iron (5 and up) **Fic**

History—Tudors, 1485-1603

Hodges, C. W. The battlement garden (6 and up) **942.05**

Shakespeare's England (6 and up) **822.3**

History—Tudors, 1485-1603—Fiction

Beatty, J. Holdfast (6 and up) **Fic**

Willard, B. The lark and the laurel (6 and up) **Fic**

History—20th century

Reynolds, Q. Winston Churchill (4 and up) **92**

History, Naval

See pages in the following book:

Hodges, C. W. The battlement garden p89-99 (6 and up) **942.05**

Industries

See pages in the following book:

Street, A. The land and the people of England p115-20 (5 and up) **942**

Kings and rulers

Fritz, J. Can't you make them behave, King George? [biography of George III, King of Great Britain] (3-5) **92**

Religion

See pages in the following book:

Hodges, C. W. The battlement garden p74-78 (6 and up) **942.05**

Social life and customs

Duggan, A. Growing up with the Norman Conquest (6 and up) **942.02**

See also pages in the following books:

Hodges, C. W. The battlement garden p35-44 (6 and up) **942.05**

Sechrist, E. H. Christmas everywhere p58-74 **394.2**

The **great** Christmas kidnaping caper. Van Leeuwen, J. **Fic**

The **great** conjure-alligator-man of Florida. Jagendorf, M. A.

In Jagendorf, M. A. Folk stories of the South p67-69 **398.2**

The **great** Constitution. Commager, H. S. **342**

Great days of the circus **791.3**

The **great** Declaration. Commager, H. S. **973.3**

Great Dismal Swamp. See Dismal Swamp

The **great** excluded. See Children's Literature **028.505**

The **great** flood. Kim, So-un

In Kim, So-un. The story bag p66-75 **398.2**

The **great** flood. Sechrist, E. H.

In Sechrist, E. H. Once in the first times p8-11 **398.2**

The **Great** Flood. Thompson, V. L.
   In Thompson, V. L. Hawaiian tales of heroes and champions p86-92 **398.2**
The **great** game of soccer. Liss, H. **796.334**
The **great** Gilly Hopkins. Paterson, K. **Fic**
The **Great** Golloping Wolf. Manning-Sanders, R.
   In Manning-Sanders, R. A book of monsters p85-97 **398.2**
Great-grandfather
   Andersen, H. C. Great-grandfather
   In Andersen, H. C. The complete fairy tales and stories p987-91 **S C**
Great-grandfather in the honey tree. Swayne, S. **Fic**
Great-Grandfather, the baby and me. Knotts, H. **E**
The **great** green Turkey Creek monster. Flora, J. **E**
The **great** hamster hunt. Blegvad, L. **Fic**
Great Lakes
   Ault, P. These are the Great Lakes (5 and up) **977**
   Barry, J. P. The Great Lakes (4-6) **977**
Fiction
   Holling, H. C. Paddle-to-the-sea (4-6) **Fic**
Great Lakes region
   Ault, P. These are the Great Lakes (5 and up) **977**
   Barry, J. P. The Great Lakes (4-6) **977**
The **great** lizard of Nimple. Courlander, H.
   In Courlander, H. The tiger's whisker, and other tales and legends from Asia and the Pacific p140-43 **398.2**
Great monsters of the movies. Edelson, E. **791.43**
Great movie spectaculars. Edelson, E. **791.43**
Great peace. Hooke, H. M.
   In Hooke, H. M. Thunder in the mountains p93-98 **398.2**
The **great** perpetual learning machine. Blake, J. **372.1**
The **great** Pete Penney. Tolle, J. B. **Fic**
Great pets! Stein, S. **636.08**
Great Plains
   See pages in the following book:
   Coburn, D. A spit is a piece of land p39-42 (4-6) **551.4**
Bibliography
   Laughlin, M. Reading for young people: The Great Plains **016.978**
The **great** Proclamation. Commager, H. S. **326**
The **great** Quillow. Thurber, J. **Fic**
The **great** river monster. Marriott, A.
   In Marriott, A. American Indian mythology **398.2**
Great Roving Uhu. Thompson, V. L.
   In Thompson, V. L. Hawaiian tales of heroes and champions p109-21 **398.2**
The **great** Samurai sword. Winther, B.
   In Dramatized folk tales of the world p306-16 **812.08**
The **great** science magic show. Arnold, N. **793.8**
The **great** sea serpent. Andersen, H. C.
   In Andersen, H. C. The complete fairy tales and stories p1006-14 **S C**

Great Smoky Mountains National Park
   See pages in the following book:
   National Geographic Society. The new America's wonderlands **917.3**
The **Great** song book **784.6**
Great Swedish fairy tales. Olenius, E. comp. **398.2**
Great thumbprint drawing book, Ed Emberley's. Emberley, E. **743**
The **great** traveler of Chelm. Jagendorf, M. A.
   In Jagendorf, M. A. Noodlehead stories from around the world p53-58 **398.2**
The **great** tug-of-war. Sturton, H.
   In The Arbuthnot Anthology of children's literature p318-21 **808.8**
   In Time for old magic p195-98 **398.2**
Great White bear
   Lindsay, M. The great white bear
   In Harper, W. comp. Ghosts and goblins p201-04 **398.2**
The **greatest** Christmas gift. Murray, J.
   In On stage for Christmas p227-50 **812.08**
The **greatest** guessing game. Froman, R. **513**
Greaves, Margaret
   A net to catch the wind (2-4) **Fic**
Greaves, Red Legs
   See pages in the following book:
   Whipple, A. B. C. Famous pirates of the New World p118-20 (5 and up) **910.4**
Greece
   Gianakoulis, T. The land and people of Greece **949.5**
Antiquities
   Robinson, C. A. The first book of ancient Greece (4-6) **938**
   Van Duyn, J. The Greeks (5 and up) **938**
   See pages in the following book:
   Goode, R. People of the first cities p127-38 (5 and up)
Civilization
   See Civilization, Greek
Fiction
   Walsh, J. P. Children of the fox (5 and up) **S C**
   Yolen, J. The boy who had wings (3-5) **Fic**
Folklore
   See Folklore—Greece
History
   Asimov, I. The Greeks: a great adventure (6 and up) **938**
   Coolidge, O. The golden days of Greece (4-6) **938**
   Rutland, J. See inside an ancient Greek town (4 and up) **938**
   See also pages in the following book:
   Unstead, R. J. Looking at ancient history p46-73 (4-6) **930**
History—Peloponnesian War, 431-404 B.C.
   See pages in the following book:
   Van Duyn, J. The Greeks p155-66 (5 and up) **938**
Legends
   See Legends—Greece

Greece, Modern
Gianakoulis, T. The land and people of Greece (5 and up) **949.5**
Warren, R. Modern Greece (4-6) **949.5**

Description and travel
Sasek, M. This is Greece (3-6) **914.95**

Fiction
Zei, A. Petros' war (5 and up) **Fic**

Folklore
See Folklore—Greece, Modern

The **greedy** crow
In Jataka tales p62-65 **398.2**
Greedy Mariani. Carter, D. S.
In Carter, D. S. Greedy Mariani, and other folktales of the Antilles p99-105 **398.2**
Greedy Mariani, and other folktales of the Antilles. Carter, D. S. **398.2**
The **greedy** red lobster. Simon, S.
In Simon, S. The wisemen of Helm and their merry tales p29-34 **398.2**

Greek Americans
Jones, J. C. The Greeks in America (5 and up) **305.8**
Greek architecture. See Architecture, Greek
Greek art. See Art, Greek
Greek civilization. See Civilization, Greek
Greek drama

History and criticism
See pages in the following book:
Van Duyn, J. The Greeks p121-35 (5 and up) **938**
The **Greek** king and the physician Douban
In The Arabian nights entertainment p29-31 **398.2**
Greek mythology. See Mythology, Classical
The **Greeks.** Van Duyn, J. **938**
The **Greeks:** a great adventure. Asimov, I. **938**
The **Greeks** in America. Jones, J. C. **305.8**
Greeley, Horace
See pages in the following book:
Ault, P. "All aboard!" p34-38 (5 and up) **385.09**

Green, Elizabeth
(illus.) Severn, B. Magic with coins and bills **793.8**
Green, Jane
(jt. auth.) Choate, J. Patchwork **746.46**
Green, Melinda
Rachel's recital (2-4) **Fic**
Green, Norma
The hole in the dike **E**
The **green** and burning tree. Cameron, E. **028.5**
Green bird
Manning-Sanders, R. The green bird
In Manning-Sanders, R. A book of ogres and trolls p80-90 **398.2**
Green blades rising. Crossley-Holland, K. **942.01**
The **green** children. Colwell, E.
In Colwell, E. Round about and long ago p70-73 **398.2**
Green eyes. Birnbaum, A. **E**
Green fairy book **398.2**

Green gourd
Green gourd
In Grandfather tales p213-21 **398.2**
The **green** hero. Evslin, B. **398.2**
The **Green** Knight. Kristensen, E. T.
In The Andrew Lang Fairy tale treasury p460-73 **398.2**
The **green** leaf. Kim, So-un
In Kim, So-un. The story bag p129-37 **398.2**
Green Mountain Boys
Brown, S. Ethan Allen and the Green Mountain Boys (5 and up) **92**
Holbrook, S. H. America's Ethan Allen (5 and up) **92**
Green Mountain hero. Jagendorf, M. A.
In Jagendorf, M. A. New England bean-pot p89-94 **398.2**
Green pea John
Duvoisin, R. Green Pea John
In The three sneezes, and other Swiss tales p8-15 **398.2**
Green says go. Emberly, E. **535.6**
Green turtle mysteries. Waters, J. F. **597.9**
Greenaway, Kate
A Apple pie **E**
also in Greenaway, K. The Kate Greenaway treasury p228-48 **828**
Alphabet
In Greenaway, K. The Kate Greenaway treasury p220-27 **828**
The Kate Greenaway treasury **828**
Kate Greenaway's Book of games **796.1**
Marigold garden (k-2) **821**
Under the window (k-2) **821**
(illus.) Browning, R. The Pied Piper of Hamelin **821**
(illus.) Mother Goose. See Mother Goose **398**

About
See pages in the following books:
A Horn Book Sampler on children's books and reading p41-49 **028.5**
Illustrators of children's books: 1744-1945 p75-86 **741.64**
Lanes, S. G. Down the rabbit hole p31-43 **028.5**
Greene, Bette
Philip Hall likes me. I reckon maybe (4-6) **Fic**
Summer of my German soldier (6 and up) **Fic**
Greene, Constance C.
Beat the turtle drum (5 and up) **Fic**
The ears of Louis (4-6) **Fic**
A girl called A1 (5 and up) **Fic**
I and Sproggy (5 and up) **Fic**
I know you, A1. See note under Greene, C. C. A girl called A1 **Fic**
Isabelle the itch (4-6) **Fic**
Leo the lioness (6 and up) **Fic**
The unmaking of Rabbit (5 and up) **Fic**
Your old pal, A1. See note under Greene, C. C. A girl called A1 **Fic**
Greene, Ellin
(comp.) Clever cooks (3-6) **398.2**
(comp.) Midsummer magic. See Midsummer magic **398.2**
(ed.) A Multimedia approach to children's literature. See A Multimedia approach to children's literature **011**

Grimm, Jacob—*Continued*

Three-eyes; Fair Katrinelje and Pif-Paf-Poltrie; The fox and the horse; The shoes that were danced to pieces; The six servants; The white bride and the black bride; Iron Hans; The three black princesses; Knoist and his three sons; The maid of Brakel; My household; The lambkin and the little fish; Simeli mountain; Going a traveling; The donkey; The ungrateful son; The turnip; The old man made young again; The Lord's animals and the Devil's; The beam; The old beggar-woman; The three sluggards; The twelve idle servants; The shepherd boy; The star money; The stolen farthings; Looking for a bride; The hurds; The sparrow and his four children; The story of Schlauraffen land; The Ditmars tale of wonders; A riddling tale; Snow-White and Rose-Red; The wise servant; The glass coffin; Lazy Harry; The griffin; Strong Hans; The peasant in heaven; Lean Lisa; The hut in the forest; Sharing joy and sorrow; The willow-wren; The sole; The bittern and the hoopoe; The owl; The moon; The duration of life; Death's messengers; Master Pfriem; The goose-girl at the well; Eve's various children; The nixie of the mill-pond; The little folks' presents; The giant and the tailor; The nail; The poor boy in the grave; The true bride; The hare and the hedgehog; The spindle, the shuttle, and the needle; The peasant and the Devil; The crumbs on the table; The sea-hare; The master-thief; The drummer; The ear of corn; The grave-mound; Old rinkrank; The crystal ball; Maid Maleen; The boots of buffalo leather; The golden key; St Joseph in the forest; The twelve apostles; The rose; Poverty and humility lead to heaven; God's food; The three green twigs; Our Lady's little glass; The aged mother; The heavenly wedding; The hazel-branch

The crystal coffin
  In Green fairy book p333-40   398.2
The devil and his grandmother
  In Yellow fairy book p46-49   398.2
The donkey cabbage
  In The Andrew Lang Fairy tale treasury p266-73   398.2
The elves and the shoemaker
  In The Arbuthnot Anthology of children's literature p199-200   808.8
  In The Fairy tale treasury p118-21   398.2
  In Stories to dramatize p49-50   372.6
  In Time for old magic p47-48   398.2
The elves and the shoemaker; dramatization. See Thane, A. The elves and the shoemaker
Fairy tales of the Brothers Grimm (4 and up)   398.2
Contents: Snowdrop; Hansel and Gretel; Cherry, or The frog bride; The fisherman and his wife; Rosebud; The goose girl; Catskin; Rumpelstiltskin; The valiant little tailor; The six swans; The juniper tree; The two brothers
The fisherman and his wife (1-4)   398.2
  also in The Arbuthnot Anthology of children's literature p193-97   808.8
  also in The Golden Treasury of children's literature p187-92   808.8
  also in Time for old magic p68-72   398.2
  also in Told under the green umbrella p88-100   398.2
The four musicians
  In The Arbuthnot Anthology of children's literature p200-02   808.8
  In Time for old magic p48-50   398.2
The frog-king
  In Time for old magic p55-56   398.2
The frog-prince
  In The Classic fairy tales p185-87   398.2
  In Darrell, M. ed. Once upon a time p43-46   808.8
  In The Fairy tale treasury p114-17   398.2
  In Gruenberg, S. M. ed. Favorite stories old and new p295-98   808.8

The golden goose
  In The Fairy tale treasury p58-65   398.2
  In Red fairy book p337-42   398.2
The golden goose; dramatization. See Thane, A. Dummling and the Golden Goose
The golden lads
  In Green fairy book p352-59   398.2
The goose girl (2-4)   398.2
  also in Blue fairy book p278-85   398.2
  also in Time for old magic p78-81   398.2
Grimm's Fairy tales (3-6)   398.2
Contents: Snowdrop; The white snake; The golden goose; The three languages; The goose-girl; Rumpelstiltskin; The valiant tailor; The twelve dancing princesses; The mouse, the bird and the sausage; The queen bee; The robber bridegroom; Fundevogel; The King of the Golden Mountain; Jorinda and Joringel; Clever Elsa; Tom Thumb; Sweetheart Roland; The fisherman and his wife; The Bremen town musicians; The golden bird

Hans in luck (k-2)   398.2
Hans my hedgehog
  In Green fairy book p382-89   398.2
Hansel and Gretel
  In The Classic fairy tales p238-44   398.2
  In The Golden Treasury of children's literature p142-56   808.8
Hansel and Gretel; illus. by A. Adams (k-3)   398.2
Hansel and Gretel; illus. by A. Lobel (1-3)   398.2
Hansel and Gretel; illus. by L. Zwerger (k-3)   398.2
Hansel and Gretel; dramatization. See Thane, A. Hansel and Gretel
Hansel and Grethel
  In The Arthur Rackham Fairy book p269-77   398.2
  In Darrell, M. ed. Once upon a time p59-65   808.8
  In Giants & witches and a dragon or two p126-37   398.2
Hansel and Grettel
  In The Andrew Lang Fairy tale treasury p91-98   398.2
  In The Arbuthnot Anthology of children's literature p185-88   808.8
  In Blue fairy book p259-68   398.2
  In Time for old magic p57-60   398.2
Household stories (4-6)   398.2
Contents: The rabbit's bride; Six soldiers of fortune; Clever Grethel; The death of the hen; Hans in luck; The goose girl; The raven; The frog prince; Cat & mouse in partnership; The wolf and the seven little goats; Faithful John; The wonderful musician; The twelve brothers; The vagabonds; The brother and sister; Rapunzel; The three little men in the wood; The three spinsters; Hansel and Grethel; The white snake; The straw, the coal, and the bean; The fisherman and his wife; The gallant tailor; Aschenputtel; The mouse, the bird, and the sausage; Mother Hulda; Little Red Cap; The Bremen Town musicians; Prudent Hans; Clever Else; The table, the ass, and the stick; Tom Thumb; How Mrs Fox married again; The elves (I); The elves (II); The elves (III); The robber bridegroom; Mr Korbes; Tom Thumb's travels; The almond tree; Old Sultan; The six swans; The sleeping beauty; King Thrushbeard; Snow-White; The knapsack, the hat, and the horn; Rumpelstiltskin; Roland; The golden bird; The dog and the sparrow; Fred and Kate; The little farmer; The queen bee; The golden goose

How six men travelled through the wide world
  In The Andrew Lang Fairy tale treasury p229-304   398.2

Grizzly bear
Annixter, J. The year of the she-grizzly (4-6)
599.74
Dixon, P. The young grizzly (4-6)   599.74
Freschet, B. Grizzly bear (2-4)   599.74
Groac'h of the Isle of Loc
Masson, E. The witch of Lok Island
In Harper, W. comp. Ghosts and goblins
p176-91   398.2
In Witches, witches, witches p206-18 808.8
Groat, Diane de. See De Groat, Diane
Grooming, Personal
Kozuszek, J. E. Hygiene (4-6)   613
Grose, Helen Mason
(illus.) Wiggin, K. D. Rebecca of Sunny-brook Farm   Fic
Gross, Nathalie F.
The mystery ring
In Fifty plays for junior actors p236-44
812.08
Grossman, Myron
(illus.) Williams, J. Science puzzles   793.7
Grossman, Nancy
(illus.) Caudill, R. Did you carry the flag today, Charley?   Fic
Grossman, Robert
(illus.) Byars, B. The 18th emergency   Fic
Grossman, Ronald P.
The Italians in America (5 and up)   305.8
Gross, Ruth Belov
Alligators and other crocodilians (2-5) 597.9
A book about your skeleton (k-2)   612
Snakes (3-5)   597.9
Grossenheider, Richard Philip
(illus.) Burt, W. H. A field guide to the mammals   599
Grossman, Nancy
(illus.) Hill, E. S. Evan's corner   E
Grosvenor, Donna K.
The blue whale (k-3)   599.5
Pandas (k-3)   599.74
Zoo babies (k-3)   590.74
(illus.) Bridge, L. M. Cats: little tigers in your house   636.8
Groth, John
(illus.) Dickens, C. A Christmas carol in prose   Fic
(illus.) Sewell, A. Black Beauty   Fic
The **grouchy** ladybug. Carle, E.   E
Ground-hogs. See Marmots
Ground-nuts. See Peanuts
Groundhog's horse. Rockwood, J.   Fic
Group discussion. See Discussion groups
Groups, Ethnic. See Ethnic groups
Grove, Elaine
(illus.) Greenfeld, H. Passover   296.4
(illus.) Greenfeld, H. Rosh Hashanah and Yom Kippur   296.4
Grover, Eulalie Osgood
(ed.) Mother Goose; illus. by F. Richardson.
See Mother Goose; illus. by F. Richardson
398
Grover. Cleaver, V.   Fic
Growing a garden, indoors or out. Cutler, K. N.   635
Growing anyway up. Heide, F. P.   Fic
Growing older. Ancona, G.   305.2
Growing Point   028.505

The **growing** story. Krauss, R.   E
Growing up. De Schweinitz, K.   612
Growing up. Singer, I. B.
In Singer, I. B. Naftali the storyteller and his horse, Sus, and other stories p113-29   S C
Growing up chimpanzee. Alston, E.   599.88
Growing up with the Norman Conquest. Duggan, A.   942.02
Growth
Meeks, E. K. How new life begins (k-3)
574.1
Selsam, M. E. When an animal grows (k-3)
591.3
See also pages in the following books:
Riedman, S. R. Hormones: how they work p43--57 (6 and up)   612
Silverstein, A. The endocrine system p14-18 (4 and up)   612
Wilson, R. How the body works p62-71 (4 and up)   612
See also Growth (Plants)

Fiction
Kraus, R. The growing story   E
Growth (Plants)
Rahn, J. E. More about what plants do (5 and up)   581.3
Rahn, J. E. Watch it grow, watch it change (5 and up)   581.3
Gruber, Franz Xaver
Pauli, H. Silent night (4 and up)   783.6
Gruenberg, Sidonie Matsner
(ed.) Favorite stories old and new   808.8
(comp.) Let's hear a story   808.8
Grumbling old woman
Afanas'ev, A. The grumbling old woman
In Afanas'ev, A. Russian fairy tales p340-41
Grumpy Timothy Crumb. Jagendorf, M. A.
In Jagendorf, M. A. New England bean-pot p248-55   398.2
Grundtvig, Svendt
The most obedient wife
In The Arbuthnot Anthology of children's literature p232-35   808.8
In Time for old magic p112-15   398.2
Guaní. Belpré, P.
In Belpré, P. Once in Puerto Rico p18-24
398.2
The **guard** mouse. Freeman, D.   E
Guardians of the gate
Carpenter, F. Guardians of the gate
In Carpenter, F. Tales of a Chinese grand-mother p47-55   398.2
Guardians of tomorrow. Hirsch, S. C.   920
Guatemala
Fiction
Buff, M. Magic maize (3-6)   Fic
Social conditions
Jenness, A. A life of their own (5 and up)
972.81
Gudbrand on the hill-side. Asbjörnsen, P. C.
In The Arbuthnot Anthology of children's literature p244-46   808.8
In Time for old magic p127-29   398.2
Gudbrand on the Hillside. Dasent, G.
In Time to laugh p168-74   S C

Gutenberg, Johann
See pages in the following books:
Barker, A. Black on white and read all over p16-23 (4-6)   **686.2**
Cottler, J. Heroes of civilization p207-16 (5 and up)   **920**
Guthrie, Janet
Olney, R. R. Janet Guthrie: first woman at Indy (4 and up)   **92**
Gutman, Bill
(ed.) Brewster, B. Baseball   **796.357**
Guyer, Carol
(illus.) Glubok, S. The art of India   **709.54**
Guynemer, Georges Marie Ludovic
See pages in the following book:
Gurney, G. Flying aces of World War I p22-39 (4-6)   **920**
Gymnastics
Dolan, E. F. The complete beginner's guide to gymnastics (5 and up)   **796.4**
Krementz, J. A very young gymnast   **796.4**
Resnick, M. Gymnastics and you (4-6)   **796.4**
Sullivan, G. Better gymnastics for girls (4 and up)   **796.4**
Traetta, J. Gymnastics basics (4 and up)   **796.4**
Gymnastics and you. Resnick, M.   **796.4**
Gymnastics basics. Traetta, J.   **796.4**
Gypsies
Greenfeld, H. Gypsies (5 and up)   **305.8**
The **gypsies'** fiddle. Jagendorf, M. A.
In Jagendorf, M. A. The gypsies' fiddle, and other gypsy tales p102-06   **398.2**
The **gypsies'** fiddle, and other gypsy tales. Jagendorf, M. A.   **398.2**
The **gypsy** and the snake. Jagendorf, M. A.
In Jagendorf, M. A. The gypsies' fiddle, and other gypsy tales p24-34   **398.2**
Gypsy folklore. See Folklore, Gypsy
The **gypsy** in the ghost house. Jagendorf, M. A.
In Jagendorf, M. A. The gypsies' fiddle, and other gypsy tales p111-17   **398.2**
The **gypsy** look. Heath, A. L.
In Fifty plays for junior actors p245-56   **812.08**

H

Ha! ha! ha! Manning-Sanders, R.
In Manning-Sanders, R. A book of spooks and spectres p126-[28]   **398.2**
Haar, Jaap ter
Boris (5 and up)   **Fic**
Haas, Irene
The Maggie B.   **E**
(illus.) Craft, R. Carrie Hepple's garden   **E**
(illus.) De Regniers, B. S. A little house of your own   **E**
(illus.) De Regniers, B. S. Something special   **811**
(illus.) Joslin, S. There is a dragon in my bed   **448**
Habitations, Human. See Houses
Habitations of animals. See Animals—Habitations
Habits of animals. See Animals—Habits and behavior

Habsburg, House of
See pages in the following books:
Rothkopf, C. Z. Austria p52-59 (4 and up)   **943.6**
Wohlrabe, R. A. The land and people of Austria p33-40 (5 and up)   **943.6**
Hackett, Walter
A Christmas carol
In Popular plays for classroom reading p337-53   **808.82**
A merry Christmas
In On stage for Christmas p429-45   **812.08**
Haddad, George A.
(illus.) Ross, F. Antique car models   **629.2**
Haddam witches. Jagendorf, M. A.
In Jagendorf, M. A. New England bean-pot p206-11   **398.2**
In Witches, witches, witches p187-91   **808.8**
Hader, Berta
The big snow   **E**
Caldecott Medal acceptance paper
In Caldecott Medal books: 1938-1957 p185-91   **028.5**
About
See pages in the following books:
Authors and illustrators of children's books p180-85   **028.5**
Caldecott Medal books: 1938-1957 p192-99   **028.5**
Hader, Elmer
Caldecott Medal acceptance paper
In Caldecott Medal books: 1938-1957 p185-91   **028.5**
(jt. auth.) Hader, B. The big snow   **E**
About
See pages in the following books:
Authors and illustrators of children's books p180-85   **028.5**
Caldecott Medal books: 1938-1957 p192-99   **028.5**
Hafiz, the stone-cutter. Shedlock, M. L.
In Shedlock, M. L. The art of the story-teller p179-82   **372.6**
See also Stone cutter
Hafner, Marilyn
(illus.) Gage, W. Mrs Gaddy and the ghost   **E**
(illus.) Prelutsky, J. It's Halloween   **811**
(illus.) Schulman, J. Camp KeeWee's secret weapon   **E**
Hague, Michael R.
(illus.) Grahame, K. The wind in the willows   **Fic**
(illus.) Hilgartner, B. A necklace of fallen stars   **Fic**
Hahn, Emily
See pages in the following book:
Young and female p37-56 (6 and up)   **920**
Haiku
Atwood, A. Haiku: the mood of earth (5 and up)   **811**
Atwood, A. My own rhythm (5 and up)   **811**
Cricket songs (4 and up)   **895.6**
Lewis, R. ed. In a spring garden (k-3)   **895.6**
Mizumura, Kazue. Flower, moon, snow (2-4)   **811**
More Cricket songs (4 and up)   **895.6**
See also pages in the following book:
Cosman, A. How to read and write poetry p31-44 (5 and up)   **808.1**

Handicraft—*Continued*

Pettit, F. H. Christmas all around the house (5 and up) **745.59**

Pettit, F. H. How to make whirligigs and whimmy diddles, and other American folkcraft objects (5 and up) **745.5**

A Pumpkin in a pear tree (1-4) **745.59**

Purdy, S. Christmas gifts for you to make (4-6) **745.59**

Purdy, S. Holiday cards for you to make (5 and up) **745.594**

Purdy, S. G. Jewish holidays (4 and up) **394.2**

Roche, P. K. Dollhouse magic (2-4) **745.592**

Rockwell, H. I did it (1-3) **745.5**

Seidelman, J. E. Creating with wood (4 and up) **745.51**

Temko, F. Folk crafts for world friendship **745.59**

Thomson, N. Fairground games to make and play (3-5) **745.592**

Tichenor, T. Christmas tree crafts (6 and up) **745.594**

Wilkins, M. The long ago lake (5 and up) **500**

Wirtenberg, P. Z. All-round-the-house art and craft book (4 and up) **745.5**

Wiseman, A. Making musical things (3-6) **781.91**

Wiseman, A. Making things (5 and up) **745.5**

Zubrowski, B. Milk carton blocks (3-5) **693**

See also pages in the following book:

Cassell, S. Indoor games and activities p 1-22, 84-100 (3-6) **793**

See also names of crafts, e.g. Egg decoration; Weaving

Equipment and supplies

Sattler, H. R. Recipes for art and craft materials (4 and up) **745.5**

The **handsomest** father. Hautzig, D. **E**

Handtalk. Charlip, R. **419**

Handville, Robert

(illus.) Gates, D. Lord of the sky: Zeus **292**

Handy, William Christopher

Montgomery, E. R. William C. Handy: father of the blues (3-4) **92**

See also pages in the following book:

Rollins, C. H. They showed the way p75-79 (5 and up) **920**

Handy key to your "National Geographics". Underhill, C. S. comp. **910.5**

Hang tough, Paul Mather. Sloate, A. **Fic**

Hangin' out with Cici. Pascal, F. **Fic**

Hanging on. Freedman, R. **591.5**

The **hangman's** ghost trick. Corbett, S. See note under Corbett, S. The lemonade trick **Fic**

Hankey, Peter

(ed.) The Great song book. See The Great song book **784.6**

Hanlon, Emily

The swing (5 and up) **Fic**

Hannibal

See pages in the following book:

Brooks, P. S. When the world was Rome, 753 B.C. to A.D. 476 p29-51 (6 and up) **937**

Hannigan, Jane Anne

(ed.) Media center facilities design. See Media center facilities design **027.8**

Hans and his master. Manning-Sanders, R.
In Haunting tales p33-39 **S C**
In Manning-Sanders, R. A book of ghosts & goblins p55-61 **398.2**

Hans Andersen: his classic fairy tales. Andersen, H. **S C**

Hans Brinker

Thane, A. A gift for Hans Brinker
In Dramatized folk tales of the world p200-11 **812.08**

Hans Christian Andersen's The fir tree. Andersen, H. C. **Fic**

Hans Clodhopper

Andersen, H. C. Blockhead-Hans
In Yellow fairy book p309-13 **398.2**

Andersen, H. C. Clod Hans
In Andersen, H. C. The complete fairy tales and stories p479-82 **S C**

Hans Hecklemann's luck

Pyle, H. Hans Hecklemann's luck
In Pyle, H. Pepper & salt p57-68 **398.2**

Hans Humdrum

Hatch, M. C. Hans Humdrum
In Hatch, M. C. 13 Danish tales p148-69 **398.2**

Hans in luck

Grimm, J. Hans in luck **398.2**
also in Grimm, J. The complete Grimm's fairy tales p381-86 **398.2**
also in Grimm, J. Household stories p14-19 **398.2**

See also Barter

Hans Kuhschwanz

Duvoisin, R. Hans Kuhschwanz
In Duvoisin, R. The three sneezes, and other Swiss tales p162-66 **398.2**

Hans married

Grimm, J. Hans married
In Grimm, J. The complete Grimm's fairy tales p387-88 **398.2**

Hans my hedgehog

Grimm, J. Hans my hedgehog
In Green fairy book p382-89 **398.2**
In Grimm, J. The Brothers Grimm: popular folk tales p151-57 **398.2**
In Grimm, J. The juniper tree, and other tales from Grimm v 1 p11-22 **398.2**

Grimm, J. Hans the Hedgehog
In Grimm, J. The complete Grimm's fairy tales p497-502 **398.2**
In Grimm, J. The complete Grimm's fairy tales p497-502 **398.2**

Hans the Hedgehog. Grimm, J.
In Grimm, J. The complete Grimm's fairy tales p497-502 **398.2**

See also Hans my hedgehog

Hans, who made the princess laugh

Haviland, V. Taper Tom
In Haviland, V. Favorite fairy tales told in Norway p50-64 **398.2**

Thorne-Thomsen, G. Taper Tom
In Stories to dramatize p105-09 **372.6**

Hans, who made the Princess laugh; play. Rowland, E.
In One hundred plays for children p726-33 **808.82**

Hansel and Gretel. See Hansel and Grethel

Hardy Hardhead
Hardy Hardhead
In The Jack tales p96-105   398.2
The hare. Carrick, M.
In Carrick, M. The wise men of Gotham
398.2
Hare and the corn bins. Arnott, K.
In Arnott, K. African myths and legends
p101-04   398.2
Hare and the hedgehog
Grimm, J. The hare and the hedgehog
In Grimm, J. The complete Grimm's fairy
tales p760-64   398.2
Grimm, J. The hedgehog and the rabbit
In Grimm, J. More Tales from Grimm
p163-70   398.2
Grimm, J. The race between the hare and
the hedgehog
In The Golden Treasury of children's
literature p403-05   808.8
The Race between Hare and Hedgehog
In Told under the green umbrella p30-35
398.2
Hare and the Hyena. Arnott, K.
In Arnott, K. African myths and legends
p108-11   398.2
The Hare and the tortoise   398.2
The hare and the tortoise. Bennett, R.
In Bennett, R. Creative plays and programs
for holidays p186-92   812
Hare in the moon
The Rabbit in the moon
In Sakade, F. ed. Japanese children's
favorite stories p35-37   398.2
Shedlock, M. L. The true spirit of a festival
day
In Shedlock, M. L. The art of the story-
teller p225-28   372.6
The hare that ran away. Shedlock, M.
In The Arbuthnot Anthology of children's
literature p347-48   808.8
In Time for old magic p226-27   398.2
See also Timid hare
Hare that was sent to York
Carrick, M. The hare
In Carrick, M. The wise men of Gotham
398.2
Hares. See Rabbits
The hare's bride. Grimm, J.
In Grimm, J. The complete Grimm's fairy
tales p332-33   398.2
See also Rabbit's bride
Hari Raya
See pages in the following book:
More Festivals in Asia p29-34 (2-5)   394.2
Harisarman
Harisarman
In Indian fairy tales p85-89   398.2
Hark, Mildred
Christmas recaptured
In On stage for Christmas p162-82   812.08
The magic egg
In One hundred plays for children p324-
35   808.82
Merry Christmas, Crawfords!
In A Treasury of Christmas plays p21-44
812.08
Merry Christmas customs
In A Treasury of Christmas plays p376-82
812.08

Off the shelf
In One hundred plays for children p423-32
808.82
Reindeer on the roof
In On stage for Christmas p3-27   812.08
What, no Santa Claus?
In On stage for Christmas p272-84   812.08
Hark! Hark! The dogs do bark, and other
rhymes about dogs   398
Harker, Doug
(illus.) Rutland, J. See inside an oil rig
and tanker   338.2
Harkness, Ruth
See pages in the following book:
Facklam, M. Wild animals, gentle women
p27-38 (5 and up)   920
Harlem Globetrotters
Gault, C. The Harlem Globetrotters and
basketball's funniest games (3-6)   796.32
The Harlem Globetrotters and basketball's
funniest games. Gault, C.   796.32
Harlem, New York (City)

Fiction
Childress, A. A hero ain't nothin' but a
sandwich (6 and up)   Fic
Myers, W. D. Fast Sam, Cool Clyde &
Stuff (6 and up)   Fic
Myers, W. D. Mojo and the Russians (6
and up)   Fic
Wagner, J. J. T. (3-6)   Fic
Weik, M. H. The Jazz Man (3-5)   Fic
The harlequin moth. Selsam, M. E.   595.7
Harman, Carter
Skyscraper goes up (5 and up)   690
Harmon, Seth
Pink petunia
In Harper, W. comp. Easter chimes
p118-28   S C
Harmonica, Mouth. See Mouth-organ
Harnessing the sun. Knight, D. C.   621.47
Haro
(illus.) Jokes, giggles & guffaws. See Jokes,
giggles & guffaws   808.87
Harold and the purple crayon. Johnson, C.   E
Harold's ABC. Johnson, C. See note under
Johnson, C. Harold and the purple crayon
E
Harold's circus. Johnson, C. See note under
Johnson, C. Harold and the purple crayon
E
Harold's trip to the sky. Johnson, C. See note
under Johnson, C. Harold and the purple
crayon   E
Harper, Frances Ellen (Watkins)
See pages in the following books:
Rollins, C. Famous American Negro poets
p22-27 (5 and up)   920
Rollins, C. H. They showed the way p80-82
(5 and up)   920
Harper, Richard
The samaritan
In Universe ahead: stories of the future
p194-207 (6 and up)   S C
Harper, Wilhelmina
(comp.) Easter chimes   S C
(comp.) Ghosts and goblins   398.2
The Gunniwolf (k-1)   398.2
(comp.) The harvest feast   S C
(comp.) Merry Christmas to you   S C

Harper's Round Table
See pages in the following book:
Yankee Doodle's literary sampler of prose, poetry, and pictures p437-45   028.5

Harper's Young People. See Harper's Round Table

Harpist in the wind. McKillip, P. A. See note under McKillip, P. A. The riddlemaster of Hed   **Fic**

The **harps** of Heaven. Babbitt, N.
In Babbitt, N. The Devil's storybook p21-35   **S C**

Harriet and the promised land. Lawrence, J.   811

Harriet and the runaway book; the story of Harriet Beecher Stowe and Uncle Tom's cabin. Johnston, J.   92

Harriet changes her mind. Fitzhugh, L.
In The Arbuthnot Anthology of children's literature p676-79   808.8

Harriet goes to the circus. Maestro, B.   **E**

Harriet reads signs and more signs. Maestro, B. See note under Maestro, B. Harriet goes to the circus   **E**

Harriet the spy. Fitzhugh, L.   **Fic**

Harriet the spy; excerpt. Fitzhugh, L.
In The Arbuthnot Anthology of children's literature p676-79   808.8

Harriet Tubman: guide to freedom. Epstein, S.   92

Harrington, Lyn
The polar regions (5 and up)   998

Harris, Christie
Mouse Woman and the mischief-makers (4 and up)   398.2
Contents: Mouse woman and porcupine hunter; Mouse woman and the vanished princes; Mouse woman and the snee-nee-ig; Mouse woman and the wooden wife; Mouse woman and the monster killer whale; Mouse woman and the daughter of the sun; Mouse woman and the tooth
Mouse Woman and the muddleheads (4 and up)   398.2
Contents: The mink being who wanted to marry a princess; The sea hunters who were swallowed by a whirlpool; Robin Woman and Sawbill Duck Woman; The rumor; The princess and Copper Canoeman; Asdilda and Omen; The princess who rejected her cousin
Mouse Woman and the vanished princesses (4 and up)   398.2
Contents: The princess and the feathers; The princess and the bears; The princess and the magic plume; The princess and the snails; The princess and the geese; The princess and the magical hat
Once more upon a totem (4 and up)   398.2
Contents: The prince who was taken away by the salmon; Raven traveling; Ghost story

Harris, Isabel Sherwin
(illus.) Hussey, L. J. Collecting cocoons   595.7

Harris, Joel Chandler
Brer Rabbit grossly deceives Brer Fox
In The Golden Treasury of children's literature p226-28   808.8
How Brer Rabbit was too sharp for Brer Fox
In The Golden Treasury of children's literature p224-25   808.8
Old Mr Rabbit, he's a good fisherman
In The Arbuthnot Anthology of children's literature p385-86   808.8

The wonderful tar-baby story
In The Arbuthnot Anthology of children's literature p383-84   808.8
In The Golden Treasury of children's literature p221-23   808.8
In Gruenberg, S. M. ed. Favorite stories old and new p336-38   808.8
In Stories to dramatize p50-53   372.6
In Time for old magic p256-57   398.2

Harris, Karen H.
(ed.) The Special child in the library. See The Special child in the library   027.62
(jt. auth.) Baskin, B. H. Notes from a different drummer   016.8

Harris, John
Endangered predators (5 and up)   599.74

Harris, Lorle
Biography of a river otter (3-5)   599.74
Biography of a whooping crane (2-4)   598

Harris, Robie H.
Before you were three   155.4

Harris, Rosemary
Beauty and the beast (2-4)   398.2

Harris, Susan
Helicopters (2-4)   629.133

Harrisburg Seven (Trial)
See pages in the following book:
Aymar, B. Laws and trials that created history p103-201 (6 and up)   345

Harrison, Elizabeth
The legend of the Christ child
In Harper, W. comp. Merry Christmas to you p87-93   **S C**
Little Gretchen and the wooden shoe
In Harper, W. comp. Merry Christmas to you p111-23   **S C**

Harrison, Ted
Children of the Yukon (2-4)   971.9

Harrison, William Henry, President U.S.
See pages in the following book:
Schraff, A. Tecumseh p29-47 (5 and up)   92

Harry and Shellburt. Van Woerkom, D. O.   **E**

Harry and the lady next door. Zion, G. See note under Zion, G. Harry the dirty dog   **E**

Harry and the terrible Whatzit. Gackenbach, D.   **E**

Harry by the sea. Zion, G. See note under Zion, G. Harry the dirty dog   **E**

Harry Cat's pet puppy. Selden, G. See note under Selden, G. The cricket in Times Square   **Fic**

Harry the dirty dog. Zion, G.   **E**

Harsh words
In Jakata tales p29-31   398.2

Hart, Johan
The king's rijstepap
In It's time for story hour p66-68   372.6
The magic cap
In It's time for story hour p117-20   372.6

Hartelius, Margaret A.
(illus.) Camp Fire Girls, Inc. The Blue Bird wish   369.47
(illus.) Camp Fire Girls, Inc. The Camp Fire Blue Bird Series   369.47
(illus.) Chernoff, G. T. Clay-dough play-dough   745.5
(illus.) Chernoff, G. T. Easy costumes you don't have to sew   391

Harter, Walter
Osceola's head, and other American ghost stories (4-6)   **S C**
Contents: The ghost at Valley Forge; Bloody handprints on the wall; Jamie Dawkin's drum; Osceola's head; The house that hated war; The actor who won't stay dead; The ghosts of Foley Square; The ghostly inhabitants of Fort Monroe; The witch in the pond; The mystery of the gold doubloons

Hartley, Carol
Children of the calendar
In One hundred plays for children p122-26   **808.82**

Hartley, L. P.
The crossways
In Haunting tales p246-55 (5 and up)   **S C**

Härtling, Peter
Oma (3-5)   **Fic**

The **harvest** feast. Harper, W. comp.   **S C**

Harvest home. Perkins, L. F.
In Thanksgiving p117-24   **394.2**

A **Harvest** of Russian children's literature   **891.7**

Harvest time the world around. Lockhardt, M. C.
In Thanksgiving p319-26   **394.2**

Harvestmen. See Daddy longlegs

Harvey, William
See pages in the following book:
Cottler, J. Heroes of civilization p279-88 (5 and up)   **920**

Hashepsowe, Queen of Egypt. See Hatshepsut, Queen of Egypt

Haskins, James
Fighting Shirley Chisholm (6 and up)   **92**
The life and death of Martin Luther King, Jr. (5 and up)   **92**
Pelé [biography of Edson Arantes do Nascimento] (6 and up)   **92**
The quiet revolution (5 and up)   **362.4**

Hassall, Joan
(illus.) The Oxford Nursery rhyme book. See The Oxford Nursery rhyme book   **398**

Hasselriis, Else
(illus.) Chrisman, A. B. Shen of the sea   **S C**

Hasselriis, Malthé
(illus.) Carpenter, F. Tales of a Chinese grandmother   **398.2**

The **hat.** Manning-Sanders, R.
In Manning-Sanders, R. A book of charms and changelings p51-55   **398.2**

The **hat**-shaking dance, and other tales from the Gold Coast. Courlander, H.   **398.2**

The **hatbox** cake. Potter, M. C.
In Gruenberg, S. M. comp. Let's hear a story p53-61   **808.8**

Hatch, Mary C.
The talking pot
In The Arbuthnot Anthology of children's literature p235-37   **808.8**
13 Danish tales (3-5)   **398.2**
Contents: James the huntsman; Talking pot; Mother's pet; Foolish lad; Mistress Good Luck and Dame Know-all; Three tailors and the white goose; The suitor; Wonderful knapsack; Doctor and detective, too; Peter Humbug and the white cat; Brave in spite of himself; Princess who always believed what she heard; Hans Humdrum

The **hating** book. Zolotow, C.   **E**

Hats
Fiction
Keats, E. J. Jennie's hat   **E**
Seuss, Dr. The 500 hats of Bartholomew Cubbins   **E**

Hatshepsut, Queen of Egypt
See pages in the following book:
Payne, E. The pharaohs of ancient Egypt p87-103 (5 and up)   **932**

Hatsuno's great-grandmother. Means, F. C.
In The Arbuthnot Anthology of children's literature p679-84   **808.8**

Hauff, Wilhelm
The story of Caliph Stork
In Green fairy book p 1-15 (4-6)   **398.2**

Haufrecht, Herbert
The Laura Ingalls Wilder songbook. See The Laura Ingalls Wilder songbook   **784**

Haugaard, Erik Christian
Hakon of Rogen's saga (6 and up)   **Fic**
The little fishes (6 and up)   **Fic**
Orphans of the wind (6 and up)   **Fic**
A slave's tale. See note under Haugaard, E. C. Hakon of Rogen's saga   **Fic**

Hauman, Doris
(illus.) Dickinson, E. Poems for youth   **811**

Hauman, George
(illus.) Dickinson, E. Poems for youth   **811**

Haunted Alp
Duvoisin, R. Haunted Alp
In Duvoisin, R. The three sneezes, and other Swiss tales p196-202   **398.2**

Haunted houses. See Ghosts

Haunted houses. Kettelkamp, L.   **133.1**

The **haunted** mountain. Hunter, M.   **Fic**

Haunted Subalterns. Kipling, R.
In Sechrist, E. H. ed. 13 ghostly yarns p131-40   **S C**

The **haunting** of America. Anderson, J.   **398.2**

Haunting tales (5 and up)   **S C**

The **haunted** trailer. Arthur, R.
In Haunting tales p40-62 (5 and up)   **S C**

Haunts, haunts, haunts (5 and up)   **S C**

Hauptmann, Bruno Richard
See pages in the following book:
David, A. Famous criminal trials p64-69 (5 and up)   **345**

Hausas
See pages in the following book:
Jenness, A. Along the Niger River p83-92 (5 and up)   **966.9**

Haussas. See Hausas

Hauserr, Rosmarie
(illus.) Bernstein, J. E. When people die   **128**

Hautzig, Deborah
The handsomest father   **E**

Hautzig, Esther
At home (k-3)   **410**
The case against the wind, and other stories (4 and up)   **S C**
Contents: The treasure; The obsession with clothes; The seven good years; Revealed; If not still higher; The fast; The match; Miracles on the sea; Bontche the silent; The case against the wind
Cool cooking (2-5)   **641.5**
In school (k-3)   **410**
In the park (k-3)   **410**
Let's make gifts (3 and up)   **745.5**
Let's make more presents (4 and up)   **745.5**
Life with working parents: practical hints for everyday situations (5 and up)   **649**

Have you seen roads? Oppenheim, J.   **625.7**

Haviland, Laura (Smith)
See pages in the following book:
As I saw it: women who lived the American adventure p86-89 (6 and up)   973

Haviland, Virginia
(comp.) Children and literature. See Children and literature   028.5
(comp.) Children & poetry: a selective, annotated bibliography. See Children & poetry: a selective, annotated bibliography   016.8
(comp.) Children's books. See Children's books   011
(ed.) Children's books of international interest. See Children's books of international interest   011
(comp.) Children's literature; a guide to reference sources. See Children's literature; a guide to reference sources   011
(comp.) Children's literature; a guide to reference sources; first supplement. See Children's literature; a guide to reference sources; first supplement   011
(comp.) Children's literature; a guide to reference sources; second supplement. See Children's literature; a guide to reference sources; second supplement   011
(comp.) The Fairy tale treasury. See The Fairy tale treasury   398.2
Favorite fairy tales told in Czechoslovakia (2-5)   398.2
Contents: The twelve months; Kuratko the terrible; The wood fairy; The shepherd's nosegay; The three golden hairs of Grandfather Know All
Favorite fairy tales told in Denmark (3-5)   398.2
Contents: The wonderful pot; Ee-aw! Ee-aw; The knapsack; Grayfoot; The tree of health; A legend of Christmas Eve
Favorite fairy tales told in France (2-5)   398.2
Contents: Twelve dancing princesses; Puss in Boots; Beauty and the beast; Sleeping Beauty in the wood; Drakestail
Favorite fairy tales told in Greece (2-5)   398.2
Contents: Constantes and the dragon; The princess who loved her father like salt; The foolish wife and her three foolish daughters; The fairy wife; The wonders of Skoupa; Fairy gardens; The first of May; Fairy mother
Favorite fairy tales told in India (2-5)   398.2
Contents: The valiant chattee-maker; The little jackals and the lion; The cat and the parrot; The blind man, the deaf man, and the donkey; The alligator and the jackal; Sir Buzz; The tiger, the Brahman, and the jackal; Banyan Deer
Favorite fairy tales told in Ireland (2-5)   398.2
Contents: The bee, the harp, the mouse, and the bumclock; The old hag's long leather bag; Billy Beg and the bull; The widow's lazy daughter; Patrick O'Donnell and the leprechaun
Favorite fairy tales told in Italy (2-5)   398.2
Contents: Cenerentola; The story of Bensurdatu; The stone in the cock's head; Bastianelo; The three goslings; The golden lion
Favorite fairy tales told in Japan (2-5)   398.2
Contents: One-Inch Fellow; The good fortune kettle; The tongue-cut sparrow; Momotaro; The white hare and the crocodiles
Favorite fairy tales told in Norway (2-5)   398.2
Contents: The Princess on the glass hill; Why the sea is salt; The three billy goats Gruff; Taper Tom; Why the bear is stumpy-tailed; The lad and the North Wind; Boots and the Troll

Favorite fairy tales told in Scotland (2-5)   398.2
Contents: The page boy and the silver goblet; The wee bannock; Peerifool; The Brownie o' Ferne-Den; The good housewife and her night labors; Assipattle and the giant sea serpent
Favorite fairy tales told in Spain (2-5)   398.2
Contents: The flea; Four brothers who were both wise and foolish; The half-chick; The Carlanco; Juan Cigarron; The enchanted mule
Favorite fairy tales told in Sweden (2-5)   398.2
Contents: The boy and the water-sprite; The old woman and the tramp; The lad and the fox; Pinkel; The old woman and the fish; Lars, by lad
The good housewife and her night labors
In Time for old magic p29-31   398.2
(ed.) North American legends. See North American legends   398.2
The old woman and the tramp
In Time for old magic p140-42   398.2
One-Inch Fellow
In The Fairy tale treasury p162-69   398.2
Poor Turkey Girl
In North American legends p76-82   398.2
Star maiden
In North American legends p97-100   398.2
(ed.) Yankee Doodle's literary sampler of prose, poetry, and pictures. See Yankee Doodle's literary sampler of prose, poetry and pictures   028.5
(comp.) Bechtel, L. S. Books in search of children   028.5

Hawaii
Folklore
See Folklore—Hawaii
Natural history
See Natural history—Hawaii
Hawaiian mythology. See Mythology, Hawaiian
Hawaiian myths of earth, sea, and sky. Thompson, V. L.   398.2
Hawaiian tales of heroes and champions. Thompson, V. L.   398.2
Hawes, Charles Boardman
See pages in the following book:
Newbery Medal books: 1922-1955 p30-32   028.5
Hawes, Dorothea Cable
Newbery Medal acceptance paper
In Newbery Medal books: 1922-1955 p31-32   028.5
Hawes, Judy
Bees and beelines (k-2)   595.7
Fireflies in the night (k-3)   595.7
Ladybug, ladybug, fly away home (k-2)   595.7
My daddy longlegs (1-3)   595.4
What I like about toads (k-3)   597.8
Why frogs are wet (k-3)   597.8
The **hawk** and the wildcat. Sechrist, E. H.
In Sechrist, E. H. Once in the first times p54-56   398.2
Hawk, I'm your brother. Baylor, B.   E
Hawkesworth, Eric
Paper cutting (4-6)   736
Hawkesworth, Margaret
(illus.) Hawkesworth, E. Paper cutting   736
Hawkins, Arthur
(jt. auth.) Paul, A. Kids cooking   641.5
(illus.) Paul, A. Kids gardening   635.9

Hawkinson, John
Collect, print and paint from nature (3-6)
751.42
Pastels are great! (3-6)   741.2
Rhythms, music and instruments to make
(3-6)   781

Hawks
See pages in the following book:
Brady, I. Wild babies p32-41 (4-6)   591.3

Fiction
Baylor, B. Hawk, I'm your brother   E

Hawthorne, Nathaniel
The golden touch; adaptation
In Stories to dramatize p159-63   372.6
The Gray Champion
In Sechrist, E. H. ed. 13 ghostly yarns
p141-54   **S C**
Tanglewood tales
In Hawthorne, N. A wonder-book, and
Tanglewood tales p201-421   292
A wonder book
In Hawthorne, N. A wonder-book, and
Tanglewood tales p15-198   292
A wonder-book, and Tanglewood tales (5
and up)   292

Hay fever
See pages in the following book:
Silverstein, A. Allergies p40-51 (5 and up)
616.97

Haycock, Ken
(comp.) Sears List of subject headings:
Canadian companion. See Sears List of
subject headings: Canadian companion
025.4

Haycraft, Howard
(ed.) The Junior book of authors. See The
Junior book of authors   920.03

Hayden, Robert C.
Eight black American inventors (5 and up)
920
Seven black American scientists (5 and up)
920

Haydn, Franz Joseph
Lasker, D. The boy who loved music
(2-5)   92

Hayes, R. Chetwynd- See Chetwynd-Hayes, R.
Haym Salomon, liberty's son. Milgrim, S.   92
Hays, James D.
Our changing climate (5 and up)   551.6
Hays, R. Vernon
(jt. auth.) Hays, W. P. Foods the Indians
gave us   641.3
Hays, Wilma Pitchford
Foods the Indians gave us (5 and up)   641.3
Paying for the Indian corn
In Thanksgiving p106-13   394.2
Pilgrim Thanksgiving (3-5)   **Fic**
Haystack cricket and how things are different
up in the moon towns. Sandburg, C.
In Sandburg, C. Rootabaga stories v2 p153-
59   **S C**
In Sandburg, C. The Sandburg treasury
p139-42   818
Haywood, Carolyn
Annie Pat and Eddie. See note under Hay-
wood, C. Little Eddie   **Fic**
"B" is for Betsy (2-4)   **Fic**
Back to school with Betsy. See note under
Haywood, C. "B" is for Betsy   **Fic**

Betsy and Billy. See note under Haywood, C.
"B" is for Betsy   **Fic**
Betsy and Mr Kirkpatrick. See note under
Haywood, C. "B" is for Betsy   **Fic**
Betsy and the boys. See note under Hay-
wood, C. "B" is for Betsy   **Fic**
Betsy and the circus. See note under Hay-
wood, C. "B" is for Betsy   **Fic**
Betsy's busy summer. See note under
Haywood, C. "B" is for Betsy   **Fic**
Betsy's little Star. See note under Hay-
wood, C. "B" is for Betsy   **Fic**
Betsy's play school. See note under Hay-
wood, C. "B" is for Betsy   **Fic**
Betsy's winterhouse. See note under
Haywood, C. "B" is for Betsy   **Fic**
The children's theater
In Friends are like that! p32-45   **S C**
Eddie and Gardenia. See note under Hay-
wood, C. Little Eddie   **Fic**
Eddie and his big deals. See note under
Haywood, C. Little Eddie   **Fic**
Eddie and Louella. See note under Hay-
wood, C. Little Eddie   **Fic**
Eddie and the fire engine. See note under
Haywood, C. Little Eddie   **Fic**
Eddie goes to dancing school
In The Arbuthnot Anthology of children's
literature p608-11   808.8
Eddie makes music. See note under Hay-
wood, C. Little Eddie   **Fic**
Eddie, the dog holder. See note under
Haywood, C. Little Eddie   **Fic**
Eddie's green thumb. See note under Hay-
wood, C. Little Eddie   **Fic**
Eddie's happenings. See note under Hay-
wood, C. Little Eddie   **Fic**
Eddie's menagerie. See note under Hay-
wood, C. Little Eddie   **Fic**
Eddie's pay dirt. See note under Haywood, C.
Little Eddie   **Fic**
Eddie's valuable property. See note under
Haywood, C. Little Eddie   **Fic**
Ever-ready Eddie. See note under Hay-
wood, C. Little Eddie   **Fic**
Little Eddie (2-4)   **Fic**
Little Eddie goes to town
In Gruenberg, S. M. ed. Favorite stories
old and new p29-36   808.8
Merry Christmas from Betsy. See note under
Haywood, C. "B" is for Betsy   **Fic**
Snowbound with Betsy. See note under
Haywood, C. "B" is for Betsy   **Fic**

About
See pages in the following book:
Authors and illustrators of children's books
p193-96   028.5
Hazard, Eleanor
(illus.) Krauss, R. Somebody spilled the
sky   811
Hazard, Paul
Books, children & men   028.5
The **hazel**-branch. Grimm, J.
In Grimm, J. The complete Grimm's fairy
tales p830   398.2
Hazel-nut child
The Hazel-nut child
In Yellow fairy book p206-09   398.2
Hazeltine, Alice I.
(comp.) The Year around. See The Year
around   808.81

Hazeltine, Mary Emogene
Gregory, R. W. Anniversaries and holidays
394.2
Hazen, Barbara Shook
The gorilla did it **E**
Gorilla wants to be the baby. See note under Hazen, B. S. The gorilla did it **E**
Where do bears sleep? **E**
Why couldn't I be an only kid like you, Wigger **E**
He came down. Paterson, K.
In Paterson, K. Angels & other strangers p81-89 **S C**
He is our guest, let's not see his mistakes. Patri, A.
In Gruenberg, S. M. ed. Favorite stories old and new p250-52 **808.8**
He won't be home for Christmas. Moessinger, W.
In On stage for Christmas p316-30 **812.08**
Head, Faye E.
The second shepherd's play
In On stage for Christmas p465-75 **812.08**
A spouse for Susie Mouse
In Dramatized folk tales of the world p317-23 **812.08**
Head
See also Brain; Eye
The **head**. Leach, M.
In Leach, M. The thing at the foot of the bed, and other scary tales p63-64 **S C**
Headache
See pages in the following book:
Silverstein, A. Allergies p92-94 (5 and up) **616.97**
The **headless** cupid. Snyder, Z. K. **Fic**
The **headless** horseman. Manning-Sanders, R.
In Manning-Sanders, R. A book of ghosts & goblins p80-86 **398.2**
Heady, Eleanor B.
Make your own dolls (3-5) **745.592**
Men of different colors
In The Arbuthnot Anthology of children's literature p316-18 **808.8**
Son of the long one
In The Arbuthnot Anthology of children's literature p314-16 **808.8**
In Time for old magic p193-95 **398.2**
Heady, Harold F.
(illus.) Heady, E. B. Make your own dolls **745.592**
Healing, Mental. See Mental healing
The **healing** arts. Kettelkamp, L. **615.5**
Health. See Hygiene
Health, Public. See Public health
Health care. See Medical care
Health food. See Food, Natural
Heaps, Willard A.
Superstition! (6 and up) **398**
(ed.) Browne, C. A. The story of our national ballads **784.7**
Hear your heart. Showers, P. **612**
Hearing
See pages in the following book:
Silverstein, A. The sense organs p27-35 (4 and up) **612**
See also Deafness
Hearing aids
Litchfield, A. B. A button in her ear (1-3) **617.8**

Hearn, Lafcadio
The boy who drew cats
In A Chilling collection p63-66 **S C**
In The Golden Treasury of children's literature p525-27 **808.8**
In Gruenberg, S. M. ed. Favorite stories old and new p373-76 **808.8**
The old woman and her dumpling; adaptation. See Mosel, A. The funny little woman **398.2**
The soul of the great bell
In Sechrist, E. H. ed. 13 ghostly yarns p25-33 **S C**
Hodges, M. The wave **398.2**
Heart
Elgin, K. The human body: the heart (3-5) **612**
Showers, P. Hear your heart (k-3) **612**

Surgery—Fiction
Singer, M. It can't hurt forever (4 and up) **Fic**
Heart of ice
Caylus, Comte de. Heart of ice
In The Andrew Lang Fairy tale treasury p190-219 **398.2**
In Green fairy book p114-46 **398.2**
Hearts, cupids, and red roses. Barth, E. **394.2**
Hearts of oak. Hall, M. E.
In One hundred plays for children p821-27 **808.82**
Hearts, tarts and valentines. Fisher, A.
In Fisher, A. Holiday programs for boys and girls p207-17 **812**
Heat
Adler, I. Hot and cold (4-6) **536**
Balestrino, P. Hot as an ice cube (k-3) **536**
See also Fire; Temperature
Heat engines
See pages in the following book:
Weiss, H. Motors and engines and how they work p42-50 (5 and up) **621.4**
Heath, Anna Lenington
The Gypsy look
In Fifty plays for junior actors p245-56 **812.08**
Much ado about ants
In One hundred plays for children p127-34 **808.82**
Heaven forbid! Manning-Sanders, R.
In Manning-Sanders, R. A book of spooks and spectres p123-35 **398.2**
Heaven to Betsy; a Betsy-Tacy high school story. Lovelace, M. H. See note under Lovelace, M. H. Betsy-Tacy **Fic**
The **heavenly** jam. Freshman, E.
In Thanksgiving p311-17 **394.2**
The **heavenly** wedding. Grimm, J.
In Grimm, J. The complete Grimm's fairy tales p828-29 **398.2**
Heavy is a hippopotamus. Schlein, M. **E**
Hebrew literature
See also Jewish literature
Hechtlinger, David
(illus.) Berger, T. Special friends **305.2**
Hector Protector, and As I went over the water. Sendak, M. **398**
Hedder, Mairi
(illus.) Duncan, J. Brave Janet Reachfar **E**

The **hedgehog** and the rabbit. Grimm, J.
In Grimm, J. More Tales from Grimm
p163-70   398.2
See also Hare and the hedgehog

Hedgehogs

Fiction

Potter, B. The tale of Mrs Tiggy-Winkle
                                                          E
Hedin, Don
(illus.) Carr, R. Be a frog, a bird, or a tree
                                                      613.7
Hedley Kow
The Hedley Kow
In Tatterhood, and other tales p13-16
                                                      398.2
Heide, Florence Parry
Banana twist (4-6)   Fic
Growing anyway up (6 and up)   Fic
The shrinking of Treehorn   E
Heiderstadt, Dorothy
Indians for Thanksgiving
In Harper, W. comp. The harvest feast
p50-63   S C
In It's time for Thanksgiving p60-69   394.2
Heidi. Spyri, J.   Fic
Heidi; excerpt. Spyri, J.
In The Arbuthnot Anthology of children's
literature p708-12   808.8
Heidi. Thane, A.
In Thane, A. Plays from famous stories
and fairy tales p315-34   812
Heifer hide
The heifer hide
In The Jack tales p161-71   398.2
Heighway, Richard
Jacobs, J. The fables of Aesop   398.2
Heilbroner, Joan
This is the house where Jack lives   E
Heinlein, Robert
Space ship Bifrost
In The Arbuthnot Anthology of children's
literature p591-94   808.8
Heinly, John
(illus.) Foley, L. M. Tackle 22   Fic
Heins, Paul
Jordan, A. M. Children's classics   011
Heir of sea & fire. McKillip, P. A. See note
under McKillip, P. A. The riddle-master
of Hed   Fic
Helbig, Alethea
(comp.) Straight on till morning. See
Straight on till morning   821.08
Heldman, Max
(illus.) Hunt, S. E. Games and sports the
world around   796.1
The **Helen** Keller story. Peare, C. O.   92
Helfman, Elizabeth S.
Maypoles and wood demons (3-6)   398
Signs & symbols of the sun (5 and up)   398
(jt. auth.) Helfman, H. Strings on your
fingers   793
Helfman, Harry
Creating things that move (4-6)   745.5
Strings on your fingers (3-6)   793
Tricks with your fingers (3-6)   793.8
Helga's dowry. De Paola, T.   E
Helicopters
Delear, F. J. Helicopters and airplanes of
the U.S. Army (5 and up)   623.74
Harris, S. Helicopters (2-4)   629.133
See also pages in the following books:
Bendick, J. The first book of airplanes p52-
55 (3-5)   629.13

Helicopters and airplanes of the U.S. Army.
Delear, F. J.   623.74
Hellender, Isobel Millier
Erika's two guests
In Christmas stories round the world p13-
17   S C
Hellman, Hal
The lever and the pulley (3-5)   531
Transportation in the world of the future
(5 and up)   380.5
Hellman, Harold. See Hellman, Hal
Hello, Aurora; excerpt. Vesty, A. C.
In The Arbuthnot Anthology of children's
literature p701-05   808.8
Hello, Mrs Piggle-Wiggle. MacDonald, B. See
note under MacDonald, B. Mrs. Piggle-
Wiggle   Fic
The **Helmites** capture the moon. Simon, S.
In Simon, S. The wisemen of Helm and
their merry tales p35-42   398.2
The **helmsman.** Kafka, F.
In Haunts, haunts, haunts p52   S C
Help! Emergencies that could happen to you,
and how to handle them. Vandenburg,
M. L.   616.02
Help, thieves in Helm! Simon, S.
In Simon, S. The wisemen of Helm and
their merry tales p55-66   398.2
Helpers. See Hughes, S. George the babysitter
                                                          E
Helping children cope. Fassler, J.   016.3627
Helsinki
See pages in the following book:
Berry, E. The land and people of Finland
p63-79 (5 and up)   948.97
Helweg, Hans
(illus.) Bond, M. The tales of Olga da Polga
                                                         Fic
(illus.) Jagendorf, M. A. The gypsies' fiddle,
and other gypsy tales   398.2
The **hemp** smoker and the hemp grower. Cour-
lander, H.
In Courlander, H. The king's drum, and
other African stories p101-05   398.2
Henbest, Nigel
(jt. auth.) Couper, H. Space frontiers   500.5
Henderson, Bernard
The ghosts of Kahlberg
In Harper, W. comp. Ghosts and goblins
p234-49   398.2
Henderson, Le Grand
Almost an ambush
In Gruenberg, S. M. ed. Favorite stories
old and new p189-97   808.8
Henderson, Nancy
Celebrate America (5 and up)   812
Contents: Soul force; Hail the lucky year;
Legend for our time; "John Muir, Earth-Planet.
Universe"; Honor the brave; Casey at the bat;
Moonlife 2069; Come to the fair; Little Turtle;
The land we love; M.D. in petticoats; Keeping
Christmas merry; Popcorn whoppers
Henderson, R. A.
(jt. auth.) Henderson, W. F. Looking at
Australia   994
Henderson, Richard
See pages in the following book:
Steele, W. O. Westward adventure p122-58
(5 and up)   920
Henderson, W. F.
Looking at Australia (4-6)   994

Hightower, Florence
   The ghost of Follonsbee's Folly (5 and up)
                                       Fic
Highway construction. See Roads
Highway engineering
   See also Roads
Highway transportation. See Transportation,
   Highway
Highways. See Roads
Higuera, Prudencia
   See pages in the following book:
   As I saw it: women who lived the American
     adventure p21-23 (6 and up)   973
Hiking
   See also Backpacking; Walking
Hildebrandt, Greg
   (illus.) Hiss, A. The giant panda book
                              599.74
Hildebrandt, Tim
   (illus.) Hiss, A. The giant panda book
                              599.74
Hildick, E. W.
   Louie's lot (6 and up)   Fic
   Louie's ransom. See note under Hildick,
     E. W. Louie's lot   Fic
   Manhattan is missing (4-6)   Fic
Hildilid's night. Ryan, C. D.   E
Hilgartner, Beth
   A necklace of fallen stars (4-6)   Fic
Hilgerdt, Erik
   (illus.) Schlein, M. I, Tut: the boy who
     became pharaoh   92
Hill, Donna
   (ed.) Third book of junior authors. See
     Third book of junior authors   920.03
Hill, Elizabeth Starr
   Evan's corner   E
Hill, Eric
   (illus.) Hoke, H. Hoke's Jokes, cartoons &
     funny things   793.7
Hill, Helen
   Charlie rides in the engine of a real train
    In Gruenberg, S. M. ed. Favorite stories
      old and new p88-91   808.8
   (comp.) Straight on till morning. See
     Straight on till morning   821.08
   Toys and Christmas
    In Dalgliesh, A. comp. Christmas p137-46
                           S C
Hill, James Jerome
   See pages in the following book:
   Captains of industry p51-60 (5 and up) 920
Hill, Janet
   Children are people   027.62
Hill, Kay
   Midnight burial
    In One hundred plays for children p135-39
                       808.82
Hill of fire. Lewis, T. P.   E
The hill of the elves. Andersen, H. C.
   In Andersen, H. C. The complete fairy
     tales and stories p282-88   S C
Hillbrand, Percie V.
   The Norwegians in America (5 and up)
                          305.8
   The Swedes in America (5 and up) 305.8
Hillcourt, William
   Boy Scouts of America. The official Boy
     Scout handbook   369.43

Hiller, Carl E.
   Caves to cathedrals (5 and up)   726
Hillman and the housewife
   Ewing, J. H. The hillman and the housewife
    In Stories to dramatize p102-03   372.6
Hills End. Southall, I.   Fic
Hilton, Suzanne
   The way it was—1876 (6 and up)   973.8
Himler, Ronald
   Wake up, Jeremiah   E
   (illus.) Adoff, A. I am the running girl 811
   (illus.) Adoff, A. Under the early morning
     trees   811
   (illus.) Bulla, C. R. Conquista   Fic
   (illus.) Burgess, R. F. Exploring a coral
     reef   574.92
   (illus.) Byars, B. After the Goat Man Fic
   (illus.) Caines, J. Daddy   E
   (illus.) Coerr, E. Sadako and the thousand
     paper cranes [a biography of Sadako
     Sasaki]   92
   (illus.) Gipson, F. Curly and the wild boar
                             Fic
   (illus.) Glazer, T. Eye winker, Tom Tinker,
     chin chopper   796.1
   (illus.) Jewell, N. Bus ride   E
   (illus.) Kennedy, R. The blue stone Fic
Hinamatsuri
   See pages in the following book:
   Festivals in Asia p23-30 (2-5)   394.2
Hincks, Gary
   (illus.) Stonehouse, B. A closer look at
     plant life   581
   (illus.) Stonehouse, B. A closer look at
     reptiles   597.9
Hind in the forest
   Jagendorf, M. A. The white doe
    In Jagendorf, M. A. Folk stories of the
     South p178-80   398.2
Hinds, Lorna
   Looking at Great Britain (4-6)   941
Hinds, Robert William
   (illus.) Seidelman, J. Creating with clay
                           731.4
Hinduism
   Edmonds, I. G. Hinduism (5 and up) 294.5
   See also pages in the following books:
   Bothwell, J. The first book of India p24-30
     (4-6)   954
   Fitch, F. M. Their search for God p11-51
     (4 and up)   291
   Helfman, E. S. Signs & symbols of the sun
     p81-87 (5 and up)   398
   Kettelkamp, L. Religions, East and West
     p27-37 (5 and up)   291
   Rawding, F. W. The Buddha p16-26 (5 and
     up)   294.3
   Seeger, E. Eastern religions p7-56 (6 and
     up)   291
Hine, Al
   (ed.) This land is mine (5 and up) 811.08
Hines, Bob
   (illus.) McClung, R. M. Lost wild worlds
                          591.9
Hinman, Dorothy
   Reading for young people: the Midwest
                        016.977
Hinton, S. E
   The outsiders (5 and up)   Fic

Hippopotamus

Fiction

Brown, M. How, Hippo! **E**
Duvoisin, R. Veronica **E**
Mahy, M. The boy who was followed home **E**
Marshall, J. George and Martha **E**
Hiroko. Wolkstein, D.
  In Wolkstein, D. Lazy stories p7-13 **398.2**
Hiroshige
  (illus.) Buck, P. S. The big wave **Fic**
Hirsch, S. Carl
  Guardians of tomorrow (5 and up) **920**
  Meter means measure (5 and up) **389**
  Stilts (4 and up) **685**
Hirsh, Marilyn
  Could anything be worse? (k-3) **398.2**
  The Hanukkah story (1-3) **296.4**
  One little goat (k-2) **296.4**
  Potato pancakes all around **E**
  (illus.) Pine, T. S. The Polynesians knew **996**
Hirzel, Bertha M.
  (jt. auth.) Withrow, D. E. Gateways to readable books **011**
His first bronc. James, W.
  In Gruenberg, S. M. ed. Favorite stories old and new p155-59 **808.8**
His mother's dog. Skorpen, L. M. **E**
Hispanic-American literature. See Latin American literature
Hispano-American War, 1898. See United States—History—War of 1898
Hiss, Anthony
  The giant panda book (3-5) **599.74**
Historic models of early America, and how to make them. Maginley, C. J. **688**
Historic plane models. Ross, F. **629.133**
Historic racing car models. Ross, F. **629.2**
Historic sites
  National Geographic Society. Visiting our past: America's historylands (5 and up) **917.3**
Historical catastrophes: earthquakes. Brown, B. W. **551.2**
Historical catastrophes: hurricanes & tornadoes. Brown, B. W. **551.5**
Historical fiction
  See pages in the following books:
  Children and literature p298-312 **028.5**
  Egoff, S. The republic of childhood p95-130 **028.5**
  Horn Book Reflections on children's books and reading p137-50 **028.5**
  Only connect p233-64 **028.5**
  Sutherland, Z. Children & books p370-94 **028.5**
  Townsend, J. R. Written for children p219-37 **028.5**
Bibliography
  Meztner, S. World history in juvenile books: a geographical and chronological guide **016.9**
  See also pages in the following book:
  Sutherland, Z. Children & books p395-401 **028.5**
History
Bibliography
  Metzner, S. World history in juvenile books: a geographical and chronological guide **016.9**

Fiction
See pages in the following book:
The Arbuthnot Anthology of children's literature p736-75 **808.8**
Poetry
See pages in the following book:
One thousand poems for children p319-60 **821.08**
History, Ancient
  Unstead, R. J. Looking at ancient history (4-6) **930**
History, Local. See names of countries, states, etc. with the subdivision History, Local, e.g. United States—History, Local
History, Naval. See names of countries with the subdivision History, Naval, e.g. United States—History, Naval
History of Codabad and his brothers
  In The Arabian nights p264-89 **398.2**
The **History** of Dwarf Long Nose
  In The Andrew Lang Fairy tale treasury p534-56 **398.2**
  See also Longnose, the dwarf
The **History** of Jack and the beanstalk
  In The Classic fairy tales p164-74 **398.2**
  See also Jack and the bean-stalk
The **History** of Jack and the giants
  In The Classic fairy tales p51-65 **398.2**
  See also Jack the giant-killer
The **History** of Jack the giant-killer
  In Blue fairy book p328-36 **398.2**
  See also Jack the giant-killer
History of the young king of the Black Isles
  In The Arabian nights p67-80 **398.2**
The **History** of Tom Thumb
  In The Classic fairy tales p33-46 **398.2**
  See also Tom Thumb
The **history** of Tom Thumb. Jacobs, J.
  In The Fairy tale treasury p72-77 **398.2**
  In Jacobs, J. English fairy tales p140-47 **398.2**
  See also Tom Thumb
The **History** of Whittington
  In Blue fairy book p217-26 **398.2**
  See also Dick Whittington and his cat
Hitchcock, Alfred
  (comp.) Alfred Hitchcock's Supernatural tales of terror and suspense. See Alfred Hitchcock's Supernatural tales of terror and suspense **S C**
Hitler, Adolf
  Goldston, R. The life and death of Nazi Germany (5 and up) **943.086**
  See also pages in the following book:
  Hall, E. The land and people of Czechoslovakia p93-99 (5 and up) **943.7**
Hitopadésa
  Brown, M. Once a mouse **398.2**
Hitopadesa; excerpts. Gaer, J.
  In Gaer, J. The fables of India p53-116 **398.2**
Hitty: her first hundred years. Field, R. **Fic**
Hoag, Edwin
  American houses: colonial, classic, and contemporary (6 and up) **728**
Hoban, Lillian
  Arthur's Christmas cookies **E**
  Arthur's honey bear. See note under Hoban, L. Arthur's Christmas cookies **E**

Hoban, Lillian—*Continued*

Arthur's pen pal. See note under Hoban, L. Arthur's Christmas cookies **E**

Arthur's prize reader. See note under Hoban, L. Arthur's Christmas cookies **E**

The sugar snow spring **E**

(illus.) Cohen, M. Will I have a friend? **E**

(illus.) Delton, J. The new girl at school **E**

(illus.) Feder, P. K. Where does the teacher live? **E**

(illus.) Fisher, A. In one door and out the other **811**

(illus.) Hoban, R. Egg thoughts, and other Frances songs **811**

(illus.) Hoban, R. Emmet Otter's Jug-Band Christmas **E**

(illus.) Hoban, R. The little Brute family **E**

(illus.) Hoban, R. The Mole family's Christmas **E**

(illus.) Hoban, R. The mouse and his child **Fic**

(illus.) Hoban, R. Nothing to do **E**

(illus.) Hoban, R. The sorely trying day **E**

(illus.) Willard, N. Papa's panda **E**

Hoban, Russell

Arthur's new power. See note under Hoban, R. Dinner at Alberta's **E**

A baby sister for Frances. See note under Hoban, R. Bedtime for Frances **E**

A bargain for Frances. See note under Hoban, R. Bedtime for Frances **E**

Bedtime for Frances **E**

Best friends for Frances. See note under Hoban, R. Bedtime for Frances **E**

A birthday for Frances. See note under Hoban, R. Bedtime for Frances **E**

Bread and jam for Frances. See note under Hoban, R. Bedtime for Frances **E**

Dinner at Alberta's **E**

Egg thoughts, and other Frances songs (k-2) **811**

Emmet Otter's Jug-Band Christmas **E**

How Tom beat Captain Najork and his hired sportsmen **E**

The little Brute family **E**

The Mole famliy's Christmas **E**

The mouse and his child (4-6) **Fic**

A near thing for Captain Najork. See note under Hoban, R. How Tom beat Captain Najork and his sportsmen **E**

Nothing to do **E**

The sorely trying day **E**

The stone doll of Sister Brute. See note under Hoban, R. The little Brute family **E**

Hoban, Tana

Circles, triangles and squares **E**

Big ones, little ones **E**

Count and see **E**

Dig, drill, dump, fill (k-2) **621.8**

Is it red? Is it yellow? Is it blue? (k-2) **535.6**

Look again! **E**

One little kitten **E**

Over, under & through, and other spatial concepts **E**

Push pull, empty full **E**

Shapes and things **E**

Where is it? **E**

Hobberdy Dick. Briggs, K. M. **Fic**

The **hobbit.** Tolkien, J. R. R. **Fic**

The **hobbit;** excerpt. Tolkien, J. R. R.
In The Arbuthnot Anthology of children's literature p555-57 **808.8**

Hoberman, Mary Ann

Nuts to you & nuts to me (k-2) **811**

A **hobo** adventure. Carlson, N. S.
In The Arbuthnot Anthology of children's literature p712-16 **808.8**

Hoboes. See Tramps

The **Hoboken** chicken emergency. Pinkwater, D. M. **Fic**

Hobson, Burton

(ed.) Reinfeld, F. How to build a coin collection **737.4**

Hobyahs

The Hobyahs
In Juba this and Juba that p51-54 **372.6**

Jacobs, J. The Hobyahs
In Giants & witches and a dragon or two p174-77 **398.2**

Stern, S. Hobyahs **398.2**

Hockey. See Ice hockey

Hockey talk for beginners. Liss, H. **796.96**

The **hockey** trick. Corbett, S. See note under Corbett, S. The lemonade trick **Fic**

The **hodgepodge** book. Emrich, D. comp. **398**

Hodges, C . Walter

The battlement garden (6 and up) **942.05**

(illus.) Serraillier, I. The silver sword **Fic**

(illus.) Twain, M. The adventures of Huckleberry Finn **Fic**

(illus.) Twain, M. The adventures of Tom Sawyer **Fic**

Hodges, David

(illus.) Blassingame, W. Story of the Boy Scouts **369.43**

(illus.) Clayton, E. Martin Luther King: the peaceful warrior **92**

(illus.) Montgomery, E. R. William C. Handy: father of the blues **92**

Hodges, Margaret

Baldur and the mistletoe (4-6) **293**

The Fire Bringer (2-4) **398.2**

The freewheeling Joshua Cobb (4 and up) **Fic**

Persephone and the springtime (k-3) **292**

The wave (3-5) **398.2**

also in Time for old magic p217-19 **398.2**

Hodgson, Mary Anne

Fast and easy needlepoint (3-6) **746.44**

Hodgson, Richard

See pages in the following book:

Cohen, D. In search of ghosts p120-27 (6 and up) **133**

Hodgson, Sheila

Slip stream
In Alfred Hitchcock's Supernatural tales of terror and suspense p68-75 **S C**

The whistling room
In Haunts, haunts, haunts p140-59 **S C**

Hodson, Haro. See Haro

Hoff, Syd

Barkley **E**

Danny and the dinosaur **E**

Gentleman Jim [Corbett] and the great John L. (1-3) **92**

Irving and me (5 and up) **Fic**

(illus.) Lexau, J. M. The homework caper **E**

(illus.) Lexau, J. M. I should have stayed in bed **E**

(illus.) Lexau, J. M. The rooftop mystery **E**

Horses—Fiction—*Continued*

Henry, M. King of the Wind (4 and up)   **Fic**

Henry, M. San Domingo: The medicine hat stallion (4-6)   **Fic**

James, W. Smoky, the cow horse (6 and up)   **Fic**

Lawson, R. Mr Revere and I (5 and up)   **Fic**

Merrill, J. The superlative horse (4-6)   **Fic**

Peet, B. Cowardly Clyde   **E**

Rockwood, J. Groundhog's horse (4-6)   **Fic**

Sewell, A. Black Beauty   **Fic**

Ward, L. The silver pony   **Fic**

Wormser, R. The black mustanger (5 and up)   **Fic**

History

Burt, O. W. The horse in America (5 and up)   **636.1**

Darling, L. Sixty million years of horses (4 and up)   **636.1**

Infancy

Isenbart, H. H. A foal is born (k-3)   **636.1**

Law and legislation

Weiss, A. E. Save the mustangs! (3-5)   **328.73**

Hort, Pamela

(illus.) Schnurnberger, L. E. Kings, queens, knights & jesters: making medieval costumes   **391.09**

Horticulture

See also Gardening

Horton hatches the egg. Seuss, Dr   **E**

Horton hears a Who! Seuss, Dr. See note under Seuss, Dr. Horton hatches the egg   **E**

Horvath, Joan

Filmmaking for beginners (6 and up)   **778.5**

Hosford, Dorothy G.

Thunder of the gods (5 and up)   **293**

Hosie's alphabet   **E**

Hosie's aviary   **598**

Hospital ships. See Hope (ship)

Hospitals

Beame, R. Emergency! (3-6)   **362.1**

Marino, B. P. Eric needs stitches (k-3)   **362.1**

Sobol, H. L. Jeff's hospital book (k-3)   **362.1**

Weber, A. Elizabeth gets well (k-3)   **362.1**

Bibliography

See pages in the following book:

Fassler, J. Helping children cope p51-85   **016.3627**

Fiction

Singer, M. It can't hurt forever (4 and up)   **Fic**

The **hoss**-mackerel and Bassoon Bobby. Stoutenburg, A.

In Stoutenburg, A. American tall-tale animals p68-79   **398.2**

Hot Air Engines. See Heat engines

Hot and cold. Adler, I.   **536**

Hot as an ice cube. Balestrino, P.   **536**

Hot cross buns, and other old street cries   **398**

Hotchkiss, Jeanette

American historical fiction and biography for children and young people   **016.8**

European historical fiction and biography for children and young people   **016.8**

The **hotel** cat. Averill, E. See note under Averill, E. The school for cats   **E**

Hotels, motels, etc.

Fiction

Burch, R. Skinny (4-6)   **Fic**

Cohen, B. The innkeeper's daughter (6 and up)   **Fic**

Houck, Carter

Warm as wool, cool as cotton (3-6)   **677**

Houdini: master of escape. Kendall, L.   **92**

Houdini, Harry

Ernst, J. Escape king: the story of Harry Houdini (4 and up)   **92**

Kendall, L. Houdini: master of escape (6 and up)   **92**

Hough, Richard

The Battle of Britain (5 and up)   **940.54**

Hound and Bear. Gackenbach, D.   **E**

The **house** at Pooh Corner. Milne, A. A.   **Fic**

also in Milne, A. A. The world of Pooh p153-314 (1-4)   **Fic**

The **house** in the middle of the road. Aardema, V.

In Aardema, V. Behind the back of the mountain p74-80   **398.2**

House in the wood

Grimm, J. The hut in the forest

In Grimm, J. The complete Grimm's fairy tales p698-704   **398.2**

In Time for old magic p52-54   **398.2**

The **house** in the woods. Sechrist, E. H.

In Sechrist, E. H. Once in the first times p128-31   **398.2**

House of Bourbon. See Bourbon, House of

The **house** of Dies Drear. Hamilton, V.   **Fic**

The **house** of Dies Drear; excerpt. Hamilton, V.

In The Arbuthnot Anthology of children's literature p646-55   **808.8**

The **house** of ice and the house of wood. Riordan, J.

In Riordan, J. Tales from Central Russia p112-14   **398.2**

A **house** of promegranates. See Wilde, O. The Happy Prince, and other stories   **S C**

The **house** of sixty fathers. DeJong, M.   **Fic**

The **house** of wings. Byars, B.   **Fic**

The **house** on East 88th Street. Waber, B.   **E**

The **house** on Parchment Street. McKillip, P. A.   **Fic**

House painting

Fiction

Spier, P. Oh, were they ever happy!   **E**

House plans. See Architecture, Domestic—Designs and plans

House plants

Baker, S. S. The indoor and outdoor grow-it book (1-6)   **635**

Cutler, K. N. Growing a garden, indoors or out (4 and up)   **635**

Kramer, J. Plant sculptures (4-6)   **635.9**

Millard, A. Plants for kids to grow indoors (4-6)   **635.9**

Paul, A. Kids gardening (3-6)   **635.9**

Selsam, M. E. How to grow house plants (4-6)   **635.9**

See also pages in the following book:

Limburg, P. R. Poisonous plants p11-20 (4 and up)   **681.6**

The **house** surgeon. Kipling, R.
In Haunts, haunts, haunts p24-51 **S C**
The **house** that hated war. Harter, W.
In Harter, W. Osceola's head, and other American ghost stories p31-37 **S C**
The **House** that Jack built **398**
The **house** that Jack built. Caldecott, R.
In Caldecott, R. The Randolph Caldecott treasury p165-204 **741.9**
In Randolph Caldecott's John Gilpin and other stories **398**
The **house** that Jack built. Rockwell, A.
In Rockwell, A. The three bears & 15 other stories p45-52 **398.2**
House that Jack built; adaptation. See Heilbroner, J. This is the house where Jack lives **E**
The **house** with a clock in its walls. Bellairs, J. **Fic**
The **house** that lacked a bogle. Nic Leodhas, S.
In A-haunting we will go p95-105 **S C**
Housebuilding for children. Walker, L. **690**
Household, Geoffrey
Escape into daylight (6 and up) **Fic**
Household employees
See pages in the following book:
Sandler, M. W. The way we lived p90-95 (4 and up) **331.09**
Household moving. See Moving, Household
Household stories. Grimm, J. **398.2**
Housekeeping. See Home economics
Housemaids. See Household employees
Houses
Hoag, E. American houses: colonial, classic, and contemporary (6 and up) **723**
Huntington, L. P. Simple shelters (3-5) **728**
Myller, R. From idea into house (5 and up) **728**
Siberell, A. Houses (2-4) **728**
Sobol, H. L. Pete's house (3-5) **690**
Walker, L. Housebuilding for children **690**
See also pages in the following books:
Caney, S. Steven Caney's Kids' America p66-93 (4 and up) **790.1**
Kirk, R. Hunters of the whale p149-54 (5 and up) **970.004**
See also Apartment houses

Fiction
Burton, V. L. The little house **E**
Calhoun, M. Katie John (4-6) **Fic**
Houses, Sod. See Sod houses
Houses from the sea. Goudey, A. E. **594**
Houses of animals. See Animals—Habitations
Housman, Laurence
The rat-catcher's daughter (4 and up) **S C**
Contents: The rat-catcher's daughter; Rocking-Horse Land; Gammelyn, the dressmaker; The traveller's shoes; The wooing of the maze; Moozipoo; The Cloak of Friendship; The Prince with the nine sorrows; The white doe; A Chinese fairy tale; Happy returns; Knoonie in the sleeping palace
Rocking-Horse Land
In Told under the magic umbrella p180-88 **S C**
Houston, James
Frozen fire (6 and up) **Fic**
Ghost paddle (4-6) **Fic**
Kiviok's magic journey **398.2**
(ed.) Songs of the dream people. See Songs of the dream people **897**
Tikta'liktak (4-6) **398.2**

Hou-tien, Cheng. See Cheng, Hou-tien
How a fish swam in the air and a hare in water
Afanas'ev, A. The indiscreet wife
In Afanas'ev, A. Russian fairy tales p226-27 **398.2**
How a husband weaned his wife from fairy tales. Afanas'ev, A.
In Afanas'ev, A. Russian fairy tales p308 **398.2**
See also Cure for story-telling
How a law is made. Stevens, L. A. **328.73**
How a peasant cured his wife of telling tales. Riordan, J.
In Riordan, J. Tales from Central Russia p233-37 **398.2**
See also Cure for story-telling
How a rock came to be in a fence on a road near a town. Ruchlis, H. **552**
How a seed grows. Jordan, H. J. **582**
How a skyscraper and a railroad train got picked up and carried away from Pig's Eye Valley far in the Pickax Mountains. Sandburg, C.
In Sandburg, C. Rootabaga stories v2 p191-97 **S C**
In Sandburg, C. The Sandburg treasury p152-54 **818**
How a wolf reforms
In Jataka tales p60-61 **398.2**
How animals brought fire to man. Fisher, A. B.
In Fisher, A. B. Stories California Indians told p46-53 **398.2**
How animals communicate. Dean, A. **591.5**
How animals defend their young. Freedman, R. **591.5**
How animals hide. McClung, R. M. **591.5**
How animals learn. Freedman, R. **591.5**
How animals live together. Selsam, M. E. **591.5**
How the animals lost their tails and got them back traveling from Philadelphia to Medicine Hat. Sandburg, C.
In Sandburg, C. The Sandburg treasury p81-86 **818**
How animals tell time. Selsam, M. E. **591.5**
How autumn came to the earth; play. Woolsey, J.
In It's time for Thanksgiving p164-74 **394.2**
How babies are made. Andry, A. C. **612**
How Bimbo the Snip's thumb stuck in his nose when the wind changed. Sandburg, C.
In Sandburg, C. Rootabaga stories v 1 p123-28 **S C**
In Sandburg, C. The Sandburg treasury p51-54 **818**
How birds fly. Freedman, R. **598**
How birds learn to sing. Ford, B. **598**
How Blue Crane taught Jackal to fly. Aardema, V.
In Aardema, V. Behind the back of the mountain p26-33 **398.2**
How Bobtail beat the Devil
In Grandfather tales p88-98 **398.2**
How Boots befooled the king
Pyle, H. How Boots befooled the king
In It's time for story hour p146-53 **372.6**
In Pyle, H. The wonder clock p135-47 **398.2**

How Bozo the Button Buster busted all his buttons when a mouse came. Sandburg, C.
In Sandburg, C. Rootabaga stories v2 p63-71 **S C**
In Sandburg, C. The Sandburg treasury p110-12 **818**

How Brer Rabbit was too sharp for Brer Fox. Harris, J. C.
In The Golden Treasury of children's literature p224-25 **808.8**

How Brother Rabbit fooled the whale and the elephant. Bryant, S. C.
In It's time for story hour p132-35 **372.6**

How California was made. Fisher, A. B.
In Fisher, A. B. Stories California Indians told p10-15 **398.2**

How come Christmas. Bradford, R.
In Rollins, C. comp. Christmas gif' p26-32 **394.2**

How Coyote became a friend to man. Fisher, A. B.
In Fisher, A. B. Stories California Indians told p74-79 **398.2**

How Coyote got his voice. Fisher, A. B.
In Fisher, A. B. Stories California Indians told p36-45 **398.2**

How Coyote helped to light the world. Fisher, A. B.
In Fisher, A. B. Stories California Indians told p16-23 **398.2**

How Coyote put fish in Clear Lake. Fisher, A. B.
In Fisher, A. B. Stories California Indians told p80-86 **398.2**

How Coyote put salmon in the Klamath River. Fisher, A. B.
In Fisher, A. B. Stories California Indians told p96-102 **398.2**

How Coyote stole fire. Robinson, G.
In North American legends p52-56 **398.2**

How crab got a hard back. Sherlock, P.
In Sherlock, P. West Indian folk-tales p86-92 **398.2**

How Dame Margery Twist saw more than was good for her
Pyle, H. How Dame Margery Twist saw more than was good for her
In Pyle, H. Pepper & salt p28-42 **398.2**

How death came to the world (Kiowa). Marriott, A.
In Marriott, A. American Indian mythology **398.2**

How death came to the world (Modoc). Marriott, A.
In Marriott, A. American Indian mythology **398.2**

How Deep Red Roses goes back and forth between the clock and the looking glass. Sandburg, C.
In Sandburg, C. Rootabaga stories v2 p97-104 **S C**
In Sandburg, C. The Sandburg treasury p121-23 **818**

How democracy failed. Switzer, E. **943.085**

How did numbers begin? Sitomer, M **513**

How did we find out about Antarctica? Asimov, I. **998**

How did we find out about black holes? Asimov, I. **523.8**

How did we find out about earthquakes? Asimov, I. **551.2**

How did we find out about germs? Asimov, I. **616**

How did we find out about nuclear power? Asimov, I. **539.7**

How did we find out about our human roots? Asimov, I. **573.2**

How did we find out about outer space? Asimov, I. **629.4**

How did we find out about vitamins? Asimov, I. **613.2**

How did we find out the earth is round? Asimov, I. **525**

How Dippy the Wisp and Slip me Liz came in the moonshine where the Potato Face Blind Man sat with his accordion. Sandburg, C.
In Sandburg, C. Rootabaga stories v2 p115-26 **S C**
In Sandburg, C. The Sandburg treasury p127-31 **818**

How Djadja-em-ankh saved the day **398.2**

How do I put it on? Getting dressed. Watanabe, Shigeo **E**

How do you hide a monster? Kahl, V. **E**

How does it feel to be old? Farber, N. **811**

How does it feel when your parents get divorced? Berger T. **306.8**

How Dog outwitted Leopard. Aardema, V.
In Aardema, V. Tales from the story hat p49-52 **398.2**

How El Bizarrón fooled the Devil. Carter, D. S.
In Carter, D. S. Greedy Mariani, and other folktales of the Antilles p23-29 **398.2**

How far is it to Jacob Cooper's? Jagendorf, M. A.
In Jagendorf, M. A. Folk stories of the South p17-19 **398.2**

How fear came. Kipling, R.
In Kipling, R. The second jungle book p 1-22 **S C**

How footbinding started
Carpenter, F. Big feet of the Empress Tu Chin
In Carpenter, F. Tales of a Chinese grandmother p81-88 **398.2**

How Gimme the Ax found out about the zigzag railroad and who made it zigzag. Sandburg, C.
In Sandburg, C. Rootabaga stories v 1 p65-70 **S C**
In Sandburg, C. The Sandburg treasury p31-32 **818**

How Glooskap found the summer. Leland, C.
In North American legends p57-59 **398.2**

How Googler and Gaggler, the two Christmas babies, came home with monkey wrenches. Sandburg, C.
In Sandburg, C. Rootabaga stories v2 p75-85 **S C**
In Sandburg, C. The Sandburg treasury p113-17 **818**

How grandpa mowed the lord's meadow. Ginsburg, M.
In Ginsburg, M. The twelve clever brothers, and other fools p20-23 **398.2**

How Henry Hagglyhoagly played the guitar with his mittens on. Sandburg, C.
In Sandburg, C. Rootabaga stories v 1 p175-83 **S C**
In Sandburg, C. The Sandburg treasury p69-71 **818**

How, Hippo! Brown, M.   **E**

How Horace learned to moan. Ireland, E.
  In A-haunting we will go p20-27   **S C**

How horses came to the Navaho. Marriott, A.
  In Marriott, A. American Indian mythology   **398.2**

How Hot Balloons and his pigeon daughters crossed over into the Rootabaga country. Sandburg, C.
  In Sandburg, C. Rootabaga stories v2 p127-37   **S C**
  In Sandburg, C. The Sandburg treasury p131-34   **818**

How I crossed the street for the first time all by myself. Gardner, H.
  In Free to be . . . you and me p100-11
                                    810.8

How I hunted the little fellows. Zhitkov, B.
                                    Fic

How ice cream came. Bailey, C. S.
  In Gruenberg, S. M. ed. Favorite stories old and new p223-25   **808.8**

How Ijapa, who was short, became long. Courlander, H.
  In Courlander, H. Olode the hunter, and other tales from Nigeria p37-39
                                    398.2

How Indians really lived. Baldwin, G. C.
                                    970.004

How it works. Papallo, G.
  In Papallo, G. What makes it work   **600**

How Jack went to seek his fortune
Jacobs, J. How Jack went to seek his fortune
  In Jacobs, J. English fairy tales p24-27
                                    398.2
Palmer, F. L. How Jack went to seek his fortune
  In North American legends p141-43   **398.2**

How Jahdu became himself. Hamilton, V.
  In Hamilton, V. The time-ago tales of Jahdu   **S C**

How Jahdu discovered the light and found enough time. Hamilton, V.
  In Hamilton, V. Time-ago lost: more tales of Jahdu p41-68   **S C**

How Jahdu found a fire to light his way. Hamilton, V.
  In Hamilton, V. Time-ago lost: more tales of Jahdu p22-40   **S C**

How Jahdu found his power. Hamilton, V.
  In Hamilton, V. The time-ago tales of Jahdu   **S C**

How Jahdu ran through darkness in no time at all. Hamilton, V.
  In Hamilton, V. Time-ago lost: more tales of Jahdu p 1-21   **S C**

How Jahdu took care of trouble. Hamilton, V.
  In Hamilton, V. The time-ago tales of Jahdu   **S C**

How Joe became Snaky Joe. Jagendorf, M. A.
  In Jagendorf, M. A. Folk stories of the South p271-75   **398.2**

How Johnny the Whan sleeps in money all the time and Joe the Wimp shines and sees things. Sandburg, C.
  In Sandburg, C. Rootabaga stories v2 p87-84   **S C**
  In Sandburg, C. The Sandburg treasury p117-20   **818**

How Juan married a princess. Sechrist, E. H.
  In Sechrist, E. H. Once in the first times p135-40   **398.2**

How kittens grow. Selsam, M. E.   **636.8**

How Lee Edward went running along with Jahdu. Hamilton, V.
  In Hamilton, V. Time-ago lost: more tales of Jahdu p69-85   **S C**

How little and how much. Branley, F M.   **389**

How Little Pear wanted both a top and a tang-hulur. Lattimore, E. F.
  In Gruenberg, S. M. ed. Favorite stories old and new p72-74   **808.8**

How locusts came to be. Sechrist, E. H.
  In Sechrist, E. H. Once in the first times p34-37   **398.2**

How many donkeys?
Kelsey, A. G. How many donkeys?
  In The Arbuthnot Anthology of children's literature p300-01   **808.8**
  In Time for old magic p179-80   **398.2**

How many miles to Babylon? Fox, P.   **Fic**

How many miles to Babylon? excerpt. Fox, P.
  In The Arbuthnot Anthology of children's literature p633-38   **808.8**

How many miles to sundown. Beatty, P.   **Fic**

How Mrs Fox married again. Grimm, J.
  In Grimm, J. Household stories p167-70
                                    398.2

  See also Wedding of Mrs Fox

How Moremi saved the town of Ife. Courlander, H.
  In Courlander, H. Olode the hunter, and other tales from Nigeria p113-17
                                    398.2

How much land does a man need? Leech, M. T.
  In Popular plays for classroom reading p284-99   **808.82**

How new life begins. Meeks, E. K.   **574.1**

How ol' Paul changed the map of America. Malcolmson, A.
  In Malcolmson, A. Yankee Doodle's cousins p251-60   **398.2**

How Old Stormalong captured Mocha Dick. Shapiro, I.
  In Shapiro, I. Heroes in American folklore p58-104   **398.2**

How Ole Woodpecker got Ole Rabbit's conjure bag. Owen, M. A.
  In North American legends p115-21
                                    398.2

How Ologbon-Ori sought wisdom. Courlander, H.
  In Courlander, H. Olode the hunter, and other tales from Nigeria p65-68
                                    398.2

How one turned his troubles to some account
Pyle, H. How one turned his troubles to some account
  In Pyle, H. The wonder clock p27-38
                                    398.2

How Pa learned to grow hot peppers. Credle, E.
  In Credle, E. Tales from the high hills, and other stories p67-81   **398.2**

How Pan Ku made the world
Carpenter, F. How Pan Ku made the world
  In Carpenter, F. Tales of a Chinese grandmother p14-21   **398.2**

How Pat got good sense. Finger, C. J.
  In Time to laugh p3-16   **S C**

How Paul Bonjean became Paul Bunyan. Malcolmson, A.
  In Malcolmson, A. Yankee Doodle's cousins p231-40   **398.2**

How Pink Peony sent Spuds, the ballplayer, up to pick four moons. Sandburg, C.
In Sandburg, C. Rootabaga stories v2 p105-11 **S C**
In Sandburg, C. The Sandburg treasury p124-26 **818**

How plants are pollinated. Rahn, J. E. **581.1**

How poverty was revealed to the King of Adja. Courlander, H.
In Courlander, H. The king's drum, and other African stories p45-49 **398.2**

How puppies grow. Selsam, M. E. **636.7**

How Rag Bag Mammy kept her secret while the wind blew away the Village of Hat Pins. Sandburg, C.
In Sandburg, C. Rootabaga stories v2 p33-40 **S C**
In Sandburg, C. The Sandburg treasury p100-02 **818**

How red strawberries brought peace in the woods. Jagendorf, M. A.
In Jagendorf, M. A. Folk stories of the South p33-35 **398.2**

How Saynday brought the buffalo
In Winter-telling stories p12-24 **398.2**

How Saynday got caught in a buffalo skull
In Winter-telling stories p39-46 **398.2**

How Saynday got caught in a tree
In Winter-telling stories p54-60 **398.2**

How Saynday got the sun
In North American legends p65-70 **398.2**
In Winter-telling stories p3-12 **398.2**

How Saynday ran a foot race with Coyote
In Winter-telling stories p47-54 **398.2**

How Saynday tried to marry the whirlwind
In Winter-telling stories p70-74 **398.2**

How she brightened her home. Newell, H.
In Newell, H. The little woman who used her head, and other stories p105-12 **S C**

How she did her marketing. Newell, H.
In Newell, H. The little old woman who used her head, and other stories p33-39 **S C**

How she finished her red muffler. Newell, H.
In Newell, H. The little old woman who used her head, and other stories p27-32 **S C**

How she got a feather bed. Newell, H.
In Newell, H. The little old woman who used her head, and other stories p12-16 **S C**

How she got her fortune told. Newell, H.
In Newell, H. The little old woman who used her head, and other stories p69-76 **S C**

How she kept her geese warm. Newell, H.
In Newell, H. The little old woman who used her head, and other stories p22-26 **S C**

How she kept herself cheerful. Newell, H.
In Newell, H. The little old woman who used her head, and other stories p64-68 **S C**

How she made the baby elephant happy. Newell, H.
In Newell, H. The little old woman who used her head, and other stories p57-63 **S C**

How she put up her Christmas tree. Newell, H.
In Newell, H. The little old woman who used her head, and other stories p113-18 **S C**

How she rested her head. Newell, H.
In Newell, H. The little old woman who used her head, and other stories p40-43 **S C**

How she saved her corn. Newell, H.
In Newell, H. The little old woman who used her head, and other stories p17-21 **S C**

How she saved her pennies. Newell, H.
In Newell, H. The little old woman who used her head, and other stories p98-104 **S C**

How she saw the circus come to town. Newell, H.
In Newell, H. The little old woman who used her head, and other stories p52-56 **S C**

How she spent Christmas Eve. Newell, H.
In Newell, H. The little old woman who used her head, and other stories p126-27 **S C**

How she took things easy. Newell, H.
In Newell, H. The little old woman who used her head, and other stories p44-51 **S C**

How she traveled on land. Newell, H.
In Newell, H. The little old woman who used her head, and other stories p77-85 **S C**

How she traveled on water. Newell, H.
In Newell, H. The little old woman who used her head, and other stories p86-97 **S C**

How she trimmed her tree. Newell, H.
In Newell, H. The little old woman who used her head, and other stories p119-25 **S C**

How six men got on in the world. Grimm, J.
In Grimm, J. The complete Grimm's fairy tales p344-49 **398.2**
See also How six men travelled through the wide world

How six men travelled through the wide world
Grimm, J. How six men got on in the world
In Grimm, J. The complete Grimm's fairy tales p344-49 **398.2**
Grimm, J. How six men travelled through the wide world
In The Andrew Lang Fairy tale treasury p299-304 **398.2**
Grimm, J. Six men who go far together in the wide world
In Grimm, J. The Brothers Grimm: popular folk tales p139-45 **398.2**
In Yellow fairy book p95-100 **398.2**
Grimm, J. Six soldiers of fortune
In Grimm, J. Household stories p3-8 **398.2**
Grimm, J. The soldier and his magic helpers
In Grimm, J. More Tales from Grimm p63-75 **398.2**

How six pigeons came back to Hatrack the Horse after many accidents and six telegrams. Sandburg, C.
In Sandburg, C. Rootabaga stories v2 p41-48 **S C**
In Sandburg, C. The Sandburg treasury p103-06 **818**

How six umbrellas took off their straw hats to show respect to the one big umbrella. Sandburg, C.
In Sandburg, C. Rootabaga stories v2 p55-62   **S C**
In Sandburg, C. The Sandburg treasury p107-10   **818**

How Sly-Fox was fooled. Soyer, A.
In Soyer, A. The adventures of Yemima, and other stories p14-20   **S C**

How Spider got a bald head. Arkhurst, J. C.
In Arkhurst, J. C. The adventures of Spider p21-30   **398.2**

How Spider got a thin waist. Arkhurst, J. C.
In Arkhurst, J. C. The adventures of Spider p5-10   **398.2**

How Spider helped a fisherman. Arkhurst, J. C.
In Arkhurst, J. C. The adventures of Spider p32-38   **398.2**

How straws were invented
In Jataka tales p51-53   **398.2**

How summer came to Canada. Toye, W.   **398.2**

How Sun, Moon, and Wind went out to dinner
In Indian fairy tales p218-20   **398.2**

How Susan became rich. Sechrist, E. H.
In Sechrist, E. H. Once in the first times p177-84   **398.2**

How the alphabet was made. Kipling, R.
In Kipling, R. Just so stories   **S C**

How the animals came to North America. May, J.   **591.5**

How the animals got their fur coats. Hooke, H. M.
In Hooke, H. M. Thunder in the mountains p5-15   **398.2**

How the animals lost their tails and got them back traveling from Philadelphia to Medicine Hat. Sandburg, C.
In Sandburg, C. Rootabaga stories v 1 p213-30   **S C**

How the bear lost his tail and the bees gained a friend. Riordan, J.
In Riordan, J. Tales from Tartary p44-45   **398.2**

How the birds got their colours. Hooke, H. M.
In Hooke, H. M. Thunder in the mountains p17-26   **398.2**

How the bobcat got his spots
In Winter-telling stories p62-70   **398.2**

How the body works. Wilson, R.   **612**

How the brothers joined the Cat Club. Averill, E.
In Averill, E. Jenny and the Cat Club   **S C**

How the camel got his hump. Kipling, R.
In Kipling, R. Just so stories   **S C**

How the cat swallowed thunder. Alexander, L.
In Just for fun p3-12   **S C**

How the clever doctor tricked death. Carter, D. S.
In Carter, D. S. Greedy Mariani, and other folktales of the Antilles p9-13   **398.2**

How the cock got his red crown. Hume, L. C.
In Hume, L. C. Favorite children's stories from China and Tibet p27-32   **398.2**

How the cow went under the ground. Faulkner, W. J.
In Faulkner, W. The days when the animals talked p152-57   **398.2**

How the cows flew across the sea. Jagendorf, M. A.
In Jagendorf, M. A. The gypsies' fiddle, and other gypsy tales p164-69   **398.2**

How the crow came to be black
In The Sound of flutes, and other Indian legends p57-59   **398.2**

How the deer lost his tail. Hume, L. C.
In Hume, L. C. Favorite children's stories from China and Tibet p109-14   **398.2**

How the doctor knows you're fine. Cobb, V.   **616**

How the dragon lost his tail. Cheney, C.
In Cheney, C. Tales from a Taiwan kitchen p13-14   **398.2**

How the eight old ones crossed the sea. Carpenter, F.
In Carpenter, F. Tales of a Chinese grandmother p150-58   **398.2**

How the elephant and the whale were tricked
Bryant, S. C. How Brother Rabbit fooled the whale and the elephant
In It's time for story hour p132-35   **372.6**

How the fiddler crabs came to be. Sechrist, E. H.
In Sechrist, E. H. Once in the first times p31-34   **398.2**

How the first letter was written. Kipling, R.
In Kipling, R. Just so stories   **S C**

How the first rainbow was made. Fisher, A. B.
In Fisher, A. B. Stories California Indians told p60-73   **398.2**

How the five rusty rats helped find a new village. Sandburg, C.
In Sandburg, C. Rootabaga stories v 1 p29-37   **S C**
In Sandburg, C. The Sandburg treasury p19-23   **818**

How the good gifts were used by two
Pyle, H. How the good gifts were used by two
In Pyle, H. The wonder clock p121-33   **398.2**

How the great rocks grew. Fisher, A. B.
In Fisher, A. B. Stories California Indians told p88-95   **398.2**

How the Grinch stole Christmas. Seuss, Dr   **E**

How the gypsy boy outsmarted death. Jagendorf, M. A.
In Jagendorf, M. A. The gypsies' fiddle, and other gypsy tales p129-33   **398.2**

How the half boys came to be. Marriott, A.
In Marriott, A. American Indian mythology   **398.2**

How the Helmites bought a barrel of justice. Simon S.
In Simon, S. The wisemen of Helm and their merry tales p67-76   **398.2**

How the hot ashes shovel helped Snoo Foo. Sandburg, C.
In Sandburg, C. Rootabaga stories v 1 p105-08   **S C**
In Sandburg, C. The Sandburg treasury p45-46   **818**

How the kakok bird came to be. Sechrist, E. H.
In Sechrist, E. H. Once in the first times p22-24   **398.2**

How the leopard got his claws. Achebe, C.   **Fic**

How the leopard got his spots. Kipling, R.   **Fic**
also in Kipling, R. Just so stories   **S C**

How the little owl's name was changed
Gillham, C. E. How the little owl's name was changed
In Time for old magic p263-65　**398.2**
How the little owl's name was changed. Gillham, C.
In The Arbuthnot Anthology of children's literature p394-96　**808.8**
In Time for old magic p263-65　**398.2**
How the lizard lost and regained his farm. Courlander, H.
In Courlander, H. The hat-shaking dance, and other tales from the Gold Coast p70-76　**398.2**
How the lizards got their markings. Sechrist, E. H.
In Sechrist, E. H. Once in the first times p49-51　**398.2**
How the millstones drowned. Simon, S.
In Simon, S. The wisemen of Helm and their merry tales p23-28　**398.2**
How the monkey came to be. Sechrist, E. H.
In Sechrist, E. H. Once in the first times p37-38　**398.2**
How the Moolah was taught a lesson. Titiev, E.
In Titiev, E. How the Moolah was taught a lesson & other tales from Russia p 1-8　**398.2**
How the Moolah was taught a lessson & other tales from Russia. Titiev, E.　**398.2**
How the moon and stars came to be. Sechrist, E. H.
In Sechrist, E. H. Once in the first times p12-13　**398.2**
How the moonfish came to be. Carter, D. S.
In Carter, D. S. Greedy Mariani, and other folktales of the Antilles p3-8　**398.2**
How the people came to the middle place. Marriott, A.
In Marriott, A. American Indian mythology　**398.2**
How the people of Ife became scattered. Courlander, H.
In Courlander, H. Olode the hunter, and other tales from Nigeria p110-12　**398.2**
How the Pilgrims built their towne in New England. Daugherty, J.
In Thanksgiving p99-103　**394.2**
How the Potato Face Man enjoyed himself on a fine spring morning. Sandburg, C.
In Sandburg, C. Rootabaga stories v 1 p45-51　**S C**
In Sandburg, C. The Sandburg treasury p25-26　**818**
How the princess' pride was broken
Pyle, H. How the princess' pride was broken
In Pyle, H. The wonder clock p267-78　**398.2**
How the Raja's son won the Princess Labam
How the Raja's son won the Princess Labam
In Indian fairy tales p3-16　**398.2**
How the rhinoceros got his skin. Kipling, R.　**Fic**
also in Kipling, R. Just so stories　**S C**
How the robber band was tricked
Duvoisin, R. How the robber band was tricked
In Duvoisin, R. The three sneezes, and other Swiss tales p223-29　**398.2**
How the robin's breast became red. Cooke, F. J.
In Stories to dramatize p77-78　**372.6**

How the rooster saved the day. Lobel, A.　**E**
How the seven brothers saved their sister. Penney, G. J.
In North American legends p33-39　**398.2**
How the singing water got to the tub
In Gruenberg, S. M. ed. Favorite stories old and new p40-44　**808.8**
How the Sioux Nation came into being
In The Sound of flutes, and other Indian legends p72-73　**398.2**
How the storm changed the signs. Andersen, H. C.
In Andersen, H. C. The complete fairy tales and stories p840-44　**S C**
How the sun was brought back to the sky. Ginsburg, M.　**398.2**
How the Swiss came to use the Alpine horn
Duvoisin, R. The alphorn
In Duvoisin, R. The three sneezes, and other Swiss tales p218-22　**398.2**
How the three wild Babylonian Baboons went away in the rain eating bread and butter. Sandburg, C.
In Sandburg, C. Rootabaga stories v2 p49-53　**S C**
In Sandburg, C. The Sandburg treasury p106-07　**818**
How the Thunder-Bird lost his courage. Hooke, H. M.
In Hooke, H. M. Thunder in the mountains p45-55　**398.2**
How the turtle saved his own life
Babbitt, E. C. How the turtle saved his own life
In Babbitt, E. C. Jataka tales p10-12　**398.2**
How the twelve clever brothers got their feet mixed up. Ginsburg, M.
In Ginsburg, M. The twelve clever brothers, and other fools p82-89　**398.2**
How the whale got his throat. Kipling, R.
In The Golden Treasury of children's literature p8-11　**808.8**
In Kipling, R. Just so stories　**S C**
How the wicked sons were duped
Knowles, J. H. How the wicked sons were duped
In Indian fairy tales p221-22　**398.2**
How the world got wisdom. Arkhurst, J. C.
In Arkhurst, J. C. The adventures of Spider p50-58　**398.2**
How the world was made (Cheyenne). Marriott, A.
In Marriott, A. American Indian mythology　**398.2**
How the world was made (Modoc). Marriott, A.
In Marriott, A. American Indian mythology　**398.2**
How the world was saved. Curtis, E. S.
In Curtis, E. S. The girl who married a ghost, and other tales from the north American Indian p81-95　**398.2**
How the world's first cities began. Gregor, A. S.　**935**
How they bring back the Village of Cream Puffs when the wind blows it away. Sandburg, C.
In The Arbuthnot Anthology of children's literature p570-71　**808.8**
In Sandburg, C. Rootabaga stories v 1 p19-27　**S C**
In Sandburg, C. The Sandburg treasury p17-19　**818**

How they broke away to go to the Rootabaga country. Sandburg, C.
In Sandburg, C. Rootabaga stories v 1 p3-17   **S C**
In Sandburg, C. The Sandburg treasury p10-16   **818**

How things work. Pollard, M.   **600**

How three went out into the wide world
Pyle, H. How three went out into the wide world
In Pyle, H. The wonder clock p39-48   **398.2**

How to be a clown. Meyer, C. R.   **791.3**

How to become a dragon. Cheney, C.
In Cheney, C. Tales from a Taiwan kitchen p75-78   **398.2**

How to become a witch. Leach, M.
In Leach, M. Whistle in the graveyard p98-99   **398.2**

How to bring up your pet dog. Unkelbach, K.   **636.7**

How to build a better mousetrap car—and other experimental science fun. Renner, A. G.   **507**

How to build a coin collection. Reinfeld, F.   **737.4**

How to cook soup upon a sausage pin. Andersen, H. C.
In Andersen, H. C. The complete fairy tales and stories p516-27   **S C**

How to count like a Martian. St John, G.   **513**

How to dig a hole to the other side of the world. McNulty, F.   **551.1**

How to do a science project. Webster, D.   **507**

How to draw with pen & brush. Zaidenberg, A.   **741.2**

How to eat a poem & other morsels (3-5) **821.08**

How to eat fried worms. Rockwell, T.   **Fic**

How to get it together when your parents are coming apart. Richards, A.   **306.8**

How to give a party. Frame, J.   **793.2**

How to grow house plants. Selsam, M. E.   **635.9**

How to improve your written English. Brandt, S. R.   **808**

How to keep a secret. James, E.   **652**

How to make a cloud. Bendick, J.   **551.5**

How to make & fly paper airplanes. Barnaby, R. S.   **629.133**

How to make and use electric motors. Renner, A. G.   **621.46**

How to make play places and secret hidy holes. Lane, J.   **745.592**

How to make snop snappers, and other fine things. Lopshire, R.   **745.592**

How to make whirligigs and whimmy diddles, and other American folkcraft objects. Pettit, F. H.   **745.5**

How to make your own books. Weiss, H.   **686**

How to make your own movies. Weiss, H.   **778.5**

How to make your science project scientific. Moorman, T.   **507**

How to paint with water colors. Zaidenberg, A.   **751.42**

How to photograph your world. Holland, V.   **770.28**

How to play better football. Jackson, C. P.   **796.332**

How to play better soccer. Jackson, C. P.   **796.334**

How to play drums. Rothman, J.   **789**

How to raise mice, rats, hamsters, and gerbils. Stein, S. B.   **636.08**

How to read and write poetry. Cosman, A.   **808.1**

How to run a railroad. Weiss, H.   **625.1**

How to tell corn fairies if you see 'em. Sandburg, C.
In Sandburg, C. Rootabaga stories v 1 p205-12   **S C**
In Sandburg, C. The Sandburg treasury p78-80   **818**
In Told under the magic umbrella p127-32   **S C**

How to understand auto racing. Olney, R. R.   **796.7**

How to use the Readers' guide to periodical literature   **051**

How to write a report. Brandt, S. R.   **808**

How to write codes and send secret messages. Peterson, J.   **652**

How Tom beat Captain Najork and his hired sportsmen. Hoban, R.   **E**

How two brothers improved their luck. Ginsburg, M.
In Ginsburg, M. The twelve clever brothers, and other fools p36-43   **398.2**

How two sweetheart dippies sat in the moonlight on a lumber yard fence and heard about the sooners and boomers. Sandburg, C.
In Sandburg, C. Rootabaga stories v2 p139-50   **S C**
In Sandburg, C. The Sandburg treasury p134-39   **818**

How two went into partnership
Pyle, H. How two went into partnership
In Pyle, H. The wonder clock p279-90   **398.2**

How was I born? Nilsson, L.   **612**

How we choose a President. Gray, L. L.   **324.6**

How we got our numbers. Kane, E. B.
In One hundred plays for children p144-50   **808.82**

How we named our states. Arnold, P.   **917.3**

How wild animals fight. Shuttlesworth, D. E.   **591.5**

How wise were the old men. Chrisman, A. B.
In Chrisman, A. B. Shen of the sea p42-57   **S C**

How you talk. Showers, P.   **612**

How Young Owl and almost everybody got tired of Jahdu. Hamilton, V.
In Hamilton, V. The time-ago tales of Jahdu   **S C**

How young Will Bradford made a great decision. Daugherty, J.
In Thanksgiving p45-48   **394.2**

Howard, Helen Littler
Candles for Christmas
In A Treasury of Christmas plays p372-75   **812.08**

Doctor Know All
In Popular plays for classroom reading p69-77   **808.82**
I'll share my fare
In One hundred plays for children p460-62   **808.82**

Hughes, Shirley
David and Dog E
George the babysitter E
Moving Molly E
(illus.) Stewart, M. The little broomstick Fic
Hughes, Ted
Moon-whales, and other Moon poems (6 and up) 821
Season songs (6 and up) 821
Hugo, Victor
The bishop's candlesticks
In Stories to dramatize p323-29 372.6
Hugo and Josephine. Gripe, M. Fic
Hull House, Chicago
Keller, G. F. Jane Addams (1-3) 92
See also pages in the following book:
Sechrist, E. H. It's time for brotherhood p47-52 (5 and up) 361
Hülsmann, Eva
(illus.) Rau, M. The giant panda at home 599.74
(illus.) Rau, M. The gray kangaroo at home 599.2
(illus.) Rau, M. The snow monkey at home 599.8
Hulton, Ann
See pages in the following book:
As I saw it: women who lived the American adventure p27-32 (6 and up) 973
Human anatomy. See Anatomy, Human
Human—and anti-human—values in children's books. Council on Interracial Books for Children. Racism and Sexism Resources Center for Educators 028.5
Human behavior
Burns, M. I am not a short adult! (3-6) 305.2
Bibliography
See pages in the following books:
Gillis, R. J. Children's books for times of stress p5-24 016.3627
Human body. See Anatomy, Human; Physiology
The **human** body: the brain. Elgin, K. 612
The **human** body: the digestive system. Elgin, K. 612
The **human** body: the heart. Elgin, K. 612
The **human** body: the muscles. Elgin, K. 612
The **human** body: the skeleton. Elgin, K. 612
Human color. See Color of people
Human ecology
Gregor, A. S. Man's mark on the land (4 and up) 304.2
See also Man—Influence on nature; Population
Human figure in art. See Anatomy, Artistic; Figure drawing
Human race. See Anthropology; Man
Human relations
Kalb, J. What every kid should know (5 and up) 158
Sechrist, E. H. It's time for brotherhood (5 and up) 361
See also Conflict of generations; Discrimination; Family; Human behavior; and interpersonal relations between individuals or group of individuals, e.g. Jews and Gentiles; Parent and child
Bibliography
Reading ladders for human relations 016.302

Human rights. See Civil rights
The **human** rights book. Meltzer, M. 323.4
The **humblest** place. DuBois, G.
In A Treasury of Christmas plays p112-28 812.08
Humboldt, Alexander, Freiherr von
See pages in the following book:
Shuttlesworth, D. E. The wildlife of South America p27-32 (5 and up) 591.9
Humbug Mountain. Fleischman, S. Fic
Humbug witch. Balian, L. E
Hume, Lotta Carswell
Favorite children's stories from China and Tibet (3-6) 398.2
Contents: Soo Tan the tiger and the little green frog; A Chinese Cinderella; The fox, the hare, and the toad have an argument; How the cock got his red crown; The cricket fight; The story of the tortoise and the monkey; The wishing cup; A hungry wolf; The tower that reached from Earth to Heaven; The fox outwits the tiger; The story of the fairy boat; The tiger in court; The magic pancakes at the Footbridge Tavern; The King of the Mountain; The jackals and the tiger; The fox turns a somersault; The country of the mice; How the deer lost his tail; The little hare's clever trick
The **hummingbird** and the carabao. Sechrist, E. H.
In Sechrist, E. H. Once in the first times p43-46 398.2
Hummingbird and the flower
Finger, C. Humming-bird and the flower
In Finger, C. Tales from silver lands p43-47 398.2
Hummingbirds
Gans, R. Hummingbirds in the garden (1-3) 598
Hummingbirds in the garden. Gans, R. 598
Humor. See Wit and humor
Humorous poetry
Ciardi, J. You read to me, I'll read to you (1-4) 811
Cole, W. comp. Humorous poetry for children (5 and up) 821.08
Fowke, E. comp. Ring around the moon 784.4
My tang's tungled and other ridiculous situations (3-6) 821.08
Silverstein, S. Where the sidewalk ends (3 and up) 811
What a wonderful bird the frog are (5 and up) 808.81
See also pages in the following book:
The Arbuthnot Anthology of children's literature p70-85 808.8
See also Nonsense verses
Collections
Love, K. comp. A little laughter (3-6) 821.08
Humorous poetry for children. Cole, W. comp. 821.08
Humorous stories. See Wit and humor
Humperdinck, Engelbert
Grimm, W. Hansel and Gretel 782.1
Humphrey, Grace
The last Thursday in November
In Harper, W. comp. The harvest feast p247-55 S C
The **hundred** dresses. Estes, E. Fic
The **hundred** penny box. Mathis, S. B. E

Hyde, Bruce G.
(jt. auth.) Hyde, M. O. Everyone's trash problem: nuclear wastes (4 and up)   **621.48**
(jt. auth.) Hyde, M. O. Know about drugs   **613.8**

Hyde, Douglas
Guleesh
In Fairy tales from many lands p34-51   **398.2**

Hyde, Margaret O.
Alcohol: drink or drug? (6 and up)   **613.8**
Everyone's trash problem: nuclear wastes (4 and up)   **621.48**
Know about alcohol (4 and up)   **613.8**
Know about drugs (4-6)   **613.8**
VD: the silent epidemic (5 and up)   **616.95**

Hydras. See Hydrozoa

Hydraulic engineering
See also Hydrodynamics

Hydraulic structures
See also Dams

Hydraulics
See also Hydrodynamics

Hydrodynamics
Branley, F. M. Floating and sinking (1-3)   **532**
Corbett, S. What makes a boat float? (3-5)   **532**
Kaufmann, J. Streamlined (2-4)   **531**

Hydroelectric power. See Water power

Hydrofoil boats
See pages in the following book:
Hellman, H. Transportation in the world of the future p130-45 (5 and up)   **380.5**

Hydrology. See Water

Hydroponics. See Plants—Soilless culture

Hydrozoa
See pages in the following book:
Simon, S. Pets in a jar p19-25 (4 and up)   **639**

Hyenas

Fiction
Prelutsky, J. The mean old mean hyena   **E**

Hygiene
Kozuszek, J. E. Hygiene (4-6)   **613**
See also Exercise

Hygiene, Social. See Venereal diseases

Hyman, Linda
Winslow Homer: America's old master (5 and up)   **92**

Hyman, Trina Schart
(illus.) Barrie, J. M. Peter Pan   **Fic**
(illus.) Brink, C. R. The bad times of Irma Baumlein   **Fic**
(illus.) Brink, C. R. Caddie Woodlawn   **Fic**
(illus.) Cameron, E. A room made of windows   **Fic**
(illus.) Carter, D. S. Greedy Mariani, and other folktales of the Antilles   **398.2**
(illus.) Farber, N. How does it feel to be old?   **811**
(illus.) Fritz, J. Why don't you get a horse, Sam Adams?   **92**
(illus.) Fritz, J. Will you sign here, John Hancock? (3-5)   **92**
(illus.) Gates, D. Two queens of heaven: Aphrodite [and] Demeter   **292**
(illus.) Gauch, P. L. On to Widecombe Fair   **398.2**

(illus.) Greene, E. comp. Clever cooks   **398.2**
(illus.) Grimm, J. Snow White   **398.2**
(illus.) Haviland, V. Favorite fairy tales told in Czechoslovakia   **398.2**
(illus.) Hunter, M. The walking stones   **Fic**
(illus.) Kimmel, M. M. Magic in the mist   **Fic**
(illus.) Livingston, M. C. ed. Listen, children, listen   **821.08**
(illus.) Meyer, C. The bread book   **641.8**
(illus.) Moeri, L. Star Mother's youngest child   **E**
(illus.) Nichols, R. The marrow of the world   **Fic**
(illus.) Nichols, R. A walk out of the world   **Fic**
(illus.) Pyle, H. King Stork   **398.2**
(illus.) St John, W. F. The ghost next door (4 and up)   **Fic**
(illus.) Sawyer, R. Joy to the world (3-6)   **394.2**
(illus.) Stearns, P. The mechanical doll   **Fic**
(illus.) Witch poems. See Witch poems   **811.08**

Hymenoptera. See Ants; Bees

Hymns
See pages in the following books:
Fireside book of folk songs p278-97   **784.4**
It's time for Easter p103-37 (4 and up)   **394.2**
Yolen, J. Simple gifts p81-88 (5 and up)   **289**
See also Carols

Hyndman, Robert Utley. See Wyndham, Robert

I

I am adopted. Lapsley, S.   **E**
I am an Orthodox Jew. Greene, L.   **296.7**
I am here: yo estoy aqui. Blue, R.   **E**
I am not a short adult! Burns, M.   **305.2**
I am the darker brother. Adoff, A. ed.   **811.08**
I am the running girl. Adoff, A.   **811**
I and Sproggy. Greene, C. C.   **Fic**
I can dance. Bullard, B.   **792.8**
I can do lots of things!
In Camp Fire Girls, Inc. The Camp Fire Blue Bird Series bk.3   **369.47**
I can do it by myself. Little, L. J.   **E**
I can fly. Brock, B.
In The Arbuthnot Anthology of children's literature p523-26   **808.8**
I can't said the ant. Cameron, P.   **E**
I carve stone. Fine, J.   **731.4**
I caught a lizard. Conklin, G.   **639**
I, Charlotte Forten, black and free. Longsworth, P.   **92**
I did it. Rockwell, H.   **745.5**
I greet the dawn. Dunbar, P. L.   **811**
The I hate mathematics! book. Burns, M.   **793.7**
I hate Red Rover. Lexau, J. M.   **E**
I have a sister—my sister is deaf. Peterson, J. W.   **362.4**
I heard a scream in the street. Larrick, N. comp.   **811.08**

Index to children's poetry; second supplement. Brewton, J. E. comp. **808.81**

Index to children's poetry; third supplement. See Brewton, J. E. comp. Index to poetry for children and young people, 1964-1969 **808.81**

Index to children's songs. Peterson, C. S. comp. **784.6**

Index to collective biographies for young readers. Silverman, J. **920**

Index to educational audio tapes
In National Information Center for Educational Media [NICEM Indexes to nonbook media] **016.3713**

Index to educational overhead transparencies
In National Information Center for Educational Media [NICEM indexes to nonbook media] **016.3713**

Index to educational records
In National Information Center for Educational Media [NICEM Indexes to nonbook media] **016.3713**

Index to educational slides
In National Information Center for Educational Media [NICEM Indexes to nonbook media] **016.3713**

Index to educational video tapes
In National Information Center for Educational Media [NICEM Indexes to nonbook media] **016.3713**

Index to 8mm motion cartridges
In National Information Center for Educational Media [NICEM Indexes to nonbook media] **016.3713**

Index to environmental studies—multimedia
In National Information Center for Educational Media [NICEM Indexes to nonbook media] **016.3713**

Index to fairy tales, myths and legends **398.2**

Index to fairy tales, myths and legends; supplement **398.2**

Index to fairy tales, myths and legends; second supplement **398.2**

Index to fairy tales, 1949-1972 **398.2**

Index to fairy tales, 1973-1977 **398.2**

Index to health and safety education—multimedia
In National Information Center for Educational Media [NICEM Indexes to nonbook media] **016.3713**

Index to nonprint special education materials—multimedia (learner volume)
In National Information Center for Educational Media [NICEM Indexes to nonbook media] **016.3713**

Index to nonprint special education materials—multimedia (professional volume)
In National Information Center for Educational Media [NICEM Indexes to nonbook media] **016.3713**

Index to poetry for children and young people, 1964-1969. Brewton, J. E. comp. **808.81**

Index to poetry for children and young people, 1970-1975. Brewton, J. E. comp. **808.81**

Index to producers and distributors
In National Information Center for Educational Media [NICEM Indexes to nonbook media] **016.3713**

Index to psychology—multimedia
In National Information Center for Educational Media [NICEM Indexes to nonbook media] **016.3713**

Index to 16mm educational films
In National Information Center for Educational Media [NICEM Indexes to nonbook media] **016.3713**

Index to 35mm educational filmstrips
In National Information Center for Educational Media [NICEM Indexes to nonbook media] **016.3713**

Index to vocational and technical education—multimedia
In National Information Center for Educational Media [NICEM Indexes to nonbook media] **016.3713**

An **index** to young readers' collective biographies. See Silverman, J. Index to collective biographies for young readers **920**

Indexes
See also Subject headings; and subjects with the subdivision Indexes, e.g. Biography—Indexes

Indexing
See also Cataloging

India
Bothwell, J. The first book of India (4-6) **954**

Art
See Art, Indic

Cities and towns
See Cities and towns—India

Civilization
See pages in the following book:
Rawding, F. W. The Buddha p16-26 (5 and up) **294.3**

Economic conditions
See pages in the following book:
Archer, J. Hunger on planet Earth p65-74 (6 and up) **338.1**

Fiction
Kipling, R. The jungle book (4 and up) **S C**
Kipling, R. Just so stories (3-6) **S C**
Kipling, R. The second jungle book (4 and up) **S C**
Mukerji, D. G. Gay-Neck: the story of a pigeon (6 and up) **Fic**
Rose, G. The tiger-skin rug **E**

Folklore
See Folklore—India

History
See pages in the following book:
Sechrist, E. H. It's time for brotherhood p78-83 (5 and up) **361**

Social life and customs
Bergman Sucksdorff, A. Chendru: the boy and the tiger (3-6) **954**

The **Indian** and his horse. Hofsinde, R. **970.004**

Indian arts. Hofsinde, R. **709.01**

Indian beadwork. Hofsinde, R. **746.5**

The **Indian** boy without a name. Vahl, R.
In Dramatized folk tales of the world p526-36 **812.08**

Indian captive; the story of Mary Jemison. Lenski, L. **92**

The **Indian** Cinderella. Macmillan, C.
In North American legends p94-96   398.2
Indian corn and other gifts. Lavine, S. A.
641.3
Indian costumes. Hofsinde, R.   391
Indian crafts. D'Amato, J.   745.5
Indian fairy tales (4-6)   398.2
Indian festivals. Showers, P.   394.2
Indian fishing and camping. Hofsinde, R.
799.1
Indian folk and fairy tales. See Indian fairy
tales   398.2
Indian folklore. See Folklore, Indian
Indian games and crafts. Hofsinde, R.   790.1
Indian hunting. Hofsinde, R.   799.2
Indian Knoll site, Ky.
See pages in the following book:
Steele, W. O. Talking bones p23-31 (3-5)
970.004
The **Indian** medicine man. Hofsinde, R.
970.004
Indian music makers. Hofsinde, R.   781.7
Indian poetry. See American poetry—American Indian authors
Indian Saynday and White Man Saynday
In Winter-telling stories p74-82   398.2
Indian sign language. Hofsinde, R.   001.56
Indian signs and signals. Fronval, G.   001.56
Indian summer
Meigs, C. Indian summer
In Harper, W. comp. The harvest feast
p37-49   S C
Indian tribes of America. Gridley, M. E.
970.004
Indian warriors and their weapons. Hofsinde, R.   970.004
Indiana
Fiction
Thrasher, C. The dark didn't catch me (5
and up)   Fic
Indianapolis Speedway Race
Olney, R. R. Janet Guthrie: first woman at
Indy (4 and up)   92
Indians
Hays, W. P. Foods the Indians gave us (5
and up)   641.3
Lavine, S. A. Indian corn and other gifts
(4 and up)   641.3
See also pages in the following book:
Discoverers of the New World p88-91 (5
and up)   970.01
Games
Lavine, S. A. The games the Indians played
(5 and up)   790.1
Indians. Tunis, E.   970.004
Indians at home. Hofsinde, R.   728
Indians for Thanksgiving. Heiderstadt, D.
In Harper, W. comp. The harvest feast
p50-63   S C
In It's time for Thanksgiving p60-69   394.2
Indians in the house. Wilder, L. I.
In Gruenberg, S. M. ed. Favorite stories
old and new p116-22   808.8
Indians of Central America
Guatemala
Jenness, A. A life of their own (5 and up)
972.81

Indians of Mexico
See also Aztecs; Mayas
Art
Glubok, S. The art of ancient Mexico (4
and up)   709.01
Legends
Traven, B. The creation of the sun and the
moon (5 and up)   398.2
Indians of North America
Baylor, B. They put on masks (1-4)   391
Boesen, V. Edward S. Curtis, photographer
of the North American Indian (5 and up)
92
D'Amato, J. Indian crafts (4 and up)   745.5
Gridley, M. E. Indian tribes of America (4-6)
970.004
Hofsinde, R. The Indian and his horse (4-6)
970.004
Hofsinde, R. Indian fishing and camping
(3-6)   799.1
Hofsinde, R. Indian hunting (3-6)   799.2
Hofsinde, R. The Indian medicine man (4-7)
970.004
Hofsinde, R. Indian warriors and their
weapons (3-6)   970.004
Parish, P. Let's be Indians (2-5)   745.5
Sheppard, S. Indians of the eastern woodlands (5 and up)   970.004
Tamarin, A. We have not vanished (6 and
up)   970.004
Tunis, E. Indians (5 and up)   970.004
See also pages in the following books:
Lengyel, E. The colony of Pennsylvania
p48-55 (5 and up)   974.4
Sechrist, E. H. It's time for brotherhood
p110-21 (5 and up)   361
See also names of peoples and linguistic
families, e.g. Teton Indians
Amusements
See Indians of North America—Games
Antiquities
Steele, W. O. Talking bones (3-5)   970.004
See also Makah Indians—Antiquities
Art
Baylor, B. Before you came this way (1-4)
709.01
Baylor, B. When clay sings (1-4)   970.004
Glubok, S. The art of the North American
Indian (4 and up)   709.01
Glubok, S. The art of the Northwest coast
Indians (4 and up)   709.01
Glubok, S. The art of the Plains Indians
(4 and up)   709.01
Glubok, S. The art of the Southeastern Indians (4 and up)   709.01
Glubok, S. The art of the Southwest Indians
(4 and up)   709.01
Hofsinde, R. Indian arts (4-6)   709.01
See also pages in the following book:
Batterberry, A. R. The Pantheon Story of
American art for young people p9-29 (5
and up)   709.73
Bibliography
Books on American Indians and Eskimos
016.970004
Stensland, A. L. Literature by and about
the American Indian   016.970004
See also pages in the following book:
Issues in children's book selection p136-41
028.5

Io (Greek mythology)
See pages in the following book:
Gates, D. Lord of the sky: Zeus p11-26 (4 and up)   **292**
Ira sleeps over. Waber, B.   **E**
Iran
Folklore
See Folklore—Iran
Iraq
Fichter, G. S. Iraq (4 and up)   **956.7**
Ireland, Elizabeth
How Horace learned to moan
In A-haunting we will go p20-27   **S C**
Ireland, Norma Olin
(comp.) Index to fairy tales, 1949-1972. See Index to fairy tales, 1949-1972.   **398.2**
(comp.) Index to fairy tales, 1973-1977. See Index to fairy tales, 1973-1977   **398.2**
Ireland
Ireland in pictures (4 and up)   **941.5**
O'Brien, E. The land and people of Ireland (5 and up)   **941.5**
Sasek, M. This is Ireland (3-6)   **914.15**

Agriculture
See Agriculture—Ireland

Church history
Corfe, T. St Patrick and Irish Christianity (5 and up)   **274.15**

Description and travel
Sasek, M. This is Ireland (3-6)   **914.15**

Fiction
Kennedy, R. The leprechaun's story   **E**
Macken, W. The flight of the Doves (4-6)   **Fic**

Folklore
See Folklore—Ireland

History
See pages in the following book:
Carter, S. Vikings bold: their voyages & adventures p90-100 (5 and up)   **948**
Ireland in pictures   **941.5**
Ireson, Barbara
(ed) Haunting tales. See Haunting tales **S C**
Irish Americans
Johnson, J. E. The Irish in America (5 and up)   **305.8**
Irish fairy tales. Stephens, J.   **398.2**
The Irish in America. Johnson, J. E.   **305.8**
Irish Red. Kjelgaard, J. See note under Kjelgaard, J. Big Red   **Fic**
Iroaganachi, John
Achebe, C. How the leopard got his claws   **Fic**
Iron
See also Ironwork
Iron Hans
Grimm, J. Iron Hans
In Grimm, J. The complete Grimm's fairy tales p612-20   **398.2**
In Grimm, J. More Tales from Grimm p207-28   **398.2**
The iron lily. Willard, B. See note under Willard, B. The lark and the laurel   **Fic**
The iron road. Snow, R. F.   **385.09**

Iron stove
Grimm, J. The iron stove
In Grimm, J. The complete Grimm's fairy tales p571-77   **398.2**
In Yellow fairy book p40-45   **398.2**
Ironclad! Reit, S.   **973.7**
Ironwork
See pages in the following book:
Tunis, E. Colonial craftsmen and the beginnings of American industry p147-54 (5 and up)   **670**
Iroquois Indians
Sheppard, S. Indians of the eastern woodlands (5 and up)   **970.004**
See also pages in the following books:
Hofsinde, R. Indian costumes p40-48 (3-6)   **391**
Hofsinde, R. The Indian medicine man p33-42 (4-7)   **970.004**
Hofsinde, R. Indian warriors and their weapons p27-34 (3-6)   **970.004**
Hofsinde, R. Indians at home p25-38 (4 and up)   **728**
Tunis, E. Indians p58-69 (5 and up)   **970.004**

Social life and customs
D'Amato, J. Algonquian and Iroquois crafts for you to make (4-6)   **745.5**
Irraweka, mischief-maker. Sherlock, P.
In Sherlock, P. West Indian folk-tales p21-26   **398.2**
Irrigation
See also Dams
Irving, James Gordon
(illus.) Zim, H. S. Birds   **598**
(illus.) Zim, H. S. Fishes   **597**
(illus.) Zim, H. S. Homing pigeons   **636.5**
(illus.) Zim, H. S. Insects   **595.7**
(illus.) Zim, H. S. Mammals   **599**
(illus.) Zim, H. S. Owls   **598**
(illus.) Zim, H. S. Stars   **523**
Irving, Washington
The bold dragoon
In Sechrist, E. H. ed. 13 ghostly yarns p61-74   **S C**
The legend of Sleepy Hollow
In Irving, W. Rip Van Winkle, The legend of Sleepy Hollow, and other tales p45-98   **S C**
The legend of the Moor's legacy; adaptation
In Stories to dramatize p236-43   **372.6**
Rip Van Winkle (5 and up)   **Fic**
also in The Arthur Rackham Fairy book p246-65   **398.2**
also in Darrell, M. ed. Once upon a time p13-36   **808.8**
also in Irving, W. Rip Van Winkle, The legend of Sleepy Hollow, and other tales p9-44   **S C**
Rip Van Winkle; adaptation
In Stories to dramatize p249-59   **372.6**
Rip Van Winkle; dramatization. See Thane, A. Rip Van Winkle
Rip Van Winkle, The legend of Sleepy Hollow, and other tales (4-6)   **S C**
Short stories included are: The spectre bridegroom; The Moor's legacy
The Spectre Bridegroom
In Sechrist, E. H. ed. 13 ghostly yarns p109-30   **S C**
Irving and me. Hoff, S.   **Fic**

It all came out of an egg
Duvoisin, R. It all came out of an egg
In Duvoisin, R. The three sneezes, and other Swiss tales p30-37   **398.2**

It can't hurt forever. Singer, M.   **Fic**

It could always be worse. Zemach, M.   **398.2**

It does not say meow, and other animal riddle rhymes. De Regniers, B. S.   **793.7**

It doesn't always have to rhyme. Merriam, E.   **811**

It is perfectly true! Andersen, H. C.
In Andersen, H. C. The complete fairy tales and stories p405-07   **S C**
See also It is quite true

It is quite true
Andersen, H. C. It is perfectly true!
In Andersen, H. C. The complete fairy tales and stories p405-07   **S C**
Andersen, H. C. It's absolutely true
In Andersen, H. C. Seven tales p105-13   **S C**

"It is you the fable is about." Andersen, H. C.
In Andersen, H. C. The complete fairy tales and stories p1004-05   **S C**

It looked like spilt milk. Shaw, C. G.   **E**

Italian Americans
Grossman, R. P. The Italians in America (5 and up)   **305.8**
Fiction
De Paola, T. Watch out for the chicken feet in your soup   **E**

Italian architecture. See Architecture, Italian

Italian art. See Art, Italian

Italian literature
See pages in the following book:
Winwar, F. The land and people of Italy p78-86 (5 and up)   **945**

The Italians in America. Grossman, R. P.   **305.8**

Italic handwriting for young people. Eager, F.   **745.6**

Italy
Epstein, S. The first book of Italy (4 and up)   **945**
Winwar, F. The land and people of Italy (5 and up)   **945**
See also pages in the following book:
National Geographic Society. The Alps p120-51 (6 and up)   **914.94**
Fascism
See Fascism—Italy
Fiction
De Paola, T. Big Anthony and the magic ring   **E**
Haugaard, E. C. The little fishes (6 and up)   **Fic**
Folklore
See Folklore—Italy
Industries
See pages in the following book:
Winwar, F. The land and people of Italy p43-49 (5 and up)   **945**
Social life and customs
See pages in the following book:
Sechrist, E. H. Christmas everywhere p126-36   **394.2**

Itch, sniffle & sneeze. Silverstein, A.   **616.97**

It'll all come out in the wash. Gray, N.   **E**

It's a —; play. Carlson, B. W.
In Carlson, B. W. The right play for you p94-96   **792**

It's a baby. Ancona, G.   **612**

It's a gingerbread house. Williams, V. B.   **641.8**

It's absolutely true. Andersen, H. C.
In Andersen, H. C. Seven tales p105-13   **S C**
See also It is quite true

It's all about me
In Camp Fire Girls, Inc. The Camp Fire Blue Bird Series bk.1   **369.47**

It's easy to sew with scraps and remnants. Inouye, C.   **646.2**

It's Halloween. Prelutsky, J.   **811**

It's like this, Cat. Neville, E.   **Fic**

It's magic? Lopshire, R.   **793.8**

It's nesting time. Gans, R.   **598**

It's not the end of the world. Blume, J.   **Fic**

It's raining, said John Twaining. Bodecker, N. M.   **398**

It's so nice to have a wolf around the house. Allard, H.   **E**

It's such a beautiful day. Asimov, I.
In Universe ahead: stories of the future p29-59   **S C**

It's time for brotherhood. Sechrist, E. H.   **361**

It's time for Christmas (4 and up)   **394.2**

It's time for Easter (4 and up)   **394.2**

It's time for story hour   **372.6**

It's time for Thanksgiving (4 and up)   **394.2**

It's time now! Tresselt, A.   **525**

Ivan IV, the Terrible, Czar of Russia
See pages in the following book:
Nazaroff, A. The land and people of Russia p102-11 (5 and up)   **947**

Ivan and the grey wolf
Afanas'ev, A. Prince Ivan, the firebird, and the gray wolf
In Afanas'ev, A. Russian fairy tales p612-24   **398.2**

Ivan Bear's Ear. Riordan, J.
In Riordan, J. Tales from Central Russia p59-62   **398.2**

Ivan the Cow's Son
Afanas'ev, A. Ivan the Cow's Son
In Afanas'ev, A. Russian fairy tales p234-49   **398.2**

Ivan the peasant's son and the little man, himself one finger tall, his mustache seven versts in length
Afanas'ev, A. Ivan the peasant's son and the thumb-sized man
In Afanas'ev, A. Russian fairy tales p262-68   **398.2**

Ivan the peasants son and the three dragons. Riordan, J.
In Riordan, J. Tales from Central Russia p96-105   **398.2**

Ivan the peasant's son and the thumb-sized man. Afanas'ev, A.
In Afanas'ev, A. Russian fairy tales p262-68   **398.2**

Ivan the Rich and Ivan the Poor. Riordan, J.
In Riordan, J. Tales from Central Russia p23-30   **398.2**

Jagendorf, M. A.—*Continued*

The gypsies' fiddle, and other gypsy tales (5 and up) **398.2**

Contents: The silly fellow who sold his beard; The gypsy and the snake; The summer of the big snow; The peasant's strong wife; Saint Peter and his trombone; Noodlehead and the flying horse; The tale of the gypsy and his strange love; The gypsies' fiddle; The old gypsy woman and the good Lord; The gypsy in the ghost house; Traveling through the chimney; The silly men of Russia; How the gypsy boy outsmarted death; Fishing for pots in the pond; Prop for the tree; Flaming tales; The husband, the wife, and the Devil; How the cows flew across the sea; Fording the river in a copper cauldron

The Haddam witches
In Witches, witches, witches p187-91 **808.8**

King clothes
In The Arbuthnot Anthology of children's literature p272-73 **808.8**
In Time for old magic p155-56 **398.2**

The king of the mountains
In The Arbuthnot Anthology of children's literature p405-06 **808.8**

Mike Hooter and the smart bears in Mississippi
In The Arbuthnot Anthology of children's literature p380-81 **808.8**

New England bean-pot (5 and up) **398.2**

Contents: Young Paul; Skipper and the witch; Stubbornest man in Maine; Corsair of Spouting Horn; Smart woman of Kennebunkport; Tall Barney Beal; Cinderella of New Hampshire; Three times and out; Fairies in the White Mountains; Holding the bag; Giant of the Hills; Becky's garden; Old Ave Henry and the smart logger man; Lucky Rose Tuttle; Devil in the barrel; Green Mountain hero; Ride in the night; Tale of the tail of a bear; Well-Done-Peter-Parker; Strange adventure of the cowboy-sailor; Golden horse with the silver mane; Jingling rhymes and jingling money; Magic in Marblehead; Lord of Massachusetts; Devil in the steeple; Merry tale of Merrymount; Sacred cod and the striped haddock; Tiny Perry; Smart husband and the smarter wife; Giant Kingfisher of Mount Riga; Wise men of Hebron; Bee man and the boundary man; Frogs of Windham Town; Haddam witches; Diamond Jim and Big Bill; Puffing Potter's powerful puff; Rich lady and the ring in the sea; Cat Inspector; Devil in red flannel; Mysteries of the sea; Old man Elias and the dancing sheriff; New way to cure old witch-hunting; Grumpy Timothy Crumb; Weaver-woman's monument; Little Annie and the whaler captain; Tale of Godfrey Malbone

Noodlehead stories from around the world (4-6) **398.2**

Contents: The horse-egg; Don't marry two wives; The Noodlehead tiger; There are such people; Do you know; The donkey of Abdera; Barefoot in bed; The fox in the hole; The golden shoes; The great traveler of Chelm; Figs for gold, figs for folly; Donkeys all; The cow and the thread; Ceylon sillies; Like master, like servant; The sad victory; When Noodlehead marries Noodlehead; The foolish lion and the silly rooster; Who is who; Magic! Silly magic; The farmer's secret; The wisdom of the Lord; The costly feast; The flying fool; The wise men of Gotham; The brave men of Austwick; Knucklehead John; A sheep can only bleat; A new way to boil eggs; The needle crop of Sainte-Dodo; Bahh; Tales from Tartari-Barbari; Peter's adventures; Faithful legs and lazy head; The man, the woman, and the fly; Fools' bells ring in every town; Giufá and the judge; Donkey and scholars; Silly Matt; The Schilda town hall; The stove and the town hall; The tailor from the sea; Aili's quilt; Kultani, the noodle gossip; The obedient servant; The hero; Luck for fools; Tandala and Pakala; Belmont antics; Lutonya; The tale of the men of Prach; Smartness for sale; The moon in the donkey; Not on the Lord's Day; The wolf in the sack; Juan Bobo; Noodlehead Pat; The sombreros of the men of Lagos; The "Foolish People"; Little head, big medicine; Sam'l Dany, Noodlehead; Noodlehead luck; John in the storeroom; Kibbe's shirt

Oversmart is bad luck
In The Arbuthnot Anthology of children's literature p408-09 **808.8**

Pancho Villa and the Devil
In The Arbuthnot Anthology of children's literature p413 **808.8**

The sacred drum of Tepozteco
In The Arbuthnot Anthology of children's literature p411-13 **808.8**

The stubbornest man in Maine
In A-haunting we will go p106-10 **S C**

Tyll Ulenspiegel
In Stories to dramatize p176-81 **372.6**

Tyll Ulenspiegel's merry pranks (4-6) **398.2**

Who rules the roost?
In The Arbuthnot Anthology of children's literature p401-03 **808.8**

Jagendorf, Moritz Adolf. See Jagendorf, M. A.

Jagr, Miloslav
(illus.) Seeger, P. The foolish frog **784.4**

The **jaguar** and the crested curassow. Sherlock, P.
In Sherlock, P. West Indian folk-tales p27-33 **398.2**

Jahsmann, Allan Hart
(ed.) Bible. Selections. The Holy Bible for children **220.5**

Jake. Slote, A. **Fic**

Jakes, John
Ranging
In Universe ahead: stories of the future p281-300 (6 and up) **S C**

Jamaica
Folklore
See Folklore—Jamaica

Jambo means hello. Feelings, M. **E**

Jambor, Louis
(illus.) Alcott, L. M. Little women **Fic**

James, Elizabeth
How to keep a secret (4-6) **652**
What do you mean by "average?" (4-6) **519.5**
(jt. auth.) Arthur, L. Sportsmath: how it works **796**

James, Jesse Woodson
See pages in the following book:
Ault, P. "All aboard!" p123-26 (5 and up) **385.09**

James, Laurie
Camp Fire Girls, Inc. Adventure **369.47**
Camp Fire Girls, Inc. The Blue Bird wish **369.47**
Camp Fire Girls, Inc. Discovery **369.47**

James, Will
His first bronc
In Gruenberg, S. M. ed. Favorite stories old and new p155-59 **808.8**
Smoky, the cow horse (6 and up) **Fic**

About
See pages in the following book:
Newbery Medal books: 1922-1955 p47-48 **028.5**

James and the giant peach. Dahl, R. **Fic**

James Marshall's Mother Goose **398**

James the huntsman
Hatch, M. C. James the huntsman
In Hatch, M. C. 13 Danish tales p3-15 **398.2**

Jameson, Cynthia
The clay pot boy (k-2) **398.2**

Jameson, Helen D.
(illus.) Aldis, D. All together **811**

Jewett, Eleanore M.
Even unto the end of the world
In It's time for Easter p159-69   **394.2**
Which was witch?
In The Arbuthnot Anthology of children's
literature p343-44   **808.8**
In Time for old magic p220-21   **398.2**
In Witches, witches, witches p172-75   **808.8**

Jewish-Arab relations. See Israeli-Arab relations

Jewish cookery. See Cookery, Jewish

The **Jewish** holiday book. Lazar, W.   **394.2**

Jewish holiday cookbook. Purdy, S. G.   **641.5**

Jewish holiday crafts. Becker, J.   **745.5**

Jewish holidays. See Fasts and feasts—Judaism

Jewish holidays. Cuyler, M.   **394.2**

Jewish holidays. Purdy, S. G.   **394.2**

Jewish holocaust (1939-1945) See Holocaust, Jewish (1939-1945)

Jewish legends. See Legends, Jewish

Jewish literature
See also Yiddish literature
History and criticism
See pages in the following book:
Meltzer, M. World of our fathers p155-75
(6 and up)   **305.8**

Jewish maiden
Andersen, H. C. The servant
In Andersen, H. C. The complete fairy
tales and stories p487-91   **S C**

Jewish New Year. See Rosh ha-Shanah

The **Jewish** New Year. Cone, M.   **296.4**

Jewish refugees. See Refugees, Jewish

Jewish religion. See Judaism

Jews
Biography
Milgrim, S. Haym Salomon, liberty's son
(5 and up)   **92**
Noble, I. Nazi hunter: Simon Wiesenthal
(5 and up)   **92**
Customs
See Jews—Social life and customs
Education
See pages in the following book:
Meltzer, M. World of our fathers p112-29
(6 and up)   **305.8**
Festivals
See Fasts and feasts—Judaism
Fiction
Aleichem, S. Holiday tales of Sholom Alei-
chem (5 and up)   **S C**
Hautzig, E. The case against the wind, and
other stories (4 and up)   **S C**
Ish-Kishor, S. Our Eddie (6 and up)   **Fic**
Levitin, S. A sound to remember   **E**
Shulevitz, U. Hanukah money   **E**
Singer, I. B. The fools of Chelm and their
history (3-6)   **Fic**
Folklore
See Folklore, Jewish
Legends
See Legends, Jewish
Literature
See Jewish literature

Persecutions
See pages in the following book:
Meltzer, M. World of our fathers p36-62,
196-218, 232-52 (6 and up)   **305.8**
See also Holocaust, Jewish (1939-1945)
Relations with Gentiles
See Jews and Gentiles
Religion
See Judaism
Rites and ceremonies
Greene, L. I am an Orthodox Jew (2-4)   **296.7**
Social conditions
Meltzer, M. Taking root (6 and up)   **305.8**
Social life and customs
Greene, L. I am an Orthodox Jew (2-4)   **296.7**
Songs and music
Hirsh, M. One little goat (k-3)   **296.4**

Jews and Gentiles
See pages in the following book:
Meltzer, M. Taking root p5-13, 51-60, 237-47
(6 and up)   **305.8**
Fiction
Neville, E. C. Berries Goodman (5 and up)   **Fic**

The **Jews** helped build America. Kurtis, A. H.   **305.8**

Jews in Austria
Fiction
Orgel, D. The devil in Vienna (6 and up)   **Fic**

Jews in Bohemia
Fiction
Ish-Kishor, S. A boy of old Prague (5
and up)   **Fic**
Ish-Kishor, S. The Master of Miracle (5
and up)   **Fic**

Jews in Canada
Fiction
Kaplan, B. The empty chair (6 and up)   **Fic**

Jews in Eastern Europe
Meltzer, M. World of our fathers (6 and up)   **305.8**

Jews in France
Fiction
Sachs, M. A pocket full of seeds (5 and up)   **Fic**

Jews in Germany
Koehn, I. Mischling, second degree (6 and up)   **92**
Fiction
Kay, M. In face of danger (6 and up)   **Fic**
Richter, H. P. Friedrich (5 and up)   **Fic**

Jews in literature
See pages in the following book:
Issues in children's book selection p102-06   **028.5**

Jews in New York (City)
Fiction
Chaikin, M. I should worry, I should care
(3-5)   **Fic**
Cohen, B. The carp in the bathtub (2-4)   **Fic**

K

Kara Khan's daughter. Baumann, H.
In Baumann, H. The stolen fire p33-37
                   398.2

Karagiosis and the dragon; puppet play.
  Cochrane, L.
In Cochrane, L. Shadow puppets in color
  p26-35   **791.5**

The **Karankawa** from the great gleaming
  oyster shells. Jagendorf, M. A.
In Jagendorf, M. A. Folk stories of the
  South p269-70   **398.2**

Karasz, Ilonka
  (illus.) The Twelve days of Christmas. See
  The Twelve days of Christmas   **783.6**

Karate
  Kozuki, R. Junior karate (5 and up) **796.8**
    See also pages in the following books:
  Reisberg, K. The martial arts p29-47 (4
    and up)   **796.8**
  Ribner, S. The martial arts p10-41, 83-120
    (5 and up)   **796.8**

Karen, Ruth
  Feathered serpent (6 and up)   **972**

Kari Woodengown
  Asbjørnsen, P. C. Katie Woodencloak
  In Red fairy book p205-19   **398.2**

Karl, Jean E.
  Beloved Benjamin is waiting (4-6)   **Fic**
  From childhood to childhood   **028.5**
  The turning place (6 and up)   **S C**
  Contents: The turning place; Over the hill;
Enough; Accord; Catabilid conquest; Quiet and
a white bush; The talkaround; A central ques-
tion; Out for the flicker path

Karle, Isabella Lugoski
    See pages in the following book:
  Noble, I. Contemporary women scientists of
    America p107-22 (5 and up)   **920**

Karlin, Eugene
  (illus.) Church, A. J. The Aeneid for boys
  and girls   **873**

Karlsefni,Thorfinn. See Thorfinn Karlsefni

Karoo, the kangaroo. Wiese, K.
  In Gruenberg, S. M. ed. Favorite stories
  old and new p182-88   **808.8**

Kashmir
    See pages in the following book:
  Lang, R. The land and people of Pakistan
  p138-46 (5 and up)   **954.9**

Kassim's shoes. Berson, H.   **398.2**

Kastner, Erich
  Emil and the detectives (4-6)   **Fic**
  The little man (4-6)   **Fic**

Kate. Little, J. See note under Little, J. Look
  through my window   **Fic**

Kate Crackernuts
  In Tatterhood, and other tales p33-38
                   398.2
    See also Katherine Crackernuts

Kate Crackernuts. Jacobs, J.
  In Jacobs, J. English fairy tales p198-202
                   398.2
    See also Katherine Crackernuts

The **Kate** Greenaway treasury. Greenaway, K.
                   828

Kate Greenaway's Book of games. Greenaway, K.   **796.1**

Kate, the Bell Witch. Jagendorf, M. A.
  In Jagendorf, M. A. Folk stories of the
  South p231-34   **398.2**

Katherine Crackernuts
  Jacobs, J. Kate Crackernuts
  In Jacobs, J. English fairy tales p198-202
                   398.2
  Kate Crackernuts
  In Tatterhood, and other tales p33-38
                   398.2

Katherine of Aragon. See Catherine of Aragon,
  consort of Henry VIII, King of England

Katie John. Calhoun, M.   **Fic**

Katie John and Heathcliff. See note under
  Calhoun, M. Katie John   **Fic**

Katie Woodencloak. Asbjørnsen, P. C.
  In Red fairy book p205-19   **398.2**

Katy and the big snow. Burton, V. L.   **E**

Katy No-Pocket. Payne, E.   **E**

Katydids
    See pages in the following books:
  Ricciuti, E. R. Shelf pets p92-97 (5 and up)
                   639
  Ricciuti, E. R. Sounds of animals at night
    p31-39 (3-5)   **591.5**

Katz, William Loren
  An album of the Great Depression (5 and
    up)   **330.973**
  The Constitutional amendments (4 and up)
                   342

Katzman, Marylyn
  (illus.) Kerina, J. African crafts   **745.5**

Kaufman, Ted
  Piffle! It's only a sniffle!
  In One hundred plays for children p151-58
                 808.82

Kaufmann, John
  Bats in the dark (1-3)   **599.4**
  Birds are flying (2-4)   **598**
  Birds in flight (5 and up)   **598**
  Flying reptiles in the age of dinosaurs (1-4)
                 567.9
  Insect travelers (6 and up)   **595.7**
  Little dinosaurs and early birds (1-3) **568**
  Robins fly north, robins fly south (3-5) **598**
  Streamlined (2-4)   **531**
  (illus.) Carlson, N. S. The empty school-
    house   **Fic**
  (illus.) Selsam, M. E. How animals tell
    time   **591.5**
  (illus.) Selsam, M. E. When an animal
    grows   **591.3**

Kaula, Edna Mason
  The land and people of New Zealand (5
    and up)   **993**
  The land and people of Tanzania (5 and
    up)   **967.8**

Kavaler, Lucy
  The wonders of fungi (5 and up)   **589.2**

Kavcic, Vladimir
  The miller, his cook and the king
  In Greene, E. comp. Clever cooks p101-07
    (3-6)   **398.2**

Kay, Helen
  One mitten Lewis   **E**

Kay, Mara
  In face of danger (6 and up)   **Fic**

Kaye, Evelyn
  The ACT Guide to children's television.
  See The ACT Guide to children's tele-
  vision   **791.45**

Keane, Richard
  (illus.) Schaller, G. Wonders of lions **599.74**

Keasey, Merritt S.
(illus.) Brenner, B. Lizard tails and cactus
spines 597.9
Keaton, Buster
See pages in the following book:
Edelson, E. Funny men of the movies p32-
40 (6 and up) 791.43
Keats, Ezra Jack
Apt. 3 E
Caldecott Medal acceptance paper
In Newbery and Caldecott Medal books:
1956-1965 p239-40 028.5
Dreams E
Goggles! See note under Keats, E. J. The
snowy day E
Hi, cat! See note under Keats, E. J. The
snowy day E
Jennie's hat E
John Henry (k-3) 398.2
A letter to Amy. See note under Keats,
E. J. The snowy day E
(illus.) Over in the meadow. See Over in
the meadow E
Pet show! See note under Keats, E. J. The
snowy day E
Peter's chair. See note under Keats, E. J.
The snowy day E
The snowy day E
Whistle for Willie. See note under Keats,
E. J. The snowy day E
(illus.) Alexander, L. The king's fountain E
(illus.) Davis, K. The little drummer boy
783.6
(illus.) Freedman, F. B. Two tickets to
freedom; the true story of Ellen and
William Craft, fugitive slaves 92
(illus.) Hautzig, E. In the park 410
(illus.) Martin, P. M. The rice bowl pet E
(illus.) Williams, J. Danny Dunn and the
homework machine Fic

About
See pages in the following books:
Authors and illustrations of children's books
p230-42 028.5
Newbery and Caldecott Medal books: 1956-
1965 p241-45 028.5
Keen, Martin L.
Be a rockhound (4 and up) 549
The world beneath our feet (4-6) 631.4
Keep running, Allen! Bulla, C. R. E
Keep stompin' till the music stops. Pevsner, S.
Fic
Keeping, Charles
(illus.) Haunts, haunts, haunts S C
(illus.) Newman, R. The twelve labors of
Hercules 292
Keeping amphibians and reptiles as pets.
Fichter, G. S. 639
Keeping Christmas. Peacock, M.
In A Treasury of Christmas plays p297-
303 812.08
Keeping Christmas merry. Henderson, N.
In Henderson, N. Celebrate America p113-
21 812
Kefala's secret something. Robinson, A.
In Robinson, A. Three African tales 398.2
Keifer, Irene
Energy for America (6 and up) 333.79
Keith, Eros
(illus.) Aiken, J. The faithless lollybird S C
(illus.) Fox, P. The slave dancer Fic

(illus.) Hamilton, V. The house of Dies
Drear Fic
(illus.) Latham, J. L. Anchor's aweigh; the
story of David Glasgow Farragut 92
(illus.) The Moon is like a silver sickle.
See The Moon is like a silver sickle 891.7
Keith, Hal
(illus.) Math, I. Morse, Marconi and you
621.38
Keith, Harold
Newbery Medal acceptance paper
In Newbery and Caldecott Medal books:
1956-1965 p53-62 028.5
Rifles for Watie (6 and up) Fic
Sports and games (5 and up) 796

About
See pages in the following book:
Newbery and Caldecott Medal books: 1956-
1965 p63-68 028.5
Keller, Charles
(comp.) The star spangled banana, and
other revolutionary riddles (3-5) 793.7
Keller, Gail Faithfull
Jane Addams (1-3) 92
Keller, Gottfried
Hungry Hans
In The Golden Treasury of children's
literature p487-93 808.8
Keller, Helen Adams
Brown, M. M. The silent storm [biography
of Anne Sullivan Macy] (5 and up) 92
Malone, M. Annie Sullivan [biography of
Anne Sullivan Macy] (2-4) 92
Peare, C. O. The Helen Keller story (5 and
up) 92
See also pages in the following book:
The Arbuthnot Anthology of children's
literature p841-48 808.8
Keller, Ronald
(illus.) Millay, E. St V. Edna St Vincent
Millay's Poems selected for young people
811
Kellogg, Steven
(illus.) Sleator, W. Once, said Darlene E
(illus.) Van Leeuwen, J. The great Christ-
mas kidnaping caper Fic
Kelley, Alberta
Lenses, spectacles, eyeglasses, and contacts
(5 and up) 617.7
Kelley, True
(illus.) I saw a purple cow, and 100 other
recipes for learning. See I saw a purple
cow, and 100 other recipes for learning
372.1
Kellner, Esther
Animals come to my house (5 and up) 639
Kellogg, Elijah
See pages in the following book:
Jordan, A. M. From Rollo to Tom Sawyer,
and other papers p102-12 028.5
Kellogg, Steven
Can I keep him? E
Much bigger than Martin E
The mystery of the missing red mitten E
The mysterious tadpole E
Pinkerton, behave! E
(illus.) Bangs, E. Steven Kellogg's Yankee
Doodle 784.7
(illus.) Caines, J. Abby E
(illus.) Mahy, M. The boy who was fol-
lowed home E
(illus.) Nodset, J. L. Come here, cat E

King Alfred and the cakes. Thane, A.
In Thane, A. Plays from famous stories and fairy tales p143-52 **812**

The **king** and the bee. Whitworth, V. P.
In Dramatized folk tales of the world p250-57 **812.08**

King and the corn. Farjeon, E.
In Farjeon, E. The little bookroom p 1-6 **S C**

The **king** and the witch. Colwell, E.
In Colwell, E. Round about and long ago p77-81 **398.2**

King Arthur. See Arthur, King

King Arthur and his knights. Morley, O. J.
In Dramatized folk tales of the world p106-27 **812.08**

The **King** at the door. Cole, B. **E**

King Bartek
Borski, L. M. King Bartek
In The Arbuthnot Anthology of children's literature p274-76 **808.8**
In Time for old magic p157-59 **398.2**

King Bear
Afanas'ev, A. King Bear
In Afanas'ev, A. Russian fairy tales p393-98 **398.2**

King clothes. Jagendorf, M. A.
In The Arbuthnot Anthology of children's literature p272-73 **808.8**
In Time for old magic p155-56 **398.2**

King Coal. Malcolmson, A.
In Malcolmson, A. Yankee Doodle's cousins p45-52 **398.2**

King Dragon
Manning-Sanders, R. Prince Lindworm
In Manning-Sanders, R. A book of monsters p49-59 **398.2**

King Eagle. Manning-Sanders, R.
In Manning-Sanders, R. A book of kings and queens p37-53 **398.2**

King Frost
Afanas'ev, A. Jack Frost
In Afanas'ev, A. Russian fairy tales p366-69 **398.2**
Riordan, J. Grandfather Frost
In Riordan, J. Tales from Central Russia p86-90 **398.2**
The Story of Old Frost
In Yellow fairy book p192-95 **398.2**

King George's head was made of lead. Monjo, F. N. **Fic**

King Grisly-Beard. Grimm, J. **398.2**
See also King Thrushbeard

King Josef. Manning-Sanders, R.
In Manning-Sanders, R. A book of kings and queens p66-71 **398.2**

King Kojata
King Kojata
In Green fairy book p207-20 **398.2**

King Krakus and the dragon. Domanska, J. **398.2**

King Midas, Gardner, M.
In Dramatized folk tales of the world p177-90 **812.08**

King Midas and the golden touch
In Gruenberg, S. M. ed. Favorite stories old and new p408-10 **808.8**

The **King** o' the Cats. Jacobs, J.
In Harper, W. comp. Ghosts and goblins p57-59 **398.2**

The **King** of Colchester's daughter
In The Classic fairy tales p159-61 **398.2**
See also Three heads of the well

King of his turf
In Jataka tales p68-70 **398.2**

The **King** of Sedo. Courlander, H.
In Courlander, H. The king's drum, and other African stories p19-21 **398.2**

The **king** of the animals. Courlander, H.
In Courlander, H. The piece of fire, and other Haitian tales p97-100 **398.2**

King of the cats
Jacobs, J. The King o' the cats
In Harper, W. comp. Ghosts and goblins p57-59 **398.2**

The **king** of the forest. Courlander, H.
In Courlander, H. The tiger's whisker, and other tales and legends from Asia and the Pacific p46-48 **398.2**

King of the Golden Mountain
Grimm, J. The King of the Golden Mountain
In Grimm, J. The complete Grimm's fairy tales p425-30 **398.2**
In Grimm, J. Grimm's Fairy tales p75-81 **398.2**

King of the Golden River
Ruskin, J. The king of the Golden River
In The Golden Treasury of children's literature p330-47 **808.8**

King of the monkeys. Carpenter, F.
In Carpenter, F. Tales of a Chinese grandmother p107-16 **398.2**

The **King** of the Mountain. Hume, L. C.
In Hume, L. C. Favorite children's stories from China and Tibet p85-92 **398.2**

The **king** of the mountains. Jagendorf, M. A.
In The Arbuthnot Anthology of children's literature p405-06 **808.8**
In Time for old magic p271-72 **398.2**

King of the Wind. Henry, M. **Fic**

King O'Toole and his goose
Jacobs, J. King O'Toole and his goose
In Time for old magic p38-40 **398.2**
King O'Toole and his goose
In The Arbuthnot Anthology of children's literature p177-80 **808.8**

King Rooster, Queen Hen. Lobel, A. **398.2**

King Solomon's answer
Whitworth, V. P. The king and the bee
In Dramatized folk tales of the world p250-57 **812.08**

King Stork
Pyle, H. King Stork **398.2**
also in Giants & witches and a dragon or two p3-17 **398.2**
also in Pyle, H. The wonder clock p291-304 **398.2**
also in Ross, E. S. ed. The lost half-hour p106-19 **372.6**

The **king**, the mice and the cheese. Gurney, N. **E**

King Throstlebeard. Grimm, J.
In Grimm, J. The Brothers Grimm: popular folk tales p118-23 **398.2**
See also King Thrushbeard

King Thrushbeard
Grimm, J. King Grisly-Beard **398.2**
Grimm, J. King Throstlebeard
In Grimm, J. The Brothers Grimm: popular folk tales p118-23 **398.2**

King Thrushbeard—*Continued*

Grimm, J. King Thrushbeard 398.2
also in Grimm, J. About wise men and
simpletons p91-95 398.2
also in Grimm, J. The complete Grimm's
fairy tales p244-48 398.2
In Grimm, J. Household stories p208-12
398.2

See also Greyfoot

The **king** who ate chaff. Courlander, H.
In Courlander, H. The tiger's whisker,
and other tales and legends from
Asia and the Pacific p33-34 398.2

The **king** who was a gentleman. MacManus, S.
In MacManus, S. Hibernian nights p36-47
398.2

The **king** who was bored. Thane, A.
In Dramatized folk tales of the world
p334-45 812.08

King who would be stronger than fate
Story of the king who would be stronger
than fate
In The Andrew Lang Fairy tale treasury
p513-27 398.2

The **king** with a terrible temper
In With a deep sea smile p61-63 372.6

King Wren
Grimm, J. The willow-wren
In Grimm, J. The complete Grimm's fairy
tales p705-08 398.2

Kingdom of the greedy
Stahl, P. J. The Kingdom of the Greedy
In Harper, W. comp. The harvest feast
p110-34 S C

The **kingdom** of wolves. Barry, S. 599.74

The **kingdoms** of copper, silver and gold.
Riordan, J.
In Riordan, J. Tales from Central Russia
p264-68 398.2

Kingham, David
(illus.) Lyons, G. The Creek Indians
970.004

Kingman, Lee
(ed.) The Illustrator's notebook. See The
Illustrator's notebook 741.64
(comp.) Illustrators of children's books:
1957-1966. See Illustrators of children's
books: 1957-1966 741.64
(comp.) Illustrators of children's books:
1967-1976. See Illustrators of children's
books: 1967-1976 741.64
The magic pumpkin
In One hundred plays for children p403-
11 808.82
Mr Thanks has his day
In One hundred plays for children p467-
74 808.82
(ed.) Newbery and Caldecott Medal books:
1956-1965. See Newbery and Caldecott
Medal books: 1956-1965 028.5
(ed.) Newbery and Caldecott Medal books:
1966-1975. See Newbery and Caldecott
Medal books: 1966-1975 028.5
Peter's long walk E
The year of the raccoon (6 and up) Fic

Kings and rulers
See also names of countries with the
subdivision Kings and rulers, e.g. Great
Britain—Kings and rulers; and names of
individual kings and rulers, e.g. Philip II,
King of Spain

Fiction

Anno, M. The King's flower E
Cole, B. The King at the door E
Gripe, M. In the time of the bells (5 and
up) Fic
Manning-Sanders, R. A book of kings and
queens (3-6) 398.2

The **king's** ankus. Kipling, R.
In Kipling, R. The second jungle book
p117-39 S C

The **King's** calendar. Oser, J. A.
In Fifty plays for junior actors p450-59
812.08

The **king's** choice. Wahlenberg, A.
In Olenius, E. comp. Great Swedish fairy
tales p50-58 398.2

The **King's** creampuffs. Swintz, M.
In One hundred plays for children p237-
52 808.82

King's daughter cries for the moon. Far-
jeon, E.
In Farjeon, E. The little bookroom p7-31
S C

The **king's** drum. Courlander, H.
In Courlander, H. The king's drum, and
other African stories p32-35 398.2

The **king's** drum, and other African stories.
Courlander, H. 398.2

The **King's** fifth. O'Dell, S. Fic

King's flea
Haviland, V. The flea
In Haviland, V. Favorite fairy tales told
in Spain p3-17 398.2

The **King's** flower. Anno, M. E

The **King's** fountain. Alexander, L. E

The **king's** holiday. Bennett, R.
In Bennett, R. Creative plays and programs for holidays p352-58 812

Kings, queens, knights & jesters: making
medieval costumes. Schnurnberger, L. E.
391.09

King's rijstepap
Hart, J. The king's rijstepap
In It's time for story hour p66-68 372.6

The **king's** rival. Robinson, A.
In Robinson, A. Three African tales 398.2

The **king's** son who feared nothing. Grimm, J.
In Grimm, J. The complete Grimm's fairy
tales p545-50 398.2

The **King's** white elephant. Babbitt, E. C.
In Babbitt, E. C. Jataka tales p69-73
398.2

Kinkajou
See pages in the following book:
Patent, D. H. Raccoons, coatimundis, and
their family p84-93 (5 and up) 599.74

Kiowa Indians
Legends
Winter-telling stories (3-6) 398.2

Kipling, J. Lockwood
(illus.) Kipling, R. The second jungle book
S C

Kipling, Rudyard
The elephant's child (1-4) Fic
also in The Arbuthnot Anthology of children's literature p484-87 808.8
also in Gruenberg, S. M. ed. Favorite
stories old and new p456-63 808.8
also in Ross, E. S. ed. The lost half-
hour p50-60 372.6

Krush, Beth
(illus.) Cameron, E. The terrible churna-dryne   Fic
(illus.) Courlander, H. The piece of fire, and other Haitian tales   398.2
(illus.) Enright, E. Gone-Away Lake   Fic
(illus.) Norton, M. The Borrowers   Fic
(illus.) Sorensen, V. Miracles on Maple Hill   Fic

Krush, Joe
(illus.) Cameron, E. The terrible churna-dryne   Fic
(illus.) Courlander, H. The piece of fire, and other Haitian tales   398.2
(illus.) Enright, E. Gone-Away Lake   Fic
(illus.) Norton, M. The Borrowers   Fic
(illus.) Sorensen, V. Miracles on Maple Hill   Fic

Krüss, James
3 x 3: three by three   E
K'tonton arrives. Weilerstein, S. R.
In Association for Childhood Education International. Told under the Christmas tree p255-58   808.8
K'tonton takes a ride on a runaway trendle. Weilerstein, S. R.
In Association for Childhood Education International. Told under the Christmas tree p259-63   808.8

Kubie, Nora Benjamin
Israel (4 and up)   956.94

Kubinyi, Laszlo
(illus.) Alexander, L. The town cats, and other tales   S C
(illus.) Alexander, L. The wizard in the tree   Fic
(illus.) Belting, N. comp. Our fathers had powerful songs   897
(illus.) Hardendorff, J. B. Witches, wit, and a werewolf   S C
(illus.) Hunter, M. The haunted mountain   Fic

Kueker, Don
(illus.) Bible. Selections. The Holy Bible for children   220.5

Kuhn, Bob
(illus.) Carr, M. J. Children of the covered wagon   Fic
(illus.) Kjelgaard, J. Big Red   Fic

Kultani, the noodle gossip. Jagendorf, M. A.
In Jagendorf, M. A. Noodlehead stories from around the world p202-06   398.2

Kung-fu. See Karate

Kunitz, Stanley J.
(ed.) The Junior book of authors. See The Junior book of authors   920.03

Kunstler, Mort
(illus.) Cole, J. Dinosaur story   567.9

Kunz, Virginia Brainard
The French in America (5 and up)   305.8
The Germans in America (5 and up)   305.8

Kupti and Imani
Kupti and Imani
In Tatterhood, and other tales p93-102   398.2

A kupua plays tricks. Thompson, V. L.
In Thompson, V. L. Hawaiian myths of earth p45-52   398.2

Kuratko the terrible
Haviland, V. Kuratko the terrible
In Haviland, V. Favorite fairy tales told in Czechoslovakia p21-33   398.2

Kurelek, William
Lumberjack (3-5)   634.9
A northern nativity (4 and up)   232.9
A prairie boy's summer (3-5)   971.27
A prairie boy's winter (3-5)   971.27

Kuropas, Myron B.
The Ukrainians in America (5 and up)   305.8

Kurosaki, Yoshisuke
(illus.) Sakade, F. ed. Japanese children's favorite stories   398.2

Kurtis, Arlene Harris
The Jews helped build America (4 and up)   305.8

Kurtz, Henry Ira
John and Sebastian Cabot (4-6)   92

Kuskin, Karla
Any me I want to be (1-4)   811
Near the window tree (2-5)   811
Roar and more   E
(illus.) What shall we do and Allee galloo! See What shall we do and Allee galloo!   796.1

Kutune, Shirka and the golden otter. Baumann, H.
In Baumann, H. The stolen fire p87-92   398.2

Kuwait (State)
See pages in the following book:
Berger, G. Kuwait and the rim of Arabia p19-56 (4 and up)   953

Kuwait and the rim of Arabia. Berger, G.   953

Kwangchow. See Canton, China

Kyle, Anne D.
Easter lambs
In Harper, W. comp. Easter chimes p45-62   S C

Kyrie. Anderson, P.
In Universe ahead: stories of the future p252-67   S C

L

LMP. See Literary market place: LMP   070.5025

LSD. See Lysergic acid diethylamide

Labastida, Aurora
(jt. auth.) Ets, M. H. Nine days to Christmas   E

Labor, Migratory. See Migrant labor

Labor and laboring classes
See also Child labor; Migrant labor; and names of countries, cities, etc. with the subdivision Social conditions, e.g. United States—Social conditions

Law and legislation
See pages in the following book:
Burns, M. I am not a short adult! p65-74 (3-6)   305.2
United States
Sandler, M. W. The way we lived (4 and up)   331.09

Labor unions
United States
See pages in the following book:
Meltzer, M. Taking root p219-35 (6 and up)   305.8

Laidly Worm of Spindleston Heugh. Jacobs, J.
  In Jacobs, J. English fairy tales p182-87
  398.2

Laimgruber, Monika
  (illus.) Grimm, J. The fisherman and his wife
  398.2

The **Laird's** lass and the gobha's son
  In Tatterhood, and other tales p65-78
  398.2

Laite, Gordon
  (illus.) Epstein, S. A year of Japanese festivals
  394.2

Lake, Herbert E.
  (illus.) Kelly, J. E. The dam builders   627
  (illus.) Kelly, J. E. The tunnel builders   624

The **lake**. Manning-Sanders, R.
  In Manning-Sanders, R. A book of spooks and spectres p112-14   398.2

Lake Erie. See Erie, Lake

Lake that flew. Credle, E.
  In Credle, E. Tall tales from high hills, and other stories p96-99   398.2

Lake Victoria. See Victoria, Lake

Lakes
  See pages in the following book:
  Wyckoff, J. The story of geology p70-77 (5 and up)   551

Lakota Indians. See Teton Indians

The **Lakota** woman. Yellow Robe, R.
  In Yellow Robe, R. Tonweya and the eagles, and other Lakota Indian tales p94-101   398.2

La-lee-lu. Manning-Sanders, R.
  In Manning-Sanders, R. A book of spooks and spectres p15-16   398.2

Laliberte, Norman
  (illus.) Hieatt, C. The Castle of Ladies
  398.2

Lamb, Charles
  A midsummer night's dream
  In Darrell, M. ed. Once upon a time p147-57   808.8
  Romeo and Juliet
  In Darrell, M. ed. Once upon a time p158-69   808.8
  Tales from Shakespeare   822.3
  The taming of the shrew
  In Darrell, M. ed. Once upon a time p140-46   808.8

Lamb, Geoffrey
  Secret writing tricks (5 and up)   652

Lamb, Mary
  (jt. auth.) Lamb, C. Tales from Shakespeare   822.3

Lamb, Pompey
  See pages in the following book:
  Rollins, C. H. They showed the way p100-02 (5 and up)   920

Lamb and the fish
  Grimm, J. The lambkin and the little fish
  In Grimm, J. The complete Grimm's fairy tales p625-27   398.2

Lamb that went to Fairyland. Fyleman, R.
  In Told under the magic umbrella p30-32   S C

Lambert, Eloise
  Our names (5 and up)   929.4

Lambie, Laurie Jo
  (illus) Adler, I. Integers: positive and negative   513
  (illus.) Adler, I. Language and man   410

Lambikin. Rockwell, A.
  In Rockwell, A. The old woman and her pig, & 10 other stories p37-47   398.2

The **lambikin.** Steel, F. A.
  In Indian fairy tales p17-20   398.2

The **lambkin** and the little fish. Grimm, J.
  In Grimm, J. The complete Grimm's fairy tales p625-27   398.2

The **lame** turkey. Kelsey, A. G.
  In Thanksgiving p274-80   394.2

Lament of Cadieux. Hooke, H. M.
  In Hooke, H. M. Thunder in the mountains p199-209   398.2

Lamorisse, Albert
  The red balloon (1-4)   Fic

Lampman, Evelyn Sibley
  The shy stegosaurus of Cricket Creek (5 and up)   Fic
  Squaw Man's son (5 and up)   Fic
  White captives (5 and up)   Fic

Lampreys
  See pages in the following book:
  Ault, P. These are the Great Lakes p134-40 (5 and up)   977

Lamps
  Fiction
  Goffstein, M. B. Goldie the dollmaker (3-5)   Fic

Lancaster, Fidelity
  The Bedouin (4 and up)   953

Lancelot
  Hieatt, C. The knight of the cart (4-7)   398.2
  See also pages in the following book:
  Reeves, J. The shadow of the hawk, and other stories p49-83 (5 and up)   398.2

The **land** and people of Argentina. Hall, E.   982

The **land** and people of Australia. Blunden, G.   994

The **land** and people of Austria. Wohlrabe, R. A.   943.6

The **land** and people of Belgium. Loder, D.   949.3

The **land** and people of Bolivia. Warren, L. F.   984

The **land** and people of Brazil. Brown, R.   981

The **land** and people of Ceylon. Wilbur, D. N.   954.9

The **land** and people of Cuba. Ortiz, V.   972.91

The **land** and people of Czechoslovakia. Hall, E.   943.7

The **land** and people of Denmark. Wohlrabe, R. A.   948.9

The **land** and people of Egypt. Mahmoud, Z. N.   962

The **land** and people of England. Street, A.   942

The **land** and people of Finland, Berry, E.   948.97

The **land** and people of France. Bragdon, L. J.   944

The **land** and people of Germany. Wohlrabe, R. A.   943

The **land** and people of Ghana. Sale, J. K.   966.7

The **land** and people of Greece. Gianakoulis, T.   949.5

The **land** and people of Holland. Barnouw, A. J.   949.2

Lawson, Robert—*Continued*
Rabbit Hill (3-6)   **Fic**
Rabbit Hill: excerpt
  In The Arbuthnot Anthology of children's
   literature p481-83   **808.8**
The tough winter. See note under Lawson, R. Rabbit Hill   **Fic**
(illus.) Under the tent of the sky. See Under the tent of the sky   **808.81**
Watchwords of liberty (3-6)   **973**
Willie's bad night
  In The Arbuthnot Anthology of children's
   literature p481-83   **808.8**
(illus.) Atwater, R. Mr Popper's penguins
    Fic
(illus.) Godolphin, M. Pilgrim's progress
    Fic
(illus.) Gray, E. J. Adam of the road   **Fic**
(illus.) Leaf, M. The story of Ferdinand   **E**
(illus.) Leaf, M. Wee Gillis   **E**

About
See pages in the following books:
Authors and illustrators of children's books
  p256-67   **028.5**
Caldecott Medal books: 1938-1957 p75-78
    028.5
Newbery Medal books: 1922-1955 p258-60
    028.5

Lawson, Roberta Campbell
See pages in the following book:
Gridley, M. E. American Indian women p88-
  93 (5 and up)   **920**

Laybourne, Kit
(ed.) Center for Understanding Media. Doing the media   **371.3**

Laycock, George
Beyond the Arctic Circle (5 and up)   **998**
Caves (5 and up)   **551.4**
The complete beginner's guide to photog-
  raphy (5 and up)   **770.28**
Exploring the great swamp (4-6)   **574.5**
Islands and their mysteries (5 and up)
    574.5
Tornadoes, killer storms (4 and up)   **551.5**

Layout and typography. See Printing

Lazar, Wendy
The Jewish holiday book (3-6)   **394.2**

Lazare, Jerry
(illus.) Burch, R. Queenie Peavy   **Fic**
(illus.) Little, J. One to grow on   **Fic**
(illus.) Little, J. Take wing   **Fic**

The Lazies   **398.2**

Laziness

Fiction
Lobel, A. A treeful of pigs   **E**

Lazy 'Arry. Grimm, J.
  In Grimm, J. The Brothers Grimm: popu-
   lar folk tales p87-89   **398.2**
   See also Lazy Heinz

The Lazy daughter
  In The Lazies p49-55   **398.2**

The lazy farmer. Prescott, J.
  In Gruenberg, S. M. ed. Favorite stories
   old and new p394-95   **808.8**

The lazy farmer's tale. Carrick, M.
  In Carrick, M. The wise men of Gotham
    398.2

Lazy Hans. Manning-Sanders, R.
  In Manning-Sanders, R. A book of
   witches p27-37   **398.2**
   See also Lazy Heinz

Lazy Harry. Grimm, J.
  In Grimm, J. The complete Grimm's fairy
   tales p678-81   **398.2**
   See also Lazy Heinz

Lazy Heinz
Grimm, J. Lazy 'Arry
  In Grimm, J. The Brothers Grimm: popu-
   lar folk tales p87-89   **398.2**
Grimm, J. Lazy Harry
  In Grimm, J. The complete Grimm's fairy
   tales p678-81   **398.2**
  In Grimm, J. Tales from Grimm p191-200
    398.2

Manning-Sanders, R. Lazy Hans
  In Manning-Sanders, R. A book of
   witches p27-37   **398.2**

Lazy Jack
Jacobs, J. Lazy Jack
  In Jacobs, J. English fairy tales p152-54
    398.2

Lazy Jack
  In It's time for story hour p94-96   **372.6**
  In The Tall book of nursery tales p71-73
    398.2

The story of Ferdinand   **E**
Rockwell, A. Lazy Jack
  In Rockwell, A. The three bears & 15
   other stories p92-99   **398.2**
  See also Jack and the king's girl

The lazy maiden. Afanas'ev, A.
  Afanas'ev, A. Russian fairy tales p423-25
    398.2

Lazy people, Tale of the. See Tale of the lazy
people

Lazy spinner
Grimm, J. The lazy spinner
  In Grimm, J. The complete Grimm's fairy
   tales p577-79   **398.2**

Lazy stories. Wolkstein, D.   **398.2**

Leach, Maria
Here we go!
  In A-haunting we will go p92-94   **S C**
Here we go!
  In Harper, W. comp. Ghosts and goblins
   p222-24   **398.2**
The lion sneezed (4-6)   **398.2**
Includes the following tales: The lion sneezed;
Take along the little cat; The cat and Nirantali;
The cat and Mahadeo; What's that?; Why Cat
eats first and washes afterward; The mouser;
Why Goat cannot climb a tree; Kitten and
Little Rat; Why Cat sleeps by the fire or keeps
the chimney corner; The manx cat and the
governor's lady; The good child and the bad
child, and Gattomammone, and what the kittens
said
Noodles, nitwits, and numskulls (4 and up)
    398
Riddle me, riddle me, ree (3-6)   **398**
The thing at the foot of the bed, and other
  scary tales (3-6)   **S C**
Contents: Here we go; Ghost race; Wait till
Martin comes; Big Fraid and Little Fraid; The
lucky man; The golden arm; The dare; I'm in
the room; No head; As long as this; The legs;
Talk; Milk bottles; The head; The lovelorn pig;
The ghostly hitchhiker; Aunt Tilly; The cradle
that rocked by itself; The gangster in the back
seat; Witch cat; Sop, doll; Singing bone

Leach, Maria—*Continued*

Whistle in the graveyard (4-6)   **398.2**

Contents: White House ghosts; Earl Gerald; Anne Boleyn; White ghosts; Skull race; Nobody here but you and me; What's the matter?; Old Tom comes home; 'Tain't so; One handful; Can't rest; Blackbeard's treasure; The tired ghost; Cauld, cauld, cauld, forever cauld; The outside man; I'm coming up the stairs; The man on Morvan's Road; Staring at you; The sea captain at the door; Grandpa Joe's brother; Bill is with me now; Tony and his harp; Crossing the bridge; The ghostly spools; Tick, tick, tick; Pumpkin; Jenny Green Teeth; Baba Yaga; Nuimumma-Kwiten; Pot-Tilter; Willie Winkie; Raw Head and Bloody Bones; The black cat's eyes; How to become a witch; Next turn to the right; A breath of air; The ghost on Brass's Hill; Sunrise; Dead man

Twist-mouth family

In North American legends p144-46 **398.2**

Leacroft, Helen

The buildings of ancient Egypt (5 and up)   **722**

The buildings of ancient Greece (5 and up)   **722**

The buildings of ancient man (5 and up)   **722**

The buildings of ancient Rome (5 and up)   **722**

Buildings of early Islam (5 and up)   **722**

Leacroft, Richard

(jt. auth.) Leacroft, H. The buildings of ancient Egypt   **722**

(jt. auth.) Leacroft, H. The buildings of ancient Greece   **722**

(jt. auth.) Leacroft, H. The buildings of ancient man   **722**

(jt. auth.) Leacroft, H. The buildings of ancient Rome   **722**

(jt. auth.) Leacroft, H. Buildings of early Islam (5 and up)   **722**

Leaf, Munro

Metric can be fun! (2-4)   **389**

also in Gruenberg, S. M. ed. Favorite stories old and new p469-72 **808.8**

Wee Gillis   **E**

Leaf from Heaven

Andersen, H. C. A leaf from heaven

In Andersen, H. C. The complete fairy tales and stories p449-51   **S C**

Leak in the dike

The Dutch boy and the dike

In Gruenberg, S. M. ed. Favorite stories old and new p363-66 **808.8**

Lewis, M. The boy who kept his finger in the dike

In The Golden Treasury of children's literature p522-23   **808.8**

Lean Liesl and Lanky Lenz

Grimm, J. Lean Liesl and Lanky Lenz

In Grimm, J. Tales from Grimm p201-03   **398.2**

Grimm, J. Lean Lisa

In Grimm, J. The complete Grimm's fairy tales p696-98   **398.2**

Grimm, J. Skinny Lizzie

In Grimm, J. The Brothers Grimm: popular folk tales p90-92   **398.2**

Lean Lisa. Grimm, J.

In Grimm, J. The complete Grimm's fairy tales p696-98   **398.2**

See also Lean Liesl and Lanky Lenz

The **leaning** silver birch. Riordan, J.

In Riordan, J. Tales from Tartary p129-30   **398.2**

Leap the elk and little Princess Cottongrass. Kjellin, H.

In Olenius, E. comp. Great Swedish fairy tales p123-24   **398.2**

Leaping match

Andersen, H. C. The jumping competition

In Andersen, H. C. The complete fairy tales and stories p295-96   **S C**

Andersen, H. C. The leaping match

In The Golden Treasury of children's literature p528-29   **808.8**

Lear, Edward

The complete nonsense of Edward Lear **821**

Edward Lear's The Scroobious Pip (2-6)   **821**

The Jumblies, and other nonsense verses (2-6)   **821**

The owl and the pussy-cat; illus. by Barbara Cooney (k-3)   **821**

The owl and the pussy-cat; illus. by Gwen Fulton (k-3)   **821**

The pelican chorus & other nonsense verses (2-6)   **821**

About

See pages in the following books:

Jan, I. On children's literature p56-59   **028.5**

Only connect p279-85   **028.5**

Learn and live

In Jataka tales p35-37   **398.2**

The **learned** men. Courlander, H.

In Courlander, H. The tiger's whisker, and other tales and legends from Asia and the Pacific p122-26   **398.2**

Learning (Periodical)   **370.5**

Learning and scholarship

See also Education

Learning disabilities

See pages in the following books:

Adams, B. Like it is: facts and feelings about handicaps from kids who know p53-68 (4-6)   **362.4**

Kamien, J. What if you couldn't. . . . ? p73-83 (4-6)   **362.4**

Fiction

Pevsner, S. Keep stompin' till the music stops (3-6)   **Fic**

Smith, D. B. Kelly's creek (4-6)   **Fic**

Learning disorders. See Learning disabilities

Learning resource centers. See Instructional materials centers

Learning to say good-by. LeShan, E.   **155.9**

Leather

See also Tanning

Leather industry and trade

See also Shoes and shoe industry

Leathers, Noel L.

The Japanese in America (5 and up) **305.8**

Leave Horatio alone. Clymer, E. See note under Clymer, E. Horatio   **E**

"**Leave** it there!" Robinson, A.

In Robinson, A. Singing tales of Africa p50-64   **398.2**

Leave well enough alone

In Jataka tales p41-42   **398.2**

Leaving paradise. Farjeon, E.

In Farjeon, E. The little bookroom p149-73   **S C**

Legend of the first Filipinos. Sechrist, E. H
  In Sechrist, E. H. Once in the first times
  p3-7   398.2

The **legend** of the hummingbird. Belpré, P.
  In Belpré, P. Once in Puerto Rico p25-28
       398.2

The **legend** of the Moor's legacy; adaptation.
  Irving, W.
  In Stories to dramatize p236-43   372.6

The **legend** of the Royal Palm. Belpré, P.
  In Belpré, P. Once in Puerto Rico p13-17
       398.2

Legend of the sleeping giant. Hooke, H. M.
  In Hooke, H. M. Thunder in the mountain
  p101-10   398.2

Legend of the wishing well. Hooke, H. M.
  In Hooke, H. M. Thunder in the mountains p71-81   398.2

Legends
  Baumann, H. The stolen fire (4-6)   398.2
  De Paola, T. The clown of God (k-3)   398.2
  Sawyer, R. Joy to the world (3-6)   394.2
  See also Fables; Folklore; Mythology

Africa
Arnott, K. African myths and legends (4
  and up)   398.2

Canada
Hooke, H. M. Thunder in the mountains
  (5 and up)   398.2
Toye, W. How summer came to Canada
  (k-3)   398.2

Finland
Synge, U. Land of heroes (5 and up)   398.2

Flanders
Jagendorf, M. A. Tyll Ulenspiegel's merry
  pranks (4-6)   398.2
Williams, J. The wicked tricks of Tyl Uilenspiegel (3-5)   398.2

France
Baldwin, J. The story of Roland (6 and up)
       398.2
Holman, F. The Drac (5 and up)   398.2
Scribner, C. The devil's bridge (2-4)   398.2
Valen, N. The Devil's tail (2-4)   398.2

Germany
Jagendorf, M. A. Tyll Ulenspiegel's merry
  pranks (4-6)   398.2

Great Britain
Brown, M. Dick Whittington and his cat
  (k-3)   398.2
Picard, B. L. Stories of King Arthur and
  his knights (5 and up)   398.2
Pyle, H. The merry adventures of Robin
  Hood of great renown in Nottinghamshire
  (5 and up)   398.2
Pyle, H. Some merry adventures of Robin
  Hood of great renown in Nottingham-
  shire (5 and up)   398.2

Greece
Anderson, L. Arion and the dolphin (k-3)
       398.2

Hawaii
Williams, J. The surprising things Maui did
  (1-3)   398.2

Indexes
Index to fairy tales, myths and legends
       398.2
Index to fairy tales, myths and legends;
  supplement   398.2

Index to fairy tales, myths and legends;
  second supplement   398.2
Index to fairy tales, 1949-1972   398.2
Index to fairy tales, 1973-1977   398.2

Ireland
Fritz, J. Brendan the Navigator (3-5)   398.2
Stephens, J. Irish fairy tales (6 and up)
       398.2

Mexico
De Paola, T. The Lady of Guadalupe (k-3)
       232.9

New England
Jagendorf, M. A. New England bean-pot
  (5 and up)   398.2
Lent, B. John Tabor's ride (k-3)   398.2

Poland
See pages in the following book:
Kelly, E. P. The land and people of Poland
  p21-28 (5 and up)   943.8

Russia
Downing, C. Russian tales and legends (4
  and up)   398.2
Robbins, R. Baboushka and the three kings
  (1-4)   398.2

Southern States
Jagendorf, M. A. Folk stories of the South
  (4 and up)   398.2

United States
Anderson, J. The haunting of America (5
  and up)   398.2
Felton, H. W. John Henry and his hammer
  (5 and up)   398.2
Keats, E. J. John Henry (k-3)   398.2
McCormick, D. J. Paul Bunyan swings his
  axe (4-6)   398.2
Malcolmson, A. Yankee Doodle's cousins
  (4 and up)   398.2
Rounds, G. Ol' Paul, the mighty logger
  (3-6)   398.2
Shapiro, I. Heroes in American folklore (4
  and up)   398.2

Wales
Robbins, R. Taliesin and King Arthur (3-5)
       398.2

Legends, Celtic
  Reeves, J. The shadow of the hawk, and
  other stories (5 and up)   398.2

Legends, Eskimo
  Houston, J. Kiviok's magic journey   398.2
  Houston, J. Tikta'liktak (4-6)   398.2

Legends, Germanic
  Baldwin, J. The story of Siegfried (6 and
  up)   398.2

Legends, Indian. See Indians of North America—Legends

Legends, Jewish
  Ish-Kishor, S. The carpet of Solomon (4-6)
       398.2
  McDermott, B. B. The Golem (2-5)   398.2
  Shulevitz, U. The magician (k-2)   398.2

Legends of Charlemagne. Bulfinch, T.
  In Bulfinch, T. Bulfinch's Mythology   291

Legends of the flowers. Woolsey, J.
  In It's time for Christmas p43-48   394.2

Legends of the trees. Woolsey, J.
  In It's time for Christmas p49-53   394.2

Legends of the underground bells. Woolsey, J.
  In It's time for Christmas p42-43   394.2

Lenski, Lois—*Continued*
Newbery Medal acceptance paper
  In Newbery Medal books: 1922-1955 p278-87   028.5
Strawberry girl (4-6)   Fic
(illus.) Barksdale, L. The first Thanksgiving   394.2
(illus.) Lovelace, M. H. Betsy-Tacy   Fic

About
See pages in the following books:
Authors and illustrators of children's books p268-74   028.5
Newbery Medal books: 1922-1955 p270-77   028.5

Lent, Blair
Caldecott Medal acceptance paper
  In Newbery and Caldecott Medal books: 1966-1975 p244-49   028.5
John Tabor's ride (k-3)   398.2
(illus.) Andersen, H. C. The little match girl   Fic
(illus.) Dayrell, E. Why the sun and the moon live in the sky   398.2
(illus.) Fisher, A. I stood upon a mountain   113
(illus.) Haviland, V. Favorite fairy tales told in India   398.2
(illus.) Hodges, M. The wave   398.2
(illus.) Mosel, A. The funny little woman   398.2
(illus.) Mosel, A. Tikki Tikki Tembo   398.2
(illus.) Sleator, W. The angry moon   398.2
(illus.) Small, E. Baba Yaga   398.2

About
See pages in the following book:
Newbery and Caldecott Medal books: 1966-1975 p250-55   028.5

Lentil. McCloskey, R.   E
Leo the lioness. Greene, C. C.   Fic
Leodhas, Sorche Nic. See Nic Leodhas, Sorche
Leonard, Marcia
(comp.) Cricket's Jokes, riddles and other stuff. See Cricket's Jokes, riddles and other stuff   793.7
The **leopard.** Baumann, H.
  In Baumann, H. The stolen fire p66-69   398.2
The **leopard.** Bodker, C.   Fic
Leopards
Schick, A. Serengeti cats (4 and up)   599.74

Fiction
Kipling, R. How the leopard got his spots (1-4)   Fic
The **leopard's** daughter. Courlander, H.
  In With a deep sea smile p56-60   372.6
Leopard's prey. Wibberley, L.   Fic
Leopold, Aldo
See pages in the following book:
Hirsch, S. C. Guardians of tomorrow p138-57 (5 and up)   920
Leopold, Nathan Freudenthal
See pages in the following book:
David, A. Famous criminal trials p20-37 (5 and up)   345
Leopold III, King of the Belgians
See pages in the following book:
Loder, D. The land and people of Belgium p64-68 (5 and up)   949.3

Lepidoptera. See Butterflies; Moths
Lepman, Jella
A bridge of children's books   028.5
Leppä Pölkky and the blue cross. Bowman, J. C.
  In Bowman, J. C. Tales from a Finnish tupa p171-86   398.2
  See also Log
The **leprechaun** shoemakers. Watts, F. B.
  In Dramatized folk tales of the world p239-49   812.08
The **leprechaun's** story. Kennedy, R.   E
Le Prince de Beaumont, Marie
Beauty and the beast   398.2
  also in The Classic fairy tales p139-50   398.2
  also in Perrault, C. Perrault's Complete fairy tales p115-34   398.2
Prince Dorus
  In Blue fairy book p227-35   398.2
The tale of the three wishes
  In The Classic fairy tales p153-55   398.2
Lerner, Carol
On the forest edge (3-5)   574.5
(illus.) McClung, R. M. Peeper, first voice of spring   597.8
Leroy, Gen
Emma's dilemma (4-6)   Fic
LeShan, Eda
Learning to say good-by (4 and up)   155.9
What makes me feel this way? (3-6)   152.4
What's going to happen to me? (4-6)   306.8
You and your feelings (6 and up)   155.5
A **lesson** for kings
  In Indian fairy tales p127-31   398.2
Lester, Julius
The knee-high man, and other tales (k-3)   398.2
To be a slave (6 and up)   326

About
See pages in the following book:
Authors and illustrators of children's books p275-79   028.5
Les Tina, Dorothy
May Day (1-3)   394.2
Leto
See pages in the following book:
Gates, D. The golden god: Apollo p7-11 (4 and up)   292
Let's bake bread. Johnson, H. L.   641.8
Let's be early settlers with Daniel Boone. Parish, P.   745.5
Let's be enemies. Udry, J. M.   E
Let's be Indians. Parish, P.   745.5
Let's celebrate: holiday decorations you can make. Parish, P.   745.59
Let's do fingerplays. Grayson, M.   796.1
Let's find out about the sun. Shapp, M.   523.8
Let's go to the moon. Wheat, J. K.   629.45
Let's hear a story. Gruenberg, S. M. comp.   808.8
Let's look at reptiles. Huntington, H. E.   597.9
Let's make gifts. Hautzig, E.   745.5
Let's make more presents. Hautzig, E.   745.5
Let's marry said the cherry, and other nonsense poems. Bodecker, N. M.   811

The letter, the witch, and the ring. Bellairs, J. See note under Bellairs, J. The house with the clock in its walls **Fic**

A letter to Amy. Keats, E. J. See note under Keats, E. J. The snowy day **E**

A letter to Lincoln. Barbee, L.
  In One hundred plays for children p268-76 **808.82**

Lettering
  See pages in the following book:
Kemp, J. E. Planning and producing audio-visual materials p120-31 **371.3**

Letters to Horseface. Monjo, F. N. **Fic**

Letting in the jungle. Kipling, R.
  In Kipling, R. The second jungle book p48-83 **S C**

Leukemia
Coerr, E. Sadako and the thousand paper cranes [a biography of Sadako Sasaki] (3-6) **92**

Fiction
Slote, A. Hang tough, Paul Mather (4 and up) **Fic**

Leuser, Eleanore
  The Christmas sampler
    In A Treasury of Christmas plays p288-96 **812.08**
  The Courage Piece
    In Fifty plays for junior actors p280-92 **812.08**
  The honored one
    In Fifty plays for junior actors p293-301 **812.08**
  The legend of the Christmas rose
    In A Treasury of Christmas plays p349-54 **812.08**
  The magic grapes
    In Dramatized folk tales of the world p258-64 **812.08**
  The mixing stick
    In One hundred plays for children p701-05 **808.82**
  The secret of the wishing well
    In Dramatized folk tales of the world p15-22 **812.08**
  Tommy's adventure
    In One hundred plays for children p159-63 **808.82**
  The wise people of Gotham
    In Dramatized folk tales of the world p88-97 **812.08**

Levenson, Dorothy
  Women of the West (4 and up) **305.4**

The lever and the pulley. Hellman, H. **531**

Levine, Barbara
  (illus.) Kiefer, I. Global jigsaw puzzle (6 and up) **551.1**

Levine, Edna S.
  Lisa and her soundless world (1-3) **617.8**

Levine, Joseph
  (jt. auth.) Pine, T. S. Measurements and how we use them **389**
  (jt. auth.) Pine, T. S. The Polynesians knew **996**
  (jt. auth.) Pine, T. S. Simple machines and how we use them **621.8**

Levinger, Elma Ehrlich
  The cruse of oil—165 B. C.
    In Association for Childhood Education International. Told under the Christmas tree p290-95 **808.8**

Levitin, Sonia
  The mark of Conte (6 and up) **Fic**
  A single speckled egg. See note under Levitin, S. Who owns the moon? **E**
  A sound to remember **E**
  Who owns the moon? **E**

Levoy, Myron
  Alan and Naomi (6 and up) **Fic**
  The witch of Fourth Street, and other stories (4-6) **S C**

Levy, Elizabeth
  Something queer at the ballpark. See note under Levy, E. Something queer is going on (a mystery) **E**
  Something queer at the library. See note under Levy, E. Something queer is going on (a mystery) **E**
  Something queer is going on (a mystery) **E**
  Something queer on vacation. See note under Levy, E. Something queer is going on (a mystery) **E**
  (jt. auth.) Harris, R. H. Before you were three **155.4**

Lewin, Ted
  World within a world: Baja (4-6) **574.9**
  (illus.) Blue, R. Grandma didn't wave back **Fic**
  (illus.) Blue, R. A month of Sundays **Fic**
  (illus.) MacKellar, W. The witch of Glen Gowrie **Fic**
  (illus.) Pringle, L. Listen to the crows **598**
  (illus.) Stemple, D. High ridge gobbler **598**
  (illus.) Straight on till morning. See Straight on till morning **821.08**

Lewis, Allen
  (illus.) Field, R. Calico bush **Fic**

Lewis, Bruce
  Meet the computer (3-5) **001.64**
  What is a laser? (4 and up) **535.5**

Lewis, C. S.
  The horse and his boy. See note under Lewis, C. S. The lion, the witch and the wardrobe **Fic**
  The last battle. See note under Lewis, C. S. The lion, the witch and the wardrobe **Fic**
  The lion, the witch and the wardrobe (4 and up) **Fic**
  The lion, the witch and the wardobe; excerpt
    In The Arbuthnot Anthology of children's literature p526-31 **808.8**
  The magician's nephew. See note under Lewis, C. E. The lion, the witch and the wardrobe **Fic**
  Prince Caspian. See note under Lewis, C. S. The lion, the witch and the wardrobe **Fic**
  The silver chair. See note under Lewis, C. S. The lion, the witch and the wardrobe **Fic**
  The voyage of the Dawn Treader. See note under Lewis, C. S. The lion, the witch and the wardrobe **Fic**

About
  See pages in the following books:
Authors and illustrators of children's books p280-96 **028.5**
Horn Book Reflections on children's books and reading p225-37 **028.5**
Only connect p170-75 **028.5**

Lewis, Clive Staples. See Lewis, C. S.

The life of Annie Christmas. Jagendorf, M. A.
In Jagendorf, M. A. Folk stories of the
South p128-33   **398.2**
A life of their own. Jenness, A.   **972.81**
Life on other planets
See pages in the following book:
Branley, F. M. A book of flying saucers
for you p60-64   **001.9**
Fiction
Karl, J. E. Beloved Benjamin is waiting
(4-6)   **Fic**
Life sciences
See also Medicine
Life with working parents: practical hints
for everyday situations. Hautzig, E.   **649**
Lifesaving
See pages in the following book:
Clemens, V. P. Super animals and their un-
usual careers p140-54 (4 and up)   **636.08**
Lifton, Betty Jean
Children of Vietnam (6 and up)   **959.704**
Lifts. See Hoisting machinery
Light
Branley, F. M. Light and darkness (1-3)
    535
Schneider, H. Science fun with a flashlight
(1-4)   **535**
See also Lasers
Light, Zodiacal. See Zodiacal light
**Light amplification by stimulated emission of
radiation.** See Lasers
Light and darkness. Branley, F. M.   **535**
Light and shade. See Shades and shadows
Light in the forest. Richter, C.   **Fic**
The **light** princess. Macdonald, G.   **Fic**
also in MacDonald, G. The complete fairy
tales of George MacDonald p13-63
    S C
The **light** princess, and other tales. See Mac-
Donald, G. The complete fairy tales of
George MacDonald   **S C**
Light ships. See Lightships
Lightbody, Donna M.
Braid craft (4 and up)   **746.42**
The **lighthouse** book. Berenstain, M.   **387.1**
The **lighthouse** keeper's lunch. Armitage, R.
    E
Lighthouses
Berenstain, M. The lighthouse book (2-4)
    387.1
Smith, A. Lighthouses (5 and up)   **387.1**
Fiction
Armitage, R. The lighthouse keeper's lunch
    E
Swift, H. H. The little red lighthouse and
the great gray bridge   **E**
Lightner, Alice M. See Hopf, Alice L.
Lightning
Branley, F. M. Flash, crash, rumble, and
roll (k-3)   **551.5**
See also pages in the following books:
Vandenburg, M. L. Help! Emergencies that
could happen to you, and how to handle
them p23-29 (2-5)   **616.02**
Weiss, M. E. Storms—from the inside out
p36-43 (4-6)   **551.5**

Lightships
See pages in the following book:
Smith, A. Lighthouses p127-46 (5 and up)
    387.1
Liisa and the prince
Bowman, J. C. Liisa and the prince
In Bowman, J. C. Tales from a Finnish
tupa p187-98   **398.2**
Like it is: facts and feelings about handicaps
from kids who know. Adams, B.   **362.4**
Like master, like servant. Jagendorf, M. A.
In Jagendorf, M. A. Noodlehead stories
from around the world p75-77
    398.2
Like meat loves salt
Like meat loves salt
In Grandfather tales p124-29   **398.2**
Lilacs
See pages in the following book:
Rahn, J. E. Watch it grow, watch it change
p7-32 (5 and up)   **581.3**
Liley, Margaret
(jt. auth.) Day, B. The secret world of
the baby   **612**
Lilies, rabbits, and painted eggs. Barth, E.
    394.2
The **Lilith** summer. Irwin, H.   **Fic**
Liliúokalani, Queen of the Hawaiian Islands
See pages in the following book:
As I saw it: women who lived the Ameri-
can adventure p168-71 (6 and up)   **973**
Lillie, Amy Morris
Land of the Pilgrims' pride
In Thanksgiving p176-88   **394.2**
Lilly, Charles
(illus.) Childress, A. When the rattlesnake
sounds   **812**
(illus.) Greene, B. Philip Hall likes me. I
reckon maybe   **Fic**
Limburg, Peter R.
Poisonous plants (4 and up)   **581.6**
Watch out, it's poison ivy! (3-6)   **581.6**
Limericks
Laughable limericks (4 and up)   **821.08**
Livingston, M. C. A lollygag of limericks
    811
They've discovered a head in the box for
the bread, and other laughable limericks
(5 and up)   **821.08**
See also Nonsense verses
Lin Tachian. Cheney, C.
In Cheney, C. Tales from a Taiwan kitchen
p150-56   **398.2**
Lincoln, Abraham, President U.S.
The Gettysburg Address
In Foster, G. Year of Lincoln, 1861 p28-29
    909.81
About
Aulaire, I. d'. Abraham Lincoln (2-4)   **92**
Commager, H. S. The great Proclamation
(6 and up)   **326**
De Regniers, B. S. The Abraham Lincoln
joke book (4-6)   **817.08**
Foster, G. Year of Lincoln, 1861 (3-6)
    909.81
McNeer, M. America's Abraham Lincoln
(5 and up)   **92**

Lincoln, Abraham, President U.S.—About
—*Continued*

Phelan, M. K. Mr Lincoln's inaugural journey (5 and up)   92

See also pages in the following books:

Anderson, J. The haunting of America p40-48 (5 and up)   398.2

The Arbuthnot Anthology of children's literature p806-09   808.8

Holiday ring p28-39 (4 and up)   394.2

National Geographic Society. Visiting our past: America's historylands p304-17 (5 and up)   917.3

Sandburg, C. The Sandburg treasury p383-477 (5 and up)   818

Fiction

Davis, B. Mr Lincoln's whiskers (4-6)   **Fic**

See also pages in the following books:

The Arbuthnot Anthology of children's literature p756-61   808.8

Stories to dramatize p265-70   372.6

Poetry

See pages in the following books:

O frabjous day! p63-71 (5 and up)   808.81

Sechrist, E. H. comp. Poems for red letter days p44-51   821.08

The **Lincoln** coat. Sealock, T. W.
In One hundred plays for children p277-87   808.82

Lincoln Library encyclopedia, The New   031

The **Lincoln** Library of essential information. See The New Lincoln Library encyclopedia   031

Lincoln's Birthday

See pages in the following book:

Sechrist, E. H. Red letter days p31-41   394.2

Drama

See pages in the following book:

Fisher, A. Holiday programs for boys and girls p172-93 (4 and up)   812

Linda-Gold and the old king. Wahlenberg, A.
In The Arbuthnot Anthology of children's literature p257-60   808.8
In Olenius, E. comp. Great Swedish fairy tales p195-202   398.2

Linda Richards: first American trained nurse. Collins, D. R.   92

Lindbergh, Charles Augustus, 1902-1974

Foster, J. T. The flight of the Lone Eagle (5 and up)   629.13

Grierson, J. I remember Lindbergh (6 and up)   92

See also pages in the following book:

Ross, F. Historic plane models p119-25 (5 and up)   629.133

Lindbergh, Charles Augustus, 1930-1932

See pages in the following book:

David, A. Famous criminal trials p54-69 (5 and up)   345

Lindblom, Steven

The fantastic bicycles book (5 and up)   629.2

Linden Artists

(illus.) Rutland, J. See inside an ancient Greek town   938

Linder, Enid

Potter, B. The art of Beatrix Potter   741.64

Linder, Leslie

Potter, B. The art of Beatrix Potter   741.64

Lindgren, Astrid

Boys just can't keep a secret
In Friends are like that! p20-31   **S C**

Christmas in the stable (k-2)   232.9

Pippi celebrates her birthday
In Holiday ring p158-68   394.2

Pippi goes on board. See note under Lindgren, A. Pippi Longstocking   **Fic**

Pippi in the South Seas. See note under Lindgren, A. Pippi Longstocking   **Fic**

Pippi Longstocking (3-6)   **Fic**

Pippi on the run. See note under Lindgren, A. Pippi Longstocking   **Fic**

The Tomten   **E**

The Tomten and the fox   **E**

About

See pages in the following book:

Authors and illustrators of children's books p297-301   028.5

Lindholm, P. A.

Stalo and Kauras
In Olenius, E. comp. Great Swedish fairy tales p170-73   398.2

Lindop, Edmund

The first book of elections (4 and up)   324.6

Lindquist, Jennie D.

The golden name day (3-5)   **Fic**

Lindroth, David

(illus.) Gore, H. M. What to do when there's no one but you   616.02

Lindsay, Maud

The great white bear
In Harper, W. comp. Ghosts and goblins p201-04   398.2

The jar of rosemary
In Harper, W. comp. Merry Christmas to you p178-84   **S C**

Little Dog and Big Dog
In Told under the magic umbrella p33-38   **S C**

The wishing well
In Harper, W. comp. Ghosts and goblins p166-72   398.2

Line, Les

(illus.) Graham, A. The milkweed and its world of animals   574.5

(illus.) Selsam, M. E. Land of the giant tortoise   500

Linen

See pages in the following book:

Houck, C. Warm as wool, cool as cotton p23-26 (3-6)   677

Lines and shapes. Russell, S. P.   516

The **lines** are coming. Rauch, H. G.   741.2

Lingnell, Lois

(illus.) Bulla, C. R. A tree is a plant   582.16

Linguistics. See Language and languages

Link, Martin

(jt. auth.) Blood, C. L. The goat in the rug   **E**

Linn, Charles F.

Estimation (2-4)   513

Probability (2-4)   519.2

Linoleum block printing

See pages in the following book:

Rockwell, H. Printmaking p42-51 (4-6)   760.2

Linsner, Kenneth Jay
(illus.) Huffman, T. Wrapped for eternity
393

The **Lion** and the crane
In Indian fairy tales p 1-2   398.2

Lion and the mouse
In The Tall book of nursery tales p108-09
398.2

The **lion** and the mouse. Rockwell, A.
In Rockwell, A. The three bears & 15 other
stories p14-16   398.2

The **lion** and the mouse; play. Bennett, R.
In Bennett, R. Creative plays and programs
for holidays p193-97   812
In One hundred plays for children p605-08
808.82

Lion cubs. National Geographic Society
599.74

The **Lion**-hearted kitten. Bacon, P.
In Gruenberg, S. M. ed Favorite stories
old and new p228-31   808.8

The **Lion** hunt
In Juba this and Juba that p62-70   372.6

Lion on the mountain. Dixon, P.   Fic

The **lion** sneezed. Leach, M.   398.2

The **lion** sneezed; folktale. Leach, M.
In Leach, M. The lion sneezed p6-7   398.2

The **lion**, the witch and the wardrobe. Lewis,
C. S.   Fic

The **lion**, the witch, and the wardrobe; excerpt.
Lewis, C. S.
In The Arbuthnot Anthology of children's
literature p526-31   808.8

Lion to lamb. Boiko, C.
In Boiko, C. Children's plays for creative
actors p230-38   812

Lionni, Leo
Alexander and the wind-up mouse   E
The biggest house in the world   E
Fish is fish   E
Frederick   E
Inch by inch   E
Little blue and little yellow   E
Swimmy   E
About
See pages in the following book:
Authors and illustrators of children's books
p302-07   028.5

Lions
Adamson, J. Elsa (2-5)   599.74
National Geographic Society. Lion cubs (k-3)
599.74
Schaller, G. Wonders of lions (5 and up)
599.74
Schick, A. Serengeti cats (4 and up)   599.74

Fiction
Fatio, L. The happy lion   E
Freeman, D. Dandelion   E
Hurd, E. T. Johnny Lion's book   E
Peet, B. Eli   E

The **lion's** share. Courlander, H.
In Courlander, H. The king's drum, and
other African stories p78-79   398.2

Lip reading. See Deaf—Means of communication

Lipkind, William
Nubber bear   E

Lipnick, Esther
Angel of mercy
In Fifty plays for junior actors p302-12
812.08
A son of liberty
In One hundred plays for children p828-37
808.82

Lippincott, Joseph Wharton
The Wahoo bobcat (5 and up)   Fic
Wilderness champion (5 and up)   Fic

Lippincott, Sara Lee
(jt. auth.) Joseph, J. M. Point to the stars
523.8

Lippizaner horse
Fiction
Henry, M. White stallion of Lipizza (5 and
up)   Fic

Lippman, Peter
(illus.) Cobb, V. Arts and crafts you can eat
745.5
(illus.) Cobb, V. Science experiments you can
eat   507
(illus.) Cobb, V. Supersuits   613

Lippo and Tapio
Bowman, J. C. Lippo and Tapio
In Bowman, J. C. Tales from a Finnish
tupa p65-72   398.2

Lipsyte, Robert
Free to be Muhammad Ali (5 and up)   92
One fat summer (6 and up)   Fic

Liquor problem
See also Alcoholism

Lisa and her soundless world. Levine, E. S.
617.8

Lisa's song. Kennell, R.
In Gruenberg, S. M. ed. Favorite stories
old and new p92-97   808.8

Lisker, Sonia O.
(illus.) Blume, J. Freckle juice   Fic

Lisowski, Gabriel
(illus.) Blaine, M. Dvora's journey   Fic
(illus.) Levitin, S. A sound to remember   E
(illus.) Levoy, M. The witch of Fourth
Street, and other stories   S C

Liss, Howard
Basketball talk for beginners (4 and up)
796.32
Fishing talk for beginners (5 and up)   799.1
The great game of soccer (5 and up)   796.334
Hockey talk for beginners (4 and up)   796.96

List, Albert
A walk in the forest (5 and up)   574.5

List, Ely
(ed.) Girl Scouts of the United States of
America. Girl Scout cookbook   641.5

List, Ilka
(jt. auth.) List, A. A walk in the forest
574.5

List of subject headings: Canadian companion,
Sears   025.4

List of subject headings, Sears   025.4

Listen! And help tell the story. Carlson, B. W.
372.6

Listen, children, listen. Livingston, M. C. ed.
821.08

Listen for the singing. Little, J. See note under
Little, J. From Anna   Fic

Listen, rabbit. Fisher, A.   E

Listen to a shape. Brown, M.   500

Listen to the crows. Pringles, L.   598

The **listening** walk. Showers, P.   **E**

Lister, Joseph Lister, 1st Baron
See pages in the following book:
Cottler, J. Heroes of civilization p325-36 (5 and up)   **920**

Liston, Robert A.
Who shall pay? (5 and up)   **336.2**

Litchfield, Ada B.
A button in her ear (1-3)   **617.8**

Literary awards. See Literary prizes; and names of literary prizes, e.g. Newbery Medal books

Literary characters. See Characters and characteristics in literature

Literary criticism. See Criticism

Literary market place: LMP   **070.5025**

Literary prizes
See pages in the following books:
The Arbuthnot Anthology of children's literature p979-83   **808.8**
Children and literature p439-56   **028.5**
Sutherland, Z. Children & books p631-38   **028.5**

See also names of literary prizes, e.g. Caldecott Medal books

Bibliography
Children's books: awards and prizes   **016.8**

Literature
See also Children's literature; Drama; Fables; Fairy tales; Legends; Poetry; Sagas; Wit and humor; and names of literatures, e.g. American literature

Collections
The Arbuthnot Anthology of children's literature   **808.8**
Association for Childhood Education International. Told under the Christmas tree (3-6)   **808.8**
Carlson, B. W. Listen! And help tell the story   **372.6**
Darrell, M. ed. Once upon a time (4 and up)   **808.8**
The Golden Treasury of children's literature   **808.8**
Gruenberg, S. M. ed. Favorite stories old and new   **808.8**
Gruenberg, S. M. comp. Let's hear a story   **808.8**
It's time for story hour   **372.6**
Juba this and Juba that   **372.6**
Ross, E. S. ed. The lost half-hour   **372.6**
Sawyer, R. The way of the storyteller   **372.6**
Shedlock, M. L. The art of the story-teller   **372.6**
Stories to dramatize   **372.6**
Witches, witches, witches (5 and up)   **808.8**
With a deep sea smile   **372.6**
Yankee Doodle's literary sampler of prose, poetry, and pictures   **028.5**
See also Quotations; Short stories; and names of literatures and literary forms with subdivision Collections, e.g. Russian literature — Collections; Poetry — Collections

Encyclopedias
Brewer's Dictionary of phrase and fable   **803**

Evaluation
See Books—Reviews

History and criticism
See also Criticism

Prizes
See Literary prizes; and names of literary prizes, e.g. Caldecott Medal books

Selections
See Literature—Collections

Stories, plots, etc.
Gillespie, J. Introducing books   **028.1**
Gillespie, J. Juniorplots   **028.1**
Gillespie, J. T. More Juniorplots   **028.1**
Spirt, D. L. Introducing more books   **028.1**

Literature and young children   **028.5**

Literature by and about the American Indian Stensland, A. L.   **016.970004**

Literature for children: enrichment ideas. See Carlson, R. K. Enrichment ideas   **028.5**

Lithography
See pages in the following books:
Barker, A. Black on white and read all over p42-53 (4-6)   **686.2**
The Illustrator's notebook p109-14   **741.64**

Litsky, Frank
The winter Olympics (4-6)   **796.9**

Litterbug convention; play. Carlson, B. W.
In Carlson, B. W. The right play for you p97-100   **792**

Littering. See Refuse and refuse disposal

Little, Jean
From Anna (4 and up)   **Fic**
Kate. See note under Little, J. Look through my window   **Fic**
Listen for the singing. See note under Little, J. From Anna   **Fic**
Look through my window (4-6)   **Fic**
Mine for keeps (4-6))   **Fic**
One to grow on (4-6)   **Fic**
The second day
In The Arbuthnot Anthology of children's literature p705-08   **808.8**
Take wing (4-6)   **Fic**

Little, Lessie Jones
I can do it by myself   **E**
(jt. auth.) Greenfield, E. Childtimes   **920**

Little, Malcolm. See Malcolm X

Little Annie and the whaler captain. Jagendorf, M. A.
In Jagendorf, M. A. New England beanpot p261-66   **398.2**

Little apes. Conklin, G.   **599.88**

Little Bear. Minarik, E. H.   **E**

Little Bear's friend. Minarik, E. H. See note under Minarik, E. H. Little Bear   **E**

Little bear's son
Afanas'ev, A. Ivanko the bear's son
In Afanas'ev, A. Russian fairy tales p221-23   **398.2**

Little Bear's visit. Minarik, E. H. See note under Minarik, E. H. Little Bear   **E**

Little Big Horn, Battle of the, 1876
Goble, P. Red Hawk's account of Custer's last battle (4 and up)   **973.8**
Reynolds, Q. Custer's last stand (5 and up)   **92**

Little black ant
Gall, A. The sandy mound by the thicket
In Gruenberg, S. M. ed. Favorite stories old and new p164-69   **808.8**

The **little** shepherd boy. Grimm, J.
In Grimm, J. More Tales from Grimm p47-49 **398.2**
See also Shepherd boy and the king

Little sister
Bowman, J. C. Girl who sought her nine brothers
In Bowman, J. C. Tales from a Finnish tupa p116-25 **398.2**

Little Sister and the Month Brothers. De Regniers, B. S. **398.2**
See also Twelve months

Little Sister Fox and Brother Wolf. Riordan, J.
In Riordan, J. Tales from Central Russia p20-22 **398.2**
See also Little Sister Fox and the wolf

Little Sister Fox and the wolf
Afanas'ev, A. Little Sister Fox and the wolf
In Afanas'ev, A. Russian fairy tales p371-75 **398.2**
Riordan, J. Little Sister Fox and Brother Wolf
In Riordan, J. Tales from Central Russia p20-22 **398.2**

Little Snow-White. Grimm, J.
In Grimm, J. The Brothers Grimm: popular folk tales p61-71 **398.2**
In Grimm, J. The complete Grimm's fairy tales p249-58 **398.2**
See also Snow-White and the seven dwarfs

Little Snowdrop. Grimm, J.
In Red fairy book p324-36 **398.2**
See also Snow White and the seven dwarfs

Little soldier
Deulin, C. The little soldier
In The Andrew Lang Fairy tale treasury p243-59 **398.2**
In Green fairy book p166-87 **398.2**

The **little** swineherd, Fox, P.
In Fox, P. The little swineherd, and other tales p7-47 **S C**

The **little** swineherd, and other tales. Fox, P. **S C**

The **little** tailor and the three dogs. Manning-Sanders, R.
In Manning-Sanders, R. A book of ogres and trolls p101-09 **398.2**

Little Thumb. Perrault, C.
In Blue fairy book p236-47 **398.2**
See also Hop-o'-my Thumb

Little Tim and the brave sea captain. Ardizzone, E. **E**

A **little** time. Baldwin, A. N. **Fic**

The **little** toe bone. Hardendorff, J. B.
In Hardendorff, J. B. Witches, wit, and a werewolf p64-66 **S C**

Little Tom Thumb. Perrault, C.
In Perrault, C. Perrault's Complete fairy tales p26-41 **398.2**
See also Hop-o'-my-Thumb

Little Toot. Gramatky, H. **E**
also in Gruenberg, S. M. comp. Let's hear a story p15-24 **808.8**

Little Toot on the Mississippi. Gramatky, H.
See note under Gramatky, H. Little Toot **E**

Little Toot on the Thames. Gramatky, H. See note under Gramatky, H. Little Toot **E**

Little Toot through the Golden Gate. Gramatky, H. See note under Gramatky, H. Little Toot **E**

Little town on the prairie. Wilder, L. I. See note under Wilder, L. I. Little house in the big woods **Fic**

Little Tuck. Andersen, H. C.
In Andersen, H. C. The complete fairy tales and stories p330-33 **S C**

Little Tuk
Andersen, H. C. Little Tuck
In Andersen, H. C. The complete fairy tales and stories p330-33 **S C**

Little Turtle. Henderson, N.
In Henderson, N. Celebrate America p86-94 **812**

Little whale. McGovern, A. **599.5**

The **little** white lily: story of the Easter seal. Sechrist, E. H.
In It's time for Easter p242-47 **394.2**

Little witch. Bennett, A. E. **Fic**

Little women. Alcott, L. M. **Fic**

Little women. Morley, O. J.
In A Treasury of Christmas plays p129-46 **812.08**

The **little** wood duck. Wildsmith, B. **E**

The **little** wooden doll. Bianco, W. M. **Fic**

Littledale, Freya
The elves and the shoemaker (k-3) **398.2**

The **littlest** artist. Bennett, R.
In Bennett, R. Creative plays and programs for holidays p45-50 **812**

Litzinger, Roseanne
(illus.) Masterman-Smith, V. The treasure trap **Fic**

Livaudais, Madeleine
The skeleton book (3-6) **596**

Live polio-virus vaccine. See Poliomyelitis vaccine

Lively, Penelope
The ghost of Thomas Kempe (4-6) **Fic**
The ghost of Thomas Kempe; excerpt
In The Arbuthnot Anthology of children's literature p557-62 **808.8**
Messages from a sorcerer
In The Arbuthnot Anthology of children's literature p557-62 **808.8**
A stitch in time (4-6) **Fic**
The voyage of QV 66 (4-6) **Fic**

About
See pages in the following book:
Townsend, J. R. A sounding of storytellers p125-38 **028.5**

Liverworts
See pages in the following book:
Hutchins, R. E. Plants without leaves p111-16 (5 and up) **586**

The **lives** of my cat Alfred. Zimelman, N. **E**

Livestock
See pages in the following book:
Dobler, L. The land and people of Uruguay p71-81 (5 and up) **989.5**
See also Domestic animals

The **living** colors of the Twenty-first. Jagendorf, M. A.
In Jagendorf, M. A. Folk stories of the South p151-53 **398.2**

London—Fiction—*Continued*

King, C. Me and my million (5 and up) **Fic**
Newman, R. The case of the Baker Street Irregular (5 and up) **Fic**
Roach, M. K. Presto: or, The adventures of a turnspit dog (4 and up) **Fic**
Streatfeild, N. Ballet shoes (4-6) **Fic**
London Bridge is falling down! (k-2) **784.4**
The **Lone** Arthur. Coren, A. See note under Coren, A. Arthur the Kid **Fic**
Lone Bull's horse raid. Goble, P. **Fic**
The **lone** hunt. Steel, W. O. **Fic**
Lone Wolf
(illus.) Gridley, M. E. Indian tribes of America **970.004**
Lonely Veronica. Duvoisin, R. See note under Duvoisin, R. Veronica **E**
The **loner**. Wier, E. **Fic**
Lonette, Reisie
(illus.) It's time for Christmas. See It's time for Christmas **394.2**
The **long** ago lake. Wilkins, M. **500**
A **long** day without water. Aiken, J.
In Haunting tales p132-55 **S C**
Long-life name
Mosel, A. Tikki Tikki Tembo **398.2**
The **long** lost coelacanth: and other living fossils. Aliki **597**
A **long** night of terror. Kendall, C.
In The Arbuthnot Anthology of children's literature p518-23 **808.8**
The **Long**-nosed goblins
In Sakade, F. ed. Japanese children's favorite stories p29-34 **398.2**
Long Sash and his people. Marriott, A.
In Marriott, A. American Indian mythology **398.2**
The **long** secret. Fitzhugh, L. See note under Fitzhugh, L. Harriet the spy **Fic**
The **long** view into space. Simon, S. **523.1**
A **long** way from Verona. Gardam, J. **Fic**
The **long** winter. Wilder, L. I. See note under Wilder, L. I. Little house in the big woods **Fic**
Longfellow, Henry Wadsworth
The children's own Longfellow (5 and up) **811**
Paul Revere's ride
In The Arbuthnot Anthology of children's literature p26-27 **808.8**
In Longfellow, H. W. The children's own Longfellow **811**
Longnose, the dwarf
Dwarf Long Nose
In Greene, E. comp. Clever cooks p56-86 **398.2**
The History of Dwarf Long Nose
In The Andrew Lang Fairy tale treasury p534-56 **398.2**
Longsworth, Polly
I, Charlotte Forten, black and free (6 and up) **92**
Longtemps, Ken
(illus.) Baylor, B. Sometimes I dance mountains **792.8**
Longworth, Florence
(illus.) Klots, A. B. A field guide to the butterflies of North America, east of the Great Plains **595.7**

Lontoft, Ruth Giles
(comp.) Illustrators of children's books: 1957-1966. See Illustrators of children's books: 1957-1966 **741.64**
Look again! Hoban, T. **E**
Look at a colt. Wright, D. **636.1**
Look at a flower. Dowden, A. O. **582.13**
A **look** at ants. Hutchins, R. E. **595.7**
Look at castles. See Duggan, A. The castle book **728.8**
Look at your eyes. Showers, P. **612**
Look behind as well as before
Burton, W. F. P. Look behind as well as before
In The Arbuthnot Anthology of children's literature p326 **808.8**
In Time for old magic p203 **398.2**
Look how many people wear glasses. Brindze, R. **617.7**
Look through my window. Little, J. **Fic**
Look to a new day. Fisher, A.
In Fisher, A. Holiday programs for boys and girls p347-67 **812**
Look to the night sky. Simon, S. **523**
Look what I can do. Aruego, J. **E**
Looking at ancient history. Unstead, R. J. **930**
Looking at architecture. Paine, R. M. **720.9**
Looking at art. Chase, A. E. **701**
Looking at Australia. Henderson, W. F. **994**
Looking at Brazil. Kendall, S. **981**
Looking at China. Gray, N. **951**
Looking at Great Britain. Hinds, L. **941**
Looking at maps. Fuchs, E. **912**
Looking at Russia. Hewitt, P. **947**
Looking at Sweden. Arbman, J. **948.5**
Looking for a bride. Grimm, J.
In Grimm, J. The complete Grimm's fairy tales p655-56 **398.2**
The **looking**-glass tree. Aiken, J.
In Aiken, J. The faithless lollybird p209-35 **S C**
The **loon's** necklace. Toye, W. **398.2**
López, Francisco Solano
See pages in the following book:
Dobler, L. The land and people of Uruguay p54-59 (5 and up) **989.5**
Lopez, Gretchen
(illus.) Olney, R. Pocket calculator fun & games **793.7**
Lopshire, Robert
A beginner's guide to building and flying model airplanes (5 and up) **629.133**
How to make snop snappers, and other fine things (1-3) **745.592**
It's magic? (k-2) **793.8**
(illus.) Baker, B. The Pig War **973.6**
(illus.) Platt, K. Big Max **E**
Lord, John Vernon
The giant jam sandwich **E**
Lord Bag of Rice
Manning-Sanders, R. My Lord Bag of Rice
In Manning-Sanders, R. A book of dragons p38-42 **398.2**
Lord of Massachusetts. Jagendorf, M. A.
In Jagendorf, M. A. New England beanpot p147-52 **398.2**

Lovecraft, H. P.
The music of Erich Zann
In Haunts, haunts, haunts p160-70 **S C**
Lovejoy, Elijah Parish
See pages in the following books:
Chittenden, E. F. Profiles in black and white
p142-58 (5 and up) **920**
Fincher, E. B. The Bill of rights p 1-4
(5 and up) **342**
Lovelace, Maud Hart
Betsy and Joe, a Betsy-Tacy high school
story. See note under Lovelace, M. H.
Betsy-Tacy **Fic**
Betsy and the great world. See note under
Lovelace, M. H. Betsy-Tacy **Fic**
Betsy in spite of herself. See note under
Lovelace, M. H. Betsy-Tacy **Fic**
Betsy was a junior, a Betsy-Tacy high school
story. See note under Lovelace, M. H.
Betsy-Tacy **Fic**
Betsy-Tacy (2-4) **Fic**
Betsy-Tacy and Tib. See note under Love-
lace, M. H. Betsy-Tacy **Fic**
Betsy's wedding. See note under Lovelace,
M. H. Betsy-Tacy **Fic**
Down town, a Betsy-Tacy story. See note
under Lovelace, M. H. Betsy-Tacy **Fic**
Heaven to Betsy; a Betsy-Tacy high school
story. See note under Lovelace, M. H.
Betsy-Tacy **Fic**
Over the big hill, a Betsy-Tacy story. See
note under Lovelace, M. H. Betsy-Tacy
Fic
Loveliest rose in the world
Andersen, H. C. The loveliest rose in the
world
In Harper, W. comp. Easter chimes p129-
33 **S C**
In It's time for Easter p198-201 **304.2**
Andersen, H. C. The world's most beautiful
rose
In Andersen, H. C. The complete fairy
tales and stories p390-92 **S C**
The **lovelorn** pig. Leach, M.
In Leach, M. The thing at the foot of the
bed, and other scary tales p65-67
S C
"Lovely." Andersen, H. C.
In Andersen, H. C. The complete fairy
tales and stories p650-56 **S C**
Loving Laili
Loving Laili
In Indian fairy tales p51-65 **398.2**
Low, Edward
See pages in the following book:
Stockton, F. R. Buccaneers & pirates of our
coasts p202-11 (5 and up) **910.4**
Low, Joseph
Five men under one umbrella, and other
ready-to-read riddles p(1-3) **793.7**
A mad wet hen, and other riddles (1-3)
793.7
(illus.) Branley, F. M. Roots are food finders
581.1
(illus.) Goldin, A. Spider silk **595.4**
(illus.) Jordan, H. J. How a seed grows
582
(illus.) Livingston, M. C. A lollygag of
limericks **811**
(illus.) Showers, P. Hear your heart **612**
(illus.) Thomson, P. Museum people **069**

(illus.) Van Woerkom, D. Meat pies &
sausage **E**
(illus.) Wright, W. W. The rainbow dic-
tionary **423**
Lowe, Kurt E.
(jt. auth.) Chesterman, C. W. The Audubon
Society Field guide to North American
rocks and minerals **549**
Lowe, Patricia Tracy
The tale of Czar Saltan (3-5) **398.2**
The tale of the golden cockerel (3-5) **398.2**
Lowenheim, Alfred
(illus.) Gardner, R. The boys and girls
book about divorce **306.8**
Lowenstein, Dyno
Graphs (5 and up) **511**
Lower than angels. Budrys, A.
In Universe ahead: stories of the future
p208-51 **S C**
Lownsbery, Eloise
The boy knight of Reims; excerpt
In Stories to dramatize p214-18 **372.6**
Lowrey, Janette Sebring
Six silver spoons **E**
Lowrie, Jean Elizabeth
Elementary school libraries **027.8**
Lowry, Lois
Anastasia Krupnik (4-6) **Fic**
A summer to die (5 and up) **Fic**
Loy Krathong
See pages in the following book:
More Festivals in Asia p55-60 (2-5) **394.2**
Loyalists, American. See American Loyalists
Lubell, Cecil
(jt. auth.) Lubell, W. Picture signs & sym-
bols **001.56**
Lubell, Winifred
Picture signs & symbols (2-4) **001.56**
(jt. auth.) Miller, I. P. The stitchery book
746.44
(illus.) Selsam M. See through the sea
591.92
Lubin, Leonard B.
The white cat (1-3) **398.2**
(illus.) Fox, P. The little swineherd, and
other tales **S C**
Lu-bo-bo. Manning-Sanders, R.
In Manning-Sanders, R. A book of mon-
sters p41-48 **398.2**
Lucas the strong. Sechrist, E. H.
In Sechrist, E. H. Once in the first times
p196-204 **398.2**
Lucia Bride. Reel, A.
In Christmas stories round the world
p89-93 **S C**
Luck can be found in a stick. Andersen, H. C.
In Andersen, H. C. The complete fairy
tales and stories p975-77 **S C**
Luck for fools. Jagendorf, M. A.
In Jagendorf, M. A. Noodlehead stories
from around the world p216-21
398.2
Luck may lie in a pin
Andersen, H. C. Luck can be found in a
stick
In Andersen, H. C. The complete fairy
tales and stories p975-77 **S C**
The **luck** of Pokey Bloom. Conford, E. **Fic**
Luckhardt, Mildred Corell
The daring venture
In Thanksgiving p21-43 **394.2**
Happy Thanksgiving!
In Thanksgiving p94-98 **394.2**

A lying story. Manning-Sanders, R.
   In Manning-Sanders, R. A book of enchantments and curses p50-55 **398.2**
Lyle and the birthday party. Waber, B. See note under Waber, B. The house on East 88th Street **E**
Lyle finds his mother. Waber, B. See note under Waber, B. The house on East 88th Street **E**
Lyle, Lyle, crocodile. Waber, B. See note under Waber, B. The house on East 88th Street **E**
Lynch, Brendan
   (illus.) May, J. A new baby comes **612**
Lynch, Lorenzo
   (illus.) Adoff, A. Big Sister tells me that I'm black **811**
Lynch, Marietta
   (jt. auth.) Perry, P. Mommy and Daddy are divorced **E**
Lynch, May
   Finn McCool
   In Dramatized folk tales of the world p218-26 **812.08**
Lynch, Patricia
   See pages in the following book:
   Horn Book Reflections on children's books and reading p260-64 **028.5**
Lynn, Ruth Nadelman
   Fantasy for children **016.8**
Lynx. See Bobcat
Lyon, Fred H.
   (illus.) Beeler, N. F. Experiments in optical illusion **535**
Lyons, Grant
   The Creek Indians (4-6) **970.004**
Lyons, John Henry
   Stories of our American patriotic songs (4 and up) **784.7**
Lysbet and the fire kittens. Moskin, M. **Fic**
Lysergic acid diethylamide
   See pages in the following book:
   Gorodetzky, C. W. What you should know about drugs p44-57 (5 and up) **613.8**
Lyttle, Richard B.
   The complete beginner's guide to backpacking (5 and up) **796.5**
   Jogging and running (5 and up) **796.4**

M

M. C. Higgins, the great. Hamilton, V. **Fic**
M. D. in petticoats. Henderson, N.
   In Henderson, N. Celebrate America p103-12 **812**
Ma Liang and his magic brush. Wyndham, R.
   In Wyndham, R. Tales the people tell in China p73-82 **398.2**
Ma nda La. Adoff, A. **E**
Maas, Selve
   The old traveler
   In The Arbuthnot Anthology of children's literature p285-87 **808.8**
Mabinogion
   Bulfinch, T. Bulfinch's Mythology (6 and up) **291**
MacAgy, Douglas
   Going for a walk with a line (3 and up) **709.04**

MacAgy, Elizabeth
   (jt. auth.) MacAgy, D. Going for a walk with a line **709.04**
McArthur, Jean A.
   Fiesta the first
   In Fifty plays for junior actors p313-21 **812.08**
Macaulay, David
   Castle (5 and up) **728.8**
   Cathedral: the story of its construction (4 and up) **726**
   City (4 and up) **711**
   Pyramid (5 and up) **726**
   Underground (5 and up) **624**
McBride, Kathy Fritz
   (illus.) Herda, D. J. Vegetables in a pot **635**
MacBride, Roger Lea
   (ed.) Wilder, L. I. West from home; letters of Laura Ingalls Wilder to Almanzo Wilder, San Francisco, 1915 **92**
McBroom and the beanstalk. Fleischman. S. See note under Fleischman, S. McBroom tells a lie **Fic**
McBroom and the great race. Fleischman, S. See note under Fleischman, S. McBroom tells a lie **Fic**
McBroom tells a lie. Fleischman, S. **Fic**
Maccabees
   Greenfeld, H. Chanukah (4 and up) **296.4**
   Hirsh, M. The Hanukkah story (1-3) **296.4**
McCaffery, Janet
   (illus.) Still, J. Way down yonder on Troublesome Creek **398**
McCaffrey, Anne
   Dragondrums. See note under McCaffrey, A. Dragonsong **Fic**
   Dragonsinger. See note under McCaffrey, A. Dragonsong **Fic**
   Dragonsong (6 and up) **Fic**
MacCann, Donnarae
   (ed.) The Black American in books for children: readings in racism. See The Black American in books for children: readings in racism **028.5**
   The child's first books **028.5**
McCarty, E. Clayton
   The little cake
   In One hundred plays for children p518-27 **808.82**
MacClain, George
   (illus.) I'm mad at you. See I'm mad at you **811.08**
McClenathan, Louise
   My mother sends her wisdom **E**
McCloskey, Robert
   Blueberries for Sal **E**
   Burt Dow, deep-water man **E**
   Caldecott Medal acceptance paper [1942]
   In Caldecott Medal books: 1938-1957 p80-84 **028.5**
   Caldecott Medal acceptance paper [1958]
   In Newbery and Caldecott Medal books: 1956-1965 p188-93 **028.5**
   The Centerburg tales. See note under McCloskey, R. Homer Price **Fic**
   The doughnuts
   In The Arbuthnot Anthology of children's literature p687-91 **808.8**
   Homer Price (4 and up) **Fic**
   Homer Price; excerpt
   In The Arbuthnot Anthology of children's literature p687-91 **808.8**

AUTHOR, TITLE, SUBJECT, AND ANALYTICAL INDEX
FOURTEENTH EDITION, 1981

Maestro, Giulio
- (illus.) Berger, M. Energy from the sun **621.47**
- (illus.) Branley, F. M. The beginning of the earth **551**
- (illus.) Charosh, M. Number ideas through pictures **513**
- (illus.) Cobb, V. More Science experiments you can eat **507**
- (illus.) Cutler, K. N. Creative shellcraft **745.55**
- (illus.) Cutler, K. N. From petals to pine-cones **745.58**
- (illus.) Delton, J. Two good friends **E**
- (illus.) Gans, R. Caves **551.4**
- (illus.) Gans, R. Millions and millions of crystals **548**
- (illus.) Ginsburg, M. Three kittens **E**
- (illus.) Haines, G. K. Natural and synthetic poisons **615.9**
- (jt. auth.) Maestro, B. Busy day: a book of action words **E**
- (jt. auth.) Maestro, B. Harriet goes to the circus **E**
- (illus.) Meyer, C. Milk, butter, and cheese **641.3**
- (illus.) Milgrom, H. Egg-ventures **500**
- (illus.) Riedman, S. R. Trees alive **582.16**
- (illus.) Sommer, E. The bread dough craft book **745.5**
- (illus.) Sommer, E. A patchwork, appliqué, and quilting primer **746.46**
- (illus.) Trivett, D. Time for clocks **529**

Maffia, Daniel
- (illus.) Branley, F. M. Shakes, quakes, and shifts: earth tectonics **551.1**

Magarac, Joe
- *See pages in the following books:*
- Malcolmson, A. Yankee Doodle's cousins p29-35 (4 and up) **398.2**
- Shapiro, I. Heroes in American folklore p199-256 (4 and up) **398.2**

Magazines. See Periodicals

Magellan, Ferdinand
- Syme, R. Magellan, first around the world (4-6) **92**
- *See also pages in the following books:*
- Cottler, J. Heroes of civilization p26-36 (5 and up) **920**
- Discoverers of the New World p53-63 (5 and up) **970.01**
- Hall, E. The land and people of Argentina p68-72 (5 and up) **982**

Magellan, first around the world. Syme, R. **92**

The **Maggie** B. Haas, I. **E**

Maggie Marmelstein for president. Sharmat, M. W. See note under Sharmat, M. W. Getting something on Maggie Marmelstein **Fic**

Maggie's gift. Paterson, K.
- *In* Paterson, K. Angels & other strangers p49-63 **S C**

Magi
- Blanco, T. The Child's gifts (5 and up) **232.9**

Fiction
- Menotti, G. C. Gian-Carlo Menotti's Amahl and the night visitors (4 and up) **Fic**

Magic
- Arnold, N. The great science magic show (5 and up) **793.8**
- Cobb, V. Magic . . . naturally! Science entertainments & amusements (4 and up) **793.8**
- Fleischman, S. Mr Mysterious's secrets of magic (3-6) **793.8**
- Helfman, H. Tricks with your fingers (3-6) **793.8**
- Hutton, D. Ventriloquism p63-75 (6 and up) **793.8**
- Kettelkamp, L. Magic made easy (4 and up) **793.8**
- Kettelkamp, L. Spooky magic (3-6) **793.8**
- Lopshire, R. It's magic? (k-2) **793.8**
- McGovern, A. Squeals & squiggles & ghostly giggles (2-5) **394.2**
- Marks, B. Give a magic show! (3-5) **793.8**
- Permin, I. Hokus pokus: with wands, water & glasses (5 and up) **793.8**
- Severn, B. Bill Severn's Big book of magic (6 and up) **793.8**
- Severn, B. Magic with coins and bills (6 and up) **793.8**
- Stoddard, E. The first book of magic (4-6) **793.8**
- Van Rensselaer, A. Fun with magic (4 and up) **793.8**
- White, L. B. So you want to be a magician? (5 and up) **793.8**
- Wyler, R. Magic secrets (1-3) **793.8**
- Wyler, R. Spooky tricks (1-3) **793.8**
- *See also* Tricks

Fiction
- Fleischman, S. Mr Mysterious & Company (4-6) **Fic**
- Van Allsburg, C. The garden of Abdul Gasazi **E**

Magic. Afanas'ev, A.
- *In* Afanas'ev, A. Russian fairy tales p399-404 **398.2**

The **magic** amulet. Steele, W. O. **Fic**

Magic ball
- Finger, C. Magic ball
  - *In* Finger, C. Tales from silver lands p48-58 **398.2**
  - *In* Witches, witches, witches p56-64 **808.8**

The **magic** bed-knob. Norton, M.
- *In* Norton, M. Bed-knob and broomstick p11-94 **Fic**

The **magic** bookshelf. Clapp, P.
- *In* Fifty plays for junior actors p136-50 **812.08**

Magic box
- Afanas'ev, A. The magic box
  - *In* Afanas'ev, A. Russian fairy tales p164-68 **398.2**
- Sawyer, R. The magic box
  - *In* Sawyer, R. The way of the storyteller **372.6**

The **magic** box. Peterson, M. N.
- *In* Dramatized folk tales of the world p265-77 **812.08**

The **magic** bridle. Manning-Sanders, R.
- *In* Manning-Sanders, R. A book of charms and changelings p11-15 **398.2**

Magic by the lake. Eager, E. See note under Eager, E. Half magic **Fic**

Magic cap
Bowman, J. C. Pekka and the rogues
In Bowman, J. C. Tales from a Finnish
tupa p231-36   **398.2**
Hart, J. The magic cap
In It's time for story hour p117-20   **372.6**
The **magic** cloak. Whitworth, V. P.
In Dramatized folk tales of the world
p435-46   **812.08**
The **magic** cookie jar. Miller, H. L.
In One hundred plays for children p706-17
808.82

Magic dog
Finger, C. Magic dog
In Finger, C. Tales from silver lands p14-
22   **398.2**
The **magic** drum. Arnott, K.
In Arnott, K. African myths and legends
p124-32   **398.2**
The **magic** drum. Kirkup, J.   **398.2**
The **magic** dumplings. Olcott, F. J.
In It's time for story hour p97-102   **372.6**
See also Why the dog and cat are ene-
mies
The **magic** egg. Hark, M.
In One hundred plays for children p324-35
808.82

Magic fiddle
The Magic fiddle
In Indian fairy tales p40-45   **398.2**
The **magic** fishbone. Dickens, C.   **Fic**
also in The Golden Treasury of children's
literature p349-54   **808.8**
also in Gruenberg, S. M. ed. Favorite sto-
ries old and new p299-309   **808.8**
also in It's time for story hour p194-205
372.6
The **magic** fishbone. Peterson, M. N.
In Fifty plays for junior actors p471-80
812.08
The **magic** galoshes. Andersen, H. C.
In Andersen, H. C. The complete fairy
tales and stories p82-107   **S C**
The **magic** gem. Kim, So-un
In Kim, So-un. The story bag p99-115
398.2
The **magic** glass. Hughes, R.
In Gruenberg, S. M. ed. Favorite stories
old and new p253-57   **808.8**
The **magic** grandfather. Williams, J.   **Fic**
The **magic** grapes. Leuser, E. D.
In Dramatized folk tales of the world
p258-64   **812.08**
The **magic** hood. Kim, So-un
In Kim, So-un. The story bag p180-85
398.2
A **magic** hood. Sano, Masayuki
In Siks, G. B. Drama with children p215-
31   **372.6**
The **magic** horns. Arnott, K.
In Arnott, K. African myths and legends
p78-84   **398.2**
Magic house of numbers. Adler, I.   **793.7**
Magic in Marblehead. Jagendorf, M. A.
In Jagendorf, M. A. New England bean-
pot p139-46   **398.2**
Magic in the mist. Kimmel, M. M.   **Fic**
The **magic** jack-o-lantern. Howard, H. L.
In One hundred plays for children p399-
402   **808.82**

Magic knot
Finger, C. Magic knot
In Finger, C. Tales from silver lands
p122-33   **398.2**
The **magic** listening cap. Uchida, Yoshiko **398.2**
The **magic** listening cap; story. Uchida, Yoshiko
In Uchida, Yoshiko. The magic listening
cap p3-10   **398.2**
Magic made easy. Kettelkamp, L.   **793.8**
Magic maize. Buff, M.   **Fic**
Magic Michael. Slobodkin, L.   **E**
The **magic** mill. Huggins, E.
In The Arbuthnot Anthology of children's
literature p287-89   **808.8**
Magic mortar. Uchida, Yoshiko
In Uchida. Yoshiko. The magic listening
cap p33-41   **398.2**
Magic . . . naturally! Science entertainments
& amusements. Cobb, V.   **793.8**
The **magic** nutmeg-grater. Thane, A.
In Thane, A. Plays from famous stories
and fairy tales p198-215   **812**
The **magic** of the Glits. Adler, C. S.   **Fic**
Magic or not? Eager, E. See note under
Eager, E. Half magic   **Fic**
The **magic** pancakes at the Footbridge Tavern.
Hume, L. C.
In Hume, L. C. Favorite children's stories
from China and Tibet p79-84   **398.2**
The **magic** pot. Coombs, P.   **398.2**
See also Wonderful pot
The **magic** pumpkin. Kingman, L.
In One hundred plays for children p403-
11   **808.82**

Magic ring
The Magic ring
In Yellow fairy book p158-72   **398.2**
Magic secrets. Wyler, R.   **793.8**

Magic shirt
Afanas'ev, A. The magic shirt
In Afanas'ev, A. Russian fairy tales p110-13
398.2
The **magic** shop. Wells, H. G.
In Haunting tales p63-77   **S C**
Magic! Silly magic! Jagendorf, M. A.
In Jagendorf, M. A. Noodlehead stories
from around the world p97-99   **398.2**
The **magic** spell. Cooper, E.
In One hundred plays for children p382-85
808.82

Magic swan geese
Afanas'ev, A. The magic swan geese
In Afanas'ev, A. Russian fairy tales p349-
51   **398.2**
Riordan, J. The Swan Geese
In Riordan, J. Tales from Central Russia
p175-78   **398.2**
The **magic** tabo. Sechrist, E. H.
In Sechrist, E. H. Once in the first times
p184-88   **398.2**
The **Magic** teakettle
In Sakade, F. ed. Japanese children's fa-
vorite stories p17-24   **398.2**
See also Accomplished and lucky tea
kettle
The **magic** tree. McDermott, G.   **398.2**
The **magic** weaver. Bennett, R.
In Bennett, R. Creative plays and programs
for holidays p315-20   **812**
Magic with coins and bills. Severn, B. **793.8**

Maize. See Corn
Majeski, Bill
Whatever happened to good old Ebenezer Scrooge?
In On stage for Christmas p47-64 **812.08**
The **majesty** of Grace. See Langton, J. Her Majesty, Grace Jones **Fic**
Makah Indians

Antiquities
Kirk, R. Hunters of the whale (5 and up) **970.004**
Make a joyful noise unto the Lord! The life of Mahalia Jackson, queen of gospel singers. Jackson, J. **·92**
Make a world. See Emberley, E. Ed Emberley's Drawing book: make a world **743**
Make him smile. Arnold, E. W.
In One hundred plays for children p 1-9 **808.82**
Make it and ride it. Maginley, C. J. **688.6**
Make it with felt. Newsome, A. J. **745.5**
Make way for ducklings. McCloskey, R. **E**
Make your own animated movies. Andersen, Y. **778.5**
Make your own comics for fun and profit. Cummings, R. **741.5**
Make your own dolls. Heady, E. B. **745.592**
Make your own model forts & castles. Cummings, R. **623**
Make your own musical instruments. Mandell, M. **781.91**
Makeup, Theatrical
Barwell, E. Disguises you can make (4-6) **391**
Making costumes for parties, plays, and holidays. Gilbreath, A. **391**
Making musical things. Wiseman, A. **781.91**
Making puppets come alive. Engler, L. **791.5**
Making things. Wiseman, A. **745.5**
Malaria
See pages in the following book:
Selsam, M. E. Plants that heal p37-42 (4-6) **581.6**
Malati and the prince. Picard, B. L.
In Picard, B. L. The faun and the woodcutter's daughter p59-72 **S C**
Malawi
See pages in the following book:
Newlon, C. Southern Africa: the critical land p204-09 (5 and up) **968**
Malay Archipelago

Animals
See Animals—Malay Archipelago
Malaysia
Poole, F. K. Malaysia & Singapore (4 and up) **959.5**
Malaysia & Singapore. Poole, F. K. **959.5**
Malcolm, Heather
See pages in the following book:
Facklam, M. Wild animals, gentle women p113-23 (5 and up) **920**
Malcolm X
Adoff, A. Malcolm X (2-5) **92**
See also pages in the following book:
Alexander, R. P. comp. Young and black in America p59-68 (6 and up) **920**

Malcolmson, Anne
Stormalong fights the kraken
In North American legends p184-91 **398.2**
Yankee Doodle's cousins (4 and up) **398.2**
Contents: John Darling; The gift of Saint Nicholas; Captain Kidd; Joe Magarac; The ghost of Dark Hollow Run; King Coal; Ichabod Paddock; Stormalong; Ole massa and his chillun; Mule Humans; Blackbeard; John Henry; Tony Beaver; Johnny Appleseed; Mike Fink; Dan'l Boone; Davy Crockett; The big bear of Arkansas; Pirate Jean Lafitte; Febold Feboldson; Kemp Morgan; The white mustang; The golden cities of Cibola; Pecos Bill; Pecos Bill and his bouncing bride; How Paul Bonjean became Paul Bunyan; Ol' Paul's camp on the Big Onion River; How ol' Paul changed the map of America
Male, Alan
(illus.) Stonehouse, B. A closer look at reptiles **597.9**
The **Malibu,** and other poems. Livingston, M. C. **811**
Malice, Bouki and Momplaisir. Carter, D. S.
In Carter, D. S. Greedy Mariani, and other folktales of the Antilles p91-98 **398.2**
Malkus, Alida Sims
The goblin of the pitcher
In Harper, W. comp. Ghosts and goblins p103-09 **398.2**
Malone, Mary
Annie Sullivan [biography of Anne Sullivan Macy] (2-4) **92**
Manatees
See pages in the following book:
McClung, R. M. Hunted mammals of the sea p71-86 (5 and up) **599**
Mammals
Burt, W. H. A field guide to the mammals **599**
Jordan, E. L. Animal atlas of the world **599**
McClung, R. M. Hunted mammals of the sea (5 and up) **599**
National Geographic Society. Wild animals of North America **599**
Weber, W. J. Wild orphan babies: mammals and birds (4 and up) **639**
Zim, H. S. Mammals **599**
See also pages in the following books:
Buck, M. W. Where they go in winter p57-69 (3-6) **591.5**
Boy Scouts of America. Fieldbook p464-79 **369.43**
Clement, R. C. Hammond Nature atlas of America p112-39 **500**
Merrill, M. W. Skeletons that fit p40-45 (4-6) **575**
Sarasy, P. Winter-sleepers p17-35 (3-5) **591.5**
Shuttlesworth, D. E. The wildlife of South America p39-56 (5 and up) **591.9**
See also names of mammals, e.g. Bats

Pictorial works
Wildsmith, B. Wild animals **E**
Mammals, Fossil
McGowen, T. Dinosaurs & other prehistoric animals (3-6) **567.9**
See also Mastodon
Mammoth
Aliki. Wild and wooly mammoths (1-3) **569**
Mammoth Cave
See pages in the following book:
Laycock, G. Caves p38-44 (5 and up) **551.4**

Mammoth Cave National Park
See pages in the following book:
Laycock, G. Caves p45-52 (5 and up)　**551.4**

Man
See also Anthropology

Color
See Color of people

Influence of environment
Bova, B. The weather changes man (5 and up)　**551.6**
See also pages in the following book:
Hays, J. Our changing climate p91-97 (5 and up)　**551.6**

Influence on nature
Gregor, A. S. Man's mark on the land (4 and up)　**304.2**
McClung, R. M. Lost wild worlds (6 and up)　**591.9**
Müller, J. The changing countryside　**307.7**
See also pages in the following book:
Hays, J. Our changing climate p85-90 (5 and up)　**551.6**
See also Pollution

Origin and antiquity
Asimov, I. How did we find out about our human roots? (4 and up)　**573.2**
Goode, R. People of the Ice Age (5 and up)　**573.3**

Man, Prehistoric
Asimov, I. How did we find out about our human roots? (4 and up)　**573.2**
Baumann, H. The caves of the great hunters (5 and up)　**930.1**
Goode, R. People of the Ice Age (5 and up)　**573.3**
May, J. Before the Indians (2-4)　**970.01**
See also pages in the following book:
Weatherbee, D. E. Ancient Indonesia and its influence in modern times p4-16 (4 and up)　**959.8**

Fiction
Millstead, T. Cave of the moving shadows (5 and up)　**Fic**
Steele, W. O. The magic amulet (4-6)　**Fic**

Man-crow. Carter, D. S.
In Carter, D. S. Greedy Mariani, and other folktales of the Antilles p73-78　**398.2**

The **man** from Kailasa. Courlander, H.
In Courlander, H. The tiger's whisker, and other tales and legends from Asia and the Pacific p58-62　**398.2**

The **man** in the Moon as he sails the sky, and other Moon verse　**821.08**

Man O'War (Race horse)
See pages in the following book:
Anderson, C. W. C. W. Anderson's Complete book of horses and horsemanship p111-18 (5 and up)　**636.1**

Man of the Monitor; the story of John Ericsson. Latham, J. L.　**92**

The **man** on Morvan's Road. Leach, M.
In Leach, M. Whistle in the graveyard p59-60　**398.2**

Man, the boy, and the donkey
Jacobs, J. The miller, his son, and their donkey
In The Fairy tale treasury p102-03　**398.2**

The **man**, the white steed, and the wondrous wood. Jagendorf, M. A.
In Jagendorf, M. A. Folk stories of the South p193-98　**398.2**

The **man**, the woman, and the fly. Jagendorf, M. A.
In Jagendorf, M. A. Noodlehead stories from around the world p161-63　**398.2**

The **man** who bought a dream. Uchida. Yoshiko
In Uchida, Yoshiko. The magic listening cap p93-100　**398.2**

Man who did not know fear
Afanas'ev, A. The man who did not know fear
In Afanas'ev, A. Russian fairy tales p325-27　**398.2**

The **man** who didn't believe in ghosts. Nic Leodhas, S.
In Haunting tales p25-32　**S C**

The **man** who didn't wash his dishes. Krasilovsky, P.　**E**

The **man** who learned the language of the animals. Arnott, K.
In Arnott, K. African myths and legends p5-12　**398.2**

The **man** who looked for death. Courlander, H.
In Courlander, H. Olode the hunter, and other tales from Nigeria p15-18　**398.2**

The **man** who lost his head. Bishop, C. H.　**E**

The **man** who loved tiny creatures. Cheney, C.
In Cheney, C. Tales from a Taiwan kitchen p37-52　**398.2**

The **man** who loved to laugh. Korty, C.
In Korty, C. Plays from African folktales p17-36　**812**

The **man** who pinched God's letter. Aiken, J.
In Aiken, J. The faithless lollybird p38-60　**S C**

The **man** who planted onions. Kim, So-un
In Kim, So-un. The story bag p11-16　**398.2**

Man who rode the bear. Credle, E.
In Credle, E. Tall tales from the high hills, and other stories p100-14　**398.2**

The **man** who sang the sillies. Ciardi, J.　**811**

The **man** who sold a ghost. Wyndham, R.
In Wyndham, R. Tales the people tell in China p48-51　**398.2**

The **man** who stole a rope. Wyndham, R.
In Wyndham, R. Tales the people tell in China p38-39　**398.2**

The **man** who tried to save time. Krasilovsky, P.　**E**

Man who was going to mind the house
Asbjörnsen, P. C. The husband who was to mind the house
In The Arbuthnot Anthology of children's literature p246-47　**808.8**
In Time for old magic p129-30　**398.2**
Gág, W. Gone is gone　**398.2**
also in The Fairy tale treasury p48-55　**398.2**
Wiesner, W. Turnabout　**398.2**

The **man** who would know magic. Wyndham, R.
In Wyndham, R. Tales the people tell in China p67-72　**398.2**

Man whose trade was tricks
Papashvily, G. The man whose trade was tricks
In It's time for story hour p106-10　**372.6**

Mancrow, bird of darkness. Sherlock, P.
In Sherlock, P. West Indian folk-tales p65-70　**398.2**

Many, many weddings in one corner house. Sandburg, C.
In Sandburg, C. Rootabaga stories v2 p19-25 **S C**
In Sandburg, C. The Sandburg treasury p95-97 **818**

Many moons. Thurber, J. **Fic**

Many wives. Chrisman, A. B.
In Chrisman, A. B. Shen of the sea p111-21 **S C**

Mao, Tsê-tung
See pages in the following book:
Rau, M. Our world: the People's Republic of China p29-42, 53-57 (6 and up) **951.05**

Maoris
See pages in the following book:
Kaula, E. M. The land and people of New Zealand p78-85, 94-98 (5 and up) **993**

Map drawing
Brown, L. A. Map making (5 and up) **526**
Cartwright, S. What's in a map? (k-2) **912**
Oliver, J. E. What we find when we look at maps (3-5) **526**

Map making. Brown, L. A. **526**

Maple
Selsam, M. E. Maple tree (2-4) **582.16**

Maple harvest. Gemming, E. **633.6**

Maple sugar
Gemming, E. Maple harvest (4-6) **633.6**
See also pages in the following book:
Lavine, S. A. Indian corn and other gifts p29-36 (4 and up) **641.3**

Maple tree. Selsam, M. E. **582.16**

Mapp, Frances
The ogre who built a bridge
In Dramatized folk tales of the world p278-87 **812.08**

Maps
Brown, L. A. Map making (5 and up) **526**
Cartwright, S. What's in a map? (k-2) **912**
Fuchs, E. Looking at maps (2-4) **912**
Oliver, J. E. What we find when we look at maps (3-5) **526**
See also pages in the following book:
Boy Scouts of America. Fieldbook p15-27 **369.43**

Maps, tracks, and the bridges of Königsberg. Holt, M. **514**

Mara, Thalia
First steps in ballet (4 and up) **792.8**

Mara, daughter of the Nile. McGraw, E. J. **Fic**

Marais, Josef
Windbird and the Sun
In The Arbuthnot Anthology of children's literature p326-29 **808.8**
In Time for old magic p203-06 **398.2**

Maraslis, Demetra
(illus.) Yolen, J. The seeing stick **Fic**

Marcellin, Jean
(illus.) Fronval, G. Indian signs and signals **001.56**

March and the shepherd
Vittorini, D. March and the shepherd
In The Arbuthnot Anthology of children's literature p269-70 **808.8**
In Time for old magic p152-53 **398.2**

The **march** of the lemmings. Newton, J. R. **599.32**

Marches for black civil rights. See Blacks—Civil rights

Marchiori, Carlos
Fowke, E. comp. Sally go round the sun **796.1**

Marco Polo's adventures in China **92**

Marco the Rich and Vasily the Luckless. Afanas'ev, A.
In Afanas'ev, A. Russian fairy tales p213-20 **398.2**

Marconi, Guglielmo, Marchese
See pages in the following books:
Cottler, J. Heroes of civilization p260-64 (5 and up) **920**
Foster, G. The year of the flying machine, 1903 p24-32 (3-6) **909.82**

Marcos, Ferdinand Edralin, President Philippines
See pages in the following book:
Nance, J. The land and people of the Philippines p154-78 (5 and up) **959.9**

Marcus, Rebecca B.
The first book of volcanoes & earthquakes (5 and up) **551.2**
Survivors of the stone age (5 and up) **306**

Marelles, Charles
Drakestail
In Red fairy book p220-27 **398.2**
The true history of Little Golden-hood
In The Andrew Lang Fairy tale treasury p132-36 **398.2**

Margai, Milton
See pages in the following book:
Clifford, M. L. The land and people of Sierra Leone p78-88 (5 and up) **966**

Marguerite de Angeli's Book of nursery and Mother Goose rhymes **398**

Mari, Enzo
(jt. auth.) Mari, I. The apple and the moth **E**
(jt. auth.) Mari, I. The chicken and the egg **E**

Mari, Iela
The apple and the moth **E**
The chicken and the egg **E**

Maria Morevna
In The Firebird, and other Russian fairy tales p29-47 **398.2**
See also Marya Morevna

Maria Morevna. Afanas'ev, A.
In Afanas'ev, A. Russian fairy tales p553-62 **398.2**
See also Marya Morevna

Marian Anderson: lady from Philadelphia. Newman, S. P. **92**

Maria's Christmas song. Meyer, E. P.
In Christmas stories round the world p81-86 **S C**

Marie de France
Reeves, J. The shadow of the hawk, and other stories **398.2**

Marigold garden. Greenaway, K. **821**

Marihuana
Stwertka, E. Marijuana (5 and up) **613.8**
See also pages in the following book:
Gorodetzky, C. W. What you should know about drugs p30-43 (5 and up) **613.8**

Marijuana. See Marihuana

Marijuana. Stwertka, E. **613.8**

Marika
(illus.) Parker, A. Terrariums   635.9
Marine animals
Holling, H. C. Pagoo (4 and up)   595.3
Jacobs, F. Sounds in the sea (4-6)   591.92
McClung, R. M. Hunted mammals of the sea (5 and up)   599
Selsam, M. See through the sea (2-4)   591.92
Straker, J. A. Animals that live in the sea (1-3)   591.92
Zim, H. S. Sea stars and their kin (4 and up)   593.9
Zim, H. S. Seashores (5 and up)   574.92
  See also pages in the following books:
Silverstein, A. The excretory system p46-53 (4-6)   574.1
Simon, S. Tropical saltwater aquariums p68-72 (4 and up)   639.3
  See also Corals; Fishes; Fresh water animals
Marine aquariums
Simon, S. Tropical saltwater aquariums (4 and up)   639.3
  See also pages in the following book:
Discovering nature indoors p22-28 (5 and up)   591
Marine biology
Buck, M. W. Along the seashore (3-6)   574.92
Cooper, E. K. Science on the shores and banks (5 and up)   574.92
Goldin, A. The sunlit sea (1-3)   574.92
Kohn, B. The beachcomber's book (3-6)   745.5
McGovern, A. The underwater world of the coral reef (2-4)   574.92
Selsam, M. E. See along the shore (3-5)   574.92
  See also pages in the following books:
Burgess, R. F. Exploring a coral reef p17-39 (4-6)   574.92
Pringle, L. This is a river p17-39 (4-6)   574.5
  See also Marine animals; Marine plants
Marine ecology
Goldin, A. The sunlit sea (1-3)   574.92
Straker, J. A. Animals that live in the sea (1-3)   591.92
  See also Coral reef ecology; Estuarine ecology
Marine engineering
Corbett, S. What makes a boat float? (3-5)   532
Marine fauna. See Marine animals
Marine flora. See Marine plants
Marine plants
Zim, H. S. Seashores (5 and up)   574.92
  See also Algae; Fresh-water plants
Marine pollution
  See also types of water pollution, e.g. Petroleum pollution of water
Marine resources
Berger, M. Oceanography lab p66-70 (4-6)   551.46
  See also Fisheries
Marine transportation. See Shipping
Marine zoology. See Marine animals
Mariners. See Sailors

Marino, Barbara Pavis
Eric needs stitches (k-3)   362.1
Marionettes. See Puppets and puppet plays
Mariott, John
(illus.) Kerrod, R. Rocks and minerals   549
Mark, Jan
Thunder and Lightnings (5 and up)   Fic
Under the autumn garden (4-6)   Fic
The **mark** of Conte. Levitin, S.   Fic
Markham, R. L.
(illus.) Vandenburg, M. L. Help! Emergencies that could happen to you, and how to handle them   616.02
Marking the boat to locate the sword. Wyndham, R.
  In Wyndham, R. Tales the people tell in China p66   398.2
Marks, Burton
Give a magic show! (3-5)   793.8
Marks, Mickey Klar
Op-tricks (5 and up)   702.8
Marks, Rita
(jt. auth.) Marks, B. Give a magic show!   793.8
Markun, Patricia Maloney
The Panama Canal (5 and up)   972.87
Marley's ghost. Dickens, C.
  In Sechrist, E. H. ed. 13 ghostly yarns p177-97   S C
Marmots
McNulty, F. Woodchuck (1-3)   599.32
  See also pages in the following books:
Cartwright, S. Animal homes p25-33 (1-3)   591.5
Shuttlesworth, D. E. The story of rodents p47-54 (3-6)   599.32
Marokvia, Arthur
(illus.) Conklin, G. I caught a lizard   639
(illus.) Haviland, V. Favorite fairy tales told in Ireland   398.2
Marquardt, Dorothy A.
(jt. auth.) Ward, M. E. Authors of books for young people   920.03
(jt. auth.) Ward, M. E. Authors of books for young people; supplement to the 2d ed.   920.03
(jt. auth.) Ward, M. E. Illustrators of books for young people   920.03
Marquette, Jacques
Kjelgaard, J. Explorations of Père Marquette (4-6)   92
Marrakech, Morocco
  See pages in the following book:
Spencer, W. The land and people of Morocco p134-42 (5 and up)   964
Marra's world. Coatsworth, E.   Fic
Marriage
  See also Divorce

Fiction
Hogrogian, N. Carrot cake   E
Zemach, K. The beautiful rat (k-3)   398.2

Poetry
  See pages in the following book:
Life hungers to abound p 1-36 (6 and up)   808.81
Marriage, Mixed. See Intermarriage

Master thief
Afanas'ev, A. The thief
In Afanas'ev, A. Russian fairy tales p590-93   **398.2**
Asbjørnsen, P. C. The master thief
In Red fairy book p129-46   **398.2**
Grimm, J. The master-thief
In Grimm, J. The complete Grimm's fairy tales p773-80   **398.2**
In Grimm, J. The juniper tree, and other tales from Grimm v 1 p113-28   **398.2**
See also Jack and the doctor's girl

Master wizard, Pan Twardowski, and his spider
Turska, K. The magician of Cracow (k-3)   **398.2**

Mastermaid
In Tatterhood, and other tales p149-55   **398.2**
The **mastermaid**. Asbjørnsen, P. C.
In Blue fairy book p130-47   **398.2**

Masterman-Smith, Virginia
The treasure trap (4-6)   **Fic**

Masters, Kelley R. See Ball, Zachary

Masters, Robert V.
Japan in pictures (4 and up)   **952**

Mastodon
See pages in the following book:
McHargue, G. Mummies p18-32 (5 and up)   **393**

The **match**. Hautzig, E.
In Hautzig, E. The case against the wind, and other stories p45-53   **S C**
The **matchlock** gun. Edmonds, W. D.   **Fic**

Materia medica
See also Drugs
Math, Irwin
Morse, Marconi and you (6 and up)   **621.38**
Math puzzles. Adler, P.   **793.7**
Mathematical drawing. See Geometrical drawing
Mathematical games for one or two. Charosh, M.   **793.7**

Mathematical recreations
Adler, I. Magic house of numbers (6 and up)   **793.7**
Adler, P. Math puzzles (4-6)   **793.7**
Barr, G. Entertaining with number tricks (5 and up)   **793.7**
Burns, M. The I hate mathematics! book (5 and up)   **793.7**
Charosh, M. Mathematical games for one or two (1-4)   **793.7**
Olney, R. Pocket calculator fun & games (5 and up)   **793.7**
See also pages in the following books:
Mosler, G. The puzzle school p3-12 (5 and up)   **793.7**
Mulac, M. E. Educational games for fun p 1-47   **372.1**
See also Scientific recreations

Mathematical sets. See Set theory
Mathematics
Bendick, J. Names, sets and numbers (2-5)   **511**
James, E. What do you mean by "average"? (4-6)   **519.5**

Srivastava, J. J. Averages (2-4)   **519.5**
See also Arithmetic; Binary system (Mathematics); Geometry; Measurement; Number theory

Bibliography
Matthias, M. Children's mathematics books   **016.51**

Matheson, Richard
Deadline
In Haunts, haunts, haunts p171-77   **S C**
Mathiesen, Egon
The blue-eyed pussy
In Gruenberg, S. M. ed. Favorite stories old and new p152-55   **808.8**
Mathis, Sharon Bell
The hundred penny box   **E**
Ray Charles (2-5)   **92**
Teacup full of roses (6 and up)   **Fic**
Matilda, Princess of England, consort of Geoffrey, count of Anjou
See pages in the following book:
The Arbuthnot Anthology of children's literature p778-81   **808.8**
Matsuda, Minn
(illus.) Nelson, E. L. Singing and dancing games for the very young   **796.1**
Matt Gargan's boy. Slote, A.   **Fic**
Matter of brogues
Sawyer, R. A matter of brogues
In Sawyer, R. The way of the storyteller   **372.6**
Matternes, Jay H.
(illus.) Jackson, K. Dinosaurs   **567.9**
Matthews, Ellen
The trouble with Leslie (4-6)   **Fic**
Matthews, William H.
The story of glaciers and the ice age (5 and up)   **551.3**
Matthias, Margaret
Children's mathematics books   **016.51**
Matthiesen, Thomas
ABC   **E**
Things to see   **E**
Matulay, Laszlo
(illus.) Carlson, B. W. Do it yourself!   **793**
Matzeliger, Jan Ernest
See pages in the following books:
Hayden, R. C. Eight black American inventors p60-77 (5 and up)   **920**
Rollins, C. H. They showed the way p93-96 (5 and up)   **920**
Maud, consort of Henry V, Emperor of the Holy Roman Empire. See Matilda, Princess of England, consort of Geoffrey, count of Anjou
Maui (Polynesian deity)
Williams, J. The surprising things Maui did (1-3)   **398.2**
Maui the great. Courlander, H.
In Courlander, H. The tiger's whisker, and other tales and legends from Asia and the Pacific p132-39   **398.2**
Maui traps Sun. Thompson, V. L.
In Thompson, V. L. Hawaiian myths of earth p60-64   **398.2**
Maupassant, Guy de
On the river; adaptation. See Handendorff, J. B. On the river
Maury, Jean West
(comp.) Bible. Selections. A first Bible   **220.5**

Mentally ill children
See pages in the following book:
Kamien, J. What if you couldn't . . . ? p62-72 (4-6)   362.4
Fiction
Heide, F. P. Growing anyway up (6 and up)   **Fic**

Mentally retarded
Dunbar, R. E. Mental retardation (4 and up)   362.3
See also pages in the following books:
Adams, B. Like it is: facts and feelings about handicaps from kids who know p43-52 (4-6)   362.4
Kamien, J. What if you couldn't . . . ? p24-34 (4-6)   362.4
Fiction
Bridgers, S. E. All together now (6 and up)   **Fic**

Mentally retarded children
Sobol, H. L. My brother Steve is retarded (3-5)   362.3
Fiction
Baldwin, A. N. A little time (4-6)   **Fic**
Byars, B. The summer of the swans (5 and up)   **Fic**
Little, J. Take wing (4-6)   **Fic**
Wrightson, P. A racecourse for Andy (5 and up)   **Fic**

Menus
Blanchard, M. P. The outdoor cookbook (6 and up)   641.5
See also pages in the following books:
Betty Crocker's Cookbook for boys & girls p141-54 (3-6)   641.5
Schwartz, P. D. You can cook p183-87 (5 and up)   641.5

Mercantile marine. See Merchant marine

Mercer, Charles
Monsters in the earth (5 and up)   551.2

Merchandising. See Retail trade

Merchant marine
Zim, H. S. Cargo ships (3-6)   387.2

The **merchant** of Seri. Babbitt, E. C.
In Babbitt, E. C. Jataka tales p13-17   398.2

Merchant's daughter and the maidservant
Afanas'ev, A. The merchant's daughter and the maidservant
In Afanas'ev, A. Russian fairy tales p327-31   398.2

Merchant's daughter and the slanderer
Afanas'ev, A. The merchant's daughter and the slanderer
In Afanas'ev, A. Russian fairy tales p415-18   398.2

Mercury. See Hermes

Mercury (Planet)
See pages in the following book:
Branley, F. M. The nine planets p26-34 (6 and up)   523.4

Meredith, Robert
(jt. ed.) Smith, E. B. ed. Pilgrim courage   974.4

Mergenthaler, Ottmar
See pages in the following book:
Barker, A. Black on white and read all over p68-75 (4-6)   686.2

Merisier, stronger than the elephants. Courlander, H.
In Courlander, H. The piece of fire, and other Haitian tales p9-14   398.2
Merit students encyclopedia   031
Merit students year book. See Merit students encyclopedia   031
Merlin
See pages in the following book:
Aylesworth, T. G. The alchemists: magic into science p13-17 (6 an up)   540.1

Mermaids
Fiction
Oppenheim, S. The selchie's seed (4-6)   **Fic**

Merriam, Eve
It doesn't always have to rhyme (4 and up)   811
Rainbow writing (4 and up)   811
There is no rhyme for silver (2-5)   811
The **Merriam**-Webster Dictionary for large print users   423

Merrill, Jean
The pea shooter campaign—phase I
In The Arbuthnot Anthology of children's literature p573-76   808.8
The pushcart war (5 and up)   **Fic**
The pushcart war; excerpt
In The Arbuthnot Anthology of children's literature p573-76   808.8
The superlative horse (4-6)   **Fic**
The toothpaste millionaire (4-6)   **Fic**

Merrill, Margaret W.
Skeletons that fit (4-6)   575

Merrimac (Frigate)
Reit, S. Ironclad! (4-6)   973.7
The **merry** adventures of Robin Hood of great renown in Nottinghamshire. Pyle, H.   398.2
A **Merry** Christmas. Alcott, L. M.
In Association for Childhood Education International. Told under the Christmas tree p138-52   808.8
A **merry** Christmas. Hackett, W.
In On stage for Christmas p429-45   812.08
Merry Christmas, Crawfords! Hark, M.
In A Treasury of Christmas plays p21-44   812.08
Merry Christmas customs. Hark, M.
In A Treasury of Christmas plays p376-82   812.08
Merry Christmas from Betsy. Haywood, C.
See note under Haywood, C. "B" is for Betsy   **Fic**
Merry Christmas to you. Harper, W. comp.   **S C**
Merry ever after. Lasker, J.   392
The **merry**-go-round and the Griggses. Emerson, C. D.
In Gruenberg, S. M. ed. Favorite stories old and new p463-66   808.8
In Told under the magic umbrella p18-22   **S C**
Merry merry FIBruary. Orgel, D.   811
Merry, merry, merry. Carroll, G. H.
In One hunded plays for children p492-506   808.82
The **merry** tale of Belle Boyd. Jagendorf, M. A.
In Jagendorf, M. A. Folk stories of the South p304-06   398.2
Merry tale of Merrymount. Jagendorf, M. A.
In Jagendorf, M. A. New England beanpot p158-62   398.2

Mills, Grace Evelyn
Christmas comes to Hamelin
In One hundred plays for children p528-39
808.82

Mills, Yaroslava
(illus.) Borghese, A. The international cookie jar cookbook **641.8**

Millstead, Thomas
Cave of the moving shadows (5 and up) **Fic**

Milne, A. A.
The Christopher Robin story book (k-3) **828**
The house at Pooh Corner (1-4) **Fic**
also in Milne, A. A. The house at Pooh Corner p153-314 **Fic**
In which Eeyore has a birthday and gets two presents
In The Golden Treasury of children's literature p56-63 **808.8**
In which Pooh goes visiting and gets into a tight place
In The Arbuthnot Anthology of children's literature p494-96 **808.8**
Now we are six (k-3) **821**
also in Milne, A. A. The world of Christopher Robin p119-234 **821**
Pooh goes visiting and gets into a tight place
In Gruenberg, S. M. ed. Favorite stories old and new p451-55 **808.8**
The Pooh story book (1-4) **Fic**
Tigger has breakfast
In Stories to dramatize p69-76 **372.6**
When we were very young (k-3) **821**
also in Milne, A. A. The world of Christopher Robin p 1-118 **821**
Winnie-the-Pooh (1-4) **Fic**
also in Milne, A. A. The world of Pooh p7-149 **Fic**
Winnie-the-Pooh; excerpt
In The Arbuthnot Anthology of children's literature p493-96 **808.8**
The world of Christopher Robin (k-3) **821**
The world of Pooh (1-4) **Fic**
Ellison, V. H. The Pooh cook book **641.5**

Milne, Alan Alexander. See Milne, A. A.

Milne, Lorus J.
Because of a flower (5 and up) **582.13**

Milne, Margery
(jt. auth.) Milne, L. J. Because of a flower **582.13**

Mimosa, the sensitive plant. Selsam, M. E. **583**

Mimosas
Selsam, M. E. Mimosa, the sensitive plant (3-5) **583**

Minarik, Else Holmelund
Father Bear comes home. See note under Minarik, E. H. Little Bear **E**
A kiss for Little Bear. See note under Minarik, E. H. Little Bear **E**
Little Bear **E**
Little Bear's friend. See note under Minarik, E. H. Little Bear **E**
Little Bear's visit. See note under Minarik, E. H. Little Bear **E**
No fighting, no biting **E**

Mind and body
Kettelkamp, L. A partnership of mind and body: biofeedback (5 and up) **152.1**
See also Mental healing; Nervous system

Mind reading
Fiction
Butterworth, O. The trouble with Jenny's ear (4 and up) **Fic**

Mine for keeps. Little, J. **Fic**

Mineral resources. See Mines and mineral resources

Mineralogy
Chesterman, C. W. The Audubon Society Field guide to North American rocks and minerals (2-4) **549**
Fenton, C. L. Rocks and their stories (2-4) **549**
Keen, M. L. Be a rockhound (4 and up) **549**
Kerrod, R. Rocks and minerals (5 and up) **549**
Pough, F. H. A field guide to rocks and minerals **549**
Shuttlesworth, D. The story of rocks (5 and up) **549**
Simon, S. The rock-hound's book (4 and up) **549**
Zim, H. S. Rocks and minerals (4 and up) **549**
See also pages in the following books:
Clement, R. C. Hammond Nature atlas of America p20-39 **500**
Wyckoff, J. The story of geology p144-51 (5 and up) **551**

Minerals. See Minerology

Miners
See pages in the following book:
Sandler, M. W. The way we lived p20-25 (4 and up) **331.09**

Mines and mineral resources
See also Mineralogy; and specific types of mines and mining, e.g. Coal mines and mining

Australia
See pages in the following book:
Blunden, G. The land and people of Australia p78-88 (5 and up) **994**

Bolivia
See pages in the following book:
Warren, L. F. The land and people of Bolivia p67-81 (5 and up) **984**

Sierra Leone
See pages in the following book:
Clifford, M. L. The land and people of Sierra Leone p137-43 (5 and up) **966**

United States—History
See pages in the following book:
Sandler, M. W. The way we lived p20-25 (4 and up) **331.09**

Mine's the best. Bonsall, C. **E**

Miniature gardens. See Gardens, Miniature

Miniature objects. See names of miniature objects, e.g. Dollhouses; and names of objects with the subdivision Models, e.g. Airplanes—Models

Minibikes and small cycles. Stambler, I. **629.2**

Mining. See Mines and mineral resources

The **mink** being who wanted to marry a princess. Harris, C.
In Harris, C. Mouse Woman and the muddleheads p5-25 **398.2**

A month of Sundays. Blue, R.   **Fic**

Montresor, Beni

Caldecott Medal acceptance paper

In Newbery and Caldecott Medal books: 1956-1965 p259-65   **028.5**

Cinderella (2-4)   **782.1**

(illus.) De Regniers, B. S. May I bring a friend?   **E**

(illus.) Stolz, M. Belling the tiger   **Fic**

About

See pages in the following book:

Newbery and Caldecott Medal books: 1956-1965 p266-69   **028.5**

Montreville, Doris de. See De Montreville, Doris

Monty. Stevenson, J.   **E**

Monuments

See also Pyramids; Tombs

Mooch the messy. Sharmat, M. W.   **E**

Moody, Anne

See pages in the following book:

Alexander, R. P. comp. Young and black in America p85-102 (6 and up)   **920**

Moominland midwinter. Jansson, T. See note under Jansson, T. Comet in Moominland   **Fic**

Moominpapa at sea. Jansson, T. See note under Jansson, T. Comet in Moominland   **Fic**

Moominsummer madness. Jansson, T. See note under Jansson, T. Comet in Moominland   **Fic**

Moominvalley in November. Jansson, T. See note under Jansson, T. Comet in Moominland   **Fic**

Moon, Elzia

(illus.) Towne, P. George Washington Carver   **92**

Moon (as subject)

Shuttlesworth, D. E. The moon (5 and up)   **523.3**

See also pages in the following books:

Freeman, M. The sun, the moon, and the stars p16-21 (2-4)   **523**

Simon, S. Look to the night sky p36-42 (4 and up)   **523**

See also Tides

Fiction

Asch, F. Moon Bear   **E**

Dayrell, E. Why the sun and the moon live in the sky (k-2)   **398.2**

Levitin, S. Who owns the moon?   **E**

Preston, E. M. Squawk to the moon, Little Goose   **E**

Talbot, T. A bucketful of moon   **E**

Poetry

Hughes, T. Moon-whales, and other Moon poems (6 and up)   **821**

The Man in the Moon as he sails the sky, and other Moon verse (k-3)   **821.08**

Moon, Voyages to. See Space flight to the moon

The **moon.** Grimm, J.

In Grimm, J. The Brothers Grimm: popular folk tales p93-96   **398.2**

In Grimm, J. The complete Grimm's fairy tales p713-15   **398.2**

Moon Bear. Asch, F.   **E**

Moon Dragon; puppet play. Cochrane, L.

In Cochrane, L. Shadow puppets in color p18-25   **791.5**

The **moon** in the donkey. Jagendorf, M. A.

In Jagendorf, M. A. Noodlehead stories from around the world p249-52   **398.2**

The **moon** is like a silver sickle. Morton, M. ed.   **891.7**

The **moon** jumpers. Udry, J. M.   **E**

The **Moon** Maiden. Chrisman, A. B.

In Chrisman, A. B. Shen of the sea p134-45   **S C**

Moon Man. Ungerer, T.   **E**

The **moon** of Gomrath. Garner, A. See note under Garner, A. The Weirdstone of Brisingamen   **Fic**

The **moon** on the one hand. Crofut, W.   **784.6**

Moon rocks. See Lunar petrology

Moon shot. Korty, C.

In Korty, C. Silly soup p102-20   **812**

Moon-whales, and other Moon poems. Hughes, T.   **821**

Moonlife 2069. Henderson, N.

In Henderson, N. Celebrate America p63-75   **812**

The **moon's** escape. Sechrist, E. H.

In Sechrist, E. H. Once in the first times p75-78   **398.2**

The **Moon's** the North Wind's cooky (k-3)   **811.08**

Moonshine in the mustard pot. Aiken, J.

In Aiken, J. The faithless lollybird p149-70   **S C**

Moore, Clement C.

A visit from St Nicholas

In The Arbuthnot Anthology of children's literature p120   **808.8**

A visit from St Nicholas; dramatization. See Chermak, S. A visit from St Nicholas

Moore, Edna G.

Mr Longfellow observes Book Week

In One hundred plays for children p433-38   **808.82**

Moore, Eva

The cookie book (3-5)   **641.8**

The Seabury Cook book for boys and girls (1-3)   **641.5**

Moore, Lilian

(ed.) Go with the poem. See Go with the poem   **811.08**

Little raccoon and poems from the woods (k-3)   **811**

Little raccoon and the thing in the pool   **E**

The "now-really" time

In Gruenberg, S. M. comp. Let's hear a story p68-73   **808.8**

See my lovely poison ivy, and other verses about witches, ghosts and things (1-4)   **811**

The snake that went to school (2-4)   **Fic**

Moore, Vardine

Pre-school story hour   **372.6**

Moorman, Thomas

How to make your science project scientific (5 and up)   **507**

What is it really like out there? (6 and up)   **121**

Moors
See pages in the following book:
Loder, D. The land and the people of Spain p23-31 (5 and up) **946**
The **Moor's** legacy. Irving, W.
In Irving, W. Rip Van Winkle, The legend of Sleepy Hollow, and other tales p129-58 **S C**
Moor's legacy, Legend of the. See The legend of the Moor's legacy
Moose
Eberle, I. Moose live here (1-3) **599.73**

Fiction
Pinkwater, M. Blue moose (1-3) **Fic**
Moose live here. Eberle, I. **599.73**
Moote, Al
(illus.) Weir, L. Skateboards and skateboarding **796.2**
Moozipoo. Housman, L.
In Housman, L. The rat-catcher's daughter p68-85 **S C**
Mopeding. Coombs, C. **629.2**
Mopeds
Coombs, C. Mopeding (5 and up) **629.2**
A **moral** alphabet. Belloc, H.
In Belloc, H. The bad child's book of beasts, and More beasts for worse children and A moral alphabet **821**
Mordvinoff, Nicolas
Caldecott Medal acceptance paper
In Caldecott Medal books: 1938-1957 p230-36 **028.5**
About
See pages in the following book:
Caldecott Medal books! 1938-1957 p237-41 **028.5**
For a book illustrated by this artist see Nicolas
More about Paddington. Bond, M. See note under Bond, M. A bear called Paddington **Fic**
More about what plants do. Rahn, J. E. **581.3**
More adventures of the Great Brain. Fitzgerald, J. D. See note under Fitzgerald, J. D. The Great Brain **Fic**
More All-of-a-kind family. Taylor, S. See note under Taylor, S. All-of-a-kind family **Fic**
More beasts for worse children. Belloc, H.
In Belloc, H. The bad child's book of beasts, and More beasts for worse children, and A moral alphabet **821**
More beginning crafts for beginning readers. Gilbreath, A. **745.5**
More brain-boosters. Webster, D. **507**
More Codes for kids. Albert, B. **652**
More Colonial crafts for you to make. D'Amato, J. **745.5**
More Cricket songs (4 and up) **895.6**
More Festivals in Asia (2-5) **394.2**
More Films kids like. Gaffney, M. comp. **016.3713**
More Fun with Spanish. Cooper, L. **468**
More How it works. Papallo, G.
In Papallo, G. What makes it work **600**
More junior authors **920.03**
More Juniorplots Gillespie, J. T. **028.1**

More potatoes! Selsam, M. E. **635**
More Science experiments you can eat. Cobb, V. **507**
More Silver pennies. See Thompson, B. J. ed. All the Silver pennies **821.08**
More Small poems. Worth, V. **811**
More Tales from Grimm. Grimm, J. **398.2**
More Words of science. Asimov, I. **503**
Morey, Walt
Gentle Ben (5 and up) **Fic**
Operation blue bear (4-6) **599.74**
Year of the black pony (5 and up) **Fic**
Morgan Alfred
First chemistry book for boys and girls (5 and up) **540**
Morgan, Alison
A boy called Fish (5 and up) **Fic**
Morgan, Ava
(illus.) Hautzig, E. Let's make gifts **745.5**
(illus.) Pels, G. The care of water pets **639.3**
Morgan, Garrett A.
See pages in the following book:
Hayden, R. C. Eight black American inventors p16-29 (5 and up) **920**
Morgan, Sir Henry
See pages in the following book:
Stockton, F. R. Buccaneers & pirates of our coasts p101-31 (5 and up) **910.4**
Morgan, John Pierpont, 1837-1913
See pages in the following book:
Captains of industry p89-105 (5 and up) **920**
Morgan, Kemp
See pages in the following book:
Malcolmson, A. Yankee Doodle's cousins p185-94 (4 and up) **398.2**
Morgan, Roy
(illus.) Picard, B. L. Stories of King Arthur and his knights **398.2**
Morgan horse
Fiction
Henry, M. Justin Morgan had a horse (4 and up) **Fic**
Morley, Christopher
Gissing and the telephone
In Told under the magic umbrella p79-85 **S C**
The tree that didn't get trimmed
In It's time for Christmas p238-42 **394.2**
Morley, Olive J.
King Arthur and his knights
In Dramatized folk tales of the world p106-27 **812.08**
Little women
In A Treasury of Christmas plays p129-46 **812.08**
O little town of Bethlehem
In A Treasury of Christmas plays p211-21 **812.08**
Morocco
Spencer, W. The land and people of Morocco (5 and up) **964**
See also pages in the following book:
Lawson, D. Morocco, Algeria, Tunisia, and Libya p4-17 (4 and up) **961**
Folklore
See Folklore—Morocco

My backyard history book. Weitzman, D. 973
My black me. Adoff, A. ed. 811.08
My brother Sam is dead. Collier, J. L. Fic
My brother Steve is retarded. Sobol, H. L. 362.3
My brother Stevie. Clymer, E. Fic
My cat has eyes of sapphire blue. Fisher, A. 811
My dad lives in a downtown hotel. Mann, P. Fic
My daddy longlegs. Hawes, J. 595.4
My dentist. Rockwell, H. 617.6
My doctor. Rockwell, H. 610.69
My father's dragon. Gannett, R. S. Fic
My five senses. Aliki 612
My friend John. Zolotow, C. E
My goldfish. Wong, H. H. 597
My grandfather, Hendry Watty. Quiller-Couch, Sir A.
In Sechrist, E. H. ed. 13 ghostly yarns p35-44 S C
My grandson Lew. Zolotow, C. E
My household
Grimm, J. My household
In Grimm, J. The complete Grimm's fairy tales p624 398.2
My island grandma. Lasky, K. E
My journals and sketchbooks. [Politzer, A.] Fic
My Lord Bag of Rice. Manning-Sanders, R.
In Manning-Sanders, A. A book of dragons p38-42 398.2
My mama says there aren't any zombies, ghost, vampires, creatures, demons, monsters, fiends, goblins, or things. Viorst, J. E
My mom got a job. Smith, L. B. E
My mother is the most beautiful woman in the world. Reyher, B. 398.2
My mother sends her wisdom. McClenathan, L. E
My name is Emily. Hamilton, M. E
My Noah's ark. Goffstein, M. B. E
My nursery school. Rockwell, H. E
My other-mother, my other-father. Sobol, H. L. 306.8
My own rhythm. Atwood, A. 811
My own true ghost story. Kipling, R.
In Sechrist, E. H. ed. 13 ghostly yarns p199-221 S C
My poetry book (5 and up) 821.08
My puppy is born. Cole, J. 636.7
My red umbrella. Bright, R. E
My side of the mountain. George, J. C. Fic
My side of the mountain; excerpt. George, J. C.
In The Arbuthnot Anthology of children's literature p660-65 808.8
My tang's tungled and other ridiculous situations (3-6) 821.08
My teddy bear. Nakatani, Chiyoko E
My treasure. Carlson, B. W.
In Carlson, B. W. Funny-bone dramatics p60-64 812
My village in Hungary. Gidal, S. 943.9
My village, Sturbridge. Bowen, G. 974.4

My visit to the dinosaurs. Aliki 567.9
Myaskovsky, Nicholas. See Miaskovskiĭ, Nikolai
Mycenae
See pages in the following book:
Hall, J. Buried cities p101-16 (5 and up) 930.1
Myers, Bernice
(illus.) Peterson, J. How to write codes and send secret messages 652
(illus.) Pine, T. S. Simple machines and how we use them 621.8
Myers, Elisabeth P.
Langston Hughes: poet of his people (4-6) 92
Myers, Steven J.
The enchanted sticks (3-5) Fic
Myers, Walter Dean
The dragon takes a wife E
Fast Sam, Cool Clyde & Stuff (6 and up) Fic
Mojo and the Russians (6 and up) Fic
The young landlords (6 and up) Fic
Social welfare (4 and up) 361.6
Myller, Rolf
From idea into house (5 and up) 728
Symbols & their meaning (4 and up) 001.56
Myrick, Mildred
The Secret Three E
Myrick, Norman
The day is bright
In One hundred plays for children p253-67 808.82
Mysteries of the sea. Jagendorf, M. A.
In Jagendorf, M. A. New England beanpot p236-39 398.2
The mysterious disappearance of Leon (I mean Noel). Raskin, E. Fic
The mysterious rays: Marie Curie's world. Veglahn, N. 92
The mysterious schoolmaster. Anckarsvärd, K. Fic
The mysterious stranger. Nicholson, J.
In Fifty plays for junior actors p418-34 812.08
The mysterious tadpole. Kellogg, S. E
The mysterious traveller. Colwell, E.
In Colwell, E. Round about and long ago p43-45 398.2
Mystery and detective stories
Anckarsvärd, K. The mysterious schoolmaster (5 and up) Fic
Babbitt, N. Goody Hall (4-6) Fic
Berends, P. B. The case of the elevator duck (3-5) Fic
Bonham, F. Mystery of the fat cat (5 and up) Fic
Bonsall, C. The case of the hungry stranger E
Brookins, D. Alone in Wolf Hollow (5 and up) Fic
Brooks, W. R. Freddy, the detective (3-5) Fic
Cameron, E. The court of the stone children (5 and up) Fic
Cameron, E. The terrible churndryne (4-6) Fic
Curry, J. L. The Bassumtyte treasure (5 and up) Fic
Curry, J. L. Ghost Lane (5 and up) Fic
Curry, J. L. The ice ghosts mystery (4 and up) Fic

Naturecraft. Inouye, C. **745.58**
Nature's pretenders. Hopf, A. L. **591.5**
Nature's weather forecasters. Sattler, H. R. **551.6**
Naughty boy
Andersen, H. C. The naughty boy
In Anderson, H. C. The complete fairy tales and stories p38-39 **S C**
Navaho Indians
Erdoes, R. The native Americans: Navajos (4 and up) **970.004**
Reit, S. Child of the Navajos (2-4) **970.004**
See also pages in the following books:
Baldwin, G. C. The Apache Indians p167-72 (6 and up) **970.004**
Ehrlich, A. Wounded Knee: an Indian history of the American West p3-18 (6 and up) **970.004**
Hofsinde, R. The Indian medicine man p56-68 (4 and up) **970.004**
Hofsinde, R. Indian warriors and their weapons p89-96 (3-6) **970.004**

Fiction
Armer, L. A. Waterless Mountain (5 and up) **Fic**
Blood, C. L. The goat in the rug **E**
Miles, M. Annie and the Old One (1-4) **Fic**
O'Dell, S. Sing down the moon (5 and up) **Fic**
Navajo Indians. See Navaho Indians
Naval airplanes. See Fighter planes
Naval architecture
See also Marine engineering; Shipbuilding
Naval engineering. See Marine engineering
Navarra, John Gabriel
Superboats (4 and up) **387.2**
Supercars (4 and up) **629.2**
Superplanes (5 and up) **629.133**
Supertrains (3-6) **385**
Navigation
See also Compass; Lighthouses
Naw, Jacques Jean. See L'Olonnois, Francis
Nawasi goes to war. Courlander, H.
In Courlander, H. The king's drum, and other African stories p80-86 **398.2**
Naylor, Phyllis Reynolds
Getting along in your family (4 and up) **306.8**
Nayman, Jacqueline
Atlas of wildlife (5 and up) **591.9**
Nazaroff, Alexander
The land and people of Russia (5 and up) **947**
Nazi hunter: Simon Wiesenthal. Noble, I. **92**
Nazi movement. See National socialism
Neal, Harry Edward
Communication (5 and up) **001.51**
Near East. See Middle East
Near mutiny on the "Santa Maria"; play. Carlson, B. W.
In Carlson, B. W. The right play for you p122-26 **792**
Near the window tree. Kuskin, K. **811**

A **near** thing for Captain Najork. Hoban, R. See note under Hoban, R. How Tom beat Captain Najork and his sportsmen **E**
Nebel, Gustave E.
(illus.) Lindop, E. The first book of elections **324.6**
Nebraska

Fiction
Talbot, C. J. An orphan for Nebraska (4-6) **Fic**
A **necklace** of fallen stars. Hilgartner, B. **Fic**
The **needle** crop of Sainte-Dodo. Jagendorf, M. A.
In Jagendorf, M. A. Noodlehead stories from around the world p133-35 **398.2**
Needlepoint
Hodgson, M. A. Fast and easy needlepoint (3-6) **746.44**
Needlework
Enthoven, J. Stitchery for children **746.44**
Meyer, C. Yarn—the things it makes and how to make them (4 and up) **746.4**
See also types of needlework, e.g. Embroidery
Negri, Rocco
(illus.) Byars, B. Trouble River **Fic**
(illus.) Johnston, J. The Indians and the strangers **920**
(illus.) Monjo, F. N. The one bad thing about father
Negroes. See Blacks
Negroes in the early West. Burt, O. W. **920**
Negron, Bill
(illus.) Levitin, S. The mark of Conte **Fic**
Neighboring families
Andersen, H. C. The neighbors
In Andersen, H. C. The complete fairy tales and stories p320-29 **S C**
The **neighbors** Andersen, H. C.
In Andersen, H. C. The complete fairy tales and stories p320-29 **S C**
Neighbors. Goffstein, M. B. **E**
Neilson, William Allan
(ed.) Webster's Biographical dictionary. See Webster's Biographical dictionary **920.03**
Neimark, Anne E.
Touch of light; the story of Louis Braille (4 and up) **92**
Nell, William Cooper
See pages in the following book:
Chittenden, E. F. Profiles in black and white p3-17 (5 and up) **920**
Nelson, Esther L.
Singing and dancing games for the very young **796.1**
Neptune (Planet)
See pages in the following book:
Branley, F. M. The nine planets p79-82 (6 and up) **523.4**
Nerves
See also Nervous system
Nervous system
Elgin, K. The human body: the brain (3-5) **612**
Kalina, S. Your nerves and their messages (3-5) **612**
Showers, P. Use your brain (1-3) **612**

New York (City)—Fiction—*Continued*

Selden, G. The cricket in Times Square (3-6) **Fic**
Snyder, C. Ike and Mama and the once-a-year suit (2-4) **Fic**
Stevenson, J. Howard **E**
Steptoe, J. Train ride (3-6) **Fic**
Stolz, M. The noonday friends (4-6) **Fic**
Stolz, M. A wonderful, terrible time (4-6) **Fic**
Taylor, S. All-of-a-kind family (4-6) **Fic**
Waber, B. The house on East 88th Street **E**
Will. The two Reds **E**

Finance
See Finance—New York (City)

Fires and fire prevention
Beame, R. Ladder Company 108 (3-5) **363.3**

History
Spier, P. The legend of New Amsterdam (1-4) **974.7**

See also pages in the following book:
Tunis, E. The young United States, 1783 to 1830 p113-21 (6 and up) **973**

History—Fiction
Lobel, A. On the day Peter Stuyvesant sailed into town **E**
Moskin, M. Lysbet and the fire kittens (2-4) **Fic**

Metropolitan Museum of Art
Bible. New Testament. Selections. The Christmas story from the Gospels of Matthew & Luke **232.9**
Schnurnberger, L. E. Kings, queens, knights & jesters: making medieval costumes **391.09**

Metropolitan Museum of Art (as subject)—
Fiction
Konigsburg, E. L. From the mixed-up files of Mrs Basil E. Frankweiler (4 and up) **Fic**

Police
Demuth, J. City horse (3-6) **363.2**

Public Library
The Black experience in children's audio-visual materials **016.3058**
The Black experience in children's books **016.3058**

Social life and customs
Spier, P. The legend of New Amsterdam (1-4) **974.7**

Zoological Park
Scott, J. D. City of birds and beasts (6 and up) **590.74**

New York (State)
Fiction
Edmonds, W. D. Bert Breen's barn (6 and up) **Fic**
Edmonds, W. D. The matchlock gun (4-6) **Fic**
Irving, W. Rip Van Winkle (5 and up) **Fic**
Pope, E. M. The Sherwood ring (6 and up) **Fic**
Wilder, L. I. Farmer boy (4-6) **Fic**

New York Library Association. Children's and Young Adult Services Section
Films for children **016.3713**
Recordings for children **016.7899**
The New York Times Book Review **028.1**

New Zealand
Kaula, E. M. The land and people of New Zealand (5 and up) **993**

Animals
See Animals—New Zealand

Newbery, John
See pages in the following books:
Newbery Medal books: 1922-1955 p6-9 **028.5**
Townsend, J. R. Written for children p29-39 **028.5**

Newbery and Caldecott Medal books: 1956-1965 **028.5**

Newbery and Caldecott Medal books: 1966-1975 **028.5**

Newbery Medal books
Alexander, L. The High King (1969) **Fic**
Armer, L. A. Waterless Mountain (1932) **Fic**
Armstrong, W. H. Sounder (1970) **Fic**
Bailey, C. S. Miss Hickory (1947) **Fic**
Blos, J. W. A gathering of days (1980) **Fic**
Brink, C. R. Caddie Woodlawn (1936) **Fic**
Byars, B. The summer of the swans (1971) **Fic**
Chrisman, A. B. Shen of the sea (1926) **S C**
Clark, A. N. Secret of the Andes (1953) **Fic**
Coatsworth, E. The cat who went to heaven (1931) **Fic**
Cooper, S. The grey king (1976) **Fic**
De Angeli, M. The door in the wall (1950) **Fic**
DeJong, M. The wheel on the school (1955) **Fic**
Du Bois, W. P. The twenty-one balloons (1948) **Fic**
Edmonds, W. D. The matchlock gun (1942) **Fic**
Enright, E. Thimble summer (1939) **Fic**
Estes, E. Ginger Pye (1952) **Fic**
Field, R. Hitty: her first hundred years (1930) **Fic**
Finger, C. Tales from silver lands (1925) **398.2**
Forbes, E. Johnny Tremain (1944) **Fic**
Fox, P. The slave dancer (1974) **Fic**
George, J. C. Julie of the wolves (1973) **Fic**
Gray, E. J. Adam of the road (1943) **Fic**
Hamilton, V. M. C. Higgins, the great (1975) **Fic**
Henry, M. King of the Wind (1949) **Fic**
Hunt, I. Up a road slowly (1967) **Fic**
James, W. Smoky, the cow horse (1927) **Fic**
Keith, H. Rifles for Watie (1958) **Fic**
Kelly, E. P. The trumpeter of Krakow (1929) **Fic**
Konigsburg, E. L. From the mixed-up files of Mrs Basil E. Frankweiler (1968) **Fic**
Krumgold, J. . . . and now Miguel (1954) **Fic**
Krumgold, J. Onion John (1960) **Fic**
Lawson, R. Rabbit Hill (1945) **Fic**
L'Engle, M. A wrinkle in time (1963) **Fic**
Lenski, L. Strawberry girl (1946) **Fic**
Lewis, E. F. Young Fu of the upper Yangtze (1933) **Fic**
Mukerji, D. G. Gay-Neck: The story of a pigeon (1928) **Fic**
Neville, E. It's like this, Cat (1964) **Fic**
O'Brien, R. C. Mrs Frisby and the rats of NIMH (1972) **Fic**
O'Dell, S. Island of the Blue Dolphins (1961) **Fic**

Newbery Medal books—*Continued*

Paterson, K. Bridge to Terabithia (1978)
    Fic

Raskin, E. The Westing game (1979)   **Fic**

Seredy, K. The white stag (1938)   **Fic**

Sorensen, V. Miracles on Maple Hill (1957)
    Fic

Speare, E. G. The bronze bow (1962)   **Fic**

Speare, E. G. The witch of Blackbird Pond (1959)
    Fic

Sperry, A. Call it courage (1941)   **Fic**

Taylor, M. D. Roll of thunder, hear my cry (1977)
    Fic

Trevino, E. B. de. I, Juan de Pareja (1966)
    Fic

Wojciechowska, M. Shadow of a bull (1965)
    Fic

Yates, E. Amos Fortune, free man (1951)
    92

Newbery Medal books (as subject)

Newbery and Caldecott Medal books: 1956-1965
    028.5

Newbery and Caldecott Medal boks: 1966-1975
    028.5

Newbery Medal books: 1922-1955   **028.5**

See also pages in the following books:

The Black American in books for children: readings in racism p78-106   **028.5**

Children and literature p416-35   **028.5**

Issues in children's book selection p31-34
    028.5

Newbery Medal books: 1922-1955   **028.5**

Newberry, Clare Turlay

The kittens' ABC   **E**

Marshmallow   **E**

Newell, Hope

The little Old Woman and how she kept her geese warm

In Told under the magic umbrella p55-58
    S C

The little old woman who used her head, and other stories (1-3)   **S C**

Contents: The little old woman; How she got a feather bed; How she saved her corn; How she kept her geese warm; How she finished her red muffler; How she did her marketing; How she rested her head; How she took things easy; How she saw the circus come to town; How she made the baby elephant happy; How she kept herself cheerful; How she got her fortune told; How she traveled on land; How she traveled on water; How she saved her pennies; How she brightened her home; How she put up her Christmas tree; How she trimmed her tree; How she spent Christmas Eve

Newer and better organic gardening. Davis, B.
    635

Newfeld, Frank

(illus.) Lee, D. Alligator pie   **811**

(illus.) Lee, D. Garbage delight   **811**

Newfield, Marcia

A book for Jodan (3-5)   **Fic**

Newfoundland dogs

See pages in the following book:

Clemens, V. P. Super animals and their unusual careers p140-54 (4 and up)   **636.08**

Newlon, Clarke

Southern Africa: the critical land (6 and up)
    968

Newman, Deborah

Plum Blossom and the dragon

In Dramatized folk tales of the world p38-46   **812.08**

The rebellious robots

In Fifty plays for junior actors p407-17
    812.08

Newman, Dora Lee

The tar baby

In North American legends p109-14   **398.2**

Newman, Gerald

The changing Eskimos (2-4)   **970.004**

(ed.) The Concise encyclopedia of sports. See The Concise encyclopedia of sports
    796.03

Lebanon (4 and up)   **956.92**

Newman, Robert

The case of the Baker Street Irregular (5 and up)   **Fic**

Night spell (5 and up)   **Fic**

The twelve labors of Hercules (4-6)   **292**

Newman, Shirlee P.

Marian Anderson: lady from Philadelphia (5 and up)   **92**

News or not? Weiss, A. E.   **070.4**

Newsletter on Intellectual Freedom   **323.44**

Newsome, Arden J.

Make it with felt (4 and up)   **745.5**

Newsome, Effie Lee

See pages in the following book:

Rollins, C. Famous American Negro poets p56-60 (5 and up)   **920**

Newspaper work. See Journalism

Newspapers

See also American newspapers; Journalism

Newton, Sir Isaac

See pages in the following books:

Cottler, J. Heroes of civilization p140-49 (5 and up)   **920**

Foster, G. The world of William Penn p103-13 (5 and up)   **909.08**

Newton, James R.

The march of the lemmings (2-4)   **599.32**

Newts

See pages in the following book:

Ommanney, F. D. Frogs, toads & newts p29-36 (4-6)   **597.6**

Next turn to the right. Leach, M.

In Leach, M. Whistle in the graveyard p103-04   **398.2**

Nez Percé Indians

Biography

Davis, R. Chief Joseph: war chief of the Nez Percé (5 and up)   **92**

Nibble, nibble. Brown, M. W.   **811**

Nice new neighbors. Brandenberg, F.   **E**

Nicholas II, Emperor of Russia

See pages in the following book:

Nazaroff, A. The land and people of Russia p145-49 (5 and up)   **947**

Nichols, Ruth

The marrow of the world (5 and up)   **Fic**

A walk out of the world (4-6)   **Fic**

Nicholson, Jessie

Holiday for Santa

In A Treasury of Christmas plays p241-53
    812.08

The mysterious stranger

In Fifty plays for junior actors p418-34
    812.08

Teapot trouble

In Fifty plays for junior actors p435-49
    812.08

Nicholson, Mary Ann
The price of eggs
In Dramatized folk tales of the world
p149-54   **812.08**
Nicholson, William
Clever Bill   **E**
(illus.) Williams, M. The velveteen rabbit
    Fic
Nickel, Mildred L.
Steps to service   **027.8**
Nicklaus, Carol
(illus.) Carlson, D. Girls are equal too
    305.4
(illus.) Nostlinger, C. Konrad   **Fic**
Nicknames
Shankle, G. E. American nicknames   **929.4**
Nic Leodhas, Sorche
Always room for one more (k-3)   **784.4**
The bride who out talked the water kelpie
In The Arbuthnot Anthology of children's
literature p166-70   **808.8**
The house that lacked a bogle
In A-haunting we will go p95-105   **S C**
The man who didn't believe in ghosts
In Haunting tales p25-32 (5 and up)   **S C**
The woman who flummoxed the fairies
In Greene, E. comp. Clever cooks p13-24
    398.2
Nicola Bayley's Book of nursery rhymes
    398
Nicolas
(illus.) Will. Finders keepers   **E**
(illus.) Will. The two Reds   **E**
*For other material by and about this
illustrator see* Mordvinoff, Nicolas
Nidden and Didden and Donald Beg O'Neary.
MacManus, S.
In MacManus, S. Hibernian nights p141-47
    398.2
Nielsen, Kay
(illus.) Asbjörnsen, P. C. East of the sun
and west of the moon   **398.2**
(illus.) Grimm, J. Fairy tales of the Brothers
Grimm   **398.2**
The **Niger**: Africa's river of mystery. Watson, J.   **966**
Niger River
Watson, J. The Niger: Africa's River of
mystery (4-6)   **966**
Nigeria
Forman, B. The land and people of Nigeria
(5 and up)   **966.9**
Folklore
See Folklore—Nigeria
Social life and customs
Jenness, A. Along the Niger River (5 and
up)   **966.9**
Nigerian arts. See Arts, Nigerian
Night
Fiction
Babbitt, N. The something   **E**
Brown, M. W. A child's good night book
    E
Brown, M. W. Goodnight moon   **E**
Brown, M. W. Wait till the moon is full
    E
Crowe, R. L. Clyde monster   **E**
Ryan, C. D. Hildilid's night   **E**
Poetry
The Moon's the North Wind's cooky (k-3)
    811.08

Night animals. Cohen, D.   **591.5**
The **night** before Christmas. Moore, C. C.
    811
The **night** daddy. Gripe, M.   **Fic**
Night journeys. Avi   **Fic**
Night noises, and other Mole and Troll stories.
Johnston, T.   **E**
The **night** of the comet. Garfield, L.   **Fic**
The **night** of the Leonids. Konigsburg, E. L.
In Konigsburg, E. L. Altogether, one at a
time p13-28   **S C**
The **night** sky book. Jobb, J.   **523**
Night spell. Newman, R.   **Fic**
The **night** the stars were gone. Aiken, J.
In Aiken, J. The faithless lollybird p93-103
    S C
Nightingale, Florence
See pages in the following book:
McNeer, M. Armed with courage p7-22
(4-6)   **920**
The **nightingale**. Andersen, H. C.   **Fic**
also in Andersen, H. C. Ardizzone's Hans
Andersen: fourteen classic tales p179-
91   **S C**
also in Andersen, H. C. The complete fairy
tales and stories p203-12   **S C**
also in Andersen, H. Dulac's The Snow
Queen, and other stories from Hans
Andersen p94-107   **S C**
also in Andersen, H. Hans Andersen: his
classic fairy tales p19-28   **S C**
also in The Andrew Lang Fairy tale treasury p317-26   **398.2**
also in It's time for story hour p249-58
    372.6
also in Shedlock, M. L. The art of the
storyteller p243-58   **372.6**
also in Yellow fairy book p282-93   **398.2**
The **nightingale**. Reeves, J.
In Reeves, J. The shadow of the hawk, and
other stories p85-95   **398.2**
The **nightingale** and the rose. Wilde, O.
In Wilde, O. The Happy Prince, and other
stories p13-20   **S C**
The **Nightingale** and the turkey
In Laughing together p100   **808.87**
Nightingales
Fiction
Andersen, H. C. The nightingale (3-5)   **Fic**
The **nightingale's** song. Riordan, J.
In Riordan, J. Tales from Tartary p33-36
    398.2
Nightmare brother. Nourse, A. E.
In Universe ahead: stories of the future
p163-93   **S C**
The **nightmare** world of the shark. Cook, J. J.
    597
Nightmares. Prelutsky, J.   **811**
Nigognossian, Christine Willis
(illus.) Andersen, H. C. Thumbelina   **Fic**
Niilo and the wizard. Bowman, J. C.
In Bowman, J. C. Tales from a Finnish
tupa p141-46   **398.2**
Nikita the Tanner
Afanas'ev, A. Nikita the Tanner
In Afanas'ev, A. Russian fairy tales p310-11
    398.2
Nilda. Mohr, N.   **Fic**

Nile River
See pages in the following books:
Mahmoud, Z. N. The land and people of
Egypt p11-19 (5 and up) **962**
Perl, L. East Africa p62-68 (4-6) **967.6**
Nils in the forest. Manning-Sanders, R.
In Manning-Sanders, R. A book of ogres
and trolls p123-27 **398.2**
Nilsson, Lennart
How was I born? (3-6) **612**
(illus.) Day, B. The secret world of the
baby **612**
Nine cheers for Christmas. Fisher, A.
In A Treasury of Christmas plays p330-38
812.08
Nine days to Christmas. Ets, M. H. **E**
The **nine** doves. Manning-Sanders, R.
In Manning-Sanders, R. A book of
dragons p43-54 **398.2**
The **nine** planets. Branley, F. M. **523.4**
Nine times Christmas. Olfson, L.
In On stage for Christmas p298-315
812.08
Nineteenth century
Foster, G. Year of Lincoln, 1861 (3-6)
909.81
Foster, G. The year of the horseless carriage,
1801 (3-6) **909.81**
The **ninety**-sixth ghost. Hopkins, L. B.
In A-haunting we will go p42-49 **S C**
Ninjitsu. See Ninjutsu
Ninjutsu
See pages in the following book:
Ribner, S. The martial arts p174-80 (5 and up)
796.8
Ninon
(illus.) For a child. See For a child **821.08**
Niobe
See pages in the following book:
Gates, D. The golden god: Apollo p12-18
(4 and up) **292**
Nippy and the Yankee Doodle. Roberts, L.
In North American legends p155-59 **398.2**
Nis and the dame
Andersen, H. C. The pixy and the grocer
wife
In Andersen, H. C. The complete fairy
tales and stories p853-56 **S C**
Nis at the grocer's
Andersen, H. C. the pixy and the grocer
In Andersen, H. C. The complete fairy
tales and stories p424-27 **S C**
Nivola, Claire A.
(illus.) Miles, B. Save the earth! **363.7**
Nix in the pond
Grimm, J. The nixie of the mill-pond
In Grimm, J. The complete Grimm's fairy
tales p736-42 **398.2**
The Nixy
In Yellow fairy book p101-05 **398.2**
Nix Nought Nothing
Jacobs, J. Nix Nought Nothing
In Jacobs, J. English fairy tales p33-39
398.2
The **nixie** of the mill-pond. Grimm, J.
In Grimm, J. The complete Grimm's fairy
tales p736-42 **398.2**
See also Nix in the pond
Nixon, Joan Lowery
(jt. auth.) Nixon, H. H. Volcanoes **551.2**

Nixon, Hershell H.
Volcanoes (3-5) **551.2**
The **Nixy**
In Yellow fairy book p101-05 **398.2**
See also Nix in the pond
Nkrumah, Kwame, President Ghana
See pages in the following book:
Sale, J. K. The land and people of Ghana
p91-120 (5 and up) **966.7**
No braver soldier. Bierling, J. C. E.
In One hundred plays for children p803-12
808.82
No fighting, no biting! Minarik, E. H. **E**
No flying in the house; excerpt. Brock, B.
In The Arbuthnot Anthology of children's
literature p523-26 **808.8**
No good in art. Cohen, M. See Cohen, M. Will
I have a friend? **E**
No head. Leach, M.
In Leach, M. The thing at the foot of the
bed, and other scary tales p41-43
S C
No one can fool a Helmite. Simon, S.
In Simon, S. The wisemen of Helm and
their merry tales p17-22 **398.2**
No one noticed Ralph. Bishop, B. **E**
No room at the inn. Patterson, E. L.
In One hundred plays for children p551-59
808.82
No roses for Harry. Zion, G. See note under
Zion, G. Harry the dirty dog **E**
No school today! Brandenberg, F. See note
under Brandenberg, F. I wish I was sick,
too! **E**
Noah and the great flood. Hutton, W. **221.9**
Noah and the rainbow. Bolliger, M. **221.9**
Noah's Ark
Bolliger, M. Noah and the rainbow (k-3)
221.9
Duvoisin, R. A for the Ark **E**
Emberley, B. One wide river to cross (k-3)
784.4
Hutton, W. Noah and the great flood (k-3)
221.9
Noah's Ark **E**
Poetry
Nash, O. The cruise of the Aardvark (3-5)
811
Noah's castle. Townsend, J. R. **Fic**
Nobel prizes
See pages in the following book:
Sechrist, E. H. It's time for brotherhood
p184-88 (5 and up) **361**
Noble, Iris
Contemporary women scientists of America
(5 and up) **920**
Nazi hunter: Simon Wiesenthal (5 and up)
92
Susan B. Anthony (5 and up) **92**
Nobleman and the peasant
Afanas'ev, A. The nobleman and the peasant
In Afanas'ev, A. Russian fairy tales p59-61
398.2
Nobody asked me if I wanted a baby sitter.
Alexander, M. **E**
Nobody here but you and me. Leach, M.
In Leach, M. Whistle in the graveyard
p28-29 **398.2**

Nobody sees a mockingbird on Friday. Jagendorf, M. A.
In Jagendorf, M. A. Folk stories of the South p69-71 **398.2**

Nobody's cat. Miles, M. **Fic**

Nobody's family is going to change. Fitzhugh, L. **Fic**

Nocella, Samuel
(illus.) Schwartz, A. Stores **381**

Nockels, David
(illus.) Nayman, J. Atlas of wildlife (5 and up) **591.9**

The **nocturnal** world of the lobster. Cook, J. J. **595.3**

Nodey, the priest's grandson
Afanas'ev, A. Nodey, the priest's grandson
In Afanas'ev, A. Russian fairy tales p173-77 **398.2**

Nødset, Joan L.
Come here, cat **E**
Go away, dog **E**
Who took the farmer's [hat]? **E**
For other titles by this author see Lexau, Joan M.

Noel, J.
(illus.) Huntington, H. E. Let's look at reptiles **597.9**

Noël for Jeanne-Marie. Françoise. See note under Françoise. Jeanne-Marie counts her sheep **E**

Noguchi, Isamu
Tobias, T. Isamu Noguchi: the life of a sculptor (3-6) **92**

Noise
See pages in the following book:
Webster, D. More brain-boosters p69-72 (4 and up) **507**

Noisy Nancy and Nick. Gaeddert, L. See note under Gaeddert, L. Noisy Nancy Norris **E**

Noisy Nancy Norris. Gaeddert, L. **E**

Noisy Nora. Wells, R. **E**

Nolan, Jeannette Covert
Happy Christmas to all
In One hundred plays for children p540-50 **808.82**

Nolan, Paul T.
The trouble with Christmas
In On stage for Christmas p128-44 **812.08**
In A Treasury of Christmas plays p95-111 **812.08**

Nollichucky Jack. Jagendorf, M. A.
In Jagendorf, M. A. Folk stories of the South p184-87 **398.2**

Nomination of Presidents. See Presidents—United States—Nomination

Nonbook materials. See Audio-visual materials

Nonbook materials: the organization of integrated collections. Weihs, J. **025.3**

Nonna. Bartoli, J. **E**

Nonnast, Marie
(illus.) Dalgliesh, A. The Fourth of July story **973.3**

Nonobjective art. See Art, Abstract

Nonprint materials. See Audio-visual materials

The **nonsense** book of riddles, rhymes, tongue twisters, puzzles and jokes from American folklore. Emrich, D. comp. **398**

Nonsense verses
Belloc, H. The bad child's book of beasts, and More beasts for worse children, and A moral alphabet (1-4) **821**
Bodecker, N. M. Hurry, hurry, Mary dear! And other nonsense poems (2-5) **811**
Bodecker, N. M. Let's marry said the cherry, and other nonsense poems (2-5) **811**
Cameron, P. I can't said the ant **E**
Carroll, L. The hunting of the snark (4 and up) **821**
Carroll, L. Lewis Carroll's Jabberwocky (1-3) **821**
Ciardi, J. I met a man (1-3) **811**
Ciardi, J. The man who sang the sillies (2-5) **811**
A Great big ugly man came up and tied his horse to me (k-3) **821.08**
Heilbroner, J. This is the house where Jack lives **E**
Kennedy, S. J. The phantom ice cream man (3-6) **811**
Lear, E. The complete nonsense of Edward Lear **821**
Lear, E. Edward Lear's The Scroobious Pip (2-6) **821**
Lear, E. The Jumblies, and other nonsense verses (2-6) **821**
Lear, E. The owl and the pussy-cat; illus. by Barbara Cooney (k-3) **821**
Lear, E. The owl and the pussy-cat; illus. by Gwen Fulton (k-3) **821**
Lear, E. The pelican chorus & other nonsense verses (2-6) **821**
Lee, D. Alligator pie (k-3) **811**
Lee, D. Garbage delight (3-6) **811**
Morrison, B. Squeeze a sneeze (k-3) **811**
Oh, how silly! (3-6) **821.08**
Oh, such foolishness! (3 and up) **811.08**
Oh, that's ridiculous! (3-6) **821.08**
Oh, what nonsense! (3-6) **821.08**
Orgel, D. Merry merry FIBruary (k-3) **811**
Prelutsky, J. The Queen of Eene (k-3) **811**
Prelutsky, J. The snopp on the sidewalk, and other poems (k-4) **811**
Richards, L. E. Tirra lirra (3-5) **811**
Seuss, Dr. The cat in the hat **E**
Seuss, Dr. Horton hatches the egg **E**
Seuss, Dr. How the Grinch stole Christmas **E**
Seuss, Dr. If I ran the circus **E**
Seuss, Dr. If I ran the zoo **E**
Silverstein, S. Where the sidewalk ends (3 and up) **811**
Smith, W. J. Laughing time **811**
Watson, C. Father Fox's pennyrhymes (k-3) **811**
Zemach, H. The judge **E**
See also pages in the following books:
Piping down the valleys wild p21-36 **808.81**
Rainbow in the sky p351-82 (k-4) **821.08**
See also Humorous poetry; Limericks; Tongue twisters

Nonverbal communication
Castle, S. Face talk, hand talk, body talk (k-2) **153.6**
See also pages in the following book:
Pellowski, A. The world of storytelling p108-23 **372.6**

Nonword stories. See Stories without words

The **noodle.** Kendall, C.
In Kendall, C. Sweet and sour p100-05 **398.2**

Paperback books

Gillespie, J. T. The young phenomenon: paperbacks in our schools   **027.8**

See also pages in the following book:

Larrick, N. A parent's guide to children's reading p235-42   **028.5**

Directories

Gillespie, J. T. Paperback books for young people   **070.5025**

Paperback books for young people. Gillespie, J. T.   **070.5025**

The **papermakers.** Fisher, L. E.   **676**

Papier-mâché. See Paper crafts

Pappa Greatnose. Manning-Sanders, R.

In Manning-Sanders, R. A book of ghosts & goblins p47-54   **398.2**

Papuans

Marcus, R. B. Survivors of the stone age (5 and up)   **306**

Papyrus Westcar

How Djadja-em-ankh saved the day. See How Djadja-em-ankh saved the day   **398.2**

Paracelsus

See pages in the following book:

Aylesworth, T. G. The alchemists: magic into science p17-24 (6 and up)   **540.1**

Paradis, Adrian A.

From trails to superhighways (3-6)   **625.7**

Parakeets. See Budgerigars

Paramecium. See Protozoa

Paramedical personnel. See Applied health personnel

Paraprofessions and paraprofessionals

See also Allied health personnel

Parapsychology. See Psychical research

Pareja, Juan de

Fiction

Treviño, E. B. I, Juan De Pareja (6 and up)   **Fic**

Parent and child

Hautzig, E. Life with working parents: practical hints for everyday situations (5 and up)   **649**

See also pages in the following books:

Kalb, J. What every kid should know p28-51 (5 and up)   **158**

LeShan, E. What makes me feel this way? p79-89 (3-6)   **152.4**

LeShan, E. You and your feelings p12-42 (6 and up)   **155.5**

Seixas, J. S. Living with a parent who drinks too much (4 and up)   **362.8**

See also Stepchildren

Fiction

Blume, J. It's not the end of the world (4-6)   **Fic**

Burch, R. Queenie Peavy (5 and up)   **Fic**

Caines, J. Daddy   **E**

Clifton, L. Amifika   **E**

Ewing, K. A private matter (4-6)   **Fic**

Gray, N. It'll all come out in the wash   **E**

Hautzig, D. The handsomest father   **E**

Hurwitz, J. The law of gravity (4-6)   **Fic**

Johnson, A. The grizzly (5 and up)   **Fic**

Lexau, J. M. Emily and the klunky baby and the next-door dog   **E**

Mann, P. There are two kinds of terrible (5 and up)   **Fic**

Nostlinger, C. Konrad (4-6)   **Fic**

Pascal, F. Hangin' out with Cici (5 and up)   **Fic**

Scott, A. H. On mother's lap   **E**

Snyder, C. Ike and Mama and the once-a-year suit (2-4)   **Fic**

Townsend, J. R. Noah's castle (6 and up)   **Fic**

Yep, L. Sea glass (6 and up)   **Fic**

Zei, A. The sound of the dragon's feet (5-6)   **Fic**

Poetry

Clifton, L. Everett Anderson's 1 2 3 (k-3)   **811**

See also pages in the following book:

Life hungers to abound p37-71, 131-70 (6 and up)   **808.81**

A **parent's** guide to children's reading. Larrick, N.   **028.5**

Parents' Nursery School

Kids are natural cooks (3-6)   **641.5**

Parents without partners. See Single parent family

Pargment, Lila

(jt. auth.) Titiev, E. How the Moolah was taught a lesson & other tales from Russia   **398.2**

Paricutin (Volcano)

Fiction

Lewis, T. P. Hill of fire   **E**

Paris

See pages in the following book:

Bragdon, L. J. The land and people of France p120-29 (5 and up)   **944**

Fiction

Bemelmans, L. Madeline's rescue   **E**

Carlson, N. S. The family under the bridge (3-5)   **Fic**

Lamorisse, A. The red balloon (1-4)   **Fic**

Parish, Peggy

Amelia Bedelia   **E**

Amelia Bedelia and the surprise shower. See note under Parish, P. Amelia Bedelia   **E**

Amelia Bedelia helps out. See note under Parish, P. Amelia Bedelia   **E**

Beginning mobiles (1-3)   **731**

Come back, Amelia Bedelia. See note under Parish, P. Amelia Bedelia   **E**

Costumes to make (4-6)   **391**

December decorations (1-3)   **745.59**

Dinosaur time (k-2)   **567.9**

Good work, Amelia Bedelia. See note under Parish, P. Amelia Bedelia   **E**

Let's be early settlers with Daniel Boone (2-5)   **745.5**

Let's be Indians (2-5)   **745.5**

Let's celebrate: holiday decorations you can make (3-6)   **745.59**

Play ball, Amelia Bedelia. See note under Parish, P. Amelia Bedelia   **E**

Teach us, Amelia Bedelia. See note under Parish, P. Amelia Bedelia   **E**

Thank you, Amelia Bedelia. See note under Parish, P. Amelia Bedelia   **E**

Park, William R.
(jt. auth.) Kelly, J. E. The dam builders
627
(jt. auth.) Kelly, J. E. The tunnel builders
624

Parker, Alice
Terrariums (2-4)				635.9

Parker, Eli Samuel, Seneca chief
See pages in the following book:
Ehrlich, A. Wounded Knee: an Indian history of the American West p121-28 (6 and up)				970.004

Parker, Elinor
(ed.) 100 more story poems (6 and up)
821.08

Parker, Lewis
(illus.) Little, J. Mine for keeps			Fic

Parker, Nancy Winslow
(illus.) Hot cross buns, and other old street cries. See Hot cross buns, and other old street cries				398
Poofy loves company			E
The President's Cabinet and how it grew (3-5)				353.04
(illus.) Sweetly sings the donkey. See Sweet sings the donkey			784.1
(illus.) Blood, C. L. The goat in the rug		E
(illus.) Houck, C. Warm as wool, cool as cotton				677
(illus.) Kantrowitz, M. Willy Bear		E
(illus.) Langstaff, J. Oh, a-hunting we will go
784.4

Parker, Robert
(illus.) Gardner, J. L. Mary Jemison: Seneca captive				92
(illus.) Neimark, A. E. Touch of light; the story of Louis Braille				92

Parker, Robert Andrew
(illus.) Baylor, B. Guess who my favorite person is			E
(illus.) Crompton, A. E. The winter wife
398.2
(illus.) Gauch, P. L. The impossible Major Rogers				92
(illus.) Jones, H. comp. The trees stand shining				897
(illus.) Taylor, T. Battle in the Arctic seas
940.54

Parker, Stephen
Life before birth: the story of the first nine months (3-6)				612

Parker, Theodore
See pages in the following book:
Chittenden, E. F. Profiles in black and white p88-106 (5 and up)				920

Parker, Xenia Ley
A beginner's book of knitting and crocheting (5 and up)				746.43

Parkin, Rex
The red carpet			E

Parks, David
(illus.) Hopkins, L. B. comp. On our way
811.08

About
See pages in the following book:
Alexander, R. P. comp. Young and black in America p123-37 (6 and up)				920

Parks, Gordon
(illus.) Wagner, J. J. T.			Fic

Parks, Michael
(illus.) Jagendorf, M. A. Folk stories of the South				398.2

Parks, Peter
(illus.) The Chicken and the egg. See The Chicken and the egg				636.5

Parks, Rosa Lee
Greenfield, E. Rosa Parks (2-4)			92

Parks
Hautzig, E. In the park (k-3)			410
See also Zoological gardens

Parley, Peter. See Goodrich, Samuel Griswold

Parliamentary practice
Robert, H. M. Robert's Rules of order   060.4

Parnall, Peter
(illus.) The Fireside song book of birds and beasts. See The Fireside song book of birds and beasts				784.4
The mountain				E
(illus.) Baylor, B. The desert is theirs	574.5
(illus.) Baylor, B. Everybody needs a rock
E
(illus.) Baylor, B. Hawk, I'm your brother
E
(jt. auth.) Baylor, B. The other way to listen			E
(illus.) Baylor, B. The way to start a day
291.4
(jt. auth.) Baylor, B. Your own best secret place			E
(illus.) Hodges, M. The Fire Bringer		398.2
(illus.) Miles, M. Annie and the Old one
Fic
(illus.) Miles, M. Apricot ABC			E
(illus.) Pringle, L. Twist, wiggle, and squirm
595.1
(illus.) Schick, A. The peregrine falcons
598

Parrakeets. See Budgerigars
Parrakeets. Zim, H. S.				636.6

Parrish, Anne
See pages in the following book:
A Horn Book Sampler on children's books and reading p4-7				028.5

Parrish, Dillwyn
See pages in the following book:
A Horn Book Sampler on children's books and reading p4-7				028.5

Parrish, George Dillwyn. See Parrish, Dillwyn

Parrish, Maxfield
(illus.) The Arabian nights. See The Arabian nights				398.2

Parrish, Thomas
The American flag (4 and up)			929.9

Parrot that fed his parents
Shedlock, M. L. Filial piety
In Shedlock, M. L. The art of the storyteller p229-32				372.6

The **parrot** who wouldn't say Cataño. Belpré, P.
In Belpré, P. Once in Puerto Rico p85-90
398.2

Parrots
Fiction
Bishop, B. No one noticed Ralph		E

Parry, Marian
(illus.) The Lazies. See The Lazies		398.2

Parson Weems. See Weems, Mason Locke

Peking—Description—*Continued*

Rau, M. The people of new China p107-25 (4-6)   **951.05**

Sidel, R. Revolutionary China: people politics, and ping-pong p99-118 (6 and up)   **951.05**

Social life and customs
See pages in the following book:

Rau, M. Our world: the People's Republic of China p67-80 (6 and up)   **951.05**

Pekka and the rogues. Bowman, J. C.
In Bowman, J. C. Tales from a Finnish tupa p231-36   **398.2**

See also Magic cap

Pelé. See Nascimento, Edson Arantes do

Pelé [biography of Edson Arantes do Nascimento]. Haskins, J. S.   **92**

The **pelican** chorus & other nonsense verses. Lear, E.   **821**

Pelicans

Cook, J. J. Wonders of the pelican world (4 and up)   **598**

Scott, J. D. That wonderful pelican (5 and up)   **598**

Fiction

Thiele, C. Storm Boy (3-5)   **Fic**

Pelle's new suit. Beskow, E.   **E**
also in Gruenberg, S. M. ed. Favorite stories old and new p57-58   **808.8**

Pellowski, Anne
The world of storytelling   **372.6**

Peloponnesian War. See Greece—History—Peloponnesian War, 431-404 B.C.

Pels, Albert
(illus.) Pels, G. Easy puppets   **791.5**

Pels, Gertrude
The care of water pets (4-6)   **639.3**
Easy puppets (3-6)   **791.5**

Pelta, Kathy
What does a paramedic do? (4-6)   **610.69**

Pen and the ink stand
Andersen, H. C. The pen and the inkwell
In Andersen, H. C. The complete fairy tales and stories p639-41   **S C**

The **pen** and the inkwell. Andersen, H. C.
In Andersen, H. C. The complete fairy tales and stories p639-41   **S C**

Pen drawing
Rauch, H. G. The lines are coming (2-6)   **741.2**

Zaidenberg, A. How to draw with pen & brush (3 and up)   **741.2**

Pencil, pen and brush. Weiss, H.   **741.2**

Pendleton, Andrew Sherburne
See pages in the following book:
Lasky, K. Tall ships p47-55 (5 and up)   **387.2**

Pène du Bois, William
(illus.) Tobias, T. Moving day   **E**

Penguins
Eberle, I. Penguins live here (3-5)   **598**
Mizumura, K. The emperor penguins (k-3)   **598**
Stonehouse, B. Penguins (4 and up)   **598**
See also Gentoo penguin

Fiction

Atwater, R. Mr Popper's penguins (3-5)   **Fic**

Penguins live here. Eberle, I.   **598**

Penmanship
See also Calligraphy

Penn, William
Foster, G. The world of William Penn (5 and up)   **909.08**
See also pages in the following books:
The Arbuthnot Anthology of children's literature p781-86   **808.8**
Lengyel, E. The colony of Pennsylvania p12-26, 39-47, 49-61 (5 and up)   **974.4**

Penner, Lucille Recht
The colonial cookbook (5 and up)   **641.5**

Penney, Grace Jackson
How the seven brothers saved their sister
In North American legends p33-39   **398.2**

Pennsylvania

Fiction

Avi. Night journeys (5 and up)   **Fic**
Fritz, J. Brady (4 and up)   **Fic**
Fritz, J. The cabin faced west (3-6)   **Fic**
Holman, F. The murderer (5 and up)   **Fic**

History

Lengyel, E. The colony of Pennsylvania (5 and up)   **974.4**

History—Fiction

Collier, J. L. The country (6 and up)   **Fic**

Pennsylvania Canal
See pages in the following book:
Franchere, R. Westward by canal p112-18 (5 and up)   **386**

Pennsylvania Dutch

Fiction

Milhous, K. The egg tree   **E**

A **penny** a look. Zemach, H.   **398.2**

Penny whistles. See Stevenson, R. L. A child's garden of verses   **821**

Penny wise. Boiko, C.
In Boiko, C. Children's plays for creative actors p66-74   **812**

Pennyworth. Farjeon, E.
In Farjeon, E. The little bookroom p208-15   **S C**

Pentalina. Manning-Sanders, R.
In Manning-Sanders, R. A book of monsters p118-28   **398.2**

The **people** of new China. Rau, M.   **951.05**

People of the Bible. Northcott, C.   **220.9**

People of the first cities. Goode, R.   **930**

People of the Ice Age. Goode, R.   **573.3**

Pepe and the cornfield bandit. Boiko, C.
In Dramatized folk tales of the world p324-33   **812.08**

Pepito. Manning-Sanders, R.
In Manning-Sanders, R. A book of dragons p62-75   **398.2**

Peppé, Rodney
Circus numbers   **E**
Odd one out   **E**

Pepper & salt. Pyle, H.   **398.2**

The **peppermint** pig. Bawden, N.   **Fic**

Peppi. Manning-Sanders, R.
In Manning-Sanders, R. A book of charms and changelings p85-97   **398.2**

Perambulatin' pumpkin. Credle, E.
In Credle, E. Tall tales from the high hills, and other stories p16-20 **398.2**
In Greene, E. comp. Clever cooks p137-42   **398.2**

Perrault, Charles—*Continued*
The master cat
In The Andrew Lang Fairy tale treasury
p 1-7   398.2
In The Arbuthnot Anthology of children's
literature p213-16   808.8
In Blue fairy book p154-60   398.2
In The Classic fairy tales p113-16   398.2
In Time for old magic p90-92   398.2
Perrault's Complete fairy tales (4-6)   398.2
The tales by Perrault are: The sleeping beauty
in the wood; Puss in boots; Little Tom Thumb;
The fairies; Ricky of the Tuft; Cinderella; Little
Red Riding Hood; Blue Beard; The ridiculous
wishes; Donkey-skin; Patient Griselda
Puss in Boots (k-3)   398.2
also in The Arthur Rackham Fairy book
p233-39   398.2
also in The Fairy tale treasury p122-27
398.2
also in The Golden Treasury of children's
literature p96-105   808.8
Puss in Boots; dramatization. See Thane, A.
Puss in boots
Sleeping Beauty
In The Arthur Rackham Fairy book p182-
89   398.2
In Fairy tales from many lands p52-65
398.2
In The Golden Treasury of children's liter-
ature p76-87   808.8
Sleeping Beauty; dramatization. See Thane,
A. The Sleeping Beauty
The sleeping beauty in the wood
In The Andrew Lang Fairy tale treasury
p8-17   398.2
In The Arbuthnot Anthology of children's
literature p207-10   808.8
In Blue fairy book p54-65   398.2
In The Classic fairy tales p85-92   398.2
In Time for old magic p84-87   398.2
Toads and diamonds
In The Andrew Lang Fairy tale treasury
p106-09   398.2
In The Arthur Rackham Fairy book p196-
98   398.2
In Blue fairy book p286-89   398.2
Galdone, P. Cinderella   398.2
Galdone, P. Puss in Boots   398.2
Perrault's Complete fairy tales. Perrault, C.
398.2
Perrifool
Haviland, V. Peerifool
In Haviland, V. Favorite fairy tales told
in Scotland p25-48   398.2
Perrott, Jennifer
(illus.) Meyer, C. Yarn—the things it makes
and how to make them   746.4
Perry, Oliver Hazard
See pages in the following book:
Ault, P. These are the Great Lakes p73-81
(5 and up)   977
Perry, Patricia
Mommy and Daddy are divorced   E
Persecution
See also Jews—Persecutions
Persephone
Farmer, P. The story of Persephone (3-5)
292
Hodges, M. Persephone and the springtime
(k-3)   292
Persephone and the springtime. Hodges, M.
292

Perseus
See pages in the following books:
Blue fairy book p190-201 (4-6)   398.2
Gates, D. The warrior goddess: Athena
p24-50 (4 and up)   292
Hamilton, E. Mythology p197-208 (6 and
up)   292
Persian folk and fairy tales. Mehdevi, A. S.
398.2
Persian gold. Walsh, J. P.
In Walsh, J. P. Children of the fox   S C
Persian Gulf States
Berger, G. Kuwait and the rim of Arabia
(4 and up)   953
Clifford, M. L. The land and people of the
Arabian Peninsula (5 and up)   953
Personal finance. See Finance, Personal
Personal grooming. See Grooming, Personal
Personality
See also Self
Perspective
See pages in the following book:
Weiss, H. Pencil, pen and brush p44-45
741.2
See also Drawing
Personal names. See Names, Personal
Peru
Antiquities
Gemming, E. Lost city in the clouds (5
and up)   985
Fiction
Clark, A. N. Secret of the Andes (4 and up)
Fic
Social life and customs
Mangurian, D. Children of the Incas (4-6)
985
Pessino, Catherine
(jt. auth.) Hussey, L. J. Collecting cocoons
595.7
(jt. auth.) Hussey, L. J. Collecting small
fossils   560
Pest control. See Pests—Control
Pesticide pollution. See Pesticides—Environ-
mental aspects
Pesticides
Environmental aspects
Pringle, L. Pests and people (5 and up)
632
Pests
See also types of pests, e.g. Agricultural
pests
Biological control
Graham, A. Bug hunters (5 and up)   632
Hogner, D. C. Good bugs and bad bugs in
your garden (5 and up)   632
Pringle, L. Pests and people (5 and up)
632
See also pages in the following book:
Fenten, D. X. Gardening . . . naturally p60-
70 (4 and up)   635
Control
Pringle, L. Pests and people (5 and up)
632
See also names of specific pests with the
subdivision Control, e.g. Rats—Control
Pests and people. Pringle, L.   632
A pet for the orphelines. Carlson, N. S. See
note under Carlson, N. S. The happy orphelines   Fic

Pettit, Robert M.
(illus.) Pettit, F. H. The stamp-pad printing book   761

Petunia. Duvoisin, R.   **E**

Petunia, beware! Duvoisin, R. See note under Duvoisin, R. Petunia   **E**

Petunia, I love you. Duvoisin, R. See note under Duvoisin, R. Petunia   **E**

Petunia takes a trip. Duvoisin, R. See note under Duvoisin, R. Petunia   **E**

Petunia's Christmas. Duvoisin, R. See note under Duvoisin, R. Petunia   **E**

Petunia's treasure. Duvoisin, R. See note under Duvoisin, R. Petunia   **E**

Pevsner, Stella
And you give me a pain, Elaine (5 and up)   **Fic**
Keep stompin' till the music stops (3-6)   **Fic**
A smart kid like you (4 and up)   **Fic**

The **peyote** religion. Marriott, A.
In Marriott, A. American Indian mythology   398.2

Peyton, K. M.
See pages in the following book:
Townsend, J. R. A sounding of storytellers p166-78   028.5

Peyton, Kathleen Wendy. See Peyton, K. M.

Pflug, Betsy
Egg-speriment (1-3)   745.5
Funny bags (k-3)   745.54

Phaedrus   028.505

Phaethon
See pages in the following book:
Gates, D. The golden god: Apollo p81-89 (4 and up)   292

Phalangers, Ring-tailed. See Ring-tailed phalangers

Phantasmagoria, and other poems. Carroll, L.
In Carroll, L. The complete works of Lewis Carroll p827-900   828

The **phantom** ice cream man. Kennedy, X. J.   811

The **phantom** tollbooth. Juster, N.   **Fic**

Phantoms. See Ghosts

The **pharaohs** of ancient Egypt. Payne, E.   932

Pharmaceuticals. See Drugs

The **pheasant,** the dove, and the magpie. Kim, So-un
In Kim, So-un. The story bag p19-22   398.2

Pheasants
See pages in the following book:
Silverstein, A. Animal invaders p13-20 (5 and up)   591.5

The **pheasant's** bell. Kim, So-un
In Kim, So-un. The story bag p123-28   398.2

Phelan, Mary Kay
The burning of Washington: August 1814 (5 and up)   975.3
Four days in Philadelphia, 1776 (5 and up)   973.3
The Fourth of July (1-3)   394.2
Martha Berry (2-4)   92
Midnight alarm (3-6)   973.3

Mr Lincoln's inaugural journey (5 and up)   92
The story of the Boston Massacre (6 and up)   973.3
The story of the Boston Tea Party (4-6)   973.3
The story of the great Chicago fire, 1871 (5 and up)   977.3
The story of the Louisiana Purchase (5 and up)   973.4

Phelps, Ethel Johnston
(ed.) Tatterhood, and other tales. See Tatterhood, and other tales   398.2

Phenician antiquities
See pages in the following book:
Goode, R. People of the first cities p89-94 (5 and up)   930

Phenicians
See pages in the following book:
Newman, G. Lebanon p5-13 (4 and up)   956.92

Philadelphia

Centennial Exhibition, 1876
See pages in the following book:
Hilton, S. The way it was—1876 p176-204 (6 and up)   973.8

Fiction
Finlayson, A. Rebecca's war (5 and up)   **Fic**
Vining, E. The taken girl (5 and up)   **Fic**

History
Miller, N. The history of the Liberty Bell (2-4)   974.8
See also pages in the following books:
Lengyel, E. The colony of Pennsylvania p39-47 (5 and up)   974.4
National Geographic Society. Visiting our past: America's historylands p154-66 (5 and up)   917.3

Independence Hall
Milhous, K. Through these arches (5 and up)   974.8

Philanthropy. See Endowments

Philbert the Fearful. Williams, J.
In Williams, J. The practical princess, and other liberating fairy tales p81-99   **S C**

Philemon
See pages in the following book:
Gates, D. Lord of the sky: Zeus p37-42 (4 and up)   292

Philip, King (Metacomet) Sachem of the Wampanoags
See pages in the following book:
In Johnston, J. The Indians and the strangers p35-41 (2-5)   920

Philip II, King of Macedonia
See pages in the following book:
Coolidge, O. The golden days of Greece p160-77 (4-6)   938

Philip II, King of Spain
See pages in the following book:
Loder, D. The land and people of Spain p53-57 (5 and up)   946

Philip Hall likes me. I reckon maybe. Greene, B.   **Fic**

Poetry—*Continued*
Collections

Beastly boys and ghastly girls (5 and up) **808.81**

Bridled with rainbows (3-6) **808.81**

Cakes and custard: children's rhymes (k-2) **398**

Callooh! Callay! (4-6) **808.81**

Crofut, W. The moon on the one hand (3-6) **784.6**

Dinosaurs and beasts of yore **808.81**

Favorite poems, old and new (4-6) **808.81**

I went to the animal fair (k-3) **808.81**

Lewis, R. comp. Miracles **808.81**

Life hungers to abound (6 and up) **808.81**

Morrison, L. comp. Sprints and distances (5 and up) **808.81**

O frabjous day! (5 and up) **808.81**

Piping down the valleys wild **808.81**

Poetry of earth (3-6) **808.81**

Room for me and a mountain lion (5 and up) **808.81**

Some haystacks don't even have any needle, and other complete modern poems (6 and up) **808.81**

A Tune beyond us (6 and up) **808.81**

Under the tent of the sky (3-6) **808.81**

What a wonderful bird the frog are (5 and up) **808.81**

The Year around (4 and up) **808.81**

Zero makes me hungry **808.81**

See also pages in the following books:

The Arbuthnot Anthology of childrens' literature p2-145 **808.8**

Carlson, B. W. Listen! And help tell the story p41-62, 79-98, 125-72 **372.6**

With a deep sea smile p15-40 **372.6**

See also American poetry—Collections; Christmas—Poetry; English poetry—Collections; Nonsense verses; Patriotic poetry; Religious poetry; Sea poetry; Songs; War poetry

Indexes

Brewton, J. E. comp. Index to children's poetry **808.81**

Brewton, J. E. comp. Index to children's poetry; first supplement **808.81**

Brewton, J. E. comp. Index to children's poetry; second supplement **808.81**

Brewton, J. E. comp. Index to poetry for children and young people, 1964-1969 **808.81**

Brewton, J. E. comp. Index to poetry for children and young people, 1970-1975 **808.81**

Granger's Index to poetry **808.81**

Granger's Index to poetry, 1970-1977 **808.81**

Subject index to poetry for children and young people, 1957-1975 **808.81**

Technique
See Poetics

Poetry for children. See Children's poetry; Nursery rhymes

Poetry for holidays. Larrick, N. comp. **811.08**

Poetry of earth (3-6) **808.81**

Poetry of nature. See Nature in poetry

The Poetry troupe **821.08**

Poets
Fiction
Jarrell, R. The bat-poet (2-4) **Fic**

Poets, American
Barth, E. I'm nobody! Who are you? The story of Emily Dickinson (5 and up) **92**

Fuller, M. M. Phillis Wheatley, America's first black poetess (3-6) **92**

Myers, E. P. Langston Hughes: poet of his people (4-6) **92**

Rollins, C. Famous American Negro poets (5 and up) **920**

Schultz, P. H. Paul Laurence Dunbar: Black poet laureate (4 and up) **92**

Walker, A. Langston Huges, American poet (2-4) **92**

Poet's nightmare. Hoppenstedt, E. M.
In Fifty plays for junior actors p257-70 **812.08**

Pogany, Nandor
The wonderful lamb
In Harper, W. comp. ghosts and goblins p212-21 **398.2**

Pogány, Willy
(illus.) Colum, P. The Golden Fleece and the heroes who lived before Achilles **292**

(illus.) My poetry book. See My poetry book **821.08**

Point to the stars. Joseph, J. M. **523.8**

Pointe de Sable, Jean Baptiste
See pages in the following books:

Burt, O. W. Negroes in the early West p36-41 (4-6) **920**

Rollins, C. H. They showed the way p63-67 (5 and up) **920**

The pointing finger. Kendall, C.
In Kendall, C. Sweet and sour p60-62 **398.2**

Poison ivy
Limburg, P. R. Watch out, it's poison ivy! (3-6) **581.6**

Poisonous animals
Brenner, B. Beware! These animals are poison (3-5) **591.6**

Poisonous plants
Limburg, P. R. Poisonous plants (4 and up) **581.6**

Poisons
Haines, G. K. Natural and synthetic poisons (4-6) **615.9**

See also pages in the following books:

Berger, M. Disease detectives p39-47 (5 and up) **614.4**

Selsam, M. E. Plants that heal p68-81 (4-6) **581.6**

Poker Face the Baboon and Hot Dog the tiger. Sandburg, C.
In Sandburg, C. Rootabaga stories v 1 p53-58 **S C**

In Sandburg, C. The Sandburg treasury p27-29 **818**

Poland
Fiction
Kelly, E. P. The trumpeter of Krakow (5 and up) **Fic**

Singer, I. B. Naftali the storyteller and his horse, Sus, and other stories (4-6) **S C**

Folklore
See Folklore—Poland

Polar bear. McDearmon, K. **599.74**

Polar bears
McDearmon, K. Polar bear (3-5)   **599.74**
See also pages in the following book:
McClung, R. M. Hunted mammals of the sea p157-69 (5 and up)   **599**

Polar expeditions. See Arctic regions; Polar regions

Polar regions
Harrington, L. The polar regions (5 and up)   **998**
See also Antarctic regions; Arctic regions

The Poles in America. Wytrwal, J. A.   **305.8**

Polette, Nancy
E is for everybody: a manual for bringing fine picture books into the hands and hearts of children   **028.5**

Polgreen, Cathleen
(jt. auth.) Polgreen, J. Sunlight and shadows   **525**

Polgreen, John
Sunlight and shadows (1-3)   **525**
(illus.) Lauber, P. This restless earth   **551**

Police
See also names of cities with the subdivision Police, e.g. New York (City)—Police

Police dogs
See pages in the following books:
Clemens, V. P. Super animals and their unusual careers p11-29 (4 and up)   **636.08**
Fichter, G. S. Working dogs p46-55 (4-6)   **636.7**

Poliomyelitis vaccine
See pages in the following book:
Nourse, A. E. Viruses p45-49 (5 and up)   **576**

Polish Americans
Wytrwal, J. A. The Poles in America (5 and up)   **305.8**

Politeness. See Etiquette

Politi, Leo
The butterflies come   **E**
Caldecott Medal acceptance paper
In Caldecott Medal books: 1938-1957 p201-03   **028.5**
Moy Moy   **E**
Pedro, the angel of Olvera Street   **E**
Song of the swallows   **E**

About
See pages in the following books:
Authors and illustrators of children's books p348-52   **028.5**
Caldecott Medal books: 1938-1957 p204-11   **028.5**

Political parties
Cook, F. J. The rise of American political parties (5 and up)   **324.273**
See also pages in the following book:
Lindop, E. The first book of elections p37-47 (4 and up)   **324.6**

Political prisoners
Meltzer, M. The human rights book (6 and up)   **323.4**

Political science
See also Political parties; World politics; and names of countries, cities, etc. with the subdivision Politics and government, e.g. United States—Politics and government

Yearbooks
The Statesman's yearbook   **310.5**

Politicians, American
Faber, D. Bella Abzug (5 and up)   **92**
Goodsell, J. Daniel Inouye (3-5)   **92**

Politicians, British
Reynolds, Q. Winston Churchill (4 and up)   **92**

[Politzer, Anie]
My journals and sketchbooks (4 and up)   **Fic**

Pollard, Michael
How things work (5 and up)   **600**

Pollination. See Fertilization of plants

Pollution
Miles, B. Save the Earth! (4 and up)   **363.7**
Milgrom, H. ABC of ecology (k-2)   **363.7**
Parnall, P. The mountain   **E**
See also pages in the following books:
Archer, J. Hunger on planet Earth p155-64 (6 and up)   **338.1**
Gregor, A. S. Man's mark on the land p78-90 (4 and up)   **304.2**
See also types of pollution, e.g. Water—Pollution

Pollution of air. See Air—Pollution

Pollution of water. See Water—Pollution

Polo, Marco
Marco Polo's adventures in China (5 and up)   **92**
See also pages in the following books:
Cottler, J. Heroes of civilization p3-13 (5 and up)   **920**
Winwar, F. The land and people of Italy p61-65 (5 and up)   **945**

Polseno, Jo
(illus.) Bertol, R. Charles Drew   **92**
(illus.) Gans, R. Bird talk   **598**

Poltergeists. See Ghosts

Polushkin, Maria
The little hen and the giant   **E**

Polynesia
Pine, T. S. The Polynesians knew (4-6)   **996**
See also pages in the following book:
May, C. P. Oceania: Polynesia, Melanesia, Micronesia p73-95 (5 and up)   **990**

Fiction
Sperry, A. Call it courage (5 and up)   **Fic**
The **Polynesians** knew. Pine, T. S.   **996**

Pomerantz, Charlotte
The piggy in the puddle   **E**
Why you look like you, whereas I tend to look like me (4-6)   **575.1**

Pompeii
See pages in the following book:
Hall, J. Buried cities p2-46 (5 and up)   **930.1**

Pompey. See Lamb, Pompey

Ponce de León, Juan
See pages in the following book:
Discoverers of the New World p64-69 (5 and up)   **970.01**

Pond and marsh plants. Earle, O. L. **581.92**
Pond ecology
Kane, H. B. The tale of a pond (4 and up)
574.5
Tresselt, A. The beaver pond (k-3) **574.5**
Pond life. Reid, G. K. **574.92**
Ponds
See also Pond ecology
Ponies
Brady, I. America's horses and ponies (5 and up) **636.1**
Hess, L. A pony to love (3-6) **636.1**
Hess, L. Shetland ponies (k-3) **636.1**
Slaughter, J. Pony care (5 and up) **636.1**
See also pages in the following book:
Henry, M. Album of horses p86-97 (4 and up) **636.1**
See also Chincoteague pony

Fiction
Anderson, C. W. Billy and Blaze **E**
Doty, J. S. The crumb (6 and up) **Fic**
Morey, W. Year of the black pony (5 and up) **Fic**
Rounds, G. The blind colt (4-6) **Fic**

Infancy
Miller, J. Birth of a foal (1-3) **636.1**
Pontiac, Ottawa chief
See pages in the following book:
Johnston, J. The Indians and the strangers p51-58 (2-5) **920**
Pontius Pilate. Duvoisin, R.
In Duvoisin, R. The three sneezes, and other Swiss tales p138-45 **398.2**
Pony care. Slaughter, J. **636.1**
Pony express
Adams, S. H. The pony express (5 and up)
383
Pony Penning Day. Henry, M.
In Gruenberg, S. M. ed. Favorite stories old and new p198-206 **808.8**
A pony to love. Hess, L. **636.1**
The pony tree. Brate, C.
In Told under the magic umbrella p59-63
S C
Poofy loves company. Parker, N. W. **E**
The Pooh cook book. Ellison, V. H. **641.5**
The Pooh craft book. Friedrichsen, C. S.
745.592
Pooh goes visiting and gets into a tight place. Milne, A. A.
In Gruenberg, S. M. ed. Favorite stories old and new p451-55 **808.8**
The Pooh story book. Milne, A. A. **Fic**
The pool of fire. Christopher, J. See note under Christopher, J. The White Mountain **Fic**
Poole, Frederick King
Jordan (4 and up) **956.95**
Malaysia & Singapore (4 and up) **959.5**
Poole, Josephine
Catch as catch can (5 and up) **Fic**
Poo-Poo brings the dragon home. Forester, C. S.
In The Golden Treasury of children's literature p29-31 **808.8**
Poo-Poo finds a dragon Forester, C. S.
In The Golden Treasury of children's literature p25-28 **808.8**

Poor
See pages in the following book:
Myers, W. D. Social welfare p 1-7 (4 and up)
361.6
The poor boy and the princess. Sechrist, E. H.
In Sechrist, E. H. Once in the first times p168-73 **398.2**
Poor boy in the grave
Grimm, J. The poor boy in the grave
In Grimm, J The complete Grimm's fairy tales p749-52 **398.2**
Poor Count's Christmas
Stockton, F. R. The poor Count's Christmas
In Harper, W. Comp. Merry Christmas to you p44-54 **S C**
Poor Goose: a French folktale. Rockwell, A.
398.2
The poor man and his thousand tanga. Riordan, J.
In Riordan, J. Tales from Tartary p125-28
398.2
Poor man and the rich man
Grimm, J. The poor man and the rich man
In Grimm, J. The complete Grimm's fairy tales p394-98 **398.2**
The poor miller's boy and the cat. Grimm, J.
In Grimm, J. The complete Grimm's fairy tales p482-85 **398.2**
See also Miller's boy and his cat
The poor miller's boy and the little cat. Grimm, J.
In Grimm, J. The juniper tree, and other tales from Grimm v2 p178-86 **398.2**
See also Miller's boy and his cat
Poor relief. See Public welfare
Poor Richard [biography of Benjamin Franklin]. Daugherty, J. **92**
Poor Stainless. Norton, M. See note under Norton, M. The Borrowers **Fic**
Poor Tom's ghost. Curry, J. L. **Fic**
Poor Turkey Girl. Haviland, V.
In North American legends p76-82 **398.2**
Poor wretch
Afanas'ev, A. The poor wretch
In Afanas'ev, A. Russian fairy tales p177-79
398.2
Poortvliet, Rien
(illus.) Haar, J. ter. Boris **Fic**
Pop art
See pages in the following book:
Batterberry, A. R. The Pantheon Story of American art for young people p155-57 (5 and up) **709.73**
Popcorn
De Paola, T. The popcorn book (k-3) **641.6**
Selsam, M. E. Popcorn (3-5) **584**
The popcorn book. De Paola, T. **641.6**
Popcorn patch. Credle, E.
In Credle, E. Tall tales from the high hills, and other stories p53-54 **398.2**
Popcorn Whoppers. Henderson, N.
In Henderson, N. Celebrate America p122-28 **812**
Pope, Elizabeth Marie
The Perilous Gard (6 and up) **Fic**
The Sherwood ring (6 and up) **Fic**
Popé, Pueblo Indian
See pages in the following book:
Folsom, F. Red power on the Rio Grande p59-91 (5 and up) **970.004**

Rachel's recital. Green, M. Fic

Rachev, E.
Tresselt, A. The mitten 398.2

Rachlin, Carol K.
(jt. auth.) Marriott, A. American Indian mythology 398.2

Rachmaninoff, Sergei
See pages in the following book:
Posell, E. Z. Russian composers p82-98 (5 and up) 920

Rachmaninov, Sergei Vassilievich. See Rachmaninoff, Sergei

Racing. See names of types of racing, e.g. Automobile racing

Racing car models, Historic. Ross, F. 629.2

Racism in literature
The Black American in books for children: readings in racism 028.5
Interracial Books for Children Bulletin 028.505

Raciti, Salvatore
(illus.) Cole, J. Twins 612

Rackham, Arthur
(illus.) The Arthur Rackham Fairy book. See The Arthur Rackham Fairy book 398.2
(illus.) Fairy tales from many lands. See Fairy tales from many lands 398.2
(illus.) Mother Goose nursery rhymes. See Mother Goose nursery rhymes 398
(illus.) Darrell, M. ed. Once upon a time 808.8
(illus.) Dickens, C. A Christmas carol in prose Fic
(illus.) Evans, C. S. Cinderella 398.2
(illus.) Evans, C. S. The sleeping beauty 398.2
(illus.) Grimm, J. Grimm's Fairy tales 398.2
(illus.) Irving, W. Rip Van Winkle Fic
(illus.) Lamb, C. Tales from Shakespeare 822.3
(illus.) Moore, C. C. The night before Christmas 811
(illus.) Stephens, J. Irish fairy tales 398.2

About
See pages in the following books:
Darrell, M. ed. Once upon a time p7-12 (4 and up) 808.8
A Horn Book Sampler on children's books and reading p50-59 028.5
Lanes, S. G. Down the rabbit hole p66-78 028.5

Racquetball
Boccaccio, T. Racquetball basics (4 and up) 796.34
Fichter, G. S. Racquetball (4 and up) 796.34

Racquetball basics. Boccaccio, T. 796.34

Radiation
Physiological effect
See also Atomic bomb—Physiological effect

Radiation, Solar. See Solar radiation

Radio
See pages in the following book:
Neal, H. E. Communication p153-59 (5 and up) 001.51

Apparatus and supplies
See pages in the following book:
Math, I. Morse, Marconi and you p50-61 (6 and up) 621.38

Radio, Short wave
Apparatus and supplies
See pages in the following book:
Math, I. Morse, Marconi and you p62-67 (6 and up) 621.38

Radio broadcasting
See pages in the following book:
Weiss, A. E. News or not? p51-64 (6 and up) 070.4

Radioactive substance. See Radioactivity

Radioactivity
Hyde, M. O. Everyone's trash problem: nuclear wastes (4 and up) 621.48

Radiocarbon dating
See pages in the following book:
Wyckoff, J. The story of geology p171-75 (5 and up) 551

Radiography. See X-rays

Radio waves. See Electric waves

Rags
Andersen, H. C. The rags
In Andersen, H. C. The complete fairy tales and stories p925-26 S C

Rags and Tatters
Macdonnell, A. Rags-and-Tatters
In It's time for story hour p236-42 372.6

Rags, rugs and wool pictures. Wiseman, A. 746.7

Rahn, Joan Elma
Alfalfa, beans & clover (6 and up) 583
How plants are pollinated (5 and up) 581.1
The metric system (6 and up) 389
More about what plants do (5 and up) 581.3
Seeing what plants do (3-5) 581
Seven ways to collect plants (4 and up) 579
Watch it grow, watch it change (5 and up) 581.3

Raible, Alton
(illus.) Snyder, Z. K. Below the root Fic
(illus.) Snyder, Z. K. The changeling Fic
(illus.) Snyder, Z. K. The Egypt game Fic
(illus.) Snyder, Z. K. The headless cupid Fic
(illus.) Snyder, Z. K. The velvet room (4-6) Fic
(illus.) Snyder, Z. K. The witches of Worm Fic

Railroad Arthur. Coren, A. See note under Coren, A. Arthur the Kid Fic

Railroad Bill. Jagendorf, M. A.
In Jagendorf, M. A. Folk stories of the South p13-15 398.2

Railroad stations. See Railroads—Stations

Railroads
Crews, D. Freight train E
Navarra, J. G. Supertrains (3-6) 385
See also pages in the following book:
Hellman, H. Transportation in the world of the future p19-58, 112-29 (5 and up) 380.5

Depots
See Railroads—Stations

Fiction
Bontemps, A. The fast Sooner hound (2-5) Fic
Felton, H. W. John Henry and his hammer (5 and up) 398.2
McPhail, D. The train E

Rats—*Continued*

Control

See pages in the following book:

Silverstein, A. Animal invaders p42-49 (5 and up) **591.5**

Fiction

O'Brien, R. C. Mrs Frisby and the rats of NIMH (4 and up) **Fic**

Potter, B. The sly old cat **E**

Sharmat, M. W. Mooch the messy **E**

Zemach, K. The beautiful rat (k-3) **398.2**

Rats. Haldane, J. B. S.
In Time to laugh p175-91 **S C**

Rattlers and rollers. Stoutenburg, A.
In Stoutenburg, A. American tall-tale animals p19-33 **398.2**

Rau, Margaret

The giant panda at home (5 and up) **599.74**

The gray kangaroo at home (5 and up) **599.2**

Our world: the People's Republic of China (6 and up) **951.05**

The people of new China (4-6) **951.05**

The snow monkey at home (5 and up) **599.8**

The Yangtze River (4-6) **951**

Rauch, Hans-Georg

The lines are coming (2-6) **741.2**

Raven

Grimm, J. The raven
In Grimm, J. The complete Grimm's fairy tales p431-36 **398.2**
In Grimm, J. Household stories p26-31 **398.2**

The **raven** and the lobster. Afanas'ev, A.
In Afanas'ev, A. Russian fairy tales p612 **398.2**

Raven lets out the daylight. Martin, F.
In North American legends p44-51 **398.2**

Raven traveling. Harris, C.
In Harris, C. Once more upon a totem p67-146 **398.2**

Ravens

Fiction

Aiken, J. Arabel's raven (4-6) **Fic**

Ravielli, Anthony

What is bowling? (3-5) **794.6**

What is golf? (3-6) **796.352**

(illus.) Cobb, V. How the doctor knows you're fine **616**

Raw Head and Bloody Bones. Leach, M.
In Leach, M. Whistle in the graveyard p91 **398.2**

Rawding, F. W.

The Buddha (5 and up) **294.3**

Rawlings, Marjorie Kinnan

A boy and his pa
In Holiday ring p122-30 **394.2**

The yearling (6 and up) **Fic**

Rawlinson, Sir Henry Creswicke, 1st bart.

See pages in the following books:

Baumann, H. In the land of Ur p23-26 (5 and up) **935**

Cottler, J. Heroes of civilization p51-66 (5 and up) **920**

Rawls, Wilson

Where the red fern grows (6 and up) **Fic**

Ray, Deborah

(illus.) Peterson, J. W. I have a sister—my sister is deaf **362.4**

(illus.) Welber, R. The winter picnic **E**

Ray, Dixy Lee

See pages in the following book:

Noble, I. Contemporary women scientists of America p92-106 (5 and up) **920**

Ray, James Earl

Faber, D. The assassination of Martin Luther King, Jr. (5 and up) **92**

See also pages in the following book:

David, A. Famous criminal trials p113-26 (5 and up) **345**

Raymer, Steve

(illus.) Gray, W. R. Camping adventure **796.54**

Rayner, Mary

Garth Pig and the icecream lady. See note under Rayner, M. Mr and Mrs Pig's evening out **E**

Mr and Mrs Pig's evening out **E**

Rays (Fishes)

Fiction

O'Dell, S. The black pearl (6 and up) **Fic**

Reactors (Nuclear physics). See Nuclear reactors

Read, Herbert

(ed.) This way, delight. See This way, delight **821.08**

Read, Mary

See pages in the following books:

Stockton, F. R. Buccaneers & pirates of our coasts p194-98 (5 and up) **910.4**

Whipple, A. B. C. Famous pirates of the New world p134-37 (5 and up) **910.4**

Read about the brain. See Elgin, K. The human body: the brain **612**

Readers. See Primers; Reading materials

Readers' guide to periodical literature **051**

Readers' guide to periodical literature

How to use the Readers' guide to periodical literature. See How to use the Readers' guide to periodical literature **051**

Readers' guide to periodical literature, Abridged **051**

Reading

Chambers, A. Introducing books to children **028.5**

Cleary, F. D. Blueprints for better reading **028.5**

See also pages in the following book:

Larrick, N. A parent's guide to children's reading p205-31 **028.5**

See also Books and reading

Periodicals

The Reading Teacher **372.405**

Study and teaching

See Reading

Reading. Boy Scouts of America **028.5**

Reading for young people: The Great Plains. Laughlin, M. **016.978**

Reading for young people: the Midwest. Hinman, D. **016.977**

Reading ladders for human relations **016.302**

Reading materials

McGuffey, W. H. Old favorites from the McGuffey readers, 1836-1936 **372.4**

The **Reading** Teacher **372.405**

Reichert, E. C.
Space ship to the moon
In Gruenberg, S. M. ed. Favorite stories old and new p263-69   **808.8**

Reid, George K.
Pond life (6 and up)   **574.92**

Reid, Jon
Piatti, C. Celestino Piatti's Animal ABC   **E**

Reid, Virginia M.
(ed.) Reading ladders for human relations.
See Reading ladders for human relations   **016.302**

Reindeer
See pages in the following book:
Berry, E. The land and people of Finland p126-30 (5 and up)   **948.97**

Reindeer on the roof. Hark, M.
In On stage for Christmas p3-27   **812.08**

Reinfeld, Beatrice
Reinfeld, F. Coin collectors' handbook   **737.4**

Reinfeld, Fred
Chess for children (5 and up)   **794.1**
Coin collectors' handbook   **737.4**
How to build a coin collection   **737.4**

Reisberg, Ken
Card games (4 and up)   **795.4**
The martial arts (4 and up)   **796.8**

Reiss, Johanna
The journey back   **92**
The upstairs room   **92**

Reiss, John J.
Colors   **E**
Numbers   **E**
Shapes   **E**
(illus.) Srivastava, J. J. Statistics   **519.5**

Reiss, Winold
(illus.) Neuberger, R. L. The Lewis and Clark Expedition   **973.4**

Reit, Seymour
Child of the Navajos (2-4)   **970.004**
Ironclad! (4-6)   **973.7**

Religion
Moskin, M. D. In search of God (6 and up)   **291**
See also God; Religions; Superstition; Worship; and names of peoples, ethnic groups, countries, states, etc. with the subdivision Religion, e.g. Indians of North America—Religion

Egypt
See Egypt—Religion

Religions
Fitch, F. M. Their search for God (4 and up)   **291**
Kettelkamp, L. Religions, East and West (5 and up)   **291**
Moskin, M. D. In search of God (6 and up)   **291**
Seeger, E. Eastern religions (6 and up)   **291**
See also Buddhism; Christianity; Confucianism; Hinduism; Islam; Judaism; Religion

Fiction
Blume, J. Are you there God? It's me, Margaret (5 and up)   **Fic**

Religions, East and West. Kettelkamp, L.   **291**

Religious art. See Art, Medieval

Religious art and symbolism
See also Christian art and symbolism

Religious festivals. See names of festivals, e.g. Christmas

Religious freedom
See pages in the following book:
Kohn, B. The spirit and the letter p35-47 (5 and up)   **323.4**

Religious literature
Bibliography
See pages in the following book:
Sutherland, Z. Children & books p494-96   **028.5**

Religious poetry
See pages in the following book:
One thousand poems for children p187-93, 489-510   **821.08**

The **reluctant** dragon. Grahame, K.   **Fic**

The **reluctant** dragon; play. Thane, A.
In Thane, A. Plays from famous stories and fairy tales p267-82   **812**

The **Remaking** of the world
In The Sound of flutes, and other Indian legends p126-29   **398.2**

The **remarkable** return of Winston Potter Crisply. Rice, E.   **Fic**

The **remarkable** rocket. Wilde, O.
In Wilde, O. The Happy Prince, and other stories p40-51   **S C**

Remember me when this you see. Morrison, L. comp.   **808.88**

Remember the days. Meltzer, M.   **305.8**

Renaissance
See pages in the following books:
Bragdon, L. J. The land and people of France p52-56 (5 and up)   **944**
Winwar, F. The land and people of Italy p71-77 (5 and up)   **945**
See also Architecture, Renaissance; Art, Renaissance

Renfro, Nancy
A puppet corner in every library   **027.62**

Renner, Al G.
Experimental fun with the yo-yo, and other science projects (3-6)   **507**
How to build a better mousetrap car—and other experimental science fun (4-6)   **507**
How to make and use electric motors (5 and up)   **621.46**

Report writing
Brandt, S. R. How to write a report (6 and up)   **808**

Reporters and reporting
Weiss, A. E. News or not? (6 and up)   **070.4**

Reproduction
Andry, A. C. How babies are made (k-3)   **612**
Brady, I. Wild mouse (2-4)   **599.32**
Cole, J. A calf is born (k-2)   **636.2**
Cole, J. A chick hatches (k-3)   **636.5**
Cole, J. My puppy is born (k-3)   **636.7**
De Schweinitz, K. Growing up (2-5)   **612**
Freedman, R. Getting born (2-4)   **591.1**
Hess, L. Life begins for puppies (4-6)   **636.7**
Isenbart, H. H. A foal is born (k-3)   **636.1**
Lauber, P. What's hatching out of that egg? (2-4)   **591.3**
May, J. Living things and their young (4-6)   **591.1**

Rounds, Glen—*Continued*
(illus.) Conklin, G. Tarantula: the giant spider **595.4**
(illus.) Freschet, B. Elephant & friends **E**
(illus.) Freschet, B. The happy dromedary **E**
(illus.) Freschet, B. Lizard lying in the sun **597.9**
(illus.) Gage, W. Down in the boondocks **E**
(illus.) Gage, W. Squash pie **E**
(illus.) Gilchrist, T. E. Halfway up the mountain **E**
(illus.) Schwartz, A. comp. Cross your fingers, spit in your hat **398**
(illus.) Schwartz, A. comp. Kickle snifters gers, spit in your hat **398**
(illus.) Schwartz, A. comp. Tomfoolery **398**
(illus.) Schwartz, A. comp. A twister of twists, a tangler of tongues (4 and up) **808.88**
(illus.) Schwartz, A. comp. Whoppers **398.2**
(illus.) Schwartz, A. comp. Witcracks **398**
(illus.) Stoutenburg, A. American tall-tale animals **398.2**

Rounds about rounds **784.1**

Rouse, W. H. D.
The wise old shepherd
In Shedlock, M. L. The art of the storyteller p216-21 **372.6**

Rousseau, Jean Jacques
See pages in the following book:
Jan, I. On children's literature p18-24, 90-94 **028.5**

Rowand, Phyllis
(illus.) Krauss, R. The growing story **E**

Rowland, Elsi
Hans, who made the Princess laugh
In One hundred plays for children p726-33 **808.82**
A precedent in pastries
In One hundred plays for children p734-40 **808.82**
The three aunts
In One hundred plays for children p741-50 **808.82**

Rowland, Florence Wightman
Snowbound at Easter
In Harper, W. comp. Easter chimes p209-15 **S C**

Rowlandson, Mary (White)
See pages in the following book:
As I saw it: women who lived the American adventure p9-16 (6 and up) **973**

Roy, Ron
Three ducks went wandering **E**

Royal Ballet School, London
Jessel, C. Life at the Royal Ballet School (5 and up) **792.8**

Roybal, J. D.
(illus.) Folsom, F. Red power on the Rio Grande **970.004**

Royce, Sarah (Bayliss)
See pages in the following book:
As I saw it: women who lived the American adventure p60-62 (6 and up) **973**

Royt, Kevin
(illus.) Bauer, C. F. Handbook for storytellers **372.6**

Ruba and the Stork. Mehdevi, A. S.
In Mehdevi, A. S. Persian folk and fairy tales p44-50 **398.2**

Rubber bands, baseballs and doughnuts. Froman, R. **514**

The **rubber** man. Arnott, K.
In Arnott, K. African myths and legends p16-21 **398.2**

Rubber stamp printing
Pettit, F. H. The stamp-pad printing book (5 and up) **761**

Rubel, Nicole
(illus.) Gantos, J. Rotten Ralph **E**

Rubel, Reina
(illus.) Thurman, J. Flashlight, and other poems **811**

Rubens, Sir Peter Paul
See pages in the following book:
Loder, D. The land and people of Belgium p78-82 (5 and up) **949.3**

Rubenstone, Jessie
Crochet for beginners (3-5) **746.43**
Knitting for beginners (4 and up) **746.43**
Weaving for beginners (4 and up) **746.1**

Rubezahl
Manning-Sanders, R. Rubizal
In Manning-Sanders, R. A book of charms and changelings p114-19 **398.2**
Manning-Sanders, R. Rubizal and the miller's daughter
In Manning-Sanders, R. A book of spooks and spectres p51-61 **398.2**
Rubezahl
In The Andrew Lang Fairy tale treasury p497-512 **398.2**

Rubin, Eva Johanna
(illus.) Krüss, J. 3 x 3: three by three **E**

Rubin, Robert
Lou Gehrig: courageous star (5 and up) **92**

Rubizal. Manning-Sanders, R.
In Manning-Sanders, R. A book of charms and changelings p114-19 **398.2**
See also Rubezahl

Rubizal and the miller's daughter. Manning-Sanders, R.
In Manning-Sanders, R. A book of spooks and spectres p51-61 **398.2**
See also Rubezahl

Ruchlis, Hy
How a rock came to be in a fence on a road near a town (2-4) **552**
Your changing earth (2-4) **551**

Rucks, Meredith
(jt. auth.) Teleki, G. Aerial apes **599.88**

Ruda, the quick thinker. Courlander, H.
In Courlander, H. The king's drum, and other African stories p87-89 **398.2**

Rudeen, Kenneth
Jackie Robinson (2-4) **92**
Roberto Clemente (2-4) **92**
Wilt Chamberlain (2-5) **92**

Rudinski, Richard
(illus.) Marino, B. P. Eric needs stitches **362.1**

Rudolph, Marguerita
Yolka (a little fir tree)
In Association for Childhood Education International. Told under the Christmas tree p217-22 **808.8**

Savitt, Sam
(illus.) Sports Illustrated Horseback riding. See Sports Illustrated Horseback riding   **798.2**

(illus.) Unkelbach, K. How to bring up your pet dog   **636.7**

Savitz, Harriet May
Wheelchair champions (5 and up)   **790.1**

Sawyer, Ruth
The caravan
   In Take joy! p43-46   **394.2**
The Christmas apple
   In Harper, W. comp. Merry Christmas to you p57-65   **S C**
   In Ross, E. S. ed. The lost half-hour p172-80   **372.6**
   In Stories to dramatize p340-44   **372.6**
A Christmas promise
   In Stories to dramatize p227-32   **372.6**
Fiddler, play fast, play faster
   In Haunting tales p203-10 (5 and up)   **S C**
Gifts for the first birthday
   In It's time for Christmas p194-97   **394.2**
Journey cake, ho! (k-2)   **398.2**
   also in The Arbuthnot Anthology of children's literature p365-67   **808.8**
   also in Time for old magic p241-43   **398.2**
Joy to the world (3-6)   **394.2**
Stories included are: The two lambs; This is the Christmas; The precious herbs of Christmas; What the Three Kings brought; San Froilan of the Wilderness; The miracle of Saint Cumgall
Juan Cigarron
   In Time to laugh p200-08   **S C**
Newberry Medal acceptance paper
   In Newbery Medal books: 1922-1955 p153-56   **028.5**
The peddler of Ballaghadereen
   In The Arbuthnot Anthology of children's literature p181-84   **808.8**
   also in Holiday ring p67-74   **394.2**
   also in Time for old magic p42-45   **398.2**
The sack of truth
   In It's time for story hour p243-48   **372.6**
Schnitzle, Schnotzle, and Schnootzle
   In Holiday ring p235-44   **394.2**
The Voyage of the wee red cap
   In Association for Childhood Education International. Told under the Christmas tree p163-71   **808.8**
   In Stories to dramatize p219-24   **372.6**
The way of the storyteller   **372.6**
Stories included are: Wee Meg Barnileg and the fairies; The magic box; Señora, will you snip? Señora, will you sew?; The peddler of Ballaghadereen; Where one is fed a hundred can dine; A matter of brogues; The juggler of Notre Dame; The deserted mine; The bird who spoke three times; The legend of Saint Elizabeth; The Princess and the vagabone

About
See pages in the following book:
Newbery Medal books: 1922-1955 p149-52   **028.5**

Saxon, Gladys R.
Rosina's chickens
   In Harper, W. comp. Easter chimes p153-61   **S C**

Saxons. See Anglo-Saxons

Say, Allen
The ink-keeper's apprentice (6 and up)   **Fic**
Once under the cherry blossom tree (1-3)   **398.2**

Sayings. See Epigrams; Proverbs; Quotations

Saynday and Smallpox: the white man's gift. Marriott, A.
   In Marriott, A. American Indian mythology   **398.2**

Scagell, Robin
(jt. auth.) Wilson, M. Jet journey   **387.7**

Scale-insects
   See pages in the following book:
Hutchins, R. E. The bug clan p42-46 (5 and up)   **595.7**

Scandinavian mythology. See Mythology, Norse

Scandinavians
   See also Vikings

The **scarecrow** and the witch. Bennett, R.
   In Bennett, R. Creative plays and program for holidays p112-22   **812**

Scaredy cat. Boiko, C.
   In Boiko, C. Children's plays for creative actors p75-85   **812**

Scarf, Maggie
Antarctica: exploring the frozen continent (3-6)   **998**

Scarface. Grinnell, G. B.
   In North American legends p83-93   **398.2**

The **Scarlet** Pimpernel. Leech, M. T.
   In Popular plays for classroom reading p300-24   **808.82**

Schackburg, Richard
Yankee Doodle (k-3)   **784.7**

Schaefer, Jack
Old Ramon (5 and up)   **Fic**

Schaeffer, Elizabeth
Dandelion, pokeweed, and goosefoot (4 and up)   **581.6**

Schaller, George B.
The tiger (5 and up)   **599.74**
Wonders of lions (5 and up)   **599.74**

Schaller, Kay
(jt. auth.) Schaller, G. Wonders of lions   **599.74**

Scharl, Josef
(illus.) Grimm, J. The complete Grimm's fairy tales   **398.2**

Scheer, Julian
Rain makes applesauce   **E**

Scheffer, Victor B.
Little Calf (5 and up)   **599.5**

Schepp, Steven
(jt. auth.) Andry, A. C. How babies are made   **612**

Scherer, Fred F.
(illus.) Selsam, M. E. Play with trees   **582.16**

Scherf, Walter
(ed.) The Best of the best. See The Best of the best   **011**

Shick, Alice
The peregrine falcons (5 and up)   **598**
Serengeti cats (4 and up)   **599.74**

Schick, Eleanor
One summer night   **E**
Peggy's new brother   **E**
Summer at the sea   **E**

Schick, Joel
(illus.) James, E. How to keep a secret   **652**
(illus.) James, E. What do you mean by "average?"   **519.5**
(illus.) Knight, D. C. Dinosaur days   **567.9**
(illus.) Riley, J. W. The gobble-uns'll git you ef you don't watch out!   **811**
(illus.) Schick, A. Serengeti cats   **599.74**

Schwartz, Daniel
(illus.) Byars, B. The house of wings   Fic

Schwartz, Lynne Sharon
The Wizard of Oz
In Fifty plays for junior actors p530-53
812.08
In Popular plays for classroom reading
p246-64   808.82

Schwartz, Morton K.
All in favor
In One hundred plays for children p218-27
808.82
Twin cousins
In One hundred plays for children p228-36
808.82

Schwartz, Paula Dunaway
You can cook (5 and up)   641.5

Schweitzer, Albert
See pages in the following books:
McNeer, M. Armed with courage p99-112
(4-6)   920
Sechrist, E. H. It's time for brotherhood
p68-75 (5 and up)   361

Schweitzer, Byrd Baylor
Amigo   E
For other titles by this author see
Baylor, Byrd

Schweitzer, Marilyn
(illus.) Baylor, B. We walk in sandy places
591.5

Schweninger, Ann
(comp.) The Man in the Moon as he sails
the sky, and other Moon verse. See The
Man in the Moon as he sails the sky, and
other Moon verse   821.08

Science
Allison, L. The wild inside (5 and up)   500
See also Astronomy; Bacteriology; Biology; Botany; Chemistry; Crystallography;
Fossils; Geology; Meteorology; Mineralogy; Natural history; Physics; Physiology;
Space sciences; Zoology

Bibliography
See pages in the following books:
Meacham, M. Information sources in children's literature p56-66   011
Sutherland, Z. Children & books p482-88
028.5
Withrow, D. E. Gateways to readable books
p132-44   011

Bibliography—Periodicals
Appraisal   016.5
Science Books & Films   016.5

Denmark
See pages in the following book:
Wohlrabe, R. A. The land and people of
Denmark p137-44 (5 and up)   948.9

Encyclopedias
The New Book of popular science   503

Experiments
Allison, L. The wild inside (5 and up)   500
Cobb, V. Science experiments you can eat
(5 and up)   507
Cobb, V. More Science experiments you
can eat (5 and up)   507
Milgrom, H. Adventures with a cardboard
tube (k-2)   507

Milgrom, H. Adventures with a straw (k-2)
507
Milgrom, H. Egg-ventures (1-3)   507
Moorman, T. How to make your science
project scientific (5 and up)   507
Pine, T. S. The Polynesians knew (4-6)
996
Renner, A. G. Experimental fun with the
yo-yo, and other science projects (3-6)
507
Renner, A. G. How to build a better mousetrap car—and other experimental science
fun (4-6)   507
Schneider, H. Science fun for you in a
minute or two (2-4)   507
Schneider, H. Science fun with a flashlight
(1-4)   535
Webster, D. How to do a science project
(4 and up)   507
Webster, D. More brain-boosters (4 and up)
507
White, L. B. Investigating science with
coins (4 and up)   507
White, L. B. Investigating science with
nails (4 and up)   507
White, L. B. Investigating science with
rubber bands (4 and up)   507
White, L. B. Science puzzles (k-3)   507
Wyler, R. Prove it! (1-3)   507
See also pages in the following books:
Cassell, S. Indoor games and activities p64-
83 (3-6)   793
Gardner, R. Shadow science p86-102 (4-6)
535
See also particular branches of science
with the subdivision Experiments, e.g.
Chemistry—Experiments

Greece
See pages in the following book:
Van Duyn, J. The Greeks p137-54 (5 and
up)   938

Methodology
Moorman, T. How to make your science
project scientific (5 and up)   507

Motion pictures—Catalogs
AAAS Science film catalog   016.5

Motion pictures—Periodicals
Science Books & Films   016.5

Netherlands
See pages in the following book:
Barnouw, A. J. The land and people of
Holland p79-82 (5 and up)   949.2

Pictorial works
Grillone, L. Smalls worlds close up (5 and
up)   500

Study and teaching
See also Nature study

Study and teaching—Periodicals
The Science Teacher   507.05

Terminology
Asimov, I. More Words of science (6 and
up)   503
Asimov, I. Words of science and the history
behind them (6 and up)   503

Yearbooks
Science year   505

The **sea** hunters who were swallowed by a whirlpool. Harris, C.
  In Harris, C. Mouse Woman and the muddleheads p26-43   **398.2**
The **Sea** King and Vasilisa the Wise. Afanas'ev, A.
  In Afanas'ev, A. Russian fairy tales p427-37   **398.2**
Sea life. See Sailors; Seafaring life; and names of countries with the subhead Navy, e.g. United States. Navy
Sea lions. See Seals (Animals)
The **Sea**-Mammy. Sherlock, P.
  In Sherlock, P. West Indian folk-tales p130-34   **398.2**
Sea monsters

Fiction
Kahl, V. How do you hide a monster?   **E**
Sea monsters of long ago. Selsam, M. E.   **567.9**
Sea mosses. See Algae
Sea otters
  See pages in the following book:
McClung, R. M. Hunted mammals of the sea p87-101 (5 and up)   **599**
Sea poetry
  See pages in the following books:
Field, R. Poems p85-92 (2-5)   **811**
Gaily we parade p73-79 (3-6)   **821.08**
Sea shells. See Shells
Sea shells of the world. Abbott, R. T.   **594**
Sea-shore. See Seashore
Sea star. McClung, R. M.   **593.9**
Sea Star, orphan of Chincoteague. Henry, M. See note under Henry, M. Misty of Chincoteague   **Fic**
Sea stars and their kin. Zim, H. S.   **593.9**
Sea stories
Ardizzone, E. Little Tim and the brave sea captain   **E**
Babbitt, N. The eyes of the Amaryllis (5 and up)   **Fic**
Fisher, L. E. The death of Evening Star (5 and up)   **Fic**
Fox, P. The slave dancer (6 and up)   **Fic**
Haugaard, F. C. Orphans of the wind (6 and up)   **Fic**
Holling, H. C. Seabird (4-6)   **Fic**
Lent, B. John Tabor's ride (k-3)   **398.2**
McCloskey, R. Burt Dow, deep water man   **E**
Thiele, C. Blue Fin (6 and up)   **Fic**
Verne, J. Twenty thousand leagues under the sea (5 and up)   **Fic**
Wibberley, L. Leopard's prey (6 and up)   **Fic**
The **Sea** View Hotel. Stevenson, J.   **E**
Sea water aquariums. See Marine aquariums
Sea waves. See Ocean waves
Seabird. Holling, H. C.   **Fic**
The **Seabury** Cook book for boys and girls. Moore, E.   **641.5**
Seafaring life
Lasky, K. Tall ships (5 and up)   **387.2**
  See also pages in the following books:
Heaps, W. A. Superstition! p122-32 (6 and up)   **398**
Tunis, E. The young United States, 1783 to 1830 p81-95 (6 and up)   **973**
  See also Sailors
Seafood. See Sea food

Seahorses. See Sea horses
Sealock, Thelma W.
The Lincoln coat
  In One hundred plays for children p277-87   **808.82**
Seals (Animals)
  See pages in the following books:
Lewin, T. World within a world: Baja p13-55 (4-6)   **574.9**
McClung, R. M. Hunted mammals of the sea p103-20, 135-56 (5 and up)   **599**
National Geographic Society. Wild animals of North America p283-307   **599**
  See also Elephant seals

Fiction
Coatsworth, E. Marra's world (2-5)   **Fic**
Oppenheim, S. The selchie's seed (4-6)   **Fic**
Sealth [biography of Seattle, Chief of the Suquamish and allied tribes] Boring, M.   **92**
Seamen. See Sailors
The **search.** Byars, B.
  In The Arbuthnot Anthology of children's literature p638-41   **808.8**
The **search** for delicious. Babbitt, N.   **Fic**
The **Search** for the magic lake
  In Tatterhood, and other tales p121-28   **398.2**
The **search:** who gets the chief's daughter. Courlander, H.
  In Courlander, H. The king's drum, and other African stories p28-31   **398.2**
  In With a deep sea smile p70-74   **372.6**
Searching for Shona. Anderson, M. J.   **Fic**
Sears, Bill
(illus.) Baylor, B. Sometimes I dance mountains   **792.8**
Sears List of subject headings   **025.4**
Sears List of subject headings: Canadian companion   **025.4**
Seas. See Ocean
Seashore
Buck, M. W. Along the seashore (3-6)   **574.92**
Kohn, B. The beachcomber's book (3-6)   **745.5**
Selsam, M. E. See along the shore (3-5)   **574.92**
Zim, H. S. Seashores (5 and up)   **574.92**
  See also Beaches

Fiction
Boston, L. M. The sea egg (3-5)   **Fic**
Myrick, M. The Secret Three   **E**
Schick, E. Summer at the sea   **E**
Seashore story. Yashima, Taro   **E**
Seashores. Zim, H. S.   **574.92**
The **Season** for singing (4 and up)   **783.6**
Season songs. Hughes, T.   **821**
Seasons
Allison, L. The reasons for seasons (5 and up)   **500**
Branley, F. M. Sunshine makes the seasons (2-4)   **525**
Provensen, A. A book of seasons   **E**
Tresselt, A. It's time now (k-2)   **525**
  See also pages in the following books:
Simon, S. Look to the night sky p21-35 (4 and up)   **523**

Sending messages. Stewig, J. W.   001.51

Seneca Indians
Gardner, J. L. Mary Jemison: Seneca captive (4-6)   92
Lenski, L. Indian captive; the story of Mary Jemison (5 and up)   92

Seneferu, King of Egypt. See Snofru, King of Egypt

Senior citizens. See Elderly

Sennett, Mack
See pages in the following book:
Edelson, E. Funny men of the movies p11-20 (6 and up)   791.43

Señora, will you snip? Señora, will you sew?
Sawyer, R. Señora, will you snip? Señora, will you sew?
In Sawyer, R. The way of the storyteller   372.6

A **sense** of story. See Townsend, J. R. A sounding of storytellers   028.5

The **sense** organs. Silverstein, A.   612

Senses and sensation
Adler, I. Taste, touch and smell (3-5)   612
Aliki. My five senses (k-2)   612
Brenner, B. Faces (k-2)   152.1
Kohl, J. The view from the oak (6 and up)   591.5
Silverstein, A. The sense organs (4 and up)   612
Zim, H. S. Our senses and how they work (4 and up)   612
See also pages in the following book:
Wilson, R. How the body works p38-49 (4 and up)   612
See also Touch; Vision

Separation (Law) See Divorce

Separation and loss, Books to help children cope with. Bernstein, J. E.   016.3627

Sequoya, Cherokee Indian
See pages in the following book:
Johnston, J. The Indians and the strangers p89-96 (2-5)   920
Fiction
Jones, W. Edge of two worlds (5 and up)   Fic

Serage, Nancy
The prince who gave up a throne [biography of Gautama Buddha] (4-6)   92

Serbia
Social life and customs
See pages in the following book:
Sechrist, E. H. Christmas everywhere p154-64   394.2

Seredy, Kate
Christmas
In Association for Childhood Education International. Told under the Christmas tree p111-18   808.8
The Good Master (4-6)   Fic
The little rooster and the Turkish sultan
In Gruenberg, S. M. ed. Favorite stories old and new p369-73   808.8
The little rooster, the diamond button and the Turkish sultan
In Ross, E. S. ed. The lost half-hour p45-49   372.6
Newbery Medal acceptance paper
In Newbery Medal books: 1922-1955 p163-65   028.5

The singing tree; excerpt
In Holiday ring p197-201   394.2
The white stag (4-6)   Fic
(illus.) Daringer, H. F. Adopted Jane   Fic
About
See pages in the following books:
Authors and illustrators of children's books p378-93   028.5
Newbery Medal books: 1922-1955 p161-62   028.5

Serengeti cats. Schick, A.   599.74

Serengeti National Park
Schick, A. Serengeti cats (4 and up)   599.74

The **serpent**-slayer. Kendall, C.
In Kendall, C. Sweet and sour p33-38   398.2

Serpents. See Snakes

Serpent's bride
Berger, T. The serpent's bride
In Berger, T. Black fairy tales p15-32   398.2

Serraillier, Ian
A fall from the sky (4-6)   292
The silver sword (5 and up)   Fic
Suppose you met a witch   E

The **servant.** Andersen, H. C.
In Andersen, H. C. The complete fairy tales and stories p487-91   S C

Servants. See Household employees

Servants, Indentured. See Indentured servants

The **servants** of the Queen. Kipling, R.
In Kipling, R. The jungle book   S C

Servello, Joe
(illus.) Bierhorst, J. comp. Songs of the Chippewa   781.7

Serwadda, W. Moses
Songs and stories from Uganda   784.4

Set theory
Bendick, J. Names, sets and numbers (2-5)   511
See also Number theory

Sets (Mathematics) See Set theory

Settlers and strangers. Baker, B.   970.004

Seuling, Barbara
The teeny tiny woman (k-2)   398.2
You can't eat peanuts in church and other little-known laws (4 and up)   349

Seuss, Dr
And to think that I saw it on Mulberry Street   E
also in Gruenberg, S. M. ed. Favorite stories old and new p217-21   808.8
Bartholomew and the oobleck. See note under Seuss, Dr. The 500 hats of Bartholomew Cubbins   E
The cat in the hat   E
The Cat in the hat Beginner book dictionary. See The Cat in the hat Beginner book dictionary   423
The cat in the hat comes back! See note under Seuss, Dr. The cat in the hat   E
The 500 hats of Bartholomew Cubbins   E
Horton hatches the egg   E
Horton hears a Who! See note under Seuss, Dr. Horton hatches the egg   E
How the Grinch stole Christmas   E
If I ran the circus   E
If I ran the zoo   E
McElligot's pool. See note under Seuss, Dr. And to think that I saw it on Mulberry Street   E
For material about this author see Geisel, Theodor Seuss

Siksika Indians—*Continued*
Legends
San Souci, R. The legend of Scarface (2-4)
398.2
Silas and Ben-Godik. Bødker, C. See note under Bødker, C. Silas and the black mare
Fic
Silas and Con. Stewart, A. C. Fic
Silas and the black mare. Bødker, C. Fic
Silas and the runaway coach. Bødker, C. See note under Bødker, C. Silas and the black mare
Fic
The **silent** album. Andersen, H. C.
In Andersen, H. C. The complete fairy tales and stories p381-82 S C
Silent Bianca. Yolen, J.
In Yolen, J. The girl who cried flowers, and other tales p46-55 S C
Silent night. Crichton, M.
In On stage for Christmas p251-61 812.08
Silent night. Pauli, H. 783.6
The **silent** storm [biography of Anne Sullivan Macy] Brown, M. M. 92
Silk
See pages in the following book:
Houck, C. Warm as wool, cool as cotton p27-31 (3-6) 677
The **silly** fellow who sold his beard. Jagendorf, M. A.
In Jagendorf, M. A. The gypsies' fiddle, and other gypsy tales p17-23 398.2
Silly Jean
Duvoisin, R. Silly Jean
In Duvoisin, R. The three sneezes, and other Swiss tales p38-43 398.2
Silly Matt
Jagendorf, M. A. Silly Matt
In Jagendorf, M. A. Noodlehead stories from around the world p180-83 398.2
Silly men and cunning wives
Two old women's bet
In Grandfather tales p156-61 398.2
The **silly** men of Russia. Jagendorf, M. A.
In Jagendorf, M. A. The gypsies' fiddle, and other gypsy tales p122-28 398.2
Silly Saburo
In Sakade, F. ed. Japanese children's favorite stories p45-48 398.2
Silly soup. Korty, C. 812
Silver
See also Silverwork
The **silver** bell of Chênière Caminada. Jagendorf, M. A.
In Jagendorf, M. A. Folk stories of the South p140-43 398.2
Silver bullet. Hooke, H. M.
In Hooke, H. M. Thunder in the mountains p149-65 398.2
The **silver** chair. Lewis, C. S. See note under Lewis, C. S. The lion, the witch and the wardrobe
Fic
The **silver** coach. Adler, C. S. Fic
The **silver** crest. Chukovsky, K. 92
The **silver** flower. Wells, R.
In Gruenberg, S. M. ed. Favorite stories old and new p144-45 808.8
Silver hen
Wilkins, M. E. The silver hen
In Ross, E. S. ed. The lost half-hour p158-71 372.6

Silver on the tree. Cooper, S. See note under Cooper, S. Over sea, under stone Fic
Silver pennies. See Thompson, B. J. ed. All the silver pennies 821.08
The **silver** pony. Ward, L. Fic
Silver shilling
Andersen, H. C. The silver shilling
In Andersen, H. C. The complete fairy tales and stories p815-19 S C
The **silver** snake of Louisiana. Jagendorf, M. A.
In Jagendorf, M. A. Folk stories of the South p123-24 398.2
The **silver** spoon. Kim, So-un
In Kim, So-un. The story bag p215-29 398.2
The **silver** sword. Serraillier, I. Fic
Silver Wolf. Dixon, P. 599.74
Silverman, Judith
Index to collective biographies for young readers 920
Silversmithing. See Silverwork
The **silversmiths**. Fisher, L. E. 739.2
Silverstein, Alvin
Aging (5 and up) 305.2
Alcoholism (5 and up) 613.8
Allergies (5 and up) 616.97
Animal invaders (5 and up) 591.5
Cats: all about them (4 and up) 636.8
Cells: building blocks of life (4 and up) 574.8
The code of life (6 and up) 575.1
The digestive system (4 and up) 612
The endocrine system (4 and up) 612
Epilepsy (5 and up) 616.8
The excretory system (4-6) 574.1
Gerbils: all about them (4 and up) 599.32
Guinea pigs: all about them (3 and up) 599.32
Hamsters: all about them (4 and up) 599.32
Itch, sniffle & sneeze (3-5) 616.97
The left-hander's world (4 and up) 152.3
The muscular system (4-6) 574.1
The nervous system (4 and up) 612
Rabbits: all about them (4 and up) 599.32
The respiratory system (4-6) 574.1
The sense organs (4 and up) 612
The skeletal system (4 and up) 612
The skin (4-6) 574.1
Sleep and dreams (6 and up) 154.6
So you're getting braces: a guide to orthodontics (5 and up) 617.6
The sugar disease: diabetes (5 and up) 616.4
A world in a drop of water (3-5) 576
The world of bionics (5 and up) 001.53
Silverstein, Glenn
(jt. auth.) Silverstein, A. Aging 305.2
Silverstein, Shel
Ladies first; adaptation. See Rodgers, M. Ladies first
Where the sidewalk ends (3 and up) 811
Silverstein, Virginia B.
(jt. auth.) Silverstein, A. Aging 305.2
(jt. auth.) Silverstein, A. Alcoholism 613.8
(jt. auth.) Silverstein, A. Allergies 616.97
(jt. auth.) Silverstein, A. Animal invaders 591.5
(jt. auth.) Silverstein, A. Cats: all about them 636.8
(jt. auth.) Silverstein, A. Cells: building blocks of life 574.8
(jt. auth.) Silverstein, A. The code of life 575.1

Social settlements
    See also names of settlements, e.g. Hull House, Chicago

Social studies. See Geography; History; Social sciences

Social welfare. See Public welfare; Social work

Social welfare. Myers, W. D.   **361.6**

Social work
    Sechrist, E. H. It's time for brotherhood (5 and up)   **361**
    See also Public welfare

Biography
    Keller, G. F. Jane Addams (1-3)   **92**

Socialism
    See also Utopias

Socially handicapped children
    See pages in the following book:
    Chicago. University. Graduate Library School. A critical approach to children's literature p32-45   **028.5**

Socially handicapped children, Books for

Bibliography
    Spache, G. D. Good reading for the disadvantaged reader   **011**

Society, Nonliterate folk
    Marcus, R. B. Survivors of the stone age (5 and up)   **306**

Society of Friends. See Friends, Society of

Sociology, Urban
    See also City life

Socks. Cleary, B.   **Fic**

Socrates
    See pages in the following books:
    Aymar, B. Laws and trials that created history p 1-11 (6 and up)   **345**
    Coolidge, O. The golden days of Greece p113-27 (4-6)   **938**
    Gianakoulis, T. The land and people of Greece p123-26 (5 and up)   **949.5**

Sod houses
    Rounds, G. The treeless plains (4-6)   **978**

Sodom
    Singer, I. B. The wicked city (3-6)   **221.9**

Sody saleratus
    In Juba this and Juba that p55-59   **372.6**
    See also Sody Sallyraytus

Sody sallyraytus
    Sody saleratus
    In Juba this and Juba that p55-59   **372.6**
    Sody Sallyraytus
    In Grandfather tales p75-80   **398.2**

Soelen, Philip Van. See Van Soelen, Philip

Sofo's escape from the leopard. Courlander, H.
    In Courlander, H. Olode the hunter, and other tales from Nigeria p61-64   **398.2**

Softball
    See pages in the following books:
    Antonacci, R. J. Baseball for young champions p108-19 (4 and up)   **796.357**
    Keith, H. Sports and games p200-09 (5 and up)   **796**

Fiction
    Schulman, J. Camp KeeWee's secret weapon   **E**

Softly, Barbara
    Master ghost and I
    In Haunting tales p256-79 (5 and up)   **S C**

Soil conservation
    Keen, M. L. The world beneath our feet (4-6)   **631.4**

Soil ecology
    Rhine, R. Life in a bucket of soil (5 and up)   **595**

Soil fertility. See Soils

Soilless agriculture. See Plants—Soilless culture

Soils
    Goldin, A. Where does your garden grow? (1-3)   **631.4**
    Keen, M. L. The world beneath our feet (4-6)   **631.4**
    Lauber, P. Earthworms, underground farmers (3-5)   **595.1**
    See also pages in the following book:
    Mintz, L. M. Vegetables in patches and pots p12-15 (3-6)   **635**
    See also Fertilizers and manures

Sojo. Berry, E.
    In Told under the magic umbrella p39-49   **S C**

Sojourner Truth, a self-made woman. Oritz, V.   **92**

Solar batteries
    See pages in the following books:
    Branley, F. M. Solar energy p92-102 (5 and up)   **621.47**

Solar cells. See Solar batteries

Solar eclipses. See Eclipses, Solar

Solar energy
    Bendick, J. Putting the sun to work (3-5)   **621.47**
    Berger, M. Energy from the sun (1-3)   **621.47**
    Branley, F. M. Solar energy (5 and up)   **621.47**
    Gadler, S. J. Sun power: facts about solar energy (6 and up)   **621.47**
    Knight, D. C. Harnessing the sun (6 and up)   **621.47**
    Smith, N. F. Sun power (1-3)   **333.79**
    See also pages in the following books:
    Gallant, R. A. Fires in the sky p41-51, 58-68 (5 and up)   **523.8**
    Kiefer, I. Energy for America p87-110 (6 and up)   **333.79**
    Shuttlesworth, D. E. Disappearing energy p68-74 (5 and up)   **333.79**
    Watson, J. W. Alternate energy sources p5-20 (4 and up)   **333.79**

Solar engines
    See pages in the following book:
    Branley, F. M. Solar energy p76-80 (5 and up)   **621.47**

Solar heating
    See also Solar homes

Solar homes
    See pages in the following book:
    Branley, F. M. Solar energy p36-56 (5 and up)   **621.47**

Solar physics. See Sun

Solar power. See Solar energy

Sri Lanka
Wilber, D. N. The land and people of Ceylon (5 and up)   **954.9**

Agriculture
See Agriculture—Sri Lanka

Education
See Education—Sri Lanka

Srivastava, Jane Jonas
Area (2-4)   **516**
Averages (2-4)   **519.5**
Computers (2-4)   **001.64**
Number families (2-4)   **513**
Statistics (2-4)   **519.5**
Weighing & balancing (1-3)   **389**

Sroda, Anne
Santa changes his mind
In On stage for Christmas p363-70   **812.08**

The **staff** and the fiddle. Pyle, H.
In Pyle, H. The wonder clock p253-66   **398.2**

The **staff** of Oranmiyan. Courlander, H.
In Courlander, H. Olode the hunter, and other tales from Nigeria p118-20   **398.2**

Staffan, Alvin E.
(illus.) Cooper, K. All about goldfish as pets   **639.3**
(illus.) Cooper, K. All about rabbits as pets   **636.08**

Stagecoaches. See Carriages and carts

Stahl, Ben F.
(illus.) Cartwright, S. Animal homes (1-3)   **591.5**
(illus.) Peck, R. N. Mr Little   **Fic**
(illus.) Sachs, M. A pocket full of seeds   **Fic**
(illus.) Syme, R. Geronimo, the fighting Apache   **92**
(illus.) Syme, R. Osceola, Seminole leader   **92**

Stahl, P. J.
The Kingdom of the Greedy
In Harper, W. comp. The harvest feast p110-34   **S C**

Stalder, Valerie
Even the devil is afraid of a shrew (k-3)   **398.2**

Stallion, Bill
(illus.) Rutland, J. See inside an ancient Greek town   **938**

Stalo and Kauras. Lindholm, P. A.
In Olenius, E. comp. Great Swedish fairy tales p170-73   **398.2**

Stambler, Irwin
Minibikes and small cycles (5 and up)   **629.2**

Stamina, Physical. See Physical fitness

The **stamp**-pad printing book. Pettit, F. H.   **761**

Stamps, Postage. See Postage stamps

Stan, Susan
(illus.) Ellison, E. C. Fun with lines and curves   **745.4**

Stan Bolovan
Manning-Sanders, R. Stan Bolovan
In Manning-Sanders, R. A book of dragons p25-37   **398.2**

Standard time. See Time

Standards for school media programs. See Media programs: district and school   **371.3**

Stanfield, James
(illus.) Adams, B. Like it is: facts and feelings about handicaps from kids who know   **362.4**
(illus.) Foster, J. Dogs working for people   **636.7**

Stanley, Sir Henry Morton
See pages in the following book:
Perl, L. East Africa p66-69 (4-6)   **967.6**

Stanton, Elizabeth (Cady)
See pages in the following book:
As I saw it: women who lived the American adventure p181-83 (6 and up)   **973**

Star bright. Boiko, C.
In Boiko, C. Children's plays for creative actors p148-54   **812**

The **Star**-child. Wilde, O.
In Wilde, O. The Happy Prince, and other stories p135-54   **S C**

Star dollars
Grimm, J. The star dollars
In Grimm, J. More Tales from Grimm p85-86   **398.2**
Grimm, J. The star-money
In Grimm, J. The complete Grimm's fairy tales p652-54   **398.2**
Rockwell, A. The star money
In Rockwell, A. The three bears & 15 other stories p113-17   **398.2**

Star for Hansi. Vance, M.
In Association for Childhood Education International. Told under the Christmas tree p185-97   **808.8**

The **star** husband. Mobley, J.   **398.2**

The **star** in the pail. McCord, D.   **811**

Star maiden. Haviland, V.
In North American legends p97-100   **398.2**

The **star**-money. Grimm, J.
In Grimm, J. The complete Grimm's fairy tales p652-54   **398.2**
See also Star dollars

The **star** money. Rockwell, A.
In Rockwell, A. The three bears & 15 other stories p113-17   **398.2**
See also Star dollars

Star Mother's youngest child. Moeri, L.   **E**

Star of night. Paterson, K.
In Paterson, K. Angels & other strangers p64-80   **S C**

Star over Bethlehem. Dubois, G.
In On stage for Christmas p88-106   **812.08**

The **star** spangled banana, and other revolutionary riddles. Keller, C. comp.   **793.7**

The **Star**-spangled Banner. Key, F. S.   **784.7**

Starbird, Kaye
The covered bridge house, and other poems (3-6)   **811**

Starfish. Hurd, E. T.   **593.9**

Starfishes
Hurd, E. T. Starfish (k-3)   **593.9**
McClung, R. M. Sea star (2-4)   **593.9**
Zim, H. S. Sea stars and their kin (4 and up)   **593.9**
See also pages in the following book:
Cooper, E. K. Science on the shores and banks p83-89 (5 and up)   **574.92**

The **stones** of Green Knowe. Boston, L. M. See
note under Boston, L. M. The children of
Green Knowe   **Fic**

Stonewall [biography of Thomas Jonathan
Jackson] Fritz, J.   **92**

Stopping by woods on a snowy evening. Frost,
R.   **811**

Storage batteries
See also Electric batteries

Stores. Schwartz, A.   **381**

Stories. See Bible stories; School stories; Sea
stories; Stories without words; Storytelling; also literary and musical forms with
the subdivision Stories, plots, etc. e.g.
Ballets—Stories, plots, etc.; Operas—
Stories, plots, etc.; also subjects with the
subdivision Fiction, e.g. Slavery in the
United States—Fiction

Stories California Indians told. Fisher, A. B.
   398.2

Stories from the Bible. De La Mare, W.   **221.9**

Stories in rhyme
Adoff, A. Black is brown is tan   **E**
Adoff, A. Where wild Willie   **E**
Ahlberg, J. Each peach pear plum   **E**
Bemelmans, L. Madeline's rescue   **E**
Brooke, L. L. Johnny Crow's garden   **E**
Brown, M. W. Goodnight moon   **E**
Craft, R. Carrie Happle's garden   **E**
Craft, R. The winter bear   **E**
De Regniers, B. S. Red Riding Hood (1-3)
   398.2
Domanska, J. What do you see?   **E**
Fisher, A. Going barefoot   **E**
Fisher, A. I like weather   **E**
Fisher, A. Listen, rabbit   **E**
Gág, W. The A B C bunny   **E**
Gage, W. Down in the boondocks   **E**
Hoban, T. One little kitten   **E**
Hoban, T. Where is it?   **E**
Hutchins, P. The wind blew   **E**
Kahl, V. The Duchess bakes a cake   **E**
Kahl, V. How do you hide a monster?   **E**
Kraus, R. Whose mouse are you?   **E**
Lipkind, W. Nubber Bear   **E**
Lobel, A. On the day Peter Stuyvesant
sailed into town   **E**
Lord, J. V. The giant jam sandwich   **E**
Mayer, M. What do you do with a kangaroo?
   E
Miles, M. Apricot ABC   **E**
Noah's Ark   **E**
Over in the meadow   **E**
Oxenbury, H. Pig tale   **E**
Parkin, R. The red carpet   **E**
Peet, B. Huge Harold   **E**
Pomerantz, C. The piggy in the puddle   **E**
Prelutsky, J. The mean old mean hyena   **E**
Raskin, E. Who, said Sue, said Whoo?   **E**
Schweitzer, B. B. Amigo   **E**
Serraillier, I. Suppose you met a witch   **E**
Seuss, Dr. And to think that I saw it on
Mulberry Street   **E**
Seuss, Dr. The cat in the hat   **E**
Seuss, Dr. Horton hatches the egg   **E**
Seuss, Dr. How the Grinch stole Christmas
   E

Seuss, Dr. If I ran the circus   **E**
Seuss, Dr. If I ran the zoo   **E**
Wells, R. Noisy Nora   **E**
Zemach, H. The judge   **E**
See also pages in the following book:
The Home book of verse for young folks
p395-474   **821.08**

Stories of King Arthur and his knights. Picard,
B. L.   **398.2**

Stories of our American patriotic songs.
Lyons, J. H.   **784.7**

Stories of the gods and heroes. Benson, S.
   292

Stories to dramatize   **372.6**

Stories to tell to children   **016.3726**

Stories without words
Alexander, M. Bobo's dream   **E**
Anno, M. Anno's journey   **E**
Briggs, R. The snowman   **E**
Carle, E. Do you want to be my friend?   **E**
Charlip, R. Thirteen   **E**
De Groat, D. Alligator's toothache   **E**
Emberley, E. A birthday wish   **E**
Goodall, J. S. The adventures of Paddy Pork
   E
Goodall, J. S. Creepy castle   **E**
Goodall, J. S. Shrewbettina's birthday   **E**
Goodall, J. S. The surprise picnic   **E**
Hogrogian, N. Apples   **E**
Hutchins, P. Changes, changes   **E**
Krahn, F. The biggest Christmas tree on
earth   **E**
Krahn, F. Who's seen the scissors?   **E**
Mayer, M. A boy, a dog, and a frog   **E**
Rockwell, A. Albert B. Cub & Zebra   **E**
Turkle, B. Deep in the forest   **E**
Ward, L. The silver pony   **E**

Storks (as subject)
Fiction
Brown, M. W. Wheel on the chimney   **E**
DeJong, M. The wheel on the school (4-6)
   Fic

Storks
Andersen, H. C. The storks
In Andersen, H. C. The complete fairy
tales and stories p151-55   **S C**

Storm Boy. Thiele, C.   **Fic**

Storm from the west. Willard, B.   **Fic**

Storm moves the sign-boards
Andersen, H. C. How the storm changed
the signs
In Andersen, H. C. The complete fairy
tales and stories p840-44   **S C**

Storm warning. Buehr, W.   **551.5**

Storm warning. See Kay, M. In face of danger
   Fic

Stormalong. See Stormalong, Alfred Bulltop

Stormalong, Alfred Bulltop
See pages in the following books:
Malcolmson, A. Yankee Doodle's cousins
p63-70 (4 and up)   **398.2**
North American legends p184-91 (5 and up)
   398.2
Shapiro, I. Heroes in American folklore
p58-104 (4 and up)   **398.2**

Stormalong. Malcolmson, A.
In Malcolmson, A. Yankee Doodle's cousins
p63-69   **398.2**

The **tale** of the Daughters of the Sun. Jagendorf, M. A.
In Jagendorf, M. A. Folk stories of the South p97-99 **398.2**
The **tale** of the faithful dove. Potter, B. **E**
The **tale** of the flopsy bunnies. Potter, B. See note under Potter, B. The tale of Peter Rabbit **E**
Tale of the Gentle Folk
Finger, C. Tale of the Gentle Folk
In Finger, C. Tales from silver lands p99-106 **398.2**
The **tale** of the golden cockerel. Lowe, P. T. **398.2**
The **tale** of the gypsy and his strange love. Jagendorf, M. A.
In Jagendorf, M. A. The gypsies' fiddle, and other gypsy tales p93-101 **398.2**
The **tale** of the hairy toe. Jagendorf, M. A.
In Jagendorf, M. A. Folk stories of the South p180-82 **398.2**
The **tale** of the hunchback. Dawood, N. J.
In Dawood, N. J. Tales from the Arabian nights p243-304 **398.2**
The **tale** of the kurai. Riordan, J.
In Riordan, J. Tales from Tartary p46-49 **398.2**
Tale of the lazy people
Finger, C. Tale of the lazy people
In Finger, C. Tales from silver lands p170-87 **398.2**
The **tale** of the men of Prach. Jagendorf, M. A.
In Jagendorf, M. A. Noodlehead stories from around the world p241-43 **398.2**
A **tale** of the pie and the patty-pan. See Potter, B. The pie and the patty-pan **E**
The **tale** of the Superman. Arnott, K.
In Arnott, K. African myths and legends p43-55 **398.2**
Tale of the tail of a bear. Jagendorf, M. A.
In Jagendorf, M. A. New England bean-pot p100-05 **398.2**
The **tale** of the three talismans. Riordan, J.
In Riordan, J. Tales from Tartary p83-93 **398.2**
The **tale** of the three wishes. Le Prince de Beaumont, M.
In The Classic fairy tales p153-55 **398.2**
Tale of the Tontlawald
A Tale of the Tontlawald
In The Andrew Lang Fairy tale treasury p557-70 **398.2**
Tale of three tails
Finger, C. Tale of three tails
In Finger, C. Tales from the silver lands p 1-13 **398.2**
The **tale** of Tom Kitten. Potter, B. See note under Potter, B. The story of Miss Moppet **E**
The **tale** of Tuppenny. Potter, B. **E**
The **tale** of two bad mice. Potter, B. **E**
A **tale** of two drummers. Boiko, C.
In Boiko, C. Children's plays for creative actors p211-21 **812**
Tale that cost a dollar
Finger, C. Tale that cost a dollar
In Finger, C. Tales from silver lands p107-21 **398.2**
Talent is not enough. Hunter, M. **808.06**
The **Talent** Tree. Brown, T. L.
In One hundred plays for children p31-36 **808.82**

Tales. See Fables; Fairy tales; Folklore; Legends
Tales from a Finnish tupa. Bowman, J. C. **398.2**
Tales from a Taiwan kitchen. Cheney, C. **398.2**
Tales from Central Russia. Riordan, J. **398.2**
Tales from Grimm. Grimm, J. **398.2**
Tales from Moominvalley. Jansson, T. See note under Jansson, T. Comet in Moominland **Fic**
Tales from Shakespeare. Lamb, C. **822.3**
Tales from silver lands. Finger, C. **398.2**
Tales from Tartari-Barbari. Jagendorf, M. A.
In Jagendorf, M. A. Noodlehead stories from around the world p142-46 **398.2**
Tales from Tartary. Riordan, J. **398.2**
Tales from the Arabian nights. Dawood, N. J. **398.2**
Tales from the story hat. Aardema, V. **398.2**
Tales of a Chinese grandmother. Carpenter, F. **398.2**
Tales of a fourth grade nothing. Blume, J. **Fic**
The **tales** of Olga da Polga. Bond, M. **Fic**
Tales of Oliver Pig. Van Leeuwen, J. **E**
Tales of the paddock. Grimm, J.
In Grimm, J. The complete Grimm's fairy tales p480-82 **398.2**
See also Toad
Tales the people tell in China. Wyndham, R. **398.2**
Taliesin
Robbins, R. Taliesin and King Arthur (3-5) **398.2**

Fiction
Bond, N. A string in the harp (6 and up) **Fic**
Taliesin and King Arthur. Robbins, R. **398.2**
The **talisman.** Andersen, H. C.
In Andersen, H. C. The complete fairy tales and stories p550-52 **S C**
Talismans. See Charms
Talk. Courlander, H.
In Gruenberg, S. M. ed. Favorite stories old and new p354-57 **808.8**
Talk. Leach, M.
In Leach, M. The thing at the foot of the bed, and other scary tales p49-50 **S C**
Talk about a family. Greenfield, E. **Fic**
The **talkaround.** Karl, J. E.
In Karl, J. E. The turning place: stories of a future past p143-60 **S C**
Talkative tortoise
Babbitt, E. C. The turtle who couldn't stop talking
In Babbitt, E. C. Jataka tales p18-20 **398.2**
In Gruenberg, S. M. ed. Favorite stories old and new p222 **808.8**
Talkative tortoise
In Indian fairy tales p100-02 **398.2**
Talking. See Speech
Talking bird, the singing tree, and the golden water
In The Arabian nights p3-51 **398.2**
Talking bones. Steele, W. O. **970.004**
Talking books
For younger readers: braille and talking books **011**

Thief and his master
Grimm, J. The thief and his master
  In Grimm, J. The complete Grimm's fairy
    tales p337-38   398.2
The thief who kept his hands clean. Kendall, C.
  In Kendall, C. Sweet and sour p30-32   398.2
Thiele, Colin
  Blue Fin (6 and up)   Fic
  Fight against Albatross Two (6 and up)   Fic
  The shadow on the hills (6 and up)   Fic
  Storm Boy (3-5)   Fic
Thiessen, Diane
  (jt. auth.) Matthias, M. Children's mathe-
    matics books   016.51
Thievery. Kendall, C.
  In Kendall, C. Sweet and sour p78-79 398.2
Thieves. See Robbers and outlaws
Thimble summer. Enright, E.   Fic
The thing. Caudill, R.
  In The Arbuthnot Anthology of children's
    literature p605-08   808.8
The thing at the foot of the bed. Leach, M.
  In Leach, M. The thing at the foot of the
    bed, and other scary tales p15-16   S C
The thing at the foot of the bed, and other
  scary tales. Leach, M.   S C
Things to make and do for Valentine's Day. De
  Paola, T.   394.2
Things to see. Matthiesen, T.   E
Thingyan
  See pages in the following book:
  Festivals in Asia p37-42 (2-5)   394.2
Think metric! Branley, F. M.   389
Thinking. See Thought and thinking
Third book of junior authors   920.03
The third eye. Hunter, M.   Fic
The third gift. Carew, J.   Fic
The third witch. Picard, B. L.
  In Picard, B. L. The faun and the wood-
    cutter's daughter p89-108   S C
Thirteen. Charlip, R.   E
Thirteen. Martens, A. C.
  In Fifty plays for junior actors p355-71
                                          812.08
  In Popular plays for classroom reading
    p158-72   808.82
The 13 clocks. Thurber, J.   Fic
13 Danish tales. Hatch, M. C.   398.2
13 ghostly yarns. Sechrist, E. H. ed.   S C
Thirteenth century
Fiction
  Skurzynski, G. What happened in Hamelin
    (5 and up)   Fic
Thirteenth son of the King of Erin
  Manning-Sanders, R. The thirteenth son of
    the King of Erin
    In Manning-Sanders, R. A book of dra-
      gons p87-94   398.2
This book is about time. Burns, M.   529
This for that. Aardema, V.
  In Aardema, V. Behind the back of the
    mountain p48-56   398.2
This is a river. Pringle, L.   574.5
This is an orchestra. Posell, E. Z.   781.91
This is Australia. Sasek, M.   919.4
This is Edinburgh. Sasek, M.   914.11
This is Greece. Sasek, M.   914.95

This is historic Britain. Sasek, M.   914.1
This is Hong Kong. Sasek, M.   915.1
This is Ireland. Sasek, M.   914.15
This is London. Sasek, M.   914.21
This is New York. Sasek, M.   917.47
This is pro basketball. Sullivan, G.   796.32
This is pro soccer. Sullivan, G.   796.334
This is Rome. Sasek, M.   914.5
This is San Francisco. Sasek, M.   917.94
This is Texas. Sasek, M.   917.64
This is the Christmas. Sawyer, R.
  In Sawyer, R. Joy to the world p7-21   394.2
This is the house where Jack lives. Heil-
  broner, J.   E
This is the United Nations. Sasek, M.   341.23
This is Venice. Sasek, M.   914.5
This is Washington, D. C. Sasek, M.   917.53
This land is mine. Hine, A. ed.   811.08
This little pig-a-wig, and other rhymes about
  pigs (k-2)   398
This noble harvest. Dowden, A. O.   635
This restless earth. Lauber, P.   551
This star shall abide. Engdahl, S. L.   Fic
This time, Tempe Wicke? Gauch, P. L.   Fic
This way, delight (5 and up)   821.08
Thomas, Carol H.
  (illus.) Thomas, J. L. Turning kids on to
    print using nonprint   371.3
Thomas, Ianthe
  Hi, Mrs Mallory! (2-5)   Fic
  Walk home tired, Billy Jenkins   E
Thomas, James L.
  Turning kids on to print using nonprint
                                           371.3
Thomas, Marlo
  Free to be . . . you and me. See Free to be
    . . . you and me   810.8
Thomas, W. Jenkyn
  Arthur in the cave
    In Shedlock, M. L. The art of the story-
      teller p173-78   372.6
Thomas and Clem. Stevenson, J.
  In Stevenson, J. Fast friends p38-64   E
Thomas Berennikov
  Afanas'ev, A. Foma Berennikov
    In Afanas'ev, A. Russian fairy tales p284-87
                                           398.2
Thompson, Blanche Jennings
  (ed.) All the Silver pennies (3-6)   821.08
Thompson, David
  (illus.) Bees and honey. See Bees and honey
                                           595.7
Thompson, George Selden. See Selden, George
Thompson, Gregory
  (illus.) Millard, A. Plants for kids to grow
    indoors   635.9
Thompson, S. C.
  (jt. auth.) Turkin, H. The official encyclo-
    pedia of baseball   796.357
Thompson, Vivian L.
  Hawaiian myths of earth, sea, and sky (3-6)
                                           398.2
  Contents: The Time of Deep Darkness; A battle
  nobody won; Spears of lightning; A strange sled
  race: The lost Sun, Moon, and Stars; The Shark
  in the Milky Way; A kupua play tricks; The
  gift of The Hairy One; Maui traps Sun; The
  monster mo-o; Calabash of the winds;; The
  woman in Moon

Three bears—*Continued*

Southey, R. The story of the three bears
In The Classic fairy tales p201-05   **398.2**
In Green fairy book p236-41   **398.2**
In Time for old magic p5-7   **398.2**

Steel, F. A. The story of the three bears
In The Fairy tale treasury p36-43   **398.2**

The story of the three bears
In The Arbuthnot Anthology of children's literature p150-52   **808.8**

Three Bears
In The Arthur Rackham Fairy book p200-05   **398.2**
In Gruenberg, S. M. ed. Favorite stories old and new p270-75   **808.8**
In The Tall book of nursery tales p37-45   **398.2**

See also Scrapefoot

The **three** bears & 15 other stories. Rockwell, A.   **398.2**

Three big sillies
In The Tall book of nursery tales p98-104   **398.2**

See also Three sillies

Three billy goats gruff

Asbjörnsen, P. C. The three Billy Goats Gruff   **398.2**
also in The Arbuthnot Anthology of children's literature p237-38   **808.8**
also in The Fairy tale treasury p56-57   **398.2**
also in Time for old magic p115-16   **398.2**

Dasent, G. Three Billy Goats Gruff
In Stories to dramatize p21-23   **372.6**

Galdone, P. The three Billy Goats Gruff   **398.2**

Haviland, V. The three billy goats Gruff
In Haviland, V. Favorite fairy tales told in Norway p45-49   **398.2**

Rockwell, A. The three billy goats gruff
In Rockwell, A. The three bears & 15 other stories p56-62   **398.2**

Thorne-Thomsen, G. The three Billy Goats Gruff
In Told under the green umbrella p21-23   **398.2**

Three Billy Goats Gruff
In The Tall book of nursery tales p46-48   **398.2**

Three black princesses

Grimm, J. The three black princesses
In Grimm, J. The complete Grimm's fairy tales p620-21   **398.2**

Three blind mice. See Ivimey, J. W. Complete version of Ye three blind mice   **398**

Three boys with jugs of molasses and secret ambitions. Sandburg, C.
In Sandburg, C. Rootabaga stories v 1 p109-22   **S C**
In Sandburg, C. The Sandburg treasury p46-51   **818**

Three brothers

Grimm, J. The three brothers
In Grimm, J. The complete Grimm's fairy tales p561-62   **398.2**
In Grimm, J. Tales from Grimm p171-78   **398.2**

The Three brothers
In Yellow fairy book p119-22   **398.2**

The **three** brothers and the black hen. Picard, B. L.
In Picard, B. L. The faun and the woodcutter's daughter p111-20   **S C**

3 x 3: three by three. Krüss, J.   **E**

Three chests

Bowman, J. C. Jurma and the sea god
In Bowman, J. C. Tales from a Finnish tupa p81-90   **398.2**

Three copecks

Afanas'ev, A. The three pennies
In Afanas'ev, A. Russian fairy tales p113-14   **398.2**

Manning-Sanders, R. The good ogre
In Manning-Sanders, R. A book of ogres and trolls p9-19   **398.2**

3D, 2D, 1D. Adler, D. A.   **530.8**

The **three** daughters. Riordan, J.
In Riordan, J. Tales from Tartary p104-05   **398.2**

Three dogs

Bechstein, L. The three dogs
In Green fairy book p294-300   **398.2**

Manning-Sanders, R. The three dogs
In Manning-Sanders, R. A book of dragons p114-22   **398.2**

Three ducks went wandering. Roy, R.   **E**

The **three** dwarfs. Grimm, J.
In Red fairy book p228-34   **398.2**

See also Three little men in the wood

The **three** elevators. Burgess, G.
In Told under the magic umbrella p64-67   **S C**

The **three** fairies. Carter, D. S.
In The Arbuthnot Anthology of children's literature p403-04   **808.8**
In Carter, D. S. Greedy Mariani, and other folktales of the Antilles p106-11   **398.2**

Three fast men. Courlander, H.
In Courlander, H. The king's drum, and other African stories p17-18   **398.2**

Three feathers

Grimm, J. The three feathers
In Grimm, J. About wise men and simpletons p58-61   **398.2**
In Grimm, J. The complete Grimm's fairy tales p319-22   **398.2**
In Grimm, J. The juniper tree, and other tales from Grimm v 1 p3-10   **398.2**

The **three** foolish brides. Kim, So-un
In Kim, So-un. The story bag p56-57   **398.2**

Three friends find spring. See Delton, J. Two good friends   **E**

The **three** goats. Poulsson, E.
In Told under the green umbrella p78-80   **398.2**

Three gold pieces. Aliki   **398.2**

Three golden eggs

MacManus, S. The three golden eggs
In MacManus, S. Hibernian nights p25-35   **398.2**

The **three** golden hairs of Grandfather Know All. Haviland, V.
In Haviland, V. Favorite fairy tales told in Czechoslovakia p67-90   **398.2**

See also Giant with the golden hair

The **three** golden hairs of the Devil. Grimm, J.
In Grimm, J. The Brothers Grimm: popular folk tales p170-77   **398.2**

See also Giant with the golden hair

The **three** goslings. Haviland, V.
In Haviland, V. Favorite fairy tales told in Italy p67-77   **398.2**

Travel

See also Voyages and travels; Voyages around the world

Fiction

Jewell, N. Bus ride   **E**

The **traveler** and the net tree. Courlander, H.
In Courlander, H. The tiger's whisker, and other tales and legends from Asia and the Pacific p76   **398.2**

Traveling companion
Andersen, H. C. The traveling companion
In Andersen, H. C. The complete fairy tales and stories p40-56   **S C**

Traveling through the chimney. Jagendorf, M. A.
In Jagendorf, M. A. The gypsies' fiddle, and other gypsy tales p118-21   **398.2**

The **traveller's** shoes. Housman, L.
In Housman, L. The rat-catcher's daughter p33-56   **S C**

Travels. See Overland journeys to the Pacific (U.S.); Voyages and travels

The **Travels** of a fox
In Time for old magic p12-14   **398.2**
In Told under the green umbrella p40-46   **398.2**

The **travels** of a fox. Rockwell, A.
In Rockwell, A. The old woman and her pig, & 10 other stories p23-33   **398.2**

The **travels** of Babar. Brunhoff, J. de. See note under Brunhoff, J. de. The story of Babar, the little elephant   **E**

Traven, B.
The creation of the sun and the moon (5 and up)   **398.2**

Travers, P. L.
Laughing gas
In The Golden Treasury of children's literature p41-49   **808.8**
Mary Poppins (4-6)   **Fic**
Mary Poppins comes back. See note under Travers, P. L. Mary Poppins   **Fic**
Mary Poppins from A to Z. See note under Travers, P. L. Mary Poppins   **Fic**
Mary Poppins in the park. See note under Travers, P. L. Mary Poppins   **Fic**
Mary Poppins opens the door. See note under Travers, P. L. Mary Poppins   **Fic**

Tray gardens. See Gardens, Miniature

The **treasure.** Hautzig, E.
In Hautzig, E. The case against the wind, and other stories p3-7   **S C**

The **treasure.** Shulevitz, U.   **398.2**

Treasure hunt. Fisher, A.
In Fisher, A. Holiday programs for boys and girls p81-91   **812**

Treasure in the Smith house. Barnett, G. T.
In Fifty plays for junior actors p3-18 **812.08**

Treasure Island. Stevenson, R. L.   **Fic**

Treasure Island. York, M. A.
In Popular plays for classroom reading p218-30   **808.82**

The **treasure** of Alpheus Winterborn. Bellairs, J.   **Fic**

Treasure of Green Knowe. Boston, L. M. See note under Boston, L. M. The children of Green Knowe   **Fic**

The **treasure** of Li-Po. Ritchie, A.   **S C**

The **treasure** of Li-Po; short story. Ritchie, A.
In Ritchie, A. The treasure of Li-Po p3-39   **S C**

The **treasure** trap. Masterman-Smith, V.   **Fic**

Treasure trove. See Buried treasure

Treasure-trove. Afanas'ev, A.
In Afanas'ev, A. Russian fairy tales p550-52   **398.2**

Treasures in the sea. McClung, R. M.   **910.4**

Treasures of Morrow. Hoover, H. M.   **Fic**

Treasures to see. Weisgard, L.   **708**

A **Treasury** of Christmas plays   **812.08**

A **Treasury** of Christmas songs and carols **783.6**

Treasury of poetry, The Golden   **821.08**

Tredrill. Manning-Sanders, R.
In Manning-Sanders, R. A book of charms and changelings p120-24   **398.2**

Tree-dwellings
Stiles, D. The tree house book (6 and up)   **690**

The **tree** house book. Stiles, D.   **690**

Tree houses. See Tree-dwellings

Tree in the trail. Holling, H. C.   **Fic**

A **tree** is a plant. Bulla, C. R.   **582.16**

A **tree** is nice. Udry, J. M.   **E**

Tree of freedom; excerpt. Caudill, R.
In Stories to dramatize p259-65   **372.6**

Tree of health
Haviland, V. The tree of health
In Haviland, V. Favorite fairy tales told in Denmark p65-76   **398.2**

The **tree** that didn't get trimmed. Morley, C.
In It's time for Christmas p238-42   **394.2**

The **tree** that trimmed itself. Bailey, C. S.
In Association for Childhood Education International. Told under the Christmas tree p41-44   **808.8**

Treece, Henry
See pages in the following book:
Only connect p256-64   **028.5**

A **treeful** of pigs. Lobel, A.   **E**

Treehoppers
See pages in the following book:
Hutchins, R. E. The bug clan p63-66 (5 and up)   **595.7**

The **treeless** plains. Rounds, G.   **978**

Trees
Budbill, D. Christmas tree farm (k-2)   **634.9**
Bulla, C. R. A tree is a plant (k-2)   **582.16**
Cole, J. Plants in winter (1-3)   **581**
Helfman, E. S. Maypoles and wood demons (3-6)   **398**
Petrides, G. A. A field guide to trees and shrubs   **582.1**
Riedman, S. R. Trees alive (5 and up)   **582.16**
Selsam, M. E. The apple and other fruits (3-5)   **583**
Selsam, M. E. Play with trees (3-5)   **582.16**
Udry, J. M. A tree is nice (3-5)   **E**
Zim, H. S. Trees   **582.16**
See also pages in the following book:
Webster, D. More brain-boosters p91-98 (4 and up)   **507**
See also Nuts; Plants; State trees; and names of trees, e.g. Maple

Trees—*Continued*

Fiction

Fleischman, P. The birthday tree (2-4)   **Fic**

Holling, H. C. Tree in the trail (4 and up)   **Fic**

Norris, L. An oak tree dies and a journey begins   **E**

Taylor, M. D. Song of the trees (4-6)   **Fic**

Poetry

Adoff, A. Under the early morning trees (4-6)   **811**

See also pages in the following book:

My poetry book p266-82 (5 and up)   **821.08**

United States

Anderson, M. J. Exploring city trees and the need for urban forests (4-6)   **582.16**

Collingwood, G. H. Knowing your trees   **582.16**

Dowden, A. O. The blossom on the bough (5 and up)   **582.15**

See also pages in the following book:

Clement, R. C. Hammond Nature atlas of America p40-69   **500**

Trees alive. Riedman, S. R.   **582.16**

The **trees** stand shining. Jones, H. comp.   **897**

Trefoil round the world. World Association of Girl Guides and Girl Scouts   **369.463**

Tregarthen, Enys

The doll who came alive (3-5)   **Fic**

Skerry-Werry

In The Arbuthnot Anthology of children's literature p171-77   **808.8**

In Time for old magic p32-38   **398.2**

About

See pages in the following book:

A Horn Book Sampler on children's books and reading p23-27   **028.5**

Tregaskis, Richard

See pages in the following book:

John F. Kennedy and PT-109 (5 and up)   **940.54**

Tremain, Ruthven

Fooling around with words (2-4)   **793.7**

The **trenches.** Hoobler, D.   **940.4**

Trenton, Battle of, 1776

See pages in the following book:

Tunis, E. The tavern at the ferry p94-99 (5 and up)   **973.2**

Tresselt, Alvin

Autumn harvest   **E**

The beaver pond (k-3)   **574.5**

Follow the wind   **E**

"Hi, Mister Robin!"   **E**

Hide and seek fog   **E**

also in The Arbuthnot Anthology of children's literature p860-61   **808.8**

It's time now! (k-2)   **525**

The mitten (k-2)   **398.2**

Rain drop splash   **E**

Sampson, the fire dog

In Gruenberg, S. M. comp. Let's hear a story p132-35   **808.8**

White snow, bright snow   **E**

The world in the candy egg   **E**

Treviño, Elizabeth Borton de

I, Juan de Pareja (6 and up)   **Fic**

Newbery Medal acceptance paper

In Newbery and Caldecott Medal books 1966-1975 p5-11   **028.5**

About

See pages in the following books:

Authors and illustrators of children's books p122-24   **028.5**

Newbery and Caldecott Medal books: 1966-1975 p12-19   **028.5**

The **trial** of Avichára-pura. Courlander, H.

In Courlander, H. The tiger's whisker, and other tales and legends from Asia and the Pacific p49-51   **398.2**

The **trial** of Billy Scott. Hall, M.

In One hundred plays for children p113-21   **808.82**

Trial of brides

Grimm, J. Looking for a bride

In Grimm, J. The complete Grimm's fairy tales p655-56   **398.2**

The **trial** of the stone. Courlander, H.

In Courlander, H. The tiger's whisker, and other tales and legends from Asia and the Pacific p24-28   **398.2**

Trial Valley. Cleaver, V. See note under Cleaver, V. Where the lilies bloom   **Fic**

Trials

Aymar, B. Laws and trials that created history (6 and up)   **345**

David, A. Famous criminal trials (5 and up)   **345**

The **trick** on the trek. Aardema, V.

In Aardema, V. Behind the back of the mountain p11-18   **398.2**

Trickery

In Jataka tales p54-55   **398.2**

Tricks

Carlson, B. W. Do it yourself! (4 and up)   **793**

Fleischman, S. Mr Mysterious's secrets of magic (3-6)   **793.8**

Helfman, H. Tricks with your fingers (3-6)   **793.8**

Kettelkamp, L. Magic made easy (4 and up)   **793.8**

Kettelkamp, L. Spooky magic (3-6)   **793.8**

Lopshire, R. It's magic? (k-2)   **793.8**

Marks, B. Give a magic show! (3-5)   **793.8**

Permin, I. Hokus pokus: with wands, water & glasses (5 and up)   **793.8**

Severn, B. Bill Severn's book of magic (6 and up)   **793.8**

Severn, B. Magic with coins and bills (6 and up)   **793.8**

Stoddard, E. The first book of magic (4-6)   **793.8**

Van Rensselaer, A. Fun with magic (4 and up)   **793.8**

White, L. B. So you want to be a magician? (5 and up)   **793.8**

Wyler, R. Magic secrets (1-3)   **793.8**

Wyler, R. Spooky tricks (1-3)   **793.8**

See also Magic

Tricks of eye and mind. Kettelkamp, L.   **535**

Tricks with your fingers. Helfman, H.   **793.8**

Tricksy Rabbit. Aardema, V.

In Aardema, V. Tales from the story hat p9-17   **398.2**

United States—*Continued*

Library of Congress

Children's literature; a guide to reference sources. See Children's literature; a guide to reference sources **011**

Children's literature; a guide to reference sources; first supplement. See Children's literature; a guide to reference sources; first supplement **011**

Children's literature; a guide to reference sources; second supplement. See Children's literature; a guide to reference sources; second supplement **011**

Library of Congress. Children's Book Section

Creating independence, 1763-1789. See Creating independence, 1763-1789 **016.9733**

Folklore from Africa to the United States. See Folklore from Africa to the United States **016.398**

Folklore of the North American Indians. See Folklore of the North American Indians **016.398**

See also United States. Library of Congress. Children's Literature Center

Library of Congress. Children's Literature Center

Children & poetry: a selective, annotated bibliography. See Children & poetry: a selective, annotated bibliography. **016.8**

Children's books. See Children's books **011**

See also United States. Library of Congress. Children's Book Section

Library of Congress. National Library Service for the Blind and Physically Handicapped

For younger readers: braille and talking books. See For younger readers: braille and talking books **011**

Mail

See Postal service—United States

Manners and customs

See United States—Social life and customs

Manufactures

See United States—Industries

Maps

National Geographic Society. National Geographic Picture atlas of our fifty states (4-6) **912**

Music

See Music, American

Names, Geographical

See Names, Geographical—United States

National songs

See National songs, American

Natural monuments

See Natural monuments—United States

Natural resources

See Natural resources—United States

Navy

Cooke, D. C. Famous U.S. Navy fighter planes (5 and up) **623.74**

Van Orden, M. D. The book of United States Navy ships (5 and up) **359.3**

Naval history

See United States—History, Naval

Painters

See Painters, American

Physical geography

See Physical geography—United States

Plants, Cultivated

See Plants, Cultivated—United States

Poets

See Poets, American

Politics and government

Cook, F. J. The rise of American political parties (5 and up) **324.273**

Eichner, J. A. The first book of local government (4 and up) **352**

Politics and government— 1933-1945—Biography

Franklin Delano Roosevelt (5 and up) **92**

Postal service

See Postal service—United States

Presidents

See Presidents—United States

Race relations

Griffin, J. H. A time to be human (5 and up) **305.8**

Schools

See Schools—United States

Sculpture

See Sculpture, American

Shipping

See Shipping—United States

Social conditions

Katz, W. L. An album of the Great Depression (5 and up) **330.973**

Sandler, M. W. The way we lived (4 and up) **331.09**

Social life and customs

Caney, S. Steven Caney's Kids' America (4 and up) **790.1**

Cook, A. What was it like? When your grandparents were your age (3-6) **973.91**

Hilton, S. The way it was—1876 (6 and up) **973.8**

Loeper, J. J. Going to school in 1776 (3-6) **973.3**

Tunis, E. The young United States, 1783 to 1830 (6 and up) **973**

See also pages in the following book:

Sechrist, E. H. Christmas everywhere p15-35 **394.2**

Social life and customs— Colonial period, 1600-1775

Colby, C. B. Early American crafts (4 and up) **670**

D'Amato, J. Colonial crafts for you to make (4 and up) **745.5**

D'Amato, J. More Colonial crafts for you to make (4 and up) **745.5**

DePauw, L. G. Founding mothers (6 and up) **305.4**

Fisher, L. E. The blacksmiths (4 and up) **682**

Fisher, L. E. The cabinetmakers (4 and up) **684.1**

W

Wabash and Erie Canal
See pages in the following book:
Franchere, R. Westward by canal p129-31 (5 and up)   386

Waber, Bernard
An anteater named Arthur   E
A firefly named Torchy   E
Good-bye, funny dumpy-lumpy   E
The house on East 88th Street   E
I was all thumbs   E
Ira sleeps over   E
Lovable Lyle. See note under Waber, B. The house on East 88th Street   E
Lyle and the birthday party. See note under Waber, B. The house on East 88th Street E
Lyle finds his mother. See note under Waber, B. The house on East 88th Street   E
Lyle, Lyle, crocodile. See note under Waber, B. The house on East 88th Street   E

Wachs, Stanley R.
(illus.) Zappler, G. From one cell to many cells   574.8

Wadsworth, Olive A.
Over in the meadow. See Over in the meadow   E

WAGGGS. See World Association of Girl Guides and Girl Scouts

Wagner, Jane
J. T. (3-6)   Fic

Wagner, Jenny
The Bunyip of Berkeley's Creek   E

Wagner, Richard
The Ring of the Nibelung; adaptation. See Updike, J. The Ring   782.1

Wagon wheels. Brenner, B.   Fic

Wagons. See Carriages and carts

Wahlenberg, Anna
The barrel bung
In Olenius, E. comp. Great Swedish fairy tales p29-37   398.2
The king's choice
In Olenius, E. comp. Great Swedish fairy tales p50-58   398.2
Linda-Gold and the old king
In The Arbuthnot Anthology of children's literature p257-60   808.8
In Olenius, E. comp. Great Swedish fairy tals p195-202   398.2
The magician's cape
In Olenius, E. comp. Great Swedish fairy tales p19-28   398.2
The magpie with salt on her tail
In Olenius, E. comp. Great Swedish fairy tales p136-41   398.2
The old troll of Big Mountain
In Olenius, E. comp. Great Swedish fairy tales p114-21   398.2
Peter and the witch of the wood
In Harper, W. comp. Ghosts and goblins p67-82   398.2
In Witches, witches, witches p112-24   808.8
The queen
In Olenius, E. comp. Great Swedish fairy tales p230-38   398.2
The troll ride
In Olenius, E. comp. Great Swedish fairy tales p78-86   398.2

The **Wahoo** bobcat. Lippincott, J. W.   **Fic**
The **waif** woman. Stevenson, R. L.
In Mayne, W. ed. Ghosts p67-86   820.8
Wait till Martin comes. Leach, M.
In Leach, M. The thing at the foot of the bed, and other scary tales p23-26
                                             S C
Wait till Martin comes. Wickes, F. G.
In Harper, W. comp. Ghosts and goblins p195-98   398.2
Wait till the moon is full. Brown, M. W.   **E**

Waite, Helen E.
Christmas House
In One hundred plays for children p560-69
                                             808.82
The master of the strait
In A Treasury of Christmas plays p198-208   812.08
Not only the strong
In One hundred plays for children p848-61
                                             808.82

Waiting for a turkey. Courlander, H.
In Courlander, H. the piece of fire, and other Haitian tales p111-12   398.2
Waiting for mama. Moskin, M.   **Fic**
Waiting for rabbits. Cheney, C.
In Cheney, C. Tales from a Taiwan kitchen p115-18   398.2

Waitley, Douglas
(jt. auth.) Ogilvie, B. Rand McNally Picture atlas of the world   912

Wakaima and the clay man
Kalibala, E. B. Wakaima and the clay man
In The Fairy tale treasury p104-09   398.2
Wake up, Jeremiah. Himler, R.   **E**

Wakefield, Edward Gibbon
See pages in the following book:
Kaula, E. M. The land and people of New Zealand p69-75 (5 and up)   993

Wakefield, H. Russell
Mr Ash's studio
In Alfred Hitchcock's Supernatural tales of terror and suspense p156-72   **S C**
The triumph of death
In Alfred Hitchcock's Supernatural tales of terror and suspense p2-19   **S C**

Wakin, Edward
Black fighting men in U.S. history (5 and up)   355

Waking the daffodil. Bennett, R.
In Bennett, R. Creative plays and programs for holidays p327-30   812

Wald, Lillian D.
See pages in the following book:
Sechrist, E. H. It's time for brotherhood p53-57 (5 and up)   361

Waldman, Neil
(illus.) Harter, W. Osceola's head, and other American ghost stories   **S C**

Waldron, Ann
The integration of Mary-Larkin Thornhill (6 and up)   **Fic**

Wales
See pages in the following book:
Hinds, L. Looking at Great Britain p32-35 (4-6)   941
Description and travel
See pages in the following book:
Sasek, M. This is historic Britain p46-53 (3-6)   914.1

Wales—*Continued*

Fiction

Bawden, N. Carrie's war (4 and up)   **Fic**
Bond, N. A string in the harp (6 and up)   **Fic**
Garner, A. The owl service (5 and up)   **Fic**
Kimmel, M. M. Magic in the mist (1-4)   **Fic**
Morgan, A. A boy called Fish (5 and up)   **Fic**

Walk home tired, Billy Jenkins. Thomas, I.   **E**
A **walk** in the forest. List, A.   **574.5**
A **walk** in the snow. Busch, P. S.   **551.57**
A **walk** out of the world. Nicholas, R.   **Fic**
Walk the world's rim. Baker, B.   **Fic**
Walk together children   **784.7**
Walk with your eyes. Brown, M.   **500**
Walker, Alice
Langston Hughes, American poet (2-4)   **92**
Walker, Barbara K.
(comp.) Laughing together. See Laughing together   **808.87**
Teeny-Tiny and the witch-woman (k-3)   **398.2**
Walker, Barbara Muhs
The Little House cookbook (5 and up)   **641.5**
Walker, Charles W.
(illus.) Phelan, M. K. Four days in Philadelphia, 1776   **973.3**
(illus.) Phelan, M. K. Martha Berry   **92**
Walker, David
Big Ben (3-5)   **Fic**
Walker, Gil
(illus.) MacLean, A. Lawrence of Arabia   **92**
Walker, Les
Housebuilding for children (2 and up)   **690**
Walker, Maggie Lena (Mitchell)
See pages in the following book:
Rollins, C. H. They showed the way p138-40 (5 and up)   **920**
Walker, Margaret
See pages in the following book:
Rollins, C. Famous American Negro poets p80-86 (5 and up)   **920**
Walker, Stephen
(illus.) Holman, F. The Drac   **398.2**
Walking
See pages in the following books:
Antonacci, R. J. Physical fitness for young champions p112-20 (5 and up)   **613.7**
Antonacci, R. J. Track and field for young champions p163-69 (4 and up)   **796.4**
Boy Scouts of America. Fieldbook p5-31   **369.43**

Fiction

Sharmat, M. W. Burton and Dudley   **E**
The **walking** stones. Hunter, M.   **Fic**
Wallace, Daisy
(ed.) Ghost poems. See Ghost poems   **811.08**
(ed.) Giant poems. See Giant poems   **811.08**
(ed.) Monster poems. See Monster poems   **811.08**
(ed.) Witch poems. See Witch poems   **811.08**
Wallace, Roy
(illus.) Coskey, E. Christmas crafts for everyone   **745.59**

Wallner, John C.
(illus.) Blaine, M. The terrible thing that happened at our house   **E**
(illus.) Hurwitz, J. Much ado about Aldo   **Fic**
(illus.) A January fog will freeze a hog, and other weather folklore. See A January fog will freeze a hog, and other weather folklore   **551.6**
(illus.) Tompert, A. Charlotte & Charles   **E**
(illus.) Tompert, A. Little fox goes to the end of the world   **E**
The **walls** of Athens. Walsh, J. P.
In Walsh, J. P. Children of the fox   **S C**
Walruses
See pages in the following book:
McClung, R. M. Hunted mammals of the sea p123-33 (5 and up)   **599**
Walsh, Anne Batterberry
A gardening book: indoors and outdoors (4-6)   **635**
Walsh, Jill Paton
A chance child (5 and up)   **Fic**
Children of the fox (5 and up)   **S C**
Contents: Crossing to Salamis; The walls of Athens; Persian gold
Fireweed (5 and up)   **Fic**
Goldengrove (6 and up)   **Fic**
Unleaving. See note under Walsh, J. P. Goldengrove   **Fic**

About

See pages in the following book:
Townsend, J. R. A sounding of storytellers p153-65   **028.5**
Walt Disney: master of make-believe. Montgomery, E. R.   **92**
Walter the lazy mouse. Flack, M.   **Fic**
Waltrip, Mildred
(illus.) Barr, G. Entertaining with number tricks   **793.7**
(illus.) Barr, G. Young scientist and sports   **796**
Waltz, Jean Jacques. See Hansi, L'Oncle
Walworth, Nancy Zinsser
(jt. auth.) Brooks, P. S. When the world was Rome   **937**
Walz, Lila Philips
Camp Fire Girls, Inc. The Camp Fire Blue Bird Series   **369.47**
Wampanoag Indians

Biography

Bulla, C. R. Squanto, friend of the Pilgrims (2-4)   **92**
Wanda Gág's Jorinda and Joringel. Grimm, J.   **398.2**
See also Jorinde and Joringel
Wanda Gág's The sorcerer's apprentice. Gág, W.   **398.2**
See also Master and his pupil
Wang, C. C.
(illus.) Wolff, D. Chinese writing   **495.1**
War

Fiction

Davies, A. Conrad's war (5 and up)   **Fic**
War crime trials
Noble, I. Nazi hunter; Simon Wiesenthal (5 and up)   **92**
War of 1812. See United States—History—War of 1812

War of the American Revolution. See United States—History—Revolution, 1775-1783

War of the wolf and the fox
The war of the wolf and the fox
In Green fairy book p280-85   398.2

The war of the plants. Courlander, H.
In Courlander, H. The tiger's whisker, and other tales and legends from Asia and the Pacific p127-31   398.2

War poetry
See pages in the following book:
The Home book of verse for young folks p517-48   821.08

The Warau people discover the earth. Sherlock, P.
In Sherlock, P. West Indian folk-tales p39-44   398.2

Warblers. See Wood warblers

Ward, Charles Forbes
(illus.) Rubenstone, J. Weaving for beginners   746.1

Ward, Don
Cowboys and cattle country. See Cowboys and cattle country   978

Ward, Keith
(illus.) Farley, W. The Black Stallion   Fic

Ward, Lynd
The biggest bear   E
Caldecott Medal acceptance paper
In Caldecott Medal books: 1938-1957 p243-48   028.5
The silver pony   Fic
(illus.) Coatsworth, E. The cat who went to heaven   Fic
(jt. auth.) Commager, H. S. America's Robert E. Lee   92
(illus.) Forbes, E. Johnny Tremain   Fic
(illus.) Fritz, J. Brady   Fic
(illus.) Fritz, J. Early thunder   Fic
(illus.) Holbrook, S. H. America's Ethan Allen   92
(illus.) McNeer, M. America's Abraham Lincoln   92
(illus.) McNeer, M. America's Mark Twain   92
(jt. auth.) McNeer, M. Armed with courage   920
(jt. auth.) Swift, H. H. The little red lighthouse and the great gray bridge   E
(illus.) Swift, H. H. North star shining   305.8
(illus.) Wyss, J. D. The Swiss family Robinson   Fic
About
See pages in the following books:
Authors and illustrators and children's books p403-06   028.5
Caldecott Medal books: 1938-1957 p249-53   028.5

Ward, Mrs May (McNeer). See McNeer, May Yonge

Ward, Martha E.
Authors of books for young people   920.03
Authors of books for young people; supplement to the 2d ed.   920.03
Illustrators of books for young people   920.03
Mr Lazy Man's family
In Fifty plays for junior actors p606-26   812.08

Ward, Nancy
See pages in the following book:
Gridley, M. E. American Indian women p39-46 (5 and up)   920

Ward, Winifred
(ed.) Stories to dramatize. See Stories to dramatize   372.6

Wardle, Ross
(illus.) Kerrod, R. Rocks and minerals   549

Waring, Ruth Ann
Puddle: the real story of a baby hippo
In Gruenberg, S. M. ed. Favorite stories old and new p146-48   808.8

The warlock of Westfall. Fisher, L. E.   Fic

Warm as wool, cool as cotton. Houck, C.   677

Warm Spring Apache Indians
See pages in the following book:
Baldwin, G. C. The Apache Indians p70-84 (6 and up)   970.004

Warner, Oliver
Captain Cook and the South Pacific. See Captain Cook and the South Pacific   990

Warner, Susan
See pages in the following book:
Jordan, A. M. From Rollo to Tom Sawyer, and other papers p82-91   028.5
For a work by this author see Wetherell, Elizabeth

A warning from the gods, Wyndham, R.
In Wyndham, R. Tales the people tell in China p52-54   398.2

Warren, Betsy
(illus.) Miller, N. The story of the Liberty Bell   974.8

Warren, Leslie F.
The land and people of Bolivia (5 and up)   984
Brown, R. The land and people of Brazil   981

Warren, Maude R.
The first New England dinner
In Harper, W. comp. The harvest feast p27-36   S C

Warren, Ruth
Modern Greece (4-6)   949.5
A pictorial history of women in America (6 and up)   305.4

The warrior goddess: Athena. Gates, D.   292

Warsaw
See pages in the following book:
Kelly, E. P. The land and people of Poland p79-93 (5 and up)   943.8

Warshaw, Jerry
(illus.) Albert, B. More Codes for kids   001.54
(illus.) Rothman, J. How to play drums   789

Warships
Van Orden, M. D. The book of United States Navy ships (5 and up)   359.3

The Wart meets a giant. White, T. H.
In The Golden Treasury of children's literature p496-505   808.8

Wartik, Herschel
(illus.) Zim, H. S. Our senses and how they work   612
(illus.) Zim, H. S. What's inside of animals?   591.4
(illus.) Zim, H. S. What's inside of plants?   581.4

Warton and Morton. Erickson, R. E. See note under Erickson, R. E. A toad for Tuesday   Fic

Warton and the king of the skies. Erickson, R. E. See note under Erickson, R. E. A toad for Tuesday **Fic**

Warton and the traders. Erickson, R. E. See note under Erickson, R. E. A toad for Tuesday **Fic**

Warton's Christmas Eve adventure. Erickson, R. E. See note under Erickson, R. E. A toad for Tuesday **Fic**

Washburn, James K.
(illus.) Berends, P. B. The case of the elevator duck **Fic**

Washington, Booker Taliaferro
Graham, S. Booker T. Washington: educator of hand, head, and heart (5 and up) **92**
See also pages in the following books:
Rollins, C. H. They showed the way p141-42 (5 and up) **920**
Johnston, J. A special bravery p51-54 (2-5) **920**

Washington, George, President U.S.
Aulaire, I. d'. George Washington (2-4) **92**
Griffin, J. B. Phoebe and the General (2-5) **973.3**
See also pages in the following books:
The Arbuthnot Anthology of children's literature p790-97 **808.8**
Davis, B. Heroes of the American Revolution p127-43 (5 and up) **920**
Holiday ring p55-62 (4 and up) **394.2**
National Geographic Society. Visiting our past: America's historylands p168-80 (5 and up) **917.3**
Fiction
Fritz, J. George Washington's breakfast (2-4) **Fic**
Poetry
See pages in the following books:
O frabjous day! p72-83 (5 and up) **808.81**
Sechrist, E. H. comp. Poems for red letter days p56-60 **821.08**

Washington, D.C.
See pages in the following book:
National Geographic Society. Visiting our past: America's historylands p378-91 (5 and up) **917.3**
Description
Sasek, M. This is Washington, D. C. (3-6) **917.53**
Shaw, R. Washington for children **917.53**
Fiction
Brady, E. W. The toad on Capitol Hill (4-6) **Fic**
Fife, D. Who's in charge of Lincoln? (2-4) **Fic**
History
Phelan, M. K. The burning of Washington: August 1814 (5 and up) **975.3**

Washington for children. Shaw, R. **917.53**
Washington marches on. Fisher, A.
In Fisher, A. Holiday programs for boys and girls p223-44 **812**

Washington's Birthday
See pages in the following books:
Araki, C. Origami in the classroom: Book II p14-16 (4 and up) **736**
Sechrist, E. H. Red letter days p50-56 **394.2**

Drama
See pages in the following book:
Fisher, A. Holiday programs for boys and girls p223-44 (4 and up) **812**
Wasps
Hughes, J. A closer look at bees and wasps (4 and up) **595.7**
McClung, R. M. Bees, wasps, and hornets and how they live (3-6) **595.7**
See also pages in the following books:
Graham, A. Bug hunters p58-64 (5 and up) **632**
Rounds, G. Wildlife at your doorstep p36-56 (4 and up) **591.5**
Teale, E. W. The junior book of insects p121-30 (6 and up) **595.7**
Fiction
Lord, J. V. The giant jam sandwich **E**

Wasson, Valentina P.
The chosen baby **E**

Waste disposal. See Refuse and refuse disposal; Waste products

Waste products
Hyde, M. O. Everyone's trash problem: nuclear wastes (4 and up) **621.48**
See also Recycling (Waste, etc.); Refuse and refuse disposal

Recycling
See Recycling (Waste, etc.)

Waste reclamation. See Recycling (Waste, etc.)

Wastewin and the beaver. Yellow Robe, R.
In Yellow Robe, R. Tonweya and the eagles, and other Lakota Indian tales p52-58 **398.2**

Watanabe, Shigeo
How do I put it on? Getting dressed **E**

The **Watch** House. Westall, R. **Fic**

Watch it grow, watch it change. Rahn, J. E. **581.3**

Watch out, it's poison ivy! Limburg, P. R. **581.6**

Watch out for the chicken feet in your soup. De Paola, T. **E**

The **watchers.** Curry, J. L. **Fic**

Watches. See Clocks and watches

Watching the new baby. Samson, J. **649**

Watching the wild apes. Kevles, B. **599.88**

Watching them grow. Hewett, J. **590.74**

The **watchman** of the tower. Andersen, H. C.
In Andersen, H. C. The complete fairy tales and stories p614-19 **S C**

Watchwords of liberty. Lawson, R. **973**

Water
Berger, M. The new water book (4-6) **553.7**
Gans, R. Water for dinosaurs and you (1-3) **551.48**
See also pages in the following books:
Allison, L. The wild inside p98-115 (5 and up) **500**
Cooper, E. K. Science in your own back yard p49-57 (5 and up) **507**
Milgrom, H. Understanding weather p23-29 (5 and up) **551.6**
Webster, D. More brain-boosters p19-25, 43-52 (4 and up) **507**
Wyler, R. Prove it! p5-24 (1-3) **507**
See also Ocean

Water—*Continued*

Petroleum pollution

See Petroleum pollution of water

Pollution

Berger, M. The new water book (4-6)   **553.7**
Elliott, S. M. Our dirty water (4-6)   **363.7**
Pringle, L. This is a river (4-6)   **574.5**
    See also pages in the following books:
Ault, P. These are the Great Lakes p146-57
    (5 and up)   **977**
Gans, R. Water for dinosaurs and you p26-32
    (1-3)   **551.48**
Miles, B. Save the earth! p55-73 (4 and up)   **363.7**
    See also Petroleum pollution of water

Water; play. Carlson, B. W.
    In Carlson, B. W. The right play for you
        p25   **792**

Water animals. See Fresh water animals;
    Marine animals

Water birds

National Geographic Society. Water, prey,
    and game birds of North America   **598**
    See also names of water birds, e.g. Albatrosses

Water boatman

    See pages in the following book:
Hutchins, R. E. The bug clan p89-93 (5
    and up)   **595.7**

Water buffalo

Fiction

Aruego, J. Look what I can do   **E**

Water bugs

    See pages in the following book:
Hutchins, R. E. The bug clan p95-98 (5 and
    up)   **595.7**

Water color painting

Technique

Hawkinson, J. Collect, print and paint from
    nature (3-6)   **751.42**
Zaidenberg, A. How to paint with water
    colors (4 and up)   **751.42**

Water colors

    See pages in the following book:
Weiss, H. Paint, brush and palette p52-57
    (5 and up)   **751.4**

Water drops. Manning-Sanders, R.
    In Manning-Sanders, R. A book of ghosts
        & goblins p90-94   **398.2**

Water farming. See Plants—Soilless culture

Water festival. See Thingyan

Water for dinosaurs and you. Gans, R.   **551.48**

The **water** ghost of Harrowby Hall. Bangs,
    J. K.
    In Sechrist, E. H. ed. 13 ghostly yarns
        p45-59   **S C**

The **Water**-lily: the gold spinners
    In Blue fairy book p180-89   **398.2**

The **water**-nixie. Grimm, J.
    In Grimm, J. The complete Grimm's fairy
        tales p364-65   **398.2**
    In Grimm, J. More Tales from Grimm
        p23-25   **398.2**

The **water**-nixie. Rockwell, A.
    In Rockwell, A. The three bears & 15 other
        stories p53-55   **398.2**

The **water** nixie. Tennant, P.
    In Shedlock, M. L. The art of the storyteller p198-203   **372.6**

The **water** of life. Grimm, J.
    In Grimm, J. About wise men and simpletons p65-73   **398.2**
    In Grimm, J. The complete Grimm's fairy
        tales p449-55   **398.2**

The **water** of life. Maspons y Labrós, F.
    In The Andrew Lang Fairy tale treasury
        p362-68   **398.2**

Water of life. Pyle, H.
    In Pyle, H. The wonder clock p15-26   **398.2**

Water pets, The care of. Pels, G.   **639.3**

Water plants. See Fresh water plants; Marine
    plants

Water plants. Pringle, L.   **581.92**

Water pollution. See Water—Pollution

Water power

    See pages in the following books:
Shuttlesworth, D. E. Disappearing energy
    p20-27 (5 and up)   **333.79**
Watson, J. W. Alternate energy sources p42-
    48 (4 and up)   **333.79**
    See also Dams

Water, prey, and game birds of North America. National Geographic Society   **598**

Water resources development

    See pages in the following book:
Wilber, D. N. The land and people of Ceylon
    p39-53, 138-41 (5 and up)   **954.9**

Water spider

    See pages in the following book:
Hutchins, R. E. The bug clan p86-89 (5 and
    up)   **595.7**

Water sports

    See also names of water sports, e.g.
    Swimming

Water supply

Gans, R. Water for dinosaurs and you (1-3)   **551.48**
    See also pages in the following book:
Berger, M. The new water book p59-69 (4-6)   **551.4**
    See also Dams; Water—Pollution

Waterhouse, Charles
    (illus.) Shalit, N. Cup and saucer chemistry   **540.7**

Waterless Mountain. Armer, L. A.   **Fic**

The **watermill** that wouldn't work. Simon, S.
    In Simon, S. The wisemen of Helm and
        their merry tales p7-16   **398.2**

Waters, G. W.
Cesarino and the dragon
    In Fairy tales from many lands p66-76   **398.2**

Waters, John F.
Camels: ships of the desert (1-3)   **599.73**
Green turtle mysteries (1-3)   **597.9**
Hungry sharks (1-3)   **597**
A jellyfish is not a fish (2-4)   **593.7**

Waters, Lydia
    See pages in the following book:
As I saw it: women who lived the American
    adventure p63-65 (6 and up)   **973**

Watership Down. Adams, R.   **Fic**

Watership Down; excerpt. Adams, R.
    In The Arbuthnot Anthology of children's
        literature p553-55   **808.8**

Waterways
See also Canals; Rivers
Waterworks. See Water supply
Watie, Stand
Fiction
Keith, H. Rifles for Watie (6 and up) Fic
Watkins, Frances Ellen. See Harper, Frances Ellen (Watkins)
Watling, James
(illus.) Andersen, H. C. The nightingale Fic
Watson, Aldren A.
(illus.) Felton, H. W. John Henry and his hammer 398.2
(illus.) Wong, H. H. Our terrariums 639
Watson, Clyde
Binary numbers (2-4) 513
Catch me & kiss me & say it again (k-1) 811
Father Fox's pennyrhymes (k-3) 811
Tom Fox and the apple pie E
Watson, Jane Werner
Alternate energy sources (4 and up) 333.79
The Niger: Africa's river of mystery (4-6) 966
Watson, Nancy Dingman
The birthday goat E
Blueberries lavender (3-5) 811
Watson, Wendy
(illus.) Holt, M. Maps, tracks, and the bridges of Königsberg 514
(illus.) Linn, C. F. Probability 519.2
(illus.) Miles, M. Jenny's cat Fic
(illus.) Nash, O. The cruise of the Aardvark 811
(illus.) Pettit, F. H. Christmas all around the house 745.59
(illus.) Showers, P. Sleep is for everyone 613.7
(illus.) Watson, C. Binary numbers 513
(illus.) Watson, C. Catch me & kiss me & say it again 811
(illus.) Watson, C. Father Fox's pennyrhymes 811
(illus.) Watson, C. Tom Fox and the apple pie E
(illus.) Watson, N. D. The birthday goat E
Watt, James
See pages in the following book:
Cottler, J. Heroes of civilization p161-68 (5 and up) 920
Watts, Frances B.
The bridge to Killybog Fair
In Dramatized folk tales of the world p227-38 812.08
The crimson feather
In Fifty plays for junior actors p627-34 812.08
Grandma and the pampered boarder
In One hundred plays for children p95-105 808.82
The leprechaun shoemakers
In Dramatized folk tales of the world p239-49 812.08
Miss Louisa and the outlaws
In Fifty plays for junior actors p635-44 812.08
In Popular plays for classroom reading p132-41 808.82
Watts, Marjorie-Ann
(illus.) Storr, C. Clever Polly and the stupid wolf Fic

Wauneka, Annie Dodge
See pages in the following book:
Gridley, M. E. American Indian women p119-30 (5 and up) 920
The wave. Hodges, M. 398.2
also in Time for old magic p217-19 398.2
Waves
See pages in the following book:
Bendick, J. Electronics for young people p50-59 (5 and up) 621.381
See also Electric waves; Ocean waves
Waves. Zim, H. S. 551.47
Waves, tides, and currents. Clemons, E. 551.47
The way. Runnette, H. V.
In A Treasury of Christmas plays p304-12 812.08
Way deep down in the Okefenokee Swamps. Jagendorf, M. A.
In Jagendorf, M. A. Folk stories of the South p79-81 398.2
Way down yonder on Troublesome Creek. Still, J. 398
The way it was—1876. Hilton, S. 973.8
The way of an ant. Mizumura, Kazue E
The way of the storyteller. Sawyer, R. 372.6
The way to Norwich. Fisher, A.
In One hundred plays for children p80-86 808.82
The way to start a day. Baylor, B. 291.4
The way we lived. Sandler, M. W. 331.09
The ways of the Lord. Jagendorf, M. A.
In Jagendorf, M. A. Folk stories of the South p190-92 398.2
The wayward witch. Boiko, C.
In Boiko, C. Children's plays for creative actors p86-94 812
We all come from someplace: children of Puerto Rico. Singer, J. 972.95
We are having a baby. Holland, V. E
We elect a President. Weingast, D. E. 324.6
We have not vanished. Tamarin, A. 970.004
We hide, you seek. Aruego, J. E
We interrupt this program. Boiko, C.
In On stage for Christmas p285-97 812.08
We interrupt this semester for an important bulletin. Conford, E. See note under Conford, E. Dear Lovey Hart, I am desperate Fic
We never get to do anything. Alexander, M. E
We remember Philip. Simon, N. Fic
We walk in sandy places. Baylor, B. 591.5
Wealth
See also Capitalists and financiers
Weapons. Tunis, E. 623.4
Weapons and weaponry. See Arms and armor; Firearms
Weare, Philip
(illus.) Stonehouse, B. A closer look at plant life 581
(illus.) Stonehouse, B. A closer look at reptiles 597.9
Weasels
See pages in the following book:
Patent, D. H. Weasels, otters, skunks, and their family p23-31 (3-6) 599.74
Weasels, otters, skunks, and their family. Patent, D. H. 599.74

Witchcraft—Fiction—*Continued*

Preussler, O. The Satanic mill (6 and up) **Fic**

Snyder, Z. K. The witches of Worm (4 and up) **Fic**

Speare, E. G. The witch of Blackbird Pond (6 and up) **Fic**

Williams, J. The magic grandfather (4-6) **Fic**

Witches

Witches, witches, witches (5 and up) **808.8**

Fiction

Adams, A. A woggle of witches **E**

Balian, L. Humbug witch **E**

Calhoun ,M. The witch's pig (k-3) **398.2**

De Paola, T. Big Anthony and the magic ring **E**

Embry, M. The blue-nosed witch (1-4) **Fic**

Estes, E. The witch family (1-4) **Fic**

Jones, D. W. Charmed life (5 and up) **Fic**

Kimmel, M. M. Magic in the mist (1-4) **Fic**

MacKellar, W. The witches of Glen Gowrie (5 and up) **Fic**

Mahy, M. The boy who was followed home **E**

Manning-Sanders, R. A book of witches (3-6) **398.2**

Nichols, R. The marrow of the world (5 and up) **Fic**

Norton, M. Bed-knob and broomstick (3-5) **Fic**

Peet, B. Big bad Bruce **E**

Peet, B. The whingdingdilly **E**

Serraillier, I. Suppose you met a witch **E**

Steig, W. Caleb & Kate **E**

Stewart, M. The little broomstick (3-6) **Fic**

Poetry

Witch poems (2-5) **811.08**

The **witches** of Worm. Snyder, Z. K. **Fic**

Witches, pumpkins and grinning ghosts. Barth, E. **394.2**

The **witches'** ride. De Osma, L.

In The Arbuthnot Anthology of children's literature p407-08 **808.8**

In Harper, W. comp. Ghosts and goblins p228-33 **398.2**

In Time for old magic p273-74 **398.2**

Witches, wit, and a werewolf. Hardendorff, J. B. **S C**

Witches, witches, witches (5 and up) **808.8**

The **witch's** daughter. Bawden, N. **Fic**

The **witch's** pig. Calhoun, M. **398.2**

The **witch's** pumpkin. Cooper, E.

In One hundred plays for children p386-89 **808.82**

The **witch's** shoes. Olcott, F. J.

In Harper, W. comp. Ghosts and goblins p192-94 **398.2**

In Witches, witches, witches p219-20 **808.8**

Witcracks. Schwartz, A. comp. **398**

With a deep sea smile **372.6**

With a wig, with a wag. Cothran, J.

In With a deep sea smile p86-92 **372.6**

With Bert & Ray. Konigsburg, E. L.

In Konigsburg, E. L. Throwing shadows p121-51 **S C**

Withers, Carl

(comp.) The American riddle book. See The American riddle book **398**

(comp.) Riddles of many lands. See Riddles of many lands **398**

Within the gates. Zei, A.

In The Arbuthnot Anthology of children's literature p772-75 **808.8**

Withrow, Dorothy E.

Gateways to readable books **011**

Witsen, Betty van. See Van Witsen, Betty

Wittig, Alice J.

U.S. Government publications for the school media center **015.73**

Wittman, Sally

A special trade **E**

Wives of presidents

United States

See Presidents—United States—Wives

The **wives'** tale. Carrick, M.

In Carrick, M. The wise men of Gotham **398.2**

Wizard and his pupil

Bowman, J. C. Niilo and the wizard

In Bowman, J. C. Tales from a Finnish tupa p141-46 **398.2**

The **wizard** in the tree. Alexander, L. **Fic**

The **wizard** islands. Yolen, J. **910**

The **wizard** of Alderley Edge. Colwell, E.

In Colwell, E. Round about and long ago p15-18 **398.2**

A **wizard** of Earthsea. LeGuin, U. K. **Fic**

The **wizard** of Long Sleddale. Colwell, E.

In Colwell, E. Round about and long ago p27-29 **398.2**

The **wizard** of Op. Emberley, E. **E**

The **Wizard** of Oz. Baum, L. F. **Fic**

The **wizard** of Oz. Schwartz, L. S.

In Fifty plays for junior actors p530-53 **812.08**

In Popular plays for classroom reading p246-64 **808.82**

Wizardry. See Witchcraft

Wizards. See Witches

Woe. Riordan, J.

In Riordan, J. Tales from Tartary p54-58 **398.2**

Woerkom, Dorothy van. See Van Woerkom, Dorothy

A **woggle** of witches. Adams, A. **E**

Wohlrabe, Raymond

The land and people of Austria (5 and up) **943.6**

The land and people of Denmark (5 and up) **948.9**

The land and people of Germany (5 and up) **943**

(jt. auth.) Barnouw, A. J. The land and people of Holland **949.2**

Wojcicki, Kazimierz Władysław

The crow

In Yellow fairy book p92-94 **398.2**

Wojciechowska, Maia

Newbery Medal acceptance paper

In Newbery and Caldecott Medal books: 1956-1965 p142-46 **028.5**

Shadow of a bull (6 and up) **Fic**

About

See pages in the following books:

Authors and illustrators of children's books p417-20 **028.5**

Newbery and Caldecott Medal books: 1956-1965 p147-52 **028.5**

World War, 1939-1945—*Continued*
Poland
See pages in the following book:
Kelly, E. P. The land and people of Poland p105-16 (5 and up)   **943.8**

Russia
See also Leningrad—Siege, 1941-1944

United States
Colby, C. B. Fighting gear of World War II (4 and up)   **355.8**
World within a world: Baja. Lewin, T. **574.9**
Worldmark Encyclopedia of the nations   **910.3**
The **world's** most beautiful rose. Andersen, H. C.
In Andersen, H. C. The complete fairy tales and stories p390-92   **S C**
The **world's** most famous ghosts. Cohen, D.   **133.1**
Worlds to explore: handbook for Brownie and Junior Girl Scouts. Girl Scouts of the United States of America   **369.463**
Worms
See pages in the following books:
Cooper, E. K. Science on the shores and banks p94-103 (5 and up)   **574.92**
Rhine, R. Life in a bucket of soil p23-35 (5 and up)   **595**
See also Earthworms

Fiction
Lionni, L. Inch by inch   **E**
Rockwell, T. How to eat fried worms (3-6)   **Fic**
Worms. Darling, L.   **595.1**
Wormser, Richard
The black mustanger (5 and up)   **Fic**
Worrall, Ambrose A.
See pages in the following book:
Kettelkamp, L. Investigating psychics p67-84 (5 and up)   **133.8**
Worrall, Olga Nathalie Ripich
See pages in the following book:
Kettelkamp, L. Investigating psychics p67-84 (5 and up)   **133.8**
Worship
Baylor, B. The way to start a day (1-3)   **291.4**
See also pages in the following book:
Yolen, J. Simple gifts p 1-5 (5 and up) **289**
The **worst** person in the world. Stevenson, J.   **E**
Worstell, Emma Victor
(comp.) Jump the rope jingles. See Jump the rope jingles   **796.1**
Worth, Valerie
More Small poems (3-5)   **811**
Small poems (3-5)   **811**
Still More Small poems (3-5)   **811**
Woster, Alice
Hubbub on the bookshelf
In One hundred plays for children p439-54   **808.82**
Wounded, First aid to. See First aid
Wounded Knee: an Indian history of the American West. Ehrlich, A.   **970.004**

Wounded lion
Maspons y Labrós, F. The wounded lion
In The Andrew Lang Fairy tale treasury p385-93   **398.2**
The **wounded** wolf. George, J. G.   **Fic**
Woycicki, K. W. See Wojcicki, Kazimierz Władysław
Wrapped for eternity. Pace, M. M.   **393**
Wrapping. See Gift wrapping
A **wreath** of Christmas legends. McGinley, P.   **811**
Wrekin
Colwell, E. E. The giant and the Wrekin
In Colwell, E. Round about and long ago p95-96   **398.2**
Wren and the bear
Grimm, J. The bear and the kingbird (k-3)   **398.2**
Grimm, J. The willow-wren and the bear
In Grimm, J. The complete Grimm's fairy tales p472-74   **398.2**
The **wrestler** of Kyushu. Courlander, H.
In Courlander, H. The tiger's whisker, and other tales and legends from Asia and the Pacific p83-86   **398.2**
The **wrestlers.** Courlander, H.
In Courlander, H. Olode the hunter, and other tales from Nigeria p107-09   **398.2**
Wrestling
See pages in the following book:
Keith, H. Sports and games p292-302 (5 and up)   **796**
The **wrestling** match of the two Buddhas. Uchida, Yoshiko
In Uchida, Yoshiko. The magic listening cap p23-31   **398.2**
Wright, Blanche Fisher
(illus.) The Real Mother Goose. See The Real Mother Goose   **398**
Wright, Dare
Look at a colt (k-2)   **636.1**
Wright, Doris G.
The twelve days of Christmas
In A Treasury of Christmas plays p339-45   **812.08**
Wright, Gordon
Sports Illustrated Horseback riding. See Sports Illustrated Horseback riding   **798.2**
Wright, Nicolas
The Red Baron [biography of Richthofen, Manfred Albrecht, Freiherr von] (5 and up)   **92**
Wright, Orville
Reynolds, Q. The Wright brothers (3-6)   **92**
See also pages in the following books:
Cottler, J. Heroes of civilization p265-75 (5 and up)   **920**
Foster, G. The year of the flying machine, 1903 p13-19, 46-50, 68-72, 91-93 (3-6)   **909.82**
Ross, F. Historic plane models p20-26 (5 and up)   **629.133**
Wright, Richard
See pages in the following book:
Alexander, R. P. comp. Young and black in America p19-36 (6 and up)   **920**
Wright, Wendell W.
The rainbow dictionary (1-4)   **423**
Schulz, C. M. The Charlie Brown dictionary   **423**

DIRECTORY OF PUBLISHERS AND DISTRIBUTORS

A.L.A. American Library Association, 50 E Huron St, Chicago, Ill. 60611

APS Publications. APS Publications, Inc, 150 5th Ave, New York, N.Y. 10011

Abelard-Schuman. See Harper

Abingdon Press. Abingdon Press, 201 8th Ave, S, Nashville, Tenn. 37202

Abrams. Harry N. Abrams, Inc, 110 E 59th St, New York, N.Y. 10022

Addison-Wesley. Addison-Wesley Publishing Company, Inc, Reading, Mass. 01867

Airmont. Airmont Publishing Company, Inc, 22 E 60th St, New York, N.Y. 10022

Am. Assn. for the Advancement of Science. American Association for the Advancement of Science, 1515 Massachusetts Ave, N.W, Washington, D.C. 20005

Am. Bibl. Center-Clio Press. American Bibliographical Center-Clio Press, Inc, Riviera Campus, 2040 A.P.S, Box 4397, Santa Barbara, Calif. 93103

Am. Council on Educ. American Council on Education, 1 Dupont Circle, N.W, Washington, D.C. 20036

Am. Forestry Assn. American Forestry Association, Book Edit Dept, 1319 18th St, N.W, Washington, D.C. 20036

Am. Guidance Service. American Guidance Service, Inc, Publishers' Bldg, Circle Pines, Minn. 55014

Am. Heritage. American Heritage Publishing Company, Inc, 10 Rockefeller Plaza, New York, N.Y. 10020

Am. Mus. of Natural Hist. American Museum of Natural History, Central Park W, at 79th St, New York, N.Y. 10024

Anchorage Press. Anchorage Press, P.O. Box 8067, New Orleans, La. 70182

Arco. Arco Publishing, Inc, 219 Park Ave, S, New York, N.Y. 10003

Arno Press. Arno Press, Inc, 3 Park Ave, New York, N.Y. 10016

Associated Booksellers. Associated Booksellers, 147 McKinley Ave, Bridgeport, Conn. 06606

Assn. for Childhood Educ. Association for Childhood Education International, 3615 Wisconsin Ave, N.W, Washington, D.C. 20016

Assn. for Educational Communications & Technology. Association for Education Communications & Technology, 1126 16th St, N.W, Washington, D.C. 20036

Astor-Honor. Astor-Honor, Inc, 48 E 43d St, New York, N.Y. 10017

Atheneum Pubs. Atheneum Publishers, 597 5th Ave, New York, N.Y. 10017

Avenel Bks. See Crown

Avon. Avon Books, 959 8th Ave, New York, N.Y. 10019

Barnes A.S. A. S. Barnes & Company, Inc, Service, Inc, Publishers' Bldg, Circle Pines, 11175 Flintkote Ave, Suite C, San Diego, Calif. 92121

Beacon Press. Beacon Press, 25 Beacon St, Boston, Mass. 02108

Beginner Bks. See Random House

Bell Bks. See Farrar, Straus

Biblio. Biblio Distribution Center, 81 Adams Dr, P.O. Box 327, Totowa, N.J. 07511

Bobbs. Bobbs-Merrill Company, Inc, 4300 W 62d St, Indianapolis, Ind. 46206

Bonim Bks. See Hebrew Pub.

Bowker. R. R. Bowker Company, 1180 Ave. of the Americas, New York, N.Y. 10036

Boy Scouts of America. Boy Scouts of America, Supply Division, P.O. Box 61030, Dallas/Ft. Worth Airport, Texas 75261

Boyars, M. Marion Boyars, Inc, 99 Main St, Salem, N.H. 03079

Bradbury Press. Bradbury Press, Inc, 2 Overhill Rd, Scarsdale, N.Y. 10583

Bro-Dart Foundation. Bro-Dart Foundation, 1807 Pembroke Rd, Greensboro, N.C. 27408

Brown, W.C. William C. Brown Company, Publishers, 2460 Kerper Blvd, Dubuque, Iowa 52001

Cambridge. Cambridge University Press, 32 E 57th St, New York, N.Y. 10022

Camp Fire Girls. Camp Fire Girls, Inc, 4601 Madison, Kansas City, Mo. 64112

Canadian Lib. Assn. Canadian Library Association, 151 Sparks St, Ottawa, ON KIP 5E3, Canada

Cavanagh. Gladys Cavanagh, 2020 University Ave, Suite 6, Madison, Wis. 53705

Caxton Ptrs. The Caxton Printers, Ltd, Box 700, Caldwell, Idaho 83605

Center for Applied Res. in Educ. Center for Applied Research in Education, Route 9W, Englewood Cliffs, N.J. 07632

Childrens Bk. Council. Children's Book Council, Inc, 67 Irving Place, New York, N.Y. 10003

Childrens Press. Children's Press, 1224 W Van Buren St, Chicago, Ill. 60607

Childrens Science Bk. Rev. Committee. Children's Science Book Review Committee, Boston University School of Education, Department of Science and Mathematic Education, 36 Cunnington St, Boston, Mass. 02215

The Childrens Theatre Press. See Anchorage Press

Chilton Bk. Co. Chilton Book Company, Chilton Way, Radnor, Pa. 19089

Choice. Choice, 100 Riverview Center, Middletown, Conn. 06457

Clarendon Press. See Oxford

Collier Bks. See Macmillan Pub. Co.

Columbia Univ. Press. Columbia University Press, 562 W 113th St, New York, N.Y. 10025

Compton. F. E. Compton Company, 425 N Michigan Ave, Chicago, Ill. 60611

Concordia. Concordia Publishing House, 3558 S Jefferson Ave, St Louis, Mo. 63118

Contemporary Bks. Contemporary Books, Inc, 180 N Michigan Ave, Chicago, Ill. 60601

Cook. David C. Cook Publishing Company, 850 N Grove Ave, Elgin, Ill. 60120

Council for Exceptional Children. Council for Exceptional Children, 1920 Association Dr, Reston, Va. 22091

Council on Interracial Bks. for Children. Council on Interracial Books for Children, 1841 Broadway, New York, N.Y. 10023

Coward-McCann. See Coward, McCann & Geoghegan

Coward, McCann & Geoghegan. Coward, McCann & Geoghegan, Inc, 200 Madison Ave, New York, N.Y. 10016

Creative Arts Bk. Co. Creative Arts Book Company, 833 Bancroft Way, Berkeley, Calif. 94710

Creative Educ. Creative Education Society, 123 S Broad St, Mankato, Minn. 56001

Criterion Bks. See Lippincott & Crowell

Crowell. See Harper

Crowell-Collier Press. See Macmillan Pub. Co.

Crown. Crown Publishers, Inc, 1 Park Ave, New York, N.Y. 10016

Day. See Harper

Delacorte Press. See Dell

Dell. Dell Publishing Company, Inc, 1 Dag Hammarskjold Plaza, 245 E 47th St, New York, N.Y. 10017

Denison. T. S. Denison & Company, Inc, 9601 Newton Ave, S, Minneapolis, Minn. 55431

Dent. J. M. Dent & Sons, Ltd, Biblio Distribution Center, 81 Adams Dr, Totowa, N.J. 07512

Deutsch. See Elsevier-Dutton

Devin-Adair. Devin-Adair Company, Inc, 143 Sound Beach Ave, Old Greenwich, Conn. 06870

Dial Press. The Dial Press, 1 Dag Hammarskjold Plaza, 245 E 47th St, New York, N.Y. 10017

Dillon Press. Dillon Press, Inc, 500 S 3d St, Minneapolis, Minn. 55415

Dodd. Dodd, Mead & Company, 79 Madison Ave, New York, N.Y. 10016

Doubleday. Doubleday & Company, Inc, 245 Park Ave, New York, N.Y. 10017

Dover. Dover Publications, Inc, 180 Varick St, New York, N.Y. 10014

Dutton. See Elsevier-Dutton

Educ. Today. Education Today Company, Inc, 530 University Ave, Palo Alto, Calif. 94301

Educational Film Library Assn. Educational Film Library Association, Inc, 43 W 61st St, New York, N.Y. 10023

Educators Progress Service. Educators Progress Service, Inc, 214 Center St, Randolph, Wisconsin 53956

Elsevier-Dutton. Elsevier-Dutton Publishing Company, Inc, 2 Park Ave, New York, N.Y. 10016

Elsevier/Nelson Bks. See Elsevier-Dutton

Encyclopaedia Britannica Educ. Corp. Encyclopaedia Britannica Educational Corporation, 425 N Michigan Ave, Chicago, Ill. 60611

Enslow Pubs. Enslow Publishers, Bloy St & Ramsey Ave, Hillside, N.J. 07205

Evans, M.&Co. See Elsevier-Dutton

Faber & Faber. Faber & Faber, 99 Main St, Salem, N.H. 03079

Farrar, Straus. Farrar, Straus & Giroux, Inc, 19 Union Sq, W, New York, N.Y. 10003

Faxon. F. W. Faxon Company, Inc, 15 Southwest Park, Westwood, Mass. 02090

Fell. Frederick Fell Publishers, Inc, 386 Park Ave, S, New York, N.Y. 10016

Feminist Press. The Feminist Press, Box 334, Old Westbury, N.Y. 11568

Field Enterprises. Field Enterprises Educational Corporation, 510 Merchandise Mart Plaza, Chicago, Ill. 60654

Fleet Press. Fleet Press Corporation, 160 5th Ave, New York, N.Y. 10010

Follett. Follett Publishing Company, 1010 W Washington Blvd, Chicago, Ill. 60607

Forest Press. Forest Press, Inc, 85 Watervliet Ave, Albany, N.Y. 12206

Fortress Press. Fortress Press, 2900 Queens Lane, Philadelphia, Pa. 19129

Four Winds. Four Winds Press, 50 W 44th St, New York, N.Y. 10036

Free Press. The Free Press, 866 3d Ave, New York, N.Y. 10022

Friendship Press. Friendship Press, 475 Riverside Dr, New York, N.Y. 10027

Frontier Press. The Frontier Press Company, Box 1098, Columbus, Ohio 43216

Gale Res. Gale Research Company, Book Tower, Detroit, Mich. 48226

Gambit. Gambit, 27 N Main St, Meeting House Green, Ipswich, Mass. 01938

Garrard. Garrard Publishing Company, 1607 N Market St, Champaign, Ill. 61820

Gaylord. Gaylord Professional Publications, Box 4901, Syracuse, N.Y. 13221

Girl Scouts of the United States of America. Girl Scouts of the United States of America, National Equipment Service, 830 3d Ave, New York, N.Y. 10022

Gloucester Press. See Watts, F.

Godine. David R. Godine Publisher, Inc, 306 Dartmouth St, Boston, Mass. 02116

Golden Press Bk. See Western Pub. Co.

Greenwillow Bks. See Morrow

Greenwood Press. Greenwood Press, 88 Post Rd, W, Westport, Conn. 06881

Grolier. Grolier, Inc, Sherman Turnpike, Danbury, Conn. 06816

Grosset. Grosset & Dunlap, Inc, 51 Madison Ave, New York, N.Y. 10010

Hall, G.K.&Co. G. K. Hall & Company, 70 Lincoln St, Boston, Mass. 02111

Hammond. Hammond, Inc, 515 Valley St, Maplewood, N.J. 07040

Harcourt. Harcourt Brace Jovanovich, Inc, 757 3d Ave, New York, N.Y. 10017

Harper. Harper & Row, Publishers, Inc, 10 E 53d St, New York, N.Y. 10022

Hart. Hart Publishing Company, Inc, 12 E 12th St, New York, N.Y. 10003

Harvey House. Harvey House, Publishers, 20 Waterside Plaza, New York, N.Y. 10010

Hastings House. Hastings House, Publishers, Inc, 10 E 40th St, New York, N.Y. 10016

Hawthorn Bks. See Elsevier-Dutton

Hebrew Pub. Hebrew Publishing Company, 80 5th Ave, New York, N.Y. 10011

Hermann Schaffstein Verlag. Hermann Schaffstein Verlag, Degginstrasse 93, 4600 Dortmund 1, Federal Republic of Germany

Hill. Lawrence Hill & Company, Publishers, Inc, 520 Riverside Ave, Westport, Conn. 06880

Hill & Wang. See Farrar, Straus

Holiday House. Holiday House, Inc, 18 E 53d St, New York, N.Y. 10022

Holt. Holt, Rinehart & Winston, Inc, 383 Madison Ave, New York, N.Y. 10017

Horn Bk. The Horn Book, Inc, Park Sq. Bldg, 31 St James Ave, Boston, Mass. 02116

Houghton. Houghton Mifflin Company, 1 Beacon St, Boston, Mass. 02107

Howell Bk. House. Howell Book House, Inc, 230 Park Ave, New York, N.Y. 10017

Hubbard Press. See Rand McNally

Human Sciences Press. Human Sciences Press, Inc, 72 5th Ave, New York, N.Y. 10011

Incentive Pubs. Incentive Publishers, Inc, Box 12522, Nashville, Tenn. 37212

Indiana Univ. Press. Indiana University Press, 10th & Morton Sts, Bloomington, Ind. 47405

Instructor. Instructor Publications, P.O. Box 6099, Duluth, Minn. 55806

Int. Reading Assn. International Reading Association, 800 Barksdale Rd, Box 8139, Newark, Del. 19711

Jewish Publication Soc. of America. Jewish Publication Society of America, 117 S 17th St, Philadelphia, Pa. 19103

Johnson Pub. Co. Johnson Publishing Company, 1880 S 57th Court, Boulder, Colo. 80301

Kirkus Service. The Kirkus Service, Inc, 200 Park Ave, S, New York, N.Y. 10003

Knopf. Alfred A. Knopf, Inc, 201 E 50th St, New York, N.Y. 10022

Kraus Reprint Corp. Kraus Reprint Corporation, Rt. 100, Millwood, N.Y. 10546

Ktav. Ktav Publishing House, Inc, 75 Varick St, New York, N.Y. 10013

Landers Associates. Landers Associates, P.O. Box 69760, Los Angeles, Calif. 90069

Larousse. Larousse & Company, Inc, 572 5th Ave, New York, N.Y. 10036

Lerner Publications. Lerner Publications Company, 241 1st Ave, N, Minneapolis, Minn. 55401

Libs. Unlimited. Libraries Unlimited, Inc, Box 263, Littleton, Colo. 80160

Lion. Lion Books, 111 E 39th St, New York, N.Y. 10016

Lippincott. See Harper

Little. Little, Brown & Company, 34 Beacon St, Boston, Mass. 02106

London House & Maxwell. See Pergamon Press

Lothrop. See Morrow

McGraw. McGraw-Hill, Inc, 1221 Ave. of the Americas, New York, N.Y. 10020

McKay. David McKay Company, Inc, 2 Park Ave, New York, N.Y. 10016

Macmillan Pub. Co. Macmillan Publishing Company, Inc. 866 3d Ave, New York, N.Y. 10022

Macrae Smith Co. Macrae Smith Company, Routes 54 & Old 147, Turbotville, Pa. 17772

Marsh Hall. Marsh Hall, Thurstonland, Huddersfield, HD4 6XB, Yorkshire, England

Meredith. Meredith Corp, 1716 Locust St, Des Moines, Iowa 50336

Merriam. G. & C. Merriam Company, 47 Federal St, Springfield, Mass. 01101

Merrimack Bk. Service. Merrimack Book Service, Inc, 99 Main St, Salem, N.H. 03079

Merrimack Pub. Corp. See Associated Booksellers

Messner. Julian Messner, The Simon & Schuster Bldg, 1230 Ave. of the Americas, New York, N.Y. 10020

Methuen. Methuen, Inc, 733 3d Ave, New York, N.Y. 10017

Metropolitan Mus. of Art. The Metropolitan Museum of Art, 5th Ave & 82d St, New York, N.Y. 10028

Modern Lib. Modern Library, Inc, 201 E 50th St, New York, N.Y. 10022

Morrow. William Morrow & Company, Inc, 105 Madison Ave, New York, N.Y. 10016

Nancy Renfro Studios, Nancy Renfro Studios, 1117 W 9th St, Austin, Texas 78703

Natl. Council of Teachers of English. National Council of Teachers of English, 111 Kenyon Rd, Urbana, Ill. 61801

Natl. Geographic Soc. National Geographic Society, 17th & M Sts, N.W, Washington, D.C. 20036

Natl. Information Center for Educational Media. National Information Center for Educational Media, University of Southern California, University Park, Los Angeles, Calif. 90007

Natl. Wildlife Federation. National Wildlife Federation, Inc, 1412 16th St, N.W, Washington, D.C. 20036

Natl. Science Teachers Assn. National Science Teacher's Association, 1742 Connecticut Ave, N.W, Washington, D.C. 20009

Natural Hist. Press. Natural History Press, 245 Park Ave, New York, N.Y. 10017

Nelson. Thomas Nelson, Inc, 405 7th Ave, S, Nashville, Tenn. 37203

New Am. Lib. New American Library, Inc, 1633 Broadway, New York, N.Y. 10019

N.Y. Graphic. N.Y. Graphic Society Books, 41 Mt Vernon St, Boston, Mass. 02106

N.Y. Library Assn. New York Library Association, 60 E 42d St, New York, N.Y. 10017

N.Y. Pub. Library. New York Public Library, Public Relations Office, 5th Ave. & 42d St, New York, N.Y. 10018

N.Y. Times Co. New York Times Company, 229 W 43d St, New York, N.Y. 10036

North American Pub. Co. North American Publishing Company, 401 N Broad St, Philadelphia, Pa. 19108

Obolensky. See Astor-Honor

Oceana. Oceana Publications, Inc, Dobbs Ferry, New York 10522

Open Court. Open Court Publishing Company, La Salle, Ill. 61301

Oryx Press. The Oryx Press, 2214 N Central at Encanto, Phoenix, Ariz. 85004

Overlook Press. The Overlook Press, 667 Madison Ave, New York, N.Y. 10021

Oxford. Oxford University Press, Inc, 200 Madison Ave, New York, N.Y. 10016

Pantheon Bks. Pantheon Books, Inc, 201 E 50th St, New York, N.Y. 10022

Parents Mag. Press. Parents Magazine Press, 685 3d Ave, New York, N.Y. 10017

Parnassus Press. See Houghton

Penguin Bks. Penguin Books, 625 Madison Ave, New York, N.Y. 10022

Pergamon Press. Pergamon Press, Inc, Maxwell House, Fairview Park, Elmsford, N.Y. 10523

Phaedrus. Phaedrus, Inc, Box 1166, Marblehead, Mass. 01945

Phillips. S. G. Phillips, Inc, 305 W 86th St, New York, N.Y. 10024

Philomel Bks. See Putnam

Platt & Munk. See Grosset

Plays, Inc. Plays, Inc, 8 Arlington St, Boston, Mass. 02116

Potter, C.N. Clarkson N. Potter, Inc, 1 Park Ave, New York, N.Y. 10016

Prentice-Hall. Prentice-Hall, Inc, Route 9W, Englewood Cliffs, N.J. 07632

Puffin Bks. See Penguin Bks.

Putnam. G. P. Putnam's Sons, 200 Madison Ave, New York, N.Y. 10016

Raintree Pubs. Raintree Publishers, Inc, 205 W Highland Ave, Milwaukee, Wis. 53203

Rand McNally. Rand McNally & Company, 8255 Central Park Ave, Skokie, Ill. 60076

Random House. Random House, Inc, 201 E 50th St, New York, N.Y. 10022

Raymond, A. Allen Raymond, 11 Hale Lane, Box 1266, Darien, Conn. 06820

Regnery/Gateway. Regnery/Gateway, Inc, 116 S Michigan Ave, Suite 300, Chicago, Ill. 60603

Rinehart. See Holt

Rodale. Rodale Press, Inc, 33 E Minor St, Emmaus, Pa. 18049

Ronald. See Wiley

St Martins. St Martins Press, Inc, 175 5th Ave, New York, N.Y. 10010

Scarecrow. Scarecrow Press, Inc, 52 Liberty St, Metuchen, N.J. 08840

Schocken. Schocken Books, Inc, 200 Madison Ave, New York, N.Y. 10016

Scholastic. Scholastic Book Services, 50 W 44th St, New York, N.Y. 10036

School Library Assn. School Library Association, Victoria House, 29-31 George St, Oxford 0X1, 2AY, England

Scott. Scott, Foresman & Company, 1900 E Lake Ave, Glenview, Ill. 60025

Scribner. Charles Scribner's Sons, 597 5th Ave, New York, N.Y. 10017

Scroll Press. Scroll Press, Inc, 559 W 26th St, New York, N.Y. 10001

Seabury. The Seabury Press, Inc, 815 2d Ave, New York, N.Y. 10017

Sierra Club Bks. See Scribner

Simon & Schuster. Simon & Schuster, Inc, The Simon & Schuster Bldg, 1230 Ave. of of the Americas, New York, N.Y. 10020

Singing Tree Press. See Gale Res.

Smith, P. Peter Smith, 6 Lexington Ave, Magnolia, Mass. 01930

Sniffen Court Bks. Sniffen Court Books, 595 5th Ave, New York, N.Y. 10017

Stemmer House. Stemmer House Publishers, Inc, 2627 Caves Rd, Owings Mills, Md. 21117

Stephen Greene. The Stephen Greene Press, Fessenden Rd, Brattleboro, Vt. 05301

Sterling. Sterling Publishing Company, 2 Park Ave, New York, N.Y. 10016

Supt. of Docs. Superintendent of Documents, Government Printing Office, Washington, D.C. 20402

Taplinger. Taplinger Publishing Company, Inc, 200 Park Ave, S, New York, N.Y. 10003

Thimble Press. The Thimble Press, Lockwood Station Rd, South Woodchester, Stroud, Glos GL5 5EQ, United Kingdom

Third Press. Third Press Review of Books Company, 1995 Broadway, New York, N.Y. 10023

Time-Life Bks. Time-Life Books, Inc, 777 Duke St, Alexandria, Va. 22314

Triad Scientific Pubs. Triad Scientific Publishers, Box 13096, University Sta, Gainesville, Fla. 32604

Troll Assocs. Troll Associates, 320 Route 17, Mahwah, N.J. 07430

Tundra Bks. Tundra Books of Northern N.Y, Box 1030, 51 Clinton St, Plattsburgh, N.Y. 12901

Tuttle. Charles E. Tuttle Company, Inc, 28 S Main St, Rutland, Vt. 05701

U.S. Govt. Ptg. Off. See Supt. of Docs.

Underhill, C. S. Charles S. Underhill, P.O. Box 127, East Aurora, N.Y. 14052

Univ. of Calif. Press. University of California Press, 2223 Fulton St, Berkeley, Calif. 94720

Univ. of Chicago Press. University of Chicago Press, 5801 Ellis Ave, Chicago, Ill. 60637

Univ. of Ill. Graduate Sch. of Library Science. University of Illinois. Graduate School of Library Science, Publications Office, 249 Armory Bldg, Champaign, Ill. 61820

Univ. of Pittsburgh Press. University of Pittsburgh Press, 127 N Bellefield Ave, Pittsburgh, Pa. 15260

Univ. of Toronto Press. University of Toronto Press, 5201 Dufferin St, Downsview, Ontario, M3H 5T8, Canada

Univ. Press Bk. Service. University Press Book Service, UPBS Inc, 301 5th Ave, New York, N.Y. 10001

Van Nostrand. Van Nostrand Reinhold Company, 135 W 50th St, New York, N.Y. 10020

Vanguard. Vanguard Press, Inc, 424 Madison Ave, New York, N.Y. 10017

Viking. The Viking Press, 625 Madison Ave, New York, N.Y. 10022

Vintage Bks. See Random House

Walck, H.Z. See McKay

Walker & Co. Walker & Company, 720 5th Ave, New York, N.Y. 10019

Wanderer Bks. See Simon & Schuster

Warne. Frederick Warne & Company, Inc, 2 Park Ave, New York, N.Y. 10016

Warwick Press. See Watts, F.

Washburn. Washburn, Ives, Inc, 750 3d Ave, New York, N.Y. 10017

Watts, F. Franklin Watts, Inc, 730 5th Ave, New York, N.Y. 10019

Western Pub. Co. Western Publishing Company, Inc, 1220 Mound Ave, Racine, Wis. 53404

Westminster Press. The Westminster Press, 925 Chestnut St, Philadelphia, Pa. 19107

White, D. David White, Inc, 14 Vanderventer Ave, Port Washington, N.Y. 11050

Whitman, A. Albert Whitman & Company, 560 W Lake St, Chicago, Ill. 60606

Wiley. John Wiley & Sons, Inc, 605 3d Ave, New York, N.Y. 10016

Wilson, H.W. The H. W. Wilson Company, 950 University Ave, Bronx, N.Y. 10452

Workman Pub. Workman Publishing Company, Inc, 1 W 39th St, New York, N.Y. 10018

World Book-Childcraft Int. World Book-Childcraft International, Inc, 510 Merchandise Mart Plaza, Chicago, Ill. 60654

Worldmark Press. Worldmark Press, Inc, 242 E 50th St, New York, N.Y. 10022

Writer. The Writer, Inc, 8 Arlington St, Boston, Mass. 02116

Yale Univ. Press. Yale University Press, 302 Temple St, New Haven, Conn. 06511

The Young Naturalist Foundation. The Young Naturalist Foundation, 59 Front St, E, Toronto, Ontario M5E 1B3, Canada

Young Scott Bks. See Addison-Wesley

NOTES

NOTES

NOTES

NOTES

NOTES

NOTES